2014

CATHOLIC ALMANAC

Our Sunday Visitor Publishing Division
Our Sunday Visitor, Inc.
Huntington, Indiana 46750

OUR SUNDAY VISITOR'S CATHOLIC ALMANAC
2014 EDITION

STAFF

Greg Erlandson
Editor-in-Chief

Matthew E. Bunson, M.Div., D.Min.
General Editor

Murray W. Hubley
Production Editor

Cathy Dee
Web Editor

Contributors to the 2014 Edition
Gerald Korson
Msgr. C. Eugene Morris
Rev. Bernard O'Connor, S.T.D., J.C.D.
Rev. Ronald Roberson, C.S.P.
Russell Shaw

Carrie Bannister, Assistant
Becky Heaston, Design

ACKNOWLEDGMENTS: Catholic News Service, for coverage of news and documentary texts; *The Documents of Vatican II*, ed. W. M. Abbott (Herder and Herder, America Press: New York 1966), for quotations of Council documents; *Annuario Pontificio* (2012); *Statistical Yearbook of the Church* (2013); *L'Osservatore Romano* (English editions); *The Official Catholic Directory* — Excerpts of statistical data and other material, reprinted with permission of *The Official Catholic Directory*, © 2013 by Reed Reference Publishing, a division of Reed Publishing (USA) Inc. Trademark used under license from Reed Publishing (Nederland) B.V.; *The Papal Encyclicals*, 5 vols., ed. C. Carlen (Pierian Press, Ann Arbor, MI); *Newsletter of the U.S. Bishops' Committee on the Liturgy*; Kathleen Bullock, Associate for Operations, The United States Catholic Mission Assoc. (3029 Fourth St. N.E., Washington, DC 20017), for U.S. overseas-mission compilations and statistics; *Catholic Press Directory* (2013); *Annuaire Directoire*, Canadian Conference of Catholic Bishops, for latest available Canadian Catholic statistics; other sources as credited in particular entries.

Special thanks are owed to Secretariat for Pro-Life Activities, USCCB; Rev. Mr. William Kokesch, Dir.-Communications Service, Canadian Conference of Catholic Bishops; Msgr. Michael Servinsky; and Rev. Jorge Francisco Vázquez Moreno, adjunct secretary of the *Conferencia del Episcopado Mexicano*.

2014 Catholic Almanac

Copyright © 2014 Our Sunday Visitor Publishing Division, Our Sunday Visitor, Inc.
Published annually by Our Sunday Visitor Publishing Division, Our Sunday Visitor, Inc., 200 Noll Plaza, Huntington, IN 46750
ISBN: 978-1-61278-692-6
ID: T1402
Library of Congress Catalog Card No. 73-641001
International Standard Serial Number (ISSN) 0069-1208

Editorial Note: Comments, corrections, and suggestions should be addressed to the editorial offices of the *Catholic Almanac*: 200 Noll Plaza, Huntington, IN 46750; (800) 348-2440; E-mail: almanac@osv.com.

Visit us online at www.CatholicAlmanac.com, and at the Our Sunday Visitor website at www.OSV.com.

CONTENTS

Year In Review September 2012 to August 2013

SEPTEMBER 2012

VATICAN

African Catholics On Sept. 1, Pope Benedict XVI sent a written message to 300 delegates to the Pan-African Congress of Lay Catholics, meeting in Yaounde, Cameroon, from Sept. 4-9. The pontiff used the message to give encouragement to African Catholics in their faith and urged them to defend the traditional values of Africa. The Pope wrote, "The most valid traditional values of African culture are threatened today by secularization…tribalism, violence, corruption in public life, the humiliation and exploitation of women and children, and the growth of poverty and hunger." The pope added, "If we look at the heart of the African people, we discover a great richness of spiritual resources that are precious for our age."

"God speaks to us" In his general audience at Castel Gandolfo – where he was completing his vacation – Pope Benedict XVI continued his catechesis on the "school of prayer," focusing on prayer in the Book of Revelation, "which, as you know, is the last one in the New Testament. It is a complex book, but one containing great richness. It puts us in touch with the vital, vibrant prayer of the Christian assembly, gathered 'on the Lord's day' (Rv 1:10): indeed, the text unfolds into this basic premise." He taught especially on the opening chapter of Revelation, in which God reveals himself as "the Alpha and the Omega" in which God shows himself to be "the beginning and end of history. He takes to heart the requests of the assembly. He was, is and will be present and active with his love in the midst of the events of humanity."

Mary, Model Faith On Sept. 8, Pope Benedict XVI sent a message to a conference of Marian experts in Rome and placed the upcoming Year of Faith under Mary's protection, calling her "an exemplary model of the faith" and "blessed because she believed." The participants were in Rome from Sept. 4-9 as part of the Mariological Marian International Congress, sponsored by the Pontifical Marian International Academy. The pontiff added that he hoped the conference would be "a true moment of grace in which Mary's faith precedes us and accompanies us as a bright beacon and as a model of fullness and Christian maturity."

Global Norms On Sept. 9, the Holy See announced that it had hired an outside expert in combating money laundering and financing terrorism and to assist in conforming more fully with international standards against financial crime. Rene Brulhart, a 40-year-old Swiss international lawyer, was brought in to oversee the Vatican's efforts in "all matters related to anti-money laundering and financing of terrorism." According to Vatican Radio,

Brulhart will "assist the Holy See in strengthening its framework to fight financial crimes. The decision comes as part of the on-going efforts by the Vatican to conform properly with the new tighter norms regarding financial transparency. In July, the Holy See passed a major test as administered by European finance experts, although there was still progress needed in closing crucial loopholes, according to Moneyval – the Council of Europe's Committee of Experts on the Evaluation of Anti-Money Laundering Measures and the Financing of Terrorism.

Pope Benedict XVI in Lebanon Pope Benedict XVI made an apostolic visit to Lebanon from Sept. 14-16. At the welcoming ceremony at Beirut's airport, Pope Benedict stressed the heritage of Lebanon as a model for coexistence and respectful dialogue between Catholics and Muslims, even as he noted that Lebanese society has a delicate "equilibrium, which is presented everywhere as an example, is extremely delicate. Sometimes it seems about to snap like a bow which is overstretched or submitted to pressures." He also praised the so-called Arab Spring, the effort toward democratization that began in December 2010 and hastened the collapse of dictatorships in Tunisia, Egypt, Libya, and Yemen, and that has impacted also the political upheaval in Syria.

On Sept. 14, the pontiff signed a post-synodal apostolic exhortation that reflects on the work of the 2010 special Synod of Bishops that was dedicated to the challenges facing Christians in the Middle East. Signed in a ceremony at the Melkite Catholic Basilica of St. Paul in Harissa, the exhortation, "*Ecclesia in Medio Oriente*," is 90-pages long and is the pope's reflections on the conclusions of the synod. In his introduction, he wrote: "All who took part in the Synod assembly had an experience of the unity which exists within the Catholic Church in a broad spectrum of geographical, religious, cultural and sociopolitical contexts. The common faith is practiced and made admirably evident in the diversity of its theological, spiritual, liturgical and canonical expressions…I likewise assure my Latin brothers and sisters of my affection and my concern for their needs and necessities, in accordance with the commandment of charity which presides over all, and the norms of law. [For details see under **News in Depth**, page 62.]

On May 15, the pope met with young people in the square across from the Maronite Patriarchate of Bkerké. He told them: "you are living today in this part of the world which witnessed the birth of Jesus and the growth of Christianity. It is a great honor! It is also a summons to fidelity, to love of this region and, above all, to your calling to be witnesses and messengers of the joy of Christ. The faith handed down from the Apostles leads to complete freedom and joy, as the many Saints and Blesseds of this country have shown. Their message lights up the universal Church. It can light up your lives as well. Many of the Apostles and saints lived in troubled times and their faith was the source of their courage and their witness. Find in their example and intercession the inspiration and support that you need!"

On Sept. 16, the pope celebrated an outdoor Mass at Beirut's City Center Waterfront and exhorted a crowd of more than 350,000, "Remain ever hopeful because of Christ." He focused his homily on the Gospel of St. Mark, describing Jesus as a "Messiah who suffers, a Messiah who serves, and not some triumphant political savior." He added: "Dear brothers and sisters, I pray in particular that the Lord will grant to this region of the Middle East servants of peace and reconciliation, so that all people can live in peace and with dignity. This is an essential testimony which Christians must render here, in cooperation with all people of good will. I appeal to all of you to be peacemakers, wherever you find yourselves.

"Service must also be at the heart of the life of the Christian community itself. Every ministry, every position of responsibility in the Church, is first and foremost a service to God and to our brothers and sisters. This is the spirit which should guide the baptized among themselves, and find particular expression in an effective commitment to serving the poor, the outcast and the suffering, so that the inalienable dignity of each person may be safeguarded.

"Dear brothers and sisters who are suffering physically or spiritually, your sufferings are not in vain! Christ the Servant wished to be close to the suffering. He is always close to you. Along your own path, may you always find brothers and sisters who are concrete signs of His loving presence which will never forsake you! Remain ever hopeful because of Christ! And may all of you, my brothers and sisters who have come to take part in this celebration, strive to be ever more fully conformed to the Lord Jesus, who became the Servant of all for the life of the world. May God bless Lebanon; may he bless all the peoples of this beloved region of the Middle East, and may He grant them the gift of His peace."

On Sept. 16, Pope Benedict held an ecumenical meeting at the Hall of Honor of the Syrian Catholic Patriarchate of Charfet. He declared: "Let us work without ceasing so that the love of Christ may lead us little by little into full communion with each other. In this regard, by means of common prayer and mutual commitment, we must constantly return to our one Lord and Savior…I entrust each one of you and all the members of your Churches and ecclesial communities to the Virgin Mary. May she intercede with her Son for us, so that we may be delivered from every evil and from all forms of violence, and so that the Middle East may at last know a time of reconciliation and peace."

VatiLeaks Trial On Sept. 17, a Vatican magistrate set a trial date for Sept. 29 for two men formally indicted for their role in the so-called "VatiLeaks" scandal. The first defendant, Paolo Gabriele, had served as Pope Benedict XVI's personal assistant but was indicted in August on charges of aggravated theft of a large number of secret papal documents. The second defendant, Claudio Sciarpelletti, a computer technician from the Vatican Secretariat of State, was indicted on lesser charges of aiding Gabriele. Gabriele and Sciarpelleti were to face a panel of three Vatican judges; all of the judges were to be laymen and professors at several Italian universities. Gabriele faced a sentence of one to six years in prison. By the terms

of the 1929 Lateran Treaty between the Holy See and Italy, anyone convicted by a Vatican court and sentenced to prison serves the term in an Italian prison. The VatiLeaks controversy began when secret papal letters and documents were leaked to a journalist, Gianluigi Nuzzi, who featured them on an Italian television program in January.

Jesus of Nazareth On Sept. 21, the Vatican announced that the third volume of Pope Benedict XVI's series of books on Jesus of Nazareth would be published before Christmas. The third volume would concentrate on the Gospel accounts of Jesus' infancy and childhood; it was intended to be the final part of the trilogy. According to the Vatican statement, the volume would be intended "to make known the figure and message of Jesus." The first volume of "Jesus of Nazareth," covering the period from Jesus' baptism to his Transfiguration, was published in 2007; it was followed in 2011by the second volume that covered Christ's Passion. The books were international bestsellers and were hailed by biblical scholars for their insights. Notably, they were published under the name Joseph Ratzinger and not Pope Benedict XVI.

Pope John Paul I Cause On Sept. 26, it was announced that the cause for canonization of Pope John Paul I was progressing. Albino Luciani, then cardinal of Venice, Italy, was elected on Aug. 26, 1978, as successor to Pope Paul VI; served for less than a month until his unexpected death on Sept. 28. His cause for canonization began on the diocesan level in 2003. Bp. Giuseppe Andrich of Belluno and Feltre, Italy, the diocese in which the late pope was born and where the cause was officially launched, and Bp. Enrico Dal Covolo, the postulator of the cause, announced that the positio, or major document attesting to the heroic virtues and sanctity of a candidate for canonization, would be officially submitted to the Congregation for the Causes of Saints on Oct. 17, the 100th anniversary of the late pope's birth. The positio also includes all related historical materials, a detailed biography, and historical and theological reports by relevant commissions. Notably, the postulator, Bp. Dal Covolo, serves also as rector of Rome's Pontifical Lateran University.

Consecrated Life On Sept. 24, the Vatican's Congregation for Institutes of Consecrated Life and Societies of Apostolic Life announced that it would implement its course on religious life to mark the 50th anniversary of the Second Vatican Council. The course includes both theology and canon law and would reflect on the impact of the council on consecrated life, including the call for the Church's women and men religious to return to the founding spirit and inspiration of their orders and communities.

Beatifications Two beatifications were held in September for Bl. Louis Brisson and Bl. Gabriela Maria Allegra. Bl. Louis (1817-1908) was a French priest and founder of the Oblate Sisters of St. Francis de Sales and the Oblates of St. Francis de Sales. He founded the Oblate Sisters with St. Leonie de Sales Aviat and was also the creator of an astronomic clock that was so accurate it was later studied by NASA. He was beatified on Sept. 22, 2012, at Troyes, France, in a ceremony presided over by Card. Angelo Amato, prefect of the Congregation for the Causes of the Saints. Bl. Gabriele (1907-1976) was an Italian Franciscan priest and biblical scholar, best known for his translation of the Catholic Bible into Chinese. He was beatified on Sept. 29, 2012, at Acireale, Sicily, in a ceremony presided by Card. Angelo Amato, prefect of the Congregation for the Causes of the Saints.

Vatican tribunal On Sept. 29, a Vatican tribunal overseeing the impending trial of two individuals charged with stealing Vatican documents determined that the trials should go forward, although separately. There would be two trials for the so-called VatiLeaks scandal, one for Paolo Gabriele, the papal assistant charged with aggravated theft, and one for Claudio Sciarpelletti, a computer technician in the Vatican Secretariat of State, on charges of aiding and abetting Gabriele. Gabriele appeared before the tribunal on Sept. 29.

Congo Plea On Sept. 30, Pope Benedict XVI used his weekly general audience to issue an appeal for an end to the violence in eastern Congo. The pontiff expressed his hope that peaceful settlement might be accomplished, and added his "love and concern" for the people. The bloodshed has been caused by a rebel military group, "M23," made up of former members of the Congolese military and its clash with the army. Hundreds of thousands of Congolese have fled their homes, and United Nations officials are concerned that elements of the Rwandan military are assisting M23. The pope added that his prayers were with the "refugees, women and children, who because of prolonged armed clashes are subjected to suffering, violence and deep distress."

Justice and Peace On Sept. 29, Pope Benedict XVI appointed two Catholic professors from the United States to the Pontifical Council for Justice and Peace. The professors are: Roza Pati, a professor of law at St. Thomas University School of Law in Miami, who was named a member of the Pontifical Council, and Msgr. Martin Schlag, a professor at Rome's Pontifical University of the Holy Cross, who was named a consultant to the council. Pati also serves as executive director of the graduate program in intercultural human rights, and Msgr. Schlag, is a specialist in moral theology and Catholic social teaching.

GENERAL AUDIENCE

Sept. 5, Prayer in the first part of the Book of Revelation (Rv 1:4-3:22)

Sept. 12, Prayer in the second part of the Book of Revelation (Rv 4:1-22:21)

Sept. 19, Apostolic Journey to Lebanon

Sept. 26, Prayer and the Liturgy

INTERNATIONAL

Pakistan cleric On Sept 2, a Pakistani court ordered the arrest of a Muslim cleric on suspicion of fabricating evidence against Rimsha Masih, an 11 year-old girl with Down Syndrome. She was accused by the imam Khalid Jadoon Chishti, of burning pages of the Koran, the Muslim holy book. Witnesses testified that they saw the imam take torn pages from a Koran and plant them in the little girl's bag along with some burned papers. Based on his testimony, Rimsha was arrested on Aug. 18. A Pakistan court delayed her bail hearing until Sept. 1, but it was then postponed again with the arrest of the Muslim cleric.

Abuse Conference The subject of clergy sexual abuse was the focus of a conference held from Sept. 4-5 in England, titled "Redeeming Power: Overcoming Abuse in Church and Society." The conference was sponsored by the European Society of Catholic Theology and held at St. Mary's University College in Twickenham as part of the International Network of Societies for Catholic Theology's three-year research project on "the power of theology to overcome power abuse in church and society."

Irish abuse audits On Sept. 5, the National Board for Safeguarding Children – the independent review board overseeing issues of safety in the Irish Church in the wake of the clergy sexual abuse scandal – released the results of the latest audits of the Irish dioceses' handling of abuse allegations. The report found that much progress has been made across Ireland but there were still areas of noncompliance

with agreed-upon procedures. The chief failing had to do with reporting new cases, including the lamentable fact that as recently as 2011, religious congregation were still failing to implement properly the procedure on reporting all allegations to the Congregation for the Doctrine of the Faith in Rome.

Bail for Rimsha On Sept. 7, a Pakistani court granted bail to Rimsha Masih, a young Christian girl accused of blasphemy. She was released on a bail of about $5,282, on the basis that there was insufficient evidence to justify continuing to hold her; the charges remain, however, that she blasphemed Islam by supposedly burning pages form the Koran. The case had fallen into considerable disarray owing to accusations that that the Imam Khalid Jadoon Chishti had fabricated the evidence. He was arrested on Sept. 2. Rimsha's case garnered international attention because of the accusations and also because she is an 11 year old girl with Down syndrome.

Ukrainian Catholic Bishops On Sept. 10, Ukrainian Catholic bishops from around the world assembled in Canada to discuss approaches in how to make their parishes more active, especially with regard to laypeople. There are some 4 million Ukrainian Catholics around the world, and the bishops have begun work on a strategic plan to assist pastoral care and revitalize their often far-flung parishes. The plan, "Vision 2020," examines the many challenges faced by the parish communities, including an aging population, priest morale, and outreach to young people. The strategic plan was approved by the synod of Ukrainian bishops during their 2011 gathering in Brazil.

Laypeople at funerals On Sept. 15, Abp. Patrick Kelly, the head of the Archdiocese of Liverpool gave his formal permission for lay people to preside at funerals; Liverpool that became the first diocese in England and Wales to commission laypeople to preside at funerals. Abp. Kelly formally commissioned 22 lay ministers to celebrate funeral ceremonies, The decision was taken to assist priests who are being forced to celebrate multiple funeral Masses every week. The details of the plan were revealed in a brochure, "Planning a Catholic Funeral," published by the archdiocese and that described a funeral as the "community's main celebration and prayer for the deceased. This could be a funeral Mass but ... it may be a funeral service led by a lay funeral minister or a deacon." The plan is also a reaction to the declining priest population in the archdiocese, a trend that is expected to continue over the next years.

Uruguay and Abortion On Sept. 26, the Uruguayan Chamber of Deputies approved legislation that would legalize abortion during the first trimester of pregnancy. The bill was passed by a vote of 50-49 and was to go back to the Senate for approval where it was expected to pass. President Jose Mujica stated publicly that he would not veto the bill. It stipulates that a woman would need to be interviewed by at least three health professionals and wait at a minimum of five days before confirming her decision. The approval meant that Uruguay was poised to become the second Latin American country, after Cuba, to decriminalize abortion in the first trimester of pregnancy. Elsewhere in Latin America, Argentina allows for abortions in case of rape and Colombia and Brazil permit it in the event of rape or there is the risk of death for the mother.

NATIONAL

Pro-Life Democrat? On Sept. 4, Pro-Life Democrats attending their party's national convention in Charlotte, NC, distributed buttons saying, "Do We Count?" The Democrats who feel increasingly isolated within their own party, asked at a public forum, "Can you be pro-life in a pro-choice party?"

The hopes of the Pro-Life Democrats to convince the party to soften its radical position on abortion were effectively dashed by the platform adopted by the party at the convention, and the group, Democrats for Life admitted failure but remained committed to changing the platform and the mindset of the party. Complicating the challenges of the group was the fierce opposition it has faced by the extreme pro-abortion groups, Planned Parenthood and NARAL, that are major donors and power brokers within the party.

Bart Stupak On Sept. 4, former U.S. Rep. Bart Stupak, D-Mich., spoke to a meeting of pro-life Democrats in Charlotte, NC, during the party's national convention and declared that the Department of Health and Human Services' infamous contraceptive mandate was illegal. The mandate would force many religious institutions to provide free contraceptives against their consciences. The Democrat, who provided a crucial last minute vote in favor of the 2010 Patient Protection and Affordable Care Act by negotiating an executive order with the Obama administration that guaranteed the act would not violate the Hyde Amendment, observed that the HHS mandate violates that executive order, as well as the Hyde Amendment. The mandate, imposed by HHS Secretary Kathleen Sebelius, declares that nearly all employers must include free contraception, sterilization services and abortion-inducing drugs in their health insurance policies. The extremely narrow exemptions for religious employers who object has proven so impractical that it forces Catholic employers to choose between providing coverage in violation of Catholic teaching, pay crushing annual fines in order to providing health insurance to their employees and students, or stop providing health insurance entirely.

Bishop Finn On Sept. 6, Bp. Robert W. Finn of Kansas City-St. Joseph was convicted on one count of failing to report suspected child abuse and acquitted on another count in a brief bench trial. Jackson County Circuit Judge John M. Torrence issued the verdict and gave the bishop a suspended sentence of two years' probation. The charges initially carried a possible maximum sentence of one year in jail and a fine of up to $1,000. The bishop was indicted last October on the misdemeanor charges of failing to report suspected child abuse to state authorities and was the result of the 2010 case against Fr. Shawn Ratigan who was found to have illegal images on his computer. The diocese failed to report the incident for six months. Bp. Finn issued a formal apology.

Cardinal Dolan On Sept. 6, Card. Timothy M. Dolan of New York offered the closing benediction at the Democratic National Convention in Charlotte. The Cardinal had also offered the closing benediction at the Republican National Convention and used the opportunity in both events to make a plea for religious liberty. In his benediction at the DNC, Card. Dolan pleaded, "Renew in all our people a profound respect for religious liberty: the first, most cherished freedom bequeathed upon us at our founding." His reference to religious liberty was seen as a reminder of the on-going efforts by the U.S. bishops to defend religious liberty in the face of the infamous HHS mandate from the Department of Health and Human Services that would require religious employers to offer contraceptive coverage, sterilization, and abortion-inducing drugs. Card. Dolan added: "We ask your benediction on those waiting to be born, that they may be welcomed and protected."

Philadelphia archbishop's residence On Sept. 7, St. Joseph's University announced that it would buy the archbishop of Philadelphia's residence for $10 million. The archdiocese of Philadelphia signed a letter of intent for the university to acquire the 8.9-acre property and its three-story, 23,350-square-foot mansion. The residence had been the home of the archbishops of Philadelphia since 1935. St. Joseph's president, Jesuit Fr. C. Kevin Gillespie announced, "Acquiring this adjacent property presents an opportunity that will be integral to the university's long-term strategic planning. As we look to the future, this opens exciting possibilities for the university community, and it will further enhance our students' experience for decades to come." Abp. Charles J. Chaput, the current archbishop of Philadelphia chose to reside at St. Charles Borromeo Seminary and to sell the residence as part of the effort to restore archdiocesan finances.

Missouri Legislature On Sept. 12, both houses of the Missouri Legislature voted by wide margins to override the veto of Missouri Gov. Jay Nixon of a religious liberty bill regarding the HHS contraception mandate. The legislation, SB 749, stipulates that no one should be forced to pay for contraception, sterilization, and abortion-inducing drugs as part of a health insurance plans. During a special veto session, the Missouri Senate voted 26-6 to override the veto and the House voted 109-45. Twenty-eight out of 34 senators and 105 out of 163 state representatives originally had voted for the bill. The actions of the Legislature were heavily supported by the bishops of the state and the Missouri Catholic Conference that declared that the bill "upholds religious liberty in a very practical way. Under this bill, no one can be forced to pay for surgical abortions, abortion-inducing drugs, contraceptives or sterilizations when this violates their moral or religious beliefs."

Home for priests On Sept. 15, the archdiocese of Philadelphia announced that a vacation house at the South Jersey shore used by elderly priests had been sold at auction by the archdiocese for $4.5 million. The property, Villa St. Joseph by the Sea, is a 19-room, 9,800-square-foot mansion in Ventnor, N.J., and had been owned by the archdiocese since 1963. Donna Farrell, Philadelphia's archdiocesan spokesperson, said, "An auction like this is certainly a new experience for the archdiocese. We're very pleased with the outcome." The sale of the house was part of the effort to improve the finances of the archdiocese that had a projected $6 million budget gap for the year.

Our Sunday Visitor 100th On Sept. 28, Our Sunday Visitor celebrated 100 years of "serving the church." Founded in 1912 by Fr. (later Abp.) John F. Noll to resist anti-Catholic bigotry, OSV has grown over the decades into the largest Catholic publishing and offering envelope companies in the country; there is also the OSV Institute that supports efforts at evangelization. To mark the anniversary, OSV celebrated with a centennial issue of the *OSV Newsweekly*, 128 pages in length with coverage of every year and key events in Catholicism over the century. OSV also had a special open house on May 5 to mark the actual 100th anniversary date of the first issue. Our Sunday Visitor also co-sponsored the 2012 Catholic Media Convention, held in Indianapolis, with *The Criterion*, newspaper of the Archdiocese of Indianapolis. The anniversary concluded with a series of events on the 28th including a symposium featuring Cardinal Francis E. George of Chicago, Scott Hahn, and Helen Alvaré. Following the symposium was a "Mass of rededication and thanksgiving" for Our Sunday Visitor's staff and commitment to work for the good of the Church, celebrated by Bp. Kevin C. Rhoades of Ft. Wayne-South Bend at the Cathedral of the Immaculate Conception in Ft. Wayne. After Mass, there was a dinner that featured a talk by Abp. Claudio Mari Celli, president of the Pontifical for Social Communications.

OCTOBER 2012

VATICAN

Arabic Language On Oct. 10, Pope Benedict XVI added the Arabic language to those in use during his Wednesday General Audiences. This mean as well that Arabic would be utilized during the general audience and also in all media versions emanating from the Vatican Press Office. According to Fr. Federico Lombardi, SJ, director of the Holy See Press Office, starting on Oct. 10 "a commentator will summarize in Arabic the contents of the Pope's catechesis and will translate his greetings" to the pilgrim belonging to different language groups. The decision was made in the wake of the pope's visit to Lebanon in September and the desire to expand the outreach in the Arabic language "to show his continued interest in and encouragement to Christians of the Middle East, and also to remind all of the duty to pray for peace in the Middle East."

Archbishop Tomasi on Refugees On Oct. 10, Abp. Silvano S. Tomasi, the Permanent Observer of the Holy See to the United Nations in Geneva, delivered a speech for the 63rd Session of the Executive Committee of the United Nations High Commissioner for Refugees (UNHCR), focused on the "futility of violence" and addressed the "price in suffering that hundreds of thousands of persons, mostly women and children, are paying as a consequence of political decisions that disregard their human impact." He also looked at issues of maintaining open borders for refugees who are fleeing neighboring states to escape violence and recent economic crises that are impacting food prices which in turn have a severe impact on the care of refugees. International cooperation is crucial to the easing the situation of refugees, adding that such cooperation "is a grave and unconditional moral responsibility, founded on the unity of the human race, and on the common dignity and shared destiny of rich and poor alike, who are drawn ever closer by the process of globalization."

Vatican II Booklet The Vatican newspaper "*L'Osservatore Romano*" announced on Oct. 10 that it would publish a special booklet to commemorate the 50th anniversary of the Second Vatican Council. The publication will utilize previously unpublished material, as well as photos of the then current and future popes who were present at the Council, including Karol Wojtyla, then a young bishop and the future Pope Bl. John Paul II, and then Fr. Joseph Ratzinger, the future Pope Benedict XVI, who took part as a peritus, or theological expert to the German bishops. Also included will be the introduction by Pope Benedict that were first published in the German edition of his conciliar writings.

Year of Faith Begins On Oct. 11, Pope Benedict XVI officially opened the Year of Faith with a Mass that also commemorated the 50th anniversary of the opening of the Second Vatican Council. In his homily at the opening Mass of the Year of Faith, the pontiff noted that the council gave a series of important signs: "These signs help us not only to remember, they also offer us the possibility of going beyond commemorating. They invite us to enter more deeply into the spiritual movement which characterized Vatican II, to make it ours and to develop it according to its true meaning. And its true meaning was and remains faith in Christ, the apostolic faith, animated by the inner desire to communicate Christ to individuals and all people, in the Church's pilgrimage along the pathways of history." He added that the Year of Faith is "linked harmoniously with the Church's whole path over the last 50 years: from the Council, through the Magisterium of the Servant of God Paul VI, who proclaimed a Year of Faith in 1967, up to the Great Jubilee of the year 2000, with which Blessed John Paul II re-proposed to all humanity Jesus Christ as the one Savior, yesterday, today and forever. Between these two Popes, Paul VI and John Paul II, there was a deep and profound convergence, precisely upon Christ as the center of the cosmos and of history, and upon the apostolic eagerness to announce him to the world."

Connecting the anniversary of the council with the Year of Faith and the immense project of the New Evangelization, the pope taught that the task before the Church is "is to revive in the whole Church that positive tension, that yearning to announce Christ again to contemporary man. But, so that this interior thrust towards the new evangelization neither remain just an idea nor be lost in confusion, it needs to be built on a concrete and precise basis, and this basis is the documents of the Second Vatican Council, the place where it found expression…If today the Church proposes a new Year of Faith and a new evangelization," the Holy Father continued, "it is not to honor an anniversary, but because there is more need of it, even more than there was 50 years ago! And the reply to be given to this need is the one desired by the Popes, by the Council Fathers, and contained in its documents."

Legion of Christ On Oct. 11, the Legion of Christ released a statement that the current General Director of the Legion of Christ, Fr. Alvaro Corcuera, LC, had requested a sabbatical for health reasons. In response to the request, Card. Velasio De Paolis, the Delegate of the Pope for Regnum Christi and the Legion of Christ, had temporarily relieved him of his duties as General Director which would be assumed by the current Vicar General, Fr. Sylvester Heereman, LC; this state of affairs would continue until the General Chapter which was expected to be held at the end of 2013 or the beginning of 2014. In a letter regarding the sabbatical, Card. De Paolis, wrote, Fr. Alvaro's "efforts carried out in a climate that was frequently one of suffering and misunderstanding, have weakened his energies to the point of causing us to fear that if he continued his efforts, especially in this year leading up to the General Chapter we might have compromised his health." Fr. Alvaro assumed the post in the horrendous aftermath of the scandal of the Legion's founder, the late Fr. Maciel.

Torchlight Procession On Oct. 12, Pope Benedict XVI addressed tens of thousands of pilgrims who had gathered in St. Peter's Square for a Torchlight Procession organized by Italian Catholic Action to commemorate the 50th Anniversary of the Second Vatican Council. The event gave the pontiff an opportunity to reflect on the council and its start half a century before. He said that Pope Blessed John XXIII, had spoken then with "unforgettable words, words full of poetry, of kindness; words of the heart…We were happy – I would say – and full of enthusiasm. The great Ecumenical Council had begun; we were sure that a new springtime for the Church was coming, a new Pentecost, with a new strong presence of the liberating grace of the Gospel. He added that in the intervening 50 years, the Church has seen that "in the field of the Lord there are always weeds…We have seen that human frailty is present in the Church as well, that the ship of the Church is sailing against the current, with storms that threaten the ship and sometimes we thought: 'The Lord sleeps and he has forgotten us.'" And yet, he added, Christ is always present: "Yes, Christ lives, and he is with us today as well, and we can also be happy today because his goodness does not extinguish, it is strong even today."

Holy See- Equatorial Guinea Accord On Oct. 15, an official accord was signed between the Holy See and the Republic of Equatorial Guinea that recognizes the juridical personality of the Church and its institutions, among them canonical marriage, places of worship and spiritual care of the sick and imprisoned. The accord was signed in the city of Mongomo, and in attendance were the President of the Republic, Mr. Theodore Obiang Nguema Mbasogo, along with the Minister of Foreign Affairs Mr. Agapito Mba Mokuy, as well as Abp. Piero Pioppo, titular archbishop of Torcello and Apostolic Nuncio of Equatorial Guinea. The accord included 19 articles and an additional protocol.

Seven New Saints On Oct. 22, Pope Benedict XVI presided at the canonization of seven new saints for the Church, including two saints of great importance to the Church in the United States, St. Kateri Tekakwitha, the first Native American to be canonized by the Church, and St. Marianne Cope, Mother Marianne, a member of the Sisters of the Third Order of St. Francis in Syracuse who devoted her life to care of lepers in the islands of Hawaa and who cared for St. Damien of Molokai (canonized in Oct. 2009) in his last years as he died from leprosy. In addition, the other saints were: St. Pedro Calungsod, a young Filipino catechist; St. Jacques Berthieu, a priest of the society of Jesus; St. Giovanni Battista Piamarta, Italian priest and founder of the Congregation of the Holy Family of Nazareth and of the Congregation of the Humble Sister Servants of the Lord; St. Maria del Carmen, Spanish foundress of the Conceptionist Missionary Sisters of Teaching; and St. Anna Schäffer, a German laywoman. Speaking of Kateri Tekakwitha, he proclaimed, "Kateri impresses us by the action of grace in her life in spite of the absence of external help and by the courage of her vocation, so unusual in her culture. In her, faith and culture enrich each other! May her example help us to live where we are, loving Jesus without denying who we are. St. Kateri, Protectress of Canada and the first native American saint, we entrust to you the renewal of the faith in the first nations and in all of North America! May God bless the first nations!"

Regarding Mother Marianne, the pope said, "Only one year old when taken to the United States, in 1862 she entered the Third Order Regular of St. Francis at Syracuse, New York. Later, as Superior General of her congregation, Mother Marianne willingly embraced a call to care for the lepers of Hawaii after many others had refused. She personally went, with six of her fellow sisters, to manage a hospital on Oahu, later founding Malulani Hospital on Maui and opening a home for girls whose parents were lepers. Five years after that she accepted the invitation to open a home for women and girls on the island of Molokai itself, bravely going there herself and effectively ending her contact with the outside world. There she looked after Father Damien, already famous for his heroic work among the lepers, nursed him as he died and took over his work among male lepers. At a time when little could be done for those suffering from this terrible disease, Marianne Cope showed the highest love,

courage and enthusiasm. She is a shining and energetic example of the best of the tradition of Catholic nursing sisters and of the spirit of her beloved St. Francis."

Pope Benedict noted also that the canonization Mass came during the Synod of Bishops on the New Evangelization and World Mission Sunday, adding that the new saints show us how "to bear witness and to proclaim the Christian message, configuring ourselves to Christ and following His same way of life. This is true both for the '*missio ad Gentes*' and for the New Evangelization in places with ancient Christian roots. The Son of Man came to serve, and to give His life as a ransom for many. These words were the existential blueprint of the seven blessed men and women that the Church solemnly enrolls this morning in the glorious ranks of the saints. They are sons and daughters of the Church who chose a life of service following the Lord. Holiness always rises up in the Church from the well-spring of the mystery of redemption."

Reflecting on the passage from the Gospel of Mark, "The Son of Man came to serve, and to give his life as a ransom for many" (cf. Mk 10:45), the pope taught: "These words were the blueprint for living of the seven Blessed men and women that the Church solemnly enrols this morning in the glorious ranks of the saints. With heroic courage they spent their lives in total consecration to the Lord and in the generous service of their brethren. They are sons and daughters of the Church who chose a life of service following the Lord. Holiness always rises up in the Church from the well-spring of the mystery of redemption, as foretold by the prophet Isaiah in the first reading: the Servant of the Lord is the righteous one who "shall make many to be accounted as righteous; and he shall bear their iniquities" (Is 53:11); this Servant is Jesus Christ, crucified, risen and living in glory. Today's canonization is an eloquent confirmation of this mysterious saving reality. The tenacious profession of faith of these seven generous disciples of Christ, their configuration to the Son of Man shines out brightly today in the whole Church."

Ratzinger Prize On Oct. 22, Pope Benedict XVI bestowed the Ratzinger Prize on two recipients for their work in advancing theology and philosophy. During a ceremony held in the Clementine Hall of the Vatican Apostolic Palace and in the presence of the heads of the Synod of Bishops, the pontiff awarded the prize to Prof. Rémi Brague of France, a layman and a scholar of the philosophy of religions, and Fr. Brian E. Daley, S.J., of the United States, an expert in historical theology with the specialization in patristic theology. The award was established by the "Joseph Ratzinger-Benedict XVI Vatican Foundation," founded in 2010 to "promote the publication, distribution and study of the writings of former university professor Joseph Ratzinger."

Paolo Gabriele Sentence On Oct. 23, the Vatican tribunal holding the trial of the former papal butler, Paolo Gabriele, who had been charged with the aggravated theft of private documents belonging to Pope Benedict XVI published its verdict. At a press conference on the matter, Fr. Federico Lombardi, Director of the Holy See Press Office, discussed the sentence and stressed that the tribunal had defined "the juridical terms of the offence of theft; i.e., the removal and appropriation of an object without the consent of its owner with the intent of obtaining some benefit...the benefit Gabriele sought to gain was not economic in nature, but intellectual and moral." There was an expectation that Pope Benedict would ultimately pardon Gabriele or reduce the sentence.

New Cardinals On Oct 26, Pope Benedict made the surprise announcement that he had appointed six new members of the College of Cardinals and would install them in the College in a consistory of Nov. 24. The appointments were unexpected, especially as a consistory had been held last February. The new Cardinals were: Abp. Michael James Harvey, Prefect of the Papal Household, who was also named Archpriest of the Papal Basilica of St. Paul Outside the Walls; His Beatitude Bechara Boutros Rai, Patriarch of Antioch of the Maronites (Lebanon); His Beatitude Baselios Cleemis Thottunkal, Major Archbishop of Trivandrum of the Syro-Malankars (India); Abp. John Olorunfemi Onaiyekan, Abp. of Abuja (Nigeria); Abp. Rubén Salazar Gomez, Archbishop of Bogotá (Colombia); Abp. Luis Antonio Tagle, Abp. of Manila (Philippines). The new Cardinals represented a clear effort to advance internationalization in the College, most so after the consistory in February that was comprised chiefly of Europeans in general and Italians in particular. In his announcement, Pope Benedict XVI taught, "Cardinals have the task of helping the Successor of Peter in carrying out his Ministry of strengthening his brethren in the faith and of being the principle and foundation of the unity and communion of the Church."

Final Message of the Synod On Oct. 26, the Bishops participating in the Synod of Bishops on the New Evangelization presented their final message that examined the theme: "The New Evangelization for the Transmission of the Christian Faith." A press conference was to issue the final message presided over by Card. Giuseppe Bertori, Abp. of Florence and present of the Commission for the Message; Abp. Pierre-Marie Carre of Montpellier, France, special secretary, and Card.-elect Luis Antonio G. Tagle of Manila, Philippines, secretary of the Commission for the Message. In its introduction, the message declares: "Leading the men and women of our time to Jesus, to an encounter with him is a necessity that touches all the regions of the world, those of the old and those of the recent evangelization. Everywhere indeed we feel the need to revive a faith that risks eclipse in cultural contexts that hinders its taking root in persons and its presence in society, the clarity of its content and the coherence of its fruits. It is not a matter of starting again, but of entering into the long path of proclaiming the Gospel with the apostolic courage of Paul who would go so far as to say "Woe to me if I do not preach the Gospel!" (1 Cor 9:16). Throughout history, from the first centuries of the Christian era to the present, the Gospel has edified communities of believers in all parts of the world. Whether small or great, these are the fruit of the dedication of generations of witnesses to Jesus – missionaries and martyrs – whom we remember with gratitude.

In his Mass closing the Synod, Pope Benedict taught, "The new evangelization applies to the whole of the Church's life. It applies, in the first instance, to the ordinary pastoral ministry that must be more animated by the fire of the Spirit, so as to inflame the hearts of the faithful who regularly take part in community worship and gather on the Lord's day to be nourished by his word and by the bread of eternal life. I would like here to highlight three pastoral themes that have emerged from the Synod. The first concerns the sacraments of Christian initiation. It has been reaffirmed that appropriate catechesis must accompany preparation for Baptism, Confirmation and Eucharist. The importance of Confession, the sacrament of God's mercy, has also been emphasized. This sacramental journey is where we encounter the Lord's call to holiness, addressed to all Christians. In fact it has often been said that the real protagonists of the new evangelization are the saints: they speak a language intelligible to all through the example of their lives and their works of charity. Second, the new evangelization is essentially linked to the *Missio ad Gentes*. The Church's task is to evangelize, to proclaim the message of salvation to those who do not yet know Jesus Christ. During the Synod, it was emphasized that there are still many regions in Africa, Asia and Oceania whose inhabitants await with lively expectation, sometimes without being fully aware of it, the first proclamation of the Gospel. So we must ask the Holy Spirit to arouse in the Church a new missionary dynamism, whose progatonists are, in particular, pastoral workers and the lay faithful. Globalization has led to a remarkable migration of peoples. So the first proclamation is needed even in countries that were evangelized long ago. All people have a right to know Jesus Christ and His Gospel: and Christians, all Christians – priests, religious and lay faithful – have a corresponding duty to proclaim the Good News. A third aspect concerns the baptized whose lives do not reflect the demands of Baptism. [See also **News in Depth**, page 75, for full coverage of the Synod.]

Pope and Cypriot President On Oct. 26, Pope Benedict XVI received in audience Demetris Christofias, president of the Republic of Cyprus at the Vatican Apostolic Palace. The president also met with Vatican Secretary of State Cardinal Tarcisio Bertone and Abp. Dominique Mamberti, secretary for Relations with States. In a communique released by the Holy See, discussions were cordial and noted the excellent relations between the Holy See and the Republic of Cyprus. There was also discussion of "issues of mutual interest, in particular the importance of dialogue and of respect for human rights, including the right to religious freedom... The hope was expressed that initiatives for dialogue and peace between the sides in conflict in the Middle East would achieve a positive outcome with the contribution of the international community.

Bertone on the Gabriele Sentence On Oct. 26, the Vatican Secretariat of State issued a communique regarding the sentence of Paolo Gabriele, the former papal butler who was convicted of stealing private papal documents and began serving his 18-month prison term. The statement stressed the seriousness of the offenses: "A personal offense was done to the Holy Father; the right to privacy of the many people [...] was violated [...] and scandal was caused among the community of the faithful...The accused admitted his guilt at the end of a judicial process which took place transparently and justly, and with full respect for the rights of the defense." The statement also noted that there was still a possibility of a pardon.

General Audiences

Oct. 3, "Do I leave enough room for prayer?"
Oct. 10, 50th Anniversary of the Council
Oct. 17, Catechesis on the Year of Faith
Oct. 24, Catechesis on the Year of Faith
Oct. 31, Catechesis on the Year of Faith

INTERNATIONAL

Syrian Orthodox School Attack On Oct. 22, a Syrian Orthodox School in Aleppo was attacked by a homemade mortar, an ominous event that pointed to potentially deteriorating conditions in Syria which is in the grips of a deepening civil war. The mortar struck the Bani Taghieb I School, which includes kindergarten classes. A statement made by the Abp. of Aleppo declared: "At this juncture it is rather difficult and frankly irrelevant to know the source of the mortar. Missiles fall relentlessly and indiscriminately, day and night over all residential districts of Aleppo. Considering that the Sulaimania District is one of the hot spots of the city of Aleppo, it has its fair share. The missiles cause an untold toll of martyrdom, fatalities, injuries and great damages to utilities, infrastructure and antiquities of the oldest inhabited city in the World...

"We believe it is high time that belligerent brothers should get together to discuss the need to bring about ceasefire, co-operate to re-establish security and bring back the life to our beloved city, so Aleppians can celebrate Eid and festivities in the usual joyful customary ways and usher the start of a new era of reform and justice."

Priests Kidnapped in Congo On Oct. 23, it was announced that three priests had been kidnapped from their parish of Notre-Dame des Pauvres in Mbau, in the north-eastern side of the Democratic Republic of Congo. The priests, Jean-Pierre Ndulani, Anselme Wasikundi and Edmond Bamutute, are members of the Assumptionist Fathers and are all natives of the Congo. The announcement was made by the Secretary of the Commission for social communications of the National Episcopal Conference of the Congo (CENCO), Bp. Melchisedec Sikuli Paluku of Butembo-Beni, who made a plea for the release of the priests even as he discussed the growing crisis in parts of Congo in which rebel groups and government forces have been engaged in a fierce struggle since 2004. He observed, "We have appealed to the general mobilization not only of the police and other security forces, but also to the population of the area to provide us with information on the kidnappers' movements. We have asked the faithful to pray so that God touches the hearts of the kidnappers and release our fathers."

NATIONAL

Decline in Institutional Religion On Oct. 12, the Pew Forum on Religion and Public Life published a survey bringing together a number of studies and polls titled, "Nones on the Rise: One-in-Five Adults Have No Religious Affiliation." The report confirmed that religious affiliation has declined significantly in the United States and used the term "religiously unaffiliated" instead of "nones" while noting that those who declare no affiliation do believe in God and describe themselves as religious or spiritual. According to the report, in the last five years, the percentage of those religiously unaffiliated has risen from 15.3 to 19.6% of the adult population. This increases to a third for adults under 30 years of age, while only 9% among those 65 and over are religiously unaffiliated. The report points to a serious generational change taking place, with young adults trending toward a status of being religiously unaffiliated.

In a related issue, the study found that for the first time since the Pew surveys started the Protestant share of the adult population has dipped below 50%. In 2007, 53% of adults in Pew Research Center surveys described themselves as Protestants. By the first half of 2012 only 48% of American adults said they are Protestant. The decline was especially significant among white Protestants, both evangelical and mainline. The result is that while one-fifth of whites now see themselves as religiously unaffiliated, the percentage of blacks and Hispanics who are religiously unaffiliated has not changed by a statistically significant margin in recent years.

In contrast, the Catholic share of the population has held steady in recent years, although the findings note that this is due to the continuing number of immigrants from Latin America.

While many in the media suggested that the Pew Poll pointed to a decline in religion in the United States the report found that the United States remains a highly religious country as the number of Americans who say religion is very important in their lives is at 58%, only a marginal decline from recent years. The number is also significantly higher than in Britain (17%), France (13%), Germany (21%) or Spain (22%).

Of the 46 million adults who describe themselves as unaffiliated, 68% say they believe in God. Equally, the number of declared atheists or agnostics is only 6% of adults. More than a third of respondents declare that they are spiritual, but not religious, and 21% say they pray every day. Moreover, the report found that a majority of respondents among the religiously unaffiliated think that religion is a positive force, and 78% say that religious organizations bring people together and help strengthen community bonds; a similar number saying religious organizations play an important role in helping the poor and needy.

One cautionary note is that two-thirds of American adults, including 63% of the religiously unaffiliated, say religion as a whole is losing its influence on American life, while a large majority of those who think religion's influence is on the decline see this as a bad thing.

In the area of social policy, the Pew Poll found that religiously unaffiliated Americans are about twice as likely to describe themselves as political liberals and are generally in favor of legalized abortion and same-sex marriage. This has also meant that the religiously unaffiliated vote in majority numbers for the Democratic Party. This is also consistent with the trends in recent elections in which religiously unaffiliated tend to be younger. A third of unaffiliated adults, 35%, are under age 30, compared with 22% of the general population. There are more men, 56%, than women, 44%. And only 39% of the unaffiliated are married, compared with 51% of the general public.

Memorial of Blessed John Paul II On Oct. 22, the Vatican Congregation for Divine Worship gave its formal approval to the insertion of the optional memorial of Bl. John Paul II in the proper calendar of the dioceses of the United States and provided the proper liturgical texts for observance of the Memorial in the Mass and Divine Office. Last Nov., the U.S. bishops at their meeting in Baltimore, MD, voted overwhelmingly to request the addition of the memorial of the beloved late pope to the U.S. liturgical calendar. The Office of Readings includes an excerpt from Pope John Paul's homily at his inauguration as pope in 1978, "Do not be afraid, Open, I say open wide the doors for Christ."

NOVEMBER 2012

VATICAN

Communion with the Living God On Nov. 4, Pope Benedict XVI used his homily at Mass in honor of the cardinals, archbishops and bishop who had died over the past year to speak about death and life. He taught: "The atmosphere of the Communion of Saints and the Commemoration of the Faithful Departed is present and alive in our hearts. The liturgy has enabled us to live it intensely in the celebrations of the past few days. In particular, visiting cemeteries has allowed us to renew our bond with those loved ones who have left us; death, paradoxically, preserves what life cannot retain. We discover how our deceased lived, what they loved, feared and hoped, what they rejected, in a singular way from their tombs, that have remained almost as a mirror of their existence, of their world — challenging us and inducing us to reestablish a dialogue that death has put in jeopardy. Thus, the burial places are a kind of assembly, in which the living meet their dead and reaffirm the bonds of communion that death was unable to stop. And here in Rome, in these singular cemeteries, namely the catacombs, we see, as in no other place, the deep links to early Christianity, that we feel so close. When we step into the corridors of the catacombs in Rome — as in those cemeteries in our cities and in our towns — it is as though we were crossing an immaterial threshold and entering into communication with those who guard their past, made of joy and sorrow, of loss and of hope there. This happens because death concerns man today just as it did then; and even if many things of the past have become estranged to us, death remains the same."

Among the deceased prelates who had died in the previous year were: Cardinals John Patrick Foley, Anthony Bevilacqua, José Sánchez, Ignace Moussa Daoud, Luis Aponte Martínez, Rodolfo Quezada Toruño, Eugênio de Araújo Sales, Paul Shan Kuo-hsi, Carlo Maria Martini, and Fortunato Baldelli.

Vatican Trial On Nov. 5, a Vatican tribunal opened a second criminal trial related to the so-called VatiLeaks scandal involving the theft of papal papers. The trial of Claudio Sciarpelletti, 48, a computer technician in the Vatican Secretariat of State, centered around his aiding and abetting Paolo Gabriele, the papal butler, who was convicted in October of aggravated theft for stealing or photocopying private Vatican correspondence. Gabriele was sentenced to 18 months in jail.

Pope and Obama On Nov. 7, Pope Benedict XVI sent a telegram of congratulations to Pres. Barack Obama on his re-election. The telegram, sent via Abp. Carlo Maria Vigano, the apostolic nuncio to the United States, declared, "In the message, the Holy Father sent his best wishes to the president for his new term and assured him of his prayers that God might assist him in his very great responsibility before the country and the international community." The pope added that he hoped that "the ideals of liberty and justice that guided the founders of the United States of America might continue to shine."

Aid for Syria On Nov. 7, the Holy See announced that the planned visit by a papal delegation to Syria was cancelled owing to safety concerns and that in its place a smaller group would visit to Lebanon and deliver a $1 million donation to assist the humanitarian response to the mounting crisis. Pope Benedict XVI also spoke of the crisis in his general audience, saying, "We have to do everything possible because one day it could be too late. I renew my invitation to the parties in conflict, and to all those who have the good of Syria at heart, to spare no effort in the search for peace and to pursue through dialogue the path to a just coexistence, in view of a suitable political solution of the conflict. I continue to follow with great concern the tragic situation of violent conflict in Syria, where the fighting has not ceased and each day the toll of victims rises, accompanied by the untold suffering of many civilians, especially those who have been forced to abandon their homes.

INTERPOL On Nov. 6, Abp. Dominique Mamberti, Secretary for Relations with States, addressed the eighty-first session of the general assembly of the International Criminal Police Organization (INTERPOL), which was being held in Rome on the theme: "Challenges for police facing contemporary criminal violence." In his address, the archbishop observed, "crime has undergone a substantial increase, both in quantitative terms and as regards the use of violence. The characteristics of criminal activity have evolved in a worrying fashion, as the aggression and atrocity of incidents has augmented dangerously. Furthermore, criminal activities have now assumed a planetary scale, with systems of coordination and criminal pacts which traverse national frontiers. The struggle against all forms of violence, especially in its most brutal forms, presupposes a moral duty to help create the conditions necessary to ensure violence does not arise and develop. People who work with the forces of law and order, and the police organizations you represent, are well aware that the most effective antibody to any form of criminality is a country's citizens. Alliance and solidarity between citizens and police is the strongest bastion against criminality."

Burundi and the Holy See On Nov. 8, a framework agreement was signed between the Holy See and the Republic of Burundi on "matters of common interest" in Bujumbura, Burundi. The agreement was signed by the Head of State, Pierre Nkurunziza and Abp. Franco Coppola, the apostolic nuncio of Burundi. It notes that diplomatic ties between Burundi and the Holy See have been historically friendly and guaranteed the legal status of the Church in Burundi, including canonical marriage, places of worship, schools and religion in schools, and pastoral care in the armed forces, prisons, and hospitals.

Christians and Hindus On Nov. 8, Card. Jean-Louis Tauran and Fr. Miguel Ayuso Guixot, respectively the president and secretary of the Pontifical Council for Interreligious Dialogue issued their annual letter to Hindus for the feast of Diwali that would begin on Nov. 13. The letter called on Hindus and Christians "form young men and women into people of peace and builders of peace is an urgent summons to collective engagement and common action. If peace is to be authentic and enduring, it must be built on the pillars of truth, justice, love and freedom (cf. John XXIII, *Pacem in Terris*, No. 35), and all young men and women need to be taught above all to act truthfully and justly in love and freedom. Furthermore, in all education for peace, cultural differences ought surely to be treated as a richness rather than a threat or danger.

"The family is the first school of peace and the parents the primary educators for peace. By their example and teachings, they have the unique privilege of forming their children in values that are essential for peaceful living: mutual trust, respect, understanding, listening, sharing, caring and forgiving. In schools, colleges and universities, as young people mature by relating, studying and working with others from different religions and cultures, their teachers and others responsible for their training have the noble task of ensuring an education that respects and celebrates the innate dignity of all human beings and promotes friendship, justice, peace and cooperation for integral human development. With spiritual and moral values as the bedrock of education, it becomes their ethical imperative also to caution the students against ideologies that cause discord and division."

Pontifical Academy of Sciences On Nov. 9, Pope Benedict XVI addressed the members of the Pontifical Academy of Sciences who gathered in Rome for a plenary assembly on the theme: "Complexity and Analogy in Science: Theoretical, Methodological and Epistemological Aspects." Speaking on the theme, the pontiff noted that it "touches on an important subject which opens up a variety of perspectives pointing towards a new vision of the unity of the sciences. Indeed, the significant discoveries and advances of recent years invite us to consider the great analogy of physics and biology which is clearly manifested every time that we achieve a deeper understanding of the natural order. If it is true that some of the new notions obtained in this way can also allow us to draw conclusions about processes of earlier times, this extrapolation points further to the great unity of nature in the complex structure of the cosmos and to the mystery of man's place within it. The complexity and greatness of contemporary science in all that it enables man to know about nature has direct repercussions for human beings. Only man can constantly expand his knowledge of truth and order it wisely for his good and that of his environment.

"In our time, the availability of powerful instruments of research and the potential for highly complicated and precise experiments have enabled the natural sciences to approach the very foundations of corporeal reality as such, even if they do not manage to understand completely its unifying structure and ultimate unity. The unending succession and the patient integration of various theories, where results once achieved serve in turn as the presuppositions for new research, testify both to the unity of the scientific process and to the constant impetus of scientists towards a more appropriate understanding of the truth of nature and a more inclusive vision of it."

The Holy Father ended by saying, "In the great human enterprise of striving to unlock the mysteries of man and the universe, I am convinced of the urgent need for continued dialogue and cooperation between the worlds of science and of faith in the building of a culture of respect for man, for human dignity and freedom, for the future of our human family and for the long-term sustainable development of our planet. Without this necessary interplay, the great questions of humanity leave the domain of reason and truth, and are abandoned to the irrational, to myth, or to indifference, with great damage to humanity itself, to world peace and to our ultimate destiny."

Vatican Trial Verdict On Nov. 10, a Vatican tribunal convicted Claudio Sciarpelletti, a computer expert in the Secretariat of State, of aiding and abetting the papal butler, Paolo Gabriele who was convicted of stealing papal and Vatican correspondence in October. The three-judge tribunal sentenced Sciarpelletti to four months in jail, but the sentence was reduced to two months owing to the decision that Sciarpelletti had no prior record. The Vatican court had indicted Sciarpelletti in August.

Latin Academy On Nov. 10, it was announced that Pope Benedict XVI had established a new Pontifical Academy of Latinity to promote the study of the Latin language and culture. In his *motu proprio* founding the academy, the pope wrote, "Even in our own time the knowledge of the Latin language and culture is more necessary than ever for the study of the sources from which, among others, numerous ecclesiastical disciplines draw, for example, theology, liturgy, patristics and canon law, as the Second Vatican Ecumenical Council teaches…precisely in our world in which science and technology play such a prominent role, we find a renewed interest for the Latin culture and language, not only on those continents that have their roots in the Greco-Roman legacy. Such attention appears more important not only insofar as it involves academic and institutional spheres, but as it regards young people and scholars from nations of very different traditions." The academy is intended to reach out beyond even the Church – whose official language remains Latin – to the wider world. In his decree founding the academy the pope declared that it should promote the study of Latin, particularly in Catholic schools, universities and seminaries and assist new generations to learn Latin, "including through the use of modern means of communications." Pope Benedict appointed Ivano Dionigi, 64, a Latinist and rector of the Alma Mater Studiorum at the University of Bologna, as the new head of the academy; Fr. Roberto Spataro, S.D.B., secretary of the Pontifical Institute for Higher Latin Studies at the Pontifical Salesian University in Rome was named secretary. The academy is under the authority of the Pontifical Council for Culture, headed by Card. Gianfranco Ravasi.

Benedict and the Elderly On Nov. 12, Pope Benedict XVI visited a Rome residence for the elderly and urged the residents to understand their old age as a sign of God's blessing. The pontiff expressed his solidarity with the elderly being advanced in years himself. He declared, "Though I know the difficulties that come with being our age, I want to say, it's wonderful being old."

Liturgical art, architecture, and music On Nov. 14, the Congregation for Divine Worship and the Sacraments announced that it had established an office to promote the development and use of appropriate liturgical art, architecture, and music. The office is intended to provide advice, encouragement, and guidance, but it would not be expected to impose specific forms or styles of music and architecture in the area of liturgy.

College of Cardinals On Nov. 24, Pope Benedict XVI created six new cardinals during a consistory held at the Vatican. The new Cardinals were: Luis Tagle of Manila, Philippines; Lebanon's Maronite Patriarch of Bechara Rai; James M. Harvey; Baselios Cleemis Thottunkal of India, head of the Syro-Malankara Catholic Church; John Olorunfemi Onaiyekan of Nigeria; and Ruben Salazar Gomez of Colombia. In his homily, Pope Benedict focused on the teaching that the Church is "one, holy, catholic, and apostolic." He declared: "Jesus sends his Church not to a single group, then, but to the whole human race, and thus he unites it, in faith, in one people, in order to save it. The Second Vatican Council expresses this succinctly in the Dogmatic Constitution *Lumen Gentium*: "All men are called to belong to the new people of God. Therefore this people, while remaining one and unique, is to be spread throughout the whole world and through every age, so that the design of God's will may be fulfilled" (No. 13). Hence the universality of the Church flows from the universality of God's unique plan of salvation for the world. This universal character emerges clearly on the day of Pentecost, when the Spirit fills the first Christian community with his presence, so that the Gospel may spread to all nations, causing the one People of God to grow in all peoples. From its origins, then, the Church is oriented *kat'holon*, it embraces the whole universe. The Apostles bear witness to Christ, addressing people from all over the world, and each of their hearers understands them as if they were speaking his native language (cf. Acts 2:7-8). From that day, in the "power of the Holy Spirit," according to Jesus' promise, the Church proclaims the dead and risen Lord "in Jerusalem and in all Judea and Samaria and to the end of the earth" (Acts 1:8). The Church's universal mission does not arise from below, but descends from above, from the Holy Spirit: from the beginning it seeks to express itself in every culture so as to form the one People of God. Rather than beginning as a local community that slowly grows and spreads outwards, it is like yeast oriented toward a universal horizon, toward the whole: universality is inscribed within it."

The pope said to the Cardinals, "From now on, you will be even more closely and intimately linked to the See of Peter: the titles and deaconries of the churches of Rome will remind you of the bond that joins you, as members by a very special title, to this Church of Rome, which presides in universal charity. Particularly through the work you do for the Dicasteries of the Roman Curia, you will be my valued co-workers, first and foremost in my apostolic ministry for the fullness of catholicity, as Pastor of the whole flock of Christ and prime guarantor of its doctrine, discipline and morals."

General Audiences

Nov. 7, Catechesis on the Year of Faith
Nov. 14, Catechesis on the Year of Faith
Nov. 21, Catechesis on the Year of Faith
Nov. 28, Catechesis on the Year of Faith

INTERNATIONAL

Nigerian Peace On Nov. 2, Abp. Felix Job of Ibadan, Nigeria, criticized a government plan to open dialogue with the radical Boko Haram Islamic sect that has killed thousands of Nigerians over the last years. The archbishop questioned the logic of negotiating with the violent sect and giving credibility to it.

Same-sex marriage in France On Nov. 8, French bishops and prominent leaders in the family life movement of France stated publicly that they would resist all efforts to advance legislation allowing same-sex couples to marry and adopt. Card. André Vingt-Trois, president of the French Bishops' Conference and archbishop of Paris, met with Antoine Renard, president of France's National Federation of Catholic Family Associations, to try and slow the advance of the legislation.

Irish children On Nov. 10, voters in Ireland approved a referendum that delineates rights for children, a first in the country's history. The referendum was supported by 58 percent of voters, with 42 percent voting against it. Prime Minister Enda Kenny, speaking on the vote, said in a statement, "It is a historic day for the children of Ireland as it is the first time the constitution of this republic will recognize them as citizens in their own right. The passing of this amendment will help make childhood a good, secure and loving space for all our children. It will also give hope, reassurance and confidence to parents, foster parents and vulnerable children." The Irish bishops gave their guarded support to the referendum.

Australian child sexual abuse On Nov. 13, Card. George Pell of Sydney expressed his full cooperation and support for a royal commission examining the issue of sexual abuse of children in the country, including the history of the failures in Church leadership in the area. Australia's Prime Minister, Julia Gillard, announced that the federal government will convoke a royal commission to investigate institutions, including the Church, as well as government institutions, non-profit organizations, and other churches. A statement issued by the president of the Australian Catholic Bishops Conference, Abp. Denis Hart, and the permanent committee of the conference welcomed the announcement of the royal commission, stating, "As Catholic bishops and as individuals we share the feelings of horror and outrage which all decent people feel when they read the reports of sexual abuse and allegations of cover ups...Over the past 20 years, there have been major developments in the way the Church responds to victims, deals with perpetrators and puts in place preventive measures. Sexual abuse of children is not confined to the Catholic Church. Tragically, it occurs in families, churches, community groups, schools and other organizations. We believe a Royal Commission will enable an examination of the issues associated with child abuse nationally, and identify measures for better preventing and responding to child abuse in our society.

Card. Pell added in statement, "Public opinion remains unconvinced that the Catholic Church has dealt adequately with sexual abuse. Ongoing and at times one sided media coverage has deepened this uncertainty. This is one of the reasons for my support for this Royal Commission. I welcome the Prime Minister's announcement. I believe the air should be cleared and the truth uncovered."

NATIONAL

HHS mandate suit On Nov. 1, a federal district court judge in Ann Arbor granted a Michigan business, Weingartz Supply Co., a temporary injunction from the Health and Human Services' contraceptive mandate. The judge also dismissed a lawsuit filed by a nonprofit Catholic group, Legatus, because he found that the religious organization qualified for the Obama administration's temporary so-called "safe harbor" from complying with the mandate. The judge did also rule, however, that the federal government had to provide monthly updates on the status of the process for amending final regulations. The HHS mandate requires all employers, including most religious employers, to cover the costs of contraceptives, sterilizations, and abortion-inducing drugs.

Obama Re-election On Nov. 7, Card. Timothy M. Dolan of New York, president of the U.S. Conference of Catholic Bishops, gave his congratulations to Pres. Barack Obama on his re-election. In a letter, Dolan wrote, "The people of our country have again entrusted you with a great responsibility. The Catholic bishops of the United States offer our prayers that God will give you strength and wisdom to meet the difficult challenges that face America." Card. Dolan also assured him of the bishops' prayers that Obama would "help restore a sense of civility to the public order, so our public conversations may be imbued with respect and charity toward everyone. In particular, we pray that you will exercise your office to pursue the common good, especially in care of the most vulnerable among us, including the unborn, the poor, and the immigrant. We will continue to stand in defense of life, marriage and our first, most cherished liberty, religious freedom."

Ballot Initiatives The 2012 election brought a variety of ballot measures that impacted the defense of life. By a very narrow margin, voters in Massachusetts narrowly defeated a "death with dignity" measure that halted efforts to legalize assisted suicide. The Massachusetts initiative, known as Question 2, was defeated by fewer than 39,000 votes, a result that indicated the divisive nature of the proposed measure. In an e-mail statement, Card. Sean P. O'Malley of Boston expressed his satisfaction with the outcome, writing, "The campaign against physician assisted suicide brought together a diverse coalition from medical, disability rights and interfaith communities, all dedicated to ensuring that our residents were well informed on the issue." In California, an initiative to end the use of the death penalty was defeated, but four states, Maine, Maryland, Minnesota, and Washington, all approved ballot measures legalizing same-sex marriage. The ballot measures marked setbacks for the Catholic bishops in each state and the efforts of many organizations to defeat the ballots.

Religious Liberty On Nov. 4, Abp. Carlo Maria Viganó, the apostolic nuncio to the United States, gave a speech at the University of Notre Dame and warned that the "menace to religious liberty is concrete on many fronts," including the United States. The address was given during the "Seed of the Church: Telling the Story of Today's Christian Martyrs" Conference, held at the University of Notre Dame, and it was entitled "Religious Freedom, Persecution of the Church, and Martyrdom."

The archbishop pointed to the Health and Human Services' contraceptive mandate as an example of a threat to religious liberty, but he added that this is just one of various attacks on "authentic and legitimate exercise of religious freedom" in the country. He listed, for example, threats to religious liberty when Catholic Charities agencies across the country are "being removed from vital social services that advance the common good because the upright people administering these programs would not adopt policies or engage in procedures that violate fundamental moral principles of the Catholic faith."

He added: "We must all be mindful that our Lord noted, time and again, that each member of the Church – clerical, religious, and lay – is a branch on the vine of Christ. In our unity with Him, we are a part of something universal – one faith, one belief displayed through a variety of talents, in a multiplicity of places. This is what our Lord asks us to do, and, therefore, this is what we must do: to preach and live the Good News and to do so in communion with our Lord, with the successors of His apostles, and with His Vicar. It is our faith, and it is our duty to live and proclaim the Gospel through the Church's teachings so that by reasoned proposition, not imposition, God's will and our discipleship can advance the common good for every member of the human family... And so, let us go into the Lord's vineyard together, with love, hope, freedom, the firmness of the convictions of our faith, and the help that God so willingly extends to us. We have been appointed by God and His holy Church to go forth and bear much fruit. Let us do so with the freedom and its necessary complement, responsibility, which God has given us. We further know that Christ is the way, the truth, and the life. What God has given, the servant state does not have the competence to remove. And God has given us the truth of His Son, the truth who gives us the most precious freedom of all, which is the desire to be with God forever! This is our destiny, and this is why religious freedom as I have explained it is of paramount importance. It is essential to the exercise of our other rights and responsibilities as citizens of the Two Cities.

LCWR Reform On Nov. 12, three bishops met with the heads of the Leadership Conference of Women Religious to discuss the mandated reform of the organization of women religious. The meeting was held in Baltimore just before the start of the U.S. Bishops' annual fall general assembly.

New Preaching Document On Nov. 12, the U.S. bishops at their fall meeting in Baltimore approved the first new document in 30 years on preaching. The document, "Preaching the Mystery of Faith: The Sunday Homily," encourages homilists to engage in a pastoral style that makes the connection between the homily and the lives of their flocks. Prepared by the U.S. Conference of Catholic Bishops' Committee on Clergy, Consecrated Life and Vocations, chaired by Abp. Robert J. Carlson of St. Louis, with subsequent review and comment by eight other USCCB committees, the document says: "The homily is intended to establish a 'dialogue' between the sacred biblical text and the Christian life of the hearer. Preachers should be aware, in an appropriate way, of what their people are watching on television, what kind of music they are listening to, which websites they find appealing, and which films they find compelling." The vote was 227-11, with four abstentions; approval required two-thirds of the membership of the U.S. Conference of Catholic Bishops, or 182 votes.

Sacrament of Penance On Nov. 12, the U.S. Bishops at their fall general meeting approved a document that would encourage Catholics to take advantage of the sacrament of penance. The text was prepared by the Bishops' Committee on Evangelization and Catechesis, chaired by Bp. David L. Ricken of Green Bay and is based on the Gospel of John after Jesus arose and told the Apostles: "Receive the Holy Spirit. Whose sins you forgive are forgiven them." The vote was 236-1 and required approval of two-thirds of the bishops.

Blessed Francis Seelos On Nov. 13, the U.S. Bishops during their annual fall general assembly in Baltimore approved by a vote of 213-1 with one abstention to expand a liturgical memorial for Blessed Francis Xavier Seelos, a German-born Redemptorist priest who served in the United States; approval required a two-thirds vote of the Latin-rite bishops with subsequent confirmation by the Vatican Congregation for Divine Worship and the Sacraments. Seelos was beatified in 2000, and his feast day is Oct. 5.

Dorothy Day On Nov. 13, the U.S. Bishops, on a voice vote, endorsed the cause for canonization of Dorothy Day, the co-founder of the Catholic Worker movement. The endorsement was required canonical consultation for a new cause, according to the 2007 Vatican document "*Sanctorum Mater.*"

DECEMBER 2012

VATICAN

Benedict on Advent On Dec. 2, Pope Benedict XVI gave his Sunday Angelus and reflected on Advent, noting that it marked the start of a new liturgical year, "a journey that is subsequently enriched by the Year of Faith, which we observe 50 years after the opening of the Second Vatican Council." He taught that, "The first part of this journey is Advent, constituted, in the Roman Rite, by the four weeks that precede the Christmas of the Lord, that is, the mystery of the Incarnation. The word 'advent' means 'coming' or 'presence.' In the ancient world it indicated the visit of the king or emperor to a province; in the language of Christianity it refers to the coming of God, to His presence in the world; a mystery that involves the entire cosmos and all of history, but that knows two culminating moments: the first and the second coming of Jesus Christ. The first is precisely the Incarnation; the second His glorious return at the end of time.

These two moments that are chronologically distant – and it is not given to us to know how distant – touch each other in their depths, because with his death and resurrection Jesus has already realized that transformation of man and the cosmos that is the final goal of creation. But before the end, it is necessary that the Gospel be preached to all nations, Jesus says in the Gospel of St. Mark (cf. Mk 13:10). The Lord's coming continues, the world must be penetrated by his presence.

@Pontifex On Dec. 3, the Holy See Press Office officially announced Pope Benedict XVI's presence on Twitter and that the Holy Father would send out his first tweet on Dec. 12, Feast of Our Lady of Guadalupe, under the username @pontifex. At the press conference were Fr. Federico Lombardi, director of the Holy See Press Office; Abp. Claudio Maria Celli, pres. of the Pontifical Council for Social Communication; Professor Gian Maria Vian, director of *L'Osservatore Romano*; and Dr. Greg Burke, Media Advisor to the Vatican Secretary of State. Also present at the press conference was Dr. Claire Diaz-Ortiz, Director of Social Innovation for Twitter. Abp. Celli declared, "The desire of this Pontiff is to enter into dialogue with the man and woman of today, and to speak with them in places where they are found…The problem is not 140 characters; the main concern is to give profound human expression to the words that are given." Celli likewise announced a variety of other initiatives by the Pontifical Council for Social Communication, including a YouTube page for news.va, an e-book on the Year of Faith, and a mobile app, called "The Pope App" available on smartphones and iphones.

First Indian Martyr Beatified On Dec. 4, Devasahayam Pillai (1712-52) was beatified in his native diocese of Kottar, in the state of Tamil Nadu, in India, exactly 300 years after his birth; he is the first Indian lay martyr to be beatified. The beatification Mass was celebrated by Card. Angelo Amato, prefect of the Congregation for the Causes of Saints, along with Cards. Oswald Gracias and Telesphore Toppo, both from India. Pillai converted to the Christian faith and was baptized in 1745; he took the name Devasahayam, the Tamil translation of the biblical name Lazarus, which means "God has helped." He subsequently suffered horrendous tortures from Hindu authorities who arrested him in 1749 and demanded he renounce his new faith. He died at the hands of his captors.

Peace in the Congo On Dec. 5, Pope Benedict XVI made a public plea for peace in the Democratic Republic of Congo. The country has been plagued in recent months with renewed violence, the residents of the region around the provincial capital of Goma reported rebels had been responsible for mass killings, child soldier recruitment and mass rapes. According to Vatican Radio, the U.N. humanitarian agency OCHA reported that at least 130,000 people had been displaced. The Holy Father implored: "I therefore renew my call for dialogue and reconciliation and ask the international community to work to provide for the needs of the population."

President of Germany On Dec. 6, Pope Benedict XVI received in audience Joachim Gauck, president of the Federal Republic of Germany at the Vatican Apostolic Palace. The German president also met with Vatican Secretary of State Card. Tarcisio Bertone and Msgr. Ettore Balastrero, under-secretary for Relations with States. In a communique released by the Holy See, stress was placed on the cordial relations between the Holy See and the Federal Republic of Germany, and it noted that the discussions included the issues being raised by globalization and the secularization of society and "a fruitful exchange of opinions on the international situation and the current economic crisis, especially in relation to its consequences in Europe, and the contribution that the Catholic Church may offer."

Archbishop Georg Gänswein It was announced on Dec. 7 that Pope Benedict XVI had named Msgr. Georg Gänswein, personal secretary of the Holy Father, as Prefect of the Pontifical Household, at the same time elevating him to the titular see of Urbisaglia with the title of Archbishop. The archbishop-elect had served as the personal secretary to then-Card. Ratzinger from 1996 and became papal secretary in 2005 with the election of Ratzinger as Pope Benedict XVI. Archbishop-elect Gänswein was born in Waldshut, Germany, in 1956 and was ordained a priest in 1984 for the Archdiocese of Freiburg im Breisgau. He was named to the Congregation for Divine Worship and the Discipline of the Sacraments in 1995. It was noted in the announcement that Archbishop-elect Gänswein would continue to serve as papal secretary.

Religious Freedom in Europe On Dec. 7, Abp. Dominique Mamberti, secretary for Relations with States, addressed the 29th meeting of the Council of Ministers of the Organization for Security and Cooperation in Europe (OSCE), held in Dublin, Ireland. In his address, Abp. Mamberti spoke of religious freedom, noting, "Among the fundamental freedoms, the right to freedom of religion figures prominently for the Holy See. The OSCE has always emphasized the positive contributions of religious communities to society. In this sense, the activity of the OSCE has ensured that public debate gives space to viewpoints inspired by a religious vision in all its dimensions, including ritual, worship, education, dissemination of information and the freedom to profess and choose one's religion. In fact, the rights associated with religion are all the more in need of protection if they are considered to clash with a prevailing secular ideology or with majority religious positions of an exclusive nature." He also pointed to the discrimination being faced by Christians who "are frequently targets of prejudice and threats of violence, perhaps on account of their active participation in public conversations to form societies more respectful of human life and dignity."

International Congress on "Ecclesia in America" On

Dec. 10, Pope Benedict XVI addressed the participants of the International Congress "Ecclesia in America" on the Church in the American continent that had been organized by the Pontifical Commission for Latin America and the Knights of Columbus in collaboration with the Institute for Guadalupan Studies; it took as its purpose to reflect on the work of the Synod of Bishops in 1997 under the title of "Encounter with the living Jesus Christ: The way to conversion, communion and solidarity in America." The Holy Father spoke to the participants on the themes, declaring, "Today these themes merit review in order to put Christ's redeeming message into practice with greater diligence, in the hope of reaping abundant rewards of sanctity and ecclesial renewal…In effect, Jesus Christ's love and the power of His grace must take root ever more intensely in the hearts of the people, families and Christian communities of your nations, to allow them to progress with dynamism along the paths of harmony and fair progress." He pointed especially to the contemporary challenges of secularism.

The First Papal Tweet On Dec. 12, Pope Benedict XVI sent out his first tweet on Twitter using the account @ pontifex. The tweet, sent via iPad, said: "Dear friends, I am pleased to get in touch with you through Twitter. Thank you for your generous response. I bless all of you from my heart. In a communique from the Holy See Press Office, the Holy Father was assisted by Thaddeus Jones, a representative of the Pontifical Council for Social Communication, and Claire Díaz-Ortiz, director of Social Innovation for Twitter. Since the announcement on Dec. 3, the Twitter account gained 700,000 followers in multiple languages. A second tweet asked: "How can we celebrate the Year of Faith better in our daily lives?" A third tweet said: "By speaking with Jesus in prayer, listening to what he tells you in the Gospel and looking for him in those in need."

New Ambassadors On Dec. 13, Pope Benedict XVI received in audience six new ambassadors and non-resident ambassadors to the Holy See today. They were: Bizwayo Newton Nkunika of Zambia, Chalermpol Thanchitt of Thailand, Ravinatha Pandukabhaya Aryasinha of Sri Lanka, Wafic Rida Said of St. Vincent and the Grenadines, Aminatou Batoure Gaoh of Niger and Ibrahima Sory Sow of Guinea. The Pope, focusing on education, said to them: "Schools and universities seem to have become incapable of creative projects leading to a transcendental teleology able to attract young people in the very depths of their being. Today's world and its responsible adults are not able to provide them with the necessary points of reference. I again urge your governments to have the courage to strengthen and consolidate the moral authority – the call to a coherent way of life – necessary for a genuine and healthy education for the younger generations."

Message for World Day of Peace On Dec. 14, Card. Peter Kodwo Appiah Turkson, president of the Pontifical Council for Justice and Peace along with Bp. Mario Toso, secretary of the same Council, presented Pope Benedict XVI's Message for the 46th World Day of Peace. The message was written under the theme, "Blessed are the peacemakers." Reflecting on it, Card. Turkson observed, "It states a fact – the existence, in the midst of conflicts, tension and violence, of numerous peacemakers; in the explanation of the Gospel beatitude it explains that this is a promise that is guaranteed, in that it is made by God and does not refer merely to the future but already finds fulfillment in this life."

Pope and Newtown Victims On Dec. 17, Pope Benedict XVI expressed his spiritual closeness to the victims of a shooting at an elementary school in Newtown, CT. A gun-man opened fire at Sandy Hook Elementary School on Dec. 14, killing 26 people, 20 of them children, before committing suicide. The suspect in the killings had also murdered his mother before proceeding to the school. The pope said, "I was deeply saddened by Friday's senseless violence in Newtown, Connecticut. I assure the families of the victims, especially those who lost a child, of my closeness in prayer. May the God of consolation touch their hearts and ease their pain…Upon those affected by this tragedy, and upon each of you, I invoke God's abundant blessings!"

In the immediate aftermath of the shooting, the papal Secretary of State, Card. Tarcisio Bertone, released a message on the Pope's behalf: "The Holy Father was promptly informed of the shooting at Sandy Hook Elementary School in Newtown and he has asked me to convey his heartfelt grief and the assurance of this closeness in prayer to the victims and their families, and to all affected by the shocking event. In the aftermath of this senseless tragedy he asks God, our Father, to console all those who mourn and to sustain the entire community with the spiritual strength which triumphs over violence by the power of forgiveness, hope and reconciling love."

Benedict XVI and Mahmoud Abbas On Dec. 17, Pope Benedict XVI received in audience Mahmoud Abbas, president of the Palestinian Authority, at the Vatican Apostolic Palace. After the meeting, Abbas had a meeting with the papal Secretary of State, Card. Tarcisio Bertone, and Abp. Dominique Mamberti, secretary for Relations with States. In a communique released by the Holy See, it was reported that discussions focused on the recent resolution approved by the United Nations General Assembly that recognized Palestine as a Non-member Observer State.

Papal Twitter Account On Dec. 18, it was announced that Pope Benedict XVI's Twitter account, @Pontifex, had surpassed two million followers since the account was opened on Dec. 3. The first papal tweets were sent out in eight languages following the Dec. 12 General Audience.

Financial Times On Dec. 20, the *Financial Times* of London, England, published an article written by Pope Benedict XVI which appeared in the *Financial Times*. The editorial staff of the *Times* had made the invitation to the pope, and he had accepted. The article presented a meditation on Christmas, the politicization of religion, the deification of temporal power, and authentic liberation. The Pope wrote, "The birth of Christ challenges us to reassess our priorities, our values, our very way of life. While Christmas is undoubtedly a time of great joy, it is also an occasion for deep reflection, even an examination of conscience. At the end of a year that has meant economic hardship for many, what can we learn from the humility, the poverty, the simplicity of the crib scene? Christmas can be the time in which we learn to read the Gospel, to get to know Jesus not only as the child in the manger, but as the one in whom we recognize that God made man. It is in the Gospel that Christians find inspiration for their daily lives and their involvement in worldly affairs – be it in the Houses of Parliament or the stock exchange. Christians should not shun the world; they should engage with it. But their involvement in politics and economics should transcend every form of ideology." In its byline, the *Financial Times* described the pontiff: "The writer is the Bishop of Rome and author of *Jesus of Nazareth: The Infancy Narratives*."

Decrees for Saint Causes On Dec. 20, Pope Benedict XVI received Card. Angelo Amato, Prefect of the Congregation for the Causes of Saints in a private audience and authorized the decree regarding over 30 Blesseds, Venerables, and

Servants of God, meaning that their causes could proceed to the next relevant stages. Notably, among the decrees was one that recognized the Heroic Virtue of the Servant of God, Pope Paul VI, who died in 1978.

Pope's Address to the Curia On Dec. 21, Pope Benedict XVI met with Cardinals, members of the Roman Curia, and the Governorate of Vatican City State and delivered the annual Christmas address and New Years greetings. In his remarks, the pope reflected on his travel during the year, including the trip to Mexico and Cuba and Lebanon, the Meeting of Families that had taken place in Milan, the need for religious dialogue, and the urgency of the New Evangelization. Speaking of dialogue, the pope declared, "the search for knowledge and understanding always has to involve drawing closer to the truth. Both sides in this piece-by-piece approach to truth are therefore on the path that leads forward and towards greater commonality, brought about by the oneness of the truth. We do not possess the truth, the truth possesses us: Christ, Who is the truth, has taken us by the hand, and we know that His hand is holding us securely on the path of our quest for knowledge."

Pope Benedict XVI's Urbi et Orbi Message On Christmas Day, Pope Benedict XVI delivered his annual *Urbi et Orbi* message. It took as its theme, *"Veritas de terra orta est!"* – "Truth has sprung out of the earth"(Ps 85:12): "'If we believe.' Here we see the power of faith! God has done everything; he has done the impossible: he was made flesh. His all-powerful love has accomplished something which surpasses all human understanding: the Infinite has become a child, has entered the human family. And yet, this same God cannot enter my heart unless I open the door to him. *Porta fidei!* The door of faith! We could be frightened by this, our inverse omnipotence. This human ability to be closed to God can make us fearful. But see the reality which chases away this gloomy thought, the hope that conquers fear: truth has sprung up! God is born! "The earth has yielded its fruits" (Ps 67:7).

General Audiences

Dec. 5, Catechesis on the Year of Faith
Dec. 12, Catechesis on the Year of Faith
Dec. 19, Mary in Advent

INTERNATIONAL

Christian Attacked in Pakistan On Dec. 4, a lay Protestant Christian missionary was attacked in Lahore, capital of the province of Punjab, in Pakistan. The victim, Bargeeta Almby, a 72-year-old missionary from Sweden, was shot at in her car by two men on a motorcycle, according to the Fides News Agency. She was struck at least once in the chest. Almby has served in Pakistan for the last 38 years.

"Ecclesia in America" On Dec. 10, Card. Marc Ouellet, Prefect for the Congregation of Bishops and president of the Pontifical Council for Latin America, celebrated Mass at the opening of a three day International Congress on the post-synodal exhortation, Ecclesia in America, that was issued by Pope John Paul II in 1999. The congress marks the 15th anniversary of the Synod of Bishops for America. In his homily, Card. Ouellet noted the words of John Paul in the exhortation: "On the threshold of the third Christian millennium and at a time when many walls and ideological barriers have fallen, the Church feels absolutely duty-bound to bring into still deeper spiritual union the peoples who compose this great continent and also, prompted by the religious mission which is proper to the Church, to stir among these peoples a spirit of solidarity."

United Kingdom Same-Sex Marriage On Dec. 12, Abp. Vincent Nichols and Abp. Peter Smith, president and vice-president of the Catholic Bishops' Conference of England and Wales respectively, issued a joint statement following the British government's publication of a response to the "Equal Civil Marriage" consultation; the government announced that it would press ahead in 2013 with legislation to redefine marriage in law to permit same-sex couples to marry. The statement by the archbishops declared in part: "The meaning of marriage matters. It derives that meaning from its function as the foundation of the family. The union of one man and one woman for love and mutual support and open to procreation has over the centuries formed a stable unit we call the family. Marriage is the enduring public recognition of this commitment and has been rightly recognized as unique and worthy of legal protection…We strongly oppose such a Bill."

Drop in Christians On December 12, the British Office for National Statistics released a new survey that revealed that the number of people self-identifying as Christian has declined from 37.3 million (72%) in 2001 to 33.2 million (59%), in 2011. The Conference of Catholic Bishops of England and Wales issued a statement that, "The overall decrease in the number of self-identifying Christians is consistent with recent social attitude and social value surveys. While this is a challenge, the fact that six out of 10 people in England and Wales self-identify as Christians is not discouraging. Christianity is no longer a Religion of culture, but a Religion of decision and commitment. People are making a positive choice in self-identifying as Christians. While precise figures are difficult to determine, polling shows that the Catholic population has remained consistent at 9% of the total population for many years."

"Reproductive Health" Bill On Dec. 13, the Philippine House and Senate narrowly approved the controversial RH (reproductive health) bill. Approval was by a vote of 113-104. Card. Luis Tagle, archbishop of Manila, issued a statement that "aside from promoting the use of artificial contraceptives, the measure also imposes a condition, which according to critics, discriminates poor people…The vote in favor of the RH bill in Congress is unfortunate and tragic…We do not take it as a defeat of truth – for truth shall prevail, especially the truth about human life, marriage and the family. This vote leads us to further commit the Church, specifically the Archdiocese of Manila, to the service of the poor, of the family, of women, of infants and children," the cardinal added. "We will work harder to promote the sanctity of human life and of the human person, the integral education of the youth, the access of the poor to social and medical services, the preservation of the true meaning of marriage, and stewardship of creation."

Nuns Join Ordinariate On Dec. 13, eleven nuns from an Anglican community of women were received into the Catholic Church in the Personal Ordinariate of Our Lady of Walsingham in England. The sisters are members of the Community of St. Mary the Virgin (CSMV) in Wantage, Oxfordshire. The Personal Ordinariate of Our Lady of Walsingham was established by then-Pope Benedict XVI to ease the process by which Anglicans and Episcopalians can enter the Church.

NATIONAL

Supreme Court on Marriage On Dec. 10, the U. S. Supreme Court decision to hear the case challenging California's Proposition 8 and a case challenging the federal Defense of Marriage Act (DOMA). A statement issued by Abp. Salvatore Cordileone of San Francisco, chairman of the U.S. Bishops' Subcommittee for the Promotion and Defense of Marriage, declared: "The U.S. Supreme Court's decision to hear these cases is a significant moment for our nation. I pray the Court will affirm the fact that the institution of marriage, which is as old as humanity and written in our very nature, is the union of one man and one woman. Marriage is the foundation of a just society, as it protects the most vulnerable among us, children. It is the only institution that unites children with their mothers and fathers together. We pray for the Court, that its deliberations may be guided by truth and justice so as to uphold marriage's true meaning and purpose." In 2008, California voters passed Proposition 8, defining marriage in California's State Constitution as the union of one man and one woman. DOMA was passed by Congress and signed into law by Pres. Bill Clinton in 1996; it defined marriage as the union of one man and one woman for purposes of federal law. The Supreme Court is expected to rule by next June.

Connecticut Shooting On Dec. 14 the town of Newtown, in the diocese of Bridgeport, was shattered by the massacre of 20 six- and seven-year-old school children and six staff from Sandy Hook Elementary School; the alleged shooter also killed his mother and himself. Catholic parishes and officials issued a variety of statements, including one by Abp. William Lori of Baltimore, the former bishop of Bridgeport, that stated in part: "Along with you, and along with the rest of our nation and, indeed, the rest of the world, I was shocked and horrified to learn of what had taken place in Newtown so suddenly and terribly on Friday morning. I was in Rome for meetings, and it was early evening there when I heard. Since that moment, my heart has been heavy, and I can't stop thinking about everyone in Newtown, especially the victims, the children, and their families. So I just wanted to say very sincerely and simply that I am close to all of you in my thoughts and prayers right now. We cannot allow ourselves to lose hope, but indeed, now more than ever, must strengthen one another through our friendships in Christ, and our unity of faith in him and his resurrection."

Call for Action On Dec. 21, Bps. Stephen E. Blaire of Stockton, John C. Wester of Salt Lake City, and Kevin C. Rhoades of Fort Wayne-South Bend issued a statement calling for action in the aftermath of the terrible shooting in Newtown, CT. The statement read in part: "In the face of the horrific evil that occurred at Sandy Hook Elementary School on Dec. 14, 2012, as people of faith we first and foremost turn to God and pray. We pray for those whose lives were robbed from them. As Catholic Bishops, we join together with the President of our Conference, Card. Timothy Dolan, who on the day of the horrible tragedy expressed his profound solidarity with and prayers for the families, friends, neighbors, and communities whose hearts have been rent by the loss of a child or loved one. No words can capture their suffering. We look to Christ, his words and deeds, and ultimately to his Cross and Resurrection. It is in Jesus that we place our hope.

The Sandy Hook tragedy has caused great anguish for parents and others who attempt to safeguard our children. In addition to the outpouring of prayers and support from around the nation, understandably this tragedy has given rise to discussions about national policies and steps that can be taken to foster a culture that protects the innocent and those most vulnerable among us. It is time for our nation to renew a culture of life in our society.

Sacred Scripture reminds us time and again to "be not afraid." Indeed, we must find within ourselves the faith-filled courage to address the challenges our nation faces, both in our homes and in our national policies. These challenges encompass many areas with various complexities. Here, we offer particular words regarding the issue of the regulation of fire arms, the standards for the entertainment industry, and our service to those with mental health needs. As religious leaders, we are compelled to call on all Americans, especially elected leaders, to address these issues.

With regard to the regulation of fire arms, first, the intent to protect one's loved ones is an honorable one, but simply put, guns are too easily accessible. The Vatican's Pontifical Council for Justice and Peace, in their document, "The International Arms Trade (2006)," emphasized the importance of enacting concrete controls on handguns, for example, noting that "limiting the purchase of such arms would certainly not infringe on the rights of anyone."

Second, our entertainers, especially film producers and video game creators, need to realize how their profit motives have allowed the proliferation of movies, television programs, video games and other entertainment that glorify violence and prey on the insecurities and immaturity of our young people. Such portrayals of violence have desensitized all of us. The massacre of 20 little children and seven adults causes each of us to reflect on our own understanding of the value of human life. We must improve our resources for parents, guardians and young people, so that they can evaluate entertainment products intelligently. We need to admit that the viewing and use of these products has negative emotional, psychological and spiritual effects on people.

We must also reflect on our own fears as we grapple with our prejudices toward those with mental health needs. Our society must provide health services and support to those who have mental illnesses and to their families and caregivers. As a community we need to support one another so no one feels unable to get help for a mentally ill family member or neighbor in need. Burdensome healthcare policies must be adjusted so people can get help for themselves or others in need. Just as we properly reach out to those with physical challenges we need to approach mental health concerns with equal sensitivity. There is no shame in seeking help for oneself or others; the only shame is in refusing to provide care and support.

The events in Newtown call us to turn to our Lord in prayer and to witness more profoundly Christ's perfect love, mercy and compassion. We must confront violence with love.

There are glimmers of hope in this tragedy. Many people, including some of the victims, made extraordinary efforts to protect life. In particular, the teachers, the principal, the children, the first responders and other leaders showed tremendous courage during the tragedy. Some sacrificed their own lives protecting others.

In their memory and for the sake of our nation, we reiterate our call made in 2000, in our statement, Responsibility, Rehabilitation and Restoration: A Catholic Perspective on Crime and Criminal Justice, for all Americans, especially legislators, to: 1.Support measures that control the sale and use of firearms 2.Support measures that make guns safer (especially efforts that prevent their unsupervised use by children and anyone other than the owner) 3.Call for sensible regulations of handguns 4.Support legislative efforts that seek to protect society from the violence associated with easy access to deadly weapons including assault weapons 5.Make a serious commitment to confront the pervasive role of addiction and mental illness in crime. As we long for the arrival of the Prince of Peace in this Advent and Christmas season, we call on all people of goodwill to help bring about a culture of life and peace."

JANUARY 2013

VATICAN

Solemnity of the Mother of God On Jan. 1, Pope Benedict XVI celebrated the Solemnity of Mary, the Mother of God with a Mass at St. Peter's Basilica. The celebration also marked the 46thWorld Day of Peace under the theme: "Blessed are the Peacemakers." The concelebrants for the Mass were Card. Tarcisio Bertone, Vatican Secretary of State; Card. Peter Kodwo Appiah Turkson, President of the Pontifical Council for Justice and Peace, and Abp. Dominique Mamberti, Secretary for Relations with States. In his homily, the pontiff spoke of the vocation to peace, adding: "In every person the desire for peace is an essential aspiration which coincides in a certain way with the desire for a full, happy and successful human life. In other words, the desire for peace corresponds to a fundamental moral principle, namely, the duty and right to an integral social and communitarian development, which is part of God's plan for mankind. Man is made for the peace which is God's gift. All of this led me to draw inspiration for this Message from the words of Jesus Christ: 'Blessed are the peacemakers, for they will be called children of God' (Mt 5:9)."

The Holy Father went on to say that the beatitude in particular is both a divine gift as well as one brought by the fruit of human effort. Citing the readings of the day, Pope Benedict said that the root of how one can obtain peace can be found in the Gospel of Luke. The Holy Father recalled the Virgin Mary's "even tempered" demeanor though not finding room at the inn. The pope added, "This is the interior peace which we ought to have amid the sometimes tumultuous and confusing events of history, events whose meaning we often do not grasp and which disconcert us." The Holy Father called on the faithful to contemplate on Jesus Christ. By doing so, he said, one may feel the "same security that a child feels in the arms of a loving and all-powerful Father. The splendor of the face of God, shining upon us and granting us peace, is the manifestation of his fatherhood: the Lord turns his face to us, he reveals himself as our Father and grants us peace. Here is the principle of that profound peace – 'peace with God' – which is firmly linked to faith and grace, as St. Paul tells the Christians of Rome."

Pope Benedict also said that this peace cannot be taken from believers, even in the most difficult circumstances of one's life. Concluding his homily, the Holy Father invoked the Virgin Mary to aid all in contemplating the face of Christ. "May she sustain us and accompany us in this New Year: and may she obtain for us and for the whole world the gift of peace," the Pope said.

Pope Benedict XVI Baptizes 20 Infants On Jan. 14, Pope Benedict XVI celebrated the Feast of the Baptism of the Lord and used the occasion to baptize 20 children. In his homily, the pontiff focused on Jesus' own baptism of penance and conversion in the River Jordan. "Was Jesus," he asked, "in need of penitence and conversion? Certainly not; And yet ... he wanted to place himself alongside the sinners ... expressing God's nearness. ... He demonstrates solidarity with us, with the weariness we feel in trying to convert, trying to leave aside our selfishness, trying to tear ourselves away from our sins, in order to tell us that, if we accept Him in our lives, He is capable of lifting us back up and leading us to the height of God the Father." Addressing the baptism of the 20 children, the Pope taught: "The heavens have also opened over your children and God says: these are my children with whom I am well pleased," the Holy Father said to the parents of those baptized. "Included in this relationship and freed from original sin they become living members of the one body that is the Church and become capable of fully living their call to holiness so that they might inherit the eternal life obtained for us through Jesus' resurrection."

Freedom of Conscience On Jan. 16, Abp. Dominique Mamberti, secretary for the Holy See's Relations with States, spoke on Vatican Radio about the recent decisions of the European Court of Human Rights regarding freedom of conscience and religion on the part of several employees in the United Kingdom. The cases centered around employees who were dismissed from their workplace for refusing to remove small crosses around their necks and freedom to object in conscience to the celebration of a civil union between people of the same sex and to conjugal counseling for same sex counseling. Abp. Mamberti declared: "In both cases, the rights to freedom of association and freedom of expression were invoked in order to constrain religious communities to act in a manner contrary to their canonical status and the Magisterium. Thus, these cases call into question the Church's freedom to function according to her own rules and not to be subject to civil rules other than those necessary to ensure that the common good and just public order are respected." He added the need to protect religious freedom in its social dimension: "This dimension corresponds to the essentially social nature both of the person and of the religious fact in general. The Church does not ask that religious communities be lawless zones but that they be recognized as spaces for freedom, by virtue of the right to religious freedom, while respecting just public order. This teaching is not reserved to the Catholic Church; the criteria derived from it are founded in justice and are therefore of general application."

Manual for Mass On Jan. 16, the Congregation for Divine Worship and the Sacraments announced that it was preparing a booklet to assist priests in the celebration of Mass properly and to help the faithful to participate more fully. Card. Antonio Cañizares, prefect of the congregation, announced the title of the booklet would be "Catholic Liturgy since Vatican II: Continuity and Evolution."

Georg's 89th Birthday On Jan. 15, the Pope's older brother, Georg Ratzinger, celebrated his 89th birthday. Georg was born Jan. 15, 1924, at Pleiskirchen, in Bavaria, Germany. Ordained with his brother Joseph on June 29, 1951, Georg became choirmaster at Traunstein in 1957, and then director of the *voix blanches* choir at Regensburg in 1964, the famed *Regensburger Domspatzen*, a post he held until his retirement in 1994. In 2011, a book-length interview was published with him, titled *My Brother the Pope*.

Vietnamese Leader On Jan. 22, Nguyen Phu Trong, the general secretary of the Central Committee of the Communist Party of Vietnam, visited Benedict XVI in the Vatican. He also met with the papal Secretary of State, Card. Tarcisio Bertone, and Abp. Dominique Mamberti, secretary for Relations with States. The meeting with the pope was the first time that a general secretary of the Communist Party of Vietnam had met with the Supreme Pontiff and other officials of the Secretariat of State. In a communique, the Holy See noted the "cordial discussions on topics of interest to Vietnam and the Holy See ... expressing the hope that some pending situations may be resolved and that the existing fruitful cooperation may be strengthened."

Papal Tweet On Jan. 25, Pope Benedict XVI tweeted a message of support to the hundreds of thousands of pro-lifers who marched in Washington, D.C., to mark the anniversary of the infamous Supreme Court decision in 1973 that legalized abortion. The march was held on the 40th anniversary of *Roe vs. Wade*. The Pontiff tweeted: "I join all those marching for life from afar, and pray that political leaders will protect the unborn and promote a culture of life." Abp. Carlo Viganò, apostolic nuncio to the United States, announced that he would take part in the west coast Walk for Life in San Francisco.

Curial Changes On Jan. 25, Pope Benedict XVI issued two documents that changed the oversight of seminaries and Catechesis within the Roman Curia. The first document, *"Ministrorum Institution"* modifies the 1988 apostolic constitution *Pastor Bonus*, transferring oversight of seminaries from the Congregation for Catholic Education to the Congregation for the Clergy. The pope declared that he found it opportune "to assign the promotion and governance of everything regarding the formation, the life, and the ministry of priests and deacons to the Congregation for the Clergy: from the pastoral care for vocations and the selection of candidates for Holy Orders – including their personal, spiritual, doctrinal, and pastoral formation in seminaries and special centers for permanent deacons – to their permanent formation–including living conditions and procedures for exercising their ministry and their welfare and social assistance."

The second document, *"Fides per doctrinam,"* transferred responsibility for catechesis from the Congregation for the Clergy to the Pontifical Council for Promoting New Evangelization. In his letter, the pontiff wrote: "Faith needs to be supported by doctrine that is capable of illuminating the minds and hearts of believers. This particular historical moment in which we are living, marked among other things by a dramatic crisis of faith, requires an awareness that is able to respond to the high expectations that arise in the hearts of believers when facing the new questions that challenge the world and the Church. Understanding faith, therefore, always requires that its content be expressed in a new language, one capable of presenting the living hope of believers to those inquiring into its purpose."

World Day of Sick On Jan. 29, Abp. Zygmunt Zimowski, president of Pontifical Council for Pastoral Assistance to Health Care Workers, held a press conference at which he presented Pope Benedict XVI's message for the 21st World Day of the Sick. It was announced also that the celebrations for the World Day would take place in Altotting, Bavaria, Germany. The Message of the Holy Father for the World Day of the Sick was entitled: "Go and Do Likewise." Abp. Zimowski observed that in his message for the World Day of Sick, the pope "emphasizes that its celebration should be strongly characterized by prayer, sharing, and offering up suffering for the good of the Church, as well as serving as a call so that everyone might recognize, in the face of their sick brother or sister, the face of Christ who, suffering, dying, and rising, saved humanity."

Holy See-Israeli Commission On Jan. 30, it was announced that the Bilateral Permanent Working Commission between the Holy See and the State of Israel had held a plenary meeting in Jerusalem. The meeting occurred as part of the desire to continue negotiations according to Art. 10, No. 2, of the Fundamental Agreement between the Holy See and the State of Israel. The meeting was attended by Mr. Daniel Ayalon, deputy minister of Foreign Affairs and by Msgr. Ettore Balestrero, under-secretary of the Holy See for the Relations with States. The Holy See and Israel agreed to hold the next plenary meeting in June 2013 in Vatican City.

Holy See and State of Palestine On Jan. 31, a meeting was held at the Ministry of Foreign Affairs of the State of Palestine in Ramallah; it was a continuation of on-going bilateral negotiations between the Palestine Liberation Organization (PLO) and the Holy See. The participants included Dr. Riad Al-Malki, minister of Foreign Affairs of the State of Palestine and Msgr. Ettore Balestrero, under-secretary for the Holy See's Relations with States. In a joint communique, the two parties stated that the talks "were held in an open and cordial atmosphere, the expression of the existing good relations between the Holy See and the State of Palestine. The Delegations expressed the wish that negotiations be accelerated and brought to a speedy conclusion. It was thus agreed that a joint technical group will meet to follow-up."

General Audiences

Jan. 2 , Where is Jesus From?
Jan. 9, The Mystery of God
Jan. 16, The Revelation of God
Jan. 23, I believe in God
Jan. 30, I believe in God: the almighty Father

INTERNATIONAL

Madrid Holy Family On Jan 2, Card. Antonio Maria Rouco Varela, Abp. of Madrid, presided over a solemn Mass in Plaza de Colón in Madrid, Spain, on the feast of the Holy Family. The Mass was concelebrated by Cardinal Luis Maria Sistach of Barcelona, Card. Antonio Cañizares, prefect of the Congregation for Divine Worship and the Discipline of the Sacraments and, and Card. Vicenzo Paglia, president of the Pontifical Council for the Family. In his homily, Card. Rouco observed, "the Feast of the Holy Family brings us together today, again, in this year that is ending, 2012, a critical and painful year for so many reasons, to give thanks to God for our families rooted in faith in Jesus Christ, in the Redeemer of man, and to beseech Him for the good of the Christian family, the true hope for today…We meet on this bright Sunday morning of the Holy Family in Madrid's Plaza de Colón, reminiscent of many memorable ecclesial gatherings, to form the great Family of the Children of God, to profess before the world, in the light of the divine Word and realizing 'eucharistically' the Mystery of our Redemption, our faith in the Truth of the Christian Family reflected, made possible and fully and definitively founded in the Holy Family of Nazareth: in the Family of Jesus, Joseph and Mary."

Augustinian Sister Honored It was announced on Jan. 2 that Sr. Mary Thomas, an Augustinian Sister and Irish native, had been awarded an MBE (Most Excellent Order of the British Empire) by Queen Elizabeth II in the New Year's Honor's List for her services to St. George's Park Retirement Village," a facility for the elderly. When informed of the award, Sr. Thomas told the press: "I accept this MBE on behalf of the community of the Sisters of St. Augustine and all those we are privileged to serve in our care homes. I recognize that the award is given not just to myself but in recognition, too, of my own religious community and many other professionals who have worked with us over these years to assist the elderly and most vulnerable in our society."

Syrian Archbishop Appeal On Jan. 3, Syrian Catholic Abp. Jacques Behnan Hindo of Hassaké-Nisibis, Syria, appealed to both the presidency of the United Nations Organization for Food and Agriculture (FAO) and to Iraqi Prime Minister Nuri al-Maliki, for immediate humanitarian aid to thousands of Syrian refugees in the region of Jazira in Syria. In the wake of the deteriorating situation in Syria, the people in the region are moving quickly to starvation, especially as badly need food supplies were being cut off. Also endangered were vital supplies of medicines, including antibiotics.

Tanzanian Attacks It was reported on Jan. 4 that Fr. Ambrose Mkenda, a Tanzanian priest had been attacked on Christmas Day by unknown gunmen on the island of Zanzibar off the Tanzanian coast. He had been shot by two men on a motorcycle. Fr. Mkenda was reportedly in serious condition but would likely recover. The president of Tanzania, Jakaya Kikwete, visited the priest in the hospital.

Philippine Petition On Jan. 4, two Filipino lawyers, James and Lovely-Ann Imbong, filed a petition with the Supreme Court of the country to stop the implementation of the recently passed Reproductive Health (RH) bill, Republic Act (RA) 10354, that had been signed by Pres. Benigno Aquino III of the Philippines at the end of 2012. The petition was made on the basis of Article 12, Sec. 2 of the Philippine Constitution, that recognizes the State's duty to protect the family, the life of mothers and their unborn children, and to support the primary right of parents in rearing their children. According to the Constitution, "The State recognizes the sanctity of family life and shall protect and strengthen the family as a basic autonomous social institution. It shall equally protect the life of the mother and the life of the unborn from conception. The natural and primary right and duty of parents in the rearing of the youth for civic efficiency and the development of moral character shall receive the support of the government."

Coptic Bishops Protest On Jan. 7, Bp. Kyrillos William, administrator of the Coptic Catholic Patriarchate of Alexandria, and two other bishops issued a public condemnation of the new Egyptian Constitution as an attack on human rights; the constitution was signed into law on Dec. 26. The bishops noted that the new law governing the country is narrowly interested in the Islamic inhabitants of the country and paves the way for a Muslim Caliphate and the imposition of Sharia law on Egypt. In a statement to the organization Aid to the Church in Need, Bp. William said, "Everywhere in the constitution there are clauses saying everything should be in accordance with Islamic law. The president [Mohammed Morsi] promised to build a civic, modern and democratic state but we do not think that this constitution is in any way in accordance with that…The people should fight for their rights. The Church cannot speak in their name but we can make people aware of the issues through our Justice and Peace committees."

European Court Rules On Jan. 17, the European Court of Human Rights (ECHR) ruled that British Airways violated the religious rights of one of its employees, Nadia Ewieda, in 2006 by telling her that she could not wear a cross to work. While the airline changed its policy in 2007 to allow employees to wear symbols of faith, the court nevertheless ruled that Eweida's religious rights had been violated. In other decisions, the court ruled against three other religious discrimination cases, including that of Shirley Chaplin, a nurse, who was transferred to a desk job in a hospital when she refused to remove a cross necklace, one which she had worn to work for 30 years. The court declared that the hospital had the right to impose such a demand in order to protect the health and safety of nurses and patients.

Dublin Pro-Life Rally On Jan. 21, 25,000 people gathered in Dublin's Merrion square to call for the protection of the unborn in Ireland. The rally, "Unite for Life," was organized by the Pro Life Campaign, Youth Defense, the Life Institute, and Family and Life, to protest the apparent efforts by the Irish government to implement legislation that would permit abortions in cases where the mother is at risk of suicide. The move by the government would open the door to abortion in the country.

British Same-Sex Marriage On Jan. 30, the Catholic Bishops of Great Britain called upon members of Parliament to oppose a bill that would allow same-sex couples to marry under civil law. The bishops noted that the bill "fundamentally seeks to break the existing legal link between the institution of marriage and sexual exclusivity, loyalty and responsibility for the children of the marriage…The British public, as a whole, did not seek this change; none of the mainstream political parties promised it in their last election manifestos; there has been no referendum; there was no Green or White Paper and the Government consultation did not ask whether the law would be changed, but how the law should be changed."

NATIONAL

Joint Pastoral Letter On Jan. 6 the start of National Migration Week was observed in dioceses around the country under the theme this year of "We are Strangers No Longer: Our Journey of Hope Continues." The theme was chosen by the U.S. Bishops to celebrate the tenth anniversary of the joint pastoral letter, "Strangers No Longer: Together on a Journey of Hope," that was issued by the U.S. Conference of Catholic Bishops (USCCB) and the Conferencia del Episcopado Mexicano in 2003. In the original pastoral letter the bishops reflected on migration between Mexico and the United States as a "sign of the times," stressing that such movements of people should be seen as both necessary and beneficial. Abp. José Gomez of Los Angeles, chairman of the USCCB Committee on Migration, wrote, "Catholics have a responsibility to welcome newcomers into our communities and parishes, help them integrate and provide material and spiritual support that will allow them to flourish. National Migration Week is an opportunity for the Church to remember and reflect on these obligations. The Administration and Congress should work together to secure legislation that will provide a path to citizenship for undocumented immigrants, provide legal means for migrants to enter our nation to work, and reform the system to allow family reunification.

To mark National Migration Week, the USCCB Migration and Refugee Services launched a postcard campaign calling on Congress to enact comprehensive immigration reform with clear objectives: Provide a path to citizenship for undocumented persons in the country; Preserve family unity as a cornerstone of our national immigration system; Provide legal paths for low-skilled immigrant workers to come and work in the United States; Restore due process protections to immigration enforcement policies; Address the root causes of migration caused by persecution and economic disparity.

HHS Mandate On Jan. 4, it was announced that Dominos Pizza founder Tom Monaghan had succeeded in securing an emergency motion for a Temporary Restraining Order (TRO) to halt enforcement of the controversial HHS mandate on the grounds of the mandate's violation of the employer's First Amendment religious rights. The Health and Human Services (HHS) federal mandate requires employers of religious institutions to pay for insurance that provides abortion-inducing drugs, contraception, and sterilization procedures to employees. The mandate, part of the Affordable Care Act – so-called Obamacare – and took effect Jan. 1, 2013. The Thomas More Law Center (TMLC) filed the motion, and U.S. District Judge Lawrence Zatkoff ruled in favor of the motion, citing the government's failure to "satisfy its burden of showing that its actions were narrowly tailored to serve a compelling interest." As of early January, there were more than 40 separate lawsuits challenging the HHS mandate, including suits from Hobby Lobby, Wheaton College, East Texas Baptist University, Houston Baptist University, Belmont Abbey College, Colorado Christian University, the Eternal Word Television Network (EWTN), Ave Maria University, and Our Sunday Visitor.

West Coast March for Life Abp. Carlo Maria Viganò, the Holy See's ambassador to the United States, took part in the 9th Annual Walk for Life West Coast in San Francisco on Jan. 26. The event on the West Coast was held to coordinate with the longstanding annual march held in Washington, D.C., to commemorate the Supreme Court decision legalizing abortion in the United States in 1973. Abp. Viganò was appointed nuncio to the United States on Oct. 19, 2011. Other speakers included: actress Jennifer O'Neill; Lacey Buchanan, a young mother whose YouTube video about her blind son went viral and has touched over 11 million viewers; Elaine Riddick, a woman who was forcibly sterilized at the age of 14 by the North Carolina Eugenics Board; Rev. Clenard Childress, the founder and director of www.blackgenocide.org; Kelly and Matthew Clinger, a post-abortive couple.

Archbishop Viganò was welcomed at the rally by Abp. Salvatore Cordileone of San Francisco, who said he was grateful for the nuncio's support. In an interview with the *National Catholic Register*, the nuncio observed, "One of the duties of the mission of the apostolic nuncio and his staff is to provide and offer [information] to the Pope about the situation of the Church in the United States and to present to him suitable candidates to be bishops. This is a very important responsibility, and, since the country is so large, I try to be present at any occasion or for an important meeting... Every one of us brings to these gatherings the experience of their years of life and mission. I was affected by my first diplomatic assignment in 1973

in Iraq ... before the first Gulf War ... [under] the dictatorship of Saddam Hussein. A democracy is not something that is won forever. As Blessed John Paul II and Pope Benedict have said, 'A democracy that is deprived from values very soon will become a dictatorship and a situation of persecution.'"

Novena to End Abortion On Jan. 16, it was announced that the U.S. bishops were calling for a national novena to end abortion. The nine days of prayer, penance, and pilgrimage ran from Jan. 19 to 27 and coincided with the marking of the anniversary of the infamous *Roe v. Wade* decision in 1973. The annual March for Life began in response to to the Jan. 22 decision, and 2013 was the 40th anniversary of *Roe vs. Wade*. Marches were held in Washington, D.C., and in San Francisco on Jan. 25 and 26 respectively. The bishops noted, "Since that tragic [Supreme Court] decision, more than 55 million children's lives have been lost to abortion, and the lives of millions of their parents have been shattered." a statement on the bishops' website noted.

National Prayer Vigil On Jan. 23, as part of the preparation for the annual March for Life to protests the *Roe v. Wade* by the U.S. Supreme Court in 1973, a prayer vigil was held at the National Shrine of the Immaculate Conception in Washington, D.C. It began with Mass celebrated by Card. Seán O'Malley, chairman of the Secretariat of pro-life activities for the United States Conference of Catholic Bishops (USCCB). Pilgrims then took part in various activities, including Eucharistic Adoration, the sacrament of reconciliation, Compline, and the National Rosary for Life. The vigil concluded the following morning with Mass celebrated by Bp. Kevin Ferrell of Dallas, Texas.

Gift of Forgiveness On Jan. 23, the U.S. Bishops issued a statement promoting a return to the sacrament of reconciliation by Catholics, especially during Lent. The Pastoral Exhortation on the Sacrament of Penance and Reconciliation was approved in Nov. 2012 by the bishops during their annual Fall General Assembly in Baltimore. In a statement on the initiative, Bp. David Ricken of Green Bay, chairman of the bishops' Committee on Evangelization and Catechesis, said: "Pope Benedict XVI and Card. Timothy Dolan have both stressed the importance of confession in strengthening our witness during the Year of Faith. The document itself teaches: "'Receive the Holy Spirit. Whose sins you forgive are forgiven them' (Jn 20:19-23). What an extraordinary gift! He wanted them to become apostles of this forgiveness to others... In the Sacrament of Penance and Reconciliation, also called confession, we meet the Lord, who wants to grant forgiveness and the grace to live a renewed life in him...The Church also encourages frequent confession in order to grow closer to Christ Jesus and his Body, the Church. We bishops and priests are eager to help you if you experience difficulty, hesitation, or uncertainty about approaching the Lord in this sacrament. If you have not received this healing sacrament in a long time, we are ready to welcome you. We pray that through the work of the Holy Spirit, all Catholics—clergy and laity—will respond to the call of the New Evangelization to encounter Christ in the Sacrament of Penance and Reconciliation."

FEBRUARY 2013

VATICAN

Lenten Message On Feb. 1, Pope Benedict XVI's Lenten Message for 2013 was presented by the Sala Stampa, or Press Office, of the Holy See. The message had the title: "Believing in Charity Calls Forth Charity: 'We have come to know and to believe in the love God has for us,' (1 Jn 4:16)." A press conference was held at the Press Office with the participation of Card. Robert Sarah, president of the Pontifical Council "Cor Unum"; Msgr. Giampietro Dal Toso and Msgr. Segundo Tejado Munoz, respectively secretary and undersecretary of that dicastery; and Dr. Michael Thio, president general of the International Confederation-Society of St. Vincent de Paul. In his statement regarding the message, Card. Sarah said, "This year the theme of the message focuses on the compelling relationship between faith and charity ... between believing in God, the God revealed by Jesus Christ, and the charity that is the fruit of the Holy Spirit and that leads us to the horizon of a deeper openness to God and neighbor. The center of this Lenten Message is certainly the indissoluble interrelation of faith and charity. We can never separate, let alone oppose, faith and charity.' However, this separation or opposition can take different forms. It is a misunderstanding to emphasize the faith, and the liturgy as its privileged channel, so strongly as to forget that they are intended for actual persons who have their own needs, human as they may be their own history, their own relationships."

Lateran Pact On Feb. 4, Pope Benedict XVI and Italian President Giorgio Napolitano were guests of honor at a special concert in the Paul VI Hall that was sponsored by the Italian Embassy to the Holy See. The Orchestra of the Maggio Musicale Fiorentino, conducted by Maestro Zubin Mehta, performed Beethoven's Symphony No.3 and "La forza del Destino" by Giuseppe Verdi. The concert was funded by the founder members of the Flying Angels Foundation, chaired by the Ambassador of Italy to the Holy See that provides free airline tickets for disadvantaged children in need of medical care. The event marked the 84th anniversary of the Lateran Pacts that were signed in 1929 to recognize the sovereignty of the Holy See in Vatican City.

Pope Benedict XVI Resigns On Feb. 11, Pope Benedict XVI announced that he would resign the See of Rome on Feb. 28. Meeting with the Cardinals in Rome who were present for a consistory. In a statement in Latin, the Holy Father said: "After having repeatedly examined my conscience before God, I have come to the certainty that my strengths, due to an advanced age, are no longer suited to an adequate exercise of the Petrine ministry. I am well aware that this ministry, due to its essential spiritual nature, must be carried out not only with words and deeds, but no less with prayer and suffering. However, in today's world, subject to so many rapid changes and shaken by questions of deep relevance for the life of faith, in order to govern the bark of St. Peter and proclaim the Gospel, both strength of mind and body are necessary, strength which in the last few months, has deteriorated in me to the extent that I have had to recognize my incapacity to adequately fulfill the ministry entrusted to me."

Pope Benedict announced that on Feb. 28, at 8:00 p.m., the See of St. Peter would be vacant. Whereupon a Conclave would gather to elect a new Supreme Pontiff.

Pope Benedict concluded: "And now, let us entrust the Holy Church to the care of Our Supreme Pastor, Our Lord Jesus Christ, and implore his holy Mother Mary, so that she may assist the Cardinal Fathers with her maternal solicitude, in electinga new Supreme Pontiff. With regard to myself, I wish to also devotedly serve the Holy Church of God in the future through a life dedicated to prayer."

Lombardi Reaction On Feb. 11, in the immediate aftermath of the stunning announcement by Pope Benedict XVI that he was resigning the papacy, Fr. Federico Lombardi, S.J., director of the Vatican press office, held a press conference to address the media crush. "Among the reasons for the Pope's resignation, as he noted in his own words are the circumstances of today's world that, in relation to the past, are particularly difficult, both because of the speed as well as the number of events and problems that arise that, therefore, need a vigor, perhaps stronger than in the past. It is a vigor that the Pope says he has felt diminish in him in recent months. The phrase: 'well aware of the seriousness of this act, with full freedom I declare that I renounce the ministry of Bishop of Rome, Successor of St. Peter,' is very significant. This is the formal declaration, which is important from a juridical point of view. In paragraph 2 of canon 332 of the Code of Canon Law, we read: 'Should it happen that the Roman Pontiff resigns from his office, it is required for validity that the resignation be freely made and properly manifested, but it is not necessary that it be accepted by anyone.' The two fundamental points are, therefore, freedom and due manifestation. Freedom and public manifestation, and the consistory in which the Pope manifested his will is public.

"Benedict XVI will continue to fully carry out his functions and his service until Feb. 28, at 8:00 p.m. [Rome time]. From that moment on the situation of *Sede Vacante* will begin, regulated, from a legal and canonical standpoint, by the texts referring to *Sede Vacante* in the Code of Canon Law and the Apostolic Constitution '*Universi Dominici Gregis*' by John Paul II, regarding the *Sede Vacante* of the Apostolic See. The Pope's announcement is consistent with what he declared in the book *Light of the World* by Peter Seewald, based on interviews with Benedict XVI. Seewald posed two precise questions on the hypothesis of resignation. In the first, he asked the Holy Father whether, in difficult situations that weigh on the pontificate in progress, the Pope would consider resigning. Benedict's response was: 'When the danger is great, one cannot escape. For this reason, surely, this would not be the time to resign' (he was referring to the question of sexual abuse, etc.). Moments like this are the times when one has to be strong and face the difficult situation. This is what I think. One can resign in a time of peace, or when one simply no longer has the strength, but one cannot escape in a moment of danger saying 'someone else take care of it.' In any case, the Pope said that the difficulties would not be, for him, a motive for resignation; rather, they would be a reason not to. Seewald's second question was: 'Well then, can you imagine a situation in which you would think that a Pope could resign?' The Holy Father responded: 'When a Pope realizes clearly that he is no longer physically, mentally, and spiritually capable of carrying out his role, then there is legally the possibility, and also the obligation, to resign.'"

Benedict XVI's Last Public Liturgy On Feb. 13, Pope Benedict XVI celebrated the last public liturgy of his pontificate with Mass in St. Peter's Basilica. As he processed out of the basilica, he received a tumultuous greeting from the large crowd in the basilica and St. Peter's Square. In his homily, the pontiff declared, "Tonight we are great in number around the tomb of the Apostle Peter, also to request his intercession for the Church's journey at this particular time, renewing our faith in the Supreme Pastor, Christ the Lord. For me it is a good opportunity to thank everyone, especially the faithful of the Diocese of Rome, as I prepare to conclude my Petrine ministry, and ask for a special remembrance in prayer."

Benedict XVI's General Audience On Feb. 13, Pope Benedict XVI used his weekly general audience address to address his impending retirement. The audience was attended by thousands of pilgrims who assembled in the Paul VI Audience Hall. The pope spoke chiefly about the start of Lent, but he also addressed his impending resignation: "As you know, I have decided – thank you for your kindness – to renounce the ministry which the Lord entrusted to me on April, 19, 2005. I have done this in full freedom for the good of the Church, after much prayer and having examined my conscience before God, knowing full well the seriousness of this act, but also realizing that I am no longer able to carry out the Petrine ministry with the strength which it demands. I am strengthened and reassured by the certainty that the Church is Christ's, who will never leave her without his guidance and care. I thank all of you for the love and for the prayers with which you have accompanied me. Thank you; in these days which have not been easy for me, I have felt almost physically the power of prayer – your prayers – which the love of the Church has given me. Continue to pray for me, for the Church and for the future Pope. The Lord will guide us."

Pope Meets Roman Priests On Feb. 14, Pope Benedict XVI met with the priests of the Diocese of Rome. While an annual gathering, this year's session has particular meaning because of the pontiff's impending resignation. The pope received an intense welcome by the priests; he delivered a lengthy discourse on his experiences at the Second Vatican Council. He assured the priests, "Even as I leave, I will remain close to you in prayer, and I'm sure that all of you will be close to me, though I will be hidden from the world." At the end of the audience, Card. Agostino Vallini, vicar for Rome, spoke to the Holy Father: "We give you our emotional greeting with great filial affection. Allow me, Holy Father, to tell you that in our hearts this morning we have sentiments that in some way are similar to those of the elders of Ephesus, called by Paul to Miletus to hear his words of farewell before his departure for Jerusalem…You have taught us many things to be credible disciples of Christ and good pastors with your indomitable faith full of courage, your humility in service, your passion for the truth in your endeavor to proclaim the Gospel in a world in which the faith is being proposed again as well as the care of the weak and the poor that you have always defended and helped."

Ash Wednesday On Feb. 14, Pope Benedict XVI delivered a homily for Ash Wednesday, what was his last public liturgy. So great was the interest in the Mass that it was moved from the traditional site of the Basilica of Santa Sabina to St. Peter's Basilica. Pope Benedict said, "The circumstances have suggested that we gather in St. Peter's Basilica. Tonight we are great in number around the tomb of the Apostle Peter, also to request his intercession for the Church's journey at this particular time, renewing our faith in the Supreme Pastor, Christ the Lord. For me it is a good opportunity to thank everyone, especially the faithful of the Diocese of Rome, as I prepare to conclude my Petrine ministry, and ask for a special remembrance in prayer."

New IOR President On Feb. 15, the Vatican Press Office issued a communique that the Holy See's Commission of Cardinals had selected a a new president of the Institute for the Works of Religion's (IOR) Supervisory Board, Ernst von Freyburg, a 54-year-old German lawyer. The appointment marks a new turn in recent efforts by the Holy See to improve the leadership and administration of the so-called Vatican Bank that has struggled to implement needed reforms to bring Vatican finances into line with new international standards for transparency and the prevention of financial fraud. The communique stressed that von Freyberg has "a vast experience of financial matters and the financial regulatory process."

Holy See and South Sudan On Feb. 22, the Holy See and the Republic of South Sudan established formal diplomatic relations. South Sudan was created in 2011 after breaking off from Sudan thereby ending many years of civil strife, including two civil wars. The new country has approximately 2 million Christians – most are Catholics – among a total population of 8.2 million. The communiqué noted that the Holy See would establish an apostolic nunciature and that the two states, "being desirous of promoting bonds of mutual friendship, have decided by common accord to establish diplomatic relations at the level of Apostolic Nunciature on the part of the Holy See and of Embassy on the part of the Republic of South Sudan."

Motu Proprio on the Conclave On Feb. 25, Pope Benedict XVI issued a *motu proprio* (Latin for "on one's own initiative"), that permitted several changes to the law governing the election of the Roman pontiff. Under the title *Normas Nonnullas* ("Some Norms") clarified several points from the Apostolic Constitution *Universi Dominici Gregi* of Pope John Paul II and also reflected the document issued in 2007 that further clarified papal elections. Notably, the pontiff granted the Cardinals the right to change the date of the start of the conclave. The constitution stipulates that a conclave must be held 15 to 20 days after the vacant see begins, so the *motu proprio* permits the college of cardinals to change the start if all the electors are present in Rome a majority agree. It also allowed the cardinals to postpone it in case of serious events. A second point notes that if the number of cardinals is not divisible by three, or a multiple of three, dividing two-thirds of the votes to elect the pontiff becomes mathematically difficult, and so at least two-thirds of the votes of the electors present and voting is required. The new document stresses that secrecy is needed on all matters relating to the election of the Roman pontiff and that cardinals are required to maintain it and violators will be subject to latae sententiae [automatic] excommunication."

Pope Benedict's Final Audience On Feb. 27, Pope Benedict XVI held the final General Audience of his pontificate, attended by an estimated 150,000 pilgrims gathered in St. Peter's Square. The scene was a tear-filled one, and the pontiff was greeted by shouts of "*Benedetto*" (Benedict) and "*Viva il Papa*" (Long live the Pope). The pope was scheduled to resign the papacy the next day and spoke to his imminent departure: "When, on April 19 almost eight years ago, I agreed to take on the Petrine ministry, I felt this certainty firmly, and it has always accompanied me. At that moment, as I have already stated several times, the words that resounded in my heart were: Lord, why are you asking this of me and what are you asking of me? It is a great weight you are placing on my shoulders, but if this is what You ask, at your word I will let down the nets, confident that You will guide me, even with my weaknesses. And eight years later I can say that the Lord has truly guided me…I always knew that the Lord is in the boat, and I always knew that the boat of the Church is not mine, not ours, but it is His. And He will not let her sink, it is He who leads it, certainly also through the men he has chosen, because so He has willed it. This was and is a certainty, that nothing can obscure. And that is why today my heart is filled with gratitude to God because He has never left me or the Church without His consolation, His light, His love."

Benedict's Final Farewell On Feb. 28, Benedict XVI ended his pontificate with a ceremonial meeting with the members of the College of Cardinals followed by a departure from the Vatican. The pontiff met with 144 of the Cardinals in the morning and pledged his fidelity and obedience to his successor. After an address by the Dean of the College, Card. Angelo Sodano, Pope Benedict said, "As I said yesterday, in front of the thousands of faithful filling St. Peter's Square, your closeness, your advice have been of great help to me in my ministry. In these eight years we have lived with faith beautiful moments of radiant light in the path of the Church, along with times when a few clouds have formed in the sky. We have tried to serve Christ and his Church with deep and total love, which is the soul of our ministry. We have given hope, that which comes to us from Christ, and that alone can enlighten the way. Together we can thank the Lord, who has made us grow in communion; together we can beseech Him to help you grow still in this profound unity, so that the College of Cardinals may be like an orchestra, where the diversities, an expression of the universal Church, may always contribute to the greater, unifying harmony."

The pontiff then added: "Among you, among the College of Cardinals, there is also the future pope, to whom already today I promise my unconditional reverence and obedience.

The pope left the apostolic palace by car and was taken to the Vatican heliport, where he lifted off at 5:07 Rome time. Vatican Television transmitted coverage of the flight, which was then broadcast by every major network in the world. The helicopter arrived at Castel Gandolfo at 5:24, where he was scheduled to remain for several weeks before taking up residence at the Mater Ecclesiae monastery within the Vatican walls. His pontificate ended officially at 8 p.m., an event that was marked by the Swiss Guard formally closing the doors of the papal residence. After arriving at Castel Gandolfo, the pope held a brief audience with the many pilgrims gathered there to say farewell. He declared: "Thank you, thank you from my heart. I am happy to be here with you, surrounded by the beauty of Creation and your friendship that does me so much good, thank you for your friendship, for caring. You know that today is different from others…as of 8 p.m., I will no longer be the Supreme Pontiff of the Catholic Church. I will simply be a pilgrim who is beginning the last part of his pilgrimage on earth. But with my heart, my love, my prayer, with all my interior strength, I will work for the common good and the good of the Church and all humanity. And I feel greatly supported by your affection. Let us move forward together with the Lord for the good of the Church and the world. I will now impart upon you all my Apostolic Blessing. Thank you and good night. Thank you all!"

General Audience

Feb. 6, Catechesis on the Year of Faith
Feb. 13, Papal Resignation
Feb. 27, Final Audience of the Pontificate

INTERNATIONAL

New Patriarch for Iraq On Feb. 5, it was announced that Pope Benedict XVI had confirmed the appointment of Abp. Louis Sako, 64, as Patriarch Raphael I of Baghdad of the Chaldeans; he had been elected two days before. Patriarch Raphael had served previously as archbishop of Kirkuk. His election as successor to Patriarch Card. Emmanuel III Delly, 85, who resigned for reasons of age, found the Christians in Iraq continuing to live in a state of crisis because of attacks by radical Islamist elements. The Christian population in the last decade has plummeted to 300,000, down from below 800,000; there were 1.4 million in the last census in 1987.

World Reacts to Resignation The shocking announcement on Feb. 11 that Pope Benedict XVI was resigning the papacy was met with a host of reactions from around the world. Card. Timothy Dolan, president of the United States Conference of Catholic Bishops (USCCB) stated: "We are sad that he will be resigning but grateful for his eight years of selfless leadership as successor of St. Peter. Pope Benedict often cited the significance of eternal truths and he warned of a dictatorship of relativism. Some values, such as human life, stand out above all others, he taught again and again. It is a message for eternity…Our experience impels us to thank God for the gift of Pope Benedict. Our hope impels us to pray that the College of Cardinals under the inspiration of the Holy Spirit choose a worthy successor to meet the challenges present in today's world."

Saints Cyril and Methodius On Feb. 14, Sts. Cyril and Methodius, the saints, brothers and co-patrons of Europe, were honored by an International Congress, "Sts. Cyril and Methodius among the Slavs: 1,150 years since the beginning of the mission" held on Feb. 14 and 26 at the Pontifical Oriental Institute and the Pontifical Gregorian University. The event was organized by Card. Jozef Tomko, Prefect Emeritus of the Congregation for the Evangelization of Peoples, and Abp. Cyril Vasil, Secretary of the Congregation for the Oriental Churches.

Israeli Gratitude On Feb. 14, Israeli Prime Minister, Benjamin Netanyahu sent a letter to Pope Benedict XVI to express thanks to the Holy Father for his efforts to improve relations between Jews and Christians. He wrote: "On behalf of the people of Israel, I want to thank you for all you have done as Pope to strengthen relations between Christians and Jews and between the Vatican and the Jewish State. I thank you also for courageously defending Judeo-Christian values and the roots of our common civilization during your time as pontiff. I have no doubt that these values, which were so essential to building the modern world, are no less critical to securing a future of security, prosperity and peace."

Priests in Syria On Feb. 19, the Fides News Agency reported that two priests in the Syrian town of Aleppo had been kidnapped: Fr. Michel Kayyal of the Armenian Catholic Church and Fr. Maher Mahfouz of the Greek Orthodox Church. Abp. Bourtros Marayati, the Armenian Catholic Abp. of Aleppo, told Fides that the kidnappers had contacted the brother of one of the priests. At the time of their abduction, Frs. Kayyal and Mahfouz were on a public bus for the Salesian house in Kafrun. The kidnappers removed them from the bus.

African Bishops On Feb. 20, the Bishops of Africa belonging to SECAM (the Symposium of Episcopal Conferences in Africa and Madagascar) issued a pastoral letter, "Governance, Common Good, and Democratic Transitions in Africa." The letter was presented in Accra, Ghana, by Card. Polycarp Pengo, archbishop of Dar-es-Salaam, Tanzania and president of SECAM. It was drafted in light of Pope Benedict XVI's post-synodal Apostolic Exhortation "*Africae Munus*," and its call that the Church cannot remain indifferent and isolated in the face of Africa's socio-political and economic challenges. The bishops noted, "The justice that the prophets demanded is not abstract; it is very practical, down-to-earth actions, which take place to ensure that the weak are protected from abuse, that the poor have what they need, and that the socially disadvantaged are cared for. It means giving to everyone what God has intended for them regardless of any distinction."

Cardinal Keith O'Brien On Feb. 25, Pope Benedict XVI

accepted the resignation of Card. Keith Michael Patrick O'Brien, Abp. of St. Andrews and Edinburgh in Scotland. A communique released by the Holy See Press Office stated that the Pope accepted Card. O'Brien's resignation in conformity with canon 401 § 1, which requires prelates to tender their resignation upon reaching the age of 75. The Cardinal had become the center of a firestorm owing to allegations of sexual impropriety. He was expected to depart his see, especially because of the scrutiny cause by the impending conclave to elect a successor to Pope Benedict who was scheduled to resign on Feb. 28. Fr. Federico Lombardi, S.J., director of the Holy See Press Office, noted that Card. O'Brien's resignation was accepted *nunc pro tunc* (meaning effective at a later date) to November of last year in anticipation of his 75th birthday. Card. O'Brien issued a statement on the matter, saying "Looking back over my years of ministry: For any good I have been able to do, I thank God. For any failures, I apologize to all whom I have offended…I also ask God's blessing on my brother Cardinals who will soon gather in Rome to elect his successor. I will not join them for this Conclave in person. I do not wish media attention in Rome to be focused on me – but rather on Pope Benedict XVI and on his successor. However, I will pray with them and for them that, enlightened by the Holy Spirit, they will make the correct choice for the future good of the Church."

NATIONAL

Clergy Abuse Files On Feb. 1, Abp. José Gomez of Los Angeles issued a statement on the release of thousands of clergy files pertaining to the sexual abuse of children. The archbishop stated, "I find these files to be brutal and painful reading. The behavior described in these files is terribly sad and evil. There is no excuse, no explaining away what happened to these children. The priests involved had the duty to be their spiritual fathers and they failed. To every victim of child sexual abuse by a member of our Church: I want to help you in your healing. I am profoundly sorry for these sins against you. To every Catholic in the Archdiocese of Los Angeles, I want you to know: We will continue, as we have for many years now, to immediately report every credible allegation of abuse to law enforcement authorities and to remove those credibly accused from ministry. We will continue to work, every day, to make sure that our children are safe and loved and cared for in our parishes, schools and in every ministry in the Archdiocese. Today is a time for prayer and reflection and deep compassion for the victims of child sexual abuse. I entrust all of us and our children and families to the tender care and protection of our Blessed Mother Mary, Our Lady of Guadalupe and Our Lady of the Angels."

Reformed Baptisms On Feb. 1, it was announced that representatives of the U.S. Conference of Catholic Bishops (USCCB) and four Reformed Christian denominations had held a public signing of an agreement on baptism that affirmed the mutual recognition of the validity of each other's baptisms. The signing occurred at the opening of the annual meeting of the ecumenical association Christian Churches Together (CCT), that includes more than 40 Christian communions and groups. Fr. John Crossin, O.S.F.S., executive director of USCCB's Secretariat for Ecumenical and Interreligious Affairs, declared in a statement, "There has already been a strong response from CCT members who have said this represents healing. In the past, there has been much confusion, and even pain, over the failure to reach an understanding on this question. Our hope is that this would be a model for similar agreements." Bp. Denis Madden, auxiliary bishop of Baltimore and chairman

of the USCCB Committee on Ecumenical and Interreligious Affairs, said, "We are overjoyed at this historic recognition of one another's baptism and are committed to move forward in a new round exploring a common vision of the church." The Common Agreement on the Mutual Recognition of Baptism is the result of the seventh round of the Catholic-Reformed Dialogue in the United States, from 2003-2010. The key provision in the Common Agreement is that only those baptisms performed "with flowing water in the name of the Father and of the Son and of the Holy Spirit," will be considered valid by the signatories. Proof of baptism will be accomplished by the use of common wording on baptismal certificates for baptisms performed after the effective date of the agreement. The U.S. bishops voted to accept the agreement at the annual Fall General Assembly in Baltimore in November 2010. In 2011, members of the Catholic-Reformed Dialogue privately signed the agreement. The public signing was a ceremonial representation of the growing unity between Christians and the progress of the ecumenical movement. While other episcopal conferences around the world have similar agreements with Protestant communities, this is the first such agreement into which USCCB has entered.

Papal resignation On Feb. 11, the leaders of the Church in the United States responded to the news that Pope Benedict XVI would resign. Card. Timothy Dolan of New York, president of the U.S. Conference of Catholic Bishops, issued a statement: "The Holy Father brought the tender heart of a pastor, the incisive mind of a scholar and the confidence of a soul united with His God in all he did. His resignation is but another sign of his great care for the Church. We are sad that he will be resigning but grateful for his eight years of selfless leadership as successor of St. Peter. Though 78 when he elected pope in 2005, he set out to meet his people – and they were of all faiths – all over the world. He visited the religiously threatened – Jews, Muslims and Christians in the war-torn Middle East, the desperately poor in Africa, and the world's youth gathered to meet him in Australia, Germany, Spain and Brazil. He delighted our beloved United States of America when he visited Washington and New York in 2008. As a favored statesman he greeted notables at the White House. As a spiritual leader he led the Catholic community in prayer at Nationals Park, Yankee Stadium and St. Patrick's Cathedral. As a pastor feeling pain in a stirring, private meeting at the Vatican nunciature in Washington, he brought a listening heart to victims of sexual abuse by clerics.

"Pope Benedict often cited the significance of eternal truths and he warned of a dictatorship of relativism. Some values, such as human life, stand out above all others, he taught again and again. It is a message for eternity. He unified Catholics and reached out to schismatic groups in hopes of drawing them back to the church. More unites us than divides us, he said by word and deed. That message is for eternity. He spoke for the world's poor when he visited them and wrote of equality among nations in his peace messages and encyclicals. He pleaded for a more equitable share of world resources and for a respect for God's creation in nature. Those who met him, heard him speak and read his clear, profound writings found themselves moved and changed. In all he said and did he urged people everywhere to know and have a personal encounter with Jesus Christ. The occasion of his resignation stands as an important moment in our lives as citizens of the world. Our experience impels us to thank God for the gift of Pope Benedict. Our hope impels us to pray that the College of Cardinals under the inspiration of the Holy Spirit choose a worthy successor to meet the challenges present in today's world."

MARCH 2013

VATICAN

Sede Vacante With the resignation of Pope Benedict XVI on Feb. 28, the Church officially entered into the sede vacante. On March 1, Card. Angelo Sodano, Dean of the College of Cardinals, sent a letter summoning the members of the College of Cardinals to the first General Congregation to begin on March 4 at the Synod of Bishops Hall. The Cardinal Dean wrote: "The General Congregations will then continue regularly, until the complete number of Cardinal electors has been reached and the College of Cardinals then decides the date of entrance into Conclave of those Cardinal electors as prescribed by the recent *Motu Proprio* of this past Feb. 22 concerning some changes to the rules regarding the election of the Roman Pontiff."

Vatican Stamps On March 1, the Philatelic and Numismatic Office of the Governorate of Vatican City State issued four stamps with the image of an angel raising the pavilion ("*umbraculum*") of the Apostolic Camera, the work of Italian artist Daniela Longo. The stamps marked the fact that the Holy See was vacant and that the Church had entered into a sede vacante. The stamps cost: €0.70 for mail to Italy, with a light green background; €0.85 for mail to Europe, with a blue background; €2.00 for mail to the Americas, with a grey background; and €2.50 for mail to Oceania, on a yellow background.

1st General Congregation On March 4, the members of the College of Cardinals held the first General Congregation of Cardinals in the Synod Hall, located in the Paul VI Audience Hall. The Congregation was presided over by Card. Angelo Sodano, Dean of the College of Cardinals, along with Cardinal Tarcisio Bertone, the Camerlengo of the Apostolic Chamber, and Abp. Lorenzo Baldisseri, secretary of the Congregation of Bishops. There were 142 Cardinals present, with 103 of them Cardinal electors, meaning they were eligible to elect the new Roman Pontiff.

Telegram to Benedict XVI On March 5, during the second day of the General Congregation Meetings of the College of Cardinals, the Cardinal Fathers sent a telegram to Pope Emeritus Benedict XVI. The telegram read: "The Cardinal Fathers, gathered at the Vatican for the General Congregations in view of the next Conclave, send you their devoted greetings and express their renewed gratitude for all your brilliant petrine ministry and for your example of generous pastoral care for the good of the Church and of the world. With their gratitude they hope to represent the recognition of the entire Church for your tireless work in the vineyard of the Lord."

Cardinals Pray for the Church On March 6, the College of Cardinals gathered to pray for the Church at St. Peter's Basilica. The liturgy was held at the Altar of the Cathedra and began with the recitation of the Glorious Mysteries of the Rosary in Italian and Latin. Following the Rosary there was Exposition of the Blessed Sacrament and Adoration. The rosary and Adoration were followed by Vespers, presided over by Card. Angelo Comastri, archpriest of St. Peter's Basilica. The rite concluded with Eucharistic Benediction offered by Card. Comastri.

Conclave Date On March 8, the Cardinals gathered at the afternoon Session of the General Congregation issued a communique that the Conclave would begin on Tuesday, Mar. 12. According to the communique, the '*pro eligendo Romano Pontifice*' Mass would be celebrated in St. Peter's Basilica in the morning.

Final General Congregation On March 11, the Cardinals held the tenth and final General Congregation of Cardinals prior to the commencement of the Conclave the next day. There were 152 Cardinals at the congregation. A total of 28 Cardinals spoke, making a total of 161 interventions given throughout the General Congregation. The Cardinals then voted not to hold another congregation to permit the Cardinal electors to move to the Domus Santa Marta in preparation for the Conclave.

The Conclave Begins At 5:35 Local Rome Time the Cardinal electors were sealed into the Sistine Chapel and commenced the Conclave for the election of a new pontiff. The conclave is governed by the Book of Rites of the Conclave. The morning had begun with the '*pro eligendo Romano Pontifice*' Mass, the Mass for the Election of a Roman Pontiff, with the chief celebrant Card. Angelo Sodano, Dean of the College. The Cardinals then processed into the Sistine Chapel while singing the Litany of Saints and concluding with the hymn "*Veni Creator Spiritus*." Each Cardinal then took a solemn oath, placing his hand on the Gospels and reading in Latin the formula. When the last of the Cardinal electors had taken the oath, the Master of Ceremonies recited the traditional formula "Extra omnes" calling on those not taking part to depart the Chapel. The doors were then closed. In addition to the Cardinals, the Master of Ceremonies and Card. Prospero Grech, O.S.A., who preached the second meditation concerning the grave duty upon the Cardinals were allowed to remain.

Pope Francis On March 13, a little after 7 p.m. Rome time, Card. Jorge Mario Bergoglio, 76, archbishop of Buenos Aires, was elected the 267th Successor of St. Peter and took the name Francis. He was chosen on the fifth ballot on the second day. Francis is a pope of many firsts, including the first Latin American pope, the first Jesuit, the first pope of the Southern Hemisphere, and the first non-European pope since 741 and Pope Gregory III, a Syrian.

The signal of white smoke at 7:06 p.m. from the Sistine Chapel was marked by wild celebrations in St. Peter's Square, and the crowd soon grew to more than 150,000. Card. Jean-Louis Tauran, Proto-Cardinal Deacon, made the announcement of "*Habemus papam!*" ("We have a pope!"). Pope Francis then delivered his *urbi et orbi*, an address to the "city and the world."

"Brothers and sisters, good evening! You know that the duty of the Conclave was to give a bishop to Rome. It seems as though my brother cardinals went almost to the end of the world to get him. But here we are. I thank you for your welcome. The diocesan community of Rome has a bishop. Thank you!

"Before all else, I would like to say a prayer for our Bishop Emeritus Benedict XVI. Let us all pray together for him, that the Lord may bless him and that Our Lady may watch over him …

[Our Father … Hail Mary … Glory be]

"And now let us begin this journey, [together] as bishop and people. This journey of the Church of Rome, which is to preside over all the Churches in charity. It is a journey of fraternity, of love, of trust between us. Let us always pray for one another. Let us pray for the world, so that a great brotherhood may be created. I hope that this journey of the Church, which we begin today and in which my Cardinal Vicar who is present here will assist me, will be fruitful for the Evangelization of this beautiful city.

"And now I would like to give you my blessing. But

before I do, I would like to ask you a favor: before the bishop blesses the people, I ask you to pray to the Lord that He bless me…. the prayer of the people for a blessing upon their bishop. Let us take a moment of silence for you to offer your prayer for me."

[Silence … the Holy Father bows]

[Cardinal N. says … "The Holy Father, Francesco …"]

"Now I will give you my blessing and to the whole world, to all men and women of good will."

[Pope's blessing]

Brothers and Sisters,

I leave you now. Thank you for your welcome. Pray for me. And we'll see one another again soon. Tomorrow I want to go and pray to Our Lady, asking her to watch over Rome. Good night and have a good rest.

Mass With Cardinals On March 14, Pope Francis celebrated Mass with the members of the College of the Cardinals who had elected him the day before. The Mass was celebrated in the Sistine Chapel. The new pontiff delivered a homily without a text and in Italian focusing on the readings: "There is something that I see that these three readings have in common: movement. In the first reading it is the movement of a journey; in the second reading it is the movement in building the Church; in the third, the Gospel, it is the movement of confession. Journeying, building, confessing."

Saint Mary Major On March 14, Pope Francis made his first non-official act outside of Vatican City by going to the Basilica of Santa Maria Maggiore where he placed a bouquet of flowers at the feet of the image of Santa Maria Salus Populi Romani (Protectress of the Roman People), the Virgin of Snows. The pope then departed the basilica after prayer and blessed a pregnant woman.

Francis' Inauguration Mass On March 19, Pope Francis celebrated the Inauguration of the Petrine Ministry Mass celebrated for a crowd in excess of 200,000 people in St. Peter's Square. The Mass was celebrated on the Feast of St. Joseph, patron saint of the Universal Church. Card. Jean Louis Tauran, the proto deacon who announced the election of Pope Francis last week, invested the Holy Father with the pallium and Card. Angelo Sodano, dean of the College of Cardinals, placed the Ring of the Fisherman on the Pope's finger. The Holy Father focused his homily on being protectors through the example of St. Joseph: to "protect Christ in our lives, so that we can protect others, so that we can protect creation!" The pope taught: "The vocation of being a 'protector,' however, is not just something involving us Christians alone; it also has a prior dimension which is simply human, involving everyone. It means protecting all creation, the beauty of the created world, as the Book of Genesis tells us and as St. Francis of Assisi showed us. It means respecting each of God's creatures and respecting the environment in which we live. It means protecting people, showing loving concern for each and every person, especially children, the elderly, those in need, who are often the last we think about. It means caring for one another in our families: husbands and wives first protect one another, and then, as parents, they care for their children, and children themselves, in time, protect their parents. It means building sincere friendships in which we protect one another in trust, respect, and goodness. In the end, everything has been entrusted to our protection, and all of us are responsible for it. Be protectors of God's gifts!

Different Faiths On March 20, Pope Francis received in audience representatives of Churches, ecclesial communities, and international ecumenical and interreligious organizations. The delegations came to Rome for the inauguration of Francis' ministry as Bishop of Rome and Successor of the Apostle Peter. Notably, in attendance was the Ecumenical Patriarch of Constantinople, Bartholomew I, who was the first ecumenical patriarch to attend a papal inauguration since the Schism of 1054. The Holy Father declared: "I begin my Apostolic Ministry in this year which my venerable predecessor, Pope Benedict XVI, with truly inspired insight, proclaimed the Year of Faith for the Catholic Church. With this initiative, which I want to continue and hope is a stimulus for the faith journey of all, he wished to mark the 50th anniversary of the beginning of the Second Vatican Council, proposing a sort of pilgrimage towards that which is most essential for every Christian: the personal and transforming relationship with Jesus Christ, Son of God, who died and rose for our salvation."

Diplomatic Corps On March 22, Pope Francis met with the diplomatic corps accredited to the Holy See. He spoke in Italian and focused on his priorities for the new pontificate. He also revealed some details about his election, saying "One of the first reasons [I chose the name] was Francis' love for the poor," he explained. "How many poor people there still are in the world! An what great suffering they have to endure!" He then spoke of poverty noting that the Church helps those who suffer: "But there is another form of poverty! It is the spiritual poverty of our time, which afflicts the so-called richer countries particularly seriously. It is what my much-loved predecessor, Benedict XVI, called the 'tyranny of relativism,' which makes everyone his own criterion and endangers the coexistence of peoples. And that brings me to a second reason for my name. Francis of Assisi tells us we should work to build peace. But there is no true peace without truth! There cannot be true peace if everyone is his own criterion, if everyone can always claim exclusively his own rights, without at the same time caring for the good of others, of everyone, on the basis of the nature that unites every human being on this earth."

He added: "My own origins impel me to work for the building of bridges. As you know, my family is of Italian origin; and so this dialogue between places and cultures a great distance apart matters greatly to me, this dialogue between one end of the world and the other. It is not possible to build bridges between people while forgetting God. But the converse is also true: it is not possible to establish true links with God, while ignoring other people. Hence it is important to intensify dialogue among the various religions, and I am thinking particularly of dialogue with Islam…Fighting poverty, both material and spiritual, building peace and constructing bridges: these, as it were, are the reference points for a journey that I want to invite each of the countries here represented to take up. But it is a difficult journey, if we do not learn to grow in love for this world of ours. Here too, it helps me to think of the name of Francis, who teaches us profound respect for the whole of creation and the protection of our environment, which all too often, instead of using for the good, we exploit greedily, to one another's detriment."

Palm Sunday On March 25, Pope Francis celebrated Palm Sunday with a Mass for an estimated 250,000 in St. Peter's Square. In his homily, the Holy Father focused on Christ's triumphant entry into Jerusalem: "Crowds, celebrating, praise, blessing, peace: joy fills the air. Jesus has awakened great hopes, especially in the hearts of the simple, the humble, the poor, the forgotten, those who do not matter in the eyes of the world. He understands human sufferings, he has shown the face of God's mercy, and he has bent down to heal body and soul. This is Jesus. This is his heart which looks to all of us, to our sicknesses, to our sins. The love of Jesus is great. And thus he enters Jerusalem, with this love, and looks at us. It is a beautiful scene, full of light – the light of the love of Jesus, the love of his heart – of joy, of celebration."

Francis added: "Jesus does not enter the Holy City to receive the honours reserved to earthly kings, to the powerful, to rulers; he enters to be scourged, insulted and abused, as Isaiah foretold in the First Reading. He enters to receive a crown of thorns, a staff, a purple robe: his kingship becomes an object of derision. Why the Cross? Because Jesus takes upon himself the evil, the filth, the sin of the world, including the sin of all of us, and he cleanses it, he cleanses it with his blood, with the mercy and the love of God. Let us look around: how many wounds are inflicted upon humanity by evil! Wars, violence, economic conflicts that hit the weakest, greed for money that you can't take with you and have to leave."

Pope Francis and Benedict XVI Meet On March 25, Francis traveled by helicopter to Castel Gandolfo to meet with Pope Emeritus Benedict XVI. The first such meeting in the history of the Church, was a cordial and prayerful one. Benedict XVI greeted the new pontiff at the heliport and then showed Francis around the Apostolic Palace, where they prayed in the chapel dedicated to Our Lady of Czestochowa. Pope Francis and Benedict XVI had a private discussion that lasted for 45 minutes.

Francis' First General Audience On March 27, Pope Francis held the first general audience of his pontificate. Speaking in Italian, the pontiff meditated on Holy Week and promised to continue Pope Benedict XVI's on-going catechesis on the Year of Faith. The pope noted: "What does it mean to follow Jesus in his path toward the Cross on Calvary and the Resurrection? Jesus spoke to everyone, without distinction, to the great and the humble, to the rich young man and the poor widow, to the powerful and the weak; he brought the mercy and forgiveness of God; he healed, he consoled, he understood; he gave hope; he brought to all the presence of God who is interested in every man and every woman, as a good father and a good mother is in each of their children. God did not wait for everyone to go to Him, but it was He who moved toward us, without calculating, without measure. God is like this: He always takes the first step, He moves towards us."

First Chrism Mass On March 28, Pope Francis celebrated the first Chrism Mass of his pontificate and used his homily to focus on anointing and the priesthood. The readings were on God's anointed ones: the suffering Servant of Isaiah, King David and Jesus Christ, and the anointing of all three was meant "in turn to anoint God's faithful people," meaning, the poor, prisoners, and the oppressed. He noted especially the image of the oil of anointing: "The image of spreading oil," the pope said, "flowing down from the beard of Aaron upon the collar of his sacred robe, is an image of the priestly anointing which, through Christ, the Anointed One, reaches the ends of the earth, represented by the robe. From the beauty of all these liturgical things, which is not so much about trappings and fine fabrics than about the glory of our God resplendent in his people, alive and strengthened, we turn to a consideration of activity, action. The precious oil which anoints the head of Aaron does more than

simply lend fragrance to his person; it overflows down to the edges...a good priest can be recognized by the way his people are anointed...Our people like to hear the Gospel preached with unction, they like it when the Gospel we preach touches their daily lives, when it runs down like the oil of Aaron to the edges of reality, when it brings light to moments of extreme darkness, to the outskirts where people of faith are most exposed to the onslaught of those who want to tear down their faith. People thank us because they feel that we have prayed over the realities of their everyday lives, their troubles, their joys, their burdens and their hopes...We need to go out, then, in order to experience our own anointing, its power and its redemptive efficacy: to the outskirts where there is suffering, bloodshed, blindness that longs for sight, and prisoners in thrall to many evil masters. It is not in soul-searching or constant introspection that we encounter the Lord: self-help courses can be useful in life, but to live by going from one course to another, from one method to another, leads us to become pelagians and to minimize the power of grace, which comes alive and flourishes to the extent that we, in faith, go out and give ourselves and the Gospel to others, giving what little ointment we have to those who have nothing, nothing at all."

General Audiences
March 17, 2013 Holy Week.

INTERNATIONAL
Card. O'Brien Statement On March 4, recently retired Card. Keith O'Brien, archbishop emeritus of St. Andrews and Edinburgh in Scotland, issued a statement on the various allegations of impropriety that had surfaced in recent weeks. Card. O'Brien noted that the allegations were "anonymous and non-specific," but he added: "However, I wish to take this opportunity to admit that there have been times that my sexual conduct has fallen below the standards expected of me as a priest, archbishop and cardinal. To those I have offended I apologize and ask forgiveness. To the Catholic Church and people of Scotland, I also apologize." He pledged to retire completely from public life and would play "no further part in the life of the Catholic Church in Scotland."

Religious Freedom On March 6, Abp. Silvano Tomasi, the Holy See's Permanent Observer to the United Nations in Geneva, addressed the 22nd Session of the Human Rights Council today and spoke on the report of the Special Rapporteur on freedom of religion or belief. He observed: "Lately this worrying situation has caught the attention of some Governments and segments of civil society. Thus awareness about this serious problem has become more evident. On the other hand, widespread discrimination affecting religious minorities persists and even increases...The legal recognition of a minority is the starting point for the necessary harmony between individual and group freedom. By adopting such a realistic approach to this issue the coexistence of communities is facilitated in a climate of relative tolerance...Only through respect for this balance can both peaceful coexistence and the advancement of all human rights be attained. The recognition of the religious freedom of individuals and social groups implies that they should act by the same standards of the freedom they enjoy and such a condition justifies their presence as important and authentic actors in the public square.

Hugo Chavez On March 6, Hugo Chavez, president

of Venezuela, died of cancer at the age of 58. It was announced that Card. Jorge Urosa Savino, archbishop of Caracas and Primate of Venezuela, would celebrate a "solemn Mass" in Rome in honor of deceased leader. A communique issued from Rome – where the Venezuelan Cardinal was attending the preparations for the conclave – stated: "Card. Urosa, archbishop of Caracas, will celebrate a solemn funeral Mass in Rome at a date and place to be announced shortly. All Venezuelans who wish to do so, are invited to attend the religious ceremony to pray for the eternal rest of President Chavez." Relations between the Church in Venezuela and the radical left-wing president had been difficult over the years, but throughout Chavez's illness, Card. Urosa had encouraged the faithful to pray for his recovery.

Cuba's Good Friday On March 22, the Communist Cuban government announced that Good Friday would be a public holiday in Cuba, an apparent response to the appeal made to Cuban authorities by Pope Benedict XVI during his visit in 2012. In 1998, following Pope John Paul II's visit, the Cuban regime declared Christmas a public holiday, and the date was made official the following year. The measure was seen as another step forward by the once atheist regime that has controlled Cuba for more than a half century under the dictator Fidel Castro. The Communist government effectively banned Christmas and Good Friday as public holidays and brought considerable oppression to the Church. Changes began in the wake of the collapse of the Soviet Union, and in 1993, Cuba ceased to refer to itself as an atheist state.

NATIONAL

Conscience Protection On March 7, a bill was introduced in the U.S. House of Representatives to protect the conscience rights of Americans, the Health Care Conscience Rights Act of 2013. The proposed measure was welcomed by the U.S. bishops, and in a statement by Abp. William Lori of Baltimore, chairman of the US bishops' Ad Hoc Committee for Religious Liberty, declared: "I am grateful to Congresswoman Black and other sponsors for their leadership today. I welcome the Health Care Conscience Rights Act and call for its swift passage into law. While federal laws are on the books protecting conscience rights in health care, this Act would make such protection truly effective. This overdue measure is especially needed in light of new challenges to conscience rights arising from the federal health care reform act."

Poll of U.S. Catholics On March 8, a Knights of Columbus-Marist poll was released, and its findings indicated that American Catholics approved by a large majority of the pontificate of Pope Emeritus Benedict XVI. According to the poll, more than three quarters of Catholics (77%) and more than 8 in 10 practicing Catholics (82%) have a very positive or positive impression of Pope Benedict XVI's pontificate. In addition, 68% of Catholics and 77% of practicing Catholics believed that Pope Benedict had a "very positive" or "positive" impact on their lives. Only 13% of Catholics and 12% of practicing Catholics had a negative view. Remarkably, 70% of Catholics and 75% of practicing Catholics believe he had a "very positive" or "positive" impact on the direction of the Catholic Church. Regarding the moral direction of the world, 65% of Catholics and 69% of practicing Catholics said he had a "very positive" or "positive" impact on the moral direction of the world. Only 23 and 22% respectively said his impact was negative or very negative. Overall, 69% of Catholics and 75% of practicing Catholics had a very favorable or favorable view of Pope Benedict XVI. Only 16% of Catholics and 14% of practicing Catholics had an unfavorable view. The survey was of 2,000 American adults including 515 Catholics was conducted from March 2 through 5. The margin of error for Catholics was +/- 4.3 percentage points.

Pope Francis On March 13, Card. Timothy Dolan of New York, president of the U.S. Conference of Catholic Bishops (USCCB), congratulated the newly elected Pope Francis, Card. Jorge Mario Bergoglio of Argentina. Card. Dolan wrote, "The election of Card. Jorge Mario Bergoglio, who has taken the name Francis, marks a great milestone in our church. As successor to Peter, our first pope, Pope Francis stands as the figure of unity for all Catholics wherever they reside. The bishops of the United States and the people of our 195 dioceses offer prayers for our new leader and promise allegiance to him. Intense prayer from all around the world surrounded the election of Pope Francis. The bishops of the United States thank God for the guidance of the Holy Spirit and the inspired choice of the College of Cardinals. With joy in our hearts, we declare "*Ad Multos Annos!*" (For many years!)" On March 19, after the Installation Mass of Pope Francis in St. Peter's Square, Card. Dolan wrote, "Since your election as Roman Pontiff on Mar. 13, the Church in our country has felt a renewed sense of unity, hope and love of Jesus Christ and His Church. Your messages of mercy and forgiveness spur us on to continue the faithful work of the new evangelization in our country and our world. The inauguration of your Petrine ministry, occurring as it does on the Feast of St. Joseph, Patron of the Universal Church, inspires us with the profound awareness that we stand as one before God and before the world united with you as our beloved Shepherd."

Budget Cuts On March 20, a statement was issued by Bp. Stephen Blaire of Stockton, chairman of the USCCB Committee on Domestic Justice and Human Development, and Bp. Richard Pates of Des Moines, chairman of the USCCB Committee on International Justice and Peace that called for Congress to address the moral and human dimensions of the federal budget and to protect the poor against the impending budget discussions. The bishops wrote: "We support the goal of reducing future unsustainable deficits, but insist that this worthy goal be pursued in ways that protect poor and vulnerable people at home and abroad. The moral measure of this budget debate is not which party wins or which powerful interests prevail, but rather how those who are jobless, hungry, homeless or poor are treated. Their voices are too often missing, but they have the most compelling moral claim on our consciences and our common resources. The bishops stand ready to work with leaders of both parties for a budget that reduces future deficits, protects poor and vulnerable people, advances the common good, and promotes human life and dignity. The bishops also pushed for the embrace of three moral criteria to guide budgetary decisions: Every budget decision should be assessed by whether it protects or threatens human life and dignity; Every budget proposal should be measured by how it affects 'the least of these' (Mt 25). The needs of those who are hungry and homeless, without work or in poverty should come first; Government and other institutions have a shared responsibility to promote the common good of all, especially ordinary workers and families who struggle to live in dignity in difficult economic times."

APRIL 2013

VATICAN

Papal Tombs On Apr. 2, Pope Francis visited the tomb of his predecessors in St. Peter's Basilica, including the Scavi to see the tomb of St. Peter and the tomb of Blessed Pope John Paul II, on the eighth anniversary of his death. The Pope was accompanied by Card. Angelo Comastri, archpriest of the Vatican Basilica, and by his personal secretary, Msgr. Alfred Xuereb. Francis was the first Pope to visit the excavations of the Vatican necropolis, the Scavi. He then visited the Vatican Grottoes, where the tombs of numerous popes are located, and Francis stopped to pray at the tombs of Benedict XV, Pius XI, Pius XII, Paul VI, and John Paul I.

Sex Abuse Scandal On Apr. 5, Pope Francis reiterated his firm commitment to pushing ahead with reforms against clergy sexual abuse that had been successful under Pope Benedict XVI. Pope Francis met with Abp. Gerhard Ludwig Müller, prefect for the Congregation of the Doctrine of the Faith and discussed various issues including sexual abuse cases that are the purview of the congregation. In a communique issued after the meeting, it was noted: "In particular the Holy Father recommended that the Congregation, continuing along the lines set by Benedict XVI, act decisively with regard to cases of sexual abuse, first of all by promoting measures for the protection of minors, as well as in offering assistance to those who have suffered abuse, carrying out due proceedings against the guilty, and in the commitment of bishops' conferences to formulate and implement the necessary directives in this area that is so important for the Church's witness and credibility." It also stressed that Pope Francis was praying for the victims of abuse.

Francis and Ban Ki-moon On Apr. 9, Pope Francis met with United Nations Secretary General Ban Ki-moon along with his wife and members of his entourage at the Apostolic Palace of the Vatican. Secretary-General Ban also had a meeting with Cardinal Tarcisio Bertone, the Vatican Secretary of State, along with Abp. Antoine Camilleri, under-Secretary for the Holy See's Relations with States. According to a communique released by the Holy See, "During the course of the cordial conversations, issues of mutual interest were discussed, in particular: situations of conflict and serious humanitarian emergency, especially in Syria and other places such as the Korean peninsula and the African continent, where peace and stability are threatened...Pope Francis also recalled the Catholic Church's contribution, beginning with her identity and through the means proper to her, in support of the entirety of human dignity and in promoting a Culture of Encounter that helps to realize the UN's highest institutional goals."

In a press conference with reporters after the meeting with Pope Francis, the Secretary General praised Pope Francis as "a man of peace and purpose." He added, "He speaks loudly of his commitment to the poor, he has a deep sense of humility, his passion and compassion to improve the human condition. I was especially privileged to meet Pope Francis as we mark 1,000 days to the deadline to the Millennium Development Goals (MDGs). We discussed the need to advance social justice and accelerate work to meet with the MDG's this is vital if we are to meet the Millennium promise to the world's poorest. He is a voice for the voiceless. I look forward to continuing our conversation. In this period and following in the tradition of his predecessor I was delighted to invite Pope Francis to visit the United Nations at his earliest convenience."

Prime Minister of Mozambique On Apr. 11, Pope Francis met with Prime Minister Alberto Clementino Vaquina of Mozambique. The prime minister also met with Card. Tarcisio Bertone, the papal secretary of state, and with Abp. Dominique Mamberti, Vatican secretary for relations with states. In a communique issued after the meeting, the Vatican Sala Stampa, press office, noted that "the Prime Minister repeated to the Holy Father the congratulations of the people of Mozambique on his election as Pope." It stated as well that the two were pleased "with the good relations existing between the Holy See and Mozambique, which have been further strengthened by the bilateral agreement between the two, which were signed on Dec. 7, 2011, and were ratified last year. In particular, the Catholic Church's positive contribution to the peace and development of the country, especially through her initiatives in education and charitable assistance, was highlighted."

Papal Foundation On Apr. 11, Pope Francis received members of the Papal Foundation who were visiting Rome for their annual pilgrimage; the members presented the pontiff with $8.6 million to support the charitable work of the Holy See. The foundation was established in Pennsylvania by the late Card. John Krol to provide funds to the Holy See. Pope Francis thanked the members of the Papal Foundation, saying: "In these years, you have contributed significantly to the growth of local Churches in developing countries by supporting, among other things, the continuing formation of their clergy and religious, the provision of shelter, medical assistance and care to the poor and needy, and the creation of much-needed educational and employment opportunities." He noted as well the 50th anniversary of John XXIII's encyclical "*Pacem in Terris*" and called on the member to use it to "serve as an incentive for your commitment to promoting reconciliation and peace at every level."

Pontifical Biblical Commission On Apr. 12, Pope Francis received in audience the members of the Pontifical Biblical Commission. The commission was led by its president, Abp. Gerhard Ludwig Muller, prefect of the Congregation for the Doctrine of the Faith who is therefore *ex officio* of the PBC. The commission had just completed their Plenary Assembly on the theme: "Inspiration and Truth of the Bible." Pope Francis spoke on the wok of the commission, saying, "As we know, the Holy Scriptures are the testimony in written form of God's Word, the canonical memorial that attests to the event of Revelation. The Word of God, therefore, precedes and exceeds the Bible. It is for this reason that the center of our faith is not only a book, but a history of salvation and especially a Person, Jesus Christ, the Word of God made flesh. Precisely because the Word of God embraces and extends beyond Scripture to understand it properly we need the constant presence of the Holy Spirit who 'guide us to all truth.'"

Addressing the Vatican II Constitution, *Dei Verbum*, Pope Francis discussed the role of the exegete, saying, "The interpretation of the Holy Scriptures cannot be only an individual scientific effort, but must always confront itself with, be inserted within and authenticated by the living tradition of the Church."

Secretariat of State On Apr. 12, Pope Francis visited the Secretariat of State, in the Apostolic Palace under the direction of Card. Tarcisio Bertone, the Vatican Secretary of State. According to Vatican Radio, Card. Bertone welcomed the Holy Father to the offices of the Secretariat of State, saying: "Here is the great family of your closest collaborators; the Secretariat of State that is, in fact, the real papal secretariat in the two sections: the General Affairs and the Section for Relations with States, with superiors and with all those responsible for the different sectors, with all employees. So you also see a variety of vocations that are represented here. We are grateful for your visit," he continued, "we are excited by the momentum that you have given to the Petrine ministry and we hope that it will pervade, that it will animate us too in carrying out our mission not only with diligence, but above all with love and dedication for the good of the Church. We ask you for your blessing and pledge our devotion, our loyalty and our daily prayer."

Pope Francis spoke to the members of the Secretariat and thanked them for their efforts: "Why am I here today? To thank you, because I know that these days – tomorrow marks one month – you have worked a lot more, many hours more, and that you are not paid for this, because you have worked with your heart and this can only be repaid with a "thank you" but a "thank you" from the heart, no? So I wanted to come to greet you and thank you personally for all this work you have done. Thank you very much, from my heart. Thank you."

Cardinal Advisors On Apr. 15, Pope Francis established an informal commission of eight Cardinals from around the world to advise him in the government of the Universal Church and "to study a plan for revising the Apostolic Constitution on the Roman Curia, '*Pastor Bonus*.'" The commission is a response in part to the calls by the Cardinals during the General Congregations prior to the conclave that a reform of the Curia be undertaken. The group of Cardinals consists of: Card. Giuseppe Bertello, President of the Governorate of Vatican City State; Card. Francisco Javier Errázuriz Ossa, Abp. emeritus of Santiago de Chile, Chile; Card. Oswald Gracias, Abp. of Bombay, India; Card. Reinhard Marx, Abp. of Munich and Freising, Germany; Card. Laurent Monsengwo Pasinya, Abp. of Kinshasa, Democratic Republic of Congo; Card. Sean Patrick O'Malley, O.F.M. Cap., Arbp. of Boston, USA; Card. George Pell, Abp. of Sydney, Australia; Card. Oscar Andrés Rodríguez Maradiaga, S.D.B., Abp. of Tegucigalpa, Honduras, who will serve as coordinator; and Bp. Marcello Semeraro of Albano, Italy, who will serve as secretary.

According to the Holy See Sala Stampa, Press Office, the informal body "is a group, not a commission, committee, or council. The Group has no legislative power and its main function is to advise the Pope. The Group will not in any way interfere in the normal functions of the Roman Curia, which helps the Pope in the daily governance of the Church." The group's first meeting was scheduled for Oct. 1-3, 2013.

Birthday Greetings On Apr. 16, Pope Francis sent birthday best wishes to Pope Emeritus Benedict XVI, who celebrated his 86th birthday. During his Mass in the Domus Sanctae Marthae, Pope Francis said, "Today is Benedict XVI's birthday. We offer the Mass for him, so that the Lord be with him, comfort him, and give him much consolation." Pope Francis also telephoned his predecessor who was still residing at the Apostolic Palace in Castel Gandolfo.

Prime Minister of Spain On Apr. 16, Pope Francis met with Mariano Rajoy Brey, prime minister of Spain at the Vatican Apostolic Palace. The Spanish Prime Minister also met with Card. Tarcisio Bertone, the papal Secretary of State, as well as Abp. Dominique Mamberti, secretary for Relations with States. A communique was issued by the Holy See Sala Stampa, Press Office, that noted that the Holy Father and Prime Minister Rajoy Brey discussed the on-going crises in both Spain and Europe.

Earthquake Victims On Apr. 17, Pope Francis used his General Audience to ask for prayers for prayers for the victims of a 7.8 magnitude earthquake that struck the border between the Iran and Pakistan and killed 34 people and injured almost 80 in the Mashkel district of Balochistan province in Pakistan. Pope Francis declared, "I raise a prayer to God for the victims and for all those who are in pain and I wish to express my closeness to the Iranian and the Pakistani people."

Texas Explosion On Apr. 18, Pope Francis tweeted his prayers for the victims and their families after an explosion at a fertilizer plant in Texas that killed as many as 15 people and wounded more than 160 others. The Holy Father tweeted from his Twitter account, @pontifex: "Please join me in praying for the victims of the explosion in Texas and their families."

President of Ecuador On Apr. 19, Pope Francis received Rafael Correa Delgado, president of the Republic of Ecuador, in audience at the Vatican Apostolic Palace. The president also met with Abp. Dominique Mamberti, secretary for Relations with States. A communique was issued after the meeting that stressed the "atmosphere of cordiality…The centrality of social justice and the value of solidarity and subsidiarity in seeking the common good were emphasized" including "Issues regarding current events in the region, respect for indigenous peoples and their culture, as well as environmental protection."

President of the Italian Republic On Apr. 22, Pope Francis sent his congratulations to Giorgio Napolitano following his re-election as president of the Italian Republic. Pope Francis wrote, "As I wish for you to continue your enlightened and wise work supported by everyone's responsible cooperation, I invoke constant divine assistance on your behalf and for your great service to the country."

Violence in Syria On Apr. 24, Pope Francis concluded his weekly general audience to make a plea for an end to the violence in Syria. He said, "The kidnapping of the Greek Orthodox and Siro-Orthodox Metropolitans of Aleppo, about which there are conflicting news releases, is a further sign of the tragic situation that is enveloping the dear Syrian nation, where violence and weapons continue to sow death and suffering. I ask God to enlighten the hearts and I renew the pressing invitation that I made on the day of Easter to stop the bloodshed, that the necessary humanitarian assistance may be given to the population and that a political solution to the crisis is found as soon as possible."

Confirmation Candidates On Apr. 29, Pope Francis confirmed 44 young people from around the world during a Mass at St. Peter's Square that drew more than 100,000 faithful. In his homily, the pontiff meditated on the Sunday readings and spoke especially to the youths: "How beautiful it would be if each of you, every evening, could say: Today at school, at home, at work, guided by God, I showed a sign of love towards one of my friends, my parents, an older person! How beautiful!...But difficulties and trials are part of the path that leads to God's glory, just as they were for Jesus, who was glorified on the cross; we will always encounter them in life! Do not be discouraged! We have the power of the Holy Spirit to overcome these trials!"

The pope added: "Pay attention, my young friends, to go against the current; this is good for the heart, but we need courage to swim against the tide. Jesus gives us this courage! There are no difficulties, trials or misunderstandings to fear, provided we remain united to God as branches to the vine, provided we do not lose our friendship with him, provided we make ever more room for him in our lives. We Christians were not chosen by the Lord for little things; push onwards toward the highest principles. Stake your lives on noble ideals, my dear young people: the new things of God, the trials of life, remaining steadfast in the Lord."

Italian Prime Minister On Apr. 29, Pope Francis met with Italian Prime Minister Mario Monti at the Domus Sanctae Marthae in Vatican City. A communique was issued after the meeting that detailed the 20 minute encounter. According to Fr. Federico Lombardi, S.J., director of the Holy See Press Office Pope Francis and Prime Minister Monti discussed important topics. The Prime Minister gave the Holy Father a triptych of pens, identical to those he gave to Pope Emeritus Benedict XVI, and two books: one on the Cathedrals of Europe and an autographed copy of a book on Democracy in Europe, co-authored oy Monti and Sylvie Goulard. The Holy Father gave Monti an autographed book wthat contained the first discourses of his pontificate, along with a set of Vatican coins and a rosary.

President of Israel On Apr. 30, Pope Francis met with Israeli President Shimon Peres at the Vatican Apostolic Palace; after the meeting, President Peres met with Cardinal Tarcisio Bertone, the papal Secretary of State, as well as Abp. Dominique Mamberti, secretary for Relations with States. The Holy Father and Pres. Peres discussed various issues, most so the crisis in the Middle East. In a communique released by the Holy See, attention was paid to the hope for a "speedy resumption of negotiations between Israelis and Palestinians" and that "an agreement may be reached that respects the legitimate aspirations of the two Peoples, thus decisively contributing to the peace and stability of the region."

General Audiences

Apr. 3, Catechesis on the Year of Faith.
Apr. 10, Catechesis on the Year of Faith.
Apr. 17, He ascended into heaven and is seated at the right hand of the Father.
Apr. 24, Jesus "will come again in glory to judge the living and the dead."

INTERNATIONAL

Adult Stem Cell Therapy On Apr. 11, the opening session was held for the Second International Vatican Adult Stem Cell Conference, that brought together scientists, doctors and patients involved in the advances in adult stem cell research; the conference was held in the Paul VI Hall in Vatican City. The conference was sponsored by the Pontifical Council for Culture, as well as NeoStem, a developer cellular therapy. Underlying the work of the conference are the related themes of progress in the field and also the relationship between science and faith. The conference was opened by Cardinal Gianfranco Ravasi, president of the Pontifical Council. In his address, he examined three key themes: culture, anthropology, and faith. Another address was given by Bp. Ignacio Carrasco de Paula, president of the Pontifical Academy for Life, who spoke of the subject of the therapeutical use of adult stem cells, describing it "a difficult challenge with clinical economic and ethical consequences. And right now, the problems I have seen that are insurmountable are of those that are embryonic." Speaking of faith and science, he said, "There is room for a possible friendship between science and faith. Faith is based on words, on confidence; science is based on verification of facts. They are quite different but not enemies. The Catholic faith has nothing against stem cells. They are a part of the biological world we live in. They are a demonstration of God's power, of human potential. I think that this must become a real benchmark for our society. We must build

an alliance between heart and mind. Our patients will be deeply grateful to us."

Peace in Syria On Apr. 15, the Melkite Greek Catholic Patriarch, Gregorios III Laham, made a plea for peace in Syria. According to the patriarchate, approximately 400,000 Syrian Christians have been displaced or forced to flee the country. A statement issued by the patriarchate pointed out that since the start of 2011 more than 1,000 Christians have been killed and more than 40 churches and other Christian schools, orphanages and care homes have been attacked or damaged. The patriarch wrote: "The whole of Syria has become a battlefield... Every aspect of democracy, human rights, freedom, secularism and citizenship is lost from view and no-one cares...Suffering has gone beyond all bounds. The crisis has mown down thousands upon thousands of soldiers, opponents, civilians, men, women, children, Muslim sheikhs and Christian priests...The future of Christians in Syria is threatened not by Muslims but by ... chaos ... and the infiltration of uncontrollable fanatical, fundamentalist groups."

Bishops of England and Wales On Apr. 17, the bishops of England and Wales met with Pope Francis during the Holy Father's General Audience and took part in a conference on Scripture in Rome. Card. Cormac Murphy-O'Connor, archbishop-emeritus of Westminster, delivered a brief address on behalf of his fellow bishops. In advance of the audience, the bishops celebrated Mass at the tomb of St. Peter beneath the Basilica for the repose of the soul of Margaret Thatcher, the former British Prime Minister who had recently died and was scheduled to receive her funeral that day in London's St Paul's Cathedral. Speaking to Vatican Radio, Abp. Vincent Nichols of Westminster said, "We were privileged to meet Pope Francis this morning and in a few short remarks, Card. Cormac said to him that these weeks of his pontificate have given a fresh joy and hope to the Church. ... There's a fresh spring about the Church at the moment and I think that's from the Pope's eloquence in gesture and his words when he preaches and at his audiences. I think what is most remarkable in the UK is that everybody seems to have been touched by his eloquence, by his gentleness and by the humility of Pope Francis."

The bishops through the Bishops' Conference for England and Wales sponsored "The Word of the Lord" conference, looking at three elements of Scripture studies: Catholic Biblical Theology; the Scriptures in the Church's pastoral ministry; and the Bible in mission and dialogue. Among the speakers were Fr. Timothy Radcliffe, O.P., Michelle Moran, and Fr. Henry Wansbrough, O.S.B.

NATIONAL

HHS Mandate On Apr. 8, Abp. William E. Lori of Baltimore, chairman of the U.S. Bishops' Ad Hoc Committee for Religious Liberty, issued a statement expressing "solidarity and appreciation" for litigants challenging the U.S. Department of Health and Human Services (HHS) mandate, that forces employers to pay for contraceptive services, sterilizations, and abortion-inducing drugs to employees. Abp. Lori said, "Their goal is nothing less than securing the freedom of the Church to continue to obey the Lord's command—and, in turn, to serve the common good–by providing charitable ministries in health care, education, and service to the poor, all without compromising Catholic beliefs...We continue to pray for the success of all of these lawsuits...in our Catholic tradition, the right to religious freedom proceeds from the inherent dignity of each and every human person. Accordingly, our concern for religious freedom extends well beyond our own ministries of service... Their actions have been a source of encouragement, particularly because of their high rate of success in obtaining early injunctions to block the mandate... Catholics in America have long been advocates for religious liberty, and we continue to affirm this basic right today...We have consistently supported the rights of individuals not to act against their religious beliefs or moral convictions, especially when individuals seek to protect the dignity of human life...I would like to urge all people of good will to pray that our leaders, and all people of this great country, will promote and protect religious liberty and its fundamental place in society."

Gun Control On Apr. 9, Bp. Stephen Blaire of Stockton, California, chairman of the U.S. Bishops' Committee on Domestic Justice and Human Development for the United States Conference of Catholic Bishops sent a letter to the U.S. Senate to promote policies that "reduce gun violence and save people's lives in homes and communities throughout our nation." Bp. Blaire declared: "I also urge you to resist amendments that would expand the use of minimum mandatory sentences as punishment for gun violations. The rising rate of incarceration partially stems from the pervasive use of minimum mandatory sentencing. One-size-fits-all policies are counterproductive, inadequate and replace judges' assessments with rigid formulations. Punishment for its own sake is never justified. In the USCBB's pastoral statement, *Responsibility, Rehabilitation, and Restoration: A Catholic Perspective on Crime and Criminal Justice* (2000), the bishops wrote, "We support measures that control the sale and use of firearms and make them safer (especially efforts that prevent their unsupervised use by children or anyone other than the owner), and we reiterate our call for sensible regulation of handguns. Sadly, gun violence is too common a reality. Tragic events, such as the recent event in Newton, Connecticut and the violence that occurs daily in our homes and communities, should lead us to answer the call of Pope Francis to "change hatred into love, vengeance into forgiveness, war into peace. Therefore, we urge Congress to act and support policies that promote a culture of life by helping reduce gun violence and save lives. In a letter Monday, addressed provisions in legislation before the Senate, including the expansion of background checks for all gun purchases and strengthening of gun trafficking provisions, which the bishops deem a positive step in the right direction."

Immigration Reform On Apr. 17, the U.S. Bishops responded to the Congressional introduction of bipartisan legislation to reform the U.S. immigration system. Abp. José Gomez of Los Angeles, chairman of the United States Conference of Catholic Bishops' (USCCB) Committee on Migration, said that he welcomed the introduction of the legislation, saying, "The U.S. bishops look forward to carefully examining the legislation and working with Congress to fashion a final bill that respects the basic human rights and dignity of newcomers to our land – migrants, refugees, and other vulnerable populations." Card. Timothy Dolan, archbishop of New York and president of the Bishops' Conference, in a press conference on Apr. 22, said, "Let me say that now is the time to address this issue. As we speak, persons are being deported and an untold number of families are being divided. Human beings continue to die in the American desert. This suffering must end...As the pastor of the archdiocese of perhaps the greatest immigrant city in the world, I know first-hand of the many efforts that have been made by the Catholic community on behalf of immigrants." Abp. Gomez added: "If the goal [of the legislation] is to solve the problem in a humane manner, then all undocumented persons should be able to participate. This is an important and historic moment for our country and for the Church. We hope to see the legislation improve and advance, and we will work toward that end. The lives of millions of our fellow human beings depend upon it.This is an important and historic moment for our country and for the Church," Abp. Gomez concluded. "We hope to see the legislation improve and advance, and we will work toward that end. The lives of millions of our fellow human beings depend upon it."

Gun Regulations On Apr. 22, Bp. Stephen Blaire of Stockton, California, chairman of committee for domestic justice for the United States Conference of Catholic Bishops, issued a letter to Senate Majority Leader Harry Reid and Senate Minority Leader Mitch McConnell. He wrote: "The USCCB has been working with other faith leaders and organizations urging Congress to support legislation that builds a culture of life by promoting policies that reduce gun violence and save people's lives in homes and communities throughout our nation. In the wake of tragic events such as the shooting at Sandy Hook Elementary, the failure to support even modest regulations on firearms is a failure in moral leadership to promote policies which protect and defend the common good. Though we are disappointed, we will continue our efforts to work with Congress and other people of good will to advocate for policies that create a safer and more peaceful society."

Budget Concerns On Apr. 25, Bps. Leonard Blaire of Stockton and Richard Pates of Des Moines, chairs the USCCB Committees on Domestic Justice and Human Development and International Justice and Peace, respectively, issued letters to Congress on the proposed budget decisions facing the country. The bishops wrote: "As persistently high poverty and unemployment plague our nation, and war and crushing poverty tear families apart around the world, a just framework for future budgets cannot rely on disproportionate cuts to programs that help people live in a manner worthy of their human dignity. It demands a 'Circle of Protection' around our brothers and sisters at home and abroad who are poor and vulnerable, and it requires shared sacrifice by all. This will include raising adequate revenues, eliminating unnecessary military and other spending, and addressing the long-term costs of health insurance and retirement programs fairly. As Catholic pastors, we continue to emphasize that while these choices may seem merely economic and political, they have clear moral and human consequences. We offer the following timeless moral criteria to guide you in the decisions that lie ahead: 1. Every budget decision should be assessed by whether it protects or threatens human life and dignity. 2. A central moral measure of any budget proposal is how it affects 'the least of these' (Mt 25). The needs of those who are hungry and homeless, without work or in poverty should come first. 3. Government and other institutions have a shared responsibility to promote the common good of all, especially ordinary workers and families who struggle to live in dignity in difficult economic times. While we acknowledge that raising adequate revenue is a necessary component of responsible deficit reduction, how the country accomplishes that is just as important. Placing limits on some personal income tax deductions could unintentionally harm charitable giving by eroding or eliminating, in some cases, the value of the charitable tax deduction. Our Catholic community defends the unborn, feeds the hungry, shelters the homeless, educates the young, and cares for the sick, both at home and abroad."

MAY 2013

VATICAN

Francis Welcomes Benedict On May 2, Pope Emeritus Benedict XVI traveled back to the Vatican City State and was welcomed at the door of the Mater Ecclesiae Monastery by Pope Francis, his successor. The pope emeritus had resided at the papal summer residence of Castel Gandolfo since his resignation of the papacy on Feb. 28 and wile the monastery in the Vatican State was being finished as his place of residence. The retired pontiff was greeted by Cardinals Giuseppe Bertello, president of the Governatorate of Vatican City State, Tarcisio Bertone, secretary of state, and Angelo Sodano, dean of the College of Cardinals. He was then greeted personally by Pope Francis. The pope emeritus chose Mater Ecclesiase as his residence prior to his resignation.

President of Lebanon On May 3, Pope Francis received President Michel Sleiman of Lebanon in the Apostolic Palace. The Lebanese President also met with Card. Tarcisio Bertone, the papal Secretary of State, as well as Abp. Dominique Mamberti, the secretary for Relations with States. A communique was released by the Holy See Press Office, pointing to the discussions on a variety of issues, including the importance of dialogue, adding, "Likewise, the common good, development, and the nation's stability were also considered. In that regard, best wishes were expressed for the formation of a new government that will have to face the important challenges in the national arena as well as in the international sphere." Talks also encompassed the need for "greater humanitarian assistance , with the help of the international community" and "the desire for a rapid and beneficial resumption of negotiations between Israelis and Palestinians, evermore necessary for the peace and stability of the region, was expressed."

Swiss Guards On May 6, Pope Francis welcomed 35 new recruits of the Pontifical Swiss Guards who were sworn in on the day commemorating the death of 147 Swiss soldiers who died protecting Pope Clement during the Sack of Rome in 1527 by the forces of Emperor Charles V, the Catholic ruler of the Holy Roman Empire. The oath was administered by Abp. Giovanni Angelo Becciu, substitute of the Secretariat of State; the new members also met with Pope Francis during a private audience at the Vatican Apostolic Palace. The pontiff observed: "Every day, I am able to experience the dedication, professionalism and love with which you conduct your service. And for this I thank you! In particular, I would like to thank your families, who have graciously accepted your choice to live this service at the Vatican and support you with their affection and their prayers."

Basilica of St. Mary Major On May 6, Pope Francis officially took possession of the Papal Basilica of Santa Maria Maggiore (St. Mary Major) in Rome. The oldest Marian Shrine in the West, the basilica was first visited by the pontiff the day after his election, when he placed pontificate under the Blessed Mother's protection. In his meditation, the pope focused on the Blessed Virgin Mary, saying, "Mary is mother, and a mother concerns herself above all with the health of her children, she knows how to care for it with great and tender love. Our Lady protects our health. What does it mean to say that the Our Lady protects our health? I think above all of three aspects: she helps us to grow, face life, to be free…The mother cares for the children so that they grow more, they grow strong, able to take responsibility, to commit themselves in life, to pursue grand ideals.

Explosion in Mexico On May 8, Pope Francis sent his condolences to the victims of a gas tanker explosion in Ecatepec, Mexico in a message sent by Card. Tarcisio Bertone, the Vatican Secretary of State. The message read: "His Holiness Pope Francis wishes to send, through Your Excellency, his condolences to the families of the deceased, together with expressions of consolation and affection for all those wounded, with the strong desire for their quick and complete recovery."

Money Laundering On May 8, the Financial Intelligence Authority of the Holy See and Vatican City State (AIF), signed a Memorandum of Understanding today in Washington, D.C., with the Financial Crimes Enforcement Network (FinCEN), part of the U.S. Department of Treasury. The agreement is intended to strengthen efforts to fight money laundering and the funding of international terrorism. The signatories were René Brülhart, Director of the AIF, and Jennifer Shasky Calvery, director of FinCEN. According to a communique released by the Holy See, the AIF "was established in 2010 and became operational in April 2011. It is the competent authority of the Holy See and Vatican City State for financial intelligence and for supervision and regulation in the prevention and countering of money laundering and financing of terrorism."

Pope Tawadros II On May 9, Pope Francis met with the head of the Coptic Orthodox Church of Egypt, His Holiness Pope Tawadros II, the Pope of Alexandria and Patriarch of the See of St. Mark. A communique was issued by the Holy See Press Office noting that the last visit of a Coptic Pope took place in May 1973 when Pope Shenouda II met with Pope Paul VI and signed an" an important Christological Declaration in common and initiated bilateral ecumenical dialogue between the two Churches." The encounter between Pope Francis and the head of the Coptic Orthodox Church was seen as an event of considerable ecumenical significance. Pope Tawadros was also scheduled to visit the Pontifical Council for Promoting Christian Unity and other offices of the Roman Curia.

In his address to Pope Francis, Pope Tawadros II said, "May this visit of love and brotherhood be the first of a long series between our two great Churches. Therefore, I propose that the 10th of May of each year should be considered as a celebration of brotherly love between the Catholic Church and the Coptic Orthodox Church. Both Churches, the Catholic and the Coptic, have always worked together, in the Middle East and in the Western World, to make peace prevail. The most important aim for both is the promotion of ecumenical dialogue in order to get to the most pursued goal: unity." Pope Francis said, "Today's visit strengthens the bonds of friendship and brotherhood that already exist between the See of Peter and the See of Mark, heir to an inestimable heritage of martyrs, theologians, holy monks and faithful disciples of Christ, who have borne witness to the Gospel from generation to generation, often in situations of great adversity. We are glad to be able to confirm today what our illustrious predecessors solemnly declared, we are glad to recognize that we are united by one Baptism, of which our common prayer is a special expression, and we long for the day when, in fulfilment of the Lord's desire, we will be able to communicate from the one chalice. I am convinced that – under the guidance of the Holy Spirit – our persevering prayer, our dialogue and the will to build communion day by day in mutual love will allow us to take important further steps towards full unity."

New Saints On May 12, Pope Francis presided over the first canonizations of his pontificate with a Mass in St. Peter's Square during which he raised to the altars 802 new saints, the largest number of saints to be canonized at the same time in the history of the Church. The new saints included Mother Laura Montoya, the first saint from Colombia; Mother María Guadalupe García Zavala of Mexico; and the 800 martyrs of Otranto, who were put to death in 1480 during the little-known invasion of Italy by the Ottoman Turks. Speaking of the Martyrs of Otranto who died rather than convert to Islam, the pope said, "As we venerate the martyrs of Otranto, let us ask God to sustain the many Christians who, in our own time and in many parts of the world, now still suffer from violence, and to give them the courage of fidelity and to answer evil with good." Speaking of St. Maria Laura Montoya, the pontiff said, "This first saint born in the beautiful country of Colombia teaches us to be generous with God, not to live our faith alone – as if it were possible to live the faith in an isolated way – but to communicate it, to convey the joy of the Gospel with words and the witness of life in every place in which we find ourselves." Regarding St. Maria Guadalupe García Zavala, the pope declared, "This new Mexican saint invites us to love as Jesus did, and this means to not shut up in ourselves, in our own problems, our own ideas, our own interests, in this little world that does so much damage to us, but going out and caring for those who need attention, understanding, help, to bring them the warmth and nearness of God's love, through delicate gestures of sincere affection and love."

President of Colombia On May 13, Pope Francis received Mr. Juan Manuel Santos Calderon, President of Colombia in audience at the Vatican Apostolic Palace. Pres. Santos Calderon was in Rome to attend the canonization of Mother Laura Montoya Upegui, the first Colombian saint. In a communique released by the Holy See Press Office, the Holy Father and the president spoke of pressing issues for the country and region: "The challenges that the country must face were taken into consideration, especially in regard to social inequalities. Reference to the undergoing process of peace and the victims of conflict was not overlooked, with the wishes that the parties involved carry on negotiations, inspired by a sincere search for the common good and for reconciliation. Finally, the Church's commitment in favor of life and of families was emphasized." The president also met with Vatican Secretary of State, Card. Tarcisio Bertone and Abp. Dominique Mamberti, secretary for Relations with States.

New Ambassadors On May 16, Pope Francis received the letters of credential from four new ambassadors to the Holy See: Bolot Iskovich Otunbaev from Kyrgyzstan; David Shoul from Antigua and Barbuda; Jean-Paul Senninger from Luxembourg; and Lameck Nthekela from Botswana. He used the occasion to speak to the new ambassadors, declaring, "Our human family is presently experiencing something of a turning point in its own history, if we consider the advances made in various areas. We can only praise the positive achievements which contribute to the authentic welfare of mankind, in fields such as those of health, education and communications. At the same time, we must also acknowledge that the majority of the men and women of our time continue to live daily in situations of insecurity, with dire consequences. Certain pathologies are increasing, with their psychological consequences; fear and desperation grip the hearts of many people, even in the so-called rich countries; the joy of life is diminishing; indecency and violence are on the rise; poverty is becoming more and more evident. People have to struggle to live and, frequently, to live in an undignified way…The worldwide financial and economic crisis seems to highlight their distortions and above all the gravely deficient human perspective, which reduces men and women to just one of their needs alone, namely, consumption. Worse yet, human beings themselves are nowadays considered as consumer goods which can be used and thrown away. We have started down the path of a disposable culture."

Caritas Internationalis On May 16, Pope Francis met with the executive committee of Caritas Internationalis, including its president, Card. Oscar Andrés Rodríguez Maradiaga, abp. of Tegucigalpa, Honduras. The Holy Father said, "Caritas is not just for emergency situations as a first aid agency. In the situation of war or during a crisis, there is a need to look after the wounded, to help the ill … but there is also a need to support them, to care for their development. Caritas is the caress of the Church to its people, the caress of the Mother Church to her children, her tenderness and closeness."

Pontifical Missionary Works On May 17, Pope Francis met with directors of the Pontifical Missionary Works (POM), also known as the Pontifical Mission Societies, who had gathered in Rome for their annual assembly. The POM includes the Society for the Propagation of the Faith, the Society of St. Peter the Apostle, the Missionary Childhood Association and the Missionary Union of Priests and Religious. Speaking to the directors, Pope Francis said, "Certainly the mission that awaits us is difficult but, with the guidance of the Holy Spirit, it becomes an exciting mission. This is what we should always draw courage from: knowing that the strength of evangelization comes from God; belongs to him. We are called to open ourselves more and more to the Holy Spirit's work, to be instruments of God's mercy, his tenderness, his love for every man and woman, and especially for the poor, the excluded and the marginalized. And this holds for every Christian, for the whole Church. It isn't an optional mission but an essential one…Faced with the temptations communities have, to become wrapped up in themselves, worried about their own problems, your job is to recall the 'missio ad gentes', to prophetically witness that the life of the Church and the churches is a mission, and it is a universal mission."

Pentecost Mass On May 20, Pope Francis celebrated the Solemnity of Pentecost with Mass for a crowd of approximately 200,000 faithful. In his homily, Holy Father spoke of the newness brought by the Holy Spirit. "Newness always makes us a bit fearful, because we feel more secure if we have everything under control, if we are the ones who build, program, and plan our lives. This is also the case when it comes to God. It is hard to abandon ourselves to him with complete trust, allowing the Holy Spirit to be the soul and guide of our lives…The Holy Spirit would appear to create disorder in the Church, since he brings the diversity of charisms and gifts; yet all this, by his working, is a great source of wealth, for the Holy Spirit is the Spirit of unity, which does not mean uniformity, but which leads everything back to harmony."

German Chancellor On May 20, Pope Francis met with German Chancellor Angela Merkel at the Vatican Apostolic Palace. The German leader also met with Abp. Dominique Mamberti, secretary for Relations with States. A communique, released by the Holy See, stated that Pope Francis and Chancellor Merkel used their discussions to cover several important, including the current conditions in European culture, society and politics. "In particular the protection of human rights, the persecution of Christians, religious freedom, and international collaboration for the promotion of peace were discussed."

Missionaries of Charity On May 21, Pope Francis made a private visit to the Casa Dono di Maria ("Gift of Mary

House"), a soup kitchen located within the Vatican City State and maintained by the Missionaries of Charity and that cares for young women in difficult situations. Pope Francis marked the 25th anniversary of Pope John Paul II's decision to grant custody of the house to Blessed Teresa of Calcutta. Pope Francis said, "You, dear Sisters, together with the Missionaries of Charity [Brothers and Fathers] and your collaborators, make present the love of the Church for the poor. With your daily service you are – as the Psalm says – the hand of God that satisfies the hunger of every living being. This is a 'home.' And this is what this House has tried to be for 25 years! At the border between the Vatican and Italy, it is a strong appeal to us all, to the Church, to the City of Rome to be always more family, 'home' in which one is open to hospitality, care and fraternity."

Oklahoma Tornado Victims On May 21, Pope Francis sent a message via Twitter to express his sympathy to the victims of a tornado that struck Oklahoma and killed 51, including 20 children, in Oklahoma City. In his tweet, the Holy Father stated: "I am close to the families of all who died in the Oklahoma tornado, especially those who lost young children. Join me in praying for them."

Catholics in China On May 22, at the end of his weekly General Audience, Pope Francis made an appeal to Catholics everywhere to pray for Catholics in China. He said, "I invite all Catholics around the world to join in prayer with our brothers and sisters who are in China to implore from God the grace to announce with humility and joy Christ who died and is risen, to be faithful to his Church and to the successor of Peter and to live daily life in service to their country and their fellow citizens in a manner consistent with the faith they profess."

Report on Money Laundering On May 22, the Vatican's Financial Information Authority (AIF) published its first annual report looking at the state of the Holy See's financial activities. The report was presented at the Holy See Press Office, by AIF's director, Rene Brulhart, who spoke of the moral obligation to resist money laundering. The AIF authority of the Holy See and of Vatican City State was instituted by then-Pope Benedict XVI in Dec. 2012 to fight against money laundering and financing of terrorism.

President of El Salvador On May 23, Pope Francis met with Carlos Mauricio Funes Cartagena, President of El Salvador at the Apostolic Palace. After the meeting the president met with Card. Tarcisio Bertone, the Vatican Secretary of State, as well as Abp. Dominique Mamberti, Secretary for Relations with States. A communique issued by the Holy See after the meeting said: "During the cordial talks, satisfaction was express for the good relations between the Holy See and the nation of El Salvador. In particular, Servant of God Abp. Óscar Arnulfo Romero y Galdámez of San Salvador was spoken of and the importance of his witness for the entire nation."

Forced Migrations On May 24, Pope Francis addressed the plenary assembly of the Pontifical Council for Migrants and Travelers and spoke on its theme of "The Pastoral Concern of the Church in the Context of Forced Migrations." The pontiff called human trafficking "a disgrace for our societies that call themselves civilized! Exploiters and clients at all levels should make a serious examination of conscience before themselves and before God! In a world where there is much talk of rights, how many times human dignity is trampled. In a world where there is so much talk of rights, it seems the only one that has them is money. Dear brothers and sisters, we live in a world where money commands. We live in a world, in a culture where the fetishism of money reigns. We are in fact only one human family that, in the

multiplicity of its differences, walks toward unity, valuing solidarity and dialogue between peoples."

Roman Parish On May 27, Pope Francis marked the Solemnity of the Holy Trinity with a Mass and visit to the parish of Sts. Elizabeth and Zechariah in Rome, his first parish visit in the diocese of Rome. In his homily, Pope Francis taught, "When Our Lady, just having received the announcement that she would be the mother of Jesus, and the announcement that her cousin Elizabeth was expecting, the Gospel says, she set out in haste; she did not wait. She did not say to herself, 'But I'm pregnant now, so I had better look after my health. My cousin will have friends who perhaps will help her.' She heard something and she 'set out in haste.' It is lovely to think about these actions of Our Lady, our Mother, who sets out in haste, because it tells us about helping. She goes to help, she does not go to boast and say to her cousin: 'Now listen, I'm in charge now because I am God's mamma!' No she did not do that. She went to help! And Our Lady is always like this. She is our Mother, who always comes in haste when we need help."

Centesimus Annus – Pro Pontefice On May 27, Pope Francis met with the members of the "Centesimus Annus – Pro Pontefice" Foundation, which was established 20 years ago by Pope John Paul II. The gathering for 2013 was "Rethinking Solidarity for Work: Challenges of the 21st Century. Rethinking solidarity doesn't mean questioning the recent Magisterium that, in fact, demonstrates ever more its vision and its relevance. Rather, 'rethinking' seems to me to mean two things: first of all combining the Magisterium with socio-economic development that, being constant and quick, always presents new aspects and second, 'rethinking' means going more in depth, reflecting further, to make all of a value's worth emerge–solidarity in this case–which draws upon the Gospel profoundly, that is, upon Jesus Christ and thus contains inexhaustible potential. The current economic and social crisis adds urgency to this 'rethinking.'"

Cardinal Velasio De Paolis On May 30, Pope Francis met with Card. Velasio De Paolis, C.S., Papal Delegate for the Legion of Christ and the Regnum Christi in audience at the Vatican Apostolic Palace. The meeting was devoted chiefly to an update by the Cardinals of the reform of the Legion of Christ, including the elaboration of new Constitutions of the Legion to be presented at an Extraordinary General Chapter in early 2014.

U.N. General Assembly On May 31, Pope Francis met with His Excellency Mr. Vuk Jeremic, the president for the 67th session of the United Nations General Assembly; Jeremic also met with the papal Secretary of State, Card.Tarcisio Bertone, S.D.B., as well as Abp. Dominique Mamberti, secretary for Relations with States. The meeting between the pope and the president covered a variety of topics, including the Middle East, the problem of human trafficking, and refugees and migrants, and the global economic crisis.

General Audiences

May 1, St. Joseph the Worker
May 8, "I believe in the Holy Spirit."
May 15, "The Holy Spirit's action in guiding the Church."
May 22, "I believe in one, holy, catholic and apostolic Church"
May 29, "the Church as God's family."

INTERNATIONAL

Nigeria in Crisis On May 3, Card. John Onaiyekan, archbishop of Abuja, and Bp. Matthew Hassan Kukah of Sokoto met with officers of the European Union to discuss the problems facing Nigeria. Card. Onaiyekan spoke of growing corruption and religious violence and warned of "the twin monsters of corruption and insecurity." Card. Onaiyekan also noted that poverty and the instability in nearby Libya had exacerbated the situation.

March Against Gay Marriage On May 26, the city of Paris witnessed a proest march by more than one million people against the recently approved same-sex "marriage" law signed by Pres. François Hollande. The law was approved by the National Assembly, which is controlled by Hollande's party, the Socialists, who have implemented a radical left-wing agenda since their victory in last year's election. The protesters also protested what were likely new initiatives in such areas as the adoption of children by homosexual couples.

Filipino Elections On May 28, the National Secretariat for Social Justice and Peace, the office in the Philippines for the promotion of Catholic social teachings, issued a statement calling on the country's Election Commission to explain the severe irregularities in the recent election that included charges of voter fraud, malfunctions of voting machines, and deliberate transmission failures. The statement noted that the Secretariat "is not blind to the glaring discrepancies and election violations, the highly-suspicious interventions during the canvassing, and the possible manipulation of election result during the lull hours of transmission, canvassing and consolidation of votes."

100,000 Christians Killed On May 29, Abp. Silvano M. Tomasi, Permanent Observer of the Holy See to the United Nations in Geneva, spoke to the U.N.'s Human Rights Council and noted every year at least 100,000 Christians are killed around the world because of their faith. He added: "The serious violations of the right to freedom of religion in general and the recent continuing discrimination and systematic attacks inflicted on some Christian communities in particular, deeply concern the Holy See and many democratic Governments whose population embrace various religious and cultural traditions." He pointed especially to the dire situation in such places as Syria where two Bishops were abducted in Aleppo: Syrian Orthodox Metropolitan Mar Gregorios Yohanna Ibrahim and Greek-Orthodox Bp. Boulos al-Yazigi.

NATIONAL

Repeal of Death Penalty On May 3, Bp. Stephen E. Blaire of Stockton, chair the U.S. Conference of Catholic Bishops' (USCCB) Committee on Domestic Justice and Human Development, issued a statement on the repeal of the death penalty in Maryland and called it a courageous step toward a culture of life. He wrote, "We must lift up the dignity of all human life even for those convicted of the worst crimes, and work to transform our culture so that it respects the inherent dignity and value of all people. Americans are beginning to realize that we can do better than the death penalty both to punish crime and keep our society safe. We welcome the decision by the Maryland legislature and Governor O'Malley to abolish the use of the death penalty in Maryland. This is a courageous step toward a culture of life.

LCWR On May 7, the Sala Stampa, or Holy See Press Office, released a statement affirming that both the Congregation for the Doctrine of the Faith and the Congregation for Institutes of Consecrated Life and Societies of Apostolic Life were collaborating on a "renewed theological vision of Religious Life in the Church." The statement added, "The concern of the Holy See, expressed partially in the Doctrinal Assessment of the Leadership Conference of Women Religious in the United States, is motivated by a desire to support the noble and beautiful vocation of Religious so that the eloquent witness of Religious Life may prosper in the Church to the benefit of future generations...The Prefects of these two Congregations work closely together according to their specific responsibilities and have collaborated throughout the process of the Doctrinal Assessment of the LCWR."

Same-Sex Marriage On May 8, the Delaware Senate passed a bill to redefine marriage that was signed into law by the governor, making Delaware the eleventh state to approve same-sex "marriage." Abp. Salvatore Cordileone of San Francisco, chairman of the U.S. bishops' Subcommittee for the Promotion and Defense of Marriage, issued a statement on the unfortunate decision, writing, "The claim of this bill to redefine marriage is in vain; marriage cannot be redefined, because its unique meaning lies in our very nature. It is also a serious injustice to the most vulnerable among us: children. Marriage is the only institution that unites a man and a woman to each other and to any child conceived of their union. Our society either preserves laws that respect the fundamental right of children to be raised by their moms and dads together in marriage, or it does not."

Sex Abuse Allegations On May 9, the audit of dioceses in the U.S. was releasedregarding allegations of clergy sexual abuse. The audit was conducted by StoneBridge Business Partners, and it determined that there was a grand total of six credible cases among 34 allegations of abuse of minors in 2012; the credibility of 15 of the allegations was still under investigation. This marks the lowest number of cases since 2004. Most of the allegations reported were from the 70s and 80s.

The audit likewise found that "over 99 percent of clerics and over 96 percent of employees and volunteers were trained in safe environment programs. In addition, over 4.6 million children received safe environment training. Background evaluations were conducted on over 99 percent of clerics; 98 percent of educators; 96 percent of employees; and 96 percent of volunteers." Dioceses and eparchies that responded to the survey reported costs related to allegations at $112,966,427 in 2012.

Fortnight for Freedom On May 14, the United States Conference of Catholic Bishops announced that the second annual Fortnight for Freedom would take place between June 21 to July 4, and was scheduled to include both national and local efforts to educate Americans both Catholic and non-Catholic about the dangers to religious liberty in the country and around the world. Abp. William Lori of Baltimore, chairman of the U.S. bishops' Ad Hoc Committee for Religious Liberty, was scheduled to open the 2013 Fortnight for Freedom by celebrating Mass at Baltimore's National Shrine of the Assumption.

The Fortnight was to be closed on July 4 with a Mass celebrated by Card. Donald Wuerl of Washington at the Basilica of the National Shrine of the Immaculate Conception in Washington. Abp. Lori wrote in a statement, "The need for prayer, education, and action in defense of religious liberty has never been greater. The Fortnight for Freedom exists to meet that need. This year's Fortnight occurs just weeks before Aug. 1, when the administration's mandate coercing us to violate our deeply-held beliefs will be enforced against most religious non-profits. During the Fortnight the Supreme Court's decisions on the definition of marriage will likely be handed down as well. Those decisions could have a profound impact on religious freedom for generations to come."

JUNE 2013

VATICAN

A Model of Sanctity On June 3, Pope Francis spoke of Pope Blessed John XXIII on the 50th anniversary of the late pontiff's death during his homily at morning Mass in the chapel of the Domus Sanctae Marthae. He referred to Pope John as a "model of sanctity" and prayed at the tomb of the pontiff who convoked the Second Vatican Council in 1962 and was pontiff from 1958-1963. The Holy Father also met in St. Peter's Basilica with 3,000 pilgrims from the Italian diocese of Bergamo, the birthplace of Blessed John. Pope John Paul II beatified John on Sept. 3, 2000.

President of Cape Verde On June 3, Pope Francis received Pres. Jorge Carlos de Almeida Fonseca of the Republic of Cape Verde in an audience at the Vatican Apostolic Palace. Pres. Fonseca also met with the papal Secretary of State, Card. Tarcisio Bertone, S.D.B., along with Abp. Dominique Mamberti, secretary for Relations with States. A communique issued by the Holy See after the meeting noted the cordial discussions and the warm relations between the Holy See and the Republic of Cape Verde.

Worldwide Eucharistic Adoration On June 4, Pope Francis presided over Eucharistic Adoration at 5 p.m. in St. Peter's Basilica and asked that churches all over the world hold adoration at the same time. The Holy Father made the request for two intentions. The first: "For the Church spread throughout the world and united today in the adoration of the Most Holy Eucharist as a sign of unity. May the Lord make her ever more obedient to hearing his Word in order to stand before the world 'ever more beautiful, without stain or blemish, but holy and blameless.' That through her faithful announcement, the Word that saves may still resonate as the bearer of mercy and may increase love to give full meaning to pain and suffering, giving back joy and serenity." The second intention was for those suffering around the world, especially victims of slavery, war, human trafficking, drug running, and violence: "For the children and women," the Holy Father's intention continues, "who are suffering from every type of violence. May their silent scream for help be heard by a vigilant Church so that, gazing upon the crucified Christ, she may not forget the many brothers and sisters who are left at the mercy of violence. Also, for all those who find themselves in economically precarious situations, above all for the unemployed, the elderly, migrants, the homeless, prisoners, and those who experience marginalization. That the Church's prayer and its active nearness give them comfort and assistance in hope and strength and courage in defending human dignity."

Suffering in Syria On June 5, Pope Francis met with representatives of various humanitarian and relief organizations that are trying to bring aid and relief to Syria. The meeting was arranged by the Pontifical Council Cor Unum and included representatives from Catholic charities such as Aid to the Church in Need International, the AVSI foundation, CAFOD, and Caritas Internationalis. Also taking part were the Catholic Near East Welfare Association, Catholic Relief Services, the International Catholic Migration Commission, the International Confederation of the Society of St. Vincent de Paul, the Jesuit Refugee Service, and the Sovereign Military Order of Malta. Pope Francis addressed the gathering and noted, "The Holy See's concern for the crisis in Syria, and in a particular way, for the people, often defenceless, who are suffering as a result of it, is well known. Benedict XVI repeatedly called for a ceasefire and for a search for a resolution through dialogue in order to achieve a profound reconciliation between sides. Let the weapons be silent!...The destiny of the Syrian people is a concern that is close to my heart also. On Easter Sunday I asked for peace: 'above all for dear Syria,' I said, 'for its people torn by conflict, and for the many refugees who await help and comfort. How much blood has been shed! And how much suffering must there be before a political solution to the crisis is found.'"

Careerism is a Leprosy On June 6, Pope Francis spoke to members of the Pontifical Ecclesiastical Academy, the training center for priests who serve in the diplomatic corps and the Secretariat of State of the Holy See. He thanked them for the dedication and service to the Church and then gave some reflections of authentic service and urged them to avoid all forms of ambition and careerism. He said, "Careerism is leprosy! Leprosy! Please, no careerism!...You can make a precious treasure of the instruments of conforming your priestly spirituality to Christ himself, cultivating a life of prayer and making your daily work the gymnasium of your sanctification...When in the Nunciature there is a secretary or a nuncio that doesn't go along the way of sanctity, and gets involved in so many forms, in so many kinds of spiritual worldliness, he looks ridiculous, and everyone laughs at him! Please don't be ridiculous: either [be] saints or go back to the diocese and be a pastor, but don't be ridiculous in the diplomatic [service], in the diplomatic life, where there is so much danger of becoming worldly in spirituality."

Papal Vacation On June 6, the Prefecture of the Pontifical Household announced that the papal general audiences would be suspended for the month of July, a shorter time than traditional. Moreover, Pope Francis had decided not to spend the traditional papal vacation at the summer residence of Castel Gandolfo but to remain in the Vatican City State in the Domus Sanctae Marthae; it added that he would make several visits to Castel Gandolfo during the summer.

Human and Environmental Ecology On June 6, Pope Francis devoted his weekly general audience to the issue of the environment, noting the commemoration of World Environment Day, a United Nations initiative. The Holy Father spoke of the meaning of the word "cultivate," adding, "Nurturing and cherishing creation is a command God gives not only at the beginning of history, but to each of us. It is part of his plan; it means causing the world to grow responsibly, transforming it so that it may be a garden, a habitable place for everyone. We are experiencing a moment of crisis; we see it in the environment, but mostly we see it in man. The human being is at stake: here is the urgency of human ecology! And the danger is serious because the cause of the problem is not superficial, but profound: it's not just a matter of economics, but of ethics and anthropology... This scrap culture has also made us insensitive to waste, including food waste, which is even more reprehensible when in every part of the world, unfortunately, many people and families are suffering from hunger and malnutrition."

Pope Speaks With Students On June 7, Pope Francis met with 9,000 students from Jesuit schools in Italy and Albania at the Paul VI Audience Hall. The pontiff surprised the students by dismissing his prepared text and taking questions from the young people. He said, "I've prepared a text but it's five pages and that's a little long. Let's do this: I'll give it to the Provincial Father and Fr. Federico Lombardi [director of the Holy See Press Office] so that you all can have it written and then some of you will ask me questions and I'll answer them. That way we can talk."

Protection of Migrants and Refugees On June 7, the Holy See presented the document "Welcoming Christ in Refugees and Forcibly Displaced Persons" focusing on the problems of migration. The document was presented at the Holy See Press Office by various officials of the Holy See, including Card. Antonio Maria Veglio, president of the Pontifical Council for the Pastoral Care of Migrants and Itinerant People; Card. Robert Sarah, president of the Pontifical Council "Cor Unum"; Johan Ketelers, secretary general of the Catholic International Commission for Migrations (CICM); and Katerine Camilleri, vice-director of the Jesuit Refugee Service in Malta. The document calls for an end to the trafficking of human beings, the sex industry, forced labor, the traffic of organs for transplants; slavery, and the use of children for armed conflicts.

Adequate Health Care For All On June 10, Abp. Silvano M. Tomasi, Permanent Observer of the Holy See to the United Nations in Geneva, addressed the XXIII Ordinary Session of the Human Rights Council on Access to Medicines. Abp. Tomasi focused on the availability of medical care and medicines around the globe, declaring "a comprehensive analysis of this crucial topic must reach beyond legal frameworks to include an examination of the social and political realities that deprive millions of people from enjoyment of the highest attainable standard of physical and mental health because of the obstacles that they place on access to medicines…optimal facilitation of access to medicine is a complex endeavor and deserves comprehensive analysis and acknowledgement of all factors contributing to its promotion, rather than a more restricted analysis of legal, economic, and political frameworks."

Filipino Catholics On June 11, Card. Tarcisio Bertone, the Vatican Secretary of State, sent a message to Abp. Jose Palma, President of the Catholic Bishops Conference of the Philippines on behalf of Pope Francis thanking Filipino Catholics for the national consecration to the Immaculate Heart of Mary that took place in June across the country. Card. Bertone wrote, "The Holy Father unites himself spiritually with you on this important occasion, praying that the Most Pure Heart of our Blessed Mother Mary may inspire all Filipinos to devote themselves through her, to Jesus her divine Son…[The Holy Father] hopes that devotion to Mary's Immaculate Heart, beating in unison with that of her unborn child, may inspire an ever greater appreciation and attention to all human life, from conception through natural death, and lead to greater service to the poorest and the weakest, those who are closest to God himself."

Francis and the Italian President On June 11, Pope Francis met with Italian Pres. Giorgio Napolitano. During their meeting, the pontiff said, "In Italy the collaboration between State and Church, is always geared to the interest of the people and of society; it is realized in the daily relations between civil entities and those of the Catholic community, represented by Bishops and their organizations, and in an altogether particular way by the Bishop of Rome. So, also this first visit of the President to the Pope – after your participation at the Mass for the beginning of the Petrine ministry – can be expressed effectively with the image of two hills, the Quirinale and the Vatican, which regard one another with esteem and sympathy…In today's world religious liberty is more often affirmed than fulfilled. In fact, it is constrained to suffer threats of various sorts and not rarely is violated. The grave outrages inflicted on such a primary right are a source of serious concern and must elicit the unanimous reaction of the countries of the world in reaffirming, against any attack, the intangible dignity of the human person. It is a duty of everyone to defend religious liberty and to have it promoted by all. Found, moreover, in the shared protection of such a moral good is, also, a guarantee of growth and of development of the whole community."

Italian Association of the Blind and the Visually Impaired On June 11, Pope Francis met with the Italian Association of the Blind and the Visually Impaired. The pope said, "The Gospel tells us that Jesus had a special care for the blind. He healed many of them, along with so many other sick people. However, the healing of the person deprived of sight has a particular symbolic meaning: it represents the gift of faith. And it is a sign that concerns all, because we all have need of the light of faith to journey on the path of life. Because of this, Baptism, which is the first Sacrament of the faith, in times past, was also called 'illumination.' I pray to the Lord to renew in each one of you the gift of faith, so that the light of God will always be in your spirit, the light of love, which gives meaning to our life, illumines it, gives us hope, and makes us be good and be at the disposition of our brothers."

Love of God and Neighbor On June 12, Pope Francis used his weekly General Audience to the Church as the People of God, part of the Holy Father's continuing catechesis on the Creed. The pope taught, "Jesus does not say to the Apostles and to us to form an exclusive group, an elite. Jesus says: go and make disciples of all Nations. St. Paul states that in the people of God, in the Church, 'there is no longer Jew nor Greek … since you are all one in Christ Jesus' I would also say to those who feel far away from God and the Church, the one who is fearful or indifferent, who thinks he can no longer change: the Lord calls you to join his people and does so with great respect and love!"

President of Venezuela On June 17, Pope Francis received President Nicolas Maduro Moros, president of the Bolivarian Republic of Venezuela at the Vatican Apostolic Palace. Pres. Maduro later met with Card. Tarcisio Bertone, the papal Secretary of State, as well as Abp. Dominique Mamberti, secretary for Relations with States. According to a communique issued by the Holy See Press Office, the meetings "focused on included the country's social and political situation after the recent death of Pres. Hugo Chavez Frias, as well as current issues such as poverty and the fight against crime and drug trafficking. As the talks continued, reference was made to the Catholic Church's historical presence in the country and her decisive contribution to charity, health care, and education, and the need for constant and sincere dialogue between the Episcopal Conference and the State for the development of the entire nation was agreed upon."

Prime Minister David Cameron On June 17, Pope Francis made public a letter he sent to the British Prime Minister David Cameron prior to the G8 summit being held in Northern Ireland. The letter was sent in response to a message sent by Prime Minister Cameron to the Holy Father on June 5. Pope Francis wrote on the theme of the G8 Summit: "A G8 Meeting that Goes Back to First Principles," telling the PM, "If this topic is to attain its broadest and deepest resonance," Pope Francis wrote, "it is necessary to ensure that all political and economic activity, whether national or international, makes reference to man. Indeed, such activity must, on the one hand, enable the maximum expression of freedom and creativity, both individual and collective, while on the other hand it must promote and guarantee their responsible exercise in solidarity, with particular attention to the poorest."

French Senate And National Assembly On June 17, Pope Francis received members of the French Parliament at the Vatican Apostolic Palace at the request of the French leaders during a time of social and moral crisis in France because of the radical agenda of the Socialist government of Prime Minister François Hollande. Speaking to the French leaders, the pope said, "The principle of secularism that governs the relations between the French state and the different religious confessions need not in itself mean hostility to religion or an exclusion of religions from the public square and the debates that animate it. We can rejoice in the fact that the proposals of the Church are among those that are valued in French society, in particular the Church's vision of the human person and his dignity in view of the common good. The Church thus desires to offer her own specific contribution to the profound questions that require a more complete vision of the person and his destiny and of society and its destiny. This contribution situates itself not only in the anthropological and social sphere but also in the political, economic and cultural spheres."

Eucharistic Prayer Addition On June 19, the Congregation of Divine Worship and the Discipline of the Sacraments issued a decree that the name of St. Joseph, spouse of the Blessed Virgin Mary, would be added to the Eucharistic Prayer II, III, and IV in the *Roman Missal*. The change had been desired by Pope Francis, and the decree states that St. Joseph exercised paternal care over Jesus with grace and that Joseph adhered "firmly to the mystery of God's design of salvation in its very beginnings" as well as standing as "an exemplary model of the kindness and humility that the Christian faith raises to a great destiny." The decree added: "Through these virtues, this Just man, caring most lovingly for the Mother of God and happily dedicating himself to the upbringing of Jesus Christ, was placed as guardian over God the Father's most precious treasures. Therefore he has been the subject of assiduous devotion on the part of the People of God throughout the centuries, as the support of that mystical body, which is the Church." The decree stated that the new formulas for the addition of St. Joseph in the Eucharistic prayers would follow after the name of the Blessed Virgin Mary.

U.N. Food and Agriculture Organization On June 20, Pope Francis met with participants gathered in Rome for the 38th Conference of the UN Food and Agriculture Organization (FAO). The Holy Father spoke of the present-day problems facing the world, including security, continuing conflicts, climate change, and the preservation of biological diversity. He then stressed human dignity, noting, "This, I believe, is the significance of our meeting today: to share the idea that something more can and must be done in order to provide a new stimulus to international activity on behalf of the poor, inspired by something more than mere goodwill or, worse, promises which all too often have not been kept…Human dignity should be instead the pillars for creating shared rules and structures capable of passing beyond purely pragmatic or technical approaches in order to eliminate divisions and to bridge existing differences. The Catholic Church, with all her structures and institutions, is at your side in this effort, which is aimed at building concrete solidarity, and the Holy See follows with interest and encourages the initiatives and activities undertaken by FAO."

Pontifical Representatives and Apostolic Nuncios On June 21, Pope Francis met with the Pontifical Representatives and Apostolic Nuncios in the Vatican, his first encounter with the Church's ambassadors since his election. He said to them, "You represent me in Churches spread throughout the world and with the Governments, but seeing so many of you today also gives me the sense of the catholicity of the Church, of its universality. I thank you wholeheartedly!" The Pope spoke of Abraham as a model for their lives:

"God asks him to leave his country, his security, to go, trusting in a promise, which he does not see, but which he simply keeps in his heart like the hope which God offers him."

Aid Agencies for the Oriental Churches On June 21, Pope Francis met with the Reunion of Aid Agencies for the Oriental Churches (ROACO) at the conclusion of their 86th Plenary Assembly in Rome. The pontiff thanked the representatives for their work, saying, "As my Predecessors, I wish to encourage and support you in the exercise of charity, which is the only reason to boast for the disciples of Jesus. This charity flows from the love of God in Christ: the Cross is the summit, luminous sign of the mercy and charity of God toward all, which was poured into our hearts through the Holy Spirit."

Children's Train On June 24, Pope Francis met with hundreds of children who took part in the "Children Train: A Journey Through Beauty," an event promoted by the Pontifical Council for Culture. The event was part of the initiative of the Courtyard of the Gentiles, called the Courtyard of the Children designed to foster universal values through education and formation. The children arrived on a special train that made stops in Milan, Bologna, Florence, and finally the Vatican Train Station where they were received by the Holy Father. He pontiff greeted the children and spoke with them for more than 20 minutes.

International Jewish Committee on Interreligious Consultations On June 26, Pope Francis met with a delegation from the International Jewish Committee on Interreligious Consultations (IJCIC) during a private audience held at the Vatican Apostolic Palace. The committee works to promote dialogue and relations with various international religious bodies such as the Holy See's Commission on Religious Relations with the Jews, the Orthodox Christian Church, and the World Council of Churches. Speaking to the members, Pope Francis said, "The 21 meetings held until today have certainly helped to reinforce mutual understanding and the links of friendship between Jews and Catholics. I know that you are preparing the next meeting in October in Madrid and that it will have as its theme Challenges to Faith in Contemporary Society. Thank you for your commitment to this!"

New Pontifical Commission On June 27, Pope Francis issued a chirography that established a new Pontifical Commission charged with assessing the legal position and various activities of the Institute for Religious Works (IOR), the Vatican's financial institution. Pope Francis wrote that the commission's findings will allow for "a better harmonization of the [IOR] with the universal mission of the Apostolic See. The Pontifical Commission will be composed of five people. Card. Raffaele Farina, S.D.B., the Archivist Emeritus of the Vatican Secret Archives, will serve as president of the commission, as will Card. Jean-Louis Tauran, president of the Pontifical Council for Interreligious Dialogue, Bp. Juan Ignacio Arrieta Ochoa de Chinchetru, Secretary of the Pontifical Council for Legislative Texts, Msgr. Peter Bryan Wells, Assessor for General Affairs for the Secretariat of State, and Dr. Mary Ann Glendon, a Harvard Law professor and former US Ambassador to the Holy See.

Ecumenical Patriarchate of Constantinople On June 28, Pope Francis welcomed a delegation of the Ecumenical Patriarchate of Constantinople who were in Rime to attend the Solemnity of Sts. Peter and Paul. The traditional visit began in 1969 and was described by the pontiff as part of the search for unity a task "from which, today more than ever, we cannot prescind. In our world that hungers and thirsts for truth, love, hope, peace, and unity, our witness demands that we should at last be able to proclaim, with one voice, the good news of the Gospel and celebrate together the Divine Mysteries of our new life in Christ. We are well aware that unity is primarily a gift from Gift that we must pray for unceasingly, but we all have the task of preparing the conditions, of cultivating the soil of the heart so that this extraordinary grace may be received."

Arrest of Vatican Official On June 28, the Holy See pledged its full cooperation with Italian authorities in the wake of the arrest of Msgr. Nunzio Scarano, a Vatican finance official who was arrested as part of a wider financial scheme; the prelate allegedly attempted to transport 20 million euros on a private jet from Switzerland into Italy. Msgr. Scarano works with the Institute for Religious Works (IOR) and is a senior accountant for the Administration of the Patrimony of the Apostolic See (APSA).The Vatican announced that Scarano had been suspended from duty at APSA for over a month as soon as Superiors were informed that he was under investigation, pursuant to the Rules of the Roman Curia.

General Audiences
June 5, The Environment
June 12, People of God
June 19, Body of Christ
June 26, The Temple

INTERNATIONAL

British Marriage Bill On June 6, the Catholic Bishops' Conference of England and Wales reiterated its objections to the Marriage (Same Sex Couples) Bill before the Houses of Parliament. The statement read: "The Church's principled objection to the legal re-definition of marriage is consistently and clearly set out. Following the Bill's second reading in the House of Lords, the Church's aim is to ensure the Bill, as it goes to committee stage, is amended so that it effectively delivers the protections that the Government promised to provide for schools, religious organisations and individuals."

Statement by Irish Bishops On June 11, the Catholic Bishops of Ireland issued a statement on upholding life in Ireland. The message said in part: "We are at a defining moment for our country...The right to life is the most fundamental of all rights; it is the foundation of all other rights. No individual has the right to destroy life and no State has the right to undermine the right to life. Yet the Irish Government is proposing abortion legislation that will fundamentally change the culture of medical practice in Ireland. For the first time legislation will be enacted permitting the deliberate and intentional killing of an unborn child. This represents a radical change. Every citizen, not just people of faith, should be deeply concerned...Freedom of conscience is a fundamental human right. A State that truly cherishes freedom will respect the conscience of its citizens, including its public representatives, on such an important human value as the right to life...Every human life is precious, every human life is beautiful, every human life is sacred. Choose life!

NATIONAL

G8 Letter On June 3, Card. Timothy M. Dolan of New York, president of the U.S. Conference of Catholic Bishops, joined the Catholic Bishops' Conferences of the Group of 8 nations (G8) in urging leaders to protect the poor and assist developing countries at the upcoming G8 Summit in the United Kingdom. Card. Dolan wrote, "In a world that has made great strides in improving food production and distribution, far too many of God's children still go to bed hungry or suffer from a lack of nutrition, a tragedy that has lifelong consequences for health and educational achievement. In particular, there is a need to strengthen assistance to African countries in order to improve local agriculture...Trade and trade rules must serve the universal common good of the whole human family and the special needs of the most vulnerable nations. It is counterproductive to provide agricultural development assistance on the one hand and then to use unfair agricultural trade policies that harm the agricultural economics of poorer nations on the others."

Holy See Ambassador On June 15, the White House announced Barack Obama had nominated Ken Hackett, the former president of Catholic Relief Services, to the post of U.S. ambassador to the Holy See. Hackett retired from CRS in 2012, after 40 years of service and when he had been the President and CEO from 1993 to 2012. Hackett was also North American Vice President of Caritas Internationalis from 1996 to 2004 and from 1996 to 2011 served as a member of the Pontifical Commission, Cor Unum.

Supreme Court Rulings On June 26, the U.S. Supreme Court struck down parts of the federal Defense of Marriage Act (DOMA), that barred federal recognition of same-sex marriage contracts and that had been signed by Pres. Bill Clinton in 1996. The Supreme Court also declined to rule on a case regarding California's Proposition 8 in which citizens voted to ban same-sex marriages in California; the ban was later rejected by the left-leaning 9th Circuit Court. In a statement, the United States Conference of Catholic Bishops declared: "The common good of all, especially our children, depends upon a society that strives to uphold the truth of marriage. Now is the time to redouble our efforts in witness to this truth. These decisions are part of a public debate of great consequence. The future of marriage and the well-being of our society hang in the balance...marriage is the only institution that brings together a man and a woman for life, providing any child who comes from their union with the secure foundation of a mother and a father. Our culture has taken for granted for far too long what human nature, experience, common sense, and God's wise design all confirm: the difference between a man and a woman matters, and the difference between a mom and a dad matters. While the culture has failed in many ways to be marriage-strengthening, this is no reason to give up. Now is the time to strengthen marriage, not redefine it."

Senate Immigration Bill On June 28, the U.S. Senate passed S. 744, the Border Security, Economic Competitiveness, and Immigration Modernization Act of 2013, by a vote of 68-32; 14 Republicans joined with every Democratic Senator to pass the bill. Abp. José Gomez of Los Angeles, chairman of the U.S. bishops' Committee on Migration, issued a statement after the vote, saying, "I commend the U.S. Senate on the vote and for the bipartisan cooperation displayed during the legislative process. I urge the House of Representatives to follow the U.S. Senate's lead and pass a comprehensive reform bill as soon as possible. The status quo of our current system causes much suffering among immigrants and their families and must end. The Senate legislation would allow immigrants and their families to come out of the shadows and into the light and would protect families from separation. Our work is not finished. The Church will continue to fight for the rights of migrants."

JULY 2013

VATICAN

Message to the Youth of Lithuania On July 1, Pope Francis sent a message to the youth gathered in Kaunas, Lithuania for the "Sixth Day of Youth of Lithuania" (June 28-30) on the theme: "I have called you friends" (Jn 15:15). The pope encouraged young people to follow Christ and to cultivate His friendship, adding, "And this friendship of Jesus that brought us mercy, the love of God, is 'free,' a pure gift. He doesn't ask you for anything in return, but asks you only to receive it. Jesus wants to love you for what you are, even in your frailty and weakness because, touched by His love, you will be able to be renewed."

IOR Officials Resign On July 1, Paolo Cipriani and Masimo Tulli, Director and Deputy Director of the Institute for Religious Works (IOR) respectively, resigned their posts, according to a communique released by the Holy See Press Office. The communique stated: "After many years of service both have decided that this decision would be in the best interest of the Institute and the Holy See. The Oversight Council along with the Commission of Cardinals that maintain oversight for the IOR accepted the resignations and named Ernst von Freyberg as the interim General Director. Further reforms were expected from the Special Commission established by Pope Francis at the end of June to study the functioning of the IOR.

Vatican Financial Intelligence Authority On July 3, the Egmont Group, a network of Financial Intelligence Units (FIUs) around the globe announced that it had admitted the Financial Intelligence Authority of the Holy See/Vatican City State (AIF) as a full member at its 21st Group Plenary in Sun City, South Africa. The group is intended to assist the flow of information and encourage cooperation against financial crime and fraud and was founded in 1995. It currently consists of more than 130 national FIUs.

New Popemobile On July 3, Pope Francis received Dieter Zetsche, president of Daimler AG, who symbolically presented the Holy Father with the keys to the new "Popemobile" that was to be used at World Youth Day in Rio de Janeiro, Brazil. In a press release, Zetsche said, "It was a great joy for me to meet with Pope Francis. We will accompany Pope Francis in his first apostolic trip to Brazil, continuing a tradition that fills our employees with pride." Mercedes-Benz has a long tradition of providing transportation for the popes over the last 80 years, starting with the Nurburg 460 limousine delivered to Pope Pius XI in 1930.

Italian Prime Minister On July 4, Pope Francis met this morning with Enrico Letta, Prime Minister of the Italian Republic. After the meeting, the Italian leader met with Card. Tarcisio Bertone, the papal Secretary of State, as well as Abp. Dominique Mamberti, Secretary of Relations with States. According to a communique issued by the Holy See, the encounters included discussions on the social, economic, and political situations in Italy and the European Union as well as the situation in the Middle East.

Lumen Fidei On July 5, Pope Francis officially published the first encyclical of his pontificate, entitled *Lumen Fidei* ("The Light of Faith"). The encyclical reflects on the theological virtue of Faith and is intended for the Year of Faith. It is also the final encyclical of the trilogy on the theological virtues started by Pope Benedict XVI with *Deus Caritas Est* (2005) and *Spe Salvi* (2007) on the virtues of Love and Hope respectively. Pope Francis received a draft of the encyclical from Pope Emeritus Benedict and decided to incorporate it in his own encyclical. (For details, see under **News in Depth**, page 71.)

Monument to St. Michael On July 5, Pope Francis dedicated a new statue to St. Michael the Archangel in the Vatican Gardens; at the presentation was Pope Emeritus Benedict XVI, who, according to communique released by the Holy See, "was specially invited by Pope Francis." Pope Francis spoke on the new statue, saying, "In the Vatican Gardens there are many works of art, joined today by this one which however takes a position of particular importance, both for its location and for the meaning it expresses. Indeed, it is not merely a celebratory work, but rather an invitation to reflection and prayer, which fits well into this Year of Faith. Michael, which means 'Who is like God,' is the example of God's primacy, of his transcendence and power. Michael fights to re-establish divine justice; he defends the People of God from enemies and above all from the greatest enemy of all, the devil. And St. Michael is victorious because God acts in him. This sculpture reminds us that evil is vanquished. The Holy Father then consecrated the Vatican City State to St. Michael "asking him to defend us against evil and to banish it." He also consecrated Vatican City to St. Joseph so that his presence "strengthens us and gives us the courage to make space for God in our lives in order that good may always vanquish evil."

New Saints On July 5, Pope Francis received Card. Angelo Amato, Prefect of the Congregation for the Causes of Saints and gave his approval to the advancement of the causes for canonization of Blesseds John Paul II and John XXIII. The Holy Father approved the second miracle attributed to the intercession of the late John Paul II; the miracle in question involved a Costa Rican woman who was cured from a severe brain aneurism through the intercession of the late pontiff. More surprising was the pope's decision to approve the canonization of John XXIII without the typically required second miracle by accepting the favorable votes made by the Ordinary Session of the Congregation of Cardinals and Bishops to elevate Blessed John to the "altars of sainthood." It was expected that a special consistory would be convoked in September to decide on a date for the canonization of both Blessed John Paul II and Blessed John XXIII. (See also **News in Depth**, page 71, for details.)

Francis Meets With Seminarians On July 8, Pope Francis met in the Paul VI Audience Hall with 6,000 seminarians, novices and people on a vocational path from some 66 countries to celebrate the Year of Faith. The meeting was a jubilant one, but Francis also sounded a somber tone, saying to the young people, "Does the joy of a seminarian come from going out to dance on the weekend with friends? Or does it center in owning, or for example, obtaining the latest smartphone model or the fastest motorbike. An attention-grabbing automobile, I tell you sincerely, it pains me when I see a priest or a nun with the latest automobile. This cannot be! A car is necessary, but a more humble one and if you like a nice car, think only of how many children die of hunger in the world…When one meets with a seminarian or a novice that is very sad, one thinks that something isn't right, because the joy of the Lord is lacking, who carries out the service, the encounter with Jesus that brings you to meet with other."

Lampedusa Visit On July 8, Pope Francis travelled to the Italian island of Lampedusa, approximately 75 miles from the coast of Tunisia and said Mass on behalf of the thousands of African migrants who enter Italy through the island. Prior to his arrival via ferry, the pontiff laid a wreath in the sea to commemorate the almost 20,000 people who have lost their lives trying to enter the country. He then had an encounter with a group of migrants before saying Mass.

In his homily he focused on the importance love of neighbor and welcoming the stranger.

Plenary Indulgence for World Youth Day On July 9, the Apostolic Penitentiary issued a decree by which Pope Francis granted an indulgence to all who participate in the 28th World Youth Day celebrations in Rio de Janeiro. The decree was signed by Card. Manuel Monteiro de Castro, the Major Penitentiary, along with Bp. Krysztof Nykiel, regent of the Apostolic Penitentiary. A plenary indulgence was also granted for those could not attend World Youth Day: "The faithful who on account of a legitimate impediment cannot attend the aforementioned celebrations may obtain Plenary Indulgence under the usual spiritual, sacramental and prayer conditions, in a spirit of filial submission to the Roman Pontiff, by participation in the sacred functions on the days indicated, following the same rites and spiritual exercises as they occur via television or radio or, with due devotion, via the new means of social communication." It also granted a partial indulgence for those who, "with a contrite heart" who pray for youth during the time of the celebrations.

New Vatican Laws On July 11, it was announced that Pope Francis had issued a *Motu Proprio* that updated the Laws of the Vatican City State to conform with current international conventions. The laws that were adopted by the Pontifical Commission for Vatican City State were: Law No. VIII containing Supplementary Norms on Criminal Law Matters; Law No. IX containing Amendments to the Criminal Code and the Criminal Procedure Code; and Law No. X containing General Provisions on Administrative Sanctions. In a statement issued by Abp. Dominique Mamberti, secretary for Relations with States, the new laws were intended to give a clearer definition of laws that are already established. (See News in Depth, page 72, for other details.)

Vatican Prelate Investigated On July 12, Fr. Federico Lombardi, S.J., director of the Holy See Press Office, updated journalists on the investigation by Vatican authorities into the activities of Msgr. Nunzio Scarano, an official in the Vatican finance system. Scarano had been arrested in June by Italian authorities along with a broker and a secret service agent for allegedly attempting to transport 20 million euros on a private jet from Switzerland into Italy. Scarano worked as a senior accountant for the Administration of the Patrimony of the Apostolic See (APSA). According to Fr. Lombardi, the Vatican Promoter of Justice had frozen "funds at the Institute for Religious Works (IOR) attributed to suspended Vatican employee Nunzio Scarano as part of an ongoing investigation by the Vatican judicial authorities."

World Tourism Day On July 12, Card. Antonio Maria Veglio, president of the Pontifical Council for Migrants and Itinerant Peoples, published a message marking the celebration of World Tourism Day, scheduled for Sept. 27, 2013. The theme of this year's World Tourism Day was "Tourism and water: protecting our common future." The message read in part: "The Holy See also wishes to join in this commemoration, bringing its contribution from its own perspective, aware of the importance of the phenomenon of tourism at the present time and the challenges and opportunities it provides to our mission of evangelization. This is one of the economic sectors with the largest and fastest growth in the world. We must not forget that last year it was exceeded the milestone of one billion international tourists, to which we must add the even higher figures of local tourism."

Massacre of Volhynia On July 15, Pope Francis commemorated the massacres of Volhynia in June 1943, that brought the during World War II of tens of thousands of lives. The pope declared, "I join in prayer with the prelates and faithful of the Church in Ukraine, gathered in the cathedral of Lutsk for the Holy Mass of the souls of the deceased on the seventieth anniversary of the massacres at Volhynia. Those actions, provoked by nationalist ideology in the tragic context of the Second World War, claimed tens of thousands of victims and damaged the fraternity between the two peoples, the Polish and the Ukrainian. I entrust to the mercy of God the souls of the victims and, for their people, I ask the grace of profound reconciliation and of a peaceful future in hope and in sincere collaboration in building together the Kingdom of God."

Pope at Castel Gandolfo On July 15, Pope Francis visited the Papal residence of Castel Gandolfo; he took the opportunity to speak to employees and then delivered his Sunday Angelus address. Welcome was given to the pope by Bp. Marcello Semeraro of Albano, Dr. Saverio Petrillo, director of the Pontifical Residence, and Milva Monachesi, the mayor of Castel Gandolfo. In his Angelus address to a crowd of some 10,000 people, the pontiff spoke on the Sunday Gospel and the parable of the Good Samaritan, using it to reflect on mercy.

Day for Life On July 16, Pope Francis sent a special message to Catholics across Ireland and Great Britain in anticipation of the Church's annual Day for Life in October. The 2013 Day for Life message focused on care for unborn children and their mothers; care for people who are elderly; and care for those who are suicidal and their families. In his message, Pope Francis spoke of the value of all life, "even the weakest and most vulnerable, the sick, the old, the unborn and the poor, are masterpieces of God's creation, made in his own image, destined to live forever, and deserving of the utmost reverence and respect. He has promised his prayers that Day for Life will help to ensure that human life always receives the protection that it is due." The theme of this year's Day for Life is "Care for Life – It's Worth It." The message read: "Calling to mind the teaching of St. Irenaeus that the glory of God is seen in a living human being, the Holy Father encourages all of you to let the light of that glory shine so brightly that everyone may come to recognise the inestimable value of all human life. Even the weakest and most vulnerable, the sick, the old, the unborn and the poor, are masterpieces of God's creation, made in his own image, destined to live for ever, and deserving of the utmost reverence and respect. His Holiness prays that the Day for Life will help to ensure that human life always receives the protection that is its due, so that 'everything that breathes may praise the Lord' (Ps 150:6)."

New Pontifical Commission On July 19, Pope Francis issued a chirograph establishing a new Pontifical Commission for Holy See Finances. The new commission includes financial and legal experts, all laypeople. According to the document, the Commission will gather information, report to the Holy Father, and cooperate with the Council of Cardinals for the study of the organizational and economic problems of the Holy See, with the intention of drafting reforms of the institutions of the Holy See, toward a "simplification and rationalization of the existing bodies and more careful planning of the economic activities of all the Vatican Administrations." The chirograph also stated that the Committee will "offer the technical support of specialist advice and develop strategic solutions for improvement, so as to avoid the misuse of economic resources, to improve transparency in the processes of purchasing goods and services; to refine the administration of goods and real estate; to work with ever greater prudence in the financial sphere; to ensure correct application of accounting principles; and to guarantee healthcare and social security benefits to all those eligible." The Commission will also collaborate, on request, with the working Group of eight Cardinals in drafting a plan for the reform of the Apostolic Constitution *Pastor Bonus* on the Roman Curia. (See under **News in Depth**, page 71,for details.)

World Youth Day On the first Apostolic Visit outside of Italy of his pontificate, Pope Francis journeyed to Brazil to take part in the 28th World Youth Day in Rio de Janeiro, from July 22-29. The pontiff returned to Latin America for the first time since his election as pope in March. His schedule of events included Holy Mass in the Basilica of the Shrine of Our Lady of the Conception in Aparecida, on July 24; a visit to the impoverished Community of Varginha in Rio de Janeiro, on July 25; the Way of the Cross with the young people on the waterfront of Copacabana on July 26; Holy Mass for the 28th World Youth Day in Rio de Janeiro, on July 28; and a memorable Press Conference during the return flight on July 28. The celebration of World Youth Day culminated on July 28 with a Mass that drew more than three million people to Copacabana Beach. Throughout his visit, the pontiff was met by enormous and enthusiastic crowds. At the end of World Youth Day, the announcement was made that the next celebration would be held in Krakow, Poland, in 2016. (For details, see under **News in Depth**, page 64.)

Vatican Financial Information Authority On July 26, the Financial Intelligence Authority (AIF) of the Holy See and Vatican City State signed a Memorandum of Understanding (MOU) with its Italian counterpart, the Financial Information Unit (UIF) of the Bank of Italy. The Memorandum was signed in Rome by Card. Attilio Nicora, President of the AIF, and Dr. Claudio Clemente, director of UIF. A communique released by the Holy See Press Office noted that the Memorandum of Understanding is a "standard practice and formalizes the cooperation and exchange of financial information to fight money laundering and terrorist financing across borders between the competent authorities of both countries. It is based on the model Memorandum of Understanding prepared by the Egmont Group, the global organization of national Financial Intelligence Units, and contains clauses on reciprocity, permitted uses of information and confidentiality."

General Audience

None Scheduled

INTERNATIONAL

European Congress on Vocations On July 1, the European Vocation Service Commission of the Council of Catholic Bishops' Conferences of Europe (CCEE) began hosting the annual meeting on the priesthood in Rome that was scheduled to continue until July 4. Bishops and delegates from 22 Catholic Bishops' Conferences in Europe attended the meeting, along with delegates of the religious in Europe and North America. A communique released by the CCEE stated that the meeting would "discuss the vocation to priesthood today in the light of the document of the Congregation for Catholic Education 'Pastoral Guidelines for the promotion of vocations to the ministerial priesthood.'"

Coptic Patriarch On July 4, the Patriarch of Alexandria of the Catholic Copts Ibrahim Isaac Sidrak expressed his support for the removal of Mohamed Morsy as president of Egypt by the Egyptian military. Speaking to the Fides News Agency, Patriarch Sidrak said, "We have been celebrating since yesterday evening. We did not sleep. The people of Egypt have peacefully regained their country. And therefore showed the world that they are civilized people, in spite of the great problems they face. Several signals show that we

are on the right track. We will not repeat the mistakes made in the past. This time, they have well prepared the next steps, today the new interim Pres. Adly Mansour swears in, and gradually steps will be taken toward the full restoration of democratic order."

Pandoras Box On July 9, Bp. Gabriel Reyes of Antipolo in the Philippines spoke against the controversial Reproductive Health (RH) Law in the Philippines and called it a "Pandora's Box." During a homily at the Archdiocesan Shrine of Nuestra Señora de Guia, Bp. Reyes said that the approval of the law opens the door for euthanasia, and he cited the example of Belgium. He asked, "Aren't we like animals this way? When a leg gets broken, we just end its life. But we are not animals, we are human beings…It's unimaginable… Where will it end?"

Caritas Africa On July 9, the secretaries and national directors of Caritas Africa held a meeting Nairobi, Kenya where they called for aid for the Central African Republic in the face of severe political upheaval. In a statement, the participants declared, "We welcome and support the courageous and prophetic efforts undertaken by the Church of the Central African Republic to restore hope to the people who are suffering and to work to prevent the extension of this crisis as well as prevent its insidious transformation into a religious conflict."

Symposium of Episcopal Conferences On July 15, the 26th plenary meeting of the Symposium of Episcopal Conferences of Africa and Madagascar (SECAM) completed its plenary meeting and issued a call for political leaders in Africa to work for the common good. The theme of the plenary was "The Church, the family of God in Africa at the service of reconciliation, justice and peace," and the bishops had gathered in Kinshasa, Congo, from July 9-14. In their statement, they declared, "We cannot remain silent before a drama which appears to have been forgotten," the bishops stated. "We launch an urgent appeal to the United Nations, the European Union, the African Union and the governments of other countries in any way involved to take resolute action to bring an end to this war which has already lasted too long."

Family Meeting in Havana On July 16 the first national meeting of the Pastoral of the Family was held in Havana under the theme: "The Family: Path of Hope for Cuba." The meeting was chaired by Bp. Arturo Gonzalez of Santa Clara, who quoted Pope John Paul II when he visited Cuba during his pontificate: "Cuba: care for your families, in order to keep your heart pure!" The meeting looked at the current situation of families in Cuba and the future for the families of the island nation.

Same-Sex "Marriage" Bill On July 17, Queen Elizabeth II approved a bill that legalized same-sex marriage in Britain. The royal approval was the final step in the process of legalization under British law. The new law will enable same-sex couples to "marry" in both civil and religious ceremonies and will allow same-sex couples who had entered into civil partnerships to obtain the legal status of "marriage." The Catholic Bishops Conference of England and Wales issued a statement: "In receiving Royal Assent, the Marriage (Same Sex Couples) Act marks a watershed in English law and heralds a profound social change. This fact is acknowledged by both advocates and opponents of the Act. Marriage has, over the centuries, been publicly recognized as a stable institution which establishes a legal framework for the committed relationship between a man and a woman and for the upbringing and care of their children. It has, for this reason, rightly been recognized as unique and worthy of legal protection. The new Act breaks the existing legal links between the institution of marriage and sexual complementarity. With this new legislation, marriage has now become an institution in which openness to children, and with it the responsibility on fathers and mothers to remain together to care for children born into their family unit, are no longer central. That is why we were opposed to this legislation on principle."

March For Peace On July 18, thousands of Catholics in South Korea marched near the demilitarized zones between South and North Korea as part of the 60th anniversary of the end of the Korean War. Fides News Agency reported that the event was organized by the "Commission for the Reconciliation of the Korean people" of the Korean Bishops Conference. A symposium entitled "Peace on the Korean Peninsula: How to Build It" was also organized as part of the commemoration. A statement from the commission published by Fides called for a lasting peace and not "a precarious cease-fire in force in the last 60 years." It added, "It is important to rekindle the passion of the faithful for the reconciliation and unity of the Korean people, to build genuine peace on the Korean peninsula, to prepare for the evangelization of North Korea, helping the faithful to become apostles of peace."

Coptic Pope Tawadros II On July 18, it was announced that the Coptic Orthodox Pope Tawadros II had suspended his weekly meeting of public prayer and catechesis owing to worries about security. The catechesis sessions were held every Wednesday afternoon in the Coptic Cathedral of Cairo. According to the Fides News Agency, the sessions were ended because of the current situation in the region in the wake of the removal of Pres. Mohamed Morsi on July 3.

NATIONAL

New HHS Ruling On July 3, Card. Timothy Dolan, Archbishop of New York and president of the U.S. Conference of Catholic Bishops (USCCB) issued a statement that a new 110 page update to the U.S Department of Health and Human Services mandate that requires employee health insurance for contraceptives, including abortion-causing drugs, and female sterilization failed to eliminate "the need to continue defending our rights in Congress and the courts." After careful analysis of the mandate by the officials of the USCCB, Cardinal Dolan issued a statement that declared, "Once again, the statement United for Religious Freedom–issued by the U.S. bishops' Administrative Committee in March 2012, and affirmed by the entire body of bishops in June 2012–provides the framework for examining the final form of the HHS mandate. That document identified three categories of religious freedom problems in the mandate–in short, problems with the "religious employer" exemption; problems with the 'accommodation' for employers deemed not 'religious enough' for the exemption; and problems with the lack of any exemption or 'accommodation' for individuals and for-profit businesses.That is, we are concerned as pastors with the freedom of the Church as a whole–not just for the full range of its institutional forms, but also for the faithful in their daily lives–to carry out the mission and ministry of Jesus Christ. We can already tell how the final rule fares in the first and third categories, because there have been no changes in those areas since the proposed rule of February.

Religious Liberty On July 2, Abp. William E. Lori of Baltimore, chairman of the U.S. Conference of Catholic Bishops' (USCCB) Ad Hoc Committee for Religious Liberty, Russell D. Moore, Ph.D., pres. of the Southern Baptist Convention's Ethics & Religious Liberty Commission, and more than 100 prominent national religious leaders and scholars released an open letter entitled Standing Together

for Religious Freedom that called on the Administration and Congress to respect conscience rights and religious freedom. The letter declared: "The doctrines of our respective faiths require something of us beyond the walls of our churches, synagogues, temples, and other places of worship. Those faith convictions manifest themselves through our daily interactions among family, neighbors, strangers and institutions. As the Catholic bishops have said from the very beginning, the underlying issue with the HHS Mandate is not about any specific teaching. In fact, other signatories on the letter do not share our view on contraception and probably disagree with us in many other ways, but they understand the core religious freedom issue at stake here."

Fortnight for Freedom On July 4, Catholic dioceses across the United States ended the second Fortnight for Freedom, a two-week celebration of religious liberty in America and around the world. The second annual Fortnight began on June 21, the vigil of the feast of Sts. Thomas More and John Fisher. Card. Donald Wuerl, Archbishop of Washington, celebrated the closing Mass of the Fortnight at the Basilica of the National Shrine of the Immaculate Conception in Washington. A statement issued by Abp. William Lori of Baltimore, chairman of the U.S. bishops' Ad Hoc Committee on Religious Liberty, stated, "Participation in the second Fortnight for Freedom has been an encouraging sign that Catholics take seriously their responsibility to participate in civic life and that we must all witness to the positive role faith plays in our society."

Parental Notification On July 12, the Illinois Supreme Court unanimously upheld a 1995 parental notification of abortion law. State lawmakers had approved the legislation that required a parent or legal guardian be notified when a minor seeks an abortion in order to protect children from making such a decision on their own. The measure included a waiver for those children who have been physically or sexually abused. The Catholic Conference of Illinois welcomed the decision, issuing a statement that, "With this ruling, parents across the state and the Midwest can breathe a sigh of relief with the knowledge that state law finally allows them to fully parent their children, and safeguard their lives and those of the unborn."

Fairness Act On July 29, Abp. William E. Lori of Baltimore, chairman of the U.S. Conference of Catholic Bishops' (USCCB) Ad Hoc Committee for Religious Liberty, and Bp. Denis J. Madden, auxiliary bishop of Baltimore and chairman of the USCCB Committee on Ecumenical and Interreligious Affairs, expressed pleasure over the introduction of S. 1274 by Senators Kirsten Gillibrand and Roy Blunt and urged U.S. Senators to support passage of the Federal Disaster Assistance Nonprofit Fairness Act of 2013. S. 1274 is similar to H.R. 592, which overwhelmingly passed the House of Representatives on Feb. 13, 2013. In a statement, they wrote, "Your legislation is consistent with Supreme Court jurisprudence, which recognizes the right of religious institutions to receive public financial aid in the context of a broad program administered on the basis of religion-neutral criteria. The bill is not asking for special treatment, just equal treatment that conforms to constitutional protections. It should be noted that in the aftermath of a natural disaster houses of worship often play an irreplaceable role in the recovery of a community. Discrimination that treats houses of worship as ineligible for federal assistance in the wake of a natural disaster, beyond being a legal violation, hurts the very communities most affected by the indiscriminate force of nature. The best approach to address questions of eligibility for houses of worship is a permanent clarification of federal law."

AUGUST 2013

Ramadan Message On Aug. 2, Pope Francis sent a personal message to Muslims for the end of Ramadan, a departure from Vatican tradition in which the message was sent by the president of the Pontifical Council for Interreligious Dialogue. In the message, the pope focused on the theme of common reflection "that concerns both Muslims and Christians: Promoting Mutual Respect through Education." Pope Francis invited Muslims and Christians to respect each person "first of all his life, his physical integrity, his dignity and the rights deriving from that dignity, his reputation, his property, his ethnic and cultural identity, his ideas and his political choices. We are therefore called to think, speak and write respectfully of the other, not only in his presence, but always and everywhere, avoiding unfair criticism or defamation. Families, schools, religious teaching and all forms of media have a role to play in achieving this goal."

World Youth Day Remembered On Aug. 5, Pope Francis used his Angelus address to remember World Youth Day and his closing Mass in Rio de Janeiro. The pontiff said, "Let us always remember: the youth do not follow the Pope, they follow Jesus Christ, carrying his cross. And the Pope leads them and accompanies them on this journey of faith and hope. So, I thank all the young people who participated, some of whom also made sacrifices to do so. And I thank the Lord too for the meetings I had with the Pastors and people of that great country that is Brazil, as well as with the authorities and volunteers. May the Lord repay all those who worked for this great feast of faith."

World Mission Day On Aug. 6, Pope Francis issued the annual letter for World Mission Day and centered his message on faith, which he called "God's precious gift" that is "not reserved for a few but offered with generosity." He added, "Everyone should be able to experience the joy of being loved by God, the joy of salvation…Each community is therefore challenged, and invited to make its own, the mandate entrusted by Jesus to the Apostles, to be his 'witnesses in Jerusalem, throughout Judea and Samaria and to the ends of the earth' (Acts 1:8) and this, not as a secondary aspect of Christian life, but as its essential aspect: we are all invited to walk the streets of the world with our brothers and sisters, proclaiming and witnessing to our faith in Christ and making ourselves heralds of his Gospel."

Syrian Violence On Aug. 6, the Congregation for the Eastern Churches released a statement on the crisis in Syria and the escalating violence against Christians. Of particular concern was the recent kidnapping of Fr. Paolo dall'Oglio, an Italian Jesuit priest who had worked in Syria for the 30 years and was kidnapped by the Islamic State of Iraq and Levant, a radical Islamist group with ties to Al-Qaeda. The prefect of the Congregation for the Eastern Churches, Card. Leonardo Sandri, wrote, "Together with the churches of the region, he remembers the absolute silence that weighs on the fate of two bishops and two priests kidnapped months ago, like many others, Syrian and foreign, in the same painful condition."

Tomb of Paul VI On Aug. 7, Pope Francis visited the Vatican Grottoes, located below the St. Peter's Basilica, and prayed in front of the tomb of his predecessor Pope Paul VI on the 35th anniversary of Paul's death. During the visit, the pontiff met with a group of young people from Brescia, the home diocese of Pope Paul, who were visiting Rome pilgrimage to commemorate the death of the late pontiff.

Knights of Columbus On Aug. 8, Card. Tarcisio Bertone, the papal secretary of state, sent a letter on Pope Francis' behalf to the Knights of Columbus during their 131st Supreme Convention, in San Antonio, Texas. The convention's theme, "Be Protectors of God's Gifts," was drawn from the pope's homily at the inauguration of his papal ministry on March 19. The cardinal wrote, "In this time of rapid social and cultural changes, the protection of God's gifts cannot fail to include the affirmation and defense of the great patrimony of moral truths taught by the Gospel and confirmed by right reason, which serve as the bedrock of a just and well-ordered society.

Financial Reform On Aug. 8, the Holy See announced that Pope Francis had issued a *motu proprio* on the prevention and countering of money laundering, the financing of terrorism, and the proliferation of weapons of mass destruction. The papal document was a reaffirmation of the Holy See's commitment to preventing illegal activities that was given significant foundation in the 2010 *motu proprio* issued by Pope Benedict. The new *motu proprio* includes expanding the applicability of Vatican laws to encompass all dicasteries, or offices, of the Roman Curia as well as other entities that are dependent on the Holy See.

In addition, the Vatican's Financial Information Authority (FAI) received expanded "supervisory and regulatory function," and a Financial Security Committee was established to coordinate "the competent authorities of the Holy See and the Vatican City State in the area of prevention and countering of money laundering, the financing of terrorism and the proliferation of weapons of mass destruction."

Pope on Families On Aug. 12, Pope Francis sent a message to Brazilian families on the occasion of the "National Week of the Family." The theme of the week was "The transmission and education of the Christian faith in the family." Pope Francis wrote, "Parents are called to transmit with their words, and above all, their deeds, the fundamental truth on life and human love, that receives a new light from the Revelation of God. In particular, facing a throwaway culture that relativizes the values of human life, parents are called to transmit to their children the knowledge that [life] must always be defended, from the maternal womb, recognizing it as a gift from God and a guarantee of the future of humanity, but also in the care of the elderly, especially of grandparents, that are the living memory of a people and transmit the wisdom of life."

Athletes Meet the Pope On Aug. 13, Pope Francis met with members of the Italian and Argentinian national soccer teams who had been playing a soccer match in honor of the pontiff. The said to the athletes, "Dear players, I would like to remind you especially, that you are a point of reference in life in the way you behave, both on the field as well as outside it. Last Sunday I talked on the telephone with some boys of a group. They wanted to greet me. I chatted with them for about half an hour and, of course, the great topic of those boys was tomorrow's match. They mentioned several of you and said: 'no, I like this one for this reason, this one for that, and this other one for this.' You are an example, you are points of reference. The good you do is impressive. You do good with your conduct, with your game, with your values; people look at you – take advantage of this to sow goodness. Even if you don't realize it, you are models, for good or evil, for so many people who look at you with admiration.

"Be conscious of this and give an example of loyalty, respect and altruism. You are also architects of understanding and social peace, architects of understanding and social peace that we so need. You are a reference for so many youths and model of values embodied in life. I'm confident of all the good you can do among youths."

50th Anniversary On Aug. 14, Pope Francis sent a letter to Bp. José María Rossi of the diocese of the Inmaculada Concepción (Immaculate Conception) in Argentina to celebrate its 50th anniversary. The Holy Father wrote, "In these 50 years you have walked and have made a path of disciples of Jesus and announcers of the Gospel: disciples and missionaries, so that all in the diocese may have life in abundance…To walk, to become a disciple and to announce. Three words. 'To walk': You know that I am afraid of settled Christians. They end up like still water. 'To become a disciple': I also am afraid of those who believe that they 'know it all,' the sufficient. Without knowing, they close their heart to the Lord; they end up centered in themselves. They are the Christians that we make may call 'Christians with themselves and for themselves.' When one finds themselves with Jesus, they live the wondrous awe of that encounter and feel the need to look for Him in prayer, in the reading of the Gospels. They feel the need to adore Him, to know Him… and feel the need to announce him. And this is the third word: "to announce", meaning, missionaries, to bring his name, the teachings, and the gestures of Jesus to the brothers. The Christian walks, becomes a disciple and announces. They are not settled, they come out of themselves: they come out of themselves to announce the Good News of Jesus to the brothers."

General Audiences

No Audiences

INTERNATIONAL

English Youth On Aug. 9, the fifth Annual Report on the work of the National Catholic Safeguarding Commission (NCSC) and the Catholic Safeguarding Advisory Service (CSAS) was issued and noted the significant progress made in the last years in protecting young people in the England and Wales. The report noted advances in outreach to victims, responding sensitively to victims of abuse, offering immediate support to victims, and progress with the "One Church" project.

Lebanese Maronite Bishops On Aug. 9, the Council of Maronite Bishops in Lebanon called on the country to maintain its neutrality in the bloody conflicts taking place in neighboring areas, especially Syria. The council, headed by Patriarch Bechara Boutros Rai, wrote, "The bishops express their concern and that of the Lebanese people before the political paralysis that affects the constitutional institutions because of the extreme vertical divisions of the political class, polarized into two opposite fronts, that each try to monopolize power and impose their point of view."

NATIONAL

Permanent Deaconate According to a national survey released by the U.S. Conference of Catholic Bishops (USCCB) and conducted by the Center for Applied Research in the Apostolate (CARA), the permanent diaconate continues to be on the increase in the dioceses of the United States. There are presently more than 18,000 deacons, about 3,000 of them retired, with the largest numbers found in the Archdiocese of Galveston-Houston (414), Diocese of Trenton, (383), Archdiocese of Los Angeles (344), and Archdiocese of Hartford, Connecticut (300). Ninety-three percent of active deacons are currently married; four percent are widowers, and two percent never married. Ninety-five percent of active deacons are at least 50 years old. About a quarter are in their fifties; 43 percent are in their sixties; and 25 percent are 70 or older.

Almost 90 percent of dioceses have a minimum age for deacon candidacy and half have a mandatory retirement age. In the U.S. the minimum age for ordination to the permanent deaconate is 35. The average minimum age for acceptance into a diaconate program is 33. Thirteen percent of dioceses have a mandatory retirement age of 70. Eighty percent mandate retirement at 75. Seventy-eight percent of active deacons are white. Fifteen percent are Hispanic or Latino, Three percent are African American and three percent are Asian.

Labor Day Statement On Aug. 12, the U.S. Bishops issued their 2013 annual Labor Day Statement, released under the signature of Bp. Stephen Blaire of Stockton, chairman of the U.S. bishops' Committee on Domestic Justice and Human Development. The statement noted that the current economic imbalances do not have to be inevitable, adding, "We must be bold in promoting a just economy that reduces inequality by creating jobs that pay a living wage and share with workers some profits of the company, as well as ensuring a strong safety net for jobless workers and their families and those who are incapable of work… Over four million people have been jobless for over six months, and that does not include the millions more who have simply lost hope; for every available job, there are as many as five unemployed and underemployed people actively vying for it. This gap pushes wages down – half of the jobs in this country pay less than $27,000. Over 46 million people live in poverty, 16 million of them children."

DEATHS — AUGUST 2012 TO AUGUST 2013

Ambrozic, Cardinal Aloysius M., 81, Aug. 26, 2011, abp. of Toronto, Canada, from 1990 to 2006; born in Gabrje, Slovenia, he emigrated to Austria with his family in 1945 and then to Canada in 1948; ord. a priest on June 4, 1955, for the archdiocese of Toronto, after studies in Rome, he taught Scripture at St. Augustine's Seminary from 1960-67 and New Testament exegesis at the Toronto School of Theology from 1970-76; ord. aux. bp. of Toronto on Mar. 26, 1976, he was appointed co-adjutor abp. of Toronto on May 22, 1986 and became abp. of Toronto on Mar. 17, 1990; he was named to the College of Cardinals on Feb. 21, 1998, with the titular church of Sts. Marcellinus and Peter; he retired on Jan. 30, 2007; he was well-known throughout Canada for his defense of traditional marriage.

Anderson, Bp. Moses B., 84, Jan. 7, 2013, aux. bp. of Detroit from 1983-2003; a native of Selma, AL, he studied at St. Michael's College in Winooski, VT, St. Edmund Seminary in Burlington, VT, and the University of Legon in Ghana and was ordained a priest in 1958 for the Society of St. Edmund; ordained titular bp. of Vatarba and aux. bp. of Detroit in 1983, he retired in 2003; at the time of his ordination, he was one of seven African-American bishops in the United States; in 1984, he helped draft "What We Have Seen and Heard," the first joint pastoral letter by the country's black bishops, on the topic of evangelization.

Antonetti, Cardinal Lorenzo, 90, Apr. 10, 2013, Italian cardinal and head of the Administration of the Patrimony of the Holy See from 1995 to 1998; born in Romagnano Sesia, Italy, he studied at the Pontifical University of St. Thomas and canon law from the Pontifical Gregorian University; he was ordained a priest in 1945 and, after studies at the Pontifical Ecclesiastical Academy, he entered diplomatic service and served in Lebanon, Venezuela, the first section for Extraordinary Affairs of the Secretariat of State, the U.S., and France; appointed apostolic nuncio to Nicaragua and Honduras and then Zaire, he was named secretary of the Administration of the Patrimony of the Apostolic See (APSA) in 1977; named apostolic nuncio to France in 1988, he was appointed pro-president of APSA in 1995 and president in 1998; Pope John Paul II made him a cardinal in 1998.

Baldelli, Cardinal Fortunato, 77, Sept. 20, 2012, Italian Cardinal and Major Penitentiary from 2009; a native of Valfabbrica, Italy, he studied at the Major Roman Seminary and the Pontifical Lateran University, Rome, and then diplomacy at the Pontifical Ecclesiastical Academy; ordained a priest in 1961, he entered the diplomatic service of the Holy See in 1966; after serving around the world, he was appointed titular abp. of Bevagna (Mevania) and was apostolic delegate in Angola, São Tomé and Príncipe, nuncio in the Dominican Republic and apostolic delegate in Puerto Rico, and nuncio in France; appointed Major Pentientiary in 2009, he was named a cardinal in 2010.

Billings, Dr. Evelyn, 95, Feb. 16, 2013, Australian physician who, with her husband John, helped develop a form of natural family planning supported by the Church; a native of Australia, she studied medicine at the University of Melbourne and pediatrics as a post-graduate student in London; she was also an instructor in embryology and histology within the anatomy department of the University of Melbourne and an assistant physician to the Department of Community Medicine at St Vincent's Hospital, also in Melbourne; she and her husband developed the Billings Method, a clear and teachable form of NFP; according to the World Organization of Ovulation Method Billings, known as WOOMB, women in more than 100 countries practice the method; she and her husband were among 40 founding members named by Blessed John Paul II to the Pontifical Academy for Life in 1994.

Boggs, Corine Lindy, 97, July 27, 2013, former U.S. Ambassador to the Vatican and noted public servant; after her husband, Louisiana Congressman Hale Boggs, died when the private plane he was in crashed in Alaska in 1972, she ran successfully as a Democrat for his seat in Louisiana's 2nd Congressional District, based in New Orleans; she served nine terms as the first woman from Louisiana to be elected to Congress until her retirement in 1991; in 1997 President Bill Clinton appointed her U.S. ambassador to the Vatican when she was 81 years old, and she held the post until 2001; among her many honors were the University of Notre Dame's Laetare Medal, the Pope John Paul II Award from the Catholic Foundation of the Archdiocese of New Orleans, and the Congressional Award of the Veterans of Foreign Wars.

Bork, Judge Robert, 85, Dec. 19, 2012, noted American judicial figure, U.S. solicitor general, a 1987 Supreme Court judicial nominee, and a convert to Catholicism in 2003; born in Pittsburgh, he studied at the University of Chicago and taught constitutional law at Yale University for 20 years; his first wife, Claire Davidson Bork, died in 1980, and in 1982 he married Mary Ellen Pohl, a former member of the Religious of the Sacred Heart of Jesus; he was a U.S. Circuit Court judge for the District of Columbia from 1982 until 1988; his nomination to the U.S. Supreme Court by Pres. Ronald Reagan in 1987 was met with such fury and extreme political and personal attacks by the American Left that the word "bork" was added to the Oxford English Dictionary as an example of defamation and vilification; his nomination was rejected by the Democratic-led U.S. Senate in a 58-42 vote; he authored several books, including *Slouching Towards Gomorrah: Modern Liberalism and American Decline*, and *Coercing Virtue: The Worldwide Rule of Judges*.

Bosco, Bp. Anthony G., 85, July 2, 2013, bishop of Greensburg from 1987 to 2004; born in New Castle, PA, he studied at St. Vincent Seminary in Latrobe, PA, and the Lateran University in Rome; ordained a priest for Pittsburgh In 1952, he was ordained titular bp. of Labicum and aux. of Pittsburgh in 1970; appointed bp. of Greensburg in 1987; he retired on Mar. 4, 2004; as bishop, he promoted the role of the laity and catechesis.

Brubeck, Dave, 91, Dec. 5, 2012, famous pianist and jazz performer; a native of Concord, CA, he served in World War II and formed the Dave Brubeck Quartet in 1951; his first major hit was "Take Five" and spent the rest of his life regularly touring; he performed before Pope John Paul II and eight presidents; he converted to Catholicism in 1980 after finishing commission from Our Sunday Visitor for a Mass titled "To Hope"; he received the Laetare Medal from the University of Notre Dame and the Christophers' Life Achievement Award, both in 2006, and the Grammy Lifetime Achievement Award in 1996, as well as an honorary degree in sacred theology from the University of Fribourg in Switzerland in 2004 and the Kennedy Center Honors in 2009.

Catanello, Bp. Ignatius A., 74, Mar. 11, 2013, auxiliary bp. of Brooklyn from 1994; a native of Brookly, he studied at the Cathedral Preparatory Seminary and St. Francis College, The Catholic University of America, St. John's University in Jamaica, NY, and New York University; ordained a priest for Brooklyn on May 28, 1966, he was ordained titular bp.

of Deulto and aux. bishop of Brooklyn on Aug. 22, 1994; he was known as "Bishop Iggy"; he retired In 2010 for reasons of health.

Cellucci, Gov. Paul, 65, Sept. 11, 2012, governor of Massachusetts and U.S. ambassador to Canada; born in Hudson, MA, he graduated from Boston College and received a degree from Boston College Law School in 1973; he served in the Massachusetts House of Representatives and Senate before being elected the state's lieutenant governor in 1991; he became acting governor in 1997 after Gov. William Weld resigned to become ambassador to Mexico and was then elected governor in 1998 and served until 2001 when he resigned to become ambassador to Canada, a post he held until 2005; he supported the U.S. Supreme Court's *Roe v. Wade* decision, which legalized abortion, to the sadness of Catholic leaders.

Cheli, Cardinal Giovanni, 94, Feb. 8, 2013, Italian Cardinal, longtime Vatican diplomat, and head of the Pontifical Council for Migrants and Travelers from 1986-98; a native of Turin, Italy, he was ordained a priest in 1942 and served the Secretariat of State and diplomatic service in apostolic nunciatures in Guatemala, Spain, and Rome; he served as Permanent Observer of the Holy See to the U.N., 1973-86 and was ordained titular abp. of Santa Giusta, in 1978; president of the Pontifical Council for the Pastoral Care of Migrants and Itinerant People from 1986-98, he was made a cardinal in 1998.

Cooney, Bp. Patrick R., 78, Oct. 15, 2012, bishop of Gaylord from 1989-2009; a native of Detroit, MI, he studied at Sacred Heart Seminary in Detroit, the Gregorian University in Rome, and the University of Notre Dame; ordained a priest in 1959, he was ordained titular bp. of Hodelm and aux. bp. of Detroit in 1983 and appointed bp. of Gaylord in 1989; he retired in 2009.

D'Arcy, Bp. John M., 80, Feb. 3, 2013, bishop of Fort Wayne-South Bend from 1985-2009; the son of Irish immigrants, he was born in 1932, in Brighton, MA and studied at St. John's Seminary, Brighton, and was ordained to the priesthood in 1957, for the Archdiocese of Boston; he earned a doctorate in spiritual theology at the Pontifical University of St. Thomas, known as the Angelicum, in Rome in 1968 and served as spiritual director and professor of spiritual theology at St. John's Seminary from 1968 to 1985; ordained auxiliary bp. of Boston in 1975, he was appointed to Ft. Wayne-South Bend on Feb. 26, 1985; his time as bishop was marked by progress in catechesis, education, ecumenism and social services, as well as the start of the annual Bishop's Appeal; he was also noted for his courage in warning the archdiocesan leadership about the sexual abuse crisis in Boston.

Dodds, Monica, 60, Jan. 6, 2013, noted author, editor, and longtime columnist for the Catholic News Service; a native of Seattle, WA, she was married to writer Bill Dodds and was a columnist for CNS until 1991; she wrote extensively with her husband, including columns for the Knights of Columbus magazine, *Columbia*, books such as *The Joy of Marriage* and *Encyclopedia of Mary* and editor of *My Daily Visitor* for Our Sunday Visitor; she was also author of *A Catholic Guide to Caring for Your Aging Parent* and *Praying in the Presence of Our Lord with St. Thérèse of Lisieux*.

Dorsey, Bp. Norbert M., C.P., 83, Feb. 21, 2013, bishop of Orlando from 1990-2004 and a member of the Passionists; a native of Springfield, MA, he studied at Passionist seminaries in the eastern U.S. province, and the Pontifical Institute of Sacred Music and Gregorian University in Rome, and was professed in the Passionists in 1949 and ordained a priest in 1956; assistant general of Passionists from 1976-86, he was

ordained titular bp. of Mactaris and aux. bp. of Miami in 1986; appointed bp. of Orlando in 1990, he retired in 2004.

Fitzsimons, Bp. George K., 84, July 28, 2013, bishop of Salina from 1984 to 2004; a native of Kansas City, MO, he worked in banking, served as a lieutenant junior grade in the U.S. Navy as a pilot, and was a real estate salesman before entering the seminary; he studied at Conception Seminary College and was ordained to the priesthood in 1961; in 1975 he was named auxiliary bp. of Kansas City-St. Joseph; he was appointed bp. of Salina in 1984.

Glemp, Cardinal Józef, 83, Jan. 23, 2013, archbishop of Warsaw and primate of Poland from 1981-92; born in Inowroclaw, Poland, he was assigned to forced labor on a German farm in Rycerzow during the Nazi occupation; ordained a priest in 1956, he studied in Rome from 1958 64 and received a degree in Roman and canon law from the Pontifical Lateran University; ordained bp. of Warmia in 1979, he was named abp. of Gniezno, with the title of abp. of Warsaw and primate of Poland; in 1981 and made a cardinal in 1983; he led the Polish Church during the final era of Communism and was a prominent national figure after the collapse of the Soviet Union.

Gossman, Bp. F. Joseph, 83, Aug. 12, 2013, bishop of Raleigh from 1975-2006; born in Baltimore, MD, he studied at St. Charles College in Catonsville, MD, St. Mary's Seminary in Baltimore, MD, the North American College in Rome, and the Catholic Univ. of America in Washington, DC; ord. a priest for Baltimore on Dec. 17, 1955, he was ordained titular bp. of Agunto and aux. bp. of Baltimore on Sept. 11, 1968; appointed bp. of Raleigh on Apr. 8, 1975, he served for 31 years and was shepherd during a period of phenomenal growth in the diocese; he dedicated more than 60 parishes, schools and all-purpose buildings in his tenure; he retired on June 8, 2006.

Greeley, Fr. Andrew, 85, May 29, 2013, Chicago archdiocesan priest and widely read novelist, journalist, and sociologist; born in Oak Park, IL, he was ordained a priest for the Archdiocese of Chicago in 1954 and studied sociology at the University of Chicago; he later taught sociology at University of Chicago and the University of Arizona in Tucson; he authored more than 60 novels, as well as more than 70 works of nonfiction including on sociology; his final book, *Chicago Catholics and the Struggles Within Their Church*, was published in 2010.

Honoré, Cardinal Jean, 92, Feb. 28, 2013, abp. of Tours from 1981-1997 and one of the contributors on the *Catechism of the Catholic Church*; ordained a priest on June 29, 1943, he authored his doctoral dissertation under the direction of Jean Daniélou at the Institute Catholique, Paris and taught at St. Vincent's College in Rennes and in Saint-Malo; he worked for six years at the National Religious Education Centre (CNEC) and was rector of the Catholic University of Angers; appointed bp. of Evreux on Oct. 24, 1972; appointed abp. of Tours on Aug. 13, 1981; he was made a cardinal 2001.

Hughes, Bp. Edward T., 92, Dec. 25, 2012, bishop of Metuchen from 1986-97; a native of Lansdowne, PA, he studied at St. Charles Seminary, the University of Pennsylvania in Philadelphia, and was ordained a priest in 1947; ordained titular bp. of Segia and aux. bp. of Philadelphia in 1976, he was appointed bp. of Metuchen on Dec. 11, 1986 and retired in 1997; as bishop he was a strong supporter of Catholic education.

Hughes, Bp. William A., 91, Feb. 7, 2013, bishop of Covington from 1979-1995; born in Youngstown, OH, he studied at St. Charles College in Catonsville, MD, St. Mary's Seminary in Cleveland, OH, and the University of

Notre Dame; ordained a priest for Youngstown in 1946, he was ordained titular bp. of Inis Cathaig and aux. bp. of Youngstown in 1974; appointed bp. of Covington in 1979, he retired in 1995; as bishop, he established the Permanent Diaconate Office, Office of Youth Ministry and the Diocesan Pastoral Council and reinstituted the Rite of Christian Initiation of Adults program; he also headed the U.S. Bishops' Task Force on AIDS in 1987.

Jakubowski, Bp. Thad J., 89, July 14, 2013, auxiliary bishop of Chicago from 1988-2003; a native of Chicago, IL, he studied at Mundelein Seminary, St. Mary of the Lake University, and Loyola University; ordained a priest for Chicago in 1950, he was ordained titular bp. of Plestia and aux. bp. of Chicago in 1988; he retired in 2003.

Lewis, Philip D., 82, Sept. 4, 2012, one-time Florida state senator and Catholic philanthropist; born in Omaha, NE, and raised in Chicago and Palm Beach, he attended Georgetown University and then founded Philip D. Lewis Real Estate, specializing in commercial and industrial real estate and investments; he was elected to the Florida State Senate in 1970 and served 10 years, including two years as Senate president; a daily communicant and member of various Catholic and diocesan organizations, he was named a Knight of St. Gregory by Pope Paul VI in 1965; he was also a past board chairman of Foundations and Donors Interested in Catholic Activities (FADICA).

Lotocky, Innocent Hilarius, O.S.B.M., 97, July 4, 2013, bishop of St. Nicholas of Chicago for the Ukrainians, from 1981-1993; born on Nov. 3, 1915, in Petlykiwci, Ukraine, he studied in seminaries in Ukraine, Czechoslovakia, and Austria and was ordained a priest on Nov. 24, 1940; appointed bishop of the Ukrainian Catholic Eparchy of Chicago on Dec. 22, 1980, he was ordained a bishop on Mar. 22, 1981; he retired on July 15, 1993.

Martini, Cardinal Carlo Maria, 85, Aug. 31, 2012, Jesuit Italian Cardinal, archbishop of Milan, and a renowned biblical scholar; a native of Turin, he entered the Society of Jesus in 1944 and was ordained a priest in 1952; he served as rector from 1969 78 of the Pontifical Biblical Institute and rector of the Pontifical Gregorian University from 1978 79; the author of theological, biblical and spiritual works, he was named abp. of Milan in 1980 and was named a cardinal in 1983; he retired in 2002 but was considered among the papabili in the 2005 conclave.

McFadden, Bp. Joseph P., 65, May 2, 2013, bishop of Harrisburg from 2010 who died unexpectedly while attending meetings of the Pennsylvania bishops; a native of Philadelphia, he studied at St. Joseph University in Philadelphia and was ordained a priest for the Archdiocese of Philadelphia in 1981; in 2004, he was named an auxiliary bp. of Philadelphia; he was named bp. of Harrisburg in 2010.

McFadden, Msgr. Leo F., 84, Feb. 9, 2013, award-winning columnist and former staff member of the Catholic News Service's Rome bureau; a native of Butte, Montana, he grew up in Nevada and studied in Rome before ordination as a priest for Reno in 1953; he studied journalism at the University of Nevada and was editor of Reno's diocesan newspaper, the *Nevada Register*; he joined the Rome bureau of CNS in 1969; a fellow in the John Henry Cardinal Newman Honor Society, he received the Nevada Press Association Award as "Best Columnist in all Nevada Newspapers" and was twice nominated for the Pulitzer Prize; he was also the first National Guard chaplain to be promoted to the rank of brigadier general in the U.S. Air Force.

McGeady, Sister Mary Rose, 84, Sept. 13, 2012, head of Covenant House from 1990-2003 and member of the Daughters of Charity of St. Vincent de Paul; she became head of Covenant House after its founder, Franciscan Father Bruce Ritter, departed owing to scandal, and she was credited with restoring the institution to credibility.

Musial, Stan, 92, Jan. 19, 2013, Hall of Fame baseball player for the St. Louis Cardinals, called "Stan the Man"; he grew up in Donora, PA, and played for the Cardinals for 22 years until his retirement after the 1963 season; he won seven National League batting championships, held 17 major league batting records, and won the National League's Most Valuable Player award three times and the World Series championship with the Cardinals three time; he was awarded the Medal of Freedom, considered the nation's highest civilian honor, in 2011; he was co-chair of Pope John Paul II's 1999 pastoral visit to St. Louis.

Nagy, Cardinal Stanislaw, 91, June 5, 2013, Polish cardinal, friend of Pope John Paul II, and member of the International Theological Commission; a native of Bieruñ Stary, Poland, he joined the Priests of the Sacred Heart of Jesus, also known as the Dehonians, at age 16, professed permanent vows during the Nazi occupation in 1941, and was ordained a priest in 1945; he taught with the future Pope John Paul II at Lublin University in Poland and would ski with the future pontiff near Zakopane in the Tatra Mountains; he served on the International Theological Commission and was appointed cardinal in 2003.

O'Neill, Bp. Arthur J., 95, April 27, 2013, bishop of Rockford from 1968 to 1994, the first native-born priest of the diocese to become its bishop; born in East Dubuque, IL, he studied at Loras College and St. Mary's Seminary in Baltimore; he was ordained a priest in 1943; he served as editor of *The Observer*, the diocesan newspaper, in 1954 and served in the position until 1968; as bishop he remained committed to Catholic communications and served on the U.S. Conference of Catholic Bishops Committee on Communications.

Ottenweller, Bp. Albert H., 96, Sept. 23, 2012, bishop of Steubenville from 1977-1992; a native of Stanford, Mont., he studied at The Catholic University of America and was ordained a priest for the Toledo diocese on June 19, 1943; he was ordained titular bp. of Perdices and aux. bp. of Toledo on May 29, 1974; app. bp. of Steubenville on Oct. 11, 1977 and inst., Nov. 22, 1977; he retired on Jan. 28, 1992; as head of the U.S. Bishops' Committee on the Laity from 1978 to 1981 he oversaw the writing of "Called and Gifted: American Catholic Laity 1980."

Pellegrino, Dr. Edmund, 92, June 13, 2013, a major figure in the field of bioethics; a native of Newark, NJ, he studied at St. John's University and New York University; in his immense career, he was the author of more than 575 published articles and chapters in medical science, philosophy, and ethics and author or co-author of 23 books; he served as a department chair and dean, as well as President of The Catholic University of America; a Master of the American College of Physicians, a Fellow of the American Association for the Advancement of Science and a Senior Fellow of The Center for Bioethics And Human Dignity; he was also was director of its Kennedy Institute of Ethics and founding director of its Center for Clinical Bioethics, which established the Edmund D. Pellegrino Center for Clinical Bioethics; he also received the John Carroll Society's 2013 James Cardinal Hickey Lifetime Service Award; in 1994, he was one of only four Americans named to serve on the Vatican's Pontifical Academy for Life.

Pimenta, Cardinal Simon, 93, July 19, 2013, Indian cardinal and archbishop of Mumbai from 1978 to 1996; born in

Marol, India, he was ordained a priest of Mumbai in 1949 and named an auxiliary bp. for the archdiocese in 1971 and coadjutor of Mumbai in 1977; he became archbishop in 1978 and was named a cardinal in 1988 Pope Pope John Paul II; he retired in 1996.

Plourde, Abp. Joseph-Aurele, 97, Jan. 5, 2013, abp. of Ottawa from 1967 to 1989; a native of New Brunswick, he was ordained a priest in 1944 and did graduate studies in social sciences in Paris and Ottawa; named aux. bp. of Alexandria in 1964, he was appointed to Ottawa in 1967 and was instrumental in restructuring the Canadian Catholic Conference, which was renamed the Canadian Conference of Catholic Bishops in 1977; he was president of the bishops' conference from 1969-1971.

Ries, Cardinal Julien, 92, Feb. 23, Belgian Cardinal and a leading expert on the history of religions; ordained a priest in 1945, he founded the Center for the History of Religions at the Catholic University of Louvain-la-Neuve and served as president of its Oriental Institute from 1975 to 1980; from 1979 to 1985, he was a consultant to the Vatican office that became the Pontifical Council for Interreligious Dialogue; Pope Benedict XVI appointed him to the College of Cardinals in 2012.

Shan Kuo-hsi, Cardinal Paul, S.J., 88, Aug. 22, 2012, Jesuits, bishop of Kaohsiung, Taiwan, and a cardinal; born in Puyang, China, he joined the Jesuits in 1946 and was ordained a priest in 1955; director of the Chinese section of the Sacred Heart School in Cebu, he was appointed bp. of Hualien in 1979 and then bp. of Kaohsiung, Taiwan, in 1991; Pope John Paul II named him a cardinal in 1991.

Seasoltz, Fr. R. Kevin, O.S.B., 82, Apr. 27, 2013, Benedictine priest and a noted liturgist and author; born Robert Joseph Seasoltz in Johnstown, PA, he was ordained a priest in 1956 for his home diocese of Altoona-Johnstown but entered the Benedictines in 1960, taking the name Kevin; he served as rector of the Benedictine seminary at Collegeville from 1988 to 1992 and served as a theology professor there from 1972 to 2008 and was on the faculty of The Catholic University of America in Washington for 25 years; he authored numerous books and won a Catholic Press Association book award for best book on liturgy in 2006 with *A Sense of the Sacred: Theological Foundations of Christian Architecture and Art.*

Shea, Jack, 84, Apr. 28, 2013, Catholics in Media co-founder and TV director; born in New York, NY, he grew up in Manhattan and studied at Fordham University; he then embarked on a long career in television; he directed such notable programs as "Truth or Consequences," "The Jeffersons," "The Waltons," and "The Golden Girls"; he was twice nominated for an Emmy Award and was a former member of the U.S. Conference of Catholic Bishops' Committee for Communications.

Steltemeier, Deacon Bill, 83, Feb. 15, 2013, founding president of the Eternal Word Television Network and its long-time chairman of the board; a native of Nashville, TN, he attended Chaminade College Preparatory School in St. Louis and Vanderbilt University; he married Ramona Schnupp in 1953; after graduating from Vanderbilt Law School, in 1954, he entered the U.S. Army and served for two years in France; in 1960, he co-founded the Nashville law firm of Steltemeier & Westbrook specializing in bankruptcy and commercial law; he was ordained a permanent deacon for the Diocese of Nashville in 1975 and first met Mother Angelica in 1978 and in 1980 became EWTN's first president and a founding board member. In 1985, he resigned from his law firm to work full-time for Mother Angelica and EWTN; after Mother's retirement from active leadership in 2000, he became chairman of the board and CEO; in 2009, he was awarded the Pro Ecclesia et Pontifice Cross by Pope Benedict XVI.

Sullivan, Bp. Joseph M., 83, June 7, 2013, aux bp. of Brooklyn from 1980-2005; born in Brooklyn, he studied at Immaculate Conception Seminary in Huntington, Long Island, and was ordained a priest in 1956; he then studied at Fordham University; in 1980, Pope John Paul II named him an auxiliary bishop; he retired in 2005 but remained active.

Sullivan, Bp. Walter, 84, Dec. 11, 2012, bp. of Richmond from 1974-2003; born in Washington, DC, he studied at St. Mary's Seminary in Baltimore, MD and The Catholic University of America; ordained a priest for Richmond in 1953, he was ordained titular bp. of Selsea and aux. bp. of Richmond in 1970 and appointed bp. of Richmond in 1974; he retired in 2003; as bishop he was an ardent advocate for justice and peace, including as bishop-president of Pax Christi USA.

Tonini, Cardinal Ersilio, 99, July 28, 2013, archbishop of Ravenna-Cervia from 1975-1990; born in Centovera di San Giorgio Piacentino, Italy, he was ordained a priest on Apr. 18, 1937 and later served as vice-rector and later rector of the Piacenza seminary; he taught Italian, Latin and Greek and was editor of the diocesan weekly; ordained bp. of Macerata-Tolentino in 1969, he was named abp. of Ravenna–Cervia on Nov. 22, 1975; Pope John Paul II named him a Cardinal in 1994; he retired in 1990.

Deceased Cardinals 2012-2013

The following Cardinals died between Aug. 2012 and Aug. 2013. For their individual obituaries, see above.

Ambrozic, Cardinal Aloysius M., 81, Aug. 26, 2011, abp. of Toronto, Canada, from 1990 to 2006.

Antonetti, Cardinal Lorenzo, 90, Apr. 10, 2013, Italian cardinal and head of the Administration of the Patrimony of the Holy See from 1995 to 1998.

Baldelli, Cardinal Fortunato, 77, Sept. 20, 2012, Italian Cardinal and Major Penitentiary from 2009.

Cheli, Cardinal Giovanni, 94, Feb. 8, 2013, Italian Cardinal, longtime Vatican diplomat, and head of the Pontifical Council for Migrants and Travelers from 1986-98.

Glemp, Cardinal Józef, 83, Jan. 23, 2013, archbishop of Warsaw and primate of Poland from 1981-92.

Honoré, Cardinal Jean, 92, Feb. 28, 2013, abp. of Tours from 1981-1997 and one of the contributors on the Catechism of the Catholic Church.

Martini, Cardinal Carlo Maria, 85, Aug. 31, 2012, Jesuit Italian Cardinal, archbishop of Milan, and a renowned biblical scholar.

Nagy, Cardinal Stanislaw, 91, June 5, 2013, Polish cardinal, friend of Pope John Paul II, and member of the International Theological Commission.

Pimenta, Cardinal Simon, 93, July 19, 2013, Indian cardinal and archbishop of Mumbai from 1978 to 1996.

Ries, Cardinal Julien, 92, Feb. 23, 2013, Belgian Cardinal and a leading expert on the history of religions.

Shan Kuo-hsi, Cardinal Paul, S.J., 88, Aug. 22, 2012, Jesuits, bishop of Kaohsiung, Taiwan, and a cardinal.

Tonini, Cardinal Ersilio, 99, July 28, 2013, archbishop of Ravenna-Cervia from 1975-1990.

News in Depth

THE ELECTION OF POPE FRANCIS

The Papal Transition

On Feb. 11, 2013, Pope Benedict XVI announced to a stunned gathering of Cardinals in Rome that he was planning to resign the papacy on Feb. 28, 2013. He was the first pontiff since 1415 to renounce the papacy when Pope Gregory XII stepped down to help bring an end to the Great Western Schism that had divided the Church since 1378. The Holy Father read a prepared text in Latin:

"I have convoked you to this Consistory, not only for the three canonizations, but also to communicate to you a decision of great importance for the life of the Church. After having repeatedly examined my conscience before God, I have come to the certainty that my strengths, due to an advanced age, are no longer suited to an adequate exercise of the Petrine ministry. I am well aware that this ministry, due to its essential spiritual nature, must be carried out not only with words and deeds, but no less with prayer and suffering. However, in today's world, subject to so many rapid changes and shaken by questions of deep relevance for the life of faith, in order to govern the barque of St. Peter and proclaim the Gospel, both strength of mind and body are necessary, strength which in the last few months, has deteriorated in me to the extent that I have had to recognize my incapacity to adequately fulfill the ministry entrusted to me. For this reason, and well aware of the seriousness of this act, with full freedom I declare that I renounce the ministry of Bishop of Rome, Successor of St. Peter, entrusted to me by the Cardinals on April 19, 2005, in such a way, that as from Feb. 28, 2013, at 20:00 hours, the See of Rome, the See of St. Peter, will be vacant and a Conclave to elect the new Supreme Pontiff will have to be convoked by those whose competence it is.

"Dear Brothers, I thank you most sincerely for all the love and work with which you have supported me in my ministry and I ask pardon for all my defects. And now, let us entrust the Holy Church to the care of Our Supreme Pastor, Our Lord Jesus Christ, and implore his holy Mother Mary, so that she may assist the Cardinal Fathers with her maternal solicitude, in electing a new Supreme Pontiff. With regard to myself, I wish to also devotedly serve the Holy Church of God in the future through a life dedicated to prayer."

At the end of the pope's statement, Card. Angelo Sodano, the Dean of the College of Cardinals, read a prepared text – he was, in fact, one of the few Vatican officials to know ahead of time – in which he said:

"Your Holiness, beloved and revered Successor of Peter, Your moving message has resounded in this room like a lightning bolt in a calm sky. We've listened to you with a sense of shock, rather in total disbelief. In your words we noticed the great affection that you have always had for the Holy Church of God, for this Church that you have loved so much.

"Allow me to tell you, in the name of this apostolic cenacle – the College of Cardinals – in the name of your dear collaborators, let me tell you that we are closer to you than ever before, just as we have been in these eight luminous years of your pontificate.

"On April 19, 2005, if I remember right, at the end of the Conclave I asked you, with trembling voice after all our years together, 'Do you accept your canonical election as Supreme Pontiff?' And you did not take long – albeit with trepidation – to respond by saying that you accepted with trust in the Lord and in the maternal intercession of Mary, Mother of the Church.

"With Mary, that day you gave your 'yes,' and so began your luminous pontificate with the plow of continuity, that continuity of which you have spoken to us so often in the history of the Church – continuity with your 265 predecessors in the Chair of Peter, in the course of 2,000 years of history, from the Apostle Peter, humble fisherman of Galilee, right through to the great popes of the last century, from St. Pius X to Blessed John Paul II.

"Holy Father, before Feb. 28 – the day which, as you have said, you seek to put the word 'fine' [the end] over your service as pontiff, one given with so much love, with humility – before Feb. 28, we will have a way to better express our feelings, so will many pastors and faithful throughout the world, as will so many people of good will along with the authorities of many countries. In this month to come, too, we will have the joy of hearing your shepherd's voice on Ash Wednesday, then on Thursday, with the clergy of Rome, in the Angelus of these Sundays, at the Wednesday audiences; there will thus be many opportunities still to hear your fatherly voice....

"Even beyond these, your mission will continue onward: you have said that you will always be close to us with your witness and your prayers. Sure as the stars in the sky always continue to shine, so the star of your pontificate will always shine in our midst.

"We are close to you, Holy Father – bless us."

The Resignation Pope Benedict XVI

Pope Benedict XVI's choice to renounce the papacy was clearly undertaken for what he sees as the good of the Church.

The pontiff declared in his poignant announcement Feb. 11, "In order to govern the barque of St. Peter and proclaim the Gospel, both strength of mind and body are necessary, strength which, in the last few months, has deteriorated in me to the extent that I have had to recognize my incapacity to adequately fulfill the ministry entrusted to me."

He will renounce the office of the Bishop of Rome officially at 8 p.m. Roman time on Feb. 28.

Pope Benedict's decision is not one that can be rejected

by the members of the College of Cardinals. According to Canon 332, Paragraph 2 in the Code of Canon Law, a papal resignation is valid when freely and properly manifested. But the Church's law also notes that it is not accepted by anyone, as there is no one qualified to "accept"; it occurs simply as a result of the pope freely resigning. This he did, with "full freedom."

Historical Context

In the history of the Church, papal resignations have been rare, but they are not unprecedented. The last resignation was in 1415 when Pope Gregory XII renounced his rightful claim to be pope in order to end the so-called Great Western Schism that had divided the Church since 1378.

Before that, Pope St. Celestine V resigned in 1294 when he concluded that he was unable to lead the Church.

A one-time hermit, Pope Celestine was overburdened with the demands of governing. After his resignation, he was allowed to retire to a monastery. Upon entering his new quarters, he exclaimed, "I desired nothing in the world save a cell, and a cell they have given me." He died two years later.

Pope Benedict was more than capable as pontiff, but, like Pope Celestine, he ended his pontificate for the sake of the Church. Pope Benedict will reportedly spend his final days in prayer and study in a small monastery located in the Vatican City State.

History proved a harsh judge of Pope Celestine. Dante Alighieri, in *The Divine Comedy*, consigned him to hell for "the great refusal."

The judgment on Pope Benedict XVI is likely to be very different. He accepted election with reluctance after a lifetime of service to the Church as a priest, archbishop, cardinal and one of the great theologians of the 20th century. He served as pope for nearly eight years, and when he realized that his mounting infirmities posed challenges for him to lead fully and effectively, he renounced the Petrine ministry. The decision was an act of remarkable humility and also one of extraordinary prudence. He will die Joseph Ratzinger, having given one final act of service to the Church.

Health Struggles

The signs had been there for several years that this was a possibility. In April 2009, Pope Benedict visited the central Italian town of Aquila. While there, he stopped and prayed at the tomb of Pope Celestine in the Basilica Santa Maria di Collemaggio. He then placed upon the tomb his pallium, the white woolen band of cloth adorned with six black crosses that is worn by metropolitan archbishops and the pope himself representing their authority.

The gesture was followed the next year by an interview with German journalist Peter Seewald in *Light of the World: The Pope, the Church, and the Signs of the Times* (Ignatius Press, $19.95) in which he was asked if he could imagine the circumstances in which resignation might be appropriate.

He replied, "If a pope clearly realizes he is no longer physically, psychologically and spiritually capable of handling the duties of his office, then he has a right and, under some circumstances, also an obligation to resign."

Over the next several years, speculation only increased about his health. In fall 2011, he began using the transport device that had been adopted by Blessed John Paul II to travel the football-field long floor of St. Peter's Basilica, and by the end of 2012 many papal observers pointed to fatigue and his struggle to walk, especially during long liturgies.

Planning Ahead

The pope went about his preparations methodically. He held two consistories in 2012, the first naming 22

cardinals in February and then another, naming six in November. The second set of appointments included cardinals distributed from around the world. In effect, the pope was making certain that the College of Cardinals was at or close to its limit of 120 papal electors (cardinals under the age of 80).

He met a few days before with the dean of the College of Cardinals, Angelo Sodano, and likely consulted with some of his closest advisers. Few in the Vatican apparently knew of his final decision.

The precise timing has been the source of speculation. It is probable that he plans to use the remaining weeks to prepare for his departure from the Apostolic Palace.

The conclave to find a new pope will go forward in precisely the same manner as any other. The last time a pope was elected who was not at the time a cardinal was 1376, so the odds are very high that one of the cardinals entering the Sistine Chapel in early March will be chosen.

Setting a Precedent

The new pope will have two immediate challenges. The first is to assume the enormity of the papacy. The second is to ascend to the throne of Peter with his successor still alive, an event that has not happened in six centuries.

How this will work in a practical sense is yet to be determined as this is something truly peculiar in modern Catholic history.

Pope Benedict's resignation also signals something potentially very significant for those who follow him. He has established a possible precedent, in which a pontiff faced with incapacitating illness or frailty might renounce the papacy to ensure vital and active leadership for the Church.

With modern medical care lengthening lifespans, popes will inevitably live longer, but not necessarily in a condition to provide fully for the pastoral needs of more than a billion Catholics in a world, said by Pope Benedict in his announcement, that is "subject to so many rapid changes and shaken by questions of deep relevance for the life of faith."

The decision about resignation will now become a permanent feature of future pontificates, and each pontiff will have to make similarly prudential judgments. In Pope Benedict, they have a wise and humble example.

Farewell Address of Pope Benedict XVI

On Feb. 28, 2013, Pope Benedict XVI delivered a farewell address to the members of the College of Cardinals who had gathered in Rome in anticipation of his resignation and the start of the sede vacante. The address was delivered in the Clementine Hall, in the Apostolic Palace.

Venerable and Dear Brothers,

I welcome you with great joy and I offer each one of you my most cordial greeting. I thank Cardinal Angelo Sodano who, as always, interpreted the sentiments of the entire College: *Cor ad cor loquitur* [heart speaks to heart] I warmly thank you, Your Eminence. And I would like to say – taking up your reference to the disciples of Emmaus – that for me too it has been a joy to walk with you in these years, in the light of the presence of the Risen Lord.

As I said yesterday to the thousands of faithful who filled St Peter's Square, your closeness and your advice have been of great help to me in my ministry. In these eight years we have lived with faith very beautiful moments of radiant light on the Church's journey, as well as moments when several clouds gathered in the sky. We sought to serve Christ and his Church with profound and total love, which is the heart and soul of our ministry. We gave hope, the hope that comes to us from Christ, which alone can give light to us on our journey. Together we may thank the Lord who has enabled us to grow in communion and, together, pray him to help us to grow even more in this profound unity, so that the College of Cardinals may be like an orchestra where differences – an expression of the universal Church – contribute to a superior and harmonious concord.

I would like to leave you a simple thought, which is deep in my heart: a thought about the Church, about her mystery, that constitutes for us all – we can say – the reason and passion for life.

I will allow a sentence of Romano Guardini to help me. It was written in the very same year that the Fathers of the Second Vatican Council approved the Constitution *Lumen Gentium*, in his last book, which also a personal dedication to me – which makes the words of this book particularly dear to me. Guardini says the Church "is not an institution conceived and built in theory... but a living reality.... She lives through the course of time, in becoming, like every living being, in undergoing change.... And yet in her nature she remains ever the same and her heart is Christ."

It seems to me that this was our experience yesterday in the Square: seeing that the Church is a living body, enlivened by the Holy Spirit and which is really brought to life by God's power. She is in the world but not of the world: she is of God, of Christ, of the Spirit. We saw this yesterday. That is why Guardini's other famous saying is both true and eloquent: "The Church is reawakened in souls." The Church is alive, she grows and is reawakened in souls who – like the Virgin Mary – welcome the Word of God and conceive it through the action of the Holy Spirit; they offer to God their own flesh. It is precisely in their poverty and humility that they become capable of begetting Christ in the world today. Through the Church, the Mystery of the Incarnation lives on for ever. Christ continues to walk through the epochs and in all places.

Let us stay united, dear Brothers, in this Mystery: in prayer, especially in the daily Eucharist, and in this way we shall serve the Church and the whole of humanity. This is our joy that no one can take from us.

Before I say goodbye to each one of you personally, I would like to tell you that I shall continue to be close to you with my prayers, especially in these coming days, that you may be completely docile to the action of the Holy Spirit in the election of the new pope. May the Lord show you the one whom he wants. And among you, in the College of Cardinals, there is also the future pope to whom today I promise my unconditional reverence and obedience. For this reason, with affection and gratitude, I cordially impart to you the Apostolic Blessing.

Benedict XVI and Papal Diplomacy
By Fr. Bernard O'Connor, J.C.D., S.T.D.

On Jan. 9, 2012, Pope Benedict XVI delivered his annual "Address to the Members of the Diplomatic Corps Accredited to the Holy See."

The Address may be read from the perspective of concern for tensions which afflict the community of nations; for example, "the grave ... global economic and financial crisis." Similarly, one can examine the Address for its implications for theology. We may analyze, for instance, how diplomats should be aware that "the world is gloomy wherever it is not brightened by God's light ... wherever men and women no longer acknowledge their

bond with the Creator and thereby endanger their relation to other creatures and to creation itself." Diplomacy, then, should uphold religious belief and freedom, never ignoring either.

What is evident is that papal diplomatic discourse is profound in the caliber of insights which it yields for a wide range of formal disciplines: international politics, the religious sciences, history, philosophy, sociology, education, etc.. It is the opinion of this author that the speeches and messages of the Holy Father provide a remarkable microcosm of the many levels on which the Church is engaged throughout contemporary society. Much is missed when we reduce that discourse to a literal meaning derived solely from context. What is needed is a hermeneutic of interpretation which recognizes the multiple and diverse applications embodied in that discourse. To illustrate, one should look again at the same Jan. 9 Address, and how it parallels four key aspects of the practice of mediation and conflict management. These include:

(a) Mediation experts tell us that attempts to eliminate conflict often fail because disputant parties tend to approach mediation sessions as a stage upon which to 'act out' their fixed agenda of attitudes and demands. They are predisposed to a kind of 'duel-logue,' when what is required is the flexibility of dialogue. This is exactly what Pope Benedict reinforces when he states that diplomats accredited to the Holy See participate in a "dialogue" which "favors the exchange of views and information." The word "exchange" is significant. For it denotes that there is a willingness to receive respectfully those "views" with which disagreement may be a realistic possibility. The Pontiff's choice of language implies that the overall diplomatic process preempts conflict by fostering initiatives which encourage that differences be voiced without fear of reprisal. In my near 20 years of teaching university courses on mediation praxis, a comment frequently expressed is that violence arises because one party becomes convinced that another does not or cannot hear them. And so the guarantee of an acceptance of dialogue offsets the dangers inherent in self-imposed 'deafness.' Consistently in his remarks, Pope Benedict "invites" diplomats "to dialogue" in such a manner as to "build stable and reconciled societies" in which "unjust discrimination" is eliminated. It is dialogue, the Pope insists, which may moderate "political forces" geared to "bloodshed" in Syria. And it is "dialogue" which my de-escalate "tensions between Palestinians and Israelis," and which may well encourage "the leaders of these two peoples (to) adopt courageous and farsighted decisions in favor of peace."

(b) Pope Benedict next mentions diplomatic "cooperation in areas of common interest which are bilateral or multilateral in nature." Mediators would definitely approve. For it has long been known that conflict may be prevented or diffused when 'at risk' populations are assisted to identify "common interests" in preference to emphasis upon volatile specific interests, and to adopt cooperative projects and activities which further shared commonality. This is a feature of the Pave the Way Foundation (www.ptwf.org), a New York-based organization headed by a Jewish couple, Gary and Meredith Krupp. As a member of the Foundation's Advisory Board, I have witnessed how Pave the Way has promoted active collaboration where controversy exists between Jews, Muslims, Christians and seculars. On repeated occasions, the Krupps have told me how Pope Benedict's advocacy of truth and transparency in appealing to "common interest" has inspired them to persevere in pursuit of such goals as the vindication of the reputation of Pope Pius XII and in their aim to have an anti-Pope Pius exhibit at Israel's Holocaust Memorial, Yad Vashem, revised. The latter has recently met with considerable success.

(c) When a segment of society becomes prone to conflict, victims often deduce that peace is an unobtainable outcome for them. "Our situation cannot change; we cannot make progress," is a customary mantra. In order to bring about an antidote to this negativity, conflict managers stress where concrete progress – even elsewhere – is the result of constructive negotiation. Others' ratified agreements, made familiar to persons likely to succumb to divisiveness and hostility, represent a role model for what they can attain though convinced that such is beyond their capability. What is suggested is: "Give peacemaking strategies a chance: positive results are actually within your grasp."

Mediators discern a pattern in the Pope's Jan. 9 Address. Following his endorsement to diplomats of the benefit of dialogue and of cooperative undertakings, he speaks of the relationship "between the Catholic Church and States." Both the Pope and the diplomatic corps are aware that that relationship is subject to suspicion and accusation since it is often equated with the narrower political question of the relationship between the Church and the State. The popular campaign for the absolute 'separation' of Church and State generally masks a distorted idea that Church and State are, and should be, opposed. Seldom is the Church recognized for its rejection of desire to control or manipulate the State so as to acquire power and privilege. By contrast, Pope Benedict describes a Church-State rapport in which the Church is servant within the State, not its enemy, and definitely not its competitor. And so the Holy Father reminds diplomats that in their homelands the Church facilitates extensive development in education, health care and social services.

As evidence that nations might perceive the Church according to its mission of service, the Pope recalls "Accords reached in 2011 with Azerbaijan, Montenegro and Mozambique." They are the consequence of systematic and rational "negotiation." However, "fruitful dialogue" is not limited solely to the provisions of legal agreements. The Pope notes that the nations comprising "the Association of South-East Asian Nations (ASEAN) have accepted the appointment of an Apostolic Nuncio." Likewise, the Holy See has lately been welcomed as a "full member" of "the International Organization for Migration." And the prevailing motive? To convey that the Holy See and the Catholic Church are willing, "alongside the international community," to continue "the search for suitable solutions" to dilemmas which threaten "the dignity of persons" and the centrality of the "common good."

(d) What sustains the impetus in peacemaking? Mediation research affirms that the maintenance of peace largely depends upon how disputants are challenged to jointly strive toward the realization of precisely identified objectives. Think of the aftermath of a region beset by civil war. Violence will probably resurface unless antagonists channel their energies toward a reconstruction which incorporates their respective issues and which takes into account their lingering doubts and fears. And so we are not surprised when political mediators choose to conclude peace negotiations by enumerating "what remains to be done" so as to ensure the proper restoration of social order. Pope Benedict employs the same approach. The prospects of current diplomatic and political achievement are not enough. Because obstacles to the realization of peace abound and are daunting. Therefore the Pontiff says, "we must not lose heart, but instead resolutely rediscover our way through new forms of commitment." We must steadily confront the plight of young people, especially in North Africa and the Middle East, "who are suffering from poverty and unemployment." These young yearn for political reforms which will safeguard their "fundamental rights." And they are entitled to official "policies" which support family, "based on the marriage of a man and a woman"; policies which "aid social cohesion" and reflect an "openness to life."

Pope Benedict's diplomatic address appeals for citizen status in which nobody becomes a "second-class spectator" of what is vital to their holistic and wholesome existence. Quite the contrary. And so he reminded us that, as in the case of all mediation and conflict management, diplomacy remains a viable mechanism to enhance our "sense of solidarity and responsibility towards present and future generations."

Benedict XVI and the Sex Abuse Crisis

The pontificate of Pope Benedict XVI began and ended in the shadow of the clergy sexual abuse crises that have plagued the Church. The election of Card. Joseph Ratzinger in 2005 as Pope Benedict XVI took place in the wake of the pedophilia revelations that exploded in 2002 in Boston.

In the intervening years, it spread beyond the United States to Belgium, Germany, Ireland and elsewhere. On the eve of the pope's resignation, Scottish Card. Keith O'Brien resigned after allegations from four priests that he had acted inappropriately with them decades earlier. Card. O'Brien also said he would not attend the conclave to elect the next pope.

Apostolic Letter

The persistent revelations and allegations particularly fo- cused on child sexual abuse by members of the clergy meant that for most of Pope Benedict's pontificate experts in the Church's handling of the crisis have had to spend years working to refute the thoroughly discredited claim that the pope had failed to act properly in dealing with the crisis and may even have been complicit in coverups and transferring abuser priests.

Card. Ratzinger was only made aware of the sheer scale of the sexual abuse crisis gradually. Before 2001, cases had been handled by the Vatican in a scattered fashion owing to older complexities in Church law. As the crisis erupted in the United States, Card. Ratzinger became increasingly convinced of the need to rid the Church of what he called the "filth" of abuse, and he emerged as one of the Vatican's most dedicated leaders in confronting the growing challenge.

He pushed to have Pope John Paul II assign responsibility to the Congregation for the Doctrine of the Faith (CDF) to oversee all of the cases worldwide. On May 18, 2001, the pope promulgated an apostolic letter titled *Sacramentorum Sanctita- tis Tutela* ("The Safeguarding of the Sacraments"). The document was most noteworthy for the fact that it confirmed the CDF's responsibility for disciplinary review and action regarding violations associated with abuse, including the solicitation to a sexual sin (a sin "against the Sixth Commandment") under the pretext of the confession if involving the confessor himself or the granting of absolution to "an accomplice" in a sexual sin by the confessor.

It also said that it reserved to the CDF the responsibility for reviewing sexual violations "committed by a cleric with a minor below the age of 18 years." Such acts are "to be punished according to the gravity of the offense, not excluding dismissal or deposition." In canon law, the age of a minor was listed as under 16 years. In the 1990s, the U.S. bishops had asked that the age of a minor be defined as under 18 so that it would match state law in defining the upper age of minors. The letter also addressed a long-standing request by U.S. bishops that the statute of limitations be lengthened, in this case to 10 years, rather than five, after the victim has reached his or her 18th birthday.

In short, what the apostolic letter did was require bishops to report cases of clergy sexual abuse to the CDF, marking a major change in the way the Church approached the crisis.

Assistance to U.S. Bishops

Card. Ratzinger next assisted the bishops of the United States as they dealt fully with the problem of clergy sexual abuse in 2002. The bishops introduced the so-called Dallas Charter and the imposition of the Essential Norms, by which dioceses created safe environments for children, launched a "zero tolerance" policy regarding abuse, and worked to improve the formation of priests and the seminary system. Card. Ratzinger was instrumental in streamlining the approval process by the Holy See. In the United States, the results have been nothing short of dramatic. The audits by the National Review Board found that in recent years the numbers of annually reported cases of sexual abuse of minors in the entire Church in the United States had declined to single digits.

Media Attacks

Once elected in 2005, Pope Benedict moved swiftly to enforce the reforms needed for the Church. He took action against Fr. Marcial Maciel Degollado, founder of the Legion of Christ, who had been accused of abusing minors. He brought to Rome the bishops of Ireland and Germany to receive reports on their actions to implement norms and programs to safeguard children in every area of Church life and ministry.

Even as he implemented these reforms, he fell under constant attack by the secular media. He was accused, for example, of allowing a priest-abuser into his archdiocese when he was the archbishop of Munich-Freising. The priest in question, Fr. Peter Hullermann, was later convicted of child sexual abuse by German authorities and given an 18-month suspended sentence and a fine. *The New York Times* attempted to blame then Card. Ratzinger, but the facts were that while the case exemplified the mishandling of pedophilia cases that have plagued many dioceses, then Card. Ratzinger is known only to have approved the transfer of the priest seeking psychiatric treatment for issues of a sexual nature. More attacks followed, including accusations that while head of the Congregation for the Doctrine of the Faith he had failed to act against abuser priests in the United States. Once again, the stories were debunked.

Penance, Healing

Pope Benedict was also accused of failing both to meet with victims and to apologize for the tragedy of clergy sexual abuse. In truth, Pope Benedict met with abuse victims on multiple occasions, including during his visit to the United States in 2008. He privately apologized to victims in his sessions with them. He also spoke in unmistakable terms of penance for the Church. He said plainly, "I am ashamed, and we will do everything possible to ensure that this does not happen in the future." The most pointed apology issued by the pontiff was his "Letter to the Irish," in which he wrote: "You have suffered grievously, and I am truly sorry. I know that nothing can undo the wrong you have endured. Your trust has been betrayed and your dignity has been violated."

Finally, during his time as pope the CDF mandated that every diocese implement basic norms for handling cases, subject to the specific laws of each country, and imposed time frames for their implementation. The norms for all of the world's dioceses are based on the norms first established for the Church in the United States in 2002 and that have proved successful in creating a safe environment for children and those serving the Church, and in reducing drastically the number of cases each year. Cristina Odone, a columnist for Britain's *The Daily Telegraph*, has concluded that "this pope has done more than any other churchman to address the issue of priestly child abuse."

POPE FRANCIS

On March 13, 2013, Card. Jorge Mario Bergoglio, archbishop of Buenos Aires since 1998 and a Cardinal since 2001, was elected the 265th Successor of St. Peter, Bishop of Rome, and Vicar of Christ, in succession to Pope Benedict XVI, who resigned officially on Feb. 28. He was elected on the fifth ballot of the conclave held in the Sistine Chapel by the eligible members of the College Cardinals, 115 electors in total, and took the name Francis.

Pope Francis is the first non-European pope since 731, the first Jesuit to be elected, the first pope of the Western Hemisphere, the first of the Southern Hemisphere, and the first Latin American.

The Election of Pope Francis

The election of Card. Jorge Mario Bergoglio, now Pope Francis, as successor to Pope Benedict XVI brings to an end the extraordinary events in the life of the modern Church that began Feb. 11 with Pope Benedict's resignation. The selection of the College of Cardinals was as remarkable and unexpected as the decision by Pope Benedict to step down.

A native of Buenos Aires, Argentina, and the archbishop of Buenos Aires since 1998, the 76-year-old pontiff is the first Latin American pope, the first Jesuit pope and the first successor of Peter from outside of Europe since 731 and the election of Pope Gregory III, a Syrian.

To understand the election of Pope Francis, it is vital to comprehend the dimensions of global Catholicism. Around 700 million of the world's Catholics live outside of Europe, and 450 million of them live in Latin America. His election is a stunning development, but it is also recognition of the College of Cardinals that while the Church is truly global, the center of gravity has shifted to the Southern Hemisphere. The Church in Latin America is half a millennium old, and the election of the pope from that continent is a proclamation that it has truly come into its own.

Universal Leader

The pontiff will serve as a bridge among the diverse and growing Catholic communities worldwide that were electrified by the choice of the College. Pope Francis demonstrates powerfully that the Church is, indeed, everywhere and offers a universal message of hope for the poor and the forgotten in a world struggling with the impact of globalization and transnational capitalism.

It is in Latin America, however, that he will have his most

immediate impact. He will be a vital leader in the work to preserve the Catholic culture of Latin America, where there has been a loss of zeal and numbers in the wake of the rise of Pentecostals and evangelicals, materialism, secularism and consumerism. In what was reportedly the only interview he gave to any journalists from the time he was named Archbishop of Buenos Aires in 1998 to his elevation to the College of Cardinals in 2001 – notably it was not to a major newspaper or network but to a parish news bulletin – he was asked to comment on the state of the Church in Argentina. He took exception with the assumption that Argentina was still a majority Catholic country. Why? Because the levels of corruption, the toxic messages in the media and severe social inequalities found in Argentina should not describe a Catholic country.

Francis of Assisi

Pope Francis is thus also a herald of the New Evangelization. He has spoken of the need for the New Evangelization and that it is a task for the entire Church. In that, his choice of name points to a desire to emulate St. Francis of Assisi. His election represented a powerful impulse for reform that is rooted in the Church's traditions of service and humility. His choice of papal name becomes significant because of St. Francis of Assisi, one of the great reformers in Church history. The cardinals stressed that reform must be a task for the next pope as the Roman Curia, the central government of the Church, stands in need of genuine improvement and reorganization. Francis of Assisi helped renew the Church through a thoroughgoing spiritual renewal, rooted in Christlike humility. Pope Francis will likely apply that same approach. No meaningful reform of Church institutions can be achieved without spiritual reform and renewal, and the Roman Curia is no exception. Just last year, he gave an address in which he noted the "clerical hypocrites" in the Church, so he brings as well toughness and strength of purpose.

On March 16, the new pontiff spoke to journalists in the Paul VI Hall in the Vatican and addressed specifically his choice of name. He said:

"Some people wanted to know why the Bishop of Rome wished to be called Francis. Some thought of Francis Xavier, Francis De Sales, and also Francis of Assisi. I will tell you the story. During the election, I was seated next to the Abp. Emeritus of São Paolo and Prefect Emeritus of the Congregation for the Clergy, Card. Claudio Hummes: a good friend, a good friend! When things were looking dangerous, he encouraged me. And when the votes reached two thirds, there was the usual applause, because the Pope had been elected. And he gave me a hug and a kiss, and said: "Don't forget the poor!" And those words came to me: the poor, the poor. Then, right away, thinking of the poor, I thought of Francis of Assisi. Then I thought of all the wars, as the votes were still being counted, till the end. Francis is also the man of peace. That is how the name came into my heart: Francis of Assisi. For me, he is the man of poverty, the man of peace, the man who loves and protects creation; these days we do not have a very good relationship with creation, do we? He is the man who gives us this spirit of peace, the poor man … How I would like a Church which is poor and for the poor!"

In an unprecedented gesture in the long history of popes being presented on the loggia of St. Peter's Basilica, Pope Francis prayed with the faithful and asked for their prayers and blessing, then gave his blessing to them. It was a poignant moment, but it also showed his own humility and spoke to the fact that his pontificate is something beautifully new in the 2,000 years of Church history.

POPE FRANCIS: THE LIFE OF JORGE MARIO BERGOGLIO

On March 13, the work of the cardinals in the conclave to elect a successor to Pope Benedict XVI ended with the entirely unexpected choice of the Argentinian Card. Jorge Mario Bergoglio as Pope Francis.

Over the last months, Catholics have continued to be astonished by the pontiff's humble acts of service, brief but intensely pastoral homilies and his stress on God's love and mercy.

To appreciate the direction the pope is taking the Church as the 265th successor of St. Peter, it is helpful to be reminded of where he started and the experiences that helped shape the man chosen by the College of Cardinals to lead global Catholicism.

A Child of Flores

Jorge Mario Bergoglio was born Dec. 17, 1936, in the working class Flores neighborhood of Buenos Aires, Argentina. The members of his family were considered Porteños, the name used for the inhabitants of Buenos Aires who are largely second- or third-generation descendants from immigrants, with ties to the Old World. Being of Italian origin, they were also termed Tanos, the local word for Italian immigrants. In the case of the Bergoglios, they were immigrants from Turin, in the Piedmont region of Italy. His father was Mario Bergoglio, a railway worker, and his mother Regina Sivori, a housewife who oversaw the early education of the family's five children. Bergoglio initially wanted to pursue a career in chemistry, but his academic hopes were slowed when he was teenager owing to an infection that led to the removal of a portion of his right lung. He eventually graduated in chemistry from the University of Buenos Aires and is said to have expressed hopes of being married. As a young man he was fond of the tango, Argentina's beloved traditional dance, and he has never lost his love for the San Lorenzo de Almagro soccer club of Buenos Aires.

Ultimately, Bergoglio discerned that Christ was calling him to the priesthood and the Society of Jesus. His process of discernment was shaped by an experience of God's loving mercy on Sept. 21, 1953, on the feast of St, Matthew. He entered the Jesuit novitiate at Villa Devoto, Argentina, in 1958 and after a long period of formation, he was ordained to the priesthood on Dec. 13, 1969. Fr. Bergoglio took his final vows on April 22, 1973, and was elected provincial of Argentina that same year.

Fr. Bergoglio's time as provincial from 1973 to 1979 came at a challenging time for the Church. Many priests and religious in Latin America were being drawn to the theological movement of liberation theology, and very early on Fr. Bergoglio saw it as an aberration of the Church's authentic concern for the poor and the call to authentic justice rooted in the Gospel and nurturing an encounter with Jesus Christ.

Fr. Bergoglio was confronted with the task of trying to encourage the priests of his province to defend and care for the poor, but in ways that were faithful to the teachings of the Church and grounded fully in authentic charity. His effort made him unpopular with some of his confreres, but his approach was especially important because many priests were ardent supporters of liberation theology and were becoming more and more involved in the bloody political unrest of the times.

The Dirty War

From 1976 until 1983, with the fall of the military dictatorship that had ruled for decades, Argentina was plagued by the so-called *Guerra Sucia* ("Dirty War"), an era of brutal oppression and violence during which the regime killed between 13,000 and 30,000 citizens. The chief targets of the campaign were left-leaning writers, politicians, trade-unionists and guerillas opposed to the dictatorship. Many thousands of those arrested became part of the "disappeared ones" (the *Desaparecidos*), enemies of the regime who were taken and never seen again. Democracy was finally established in Argentina only in 1983 after the regime's failed war against Great Britain over the Falkland Islands the year before.

The terrible events of the Dirty War impacted the life of Fr. Bergoglio. He had to walk a fine and dangerous line with the government. Some of his priests became targets of the dictatorship because of their associations with the guerillas and also their open opposition to the government. He urged the priests of the province not to give in to the temptation to take up arms and surrender their lives to violence and hatred.

Years later, after Bergoglio had been named the archbishop of Buenos Aires he was accused by some leftist human rights groups of not doing enough to resist the regime, and accusations even were made that he colluded with the dictators. They point to the case of the 1976 kidnapping and torture of two Jesuit priests, Orlando Yorio and Francisco Jalics, in which Bergoglio supposedly turned a blind eye. In truth, the Jesuit provincial went to extraordinary lengths behind-the-scenes to prevent their murder, and the two were subsequently released. It was later learned that Bergoglio regularly hid people on Church property to prevent their arrest and once gave his own identity papers to a man who looked liked him so that he could escape the country.

In 2000, acknowledging the failings of some Church leaders in the Dirty War, Bergoglio by then the archbishop of Buenos Aires, called on the Church in Argentina to offer public penance for the failings of the past.

Unsurprisingly, the allegations surfaced again with the election of Pope Francis. When asked about the old accusations, the Vatican spokesman, Fr. Federico Lombardi, denounced them forcefully, saying, "The campaign against Bergoglio is well-known and dates back to many years ago. It has been made by a publication that carries out sometimes slanderous and defamatory campaigns. The anticlerical cast of this campaign and of other accusations against Bergoglio is well-known and obvious."

'Father Jorge'

Completing his difficult tenure as provincial, Fr. Bergoglio settled back into teaching and a quiet life in academia. In 1980, he was named rector of the seminary in San Miguel, where he had studied. In 1986, he went to Germany to complete his doctorate, and on his return to Argentina continued to teach and serve as a spiritual director and confessor for the Society of Jesus in Córdoba. He also was well-known in the order for his expertise in Ignatian Spirituality, the school of spirituality developed by St. Ignatius Loyola.

The typical path for a Jesuit of his training and such expertise would have been to continue teaching and serving, but to his surprise, he was informed on May 20, 1992, that he been appointed by now-Blessed John Paul II as an auxiliary bishop of Buenos Aires and the titular bishop of Auca. Fr. Bergoglio was ordained a bishop on June 27, 1992.

The episcopal motto that Bishop-elect Bergoglio chose when he was first ordained a bishop in 1992 was "*miserando atque eligendo*" meaning "with mercy and choosing." It was taken from Homily 21 of the Venerable Bede, on Christ's call of St. Matthew: "He saw the tax collector and, because he saw him through the eyes of mercy and chose him, he said to him: 'Follow me.' This following meant imitating the pattern of his life – not just walking after him. St. John tells us: 'Whoever says he abides in Christ ought to walk in the same way in which he walked.'" It was tied closely to his experience of God's mercy in 1953 on the feast of St. Matthew.

While considered the auxiliary bishop with the lowest profile among his episcopal colleagues, Bp. Bergoglio was named on June 3, 1997, to be the Coadjutor Abp. of Buenos Aires. Card. Quarracino died the next year, and Abp. Bergoglio acceded to the see on Feb. 28, 1998. Pope John Paul II appointed him to the College of Cardinals Feb. 21, 2001, with the titular church in Rome of St. Robert Bellarmine. Upon learning that he had been named a Cardinal, Bp. Bergoglio issued a letter asking the faithful of Buenos Aires not to go to Rome for the consistory but instead to use the money to feed the poor.

From the start of his time as archbishop, Bergoglio made it clear that his lifelong commitment to the poor and his emphasis on humility and pastoral service were not going to end with his new office. He decided not to live in the traditional archbishop's residence but instead in a simple apartment next to the cathedral on the Plaza de Mayo in Buenos Aires. He fixed his own meals and famously took the bus and the subway to travel around the city.

In 2001, Card. Bergoglio paid a visit to AIDS patients and washed and kissed their feet. He regularly visited terminal cancer patients, baptized the children of the parishes in the city and spent a great deal of time in the city missions, soup kitchens and poorest parts of Buenos Aires.

As a bishop, of course, he was the father to his priests and an administrator. He demanded that his priests share in his own love for the poor and the defenseless, but he asked nothing of them that he was not willing to do himself. He called on his priests, as well every Catholic, to go out into the streets and homes and to speak in the public squares of the city to invite Catholics back to the Church and to promote Catholic culture.

Card. Bergoglio was likewise much praised as a fatherly and supportive presence to his presbyterate. Every priest reportedly received his private cell phone number with permission to call when they needed his help or guidance, and he set aside an hour every morning for them to call his apartment on a landline. When any of his priests were in personal crisis he was there, and when they were dying, he made it a point to sit next to their deathbeds for hours at a time, reading to them and praying with them.

A Prophetic Voice

Matching his humility in service is what Card. Bergoglio often called apostolic courage. In that sense, he was a prophetic voice as archbishop and was unafraid to stand firm in defending rights and dignity of the human person, speaking out against secularism and materialism, and proclaiming the authentic teachings of the Church in Argentina and Latin America. Two incidents were revealing. The first came in the wake of Argentina's severe financial and economic crisis in 2001-02. Pres. Néstor

Kirchner, who was elected in 2003, enacted various economic policies to restore the economy. Card. Bergoglio was not hesitant in speaking out that the policies could have a dire impact on the most vulnerable in Argentine society. As was his habit, he used the pulpit to make himself heard. As was his habit, he used the pulpit to make himself heard. In the midst of the turmoil, he gave a homily on the Ten Commandments and the Beatitudes, reminding the Argentinians of the Way of Jesus that teaches, "to trample upon the dignity of a woman, a man, a child, the elderly, is a grave sin that cries to heaven." Unhappy with the criticism, Kirchner declared Bergoglio to be the "head of the opposition," an unsuccessful effort to suggest Bergoglio had political motivations.

Kirchner chose not run for re-election in 2007, paving the way for his wife Cristina Fernández de Kirchner to become president. She launched an aggressive secularizing agenda, including the proposal to decriminalize abortion. In 2010, Argentina became the first country in Latin America to allow same-sex marriage nationwide. Card. Bergoglio spoke out directly against the legislation and the secularism, materialism and relativism threatening the whole of Latin America.

He preferred to speak out usually within the context of his homilies and pastoral letters, and his preaching was described as fiery, and his homilies made for intense reading. On Palm Sunday 2008, he told a packed Cathedral in Buenos Aires: "Today the place for Christ is the street; the place for the Christian is the street. The Lord wants us like Him: with an open heart, roaming the streets of Buenos Aires. He wants us walking the streets of Buenos Aires and carrying His message!"

Based on the experience of the Church in Argentina, Catholics can expect Pope Francis to be humble and pastoral but also ardent in his preaching and teaching. He will push for the Vatican to be truly at the service of the Petrine ministry so that the supreme pontiff can better serve the Church. And he will continue to use gestures to make key points about ecclesiastical pride and vanity. It is simplicity with a purpose: to clear away everything else so that the Church can proclaim Jesus Christ to the world.

PAPAL TRIPS, 2012-2013

Pope Benedict XVI, 2012

Lebanon, Sept. 14-16, 2012
Pope Benedict XVI, in the 24th apostolic journey of his pontificate, traveled to Lebanon from Sept. 14-16, 2012. It was the last apostolic journey of his pontificate.

Program
• Meeting of His Holiness Benedict XVI with journalists during the flight to Lebanon (Papal Flight, Sept. 14, 2012)
• Welcoming ceremony at the Beirut-Rafic Hariri International Airport (Sept. 14, 2012)
• Visit to St. Paul's Basilica in Harissa and the signing of the Post-Synodal Apostolic Exhortation (Sept. 14, 2012)
• *Ecclesia in Medio Oriente*: Post-Synodal Apostolic Exhortation on the Church in the Middle East: Communion and Witness (Sept. 14, 2012)
• Meeting with members of the government, institutions of the Republic, the diplomatic corps, religious leaders and representatives of the world of culture (May 25th Hall of the Baabda Presidential Palace, Sept. 15, 2012)
• Luncheon with the Patriarchs and Bishops of Lebanon, members of the Special Council for the Middle East of the Synod of Bishops and the papal entourage (Refectory of the Armenian Catholic Patriachate of Bzommar, Sept. 15, 2012)
• Meeting with the youth in the square across from the Maronite Patriarchate of Bkerké (Sept. 15, 2012)
• Holy Mass and the presentation of the Post-Synodal Apostolic Exhortation for the Middle East at the Beirut City Center Waterfront (Sept. 16, 2012)
• Presentation of the Post-Synodal Apostolic Exhortation for the Middle East at the Beirut City Center Waterfront (Sept. 16, 2012)
• Recitation of the Angelus (Sept. 16, 2012)
• Ecumenical Meeting in the Hall of Honor of the Syro-Catholic Patriarchate of Charfet (Sept. 16, 2012)
• Departure ceremony at the Beirut-Rafic Hariri International Airport (Sept. 16, 2012)

Excerpts from Addresses and Homilies
(*Complete texts of papal addresses, remarks and homilies can be found at www.vatican.va.*)

Welcoming ceremony at the Beirut-Rafic Hariri International Airport (Sept. 14, 2012)
Providentially, this event takes place on the Feast of the Exaltation of the Holy Cross, a celebration originating in the East in 335, following the dedication of the Basilica of the Resurrection built over Golgotha and our Lord's tomb by the Emperor Constantine the Great, whom you venerate as saint. A month from now we will celebrate the 1,700th anniversary of the appearance to Constantine of the Chi-Rho, radiant in the symbolic night of his unbelief and accompanied by the words: "In this sign you will conquer!" Later, Constantine signed the Edict of Milan, and gave his name to Constantinople. It seems to me that the Post-Synodal Exhortation can be read and understood in the light of this Feast of the Exaltation of the Cross, and more particularly in the light of the Chi-Rho, the two first letters of the Greek word "Christos." Reading it in this way leads to renewed appreciation of the identity of each baptized person and of the Church, and is at the same time a summons to witness in and through communion. Are not Christian communion and witness grounded in the Paschal Mystery, in the crucifixion, death and resurrection of Christ? Is it not there that they find their fulfilment? There is an inseparable bond between the cross and the resurrection which Christians must never forget. Without this bond, to exalt the cross would mean to justify suffering and death, seeing them merely as our inevitable fate. For Christians, to exalt the cross means to be united to the totality of God's unconditional love for mankind. It means making an act of faith! To exalt the cross, against the backdrop of the resurrection, means to desire to experience and to show the totality of this love. It means making an act of love! To exalt the cross means to be a committed herald of fraternal and ecclesial communion, the source of authentic Christian witness. It means making an act of hope!

In examining the present situation of the Church in the Middle East, the Synod Fathers reflected on the joys and struggles, the fears and hopes of Christ's disciples in these lands. In this way, the entire Church was able to hear the troubled cry and see the desperate faces of many men and women who experience grave human and material difficulties, who live amid powerful tensions in fear and uncertainty, who desire to follow Christ – the One who gives meaning to their existence – yet often find themselves prevented from doing so. That is why I wanted the First Letter of St. Peter to serve as the framework of the document. At the same time, the Church was able to admire all that is beautiful and noble in the Churches in these lands. How can we fail to thank God at every moment for all of you (cf. 1 Th 1:2; Part One of the Post-Synodal Exhortation), dear Christians of the Middle East! How can we fail to praise him for your courage and faith? How can we fail to thank him for the flame of his infinite love which you continue to keep alive and burning in these places which were the first to welcome his incarnate Son? How can we fail to praise and thank him for your efforts to build ecclesial and fraternal communion, and for the human solidarity which you constantly show to all God's children?

Meeting with members of the government, institutions of the Republic, the diplomatic corps, religious leaders and representatives of the world of culture (May 25th Hall of the Baabda Presidential Palace, Sept. 15, 2012)

The wealth of any country is found primarily in its inhabitants. The country's future depends on them, individually and collectively, as does its capacity to work for peace. A commitment to peace is possible only in a unified society. Unity, on the other hand, is not the same as uniformity. Social cohesion requires unstinting respect for the dignity of each person and the responsible participation of all in contributing the best of their talents and abilities. The energy needed to build and consolidate peace also demands that we constantly return to the wellsprings of our humanity. Our human dignity is inseparable from the sacredness of life as the gift of the Creator. In God's plan, each person is unique and irreplaceable. A person comes into this world in a family, which is the first locus of humanization, and above all the first school of peace. To build peace, we need to look to the family, supporting it and facilitating its task, and in this way promoting an overall culture of life. The effectiveness of our commitment to peace depends on our understanding of human life. If we want peace, let us defend life! This approach leads us to reject not only war and terrorism, but every assault on innocent human life, on men and women as creatures willed by God. Wherever the truth of human nature is ignored or denied, it becomes impossible to respect that grammar which is the natural law inscribed in the human heart (cf. Message for the 2007 World Day of Peace, No. 3). The grandeur and the raison d'être of each person are found in God alone. The unconditional acknowledgement of the dignity of every human being, of each one of us, and of the sacredness of human life, is linked to the responsibility which we all have before God. We must combine our efforts, then, to develop a sound vision of man, respectful of the unity and integrity of the human person. Without this, it is impossible to build true peace...

In order to make possible a future of peace for coming generations, our first task is to educate for peace in order to build a culture of peace. Education, whether it takes place in the family or at school, must be primarily an education in those spiritual values which give the wisdom and traditions of each culture their ultimate meaning and power. The human spirit has an innate yearning for beauty, goodness and truth. This is a reflection of the divine, God's mark on each person! This common aspiration is the basis for a sound and correct notion of morality, which is always centred on the person. Yet men and women can turn toward goodness only of their own free will, for "human dignity requires them to act out of a conscious and free choice, as moved in a personal way from within, and not by their own blind impulses or by exterior constraint" (*Gaudium et Spes*, No. 17). The goal of education is to guide and support the development of the freedom to make right decisions, which may run counter to widespread opinions, the fashions of the moment, or forms of political and religious ideology. This is the price of building a culture of peace! Evidently, verbal and physical violence must be rejected, for these are always an assault on human dignity, both of the perpetrator and the victim. Emphasizing peacemaking and its positive effect for the common good also creates interest in peace. As history shows, peaceful actions have a significant effect on local, national and international life. Education for peace will form men and women who are generous and upright, attentive to all, especially those most in need. Thoughts of peace, words of peace and acts of peace create an atmosphere of respect, honesty and cordiality, where faults and offences can be truthfully acknowledged as a means of advancing together on the path of reconciliation. May political and religious leaders reflect on this!

We need to be very conscious that evil is not some nameless, impersonal and deterministic force at work in the world. Evil, the devil, works in and through human freedom, through the use of our freedom. It seeks an ally in man. Evil needs man in order to act. Having broken the first commandment, love of God, it then goes on to distort the second, love of neighbor. Love of neighbour disappears, yielding to falsehood, envy, hatred and death. But it is possible for us not to be overcome by evil but to overcome evil with good (cf. Rom 12:21). It is to this conversion of heart that we are called. Without it, all our coveted human "liberations" prove disappointing, for they are curtailed by our human narrowness, harshness, intolerance, favouritism and desire for revenge. A profound transformation of mind and heart is needed to recover a degree of clarity of vision and impartiality, and the profound meaning of the concepts of justice and the common good. A new and freer way of looking at these realities will enable us to evaluate and challenge those human systems which lead to impasses, and to move forward with due care not to repeat past mistakes with their devastating consequences. The conversion demanded of us can also be exhilarating, since it creates possibilities by appealing to the countless resources present in the hearts of all those men and women who desire to live in peace and are prepared to work for peace. True, it is quite demanding: it involves rejecting revenge, acknowledging one's faults, accepting apologies without demanding them, and, not least, forgiveness. Only forgiveness, given and received, can lay lasting foundations for reconciliation and universal peace (cf. Rom 12:16b,18).

Only in this way can there be growth in understanding and harmony between cultures and religions, and in genuine mutual esteem and respect for the rights of all. In Lebanon, Christianity and Islam have lived side by side for centuries. It is not uncommon to see the two religions within the same family. If this is possible within the same family, why should it not be possible at the level of the whole of society? The particular character of the Middle East consists in the centuries-old mix of diverse elements. Admittedly, they have fought one another, sadly that is also true. A pluralistic society can only exist on the basis of mutual respect, the desire to know the other, and continuous dialogue. Such dialogue is only possible when the parties are conscious of the existence of values which are common to all great cultures because they are rooted in the nature of the human person. This substratum of values expresses man's true humanity. These values are inseparable from the rights of each and every human being.

POPE FRANCIS, 2013

Rio de Janeiro, Brazil, July 22-29, 2013

Pope Francis, on the 24th apostolic journey of his pontificate, traveled to Rio de Janeiro, Brazil, to celebrate World Youth Day. The most notable highlight of the trip was Mass at Copacabana Beach in Rio for an estimated crowd of three million, one of the largest Masses on historical record.

Program

• Meeting with journalists during the flight to Brazil (July 22, 2013)
• Welcome Ceremony at the Garden of Guanabara Palace (Rio de Janeiro, July 22, 2013)
• Holy Mass in the Basilica of the Shrine of Our Lady of the Conception (Aparecida, July 24, 2013)
• Impromptu address of Pope Francis from the balcony of the Basilica of the Shrine of Our Lady of Aparecida after the celebration of Holy Mass (July 24, 2013)
• Visit to the St. Francis of Assisi of the Providence of God Hospital – V.O.T. (Rio de Janeiro, July 24, 2013)
• Greeting to the young people from Italy at the conclusion of the visit to the St. Francis of Assisi of the Providence of God Hospital – V.O.T. (Rio de Janeiro, July 24, 2013)
• Blessing of the olympic flags at the City Palace of Rio de Janeiro (July 25, 2013)
• Visit to the Community of Varginha [Manguinhos] (Rio de Janeiro, July 25, 2013)
• Meeting with the youth from Argentina gathered in the Cathedral of San Sebastián (July 25, 2013)
• Welcoming Ceremony by the young people on the waterfront of Copacabana (Rio de Janeiro, July 25, 2013)
• Recital of the Angelus Domini from the central balcony of the Archbishopric of St. Joaquin (Rio de Janeiro, July 26, 2013)
• Way of the Cross with the young people on the waterfront of Copacabana (Rio de Janeiro, July 26, 2013)
• Holy Mass with the Bishops of the 28th WYD and with Priests, Religious and Seminarians in the Cathedral of St Sebastian (Rio de Janeiro, July 27, 2013)
• Meeting with the Brazil's leaders gathered at the Municipal Theatre (Rio de Janeiro, July 27, 2013)
• Meeting with the Bishops of Brazil in the Archbishop's House of Rio de Janeiro (July 27, 2013)
• Interview with Pope Francis for the radio of the Archdiocese of Rio ("Radio Catedral" Studios – Rio de Janeiro, July 27, 2013)
• Prayer Vigil with the young people (Rio de Janeiro, July 27, 2013)
• Holy Mass for the 28th World Youth Day (Rio de Janeiro, July 28, 2013)
• Recital of the Angelus Domini (Rio de Janeiro, July 28, 2013)
• Meeting with the Coordinating Committee of CELAM at the Sumaré Study Center (Rio de Janeiro, July 28, 2013)
• Meeting with the Volunteers of the 28th WYD at the Pavillon 5 of the Rio Center (Rio de Janeiro, July 28, 2013)
• Farewell Ceremony at the Galeão/Antonio Carlos Jobim International Airport (Rio de Janeiro, July 28, 2013)

• Press Conference of the Holy Father during the return flight (July 28, 2013)

Excerpts from Addresses and Homilies

(Complete texts of papal addresses, remarks and homilies can be found at www.vatican.va.)

Holy Mass in the Basilica of the Shrine of Our Lady of the Conception (Aparecida, July 24, 2013)

What joy I feel as I come to the house of the Mother of every Brazilian, the Shrine of our Lady of Aparecida! The day after my election as Bishop of Rome, I visited the Basilica of St. Mary Major in Rome, in order to entrust my ministry to Our Lady. Today I have come here to ask Mary our Mother for the success of World Youth Day and to place at her feet the life of the people of Latin America.

There is something that I would like to say first of all. Six years ago the Fifth General Conference of the Bishops of Latin America and the Caribbean was held in this Shrine. Something beautiful took place here, which I witnessed at first hand. I saw how the Bishops – who were discussing the theme of encountering Christ, discipleship and mission – felt encouraged, supported and in some way inspired by the thousands of pilgrims who came here day after day to entrust their lives to Our Lady. That Conference was a great moment of Church. It can truly be said that the Aparecida Document was born of this interplay between the labours of the Bishops and the simple faith of the pilgrims, under Mary's maternal protection. When the Church looks for Jesus, she always knocks at his Mother's door and asks: "Show us Jesus". It is from Mary that the Church learns true discipleship. That is why the Church always goes out on mission in the footsteps of Mary.

Today, looking forward to the World Youth Day which has brought me to Brazil, I too come to knock on the door of the house of Mary – who loved and raised Jesus – that she may help all of us, pastors of God's people, parents and educators, to pass on to our young people the values that can help them build a nation and a world which are more just, united and fraternal. For this reason I would like to speak of three simple attitudes: hopefulness, openness to being surprised by God, and living in joy.

1. Hopefulness. The second reading of the Mass presents a dramatic scene: a woman – an image of Mary and the Church – is being pursued by a Dragon – the devil – who wants to devour her child. But the scene is not one of death but of life, because God intervenes and saves the child (cf. Rv 12:13a,15-16a). How many difficulties are present in the life of every individual, among our people, in our communities; yet as great as these may seem, God never allows us to be overwhelmed by them. In the face of those moments of discouragement we experience in life, in our efforts to evangelize or to embody our faith as parents within the family, I would like to say forcefully: Always know in your heart that God is by your side; he never abandons you! Let us never lose hope! Let us never allow it to die in our hearts! The "dragon," evil, is present in our history, but it does not have the upper hand. The one with the upper hand is God, and God is our hope! It is true that nowadays, to some extent, everyone, including our young people, feels attracted by the many idols which take the place of God and appear to offer hope: money, success, power, pleasure. Often a growing sense of loneliness and emptiness in the hearts of many people leads them to seek satisfaction in these ephemeral idols. Dear brothers and sisters, let us be lights of hope! Let us maintain a positive outlook on reality. Let us encourage the generosity which is typical of the young and help them to

work actively in building a better world. Young people are a powerful engine for the Church and for society. They do not need material things alone; also and above all, they need to have held up to them those non-material values which are the spiritual heart of a people, the memory of a people. In this Shrine, which is part of the memory of Brazil, we can almost read those values: spirituality, generosity, solidarity, perseverance, fraternity, joy; they are values whose deepest root is in the Christian faith.

2. The second attitude: openness to being surprised by God. Anyone who is a man or a woman of hope – the great hope which faith gives us – knows that even in the midst of difficulties God acts and he surprises us. The history of this Shrine is a good example: three fishermen, after a day of catching no fish, found something unexpected in the waters of the Parnaíba River: an image of Our Lady of the Immaculate Conception. Whoever would have thought that the site of a fruitless fishing expedition would become the place where all Brazilians can feel that they are children of one Mother? God always surprises us, like the new wine in the Gospel we have just heard. God always saves the best for us. But he asks us to let ourselves be surprised by his love, to accept his surprises. Let us trust God! Cut off from him, the wine of joy, the wine of hope, runs out. If we draw near to him, if we stay with him, what seems to be cold water, difficulty, sin, is changed into the new wine of friendship with him.

3. The third attitude: living in joy. Dear friends, if we walk in hope, allowing ourselves to be surprised by the new wine which Jesus offers us, we have joy in our hearts and we cannot fail to be witnesses of this joy. Christians are joyful, they are never gloomy. God is at our side. We have a Mother who always intercedes for the life of her children, for us, as Queen Esther did in the first reading (cf Est 5:3). Jesus has shown us that the face of God is that of a loving Father. Sin and death have been defeated. Christians cannot be pessimists! They do not look like someone in constant mourning. If we are truly in love with Christ and if we sense how much he loves us, our heart will "light up" with a joy that spreads to everyone around us. As Benedict XVI said here, in this Shrine: "the disciple knows that without Christ, there is no light, no hope, no love, no future" (Inaugural Address, Fifth General Conference of the Bishops of Latin America and the Caribbean, Aparecida, May 13, 2007, No. 3).

Dear friends, we have come to knock at the door of Mary's house. She has opened it for us, she has let us in and she shows us her Son. Now she asks us to "do whatever he tells you" (Jn 2:5). Yes, Mother, we are committed to doing whatever Jesus tells us! And we will do it with hope, trusting in God's surprises and full of joy. Amen.

Holy Mass with the Bishops of the 28th WYD and with Priests, Religious and Seminarians in the Cathedral of St. Sebastian (Rio de Janeiro, July 27, 2013)

Seeing this Cathedral full of Bishops, priests, seminarians, and men and women religious from the whole world, I think of the Psalmist's words from today's Mass: "Let the peoples praise you, O God" (Ps 66). We are indeed here to praise the Lord, and we do so reaffirming our desire to be his instruments so that not only some peoples may praise God, but all. With the same parrhesia of Paul and Barnabas, we want to proclaim the Gospel to our young people, so that they may encounter Christ and build a more fraternal world. I wish to reflect with you on three aspects of our vocation: we are called by God, called to proclaim the Gospel, and called to promote the culture of encounter.

1. Called by God – I believe that it is important to rekindle constantly an awareness of our divine vocation, which we often take for granted in the midst of our many daily responsibilities: as Jesus says, "You did not choose me, but I chose you" (Jn 15:16). This means returning to the source of our calling. For this reason, a Bishop, a priest, a consecrated person, a seminarian cannot be "forgetful": it would mean losing the vital link to that first moment of our journey. Ask for the grace, ask the Virgin for the grace, she who had a good memory; ask for the grace to preserve the memory of this first call. We were called by God and we were called to be with Jesus (cf. Mk 3:14), united with him. In reality, this living, this abiding in Christ marks all that we are and all that we do. It is precisely this "life in Christ" that ensures our apostolate is effective, that our service is fruitful: "I appointed you that you should go and bear fruit and that your fruit be authentic" (cf. Jn 15:16). It is not creativity, however pastoral it may be, or meetings or planning that ensure our fruitfulness, even if these are greatly helpful. But what assures our fruitfulness is our being faithful to Jesus, who says insistently: "Abide in me and I in you" (Jn 15:4). And we know well what that means: to contemplate him, to worship him, to embrace him, in our daily encounter with him in the Eucharist, in our life of prayer, in our moments of adoration; it means to recognize him present and to embrace him in those most in need. "Being with" Christ does not mean isolating ourselves from others. Rather, it is a "being with" in order to go forth and encounter others. Here I wish to recall some words of Blessed Mother Teresa of Calcutta. She said: "We must be very proud of our vocation because it gives us the opportunity to serve Christ in the poor. It is in thefavelas, ... in the villas miseria, that one must go to seek and to serve Christ. We must go to them as the priest presents himself at the altar, with joy" (Mother's Instructions, I, p. 80). Jesus is the Good Shepherd; he is our true treasure. Please, let us not erase Jesus from our lives! Let us ground our hearts ever more in him (cf. Lk 12:34).

2. Called to proclaim the Gospel – Many of you, dear Bishops and priests, if not all, have accompanied your young people to World Youth Day. They too have heard the mandate of Jesus: "Go and make disciples of all nations" (cf.Mt 28:19). It is our responsibility as Pastors to help kindle within their hearts the desire to be missionary disciples of Jesus. Certainly, this invitation could cause many to feel somewhat afraid, thinking that to be missionaries requires leaving their own homes and countries, family and friends. God asks us to be missionaries. But where – where he himself places us, in our own countries or wherever he chosen for us. Let us help the young. Let us have an attentive ear to listen to their dreams – they need to be heard – to listen to their successes, to pay attention to their difficulties. You have to sit down and listen to the same libretto, but accompanied by diverse music, with different characteristics. Having the patience to listen! I ask this of you with all my heart! In the confessional, in spiritual direction, in accompanying. Let us find ways to spend time with them. Planting seeds is demanding and very tiring, very tiring! It is much more rewarding to enjoy the harvest! How cunning! Reaping is more enjoyable for us! But Jesus asks us to sow with care and responsibility.

Let us spare no effort in the formation of our young people! Saint Paul uses an expression that he embodied in his own life, when he addressed the Christian community: "My little children, with whom I am again in travail until Christ be formed in you" (Gal 4:19). Let us embody this also in our own ministry! To help our young people to discover the courage and joy of faith, the joy of being loved personally by God, is very difficult. But when young people understand it, when young people experience it through the anointing of the Holy Spirit, this "being personally loved by God" accompanies them for the rest of their lives. They rediscover the joy that God gave his Son Jesus for our salvation. Let us form them in mission, to go out, to go forth, to be itinerants who communicate the faith. Jesus did this with his own disciples: he did not keep them under his wing like a hen with her chicks. He sent them out! We cannot keep ourselves shut up in parishes, in our communities, in our parish or diocesan institutions, when so many people are waiting for the Gospel! To go out as ones sent. It is not enough simply to open the door in welcome because they come, but we must go out through that door to seek and meet the people! Let us urge our young people to go forth. Of course, they will make mistakes, but let us not be afraid! The Apostles made mistakes before us. Let us urge them to go forth. Let us think resolutely about pastoral needs, beginning on the outskirts, with those who are farthest away, with those who do not usually go to church. They are the VIPs who are invited. Go and search for them at the crossroads.

3. To be called by Jesus, to be called to evangelize, and third: to be Called to promote the culture of encounter – In many places, generally speaking, due to the economic humanism that has been imposed in the world, the culture of exclusion, of rejection, is spreading. There is no place for the elderly or for the unwanted child; there is no time for that poor person in the street. At times, it seems that for some people, human relations are regulated by two modern "dogmas": efficiency and pragmatism. Dear Bishops, priests, religious and you, seminarians who are preparing for ministry: have the courage to go against the tide of this culture. Be courageous! Remember this, which helps me a great deal and on which I meditate frequently: take the First Book of Maccabees, and recall how many of the people wanted to adapt to the culture of the time: "No …! Leave us alone! Let us eat of everything, like the others do… Fine, yes to the Law, but not every part of it…" And they ended up abandoning the faith and placing themselves in the current of that culture. Have the courage to go against the tide of this culture of efficiency, this culture of waste. Encountering and welcoming everyone, solidarity – a word that is being hidden by this culture, as if it were a bad word – solidarity and fraternity: these are what make our society truly human.

Holy Mass for the 28th World Youth Day (Rio de Janeiro, July 28, 2013)

"Go and make disciples of all nations." With these words, Jesus is speaking to each one of us, saying: "It was wonderful to take part in World Youth Day, to live the faith together with young people from the four corners of the earth, but now you must go, now you must pass on this experience to others." Jesus is calling you to be a disciple with a mission! Today, in the light of the word of God that we have heard, what is the Lord saying to us? What is the Lord saying to us? Three simple ideas: Go, do not be afraid, and serve.

1. Go. During these days here in Rio, you have been able to enjoy the wonderful experience of meeting Jesus, meeting him together with others, and you have sensed the joy of faith. But the experience of this encounter must not remain locked up in your life or in the small group of your parish, your movement, or your community. That would be like withholding oxygen from a flame that was burning strongly. Faith is a flame that grows stronger the more it is shared and passed on, so that everyone may know, love and confess Jesus Christ, the Lord of life and history (cf. Rom 10:9).

Careful, though! Jesus did not say: "go, if you would like to, if you have the time," but he said: "Go and make disciples of all nations." Sharing the experience of faith, bearing witness to the faith, proclaiming the Gospel: this is a command that the Lord entrusts to the whole Church, and that includes you; but it is a command that is born not from a desire for domination, from the desire for power, but from the force of love, from the fact that Jesus first came into our midst and did not give us just a part of himself, but he gave us the whole of himself, he gave his life in order to save us and to show us the love and mercy of God. Jesus does not treat us as slaves, but as people who are free, as friends, as brothers and sisters; and he not only sends us, he accompanies us, he is always beside us in our mission of love.

Where does Jesus send us? There are no borders, no limits: he sends us to everyone. The Gospel is for everyone, not just for some. It is not only for those who seem closer to us, more receptive, more welcoming. It is for everyone. Do not be afraid to go and to bring Christ into every area of life, to the fringes of society, even to those who seem farthest away, most indifferent. The Lord seeks all, he wants everyone to feel the warmth of his mercy and his love.

In particular, I would like Christ's command: "Go" to resonate in you young people from the Church in Latin America, engaged in the continental mission promoted by the bishops. Brazil, Latin America, the whole world needs Christ! St. Paul says: "Woe to me if I do not preach the Gospel!" (1 Cor 9:16). This continent has received the proclamation of the Gospel which has marked its history and borne much fruit. Now this proclamation is entrusted also to you, that it may resound with fresh power. The Church needs you, your enthusiasm, your creativity and the joy that is so characteristic of you. A great Apostle of Brazil, Blessed José de Anchieta, set off on the mission when he was only 19 years old. Do you know what the best tool is for evangelizing the young? Another young person. This is the path for all of you to follow!

2. Do not be afraid. Some people might think: "I have no particular preparation, how can I go and proclaim the Gospel?" My dear friend, your fear is not so very different from that of Jeremiah, as we have just heard in the reading, when he was called by God to be a prophet. "Ah, Lord God! Behold, I do not know how to speak, for I am only a youth". God says the same thing to you as he said to Jeremiah: "Be not afraid … for I am with you to deliver you" (Jer 1:7,8). He is with us!

"Do not be afraid!" When we go to proclaim Christ, it is he himself who goes before us and guides us. When he sent his disciples on mission, he promised: "I am with you always" (Mt 28:20). And this is also true for us! Jesus never leaves anyone alone! He always accompanies us.

And then, Jesus did not say: "One of you go," but "All of you go": we are sent together. Dear young friends, be aware of the companionship of the whole Church and also the communion of the saints on this mission. When we face challenges together, then we are strong, we discover resources we did not know we had. Jesus did not call the Apostles to live in isolation, he called them to form a group, a community. I would like to address you, dear priests concelebrating with me at this Eucharist: you have come to accompany your young people, and this is wonderful, to share this experience of faith with them! Certainly he has rejuvenated all of you. The young make everyone feel young. But this experience is only a stage on the journey. Please, continue to accompany them with generosity and joy, help them to become actively engaged in the Church; never let them feel alone! And here I wish to thank from the heart the youth ministry teams from the movements and new communities that are accompanying the young people in their experience of being Church, in such a creative and bold way. Go forth and don't be afraid!

3. The final word: serve. The opening words of the psalm that we proclaimed are: "Sing to the Lord a new song" (Ps 95:1). What is this new song? It does not consist of words, it is not a melody, it is the song of your life, it is allowing our life to be identified with that of Jesus, it is sharing his sentiments, his thoughts, his actions. And the life of Jesus is a life for others. The life of Jesus is a life for others. It is a life of service.

Farewell Ceremony at the Galeão/Antonio Carlos Jobim International Airport (Rio de Janeiro, July 28, 2013)

I am about to leave your country to return to Rome. I depart with many happy memories which I know will nourish my prayers. Already I am beginning to miss Brazil, this great people showing so much affection and friendship. I shall miss the natural and warm smiles I have seen in so many faces, and the enthusiasm shown by the volunteers. I shall miss the hope filling the eyes of the young people in the Hospital of St. Francis. I shall miss the faith and joy shown by the residents of Varginha in the midst of their hardship. I know that Christ is truly present in the lives of countless young people and in the lives of many whom I have met during this unforgettable week. Thank you for the warm welcome and the friendship that have been offered to me. This too I shall miss.

In particular, I would like to thank Madam President, represented here by the Vice-President, for having expressed the sentiments of the entire population of Brazil towards the Successor of Peter. I warmly extend gratitude to my brother Bishops and to their many collaborators for making this week a splendid celebration of the richness and joy of our faith in Jesus Christ. I wish to thank, in a particular way, Abp. Orani Tempesta of Rio de Janeiro, his Aux. Bps., and Card. Raymundo Damasceno, President of the Bishops' Conference. I thank all those who took part in the eucharistic celebrations and other events, and I thank those who organized them and those who worked to broadcast them through the media. Finally, I wish to thank all those who in one way or another rose to the challenge of hosting and organizing the large numbers of young people. And not least my gratitude goes to the many people who prayed, often in silence and simplicity, for this World Youth Day to be an authentic experience of growth in faith. May God reward all of you, as only he can!

As I express my thanks and bid farewell, my thoughts turn to those who are at the heart of these celebrations: the young people! May God bless you for the beautiful witness of your lives and for your intense and joyful participation over these last few days. Many of you came here as disciples; I have no doubt that all of you will leave as missionaries. Through your joyful witness and service, help to build a civilization of love. Show, by your life, that it is worth giving your time and talents in order to attain high ideals, it is worth recognizing the dignity of each human person, and it is worth taking risks for Christ and his Gospel. It is he that we have come to seek because he first sought us. It is he who has inflamed our hearts with the desire to take the Good News to the large cities and to the small communities, to the countryside and to all the corners of this vast planet. I will always place my hopes in the young people of Brazil and in the young around the world: through them, Christ is preparing a new springtime all over the earth. I have seen its first fruits and I know that others will joyfully reap the full harvest.

Finally, my thoughts turn to Our Lady of Aparecida, to whom I also bid farewell. In that beloved Shrine I knelt to pray for the entire human family and in particular for all Brazilians. I implored Mary to strengthen you in the Christian faith, which forms part of the noble soul of Brazil, as indeed of many other countries; this faith is your culture's treasure and serves as encouragement and support in the task of building a renewed humanity in harmony and solidarity.

As he departs, the Pope says to all of you affectionately: "see you soon." He asks you not to forget to pray for him. The Pope needs the prayers of all of you. I offer you an affectionate embrace. May God bless you!

Press Conference of the Holy Father during the return flight (July 28, 2013)

Father Lombardi: Now, my friends, we are delighted to have the Holy Father, Pope Francis, with us on this return flight. He has been good enough to allow plenty of time to review the visit with us and to respond in complete freedom to your questions. I shall ask him to give us a brief introduction and then we will begin with the list of those who have asked to speak, and we will take them from different national groups and language groups. So, over to you, Your Holiness, for your words of introduction.

Pope Francis: Good evening, and thank you very much. I am pleased. It has been a good journey, spiritually it has done me good. I am quite tired, but my heart is joyful, and I am well, really well: this has done me good spiritually. Meeting people does me good, because the Lord works in each one of us, he works in our hearts, and the Lord's riches are so great that we can always receive many wonderful things from others. And this does me good. So that is my first reflection. Then, I would say that the goodness, the hearts of the Brazilian people, are big, really big. They are a very lovable people, a people who like to celebrate, who even amid suffering always find a path to seek out the good somewhere. And this is good: they are lively people, and they have suffered greatly! The liveliness of the Brazilians is contagious, it really is! And these people have big hearts. Then, I would say of the organizers, both at our end and those at the Brazilian end, well! I felt as if I was sitting in front of a computer, an incarnate computer ... no, really! Everything was timed so well, wasn't it? It was wonderful. Then, we had problems with the plans for security: security here, security there; there wasn't a single accident in the whole of Rio de Janeiro during these days, and everything was spontaneous. With less security, I could have been with the people, I could have embraced them, greeted them, without armoured cars ... there is security in trusting a people. It is true that there is always the danger of some mad person ... the danger that some mad person will do something, but then there is the Lord! But to make an armed space between the bishop and the people is madness, and I prefer the other madness: away with it! And run the risk of the other madness! I prefer this madness: away with it! Closeness is good for us all.

Then, the organization of WYD, not any particular aspect, but overall: the artistic element, the religious element, the catechetical element, the liturgical element ... it was all wonderful! They have the capacity to express themselves in art. Yesterday, for example, they did really lovely things, really lovely! Then, Aparecida: Aparecida for me was a powerful religious experience. I remember the Fifth Conference, I went there to pray, to pray. I wanted to go alone, somewhat hidden, but there was an impressive crowd! But it is not possible, as I knew before I arrived. And we prayed. I don't know ... one thing ... but on your part as well, your work, they tell me – I didn't read the newspapers during these days, I didn't have time, I didn't see the television, nothing – but they tell me that good work was done, really good work. Thank you, thank you for your collaboration, thank you for doing all this. Then the number, the number of young people. Today – I can hardly believe it – but today, the Governor spoke of three million. I cannot believe it. But from the altar – it's true! I don't know whether you, or some of you, were at the altar. From the altar, at the end of Mass, the whole beach was full, as far as the curve; more than four kilometres. There were so many young people. And they say, Abp. Tempesta said, they came from 178 countries: 178! The Vice-President gave me the same figure, so it's certain. It is important! Amazing!

Father Lombardi: Thank you. Now we invite Juan de Lara to speak first, from EFE, he is Spanish, and it is the last journey he will make with us. So we are pleased to give him this opportunity.

Juan de Lara: Your Holiness, good evening. On behalf of all our colleagues, we want to thank you for these days that you have given us in Rio de Janeiro, for the work that you have done and the effort you have made. And also, on behalf of all the Spanish journalists, we want to thank you for your prayers for the victims of the train accident in Santiago de Compostela. Thank you very much indeed. The first question does not have much to do with the journey, but we take the opportunity that this occasion gives us, and I would like to ask you: Your Holiness, in these four months of pontificate, we see that you have created various commissions to reform the Curia. I want to ask you: what kind of reform do you have in mind, do you foresee the possibility of suppressing the IOR, the so-called Vatican Bank? Thank you.

Pope Francis: The steps I have taken during these four and a half months come from two sources: the content of what had to be done, all of it, comes from the General Congregations of the Cardinals. There were certain things that we Cardinals asked of the one who was to be the new Pope. I remember that I asked for many things, thinking that it would be someone else... We asked, for example, for the Commission of eight Cardinals, we know that it is important to have an outside body of consultors, not the consultation bodies that already exist, but one on the outside. This is entirely in keeping – here I am making a mental abstraction, but it's the way I try to explain it – in keeping with the maturing of the relationship between synodality and primacy. In other words, having these eight Cardinals will favor synodality, they will help the various episcopates of the world to express themselves in the very government of the Church. There were many proposals made that have yet to be implemented, such as the reform of the Secretariat of the Synod and its methodology; the Post-Synodal commission, which would have a permanent consultative character; the consistories of Cardinals with less formal agendas, canonization, for example, but also other items, etc. So the source of the content is to be found there! The second source has to do with present circumstances. I admit that it was no great effort for me, during the first month of the pontificate, to organize the Commission of the eight Cardinals, which is an initial step. The financial part I was planning to address next year, because it is not the most important thing that needed to be done. But the agenda changed on account of circumstances that you know about, that are in the public domain. Problems arose that had to be dealt with. The first is the problem of the IOR, that is to say, how to manage it, how to conceptualize it, how to reformulate it, how to put right what needs to be put right, hence the first Commission of Reference, as it is called. You are familiar with the chirograph, what the aims are, who the members are, etc. Then we had the meeting of the Commission of 15 Cardinals who follow the economic affairs of the Holy See. They come from all over the world. And then, while we were preparing for this meeting, we saw the need to make a single Commission of Reference for the whole economy of the Holy See. That is to say, the economic problem was not on the agenda when it had to be addressed, but these things happen when you're in governance: you try to go in one direction, but then someone throws you a ball from another direction, and you have to bat it back. Isn't that the way it is? So, life is like that, but this too is part of the wonder of life. I repeat the question that you asked me about the IOR, excuse me, I'm speaking Spanish. Excuse me, the answer came to me in Spanish.

Returning to the question you asked about the IOR, I don't know how the IOR will end up. Some say perhaps it would be better as a bank, others say it should be an aid fund, others say it should be shut down. Well! That's what people are saying. I don't know. I trust the work done by the IOR personnel, who are working on this, and the Commission personnel too. The President of the IOR is staying, the same one as before, whereas the Director and Vice-Director have resigned. But I don't know how all this is going to end up, and that's fine, because we keep looking and we will come up with something. We are human in all this. We must find the best solution, no doubt about that. But the hallmarks of the IOR – whether it be a bank, an aid fund, or whatever else – have to be transparency and honesty, they have to be. Thank you.

Father Lombardi: Many thanks, Your Holiness. So, now we move on to a person from the representatives of the Italian group, and we have someone you know well: Andrea Tornielli, who is going to ask you a question on behalf of the Italian group.

Andrea Tornielli: Holy Father, I want to ask something perhaps a little indiscreet: there was a photograph that went all over the world when we set off, of you climbing the steps of the airplane carrying a black brief-case, and there have been articles all over the world commenting on this new departure. Yes, about the Pope climbing the steps – let's say it had never happened before that the Pope should climb on board with his own hand-luggage. So, there have been various suggestions about what the black bag contained. So my questions are these: first, why was it you carrying the black bag, and not one of your entourage, and second, could you tell us what was in it? Thank you.

Pope Francis: It wasn't the key for the atom bomb! Well! I was carrying it because that's what I've always done. When I travel, I carry it. And inside, what was there? There was a razor, a breviary, an appointment book, a book to read, I brought one about St. Thérèse, to whom I have a devotion. I have always taken a bag with me when travelling – it's normal. But we must be normal ... I don't know ... what you say is a bit strange for me, that the photograph went all over the world. But we must get used to being normal. The normality of life. I don't know, Andrea, whether I have answered your question.

Jean-Marie Guénois: Holy Father, one question, with

my colleague from *La Croix*: You have said that without women, the Church grows barren. What concrete measures will you take? For example, the diaconate for women or a woman as a head of dicastery? Also, a little technical question: you said you were tired. Have special arrangements been made for the return flight? Thank you, Your Holiness.

Pope Francis: Let's begin with the last question. This plane doesn't have any special arrangements. I am up front, I have a nice seat, a normal one, the same as everyone else has. I had them write a letter and make a phone call to say that I did not want special arrangements on the plane: is that clear? Second, about women. A Church without women is like the college of the Apostles without Mary. The role of women in the Church is not simply that of maternity, being mothers, but much greater: it is precisely to be the icon of the Virgin, of Our Lady; what helps make the Church grow! But think about it, Our Lady is more important than the Apostles! She is more important! The Church is feminine. She is Church, she is bride, she is mother. But women, in the Church, must not only… I don't know how to say this in Italian… the role of women in the Church must not be limited to being mothers, workers, a limited role… No! It is something else! But the Popes… Paul VI wrote beautifully of women, but I believe that we have much more to do in making explicit this role and charism of women. We can't imagine a Church without women, but women active in the Church, with the distinctive role that they play. I think of an example which has nothing to do with the Church, but is an historical example: in Latin America, Paraguay. For me, the women of Paraguay are the most glorious women in Latin America. Are you paraguayo? After the war, there were eight women for every man, and these women made a rather difficult decision: the decision to bear children in order to save their country, their culture, their faith, and their language. In the Church, this is how we should think of women: taking risky decisions, yet as women. This needs to be better explained. I believe that we have not yet come up with a profound theology of womanhood, in the Church. All we say is: they can do this, they can do that, now they are altar servers, now they do the readings, they are in charge of Caritas (Catholic charities). But there is more! We need to develop a profound theology of womanhood. That is what I think.

Ana Fereira: Good evening, Holy Father. Thanks. I would like to say any number of "thanks." Thanks for having brought so much joy to Brazil, and thanks also for responding to our questions. We journalists really like to ask questions. I would like to know, since yesterday you spoke to the Brazilian bishops about the participation of women in our Church… I would like to understand better, what this participation of us women in the Church would be like. Also, what do you think of women's ordination? What should our position in the Church be like?

Pope Francis: I would like to explain a bit more what I said about women's participation in the Church. It can't just be about their acting as altar servers, heads of Caritas, catechists… No! They have to be more, profoundly more, even mystically more, along with everything I said about the theology of womanhood. And, as far as women's ordination is concerned, the Church has spoken and said: "No." John Paul II said it, but with a definitive formulation. That door is closed, but on this issue I want to tell you something. I have said it, but I repeat it. Our Lady, Mary, was more important than the Apostles, than bishops and deacons and priests. Women, in the Church, are more important than bishops and priests; how, this is something we have to try to explain better, because I believe that we lack a theological explanation of this. Thank you.

Father Lombardi: Gianguido Vecchi, from Corriere della Sera: then I would ask Mrs Pigozzi and Nicole to come forward.

Gianguido Vecchi: Holy Father, during this visit too, you have frequently spoken of mercy. With regard to the reception of the sacraments by the divorced and remarried, is there the possibility of a change in the Church's discipline? That these sacraments might be an opportunity to bring these people closer, rather than a barrier dividing them from the other faithful?

Pope Francis: This is an issue which frequently comes up. Mercy is something much larger than the one case you raised. I believe that this is the season of mercy. This new era we have entered, and the many problems in the Church – like the poor witness given by some priests, problems of corruption in the Church, the problem of clericalism for example – have left so many people hurt, left so much hurt. The Church is a mother: she has to go out to heal those who are hurting, with mercy. If the Lord never tires of forgiving, we have no other choice than this: first of all, to care for those who are hurting. The Church is a mother, and she must travel this path of mercy. And find a form of mercy for all. When the prodigal son returned home, I don't think his father told him: "You, sit down and listen: what did you do with the money?" No! He celebrated! Then, perhaps, when the son was ready to speak, he spoke. The Church has to do this, when there is someone… not only wait for them, but go out and find them! That is what mercy is. And I believe that this is a *kairos*: this time is a *kairos* of mercy. But John Paul II had the first intuition of this, when he began with Faustina Kowalska, the Divine Mercy… He had something, he had intuited that this was a need in our time. With reference to the issue of giving communion to persons in a second union (because those who are divorced can receive communion, there is no problem, but when they are in a second union, they can't…), I believe that we need to look at this within the larger context of the entire pastoral care of marriage. And so it is a problem. But also – a parenthesis – the Orthodox have a different practice. They follow the theology of what they call *oikonomia*, and they give a second chance, they allow it. But I believe that this problem – and here I close the parenthesis – must be studied within the context of the pastoral care of marriage. And so, two things: first, one of the themes to be examined with the eight members of the Council of Cardinals with whom I will meet on Oct. 1-3 is how to move forward in the pastoral care of marriage, and this problem will come up there. And a second thing: two weeks ago the Secretary of the Synod of Bishops met with me about the theme of the next Synod. It was an anthropological theme, but talking it over, going back and forth, we saw this anthropological theme: how does the faith help with one's personal life-project, but in the family, and so pointing towards the pastoral care of marriage. We are moving towards a somewhat deeper pastoral care of marriage. And this is a problem for everyone, because there are so many of them, no? For example, I will only mention one: Card. Quarracino, my predecessor, used to say that as far as he was concerned, half of all marriages are null. But why did he say this? Because people get married lacking maturity, they get married without realizing that it is a life-long commitment, they get married because society tells them they have to get married. And this is where the pastoral care of marriage also comes in. And then there is the legal problem of matrimonial nullity, this has to be reviewed, because ecclesiastical tribunals are not sufficient for this. It is complex, the problem of the pastoral care of marriage. Thank you.

Father Lombardi: Thank you, Your Holiness. Who is still to come? Ilze? Then everyone will have had a turn, even more than had signed up before ...

Ilze Scamparini: I would like permission to ask a delicate question: another image that has been going around the world is that of Msgr. Ricca and the news about his private life. I would like to know, Your Holiness, what you intend to do about this? How are you confronting this issue and how does Your Holiness intend to confront the whole question of the gay lobby?

Pope Francis: About Msgr. Ricca: I did what canon law calls for, that is a preliminary investigation. And from this investigation, there was nothing of what had been alleged. We did not find anything of that. This is the response. But I wish to add something else: I see that many times in the Church, over and above this case, but including this case, people search for "sins from youth," for example, and then publish them. They are not crimes, right? Crimes are something different: the abuse of minors is a crime. No, sins. But if a person, whether it be a lay person, a priest or a religious sister, commits a sin and then converts, the Lord forgives, and when the Lord forgives, the Lord forgets and this is very important for our lives. When we confess our sins and we truly say, "I have sinned in this," the Lord forgets, and so we have no right not to forget, because otherwise we would run the risk of the Lord not forgetting our sins. That is a

danger. This is important: a theology of sin. Many times I think of St. Peter. He committed one of the worst sins, that is he denied Christ, and even with this sin they made him Pope. We have to think a great deal about that. But, returning to your question more concretely. In this case, I conducted thepreliminary investigation and we didn't find anything. This is the first question. Then, you spoke about the gay lobby. So much is written about the gay lobby. I still haven't found anyone with an identity card in the Vatican with "gay" on it. They say there are some there. I believe that when you are dealing with such a person, you must distinguish between the fact of a person being gay and the fact of someone forming a lobby, because not all lobbies are good. This one is not good. If someone is gay and is searching for the Lord and has good will, then who am I to judge him? The Catechism of the Catholic Church explains this in a beautiful way, saying ... wait a moment, how does it say it ... it says: "no one should marginalize these people for this, they must be integrated into society." The problem is not having this tendency, no, we must be brothers and sisters to one another, and there is this one and there is that one. The problem is in making a lobby of this tendency: a lobby of misers, a lobby of politicians, a lobby of masons, so many lobbies. For me, this is the greater problem. Thank you so much for asking this question. Many thanks.

Father Lombardi: Thank you. It seems to me that we cannot do more than we have done. We have kept the Pope too long, after he already said he was a little tired. We wish him now some time of rest.

Pope Francis: Thank you. Goodnight, have a good trip and rest well.

NEWS AND DOCUMENTS

Holy See Finances

On July 2-3, 2013, the meeting of the Council of Cardinals for the Study of Organizational and Economic Problems of the Holy See was held in Vatican City, presided over by Cardinal Secretary of State Tarcisio Bertone.

The meeting was attended by Cards. Joachim Meisner, archbishop of Köln (Germany), Antonio María Rouco Varela, archbishop of Madrid (Spain), Polycarp Pengo, archbishop of Dar-el-Salaam (Tanzania), Norberto Rivera Carrera, archbishop of México (México), Wilfrid Fox Napier, O.F.M., archbishop of Durban (South Africa), Angelo Scola, archbishop of Milan (Italy), Telesphore Placidus Toppo, archbishop of Ranchi (India), George Pell, archbishop of Sydney (Australia), Agostino Vallini, vicar general of His Holiness for the diocese of Rome, John Tong Hon, bishop of Hong Kong (China), Jorge Liberato Urosa Savino, archbishop of Caracas (Venezuela), and Odilo Pedro Scherer, archbishop of São Paulo (Brazil).

The Prefecture for the Economic Affairs of the Holy See was represented by the president, Card. Giuseppe Versaldi, the secretary, Msgr. Lucio Angel Vallejo Balda, and the Accountant General, Stefano Fralleoni.

The Governorate of Vatican City State and the Administration of the Patrimony of the Apostolic See (APSA) were represented by: Card. Giuseppe Bertello and Msgr. Giuseppe Sciacca, president of the Commission of Cardinals for Vatican City State and the secretary general of the Governorate of Vatican City State respectively, Card. Domenico Calcagno and Msgr. Luigi Misto, president and secretary of APSA respectively.

Pope Francis addressed the council on July 3, stressing the aims of the Council.

The meeting was intended chiefly to present the report on the consolidated financial statement of the Holy See for the year 2012 and subsequently that of the Governorate of Vatican City State.

The consolidated financial statement for the Holy See for the year 2012 showed a profit of €2,185,622, due chiefly to good performance in financial management. The most significant categories of expenditure are those regarding the cost of personnel, means of social communication considered in their entirety, and the new property taxes (IMU) which resulted in an increase in expenditure of €5,000,000 compared to previous figures.

The Governorate's 2012 financial statement, while impacted by the global economic climate, closed with a profit of €23,079,800, an increase of over a million euros compared to that of the previous year.

Peter's Pence, the contributions offered by the faithful in support of the Holy Father's charity, declined from USD 69,711,722.76 in 2011, to USD 65,922,637.08, registering a reduction of 11.91%. Further contributions to the Holy See on the part of the Institutes of Consecrated Life, Societies of Apostolic Life and Foundations passed from USD 1,194,217.78, in 2011, to USD 1,133,466.91, with a reduction of 5.09%. In total, therefore, there has been a decrease of 7.45% compared to the total in US dollars recorded in 2011.

The Institute for the Works of Religion (IOR), as each year, offered the Holy Father a significant sum in support of his apostolic and charitable ministry. For 2012 this was a sum of €50,000,000, to which €1,000,000 is to be added for the Amazon Fund, €1,500,000 for the Pro-orantibus Fund (support for cloistered monasteries), € 1,500,000 for the San Sergio Fund (support for the Church in the former Soviet Union), €1,000,000 for the Commission for Latin America, and other minor donations.

Papal Encyclical: *Lumen Fidei*

On July 5, Pope Francis issued the first encyclical of his pontificate, Lumen Fidei *("Light of Faith"), examining the theological virtue of faith.*

Presented in four chapters with an introduction, and around 19,000 words in length, the encyclical represents the final piece of a papal triptych on the theological virtues, Faith, Hope and Love that began under Pope Benedict XVI with *Deus Caritas Est* ("God is Love") in 2005 and that was followed by *Spe Salvi* ("Saved in Hope") in 2007. Francis stresses the essential relationship among the theological virtues in his encyclical, writing, "Thus wonderfully interwoven, faith, hope and charity are the driving force of the Christian life as it advances towards full communion with God. But what is it like, this road which faith opens up before us?"

Lumen Fidei was begun by Pope Benedict, but he resigned the papacy in February 2013 before its completion. Francis notes in the introduction to the encyclical that Benedict "had almost completed a first draft of an encyclical on faith. For this I am deeply grateful to him, and as his brother in Christ I have taken up his fine work and added a few contributions of my own."

While there might be a temptation to study the encyclical paragraph by paragraph to discern what was penned by Benedict or by Francis, the papal teaching is strikingly harmonized, and the result is not a hybrid document of two competing minds but a product of nearly seamless continuity among the modern popes, in particular Bl. John XXIII, Bl. John Paul II, Benedict XVI and Francis. Interestingly, on the very day the encyclical was promulgated Francis and Benedict were together in the Vatican Gardens for the unveiling of a statue dedicated to the Archangel Michael as protector of the Vatican. That same morning came the announcement that both John XXIII and John Paul II would be canonized in the coming months, and then there is the important context of the encyclical's release in the middle of the Year of Faith and during the events marking the 50th anniversary of the Second Vatican Council.

The encyclical is thus taken up from the start with the concern of the Church, especially since the council, of a dialogue with modernity that nurtures an encounter with the light of faith, that great gift brought by Jesus Christ. Francis writes in his introduction, "In modernity, that light might have been considered sufficient for societies of old, but was felt to be of no use for new times, for a humanity come of age." Francis shows through his encyclical, however, that, "There is an urgent need…to see once again that faith is a light, for once the flame of faith dies out, all other lights begin to dim."

Each chapter reflects a different aspect of faith in light of this greater purpose: "We have believed in Love (1 Jn 4:16)," on faith in Salvation History; "Unless you believe you will not understand" (cf. Is 7:9) on the relationship between faith and truth, the dialogue between faith and reason and the search for God; "I delivered to you what I also received" (cf. 1 Cor 15:3), on the safeguarding and transmission of the faith; and "God prepares a city for them" (cf. Heb 11:16), on the social dimensions of faith and of faith and the common good, in the family, in society and in the midst of suffering.

Francis writes that "if we want to understand what faith is, we need to follow the route it has taken, the path trodden by believers," that is, that we see the role of faith in the fulfillment of Salvation History – in the journey of Abraham, the people of Israel and Moses. It is a journey that is historical but that also anticipates a future promise, a "memory of the future" (*memoria futuri*) that sees beyond this world and to the source of our hope, the culmination of Salvation History in Christ Jesus, who is "the definitive 'Yes' to all the promises, the ultimate basis of our 'Amen' to God (cf. 2 Cor 1:20)."

For Francis, too, the history that culminates in Jesus "is the complete manifestation of God's reliability," but in our modern era, "culture has lost its sense of God's tangible presence and activity in our world. We think that God is to be found in the beyond, on another level of reality, far removed from our everyday relationships."

In the relationship between faith and truth, Francis notes the need for a proper setting for faith: the Church. "Faith," he declares, "in fact, needs a setting in which it can be witnessed to and communicated, a means which is suitable and proportionate to what is communicated."

But what is communicated in the Church, the pope teaches, remains "an encounter with the true God, a light which touches us at the core of our being and engages our minds, wills and emotions, opening us to relationships lived in communion."

The Church hands down this faith through the four elements that comprise "the storehouse of memory" – the profession of faith, the celebration of the sacraments, the Decalogue and prayer.

This handing down of faith, of course, points to the truth that "the unity of the Church in time and space is linked to the unity of the faith: 'there is one body and one Spirit… one faith' (Eph 4:4-5)." But, Francis sees that if the faith is one, it must be professed in all its purity and integrity, which is another way that every generation can see and attest to the reliability of God.

This reliability is seen in practical terms in the way that "the light of faith is concretely placed at the service of justice, law and peace." It has a vital social dimension, and allows us to proclaim that "God, by his concrete actions, makes a public avowal that he is present in our midst and that he desires to solidify every human relationship." This is especially important in the face of a modern world that struggles with suffering and a tragic absence of hope. "Suffering," Francis, writes, "reminds us that faith's service to the common good is always one of hope — a hope which looks ever ahead in the knowledge that only from God, from the future which comes from the risen Jesus, can our society find solid and lasting foundations."

Pope Francis ends his reflections on faith with Mary, the great role model in faith, who received the word into her heart, "so that in her womb it could take flesh and be born as light for humanity."

New Vatican Bank Commission

On June 24, 2013, Pope Francis issued a chirography that established a new Pontifical Commission charged with assessing the legal position and various activities of the Institute for Religious Works (IOR), the Vatican's financial institution.

Pope Francis wrote that the commission's findings will allow for "a better harmonization of the [IOR] with the universal mission of the Apostolic See. The Pontifical Commission will be composed of 5 people. Card. Raffaele

Farina, S.D.B., the Archivist Emeritus of the Vatican Secret Archives, will serve as president of the commission, as will Card. Jean-Louis Tauran, president of the Pontifical Council for Interreligious Dialogue, Bp. Juan Ignacio Arrieta Ochoa de Chinchetru, Secretary of the Pontifical Council for Legislative Texts, Msgr. Peter Bryan Wells, Assessor for General Affairs for the Secretariat of State, and Dr. Mary Ann Glendon, a Harvard Law professor and former U.S. Ambassador to the Holy See.

Chirograph Establishing a Pontifical Commission for Reference on the Institute for Works of Religion

With a Chirograph dated March 1, 1990, Blessed John Paul II established the Institute for Works of Religion as an entity with a public juridical personality. He gave the Institute a new configuration while preserving its name and purpose. In the same perspective, mindful that he wished to bring the Institute's structures and activities more into line with the needs of the times; taking up the invitation of our Predecessor Benedict XVI to ensure that economic and financial activities be permeated by the Gospel principles; having heard the opinion of various Cardinals and other Brothers in the Episcopate, as well as other collaborators, and in light of the need to introduce reforms in the Institutions that offer assistance to the Apostolic See, We have decided to establish a Commission for Reference on the Institute for the Works of Religion that will gather accurate information on the legal status and various activities of the Institute to permit, when necessary, a better harmonization of the said Institute with the universal mission of the Apostolic See. The Commission is to carry out its duties in accordance with this Chirograph and with our provisions currently in force.

1. The Commission shall consist of a minimum of five Members, including a President, who is its legal representative; a Coordinator, who has the ordinary powers of a delegate and acts on behalf of and for the Commission, collecting documents, data, and the necessary information; as well as a Secretary, who assists Members and takes care of the proceedings.

2. The Commission shall be endowed with the appropriate powers and faculties to carry out its institutional duties within the limits established by this Chirograph and by the regulations of the juridical system. The Commission shall collect the documents, data, and information necessary in order to carry out its institutional duties. Professional secrecy and other possible restrictions established by the juridical system shall neither curtail nor restrict the access of the Commission to documents, data and information, with the exception of the norms which protect the autonomy and independence of the Authorities who oversee and regulate the Institute, which will remain in force.

3. The Commission shall have at its disposal the appropriate human and material resources for its institutional functions. If necessary, it shall avail itself of qualified staff and consultants.

4. The governance of the Institute shall continue to function in accordance with the Chirograph which established it, unless we provide otherwise.

5. The Commission shall avail itself of the prompt cooperation of the Bodies of the Institute, as well as of its entire staff. In addition, the Superiors, Members and Officials of the Dicasteries of the Roman Curia, and of the other Agencies connected with it, as well as of Vatican City State, shall likewise cooperate with the Commission. Further, the Commission shall enlist the cooperation of others, either spontaneously or when requested.

6. The Commission shall keep Us informed of its activities in the course of its work.

7. The Commission shall deliver to Us promptly, upon the conclusion of its tasks, the results of its work, as well as its entire archives.

8. The Commission's activities shall take effect as from the date of this Chirograph.

9. The dissolution of the Commission will be announced.

Given in the Vatican on June 24, 2013, in the first year of my Pontificate.

New Vatican Laws

On July 11, 2013, Pope Francis issued a motu proprio *that updated the Laws of the Vatican City State to conform with current international conventions.*

The laws that were adopted by the Pontifical Commission for Vatican City State were: Law No. VIII containing Supplementary Norms on Criminal Law Matters; Law No. IX containing Amendments to the Criminal Code and the Criminal Procedure Code; and Law No. X containing General Provisions on Administrative Sanctions.

Motu Proprio on the Jurisdiction of Judicial Authorities of Vatican City State in Criminal Matters

In our times, the common good is increasingly threatened by transnational organized crime, the improper use of the markets and of the economy, as well as by terrorism.

It is therefore necessary for the international community to adopt adequate legal instruments to prevent and counter criminal activities, by promoting international judicial cooperation on criminal matters.

In ratifying numerous international conventions in these areas, and acting also on behalf of Vatican City State, the Holy See has constantly maintained that such agreements are effective means to prevent criminal activities that threaten human dignity, the common good and peace.

With a view to renewing the Apostolic See's commitment to cooperate to these ends, by means of this Apostolic Letter issued *Motu Proprio*, I establish that:

1. The competent Judicial Authorities of Vatican City State shall also exercise penal jurisdiction over:

a) crimes committed against the security, the fundamental interests or the patrimony of the Holy See;

b) crimes referred to:

• in Vatican City State Law No. VIII, of July 11, 2013, containing Supplementary Norms on Criminal Law Matters;

• in Vatican City State Law No. IX, of July 11, 2013, containing Amendments to the Criminal Code and the Criminal Procedure Code;

when such crimes are committed by the persons referred to in paragraph 3 below, in the exercise of their functions;

c) any other crime whose prosecution is required by an international agreement ratified by the Holy See, if the perpetrator is physically present in the territory of Vatican City State and has not been extradited.

2. The crimes referred to in paragraph 1 are to be judged pursuant to the criminal law in force in Vatican City State at the time of their commission, without prejudice to the general principles of the legal system on the temporal application of criminal laws.

3. For the purposes of Vatican criminal law, the following persons are deemed "public officials."

a) members, officials and personnel of the various organs of the Roman Curia and of the Institutions connected to it.

b) papal legates and diplomatic personnel of the Holy See.

c) those persons who serve as representatives, managers or directors, as well as persons who even de facto manage or exercise control over the entities directly dependent on the Holy See and listed in the registry of canonical juridical persons kept by the Governorate of Vatican City State;

d) any other person holding an administrative or judicial mandate in the Holy See, permanent or temporary, paid or unpaid, irrespective of that person's seniority.

4. The jurisdiction referred to in paragraph 1 comprises also the administrative liability of juridical persons arising from crimes, as regulated by Vatican City State laws.

5. When the same matters are prosecuted in other States, the provisions in force in Vatican City State on concurrent jurisdiction shall apply.

6. The content of article 23 of Law No. CXIX of Nov. 21, 1987, which approves the Judicial Order of Vatican City State remains in force.

This I decide and establish, anything to the contrary notwithstanding.

I establish that this Apostolic Letter issued Motu Proprio will be promulgated by its publication in L'Osservatore Romano, entering into force on Sept. 1, 2013.

Given in Rome, at the Apostolic Palace, on July 11, 2013, the first of my Pontificate.

New Pontifical Commission

On July 18, 2013, Pope Francis issued a chirograph establishing a new Pontifical Commission for Holy See Finances.

The new commission includes financial and legal experts, all laypeople. According to the document, the Commission will gather information, report to the Holy Father, and cooperate with the Council of Cardinals for the study of the organizational and economic problems of the Holy See, with the intention of drafting reforms of the institutions of the Holy See, toward a "simplification and rationalization of the existing bodies and more careful planning of the economic activities of all the Vatican Administrations." The chirograph also stated that the Committee will "offer the technical support of specialist advice and develop strategic solutions for improvement, so as to avoid the misuse of economic resources, to improve transparency in the processes of purchasing goods and services; to refine the administration of goods and real estate; to work with ever greater prudence in the financial sphere; to ensure correct application of accounting principles; and to guarantee healthcare and social security benefits to all those eligible." The Commission will also collaborate, on request, with the working Group of eight Cardinals in drafting a plan for the reform of the Apostolic Constitution *Pastor Bonus* on the Roman Curia. The following is the text of the Chirograph:

Chirograph for the Institution of a Pontifical Commission for Reference on the Organization of the Economic-Administrative Structure of the Holy See

Communique from the Secretary of State

The Holy Father, by a chirograph dated July 18, has established a Pontifical Commission for Reference on the Organisation of the economic-administrative structure of the Holy See.

The Commission will gather information, report to the Holy Father and co-operate with the Council of Cardinals for the study of the organisational and economic problems of the Holy See, in order to draft reforms of the institutions of the Holy See, with the aim of a "simplification and rationalisation of the existing bodies and more careful planning of the economic activities of all the Vatican Administrations."

As explained in the Chirograph, the Committee will "offer the technical support of specialist advice and develop stra-

tegic solutions for improvement, so as to avoid the misuse of economic resources, to improve transparency in the processes of purchasing goods and services; to refine the administration of goods and real estate; to work with ever greater prudence in the financial sphere; to ensure correct application of accounting principles; and to guarantee healthcare and social security benefits to all those eligible."

The Commission will be able to collaborate, on request, with the working Group of eight Cardinals in drafting a plan for the reform of the Apostolic Constitution *Pastor Bonus* on the Roman Curia.

The aims and the appointments of the Commission are described in detail in the Chirograph itself.

The members of the Commission are laypeople, experts in "legal, economic, financial and organisational matters," currently eminent consultants or reviewers for Vatican or ecclesiastical economic institutions. The only member of the clergy is the Secretary.

The eight members are:

Dr. Joseph FX Zahra (Malta), President

Msgr. Lucio Angel Vallejo Balda (Secretary of the Prefecture for Economic Affairs), Secretary

Mr. Jean-Baptiste de Franssu (France)

Dr. Enrique Llano (Spain)

Dr. Jochen Messemer (Germany)

Ms. Francesca Immacolata Chaouqui (Italy)

Mr. Jean Videlain-Sevestre (France)

Mr. George Yeo (Singapore)

Dr. Zahra and Dr. Messemer are International reviewers of the Prefecture of Economic Affairs of the Holy See.

Chirograph of the Holy Father

The reflections of recent days on the positive economic data communicated by the Council of Cardinals for the Study of Organizational and Economic Questions of the Holy See (Consolidated Financial Statement of the Holy See and Consolidated Financial Statement of the Governorate of Vatican City State for the year 2012) have led us, after due consultation with Cardinals, Brother Bishops and expert advisors, to proceed with the introduction of reforms in the Institutions of the Holy See, with a view to simplifying and rationalizing the existing structures and programming more attentively the economic activities of all the Vatican's administrative bodies.

To this end, we have decided to institute a Commission of Reference charged with the task of gathering detailed information on economic questions concerning the Vatican's administrative bodies and cooperating with the aforementioned Council of Cardinals in its valued work, by offering technical support and expert advice and working out strategic solutions for improvement, designed to avoid depletion of economic resources, to favour transparency in the acquisition of goods and services, to fine-tune the administration of movable and immovable patrimony, to operate with ever greater prudence in financial matters, to ensure the correct application of accounting principles and to guarantee health assistance and social welfare to all who are entitled to it.

The Commission carries out its assigned tasks according to the norms of this Chirograph and our operational rules:

1. The Commission is composed of a minimum of eight members, from whom a President is chosen who is its legal representative, as well as a Coordinating Secretary with delegated powers who acts in the name and on behalf of the Commission when gathering documents, data and information necessary for the execution of its institutional functions.

2. The Members, all appointed by the Supreme Pontiff, are

experts in the juridical, economic, financial and organizational matters dealt with by the Commission.

3. The Commission's institutional functions do not trespass on the areas of competence of the government or the activities of the administrative bodies concerned, which are required to cooperate readily with the Commission. The official secret and any other restrictions established by juridical norms do not impede or limit the Commission's access to documents, data and information necessary for the execution of the tasks entrusted to it.

4. The Commission keeps us informed regarding its work and hands over its findings to us. It is required to deposit with us the entire paper and digital archive at the conclusion of its mandate.

5. The Commission is equipped with resources, including interpreters and translators, and with instruments suited to its institutional functions. It may avail itself of expert assistance and of consultancies to be identified both outside the Holy See, from any part of the world, and within the Holy See, as long as there is no conflict of interest regarding the exercise of professions, functions or offices connected with the activities of the Vatican administrative bodies.

6. The Commission cooperates, when requested, with the working group of eight Cardinals charged with the study of a reform proposal for the Apostolic Constitution *Pastor Bonus* on the Roman Curia.

7. The Commission is instituted from the date of the present Chirograph. It will be dissolved when we so dispose.

Given in the Vatican on July 18, 2013, the first year of my Pontificate.

Vatican Financial Security Committee

On Aug. 8, the Holy See announced that Pope Francis had issued a motu proprio on the prevention and countering of money laundering, the financing of terrorism, and the proliferation of weapons of mass destruction.

The papal document was a reaffirmation of the Holy See's commitment to preventing illegal activities that was given significant foundation in the 2010 *motu proprio* issued by Pope Benedict. The new motu proprio includes expanding the applicability of Vatican laws to encompass all dicasteries, or offices, of the Roman Curia as well as other entities that are dependent on the Holy See. In addition, the Vatican's Financial Information Authority (FAI) received expanded "supervisory and regulatory function," and a Financial Security Committee was established to coordinate "the competent authorities of the Holy See and the Vatican City State in the area of prevention and countering of money laundering, the financing of terrorism and the proliferation of weapons of mass destruction."

Msgr. Peter B. Wells, assessor in the Vatican Secretariat of State and the highest ranking American in the Secretariat, will serve as committee president. The other members are: undersecretary for relations with states in the Secretariat of State; secretary of the Prefecture for the Economic Affairs of the Holy See; vice-secretary general of the commission governing Vatican City; the Vatican City prosecuting attorney; the director of the Financial Intelligence Authority; and the head of the Vatican police.

INTERNATIONAL NEWS 2012-2013

Year of Faith

On Oct. 11, 2012, Pope Benedict XVI officially opened the Year of Faith with a Mass that also commemorated the 50th anniversary of the opening of the Second Vatican Council. In his homily at the opening Mass of the Year of Faith, the pope taught:

Today, 50 years from the opening of the Second Vatican Ecumenical Council, we begin with great joy the Year of Faith. I am delighted to greet all of you, particularly His Holiness Bartholomaois I, Patriarch of Constantinople, and His Grace Rowan Williams, Archbishop of Canterbury. A special greeting goes to the Patriarchs and Major Archbishops of the Eastern Catholic Churches, and to the Presidents of the Bishops' Conferences. In order to evoke the Council, which some present had the grace to experience for themselves – and I greet them with particular affection – this celebration has been enriched by several special signs: the opening procession, intended to recall the memorable one of the Council Fathers when they entered this Basilica; the enthronement of the Book of the Gospels with the same book that was used at the Council; the consignment of the seven final Messages of the Council, and of the *Catechism of the Catholic Church*, which I will do before the final blessing. These signs help us not only to remember, they also offer us the possibility of going beyond commemorating. They invite us to enter more deeply into the spiritual movement which characterized Vatican II, to make it ours and to develop it according to its true meaning. And its true meaning was and remains faith in Christ, the apostolic faith, animated by the inner desire to communicate Christ to individuals and all people, in the Church's pilgrimage along the pathways of history.

The Year of Faith which we launch today is linked harmoniously with the Church's whole path over the last 50 years: from the Council, through the Magisterium of the Servant of God Paul VI, who proclaimed a Year of Faith in 1967, up to the Great Jubilee of the year 2000, with which Blessed John Paul II re-proposed to all humanity Jesus Christ as the one Savior, yesterday, today and forever. Between these two Popes, Paul VI and John Paul II, there was a deep and complete convergence, precisely upon Christ as the center of the cosmos and of history, and upon the apostolic eagerness to announce him to the world. Jesus is the center of the Christian faith. The Christian believes in God whose face was revealed by Jesus Christ. He is the fulfilment of the Scriptures and their definitive interpreter. Jesus Christ is not only the object of the faith but, as it says in the Letter to the Hebrews, he is "the pioneer and the perfecter of our faith" (12:2).

Today's Gospel tells us that Jesus Christ, consecrated by the Father in the Holy Spirit, is the true and perennial subject of evangelization. "The Spirit of the Lord is upon me, because he has anointed me to preach the good news to the poor" (Lk 4:18). This mission of Christ, this movement of his continues in space and time, over centuries and continents. It is a movement which starts with the Father and, in the power of the Spirit, goes forth to bring the good news to the poor, in both a material and a spiritual sense. The Church is the first and necessary instrument of this work of Christ because it is united to him as a body to its head. "As the Father has sent me, even so I send you" (Jn 20:21), says the Risen One to his disciples, and breathing upon them, adds, "Receive the Holy Spirit" (v. 22). Through Christ, God is the principal subject of evangelization in the world; but Christ himself wished to pass on his own mission to the Church; he did so, and continues to do so, until the end of time pouring out his Spirit upon the disciples, the same Spirit who came upon him and remained in him during all his earthly life, giving him the strength "to proclaim release to the captives and recovering of sight to the blind, to set at liberty those who are oppressed" and "to proclaim the acceptable year of the Lord" (Lk 4:18-19).

The Second Vatican Council did not wish to deal with the theme of faith in one specific document. It was, however, animated by a desire, as it were, to immerse itself anew in the Christian mystery so as to re-propose it fruitfully to contemporary man. The Servant of God Paul VI, two years after the end of the Council session, expressed it in this way: "Even if the Council does not deal expressly with the faith, it talks about it on every page, it recognizes its vital and supernatural character, it assumes it to be whole and strong, and it builds upon its teachings. We need only recall some of the Council's statements in order to realize the essential importance that the Council, consistent with the doctrinal tradition of the Church, attributes to the faith, the true faith, which has Christ for its source and the Church's Magisterium for its channel" (General Audience, Mar. 8, 1967).

We now turn to the one who convoked the Second Vatican Council and inaugurated it: Blessed John XXIII. In his opening speech, he presented the principal purpose of the Council in this way: "What above all concerns the Ecumenical Council is this: that the sacred deposit of Christian doctrine be safeguarded and taught more effectively [...] Therefore, the principal purpose of this Council is not the discussion of this or that doctrinal theme... a Council is not required for that... [but] this certain and immutable doctrine, which is to be faithfully respected, needs to be explored and presented in a way which responds to the needs of our time" (AAS 54 [1962], 790,791-792). So said Pope John at the inauguration of the Council.

In the light of these words, we can understand what I myself felt at the time: during the Council there was an emotional tension as we faced the common task of making the truth and beauty of the faith shine out in our time, without sacrificing it to the demands of the present or leaving it tied to the past: the eternal presence of God resounds in the faith, transcending time, yet it can only be welcomed by us in our own unrepeatable today. Therefore I believe that the most important thing, especially on such a significant occasion as this, is to revive in the whole Church that positive tension, that yearning to announce Christ again to contemporary man. But, so that this interior thrust towards the new evangelization neither remain just an idea nor be lost in confusion, it needs to be built on a concrete and precise basis, and this basis is the documents of the Second Vatican Council, the place where it found expression. This is why I have often insisted on the need to return, as it were, to the "letter" of the Council – that is to its texts – also to draw from them its authentic spirit, and why I have repeated that the true legacy of Vatican II is to be found in them. Reference to the documents saves us from extremes of anachronistic nostalgia and running too far ahead, and allows what is new to be welcomed in a context of continuity. The Council did not formulate anything new in matters of faith, nor did it wish to replace what was ancient. Rather, it concerned itself with seeing that the same faith might continue to be lived in the present day, that it might remain a living faith in a world of change.

If we place ourselves in harmony with the authentic approach which Blessed John XXIII wished to give to Vatican II, we will be able to realize it during this Year of Faith, following the same path of the Church as she continuously endeavours to deepen the deposit of faith entrusted to her by Christ. The Council Fathers wished to present the faith in a meaningful way; and if they opened themselves trustingly to dialogue with the modern world it is because they were certain of their faith, of the solid rock on which they stood. In the years following, however, many embraced uncritically the dominant mentality, placing in doubt the very foundations of the deposit of faith, which they sadly no longer felt able to accept as truths.

If today the Church proposes a new Year of Faith and a new evangelization, it is not to honour an anniversary, but because there is more need of it, even more than there was 50 years ago! And the reply to be given to this need is the one desired by the Popes, by the Council Fathers and contained in its documents. Even the initiative to create a Pontifical Council for the promotion of the new evangelization, which I thank for its special effort for the Year of Faith, is to be understood in this context. Recent decades have seen the advance of a spiritual "desertification." In the Council's time it was already possible from a few tragic pages of history to know what a life or a world without God looked like, but now we see it every day around us. This void has spread. But it is in starting from the experience of this desert, from this void, that we can again discover the joy of believing, its vital importance for us, men and women. In the desert we rediscover the value of what is essential for living; thus in today's world there are innumerable signs, often expressed implicitly or negatively, of the thirst for God, for the ultimate meaning of life. And in the desert people of faith are needed who, with their own lives, point out the way to the Promised Land and keep hope alive. Living faith opens the heart to the grace of God which frees us from pessimism. Today, more than ever, evangelizing means witnessing to the new life, transformed by God, and thus showing the path. The first reading spoke to us of the wisdom of the wayfarer (cf. Sir 34:9-13): the journey is a metaphor for life, and the wise wayfarer is one who has learned the art of living, and can share it with his brethren – as happens to pilgrims along the Way of St. James or similar routes which, not by chance, have again become popular in recent years. How come so many people today feel the need to make these journeys? Is it not because they find there, or at least intuit, the meaning of our existence in the world? This, then, is how we can picture the Year of Faith, a pilgrimage in the deserts of today's world, taking with us only what is necessary: neither staff, nor bag, nor bread, nor money, nor two tunics – as the Lord said to those he was sending out on mission (cf. Lk 9:3), but the Gospel and the faith of the Church, of which the Council documents are a luminous expression, as is the *Catechism of the Catholic Church*, published 20 years ago.

Synod of Bishops

On Oct. 5, 2012, the XIII Ordinary General Assembly of the Synod of Bishops opened under the title of "New Evangelization for the Transmission of the Christian Faith." The synod met in the Vatican City State from Oct. 7-26.

Pope Benedict XVI opened the synod with a Mass on Oct. 7 that included the proclamation of two new Doctors of the Church, St. John of Ávila and Hildegard of Bingen. The Holy Father declared:

With this solemn concelebration we open the thirteenth Ordinary General Assembly of the Synod of Bishops on the theme The New Evangelization for the Transmission of the Christian Faith. This theme reflects a programmatic direction for the life of the Church, its members, families, its communities and institutions. And this outline is reinforced by the fact that it coincides with the beginning of the Year of Faith, starting on Oct. 11, on the 50th anniversary of the opening of the Second Vatican Ecumenical Council. I give a cordial and grateful welcome to you who have come to be part of the Synodal Assembly, in particular to the Secretary-General of the Synod of Bishops, and to his colleagues. I salute the fraternal delegates of the other churches and ecclesial communities as well as all present, inviting them to accompany in daily prayer the deliberations which will take place over the next three weeks.

The readings for this Sunday's Liturgy of the Word propose to us two principal points of reflection: the first on matrimony, which I will touch shortly; and the second on Jesus Christ, which I will discuss now. We do not have time to comment upon the passage from the Letter to the Hebrews but, at the beginning of this Synodal Assembly, we ought to welcome the invitation to fix our gaze upon the Lord Jesus, "crowned with glory and honour, because of the suffering of death (2:9). The word of God places us before the glorious One who was crucified, so that our whole lives, and in particular the commitment of this Synodal session, will take place in the sight of him and in the light of his mystery. In every time and place, evangelization always has as its starting and finishing points Jesus Christ, the Son of God (cf. Mk 1:1); and the Crucifix is the supremely distinctive sign of him who announces the Gospel: a sign of love and peace, a call to conversion and reconciliation. My dear Brother Bishops, starting with ourselves, let us fix our gaze upon him and let us be purified by his grace.

I would now like briefly to examine the new evangelization, and its relation to ordinary evangelization and the mission ad Gentes. The Church exists to evangelize. Faithful to the Lord Jesus Christ's command, his disciples went out to the whole world to announce the Good News, spreading Christian communities everywhere. With time, these became well-organized churches with many faithful. At various times in history, divine providence has given birth to a renewed dynamism in the Church's evangelizing activity. We need only think of the evangelization of the Anglo-Saxon peoples or the Slavs, or the transmission of the faith on the continent of America, or the missionary undertakings among the peoples of Africa, Asia and Oceania. It is against this dynamic background that I like to look at the two radiant figures that I have just proclaimed Doctors of the Church, St. John of Avila and St. Hildegard of Bingen. Even in our own times, the Holy Spirit has nurtured in the Church a new effort to announce the Good News, a pastoral and spiritual dynamism which found a more universal expression and its most authoritative impulse in the Second Vatican Ecumenical Council. Such renewed evangelical dynamism produces a beneficent influence on the two specific "branches" developed by it, that is, on the one hand the Missio ad Gentes or announcement of the Gospel to those who do not yet know Jesus Christ and his message of salvation, and on the other the New Evangelization, directed principally at those who, though baptized, have drifted away from the Church and live without reference to the Christian life. The Synodal Assembly which opens today is dedicated to this new evangelization, to help these people encounter the Lord, who alone who fills our existence with deep meaning and peace; and to favor the rediscovery of the faith, that source of grace which brings joy and hope to personal, family and social life.

Obviously, such a special focus must not diminish either missionary efforts in the strict sense or the ordinary activity of evangelization in our Christian communities, as these are three aspects of the one reality of evangelization which complement and enrich each other.

The theme of marriage, found in the Gospel and the first reading, deserves special attention. The message of the word of God may be summed up in the expression found in the Book of Genesis and taken up by Jesus himself: "Therefore a man leaves his father and his mother and cleaves to his wife, and they become one flesh" (Gn 2:24; Mk 10:7-8). What does this word say to us today? It seems to me that it invites us to be more aware of a reality, already well known but not fully appreciated: that matrimony is a Gospel in itself, a Good News for the world of today, especially the dechristianized world. The union of a man and a woman, their becoming "one flesh" in charity, in fruitful and indissoluble love, is a sign that speaks of God with a force and an eloquence which in our days has become greater because unfortunately, for various reasons, marriage, in precisely the oldest regions evangelized, is going through a profound crisis. And it is not by chance. Marriage is linked to faith, but not in a general way. Marriage, as a union of faithful and indissoluble love, is based upon the grace that comes from the triune God, who in Christ loved us with a faithful love, even to the Cross. Today we ought to grasp the full truth of this statement, in contrast to the painful reality of many marriages which, unhappily, end badly. There is a clear link between the crisis in faith and the crisis in marriage. And, as the Church has said and witnessed for a long time now, marriage is called to be not only an object but a subject of the new evangelization. This is already being seen in the many experiences of communities and movements, but its realization is also growing in dioceses and parishes, as shown in the recent World Meeting of Families.

One of the important ideas of the renewed impulse that the Second Vatican Council gave to evangelization is that of the universal call to holiness, which in itself concerns all Christians (cf. Lumen Gentium, Nos. 39-42). The saints are the true actors in evangelization in all its expressions. In a special way they are even pioneers and bringers of the new evangelization: with their intercession and the example of lives attentive to the inspiration of the Holy Spirit, they show the beauty of the Gospel to those who are indifferent or even hostile, and they invite, as it were tepid believers, to live with the joy of faith, hope and charity, to rediscover the taste for the word of God and for the sacraments, especially for the bread of life, the Eucharist. Holy men and women bloom among the generous missionaries who announce the Good News to non-Christians, in the past in mission countries and now in any place where there are non-Christians. Holiness is not confined by cultural, social, political or religious barriers. Its language, that of love and truth, is understandable to all people of good will and it draws them to Jesus Christ, the inexhaustible source of new life.

At this point, let us pause for a moment to appreciate the two saints who today have been added to the elect number of Doctors of the Church. St. John of Avila lived in the 16th century. A profound expert on the sacred Scriptures, he was gifted with an ardent missionary spirit. He knew how to penetrate in a uniquely profound way the mysteries of the redemption worked by Christ for humanity. A man of God, he united constant prayer to apostolic action. He dedicated himself to preaching and to the more frequent practice of the sacraments, concentrating his commitment on improving the formation of candidates for the priesthood, of religious and of lay people, with a view to a fruitful reform of the Church.

St. Hildegard of Bingen, an important female figure of the twelfth century, offered her precious contribution to the growth of the Church of her time, employing the gifts received from God and showing herself to be a woman of brilliant intelligence, deep sensitivity and recognized spiritual authority. The Lord granted her a prophetic spirit and fervent capacity to discern the signs of the times. Hildegard nurtured an evident love of creation, and was learned in medicine, poetry and music. Above all, she maintained a great and faithful love for Christ and his Church.

This summary of the ideal in Christian life, expressed in the call to holiness, draws us to look with humility at the fragility, even sin, of many Christians, as individuals and communities, which is a great obstacle to evangelization and to recognizing the force of God that, in faith, meets human weakness. Thus, we cannot speak about the new evangelization without a sincere desire for conversion. The best path to the new evangelization is to let ourselves be reconciled with God and with each other (cf. 2 Cor 5:20). Solemnly purified, Christians can regain a legitimate pride in their dignity as children of God, created in his image and redeemed by the precious blood of Jesus Christ, and they can experience his joy in order to share it with everyone, both near and far.

Dear brothers and sisters, let us entrust the work of the Synod meeting to God, sustained by the communion of saints, invoking in particular the intercession of great evangelizers, among whom, with much affection, we ought to number Blessed Pope John Paul II, whose long pontificate was an example of the new evangelization. Let us place ourselves under the protection of the Blessed Virgin Mary, Star of the New Evangelization. With her let us invoke a new outpouring of the Holy Spirit, that from on high he may illumine the Synodal Assembly and make it fruitful for the Church's journey today, in our time. Amen.

Conclusion

At the end of the synod, the Bishops issued a Final Message For the People of God of the Synod of Bishops on the New Evangelization for the Transmission of the Christian Faith. The following is the official summary of the Final Message issued by the Press Office of the Holy See:

"At the beginning of the document, the bishops recalled the evangelical passage from John which tells about the encounter of Jesus with the Samaritan woman at the well: this is the image of contemporary man with an empty vessel, who is thirsting and is nostalgic for God, and to whom the Church must turn to make the Lord present to him. And just like the Samaritan woman, who encounters Jesus, he can but become a witness of the proclamation of salvation and hope of the Gospel.

"Looking specifically at the context of new evangelization, the Synod therefore reminds of the necessity to revive faith, which risks being made obscure in the context of today's cultures, also faced with the weakening of the faith by many baptized persons. The encounter with the Lord, which reveals God as love, can only come about in the Church, as the form of receptive community and experience of communion; from this, then, Christians become its witnesses also in other places. However, the Church reasserts that to evangelize one must be evangelized first of all, and sends out a plea – starting with herself – for conversion, because the weaknesses of Jesus' disciples weigh upon the credibility of the mission. Conscious of the fact that the Lord is the guide of history and therefore that evil will not have the last word, the bishops invite Christians to overcome fear with faith and to look at the world with serene courage because, while full of contradictions and challenges, this is still the world God loves. Therefore no pessimism: globalization, secularization and the new scenarios of society, migration, even with the difficulties and suffering they entail, they must be seen as opportunities for evangelization. Because this is not a question of finding new strategies as if the Gospel was to be spread like a market product, but rediscovering the ways in which individuals come close to Jesus.

"The Message looks at the family as the natural place for evangelization and reasserts that it should be supported by the Church, by politics and by society. Within the family, the special role of women is underlined and there is a reminder about the painful situation of divorced and remarried persons: while reconfirming the discipline with regards to access to the sacraments, it is reasserted that they are in no way abandoned by the Lord and that the Church is the welcoming house for all. The Message also mentions consecrated life, witness of the ultra-earthly sense of human existence, and the parishes as centers for evangelization; it recalls the importance of permanent formation for priests and religious men and women and invites the laity (movements and new ecclesial realities) to evangelize, remaining in communion with the Church. New evangelization finds a welcome cooperation with the other Churches and ecclesial communities, they too moved by the same spirit of proclamation of the Gospel. Special attention is focused on the young persons in a perspective of listening and dialogue to redeem and not mortify their enthusiasm.

"Then, the Message looks at dialogue, seen in many ways: with culture, which needs a new alliance between faith and reason; with education; with science which, when it doesn't close man in materialism it becomes an ally for the humanization of life; with art; with the world of economy and work; with the ill and the suffering; with politics, where an uninterested and transparent involvement towards the common good is asked for; with other religions. In particular, the Synod emphasizes that interreligious dialogue contributes to peace, refutes fundamentalism and denounces any violence against believers. The Message recalls the possibilities offered by the Year of the Faith, by the memory of Vatican Council II and by the *Catechism of the Catholic Church*. Finally, it indicates two expressions of a life of faith, which are especially meaningful for new evangelization: contemplation, where silence allows for the better reception of the Word of God, and service to the poor, in the view of recognizing Christ in their faces.

"In the last part, the Message looks at the Church in the various regions of the world and addresses a word of encouragement for the proclamation of the Gospel to each of them: to the Eastern Churches wishing to be able to practice faith in conditions of peace and religious freedom; to the African Church asking for develop evangelization in the encounter of ancient and new cultures, calling then upon the governments to cease the conflicts and violence. The Christians of North America, who live in a culture with many expressions distant from the Gospel, must look towards conversion, to being open to welcoming immigrants and refugees. Latin America is invited to live the permanent mission to face today's challenges such as poverty, violence, even the new conditions of religious pluralism. The Church in Asia, even while being a small minority, often placed at the edges of society and persecuted, is encouraged and exhorted to the steadfastness of faith. Europe, marked by an even aggressive secularization and wounded by past regimes, has nevertheless created a humanistic culture capable of giving a face to the dignity of man and to the building of the common good; today's difficulties therefore must not dishearten the European Christians, but must be perceived as a challenge. Oceania is asked to feel once again the involvement of preaching the Gospel. Finally, the Message closes with trust in Mary, the Star of New Evangelization."

NATIONAL NEWS 2012-2013

Religious Liberty and the HHS Mandate

The issue of religious liberty remained a significant one in the concerns of the Bishops of the United States and among both Catholics and non-Catholics.

The issue was much discussed in the lead up to the 2012 presidential election, and the Bishops continued to press for a resolution to the on-going HHS Mandate that requires that religious groups provide insurance coverage to employees that includes contraception, sterilization, and abortion-inducing drugs.

On June 28, 2013, the U.S. Department of Health and Human Services issued its final rule on the mandate. After analysis, the conference was compelled to declare that it fails to provide the necessary exemption for religious employers and thus will force the Church and other religious bodies to pursue a defense of rights in Congress and the courts.

On July 3, 2013, Card. Timothy Dolan, president of the U.S. Conference of Catholic Bishops, issued a statement on the mandate and listed three areas of concern based on the original March 2012 statement of the Administrative Committee, United for Religious Freedom: (1) the narrow definition of "religious employers" that are exempted, (2) the "accommodation" of religious ministries excluded from that definition, and (3) the treatment of businesses run by people who seek to operate their companies according to their religious principles. The full statement follows:

Statement of Card. Timothy Dolan Responding to June 28 Final Rule on HHS Mandate

Last Friday, the Administration issued its final rule regarding the HHS mandate, which requires healthcare coverage for sterilization, contraception, and drugs and devices that may cause abortions. That same day, I issued a brief statement indicating that the Conference would take the time necessary to analyze the 110-page regulation carefully and offer a fuller statement in due course. As I noted then, we appreciate the five-month delay in enforcement, in part because it affords us the time for that necessary analysis and response.

Although the Conference has not completed its analysis of the final rule, some basic elements of the final rule have already come into focus.It is useful to report promptly on what we do know, and also to identify where further study is needed.

Once again, the statement United for Religious Freedom–issued by the U.S. bishops' Administrative Committee in March 2012, and affirmed by the entire body of bishops in June 2012–provides the framework for examining the final form of the HHS mandate.

That document identified three categories of religious freedom problems in the mandate–in short, problems with the "religious employer" exemption; problems with the "accommodation" for employers deemed not "religious enough" for the exemption; and problems with the lack of any exemption or "accommodation" for individuals and for-profit businesses. That is, we are concerned as pastors with the freedom of the Church as a whole–not just for the full range of its institutional forms, but also for the faithful in their daily lives–to carry out the mission and ministry of Jesus Christ.

We can already tell how the final rule fares in the first and third categories, because there have been no changes in those areas since the proposed rule of February. At that time, we made clear that all but one of the problems we originally identified with the definition of "religious employer" remained in place, and that the proposed rule actually made matters more troubling by preventing dioceses and other exempt employers from extending their coverage to the employees of service ministries that are not exempt. We also made clear in February that the proposed rule, like earlier versions, made no provision at all for individuals and for-profit businesses. Because the final rule remains the same in these areas, so do our concerns.

In the second category–the "accommodation" for religious charities, schools, and hospitals–the overall structure remains the same as under the proposed rule. There are, however, some relatively small changes to the "accommodation" that will take more time to evaluate. But even now, it is clear that the final rule does at least three things differently from the proposed rule.

Two developments related to insured plans, and one to self-insured plans:

For insured plans, the proposed rule would have established separate insurance policies for coverage of sterilization, contraception, and abortifacients; but the final rule does not.Now, there is only one policy, and it is the one sponsored by the Catholic employer.The objectionable items will still be paid for by virtue of the fact that an employee belongs to the Catholic employer's plan, but these amounts are described as "payments" rather than "coverage."

Also regarding insured plans, the final rule proposes to segregate funds in a way not specified in the proposed rule. This seems intended to strengthen the claim that objectionable items will not ultimately be paid by the employer's premium dollars. But it is unclear whether the proposal succeeds in identifying a source of funds that is genuinely separate from the objecting employer, and if so, whether it is workable to draw from that separate source. Regarding self-insured plans, the proposed rule described three alternative roles for the third-party administrator in securing coverage of sterilization, contraception, and abortifacients. The final rule selects the alternative that treats the employer's very act of objecting to coverage of sterilization, contraception, and abortifacients as the legal authorization for a third-party administrator to secure the objectionable coverage. In our comments to HHS on the proposed rule, we identified this alternative as the most objectionable of the three.

Following United for Religious Freedom, we will continue to examine the extent to which these changes tend to "force [these religious ministries of service] to violate their own teachings within their very own institutions," in turn "undermin[ing] the effective proclamation of those teachings to the faithful and to the world." We will have more to say when this aspect of our analysis is completed. At this point, however, our study has not discovered any new change that eliminates the need to continue defending our rights in Congress and the courts.

Update on the Sex Abuse Scandal
By Russell Shaw

Specifics were different in 2012-2013, but the large picture of the clergy sex abuse scandal in the Catholic Church in the United States looked much the same during the year as it has for several years past.

Evidence of significant progress in dealing with the problem was repeatedly overshadowed by a handful of isolated new incidents along with fallout from events in the past.

On the positive side, the annual audit of diocesan compliance with the U.S. bishops' Charter for the Protection of Children and Young People found what the Center for Applied Research in the Apostolate said was "the fewest allegations and victims reported since the data collection...began in 2004."

StoneBridge Business Partners, which conducted the audit, said that among 34 allegations of abuse of minors in 2012, law enforcement agencies found only six to be credible. Fifteen others were still under investigation, 12 were unfounded or could not be proven, and one was a "boundary violation."

Overall, CARA said, the audit found 397 allegations against 313 priests or deacons involving 390 individuals. Most cases were from the 1970s and 1980s, and in many instances the alleged offenders were deceased or had already been removed from ministry. Of the victims, about 84% were male. At the time the abuse began, half were between the ages of 10 and 14, 17% between 15 and 17, and 19% younger than 10.

Dioceses, eparchies, and religious orders spent $148,338,437 in 2012 on settlements, attorneys' fees, therapy for victims, and support for offenders. Another $26,583,087 went for child protection programs. The total cost of the abuse scandal to U.S. dioceses, eparchies, and religious communities between 2004 and 2012 rose to $2,621,516,566.

The audit found that in cooperating dioceses, over 99% of clerics and over 96% of employees and volunteers had been trained in safe environment programs, as had more than 4.6 million children. Background evaluations had been carried out on over 99% of clerics, 98% of educators, 96% of employees, and 96% of volunteers.

Among limitations of its findings, the StoneBridge firm cited the "unwillingness of most dioceses and eparchies" to have parish audits carried out, obliging it to rely on information supplied by the dioceses and eparchies. In a letter to Card. Timothy Dolan of New York, president of the U.S. Conference of Catholic Bishops, Al J. Notzon III, chairman of the bishops' National Review Board, which oversees the audit process, seconded this concern.

"Protecting children from sexual abuse is a race without a finish and more rather than less effort is necessary to keep this sacred responsibility front and center," Notzon added.

The audit found almost all participating dioceses fully compliant with the bishops' Charter. The Diocese of Lincoln, Neb., and five Eastern rite eparchies declined to be audited. The Lincoln diocese and one eparchy also did not respond to an accompanying 2012 survey of allegations and costs.

Among other developments of the past year were these.

In September 2012, Bp. Robert Finn of Kansas City, Mo., was found guilty of one of two charges of failing to report evidence of sexual abuse by a priest of his diocese. After a brief bench trial, Judge John Torrence sentenced Bp. Finn to two years on probation. He thus became the first American bishop convicted of a criminal offense in such a case.

The case began in December 2010 when a computer repairman found pornographic photographs of young girls on a laptop computer belonging to Fr. Shawn Ratigan, a Kansas City priest. Five months then passed before the priest was reported to authorities. He subsequently pleaded guilty to child pornography charges. "I truly regret and am sorry for the hurt that these events have caused," Bp. Finn said at the time of his sentencing.

In May 2013 the diocese reached a $600,000 settlement with the family of a girl involved in a case against Fr. Ratigan, but less than a week later two other lawsuits were filed against him, Bp. Finn, and the diocese.

In July, the Archdiocese of Milwaukee released thousands of pages of documents reflecting the response of archdiocesan authorities to sex abuse complaints over several decades. The documents, which included personnel files of accused priests, were released as part of an agreement with abuse victims worked out with the bankruptcy court which is supervising the archdiocese's bankruptcy.

The 6,000 pages of documentation showed a pattern of attempts to cover up evidence of abuse and moving priests to new parish assignments during the tenure of some previous archbishops. They also showed a change under then-Abp. Dolan, who as Archbishop of Milwaukee from 2002 to 2009 pressed for prompt and decisive action against priests guilty of abuse.

To complaints that he shifted cemetery funds to a trust to protect them from creditors, Abp. Dolan said he acted to keep cemetery money separate as required by state law. In a ruling in July, a federal judge said the archdiocese had acted rightly.

Notable settlements of abuse cases during the year included the following.

The Chicago province of the Society of Jesus agreed to pay $19.6 million to six men who were abused by Donald McGuire. McGuire, who has been dismissed from the Jesuits and from the priesthood, was convicted of abuse by a Wisconsin court in 2006 and, on separate charges, by a federal court in 2008, and is now serving a 25-year-prison term.

The U.S. Christian Brothers, who filed for bankruptcy protection in 2011, agreed to pay $16.5 million to settle claims involving members of the order. The settlement, which the bankruptcy court approved, will be divided among more than 400 people who say they were abused.

The Archdiocese of Los Angeles agreed to pay $10 million to four men who say they were abused by Michael Baker, formerly a priest of the archdiocese who was laicized in 2000.

This is in addition to the archdiocese's $660 million settlement with over 500 abuse victims in 2007.

As part of that settlement, the Los Angeles archdiocese

last January released voluminous files dating as far back as the 1940s and documenting the handling of accused priests by archdiocesan officials. Among other things, the files showed that in 1986 and 1987, Card. Roger Mahony, Archbishop of Los Angeles at the time, and Father–later, Aux. Bishop–Thomas Curry, vicar for clergy, had discussed steps for shielding several priests from prosecution.

Following the new revelations, Bp. Curry resigned as regional bishop for Santa Barbara, Calif., and Abp. Jose H. Gomez, now Archbishop of Los Angeles, relieved now-retired Card. Mahony of all administrative and public duties in the archdiocese. The Cardinal and the Bishop both apologized for their actions. "Nothing in my own background or education equipped me to deal with this grave problem," Card. Mahony said in an open letter to Abp. Gomez, adding that he acted according to the best thinking at the time.

In August, the first set of religious order files on abuse by their members in Los Angeles was released. The files, covering incidents ranging from the 1950s to the 1980s, covered three orders of men and two of women and concerned 10 priests or brothers and two nuns and 21 alleged victims.

In April, Abp. Charles Chaput, O.F.M. Cap., of Philadelphia permanently removed three more priests from ministry based on allegations of abuse. Of 26 priests placed on administrative leave following a 2011 report by a Philadelphia grand jury, eight later were declared suitable for ministry, nine unsuitable, one has died, and seven cases remained unresolved.

In April, too, questions were raised concerning the reliability of testimony by a key witness in a case that resulted a year earlier in the conviction of Msgr. William J. Lynn, former Philaelphia archdiocesan secretary for clergy, for endangering the welfare of a 10-year-old boy. Former priest Edward V. Avery said he had not abused the boy but had pleaded guilty in return for a relatively light jail sentence. Msgr. Lynn, the first U.S. Church official to be tried on charges relating to sex abuse, is now serving time in prison.

In May, Michael Fugee, a priest of the Archdiocese of Newark, resigned from ministry amid a controversy over the archdiocese's handling of his case. Fugee, who admitted sexual abuse, had violated an agreement with prosecutors not to have unsupervised contact with young people. When complaints surfaced, the archdiocese first defended him but later said it had been unaware of the agreement's violation.

Fr. Robert Oliver, an official of the Boston archdiocese with responsibility for canonical affairs, in December was named "promoter of justice" at the Vatican's Congregation for the Doctrine of the Faith. In that capacity he will serve as prosecutor in clergy sex abuse cases. He succeeded Msgr. Charles Scicluna, who was named an auxiliary bishop in his native Malta. Fr. Oliver helped draft new sex abuse policies adopted in the Boston archdiocese in 2003.

Defense of Marriage

On June 26, 2013, the U.S. Supreme Court struck down parts of the federal Defense of Marriage Act (DOMA), that barred federal recognition of same-sex marriage contracts and that had been signed by Pres. Bill Clinton in 1996.

The Supreme Court also declined to rule on a case regarding California's Proposition 8 in which citizens voted to ban same-sex marriages in California; the ban was later rejected by the left-leaning 9th Circuit Court. Card. Timothy Dolan of New York, president of the U.S. Conference of Catholic Bishops, and Abp. Salvatore Cordileone of San Francisco, chair of the U.S. bishops' Subcommittee for the Promotion and Defense of Marriage issued a statement on the Supreme Court decision. The statement read:

"Today is a tragic day for marriage and our nation. The Supreme Court has dealt a profound injustice to the American people by striking down in part the federal Defense of Marriage Act. The Court got it wrong. The federal government ought to respect the truth that marriage is the union of one man and one woman, even where states fail to do so. The preservation of liberty and justice requires that all laws, federal and state, respect the truth, including the truth about marriage. It is also unfortunate that the Court did not take the opportunity to uphold California's Proposition 8 but instead decided not to rule on the matter. The common good of all, especially our children, depends upon a society that strives to uphold the truth of marriage. Now is the time to redouble our efforts in witness to this truth. These decisions are part of a public debate of great consequence. The future of marriage and the well-being of our society hang in the balance.

"Marriage is the only institution that brings together a man and a woman for life, providing any child who comes from their union with the secure foundation of a mother and a father.

"Our culture has taken for granted for far too long what human nature, experience, common sense, and God's wise design all confirm: the difference between a man and a woman matters, and the difference between a mom and a dad matters. While the culture has failed in many ways to be marriage-strengthening, this is no reason to give up. Now is the time to strengthen marriage, not redefine it. When Jesus taught about the meaning of marriage – the lifelong, exclusive union of husband and wife – he pointed back to "the beginning" of God's creation of the human person as male and female (see Mt 19). In the face of the customs and laws of his time, Jesus taught an unpopular truth that everyone could understand. The truth of marriage endures, and we will continue to boldly proclaim it with confidence and charity. Now that the Supreme Court has issued its decisions, with renewed purpose we call upon all of our leaders and the people of this good nation to stand steadfastly together in promoting and defending the unique meaning of marriage: one man, one woman, for life. We also ask for prayers as the Court's decisions are reviewed and their implications further clarified."

Labor Day

On Sept. 2, 2013, Bp. Stephen E. Blaire of Stockton, Chairman of the Committee on Domestic Justice and Human Development United States Conference of Catholic Bishops, issued the annual Labor Day statement. The statement read:

Every human being enjoys a basic right to be respected, not because of any title, position, prestige, or accomplishment but first of all because we are created in the image and likeness of God. From an ethical and moral perspective we embrace the exhortation of St. Paul "to anticipate one another in showing honor" (Rom 12:10). Today's competitive culture challenges us to strive for victory and advantage, but for St. Paul the challenge is to build each other up and honor one another's innate dignity.

Labor Day is an opportunity to take stock of the ways workers are honored and respected. Earlier this year, Pope Francis pointed out, "Work is fundamental to the dignity of a person. . . . It gives one the ability to maintain oneself, one's family, to contribute to the growth of one's own nation." Unfortunately, millions of workers today are denied this honor and respect as a result of unemployment, underemployment, unjust wages, wage theft, abuse, and exploitation.

Even with new indicators of some modest progress in recovery, the economy still has not improved the standard of living for many people, especially for the poor and the working poor, many of whom are unemployed or underemployed. More than four million people have been jobless for over six months, and that does not include the millions more who have simply lost hope. For every available job, there are often five unemployed and underemployed people actively vying for it. This jobs gap pushes wages down. Half of the jobs in this country pay less than $27,000 per year. More than 46 million people live in poverty, including 16 million children. The economy is not creating an adequate number of jobs that allow workers to provide for themselves and their families. Jobs, wages, and poverty are interrelated. The only way to reduce the widening gap between the affluent and the poorest people in our nation is by creating quality jobs that provide a just compensation that enables workers to live in the dignity appropriate for themselves and their families.

Growing Inequality Hurts Families and Communities

High unemployment and underemployment are connected to the rise in income inequality. The prophetic words of Pope Emeritus Benedict XVI in *Caritas in Veritate* warn us of the dangers of inequality:

"The dignity of the individual and the demands of justice require, particularly today, that economic choices do not cause disparities in wealth to increase in an excessive and morally unacceptable manner, and that we continue to prioritize the goal of access to steady employment for everyone. . . . Through the systemic increase of social inequality . . . not only does social cohesion suffer, thereby placing democracy at risk, but so too does the economy, through the progressive erosion of 'social capital' ... indispensable for any form of civil coexistence" (No. 32).

Is it possible that this is happening here in the United States? In many places, wealth and basic needs are separated by only a few blocks or subway stops. We only have to look under bridges and in alleyways. The words from *Gaudium et Spes* (No. 63) from the Second Vatican Council of 50 years ago seem to be just as true today: "While an immense number of people still lack the absolute necessities of life, some, even in less advanced areas, live in luxury or squander wealth." How can it be said that persons honor one another when such "extravagance and wretchedness exist side by side"?

Who Do We Hope to Be As a Nation?

Most people want to live in a more equal society that provides opportunities for growth and development. The current imbalances are not inevitable, but demand boldness in promoting a just economy that reduces inequality by creating jobs that pay a living wage and share with workers some profits of the company. It also requires ensuring a strong safety net for jobless workers and their families and those who are incapable of work. As individuals and families, as the Church, as community organizations, as businesses, as government, we all have a responsibility to promote the dignity of work and to honor workers' rights.

Since the end of the Civil War, unions have been an important part of our economy because they provide protections for workers and more importantly a way for workers to participate in company decisions that affect them. Catholic teaching has consistently affirmed the right of workers to choose to form a union. The rise in income inequality has mirrored a decline in union membership. Unions, like all human institutions, are imperfect, and they must continue to reform themselves so they stay focused on the important issues of living wages and appropriate benefits, raising the minimum wage, stopping wage theft, standing up for safe and healthy working conditions, and other issues that promote the common good. The Church, in accord with her principles on the life and dignity of the human person, wishes to collaborate with unions in securing the rights and dignity of workers.

Private enterprises, at their best, create decent jobs, contribute to the common good, and pay just wages. Ethical and moral business leaders know that it is wrong to chase profits and success at the expense of workers' dignity. They know that they have a vocation to build the kind of solidarity that honors the worker and the least among us. They remember that the economy is "for people." They know that great harm results when they separate their faith or human values from their work as business leaders.

Whenever possible we should support businesses and enterprises that protect human life and dignity, pay just wages, and protect workers' rights. We should support immigration policies that bring immigrant workers out of the shadows to a legal status and offer them a just and fair path to citizenship, so that their human rights are protected and the wages for all workers rise.

We honor the immigrant worker by remembering that the building of America has been carried out by so many who fled persecution, violence, and poverty elsewhere, coming to America to offer their talents and gifts to support themselves and their families. We welcome the stranger, the refugee, the migrant, and the marginalized, because they are children of God and it is our duty to do so. But at the same time it is important to end the political, social, and economic conditions that drive people from their homelands and families. Solidarity calls us to honor workers in our own communities and around the world. The pain of the poor and those becoming poor in the rising economic inequality of our society is mounting. Therefore, on this Labor Day 2013, let us renew our commitment to promote the dignity of the human person through work that is honorable, pays just wages, and recognizes the God-given dignity of the working person.

LIFE ISSUES 2012-2013

By Gerald Korson

The key concerns regarding life issues in late 2012 and 2013 included the debate over implementation of the Affordable Care Act, the controversy regarding unrestricted sale of emergency contraceptives, the murder trial of notorious abortion provider Dr. Kermit Gosnell, abortion legislation at the state and national levels, and the decline in the use of capital punishment.

Catholics (and Others) vs. Obamacare

The Catholic Church has long been one of the most vocal proponents of health care as a fundamental human right. While Church officials applaud the efforts of the Affordable Care Act to reduce the number of uninsured Americans and increase access to health services, they have been just as vocal in opposing particular aspects of the Obama Administration's healthcare reform plan that run counter to the principles of respect for human life, conscience rights, and religious freedom. The primary issue in the implementation of the so-called Obamacare system is the requirement issued by the U.S. Department of Health and Human Services that all employers, with a few very narrow exceptions, must provide coverage for sterilization and contraception (including certain abortion-inducing drugs) through their employee health plans free of charge. The churches had until Aug. 1, 2013, to comply with the new law.

As Catholic leaders protested this stipulation and a large number of Catholic dioceses, universities, and other institutions filed lawsuits, the Obama Administration provided a narrow "accommodation" that amounted to little more than a paperwork shift but did not relieve Catholic institutions from the offensive HHS mandate or "contraceptive mandate." Many private business owners who objected on religious grounds to providing such coverage likewise filed their own lawsuits. Some businesses, including the owners of the national arts-and-crafts chain Hobby Lobby, won injunctions against the healthcare plan; others did not.

President Obama's re-election in November 2012 put a damper on Republican efforts to repeal the Affordable Care Act and provided little motivation for the administration to offer any further compromise to the contraceptive mandate. When HHS issued its final rules on June 28, 2013, its onerous stipulations had changed little. The mandate still required religious employers to provide coverage for contraceptives, abortifacients, and sterilizations, and does not allow any exemptions based on conscience for nonprofit or for-profit employers. The "accommodated" religious institutions would have their contraceptive coverage provided separately through third-party administrators or health insurance companies using funds obtained through other than the organization's own premiums — a technicality that does not satisfy the Catholic bishops' objections to the mandate.

Noting that the final rules varied minimally from the previous form of the HHS mandate, Card. Timothy Dolan of New York, president of the U.S. Conference of Catholic Bishops, issued a statement concluding that "our study has not discovered any new change that eliminates the need to continue defending our rights in Congress and the courts."

'Morning-after' Pill Goes Unrestricted

After a dozen years of legal maneuvers and controversy, the emergency contraceptive called Plan B One-Step became available on retail shelves – without a prescription and without age restrictions – in the spring of 2013.

Plan B and other morning-after pharmaceuticals containing the synthetic hormone levonorgestrel are designed to be taken by a woman soon after unprotected sex because they help delay ovulation and inhibit fertilization. Levonorgestrel also makes it more difficult for an already-fertilized ovum to become implanted in the lining of the woman's uterus. Since Catholic teaching defines abortion as the destruction of a fertilized human egg, this would mean Plan B could act as an abortifacient, or an abortion-inducing drug. (Under the American Medical Association definition, abortion is the destruction of an embryo after its implanation, which typically takes place about seven days after fertilization.)

Furthermore, the expanded and easy availability of the morning-after pill to teenagers and adolescents, opponents say, sends a message that encourages and facilitates premarital sex. In this regard, Deirdre McQuade, spokeswoman for the USCCB's Secretariat for Pro Life Activities, said in a June 2013 email to Catholic News Service: "Many studies have shown that wider access to 'emergency contraception' among young people does not reduce pregnancy or abortion rates, but can contribute to higher rates of sexually transmitted disease. No public health consideration justifies the unregulated distribution of such drugs to children."

In 2011, the U.S. Food and Drug Administration had sought to allow over-the-counter sales of Plan B to all ages, but Health and Human Services Secretary Kathleen Sibelius blocked that action, stating uncertainty over the safety of the drug. But in April 2013, Federal Judge Edward Korman issued an order to permit unrestricted sales of Plan B One-Step to all ages. Previously, the drug had been available only to women 17 and older and only with a prescription. In response, the FDA approved such sales to persons 15 years of age and older whle the Obama Administration initially filed an appeal of the judge's order. That appeal was soon dropped, however, and the FDA approved sale of Plan B in compliance with the order in June.

The Catholic Church has long allowed for the use of levonorgestrel drugs in cases of rape when there is moral certainty fertilization has not taken place. In 2001, the U.S. Conference of Catholic Bishops issued directives for Catholic health care that said raped women could be treated with "medications that prevent ovulation, sperm capacitation or fertilization" when conception had not occurred, but ruled out treatments aimed at "the removal, destruction or interference with the implantation of a fertilized ovum."

In February 2013, a statement by the Catholic bishops of Germany said morning-after pills like Plan B can be dispensed at church-run hospitals to prevent rape victims from becoming pregnant. "Women who have been victims of rape will, of course, receive human, medical, psychological and pastoral help in Catholic hospitals – this can include administration of the 'morning-after pill' as long as it has a preventive rather than abortive effect," the bishops' conference said.

However, "Medical and pharmaceutical methods that result in the death of an embryo may still not be used," the statement continued. "The German bishops trust that, in facilities run by the Catholic Church, decisions on practical treatment will be based on moral and theological guidelines."

Gosnell Convicted in Abortion Murder Trial

A Philadelphia doctor was found guilty Monday of murdering three babies born alive in an abortion clinic, Fox News confirms. He was acquitted in the fourth baby's death, and found guilty of involuntary manslaughter in the overdose death of an adult patient.

On May 13, 2013, Dr. Kermit Gosnell, who operated a Philadelphia abortion clinic for more than two decades, was convicted of first-degree murder in the deaths of three babies who were born alive during abortions. Authorities say Gosnell killed the newborns with scissors after finding they had survived the late-term abortion procedure. In addition, Gosnell was convicted of involuntary manslaughter in the death of an adult patient, a Bhutanese refugee named Karnamaya Mongar, who died of a drug overdose administered after she had undergone an abortion at his clinic.

Gosnell was given three consecutive life sentences plus 2.5 years for the murders and manslaughter charges. His wife, Pearl, who assisted in the business and in one abortion, was sentenced to 23 months. Several other clinic workers pled guilty to various charges and were also given sentences.

Gosnell was cleared of murder charges involving a fourth baby, and three other murder charges were dropped earlier in the two-month trial. In reality, prosecutors say, hundreds of such born-alive babies were killed at the clinic over the years. In his lucrative practice, Gosnell generally had staff members administer abortion-inducing drugs during the day, and he would arrive at the clinic in the evening. Many mothers delivered live babies, whose spinal cords Gosnell and his staff would "snip" as a way of "ensuring fetal demise," in Gosnell's own words. Many of his patients were well beyond the 24-week limit on abortions under Pennsylvania law. A clinic worker testified that Gosnell, as he snipped the neck of a 30-week-old fetus, joked that the fetus was big enough to "walk to the bus stop."

The case became notorious for several factors: The long history of abuses and violations at the unsanitary but legal clinic, the slowness of authorities to inspect and investigate the clinic, the reticence of the secular media to report news of the charges against Gosnell and his trial, the apparent indifference of Gosnell to human life.

The investigation began in February 2010 – three months after Mongar's death – as police entered the clinic with a search warrant after reports of illegal drug activity. (Gosnell reportedly also conducted a "prescription mill" and would freely prescribe Oxycontin and other controlled drugs, leaving blank, pre-signed prescription pads for his staff to fill orders.) Investigators said the clinic smelled strongly of urine and found bottles and bags that stored fetus and fetal parts (such as jars of baby genitals or severed feet), bloodstained furniture, and unsanitary medical instruments. Women patients moaned in pain in various rooms, and numerous cats roaming the clinic freely. The drug charges against Gosnell are still pending.

State health authorities had not conducted routine inspections of its abortion clinics for the previous 15 years before that raid. Two top health-department officials have since been fired, and the state has passed tougher regulations for abortion clinics.

After Gosnell's conviction, Abp. Charles Chaput of Philadelphia released this statement:

"The trial of Kermit Gosnell is over. His convictions will surprise very few. But nothing can bring back the innocent children he killed, or make up for the vulnerable women he exploited. We should keep the repugnance of his clinic conditions sharp in our memories, and we should remember the media's inadequacy in covering his case, because Kermit Gosnell is not an exception. Others just like him run abortion mills throughout our country…. We need to stop cloaking the ugliness of abortion with misnomers like 'proper medical coverage' or 'choice.' It's violence of the most intimate sort, and it needs to end."

States Take Steps to Restrict Abortion

The year 2012 saw the enactment of 43 new state-level abortion restrictions in the United States, second only to the 92 laws that took effect in 2011, according to the Guttmacher Institute, a leading pro-abortion organization once affiliated with Planned Parenthood. The institute also reports that no state laws loosening abortion restrictions were enacted in 2012.

Most of the new 2012 restrictions set limits on late-term abortions, limited abortion coverage in health-insurance exchanges under the Affordable Care Act, or the use and availability of abortifacient drugs. Many required that women undergo an ultrasound and/or be allowed to see the ultrasound image of their unborn child prior to abortion; others required abortion clinics to the same health and safety laws as other medical clinics. Three states – Arizona, Georgia, and Louisiana – enacted laws banning abortions after 20 weeks of pregnancy. A few states addressed issues involving parental involvement in abortions involving minors.

Despite the defeat of key national pro-life candidates in the U.S. general election in November, the movement toward tightening abortion law continued at the state and national level in 2013. Among the highlights of pro-life legislation:

• In Texas, God. Rick Perry signed tougher aborton regulations into law July 17. The new law prohibits abortions beginning with the 20th week of pregnancy. It also stipulates that abortion clinics must be certified as surgical centers, requires that doctors follow prescription guidelines when administering the RU-486 abortion drug, and mandates that doctors who perform abortions have hospital privileges within 30 miles of the abortion facility.

The bill's passage came after a long and heated debate that drew national and international attention as pro-abortion protesters noisily disrupted the Legislature at one point in order to thwart the measure's imminent passage.

"Twenty weeks is five months – that's late term and a point where babies can feel pain," said Jeff Patterson, executive director of the Texas Catholic Conference, which represents the Catholic bishops of the state on legislative matters. "The higher standards for abortion clinics are in case there are complications or problems that occur when providing abortions."

• On July 5, Wisconsin Gov. Scott Walker signed into law a bill requiring that women who wish to have an abortion get an ultrasound of their unborn child. It also has similar hospital-admitting requirements as the Texas law.

That same day, Planned Parenthood of Wisconsin and a Milwaukee abortion clinic filed a lawsuit challenging the new law, claiming it would limit abortion access – in part because Catholic hospitals have said they would not grant admitting privileges to abortion providers. In response, the state Department of Justice said that any hospital that accepts federal funds hospitals that accept federal funds "may not discriminate against a physician because that physician has participated in or refused to participate in abortions." U.S. District Judge William M. Conley in Madison immediately put a freeze on the admitting-privileges provision.

• Republican Gov. Pat McCrory of North Carolina signed into law a bill that tightens regulations on the state's 16 abortion clinics, bans gender-selective abortions, and broadens conscience protections for health care providers. It also requires that the physician be physically present in the room when a patient is administered abortion-inducing drugs instead of simply watching the procedure on a webcam or closed-circuit monitor. The measure was to take effect Oct. 1.

The new clinic regulations, which make abortion facilities comply with the same safety standards as outpatient surgery centers, is the first such revision in the state since 1994.

North Carolina's two Catholic bishops, Bp. Michael F. Burbidge of Raleigh and Bp. Peter J. Jugis of Charlotte, supported the proposals in the measure, calling them "significant protections for the unborn in North Carolina."

• North Dakota Gov. Jack Dalrymple signed three abortion bills into law in March, variously governing admitting privileges, banning abortions for sex-selection or genetic abnormality, and prohibiting abortion after the detection of a fetal heartbeat. In July, U.S. District Court Judge Daniel Hovland blocked the fetal-heartbeat provision after a suit was filed by the state's sole abortion clinic. All three laws were slated to become effective Aug. 1.

• In New York, Democratic Gov. Andrew Cuomo had included a "Reproductive Health Act" as part of his 10-point "women's equality bill" he sought to push through the state Legislature. In June, the state Senate rejected that plank in what the New York State Catholic Conference called a "remarkable victory for unborn children." The act, the Catholic conference had said, represented "the most radical expansion of abortion since the state legalized it in 1970."

What transpired in the state Legislature is, "quite literally, the answer to prayer," said a June 21 statement by the conference. "More accurately, it is the answer to millions of prayers by men, women and children of every faith from every section of the state who believe in the inalienable right to life of the baby in the womb."

The statement went on: "The movement to pass this bill awoke a sleeping giant, a silent pro-life majority that had been discouraged and disheartened from living in the state with the highest abortion rate in the country."

Death penalty use on the wane

The use of capital punishment continued to diminish in the United States during 2012 and 2013.

In 2012, there were 43 executions, the same number as in 2011. By the first week of August, there had been just 23 executions carried out in 2013, with only 14 more scheduled before the end of the year. Of these death-row inmates, three had already been issued stays of execution. So 2013 may well end as the year with the fewest executions since 1994, when only 31 convicts received the death penalty.

In May 2013, Maryland Gov. Martin O'Malley signed into law a bill that repealed capital punishment in the state. Bp. Stephen E. Blaire of Stockton, Calif., chairman of the U.S. bishops' Committee on Domestic Justice and Human Development, called the measure "a courageous step toward a culture of life."

Bp. Blaire said in his statement: "We must lift up the dignity of all human life – even for those convicted of the worst crimes, and work to transform our culture so that it respects the inherent dignity and value of all people."

Maryland thus became the 18th state to abolish the death penalty and the sixth to do so since 2007. The others, in alphabetical order, include Alaska, Connecticut, Hawaii, Illinois, Iowa, Maine, Massachusetts, Michigan, Minnesota, New Jersey, New Mexico, New York, North Dakota, Rhode Island, Vermont, West Virginia and Wisconsin. Capital punishment also is banned in the District of Columbia.

Six states have banished the use of the death penalty in the 21st century. Maryland joins Connecticut, Illinois, New Jersey, New Mexico and New York with that distinction. As with some of the other states, Maryland's law is not applied retroactively, so five inmates remain on death row. O'Malley has promised to review their cases individually.

The last person executed in 2013 at press time was John Errol Ferguson, killed via lethal injection by the State of Florida. Convicted of eight murders, Ferguson had been on death row for 35 years. The Catholic bishops of Florida had appealed to Gov. Rick Scott for clemency on Ferguson's behalf.

MEETINGS OF U.S. BISHOPS 2012-2013

November 12-13, 2012

The Bishops of the United States Catholic Conference in Baltimore, gathered for their Nov. 12-13 fall general meeting.

Agenda:

The bishops acted on a variety of issues:

• Approved "Preaching the Mystery of Faith: The Sunday Homily," the first document on preaching to be approved in thirty years.

• Approved an exhortation to give encouragement to Catholics to utilize the sacrament of penance.

• Approved a budget for 2013 of $220.4 million and approved a national collection for the U.S. Archdiocese for Military Services.

• Approved the endorsement of the cause of canonization of Dorothy Day, co-founder of the Catholic Worker movement.

• Approved an expanded memorial for the German Redemptorist priest Bl. Francis Xavier Seelos.

• Approved a revision to the Liturgy of the Hours to update hymns, psalms, canticles and psalm prayers, some antiphons, scriptural readings, and other elements.

• Approved the hiring of a public affairs director to assist the Communications Department.

• Adopted a strategic plan for the next four years for improved development of the conference.

• Participated in a pre-meeting workshop on the use of all forms of social media, including Twitter, blogs, and Facebook.

• Elected a new treasurer-elect, along with the chairmen-elect of five committees and new members of the board of Catholic Relief Services (CRS).

President's Address

Cardinal Timothy Dolan of New York, president of

the U.S. Conference of Catholic Bishops (USCCB) delivered the annual address given at the USCCB General Assembly Fall meeting on Nov. 12, 2012.

My brother bishops,

Yes, we have "a lot on our plate" as we commence our meeting, urgent issues very worthy of our solicitude as pastors – the suffering in vast areas not far from here caused by the Hurricane of two weeks ago, the imperative to the New Evangelization, the invitation offered by the Year of Faith, and our continued dialogue, engagement, and prophetic challenge to our culture over urgent issues such as the protection of human life, the defense of marriage, the promotion of human dignity in the lives of the poor, the immigrant, those in danger from war and persecution throughout the world, and our continued efforts to defend our first and most cherished freedom – all issues calling for our renewed and enthusiastic commitment.

But I stand before you this morning to say simply: first things first. We gather as disciples of, as friends of, as believers in Jesus Christ, our Lord and Savior, "the Way, the Truth and the Life," who exhorted us to "seek first the Kingdom of God."

We cannot engage culture unless we let Him first engage us; we cannot dialogue with others unless we first dialogue with Him; we cannot challenge unless we first let Him challenge us.

The Venerable Servant of God, Fulton J. Sheen, once commented, "The first word of Jesus in the Gospel was 'come'; the last word of Jesus was 'go.'"

Fifty years ago, on Oct. 11, 1962, Blessed John XXIII courageously convened the Second Vatican Council "the greatest concern of which," he insisted, "is that the sacred deposit of Christian doctrine should be guarded and taught more efficaciously." (Allocution on the occasion of the opening of the Second Vatican Council, *Gaudet Mater Ecclesia*).

We gather for our plenary assembly in our nation"s premiere see, at the close of the XIII Ordinary General Synod of Bishops, still near the beginning of the Year of Faith. Both occasions have the same origin, the same goal expressed by Blessed John XXIII: the effective transmission of the faith for the transformation of the world.

A year ago we began our visits *ad limina Petri et Pauli*. I know you join me in expressing deep gratitude for the extraordinary affection, warmth and fraternal care with which our Holy Father welcomed us.

But Pope Benedict did not stop with his gracious hospitality. No. He also gave us plenty of fatherly advice – for our ministry as pastors of the Church and our personal role in the New Evangelization.

Here's an especially striking example from his first *ad limina* address: "Evangelization," the Successor of St. Peter noted, ". . . appears not simply a task to be undertaken ad extra; we ourselves are the first to need re-evangelization. As with all spiritual crises, whether of individuals or communities, we know that the ultimate answer can only be born of a searching, critical and ongoing self-assessment and conversion in the light of Christ"s truth."

As we bishops at the just concluded Synod of Bishops confessed in our closing message:

"We, however, should never think that the new evangelization does not concern us as bishops personally. In these days voices among the bishops were raised to recall that the Church must first of all heed the Word before she can evangelize the world. The invitation to evangelize becomes a call to conversion."

"We bishops firmly believe that we must convert ourselves

first to the power of Jesus Christ who alone can make all things new, above all our poor existence. With humility we must recognize that the poverty and weaknesses of Jesus" disciples, especially us, his ministers, weigh on the credibility of the mission. We are certainly aware – we bishops first of all – that we can never really be equal to the Lord"s calling and mandate to proclaim His Gospel to the nations. We... do not hesitate to recognize our personal sins. We are, however, also convinced that the Lord"s Spirit is capable of renewing His Church and rendering her garment resplendent if we let Him mold us."(Final Message of the Synod of Bishops to the People of God, Oct. 28, 2012)

The New Evangelization reminds us that the very agents of evangelization – you and me – will never achieve that abundant harvest Blessed John XXIII described unless we are willing and eager to first be evangelized themselves. Only those themselves first evangelized can then evangelize. As St. Bernard put it so well, "If you want to be a channel, you must first be a reservoir."

I would suggest this morning that this reservoir of our lives and ministry, when it comes especially to the New Evangelization, must first be filled with the spirit of interior conversion born of our own renewal. That"s the way we become channels of a truly effective transformation of the world, through our own witness of a penitential heart, and our own full embrace of the Sacrament of Penance.

II. "To believers also the Church must ever preach faith and penance," declared the council fathers in the very first of the documents to appear, Constitution on the Sacred Liturgy. (SC, No. 9)

To be sure, the sacraments of initiation – Baptism, Confirmation, the Eucharist – charge, challenge, and equip the agents of evangelization. Without those sacraments, we remain isolated, unredeemed, timid and unfed.

But, the Sacrament of Reconciliation evangelizes the evangelizers, as it brings us sacramentally into contact with Jesus, who calls us to conversion of heart, and allows us to answer his invitation to repentance – a repentance from within that can then transform the world without.

What an irony that despite the call of the Second Vatican Council for a renewal of the Sacrament of Penance, what we got instead was its near disappearance.

We became very good in the years following the Council in calling for the reform of structures, systems, institutions, and people other than ourselves.That, too, is important; it can transform our society and world. But did we fail along the way to realize that in no way can the New Evangelization be reduced to a program, a process, or a call to structural reform; that it is first and foremost a deeply personal conversion within? "The Kingdom of God is within," as Jesus taught.

The premier answer to the question "What's wrong with the world?" "What's wrong with the Church?" is not politics, the economy, secularism, sectarianism, globalization or global warming . . .none of these, as significant as they are. As Chesterton wrote, "The answer to the question 'What's wrong with the world?' is just two words: 'I am.'"

I am! Admitting that leads to conversion of heart and repentance, the marrow of the Gospel-invitation. I remember the insightful words of a holy priest well known to many of us from his long apostolate to priests and seminarians in Rome, Msgr. Charles Elmer, wondering aloud from time to time if, following the close of the Council, we had sadly become a Church that forgot how to kneel.If we want the New Evangelization to work, it starts on our knees.

Remember a few years back, when Card. Cahal Daly led

us in our June retreat? Speaking somberly of the Church in his home country, he observed, "The Church in Ireland is in the dirt on her knees." Then he paused, and concluded, "Maybe that's where the Church is at her best."

We kneel in the Sacrament of Penance because we are profoundly sorry for our faults and our sins, serious obstacles to the New Evangelization. But then we stand forgiven, resolute to return to the work entrusted to us – as evangelizers of the Gospel of Mercy.

I recall a conversation about a year ago with one of our brother bishops, newly ordained, attending his first plenary assembly. I asked his impressions of the meeting. "Well organized, informative, enjoyable," he replied, but he went on to observe that it was one moment in particular that had the greatest impact on him. It was during our closing Holy Hour, as he entered the large room next to the chapel, to see dozens and dozens of bishops lined up to approach the Sacrament of Penance. This new bishop told me that he felt that moment had more of an influence upon him than anything else at the meeting.

Who can forget the prophetic words of repentance from Blessed John Paul II, during the Great Jubilee, as he expressed contrition – publically and repeatedly – for the sins of the past? He mentioned the shame of the slave trade, the horrors of the holocaust, the death and destruction wrought by the crusades, the injustices of the conquest of the new world, and the violence of religious wars, to name only a few.

I remember during the celebration of the 50th International Eucharistic Congress in Ireland last June, when Card. Marc Ouellet, the Papal Legate, expressed this so forcefully as he spoke on behalf of the Holy Father at the penitential shrine of St. Patrick's Purgatory: "I come here with the specific intention of seeking forgiveness, from God and from the victims, for the grave sin of sexual abuse of children by clerics. . . In the name of the Church, I apologize once again to the victims, some of which I have met here in Lough Derg."

And so it turns to us, my brothers. How will we make the Year of Faith a time to renew the Sacrament of Penance, in our own lives and in the lives of our beloved people whom we serve? Once again, we will later this week approach the Sacrament of Penance.

And we"ll have the opportunity during this meeting to approve a simple pastoral invitation to all our faithful to join us in renewing our appreciation for and use of the Sacrament. We will "Keep the Light On" during the upcoming Advent Season!

The work of our Conference during the coming year includes reflections on re-embracing Friday as a particular day of penance, including the possible re-institution of abstinence on all Fridays of the year, not just during Lent. Our pastoral plan offers numerous resources for catechesis on the Sacrament of Penance, and the manifold graces that come to us from the frequent use of confession. Next June we will gather in a special assembly as brother bishops to pray and reflect on the mission entrusted to us by the Church, including our witness to personal conversion in Jesus Christ, and so to the New Evangelization.

We work at giving our people good examples of humble, repentant pastors, aware of our own personal and corporate sins, constantly responding to the call of Jesus to interior conversion. Remember the Curé of Ars? When a concerned group of his worried supporters came to him with a stinging protest letter from a number of parishioners, demanding the bishop to remove John Vianney as their curé, claiming he was a sinner, ignorant, and awkward, St. John Vianney took the letter, read it carefully ... and signed the petition!

III. As I began my talk this morning, my brothers, so I would like to end it, with Blessed John XXIII.

It was the Sunday angelus of Oct. 28, 1962. The message the Holy Father delivered on that bright Roman afternoon never even mentions the phrase New Evangelization. But it strikes right at the heart of the mission entrusted to each of us as shepherds.

"I feel something touching my spirit that leads to serenity," Good Pope John remarked. "The word of the Gospel is not silent. It resonates from one end of the world to the other, and finds the way of the heart. Dangers and sorrows, human prudence and wisdom, everything needs to dissolve into a song of love, into a renewed invitation, pleading all to desire and wish for the establishment of the Kingdom of Christ. A kingdom of truth and life; a kingdom of holiness and grace; a kingdom of justice, love and peace."

How could we not see it alive in those holy men and women of every time and place, the heroic evangelizers of our faith, including most recently St. Kateri Tekakwitha and St. Marianne Cope?

We have beheld it in the Church's unrelenting corporal and spiritual works of mercy, in the heroic witness of persecuted Christians, in the Church's defense of unborn human life, the care of our elders and the terminally ill, advocacy for the unemployed, those in poverty, our immigrant brothers and sisters, victims of terror and violence throughout our world, of all faiths and creeds, and in our defense of religious freedom, marriage and family. And, I have suggested today, that as we "come and go" in response to the invitation of Jesus, we begin with the Sacrament of Penance. This is the sacrament of the New Evangelization, for as Pope Benedict reminds us, "We cannot speak about the new evangelization without a sincere desire to conversion." (Homily for the Opening of the XIII Ordinary General Synod of Bishops).

With this as my presidential address, I know I risk the criticism. I can hear it now: "With all the controversies and urgent matters for the Church, Card. Dolan spoke of conversion of heart through the Sacrament of Penance. Can you believe it?"

To which I reply, "You better believe it!" First things first!

June 10-14, 2013

The Bishops gathered for their annual Spring Assembly from June 10-14, 2013, at the Loews Coronado Springs resort near San Diego, CA.

Doctrine of the Catholic Church

THE CATECHISM OF THE CATHOLIC CHURCH

By Russell Shaw

"The Catechism of the Catholic Church ... is a statement of the Church's faith and of Catholic doctrine, attested to or illumined by Sacred Scripture, the Apostolic Tradition, and the Church's Magisterium. I declare it to be a sure norm for teaching the faith and thus –a valid and legitimate instrument for ecclesial communion."

Thus Pope John Paul II in the Apostolic Constitution *Fidei Depositum* ("The Deposit of Faith") formally presented the first official catechism or compendium of doctrine for the universal Church to have been published since the 16th century.

Fidei Depositum is dated Oct. 11, 1992, the 30th anniversary of the opening of the Second Vatican Council (1962-65), and that date is significant. The predecessor of the Catechism of the Catholic Church is the Roman Catechism or Catechism of the Council of Trent, which was published by Pope St. Pius V in 1566 following the great reforming council held from 1545 to 1563. As the Roman Catechism sets forth the doctrine of the Church in light of the Council of Trent, so the Catechism of the Catholic Church sets forth the Church's teaching against the background of Vatican Council II.

History of the Catechism

In development since 1986, the definitive text of the *Catechism of the Catholic Church* was officially approved by Pope John Paul on June 25, 1992, with Dec. 8 the date of formal promulgation.

Nine separate drafts of the *Catechism* were prepared. The document was written in French. In November 1989, the commission of cardinals sent a draft text to all the bishops of the world asking for their comments and suggestions. Although this consultation produced a reaction generally favorable to the text, more than 24,000 individual amendments were submitted by the bishops, and these were reviewed by the commission, and helped to shape the further revision of the document.

The pope in *Fidei Depositum* described the *Catechism* as "a sure and authentic reference text" both for the teaching of Catholic doctrine and particularly for the preparation of local catechisms; he said the *Catechism* was presented to "all the Church's Pastors and the Christian faithful" with these ends in view. Other purposes mentioned included helping Catholics to deepen their knowledge of the faith, supporting ecumenical efforts by "showing carefully the content and wondrous harmony of the Catholic faith," and providing authoritative answers to anyone who wishes to know "what the Catholic Church believes."

Structure and Contents of the Catechism

The *Catechism* adopts the four-fold division of the *Roman Catechism*. The four parts or "pillars" deal with the Creed; the Sacred Liturgy, with special emphasis on the sacraments; the Christian way of life, analyzed according to the Ten Commandments; and prayer, considered in the framework of the petitions of the Our Father.

Describing this organizational scheme, Pope John Paul said: "The four parts are related one to another: the Christian mystery is the object of faith (first part); it is celebrated and communicated in liturgical actions (second part); it is present to enlighten and sustain the children of God in their actions (third part); it is the basis of our prayer, the privileged expression of which is the Our Father, and it represents the object of our supplication, our praise and our intercession (fourth part)."

The pope also stressed the Christocentric nature of Christian faith as it is presented in the *Catechism*. "In reading the *Catechism of the Catholic Church* we can perceive the wonderful unity of the mystery of God, his saving will, as well as the central place of Jesus Christ, the only-begotten Son of God, sent by the Father, made man in the womb of the Blessed Virgin Mary by the power of the Holy Spirit, to be our Savior. Having died and risen, Christ is always present in his Church, especially in the sacraments; he is the source of our faith, the model of Christian conduct, and the Teacher of our prayer."

The text of the *Catechism of the Catholic Church*, with extensive cross-references and sectional summaries, consists of 2,865 numbered paragraphs. Passages in large print set out its more substantive contents, while passages in small print provide background information and explanations; there are numerous cross-references in the margins directing readers to other passages that treat the same theme or related themes. Among the features of the *Catechism* are the "In Brief" sections found throughout, which sum up the teaching of the preceding unit.

OUTLINE OF THE CATECHISM

Prologue (1-25)

The nature of catechesis is described, along with the aim of the present *Catechism* and its intended readership, its structure, its use, and the desirability of adaptations for different cultures, age groups, etc.

Part One: The Profession of Faith (26-1065)

Section One discusses the nature of faith. "Faith is man's response to God, who reveals himself and gives himself to man, at the same time bringing man a superabundant light as he searches for the ultimate meaning of his life. Thus we shall consider first that search (Chapter One), then the divine Revelation by which God comes to meet man (Chapter Two), and finally the response of faith (Chapter Three)" (26). The topics discussed include knowledge of God; Divine Revelation and its transmission; Sacred Scripture; and faith as the human response to God. "We do not believe in formulas, but in those realities they express, which faith allows us to touch.... All the same, we do approach these realities with the help of formulations of the faith which permit us to express the faith and to hand it on, to celebrate it in community, to assimilate and live on it more and more" (170).

Section Two deals with the profession of Christian faith, with the treatment organized according to the articles of the Creed. The Creed used is the Apostles' Creed; its "great authority," says the *Catechism*, quoting St. Ambrose, arises from its being "the Creed of the Roman Church, the See of Peter, the first of the apostles" (194). Among the doctrines covered in the three chapters of this section are the Trinity, creation, the angels, the creation of man, original sin, the Incarnation, the virgin birth, redemption, the Resurrection of Christ, the work of the Holy Spirit, the Church, the hierarchical constitution of the Church, the communion of saints, the Virgin Mary as Mother of Christ and Mother of the Church, the resurrection of the dead, judgment, heaven, and hell. "[T]he Creed's final 'Amen' repeats and confirms its first words: 'I believe.' To believe is to say 'Amen' to God's words, promises and commandments; to entrust oneself completely to him who is the 'Amen' of infinite love and perfect faithfulness. The Christian's everyday life will then be the 'Amen' to the 'I believe' of our baptismal profession of faith" (1064).

Part Two: The Celebration of the Christian Mystery (1066-1690)

Section One considers the sacramental economy. It explains that in this present "age of the Church," begun on Pentecost, "Christ now lives and acts in his Church, in a new way appropriate to this new age. He acts through the sacraments in what the common Tradition of the East and the West calls 'the sacramental economy'... the communication (or 'dispensation') of the fruits of Christ's Paschal Mystery in the celebration of the Church's 'sacramental' liturgy" (1076). Topics treated here are the Paschal Mystery and its sacramental celebration.

Section Two covers the seven sacraments of the Church. "Christ instituted the sacraments of the new law.... The seven sacraments touch all the stages and all the important moments of Christian life: they give birth and increase, healing and mission to the Christian's life of faith. There is thus a certain resemblance between the stages of natural life and the stages of the spiritual life" (1210). The presentation is organized in four chapters. These are: the sacraments of Christian initiation (Baptism, Confirmation, the Eucharist) in chapter one; the sacraments of healing (Penance and Reconciliation, the Anointing of the Sick) in chapter two; the "sacraments at the service of communion" (Holy Orders and Matrimony) in chapter three; and sacramentals and Christian funerals in chapter four.

Part Three: Life in Christ (1691-2557)

Section One is entitled "Man's Vocation: Life in the Spirit." Its three chapters discuss the dignity of the human person, the human community, and "God's Salvation: Law and Grace" (the moral law, grace and justification, the Church as teacher of moral truth). "Catechesis has to reveal in all clarity the joy and the demands of the way of Christ.... The first and last point of reference of this catechesis will always be Jesus Christ himself, who is 'they way, and the truth, and the life'" (1697-1698).

Section Two reflects on the contents of Christian moral life. The treatment is organized according to the Ten Commandments, with a chapter devoted to each commandment and its concrete applications. While the commandments admit of what is traditionally called light matter (venial sin), nevertheless, the text says: "Since they express man's fundamental duties towards God and towards his neighbor, the Ten Commandments reveal, in their primordial content, grave obligations. They are fundamentally immutable, and they oblige always and everywhere. No one can dispense from them. The Ten Commandments are engraved by God in the human heart" (2072).

Part Four: Christian Prayer (2558-2865)

Section One considers prayer in Christian life, underlining the relationship of this topic to the rest of the *Catechism*: "The Church professes this mystery [of faith] in the Apostles' Creed (Part One) and celebrates it in the sacramental liturgy (Part Two), so that the life of the faithful may be conformed to Christ in the Holy Spirit to the glory of God the Father (Part Three). This mystery, then, requires that the faithful believe in it, that they celebrate it, and that they live from it in a vital and personal relationship with the living and true God. This relationship is prayer" (2558). The section then discusses the "revelation of prayer" in the Old Testament and now in the age of the Church, the tradition of prayer, and the life of prayer (kinds of prayer, problems and perseverance in prayer).

Section Two presents an extended reflection on the Our Father, considered as the model of prayer. Quoting Tertullian, the *Catechism* says: "The Lord's Prayer 'is truly the summary of the whole Gospel.' 'Since the Lord ... after handing over the practice of prayer, said elsewhere, 'Ask and you will receive,' and since everyone has petitions which are peculiar to his circumstances, the regular and appropriate prayer [the Lord's Prayer] is said first, as the foundation of further desires'" (2761).

Reception of the Catechism

Following the publication of the *Catechism of the Catholic Church*, Pope John Paul established an Interdicasterial Commission for the Catechism, under the chairmanship of Cardinal Ratzinger, responsible for overseeing translations of the volume and reviewing and approving suggested changes in the text. The commission approved the English translation of the *Catechism* in February 1994, and it was published on June 22 of that year — in the United States, under the auspices of the National Conference of Catholic Bishops.

Pope John Paul presented the *editio typica* or normative Latin version of the *Catechism* in a formal ceremony on Sept. 8, 1997.

The following day, Cardinal Ratzinger presented the *editio typica* at a Vatican news conference. At the same time, he also introduced more than a hundred changes which had been approved for incorporation into the text. Most of the changes were of a minor, editorial nature. The most important was in paragraphs 2265-2267 of the *Catechism*, where the treatment of capital punishment had been strengthened to reflect the discussion of the same topic in Pope John Paul's 1995 encyclical letter *Evangelium Vitae* ("*The Gospel of Life*").

In the United States, the National Conference of Catholic Bishops in 1994 established an Ad Hoc Committee to Oversee the Use of the Catechism. It has an office and staff at NCCB headquarters in Washington, DC. The committee reviews and approves materials that seek to make substantial direct use of the text of the *Catechism of the Catholic Church*, and also reviews catechetical series for their conformity with the *Catechism*. In addition, the committee was mandated to conduct a feasibility study of a national catechism or catechetical series for the United States.

Compendium of the Catechism

On June 28, 2005, Pope Benedict XVI issued a *motu proprio* for the approval and publication of the *Compendium of the Catechism of the Catholic Church*. The Holy Father declared in his *motu proprio*:

"The *Compendium*, which I now present to the Universal Church, is a faithful and sure synthesis of the *Catechism of the Catholic Church*. It contains, in concise form, all the essential and fundamental elements of the Church's faith, thus constituting, as my Predecessor had wished, a kind of *vademecum* which allows believers and non-believers alike to behold the entire panorama of the Catholic faith.

"In its structure, contents and language, the *Compendium* faithfully reflects the *Catechism of the Catholic Church* and will thus assist in making the Catechism more widely known and more deeply understood."

The Introduction to the *Compendium*, written by Joseph Cardinal Ratzinger prior to his election as pope, described the process by which the text came about, namely to realize more fully the potential of the *Catechism* and to provide a synthesis of the vast treasure of its teachings. Then Cardinal Ratzinger noted its three principal characteristics: "the close reliance on the *Catechism of the Catholic Church*; the dialogical format; the use of artistic images in the catechesis."

Like the *Catechism*, the Compendium offers four parts, corresponding to the fundamental laws of life in Christ. Part one is "The Profession of Faith"; part two is "The Celebration of the Christian Mystery"; part three is "Life in Christ"; and the fourth part is "Christian Prayer."

DOGMATIC CONSTITUTION ON THE CHURCH — LUMEN GENTIUM

Following are excerpts from the first two chapters of the "Dogmatic Constitution on the Church" (*Lumen Gentium*) promulgated by the Second Vatican Council. They describe the relation of the Catholic Church to the Kingdom of God, the nature and foundation of the Church, the People of God, the necessity of membership and participation in the Church for salvation. Additional subjects in the constitution are treated in other *Almanac* entries.

I. MYSTERY OF THE CHURCH

By her relationship with Christ, the Church is a kind of sacrament or sign of intimate union with God, and of the unity of all mankind (No. 1).

He (the eternal Father) planned to assemble in the holy Church all those who would believe in Christ. Already from the beginning of the world the foreshadowing of the Church took place. She was prepared for in a remarkable way throughout the history of the people of Israel and by means of the Old Covenant. Established in the present era of time, the Church was made manifest by the outpouring of the Spirit. At the end of time she will achieve her glorious fulfillment. Then all just men from the time of Adam, "from Abel, the just one, to the last of the elect," will be gathered together with the Father in the universal Church (No. 2).

When the work which the Father had given the Son to do on earth (cf. Jn 17:4) was accomplished, the Holy Spirit was sent on the day of Pentecost in order that he might forever sanctify the Church, and thus all believers would have access to the Father through Christ in the one Spirit (cf. Eph 2:18).

The Spirit dwells in the Church and in the hearts of the faithful as in a temple (cf. 1 Cor 3:16; 6:19).... The Spirit guides the Church into the fullness of truth (cf. Jn 16:13) and gives her a unity of fellowship and service. He furnishes and directs her with various gifts, both hierarchical and charismatic, and adorns her with the fruits of His grace (cf. Eph 4:11-12; 1 Cor 12:4; Gal 5:22). By the power of the Gospel he makes the Church grow, perpetually renews her, and leads her to perfect union with her Spouse (No. 4).

Foundation of the Church

The mystery of the holy Church is manifest in her very foundation, for the Lord Jesus inaugurated her by preaching the Good News, that is, the coming of God's Kingdom, which, for centuries, had been promised in the Scriptures.... In Christ's word, in his works, and in his presence this Kingdom reveals itself to men.

The miracles of Jesus also confirm that the Kingdom has already arrived on earth.

Before all things, however, the Kingdom is clearly visible in the very Person of Christ, Son of God and Son of Man.

When Jesus rose up again after suffering death on the cross for mankind, he manifested that he had been appointed Lord, Messiah, and Priest forever (cf. Acts 2:36; Heb 5:6; 7:17-21), and he poured out on his disciples the Spirit promised by the Father (cf. Acts 2:33). The Church, consequently, equipped with the gifts of her Founder and faithfully guarding his precepts receives the mission to proclaim and to establish among all peoples the Kingdom of Christ and of God. She becomes on earth the initial budding forth of that Kingdom. While she slowly grows, the Church strains toward the consummation of the Kingdom and, with all her strength, hopes and desires to be united in glory with her King (No. 5).

Figures of the Church

In the Old Testament the revelation of the Kingdom had often been conveyed by figures of speech. In the same way the inner nature of the Church was now to be made known to us through various images.

The Church is a sheepfold ... a flock ... a tract of land to be cultivated, the field of God ... his choice vineyard ... the true vine is Christ ... the edifice of God ... the house of God ... the holy temple (whose members are) living stones ... this holy city ... a bride ... our Mother ... the spotless spouse of the spotless Lamb ... an exile (No. 6).

In the human nature which he united to himself, the Son of God redeemed man and transformed him into a new creation (cf. Gal 6:15; 2 Cor 5:17) by overcoming death through his own death and resurrection. By communicating his Spirit to his brothers, called together from all peoples, Christ made them mystically into his own body.

In that body, the life of Christ is poured into the believers, who, through the sacraments, are united in a hidden and real way to Christ who suffered and was glorified. Through baptism we are formed in the likeness of Christ.

Truly partaking of the body of the Lord in the breaking of the eucharistic bread, we are taken up into communion with him and with one another (No. 7).

One Body in Christ

As all the members of the human body, though they are many, form one body, so also are the faithful in Christ (cf. 1 Cor 12:12). Also, in the building up of Christ's body there is a flourishing variety of members and functions. There is only one Spirit who distributes his different gifts for the welfare of the Church (cf. 1 Cor 12:1-11). Among these gifts stands out the grace given to the apostles. To their authority, the Spirit himself subjected even those who were endowed with charisms (cf. 1 Cor 14). The head of this body is Christ (No. 7).

Mystical Body of Christ

Christ, the one Mediator, established and ceaselessly sustains here on earth his holy Church, the community of faith, hope, and charity, as a visible structure. Through her he communicates truth and grace to all. But the society furnished with hierarchical agencies and the Mystical Body of Christ are not to be considered as two realities, nor are the visible assembly and the spiritual community, nor the earthly Church and the Church enriched with heavenly things. Rather they form one interlocked reality which is comprised of a divine and a human element. For this reason, this reality is compared to the mystery of the incarnate Word. Just as the assumed nature inseparably united to the divine Word serves him as a living instrument of salvation, so, in a similar way, does the communal structure of the Church serve Christ's Spirit, who vivifies it by way of building up the body (cf. Eph 4:16).

This is the unique Church of Christ which in the Creed we avow as one, holy, catholic, and apostolic. After his Resurrection our Savior handed her over to Peter to be shepherded (Jn 21:17), commissioning him and the other apostles to propagate and govern her (cf. Mt 28:18, ff.). Her he erected for all ages as "the pillar and mainstay of the truth" (1 Tm 3:15). This Church, constituted and organized in the world as a society, subsists in the Catholic Church, which is governed by the successor of Peter and by the bishops in union with that successor, although many elements of sanctification and of truth can be found outside of her visible structure. These elements, however, as gifts properly belonging to the Church of Christ, possess an inner dynamism toward Catholic unity.

The Church, embracing sinners in her bosom, is at the same time holy and always in need of being purified, and incessantly pursues the path of penance and renewal.

The Church, "like a pilgrim in a foreign land, presses forward, announcing the cross and death of the Lord until he comes" (cf. 1 Cor 11:26) (No. 8).

II. THE PEOPLE OF GOD

At all times and among every people, God has given welcome to whosoever fears him and does what is right (cf. Acts 10:35). It has pleased God, however, to make men holy and save them not merely as individuals without any mutual bonds, but by making them into a single people, a people which acknowledges him in truth and serves him in holiness. He therefore chose the race of Israel as a people unto himself. With it he set up a covenant. Step by step he taught this people by manifesting in its history both himself and the decree of his will, and by making it holy unto himself. All these things, however, were done by way of preparation and as a figure of that new and perfect covenant which was to be ratified in Christ.

Christ instituted this New Covenant, that is to say, the New Testament, in his blood (cf. 1 Cor 11:25), by calling together a people made up of Jew and Gentile, making them one, not according to the flesh but in the Spirit.

This was to be the new People of God ... reborn ... through the Word of the living God (cf. 1 Pt 1:23). from water and the Holy Spirit (cf. Jn 3:5-6) ... "a chosen race, a royal priesthood, a holy nation, a purchased people. You who in times past were not a people, but are now the People of God" (1 Pt 2:9-10).

That messianic people has for its head Christ. Its law is the new commandment to love as Christ loved us (cf. Jn 13:34). Its goal is the Kingdom of God, which has been begun by God himself on earth, and which is to be further extended until it is brought to perfection by him at the end of time.

This messianic people, although it does not actually include all men, and may more than once look like a small flock, is nonetheless a lasting and sure seed of unity, hope, and salvation for the whole human race. Established by Christ as a fellowship of life, charity, and truth, it is also used by him as an instrument for the redemption of all, and is sent forth into the whole world as the light of the world and the salt of the earth (cf. Mt 5:13-16).

Israel according to the flesh ... was already called the Church of God (Neh 13:1; cf. Nm 20:4; Dt 23:1, ff.). Likewise the new Israel ... is also called the Church of Christ (cf. Mt 16:18). For he has bought it for himself with his blood (cf. Acts 20:28), has filled it with his Spirit, and provided it with those means which befit it as a visible and social unity. God has gathered together as one all those who in faith look upon Jesus as the author of salvation and the source of unity and peace, and has established them as the Church, that for each and all she may be the visible sacrament of this saving unity (No. 9).

Priesthood

The baptized, by regeneration and the anointing of the Holy Spirit, are consecrated into a holy priesthood.

[All members of the Church participate in the priesthood of Christ, through the common priesthood of the faithful. See **Priesthood of the Laity**.]

Though they differ from one another in essence and not only in degree, the common priesthood of the faithful and the ministerial or hierarchical priesthood are nonetheless interrelated. Each of them in its own special way is a participation in the one priesthood of Christ (No. 10).

It is through the sacraments and the exercise of the virtues that the sacred nature and organic structure of the priestly community is brought into operation (No. 11). (*See* **Role of the Sacraments**.)

Prophetic Office

The holy People of God shares also in Christ's prophetic office. It spreads abroad a living witness to him, especially by means of a life of faith and charity and by offering to God a sacrifice of praise…. The body of the faithful as a whole, anointed as they are by the Holy One (cf. Jn 2:20, 27), cannot err in matters of belief. Thanks to a supernatural sense of faith which characterizes the People as a whole, it manifests this unerring quality when, "from the bishops down to the last member of the laity," it shows universal agreement in matters of faith and morals.

God's People accepts not the word of men but the very Word of God (cf. 1 Thes 2:13). It clings without fail to the faith once delivered to the saints (cf. Jude 3), penetrates it more deeply by accurate insights, and applies it more thoroughly to life. All this it does under the lead of a sacred teaching authority to which it loyally defers.

It is not only through the sacraments and Church ministries that the same Holy Spirit sanctifies and leads the People of God…. He distributes special graces among the faithful of every rank. By these gifts he makes them fit and ready to undertake the various tasks or offices advantageous for the renewal and upbuilding of the Church. These charismatic gifts … are to be received with thanksgiving and consolation, for they are exceedingly suitable and useful for the needs of the Church.

Judgment as to their genuineness and proper use belongs to those who preside over the Church, and to whose special competence it belongs … to test all things and hold fast to that which is good (cf. 1 Thes 5:12; 19-21) (No. 12).

All Are Called

All men are called to belong to the new People of God. Wherefore this People, while remaining one and unique, is to be spread throughout the whole world and must exist in all ages, so that the purpose of God's will may be fulfilled. In the beginning God made human nature one. After his children were scattered, he decreed that they should at length be united again (cf. Jn 11:52). It was for this reason that God sent his Son…. that he might be Teacher, King, and Priest of all, the Head of the new and universal People of the sons of God. For this God finally sent his Son's Spirit as Lord and Lifegiver. He it is who, on behalf of the whole Church and each and every one of those who believe, is the principle of their coming together and remaining together in the teaching of the apostles and in fellowship, in the breaking of bread and in prayers (cf. Acts 2:42) (No. 13).

One People of God

It follows that among all the nations of earth there is but one People of God, which takes its citizens from every race, making them citizens of a Kingdom which is of a heavenly and not an earthly nature. For all the faithful scattered throughout the world are in communion with each other in the Holy Spirit…. the Church or People of God foster(s) and take(s) to herself, insofar as they are good, the ability, resources and customs of each people. Taking them to herself, she purifies, strengthens, and ennobles them…. This characteristic of universality which adorns the People of God is a gift from the Lord himself. By reason of it, the Catholic Church strives energetically and constantly to bring all humanity with all its riches back to Christ its Head in the unity of his Spirit.

In virtue of this catholicity each individual part of the Church contributes through its special gifts to the good of the other parts and of the whole Church. Thus through the common sharing of gifts. The whole and each of the parts receive increase.

All men are called to be part of this catholic unity of the People of God. And there belong to it or are related to it in various ways, the Catholic faithful as well as all who believe in Christ, and indeed the whole of mankind. For all men are called to salvation by the grace of God (No. 13).

The Catholic Church

This sacred Synod turns its attention first to the Catholic faithful. Basing itself upon sacred Scripture and tradition, it teaches that the Church is necessary for salvation. For Christ, made present to us in his Body, which is the Church, is the one Mediator and the unique Way of salvation. In explicit terms he himself affirmed the necessity of faith and baptism (cf. Mk 16:16; Jn 3:5) and thereby affirmed also the necessity of the Church, for through baptism as through a door men enter the Church. Whosoever, therefore, knowing that the Catholic Church was made necessary by God through Jesus Christ, would refuse to enter her or to remain in her could not be saved.

They are fully incorporated into the society of the Church who, possessing the Spirit of Christ, accept her entire system and all the means of salvation given to her, and through union with her visible structure are joined to Christ, who rules her through the Supreme Pontiff and the bishops. This joining is effected by the bonds of professed faith, of the sacraments, of ecclesiastical government, and of communion. He is not saved, however, who, though he is part of the body of the Church, does not persevere in charity. He remains indeed in the bosom of the Church, but only in a "bodily" manner and not "in his heart."

Catechumens who, moved by the Holy Spirit, seek with

explicit intention to be incorporated into the Church, are by that very intention joined to her. Mother Church already embraces them as her own (No. 14).

Other Christians, The Unbaptized

The Church recognizes that in many ways she is linked with those who, being baptized, are honored with the name of Christian, though they do not profess the faith in its entirety or do not preserve unity of communion with the successor of Peter.

We can say that in some real way they are joined with us in the Holy Spirit, for to them also he gives his gifts and graces, and is thereby operative among them with his sanctifying power (No. 15).

Finally, those who have not yet received the Gospel are related in various ways to the People of God. In the first place there is the people to whom the covenants and the promises were given and from whom Christ was born according to the flesh (cf. Rom 9:4-5). On account of their fathers, this people remains most dear to God, for God does not repent of the gifts he makes nor of the calls he issues (cf. Rom 11:28-29).

But the plan of salvation also includes those who acknowledge the Creator. In the first place among these are the Moslems. Nor is God himself far distant from those who in shadows and images seek the unknown God.

Those also can attain to everlasting salvation who through no fault of their own do not know the Gospel of Christ or his Church, yet sincerely seek God and, moved by grace, strive by their deeds to do his will as it is known to them through the dictates of conscience. Nor does divine Providence deny the help necessary for salvation to those who, without blame on their part, have not yet arrived at an explicit knowledge of God, but who strive to live a good life, thanks to his grace. Whatever goodness or truth is found among them is looked upon by the Church as a preparation for the Gospel. She regards such qualities as given by him who enlightens all men so that they may finally have life. (No. l6).

THE POPE, TEACHING AUTHORITY, COLLEGIALITY

The Roman Pontiff — the successor of St. Peter as the bishop of Rome and head of the Church on earth — has full and supreme authority over the universal Church in matters pertaining to faith and morals (teaching authority), discipline and government (jurisdictional authority).

The primacy of the pope is real and supreme power. It is not merely a prerogative of honor — that is, of his being regarded as the first among equals. Neither does primacy imply that the pope is just the presiding officer of the collective body of bishops. The pope is the head of the Church.

Catholic belief in the primacy of the pope was stated in detail in the dogmatic constitution on the Church, *Pastor Aeternus*, approved in 1870 by the fourth session of the First Vatican Council. Some elaboration of the doctrine was made in the Dogmatic Constitution on the Church which was approved and promulgated by the Second Vatican Council Nov. 21, 1964. The entire body of teaching on the subject is based on Scripture and tradition and the centuries-long experience of the Church.

Infallibility

The essential points of doctrine concerning infallibility in the Church and the infallibility of the pope were stated by the Second Vatican Council in the Dogmatic Constitution on the Church, as follows:

"This infallibility with which the divine Redeemer willed his Church to be endowed in defining a doctrine of faith and morals extends as far as extends the deposit of divine revelation, which must be religiously guarded and faithfully expounded. This is the infallibility which the Roman Pontiff, the head of the college of bishops, enjoys in virtue of his office, when, as the supreme shepherd and teacher of all the faithful who confirms his brethren in their faith (cf. Lk 22:32), he proclaims by a definitive act some doctrine of faith or morals. Therefore his definitions, of themselves, and not from the consent of the Church, are justly styled irreformable, for they are pronounced with the assistance of the Holy Spirit, an assistance promised to him in blessed Peter. Therefore they need no approval of others, nor do they allow an appeal to any other judgment. For then the Roman Pontiff is not pronouncing judgment as a private person. Rather, as the supreme teacher of the universal Church, as one in whom the charism of the infallibility of the Church herself is individually present, he is expounding or defending a doctrine of Catholic faith.

"The infallibility promised to the Church resides also in the body of bishops when that body exercises supreme teaching authority with the successor of Peter. To the resultant definitions the assent of the Church can never be wanting, on account of the activity of that same Holy Spirit, whereby the whole flock of Christ is preserved and progresses in unity of faith.

"But when either the Roman Pontiff or the body of bishops together with him defines a judgment, they pronounce it in accord with revelation itself. All are obliged to maintain and be ruled by this revelation, which, as written or preserved by tradition, is transmitted in its entirety through the legitimate succession of bishops and especially through the care of the Roman Pontiff himself.

"Under the guiding light of the Spirit of truth, revelation is thus religiously preserved and faithfully expounded in the Church. The Roman Pontiff and the bishops, in view of their office and of the importance of the matter, strive painstakingly and by appropriate means to inquire properly into that revelation and to give apt expression to its contents. But they do not allow that there could be any new public revelation pertaining to the divine deposit of faith" (No. 25).

Authentic Teaching

The pope rarely speaks *ex cathedra* — that is, "from the chair" of St. Peter — for the purpose of making an infallible pronouncement. More often and in various ways he states authentic teaching in line with Scripture, tradition, the living experience of the Church, and the whole analogy of faith. Of such teaching, the Second Vatican Council said in its Dogmatic Constitution on the Church (No. 25):

"Religious submission of will and of mind must be shown in a special way to the authentic teaching authority of the Roman Pontiff, even when he is not speaking *ex cathedra*. That is, it must be shown in such a way that his supreme magisterium is acknowledged with reverence, the judgments made by him are sincerely adhered to, according to his manifest mind and will. His mind and will in the matter may be known chiefly either from the character of the documents, from his frequent repetition of the same doctrine, or from his manner of speaking."

Bishops "are authentic teachers, that is, teachers endowed with the authority of Christ, who preach to the people committed to them the faith they must believe and put into practice. By the light of the Holy Spirit, they make that faith clear, bringing forth from the treasury of revelation new things and old (cf. Mt 13:52), making faith bear fruit and vigilantly warding off any errors which threaten their flock (cf. 2 Tm 4:1-4).

"Bishops, teaching in communion with the Roman Pontiff, are to be respected by all as witnesses to divine and Catholic truth. In matters of faith and morals, the bishops speak in the name of Christ and the faithful are to accept their teaching and adhere to it with a religious assent of soul."

Magisterium — Teaching Authority

Responsibility for teaching doctrine and judging orthodoxy belongs to the official teaching authority of the Church.

This authority is personalized in the pope, the successor of St. Peter as head of the Church, and in the bishops together and in union with the pope, as it was originally committed to Peter and to the whole college of apostles under his leadership. They are the official teachers of the Church.

Others have auxiliary relationships with the magisterium: theologians, in the study and clarification of doctrine; teachers — priests, religious, lay persons — who cooperate with the pope and bishops in spreading knowledge of religious truth; the faithful, who by their sense of faith and personal witness contribute to the development of doctrine and the establishment of its relevance to life in the Church and the world.

The magisterium, Pope Paul VI noted in an address at a general audience Jan. 11, 1967, "is a subordinate and faithful echo and secure interpreter of the divine word." It does not reveal new truths, "nor is it superior to sacred Scripture." Its competence extends to the limits of divine revelation manifested in Scripture and tradition and the living experience of the Church, with respect to matters of faith and morals and related subjects. Official teaching in these areas is infallible when it is formally defined, for belief and acceptance by all members of the Church, by the pope, acting in the capacity of supreme shepherd of the flock of Christ; also, when doctrine is proposed and taught with moral unanimity of bishops with the pope in a solemn collegial manner, as in an ecumenical council, and/or in the ordinary course of events. Even when not infallibly defined, official teaching in the areas of faith and morals is authoritative and requires religious assent.

The teachings of the magisterium have been documented in creeds, formulas of faith, decrees and enactments of ecumenical and particular councils, various kinds of doctrinal statements, encyclical letters and other teaching instruments. They have also been incorporated into the liturgy, with the result that the law of prayer is said to be a law of belief.

Collegiality

The bishops of the Church, in union with the pope, have supreme teaching and pastoral authority over the whole Church in addition to the authority of office they have for their own dioceses.

This collegial authority is exercised in a solemn manner in an ecumenical council and can be exercised in other ways as well, "provided that the head of the college calls them to collegiate action, or at least so approves or freely accepts the united action of the dispersed bishops that it is made a true collegiate act."

This doctrine is grounded on the fact that: "Just as, by the Lord's will, St. Peter and the other apostles constituted one apostolic college, so in a similar way the Roman Pontiff as the successor of Peter, and the bishops as the successors of the apostles are joined together."

Doctrine on collegiality was stated by the Second Vatican Council in the Dogmatic Constitution on the Church (Nos. 22 and 23).

(For coverage of the Role of Mary in the Mystery of Christ and the Church, Chapter VIII, Lumen Gentium, see the section on the Blessed Virgin Mary.)

REVELATION

Following are excerpts from the "Dogmatic Constitution on Divine Revelation" (Dei Verbum) promulgated by the Second Vatican Council. They describe the nature and process of divine revelation, inspiration and interpretation of Scripture, the Old and New Testaments, and the role of Scripture in the life of the Church.

I. REVELATION ITSELF

God chose to reveal himself and to make known to us the hidden purpose of his will (cf. Eph. 1:9) by which through Christ, the Word made flesh, man has access to the Father in the Holy Spirit and comes to share in the divine nature (cf. Eph 2:18; 2 Pt 1:4). Through this revelation, therefore, the invisible God (cf. Col 1:15; 1 Tm 1:17). speaks to men as friends (cf. Ex 33:11; Jn 15:14-15) and lives among them (cf. Bar 3:38) so that he may invite and take them into fellowship with himself. This plan of revelation is realized by deeds and words having an inner unity: the deeds wrought by God in the history of salvation manifest and confirm the teaching and realities signified by the words, while the words proclaim the deeds and clarify the mystery contained in them. By this revelation then, the deepest truth about God and the salvation of man is made clear to us in Christ, who is the Mediator and at the same time the fullness of all revelation (No. 2).

God from the start manifested himself to our first parents. Then after their fall his promise of redemption aroused in them the hope of being saved (cf. Gn 3:15), and from that time on he ceaselessly kept the human race in his care, in order to give eternal life to those who perseveringly do good in search of salvation (cf. Rom 2:6-7). He called Abraham in order to make of him a great nation (cf. Gn 12:2). Through the patriarchs, and after them through Moses and the prophets, he taught this nation to acknowledge himself as the one living and true God and to wait for the Savior promised by him. In this manner he prepared the way for the Gospel down through the centuries (No. 3).

Revelation in Christ

Then, after speaking in many places and varied ways through the prophets, God "last of all in these days has spoken to us by his Son" (Heb 1:1-2). Jesus perfected revelation by fulfilling it through his whole work of making himself present and manifesting himself: through his words and deeds, his signs and wonders, but especially through his death and glorious resurrection from the dead and final sending of the Spirit of truth. Moreover, he confirmed with divine testimony what revelation proclaimed: that God is with us to free us from the darkness of sin and death, and to raise us up to life eternal.

The Christian dispensation, therefore, as the new and definitive covenant, will never pass away, and we now await no further new public revelation before the glorious manifestation of our Lord Jesus Christ (cf. 1 Tm 6:14; Ti 2:13) (No. 4).

II. TRANSMISSION OF REVELATION

God has seen to it that what he had revealed for the salvation of all nations would abide perpetually in its full integrity and be handed on to all generations. Therefore Christ the Lord, in whom the full revelation of the supreme God is brought to completion (cf. 2 Cor 1:20; 3:16; 4:6), commissioned the apostles to preach to all men that Gospel which is the source of all saving truth and moral teaching, and thus to impart to them divine gifts. This Gospel had been promised in former times through the prophets, and Christ himself fulfilled it and promulgated it with his own lips. This commission was faithfully fulfilled by the apostles who, by their oral preaching, by example, and by ordinances, handed on what they had received from Christ or what they had learned through the prompting of the Holy Spirit. The commission was fulfilled, too, by those apostles and apostolic men who under the inspiration of the same Holy Spirit committed the message of salvation to writing (No. 7).

Tradition

But in order to keep the Gospel forever whole and alive within the Church, the apostles left bishops as their successors, "handing over their own teaching role" to them. This sacred tradition, therefore, and sacred Scripture of both the Old and the New Testament are like a mirror in which the pilgrim Church on earth looks at God (No. 7).

The apostolic preaching, which is expressed in a special way in the inspired books, was to be preserved by a continuous succession of preachers until the end of time. Therefore the apostles, handing on what they themselves had received, warn the faithful to hold fast to the traditions which they have learned. Now what was handed on by the apostles includes everything which contributes to the holiness of life, and the increase in faith of the People of God; and so the Church, in her teaching, life, and worship, perpetuates and hands on to all generations all that she herself is, all that she believes (No. 8).

Development of Doctrine

This tradition which comes from the apostles develops in the Church with the help of the Holy Spirit. For there is a growth in the understanding of the realities and the words which have been handed down. This happens through the contemplation and study made by believers through the intimate understanding of spiritual things they experience, and through the preaching of those who have received through episcopal succession the sure gift of truth. For, as the centuries succeed one another, the Church constantly moves forward toward the fullness of divine truth until the words of God reach their complete fulfillment in her.

The words of the holy Fathers witness to the living presence of this tradition, whose wealth is poured into the practice and life of the believing and praying Church. Through the same tradition the Church's full canon of the sacred books is known, and the sacred writings themselves are more profoundly understood and unceasingly made active in her; ... and the Holy Spirit, through whom the living voice of the Gospel resounds in the Church, and through her, in the world, leads unto all truth those who believe and makes the word of Christ dwell abundantly in them (cf. Col 3:16) (No. 8).

Tradition and Scripture

Hence there exist a close connection and communication between sacred tradition and sacred Scripture. For both of them, flowing from the same divine wellspring, in a certain way merge into a unity and tend toward the same end. For sacred Scripture is the word of God inasmuch as it is consigned to writing under the inspiration of the divine Spirit. To the successors of the apostles, sacred tradition hands on in its full purity God's word, which was entrusted to the apostles by Christ the Lord and the Holy Spirit. Thus, led by the light of the Spirit of truth, these successors can in their preaching preserve this word of God faithfully, explain it, and make it more widely known. Consequently, it is not from sacred Scripture alone that the Church draws her certainty about every thing which has been revealed. Therefore both sacred tradition and sacred Scripture are to be accepted and venerated with the same sense of devotion and reverence (No. 9).

Sacred tradition and sacred Scripture form one sacred deposit of the word of God, which is committed to the Church (No. 10).

Teaching Authority of Church

The task of authentically interpreting the word of God, whether written or handed on, has been entrusted exclusively to the living teaching office of the Church, whose authority is exercised in the name of Jesus Christ. This teaching office is not above the word of God, but serves it, teaching only what has been handed on ... it draws from this one deposit of faith everything which it presents for belief as divinely revealed.

It is clear, therefore, that sacred tradition, sacred Scripture, and the teaching authority of the Church ... are so linked and joined together that one cannot stand without the others, and that all together and each in its own way under the action of the one Holy Spirit contribute effectively to the salvation of souls (No. 10).

III. INSPIRATION, INTERPRETATION

Those revealed realities contained and presented in sacred Scripture have been committed to writing under the inspiration of the Holy Spirit. Holy Mother Church, relying on the belief of the apostles, holds that the books of both the Old and New Testament in their entirety, with all their parts, are sacred and canonical because, having been written under the inspiration of the Holy Spirit (cf. Jn 20:31; 2 Tm 3:16; 2 Pt 1:19-21, 3:15-16) they have God as their author and have been handed on as such to the Church herself. In composing the sacred books, God chose men and, while employed by him, they made use of their powers and abilities, so that, with him acting in them and through them, they, as true authors, consigned to writing everything and only those things which he wanted (No. 11).

Inerrancy

Therefore, since everything asserted by the inspired authors or sacred writers must be held to be asserted by the Holy Spirit, it follows that the books of Scripture must be acknowledged as teaching firmly, faithfully, and without error that truth which God wanted put into the sacred writings for the sake of our salvation. Therefore "all Scripture is inspired by God and useful for teaching, for reproving, for correcting, for instruction in justice; that the man of God may be perfect, equipped for every good work" (2 Tm 3:16-17) (No. 11).

Literary Forms

However, since God speaks in sacred Scripture through men in human fashion, the interpreter of sacred Scripture, in order to see clearly what God wanted to communicate to us, should carefully investigate what meaning the sacred writers really intended, and what God wanted to manifest by means of their words.

The interpreter must investigate what meaning the sacred writer intended to express and actually expressed in particular circumstances as he used contemporary literary forms in accordance with the situation of his own time and culture. For the correct understanding of what the sacred author wanted to assert, due attention must be paid to the customary and characteristic styles of perceiving, speaking, and narrating which prevailed at the time of the sacred writer, and to the customs men normally followed at that period in their everyday dealings with one another (No. 12).

Analogy of Faith

No less serious attention must be given to the content and unity of the whole of Scripture, if the meaning of the sacred texts is to be correctly brought to light. The living tradition of the whole Church must be taken into account along with the harmony which exists between elements of the faith. All of what has been said about the way of interpreting Scripture is subject finally to the judgment of the Church, which carries out the divine commission and ministry of guarding and interpreting the word of God (No. 12).

IV. THE OLD TESTAMENT

In carefully planning and preparing the salvation of the whole human race, the God of supreme love, by a special dispensation, chose for himself a people to whom he might entrust his promises. First he entered into a covenant with Abraham (cf. Gn 15:18) and, through Moses, with the people of Israel (cf. Ex 24:8). To this people which he had acquired for himself, he so manifested himself through words and deeds as the one true and living God that Israel came to know by experience the ways of God with men. The plan of salvation, foretold by the sacred authors, recounted and explained by them, is found as the true word of God in the books of the Old Testament: these books, therefore, written under divine inspiration, remain permanently valuable (No. 14).

Principal Purpose

The principal purpose to which the plan of the Old Covenant was directed was to prepare for the coming both of Christ, the universal Redeemer, and of the messianic Kingdom. Now the books of the Old Testament, in accordance with the state of mankind before the time of salvation established by Christ, reveal to all men the knowledge of God and of man and the ways in which God deals with men. These books show us true divine pedagogy (No. 15).

The books of the Old Testament with all their parts, caught up into the proclamation of the Gospel, acquire and show forth their full meaning in the New Testament (cf. Mt 5:17; Lk 24:27; Rom 16:25-26; 2 Cor 3:14-16) and in turn shed light on it and explain it (No. 16).

V. THE NEW TESTAMENT

The word of God is set forth and shows its power in a most excellent way in the writings of the New Testament. For when the fullness of time arrived (cf. Gal 4:4), the Word was made flesh and dwelt among us in the fullness of grace and truth (cf. Jn 12:32). This mystery had not been manifested to other generations as it was now revealed to his holy apostles and prophets in the Holy Spirit (cf. Eph 3:4-6), so that they might preach the Gospel, stir up faith in Jesus, Christ and Lord, and gather the Church together. To these realities, the writings of the New Testament stand as a perpetual and divine witness (No. 17).

The Gospels and Other Writings

The Gospels have a special preeminence for they are the principal witness of the life and teaching of the incarnate Word, our Savior.

The Church has always and everywhere held and continues to hold that the four Gospels are of apostolic origin. For what the apostles preached afterwards they themselves and apostolic men, under the inspiration of the divine Spirit, handed on to us in writing: the foundation of faith, namely, the fourfold Gospel, according to Matthew, Mark, Luke, and John (No. 18).

The four Gospels ... whose historical character the Church unhesitatingly asserts, faithfully hand on what Jesus Christ, while living among men, really did and taught for their eternal salvation until the day he was taken up into heaven (see Acts 1:1-2). Indeed, after the ascension of the Lord the apostles handed on to their hearers what he had said and done. The sacred authors wrote the four Gospels, selecting some things from the many which had been handed on by word of mouth or in writing, reducing some of them to a synthesis, explicating some things in view of the situation of their churches, and preserving the form of proclamation but always in such fashion that they told us the honest truth about Jesus. For their intention in writing was that we might know "the truth" concerning those matters about which we have been instructed (cf. Lk 1:2-4) (No. 19).

Besides the four Gospels, the canon of the New Testament also contains the Epistles of St. Paul and other apostolic writings, composed under the inspiration of the Holy Spirit. In these writings those matters which concern Christ the Lord are confirmed, his true teaching is more and more fully stated, the saving power of the divine work of Christ is preached, the story is told of the beginnings of the Church and her marvelous growth, and her glorious fulfillment is foretold (No. 20).

VI. SCRIPTURE IN CHURCH LIFE

The Church has always venerated the divine Scriptures just as she venerates the body of the Lord. She has always regarded the Scriptures together with sacred tradition as the supreme rule of faith, and will ever do so. For, inspired by God and committed once and for all to writing, they impart the word of God himself without change, and make the voice of the Holy Spirit resound in the words of the prophets and apostles. Therefore, like the Christian religion itself, all the preaching of the Church must be nourished and ruled by sacred Scripture (No. 21).

Easy access to sacred Scripture should be provided for all the Christian faithful. That is why the Church from the very beginning accepted as her own that very ancient Greek translation of the Old Testament which is named after 70 men (the Septuagint); and she has always given a place of honor to other translations, Eastern and Latin, especially the one known as the Vulgate. But since the word of God should be available at all times, the Church with maternal concern sees to it that suitable and correct translations are made into different languages, especially from the original texts of the sacred books. And if, given the opportunity and the approval of Church authority, these translations are produced in cooperation with the separated brethren as well, all Christians will be able to use them (No. 22).

Biblical Studies, Theology

The constitution encouraged the development and progress of biblical studies "under the watchful care of the sacred teaching office of the Church."

It also noted: "Sacred theology rests on the written word of God, together with sacred tradition, as its primary and perpetual foundation," and that "the study of the sacred page is, as it were, the soul of sacred theology" (Nos. 23, 24).

(*See separate article,* **Interpretation of the Bible**.)

THE BIBLE

The Canon of the Bible is the Church's official list of sacred writings. These works, written by men under the inspiration of the Holy Spirit, contain divine revelation and, in conjunction with the tradition and teaching authority of the Church, constitute the rule of Catholic faith. The Canon was fixed and determined by the tradition and teaching authority of the Church.

The Catholic Canon

The Old Testament Canon of 46 books is as follows.
• **The Pentateuch**, the first five books: Genesis (Gn), Exodus (Ex), Leviticus (Lv), Numbers (Nm), Deuteronomy (Dt).
• **Historical Books**: Joshua (Jos), Judges (Jgs), Ruth (Ru) 1 and 2 Samuel (Sm), 1 and 2 Kings (Kgs), 1 and 2 Chronicles (Chr), Ezra (Ezr), Nehemiah (Neh), Tobit (Tb), Judith (Jdt), Esther (Est), 1 and 2 Maccabees (Mc).
• **Wisdom Books**: Job (Jb), Psalms (Ps), Proverbs (Prv), Ecclesiastes (Eccl), Song of Songs (Song), Wisdom (Wis), Sirach (Sir).
• **The Prophets**: Isaiah (Is), Jeremiah (Jer), Lamentations (Lam), Baruch (Bar), Ezekiel (Ez), Daniel (Dn), Hosea (Hos), Joel (Jl), Amos (Am), Obadiah (Ob), Jonah (Jon), Micah (Mi), Nahum (Na), Habakkuk (Hb), Zephaniah (Zep), Haggai (Hg), Zechariah (Zec) Malachi (Mal).

The New Testament Canon of 27 books is as follows.
• **The Gospels**: Matthew (Mt), Mark (Mk), Luke (Lk), John (Jn).
• **The Acts of the Apostles** (Acts).
• **The Pauline Letters**: Romans (Rom), 1 and 2 Corinthians (Cor), Galatians (Gal), Ephesians (Eph), Philippians (Phil), Colossians (Col), 1 and 2 Thessalonians (Thes) 1 and 2 Timothy (Tm), Titus (Ti), Philemon (Phlm), Hebrews (Heb).
• **The Catholic Letters**: James (Jas), 1 and 2 Peter (Pt), 1, 2, and 3 John (Jn), Jude (Jude).
• **Revelation** (Rv).

Developments

The Canon of the Old Testament was firm by the fifth century despite some questioning by scholars. It was stated by a council held at Rome in 382, by African councils held in Hippo in 393 and in Carthage in 397 and 419, and by Innocent I in 405.

All of the New Testament books were generally known and most of them were acknowledged as inspired by the end of the second century. The Muratorian Fragment, dating from about 200, listed most of the books recognized as canonical in later decrees. Prior to the end of the fourth century, however, there was controversy over the inspired character of several works — the Letter to the Hebrews, James, Jude, 2 Peter, 2 and 3 John and Revelation. Controversy ended in the fourth century and these books, along with those about which there was no dispute, were enumerated in the canon stated by the councils of Hippo and Carthage and affirmed by Innocent I in 405.

The Canon of the Bible was solemnly defined by the Council of Trent in the dogmatic decree *De Canonicis Scripturis*, Apr. 8, 1546.

Hebrew and Other Canons

The Hebrew Canon of sacred writings was fixed by tradition and the consensus of rabbis, probably by about 100 A.D. by the Synod or Council of Jamnia and certainly by the end of the second or early in the third century. It consists of the following works in three categories.
• **The Law** (Torah): the five books of Moses: Genesis, Exodus, Leviticus, Numbers, Deuteronomy.
• **The Prophets**: former prophets — Joshua, Judges, 1 and 2 Samuel, 1 and 2 Kings; latter prophets — Isaiah, Jeremiah, Ezekiel, and 12 minor prophets (Hosea, Joel, Amos, Obadiah, Jonah, Micah, Nahum, Habakkuk, Zephaniah, Haggai, Zechariah, Malachi).
• **The Writings**: 1 and 2 Chronicles, Ezra, Nehemiah, Job, Psalms, Proverbs, Ecclesiastes, Song of Songs, Ruth, Esther, Daniel.

This Canon, embodying the tradition and practice of the Palestine community, did not include a number of works contained in the Alexandrian version of sacred writings translated into Greek between 250 and 100 B.C. and in use by Greek-speaking Jews of the Dispersion (outside Palestine). The rejected works, called apocrypha and not regarded as sacred, are: Tobit, Judith, Wisdom, Sirach, Baruch, 1 and 2 Maccabees, the last six chapters of Esther and three passages of Daniel (3:24-90; 13; 14). These books have also been rejected from the Protestant Canon, although they are included in Bibles under the heading "*Apocrypha.*"

The aforementioned books are held to be inspired and sacred by the Catholic Church. In Catholic usage, they are called deuterocanonical because they were under discussion for some time before questions about their canonicity were settled. Books regarded as canonical with little or no debate were called protocanonical. The status of both categories of books is the same in the Catholic Bible.

The Protestant Canon of the Old Testament is the same as the Hebrew.

The Old Testament Canon of some separated Eastern churches differs from the Catholic Canon. Christians are in agreement on the Canon of the New Testament.

Languages

Hebrew, Aramaic and Greek were the original languages of the Bible. Most of the Old Testament books were written in Hebrew. Portions of Daniel, Ezra, Jeremiah, Esther, and probably the books of Tobit and Judith were written in Aramaic. The Book of Wisdom, 2 Maccabees and all the books of the New Testament were written in Greek (although there are traditions that Matthew's Gospel may have been based in part on materials in Aramaic).

Manuscripts and Versions

The original writings of the inspired authors have been lost. The Bible has been transmitted through ancient copies called manuscripts and through translations or versions.

Authoritative Greek manuscripts include the Sinaitic and Vatican manuscripts of the fourth century and the Alexandrine of the fifth century A.D. The Septuagint and Vulgate translations are in a class by themselves.

The Septuagint version, a Greek translation of the Old Testament for Greek-speaking Jews, was begun about 250 and completed about 100 B.C. The work of several Jewish translators at Alexandria, it differed from the Hebrew Bible in the arrangement of books and included several, later called deuterocanonical, which were not acknowledged as sacred by the community in Palestine.

The Vulgate was a Latin version of the Old and New Testaments produced from the original languages by St. Jerome from about 383 to 404. It became the most widely used Latin text for centuries and was regarded as basic long before the Council of Trent designated it as authentic and suitable for use in public reading, controversy, preaching and teaching. Because of its authoritative character, it became the basis for many translations into other languages. A critical revision was com-

pleted by a pontifical commission in 1977.

Hebrew and Aramaic manuscripts of great antiquity and value have figured more significantly than before in recent scriptural work by Catholic scholars, especially since their use was strongly encouraged, if not mandated, in 1943 by Pius XII in the encyclical *Divino Afflante Spiritu.*

The English translation of the Bible in general use among Catholics until well into the 20th century was the Douay-Rheims, so-called because of the places where it was prepared and published, the New Testament at Rheims in 1582 and the Old Testament at Douay in 1609. The translation was made from the Vulgate text. As revised and issued by Bp. Richard Challoner in 1749 and 1750, it became the standard Catholic English version for about 200 years.

A revision of the Challoner New Testament, made on the basis of the Vulgate text by scholars of the Catholic Biblical Association of America, was published in 1941 in the United States under the sponsorship of the Episcopal Committee of the Confraternity of Christian Doctrine.

New American Bible

A new translation of the entire Bible, the first ever made directly into English from the original languages under Catholic auspices, was projected in 1944 and completed in the fall of 1970 with publication of the *New American Bible.* The Episcopal Committee of the Confraternity of Christian Doctrine sponsored the NAB. The translators were members of the Catholic Biblical Association of America and scholars of other faiths. The typical edition was produced by St. Anthony Guild Press, Paterson, NJ.

The *Jerusalem Bible*, published by Doubleday & Co., Inc., is an English translation of a French version based on the original languages.

Biblical translations approved for liturgical use by the National Conference of Catholic Bishops and the Holy See are the *New American Bible* (1970 edition), the *Revised Standard Version-Catholic Edition*, and the *Jerusalem Bible* (1966).

The Protestant counterpart of the *Douay-Rheims Bible* was the *King James Bible*, called the *Authorized Version* in England. Originally published in 1611 and in general use for more than three centuries, its several revisions include the *Revised Standard Version* and the *New Revised Standard Version.*

Biblical Federation

In November 1966, Pope Paul VI commissioned the Secretariat for Promoting Christian Unity to start work for the widest possible distribution of the Bible and to coordinate endeavors toward the production of Catholic-Protestant Bibles in all languages.

The World Catholic Federation for the Biblical Apostolate, established in 1969, sponsors a program designed to create greater awareness among Catholics of the Bible and its use in everyday life.

The U. S. Center for the Catholic Biblical Apostolate is related to the Secretariat for Pastoral Research and Practices, National Conference of Catholic Bishops, 3211 Fourth St. N.E., Washington, DC, 20017.

APOCRYPHA

In Catholic usage, Apocrypha are books which have some resemblance to the canonical books in subject matter and title but which have not been recognized as canonical by the Church. They are characterized by a false claim to divine authority; extravagant accounts of events and miracles alleged to be supplemental revelation; material favoring heresy (especially in "New Testament" apocrypha); minimal, if any, historical value. Among examples of this type of literature itemized by J. McKenzie, S.J., in *Dictionary of the Bible* are: the Books of Adam and Eve, Martyrdom of Isaiah, Testament of the Patriarchs, Assumption of Moses, Sibylline Oracles; Gospel of James, Gospel of Thomas, Arabic Gospel of the Infancy, History of Joseph the Carpenter; Acts of John, Acts of Paul, Acts of Peter, Acts of Andrew, and numerous epistles.

Books of this type are called "pseudepigrapha" by Protestants.

In Protestant usage, some books of the Catholic Bible (deuterocanonical) are called apocrypha because their inspired character is rejected.

DEAD SEA SCROLLS

The Qumran Scrolls, popularly called the Dead Sea Scrolls, are a collection of manuscripts, all but one of them in Hebrew, found since 1947 in caves in the Desert of Juda west of the Dead Sea.

Among the findings were a complete text of Isaiah dating from the second century B.C., more or less extensive fragments of other Old Testament texts (including the deuterocanonical Tobit), and a commentary on Habakkuk. Until the discovery of these materials, the oldest known Hebrew manuscripts were from the A.D. 10th century.

Also found were messianic and apocalyptic texts, and other writings describing the beliefs and practices of the Essenes, a rigoristic Jewish sect.

The scrolls, dating from about the first century before and after Christ, are important sources of information about Hebrew literature, Jewish history during the period between the Old and New Testaments, and the history of Old Testament texts. They established the fact that the Hebrew text of the Old Testament was fixed before the beginning of the Christian era and have had definite effects in recent critical studies and translations of the Old Testament. Together with other scrolls found at Masada, they are still the subject of intensive study.

BOOKS OF THE BIBLE

Old Testament Books

Pentateuch

The Pentateuch is the collective title of the first five books of the Bible. Substantially, they identify the Israelites as Yahweh's Chosen People, cover their history from Egypt to the threshold of the Promised Land, contain the Mosaic Law and Covenant, and disclose the promise of salvation to come. Principal themes concern the divine promise of salvation, Yahweh's fidelity and the Covenant. Work on the composition of the Pentateuch

was completed in the sixth century.

Genesis: The book of origins, according to its title in the Septuagint. In two parts, covers: religious prehistory, including accounts of the origin of the world and man, the original state of innocence and the fall, the promise of salvation, patriarchs before and after the deluge, the Tower of Babel narrative, genealogies (first 11 chapters); the covenant with Abraham and patriarchal history from Abraham to Joseph (balance of the 50 chapters). Significant are the themes of Yahweh's universal sovereignty and mercy.

Exodus: Named with the Greek word for departure, is a religious epic which describes the oppression of the 12 tribes in Egypt and their departure, liberation or passover therefrom under the leadership of Moses; Yahweh's establishment of the covenant with them, making them his chosen people, through the mediation of Moses at Mt. Sinai; instructions concerning the tabernacle, the sanctuary and Ark of the Covenant; the institution of the priesthood. The book is significant because of its theology of liberation and redemption. In Christian interpretation, the Exodus is a figure of baptism.

Leviticus: Mainly legislative in theme and purpose, contains laws regarding sacrifices, ceremonies of ordination and the priesthood of Aaron, legal purity, the holiness code, atonement, the redemption of offerings and other subjects. Summarily, Levitical laws provided directives for all aspects of religious observance and for the manner in which the Israelites were to conduct themselves with respect to Yahweh and each other. Leviticus was the liturgical handbook of the priesthood.

Numbers: Taking its name from censuses recounted at the beginning and near the end, is a continuation of Exodus. It combines narrative of the Israelites' desert pilgrimage from Sinai to the border of Canaan with laws related to and expansive of those in Leviticus.

Deuteronomy: The concluding book of the Pentateuch, recapitulates, in the form of a testament of Moses, the Law and much of the desert history of the Israelites; enjoins fidelity to the Law as the key to good or bad fortune for the people; gives an account of the commissioning of Joshua as the successor of Moses. Notable themes concern the election of Israel by Yahweh, observance of the Law, prohibitions against the worship of foreign gods, worship of and confidence in Yahweh, the power of Yahweh in nature. The Deuteronomic Code or motif, embodying all of these elements, was the norm for interpreting Israelite history.

Joshua, Judges, Ruth

Joshua: Records the fulfillment of Yahweh's promise to the Israelites in their conquest, occupation and division of Canaan under the leadership of Joshua. It also contains an account of the return of Transjordanian Israelites and of a renewal of the Covenant. It was redacted in final form probably in the sixth century or later.

Judges: Records the actions of charismatic leaders, called judges, of the tribes of Israel between the death of Joshua and the time of Samuel, and a crisis of idolatry among the people. The basic themes are sin and punishment, repentance and deliverance; its purpose was in line with the Deuteronomic motif, that the fortunes of the Israelites were related to their observance or non-observance of the Law and the Covenant. It was redacted in final form probably in the sixth century.

Ruth: Named for the Gentile (Moabite) woman who, through marriage with Boaz, became an Israelite and an ancestress of David (her son, Obed, became his grandfather). Themes are filial piety, faith and trust in Yahweh, the universality of messianic salvation. Dates ranging from c. 950 to the seventh century have been assigned to the origin of the book, whose author is unknown.

Historical Books

These books, while they contain a great deal of factual material, are unique in their preoccupation with presenting and interpreting it, in the Deuteronomic manner, in primary relation to the Covenant on which the nation of Israel was founded and in accordance with which community and personal life were judged.

The books are: Samuel 1 and 2, from the end of Judges (c. 1020) to the end of David's reign (c. 961); Kings 1 and 2, from the last days of David to the start of the Babylonian exile and the destruction of the Temple (587); Chronicles 1 and a major theological work for the 21st century that has had center stage since the mid-20th century 2, from the reign of Saul (c. 1020-1000) to the return of the people from the exile (538); Ezra and Nehemiah, covering the reorganization of the Jewish community after the exile (458-397); Maccabees 1 and 2, recounting the struggle against attempted suppression of Judaism (168-142).

Three of the books listed below — Tobit, Judith, and Esther — are categorized as religious novels.

Samuel 1 and 2: A single work in concept and contents, containing episodic history of the last two Judges, Eli and Samuel, the establishment and rule of the monarchy under Saul and David, and the political consequences of David's rule. The royal messianic dynasty of David was the subject of Nathan's oracle in 2 Sm. 7. The books were edited in final form probably late in the seventh century or during the exile.

Kings 1 and 2: Cover the last days of David and the career of Solomon, including the building of the Temple and the history of the kingdom during his reign; stories of the prophets Elijah and Elisha; the history of the divided kingdom to the fall of Israel in the North (721) and the fall of Judah in the South (587), the destruction of Jerusalem and the Temple. They reflect the Deuteronomic motif in attributing the downfall of the people to corruption of belief and practice in public and private life. They were completed probably in the sixth century.

Chronicles 1 and 2: A collection of historical traditions interpreted in such a way as to present an ideal picture of one people governed by divine law and united in one Temple worship of the one true God. Contents include genealogical tables from Adam to David, the careers of David and Solomon, coverage of the kingdom of Judah to the exile, and the decree of Cyrus permitting the return of the people and rebuilding of Jerusalem. Both are related to and were written about 400 by the same author, the Chronicler, who composed Ezra and Nehemiah.

Ezra and Nehemiah: A running account of the return of the people to their homeland after the exile and of practical efforts, under the leadership of Ezra and Nehemiah, to restore and reorganize the religious and political community on the basis of Israelite traditions, divine worship and observance of the Law. Events of great significance were the building of the second Temple, the building of a wall around Jerusalem and the proclamation of the Law by Ezra. This restored community was the start of Judaism. Both are related to and were written about 400 by the same author, the Chronicler, who composed Chronicles 1 and 2.

Tobit: Written in the literary form of a novel and having greater resemblance to wisdom than to historical literature, narrates the personal history of Tobit, a devout and charitable Jew in exile, and persons connected with him, viz., his son Tobiah, his kinsman Raguel and Raguel's daughter Sarah. Its purpose was to teach people how to be good Jews. One of its principal themes is patience under trial, with trust in divine Providence which is symbolized by the presence and action of the angel Raphael. It was written about 200.

Judith: Recounts, in the literary form of a historical novel or romance, the preservation of the Israelites from conquest and ruin through the action of Judith. The essential themes are trust in God for deliverance from danger and emphasis on observance of the Law. It was written probably during the Maccabean period.

Esther: Relates, in the literary form of a historical novel or romance, the manner in which Jews in Persia were saved from annihilation through the central role played by Esther, the Jewish wife of Ahasuerus; a fact commemorated by the Jewish feast of Purim. Like Judith, it has trust in Divine Providence as its theme and indicates that God's saving will is sometimes realized by persons acting in unlikely ways. It may have been written near the end of the fourth century.

Maccabees 1 and 2: While related to some extent because of common subject matter, are quite different from each other.

The first book recounts the background and events of the 40-year (175-135) struggle for religious and political freedom led by Judas Maccabaeus and his brothers against the Hellenist Seleucid kings and some Hellenophiles among the Jews. Victory was symbolized by the rededication of the Temple. Against the background of opposition between Jews and Gentiles, the author equated the survival of belief in the one true God with survival of the Jewish people, thus identifying religion with patriotism. It was written probably near the year 100.

The second book supplements the first to some extent, covering and giving a theological interpretation to events from 180 to 162. It explains the feast of the dedication of the Temple, a key event in the survival of Judaism which is commemorated in the feast of Hanukkah; stresses the primacy of God's action in the struggle for survival; and indicates belief in an afterlife and the resurrection of the body. It was completed probably about 124.

Wisdom Books

With the exceptions of Psalms and the Song of Songs, the titles listed under this heading are called "wisdom books" because their purpose was to formulate the fruits of human experience in the context of meditation on sacred Scripture and to present them as an aid toward understanding the problems of life. Hebrew wisdom literature was distinctive from pagan literature of the same type, but it had limitations; these were overcome in the New Testament, which added the dimensions of the New Covenant to those of the Old. Solomon was regarded as the archetype of the wise man.

Job: A dramatic, didactic poem consisting mainly of several dialogues between Job and his friends concerning the mystery involved in the coexistence of the just God, evil and the suffering of the just. It describes an innocent man's experience of suffering and conveys the truth that faith in and submission to God rather than complete understanding, which is impossible, make the experience bearable; also, that the justice of God cannot be defended by affirming that it is realized in this world. Of unknown authorship, it was composed between the seventh and fifth centuries.

Psalms: A collection of 150 religious songs or lyrics reflecting Israelite belief and piety dating from the time of the monarchy to the post-Exilic period, a span of well over 500 years. The psalms, which are a compendium of Old Testament theology, were used in the temple liturgy and for other occasions. They were of several types suitable for the king, hymns, lamentations, expressions of confidence and thanksgiving, prophecy, historical meditation and reflection, and the statement of wisdom. About one-half of them are attributed to David; many were composed by unknown authors.

Proverbs: The oldest book of the wisdom type in the Bible, consisting of collections of sayings attributed to Solomon and other persons regarding a wide variety of subjects including wisdom and its nature, rules of conduct, duties with respect to one's neighbor, the conduct of daily affairs. It reveals many details of Hebrew life. Its nucleus dates from the period before the exile. The extant form of the book dates probably from the end of the fifth century.

Ecclesiastes: A treatise about many subjects whose unifying theme is the vanity of strictly human efforts and accomplishments with respect to the achievement of lasting happiness; the only things which are not vain are fear of the Lord and observance of his commandments. The pessimistic tone of the book is due to the absence of a concept of afterlife. It was written by an unknown author probably in the third century.

Song of Songs: A collection of love lyrics reflecting various themes, including the love of God for Israel and the celebration of ideal love and fidelity between man and woman. It was written by an unknown author after the exile.

Wisdom: Deals with many subjects including the reward of justice; praise of wisdom, a gift of Yahweh proceeding from belief in him and the practice of his Law; the part played by him in the history of his people, especially in their liberation from Egypt; the folly and shame of idolatry. Its contents are taken from the whole sacred literature of the Jews and represent a distillation of its wisdom based on the law, beliefs and traditions of Israel. The last of the Old Testament books, it was written in the early part of the first century before Christ by a member of the Jewish community at Alexandria.

Sirach: Resembling Proverbs, is a collection of sayings handed on by a grandfather to his grandson. It contains a variety of moral instruction and eulogies of patriarchs and other figures in Israelite history. Its moral maxims apply to individuals, the family and community, relations with God, friendship, education, wealth, the Law, divine worship. Its theme is that true wisdom consists in the Law. (It was formerly called Ecclesiasticus, the Church Book, because of its extensive use by the Church for moral instruction.) It was written in Hebrew between 200 and 175, during a period of strong Hellenistic influence, and was translated into Greek after 132.

The Prophets

These books and the prophecies they contain "express judgments of the people's moral conduct, on the basis of the Mosaic alliance between God and Israel. They teach sublime truths and lofty morals. They contain exhortations, threats, announcements of punishment, promises of deliverance. In the affairs of men, their prime concern is the interests of God, especially in what pertains to the Chosen People through whom the Messiah is to come; hence their denunciations of idolatry and of that externalism in worship which exclude the interior spirit of religion. They are concerned also with the universal nature of the moral law, with personal responsibility, with the person and office of the Messiah, and with the conduct of foreign nations" (*The Holy Bible*, Prophetic Books, CCD Edition, 1961; Preface). There are four major (Isaiah, Jeremiah, Ezekiel, Daniel) and twelve minor prophets (distinguished by the length of books), Lamentations and Baruch. Earlier prophets, mentioned in historical books, include Samuel, Gad, Nathan, Elijah, and Elisha.

Before the exile, prophets were the intermediaries through whom God communicated revelation to the people. Afterwards, prophecy lapsed and the written word of the Law served this purpose.

Isaiah: Named for the greatest of the prophets whose career spanned the reigns of three Hebrew kings from 742 to the beginning of the seventh century, in a period of moral breakdown in Judah and threats of invasion by foreign enemies. It is an anthology of poems and oracles credited to him and a number of followers deeply influenced by him. Of special importance are the prophecies concerning Immanuel (6 to 12), including the prophecy of the virgin birth (7:14). Chapters 40 to 55, called Deutero-Isaiah, are attributed to an anonymous poet toward the end of the exile; this portion contains the Songs of the Servant. The concluding part of the book (56-66) contains oracles by later disciples. One of many themes in Isaiah concerned the saving mission of the remnant of Israel in the divine plan of salvation.

Jeremiah: Combines history, biography and prophecy in a setting of crisis caused by internal and external factors, viz., idolatry and general infidelity to the Law among the Israelites and external threats from the Assyrians, Egyptians and Babylonians. Jeremiah prophesied the promise of a new covenant as well as the destruction of Jerusalem and the Temple. His career began in 626 and ended some years after the beginning of the exile. The book, the longest in the Bible, was edited in final form after the exile.

Lamentations: A collection of five laments or elegies over the fall of Jerusalem and the fate of the people in exile, written by an unknown eyewitness. They convey the message that Yahweh struck the people because of their sins and reflect confidence in his love and power to restore his converted people.

Baruch: Against the background of the already-begun

exile, it consists of an introduction and several parts: an exile's prayer of confession and petition for forgiveness and the restoration of Israel; a poem praising wisdom and the Law of Moses; a lament in which Jerusalem, personified, bewails the fate of her people and consoles them with the hope of blessings to come; and a polemic against idolatry. Although ascribed to Baruch, Jeremiah's secretary, it was written by several authors, probably in the second century.

Ezekiel: Named for the priest-prophet who prophesied in Babylon from 593 to 571, during the first phase of the exile. To prepare his fellow early exiles for the impending fall of Jerusalem, he reproached the Israelites for past sins and predicted woes to come upon them. After the destruction of the city, the burden of his message was hope and promise of restoration. Ezekiel had great influence on the religion of Israel after the exile.

Daniel: The protagonist is a young Jew, taken early to Babylon where he lived until about 538, who figured in a series of edifying stories which originated in Israelite tradition. The stories, whose characters are not purely legendary but rest on historical tradition, recount the trials and triumphs of Daniel and his three companions, and other episodes including those concerning Susannah, Bel, and the Dragon. The book is more apocalyptic than prophetic: it envisions Israel in glory to come and conveys the message that men of faith can resist temptation and overcome adversity. It states the prophetic themes of right conduct, divine control of men and events, and the final triumph of the kingdom. It was written by an unknown author in the 160s to give moral support to Jews during the persecutions of the Maccabean period.

Hosea: Consists of a prophetic parallel between Hosea's marriage and Yahweh's relations with his people. As the prophet was married to a faithless wife whom he would not give up, Yahweh was bound in Covenant with an idolatrous and unjust Israel whom he would not desert but would chastise for purification. Hosea belonged to the Northern Kingdom of Israel and began his career about the middle of the eighth century. He inaugurated the tradition of describing Yahweh's relation to Israel in terms of marriage.

Joel: Is apocalyptic and eschatological regarding divine judgment, the Day of the Lord, which is symbolized by a ravaging invasion of locusts, the judgment of the nations in the Valley of Josaphat and the outpouring of the Spirit in the messianic era to come. Its message is that God will vindicate and save Israel, in view of the prayer and repentance of the people, and will punish their enemies. It was composed about 400.

Amos: Consists of an indictment against foreign enemies of Israel; a strong denunciation of the people of Israel, whose infidelity, idolatry and injustice made them subject to divine judgment and punishment; and a messianic oracle regarding Israel's restoration. Amos prophesied in the Northern Kingdom of Israel, at Bethel, in the first half of the eighth century; chronologically, he was the first of the canonical prophets.

Obadiah: A 21-verse prophecy, the shortest and one of the sternest in the Bible, against the Edomites, invaders of southern Judah and enemies of those returning from the exile to their homeland.

It was probably composed in the fifth century.

Jonah: A parable of divine mercy with the theme that Yahweh wills the salvation of all, not just a few, men who respond to his call. Its protagonist is a disobedient prophet; forced by circumstances beyond his control to preach penance among Gentiles, he is highly successful in his mission but baffled by the divine concern for those who do not belong to the Chosen People. It was written after the exile, probably in the fifth century.

Micah: Attacks the injustice and corruption of priests, false prophets, officials and people; announces judgment and punishment to come; foretells the restoration of Israel; refers to the saving remnant of Israel. Micah was a contemporary of Isaiah.

Nahum: Concerns the destruction of Nineveh in 612 and the overthrow of the Assyrian Empire by the Babylonians.

Habakkuk: Dating from about 605-597, concerns sufferings to be inflicted by oppressors on the people of Judah because of their infidelity to the Lord. It also sounds a note of confidence in the Lord, the Savior, and declares that the just will not perish.

Zephaniah: Exercising his ministry in the second half of the seventh century, during a time of widespread idolatry, superstition and religious degradation, he prophesied impending judgment and punishment for Jerusalem and its people. He prophesied too that a holy remnant of the people (*anawim*, mentioned also by Amos) would be spared. Zephaniah was a forerunner of Jeremiah.

Haggai: One of the first prophets after the exile, Haggai in 520 encouraged the returning exiles to reestablish their community and to complete the second Temple (dedicated in 515), for which he envisioned greater glory, in a messianic sense, than that enjoyed by the original Temple of Solomon.

Zechariah: A contemporary of Haggai, he prophesied in the same vein. A second part of the book, called Deutero-Zechariah and composed by one or more unknown authors, relates a vision of the coming of the Prince of Peace, the Messiah of the Poor.

Malachi: Written by an anonymous author, presents a picture of life in the post-Exilic community between 516 and the initiation of reforms by Ezra and Nehemiah about 432. Blame for the troubles of the community is placed mainly on priests for failure to carry out ritual worship and to instruct the people in the proper manner; other factors were religious indifference and the influence of doubters who were scandalized at the prosperity of the wicked. The vision of a universal sacrifice to be offered to Yahweh (1:11) is interpreted in Catholic theology as a prophecy of the sacrifice of the Mass. Malachi was the last of the minor prophets.

DATES of the OLD TESTAMENT

c. 1800 – c. 1600 B.C.: Period of the patriarchs (Abraham, Isaac, Jacob).

c. 1600: Israelites in Egypt.

c. 1250: Exodus of Israelites from Egypt.

c. 1210: Entrance of Israelites in Canaan.

c. 1210 – c. 1020: Period of the Judges.

c. 1020 – c. 1000: Reign of Saul, first king.

c. 1000 – c. 961: Reign of David.

c. 961 – 922: Reign of Solomon. Temple built dur-

ing his reign.
922: Division of the Kingdom into Israel (North) and Judah (South).
721: Conquest of Israel by Assyrians.
587-538: Conquest of Judah by Babylonians.
Babylonian Captivity and Exile: Destruction of Jerusalem and the Temple, 587. Captivity ended with the return of exiles, following the decree of Cyrus permitting the rebuilding of Jerusalem.
515: Dedication of the second Temple.
458-397: Restoration and reform of the Jewish religious and political community; building of the Jerusalem wall, 439. Leaders in the movement were Ezra and Nehemiah.
168-142: Period of the Maccabees; war against Syrians.
142: Independence granted to Jews by Demetrius II of Syria.
135-37: Period of the Hasmonean dynasty.
63: Beginning of Roman rule.
37-4: Period of Herod the Great.

NEW TESTAMENT BOOKS

Gospels

The term "Gospel" is derived from the Anglo-Saxon *god-spell* and the Greek *euangelion*, meaning good news, good tidings. In Christian use, it means the good news of salvation proclaimed by Christ and the Church, and handed on in written form in the Gospels of Matthew, Mark, Luke and John.

The initial proclamation of the coming of the kingdom of God was made by Jesus in and through his Person, teachings and actions, and especially through his Passion, death and resurrection. This proclamation became the center of Christian faith and the core of the oral Gospel tradition with which the Church spread the good news by apostolic preaching for some 30 years before it was committed to writing by the Evangelists.

Nature of the Gospels

The historical truth of the Gospels was the subject of an instruction issued by the Pontifical Commission for Biblical Studies Apr. 21, 1964.

• The sacred writers selected from the material at their disposal (the oral Gospel tradition, some written collections of sayings and deeds of Jesus, eyewitness accounts) those things which were particularly suitable to the various conditions (liturgical, catechetical, missionary) of the faithful and the aims they had in mind, and they narrated these things in such a way as to correspond with those circumstances and their aims.

• The life and teaching of Jesus were not simply reported in a biographical manner for the purpose of preserving their memory but were "preached" so as to offer the Church the basis of doctrine concerning faith and morals.

• In their works, the Evangelists presented the true sayings of Jesus and the events of his life in the light of the better understanding they had following their enlightenment by the Holy Spirit. They did not transform Christ into a "mythical" Person, nor did they distort his teaching. Passion narratives are the core of all the Gospels, covering the suffering, death and resurrection of Jesus as central events in

bringing about and establishing the New Covenant. Leading up to them are accounts of the mission of John the Baptizer and the ministry of Jesus, especially in Galilee and finally in Jerusalem before the Passion. The infancy of Jesus is covered by Luke and Matthew with narratives inspired in part by appropriate Old Testament citations.

Matthew, Mark and Luke, while different in various respects, have so many similarities that they are called Synoptic; their relationships are the subject of the Synoptic Problem.

Matthew: Written probably between 80 and 100 for Jewish Christians with clear reference to Jewish background and identification of Jesus as the divine Messiah, the fulfillment of the Old Testament. Distinctive are the use of Old Testament citations regarding the Person, activity and teaching of Jesus, and the presentation of doctrine in sermons and discourses.

Mark: Most likely the first of the Gospels, dating from about 70. Written for Gentile Christians, it is noted for the realism and wealth of concrete details with which it reveals Jesus as Son of God and Savior more by his actions and miracles than by his discourses. Theologically, it is less refined than the other Gospels.

Luke: Written about 75 for Gentile Christians. It is noted for the universality of its address, the insight it provides into the Christian way of life, the place it gives to women, the manner in which it emphasizes Jesus' friendship with sinners and compassion for the suffering.

John: Edited and arranged in final form probably between 90 and 100, this is the most sublime and theological of the Gospels, and is different from the Synoptics in plan and treatment. Combining accounts of signs with longer discourses and reflections, it progressively reveals the Person and mission of Jesus — as Word, Way, Truth, Life, Light — in line with the purpose, "to help you believe that Jesus is the Messiah, the Son of God, so that through this faith you may have life in his name" (Jn 20:31). There are questions about the authorship but no doubt about the Johannine authority and tradition behind the Gospel.

Acts of the Apostles

Written by Luke about 75 as a supplement to his Gospel. It describes the origin and spread of Christian communities through the action of the Holy Spirit from the resurrection of Christ to the time when Paul was placed in custody in Rome in the early 60s.

Letters (Epistles)

These letters, many of which antedated the Gospels, were written in response to existential needs of the early Christian communities for doctrinal and moral instruction, disciplinary action, practical advice, and exhortation to true Christian living.

Pauline Letters

These letters, which comprise approximately one-fourth of the New Testament, are primary and monumental sources of the development of Christian theology. Several of them may not have had Paul as their actual author, but evidence of the

Pauline tradition behind them is strong. The letters to the Colossians, Philippians, Ephesians and Philemon have been called the "Captivity Letters" because of a tradition that they were written while Paul was under house arrest or another form of detention.

Romans: Written about 57, probably from Corinth, on the central significance of Christ and faith in him for salvation, and the relationship of Christianity to Judaism; the condition of mankind without Christ; justification and the Christian life; duties of Christians.

Corinthians 1: Written near the beginning of 57 from Ephesus to counteract factionalism and disorders, it covers community dissension, moral irregularities, marriage and celibacy, conduct at religious gatherings, the Eucharist, spiritual gifts (charisms) and their function in the Church, charity, the resurrection of the body.

Corinthians 2: Written later in the same year as 1 Cor, concerning Paul's defense of his apostolic ministry, and an appeal for a collection to aid poor Christians in Jerusalem.

Galatians: Written probably between 54 and 55 to counteract Judaizing opinions and efforts to undermine his authority, it asserts the divine origin of Paul's authority and doctrine, states that justification is not through Mosaic Law but through faith in Christ, insists on the practice of evangelical virtues, especially charity.

Ephesians: Written probably between 61 and 63, mainly on the Church as the Mystical Body of Christ.

Philippians: Written between 56 and 57 or 61 and 63 to warn the Philippians against enemies of their faith, to urge them to be faithful to their vocation and unity of belief, and to thank them for their kindness to him while he was being held in detention.

Colossians: Written probably while he was under house arrest in Rome from 61 to 63, to counteract the influence of self-appointed teachers who were watering down doctrine concerning Christ. It includes two highly important Christological passages, a warning against false teachers, and an instruction on the ideal Christian life.

Thessalonians 1 and 2: Written within a short time of each other probably in 51 from Corinth, mainly on doctrine concerning the *Parousia*, the second coming of Christ.

Timothy 1 and 2, Titus: Written between 65 and 67, or perhaps in the 70s, giving pastoral counsels to Timothy and Titus, who were in charge of churches in Ephesus and Crete, respectively. 1 Tm emphasizes pastoral responsibility for preserving unity of doctrine; 2 Tm describes Paul's imprisonment in Rome.

Philemon: A private letter written between 61 and 63 to a wealthy Colossian concerning a slave, Onesimus, who had escaped from him; Paul appealed for kind treatment of the man.

Hebrews: Dating from sometime between 70 and 96, a complex theological treatise on Christology, the priesthood and sacrifice of Christ, the New Covenant, and the pattern for Christian living. Critical opinion is divided as to whether it was addressed to Judaeo or Gentile Christians.

Catholic Letters

These seven letters have been called "catholic" because it was thought for some time, not altogether correctly, that they were not addressed to particular communities.

James: Written sometime before 62 in the spirit of Hebrew wisdom literature and the moralism of Tobit. An exhortation to practical Christian living, it is also noteworthy for the doctrine it states on good works and its citation regarding anointing of the sick.

Peter 1 and 2: The first letter may have been written between 64 and 67 or between 90 and 95; the second may date from 100 to 125. Addressed to Christians in Asia Minor, both are exhortations to perseverance in the life of faith despite trials and difficulties arising from pagan influences, isolation from other Christians and false teaching.

John 1: Written sometime in the 90s and addressed to Asian churches, its message is that God is made known to us in the Son and that fellowship with the Father is attained by living in the light, justice and love of the Son.

John 2: Written sometime in the 90s and addressed to a church in Asia, it commends the people for standing firm in the faith and urges them to perseverance.

John 3: Written sometime in the 90s, it appears to represent an effort to settle a jurisdictional dispute in one of the churches.

Jude: Written probably about 80, it is a brief treatise against erroneous teachings and practices opposed to law, authority and true Christian freedom.

Revelation

Written in the 90s along the lines of Johannine thought, it is a symbolic and apocalyptic treatment of things to come and of the struggle between the Church and evil combined with warning but hope and assurance to the Church regarding the coming of the Lord in glory.

INTERPRETATION OF THE BIBLE

According to the Dogmatic Constitution on Divine Revelation (*Dei Verbum*) issued by the Second Vatican Council, "the interpreter of Sacred Scripture, in order to see clearly what God wanted to communicate to us, should carefully investigate what meaning the sacred writers really intended, and what God wanted to manifest by means of their words" (No. 12).

Hermeneutics, Exegesis

This careful investigation proceeds in accordance with the rules of hermeneutics, the normative science of biblical interpretation and explanation. Hermeneutics in practice is called exegesis.

The principles of hermeneutics are derived from various disciplines and many factors which have to be considered in explaining the Bible and its parts. These include: the original languages and languages of translation of the sacred texts, through philology and linguistics; the quality of texts, through textual criticism; literary forms and genres, through literary and form criticism; cultural, historical, geographical and other conditions which influenced the writers, through related studies; facts and truths of salvation history; the truths and analogy of faith.

Distinctive to biblical hermeneutics, which differs

in important respects from literary interpretation in general, is the premise that the Bible, though written by human authors, is the work of divine inspiration in which God reveals his plan for the salvation of men through historical events and persons, and especially through the Person and mission of Christ.

Textual, Form Criticism

Textual criticism is the study of biblical texts, which have been transmitted in copies several times removed from the original manuscripts, for the purpose of establishing the real state of the original texts. This purpose is served by comparison of existing copies; by application to the texts of the disciplines of philology and linguistics; by examination of related works of antiquity; by study of biblical citations in works of the Fathers of the Church and other authors; and by other means of literary study.

Since about 1920, the sayings of Christ have been a particular object of New Testament study, the purpose being to analyze the forms of expression used by the Evangelists in order to ascertain the words actually spoken by him.

Literary Criticism

Literary criticism aims to determine the origin and kinds of literary composition, called forms or genres, employed by the inspired authors. Such determinations are necessary for decision regarding the nature and purpose and, consequently, the meaning of biblical passages. Underlying these studies is the principle that the manner of writing was conditioned by the intention of the authors, the meaning they wanted to convey, and the then-contemporary literary style, mode or medium best adapted to carry their message — e.g., true history, quasi-historical narrative, poems, prayers, hymns, psalms, aphorisms, allegories, discourses. Understanding these media is necessary for the valid interpretation of their message.

Literal Sense

The key to all valid interpretation is the literal sense of biblical passages. Regarding this matter and the relevance to it of the studies and procedures described above, Pius XII wrote the following in the encyclical *Divino Afflante Spiritu:*

"What the literal sense of a passage is, is not always as obvious in the speeches and writings of ancient authors of the East as it is in the works of our own time. For what they wished to express is not to be determined by the rules of grammar and philology alone nor solely by the context; the interpreter must, as it were, go back wholly in spirit to those remote centuries of the East and with the aid of history, archeology, ethnology, and other sciences accurately determine what modes of writing, so to speak, the authors of that ancient period would be likely to use and in fact did use. In explaining the Sacred Scripture and in demonstrating and proving its immunity from all error [the Catholic interpreter] should make a prudent use of this means, determine to what extent the manner of expression or literary mode adopted by the sacred writer may lead to a correct and genuine interpretation; and let him be convinced that this part of his office cannot be neglected without serious detriment to Catholic exegesis."

The literal sense of the Bible is the meaning in the mind of and intended by the inspired writer of a book or passage of the Bible. This is determined by the application to

texts of the rules of hermeneutics. It is not to be confused with word-for-word literalism.

Typological Sense

The typological sense is the meaning which a passage has not only in itself but also in reference to something else of which it is a type or foreshadowing. A clear example is the account of the Exodus of the Israelites: in its literal sense, it narrates the liberation of the Israelites from death and oppression in Egypt; in its typical sense, it foreshadowed the liberation of men from sin through the redemptive death and resurrection of Christ. The typical sense of this and other passages emerged in the working out of God's plan of salvation history. It did not have to be in the mind of the author of the original passage.

Accommodated Senses

Accommodated, allegorical and consequent senses are figurative and adaptive meanings given to books and passages of the Bible for moral and other purposes. Such interpretations involve the danger of stretching the literal sense beyond proper proportions. Hermeneutical principles require that interpretations like these respect the integrity of the literal sense of the passages in question.

In the Catholic view, the final word on questions of biblical interpretation belongs to the teaching authority of the Church. In other views, generally derived from basic principles stated by Martin Luther, John Calvin and other reformers, the primacy belongs to individual judgment acting in response to the inner testimony of the Holy Spirit, the edifying nature of biblical subject matter, the sublimity and simplicity of the message of salvation, the intensity with which Christ is proclaimed.

Biblical Studies

The first center for biblical studies, in some strict sense of the term, was the School of Alexandria, founded in the latter half of the second century. It was noted for allegorical exegesis. Literal interpretation was a hallmark of the School of Antioch.

St. Jerome, who produced the Vulgate, and St. Augustine, author of numerous commentaries, were the most important figures in biblical studies during the patristic period. By the time of the latter's death, the Old and New Testament canons had been stabilized. For some centuries afterwards, there was little or no progress in scriptural studies, although commentaries were written, collections were made of scriptural excerpts from the writings of the Fathers of the Church, and the systematic reading of Scripture became established as a feature of monastic life.

Advances were made in the 12th and 13th centuries with the introduction of new principles and methods of scriptural analysis stemming from renewed interest in Hebraic studies and the application of dialectics.

By the time of the Reformation, the Bible had become the first book set in movable type, and more than 100 vernacular editions were in use throughout Europe.

The Council of Trent

In the wake of the Reformation, the Council of Trent formally defined the Canon of the Bible; it also reasserted the authoritative role of tradition and the teaching authority of the Church as well as Scripture with respect to the rule of faith. In the heated atmosphere of the 16th and 17th centuries, the Bible was turned into a polemical weapon; Protestants used it to defend their doctrines, and Catholics countered with citations in support of the dogmas of the Church. One result of this state of affairs was a lack of substantial progress in biblical studies during the period.

Rationalists from the 18th century on and later Modernists denied the reality of the supernatural and doctrine concerning inspiration of the Bible, which they generally regarded as a strictly human production expressive of the religious sense and experience of mankind. In their hands, the tools of positive critical research became weapons for biblical subversion. The defensive Catholic reaction to their work had the temporary effect of alienating scholars of the Church from solid advances in archeology, philology, history, textual and literary criticism.

Catholic Developments

Major influences in bringing about a change in Catholic attitude toward use of these disciplines in biblical studies were two papal encyclicals and two institutes of special study, the *École Biblique*, founded in Jerusalem in 1890, and the Pontifical Biblical Institute established in Rome in 1909. The encyclical *Providentissimus Deus*, issued by Leo XIII in 1893, marked an important breakthrough; in addition to defending the concept of divine inspiration and the formal inspiration of the Scriptures, it encouraged the study of allied and ancillary sciences and techniques for a more fruitful understanding of the sacred writings. The encyclical *Divino Afflante Spiritu*, by Pope Pius XII 50 years later, gave encouragement for the use of various forms of criticism as tools of biblical research. A significant addition to documents on the subject is "The Interpretation of the Bible in the Church," published by the Pontifical Biblical Commission in November 1993. It presents an overview of approaches to the Bible and probes the question: "Which hermeneutical theory best enables a proper grasp of the profound reality of which Scripture speaks and its meaningful expression for people today?"

The documents encouraged the work of scholars and stimulated wide communication of the fruits of their study.

Great changes in the climate and direction of biblical studies have occurred in recent years. One of them has been an increase in cooperative effort among Catholic, Protestant, Orthodox and Jewish scholars. Their common investigation of the Dead Sea Scrolls is well-known. Also productive has been the collaboration of Catholics and Protestants in turning out various editions of the Bible.

The development and results of biblical studies in this century have directly and significantly affected all phases of the contemporary renewal movement in the Church. Their influence on theology, liturgy, catechetics, and preaching indicate the importance of their function in the life of the Church.

On Sept. 30, 2010, Pope Benedict XVI issued *Verbum Domini: a Post-Synodal Apostolic Exhortation on the Word of God in the Life and Mission of the Church.* For details on this document, see under **News in Depth**.

APOSTLES AND EVANGELISTS

The Apostles were the men selected, trained, and commissioned by Christ to preach the Gospel, to baptize, to establish, direct and care for his Church as servants of God and stewards of his mysteries. They were the first bishops of the Church.

St. Matthew's Gospel lists the Apostles in this order: Peter, Andrew, James the Greater, John, Philip, Bartholomew, Thomas, Matthew, James the Less, Jude, Simon, and Judas Iscariot. Matthias was elected to fill the place of Judas. Paul became an Apostle by a special call from Christ. Barnabas was called an Apostle.

Two of the Evangelists, John and Matthew, were Apostles. The other two, Luke and Mark, were closely associated with the apostolic college.

Andrew: Born in Bethsaida, brother of Peter, disciple of John the Baptist, a fisherman, the first Apostle called; according to legend, preached the Gospel in northern Greece, Epirus and Scythia, and was martyred at Patras about 70; in art, is represented with an X-shaped cross, called St. Andrew's Cross; is honored as the patron of Russia and Scotland; Nov. 30.

Barnabas: Originally called Joseph but named Barnabas by the Apostles, among whom he is ranked because of his collaboration with Paul; a Jew of the Diaspora, born in Cyprus; a cousin of Mark and member of the Christian community at Jerusalem, influenced the Apostles to accept Paul, with whom he became a pioneer missionary outside Palestine and Syria, to Antioch, Cyprus, and southern Asia Minor; legend says he was martyred in Cyprus during the Neronian persecution; June 11.

Bartholomew (Nathaniel): A friend of Philip; according to various traditions, preached the Gospel in Ethiopia, India, Persia, and Armenia, where he was martyred by being flayed and beheaded; in art, is depicted holding a knife, an instrument of his death; Aug. 24 (Roman Rite), Aug. 25 (Byzantine Rite).

James the Greater: A Galilean, son of Zebedee, brother of John (with whom he was called a "Son of Thunder"), a fisherman; with Peter and John, witnessed the raising of Jairus's daughter to life, the transfiguration, the agony of Jesus in the Garden of Gethsemane; first of the Apostles to die, by the sword in 44 during the rule of Herod Agrippa; there is doubt about a journey legend says he made to Spain and also about the authenticity of relics said to be his at Santiago de Compostela; in art, is depicted carrying a pilgrim's bell; July 25 (Roman Rite), Apr. 30 (Byzantine Rite).

James the Less: Son of Alphaeus, called "Less" because he was younger in age or shorter in stature than James the Greater; one of the Catholic Epistles bears his name; was stoned to death in 62 or thrown from the top of the temple in Jerusalem and clubbed to death in 66; in art, is depicted with a club or heavy staff; May 3 (Roman Rite), Oct. 9 (Byzantine Rite).

John: A Galilean, son of Zebedee, brother of James the Greater (with whom he was called a "Son of Thunder"), a fisherman, probably a disciple of John the Baptist, one of the Evangelists, called the "Beloved Disciple"; with Peter and James the Greater, witnessed the raising of Jairus's daughter to life, the transfiguration, the agony of Jesus in the Garden of Gethsemane; Mary was commended to his special care by Christ; the fourth Gospel, three Catholic Epistles, and Revelation bear his name; according to various accounts, lived at Ephesus in Asia Minor for some time and died a natural death about 100; in art, is represented by an eagle, symbolic of the sublimity of the contents of his Gospel; Dec. 27 (Roman Rite), May 8 (Byzantine Rite).

Jude Thaddeus: One of the Catholic Epistles, the shortest, bears his name; various traditions say he preached the Gospel in Mesopotamia, Persia, and elsewhere, and was martyred; in art, is depicted with a halberd, the instrument of his death; Oct. 28 (Roman Rite), June 19 (Byzantine Rite).

Luke: A Greek convert to the Christian community, called "our most dear physician" by Paul, of whom he was a missionary companion; author of the third Gospel and Acts of the Apostles; the place — Achaia, Bithynia, Egypt — and circumstances of his death are not certain; in art, is depicted as a man, a writer, or an ox (because his Gospel starts at the scene of temple sacrifice); Oct. 18.

Mark: A cousin of Barnabas and member of the first Christian community at Jerusalem; a missionary companion of Paul and Barnabas, then of Peter; author of the Gospel which bears his name; according to legend, founded the Church at Alexandria, was bishop there and was martyred in the streets of the city; in art, is depicted with his Gospel and a winged lion, symbolic of the voice of John the Baptist crying in the wilderness, at the beginning of his Gospel; Apr. 25.

Matthew: A Galilean, called Levi by Luke and John and the son of Alphaeus by Mark, a tax collector, one of the Evangelists; according to various accounts, preached the Gospel in Judea, Ethiopia, Persia and Parthia, and was martyred; in art, is depicted with a spear, the instrument of his death, and as a winged man in his role as Evangelist; Sept. 21 (Roman Rite), Nov. 16 (Byzantine Rite).

Matthias: A disciple of Jesus whom the faithful 11 Apostles chose to replace Judas before the Resurrection; uncertain traditions report that he preached the Gospel in Palestine, Cappadocia or Ethiopia; in art, is represented with a cross and a halberd, the instruments of his death as a martyr; May 14 (Roman Rite), Aug. 9 (Byzantine Rite).

Paul: Born at Tarsus, of the tribe of Benjamin, a Roman citizen; participated in the persecution of Christians until the time of his miraculous conversion on the way to Damascus; called by Christ, who revealed himself to him in a special way; became the Apostle of the Gentiles, among whom he did most of his preaching in the course of three major missionary journeys through areas north of Palestine, Cyprus, Asia Minor, and Greece; 14 epistles bear his name; two years of imprisonment at Rome, following initial arrest in Jerusalem and confinement at Caesarea, ended with martyrdom, by beheading, outside the walls of the city in 64 or 67 during the Neronian persecution; in art, is depicted in various ways with St. Peter, with a sword, in the scene of his conversion; June 29 (with St. Peter), Jan. 25 (Conversion).

Peter: Simon, son of Jonah, born in Bethsaida, brother of Andrew, a fisherman; called Cephas or Peter by Christ who made him the chief of the Apostles and head of the Church as his vicar; named first in the listings of Apostles in the Synoptic Gospels and the Acts of the Apostles; with James the Greater and John, witnessed the raising of Jairus's daughter to life, the transfiguration, the agony of Jesus in the Garden of Gethsemane; was the first to preach the Gospel in and around Jerusalem and was the leader of the first Christian community there; established a local church in Antioch; presided over the Council of Jerusalem in 51; wrote two Catholic Epistles

to the Christians in Asia Minor; established his see in Rome where he spent his last years and was martyred by crucifixion in 64 or 65 during the Neronian persecution; in art, is depicted carrying two keys, symbolic of his primacy in the Church; June 29 (with St. Paul), Feb. 22 (Chair of Peter).

Philip: Born in Bethsaida; according to legend, preached the Gospel in Phrygia where he martyeded by crucifixion; May 3 (Roman Rite), Nov. 14 (Byzantine Rite).

Simon: Called the Cananean or the Zealot; according to legend, preached in various places in the Middle East and suffered martyrdom by being sawed in two; in art, is depicted with a saw, the instrument of his death, or a book, symbolic of his zeal for the Law; Oct. 28 (Roman Rite), May 10 (Byzantine Rite).

Thomas (Didymus): Notable for his initial incredulity regarding the Resurrection and his subsequent forthright confession of the divinity of Christ risen from the dead; according to legend, preached the Gospel in places from the Caspian Sea to the Persian Gulf and eventually reached India where he was martyred near Madras; Thomas Christians trace their origin to him; in art, is depicted kneeling before the risen Christ, or with a carpenter's rule and square; feast, July 3 (Roman Rite), Oct. 6 (Byzantine Rite).

* * *

Judas: The Gospels record only a few facts about Judas, the Apostle who betrayed Christ. The only non-Galilean among the Apostles, he was from Carioth, a town in southern Judah. He was keeper of the purse in the apostolic band. He was called a petty thief by John. He voiced dismay at the waste of money, which he said might have been spent for the poor, in connection with the anointing incident at Bethany. He took the initiative in arranging the betrayal of Christ. Afterwards, he confessed that he had betrayed an innocent man and cast into the Temple the money he had received for that action. Of his death, Matthew says that he hanged himself; the Acts of the Apostles states that he swelled up and burst open; both reports deal more with the meaning than the manner of his death — the misery of the death of a sinner.

The consensus of speculation over the reason why Judas acted as he did in betraying Christ focuses on disillusionment and unwillingness to accept the concept of a suffering Messiah and personal suffering of his own as an Apostle.

APOSTOLIC FATHERS, FATHERS, DOCTORS OF THE CHURCH

The writers listed below were outstanding and authoritative witnesses to authentic Christian belief and practice, and played significant roles in giving them expression.

Apostolic Fathers

The Apostolic Fathers were Christian writers of the first and second centuries whose writings echo genuine apostolic teaching. Chief in importance are: St. Clement (d. c. 97), bishop of Rome and third successor of St. Peter in the papacy; St. Ignatius (50-c. 107), bishop of Antioch and second successor of St. Peter in that see, reputed to be a disciple of St. John; St. Polycarp (69-155), bishop of Smyrna and a disciple of St. John. The authors of the Didache and the Epistle of Barnabas are also numbered among the Apostolic Fathers.

Other early ecclesiastical writers included: St. Justin,

martyr (100-165), of Asia Minor and Rome, a layman and apologist; St. Irenaeus (130-202), bishop of Lyons, who opposed Gnosticism; and St. Cyprian (210-258), bishop of Carthage, who opposed Novatianism.

Fathers and Doctors

The Fathers of the Church were theologians and writers of the first eight centuries who were outstanding for sanctity and learning. They were such authoritative witnesses to the belief and teaching of the Church that their unanimous acceptance of doctrines as divinely revealed has been regarded as evidence that such doctrines were so received by the Church in line with apostolic tradition and Sacred Scripture. Their unanimous rejection of doctrines branded them as heretical. Their writings, however, were not necessarily free of error in all respects.

The greatest of these Fathers were: Sts. Ambrose, Augustine, Jerome, and Gregory the Great in the West; Sts. John Chrysostom, Basil the Great, Gregory of Nazianzus, and Athanasius in the East.

The Doctors of the Church were ecclesiastical writers of eminent learning and sanctity who have been given this title because of the great advantage the Church has derived from their work. Their writings, however, were not necessarily free of error in all respects.

Albert the Great, St. (c. 1200-1280): Born in Swabia, Germany; Dominican; bishop of Regensburg (1260-1262); wrote extensively on logic, natural sciences, ethics, metaphysics, Scripture, systematic theology; contributed to development of Scholasticism; teacher of St. Thomas Aquinas; canonized and proclaimed doctor, 1931; named patron of natural scientists, 1941; called *Doctor Universalis, Doctor Expertus;* Nov. 15.

Alphonsus Liguori, St. (1696-1787): Born near Naples, Italy; bishop of Saint Agatha of the Goths (1762-1775); founder of the Redemptorists; in addition to his principal work, *Theologiae Moralis,* wrote on prayer, the spiritual life and doctrinal subjects in response to controversy; canonized, 1839; proclaimed doctor, 1871; named patron of confessors and moralists, 1950; Aug. 1.

Ambrose, St. (c. 340-397): Born in Trier, Germany; bishop of Milan (374-397); one of the strongest opponents of Arianism in the West; his homilies and other writings — on faith, the Holy Spirit, the Incarnation, the sacraments and other subjects — were pastoral and practical; influenced the development of a liturgy at Milan which was named for him; Father and Doctor of the Church; Dec. 7.

Anselm, St. (1033-1109): Born in Aosta, Piedmont, Italy; Benedictine; archbishop of Canterbury (1093-1109); in addition to his principal work, *Cur Deus Homo,* on the atonement and reconciliation of man with God through Christ, wrote about the existence and attributes of God and defended the *Filioque* explanation of the procession of the Holy Spirit from the Father and the Son; proclaimed doctor, 1720; called Father of Scholasticism; Apr. 21.

Anthony of Padua, St. (1195-1231): Born in Lisbon, Portugal; first theologian of the Franciscan Order; preacher; canonized, 1232; proclaimed doctor, 1946; called Evangelical Doctor; June 13.

Athanasius, St. (c. 297-373): Born in Alexandria, Egypt; bishop of Alexandria (328-373); participant in the Council of Nicaea I while still a deacon; dominant opponent of Arians whose errors regarding Christ he refuted in *Apology Against the Arians,* Discourses against the Arians and other works; Father and Doctor of the Church; called

Father of Orthodoxy; May 2.

Augustine, St. (354-430): Born in Tagaste, North Africa; bishop of Hippo (395-430) after conversion from Manichaeism; works include the autobiographical and mystical *Confessions, City of God,* treatises on the Trinity, grace, passages of the Bible and doctrines called into question and denied by Manichaeans, Pelagians, and Donatists; had strong and lasting influence on Christian theology and philosophy; Father and Doctor of the Church; called Doctor of Grace; Aug. 28.

Basil the Great, St. (c. 329-379): Born in Caesarea, Cappadocia, Asia Minor; bishop of Caesarea (370-379); wrote three books; *Contra Eunomium,* in refutation of Arian errors; a treatise on the Holy Spirit; many homilies; and several rules for monastic life, on which he had lasting influence; Father and Doctor of the Church; called Father of Monasticism in the East; Jan. 2.

Bede the Venerable, St. (c. 673-735): Born in Northumberland, England; Benedictine; in addition to his principal work, *Ecclesiastical History* of the English Nation (covering the period 597-731), wrote scriptural commentaries; regarded as probably the most learned man in Western Europe of his time; called Father of English History; May 25.

Bernard of Clairvaux, St. (c. 1090-1153): Born near Dijon, France; abbot; monastic reformer, called the second founder of the Cistercian Order; mystical theologian with great influence on devotional life; opponent of the rationalism brought forward by Abélard and others; canonized, 1174; proclaimed doctor, 1830; called Mellifluous Doctor because of his eloquence; Aug. 20.

Bonaventure, St. (c. 1217-1274): Born near Viterbo, Italy; Franciscan; bishop of Albano (1273-1274); cardinal; wrote *Itinerarium Mentis in Deum, De Reductione Artium ad Theologiam, Breviloquium,* scriptural commentaries, additional mystical works affecting devotional life, and a life of St. Francis of Assisi; canonized, 1482; proclaimed doctor, 1588; called Seraphic Doctor; July 15.

Catherine of Siena, St. (c. 1347-1380): Born in Siena, Italy; member of the Third Order of St. Dominic; mystic; authored a long series of letters, mainly concerning spiritual instruction and encouragement, to associates, and *Dialogue,* a spiritual testament in four treatises; was active in support of a crusade against the Turks and efforts to end war between papal forces and the Florentine allies; had great influence in inducing Gregory XI to return himself and the Curia to Rome in 1377, to end the Avignon period of the papacy; canonized, 1461; proclaimed second woman doctor, Oct. 4, 1970; Apr. 29; named a co-patroness of Europe, with St. Edith Stein and St. Bridget of Sweden, on Oct. 1, 1999.

Cyril of Alexandria, St. (c. 376-444): Born in Egypt; bishop of Alexandria (412-444); wrote treatises on the Trinity, the Incarnation and other subjects, mostly in refutation of Nestorian errors; made key contributions to the development of Christology; presided at the Council of Ephesus, 431; proclaimed doctor, 1882; June 27.

Cyril of Jerusalem, St. (c. 315-386): Bishop of Jerusalem from 350; vigorous opponent of Arianism; principal work, *Catecheses,* a pre-baptismal explanation of the creed of Jerusalem; proclaimed doctor, 1882; Mar. 18.

Ephraem, St. (c. 306-373): Born in Nisibis, Mesopotamia; counteracted the spread of Gnostic and Arian errors with poems and hymns of his own composition; wrote also on the Eucharist and Mary; proclaimed doctor, 1920; called

Deacon of Edessa and Harp of the Holy Spirit; June 9.

Francis de Sales, St. (1567-1622): Born in Savoy; bishop of Geneva (1602-1622); spiritual writer with strong influence on devotional life through treatises such as *Introduction to a Devout Life*, and *The Love of God*; canonized, 1665; proclaimed doctor, 1877; patron of Catholic writers and the Catholic press; Jan. 24.

Gregory Nazianzen, St. (c. 330-c. 390): Born in Arianzus, Cappadocia, Asia Minor; bishop of Constantinople (381-390); vigorous opponent of Arianism; in addition to five theological discourses on the Nicene Creed and the Trinity for which he is best known, wrote letters and poetry; Father and Doctor of the Church; called the Christian Demosthenes because of his eloquence and, in the Eastern Church, the Theologian; Jan. 2.

Gregory I, the Great, St. (c. 540-604): Born in Rome; pope (590-604): wrote many scriptural commentaries, a compendium of theology in the *Book of Morals* based on Job, Dialogues concerning the lives of saints, the immortality of the soul, death, purgatory, heaven and hell, and fourteen books of letters; enforced papal supremacy and established the position of the pope vis-á-vis the emperor; worked for clerical and monastic reform and the observance of clerical celibacy; Father and Doctor of the Church; Sept. 3.

Hilary of Poitiers, St. (c. 315-368): Born in Poitiers, France; bishop of Poitiers (c. 353-368); wrote *De Synodis*, with the Arian controversy in mind, and *De Trinitate*, the first lengthy study of the doctrine in Latin; introduced Eastern theology to the West; contributed to the development of hymnology; proclaimed doctor, 1851; called the Athanasius of the West because of his vigorous defense of the divinity of Christ against Arians; Jan. 13.

Hildegard of Bingen, St. (1098-1179) German mystic and abbess, called the "Sibyl of the Rhine" because of her many visions; she wrote the *Scivias*, a collection of visions, divided into three books; other works included hymns, scientific treatises, letters, and theological writings; given equivalent canonization by Pope Benedict XVI, she was proclaimed a doctor in 2012; Sept. 17.

Isidore of Seville, St. (c. 560-636): Born in Cartagena, Spain; bishop of Seville (c. 600-636); in addition to his principal work, *Etymologiae*, an encyclopedia of the knowledge of his day, wrote on theological and historical subjects; regarded as the most learned man of his time; proclaimed doctor, 1722; Apr. 4.

Jerome, St. (c. 343-420): Born in Stridon, Dalmatia; translated the Old Testament from Hebrew into Latin and revised the existing Latin translation of the New Testament to produce the Vulgate version of the Bible; wrote scriptural commentaries and treatises on matters of controversy; regarded as Father and Doctor of the Church from the eighth century; called Father of Biblical Science; Sept. 30.

John Chrysostom, St. (c. 347-407): Born in Antioch, Asia Minor; archbishop of Constantinople (398-407); wrote homilies, scriptural commentaries and letters of wide influence in addition to a classical treatise on the priesthood; proclaimed doctor by the Council of Chalcedon, 451; called the greatest of the Greek Fathers; named patron of preachers, 1909; called Golden-Mouthed because of his eloquence; Sept. 13.

John Damascene, St. (c. 675-c. 749): Born in Damascus, Syria; monk; wrote *Fountain of Wisdom*, a three-part work including a history of heresies and an exposition of the Christian faith, three discourses against the Iconoclasts, homilies on Mary, biblical commentaries,

and treatises on moral subjects; proclaimed doctor, 1890; called Golden Speaker because of his eloquence; Dec. 4.

John of the Cross, St. (1542-1591): Born in Old Castile, Spain; Carmelite; founder of Discalced Carmelites; one of the greatest mystical theologians, wrote *The Ascent of Mt. Carmel; The Dark Night of the Soul, The Spiritual Canticle, The Living Flame of Love*; canonized, 1726; proclaimed doctor, 1926; called Doctor of Mystical Theology; Dec. 14.

John of Ávila, St. (1500-1569) Apostle of Andalusia, a Spanish mystic reformer, and preacher, the patron of priests in Spain; Jewish-born near Toledo, he initially prepared for missionary work in Mexico, but he was sent to revive the faith in Andalusia; renowned for his sermons, he was an ardent proponent of clerical reform; canonized in 1970 by Pope Paul VI; proclaimed doctor in 2012; May 10.

Lawrence of Brindisi, St. (1559-1619): Born in Brindisi, Italy; Franciscan (Capuchin); vigorous preacher of strong influence in the post-Reformation period; 15 tomes of collected works include scriptural commentaries, sermons, homilies and doctrinal writings; canonized, 1881; proclaimed doctor, 1959; July 21.

Leo I, the Great, St. (c. 400-461): Born in Tuscany, Italy; pope (440-461); wrote the *Tome* of Leo, to explain doctrine concerning the two natures and one Person of Christ, against the background of the Nestorian and Monophysite heresies; other works included sermons, letters and writings against the errors of Manichaeism and Pelagianism; was instrumental in dissuading Attila from sacking Rome in 452; proclaimed doctor, 1574; Nov. 10.

Peter Canisius, St. (1521-1597): Born in Nijmegen, Holland; Jesuit; wrote popular expositions of the Catholic faith in several catechisms which were widely circulated in 20 editions in his lifetime alone; was one of the moving figures in the Counter-Reformation period, especially in southern and western Germany; canonized and proclaimed doctor, 1925; Dec. 21.

Peter Chrysologus, St. (c. 400-450): Born in Imola, Italy; served as archbishop of Ravenna (c. 433-450); his sermons and writings, many of which were designed to counteract Monophysitism, were pastoral and practical; proclaimed doctor, 1729; July 30.

Peter Damian, St. (1007-1072): Born in Ravenna, Italy; Benedictine; cardinal; his writings and sermons, many of which concerned ecclesiastical and clerical reform, were pastoral and practical; proclaimed doctor, 1828; Feb. 21.

Robert Bellarmine, St. (1542-1621): Born in Tuscany, Italy; Jesuit; archbishop of Capua (1602-1605); wrote *Controversies*, a three-volume exposition of doctrine under attack during and after the Reformation, two catechisms and the spiritual work, *The Art of Dying Well*; was an authority on ecclesiology and Church-state relations; canonized, 1930; proclaimed doctor, 1931; Sept. 17.

Teresa of Jesus (Ávila), St. (1515-1582): Born in Ávila, Spain; entered the Carmelite Order, 1535; in the early 1560s, initiated a primitive Carmelite reform which greatly influenced men and women religious, especially in Spain; wrote extensively on spiritual and mystical subjects; principal works included her *Autobiography, Way of Perfection, The Interior Castle, Meditations on the Canticle, The Foundations, Visitation of the Discalced Nuns*; canonized, 1622; proclaimed first woman doctor, Sept. 27, 1970; Oct. 15.

Thérèse of Lisieux, St. (1873-1897): Born in Alençon, Normandy, France; entered the Carmelites at Lisieux in

1888, lived for only nine more years, dying on September 30, 1897 from tuberculosis. Trusting completely in God, a path she described as the "little way," she lived a seemingly ordinary life of a nun, but her spiritual advancement was such that her superiors instructed her to write an autobiography in 1895 (*The Story of a Soul*). One of the most popular and respected saints throughout the 20th century, she was canonized on May 17, 1925. Pope John Paul II declared her the third woman doctor on Oct. 20, 1997 in the letter *Divini amoris scientia*; her relics also toured the United States, attracting huge crowds, Sept.–Oct. 2013.

Thomas Aquinas, St. (1225-1274): Born near Naples, Italy; Dominican; teacher and writer on virtually the whole range of philosophy and theology; principal works were *Summa contra Gentiles*, a manual and systematic defense of Christian doctrine, and *Summa Theologiae*, a new (at that time) exposition of theology on philosophical principles; canonized, 1323; proclaimed doctor, 1567; called *Doctor Communis, Doctor Angelicus*, the Great Synthesizer because of the way in which he related faith and reason, theology and philosophy (especially that of Aristotle), and systematized the presentation of Christian doctrine; named patron of Catholic schools and education, 1880; Jan. 28.

CREEDS

Creeds are formal and official statements of Christian doctrine. As summaries of the principal truths of faith, they are standards of orthodoxy and are useful for instructional purposes, for actual profession of the faith and for expression of the faith in the liturgy.

The classical creeds are the Apostles' Creed and the Creed of Nicaea-Constantinople. Two others are the Athanasian Creed and the Creed of Pius IV.

Apostles' Creed

Text: *I believe in God, the Father almighty, Creator of heaven and earth.*

And in Jesus Christ, his only Son, our Lord; who was conceived by the Holy Spirit, born of the Virgin Mary, suffered under Pontius Pilate, was crucified, died, and was buried. He descended into hell; the third day he arose again from the dead; he ascended into heaven, sits at the right hand of God, the Father almighty; from thence he shall come to judge the living and the dead.

I believe in the Holy Spirit, the holy Catholic Church, the communion of saints, the forgiveness of sins, the resurrection of the body, and life everlasting. Amen.

Background: The Apostles' Creed reflects the teaching of the Apostles but is not of apostolic origin. It probably originated in the second century as a rudimentary formula of faith professed by catechumens before the reception of baptism. Baptismal creeds in fourth-century use at Rome and elsewhere in the West closely resembled the present text, which was quoted in a handbook of Christian doctrine written between 710 and 724. This text was in wide use throughout the West by the ninth century. The Apostles' Creed is common to all Christian confessional churches in the West, but is not used in Eastern Churches.

Nicene Creed

The following translation of the Latin text of the Creed was prepared by the International Committee on English in the Liturgy.

Text: *I believe in one God, the Father almighty, maker of heaven and earth, of all things visible and invisible.*

I believe in one Lord Jesus Christ, the Only Begotten Son of God, born of the Father before all ages.

God from God, Light from Light, true God from true God, begotten, not made, consubstantial with the Father; through him all things were made.

For us men and for our salvation he came down from heaven, and by the Holy Spirit was incarnate of the Virgin Mary, and became man.

For our sake he was crucified under Pontius Pilate, he suffered death and was buried, and rose again on the third day in accordance with the Scriptures.

He ascended into heaven and is seated at the right hand of the Father.

He will come again in glory to judge the living and the dead and his kingdom will have no end.

I believe in the Holy Spirit, the Lord, the giver of life, who proceeds from the Father and the Son, who with the Father and the Son is adored and glorified, who has spoken through the prophets.

I believe in one, holy, catholic and apostolic Church.

I confess one Baptism for the forgiveness of sins and I look forward to the resurrection of the dead and the life of the world to come. Amen

Background: The Nicene Creed (Creed of Nicaea-Constantinople) consists of elements of doctrine contained in an early baptismal creed of Jerusalem and enactments of the Council of Nicaea (325) and the Council of Constantinople (381).

Its strong trinitarian content reflects the doctrinal errors, especially of Arianism, it served to counteract. Theologically, it is much more sophisticated than the Apostles' Creed.

Since late in the fifth century, the Nicene Creed has been the only creed in liturgical use in the Eastern Churches. The Western Church adopted it for liturgical use by the end of the eighth century.

The Athanasian Creed

The Athanasian Creed, which has a unique structure, is a two-part summary of doctrine concerning the Trinity and the Incarnation-Redemption bracketed at the beginning and end with the statement that belief in the cited truths is necessary for salvation; it also contains a number of anathemas or condemnatory clauses regarding doctrinal errors. Although attributed to St. Athanasius, it was probably written after his death, between 381 and 428, and may have been authored by St. Ambrose. It is not accepted in the East; in the West, it formerly had place in the Roman-Rite Liturgy of the Hours and in the liturgy for the Solemnity of the Holy Trinity.

Creed of Pius IV

The Creed of Pius IV, also called the Profession of Faith of the Council of Trent, was promulgated in the bull *Injunctum Nobis*, Nov. 13, 1564. It is a summary of doctrine defined by the council concerning: Scripture and tradition, original sin and justification, the Mass and sacraments, veneration of the saints, indulgences, the primacy of the See of Rome. It was slightly modified in 1887 to include doctrinal formulations of the First Vatican Council.

CHRISTIAN MORALITY

By Fr. Alfred McBride, O.Praem.

"Incorporated into Christ by Baptism, Christians are 'dead to sin and alive in Christ Jesus ... '" (Rom 6:11).

CHRISTIAN MORALITY IS LIFE IN CHRIST

The third part of the *Catechism* focuses on Christian morality. After the Creed as faith professed, and sacraments as faith celebrated, the *Catechism* turns our attention to the faith lived. It deals with this issue in two major sections. The first section establishes the context for Christian morality. The second section analyzes the ten commandments. This approach preserves the *Catechism's* resolute insistence on the primacy of God's initiative through Revelation, salvation, and grace followed by our human response in faith, celebration, and Christian witness. Hence morality does not begin with the rules but with the call to life in Christ and the Holy Spirit. Covenant love comes first, then the response of Christian affection in the life of the commandments. This saves us both from legalism and from piety without practical witness.

The following excerpt from the *Catechism of the Catholic Church* sets the vision for the Christian moral life:

LIFE IN CHRIST

1691 "Christian, recognize your dignity and, now that you share in God's own nature, do not return to your former base condition by sinning. Remember who is your head and of whose body you are a member. Never forget that you have been rescued from the power of darkness and brought into the light of the Kingdom of God."[1]

1692 The Symbol of the faith confesses the greatness of God's gifts to man in his work of creation, and even more in redemption and sanctification. What faith confesses, the sacraments communicate: by the sacraments of rebirth, Christians have become "children of God,"[2] "partakers of the divine nature."[3] Coming to see in the faith their new dignity, Christians are called to lead henceforth a life "worthy of the gospel of Christ."[4] They are made capable of doing so by the grace of Christ and the gifts of his Spirit, which they receive through the sacraments and through prayer.

1693 Christ Jesus always did what was pleasing to the Father,[5] and always lived in perfect communion with him. Likewise Christ's disciples are invited to live in the sight of the Father "who sees in secret,"[6] in order to become "perfect as your heavenly Father is perfect."[7]

1694 Incorporated into Christ by Baptism, Christians are "dead to sin and alive to God in Christ Jesus" and so participate in the life of the Risen Lord.[8] Following Christ and united with him,[9] Christians can strive to be "imitators of God as beloved children, and walk in love"[10] by conforming their thoughts, words and actions to the "mind ... which is yours in Christ Jesus,"[11] and by following his example.[12]

1695 "Justified in the name of the Lord Jesus Christ and in the Spirit of our God,"[13] "sanctified ... [and] called to be saints,"[14] Christians have become the temple of the Holy Spirit.[15] This "Spirit of the Son" teaches them to pray to the Father[16] and, having become their life, prompts them to act so as to bear "the fruit of the Spirit"[17] by charity in action. Healing the wounds of sin, the Holy Spirit renews us interiorly through a spiritual transformation.[18] He enlightens and strengthens us to live as "children of light"

through "all that is good and right and true."[19]

1696 The way of Christ "leads to life"; a contrary way "leads to destruction."[20] The Gospel parable of the two ways remains ever present in the catechesis of the Church; it shows the importance of moral decisions for our salvation: "There are two ways, the one of life, the other of death; but between the two, there is a great difference."[21]

1697 Catechesis has to reveal in all clarity the joy and the demands of the way of Christ.[22] Catechesis for the "newness of life"[23] in him should be:

• a catechesis of the Holy Spirit, the interior Master of life according to Christ, a gentle guest and friend who inspires, guides, corrects, and strengthens this life;

• a catechesis of grace, for it is by grace that we are saved and again it is by grace that our works can bear fruit for eternal life;

• a catechesis of the beatitudes, for the way of Christ is summed up in the beatitudes, the only path that leads to the eternal beatitude for which the human heart longs;

• a catechesis of sin and forgiveness, for unless man acknowledges that he is a sinner he cannot know the truth about himself, which is a condition for acting justly; and without the offer of forgiveness he would not be able to bear this truth;

• a catechesis of the human virtues which causes one to grasp the beauty and attraction of right dispositions toward goodness;

• a catechesis of the Christian virtues of faith, hope, and charity, generously inspired by the example of the saints; a catechesis of the twofold commandment of charity set forth in the Decalogue;

• an ecclesial catechesis, for it is through the manifold exchanges of "spiritual goods" in the "communion of saints" that Christian life can grow, develop, and be communicated.

1698 The first and last point of reference of this catechesis will always be Jesus Christ himself, who is "the way, and the truth, and the life."[24] It is by looking to him in faith that Christ's faithful can hope that he himself fulfills his promises in them, and that, by loving him with the same love with which he has loved them, they may perform works in keeping with their dignity: "I ask you to consider that our Lord Jesus Christ is your true head, and that you are one of his members. He belongs to you as the head belongs to its members; all that is his is yours: his spirit, his heart, his body and soul, and all his faculties. You must make use of all these as of your own, to serve, praise, love, and glorify God. You belong to him, as members belong to their head. And so he longs for you to use all that is in you, as if it were his own, for the service and glory of the Father."[25] "For to me, to live is Christ."[26]

Footnotes

1. St. Leo the Great, *Sermo* 22 in nat. Dom. 3: PL 54, 192C. [2] Jn 1:12; 1 Jn 3:1. [3] 2 Pt 1:4. [4] Phil 1:27. [5] Cf. Jn 8:29. [6] Mt 6:6. [7] Mt 5:48. [8] Rom 6:11 and cf. 6:5; cf. Col 2:12. [9] Cf. Jn 15:5. [10] Eph 5:1-2. [11] Phil 2:5. [12] Cf. Jn 13:12-16. [13] 1 Cor 6:11. [14] 1 Cor 1:2. [15] Cf. 1 Cor 6:19. [16] Cf. Gal 4:6. [17] Gal 5:22,25. [18] Cf. Eph 4:23. [19] Eph 5:8,9. [20] Mt 7:13; cf. Dt 30:15-20. [21] Didache 1, 1: SCh 248, 140. [22] Cf. John Paul II, CT 29. [23] Rom 6:4. [24] Jn 14:6. [25] St. John Eudes, *Tract. de admirabili corde Jesu*, 1, 5. [26] Phil 1:21.

THE TEN COMMANDMENTS

Any discussions of the commandments should begin with the scene at Sinai where God gave them to us. Read Ex 19:3-6; 20:1-17. The first event is a covenant experience. God tells Moses how much he has loved the Israelites, is delivering them from slavery by "raising them up on eagles' wings," and is bringing them to freedom. God then offers them a binding covenant of love. He will be their only God and they will be his chosen people. It's like a marriage experience, an exchange of vows between God and Israel.

The next section shows God telling them how to live out the love they have pledged. He gives them the Ten Commandments as the means to live the covenant, to express the love they have promised. The *Catechism* points out that the Ten Commandments are privileged expressions of the natural law, made known to us by reason as well as Divine Revelation. We are obliged in obedience to observe these laws of love, both in serious and light matters. Love is in the details as well as the large matters. We must remember that what God has commanded, he makes possible by his grace.

Jesus set the tone for understanding the importance of the commandments. When a rich young man came to him and asked him what he should do to enter eternal life, Jesus replied, "if you wish to enter into life, keep the commandments" (Mt 19:17). In another case, someone asked him which were the greatest commandments, Jesus replied, "you shall love the Lord, your God, with all your heart, with all your soul, and with all your mind. This is the greatest and first commandment. The second is like it: You shall love your neighbor as yourself" (Mt 22:37-39). The first three commandments deal with Christ's call to God with all our being. The last seven commandments show us how to love our neighbors as we love ourselves.

The following excerpt from the *Catechism of the Catholic Church* shows how Jesus taught the importance of the Ten Commandments:

"Teacher, what must I do . . .?"

2052 "Teacher, what good deed must I do, to have eternal life?" To the young man who asked this question, Jesus answers first by invoking the necessity to recognize God as the "One there is who is good," as the supreme Good and the source of all good. Then Jesus tells him: "If you would enter life, keep the commandments." And he cites for his questioner the precepts that concern love of neighbor: "You shall not kill, You shall not commit adultery, You shall not steal, You shall not bear false witness, Honor your father and mother." Finally Jesus sums up these commandments positively: "You shall love your neighbor as yourself."[1]

2053 To this first reply Jesus adds a second: "If you would be perfect, go, sell what you possess and give to the poor, and you will have treasure in heaven; and come, follow me."[2] This reply does not do away with the first: following Jesus Christ involves keeping the Commandments. The Law has not been abolished,[3] but rather man is invited to rediscover it in the person of his Master who is its perfect fulfillment. In the three synoptic Gospels, Jesus' call to the rich young man to follow him, in the obedience of a disciple and in the observance of the Commandments, is joined to the call to poverty and chastity.[4] The evangelical counsels are inseparable from the Commandments.

2054 Jesus acknowledged the Ten Commandments, but he also showed the power of the Spirit at work in their letter. He preached a "righteousness [which] exceeds that of the scribes and Pharisees"[5] as well as that of the Gentiles. [6] He unfolded all the demands of the Commandments. "You have heard that it was said to the men of old, 'You shall not kill.' … But I say to you that every one who is angry with his brother shall be liable to judgment."[7]

2055 When someone asks him, "Which commandment in the Law is the greatest?"[8] Jesus replies: "You shall love the Lord your God with all your heart, and with all your soul, and with all your mind. This is the greatest and first commandment. And a second is like it: You shall love your neighbor as yourself. On these two commandments hang all the Law and the prophets."[9] The Decalogue must be interpreted in light of this twofold yet single commandment of love, he fullness of the Law: "The commandments: 'You shall not commit adultery, You shall not kill, You shall not steal, You shall not covet,' and any other commandment, are summed up in this sentence: 'You shall love your neighbor as yourself.' Love does no wrong to a neighbor; therefore love is the fulfilling of the law."[10]

Footnotes

[1] Mt 19:16-19. [2] Mt 19:21. [3] Cf. Mt 5:17. [4] Cf. Mt 19:6-12,21,23-29. [5] Mt 5:20. [6] Cf. Mt 5:46-47. [7] Mt 5:21-22. [8] Mt 22:36. [9] Mt 22:37-40; cf. Dt 6:5; Lv 19:18. [10] Rom 13:9-10.

In the traditional Catholic enumeration and according to Dt. 5:6-21, the Commandments are:
1. "I, the Lord, am your God You shall not have other gods besides me. You shall not carve idols."
2. "You shall not take the name of the Lord, your God, in vain."
3. "Take care to keep holy the Sabbath day."
4. "Honor your father and your mother."
5. "You shall not kill."
6. "You shall not commit adultery."
7. "You shall not steal."
8. "You shall not bear dishonest witness against your neighbor."
9. "You shall not covet your neighbor's wife."
10. "You shall not desire your neighbor's house or field, nor his male or female slave, nor his ox or ass, nor anything that belongs to him" (summarily, his goods).

Another version of the Commandments, substantially the same, is given in Ex 20:1-17.

The traditional enumeration of the Commandments in Protestant usage differs from the above. Thus: two commandments are made of the first, as above; the third and fourth are equivalent to the second and third, as above, and so on; and the 10th includes the ninth and 10th, as above.

Love of God and Neighbor

The first three of the commandments deal directly with man's relations with God, viz.: acknowledgment of one true God and the rejection of false gods and idols; honor due to God and his name; observance of the Sabbath as the Lord's day.

The rest cover interpersonal relationships, viz.: the obedience to parents and, logically, to other persons in authority, and the obligations of parents to children and of persons in authority to those under their care; respect for life and physical integrity; fidelity in marriage, and chastity; justice and rights; truth; internal respect for faithfulness in marriage, chastity, and the goods of others.

Perfection in Christian Life

The moral obligations of the Ten Commandments are complemented by others flowing from the twofold law of love, the whole substance and pattern of Christ's teaching, and everything implied in full and active membership and participation in the community of salvation formed by Christ in his Church. Some of these matters are covered in other sections of the *Almanac* under appropriate headings.

Precepts of the Church

The purpose of the precepts of the Church, according to the *Catechism of the Catholic Church*, is "to guarantee to the faithful the indispensable minimum in the spirit of prayer and moral effort, in the growth and love of God and neighbor" (No. 2041).

1. Attendance at Mass on Sundays and holy days of obligation. (Observance of Sundays and holy days of obligation involves refraining from work that hinders the worship due to God.)

2. Confession of sins at least once a year. (Not required by the precept in the absence of serious sin.)

3. Reception of the Eucharist at least during the Easter season (in the U.S., from the first Sunday of Lent to Trinity Sunday).

4. Keep holy the holy days of obligation.

5. Observance of specified days of fasting and abstinence.

There is also an obligation to provide for the material needs of the Church.

CATHOLIC MORAL TEACHINGS OF POPE JOHN PAUL II

On Aug. 6, 1993, Pope John Paul II published his tenth encyclical, Veritatis Splendor *("The Splendor of the Truth") regarding the fundamental truths of the Church's moral teachings. On Mar. 25, 1995, he published his eleventh encyclical,* Evangelium Vitae *("The Gospel of Life"), concerning the value and inviolability of human life. The following material is adapted from* The Encyclicals of John Paul II, *with the kind permission of Most Rev. J. Michael Miller, C.S.B.*

Veritatis Splendor ("The Splendor of the Truth")

On Aug. 6, 1993, John Paul II signed his 10th encyclical, *Veritatis Splendor,* regarding certain fundamental truths of the Church's moral teaching.[1] Undoubtedly it is the pope's most complex and most discussed document. Since its publication, the encyclical has generated a great deal of comment in the media and among theologians. This is not surprising, since *Veritatis Splendor* is the first-ever papal document on the theological and philosophical foundations of Catholic moral teaching. In this encyclical the pope affirms that divine revelation contains "a specific and determined moral content, universally valid and permanent" (§37.1), which the Magisterium has the competence to interpret and teach.

Six years before, in the apostolic letter *Spiritus Domini* (1987), John Paul had publicly announced his intention to publish a document that would treat "more fully and more deeply the issues regarding the very foundations of moral theology" (§5.1). For several reasons the encyclical's preparation took longer than was first anticipated. First, the pope widely consulted bishops and theologians throughout the world, and various drafts were drawn up. Second, he thought that it was fitting for the encyclical "to be preceded by the *Catechism of the Catholic Church,*" which contains a complete and systematic exposition of

Christian moral teaching" (§5.3). The *Catechism,* published in 1992, gives a full presentation of the Church's moral doctrine, including that on particular questions, and expounds it in a positive way. *Veritatis Splendor,* on the other hand, limits itself to dealing with the fundamental principles underlying all moral teaching.

But why does John Paul think that an encyclical on moral issues will serve the Church and the world on the threshold of the third millennium? According to him, reflection on the ethical implications of Christian faith, lived from the beginning as the "way" (Acts 22:4), belongs to the full proclamation of the Gospel. Moreover, he is convinced that society is in the throes of a *"crisis of truth"* (§32.2). This crisis has the "most serious implications for the moral life of the faithful and for communion in the Church, as well as for a just and fraternal social life" (§5.2).

The deChristianization of many cultures involves not only a loss of faith but also *"a decline or obscuring of the moral sense"* (§106.2). This new moral situation brings with it "the *confusion between good and evil,* which makes it impossible to build up and to preserve the moral order" (§93.1). The ethical bewilderment of some Catholics has led to "the spread of numerous doubts and objections of a human and psychological, social and cultural, religious and even properly theological nature, with regard to the Church's moral teachings" (§4.2). In an increasingly secular world, believers are "making judgments and decisions [that] often appear extraneous or even contrary to those of the Gospel" (§88.2). Moreover, dissent from Catholic moral teaching often entails "an overall and systematic calling into question of traditional moral doctrine" (§4.2). Thus, as a service to the ethical and spiritual welfare of individuals and cultures, John Paul addresses the basic moral principles handed down by the Christian Tradition.

In order to meet his goal, the pope responds in a constructive way to the contemporary moral crisis by proclaiming "the splendor of the truth." When he announced the forthcoming publication of *Veritatis Splendor,* he described the encyclical's purpose: "It reaffirms the dignity of the human person, created in God's image, and proposes anew the genuine concept of human freedom, showing its essential and constitutive relationship with the truth in accordance with Christ's words: 'The truth will make you free!' (Jn 8:32)."[2] On another occasion, John Paul said that he intended the encyclical to be "a proclamation of truth and a hymn to freedom: values felt strongly by contemporary man and deeply respected by the Church."[3] His primary aim, then, is not to censure specific dissident moral opinions but to proclaim that Christ is "the true and final answer to the problem of morality" (§85).

John Paul sets several specific objectives for the encyclical. First, he wishes "*to reflect on the whole of the Church's moral teaching,* with the precise goal of recalling certain fundamental truths of Catholic doctrine which, in the present circumstances, risk being distorted or denied" (§4.2, cf. §30.1). Second, he aims to show the faithful "the inviting splendor of that truth which is Jesus Christ himself" (§83.2). Christ alone is the answer to humanity's questions, "the only response fully capable of satisfying the desire of the human heart" (§7.1). Third, if the present crisis is to be successfully resolved, the Magisterium must authoritatively discern "*interpretations of Christian morality which are not consistent with 'sound teaching'* (2 Tm 4:3)" (§29.4, cf. §27.4). This pastoral discernment of the pope and bishops is necessary as a way of assuring "*the right of the faithful* to receive Catholic doctrine in its purity and integrity" (§113.2).

The pope addresses *Veritatis Splendor* specifically to his brother bishops. He intends them to be the first, but not exclusive, recipients of the encyclical. John Paul reminds them of their responsibility to safeguard and find "ever new ways of speaking with love and mercy" about *"the path of the moral life"* (§3.1,2).

John Paul II's training in ethics and moral theology is clearly evident in *Veritatis Splendor*. The encyclical's exposition is sometimes highly technical, especially in its analyses and responses to opinions contrary to Church teaching. While some commentators have voiced disagreement about the accuracy of the pope's descriptions of the ethical positions with which he disagrees, they respect his desire to be fair-minded. As we shall see, whenever John Paul deals with an opinion he disagrees with, he first takes great pains to point out what is positive in the view. Only after doing this does he then examine its weaknesses. When unmasking theological and philosophical ideas incompatible with revealed truth, he scrupulously avoids imposing "any particular theological system, still less a philosophical one" (§29.4).

Throughout the encyclical the pope repeatedly draws inspiration from the Bible. Chapter one, structured around the encounter of Jesus with the rich young man (Mt 19:16-21), establishes a biblical foundation for fundamental moral principles. In this chapter the pope wishes to apply the theological method proposed by the Second Vatican Council: "Sacred Scripture remains the living and fruitful source of the Church's moral doctrine" (§28.2, cf. §5.3). Chapter two, on the other hand, uses Scripture chiefly to corroborate positions advanced on the basis of the natural moral law. The beginning of chapter three returns to a more biblical approach; it discusses discipleship in terms of the Paschal Mystery and of martyrdom as the supreme expression of following Christ.

More so than in his other encyclicals, in *Veritatis Splendor* John Paul relies considerably on the teaching of St. Thomas Aquinas, referring to him directly at least 20 times, and on the teaching of St. Augustine, citing him 16 times. The pope also mines extensively the documents of Vatican II, especially *Gaudium et Spes*, which he cites more than 25 times. Except for one reference to St. Alphonsus Liguori and a single direct citation of John Henry Newman, the pope mentions no moral philosopher or theologian after the Middle Ages.

Footnotes

[1] *Acta Apostolicae Sedis,* 85 (1993), 1133-1228. [2] *Angelus,* Oct. 3, 1993, *L'Osservatore Romano,* 40 (1993), 1. [3] *Angelus,* Oct. 17, 1993, *L'Osservatore Romano,* 42 (1993), 1.

Evangelium Vitae ("The Gospel of Life")

"The *Gospel of life* is at the heart of Jesus' message" (§1.1). With these words Pope John Paul II begins his eleventh encyclical, *Evangelium Vitae,* published on Mar. 25, 1995.[1] He aptly chose the feast of the Annunciation, which celebrates Mary's welcoming of the Son of God who took flesh in her womb, to issue a document dedicated to the value and inviolability of human life. By taking up the cause of the "great multitude of weak and defenseless human beings" (§5.4), especially unborn children and those at the end of life, the pope continues the defense of human dignity dealt with in his three social encyclicals. *Evangelium Vitae* is an anguished and vigorous response to *"scientifically and systematically programmed threats"* against life (§17.2), assaults which have repercussions on Church teaching, touching upon "the core of her faith in the redemptive Incarnation of the Son of God" (§3.1).

For John Paul II, the cause of life is the cause of the Gospel entrusted to the Church, which is duty-bound to raise her voice in the defense of life. His encyclical is a "pressing appeal addressed to each and every person, in the name of God: *respect, protect, love and serve life, every human life!*" (§5.5).

Preparations for the encyclical began in Apr. 1991, when the pope called a special meeting in Rome of the College of Cardinals to discuss current threats to human life. After their deliberations, the cardinals asked him "to reaffirm with the authority of the Successor of Peter the value of human life and its inviolability" (§5.1). As a first response to their request, the pope wrote a personal letter to every bishop, seeking contributions to the planned document. They replied with valuable suggestions, and he incorporated many of their proposals into the encyclical. *Evangelium Vitae,* then, is the fruit of genuine episcopal collegiality. By taking an active part in its preparation, the bishops "bore witness to their unanimous desire to share in the doctrinal and pastoral mission of the Church with regard to the *Gospel of life*" (§5.2).

Unlike *Veritatis Splendor,* which was directed primarily to bishops, John Paul intends *Evangelium Vitae* to be read also by the lay faithful, indeed by all people of good will. Concern for the sacredness of human life is not just a matter for Catholics. "The value at stake," writes the pope, "is one which every human being can grasp by the light of reason" (§101.2). The essential truths of the Gospel of life "are written in the heart of every man and woman," echoing in every human conscience "from the time of creation itself" (§29.3). He insists that anyone who is sincerely open to truth and goodness can discover "the sacred value of human life from its very beginning until its end, and can affirm the right of every human being to have this primary good respected to the highest degree" (§2.2).

The encyclical's style is typically Wojtylan. It intersperses rigorous analysis with prayers and exhortations. As can be seen from the more than 300 biblical quotations and references, Scripture accompanies the pope's presentation from start to finish, giving *Evangelium Vitae* an inspirational tone and familiar style. He also relies heavily on the Church Fathers. The 18 patristic quotations that appear in the encyclical reinforce the truths that God is the origin of life, that human beings share in divine life, and that Jesus gave his life so that others might live. As is customary, John Paul frequently cites the documents of the Second Vatican Council — here, more than 25 times. He also makes use of the *Catechism of the Catholic Church,* citing it on 10 occasions.

Of particular significance in *Evangelium Vitae* are the pope's three authoritative doctrinal pronouncements: on the direct and voluntary killing of innocent human life (cf. §57.4), on abortion (cf. §62.3), and on euthanasia (cf. §65.3). In each of these formal statements John Paul recalls, through his ordinary magisterium, that a specific proposition is taught infallibly by the ordinary and universal Magisterium of the College of Bishops in communion with the Successor of Peter. He does not, therefore, call upon the charism which belongs to the Petrine ministry to teach infallibly, as this was defined at the First Vatican Council (1870). Rather, the pope "confirms" or "declares" (as in the case of abortion) a doctrine already taught by the bishops as belonging to the Catholic faith. Thus, there is nothing "new" in the Pope's affirmations, but merely the reiteration of teaching about which a consensus exists in the Episcopal College.

Footnotes: [1] *Acta Apostolicae Sedis,* 87 (1995), 401-522.

CATHOLIC SOCIAL DOCTRINE

Nature of the Doctrine

Writing in *Christianity and Social Progress*, Pope John XXIII made the following statement about the nature and scope of the Church's social doctrine as stated in the encyclicals in particular and related writings in general:

"What the Catholic Church teaches and declares regarding the social life and relationships of men is beyond question for all time valid.

"The cardinal point of this teaching is that individual men are necessarily the foundation, cause, and end of all social institutions insofar as they are social by nature, and raised to an order of existence that transcends and subdues nature.

"Beginning with this very basic principle whereby the dignity of the human person is affirmed and defended, Holy Church — especially during the last century and with the assistance of learned priests and laymen, specialists in the field — has arrived at clear social teachings whereby the mutual relationships of men are ordered. Taking general norms into account, these principles are in accord with the nature of things and the changed conditions of man's social life, or with the special genius of our day. Moreover, these norms can be approved by all."

Background

While social concerns have always been a part of the Church's teachings, Catholic social doctrine has been the subject of much consideration since the end of the last century and has been formulated in a progressive manner in a number of authoritative documents starting with the encyclical *Rerum Novarum* ("On Capital and Labor") issued by Leo XIII in 1891. Owing to its significance, the encyclical was called by Pope John XXIII the *magna carta* of Catholic social doctrine.

Other outstanding examples are the encyclicals: *Quadragesimo Anno* ("On Reconstruction of the Social Order") by Pius XI in 1931; *Mater et Magistra* ("Christianity and Social Progress") and *Pacem in Terris* ("Peace on Earth"), by John XXIII in 1961 and 1963, respectively; *Populorum Progressio* ("Development of Peoples"), by Paul VI in 1967; *Laborem Exercens* ("On Human Work"), *Sollicitudo Rei Socialis* ("On Social Concerns") and *Centesimus Annus* ("The 100th Year") by John Paul II in 1981, 1987 and 1991, respectively. Among many other accomplishments of ideological importance in the social field, Pius XII made a distinctive contribution with his formulation of a plan for world peace and order in Christmas messages from 1939 to 1941, and in other documents.

Of particular significance to the contemporary application of social doctrine are the document *Gaudium et Spes* (Pastoral Constitution on the Church in the Modern World) issued by the Second Vatican Council and Pope John Paul II's encyclical letters, *Laborem Exercens* ("On Human Work"), *Sollicitudo Rei Socialis* ("On Social Concerns"), and *Centesimus Annus* ("The 100th Year").

These documents represent the most serious attempts in modern times to systematize the social implications of divine revelation as well as the socially relevant writings of the Fathers and Doctors of the Church. Their contents are theological penetrations into social life, with particular reference to human rights, the needs of the poor and those in underdeveloped countries, and humane conditions of life, freedom, justice and peace. In some respects, they read like juridical documents; essentially, however, they are Gospel-oriented and pastoral in intention.

Gaudium et Spes

Gaudium et Spes ("Pastoral Constitution on the Church in the Modern World") was the last document issued by Vatican Council II (Dec. 7, 1965). The document has as its purpose to search out the signs of God's presence and meaning in and through the events of this time in human history. Accordingly, it deals with the situation of men in present circumstances of profound change, challenge and crisis on all levels of life. It is evenly divided into two main parts: the Church's teaching on humanity in the modern era and urgent problems of the times.

Part One

The first part begins: "The joys and the hopes, the griefs and the anxieties of this age" (No. 1) — a clear indication that the Council Fathers were aware both of the positive nature of the modern world and its many dangers and travails. Further, the council places great emphasis throughout on the human existence, a stress that was quite innovative in its presentation: "According to the almost unanimous opinion of believers and unbelievers alike, all things on earth should be related to man as their center and crown" (No. 12). Having developed an analysis of humanity, the document then offered a thorough summary of traditional Church teaching on human life, complete with discussion of sin, the union of body and soul, and the moral conscience.

There is, as well, a genuinely realistic appraisal of contemporary society, noting the pervasiveness of atheism, adding that its spread can be attributed in part to the fault and carelessness of those within the Church whose actions and failures "must be said to conceal rather than reveal the authentic face of God and religion" (No. 19). Toward the fuller understanding of the place of the Church in the modern world, *Gaudium et Spes* emphasizes the harmony that should exist between the Catholic faith and scientific progress because "earthly matters and the concerns of faith derive from the same God" (No. 36). This does not mean, however, that there ought to be no qualifying elements or restraints to science; the Council Fathers add to this positive statement the provision that such research, "within every branch of learning," must be "carried out in a genuinely scientific manner and in accord with moral norms" (No. 36). Finally, the first part makes an ecumenical gesture, noting that the Church "holds in high esteem the things which other Christian Churches or ecclesial communities have done…" (No. 40).

Part Two

Part Two offers the practical application of the Church's teaching and message enunciated in Part One. Most pressing is the council's concern for the family, and its treatment of family life and marriage is the most detailed and extensive in the history of the councils of the Church. This leads to study of the deeply troubling presence of contraception. The council reiterates Church instruction in an affirmation of opposition to contraception that would receive even fuller expression in three years in the encyclical *Humanae Vitae*. In the matter of abortion, the document states clearly: "… from the moment of its conception life must be guarded with the greatest care, while abortion and infanticide are unspeakable crimes" (No. 51). In its study of culture, in which the council reminds all humanity that culture and civilization are creations of man, it points out his responsibility for work and his duty to seek that which is above, which entails an "obligation to work with all men in constructing a more human world" (No. 57). Here we have a powerful preface or introduction to the next concerns voiced in *Gaudium et Spes*: the questions of economic life, political systems, and war. In building upon earlier social encyclicals, *Gaudium et Spes* discusses economics as vital to human progress and social development, striking the important balance (developed so masterfully in the later writings of Pope John Paul II) between the rights of an individual to possess goods and the obligation to aid the poor (Nos. 63-72). While declaring the autonomous and independent nature of the Church and politics, the Council Fathers do acknowledge: "There are, indeed, close links between earthly affairs and those aspects of man's condition which transcend this world. The Church herself employs the things of time to the degree that her own proper mission demands" (No. 76). The document goes on to state that "the arms race is an utterly treacherous trap for humanity" (No. 81) and "It is our clear duty, then, to strain every muscle as we work for the time when all war can be completely outlawed by international consent" (No. 82).

SOCIAL DOCTRINE UNDER POPE JOHN PAUL II

Throughout his pontificate, Pope John Paul II has traveled the globe speaking out on all matters of the Church's social teachings and has written a number of important encyclicals that are reflective not only of the Church's traditions of social doctrine but that seek to utilize the teachings of the faith to offer specific points of reflection and solutions to the many pressing problems of the late 20th century. Rooted in Christian anthropology and Tradition, Scripture, and Magisterium, John Paul's writings have encompassed economic ethics, the rights and dignity of the worker, the primacy of the human person, the place of the family in society and the Church, and the integrative teachings of the Church in the areas of moral and pastoral theology. The three main expressions of his social teachings have been the encyclicals: *Laborem Exercens* (1981); *Sollicitudo Rei Socialis* (1987); and *Centesimus Annus* (1991).

SOCIAL ENCYCLICALS OF POPE JOHN PAUL II AND POPE BENEDICT XVI

The following material on the encyclicals of John Paul II is adapted from The Encyclicals of John Paul II, *with the kind permission of the Most Rev. J. Michael Miller, C.S.B.*

Laborem Exercens

Fascinated as he is by commemorative events, Pope John Paul II marked the ninetieth anniversary of Leo XIII's *Rerum Novarum* (1891) by publishing his first social encyclical, *Laborem Exercens*, on Sept. 14, 1981.[1] Before

him, Pius XI in *Quadragesimo Anno* (1931), John XXIII in *Mater et Magistra* (1961), and Paul VI in *Octogesima Adveniens* (1971) had observed the anniversary of Leo's ground-breaking encyclical with documents of their own.

Laborem Exercens is a very personal document. The encyclical has solid roots in the pope's own experience as a worker. It reflects his familiarity with various worlds of work: in mines and factories, in artistic and literary production, in scholarship and pastoral ministry. More particularly, *Laborem Exercens* has its origins in the long debate carried on by the Archbishop of Kracow with Marxist intellectuals. The topics chosen, which include the struggle between capital and labor, ownership of the means of production, and solidarity, as well as the terminology of the encyclical, bear ample witness to this background of controversy. Here, however, he is less concerned with economic systems than with the human person as a "worker." Furthermore, John Paul intended his letter to encourage the Solidarity union movement, which in the early 1980s was the primary motor for effecting social and political change in a Poland under a totalitarian regime.

The style of encyclical is distinctively Wojtylan. It reveals the pope's preference for combining a phenomenological description of experience with philosophical-theological meditation. While he cites the Second Vatican Council's *Gaudium et Spes*, John Paul never directly quotes from any previous social encyclical, not even from *Rerum Novarum*. The encyclical's footnotes are almost entirely biblical, indicating that its primary inspiration is Sacred Scripture. As in his two previous encyclicals, *Redemptor Hominis* (1979) and *Dives in Misericordia* (1980), the pope relies heavily upon the plastic and descriptive language of the Bible, especially from the opening chapters of Genesis, to develop his theme. The encyclical unfolds the meaning of the human vocation to work in light of the biblical text on "subduing the earth" (cf. Gn 1:28). This call to exercise dominion is to be carried out by those created "in the image of God" (Gn 1:27) through their work, which the pope qualifies as *"one of the characteristics that distinguish* man *from the rest of creatures"* (preface).

Unlike earlier social encyclicals which dealt with a wide range of different questions, *Laborem Exercens* is sharply focused. John Paul chooses a very specific theme — the dignity and role of human work — and explores its many ramifications: "Through work man must earn his daily bread and contribute to the continual advance of science and technology and, above all, to elevating unceasingly the cultural and moral level of the society within which he lives in community with those who belong to the same family" (preface). At the present moment, he believes, the world is faced with important choices. It is "on the eve of new developments in technological, economic, and political conditions which, according to many experts, will influence the world of work and production no less than the industrial revolution of the last century" (§1.3).

A crisis in the meaning of human work is a crucial factor contributing to society's current plight. "Work, as human issue, is at the very center of the 'social question'" (§2.1). Moreover, the pope adds, "human work is *a key*, probably *the essential key*, to the whole social question" (§3.2). It is a problem with ramifications which extend beyond the so-called "working class"; the dimensions of the crisis are universal. Therefore he does not confine his encyclical to a reflection on the work only of industrial or agricultural workers. Instead, he extends it to encompass the work done by every sector of society: management, white-collar workers, scientists, intellectuals, artists, women in the home. "Each and every individual, to the proper extent and in an incalculable number of ways, takes part in the giant process whereby man 'subdues the earth' through his work" (§4.4). To use a favorite expression of the pope's, the world's "workbench" includes all those who labor for their daily bread — all men and women.

As in his two previous encyclicals, John Paul takes up the "way" of the human person, this time with regard to his fundamental activity of work. *Laborem Exercens* is yet another chapter in the pope's book on Christian anthropology. Moreover, since work is a great gift and good for humanity, his tone throughout the encyclical is constructive and exhortatory.

Footnote
1. *Acta Apostolicae Sedis*, 73 (1981), 577-647.

Sollicitudo Rei Socialis

Although signed on Dec. 30, 1987, Pope John Paul II's encyclical "on social concern" was not officially published until Feb. 19, 1988.[1] Like *Laborem Exercens* (1981), this second social encyclical commemorates a previous papal document. *Sollicitudo Rei Socialis* marks the twentieth anniversary of Paul VI's *Populorum Progressio* (1967). But more than merely recalling the relevance and doctrine of Pope Paul's encyclical, it highlights new themes and responds to the problems of development in the Third World which had emerged in the intervening 20 years.

John Paul writes as a teacher, explaining why the proclamation of the Church's social doctrine belongs to her evangelizing mission. He also writes as an informed witness to the increasing injustice and poverty in the world. Lastly, he writes as a defender of human dignity and inalienable rights, and of every person's transcendent vocation to communion with the Triune God.

In some ways *Sollicitudo Rei Socialis* echoes *Laborem Exercens* (1981). John Paul's use of Sacred Scripture, for example, is similar in that he frequently quotes from the opening chapters of Genesis. The differences between the two social encyclicals, however, are noteworthy. Whereas in *Laborem Exercens* (1981) the pope never directly cites *Rerum Novarum* (1891), the encyclical of Leo XIII which it commemorates, throughout *Sollicitudo Rei Socialis* John Paul quotes or refers to *Populorum Progressio* more than forty times. It is his constant point of reference. Second, to support his presentation, the pope marshals statements taken from earlier writings and discourses of his own pontificate, as well as the social teaching of the Second Vatican Council expressed in *Gaudium et Spes*. Third, more than in any other encyclical, John Paul makes use of documents published by the Roman Curia. Especially notable are his six references to the *Instruction on Christian Freedom and Liberation* (1986) issued by the Congregation for the Doctrine of the Faith. He also cites two publications of the Pontifical Commission "Iustitia et Pax": *At the Service of the Human Community: An Ethical Approach to the International Debt Question* (1986) and *The Church and the Housing Problem* (1987).

While *Sollicitudo Rei Socialis* perceptively analyzes the economic, political, social, and cultural dimensions of world development, its perspective is primarily ethical and theological. John Paul rereads *Populorum Progressio* through a moral-spiritual lens. His main concern is to form the consciences of individual men and women, to help them

in their task of promoting authentic development "in the light of faith and of the Church's Tradition" (§41.7).

Footnote
1. *Acta Apostolicae Sedis*, 80 (1988), 513-586.

Centesimus Annus

Pope John Paul II issued his ninth encyclical, *Centesimus Annus*, on May 1, 1991.[1] Not surprisingly, the pope chose to mark the centenary of Leo XIII's *Rerum Novarum* (1891) with a document of his own. In the four years since the signing of *Sollicitudo Rei Socialis* (1987) the Berlin Wall had collapsed, and in the light of this event John Paul offers his "rereading" of *Rerum Novarum*. His purpose is twofold. He wishes to recall Leo's contribution to the development of the Church's social teaching and to honor the popes who drew upon the encyclical's "vital energies" in their social teaching.

Centesimus Annus has some interesting peculiarities. First, among all John Paul's encyclicals, it relies the least on citing Sacred Scripture. Its few biblical references are primarily exhortatory or illustrative. For his sources the pope depends mostly on *Rerum Novarum* and on the social encyclicals of his predecessors, as well as on earlier documents and discourses of his own Magisterium. Second, much of the encyclical's content is conditioned by current geopolitical affairs. Indeed, the encyclical reads as if the pope had *Rerum Novarum* in one hand and a diary of the 1989 events sweeping eastern Europe in the other.

Despite the opinions of some commentators, John Paul's primary interest is not to pass judgment on either failed socialism or contemporary capitalism. Above all, in keeping with his desire to articulate a Christian anthropology, he recalls the need for Catholic social doctrine to have a *"correct view of the human person* and of his unique value" (§11.3). Without such a view, he believes, it is impossible to solve today's social, economic, and political problems. The Church's distinctive contribution to meeting these challenges is her vision of the transcendent dignity of the human person created in God's image and redeemed by Christ's blood.

The pope's rereading of Leo XIII encompasses three time frames: "looking back" at *Rerum Novarum* itself, "looking around" at the contemporary situation, and "looking to the future" (§3.1). In looking back, John Paul confirms the enduring principles of Leo's encyclical, principles that belong to the Church's doctrinal inheritance. His "pastoral solicitude" also impels the pope to analyze recent political events from the perspective of the Gospel "in order to discern the new requirements of evangelization" (§3.5).

Even more clearly than in his two previous social encyclicals, *Laborem Exercens* (1981) and *Sollicitudo Rei Socialis* (1987), John Paul clearly distinguishes the authentic doctrine contained in the Church's social teaching from the analysis of contingent historical events. This analysis, he states, "is not meant to pass definitive judgments, since this does not fall *per se* within the Magisterium's specific domain" (§3.5). Whatever comes within the doctrinal sphere, however, "pertains to the Church's evangelizing mission and is an essential part of the Christian message" (§5.5).

Footnote
Acta Apostolicae Sedis, 83 (1991), 793-867.

Caritas in Veritate

On July 7, 2009, Pope Benedict XVI issued the third encyclical since his election in 2005 and his first social encyclical, *Caritas in Veritate* (Love in Truth). Within hours of its publication, media outlets and pundits weighed in with their own interpretations of what the Holy Father had written or what they thought the pontiff really meant to say. Some saw in the encyclical a rejection of capitalism, others a call for a one-world government to regulate corporations. Still others saw a demand for the environment to become the main priority for the Church's theologians. There is always a tendency to impose upon a major papal document what we want to see in it, but through a proper understanding of Pope Benedict and the goals he has set for the Church, it is possible to appreciate his true hopes for *Caritas in Veritate*.

Pope Benedict chose for his third encyclical a concern for the Church that is very much in tune with the "signs of the times." In the face of a global financial meltdown, the pope reiterates Catholic social teaching and then makes even more manifest the essential links between truth, the moral good, and the real world. As he writes, "Each person finds his good by adherence to God's plan for him, in order to realize it fully: in this plan, he finds truth, and through adherence to this truth he becomes free" (CV, Introduction). The love of truth is symphonic in the way that the pontiff makes a direct link between scientific and technological progress with the imposition of a culture of death on the developing world. The encyclical, of course, does not propose technical solutions to the vast social problems of the contemporary world as these lie outside the competence of the Magisterium of the Church. Still, it offers principles that are crucial to building human development, if the world has the wisdom to listen.

The foundation for this remarkable project is Benedict's wider concern about applying the social teachings of the Church. For some years, there has been a tendency by some theologians to think that there are two functional and rival approaches in Catholic social doctrine, one rooted in the time before the Second Vatican Council and a better one that came afterward. For Benedict, Catholics must have a commitment to continuity in Church teachings. There is only one Catholic social teaching – not two – and to make his point, he quotes from every social encyclical since Leo XIII's *Rerum Novarum* in 1891 and quotes Pope John Paul II that "there is a single teaching, consistent and at the same time ever new" (*Sollicitudo Rei Socialis*, 3). This permits Benedict to pull together the whole framework of Catholic social thought, especially its pillars of the defense of human dignity, of solidarity, and of subsidiarity as they apply to human development.

The encyclical does not merely repeat the thought of previous popes. Rather, the pontiff builds on the legacy of his predecesssors and applies the timeless teachings of the Church in a timely way. Even as he restates traditional Catholic social thought, the pontiff makes several significant innovations, such as the link between the culture of life and human development and the connection between justice and concern for the environment.

The world situation of today, the pope declares, is clearly one of increasing globalization, a shrinking of the earth in the face of advances of communication, travel, and technology. This is an opportunity for the whole global community, but it brings with it grave social and economic imbalances that can be remedied only by genuine reform and moral and cultural renewal. Business decisions and finance cannot be separated from the priority of the human person. Here continuity again becomes crucial. Where Pope John XXIII stressed peace in his 1958 social encyclical *Pacem in Terris*, and Pope Paul VI urged justice in his 1967 social encyclical *Populorum Progressio*, Pope Benedict ties them to the defense of human life in every form.

The encyclical makes the link "between life ethics and social ethics" (No. 15), especially in its tribute to the late Pope Paul VI's prophetic encyclicals *Populorum Progressio* and *Humanae Vitae* (1968). In *Populorum Progressio*, Paul VI anticipated the problems that have attended globalization, and in *Humanae Vitae*, he predicted with searing accuracy the long-term social effects of a contraceptive culture. Reflecting on both of these earlier documents, *Caritas in Veritate* proclaims that true development must encompass the rights of all human persons, including the unborn. The Holy Father notes that economic development and humanitarian aid from the West are too often accompanied by the imposition of dehumanizing programs and exploitation of labor and natural resources, but they can also entail an obligation to embrace of the culture of death through the same toxic reproductive and technological policies that are eroding the social fabric of the first world. Benedict XVI argues that not only do abortion, contraception, and euthanasia inherently trample upon the dignity of the human person and responsible human freedom, they are bad economics because of the strains they places on social welfare systems and labor resources, not to mention the wider impoverishment of culture. The Pope writes, "Openness to life is at the center of true development. When a society moves toward the denial or suppression of life, it ends up no longer finding the necessary motivation and energy to strive for man's true good" (No. 28). There is also a practical economic advantage to this openness. Populous nations are able to emerge from poverty in part because of the talents of their people, while one-time prosperous nations that are plagued by falling birth rates witness strains on social welfare systems, increased costs, and dwindling "brain pool."

Human development, most so in light of globalization, is a reminder that we are deeply and innately connected to each other. Pope Benedict describes this reality when he calls upon all people to remember that "the development of peoples depends above all on a recognition that the human race is a single family." The decisions that are made in board rooms in the first world have a direct impact upon the lives and the destinies of men, women, and children in far flung corners of the earth. By thinking and acting in solidarity with the poor, the helpless, and the developing parts of the world, we will be able to embrace "the interconnection between the impetus toward the unification of humanity and the Christian ideal of a single family of peoples in solidarity and fraternity" (No. 13).

The Pope also examines the principle of subsidiarity, the idea that the most people can be helped when functions of government are handled at a more immediate or local level. A key teaching in Catholic social thought, subsidiarity rejects the dangers of the vast social welfare state in favor of a real development that does not lose focus on the human person. There are those who claimed that the encyclical condemned capitalism and called for a socialist model for global economic management. Such claims were made falsely about Pope John Paul II's encyclical *Centessimus Annus*, and they were just as erroneous regarding *Caritas in Veritate*. Benedict calls for proper government intervention in the economy when needed, but he also demands a thorough reform of the United Nations and the "economic institutions and international finance."

Likewise, the connection between the development of people and the environment has long-term consequences for everyone. Nature is a gift from God that signifies "a design of love and truth" (No. 48), meaning that humanity has an obligation to use it responsibly. That entails the proper use of energy resources and with a sense of solidarity that reflects the vision of a human family. Technologically advanced societies must find ways to reduce their energy consumption, encourage new and alternative forms of energy, and assist developing societies with their own energy needs. The imperative is to establish decisively what the pontiff terms "the overall moral tenor of society," and the environment is related to the culture of life. The pope writes, "The book of nature is one and indivisible: it takes in not only the environment but also life, sexuality, marriage, the family, social relations: in a word, integral human development. Our duties toward the environment are linked to our duties toward the human person, considered in himself and in relation to others. It would be wrong to uphold one set of duties while trampling on the other" (No. 51). While a complicated and lengthy document, the pope's social encyclical is a welcome opportunity to meditate in a new way on the priorities of the current pontificate. The Holy Father is not proposing some supposed middle way between capitalism and socialism. In restating eloquently the clear development of Catholic social teachings from *Rerum Novarum* in 1891 to *Quadragesimo Anno* in 1940, to *Populorum Progressio*, and then to *Sollicitudo Rei Socialis* in 1987 and *Centessimus Annus*, Pope Benedict is reminding the world that the Church offers only one Way: Christ, who is the Way, the Truth, and the Life.

SOCIO-ECONOMIC STATEMENTS BY U.S. BISHOPS

Over a period of nearly 80 years, the bishops of the United States have issued a great number of socio-economic statements reflecting papal documents in a U.S. context.

One such statement, entitled "Economic Justice for All: Social Teaching and the U.S. Economy" was issued in November, 1986. Its contents are related in various ways with the subsequently issued encyclical letter, *Centesimus Annus*. Principles drawn from the bishops' document are given in the following excerpt entitled "A Catholic Framework for Economic Life." Another significant statement, entitled "The Harvest of Justice Is Sown in Peace" (1993) follows.

A Catholic Framework for Economic Life

As followers of Jesus Christ and participants in a powerful economy, Catholics in the United States, are called to work for greater economic justice in the face of persistent poverty, growing income gaps and increasing discussion of economic issues in the United States and around the world. We urge Catholics to use the following ethical framework for economic life as principles for reflection, criteria for judgment and directions for action. These principles are drawn directly from Catholic teaching on economic life.

1. The economy exists for the person, not the person for the economy.

2. All economic life should be shaped by moral principles. Economic choices and institutions must be judged by how they protect or undermine the life and dignity of the human person, support the family and serve the common good.

3. A fundamental moral measure of an economy is how the poor and vulnerable are faring.

4. All people have a right to life and to secure the basic necessities of life (e.g., food, clothing, shelter, education, health care, safe environment, economic security).

5. All people have the right to economic initiative, to productive work, to just wages and benefits, to decent working conditions as well as to organize and join unions or other associations.

6. All people, to the extent they are able, have a corresponding duty to work, a responsibility to provide for the needs of their families and an obligation to contribute to the broader society.

7. In economic life, free markets have both clear advantages and limits; government has essential responsibilities and limitations; voluntary groups have irreplaceable roles, but cannot substitute for the proper working of the market and the just policies of the state.

8. Society has a moral obligation, including governmental action where necessary, to assure opportunity, meet basic human needs and pursue justice in economic life.

9. Workers, owners, managers, stockholders and consumers are moral agents in economic life. By our choices, initiative, creativity and investment, we enhance or diminish economic opportunity, community life and social justice.

10. The global economy has moral dimensions and human consequences. Decisions on investment, trade, aid and development should protect human life and promote human rights, especially for those most in need wherever they might live on this globe.

The Harvest of Justice Is Sown in Peace

The National Conference of Catholic Bishops, at a meeting Nov. 17, 1993, issued a statement entitled "The Harvest of Justice Is Sown in Peace," marking the 10th anniversary of their earlier pastoral letter, "The Challenge of Peace: God's Promise and Our Response."

The Challenge of Peace

"The challenge of peace today is different, but no less urgent" than in 1983, and the threat of global nuclear war "may seem more remote than at any time in the nuclear age." Questions of peace and war, however, cannot be addressed "without acknowledging that the nuclear question remains of vital political and moral significance."

The statement outlines an agenda for action to guide future advocacy efforts of the bishops' national conference. It also urges that the cause of peace be reflected constantly in liturgical prayers of petition, preaching and Catholic education at all levels.

Confronting the temptation to isolationism in U.S. foreign policy is among "the major challenges peacemakers face in this new era."

Factors in a vision for peace include a commitment to the universal common good and recognition of the imperative of human solidarity.

Nonviolent revolutions in some countries "challenge us to find ways to take into full account the power of organized, active nonviolence."

With respect to just war criteria, the statement says that "important work needs to be done in refining, clarifying and applying the just war tradition to the choices facing our decision-makers in this still violent and dangerous world."

Subjects of concern include humanitarian intervention, deterrence, conscientious objection and the development of peoples.

Presumption against Force

"Our conference's approach, as outlined in 'The Challenge of Peace,' can be summarized in this way:

"1) In situations of conflict our constant commitment ought to be, as far as possible, to strive for justice through nonviolent means.

"2) But when sustained attempts at nonviolent action fail to protect the innocent against fundamental injustice, then legitimate political authorities are permitted as a last resort to employ limited force to rescue the innocent and establish justice."

Lethal Force

"Whether lethal force may be used is governed by the following criteria:

• "Just cause: Force may be used only to correct a grave, public evil, i.e., aggression or massive violation of the basic rights of whole populations.

• "Comparative justice: While there may be rights and wrongs on all sides of a conflict, to override the presumption against the use of force, the injustice suffered by one party must significantly outweigh that suffered by the other.

• "Legitimate authority: Only duly constituted public authorities may use deadly force or wage war.

• "Right intention: Force may be used only in a truly just cause and solely for that purpose.

• "Probability of Success: Arms may not be used in a futile cause or in a case where disproportionate measures are required to achieve success.

• "Proportionality: The overall destruction expected from the use of force must be outweighed by the good to be achieved.

• "Last Resort: Force may be used only after all peaceful alternatives have been seriously tried and exhausted.

"These criteria [of just war], taken as a whole, must be satisfied in order to override the strong presumption against the use of force."

Just War

"The just-war tradition seeks also to curb the violence of war through restraint on armed combat between the contending parties by imposing the following moral standards for the conduct of armed conflict:

• "Noncombatant Immunity: Civilians may not be the object of direct attack, and military personnel must take due care to avoid and minimize indirect harm to civilians

• "Proportionality: In the conduct of hostilities, efforts must be made to attain military objectives with no more force than is militarily necessary and to avoid disproportionate collateral damage to civilian life and property.

• "Right Intention: Even in the midst of conflict, the aim of political and military leaders must be peace with justice so that acts of vengeance and indiscriminate violence, whether by individuals, military units or governments, are forbidden."

Structures for Justice and Peace

Quoting an address given by Pope John Paul in Aug. 1993 in Denver, the statement said:

" 'The international community ought to establish more effective structures for maintaining and promoting justice and peace. This implies that a concept of strategic interest should evolve which is based on the full development of peoples – out of poverty and toward a more dignified existence, out of injustice and exploitation toward fuller respect for the human person and the defense of universal rights.'

"As we consider a new vision of the international community, five areas deserve special attention: (1) strengthening global institutions; (2) securing human rights; (3) promoting human development; (4) restraining nationalism and eliminating religious violence; and (5) building cooperative security."

Humanitarian Intervention

"Pope John Paul, citing the 'conscience of humanity and international humanitarian law,' has been outspoken in urging that 'humanitarian intervention be obligatory where the survival of populations and entire ethnic groups is seriously compromised. This is a duty for nations and the international community.' He elaborated on this right and duty of humanitarian intervention in his 1993 annual address to the diplomatic corps (accredited to the Holy See): " 'Once the possibilities afforded by diplomatic negotiations and the procedures provided for by international agreements and organizations have been put into effect, and that [sic], nevertheless, populations are succumbing to the attacks of an unjust aggressor, states no longer have a 'right to indifference.' It seems clear that their duty is to disarm this aggressor if all other means have proved ineffective. The principles of the sovereignty of states and of noninterference in their internal affairs — which retain all their value — cannot constitute a screen behind which torture and murder may be carried out.'"

THE BLESSED VIRGIN MARY

ROLE OF MARY IN THE MYSTERY OF CHRIST AND THE CHURCH

The following excerpts are from Chapter VIII of the Second Vatican Council's "Constitution on the Church," Lumen Gentium.

Preface

Wishing in his supreme goodness and wisdom to effect the redemption of the world, "when the fullness of time came, God sent his Son, born of a woman, that we might receive the adoption of sons" (Gal 4:4-5). "He for us men and for our salvation, came down from heaven, and was incarnate by the Holy Spirit from the Virgin Mary." This divine mystery of salvation is revealed to us and continued in the Church, which the Lord established as his own body. In this Church, adhering to Christ the head and having communion with all his saints, the faithful must also venerate the memory "above all of the glorious and perpetual Virgin Mary. Mother of our God and Lord Jesus Christ." (52)

At the message of the angel, the Virgin Mary received the Word of God in her heart and in her body, and gave Life to the world. Hence, she is acknowledged and honored as being truly the Mother of God and Mother of the Redeemer. Redeemed in an especially sublime manner by reason of the merits of her Son, and united to him by a close and indissoluble tie, she is endowed with the supreme office and dignity of being the Mother of the

Son of God. As a result, she is also the favorite daughter of the Father and the temple of the Holy Spirit. Because of this gift of sublime grace, she far surpasses all other creatures, both in heaven and on earth.

At the same time, however, because she belongs to the offspring of Adam, she is one with all human beings in their need for salvation. Indeed, she is "clearly the Mother of the members of Christ since she cooperated out of love so that there might be born in the Church the faithful, who are members of Christ their head. Therefore, she is also hailed as a pre-eminent and altogether singular member of the Church, and as the Church's model and excellent exemplar in faith and charity. Taught by the Holy Spirit, the Catholic Church honors her with filial affection and piety as a most beloved Mother. (53)

This sacred synod intends to describe with diligence the role of the Blessed Virgin in the mystery of the Incarnate Word and the Mystical Body. It also wishes to describe the duties of redeemed mankind toward the Mother of God, who is the Mother of Christ and Mother of men, particularly of the faithful.

The synod does not, however, have it in mind to give a complete doctrine on Mary, nor does it wish to decide those questions which have not yet been fully illuminated by the work of theologians. (54)

II. The Role of the Blessed Virgin in the Economy of Salvation

The Father of mercies willed that the consent of the pre-destined Mother should precede the Incarnation so that, just as a woman contributed to death, so also a woman should contribute to life. This contrast was verified in outstanding fashion by the Mother of Jesus. She gave to the world that very Life which renews all things, and she was enriched by God with gifts befitting such a role.

It is no wonder, then, that the usage prevailed among the holy Fathers whereby they called the Mother of God entirely holy and free from all stain of sin, fashioned by the Holy Spirit into a kind of new substance and new creature. Adorned from the first instant of her conception with the splendors of an entirely unique holiness, the Virgin of Nazareth is, on God's command, greeted by an angel messenger as "full of grace" (cf. Lk 1:28). To the heavenly messenger she replies: "Behold the handmaid of the Lord; be it done to me according to thy word" (Lk 1:38).

By thus consenting to the divine utterance, Mary, a daughter of Adam, became the Mother of Jesus. Embracing God's saving will with a full heart and impeded by no sin, she devoted herself totally as a hand-maid of the Lord to the person and work of her Son. In subordination to him and along with him, by the grace of almighty God she served the mystery of redemption.

Rightly, therefore, the holy Fathers see her as used by God not merely in a passive way but as cooperating in the work of human salvation through free faith and obedience. (56)

This union of the Mother with the Son in the work of salvation was manifested from the time of Christ's virginal conception up to his death. It is shown first of all when Mary, arising in haste to go a major theological work for the 21st century that has had center stage since the mid-20th century to visit Elizabeth, was greeted by her as blessed because of her belief in the promise of salvation, while the precursor leaped for joy in the womb of his mother (cf. Lk 1:41-45). This association was shown

also at the birth of our Lord, who did not diminish his Mother's virginal integrity but sanctified it, when the Mother of God joyfully showed her first-born Son to the shepherds and the Magi.

When she presented him to the Lord in the Temple, making the offering of the poor, she heard Simeon fore-telling at the same time that her Son would be a sign of contradiction and that a sword would pierce the Mother's soul, that out of many hearts thoughts might be revealed (cf. Lk 2:34-35). When the Child Jesus was lost and they had sought him sorrowing, his parents found him in the temple, taken up with things which were his Father's business. They did not understand the reply of the Son. But his Mother, to be sure, kept all these things to be pondered over in her heart (cf. Lk 2:41-51). (57)

In the public life of Jesus, Mary made significant appearances. This was so even at the very beginning, when she was moved with pity at the marriage feast of Cana, and her intercession brought about the beginning of the miracles by Jesus the Messiah (Cf. Jn 2:1-11). In the course of her Son's preaching, she received his praise when, in extolling a kingdom beyond the calculations and bonds of flesh and blood, he declared blessed (cf. Mk 3:35 par.; Lk 11:27-28) those who heard and kept the word of the Lord as she was faithfully doing (cf. Lk 2:19,51).

Thus, the Blessed Virgin advanced in her pilgrimage of faith and loyally persevered in her union with her Son unto the cross. There she stood, in keeping with the divine plan (cf. Jn 19:25), suffering grievously with her only-begotten Son. There she united herself with a maternal heart to his sacrifice, and lovingly consented to the immolation of this Victim whom she herself had brought forth. Finally, the same Christ Jesus dying on the cross gave her as a mother to his disciple. This he did when he said: "Woman, behold your son" (Jn 19:26-27). (58)

But since it pleased God not to manifest solemnly the mystery of the salvation of the human race until he poured forth the Spirit promised by Christ, we see the apostles before the day of Pentecost "continuing with one mind in prayer with the women and Mary, the Mother of Jesus, and with his brethren" (Acts 1:14). We see Mary prayerfully imploring the gift of the Spirit, who had already overshadowed her in the Annunciation.

Finally, preserved free from all guilt of original sin, the Immaculate Virgin was taken up body and soul into heavenly glory upon the completion of her earthly sojourn. She was exalted by the Lord as Queen of all, in order that she might be the more thoroughly conformed to her Son, the Lord of lords (cf. Rv 19:16) and the conqueror of sin and death. (59)

III. The Blessed Virgin and the Church

We have but one Mediator, as we know from the words of the Apostle: "For there is one God, and one Mediator between God and men, himself man, Christ Jesus, who gave himself as a ransom for all" (1 Tm 2:5-6). The maternal duty of Mary toward men in no way obscures or diminishes this unique mediation of Christ, but rather shows its power. For all the saving influences of the Blessed Virgin on men originate, not from some inner necessity, but from the divine pleasure. They flow forth from the superabundance of the merits of Christ, rest on his mediation, depend entirely on it, and draw all their power from it. In no way do they impede the immediate union of the faithful with Christ. Rather, they foster this union. (60)

In an utterly singular way, she (Mary) cooperated by her obedience, faith, hope and burning charity in the Savior's work of restoring supernatural life to souls. For this reason she is a mother to us in the order of grace. (61)

This maternity of Mary in the order of grace began with the consent which she gave in faith at the Annunciation and which she sustained without wavering beneath the cross. This maternity will last without interruption until the eternal fulfillment of all the elect. For, taken up to heaven, she did not lay aside this saving role, but by her manifold acts of intercession continues to win for us gifts of eternal salvation.

By her maternal charity, Mary cares for the brethren of her Son who still journey on earth surrounded by dangers and difficulties until they are led to their happy fatherland. Therefore, the Blessed Virgin is invoked by the Church under the titles of Advocate, Auxiliatrix, Adjutrix and Mediatrix. These, however, are to be so understood that they neither take away nor add anything to the dignity and efficacy of Christ the one Mediator.

For no creature could ever be classed with the Incarnate Word and Redeemer. But, just as the priesthood of Christ is shared in various ways both by sacred ministers and by the faithful; and as the one goodness of God is in reality communicated diversely to his creatures: so also the unique mediation of the Redeemer does not exclude but rather gives rise among creatures to a manifold cooperation which is but a sharing in this unique source.

The Church does not hesitate to profess this subordinate role of Mary. She experiences it continuously and commends it to the hearts of the faithful so that, encouraged by this maternal help, they may more closely adhere to the Mediator and Redeemer. (62)

Through the gift and role of divine maternity, Mary is united with her Son, the Redeemer, and with his singular graces and offices. By these, the Blessed Virgin is also intimately united with the Church. As St. Ambrose taught, the Mother of God is a model of the Church in the matter of faith, hope and charity, and perfect union with Christ. For in the mystery of the Church, herself rightly called Mother and Virgin, the Blessed Virgin stands out in eminent and singular fashion as exemplar of both virginity and motherhood. (63)

In the most holy Virgin, the Church has already reached that perfection whereby she exists without spot or wrinkle (cf. Eph 5:27). Yet, the followers of Christ still strive to increase in holiness by conquering sin. And so they raise their eyes to Mary who shines forth to the whole community of the elect as a model of the virtues. Devoutly meditating on her and contemplating her in the light of the Word made man, the Church with reverence enters more intimately into the supreme mystery of the Incarnation and becomes ever increasingly like her Spouse. (64)

The Church in her apostolic work looks to her who brought forth Christ, conceived by the Holy Spirit and born of the Virgin, so that through the Church Christ may be born and grow in the hearts of the faithful also. The Virgin Mary in her own life lived as an example of that maternal love by which all should be fittingly animated who cooperate in the apostolic mission of the Church on behalf of the rebirth of men. (65)

IV. Devotion to the Blessed Virgin in the Church

Mary was involved in the mystery of Christ. As the most holy Mother of God she was, after her Son, exalted by divine grace above all angels and men. Hence, the Church appropriately honors her with special reverence. Indeed, from most ancient times the Blessed Virgin has been venerated under the title of "God-bearer." In all perils and needs, the faithful; have fled prayerfully to her protection. Especially after the Council of Ephesus the cult of the people of God toward Mary wonderfully increased in veneration and love, in invocation and imitation, according to her own prophetic words: "All generations shall call me blessed; because he who is mighty has done great things for me" (Lk 1:48).

As it has always existed in the Church, this cult (of Mary) is altogether special, Still, it differs essentially from the cult of adoration which is offered to the Incarnate Word, as well as to the Father and the Holy Spirit. Yet, devotion to Mary is most favorable to this supreme cult. The Church has endorsed many forms of piety toward the Mother of God, provided that they were within the limits of sound and orthodox doctrine. These forms have varied according to the circumstances of time and place, and have reflected the diversity of native characteristics and temperament among the faithful. While honoring Christ's Mother, these devotions cause her Son to be rightly known, loved and glorified, and all his commands observed. Through him all things have their beginning (cf. Col 1:15-16) and in him "it has pleased (the eternal Father) that all his fullness should dwell" (Col 1:19). (66)

This most holy synod deliberately teaches this Catholic doctrine. At the same time, it admonishes all the sons of the Church that the cult, especially the liturgical cult, of the Blessed Virgin, be generously fostered. It charges that practices and exercises of devotion toward her be treasured as recommended by the teaching authority of the Church in the course of centuries.

This synod earnestly exhorts theologians and preachers of the divine word that, in treating of the unique dignity of the Mother of God, they carefully and equally avoid the falsity of exaggeration on the one hand and the excess of narrow-mindedness on the other.

Let the faithful remember, moreover, that true devotion consists neither in fruitless and passing emotion, nor in a certain vain credulity. Rather, it proceeds from the true faith, by which we are led to know the excellence of the Mother of God, and are moved to a filial love toward our Mother and to the imitation of her virtues. (67)

REDEMPTORIS MATER

Redemptoris Mater (*Mother of the Redeemer*), Pope John Paul II's sixth encyclical letter, is a "reflection on the role of Mary in the mystery of Christ and on her active and exemplary presence in the life of the Church." The letter was published Mar. 25, 1987.

Central to consideration of Mary is the fact that she is the Mother of God (*Theotokos*), since by the power of the Holy Spirit she conceived in her virginal womb and brought into the world Jesus Christ, the Son of God, who is of one being with the Father and the Holy Spirit.

Mary was preserved from original sin in view of her calling to be the Mother of Jesus. She was gifted in grace beyond measure. She fulfilled her role in a unique pilgrimage of faith. She is the Mother of the Church and the spiritual mother of all people.

The following excerpts are from the English text

provided by the Vatican and circulated by the CNS Documentary Service, *Origins*, Apr. 9, 1987 (Vol. 16, No. 43). Subheads have been added. Quotations are from pertinent documents of the Second Vatican Council.

Mary's Presence in the Church

Mary, through the same faith which made her blessed, especially from the moment of the Annunciation, is present in the Church's mission, present in the Church's work of introducing into the world the kingdom of her Son.

This presence of Mary finds as many different expressions in our day just as it did throughout the Church's history. It also has a wide field of action: through the faith and piety of individual believers; through the traditions of Christian families or "domestic churches," of parish and missionary communities, religious institutes and dioceses; through the radiance and attraction of the great shrines where not only individuals or local groups, but sometimes whole nations and societies, even whole continents, seek to meet the Mother of the Lord, the one who is blessed because she believed, is the first among believers, and therefore became the Mother of Emmanuel.

This is the message of the land of Palestine, the spiritual homeland of all Christians, because it was the homeland of the Savior of the world and of his Mother.

This is the message of the many churches in Rome and throughout the world which have been raised up in the course of the centuries by the faith of Christians. This is the message of centers like Guadalupe, Lourdes, Fátima and others situated in the various countries. Among them, how could I fail to mention the one in my own native land, Jasna Gora? One could perhaps speak of a specific "geography" of faith and Marian devotion which includes all of these special places of pilgrimage where the people of God seek to meet the Mother of God in order to find, within the radius of the maternal presence of her "who believed," a strengthening of their own faith.

Mary and Ecumenism

"In all of Christ's disciples the Spirit arouses the desire to be peacefully united, in the manner determined by Christ, as one flock under one shepherd." The journey of the Church, especially in our own time, is marked by the sign of ecumenism: Christians are seeking ways to restore that unity which Christ implored from the Father for his disciples on the day before his passion.

Christians must deepen in themselves and each of their communities that "obedience of faith" of which Mary is the first and brightest example.

Christians know that their unity will be truly rediscovered only if it is based on the unity of their faith. They must resolve considerable discrepancies of doctrine concerning the mystery and ministry of the Church, and sometimes also concerning the role of Mary in the work of salvation.

Mary, who is still the model of this pilgrimage, is to lead them to the unity which is willed by their one Lord, and which is so much desired by those who are attentively listening to what "the Spirit is saying to the churches" today.

A Hopeful Sign

Meanwhile, it is a hopeful sign that these churches and ecclesial communities are finding agreement with the Catholic Church on fundamental points of Christian belief, including matters relating to the Virgin Mary. For they recognize her as the Mother of the Lord and hold that this forms part of our faith in Christ, true God and true man. They look to her who at the foot of the cross accepted as her son the Beloved Disciple (John), the one who in his turn accepted her as his Mother.

On the other hand, I wish to emphasize how profoundly the Catholic Church, the Orthodox Church and the ancient churches of the East feel united by love and praise of the *Theotokos*. Not only "basic dogmas of the Christian faith concerning the Trinity and God's Word made flesh of the Virgin Mary were defined in ecumenical councils held in the East," but also in their liturgical worship "the Eastern Christians pay high tribute, in very beautiful hymns, to Mary ever-Virgin. God's most holy Mother."

The churches which profess the doctrine of Ephesus proclaim the Virgin as "true Mother of God" since "our Lord Jesus Christ, born of the Father before time began according to his divinity, in the last days he himself, for our sake and for our salvation, was begotten of Mary the Virgin Mother of God according to his humanity." The Greek Fathers and the Byzantine tradition, contemplating the Virgin in the light of the Word made flesh, have sought to penetrate the depth of that bond which unites Mary, as the Mother of God, to Christ and the Church. The Virgin is a permanent presence in the whole reality of the salvific mystery.

Marian Mediation

The Church knows and teaches with St. Paul that there is only one mediator: "For there is one God, and there is one mediator between God and men, the man Christ Jesus, who gave himself as a ransom for all" (1 Tm 2:5-6). "The maternal role of Mary toward people in no way obscures or diminishes the unique mediation of Christ, but rather shows its power." It is mediation in Christ.

The Church knows and teaches that "all the saving influences of the Blessed Virgin on mankind originate from the divine pleasure. They flow forth from the superabundance of the merits of Christ, rest on his mediation, depend entirely on it and draw all their power from it. In no way do they impede the immediate union of the faithful with Christ. Rather, they foster this union." This saving influence is sustained by the Holy Spirit, who, just as he overshadowed the Virgin Mary when he began in her the divine motherhood, in a similar way constantly sustains her solicitude for the brothers and sisters of her Son.

Mediation and Motherhood

In effect, Mary's mediation is intimately linked with her motherhood. It possesses a specifically maternal character, which distinguishes it from the mediation of the other creatures who in various and always subordinate ways share in the one mediation of Christ, although her own mediation is also a shared mediation. In fact, while it is true that "no creature could ever be classed with the Incarnate Word and Redeemer," at the same time "the unique mediation of the Redeemer does not exclude but rather gives rise among creatures a manifold cooperation which is but a sharing in this unique source." Thus "the one goodness of God is in reality communicated diversely to his creatures."

Subordinate Mediation

The teaching of Vatican II presents the truth of Mary's mediation as "a sharing in the one unique source that is the mediation of Christ himself." Thus we read: "The Church does not hesitate to profess this subordinate role of Mary. She experiences it continuously and commends it to the hearts of the faithful so that, encouraged by this maternal help, they may more closely adhere to the

Mediator and Redeemer."

This role is at the same time special and extraordinary. It flows from her divine motherhood and can be understood and lived in faith only on the basis of the full truth of this motherhood. Since by virtue of divine election Mary is the earthly Mother of the Father's consubstantial Son and his "generous companion" in the work of redemption, "she is a Mother to us in the order of grace." This role constitutes a real dimension of her presence in the saving mystery of Christ and the Church.

Mary is honored in the Church "with special reverence. Indeed, from most ancient times the Blessed Virgin Mary has been venerated under the title of 'God-bearer.' In all perils and needs, the faithful have fled prayerfully to her protection." This cult is altogether special; it bears in itself and expresses the profound link which exists between the Mother of Christ and the Church. As Virgin and Mother, Mary remains for the Church a "permanent model." It can therefore be said that, especially under this aspect, namely, as a model or rather as a "figure," Mary, present in the mystery of Christ, remains constantly present also in the mystery of the Church. For the Church too is "called mother and virgin," and these names have a profound biblical and theological justification.

Mary and Women

This Marian dimension of Christian life takes on special importance in relation to women and their status. In fact, femininity has a unique relationship with the Mother of the Redeemer, a subject which can be studied in greater depth elsewhere…. The figure of Mary of Nazareth sheds light on womanhood as such by the very fact that God, in the sublime event of the incarnation of his Son, entrusted himself to the ministry, the free and active ministry, of a woman.

… Women, by looking to Mary, find in her the secret of living their femininity with dignity and of achieving their own true advancement. In the light of Mary, the Church sees in the face of women the reflection of a beauty which mirrors the loftiest sentiments of which the human heart is capable: the self-offering totality of love; the strength that is capable of bearing the greatest sorrows; limitless fidelity and tireless devotion to work; the ability to combine penetrating intuition with words of support and encouragement.

APPARITIONS OF THE BLESSED VIRGIN MARY

The Bessed Virgin Mary has appeared historically in places all over the world. Eight of the best-known apparitions are described.

Banneux, near Liège, Belgium: Mary appeared eight times between Jan. 15 and Mar. 2, 1933, to an 11-year-old peasant girl, Mariette Beco, in a garden behind the family cottage in Banneux. She called herself the Virgin of the Poor, and has since been venerated as Our Lady of the Poor, the Sick, and the Indifferent. A small chapel was blessed Aug. 15, 1933. Approval of devotion to Our Lady of Banneux was given in 1949 by Bp. Louis J. Kerkhofs of Liège, and a statue of that title was solemnly crowned in 1956.

Beauraing, Belgium: Mary appeared 33 times between Nov. 29, 1932, and Jan. 3, 1933, to five children in the garden of a convent school in Beauraing. A chapel was erected on the spot. Reserved approval of devotion to Our Lady of Beauraing was given Feb. 2, 1943, and final approbation July 2, 1949, by Bp. Charue of Namur (d. 1977).

Fátima, Portugal: Mary appeared six times between May 13 and Oct. 13, 1917, to three children (Lucia dos Santos, 10, who became a Carmelite nun, died in 2005; Francisco Marto, 9, who died in 1919; and his sister Jacinta, 7, who died in 1920; Jacinta and Francisco were beatified by Pope John Paul II in 2000) in a field called Cova da Iria near Fátima. She recommended frequent recitation of the Rosary; urged works of mortification for conversion of sinners; called for devotion to herself under the title of her Immaculate Heart; asked that the people of Russia be consecrated to her under this title, and that the faithful make a Communion of reparation monthly on the first Saturday.

The apparitions were declared worthy of belief in Oct. 1930, and devotion to Our Lady of Fátima was authorized under the title of Our Lady of the Rosary. In Oct. 1942, Pius XII consecrated the world to Mary under the title of her Immaculate Heart. Ten years later, in the first apostolic letter addressed directly to the peoples of Russia, he consecrated them in a special manner to Mary. For more on the Third Secret of Fátima, see below.

Guadalupe, Mexico: Mary appeared four times in 1531 to an Indian, Juan Diego (beatified in 1990 and canonized in 2002), on Tepeyac hill outside of Mexico City, and instructed him to tell Bishop Zumarraga of her wish that a church be built there. The bishop complied with the request about two years later, after being convinced of the genuineness of the apparition by the evidence of a miraculously painted life-size figure of the Virgin on the mantle of the Indian. The mantle bearing the picture has been preserved and is enshrined in the Basilica of Our Lady of Guadalupe. The shrine church, originally dedicated in 1709 and subsequently enlarged, has the title of basilica.

Benedict XIV, in a 1754 decree, authorized a Mass and Office under the title of Our Lady of Guadalupe for celebration on Dec. 12, and named Mary the patroness of New Spain. Our Lady of Guadalupe was designated patroness of Latin America by St. Pius X in 1910 and of the Americas by Pius XII in 1945.

La Salette, France: Mary appeared as a sorrowing and weeping figure Sept. 19, 1846, to two peasant children, Melanie Matthieu, 15, and Maximin Giraud, 11, at La Salette. The message she confided to them, regarding the necessity of penance, was communicated to Pius IX in 1851 and has since been known as the "secret" of La Salette. Bp. de Bruillard of Grenoble declared in 1851 that the apparition was credible, and devotion to Mary under the title of Our Lady of La Salette was authorized. A Mass and Office with this title were authorized in 1942. The shrine church was given the title of minor basilica in 1879.

Lourdes, France: Mary, identifying herself as the Immaculate Conception, appeared 18 times between Feb. 11 and July 16, 1858, to 14-year-old Bernadette Soubirous (canonized in 1933) at the grotto of Massabielle near Lourdes. Her message concerned the necessity of prayer and penance for the conversion of peoples. Mary's request that a chapel be built at the grotto and spring was fulfilled in 1862. Devotion under the title of Our Lady of Lourdes was authorized, and a Feb. 11 feast commemorating the apparitions was instituted by Leo XIII. St. Pius X extended this feast throughout the Church in 1907. The Church of Notre Dame was made a basilica in 1870, and the Church of the Rosary was built later. The underground Church of St. Pius X, with a capacity of 20,000 persons, was consecrated Mar. 25, 1958. Plans were announced in 1994 for renovation and reconstruction of the Lourdes sanctuary.

Notre Dame du Laus, France: Mary appeared to the

young girl Benôite Rencurel between 1664 and 1718. After four months of daily apparitions starting in May 1664, the Virgin Mary asked Rencurel to build a church and a sanctuary to receive priests. The apparitions received formal approval on May 4, 2008, after years of study by theologians. The shrine is located in the French Alps, near the southeastern French town of Gap.

Our Lady of the Miraculous Medal, France: Mary appeared three times in 1830 to Catherine Labouré (canonized in 1947) in the chapel of the motherhouse of the Daughters of Charity of St. Vincent de Paul, Rue de Bac, Paris. She commissioned Catherine to have made the medal of the Immaculate Conception, now known as the Miraculous Medal, and to spread devotion to her under this title. In 1832, the medal was struck.

Other approved apparitions include Pontmain, France (1871), Knock, Ireland (1879), and Akita (1984).

THE THIRD SECRET OF FÁTIMA

Courtesy Vatican Information Service.
On June 26, 2000, the Holy See Press Office issued the document "The Message Of Fátima" that had been prepared by the Congregation for the Doctrine of the Faith and carried the signatures of Card. Joseph Ratzinger and Abp. Tarcisio Bertone S.D.B., respectively prefect and secretary of the congregation.

The document, which is over 40 pages long, was published in English, French, Italian, Spanish, German, Portuguese and Polish. It was made up of an introduction by Abp. Bertone; the first and second parts of the "secret" of Fátima in Sr. Lucia's original text dated Aug. 31, 1941, and addressed to the bishop of Leiria-Fátima, and a translation; the photostatic reproduction of the original manuscript of the third part of the "secret" and a translation; John Paul II's letter to Sr. Lucia dated Apr. 19, 2000, and a translation; a summary of Sr. Lucia's conversation with Abp. Bertone and Bp. Serafim de Sousa Ferreira e Silva of Leiria-Fátima which took place on Apr. 27, 2000, in the Carmel Monastery of St. Teresa of Coimbra, Portugal; the words of Cardinal Secretary of State Angelo Sodano at the end of the beatification of Jacinta and Francisco on May 13, 2000; a theological commentary by Card. Ratzinger.

In his introduction, Abp. Bertone affirms that "Fátima is undoubtedly the most prophetic of modern apparitions.... In 1917 no one could have imagined all this: the three *'pastorinhos'* of Fátima see, listen and remember, and Lucia, the surviving witness, commits it all to paper when ordered to do so by the Bishop of Leiria and with Our Lady's permission."

He continues: "The third part of the 'secret' was written ... on Jan. 3, 1944. There is only one manuscript, which is here reproduced photostatically. The sealed envelope was initially in the custody of the Bishop of Leiria. To ensure better protection for the 'secret' the envelope was placed in the secret archives of the Holy Office on Apr. 4, 1957. The Bishop of Leiria informed Sr. Lucia of this."

The secretary of the Congregation for the Doctrine of the Faith indicates that "according to the records of the Archives, the Commissary of the Holy Office, Fr. Pierre Paul Philippe, O.P., with the agreement of Card. Alfredo Ottaviani, brought the envelope containing the third part of the 'secret of Fátima' to Pope John XXIII on Aug. 17, 1959. 'After some hesitation,' His Holiness said: 'We shall

wait. I shall pray. I shall let you know what I decide.' In fact Pope John XXIII decided to return the sealed envelope to the Holy Office and not to reveal the third part of the 'secret.' Paul VI read the contents with the Substitute, Abp. Angelo Dell'Acqua, on Mar. 27, 1965, and returned the envelope to the Archives of the Holy Office, deciding not to publish the text. John Paul II, for his part, asked for the envelope containing the third part of the 'secret' following the assassination attempt on May 13, 1981," and this was given to Abp. Eduardo Martinez Somalo, Substitute of the Secretariat of State, on July 18 of the same year. On Aug. 11 it was returned to the Archives of the Holy Office.

"As is well known," added Abp. Bertone, "Pope John Paul II immediately thought of consecrating the world to the Immaculate Heart of Mary and he himself composed a prayer for what he called an 'Act of Entrustment' which was to be celebrated in the Basilica of St. Mary Major on June 7 1981."

"In order to respond more fully to the requests of 'Our Lady,' the Holy Father desired to make more explicit during the Holy Year of the Redemption the Act of Entrustment of June 7, 1981, which had been repeated in Fátima on May 13, 1982."

"Sr. Lucia," continued the archbishop, "personally confirmed that this solemn and universal act of consecration corresponded to what Our Lady wished. Hence any further discussion or request is without basis."

Sr. Lucia had already hinted at the interpretation of the third part of the "secret" in a letter to the Holy Father dated May 12, 1982. That letter is also published in the document.

Finally, Abp. Tarcisio Bertone indicates that "the decision of His Holiness Pope John Paul II to make public the third part of the 'secret' of Fátima brings to an end a period of history marked by tragic human lust for power and evil, yet pervaded by the merciful love of God and the watchful care of the Mother of Jesus and of the Church."

TRANSLATION OF THE THIRD SECRET OF FÁTIMA

On June 26, 2000, the Holy See issued the complete translation of the original Portuguese text of the third part of the secret of Fátima, revealed to the three shepherd children at Cova da Iria-Fátima on July 13, 1917, and committed to paper by Sr. Lucia on Jan. 3, 1944:

"I write in obedience to you, my God, who command me to do so through his Excellency the Bishop of Leiria and through your Most Holy Mother and mine.

"After the two parts which I have already explained, at the left of Our Lady and a little above, we saw an Angel with a flaming sword in his left hand; flashing, it gave out flames that looked as though they would set the world on fire; but they died out in contact with the splendor that Our Lady radiated toward him from her right hand: pointing to the earth with his right hand, the Angel cried out in a loud voice: 'Penance, Penance, Penance!' And we saw in an immense light that is God: 'something similar to how people appear in a mirror when they pass in front of it' a Bishop dressed in White 'we had the impression that it was the Holy Father.' Other Bishops, Priests, men and women Religious going up a steep mountain, at the top of which there was a big Cross of rough-hewn trunks as of a cork-tree with the bark; before reaching there the Holy Father passed through a big city half in ruins and half trembling with halting step, afflicted with pain and sorrow, he prayed for the souls of the corpses he met on his way; having reached the top of the mountain, on his knees at the foot of the big Cross he was killed by a group of soldiers who fired bullets and arrows at him, and in the same way there died one after another the other Bishops, Priests, men and women Religious, and various lay people of different ranks and positions. Beneath the two arms of the Cross there were two Angels each with a crystal aspersorium in his hand, in which they gathered up the blood of the Martyrs and with it sprinkled the souls that were making their way to God."

EVENTS AT MEDJUGORJE

The alleged apparitions of the Blessed Virgin Mary to six young people of Medjugorje, Bosnia-Herzogovina, have been the source of interest and controversy since they were first reported in June 1981, initially in the neighboring hillside field, subsequently in the village church of St. James and even in places far removed from Medjugorje.

Reports say the alleged visionaries have seen, heard, and even touched Mary during visions, and that they have variously received several or all of 10 secret messages related to coming world events and urging a quest for peace through penance and personal conversion. An investigative com-

mission appointed by former local Bp. Pavao Zanic of Mostar-Duvno reported in Mar. 1984 that the authenticity of the apparitions had not been verified. He called the apparitions a case of "collective hallucination" exploited by local Franciscan priests at odds with him over control of a parish.

Former Abp. Frane Franic of Split-Makarska, on the other hand, said in Dec. 1985: "Speaking as a believer and not as a bishop, my personal conviction is that the events at Medjugorje are of supernatural inspiration." He based his conviction on the observations of spiritual benefits related to the reported events, such as the spiritual development of the six young people, the increases in Mass attendance and sacramental practice at the scene of the apparitions, and the incidence of reconciliation among people.

On Jan. 29, 1987, the bishops of Yugoslavia declared: "On the basis of research conducted so far, one cannot affirm that supernatural apparitions are involved" at Medjugorje. Currently, the events at Medjugorje are under on-going investigation by the Holy See to determine their authenticity. Nevertheless, the site of Medjugorje remains a popular destination for Catholic pilgrims from Europe and the United States. On Mar. 17, 2010, the Vatican announced that it was launching a formal inquiry into Medjugorje under the authority of the Congregation for the Doctrine of the Faith.

THE CODE OF CANON LAW

Canon Law is the term that denotes the body of laws governing the Catholic Church. The name is derived from the Greek word *kanon* (rule, i.e., rule of practical direction), which, from the fourth century, was used to denote the ordinances and regulations promulgated by the various Church councils that were convened to discuss problems or important topics. The actual term "canon law" (*ius canonicum*) came into use in the 1100s and was intended to differentiate ecclesiastical law from civil law (*ius civile*).

History of Canon Law

In a practical sense, the laws and regulations began to take shape as early as apostolic times and were evident in their nascent form in the Didache, the Didscalia and the Apostolic Tradition. Owing to the persecution of the Church, however, there was little effort to gather laws together, and certainly less time was devoted to systematizing them.

The fourth century brought the Church freedom from persecution and the resulting rapid growth in membership that was a concomitant of the favors bestowed upon the faith by the rulers of the Roman Empire. New laws were naturally needed and desired. Local regulations were soon established through the decrees of the councils, although these most often had only a local authority and adherence. The general (or ecumenical) councils made laws for the whole Church, and the custom developed of carrying on the decrees of previous assemblies by having them read before the start of a new council. Collections of these laws or canons were then undertaken, but these did not bear the weight of being an official code as they were gathered under private authority.

The earliest efforts at collecting Church laws were centered around the private compilation of the decrees of the Eastern councils to which were added

those of the Western Church. The councils of the African Church also made lasting contributions, the most significant coming out of the Seventeenth Council of Carthage (419), which accepted the book of canons later adopted into the canon law of both the Eastern and Western Churches. An official Code of Canon Law was recognized in the seventh century under the Isidorian Collection. Other important influences were the writings of monks in England and Ireland. The monks compiled lists of sins and various offenses to which confessors applied the proper fines or penances. The resulting books were called Penitentials, and they offer scholars an invaluable glimpse into the state of Church law in early medieval England and the development of moral theology.

The Carolingian Reforms of the Church under Charlemagne facilitated the enactment of much legislation that was beneficial to the faith, but it also signaled a long period of secular interference in ecclesiastical affairs. Two by-products of this lay intrusion were the creation of the forged but interesting False Decretals (collections of false canons and decrees of the popes used to falsify the Church's position) and the application of legal arguments by Churchmen that could protect the Church from abuse. Efforts at revitalization would become heightened under the Gregorian Reform, in particular with the reign of Pope St. Gregory VII (1073-1085). From that time, throughout the Middle Ages, laws from the Church would be centered in and produced by the papacy, assisted in running the administration of the Church by the Roman Curia.

Gradually, legal experts collected the decrees of popes, enactments of councils, and sources of older, ancient canons. To these were added glosses, or commentaries, to assist in the teaching of the details of the subject. Still, the study of canon law was severely handicapped by the sheer number of collections, the contradiction between many points of law, and the inability to find specific laws because of the chronological arrangements of the material. Thus can be seen the major significance of the *Decretum* of Gratian, published around 1148 in Bologna. Compiled by the legal expert Gratian, the *Decretum* (in full, *Concordantia discordantum canonum*) was not a formal collection of canons but sought to provide a juridical system for its readers. Toward this end, though, Gratian examined (and excerpted) virtually every canon ever published. The *Decretum* was quickly adopted as the textbook of canon law, despite the fact that it was a private collection and not codified.

Over the next centuries, the popes added to the body of laws by giving rulings to those questions posed to them by bishops from around the Church. These decretal letters were then brought together and, for purposes of comprehensiveness, added to the *Decretum Gratiani*. The most important of these was the *Liber extra*, the collection made by St. Raymond Peñafort for Pope Gregory IX. This received official approval and was to be a vital source for the *Corpus Juris Canonici*. Other remarkable contributors to canon law in the late Middle Ages were Zenzelinus de Cassanis, Jean Chappuis, Guido de Baysio, John the Teuton (or Joannes Teutonicus), Stephen of Tournai, and most of all, Joannes Andreae (d. 1348).

Considerable activity was initiated by the Council of Trent (1545-1563), which sought to reform and reinvigorate the Church in the wake of the Protestant Reformation. The same century brought the formation in 1588 of the Sacred Congregation of the Curia by Pope Sixtus V (r. 1585-1590), which became the main means of implementing new laws and examining facets of established ones.

The final decision to codify the laws of the Church was made by Pope St. Pius X who, in 1903, issued *Arduum*, the *motu proprio* ordering the complete reform and codification of all canon law. It was completed and promulgated in 1917 as the *Codex Juris Canonici*, the first official guide to the laws of the Catholic Church. A new Code of Canon Law was issued by Pope John Paul II in 1983, the final result of a call for a new code dating back to Pope John XXIII (r. 1958-1963) and continued by Pope Paul VI (r. 1963-1978).

The 1983 Code of Canon Law

Pope John Paul II promulgated a revised Code of Canon Law for the Latin Rite on Jan. 25, 1983, with the apostolic constitution *Sacrae Disciplinae Legis* ("Of the Sacred Discipline of Law") and ordered it into effect as of the following Nov. 27. Promulgation of the Code marked the completion of the last major reform in the Church stemming from the Second Vatican Council.

The 1983 Code of Canon Law replaced the one which had been in effect since 1918. The new Code incorporates into law the insights of Vatican Council II. These 1,752 canons focus on the People of God and the threefold ministries of sanctifying, teaching and governance. Also included are general norms, temporalities, sanctions and procedures.

Guiding Principles

When Pope John XXIII announced on Jan. 25, 1959, that he was going to convoke the Second Vatican Council, he also called for a revision of the existing Code of Canon Law. His successor, Paul VI, appointed a commission for this purpose in 1963 and subsequently enlarged it. The commission, which began its work after the conclusion of the Council in 1965, was directed by the 1967 Synod of Bishops to direct its efforts in line with 10 guiding principles. The bishops said the revised Code should:
- be juridical in character, not just a set of broad moral principles;
- be intended primarily for the external forum (regarding determinable fact, as opposed to the internal forum of conscience);
- be clearly pastoral in spirit;
- incorporate most of the faculties bishops need in their ministry;
- provide for subsidiarity or decentralization;
- be sensitive to human rights;
- state clear procedures for administrative processes and tribunals;
- be based on the principle of territoriality;
- reduce the number of penalties for infraction of law;
- have a new structure.

The commission carried out its mandate with the collegial collaboration of bishops all over the world and in consultation and correspondence with individuals and experts in canon law, theology, and related disciplines. The group finished its work in 1981 and turned its final draft over to Pope John Paul II at its final plenary meeting in October of that year.

Features

The revised code is shorter (1,752 canons) than the one it replaced (2,414 canons) and has a number of important features:

It is more pastoral and flexible, as well as more theologically oriented than the former Code. It gives greater emphasis than its predecessor to a number of significant facets and concepts in church life.

In the apostolic constitution with which he promulgated the Code, Pope John Paul II called attention to its nature and some of its features, as follows:

Prime Legislative Document

"Since this is so, it seems clear enough that the Code in no way has its scope to substitute for faith, grace, the charisms, and especially charity in the life of the Church of the faithful. On the contrary, its end is rather to create such order in ecclesial society that, assigning primacy to love, grace and charisms, it at the same time renders more active their organic developments in the life both of the ecclesial society and of the individuals belonging to it. Inasmuch as it is the Church's prime legislative document, based on the juridical and legislative heritage of revelation and tradition, the Code must be regarded as the necessary instrument whereby due order is preserved in both individual and social life and in the Church's activity. Therefore, besides containing the fundamental elements of the hierarchical and organic structure of the Church, laid down by her divine Founder and founded on apostolic or at any rate most ancient tradition, and besides outstanding norms concerning the carrying out of the task mandated to the Church herself, the Code must also define a certain number of rules and norms of action."

Suits the Nature of the Church

"The instrument the Code is fully suits the Church's nature, for the Church is presented, especially through the magisterium of the Second Vatican Council, in her universal scope, and especially through the Council's ecclesiological teaching. In a certain sense, indeed, this new Code may be considered as a great effort to transfer that same ecclesiological or conciliar doctrine into canonical language. And, if it is impossible for the image of the Church described by the Council's teaching to be perfectly converted into canonical language, the Code nonetheless must always be referred to that very image, as the primary pattern whose outline the Code ought to express as well as it can by its own nature.

"From this derive a number of fundamental norms by which the whole of the new Code is ruled, of course within the limits proper to it as well as the limits of the very language befitting the material.

"It may rather be rightly affirmed that from this comes that note whereby the Code is regarded as a complement to the magisterium expounded by the Second Vatican Council.

"The following elements are most especially to be noted among those expressing a true and genuine image of the Church: the doctrine whereby the Church is proposed as the People of God and the hierarchical authority is propounded as service; in addition, the doctrine which shows the Church to be a 'communion' and from that lays down the mutual relationships which ought to exist between the particular and universal Church and between collegiality and primacy; likewise, the doctrine whereby all members of the People of God, each in the manner proper to him, share in Christ's threefold office of priest, prophet and king; to this doctrine is also connected that regarding the duties and rights of the Christian faithful, particularly the laity; then there is the effort which the Church has to make for ecumenism."

Code Necessary for the Church

"Indeed, the Code of Canon Law is extremely necessary for the Church ... The Church needs it for her hierarchichal and organic structure to be visible: so that exercise of the offices and tasks divinely entrusted to her, especially her sacred power and administration of the sacraments, should be rightly ordered; so that mutual relations of the Christian faithful may be carried out according to justice based on charity, with the rights of all being safeguarded and defined; so that we may then prepare and perform our common tasks, and that these, undertaken in order to live a Christian life more perfectly, may be fortified by means of the canonical laws.

"Thus, canonical laws need to be observed because of their very nature. Hence it is of the greatest importance that the norms be carefully expounded on the basis of solid juridical, canonical and theological foundations."

BOOKS OF THE CODE

Book I, General Norms (Canons 1-203): Canons in this book cover Church laws, in general, custom and law, general decrees and instructions, administrative acts, statutes, physical and juridical persons, juridical acts, the power of governing, ecclesiastical offices, prescription (statutes of limitations), the reckoning of time.

Book II, The People of God (Canons 204-746): Canons in Part I cover the obligations and rights of all the faithful, the obligations and rights of lay persons, sacred ministers and clerics, personal prelatures and associations of the faithful.

Canons in Part II cover the hierarchic constitution of the Church under the headings: the supreme authority of the Church and the college of bishops, diocesan churches and the authority constituted in them, councils of diocesan churches and the internal order of diocesan churches.

Canons in Part III cover institutes of consecrated life and societies of apostolic life.

Book III: The Teaching Office of the Church (Canons 747-833): Canons under this heading cover: the ministry of the divine word, the missionary action of the Church, Catholic education, the instruments of social communication and books in particular, and the profession of faith.

Book IV, The Sanctifying Office of the Church (Canons 834-1252): Canons under this heading cover each of the seven sacraments – baptism, confirmation, the Eucharist, penance, anointing of the sick, holy orders and matrimony; other acts of divine worship including sacramentals, the Liturgy of the Hours, ecclesiastical burial; the veneration of saints, sacred images and relics, vows and oaths.

Book V, Temporal Goods of the Church (Canons 1254-1310): Canons under this heading cover: the acquisition and administration of goods, contracts, the alienation of goods, wills and pious foundations.

Book VI, Sanctions in the Church (Canons 1311-1399): Canons in Part I cover crimes and penalties in general: the punishment of crimes in general, penal law and penal precept, persons subject to penal sanctions, penalties and other punishments, the application and cessation of penalties.

Canons in Part II cover penalties for particular crimes: crimes against religion and the unity of the Church; crimes against the authority of the Church and the liberty of the Church; the usurpation of Church offices and crimes in exercising office; false accusation of a confessor; crimes against special obligations; crimes against human life and liberty; a general norm regarding the punishment of external violations of divine law not specifically covered in the Code.

Book VII, Procedures (Canons 1400-1752): Judicial proceedings are the principal subjects of canons under this heading: tribunals and their personnel, parties to proceedings, details regarding litigation and the manner in which it is conducted, special proceedings – with emphasis on matrimonial cases.

Glossary

A

Abbacy Nullius: A non-diocesan territory whose people are under the pastoral care of an abbot acting in general in the manner of a bishop.

Abbess: The female superior of a monastic community of nuns; e.g., Benedictines, Poor Clares, some others. Elected by members of the community, an abbess has general authority over her community but no sacramental jurisdiction.

Abbey: *See* **Monastery**.

Abbot: The male superior of a monastic community of men religious; e.g., Benedictines, Cistercians, some others. Elected by members of the community, an abbot has ordinary jurisdiction and general authority over his community. Eastern Rite equivalents of an abbot are a hegumen and an archimandrite. A regular abbot is the head of an abbey or monastery. An abbot general or archabbot is the head of a congregation consisting of several monasteries. An abbot primate is the head of the modern Benedictine Confederation.

Abiogenesis: The term used to describe the spontaneous generation of living matter from non-living matter.

Ablution: A term derived from Latin, meaning washing or cleansing, and referring to the cleansing of the hands of a priest celebrating Mass, after the offering of gifts; and to the cleansing of the chalice with water and wine after Communion.

Abnegation: The spiritual practice of self-denial (or mortification), in order to atone for past sins or in order to join oneself to the passion of Christ. Mortification can be undertaken through fasting, abstinence, or refraining from legitimate pleasure.

Abortion: Abortion is not only "the ejection of an immature fetus" from the womb, but is "also the killing of the same fetus in whatever way at whatever time from the moment of conception it may be procured." (This clarification of Canon 1398, reported in the Dec. 5, 1988, edition of *L'Osservatore Romano*, was issued by the Pontifical Council for the Interpretation of Legislative Texts — in view of scientific developments regarding ways and means of procuring abortion.) Accidental expulsion, as in cases of miscarriage, is without moral fault. Direct abortion, in which a fetus is intentionally removed from the womb, constitutes a direct attack on an innocent human being, a violation of the Fifth Commandment. A person who procures a completed abortion is automatically excommunicated (Canon 1398 of the *Code of Canon Law*); also excommunicated are all persons involved in a deliberate and successful effort to bring about an abortion. Direct abortion is not justifiable for any reason, e.g.: therapeutic, for the physical and/or psychological welfare of the mother; preventive, to avoid the birth of a defective or unwanted child; social, in the interests of family and/ or community. Indirect abortion, which occurs when a fetus is expelled during medical or other treatment of the mother for a reason other than procuring expulsion, is permissible under the principle of double effect for a proportionately serious reason; e.g., when a medical or surgical procedure is necessary to save the life of the mother. Such a procedure should not be confused with the purportedly "medical" procedure of the partial-birth abortion, a particularly cruel form of abortion.

Abrogation: The Abolition or elimination of a law by some official action. In Canon Law, abrogation occurs through a direct decree of the Holy See or by the enactment of a later or subsequent law contrary to the former law.

Absolute: (1) A term in philosophy, first introduced at the end of the 18th century and used by Scholasticism, that signifies the "perfect being" (i.e., God), who relies upon no one for existence. Modern philosophical thought has added two new concepts: a) the Absolute is the sum of all being; b) the Absolute has no relationship with any other things; the Absolute is thus unknowable. These concepts are agnostic and contrary to Catholicism, which holds that God is the cause of all being (and hence not the sum) and is knowable by his creatures, at least in part. (2) Certain truths, revealed by God, which are unchanging.

Absolution, Sacramental: The act by which bishops and priests, acting as agents of Christ and ministers of the Church, grant forgiveness of sins in the sacrament of penance. The essential formula of absolution is: "I absolve you from your sins; in the name of the Father, and of the Son, and of the Holy Spirit. Amen." The power to absolve is given with ordination to the priesthood and episcopate. Priests exercise this power in virtue of authorization (faculties) granted by a bishop, a religious superior or canon law. Authorization can be limited or restricted regarding certain sins and penalties or censures. In cases of necessity, and also in cases of the absence of their own confessors, Eastern and Latin Rite Catholics may ask for and receive sacramental absolution from an Eastern or Latin Rite priest; so may Polish National Catholics, according to a Vatican decision issued in May 1993. Any priest can absolve a person in danger of death; in the absence of a priest with the usual faculties, this includes a laicized priest or a priest under censure. (*See* additional entry under **Sacraments**, pp. 190, 185.)

Abstinence: 1. The deliberate deprivation by a person of meat or of foods prepared with meat on those days prescribed by the Church as penitential (Ash Wednesday, Good Friday, and all Fridays of the year which are not solemnities — in the United States, not all Fridays of the year but only the Fridays of Lent). Those 14 years of age and above are bound by the discipline. (2) Sexual abstinence is the willing refrain from sexual intercourse;

total abstinence is observed in obedience to the Sixth Commandment by single persons and couples whose marriages are not recognized by the Church as valid; periodic abstinence or periodic continence is observed by a married couple for regulating conception by natural means or for ascetical motives.

Adoration: The highest act and purpose of religious worship, which is directed in love and reverence to God alone in acknowledgment of his infinite perfection and goodness, and of his total dominion over creatures. Adoration, which is also called latria, consists of internal and external elements, private and social prayer, liturgical acts and ceremonies, and especially sacrifice.

Adultery: Marital infidelity. Sexual intercourse between a married person and another to whom one is not married, a violation of the obligations of the marital covenant, chastity and justice; any sin of impurity (thought, desire, word, action) involving a married person who is not one's husband or wife has the nature of adultery.

Advent Wreath: A wreath of laurel, spruce, or similar foliage with four candles which are lighted successively in the weeks of Advent to symbolize the approaching celebration of the birth of Christ, the Light of the World, at Christmas. The wreath originated among German Protestants.

Agape: A Greek word, meaning love, love feast, designating the meal of fellowship eaten at some gatherings of early Christians. Although held in some places in connection with the Mass, the agape was not part of the Mass, nor was it of universal institution and observance. It was infrequently observed by the fifth century and disappeared altogether between the sixth and eighth centuries.

Age of Reason: (1) The time of life when one begins to distinguish between right and wrong, to understand an obligation and take on moral responsibility; seven years of age is the presumption in church law. (2) Historically, the 18th century period of Enlightenment in England and France, the age of the Encyclopedists and Deists. According to a basic thesis of the Enlightenment, human experience and reason are the only sources of certain knowledge of truth; consequently, faith and revelation are discounted as valid sources of knowledge, and the reality of supernatural truth is called into doubt and/or denied.

Aggiornamento: An Italian word having the general meaning of bringing up to date, renewal, revitalization, descriptive of the processes of spiritual renewal and institutional reform and change in the Church; fostered by the Second Vatican Council.

Agnosticism: A theory which holds that a person cannot have certain knowledge of immaterial reality, especially the existence of God and things pertaining to him. Immanuel Kant, one of the philosophical fathers of agnosticism, stood for the position that God, as well as the human soul, is unknowable on speculative grounds; nevertheless, he found practical imperatives for acknowledging God's existence, a view shared by many agnostics. The First Vatican Council declared that the existence of God and some of his attributes can be known with certainty by human reason, even without divine revelation. The word agnosticism was first used, in the sense given here, by T. H. Huxley in 1869.

Agnus Dei: A Latin phrase, meaning Lamb of God. (1) A title given to Christ, the Lamb (victim) of the Sacrifice of the New Law (on Calvary and in Mass). (2) A prayer said at Mass before the reception of Holy Communion. (3) A sacramental. It is a round paschal-candle fragment blessed by the pope. On one side it bears the impression of a lamb, symbolic of Christ. On the reverse side, there may be any one of a number of impressions; e.g., the figure of a saint, the name and coat of arms of the reigning pope. The *agnus dei* may have originated at Rome in the fifth century. The first definite mention of it dates from about 820.

Akathist Hymn: The most profound and famous expression of Marian devotion in churches of the Byzantine Rite. It consists of 24 sections, 12 of which relate to the Gospel of the Infancy and 12 to the mysteries of the Incarnation and the virginal motherhood of Mary. In liturgical usage, it is sung in part in Byzantine churches on the first four Saturdays of Lent and in toto on the fifth Saturday; it is also recited in private devotion. It is of unknown origin prior to 626, when its popularity increased as a hymn of thanksgiving after the successful defense and liberation of Constantinople, which had been under siege by Persians and Avars. Akathist means "without sitting," indicating that the hymn is recited or sung while standing. Pope John Paul, in a decree dated May 25, 1991, granted a plenary indulgence to the faithful of any rite who recite the hymn in a church or oratory, as a family, in a religious community or in a pious association — in conjunction with the usual conditions of freedom from attachment to sin, reception of the sacraments of penance and the Eucharist, and prayers for the intention of the pope (e.g., an Our Father, the Apostles' Creed and an aspiration). A partial indulgence can be gained for recitation of the hymn in other circumstances.

Alchemy: Ancient mystical science, defined in its strictest sense as the transmuting of base metals into gold; it is considered a predecessor of chemistry. Alchemy is a truly old field of study, found among the Egyptians, Chinese, Greeks, and Indians, transmitted by tradition and often secret writings to the Arabs, Byzantines, and Europeans. It was called during the Middle Ages the "Great Work" or the "Art," and its study entailed complex experimentation with large numbers of compounds, elixirs, and elements. The aim was to find the elixir that could add to the life-span – perhaps even obtain immortality – through the elixir vitae, the Philosopher's Stone that could transmute metals into gold. While the Church condemned false alchemists, especially those who preyed upon the gullible, a number of major Church figures either examined alchemy or were reputed alchemists themselves. St. Thomas Aquinas discussed it in his *Summa Theologiae* and was the reputed author of several alchemy treatises. So too were St. Albertus Magnus (with the dubious work *De Alchimia*), Roger Bacon, Arnold of Villanova, Vincent of Beauvais, and Pope John XXII. That pontiff issued the bull *Spondent quas non exhibent* in 1317 against dishonest alchemists.

Alleluia: An exclamation of joy derived from Hebrew, "All hail to him who is, praise God," with various use in the liturgy and other expressions of worship.

Allocution: A formal type of papal address, as distinguished from an ordinary sermon or statement of views.

Alms: An act, gift or service of compassion, motivated by love of God and neighbor, for the help of persons in need; an obligation of charity, which is measurable by the ability of one person to give assistance and by the degree of another's need. Almsgiving, along with prayer and fasting, is regarded as a work of penance as well as an exercise of charity. (*See* **Mercy, Works of**.)

Alpha and Omega: The first and last letters of the Greek alphabet, used to symbolize the eternity of God (Rv 1:8) and the divinity and eternity of Christ, the beginning and end of all things (Rv 21:6; 22:13). Use of the letters as a monogram of Christ originated in the fourth century or earlier.

Amen: A Hebrew word meaning truly, it is true. In the Gospels, Christ used the word to add a note of authority to his statements. In other New Testament writings, as in Hebrew usage, it was the concluding word to doxologies. As the concluding word of prayers, it expresses assent to and acceptance of God's will.

Anamnesis: A prayer recalling the saving mysteries of the death and resurrection of Jesus, following the consecration at Mass in the Latin Rite.

Anaphora: A Greek term for the Canon or Eucharistic Prayer of the Mass.

Anathema: A Greek word with the root meaning of cursed or separated and the adapted meaning of excommunication, used in church documents, especially the canons of ecumenical councils, for the condemnation of heretical doctrines and of practices opposed to proper discipline.

Anchorite: A kind of hermit living in complete isolation and devoting himself exclusively to exercises of religion and severe penance according to a rule and way of life of his own devising. In early Christian times, anchorites were the forerunners of the monastic life. The closest contemporary approach to the life of an anchorite is that of Carthusian and Camaldolese hermits.

Angels: Purely spiritual beings with intelligence and free will whose name indicates their mission as servants and messengers of God. They were created before the creation of the visible universe. Good angels enjoy the perfect good of the beatific vision. They can intercede for persons. The doctrine of guardian angels, although not explicitly defined as a matter of faith, is rooted in long-standing tradition. No authoritative declaration has ever been issued regarding choirs or various categories of angels: seraphim, cherubim, thrones, dominations, principalities, powers, virtues, archangels and angels. Archangels commemorated in the liturgy are: Michael, leader of the angelic host and protector of the synagogue; Raphael, guide of Tobiah and healer of his father; Gabriel, angel of the Incarnation. Fallen angels, the chief of whom is called the Devil or Satan, rejected the love of God and were therefore banished from heaven to hell. They can tempt persons to commit sin.

Angelus: A devotion which commemorates the Incarnation of Christ. It consists of three versicles, three Hail Marys and a special prayer, and recalls the announcement to Mary by the Archangel Gabriel that she was chosen to be the Mother of Christ, her acceptance of the divine will, and the Incarnation (Lk 1:26-38). The Angelus is recited in the morning, at noon and in the evening. The practice of reciting the Hail Mary in honor of the Incarnation was introduced by the Franciscans in 1263. The *Regina Caeli*, commemorating the joy of Mary at Christ's Resurrection, replaces the Angelus during the Easter season.

Anger (Wrath): Passionate displeasure arising from some kind of offense suffered at the hands of another person, frustration or other cause, combined with a tendency to strike back at the cause of the displeasure; a violation of the Fifth Commandment and one of the capital sins if the displeasure is out of proportion to the cause and/or if the retaliation is unjust.

Anglican Orders: Holy orders conferred according to the rite of the Anglican Church, which Leo XIII declared null and void in the bull *Apostolicae Curae*, Sept. 13, 1896. The orders were declared null because they were conferred according to a rite that was substantially defective in form and intent, and because of a break in apostolic succession that occurred when Matthew Parker became head of the Anglican hierarchy in 1559. In making his declaration, Pope Leo cited earlier arguments against validity made by Julius III in 1553 and 1554 and by Paul IV in 1555. He also noted related directives requiring absolute ordination, according to the Catholic ritual, of convert ministers who had been ordained according to the Anglican Ordinal.

Anglican Use Parishes: In line with Vatican-approved developments since 1980, several Anglican use parishes have been established in the United States with the right to continue using some elements of Anglican usage in their liturgical celebrations. A Vatican document dated Mar. 31, 1981, said: "In June, 1980, the Holy See, through the Congregation for the Doctrine of the Faith, agreed to the request presented by the bishops of the United States of America in behalf of some clergy and laity formerly or actually belonging to the Episcopal (Anglican) Church for full communion with the Catholic Church. The Holy See's response to the initiative of these Episcopalians includes the possibility of a 'pastoral provision' which will provide, for those who desire it, a common identity reflecting certain elements of their own heritage."

Animals: Creatures of God, they are entrusted to human stewardship for appropriate care, use for human needs, as pets, for reasonable experimentation for the good of people. They should not be subject to cruel treatment.

Annulment: A decree issued by an appropriate Church authority or tribunal that a sacrament or ecclesiastical act is invalid and therefore lacking in all legal or canonical consequences.

Antichrist: The "deceitful one," the "antichrist" (2 Jn 7), adversary of Christ and the kingdom of God, especially in the end time before the second coming of Christ. The term is also used in reference to anti-Christian persons and forces in the world.

Antiphon: (1) A short verse or text, generally from Scripture, recited in the Liturgy of the Hours before and after psalms and canticles. (2) Any verse sung or recited by one part of a choir or congregation in response to the other part, as in antiphonal or alternate chanting.

Anti-Semitism: A prejudice against Jews, and often accompanied by persecution. The prejudice has existed historically from the time of the ancient Persian Empire and survives even to the present day. It has been condemned consistently by the Church as being in opposition to scriptural principles and Christian charity.

Apologetics: The science and art of developing and presenting the case for the reasonableness of the Christian faith, by a wide variety of means including facts of experience, history, science, philosophy. The constant objective of apologetics, as well as of the total process of pre-evangelization, is preparation for response to God in faith; its ways and means, however, are subject to change in accordance with the various needs of people and different sets of circumstances.

Apostasy: (1) The total and obstinate repudiation of the Christian faith. An apostate automatically incurs a penalty of excommunication. (2) Apostasy from orders is the unlawful withdrawal from or rejection of the obligations of the clerical state by a man who has received major orders. An apostate from orders is subject to a canonical penalty. (3) Apostasy from the religious life occurs when a Religious with perpetual vows unlawfully leaves the community with the intention of not returning, or actually remains outside the community without permission. An apostate from religious life is subject to a canonical penalty.

Apostolate: The ministry or work of an apostle. In Catholic usage, the word is an umbrella-like term covering all kinds and areas of work and endeavor for the service of God and the Church and the good of people. Thus, the apostolate of bishops is to carry on the mission of the Apostles as pastors of the People of God: of priests, to preach the word of God and to carry out the sacramental and pastoral ministry for which they are ordained; of religious, to follow and do the work of Christ in conformity with the evangelical counsels and their rule of life; of lay persons, as individuals and/or in groups, to give witness to Christ and build up the kingdom of God through practice of their faith, professional competence and the performance of good works in the concrete circumstances of daily life. Apostolic works are not limited to those done within the Church or by specifically Catholic groups, although some apostolates are officially assigned to certain persons or groups and are under the direction of church authorities. Apostolate derives from the commitment and obligation of baptism, confirmation, holy orders, matrimony, the duties of one's state in life, etc.

Apostolic Succession: Bishops of the Church, who form a collective body or college, are successors to the Apostles by ordination and divine right; as such they carry on the mission entrusted by Christ to the Apostles as guardians and teachers of the deposit of faith, principal pastors and spiritual authorities of the faithful. The doctrine of apostolic succession is based on New Testament evidence and the constant teaching of the Church, reflected as early as the end of the first century in a letter of Pope St. Clement to the Corinthians. A significant facet of the doctrine is the role of the pope as the successor of St. Peter, the vicar of Christ and head of the college of bishops. The doctrine of apostolic succession means more than continuity of apostolic faith and doctrine; its basic requisite is ordination by the laying on of hands in apostolic succession.

Archives: Documentary records, and the place where they are kept, of the spiritual and temporal government and affairs of the Church, a diocese, church agencies like the departments of the Roman Curia, bodies like religious institutes, and individual parishes. The collection, cataloguing, preserving, and use of these records are governed by norms stated in canon law and particular regulations. The strictest secrecy is always in effect for confidential records concerning matters of conscience, and documents of this kind are destroyed as soon as circumstances permit.

Ark of the Covenant: The sacred chest of the Israelites in which were placed and carried the tablets of stone inscribed with the Ten Commandments, the basic moral precepts of the Old Covenant (Ex 25: 10-22;37:1-9). The Ark was also a symbol of God's presence. The Ark was probably destroyed with the Temple in 586 B.C.

Asceticism: The practice of self-discipline. In the spiritual life, asceticism — by personal prayer, meditation, self-denial, works of mortification, and outgoing interpersonal works — is motivated by love of God and contributes to growth in holiness.

Ashes: Religious significance has been associated with their use as symbolic of penance since Old Testament times. Thus, ashes of palm blessed on the previous Sunday of the Passion are placed on the foreheads of the faithful on Ash Wednesday to remind them to do works of penance, especially during the season of Lent, and that they are dust and unto dust will return. Ashes are a sacramental.

Aspergillum: A vessel or device used for sprinkling holy water. The ordinary type is a metallic rod with a bulbous tip which absorbs the water and discharges it at the motion of the user's hand.

Aspersory: A portable metallic vessel, similar to a pail, for carrying holy water.

Aspiration (Ejaculation): Short exclamatory prayer; e.g., My Jesus, mercy.

Atheism: Denial of the existence of God, finding expression in a system of thought (speculative atheism) or a manner of acting (practical atheism) as though there were no God. The Second Vatican Council, in its Pastoral Constitution on the Church in the Modern World (*Gaudium et Spes*, Nos. 19 to 21), noted that a profession of atheism may represent an explicit denial of God, the rejection of a wrong notion of God, an affirmation of man rather than of God, an extreme protest against evil. It said that such a profession might result from acceptance of such propositions as: there is no absolute truth; man can assert nothing, absolutely nothing, about God; everything can be explained by scientific reasoning alone; the whole question of God is devoid of meaning.

Atonement: The redemptive activity of Christ, who reconciled man with God through his Incarnation and entire life, and especially by his suffering and Resurrection. The word also applies to prayer and good works by which persons join themselves with and take part in Christ's work of reconciliation and reparation for sin.

Attributes of God: Perfections of God. God possesses — and is — all the perfections of being, without limitation. Because he is infinite, all of these perfections are one, perfectly united in him. Because of the limited power of human intelligence, divine perfections — such as omnipotence, truth, love, etc. — are viewed separately, as distinct characteristics, even though they are not actually distinct in God.

Authority, Ecclesiastical: The authority exercised by the Church, and particularly by the pope and the bishops; it is delegated by Jesus Christ to St. Peter. This authority extends to all those matters entrusted to the Apostles by

Christ, including teaching of the Faith, the liturgy and sacraments, moral guidance, and the administration of discipline.

Avarice (Covetousness): A disorderly and unreasonable attachment to and desire for material things; called a capital sin because it involves preoccupation with material things to the neglect of spiritual goods and obligations of justice and charity.

Ave Maria: See **Hail Mary**.

B

Baldacchino: A canopy over an altar.

Baptism: *See* **Sacraments**, p. 190.

Beatification: A preliminary step toward canonization of a saint. It begins with an investigation of the candidate's life, writings and heroic practice of virtue, and, except in the case of martyrs and exceptional circumstances, the certification of one miracle worked by God through his or her intercession. If the findings of the investigation so indicate, the pope decrees that the Venerable Servant of God may be called Blessed and may be honored locally or in a limited way in the liturgy. Additional procedures lead to canonization (*see* separate entry), chiefly the certification of a second miracle.

Beatific Vision: The intuitive, immediate and direct vision and experience of God enjoyed in the light of glory by all the blessed in heaven. The vision is a supernatural mystery.

Beatitude: A literary form of the Old and New Testaments in which blessings are promised to persons for various reasons. Beatitudes are mentioned 26 times in the Psalms, and in other books of the Old Testament. The best known Beatitudes — identifying blessedness with participation in the kingdom of God and his righteousness, and descriptive of the qualities of Christian perfection — are those recounted in Mt 5:3-12 and Lk 6:20-23. The Beatitudes are of central importance in the teaching of Jesus.

Benedictus: The canticle or hymn of Zechariah at the circumcision of St. John the Baptist (Lk 1:68-79). It is an expression of praise and thanks to God for sending John as a precursor of the Messiah. The Benedictus is recited in the Liturgy of the Hours as part of the Morning Prayer.

Biglietto: A papal document of notification of appointment to the cardinalate.

Biretta: A stiff, square hat with three ridges on top worn by clerics in church and on other occasions.

Blasphemy: Any internal or external expression of hatred, reproach, insult, defiance or contempt with respect to God and the use of his name, principally, and to the Church, saints and sacred things, secondarily; a serious sin, directly opposed to the second commandment. Blasphemy against the Spirit is the deliberate refusal to accept divine mercy, rejection of forgiveness of sins and of the promise of salvation. The sin that is unforgivable because a person refuses to seek or accept forgiveness.

Blessing: Invocation of God's favor, by official ministers of the Church or by private individuals. Blessings are recounted in the Old and New Testaments, and are common in the Christian tradition. Many types of blessings are listed in the Book of Blessings of the Roman Ritual. Private blessings, as well as those of an official kind, are efficacious. Blessings are imparted with the Sign of the Cross and appropriate prayer.

Bride of Christ: A metaphorical title that denotes the intimate union that Christ enjoys with his Church; the title is mentioned specifically in the NT (2 Cor 11:2).

Brief, Apostolic: A papal letter, less formal than a bull, signed for the pope by a secretary and impressed with the seal of the Fisherman's Ring. Simple apostolic letters of this kind are issued for beatifications and with respect to other matters.

Bull, Apostolic: Apostolic letter, a solemn form of papal document, beginning with the name and title of the pope (e.g., John Paul II, Servant of the Servants of God), dealing with an important subject, sealed with a *bulla* or red-ink imprint of the device on the *bulla*. Bulls are issued to confer the titles of bishops and cardinals, to promulgate canonizations, to proclaim Holy Years and for other purposes. A collection of bulls is called a *bullarium*.

Burial, Ecclesiastical: Interment with ecclesiastical rites, a right of the Christian faithful. The Church recommends burial of the bodies of the dead, but cremation is permissible if it does not involve reasons against Church teaching. Ecclesiastical burial is in order for catechumens; for unbaptized children whose parents intended to have them baptized before death; and even, in the absence of their own ministers, for baptized non-Catholics unless it would be considered against their will.

Burse, Financial: A special fund maintained by a diocese, religious institute, or private foundation usually endowed by a private benefactor; it often has the purpose of making possible the education of candidates for the priesthood.

C

Calumny (Slander): Harming the name and good reputation of a person by lies; a violation of obligations of justice and truth. Restitution is due for calumny.

Calvary: A knoll about 15 feet high just outside the western wall of Jerusalem where Christ was crucified, so called from the Latin *calvaria* (skull) which described its shape.

Canon: A Greek word meaning rule, norm, standard, measure. (1) The word designates the Canon of Sacred Scripture, which is the list of books recognized by the Church as inspired by the Holy Spirit. (2) The term also designates the canons (Eucharistic Prayers, anaphoras) of the Mass, the core of the eucharistic liturgy. (3) Certain dignitaries of the Church have the title of Canon, and some religious are known as Canons. (*See* **Bible**, p. 96.)

Canonization: An infallible declaration by the pope that a person, who died as a martyr and/or practiced Christian virtue to a heroic degree, is now in heaven and is worthy of honor and imitation by all the faithful. [For details, see **Process of Canonization** under **Communion of Saints**, p. 204; *See also* **Beatification, Saints, Canonizations by Leo XIII and His Successors**, p. 251.]

Canon Law: *See* under **Canon Law**, p. 125.

Canticle: A scriptural chant or prayer differing from the psalms. Three of the canticles prescribed for use in the Liturgy of the Hours are: the *Magnificat*, the Canticle of Mary (Lk 1:46-55); the *Benedictus*, the Canticle of

Zechariah (Lk 1:68-79); and the *Nunc Dimittis*, the Canticle of Simeon (Lk 2:29-32).

Capital Punishment: Punishment for crime by means of the death penalty. The political community, which has authority to provide for the common good, has the right to defend itself and its members against unjust aggression and may in extreme cases punish with the death penalty persons found guilty before the law of serious crimes against individuals and a just social order. Such punishment is essentially vindictive. Its value as a crime deterrent is a matter of perennial debate. The prudential judgment as to whether or not there should be capital punishment belongs to the civic community. The U.S. Supreme Court, in a series of decisions dating from June 29, 1972, ruled against the constitutionality of statutes on capital punishment except in specific cases and with appropriate consideration, with respect to sentence, of mitigating circumstances of the crime. Pope John Paul II, in his encyclical letter *Evangelium Vitae* ("The Gospel of Life"), wrote: "There is a growing tendency, both in the Church and in civil society, to demand that it (capital punishment) be applied in a very limited way or even that it be abolished completely." Quoting the *Catechism of the Catholic Church*, the pope wrote: " 'If bloodless means are sufficient to defend human lives against an aggressor and to protect public order and the safety of persons, public authority must limit itself to such means, because they better correspond to the concrete conditions of the common good and are more in conformity to the dignity of the human person.'"

Capital Sins: Sins which give rise to other sins: pride, avarice, lust, wrath (anger), gluttony, envy, sloth.

Cardinal Virtues: The four principal moral virtues are prudence, justice, temperance and fortitude.

Casuistry: In moral theology, the application of moral principles to specific cases. Casuistry can be of assistance because it takes the abstract and makes it practical in a particular situation. It has definite limitations and does not replace the conscience in the decision-making process; additionally, it must be aligned with the cardinal virtue of prudence.

Catacombs: Underground Christian cemeteries in various cities of the Roman Empire and Italy, especially in the vicinity of Rome; the burial sites of many martyrs and other Christians.

Catechesis: The whole complex of church efforts to make disciples of Christ, involving doctrinal instruction and spiritual formation through practice of the faith.

Catechism: A systematic presentation of the fundamentals of Catholic doctrine regarding faith and morals. Sources are Sacred Scripture, tradition, the magisterium (teaching authority of the Church), the writings of Fathers and Doctors of the Church, liturgy. The new *Catechism of the Catholic Church*, published Oct. 11, 1992, consists of four principal sections: the profession of faith, (the Creed), the sacraments of faith, the life of faith (the Commandments) and the prayer of the believer (the Lord's Prayer). The 16th century Council of Trent mandated publication of the *Roman Catechism*. Catechisms such as these two are useful sources

for other catechisms serving particular needs of the faithful and persons seeking admission to the Catholic Church.

Catechumen: A person preparing in a program (catechumenate) of instruction and spiritual formation for baptism and reception into the Church. The Church has a special relationship with catechumens. It invites them to lead the life of the Gospel, introduces them to the celebration of the sacred rites, and grants them various prerogatives that are proper to the faithful (one of which is the right to ecclesiastical burial). (*See* **Rite of Christian Initiation of Adults**, under **Baptism**, p. 192.)

Cathedra: A Greek word for chair, designating the chair or seat of a bishop in the principal church of his diocese, which is therefore called a cathedral.

Cathedraticum: The tax paid to a bishop by all churches and benefices subject to him for the support of episcopal administration and for works of charity.

Catholic: A Greek word, meaning universal, first used in the title Catholic Church in a letter written by St. Ignatius of Antioch about 107 to the Christians of Smyrna.

Celebret: A Latin word, meaning "Let him celebrate," the name of a letter of recommendation issued by a bishop or other superior stating that a priest is in good standing and therefore eligible to celebrate Mass or perform other priestly functions.

Celibacy: The unmarried state of life, required in the Roman Church of candidates for holy orders and of men already ordained to holy orders, for the practice of perfect chastity and total dedication to the service of people in the ministry of the Church. Celibacy is enjoined as a condition for ordination by church discipline and law, not by dogmatic necessity. In the Roman Church, a consensus in favor of celibacy developed in the early centuries while the clergy included both celibates and men who had been married once. The first local legislation on the subject was enacted by a local council held in Elvira, Spain, about 306; it forbade bishops, priests, deacons and other ministers to have wives. Similar enactments were passed by other local councils from that time on, and by the 12th century particular laws regarded marriage by clerics in major orders to be not only unlawful but also null and void. The latter view was translated by the Second Lateran Council in 1139 into what seems to be the first written universal law making holy orders an invalidating impediment to marriage. In 1563 the Council of Trent ruled definitely on the matter and established the discipline in force in the Roman Church. Some exceptions to this discipline have been made in recent years. A number of married Protestant and Episcopalian (Anglican) clergymen who became converts and were subsequently ordained to the priesthood have been permitted to continue in marriage. Married men over the age of 35 can be ordained to the permanent diaconate. Eastern Church discipline on celibacy differs from that of the Roman Church. In line with legislation enacted by the Synod of Trullo in 692 and still in force, candidates for holy orders may marry before becoming deacons and may continue in marriage thereafter, but marriage after ordination is forbidden. Bishops of Eastern Catholic Churches in the U.S., however, do not ordain married candidates for the priesthood. Bishops of Eastern Catholic Churches are unmarried.

Cenacle: The upper room in Jerusalem where Christ ate the Las Supper with his Apostles.

Censer: A metal vessel with a perforated cover and suspended by chains, in which incense is burned. It is used at some Masses, Benediction of the Blessed Sacrament and other liturgical functions.

Censorship of Books: An exercise of vigilance by the Church for safeguarding authentic religious teaching. Pertinent legislation in a decree issued by the Congregation for the Doctrine of the Faith Apr. 9, 1975, is embodied in the Code of Canon Law (Book III, Title IV). The legislation deals with requirements for pre-publication review and clearance of various types of writings on religious subjects. Permission to publish works of a religious character, together with the apparatus of reviewing them beforehand, falls under the authority of the bishop of the place where the writer lives or where the works are published. Clearance for publication is usually indicated by the terms *Nihil obstat* ("Nothing stands in the way") issued by the censor and *Imprimatur* ("Let it be printed") authorized by the bishop. The clearing of works for publication does not necessarily imply approval of an author's viewpoint or his manner of handling a subject.

Censures: Sanctions imposed by the Church on baptized Roman Catholics 18 years of age or older for committing certain serious offenses and for being or remaining obstinate therein: (1) excommunication (exclusion from the community of the faithful, barring a person from sacramental and other participation in the goods and offices of the community of the Church), (2) suspension (prohibition of a cleric to exercise orders) and (3) interdict (deprivation of the sacraments and liturgical activities). The intended purposes of censures are to correct and punish offenders; to deter persons from committing sins which, more seriously and openly than others, threaten the common good of the Church and its members; and to provide for the making of reparation for harm done to the community of the Church. Censures may be incurred automatically (*ipso facto*) on the commission of certain offenses for which fixed penalties have been laid down in Church law (*latae sententiae*); or they may be inflicted by sentence of a judge (*ferendae sententiae*). Automatic excommunication is incurred for the offenses of abortion, apostasy, heresy and schism. Obstinacy in crime — also called contumacy, disregard of a penalty, defiance of Church authority — is presumed by law in the commission of offenses for which automatic censures are decreed. The presence and degree of contumacy in other cases, for which judicial sentence is required, is subject to determination by a judge. Absolution can be obtained from any censure, provided the person repents and desists from obstinacy. Absolution may be reserved to the pope, the bishop of a place, or the major superior of an exempt clerical religious institute. In danger of death, any priest can absolve from all censures; in other cases, faculties to absolve from reserved censures can be exercised by competent authorities or given to other priests. The penal law of the Church is contained in Book VI of the Code of Canon Law.

Ceremonies, Master of: One who directs the proceedings of a rite or ceremony during the function.

Chamberlain (*Camerlengo*): (1) the Chamberlain of the Holy Roman Church is a cardinal with special responsibilities, especially during the time between the death of one pope and the election of his successor; among other things, he safeguards and administers the goods and revenues of the Holy See and heads particular congregations of cardinals for special purposes. (*See* also **Papal Election**, p. 150.) (2) the Chamberlain of the College of Cardinals has charge of the property and revenues of the College and keeps the record of business transacted in consistories. (3) the Chamberlain of the Roman Clergy is the president of the secular clergy of Rome.

Chancellor: Notary of a diocese, who draws up written documents in the government of the diocese; takes care of, arranges and indexes diocesan archives, records of dispensations and ecclesiastical trials.

Chancery: (1) A branch of church administration that handles written documents used in the government of a diocese. (2) The administrative office of a diocese, a bishop's office.

Chant: A type of sacred singing. It is either recitative in nature with a short two-to-six tones for an accentus, or melodic in one of three styles (syllabic, neumatic, or melismatic).

Chapel: A building or part of another building used for divine worship; a portion of a church set aside for the celebration of Mass or for some special devotion.

Chaplain: A priest — or, in some instances, a properly qualified religious or lay person — serving the pastoral needs of particular groups of people and institutions, such as hospitals, schools, correctional facilities, religious communities, the armed forces, etc.

Chaplet: A term, meaning little crown, applied to a rosary or, more commonly, to a small string of beads used for devotional purposes; e.g., the Infant of Prague chaplet.

Chapter: A general meeting of delegates of religious orders for elections and the handling of other important affairs of their communities.

Charismatic Renewal: A movement which originated with a handful of Duquesne University students and faculty members in the 1966-67 academic year and spread from there to Notre Dame, Michigan State University, the University of Michigan, other campuses and cities throughout the U.S., and to well over 125 other countries. Scriptural keys to the renewal are: Christ's promise to send the Holy Spirit upon the Apostles; the description, in the Acts of the Apostles, of the effects of the coming of the Holy Spirit upon the Apostles on Pentecost; St. Paul's explanation, in the Letter to the Romans and 1 Corinthians, of the charismatic gifts (for the good of the Church and persons) the Holy Spirit would bestow on Christians; New Testament evidence concerning the effects of charismatic gifts in and through the early Church. The personal key to the renewal is baptism in the Holy Spirit. This is not a new sacrament but the personally experienced actualization of grace already sacramentally received, principally in baptism and confirmation. The experience of baptism in the Holy Spirit is often accompanied by the reception of one or more charismatic gifts. A characteristic form of the renewal is the weekly prayer meeting, a gathering which includes periods of spontaneous prayer, singing, sharing of experience and testimony, fellowship and teaching. (*See* also **Index**.)

Charisms: Gifts or graces given by God to persons for the good of others and the Church. Examples are special gifts for apostolic work, prophecy, healing, discernment of spirits, the life of evangelical poverty, here-and-now witness to faith in various circumstances of life. The Second Vatican Council made the following statement about charisms in the Dogmatic Constitution on the Church (No. 12): "It is not only through the sacraments and Church ministries that the same Holy Spirit sanctifies and leads the People of God and enriches it with virtues. Allotting his gifts 'to everyone according as he will' (1 Cor 12:11), he distributes special graces among the faithful of every rank. By these gifts he makes them fit and ready to undertake the various tasks or offices advantageous for the renewal and upbuilding of the Church, according to the words of the Apostle: 'The manifestation of the Spirit is given to everyone for profit' (1 Cor 12:7). These charismatic gifts, whether they be the most outstanding or the more simple and widely diffused, are to be received with thanksgiving and consolation, for they are exceedingly suitable and useful for the needs of the Church. Still, extraordinary gifts are not to be rashly sought after, nor are the fruits of apostolic labor to be presumptuously expected from them. In any case, judgment as to their genuineness and proper use belongs to those who preside over the Church, and to whose special competence it belongs, not indeed to extinguish the Spirit, but to test all things and hold fast to that which is good" (cf. 1 Thes 5:12; 19-21).

Charity: Love of God above all things for his own sake, and love of one's neighbor as oneself because and as an expression of one's love for God; the greatest of the three theological virtues. The term is sometimes also used to designate sanctifying grace.

Chastity: Properly ordered behavior with respect to sex. In marriage, the exercise of the procreative power is integrated with the norms and purposes of marriage. Outside of marriage, the rule is self-denial of the voluntary exercise and enjoyment of the procreative faculty in thought, word or action. The vow of chastity, which reinforces the virtue of chastity with the virtue of religion, is one of the three vows professed publicly by members of institutes of consecrated life.

Chirograph or Autograph Letter: A letter written by a pope himself, in his own handwriting.

Chrism: A mixture of olive or other vegetable oil and balsam (or balm), that is consecrated by a bishop for use in liturgical anointings: Baptism, Confirmation, Holy Orders, the blessing of an altar.

Christ: The title of Jesus, derived from the Greek translation *Christos* of the Hebrew term Messiah, meaning the Anointed of God, the Savior and Deliverer of his people. Christian use of the title is a confession of belief that Jesus is the Savior.

Christianity: The sum total of things related to belief in Christ — the Christian religion, Christian churches, Christians themselves, society based on and expressive of Christian beliefs, culture reflecting Christian values.

Christians: The name first applied about the year 43 to followers of Christ at Antioch, the capital of Syria. It was used by the pagans as a contemptuous term. The word applies to persons who profess belief in the divinity and teachings of Christ and who give witness to him in life.

Circumcision: A ceremonial practice symbolic of initiation and participation in the covenant between God and Abraham.

Circumincession: The indwelling of each divine Person of the Holy Trinity in the others.

Clergy: Men ordained to holy orders and commissioned for sacred ministries and assigned to pastoral and other duties for the service of the people and the Church. (1) Diocesan or secular clergy are committed to pastoral ministry in parishes and in other capacities in a particular church (diocese) under the direction of their bishop, to whom they are bound by a promise of obedience. (2) Regular clergy belong to religious institutes (orders, congregations, societies — institutes of consecrated life) and are so called because they observe the rule (*regula*, in Latin) of their respective institutes. They are committed to the ways of life and apostolates of their institutes. In ordinary pastoral ministry, they are under the direction of local bishops as well as their own superiors.

Clericalism: A term generally used in a derogatory sense to mean action, influence and interference by the Church and the clergy in matters with which they allegedly should not be concerned. Anticlericalism is a reaction of antipathy, hostility, distrust and opposition to the Church and clergy arising from real and/or alleged faults of the clergy, overextension of the role of the laity, or for other reasons.

Cloister: Part of a monastery, convent or other house of religious reserved for use by members of the institute. Houses of contemplative Religious have a strict enclosure.

Code: A digest of rules or regulations, such as the Code of Canon Law.

Code of Canon Law: *See* **Canon Law**, p. 125.

Collegiality: A term in use especially since the Second Vatican Council to describe the authority exercised by the College of Bishops. The bishops of the Church, in union with and subordinate to the pope — who has full, supreme and universal power over the Church which he can always exercise independently — have supreme teaching and pastoral authority over the whole Church. In addition to their proper authority of office for the good of the faithful in their respective dioceses or other jurisdictions, the bishops have authority to act for the good of the universal Church. This collegial authority is exercised in a solemn manner in an ecumenical council and can also be exercised in other ways sanctioned by the pope. Doctrine on collegiality was set forth by the Second Vatican Council in *Lumen Gentium* (the Dogmatic Constitution on the Church). (*See* separate entry.) By extension, the concept of collegiality is applied to other forms of participation and co-responsibility by members of a community.

Communicatio in Sacris: The reception of the Church's sacraments by non-members or the reception by Catholics of sacraments in non-Catholic Churches.

Communion of Saints: "The communion of all the faithful of Christ, those who are pilgrims on earth, the dead who are being purified, and the blessed in heaven, all together forming one Church; in this communion, the merciful love of God and his saints is always (attentive) to our prayers" (Paul VI, *Creed of the People of God*).

Communism: The substantive principles of modern communism, a theory and system of economics and social organization, were stated about the middle of the 19th century by Karl Marx, author of *The Communist Manifesto* and, with Friedrich Engels, *Das Kapital*. The elements of communist theory include: radical materialism; dialectical determinism; the inevitability of class struggle and conflict, which is to be furthered for the ultimate establishment of a worldwide, classless society; common ownership of productive and other goods; the subordination of all persons and institutions to the dictatorship of the collective; denial of the rights, dignity and liberty of persons; militant atheism and hostility to religion, utilitarian morality. Communism in theory and practice has been the subject of many papal documents and statements. Pius IX condemned it in 1846. Leo XIII dealt with it at length in the encyclical letter *Quod Apostolici Muneris* in 1878 and *Rerum Novarum* in 1891. Pius XI wrote on the same subject in the encyclicals *Quadragesimo Anno* in 1931 and *Divini Redemptoris* in 1937. These writings have been updated and developed in new directions by Pius XII, John XXIII, Paul VI and John Paul II.

Compline: The night prayer of the Church that completes the daily cursus (course) of the Liturgy of the Hours (Divine Office).

Concelebration: The liturgical act in which several priests, led by one member of the group, offer Mass together, all consecrating the bread and wine. Concelebration has always been common in churches of Eastern Rite. In the Roman Rite, it was long restricted, taking place only at the ordination of bishops and the ordination of priests. The Constitution on the Sacred Liturgy issued by the Second Vatican Council set new norms for concelebration, which is now relatively common in the Roman Rite.

Concordance, Biblical: An alphabetical verbal index enabling a user knowing one or more words of a scriptural passage to locate the entire text.

Concordat: A church-state treaty with the force of law concerning matters of mutual concern — e.g., rights of the Church, arrangement of ecclesiastical jurisdictions, marriage laws, education. Approximately 150 agreements of this kind have been negotiated since the Concordat of Worms in 1122.

Concupiscence: Any tendency of the sensitive appetite. The term is most frequently used in reference to desires and tendencies for sinful sense pleasure.

Confession: Sacramental confession is the act by which a person tells or confesses his sins to a priest who is authorized to give absolution in the sacrament of penance.

Confessor: A priest who administers the sacrament of penance. The title of confessor, formerly given to a category of male saints, was suppressed with publication of the calendar reform of 1969.

Confraternity: An association whose members practice a particular form of religious devotion and/or are engaged in some kind of apostolic work.

Congregation: (1) The collective name for the people who form a parish. (2) One of the chief administrative departments of the Roman Curia. (3) An unofficial term for a group of men and women who belong to a religious community or institute of consecrated life.

Conscience: Practical judgment concerning the moral goodness or sinfulness of an action (thought, word, desire). In the Catholic view, this judgment is made by reference of the action, its attendant circumstances and the intentions of the person to the requirements of moral law as expressed in the Ten Commandments, the summary law of love for God and neighbor, the life and teaching of Christ, and the authoritative teaching and practice of the Church with respect to the total demands of divine Revelation. A person is obliged: (1) to obey a certain and correct conscience; (2) to obey a certain conscience even if it is inculpably erroneous; (3) not to obey, but to correct, a conscience known to be erroneous or lax; (4) to rectify a scrupulous conscience by following the advice of a confessor and by other measures; (5) to resolve doubts of conscience before acting. It is legitimate to act for solid and probable reasons when a question of moral responsibility admits of argument (*See* **Probabiliorism** and **Probabilism**).

Conscience, Examination of: Self-examination to determine one's spiritual state before God, regarding one's sins and faults. It is recommended as a regular practice and is practically necessary in preparing for the sacrament of penance. The particular examen is a regular examination to assist in overcoming specific faults and imperfections.

Consequentialism: A moral theory, closely associated with proportionalism and utilitarianism, that holds that the preferable action is one that brings about the best consequences. Preferred results, rather than the objective truth and intentionality, are the object of actions based on consequentialism. While traditional moral theology acknowledges that consequences are important in determining the rightness of an act, importance is also placed on the intrinsic morality of the act and the agent's intention.

Consistory: An assembly of cardinals presided over by the pope.

Constitution: (1) An apostolic or papal constitution is a document in which a pope enacts and promulgates law. (2) A formal and solemn document issued by an ecumenical council on a doctrinal or pastoral subject, with binding force in the whole Church; e.g., the four constitutions issued by the Second Vatican Council on the Church, liturgy, Revelation, and the Church in the modern world. (3) The constitutions of institutes of consecrated life and societies of apostolic life spell out details of and norms drawn from the various rules for the guidance and direction of the life and work of their members.

Consubstantiation: A theory which holds that the Body and Blood of Christ coexist with the substance of bread and wine in the Holy Eucharist. This theory, also called impanation, is incompatible with the doctrine of transubstantiation.

Contraception: Anything done by positive interference to prevent sexual intercourse from resulting in conception. Direct contraception is against the order of nature. Indirect contraception — as a secondary effect of medical treatment or other action having a necessary, good, non-contraceptive purpose — is permissible under the principle of the double effect. The practice of periodic continence is not contraception because it does not involve positive interference with the order of nature. (*See Humanae Vitae*, p. 199, other entries.)

Contrition: Sorrow for sin coupled with a purpose

of amendment. Contrition arising from a supernatural motive is necessary for the forgiveness of sin. (1) Perfect contrition is total sorrow for and renunciation of attachment to sin, arising from the motive of pure love of God. Perfect contrition, which implies the intention of doing all God wants done for the forgiveness of sin (including confession in a reasonable period of time), is sufficient for the forgiveness of serious sin and the remission of all temporal punishment due for sin. (The intention to receive the sacrament of penance is implicit — even if unrealized, as in the case of some persons — in perfect contrition.) (2) Imperfect contrition or attrition is sorrow arising from a quasi-selfish supernatural motive; e.g., the fear of losing heaven, suffering the pains of hell, etc. Imperfect contrition is sufficient for the forgiveness of serious sin when joined with absolution in confession, and sufficient for the forgiveness of venial sin even outside of confession.

Contumely: Personal insult, reviling a person in his presence by accusation of moral faults, by refusal of recognition or due respect; a violation of obligations of justice and charity.

Conversion: In a general sense, the turning away from someone or something and the moving toward another person or thing. In Christian belief, conversion is the embrace of Jesus Christ and a rejection of all that keeps one from God.

Corpus Iuris Canonici: *See* **Canon Law**, p. 125.

Council: A formal meeting of Church leaders, summoned by a bishop or appropriate Church leader, with the general purpose of assisting the life of the Church through deliberations, decrees, and promulgations. Different councils include: **diocesan** councils (synod), a gathering of the officials of an individual diocese; **provincial** councils, the meeting of the bishops of a province; **plenary** councils, the assembly of the bishops of a country; and **ecumenical** councils, a gathering of all the bishops in the world under the authority of the Bishop of Rome.

Counsels, Evangelical: Gospel counsels of perfection, especially voluntary poverty, perfect chastity and obedience, which were recommended by Christ to those who would devote themselves exclusively and completely to the immediate service of God. Religious (members of institutes of consecrated life) bind themselves by public vows to observe these counsels in a life of total consecration to God and service to people through various kinds of apostolic works.

Counter-Reformation: The period of approximately 100 years following the Council of Trent (1545-63), which witnessed a reform within the Church to stimulate genuine Catholic life and to counteract effects of the Reformation.

Covenant: A bond of relationship between parties pledged to each other. God-initiated covenants in the Old Testament included those with Noah, Abraham, Moses, Levi, David. The Mosaic (Sinai) covenant made Israel God's Chosen People on terms of fidelity to true faith, true worship, and righteous conduct according to the Decalogue. The New Testament covenant, prefigured in the Old Testament, is the bond people have with God through Christ. All people are called to be parties to this perfect and everlasting covenant, which was mediated and ratified by Christ. The marriage covenant seals the closest possible relationship between a man and a woman.

Creation: The production by God of something out of nothing. The biblical account of creation is contained in the first two chapters of Genesis.

Creator: God, the supreme, self-existing Being, the absolute and infinite First Cause of all things.

Creature: Everything in the realm of being is a creature, except God.

Cremation: The reduction of a human corpse to ashes by means of fire. Cremation is not in line with Catholic tradition and practice, even though it is not opposed to any article of faith. The Congregation for the Doctrine of the Faith, under date of May 8, 1963, circulated among bishops an instruction which upheld the traditional practices of Christian burial but modified anti-cremation legislation. Cremation may be permitted for serious reasons, of a private as well as public nature, provided it does not involve any contempt of the Church or of religion, or any attempt to deny, question, or belittle the doctrine of the resurrection of the body. In a letter dated Mar. 21, 1997, and addressed to Bishop Anthony M. Pilla, president of the National Conference of Catholic Bishops, the Congregation for Divine Worship and the Discipline of the Sacraments granted "a particular permission to the diocesan bishops of the United States of America. By this, local Ordinaries (heads of dioceses) are authorized . . . to permit that the funeral liturgy, including where appropriate the celebration of the Eucharist, be celebrated in the presence of the cremated remains instead of the natural body." Bishop Pilla asked bishops not to use this indult until appropriate texts and ritual directives are approved by the Vatican. (*See* **Burial, Ecclesiastical**).

Crib: Also Crèche, a devotional representation of the birth of Jesus. The custom of erecting cribs is generally attributed to St. Francis of Assisi, who in 1223 obtained from Pope Honorius III permission to use a crib and figures of the Christ Child, Mary, St. Joseph, and others, to represent the mystery of the Nativity.

Crosier: The bishop's staff, symbolic of his pastoral office, responsibility and authority; used at liturgical functions.

Crypt: An underground or partly underground chamber; e.g., the lower part of a church used for worship and/or burial.

Cura Animarum: A Latin phrase, meaning care of souls, designating the pastoral ministry and responsibility of bishops and priests.

Curia: The personnel and offices through which (1) the pope administers the affairs of the universal Church, the Roman Curia (*See* p. 255), or (2) a bishop the affairs of a diocese, diocesan curia. The principal officials of a diocesan curia are the vicar general of the diocese, the chancellor, officials of the diocesan tribunal or court, examiners, consultors, auditors, notaries.

Custos: A religious superior who presides over a number of convents collectively called a custody. In some institutes of consecrated life a custos may be the deputy of a higher superior.

D

Dean: (1) A priest with supervisory responsibility over a section of a diocese known as a deanery. The post-Vatican II counterpart of a dean is an episcopal vicar. (2) The senior or ranking member of a group.

Decision: A judgment or pronouncement on a

cause or suit, given by a church tribunal or official with judicial authority. A decision has the force of law for concerned parties.

Declaration: (1) An ecclesiastical document which presents an interpretation of an existing law. (2) A position paper on a specific subject; e.g., the three declarations issued by the Second Vatican Council on religious freedom, non-Christian religions, and Christian education.

Decree: An edict or ordinance issued by a pope and/or by an ecumenical council, with binding force in the whole Church; by a department of the Roman Curia, with binding force for concerned parties; by a territorial body of bishops, with binding force for persons in the area; by individual bishops, with binding force for concerned parties until revocation or the death of the bishop. The nine decrees issued by the Second Vatican Council were combinations of doctrinal and pastoral statements with executive orders for action and movement toward renewal and reform in the Church.

Dedication of a Church: The ceremony whereby a church is solemnly set apart for the worship of God. The custom of dedicating churches had an antecedent in Old Testament ceremonies for the dedication of the Temple, as in the times of Solomon and the Maccabees. The earliest extant record of the dedication of a Christian church dates from early in the fourth century, when it was done simply by the celebration of Mass. Other ceremonies developed later. A church can be dedicated by a simple blessing or a solemn consecration. The rite of consecration is generally performed by a bishop.

Deposit of the Faith: The body of saving truth, entrusted by Christ to the Apostles and handed on by them to the Church to be preserved and proclaimed. As embodied in Revelation and Tradition the term is very nearly coextensive with objective revelation, in that it embraces the whole of Christ's teaching. But the term of deposit highlights particular features of the apostolic teaching implying that this teaching is an inexhaustible store that rewards and promotes reflection and study so that new insights and deeper penetration might be made into the mystery of the divine economy of salvation. Although our understanding of this teaching can develop, it can never be augmented in its substance; the teaching is a divine trust that cannot be altered, modified, or debased. The term *depositum fidei* first entered official Catholic teaching with the Council of Trent, but its substance is well-attested in the Scriptures and the Fathers.

Despair: Abandonment of hope for salvation arising from the conviction that God will not provide the necessary means for attaining it, that following God's way of life for salvation is impossible, or that one's sins are unforgivable; a serious sin against the Holy Spirit and the theological virtues of hope and faith, involving distrust in the mercy and goodness of God and a denial of the truths that God wills the salvation of all persons and provides sufficient grace for it. Real despair is distinguished from unreasonable fear with respect to the difficulties of attaining salvation, from morbid anxiety over the demands of divine justice, and from feelings of despair.

Detraction: Revelation of true but hidden faults of a person without sufficient and justifying reason; a violation of requirements of justice and charity, involving the obligation to make restitution when this is possible without doing more harm to the good name of the offended party. In some cases, e.g., to prevent evil, secret faults may and should be disclosed.

Devil: (1) Lucifer, Satan, chief of the fallen angels who sinned and were banished from heaven. Still possessing angelic powers, he can cause such diabolical phenomena as possession and obsession, and can tempt men to sin. (2) Any fallen angel.

Devotion: (1) Religious fervor, piety; dedication. (2) The consolation experienced at times during prayer; a reverent manner of praying.

Devotions: Pious practices of members of the Church include not only participation in various acts of the liturgy but also in other acts of worship generally called popular or private devotions. Concerning these, the Second Vatican Council said in the Constitution on the Sacred Liturgy (*Sacrosanctum Concilium*, No. 13): "Popular devotions of the Christian people are warmly commended, provided they accord with the laws and norms of the Church. Such is especially the case with devotions called for by the Apostolic See. Devotions proper to the individual churches also have a special dignity. These devotions should be so drawn up that they harmonize with the liturgical seasons, accord with the sacred liturgy, are in some fashion derived from it, and lead the people to it, since the liturgy by its very nature far surpasses any of them." Devotions of a liturgical type are Exposition of the Blessed Sacrament, recitation of Evening Prayer and Night Prayer of the Liturgy of the Hours. Examples of paraliturgical devotion are a Bible Service or Vigil, and the Angelus, Rosary and Stations of the Cross, which have a strong scriptural basis.

Diocese: A particular church, a fully organized ecclesiastical jurisdiction under the pastoral direction of a bishop as local Ordinary.

Discalced: Of Latin derivation and meaning without shoes, the word is applied to religious orders or congregations whose members go barefoot or wear sandals.

Disciple: A term used sometimes in reference to the Apostles but more often to a larger number of followers (70 or 72) of Christ mentioned in Lk 10:1.

Disciplina Arcani: A Latin phrase, meaning discipline of the secret and referring to a practice of the early Church, especially during the Roman persecutions, to: (1) conceal Christian truths from those who, it was feared, would misinterpret, ridicule and profane the teachings, and persecute Christians for believing them; (2) instruct catechumens in a gradual manner, withholding the teaching of certain doctrines until the catechumens proved themselves of good faith and sufficient understanding.

Dispensation: The relaxation of a law in a particular case. Laws made for the common good sometimes work undue hardship in particular cases. In such cases, where sufficient reasons are present, dispensations may be granted by proper authorities. Bishops, religious superiors and others may dispense from certain laws; the pope can dispense from all ecclesiastical laws. No one has authority to dispense from obligations of the divine law.

Divination: Attempting to foretell future or hidden things by means of things like dreams, necromancy, spiritism, examination of entrails, astrology, augury, omens, palmistry, drawing straws, dice, cards, etc. Practices like these attribute to created things a power which belongs to God alone and are violations of the First Commandment.

Divine Praises: Fourteen praises recited or sung at Benediction of the Blessed Sacrament in reparation for sins of sacrilege, blasphemy and profanity. Some of these praises date from the end of the 18th century: *Blessed be God. / Blessed be his holy Name. / Blessed be Jesus Christ, true God and true Man. / Blessed be the Name of Jesus. / Blessed be his most Sacred Heart. / Blessed be his most Precious Blood. / Blessed be Jesus in the most holy Sacrament of the Altar. / Blessed be the Holy Spirit, the Paraclete. / Blessed be the great Mother of God, Mary most holy. / Blessed be her holy and Immaculate Conception. / Blessed be her glorious Assumption. / Blessed be the name of Mary, Virgin and Mother. / Blessed be St. Joseph, her most chaste Spouse. / Blessed be God in his Angels and in his Saints.*

Double Effect Principle: Actions sometimes have two effects closely related to each other, one good and the other bad, and a difficult moral question can arise: Is it permissible to place an action from which two such results follow? It is permissible to place the action, if: the action is good in itself and is directly productive of the good effect; the circumstances are good; the intention of the person is good; the reason for placing the action is proportionately serious to the seriousness of the indirect bad effect.

Doxology: (1) The lesser doxology, or ascription of glory to the Trinity, is the Glory be to the Father. The first part dates back to the third or fourth century, and came from the form of baptism. The concluding words, As it was in the beginning, etc., are of later origin. (2) The greater doxology, Glory to God in the highest, begins with the words of angelic praise at the birth of Christ recounted in the Infancy Narrative (Lk 2:14). It is often recited at Mass. Of early Eastern origin, it is found in the Apostolic Constitutions in a form much like the present. (3) The formula of praise at the end of the Eucharistic Prayer at Mass, sung or said by the celebrant while he holds aloft the paten containing the consecrated host in one hand and the chalice containing the consecrated wine in the other.

Dulia: A Greek term meaning the veneration or homage, different in nature and degree from that given to God, paid to the saints. It includes honoring the saints and seeking their intercession with God.

Duty: A moral obligation deriving from the binding force of law, the exigencies of one's state in life, and other sources.

E

Easter Controversy: A three-phase controversy over the time for the celebration of Easter. Some early Christians in the Near East, called Quartodecimans, favored the observance of Easter on the 14th day of Nisan, the spring month of the Hebrew calendar, whenever it occurred. Against this practice, Pope St. Victor I, about 190, ordered a Sunday observance of the feast. The Council of Nicaea, in line with usages of the Church at Rome and Alexandria, decreed in 325 that Easter should be observed on the Sunday following the first full moon of spring. Uniformity of practice in the West was not achieved until several centuries later, when the British Isles, in delayed compliance with measures enacted by the Synod of Whitby in 664, accepted the Roman date of observance. Unrelated to the controversy is the fact that some Eastern Christians, in accordance with traditional calendar practices, celebrate Easter at a different time than the Roman and Eastern Churches.

Easter Duty: The serious obligation binding Catholics of Roman Rite, to receive the Eucharist during the Easter season (in the U.S., from the first Sunday of Lent to and including Trinity Sunday).

Easter Water: Holy water blessed with special ceremonies and distributed on the Easter Vigil; used during Easter Week for blessing the faithful and homes.

Ecclesiology: Study of the nature, constitution, members, mission, functions, etc., of the Church.

Ecology: The natural environment of the total range of creation — mineral, vegetable, animal, human — entrusted to people for respect, care and appropriate use as well as conservation and development for the good of present and future generations.

Ecstasy: An extraordinary state of mystical experience in which a person is so absorbed in God that the activity of the exterior senses is suspended.

Economy, Divine: The fulfillment of God's plan of salvation. It was fully developed in his divine mind from eternity, and fully revealed in Jesus Christ. Before the Incarnation it was known only obscurely, but after the ascension of Christ and the coming of the Holy Spirit at Pentecost, it became the substance of apostolic preaching and is preserved in its integrity for each new generation.

Ecumenism: The movement of Christians and their churches toward the unity willed by Christ. The Second Vatican Council called the movement "those activities and enterprises which, according to various needs of the Church and opportune occasions, are started and organized for the fostering of unity among Christians" (Decree on Ecumenism, No. 4). Spiritual ecumenism, i.e., mutual prayer for unity, is the heart of the movement. The movement also involves scholarly and pew-level efforts for the development of mutual understanding and better interfaith relations in general, and collaboration by the churches and their members in the social area. (See **Index** for other entries.)

Elevation: The raising of the host after consecration at Mass for adoration by the faithful. The custom was introduced in the Diocese of Paris about the close of the 12th century to offset an erroneous teaching of the time which held that transubstantiation of the bread did not take place until after the consecration of the wine in the chalice. The elevation of the chalice following the consecration of the wine was introduced in the 15th century.

Encyclical: The highest form of papal teaching document. It is normally addressed to all the bishops and/or to all the faithful.

Envy: Sadness over another's good fortune because it is considered a loss to oneself or a detraction from one's own excellence; one of the seven capital sins, a violation of the obligations of charity.

Epiclesis: An invocation of the Holy Spirit, to bless the offerings consecrated at Mass; before the consecration in the Latin Rite, after the consecration in Eastern usage.

Epikeia: A Greek word meaning reasonableness and designating a moral theory and practice, a mild interpretation of the mind of a legislator who is prudently considered not to wish positive law to bind in certain circumstances.

Episcopate: (1) The office, dignity and sacramental powers bestowed upon a bishop at his ordination. (2) The body of bishops collectively.

Equivocation: (1) The use of words, phrases, or gestures having more than one meaning in order to conceal information which a questioner has no strict right to know. It is permissible to equivocate (have a broad mental reservation) in some circumstances. (2) A lie, i.e., a statement of untruth. Lying is intrinsically wrong. A lie told in joking, evident as such, is not wrong.

Eschatology: Doctrine concerning the last things: death, judgment, heaven and hell, and the final state of perfection of the people and kingdom of God at the end of time.

Eternity: The interminable, perfect possession of life in its totality without beginning or end; an attribute of God, who has no past or future but always is. Man's existence has a beginning but no end and is, accordingly, called immortal.

Ethics: Moral philosophy, the science of the morality of human acts deriving from natural law, the natural end of man, and the powers of human reason. It includes all the spheres of human activity — personal, social, economic, political, etc. Ethics is distinct from but can be related to moral theology, whose primary principles are drawn from divine revelation.

Euthanasia: Mercy killing, the direct causing of death for the purpose of ending human suffering. Euthanasia is murder and is totally illicit, for the natural law forbids the direct taking of one's own life or that of an innocent person. The use of drugs to relieve suffering in serious cases, even when this results in a shortening of life as an indirect and secondary effect, is permissible under conditions of the double-effect principle. It is also permissible for a seriously ill person to refuse to follow — or for other responsible persons to refuse to permit — extraordinary medical procedures even though the refusal might entail shortening of life.

Evangelization: Proclamation of the Gospel, the Good News of salvation in and through Christ, among those who have not yet known or received it; and efforts for the progressive development of the life of faith among those who have already received the Gospel and all that it entails. Evangelization is the primary mission of the Church, in which all members of the Church are called to participate.

Evolution: Scientific theory concerning the development of the physical universe from unorganized matter (inorganic evolution) and, especially, the development of existing forms of vegetable, animal and human life from earlier and more primitive organisms (organic evolution). Various ideas about evolution were advanced for some centuries before scientific evidence in support of the main-line theory of organic evolution, which has several formulations, was discovered and verified in the second half of the 19th century and afterwards. This evidence — from the findings of comparative anatomy and other sciences — confirmed evolution of species and cleared the way to further investigation of questions regarding the processes of its accomplishment. While a number of such questions remain open with respect to human evolution, a point of doctrine not open to question is the immediate creation of the human soul by God. For some time,

theologians regarded the theory with hostility, considering it to be in opposition to the account of creation in the early chapters of Genesis and subversive of belief in such doctrines as creation, the early state of man in grace, and the fall of man from grace. This state of affairs and the tension it generated led to considerable controversy regarding an alleged conflict between religion and science. Gradually, however, the tension was diminished with the development of biblical studies from the latter part of the 19th century onwards, with clarification of the distinctive features of religious truth and scientific truth, and with the refinement of evolutionary concepts. So far as the Genesis account of creation is concerned, the Catholic view is that the writer(s) did not write as a scientist but as the communicator of religious truth in a manner adapted to the understanding of the people of his time. He used anthropomorphic language, the figure of days and other literary devices to state the salvation truths of creation, the fall of man from grace, and the promise of redemption. It was beyond the competency and purpose of the writer(s) to describe creation and related events in a scientific manner.

Excommunication: Severe ecclesiastical penalty imposed by the Church that excludes a member of the faithful from the wider community. Excommunication is today covered in its particulars by Canon 1331 of the new Code of Canon Law, promulgated in 1983. It exists in two contemporary forms, *ferendae sententiae* and *latae sententiae*. The former is a penalty imposed after a formal proceeding presided over by at least three judges. The latter is considered an automatic penalty for certain acts, including the procuring of a successful abortion (Canon 1398), the embrace of heresy (Canon 1364), violation of the Seal of Confession (Canon 1388), and the blasphemous and sacrilegious use of the Eucharist (Canon 1367). A person under the ban of excommunication is unable to take part in all ceremonies of public worship, especially the Eucharist, to receive or celebrate the sacraments, and to discharge any ecclesiastical offices, ministries, or functions. (See **Censures**).

Ex Opere Operantis: A term in sacramental theology meaning that the effectiveness of sacraments depends on the moral rectitude of the minister or participant. This term was applied to rites of the O.T. in contrast with those of the N.T. when it was first advanced in the thirteenth century.

Ex Opere Operato: A term in sacramental theology meaning that sacraments are effective by means of the sacramental rite itself and not because of the worthiness of the minister or participant.

Exorcism: (1) Driving out evil spirits; a rite in which evil spirits are charged and commanded on the authority of God and with the prayer of the Church to depart from a person or to cease causing harm to a person suffering from diabolical possession or obsession. The sacramental is officially administered by a priest delegated for the purpose by the bishop of the place. Elements of the rite include the Litany of Saints; recitation of the Our Father, one or more creeds, and other prayers; specific prayers of exorcism; the reading of Gospel passages and use of the Sign of the Cross. On Jan. 26, 1999, the Congregation for Divine Worship and the Discipline of the Sacraments published a new rite of exorcism in the Roman Ritual. (2) Exorcisms which do not imply the conditions of either diabolical possession or obsession form part of the ceremony of baptism and are also included in formulas for various blessings; e.g., of water.

Exposition of the Blessed Sacrament: "In churches where the Eucharist is regularly reserved, it is recommended that solemn exposition of the Blessed Sacrament for an extended period of time should take place once a year, even though the period is not strictly continuous. Shorter expositions of the Eucharist (Benediction) are to be arranged in such a way that the blessing with the Eucharist is preceded by a reasonable time for readings of the word of God, songs, prayers and a period for silent prayer." So stated Vatican directives issued in 1973.

F

Faculties: Grants of jurisdiction or authority by the law of the Church or superiors (pope, bishop, religious superior) for exercise of the powers of holy orders; e.g., priests are given faculties to hear confessions, officiate at weddings; bishops are given faculties to grant dispensations, etc.

Faith: In religion, faith has several aspects. Catholic doctrine calls faith the assent of the mind to truths revealed by God, the assent being made with the help of grace and by command of the will on account of the authority and trustworthiness of God revealing. The term faith also refers to the truths that are believed (content of faith) and to the way in which a person, in response to Christ, gives witness to and expresses belief in daily life (living faith). All of these elements, and more, are included in the following statement: " 'The obedience of faith' (Rom 16:26; 1:5; 2 Cor 10:5-6) must be given to God who reveals, an obedience by which man entrusts his whole self freely to God, offering 'the full submission of intellect and will to God who reveals' (First Vatican Council, Dogmatic Constitution on the Catholic Faith, Chap. 3), and freely assenting to the truth revealed by him. If this faith is to be shown, the grace of God and the interior help of the Holy Spirit must precede and assist, moving the heart and turning it to God, opening the eyes of the mind, and giving 'joy and ease to everyone in assenting to the truth and believing it'" (Second Council of Orange, Canon 7) (Second Vatican Council, Constitution on Revelation, *Dei Verbum*, No. 5). Faith is necessary for salvation.

Faith, Rule of: The norm or standard of religious belief. The Catholic doctrine is that belief must be professed in the divinely revealed truths in the Bible and tradition as interpreted and proposed by the infallible teaching authority of the Church.

Fast, Eucharistic: Abstinence from food and drink, except water and medicine, is required for one hour before the reception of the Eucharist. Persons who are advanced in age or suffer from infirmity or illness, together with those who care for them, can receive Holy Communion even if they have not abstained from food and drink for an hour. A priest celebrating two or three Masses on the same day can eat and drink something before the second or third Mass without regard for the hour limit.

Father: A title of priests, who are regarded as spiritual fathers because they are the ordinary ministers of baptism, by which persons are born to supernatural life, and because of their pastoral service to people.

Fear: A mental state caused by the apprehension of present or future danger. Grave fear does not necessarily remove moral responsibility for an act, but may lessen it.

First Friday: A devotion consisting of the reception of Holy Communion on the first Friday of nine consecutive months in honor of the Sacred Heart of Jesus and in reparation for sin. (*See* **Sacred Heart, Promises**.)

First Saturday: A devotion tracing its origin to the apparitions of the Blessed Virgin Mary at Fátima in 1917. Those practicing the devotion go to confession and, on the first Saturday of five consecutive months, receive Holy Communion, recite five decades of the Rosary, and meditate on the mysteries for 15 minutes.

Fisherman's Ring: A signet ring (termed in Italian the *pescatorio*) engraved with the image of St. Peter fishing from a boat, and encircled with the name of the reigning pope. It is not worn by the pope. It is used to seal briefs, and is destroyed after each pope's death.

Forgiveness of Sin: Catholics believe that sins are forgiven by God through the mediation of Christ in view of the repentance of the sinner and by means of the sacrament of penance. (*See* **Penance, Contrition**).

Fortitude: Courage to face dangers or hardships for the sake of what is good; one of the four cardinal virtues and one of the seven gifts of the Holy Spirit.

Forty Hours Devotion: A Eucharistic observance consisting of solemn exposition of the Blessed Sacrament coupled with special Masses and forms of prayer, for the purposes of making reparation for sin and praying for God's blessings of grace and peace. The devotion was instituted in 1534 in Milan. St. John Neumann of Philadelphia was the first bishop in the U.S. to prescribe its observance in his diocese. For many years in this country, the observance was held annually on a rotating basis in all parishes of a diocese. Simplified and abbreviated Eucharistic observances have taken the place of the devotion in some places.

Forum: The sphere in which ecclesiastical authority or jurisdiction is exercised. (1) External: Authority is exercised in the external forum to deal with matters affecting the public welfare of the Church and its members. Those who have such authority because of their office (e.g., diocesan bishops) are called ordinaries. (2) Internal: Authority is exercised in the internal forum to deal with matters affecting the private spiritual good of individuals. The sacramental forum is the sphere in which the sacrament of penance is administered; other exercises of jurisdiction in the internal forum take place in the non-sacramental forum.

Freedom, Religious: The Second Vatican Council declared that the right to religious freedom in civil society "means that all men are to be immune from coercion on the part of individuals or of social groups and of any human power, in such wise that in matters religious no one is to be forced to act in a manner contrary to his own beliefs. Nor is anyone to be restrained from acting in accordance with his own beliefs, whether privately or publicly, whether alone or in association with others, within due limits" of requirements for the common good. The foundation of this right in civil society is the "very dignity of the human person" (Declaration on Religious Freedom, *Dignitatis Humanae*, No. 2). The conciliar statement did not deal with the subject of freedom within the Church. It noted the responsibility of the faithful "carefully to attend to the sacred and certain doctrine of the Church" (No. 14).

Freemasons: A fraternal order that originated in London in 1717 with the formation of the first Grand Lodge of Freemasons. From England, the order spread to Europe and elsewhere. Its principles and basic rituals embody a naturalistic religion, active participation in which is incompatible with Christian faith and practice. Grand Orient Freemasonry, developed in Latin countries, is atheistic, irreligious and anticlerical. In some places, Freemasonry has been regarded as subversive of the state; in Catholic quarters, it has been considered hostile to the Church and its doctrine. In the United States, Freemasonry has been widely regarded as a fraternal and philanthropic order. For serious doctrinal and pastoral reasons, Catholics were forbidden to join the Freemasons under penalty of excommunication, according to church law before 1983. Eight different popes in 17 different pronouncements, and at least six different local councils, condemned Freemasonry. The first condemnation was made by Clement XII in 1738. Eastern Orthodox and many Protestant bodies have also opposed the order. In the U.S., there was some easing of the ban against Masonic membership by Catholics in view of a letter written in 1974 by Cardinal Franjo Seper, prefect of the Congregation for the Doctrine of the Faith. The letter was interpreted to mean that Catholics might join Masonic lodges which were not anti-Catholic. This was called erroneous in a declaration issued by the Doctrinal Congregation Feb. 17, 1981. The prohibition against Masonic membership was restated in a declaration issued by the Doctrinal Congregation Nov. 26, 1983, with the approval of Pope John Paul II, as follows: "The Church's negative position on Masonic associations remains unaltered, since their principles have always been regarded as irreconcilable with the Church's doctrine. Hence, joining them remains prohibited by the Church. Catholics enrolled in Masonic associations are involved in serious sin and may not approach Holy Communion. Local ecclesiastical authorities do not have the faculty to pronounce a judgment on the nature of Masonic associations which might include a diminution of the above-mentioned judgment." This latest declaration, like the revised Code of Canon Law, does not include a penalty of excommunication for Catholics who join the Masons. Local bishops are not authorized to grant dispensations from the prohibition. The foregoing strictures against Masonic membership by Catholics were reiterated in a report by the Committee for Pastoral Research and Practice, National Conference of Catholic Bishops, released through Catholic News Service June 7, 1985.

Free Will: The faculty or capability of making a reasonable choice among several alternatives. Freedom of will underlies the possibility and fact of moral responsibility.

Friar: Term applied to members of mendicant orders to distinguish them from members of monastic orders. (*See* **Mendicants**.)

Fruits of the Holy Spirit: Charity, joy, peace, patience, kindness, goodness, generosity, gentleness, faithfulness, modesty, self-control, chastity.

Fruits of the Mass: The spiritual and temporal blessings that result from the celebration of the Holy Sacrifice of the Mass. The general fruits are shared by all the faithful, living and departed, while the special fruits are applied to the priest who celebrates it, to those for whose intention it is offered, and to all those who participate in its celebration.

Fundamental Option: The orientation of one's life either to God by obedience or against Him through disobedience. Catholic Tradition acknowledges that one free and deliberate act with knowledge renders one at odds with God. A prevalent and vague moral theory today asserts that one act cannot change one's option to God — no matter how grave — unless the action comes from the person's "center." Pope John Paul II cautioned against this ambiguous position in the encyclical *Veritatis Splendor* (1993).

G

Gehenna: Greek form of a Jewish name, Gehinnom, for a valley near Jerusalem, the site of Moloch worship; used as a synonym for hell.

Genuflection: Bending of the knee, a natural sign of adoration or reverence, as when persons genuflect with the right knee in passing before the tabernacle to acknowledge the Eucharistic presence of Christ.

Gethsemani: A Hebrew word meaning oil press, designating the place on the Mount of Olives where Christ prayed and suffered in agony the night before he died.

Gifts of the Holy Spirit: Supernatural habits disposing a person to respond promptly to the inspiration of grace; promised by Christ and communicated through the Holy Spirit, especially in the sacrament of confirmation. They are: wisdom, understanding, counsel, knowledge, fortitude, piety, and fear of the Lord.

Glorified Body: The definitive state of humanity in eternity. The risen Christ calls humanity to the glory of his resurrection; this is a theological premise that presupposes that, like Christ, all of his brothers and sisters will be transformed physically.

Gluttony: An unreasonable appetite for food and drink; one of the seven capital sins.

God: The infinitely perfect Supreme Being, uncaused and absolutely self-sufficient, eternal, the Creator and final end of all things. The one God subsists in three equal Persons, the Father and the Son and the Holy Spirit. God, although transcendent and distinct from the universe, is present and active in the world in realization of his plan for the salvation of human beings, principally through Revelation, the operations of the Holy Spirit, the life and ministry of Christ, and the continuation of Christ's ministry in the Church. The existence of God is an article of faith, clearly communicated in divine Revelation. Even without this Revelation, however, the Church teaches, in a declaration by the First Vatican Council, that human beings can acquire certain knowledge of the existence of God and some of his attributes. This can be done on the bases of principles of reason and reflection on human experience. Non-revealed arguments or demonstrations for the existence of God have been developed from the principle of causality; the contingency of human beings and the universe; the existence of design, change and movement in the universe; human awareness of moral responsibility; widespread human testimony to the existence of God.

Goods of Marriage: Three blessings — children, faithful companionship, and permanence — that were first enumerated by St. Augustine in a work on marriage.

Grace: A free gift of God to persons (and angels), grace is a created sharing or participation in the life of God. It is given to persons through the merits of Christ and is communicated by the Holy Spirit. It is necessary for salvation. The principal means of grace are the sacraments (especially the Eucharist), prayer and good works. (1) **Sanctifying or habitual grace** makes persons holy and pleasing to God, adopted children of God, members of Christ, temples of the Holy Spirit, heirs of heaven capable of supernaturally meritorious acts. With grace, God gives persons the supernatural virtues and gifts of the Holy Spirit. The sacraments of baptism and penance were instituted to give grace to those who do not have it; the other sacraments, to increase it in those already in the state of grace. The means for growth in holiness, or the increase of grace, are prayer, the sacraments, and good works. Sanctifying grace is lost by the commission of serious sin. Each sacrament confers sanctifying grace for the special purpose of the sacrament; in this context, grace is called sacramental grace. (2) **Actual grace** is a supernatural help of God which enlightens and strengthens a person to do good and to avoid evil. It is not a permanent quality, like sanctifying grace. It is necessary for the performance of supernatural acts. It can be resisted and refused. Persons in the state of serious sin are given actual grace to lead them to repentance.

Grace at Meals: Prayers said before meals, asking a blessing of God, and after meals, giving thanks to God. In addition to traditional prayers for these purposes, many variations suitable for different occasions are possible, at personal option.

Guilt: The condition of an individual who has committed some moral wrong and is liable to receive punishment.

H

Habit: (1) A disposition to do things easily, given with grace (and therefore supernatural) and/or acquired by repetition of similar acts. (2) The garb worn by Religious.

Hagiography: Writings or documents about saints and other holy persons.

Hail Mary: A prayer addressed to the Blessed Virgin Mary; also called the *Ave Maria* (Latin equivalent of Hail Mary) and the Angelic Salutation. In three parts, it consists of the words addressed to Mary by the Archangel Gabriel on the occasion of the Annunciation, in the Infancy Narrative (*Hail Mary, full of grace, the Lord is with you,* Lk 1:28); the words addressed to Mary by her cousin Elizabeth on the occasion of the Visitation (*Blessed are you among women; Blessed is the fruit of your womb;* Lk 1-42); a concluding petition (*Holy Mary, Mother of God, pray for us sinners now and at the hour of our death. Amen.*). The first two salutations were joined in Eastern rite formulas by the sixth century, and were similarly used at Rome in the seventh century. Insertion of the name of Jesus at the conclusion of the salutations was probably made

by Urban IV about 1262. The present form of the petition was incorporated into the breviary in 1514.

Heaven: The state of those who, having achieved salvation, are in glory with God and enjoy the beatific vision. The phrase, kingdom of heaven, refers to the order or kingdom of God, grace, salvation.

Hell: The state of persons who die in mortal sin, in a condition of self-alienation from God which will last forever.

Heresy: The obstinate post-baptismal denial or doubt by a Catholic of any truth which must be believed as a matter of divine and Catholic faith (Canon 751, of the Code of Canon Law). Formal heresy involves deliberate resistance to the authority of God who communicates revelation through Scripture and tradition and the teaching authority of the Church. Heretics automatically incur the penalty of excommunication (Canon 1364 of the Code of Canon Law). Heresies have been significant not only as disruptions of unity of faith but also as occasions for the clarification and development of doctrine. Heresies from the beginning of the Church to the 13th century are described in **Dates and Events in Church History**, p. 218.

Hermeneutics: *See* under the section **Interpretation of the Bible**, p. 103.

Hermit: *See* **Anchorite**.

Heroic Act of Charity: The completely unselfish offering to God of one's good works and merits for the benefit of the souls in purgatory rather than for oneself. Thus a person may offer to God for the souls in purgatory all the good works he performs during life, all the indulgences he gains, and all the prayers and indulgences that will be offered for him after his death. The act is revocable at will, and is not a vow. Its actual ratification depends on the will of God.

Heroic Virtue: The exemplary practice of the four cardinal virtues and three theological virtues; such virtue is sought in persons considered for sainthood.

Heterodoxy: False doctrine teaching or belief; a departure from truth.

Hierarchy: The hierarchy of order who carry out the sacramental, teaching, and pastoral ministry of the Church; the hierarchy consists of the pope, bishops, priests, and deacons; the pope and the bishops give pastoral governance to the faithful.

Holy Father: A title used for the pope; it is a shortened translation of the Latin title *Beatissimus Pater*, "Most Blessed Father" and refers to his position as the spiritual father of all the Christian faithful.

Holy Grail: A symbol of mystical veneration, perfection, and mystery that came to be identified as the chalice used by Christ at the Last Supper. The Holy Grail was a major element of medieval legend, lore, and literature, appearing variously as a cup, dish, a stone, or even a cauldron into which blood would drip from a bloody lance. It also became closely connected over time with the Arthurian legend. Scholars differ over the possible origins of the Grail legend, some proposing a Celtic or classical mythological origin, others a Christian or Oriental one. Gradually, however, the original elements were united with the tales told of the adventures of Joseph of Arimathea and the arrival of Christianity in the British Isles. The earliest Grail romance was composed around 1180 by Chrétien de Troyes in his *Perceval* or *Conte del*

Graal, the start of the great literary tradition that flourished in the late twelfth and early to mid-thirteenth centuries. Other famous Grail stories were written by Wolfram von Eschenbach (*Parzival*), Robert de Boron (*Roman de l'Estoire dou Graal*), and the 13th-century prose romance *L'Estoire del Saint Graal* (*History of the Holy Grail*).

Holy See: (1) The diocese of the pope, Rome. (2) The pope himself and/or the various officials and bodies of the Church's central administration at Vatican City — the Roman Curia — which act in the name and by authority of the pope.

Holy Spirit: God the Holy Spirit, third Person of the Holy Trinity, who proceeds from the Father and the Son and with whom he is equal in every respect; inspirer of the prophets and writers of sacred Scripture; promised by Christ to the Apostles as their advocate and strengthener; appeared in the form of a dove at the baptism of Christ and as tongues of fire at his descent upon the Apostles; soul of the Church and guarantor, by his abiding presence and action, of truth in doctrine; communicator of grace to human beings, for which reason he is called the sanctifier.

Holy Water: Water blessed by the Church and used as a sacramental, a practice which originated in apostolic times.

Holy Year: A year during which the pope grants the plenary Jubilee Indulgence to the faithful who fulfill certain conditions. For those who make a pilgrimage to Rome during the year, the conditions are reception of the sacraments of penance and the Eucharist, visits and prayer for the intention of the pope in the basilicas of St. Peter, St. John Lateran, St. Paul and St. Mary Major. For those who do not make a pilgrimage to Rome, the conditions are reception of the sacraments and prayer for the pope during a visit or community celebration in a church designated by the bishop of the locality. Pope Boniface VIII formally proclaimed the first Holy Year on Feb. 22, 1300, and the first three Holy Years were observed in 1300, 1350 and 1390. Subsequent ones were celebrated at 25-year intervals except in 1800 and 1850 when, respectively, the French invasion of Italy and political turmoil made observance impossible. Pope Paul II (1464-1471) set the 25-year timetable. In 1500, Pope Alexander VI prescribed the start and finish ceremonies — the opening and closing of the Holy Doors in the major basilicas on successive Christmas Eves. All but a few of the earlier Holy Years were classified as ordinary. Several — like those of 1933 and 1983-84 to commemorate the 1,900th and 1,950th anniversaries of the death and resurrection of Christ — were in the extraordinary category. Pope John Paul designated Jubilee Year 2000 to be a Holy Year ending the second and beginning the third millennium of Christianity.

Homosexuality: The condition of a person whose sexual orientation is toward persons of the same rather than the opposite sex. The condition is not sinful in itself. Homosexual acts are seriously sinful in themselves; subjective responsibility for such acts, however, may be conditioned and diminished by compulsion and related factors.

Hope: The theological virtue by which a person firmly trusts in God for the means and attainment salvation. The virtue was the subject of Pope Benedict XVI's encyclical, *Spe Salvi* in 2007.

Hosanna: A Hebrew word, meaning *O Lord, save, we pray*.

Host, The Sacred: The bread under whose appearances Christ is and remains present in a unique manner after the consecration which takes place during Mass. (*See* **Transubstantiation.**)

Human Dignity: The inherent worth of all human persons as they are made in God's image and likeness and they alone — of all God's creatures on earth — have an immortal soul.

Humanism: A world view centered on man. Types of humanism which exclude the supernatural are related to secularism.

Humility: A virtue which induces a person to evaluate himself or herself at his or her true worth, to recognize his or her dependence on God, and to give glory to God for the good he or she has and can do.

Hyperdulia: The special veneration accorded the Blessed Virgin Mary because of her unique role in the mystery of Redemption, her exceptional gifts of grace from God, and her pre-eminence among the saints. *Hyperdulia* is not adoration; only God is adored.

Hypostatic Union: The union of the human and divine natures in the one divine Person of Christ.

I

Icons: Byzantine-style paintings or representations of Christ, the Blessed Virgin and other saints, venerated in the Eastern Churches where they take the place of statues.

Idolatry: Worship of any but the true God; a violation of the First Commandment.

IHS: In Greek, the first three letters of the name of Jesus — *Iota, Eta, Sigma*.

Immaculate Conception: The doctrine that affirms that "the Blessed Virgin Mary was preserved, in the first instant of her conception, by a singular grace and privilege of God omnipotent and because of the merits of Jesus Christ the Savior of the human race, free from all stain of Original Sin," as stated by Pope Pius IX in his declaration of the dogma, Dec. 8, 1854. Thus, Mary was conceived in the state of perfect justice, free from Original Sin and its consequences, in virtue of the redemption achieved by Christ on the cross.

Immortality: The survival and continuing existence of the human soul after death.

Imprimatur: *See* **Censorship of Books.**

Impurity: Unlawful indulgence in sexual pleasure. (*See* **Chastity.**)

Imputability: A canonical term for the moral responsibility of a person for an act that he or she has performed.

Incardination: The affiliation of a priest to his diocese. Every secular priest must belong to a certain diocese. Similarly, every priest of a religious community must belong to some jurisdiction of his community; this affiliation, however, is not called incardination.

Incarnation: (1) The coming-in-flesh or taking of human nature by the Second Person of the Trinity. He became human as the Son of Mary, being miraculously conceived by the power of the Holy Spirit, without ceasing to be divine. His divine Person hypostatically unites his divine and human natures. (2) The supernatural mystery coextensive with Christ from the moment of his human conception and continuing through his life on earth; his sufferings and death; his resurrection from the dead and ascension to glory with the Father; his sending, with the Father, of the Holy Spirit upon the Apostles and the Church; and his unending mediation with the Father for the salvation of human beings.

Incense: A granulated substance which, when burnt, emits an aromatic smoke. It symbolizes the zeal with which the faithful should be consumed, the good odor of Christian virtue, the ascent of prayer to God. An incense boat is a small vessel used to hold incense which is to be placed in the censer.

Incest: Sexual intercourse with relatives by blood or marriage; a sin of impurity and also a grave violation of the natural reverence due to relatives. Other sins of impurity desire, etc., concerning relatives have the nature of incest.

Inculturation: The correct and entirely appropriate adaptation of the Catholic liturgy and institutions to the culture, language, and customs of an indigenous or local people among whom the Gospel is first proclaimed. Pope John Paul II on Feb. 15, 1982, at a meeting in Lagos with the bishops of Nigeria proclaimed: "An important aspect of your own evangelizing role is the whole dimension of the inculturation of the Gospel into the lives of your people. The Church truly respects the culture of each people. In offering the Gospel message, the Church does not intend to destroy or to abolish what is good and beautiful. In fact, she recognizes many cultural values and, through the power of the Gospel, purifies and takes into Christian worship certain elements of a people's customs."

Index of Prohibited Books: A list of books which Catholics were formerly forbidden to read, possess or sell, under penalty of excommunication. The books were banned by the Holy See after publication because their treatment of matters of faith and morals and related subjects were judged to be erroneous or serious occasions of doctrinal error. Some books were listed in the Index by name; others were covered under general norms. The Congregation for the Doctrine of the Faith declared June 14, 1966, that the Index and its related penalties of excommunication no longer had the force of law in the Church. Persons are still obliged, however, to take normal precautions against occasions of doctrinal error.

Indifferentism: A theory that any one religion is as true and good — or false — as any other religion, and that it makes no difference, objectively, what religion one professes, if any. The theory is completely subjective, finding its justification entirely in personal choice without reference to or respect for objective validity. It is also self-contradictory, since it regards as equally acceptable — or unacceptable — the beliefs of all religions, which in fact are not only not all the same but are in some cases opposed to each other.

Indulgence: According to The Doctrine and Practice of Indulgences, an apostolic constitution issued by Paul VI Jan. 1, 1967, an indulgence is the remission before God of the temporal punishment due for sins already forgiven as far as their guilt is concerned, which a follower of Christ — with the proper dispositions and under certain determined conditions — acquires through the intervention of the Church. An indulgence is partial or plenary, depending on whether it does away with either part or all of the temporal punishment due for sin. Both types of indulgences can always be applied to the dead by way of suffrage; the actual disposition of indulgences applied to the dead rests with God. Only one plenary indulgence can be gained in a single day. The Apostolic Penitentiary issued a decree Dec. 14, 1985, granting diocesan bishops the right to impart — three times a year on solemn feasts of their choice — the papal blessing with a plenary indulgence to those who cannot be physically present but who follow the sacred rites at which the blessing is imparted by radio or television transmission. In July, 1986, publication was announced of a new and simplified *Enchiridion Indulgentiarum*, in accord with provisions of the revised Code of Canon Law. A revised manual was issued by the Holy See on Sept. 17, 2000.

Indult: A favor or privilege granted by competent ecclesiastical authority, giving permission to do something not allowed by the common law of the Church.

Infallibility: 1) The inability of the Church to err in its teaching, in that she preserves and teaches the deposit of truth as revealed by Christ; 2) The inability of the Roman Pontiff to err when he teaches *ex cathedra* in matters of faith or morals, and indicates that the doctrine is to be believed by all the faithful; and 3) The inability of the college of bishops to err when speaking in union with the pope in matters of faith and morals, agreeing that a doctrine must be held by the universal Church, and the doctrine is promulgated by the Pontiff.

Infused Virtues: The theological virtues of faith, hope, and charity; principles or capabilities of supernatural action, they are given with sanctifying grace by God rather than acquired by repeated acts of a person. They can be increased by practice; they are lost by contrary acts. Natural-acquired moral virtues, like the cardinal virtues of prudence, justice, temperance, and fortitude, can be considered infused in a person whose state of grace gives them supernatural orientation.

Inquisition: A tribunal for dealing with heretics, authorized by Gregory IX in 1231 to search them out, hear and judge them, sentence them to various forms of punishment, and in some cases to hand them over to civil authorities for punishment. The Inquisition was a creature of its time when crimes against faith, which threatened the good of the Christian community, were regarded also as crimes against the state, and when heretical doctrines of such extremists as the Cathari and Albigensians threatened the very fabric of society. The institution, which was responsible for many excesses, was most active in the second half of the 13th century.

Inquisition, Spanish: An institution peculiar to Spain and the colonies in Spanish America. In 1478, at the urging of King Ferdinand, Pope Sixtus IV approved the establishment of the Inquisition for trying charges of heresy brought against Jewish (*Marranos*) and Moorish (*Moriscos*) converts. It acquired jurisdiction over other cases as well, however, and fell into disrepute because of irregularities in its functions, cruelty in its sentences, and the manner in which it served the interests of the Spanish crown more than the accused persons and the good of the Church. Protests by the Holy See failed to curb excesses of the Inquisition, which lingered in Spanish history until early in the 19th century.

I N R I: The first letters of words in the Latin inscription atop the cross on which Christ was crucified: *(I)esus (N)azaraenus, (R)ex (I)udaeorum* — Jesus of Nazareth, King of the Jews.

Insemination, Artificial: The implanting of human semen by some means other than consummation of natural marital intercourse. In view of the principle that procreation should result only from marital intercourse, donor insemination is not permissible.

In Sin: The condition of a person called spiritually dead because he or she does not possess sanctifying grace, the principle of supernatural life, action and merit. Such grace can be regained through repentance.

Instruction: A document containing doctrinal explanations, directive norms, rules, recommendations, admonitions, issued by the pope, a department of the Roman Curia or other competent authority in the Church. To the extent that they so prescribe, instructions have the force of law.

Intercommunion, Eucharistic Sharing: The common celebration and reception of the Eucharist by members of different Christian churches; a pivotal issue in ecumenical theory and practice. Catholic participation and intercommunion in the Eucharistic liturgy of another church without a valid priesthood and with a variant Eucharistic belief is out of order. Under certain conditions, other Christians may receive the Eucharist in the Catholic Church. (*See* additional Intercommunion entry.) Intercommunion is acceptable to some Protestant churches and unacceptable to others.

Interdict: A censure imposed on persons for certain violations of church law. Interdicted persons may not take part in certain liturgical services, administer or receive certain sacraments.

Intinction: A method of administering Holy Communion under the dual appearances of bread and wine, in which the consecrated host is dipped in the consecrated wine before being given to the communicant. The administering of Holy Communion in this manner, which has been traditional in Eastern-Rite liturgies, was authorized in the Roman Rite for various occasions by the Constitution on the Sacred Liturgy promulgated by the Second Vatican Council.

Irenicism: Peace-seeking, conciliation, as opposed to polemics; an important element in ecumenism, provided it furthers pursuit of the Christian unity willed by Christ without degenerating into a peace-at-any-price disregard for religious truth.

Irregularity: A permanent impediment to the lawful reception or exercise of holy orders. The Church instituted irregularities — which include apostasy, heresy, homicide, attempted suicide — out of reverence for the dignity of the sacraments.

J

Jehovah: The English equivalent of the Hebrew *Adonai* ("my Lord") used out of fear and reverence for the Holy Name of Yahweh. *Jehovah* uses the consonants YHWH and the vowels of *Adonai* (a, o, a). Scholars today maintain that *Jehovah* is a false derivation.

Jesus: The name of Jesus, meaning "God saves," expressing the identity and mission of the second Person of the Trinity become man; derived from the Aramaic and Hebrew Yeshua and Joshua, meaning Yahweh is salvation.

Jesus Prayer: A prayer of Eastern origin, dating back to the fifth century: "*Lord Jesus Christ, Son of God, have mercy on me (a sinner)."*

Judgment: (1) **Last or final judgment**: Final judgment by Christ, at the end of the world and the general resurrection. (2) **Particular judgment**: The judgment that takes place immediately after a person's death, followed by entrance into heaven, hell or purgatory.

Jurisdiction: Right, power, authority to rule. Jurisdiction in the Church is of divine institution; has pastoral service for its purpose; includes legislative, judicial and executive authority; can be exercised only by persons with the power of orders. (1) Ordinary jurisdiction is attached to ecclesiastical offices by law; the officeholders, called Ordinaries, have authority over those who are subject to them. (2) Delegated jurisdiction is that which is granted to persons rather than attached to offices. Its extent depends on the terms of the delegation.

Justice: One of the four cardinal virtues by which a person gives to others what is due to them as a matter of right. (*See* **Cardinal Virtues**.)

Justification: The act by which God makes a person just, and the consequent change in the spiritual status of a person, from sin to grace; the remission of sin and the infusion of sanctifying grace through the merits of Christ and the action of the Holy Spirit.

K

Kenosis: A term from the Greek for "emptying" that denotes Christ's emptying of himself in his free renunciation of his right to divine status, by reason of the Incarnation, particularly as celebrated in the kenotic hymn (Phil 2:6-11), where it is said that Christ "emptied himself," taking the form of a slave, born in the likeness of man totally integrated with his divinity.

Kerygma: Proclaiming the word of God, in the manner of the Apostles, as here and now effective for salvation. This method of preaching or instruction, centered on Christ and geared to the facts and themes of salvation history, is designed to dispose people to faith in Christ and/or to intensify the experience and practice of that faith in those who have it.

Keys, Power of the: Spiritual authority and jurisdiction in the Church, symbolized by the keys of the kingdom of heaven. Christ promised the keys to St. Peter, as head-to-be of the Church (Mt 16:19), and commissioned him with full pastoral responsibility to feed his lambs and sheep (Jn 21:15-17), The pope, as the successor of St. Peter, has this power in a primary and supreme manner. The bishops of the Church also have the power, in union with and subordinate to the pope. Priests share in it through holy orders and the delegation of authority. Examples of the application of the Power of the Keys are the exercise of teaching and pastoral authority by the pope and bishops, the absolving of sins in the sacrament of penance, the granting of indulgences, the imposing of spiritual penalties on persons who commit certain serious sins.

Kingdom of God: God's sovereign lordship or rule over salvation history, leading to the eschatological goal of eternal life with God.

Koinonia: A term from the Greek word for "community, fellowship, or association" that was used by St. Luke for the fellowship of believers who worshiped together and held all their possessions in common (Acts 2:42-47); it is also used of fellowship with God (1 Jn 1:3, 6), with the Son (1 Cor 1:9), and with the Holy Spirit (2 Cor 13:13; Phil 2:1). St. Paul used *koinonia* to denote the intimate union of the believer with Christ and the community that exists among all the faithful themselves (Rom 15:26; 2 Cor 6:14).

L

Laicization: The process by which a man ordained to holy orders is relieved of the obligations of orders and the ministry and is returned to the status of a lay person.

Languages of the Church: The languages in which the Church's liturgy is celebrated. These include Ge'ez, Syriac, Greek, Arabic, and Old Slavonic in the Eastern Churches. In the West, there is, of course, Latin and the various vernaculars. The Eastern Rites have always had the vernacular. The first language in church use, for divine worship and the conduct of ecclesiastical affairs, was Aramaic, the language of the first Christians in and around Jerusalem. As the Church spread westward, Greek was adopted and prevailed until the third century when it was supplanted by Latin for official use in the West. In the Western Church, Latin prevailed as the general official language until the promulgation on Dec. 4, 1963, of the Constitution on the Sacred Liturgy (*Sacrosanctum Concilium*) by the second session of the Second Vatican Council. Since that time, vernacular languages have come into use in the Mass, administration of the sacraments, and the Liturgy of the Hours. Latin, however, remains the official language for documents of the Holy See, administrative and procedural matters.

Latria: Greek-rooted Latin term that refers to that form of praise due to God alone.

Law: An ordinance or rule governing the activity of things. (1) **Natural law**: Moral norms corresponding to man's nature by which he orders his conduct toward God, neighbor, society and himself. This law, which is rooted in human nature, is of divine origin, can be known by the use of reason, and binds all persons having the use of reason. The Ten Commandments are declarations and amplifications of natural law. The primary precepts of natural law, to do good and to avoid evil, are universally recognized, despite differences with respect to understanding and application resulting from different philosophies of good and evil. (2) **Divine positive law**: That which has been revealed by God. Among its essentials are the twin precepts of love of God and love of neighbor, and the Ten Commandments. (3) **Ecclesiastical law**: That which is established by the Church for the spiritual welfare of the faithful and the orderly conduct of ecclesiastical affairs. (*See* **Canon Law**, p. 125.) (4) **Civil law**: That which is established by a socio-political community for the common good.

Liberalism: A multiphased trend of thought and movement favoring liberty, independence and progress in moral, intellectual, religious, social, economic and political life. Traceable to the Renaissance, it developed through the Enlightenment, the rationalism of the 19th century, and modernist- and existentialist-related theories of the 20th century. Evaluations of various kinds of liberalism depend on the validity of their underlying principles. Extremist positions — regarding subjectivism, libertinarianism, naturalist denials of the supernatural, and the alienation of individuals and society from God and the Church — were condemned by Gregory XVI in the 1830s, Pius IX in 1864, Leo XIII in 1899, and St. Pius X in 1907. There is, however, nothing objectionable about forms of liberalism patterned according to sound principles of Christian doctrine.

Liberation Theology: Deals with the relevance of Christian faith and salvation — and, therefore, of the mission of the Church — to efforts for the promotion of human rights, social justice and human development. It originated in the religious, social, political and economic environment of Latin America, with its contemporary need for a theory and corresponding action by the Church, in the pattern of its overall mission, for human rights and integral personal and social development. Some versions of liberation theology are at variance with the body of church teaching because of their ideological concept of Christ as liberator, and also because they play down the primary spiritual nature and mission of the Church. Instructions from the Congregation for the Doctrine of the Faith — "On Certain Aspects of the Theology of Liberation" (Sept. 3, 1984) and "On Christian Freedom and Liberation" (Apr. 5, 1986) — contain warnings against translating sociology into theology and advocating violence in social activism.

Life in Outer Space: Whether rational life exists on other bodies in the universe besides earth, is a question for scientific investigation to settle. The possibility can be granted, without prejudice to the body of revealed truth.

Limbo: The limbo of the fathers was the state of rest and natural happiness after death enjoyed by the just of pre-Christian times until they were admitted to heaven following the Ascension of Christ.

Litany: A prayer in the form of responsive petition; e.g., St. Joseph, pray for us, etc. Examples are the litanies of Loreto (Litany of the Blessed Mother), the Holy Name, All Saints, the Sacred Heart, the Precious Blood, St. Joseph, Litany for the Dying.

Logos: A Greek term for "word, speech, or reason." It is most commonly identified with the title given to Jesus in John's Gospel, though not exclusive to that Gospel; In the N.T., however, the term reflects more the influence of Hellenistic philosophy: St. Paul uses logos as interchangeable with *sophia*, wisdom (1 Cor 1:24). The *Logos* is the Wisdom of God made manifest in the Son. As a name for the Second Person of the Trinity, the Incarnate Word, the term receives new meaning in the light of the life, death, and resurrection of Jesus Christ.

Loreto, House of: A Marian shrine in Loreto, Italy, consisting of the home of the Holy Family which, according to an old tradition, was transported in a miraculous manner from Nazareth to Dalmatia and finally to Loreto between 1291 and 1294. Investigations conducted shortly after the appearance of the structure in Loreto revealed that its dimensions matched those of the house of the Holy Family missing from its place of enshrinement in a basilica at Nazareth. Among the many popes who regarded it with high honor was John XXIII, who went there on pilgrimage Oct. 4, 1962. The house of the Holy Family is enshrined in the Basilica of Our Lady.

Love: A devotion to a person or object that has been categorized by Greek philosophy into four types: *storge* (one loves persons and things close to him); *philia* (the love of friends); *eros* (sexual love and that of a spiritual nature); *agape* (a self-giving to one in need). Christian charity is love, but not all love is true charity. The virtue was the subject of study by Pope Benedict XVI's 2005 encyclical *Deus Caritas Est*.

Lust: A disorderly desire for sexual pleasure; one of the seven capital sins.

M

Magi: In the Infancy Narrative of St. Matthew's Gospel (2:1-12), three wise men from the East whose visit and homage to the Child Jesus at Bethlehem indicated Christ's manifestation of himself to non-Jewish people. The narrative teaches the universality of salvation. The traditional names of the Magi are Caspar, Melchior and Balthasar.

Magisterium: The Church's teaching authority, instituted by Christ and guided by the Holy Spirit, which seeks to safeguard and explain the truths of the faith. The Magisterium is exercised in two ways. The extraordinary Magisterium is exercised when the pope and ecumenical councils infallibly define a truth of faith or morals that is necessary for one's salvation and that has been constantly taught and held by the Church. Ordinary Magisterium is exercised when the Church infallibly defines truths of the Faith as taught universally and without dissent; which must be taught or the Magisterium would be failing in its duty; is connected with a grave matter of faith or morals; and which is taught authoritatively. Not everything taught by the Magisterium is done so infallibly; however, the exercise of the Magisterium is faithful to Christ and what He taught.

Magnificat: The canticle or hymn of the Virgin Mary on the occasion of her visitation to her cousin Elizabeth (Lk 1:46-55). It is an expression of praise, thanksgiving and acknowledgment of the great blessings given by God to Mary, the Mother of the Second Person of the Blessed Trinity made Man. The *Magnificat* is recited in the Liturgy of the Hours as part of the Evening Prayer.

Martyr: A Greek word, meaning witness, denoting one who voluntarily suffered death for the faith or some Christian virtue.

Martyrology: A catalogue of martyrs and other saints, arranged according to the calendar. The *Roman Martyrology* contains the official list of saints venerated by the Church. Additions to the list are made in beatification and canonization decrees of the Congregation for the Causes of Saints.

Mass for the People: On Sundays and certain feasts throughout the year pastors are required to offer Mass for the faithful entrusted to their care. If they cannot offer the Mass on these days, they must do so at a later date or provide that another priest offer the Mass.

Materialism: Theory that holds that matter is the only reality, and everything in existence is merely a manifestation of matter; there is no such thing as spirit, and the supernatural does not exist. Materialism is incompatible with Christian doctrine.

Meditation: Mental, as distinguished from vocal, prayer, in which thought, affections, and resolutions of the will predominate. There is a meditative element to all forms of prayer, which always involves the raising of the heart and mind to God.

Mendicants: A term derived from Latin and meaning beggars, applied to members of religious orders without property rights; the members, accordingly, worked or begged for their support. The original mendicants were Franciscans and Dominicans in the early 13th century; later, the Carmelites, Augustinians, Servites and others were given the mendicant title and privileges, with respect to exemption from episcopal jurisdiction and wide faculties for preaching and administering the sacrament of penance. The practice of begging is limited at the present time, although it is still allowed with the permission of competent superiors and bishops. Mendicants are supported by free will offerings and income received for spiritual services and other work.

Mercy, Divine: The love and goodness of God, manifested particularly in a time of need.

Mercy, Works of: Works of corporal or spiritual assistance, motivated by love of God and neighbor, to persons in need. (1) **Corporal works**: feeding the hungry, giving drink to the thirsty, clothing the naked, visiting the imprisoned, sheltering the homeless, visiting the sick, burying the dead. (2) **Spiritual works**: counseling the doubtful, instructing the ignorant, admonishing sinners, comforting the afflicted, forgiving offenses, bearing wrongs patiently, praying for the living and the dead.

Merit: In religion, the right to a supernatural reward for good works freely done for a supernatural motive by a person in the state of and with the assistance of grace. The right to such reward is from God, who binds himself to give it. Accordingly, good works, as described above, are meritorious for salvation.

Metanoia: A term from the Greek *metanoein* ("to change one's mind, repent, be converted") that is used in the NT for conversion. It entails the repentance of sin and the subsequent turning toward the Lord. *Metanoia* is fundamental to the Christian life and is necessary for spiritual growth.

Metaphysics: The branch of philosophy (from the Greek *meta* — after + *physika* — physics) dealing with first things, including the nature of being (ontology), the origin and structure of the world (cosmology), and the study of the reality and attributes of God (natural theology). Metaphysics has long been examined by Catholic philosophers, most especially in the writings of St. Augustine and St. Thomas Aquinas.

Millennium: A thousand-year reign of Christ and the just upon earth before the end of the world. This belief of the Millenarians, Chiliasts, and some sects of modern times is based on an erroneous interpretation of Rv 20.

Miracles: Observable events or effects in the physical or moral order of things, with reference to salvation, which cannot be explained by the ordinary operation of laws of nature and which, therefore, are attributed to the direct action of God. They make known, in an unusual way, the concern and intervention of God in human affairs for the salvation of men.

Mission: (1) Strictly, it means being sent to perform a certain work, such as the mission of Christ to redeem mankind, the mission of the Apostles and the Church and its members to perpetuate the prophetic, priestly and royal mission of Christ. (2) A place where: the Gospel has not been proclaimed; the Church has not been firmly established; the Church, although established, is weak. (3) An ecclesiastical territory with the simplest kind of canonical organization, under the jurisdiction of the Congregation for the Evangelization of Peoples. (4) A church or chapel without a resident priest. (5) A special course of sermons and spiritual exercises conducted in parishes for the purpose of renewing and deepening the spiritual life of the faithful and for the conversion of lapsed Catholics.

Modernism: The "synthesis of all heresies," which appeared near the beginning of the 20th century. It undermines the objective validity of religious beliefs and practices which, it contends, are products of the subconscious developed by mankind under the stimulus of a religious sense. It holds that the existence of a personal God cannot be demonstrated, the Bible is not inspired, Christ is not divine, nor did he establish the Church or institute the sacraments. A special danger lies in modernism, which is still influential, because it uses Catholic terms with perverted meanings. St. Pius X condemned 65 propositions of modernism in 1907 in the decree *Lamentabili* and issued the encyclical *Pascendi* to explain and analyze its errors.

Monastery: The dwelling place, as well as the community thereof, of monks belonging to the Benedictine and Benedictine-related orders like the Cistercians and Carthusians; also, the Augustinians and Canons Regular. Distinctive of monasteries are: their separation from the world; the enclosure or cloister; the permanence or stability of attachment characteristic of their members; autonomous government in accordance with a monastic rule, like that of St. Benedict in the West or of St. Basil in the East; the special dedication of its members to the community celebration of the liturgy as well as to work that is suitable to the surrounding area and the needs of its people. Monastic superiors of men have such titles as abbot and prior; of women, abbess and prioress. In most essentials, an abbey is the same as a monastery.

Monk: A member of a monastic order — e.g., the Benedictines, the Benedictine-related Cistercians and Carthusians, and the Basilians, who bind themselves by religious profession to stable attachment to a monastery, the contemplative life and the work of their community. In popular use, the title is wrongly applied to many men religious who really are not monks.

Monotheism: Belief in and worship of one God.

Morality: Conformity or difformity of behavior to standards of right conduct. (*See* **Moral Obligations**, p. 110; **Commandments of God**, p.111; **Precepts of the Church**, p. 112; **Conscience; Law**.)

Mortification: Acts of self-discipline, including prayer, hardship, austerities and penances undertaken for the sake of progress in virtue.

Motu Proprio: A Latin phrase designating a document issued by a pope on his own initiative. Documents of this kind often concern administrative matters.

Mystagogy: Experience of the mystery of Christ, especially through participation in the liturgy and the sacraments.

Mysteries of Faith: Supernatural truths whose existence cannot be known without revelation by God and whose intrinsic truth, while not contrary to reason, can never be wholly understood even after revelation. These mysteries are above reason, not against reason. Among them are the divine mysteries of the Trinity, Incarnation and Eucharist. Some mysteries — e.g., concerning God's attributes — can be known by reason without revelation, although they cannot be fully understood.

N

Natural Law: *See* **Law**.

Natural Theology: The field of knowledge that relies upon human reason and the observation of nature, instead of revelation, to determine the existence and attributes of God.

Necromancy: Supposed communication with the dead; a form of divination.

Neo-Scholasticism: A movement begun in the late 19th century that had as its aim the restoration of Scholasticism for use in contemporary philosophy and theology. Great emphasis was placed upon the writings of such Scholastic masters as Peter Lombard, St. Albert the Great, St. Anselm, St. Bonaventure, Bl. John Duns Scotus, and especially St. Thomas Aquinas. The movement began at the Catholic University of Louvain, in Belgium, and then found its way into theological centers in Italy, France, and Germany. Particular attention was given to the philosophical and theological works of St. Thomas Aquinas, from which arose a particular school of neo-Thomism; the movement was strongly reinforced by Pope Leo XIII who issued the encyclical *Aeterni Patris* (1879) mandating that Scholasticism, in particular Thomism, be the foundation for all Catholic philosophy and theology taught in Catholic seminaries, universities, and colleges. Neo-Scholasticism was responsible for a true intellectual renaissance in 20th-century Catholic philosophy and theology. Among its foremost modern leaders were Jacques Maritain, Étienne Gilson, M. D. Chenu, Henri de Lubac, and Paul Claudel.

Nihil Obstat: *See* **Censorship of Books**.

Non-Expedit: A Latin expression. It is not expedient (fitting, proper), used to state a prohibition or refusal of permission.

Novena: A term designating public or private devotional practices over a period of nine consecutive days; or, by extension, over a period of nine weeks, in which one day a week is set aside for the devotions.

Novice: A man or woman preparing, in a formal period of trial and formation called a novitiate, for membership in an institute of consecrated life. The novitiate lasts a minimum of 12 and a maximum of 24 months; at its conclusion, the novice professes temporary promises or vows of poverty, chastity and obedience. Norms require that certain periods of time be spent in the house of novitiate; periods of apostolic work are also required, to acquaint the novice with the apostolate(s) of the institute. A novice is not bound by the obligations of the professed members of the institute, is free to leave at any time, and may be discharged at the discretion of competent superiors. The superior of a novice is a master of novices or director of formation.

Nun: (1) Strictly, a member of a religious order of women with solemn vows (*moniales*). (2) In general, all women religious, even those in simple vows who are more properly called sisters.

Nunc Dimittis: The canticle or hymn of Simeon at the sight of Jesus at the Temple on the occasion of his presentation (Lk 2:29-32). It is an expression of joy and thanksgiving for the blessing of having lived to see the Messiah. It is prescribed for use in the Night Prayer of the Liturgy of the Hours.

O

Oath: Calling upon God to witness the truth of a statement. Violating an oath, e.g., by perjury in court, or taking an oath without sufficient reason, is a violation of the honor due to God.

Obedience: Submission to one in authority. General obligations of obedience fall under the Fourth Commandment. The vow of obedience professed by religious is one of the evangelical counsels.

Obsession, Diabolical: The extraordinary state of one

who is seriously molested by evil spirits in an external manner. Obsession is more than just temptation.

Occasion of Sin: A person, place, or thing that is a temptation to sin. An occasion may be either a situation that always leads to sin or one that usually leads to sin.

Octave: A period of eight days given over to the celebration of a major feast such as Easter.

Oils, Holy: The oils blessed by a bishop at the Chrism Mass on Holy Thursday or another suitable day, or by a priest under certain conditions. (1) The oil of catechumens (olive or vegetable oil), used at baptism; also, poured with chrism into the baptismal water blessed in Easter Vigil ceremonies. (2) Oil of the sick (olive or vegetable oil) used in anointing the sick. (3) Chrism (olive or vegetable oil mixed with balm), which is ordinarily consecrated by a bishop, for use at baptism, in confirmation, at the ordination of a priest and bishop, in the dedication of churches and altars.

Ontologism: A philosophical theory (the name is taken from the Greek for being and study) that posits that knowledge of God is immediate and intuitive; it stipulates further that all other human knowledge is dependent upon this. It was condemned in 1861 by Pope Pius IX. (*See* also **Ontology**.)

Ontology: A branch of metaphysics that studies the nature and relations of existence.

Oratory: A chapel.

Ordinariate: An ecclesiastical jurisdiction for special purposes and people. Examples are military ordinariates for armed services personnel (in accord with provisions of the apostolic constitution *Spirituali militum curae*, Apr. 21, 1986) and Eastern-Rite ordinariates in places where Eastern-Rite dioceses do not exist.

Ordination: The consecration of sacred ministers for divine worship and the service of people in things pertaining to God. The power of ordination comes from Christ and the Church, and must be conferred by a minister capable of communicating it.

Organ Transplants: The transplanting of organs from one person to another is permissible provided it is done with the consent of the concerned parties and does not result in the death or essential mutilation of the donor. Advances in methods and technology have increased the range of transplant possibilities in recent years.

Original Sin: The sin of Adam (Gn 2:8-3:24), personal to him and passed on to all persons as a state of privation of grace. Despite this privation and the related wounding of human nature and weakening of natural powers, original sin leaves unchanged all that man himself is by nature. The scriptural basis of the doctrine was stated by St. Paul in 1 Cor 15:21ff., and Rom 5:12-21. Original sin is remitted by baptism and incorporation in Christ, through whom grace is given to persons. Pope John Paul II, while describing original sin during a general audience Oct. 1, 1986, called it "the absence of sanctifying grace in nature which has been diverted from its supernatural end."

O Salutaris Hostia: The first three Latin words, *O Saving Victim*, of a Benediction hymn.

Ostpolitik: Policy adopted by Pope Paul VI in an attempt to improve the situation of Eastern European Catholics through diplomatic negotiations with their governments.

Oxford Movement: A movement in the Church of England from 1833 to about 1845 which had for its objective a threefold defense of the Church as a divine institution, the apostolic succession of its bishops, and the *Book of Common Prayer* as the rule of faith. The movement took its name from Oxford University and involved a number of intellectuals who authored a series of influential Tracts for Our Times. Some of its leading figures — e.g., F. W. Faber, John Henry Newman and Henry Edward Manning — became converts to the Catholic Church. In the Church of England, the movement affected the liturgy, historical and theological scholarship, the status of the ministry, and other areas of ecclesiastical life.

P

Paganism: A term referring to non-revealed religions, i.e., religions other than Christianity, Judaism, and Islam.

Palms: Blessed palms are a sacramental. They are blessed and distributed on the Sunday of the Passion in commemoration of the triumphant entrance of Christ into Jerusalem. Ashes of the burnt palms are used on Ash Wednesday.

Pange Lingua: First Latin words, *Sing, my tongue*, of a hymn in honor of the Holy Eucharist, used particularly on Holy Thursday and in Eucharistic processions.

Pantheism: Theory that all things are part of God, divine, in the sense that God realizes himself as the ultimate reality of matter or spirit through being and/or becoming all things that have been, are, and will be. The theory leads to hopeless confusion of the Creator and the created realm of being, identifies evil with good, and involves many inherent contradictions.

Papal Election: The pope is elected by the College of Cardinals during a secret conclave which begins no sooner than 15 days and no later than 20 days after the death of his predecessor. Cardinals under the age of 80, totaling no more than 120, are eligible to take part in the election by secret ballot. Election is by a two-thirds vote of participating cardinals. New legislation regarding papal elections and church government during a vacancy of the Holy See was promulgated by Pope John Paul II, Feb. 23, 1996, in the apostolic constitution *Universi Dominici Gregis* ("Shepherd of the Lord's Whole Flock").

Paraclete: A title of the Holy Spirit meaning, in Greek, Advocate, Consoler.

Parental Duties: All duties related to the obligation of parents to provide for the welfare of their children. These obligations fall under the Fourth Commandment.

Parish: A community of the faithful served by a pastor charged with responsibility for providing them with full pastoral service. Most parishes are territorial, embracing all of the faithful in a certain area of a diocese; some are personal or national, for certain classes of people, without strict regard for their places of residence.

Parousia: The coming, or saving presence, of Christ which will mark the completion of salvation history and the coming to perfection of God's kingdom at the end of the world.

Particular Church: A term used since Vatican II that denotes certain divisions of the Universal Church. Examples include dioceses, vicariates, and prelatures.

Paschal Candle: A large candle, symbolic of the risen Christ, blessed and lighted on the Easter Vigil and placed at the altar until Pentecost. It is ornamented with five large grains of incense, representing the wounds of Christ, inserted in the form of a cross; the Greek letters Alpha and Omega, symbolizing Christ the beginning and end of all things, at the top and bottom of the shaft of the cross; and the figures of the current year of salvation in the quadrants formed by the cross.

Paschal Precept: Church law requiring reception of the Eucharist in the Easter season (*See* separate entry) unless, for a just cause, once-a-year reception takes place at another time.

Passion of Christ: Sufferings of Christ, recorded in the four Gospels.

Pastor: An ordained minister charged with responsibility for the doctrinal, sacramental and related service of people committed to his care; e.g., a bishop for the people in his diocese, a priest for the people of his parish.

Pater Noster: The initial Latin words, *Our Father*, of the Lord's Prayer.

Patriarch: (1) The leaders of the Israelite tribes and heads of prominent families who appear in Genesis from Adam to Joseph. Among the most significant patriarchs of the Old Testament are Abraham, Isaac, and Jacob; the patriarchal narratives in Genesis associated with them constitute the prologue to Israel's salvation history, and the period during which they lived is known as the Age of the Patriarchs. It is noted that the title of patriarch that was used for David (Acts 2:29) was simply one of honor. (2) The head of a branch of the Eastern Church, corresponding to a province of the one-time Roman Empire. There are five official traditional patriarchal sees: Rome, Constantinople, Alexandria, Antioch, and Jerusalem. Presently, the autocephalous churches of the Orthodox Church comprise several of these traditional patriarchates.

Peace, Sign of: A gesture of greeting — e.g., a handshake — exchanged by the ministers and participants at Mass.

Pectoral Cross: A cross worn on a chain about the neck and over the breast by bishops and abbots as a mark of their office.

Penance or Penitence: (1) The spiritual change or conversion of mind and heart by which a person turns away from sin, and all that it implies, toward God, through a personal renewal under the influence of the Holy Spirit. Penance involves sorrow and contrition for sin, together with other internal and external acts of atonement. It serves the purposes of reestablishing in one's life the order of God's love and commandments, and of making satisfaction to God for sin. (2) Penance is a virtue disposing a person to turn to God in sorrow for sin and to carry out works of amendment and atonement. (3) The sacrament of penance and sacramental penance.

People of God: A name for the Church in the sense that it is comprised by a people with Christ as its head, the Holy Spirit as the condition of its unity, the law of love as its rule, and the kingdom of God as its destiny. Although it is a scriptural term, it was given new emphasis by the Second Vatican Council's Dogmatic Constitution on the Church (*Lumen Gentium*).

Perjury: Taking a false oath, lying under oath, a violation of the honor due to God.

Persecution, Religious: A campaign waged against a church or other religious body by persons and governments intent on its destruction. The best known campaigns of this type against the Christian Church were the Roman persecutions which occurred intermittently from about 54 to the promulgation of the Edict of Milan in 313. More Catholics have been persecuted in the 20th century than in any other period in history.

Personal Prelature: *See* under **Opus Dei**, p. 507.

Peter's Pence: A collection made each year among Catholics for the maintenance of the pope and his works of charity. It was originally a tax of a penny on each house, and was collected on St. Peter's day, whence the name. It originated in England in the 8th century.

Petition: One of the four purposes of prayer. In prayers of petition, persons ask of God the blessings they and others need.

Pharisees: Influential class among the Jews, referred to in the Gospels, noted for their self-righteousness, legalism, strict interpretation of the Law, acceptance of the traditions of the elders as well as the Law of Moses, and beliefs regarding angels and spirits, the resurrection of the dead and judgment. Most of them were laymen, and they were closely allied with the Scribes; their opposite numbers were the Sadducees. The Pharisaic and rabbinical traditions had a lasting influence on Judaism following the destruction of Jerusalem in A.D. 70.

Pious Fund: Property and money originally accumulated by the Jesuits to finance their missionary work in Lower California. When the Jesuits were expelled from the territory in 1767, the fund was appropriated by the Spanish Crown and used to support Dominican and Franciscan missionary work in Upper and Lower California. In 1842 the Mexican government took over administration of the fund, incorporated most of the revenue into the national treasury, and agreed to pay the Church interest of six percent a year on the capital so incorporated. From 1848 to 1967 the fund was the subject of lengthy negotiations between the U.S. and Mexican governments because of the latter's failure to make payments as agreed. A lump-sum settlement was made in 1967 with payment by Mexico to the U.S. government of more than $700,000, to be turned over to the Archdiocese of San Francisco.

Polytheism: Belief in and worship of many gods or divinities, especially prevalent in pre-Christian religions.

Poor Box: Alms-box; found in churches from the earliest days of Christianity.

Pope: A title from the Italian word *papa* (from Greek *pappas*, father) used for the Bishop of Rome, the Vicar of Christ and successor of St. Peter, who exercises universal governance over the Church.

Portiuncula: (1) Meaning little portion (of land), the Portiuncula was the chapel of Our Lady of the Angels near Assisi, Italy, which the Benedictines gave to St. Francis early in the 13th century. He repaired the chapel and made it the first church of the Franciscan Order. It is now enshrined in the Basilica of St. Mary of the Angels in Assisi. (2) The plenary Portiuncula Indulgence, or Pardon of Assisi, was authorized by Honorius III. Originally, it could be gained for the souls in purgatory only in the chapel of Our Lady of the Angels; by later concessions, it could be gained also in other Franciscan and parish churches. The indulgence (applicable to the souls in purgatory) can be gained from noon of Aug. 1 to midnight of Aug. 2, once each day. The conditions are, in addition to freedom from attachment to sin: reception of the sacraments of penance and the Eucharist on or near the day and a half; a visit to a parish church within the day and a half, during which the Our Father, the Creed and another prayer are offered for the intentions of the pope.

Positivism: The philosophy that teaches that the only reality is that which is perceived by the senses; the only truth is that which is empirically verified. It asserts that ideas about God, morality, or anything else that cannot be scientifically tested are to be rejected as unknowable.

Possession, Diabolical: The extraordinary state of a person who is tormented from within by evil spirits who exercise strong influence over his powers of mind and body. (*See* also Exorcism.)

Postulant: One of several names used to designate a candidate for membership in a religious institute during the period before novitiate.

Poverty: (1) The quality or state of being poor, in actual destitution and need, or being poor in spirit. In the latter sense, poverty means the state of mind and disposition of persons who regard material things in proper perspective as gifts of God for the support of life and its reasonable enrichment, and for the service of others in need. It means freedom from unreasonable attachment to material things as ends in themselves, even though they may be possessed in small or large measure. (2) One of the evangelical counsels professed as a public vow by members of an institute of consecrated life. It involves the voluntary renunciation of rights of ownership and of independent use and disposal of material goods; or, the right of independent use and disposal, but not of the radical right of ownership. Religious institutes provide their members with necessary and useful goods and services from common resources. The manner in which goods are received and/or handled by religious is determined by poverty of spirit and the rule and constitutions of their institute.

Pragmatism: Theory that the truth of ideas, concepts and values depends on their utility or capacity to serve a useful purpose rather than on their conformity with objective standards; also called utilitarianism.

Prayer: The raising of the mind and heart to God in adoration, thanksgiving, reparation and petition. Prayer, which is always mental because it involves thought and love of God, may be vocal, meditative, private and personal, social, and official. The official prayer of the Church as a worshipping community is called the liturgy.

Precepts: Commands or orders given to individuals or communities in particular cases; they establish law for concerned parties. Preceptive documents are issued by the pope, departments of the Roman Curia and other competent authority in the Church.

Presence of God: A devotional practice of increasing one's awareness of the presence and action of God in daily life.

Presumption: A sin against hope, by which a person striving for salvation (1) either relies too much on his own capabilities or (2) expects God to do things which he cannot do, in keeping with his divine attributes, or does not will to do, according to his divine plan. Presumption is the

opposite of despair.

Preternatural Gifts: Exceptional gifts, beyond the exigencies and powers of human nature, enjoyed by Adam in the state of original justice: immunity from suffering and death, superior knowledge, integrity or perfect control of the passions. These gifts were lost as the result of original sin; their loss, however, implied no impairment of the integrity of human nature.

Pride: Unreasonable self-esteem; one of the seven capital sins.

Prie-Dieu: A French phrase, meaning pray God, designating a kneeler or bench suitable for kneeling while at prayer.

Priesthood: (1) The common priesthood of the non-ordained faithful. In virtue of baptism and confirmation, the faithful are a priestly people who participate in the priesthood of Christ through acts of worship, witness to the faith in daily life, and efforts to foster the growth of God's kingdom. (2) The ordained priesthood, in virtue of the sacrament of orders, of bishops, priests and deacons, for service to the common priesthood.

Primary Option: The life-choice of a person for or against God which shapes the basic orientation of moral conduct. A primary option for God does not preclude the possibility of serious sin.

Prior: A superior or an assistant to an abbot in a monastery.

Privilege: A favor, an exemption from the obligation of a law. Privileges of various kinds, with respect to ecclesiastical laws, are granted by the pope, departments of the Roman Curia and other competent authority in the Church.

Probabiliorism: The moral system asserting that the more probable opinion of a varied set of acceptable positions regarding the binding character of a law should be accepted. If the reasons for being free from a law are more probably true, one is freed from the law's obligations. Probabiliorism, however, maintained that if it was probable that the law did not bind, one still had to follow it unless it was more probable that the law did not bind.

Probabilism: A moral system for use in cases of conscience which involve the obligation of doubtful laws. There is a general principle that a doubtful law does not bind. Probabilism, therefore, teaches that it is permissible to follow an opinion favoring liberty, provided the opinion is certainly and solidly probable. Probabilism may not be invoked when there is question of: a certain law or the certain obligation of a law; the certain right of another party; the validity of an action; something which is necessary for salvation.

Pro-Cathedral: A church used as a cathedral.

Promoter of the Faith (*Promotor fidei*): An official of the Congregation for the Causes of Saints, whose role in beatification and canonization procedures is to establish beyond reasonable doubt the validity of evidence regarding the holiness of prospective saints and miracles attributed to their intercession.

Prophecy: (1) The communication of divine revelation by inspired intermediaries, called prophets, between God and his people. Old Testament prophecy was unique in its origin and because of its ethical and religious content, which included disclosure of the saving will of Yahweh for the people, moral censures and warnings of divine punishment because of sin and violations of the Law and Covenant, in the form of promises, admonitions, reproaches and threats. Although Moses and other earlier figures are called prophets, the period of prophecy is generally dated from the early years of the monarchy to about 100 years after the Babylonian Exile. From that time on, the written Law and its interpreters supplanted the prophets as guides of the people. Old Testament prophets are cited in the New Testament, with awareness that God spoke through them and that some of their oracles were fulfilled in Christ. John the Baptist is the outstanding prophetic figure in the New Testament. Christ never claimed the title of prophet for himself, although some people thought he was one. There were prophets in the early Church, and St. Paul mentioned the charism of prophecy in 1 Cor 14:1-5. Prophecy disappeared after New Testament times. Revelation is classified as the prophetic book of the New Testament. (2) In contemporary non-scriptural usage, the term is applied to the witness given by persons to the relevance of their beliefs in everyday life and action.

Proportionalism: The moral theory that asserts that an action is judged on whether the evils resulting are proportionate to the goods that result. If the evils outweigh the goods, the act is objectionable; if the opposite is true, the act is permissible. Proportionalism differs from consequentialism in that the former admits that the inherent morality of the act and the agent's intention must also be considered. Proportionalism is rejected by critics as it does not offer an objective criterion for determining when evils are proportionate or disproportionate. It also fails to consider the intrinsic nature of human acts and does nothing to assist Christians to grow in virtue.

Province: (1) A territory comprising one archdiocese called the metropolitan see and one or more dioceses called suffragan sees. The head of the archdiocese, an archbishop, has metropolitan rights and responsibilities over the province. (2) A division of a religious order under the jurisdiction of a provincial superior.

Prudence: Practical wisdom and judgment regarding the choice and use of the best ways and means of doing good; one of the four cardinal virtues.

Punishment Due for Sin: The punishment which is a consequence of sin. It is of two kinds: (1) Eternal punishment is the punishment of hell, to which one becomes subject by the commission of mortal sin. Such punishment is remitted when mortal sin is forgiven. (2) Temporal punishment is a consequence of venial sin and/or forgiven mortal sin; it is not everlasting and may be remitted in this life by means of penance. Temporal punishment unremitted during this life is remitted by suffering in purgatory.

Purgatory: The state or condition of those who have died in the state of grace but with some attachment to sin, and are purified for a time before they are admitted to the glory and happiness of heaven. In this state and period of passive suffering, they are purified of unrepented venial sins, satisfy the demands of divine justice for temporal punishment due for sins, and are thus converted to a state of worthiness of the beatific vision.

Q

Quadragesima: From the Latin for fortieth, the name given to the forty penitential days of Lent.

Quinquennial Report: A report on the current state of a diocese that must be compiled and submitted by a bishop to the Holy See every five years in anticipation of the *ad liminal* visit.

Quinque Viae: From the Latin for the "five ways," the five proofs for the existence of God that were proposed by St. Thomas Aquinas in his *Summa Theologiae* (Part I, question 2, article 3). The five ways are: 1) all the motion in the world points to an unmoved Prime Mover; 2) the subordinate agents in the world imply the First Agent; 3) there must be a Cause Who is not perishable and Whose existence is underived; 4) the limited goodness in the world must be a reflection of Unlimited Goodness; 5) all things tend to become something, and that inclination must have proceeded from some Rational Planner.

R

Racism: A theory which holds that any one or several of the different races of the human family are inherently superior or inferior to any one or several of the others. The teaching denies the essential unity of the human race, the equality and dignity of all persons because of their common possession of the same human nature, and the participation of all in the divine plan of redemption. It is radically opposed to the virtue of justice and the precept of love of neighbor. Differences of superiority and inferiority which do exist are the result of accidental factors operating in a wide variety of circumstances, and are in no way due to essential defects in any one or several of the branches of the one human race. The theory of racism, together with practices related to it, is incompatible with Christian doctrine.

Rash Judgment: Attributing faults to another without sufficient reason; a violation of the obligations of justice and charity.

Rationalism: A theory which makes the mind the measure and arbiter of all things, including religious truth. A product of the Enlightenment, it rejects the supernatural, divine revelation, and authoritative teaching by any church.

Recollection: Meditation, attitude of concentration or awareness of spiritual matters and things pertaining to salvation and the accomplishment of God's will.

Relativism: Theory which holds that all truth, including religious truth, is relative, i.e., not absolute, certain or unchanging; a product of agnosticism, indifferentism, and an unwarranted extension of the notion of truth in positive science. Relativism is based on the tenet that certain knowledge of any and all truth is impossible. Therefore, no religion, philosophy or science can be said to possess the real truth; consequently, all religions, philosophies and sciences may be considered to have as much or as little truth as any of the others.

Relics: The physical remains and effects of saints, which are considered worthy of veneration inasmuch as they are representative of persons in glory with God. Catholic doctrine proscribes the view that relics are not worthy of veneration. In line with norms laid down by the Council of Trent and subsequent enactments, discipline concerning relics is subject to control by the Congregations for the Causes of Saints and for Divine Worship and the Discipline of the Sacraments.

Religion: The adoration and service of God as expressed in divine worship and in daily life. Religion is concerned with all of the relations existing between God and human beings, and between humans themselves because of the central significance of God. Objectively considered, religion consists of a body of truth that is believed, a code of morality for the guidance of conduct, and a form of divine worship. Subjectively, it is a person's total response, theoretically and practically, to the demands of faith; it is living faith, personal engagement, self-commitment to God. Thus, by creed, code and cult, a person orders and directs his or her life in reference to God and, through what the love and service of God implies, to all people and all things.

Reliquary: A vessel for the preservation and exposition of a relic; sometimes made like a small monstrance.

Reparation: The making of amends to God for sin committed; one of the four ends of prayer and the purpose of penance.

Requiem: A Mass offered for the repose of the soul of one who has died in Christ. Its name is derived from the first word of the Gregorian (Latin) entrance chant (or Introit) at Masses for the dead: *Requiem aeternam dona eis, Domine* ("Eternal rest grant unto them, O Lord"). The revised Rite for Funerals refers to the requiem as the Mass of Christian Burial; however, it would not be uncommon to hear people employ the former usage.

Rescript: A written reply by an ecclesiastical superior regarding a question or request; its provisions bind concerned parties only. Papal dispensations are issued in the form of rescripts.

Reserved Censure: A sin or censure, absolution from which is reserved to religious superiors, bishops, the pope, or confessors having special faculties. Reservations are made because of the serious nature and social effects of certain sins and censures.

Restitution: An act of reparation for an injury done to another. The injury may be caused by taking and/or retaining what belongs to another or by damaging either the property or reputation of another. The intention of making restitution, usually in kind, is required as a condition for the forgiveness of sins of injustice, even though actual restitution is not possible.

Ring: In the Church a ring is worn as part of the insignia of bishops, abbots, et al.; by sisters to denote their consecration to God and the Church. The wedding ring symbolizes the love and union of husband and wife.

Ritual: A book of prayers and ceremonies used in the administration of the sacraments and other ceremonial functions. In the Roman Rite, the standard book of this kind is the Roman Ritual.

Rogito: The official notarial act or document testifying to the burial of a pope.

Rosary: A form of mental and vocal prayer centered on mysteries or events in the lives of Jesus and Mary. Its essential elements are meditation on the mysteries and the recitation of a number of decades of Hail Marys, each beginning with the Lord's Prayer. Introductory prayers may include the Apostles' Creed, an initial Our Father, three Hail Marys and a Glory be to the Father; each decade is customarily concluded with a Glory be to the Father; at the end, it is customary to say the Hail, Holy Queen and a prayer from the liturgy for the feast of the Blessed Virgin Mary of the Rosary. Traditionally, the Mysteries of the Rosary, which are the subject of medita-

tion, are: (1) Joyful — the Annunciation to Mary that she was to be the Mother of Christ, her visit to Elizabeth, the birth of Jesus, the presentation of Jesus in the Temple, the finding of Jesus in the Temple. (2) Sorrowful — Christ's agony in the Garden of Gethsemani, scourging at the pillar, crowning with thorns, carrying of the cross to Calvary, and crucifixion. (3) Glorious — the Resurrection and Ascension of Christ, the descent of the Holy Spirit upon the Apostles, Mary's Assumption into heaven and her crowning as Queen of angels and men.

The complete Rosary, called the Dominican Rosary, consists of 15 decades. In customary practice, only five decades are usually said at one time. Rosary beads are used to aid in counting the prayers without distraction. The Rosary originated through the coalescence of popular devotions to Jesus and Mary from the 12th century onward. Its present form dates from about the 15th century. Carthusians contributed greatly toward its development; Dominicans have been its greatest promoters. The fifteen mysteries were standardized by Pope Pius V in 1569.

In 2002, Pope John Paul II added five new mysteries dedicated to chapters from Jesus' public life. Titled the Mysteries of Light, they are: Christ's baptism in the Jordan River; Christ's self-revelation at the marriage of Cana; Christ's announcement of the kingdom of God with the invitation to conversion; Christ's Transfiguration, when he revealed his glory to his Apostles; and the institution of the Eucharist at the Last Supper as the sacramental expression of the paschal mystery. The pope asked that the Mysteries of Light be recited especially on Thursday.

S

Sabbath: The seventh day of the week, observed by Jews and Sabbatarians as the day for rest and religious observance.

Sacrarium: A basin with a drain leading directly into the ground; standard equipment of a sacristy.

Sacred Heart, Enthronement of the: An acknowledgment of the sovereignty of Jesus Christ over the Christian family, expressed by the installation of an image or picture of the Sacred Heart in a place of honor in the home, accompanied by an act of consecration.

Sacred Heart, Promises: Twelve promises to persons having devotion to the Sacred Heart of Jesus, which were communicated by Christ to St. Margaret Mary Alacoque in a private revelation in 1675.

Sacrilege: Violation of and irreverence toward a person, place or thing that is sacred because of public dedication to God; a sin against the virtue of religion. Personal sacrilege is violence of some kind against a cleric or religious, or a violation of chastity with a cleric or religious. Local sacrilege is the desecration of sacred places. Real sacrilege is irreverence with respect to sacred things, such as the sacraments and sacred vessels.

Sacristy: A utility room where vestments, church furnishings and sacred vessels are kept and where the clergy vest for sacred functions.

Sadducees: The predominantly priestly party among the Jews in the time of Christ, noted for extreme conservatism, acceptance only of the Law of Moses, and rejection of the traditions of the elders. Their opposite numbers were the Pharisees.

Saints, Cult of: The veneration, called *dulia*, of holy persons who have died and are in glory with God in heaven; it includes honoring them and petitioning them for their intercession with God. Liturgical veneration is given only to saints officially recognized by the Church; private veneration may be given to anyone thought to be in heaven. The veneration of saints is essentially different from the adoration given to God alone; by its very nature, however, it terminates in the worship of God. (*See* also **Dulia** and **Latria**.)

Salvation: The liberation of persons from sin and its effects, reconciliation with God in and through Christ, the attainment of union with God forever in the glory of heaven as the supreme purpose of life and as the God-given reward for fulfillment of his will on earth. Salvation-in-process begins and continues in this life through union with Christ in faith professed and in action; its final term is union with God and the whole community of the saved in the ultimate perfection of God's kingdom. The Church teaches that: God wills the salvation of all men; men are saved in and through Christ; membership in the Church established by Christ, known and understood as the community of salvation, is necessary for salvation; men with this knowledge and understanding who deliberately reject this Church, cannot be saved. The Catholic Church is the Church founded by Christ. (*See* below, **Salvation outside the Church**.)

Salvation History: The facts and the record of God's relations with human beings, in the past, present and future, for the purpose of leading them to live in accordance with his will for the eventual attainment after death of salvation, or everlasting happiness with him in heaven. The essentials of salvation history are: God's love for all human beings and will for their salvation; his intervention and action in the world to express this love and bring about their salvation; the revelation he made of himself and the covenant he established with the Israelites in the Old Testament; the perfecting of this revelation and the new covenant of grace through Christ in the New Testament; the continuing action-for-salvation carried on in and through the Church; the communication of saving grace to people through the merits of Christ and the operations of the Holy Spirit in the here-and-now circumstances of daily life and with the cooperation of people themselves.

Salvation outside the Church: The Second Vatican Council covered this subject summarily in the following manner: "Those also can attain to everlasting salvation who through no fault of their own do not know the Gospel of Christ or his Church, yet sincerely seek God and, moved by grace, strive by their deeds to do his will as it is known to them through the dictates of conscience. Nor does divine Providence deny the help necessary for salvation to those who, without blame on their part, have not yet arrived at an explicit knowledge of God, but who strive to live a good life, thanks to his grace. Whatever good or truth is found among them is looked upon by the Church as a preparation for the Gospel. She regards such qualities as given by him who enlightens all men so that they may finally have life" (Dogmatic Constitution on the Church, *Lumen Gentium*, No. 16). These teachings were reiterated by the document issued by the Congregation for the Doctrine of the Faith, *Dominus Iesus*.

Sanctifying Grace: *See* **Grace**.

Satanism: Worship of the devil, a blasphemous inversion of the order of worship which is due to God alone.

Scandal: Conduct which is the occasion of sin to another person.

Scapular: (1) A part of the habit of some religious orders like the Benedictines and Dominicans; a nearly shoulder-wide strip of cloth worn over the tunic and reaching almost to the feet in front and behind. Originally a kind of apron, it came to symbolize the cross and yoke of Christ. (2) Scapulars worn by lay persons as a sign of association with religious orders and for devotional purposes are an adaptation of monastic scapulars. Approved by the Church as sacramentals, they consist of two small squares of woolen cloth joined by strings and are worn about the neck. They are given for wearing in a ceremony of investiture or enrollment. There are nearly 20 scapulars for devotional use: the five principal ones are generally understood to include those of Our Lady of Mt. Carmel (the brown Carmelite Scapular), the Holy Trinity, Our Lady of the Seven Dolors, the Passion, the Immaculate Conception.

Scapular Medal: A medallion with a representation of the Sacred Heart on one side and of the Blessed Virgin Mary on the other. Authorized by St. Pius X in 1910, it may be worn or carried in place of a scapular by persons already invested with a scapular.

Scapular Promise: According to a legend of the Carmelite Order, the Blessed Virgin Mary appeared to St. Simon Stock in 1251 at Cambridge, England, and declared that wearers of the brown Carmelite Scapular would be the beneficiaries of her special intercession. The scapular tradition has never been the subject of official decision by the Church. Essentially, it expresses belief in the intercession of Mary and the efficacy of sacramentals in the context of truly Christian life.

Schism: Derived from a Greek word meaning separation, the term designates formal and obstinate refusal by a baptized Catholic, called a schismatic, to be in communion with the pope and the Church. The canonical penalty is excommunication. One of the most disastrous schisms in history resulted in the definitive separation of the Church in the East from union with Rome about 1054.

Scholasticism: The term usually applied to the Catholic theology and philosophy which developed in the Middle Ages. (*See* also **Neo-Scholasticism**.)

Scribes: Hebrew intellectuals noted for their knowledge of the Law of Moses, influential from the time of the Exile to about A.D. 70. Many of them were Pharisees. They were the antecedents of rabbis and their traditions, as well as those o the Pharisees, had a lasting influence on Judaism following the destruction of Jerusalem in A.D. 70.

Scruple: A morbid, unreasonable fear and anxiety that one's actions are sinful when they are not, or more seriously sinful than they actually are. Compulsive scrupulosity is quite different from the transient scrupulosity of persons of tender or highly sensitive conscience, or of persons with faulty moral judgment.

Seal of Confession: The obligation of secrecy which must be observed regarding knowledge of things learned in connection with the confession of sin in the sacrament of penance. The seal covers matters whose revelation would make the sacrament burdensome. Confessors are prohibited, under penalty of excommunication, from making any direct revelation of confessional matter; this prohibition holds, outside of confession, even with respect to the person who made the confession unless the person releases the priest from the obligation. Persons other than confessors are obliged to maintain secrecy, but not under penalty of excommunication. General, non-specific discussion of confessional matter does not violate the seal.

Secularism: A school of thought, a spirit and manner of action which ignores and/or repudiates the validity or influence of supernatural religion with respect to individual and social life.

See: Another name for diocese or archdiocese.

Seminary: A house of study and formation for men, called seminarians, preparing for the priesthood. Traditional seminaries date from the Council of Trent in the middle of the 16th century; before that time, candidates for the priesthood were variously trained in monastic schools, universities under church auspices, and in less formal ways.

Sermon on the Mount: A compilation of sayings of Our Lord in the form of an extended discourse in Matthew's Gospel (5:1 to 7:27) and, in a shorter discourse, in Luke (6:17-49). The passage in Matthew, called the "Constitution of the New Law," summarizes the living spirit of believers in Christ and members of the kingdom of God. Beginning with the Beatitudes and including the Lord's Prayer, it covers the perfect justice of the New Law, the fulfillment of the Old Law in the New Law of Christ, and the integrity of internal attitude and external conduct with respect to love of God and neighbor, justice, chastity, truth, trust and confidence in God.

Seven Last Words of Christ: The Seven Last Words of Christ on the Cross were: (1) *"Father, forgive them; for they do not know what they are doing."* (Lk 23:34); (2) To the penitent thief: *"I assure you: today you will be with me in Paradise."* (Lk 23:24); (3) To Mary and his Apostle John: *"Woman, behold thy son! . . . Behold your mother."* (Jn 19:26); (4) *"Eli Eli, lama sabacthani* [*"My God, my God, why have you forsaken me?"*] (Mt 27:46; cf. Mk 15:34); (5) *"I thirst."* (Jn 19:28); (6) *"It is finished."* (Jn 19:30); (7) *"Father, into thy hands I commend my spirit."*(Lk 23:46).

Shrine, Crowned: A shrine approved by the Holy See as a place of pilgrimage. The approval permits public devotion at the shrine and implies that at least one miracle has resulted from devotion at the shrine. Among the best known crowned shrines are those of the Virgin Mary at Lourdes and Fátima. Shrines with statues crowned by Pope John Paul in 1985 in South America were those of Our Lady of Coromoto, patroness of Venezuela, in Caracas, and Our Lady of Carmen of Paucartambo in Cuzco, Peru.

Shroud of Turin: A strip of brownish linen cloth, 14 feet, three inches in length and three feet, seven inches in width, bearing the front and back imprint of a human body. A tradition dating from the 7th century, which has not been verified beyond doubt, claims that the shroud is the fine linen in which the body of Christ was wrapped for burial. The early history of the shroud is obscure. It was enshrined at Lirey, France, in 1354 and was transferred in 1578 to Turin, Italy, where it has been kept in the cathedral down to the present time. Scientific investigation, which began in 1898, seems to indicate that the markings on the shroud are those of a human body. The shroud, for the first time since 1933, was placed on public view from Aug. 27 to Oct. 8, 1978, and was seen by an estimated 3.3 million people. Scientists conducted intensive studies of it thereafter, finally determining that the material of the shroud dated from between 1260 and 1390. The shroud, which had been the possession of the House of Savoy, was willed to Pope John Paul II in 1983.

Sick Calls: When a person is confined at home by illness or other cause and is unable to go to church for reception of the sacraments, a parish priest should be informed and arrangements made for him to visit the person at home. Such visitations are common in pastoral practice, both for special needs and for providing persons with regular opportunities for receiving the sacraments. If a priest cannot make the visitation, arrangements can be made for a deacon or Eucharistic minister to bring Holy Communion to the homebound or bedridden person.

Sign of the Cross: A sign, ceremonial gesture or movement in the form of a cross by which a person confesses faith in the Holy Trinity and Christ, and intercedes for the blessing of himself or herself, other persons and things. In Roman-Rite practice, a person making the sign touches the fingers of the right hand to forehead, below the breast, left shoulder and right shoulder while saying: *"In the name of the Father, and of the Son, and of the Holy Spirit."* The sign is also made with the thumb on the forehead, the lips, and the breast. For the blessing of persons and objects, a large sign of the cross is made by movement of the right hand. In Eastern-Rite practice, the sign is made with the thumb and first two fingers of the right hand joined together and touching the forehead, below the breast, the right shoulder and the left shoulder; the formula generally used is the doxology, *"O Holy God, O Holy Strong One, O Immortal One."* The Eastern manner of making the sign was general until the first half of the 13th century; by the 17th century, Western practice involved the whole right hand and the reversal of direction from shoulder to shoulder.

Signs of the Times: Contemporary events, trends and features in culture and society, the needs and aspirations of people, all the factors that form the context in and through which the Church has to carry on its saving mission. The Second Vatican Council spoke on numerous occasions about these signs and the relationship between them and a kind of manifestation of God's will, positive or negative, and about subjecting them to judgment and action corresponding to the demands of divine revelation through Scripture, Christ, and the experience, tradition and teaching authority of the Church.

Simony: The deliberate intention and act of selling and/or buying spiritual goods or material things so connected with the spiritual that they cannot be separated therefrom; a violation of the virtue of religion, and a sacrilege, because it wrongfully puts a material price on spiritual things, which cannot be either sold or bought. In Church law, actual sale or purchase is subject to censure in some cases. The term is derived from the name of Simon Magus, who attempted to buy from Sts. Peter and John the power to confirm people in the Holy Spirit (Acts 8:4-24).

Sin: (1) Actual sin is the free and deliberate violation of God's law by thought, word or action. (a) **Mortal** sin — involving serious matter, sufficient reflection and full consent — results in the loss of sanctifying grace and alienation from God, and renders a person incapable of performing meritorious supernatural acts and subject to everlasting punishment. (b) **Venial** sin — involving less serious matter, reflection and consent — does not have such serious consequences. (2) **Original** sin is the sin of Adam, with consequences for all human beings. (*See* separate entry.)

Sins against the Holy Spirit: Despair of salvation, presumption of God's mercy, impugning the known truths of faith, envy at another's spiritual good, obstinacy in sin, final impenitence. Those guilty of such sins stubbornly resist the influence of grace and, as long as they do so, cannot be forgiven.

Sins, Occasions of: Circumstances (persons, places, things, etc.) which easily lead to sin. There is an obligation to avoid voluntary proximate occasions of sin, and to take precautions against the dangers of unavoidable occasions.

Sins That Cry to Heaven for Vengeance: Willful murder, sins against nature, oppression of the poor, widows and orphans, defrauding laborers of their wages.

Sister: Any woman religious, in popular speech; strictly, the title applies only to women religious belonging to institutes whose members never professed solemn vows. Most of the institutes whose members are properly called Sisters were established during and since the 19th century. Women religious with solemn vows, or belonging to institutes whose members formerly professed solemn vows, are properly called nuns.

Sisterhood: A generic term referring to the whole institution of the life of women religious in the Church, or to a particular institute of women religious.

Situation Ethics: A subjective, individualistic ethical theory which denies the binding force of ethical principles as universal laws and preceptive norms of moral conduct, and proposes that morality is determined only by situational conditions and considerations and the intention of the person. It has been criticized for ignoring the principles of objective ethics. (See also **Consequentialism** and **Proportionalism**.)

Slander: Attributing to a person faults which he or she does not have; a violation of the obligations of justice and charity, for which restitution is due.

Sloth (Acedia): One of the seven capital sins; spiritual laziness, involving distaste and disgust for spiritual things; spiritual boredom, which saps the vigor of spiritual life. Physical laziness is a counterpart of spiritual sloth.

Sorcery: A kind of black magic in which evil is invoked by means of diabolical intervention; a violation of the virtue of religion.

Soteriology: The division of theology which treats of the mission and work of Christ as Redeemer.

Species, Sacred: The appearances of bread and wine (color, taste, smell, etc.) which remain after the substance has been changed at the Consecration of the Mass into the Body and Blood of Christ. (See **Transubstantiation**.)

Spiritism: Attempts to communicate with spirits and departed souls by means of seances, table tapping, ouija boards, and other methods; a violation of the virtue of religion. Spiritualistic practices are noted for fakery.

Stational Churches, Days: Churches, especially in Rome, where the clergy and lay people were accustomed to gather with their bishop on certain days for the celebration of the liturgy. The 25 early titular or parish churches of Rome, plus other churches, each had their turn as the site of divine worship in practices which may have started in the third century. The observances were rather well developed toward the latter part of the 4th century, and by the fifth they included a Mass concelebrated by the pope and attendant priests. On some occasions, the stational liturgy was preceded by a procession from another church called a collecta. There were 42 Roman stational churches in the 8th century, and 89 stational services were scheduled annually in connection with the liturgical seasons. Stational observances fell into disuse toward the end of the Middle Ages. Some revival was begun by John XXIII in 1959 and continued by Paul VI and John Paul II.

Stations (Way) of the Cross: A form of devotion commemorating the Passion and death of Christ, consisting of a series of meditations (stations): (1) his condemnation to death, (2) taking up of the cross, (3) the first fall on the way to Calvary, (4) meeting his Mother, (5) being assisted by Simon of Cyrene and (6) by the woman Veronica who wiped his face, (7) the second fall, (8) meeting the women of Jerusalem, (9) the third fall, (10) being stripped and (11) nailed to the cross, (12) his death, (13) the removal of his body from the cross and (14) his burial. Depictions of these scenes are mounted in most churches, chapels and in some other places, beneath small crosses. A person making the Way of the Cross passes before these stations, or stopping points, pausing at each for meditation. If the stations are made by a group of people, only the leader has to pass from station to station. A plenary indulgence is granted to the faithful who make the stations, under the usual conditions: freedom from all attachment to sin, reception of the sacraments of penance and the Eucharist, and prayers for the intentions of the pope. Those who are impeded from making the stations in the usual manner can gain the same indulgence if, along with the aforementioned conditions, they spend at least a half hour in spiritual reading and meditation on the passion and death of Christ. The stations originated remotely from the practice of Holy Land pilgrims who visited the actual scenes of incidents in the Passion of Christ. Representations elsewhere of at least some of these scenes were known as early as the 5th century. Later, the stations evolved in connection with and as a consequence of strong devotion to the Passion in the 12th and 13th centuries. Franciscans, who were given custody of the Holy Places in 1342, promoted the devotion widely; one of them, St. Leonard of Port Maurice, became known as the greatest preacher of the Way of the Cross in the 18th century. The general features of the devotion were fixed by Clement XII in 1731.

Statutes: Virtually the same as **decrees** (See separate entry), they almost always designate laws of a particular council or synod rather than pontifical laws.

Stigmata: Marks of the wounds suffered by Christ in his crucifixion, in hands and feet by nails, and side by the piercing of a lance. Some persons, called stigmatists, have been reported as recipients or sufferers of marks like these. The Church, however, has never issued any infallible declaration about their possession by anyone, even in the case of St. Francis of Assisi whose stigmata seem to be the best substantiated and may be commemorated in the Roman-Rite liturgy. Ninety percent of some 300 reputed stigmatists have been women. Judgment regarding the presence, significance, and manner of causation of stigmata would depend, among other things, on irrefutable experimental evidence.

Stipend, Mass: An offering given to a priest for applying the fruits of the Mass according to the intention of the donor. The offering is a contribution to the support of the priest. The disposition of the fruits of the sacrifice, in line with doctrine concerning the Mass in particular and prayer in general, is subject to the will of God. Mass offerings and intentions were the subjects of a decree approved by John Paul II and made public Mar. 22, 1991: (1) Normally, no more than one offering should be accepted for a Mass; the Mass should be offered in accord with the donor's intention; the priest who accepts the offering should celebrate the Mass himself or have another priest do so. (2) Several Mass intentions, for which offerings have been made, can be combined for a "collective" application of a single Mass only if the previous and explicit consent of the donors is obtained. Such Masses are an exception to the general rule.

Stole Fee: An offering given on certain occasions; e.g., at a baptism, wedding, funeral, for the support of the clergy who administer the sacraments and perform other sacred rites.

Stoup: A vessel used to contain holy water.

Suffragan See: Any diocese, except the archdiocese, within a province.

Suicide: The taking of one's own life; a violation of God's dominion over human life. Ecclesiastical burial is denied to persons while in full possession of their faculties; it is permitted in cases of doubt.

Supererogation: Actions which go beyond the obligations of duty and the requirements enjoined by God's law as necessary for salvation. Examples of these works are the profession and observance of the evangelical counsels of poverty, chastity, and obedience, and efforts to practice charity to the highest degree.

Supernatural: Above the natural; that which exceeds and is not due or owed to the essence, exigencies, requirements, powers and merits of created nature. While human beings have no claim on supernatural things and do not need them in order to exist and act on a natural level, they do need them in order to exist and act in the higher order or economy of grace established by God for their salvation. God has freely given them certain things which are beyond the powers and rights of their human nature. Examples of the supernatural are: grace, a kind of participation by human beings in the divine life, by which they become capable of performing acts meritorious for salvation; divine revelation by which God manifests himself to them and makes known truth that is inaccessible to human reason alone; faith, by which they believe divine truth because of the authority of God who reveals it through Sacred Scripture and tradition and the teaching of his Church.

Suspension: A censure by which a cleric is forbidden to exercise some or all of his powers of orders and jurisdiction, or to accept the financial support of his benefices.

Syllabus, The: (1) When not qualified, the term refers to the list of 80 errors accompanying Pope Pius IX's encyclical *Quanta Cura*, issued in 1864. (2) The Syllabus of St. Pius X in the encyclical *Lamentabili*, issued by the Holy Office July 4, 1907, condemning 65 heretical propositions of modernism. This schedule of errors was followed shortly by that pope's encyclical *Pascendi*, the principal ecclesiastical document against modernism, issued Sept. 8, 1907.

Synod, Diocesan: Meeting of representative persons of a diocese — priests, religious, lay persons — with the bishop, called by him for the purpose of considering and taking action on matters affecting the life and mission of the Church in the diocese. Persons taking part in a synod have consultative status; the bishop alone is the legislator, with power to authorize synodal decrees. According to canon law, every diocese should have a synod every 10 years.

T

Tabernacle: The receptacle in which the Blessed Sacrament is reserved in churches, chapels, and oratories. It is to be immovable, solid, locked, and located in a prominent place.

Te Deum: The opening Latin words, Thee, God, of a hymn of praise and thanksgiving prescribed for use in the Office of Readings of the Liturgy of the Hours on many Sundays, solemnities and feasts.

Temperance: Moderation, one of the four cardinal virtues.

Temptation: Any enticement to sin, from any source: the strivings of one's own faculties, the action of the devil, other persons, circumstances of life, etc. Temptation itself is not sin. Temptation can be avoided and overcome with the use of prudence and the help of grace.

Thanksgiving: An expression of gratitude to God

for his goodness and the blessings he grants; one of the four ends of prayer.

Theism: A philosophy which admits the existence of God and the possibility of divine revelation; it is generally monotheistic and acknowledges God as transcendent and also active in the world. Because it is a philosophy rather than a system of theology derived from revelation, it does not include specifically Christian doctrines, like those concerning the Trinity, the Incarnation and Redemption.

Theodicy: From the Greek for God (theos) and judgment (dike), the study of God as he can be known by natural reason, rather than from supernatural revelation. First used by Gottfried Leibnitz (1646-1716), its primary objective is to make God's omnipotence compatible with the existence of evil.

Theological Virtues: The virtues which have God for their direct object: faith, or belief in God's infallible teaching; hope, or confidence in divine assistance; charity, or love of God. They are given to a person with grace in the first instance, through baptism and incorporation in Christ.

Theology: Knowledge of God and religion, deriving from and based on the data of divine Revelation, organized and systematized according to some kind of scientific method. It involves systematic study and presentation of the truths of divine Revelation in Sacred Scripture, tradition, and the teaching of the Church. Theology has been divided under various subject headings. Some of the major fields have been: dogmatic (systematic theology), moral, pastoral, historical, ascetical (the practice of virtue and means of attaining holiness and perfection), sacramental, and spiritual (higher states of religious experience). Other subject headings include ecumenism (Christian unity, interfaith relations), ecclesiology (the nature and constitution of the Church), and Mariology (doctrine concerning the Blessed Virgin Mary), etc.

Theotokos: From the Greek for God-bearer, the preeminent title given to the Blessed Mother in the Oriental Church. This title has very ancient roots, stretching as far back as the third century but it did not became official in the Church until the Council of Ephesus in 431.

Thomism: The philosophy based on St. Thomas Aquinas (1224/5-1274), which is mandated to be the dominant philosophy used in Catholic educational institutions. (See also **Neo-Scholasticism** and **Scholasticism**.)

Tithing: Contribution of a portion of one's income, originally one-tenth, for purposes of religion and charity. The practice is mentioned 46 times in the Bible. In early Christian times, tithing was adopted in continuance of Old Testament practices of the Jewish people, and the earliest positive Church legislation on the subject was enacted in 567. Catholics are bound in conscience to contribute to the support of their church, but the manner in which they do so is not fixed by law. Tithing, which amounts to a pledged contribution of a portion of one's income, has aroused new attention in recent years in the United States.

Titular Sees: Dioceses where the Church once flourished but which now exist only in name or title. Bishops without a territorial or residential diocese of their own; e.g., auxiliary bishops, are given titular sees. There are more than 2,000 titular sees; 16 of them are in the United States.

Transfinalization, Transignification: Terms coined to express the sign value of consecrated bread and wine with respect to the presence and action of Christ in the Eucharistic sacrifice and the spiritually vivifying purpose of the Eucharistic banquet in Holy Communion. The theory behind the terms has strong undertones of existential and "sign" philosophy, and has been criticized for its openness to interpretation at variance with the doctrine of transubstantiation and the abiding presence of Christ under the appearances of bread and wine after the sacrifice of the Mass and Communion have been completed. The terms, if used as substitutes for transubstantiation, are unacceptable; if they presuppose transubstantiation, they are acceptable as clarifications of its meaning.

Transubstantiation: "The way Christ is made present in this sacrament (Holy Eucharist) is none other than by the change of the whole substance of the bread into his Body, and of the whole substance of the wine into his Blood (in the Consecration at Mass), this unique and wonderful change the Catholic Church rightly calls transubstantiation" (encyclical *Mysterium Fidei* of Paul VI, Sept. 3, 1965). The first official use of the term was made by the Fourth Council of the Lateran in 1215. Authoritative teaching on the subject was issued by the Council of Trent.

Treasury of the Church: The superabundant merits of Christ and the saints from which the Church draws to confer spiritual benefits, such as indulgences.

Triduum: A three-day series of public or private devotions.

U-Z

Ultramontanism: The movement found primarily in France during the 19th century that advocated a strong sense of devotion and service to the Holy See. Generally considered a reaction to the antipapal tendencies of Gallicanism, its name was derived from the Latin for "over the mountains," a reference to the Alps, beyond which rested Rome and the Holy See.

Unction: From the Latin, ungere, meaning to anoint or smear, a term used to denote the Sacrament of the Sick (or the Anointing of the Sick); it was more commonly termed Extreme Unction and was given as an anointing to a person just before death.

Universal Law: See **Law**.

Urbi et Orbi: A Latin phrase meaning "To the City and to the World" that is a blessing given by the Holy Father. Normally, the first *Urbi et Orbi* delivered by a pontiff is immediately after his election by the College of Cardinals. This is a blessing accompanied by a short address to the crowds in St. Peter's Square and to the world; frequently, as with Pope John Paul II in 1978, it is delivered in as many languages as possible. The pope also delivers an *Urbi et Orbi* each year at Christmas and at Easter.

Usury: Excessive interest charged for the loan and use of money; a violation of justice.

Vagi: A Latin word meaning wanderers that is used to describe any homeless person with no fixed residence.

Veni Creator Spiritus: A Latin phrase, meaning "Come, Creator Spirit" that is part of a hymn sung to the Holy Spirit. The hymn invokes the presence of the Holy Spirit and was perhaps first composed by Rabanus Maurus (776-856). The hymn is commonly sung as part of the Divine Office, papal elections, episcopal consecrations, ordinations, councils, synods, canonical elections, and confirmations.

Venial Sin: See under **Sin**.

Veronica: A word resulting from the combination of a Latin word for true, vera, and a Greek word for image, eikon, designating a likeness of the face of Christ or the name of a woman said to have given him a cloth on which he caused an imprint of his face to appear. The veneration at Rome of a likeness depicted on cloth dates from about the end of the 10th century; it figured in a popular devotion during the Middle Ages, and in the Holy Face devotion practiced since the 19th century. A faint, indiscernible likeness said to be of this kind is preserved in St. Peter's Basilica. The origin of the likeness is uncertain, and the identity of the woman is unknown. Before the 14th century, there were no known artistic representations of an incident concerning a woman who wiped the face of Christ with a piece of cloth while he was carrying the cross to Calvary.

Vespers: From the Latin for evening, the evening service of the Divine Office, also known as Evening Prayer, or among Anglicans as Evensong.

Viaticum: Holy Communion given to those in danger of death. The word, derived from Latin, means provision for a journey through death to life hereafter.

Vicar Forane: A Latin term meaning "deputy outside" that is applied to the priest given authority by the local bishop over a certain area or region of the diocese.

Vicar General: A priest or bishop appointed by the bishop of a diocese to serve as his deputy, with ordinary executive power, in the administration of the diocese.

Vicar, Judicial: The title given to the chief judge and head of the tribunal of a diocese.

Virginity: Observance of perpetual sexual abstinence. The state of virginity, which is embraced for the love of God by religious with a public vow or by others with a private vow, was singled out for high praise by Christ (Mt 19:10-12) and has always been so regarded by the Church. In the encyclical *Sacra Virginitas*, Pius XII stated: "Holy virginity and that perfect chastity which is consecrated to the service of God is without doubt among the most perfect treasures which the founder of the Church has left in heritage to the society which he established." Paul VI approved in 1970 a rite in which women can consecrate their virginity "to Christ and their brethren" without becoming members of a religious institute. The *Ordo Consecrationis Virginum*, a revision of a rite promulgated by Clement VII in 1596, is traceable to the Roman liturgy of about 50

Virtue: A habit or established capability for performing good actions. Virtues are natural (acquired and increased by repeating good acts) and/or supernatural (given with grace by God).

Visions: A charism by which a specially chosen individual is able to behold a person or something that is naturally invisible. A vision should not be confused with an illusion or hallucination. Like other charisms, a vision is granted for the good of people; it should be noted, however, that they are not essential for holiness or salvation. Many saints throughout history have beheld visions, among them St. Thomas Aquinas, St. Teresa of Ávila, St. John of the Cross, and St. Francis of Assisi.

Vocation: A call to a way of life. Generally, the term applies to the common call of all persons, from God, to holiness and salvation. Specifically, it refers to particular states of life, each called a vocation, in which response is made to this universal call; viz., marriage, the religious life and/or priesthood, the single state freely chosen or accepted for the accomplishment of God's will. The term also applies to the various occupations in which persons make a living. The Church supports the freedom of each individual in choosing a particular vocation, and reserves the right to pass on the acceptability of candidates for the priesthood and religious life. Signs or indicators of particular vocations are many, including a person's talents and interests, circumstances and obligations, invitations of grace and willingness to respond thereto.

Vow: A promise made to God with sufficient knowledge and freedom, which has as its object a moral good that is possible and better than its voluntary omission. A person who professes a vow binds himself or herself by the virtue of religion to fulfill the promise. The best known examples of vows are those of poverty, chastity and obedience professed by religious (See **Counsels, Evangelical**; individual entries). Public vows are made before a competent person, acting as an agent of the Church, who accepts the profession in the name of the Church, thereby giving public recognition to the person's dedication and consecration to God and divine worship. Vows of this kind are either solemn, rendering all contrary acts invalid as well as unlawful; or simple, rendering contrary acts unlawful. Solemn vows are for life; simple vows are for a definite period of time or for life. Vows professed without public recognition by the Church are called private vows. The Church, which has authority to accept and give public recognition to vows, also has authority to dispense persons from their obligations for serious reasons.

Witness, Christian: Practical testimony or evidence given by Christians of their faith in all circumstances of life — by prayer and general conduct, through good example and good works, etc.; being and acting in accordance with Christian belief; actual practice of the Christian faith.

Zeal: The expression of charity that permits one to serve God and others fully with the objective of furthering the Mystical Body of Christ.

Zucchetto: A small skullcap worn by ecclesiastics, most notably prelates and derived from the popular Italian vernacular term *zucca*, meaning a pumpkin, and used as slang for head. The Holy Father wears a white zucchetto made of watered silk; cardinals use scarlet, and bishops use purple. Priests of the monsignorial rank may wear black with purple piping. All others may wear simple black. The origins of the zucchetto are traced back to the early Middle Ages when clergy adopted a skullcap to provide a covering for the part of the head that had been shaved during tonsure. It was worn especially during the winter. The zucchetto worn by cardinals is also usually of silk.

The Church Calendar

The calendar of the Roman Church consists of an arrangement throughout the year of a series of liturgical seasons, commemorations of divine mysteries and commemorations of saints for purposes of worship.

The key to the calendar is the central celebration of the Easter Triduum, commemorating the supreme saving act of Jesus in his death and resurrection to which all other observances and acts of worship are related.

The purposes of this calendar were outlined in the Constitution on the Sacred Liturgy (*Sacrosanctum Concilium*, Nos. 102-105) promulgated by the Second Vatican Council.

"Within the cycle of a year ... (the Church) unfolds the whole mystery of Christ, not only from his incarnation and birth until his ascension, but also as reflected in the day of Pentecost, and the expectation of a blessed, hoped-for return of the Lord.

"Recalling thus the mysteries of redemption, the Church opens to the faithful the riches of her Lord's powers and merits, so that these are in some way made present at all times, and the faithful are enabled to lay hold of them and become filled with saving grace (No. 102).

"In celebrating this annual cycle of Christ's mysteries, holy Church honors with special love the Blessed Mary, Mother of God" (No. 103).

"The Church has also included in the annual cycle days devoted to the memory of the martyrs and the other saints (who) sing God's perfect praise in heaven and offer prayers for us. By celebrating the passage of these saints from earth to heaven the Church proclaims the paschal mystery as achieved in the saints who have suffered and been glorified with Christ; she proposes them to the faithful as examples who draw all to the Father through Christ, and through their merits she pleads for God's favors (No. 104).

"In the various seasons of the year and according to her traditional discipline, the Church completes the formation of the faithful by means of pious practices for soul and body, by instruction, prayer, and works of penance and mercy (No. 105)."

The Roman Calendar

Norms for a revised calendar for the Western Church as decreed by the Second Vatican Council were approved by Paul VI in the *motu proprio Mysterii Paschalis* dated Feb. 14, 1969. The revised calendar was promulgated a month later by a decree of the Congregation for Divine Worship and went into effect Jan. 1, 1970, with provisional modifications. Full implementation of all its parts was delayed in 1970 and 1971, pending the completion of work on related liturgical texts. The U.S. bishops ordered the calendar into effect for 1972.

The Seasons

Advent: The liturgical year begins with the first Sunday of Advent, which introduces a season of four weeks or slightly less duration with the theme of expectation of the coming of Christ. During the first two weeks, the final coming of Christ as Lord and Judge at the end of the world is the focus of attention. From Dec. 17 to 24, the emphasis shifts to anticipation of the celebration of his Nativity on the solemnity of Christmas.

Advent has four Sundays. Since the 10th century, the first Sunday has marked the beginning of the liturgical year in the Western Church. In the Middle Ages, a kind of pre-Christmas fast was in vogue during the season.

Christmas Season: The Christmas season begins with the vigil of Christmas and lasts until the Sunday after Jan. 6, inclusive.

The period between the end of the Christmas season and the beginning of Lent belongs to the ordinary time of the year. Of variable length, the pre-Lenten phase of this season includes what were formerly called the Sundays after Epiphany and the suppressed Sundays of Septuagesima, Sexagesima and Quinquagesima.

Lent: The penitential season of Lent begins on Ash Wednesday, which occurs between Feb. 4 and Mar. 11, depending on the date of Easter, and lasts until the Mass of the Lord's Supper (Holy Thursday). It has six Sundays. The sixth Sunday marks the beginning of Holy Week and is known as Passion (formerly called Palm) Sunday.

The origin of Lenten observances dates back to the fourth century or earlier.

Easter Triduum: The Easter Triduum begins with evening Mass of the Lord's Supper and ends with Evening Prayer on Easter Sunday.

Easter Season: The Easter season whose theme is resurrection from sin to the life of grace, lasts for 50 days, from Easter to Pentecost. Easter, the first Sunday after the first full moon following the vernal equinox, occurs between Mar. 22 and Apr. 25. The terminal phase of the Easter season, between the solemnities of the Ascension of the Lord and Pentecost, stresses anticipation of the coming and action of the Holy Spirit.

Ordinary Time: The season of Ordinary Time begins on Monday (or Tuesday if the feast of the Baptism of the Lord is celebrated on that Monday) after the Sunday following Jan. 6 and continues until the day before Ash Wednesday, inclusive. It begins again on the Monday after Pentecost and ends on the Saturday before the first Sunday of Advent. It consists of 33 or 34 weeks. The last Sunday is celebrated as the Solemnity of Christ the King. The overall purpose of the season is to elaborate the themes of salvation history.

The various liturgical seasons are characterized in part by the scriptural readings and Mass prayers assigned to each of them. During Advent, for example, the readings are messianic; during the Easter season, from the Acts of the Apostles, chronicling the Resurrection and the original proclamation of Christ by the Apostles, and from the Gospel of John; during Lent, baptismal and penitential passages. Mass prayers reflect the meaning and purpose of the various seasons.

Commemorations of Saints

The commemorations of saints are celebrated concurrently with the liturgical seasons and feasts of our Lord. Their purpose is to illustrate the paschal mysteries as reflected in the lives of saints, to honor them as heroes of holiness, and to appeal for their intercession.

In line with revised regulations, some former feasts were either abolished or relegated to observance in particular places by local option for one of two reasons: (1) lack of sufficient historical evidence for observance of the feasts; or, (2) lack of universal significance.

The commemoration of a saint, as a general rule, is observed on the day of death (*dies natalis*, day of birth to glory with God in heaven). Exceptions to this rule include the feasts of St. John the Baptist, who is honored on the day of his birth; Sts. Basil the Great and Gregory Nazianzen; and the brother Saints, Cyril and Methodius, who are commemorated in joint feasts. Application of this general rule in the revised calendar resulted in date changes of some observances.

Sundays and Other Holy Days

Sunday is the original Christian feast day and holy day of obligation because of the unusually significant events of salvation history which took place and are commemorated on the first day of the week viz., the Resurrection of Christ, the key event of his life and the fundamental fact of Christianity; and the descent of the Holy Spirit upon the Apostles on Pentecost, the birthday of the Church. The transfer of observance of the Lord's Day from the Sabbath to Sunday was made in apostolic times. The Mass and Liturgy of the Hours (Divine Office) of each Sunday reflect the themes and set the tones of the various liturgical seasons.

Holy days of obligation are special occasions on which Catholics who have reached the age of reason are seriously obliged, as on Sundays, to assist at Mass: they are also to refrain from work and involvement with business that impedes participation in divine worship and the enjoyment of appropriate rest and relaxation.

The holy days of obligation observed in the U.S. are: Christmas, the Nativity of Jesus, Dec. 25; Solemnity of Mary the Mother of God, Jan. 1; Ascension of the Lord; Assumption of Blessed Mary the Virgin, Aug. 15; All Saints' Day, Nov. 1; Immaculate Conception of Blessed Mary the Virgin, Dec. 8.

The precept to attend Mass is abrogated in the U.S. whenever the Solemnity of Mary, the Assumption, or All Saints falls on a Saturday or Monday (1991 decree of U.S. bishops; approved by Holy See July 4, 1992, and effective Jan. 1, 1993).

In addition to these, there are four other holy days of obligation prescribed in the general law of the Church which are not so observed in the U.S.: Epiphany, Jan. 6; St. Joseph, Mar. 19; Corpus Christi; Sts. Peter and Paul, June 29. The solemnities of Epiphany and Corpus Christi are transferred to a Sunday in countries where they are not observed as holy days of obligation.

Solemnities, Feasts, Memorials

Categories of observances according to dignity and manner of observance are: solemnities, principal days in the calendar (observance begins with Evening Prayer I of the preceding day; some have their own vigil Mass); feasts (celebrated within the limits of the natural day); obligatory memorials (celebrated throughout the Church); optional memorials (observable by choice).

Fixed observances are those that are regularly celebrated on the same calendar day each year.

Movable observances are those that are not observed on the same calendar day each year. Examples of these are Easter (the first Sunday after the first full moon following the vernal equinox), Ascension (40 days after Easter), Pentecost (50 days after Easter), Trinity Sunday (first after Pentecost), Christ the King (last Sunday of the liturgical year).

Weekdays, Days of Prayer

Weekdays are those on which no proper feast or vigil is celebrated in the Mass or Liturgy of the Hours (Divine Office). On such days, the Mass may be that of the preceding Sunday, which expresses the liturgical spirit of the season, an optional memorial, a votive Mass, or a Mass for the dead. weekdays of Advent and Lent are in a special category of their own.

Days of Prayer: Dioceses, at times to be designated by local bishops, should observe "days or periods of prayer for the fruits of the earth, prayer for human rights and equality, prayer for world justice and peace, and penitential observance outside of Lent." So stated the Instruction on Particular Calendars (No. 331) issued by the Congregation for the Sacraments and Divine Worship June 24, 1970.

These days are contemporary equivalents of what were formerly called ember and rogation days.

Ember days originated at Rome about the fifth century, probably as Christian replacements for seasonal festivals of agrarian cults. They were observances of penance, thanksgiving, and petition for divine blessing on the various seasons; they also were occasions of special prayer for clergy to be ordained. These days were observed four times a year.

Rogation days originated in France about the fifth century. They were penitential in character and also occasions of prayer for a bountiful harvest and protection against evil.

Days and Times of Penance

Fridays throughout the year and the season of Lent are penitential times.

Abstinence: Catholics in the U.S., from the age of 14 throughout life, are obliged to abstain from meat on Ash Wednesday, the Fridays of Lent and Good Friday. The law forbids the use of meat, but not of eggs, the products of milk or condiments made of animal fat. Permissible are soup flavored with meat, meat gravy and sauces. The obligation to abstain from meat is not in force on days celebrated as solemnities (e.g., Christmas, Sacred Heart).

Fasting: Catholics in the U.S., from the day after their 18th birthday to the day after their 59th birthday, are also obliged to fast on Ash Wednesday and Good Friday. The law allows only one full meal a day, but does not prohibit the taking of some food in the morning and evening, observing as far as quantity and quality are concerned approved local custom. The order of meals is optional, i.e., the full meal may be taken in the evening instead of at midday. Also: (1) The combined quantity of food taken at the two lighter meals should not exceed the quantity taken at the full meal; (2) The drinking of ordinary liquids does not break the fast.

Obligation: There is a general obligation to do penance for sins committed and for the remission of punishment resulting from sin. Substantial observance of fasting and abstinence, prescribed for the community of the Church, is a matter of serious obligation; it allows, however, for alternate ways of doing penance (e.g., works of charity, prayer and prayer-related practices, almsgiving).

Readings at Mass

Scriptural readings for Masses on Sundays and holy days are indicated under the appropriate dates in the calendar pages for the year 2014-15. The Year A cycle is prescribed for Sunday Masses in liturgical year 2014, from Dec. 1, 2013 to Nov. 23, 2014. In Year A, most of the Gospel readings are from the Gospel of Matthew. The Year B cycle is prescribed for Sunday Masses in liturgical year 2015.

The Year II weekday cycle is prescribed for 2014, from Jan. 13, 2014. The Year I cycle is prescribed for 2015.

Monthly Prayer Intentions

Intentions chosen and recommended by Pope Benedict XVI to the prayers of the faithful and circulated by the Apostleship of Prayer are given for each month of the calendar. Pope John Paul II expressed his desire that all Catholics make these intentions their own "in the certainty of being united with the Holy Father and praying according to his intentions and desires."

Celebrations in U.S. Particular Calendar

The General Norms for the Liturgical Year and the Calendar, issued in 1969 and published along with the General Roman Calendar for the Universal Church, noted that the calendar consists of the General Roman Calendar used by the entire Church and of particular calendars used in particular churches (nations or dioceses) or in families of religious.

The particular calendar for the U.S. contains the following celebrations. **January:** 4, Elizabeth Ann Seton; 5, John Neumann; 6, André Bessette. **March:** 3, Katharine Drexel. **May:** 10, Damien DeVeuster; 15, Isidore the Farmer. **July:** 1, Bl. Junípero Serra; 4, Independence Day; 14, Kateri Tekakwitha. **August:** 18, Jane Frances de Chantal. **September:** 9, Peter Claver. **October:** 6, Bl. Marie-Rose Durocher; 19, Isaac Jogues and John de Brébeuf and Companions; 20, Paul of the Cross. **November:** 13, Frances Xavier Cabrini; 18, Rose Philippine Duchesne; 23, Bl. Miguel Agustín Pro; fourth Thursday, Thanksgiving Day. **December:** 9, Juan Diego; 12, Our Lady of Guadalupe.

TABLE OF MOVABLE FEASTS

| Year | Ash Wed. | Easter | Ascension | Pentecost | Weeks of Ordinary Time | | | | First Sunday of Advent |
| | | | | | Before Lent | | After Pentcst. | | |
					Weeks	Ends	Weeks	Begins	
2013	Feb. 13	Mar. 31	May 9	May 19	5	Feb. 12	28	May 20	Dec. 1
2014	Mar. 5	Apr. 20	May 29	June 8	8	Mar. 4	25	June 9	Nov. 30
2015	Feb. 18	Apr. 5	May 14	May 24	6	Feb. 17	27	May 25	Nov. 29
2016	Feb. 10	Mar. 27	May 5	May 15	5	Feb. 9	28	May 16	Nov. 27
2017	Mar. 1	Apr. 16	May 25	June 4	8	Feb. 28	26	June 5	Dec. 3
2018	Feb. 14	Apr. 1	May 10	May 20	6	Feb. 13	28	May 21	Dec. 2
2019	Mar. 6	Apr. 21	May 30	June 9	8	Mar. 5	25	June 10	Dec. 1
2020	Feb. 26	Apr. 12	May 21	May 31	7	Feb. 25	26	June 1	Nov. 29
2021	Feb. 17	Apr. 4	May 13	May 23	6	Feb. 16	27	May 24	Nov. 28
2022	Mar. 2	Apr. 17	May 26	June 5	8	Mar. 1	25	June 6	Nov. 27
2023	Feb. 22	Apr. 9	May 18	May 28	7	Feb. 21	27	May 29	Dec. 3
2024	Feb. 14	Mar. 31	May 9	May 19	6	Feb. 13	28	May 20	Dec. 1
2025	Mar. 5	Apr. 20	May 29	June 8	8	Mar. 4	25	June 9	Nov. 30
2026	Feb. 18	Apr. 5	May 14	May 24	6	Feb. 17	27	May 25	Nov. 29
2027	Feb. 10	Mar. 28	May 6	May 16	5	Feb. 9	28	May 17	Nov. 28
2028	Mar. 1	Apr. 16	May 25	June 4	8	Feb. 29	26	June 5	Dec. 3
2029	Feb. 14	Apr. 1	May 10	May 20	6	Feb. 13	28	May 21	Dec. 2
2030	Mar. 6	Apr. 21	May 30	June 9	9	Mar. 7	25	June 10	Dec. 1
2031	Feb. 26	Apr. 13	May 22	June 1	7	Feb. 25	26	June 2	Nov. 30
2032	Feb. 11	Mar. 28	May 6	May 16	5	Feb. 11	28	May 17	Nov. 28
2033	Mar. 2	Apr. 17	May 26	June 5	8	Mar. 1	25	June 6	Nov. 27
2034	Feb. 22	Apr. 9	May 18	May 28	7	Feb. 21	27	May 29	Dec. 3
2035	Feb. 7	Mar. 25	May 3	May 13	5	Feb. 6	29	May 14	Dec. 2
2036	Feb. 27	Apr. 13	May 22	June 1	7	Feb. 26	26	June 2	Nov. 30
2037	Feb. 18	Apr. 5	May 14	May 24	6	Feb. 17	27	May 25	Nov. 29
2038	Mar. 10	Apr. 25	June 3	June 13	9	Mar. 9	24	June 14	Nov. 28
2039	Feb. 23	Apr. 10	May 19	May 29	7	Feb. 22	26	May 30	Nov. 27

2014 CALENDAR

January 2014

Universal: That all may promote authentic economic development that respects the dignity of all peoples.

For Evangelization: That Christians of diverse denominations may walk toward the unity desired by Christ.

1 Wed. Octave of Christmas; Solemnity of the Blessed Virgin Mary, Mother of God; Holy day of obligation. (Nm 6:22-27; Gal 4:4-7; Lk 2:16-21).

2 Thurs. Sts. Basil the Great and Gregory Nazianzus, bishops and doctors of the Church; memorial.

3 Fri. Weekday.

4 Sat. St. Elizabeth Ann Seton, religious; memorial.

5 Sun. **Epiphany of Our Lord**; solemnity. (Is 60:1-6; Eph 3:2-3a,5-6; Mt 2:1-12).

6 Mon. Christmas Weekday. St. Andre Bessette, religious; optional memorial.

7 Tues. Christmas Weekday. St. Raymond of Penafort, priest; optional memorial.

8 Wed. Christmas Weekday.

9 Thurs. Christmas Weekday.

10 Fri. Christmas Weekday.

11 Sat. Christmas Weekday.

12 Sun. **Baptism of the Lord**; feast. (Is 42:1-4,6-7; Acts 10:34-38; Mt 3: 13-17).

13 Mon. First Week in Ordinary Time. St. Hilary, bishop-doctor; optional memorial.

14 Tues. Weekday.

15 Wed. Weekday.

16 Thurs. Weekday.

17 Fri. St. Anthony, abbot; memorial.

18 Sat. Weekday. The Blessed Virgin Mary, optional memorial.

19 Sun. **Second Sunday in Ordinary Time.** (Is 49:3,5-6; 1 Cor 1:1-3; Jn 1:29-34).

20 Mon. Weekday. St. Fabian, pope-martyr; St. Sebastian, martyr; optional memorials.

21 Tues. St. Agnes, virgin and martyr; memorial.

22 Wed. Day of Prayer for the legal Protection of Unborn Children; memorial.

23 Thurs. Weekday.

24 Fri. St. Francis de Sales, bishop-doctor; memorial.

25 Sat. Conversion of St. Paul, apostle; feast.

26 Sun. **Third Sunday in Ordinary Time** (Is 8:23-9:3; 1 Cor 1:10-13,17: Mt 4:12-23).

27 Mon. Weekday. St. Angela Merici, virgin; optional memorial.

28 Tues. St. Thomas Aquinas, priest-doctor; memorial.

29 Wed. Weekday.

30 Thurs. Weekday.

31 Fri. St. John Bosco, priest; memorial.

Observances: Solemnity of the Mother of God, a holy day of obligation, and a papal message for the World Day of Peace, Jan. 1; customary ordination of bishops by the Pope on the Solemnity of the Epiphany, Jan. 6. Week of Prayer for Christian Unity, Jan. 18-25 concluding with celebration of the Conversion of St. Paul, Jan. 25; National Prayer Vigil for Life and March for Life in Washington, D.C., in connection with the anniversary of the 1973 *Roe vs. Wade* and *Dole vs. Bolton* pro-abortion decisions of the U.S. Supreme Court, Jan. 21-22. Other celebrations in the month of January: Sts. Basil the Great and Gregory Nazianzen, Jan. 2; St. Elizabeth Ann Seton, Jan.4; St. Anthony, Jan. 17; St. Francis De Sales, Jan. 24; St. Thomas Aquinas, Jan. 28; St. John Bosco, Jan. 31.

February 2014

Universal: That the Church and society may respect the wisdom and experience of older people.

For Evangelization: That priests, religious, and lay people may work together with generosity for evangelization.

1 Sat. Weekday

2 Sun. **Presentation of the Lord**, feast. (Mal 3:1-4; Heb 2:14-18; Lk 2:22-40.)

3 Mon. Weekday. St. Blasé, bishop-martyr; St. Ansgar, bishop; optional memorial.

4 Tues. Weekday.

5 Weds. St. Agatha, virgin-martyr; memorial.

6 Thurs. St. Paul Miki, priest-martyr and companions, martyrs; memorial.

7 Fri. Weekday.

8 Sat. Weekday. St. Jerome Emiliani, priest; optional memorial.

9 Sun. **Fifth Sunday in Ordinary Time**. (Is 58:7-10; 1 Cor 2:1-5; Mt 5:13-16).

10 Mon. St. Scholastica, virgin; memorial.

11 Tue. Weekday. Our Lady of Lourdes; optional memorial.

12 Wed. Weekday.

13 Thurs. Weekday.

14 Fri. Sts. Cyril, monk and Methodius, bishop; memorial.

15 Sat. Weekday. The Blessed Virgin Mary, optional memorial.

16 Sun. **Sixth Sunday in Ordinary Time**. (Sir 15:15-20; 1 Cor 2:6-10; Mt 5:17-37).

17 Mon. Weekday. Seven Holy Founders of the Order of Servites; optional memorial.

18 Tues. Weekday.

19 Wed. Weekday.

20 Thurs. Weekday.

21 Fri. Weekday. St. Peter Damian, bishop-doctor; memorial.

22 Sat. Chair of St. Peter, apostle; feast.

23 Sun. **Seventh Sunday in Ordinary Time** (Lev 19:1-2, 17-18; 1 Cor 3: 16-23; Mt 5:38-48).

24 Mon. Weekday.

25 Tue. Weekday.

26 Wed. Weekday.

27 Thurs. Weekday.

28 Fri. Weekday.

Observances:

The conclusion of Catholic Schools Week (Sat., Feb.1). The Presentation of the Child Jesus in the Temple, traditional day for the blessings of candles that will be used throughout the year. Optional memorial of St. Blasé, bishop-martyr, whose intercession is sought against ailments of the throat and other evils. Optional memorial of Our Lady of Lourdes which is also World Day of the Sick, a day of prayer, healing and anointing of those who are ill. Other celebrations in the month of February: St. Agatha, Feb. 5; St. Paul Miki and Companions, Feb. 6; St. Scholastic, Feb. 10; Sts. Cyril and Methodius, Feb. 14; the Chair of Saint Peter, Feb. 22.

March 2014

Universal: That all cultures may respect the rights and dignity of women.

For Evangelization: That many young people may accept the Lord's invitation to consecrate their lives to proclaiming the Gospel.

1 Sat. Weekday. Blessed Virgin Mary, optional memorial.

2 Sun. Eighth Sunday in Ordinary Time. (Hos 2:16b,17b, 21-22; 1 Cor 3:1b-6; Mk 2:18-22).

3 Mon. Weekday. St. Katherine Drexel, virgin; optional memorial.

4 Tues. Weekday. St. Casimir; optional memorial.

5 Wed. **Ash Wednesday** (Jl 2:12-18; 2 Cor 5:20-6:2; Mt. 6: 1-6,16-18). Fast and Abstinence.

6 Thurs. Thursday after Ash Wednesday.

7 Fri. Friday after Ash Wednesday. Abstinence. Sts. Perpetua and Felicity, martyrs; optional memorial.

8 Sat. Saturday after Ash Wednesday. St. John of God, religious; optional memorial.

9 Sun. First Sunday of Lent (Gn 2:7-9;3:1-7; Rom 5:12-19; Mt 4:1-11).

10 Mon. Lenten Weekday.

11 Tues. Lenten Weekday.

12 Wed. Lenten Weekday.

13 Thurs. Lenten Weekday.

14 Fri. Lenten Weekday. Abstinence.

15 Sat. Lenten Weekday.

16 Sun. Second Sunday of Lent (Gn 12:1-4a; 2 Tm 1:8b-10; Mt 17:1-9).

17 Mon. Lenten Weekday. St. Patrick, bishop; commemoration.

18 Tues. Lenten Weekday. St. Cyril of Jerusalem, bishop-doctor; commemoration.

19 Wed. St. Joseph, Spouse of the Blessed Virgin Mary; solemnity.

20 Thurs. Lenten Weekday.

21 Fri. Lenten Weekday. Abstinence.

22 Sat. Lenten Weekday.

23 Sun. Third Sunday of Lent (Ex 17:3-7; Rom 5:1-2,5-8; Jn 4:5-42).

24 Mon. Lenten Weekday.

25 Tues. Annunciation of the Lord; solemnity.

26 Wed. Lenten Weekday.

27 Thurs. Lenten Weekday.

28 Fri. Lenten Weekday. Abstinence.

29 Sat. Lenten Weekday

30 Sun. Fourth Sunday of Lent (1 Sm 16:1b,6-7,10-13a; Eph 5:8-14; Jn 9:1-41).

31 Mon. Lenten Weekday.

Observances:

The Lenten Season begins with Ash Wednesday (Mar. 5) when ashes are blessed and imposed on the forehead of the faithful to remind them of their obligation to do penance for sins, to seek spiritual renewal by means of prayer, fasting and good works. Moreover, with patience and confidence in God's purposes, Catholics are called to bear the trials and difficulties of everyday life. As such, Catholics are reminded of the serious obligation to fast and abstain on those appointed days during the Lenten season as well as the opportunity for other acts of mortification and sacrifice. Unless otherwise indicated, all memorials celebrated during Lent are treated as commemorations. Commemorations may be celebrated during the praying of the Divine Office at Lauds and Vespers as well as the Holy Mass. The Solemnity of St. Joseph, husband of Mary, is observed Mar. 19. The Solemnity of the Annunciation is observed Mar. 25.

April 2014

Universal: That governments may foster the protection of creation and the just distribution of natural resources.

For Evangelization: That the Risen Lord may fill with hope the hearts of those who are being tested by pain and sickness.

1 Tues. Lenten Weekday.

2 Wed. Lenten Weekday. St. Francis of Paola, hermit; commemoration.

3 Thurs. Lenten Weekday.

4 Fri. Lenten Weekday. Abstinence. St. Isidore, bishop-doctor; commemoration.

5 Sat. Lenten Weekday. St. Vincent Ferrer, priest; optional memorial.

6 Sun. Fifth Sunday of Lent (Ez 37: 12-14; Rom 8: 8-11; Jn 11: 1-45).

7 Mon. Lenten Weekday. St. John Baptist de la Salle, priest; commemoration.

8 Tues. Lenten Weekday.

9 Wed. Lenten Weekday.

10 Thurs. Lenten Weekday.

11 Fri. Lenten Weekday. Abstinence. St. Stanislaus, bishop-martyr; commemoration.

12 Sat. Lenten Weekday.

13 Sun. Palm Sunday/The Lord's Passion (Mt 21:1-11/Is 50:4-7; Phil 2:6-11; Mt 26:14-27:66).

14 Mon. Monday of Holy Week.

15 Tue. Tuesday of Holy Week.

16 Wed. Wednesday of Holy Week

17 Thurs. Holy Thursday. Chrism Mass in the Morning. The Easter Triduum begins with the evening Mass of the Lord's Supper.

18 Fri. Good Friday. The Lord's Passion. Fast & Abstinence.

19 Sat. Holy Saturday. Easter Vigil.

20 Sun. Easter Sunday: Resurrection of the Lord; solemnity (Acts 10:34a,37-43; Col 3:1-4 or 1 Cor 5:6b-8; Jn 20:1-9 or Mt 28:1-10 or [at an afternoon or evening Mass – Lk 24:13-15]).

21 Mon. Monday in the Octave of Easter; solemnity.

22 Tues. Tuesday in the Octave of Easter; solemnity.

23 Wed. Wednesday in the Octave of Easter; solemnity.

24 Thurs. Thursday in the Octave of Easter; solemnity.

25 Fri. Friday in the Octave of Easter; solemnity.

26 Sat. Saturday in the Octave of Easter; solemnity.

27 Sun. Second Sunday of Easter (Acts 2:42-47; 1 Pt 1:3-9; Jn 20: 19-31).

28 Mon. Easter Weekday. St. Peter Chanel, priest-martyr; St. Louis Mary de Montfort; optional memorials.

29 Tues. St. Catherine of Siena, virgin-doctor; memorial.

30 Wed. Easter Weekday. St. Pius V, pope; optional memorial.

Observances:

Holy Week: Passion Sunday (Palm Sunday) begins these most solemn and holy celebrations of the Church Year. It is on this day that the Church blesses and distributes palms commemorating our Lord's triumphal entrance into Jerusalem and it is during this celebration that the Passion is read for the first time during Holy Week. Monday, Tuesday and Wednesday of Holy Week are preparatory days leading to the Sacred Triduum. The Sacred Triduum begins with the Mass of the Lord's Supper on Holy Thursday evening. Good Friday commemorates the Passion of Jesus. Easter Vigil which includes the Service of Light, Liturgy of the Word recounting salvation history, Liturgy of Christian Initiation. Easter Sunday is the day when the Holy Father delivers the traditional *Urbi et Orbi* address, to the City of Rome and to the World.

May 2014

Universal: That the media may be instruments in the service of truth and peace.

For Evangelization: That Mary, Star of Evangelization, may guide the Church in proclaiming Christ to all nations.

1 Thurs. Easter Weekday. St. Joseph the Worker; optional memorial.

2 Fri. St. Athanasius, bishop-doctor; memorial.

3 Sat. Sts. Philip and James, apostles; feast.

4 Sun. Third Sunday of Easter. (Acts 2:14,22-33; 1 Pt 1: 17-21; Lk 24:13-35).

5 Mon. Easter Weekday.

6 Tues. Easter Weekday.

7 Wed. Easter Weekday.

8 Thurs. Easter Weekday.

9 Fri. Easter Weekday.

10 Sat. Easter Weekday. St. Damien Joseph deVeuster of Molokai, priest; optional Memorial.

11 Sun. Fourth Sunday of Easter. (Acts 2:14a,36-41; 1 Pt 2: 20b-25; Jn 10:1-10).

12 Mon. Easter Weekday. Sts. Nereus and Achilleus, martyrs; St. Pancras, martyr; optional memorials.

13 Tues. Easter Weekday. Our Lady of Fatima; optional memorial.

14 Wed. St. Mathias, apostle; feast.

15 Thurs. Easter Weekday. St. Isidore the farmer; optional memorial.

16 Fri. Easter Weekday.

17 Sat. Easter Weekday.

18 Sun. Fifth Sunday of Easter. (Acts 6:1-7; 1 Pt 2:4-9; Jn 14:1-12).

19 Mon. Easter Weekday.

20 Tues. Easter Weekday. St. Bernardine of Siena, priest; optional memorial.

21 Wed. Easter Weekday. St. Christopher Magallanes, priest and companions, martyrs; optional memorial.

22 Thurs. Easter Weekday. St. Rita of Cascia, religious; optional memorial.

23 Fri. Easter Weekday.

24 Sat. Easter Weekday.

25 Sun. Sixth Sunday of Easter. (Acts 8: 5-8,14-17; 1 Pt 3: 15-18; Jn 14:15-21).

26 Mon. St. Philip Neri, priest; memorial.

27 Tues. Easter Weekday. St. Augustine of Canterbury, bishop; optional memorial.

28 Wed. Easter Weekday.

29 Thurs. Ascension of our Lord; solemnity. Holy Day of obligation (Acts 1:1-11; Eph 1:17-23; Mt 28:16-20).

30 Fri. Easter Weekday.

31 Sat. Visitation of the Blessed Virgin Mary to Elizabeth; feast.

Observances:

The Solemnity of the Ascension celebrated May 29 (transferred to Sunday in some dioceses) is a Holy Day of Obligation. Also, the month of May is traditionally dedicated to our Blessed Mother. Customary Marian devotions include the recitation of the Rosary and the Litany of Loretto, Marian processions, the crowning of Mary and the celebration of Votive Masses dedicated to our Blessed Mother. Other celebrations: St. Joseph the Worker, May 1; St. Athanasius, May 2; Sts. Philip & James, May 3; St. Matthias, May 14; St. Christopher Magallanes, May 21; St. Philip Neri, May 26; The Visitation of the Blessed Virgin Mary, May 31.

June 2014

Universal: That the unemployed may receive support and find the work they need to live in dignity.

For Evangelization: That Europe may rediscover its Christian roots through the witness of believers.

1 Sun. Seventh Sunday of Easter. (Acts 1:12-14; 1 Pt 4:13-16; Jn 17:1-11a).

2 Mon. Easter Weekday. Sts. Marcellinus and Peter, martyrs; optional memorial.

3 Tues. St. Charles Lwanga, martyr and companions, martyrs; memorial.

4 Wed. Easter Weekday.

5 Thurs. St. Boniface, bishop-martyr; memorial.

6 Fri. Easter Weekday. St. Norbert, bishop; optional memorial.

7 Sat. Easter Weekday.

8 Sun. Pentecost Sunday; solemnity. (Acts 2:1-11; 1 Cor 12:3b-7,12-13; or Gal 5:16-25; Jn 20:19-23 or Jn 15:26-27;16:12-15).

9 Mon. Tenth Week in Ordinary Time. St. Ephrem, deacon-doctor; optional memorial.

10 Tues. Weekday.

11 Wed. St. Barnabas, apostle; memorial.

12 Thurs. Weekday.

13 Fri. St. Anthony of Padua, priest-doctor; memorial.

14 Sat. Weekday.

15 Sun. Most Holy Trinity; solemnity. (Ex 34: 4b-6,8-9; 2 Cor 13:11-13; Jn 3:16-18).

16 Mon. Eleventh Week in Ordinary Time. Weekday.

17 Tues. Weekday.

18 Wed. Weekday.

19 Thurs. Weekday. St. Romuald, abbot; optional memorial.

20 Fri. Weekday.

21 Sat. St. Aloysius Gonzaga, religious; memorial.

22 Sun. Most Holy Body and Blood of Christ (Corpus Christi); solemnity. (Dt 8:2-3,14b-16a; 1 Cor 10:16-17; Jn 6: 51-58.)

23 Mon. Twelfth Week in Ordinary Time. Weekday.

24 Tues. Nativity of St. John the Baptist; solemnity.

25 Wed. Weekday.

26 Thurs. Weekday.

27 Fri. Most Sacred Heart of Jesus; solemnity.

28 Sat. St. Irenaeus, bishop-martyr; memorial.

29 Sun. Sts. Peter and Paul, apostles; solemnity. (Acts 12: 1-11; 2 Tm 4:6-8,17-18; Mt 16:13-19).

30 Mon. Thirteenth Week of Ordinary Time. Weekday. First Martyrs of the Church of Rome; optional memorial.

Observances:

The Easter Sunday is completed with the celebration of the Feast of Pentecost, the gift of the Holy Spirit given to the apostles and to the Church. The Feast of the Most Holy Trinity is celebrated on June 15. This great feast and solemnity of the Triune God is followed by the Feast the Body and Blood of Christ (Corpus Christi) celebrated on June 22. It is the custom in dioceses to gather for a Corpus Christi procession to venerate the Body of Christ at special altars prepared near the cathedral church. The procession concludes with Benediction. Also in June is the Feast of the Sacred Heart on June 27 and the Feast of Sts. Peter and Paul on June 29.

July 2014

Universal: That sports may always be occasions of human fraternity and growth.

For Evangelization: That the Holy Spirit may support the work of the laity who proclaim the Gospel in the poorest countries.

1 Tue. Weekday. Bl. Junipero Serra, priest; optional memorial.
2 Weds. Weekday
3 Thurs. St. Thomas, apostle; feast.
4 Fri. Weekday Proper Mass for Independence Day. St. Elizabeth of Portugal; optional memorial (perpetual transferred in the United States to July 5).
5 Sat. Weekday. St. Anthony Maria Zaccaria, priest; optional memorial.
6 Sun. **Fourteenth Sunday in Ordinary Time.** (Zec 9:9-10; Rom 8:9,11-13; Mt 11:25-30).
7 Mon. Weekday.
8 Tues. Weekday.
9 Wed. Weekday. St. Augustine Zhao Rong, priest and companions, martyrs; optional memorial.
10 Thurs. Weekday.
11 Fri. St. Benedict, abbot; memorial.
12 Sat. Weekday.
13 Sun. **Fifteenth Sunday in Ordinary Time.** (Is 55:10-11; Rom 8:18-23; Mt 13:1-23).
14 Mon. St. Kateri Tekakwitha, virgin; memorial.
15 Tues. St. Bonaventure, bishop-doctor; memorial.
16 Wed. Weekday. Our Lady of Mount Carmel; optional memorial.
17 Thurs. Weekday.
18 Fri. Weekday. St. Camillus de Lellis, priest; optional memorial.
19 Sat. Weekday.
20 Sun. **Sixteenth Sunday in Ordinary Time.** (Wis 12:13, 16-19; Rom 8:26-27; Mt 12:24-43).
21 Mon. Weekday. St. Lawrence of Brindisi, priest-doctor; optional memorial.
22 Tues. St. Mary Magdalene; memorial.
23 Weds. Weekday. St. Bridget of Sweden; optional memorial.
24 Thurs. Weekday. St. Sharbel Makhluf, priest; optional memorial.
25 Fri. St. James, apostle; feast.
26 Sat. Sts. Joachim and Anne, parents of the Blessed Virgin Mary; memorial.
27 Sun. **Seventeenth Sunday in Ordinary Time.** (1 Kgs 3:5, 7-12; Rom 8:28-30; Mt 13:44-52).
28 Mon. Weekday.
29 Tues. St. Martha; memorial.
30 Wed. Weekday. St. Peter Chrysologus, bishop-doctor; optional memorial.
31 Thurs. St. Ignatius of Loyola, priest; memorial.

Observances:

Blessed Junipero Serra, whose optional memorial may be celebrated July 1, found of the California Missions. St. Thomas the Apostle is observed on July 3; St. Maria Goretti, July 6; St. Benedict, the founder of Western monasticism and patron saint of Europe, July 11; St. Kateri Tekakwitha, July 14; St. Bonaventure, called the second found of the Franciscan Order, July 15; St. Ignatius Loyola, founder of the Society of Jesus, July 31. Independence Day, July 4, is observed with a special Mass for celebration in the United States.

August 2014

Universal: That refugees, forced by violence to abandon their homes, may find a generous welcome and the protection of their rights.

For Evangelization: That Christians in Oceania may joyfully announce the faith to all the people of that region.

1 Fri. St. Alphonsus Ligouri, bishop-doctor; memorial.
2 Sat. Weekday. St. Eusebius of Vercelli, bishop and St. Peter Julian Eymard, priest; optional memorials.
3 Sun. **Eighteenth Sunday in Ordinary Time.** (Is 55:1-3; Rom 8:35,37-39; Mt 14:13-21).
4 Mon. St. John Mary Vianney, priest; memorial.
5 Tues. Weekday. Dedication of the Basilica of St. Mary Major in Rome; optional memorial.
6 Wed. Transfiguration of the Lord; feast.
7 Thurs. Weekday. St. Sixtus III, pope-martyr, and Companions, martyrs; St. Cajetan, priest; optional memorial.
8 Fri. St. Dominic, priest; memorial.
9 Sat. Weekday. St. Teresa Benedicta of the Cross, Virgin & Martyr; optional memorial; Blessed Virgin Mary.
10 Sun. **Nineteenth Sunday in Ordinary Time.** (1Kgs 19: 9a,11-13a; Rom 9:1-5; Mt 14:22-33).
11 Mon. St. Clare, virgin; memorial.
12 Tues. Weekday. St. Jane Frances de Chantal, religious; optional memorial.
13 Wed. Weekday. St. Pontian, pope-martyr and St. Hippolytus, priest-martyr; optional memorials.
14 Thurs. St. Maximillian Mary Kolbe, priest-martyr; memorial.
15 Fri. Assumption of the Blessed Virgin Mary; solemnity. Holy Day of Obligation.
16 Sat. Weekday. St. Stephen of Hungary; optional memorial.
17 Sun. **Twentieth Sunday in Ordinary Time.** (Is 56: 1, 6-7; Rom 11:13-15,29-32; Mt 15:21-28).
18 Mon. Weekday.
19 Tues. Weekday. St. John Eudes, priest; optional memorial.
20 Wed. St. Bernard, abbot-doctor; memorial.
21 Thurs St. Pius X, pope; memorial.
22 Fri. Queenship of the Blessed Virgin Mary; memorial.
23 Sat. Weekday. St. Rose of Lima, virgin; optional memorial.
24 Sun. **Twenty-first Sunday in Ordinary Time.** (Is 22: 19-23; Rom 11:33-36; Mt 16:13-20).
25 Mon. Weekday. St. Louis and St. Joseph Calasanz; optional memorials.
26 Tues. Weekday.
27 Wed. St. Monica; memorial.
28 Thurs. St. Augustine, bishop-doctor; memorial.
29 Fri. Martyrdom of St. John the Baptist; memorial.
30 Sat. Weekday. Blessed Virgin Mary.
31 Sun. **Twenty-second Sunday of Ordinary Time.** (Jer 20: 7-9; Rom 12:1-2; Mt 16:21-27).

Observances:

St. Alphonsus Liguori, doctor of the Church and moral theologian, Aug. 1; St. John Vianney, patron saint of parish priests, Aug. 4; The Feast of the Transfiguration of the Lord, Aug. 6; St. Dominic, founder of the Dominicans, Aug, 8; St. Clare, foundress of the Poor Clares, Aug. 11; The Feast of the Assumption of the Blessed Virgin Mary, Aug. 15; St. Bernard of Clairvaux, Aug. 20; St. Monica, Aug. 27 and her son St. Augustine, the doctor of grace and father of the Church, Aug. 28.

September 2014

Universal: That the mentally disabled may receive the love and help they need for a dignified life.

For Evangelization: That Christians, inspired by the Word of God, may serve the poor and suffering.

1 Mon. Weekday. Labor Day. Special Mass for the Blessings of Human Labor.

2 Tues. Weekday.

3 Wed. St. Gregory the Great, pope-doctor; memorial.

4 Thurs. Weekday.

5 Fri. Weekday. Bl. Teresa of Calcutta, religious; optional memorial.

6 Sat. Weekday.

7 Sun. Twenty-third Sunday in Ordinary Time. (Ez. 33:7-9; Rom. 13: 8-10; Mt 18: 15-20).

8 Mon. The Birth of the Blessed Virgin Mary; feast.

9 Tues. St. Peter Claver, priest; memorial.

10 Wed. Weekday.

11 Thurs. Weekday.

12 Fri. Weekday. The Most Holy Name of Jesus; optional memorial.

13 Sat. St. John Chrysostom, bishop-doctor; memorial.

14 Sun. Exaltation of the Holy Cross. (Nm 21:4b-9; Phil 2:6-11; Jn 3:13-17).

15 Mon. Our Lady of Sorrows; memorial.

16 Tues. Sts. Cornelius, pope-martyr and Cyprian, bishop-martyr; memorial.

17 Wed. Wednesday of the Twenty-fourth week in Ordinary Time. St. Robert Bellarmine, bishop-doctor; optional memorial.

18 Thurs. Weekday.

19 Fri. Weekday. St. Januarius, bishop-martyr; optional memorial.

20 Sat. Sts. Andrew Kim Taegon, priest-martyr, Paul Chong Hasang, martyr, and Companions, martyrs; memorial.

21 Sun. Twenty-fifth Sunday in Ordinary Time. (Is 55:6-9; Phil 1:20c-24,27a; Mt 20:1-16a).

22 Mon. Weekday.

23 Tues. St. Pius of Pietrelcina (Padre Pio), priest; memorial.

24 Wed. Weekday.

25 Thurs. Weekday.

26 Fri. Weekday. Sts. Cosmas and Damian, martyrs; optional memorial.

27 Sat. St. Vincent de Paul, priest; memorial.

28 Sun. Twenty-sixth Sunday in Ordinary Time. (Ez 18: 25-28; Phil 2:1-11; Mt 21:28-32).

29 Mon. Michael, Gabriel, and Raphael, archangels; feast.

30 Tues. St. Jerome; memorial.

Observances:

Birth of the Blessed Virgin Mary, Sept. 8; St. John Chrysostom, doctor of the Church, Sept. 13; Exaltation of the Holy Cross, Sept. 14; Our Lady of Sorrows, Sept. 15; St. Robert Bellarmine, doctor of the Church, Sept. 17. Padre Pio, Sept. 23.; St. Vincent de Paul, founder of the Vincentians and Daughters of Charity, Sept. 27; Sts. Michael, Gabriel, and Raphael, archangels, Sept. 29.; St. Jerome, Sept. 30. Labor Day is celebrated Sept. 3 with a special Mass.

October 2014

Universal: That the Lord may grant peace to those parts of the world most battered by war and violence.

For Evangelization: That World Mission Day may rekindle in every believer zeal for carrying the Gospel into all the world.

1 Wed. St. Therese of the Child Jesus, virgin; memorial.

2 Thurs. Guardian Angels; memorial.

3 Fri. Weekday.

4 Sat. St. Francis of Assisi, religious; memorial.

5 Sun. Twenty-seventh of Ordinary Time. (Is 5:1-7; Phil 4: 6-9; Mt 21:33-43).

6 Mon. Weekday. St. Bruno, priest and Bl. Marie Rose Durocher, virgin; optional memorials.

7 Tues. Our Lady of the Rosary; memorial.

8 Wed. Weekday.

9 Thurs. Weekday. St. Denis, bishop-marytr; St. John Leonardi, priest; optional memorials.

10 Fri. Weekday.

11 Sat. Weekday. Bl. John XXIII, pope. Blessed Virgin Mary; optional memorials.

12 Sun. Twenty-eighth Sunday in Ordinary Time. (Is 25: 6-10a; Phil 4:12-14,19-20; Mt 22:1-14).

13 Mon. Weekday.

14 Tues. Weekday. St. Callistus I, pope-martyr; optional memorial.

15 Wed. St. Theresa of Avila, virgin-doctor; memorial.

16 Thurs. Weekday. St. Hedwig, religious; St. Margaret Mary Alacoque, virgin; optional memorials.

17 Fri. St. Ignatius of Antioch, bishop-martyr; memorial.

18 Sat. St. Luke, evangelist; feast.

19 Sun. Twenty-ninth Sunday in Ordinary Time. (Is 45:1, 4-6; 1 Thes 1:1-5b; Mt 22:15-21).

20 Mon. Weekday. St. Paul of the Cross; optional memorial.

21 Tues. Weekday.

22 Wed. Weekday. Bl. John Paul II, pope; optional memorial.

23 Thurs. Weekday. St. John of Capistrano, priest; optional memorial.

24 Fri. Weekday. St. Anthony Mary Claret, bishop; optional memorial.

25 Sat. Weekday. Blessed Virgin Mary, optional memorial.

26 Sun. Thirtieth Sunday in Ordinary Time. (Ex 22:20-26; 1 Thes 1:5c-10; Mt 22:34-40).

27 Mon. Weekday.

28 Tues. Sts. Simon and Jude, apostles; feast.

29 Wed. Weekday.

30 Thurs. Weekday.

31 Fri. Weekday.

Observances:

St. Therese of the Child Jesus, doctor of the Church, Oct.1; Guardian Angels Oct. 2; St. Francis of Assisi, founder of the Franciscan Order, Oct. 4; St. Teresa of Jesus, doctor of the Church, reformer of the Carmelite Order, Oct. 15; The North American Martyrs, while not celebrated this year, are normally celebrated Oct. 19. St. Paul of the Cross, founder of the Congregation of the Passion, Oct. 20. Bl. John Paul II, Oct. 22; Sts. Simon and Jude, Oct. 28. Mission Sunday is observed during the month, with appeals for prayer and financial support for persons and projects involved in the ministry of evangelization at home and abroad.

November 2014

Universal: That all who suffer loneliness may experience the closeness of God and the support of others.

For Evangelization: That young seminarians and religious may have wise and well-formed mentors.

1 Sat. All Saints; solemnity.

2 Sun. Commemoration of All the Faithful Departed. All Souls Day.

3 Mon. Weekday of the Thirty-first week in Ordinary Time. St. Martin de Porres, religious; optional memorial.

4 Tues. St. Charles Borromeo, bishop; memorial.

5 Wed. Weekday.

6 Thurs. Weekday.

7 Fri. Weekday.

8 Sat. Weekday. Blessed Virgin Mary; optional memorial.

9 Sun. Dedication of the Basilica of St. John Lateran in Rome; feast.

10 Mon. St. Leo the Great, pope-doctor; memorial.

11 Tues. St. Martin of Tours, bishop; memorial

12 Wed. St. Josaphat, bishop-martyr; memorial.

13 Thurs. St. Frances Xavier Cabrini; memorial.

14 Fri. Weekday.

15 Sat. Weekday. St. Albert the Great, bishop-doctor; optional memorial.

16 Sun. Thirty-third Sunday in Ordinary Time. (Prv 31: 10-13,19-20,30-31; 1 Thes 5:1-6; Mt 25:14-30).

17 Mon. St. Elizabeth of Hungary, religious; memorial.

18 Tues. Weekday. St. Rose Philippine Duchesne, virgin; Dedication of the Basilicas of St. Peter and St. Paul, apostles, in Rome; optional memorials.

19 Wed. Weekday.

20 Thurs. Weekday.

21 Fri. Presentation of the Blessed Virgin Mary; memorial.

22 Sat. St. Cecilia, virgin-martyr; memorial.

23 Sun. Our Lord Jesus Christ the King; solemnity. (Ez 34:11-12,15-17; 1 Cor 15:20-26,28; Mt 25:31-46).

24 Mon. St. Andrew Dung-Lac, priest-martyr and Companions, martyrs; memorial.

25 Tues. Weekday. St. Catherine of Alexandria, virgin-martyr; optional memorial.

26 Wed. Weekday.

27 Thurs. Thanksgiving Day; proper Mass.

28 Fri. Weekday.

29 Sat. Weekday.

30 Sun. First Sunday of Advent. (Is 63:16b-17,19b; 64:2-7; 1 Cor 1:3-9; Mk 13:33-37).

Observances:

All Saints Day, Nov. 1; All Souls Day, Nov. 2; Frances Xavier Cabrini, foundress, first U.S. citizen-saint, Nov. 13; St. Albert the Great, doctor of the Church, Nov. 15; Presentation of the Blessed Virgin Mary, Nov. 21; Christ the King, Nov. 23; Thanksgiving Day, Nov. 27; The beginning of the Church Year, the first Sunday of Advent, Nov. 30. The month of November is traditional devoted to praying for our beloved dead. Masses for Dead are offered frequently throughout the month especially at cemeteries.

The annual fall meeting of the bishops of the United States takes place this month in Washington, D.C. Its agenda covers a wide range of topics with particular attention given to doctrinal, pastoral and educational issues that impact the life of the Church in the United States.

December 2014

Universal: That the birth of the Redeemer may bring peace and hope to all people of good will.

For Evangelization: That parents may be true evangelizers, passing on to their children the precious gift of faith.

1 Mon. Advent Weekday.

2 Tues. Advent Weekday.

3 Wed. St. Francis Xavier, priest; memorial

4 Thurs. Advent Weekday. St. John Damascene, priest-doctor; optional memorial.

5 Fri. Advent Weekday.

6 Sat. Advent Weekday. St. Nicholas, bishop; optional memorial.

7 Sun. Second Sunday of Advent. (Is 40:1-5,9-11; 2 Pt 3:8-14; Mk 1:1-8).

8 Mon. Immaculate Conception of the Blessed Virgin Mary; solemnity. (Gn 3:9-15,20; Eph 1:3-6,11-12; Lk 1:26-38).

9 Tues. Advent Weekday. St. Juan Diego; optional memorial.

10 Wed. Advent Weekday.

11 Thurs. Advent Weekday. St. Damasus, pope; optional memorial.

12 Fri. Our Lady of Guadalupe; feast.

13 Sat. St. Lucy, virgin-martyr; memorial.

14 Sun. Third Sunday of Advent. (Is 61:1-2a,10-11; 1 Thes 5:16-24; Jn 1:6-8,19-28).

15 Mon. Advent Weekday.

16 Tues. Advent Weekday.

17 Wed. Advent Weekday.

18 Thurs. Advent Weekday.

19 Fri. Advent Weekday.

20 Sat. Advent Weekday.

21 Sun. Fourth Sunday of Advent. (2 Sm 7:1-5,8b-12,14a, 16; Rom 16:25-27; Lk 1: 26-38).

22 Mon. Advent Weekday.

23 Tues. Advent Weekday.

24 Wed. Advent Weekday.

25 Thurs. Nativity of the Lord, Christmas; solemnity. Holy Day of Obligation. (Vigil Mass – Is 62:1-5; Acts 13:16-17,22-25; Mt 1:1-25 or 1:18-25. Midnight Mass – Is 9:1-6; Ti 2:11-14; Lk 2:1-14. Mass at Dawn – Is 62:11-12; Ti 3:4-7; Lk 2:15-20. Mass during the day – Is 52:7-10; Heb 1:1-6; Jn 1:1-18 or 1:1-5, 9-14).

26 Fri. St. Stephen, first martyr; feast.

27 Sat. St. John, apostle-evangelist; feast.

28 Sun. Holy Family of Jesus, Mary, and Joseph. (Sir 3:2-7,12-14; Col 3:12-21; Lk 2:22-40).

29 Mon. Fifth Day in the Octave of Christmas. St. Thomas Becket, bishop-martyr; optional memorial.

30 Tues. Sixth Day in the Octave of Christmas.

31 Wed. Seventh Day in the Octave of Christmas. St. Sylvester, pope; optional memorial.

Observances:

St. Francis Xavier, missionary, Dec. 3; Sts. John Damascene, Ambrose, John of the Cross, Peter Canisius, doctors of the Church; Immaculate Conception, Dec. 8; St. Juan Diego, Dec. 9; Our Lady of Guadalupe, Dec. 12; Birth of our Lord, Dec. 25; St. Stephen, proto-martyr, Dec. 26; St. John, apostle-evangelist, Dec. 27; Holy Family, Dec. 28.

HOLY DAYS AND OTHER OBSERVANCES

The following list includes the six holy days of obligation observed in the U.S. and additional observances of devotional and historical significance. The dignity or rank of observances is indicated by the terms: solemnity (highest in rank); feast; memorial (for universal observance); optional memorial (for celebration by choice).

All Saints, Nov. 1, Holy Day of Obligation, solemnity. Commemorates all the blessed in heaven, and is intended particularly to honor the blessed who have no special feasts. The background of the feast dates to the fourth century when groups of martyrs, and later other saints, were honored on a common day in various places. In 609 or 610, the Pantheon, a pagan temple at Rome, was consecrated as a Christian church for the honor of Our Lady and the martyrs (later all saints). In 835, Gregory IV fixed Nov. 1 as the date of observance.

All Souls, Commemoration of the Faithful Departed, Nov. 2. The dead were prayed for from the earliest days of Christianity. By the sixth century it was customary in Benedictine monasteries to hold a commemoration of deceased members of the order at Pentecost. A common commemoration of all the faithful departed on the day after All Saints was instituted in 998 by St. Odilo, of the Abbey of Cluny, and an observance of this kind was accepted in Rome in the 14th century.

Annunciation of the Lord (formerly, Annunciation of the Blessed Virgin Mary), Mar. 25, solemnity. A feast of the Incarnation which commemorates the announcement by the Archangel Gabriel to the Virgin Mary that she was to become the Mother of Christ (Lk 1:26-38), and the miraculous conception of Christ by her. The feast was instituted about 430 in the East. The Roman observance dates from the seventh century, when celebration was said to be universal.

Ascension of the Lord, movable observance held 40 days after Easter, holy day of obligation, solemnity. Commemorates the Ascension of Christ into heaven 40 days after his Resurrection from the dead (Mk 16:19; Lk 24:51; Acts 1:2). The feast recalls the completion of Christ's mission on earth for the salvation of all people and his entry into heaven with glorified human nature. The Ascension is a pledge of the final glorification of all who achieve salvation. Documentary evidence of the feast dates from early in the fifth century, but it was observed long before that time in connection with Pentecost and Easter.

Ash Wednesday, movable observance, six and one-half weeks before Easter. It was set as the first day of Lent by Pope St. Gregory the Great (590-604) with the extension of an earlier and shorter penitential season to a total period including 40 weekdays of fasting before Easter. It is a day of fast and abstinence. Ashes, symbolic of penance, are blessed and distributed among the faithful during the day. They are used to mark the forehead with the Sign of the Cross, with the reminder: "Remember you are dust, and to dust you will return," or "Turn away from sin and be faithful to the Gospel."

Assumption, Aug. 15, holy day of obligation, solemnity. Commemorates the taking into heaven of Mary, soul and body, at the end of her life on earth, a truth of faith that was proclaimed a dogma by Pius XII on Nov. 1, 1950. One of the oldest and most solemn feasts of Mary, it has a history dating back to at least the seventh century when its celebration was already established at Jerusalem and Rome.

Baptism of the Lord, movable, usually celebrated on the Sunday after January 6, feast. Recalls the baptism of Christ by John the Baptist (Mk 1:9-11), an event associated with the liturgy of the Epiphany. This baptism was the occasion for Christ's manifestation of himself at the beginning of his public life.

Birth of Mary, Sept. 8, feast. This is a very old feast which originated in the East and found place in the Roman liturgy in the seventh century.

Candlemas Day, Feb. 2. See **Presentation of the Lord**.

Chair of Peter, Feb. 22, feast. The feast, which has been in the Roman calendar since 336, is a liturgical expression of belief in the episcopacy and hierarchy of the Church.

Christmas, Birth of Our Lord Jesus Christ, Dec. 25, holy day of obligation, solemnity. Commemorates the birth of Christ (Lk 2:1-20). This event was originally commemorated in the East on the feast of Epiphany or Theophany. The Christmas feast itself originated in the West; by 354 it was certainly kept on Dec. 25. This date may have been set for the observance to offset pagan ceremonies held at about the same time to commemorate the birth of the sun at the winter solstice. There are texts for three Christmas Masses at midnight, dawn, and during the day.

Christ the King, movable, celebrated on the last Sunday of the liturgical year, solemnity. Commemorates the royal prerogatives of Christ and is equivalent to a declaration of his rights to the homage, service and fidelity of all people in all phases of individual and social life. Pius XI instituted the feast Dec. 11, 1925.

Conversion of St. Paul, Jan. 25, feast. An observance mentioned in some calendars from the 8th and 9th centuries. Pope Innocent III (1198-1216) ordered its observance with great solemnity.

Corpus Christi (The Body and Blood of Christ), movable, celebrated on the Thursday (or Sunday, as in the U.S.) following Trinity Sunday, solemnity. Commemorates the institution of the Holy Eucharist (Mt 26:26-28). The feast originated at Liège in 1246 and was extended throughout the Church in the West by Urban IV in 1264. St. Thomas Aquinas composed the Liturgy of the Hours for the feast.

Cross, The Holy, Sept. 14, feast. Commemorates the finding of the Cross on which Christ was crucified, in 326 through the efforts of St. Helena, mother of Constantine; the consecration of the Basilica of the Holy Sepulchre nearly 10 years later; and the recovery in 628 or 629 by Emperor Heraclius of a major portion of the cross which had been removed by the Persians from its place of veneration at Jerusalem. The feast originated in Jerusalem and spread through the East before being adopted in the West. General adoption followed the building at Rome of the Basilica of the Holy Cross "in Jerusalem," so called because it was the place of enshrinement of a major portion of the cross of crucifixion.

Dedication of St. John Lateran, Nov. 9, feast. Commemorates the first public consecration of a church, that of the Basilica of the Most Holy Savior by Pope St. Sylvester about 324. The church, as well as the Lateran Palace, was the gift of Emperor Constantine. Since the 12th century it has been known as St. John Lateran, in honor of John the Baptist after whom the adjoining baptistery was named. It was rebuilt by Innocent X (1644-55), reconsecrated by Benedict XIII in 1726, and enlarged by Leo XIII (1878-1903). This basilica is regarded as the church of highest dignity in Rome and throughout the Roman rite.

Dedication of St. Mary Major, Aug. 5, optional memorial. Commemorates the rebuilding and dedication by Pope Sixtus III (432-40) of a church in honor of Blessed Mary the Virgin. This is the Basilica of St. Mary Major on the Esquiline Hill in Rome. An earlier building was erected during the pontificate of Liberius (352-66); according to legend, it was located on a site covered by a miraculous fall of snow seen by a nobleman favored with a vision of Mary.

Easter, movable celebration held on the first Sunday after the full moon following the vernal equinox (between Mar. 22 and Apr. 25), solemnity with an octave. Commemorates the Resurrection of Christ from the dead (Mk 16:1-7). The observance of this mystery, kept since the first days of the Church, extends throughout the Easter season which lasts until the feast of Pentecost, a period of 50 days. Every Sunday in the year is regarded as a "little" Easter. The date of Easter determines the dates of movable feasts, such as Ascension and Pentecost, and the number of weeks before Lent and after Pentecost.

Easter Vigil, called by St. Augustine the "Mother of All Vigils," the night before Easter. Ceremonies are all related to the Resurrection and renewal-in-grace theme of Easter: blessing of the new fire, procession with the Easter Candle, singing of the Easter Proclamation (Exsultet), Liturgy of the Word with at least three Old Testament readings, the Litany of Saints, blessing of water, baptism of converts and infants, renewal of baptismal promises, Liturgy of the Eucharist. The vigil ceremonies are held after nightfall on Saturday.

Epiphany of the Lord, Jan. 6 or (in the U.S.) a Sunday between Jan. 2 and 8, solemnity. Commemorates the manifestations of the divinity of Christ. It is one of the oldest Christian feasts, with an Eastern origin traceable to the beginning of the third century and antedating the Western feast of Christmas. Originally, it commemorated the manifestations of Christ's divinity — or Theophany — in his birth, the homage of the Magi, and baptism by John the Baptist. Later, the first two of these commemorations were transferred to Christmas when the Eastern Church adopted that feast between 380 and 430. The central feature of the Eastern observance now is the manifestation or declaration of Christ's divinity in his baptism and at the beginning of his public life. The Epiphany was adopted by the Western Church during the same period in which the Eastern Church accepted Christmas. In the Roman rite, commemoration is made in the Mass of the homage of the wise men from the East (Mt 2:1-12).

Good Friday, the Friday before Easter, the second day of the Easter Triduum. Liturgical elements of the observance are commemoration of the Passion and Death of Christ in the reading of the Passion (according to John), special prayers for the Church and people of all ranks, the veneration of the Cross, and a Communion service. The celebration takes place in the afternoon, preferably at 3:00 p.m.

Guardian Angels, Oct. 2, memorial. Commemorates the angels who protect people from spiritual and physical dangers and assist them in doing good. A feast in their honor celebrated in Spain in the 16th century was placed in the Roman calendar in 1615 and Oct. 2 was set as the date of observance. Earlier, guardian angels were honored liturgically in conjunction with the feast of St. Michael.

Holy Family, movable observance on the Sunday after Christmas, feast. Commemorates the Holy Family of Jesus, Mary and Joseph as the model of domestic society, holiness and virtue. The devotional background of the feast was very strong in the 17th century. In the 18th century, in prayers composed for a special Mass, a Canadian bishop likened the Christian family to the Holy Family. Leo XIII consecrated families to the Holy Family. In 1921, Benedict XV extended the Divine Office and Mass of the feast to the whole Church.

Holy Innocents, Dec. 28, feast. Commemorates the infants who suffered death at the hands of Herod's soldiers seeking to kill the child Jesus (Mt 2:13-18). A feast in their honor has been observed since the fifth century.

Holy Saturday, the day before Easter. The Sacrifice of the Mass is not celebrated, and Holy Communion may be given only as Viaticum. If possible the Easter fast should be observed until the Easter Vigil.

Holy Thursday, the Thursday before Easter. Commemorates the institution of the sacraments of the Eucharist and holy orders, and the washing of the feet of the Apostles by Jesus at the Last Supper. The Mass of the Lord's Supper in the evening marks the beginning of the Easter Triduum. Following the Mass, there is a procession of the Blessed Sacrament to a place of reposition for adoration by the faithful. Usually at an earlier Mass of Chrism, bishops bless oils (of catechumens, chrism, the sick) for use during the year. (For pastoral reasons, diocesan bishops may permit additional Masses, but these should not overshadow the principal Mass of the Lord's Supper.)

Immaculate Conception, Dec. 8, holy day of obligation, solemnity. Commemorates the fact that Mary, in view of her calling to be the Mother of Christ and in virtue of his merits, was preserved from the first moment of her conception from original sin and was filled with grace from the very beginning of her life. She was the only person so preserved from original sin. The present form of the feast dates from Dec. 8, 1854, when Pius IX defined the dogma of the Immaculate Conception An earlier feast of the Conception, which testified to long-existing belief in this truth, was observed in the East by the eighth century, in Ireland in the ninth, and subsequently in European countries. In 1846, Mary was proclaimed patroness of the U.S. under this title.

Immaculate Heart of Mary, Saturday following the second Sunday after Pentecost, memorial. On May 4, 1944, Pius XII ordered this feast observed throughout the Church in order to obtain Mary's intercession for "peace among nations, freedom for the Church, the conversion of sinners, the love of purity and the practice of virtue." Two years earlier, he consecrated the entire human race to Mary under this title. Devotion to Mary under the title of her Most Pure Heart originated during the Middle Ages. It was given great impetus in the 17th century by the preaching of St. John Eudes, who was the first to celebrate a Mass and Divine Office of Mary under this title. A feast, celebrated in various places and on different dates, was authorized in 1799.

Joachim and Ann, July 26, memorial. Commemorates

the parents of Mary. A joint feast, celebrated Sept. 9, originated in the East near the end of the sixth century. Devotion to Ann, introduced in the eighth century at Rome, became widespread in Europe in the 14th century; her feast was extended throughout the Latin Church in 1584. A feast of Joachim was introduced in the West in the 15th century.

John the Baptist, Birth of, June 24, solemnity. The precursor of Christ, whose cousin he was, was commemorated universally in the liturgy by the fourth century. He is the only saint, except the Blessed Virgin Mary, whose birthday is observed as a feast. Another feast, on Aug. 29, commemorates his passion and death at the order of Herod (Mk 6:14-29).

Joseph, Mar. 19, solemnity. Joseph is honored as the husband of the Blessed Virgin Mary, the patron and protector of the universal Church and workman. Devotion to him already existed in the eighth century in the East, and in the 11th in the West. Various feasts were celebrated before the 15th century when Mar. 19 was fixed for his commemoration; this feast was extended to the whole Church in 1621 by Gregory XV. In 1955, Pius XII instituted the feast of St. Joseph the Workman for observance May 1; this feast, which may be celebrated by local option, supplanted the Solemnity or Patronage of St. Joseph formerly observed on the third Wednesday after Easter. St. Joseph was proclaimed protector and patron of the universal Church in 1870 by Pius IX.

Michael, Gabriel and Raphael, Archangels, Sept. 29, feast. A feast bearing the title of Dedication of St. Michael the Archangel formerly commemorated on this date the consecration in 530 of a church near Rome in honor of Michael, the first angel given a liturgical feast. For a while, this feast was combined with a commemoration of the Guardian Angels. The separate feasts of Gabriel (Mar. 24) and Raphael (Oct. 24) were suppressed by the calendar in effect since 1970 and this joint feast of the three archangels was instituted.

Octave of Christmas, Jan. 1. See **Solemnity of Mary, Mother of God**.

Our Lady of Guadalupe, Dec. 12, feast (in the U.S.). Commemorates under this title the appearances of the Blessed Virgin Mary in 1531 to an Indian, Juan Diego, on Tepeyac hill outside Mexico City (see **Apparitions of the Blessed Virgin Mary**, p. 123). The celebration, observed as a memorial in the U.S., was raised to the rank of feast at the request of the National Conference of Catholic Bishops. Approval was granted in a decree dated Jan. 8, 1988.

Our Lady of Sorrows, Sept. 15, memorial. Recalls the sorrows experienced by Mary in her association with Christ: the prophecy of Simeon (Lk 2:34-35), the flight into Egypt (Mt 2:13-21), the three-day separation from Jesus (Lk 2:41-50), and four incidents connected with the Passion — her meeting with Christ on the way to Calvary, the crucifixion, the removal of Christ's body from the cross, and his burial (Mt 27:31-61; Mk 15:20-47; Lk 23:26-56; Jn 19:17-42). A Mass and Divine Office of the feast were celebrated by the Servites, especially, in the 17th century, and in 1814 Pius VII extended the observance to the whole Church.

Our Lady of the Rosary, Oct. 7, memorial. Commemorates the Virgin Mary through recall of the mysteries of the Rosary which recapitulate events in her life and the life of Christ. The feast was instituted in 1573

to commemorate a Christian victory by the Holy Alliance over the invading fleet of the Ottoman Empire at the Battle of Lepanto in 1571, and was extended throughout the Church by Clement XI in 1716.

Passion Sunday (formerly called Palm Sunday), the Sunday before Easter. Marks the start of Holy Week by recalling the triumphal entry of Christ into Jerusalem at the beginning of the last week of his life (Mt 21:1-9). A procession and other ceremonies commemorating this event were held in Jerusalem from very early Christian times and were adopted in Rome by the ninth century, when the blessing of palm for the occasion was introduced. Full liturgical observance includes the blessing of palm and a procession before the principal Mass of the day. The Passion, by Matthew, Mark or Luke, is read during the Mass.

Pentecost, also called Whitsunday, movable celebration held 50 days after Easter, solemnity. Commemorates the descent of the Holy Spirit upon the Apostles, the preaching of Peter and the other Apostles to Jews in Jerusalem, the baptism and aggregation of some 3,000 persons to the Christian community (Acts 2:1-41). It is regarded as the birthday of the Catholic Church. The original observance of the feast antedated the earliest extant documentary evidence from the third century.

Peter and Paul, June 29, solemnity. Commemorates the martyrdoms of Peter by crucifixion and Paul by beheading during the Neronian persecution. This joint commemoration of the chief Apostles dates at least from 258 at Rome.

Presentation of the Lord (formerly called Purification of the Blessed Virgin Mary, also Candlemas), Feb. 2, feast. Commemorates the presentation of Jesus in the Temple — according to prescriptions of Mosaic Law (Lv 12:2-8; Ex 13:2; Lk 2:22-32) — and the purification of Mary 40 days after his birth. In the East, where the feast antedated fourth century testimony regarding its existence, it was observed primarily as a feast of Our Lord; in the West, where it was adopted later, it was regarded more as a feast of Mary until the calendar in effect since 1970. Its date was set for Feb. 2 after the celebration of Christmas was fixed for Dec. 25, late in the fourth century. The blessing of candles, probably in commemoration of Christ who was the Light to enlighten the Gentiles, became common about the 11th century and gave the feast the secondary name of Candlemas.

Queenship of Mary, Aug. 22, memorial. Commemorates the high dignity of Mary as Queen of heaven, angels and men. Universal observance of the memorial was ordered by Pius XII in the encyclical *Ad Caeli Reginam*, Oct. 11, 1954, near the close of a Marian Year observed in connection with the centenary of the proclamation of the dogma of the Immaculate Conception and four years after the proclamation of the dogma of the Assumption. The original date of the memorial was May 31.

Resurrection. See **Easter**.

Sacred Heart of Jesus, movable observance held on the Friday after the second Sunday after Pentecost (Corpus Christi, in the U.S.), solemnity. The object of the devotion is the divine Person of Christ, whose heart is the symbol of his love for all people — for whom he accomplished the work of Redemption. The Mass and Office now used on the feast were prescribed by Pius XI in 1929. Devotion to the Sacred Heart was introduced into the liturgy in the 17th century through the efforts of St. John Eudes who composed an Office and Mass for the feast. It was furthered as the result of the revelations of St. Margaret Mary Alacoque after 1675 and by the work of St. Claude de la Colombière, S.J. In 1765, Clement XIII approved a Mass and Office for the feast, and in 1856 Pius IX extended the observance throughout the Roman rite.

Solemnity of Mary, Mother of God, Jan. 1, holy day of obligation, solemnity. The calendar in effect since 1970, in accord with Eastern tradition, reinstated the Marian character of this commemoration on the octave day of Christmas. The former feast of the Circumcision, dating at least from the first half of the sixth century, marked the initiation of Jesus (Lk 2:21) in Judaism and by analogy focused attention on the initiation of persons in the Christian religion and their incorporation in Christ through baptism. The feast of the Solemnity supplants the former feast of the Maternity of Mary observed on Oct. 11.

Transfiguration of the Lord, Aug. 6, feast. Commemorates the revelation of his divinity by Christ to Peter, James and John on Mt. Tabor (Mt 17:1-9). The feast, which is very old, was extended throughout the universal Church in 1457 by Callistus III.

Trinity, The Holy, movable observance held on the Sunday after Pentecost, solemnity. Commemorates the most sublime mystery of the Christian faith, i.e., that there are Three Divine Persons — Father, Son and Holy Spirit — in one God (Mt 28:18-20). A votive Mass of the Most Holy Trinity dates from the seventh century; an Office was composed in the 10th century; in 1334, John XXII extended the feast to the universal Church.

Visitation, May 31, feast. Commemorates Mary's visit to her cousin Elizabeth after the Annunciation and before the birth of John the Baptist, the precursor of Christ (Lk 1:39-47). The feast had a medieval origin and was observed in the Franciscan Order before being extended throughout the Church by Urban VI in 1389. It is one of the feasts of the Incarnation and is notable for its recall of the Magnificat, one of the few New Testament canticles, which acknowledges the unique gifts of God to Mary because of her role in the redemptive work of Christ. The canticle is recited at Evening Prayer in the Liturgy of the Hours.

Liturgical Life of the Church

The nature and purpose of the liturgy, along with norms for its revision, were the subject matter of *Sacrosanctum Concilium* (the Constitution on the Sacred Liturgy) promulgated by the Second Vatican Council. The principles and guidelines stated in this document, the first issued by the Council, are summarized here and/or are incorporated in other Almanac entries on liturgical subjects.

Nature and Purpose of Liturgy

The paragraphs under this and the following subhead are quoted directly from *Sacrosanctum Concilium* (Constitution on the Sacred Liturgy).

"It is through the liturgy, especially the divine Eucharistic Sacrifice, that 'the work of our redemption is exercised.' The liturgy is thus the outstanding means by which the faithful can express in their lives, and manifest to others, the mystery of Christ and the real nature of the true Church" (No. 2).

"The liturgy is considered as an exercise of the priestly office of Jesus Christ. In the liturgy the sanctification of man is manifested by signs perceptible to the senses, and is effected in a way which is proper to each of these signs; in the liturgy full public worship is performed by the Mystical Body of Jesus Christ, that is, by the Head and his members.

"From this it follows that every liturgical celebration, because it is an action of Christ the priest and of his Body the Church, is a sacred action surpassing all others. No other action of the Church can match its claim to efficacy, nor equal the degree of it" (No. 7).

"The liturgy is the summit toward which the activity of the Church is directed; at the same time it is the fountain from which all her power flows. For the goal of apostolic works is that all who are made sons of God by faith and baptism should come together to praise God in the midst of his Church, to take part in her sacrifice, and to eat the Lord's Supper.

"From the liturgy, therefore, and especially from the Eucharist, as from a fountain, grace is channeled into us; and the sanctification of men in Christ and the glorification of God, to which all other activities of the Church are directed as toward their goal, are most powerfully achieved" (No. 10).

Full Participation

"Mother Church earnestly desires that all the faithful be led to that full, conscious, active participation in liturgical celebrations which is demanded by the very nature of the liturgy. Such participation by the Christian people as 'a chosen race, a royal priesthood, a holy nation, a purchased people' (1 Pt 2:9; cf. 2:4-5), is their right and duty by reason of their baptism.

"In the restoration and promotion of the sacred liturgy, this full and active participation by all the people is the aim to be considered before all else; for it is the primary and indispensable source from which the faithful are to derive the true Christian spirit" (No. 14).

"In order that the Christian people may more securely derive an abundance of graces from the sacred liturgy, holy Mother Church desires to undertake with great care a general restoration of the liturgy itself. For the liturgy is made up of unchangeable elements divinely instituted, and elements subject to change. The latter not only may but ought to be changed with the passing of time if features have by chance crept in which are less harmonious with the intimate nature of the liturgy, or if existing elements have grown less functional.

"In this restoration, both texts and rites should be drawn up so that they express more clearly the holy things which they signify. Christian people, as far as possible, should be able to understand them with ease and to take part in them fully, actively, and as befits a community" (No. 21).

Norms

Norms regarding the reforms concern the greater use of Scripture; emphasis on the importance of the sermon or homily on biblical and liturgical subjects; use of vernacular languages for prayers of the Mass and for administration of the sacraments; provision for adaptation of rites to cultural patterns.

Approval for reforms of various kinds — in liturgical texts, rites, etc. — depends on the Holy See, regional conferences of bishops and individual bishops, according to provisions of law. No priest has authority to initiate reforms on his own. Reforms may not be introduced just for the sake of innovation, and any that are introduced in the light of present-day circumstances should embody sound tradition.

To assure the desired effect of liturgical reforms, training and instruction are necessary for the clergy, religious and the laity. The functions of diocesan and regional commissions for liturgy, music and art are to set standards and provide leadership for instruction and practical programs in their respective fields.

Most of the constitution's provisions regarding liturgical reforms have to do with the Roman rite. The document clearly respects the equal dignity of all rites, leaving to the Eastern Churches control over their ancient liturgies.

(For coverage of the Mystery of the Eucharist, *see* **The Mass**; other sacraments, *see* separate entries.)

Sacramentals

Sacramentals, instituted by the Church, "are sacred signs which bear a resemblance to the sacraments: they signify effects, particularly of a spiritual kind, which are obtained through the Church's intercession. By them men are disposed to receive the chief effect of the sacraments, and various occasions in life are rendered holy" (No. 60).

"Thus, for well-disposed members of the faithful, the liturgy of the sacraments and sacramentals sanctifies almost every event in their lives; they are given access to the stream of divine grace which flows from the paschal mystery of the passion, death, and resurrection of Christ, the fountain from which all sacraments and sacramentals draw their power. There is hardly any proper use of material things which cannot thus be directed toward the sanctification of men and the praise of God" (No. 61).

Some common sacramentals are priestly blessings, blessed palm, candles, holy water, medals, scapulars, prayers and ceremonies of the Roman Ritual.

Liturgy of the Hours

The *Liturgy of the Hours* (Divine Office) is the public prayer of the Church for praising God and sanctifying the day. Its daily celebration is required as a sacred obligation by men in holy orders and by men and women religious who have professed solemn vows. Its celebration by others is highly commended and is to be encouraged in the community of the faithful.

"By tradition going back to early Christian times, the *Divine Office* is arranged so that the whole course of the day and night is made holy by the praises of God. Therefore, when this wonderful song of praise is worthily rendered by priests and others who are deputed for this purpose by Church ordinance, or by the faithful praying together with the priest in an approved form, then it is truly the voice of the bride addressing her bridegroom; it is the very prayer which Christ himself, together with his Body, addresses to the Father" (No. 84).

"Hence all who perform this service are not only fulfilling a duty of the Church, but also are sharing in the greatest honor accorded to Christ's spouse, for by offering these praises to God they are standing before God's throne in the name of the Church their Mother" (No. 85).

Revised Hours

The *Liturgy of the Hours*, revised since 1965, was the subject of Pope Paul VI's apostolic constitution *Laudis Canticum*, dated Nov. 1, 1970. The master Latin text was published in 1971; its four volumes have been published in authorized English translation since May 1975.

One-volume, partial editions of the *Liturgy of the Hours* containing Morning and Evening Prayer and other elements, have been published in approved English translation.

The revised *Liturgy of the Hours* consists of:

• Office of Readings, for reflection on the word of God. The principal parts are three psalms, biblical and non-biblical readings.

• Morning and Evening Prayer, called the "hinges" of the *Liturgy of the Hours*. The principal parts are a hymn, two psalms, an Old or New Testament canticle, a brief biblical reading, Zechariah's canticle (the *Benedictus*, morning) or Mary's canticle (the *Magnificat*, evening), responsories, intercessions and a concluding prayer.

• Daytime Prayer. The principal parts are a hymn, three psalms, a biblical reading and one of three concluding prayers corresponding to the time of day.

• Night Prayer. The principal parts are one or two

psalms, a brief biblical reading, Simeon's canticle (*Nunc Dimittis*), a concluding prayer and an antiphon in honor of Mary.

In the revised *Liturgy of the Hours*, the hours are shorter than they had been, with greater textual variety, meditation aids, and provision for intervals of silence and meditation. The psalms are distributed over a four-week period instead of a week; some psalms, entirely or in part, are not included. Additional canticles from the Old and New Testaments are assigned for Morning and Evening Prayer. Additional scriptural texts have been added and variously arranged for greater internal unity, correspondence to readings at Mass, and relevance to events and themes of salvation history. Readings include some of the best material from the Fathers of the Church and other authors, and improved selections on the lives of the saints.

The book used for recitation of the *Office* is the *Breviary*.

For coverage of the Liturgical Year, see **Church Calendar**.

Sacred Music

"The musical tradition of the universal Church is a treasure of immeasurable value, greater even than that of any other art. The main reason for this pre-eminence is that, as sacred melody united to words, it forms a necessary or integral part of the solemn liturgy.

"Sacred music increases in holiness to the degree that it is intimately linked with liturgical action, winningly expresses prayerfulness, promotes solidarity, and enriches sacred rites with heightened solemnity. The Church indeed approves of all forms of true art, and admits them into divine worship when they show appropriate qualities" (No. 112).

The constitution decreed:

• Vernacular languages for the people's parts of the liturgy, as well as Latin, may be used.

• Participation in sacred song by the whole body of the faithful, and not just by choirs, is to be encouraged and brought about.

• Provisions should be made for proper musical training for clergy, religious and lay persons.

• While Gregorian Chant has a unique dignity and relationship to the Latin liturgy, other kinds of music are acceptable.

• Native musical traditions should be used, especially in mission areas.

• Various instruments compatible with the dignity of worship may be used.

Gregorian Chant: A form and style of chant called Gregorian was the basis and most highly regarded standard of liturgical music for centuries. It originated probably during the formative period of the Roman liturgy and developed in conjunction with Gallican and other forms of chant. Pope St. Gregory I the Great's connection with it is not clear, although it is known that he had great concern for and interest in church music. The earliest extant written versions of Gregorian Chant date from the ninth century. A thousand years later, the Benedictines of Solesmes, France, initiated a revival of chant which gave impetus to the modern liturgical movement.

Sacred Art and Furnishings

"Very rightly the fine arts are considered to rank among the noblest expressions of human genius.

This judgment applies especially to religious art and to its highest achievement, which is sacred art. By their very nature both of the latter are related to God's boundless beauty, for this is the reality which these human efforts are trying to express in some way. To the extent that these works aim exclusively at turning men's thoughts to God persuasively and devoutly, they are dedicated to God and to the cause of his greater honor and glory" (No. 122).

The objective of sacred art is "that all things set apart for use in divine worship should be truly worthy, becoming, and beautiful, signs and symbols of heavenly realities. The Church has always reserved to herself the right to pass judgment upon the arts, deciding which of the works of artists are in accordance with faith, piety, and cherished traditional laws, and thereby suited to sacred purposes. "Sacred furnishings should worthily and beautifully serve the dignity of worship" (No. 122).

According to the constitution:

• Contemporary art, as well as that of the past, shall "be given free scope in the Church, provided that it adorns the sacred buildings and holy rites with due honor and reverence" (No. 123).

• Noble beauty, not sumptuous display, should be sought in art, sacred vestments and ornaments.

• "Let bishops carefully exclude from the house of God and from other sacred places those works of artists which are repugnant to faith, morals, and Christian piety, and which offend true religious sense either by their distortion of forms or by lack of artistic worth, by mediocrity or by pretense.

• "When churches are to be built, let great care be taken that they be suitable for the celebration of liturgical services and for the active participation of the faithful" (No. 124).

• "The practice of placing sacred images in churches so that they may be venerated by the faithful is to be firmly maintained. Nevertheless, their number should be moderate and their relative location should reflect right order. Otherwise they may create confusion among the Christian people and promote a faulty sense of devotion" (No. 125).

• Artists should be trained and inspired in the spirit and for the purposes of the liturgy.

• The norms of sacred art should be revised. "These laws refer especially to the worthy and well-planned construction of sacred buildings, the shape and construction of altars, the nobility, location, and security of the Eucharistic tabernacle, the suitability and dignity of the baptistery, the proper use of sacred images, embellishments, and vestments" (No. 128).

RITES

Rites are the forms and ceremonial observances of liturgical worship coupled with the total expression of the theological, spiritual and disciplinary heritages of particular churches of the East and the West.

Different rites have evolved in the course of church history, giving to liturgical worship and church life in general forms and usages peculiar and proper to the nature of worship and the culture of the faithful in various circumstances of time and place. Thus, there has been development since apostolic times in the prayers and ceremonies of the Mass, in the celebration of the sacraments, sacramentals and the Liturgy of the Hours, and in observances of the liturgical calendar. The principal sources of rites in present use were practices within the patriarchates of Rome (for the West) and Antioch, Alexandria and Constantinople (for the East). Rites are identified as Eastern or Western on the basis of their geographical area of origin in the Roman Empire.

Eastern and Roman Rites

Eastern rites are proper to Eastern Catholic Churches (see separate entry). The principal rites are Byzantine, Alexandrian, Antiochene, Armenian and Chaldean.

The Latin or Roman rite prevails in the Western Church. It was derived from Roman practices and the use of Latin from the third century onward, and has been the rite in general use in the West since the eighth century. Other rites in limited use in the Western Church have been the Ambrosian (in the Archdiocese of Milan), the Mozarabic (in the Archdiocese of Toledo), the Lyonnais, the Braga, and rites peculiar to some religious orders like the Dominicans, Carmelites and Carthusians.

The purpose of the revision of rites in progress since the Second Vatican Council is to renew them, not to eliminate the rites of particular churches or to reduce all rites to uniformity. The Council reaffirmed the equal dignity and preservation of rites as follows.

"It is the mind of the Catholic Church that each individual church or rite retain its traditions whole and entire, while adjusting its way of life to various needs of time and place. Such individual churches, whether of the East or the West, although they differ somewhat among themselves in what are called rites (that is, in liturgy, ecclesiastical discipline and spiritual heritage), are, nevertheless, equally entrusted to the pastoral guidance of the Roman Pontiff, the divinely appointed successor of St. Peter in supreme government over the universal Church. They are, consequently, of equal dignity, so that none of them is superior to the others by reason of rite."

Determination of Rite

Determination of a person's rite is regulated by Church law. Through baptism, a child becomes a member of the rite of his or her parents. If the parents are of different rites, the child's rite is decided by mutual consent of the parents; if there is lack of mutual consent, the child is baptized in the rite of the father. A candidate for baptism over the age of 14 can choose to be baptized in any approved rite. Catholics baptized in one rite may receive the sacraments in any of the approved ritual churches; they may transfer to another rite only with the permission of the Holy See and in accordance with other provisions of the Code of Canon Law.

MASS, EUCHARISTIC SACRIFICE AND BANQUET

Declarations of Vatican II

The Second Vatican Council made the following declarations among others with respect to the Mass:

"At the Last Supper, on the night when he was betrayed, our Savior instituted the Eucharistic Sacrifice of his Body and Blood. He did this in order to perpetuate the Sacrifice of the Cross throughout the centuries until he should come again, and so to entrust to his beloved spouse, the Church, a memorial of his death and resurrection: a sacrament of love, a sign of unity, a bond of charity, a paschal banquet in which Christ is consumed, the mind is filled with grace, and a pledge of future glory is given to us" (*Sacrosanctum Concilium*, Constitution on the Sacred Liturgy, No. 47).

"... As often as the Sacrifice of the Cross in which 'Christ, our Passover, has been sacrificed' (1 Cor 5:7) is celebrated on an altar, the work of our redemption is carried on. At the same time, in the sacrament of the Eucharistic bread the unity of all believers who form one body in Christ (cf. 1 Cor 10:17) is both expressed and brought about. All men are called to this union with Christ" (*Lumen Gentium*, Dogmatic Constitution on the Church, No. 3).

"... The ministerial priest, by the sacred power he enjoys, molds and rules the priestly people. Acting in the person of Christ, he brings about the Eucharistic Sacrifice, and offers it to God in the name of all the people. For their part, the faithful join in the offering of the Eucharist by virtue of their royal priesthood" (Ibid., No. 10).

Declarations of Trent

Among its decrees on the Holy Eucharist, the Council of Trent stated the following points of doctrine on the Mass.

1. There is in the Catholic Church a true sacrifice, the Mass instituted by Jesus Christ. It is the sacrifice of his Body and Blood, Soul and Divinity, himself, under the appearances of bread and wine.

2. This Sacrifice is identical with the Sacrifice of the Cross, inasmuch as Christ is the Priest and Victim in both. A difference lies in the manner of offering, which was bloody upon the Cross and is bloodless on the altar.

3. The Mass is a propitiatory Sacrifice, atoning for the sins of the living and dead for whom it is offered.

4. The efficacy of the Mass is derived from the Sacrifice of the Cross, whose superabundant merits it applies to men.

5. Although the Mass is offered to God alone, it may be celebrated in honor and memory of the saints.

6. Christ instituted the Mass at the Last Supper.

7. Christ ordained the Apostles priests, giving them power and the command to consecrate his Body and Blood to perpetuate and renew the Sacrifice.

ORDER OF THE MASS

The Mass consists of two principal divisions called the **Liturgy of the Word**, which features the proclamation of the Word of God, and the **Eucharistic Liturgy**, which focuses on the central act of sacrifice in the Consecration and on the Eucharistic Banquet in Holy Communion. (Formerly, these were called, respectively, the **Mass of the Catechumens** and the **Mass of the Faithful**.) In addition to these principal divisions, there are ancillary introductory and concluding rites.

The following description covers the Mass as celebrated with participation by the people. This Order of the Mass was approved by Pope Paul VI in the apostolic constitution *Missale Romanum* dated Apr. 3, 1969, and promulgated in a decree issued Apr. 6, 1969, by the Congregation for Divine Worship. The assigned effective date was Nov. 30, 1969.

Introductory Rites

Entrance: The introductory rites begin with the singing or recitation of an entrance song consisting of one or more scriptural verses stating the theme of the mystery, season or feast commemorated in the Mass.

Greeting: The priest and people make the Sign of the Cross together. The priest then greets them in one of several alternative ways and they reply in a corresponding manner.

Introductory Remarks: At this point, the priest or another of the ministers may introduce the theme of the Mass.

Penitential Rite: The priest and people together acknowledge their sins as a preliminary step toward worthy celebration of the sacred mysteries.

This rite includes a brief examination of conscience, a general confession of sin and plea for divine mercy in one of several ways, and a prayer for forgiveness by the priest.

Glory to God: A doxology, a hymn of praise to God, sung or said on festive occasions.

Opening Prayer: A prayer of petition offered by the priest on behalf of the worshiping community.

I. Liturgy of the Word

Readings: The featured elements of this liturgy are readings of passages from the Bible. If three readings are in order, the first is usually from the Old Testament, the second from the New Testament (Letters, Acts, Revelation), and the third from one of the Gospels; the final reading is always a selection from a Gospel. The first reading(s) is (are) concluded with the formula, "The Word of the Lord" (effective Feb. 28, 1993; optional before that date), to which the people respond, "Thanks be to God." The Gospel reading is concluded with the formula, "The Gospel of the Lord," (effective as above), to which the people respond, "Praise to you, Lord Jesus Christ." Between the readings, psalm verses are sung or recited. A Gospel acclamation is either sung or omitted.

Homily: An explanation, pertinent to the mystery being celebrated and the special needs of the listeners, of some point in either the readings from sacred Scripture or in another text from the Ordinary or Proper parts of the Mass; it is a proclamation of the Good News for a response of faith.

Creed: The Nicene profession of faith, by priest and people, on certain occasions.

Prayer of the Faithful: Litany-type prayers of petition, with participation by the people. Called general intercessions, they concern needs of the Church, the salvation of the world, public authorities, persons in need, the local community.

II. Eucharistic Liturgy

Presentation and Preparation of Gifts: Presentation to the priest of the gifts of bread and wine, principally, by participating members of the congregation. Preparation of the gifts consists of the prayers and ceremonies with which the priest offers bread and wine as the elements of the sacrifice to take place during the Eucharistic Prayer and of the Lord's Supper to be shared in Holy Communion.

Washing of Hands: After offering the bread and wine, the priest cleanses his fingers with water in a brief ceremony of purification.

Pray, Brothers and Sisters: Prayer that the sacrifice to take place will be acceptable to God. The first part of the prayer is said by the priest; the second, by the people.

Prayer over the Gifts: A prayer of petition offered by the priest on behalf of the worshipping community.

Eucharistic Prayer

Preface: A hymn of praise, introducing the Eucharistic Prayer or Canon, sung or said by the priest following responses by the people. The Order of the Mass contains a variety of prefaces, for use on different occasions.

Holy, Holy, Holy; Blessed is He: Divine praises sung or said by the priest and people.

Eucharistic Prayer (Canon): Its central portion is the Consecration, when the essential act of sacrificial offering takes place with the changing of bread and wine into the Body and Blood of Christ. The various parts of the prayer, which are said by the celebrant only, commemorate principal mysteries of salvation history and include petitions for the Church, the living and dead, and remembrances of saints.

Doxology: A formula of divine praise sung or said by the priest while he holds aloft the chalice containing the consecrated wine in one hand and the paten containing the consecrated host in the other.

Communion Rite

Lord's Prayer: Sung or said by the priest and people.

Prayer for Deliverance from Evil: Called an embolism because it is a development of the final petition of the Lord's Prayer; said by the priest. It concludes with a memorial of the return of the Lord to which the people respond, "For the kingdom, the power, and the glory are yours, now and forever."

Prayer for Peace: Said by the priest, with corresponding responses by the people. The priest can, in accord with local custom, bid the people to exchange a greeting of peace with each other.

Lamb of God (*Agnus Dei*): A prayer for divine mercy sung or said while the priest breaks the consecrated host and places a piece of it into the consecrated wine in the chalice.

Communion: The priest, after saying a preparatory prayer, administers Holy Communion to himself and then to the people, thus completing the sacrifice-banquet of the Mass. (This completion is realized even if the celebrant alone receives the Eucharist.) On giving the Eucharist to each person under both species separately, the priest or eucharistic minister says, "The Body of Christ," "The Blood of Christ." The customary response is "Amen." If the Eucharist is given by intinction (in which the host is dipped into the consecrated wine), the priest says, "The Body and Blood of Christ."

Communion Song: Scriptural verses or a suitable hymn sung or said during the distribution of Holy Communion. After Holy Communion is received, some moments may be spent in silent meditation or in the chanting of a psalm or hymn of praise.

Prayer after Communion: A prayer of petition offered by the priest on behalf of the worshipping community.

Concluding Rite

Announcements: Brief announcements to the people are in order at this time.

Dismissal: Consists of a final greeting by the priest, a blessing, and a formula of dismissal. This rite is omitted if another liturgical action immediately follows the Mass; e.g., a procession, the blessing of the body during a funeral rite.

Some parts of the Mass are changeable with the liturgical season or feast, and are called the proper of the Mass. Other parts are said to be common because they always remain the same.

Additional Mass Notes

Catholics are seriously obliged to attend Mass in a worthy manner on Sundays and holy days of obligation. Failure to do so without a proportionately serious reason is gravely wrong.

It is the custom for priests to celebrate Mass daily whenever possible. To satisfy the needs of the faithful on Sundays and holy days of obligation, they are authorized to say Mass twice (**bination**) or even three times (**trination**). Bination is also permissible on weekdays to satisfy the needs of the faithful. On Christmas every priest may say three Masses.

The **fruits of the Mass**, which in itself is of infinite value, are: **general**, for all the faithful; **special (ministerial)**, for the intentions or persons specifically intended by the celebrant; **most special (personal)**, for the celebrant himself. On Sundays and certain other days pastors are obliged to offer Mass for their parishioners, or to have another priest do so. If a priest accepts a stipend or offering for a Mass, he is obliged in justice to apply the Mass for the intention of the donor. Mass may be applied for the living and the dead, or for any good intention.

Mass can be celebrated in several ways: e.g., with people present, without their presence (privately), with two or more priests as co-celebrants (concelebration), with greater or less solemnity.

Some of the various types of Masses are: **for the dead** (Funeral Mass or Mass of Christian Burial, Mass for the Dead — formerly called Requiem Mass); **ritual**, in connection with celebration of the sacraments, religious profession, etc.; **nuptial**, for married couples, with or after the wedding ceremony; **votive**, to honor a Person of the Trinity, a saint, or for some special intention.

Places, Altars for Mass

The ordinary place for celebrating the Eucharist is a church or other sacred place, at a fixed or movable altar.

The altar is a table at which the Eucharistic Sacrifice is celebrated.

A fixed altar is attached to the floor of the church. It should be of stone, preferably, and should be consecrated. The Code of Canon Law orders observance of the custom of placing under a fixed altar relics of martyrs or other saints.

A movable altar can be made of any solid and suitable material, and should be blessed or consecrated.

Outside of a sacred place, Mass may be celebrated in an appropriate place at a suitable table covered with a linen cloth and corporal. An altar stone containing the relics of saints, which was formerly prescribed, is not required by regulations in effect since the promulgation Apr. 6, 1969, of *Institutio Generalis Missalis Romani*.

LITURGICAL VESTMENTS

In the early years of the Church, vestments worn by the ministers at liturgical functions were the same as the garments in ordinary popular use. They became distinctive when their form was not altered to correspond with later variations in popular style. Liturgical vestments are symbolic of the sacred ministry and add appropriate decorum to divine worship.

Mass Vestments

Alb: A body-length tunic of white fabric; a vestment common to all ministers of divine worship.

Amice: A rectangular piece of white cloth worn about the neck, tucked into the collar and falling over the shoulders; prescribed for use when the alb does not completely cover the ordinary clothing at the neck.

Chasuble: Originally, a large mantle or cloak covering the body, it is the outer vestment of a priest celebrating Mass or carrying out other sacred actions connected with the Mass.

Chasuble-Alb: A vestment combining the features of the chasuble and alb; for use with a stole by concelebrants and, by way of exception, by celebrants in certain circumstances.

Cincture: A cord which serves the purpose of a belt, holding the alb close to the body.

Dalmatic: The outer vestment worn by a deacon in place of a chasuble.

Stole: A long, band-like vestment worn by a priest about the neck and falling to about the knees. A deacon wears a stole over the left shoulder, crossed and fastened at his right side.

The material, form and ornamentation of the aforementioned and other vestments are subject to variation and adaptation, according to norms and decisions of the Holy See and concerned conferences of bishops. The overriding norm is that they should be appropriate for use in divine worship. The customary ornamented vestments are the chasuble, dalmatic and stole.

The minimal vestments required for a priest celebrating Mass are the alb, stole, and chasuble.

Liturgical Colors

The colors of outer vestments vary with liturgical seasons, feasts and other circumstances. The colors and their use are:

Green: For the season of ordinary time; symbolic of hope and the vitality of the life of faith.

Violet (Purple): For Advent and Lent; may also be used in Masses for the dead; symbolic of penance. (See below, Violet for Advent.)

Red: For the Sunday of the Passion, Good Friday, Pentecost; feasts of the Passion of Our Lord, the Apostles and Evangelists, martyrs; symbolic of the supreme sacrifice of life for the love of God.

Rose: May be used in place of purple on the Third Sunday of Advent (formerly called Gaudete Sunday) and the Fourth Sunday of Lent (formerly called Laetare Sunday); symbolic of anticipatory joy during a time of penance.

White: For the seasons of Christmas and Easter; feasts and commemorations of Our Lord, except those of the Passion; feasts and commemorations of the Blessed Virgin Mary, angels, saints who are not martyrs, All Saints (Nov. 1), St. John the Baptist (June 24), St. John the Evangelist (Dec. 27), the Chair of St. Peter (Feb. 22), the Conversion of St. Paul (Jan. 25). White, symbolic of purity and integrity of the life of faith, may generally be substituted for other colors, and can be used for funeral and other Masses for the dead.

Options are provided regarding the color of vestments used in offices and Masses for the dead. The newsletter of the U.S. Bishops' Committee on the Liturgy, in line with No. 308 of the General Instruction of the Roman Missal, announced in July 1970: "In the dioceses of the U.S., white vestments may be used, in addition to violet (purple) and black, in offices and Masses for the dead."

On more solemn occasions, better than ordinary vestments may be used, even though their color (e.g., gold) does not match the requirements of the day.

Violet for Advent: Violet is the official liturgical color for the season of Advent, according to the September 1988 edition of the newsletter of the U.S. Bishops' Committee on the Liturgy. Blue was being proposed in order to distinguish between the Advent season and the specifically penitential season of Lent. The newsletter said, however, that "the same effect can be achieved by following the official color sequence of the Church, which requires the use of violet for Advent and Lent, while taking advantage of the varying shades which exist for violet. Light blue vestments are not authorized for use in the U.S."

Considerable freedom is permitted in the choice of colors of vestments worn for votive Masses.

Other Vestments

Cappa Magna: Flowing vestment with a train, worn by bishops and cardinals.

Cassock: A non-liturgical, full-length, close-fitting robe for use by priests and other clerics under liturgical vestments and in ordinary use; usually black for priests, purple for bishops and other prelates, red for cardinals, white for the pope. In place of a cassock, priests belonging to religious institutes wear the habit proper to their institute.

Cope: A mantle-like vestment open in front and fastened across the chest; worn by sacred ministers in processions and other ceremonies, as prescribed by appropriate directives.

Habit: The ordinary (non-liturgical) garb of members of religious institutes, analogous to the cassock of diocesan priests; the form of habits varies from institute to institute.

Humeral Veil: A rectangular vestment worn about the shoulders by a deacon or priest in Eucharistic processions and for other prescribed liturgical ceremonies.

Mitre: A headdress worn at some liturgical functions by bishops, abbots and, in certain cases, other ecclesiastics.

Pallium: A circular band of white wool about two inches wide, with front and back pendants, marked with six crosses, worn about the neck. It is a symbol of the fullness of the episcopal office. Pope Paul VI, in a document issued July 20, 1978, on his own initiative and entitled Inter Eximia Episcopalis, restricted its use to the pope and archbishops of metropolitan sees. In 1984, Pope John Paul II decreed that the pallium would ordinarily be conferred by the pope on the solemnity of Sts. Peter and Paul, June 29. The pallium is made from the wool of lambs blessed by the pope on the feast of St. Agnes (Jan. 21).

Rochet: A knee-length, white linen-lace garment of prelates worn under outer vestments.

Surplice: a loose, flowing vestment of white fabric

with wide sleeves. For some functions, it is interchangeable with an alb.

Zucchetto: A skullcap worn by bishops and other prelates.

SACRED VESSELS, LINENS
Vessels

Paten and Chalice: The principal sacred vessels required for the celebration of Mass are the paten (plate) and chalice (cup) in which bread and wine, respectively, are offered, consecrated and consumed. Both should be made of solid and noble material which is not easily breakable or corruptible. Gold coating is required of the interior parts of sacred vessels subject to rust. The cup of a chalice should be made of non-absorbent material.

Vessels for containing consecrated hosts (see below) can be made of material other than solid and noble metal — e.g., ivory, more durable woods — provided the substitute material is locally regarded as noble or rather precious and is suitable for sacred use.

Sacred vessels should be blessed, according to prescribed requirements.

Vessels, in addition to the paten, for containing consecrated hosts are:

Ciborium: Used to hold hosts for distribution to the faithful and for reservation in the tabernacle.

Luna, Lunula, Lunette: A small receptacle which holds the sacred host in an upright position in the monstrance.

Monstrance, Ostensorium: A portable receptacle so made that the sacred host, when enclosed therein, may be clearly seen, as at Benediction or during extended exposition of the Blessed Sacrament.

Pyx: A watch-shaped vessel used in carrying the Eucharist to the sick.

Linens

Altar Cloth: A white cloth, usually of linen, covering the table of an altar. One cloth is sufficient. Three were used according to former requirements.

Burse: A square, stiff flat case, open at one end, in which the folded corporal can be placed; the outside is covered with material of the same kind and color as the outer vestments of the celebrant.

Corporal: A square piece of white linen spread on the altar cloth, on which rest the vessels holding the Sacred Species — the consecrated host(s) and wine — during the Eucharistic Liturgy. The corporal is used whenever the Blessed Sacrament is removed from the tabernacle; e.g., during Benediction the vessel containing the Blessed Sacrament rests on a corporal.

Finger Towel: A white rectangular napkin used by the priest to dry his fingers after cleansing them following the offering of gifts at Mass.

Pall: A square piece of stiff material, usually covered with linen, which can be used to cover the chalice at Mass.

Purificator: A white rectangular napkin used for cleansing sacred vessels after the reception of Communion at Mass.

Veil: The chalice intended for use at Mass can be covered with a veil made of the same material as the outer vestments of the celebrant.

THE CHURCH BUILDING

A church is a building set aside and dedicated for purposes of divine worship, the place of assembly for a worshipping community. A Catholic church is the ordinary place in which the faithful assemble for participation in the Eucharistic Liturgy and other forms of divine worship.

In the early years of Christianity, the first places of assembly for the Eucharistic Liturgy were private homes (Acts 2:46; Rom 16:5; 1 Cor 16:5; Col 4:15) and, sometimes, catacombs. Church building began in the latter half of the second century during lulls in persecution and became widespread after enactment of the Edict of Milan in 313, when it finally became possible for the Church to emerge completely from the underground. The oldest and basic norms regarding church buildings date from about that time.

The essential principle underlying all norms for church building was reformulated by the Second Vatican Council: "When churches are to be built, let great care be taken that they be suitable for the celebration of liturgical services and for the active participation of the faithful" (*Sacrosanctum Concilium*, Constitution on the Sacred Liturgy, No. 124).

This principle was subsequently elaborated in detail by the Congregation for Divine Worship in a document entitled *Institutio Generalis Missalis Romani*, which was approved by Paul VI Apr. 3, 1969, and promulgated by a decree of the congregation dated Apr. 6, 1969. Coverage of the following items reflects the norms stated in Chapter V of the *Institutio*.

Main Features

Sanctuary: The part of the church where the altar of sacrifice is located, the place where the ministers of the liturgy lead the people in prayer, proclaim the word of God and celebrate the Eucharist. It is set off from the body of the church by a distinctive structural feature — e.g., elevation above the main floor — or by ornamentation. (The traditional communion rail, removed in recent years in many churches, served this purpose of demarcation.) The customary location of the sanctuary is at the front of the church; it may, however, be centrally located.

Altar: The main altar of sacrifice and table of the Lord is the focal feature of the sanctuary and entire church. It stands by itself, so that the ministers can move about it freely, and is so situated that they face the people during the liturgical action. In addition to this main altar, there may also be others; in new churches, these are ideally situated in side chapels or alcoves removed to some degree from the body of the church.

Adornment of the Altar: The altar table is covered with a suitable linen cloth. Required candelabra and a cross are placed upon or near the altar in plain sight of the people and are so arranged that they do not obscure their view of the liturgical action.

Seats of the Ministers: The seats of the ministers should be so arranged that they are part of the seating arrangement of the worshipping congregation and suitably placed for the performance of ministerial functions. The seat of the celebrant or chief concelebrant should be in a presiding position.

Ambo, Pulpit, Lectern: The stand at which scriptural lessons and psalm responses are read, the word of God preached, and the prayer of the faithful offered. It is so placed that the ministers can be easily seen and heard by the people.

Places for the People: Seats and kneeling benches (pews) and other accommodations for the people are so arranged that they can participate in the most appropriate way in the liturgical action and have freedom of movement for the reception of Holy Communion. Reserved seats are out of order.

Place for the Choir: Where it is located depends on the most suitable arrangement for maintaining the unity of the choir with the congregation and for providing its members maximum opportunity for carrying out their proper function and participating fully in the Mass.

Tabernacle: The best place for reserving the Blessed Sacrament is in a chapel suitable for the private devotion of the people. If this is not possible, reservation should be at a side altar or other appropriately adorned place. In either case, the Blessed Sacrament should be kept in a tabernacle, i.e., a safe-like, secure receptacle.

Statues: Images of the Lord, the Blessed Virgin Mary and the saints are legitimately proposed for the veneration of the faithful in churches. Their number and arrangement, however, should be ordered in such a way that they do not distract the people from the central celebration of the Eucharistic Liturgy. There should be only one statue of one and the same saint in a church.

General Adornment and Arrangement of Churches: Churches should be so adorned and fitted out that they serve the direct requirements of divine worship and the needs and reasonable convenience of the people.

Other Items

Ambry: A box containing the holy oils, attached to the wall of the sanctuary in some churches.

Baptistery: The place for administering baptism. Some churches have baptisteries adjoining or near the entrance, a position symbolizing the fact that persons are initiated in the Church and incorporated in Christ through this sacrament. Contemporary liturgical practice favors placement of the baptistery near the sanctuary and altar, or the use of a portable font in the same position, to emphasize the relationship of baptism to the Eucharist, the celebration in sacrifice and banquet of the death and resurrection of Christ.

Candles: Used more for symbolical than illuminative purposes, they represent Christ, the light and life of grace, at liturgical functions. They are made of beeswax. (See Index: Paschal Candle.)

Confessional, Reconciliation Room: A booth-like structure for the hearing of confessions, with separate compartments for the priest and penitents and a grating or screen between them. The use of confessionals became general in the Roman rite after the Council of Trent. Since the Second Vatican Council, there has been a trend in the U.S. to replace or supplement confessionals with small reconciliation rooms so arranged that priest and penitent can converse face-to-face.

Crucifix: A cross bearing the figure of the body of Christ, representative of the Sacrifice of the Cross.

Cruets: Vessels containing the wine and water used at Mass. They are placed on a credence table in the sanctuary.

Holy Water Fonts: Receptacles containing holy water, usually at church entrances, for the use of the faithful.

Sanctuary Lamp: A lamp which is kept burning continuously before a tabernacle in which the Blessed Sacrament is reserved, as a sign of the Real Presence of Christ.

LITURGICAL DEVELOPMENTS

The principal developments covered in this article are enactments of the Holy See and actions related to their implementation in the U.S.

Modern Movement

Origins of the modern movement for renewal in the liturgy date back to the 19th century. The key contributing factor was a revival of liturgical and scriptural studies. Of special significance was the work of the Benedictine monks of Solesmes, France, who aroused great interest in the liturgy through the restoration of Gregorian Chant. St. Pius X approved their work in a *motu proprio* of 1903 and gave additional encouragement to liturgical study and development.

St. Pius X did more than any other single pope to promote early first Communion and the practice of frequent Communion, started the research behind a revised breviary, and appointed a group to investigate possible revisions in the Mass.

The movement attracted some attention in the 1920s and '30s but made little progress.

Significant pioneering developments in the U.S. during the 1920s, however, were the establishment of the Liturgical Press, the beginning of publication of *Orate Fratres* (now *Worship*), and the inauguration of the League of the Divine Office by the Benedictines at St. John's Abbey, Collegeville, MN. Later events of influence were the establishment of the Pius X School of Liturgical Music at Manhattanville College of the Sacred Heart and the organization of a summer school of liturgical music at Mary Manse College by the Gregorian Institute of America. The turning point toward real renewal was reached during and after World War II.

Pius XII gave it impetus and direction, principally through the background teaching in his encyclicals on the Mystical Body (*Mystici Corporis Christi*, 1943), Sacred Liturgy (*Mediator Dei*, 1947), and On Sacred Music (*Musicae Sacrae*, 1955), and by means of specific measures affecting the liturgy itself. His work was continued during the pontificates of his successors. The Second Vatican Council, in virtue of *Sacrosanctum Concilium*, the Constitution on the Sacred Liturgy, inaugurated changes of the greatest significance.

Before and After Vatican II

The most significant liturgical changes made in the years immediately preceding the Second Vatican Council were the following:

1. Revision of the rites of Holy Week for universal observance from 1956.

2. Modification of the Eucharistic fast and permission for afternoon and evening Mass, in effect from 1953 and extended in 1957.

3. The Dialogue Mass, introduced in 1958.

4. Use of popular languages in administration of the sacraments.

5. Calendar-missal-breviary reform, in effect from Jan. 1, 1961.

6. Seven-step administration of baptism for adults, approved in 1962.

The Constitution on the Sacred Liturgy, *Sacrosanctum Concilium*, approved (2,174 to 4) and promulgated by the Second Vatican Council on Dec. 4, 1963, marked the beginning of a profound renewal in the Church's corporate worship. Implementation of some of its measures was ordered by Paul VI on

Jan. 25, 1964, in the *motu proprio Sacram Liturgiam*. On Feb. 29, a special commission, the Consilium for Implementing the Constitution on the Sacred Liturgy, was formed to supervise the execution of the entire program of liturgical reform. Implementation of the program on local and regional levels was left to bishops acting through their own liturgical commissions and in concert with their fellow bishops in national conferences.

Liturgical reform in the U.S. has been carried out under the direction of the Liturgy Committee, National Conference of Catholic Bishops. Its secretariat, established early in 1965, is located at 3211 Fourth St. N.E., Washington, DC 20017.

Stages of Development

Liturgical development after the Second Vatican Council proceeded in several stages. It started with the formulation of guidelines and directives, and with the translation into vernacular languages of virtually unchanged Latin ritual texts. Then came structural changes in the Mass, the sacraments, the calendar, the Divine Office and other phases of the liturgy. These revisions were just about completed with the publication of a new order for the sacrament of penance in February 1974. A continuing phase of development, in progress from the beginning, involves efforts to deepen the liturgical sense of the faithful, to increase their participation in worship and to relate it to full Christian life.

RECENT DEVELOPMENTS

'Happy Are Those Who Are Called to His Supper'

On Nov. 14, 2006, during their fall general meeting in Baltimore, the Bishops of the United States approved, by a 201-24 vote with two abstentions, "'Happy Are Those Who Are called to His Supper': On Preparing to Receive Christ Worthily in the Eucharist," a statement on the preparation needed to receive Communion worthily.

The New English Translation of the Order of the Mass

On June 15, 2006, during their spring meeting in Los Angeles, the Bishops of the United States approved the new English translations of the Order of the Mass and adopted several U.S. adaptations. The new translation was approved by a vote of 173-29, and the American adaptations comprised of prayers or ritual instructions not contained in the original Latin version were approved by a vote of 184-8.

On Mar. 25, 2010, Card. Antonio Cañizares Llovera, Prefect of the Congregation for Divine Worship and the Discipline of the Sacraments, issued a letter granting approval, or "recognitio," of the proposed U.S. version of the new edition of the *Roman Missal*. The new translation was introduced officially with the start of Advent 2011.

The United States Conference of Catholic Bishops (USCCB) undertook extensive efforts to prepare the faithful for the changes. Catholic publishers also devoted a variety of resources to publish guides to the changes as well as charts and pew sheets for use by Catholics to familiarize themselves with the new translation, especially during Mass.

New U.S. Norms for Distribution of Communion Under Both Species

New norms for the distribution and reception of Communion under the outward signs of both bread and wine by Catholics in the U.S. were approved by the U.S. bishops on June 15, 2001, and confirmed by the Holy See on Mar. 22, 2002; they were subsequently published by Bp. Wilton D. Gregory of Belleville, IL, president of the USCCB.

The norms, which replace the U.S. bishops' 1984 directory titled "This Holy and Living Sacrifice," give specific directives regarding liturgical roles, sacred vessels and the rites to be followed in distributing Communion under both kinds.

The first section of the new norms provides a theological summary of the Church's teaching on Communion under both kinds, while the following section describes the authorized procedures by which such distribution can be accomplished at Mass.

The U.S. adaptations are to be incorporated into the new *General Instruction of the Roman Missal* and have the same force of law in the U.S. as the rest of the general instruction. The General Instruction of the recently revised *Roman Missal* permits bishops' conferences to provide norms for the distribution of Communion under both kinds, meaning under the outward signs of both bread and wine.

Included among the norms is an indult — or exception to the general requirement — from the Vatican Congregation for Divine Worship and the Sacraments that provides for the cleansing of sacred vessels by special eucharistic ministers. The indult was promulgated as "particular law" for the dioceses of the U.S. at the same time as the norms and it became effective on Apr. 7, 2002.

However, the Vatican congregation declined to approve an indult authorizing special ministers to assist with the distribution of the consecrated blood to other chalices during the singing of the "Lamb of God."

In the letter confirming the norms, the congregation also made clear that special eucharistic ministers, or indeed any communicant, may assist in the consumption of what remains of the blood after distribution of Communion has been completed.

Texts and Translations

The master texts of all documents on liturgical reform are in Latin. Effective dates of their implementation have depended on the completion and approval of appropriate translations into vernacular languages. English translations were made by the International Committee for English in the Liturgy.

The principal features of liturgical changes and the effective dates of their introduction in the U.S. are covered below under topical headings. (For expanded coverage of various items, especially the sacraments, see additional entries.)

On May 7, 2001, the Congregation for Divine Worship and the Sacraments issued the new instruction, *Liturgiam Authenticam* ("The Authentic Liturgy"). The instruction set stricter rules for the translation of Latin liturgical texts into other languages and bears the subtitle, "On the Use of Vernacular Languages in the Publication of the Books of the Roman Liturgy." The instruction was welcomed by then-NCCB president, Bp. Joseph A. Fiorenza of Galveston-Houston, who said that it reflects long consultations between the Vatican and English-speaking bishops, adding that "It is now our hope and expectation that there will be a much quicker approval of liturgical texts" by the Vatican. The instruction was subsequently debated at the bishops' meeting in November 2001.

General Instruction of the Roman Missal

In spring 2001, Pope John Paul II authorized the publication of an *editio typica tertia* of the *Missale Romanum*. The much anticipated revision included a new edition of the *Institutio Generalis Missalis Romani* (*General Instruction of the Roman Missal*). On Nov. 12, 2002, the Latin Church members of the United States Conference of Catholic Bishops approved a translation of the *Institutio Generalis Missalis Romani* prepared by the International Commission on English in the Liturgy. The translation was confirmed by the Congregation for Divine Worship and the Discipline of the Sacraments on Mar. 17, 2003. This translation of the *General Instruction of the Roman Missal* is the sole translation of the *Institutio Generalis Missalis Romani, editio typica tertia* for use in the dioceses of the United States of America. Concerning the new edition, Msgr. James P. Moroney, Executive Director of the USCCB Secretariat for the Liturgy, wrote in the Foreword:

"This revised *Institutio Generalis* possesses a unique role among all the documents on the liturgy. Like its preceding editions, it has been published in order to give life to a dream. It was the dream of reformers such as St. Hippolytus, St. Gregory, and St. Leo. It was the dream of Pope Paul VI and clearly remains the vision of Pope John Paul II, who calls us to 'an ever deeper grasp of the liturgy of the Church, celebrated according to the current books and lived above all as a reality in the spiritual order' (*Vicesimus Quintus Annus*, 1988, No. 14). Likewise, this dream is shared by the Bishops' Committee on the Liturgy and the United States Conference of Catholic Bishops that it serves. Finally, it is the vision of the Church itself: the dream of God's people joined to Christ in Baptism and made 'ever more holy by conscious, active, and fruitful participation in the mystery of the Eucharist' (*General Instruction of the Roman Missal*, No. 5)."

Redemptionis Sacramentum

On Apr. 23, 2004, the Congregation for Divine Worship and the Sacraments, in collaboration with the Congregation for the Doctrine of the Faith and at the request of Pope John Paul II issued the instruction "*Redemptionis Sacramentum*: On Certain Matters to Be Observed or to Be Avoided Regarding the Most Holy Eucharist." The instruction states:

"It is not at all the intention here to prepare a compendium of the norms regarding the Most Holy Eucharist, but rather, to take up within this Instruction some elements of liturgical norms that have been previously expounded or laid down and even today remain in force in order to assure a deeper appreciation of the liturgical norms; to establish certain norms by which those earlier ones are explained and complemented; and also to set forth for bishops, as well as for priests, deacons and all the lay Christian faithful, how each should carry them out in accordance with his own responsibilities and the means at his disposal."

The Mass

A new Order of the Mass, supplanting the one authorized by the Council of Trent in the 16th century, was introduced in the U.S. Mar. 22, 1970. It had been approved by Paul VI in the apostolic constitution *Missale*

Romanum, dated Apr. 3, 1969.

Preliminary and related to it were the following developments.

Mass in English: Introduced Nov. 29, 1964. In the same year, Psalm 42 was eliminated from the prayers at the foot of the altar.

Incidental Changes: The last Gospel (prologue of John) and vernacular prayers following Mass were eliminated Mar. 7, 1965. At the same time, provision was made for the celebrant to say aloud some prayers formerly said silently.

Rubrics: An instruction entitled Tres Abhinc Annos, dated May 4 and effective June 29, 1967, simplified directives for the celebration of Mass, approved the practice of saying the canon aloud, altered the Communion and dismissal rites, permitted purple instead of black vestments in Masses for the dead, discontinued wearing of the maniple, and approved in principle the use of vernacular languages for the canon, ordination rites, and lessons of the Divine Office when read in choir.

Eucharistic Prayers (Canons): The traditional Roman Canon in English was introduced Oct. 22, 1967. Three additional Eucharistic prayers, authorized May 23, 1968, were approved for use in English the following Aug. 15.

The customary Roman Canon, which dates at least from the beginning of the fifth century and has remained substantially unchanged since the seventh century, is the first in the order of listing of the Eucharistic prayers. It can be used at any time, but is the one of choice for most Sundays, some special feasts like Easter and Pentecost, and for feasts of the Apostles and other saints who are commemorated in the canon. Any preface can be used with it.

The second Eucharistic prayer, the shortest and simplest of all, is best suited for use on weekdays and various special circumstances. It has a preface of its own, but others may be used with it. This canon bears a close resemblance to the one framed by St. Hippolytus about 215.

The third Eucharistic prayer is suitable for use on Sundays and feasts as an alternative to the Roman Canon. It can be used with any preface and has a special formula for remembrance of the dead.

The fourth Eucharistic prayer, the most sophisticated of them all, presents a broad synthesis of salvation history. Based on the Eastern tradition of Antioch, it is best suited for use at Masses attended by persons versed in Sacred Scripture. It has an unchangeable preface.

Five additional Eucharistic prayers — three for Masses with children and two for Masses of reconciliation — were approved in 1974 and 1975, respectively, by the Congregation for the Sacraments and Divine Worship.

Use of the Eucharistic Prayers for Various Needs and Occasions, was approved by the U.S. bishops in 1994, confirmed by the appropriate Vatican congregations May 9, 1995, and ratified for use beginning Oct. 1, 1995.

Lectionary: A new compilation of scriptural readings and psalm responsories for Mass was published in 1969. The Lectionary contains a three-year cycle of readings for Sundays and solemn feasts, a two-year weekday cycle, and a one-year cycle for the feasts of saints, in addition to readings for a variety of votive Masses, ritual Masses and Masses for various needs. There are also responsorial psalms to follow the first readings and Gospel or alleluia versicles.

A second edition of the Lectionary, substantially the same as the first, was published in 1981. New features included an expanded introduction, extensive scriptural references and additional readings for a number of solemnities and feasts.

Volume One of a new Lectionary for the Mass was decreed by Bp. Anthony Pilla of Cleveland, then president of the NCCB, as permissible for use as of the first Sunday of Advent, Nov. 29, 1998. The first new Lectionary since 1973, Volume One contains the readings for Sundays, solemnities and feasts of the Lord. Volume Two, containing the readings for weekdays, feasts of saints, and various other occasions, was given final approval on June 19, 1998, by the NCCB but still required confirmation by the Holy See.

Sacramentary (Missal): The Vatican Polyglot Press began distribution in June 1970, of the Latin text of a new *Roman Missal*, the first revision published in 400 years. The English translation was authorized for optional use beginning July 1, 1974; the mandatory date for use was Dec. 1, 1974.

The **Sacramentary** is the celebrant's Mass book of entrance songs, prayers, prefaces and Eucharistic prayers, including special common sets of texts for various commemorations and intentions — dedication of churches, Mary, the apostles, martyrs, doctors of the Church, virgins, holy men and women, the dead, other categories of holy persons, administration of certain sacraments, special intentions.

Study of the Mass: The Bishops' Committee on the Liturgy, following approval by the National Conference of Catholic Bishops in May 1979, began a study of the function and position of elements of the Mass, including the Gloria, the sign of peace, the penitential rite and the readings. Major phases of the study have been completed, and work is still under way toward completion of the project.

Mass for Special Groups: Reasons and norms for the celebration of Mass at special gatherings of the faithful were the subject of an instruction issued May 15, 1969. Two years earlier, the U.S. Bishops' Liturgy Committee went on record in support of the celebration of Mass in private homes under appropriate conditions.

Sunday Mass on Saturday: The Congregation for the Clergy, under date of Jan. 10, 1970, granted the request that the faithful, where bishops consider it pastorally necessary or useful, may satisfy the precept of participating in Mass in the late afternoon or evening hours of Saturdays and the days before holy days of obligation. This provision is stated in Canon 1248 of the Code of Canon Law.

Bination and Trination: Canon 905 of the Code of Canon Law provides that local ordinaries may permit priests to celebrate Mass twice a day (bination), for a just cause; in cases of pastoral need, they may permit priests to celebrate Mass three times a day (trination) on Sundays and holy days of obligation.

Mass in Latin: According to notices issued by the Congregation for Divine Worship June 1, 1971, and Oct. 28, 1974: (1) Bishops may permit the celebration of Mass in Latin for mixed-language groups; (2) bishops may permit the celebration of one or two Masses in Latin on weekdays or Sundays in any church, irrespective of mixed-language groups involved (1971); (3) priests may celebrate Mass in Latin when people are not present; (4) the approved revised Order of the Mass is to be used in Latin as well as vernacular languages; (5) by way of exception, bishops may permit older and handicapped priests to use the Council of Trent's Order of the Mass in private celebration of the holy Sacrifice. (See Permission for **Tridentine Mass**.)

Mass Obligation Waived: The Congregation for Bishops approved July 4, 1992, a resolution of the U.S. bishops to waive the Mass attendance obligation for the holy days of Mary, the Mother of God (Jan. 1), the Assumption of Mary (Aug. 15) and All Saints (Nov. 1) when these solemnities fall on Saturday or Monday.

Inter-Ritual Concelebration: The Apostolic Delegation (now Nunciature) in Washington, D.C., announced in June 1971 that it had received authorization to permit priests of Roman and Eastern rites to celebrate Mass together in the rite of the host church. It was understood that the inter-ritual concelebrations would always be "a manifestation of the unity of the Church and of communion among particular churches."

Ordo of the Sung Mass: In a decree dated June 24 and made public Aug. 24, 1972, the Congregation for Divine Worship issued a new *Ordo of the Sung Mass* — containing Gregorian chants in Latin — to replace the *Graduale Romanum*.

Mass for Children: Late in 1973, the Congregation for Divine Worship issued special guidelines for children's Masses, providing accommodations to the mentality and spiritual growth of pre-adolescents while retaining the principal parts and structures of the Mass. The Directory for Masses with Children was approved by Paul VI Oct. 22 and was dated Nov. 1, 1973. Three Eucharistic prayers for Masses with children were approved by the congregation in 1974; English versions were approved June 5, 1975. Their use, authorized originally for a limited period of experimentation, was extended indefinitely Dec. 15, 1980.

Lectionary for Children: A lectionary for Masses with children, with an announced publication date of September 1993, was authorized for use by choice beginning Nov. 28, 1993. A revised *Lectionary for Masses with Children* was approved by the bishops on Nov. 15, 2006 during their fall general meeting in Washington. The text must also be approved by the Vatican before it can be used in the liturgy in the United States. Assuming approval is given, it will replace the experimental children's Lectionary that has been in use since 1993. The new Lectionary includes stricter rules for its use.

Sacraments

The general use of English in administration of the sacraments was approved for the U.S. Sept. 14, 1964. Structural changes of the rites were subsequently made and introduced in the U.S. as follows.

Pastoral Care of the Sick: Revised rites, covering also administration of the Eucharist to sick persons, were approved Nov. 30, 1972, and published Jan. 18, 1973. The effective date for use of the provisional English prayer formula was Dec. 1, 1974. The mandatory effective date for use of the ritual, Pastoral Care of the Sick in English, was Nov. 27, 1983.

Baptism: New rites for the baptism of infants, approved Mar. 19, 1969, were introduced June 1, 1970.

Rite of Christian Initiation of Adults: Revised rites were issued Jan. 6, 1972, for the Christian initiation of adults — affecting preparation for and reception of baptism, the Eucharist and confirmation; also, for the reception of already baptized adults into full communion with the Church. These rites, which were introduced in the U.S. on the completion of English translation, nullified a seven-step baptismal process approved in 1962. On Mar. 8, 1988, the National Conference of Catholic Bishops was notified that the Congregation for Divine Worship had approved the final English translation of the Rite of Christian Initiation of Adults. The mandatory date for putting the rite into effect was Sept. 1, 1988.

Confirmation: Revised rites, issued Aug. 15, 1971, became mandatory in the U.S. Jan. 1, 1973. The use of a stole by persons being confirmed should be avoided, according to an item in the December 1984 edition of the Newsletter of the Bishops' Committee on the Liturgy. The item said: "The distinction between the universal priesthood of all the baptized and the ministerial priesthood of the ordained is blurred when the distinctive garb (the stole) of ordained ministers is used in this manner."

A decree regarding the proper age for confirmation, approved by the U.S. bishops in June 1993 was ratified by the Congregation for Bishops Feb. 8, 1994. The decree reads: "In accord with prescriptions of canon 891, the National Conference of Catholic Bishops hereby decrees that the sacrament of confirmation in the Latin rite shall be conferred between the age of discretion, which is about the age of seven, and 18 years of age, within the limits determined by the diocesan bishop and with regard for the legitimate exceptions given in canon 891, namely, when there is danger of death or where, in the judgment of the minister, grave cause urges otherwise." The decree became effective July 1, 1994, and continued in effect until July 1, 1999.

Special Ministers of the Eucharist: The designation of lay men and women to serve as special ministers of the Eucharist was authorized by Paul VI in an "Instruction on Facilitating Communion in Particular Circumstances" (Immensae Caritatis), dated Jan. 29 and published by the Congregation for Divine Worship Mar. 29, 1973. Provisions concerning them are contained in Canons 230 and 910 of the Code of Canon Law.

Qualified laypersons may serve as special ministers for specific occasions or for extended periods in the absence of a sufficient number of priests and deacons to provide reasonable and appropriate service in the distribution of Holy Communion, during Mass and outside of Mass (to the sick and shut-ins). Appointments of ministers are made by priests with the approval of the appropriate bishop.

The Newsletter of the U.S. Bishops' Committee on the Liturgy stated in its February 1988 edition: "When ordinary ministers (bishops, priests, deacons) are present during a Eucharistic celebration, whether they are participating in it or not, and are not prevented from doing so, they are to assist in the distribution of Communion. Accordingly, if the ordinary ministers are in sufficient number, special ministers of the Eucharist are not allowed to distribute Communion at that Eucharistic celebration." Pope John Paul II approved this decision and ordered it published June 15, 1987.

Holy Orders: Revised ordination rites for deacons, priests and bishops, validated by prior experimental use, were approved in 1970. The sacrament of holy orders underwent further revision in 1972 with the elimination of the Church-instituted orders of porter, reader, exorcist, acolyte and subdeacon, and of the tonsure ceremony symbolic of entrance into the clerical state. The former minor orders of reader and acolyte were changed from orders to ministries.

Matrimony: A revised rite for the celebration of marriage was promulgated by the Congregation for Divine Worship and the Discipline of the Sacraments Mar. 19, 1969, and went into effect June 1, 1970. A second typi-cal edition of the order of celebration, with revisions in accord with provisions of the Code of Canon Law promulgated in 1983, was approved and published in 1990 (Notitiae, Vol. 26, No.6). The date for implementation was reported to be dependent on the completion of required translations and appropriate formalities.

Penance: Ritual revision of the sacraments was completed with approval by Pope Paul VI on Dec. 2, 1973, of new directives for the sacrament of penance or reconciliation. The U.S. Bishops' Committee on the Liturgy set Feb. 27, 1977, as the mandatory date for use of the new rite. The committee also declared that it could be used from Mar. 7, 1976, after adequate preparation of priests and people. The Holy See gave authorization in 1968 for the omission of any reference to excommunication or other censures in the formula of absolution unless there was some indication that a censure had actually been incurred by a penitent.

Additional Developments

Music: An instruction on Music in the Liturgy, dated Mar. 5 and effective May 14, 1967, encouraged congregational singing during liturgical celebrations and attempted to clarify the role of choirs and trained singers. More significantly, the instruction indicated that a major development under way in the liturgy was a gradual erasure of the distinctive lines traditionally drawn between the sung liturgy and the spoken liturgy, between what had been called the high Mass and the low Mass.

In the same year, the U.S. Bishops' Liturgy Committee approved the use of contemporary music, as well as guitars and other suitable instruments, in the liturgy. The Holy See authorized in 1968 the use of musical instruments other than the organ in liturgical services, "provided they are played in a manner suitable to worship."

On Nov. 14, 2008 the U.S. Bishops at the fall meeting approved new guidelines for the use of music in worship, English- and Spanish-language rituals for the celebration of weekday Liturgies of the Word, and revised Lectionary readings for Lent. The music document, "Sing to the Lord: Music in Divine Worship," was accepted by the bishops in a 183-22 vote, with three abstentions.

Calendar: A revised liturgical calendar approved by Paul VI Feb. 14 and made public May 9, 1969, went into effect in the U.S. in 1972. Since that time, memorials and feasts of beatified persons and saints have been added.

Communion in Hand: Since 1969, the Holy See has approved the practice of in-hand reception of the Eucharist in regions and countries where it had the approval of the appropriate episcopal conferences. The first grant of approval was to Belgium in May 1969. Approval was granted the U.S. in June 1977.

Liturgy of the Hours: The background, contents, scope and purposes of the revised Divine Office, called the Liturgy of the Hours, were described by Paul VI in the apostolic constitution Laudis Canticum, dated Nov. 1, 1970. A provisional English version, incorporating basic features of the master Latin text, was published in 1971. The four complete volumes of the Hours in English have been published since May 1975. One-volume, partial editions have also been published in approved form. Nov. 27, 1977, was set by the Congregation for Divine Worship and the National Conference of Catholic Bishops as the effective date for exclusive use in liturgical worship of the translation of the Latin text of the Liturgy of the Hours approved by the International Committee on English in the Liturgy.

Holy Week: The English version of revised Holy Week rites went into effect in 1971. They introduced concelebration of Mass, placed new emphasis on commemorating the institution of the priesthood on Holy Thursday, and modified Good Friday prayers for other Christians, Jews and other non-Christians.

The Congregation for Divine Worship released Feb. 20, 1988, a "Circular Letter concerning the Preparation and Celebration of the Easter Feasts." It called the feasts the "summit of the whole liturgical year," and criticized practices which dilute or change appropriate norms for their celebration. Singled out for blame for the abuse or ignorance of norms was the "inadequate formation given to the clergy and the faithful regarding the paschal mystery as the center of the liturgical year and of Christian life." The document set out the appropriate norms for the Lenten season, Holy Week, the Easter Triduum, Easter and the weeks following. It was particularly insistent on the proper celebration of the Easter Vigil, to take place after nightfall on Saturday and before dawn on Sunday.

Oils: The Congregation for Divine Worship issued a directive in 1971 permitting the use of other oils — from plants, seeds or coconuts — instead of the traditional olive oil in administering some of the sacraments. The directive also provided that oils could be blessed at other times than at the usual Mass of Chrism on Holy Thursday, and authorized bishops' conferences to permit priests to bless oils in cases of necessity.

Dancing and Worship: Dancing and worship was the subject of an essay which appeared in a 1975 edition of *Notitiae* (11, pp. 202-205), the official journal of the Congregation for the Sacraments and Divine Worship. The article was called a "qualified and authoritative sketch," and should be considered "an authoritative point of reference for every discussion of the matter."

The principal points of the essay were:

• "The dance has never been made an integral part of the official worship of the Latin Church."

• "If the proposal of the religious dance in the West is really to be made welcome, care will have to be taken that in its regard a place be found outside of the liturgy, in assembly areas which are not strictly liturgical. Moreover, the priests must always be excluded from the dance."

Mass for Deceased Non-Catholic Christians: The Congregation for the Doctrine of the Faith released a decree June 11, 1976, authorizing the celebration of public Mass for deceased non-Catholic Christians under certain conditions: "(1) The public celebration of the Masses must be explicitly requested by the relatives, friends, or subjects of the deceased person for a genuine religious motive. (2) In the Ordinary's judgment, there must be no scandal for the faithful."

Built of Living Stones: Art, Architecture, and Worship: At their November 2001 meeting in Washington, DC, the Bishops approved this document by the U.S. Bishops' Committee on the Liturgy; it replaces the document *Environment and Art in Catholic Worship* issued in March 1978.

Doxology: The bishops' committee called attention in August 1978, to the directive that the Doxology concluding the Eucharistic Prayer is said or sung by the celebrant (concelebrants) alone, to which the people respond, "Amen." **Churches, Altars, Chalices**: The Newsletter of the U.S. Bishops' Committee on the Liturgy reported in November 1978, that the Congregation for Divine Worship had given provisional approval of a new English translation for the rite of dedicating churches and altars,

and of a new form for the blessing of chalices.

Eucharistic Worship: This was the subject of two documents issued in 1980. *Dominicae Coenae* was a letter addressed by Pope John Paul to bishops throughout the world in connection with the celebration of Holy Thursday; it was dated Feb. 24 and released Mar.18, 1980. It was more doctrinal in content than the "Instruction on Certain Norms concerning Worship of the Eucharistic Mystery" (*Inaestimabile Donum*, "The Priceless Gift"), which was approved by the Pope Apr. 17 and published by the Congregation for the Sacraments and Divine Worship May 23. Its stated purpose was to reaffirm and clarify teaching on liturgical renewal contained in enactments of the Second Vatican Council and in several related implementing documents.

Tridentine Mass: The celebration of Mass according to the 1962 typical (master) edition of the Roman Missal — the so-called Tridentine Mass — was authorized by Pope Benedict XVI under certain conditions according to the *motu proprio Summorum Pontificum*, issued on July 7, 2007. **See below.**

In a letter from the Congregation for Divine Worship, dated Oct. 3, 1984, Pope John Paul II wished to be responsive to priests and faithful who remained attached to the so-called Tridentine rite. The principal condition for the celebration was: "There must be unequivocal, even public, evidence that the priest and people petitioning have no ties with those who impugn the lawfulness and doctrinal soundness of the *Roman Missal* promulgated in 1970 by Pope Paul VI." (This, in particular, with reference to the followers of dissident Archbishop Marcel Lefebvre.)

Six guidelines for celebration of the Tridentine Mass were contained in the letter regarding its "wide and generous" use, for two purposes: to win back Lefebvre followers and to clear up misunderstandings about liberal permission for use of the Tridentine rite. The letter, from the Pontifical Commission *Ecclesia Dei*, said in part:

• The Tridentine Mass can be celebrated in a parish church, so long as it provides a pastoral service and is harmoniously integrated into the parish liturgical schedule.

• When requested, the Mass should be offered on a regular Sunday and holy day basis, "at a central location, at a convenient time" for a trial period of several months, with "adjustment" later if needed.

• Celebrants of the Mass should make it clear that they acknowledge the validity of the postconciliar liturgy.

• Although the commission has the authority to grant use of the Tridentine rite to all groups that request it, the commission "would much prefer that such faculties be granted by the Ordinary himself so that ecclesial communion can be strengthened."

• While the new Lectionary in the vernacular can be used in the Tridentine Mass, as suggested by the Second Vatican Council, it should not be "imposed on congregations that decidedly wish to maintain the former liturgical tradition in its integrity."

• Older and retired priests who have asked permission to celebrate Mass according to the Tridentine rite should be given the chance to do so for groups that request it.

In March 2003, the Vatican Secretariat of State issued new rules allowing the old rite to be used under very strict conditions.

Summorum Pontificum

Pope Benedict XVI issued the Apostolic Letter in the

form of a *motu proprio*, *Summorum Pontificum*, on July 7, 2007. The following is the text of the letter: It has always been the care of the Supreme Pontiffs until the present time, that the Church of Christ offer worthy worship to the Divine Majesty "for the praise and glory of his name" and "for the good of all his Holy Church."

As from time immemorial so in the future the principle shall be respected "according to which each particular Church must be in accord with the universal Church not only regarding the doctrine of the faith and sacramental signs, but also as to the usages universally handed down by apostolic and unbroken tradition. These are to be maintained not only so that errors may be avoided, but also so that the faith may be passed on in its integrity, since the Church's rule of prayer (*lex orandi*) corresponds to her rule of belief (*lex credendi*)."

Among Pontiffs who have displayed such care there excels the name of St. Gregory the Great, who saw to the transmission to the new peoples of Europe both of the Catholic faith and of the treasures of worship and culture accumulated by the Romans in preceding centuries. He gave instructions for the form of the Sacred Liturgy of both the Sacrifice of the Mass and of the Divine Office as was celebrated in the City. He made the greatest efforts to foster monks and nuns, who militating under the Rule of St. Benedict, in every place along with the proclamation of the Gospel by their life likewise exemplified that most salutary expression of the Rule "let nothing be given precedence over the work of God" (ch. 43). In this way the sacred liturgy according to the Roman manner made fertile not only the faith and piety but also the culture of many peoples. Moreover it is evident that the Latin Liturgy in its various forms has stimulated in the spiritual life very many saints in every century of the Christian age and strengthened in the virtue of religion so many peoples and made fertile their piety However, in order that the Sacred Liturgy might more efficaciously absolve its task, several others among the Roman Pontiffs in the course of the centuries have brought to bear particular concern, among whom St. Pius V is eminent, who with great pastoral zeal, at the exhortation of the Council of Trent, renewed the worship of the whole Church, ensuring the publishing of liturgical books amended and "restored according to the norm of the Fathers" and put them into use in the Latin Church It is clear that among the liturgical books of the Roman Rite the Roman Missal is eminent. It grew in the city of Rome and gradually down through the centuries took on forms which are very similar to those in vigor in recent generations.

"It was this same goal that as time passed the Roman Pontiffs pursued, adapting or establishing liturgical rites and books to new ages and then at the start of the present century undertaking a more ample restoration." It was in this manner that our Predecessors Clement VIII, Urban VIII, St Pius X, Benedict XV, Pius XII and the Blessed John XXIII acted.

In more recent time, however, the Second Vatican Council expressed the desire that with due respect and reverence for divine worship it be restored and adapted to the needs of our age. Prompted by this desire, our Predecessor the Supreme Pontiff Paul VI in 1970 approved for the Latin Church liturgical books restored and partly renewed, and that throughout the world translated into many vernacular languages, have been welcomed by the bishops and by the priests and faithful. John Paul II revised the third typical edition of the *Roman Missal*.

Thus the Roman Pontiffs have acted so that "this liturgical edifice, so to speak, …might once again appear splendid in its dignity and harmony."

However in some regions not a small number of the faithful have been and remain attached with such great love and affection to the previous liturgical forms, which had profoundly imbued their culture and spirit, that the Supreme Pontiff John Paul II, prompted by pastoral concern for these faithful, in 1984 by means of a special Indult Quattuor abhinc annos, drawn up by the Congregation for Divine Worship, granted the faculty to use the *Roman Missal* published by John XXIII in 1962; while in 1988 John Paul II once again, by means of the motu proprio *Ecclesia Dei*, exhorted the bishops to make wide and generous use of this faculty in favor of all the faithful requesting it.

Having pondered at length the pressing requests of these faithful to our Predecessor John Paul II, having also heard the Fathers of the Consistory of Cardinals held on March 23, 2006, having pondered all things, invoked the Holy Spirit and placed our confidence in the help of God, by this present Apostolic Letter we DECREE the following.

Art. 1. The Roman Missal promulgated by Paul VI is to be regarded as the ordinary expression of the law of prayer (lex orandi) of the Catholic Church of Latin Rite, while the Roman Missal promulgated by St. Pius V and published again by Blessed John XXIII as the extraordinary expression of the law of prayer (*lex orandi*) and on account of its venerable and ancient use let it enjoy due honor. These two expressions of the law of prayer (*lex orandi*) of the Church in no way lead to a division in the law of prayer (*lex orandi*) of the Church, for they are two uses of the one Roman Rite.

Hence it is licit to celebrate the Sacrifice of the Mass in accordance with the typical edition of the Roman Missal promulgated by Blessed John XXIII in 1962 and never abrogated, as the extraordinary form of the Liturgy of the Church. The conditions laid down by the previous documents *Quattuor abhinc annos* and *Ecclesia Dei* for the use of this Missal are replaced by what follows:

Art. 2. In Masses celebrated without the people, any priest of Latin rite, whether secular or religious, can use the *Roman Missal* published by Pope Blessed John XXIII in 1962 or the *Roman Missal* promulgated by the Supreme Pontiff Paul VI in 1970, on any day except in the Sacred Triduum. For celebration in accordance with one or the other Missal, a priest does not require any permission, neither from the Apostolic See nor his own Ordinary.

Art. 3. If Communities or Institutes of Consecrated Life or Societies of Apostolic Life of either pontifical or diocesan rite desire to have a celebration of Holy Mass in accordance with the edition of the *Roman Missal* promulgated in 1962 in the conventual or "community" celebration in their own oratories, this is allowed. If an individual community or the entire Institute or Society wants to have such celebrations often or habitually or permanently, the matter is to be decided by the Major Superiors according to the norm of law and the particular laws and statutes.

Art. 4. With due observance of law, even Christ's faithful who spontaneously request it, may be admitted to celebrations of Holy Mass mentioned in art. 2 above.

Art. 5, § 1. In parishes where a group of faithful attached to the previous liturgical tradition exists stably, let the pastor willingly accede to their requests for the celebration of the Holy Mass according to the rite of the *Roman Missal* published in 1962. Let him see to it that the good of these faithful be harmoniously reconciled with ordinary pastoral care of the parish, under the governance of the bishop according to canon 392, avoiding discord and fostering the unity of the whole Church.

§ 2. Celebration according to the Missal of Blessed John XXIII can take place on weekdays, while on Sundays and on feast days there may be one such celebration.

§ 3. Let the pastor permit celebrations in this extraordinary form for faithful or priests who request it, even in particular circumstances such as weddings, funerals or occasional celebrations, for example pilgrimages.

§ 4. Priests using the Missal of Blessed John XXIII must be worthy and not impeded by law.

§ 5. In churches, which are neither parochial nor conventual, it is the rector of the church who grants the above-mentioned permission.

Art. 6. In Masses celebrated with the people according to the Missal of Blessed John XXIII, the Readings can be proclaimed even in the vernacular, using editions that have received the recognitio of the Apostolic See.

Art. 7. Where some group of lay faithful, mentioned in art. 5§1 does not obtain what it requests from the pastor, it should inform the diocesan bishop of the fact. If he bishop is earnestly requested to grant their desire. If he cannot provide for this kind of celebration, let the matter be referred to the Pontifical Commission Ecclesia Dei.

Art. 8. A Bishop who desires to make provision for requests of lay faithful of this kind, but is for various reasons prevented from doing so, may refer the matter to the Pontifical Commission "Ecclesia Dei," which should give him advice and help.

Art. 9, § 1. Likewise a pastor may, all things duly considered, grant permission to use the older ritual in administering the Sacraments of Baptism, Matrimony, Penance and the Anointing of the Sick, as the good of souls may suggest.

§ 2. Ordinaries are granted the faculty to celebrate the sacrament of Confirmation using the former Roman Pontifical, as the good of souls may suggest.

§ 3. It is lawful for clerics in holy orders to use even the *Roman Breviary* promulgated by Blessed John XXIII in 1962.

Art 10. It is lawful for the local Ordinary, if he judges it opportune, to erect a personal parish according to the norm of canon 518 for celebrations according to the older form of the Roman rite or appoint a rector or chaplain, with due observance of the requirements of law.

Art. 11. The Pontifical Commission Ecclesia Dei, erected in 1988 by John Paul II, continues to carry out its function. This Commission is to have the form, duties and norm for action that the Roman Pontiff may wish to assign to it.

Art. 12. The same Commission, in addition to the faculties it already enjoys, will exercise the authority of the Holy See by maintaining vigilance over the observance and application of these dispositions.

Whatever is decreed by Us by means of this *Motu Proprio*, we order to be firm and ratified and to be observed as of Sept. 14 this year, the feast of the Exaltation of the Holy Cross, all things to the contrary notwithstanding.

Given at Rome, at St Peter's, on July 7, in the Year of Our Lord 2007, the Third of Our Pontificate.

+ BENEDICT XVI

1. *General Instruction of the Roman Missal*, third edition, 2002, No. 397

2. Pope John Paul II, ap. letter *Vicesimus quintus annus*, Dec. 4, 1988, n. 3: AAS 81 (1989) p. 899.

3. Ibidem.

4. Pope St Pius X, *motu proprio Abhinc duos annos*, Oct. 23, 1913: AAS 5 (1913) 449-450; cf. Pope John Paul II, ap. letter *Vicesimus quintus annus*, Dec. 4, 1988, No. 3: AAS 81 (1989) p. 899

5. Cf. Pope John Paul II, *motu proprio Ecclesia Dei adflicta*, July 2, 1988, No. 6: AAS 80 (1988) p. 1498. (This unofficial translation has been prepared by the United States Conference of Catholic Bishops' Secretariat for the Liturgy. Only the Latin original of the Apostolic Letter may be considered the official text.)

Universae Ecclesia

On May 13, 2011, the Pontifical Commission "Ecclesia Dei" published the Instruction on the application of Benedict XVI's Apostolic Letter *motu proprio "Summorum Pontificum."* The document, approved by the Pope, was signed by Cardinal William Levada and Msgr. Guido Pozzo, respectively president and secretary of the Pontifical Commission "Ecclesia Dei."

Spanish: In accord with decrees of the Congregation for Divine Worship, Spanish was approved as a liturgical language in the U.S. (Jan. 19, 1985). The *texto unico* of the Ordinary of the Mass became mandatory in the U.S. Dec. 3, 1989. Spanish translations of Proper-of-the-Mass texts proper to U.S. dioceses were approved Mar. 12, 1990. An approved Spanish version of the Rite for the Christian Initiation of Adults was published in 1991. The Institute of Hispanic Liturgy opened its national office June 1, 1995, on the campus of The Catholic University of America in Washington.

Funeral Rites: A revised Order of Christian Funerals became mandatory in the U.S. Nov. 2, 1989.

Permission for the presence of cremated human remains in the funeral liturgy, including the Eucharist, was granted in 1997 to local bishops in the U.S. by the Congregation for Divine Worship and the Discipline of the Sacraments. Adaptations to existing rites are under study.

Popular Piety and Liturgy: The relation of popular piety to the liturgy was the subject of remarks by Pope John Paul II at a meeting with a group of Italian bishops Apr. 24, 1986. He said, in part:

"An authentic liturgical ministry will never be able to neglect the riches of popular piety, the values proper to the culture of a people, so that such riches might be illuminated, purified and introduced into the liturgy as an offering of the people."

Extended Eucharistic Exposition: In response to queries, the Secretariat of the U.S. Bishops' Committee on the Liturgy issued an advisory stating that liturgical law permits and encourages in parish churches:

• Exposition of the Blessed Sacrament for an extended period of time once a year, with consent of the local Ordinary and only if suitable numbers of the faithful are expected to be present;

• Exposition ordered by the local Ordinary, for a grave and general necessity, for a more extended period of supplication when the faithful assemble in large numbers.

With regard to perpetual exposition, this form is generally permitted only in the case of those religious communities of men or women who have the general practice of perpetual Eucharistic adoration or adoration over extended periods of time.

The Secretariat's advisory appeared in the June-July 1986 edition of the Newsletter of the Bishops' Committee on the Liturgy.

Native American Languages: The Newsletter of the U.S. Bishops' Committee on the Liturgy reported in December 1986, and May 1987, respectively, that the Congregation for Divine Worship had authorized Mass translations in Navajo and Choctaw. Lakota was approved as a liturgical language in 1989.

Communion Guidelines: In 1986 and again in 1996, the U.S. bishops' approved the insertion of advisories in missalettes and similar publications, stating that: (1) The Eucharist is to be received by Catholics only, except in certain specific cases; (2) To receive Communion worthily, a person must be in the state of grace (i.e., free of serious sin) and observe the eucharistic fast (See separate entry).

Unauthorized Eucharistic Prayers: The May 1987 Newsletter of the U.S. Bishops' Committee on the Liturgy restated the standing prohibition against the use of any Eucharistic Prayers other than those contained in the Sacramentary. Specifically, the article referred to the 25 unauthorized prayers in a volume entitled *Spoken Visions*.

Homilist: According to the Pontifical Commission for the Authentic Interpretation of Canon Law, the diocesan bishop cannot dispense from the requirement of Canon 767, par. 1, that the homily in the liturgy be reserved to a priest or deacon. Pope John Paul approved this decision June 20, 1987.

Concerts in Churches: In a letter released Dec. 5, 1987, the Congregation for Divine Worship declared that churches might be used on a limited basis for concerts of sacred or religious music, but not for concerts featuring secular music.

Blessings: A revised *Book of Blessings* was ordered into use beginning Dec. 3, 1989.

Litany of the Blessed Virgin Mary: "Queen of Families," a new invocation, was reported by the U.S. bishops in 1996, for insertion between "Queen of the Rosary" and "Queen of Peace."

Inclusive Language: "Criteria for the Evaluation of Inclusive Language Translations of Scriptural Texts Proposed for Liturgical Use" was issued by the U.S. bishops in November 1990. The criteria distinguish between non-use of vertical inclusiveness in references to God and use of horizontal, gender-inclusive terms (he/she, man/woman and the like) where appropriate in references to persons.

THE SACRAMENTS OF THE CHURCH

The sacraments are actions of Christ and his Church (itself a kind of sacrament) that signify grace, cause it in the act of signifying it, and confer it upon persons properly disposed to receive it. They perpetuate the redemptive activity of Christ, making it present and effective. They infallibly communicate the fruit of that activity — namely grace — to responsive persons with faith. Sacramental actions consist of the union of sensible signs (matter of the sacraments) with the words of the minister (form of the sacraments).

Christ himself instituted the seven sacraments of the New Law by determining their essence and the efficacy of their signs to produce the grace they signify.

Christ is the principal priest or minister of every sacrament; human agents — an ordained priest, baptized persons contracting marriage with each other, any person conferring emergency baptism in a proper manner — are secondary ministers. Sacraments have efficacy from Christ, not from the personal dispositions of their human ministers.

Each sacrament confers sanctifying grace for the special purpose of the sacrament; this is, accordingly, called sacramental grace. It involves a right to actual graces corresponding to the purposes of the respective sacraments.

Baptism, confirmation and the Eucharist are sacraments of initiation; penance (reconciliation) and anointing of the sick, sacraments of healing; order and matrimony, sacraments for service.

While sacraments infallibly produce the grace they signify, recipients benefit from them in proportion to their personal dispositions. One of these is the intention to receive sacraments as sacred signs of God's saving and grace-giving action. The state of grace is also necessary for fruitful reception of the Holy Eucharist, confirmation, matrimony, holy orders and anointing of the sick. Baptism is the sacrament in which grace is given in the first instance and original sin is remitted. Penance is the secondary sacrament of reconciliation, in which persons guilty of serious sin after baptism are reconciled with God and the Church, and in which persons already in the state of grace are strengthened in that state.

Role of Sacraments

The Second Vatican Council prefaced a description of the role of the sacraments with the following statement concerning participation by all the faithful in the priesthood of Christ and the exercise of that priesthood by receiving the sacraments (Dogmatic Constitution on the Church, *Lumen Gentium*, Nos. 10 and 11).

"The baptized by regeneration and the anointing of the Holy Spirit are consecrated into a spiritual house and a holy priesthood. Thus through all those works befitting Christian men they can offer spiritual sacrifice and proclaim the power of him who has called them out of darkness into his marvelous light (cf. 1 Pt 2:4-10).

"Though they differ from one another in essence and not only in degree, the common priesthood of the faithful and the ministerial or hierarchical priesthood (of those ordained to holy orders) are nonetheless interrelated. Each of them in its own special way is a participation in the one priesthood of Christ. The ministerial priest, by the sacred power he enjoys, molds and rules the priestly people. Acting in the Person of Christ, he brings about the Eucharistic Sacrifice, and offers it to God in the name of all the people. For their part, the faithful join in the offering of the Eucharist by virtue of their royal priesthood. They likewise exercise that priesthood by receiving the sacraments, by prayer and thanksgiving, by the witness of a holy life, and by self-denial and active charity.

"It is through the sacraments and the exercise of the virtues that the sacred nature and organic structure of the priestly community is brought into operation."

Baptism: "Incorporated into the Church through baptism, the faithful are consecrated by the baptismal character to the exercise of the cult of the Christian religion. Reborn as sons of God, they must confess before men the faith which they have received from God through the Church."

Confirmation: "Bound more intimately to the Church by the sacrament of confirmation, they are endowed by the Holy Spirit with special strength. Hence they are more strictly obliged to spread and defend the faith both by word and by deed as true witnesses of Christ."

Eucharist: "Taking part in the Eucharistic Sacrifice, which is the fount and apex of the whole Christian life, they offer the divine Victim to God, and offer themselves along with It. Thus, both by the act of oblation and through holy Communion, all perform their proper part in this liturgical service, not, indeed, all in the same way but each in that way which is appropriate to himself. Strengthened anew at the holy table by the Body of Christ, they manifest in a practical way that unity of God's People which is suitably signified and wondrously brought about by this most awesome sacrament."

Penance: "Those who approach the sacrament of penance obtain pardon from the mercy of God for offenses committed against him. They are at the same time reconciled with the Church, which they have wounded by their sins, and which by charity, example, and prayer seeks their conversion."

Anointing of the Sick: "By the sacred anointing of the sick and the prayer of her priests, the whole Church commends those who are ill to the suffering and glorified Lord, asking that he may lighten their suffering and save them (cf. Jas. 5:14-16). She exhorts them, moreover, to contribute to the welfare of the whole People of God by associating themselves freely with the passion and death of Christ (cf. Rom 8:17; Col 1:24; 2 Tm 2:11-12; 1 Pt 4:13)."

Holy Orders: "Those of the faithful who are consecrated by holy orders are appointed to feed the Church in Christ's name with the Word and the grace of God."

Matrimony: "Christian spouses, in virtue of the sacrament of matrimony, signify and partake of the mystery of that unity and fruitful love which exists between Christ and his Church (cf. Eph 5:32). The spouses thereby help each other to attain to holiness in their married life and by the rearing and education of their children. And so, in their state and way of life, they have their own special gift among the People of God (cf. 1 Cor 7:7).

"For from the wedlock of Christians there comes the family, in which new citizens of human society are born. By the grace of the Holy Spirit received in baptism these are made children of God, thus perpetuating the People of God through the centuries. The family is, so to speak, the domestic Church. In it parents should, by their word and example, be the first preachers of the faith to their children. They should encourage them in the vocation which is proper to each of them, fostering with special care any religious vocation.

"Fortified by so many and such powerful means of salvation, all the faithful, whatever their condition or state, are called by the Lord, each in his own way, to that perfect holiness whereby the Father himself is perfect."

Baptism

Baptism is the sacrament of spiritual regeneration by which a person is incorporated in Christ and made a member of his Mystical Body, given grace, and cleansed of original sin. Actual sins and the punishment owed for

them are remitted also if the person baptized was guilty of such sins (e.g., in the case of a person baptized after reaching the age of reason). The theological virtues of faith, hope and charity are given with grace. The sacrament confers a character on the soul and can be received only once.

The matter is the pouring of water. The form is: "I baptize you in the name of the Father and of the Son and of the Holy Spirit."

The minister of solemn baptism is a bishop, priest or deacon, but in case of emergency anyone, including a non-Catholic, can validly baptize. The minister pours water on the forehead of the person being baptized and says the words of the form while the water is flowing. The water used in solemn baptism is blessed during the rite.

Baptism is conferred in the Roman rite by immersion or infusion (pouring of water), depending on the directive of the appropriate conference of bishops, according to the Code of Canon Law. The Church recognizes as valid baptisms properly performed by non-Catholic ministers. The baptism of infants has always been considered valid and the general practice of infant baptism was well established by the fifth century. Baptism is conferred conditionally when there is doubt about the validity of a previous baptism.

Baptism is necessary for salvation. If a person cannot receive the baptism of water described above, this can be supplied by baptism of blood (martyrdom suffered for the Catholic faith or some Christian virtue) or by baptism of desire (perfect contrition joined with at least the implicit intention of doing whatever God wills that people should do for salvation).

A sponsor is required for the person being baptized. (*See* **Godparents**, below.)

A person must be validly baptized before he or she can receive any of the other sacraments.

Christian Initiation of Infants: Infants should be solemnly baptized as soon after birth as conveniently possible. Anyone may baptize an infant in danger of death. If the child survives, the ceremonies of solemn baptism should be supplied.

The sacrament is ordinarily conferred by a priest or deacon of the parents' parish.

Catholics 16 years of age and over who have received the sacraments of confirmation and the Eucharist and are practicing their faith are eligible to be sponsors or godparents. Only one is required. Two, one of each sex, are permitted. A non-Catholic Christian cannot be a godparent for a Catholic child, but may serve as a witness to the baptism. A Catholic may not be a godparent for a child baptized in a non-Catholic religion, but may be a witness.

"Because of the close communion between the Catholic Church and the Eastern Orthodox churches," states the 1993 Directory on Ecumenism, "it is permissible for a just cause for an Eastern faithful to act as godparent together with a Catholic godparent at the baptism of a Catholic infant or adult, so long as there is provision for the Catholic education of the person being baptized and it is clear that the godparent is a suitable one.

"A Catholic is not forbidden to stand as godparent in an Eastern Orthodox Church if he/she is so invited. In this case, the duty of providing for the Christian education binds in the first place the godparent who belongs to the church in which the child is baptized."

The role of godparents in baptismal ceremonies is secondary to the role of the parents. They serve as representatives of the community of faith and with the parents request baptism for the child and perform other ritual functions. Their function after baptism is to serve as proxies for the parents if the parents should be unable or fail to provide for the religious training of the child.

At baptism every child should be given a name with Christian significance, usually the name of a saint, to symbolize newness of life in Christ.

Christian Initiation of Adults: According to the Ordo Initiationis Christianae Adultorum ("Rite of the Christian Initiation of Adults") issued by the Congregation for Divine Worship on Jan. 6, 1972, and put into effect in revised form Sept. 1, 1988, adults are prepared for baptism and reception into the Church in several stages:

• An initial period of inquiry, instruction and evangelization.

• The catechumenate, a period of at least a year of formal instruction and progressive formation in and familiarity with Christian life. It starts with a statement of purpose and includes a rite of election.

• Immediate preparation, called a period of purification and enlightenment, from the beginning of Lent to reception of the sacraments of initiation — baptism, confirmation, Holy Eucharist — during ceremonies of the Easter Vigil. The period is marked by scrutinies, formal giving of the creed and the Lord's Prayer, the choice of a Christian name, and a final statement of intention.

• A mystagogic phase whose objective is greater familiarity with Christian life in the Church through observances of the Easter season and association with the community of the faithful, and through extended formation for about a year.

National Statutes for the Catechumenate were approved by the National Conference of Catholic Bishops Nov. 11, 1986, and were subsequently ratified by the Vatican.

The priest who baptizes a catechumen can also administer the sacrament of confirmation.

A sponsor is required for the person being baptized.

The Ordo also provides a simple rite of initiation for adults in danger of death and for cases in which all stages of the initiation process are not necessary, and guidelines for: (1) the preparation of adults for the sacraments of confirmation and Holy Eucharist in cases where they have been baptized but have not received further formation in the Christian life; (2) the formation and initiation of children of catechetical age.The Church recognizes the right of anyone over the age of seven to request baptism and to receive the sacrament after completing a course of instruction and giving evidence of good will. Practically, in the case of minors in a non-Catholic family or environment, the Church accepts them when other circumstances favor their ability to practice the faith – e.g., well-disposed family situation, the presence of another or several Catholics in the family. Those who are not in such favorable circumstances are prudently advised to defer reception of the sacrament until they attain the maturity necessary for independent practice of the faith.

Reception of Baptized Christians: Procedure for the reception of already baptized Christians into full communion with the Catholic Church is distinguished from the catechumenate, since they have received some Christian formation. Instruction and formation are provided as necessary, however; and conditional baptism is administered if there is reasonable doubt about the validity of the person's previous baptism.

In the rite of reception, the person is invited to join the community of the Church in professing the Nicene Creed and is asked to state: "I believe and profess all that the holy Catholic Church believes, teaches, and proclaims as

revealed by God." The priest places his hand on the head of the person, states the formula of admission to full communion, confirms (in the absence of a bishop), gives a sign of peace, and administers Holy Communion during a Eucharistic Liturgy.

Confirmation

Confirmation is the sacrament by which a baptized person, through anointing with chrism and the imposition of hands, is endowed with the fullness of baptismal grace; is united more intimately to the Church; is enriched with the special power of the Holy Spirit; is committed to be an authentic witness to Christ in word and action. The sacrament confers a character on the soul and can be received only once.

According to the apostolic constitution *Divinae Consortium Naturae*, dated Aug. 15, 1971, in conjunction with the *Ordo Confirmationis* ("Rite of Confirmation"): "The sacrament of confirmation is conferred through the anointing with chrism on the forehead, which is done by the imposition of the hand (matter of the sacrament), and through the words: '*N., receive the seal of the Holy Spirit, the Gift of the Father*'" (form of the sacrament). On May 5, 1975, bishops' conferences in English-speaking countries were informed by the Congregation for Divine Worship that Pope Paul VI had approved this English version of the form of the sacrament: "*Be sealed with the gift of the Holy Spirit.*"

The ordinary minister of confirmation in the Roman rite is a bishop. Priests may be delegated for the purpose. A pastor can confirm a parishioner in danger of death, and a priest can confirm in ceremonies of Christian initiation and at the reception of a baptized Christian into union with the Church.

Ideally, the sacrament is conferred during the Eucharistic Liturgy. Elements of the rite include renewal of the promises of baptism, which confirmation ratifies and completes, and the laying on of hands by the confirming bishop and priests participating in the ceremony.

"The entire rite," according to the *Ordo*, "has a twofold meaning. The laying of hands upon the candidates, done by the bishop and the concelebrating priests, expresses the biblical gesture by which the gift of the Holy Spirit is invoked. The anointing with chrism and the accompanying words clearly signify the effect of the Holy Spirit. Signed with the perfumed oil by the bishop's hand, the baptized person receives the indelible character, the seal of the Lord, together with the Spirit who is given and who conforms the person more perfectly to Christ and gives him the grace of spreading the Lord's presence among men."

A sponsor is required for the person being confirmed. Eligible is any Catholic 16 years or older who has received the sacraments of confirmation and the Eucharist and is practicing the faith. The baptismal sponsor, preferably, can also be the sponsor for confirmation. Parents may present their children for confirmation but cannot be sponsors.

In the Roman rite, it has been customary for children to receive confirmation within a reasonable time after first Communion and confession. There is a trend, however, to defer confirmation until later when its significance for mature Christian living becomes more evident. In the Eastern rites, confirmation is administered at the same time as baptism.

Eucharist

The Holy Eucharist is a sacrifice (*see* **The Mass**) and the sacrament in which Christ is present and is received under the appearances of bread and wine.

The matter is bread of wheat, unleavened in the Roman

rite and leavened in the Eastern rites, and wine of grape. The form consists of the words of consecration said by the priest at Mass: "This is my body. This is the cup of my blood" (according to the traditional usage of the Roman rite).

Only a priest can consecrate bread and wine so they become the body and blood of Christ. After consecration, however, the Eucharist can be administered by deacons and, for various reasons, by religious and lay persons.

Priests celebrating Mass receive the Eucharist under the species of bread and wine. In the Roman rite, others receive under the species of bread only, i.e., the consecrated host, though in some circumstances they may receive under the species of both bread and wine. In Eastern-rite practice, the faithful generally receive a piece of consecrated leavened bread which has been dipped in consecrated wine (i.e., by intinction).

Conditions for receiving the Eucharist, commonly called Holy Communion, are the state of grace, the right intention and observance of the Eucharistic fast.

The faithful of Roman rite are required by a precept of the Church to receive the Eucharist at least once a year, ordinarily during the Easter time. (*See* **Eucharistic Fast, Mass, Transubstantiation, Viaticum.**)

First Communion and Confession: Children are to be prepared for and given opportunity for receiving both sacraments (Eucharist and reconciliation, or penance) on reaching the age of discretion, at which time they become subject to general norms concerning confession and Communion. This, together with a stated preference for first confession before first Communion, was the central theme of a document entitled *Sanctus Pontifex* and published May 24, 1973, by the Congregation for the Discipline of the Sacraments and the Congregation for the Clergy, with the approval of Pope Paul VI.

What the document prescribed was the observance of practices ordered by St. Pius X in the decree *Quam Singulari* of Aug. 8, 1910. Its purpose was to counteract pastoral and catechetical experiments virtually denying children the opportunity of receiving both sacraments at the same time. Termination of such experiments was ordered by the end of the 1972-73 school year.

At the time the document was issued, two- or three-year experiments of this kind – routinely deferring reception of the sacrament of penance until after the first reception of Holy Communion – were in effect in more than half of the dioceses of the U.S. They have remained in effect in many places, despite the advisory from the Vatican.

One reason stated in support of such experiments is the view that children are not capable of serious sin at the age of seven or eight, when Communion is generally received for the first time, and therefore prior reception of the sacrament of penance is not necessary. Another reason is the purpose of making the distinctive nature of the two sacraments clearer to children.

The Vatican view reflected convictions that the principle and practice of devotional reception of penance are as valid for children as they are for adults, and that sound catechetical programs can avoid misconceptions about the two sacraments.

A second letter on the same subject and in the same vein was released May 19, 1977, by the aforementioned congregations. It was issued in response to the question:

"'Whether it is allowed after the declaration of May 24, 1973, to continue to have, as a general rule, the reception of first Communion precede the reception of the sacrament of penance in those parishes in which this practice

developed in the past few years.'

"The Sacred Congregations for the Sacraments and Divine Worship and for the Clergy, with the approval of the Supreme Pontiff, reply: Negative, and according to the mind of the declaration.

"The mind of the declaration is that one year after the promulgation of the same declaration, all experiments of receiving first Communion without the sacrament of penance should cease so that the discipline of the Church might be restored, in the spirit of the decree, *Quam Singulari*."

The two letters from the Vatican congregations have not produced uniformity of practice in this country. Simultaneous preparation for both sacraments is provided in some dioceses where a child has the option of receiving either sacrament first, with the counsel of parents, priests and teachers. Programs in other dioceses are geared first to reception of Communion and later to reception of the Sacrament of Reconciliation.

Commentators on the letters note that: they are disciplinary rather than doctrinal in content; they are subject to pastoral interpretation by bishops; they cannot be interpreted to mean that a person who is not guilty of serious sin must be required to receive the sacrament of penance before (even first) Communion.

Canon 914 of the Code of Canon Law states that sacramental confession should precede first Communion.

Holy Communion under the Forms of Bread and Wine (by separate taking of the consecrated bread and wine or by intinction, the reception of the host dipped in the wine): Such reception is permitted under conditions stated in instructions issued by the Congregation for Divine Worship (May 25, 1967; June 29, 1970), the *General Instruction on the Roman Missal* (No. 242), and directives of bishops' conferences and individual bishops.

Accordingly, Communion can be administered in this way to: persons being baptized, received into communion with the Church, confirmed, receiving anointing of the sick; couples at their wedding or jubilee; religious at profession or renewal of profession; lay persons receiving an ecclesiastical assignment (e.g., lay missionaries); participants at concelebrated Masses, retreats, pastoral commission meetings, daily Masses and, in the U.S., Masses on Sundays and holy days of obligation.

A communicant has the option of receiving the Eucharist under the form of bread alone or under the forms of bread and wine. (*See* **New U.S. Norms in the Liturgy section.**)

Holy Communion More Than Once a Day: A person who has already received the Eucharist may receive it (only) once again on the same day only during a Eucharistic celebration in which the person participates. A person in danger of death who has already received the Eucharist once or twice is urged to receive Communion again as Viaticum. Pope John Paul approved this decision, in accord with Canon 917, and ordered it published July 11, 1984.

Holy Communion and Eucharistic Devotion outside of Mass: These were the subjects of an instruction (*De Sacra Communione et de Cultu Mysterii Eucharistici extra Missam*) dated June 21 and made public Oct. 18, 1973, by the Congregation for Divine Worship.

Holy Communion can be given outside of Mass to persons unable for a reasonable cause to receive it during Mass on a given day. The ceremonial rite is modeled on the structure of the Mass, consisting of a penitential act, a scriptural reading, the Lord's Prayer, a sign or gesture of peace, giving of the Eucharist, prayer and final blessing. Viaticum and Communion to the sick can be given by extraordinary ministers (authorized lay persons) with appropriate rites.

Forms of devotion outside of Mass are exposition of the Blessed Sacrament (by men or women religious, especially, or lay persons in the absence of a priest; but only a priest can give the blessing), processions and congresses with appropriate rites.

Intercommunion: Church policy on intercommunion was stated in an "Instruction on the Admission of Other Christians to the Eucharist," dated June 1 and made public July 8, 1972, against the background of the Decree on Ecumenism approved by the Second Vatican Council, and the Directory on Ecumenism issued by the Secretariat for Promoting Christian Unity in 1967, 1970 and 1993.

Basic principles related to intercommunion are:

• "There is an indissoluble link between the mystery of the Church and the mystery of the Eucharist, or between ecclesial and Eucharistic communion; the celebration of the Eucharist of itself signifies the fullness of profession of faith and ecclesial communion" (1972 Instruction).

• "Eucharistic communion practiced by those who are not in full ecclesial communion with each other cannot be the expression of that full unity which the Eucharist of its nature signifies and which in this case does not exist; for this reason such communion cannot be regarded as a means to be used to lead to full ecclesial communion" (1972 Instruction).

• The question of reciprocity "arises only with those churches which have preserved the substance of the Eucharist, the sacrament of orders and apostolic succession" (1967 Directory).

• "A Catholic cannot ask for the Eucharist except from a minister who has been validly ordained" (1967 Directory).

The policy distinguishes between separated Eastern Christians and other Christians.

With Separated Eastern Christians (e.g., Orthodox): These may be given the Eucharist (as well as penance and anointing of the sick) at their request. Catholics may receive these same sacraments from priests of separated Eastern churches if they experience genuine spiritual necessity, seek spiritual benefit, and access to a Catholic priest is morally or physically impossible. This policy (of reciprocity) derives from the facts that the separated Eastern churches have apostolic succession through their bishops, valid priests, and sacramental beliefs and practices in accord with those of the Catholic Church.

With Other Christians (e.g., members of Reformation-related churches, others): Admission to the Eucharist in the Catholic Church, according to the Directory on Ecumenism, "is confined to particular cases of those Christians who have a faith in the sacrament in conformity with that of the Church, who experience a serious spiritual need for the Eucharistic sustenance, who for a prolonged period are unable to have recourse to a minister of their own community and who ask for the sacrament of their own accord; all this provided that they have proper dispositions and lead lives worthy of a Christian." The spiritual need is defined as "a need for an increase in spiritual life and a need for a deeper involvement in the mystery of the Church and its unity."

Circumstances under which Communion may be given to other properly disposed Christians are danger of death, imprisonment, persecution, grave spiritual necessity coupled with no chance of recourse to a minister of their own community. Catholics cannot ask for the Eucharist from ministers of other Christian churches who have not been validly ordained to the priesthood.

Ecclesia de Eucharistia

On Apr. 17, 2002, Holy Thursday, during the Mass of the Lord's Supper, and within the liturgical setting of the beginning of the Paschal Triduum Pope John Paul II issued the fourteenth encyclical letter of his pontificate, *Ecclesia de Eucharistia*. The encyclical was intended to offer a theological reflection on the mystery of the Eucharist in its relationship with the Church.

Specifically, the pope uses the letter to reaffirm the traditional teaching of the Church on the real presence of Christ in the Eucharist, on the need for validly ordained ministers for its celebration, and on the importance of following the Church's liturgical norms.

The encyclical is organized into five chapters and a conclusion, beginning with the declaration: "The Church draws her life from the Eucharist. This truth does not simply express a daily experience of faith, but recapitulates the heart of the mystery of the Church. In a variety of ways she joyfully experiences the constant fulfillment of the promise." The Eucharistic Sacrifice is thus truly "the source and summit of the Christian life," as the Second Vatican Council proclaimed, and contains the Church's entire spiritual wealth: Jesus Christ, who offers himself to the Father for the redemption of the world. In celebrating this "mystery of faith," the Church presents the Paschal Triduum in a contemporary way, for men and women in every age.

Chapter One, "The Mystery of Faith," describes the sacrificial nature of the Eucharist which, through the ministry of the priest, makes sacramentally present at each Mass the body "given up" and the blood "poured out" by Christ for the salvation of the world.

Chapter Two, "The Eucharist Builds the Church," states that the Church "teaches that the celebration of the Eucharist is at the centre of the process of the Church's growth."

Chapter Three, "The Apostolicity of the Eucharist and of the Church," notes that that just as the Church is apostolic so too is the Eucharist in three ways. First, "The Eucharist too has its foundation in the Apostles, not in the sense that it did not originate in Christ himself, but because it was entrusted by Jesus to the Apostles and has been handed down to us by them and by their successors. It is in continuity with the practice of the Apostles, in obedience to the Lord's command, that the Church has celebrated the Eucharist down the centuries." Second, "it is celebrated in conformity with the faith of the Apostles." Third, just as the full reality of Church does not exist without apostolic succession, so there is no true Eucharist without the bishop.

Chapter Four, "The Eucharist and Ecclesial Communion," teaches that "the culmination of all the sacraments in perfecting our communion with God the Father by identification with his only-begotten Son through the working of the Holy Spirit."

Chapter Five, "The Dignity of the Eucharistic Celebration" is concerned with the truthful celebration of the Eucharist enunciated in the previous chapter.

Chapter Six, "At the School of Mary, 'Woman of the Eucharist,'" offers a reflection on the analogy between the Mother of God, and the Church.

In his conclusion, the pontiff quotes his Apostolic Letter *Novo Millennio Ineunte* in stating, "it is not a matter of inventing a 'new program.' The program already exists: it is the plan found in the Gospel and in the living Tradition; it is the same as ever." Clearly, the implementation of this process of a renewed impetus in Christian living passes through the Eucharist. He concludes, "In the humble signs of bread and wine, changed into his body and blood, Christ walks beside us as our strength and our food for the journey, and he enables us to become, for everyone, witnesses of hope."

Sacramentum Caritatis

On Mar. 13, 2007, Pope Benedict XVI released the post-synodal apostolic exhortation, *Sacramentum Caritatis* ("The Sacrament of Charity"), a 131-page papal reflection on the discussions and suggestions made during the 2005 world Synod of Bishops on the Eucharist.

Penance

Penance is the sacrament by which sins committed after baptism are forgiven and a person is reconciled with God and the Church.

Individual and integral confession and absolution are the only ordinary means for the forgiveness of serious sin and for reconciliation with God and the Church.

(Other than ordinary means are perfect contrition and general absolution without prior confession, both of which require the intention of subsequent confession and absolution.)

A revised ritual for the sacrament – *Ordo Paenitentiae*, published by the Congregation of Divine Worship Feb. 7, 1974, and made mandatory in the U.S. from the first Sunday of Lent, 1977 – reiterates standard doctrine concerning the sacrament; emphasizes the social (communal and ecclesial) aspects of sin and conversion, with due regard for personal aspects and individual reception of the sacrament; prescribes three forms for celebration of the sacrament; and presents models for community penitential services.

The basic elements of the sacrament are sorrow for sin because of a supernatural motive, confession (of previously unconfessed mortal or grave sins, required; of venial sins also, but not of necessity), and reparation (by means of prayer or other act enjoined by the confessor), all of which comprise the matter of the sacrament; and absolution, which is the form of the sacrament.

The traditional words of absolution – *"I absolve you from your sins in the name of the Father, and of the Son, and of the Holy Spirit"* – remain unchanged at the conclusion of a petition in the new rite that God may grant pardon and peace through the ministry of the Church.

The minister of the sacrament is an authorized priest – i.e., one who, besides having the power of orders to forgive sins, also has faculties of jurisdiction granted by an ecclesiastical superior and/or by canon law.

The sacrament can be celebrated in three ways:

• For individuals, the traditional manner remains acceptable but is enriched with additional elements including: reception of the penitent and making of the Sign of the Cross; an exhortation by the confessor to trust in God; a reading from Scripture; confession of sins; manifestation of repentance; petition for God's forgiveness through the ministry of the Church and the absolution of the priest; praise of God's mercy, and dismissal in peace. Some of these elements are optional.

• For several penitents, in the course of a community celebration including a Liturgy of the Word of God and prayers, individual confession and absolution, and an act of thanksgiving.

• For several penitents, in the course of a community celebration, with general confession and general absolution. In extraordinary cases, reconciliation may be attained by general absolution without prior individual confession as, for example, under these circumstances: (1) danger of death, when there is neither time nor priests available for hearing confessions; (2) grave necessity of a number of penitents who, because of a shortage of confessors, would be deprived of sacramental grace or Communion for a lengthy period of time through no fault of their own. Persons receiving general absolution are obliged to be properly disposed and resolved to make an individual confession of the grave sins from which they have been absolved; this confession should be made as soon as the opportunity to confess presents itself and before any second reception of general absolution.

Norms regarding general absolution, issued by the Congregation for the Doctrine of the Faith in 1972, are not intended to provide a basis for convoking large gatherings of the faithful for the purpose of imparting general absolution, in the absence of extraordinary circumstances. Judgment about circumstances that warrant general absolution belongs principally to the bishop of the place, with due regard for related decisions of appropriate episcopal conferences.

Communal celebrations of the sacrament are not held in connection with Mass.

The place of individual confession, as determined by episcopal conferences in accordance with given norms, can be the traditional confessional or another appropriate setting.

A precept of the Church obliges the faithful guilty of grave sin to confess at least once a year.

The Church favors more frequent reception of the sacrament not only for the reconciliation of persons guilty of serious sins but also for reasons of devotion. Devotional confession – in which venial sins or previously forgiven sins are confessed – serves the purpose of confirming persons in penance and conversion.

Penitential Celebrations: Communal penitential celebrations are designed to emphasize the social dimensions of Christian life – the community aspects and significance of penance and reconciliation.

Elements of such celebrations are community prayer, hymns and songs, scriptural and other readings, examination of conscience, general confession and expression of sorrow for sin, acts of penance and reconciliation, and a form of non-sacramental absolution resembling the one in the penitential rite of the Mass.

If the sacrament is celebrated during the service, there must be individual confession and absolution of sin.

Recent Developments: On May 2, 2002, officials of the Roman Curia released a motu proprio by Pope John Paul II, *Misericordia Dei* ("Mercy of God, On Certain Aspects of the Celebration of the Sacrament of Penance"). The 15-page document called for a "vigorous revitalization" of the sacrament and asked bishops to adopt stricter observance on Church law's "grave necessity" requirement as a condition for the use of general absolution. It also requested that bishops' conferences submit national norms for general absolution to the Holy See for approval "as soon as possible."

In February 2003, the Bishops' Committee on the Liturgy and the Subcommittee for the Jubilee Year 2000 of the USCCB issued a new booklet, *Celebrating the Sacrament of Penance: Questions and Answers.* The booklet provides answers to some of the frequently asked questions about the Sacrament of Penance, including "Why Do We Need the Sacrament of Penance?" "What Happens in the Sacrament of Penance?" and "What is 'General Absolution'?" The booklet is intended for use in parishes during preparation for the Sacrament of Penance, as a resource for reflection on the sacrament during particular seasons such as Lent, and as a practical tool to aid penitents as they go to confession.

(*See* **Absolution, Confession, Confessional, Confessor,**

Contrition, Faculties, Forgiveness of Sin, Power of the Keys, Seal of Confession, Sin.)

Anointing of the Sick

This sacrament, promulgated by St. James the Apostle (Jas 5:13-15), can be administered to the faithful after reaching the age of reason who are in danger because of illness or old age. By the anointing with blessed oil and the prayer of a priest, the sacrament confers on the person comforting grace; the remission of venial sins and inculpably unconfessed mortal sins, together with at least some of the temporal punishment due for sins; and, sometimes, results in an improved state of health.

The matter of this sacrament is the anointing with blessed oil (olive oil, or vegetable oil if necessary) of the forehead and hands; in cases of necessity, a single anointing of another portion of the body suffices. The form is: "Through this holy anointing and his most loving mercy, may the Lord assist you by the grace of the Holy Spirit so that, when you have been freed from your sins, he may save you and in his goodness raise you up."

Anointing of the sick, formerly called extreme unction, may be received more than once, e.g., in new or continuing stages of serious illness. Ideally, the sacrament should be administered while the recipient is conscious and in conjunction with the sacraments of penance and the Eucharist. It should be administered in cases of doubt as to whether the person has reached the age of reason, is dangerously ill or dead.

The sacrament can be administered during a communal celebration in some circumstances, as in a home for the aged.

Holy Orders

Order is the sacrament by which the mission given by Christ to the Apostles continues to be exercised in the Church until the end of time; it is the sacrament of apostolic mission. It has three grades: episcopacy, priesthood and diaconate. The sacrament confers a character on the soul and can be received only once. The minister of the sacrament is a bishop.

Order, like matrimony but in a different way, is a social sacrament. As the Second Vatican Council declared in *Lumen Gentium*, the Dogmatic Constitution on the Church: "For the nurturing and constant growth of the People of God, Christ the Lord instituted in his Church a variety of ministries, which work for the good of the whole body. For those ministers who are endowed with sacred power are servants of their brethren, so that all who are of the People of God, and therefore enjoy a true Christian dignity, can work toward a common goal freely and in an orderly way, and arrive at salvation" (No. 18).

Bishop: The fullness of the priesthood belongs to those who have received the order of bishop. Bishops, in hierarchical union with the pope and their fellow bishops, are the successors of the Apostles as pastors of the Church: they have individual responsibility for the care of the local churches they serve and collegial responsibility for the care of the universal Church (*see* Collegiality). In the ordination or consecration of bishops, the essential form is the imposition of hands by the consecrator(s) and the assigned prayer in the preface of the rite of ordination. "With their helpers, the priests and deacons, bishops have taken up the service of the community presiding in place of God over the flock whose shepherds they are, as teachers of doctrine, priests of sacred worship, and officers of good order" (No. 20).

Priests: A priest is an ordained minister with the power to celebrate Mass, administer the sacraments, preach and teach the word of God, impart blessings, and perform additional pastoral functions, according to the mandate of his ecclesiastical superior.

Concerning priests, the Second Vatican Council stated in *Lumen Gentium* (No. 28):

"The divinely established ecclesiastical ministry is exercised on different levels by those who from antiquity have been called bishops, priests, and deacons. Although priests do not possess the highest degree of the priesthood, and although they are dependent on the bishops in the exercise of their power, they are nevertheless united with the bishops in sacerdotal dignity. By the power of the sacrament of orders, and in the image of Christ the eternal High Priest (Heb 5:1-10;7:24;9:11-28), they are consecrated to preach the Gospel, shepherd the faithful, and celebrate divine worship as true priests of the New Testament.

"Priests, prudent cooperators with the episcopal order as well as its aides and instruments, are called to serve the People of God. They constitute one priesthood with their bishop, although that priesthood is comprised of different functions."

In the ordination of a priest of Roman rite, the essential matter is the imposition of hands on the heads of those being ordained by the ordaining bishop. The essential form is the accompanying prayer in the preface of the ordination ceremony. Other elements in the rite are the presentation of the implements of sacrifice – the chalice containing the wine and the paten containing a host – with accompanying prayers.

Deacon: There are two kinds of deacons: those who receive the order and remain in it permanently, and those who receive the order while advancing to priesthood. The following quotation – from Vatican II's Dogmatic Constitution on the Church (*Lumen Gentium*, No. 29) – describes the nature and role of the diaconate, with emphasis on the permanent diaconate.

"At a lower level of the hierarchy are deacons, upon whom hands are imposed 'not unto the priesthood, but unto a ministry of service.' For strengthened by sacramental grace, in communion with the bishop and his group of priests, they serve the People of God in the ministry of the liturgy, of the word, and of charity. It is the duty of the deacon, to the extent that he has been authorized by competent authority, to administer baptism solemnly, to be custodian and dispenser of the Eucharist, to assist at and bless marriages in the name of the Church, to bring Viaticum to the dying, to read the sacred Scripture to the faithful, to instruct and exhort the people, to preside at the worship and prayer of the faithful, to administer sacramentals, and to officiate at funeral and burial services. (Deacons are) dedicated to duties of charity and administration.

"The diaconate can in the future be restored as a proper and permanent rank of the hierarchy. It pertains to the competent territorial bodies of bishops, of one kind or another, to decide, with the approval of the Supreme Pontiff, whether and where it is opportune for such deacons to be appointed for the care of souls. With the consent of the Roman Pontiff, this diaconate will be able to be conferred upon men of more mature age, even upon those living in the married state. It may also be conferred upon suitable young men. For them, however, the law of celibacy must remain intact" (No. 29).

The Apostles ordained the first seven deacons (Acts 6:1-6): Stephen, Philip, Prochorus, Nicanor, Timon,

Parmenas, Nicholas.

Former Orders, Ministries: With the revision of the sacrament of order which began in 1971, the orders of subdeacon, acolyte, exorcist, lector and porter were abolished because they and their respective functions had fallen into disuse or did not require ordination. The Holy See started revision of the sacrament of order in 1971. By virtue of an indult of Oct. 5 of that year, the bishops of the U.S. were permitted to discontinue ordaining porters and exorcists. Another indult, dated three days later, permitted the use of revised rites for ordaining acolytes and lectors.

To complete the revision, Pope Paul VI abolished Sept. 14, 1972, the orders of porter, exorcist and subdeacon; decreed that laymen, as well as candidates for the diaconate and priesthood, can be installed (rather than ordained) in the ministries (rather than orders) of acolyte and lector; reconfirmed the suppression of tonsure and its replacement with a service of dedication to God and the Church; and stated that a man enters the clerical state on ordination to the diaconate.

The abolished orders were:

• Subdeacon, with specific duties in liturgical worship, especially at Mass. The order, whose first extant mention dates from about the middle of the third century, was regarded as minor until the 13th century; afterwards, it was called a major order in the West but not in the East.

• Acolyte, to serve in minor capacities in liturgical worship; a function now performed by Mass servers.

• Exorcist, to perform services of exorcism for expelling evil spirits; a function which came to be reserved to specially delegated priests.

• Lector, to read scriptural and other passages during liturgical worship; a function now generally performed by lay persons.

• Porter, to guard the entrance to an assembly of Christians and to ward off undesirables who tried to gain admittance; an order of early origin and utility but of present insignificance.

Permanent Diaconate

Restoration of the permanent diaconate in the Roman rite – making it possible for men to become deacons permanently, without going on to the priesthood – was promulgated by Pope Paul VI June 18, 1967, in a document entitled *Sacrum Diaconatus Ordinem* ("Sacred Order of the Diaconate").

The Pope's action implemented the desire expressed by the Second Vatican Council for reestablishment of the diaconate as an independent order in its own right not only to supply ministers for carrying on the work of the Church but also to complete the hierarchical structure of the Church of Roman rite.

Permanent deacons have been traditional in the Eastern Church. The Western Church, however, since the fourth or fifth century, generally followed the practice of conferring the diaconate only as a sacred order preliminary to the priesthood, and of restricting the ministry of deacons to liturgical functions.

The pope's document, issued on his own initiative, provided:

• Qualified unmarried men 25 years of age or older may be ordained deacons. They cannot marry after ordination.

• Qualified married men 35 years of age or older may be ordained deacons. The consent of the wife of a prospective deacon is required. A married deacon cannot remarry after the death of his wife.

• Preparation for the diaconate includes a course of study and formation over a period of at least three years.

• Candidates who are not members of religious institutes must be affiliated with a diocese. Reestablishment of the diaconate among religious is reserved to the Holy See.

• Deacons will practice their ministry under the direction of a bishop and with the priests with whom they will be associated. (For functions, *see* the description of deacon, under **Holy Orders**.)

Restoration of the permanent diaconate in the U.S. was approved by the Holy See in October 1968. Shortly afterwards the U.S. bishops established a committee for the permanent diaconate, which was chaired by Bp. Edward U. Kmiec of Nashville in 1997. The current head of the Committee on Clergy, Consecrated Life and Vocations is Abp. Robert Carlson of St. Louis. The committee operates offices are at 3211 Fourth St. N.E., Washington, DC 20017. Fr. William S. McKnight, S.T.D. is executive director of the committee.

Status and Functions

The 2013 *Official Catholic Directory* reports that in the U.S. there were a total of 18,121 permanent deacons (the highest total by far for any single country), an increase of 305 from the previous year and an increase of 4,105 from 2003. Worldwide, there are currently 40,914 deacons, according to the 2011 edition of the *Annuarium Statisticum Ecclesiae* (the most recent edition).

Training programs of spiritual, theological and pastoral formation are based on guidelines emanating from the National Conference of Catholic Bishops.

Deacons have various functions, depending on the nature of their assignments. Liturgically, they can officiate at baptisms, weddings, wake services and funerals, can preach and distribute Holy Communion. Some are engaged in religious education work. All are intended to carry out works of charity and pastoral service of one kind or another.

The majority of deacons, the majority of whom are married, continue in their secular work. Their ministry of service is developing in three dimensions: of liturgy, of the word, and of charity. Depending on the individual deacon's abilities and preference, he is assigned by his bishop to either a parochial ministry or to another field of service. Deacons are active in a variety of ministries including those to prison inmates and their families, the sick in hospitals, nursing homes and homes for the aged, alienated youth, the elderly and the poor, and in various areas of legal service to the indigent, of education and campus ministry.

National Association of Diaconate Directors: Membership organization of directors, vicars and other staff personnel of diaconate programs. Established in 1977 to promote effective communication and facilitate the exchange of information and resources of members; to develop professional expertise and promote research, training and self evaluation; to foster accountability and seek ways to promote means of implementing solutions to problems. The association is governed by an executive board of elected officers. Officers include Deacons: Deacon Gerald DuPont, Chairman; Deacon Thomas R. Dubois, MPS, exec. dir. Contact: 2136 12th Street - Suite 105, Rockford, IL 61104; (815) 965-2100; www.nadd.org.

"A Portrait of the Permanent Diaconate"

In June 2013, the USCCB released "A Portrait of the Permanent Diaconate: A Study for the U.S. Conference of Catholic Bishops 2012-2013," prepared by the Center for Applied Research in the Apostolate (CARA). The report was the result of a national survey of the Office of the Permanent Diaconate in arch/dioceses and arch/epar-

chies in the United States that was commissioned by the Secretary of Clergy and Consecrated Life and Vocations of the U.S. Conference of Catholic Bishops. The major findings reported in part:
• The 183 Latin Rite arch/dioceses that responded to the questionnaire report a total of 12,756 permanent deacons. The two arch/eparchies that responded report a total of 38 permanent deacons. Extrapolating to include arch/dioceses and arch/eparchies that did not respond to the survey, it can be estimated that there are as many as 18,497 permanent deacons in the United States today
• Ninety-three percent of active deacons are currently married; four percent are widowers, and two percent never married. Ninety-five percent of active deacons are at least 50 years old; about a quarter are in their fifties; 43 percent are in their sixties; and 25 percent are 70 or older. Almost 90 percent of dioceses have a minimum age for deacon candidacy and half have a mandatory retirement age. In the U.S. the minimum age for ordination to the permanent deaconate is 35. The average minimum age for acceptance into a diaconate program is 33. Thirteen percent of dioceses have a mandatory retirement age of 70. Eighty percent mandate retirement at 75. Seventy-eight percent of active deacons are white. Fifteen percent are Hispanic or Latino, three percent are African American and three percent are Asian.

Ordination of Women

The Catholic Church believes and teaches that, in fidelity to the will of Christ, it cannot ordain women to the priesthood. This position has been set out over the last quarter-century in a series of authoritative documents published by or with the authority of Pope Paul VI and Pope John Paul II.

The first of these, *Inter Insigniores* ("Among the Characteristics"), was issued by the Congregation for the Doctrine of the Faith in October 1976. Its central statement is: "The Sacred Congregation for the Doctrine of the Faith judges it necessary to recall that the Church, in fidelity to the example of the Lord, does not consider herself authorized to admit women to priestly ordination."

In support of this, the document cited the constant tradition of the Church, the fact that Christ called only men to be Apostles and the continuation of this practice by the Apostles themselves, and the sacramental appropriateness of a male priesthood acting *in persona Christi*–in the person of Christ.

In light of continuing discussion, Pope John Paul II returned to the subject in the apostolic letter *Ordinatio Sacerdotalis* ("Priestly Ordination"), issued May 29, 1994: "Wherefore, in order that all doubt may be removed regarding a matter of great importance, a matter which pertains to the Church's divine constitution itself, in virtue of my ministry of confirming the brethren (cf. Lk 22.32) I declare that the Church has no authority whatsoever to confer priestly ordination on women and that this judgment is to be definitively held by all the Church's faithful."

The Congregation for the Doctrine of the Faith followed this on Oct. 28, 1995, with a response, published over the signature of its Prefect, Card. Joseph Ratzinger, to a bishop's inquiry concerning how "to be definitively held" should be understood. The response was:

"This teaching requires definitive assent, since, founded on the written Word of God and from the beginning constantly preserved and applied in the Tradition of the Church, it has been set forth infallibly by the ordinary and universal Magisterium (cf. Second Vatican Council, Dogmatic Constitution on the Church *Lumen Gentium*, 25, 2)."

Concerning the possible ordination of women to the diaconate, the International Theological Commission in 2002 concluded that the permanent diaconate belongs to the sacrament of orders and thus is limited to men only.

MATRIMONY

Marriage Doctrine

The following excerpts, stating key points of doctrine on marriage, are from *Gaudium et Spes*, (Nos. 48 to 51) promulgated by the Second Vatican Council:

Conjugal Covenant

The intimate partnership of married life and love has been established by the Creator and qualified by his laws. It is rooted in the conjugal covenant of irrevocable personal consent.

God himself is the author of matrimony, endowed as it is with various benefits and purposes. All of these have a very decisive bearing on the continuation of the human race, on the personal development and eternal destiny of the individual members of a family, and on the dignity, stability, peace, and prosperity of the family itself and of human society as a whole. By their very nature, the institution of matrimony itself and conjugal love are ordained for the procreation and education of children, and find in them their ultimate crown.

Thus a man and a woman render mutual help and service to each other through an intimate union of their persons and of their actions. Through this union they experience the meaning of their oneness and attain to it with growing perfection day by day. As a mutual gift of two persons, this intimate union, as well as the good of the children, imposes total fidelity on the spouses and argues for an unbreakable oneness between them (No. 48).

Sacrament of Matrimony

Christ the Lord abundantly blessed this many-faceted love. The Savior of men and the Spouse of the Church comes into the lives of married Christians through the sacrament of matrimony. He abides with them thereafter so that, just as he loved the Church and handed himself over on her behalf, the spouses may love each other with perpetual fidelity through mutual self-bestowal.

Graced with the dignity and office of fatherhood and motherhood, parents will energetically acquit themselves of a duty which devolves primarily on them; namely, education, and especially religious education.

The Christian family, which springs from marriage as a reflection of the loving covenant uniting Christ with the Church, and as a participation in that covenant, will manifest to all men the Savior's living presence in the world, and the genuine nature of the Church (No. 48).

Conjugal Love

The biblical Word of God several times urges the betrothed and the married to nourish and develop their wedlock by pure conjugal love and undivided affection.

This love is an eminently human one since it is directed from one person to another through an affection of the will. It involves the good of the whole person. Therefore it can enrich the expressions of body and mind with a unique dignity, ennobling these expressions as special ingredients and signs of the friendship distinctive of marriage. This love the Lord has judged worthy of special gifts, healing, perfecting, and exalting gifts of grace and of charity.

Such love, merging the human with the divine, leads the spouses to a free and mutual gift of themselves, a gift proving itself by gentle affection and by deed. Such love pervades the whole of their lives. Indeed, by its generous activity it grows better and grows greater. Therefore it far excels mere erotic inclination, which, selfishly pursued, soon enough fades wretchedly away.

This love is uniquely expressed and perfected through the marital act. The actions within marriage by which the couple are united intimately and chastely are noble and worthy ones. Expressed in a manner which is truly human, these actions signify and promote that mutual self-giving by which spouses enrich each other with a joyful and a thankful will.

Sealed by mutual faithfulness and hallowed above all by Christ's sacrament, this love remains steadfastly true in body and in mind, in bright days or dark. It will never be profaned by adultery or divorce. Firmly established by the Lord, the unity of marriage will radiate from the equal personal dignity of wife and husband, a dignity acknowledged by mutual and total love.

The steady fulfillment of the duties of this Christian vocation demands notable virtue. For this reason, strengthened by grace for holiness of life, the couple will painstakingly cultivate and pray for constancy of love, largeheartedness, and the spirit of sacrifice (No. 49).

Fruitfulness of Marriage

Marriage and conjugal love are by their nature ordained toward the begetting and educating of children. Children are really the supreme gift of marriage and contribute very substantially to the welfare of their parents. God himself wished to share with man a certain special participation in his own creative work. Thus he blessed male and female, saying: "Increase and multiply" (Gn 1:28).

Hence, while not making the other purposes of matrimony of less account, the true practice of conjugal love, and the whole meaning of the family life which results from it, have this aim: that the couple be ready with stout hearts to cooperate with the love of the Creator and the Savior, who through them will enlarge and enrich his own family day by day.

Parents should regard as their proper mission the task of transmitting human life and educating those to whom it has been transmitted. They should realize that they are thereby cooperators with the love of God the Creator, and are, so to speak, the interpreters of that love. Thus they will fulfill their task with human and Christian responsibility (No. 50).

Norms of Judgment

They will thoughtfully take into account both their own welfare and that of their children, those already born and those who may be foreseen. For this accounting they will reckon with both the material and the spiritual conditions of the times as well as of their state in life. Finally, they will consult the interests of the family group, of temporal society, and of the Church herself.

The parents themselves should ultimately make this judgment in the sight of God. But in their manner of acting, spouses should be aware that they cannot proceed arbitrarily. They must always be governed according to a conscience dutifully conformed to the divine law itself, and should be submissive toward the Church's teaching office, which authentically interprets that law in the light of the Gospel. That divine law reveals and protects the integral meaning of conjugal love, and impels it toward a truly human fulfillment.

Marriage, to be sure, is not instituted solely for procreation. Rather, its very nature as an unbreakable compact between persons, and the welfare of the children, both demand that the mutual love of the spouses, too, be embodied in a rightly ordered manner, that it grow and ripen. Therefore, marriage persists as a whole manner and communion of life, and maintains its value and indissolubility, even when offspring are lacking — despite, rather often, the very intense desire of the couple (No. 50).

Love and Life

This Council realizes that certain modern conditions often keep couples from arranging their married lives harmoniously, and that they find themselves in circumstances where at least temporarily the size of their families should not be increased. As a result, the faithful exercise of love and the full intimacy of their lives are hard to maintain. But where the intimacy of married life is broken off, it is not rare for its faithfulness to be imperiled and its quality of fruitfulness ruined. For then the upbringing of the children and the courage to accept new ones are both endangered.

To these problems there are those who presume to offer dishonorable solutions. Indeed, they do not recoil from the taking of life. But the Church issues the reminder that a true contradiction cannot exist between the divine laws pertaining to the transmission of life and those pertaining to the fostering of authentic conjugal love.

Church Teaching

For God, the Lord of Life, has conferred on men the surpassing ministry of safeguarding life – a ministry which must be fulfilled in a manner which is worthy of men. Therefore from the moment of its conception life must be guarded with the greatest care, while abortion and infanticide are unspeakable crimes. The sexual characteristics of man and the human faculty of reproduction wonderfully exceed the dispositions of lower forms of life. Hence the acts themselves which are proper to conjugal love and which are exercised in accord with genuine human dignity must be honored with great reverence (No. 51).

Therefore when there is question of harmonizing conjugal love with the responsible transmission of life, the moral aspect of any procedure does not depend solely on the sincere intentions or on an evaluation of motives. It must be determined by objective standards. These, based on the nature of the human person and his acts, preserve the full sense of mutual self-giving and human procreation in the context of true love. Such a goal cannot be achieved unless the virtue of conjugal chastity is sincerely practiced. Relying on these principles, sons of the Church may not undertake methods of regulating procreation which are found blameworthy by the teaching authority of the Church in its unfolding of the divine law.

Everyone should be persuaded that human life and the task of transmitting it are not realities bound up with this world alone. Hence they cannot be measured or perceived only in terms of it, but always have a bearing on the eternal destiny of men (No. 51).

Humanae Vitae

Marriage doctrine and morality were the subjects of the encyclical letter *Humanae Vitae* ("Of Human Life"), issued by Pope Paul VI, July 29, 1968. *Humanae Vitae* was given reaffirmation and its teaching restated and defended by Pope John Paul II in his encyclical *Evangelium Vitae* (*The Gospel of Life*, 1995). Following are a number of key excerpts from *Humanae Vitae*, which was framed in the pattern of traditional teaching and statements by the Second Vatican Council.

Each and every marriage act ("*quilibet matrimonii usus*") must remain open to the transmission of life (No. 11).

Indeed, by its intimate structure, the conjugal act, while most closely uniting husband and wife, capacitates them for the generation of new lives according to laws inscribed in the very being of man and of woman. By safeguarding both these essential aspects, the unitive and the procreative, the conjugal act preserves in its fullness the sense of true mutual love and its ordination toward man's most high calling to parenthood (No. 12).

It is, in fact, justly observed that a conjugal act imposed upon one's partner without regard for his or her condition and lawful desires is not a true act of love, and therefore denies an exigency of right moral order in the relationships between husband and wife. Hence, one who reflects well must also recognize that a reciprocal act of love which jeopardizes the responsibility to transmit life — which God the Creator, according to particular laws, inserted therein — is in contradiction with the design constitutive of marriage and with the will of the Author of life. To use this divine gift, destroying, even if only partially, its meaning and its purpose, is to contradict the nature both of man and of woman and of their most intimate relationship, and therefore it is to contradict also the plan of God and his will (No. 13).

Forbidden Actions

The direct interruption of the generative process already begun, and, above all, directly willed and procured abortion, even if for therapeutic reasons, are to be absolutely excluded as licit means of regulating birth.

Equally to be excluded is direct sterilization, whether perpetual or temporary, whether of the man or of the woman. Similarly excluded is every action which, either in anticipation of the conjugal act, or in its accomplishment, or in the development of its natural consequences, proposes, whether as an end or as a means, to render procreation impossible.

To justify conjugal acts made intentionally infecund, one cannot invoke as valid reasons the lesser evil, or the fact that such acts would constitute a whole together with the fecund acts already performed or to follow later and hence would share in one and the same moral goodness. In truth, if it is sometimes licit to tolerate a lesser evil in order to avoid a greater evil or to promote a greater good, it is not licit, even for the gravest reasons, to do evil so that good may follow therefrom; that is, to make into the object of a positive act of the will something which is intrinsically disorder, and hence unworthy of the human person, even when the intention is to safeguard or promote individual, family or social well-being.

Consequently, it is an error to think that a conjugal act which is deliberately made infecund, and so is intrinsically dishonest, could be made honest and right by the ensemble of a fecund conjugal life (No. 14).

If, then, there are serious motives to space out births, which derive from the physical or psychological conditions of husband and wife, or from external conditions, the Church teaches that it is then licit to take into account the natural rhythms immanent in the generative functions, for the use of marriage in the infecund periods only, and in this way to regulate birth without offending earlier stated principles (No. 16).

Pastoral Concerns

We do not at all intend to hide the sometimes serious difficulties inherent in the life of Christian married persons; for them, as for everyone else, "the gate is narrow and the way is hard that leads to life." But the hope of that life must illuminate their way, as with courage they strive to live with wisdom, justice and piety in this present time, knowing that the figure of this world passes away.

Let married couples then, face up to the efforts needed, supported by the faith and hope which "do not disappoint because God's love has been poured into our hearts through the Holy Spirit, who has been given to us." Let them implore divine assistance by persevering prayer; above all, let them draw from the source of grace and charity in the Eucharist. And, if sin should still keep its hold over them, let them not be discouraged but rather have recourse with humble perseverance to the mercy of God, which is poured forth in the sacrament of penance (No. 25).

Marriage Laws

The Catholic Church claims jurisdiction over its members in matters pertaining to marriage. Church legislation on the subject is stated principally in 111 canons of the Code of Canon Law.

Marriage laws of the Church provide juridical norms in support of the marriage covenant. In 10 chapters, the revised Code covers: pastoral directives for preparing men and women for marriage; impediments in general and in particular; matrimonial consent; form for the celebration of marriage; mixed marriages; secret celebration of marriage; effects of marriage; separation of spouses; and convalidation of marriage.

Catholics are bound by all marriage laws of the Church. Non-Catholics, whether baptized or not, are not considered bound by these ecclesiastical laws except in cases of marriage with a Catholic. Certain natural laws, in the Catholic view, bind all men and women, irrespective of their religious beliefs; accordingly, marriage is prohibited before the time of puberty, without knowledge and free mutual consent, in the case of an already existing valid marriage bond, in the case of antecedent and perpetual impotence.

Formalities

These include, in addition to arrangements for the time and place of the marriage ceremony, doctrinal and moral instruction concerning marriage and the recording of data which verifies in documentary form the eligibility and freedom of the persons to marry. Records of this kind, which are confidential, are preserved in the archives of the church where the marriage takes place.

Premarital instructions are the subject matter of Pre-Cana Conferences.

Marital Consent

Matrimonial consent can be invalidated by an essential defect, substantial error, the strong influence of force and fear, the presence of a condition or intention against the nature of marriage.

Form of Marriage

A Catholic is required, for validity and lawfulness, to contract marriage – with another Catholic or with a non-Catholic – in the presence of a competent priest or deacon and two witnesses.

There are two exceptions to this law. A Roman-rite Catholic (since Mar. 25, 1967) or an Eastern-rite Catholic (since Nov. 21, 1964) can contract marriage validly in the presence of a priest of a separated Eastern-rite Church, provided other requirements of law are complied with. With permission of the competent Roman-rite or Eastern-rite bishop, this form of marriage is lawful, as well as valid. (*See* **Eastern-rite Laws**, below.)

With these two exceptions, and aside from cases covered by special permission, the Church does not regard as valid any marriages involving Catholics which take place before non-Catholic ministers of religion or civil officials.

(An excommunication formerly in force against Catholics who celebrated marriage before a non-Catholic minister was abrogated in a decree issued by the Sacred Congregation for the Doctrine of the Faith on Mar. 18, 1966.)

The ordinary place of marriage is the parish of either Catholic party or of the Catholic party in case of a mixed marriage.

Church law regarding the form of marriage does not affect non-Catholics in marriages among themselves. The Church recognizes as valid the marriages of non-Catholics before ministers of religion and civil officials, unless there are rendered null and void on other grounds.

The canonical form is not to be observed in the case of a marriage between a non-Catholic and a baptized Catholic who has left the Church by a formal act.

Impediments

Diriment Impediments to marriage are factors that render a marriage invalid.

• Age, which obtains before completion of the 14th year for a woman and the 16th year for a man

• Impotency, if it is antecedent to the marriage and permanent (this differs from sterility, which is not an impediment)

• The bond of an existing valid marriage

• Disparity of worship, which obtains when one party is a Catholic and the other party is unbaptized

• Sacred orders

• Religious profession of the perpetual vow of chastity

• Abduction, which impedes the freedom of the person abducted

• Crime, variously involving elements of adultery, promise or attempt to marry, conspiracy to murder a husband or wife

• Blood relationship in the direct line (father-daughter, mother-son, etc.) and to the fourth degree inclusive of the collateral line (brother-sister, first cousins)

• Affinity, or relationship resulting from a valid marriage, in any degree of the direct line

• Public honesty, arising from an invalid marriage or from public or notorious concubinage; it renders either party incapable of marrying blood relatives of the other in the first degree of the direct line

• Legal relationship arising from adoption; it renders either party incapable of marrying relatives of the other in the direct line or in the second degree of the collateral line.

Dispensations from impediments: Persons hindered by impediments cannot marry unless they are dispensed therefrom in view of reasons recognized in canon law. Local bishops can dispense from the impediments most often encountered (e.g., disparity of worship) as well as others.

Decision regarding some dispensations is reserved to the Holy See.

Separation

A valid and consummated marriage of baptized persons cannot be dissolved by any human authority or any cause other than the death of one of the persons.

In other circumstances:

1. A valid but unconsummated marriage of baptized persons, or of a baptized and an unbaptized person, can be dissolved:

a. by the solemn religious profession of one of the persons, made with permission of the pope. In such a case, the bond is dissolved at the time of profession, and the other person is free to marry again.

b. by dispensation from the pope, requested for a grave reason by one or both of the persons. If the dispensation is granted, both persons are free to marry again.

Dispensations in these cases are granted for reasons connected with the spiritual welfare of the concerned persons.

2. A legitimate marriage, even consummated, of unbaptized persons can be dissolved in favor of one of them who subsequently receives the sacrament of baptism. This is the Pauline Privilege, so called because it was promulgated by St. Paul (1 Cor 7:12-15) as a means of protecting the faith of converts. Requisites for granting the privilege are:

a. marriage prior to the baptism of either person;

b. reception of baptism by one person;

c. refusal of the unbaptized person to live in peace with the baptized person and without interfering with his or her freedom to practice the Christian faith. The privilege does not apply if the unbaptized person agrees to these conditions.

3. A legitimate and consummated marriage of a baptized and an unbaptized person can be dissolved by the pope in virtue of the Privilege of Faith, also called the Petrine Privilege.

Civil Divorce

Because of the unity and the indissolubility of marriage, the Church denies that civil divorce can break the bond of a valid marriage, whether the marriage involves two Catholics, a Catholic and a non-Catholic, or non-Catholics with each other.

In view of serious circumstances of marital distress, the Church permits an innocent and aggrieved party, whether wife or husband, to seek and obtain a civil divorce for the purpose of acquiring title and right to the civil effects of divorce, such as separate habitation and maintenance, and the custody of children. Permission for this kind of action should be obtained from proper Church authority. The divorce, if obtained, does not break the bond of a valid marriage.

Under other circumstances – as would obtain if a marriage was invalid (see **Annulment**, below) – civil divorce is permitted for civil effects and as a civil ratification of the fact that the marriage bond really does not exist.

Annulment

This is a decision by a competent church authority – e.g., a bishop, a diocesan marriage tribunal, the Roman Rota – that an apparently valid marriage was actually invalid from the beginning because of the unknown or concealed existence, from the beginning, of a diriment impediment, an essential defect in consent, radical incapability for marriage, or a condition placed by one or both of the parties against the very nature of marriage.

Eastern-rite Laws

Marriage laws of the Eastern Church differ in several respects from the legislation of the Roman rite. The regulations in effect since May 2, 1949, were contained in the *motu proprio Crebre Allatae* issued by Pius XII the previous February.

According to both the Roman Code of Canon Law and the Oriental Code, marriages between Roman-rite Catholics and Eastern-rite Catholics ordinarily take place in the rite of the groom and have canonical effects in that rite.

Regarding the form for the celebration of marriages between Eastern Catholics and baptized Eastern non-Catholics, the Second Vatican Council declared:

"By way of preventing invalid marriages between Eastern Catholics and baptized Eastern non-Catholics, and in the interests of the permanence and sanctity of marriage and of domestic harmony, this sacred Synod decrees that the canonical 'form' for the celebration of such marriages obliges only for lawfulness. For their validity, the presence of a sacred minister suffices, as long as the other requirements of law are honored" (Decree on Eastern Catholic Churches, No. 18).

Marriages taking place in this manner are lawful, as well as valid, with permission of a competent Eastern-rite bishop.

The Rota

The Roman Rota is the ordinary court of appeal for marriage, and some other cases, which are appealed to the Holy See from lower church courts. Appeals are made to the Rota if decisions by diocesan and archdiocesan courts fail to settle the matter in dispute. Pope John Paul II, at annual meetings with Rota personnel, speaks about the importance of the court's actions in providing norms of practice for other tribunals.

Mixed Marriages

"Mixed Marriages" (*Matrimonia Mixta*) was the subject of a letter issued under this title by Pope Paul VI, on Mar. 31, 1970, and also a statement, "Implementation of the Apostolic Letter on Mixed Marriages," approved by the National Conference of Catholic Bishops on Nov. 16, 1970.

One of the key points in the bishops' statement referred to the need for mutual pastoral care by ministers of different faiths for the sacredness of marriage and for appropriate preparation and continuing support of parties to a mixed marriage.

Pastoral experience, which the Catholic Church shares with other religious bodies, confirms the fact that marriages of persons of different beliefs involve special problems related to the continuing religious practice of the concerned persons and to the religious education and formation of their children.

Pastoral measures to minimize these problems include instruction of a non-Catholic party in essentials of the Catholic faith for purposes of understanding. Desirably, some instruction should also be given the Catholic party regarding his or her partner's beliefs.

Requirements

The Catholic party to a mixed marriage is required to declare his (her) intention of continuing practice of the Catholic faith and to promise to do all in his (her) power to share his (her) faith with children born of the marriage by having them baptized and raised as Catholics. No declarations or promises are required of the non-Catholic party, but he (she) must be informed of the declaration and promise made by the Catholic.

Notice of the Catholic's declaration and promise is an essential part of the application made to a bishop for permission to marry a baptized non-Catholic, or a dispensation to marry an unbaptized non-Catholic.

A mixed marriage can take place with a Nuptial Mass. (The bishops' statement added this caution: "To the extent that Eucharistic sharing is not permitted by the general discipline of the Church, this is to be considered when plans are being made to have the mixed marriage at Mass or not.")

The ordinary minister at a mixed marriage is an authorized priest or deacon, and the ordinary place is the parish church of the Catholic party. A non-Catholic minister may not only attend the marriage ceremony but may also address, pray with and bless the couple.

For appropriate pastoral reasons, a bishop can grant a dispensation from the Catholic form of marriage and can permit the marriage to take place in a non-Catholic church with a non-Catholic minister as the officiating minister. A priest may not only attend such a ceremony but may also address, pray with and bless the couple.

"It is not permitted," however, the bishops' statement declared, "to have two religious services or to have a single service in which both the Catholic marriage ritual and a non-Catholic marriage ritual are celebrated jointly or successively."

Pastoral Ministry for Divorced and Remarried

Ministry to divorced and remarried Catholics is a difficult field of pastoral endeavor, situated as it is in circumstances tantamount to the horns of a dilemma.

At Issue

On the one side is firm church teaching on the permanence of marriage and norms against reception of the Eucharist and full participation in the life of the Church by Catholics in irregular unions.

On the other side are men and women with broken unions followed by second and perhaps happier attempts at marriage which the Church does not recognize as valid and which may not be capable of being validated because of the existence of an earlier marriage bond.

Factors involved in these circumstances are those of the Church, upholding its doctrine and practice regarding the permanence of marriage, and those of many men and women in irregular second marriages who desire full participation in the life of the Church.

Sacramental participation is not possible for those whose first marriage was valid, although there is no bar to their attendance at Mass, to sharing in other activities of the Church, or to their efforts to have children baptized and raised in the Catholic faith.

An exception to this rule is the condition of a divorced and remarried couple living in a brother-sister relationship.

There is no ban against sacramental participation by separated or divorced persons who have not attempted a second marriage, provided the usual conditions for reception of the sacraments are in order.

Unverified estimates of the number of U.S. Catholics who are divorced and remarried vary between 6 and 8 million.

Tribunal Action

What can the Church do for them and with them in pastoral ministry, is an old question charged with new urgency because of the rising number of divorced and remarried Catholics.

One way to help is through the agency of marriage tribunals charged with responsibility for investigating and settling questions concerning the validity or invalidity of a prior marriage. There are reasons in canon law justifying the Church in declaring a particular marriage null and void from the beginning, despite the short- or long-term existence of an apparently valid union.

Decrees of nullity (annulments) are not new in the history of the Church. If such a decree is issued, a man or woman is free to validate a second marriage and live in complete union with the Church.

The 2011 Statistical Yearbook of the Church (*Annuarium Statisticum Ecclesiae*, the most recent edition) reported in 2011 that U.S. tribunals issued 27,325 annulments (in ordinary and documentary processes). The canonical reasons were: invalid consent (21,288), impotence (5), other impediments (1,620), defect of form (4,577). Worldwide, 51,246 decrees or declarations of nullity were issued in 2011.

On Feb. 8, 2005, Vatican officials issued a new instruction for Church marriage tribunals that was intended clarify Church law, defend the sacrament of marriage, and ensure the efficiency that justice requires. The new handbook for Latin-rite diocesan and interdiocesan tribunals, *Dignitas Connubii* ("The Dignity of Marriage"), details clear procedures for accepting, investigating, assessing, and appealing marriage cases.

Reasons behind Decrees

Pastoral experience reveals that some married persons, a short or long time after contracting an apparently valid marriage, exhibit signs that point back to the existence, at the time of marriage, of latent and serious personal deficiencies which made them incapable of valid consent and sacramental commitment.

Such deficiencies might include gross immaturity and those affecting in a serious way the capacity to love, to have a true interpersonal and conjugal relationship, to fulfill marital obligations, or to accept the faith aspect of marriage.

Psychological and behavioral factors like these have been given greater attention by tribunals in recent years and have provided grounds for numerous decrees of nullity.

Decisions of this type do not indicate any softening of the Church's attitude regarding the permanence of marriage. They affirm, rather, that some persons who have married were really not capable of doing so.

Serious deficiencies in the capacity for real interpersonal relationship in marriage were the reasons behind a landmark decree of nullity issued in 1973 by the Roman Rota, the Vatican high court of appeals in marriage cases. Pope John Paul referred to such deficiencies – the "grave lack of discretionary judgment," incapability of assuming "essential matrimonial rights and obligations," for example – in an address Jan. 26, 1984, to personnel of the Rota.

The tribunal way to a decree of nullity regarding a previous marriage, however, is not open to many persons in second marriages — because grounds are either lacking or, if present, cannot be verified in tribunal process.

Unacceptable Solutions

One unacceptable solution of the problem, called "good conscience procedure," involves administration of the sacraments of penance and the Eucharist to divorced and remarried Catholics unable to obtain a decree of nullity for a first marriage who are living in a subsequent marriage "in good faith."

This procedure, despite the fact that it has no standing or recognition in church law, is being advocated and practiced by some priests and remarried Catholics.

This issue was addressed by the Congregation for the Doctrine of the Faith in a letter to bishops dated Oct. 14, 1994, and published with the approval of Pope John Paul II. The letter said in part:

"Pastoral solutions in this area have been suggested according to which divorced-and-remarried members of the faithful could approach holy Communion in specific cases when they considered themselves authorized according to a judgment of conscience to do so. This would be the case, for example, when they had been abandoned completely unjustly although they sincerely tried to save the previous marriage; or when they are convinced of the nullity of their previous marriage although (they are) unable to demonstrate it in the external forum; or when they have gone through a long period of reflection and penance; or also when for morally valid reasons they cannot satisfy the obligation to separate.

"In some places it has also been proposed that, in order objectively to examine their actual situation, the divorced-and-remarried would have to consult a prudent and experienced priest. This priest, however, would have to respect their eventual decision in conscience to approach holy Communion, without this implying an official authorization.

"In these and similar cases, it would be a matter of a tolerant and benevolent pastoral solution in order to do justice to the different situations of the divorced-and-remarried.

"Even if analogous solutions have been proposed by a few fathers of the Church and in some measure were practiced, nevertheless these never attained the consensus of the fathers and in no way came to constitute the common doctrine of the Church nor to determine her discipline. It falls to the universal magisterium, in fidelity to sacred Scripture and tradition, to teach and to interpret authentically the deposit of faith."

Conditions for Receiving Communion

Practically speaking, "when for serious reasons — for example, for the children's upbringing — a man and a woman cannot satisfy the obligation to separate," they may be admitted to Communion if "they take on themselves the duty to live in complete continence, that is, by abstinence from the acts proper to married couples. In such a case they may receive holy Communion as long as they respect the obligation to avoid giving scandal."

The teaching of the Church on this subject "does not mean that the Church does not take to heart the situation of those faithful who, moreover, are not excluded from ecclesial communion. She is concerned to accompany them pastorally and invite them to share in the life of the Church in the measure that is compatible with the dispositions of divine law, from which the Church has no power to dispense. On the other hand, it is necessary to instruct these faithful so that they do not think their participation in the life of the Church is reduced exclusively to the question of the reception of the Eucharist. The faithful are to be helped to deepen their understanding of the value of sharing in the sacrifice of Christ in the Mass, or spiritual communion, of prayer, of meditation on the word of God, and of works of charity and justice."

The Communion of Saints

THE DECLARATION OF CANONIZATION

Such a declaration is preceded by the process of beatification and another detailed investigation concerning the person's reputation for holiness, writings, and (except in the case of martyrs) a miracle ascribed to his or her intercession after death. The pope can dispense from some of the formalities ordinarily required in canonization procedures (equivalent canonization), as Pope John XXIII did in the canonization of St. Gregory Barbarigo on May 26, 1960. A saint is worthy of honor in liturgical worship throughout the universal Church. From its earliest years the Church has venerated saints. Public official honor always required the approval of the bishop of the place. Martyrs were the first to be honored. St. Martin of Tours, who died in 397, was an early non-martyr venerated as a saint. The earliest canonization by a pope with positive documentation was that of St. Ulrich (Uldaric) of Augsburg by John XV in 993. Alexander III reserved the process of canonization to the Holy See in 1171. In 1588 Sixtus V established the Sacred Congregation of Rites for the principal purpose of handling causes for beatification and canonization: this function is now the work of the Congregation for the Causes of Saints. The official listing of saints and blessed is contained in the Roman Martyrology (revised, updated, and published in 2002 by the Congregation for Divine Worship and the Discipline of the Sacraments) and related decrees issued after its last publication. *Butler's unofficial Lives of the Saints* (1956 and recently updated) contains 2,565 entries. The Church regards all persons in heaven as saints, not just those who have been officially canonized.

SAINTS OF THE CHURCH

Biographical sketches of additional saints and blesseds are found in other *Almanac* entries. See **Index**, under the name of each saint for the apostles, evangelists, Doctors of the Church, and Fathers of the Church. For beatification and canonization procedures, see those entries in the **Glossary** (p. 128).

An asterisk (*) with a feast date indicates that the saint is listed in the General Roman Calendar or the proper calendar for U.S. dioceses. For rank of observances, see listing in calendar for current year on preceding pages.

Adalbert (956-97): Born in Bohemia; bishop of Prague; Benedictine; missionary in Poland, Prussia and Hungary; martyred by Prussians near Danzig; Apr. 23.*

Adjutor (d. 1131): Norman knight; fought in First Crusade; monk-recluse after his return; Apr. 30.

Agatha (d. c. 250): Sicilian virgin-martyr; her intercession credited in Sicily with stilling eruptions of Mt. Etna; patron of nurses; Feb. 5.*

Agnes (d. c. 304): Roman virgin-martyr; martyred at age of 10 or 12; patron of young girls; Jan. 21.*

Aloysius Gonzaga (1568-91): Italian Jesuit; died while nursing plague-stricken; canonized 1726; patron of youth; June 21.*

Amand (d. c. 676): Apostle of Belgium; b. France; established monasteries throughout Belgium; Feb. 6.

Andre Bessette, (Bro. Andre) (1845-1937): Canadian Holy Cross Brother; prime mover in building of St. Joseph's Oratory, Montreal; beatified May 23, 1982; canonized Oct. 17, 2010. Jan. 6.

Andre Grasset de Saint Sauveur, Bl. (1758-92): Canadian priest; martyred in France, Sept. 2, 1792, during the Revolution; one of a group called the Martyrs of Paris who were beatified in 1926; Sept. 2.

Andrew Bobola (1592-1657): Polish Jesuit; joined Jesuits at Vilna; worked for return of Orthodox to union with Rome; martyred; canonized 1938; May 16.

Andrew Corsini (1302-73): Italian Carmelite; bishop of Fiesoli; mediator between quarrelsome Italian states; canonized 1629; Feb. 4.

Andrew Dung-Lac and Companions (d. 18th-19th c.): Martyrs of Vietnam. Total of 117 included 96 Vietnamese, 11 Spanish and 10 French missionaries (8 bishops; 50 priests, including Andrew Dung-Lac; 1 seminarian, 58 lay persons). Canonized June 19, 1988; inscribed in General Roman Calendar, 1989, as a memorial. Nov. 24.*

Andrew Fournet (1752-1834): French priest; co-founder with St. Jeanne Elizabeth Bichier des Anges of the Daughters of the Holy Cross of St. Andrew; canonized 1933; May 13.

Andrew Kim, Paul Chong and Companions (d. between 1839-67): Korean martyrs (103) killed in persecutions of 1839, 1846, 1866, and 1867; among them were Andrew Kim, the first Korean priest, and Paul Chong, lay apostle; canonized May 6, 1984, during Pope John Paul II's visit to Korea. Sept. 20.*

Angela Merici (1474-1540): Italian secular Franciscan; foundress of Company of St. Ursula, 1535, the first teaching order of women Religious in the Church; canonized 1807; Jan. 27.*

Angelico, Bl. (Fra Angelico; John of Faesulis) (1387-1455): Dominican; Florentine painter of early Renaissance; proclaimed blessed by John Paul II, Feb. 3, 1982; patron of artists; Feb. 18.

Anne Marie Javouhey, Bl. (1779-1851): French virgin; foundress of Institute of St. Joseph of Cluny, 1812; beatified 1950; July 15.

Ansgar (801-65): Benedictine monk; b. near Amiens; archbishop of Hamburg; missionary in Denmark, Sweden, Norway and northern Germany; apostle of Scandinavia; Feb. 3.*

Anthony (c. 251-c. 354): Abbot; Egyptian hermit; patriarch of all monks; established communities for hermits which became models for monastic life, especially in the

East; friend and supporter of St. Athanasius in the latter's struggle with the Arias; Jan. 17.*

Anthony Claret (1807-70): Spanish bishop; founder of Missionary Sons of the Immaculate Heart of Mary (Claretians), 1849; archbishop of Santiago, Cuba, 1851-57; canonized 1950; Oct. 24.*

Anthony Gianelli (1789-1846): Italian bishop; founded the Daughters of Our Lady of the Garden, 1829; bishop of Bobbio, 1838; canonized 1951; June 7.

Anthony Zaccaria (1502-39): Italian priest; founder of Barnabites (Clerks Regular of St. Paul), 1530; canonized 1897; July 5.*

Apollonia (d. 249): Deaconess of Alexandria; martyred during persecution of Decius; her patronage of dentists and those suffering from toothaches probably rests on tradition that her teeth were broken by her persecutors; Feb. 9.

Augustine of Canterbury (d. 604 or 605): Italian missionary; apostle of the English; sent by Pope Gregory I with 40 monks to evangelize England; arrived there 597; first archbishop of Canterbury; May 27.*

Bartolomea Capitania (1807-33): Italian foundress with Vincenza Gerosa of the Sisters of Charity of Lovere; canonized 1950; July 26.

Beatrice da Silva Meneses (1424-90): Foundress, b. Portugal; founded Congregation of the Immaculate Conception, 1484, in Spain; canonized 1976; Sept. 1.

Benedict Joseph Labré (1748-83): French layman; pilgrim-beggar; noted for his piety and love of prayer before the Blessed Sacrament; canonized 1883; Apr. 16.

Benedict of Nursia (c. 480-547): Abbot; founder of monasticism in Western Europe; established monastery at Monte Cassino; proclaimed patron of Europe by Paul VI in 1964; July 11.*

Benedict the Black *(il Moro)* (1526-89): Sicilian Franciscan; born a slave; joined Franciscans as lay brother; appointed guardian and novice master; canonized 1807; Apr. 3.

Bernadette Soubirous (1844-79): French peasant girl favored with series of visions of Blessed Virgin Mary at Lourdes (*see* Lourdes Apparitions); joined Institute of Sisters of Notre Dame at Nevers, 1866; canonized 1933; Apr. 16.

Bernard of Montjoux (or Menthon) (d. 1081): Augustinian canon; probably born in Italy; founded Alpine hospices near the two passes named for him; patron of mountaineers; May 28.

Bernardine of Feltre, Bl. (1439-94): Italian Franciscan preacher; a founder of *montes pietatis*; Sept. 28.

Bernardine of Siena (1380-1444): Italian Franciscan; noted preacher and missioner; spread of devotion to Holy Name is attributed to him; represented in art holding to his breast the monogram IHS; canonized 1450; May 20.*

Blase (d. c. 316): Armenian bishop; martyr; the blessing of throats on his feast day derives from tradition that he miraculously saved the life of a boy who had half-swallowed a fish bone; Feb. 3.*

Boniface (Winfrid) (d. 754): English Benedictine; bishop; martyr; apostle of Germany; established monastery at Fulda which became center of missionary work in Germany; archbishop of Mainz; martyred near Dukkum in Holland; June 5.*

Brendan (c. 489-583): Irish abbot; founded monasteries; his patronage of sailors probably rests on a legend that he made a seven-year voyage in search of a fabled paradise; called Brendan the Navigator; May 16.

Bridget (Brigid) (c. 450-525): Irish nun; founded reli-

gious community at Kildare, the first in Ireland; patron, with Sts. Patrick and Columba, of Ireland; Feb. 1.

Bridget (Birgitta) (c. 1303-73): Swedish mystic; widow; foundress of Order of Our Savior (Brigittines); canonized 1391; patroness of Sweden; named a co-patroness of Europe, with St. Edith Stein and St. Catherine of Siena, on Oct. 1, 1999; July 23.*

Bruno (1030-1101): German monk; founded Carthusians, 1084, in France; Oct. 6.*

Cabrini, Mother: *See* Frances Xavier Cabrini.

Cajetan (Gaetano) **of Thiene** (1480-1547): Italian lawyer; religious reformer; a founder of Oratory of Divine Love, forerunner of the Theatines; canonized 1671; Aug. 7.*

Callistus I (d. 222): Pope, 217-22; martyr; condemned Sabellianism and other heresies; advocated a policy of mercy toward repentant sinners; Oct. 14.*

Camillus de Lellis (1550-1614): Italian priest; founder of Camillians (Ministers of the Sick); canonized 1746; patron of the sick and of nurses; July 14.*

Casimir (1458-84): Polish prince; grand duke of Lithuania; noted for his piety; buried at cathedral in Vilna, Lithuania; canonized 1521; patron of Poland and Lithuania; Mar. 4.*

Cassian of Tangier (d. 298): Roman martyr; an official court stenographer who declared himself a Christian; patron of stenographers; Dec. 3.

Catherine Labouré (1806-76): French Religious; favored with series of visions soon after she joined Sisters of Charity of St. Vincent de Paul in Paris in 1830; first Miraculous Medal (*see* Index) struck in 1832 in accord with one of the visions; canonized 1947; Nov. 28.

Catherine of Bologna (1413-63): Italian Poor Clare; mystic, writer, artist canonized 1712; patron of artists; May 9.

Cecilia (2nd-3rd century): Roman virgin-martyr; traditional patroness of musicians; Nov. 22.*

Charles Borromeo (1538-84): Italian cardinal; nephew of Pope Pius IV; cardinal bishop of Milan; influential figure in Church reform in Italy; promoted education of clergy; canonized 1610; Nov. 4.*

Charles Lwanga and Companions (d. between 1885 and 1887): Twenty-two Martyrs of Uganda, many of them pages of King Mwanga of Uganda, who were put to death because they denounced his corrupt lifestyle; canonized 1964; first martyrs of black Africa; June 3.*

Charles of Sezze (1616-70): Italian Franciscan lay brother who served in humble capacities; canonized 1959; Jan. 6.

Christopher (3rd cent.): Early Christian martyr inscribed in Roman calendar about 1550; feast relegated to particular calendars because of legendary nature of accounts of his life; traditional patron of travelers; July 25.

Clare (1194-1253): Foundress of Poor Clares; b. at Assisi; was joined in religious life by her sisters, Agnes and Beatrice, and eventually her widowed mother Ortolana; canonized 1255; patroness of television; Aug. 11.*

Claude de la Colombiere (1641-82): French Jesuit; spiritual director of St. Margaret Mary Alacoque; instrumental in spreading devotion to the Sacred Heart; beatified, 1929; canonized May 31, 1992; Feb. 15.

Clement Hofbauer (1751-1820): Redemptorist priest; missionary; born in Moravia; helped spread Redemptorists north of the Alps; canonized 1909; Mar. 15.

Clement I (d. c. 100): Pope, 88-97; third successor of St. Peter; wrote important letter to Church in Corinth settling disputes there; venerated as a martyr; Nov. 23.*

Columba (521-97): Irish monk; founded monasteries in

Ireland; missionary in Scotland; established monastery at Iona which became the center for conversion of Picts, Scots, and Northern English; Scotland's most famous saint; patron saint of Ireland (with Sts. Patrick and Brigid); June 9.

Columban (545-615): Irish monk; scholar; founded monasteries in England and Brittany (famous abbey of Luxeuil), forced into exile because of his criticism of Frankish court; spent last years in northern Italy where he founded abbey at Bobbio; Nov. 23.*

Conrad of Parzham (1818-94): Bavarian Capuchin lay brother; served as porter at the Marian shrine of Altotting in Upper Bavaria for 40 years; canonized 1934; Apr. 21.

Contardo Ferrini, Bl. (1859-1902): Italian secular Franciscan; model of the Catholic professor; beatified 1947; patron of universities; Oct. 20.

Cornelius (d. 253): Pope, 251-53; promoted a policy of mercy with respect to readmission of repentant Christians who had fallen away during the persecution of Decius (*lapsi*); banished from Rome during persecution of Gallus; regarded as a martyr; Sept. 16 (with Cyprian).*

Cosmas and Damian (d. c. 303): Arabian twin brothers, physicians; martyred during Diocletian persecution; patrons of physicians; Sept. 26.*

Crispin and Crispinian (3rd cent.): Early Christian martyrs; said to have met their deaths in Gaul; patrons of shoemakers, a trade they pursued; Oct. 25.

Crispin of Viterbo (1668-1750): Capuchin brother; canonized June 20, 1982; May 21.

Cyprian (d. 258): Early ecclesiastical writer; b. Africa; bishop of Carthage, 249-58; supported Pope St. Cornelius concerning the readmission of Christians who had apostatized in time of persecution; erred in his teaching that baptism administered by heretics and schismatics was invalid; wrote *De Unitate*; Sept. 16 (with St. Cornelius).*

Cyril and Methodius (9th century): Greek missionaries, bothers; venerated as apostles of the Slavs; Cyril (d. 869) and Methodius (d. 885) began their missionary work in Moravia in 863; developed a Slavonic alphabet; used the vernacular in the liturgy, a practice that was eventually approved; declared patrons of Europe with St. Benedict, Dec. 31, 1980; Feb. 14.*

Damasus I (d. 384): Pope, 366-84; opposed Arians and Apollinarians; commissioned St. Jerome to work on Bible translation; developed Roman liturgy; Dec. 11.*

Damian: *See* **Cosmas and Damian.**

Damien of Molokai (d. 1889): The so-called leper priest of Molokai; originally from Belgium, Damien devoted over 20 years to the care of the lepers in Hawaii, ultimately dying from the same disease. He was beatified by Pope John Paul II in 1995 canonized on Oct. 11, 2009.

David (5th or 6th cent.): Nothing for certain known of his life; said to have founded monastery at Menevia; patron saint of Wales; Mar. 1.

Denis and Companions (d. 3rd cent.): Denis, bishop of Paris, and two companions identified by early writers as Rusticus, a priest, and Eleutherius, a deacon; martyred near Paris; Denis is popularly regarded as the apostle and a patron saint of France; Oct. 9.*

Dismas (1st cent.): Name given to repentant thief (Good Thief) to whom Jesus promised salvation (Lk. 23:40-43); regarded as patron of prisoners; Mar. 25 (observed on second Sunday of October in U.S. prison chapels).

Dominic (Dominic de Guzman) (1170-1221): Spanish priest; founded Order of Preachers (Dominicans), 1215, in France; preached against Albigensian heresy; a contemporary of St. Francis of Assisi; canonized 1234; Aug. 8.*

Dominic Savio (1842-57): Italian youth; pupil of St. John Bosco; died before his 15th birthday; canonized 1954; patron of choir boys; May 6.

Duns Scotus, John (d. 1308): Scottish Franciscan; theologian; advanced theological arguments for doctrine of the Immaculate Conception; proclaimed blessed; cult solemnly confirmed by John Paul II, Mar. 20, 1993; Nov. 8.

Dunstan (c. 910-88): English monk; archbishop of Canterbury; initiated reforms in religious life; counselor to several kings; considered one of greatest Anglo-Saxon saints; patron of goldsmiths, locksmiths, jewelers (trades in which he is said to have excelled); May 19.

Dymphna (dates unknown): Nothing certain known of her life; according to legend, she was an Irish maiden murdered by her heathen father at Gheel near Antwerp, Belgium, where she had fled to escape his advances; her relics were discovered there in the 13th century; since that time cures of mental illness and epilepsy have been attributed to her intercession; patron of those suffering from mental illness; May 15.

Edith Stein, St. (1891-1942): German Carmelite (Teresa Benedicta of the Cross); born of Jewish parents; author and lecturer; baptized in Catholic Church, 1922; arrested with her sister Rosa in 1942 and put to death at Auschwitz; beatified 1987, by Pope John Paul II during his visit to West Germany; was canonized by Pope John Paul II on Oct. 11, 1998, and named a co-patroness of Europe, with St. Bridget of Sweden and St. Catherine of Siena, on Oct. 1, 1999. Aug. 10.

Edmund Campion (1540-81): English Jesuit; convert 1573; martyred at Tyburn; canonized 1970, one of the Forty English and Welsh Martyrs; Dec. 1.

Edward the Confessor (d. 1066): King of England, 1042-66; canonized 1161; Oct. 13.

Eligius (c. 590-660): Bishop; born in Gaul; founded monasteries and convents; bishop of Noyon and Tournai; famous worker in gold and silver; Dec. 1.

Elizabeth Ann Seton (1774-1821): American foundress; convert, 1805; founded Sisters of Charity in the U.S.; beatified 1963; canonized Sept. 14, 1975; the first American-born saint; Jan. 4 (U.S.).*

Elizabeth of Hungary (1207-31): Became secular Franciscan after death of her husband in 1227; devoted life to poor and destitute; a patron of the Secular Franciscan Order; canonized 1235; Nov. 17.*

Elizabeth of Portugal (1271-1336): Queen of Portugal; b. Spain; retired to Poor Clare convent as a secular Franciscan after the death of her husband; canonized 1626; July 4.*

Emily de Rodat (1787-1852): French foundress of the Congregation of the Holy Family of Villefranche; canonized 1950; Sept. 19.

Emily de Vialar (1797-1856): French foundress of the Sisters of St. Joseph of the Apparition; canonized 1951; June 17.

Erasmus (Elmo) (d. 303): Life surrounded by legend; martyred during Diocletian persecution; patron of sailors; June 2.

Ethelbert (552-616): King of Kent, England; baptized by St. Augustine of Canterbury, 597; issued legal code; furthered spread of Christianity; Feb. 26.

Eusebius of Vercelli (283-370): Italian bishop; exiled from his see (Vercelli) for a time because of his opposition to Arianism; considered a martyr because of sufferings he endured; Aug. 2.*

Fabian (d. 250): Pope, 236-50; martyred under Decius; Jan. 20.*

Felicity: *See* **Perpetua and Felicity**.

Ferdinand III (1198-1252): King of Castile and Leon; waged successful campaigns against the Moors in Spain; founded university at Salamanca; canonized 1671; May 30.

Fiacre (Fiachra) (d. c. 670): Irish hermit; patron of gardeners; Aug. 30.

Fidelis of Sigmaringen (Mark Rey) (1577-1622): German Capuchin; lawyer before he joined the Capuchins; missionary to Swiss Protestants; stabbed to death by peasants who were told he was an agent of the Austrian emperor; Apr. 24.*

Frances of Rome (1384-1440): Italian model for housewives and widows; happily married for 40 years; after death of her husband in 1436 joined community of Benedictine Oblates she had founded; canonized 1608; patron of motorists; Mar. 9.*

Frances Xavier Cabrini (Mother Cabrini) (1850-1917): American foundress; b. Italy; founded the Missionary Sisters of the Sacred Heart, 1877; settled in the U.S. 1889; became an American citizen at Seattle 1909; worked among Italian immigrants; canonized 1946, the first American citizen so honored; Nov. 13 (U.S.).*

Francis Borgia (1510-72): Spanish Jesuit; joined Jesuits after death of his wife in 1546; became general of the Order, 1565; Oct. 10.

Francis Caracciolo (1563-1608): Italian priest; founder with Father Augustine Adorno of the Clerics Regular Minor (Adorno Fathers); canonized 1807; declared patron of Italian chefs, 1996; June 4.

Francis Fasani (1681-1742): Italian Conventual Franciscan; model of priestly ministry, especially in service to poor and imprisoned; canonized 1986; Nov. 27.

Francis of Assisi (Giovanni di Bernardone) (1181/82-1226): Founder of the Franciscans, 1209; received stigmata 1224; canonized 1228; one of best known and best loved saints; patron of Italy, Catholic Action and ecologists; Oct. 4.*

Francis of Paola (1416-1507): Italian hermit: founder of Minim Friars; Apr. 2.*

Francis Xavier (1506-52): Spanish Jesuit; missionary to Far East; canonized 1602; patron of foreign missions; considered one of greatest Christian missionaries; Dec. 3.*

Francis Xavier Bianchi (1743-1815): Italian Barnabite; acclaimed apostle of Naples because of his work there among the poor and abandoned; canonized 1951; Jan. 31.

Frederick (d. 838): Bishop and martyr, also called Friderich; July 18.

Frederick (d. 1121): Bishop of Liège, Belgium, believed poisoned by the count of Louvain; May 27.

Gabriel of the Sorrowful Mother (Francis Possenti) (1838-62): Italian Passionist; died while a scholastic; canonized 1920; Feb. 27.

Gaspar (Caspar) **del Bufalo** (1786-1836): Italian priest; founded Missionaries of the Precious Blood, 1815; canonized 1954; Jan. 2.

Gemma Galgani (1878-1903): Italian laywoman; visionary; subject of extraordinary religious experiences; canonized 1940; Apr. 11.

Genesius (d. c. 300): Roman actor; according to legend, was converted while performing a burlesque of Christian baptism and was subsequently martyred; patron of actors; Aug. 25.

Geneviève (422-500): French nun; a patroness and protectress of Paris; events of her life not authenticated; Jan. 3.

George (d.c. 300): Martyr, probably during Diocletian persecution in Palestine; all other incidents of his life, including story of the dragon, are legendary; patron of England; Apr. 23.*

Gerard Majella (1725-55): Italian Redemptorist lay brother; noted for supernatural occurrences in his life including bilocation and reading of consciences; canonized 1904; patron of mothers; Oct. 16.

Gertrude (1256-1302): German mystic; writer; helped spread devotion to the Sacred Heart; Nov. 16.*

Gregory VII (Hildebrand) (1020?-85): Pope, 1075-85; Benedictine monk; adviser to several popes; as pope, strengthened interior life of Church and fought against lay investiture; driven from Rome by Henry IV; died in exile; canonized 1584; May 25.*

Gregory Barbarigo (1626-97): Italian cardinal; noted for his efforts to bring about reunion of separated Christians; canonized 1960; June 18.

Gregory of Nyssa (c. 335-95): Bishop; theologian; younger brother of St. Basil the Great; Mar. 9.

Gregory Thaumaturgus (c. 213-68): Bishop of Neocaesarea; missionary; famed as wonder worker; Nov. 17.

Gregory the Illuminator (257-332): Martyr; bishop; apostle and patron saint of Armenia; helped free Armenia from the Persians; Sept. 30.

Hedwig (1174-1243): Moravian noblewoman; married duke of Silesia, head of Polish royal family; fostered religious life in country; canonized 1266; Oct. 16.*

Helena (250-330): Empress; mother of Constantine the Great; associated with discovery of the True Cross; Aug. 18.

Henry (972-1024): Bavarian emperor; cooperated with Benedictine abbeys in restoration of ecclesiastical and social discipline; canonized 1146; July 13.*

Herman Joseph (1150-1241): German Premonstratensian; his visions were the subjects of artists; writer; cult approved, 1958; Apr. 7.

Hippolytus (d. c. 236): Roman priest; opposed Pope St. Callistus I in his teaching about the readmission to the Church of repentant Christians who had apostatized during time of persecution; elected antipope; exiled to Sardinia; reconciled before his martyrdom; important ecclesiastical writer; Aug. 13* (with Pontian).

Hugh of Cluny (the Great) (1024-1109): Abbot of Benedictine foundation at Cluny; supported popes in efforts to reform ecclesiastical abuses; canonized 1120; Apr. 29.

Ignatius of Antioch (d. c. 107): Early ecclesiastical writer; martyr; bishop of Antioch in Syria for 40 years; Oct. 17.*

Ignatius of Laconi (1701-81): Italian Capuchin lay brother whose 60 years of religious life were spent in Franciscan simplicity; canonized 1951; May 11.

Ignatius of Loyola (1491-1556): Spanish soldier; renounced military career after recovering from wounds received at siege of Pampeluna (Pamplona) in 1521; founded Society of Jesus (Jesuits), 1534, at Paris; wrote *The Book of Spiritual Exercises*; canonized 1622; July 31.*

Irenaeus of Lyons (130-202): Early ecclesiastical writer; opposed Gnosticism; bishop of Lyons; traditionally regarded as a martyr; June 28.*

Isidore the Farmer (d. 1170): Spanish layman; farmer; canonized 1622; patron of farmers; May 15 (U.S.).*

Jane Frances de Chantal (1572-1641): French widow; foundress, under guidance of St. Francis de Sales, of Order of the Visitation; canonized 1767; Dec. 12* (General Roman Calendar); Aug. 18* (U.S.).

Januarius (Gennaro) (d. 304): Bishop of Benevento; martyred during Diocletian persecution; fame rests on liquefaction of some of his blood preserved in a phial at Naples, an unexplained phenomenon which has occurred regularly several times each year for over 400 years; Sept. 19.*

Jeanne Delanoue (1666-1736): French foundress of Sisters of St. Anne of Providence, 1704; canonized 1982; Aug. 16.

Jeanne (Joan) **de Lestonnac** (1556-1640): French foundress; widowed in 1597; founded the Religious of Notre Dame 1607; canonized 1947; Feb. 2.

Jeanne de Valois (Jeanne of France) (1464-1505): French foundress; deformed daughter of King Louis XI; was married in 1476 to Duke Louis of Orleans who had the marriage annulled when he ascended the throne as Louis XII; Jeanne retired to life of prayer; founded contemplative Annonciades of Bourges, 1504; canonized 1950; Feb. 5.

Jeanne-Elizabeth Bichier des Ages (1773-1838): French Religious; co-founder with St. Andrew Fournet of Daughters of the Cross of St. Andrew, 1807; canonized 1947; Aug. 26.

Jeanne Jugan, Bl. (1792-1879): French Religious; foundress of Little Sisters of the Poor; beatified Oct. 3, 1982; Aug. 30.

Jerome Emiliani (1481-1537): Venetian priest; founded Somascan Fathers, 1532, for care of orphans; canonized 1767; patron of orphans and abandoned children; Feb. 8.*

Joan Antida Thouret (1765-1826): French Religious; founded, 1799, congregation now known as Sisters of Charity of St. Joan Antida; canonized 1934; Aug. 24.

Joan of Arc (1412-31): French heroine, called The Maid of Orleans, La Pucelle; led French army in 1429 against English invaders besieging Orleans; captured by Burgundians the following year; turned over to ecclesiastical court on charge of heresy, found guilty and burned at the stake; her innocence was declared in 1456; canonized 1920; patroness of France; May 30.

Joaquina de Vedruna de Mas (1783-1854): Spanish foundress; widowed in 1816; after providing for her children, founded the Carmelite Sisters of Charity; canonized 1959; Aug. 28.

John I (d. 526): Pope, 523-26; martyr; May 18.*

John XXIII, Bl.: *see* **Popes of the Twentieth Century** in **Papacy and the Holy See** (p. 241).

John Baptist de la Salle (1651-1719): French priest; founder of Brothers of the Christian Schools, 1680; canonized 1900; patron of teachers; Apr. 7.*

John Berchmans (1599-1621): Belgian Jesuit scholastic; patron of Mass servers; canonized 1888; Aug. 13.

John (Don) Bosco (1815-88): Italian priest; founded Salesians, 1859, for education of boys; cofounder of Daughters of Mary Help of Christians for education of girls; canonized 1934; Jan. 31.*

John Capistran (1386-1456): Italian Franciscan; preacher; papal diplomat; canonized 1690; declared patron of military chaplains, Feb. 10, 1984. Oct. 23.*

John de Ribera (1532-1611): Spanish bishop and statesman; archbishop of Valencia, 1568-1611, and viceroy of that province; canonized 1960; Jan. 6.

John Eudes (1601-80): French priest; founder of Sisters of Our Lady of Charity of Refuge, 1642, and Congregation of Jesus-Mary (Eudists), 1643; canonized 1925; Aug. 19.*

John Fisher (1469-1535): English prelate; theologian; martyr; bishop of Rochester, cardinal; refused to recognize validity of Henry VIII's marriage to Anne Boleyn; upheld supremacy of the pope; beheaded for refusing to acknowledge Henry as head of the Church; canonized 1935; June 22 (with St. Thomas More).*

John Francis Regis (1597-1640): French Jesuit priest; preached missions among poor and unlettered; canonized

1737; patron of social workers, particularly medical social workers, because of his concern for poor and needy and sick in hospitals; July 2.

John Gualbert (d. 1073): Italian priest; founder of Benedictine congregation of Vallombrosians, 1039; canonized 1193; July 12.

John Kanty (Cantius) (1395-1473): Polish theologian; canonized 1767; Dec. 23.*

John Leonardi (1550-1609): Italian priest; worked among prisoners and the sick; founded Clerics Regular of the Mother of God; canonized 1938; Oct. 9.*

John Nepomucene (1345-93): Bohemian priest; regarded as a martyr; canonized 1729; patron of Czechoslovakia; May 16.

John Nepomucene Neumann (1811-60): American prelate; b. Bohemia; ordained in New York 1836; missionary among Germans near Niagara Falls before joining Redemptorists, 1840; bishop of Philadelphia, 1852; first bishop in U.S. to prescribe Forty Hours devotion in his diocese; beatified 1963; canonized June 19, 1977; Jan. 5 (U.S.).*

John of Ávila (1499-1569): Spanish priest; preacher; ascetical writer; spiritual adviser of St. Teresa of Jesus (Ávila); canonized 1970; May 10.

John of Britto (1647-93): Portuguese Jesuit; missionary in India where he was martyred; canonized 1947; Feb. 4.

John of God (1495-1550): Portuguese founder; his work among the sick poor led to foundation of Brothers Hospitallers of St. John of God, 1540, in Spain; canonized 1690; patron of sick, nurses, hospitals; Mar. 8.*

John of Matha (1160-1213): French priest; founder of the Order of Most Holy Trinity, whose original purpose was the ransom of prisoners from the Muslims; Feb. 8.

John Ogilvie (1579-1615): Scottish Jesuit; martyr; canonized 1976, the first canonized Scottish saint since 1250 (Margaret of Scotland); Mar. 10.

John Paul II, Bl. (1920-2005): Pope from 1978-2005; one of the longest serving popes in history; wrote a great number of encyclicals that examined the modern world, human dignity, and eternal moral truths; his more than 120 international trips were vital moments in modern Catholic history; beatified on May 1, 2011; Oct. 22. See also **Popes of the Twentieth Century** in **Papacy and the Holy See** (p. 241).

John Vianney (Curé of Ars) (1786-1859): French parish priest; noted confessor, spent 16 to 18 hours a day in confessional; canonized 1925; patron of parish priests; Aug. 4.*

Josaphat Kuncevyc (1584-1623): Basilian monk; b. Poland; archbishop of Polotsk, Lithuania; worked for reunion of separated Eastern Christians with Rome; martyred by mob of schismatics; canonized 1867; Nov. 12.*

Josemaria Escrivá de Balaguer (1902-75) Priest and Founder of Opus Dei; the society was designed to promote holiness among individuals in the world; beatified in 1992 and canonized on Oct. 6, 2002; May 17.

Joseph Benedict Cottolengo (1786-1842): Italian priest; established Little Houses of Divine Providence (*Piccola Casa*) for care of orphans and the sick; canonized 1934; Apr. 30.

Joseph Cafasso (1811-60): Italian priest; renowned confessor; promoted devotion to Blessed Sacrament; canonized 1947; June 23.

Joseph Calasanz (1556-1648): Spanish priest; founder of Piarists (Order of Pious Schools); canonized 1767; Aug. 25.*

Joseph of Cupertino (1603-63): Italian Franciscan; noted for remarkable incidents of levitation; canonized 1767; Sept. 18.

Joseph Pignatelli (1737-1811): Spanish Jesuit; left Spain when Jesuits were banished in 1767; worked for revival of the Order; named first superior when Jesuits were reestablished in Kingdom of Naples, 1804; canonized 1954; Nov. 28.

Juan Diego (16th cent.): Mexican Indian, convert; indigenous name according to tradition Cuauhtlatohuac ("The eagle who speaks"); favored with apparitions of Our Lady (*see* **Our Lady of Guadalupe**) on Tepeyac hill; beatified, 1990; canonized July 30, 2002; Dec. 9* (U.S.).

Julia Billiart (1751-1816): French foundress; founded Sisters of Notre Dame de Namur, 1804; canonized 1969; Apr. 8.

Juliana Falconieri (1270-1341): Italian foundress of the Servite Nuns; the niece of St. Alexis Falconieri; canonized in 1737; June 19.

Justin de Jacobis (1800-60): Italian Vincentian; bishop; missionary in Ethiopia; canonized 1975; July 31.

Justin Martyr (100-65): Early ecclesiastical writer; Apologies for the Christian Religion, Dialog with the Jew Tryphon; martyred at Rome; June 1.*

Kateri Tekakwitha (1656-80): "Lily of the Mohawks." Indian maiden born at Ossernenon (Auriesville), N.Y.; baptized Christian, Easter, 1676, by Jesuit missionary Fr. Jacques de Lambertville; lived life devoted to prayer, penitential practices and care of sick and aged in Christian village of Caughnawaga near Montreal where her relics are now enshrined; beatified June 22, 1980 and canonized on Oct. 21, 2012; July 14.

Katharine Drexel, St. (1858-1955): Philadelphia-born heiress; devoted wealth to founding schools and missions for Indians and Blacks; foundress of Sisters of Blessed Sacrament for Indians and Colored People, 1891; beatified 1988; canonized on Oct. 1, 2000; Mar. 3* (U.S.).

Ladislaus (1040-1095): King of Hungary; supported Pope Gregory VII against Henry IV; canonized 1192; June 27.

Lawrence (d. 258): Widely venerated martyr who suffered death, according to a long-standing but unverifiable legend, by fire on a gridiron; Aug. 10.*

Lawrence (Lorenzo) **Ruiz and Companions** (d. 1630s): Martyred in or near the city of Nagasaki, Japan; Lawrence Ruiz, first Filipino saint, and 15 companions (nine Japanese, four Spaniards, one Italian and one Frenchman); canonized 1987; Sept. 28.*

Leonard Murialdo (1828-1900): Italian priest; educator; founder of Pious Society of St. Joseph of Turin; 1873; canonized 1970; Mar. 30.

Leonard of Port Maurice (1676-1751): Italian Franciscan; ascetical writer; preached missions throughout Italy; canonized 1867; patron of parish missions; Nov. 26.

Leopold Mandic (1866-1942): Croatian-born Franciscan priest, noted confessor; spent most of his priestly life in Padua, Italy; canonized 1983; July 30.

Louis IX (1215-70): King of France, 1226-70; participated in Sixth Crusade; patron of Secular Franciscan Order; canonized 1297; Aug. 25.*

Louis de Montfort (1673-1716): French priest; founder of Sisters of Divine Wisdom, 1703, and Missionaries of Company of Mary, 1715; wrote *True Devotion to the Blessed Virgin*; canonized 1947; Apr. 28.*

Louis Zepherin Moreau, Bl. (d. 1901): Canadian bishop; headed St. Hyacinthe, Que., diocese, 1876-1901; beatified 1987; May 24.

Louise de Marillac (1591-1660): French foundress, with St. Vincent de Paul, of the Sisters of Charity; canonized 1934; Mar. 15.

Lucy (d. 304): Sicilian maiden; martyred during Diocletian persecution; one of most widely venerated early virgin-martyrs; patron of Syracuse, Sicily; invoked by those suffering from eye diseases; Dec. 13.*

Lucy Filippini (1672-1732): Italian educator, helped improve status of women through education; considered a founder of the Religious Teachers Filippini, 1692; canonized 1930; Mar. 25.

Madeleine Sophie Barat (1779-1865): French foundress of the Society of the Sacred Heart of Jesus; canonized 1925; May 25.

Malachy (1095-1148): Irish bishop; instrumental in establishing first Cistercian house in Ireland, 1142; canonized 1190; Nov. 3.

Marcellinus and Peter (d.c. 304): Early Roman martyrs; June 2.*

Margaret Clitherow (1556-86): English martyr; convert shortly after her marriage; one of Forty Martyrs of England and Wales; canonized 1970; Mar. 25.

Margaret Mary Alacoque (1647-90): French Religious; spread devotion to Sacred Heart in accordance with revelations made to her in 1675 (*see* **Sacred Heart**); canonized 1920; Oct. 16.*

Margaret of Cortona (1247-97): Secular Franciscan; reformed her life in 1273 following the violent death of her lover; canonized 1728; May 16.

Margaret of Hungary (1242-70): Contemplative; daughter of King Bela IV of Hungary; lived a life of self-imposed penances; canonized 1943; Jan. 18.

Margaret of Scotland (1050-1093): Queen of Scotland; noted for solicitude for the poor and promotion of justice; canonized 1250; Nov. 16.*

Maria Goretti (1890-1902): Italian virgin-martyr; a model of purity; canonized 1950; July 6.*

Mariana Paredes of Jesus (1618-45): South American recluse; Lily of Quito; canonized, 1950; May 28.

Marianne Cope, See under **Missionaries to the Americas** (p. 363).

Marie-Leonie Paradis, Bl. (1840-1912): Canadian Religious; founded Little Sisters of the Holy Family, 1880; beatified 1984; May 4.

Marie-Rose Durocher, Bl. (1811-49): Canadian Religious; foundress of Sisters of Holy Names of Jesus and Mary; beatified 1982; Oct. 6* (in U.S.).

Martha (1st cent.): Sister of Lazarus and Mary of Bethany; Gospel accounts record her concern for homely details; patron of cooks; July 29.*

Martin I (d. 655): Pope, 649-55; banished from Rome by emperor in 653 because of his condemnation of Monothelites; considered a martyr; Apr. 13.*

Martin of Tours (316-97): Bishop of Tours; opposed Arianism and Priscillianism; pioneer of Western monasticism, before St. Benedict; Nov. 11.*

Mary Domenica Mazzarello (1837-81): Italian foundress, with St. John Bosco, of the Daughters of Mary Help of Christians, 1872; canonized 1951; May 14.

Mary Josepha Rossello (1811-81): Italian-born foundress of the Daughters of Our Lady of Mercy; canonized 1949; Dec. 7.

Mary Magdalen Postel (1756-1846): French foundress of the Sisters of Christian Schools of Mercy, 1807; canonized 1925; July 16.

Mary Magdalene (1st cent.): Gospels record her as devoted follower of Christ to whom he appeared after the Resurrection; her identification with Mary of Bethany (sister of Martha and Lazarus) and the woman sinner (Lk 7:36-50) has been questioned; July 22.*

Mary Magdalene dei Pazzi (1566-1607): Italian Carmelite nun; recipient of mystical experiences; canonized 1669; May 25.*

Mary Michaeli Desmaisières (1809-65): Spanish-born foundress of the Institute of the Handmaids of the Blessed Sacrament, 1848; canonized 1934; Aug. 24.

Maximilian Kolbe (1894-1941): Polish Conventual Franciscan; prisoner at Auschwitz who heroically offered his life in place of a fellow prisoner; beatified 1971, canonized 1982; Aug. 14.*

Methodius: *See* **Cyril and Methodius.**

Miguel Febres Cordero (1854-1910): Ecuadorean Christian Brother; educator; canonized 1984; Feb. 9.

Miguel Pro, Bl. (1891-1927): Mexican Jesuit; joined Jesuits, 1911; forced to flee because of religious persecution; ordained in Belgium, 1925; returned to Mexico, 1926, to minister to people despite government prohibition; unjustly accused of assassination plot against president; arrested and executed; beatified 1988. Nov. 23* (U.S.).

Monica (332-87): Mother of St. Augustine; model of a patient mother; her feast is observed in the Roman calendar the day before her son's; Aug. 27.*

Nereus and Achilleus (d.c. 100): Early Christian martyrs; soldiers who, according to legend, were baptized by St. Peter; May 12.*

Nicholas of Flüe (1417-87): Swiss layman; at the age of 50, with the consent of his wife and 10 children, he retreated from the world to live as a hermit; called Brother Claus by the Swiss; canonized 1947; Mar. 21.

Nicholas of Myra (4th cent.): Bishop of Myra in Asia Minor; one of most popular saints in both East and West; most of the incidents of his life are based on legend; patron of Russia; Dec. 6.*

Nicholas of Tolentino (1245-1305): Italian hermit; famed preacher; canonized 1446; Sept. 10.

Nicholas Tavelic and Companions (Deodatus of Aquitaine, Peter of Narbonne, Stephen of Cuneo) (d. 1391): Franciscan missionaries; martyred by Muslims in the Holy Land: canonized 1970; Nov. 14.

Norbert (1080-1134): German bishop; founded Canons Regular of Premontre (Premonstratensians, Norbertines), 1120; promoted reform of the clergy, devotion to Blessed Sacrament; canonized 1582; June 6.*

Odilia (d. c. 720): Benedictine abbess; according to legend she was born blind, abandoned by her family and adopted by a convent of nuns where her sight was miraculously restored; patroness of blind; Dec. 13.

Oliver Plunket (1629-81): Irish martyr; theologian; archbishop of Armagh and primate of Ireland; beatified 1920; canonized, 1975; July 1.

Pancras (d. c. 304): Roman martyr; May 12.*

Paola Frassinetti (1809-82): Italian Religious; foundress, 1834, of Sisters of St. Dorothy; canonized 1984; June 11.

Paschal Baylon (1540-92): Spanish Franciscan lay brother; spent life as door-keeper in various Franciscan friaries; defended doctrine of Real Presence in Blessed Sacrament; canonized 1690; patron of all Eucharistic confraternities and congresses, 1897; May 17.

Patrick (389-461): Famous missionary of Ireland; began missionary work in Ireland about 432; organized the Church there and established it on a lasting foundation; patron of Ireland, with Sts. Bridget and Columba; Mar. 17.*

Paul Miki and Companions (d. 1597): Martyrs of Japan; Paul Miki, Jesuit, and 25 other priests and laymen were martyred at Nagasaki; canonized 1862, the first canonized martyrs of the Far East; Feb. 6.*

Paul of the Cross (1694-1775): Italian Religious; founder

of the Passionists; canonized 1867; Oct 19* (Oct. 20, U.S.*).

Paulinus of Nola (d. 451): Bishop of Nola (Spain); writer; June 22.*

Peregrine (1260-1347): Italian Servite; invoked against cancer (he was miraculously cured of cancer of the foot after a vision); canonized 1726; May 1.

Perpetua and Felicity (d. 203): Martyrs; Perpetua was a young married woman; Felicity was a slave girl; Mar. 7.*

Peter Chanel (1803-41): French Marist; missionary to Oceania, where he was martyred; canonized 1954; Apr. 28.*

Peter Fourier (1565-1640): French priest; co-founder with Alice LeClercq (Mother Teresa of Jesus) of the Augustinian Canonesses of Our Lady, 1598; canonized 1897; Dec. 9.

Peter Gonzalez (1190-1246): Spanish Dominican; worked among sailors; court chaplain and confessor of King St. Ferdinand of Castile; patron of sailors; Apr. 14.

Peter Julian Eymard (1811-68): French priest; founder of the Congregation of the Blessed Sacrament (men), 1856, and Servants of the Blessed Sacrament (women), 1864; dedicated to Eucharistic apostolate; canonized 1962; Aug. 2.*

Peter Nolasco (c. 1189-1258): Born in Langueduc area of present-day France; founded the Mercedarians (Order of Our Lady of Mercy), 1218, in Spain; canonized 1628; Jan. 31.

Peter of Alcantara (1499-1562): Spanish Franciscan; mystic; initiated Franciscan reform; confessor of St. Teresa of Jesus (Ávila); canonized 1669; Oct. 22 (in U.S.).

Philip Benizi (1233-85): Italian Servite; noted preacher, peacemaker; canonized 1671; Aug. 23.

Philip Neri (1515-95): Italian Religious; founded Congregation of the Oratory; considered a second apostle of Rome because of his mission activity there; canonized 1622; May 26.*

Philip of Jesus (1517-57): Mexican Franciscan; martyred at Nagasaki, Japan; canonized 1862; patron of Mexico City; Feb. 6.*

Pio, Padre (1887-1968): Pio da Pietrelcina (Francesco Forgione), and Italian Capuchin Franciscan, mystic and stigmatic; assisted souls from all over the world who came to him for counsel and guidance; canonized on June 16, 2002; Sept. 23.

Pius V (1504-72): Pope, 1566-72; enforced decrees of Council of Trent; organized expedition against Turks resulting in victory at Lepanto; canonized 1712; Apr. 30.*

Pius IX (d. 1878): Pope, 1846-78; the second longest pontiff in the history of the Church; defined the dogma of the Immaculate Conception and convoked Vatican Council I (1870-1871); Feb. 7.

Polycarp (2nd cent.): Bishop of Smyrna; ecclesiastical writer; martyr; Feb. 23.*

Pontian (d. c. 235): Pope, 230-35; exiled to Sardinia by the emperor; regarded as a martyr; Aug. 13 (with Hippolytus).*

Rafaela Maria Porras y Ayllon (1850-1925): Spanish Religious; founded the Handmaids of the Sacred Heart, 1877; canonized 1977; Jan. 6.

Raymond Nonnatus (d. 1240): Spanish Merced-arian; cardinal; devoted his life to ransoming captives from the Moors; Aug. 31.

Raymond of Peñafort (1175-1275): Spanish Dominican; confessor of Gregory IX; systematized and codified canon law, in effect until 1917; master general of Dominicans, 1238; canonized 1601; Jan. 7.*

Rita of Cascia (1381-1457): Widow; cloistered Augustinian Religious of Umbria; invoked in impossible and desperate cases; May 22.

Robert Southwell (1561-95): English Jesuit; poet; martyred at Tyburn; canonized 1970, one of the Forty English and Welsh Martyrs; Feb. 21.

Roch (1350-79): French layman; pilgrim; devoted life to care of plague-stricken; widely venerated; invoked against pestilence; Aug. 17.

Romuald (951-1027): Italian monk; founded Camaldolese Benedictines; June 19.*

Rose of Lima (1586-1617): Peruvian Dominican tertiary; first native-born saint of the New World; canonized 1671; Aug. 23.*

Scholastica (d. c. 559): Sister of St. Benedict; regarded as first nun of the Benedictine Order; Feb. 10.*

Sebastian (3rd cent.): Roman martyr; traditionally pictured as a handsome youth with arrows; martyred; patron of athletes, archers; Jan. 20.*

Seven Holy Founders of the Servants of Mary (Buonfiglio Monaldo, Alexis Falconieri, Benedict dell'Antello, Bartholomew Amidei, Ricovero Uguccione, Gerardino Sostegni, John Buonagiunta Monetti): Florentine youths who founded Servites, 1233, in obedience to a vision; canonized 1888; Feb. 17.*

Sharbel Makhlouf (1828-98): Lebanese Maronite monk-hermit; canonized 1977; Dec. 24.

Sixtus II and Companions (d. 258): Sixtus, pope 257-58, and four deacons, martyrs; Aug. 7.*

Stanislaus (1030-79): Polish bishop; martyr; canonized 1253; Apr. 11.*

Stephen (d. c. 33): First Christian martyr; chosen by the Apostles as the first of the seven deacons; stoned to death; Dec. 26.*

Stephen (975-1038): King; apostle of Hungary; welded Magyars into national unity; canonized 1083; Aug. 16.*

Sylvester I (d. 335): Pope 314-35; first ecumenical council held at Nicaea during his pontificate; Dec. 31.*

Tarcisius (d. 3rd cent.): Early martyr; according to tradition, was martyred while carrying the Blessed Sacrament to some Christians in prison; patron of first communicants; Aug. 15.

Teresa Margaret Redi (1747-70): Italian Carmelite; lived life of prayer and austere penance; canonized 1934; Mar. 11.

Teresa of Jesus Jornet Ibars (1843-97): Spanish Religious; founded the Little Sisters of the Abandoned Aged, 1873; canonized 1974; Aug. 26.

Teresa, Mother (1910-97): Sister, foundress of the Missionaries of Charity, and Nobel Prize winner; called Mother Teresa of Calcutta; beatified by Pope John Paul II on Oct. 19, 2003; Sept. 5.

Theodore Guérin: *See* under **Missionaries to the Americas** (p. 363).

Thérèse Couderc (1805-85): French Religious; foundress of the Religious of Our Lady of the Retreat in the Cenacle, 1827; canonized 1970; Sept. 26.

Thomas Becket (1118-70): English martyr; archbishop of Canterbury; chancellor under Henry II; murdered for upholding rights of the Church; canonized 1173; Dec. 29.*

Thomas More (1478-1535): English martyr; statesman, chancellor under Henry VIII; author of Utopia; opposed Henry's divorce, refused to renounce authority of the papacy; beheaded; canonized 1935; Pope John Paul II declared him patron of politicians on Oct. 31, 2000; June 22 (with St. John Fisher).*

Timothy (d. c. 97): Bishop of Ephesus; disciple and companion of St. Paul; martyr; Jan. 26.*

Titus (d. c. 96): Bishop; companion of St. Paul; recipient of one of Paul's epistles; Jan. 26.*

Titus Brandsma, Bl. (1881-1942): Dutch Carmelite priest; professor, scholar, journalist; denounced Nazi persecution of Jews; arrested by Nazis, Jan. 19, 1942; executed by lethal injection at Dachau, July 26, 1942; beatified 1985; July 26.

Valentine (d. 269): Priest, physician; martyred at Rome; legendary patron of lovers; Feb. 14.

Vicenta Maria Lopez y Vicuna (1847-96): Spanish foundress of the Daughters of Mary Immaculate for domestic service; canonized 1975; Dec. 26.

Vincent (d. 304): Spanish deacon; martyr; Jan. 22.*

Vincent de Paul (1581?-1660): French priest; founder of Congregation of the Mission (Vincentians, Lazarists) and co-founder of Sisters of Charity; declared patron of all charitable organizations and works by Leo XIII; canonized 1737; Sept. 27.*

Vincent Ferrer (1350-1418): Spanish Dominican; famed preacher; Apr. 5.*

Vincent Pallotti (1795-1850): Italian priest; founded Society of the Catholic Apostolate (Pallottines), 1835; Jan. 22.

Vincent Strambi (1745-1824): Italian Passionist; bishop; reformer; canonized 1950; Sept. 25.

Vitus (d.c. 300): Martyr; died in Lucania, southern Italy; regarded as protector of epileptics and those suffering from St. Vitus Dance (chorea); June 15.

Walburga (d. 779): English-born Benedictine Religious; belonged to group of nuns who established convents in Germany at the invitation of St. Boniface; abbess of Heidenheim; Feb. 25.

Wenceslaus (d. 935): Duke of Bohemia; martyr; patron of Bohemia; Sept. 28.*

Zita (1218-78): Italian maid; noted for charity to poor; patron of domestics; Apr. 27.

SAINTS — PATRONS AND INTERCESSORS

A patron is a saint who is venerated as a special intercessor before God. Most patrons have been so designated as the result of popular devotion and long-standing custom. In many cases, the fact of existing patronal devotion is clear despite historical obscurity regarding its origin. The Church has made official designation of relatively few patrons; in such cases, the dates of designation are given in parentheses in the list below. The theological background of the patronage of saints includes the dogmas of the Mystical Body of Christ and the Communion of Saints. Listed are patron saints of occupations and professions, and saints whose intercession is sought for special needs.

Academics: Thomas Aquinas.
Accomodations: Gertrude of Nivelles.
Accountants: Matthew.
Actors: Genesius.
Adopted children: Clotilde; Thomas More.
Advertisers: Bernardine of Siena (May 20, 1960).
Alcoholics: John of God; Monica.
Alpinists: Bernard of Montjoux (or Menthon) (Aug. 20, 1923).
Altar servers: John Berchmans.
Anesthetists: René Goupil.

Animals: Francis of Assisi.
Archaeologists: Damasus.
Archers: Sebastian.
Architects: Thomas, Apostle.
Art: Catherine of Bologna.
Artists: Luke, Catherine of Bologna, Bl. Angelico (Feb. 21, 1984).
Astronauts: Joseph Cupertino.
Astronomers: Dominic.
Athletes: Sebastian.
Authors: Francis de Sales.
Aviators: Our Lady of Loreto (1920), Thérèse of Lisieux, Joseph of Cupertino.
Bakers: Elizabeth of Hungary, Nicholas.
Bankers: Matthew.
Barbers: Cosmas and Damian, Louis.
Barren women: Anthony of Padua, Felicity.
Basket-makers: Anthony, Abbot.
Bees: Ambrose.
Birth: Margaret.
Beggars: Martin of Tours.
Blacksmiths: Dunstan.
Blind: Odilia, Raphael.
Blood banks: Januarius.
Bodily ills: Our Lady of Lourdes.
Bookbinders: Peter Celestine.
Bookkeepers: Matthew.
Booksellers: John of God.
Boy Scouts: George.
Brewers: Augustine of Hippo, Luke, Nicholas of Myra.
Bricklayers: Stephen.
Brides: Nicholas of Myra.
Bridges: John of Nepomucene.
Broadcasters: Gabriel.
Brushmakers: Anthony, Abbot.
Builders: Vincent Ferrer.
Bus drivers: Christopher.
Butchers: Anthony (Abbot), Luke.
Butlers: Adelelm.
Cabdrivers: Fiacre.
Cabinetmakers: Anne.
Cancer patients: Peregrine.
Canonists: Raymond of Peñafort.
Carpenters: Joseph.
Catechists: Viator, Charles Borromeo, Robert Bellarmine.
Catholic Action: Francis of Assisi (1916).
Catholic Press: Francis de Sales.
Chandlers: Ambrose, Bernard of Clairvaux.
Chaplains: John of Capistrano.
Charitable societies: Vincent de Paul (May 12, 1885).
Chastity: Thomas Aquinas.
Childbirth: Raymond Nonnatus; Gerard Majella.
Children: Nicholas of Myra.
Children of Mary: Agnes, Maria Goretti.
Choirboys: Dominic Savio (June 8, 1956), Holy Innocents.
Church: Joseph (Dec. 8, 1870).
Circus people: Julian the Hospitaller.
Clerics: Gabriel of the Sorrowful Mother.
Colleges: Thomas Aquinas.
Comedians: Vitus.
Communications personnel: Bernardine.
Confessors: Alphonsus Liguori (Apr. 26, 1950), John Nepomucene.
Converts: Helena; Vladimir.
Convulsive children: Scholastica.

Cooks: Lawrence, Martha.
Coopers: Nicholas of Myra.
Coppersmiths: Maurus.
Dairy workers: Brigid.
Dancers: Vitus.
Deaf: Francis de Sales.
Dentists: Apollonia.
Desperate situations: Gregory of Neocaesarea, Jude Thaddeus, Rita of Cascia.
Dietitians (in hospitals): Martha.
Diplomats: Gabriel.
Divorce: Helena.
Drug addiction: Maximilian Kolbe.
Dyers: Maurice, Lydia.
Dying: Joseph.
Ecologists: Francis of Assisi (Nov. 29, 1979).
Ecumenists: Cyril and Methodius.
Editors: John Bosco.
Emigrants: Frances Xavier Cabrini (Sept. 8, 1950).
Endurance: Pantaleon.
Engineers: Ferdinand III.
Epilepsy, Motor Diseases: Vitus, Willibrord.
Eucharistic congresses and societies: Paschal Baylon (Nov. 28, 1897).
Expectant mothers: Raymond Nonnatus, Gerard Majella.
Eye diseases: Lucy.
Falsely accused: Raymond Nonnatus.
Farmers: George, Isidore.
Farriers: John the Baptist.
Firemen: Florian.
Fire prevention: Catherine of Siena.
First communicants: Tarcisius.
Fishermen: Andrew.
Florists: Thérèse of Lisieux.
Forest workers: John Gualbert.
Foundlings: Holy Innocents.
Friendship: John the Divine.
Fullers: Anastasius the Fuller, James the Less.
Funeral directors: Joseph of Arimathea, Dismas.
Gardeners: Adelard, Tryphon, Fiacre, Phocas.
Glassworkers: Luke.
Goldsmiths: Dunstan, Anastasius.
Gravediggers: Anthony, Abbot.
Greetings: Valentine.
Grocers: Michael.
Grooms: King Louis IX of France.
Hairdressers: Martin de Porres.
Happy meetings: Raphael.
Hatters: Severus of Ravenna, James the Less.
Headache sufferers: Teresa of Jesus (Ávila).
Heart patients: John of God.
Homeless: Margaret of Cortona; Benedict Joseph Labré.
Horses: Giles; Hippolytus.
Housekeepers: Zita.
Hospital administrators: Basil the Great, Frances X. Cabrini.
Hospitals: Camillus de Lellis and John of God (June 22, 1886), Jude Thaddeus.
Housewives: Anne.
Hunters: Hubert, Eustachius.
Infantrymen: Maurice.
Innkeepers: Amand, Martha, Julian the Hospitaller.
Innocence: Hallvard.
Invalids: Roch.
Janitors: Theobald.
Jewelers: Eligius, Dunstan.

Journalists: Francis de Sales (Apr. 26, 1923).
Jurists: John Capistran.
Laborers: Isidore, James, John Bosco.
Lawyers: Ivo (Yves Helory), Genesius, Thomas More.
Learning: Ambrose.
Librarians: Jerome.
Lighthouse keepers: Venerius (Mar. 10, 1961).
Linguists: Gottschalk.
Locksmiths: Dunstan.
Lost souls: Nicholas of Tolentino.
Lovers: Raphael; Valentine.
Lunatics: Christina.
Maids: Zita.
Marble workers: Clement I.
Mariners: Michael, Nicholas of Tolentino.
Medical record librarians: Raymond of Peñafort.
Medical social workers: John Regis.
Medical technicians: Albert the Great.
Mentally ill: Dymphna.
Merchants: Francis of Assisi, Nicholas of Myra.
Messengers: Gabriel.
Metal workers: Eligius.
Military chaplains: John Capistran (Feb. 10, 1984).
Millers: Arnulph, Victor.
Missions, foreign: Francis Xavier (Mar. 25, 1904), Thérèse of Lisieux (Dec. 14, 1927).
Missions, black: Peter Claver (1896, Leo XIII), Benedict the Black.
Missions, parish: Leonard of Port Maurice (Mar. 17, 1923).
Monks: Benedict of Nursia.
Mothers: Monica.
Motorcyclists: Our Lady of Grace.
Motorists: Christopher, Frances of Rome.
Mountaineers: Bernard of Montjoux (or Menthon).
Musicians: Gregory the Great, Cecilia, Dunstan.
Mystics: John of the Cross.
Notaries: Luke, Mark.
Nuns: Bridget.
Nurses: Camillus de Lellis and John of God (1930, Pius XI), Agatha, Raphael.
Nursing and nursing service: Elizabeth of Hungary, Catherine of Siena.
Orators: John Chrysostom (July 8, 1908).
Organ builders: Cecilia.
Orphans: Jerome Emiliani.
Painters: Luke.
Paratroopers: Michael.
Pawnbrokers: Nicholas.
Plumbers: Vincent Ferrer.
Pharmacists: Cosmas and Damian, James the Greater.
Pharmacists (in hospitals): Gemma Galgani.
Philosophers: Justin.
Physicians: Pantaleon, Cosmas and Damian, Luke, Raphael.
Pilgrims: James the Greater.
Plasterers: Bartholomew.
Poets: David, Cecilia.
Politicians: Thomas More
Poison sufferers: Benedict.
Policemen: Michael.
Poor: Lawrence, Anthony of Padua.
Poor souls: Nicholas of Tolentino.
Popes: Gregory I the Great.
Porters: Christopher.
Possessed: Bruno, Denis.
Postal employees: Gabriel.

Priests: Jean-Baptiste Vianney (Apr. 23, 1929).
Printers: John of God, Augustine of Hippo, Genesius.
Prisoners: Dismas, Joseph Cafasso.
Protector of crops: Ansovinus.
Public relations: Bernardine of Siena (May 20, 1960).
Public relations (of hospitals): Paul, Apostle.
Publishers: John the Divine.
Race relations: Martin de Porres.
Radiologists: Michael (Jan. 15, 1941).
Radio workers: Gabriel.
Refugees: Alban.
Retreats: Ignatius Loyola (July 25, 1922).
Rheumatism: James the Greater.
Saddlers: Crispin and Crispinian.
Sailors: Cuthbert, Brendan, Eulalia, Christopher, Peter Gonzalez, Erasmus, Nicholas.
Scholars: Bede the Venerable; Brigid.
Schools, Catholic: Thomas Aquinas (Aug. 4, 1880), Joseph Calasanz (Aug. 13, 1948).
Scientists: Albert (Aug. 13, 1948).
Sculptors: Four Crowned Martyrs.
Seamen: Francis of Paola.
Searchers of lost articles: Anthony of Padua.
Secretaries: Genesius.
Secular Franciscans: Louis of France, Elizabeth of Hungary.
Seminarians: Charles Borromeo.
Servants: Martha, Zita.
Shepherds: Drogo.
Shoemakers: Crispin and Crispinian.
Sick: Michael, John of God and Camillus de Lellis (June 22, 1886).
Silversmiths: Andronicus.
Singers: Gregory, Cecilia.
Single mothers: Margaret of Cortona.
Single women: Catherine of Alexandria.
Skaters: Lidwina.
Skiers: Bernard of Montjoux (or Menthon).
Social workers: Louise de Marillac (Feb. 12, 1960).
Soldiers: Hadrian, George, Ignatius, Sebastian, Martin of Tours, Joan of Arc.
Speleologists: Benedict.
Stamp collectors: Gabriel.
Stenographers: Genesius, Cassian.
Stonecutters: Clement.
Stonemasons: Stephen.
Stress: Walter of Portnoise.
Students: Thomas Aquinas.
Surgeons: Cosmas and Damian, Luke.
Swimmers: Adjutor.
Swordsmiths: Maurice.
Tailors: Homobonus.
Tanners: Crispin and Crispinian, Simon.
Tax collectors: Matthew.
Teachers: Gregory the Great, John Baptist de la Salle (May 15, 1950).
Telecommunications workers: Gabriel (Jan. 12, 1951).
Television: Clare of Assisi (Feb. 14, 1958).
Television workers: Gabriel.
Thieves: Dismas.
Theologians: Augustine, Alphonsus Liguori.
Throat ailments: Blase.
Torture victims: Alban; Eustachius; Regina; Vincent; Victor of Marseilles.
Toymakers: Claude.
Travelers: Anthony of Padua, Nicholas of Myra,

Christopher, Raphael.
Travel hostesses: Bona (Mar. 2, 1962).
Truck drivers: Christopher.
Universities: Blessed Contardo Ferrini.
Veterinarians: Blaise.
Vocations: Alphonsus.
Whales: Brendan the Voyager.
Watchmen: Peter of Alcantara.
Weavers: Paul the Hermit, Anastasius the Fuller, Anastasia.
Wine merchants: Amand.
Wineries: Morand; Vincent.
Women in labor: Anne.
Workingmen: Joseph.
Writers: Francis de Sales (Apr. 26, 1923), Lucy.
Yachtsmen: Adjutor.
Young girls: Agnes.
Youth: Aloysius Gonzaga (1729, Benedict XIII; 1926, Pius XI), John Berchmans, Gabriel of the Sorrowful Mother.

Patron Saints of Places

Albania: Our Lady of Good Counsel.
Alsace: Odilia.
Americas: Our Lady of Guadalupe, Rose of Lima.
Angola: Immaculate Heart of Mary (Nov. 21, 1984).
Argentina: Our Lady of Lujan.
Armenia: Gregory Illuminator.
Asia Minor: John, Evangelist.
Australia: Our Lady Help of Christians.
Belgium: Joseph.
Bohemia: Wenceslaus, Ludmilla.
Bolivia: Our Lady of Copacabana, *"Virgen de la Candelaria."*
Borneo: Francis Xavier.
Brazil: Nossa Señora de Aparecida, Immaculate Conception, Peter of Alcantara.
Canada: Joseph, Anne.
Chile: James the Greater, Our Lady of Mt. Carmel.
China: Joseph.
Colombia: Peter Claver, Louis Bertran.
Corsica: Immaculate Conception.
Cuba: Our Lady of Charity.
Czechoslovakia: Wenceslaus, John Nepomucene, Procopius.
Denmark: Ansgar, Canute.
Dominican Republic: Our Lady of High Grace, Dominic.
East Indies: Thomas, Apostle.
Ecuador: Sacred Heart.
El Salvador: Our Lady of Peace (Oct. 10, 1966).
England: George.
Equatorial Guinea: Immaculate Conception (May 25, 1986).
Europe: Benedict (1964), Cyril and Methodius, co-patrons (Dec. 31, 1980); Sts. Catherine of Siena, Bridget of Sweden, and Edith Stein, co-patronesses (Oct. 1, 1999).
Finland: Henry.
France: Our Lady of the Assumption, Joan of Arc, Thérèse (May 3, 1944).
Germany: Boniface, Michael.
Gibraltar: Blessed Virgin Mary, "Our Lady of Europe" (May 31, 1979).
Greece: Nicholas, Andrew.
Holland: Willibrord.
Hungary: Blessed Virgin, "Great Lady of Hungary," Stephen, King.
Iceland: Thorlac (Jan. 14, 1984).
India: Our Lady of Assumption.

Ireland: Patrick, Brigid and Columba.
Italy: Francis of Assisi, Catherine of Siena.
Japan: Peter Baptist.
Korea: Joseph and Mary, Mother of the Church.
Lesotho: Immaculate Heart of Mary.
Lithuania: Casimir, Cunegunda.
Luxembourg: Willibrord.
Malta: Paul, Our Lady of the Assumption.
Mexico: Our Lady of Guadalupe.
Monaco: Devota.
Moravia: Cyril and Methodius.
New Zealand: Our Lady Help of Christians.
Norway: Olaf.
Papua New Guinea (including northern Solomon Islands): Michael the Archangel (May 31, 1979).
Paraguay: Our Lady of Assumption (July 13, 1951).
Peru: Joseph (Mar. 19, 1957).
Philippines: Sacred Heart of Mary.
Poland: Casimir, Cunegunda, Stanislaus of Krakow, Our Lady of Czestochowa.
Portugal: Immaculate Conception, Francis Borgia, Anthony of Padua, Vincent of Saragossa, George.
Russia: Andrew, Nicholas of Myra, Thérèse of Lisieux.
Scandinavia: Ansgar.
Scotland: Andrew, Columba.
Silesia: Hedwig.
Slovakia: Our Lady of Sorrows.
South Africa: Our Lady of Assumption (Mar. 15, 1952).
South America: Rose of Lima.
Solomon Islands: Blessed Virgin Mary, Most Holy Name of Mary (Sept. 4, 1991).
Spain: James the Greater, Teresa.
Sri Lanka (Ceylon): Lawrence.
Sweden: Bridget, Eric.
Tanzania: Immaculate Conception (Dec. 8, 1964).
United States: Immaculate Conception (1846).
Uruguay: Blessed Virgin Mary, "La Virgen de los Treinte y Tres" (Nov. 21, 1963).
Venezuela: Our Lady of Coromoto.
Wales: David.
West Indies: Gertrude.

Emblems, Portrayals of Saints

Agatha: Tongs, veil.
Agnes: Lamb.
Ambrose: Bees, dove, ox, pen.
Andrew: Transverse cross.
Anne, Mother of the Blessed Virgin: Door.
Anthony of Padua: Infant Jesus, bread, book, lily.
Augustine of Hippo: Dove, child, shell, pen.
Bartholomew: Knife, flayed and holding his skin.
Benedict: Broken cup, raven, bell, crosier, bush.
Bernard of Clairvaux: Pen, bees, instruments of the Passion.
Bernardine of Siena: Tablet or sun inscribed with IHS.
Blase: Wax, taper, iron comb.
Bonaventure: Communion, ciborium, cardinal's hat.
Boniface: Oak, ax, book, fox, scourge, fountain, raven, sword.
Bridget of Sweden: Book, pilgrim's staff.
Bridget of Kildare: Cross, flame over her head, candle.
Catherine of Ricci: Ring, crown, crucifix.
Catherine of Siena: Stigmata, cross, ring, lily.
Cecilia: Organ.
Charles Borromeo: Communion, coat of arms with word "Humilitas."
Christopher: Giant, torrent, tree, Child Jesus on

his shoulders.
Clare of Assisi: Monstrance.
Cosmas and Damian: A phial, box of ointment.
Cyril of Alexandria: Blessed Virgin holding the Child Jesus, pen.
Cyril of Jerusalem: Purse, book.
Dominic: Rosary, star.
Edmund the Martyr: Arrow, sword.
Elizabeth of Hungary: Alms, flowers, bread, the poor, a pitcher.
Francis of Assisi: Wolf, birds, fish, skull, the Stigmata.
Francis Xavier: Crucifix, bell, vessel.
Genevieve: Bread, keys, herd, candle.
George: Dragon.
Gertrude: Crown, taper, lily.
Gervase and Protase: Scourge, club, sword.
Gregory I (the Great): Tiara, crosier, dove.
Helena: Cross.
Ignatius of Loyola: Communion, chasuble, book, apparition of Our Lord.
Isidore: Bees, pen.
James the Greater: Pilgrim's staff, shell, key, sword.
James the Less: Square rule, halberd, club.
Jerome: Lion.
John Berchmans: Rule of St. Ignatius, cross, rosary.
John Chrysostom: Bees, dove, pen.
John of God: Alms, a heart, crown of thorns.
John the Baptist: Lamb, head on platter, skin of an animal.
John the Evangelist: Eagle, chalice, kettle, armor.
Josaphat Kuncevyc: Chalice, crown, winged deacon.
Joseph, Spouse of the Blessed Virgin: Infant Jesus, lily, rod, plane, carpenter's square.
Jude: Sword, square rule, club.
Justin Martyr: Ax, sword.
Lawrence: Cross, book of the Gospels, gridiron.
Leander of Seville: Pen.
Liberius: Pebbles, peacock.
Longinus: In arms at foot of the cross.
Louis IX of France: Crown of thorns, nails.
Lucy: Cord, eyes on a dish.
Luke: Ox, book, brush, palette.
Mark: Lion, book.
Martha: Holy water sprinkler, dragon.
Mary Magdalene: Alabaster box of ointment.
Matilda: Purse, alms.
Matthew: Winged man, purse, lance.
Matthias: Lance.
Maurus: Scales, spade, crutch.
Meinrad: Two ravens.
Michael: Scales, banner, sword, dragon.
Monica: Girdle, tears.
Nicholas: Three purses or balls, anchor or boat, child.
Patrick: Cross, harp, serpent, baptismal font, demons, shamrock.
Paul: Sword, book or scroll.
Peter: Keys, boat, cock.
Philip, Apostle: Column.
Philip Neri: Altar, chasuble, vial.
Rita of Cascia: Rose, crucifix, thorn.
Roch: Angel, dog, bread.
Rose of Lima: Crown of thorns, anchor, city.
Sebastian: Arrows, crown.
Simon Stock: Scapular.
Teresa of Jesus (Ávila): Heart, arrow, book.
Thérèse of Lisieux: Roses entwining a crucifix.
Thomas, Apostle: Lance, ax.

Thomas Aquinas: Chalice, monstrance, dove, ox, person trampled under foot.
Vincent de Paul: Children.
Vincent Ferrer: Pulpit, cardinal's hat, trumpet, captives.

CANONIZATIONS AND BEATIFICATIONS 2012-13

Pope Benedict XVI beatified and canonized the following individuals from Sept. 2012 to Mar. 2013, and Pope Francis from Mar. 13, 2013. Included are the dates of the beatifications, as well as relevant biographical information.

BEATIFICATIONS

2012

Louis Brisson (1817-1908) French priest and founder of the Oblate Sisters of St. Francis de Sales and the Oblates of St. Francis de Sale. Ordained for the diocese of Troyes in 1840, he served as chaplain to the Sisters of the Visitation and was encouraged by the superior there, Mother Mary de Sales Chappuis, to establish the Oblate Sisters of St. Francis de Sales and the Oblates of St. Francis de Sales. He founded the Oblate Sisters with St. Leonie de Sales Aviat. He was also the creator of an astronomic clock that was so accurate it was later studied by NASA. He was beatified on Sept. 22, 2012, at Troyes, France.

Gabriele Maria Allegra (1907-1976) Italian Franciscan priest and biblical scholar, best known for his translation of the Catholic Bible into Chinese. Born in Catania, Italy, he entered the Franciscans in 1918, studied in Rome, and was ordained in 1930. He spent 40 years translating the Bible in the Chinese language. He was beatified on Sept. 29, 2012, at Acireale, Sicily.

Bedrich Bachstein and 13 Companions (d. 1611) Franciscan Martyrs who were slain in Prague by a Protestant mob during the terrible religious strife in Bohemia at the Church of Our Lady of the Snows and were dumped in a nearby field. They were given a proper burial four days later. They were beatified on Oct. 13, 2012, in Prague at the Cathedral of St. Vitus.

Maria Luisa Prosperi (1799-1847) Italian Benedictine nun and mystic. A native of Foligno, Italy, she was noted in her youth for her love of the Eucharist and was blessed with mystical experiences. She also served as abbess of her monastery. She was beatified on Nov. 10 at the Cathedral of Santa Maria Assunta, in Spoleto, Perugia, Italy.

María Crescencia Pérez (1897-1932) Argentine religious of the Daughters of Our Lady of the Garden. Born to an immigrant family from Spain in Buenos Aires, Argentina, she entered the Daughters in 1915 and took her vows in 1918. She worked in a hospital caring for sick children with tuberculosis; she declined in health and worked in a hospital in Vallenar, Chile, where she died. Her body was found incorrupt in 1966. She was beatified on Nov. 17 at Pergamino, Buenos Aires, Argentina.

Maria Troncatti (1883-1969) Italian missionary sister of the Daughters of Mary, Help of Christians (the Salesian Sisters of St. John Bosco). Born in Corteno Golgi, Brescia, Italy, spent her life caring for the native Shuar people in the Amazon and for abandoned children. She was killed in a plane crash at the age of 86 in Sucúa, Morona-Santiago, Ecuador. She was beatified on Nov. 24 at Morona Santiago, Ecuador.

Devasahayam (Lazarus) Pillai (1712-52) Indian convert from Hinduism and a martyr. Born to a high-caste Hindu family, he was married and converted to the Catholic faith in 1745 in Kottar, India, with his wife and family. He took the name Devasahayam, the Tamil equivalent of the name Lazarus. Hated for his conversion, he was seized in 1749 for being Catholic and endured three years of torture and humiliation. He died a martyr. He was beatified on Dec. 2, 2012 at Nagercoil, Kottar, India.

2013

Cristóbal of Saint Catherine Fernández de Valladolid (1638-90) Spanish member of the Third Order Regular of St. Francis and founder of the Congregation of the Franciscan Hospitallers of Jesus the Nazarene. A native of Merida, Spain, he was ordained a priest in 1663. He entered the Franciscans in 1671 and founded in 1673 the Hospital of Our Father Jesus the Nazarene and then the Hospitaller Brothers of Jesus of Nazareth. He was beatified on Apr. 7, 2013 at the Cathedral of Córdoba, Spain.

Luca Passi (1789-1866) Italian priest and the founder of the Pious Society of St. Dorothy. A member of a noble family in Bergamo, he was ordained a priest in 1813. In 1815, he established the Pious Societies of St. Raphael and St. Dorothy to promote the Christian education of children and youth. The male society (of St. Raphael) was checked in its growth by the political upheaval in Italy, but the Society of St. Dorothy soon spread to various Italian cities. He was beatified on Apr. 13, 2013.

Nicolò Rusca (1563-1618) Italian priest and martyr. A native of Bedano, Italy, he was born to a noble family of Milan and was ordained a priest in 1587 after studies at the Collegium Helveticum in Milan under the direction for a time of St. Charles Borromeo. Named archpriest in Sondrio, he proved a gifted preacher and was active in reviving the faith in the face of the Protestant Reformation. This brought him into the conflict of the time in Switzerland, and he was arrested in 1618 and imprisoned in Thusis. He was tortured to death and is honored as a martyr. He was beatified on Apr. 21, 2013 at Piazza Garibaldi, Sondrio, Italy.

Francisca de Paula de Jesus (1810-95) Called Nhá Chica, "Aunt Francie," a Brazilian layperson. A native of São João del-Rei, Brazil, she gave her life into the hands of the Blessed Mother and dedicated herself to the care of the poor and to promoting the construction of a church dedicated Mary, the Our Lady of Conception Sanctuary. She remained single and celibate and lived most of her life in Baependi, Brazil. She was beatified on May 4, 2013, in Baependi.

Luigi Novarese (1914-84) Italian priest and the founder of a number of Catholic associations for the faithful. Born at Casale Monferrato, Italy, into a peasant family, he suffered intensely in his youth from tuberculosis of the bone until the age of 17; his cure was attributed in part to prayers to Our Lady Help of Christians. Ordained in 1938, he worked for many years in the Vatican Secretary of State, Roman Rota, and Italian Bishops' Conference. During those years, he founded the Center Volunteers of Suffering, Silent Operari of the Cross, League Mariana Priests and Brothers of the sick. He was beatified on May 11, 2013, in the Basilica of St. Paul Outside-the-Walls, Rome, Italy.

Giuseppe Puglisi (1937-93) Called "Pino," Italian priest, opponent of the Mafia, and martyr. Born in Brancaccio, a working-class neighborhood in Palermo, Sicily, he was ordained a priest in 1960. Returning to Brancaccio in 1990 as pastor of San Gaetano's Parish, he emerged as an outspoken enemy of the Mafia and refused to accept Mafia money or to be silenced by their threats. He was murdered on Sept. 15, 1993, in front of his parish church. His murder shocked Italy, and in 1998 several Mafia bosses were sentenced to life in prison for the crime. His story was recounted in the book, *Don Puglisi: Vita del prete palermitano ucciso dalla mafia* (2001) and the film, *In the Sunlight* (2005). He was beatified on May 25, 2013 in Palermo, Italy.

Zofia Czeska-Maciejowska (1584-1650) Polish nun and founder of the Sisters of the Presentation of the Blessed Virgin Mary (the Presentation). Born in Krakow, Poland, she gave her life to the poor and orphaned and established the Virgin's House of the Presentation of the Blessed Virgin Mary in Krakow. A religious congregation was approved in 1660. Her congregation continues today to run kindergartens, orphanages, and houses for children with special needs. She was beatified on June 9, 2013 in Krakow, Poland.

Margaret Lucja Szewczyk (1828-1905) Polish nun and foundress of the Congregation of the Daughters of the Sorrowful Mother of God-Seraphic Sisters. Born into a family in Wolyn (modern Ukraine), she entered the Third Order of St. Francis of Assisi in 1848, but owing to the occupation of Poland by foreign powers, she was prevented from entering a formal religious congregation. In 1870 she went on a pilgrimage to the Holy Land and devoted the rest of her life to the poor, elderly, and sick. In 1881, she founded the Daughters and served as Mother Malgorzata until her death. She was beatified on June 9, 2013, in Krakow, Poland.

Odoardo Focherini (1907-44) Italian layman best known for his efforts to save Jews in Italy from the Holocaust. Born in Carpi, Italy, he married in 1930, and the happy couple had seven children. He worked for Catholic Action and then served as managing director of the Catholic newspaper *L'Avvenire d' Italia*. From 1942, he started his labors on behalf of Jews, including working to save them from the gas chambers and smuggle them into Switzerland. Arrested by the Nazis in March 1944, he was deported to Germany and the concentration camps of Flossenburg and Hersbrueck and died in prison. He was beatified on June 15, 2013, at Carpi, Modena, Italy.

Vladimir Ghika (1873-1954) Romanian priest, diplomat, and martyr. Born in Constantinople, (modern Istanbul, Turkey), he was raised as a Romanian Orthodox as a member of the princely Ghica Family of Romania and the grandson of the last ruler of Moldavia, Prince Gregory V Ghika (r.1849-56). After studies in Paris and then in Rome at the Pontifical University of Thomas Aquinas, he converted to Catholicism in 1902, an act that shocked his family, and was ordained a priest in 1923 in Paris. He returned to Romania in 1939 at the start of World War II to care for the sick and the poor. He remained there after the Communist takeover in 1945 and was arrested in Nov. 1952 on charges of treason. He died from torture in Bucharest. He was beatified on Aug. 31, 2013, in Bucharest, Romania.

Antonio Franco (1585-1626) Italian archbishop and Prelate Ordinary of the Prelature of Santa Lucia del Mela. Born in Naples, Italy, to a noble family, he earned Doctorates in Civil and Canon Law at the age of 17. Ordained a priest in 1610, he was named royal chaplain to the court of King Philip III of Spain in 1611. Five years later, he was appointed Chaplain of the Kingdom of Sicily, with the post of Prelate Ordinary of the Prelature of Santa Lucia del Mela with the approval by Pope Paul V. He was beatified on Sept. 2, 2013, in Messina, Italy.

Maria Bolognesi (1924-80) Italian layperson and mystic who endured severe spiritual torment. Born in Bosaro,

Rovigo, Italy, to a poor family, she received a vision in her youth of Christ giving her three rings and five rubies; the rubies represented the Five Wounds of Our Lord. She suffered from demonic possession but was freed in 1940 and beheld in 1942 a vision confirming the rings from Christ. Her remaining life was marked by severe physical torments, including pneumonia, anemia, rheumatism, heart disease, and stroke. She was beatified on Sept. 7, 2013, in Rovigo, Italy.

The following were scheduled for beatification:

José Gabriel del Rosario Brochero, Sept. 14, at Córdoba, Argentina.

Tommaso Olera, Sept. 21, at Bergamo, Italy.

Miroslav Buleši Sept. 28, at Istria, Croatia.

Rolando Rivi, Oct. 5, at Modena, Italy.

Martyrs of the Religious Persecution during the Spanish Civil War, Oct. 13, at Tarragona, Spain.

Sándor Istvan, Oct. 19, at Budapest, Hungary.

Maria Theresia Bonzel, Nov. 10, at Paderborn, Germany.

CANONIZATIONS

2012

Marianne Cope (1838-1918) A member of the Franciscan Sisters of Syracuse who served on Molokai, Hawaii, for 30 years caring for victims of leprosy. Born Maria Anna Barbara Koob, in Heppenheim, in what was then the Grand Duchy of Hesse (modern Germany), she came at the age of one with her family to Utica, New York. She entered the Sisters of the Third Order Regular of St. Francis based in Syracuse, New York, in 1862 and served as a teacher and later a principal at a school for immigrant children. She was also instrumental in starting the first two Catholic hospitals in central New York. She arrived in Hawaii in 1883 with six sisters and devoted the rest of her life to the needs of the people of Hawaii, especially lepers. She was canonized by Pope Benedict XVI in Rome, on Oct. 21, 2013.

Kateri Tekakwitha (1656-80) The "Lily of the Mohawks," a Mohawk convert who was baptized by the famed Jesuit missionary, Jacques de Lambertville. She was the first Native American to be beatified and the first to be canonized. Born in what became Auriesville, New York, she endured humiliation and abuse for her conversion and was forced to move to a Catholic colony near Montreal. She was a model for the faith, and at her death she was already called a saint. A patron saint for Native Americans, she was beatified in 1980 and canonized on Oct. 21, 2012 in a ceremony presided by Pope Benedict XVI.

Giovanni Battista Piamarta (d. 1913): An Italian priest and founder of the Congregation of the Holy Family of Nazareth for men and the Humble Servants of the Lord for women. Born to a poor family in Brescia, Italy, he was ordained a priest in 1841 and established with Father Pietro Capretti the Workman's Institute (*Istituto Artigianelli*), to assist young people in the cities, and with Fr. Giovanni Bonsignori the Agricultural Colony of Remedello. In 1900, he began the Congregation of the Holy Family of Nazareth and the Humble Servants of the Lord. He was canonized by Pope Benedict XVI in Rome, on Oct. 21, 2013.

Jacques Berthieu (1838-96) A French Jesuit priest who died as a martyr in Madagascar. Born in France, he entered the Jesuits in 1873 and two years later embarked on the Jesuit mission to Madagascar. He was brutally martyred with clubs after refusing to abjure the Faith. His body was thrown into a river that was soon reportedly the source of miracles. He beautified on Oct. 16, 1965 by Pope Paul VI and canonized by Pope Benedict XVI on Oct. 21, 2012 in Rome.

Carmen Salles y Barangueras (1848-1911) A Spanish woman religious and founder of the Sisters of the Immaculate Conception to assist poor girls and prostitutes. Born near Barcelona, Catalonia, Spain, she joined the Adores Sisters and made the central focus of her life the care of prostitutes and other societal victims. She founded the Order of the Sisters of the Immaculate Conception to advance her cause. She was beatified by John Paul II on March 15, 1998 and canonized by Pope Benedict XVI on Oct. 21, 2012 in Rome.

Peter Calungsod (1654-72) A layman in the Philippines who was martyred on Guam while serving with Jesuit missionaries. A native of the Philippines, Peter, or Pedro, was trained as a young catechist and joined with the Society of Jesus in its efforts to evangelize among the tribes of Guam. He died trying to protect his mentor, Father Diego Jose Luis San Vitores. He is the second Filipino saint. He was canonized on Oct. 21, 2012, by Pope Benedict XVI in Rome.

Anna Schäffer (1882-1925) A German laywoman and victim soul. Born to a carpenter's family, in 1901, she fell while working in a laundry and suffered severe burns. She never recovered and endured immense suffering for the rest of her life. She offered up her torment to Christ and conformed herself to the Cross. She was canonized by Pope Benedict XVI on Oct. 21, 2012 in Rome.

2013

Antonio Primaldo and Companions (d. 1480) The so-called Martyrs of Otranto, 800 citizens of the Italian city of Otranto who were put to death by the invading Ottoman Turks. The city fell on August 12, and the next day, 800 men, mostly fishermen, farmers, artisans, and shepherds were massacred, starting with Primaldo, the only martyr whose name is known with certainty. He was beheaded but remained standing miraculously until all of the others were murdered. One of the executioners converted on the spot and was slain. The remains of the martyrs were revered ever after. They were canonized on May 12, 2013 in a ceremony in Rome presided by Pope Francis.

Laura Montoya Upegui (1874-1949) A Colombian nun and foundress in 1914 of the Congregation of the Missionary Sisters of Mary Immaculate and St. Catherine of Siena. Born in Jericó, Antioquia, Colombia, she became a teacher at the age of 16 and was moved especially to teach the native people of South America. In 1914, with four other young women, she began working with the native tribes and so began the Missionaries of Mary Immaculate and St. Catherine of Siena. The Missionary Sisters serve in 19 countries throughout the Americas, Africa, and Europe. She was canonized on May 12, 2013 in a ceremony in Rome presided by Pope Francis.

María Guadalupe García Zavala (1878–1963) Mexican nun and foundress of the Handmaids of St. Margaret Mary and the Poor. Born in Zapopan, Mexico, she founded the Handmaids in 1901 to care for the sick in the hospitals. The community embraced strict poverty, to be "poor with the poor." She was elected the first Mother Superior, and during the severe persecution of the Church by the secularist government she hid priests in her hospital. Beatified by Pope Bl. John Paul II in 2004, she was canonized by Pope Francis on May 12, 2013.

Dates and Events in Catholic History

FIRST CENTURY

c. 33: First Christian Pentecost; descent of the Holy Spirit upon the disciples; preaching of St. Peter in Jerusalem; conversion, baptism and aggregation of some 3,000 persons to the first Christian community.

St. Stephen, deacon, was stoned to death at Jerusalem; he is venerated as the first Christian martyr.

c. 34: St. Paul, formerly Saul the persecutor of Christians, was converted and baptized. After three years of solitude in the desert, he joined the college of the apostles; he made three major missionary journeys and became known as the Apostle to the Gentiles; he was imprisoned twice in Rome and was beheaded there between 64 and 67.

39: Cornelius (the Gentile) and his family were baptized by St. Peter; a significant event signaling the mission of the Church to all peoples.

42: Persecution of Christians in Palestine broke out during the rule of Herod Agrippa; St. James the Greater, the first apostle to die, was beheaded in 44; St. Peter was imprisoned for a short time; many Christians fled to Antioch, marking the beginning of the dispersion of Christians beyond the confines of Palestine. At Antioch, the followers of Christ were called Christians for the first time.

49: Christians at Rome, considered members of a Jewish sect, were adversely affected by a decree of Claudius which forbade Jewish worship there.

51: The Council of Jerusalem, in which all the apostles participated under the presidency of St. Peter, decreed that circumcision, dietary regulations, and various other prescriptions of Mosaic Law were not obligatory for Gentile converts to the Christian community. The crucial decree was issued in opposition to Judaizers who contended that observance of the Mosaic Law in its entirety was necessary for salvation.

64: Persecution broke out at Rome under Nero, the emperor said to have accused Christians of starting the fire which destroyed half of Rome.

64 or 67: Martyrdom of St. Peter at Rome during the Neronian persecution. He established his see and spent his last years there after preaching in and around Jerusalem, establishing a see at Antioch, and presiding at the Council of Jerusalem.

70: Destruction of Jerusalem by Titus.

88-97: Pontificate of St. Clement I, third successor of St. Peter as bishop of Rome, one of the Apostolic Fathers. The First Epistle of Clement to the Corinthians, with which he has been identified, was addressed by the Church of Rome to the Church at Corinth, the scene of irregularities and divisions in the Christian community.

95: Domitian persecuted Christians, principally at Rome.

c. 100: Death of St. John, apostle and evangelist, marking the end of the Age of the Apostles and the first generation of the Church.

By the end of the century, Antioch, Alexandria and Ephesus in the East and Rome in the West were established centers of Christian population and influence.

SECOND CENTURY

c. 107: St. Ignatius of Antioch was martyred at Rome. He was the first writer to use the expression, "the Catholic Church."

112: Emperor Trajan, in a rescript to Pliny the Younger, governor of Bithynia, instructed him not to search out Christians but to punish them if they were publicly denounced and refused to do homage to the Roman gods. This rescript set a pattern for Roman magistrates in dealing with Christians.

117-38: Persecution under Hadrian. Many Acts of Martyrs date from this period.

c. 125: Spread of Gnosticism, a combination of elements of Platonic philosophy and Eastern mystery religions. Its adherents claimed that its secret-knowledge principle provided a deeper insight into Christian doctrine than divine revelation and faith. One gnostic thesis denied the divinity of Christ; others denied the reality of his humanity, calling it mere appearance (Docetism, Phantasiasm).

c. 144: Excommunication of Marcion, bishop and heretic, who claimed that there was total opposition and no connection at all between the Old Testament and the New Testament, between the God of the Jews and the God of the Christians; and that the Canon (list of inspired writings) of the Bible consisted only of parts of St. Luke's Gospel and 10 letters of St. Paul. Marcionism was checked at Rome by 200 and was condemned by a council held there about 260, but the heresy persisted for several centuries in the East and had some adherents as late as the Middle Ages.

c. 155: St. Polycarp, bishop of Smyrna and disciple of St. John the Evangelist, was martyred.

c. 156: Beginning of Montanism, a form of religious extremism. Its principal tenets were the imminent second coming of Christ, denial of the divine nature of the Church and its power to forgive sin, and excessively rigorous morality. The heresy, preached by Montanus of Phrygia and others, was condemned by Pope St. Zephyrinus (199-217).

161-80: Reign of Marcus Aurelius. His persecution, launched in the wake of natural disasters, was more violent than those of his predecessors.

165: St. Justin, an important early Christian writer, was martyred at Rome.

c. 180: St. Irenaeus, bishop of Lyons and one of the great early theologians, wrote *Adversus Haereses*.

He stated that the teaching and tradition of the Roman See was the standard for belief.

196: Easter Controversy, concerning the day of celebration — a Sunday, according to practice in the West, or the 14th of the month of Nisan (in the Hebrew calendar), no matter what day of the week, according to practice in the East. The controversy was not resolved at this time.

The *Didache*, whose extant form dates from the second century, is an important record of Christian belief, practice and governance in the first century.

Latin was introduced as a liturgical language in the West. Other liturgical languages were Aramaic and Greek.

The Catechetical School of Alexandria, founded about the middle of the century, gained increasing influence on doctrinal study and instruction and interpretation of the Bible.

THIRD CENTURY

202: Persecution under Septimius Severus, who wanted to establish a simple common religion in the Empire.

206: Tertullian, a convert since 197 and the first great ecclesiastical writer in Latin, joined the heretical Montanists; he died in 230.

215: Death of Clement of Alexandria, teacher of Origen and a founding father of the School of Alexandria.

217-35: St. Hippolytus, the first antipope; he was reconciled to the Church while in prison during persecution in 235.

232-54: Origen established the School of Caesarea after being deposed in 231 as head of the School of Alexandria; he died in 254. A scholar and voluminous writer, he was one of the founders of systematic theology and exerted wide influence for many years.

c. 242: Manichaeism originated in Persia: a combination of errors based on the assumption that two supreme principles (good and evil) are operative in creation and life, and that the supreme objective of human endeavor is liberation from evil (matter). The heresy denied the humanity of Christ, the sacramental system, the authority of the Church (and state), and endorsed a moral code which threatened the fabric of society. In the 12th and 13th centuries, it took on the features of Albigensianism and Catharism.

249-51: Persecution under Decius. Many of those who denied the faith (*lapsi*) sought readmission to the Church at the end of the persecution in 251. Pope St. Cornelius agreed with St. Cyprian that *lapsi* were to be readmitted to the Church after satisfying the requirements of appropriate penance. Antipope Novatian, on the other hand, contended that persons who fell away from the Church under persecution and/or those guilty of serious sin after baptism could not be absolved and readmitted to communion with the Church. The heresy was condemned by a Roman synod in 251.

250-300: Neo-Platonism of Plotinus and Porphyry gained followers.

251: Novatian, an antipope, was condemned at Rome.

256: Pope St. Stephen I upheld the validity of baptism properly administered by heretics, in the Rebaptism Controversy.

257: Persecution under Valerian, who attempted to destroy the Church as a social structure.

258: St. Cyprian, bishop of Carthage, was martyred.

c. 260: St. Lucian founded the School of Antioch, a center of influence on biblical studies.

Pope St. Dionysius condemned Sabellianism, a form of modalism (like Monarchianism and Patripassianism). The heresy contended that the Father, Son and Holy Spirit are not distinct divine persons but are only three different modes of being and self-manifestations of the one God. St. Paul of Thebes became a hermit.

261: Gallienus issued an edict of toleration which ended general persecution for nearly 40 years.

c. 292: Diocletian divided the Roman Empire into East and West. The division emphasized political, cultural and other differences between the two parts of the Empire and influenced different developments in the Church in the East and West. The prestige of Rome began to decline.

FOURTH CENTURY

303: Persecution broke out under Diocletian; it was particularly violent in 304.

305: St. Anthony of Heracles established a foundation for hermits near the Red Sea in Egypt.

c. 306: The first local legislation on clerical celibacy was enacted by a council held at Elvira, Spain; bishops, priests, deacons and other ministers were forbidden to have wives.

311: An edict of toleration issued by Galerius at the urging of Constantine the Great and Licinius officially ended persecution in the West; some persecution continued in the East.

313: The Edict of Milan issued by Constantine and Licinius recognized Christianity as a lawful religion in the Roman Empire.

314: A council of Arles condemned Donatism, declaring that baptism properly administered by heretics is valid, in view of the principle that sacraments have their efficacy from Christ, not from the spiritual condition of their human ministers. The heresy was condemned again by a council of Carthage in 411.

318: St. Pachomius established the first foundation of the cenobitic (common) life, as compared with the solitary life of hermits in Upper Egypt.

325: Ecumenical Council of Nicaea (I). Its principal action was the condemnation of Arianism, the most devastating of the early heresies, which denied the divinity of Christ. The heresy was authored by Arius of Alexandria, a priest. Arians and several kinds of Semi-Arians propagandized their tenets widely, established their own hierarchies and churches, and raised havoc in the Church for several centuries. The council contributed to formulation of the Nicene Creed (Creed of Nicaea-Constantinople); fixed the date for the observance of Easter; passed regulations concerning clerical discipline; adopted the civil divisions of the Empire as the model for the jurisdictional organization of the Church.

326: With the support of St. Helena, the True Cross on which Christ was crucified was discovered.

337: Baptism and death of Constantine.

c. 342: Beginning of a 40-year persecution in Persia.

343-44: A council of Sardica reaffirmed doctrine formulated by Nicaea I and declared also that bishops had the right of appeal to the pope as the highest authority in the Church.

361-63: Emperor Julian the Apostate waged an unsuccessful campaign against the Church in an attempt to restore paganism as the religion of the Empire.

c. 365: Persecution of orthodox Christians under Emperor Valens in the East.

c. 376: Beginning of the barbarian invasion in the West.

379: Death of St. Basil, the Father of Monasticism in the East. His writings contributed greatly to the development of rules for the life of Religious.

381: Ecumenical Council of Constantinople (I). It condemned various brands of Arianism as well as Macedonianism, which denied the divinity of the Holy Spirit; contributed to formulation of the Nicene Creed; approved a canon acknowledging Constantinople as the second see after Rome in honor and dignity.

382: The Canon of Sacred Scripture, the official list of the inspired books of the Bible, was contained in the Decree of Pope St. Damasus and published by a regional council of Carthage in 397; the Canon was formally defined by the Council of Trent in the 16th century.

382-c. 406: St. Jerome translated the Old and New Testaments into Latin; his work is called the Vulgate version of the Bible.

396: St. Augustine became bishop of Hippo in North Africa.

FIFTH CENTURY

410: Visigoths under Alaric sacked Rome and the last Roman legions departed Britain. The decline of imperial Rome dates approximately from this time.

430: St. Augustine, bishop of Hippo for 35 years, died. He was a strong defender of orthodox doctrine against Manichaeism, Donatism and Pelagianism. The depth and range of his writings made him a dominant influence in Christian thought for centuries.

431: Ecumenical Council of Ephesus. It condemned Nestorianism, which denied the unity of the divine and human natures in the Person of Christ; defined *Theotokos* (Bearer of God) as the title of Mary, Mother of the Son of God made Man; condemned Pelagianism. The heresy of Pelagianism, proceeding from the assumption that Adam had a natural right to supernatural life, held that man could attain salvation through the efforts of his natural powers and free will; it involved errors concerning the nature of original sin, the meaning of grace and other matters. Related Semi-Pelagianism was condemned by a council of Orange in 529.

432: St. Patrick arrived in Ireland. By the time of his death in 461 most of the country had been converted, monasteries founded and the hierarchy established.

438: The Theodosian Code, a compilation of decrees for the Empire, was issued by Theodosius II; it had great influence on subsequent civil and ecclesiastical law.

451: Ecumenical Council of Chalcedon. Its principal action was the condemnation of Monophysitism (also called Eutychianism), which denied the humanity of Christ by holding that he had only one, the divine, nature.

452: Pope St. Leo the Great persuaded Attila the Hun to spare Rome.

455: Vandals under Geiseric sacked Rome.

484: Patriarch Acacius of Constantinople was excommunicated for signing the *Henoticon*, a document which capitulated to the Monophysite heresy. The excommunication triggered the Acacian Schism which lasted for 35 years.

494: Pope St. Gelasius I declared in a letter to Emperor Anastasius that the pope had power and authority over the emperor in spiritual matters.

496: Clovis, King of the Franks, was converted and became the defender of Christianity in the West. The Franks became a Catholic people.

SIXTH CENTURY

520: Irish monasteries flourished as centers for spiritual life, missionary training, and scholarly activity.

529: The Second Council of Orange condemned Semi-Pelagianism.

c. 529: St. Benedict founded the Monte Cassino Abbey. Some years before his death in 543 he wrote a monastic rule which exercised tremendous influence on the form and style of religious life. He is called the Father of Monasticism in the West.

533: John II became the first pope to change his name. The practice did not become general until the time of Sergius IV (1009).

533-34: Emperor Justinian promulgated the *Corpus Iuris Civilis* for the Roman world; like the Theodosian Code, it influenced subsequent civil and ecclesiastical law.

c. 545: Death of Dionysius Exiguus who was the first to date history from the birth of Christ, a practice which resulted in use of the B.C. and A.D. abbreviations. His calculations were at least four years late.

553: Ecumenical Council of Constantinople (II). It condemned the Three Chapters, Nestorian-tainted writings of Theodore of Mopsuestia, Theodoret of Cyrus and Ibas of Edessa.

585: St. Columban founded an influential monastic school at Luxeuil.

589: The most important of several councils of Toledo was held. The Visigoths renounced Arianism, and St. Leander began the organization of the Church in Spain.

590-604: Pontificate of Pope St. Gregory I the Great. He set the form and style of the papacy which prevailed throughout the Middle Ages; exerted great influence on doctrine and liturgy; was strong in support of monastic discipline and clerical celibacy; authored writings on many subjects. Gregorian Chant is named in his honor.

596: Pope St. Gregory I sent St. Augustine of Canterbury and 40 monks to do missionary work in England.

597: St. Columba died. He founded an important monastery at Iona, established schools and did notable missionary work in Scotland. By the end of the century, monasteries of nuns were common; Western monasticism was flourishing; monasticism in the East, under the influence of Monophysitism and other factors, was losing its vigor.

SEVENTH CENTURY

613: St. Columban established the influential monastery of Bobbio in northern Italy; he died there in 615.

622: The *Hegira* (flight) of Mohammed from

Mecca to Medina signalled the beginning of Islam which, by the end of the century, claimed almost all of the southern Mediterranean area.

628: Heraclius, Eastern Emperor, recovered the True Cross from the Persians.

649: A Lateran council condemned two erroneous formulas (Ecthesis and Type) issued by emperors Heraclius and Constans II as means of reconciling Monophysites with the Church.

664: Actions of the Synod of Whitby advanced the adoption of Roman usages in England, especially regarding the date for the observance of Easter. (See **Easter Controversy,** p. 139.)

680-81: Ecumenical Council of Constantinople (III). It condemned Monothelitism, which held that Christ had only one will, the divine; censured Pope Honorius I for a letter to Sergius, bishop of Constantinople, in which he made an ambiguous but not infallible statement about the unity of will and/or operation in Christ.

692: Trullan Synod. Eastern-Church discipline on clerical celibacy was settled, permitting marriage before ordination to the diaconate and continuation in marriage afterwards, but prohibiting marriage following the death of the wife thereafter. Anti-Roman canons contributed to East-West alienation.

During the century, the monastic influence of Ireland and England increased in Western Europe; schools and learning declined; regulations regarding clerical celibacy became more strict in the East.

EIGHTH CENTURY

711: Muslims began the conquest of Spain.

726: Emperor Leo III, the Isaurian, launched a campaign against the veneration of sacred images and relics; called Iconoclasm (image-breaking), it caused turmoil in the East until about 843.

731: Pope Gregory III and a synod at Rome condemned Iconoclasm, with a declaration that the veneration of sacred images was in accord with Catholic tradition.

Venerable Bede issued his *Ecclesiastical History of the English People.*

732: Charles Martel defeated the Muslims at Poitiers, halting their advance in the West.

744: The Monastery of Fulda was established by St. Sturmi, a disciple of St. Boniface; it was influential in the evangelization of Germany.

754: A council of more than 300 Byzantine bishops endorsed Iconoclast errors. This council and its actions were condemned by the Lateran synod of 769.

Stephen II (III) crowned Pepin ruler of the Franks. Pepin twice invaded Italy, in 754 and 756, to defend the pope against the Lombards. His land grants to the papacy, called the Donation of Pepin, were later extended by Charlemagne (773) and formed part of the States of the Church.

c. 755: St. Boniface (Winfrid) was martyred. He was called the Apostle of Germany for his missionary work and organization of the hierarchy there.

781: Alcuin was chosen by Charlemagne to organize a palace school, which became a center of intellectual leadership.

787: Ecumenical Council of Nicaea (II). It condemned Iconoclasm, which held that the use of images was idolatry, and Adoptionism, which claimed that Christ was not the Son of God by nature but only by adoption. This was the last council regarded as ecumenical by Orthodox Churches.

792: A council at Ratisbon condemned Adoptionism. The famous *Book of Kells* ("The Great Gospel of Columcille") dates from the early eighth or late seventh century.

NINTH CENTURY

800: Charlemagne was crowned Emperor by Pope Leo III on Christmas Day.

Egbert became king of West Saxons; he unified England and strengthened the See of Canterbury.

813: Emperor Leo V, the Armenian, revived Iconoclasm, which persisted until about 843.

814: Charlemagne died.

843: The Treaty of Verdun split the Frankish kingdom among Charlemagne's three grandsons.

844: A Eucharistic controversy involving the writings of St. Paschasius Radbertus, Ratramnus and Rabanus Maurus occasioned the development of terminology regarding the doctrine of the Real Presence.

846: Muslims invaded Italy and attacked Rome.

847-52: Period of composition of the False Decretals, a collection of forged documents attributed to popes from St. Clement (88-97) to Gregory II (714-731). The Decretals, which strongly supported the autonomy and rights of bishops, were suspect for a long time before being repudiated entirely about 1628.

848: The Council of Mainz condemned Gottschalk for heretical teaching regarding predestination. He was also condemned by the Council of Quierzy in 853.

857: Photius displaced Ignatius as patriarch of Constantinople. This marked the beginning of the Photian Schism, a confused state of East-West relations which has not yet been cleared up by historical research. Photius, a man of exceptional ability, died in 891.

865: St. Ansgar, apostle of Scandinavia, died.

869: St. Cyril died and his brother, St. Methodius (d. 885), was ordained a bishop. The Apostles of the Slavs devised an alphabet and translated the Gospels and liturgy into the Slavonic language.

869-70: Ecumenical Council of Constantinople (IV). It issued a second condemnation of Iconoclasm, condemned and deposed Photius as patriarch of Constantinople and restored Ignatius to the patriarchate. This was the last ecumenical council held in the East. It was first called ecumenical by canonists toward the end of the 11th century.

871-c. 900: Reign of Alfred the Great, the only English king ever anointed by a pope at Rome.

TENTH CENTURY

910: William, duke of Aquitaine, founded the Benedictine Abbey of Cluny, which became a center of monastic and ecclesiastical reform, especially in France.

915: Pope John X played a leading role in the expulsion of Saracens from central and southern Italy.

955: St. Olga, of the Russian royal family, was baptized.

962: Otto I, the Great, crowned by Pope John XII, revived Charlemagne's kingdom, which became the Holy Roman Empire.

966: Mieszko, first of a royal line in Poland, was baptized; he brought Latin Christianity to Poland.

988: Conversion and baptism of St. Vladimir and the people of Kiev which subsequently became part of Russia.

993: John XV was the first pope to decree the official canonization of a saint — Bishop Ulrich (Uldaric) of Augsburg — for the universal Church.

997: St. Stephen became ruler of Hungary. He assisted in organizing the hierarchy and establishing Latin Christianity in that country.

999-1003: Pontificate of Sylvester II (Gerbert of Aquitaine), a Benedictine monk and the first French pope.

ELEVENTH CENTURY

1009: Beginning of lasting East-West Schism in the Church, marked by dropping of the name of Pope Sergius IV from the Byzantine diptychs (the listing of persons prayed for during the liturgy). The deletion was made by Patriarch Sergius II of Constantinople.

1012: St. Romuald founded the Camaldolese Hermits.

1025: The Council of Arras, and other councils later, condemned the Cathari (Neo-Manichaeans, Albigenses).

1027: The Council of Elne proclaimed the Truce of God as a means of stemming violence; it involved armistice periods of varying length, which were later extended.

1038: St. John Gualbert founded the Vallombrosians.

1043-59: Constantinople patriarchate of Michael Cerularius, the key figure in a controversy concerning the primacy of the papacy. His and the Byzantine synod's refusal to acknowledge this primacy in 1054 widened and hardened the East-West Schism in the Church.

1047: Pope Clement II died; he was the only pope ever buried in Germany.

1049-54: Pontificate of St. Leo IX, who inaugurated a movement of papal, diocesan, monastic and clerical reform.

1054: Start of the Great Schism between the Eastern and Western Churches; it marked the separation of Orthodox Churches from unity with the pope.

1055: Condemnation of the Eucharistic doctrine of Berengarius.

1059: A Lateran council issued new legislation regarding papal elections; voting power was entrusted to the Roman cardinals.

1066: Death of St. Edward the Confessor, king of England from 1042 and restorer of Westminster Abbey.

Defeat, at Hastings, of Harold by William, Duke of Normandy (later William I), who subsequently exerted strong influence on the life-style of the Church in England.

1073-85: Pontificate of St. Gregory VII (Hildebrand). A strong pope, he carried forward programs of clerical and general ecclesiastical reform and struggled against German King Henry IV and other rulers to end the evils of lay investiture. He introduced the Latin liturgy in Spain and set definite dates for the observance of ember days.

1077: Henry IV, excommunicated and suspended from the exercise of imperial powers by Gregory VII, sought absolution from the pope at Canossa. Henry later repudiated this action and in 1084 forced Gregory to leave Rome.

1079: The Council of Rome condemned Eucharistic errors (denial of the Real Presence of Christ under the appearances of bread and wine) of Berengarius, who retracted.

1084: St. Bruno founded the Carthusians.

1097-99: The first of several Crusades undertaken between this time and 1265. Recovery of the Holy Places and gaining free access to them for Christians were the original purposes, but these were diverted to less worthy objectives in various ways. Results included: a Latin Kingdom of Jerusalem, 1099-1187; a military and political misadventure in the form of a Latin Empire of Constantinople, 1204-1261; acquisition, by treaties, of visiting rights for Christians in the Holy Land. East-West economic and cultural relationships increased during the period. In the religious sphere, actions of the Crusaders had the effect of increasing the alienation of the East from the West.

1098: St. Robert founded the Cistercians.

TWELFTH CENTURY

1108: Beginnings of the influential Abbey and School of St. Victor in France.

1115: St. Bernard established the Abbey of Clairvaux and inaugurated the Cistercian Reform.

1118: Christian forces captured Saragossa, Spain; the beginning of the Muslim decline in that country.

1121: St. Norbert established the original monastery of the Praemonstratensians near Laon, France.

1122: The Concordat of Worms (*Pactum Callixtinum*) was formulated and approved by Pope Callistus II and Emperor Henry V to settle controversy concerning the investiture of prelates. The concordat provided that the emperor could invest prelates with symbols of temporal authority but had no right to invest them with spiritual authority, which came from the Church alone, and that the emperor was not to interfere in papal elections. This was the first concordat in history.

1123: Ecumenical Council of the Lateran (I), the first of its kind in the West. It endorsed provisions of the Concordat of Worms concerning the investiture of prelates and approved reform measures in 25 canons.

1139: Ecumenical Council of the Lateran (II). It adopted measures against a schism organized by antipope Anacletus and approved 30 canons related to discipline and other matters; one of the canons stated that holy orders is an invalidating impediment to marriage.

1140: St. Bernard met Abelard in debate at the Council of Sens. Abelard, whose rationalism in theology was condemned for the first time in 1121, died in 1142 at Cluny.

1148: The Synod of Rheims enacted strict disciplinary decrees for communities of women Religious.

1152: The Synod of Kells reorganized the Church in Ireland.

1160: Gratian, whose *Decretum* became a basic text of canon law, died.

Peter Lombard, compiler of the Four Books of Sentences, a standard theology text for nearly 200 years, died.

1170: St. Thomas Becket, archbishop of Canterbury, who clashed with Henry II over church-state relations, was murdered in his cathedral.

1171: Pope Alexander III reserved the process of

canonization of saints to the Holy See.

1179: Ecumenical Council of the Lateran (III). It enacted measures against Waldensianism and Albigensianism (see year 242 regarding Manichaeism), approved reform decrees in 27 canons, provided that popes be elected by a two-thirds vote of the cardinals.

1184: Waldenses and other heretics were excommunicated by Pope Lucius III.

THIRTEENTH CENTURY

1198-1216: Pontificate of Innocent III, during which the papacy reached its medieval peak of authority, influence and prestige in the Church and in relations with civil rulers.

1208: Innocent III called for a crusade, the first in Christendom itself, against the Albigensians; their beliefs and practices threatened the fabric of society in southern France and northern Italy.

1209: Verbal approval was given by Innocent III to a rule of life for the Order of Friars Minor, started by St. Francis of Assisi.

1212: The Second Order of Franciscans, the Poor Clares, was founded.

1215: Ecumenical Council of the Lateran (IV). It ordered annual reception of the sacraments of penance and the Eucharist; defined and made the first official use of the term transubstantiation to explain the change of bread and wine into the body and blood of Christ; adopted additional measures to counteract teachings and practices of the Albigensians and Cathari; approved 70 canons.

1216: Formal papal approval was given to a rule of life for the Order of Preachers, started by St. Dominic. The Portiuncula Indulgence was granted by the Holy See at the request of St. Francis of Assisi.

1221: Rule of the Third Order Secular of St. Francis (Secular Franciscan Order) approved verbally by Honorius III.

1226: Death of St. Francis of Assisi.

1231: Pope Gregory IX authorized establishment of the Papal Inquisition for dealing with heretics. It was a creature of its time, when crimes against faith and heretical doctrines of extremists like the Cathari and Albigenses threatened the good of the Christian community, the welfare of the state and the very fabric of society. The institution, which was responsible for excesses in punishment, was most active in the second half of the century in southern France, Italy and Germany.

1245: Ecumenical Council of Lyons (I). It confirmed the deposition of Emperor Frederick II and approved 22 canons.

1247: Preliminary approval was given by the Holy See to a Carmelite rule of life.

1270: St. Louis IX, king of France, died. Beginning of papal decline.

1274: Ecumenical Council of Lyons (II). It accomplished a temporary reunion of separated Eastern Churches with the Roman Church; issued regulations concerning conclaves for papal elections; approved 31 canons.

Death of St. Thomas Aquinas, Doctor of the Church, of lasting influence.

1280: Pope Nicholas III, who made the Breviary the official prayer book for clergy of the Roman Church, died.

1281: The excommunication of Michael Palaeologus by Pope Martin IV ruptured the union effected with the Eastern Church in 1274.

FOURTEENTH CENTURY

1302: Pope Boniface VIII issued the bull *Unam Sanctam*, concerning the unity of the Church and the temporal power of princes, against the background of a struggle with Philip IV of France; it was the most famous medieval document on the subject.

1309-77: For a period of approximately 70 years, seven popes resided at Avignon because of unsettled conditions in Rome and other reasons; see separate entry.

1311-12: Ecumenical Council of Vienne. It suppressed the Knights Templar and enacted a number of reform decrees.

1321: Dante Alighieri died a year after completing the *Divine Comedy*.

1324: Marsilius of Padua completed *Defensor Pacis*, a work condemned by Pope John XXII as heretical because of its denial of papal primacy and the hierarchical structure of the Church, and for other reasons. It was a charter for conciliarism (an ecumenical council is superior to the pope in authority).

1337-1453: Period of the Hundred Years' War, a dynastic struggle between France and England.

1338: Four years after the death of Pope John XXII, who had opposed Louis IV of Bavaria in a yearslong controversy, electoral princes declared at the Diet of Rhense that the emperor did not need papal confirmation of his title and right to rule. Charles IV later (1356) said the same thing in a *Golden Bull*, eliminating papal rights in the election of emperors.

1347-50: The Black Death swept across Europe, killing perhaps one-fourth to one-third of the total population; an estimated 40 per cent of the clergy succumbed.

1374: Petrarch, poet and humanist, died.

1377: Return of the papacy from Avignon to Rome. Beginning of the Western Schism; see separate entry.

FIFTEENTH CENTURY

1409: The Council of Pisa, without canonical authority, tried to end the Western Schism but succeeded only in complicating it by electing a third claimant to the papacy; see Western Schism.

1414-18: Ecumenical Council of Constance. It took successful action to end the Western Schism involving rival claimants to the papacy; rejected the teachings of Wycliff; condemned Hus as a heretic. One decree — passed in the earlier stages of the council but later rejected — asserted the superiority of an ecumenical council over the pope (conciliarism).

1431: St. Joan of Arc was burned at the stake.

1431-45: Ecumenical Council of Florence (also called Basle-Ferrara-Florence). It affirmed the primacy of the pope against the claims of conciliarists that an ecumenical council is superior to the pope. It also formulated and approved decrees of union with several separated Eastern Churches — Greek, Armenian, Jacobite — which failed to gain general or lasting acceptance.

1438: The Pragmatic Sanction of Bourges was enacted by Charles VII and the French

Parliament to curtail papal authority over the Church in France, in the spirit of conciliarism. It found expression in Gallicanism and had effects lasting at least until the French Revolution.

1453: The fall of Constantinople to the Turks.

c. 1456: Gutenberg issued the first edition of the Bible printed from movable type, at Mainz, Germany.

1476: Pope Sixtus IV approved observance of the feast of the Immaculate Conception on Dec. 8 throughout the Church.

1478: Pope Sixtus IV, at the urging of King Ferdinand of Spain, approved establishment of the Spanish Inquisition for dealing with Jewish and Moorish converts accused of heresy. The institution, which was peculiar to Spain and its colonies in America, acquired jurisdiction over other cases as well and fell into disrepute because of its procedures, cruelty and the manner in which it served the Spanish crown, rather than the accused and the good of the Church. Protests by the Holy See failed to curb excesses of the Inquisition, which lingered in Spanish history until early in the 19th century.

1492: Columbus discovered the Americas.

1493: Pope Alexander VI issued a Bull of Demarcation which determined spheres of influence for the Spanish and Portuguese in the Americas.

The Renaissance, a humanistic movement which originated in Italy in the 14th century, spread to France, Germany, the Low Countries and England. A transitional period between the medieval world and the modern secular world, it introduced profound changes which affected literature and the other arts, general culture, politics and religion.

SIXTEENTH CENTURY

1512-17: Ecumenical Council of the Lateran (V). It stated the relation and position of the pope with respect to an ecumenical council; acted to counteract the Pragmatic Sanction of Bourges and exaggerated claims of liberty by the Church in France; condemned erroneous teachings concerning the nature of the human soul; stated doctrine concerning indulgences. The council reflected concern for abuses in the Church and the need for reforms but failed to take decisive action in the years immediately preceding the Reformation.

1517: Martin Luther signaled the beginning of the Reformation by posting 95 theses at Wittenberg. Subsequently, he broke completely from doctrinal orthodoxy in discourses and three published works (1519 and 1520); was excommunicated on more than 40 charges of heresy (1521); remained the dominant figure in the Reformation in Germany until his death in 1546.

1519: Zwingli triggered the Reformation in Zurich and became its leading proponent there until his death in combat in 1531.

1524: Luther's encouragement of German princes in putting down the two-year Peasants' Revolt gained political support for his cause.

1528: The Order of Friars Minor Capuchin was approved as an autonomous division of the Franciscan Order; like the Jesuits, the Capuchins became leaders in the Counter-Reformation.

1530: The Augsburg Confession of Lutheran faith was issued; it was later supplemented by the Smalkaldic Articles, approved in 1537.

1533: Henry VIII divorced Catherine of Aragon, married Anne Boleyn, was excommunicated. In 1534 he decreed the Act of Supremacy, making the sovereign the head of the Church in England, under which Sts. John Fisher and Thomas More were executed in 1535. Despite his rejection of papal primacy and actions against monastic life in England, he generally maintained doctrinal orthodoxy until his death in 1547.

1536: John Calvin, leader of the Reformation in Switzerland until his death in 1564, issued the first edition of *Institutes of the Christian Religion*, which became the classical text of Reformed (non-Lutheran) theology.

1540: The constitutions of the Society of Jesus (Jesuits), founded by St. Ignatius of Loyola, were approved.

1541: Start of the 11-year career of St. Francis Xavier as a missionary to the East Indies and Japan.

1545-63: Ecumenical Council of Trent. It issued a great number of decrees concerning doctrinal matters opposed by the Reformers, and mobilized the Counter-Reformation. Definitions covered the Canon of the Bible, the rule of faith, the nature of justification, grace, faith, original sin and its effects, the seven sacraments, the sacrificial nature of the Mass, the veneration of saints, use of sacred images, belief in purgatory, the doctrine of indulgences, the jurisdiction of the pope over the whole Church. It initiated many reforms for renewal in the liturgy and general discipline in the Church, the promotion of religious instruction, the education of the clergy through the foundation of seminaries, etc. Trent ranks with Vatican II as the greatest ecumenical council held in the West.

1549: The first Anglican *Book of Common Prayer* was issued by Edward VI. Revised editions were published in 1552, 1559 and 1662 and later.

1553: Start of the five-year reign of Mary Tudor who tried to counteract actions of Henry VIII against the Roman Church.

1555: Enactment of the Peace of Augsburg, an arrangement of religious territorialism rather than toleration, which recognized the existence of Catholicism and Lutheranism in the German Empire and provided that citizens should adopt the religion of their respective rulers.

1558: Beginning of the reign (to 1603) of Queen Elizabeth I of England and Ireland, during which the Church of England took on its definitive form.

1559: Establishment of the hierarchy of the Church of England, with the consecration of Matthew Parker as archbishop of Canterbury.

1563: The first text of the 39 Articles of the Church of England was issued. Also enacted were a new Act of Supremacy and Oath of Succession to the English throne.

1570: Elizabeth I was excommunicated. Penal measures against Catholics subsequently became more severe.

1571: Defeat of the Turkish armada at Lepanto staved off the invasion of Eastern Europe.

1577: The Formula of Concord, the classical statement of Lutheran faith, was issued; it was, generally, a Lutheran counterpart of the canons of the Council of Trent. In 1580, along with other formulas of doctrine, it was included in the Book of Concord.

1582: The Gregorian Calendar, named for Pope Gregory XIII, was put into effect and was eventually adopted in most countries: England delayed adoption until 1752.

SEVENTEENTH CENTURY

1605: The Gunpowder Plot, an attempt by Catholic fanatics to blow up James I of England and the houses of Parliament, resulted in an anti-Catholic Oath of Allegiance.

1610: Death of Matteo Ricci, outstanding Jesuit missionary to China, pioneer in cultural relations between China and Europe.
Founding of the first community of Visitation Nuns by Sts. Francis de Sales and Jane de Chantal.

1611: Founding of the Oratorians.

1613: Catholics were banned from Scandinavia.

1625: Founding of the Congregation of the Mission (Vincentians) by St. Vincent de Paul. He founded the Sisters of Charity in 1633.

1642: Death of Galileo, scientist, who was censured by the Congregation of the Holy Office for supporting the Copernican theory of the sun-centered planetary system. The case against him was closed in his favor in 1992.
Founding of the Sulpicians by Jacques Olier.

1643: Start of publication of the Bollandist *Acta Sanctorum*, a critical work on lives of the saints.

1648: Provisions in the Peace of Westphalia, ending the Thirty Years' War, extended terms of the Peace of Augsburg (1555) to Calvinists and gave equality to Catholics and Protestants in the 300 states of the Holy Roman Empire.

1649: Oliver Cromwell invaded Ireland and began a severe persecution of the Church there.

1653: Pope Innocent X condemned five propositions of Jansenism, a complex theory which distorted doctrine concerning the relations between divine grace and human freedom. Jansenism was also a rigoristic movement which seriously disturbed the Church in France, the Low Countries and Italy in this and the 18th century.

1673: The Test Act in England barred from public office Catholics who would not deny the doctrine of transubstantiation and receive Communion in the Church of England.

1678: Many English Catholics suffered death as a consequence of the Popish Plot, a false allegation by Titus Oates that Catholics planned to assassinate Charles II, land a French army in the country, burn London, and turn over the government to the Jesuits.

1682: The four Gallican articles, drawn up by Bossuet, asserted political and ecclesiastical immunities of France from papal control. The articles, which rejected the primacy of the pope, were declared null and void by Pope Alexander VIII in 1690.

1689: The Toleration Act granted a measure of freedom of worship to other English dissenters but not to Catholics.

EIGHTEENTH CENTURY

1704: Chinese Rites — involving the Christian adaptation of elements of Confucianism, veneration of ancestors and Chinese terminology in religion — were condemned by Clement XI.

1720: The Passionists were founded by St. Paul of the Cross.

1724: Persecution in China.

1732: The Redemptorists were founded by St. Alphonsus Liguori.

1738: Freemasonry was condemned by Clement XII and Catholics were forbidden to join, under penalty of excommunication; the prohibition was repeated by Benedict XIV in 1751 and by later popes.

1760s: Josephinism, a theory and system of state control of the Church, was initiated in Austria; it remained in force until about 1850.

1764: Febronianism, an unorthodox theory and practice regarding the constitution of the Church and relations between Church and state, was condemned for the first of several times. Proposed by an auxiliary bishop of Trier using the pseudonym Justinus Febronius, it had the effects of minimizing the office of the pope and supporting national churches under state control.

1773: Clement XIV issued a brief of suppression against the Jesuits, following their expulsion from Portugal in 1759, from France in 1764 and from Spain in 1767. Political intrigue and unsubstantiated accusations were principal factors in these developments. The ban, which crippled the society, contained no condemnation of the Jesuit constitutions, particular Jesuits or Jesuit teaching. The society was restored in 1814.

1778: Catholics in England were relieved of some civil disabilities dating back to the time of Henry VIII, by an act which permitted them to acquire, own and inherit property. Additional liberties were restored by the Roman Catholic Relief Act of 1791 and subsequent enactments of Parliament.

1789: Religious freedom in the United States was guaranteed under the First Amendment to the Constitution.
Beginning of the French Revolution which resulted in: the secularization of church property and the Civil Constitution of the Clergy in 1790; the persecution of priests, religious and lay persons loyal to papal authority; invasion of the Papal States by Napoleon in 1796; renewal of persecution from 1797-1799; attempts to dechristianize France and establish a new religion; the occupation of Rome by French troops and the forced removal of Pius VI to France in 1798.
This century is called the age of Enlightenment or Reason because of the predominating rational and scientific approach of its leading philosophers, scientists and writers with respect to religion, ethics and natural law. This approach downgraded the fact and significance of revealed religion. Also characteristic of the Enlightenment were subjectivism, secularism and optimism regarding human perfectibility.

NINETEENTH CENTURY

1801: Concordat between Napoleon and Pope Pius VII is signed. It is soon violated by the Organic Articles issued by Napoleon in 1802.

1804: Napoleon crowns himself Emperor of the French with Pope Pius in attendance.

1809: Pope Pius VII was made a captive by

Napoleon and deported to France where he remained in exile until 1814. During this time he refused to cooperate with Napoleon who sought to bring the Church in France under his own control, and other leading cardinals were imprisoned.

The turbulence in church-state relations in France at the beginning of the century recurred in connection with the Bourbon Restoration, the July Revolution, the second and third Republics, the Second Empire and the Dreyfus case.

1814: The Society of Jesus, suppressed since 1773, was restored.

1817: Reestablishment of the Congregation for the Propagation of the Faith (Propaganda) by Pius VII was an important factor in increasing missionary activity during the century.

1820: Year's-long persecution, during which thousands died for the faith, ended in China. Thereafter, communication with the West remained cut off until about 1834. Vigorous missionary work got under way in 1842.

1822: The Pontifical Society for the Propagation of the Faith, inaugurated in France by Pauline Jaricot for the support of missionary activity, was established.

1829: The Catholic Emancipation Act relieved Catholics in England and Ireland of most of the civil disabilities to which they had been subject from the time of Henry VIII.

1832: Gregory XVI, in the encyclical *Mirari Vos*, condemned indifferentism, one of the many ideologies at odds with Christian doctrine which were proposed during the century.

1833: Start of the Oxford Movement which affected the Church of England and resulted in some notable conversions, including that of John Henry Newman in 1845, to the Catholic Church.

Bl. Frederic Ozanam founded the Society of St. Vincent de Paul in France. The society's objectives are works of charity.

1848: *The Communist Manifesto*, a revolutionary document symptomatic of socio-economic crisis, was issued.

1850: The hierarchy was reestablished in England and Nicholas Wiseman made the first archbishop of Westminster. He was succeeded in 1865 by Henry Manning, an Oxford convert and proponent of the rights of labor.

1853: The Catholic hierarchy was reestablished in Holland.

1854: Pius IX proclaimed the dogma of the Immaculate Conception in the bull *Ineffabilis Deus*.

1858: The Blessed Virgin Mary appeared to St. Bernadette at Lourdes, France.

1864: Pius IX issued the encyclical *Quanta Cura* and the *Syllabus of Errors* in condemnation of some 80 propositions derived from the scientific mentality and rationalism of the century. The subjects in question had deep ramifications in many areas of thought and human endeavor; in religion, they explicitly and/or implicitly rejected divine revelation and the supernatural order.

1867: The first volume of *Das Kapital* was published. Together with the Communist First International, formed in the same year, it had great influence on the subsequent development of communism and socialism.

1869: The Anglican Church was disestablished in Ireland.

1869-70: Ecumenical Council of the Vatican (I). It defined papal primacy and infallibility in a dogmatic constitution on the Church; covered natural religion, revelation, faith, and the relations between faith and reason in a dogmatic constitution on the Catholic faith.

1870-71: Victor Emmanuel II of Sardinia, crowned king of Italy after defeating Austrian and papal forces, marched into Rome in 1870 and expropriated the Papal States after a plebiscite in which Catholics, at the order of Pius IX, did not vote. In 1871, Pius IX refused to accept a Law of Guarantees. Confiscation of church property and hindrance of ecclesiastical administration by the regime followed.

1871: The German Empire, a confederation of 26 states, was formed. Government policy launched a *Kulturkampf* whose May Laws of 1873 were designed to annul papal jurisdiction in Prussia and other states and to place the Church under imperial control. Resistance to the enactments and the persecution they legalized forced the government to modify its anti-Church policy by 1887.

1878: Beginning of the pontificate of Leo XIII, who was pope until his death in 1903. Leo is best known for the encyclical *Rerum Novarum*, which greatly influenced the course of Christian social thought and the labor movement. His other accomplishments included promotion of Scholastic philosophy and the impetus he gave to scriptural studies.

1881: The first International Eucharistic Congress was held in Lille, France.

Alexander II of Russia was assassinated. His policies of Russification — as well as those of his two predecessors and a successor during the century — caused great suffering to Catholics, Jews and Protestants in Poland, Lithuania, the Ukraine and Bessarabia.

1882: Charles Darwin died. His theory of evolution by natural selection, one of several scientific highlights of the century, had extensive repercussions in the faith-and-science controversy.

1887: The Catholic University of America was founded in Washington, DC.

1893: The U.S. apostolic delegation was set up in Washington, DC.

TWENTIETH CENTURY

1901: Restrictive measures in France forced the Jesuits, Benedictines, Carmelites and other religious orders to leave the country. Subsequently, 14,000 schools were suppressed; religious orders and congregations were expelled; the concordat was renounced in 1905; church property was confiscated in 1906. For some years the Holy See, refusing to comply with government demands for the control of bishops' appointments, left some ecclesiastical offices vacant.

1903-14: Pontificate of St. Pius X. He initiated the codification of canon law, 1904; removed the ban against participation by Catholics in Italian national elections, 1905; issued decrees calling upon the faithful to receive Holy Communion frequently and daily, and stating that children should begin receiving the Eucharist at the age of seven, 1905 and 1910, respectively; ordered the establishment of the Confraternity of Christian Doctrine in all parishes throughout the world,

1905; condemned Modernism in the decree *Lamentabili* and the encyclical *Pascendi*, 1907.

1908: The United States and England, long under the jurisdiction of the Congregation for the Propagation of the Faith as mission territories, were removed from its control and placed under the common law of the Church.

1910: Laws of separation were enacted in Portugal, marking a point of departure in church-state relations.

1911: The Catholic Foreign Mission Society of America — Maryknoll, the first U.S.-founded society of its type — was established.

1914: Start of World War I, which lasted until 1918.

1914-22: Pontificate of Benedict XV. Much of his pontificate was devoted to seeking ways and means of minimizing the material and spiritual havoc of World War I. In 1917 he offered his services as a mediator to the belligerent nations, but his pleas for settlement of the conflict went unheeded.

1917: The Blessed Virgin Mary appeared to three children at Fatima, Portugal.

A new constitution, embodying repressive laws against the Church, was enacted in Mexico. Its implementation resulted in persecution in the 1920s and 1930s.

Bolsheviks seized power in Russia and set up a communist dictatorship. The event marked the rise of communism in Russian and world affairs. One of its immediate, and lasting, results was persecution of the Church, Jews and other segments of the population.

1918: The Code of Canon Law, in preparation for more than 10 years, went into effect in the Western Church.

1919: Benedict XV stimulated missionary work through the decree *Maximum Illud*, in which he urged the recruiting and training of native clergy in places where the Church was not firmly established.

1920-22: Ireland was partitioned by two enactments of the British government which (1) made the six counties of Northern Ireland part of the United Kingdom in 1920 and (2) gave dominion status to the Irish Free State in 1922. The Irish Free State became an independent republic in 1949.

1922-39: Pontificate of Pius XI. He subscribed to the Lateran Treaty, 1929, which settled the Roman Question created by the confiscation of the Papal States in 1871; issued the encyclical *Casti connubii*, 1930, an authoritative statement on Christian marriage; resisted the efforts of Benito Mussolini to control Catholic Action and the Church, in the encyclical *Non abbiamo bisogno*, 1931; opposed various fascist policies; issued the encyclicals *Quadragesimo anno*, 1931, developing the social doctrine of Leo XIII's *Rerum novarum*, and *Divini Redemptoris*, 1937, calling for social justice and condemning atheistic communism; condemned anti-Semitism, 1937.

1926: The Catholic Relief Act repealed virtually all legal disabilities of Catholics in England.

1931: Leftists proclaimed Spain a republic and proceeded to disestablish the Church, confiscate church property, deny salaries to the clergy, expel the Jesuits and ban teaching of the Catholic faith. These actions were preludes to the civil war of 1936-1939.

1933: Emergence of Adolf Hitler to power in Germany. By 1935 two of his aims were clear, the elimination of the Jews and control of a single national church. Six million Jews were killed in the Holocaust. The Church was subject to repressive measures, which Pius XI protested futilely in the encyclical *Mit Brennender Sorge* in 1937.

1936-39: Civil war in Spain between the leftist Loyalist and the forces of rightist leader Francisco Franco The Loyalists were defeated and one-man, one-party rule was established. Many priests, religious and lay persons fell victim to Loyalist persecution and atrocities.

1939-45: World War II.

1939-58: Pontificate of Pius XII. He condemned communism, proclaimed the dogma of the Assumption of Mary in 1950, in various documents and other enactments provided ideological background for many of the accomplishments of the Second Vatican Council. (See **Twentieth Century Popes**, p. 241.)

1940: Start of a decade of communist conquest in more than 13 countries, resulting in conditions of persecution for a minimum of 60 million Catholics as well as members of other faiths.

Persecution diminished in Mexico because of non-enforcement of anti-religious laws still on record.

1950: Pius XII proclaimed the dogma of the Assumption of the Blessed Virgin Mary.

1957: The communist regime of China established the Patriotic Association of Chinese Catholics in opposition to the Church in union with the pope.

1958-63: Pontificate of Bl. John XXIII. His principal accomplishment was the convocation of the Second Vatican Council, the twenty-first ecumenical council in the history of the Church. (See **Twentieth Century Popes**, p. 241.)

1962-65: Ecumenical Council of the Vatican (II). It formulated and promulgated 16 documents — two dogmatic and two pastoral constitutions, nine decrees and three declarations — reflecting pastoral orientation toward renewal and reform in the Church, and making explicit dimensions of doctrine and Christian life requiring emphasis for the full development of the Church and the better accomplishment of its mission in the contemporary world.

1963-78: Pontificate of Paul VI. His main purpose and effort was to give direction and provide guidance for the authentic trends of church renewal set in motion by the Second Vatican Council. (See **Twentieth Century Popes**, p. 241.)

1978: The 34-day pontificate of John Paul I. Start of the pontificate of John Paul II; see **p. 246.**

1983: The revised Code of Canon Law, embodying reforms enacted by the Second Vatican Council, went into effect in the Church of Roman Rite.

1985: Formal ratification of a Vatican-Italy concordat replacing the Lateran Treaty of 1929.

1989-91: Decline and fall of communist influence and control in Middle and Eastern Europe and the Soviet Union.

1991: The Code of Canon Law for Eastern Churches went into effect.

1992: Approval of the new *Catechism of the Catholic Church*.

The Vatican officially closed the case against Galileo Galilei.

1994: Initiation of celebration preparations of the start of the third Christian millennium in the year 2000.

1997: Pope John Paul II issued an apology for any anti-Semitism by Catholics; a conference on anti-Semitism was also held in Rome and a number of Catholic leaders in Europe issued apologies for historical anti-Semitism.

1998: Pope John Paul II visited Cuba and secured the release of over 300 political prisoners.

The Vatican issued a white paper on Anti-Semitism, entitled *We Remember: A Reflection on the Shoah.*

Twentieth anniversary of the pontificate of Pope John Paul II; he became the longest reigning pontiff elected in the 20th century.

TWENTY-FIRST CENTURY

2000: The Catholic Church celebrated the Holy Year 2000 and the Jubilee; commencement of the third Christian millennium.

Pope John Paul II issued apology for the sinful actions of the Church's members in the past. Pope John Paul II traveled to the Holy Land in an historic visit.

2001: Pope John Paul II traveled to Greece and Syria. He also named 44 new members to the College of Cardinals in an unprecedented consistory.

On September 11, the World Trade Center was destroyed and the Pentagon attacked by Islamic terrorists who hijacked several planes and used them as weapons of mass destruction. The attacks launched a global war on terror.

2003: Pope John Paul II appealed for a peaceful resolution to the Iraq War. A coalition headed by the U.S. removed Saddam Hussein.

2004: In March, Pope John Paul II became the third longest reigning pontiff in history, surpassing Pope Leo XIII (r. 1878-1903).

2005: Pope John Paul II died on Apr. 2. Cardinal Joseph Ratzinger was elected pope on Apr. 19 and took the name Benedict XVI. His first encyclical, *Deus Caritas Est,* was issued on Dec. 25, 2005.

2009: Pope Benedict XVI visited the Holy Land.

2010: The sex abuse crisis expanded to Europe, with the scandal engulfing Germany, Belgium, and especially Ireland.

2013: Pope Benedict XVI became the first pope since Gregory XII in 1415 to renounce the papacy; Cardinal Jorge Mario Bergoglio of Argentina is elected as his successor and takes the name Francis. Francis is the first pontiff from Latin America, the first Jesuit, and the first non-European pope since the 8th century.

ECUMENICAL COUNCILS

An ecumenical council is an assembly of the college of bishops, with and under the presidency of the pope, which has supreme authority over the Church in matters pertaining to faith, morals, worship and discipline.

The Second Vatican Council stated: "The supreme authority with which this college (of bishops) is empowered over the whole Church is exercised in a solemn way through an ecumenical council. A council is never ecumenical unless it is confirmed or at least accepted as such by the successor of Peter. It is the prerogative of the Roman Pontiff to convoke these councils, to preside over them, and to confirm them" (Dogmatic Constitution on the Church, *Lumen Gentium,* No. 22).

Pope Presides

The pope is the head of an ecumenical council; he presides over it either personally or through legates. Conciliar decrees and other actions have binding force only when confirmed and promulgated by him. If a pope dies during a council, it is suspended until reconvened by another pope. An ecumenical council is not superior to a pope; hence, there is no appeal from a pope to a council.

Collectively, the bishops with the pope represent the whole Church. They do this not as democratic representatives of the faithful in a kind of church parliament, but as the successors of the Apostles with divinely given authority, care and responsibility over the whole Church.

All and only bishops are council participants with deliberative vote. The supreme authority of the Church can invite others and determine the manner of their participation.

Basic legislation concerning ecumenical councils is contained in Canons 337-41 of the Code of Canon Law. Basic doctrinal considerations were stated by the Second Vatican Council in the Dogmatic Constitution on the Church.

Background

Ecumenical councils had their prototype in the Council of Jerusalem in 51, at which the Apostles under the leadership of St. Peter decided that converts to the Christian faith were not obliged to observe all the prescriptions of Old Testament law (Acts 15). As early as the second century, bishops got together in regional meetings, synods or councils to take common action for the doctrinal and pastoral good of their communities of faithful. The expansion of such limited assemblies to ecumenical councils was a logical and historical evolution, given the nature and needs of the Church.

Emperors Involved

Emperors were active in summoning or convoking the first eight councils, especially the first five and the eighth. Among reasons for intervention of this kind were the facts that the emperors regarded themselves as guardians of the faith; that the settlement of religious controversies, which had repercussions in political and social turmoil, served the cause of peace in the state; and that the emperors had at their disposal ways and means of facilitating gatherings of bishops. Imperial actions, however, did not account for the formally ecumenical nature of the councils.

Some councils were attended by relatively few bishops, and the ecumenical character of several was open to question for a time. However, confirmation and de facto recognition of their actions by popes and subsequent councils established them as ecumenical.

Role in History

The councils have played a highly significant role in the history of the Church by witnessing to and defining truths of revelation, by shaping forms of worship and discipline, and by promoting measures for the ever-necessary reform and renewal of Catholic life. In general, they have represented attempts of the Church to mobilize itself in times of crisis for self-preservation, self-purification and growth.

The first eight ecumenical councils were held in the East; the other 13, in the West. The majority of separated Eastern Churches — e.g., the Orthodox — recognize the ecumenical character of the first seven councils, which formulated a great deal of basic doctrine. Other separated Eastern Churches acknowledge only the first two or first three ecumenical councils.

The 21 Councils

The 21 ecumenical councils in the history of the Church are listed below, with indication of their names or titles (taken from the names of the places where they were held); the dates; the reigning and/or approving popes; the emperors who were instrumental in convoking the eight councils in the East; the number of bishops who attended, when available; the number of sessions. Significant actions of the first 20 councils are indicated under appropriate dates in **Dates and Events in Church History.**

Nicaea I, 325: St. Sylvester I (Emperor Constantine I); attended by approximately 300 bishops; sessions held between May 20 or June 19 to near the end of August.

Constantinople I, 381: St. Damasus I (Emperor Theodosius I); attended by approximately 150 bishops; sessions held from May to July.

Ephesus, 431: St. Celestine I (Emperor Theodosius II); attended by 150 to 200 bishops; five sessions held between June 22 and July 17.

Chalcedon, 451: St. Leo I (Emperor Marcian); attended by approximately 600 bishops; 17 sessions held between Oct. 8 and Nov. 1.

Constantinople II, 553: Vigilius (Emperor Justinian I); attended by 165 bishops; eight sessions held between May 5 and June 2.

Constantinople III, 680-681: St. Agatho, St. Leo II (Emperor Constantine IV); attended by approximately 170 bishops; 16 sessions held between Nov. 7, 680, and Sept. 6, 681.

Nicaea II, 787: Adrian I (Empress Irene); attended by approximately 300 bishops: eight sessions held between Sept. 24 and Oct. 23.

Constantinople IV, 869-870: Adrian II (Emperor Basil I); attended by 102 bishops; six sessions held between Oct. 5, 869, and Feb. 28, 870.

Lateran I, 1123: Callistus II; attended by approximately 300 bishops; sessions held between Mar. 8 and Apr. 6.

Lateran II, 1139: Innocent II; attended by 900 to 1,000 bishops and abbots; three sessions held in April.

Lateran III, 1179: Alexander III; attended by at least 300 bishops; three sessions held between Mar. 5 and 19.

Lateran IV, 1215: Innocent III; sessions held between Nov. 11 and 30.

Lyons I, 1245: Innocent IV; attended by approximately 150 bishops; three sessions held between June 28 and July 17.

Lyons II, 1274: Gregory X; attended by approximately 500 bishops; six sessions held between May 7 and July 17.

Vienne, 1311-1312: Clement V; attended by 132 bishops; three sessions held between Oct. 16, 1311, and May 6, 1312.

Constance, 1414-1418: Gregory XII, Martin V; attended by nearly 200 bishops, plus other prelates and many experts; 45 sessions held between Nov. 5, 1414, and Apr. 22, 1418.

Florence (also called Basel-Ferrara-Florence), 1431-c. 1445: Eugene IV; attended by many Latin-Rite and Eastern-Rite bishops; preliminary sessions were held at Basel and Ferrara before definitive work was accomplished at Florence.

Lateran V, 1512-1517: Julius II, Leo X; 12 sessions held between May 3, 1512, and Mar. 6, 1517.

Trent, 1545-1563: Paul III, Julius III, Pius IV; 25 sessions held between Dec. 13, 1545, and Dec. 4, 1563.

Vatican I, 1869-1870: Pius IX; attended by approximately 800 bishops and other prelates; four public sessions and 89 general meetings held between Dec. 8, 1869, and Sept. 1, 1870.

VATICAN II

The Second Vatican Council, which was forecast by Pope John XXIII Jan. 25, 1959, was held in four sessions in St. Peter's Basilica.

Pope John convoked it and opened the first session, which ran from Oct. 11 to Dec. 8, 1962. Following John's death June 3, 1963, Pope Paul VI reconvened the council for the other three sessions which ran from Sept. 29 to Dec. 4, 1963; Sept. 14 to Nov. 21, 1964; Sept. 14 to Dec. 8, 1965.

A total of 2,860 Fathers participated in council proceedings, and attendance at meetings varied between 2,000 and 2,500. For various reasons, including the denial of exit from Communist-dominated countries, 274 Fathers could not attend.

The council formulated and promulgated 16 documents — two dogmatic and two pastoral constitutions, nine decrees and three declarations — all of which reflect its basic pastoral orientation toward renewal and reform in the Church. Given below are the Latin and English titles of the documents and their dates of promulgation.

Lumen Gentium (Dogmatic Constitution on the Church), Nov. 21, 1964.

Dei Verbum (Dogmatic Constitution on Divine Revelation), Nov. 18, 1965.

Sacrosanctum Concilium (Constitution on the Sacred Liturgy), Dec. 4, 1963.

Gaudium et Spes (Pastoral Constitution on the Church in the Modern World), Dec. 7, 1965.

Christus Dominus (Decree on the Bishops' Pastoral Office in the Church), Oct. 28, 1965.

Ad Gentes (Decree on the Church's Missionary Activity), Dec. 7, 1965.

Unitatis Redintegratio (Decree on Ecumenism), Nov. 21, 1964.

Orientalium Ecclesiarum (Decree on Eastern Catholic Churches), Nov. 21, 1964.

Presbyterorum Ordinis (Decree on the Ministry and Life of Priests), Dec. 7, 1965.

Optatam Totius (Decree on Priestly Formation), Oct. 28, 1965.

Perfectae Caritatis (Decree on the Appropriate Renewal of the Religious Life), Oct. 28, 1965.

Apostolicam Actuositatem (Decree on the Apostolate of the Laity), Nov. 18, 1965.

Inter Mirifica (Decree on the Instruments of Social Communication), Dec. 4, 1963.

Dignitatis Humanae (Declaration on Religious Freedom), Dec. 7, 1965.

Nostra Aetate (Declaration on the Relationship of

the Church to Non-Christian Religions), Oct. 28, 1965. *Gravissimum Educationis* (Declaration on Christian Education), Oct. 28, 1965.

The key documents were the four constitutions, which set the ideological basis for all the others. To date, the documents with the most visible effects are those on the liturgy, the Church, the Church in the world, ecumenism, the renewal of religious life, the life and ministry of priests, the lay apostolate.

The main business of the council was to explore and make explicit dimensions of doctrine and Christian life requiring emphasis for the full development of the Church and the better accomplishment of its mission in the contemporary world.

Enactments of the Second Vatican Council have been points of departure for a wide variety of developments in the internal life of the Church and its mission in the world at large. Much effort has been made in the pontificate of Pope John Paul II to provide the interpretation and implementation of the conciliar documents with a more uniform and universal structure.

POPE BENEDICT XVI AND THE SECOND VATICAN COUNCIL

In December 2005, Pope Benedict XVI gave a reflection on the interpretation of Vatican II. The following are excerpts of his address:

The last event of this year on which I wish to reflect here is the celebration of the conclusion of the Second Vatican Council 40 years ago. This memory prompts the question: What has been the result of the Council? Was it well received? What, in the acceptance of the Council, was good and what was inadequate or mistaken? What still remains to be done? No one can deny that in vast areas of the Church the implementation of the Council has been somewhat difficult, even without wishing to apply to what occurred in these years the description that St. Basil, the great Doctor of the Church, made of the Church's situation after the Council of Nicea: he compares her situation to a naval battle in the darkness of the storm, saying among other things: "The raucous shouting of those who through disagreement rise up against one another, the incomprehensible chatter, the confused din of uninterrupted clamoring, has now filled almost the whole of the Church, falsifying through excess or failure the right doctrine of the faith..." (*De Spiritu Sancto*, XXX, 77; PG 32, 213 A; SCh 17 ff., p. 524).

We do not want to apply precisely this dramatic description to the situation of the post-conciliar period, yet something from all that occurred is nevertheless reflected in it. The question arises: Why has the implementation of the Council, in large parts of the Church, thus far been so difficult? Well, it all depends on the correct interpretation of the Council or — as we would say today — on its proper hermeneutics, the correct key to its interpretation and application. The problems in its implementation arose from the fact that two contrary hermeneutics came face to face and quarreled with each other. One caused confusion, the other, silently but more and more visibly, bore and is bearing fruit.

On the one hand, there is an interpretation that I would call "a hermeneutic of discontinuity and rupture"; it has frequently availed itself of the sympathies of the mass media, and also one trend of modern theology. On the other, there is the "hermeneutic of reform," of renewal in the continuity of the one subject-Church which the Lord has given to us. She is a subject which increases in time and develops, yet always remaining the same, the one subject of the journeying People of God.

The hermeneutic of discontinuity risks ending in a split between the pre-conciliar Church and the post-conciliar Church. It asserts that the texts of the Council as such do not yet express the true spirit of the Council. It claims that they are the result of compromises in which, to reach unanimity, it was found necessary to keep and reconfirm many old things that are now pointless. However, the true spirit of the Council is not to be found in these compromises but instead in the impulses toward the new that are contained in the texts.

These innovations alone were supposed to represent the true spirit of the Council, and starting from and in conformity with them, it would be possible to move ahead. Precisely because the texts would only imperfectly reflect the true spirit of the Council and its newness, it would be necessary to go courageously beyond the texts and make room for the newness in which the Council's deepest intention would be expressed, even if it were still vague.

In a word: it would be necessary not to follow the texts of the Council but its spirit. In this way, obviously, a vast margin was left open for the question on how this spirit should subsequently be defined and room was consequently made for every whim....

The hermeneutic of dis-continuity is countered by the hermeneutic of reform, as it was presented first by Pope John XXIII in his Speech inaugurating the Council on Oct. 11, 1962 and later by Pope Paul VI in his Discourse for the Council's conclusion on Dec. 7, 1965.

Here I shall cite only John XXIII's well-known words, which unequivocally express this hermeneutic when he says that the Council wishes "to transmit the doctrine, pure and integral, without any attenuation or distortion." And he continues: "Our duty is not only to guard this precious treasure, as if we were concerned only with antiquity, but to dedicate ourselves with an earnest will and without fear to that work which our era demands of us...." It is necessary that "adherence to all the teaching of the Church in its entirety and preciseness..." be presented in "faithful and perfect conformity to the authentic doctrine, which, however, should be studied and expounded through the methods of research and through the literary forms of modern thought. The substance of the ancient doctrine of the deposit of faith is one thing, and the way in which it is presented is another...," retaining the same meaning and message (*The Documents of Vatican II*, Walter M. Abbott, S.J., p. 715).

The Papacy and the Holy See

POPE FRANCIS

Cardinal Jorge Mario Bergolgio, archbishop of Buenos Aires, Argentina, was elected Bishop of Rome and the 265th Successor of St. Peter as Supreme Pastor of the Universal Church on Mar. 13, 2013, after five ballots over two days. He chose the name Francis in honor of St. Francis of Assisi. [For details of his election and life, *see* under **News in Depth**, page 55.]

POPE BENEDICT XVI (2005-2013)

Cardinal Joseph Ratzinger of Germany, Prefect of the Congregation for the Doctrine of the Faith since 1981 and one the great theologians in the Church over the last 50 years, was elected Bishop of Rome and the 264th successor of St. Peter as Supreme Pastor of the Universal Church on Apr. 19, 2005, after four ballots over two days. He chose the name Benedict in honor of Pope Benedict XV, an advocate of peace, and St. Benedict of Nursia, who helped to resurrect civilization in Europe during the Dark Ages. Pope Benedict XVI was invested with the pallium, the symbol of his office, on Apr. 24, 2005 in ceremonies attended by more than 500,000 people in St. Peter's Square. At the time

Coat of Arms of Pope Francis

MISERANDO ATQUE ELIGENDO

of his birthday in 2012, he became the sixth longest lived pope. Pope Leo XIII, who died at the age of 93 was the oldest living pontiff. On Feb. 28, 2013, at 8 p.m., he resigned the papacy. He was the first pope to renounce the papacy since 1415 and the resignation of Pope Gregory XII.

Early Life

Joseph Aloysius Ratzinger was born on Apr. 16, 1927 while the family was living in a three-story house in the little village of Marktl am Inn, situated in eastern Bavaria. His family moved several times in his early years owing to his father's opposition to the Nazis, and young Joseph was forced to join the Hitler Youth. He was adamantly opposed to the Nazis and made every effort to leave at the first opportunity. In 1939, he entered the minor seminary in Traunstein, his first step toward the priesthood. World War II forced a postponement of his studies, until 1945, when he re-entered

the seminary with his brother, Georg. In 1947, he entered the *Herzogliches Georgianum*, a theological institute associated with the University of Munich. Finally, on June 29, 1951, both Joseph and his brother were ordained to the priesthood by Card. Faulhaber, in the Cathedral at Freising, on the Feast of Sts. Peter and Paul.

Continuing his theological studies at the University of Munich, he received his doctorate in theology in July 1953, with a thesis entitled *Volk und Haus Gottes in Augustins Lehre von der Kirche* ("The People and House of God in Augustine's doctrine of the Church"). He fulfilled a requirement for teaching at the university level by completing a book-length treatise, "The Theology of History in St. Bonaventure." On Apr. 15, 1959, he began lectures as a full professor of fundamental theology at the University of Bonn. From 1962-1965, he was present during all four sessions of the Second Vatican Council as a *peritus,* or chief theological advisor, to Card. Josef Frings of Köln (Cologne), Germany.

In 1963, he began teaching at the University of Münster, taking, in 1966, a second chair in dogmatic theology at the University of Tübingen. A wave of student uprisings swept across Europe in 1968, and Marxism quickly became the dominant intellectual system at Tübingen. He found the radicalized environment to be unacceptable, so in 1969 he moved back to Bavaria and took a teaching position at the University of Regensburg. There, he eventually became dean and vice president. He was also a member of the International Theological Commission of the Holy See from 1969 until 1980.

In 1972, together with Hans Urs von Balthasar, Henri De Lubac and others, he launched the Catholic theological journal *Communio,* a quarterly review of Catholic theology and culture. It has been said that this was done in response to the misinterpretation of the Second Vatican Council by various theologians, as represented by the theological journal *Concilium.*

Archbishop and Cardinal

On Mar. 24, 1977, Fr. Ratzinger was appointed Archbishop of Munich and Freising by Pope Paul VI. He was ordained a bishop on May 28, 1977, taking as his

Episcopal motto a phrase from 3 John 8, *Cooperatores Veritatis* ("Fellow Worker in the Truth"). On June 27, 1977, he was elevated to Cardinal (Cardinal Priest) by Pope Paul VI, with the titular church of St. Mary of Consolation (in Tiburtina). In 1980, he was named by Pope John Paul II to chair the special Synod on the Laity. Shortly after that, the pope asked him to head the Congregation for Catholic Education. Card. Ratzinger declined, feeling he should not leave his post in Munich too soon. On Nov. 25, 1981, he accepted the post of the Prefect for the Congregation for the Doctrine of the Faith, becoming at the same time *ex officio* the President of the Pontifical Biblical Commission, and the International Theological Commission.

Cardinal Ratzinger was President of the Commission for the Preparation of the *Catechism of the Catholic Church*, and after 6 years of work (1986-92) he presented the new *Catechism* to the Holy Father. On Apr. 5, 1993, he was transferred to the order of Cardinal Bishops, with the suburbicarian see of Velletri-Signi. On Nov. 9, 1998, his election as Vice-Dean of the Sacred College of Cardinals was approved by Pope John Paul II, and the Holy Father approved his election as Dean of the College of Cardinals on Nov. 30, 2002, with the title of the suburbicarian See of Ostia added to that of Velletri-Segni.

Besides his prefecture at the Doctrine of the Faith, his curial memberships include: the Second Section of the Secretariat of State, the Congregation of Bishops, of Divine Worship and the Discipline of the Sacraments, of Catholic Education, of Evangelization of Peoples, for the Oriental Churches; and the Pontifical Councils for Christian Unity, for Culture (councils); as well as, the Commissions *Ecclesia Dei*, and for Latin America.

As Dean of the College he was a key figure during the *sede vacante* after the death of Pope John Paul II on April 2, 2005 and delivered the funeral homily for the deceased pontiff.

Foreign Pastoral Visits

2005: Cologne, Germany (World Youth Day), Aug. 18-21.
2006: Poland, May 25-28; Valencia, Spain, July 8-9;
Munich, Germany, Sept. 9-14; Turkey, Nov. 28-Dec. 1.
2007: Brazil, May 9-14; Austria, Sept. 7-9.
2008: United States, Apr. 15-21; Sydney, Australia, July 12-21; France, Sept. 12-15.
2009: Cameroon and Angola, Mar. 17-23; Holy Land, May 8-15; Czech Republic, Sept. 26-28.
2010: Malta, Apr. 17-18; Portugal, May 11-14; Cyprus, June 4-6; England and Scotland, Sept. 16-19; Spain, Nov. 6-7.
2011: Croatia, June 4-5; Madrid, Spain, Aug. 18-21; Germany, Sept. 22-25; Benin, Nov. 18-20.
2012: Mexico and Republic of Cuba, Mar. 23-29; Lebanon, Sept. 14-16.

Canonizations and Beatifications

As of Feb. 28, 2013, Pope Benedict XVI's pontificate witnessed the beatification of 843 Servants of God. Pope Benedict XVI canonized 45 beati. The total number of blesseds and saints in his pontificate was 888.

Encyclicals and Other Writings

Cardinal Joseph Ratzinger at the time of his election as Pope Benedict XVI was one of the Church's greatest theologians and author of a vast body of writings. Since his election, he has issued several documents, including several *motu proprio* and apostolic letters. His first encyclical, *Deus Caritas Est*, was issued on Dec. 25, 2005. His second encyclical, *Spe Salvi*, released Nov. 30, 2007. On Mar. 13, 2007, he released the post-synodal apostolic exhortation, *Sacramentum Caritatis* ("The Sacrament of Charity"), a reflection on the discussions and suggestions made during the 2005 world Synod of Bishops on the Eucharist. In spring 2007, he also published his first book as pope, *Jesus of Nazareth*. The second volume was published in spring 2011. On July 7, 2007, he issued the long-awaited *Motu Proprio Summorum Pontificum*, on the "Roman liturgy prior to the reform of 1970." His third encyclical, *Caritas in Veritate*, was issued on July 7, 2009. On Sept. 30, 2010, he issued the post-synodal apostolic exhortation, *Verbum Domini*, on the Word of God in the Life and Mission of the Church.

POPE BLESSED JOHN PAUL II, 1978-2005

Cardinal Karol Wojtyla of Cracow was elected Bishop of Rome and 263rd successor of St. Peter as Supreme Pastor of the Universal Church on Oct. 16, 1978. He chose the name John Paul II in honor of his predecessor, Pope John Paul I, as well as Popes Bl. John XXIII and Paul VI. He was invested with the pallium, symbol of his office, on Oct. 22 in ceremonies attended by more than 250,000 people in St. Peter's Square. He died on Apr. 2, 2005 at 9:37 p.m. in the Apostolic Palace in the Vatican. He was beatified on May 1, 2011; his canonization was approved in Sept. 2013.

From the start, Pope John Paul II labored to keep the Church faithful to its tradition and to the teaching and spirit of Vatican Council II, while positioning it to meet the challenges of the Third Millennium. He was a staunch defender of the sanctity of human life—"from conception to natural death," he often said—and of marriage and the family. Opposition to totalitarianism and support for human rights make this activist, long-reigning pope a major figure on the world political scene.

He was the first non-Italian pope since Adrian VI (1522-23) and the first Polish pope ever. At his election, he was the youngest pope since Pius IX (1846-78). On May 24, 1998, he became the longest-reigning pope elected in the 20th centu-
ry, surpassing the 19 years, seven months and seven days of Pius XII (1939-58). (Leo XIII, who died in 1903, was pope for 25 years.) His pontificate was also the third longest in the history of the Church. He surpassed Pope Leo XIII (25 years, 5 months), and is behind only Bl. Pius IX (31 years, 7 months, 21 days) and St. Peter (precise dates unknown).

He was the most-traveled pope in history. He covered over 750,000 miles during 104 pastoral visits outside Italy, over 146 within Italy, and 301 to the parishes of Rome. In all, he visited 129 countries and held talks with 1,022 heads of state or government. By the end of his pontificate, the Holy See had diplomatic relations with 174 states, as well as diplomatic relations with the European Union and Sovereign Military Order of Malta, and special relations with the Russian Federation and the PLO.

Certainly he was the pope most prolific in literary output, having issued 14 encyclicals, 14 apostolic exhortations, 11 apostolic constitutions, 45 apostolic letters and 30 *motu proprio*.

John Paul II proclaimed 1,338 Blesseds in 147 ceremonies and had proclaimed 482 Saints in 51 liturgical celebrations; his 17 predecessors from Pope Clement VIII to Pope Paul VI canonized a total of 302 people. He held nine consistories for the creation of cardinals and named a total of 231 cardinals (not including the *in pectore* cardinals).

The last consistory was October 2003. The Holy Father presided at 15 synods: the Particular Synod of Bishops of the Netherlands in 1980; six ordinary synods (1980, 1983, 1987, 1990, 1994 and 2001); one extraordinary (1985) and eight special (1980, 1991, 1994, 1995, 1997, two in 1998, and the second synod for Europe in October 1999); the most recent synod was held in October 2001.

Over the years the pope held over 1,161 weekly general audiences and has welcomed over 17 million faithful from every part of the world. Other audiences, including various groups and heads of state and government, total around 1,600. As pontiff, he consecrated 321 bishops and performed over 1,500 baptisms.

He was also the first pope ever to visit a synagogue (Rome, April 1986); the first to visit a mosque (Omayyad Great Mosque of Damascus, May 2001); the first to call for a Day of Pardon (Jubilee Year 2000); and the first to add five new mysteries to the Rosary (Oct. 2002).

Early Life

Karol Josef Wojtyla was born May 18, 1920, in Wadowice, an industrial town near Cracow. His parents were Karol Wojtyla, who had been an adminstrative officer in the Austrian army and was a lieutenant in the Polish army until his retirement in 1927, and Emilia Kaczorowska Wojtyla. His mother died in 1929 of kidney and heart failure. His sister died a few days after birth; his older brother Edmund, a physician, died in 1932, and his father in 1941.

He attended schools in Wadowice and in 1938 enrolled in the faculty of philosophy of the Jagiellonian University in Cracow, where he moved with his father. At the university he was active in the Studio 38 experimental theater group.

For young Wojtyla, as for countless others, life changed forever on Sept. 1, 1939, when World War II began. Nazi occupation forces closed the Jagiellonian University and the young man had to work in a quarry as a stone cutter and later in a chemical plant to avoid deportation to Germany. In Feb. 1940, he met Jan Tryanowski, a tailor who became his spiritual mentor and introduced him to the writings of St. John of the Cross and St. Teresa of Ávila. He also participated in underground theater groups, including the Rhapsodic Theater of Mieczyslaw Kotlarczyk.

In Oct. 1942, he began studies for the priesthood in the underground seminary maintained by Card. Adam Sapieha of Cracow. He was struck by an automobile Feb. 29, 1944, and hospitalized until Mar. 12. In Aug. of that year Card. Sapieha transferred him and the other seminarians to the Archbishop's Residence, where they lived and studied until war's end. Ordained a priest by the Cardinal on Nov. 1, 1946, he left Poland Nov. 15 to begin advanced studies in Rome at the Angelicum University (the Pontifical University of St. Thomas Aquinas).

He subsequently earned doctorates in theology and philosophy and was a respected moral theologian and ethicist.

Bishop and Cardinal

On July 4, 1958, Pope Pius XII named him auxiliary bishop to Abp. Eugeniusz Baziak, Apostolic Administrator of Cracow. His book *Love and Responsibility* was published in 1960. (Earlier, he had published poetry and several plays.) Following Abp. Baziak's death in 1962, he became Vicar Capitular and then on Jan. 13, 1964, Abp. of Cracow–the first residential head of the See permitted by the communist authorities since Card. Sapieha's death in 1951.

Abp. Wojtyla attended all four sessions of the Second Vatican Council, from 1962 to 1965, and helped draft Schema XIII, which became *Gaudium et Spes*, the Pastoral Constitution on the Church in the Modern World. He also contributed to *Dignitatis Humanae* (the "Declaration on Religious Freedom") and on the theology of the laity.

Pope Paul VI created him a cardinal in the consistory of June 26, 1967, with the titular Roman church of S. Cesario in Palatio.

Pope Paul died Aug. 6, 1978. Card. Wojtyla participated in the conclave that chose Card. Albino Luciani of Venice his successor on Aug. 26. When the new Pope, who had taken the name John Paul I, died unexpectedly on Sept. 28, Card. Wojtyla joined 110 other cardinals in that year's second conclave. He emerged on the second day of voting, Oct. 16, as Pope John Paul II.

Pontificate

Pope John Paul set out the major themes and program of his pontificate in his first encyclical, *Redemptor Hominis (The Redeemer of Man)*, dated Mar. 4, 1979, and published Mar. 15. "The Redeemer of Man, Jesus Christ, is the center of the universe and of history," he wrote. Throughout his pontificate he emphasized preparation for the year 2000–which he proclaimed a Jubilee Year–and for the Third Millennium of the Christian era, with the aim of fostering a renewed commitment to evangelization among Catholics. He also has produced a significant body of magisterial teaching in such areas as Christian anthropology, sexual morality, and social justice, while working for peace and human rights throughout the world.

His pontificate has been uncommonly active and filled with dramatic events. Among the most dramatic are those associated with the fall of communism in Eastern Europe. Many students of that complex event credit John Paul with a central role. His visits to his Polish homeland in 1979 (June 2-10) and 1983 (June 16-23) bolstered Polish Catholicism and kindled Polish resistance to communism, while his determined support for the Solidarity labor movement gave his countrymen a vehicle for their resistance. The result was a growing nonviolent liberation movement leading to the dramatic developments of 1989—the collapse of communist regimes, the emergence of democracy in Poland and other countries, the fall of the Berlin Wall, and, in time, to the breakup of the Soviet Union and the end of the Cold War.

Dramatic in a much different way was the 1981 attempt on the Pope's life. At 5:19 p.m. on May 13, as he greeted crowds in St. Peter's Square before his Wednesday general audience, a Turkish terrorist named Mehmet Ali Agca shot John Paul at close range. Whether the assassin acted alone or at the behest of others—and which others—remain unanswered questions. Following a six-hour operation, John Paul was hospitalized for 77 days at Gemelli Hospital. He visited Ali Agca in the Rebibbia prison on Dec. 27, 1983.

Although he resumed his activities vigorously after his recuperation, the pope's health and strength have declined over the years. In July 1992, he had colon surgery for the removal of a non-cancerous tumor; in Nov. 1993, his shoulder was dislocated in a fall; he suffered a broken femur in another fall in Apr. 1994; and in Oct. 1996, he had an appendectomy. For several years, too, the effects were apparent of what the Vatican acknowledges to be a neurological condition (many observers take the ailment to be Parkinson's disease).

Foreign Pastoral Visits

As noted, his pastoral visits were a striking feature

of his pontificate. Many were to nations in the Third World. His 104 trips outside Italy were as follows:

1979 Dominican Republic and Mexico, Jan. 5-Feb. 1; Poland, June 2-10; Ireland and the United States, Sept. 29-Oct. 7; Turkey, Nov. 28-30.

1980 Africa (Zaire, Congo Republic, Kenya, Ghana, Upper Volta, Ivory Coast), May 2-12; France, May 30-June 2; Brazil (13 cities), June 30-July 12; West Germany, Nov. 15-19.

1981 Philippines, Guam, and Japan, with stopovers in Pakistan and Alaska, Feb. 16-27.

1982 Africa (Nigeria, Benin, Gabon, Equatorial Guinea), Feb. 12-19; Portugal, May 12-15; Great Britain, May 28-June 2; Argentina, June 11-12; Switzerland, June 15; San Marino, Aug. 29; Spain, Oct. 31-Nov. 9.

1983 Central America (Costa Rica, Nicaragua, Panama, El Salvador, Guatemala, Belize, Honduras) and Haiti, Mar. 2-10; Poland, June 16-23; Lourdes, France, Aug. 14-15; Austria, Sept. 10-13.

1984 South Korea, Papua New Guinea, Solomon Islands, Thailand, May 12; Switzerland, June 12-17; Canada, Sept. 9-20; Spain, Dominican Republic, and Puerto Rico, Oct. 10-12.

1985 Venezuela, Ecuador, Peru, Trinidad and Tobago, Jan. 26-Feb. 6; Belgium, The Netherlands, and Luxembourg, May 11-21; Africa (Togo, Ivory Coast, Cameroon, Central African Republic, Zaire, Kenya, and Morocco), Aug. 8-19; Liechtenstein, Sept. 8.

1986 India, Feb. 1-10; Colombia and Saint Lucia, July 1-7; France, Oct. 4-7; Oceania (Australia, New Zealand, Bangladesh, Fiji, Singapore, and Seychelles), Nov. 18-Dec. 1.

1987 Uruguay, Chile, and Argentina, Mar. 31-Apr. 12; West Germany, Apr. 30-May 4; Poland, June 8-14; the United States and Canada, Sept. 10-19.

1988 Uruguay, Bolivia, Peru, and Paraguay, May 7-18; Austria, June 23-27; Africa (Zimbabwe, Botswana, Lesotho, Swaziland, and Mozambique), Sept. 10-19; France, Oct. 8-11.

1989 Madagascar, Reunion, Zambia, and Malawi, Apr. 28-May 6; Norway, Iceland, Finland, Denmark, and Sweden, June 1-10; Spain, Aug. 19-21; South Korea, Indonesia, East Timor, and Mauritius, Oct. 6-16.

1990 Africa (Cape Verde, Guinea Bissau, Mali, and Burkna Faso), Jan. 25-Feb. 1; Czechoslovakia, Apr. 21-22; Mexico and Curaçao, May 6-13; Malta, May 25-27; Africa (Tanzania, Burundi, Rwanda, and Ivory Coast), Sept. 1-10.

1991 Portugal, May 10-13; Poland, June 1-9; Poland and Hungary, Aug. 13-20; Brazil, Oct. 12-21.

1992 Africa (Senegal, The Gambia, Guinea), Feb. 10-26; Africa (Angola, São Tome, and Principe), June 4-10; Dominican Republic, Oct. 10-14.

1993 Africa (Benin, Uganda, Sudan), Feb. 2-10; Albania, Apr. 25; Spain, June 12-17; Jamaica, Mexico, Denver (United States), Aug. 9-15; Lithuania, Latvia, Estonia, Sept. 4-10.

1994 Zagreb, Croatia, Sept. 10.

1995 Philippines, Papua New Guinea, Australia, Sri Lanka, Jan. 12-21; Czech Republic and Poland, May 20-22; Belgium, June 3-4; Slovakia, June 30-July 3; Africa (Cameroon, South Africa, Kenya), Sept. 14-20; United Nations and United States, Oct. 4-8.

1996 Central America (Guatemala, Nicaragua, El Salvador), Feb. 5-11; Tunisia, Apr. 17; Slovenia, May 17-19; Germany, June 21-23; Hungary, Sept.

6-7; France, Sept. 19-22.

1997 Sarajevo, Apr. 12-13; Czech Republic, Apr. 25-27; Lebanon, May 10-11; Poland, May 31-June 10; France, Aug. 21-24; Brazil, Oct. 2-5.

1998 Cuba, Jan. 21-25; Nigeria, Mar. 21-23; Austria, June 19-21; Croatia, Oct. 3-4.

1999 Mexico, Jan. 22-25; St. Louis, United States, Jan. 26-27; Romania, May 2-5; Poland June, 5-17; Slovenia, Sept. 19; India, Nov. 6-7; Georgia, Nov. 8-9.

2000 Egypt and Mount Sinai, Feb. 24-26; Holy Land, March 20-26; Fátima, May 12-13.

2001 Greece, Syria, and Malta, May 4-9; Ukraine, June 23-27; Kazakstan and Armenia, Sept. 22-27.

2002 Azerbaijan and Bulgaria, May 22-26; Toronto, Canada, July 23-28; Guatemala City, July 29-30; Mexico City, July 31-Aug. 2; Poland, Aug. 16-19.

2003 Spain, May 3-4; Croatia, June 5-9; Bosnia-Herzegovina, June 22; Slovak Republic, Sept. 11-14.

2004 Switzerland, May 5-6; Lourdes, France, Aug. 15-16.

Encyclicals and Other Writings

As noted above, Pope John Paul's first encyclical, *Redemptor Hominis* (1979), set the tone for and in general terms indicated the subject matter of many of the documents to follow. These were infused with the pope's distinctive personalism, which emphasizes the dignity and rights of the human person, most truly understood in the light of Christ, as the norm and goal of human endeavor.

His other encyclical letters were: *Dives in Misericordia* ("On the Mercy of God"), 1980; *Laborem Exercens* ("On Human Work"), 1981; *Slavorum Apostoli* ("The Apostles of the Slavs", honoring Sts. Cyril and Methodius), 1985; *Dominum et Vivificantem* ("Lord and Giver of Life," on the Holy Spirit), 1986; *Redemptoris Mater* ("Mother of the Redeemer"), 1987; *Sollicitudo Rei Socialis* ("On Social Concerns"), 1988; *Redemptoris Missio* ("Mission of the Redeemer") and *Centesimus Annus* ("The Hundredth Year", on the anniversary of Leo XIII's *Rerum Novarum*), both 1991; *Veritatis Splendor* ("The Splendor of Truth"), 1993; *Evangelium Vitae* ("The Gospel of Life") and *Ut Unum Sint* ("That All May Be One"), 1995; *Fides et Ratio* ("Faith and Reason"), 1998; and *Ecclesia de Eucharistia* ("Church of the Eucharist"), 2003.

Among his other publications were: *Catechesi Tradendae*, a post-synodal apostolic exhortation on catechesis, 1979; apostolic letter proclaiming Sts. Cyril and Methodius, together with St. Benedict, patrons of Europe, 1980; post-synodal apostolic exhortation *Familiaris Consortio*, on the family, 1981; apostolic letter *Caritatis Christi*, for the Church in China, 1982; letter for the 500th anniversary of the birth of Martin Luther, 1983; apostolic letter *Salvifici Doloris* ("On the Christian Meaning of Suffering"), apostolic exhortation *Redemptionis Donum*, to men and women religious, apostolic letters *Redemptionis Anno*, on Jerusalem, and *Les Grands Mysteres*, on Lebanon, and post-synodal apostolic exhortation *Reconciliatio et Poenitentia* ("Reconciliation and Penance"), all 1984.

Also: apostolic letter *Dilecti Amici*, on the occasion of the United Nations' International Year of Youth, 1985; apostolic letter *Euntes in Mundum*, for the millennium of Christianity in Kievan Rus', and apostolic letter *Mulieris Dignitatem* ("On the Dignity and Vocation of Women"), all 1988; post-synodal apostolic exhortation *Christifideles Laici* ("The Lay Members of Christ's Faithful People") and apostolic exhortation *Redemptoris Custos* ("On St. Joseph"), 1989; post-synodal apostolic exhortation

Pastores Dabo Vobis ("I Give You Shepherds"), 1992; "Letter to Families," for the International Year of the Family, "Letter on the International Conference on Population and Development" in Cairo, apostolic letter *Ordinatio Sacerdotalis* ("On Reserving Priestly Ordination to Men Alone"), apostolic letter *Tertio Millennio Adveniente*, on preparation for the Jubilee Year 2000, and "Letter to Children in the Year of the Family," all 1994.

Also: apostolic letter *Orientale Lumen* ("The Light of the East"), on Catholic-Orthodox relations, "Letter to Women," post-synodal apostolic exhortations *Ecclesia in Africa, Ecclesia in Asia,* and *Ecclesia in Europa,* and apostolic letter for the fourth centenary of the Union of Brest, all 1995; apostolic constitution *Universi Dominici Gregis* ("On the Vacancy of the Apostolic See and the Election of the Roman Pontiff"), post-synodal apostolic exhortation *Vita Consecrata* ("On the Consecrated Life and Its Mission in the Church and in the World"), and apostolic letter on the 350th anniversary of the Union of Uzhorod, all 1996; post-synodal apostolic exhortation, "A New Hope for Lebanon," 1997; *Incarnationis Mysterium,* Bull of Indiction of the Great Jubilee of the Year 2000, 1998; and the apostolic letter *Misericordia Dei* ("On Certain Aspects of the Celebration of the Sacrament of Penance"), 2002.

In his years as pope he published several books, including *Crossing the Threshold of Hope* (1994), *Gift and Mystery: On the Fiftieth Anniversary of My Priestly Ordination* (1996), and *Alzatevi, andiamo (Get Up, Let Us Go,* 2004), on the pontiff's 20 years as a bishop in Poland.

Issues and Activities

Doctrinal Concerns: The integrity of Catholic doctrine was a major concern of Pope John Paul. On Nov. 25, 1981, he appointed Archbishop—later, Cardinal and Pope Benedict XVI—Joseph Ratzinger of Munich-Freising, a prominent theologian, Prefect of the Congregation for the Doctrine of the Faith. The congregation under Card. Ratzinger has published important documents on bioethics, liberation theology (1984 and 1986), the Church's inability to ordain women as priests, the latter affirming that the teaching on this matter has been "set forth infallibly" (1995), and same-sex unions (2003).

Catechism: One of Pope John Paul's most important initiatives was the *Catechism of the Catholic Church.* The idea for this up-to-date compendium was broached at the extraordinary assembly of the Synod of Bishops held in 1985 to evaluate the implementation of Vatican Council II. The pope approved, and the project went forward under a commission of cardinals headed by Card. Ratzinger. Published in 1992 by authorization of John Paul II (the original was in French, with the English translation appearing in 1994 and the authoritative Latin *editio typica* in 1997), this first catechism for the universal Church in four centuries is crucial to the hoped-for renewal of catechesis.

Canon Law: John Paul oversaw the completion of the revision of the Code of Canon Law begun in 1959 at the direction of Pope John XXIII. He promulgated the new code on Jan. 25, 1983; it went into effect on Nov. 27 of that year. In *Sacrae Disciplinae Leges,* the apostolic constitution accompanying the revised code, the pope says it has "one and the same intention" as Vatican Council II — whose convening John XXIII announced at the same time — namely, "the renewal of Christian living."

On Apr. 18, 1990, John Paul promulgated the Code of Canons for the Eastern Churches. Although particular sections of the Eastern code appeared at various times dating back to 1949, this was the first time an integrated code of law for the Eastern Churches had been issued in its entirety.

Ecumenical and Interreligious Relations: Ecumenical and interreligious relations received much attention from Pope John Paul II. Two of his major documents, the encyclical *Ut Unum Sint* and the apostolic letter *Orientale Lumen,* both published in 1995, deal with these matters. He met frequently with representatives of other religious bodies, spoke frequently about the quest for unity, and has called for Catholics and others to pray and work to this end.

Among the important actions in this area were the signings of common declarations with the Ecumenical Patriarch of Constantinople His Holiness Dimitrios (Dec. 7, 1987) and his successor Bartholomew I (June 29, 1995), with the Archbishop of Canterbury and Primate of the Anglican Communion, Dr. Robert Runcie (May 29, 1982, in Canterbury Cathedral and again Oct. 2, 1989, in Rome) and his successor Dr. George Leonard Carey (Dec. 6, 1996), with the Supreme Patriarch and Catholicos of All Armenians, His Holiness Karekin I (Dec. 14, 1996), and with His Holiness Aram I Keshishian, Catholicos of Cilicia of the Armenians (Jan. 26, 1997). On Oct. 5, 1991, for the first time since the Reformation, two Lutheran bishops joined the Pope and the Catholic bishops of Stockholm and Helsinki in an ecumenical prayer service in St. Peter's Basilica marking the sixth centenary of the canonization of St. Bridget of Sweden.

Pope John Paul II had Jewish friends since boyhood, and he worked hard to strengthen Catholic-Jewish ties. The Holy See formally initiated diplomatic relations with the State of Israel at the level of apostolic nunciature and embassy on June 15, 1994. In Mar. 1998, the Commission for Religious Relations with the Jews published an important document on the roots of the World War II Jewish Holocaust entitled *We Remember: A Reflection on the Shoah.* In a letter dated Mar. 12 to the commission chairman, Card. Edward Idris Cassidy, the Pope expressed "fervent hope" that it would "help to heal the wounds of past misunderstandings and injustices."

On Sunday, Mar. 12, 2000, Pope John Paul II presided over a day of pardon for those sins committed by members of the Church over the centuries. The Holy Father issued a formal apology for the misdeeds of the members of the Church in the past, including a renewed apology for all anti-Semitic actions by Catholics. This apology was given even greater depth by the Holy Father's trip to the Holy Land in Mar. 2000. During his historic visit to Israel, the pope placed a written apology to the Jewish people in the Wailing Wall in Jerusalem. He made further efforts at ecumenical dialogue with the Orthodox Churches during his visits to Greece, Syria, and Ukraine in 2001 and at the Day of Prayer for Peace at Assisi in Jan. 2002.

Women's Concerns: Pope John Paul's insistence that, in fidelity to the will of Christ, the Church is unable to ordain women as priests put him at odds with some feminists, as did his opposition to abortion and contraception. But it is clear from his writings that he was unusually sensitive to women's issues, and he was a strong defender of women's dignity and rights, about which he often has spoken. In 1995 he appointed a woman, Professor Mary Ann Glendon of the Harvard University Law School, head of the Holy See's delegation to the fourth U.N. conference on women, held in Beijing Sept. 4-15, the first time a woman had been named to such a post.

World Affairs: At least since Jan. 1979, when he accepted a request for mediation in a border conflict between Argentina and Chile, John Paul II worked for peace in many parts of the world. He supported efforts to achieve reconciliation between conflicting parties in troubled areas like Lebanon, the Balkans, and the Persian Gulf, where he sought to avert the Gulf War of 1991. He advocated religious liberty and human rights during pastoral visits to many countries, including Cuba and Nigeria in 1998. Among the notable ecumenical and interreligious events of the pontificate was the World Day of Prayer for Peace on Oct. 27, 1986, which he convoked in Assisi and attended along with representatives of numerous other churches and religious groups.

In 1984 the Holy See and the U.S. established diplomatic relations. (The pope has met with Presidents Jimmy Carter, Ronald Reagan, George Bush, Bill Clinton, and George W. Bush.) Relations with Poland were re-established in 1989. Diplomatic relations were established with the Soviet Union in 1990 and with the Russian Federation in 1992. Relations also have been established with other Eastern European countries and countries that were part of the former Soviet Union, with Mexico, and with other nations including Jordan, South Africa, and Libya. Working contacts of a "permanent and official character" were begun with the Palestine Liberation Organization in 1994, leading to the signing of a formal Basic Agreement with the PLO on Feb. 15, 2000. The pope also attempted to prevent the outbreak of hostilities in Iraq in 2003 and welcomed the new sovereign government in 2004.

Administration: Under Pope John Paul II the long-term financial problems of the Holy See were addressed and brought under control. Finances were on the agenda at the first plenary assembly of the College of Cardinals, Nov. 5-9, 1979, and subsequent meetings of that body. A council of cardinals for the study of organizational and economic problems of the Holy See was established in 1981. In 1988, the Holy See's financial report (for 1986)

was published for the first time, along with the 1988 budget. In Apr. 1991, a meeting of the presidents of episcopal conferences was held to discuss ways of increasing the Peter's Pence Collection taken in support of the Pope.

A reorganization of responsibilities of Vatican offices was carried out in 1984, and in 1988 an apostolic constitution, *Pastor Bonus*, on reform of the Roman Curia was issued. A Vatican labor office was instituted in 1989. Pope John Paul established a new Pontifical Academy of Social Sciences in 1994 and Pontifical Academy for Life in 1995. On Apr. 8, 1994, he celebrated Mass in the Sistine Chapel for the unveiling of the Michelangelo frescoes, which had been painstakingly cleaned and restored. The opening presentation of the Holy See's Internet site took place on Mar. 24, 1997.

As Bishop of Rome, John Paul presided over a diocesan synod that concluded May 29, 1993. He also has visited numerous Roman parishes — 301 out of 328 by the time of his passing.

His death on Apr. 2, 2005, came after two months of sharp decline from an infection. He was admitted to Gemelli Clinic, where he had been taken after the assassination attempt in 1981, on Jan. 30. Though released, he never recovered fully, was re-admitted a few weeks later and eventually needed a tracheotomy to assist his breathing. His voice never returned to normal, and his last two appearances, on Easter Sunday and at his Wednesday audience, proved heartbreaking for those in attendance as he struggled to communicate. His health collapsed completely over the next days, and he journeyed to God at 9:37 p.m. Rome time. His cause for canonization was opened soon after his passing as Pope Benedict XVI waived the customary five year waiting period. After confirmation of a miracle (a French nun was cured of Parkinson's Disease), the late pontiff was beatified in front of several million pilgrims at the Vatican on May 1, 2011. His feast day is Oct. 22.

POPES OF THE ROMAN CATHOLIC CHURCH

Information includes the name of the pope, in many cases his name before becoming pope, his birthplace or country of origin, the date of accession to the papacy, and the date of the end of reign that, in all but a few cases, was the date of death. Double dates indicate date of election and date of solemn beginning of ministry as Pastor of the universal Church. *Source*: Annuario Pontificio.

St. Peter (Simon Bar-Jona): Bethsaida in Galilee; d. c. 64 or 67.
St. Linus: Tuscany; 67-76.
St. Anacletus (Cletus): Rome; 76-88.
St. Clement: Rome; 88-97.
St. Evaristus: Greece; 97-105.
St. Alexander I: Rome; 105-115.
St. Sixtus I: Rome; 115-125.
St. Telesphorus: Greece; 125-136.
St. Hyginus: Greece; 136-140.
St. Pius I: Aquileia; 140-155.
St. Anicetus: Syria; 155-166.
St. Soter: Campania; 166-175.
St. Eleutherius: Nicopolis in Epirus; 175-189.
Up to the time of St. Eleutherius, the years indicated for the beginning and end of pontificates are not absolutely certain. Also, up to the middle of the 11th century, there are some doubts about the exact days and months given in chronological tables.
St. Victor I: Africa; 189-199.

St. Zephyrinus: Rome; 199-217.
St. Callistus I: Rome; 217-222.
St. Urban I: Rome; 222-230.
St. Pontian: Rome; July 21, 230, to Sept. 28, 235.
St. Anterus: Greece; Nov. 21, 235, to Jan. 3, 236.
St. Fabian: Rome; Jan. 10, 236, to Jan. 20, 250.
St. Cornelius: Rome; Mar. 251 to June 253.
St. Lucius I: Rome; June 25, 253, to Mar. 5, 254.
St. Stephen I: Rome; May 12, 254, to Aug. 2, 257.
St. Sixtus II: Greece; Aug. 30, 257, to Aug. 6, 258.
St. Dionysius: birthplace unknown; July 22, 259, to Dec. 26, 268.
St. Felix I: Rome; Jan. 5, 269, to Dec. 30, 274.
St. Eutychian: Luni; Jan. 4, 275, to Dec. 7, 283.
St. Caius: Dalmatia; Dec. 17, 283, to Apr. 22, 296.
St. Marcellinus: Rome; June 30, 296, to Oct. 25, 304.
St. Marcellus I: Rome; May 27, 308, or June 26, 308, to Jan. 16, 309.
St. Eusebius: Greece; Apr. 18, 309, to Aug. 17, 309 or 310.
St. Melchiades (Miltiades): Africa; July 2, 311, to Jan. 11, 314.
St. Sylvester I: Rome; Jan. 31, 314, to Dec. 31, 335.
(Most popes before St. Sylvester I were martyrs.)
St. Marcus: Rome; Jan. 18, 336, to Oct. 7, 336.
St. Julius I: Rome; Feb. 6, 337, to Apr. 12, 352.
Liberius: Rome; May 17, 352, to Sept. 24, 366.
St. Damasus I: Spain; Oct. 1, 366, to Dec. 11, 384.

St. Siricius: Rome; Dec. 15, or 22 or 29, 384, to Nov. 26, 399.

St. Anastasius I: Rome; Nov. 27, 399, to Dec. 19, 401.

St. Innocent I: Albano; Dec. 22, 401, to Mar. 12, 417.

St. Zosimus: Greece; Mar. 18, 417, to Dec. 26, 418.

St. Boniface I: Rome; Dec. 28 or 29, 418, to Sept. 4, 422.

St. Celestine I: Campania; Sept. 10, 422, to July 27, 432.

St. Sixtus III: Rome; July 31, 432, to Aug. 19, 440.

St. Leo I (the Great): Tuscany; Sept. 29, 440, to Nov. 10, 461.

St. Hilary: Sardinia; Nov. 19, 461, to Feb. 29, 468.

St. Simplicius: Tivoli; Mar. 3, 468, to Mar. 10, 483.

St. Felix III (II): Rome; Mar. 13, 483, to Mar. 1, 492. He should be called Felix II, and his successors of the same name should be numbered accordingly. The discrepancy in the numerical designation of popes named Felix was caused by the erroneous insertion in some lists of the name of St. Felix of Rome, a martyr.

St. Gelasius I: Africa; Mar. 1, 492, to Nov. 21, 496.

Anastasius II: Rome; Nov. 24, 496, to Nov. 19, 498.

St. Symmachus: Sardinia; Nov. 22, 498, to July 19, 514.

St. Hormisdas: Frosinone; July 20, 514, to Aug. 6, 523.

St. John I, Martyr: Tuscany; Aug. 13, 523, to May 18, 526.

St. Felix IV (III): Samnium; July 12, 526, to Sept. 22, 530.

Boniface II: Rome; Sept. 22, 530, to Oct. 17, 532.

John II: Rome; Jan. 2, 533, to May 8, 535. John II was the first pope to change his name. His given name was Mercury.

St. Agapitus I: Rome; May 13, 535, to Apr. 22, 536.

St. Silverius, Martyr: Campania; June 1 or 8, 536, to Nov. 11, 537 (d. Dec. 2, 537).

St. Silverius was violently deposed in Mar. 537, and abdicated Nov. 11, 537. His successor, Vigilius, was not recognized as pope by all the Roman clergy until his abdication.

Vigilius: Rome; Mar. 29, 537, to June 7, 555.

Pelagius I: Rome; Apr. 16, 556, to Mar. 4, 561.

John III: Rome; July 17, 561, to July 13, 574.

Benedict I: Rome; June 2, 575, to July 30, 579.

Pelagius II: Rome; Nov. 26, 579, to Feb. 7, 590.

St. Gregory I (the Great): Rome; Sept. 3, 590, to Mar. 12, 604.

Sabinian: Blera in Tuscany; Sept. 13, 604, to Feb. 22, 606.

Boniface III: Rome; Feb. 19, 607, to Nov. 12, 607.

St. Boniface IV: Abruzzi; Aug. 25, 608, to May 8, 615.

St. Deusdedit (Adeodatus I): Rome; Oct. 19, 615, to Nov. 8, 618.

Boniface V: Naples; Dec. 23, 619, to Oct. 25, 625.

Honorius I: Campania; Oct. 27, 625, to Oct. 12, 638.

Severinus: Rome; May 28, 640, to Aug. 2, 640.

John IV: Dalmatia; Dec. 24, 640, to Oct. 12, 642.

Theodore I: Greece; Nov. 24, 642, to May 14, 649.

St. Martin I, Martyr: Todi; July, 649, to Sept. 16, 655 (in exile from June 17, 653).

St. Eugene I: Rome; Aug. 10, 654, to June 2, 657. St. Eugene I was elected during the exile of St. Martin I, who is believed to have endorsed him as pope.

St. Vitalian: Segni; July 30, 657, to Jan. 27, 672.

Adeodatus II: Rome; Apr. 11, 672, to June 17, 676.

Donus: Rome; Nov. 2, 676, to Apr. 11, 678.

St. Agatho: Sicily; June 27, 678, to Jan. 10, 681.

St. Leo II: Sicily; Aug. 17, 682, to July 3, 683.

St. Benedict II: Rome; June 26, 684, to May 8, 685.

John V: Syria; July 23, 685, to Aug. 2, 686.

Conon: birthplace unknown; Oct. 21, 686, to Sept. 21, 687.

St. Sergius I: Syria; Dec. 15, 687, to Sept. 8, 701.

John VI: Greece; Oct. 30, 701, to Jan. 11, 705.

John VII: Greece; Mar. 1, 705, to Oct. 18, 707.

Sisinnius: Syria; Jan. 15, 708, to Feb. 4, 708.

Constantine: Syria; Mar. 25, 708, to Apr. 9, 715.

St. Gregory II: Rome; May 19, 715, to Feb. 11, 731.

St. Gregory III: Syria; Mar. 18, 731, to Nov. 741.

St. Zachary: Greece; Dec. 10, 741, to Mar. 22, 752.

Stephen II (III): Rome; Mar. 26, 752, to Apr. 26, 757. After the death of St. Zachary, a Roman priest named Stephen was elected but died (four days later) before his consecration as bishop of Rome, which would have marked the beginning of his pontificate. Another Stephen was elected to succeed Zachary as Stephen II. (The first pope with this name was St. Stephen I, 254-57.) The ordinal III appears in parentheses after the name of Stephen II because the name of the earlier elected but deceased priest was included in some lists. Other Stephens have double numbers.

St. Paul I: Rome; Apr. (May 29), 757, to June 28, 767.

Stephen III (IV): Sicily; Aug. 1 (7), 768, to Jan. 24, 772.

Adrian I: Rome; Feb. 1 (9), 772, to Dec. 25, 795.

St. Leo III: Rome; Dec. 26 (27), 795, to June 12, 816.

Stephen IV (V): Rome; June 22, 816, to Jan. 24, 817.

St. Paschal I: Rome; Jan. 25, 817, to Feb. 11, 824.

Eugene II: Rome; Feb. (May) 824 to Aug. 827.

Valentine: Rome; Aug. 827, to Sept. 827.

Gregory IV: Rome; 827, to Jan. 844.

Sergius II: Rome; Jan. 844 to Jan. 27, 847.

St. Leo IV: Rome; Jan. (Apr. 10) 847, to July 17, 855.

Benedict III: Rome; July (Sept. 29), 855, to Apr. 17, 858.

St. Nicholas I (the Great): Rome; Apr. 24, 858, to Nov. 13, 867.

Adrian II: Rome; Dec. 14, 867, to Dec. 14, 872.

John VIII: Rome; Dec. 14, 872, to Dec. 16, 882.

Marinus I: Gallese; Dec. 16, 882, to May 15, 884.

St. Adrian III: Rome; May 17, 884, to Sept. 885. Cult confirmed June 2, 1891.

Stephen V (VI): Rome; Sept. 885, to Sept. 14, 891.

Formosus: Bishop of Porto; Oct. 6, 891, to Apr. 4, 896.

Boniface VI: Rome; Apr. 896 to Apr. 896.

Stephen VI (VII): Rome; May 896 to Aug. 897.

Romanus: Gallese; Aug. 897 to Nov. 897.

Theodore II: Rome; Dec. 897 to Dec. 897.

John IX: Tivoli; Jan. 898 to Jan. 900.

Benedict IV: Rome; Jan. (Feb.) 900 to July 903.

Leo V: Ardea; July 903 to Sept. 903.

Sergius III: Rome; Jan. 29, 904, to Apr. 14, 911.

Anastasius III: Rome; Apr. 911 to June 913.

Landus: Sabina; July 913 to Feb. 914.

John X: Tossignano (Imola); Mar. 914 to May 928.

Leo VI: Rome; May 928 to Dec. 928.

Stephen VII (VIII): Rome; Dec. 928 to Feb. 931.

John XI: Rome; Feb. (Mar.) 931 to Dec. 935.

Leo VII: Rome; Jan. 3, 936, to July 13, 939.

Stephen VIII (IX): Rome; July 14, 939, to Oct. 942.

Marinus II: Rome; Oct. 30, 942, to May 946.

Agapitus II: Rome; May 10, 946, to Dec. 955.

John XII (Octavius): Tusculum; Dec. 16, 955, to May 14, 964 (date of his death).

Leo VIII: Rome; Dec. 4 (6), 963, to Mar. 1, 965.

Benedict V: Rome; May 22, 964, to July 4, 966. Confusion exists concerning the legitimacy of claims to the pontificate by Leo VIII and Benedict V. John XII was deposed Dec. 4, 963, by a Roman council. If this deposition was invalid, Leo was an antipope. If the deposition of John was valid, Leo was the legitimate pope and Benedict was an antipope.

John XIII: Rome; Oct. 1, 965, to Sept. 6, 972.

Benedict VI: Rome; Jan. 19, 973 to June 974.

Benedict VII: Rome; Oct. 974 to July 10, 983.

John XIV (Peter Campenora): Pavia; Dec., 983 to Aug. 20, 984.

John XV: Rome; Aug. 985 to Mar. 996.

Gregory V (Bruno of Carinthia): Saxony; May 3, 996, to Feb. 18, 999.

Sylvester II (Gerbert): Auvergne; Apr. 2, 999, to May 12, 1003.

John XVII (Siccone): Rome; June 1003 to Dec. 1003.

John XVIII (Phasianus): Rome; Jan. 1004, to July 1009.

Sergius IV (Peter): Rome; July 31, 1009, to May 12, 1012.

The custom of changing one's name on election to the papacy is generally considered to date from the time of Sergius IV. Before his time, several popes had changed their names. After his time, it became a regular practice, with few exceptions, e.g., Adrian VI and Marcellus II.

Benedict VIII (Theophylactus): Tusculum; May 18, 1012, to Apr. 9, 1024.

John XIX (Romanus): Tusculum; Apr. (May) 1024 to 1032.

Benedict IX (Theophylactus): Tusculum; 1032 to 1044.

Sylvester III (John): Rome; Jan. 20, 1045, to Feb. 10, 1045.

Sylvester III was an antipope if the forcible removal of Benedict IX in 1044 was not legitimate.

Benedict IX (second time): Apr. 10, 1045, to May 1, 1045.

Gregory VI (John Gratian): Rome; May 5, 1045, to Dec. 20, 1046.

Clement II (Suitger, Lord of Morsleben and Hornburg): Saxony; Dec. 24 (25), 1046 to Oct. 9, 1047.

If the resignation of Benedict IX in 1045 and his removal at the Dec. 1046, synod were not legitimate, Gregory VI and Clement II were antipopes.

Benedict IX (third time): Nov. 8, 1047, to July 17, 1048 (d. c. 1055).

Damasus II (Poppo): Bavaria; July 17, 1048, to Aug. 9, 1048.

St. Leo IX (Bruno): Alsace; Feb. 12, 1049, to Apr. 19, 1054.

Victor II (Gebhard): Swabia; Apr. 16, 1055, to July 28, 1057.

Stephen IX (X) (Frederick): Lorraine; Aug. 3, 1057, to Mar. 29, 1058.

Nicholas II (Gerard): Burgundy; Jan. 24, 1059, to July 27, 1061.

Alexander II (Anselmo da Baggio): Milan; Oct. 1, 1061, to Apr. 21, 1073.

St. Gregory VII (Hildebrand): Tuscany; Apr. 22 (June 30), 1073, to May 25, 1085.

Bl. Victor III (Dauferius; Desiderius): Benevento; May 24, 1086, to Sept. 16, 1087. Cult confirmed July 23, 1887.

Bl. Urban II (Otto di Lagery): France; Mar. 12, 1088, to July 29, 1099. Cult confirmed July 14, 1881.

Paschal II (Raniero): Ravenna; Aug. 13 (14), 1099, to Jan. 21, 1118.

Gelasius II (Giovanni Caetani): Gaeta; Jan. 24 (Mar. 10), 1118, to Jan. 28, 1119.

Callistus II (Guido of Burgundy): Burgundy; Feb. 2 (9), 1119, to Dec. 13, 1124.

Honorius II (Lamberto): Fiagnano (Imola); Dec. 15 (21), 1124, to Feb. 13, 1130.

Innocent II (Gregorio Papareschi): Rome; Feb. 14 (23), 1130, to Sept. 24, 1143.

Celestine II (Guido): Citta di Castello; Sept. 26 (Oct. 3), 1143, to Mar. 8, 1144.

Lucius II (Gerardo Caccianemici): Bologna; Mar. 12, 1144, to Feb. 15, 1145.

Bl. Eugene III (Bernardo Paganelli di Montemagno): Pisa; Feb. 15 (18), 1145, to July 8, 1153. Cult confirmed Oct. 3, 1872.

Anastasius IV (Corrado): Rome; July 12, 1153, to Dec, 3, 1154.

Adrian IV (Nicholas Breakspear): England; Dec. 4 (5), 1154, to Sept. 1, 1159.

Alexander III (Rolando Bandinelli): Siena; Sept. 7 (20), 1159, to Aug. 30, 1181.

Lucius III (Ubaldo Allucingoli): Lucca; Sept. 1 (6), 1181, to Sept. 25, 1185.

Urban III (Uberto Crivelli): Milan; Nov. 25 (Dec. 1), 1185, to Oct. 20, 1187.

Gregory VIII (Alberto de Morra): Benevento; Oct. 21 (25), 1187, to Dec. 17, 1187.

Clement III (Paolo Scolari): Rome; Dec. 19 (20), 1187, to Mar. 1191.

Celestine III (Giacinto Bobone): Rome; Mar. 30 (Apr. 14), 1191, to Jan. 8, 1198.

Innocent III (Lotario dei Conti di Segni): Anagni; Jan. 8 (Feb. 22), 1198, to July 16, 1216.

Honorius III (Cencio Savelli): Rome; July 18 (24), 1216, to Mar. 18, 1227.

Gregory IX (Ugolino, Count of Segni): Anagni; Mar. 19 (21), 1227, to Aug. 22, 1241.

Celestine IV (Goffredo Castiglioni): Milan; Oct. 25 (28), 1241, to Nov. 10, 1241.

Innocent IV (Sinibaldo Fieschi): Genoa; June 25 (28), 1243, to Dec. 7, 1254.

Alexander IV (Rinaldo, House of Ienne): Ienne (Rome); Dec. 12 (20), 1254, to May 25, 1261.

Urban IV (Jacques Pantal,on): Troyes; Aug. 29 (Sept. 4), 1261, to Oct. 2, 1264.

Clement IV (Guy Foulques or Guido le Gros): France; Feb. 5 (15), 1265, to Nov. 29, 1268.

Bl. Gregory X (Teobaldo Visconti): Piacenza; Sept. 1, 1271 (Mar. 27, 1272), to Jan. 10, 1276. Cult confirmed Sept. 12, 1713.

Bl. Innocent V (Peter of Tarentaise): Savoy; Jan. 21 (Feb. 22), 1276, to June 22, 1276. Cult confirmed Mar. 13, 1898.

Adrian V (Ottobono Fieschi): Genoa; July 11, 1276, to Aug. 18, 1276.

John XXI (Petrus Juliani or Petrus Hispanus): Portugal; Sept. 8 (20), 1276, to May 20, 1277.

There is confusion in the numerical designation of popes named John. The error dates back to the time of John XV.

Nicholas III (Giovanni Gaetano Orsini): Rome; Nov. 25 (Dec. 26), 1277, to Aug. 22, 1280.

Martin IV (Simon de Brie): France; Feb. 22 (Mar. 23), 1281, to Mar. 28, 1285.

The names of Marinus I (882-84) and Marinus II (942-46) were construed as Martin. In view of these two pontificates and the earlier reign of St. Martin I (649-55), this pope was called Martin IV.

Honorius IV (Giacomo Savelli): Rome; Apr. 2 (May 20), 1285, to Apr. 3, 1287.

Nicholas IV (Girolamo Masci): Ascoli; Feb. 22,

1288, to Apr. 4, 1292.

St. Celestine V (Pietro del Murrone): Isernia; July 5 (Aug. 29), 1294, to Dec. 13, 1294; d. May 19, 1296. Canonized May 5, 1313.

Boniface VIII (Benedetto Caetani): Anagni; Dec. 24, 1294 (Jan. 23, 1295), to Oct. 11, 1303.

Bl. Benedict XI (Niccolo Boccasini): Treviso; Oct. 22 (27), 1303, to July 7, 1304. Cult confirmed Apr. 24, 1736.

Clement V (Bertrand de Got): France; June 5 (Nov. 14), 1305, to Apr. 20, 1314. (*First of Avignon popes.*)

John XXII (Jacques d'Euse): Cahors; Aug. 7 (Sept. 5), 1316, to Dec. 4, 1334.

Benedict XII (Jacques Fournier): France; Dec. 20, 1334 (Jan. 8, 1335), to Apr. 25, 1342.

Clement VI (Pierre Roger): France; May 7 (19), 1342, to Dec. 6, 1352.

Innocent VI (Etienne Aubert): France; Dec. 18 (30), 1352, to Sept. 12, 1362.

Bl. Urban V (Guillaume de Grimoard): France; Sept. 28 (Nov. 6), 1362, to Dec. 19, 1370. Cult confirmed Mar. 10, 1870.

Gregory XI (Pierre Roger de Beaufort): France; Dec. 30, 1370 (Jan. 5, 1371), to Mar. 26, 1378. (*Last of Avignon popes.*)

Urban VI (Bartolomeo Prignano): Naples; Apr. 8 (18), 1378, to Oct. 15, 1389.

Boniface IX (Pietro Tomacelli): Naples; Nov. 2 (9), 1389, to Oct. 1, 1404.

Innocent VII (Cosma Migliorati): Sulmona; Oct. 17 (Nov. 11), 1404, to Nov. 6, 1406.

Gregory XII (Angelo Correr): Venice; Nov. 30 (Dec. 19), 1406, to July 4, 1415, when he voluntarily resigned from the papacy to permit the election of his successor. He died Oct. 18, 1417. (*See* **Western Schism**, page 240.)

Martin V (Oddone Colonna): Rome; Nov. 11 (21), 1417, to Feb. 20, 1431.

Eugene IV (Gabriele Condulmer): Venice; Mar. 3 (11), 1431, to Feb. 23, 1447.

Nicholas V (Tommaso Parentucelli): Sarzana; Mar. 6 (19), 1447, to Mar. 24, 1455.

Callistus III (Alfonso Borgia): Jativa (Valencia); Apr. 8 (20), 1455, to Aug. 6, 1458.

Pius II (Enea Silvio Piccolomini): Siena; Aug. 19 (Sept. 3), 1458, to Aug. 14, 1464.

Paul II (Pietro Barbo): Venice; Aug. 30 (Sept. 16), 1464, to July 26, 1471.

Sixtus IV (Francesco della Rovere): Savona; Aug. 9 (25), 1471, to Aug. 12, 1484.

Innocent VIII (Giovanni Battista Cibo): Genoa; Aug. 29 (Sept. 12), 1484, to July 25, 1492.

Alexander VI (Rodrigo Borgia): Jativa (Valencia); Aug. 11 (26), 1492, to Aug. 18, 1503.

Pius III (Francesco Todeschini-Piccolomini): Siena; Sept. 22 (Oct. 1, 8), 1503, to Oct. 18, 1503.

Julius II (Giuliano della Rovere): Savona; Oct. 31 (Nov. 26), 1503, to Feb. 21, 1513.

Leo X (Giovanni de' Medici): Florence; Mar. 9 (19), 1513, to Dec. 1, 1521.

Adrian VI (Adrian Florensz): Utrecht; Jan. 9 (Aug. 31), 1522, to Sept. 14, 1523.

Clement VII (Giulio de' Medici): Florence; Nov. 19 (26), 1523, to Sept. 25, 1534.

Paul III (Alessandro Farnese): Rome; Oct. 13 (Nov. 3), 1534, to Nov. 10, 1549.

Julius III (Giovanni Maria Ciocchi del Monte): Rome; Feb. 7 (22), 1550, to Mar. 23, 1555.

Marcellus II (Marcello Cervini): Montepulciano; Apr. 9 (10), 1555, to May 1, 1555.

Paul IV (Gian Pietro Carafa): Naples; May 23 (26), 1555, to Aug. 18, 1559.

Pius IV (Giovan Angelo de' Medici): Milan; Dec. 25, 1559 (Jan. 6, 1560), to Dec. 9, 1565.

St. Pius V (Antonio-Michele Ghislieri): Bosco (Alexandria); Jan. 7 (17), 1566, to May 1, 1572. Canonized May 22, 1712.

Gregory XIII (Ugo Buoncompagni): Bologna; May 13 (25), 1572, to Apr. 10, 1585.

Sixtus V (Felice Peretti): Grottammare (Ripatransone); Apr. 24 (May 1), 1585, to Aug. 27, 1590.

Urban VII (Giambattista Castagna): Rome; Sept. 15, 1590, to Sept. 27, 1590.

Gregory XIV (Niccolo Sfondrati): Cremona; Dec. 5 (8), 1590, to Oct. 16, 1591.

Innocent IX (Giovanni Antonio Facchinetti): Bologna; Oct. 29 (Nov. 3), 1591, to Dec. 30, 1591.

Clement VIII (Ippolito Aldobrandini): Florence; Jan. 30 (Feb. 9), 1592, to Mar. 3, 1605.

Leo XI (Alessandro de' Medici): Florence; Apr. 1 (10), 1605, to Apr. 27, 1605.

Paul V (Camillo Borghese): Rome; May 16 (29), 1605, to Jan. 28, 1621.

Gregory XV (Alessandro Ludovisi): Bologna; Feb. 9 (14), 1621, to July 8, 1623.

Urban VIII (Maffeo Barberini): Florence; Aug. 6 (Sept. 29), 1623, to July 29, 1644.

Innocent X (Giovanni Battista Pamfili): Rome; Sept. 15 (Oct. 4), 1644, to Jan. 7, 1655.

Alexander VII (Fabio Chigi): Siena; Apr. 7 (18), 1655, to May 22, 1667.

Clement IX (Giulio Rospigliosi): Pistoia; June 20 (26), 1667, to Dec. 9, 1669.

Clement X (Emilio Altieri): Rome; Apr. 29 (May 11), 1670, to July 22, 1676.

Bl. Innocent XI (Benedetto Odescalchi): Como; Sept. 21 (Oct. 4), 1676, to Aug. 12, 1689. Beatified Oct. 7, 1956.

Alexander VIII (Pietro Ottoboni): Venice; Oct. 6 (16), 1689, to Feb. 1, 1691.

Innocent XII (Antonio Pignatelli): Spinazzola (Venosa); July 12 (15), 1691, to Sept. 27, 1700.

Clement XI (Giovanni Francesco Albani): Urbino; Nov. 23, 30 (Dec. 8), 1700, to Mar. 19, 1721.

Innocent XIII (Michelangelo dei Conti): Rome; May 8 (18), 1721, to Mar. 7, 1724.

Benedict XIII (Pietro Francesco Vincenzo Maria Orsini): Gravina (Bari); May 29 (June 4), 1724, to Feb. 21, 1730.

Clement XII (Lorenzo Corsini): Florence; July 12 (16), 1730, to Feb. 6, 1740.

Benedict XIV (Prospero Lambertini): Bologna; Aug. 17 (22), 1740, to May 3, 1758.

Clement XIII (Carlo Rezzonico): Venice; July 6 (16), 1758, to Feb. 2, 1769.

Clement XIV (Giovanni Vincenzo Antonio Lorenzo Ganganelli): Rimini; May 19, 28 (June 4), 1769, to Sept. 22, 1774.

Pius VI (Giovanni Angelo Braschi): Cesena; Feb. 15 (22), 1775, to Aug. 29, 1799.

Pius VII (Barnaba Gregorio Chiaramonti): Cesena; Mar. 14 (21), 1800, to Aug. 20, 1823.

Leo XII (Annibale della Genga): Genga (Fabriano); Sept. 28 (Oct. 5), 1823, to Feb. 10, 1829.

Pius VIII (Francesco Saverio Castiglioni): Cingoli; Mar. 31 (Apr. 5), 1829, to Nov. 30, 1830.

Gregory XVI (Bartolomeo Alberto-Mauro-Cappellari): Belluno; Feb. 2 (6), 1831, to June 1, 1846.

Bl. Pius IX (Giovanni M. Mastai-Ferretti): Senigallia; June 16 (21), 1846, to Feb. 7, 1878.

Leo XIII (Gioacchino Pecci): Carpineto (Anagni); Feb. 20 (Mar. 3), 1878, to July 20, 1903.

St. Pius X (Giuseppe Sarto): Riese (Treviso); Aug. 4 (9), 1903, to Aug. 20, 1914. Canonized May 29, 1954.

Benedict XV (Giacomo della Chiesa): Genoa; Sept. 3 (6), 1914, to Jan. 22, 1922.

Pius XI (Achille Ratti): Desio (Milan); Feb. 6 (12), 1922, to Feb. 10, 1939.

Pius XII (Eugenio Pacelli): Rome; Mar. 2 (12), 1939, to Oct. 9, 1958.

Bl. John XXIII (Angelo Giuseppe Roncalli): Sotto il Monte (Bergamo); Oct. 28 (Nov. 4), 1958, to June 3, 1963.

Paul VI (Giovanni Battista Montini): Concessio (Brescia); June 21 (30), 1963, to Aug. 6, 1978.

John Paul I (Albino Luciani): Forno di Canale (Belluno); Aug. 26 (Sept. 3), 1978, to Sept. 28, 1978.

Bl. John Paul II (Karol Wojtyla): Wadowice, Poland; Oct. 16 (22), 1978, to April 2, 2005.

Benedict XVI (Joseph Ratzinger): Marktl Am Inn, Germany; Apr. 19 (24), 2005, to Feb. 28, 2013.

Francis (Jorge Mario Bergoglio): Buenos Aires, Argentina; Mar. 13 (19), 2013.

ANTIPOPES

This list of men who claimed or exercised the papal office in an uncanonical manner includes names, birthplaces and dates of alleged reigns. Source: Annuario Pontificio.

St. Hippolytus: Rome; 217-235; was reconciled before his death.

Novatian: Rome; 251.

Felix II: Rome; 355 to Nov. 22, 365.

Ursinus: 366-367.

Eulalius: Dec. 27 or 29, 418, to 419.

Lawrence: 498; 501-505.

Dioscorus: Alexandria; Sept. 22, 530, to Oct. 14, 530.

Theodore: ended alleged reign, 687.

Paschal: ended alleged reign, 687.

Constantine: Nepi; June 28 (July 5), 767, to 769.

Philip: July 31, 768; retired to his monastery on the same day.

John: ended alleged reign, Jan. 844.

Anastasius: Aug. 855 to Sept. 855; d. 880.

Christopher: Rome; July or Sept. 903 to Jan. 904.

Boniface VII: Rome; June 974 to July 974; Aug. 984 to July 985.

John XVI: Rossano; Apr. 997 to Feb. 998.

Gregory: ended alleged reign, 1012.

Benedict X: Rome; Apr. 5, 1058, to Jan. 24, 1059.

Honorius II: Verona; Oct. 28, 1061, to 1072.

Clement III: Parma; June 25, 1080 (Mar. 24, 1084), to Sept. 8, 1100.

Theodoric: ended alleged reign, 1100; d. 1102.

Albert: ended alleged reign, 1102.

Sylvester IV: Rome; Nov. 18, 1105, to 1111.

Gregory VIII: France; Mar. 8, 1118, to 1121.

Celestine II: Rome; ended alleged reign, Dec. 1124.

Anacletus II: Rome; Feb. 14 (23), 1130, to Jan. 25, 1138.

Victor IV: Mar. 1138, to May 29, 1138; submitted to Pope Innocent II.

Victor IV: Montecelio; Sept. 7 (Oct. 4), 1159, to Apr. 20, 1164; he did not recognize his predecessor (Victor IV, above).

Paschal III: Apr. 22 (26), 1164, to Sept. 20, 1168.

Callistus III: Arezzo; Sept., 1168, to Aug. 29, 1178; submitted to Pope Alexander III.

Innocent III: Sezze; Sept. 29, 1179, to 1180.

Nicholas V: Corvaro (Rieti); May 12 (22), 1328, to Aug. 25, 1330; d. Oct. 16, 1333.

Four antipopes of the Western Schism:

Clement VII: Sept. 20 (Oct. 31), 1378, to Sept. 16, 1394.

Benedict XIII: Aragon; Sept. 28 (Oct. 11), 1394, to May 23, 1423.

Alexander V: Crete; June 26 (July 7), 1409, to May 3, 1410.

John XXIII: Naples; May 17 (25), 1410, to May 29, 1415. (Date of deposition by Council of Constance which ended the Western Schism; d. Nov. 22, 1419.)

Felix V: Savoy; Nov. 5, 1439 (July 24, 1440), to Apr. 7, 1449; d. 1451.

AVIGNON PAPACY

Avignon was the residence (1309-77) of a series of French popes (Clement V, John XXII, Benedict XII, Clement VI, Innocent VI, Urban V and Gregory XI). Prominent in the period were power struggles over the mixed interests of Church and state with the rulers of France (Philip IV, John II), Bavaria (Lewis IV), England (Edward III); factionalism of French and Italian churchmen; political as well as ecclesiastical turmoil in Italy, a factor of significance in prolonging the stay of popes in Avignon. Despite some positive achievements, the Avignon papacy was a prologue to the Western Schism that began in 1378.

GREAT WESTERN SCHISM

The Great Western Schism was a confused state of affairs that divided Christendom into two and then three papal obediences from 1378 to 1417.

It occurred some 50 years after Marsilius theorized that a general (not ecumenical) council of bishops and other persons was superior to a pope and nearly 30 years before the Council of Florence stated definitively that no kind of council had such authority.

It was a period of disaster preceding the even more disastrous period of the Reformation.

Urban VI, following the return of the papal residence to Rome after approximately 70 years at Avignon, was elected pope Apr. 8, 1378, and reigned until his death in 1389. He was succeeded by Boniface IX (1389-1404), Innocent VII (1404-1406) and Gregory XII (1406-1415). These four are considered the legitimate popes of the period.

Some of the cardinals who chose Urban pope, dissatisfied with his conduct of the office, declared that his election was invalid. They proceeded to elect Clement VII, who claimed the papacy from 1378 to 1394. He was succeeded by Benedict XIII.

Prelates seeking to end the state of divided papal

loyalties convoked the Council of Pisa (1409) which, without authority, found Gregory XII and Benedict XIII guilty in absentia on 30-odd charges of schism and heresy, deposed them, and elected a third claimant to the papacy, Alexander V (1409-1410). He was succeeded by John XXIII (1410-1415).

The schism was ended by the Council of Constance (1414-1418). Although originally called into session in an irregular manner, the council, acquired authority

after being convoked by Gregory XII in 1415. In its early irregular phase, it deposed John XXIII whose election to the papacy was uncanonical anyway. After being formally convoked, it accepted the abdication of Gregory in 1415 and dismissed the claims of Benedict XIII two years later, thus clearing the way for the election of Martin V on Nov. 11, 1417. The Council of Constance also rejected the theories of John Wycliff and condemned Jan Hus as a heretic.

POPES OF THE TWENTIETH CENTURY

LEO XIII

Leo XIII (Gioacchino Vincenzo Pecci) was born May 2, 1810, in Carpineto, Italy. Although all but three years of his life and pontificate were in the 19th century, his influence extended well into the 20th century.

He was educated at the Jesuit college in Viterbo, the Roman College, the Academy of Noble Ecclesiastics, and the University of the Sapienza. He was ordained in 1837.

He served as an apostolic delegate to two States of the Church, Benevento from 1838 to 1841 and Perugia in 1841 and 1842. Ordained titular archbishop of Damietta, he was papal nuncio to Belgium from Jan. 1843, until May 1846; in the post, he had controversial relations with the government over education issues and acquired his first significant experience of industrialized society.

He was archbishop of Perugia from 1846 to 1878. He became a cardinal in 1853 and chamberlain of the Roman Curia in 1877. He was elected to the papacy Feb. 20, 1878. He died July 20, 1903.

Canonizations: He canonized 18 saints and beatified a group of English martyrs.

Church Administration: He established 300 new dioceses and vicariates; restored the hierarchy in Scotland and set up an English, as contrasted with the Portuguese, hierarchy in India; approved the action of the Congregation for the Propagation of the Faith in reorganizing missions in China.

Encyclicals: He issued 86 encyclicals, on subjects ranging from devotional to social. In the former category were Annum Sacrum, on the Sacred Heart, in 1899, and 11 letters on Mary and the Rosary.

Social Questions: Much of Leo's influence stemmed from social doctrine stated in numerous encyclicals, concerning liberalism, liberty, the divine origin of authority; socialism, in Quod Apostolici Muneris, 1878; the Christian concept of the family, in Arcanum, 1880; socialism and economic liberalism, relations between capital and labor, in Rerum Novarum, 1891. Two of his social encyclicals were against the African slave trade.

Interfaith Relations: He was unsuccessful in unity overtures made to Orthodox and Slavic Churches. He declared Anglican orders invalid in the apostolic bull Apostolicae Curae Sept. 13, 1896.

International Relations: Leo was frustrated in seeking solutions to the Roman Question arising from the seizure of church lands by the Kingdom of Italy in 1870. He also faced anticlerical situations in Belgium and France and in the Kulturkampf policies of Bismarck in Germany.

Scholarship: In the encyclical Aeterni Patris of Aug. 4, 1879, he ordered a renewal of philosophical and theological studies in seminaries along scholastic, and especially Thomistic, lines, to counteract influential trends of liberalism and Modernism. He issued guidelines for biblical exegesis in Providentissimus Deus Nov. 18, 1893, and established the Pontifical Biblical Commission in 1902.

In other actions affecting scholarship and study, he opened the Vatican Archives to scholars in 1883 and established the Vatican Observatory.

United States: He authorized establishment of the apostolic delegation in Washington, DC, Jan. 24, 1893. He refused to issue a condemnation of the Knights of Labor. With a document entitled Testem Benevolentiae, he eased resolution of questions concerning what was called an American heresy in 1899.

ST. PIUS X

St. Pius X (Giuseppe Melchiorre Sarto) was born in 1835 in Riese, Italy. Educated at the college of Castelfranco and the seminary at Padua, he was ordained to the priesthood Sept. 18, 1858. He served as a curate in Trombolo for nine years before beginning an eight-year pastorate at Salzano. He was chancellor of the Treviso diocese from Nov. 1875, and bishop of Mantua from 1884 until 1893. He was cardinal-patriarch of Venice from that year until his election to the papacy by the conclave held from July 31 to Aug. 4, 1903.

Aims: Pius's principal objectives as pope were "to restore all things in Christ, in order that Christ may be all and in all," and "to teach (and defend) Christian truth and law."

Canonizations, Encyclicals: He canonized four saints and issued 16 encyclicals. One of the encyclicals was issued in commemoration of the 50th anniversary of the proclamation of the dogma of the Immaculate Conception of Mary.

Catechetics: He introduced a whole new era of religious instruction and formation with the encyclical Acerbo Nimis of Apr. 15, 1905, in which he called for vigor in establishing and conducting parochial programs of the Confraternity of Christian Doctrine.

Catholic Action: He outlined the role of official Catholic Action in two encyclicals in 1905 and 1906. Favoring organized action by Catholics themselves, he had serious reservations about interconfessional collaboration.

He stoutly maintained claims to papal rights in the anticlerical climate of Italy. He authorized bishops to relax prohibitions against participation by Catholics in some Italian elections.

Church Administration: With the motu proprio

Arduum Sane of Mar. 19, 1904, he inaugurated the work that resulted in the Code of Canon Law; the code was completed in 1917 and went into effect in the following year. He reorganized and strengthened the Roman Curia with the apostolic constitution *Sapienti Consilio* of June 29, 1908.

While promoting the expansion of missionary work, he removed from the jurisdiction of the Congregation for the Propagation of the Faith the Church in the United States, Canada, Newfoundland, England, Ireland, Holland and Luxembourg.

International Relations: He ended traditional prerogatives of Catholic governments with respect to papal elections, in 1904. He opposed anti-Church and anticlerical actions in several countries: Bolivia in 1905, because of anti-religious legislation; France in 1906, for its 1901 action in annulling its concordat with the Holy See, and for the 1905 Law of Separation by which it decreed separation of Church and state, ordered the confiscation of church property, and blocked religious education and the activities of religious orders; Portugal in 1911, for the separation of Church and state and repressive measures that resulted in persecution later.

In 1912 he called on the bishops of Brazil to work for the improvement of conditions among Indians.

Liturgy: "The Pope of the Eucharist," he strongly recommended the frequent reception of Holy Communion in a decree dated Dec. 20, 1905; in another decree, *Quam Singulari*, of Aug. 8, 1910, he called for the early reception of the sacrament by children. He initiated measures for liturgical reform with new norms for sacred music and the start of work on revision of the Breviary for recitation of the Divine Office.

Modernism: Pius was a vigorous opponent of "the synthesis of all heresies," which threatened the integrity of doctrine through its influence in philosophy, theology and biblical exegesis. In opposition, he condemned 65 of its propositions as erroneous in the decree *Lamentabili*, July 3, 1907; issued the encyclical *Pascendi* in the same vein, Sept. 8, 1907; backed both of these with censures; and published the Oath against Modernism in Sept. 1910, to be taken by all the clergy. Ecclesiastical studies suffered to some extent from these actions, necessary as they were at the time.

Pius followed the lead of Leo XIII in promoting the study of scholastic philosophy. He established the Pontifical Biblical Institute May 7, 1909.

His death, Aug. 20, 1914, was hastened by the outbreak of World War I. He was beatified in 1951 and canonized May 29, 1954. His feast is observed Aug. 21.

BENEDICT XV

Benedict XV (Giacomo della Chiesa) was born Nov. 21, 1854, in Pegli, Italy.

He was educated at the Royal University of Genoa and Gregorian University in Rome. He was ordained to the priesthood Dec. 21, 1878.

He served in the papal diplomatic corps from 1882 to 1907, as secretary to the nuncio to Spain from 1882 to 1887, as secretary to the papal secretary of state from 1887, and as undersecretary from 1901.

He was ordained archbishop of Bologna Dec. 22, 1907, and spent four years completing a pastoral visitation there. He was made a cardinal just three months before being elected to the papacy

Sept. 3, 1914. He died Jan. 22, 1922. Two key efforts of his pontificate were for peace and the relief of human suffering caused by World War I.

Canonizations: Benedict canonized three saints; one of them was Joan of Arc.

Canon Law: He published the Code of Canon Law, developed by the commission set up by St. Pius X, May 27, 1917; it went into effect the following year.

Curia: He made great changes in the personnel of the Curia. He established the Congregation for the Oriental Churches May 1, 1917, and founded the Pontifical Oriental Institute in Rome later in the year.

Encyclicals: He issued 12 encyclicals. Peace was the theme of three of them. In another, published two years after the cessation of hostilities, he wrote about child victims of the war. He followed the lead of Leo XIII in *Spiritus Paraclitus*, Sept. 15, 1920, on biblical studies.

International Relations: He was largely frustrated on the international level because of the events and attitudes of the war period, but the number of diplomats accredited to the Vatican nearly doubled, from 14 to 26, between the time of his accession to the papacy and his death.

Peace Efforts: Benedict's stance in the war was one of absolute impartiality but not of uninterested neutrality. Because he would not take sides, he was suspected by both the Allies and the Central Powers, and the seven-point peace plan he offered to all belligerents, Aug. 1, 1917, was turned down. The points of the plan were: recognition of the moral force of right; disarmament; acceptance of arbitration in cases of dispute; guarantee of freedom of the seas; renunciation of war indemnities; evacuation and restoration of occupied territories; examination of territorial claims in dispute.

Relief Efforts: Benedict assumed personal charge of Vatican relief efforts during the war. He set up an international missing persons bureau for contacts between prisoners and their families, but was forced to close it because of the suspicion of warring nations that it was a front for espionage operations. He persuaded the Swiss government to admit into the country military victims of tuberculosis.

Roman Question: Benedict prepared the way for the meetings and negotiations which led to settlement of the question in 1929.

PIUS XI

Pius XI (Ambrogio Damiano Achille Ratti) was born May 31, 1857, in Desio, Italy.

Educated at seminaries in Seviso and Milan, and at the Lombard College, Gregorian University and Academy of St. Thomas in Rome. He was ordained to the priesthood in 1879.

He taught at the major seminary of Milan from 1882 to 1888. Appointed to the staff of the Ambrosian Library in 1888, he remained there until 1911, acquiring a reputation for publishing works on paleography and serving as director from 1907 to 1911. He then moved to the Vatican Library, of which he was prefect from 1914 to 1918. In 1919, he was named apostolic visitor to Poland in Apr.

nuncio in June, and was made titular archbishop of Lepanto Oct. 28. He was made archbishop of Milan and cardinal June 13, 1921, before being elected to the papacy Feb. 6, 1922. He died Feb. 10, 1939.

Aims: The objective of his pontificate, as stated in the encyclical *Ubi Arcano,* Dec. 23, 1922, was to establish the reign and peace of Christ in society.

Canonizations: He canonized 34 saints, including the Jesuit Martyrs of North America, and conferred the title of Doctor of the Church on Sts. Peter Canisius, John of the Cross, Robert Bellarmine and Albertus Magnus.

Eastern Churches: He called for better understanding of the Eastern Churches in the encyclical *Rerum Orientalium* of Sept. 8, 1928 and developed facilities for the training of Eastern-Rite priests. He inaugurated steps for the codification of Eastern Church law in 1929. In 1935 he made Syrian Patriarch Tappouni a cardinal.

Encyclicals: His first encyclical, *Ubi Arcano,* in addition to stating the aims of his pontificate, blueprinted Catholic Action and called for its development throughout the Church. *In Quas Primas,* Dec. 11, 1925, he established the feast of Christ the King for universal observance. Subjects of some of his other encyclicals were: Christian education, in *Rappresentanti in Terra,* Dec. 31, 1929; Christian marriage, in *Casti Connubii,* Dec. 31, 1930; social conditions and pressure for social change in line with the teaching in *Rerum Novarum,* in *Quadragesimo Anno,* May 15, 1931; atheistic Communism, in *Divini Redemptoris,* Mar. 19, 1937; the priesthood, in *Ad Catholici Sacerdotii,* Dec. 20, 1935.

Missions: Following the lead of Benedict XV, Pius called for the training of native clergy in the pattern of their own respective cultures, and promoted missionary developments in various ways. He ordained six native bishops for China in 1926, one for Japan in 1927, and others for regions of Asia, China and India in 1933. He placed the first 40 mission dioceses under native bishops, saw the number of native priests increase from about 2,600 to more than 7,000, and the number of Catholics in missionary areas more than double from nine million.

In the apostolic constitution *Deus Scientiarum Dominus* of May 24, 1931, he ordered the introduction of missiology into theology courses.

Interfaith Relations: Pius was negative to the ecumenical movement among Protestants but approved the Malines Conversations, 1921-1926, between Anglicans and Catholics.

International Relations: Relations with the Mussolini government deteriorated from 1931 on, as indicated in the encyclical *Non Abbiamo Bisogno,* when the regime took steps to curb liberties and activities of the Church; they turned critical in 1938 with the emergence of racist policies. Relations deteriorated in Germany also from 1933 on, resulting finally in condemnation of the Nazis in the encyclical *Mit Brennender Sorge,* March 1937. Pius sparked a revival of the Church in France by encouraging Catholics to work within the democratic framework of the Republic rather than foment trouble over restoration of a monarchy. Pius was powerless to influence developments related to the civil war that erupted in Spain in July 1936, sporadic persecution and repression by the Calles regime in Mexico, and systematic persecution of the Church in the Soviet Union. Many of the 10 concordats and two agreements reached with European countries after World War I became casualties of World War II.

Roman Question: Pius negotiated for two and a half years with the Italian government to settle the Roman Question by means of the Lateran Agreement of 1929. The agreement provided independent status for the State of Vatican City; made Catholicism the official religion of Italy, with pastoral and educational freedom and state recognition of Catholic marriages, religious orders and societies; and provided a financial payment to the Vatican for expropriation of the former States of the Church.

PIUS XII

Pius XII (Eugenio Maria Giovanni Pacelli) was born Mar. 2, 1876, in RomEducated at the Gregorian University and the Lateran University, in Rome, he was ordained to the priesthood Apr. 2, 1899.

He entered the Vatican diplomatic service in 1901, worked on the codification of canon law, and was appointed secretary of the Congregation for Ecclesiastical Affairs in 1914. Three years later he was ordained titular archbishop of Sardis and made apostolic nuncio to Bavaria. He was nuncio to Germany from 1920 to 1929, when he was made a cardinal, and took office as papal secretary of state in the following year. His diplomatic negotiations resulted in concordats between the Vatican and Bavaria (1924), Prussia (1929), Baden (1932), Austria and the German Republic (1933). He took part in negotiations that led to settlement of the Roman Question in 1929.

He was elected to the papacy Mar. 2, 1939. He died Oct. 9, 1958, at Castel Gandolfo after the 12th longest pontificate in history.

Canonizations: He canonized 34 saints, including Mother Frances X. Cabrini, the first U.S. citizen-saint.

Cardinals: He raised 56 prelates to the rank of cardinal in two consistories held in 1946 and 1953. There were 57 cardinals at the time of his death.

Church Organization and Missions: He increased the number of dioceses from 1,696 to 2,048. He established native hierarchies in China (1946), Burma (1955) and parts of Africa, and extended the native structure of the Church in India. He ordained the first black bishop for Africa.

Communism: In addition to opposing and condemning Communism on numerous occasions, he decreed in 1949 the penalty of excommunication for all Catholics holding formal and willing allegiance to the Communist Party and its policies. During his reign the Church was persecuted in some 15 countries that fell under communist domination.

Doctrine and Liturgy: He proclaimed the dogma of the Assumption of the Blessed Virgin Mary, Nov. 1, 1950 (apostolic constitution, *Munificentissimus Deus*).

In various encyclicals and other enactments, he provided background for the *aggiornamento* introduced by his successor, John XXIII: by his formulations of doctrine and practice regarding the Mystical Body of Christ, the liturgy, sacred music and biblical studies; by the revision of the Rites of Holy Week; by initiation of the work which led to the calendar-missal-breviary reform ordered into effect Jan. 1, 1961; by the first of several modifications of the Eucharistic fast; by extending the time of Mass to the evening. He instituted the feasts of Mary, Queen, and of St. Joseph the Worker, and clarified teaching concerning devotion to the Sacred Heart.

His 41 encyclicals and nearly 1,000 public addresses made Pius one of the greatest teaching popes. His concern in all his communications was to deal with specific points at issue and to bring Christian principles to bear on contemporary world problems.

Peace Efforts: Before the start of World War II, he tried unsuccessfully to get the contending nations — Germany and Poland, France and Italy — to settle their differences peaceably. During the war, he offered his services to mediate the widened conflict, spoke out against the horrors of war and the suffering it caused, mobilized relief work for its victims, proposed a five-point program for peace in Christmas messages from 1939 to 1942, and secured a generally open status for the city of Rome. He has been criticized in some quarters for not doing enough to oppose the Holocaust. This is a matter of historical debate, but it is a fact that through his direct intercession many thousands of Jews in Rome and Italy were saved from certain death, and he resisted wherever possible the threat of Nazism to human rights. Such were his contributions to assisting Jews that the rabbi of Rome, Dr. Abraham Zolli, was converted to Catholicism, and upon his death, Pius was praised by Golda Meir for his efforts. After the war, he endorsed the principles and intent of the U.N. and continued efforts for peace.

United States: Pius appointed more than 200 of the 265 American bishops resident in the U.S. and abroad in 1958, erected 27 dioceses in this country, and raised seven dioceses to archiepiscopal rank.

BL. JOHN XXIII

John XXIII (Angelo Roncalli) was born Nov. 25, 1881, at Sotto il Monte, Italy.

He was educated at the seminary of the Bergamo diocese and the Pontifical Seminary in Rome, where he was ordained to the priesthood Aug. 10, 1904.

He spent the first nine or 10 years of his priesthood as secretary to the bishop of Bergamo and as an instructor in the seminary there. He served as a medic and chaplain in the Italian army during World War I. Afterwards, he resumed duties in his own diocese until he was called to Rome in 1921 for work with the Society for the Propagation of the Faith.

He began diplomatic service in 1925 as titular archbishop of Areopolis and apostolic visitor to Bulgaria. A succession of offices followed: apostolic delegate to Bulgaria (1931-1935); titular archbishop of Mesembria, apostolic delegate to Turkey and Greece, administrator of the Latin vicariate apostolic of Istanbul (1935-1944); apostolic nuncio to France (1944-1953). On these missions, he was engaged in delicate negotiations involving Roman, Eastern Rite and Orthodox relations; the needs of people suffering from the consequences of World War II; and unsettling suspicions arising from wartime conditions.

He was made a cardinal Jan. 12, 1953, and three days later was appointed patriarch of Venice, the position he held until his election to the papacy Oct. 28, 1958. He died of stomach cancer June 3, 1963. His canonization was approved by Pope Francis in 2013.

John was a strong and vigorous pope whose influence far outmeasured both his age and the shortness of his time in the papacy. He was beatified by Pope John Paul II on Sept. 3, 2000.

Second Vatican Council: John announced Jan. 25, 1959, his intention of convoking the 21st ecumenical council in history to renew life in the Church,

to reform its structures and institutions, and to explore ways and means of promoting unity among Christians. Through the council, which completed its work two and a half years after his death, he ushered in a new era in the history of the Church.

Canon Law: He established a commission Mar. 28, 1963, for revision of the Code of Canon Law. The revised Code was promulgated in 1983.

Canonizations: He canonized 10 saints and beatified Mother Elizabeth Ann Seton, the first native of the U.S. ever so honored. He named St. Lawrence of Brindisi a Doctor of the Church.

Cardinals: He created 52 cardinals in five consistories, raising membership of the College of Cardinals above the traditional number of 70; at one time in 1962, the membership was 87. He made the college more international in representation than it had ever been, appointing the first cardinals from the Philippines, Japan and Africa. He ordered episcopal ordination for all cardinals. He relieved the suburban bishops of Rome of ordinary jurisdiction over their dioceses so they might devote all their time to business of the Roman Curia.

Eastern Rites: He made all Eastern Rite patriarchs members of the Congregation for the Oriental Churches.

Ecumenism: He assigned to the Second Vatican Council the task of finding ways and means of promoting unity among Christians. He established the Vatican Secretariat for Promoting Christian Unity June 5, 1960. He showed his desire for more cordial relations with the Orthodox by sending personal representatives to visit Patriarch Athenagoras I June 27, 1961; approved a mission of five delegates to the General Assembly of the World Council of Churches which met in New Delhi, India, in Nov. 1961; and removed a number of pejorative references to Jews in the Roman-Rite liturgy for Good Friday.

Encyclicals: Of the eight encyclicals he issued, the two outstanding ones were Mater et Magistra ("Christianity and Social Progress"), in which he recapitulated, updated and extended the social doctrine stated earlier by Leo XIII and Pius XI; and Pacem in Terris ("Peace on Earth"), the first encyclical ever addressed to all men of good will as well as to Catholics, on the natural law principles of peace.

Liturgy: In forwarding liturgical reforms already begun by Pius XII, he ordered a calendar-missal-breviary reform into effect Jan. 1, 1961. He authorized the use of vernacular languages in the administration of the sacraments and approved giving Holy Communion to the sick in afternoon hours. He selected the liturgy as the first topic of major discussion by the Second Vatican Council.

Missions: He issued an encyclical on the missionary activity of the Church; established native hierarchies in Indonesia, Vietnam and Korea; and called on North American superiors of religious institutes to have one-tenth of their members assigned to work in Latin America by 1971.

Peace: John spoke and used his moral influence for peace in 1961 when tension developed over Berlin, in 1962 during the Algerian revolt from France, and later the same year in the Cuban missile crisis. His efforts were singled out for honor by the Balzan Peace Foundation. In 1963, he was posthumously awarded the U.S. Presidential Medal of Freedom.

PAUL VI

Paul VI (Giovanni Battista Montini) was born Sept. 26, 1897, at Concesio in northern Italy.

Educated at Brescia, he was ordained to the priesthood May 29, 1920. He pursued additional studies at the Pontifical Academy for Noble Ecclesiastics and the Pontifical Gregorian University. In 1924 he began 30 years of service in the Secretariat of State; as undersecretary from 1937 until 1954, he was closely associated with Pius XII and was heavily engaged in organizing informational and relief services during and after World War II. He declined the offer of the cardinalate by Pope Pius XII.

Ordained archbishop of Milan Dec. 12, 1954, he was inducted into the College of Cardinals Dec. 15, 1958, by Pope John XXIII. Trusted by John, he was a key figure in organizing the first session of Vatican Council II and was elected to the papacy June 21, 1963, two days after the conclave began. He died of a heart attack Aug. 6, 1978.

Second Vatican Council: He reconvened the Second Vatican Council after the death of John XXIII, presided over its second, third and fourth sessions, formally promulgated the 16 documents it produced, and devoted the whole of his pontificate to the task of putting them into effect throughout the Church. The main thrust of his pontificate — in a milieu of cultural and other changes in the Church and the world — was toward institutionalization and control of the authentic trends articulated and set in motion by the council.

Canonizations: He canonized 84 saints. They included groups of 22 Ugandan martyrs and 40 martyrs of England and Wales, as well as two Americans — Elizabeth Ann Bayley Seton and John Nepomucene Neumann.

Cardinals: He created 144 cardinals, and gave the Sacred College a more international complexion than it ever had before. He limited participation in papal elections to 120 cardinals under the age of 80.

Collegiality: He established the Synod of Bishops in 1965 and called it into session five times. He stimulated the formation and operation of regional conferences of bishops, and of consultative bodies on other levels.

Creed and Holy Year: On June 30, 1968, he issued a Creed of the People of God in conjunction with the celebration of a Year of Faith. He proclaimed and led the observance of a Holy Year from Christmas Eve of 1974 to Christmas Eve of 1975.

Diplomacy: He met with many world leaders, including Soviet President Nikolai Podgorny in 1967, Marshal Tito of Yugoslavia in 1971 and President Nicolai Ceausescu of Romania in 1973. He worked constantly to reduce tension between the Church and the intransigent regimes of Eastern European countries by means of a detente type of policy called Ostpolitik. He agreed to significant revisions of the Vatican's concordat with Spain and initiated efforts to revise the concordat with Italy. More than 40 countries established diplomatic relations with the Vatican during his pontificate.

Encyclicals: He issued seven encyclicals, three of which are the best known. In Populorum Progressio ("Development of Peoples") he appealed to wealthy countries to take "concrete action" to promote human development and to remedy imbalances between richer and poorer nations; this encyclical, coupled with other documents and related actions, launched the Church into a new depth of involvement as a public advocate for human rights and for humanizing social, political and economic policies. In Sacerdotalis Caelibatus ("Priestly Celibacy") he reaffirmed the strict observance of priestly celibacy throughout the Western Church. In Humanae Vitae ("Of Human Life") he condemned abortion, sterilization and artificial birth control, in line with traditional teaching and in "defense of life, the gift of God, the glory of the family, the strength of the people."

Interfaith Relations: He initiated formal consultation and informal dialogue on international and national levels between Catholics and non-Catholics — Orthodox, Anglicans, Protestants, Jews, Muslims, Buddhists, Hindus, and unbelievers. He and Greek Orthodox Patriarch Athenagoras I of Constantinople nullified in 1965 the mutual excommunications imposed by their respective churches in 1054.

Liturgy: He carried out the most extensive liturgical reform in history, involving a new Order of the Mass effective in 1969, a revised church calendar in 1970, revisions and translations into vernacular languages of all sacramental rites and other liturgical texts.

Ministries: He authorized the restoration of the permanent diaconate in the Roman Rite and the establishment of new ministries of lay persons.

Peace: In 1968, he instituted the annual observance of a World Day of Peace on New Year's Day. The most dramatic of his many appeals for peace and efforts to ease international tensions was his plea for "No more war!" before the U.N., Oct. 4, 1965.

Pilgrimages: A "Pilgrim Pope," he made pastoral visits to the Holy Land and India in 1964, the U.N. and New York City in 1965, Portugal and Turkey in 1967, Colombia in 1968, Switzerland and Uganda in 1969, and Asia, Pacific islands and Australia in 1970. While in Manila in 1970, he was stabbed by a Bolivian artist.

Roman Curia: He reorganized the central administrative organs of the Church in line with provisions of the apostolic constitution, Regimini Ecclesiae Universae, streamlining procedures for more effective service and giving the agencies a more international perspective by drawing officials and consultors from all over the world. He also instituted a number of new commissions and other bodies. Coupled with curial reorganization was a simplification of papal ceremonies.

JOHN PAUL I

John Paul I (Albino Luciani) was born Oct. 17, 1912, in Forno di Canale (now Canale d'Agordo) in northern Italy. Educated at the minor seminary in Feltre and the major seminary of the Diocese of Belluno, he was ordained to the priesthood July 7, 1935. He pursued further studies at the Pontifical Gregorian University in Rome and was awarded a doctorate in theology. From 1937 to 1947 he was vice rector of the Belluno seminary, where he taught dogmatic and moral theology, canon law and sacred art. Ordained bishop of Vittorio Veneto Dec. 27, 1958, he attended all sessions of the Second Vatican Council, participated in three assemblies of the Synod of Bishops (1971, 1974 and 1977), and was vice president of the Italian Bishops' Conference from 1972 to 1975. He was appointed archbishop and patriarch of Venice Dec. 15, 1969, and was inducted into the College of Cardinals

Mar. 5, 1973.

He was elected to the papacy Aug. 26, 1978, on the fourth ballot cast by the 111 cardinals participating in the largest and one of the shortest conclaves in history. The quickness of his election was matched by the brevity of his pontificate of 33 days, during which he delivered 19 addresses. He died of a heart attack Sept. 28, 1978.

JOHN PAUL II

See separate entry, p. 232.

Benedict XVI

See separate entry, p. 231.

PAPAL ENCYCLICALS — BENEDICT XIV (1740) TO FRANCIS (2013-)

(*Source:* The Papal Encyclicals *[5 vols.], Claudia Carlen, I.H.M.; Pieran Press, Ann Arbor, MI. Used with permission.*)

An encyclical letter is a pastoral letter addressed by a pope to the whole Church. In general, it concerns matters of doctrine, morals or discipline, or significant commemorations. Its formal title consists of the first few words of the official text. Some encyclicals, notably *Pacem in Terris* by John XXIII, *Ecclesiam Suam* by Paul VI and several by John Paul II, have been addressed to people of good will in general as well as to bishops and the faithful in communion with the Church.

An encyclical epistle resembles an encyclical letter but is addressed only to part of the Church. The authority of encyclicals was stated by Pius XII in the encyclical *Humani Generis* Aug. 12, 1950: "Nor must it be thought that what is contained in encyclical letters does not of itself demand assent, on the pretext that the popes do not exercise in them the supreme power of their teaching authority. Rather, such teachings belong to the ordinary magisterium, of which it is true to say: 'He who hears you, hears me' (Lk 10:16); for the most part, too, what is expounded and inculcated in encyclical letters already appertains to Catholic doctrine for other reasons."

The Second Vatican Council declared: "Religious submission of will and of mind must be shown in a special way to the authentic teaching authority of the Roman Pontiff, even when he is not speaking *ex cathedra*. That is, it must be shown in such a way that his supreme magisterium is acknowledged with reverence, the judgments made by him are sincerely adhered to, according to his manifest mind and will. His mind and will in the matter may be known chiefly either from the character of the documents (one of which could be an encyclical), from his frequent repetition of the same doctrine, or from his manner of speaking" (Dogmatic Constitution on the Church, *Lumen Gentium,* No. 25).

The following list contains the titles and indicates the subject matter of encyclical letters and epistles. The latter are generally distinguishable by the limited scope of their titles or contents.

Benedict XIV (1740-58)

1740: *Ubi primum* (On the duties of bishops), Dec. 3.
1741: *Quanta cura* (Forbidding traffic in alms), June 30.
1743: *Nimiam licentiam* (To the bishops of Poland, on validity of marriages), May 18.
1745: *Vix pervenit* (To the bishops of Italy, on usury and other dishonest profit), Nov. 1.
1748: *Magnae Nobis* (To the bishops of Poland, on marriage impediments and dispensations), June 29.
1749: *Peregrinantes* (To all the faithful, proclaiming a Holy Year for 1750), May 5.
Apostolica Constitutio (On preparation for the Holy Year), June 26.
1751: *A quo primum* (To the bishops of Poland, on Jews and Christians living in the same place), June 14.

1754: *Cum Religiosi* (To the bishops of the States of the Church, on catechesis), June 26.
Quod Provinciale (To the bishops of Albania, on Christians using Mohammedan names), Aug. 1.
1755: *Allatae sunt* (To missionaries of the Orient, on the observance of Oriental rites), July 26.
1756: *Ex quo primum* (To bishops of the Greek rite, on the Euchologion), Mar. 1.
Ex omnibus (To the bishops of France, on the apostolic constitution, *Unigenitus*), Oct. 16.

Clement XIII (1758-69)

1758: *A quo die* (Unity among Christians), Sept. 13.
1759: *Cum primum* (On observing canonical sanctions), Sept. 17.
Appetente Sacro (On the spiritual advantages of fasting), Dec. 20.
1761: *In Dominico agro* (On instruction in the faith), June 14.
1766: *Christianae republicae* (On the dangers of anti-Christian writings), Nov. 25.
1768: *Summa quae* (To the bishops of Poland, on the Church in Poland), Jan. 6.

Clement XIV (1769-74)

1769: *Decet quam maxime* (To the bishops of Sardinia, on abuses in taxes and benefices), Sept. 21.
Inscrutabili divinae sapientiae (To all Christians, proclaiming a universal jubilee), Dec.12.
Cum summi (Proclaiming a universal jubilee), Dec. 12.
1774: *Salutis nostra* (To all Christians, proclaiming a universal jubilee), Apr. 30.

Pius VI (1775-99)

1775: *Inscrutabile* (On the problems of the pontificate), Dec. 25.
1791: *Charitas* (To the bishops of France, on the civil oath in France), Apr. 13.

Pius VII (1800-1823)

1800: *Diu satis* (To the bishops of France, on a return to Gospel principles), May 15.

Leo XII (1823-29)

1824: *Ubi primum* (To all bishops, on Leo XII's assuming the pontificate), May 5.
Quod hoc ineunte (Proclaiming a universal jubilee), May 24.
1825: *Charitate Christi* (Extending jubilee to the entire Church), Dec. 25.

Pius VIII (1829-30)

1829: *Traditi humilitati* (On Pius VIII's program for the pontificate), May 24.

Gregory XVI (1831-46)

1832: *Summo iugiter studio* (To the bishops of

Bavaria, on mixed marriages), May 27.

Cum primum (To the bishops of Poland, on civil obedience), June 9.

Mirari vos (On liberalism and religious indifferentism), Aug. 15.

1833: *Quo graviora* (To the bishops of the Rhineland, on the "pragmatic Constitution"), Oct. 4.

1834: *Singulari Nos* (On the errors of Lammenais), June 25.

1835: *Commissum divinitus* (To clergy of Switzerland, on Church and State), May 17.

1840: *Probe nostis* (On the Propagation of the Faith), Sept. 18.

1841: *Quas vestro* (To the bishops of Hungary, on mixed marriages), Apr. 30.

1844: *Inter praecipuas* (On biblical societies), May 8.

Pius IX (1846-78)

1846: *Qui pluribus* (On faith and religion), Nov. 9.

1847: *Praedecessores Nostros* (On aid for Ireland), Mar. 25.

Ubi primum (To religious superiors, on discipline for religious), June 17.

1849: *Ubi primum* (On the Immaculate Conception), Feb. 2.

Nostis et Nobiscum (To the bishops of Italy, on the Church in the Pontifical States), Dec. 8.

1851: *Exultavit cor Nostrum* (On the effects of jubilee), Nov. 21.

1852: *Nemo certe ignorat* (To the bishops of Ireland, on the discipline for clergy), Mar. 25.

Probe noscitis Venerabiles (To the bishops of Spain, on the discipline for clergy), May 17.

1853: *Inter multiplices* (To the bishops of France, pleading for unity of spirit), Mar. 21.

1854: *Neminem vestrum* (To clergy and faithful of Constantinople, on the persecution of Armenians), Feb. 2.

Optime noscitis (To the bishops of Ireland, on the proposed Catholic university for Ireland), Mar. 20.

Apostolicae Nostrae caritatis (Urging prayers for peace), Aug. 1.

1855: *Optime noscitis* (To the bishops of Austria, on episcopal meetings), Nov. 5.

1856: *Singulari quidem* (To the bishops of Austria, on the Church in Austria), Mar. 17.

1858: *Cum nuper* (To the bishops of the Kingdom of the Two Sicilies, on care for clerics), Jan. 20.

Amantissimi Redemptoris (On priests and the care of souls), May 3.

1859: *Cum sancta mater Ecclesia* (Pleading for public prayer), Apr. 27.

Qui nuper (On Pontifical States), June 18.

1860: *Nullis certe verbis* (On the need for civil sovereignty), Jan. 19.

1862: *Amantissimus* (To bishops of the Oriental rite, on the care of the churches), Apr. 8.

1863: Quanto conficiamur moerore (To the bishops of Italy, on promotion of false doctrines), Aug. 10.

Incredibili (To the bishops of Bogota, on persecution in New Granada), Sept. 17.

1864: *Maximae quidem* (To the bishops of Bavaria, on the Church in Bavaria), Aug. 18.

Quanta cura (Condemning current errors), Dec. 8.

1865: *Meridionali Americae* (To the bishops of South America, on the seminary for native clergy), Sept. 30.

1867: *Levate* (On the afflictions of the Church), Oct. 27.

1870: *Respicientes* (Protesting the taking of the Pontifical States), Nov. 1.

1871: *Ubi Nos* (To all bishops, on Pontifical States), May 15.

Beneficia Dei (On the 25th anniversary of his pontificate), June 4.

Saepe Venerabiles Fratres (On thanksgiving for 25 years of pontificate), Aug. 5.

1872: *Quae in Patriarchatu* (To bishops and people of Chaldea, on the Church in Chaldea), Nov. 16.

1873: *Quartus supra* (To bishops and people of the Armenian rite, on the Church in Armenia), Jan. 6.

Etsi multa (On the Church in Italy, Germany and Switzerland), Nov. 21.

1874: *Vix dum a Nobis* (To the bishops of Austria, on the Church in Austria), Mar. 7.

Gravibus Ecclesiae (To all bishops and faithful, proclaiming a jubilee for 1875), Dec. 24.

1875: *Quod nunquam* (To the bishops of Prussia, on the Church in Prussia), Feb. 5.

Graves ac diuturnae (To the bishops of Switzerland, on the Church in Switzerland), Mar. 23.

Leo XIII (1878-1903)

1878: *Inscrutabili Dei consilio* (On the evils of society), Apr. 21.

Quod Apostolici muneris (On socialism), Dec. 28.

1879: *Aeterni Patris* (On the restoration of Christian philosophy), Aug. 4.

1880: *Arcanum* (On Christian marriage), Feb. 10.

Grande munus (On Sts. Cyril and Methodius), Sept. 30.

Sancta Dei civitas (On mission societies), Dec. 3.

1881: *Diuturnum* (On the origin of civil power), June 29.

Licet multa (To the bishops of Belgium, on Catholics in Belgium), Aug. 3.

1882: *Etsi Nos* (To the bishops of Italy, on conditions in Italy), Feb. 15.

Auspicato concessum (On St. Francis of Assisi), Sept. 17.

Cum multa (To the bishops of Spain, on conditions in Spain), Dec. 8.

1883: *Supremi Apostolatus officio* (On devotion to the Rosary), Sept. 1.

1884: *Nobilissima Gallorum gens* (To the bishops of France, on the religious question), Feb. 8.

Humanum genus (On Freemasonry), Apr. 20.

Superiore anno (On the recitation of the Rosary), Aug. 30.

1885: *Immortale Dei* (On the Christian constitution of states), Nov. 1.

Spectata fides (To the bishops of England, on Christian education), Nov. 27.

Quod auctoritate (Proclamation of extraordinary Jubilee), Dec. 22.

1886: *Iampridem* (To the bishops of Prussia, on Catholicism in Germany), Jan. 6.

Quod multum (To the bishops of Hungary, on the liberty of the Church), Aug. 22.

Pergrata (To the bishops of Portugal, on the Church in Portugal), Sept. 14.

1887: *Vieben noto* (To the bishops of Italy, on the Rosary and public life), Sept. 20.

Officio sanctissimo (To the bishops of Bavaria, on the Church in Bavaria), Dec. 22.

1888: *Quod anniversarius* (On his sacerdotal jubilee), Apr. 1.

In plurimis (To the bishops of Brazil, on the abolition of slavery), May 5.

Libertas (On the nature of human liberty), June 20.

Saepe Nos (To the bishops of Ireland, on boycotting in Ireland), June 24.

Paterna caritas (To the Patriarch of Cilicia and the archbishops and bishops of the Armenian people, on reunion with Rome), July 25.

Quam aerumnosa (To the bishops of America, on Italian immigrants), Dec. 10.

Etsi cunctas (To the bishops of Ireland, on the Church in Ireland), Dec. 21.

Exeunte iam anno (On the right ordering of Christian life), Dec. 25.

1889: *Magni Nobis* (To the bishops of the United States, on the Catholic University of America), Mar. 7.

Quamquam pluries (On devotion to St. Joseph), Aug. 15.

1890: *Sapientiae Christianae* (On Christians as citizens), Jan. 10.

Dall'alto Dell'Apostolico seggio (To the bishops and people of Italy, on Freemasonry in Italy), Oct. 15.

Catholicae Ecclesiae (On slavery in the missions), Nov. 20.

1891: *In ipso* (To the bishops of Austria, on episcopal reunions in Austria), Mar. 3.

Rerum novarum (On capital and labor), May 15.

Pastoralis (To the bishops of Portugal, on religious union), June 25.

Pastoralis officii (To the bishops of Germany and Austria, on the morality of dueling), Sept. 12.

Octobri mense (On the Rosary), Sept. 22.

1892: *Au milieu des sollicitudes* (To the bishops, clergy and faithful of France, on the Church and State in France), Feb. 16.

Quarto abeunte saeculo (To the bishops of Spain, Italy, and the two Americas, on the Columbus quadricentennial), July 16.

Magnae Dei Matris (On the Rosary), Sept. 8.

Inimica vis (To the bishops of Italy, on Freemasonry), Dec. 8.

Custodi di quella fede (To the Italian people, on Freemasonry), Dec. 8.

1893: *Ad extremas* (On seminaries for native clergy), June 24.

Constanti Hungarorum (To the bishops of Hungary, on the Church in Hungary), Sept. 2. *Laetitiae sanctae* (Commending devotion to the Rosary), Sept. 8.

Non mediocri (To the bishops of Spain, on the Spanish College in Rome), Oct. 25.

Providentissimus Deus (On the study of Holy Scripture), Nov. 18.

1894: *Caritatis* (To the bishops of Poland, on the Church in Poland), Mar. 19.

Inter graves (To the bishops of Peru, on the Church in Peru), May 1.

Litteras a vobis (To the bishops of Brazil, on the clergy in Brazil), July 2.

Iucunda semper expectatione (On the Rosary), Sept. 8.

Christi nomen (On the propagation of the Faith and Eastern churches), Dec. 24.

1895: *Longinqua* (To the bishops of the United States, on Catholicism in the United States), Jan. 6.

Permoti Nos (To the bishops of Belgium, on social conditions in Belgium), July 10.

Adiutricem (On the Rosary), Sept. 5.

1896: *Insignes* (To the bishops of Hungary, on the Hungarian millennium), May 1.

Satis cognitum (On the unity of the Church), June 29.

Fidentem piumque animum (On the Rosary), Sept. 20.

1897: *Divinum illud munus* (On the Holy Spirit), May 9.

Militantis Ecclesiae (To the bishops of Austria, Germany, and Switzerland, on St. Peter Canisius), Aug. 1.

Augustissimae Virginis Mariae (On the Confraternity of the Holy Rosary), Sept. 12.

Affari vos (To the bishops of Canada, on the Manitoba school question), Dec. 8.

1898: *Caritatis studium* (To the bishops of Scotland, on the Church in Scotland), July 25.

Spesse volte (To the bishops, priests, and people of Italy, on the suppression of Catholic institutions), Aug. 5.

Quam religiosa (To the bishops of Peru, on civil marriage law), Aug. 16.

Diuturni temporis (On the Rosary), Sept. 5.

Quum diuturnum (To the bishops of Latin America, on Latin American bishops' plenary council), Dec. 25.

1899: *Annum Sacrum* (On consecration to the Sacred Heart), May 25.

Depuis le jour (To the archbishops, bishops, and clergy of France, on the education of the clergy), Sept. 8.

Paternae (To the bishops of Brazil, on the education of the clergy), Sept. 18.

1900: *Omnibus compertum* (To the Patriarch and bishops of the Greek-Melkite rite, on unity among the Greek Melkites), July 21.

Tametsi futura prospicientibus (On Jesus Christ the Redeemer), Nov. 1.

1901: *Graves de communi re* (On Christian democracy), Jan. 18.

Gravissimas (To the bishops of Portugal, on religious orders in Portugal), May 16.

Reputantibus (To the bishops of Bohemia and Moravia, on the language question in Bohemia), Aug. 20.

Urbanitatis Veteris (To the bishops of the Latin church in Greece, on the foundation of a seminary in Athens), Nov. 20.

1902: *In amplissimo* (To the bishops of the United States, on the Church in the United States), Apr. 15.

Quod votis (To the bishops of Austria, on the proposed Catholic University), Apr. 30.

Mirae caritatis (On the Holy Eucharist), May 28.

Quae ad Nos (To the bishops of Bohemia and Moravia, on the Church in Bohemia and Moravia), Nov. 22.

Fin dal principio (To the bishops of Italy, on the education of the clergy), Dec. 8.

Dum multa (To the bishops of Ecuador, on marriage legislation), Dec. 24.

St. Pius X (1903-14)

1903: *E supremi* (On the restoration of all things in Christ), Oct. 4.

1904: *Ad diem illum laetissimum* (On the Immaculate Conception), Feb. 2.

Iucunda sane (On Pope Gregory the Great), Mar. 12.

1905: *Acerbo nimis* (On teaching Christian doctrine), Apr. 15.

Il fermo proposito (To the bishops of Italy, on Catholic Action in Italy), June 11.

1906: *Vehementer Nos* (To the bishops, clergy, and people of France, on the French Law of Separation), Feb. 11.

Tribus circiter (On the Mariavites or Mystic Priests of Poland), Apr. 5.

Pieni l'animo (To the bishops of Italy, on the clergy in Italy), July 28.

Gravissimo officio munere (To the bishops of France, on French associations of worship), Aug. 10.

1907: *Une fois encore* (To the bishops, clergy, and people of France, on the separation of Church and State), Jan. 6.

Pascendi dominici gregis (On the doctrines of the Modernists), Sept. 8.

1909: *Communium rerum* (On St. Anselm of Aosta), Apr. 21.

1910: *Editae saepe* (On St. Charles Borromeo), May 26.

1911: *Iamdudum* (On the Law of Separation in Portugal), May 24.

1912: *Lacrimabili statu* (To the bishops of Latin America, on the Indians of South America), June 7.

Singulari quadam (To the bishops of Germany, on labor organizations), Sept. 24.

Benedict XV (1914-22)

1914: *Ad beatissimi Apostolorum* (Appeal for peace), Nov. 1.

1917: *Humani generis Redemptionem* (On preaching the Word of God), June 15.

1918: *Quod iam diu* (On the future peace conference), Dec. 1.

1919: *In hac tanta* (To the bishops of Germany, on St. Boniface), May 14.

Paterno iam diu (On children of central Europe), Nov. 24.

1920: *Pacem, Dei munus pulcherrimum* (On peace and Christian reconciliation), May 23.

Spiritus Paraclitus (On St. Jerome), Sept. 15.

Principi Apostolorum Petro (On St. Ephrem the Syrian), Oct. 5.

Annus iam plenus (On children of central Europe), Dec. 1.

1921: *Sacra propediem* (On the Third Order of St. Francis), Jan. 6.

In praeclara summorum (To professors and students of fine arts in Catholic institutions of learning, on Dante), Apr. 30.

Fausto appetente die (On St. Dominic), June 29.

Pius XI (1922-39)

1922: *Ubi arcano Dei consilio* (On the peace of Christ in the Kingdom of Christ), Dec. 23.

1923: *Rerum omnium perturbationem* (On St. Francis de Sales), Jan. 26.

Studiorum Ducem (On St. Thomas Aquinas), June 29.

Ecclesiam Dei (On St. Josaphat), Nov. 12.

1924: *Maximam gravissimamque* (To the bishops, clergy, and people of France, on French diocesan associations), Jan. 18.

1925: *Quas primas* (On the feast of Christ the King), Dec. 11.

1926: *Rerum Ecclesiae* (On Catholic missions), Feb. 28.

Rite expiatis (On St. Francis of Assisi), Apr. 30.

Iniquis afflictisque (On the persecution of the Church in Mexico), Nov. 18.

1928: *Mortalium animos* (On religious unity), Jan. 6.

Miserentissimus Redemptor (On reparation to the Sacred Heart), May 8.

Rerum Orientalium (On the promotion of Oriental Studies), Sept. 8.

1929: *Mens Nostra* (On the promotion of Spiritual Exercises), Dec. 20.

Quinquagesimo ante (On his sacerdotal jubilee), Dec. 23.

Rappresentanti in terra (On Christian education), Dec. 31. [Latin text, *Divini illius magistri*, pub-

lished several months later with minor changes.]

1930: *Ad salutem* (On St. Augustine), Apr. 20.

Casti connubii (On Christian Marriage), Dec. 31.

1931: *Quadragesimo anno* (Commemorating the fortieth anniversary of Leo XIII's *Rerum novarum*, on reconstruction of the soical order), May 15.

Non abbiamo bisogno (On Catholic Action in Italy), June 29.

Nova impendet (On the economic crisis), Oct. 2.

Lux veritatis (On the Council of Ephesus), Dec. 25.

1932: *Caritate Christi compulsi* (On the Sacred Heart), May 3.

Acerba animi (To the bishops of Mexico, on persecution of the Church in Mexico), Sept. 29.

1933: *Dilectissima Nobis* (To the bishops, clergy, and people of Spain, on oppression of the Church in Spain), June 3.

1935: *Ad Catholici sacerdotii* (On the Catholic priesthood), Dec. 20.

1936: *Vigilanti cura* (To the bishops of the United States, on motion pictures), June 29.

1937: *Mit brennender Sorge* (To the bishops of Germany, on the Church and the German Reich), Mar. 14.

Divini Redemptoris (On atheistic communism), Mar. 19.

Nos es muy conocida (To the bishops of Mexico: on the religious situation in Mexico), Mar. 28

Ingravescentibus malis (On the Rosary) Sept. 29.

Pius XII (1939-58)

1939: Summi Pontificatus (On the unity of human society), Oct. 20.

Sertum laetitiae (To the bishops of the United States, on the 150th anniversary of the establishment of the hierarchy in the United States), Nov. 1.

1940: *Saeculo exeunte octavo* (To the bishops of Portugal and its colonies, on the eighth centenary of the independence of Portugal), June 13.

1943: *Mystici Corporis Christi* (On the Mystical Body of Christ), June 29.

Divino afflante Spiritu (On promoting biblical studies, commemorating the 50th anniversary of *Providentissimus Deus*), Sept. 30.

1944: *Orientalis Ecclesiae* (On St. Cyril, Patriarch of Alexandria), Apr. 9.

1945: Communium interpretes dolorum (To the bishops of the world, appealing for prayers for peace during May), Apr. 15.

Orientales omnes Ecclesias (On the 350th anniversary of the reunion of the Ruthenian Church with the Apostolic See), Dec. 23.

1946: *Quemadmodum* (Pleading for the care of the world's destitute children), Jan. 6.

Deiparae Virginis Mariae (To all bishops, on the possibility of defining the Assumption of the Blessed Virgin Mary as a dogma of faith), May 1.

1947: *Fulgens radiatur* (On St. Benedict), Mar. 21.

Mediator Dei (On the sacred liturgy), Nov. 20.

Optatissima pax (Prescribing public prayers for social and world peace), Dec. 18.

1948: *Auspicia quaedam* (On public prayers for world peace and solution of the problem of Palestine), May 1.

In multiplicibus curis (On prayers for peace in Palestine), Oct. 24.

1949: *Redemptoris nostri cruciatus* (On the holy places in Palestine), Apr. 15.

1950: *Anni Sacri* (On the program for combating atheistic propaganda throughout the world), Mar. 12.

Summi maeroris (On public prayers for peace), July 19.

Humani generis (Concerning some false opinions threatening to undermine the foundations of Catholic doctrine), Aug. 12.

Mirabile illud (On the crusade of prayers for peace), Dec. 6.

1951: *Evangelii praecones* (On the promotion of Catholic missions), June 2.

Sempiternus Rex Christus (On the Council of Chalcedon), Sept. 8.

Ingruentium malorum (On reciting the Rosary), Sept. 15.

1952: *Orientales Ecclesias* (On the persecuted Eastern Church), Dec. 15.

1953: Doctor Mellifluus (On St. Bernard of Clairvaux, the last of the fathers), May 24.

Fulgens corona (Proclaiming a Marian Year to commemorate the centenary of the definition of the dogma of the Immaculate Conception), Sept. 8.

1954: *Sacra virginitas* (On consecrated virginity), Mar. 25.

Ecclesiae fastos (To the bishops of Great Britain, Germany, Austria, France, Belgium, and Holland, on St. Boniface), June 5.

Ad Sinarum gentem (To the bishops, clergy, and people of China, on the supranationality of the Church), Oct. 7.

Ad Caeli Reginam (Proclaiming the Queenship of Mary), Oct. 11.

1955: *Musicae sacrae* (On sacred music), Dec. 25.

1956: *Haurietis aquas* (On devotion to the Sacred Heart), May 15.

Luctuosissimi eventus (Urging public prayers for peace and freedom for the people of Hungary), Oct. 28.

Laetamur admodum (Renewing exhortation for prayers for peace for Poland, Hungary, and especially for the Middle East), Nov. 1.

Datis nuperrime (Lamenting the sorrowful events in Hungary and condemning the ruthless use of force), Nov. 5.

1957: *Fidei donum* (On the present condition of the Catholic missions, especially in Africa), Apr. 21.

Invicti athletae (On St. Andrew Bobola), May 16.

Le pelerinage de Lourdes (Warning against materialism on the centenary of the apparitions at Lourdes), July 2.

Miranda prorsus (On the communications field, motion picture, radio, television), Sept. 8.

1958: *Ad Apostolorum Principis* (To the bishops of China, on Communism and the Church in China), June 29.

Meminisse iuvat (On prayers for persecuted Church), July 14.

Bl. John XXIII (1958-63)

1959: *Ad Petri Cathedram* (On truth, unity, and peace, in a spirit of charity), June 29.

Sacerdotii Nostri primordia (On St. John Vianney), Aug. 1.

Grata recordatio (On the Rosary, prayer for the Church, missions, international and social problems), Sept. 26.

Princeps Pastorum (On the missions, native clergy, lay participation), Nov. 28.

1961: *Mater et Magistra* (On Christianity and social progress), May 15.

Aeterna Dei sapientia (On the 15th centenary of the death of Pope St. Leo I, the see of Peter as the center of Christian unity), Nov. 11.

1962: *Paenitentiam agere* (On the need for the practice of interior and exterior penance), July 1.

1963: *Pacem in terris* (On establishing universal peace in truth, justice, charity, and liberty), Apr. 11.

Paul VI (1963-78)

1964: *Ecclesiam Suam* (On the Church), Aug. 6.

1965: *Mense maio* (On prayers during May for the preservation of peace), Apr. 29.

Mysterium Fidei (On the Holy Eucharist), Sept. 3.

1966: *Christi Matri* (On prayers for peace during Oct.), Sept. 15.

1967: *Populorum progressio* (On the development of peoples), Mar. 26.

Sacerdotalis caelibatus (On the celibacy of the priest), June 24.

1968: *Humanae vitae* (On the regulation of birth), July 25.

John Paul II (1978-2005)

1979: *Redemptor hominis* (On redemption and dignity of the human race), Mar. 4

1980: *Dives in misericordia* (On the mercy of God), Nov. 30.

1981: *Laborem exercens* (On human work), Sept. 14.

1985: *Slavorum Apostoli* (Commemorating Sts. Cyril and Methodius, on the 11th centenary of the death of St. Methodius), June 2.

1986: *Dominum et Vivificantem* (On the Holy Spirit in the life of the Church and the world), May 18.

1987: *Redemptoris Mater* (On the role of Mary in the mystery of Christ and her active and exemplary presence in the life of the Church), Mar. 25.

Sollicitudo Rei Socialis (On social concerns, on the 20th anniversary of *Populorum progressio*), Dec. 30.

1991: *Redemptoris missio* (On the permanent validity of the Church's missionary mandate), Jan. 22.

Centesimus annus (Commemorating the centenary of *Rerum novarum* and addressing the social question in a contemporary perspective), May 1.

1993: *Veritatis Splendor* (On fundamental questions on the Church's moral teaching), Aug. 6.

1995: *Evangelium Vitae* (On the value and inviolability of human life), Mar. 25.

Ut Unum Sint (On commitment to ecumenism), May 25.

1998: *Fides et Ratio* (On faith and reason), Oct. 1.

2003: *Ecclesia de Eucharistia* (Church of the Eucharist), April 17.

Benedict XVI (2005-13)

2005: *Deus Caritas Est* (God is Love), Dec. 25.

2007: *Spe Salvi* (Saved by Hope), Nov. 30.

2009: *Caritas in Veritate* (Charity in Truth), June 29.

Francis (2013-)

2013: *Lumen Fidei* (The Light of Faith), June 29.

CANONIZATIONS BY LEO XIII AND HIS SUCCESSORS

"Canonization" (*see* **Glossary**) is an infallible declaration by the pope that a person who suffered martyrdom and/or practiced Christian virtue to a heroic degree is in glory with God in heaven and is worthy of public honor by the universal Church and of imitation by the faithful.

Biographies of some of the saints listed below are given elsewhere in the **Almanac**; *see* **Index**; for biographies of all new saints for 2012-13, *see* **Saints**.

Leo XIII (1878-1903)
1881: Clare of Montefalco (d. 1308); John Baptist de Rossi (1698-1764); Lawrence of Brindisi (d. 1619).
1883: Benedict J. Labre (1748-83).
1888: Seven Holy Founders of the Servite Order; Peter Claver (1581-1654); John Berchmans (1599-1621); Alphonsus Rodriguez (1531-1617).
1897: Anthony M. Zaccaria (1502-39); Peter Fourier of Our Lady (1565-1640).
1900: John Baptist de La Salle (1651-1719); Rita of Cascia (1381-1457).

St. Pius X (1903-14)
1904: Alexander Sauli (1534-93); Gerard Majella (1725-55).
1909: Joseph Oriol (1650-1702); Clement M. Hofbauer (1751-1820).

Benedict XV (1914-22)
1920: Gabriel of the Sorrowful Mother (1838-62); Margaret Mary Alacoque (1647-90); Joan of Arc (1412-31).

Pius XI (1922-39)
1925: Thérèse of Lisieux (1873-97); Peter Canisius (1521-97); Mary Magdalen Postel (1756-1846); Mary Magdalen Sophie Barat (1779-1865); John Eudes (1601-80); John Baptist Vianney (Curé of Ars) (1786-1859).
1930: Lucy Filippini (1672-1732); Catherine Tomas (1533-74); Jesuit North American Martyrs; Robert Bellarmine (1542-1621); Theophilus of Corte (1676-1740).
1931: Albert the Great (1206-80) (equivalent canonization).
1933: Andrew Fournet (1752-1834); Bernadette Soubirous (1844-79).
1934: Joan Antida Thouret (1765-1826); Mary Michaeli (1809-65); Louise de Marillac (1591-1660); Joseph Benedict Cottolengo (1786-1842); Pompilius M. Pirotti, priest (1710-56); Teresa Margaret Redi (1747-70); John Bosco (1815-88); Conrad of Parzham (1818-94).
1935: John Fisher (1469-1535); Thomas More (1478-1535).
1938: Andrew Bobola (1592-1657); John Leonardi (c. 1550-1609); Salvatore of Horta (1520-67).

Pius XII (1939-58)
1940: Gemma Galgani (1878-1903); Mary Euphrasia Pelletier (1796-1868).
1943: Margaret of Hungary (d. 1270) (equivalent canonization).
1946: Frances Xavier Cabrini (1850-1917).
1947: Nicholas of Flüe (1417-87); John of Britto (1647-93); Bernard Realini (1530-1616); Joseph Cafasso (1811-60); Michael Garicoits (1797-1863); Jeanne Elizabeth des Ages (1773-1838); Louis Marie Grignon de Montfort (1673-1716); Catherine Labouré (1806-76).
1949: Jeanne de Lestonnac (1556-1640); Maria Josepha Rossello (1811-80).
1950: Emily de Rodat (1787-1852); Anthony Mary Claret (1807-70); Bartolomea Capitanio (1807-33); Vincenza Gerosa (1784-1847); Jeanne de

Valois (1461-1504); Vincenzo M. Strambi (1745-1824); Maria Goretti (1890-1902); Mariana Paredes of Jesus (1618-45).
1951: Maria Domenica Mazzarello (1837-81); Emilie de Vialar (1797-1856); Anthony M. Gianelli (1789-1846); Ignatius of Laconi (1701-81); Francis Xavier Bianchi (1743-1815).
1954: Pope Pius X (1835-1914); Dominic Savio (1842-57); Maria Crocifissa di Rosa (1813-55); Peter Chanel (1803-41); Gaspar del Bufalo (1786-1837); Joseph M. Pignatelli (1737-1811).
1958: Herman Joseph, O. Praem. (1150-1241) (equivalent canonization).

Bl. John XXIII (1958-63)
1959: Joaquina de Vedruna de Mas (1783-1854); Charles of Sezze (1613-70).
1960: Gregory Barbarigo (1625-97) (equivalent canonization); John de Ribera (1532-1611).
1961: Bertilla Boscardin (1888-1922).
1962: Martin de Porres (1579-1639); Peter Julian Eymard (1811-68); Anthony Pucci, priest (1819-92); Francis Mary of Camporosso (1804-66).
1963: Vincent Pallotti (1795-1850).

Paul VI (1963-78)
1964: Charles Lwanga and Twenty-one Companions, Martyrs of Uganda (d. between 1885-87).
1967: Benilde Romacon (1805-62).
1969: Julia Billiart (1751-1816).
1970: Maria Della Dolorato Torres Acosta (1826-87); Leonard Murialdo (1828-1900); Therese Couderc (1805-85); John of Ávila (1499-1569); Nicholas Tavelic, Deodatus of Aquitaine, Peter of Narbonne and Stephen of Cuneo, martyrs (d. 1391); Forty English and Welsh Martyrs (d. 16th cent.).
1974: Teresa of Jesus Jornet Ibars (1843-97).
1975: Vicenta Maria Lopez y Vicuna (1847-90); Elizabeth Bayley Seton (1774-1821); John Masias (1585-1645); Oliver Plunket (1629-81); Justin de Jacobis (1800-60); John Baptist of the Conception (1561-1613).
1976: Beatrice da Silva (1424 or 1426-90); John Ogilvie (1579-1615).
1977: Rafaela Maria Porras y Ayllon (1850-1925); John Nepomucene Neumann (1811-60); Sharbel Makhlouf (1828-98).

John Paul II (1978-2005)
1982: Crispin of Viterbo (1668-1750); Maximilian Kolbe (1894-1941); Marguerite Bourgeoys (1620-1700); Jeanne Delanoue (1666-1736).
1983: Leopold Mandic (1866-1942).
1984: Paola Frassinetti (1809-92); 103 Korean Martyrs (d. between 1839-67); Miguel Febres Cordero (1854-1910).
1986: Francis Anthony Fasani (1681-1742); Giuseppe Maria Tomasi (1649-1713).
1987: Giuseppe Moscati (d. 1927); Lawrence (Lorenzo) Ruiz and 15 Companions, Martyrs of Japan (d. 1630s).
1988: Eustochia Calafato (1434-85); 117 Martyrs of Vietnam (96 Vietnamese, 11 Spanish, 10 French, included 8 bishops, 50 priests, 1 seminarian, 58 lay persons); Roque Gonzalez (1576-1628), Alfonso Rodriguez (1598-1628) and Juan de Castillo (1596-1628), Jesuit martyrs of Paraguay; Rose Philippine Duchesne (1796-1852); Simon de Rojas (1552-1624); Magdalen of Canossa

(1774-1835); Maria Rosa Molas y Vollve (d. 1876).

1989: Clelia Barbieri (1847-70); Gaspar Bertoni (1777-1853); Richard Pampuri, religious (1897-1930); Agnes of Bohemia (1211-82); Albert Chmielowski (1845-1916); Mutien-Marie Wiaux (1841-1917).

1990: Marguerite D'Youville (1701-77).

1991: Raphael (Jozef) Kalinowski (1835-1907).

1992: Claude La Colombiere (1641-82); Ezequiel Moreno y Diaz (1848-1905).

1993: Marie of St. Ignatius (Claudine Thevenet) (1774-1837); Teresa "de los Andes" (Juana Fernandez Solar) (1900-20); Enrique de Ossó y Cervelló (1840-96).

1995: Jan Sarkander (1576-1620); Zdislava of Lemberk (d. 1252); Marek Krizin (1588-1619), Stefan Pongracz (1582-1619), Melichar Grodziecky (1584-1619), martyrs of Kosice; Eugene de Mazenod (1782-1861).

1996: Jean-Gabriel Perboyre (1802-40); Juan Grande Roman (1546-1600); Bro. Egidio Maria of St. Joseph (1729-1812).

1997: Hedwig (1371-99); John Dukla, O.F.M. (d. 1484).

1998: Edith Stein (d. 1942).

1999: Marcellin Joseph Benoit Champagnat (1789-1840), Giovanni Calabria (1873-1954); Agostina Livia Pietrantonio (1864-94); St. Cunegunda Kinga (1224-92); Cirilo Bertrán and Eight Companion Brothers of the Christian Schools (d. Oct. 9, 1934); Inocencio de la Immaculada (d. Oct. 9, 1934); St. Jaime Hilario Barbal (1889-1937); Benedetto Menni (1841-1914); Tommaso da Cori (1655-1729).

2000: Mary Faustina Kowalska (1905-38); María Josefa of the Heart of Jesus Sancho de Guerra (1842-1912); Cristóbal Magallanes and 24 Companions (d. 1915-28); José Maria de Yermo y Parres (1851-1904); Maria de Jesús Sacramentado Venegas (1868-1959); 120 Martyrs of China (17th-20th centuries); Katherine Drexel (1858-1955); Josephine Bakhita (d. 1947).

2001: Luigi Scrosoppi (1804-84); Agostino Roscelli (1818-1902); Bernardo da Corleone (1605-67); Teresa Eustochio Verzeri (1801-52); Rafqa Petra Choboq Ar-Rayes (1832-1914); Giuseppe Marello (1844-95); Paula Montal Fornés de San José de Calasanz (1799-1889); Léonie Françoise de Sales Aviat (1844-1914); Maria Crescentia Höss (1682-1744).

2002: Alonso de Orozco (1500-91); Ignazio da Santhia (Lorenzo Maurizio Belvisotti) (1686-1770); Umile da Bisignano (Luca Antonio Pirozzo) (1582-1637); Paulina do Coracao Agonizante de Jesus (Amabile Visintainer) (1865-1942); Benedetta Cambiagio Frassinello (1791-1858); Pio da Pietrelcina (Padre Pio,1887-1968); Juan Diego Cuauhlatoatzin (16th century); Pedro de San Jose de Betancur (1619-67); Josemaria Escriva (1902-75).

2003: Pedro Poveda Castroverde (1874-1936); José María

Rubio y Peralta (1864-1929); Genoveva Torres Morales (1870-1956); Angela de la Cruz (1846-1932); María Maravillas de Jesus (1891-1974); Jozef Sebastian Pelczar (1842-1924); Urszula Ledochowska (1865-1939); Maria de Mattias (1805-66); Virginia Centurione Bracelli (1587-1651); Daniel Comboni (1831-1881); Arnold Janssen (1837-1909); Josef Freinademetz (1852-1908).

2004: Gianna Beretta Molla (1922-1962); Nimatullah Kassab al-Hardini (1828-1858); Josep Manyanet Vives (1833-1901); Luigi Orione (1872-1940); Annibale Di Francia (1851-1927); Paola Elisabetta Cerioli (1816-1865).

Benedict XVI (2005-13)

2005: Józef Bilczewski (1860-1923); Gaetano Catanoso (1879-1963); Zygmunt Gorazdowski (1845-1920); Alberto Hurtado Cruchaga (1901-1952); Felix of Nicosia (1715-1787).

2006: Rafael Guízar Valencia (1878-1938); Filippo Smaldone (1848-1923); Rosa Venerini (1656-1728); Theodore Guérin (1798-1856).

2007: Antoñio de Sant Anna Galváo (1739-1822); George Preca (1880-1962); Simon of Lipnica (c. 1435-1482); Karel Van Sint Andres Houben (1821-1893); Anne Marie Eugenie (1817-1898)

2008: Gaetano Errico (1791-1860); Mary Bernard (Verena) Bütler (1848-1924); Alphonsa of the Immaculate Conception (1910-1946); Narcisa de Jesús Martillo Morán (1832-1869).

2009: Arcangelo Tadini (1846-1912); Bernardo Tolomei (1272-1348); Nuno de Santa Maria Álvares Pereira (1360-1431); Geltrude Comensoli (1847-1903); Caterina Volpicelli (1839-1894); Zygmunt Szcznsny Felinski (1822-1895); Francisco Coll y Guitart (1812-1875) ; Josef Damien de Veuster (1840-1889); Rafael Arnáiz Barón (1911-1938); Jeanne Jugan (1792-1879).

2010: Stanislao Soltys (Kazimierczyk) (1433-1489); Andre Bessette (1845-1937); Candida Maria de Jesus Cipitria y Barriola (1845-1912); Mary of the Cross MacKillop (1842-1909); Giulia Salzano (1846-1929); Battista da Varano (1458-1524).

2011: Guido Conforti (1865-1931); Luigi Guanella (1842-1915); Bonifacia Rodriguez Castro (1837-1905).

2012: Marianne Cope (1838-1918); Kateri Tekakwitha (1656-1680); Giovanni Battista Piamarta (1841-1913); Jacques Berthieu (1838-1896); Carmen Salles y Barangueras (1848-1911); Peter Calungsod (1654-1672); Anna Schaffer (1882-1925).

Francis (2013-)

2013: Martyrs of Otranto (Antonio Primaldo and Companions, d. 1480); Laura Montoya Upegui (1874-1949); María Guadalupe García Zavala (1878–1963).

BEATIFICATIONS BY POPE JOHN PAUL II, 1979-2004

1979: Margaret Ebner (Feb. 24); Francis Coll, O.P., Jacques Laval, S.S.Sp. (Apr. 29); Enrique de Ossó y Cervelló (Oct. 14; canonized June 16, 1993).

1980: José de Anchieta, Peter of St. Joseph Betancurt (canonized July 30, 2002), Francois de Montmorency Laval, Kateri Tekakwitha, Marie Guyart of the Incarnation (June 22); Don Luigi Orione (canonized May 16, 2004), Bartolomea Longo, Maria Anna Sala (Oct. 26).

1981: Sixteen Martyrs of Japan (Lorenzo Ruiz and Companions) (Feb 18; canonized Oct. 18, 1987); Maria

Repetto, Alan de Solminihac, Richard Pampuri (canonized Nov. 1, 1989), Claudine Thevenet (canonized March 21, 1993), Aloysius (Luigi) Scrosoppi (canonized June 10, 2001) (Oct. 4).

1982: Peter Donders, C.SS.R., Marie Rose Durocher, Andre Bessette, C.S.C., Maria Angela Astorch, Marie Rivier (May 23); Fra Angelico (equivalent beatification) (July); Jeanne Jugan, Salvatore Lilli and 7 Armenian Companions (Oct. 3; Sr. Angela of the Cross (Nov. 5; canonized May 3, 2003).

1983: Maria Gabriella Sagheddu (Jan. 25); Luigi Versiglia,

Callisto Caravario (May 15); Ursula Ledochowska (canonized May 18, 2003) (June 20); Raphael (Jozef) Kalinowski (canonized Nov. 17, 1991), Bro. Albert (Adam Chmielowski), T.O.R. (June 22; canonized Nov. 12, 1989); Giacomo Cusmano, Jeremiah of Valachia, Domingo Iturrate Zubero (Oct. 30); Marie of Jesus Crucified (Marie Bouardy) (Nov. 13).

1984: Fr. William Repin and 98 Companions (Martyrs of Angers during French Revolution), Giovanni Mazzucconi (Feb. 19); Marie Leonie Paradis (Sept. 11); Federico Albert, Clemente Marchisio, Isidore of St. Joseph (Isidore de Loor), Rafaela Ybarra de Villalongo (Sept. 30); José Manyanet y Vives (canonized May 16, 2004), Daniel Brottier, C.S.Sp., Sr. Elizabeth of the Trinity (Elizabeth Catez) (Nov. 25).

1985: Mercedes of Jesus (Feb. 1); Ana de los Angeles Monteagudo (Feb. 2); Pauline von Mallinckrodt, Catherine Troiani (Apr. 14); Benedict Menni (canonized Nov. 21, 1999), Peter Friedhofen (June 23); Anwarite Nangapeta (Aug. 15); Virginae Centurione Bracelli (canonized May 18, 2003) (Sept. 21); Diego Luis de San Vitores, S.J., Jose M. Rubio y Peralta, S.J. (canonized May 4, 2003), Francisco Garate, S.J. (Oct. 6); Titus Brandsma, O.Carm. (Nov. 3); Pio Campidelli, C.P., Marie Teresa of Jesus Gerhardinger, Rafqa Ar-Rayes (canonized June 10, 2001) (Nov. 17).

1986: Alphonsa Mattathupandatu of the Immaculate Conception, Kuriakose Elias Chavara (Feb. 8); Antoine Chevrier (Oct. 4); Teresa Maria of the Cross Manetti (Oct. 19).

1987: Maria Pilar of St. Francis Borgia, Maria Angeles of St. Joseph, Card. Marcellis Spinola y Maestre, Emmanuel Domingo y Sol (Mar. 29); Teresa of Jesus "de los Andes" (canonized Mar. 21, 1993) (Apr. 3); Edith Stein (Teresa Benedicta of the Cross) (May 1; canonized, Oct. 11, 1998); Rupert Meyer, S.J. (May 3); Pierre-Francois Jamet, Cardinal Andrea Carlo Ferrari, Benedicta Cambiagio Frassinello, Louis Moreau (May 10); Carolina Kozka, Michal Kozal (June 10); George Matulaitis (Matulewicz) (June 28); Marcel Callo, Pierino Morosini, Antonia Mesina (Oct. 4); Blandina Marten, Ulricke Nische, Jules Reche (Bro. Arnold) (Nov. 1); 85 Martyrs (d. between 1584-1689) of England, Scotland and Wales (Nov. 22).

1988: Giovanni Calabria (canonized April 18, 1999), Joseph Nascimbeni (Apr. 17); Pietro Bonilli, Kaspar Stangassinger, Francisco Palau y Quer, Savina Petrilli (Apr. 24), Laura Vicuna (Sept. 3); Joseph Gerard (Sept. 11); Miguel Pro, Giuseppe Benedetto Dusmet, Francisco Faa di Bruno, Junipero Serra, Frederick Jansoone, Josefa Naval Girbes (Sept. 25); Bernardo Maria Silvestrelli, Charles Houben, Honoratus Kozminski (Oct. 16); Niels Stensen (Nicolaus Steno) (Oct. 23); Katharine Drexel (canonized Oct. 1, 2000), 3 Missionary Martyrs of Ethiopia (Liberato Weiss, Samuel Marzorati, Michele Pio Fasoli) (Nov. 20).

1989: Martin of St. Nicholas, Melchior of St. Augustine, Mary of Jesus of the Good Shepherd, Maria Margaret Caiani, Maria of Jesus Siedliska, Maria Catherine of St. Augustine (Apr. 23); Victoria Rasoamanarivo (Apr. 30); Bro. Scubilionis (John Bernard Rousseau) (May 2); Elizabeth Renzi, Antonio Lucci (June 17); Niceforo de Jesus y Maria (Vicente Diez Tejerina and 25 Companions (martyred in Spain), Lorenzo Salvi, Gertrude Caterina Comensoli, Francisca Ana Cirer Carbonell (Oct. 1); 7 Martyrs from Thailand (Philip Sipong, Sr. Agnes Phila, Sr. Lucia Khambang, Agatha Phutta, Cecilia Butsi, Bibiana Khampai, Maria Phon),

Timothy Giaccardo, Mother Maria of Jesus Deluil-Martiny (Oct. 22); Giuseppe Baldo (Oct. 31).

1990: 9 Martyrs of Astoria during Spanish Civil War (De la Salle Brothers Cirilo Bertran, Marciano Jose, Julian Alfredo, Victoriano Pio, Benjamin Julian, Augusto Andres, Benito de Jesus, Aniceto Adolfo; and Passionist priest Innocencio Inmaculada; canonized Nov. 21, 1999), Mercedes Prat, Manuel Barbal Cosan (Bro. Jaime), Philip Rinaldi, Tommaso da Cori (canonized Nov. 21, 1999) (Apr. 29); Juan Diego (confirmation of Apr. 9 decree; canonized July 31, 2002), 3 Child Martyrs (Cristobal, Antonio and Juan), Fr. Jose Maria de Yermo y Parres (May 6; canonized May 21, 2001); Pierre Giorgio Frassati (May 20); Hanibal Maria Di Francia (canonized May 16, 2004), Joseph Allamano (Oct. 7); Marthe Aimee LeBouteiller, Louise Therese de Montaignac de Chauvance, Maria Schinina, Elisabeth Vendramini (Nov. 4).

1991: Annunciata Cocchetti, Marie Therese Haze, Clara Bosatta (Apr. 21); Jozef Sebastian Pelczar (June 2; canonized May 18, 2003); Boleslava Lament (June 5); Rafael Chylinski (June 9); Angela Salawa (Aug. 13); Edoardo Giuseppe Rosaz (July 14, Susa, Italy); Pauline of the Heart of Jesus in Agony Visentainer (canonized May 19, 2002) (Oct. 18, Brazil); Adolph Kolping (Oct. 27).

1992: Josephine Bakhita (canonized Oct. 1, 2000), Josemaria Escriva de Balaguer (May 17; canonized Oct. 6, 2000); Francesco Spinelli (June 21, Caravaggio, Italy); 17 Irish Martyrs, Rafael Arnáiz Barón, Nazaria Ignacia March Mesa, Léonie Françoise de Sales Aviat (canonized Nov. 25, 2001), and Maria Josefa Sancho de Guerra (canonized Oct. 1, 2000) (Sept. 27); 122 Martyrs of Spanish Civil War, Narcisa Martillo Morán (Oct. 25); Cristóbal Magellanes and 24 companions, Mexican martyrs (Nov. 22), and Maria de Jesús Sacramentado Venegas (Nov. 22; canonized May 21, 2000).

1993: Dina Belanger (Mar. 20); John Duns Scotus (Mar. 20, cult solemnly recognized); Mary Angela Truszkowska, Ludovico of Casoria, Faustina Kowalska (canonized Apr. 30, 2000), Paula Montal Fornés (canonized Nov. 25, 2001) (Apr. 18); Stanislaus Kazimierczyk (Apr. 18, cult solemnly recognized); Maurice Tornay, Marie-Louise Trichet, Columba Gabriel and Florida Cevoli (May 16); Giuseppe Marello (Sept. 26; canonized Nov. 25, 2001); Eleven martyrs of Almeria, Spain, during Spanish Civil War (2 bishops, 7 brothers, l priest, l lay person); Victoria Diez y Bustos de Molina, Maria Francesca (Anna Maria) Rubatto; Pedro Castroverde (canonized May 4, 2003), Maria Crucified (Elisabetta Maria) Satellico (Oct. 10).

1994: Isidore Bakanja, Elizabeth Canori Mora; Dr. Gianna Beretta Molla (Apr. 24; canonized May 16, 2004); Nicolas Roland, Alberto Hurtado Cruchaga, Maria Rafols, Petra of St. Joseph Perez Florida, Josephine Vannini (Oct. 16); Magdalena Caterina Morano (Nov. 5); Hyacinthe Marie Cormier, Marie Poussepin, Agnes de Jesus Galand, Eugenia Joubert, Claudio Granzotto (Nov. 20).

1995: Peter ToRot (Jan. 17); Mother Mary of the Cross MacKillop (Jan. 19); Joseph Vaz (Jan. 21); Rafael Guizar Valencia, Modestino of Jesus and Mary, Genoveva Torres Morales (canonized May 4, 2003), Grimoaldo of the Purification (Jan. 29); Johann Nepomuk von Tschiderer (Apr. 30); Maria Helena Stollenwerk, Maria Alvarado Cordozo, Giuseppina Bonino, Maria Domenica Brun Barbantini, Agostino Roscelli (May 7; canonized June 10, 2001); Damien de Veuster (June 4);

109 Martyrs (64 from French Revolution – Martyrs of La Rochelle – and 45 from Spanish Civil War), Anselm Polanco Fontecha, Felipe Ripoll Morata, and Pietro Casini (Oct. 1); Mary Theresa Scherer, Maria Bernarda Butler and Marguerite Bays (Oct. 29).

1996: Daniel Comboni (canonized Oct. 5, 2003) and Guido Maria Conforti (Mar. 17); Card. Alfredo Ildefonso Schuster, O.S.B., Filippo Smaldone and Gennaro Sarnelli (priests) and Candida Maria de Jesus Cipitria y Barriola, Maria Raffaella Cimatti, Maria Antonia Bandres (religious) (May 12), Bernhard Lichtenberg and Karl Leisner (June 23), Wincenty Lewoniuk and 12 companions, Edmund Rice, Maria Ana Mogas Fontcuberta and Marcelina Darowska (Oct 6); Otto Neururer, Jakob Gapp and Catherine Jarrige (Nov. 24).

1997: Bp. Florentino Asensio Barroso, Sr. Maria Encarnacion Rosal of the Sacred Heart, Fr. Gaetano Catanoso, Fr. Enrico Rebuschini and Ceferino Gimenez Malla, first gypsy beatified (May 4); Bernardina Maria Jablonska, Maria Karlowska (June 6); Frédéric Ozanam (Aug. 22); Bartholomew Mary Dal Monte (Sep. 27); Elías del Socorro Nieves, Domenico Lentini, Giovanni Piamarta, Emilie d'Hooghvorst, Maria Teresa Fasce (Oct. 12); John Baptist Scalabrini, Vilmos Apor, María Vicenta of St. Dorothy Chávez Orozco (Nov. 9).

1998: Bp. Vincent Bossilkov, María Sallés, Brigida of Jesus (Mar. 15); Fr. Cyprian Tansi (Mar. 22); Nimatullah al-Hardini (canonized May 16, 2004), 11 Spanish nuns (May 10); Secondo Polla (May 23); Giovanni Maria Boccardo, Teresa Grillo Chavez, Teresa Bracco (May 24); Jakob Kern, Maria Restituta Kafka, and Anton Schwartz (June 21); Giuseppe Tovini (Sept. 20); Card. Alojzije Stepinac (Oct. 3); Antônio de Sant'Anna Galvão, Faustino Miguez, Zeferino Agostini, Mother Theodore Guérin (Oct. 25).

1999: Vicente Soler, and six Augustinian Recollect Companions, Manuel Martin Sierra, Nicolas Barre, Anna Schaeffer (Mar. 7); Padre Pio (May 2; canonized June 16, 2002); Fr. Stefan Wincenty Frelichowski (June 7); 108 Polish Martyrs, Regina Protmann, Edmund Bojanowski (June 13); Bp. Anton Slomsek (Sept. 19); Ferdinando Maria Baccilieri, Edward Maria Joannes Poppe, Arcangelo Tadini, Mariano da Roccacasale, Diego Oddi, Nicola da Gesturi (Oct. 3).

2000: André de Soveral, Ambrósio Francisco Ferro and 28 Companions, Nicolas Bunkerd Kitbamrung, Maria Stella Mardosewicz and 10 Companions, Pedro Calungsod and Andrew of Phú Yên (Mar. 5); Mariano de Jesus Euse Hoyos, Francis Xavier Seelos, Anna Rosa Gattorno, Maria Elisabetta Hesselblad, Mariam Thresia Chiramel Mankidiyan (Apr. 9); Jacinta and Francisco Marto of Fatima (May 13); Pope Pius IX, Pope John XXIII, Tommaso Reggio, Guillaume-Joseph Chaminade, Columba Marmion (Sept. 3).

2001: José Aparicio Sanz and 232 Companions of the Spanish Civil War (Mar. 11); Manuel Gonzalez Garcia, Marie-Anne Blondin, Caterina Volpicelli, Caterina Cittadini, Carlos Manuel Cecilio Rodriguez Santiago (Apr. 29); George Preca, Ignatius Falzon, Maria Adeodata Pisani (May 9); Abp. Jósef Bilczewski and Fr. Sygmunt Gorazdowski, Ukrainian martyrs (June 27).

2002: Gaetano Errico, Lodovico Pavoni, Luigi Variara, Maria del Transito de Jesus Sacramentado, Artemide Zatti, Maria Romero Meneses (Apr. 14); Kamen Vitchev, Pavel Djidjov, Josaphat Chichkov (May 26); Juan Bautista and Jacinto de Los Angeles (Aug. 1); Zygmunt Szczęsny Feliński, Jan Balicki, Jan Beyzym, Sancja Szymkowiak (Aug. 18); Daudi Okelo, Jildo Irwa, Andrea Giacinto Longhin, O.F.M. Cap., Marcantonio Durando, Marie de la Passion Hélène Marie de Chappotin de Neuville, Liduina Meneguzzi (Oct. 20).

2003: Pierre Bonhomme, María Dolores Rodríguez Sopeña, María Caridad Brader, Juana María Condesa Lluch, László Batthyány-Strattmann (Mar. 23); Eugenia Ravasco, Giacomo Alberione, Giulia Salzano, Marco d'Aviano, Maria Cristina Brando, Maria Domenica Mantovani (Apr. 27); Maria de Jesus Crucified Petkovic (June 6); Ivan Merz (June 22); Vasil' Hopko, Zdenka Schelingová (Sept. 14); Mother Teresa of Calcutta (Oct. 19); Juan Nepomuceno Zegrí y Moreno, Valentin Paquay, Luigi Maria Monti, Bonifacia Rodríguez Castro, Rosalie Rendu (Nov. 9).

2004: Luigi Talamoni, Matilde del Sagrado Corazón Téllez Robles, Piedad de la Cruz Ortiz Real, Maria Candida of the Eucharist (Mar. 21); Augusto Czartoryski, Laura Montoya, María Guadalupe García Zavala, Giulia Nemesia Valle, Eusebia Palomino Yenes, Alexandrina Maria da Costa (Apr. 25); Pere Tarrés i Claret, Alberto Marvelli, Pina Suriano (Sept. 5); Peter Vigne, Joseph-Marie Cassant, Anna Katharina Emmerick, Maria Ludovica De Angelis, Charles of Austria (Oct. 3).

BEATIFICATIONS UNDER POPE BENEDICT XVI (2005-13)

For biographical details of all those beatified in 2010-2011, please *see* under **Saints**.

2005: Ascensión of the Heart of Jesus, Marianne Cope (May 14); Wladyslaw Findysz, Bronislaw Markiewicz, Ignacy Klopotowski (June 19); Cardinal Clemens August von Galen (Oct. 9); Charles de Foucauld, Maria Pia Pastena, Maria Crocifissa Curcio, Eurosia Fabris (Nov. 13); María De Los Ángeles Ginard Martí, Josep Tàpies and six Companions (Oct. 29); Anacleto González Flores and 8 Companions, José Trinidad Rangel, Andrés Solá Molist, Leonardo Pérez, Darío Acosta Zurita (Nov. 20).

2006: Agostino Thevarparampil Kunjachan, Luigi Biraghi, Luigi Monza (Apr. 30); Maria Teresa of Saint Joseph (May 13); Sr. Maria of the Passion (May 14); Rita Amada of Jesus (May 28); Eustáquio von Lieshout (June 15); Sára Salkaházi, Moses Tovini (Sept. 17); Maria Teresa of Jesus (Oct. 8); Paul Josef

Nardini, Margarita Maria López de Maturana (Oct. 22); Mariano de la Mata Aparicio (Nov. 5); Euphrasia of the Sacred Heart of Jesus Eluvathingal (Dec. 3).

2007: Luigi Boccardo (Apr. 14); Maria Maddalena of the Passion (Apr. 15); Francesco Spoto (Apr. 21) Maria Rosa Pellesi (Apr. 29); Carmen del Niño Jesús González Ramos García Prieto (May 6); Carlo Liviero (May 27); Basile-Antoine Marie Moreau (Sept. 15), Marie-Céline de la Présentation (Jeanne Germaine Castang), Stanislaw of Jesus and Mary (Jana Papczynski) (Sept. 16), Maria Luisa Merkert (Sept. 30), Albertina Berkenbrock (Oct. 20), Emmanuel Gómez González, Adílio Daronch (Oct. 21), Franz Jägerstätter (Oct. 26), Celina Chludzinska v. Borzecka (Oct. 27), Zepherin Namuncurá (Nov. 11), Antonio Rosmini (Nov. 18), Lindalva Justo de Oliveira (Dec. 2).

2008: Sr. Giuseppina Nicoli (Feb. 3); Celestina of the Mother of God (Marianna Donati) (Mar. 30); Candelaria of St.

Joseph (Apr. 27); Mary Magdalene of the Incarnation (May 3); Margaret Flesch (May 4); Martha Wiecka (May 24); Maria Giuseppina di Gesù Crocifisso (June 1); Jacques Ghazir Haddad (June 22); Josepha Hendrina Stenmanns (June 29); Vincenza Maria Poloni (Sept. 21); Michał Sopoko (Sept. 28); Giovanni Francesco Bonifacio (Oct. 4); Luís Martin and Zélia Guérin (Oct. 19); Peter Kibe Kasui and 187 Companions (Nov. 24); José Olallo Valdés (Nov. 29).
2009: Raphael Rafiringa (June 7); Émilie de Villeneuve (July 5); Eustachio Kugler (Oct. 4); Ciriaco Maria Sancha y Hervas (Oct. 18); Carlo Gnocchi (Oct. 25); Zoltan Lajos Meszlenyi (Oct. 31); Maria Alfonsina Danil (Nov. 22);
2010: Josep Samsó y Elias (Jan. 23); Bernardo Francisco de Hoyos (Apr. 18); Angelo Paoli (Apr. 25); José Tous y Soler (Apr. 25); Teresa Manganiello (May 22); Maria Pierina De Micheli; Jerzy Popieluszko (June 6); Manuel Lozano Garrido (June 12); John Henry Newman (Sept. 19); Chiara Badano (Sept. 25); Alfona Clerici (Oct. 23); Szilárd Ignác Bogdánffy (Oct. 30); Barbara Maix (Nov. 6).
2011: John Paul II (Karol Wojtyla) (May 1); Giustino Maria Russolillo (May 7); Georg Häfner (May 15); Maria Clara Galvão Meixa de Moura Telles (May 21);

Dulce Lopes Pontes de Souza Brito (May 22); Maria Serafina Micheli (May 28); Juan de Palafox Mendoza (June 5); Alois Andritzki (June 13); Marguerite Rutan (June 19); Johannes Prassek and Two Companions (June 25); Serafino Morazzone, Clemente Vismara, Enrichetta Alfieri (June 26); Janos Scheffler (July 3); Elena Aiello (Sept. 14); Francesco Paleari (Sept. 17); Maria Jula Ivanisevic and Four Companions (Sept. 24); Antonia Maria Verna (Oct. 2); Anna Maria Janer Anglarill (Oct. 8); Maria Catalina Echegeray (Oct. 29); Carl Lampert (Nov. 13); Francisco Esteban Lacal and 21 Companions (Dec. 17).
2012: Hildegard Burjan (Jan. 29); Maria Ines Teresa Arias Espinosa (Apr. 21); Giuseppe Toniolo (Apr. 29); Pierre-Adrien Toulorge (Apr. 29); Louise-Elisabeth de Lamoignon (My 27); Jean-Jospeh Lataste (June 3); Cecilia Eusepi (June 17); Mariano Arciero (June 24); Louis Brisson (Sept. 22); Gabriele Maria Allegra (Sept. 29); Gabriele Maria Allegra (Sept. 29); Bedrich Bachstein and 13 Companions (Oct. 13); Maria Luisa Prosperi (Nov. 10); María Crescencia Pérez (Nov. 17); Maria Troncatti (Nov. 24); Devasahayam (Lazarus) Pillai (Dec. 2).

BEATIFICATIONS UNDER POPE FRANCIS (2013-)

2013: Cristóbal of Saint Catherine Fernández de Valladolid (Apr. 7); Luca Passi (Apr. 13); Nicolò Rusca (Apr. 21); Francisca de Paula de Jesus (May 4); Luigi Novarese (May 11); Giuseppe Puglisi (May 25); Zofia Czeska-Maciejowska (June 9); Margaret Lucja Szewczyk (June 9); Odoardo Focherini (June 15); Vladimir Ghika (Aug.

31); Antonio Franco (Sept. 2); Maria Bolognesi (Sept. 7); José Gabriel del Rosario Brochero (Sept. 14); Tommaso Olera (Sept. 21); Miroslav Bulešic (Sept. 28); Rolando Rivi (Oct. 5); Martyrs of the Religious Persecution during the Spanish Civil War (Oct. 13); Sándor Istvan (Oct. 19); Maria Theresia Bonzel (Nov. 10).

ROMAN CURIA

The Roman Curia is the Church's network of central administrative agencies (called dicasteries) serving the Vatican and the local churches, with authority granted by the Pope.

The Curia evolved gradually from advisory assemblies or synods of the Roman clergy with whose assistance the popes directed church affairs during the first 11 centuries. Its original office was the Apostolic Chancery, established in the fourth century to transmit documents. The antecedents of its permanently functioning agencies and offices were special commissions of cardinals and prelates. Its establishment in a form resembling what it is now dates from the second half of the 16th century.

Pope Paul VI initiated a four-year reorganization study in 1963 that resulted in the constitution *Regimini Ecclesiae Universae*. The document was published Aug. 18, 1967, and went into full effect in March 1968. Pope John Paul II, in the apostolic constitution *Pastor Bonus*, published June 28, 1988, and effective Mar. 1, 1989, ordered modifications of the Curia based on the broad outline of Paul VI's reorganization.

In accordance with Pope John Paul II's reform effective Mar. 1, 1989, and later revisions, the Curia consists of the Secretariat of State, nine congregations (governing agencies), three tribunals (judicial agencies), 11 councils (promotional agencies) and three offices (specialized service agencies). All have equal juridical status with authority granted by the pope.

SECRETARIAT OF STATE

The Secretariat of State, *Palazzo Apostolico Vaticano*,

Vatican City. Most Rev. Pietro Parolin, Secretary of State; Most Rev. Giovanni Angelo Becciu, Deputy for General Affairs; Most Rev. Dominique Mamberti, Secretary for Relations with States.

The Secretariat of State provides the pope with the closest possible assistance in the care of the universal Church. It consists of two sections:

• The Section for General Affairs assists the pope in expediting daily business of the Holy See. It coordinates curial operations, prepares drafts of documents entrusted to it by the pope, has supervisory duties over the *Acta Apostolicae Sedis, Annuario Pontificio,* the Vatican Press Office and the Central Statistics Office.

• The Section for Relations with States (formerly the Council for Public Affairs of the Church, a separate body) handles diplomatic and other relations with civil governments. Attached to it is a council of Cardinals and Bishops.

Background: Evolved gradually from secretarial offices (dating back to the 15th century) and the Congregation for Extraordinary Ecclesiastical Affairs (dating back to 1793; restructured as the Council for the Public Affairs of the Church by Paul VI in 1967). John Paul II gave it its present form in his June 28, 1988, reform of the Curia.

CONGREGATIONS
Congregation for the Doctrine of the Faith: Piazza del S. Uffizio 11, 00193 Rome, Italy. Most Rev. Gerhard Ludwig Müller, prefect; Most Rev. Luis F. Ladaria Ferrer, S.J., secretary.

Has responsibility to safeguard the doctrine of faith and

morals. Accordingly, it examines doctrinal questions and promotes studies thereon; evaluates theological opinions and, when necessary and after prior consultation with concerned bishops, reproves those regarded as opposed to principles of the faith; examines books on doctrinal matters and can reprove such works, if the contents so warrant, after giving authors the opportunity to defend themselves. It examines matters pertaining to the Privilege of Faith (Petrine Privilege) in marriage cases, and safeguards the dignity of the sacrament of penance. Attached to the congregation are the Pontifical Biblical Commission and the Theological Commission.

Background: At the beginning of the 13th century, legates of Innocent III were commissioned as the Holy Office of the Inquisition to combat heresy; the same task was entrusted to the Dominican Order by Gregory IX in 1231 and to the Friars Minor by Innocent IV from 1243 to 1254. On July 21, 1542 (apostolic constitution *Licet*), Paul III instituted a permanent congregation of cardinals with supreme and universal competence over matters concerning heretics and those suspected of heresy. Pius IV, St. Pius V and Sixtus V further defined the work of the congregation. St. Pius X changed its name to the Congregation of the Holy Office. Paul VI (*motu proprio Integrae Servandae*, Dec. 7, 1965), began reorganization of the Curia with this body, to which he gave the new title, Congregation for the Doctrine of the Faith. Its orientation is not merely negative, in the condemnation of error, but positive, in the promotion of orthodox doctrine.

Congregation for the Oriental Churches: Palazzo del Bramante, Via della Conciliazione 34, 00193 Rome, Italy. Card. Leonardo Sandri, prefect; Most Rev. Cyril Vasil', S.J., secretary. Members include all patriarchs of the Eastern Catholic Churches and major archbishops.

Has competence in matters concerning the persons and discipline of Eastern Catholic Churches. It has jurisdiction over territories in which the majority of Christians belong to Eastern Churches (i.e., Egypt, the Sinai Peninsula, Eritrea, Northern Ethiopia, Southern Albania, Bulgaria, Cyprus, Greece, Iran, Iraq, Lebanon, Palestine, Syria, Jordan, Turkey, Afghanistan); also, over minority communities of Eastern Church members no matter where they live.

Background: Established by Pius IX Jan. 6, 1862 (apostolic constitution Romani Pontifices), and united with the Congregation for the Propagation of the Faith. The congregation was made autonomous by Benedict XV May 1, 1917 (motu proprio *Dei Providentis*), and given wider authority by Pius XI Mar. 25, 1938 (motu proprio *Sancta Dei Ecclesia*).

Congregation for Divine Worship and the Discipline of the Sacraments: Piazza Pio XII 10, 00193 Rome, Italy. Card. Antonio Cañizares Llovera, prefect; Most Rev. Arthur Roche, secretary.

Supervises everything pertaining to the promotion and regulation of the liturgy, primarily the sacraments, without prejudice to the competencies of the Congregation for the Doctrine of the Faith. Attached to the congregation are special commissions treating causes of nullity of sacred ordinations and dispensations from obligations of sacred ordination of deacons and priests.

Background: Originally two separate congregations: the Congregation for Divine Worship (instituted by Paul VI, May 8, 1969) and the Congregation for the Discipline of the Sacraments (established by St. Pius X, June 29, 1908, to replace the Congregation of Rites instituted by Pope Sixtus V in 1588). They were united by Paul VI, July 11, 1975, as the Congregation for the Sacraments and Divine Worship; reestablished as separate congregations by John Paul II in an autograph letter of Apr. 5, 1984, and reunited anew by the same Pope, June 28, 1988 (apostolic constitution *Pastor Bonus*), as the Congregation for Divine Worship and the Discipline of the Sacraments.

Congregation for the Causes of Saints: Piazza Pio XII 10, 00193 Rome, Italy. Card. Angelo Amato, S.D.B., prefect; Most Rev. Marcello Bartolucci, secretary.

Handles matters connected with beatification and canonization causes (in accordance with revised procedures decreed in 1983), and the preservation of relics.

Background: Established by Sixtus V in 1588 as the Congregation of Rites; affected by legislation of Pius XI in 1930; title changed and functions defined by Paul VI, 1969 (apostolic constitution *Sacra Rituum Congregatio*). It was restructured and canonization procedures were revised by John Paul II in 1983 (apostolic constitution *Divinus Perfectionis Magister*).

Congregation for Bishops: Piazza Pio XII 10, 00193 Rome, Italy. Card. Marc Ouellet P.S.S., prefect; Most Rev. Lorenzo Baldisseri, secretary.

Has functions related in one way or another to bishops and the jurisdictions in which they serve. It supervises the Pontifical Commission for Latin America. Attached to the congregation are a central coordinating office for Military Vicars (established Feb. 2, 1985) and an office for coordinating ad limina visits (established June 29, 1988).

Background: Established by Sixtus V Jan. 22, 1588 (apostolic constitution Immensa); given an extension of powers by St. Pius X June 20, 1908, and Pius XII Aug. 1, 1952 (apostolic constitution *Exsul Familia*); given present title (was known as Consistorial Congregation) by Paul VI (Aug. 1, 1967); competencies redefined by John Paul II, June 28, 1988.

Congregation for the Evangelization of Peoples: Piazza di Spagna 48, 00187 Rome, Italy. Card. Fernando Filoni, prefect; Most Rev. Savio Hon Tai-Fai, S.D.B., secretary; Most Rev. Protase Rugambwa, adjunct secretary.

Directs and coordinates missionary work throughout the world. Accordingly, it has competence over those matters which concern all the missions established for the spread of Christ's kingdom without prejudice to the competence of other congregations. These include: fostering missionary vocations; assigning missionaries to fields of work; establishing ecclesiastical jurisdictions and proposing candidates to serve them as bishops and in other capacities; encouraging the recruitment and development of indigenous clergy; mobilizing spiritual and financial support for missionary activity. To promote missionary cooperation, the congregation has a Supreme Council for the Direction of Pontifical Missionary Works composed of the Missionary Union of the Clergy and Religious, the Society for the Propagation of the Faith, the Society of St. Peter the Apostle for Native Clergy, the Society of the Holy Childhood, and the International Center of Missionary Animation.

Background: Originated as a commission of cardinals by St. Pius V and Gregory XII for missions in East and West Indies, Italo-Greeks and for ecclesiastical affairs in Protestant territories of Europe; Clement VIII instituted a Congregation of the Propagation of the Faith in 1599 which ceased to exist after several years. Erected as a stable congregation by Gregory XV June 22, 1622 (apostolic constitution *Inscrutabili Divinae*); its functions were redefined by John Paul II, June 28, 1988.

Congregation for the Clergy: Piazza Pio XII 3, 00193 Rome, Italy. Card. Mauro Piacenza, prefect; Most Rev. Celso Morga Iruzubieta, secretary.

Has three offices with competencies concerning the life, discipline, rights and duties of the clergy; the preaching of the Word, catechetics, norms for religious education of children and adults; preservation and administration of the temporal goods of the Church. Attached to it are the International Council for Catechetics (established in 1973 by Paul VI) and the *Institute Sacrum Ministerium* for the permanent formation of the clergy (established in line with John Paul II's 1992 apostolic exhortation *Pastores Dabo Vobis*).

Background: Established by Pius IV Aug. 2, 1564 (apostolic constitution *Alias Nos*), under the title Congregation of the Cardinals Interpreters of the Council of Trent; affected by legislation of Gregory XIII and Sixtus V; known as Congregation of the Council until Aug. 15, 1967, when Paul VI renamed it the Congregation for the Clergy and redefined its competency; John Paul II gave it added responsibilities June 28, 1988.

Congregation for Institutes of Consecrated Life and Societies of Apostolic Life: Piazza Pio XII 3, 00193 Rome, Italy. Card. João Bráz de Aviz, prefect; Most Rev. Jose Rodriguez Carballo, O.F.M., secretary.

Has competence over institutes of Religious, secular institutes, societies of the apostolic life and third (secular) orders. With two sections, the congregation has authority in matters related to the establishment, general direction and suppression of the various institutes; general discipline in line with their rules and constitutions; the movement toward renewal and adaptation of institutes in contemporary circumstances; the setting up and encouragement of councils and conferences of major religious superiors for intercommunication, etc.

Background: Founded by Sixtus V May 27, 1586, with the title, Congregation for Consultations of Regulars; confirmed by the apostolic constitution Immensa Jan. 22, 1588; made part of the Congregation for Consultations of Bishops and other Prelates in 1601; made autonomous by St. Pius X in 1908 as Congregation of Religious; title changed to Congregation for Religious and Secular Institutes by Paul VI in 1967; given present title by John Paul II, June 28, 1988.

Congregation for Catholic Education (for Seminaries and Institutes of Study): Piazza Pio XII 3, 00193 Rome, Italy. Card. Zenon Grocholewski, prefect; Most Rev. Angelo Zani, secretary.

Has supervisory competence over institutions and works of Catholic education. It carries on its work through three offices. One office handles matters connected with the direction, discipline and temporal administration of seminaries, and with the education of diocesan clergy, religious and members of secular institutes. A second office oversees Catholic universities, faculties of study and other institutions of higher learning inasmuch as they depend on the authority of the Church; encourages cooperation and mutual assistance among Catholic institutions, and the establishment of Catholic hospices and centers on campuses of non-Catholic institutions. A third office is concerned in various ways with all Catholic schools below the college-university level, with general questions concerning education and studies, and with the cooperation of conferences of bishops and civil authorities in educational matters. The congregation supervises Pontifical Works for Priestly Vocations.

Background: The title (Congregation of Seminaries and Universities) and functions of the congregation were defined by Benedict XV Nov. 4, 1915; Pius XI, in 1931 and 1932, and Pius XII, in 1941 and 1949, extended its functions; Paul VI changed its title to Congregation for Catholic Education in 1967; given its present title by Pope John Paul II, June 28, 1988. Its work had previously been carried on by two other congregations erected by Sixtus V in 1588 and Leo XII in 1824.

Inter-Agency Curia Commissions

In accordance with provisions of the apostolic constitution *Pastor Bonus,* John Paul II established the following interdepartmental permanent commissions to handle matters when more than one agency of the Curia is involved in activities:

• For matters concerning appointments to local Churches and the setting up and alteration of them and their constitution (Mar. 22, 1989). Members include officials of the Secretariat of State and Congregation for Bishops. President, Abp. Pietro Parolin, Secretary of State.

• For matters concerning members, individually or as a community, of Institutes of Consecrated Life founded or working in mission territories (Mar. 22, 1989). Members include officials of the Congregations for the Evangelization of Peoples and for Institutes of Consecrated Life and Societies of Apostolic Life. President, Card. Fernando Filoni, prefect of the Congregation for the Evangelization of Peoples.

• For the formation of candidates for Sacred Orders (Mar. 22, 1989). Members include officials of the Congregations for Catholic Education, for Institutes of Consecrated Life and Societies of Apostolic Life, for Evangelization of Peoples, for Oriental Churches. President, Card. Zenon Grocholewski, prefect of the Congregation for Catholic Education.

• For promoting a more equitable distribution of priests throughout the world (July 20, 1991). Members include secretaries of congregations for Evangelization of Peoples, for the Clergy, Catholic Education, for the Institutes of Consecrated Life and Societies of Apostolic Life; and vice-president of Commission for Latin America. President, Card. Zenon Grocholewski, Prefect of the Congregation for Catholic Education.

• For the Church in Eastern Europe (Jan. 15, 1993), replacing the Pontifical Commission for Russia which was terminated. The commission is concerned with both Latin and Eastern-rite churches in territories of the former Soviet Union and other nations affected by the historical circumstances resulting from atheistic communism. It is responsible for promoting the apostolic mission of the Church and fostering ecumenical dialogue with the Orthodox and other Churches of the Eastern tradition. Members, under presidency of Cardinal Secretary of State, include the secretary and undersecretary of the Section for Relations with States and secretaries of Congregations for the Oriental Churches, for the Clergy, for Institutes of Consecrated Life and Societies of Apostolic Life, secretary of the Pontifical Council for Promoting Christian Unity. President, Abp. Pietro Parolin.

Tribunals

Apostolic Penitentiary: Piazza della Cancelleria 1, 00186 Rome, Italy. Card. Manuel Monteiro de Castro, major

penitentiary; regent, Most Rev. Krzysztof Jozef Nykiel.
Has jurisdiction for the internal forum only (sacramental and non-sacramental). It issues decisions on questions of conscience; grants absolutions, dispensations, commutations, sanations and condonations; has charge of non-doctrinal matters pertaining to indulgences.

Background: Origin dates back to the 12th century; affected by the legislation of many popes; radically reorganized by St. Pius V in 1569; jurisdiction limited to the internal forum by St. Pius X; Benedict XV annexed the Office of Indulgences to it Mar. 25, 1917.

Apostolic Signatura: Piazza della Cancelleria 1, 00186 Rome, Italy. Card. Raymond L. Burke, prefect; Most Rev. Frans Daneels, O. Praem., secretary.

The principal concerns of this supreme court of the Church are to resolve questions concerning juridical procedure and to supervise the observance of laws and rights at the highest level. It decides the jurisdictional competence of lower courts and has jurisdiction in cases involving personnel and decisions of the Rota. It is the supreme court of the State of Vatican City.

Background: A permanent office of the Supreme Tribunal of the Apostolic Signatura has existed since the time of Eugene IV in the 15th century; affected by the legislation of many popes; reorganized by St. Pius X in 1908 and made the supreme tribunal of the Church.

Roman Rota: Piazza della Cancelleria 1, 00186 Rome, Italy. Msgr. Pio Vito Pinto, Dean.

The ordinary court of appeal for cases appealed to the Holy See. It is best known for its competence and decisions in cases involving the validity of marriage.

Background: Originated in the Apostolic Chancery; affected by the legislation of many popes; reorganized by St. Pius X in 1908; further revised by Pius XI in 1934; new norms approved and promulgated by John Paul II in 1982 and 1987.

PONTIFICAL COUNCILS

Pontifical Council for the Laity: Piazza S. Calisto 16, 00153 Rome, Italy. Card. Stanislaw Rylko, president; Most Rev. Josef Clemens, secretary.

Its competence covers the apostolate of the laity and their participation in the life and mission of the Church. Members are mostly lay people from different parts of the world and involved in different apostolates.

Background: Established on an experimental basis by Paul VI Jan. 6, 1967; given permanent status Dec. 10, 1976 (*motu proprio Apostolatus Peragendi*).

Pontifical Council for Promoting Christian Unity: Via dell' Erba 1, 00193 Rome, Italy. Card. Kurt Koch, president; Most Rev. Brian Farrell, L.C., secretary.

Handles relations with members of other Christian ecclesial communities; deals with the correct interpretation and execution of the principles of ecumenism; initiates or promotes Catholic ecumenical groups and coordinates on national and international levels the efforts of those promoting Christian unity; undertakes dialogue regarding ecumenical questions and activities with churches and ecclesial communities separated from the Apostolic See; sends Catholic observer-representatives to Christian gatherings, and invites to Catholic gatherings observers of other churches; orders into execution conciliar decrees dealing with ecumenical affairs. The **Commission for Religious Relations with the Jews** is attached to the secretariat.

Background: Established by John XXIII June 5, 1960, as a preparatory secretariat of the Second Vatican Council; raised to commission status during the first session of the council in the fall of 1962; status as a secretariat confirmed and functions defined by Paul VI in 1966 and 1967; made a pontifical council by John Paul II, June 28, 1988.

Pontifical Council for the Family: Piazza S. Calisto 16, 00153 Rome, Italy. Most Rev. Vincenzo Paglia, president; Most Rev. Jean Laffitte, secretary.

Is concerned with promoting the pastoral care of families so they may carry out their educative, evangelizing and apostolic mission and make their influence felt in areas such as defense of human life and responsible procreation according to the teachings of the Church. Members, chosen by the Pope, are married couples and men and women from all parts of the world and representing different cultures. They meet in general assembly at least once a year.

Background: Instituted by John Paul II May 9, 1981, replacing the Committee for the Family established by Paul VI Jan. 11, 1973.

Pontifical Council for Justice and Peace: Piazza S. Calisto 16, 00153 Rome, Italy. Card. Peter Turkson, president; Most Rev. Mario Toso, secretary.

Its primary competence is to promote justice and peace in the world according to the Gospels and social teaching of the Church.

Background: Instituted by Paul VI Jan. 6, 1967, on an experimental basis; reconstituted and made a permanent commission Dec. 10, 1976; its competence was redefined and it was made a pontifical council June 28, 1988, by John Paul II.

Pontifical Council "Cor Unum": Piazza S. Calisto 16, 00153 Rome, Italy. Card. Robert Sarah, president; secretary, Msgr. Giovanni Pietro Dal Toso.

Its principal aims are to provide informational and coordinating services for Catholic aid and human development organizations and projects on a worldwide scale. Attached to the council are the John Paul II Foundation for the Sahel and "Populorum Progressio."

Background: Instituted by Paul VI July 15, 1971.

Pontifical Council for Pastoral Care of Migrants and Itinerant Peoples: Piazza S. Calisto 16, 00153 Rome, Italy. Card. Antonio Maria Vegliò, president; Most Rev. Joseph Kalathiparambil, secretary.

Is concerned with pastoral assistance to migrants, nomads, tourists, sea, and air travelers.

Background: Instituted by Paul VI and placed under general supervision of Congregation for Bishops, Mar. 19, 1970; made autonomous as a pontifical council and renamed by John Paul II, June 28, 1988.

Pontifical Council for Pastoral Assistance to Health Care Workers: Via della Conciliazione 3, 00193 Rome, Italy. Most Rev. Zygmunt Zimowski, president; Rev. Jean-Marie Mate Musivi Mupendawatu, secretary.

Its functions are to stimulate and foster the work of formation, study and action carried out by various international Catholic organizations in the health care field.

Background: Established in 1985 as a commission by John Paul II; made a council June 28, 1988.

Pontifical Council for the Interpretation of Legislative Texts: Piazza Pio XII 10, 00193 Rome, Italy. Card. Francesco Coccopalmerio, president; Most Rev. Juan Ignacio Arrieta Ochoa de Chinchetru, secretary.

Primary function is the authentic interpretation of the universal laws of the Church.

Background: Established by John Paul II, Jan. 2, 1984, as the Pontifical Commission for the Authentic Interpretation of the Code of Canon Law; name changed and given additional functions June 28, 1988. Its competency was extended in 1991 to include interpretation of Code of Canon Law of Oriental Church that was promulgated in 1990.

Pontifical Council for Interreligious Dialogue: Via dell' Erba 1, 00193 Rome, Italy. Card. Jean-Louis Tauran, president; Most Rev. Miguel Ángel Ayuso Guixot, M.C.C.I, secretary.

Its function is to promote studies and dialogue for the purpose of increasing mutual understanding and respect between Christians and non-Christians. The Commission for Religious Relations with Muslims is attached to the council.

Background: Established by Paul VI May 19, 1964, as the Secretariat for Non-Christians; given present title and functions by John Paul II, June 28, 1988.

Pontifical Council for Culture: Piazza S. Calisto 16, 00153 Rome, Italy. Card. Gianfranco Ravasi, president; Most Rev. Barthélemy Adoukonou, secretary.

Its functions are to foster the Church's and the Holy See's relations with the world of culture and to establish dialogue with those who do not believe in God or who profess no religion provided these are open to sincere cooperation. It consists of two sections: (1) faith and culture; (2) dialogue with cultures. Attached to it is the **Coordinating Council for Pontifical Academies.**

Background: Present council with expanded functions was instituted by John Paul II (*motu proprio* of Mar. 25, 1993) through the merger of the Pontifical Council for Culture (established May 20, 1982, by John Paul II) and the Pontifical Council for Dialogue with Non-Believers (established by Paul VI Apr. 9, 1965, as the secretariat for Non-Believers).

Pontifical Council for Social Communications: Palazzo S. Carlo, 00120 Vatican City. Most Rev. Claudio Maria Celli, president; Msgr. Paul Tighe, secretary; Msgr. Giuseppe Antonio Scotti, adjunct secretary.

Engaged in matters pertaining to instruments of social communication so that through them the message of salvation and human progress is fostered and carried forward in civil culture and mores.

Background: Instituted on an experimental basis by Pius XII in 1948; reorganized three times in the 1950s; made permanent commission by John XXIII Feb. 22, 1959; established as council and functions restated by John Paul II June 28, 1988.

Pontifical Council for Promoting the New Evangelization: Via della Conciliazione 5, 00193 Rome, Italy. Most Rev. Salvatore Fisichella, president; Most Rev. Jose Octavio Ruiz Arenas, secretary.

Intended to help rekindle the faith in the West, with a particular focus placed on the United States, Europe and South America; the title was first coined under Pope John Paul II to mean a reawakening of the faith in regions where the long-established Christian community faces declines in practice and zeal.

Background: Created by Pope Benedict XVI on June 30, 2010. The new dicastery was officially established on Oct. 12, 2010 through the *motu proprio, Ubicumque et semper.*

OFFICES

Apostolic Camera: Palazzo Apostolico, 00120 Vatican City. Card. Tarcisio Bertone, S.D.B., chamberlain of the Holy Roman Church; Abp. Pier Luigi Celata, vice-chamberlain.

Administers the temporal goods and rights of the Holy See between the death of one pope and the election of another (*sede vacante*), in accordance with special laws.

Background: Originated in the 11th century; reorganized by Pius XI in 1934; functions redefined (especially of *camerlengo*) by subsequent legislation in 1945, 1962 and 1975.

Administration of the Patrimony of the Apostolic See: Palazzo Apostolico, 00120 Vatican City. Card. Domenico Calcagno, president; Mons. Luigi Misto, secretary.

Handles the estate of the Apostolic See under the direction of papal delegates acting with ordinary or extraordinary authorization.

Background: Some of its functions date back to 1878; established by Paul VI Aug. 15, 1967.

Prefecture for the Economic Affairs of the Holy See: Largo del Colonnato 3, 00193 Rome, Italy. Card. Giuseppe Versaldi, president; Mons. Lucio Angel Vallejo Balda, secretary.

A financial office that coordinates and supervises administration of the temporalities of the Holy See. Membership includes Card. Roger M. Mahony and Card. Edward Egan.

Background: Established by Paul VI Aug. 15, 1967; functions redefined by John Paul II, June 28, 1988.

Other Curia Agencies

Prefecture of the Papal Household: Most Rev. Georg Gänswein, prefect; Most Rev. Paolo de Nicolò, regent.

Oversees the papal chapel — which is at the service of the pope in his capacity as spiritual head of the Church, and the pontifical family — which is at the service of the pope as a sovereign. It arranges papal audiences, has charge of preparing non-liturgical elements of papal ceremonies, makes all necessary arrangements for papal visits and trips, and settles questions of protocol connected with papal audiences and other formalities.

Background: Established by Paul VI, Aug. 15, 1967, under the title Prefecture of the Apostolic Palace; it supplanted the Sacred Congregation for Ceremonies founded by Sixtus V, Jan. 22, 1588. The office was updated and reorganized under the present title by Paul VI, Mar. 28, 1968.

Office for Liturgical Celebrations of the Supreme Pontiff: Palazzo Apostolico Vaticano, 00120 Vatican City. Msgr. Guido Marini, Master of Ceremonies.

Prepares everything necessary for liturgical and other sacred celebrations by the Pope or in his name; directs everything in accordance with prescriptions of liturgical law.

Background: Evolved gradually from the early office of Apostolic Master of Ceremonies; affected by legislation of Pope Paul IV in 1563 and Benedict XV in 1917; restructured by Paul VI in 1967; given its present title (formerly known as Prefecture of Pontifical Ceremonies) and constituted as an autonomous agency of the Roman Curia by John Paul II, June 28, 1988.

Vatican Press Office: Via della Conciliazione 54, 00120 Vatican City. Rev. Federico Lombardi, S.J., director; Rev. Ciro Benedettini, C.P., vice-director.

Established Feb. 29, 1968, to replace service agencies formerly operated by *L'Osservatore Romano* and an office created for press coverage of the Second Vatican Council. New directives were issued in 1986.

Vatican Information Service (VIS): Via della Conciliazione 54, 00120 Vatican City.

Established Mar. 28, 1990, within the framework but distinct from the Vatican Press Office. Furnishes information, in English, French and Spanish, on pastoral and magisterial activity of the Pope through use of electronic mail and fax.

Central Statistics Office: Palazzo Apostolico, 00120 Vatican City.

Established by Paul VI, Aug. 15, 1967; attached to the Secretariat of State. Compiles, systematizes and analyzes information on the status and condition of the Church.

COMMISSIONS AND COMMITTEES

Listed below are non-curial institutes that assist in the work of the Holy See. Some are attached to curial agencies, as indicated. Other institutes are listed elsewhere in the *Almanac*; see *Index*.

Pontifical Commission for the Cultural Heritage of the Church: Established by John Paul II, June 28, 1988, as Pontifical Commission for Preserving the Church's Patrimony of Art and History and attached to the Congregation for the Clergy; made autonomous and given present title Mar. 25, 1993. Card. Gianfranco Ravasi, president.

Pontifical Commission for Sacred Archeology: Instituted by Pius IX Jan, 6, 1852. Card. Gianfranco Ravasi, president.

Pontifical Biblical Commission: Instituted by Leo XIII Oct. 30, 1902; completely restructured by Paul VI June 27, 1971; attached to the Congregation for the Doctrine of the Faith. Most Rev. Gerhard Müller, president.

Pontifical Commission for Latin America: Instituted by Pius XII Apr. 19, 1958; attached to the Congregation for Bishops July, 1969; restructured by John Paul II in 1988. Card. Marc Ouellet, P.S.S., president; Prof. Guzmán Carriquiry, secretary.

Pontifical Commission for the Revision and Emendation of the Vulgate: Established in 1984 by John Paul II to replace the Abbey of St. Jerome instituted by Pius XI in 1933. Rev. Jean Mallet, O.S.B., director.

Pontifical Commission "Ecclesia Dei": Established by John Paul II, July 2, 1988, to facilitate the return to full ecclesial communion of priests, seminarians and religious who belonged to the fraternity founded by Marcel Lefebvre; attached to the Congregation for the Doctrine of the Faith in 2009. Most Rev. Gerhard Müller, president; Most Rev. Joseph Augustine Di Noia, O.P., vice-president.

Pontifical Commission for Reference on the Institute for Works of Religion: Established by Pope Francis on June 24, 2013, to gather accurate information on the legal status and various activities of the Institute to permit, when necessary, a better harmonization of the said Institute with the universal mission of the Apostolic See. Cardinal Raffaele Farina, president.

Pontifical Commission for Reference on the Organisation of the Economic-Administrative Structure of the Holy See: Established by Pope Francis, July 18, 2013, to gather information, report to the Holy Father and co-operate with the Council of Cardinals for the study of the organisational and economic problems of the Holy See. Dr. Joseph F.X. Zahra, president.

International Theological Commission: Instituted by Paul VI, Apr. 11, 1969, as an advisory adjunct of no more than 30 theologians to the Congregation for the Doctrine of the Faith; definitive statutes promulgated by John Paul II, Aug. 6, 1982. Most Rev. Gerhard Müller, president;

Rev. Serge Thomas Bonino, O.P., general secretary.

Commission for Religious Relations with the Jews: Instituted by Paul VI, Oct. 22, 1974, to promote and foster relations of a religious nature between Jews and Christians; attached to the Council for Promoting Christian Unity. Card. Kurt Koch, president.

Commission for Religious Relations with Muslims: Instituted by Paul VI, Oct. 22, 1974, to promote, regulate and interpret relations between Catholics and Muslims; attached to the Council for Interreligious Dialogue. Card. Jean-Louis Tauran, president.

Pontifical Committee for International Eucharistic Congresses: Instituted, 1879, by Pope Leo XIII; established as a pontifical committee with new statutes by John Paul II, Feb. 11, 1986. Most Rev. Piero Marini, president.

Pontifical Committee for Historical Sciences: Instituted by Pius XII, Apr. 7, 1954, as a continuation of a commission dating from 1883. Very Rev. Bernard Ardura, O. Praem., president.

Vatican II Archives: Preserves the documents of the Second Vatican Council.

Financial Security Committee: Established Aug. 8, 2013, for the prevention and contrast of laundering activities, financing of terrorism and proliferation of weapons of mass destruction. Msgr. Peter Wells, president.

Disciplinary Commission of the Roman Curia: Most Rev. Giorgio Corbellini, president.

Institute for Works of Religion: Instituted by Pius XII June 27, 1942, to bank and administer funds for works of religion; replaced an earlier administration established by Leo XIII in 1887; reorganized by John Paul II (chirograph of Mar. 1, 1990). Headed by a commission of cardinals, including Cards. Tarcisio Bertone, Telesphore Toppo, Jean-Louis Tauran. Ernst von Freyburg, president.

Fabric of St. Peter: Administration, care and preservation of Vatican Basilica. Card. Angelo Comastri, president.

Office of Papal Charities (Apostolic Almoner): Distributes alms and aid to those in need in the name of the pope. Most Rev. Konrad Krajewski, almoner.

Labor Office of the Apostolic See (ULSA - *Ufficio del Lavoro della Sede Apostolica*): Has competence in regard to those who work for the Apostolic See; charged with settling labor issues. Instituted by John Paul II (*motu proprio* of Jan. 1, 1989); functions reaffirmed and definitive text of statutes approved by John Paul II (*motu proprio* of Sept. 30, 1994). Most Rev. Giorgio Corbellini, president.

Papal Basilicas:

Papal Basilica of St. Peter in the Vatican: Archpriest, Card. Angelo Comastri.

Papal Archbasilica of St. John in the Lateran: Archpriest, Card. Agostino Vallini.

Papal Basilica of St. Paul Outside the Walls: Archpriest, Card. James Harvey.

Papal Basilica of Saint Mary Major: Archpriest, Card. Abril y Castello Santos.

Internationalization

As of July 1, 2013, principal officials of the Roman Curia were from the following countries: Italy (Cards. Amato, Antonelli, Baldelli, Bertone, Cacciavillan, Calcagno, Cheli, Coccopalmerio, Comastri, de Paolis, Filoni, Marchisano, Martino, Monterisi, Nicora, Piacenza, Pompedda, Ravasi, Sardi, Sebastiani, Silvestrini, Sodano, Vallini, Vegliò, Versaldi; Abps. Baldisseri, Bartolucci,

Becciu, Bertello, Celata, Celli, Cunial, de Magistris, del Blanco Prieto, di Ruberto, Fisichella, Gardin, Girotti, Marchetto, Marini, Nesti, Paglia, Salerno, Toso, Vachelli, Bps. Bertagna, Corbellini, de Nicolò, Girotti, Parolin, Pastore, Sciacca); France (Cards. Etchegaray, Poupard, Tauran, Abp. Bruguès, Mamberti); United States (Cards. Baum, Burke, Harvey, Levada, O'Brien, Stafford, Szoka, Abps. DiNoia); Spain (Cards. Abril y Castello, Cañizares Llovera, Martinez Somalo, Herranz; Abps. Arrieta Ochoa de Chinchetru, Gil Hellín, Ladaria, Morga Iruzubieta, Redrado Marchite); Argentina (Card. Sandri); Germany (Card. Cordes; Abps. Clemens, Müller); Poland (Cards. Grocholewski, Rylko, Abps.

Hoser, Kaszak, Nowak, Stankiewicz, Zimowski, Bp. Nykiel); Brazil (Cards. Cañizares Llovera, João Bráz de Aviz); Chile (Card. Medina Estévez); China (Abp. Hon Tai-Fai); French Guinea (Card. Sarah); Ghana (Card. Turkson); Great Britain (Roche); Ireland (Bp. Farrell), Hungary (Abp. Ternyák); Mexico (Card. Lozano Barrágan); Nigeria (Card. Arinze); Portugal (Cards. Saraiva Martins, Monteiro de Castro); India (Card. Dias; Bp. Kalathiparambil); Slovakia (Card. Tomko, Abp. Vasil'); Ukraine (Abp. Marusyn); Tanzania (Bp. Rugambwa); Croatia (Abp. Eterovic); Canada (Card. Ouellet); Switzerland (Card. Koch); Belgium (Bp. Daneels); Colombia (Abp. Ruiz Arenas).

VATICAN CITY STATE

The State of Vatican City (*Stato della Città del Vaticano*) is the territorial seat of the papacy. The smallest sovereign state in the world, it is situated within the city of Rome, embraces an area of 108.7 acres, and includes within its limits the Vatican Palace, museums, art galleries, gardens, libraries, radio station, post office, bank, astronomical observatory, offices, apartments, service facilities, St. Peter's Basilica, and neighboring buildings between the Basilica and Viale Vaticano. The extraterritorial rights of Vatican City extend to more than 10 buildings in Rome, including the major basilicas and office buildings of various congregations of the Roman Curia, and to the papal villas at **Castel Gandolfo** 15 miles southeast of the City of Rome. Castel Gandolfo is the summer residence of the Holy Father.

The government of Vatican City is in the hands of the reigning pope, who has full executive, legislative and judicial power. The administration of affairs, however, is handled by the **Pontifical Commission for the State of Vatican City** under Card. Giuseppe Bertello. The legal system is based on Canon Law; in cases where this code does not obtain, the laws of the City of Rome apply. The City is an absolutely neutral state and enjoys all the rights and privileges of a sovereign power. The citizens of Vatican City, and they alone, owe allegiance to the pope as a temporal head of state. On Nov. 26, 2000, Pope John Paul II promulgated the new Fundamental Law of the Vatican City State. The new law replaced that first established in 1929 by Pope Pius XI. A further change was introduced on Mar. 2, 2011, when Pope Benedict XVI issued a new law that regulates Vatican citizenship and restricts vehicle access to Vatican grounds. The new law extends the possibility of having official Vatican "residents" – those living on the grounds of Vatican City without being citizens. Vatican citizenship is usually held by cardinals, archbishops, and officials who serve in various posts in the Roman Curia and administration of the Vatican City State. Cardinals of the Roman Curia residing outside Vatican City enjoy the privileges of extraterritoriality. The Secretary General for the Governatorate of the Vatican City State is Rev. Fernando Vergez Alzaga, L.C.

The normal population is approximately 1,000. While the greater percentage is made up of priests and religious, there are several hundred laypersons living in Vatican City. They are housed in their own apartments in the City and are engaged in secretarial, domestic, trade and service occupations. Approximately 3,400 laypersons are employed by the Vatican.

Services of honor and order are performed by the Swiss Guards, who have been charged with responsibility for the personal safety of popes since 1506. The current Captain of the Swiss Guards is Col. Daniel Rudolf Anrig, who was appointed on Aug. 19, 2008. Additional police and ceremonial functions are under the supervision of a special office. These functions were formerly handled by the Papal Gendarmes, the Palatine Guard of Honor, and the Guard of Honor of the Pope (Pontifical Noble Guard); the units were disbanded by Pope Paul VI on Sept. 14, 1970.

The **Basilica of St. Peter**, built between 1506 and 1626, is the largest church in Christendom (with the exception of the Basilica of Our Lady Queen of Peace in Ivory Coast) and the site of most papal ceremonies. The pope's own patriarchal basilica, however, is **St. John Lateran**, whose origins date back to 324.

St. Ann's, staffed by Augustinian Fathers, is the parish church of Vatican City. Its pastor is appointed by the pope, following the recommendation of the prior general of the Augustinians and the archpriest of the Vatican Basilica.

The Church of **Santa Susanna** was designated as the national church for Americans in Rome by Pope Benedict XV Jan. 10, 1922, and entrusted to the Paulist Fathers, who have served there continuously since then except for several years during World War II.

Pastoral care in Vatican City State, which is separate from the diocese of Rome, is entrusted to the archpriest of St. Peter's Basilica, who is also vicar general for Vatican City and the papal villas at Castel Gandolfo (chirograph of Pope John Paul II, Jan. 14, 1991). Cardinal Angelo Comastri succeeded to the post of Archpriest of St. Peter's Basilica, vicar general for Vatican City, and President of the Fabric of St. Peter on Oct. 31, 2006.

The Vatican Library (00120 Vatican City; Msgr. Cesare Pasini, prefect; Dr. Ambrogio Piazzoni, vice-prefect) has among its holdings 150,000 manuscripts, about 1,000,000 printed books, and 7,500 incunabula. The **Vatican Secret Archives** (00120 Vatican City; Most Rev. Sergio Pagano, prefect), opened to scholars by Leo XIII in 1881, contain central church documents dating back to the time of Innocent III (1198-1216). Abp. Jean-Louis Brugues O.P., is librarian and archivist of the Holy Roman Church.

The independent temporal power of the pope, which is limited to the confines of Vatican City and small areas outside, was for many centuries more extensive than it is now. As late as the 19th century, the pope ruled 16,000 square miles of Papal States across the middle of Italy, with a population of over 3,000,000. In 1870 forces of the Kingdom of Italy occupied these lands that, with the exception of the small areas surrounding the Vatican and Lateran in Rome and the Villas of Castel Gandolfo, became part of the Kingdom by the Italian law of May 13, 1871.

The **Roman Question**, occasioned by this seizure and the voluntary confinement of the pope to the Vatican, was settled with ratification of the Lateran Agreement June 7, 1929, by the Italian government and Vatican City. The agreement recognized Catholicism as the religion of Italy and provided, among other things, a financial indemnity to the Vatican in return for the former Papal States; it became Article 7 of the Italian Constitution, Mar. 26, 1947. The Lateran Agreement was superseded by a new concordat given final approval by the Italian Chamber of Deputies Mar. 20 and formally ratified June 3, 1985.

Papal Flag

The papal flag consists of two equal vertical stripes of yellow and white, charged with the insignia of the papacy on the white stripe — triple crown or tiara over two crossed keys, one of gold and one of silver, tied with a red cord and two tassels. The divisions of the crown represent the teaching, sanctifying and ruling offices of the pope. The keys symbolize his jurisdictional authority.

The papal flag is a national flag inasmuch as it is the standard of the Supreme Pontiff as the sovereign of the state of Vatican City. It is also universally accepted by the faithful as a symbol of the supreme spiritual authority of the Holy Father.

Vatican Radio

The declared purpose of Vatican radio station HVJ is "that the voice of the Supreme Pastor may be heard throughout the world by means of the ether waves, for the glory of Christ and the salvation of souls." Designed by Guglielmo Marconi, the inventor of radio, and supervised by him until his death, the station was inaugurated by Pope Pius XI in 1931. The original purpose has been extended to a wide variety of programming.

Vatican Radio operates on international wave lengths, transmits programs in 37 languages, and serves as a channel of communication between the Vatican, church officials and listeners in general in many parts of the world. The station broadcasts about 400 hours a week throughout the world.

The daily English-language program for North America is broadcast on 6095, 7305, 9600 Khz as well as via satellite INTELSAT 325,5° East (Atlantic) – 4097.75 Mhz – LHCP polarization.

Frequencies, background information and audio files can be obtained at www.radiovaticana.org and www.vatican.va.

The staff of 415 broadcasters and technicians includes 30 Jesuits. Studios and offices are at Palazzo Pio, Piazza Pia, 3, 00193 Rome. The transmitters are situated at Santa Maria di Galeria, a short distance north of Rome. Rev. Federico Lombardi, S.J., director-general.

2012 Vatican Stamps and Coins

The Vatican Philatelic and Numismatic Office (00120 Vatican City) published the following list of stamps and coins for the Year 2013:

Stamps
1. Easter of Resurrection
2. Year of Faith 2012-2013
3. Benedict XVI - Year IX of the Pontificate- MMXIII
4. 60th World Day of Raoul Follereau for the 110th Anniversary of the birth
5. 50th Anniversary of the death of Pope John XXIII
6. 1700th Anniversary of the Edict of Milan (joint issue with Italy)
7. Europe 2013 – "The Postal Van"
8. 750th Anniversary of the Miracle of Bolsena
9. XXVIII World Youth Day in Rio de Janeiro
10. Bicentenary of the birth of Giuseppe Verdi and Richard Wagner
11. 1,150th Anniversary of the evangelization of Sts. Cyril and Methodius in Slovakia and the Czech Republic (joint issue with Slovakia and the Czech Republic)
12. The Popes of the Renaissance, Julius II and Leo X
13. Holy Christmas (joint issue with Åland)
14. The international Journeys of Pope Benedict XVI in 2012
15. Bicentenary of the Vatican Chapter
16. VI Centenary of the election of Santa Maria di Nardo as Cathedral
17. Sede Vacante: On Mar. 1, the Philatelic and Numismatic Office of the Governorate of Vatican City State issued four stamps with the image of an angel raising the pavilion ("*umbraculum*") of the Apostolic Camera, the work of Italian artist Daniela Longo.

Postal Stationery
• Postcards: 150th Anniversary of the birth of Giuseppe Gioacchino Belli
• Aerogramme: 150th Anniversary of the death of Pietro Mascagni
• Philatelic Cover 2013
• Envelope Postal Stationery: 50th Anniversary of the death of Pope John XIII

Philatelic and Numismatic Covers
• Philatelic and Numismatic Cover "XXVIII World Youth Day in Rio de Janeiro"
• Stamp and Coin Card "50th Anniversary of the death of Pope John XIII"

Year Book
• Vaticano 2013

Coins
• Coin Card 2013 – Michelangelo's St. Peter's Pietà
• Euro coin set BU Version
• Euro Coin Set Proof Version with a 20 Euro silver coin "Bicentenary of the birth of Giuseppe Verdi"
• Euro Coin Set Proof Version with a 50 Euro gold coin "Bicentenary of the birth of Richard Wagner"
• 2 Euro Bimetallic Commemorative Coin "XXVIII World Youth Day in Rio de Janeiro"
• 5 Euro Silver Commemorative Coin "XLVI World Day of Peace"
• 10 Euro silver Commemorative Coin "50th World Day of Prayer for Vocations"
• 20 Euro gold Commemorative Coin "The Popes of the Renaissance: Pope Julius II"
• 50 Euro gold Commemorative Coin "The Popes of the Renaissance: Leo X"
• 100 Euro gold Commemorative Coin "The Sistine Madonna"
• 200 Euro gold Commemorative Coin "The Theological virtues: Hope"

• Sede vacante: 125,000 coins, bearing the emblem of the Cardinal camerlengo with the pavilion of the Apostolic Camera, were issued for the papal interregnum.

Papal Audiences

General audiences are scheduled weekly, on Wednesday In Vatican City, they are held in the Audience Hall on the south side of St. Peter's Basilica or, weather permitting, in St. Peter's Square. The hall, which was opened in 1971, has a seating capacity of 6,800 and a total capacity of 12,000 Audiences have been held during the summer at Castel Gandolfo when the pope is there on a working vacation.

General audiences last from about 60 to 90 minutes, during which the pope gives a talk and his blessing. A résumé of the talk, which is usually in Italian, is given in several languages. Arrangements for papal audiences are handled by an office of the Prefecture of the Apostolic Household.

American visitors can obtain passes for general audiences by applying to the Bishops' Office for United States Visitors to the Vatican, Casa Santa Maria, Via dell'Umilita, 30, 00187 Rome. Private and group audiences are reserved for dignitaries of various categories and for special occasions.

Publications

Acta Apostolicae Sedis, 00120 Vatican City: The only "official commentary" of the Holy See, was established in 1908 for the publication of activities of the Holy See, laws, decrees and acts of congregations and tribunals of the Roman Curia. The first edition was published in Jan. 1909. St. Pius X made *AAS* an official organ in 1908. Laws promulgated for the Church ordinarily take effect three months after the date of their publication in this commentary. The publication, mostly in Latin, is printed by the Vatican Press. The immediate predecessor of this organ was *Acta Sanctae Sedis,* founded in 1865 and given official status by the Congregation for the Propagation of the Faith in 1904.

Annuario Pontificio, 00120 Vatican City: The yearbook of the Holy See. It is edited by the Central Statistics Office of the Church and is printed in Italian, with some portions in other languages, by the Vatican Press. It covers the worldwide organization of the Church, lists members of the hierarchy, and includes a wide range of statistical information. The publication of a statistical yearbook of the Holy See dates back to 1716, when a volume called *Notizie* appeared. Publication under the present title began in 1860, was suspended in 1870, and resumed again in 1872 under the title Catholic Hierarchy. This volume was printed privately at first, but has been issued by the Vatican Press since 1885. The title *Annuario Pontificio* was restored in 1912, and the yearbook was called an "official publication" until 1924.

L'Osservatore Romano, Via del Pellegrino, 00120 Vatican City: The daily newspaper of the Holy See. It began publication July 1, 1861, as an independent enterprise under the ownership and direction of four Catholic laymen headed by Marcantonio Pacelli, vice minister of the interior under Pope Pius IX and a grandfather of the late Pius XII. Leo XIII bought the publication in 1890, making it the "pope's" own newspaper.

The only official material in *L'Osservatore Romano* is what appears under the heading, "*Nostre Informazioni.*" This includes notices of appointments by the Holy See, the texts of papal encyclicals and addresses by the Holy Father and others, various types of documents, accounts of decisions and rulings of administrative bodies, and similar items. Additional material includes news and comment on developments in the Church and the world. Italian is the language most used. The editorial board is directed by Prof. Giovanni Maria Vian. A staff of about 15 reporters covers Rome news sources. A corps of correspondents provides foreign coverage.

A weekly roundup edition in English was inaugurated in 1968. Other weekly editions are printed in French (1949), Italian (1950), Spanish (1969), Portuguese (1970) and German (1971). The Polish edition (1980) is published monthly. *L'Osservatore della Domenica* is published weekly as a supplement to the Sunday issue of the daily edition.

Vatican Television Center (*Centro Televisivo Vaticano*, CTV), Palazzo Belvedere, 00120 Vatican City: Instituted by John Paul II Oct. 23, 1983, with the rescript, *Ex Audentia*. Most Rev. Claudio Maria Celli, pres. of the Pontifical Council for Social Communications, is president of the administrative council.

Vatican Press, 00120 Vatican City: The official printing plant of the Vatican. The Vatican press was conceived by Marcellus II and Pius IV but was actually founded by Sixtus V on Apr. 27, 1587, to print the Vulgate and the writings of the Fathers of the Church and other authors. A Polyglot Press was established in 1626 by the Congregation for the Propagation of the Faith to serve the needs of the Oriental Church. St. Pius X merged both presses under the title Vatican Polyglot Press. It was renamed Vatican Press July 1, 1991, by John Paul II following restructuring. The plant has facilities for the printing of a wide variety of material in about 30 languages. Dir., Rev. Sergio Pellini, S.D.B.

Vatican Publishing House (Libreria Editrice Vaticana), Piazza S. Pietro, 00120 Vatican City: Formerly an office of the Vatican Press to assist in the circulation of the liturgical and juridical publications of the Apostolic See, the congregations and later the Acta Apostolicae Sedis. In 1926, with the expansion of publishing activities and following the promulgation of the 1917 Code, the office was made an independent entity. An administrative council and editorial commission were instituted in 1983; in 1988 Pastor Bonus listed it among institutes joined to the Holy See; new statutes were approved by the Secretariat of State July 1, 1991. President, Msgr. Giuseppe Scotti.

Activities of the Holy See: An annual documentary volume covering the activities of the pope and of the congregations, commissions, tribunals and offices of the Roman Curia.

Statistical Yearbook of the Church (*Annuarium Statisticum Ecclesiae*): Issued by the Central Statistics Office of the Church, it contains principal data concerning the presence and work of the Church in the world. The first issue was published in 1972 under the title Collection of Statistical Tables, 1969. It is printed in corresponding columns of Italian, French, and Latin. Some of the introductory material is printed in other languages.

DIPLOMATIC ACTIVITIES OF THE HOLY SEE

REPRESENTATIVES OF THE HOLY SEE

Representatives of the Holy See and their functions were the subject of a document entitled *Sollicitudo Omnium Ecclesiarum* which Pope Paul VI issued on his own initiative under the date of June 24, 1969. As of Aug. 1, 2013 the Holy See maintained full diplomatic relations with 179 states around the world.

Delegates and Nuncios

Papal representatives "receive from the Roman Pontiff the charge of representing him in a fixed way in the various nations or regions of the world.

"When their legation is only to local churches, they are known as apostolic delegates. When to this legation, of a religious and ecclesial nature, there is added diplomatic legation to states and governments, they receive the title of nuncio, pro-nuncio, and internuncio." An apostolic nuncio has the diplomatic rank of ambassador extraordinary and plenipotentiary. Traditionally, because the diplomatic service of the Holy See has the longest uninterrupted history in the world, a nuncio has precedence among diplomats in the country to which he is accredited and serves as dean of the diplomatic corps on state occasions. Since 1965 pro-nuncios, also of ambassadorial rank, have been assigned to countries in which this prerogative is not recognized. In recent years, the Vatican has phased out the title of pro-nuncio. The title of nuncio (with an asterisk denoting he is not dean of the diplomatic corps) has been given to the majority of appointments of ambassadorial rank. *See* **Other Representatives**.

Service and Liaison

Representatives, while carrying out their general and special duties, are bound to respect the autonomy of local churches and bishops. Their service and liaison responsibilities include the following:
- Nomination of Bishops: To play a key role in compiling, with the advice of ecclesiastics and lay persons, and submitting lists of names of likely candidates to the Holy See with their own recommendations.
- Bishops: To aid and counsel local bishops without interfering in the affairs of their jurisdictions.
- Episcopal Conferences: To maintain close relations with them and to assist them in every possible way. (Papal representatives do not belong to these conferences.)
- Religious Communities of Pontifical Rank: To advise and assist major superiors for the purpose of promoting and consolidating conferences of men and women religious and to coordinate their apostolic activities.
- Church-State Relations: The thrust in this area is toward the development of sound relations with civil governments and collaboration in work for peace and the total good of the whole human family. The mission of a papal representative begins with appointment and assignment by the pope and continues until termination of his mandate. He acts "under the guidance and according to the instructions of the cardinal secretary of state to whom he is directly responsible for the execution of the mandate entrusted to him by the Supreme Pontiff." Normally representatives are required to retire at age 75.

NUNCIOS AND DELEGATES

(*Sources:* Annuario Pontificio, L'Osservatore Romano, Acta Apostolicae Sedis, *Catholic News Service.*) *As of July 30, 2013. Country, rank of legation (corresponding to rank of legate unless otherwise noted), name of legate (archbishop unless otherwise noted) as available. An asterisk indicates a nuncio who is not presently dean of the diplomatic corps.*

Delegate for Papal Legations: Abp. Luciano Suriani. The post was established in 1973 to coordinate papal diplomatic efforts throughout the world. The office entails responsibility for "following more closely through timely visits the activities of papal representatives ... and encouraging their rapport with the central offices" of the Secretariat of State.

Albania: Tirana, Nunciature; Ramiro Moliner Inglés.*

Algeria: Algiers, Nunciature; Thomas Yeh Shengnan* (also Nuncio* to Tunisia).

Andorra: Nunciature; Renzo Fratini (also Nuncio to Spain).

Angola: Luanda, Nunciature; Novatus Rugambwa* (also Nuncio* to São Tome and Principe). (Diplomatic relations established in 1997.)

Antigua and Barbuda: Nunciature; Nicola Girasoli* (resides in Port of Spain, Trinidad).

Antilles: Apostolic Delegation; Nicola Girasoli (resides in Port of Spain, Trinidad).

Arabian Peninsula: Apostolic Delegation; Petar Rajic. (also nuncio in Kuwait, Qatar, United Arab Emirates, and Yemen.

Argentina: Buenos Aires, Nunciature; Emil Paul Tscherrig.

Armenia: Nunciature; Marek Solczynski* (resides in Tbilisi, Georgia; also nuncio* to Georgia and Azerbaijan). (Diplomatic relations established in 1992.)

Australia: Canberra, Nunciature; Paul Richard Gallagher.

Austria: Vienna, Nunciature; Peter Stephan Zurbriggen.

Azerbaijan: Nunciature; Marek Soczynski* (resides in Tbilisi, Georgia; also nuncio* to Georgia and Armenia). (Diplomatic relations established in 1992.)

Bahamas: Nunciature; Nicola Girasoli* (resides in Port of Spain, Trinidad).

Bahrain: Manama; Nunciature; Petar Rajic. (Diplomatic relations established Jan. 12, 2000; also nuncio in Kuwait, Qatar, United Arab Emirates, and Yemen).

Bangladesh: Dhaka, Nunciature; George Kocherry.*

Barbados: Nunciature; Nicola Girasoli* (resides in Port of Spain, Trinidad).

Belarus: Nunciature; Claudio Gugerotti.*

Belgium: Brussels, Nunciature; Giacinto Berloco (also Nuncio to Luxembourg).

Belize: Nunciature; Leon Kalenga Badikebele* (resides in Port of Spain, Trinidad).

Benin (formerly Dahomey): Nunciature; Brian Udaigwe.* (resides in Accra, Ghana).

Bolivia: La Paz, Nunciature; Giambattista Diquattro.
Bosnia and Herzegovina: Sarajevo; Nunciature; Luigi Pezzuto.*
Botswana: Nunciature (Diplomatic relations established in November 2008); Mario Cassari (resides in Pretoria, South Africa; also Nuncio* to Lesotho, Namibia, South Africa, and Swaziland.).
Brazil: Brasilia, Nunciature; Vacant.
Brunei Darussalam: See Malaysia and Brunei.
Bulgaria: Sofia, Nunciature (reestablished in 1990); Janusz Bolonek (also nuncio to Macedonia).*
Burkina Faso: Ouagadougou, Nunciature; Vito Rallo* (also Nuncio* to Niger).
Burma: See Myanmar.
Burundi: Bujumbura, Nunciature; Franco Coppola.*
Cambodia: Nunciature (Diplomatic relations established in 1994); Paul Tschang In-Nam* (resides in Bangkok, Thailand).
Cameroon: Yaounde, Nunciature; Piero Pioppo (also Nuncio to Equatorial Guinea).
Canada: Ottawa, Nunciature; Pedro López Quintana.*
Cape Verde, Republic of: Nunciature; Luis Mariano Montemayor* (resides in Dakar, Senegal).
Central African Republic: Bangui, Nunciature; Jude Thaddeus Okolo* (also Nuncio* to Chad).
Chad: Nunciature; Jude Thaddeus Okolo* (resides in Bangui, Central African Republic).
Chile: Santiago, Nunciature; Ivo Scapolo.
China, Republic of: Taipei (Taiwan), Nunciature; Vacant.
Colombia: Bogota, Nunciature; Ettore Balestrero.
Comoros: See Madagascar: (formerly Zaire)
Congo (formerly Zaire): Kinshasa-Gombe, Nunciature; Jan Romeo Pawlowski.*
Congo: Brazzaville, Nunciature; Adolfo Tito Yllana* (also Nuncio* to Gabon).
Costa Rica: San Jose, Nunciature; Pierre Nguyên Van Tot.
Côte d'Ivoire (Ivory Coast): Abidjan, Nunciature; Vacant.
Croatia: Zagreb, Nunciature; Alessandro D'Errico (also nuncio to Bosnia and Herzegovina).
Cuba: Havana, Nunciature; Bruno Musarò.*
Cyprus: Nicosia, Nunciature; Giuseppe Lazzarotto (also Nuncio to Israel).
Czech Republic: Prague, Nunciature; Giueseppe Leanza.
Denmark: Copenhagen, Nunciature; Vacant* (also Nuncio* to Finland, Iceland, Norway and Sweden).
Djibouti: Nunciature (established May 2000); George Panikulam (resides in Addis Ababa, Ethiopia).
Dominica: Nunciature; Nicola Girasola* (resides in Port-of-Spain, Trinidad).
Dominican Republic: Santo Domingo, Nunciature; Józef Wesolowski (also serves as Apostolic Delegate to Puerto Rico).
East Timor: Díli, Nunciature (diplomatic relations established on May 20, 2002); Joseph Marino (also Nuncio* to Indonesia).
Ecuador: Quito, Nunciature; Giacomo Ottonello.
Egypt: Cairo, Nunciature; Jean-Paul Gobel (also delegate to the Organization of the League of Arab States).*
El Salvador: San Salvador, Nunciature; Leon Kalenga Badikebele.
Equatorial Guinea: Santa Isabel, Nunciature; Piero Pioppo* (resides in Yaounde, Cameroon).
Eritrea: Nunciature: Vacant.* (Diplomatic relations established in 1995.)
Estonia: Nunciature; Luigi Bonazzi* (resides in Vilnius, Lithuania).

Ethiopia: Addis Ababa, Nunciature; George Panikulam* (also Nuncio* to Djibouti and apostolic delegate to Somalia).
European Union: Brussels, Belgium, Nunciature; Alain Lebeaupain.
Fiji: Nunciature; Vacant* (resides in Wellington, New Zealand).
Finland: Helsinki, Nunciature; Henryk Jozef Nowacki* (resides in Denmark).
France: Paris, Nunciature; Luigi Ventura.
Gabon: Libreville, Nunciature; Jan Romeo Pawlowski* (resides in Congo).
Gambia: Nunciature; Miroslaw Adamczyk* (resides in Freetown, Sierra Leone).
Georgia: Tbilisi, Nunciature; Marek Solczynski* (also Nuncio* to Armenia and Azerbaijan). (Diplomatic relations established in 1992.)
Germany: Bonn, Nunciature; Jean-Claude Périsset.
Ghana: Accra, Nunciature; Vacant.*
Great Britain: London, Nunciature; Antonio Mennini* (also papal representative to Gibraltar).
Greece: Athens, Nunciature; Edward Joseph Adams.*
Grenada: Nunciature; Nicola Girasoli* (resides in Port of Spain, Trinidad). **Guatemala:** Guatemala City, Nunciature; Nicolas Thevenin.
Guinea: Conakry, Nunciature; Martin Krebs* (resides in Freetown, Sierra Leone).
Guinea Bissau: Nunciature; Luis Mariano Montemayor* (resides at Dakar, Senegal).
Guyana: Nunciature; Nicola Girasola (resides in Port of Spain, Trinidad).
Haiti: Port-au-Prince, Nunciature; Bernardito Auza.
Honduras: Tegucigalpa, Nunciature; Luigi Bianco.
Hungary: Budapest, Nunciature; Alberto Bottari de Castello (also Nuncio* to Moldova).
Iceland: Nunciature; Henryk Jozef Nowacki* (resides in Denmark).
India: New Delhi, Nunciature; Salvatore Pennacchio* (also Nuncio* to Nepal).
Indonesia: Jakarta, Nunciature; Antonio Guido Filipazzi (also nuncio to East Timor).*
Iran: Teheran, Nunciature; Leo Boccardi.*
Iraq: Baghdad, Nunciature; Giorgio Lingua* (also Nuncio to Jordan).
Ireland: Dublin, Nunciature; Charles Brown.
Israel: Nunciature; Giuseppe Lazzarotto (also Nuncio to Cyprus). (Diplomatic relations established June 1994.)
Italy: Rome, Nunciature; Adriano Bernardini (also Nuncio to San Marino).
Ivory Coast: See Côte d'Ivoire.
Jamaica: Nunciature; Nicola Girasoli (resides in Port of Spain, Trinidad).
Japan: Tokyo, Nunciature; Joseph Chennoth*.
Jerusalem and Palestine: Apostolic Delegation (also Nuncio to Israel): Antonio Franco.
Jordan: Nunciature; Giorgio Lingua* (also Nuncio to Iraq).
Kazakstan: Almaty, Nunciature; Miguel Maury Buendía* (also Nuncio* to Kyrgyzstan and Tajikistan).
Kenya: Nairobi, Nunciature; Charles D. Balvo.*
Kiribati: Nunciature; Vacant* (resides in Wellington, New Zealand).
Korea: Seoul, Nunciature; Osvaldo Padilla* (also Nuncio* to Mongolia).
Kuwait: Al Kuwait, Nunciature; Petar Rajic * (also nuncio in Qatar, Bahrain, the United Arab Emirates, and Yemen).
Kyrgyzstan: Nunciature; Miguel Maury Buendía* (resides in Kazakhstan; also Nuncio* to Kyrgyzstan and Tajikistan).

Laos: Apostolic Delegation; Paul Tschang In-Nam (resides in Bangkok, Thailand; also apostolic delegate to Myanmar).

Latvia: Nunciature; Luigi Bonazzi* (resides in Vilna, Lithuania).

Lebanon: Beirut, Nunciature; Gabriele Giordano Caccia.

Lesotho: Maseru, Nunciature; Mario Cassari (also Nuncio to Botswana, South Africa, Namibia, and Swaziland; resides in Pretoria, South Africa).

Liberia: Monrovia, Nunciature; Vacant* (resides in Freetown, Sierra Leone).

Libya: Nunciature; Aldo Cavalli* (resides in Malta). (Diplomatic relations established in 1997.)

Liechtenstein: Nunciature; Diego Causero (resides in Bern, Switzerland).

Lithuania: Vilnius, Nunciature; Luigi Bonazzi* (also Nuncio to Estonia and Latvia.).

Luxembourg: Nunciature; Giacinto Berloco (resides in Brussels, Belgium).

Macedonia: Nunciature; Janusz Bolonek* (also Nuncio to Slovenia; resides in Slovenia).

Madagascar: Antananarivo, Nunciature; Eugene Nugent* (also Nuncio* to Seychelles, and Mauritius and Apostolic Delegate to Comoros and Reunion).

Malawi: Lilongwe, Nunciature; Julio Murat* (resides in Lusaka, Zambia).

Malaysia and Brunei: Nunciature (diplomatic relations established in 2011); Joseph Marino (resides in Indonesia).

Mali: Nunciature; Martin Krebs* (resides in Dakar, Senegal, also nuncio to Guinea).

Malta: La Valletta, Nunciature; Aldo Cavalli(also Nuncio* to Libya).

Marshall Islands: Nunciature; Vacant* (resides in Wellington, New Zealand).

Mauritania: Nouakchott, Apostolic Delegation; Luis Mariano Montemayor (resides in Dakar, Senegal).

Mauritius: Port Louis, Nunciature; Eugene Nugent* (resides in Antananarivo, Madagascar).

Mexico: Mexico City, Nunciature; Christophe Pierre.* (Diplomatic relations established in 1992).

Micronesia, Federated States of: Nunciature; Vacant* (resides in Wellington, New Zealand).

Moldova: Nunciature; Francisco-Javier Lozano Sebastian* (resides in Bucharest, Romania). (Diplomatic relations established in 1992.)

Monaco, Principality of: Nunciature; Luigi Travaglino.

Mongolia: Nunciature; Osvaldo Padilla* (resides in Seoul, South Korea).

Montenegro: Podgorica, Nunciature; Luigi Pezzuto (Diplomatic relations established Dec. 17, 2006).

Morocco: Rabat, Nunciature; Antonio Sozzo.*

Mozambique: Maputo, nunciature; Antonio Arcari.* (Diplomatic relations established in 1995.)

Myanmar (formerly Burma): Apostolic Delegation; Paul Tschang In-Nam (resides in Bangkok, Thailand).

Namibia: Nunciature; Mario Cassari* (resides in Pretoria, South Africa).

Nauru: Nunciature; Vacant* (resides in Wellington, New Zealand).

Nepal: Nunciature; Salvatore Pennacchio* (resides in New Delhi, India).

Netherlands: The Hague, Nunciature; Andre Dupuy.*

New Zealand: Wellington, Nunciature; Vacant* (also Nuncio* to Fiji, Kiribati, Marshall Islands, Federated States of Micronesia, Tonga, Vanuatu and Western Samoa; Apostolic Delegate to Pacific Islands).

Nicaragua: Managua, Nunciature; Fortunatus Nwachukwu.

Niger: Niamey, Nunciature; Vito Rallo* (also Nuncio* to Burkina Faso.)

Nigeria: Lagos, Nunciature; Augustine Kasujja.*

Norway: Nunciature; Henryk Jozef Nowacki* (resides in Denmark).

Pacific Ocean: Nunciature; Vacant (resides in Wellington, New Zealand).

Pakistan: Islamabad, Nunciature; Edgar Pena Parra.

Palau, Republic of: Palau, Nunciature; Vacant.*

Panama: Panama City, Nunciature; Andrés Carrascosa Coso.

Papua New Guinea: Port Moresby; Nunciature; Michael W. Banach* (also Nuncio* to Solomon Islands).

Paraguay: Asuncion, Nunciature; Eliseo Antonio Ariotti.

Peru: Lima, Nunciature; James P. Green.

Philippines: Manila, Nunciature; Giuseppe Pinto.

Poland: Warsaw, Nunciature; Celestino Migliore.

Portugal: Lisbon, Nunciature; Rino Passigato.

Puerto Rico: See Dominican Republic.

Qatar: Dawhah, Nunciature; Petar Rajic (Diplomatic relations established in Nov. 2002; also nuncio in Kuwait, Bahrain, United Arab Emirates, and Yemen).

Reunion: See Madagascar.

Romania: Bucharest, Nunciature. Francisco-Javier Lozano.*

Russia (Federation of): Moscow, Nunciature; Ivan Jurkovic. Nuncio appointed Representative of the Holy See to Russian Federation, 1994.

Rwanda: Kigali, Nunciature. Vacant.

St. Vincent and the Grenadines: Nunciature; Nicola Girasoli, Nuncio (resides in Port of Spain, Trinidad).

Samoa: Nunciature; Vacant* (resides in Wellington, New Zealand).

San Marino: Nunciature; Adriano Bernardini (also nuncio to Italy).

Santa Lucia: Nunciature; Nicola Girasoli* (resides in Port of Spain, Trinidad).

São Tome and Principe: Nunciature; Novatus Rugambwa* (also Nuncio* to Angola, where he resides).

Senegal: Dakar, Nunciature; Luis Mariano Montemayor* (also Nuncio* to Cape Verde, Guinea-Bissau and Mali; Apostolic Delegate to Mauritania.)

Serbia: Belgrade, Nunciature; Orlando Antonini.

Seychelles Islands: Nunciature; Eugene Nugent* (resides in Antananrivo, Madagascar).

Sierra Leone: Freetown, Nunciature (1996); Vacant* (also Nuncio* to Gambia, Guinea and Liberia).

Singapore: Nunciature; Leopoldo Girelli* (He is also apostolic delegate to Malaysia and Brunei, and non-residential pontifical representative to Vietnam.)

Slovakia: Nunciature; Mario Giordana.

Slovenia: Ljubljana, Nunciature; Janusz Bolonek (also Nuncio to Macedonia and Kosovo).

Solomon Islands: Nunciature; Michael W. Banach (resides in Port Moresby, Papua New Guinea).

Somalia: Apostolic Delegation (est. 1992); George Panikulam (resides in Sudan).

South Africa: Pretoria, Nunciature; Mario Cassari.* (also Nuncio* to Botswana, Namibia, and Swaziland.)

Spain: Madrid, Nunciature; Renzo Fratini.

Sri Lanka: Colombo, Nunciature; Joseph Spiteri.*

Sudan: Khartoum, Nunciature; Vacant.*

Suriname: Nunciature; Nicola Girasoli* (resides in Port of Spain, Trinidad).

Swaziland: Nunciature; Mario Cassari* (resides in Pretoria, South Africa).

Sweden: Nunciature; Henryk Jozef Nowacki* (resides in Denmark).

Switzerland: Bern, Nunciature; Diego Causero (also Nuncio to Liechtenstein).

Syria: (Syrian Arab Republic): Damascus, Nunciature, Mario Zenari.*

Tajikistan: Nunciature (1996); Miguel Maury Buendía* (resides in Kazakstan; also Nuncio* to Kyrgyzstan and Kazakstan).

Tanzania: Dar-es-Salaam, Nunciature; Francesco Padilla.*

Thailand: Bangkok, Nunciature; Paul Tschang In-Nam* (also Nuncio* to Cambodia and Apostolic Delegate to Laos and Myanmar).

Togo: Lome, Nunciature; Brian Udaigwe* (resides in Accra, Ghana).

Tonga: Nunciature; Vacant* (resides in Wellington, New Zealand).

Trinidad and Tobago: Port of Spain, Trinidad, Nunciature; Nicola Girasoli, Nuncio (also Nuncio to Antigua and Barbuda, Bahamas, Barbados, Belize, Dominica, Grenada, Jamaica, Saint Lucia, Saint Vincent and the Grenadines, Suriname and Apostolic Delegate to Antilles).

Tunisia: Tunis, Nunciature; Thomas Yeh Sheng-nan* (resides in Algiers, Algeria).

Turkey: Ankara, Nunciature; Antonio Lucibello.*

Turkmenistan: Nunciature (1996); Antonio Lucibello* (resides in Ankara, Turkey).

Uganda: Kampala, Nunciature; Pro-Nuncio, Michael A. Blume, S.V.D.

Ukraine: Kiev, Nunciature; Thomas E. Gullickson.*

United Arab Emirates: Abu Dhabi, Nunciature (diplomatic relations established May 31, 2007); Petar Rajic* (also nuncio to Kuwait, Bahrain, Qatar, and Yemen).

United States of America: Washington, DC, Nunciature; Carlo Maria Viganó.*

Uruguay: Montevideo, Nunciature; Anselmo Guido Pecorari.

Uzbekistan: Nunciature; Ivan Jurkovic* (resides in Kazakstan; also Nuncio* to Kazakstan, Kyrgyzstan, and Tajikistan).

Vanuatu: Nunciature; Vacant* (resides in Wellington, New Zealand).

Venezuela: Caracas, Nunciature; Vacant.

Vietnam: Apostolic Delegation; Leopoldo Girelli (resides in Indonesia).

Western Samoa: Nunciature; Charles D. Balvo* (resides in Wellington, New Zealand).

Yemen: San'a, Nunciature; Petar Rajic* (relations established in 1998, also nuncio in Kuwait, Bahrain, United Arab Emirate, and Qatar).

Yugoslavia: Belgrade, Nunciature; Eugenio Sbarbaro.

Zaire: See Congo: Lusaka, Nunciature; Giuseppe Leanza* (also Nuncio* to Malawi).

Zambia: Lusaka, Nunciature; Vacant* (also Nuncio* to Malawi).

Zimbabwe: Harare, Nunciature; Vacant.*

The Current Nuncio to the U.S.

The post of nuncio to the United States is currently held by Abp. Carlo Maria Viganó (b. Jan. 16, 1941) who was named nuncio to the United States on Oct. 19, 2011. A native of Varese, Italy, Viganò was ordained a priest on Mar. 24, 1968 and earned a doctorate *utroque iure* (both canon and civil law). He entered the diplomatic service of the Holy See in 1973 and worked at the papal diplomatic mission in Iraq and Great Britain, and from 1978 to 1989, was an official of the Secretariat of State in Rome. He was named Special Envoy and Permanent Observer of the Holy See to the Council of Europe in Strasbourg in 1989. In 1992, he was appointed titular abp. of Ulpiana and apostolic nuncio to Nigeria and was consecrated a bishop on Apr. 26, 1992. He returned to the Secretariat of State in 1998 and served there until 2009 when he was appointed Secretary-General of the Governatorate of Vatican City State.

The U.S. Apostolic Nunciature is located at 3339 Massachusetts Ave., N.W., Washington, D.C. 20008-3687; (202) 333-7121.

A Nuncio represents the Holy Father to both the hierarchy and Church of a particular nation and to that nation's civil government.

From 1893 to 1984, papal representatives to the Church in the U.S. were apostolic delegates (all archbishops): Francesco Satolli (1893-96), Sebastiano Martinelli, O.S.A., (1896-1902), Diomede Falconio, O.F.M. (1902-1911), Giovanni Bonzano (1911-22), Pietro Fumasoni-Biondi (1922-33), Amleto Cicognani (1933-58), Egidio Vagnozzi (1958-67), Luigi Raimondi (1967-73), Jean Jadot (1973-80), and Pio Laghi (1980-90) who was the first to hold the title Pro-Nuncio, beginning in 1984 (*See* **Index, U.S.-Vatican Relations**). Abp. (now Card.) Agostino Cacciavillan was Pro-Nuncio and permanent observer to the Organization of American States from 1990–998. Abp. Gabriel Montalvo was nuncio and permanent observer to the Organization of American States from 1998–2005. Abp. Pietro Sambi served as nuncio to the United States and permanent observer to the Organization of American States from Dec. 17, 2005 until his passing after an illness on July 27, 2011.

Other Representatives

(*Sources:* Annuario Pontificio; *Catholic News Service.*)

The Holy See has representatives to or is a regular member of a number of quasi-governmental and international organizations. Most Rev. Ernesto Gallina was first appointed delegate to International Governmental Organizations Jan. 12, 1991.

Governmental Organizations:U.N. (Abp. Francis Chullikatt, permanent observer); U.N. Office in Geneva and Specialized Institutions (Abp. Silvano Maria Tomasi, permanent observer); African Union (Abp. George Panikulam); League of Arab States (Abp. Jean-Paul Gobel); International Atomic Energy Agency (Vacant, permanent representative); U.N. Office at Vienna and U.N. Organization for Industrial Development (Vacant, permanent observer); U.N. Food and Agriculture Organization (Vacant, permanent observer); U.N. Educational, Scientific and Cultural Organization (Msgr. Francesco Follo, permanent observer); World Trade Organization (Abp. Silvano Maria Tomasi); Council of Europe (Msgr. Aldo Giordano, special representative with function of permanent observer); Council for Cultural Cooperation of the Council of Europe (Vacant, delegate); Organization of American States (Abp. Carlo Maria Viganó, permanent observer, with personal title of Apostolic Nuncio); Organization for Security and Cooperation in Europe (Vacant, permanent representative); International Institute for the Unification of Private Law (Prof. Giuseppe dalla Torre del Tiempo di Sanguinetto Conte, delegate); International Committee of Military Medicine (Vacant, delegate), World Organization of Tourism (Abp. Renzo Fratini, permanent observer).

Non-Governmental Organizations: International Committee of Historical Sciences (Rev. Bernard Ardura, O.Praem.); International Committee of the History of Art (Dr. Antonio Paolucci); International Committee of Anthropological and Ethnological Sciences; Committee for the Neutrality of Medicine; International Center of Study for the Preservation and Restoration of Cultural Goods (Dr. Francesco Buranelli); International Council of Monuments and Sites (Msgr. Francesco Follo, delegate); International Alliance on Tourism; World Association of Jurists (Vacant); International Commission of the Civil State (Msgr. Paul Richard Gallagher); International Astronomical Union; International Institute of Administrative Sciences; International Technical Committee for Prevention and Extinction of Fires; World Medical Association; International Archives Council; World Trade Organization.

DIPLOMATS TO THE HOLY SEE

(*Sources:* Annuario Pontificio, L'Osservatore Romano).

Listed below are countries maintaining diplomatic relations with the Holy See, dates of establishment (in some cases) and names of Ambassadors (as of Aug. 30, 2013). Leaders (. . . . .) indicate the post was vacant.

Albania (1991): Rrok Logu.
Algeria (1972): ....
Andorra: Jaume Serra Serra.
Angola (1997): Vieira Armindo Fernandes do Espirito Santo.
Antigua and Barbuda (1986): David Shoul.
Argentina: Juan Pablo Cafiero.
Armenia (1992): Viguen Tchitetchian.
Australia (1973): John McCarthy.
Austria: Alfons M. Kloss.
Azerbaijan (1992): Elchin Oktyabr Oglu Amirbayov.
Bahamas (1979): . . . . .
Bahrain (2000): Naser Muhamed Youssef al Belooshi.
Bangladesh (1972): Abdul Hannan.
Barbados (1979): Peter Patrick Kenneth Simmons.
Belarus (1992): Sergei F. Aleinik.
Belgium (1835): Charles Ghislain.
Belize (1983): Lawrence H. Llewellyn.
Benin (formerly Dahomey) (1971): Theodore C. Loko.
Bolivia: Carlos Federico de la Riva Guerra.
Bosnia and Herzegovina (1992): . . . . .
Botswana: Lameck Nthekela.
Brazil: Franco de Sa Barbuda Almir.
Bulgaria (1990): . . . . .
Burkina Faso (1973): Joseph Pare.
Burundi (1963): . . . . .
Cambodia (1994): . . . . .
Cameroon (1966): Antoine Zanga.
Canada (1969): . . . . .
Cape Verde (1976): Domingos Dias Pereira Mascarenhas.
Central African Republic (1975): . . . . .
Chad (1988): Hissein Brahim Taha. **Chile:** Fernando Zegers Santa Cruz.
China, Republic of (Taiwan) (1966): Wang Larry Yu-yuan.
Colombia: German Cardona Gutierrez.
Congo (formerly Zaire) (1963): Jean-Pierre Hamuli Mupenda.
Congo (1977): Henri Marie Joseph Lopes.
Costa Rica: Fernando Sanchez Campos.
Côte d'Ivoire (Ivory Coast) (1971): Joseph Tebah-Klah.
Croatia (1992): Filip Vucak.
Cuba: Eduardo Delgado Bermúdez.
Cyprus (1973): Georgios F. Poulides.
Czech Republic (1929-50, reestablished, 1990, with Czech and Slovak Federative Republic; reaffirmed, 1993): Pavel Vosalík.
Denmark (1982): Hans Klingenberg.
Djibouti: (2000): Barkat Gourad Hamadou. (Diplomatic relations established May 20, 2000.)
Dominica (1981): . . . . .
Dominican Republic: Victor Manuel Grimaldi Céspedes.
East Timor (2002): . . . . . (Diplomatic relations established on May 20, 2002.)
Ecuador: Luis Dositeo Latorre Tapia.
Egypt (1966): . . . . .
El Salvador: Manuel Roberto Lopez Barrera.
Equatorial Guinea (1981): Narciso Ntugu Abeso Oyana.
Eritrea (1995): Petros Tseggai Asghedom.
Estonia (1991): Jüri Seilenthal.
Ethiopia (1969): Teshome Toga Chanaka.
European Union: Laurence Argimon-Pistre.
Fiji (1978): Naivakarurubalavu Solo Mara.
Finland (1966): . . . . .
France: Bruno Joubert.
Gabon (1967): Firmin Mboutsou.
Gambia, The (1978): Elizabeth Ya Eli Harding.
Georgia (1992): Princess Khétévane Bagration de Moukhrani.
Germany: Reinhard Scweppe.
Ghana (1976): Genevieve Delali Tsegah.
Great Britain (1982): Nigel M. Baker.
Greece (1980): Georgios Papadopoulos
Grenada (1979): . . . . .
Guatemala: Alfonso Roberto Matta Fahsen.
Guinea (1986): Ibrahima Sow.
Guinea-Bissau (1986): Hilia Garez Gomes Lima Barber.
Guyana (Cooperative Republic of): Laleshwar Kumar Narayan Singh.
Haiti: Carl-Henri Guiteau.
Honduras: Alejandro Emilio Valladares Lanza.
Hungary (1990): Gábor Gyoriványi.
Iceland (1976): Elín Flygenring.
India: Chitra Narayanan.
Indonesia (1965): Budiarman Badar
Iran (1966): . . . . .
Iraq (1966): Mohammed Hadi Ali Al-Sadr Habbeb.
Ireland: David Cooney.
Israel (1994): Zion Evrony.
Italy: Francesco Maria Greco.
Ivory Coast: See Côte d'Ivoire.
Jamaica (1979): . . . . .
Japan (1966): Hidekazu Yamaguchi.
Jordan (1994): Dina Kawar.
Kazakhstan (1992): Mukhtar Tileuberdi.
Kenya (1965): . . . . .
Kiribati (1995): . . . . .
Korea (1966): Thomas Han Hong-soon.
Kuwait (1969): Suhail Khalil Shuhaiber.
Kyrgyzstan (1992): Bolot Iskovich Otunbaev.
Latvia (1991): Einars Semanis.
Lebanon (1966): Georges Chakib El Khoury.
Lesotho (1967): . . . . .
Liberia (1966): Wesley Momo Johnson.
Libya: (1997): . . . . .
Liechtenstein (1985): Prince Nikolaus de Liechtenstein.
Lithuania: Irena Vaisvilaite.
Luxembourg (1955): Jean-Paul Senninger.
Macedonia (1994): Gioko Gjorgjevski.
Madagascar (1967): . . . . .
Malawi (1966): Isaac Chikwekwere Lamba.
Malaysia: Dato' Ho May Young.

Mali (1979): Boubacar Sidiki Toure.
Malta (1965): Antonio Ganado.
Marshall Islands (1993): . . . . .
Mauritius: Mohunlall Goburdhun.
Mexico (personal representative, 1990; diplomatic relations, 1992): Mariano Palacios Alcocer.
Micronesia, Federated States (1994): . . . . .
Moldova (1992): Stefan Gorda.
Monaco: Jean-Claude Michel.
Mongolia (1992): Luvsantersen Orgil.
Montenegro: (Diplomatic relations established Dec. 17, 2006): Antun Sbutega.
Morocco: . . . . .
Mozambique (diplomatic relations, 1995): Amadeus Paulo Samuel da Conceicao.
Namibia: (diplomatic relations established Sept. 1995): Neville Melvin Gertze.
Nauru (1992): . . . . .
Nepal (1983): Suresh Prasad Pradhan.
Netherlands (1967): Joseph Weterings.
New Zealand (1973): George Robert Furness Troup.
Nicaragua: José Cuadra Chamorro.
Niger (1971): Aminatou Batoure Gaoh.
Nigeria (1976): Francis Okeke.
Norway (1982): Rolf Trolle Andersen.
Order of Malta (see Index): Alberto Leoncini Bartoli.
Pakistan (1965): Muhammad Saleem.
Palau, Republic of (1998): . . . . .
Panama: Lawrence Christie Delia Cardenas.
Papua New Guinea (1977): . . . . .
Paraguay: Esteban Kriskovic.
Peru: . . . . .
Philippines (1951): Mercedes Arrastia Tuason.
Poland (1989): Hanna Suchocka.
Portugal: . . . . .
Qatar: (Diplomatic relations established Nov. 2002): Mohamad Jaham Abdulaziz Al-Kuwari.
Romania (1920; broken off, 1948; reestablished, 1990): Bogadan Tataru-Cazaban.
Russia (Federation of) (1989; formal diplomatic relations established in 2009): . . . . .
Rwanda (1964): Joseph Bonesha.
Saint Lucia (1984): Gilbert Ramez Chagoury.
Saint Vincent and the Grenadines (1990): . . . . .
San Marino (1986): Sante Canducci.
São Tome and Principe (1984): . . . . .
Senegal (1966): Félix Oudiane.
Serbia: Mirko Jelic.
Seychelles (1984): Vivianne Fock Tave.
Sierra Leone: (Diplomatic relations established July 1996): Christian Sheka Kargbo.
Singapore (1981): Barry Desker.
Slovak Republic (1993; when it became independent republic): Jozef Dravecký.
Slovenia (1992): Maja Lovrencic Svetek.
Solomon Islands (1984): . . . . .
South Africa (1994): George Johannes.
South Sudan (2013): . . . . .
Spain: Eduardo Gutierrez Saenz de Buruaga.
Sri Lanka (1975): Tamara Kunanayakam.
Sudan (1972): . . . . .
Suriname (1994): . . . . .
Swaziland (1992): H.R.H. Prince David M. Dlamini.
Sweden (1982): Perols Ulla Birgitta Gudmundson.
Switzerland (1992): Paul Widmer, Ambassador with special mission to Holy See.

Syria (Arab Republic) (1966): Edin Aala Hussam.
Tajikistan (1996): . . . . .
Tanzania (1968): . . . . .
Thailand (1969): Chalermpol Thanchitt.
Togo (1981): Félix Kodjo Sagbo.
Tonga (1994): . . . . .
Trinidad and Tobago (1978): Margaret King-Rousseau.
Tunisia (1972): . . . . .
Turkey (1966): Kenan Gürsoy.
Turkmenistan (1996): . . . . .
Uganda (1966): . . . . .
Ukraine (1992): Tetiana Izhevska.
United Arab Emirates (2007): Hissa Abdulla Ahmed Al-Otaiba.
United States (1984): Ken Hackett.
Uruguay: Daniel Edgardo Ramada Piendibene.
Uzbekistan (1992): . . . . .
Vanuatu (1994): . . . . .
Venezuela: . . . . .
Western Samoa (1994): . . . . .
Yemen: (1998): . . . . .
Yugoslavia: Darko Tanaskovic.
Zaire: See Congo.
Zambia (1965): Newton Kkunika Bizwayo.
Zimbabwe (1980): David Douglas Hamadziripi.

Special Representatives

United Nations (Center of Information of UN at the Holy See): Shalini Dewan, director.
Office of the League of Arab States: Ahmed Al-Shibli Ghanim Taha (a Memorandum of Understanding between the Vatican Secretariat of State and the League of Arab States was signed on Apr. 23, 2009.)
United Nations High Commission for Refugees: Laurens Jolles, delegate.
Organization for the Liberation of Palestine: Vacant, director.

U.S.-HOLY SEE RELATIONS

The U.S. and the Holy See announced Jan. 10, 1984, the establishment of full diplomatic relations, thus ending a period of 117 years in which there was no formal diplomatic relationship. The announcement followed action by the Congress in Nov. 1983 to end a prohibition on diplomatic relations enacted in 1867.

William A. Wilson, President Reagan's personal representative to the Holy See from 1981, was confirmed as the U.S. ambassador by the Senate, on Mar. 7, 1984. He presented his credentials to Pope John Paul II on Apr. 9, 1984, and served until May 1986, when he resigned. He was succeeded by Frank Shakespeare, 1986-89, and Thomas P. Melady, 1989-93. Raymond L. Flynn, Mayor of Boston, was appointed by Bill Clinton and confirmed by the Senate in July 1993. He served until 1997 when he was succeeded by Corinne Claiborne "Lindy" Boggs. She was succeeded by James Nicholson who served until 2005. On Aug. 1, 2005, Pres. George W. Bush nominated as Nicholson's successor L. Francis Rooney III, an Oklahoma and Florida businessman. On Nov. 5, 2007, President Bush nominated Mary Ann Glendon to become Ambassador to the Holy See. The U.S. Senate voted to confirm her on Dec. 19, 2007. On May 27, 2009, Barack Obama chose Miguel Diaz, a theology professor, as Ambassador to the Holy See. On June 14, 2013, Barack Obama noninated Ken Hackett, retired president of Catholic Relief Services, to be U.S. ambassador to the Holy See. He was approved by the U.S. Senate on Aug. 1, 2013.

Abp. (later Cardinal) Pio Laghi, apostolic delegate to the U.S. since 1980, was named first pro-nuncio by the Pope on Mar. 26, 1984. He served until 1990, when he was named prefect of the Congregation for Catholic Education. Abp. (now Cardinal) Agostino Cacciavillan was appointed pro-nuncio on June 13, 1990. He served until he was named president of the Administration of the Patrimony of the Apostolic See (APSA) and was succeeded on Dec. 7, 1998, by Abp. Gabriel Montalvo. Abp. Montalvo served as nuncio from 1998 to 2005. He was succeeded by Abp. Pietro Sambi, who served from 2005-2011. The current nuncio is Abp. Carlo Maria Viganó, who was named nuncio to the United States on Oct. 19, 2011.

Nature of Relations

The nature of relations was described in nearly identical statements by John Hughes, a State Department spokesman, and the Holy See. Hughes said: "The United States of America and the Holy See, in the desire to further promote the existing mutual friendly relations, have decided by common agreement to establish diplomatic relations between them at the level of embassy on the part of the United States of America, and nunciature on the part of the Holy See, as of today, Jan. 10, 1984."

The Holy See statement said: "The Holy See and the United States of America, desiring to develop the mutual friendly relations already existing, have decided by common accord to establish diplomatic relations at the level of apostolic nunciature on the side of the Holy See and of embassy on the side of the United States beginning today, Jan. 10, 1984."

The establishment of relations was criticized as a violation of the separation-of-church-and-state principle by spokesmen for the National Council of Churches, the National Association of Evangelicals, the Baptist Joint Committee on Public Affairs, Seventh Day Adventists, Americans United for Separation of Church and State, and the American Jewish Congress.

Legal Challenge Dismissed

U.S. District Judge John P. Fullam, ruling May 7, 1985, in Philadelphia, dismissed a legal challenge to U.S.-Holy See relations brought by Americans United for Separation of Church and State. He stated that Americans United and its allies in the challenge lacked legal standing to sue, and that the courts did not have jurisdiction to intervene in foreign policy decisions of the executive branch of the U.S. government. Parties to the suit brought by Americans United were the National Association of Laity, the National Coalition of American Nuns and several Protestant church organizations. Bishop James W. Malone, president of the U.S. Catholic Conference, said in a statement: "This matter has been discussed at length for many years. It is not a religious issue but a public policy question which, happily, has now been settled in this context."

Russell Shaw, a conference spokesman, said the decision to send an ambassador to the Holy See was not a church-state issue and "confers no special privilege or status on the Church."

Earlier Relations

Official relations for trade and diplomatic purposes were maintained by the U.S. and the Papal States while the latter had the character of and acted like other sovereign powers in the international community.

Consular relations developed in the wake of an announcement, made by the papal nuncio in Paris to the American mission there Dec. 15, 1784, that the Papal States had agreed to open several Mediterranean ports to U.S. shipping.

U.S. consular representation in the Papal States began with the appointment of John B. Sartori, a native of Rome, in June 1797. Sartori's successors as consuls were: Felix Cicognani, also a Roman, and Americans George W. Greene, Nicholas Browne, William C. Sanders, Daniel LeRoy, Horatio V. Glentworth, W.J. Stillman, Edwin C. Cushman, David M. Armstrong.

Consular officials of the Papal States who served in the U.S. were: Count Ferdinand Lucchesi, 1826 to 1829, who resided in Washington; John B. Sartori, 1829 to 1841, who resided in Trenton, NJ; Daniel J. Desmond, 1841 to 1850, who resided in Philadelphia; Louis B. Binsse, 1850 to 1895, who resided in New York.

U.S. recognition of the consul of the Papal States did not cease when the states were absorbed into the Kingdom of Italy in 1871, despite pressure from Baron Blanc, the Italian minister. Binsse held the title until his death Mar. 28, 1895. No one was appointed to succeed him.

Diplomatic Relations

The U.S. Senate approved a recommendation, made by President James K. Polk in Dec. 1847 for the establishment of a diplomatic post in the Papal States. Jacob L. Martin, the first charge d'affaires, arrived in Rome Aug. 2, 1848, and presented his credentials to Pius IX Aug. 19. Martin, who died within a month, was succeeded by Lewis Cass, Jr. Cass became minister resident in 1854 and served in that capacity until his retirement in 1858.

John P. Stockton, who later became a U.S. Senator from New Jersey, was minister resident from 1858 to 1861. Rufus King was named to succeed him but, instead, accepted a commission as a brigadier general in the Army. Alexander W. Randall of Wisconsin took the appointment. He was succeeded in Aug. 1862 by Richard M. Blatchford who served until the following year. King was again nominated minister resident and served in that capacity until 1867 when the ministry was ended because of objections from some quarters in the U.S. and failure to appropriate funds for its continuation. J. C. Hooker, a secretary, remained in the Papal States until the end of March, 1868, closing the ministry and performing functions of courtesy.

Personal Envoys

Myron C. Taylor was appointed by President Franklin D. Roosevelt in 1939 to serve as his personal representative to Pope Pius XII and continued serving in that capacity during the presidency of Harry S. Truman until 1951. Henry Cabot Lodge was named to the post by President Richard M. Nixon in 1970, served also during the presidency of Gerald Ford, and represented President Carter at the canonization of St. John Neumann in 1977. Miami attorney David Walters served as the personal envoy of President Jimmy Carter to the Pope from July 1977 until his resignation Aug. 16, 1978. He was succeeded by Robert F. Wagner who served from Oct. 1978 to the end of the Carter presidency in Jan. 1981. William A. Wilson, appointed by President Ronald Reagan in Feb. 1981, served as his personal envoy until 1984 when he was named ambassador to the Holy See.

None of the personal envoys had diplomatic status.

President Harry S. Truman nominated Gen. Mark Clark to be ambassador to the Holy See in 1951, but withdrew the nomination at Clark's request because of controversy over the appointment. None of Truman's three immediate successors

— Dwight D. Eisenhower, John F. Kennedy and Lyndon B. Johnson — had a personal representative to the pope.

PONTIFICAL ACADEMIES

Pontifical Academy of Sciences

(*Sources:* Annuario Pontificio, *Catholic News Service.*)

The Pontifical Academy of Sciences was constituted in its present form by Pius XI Oct. 28, 1936, in virtue of *In Multis Solaciis*, a document issued on his own initiative.

The academy is the only supranational body of its kind in the world with a pope-selected, life-long membership of outstanding mathematicians and experimental scientists regardless of creed from many countries. The normal complement of 70 members was increased to 80 in 1985-86 by John Paul II. There are additional honorary and supernumerary members.

The academy traces its origin to the *Linceorum Academia* (Academy of the Lynxes, its symbol) founded in Rome Aug. 17, 1603. Pius IX reorganized this body and gave it a new name, *Pontificia Accademia dei Nuovi Lincei*, in 1847. It was taken over by the Italian state in 1870 and called the *Accademia Nationale dei Lincei*. Leo XIII reconstituted it with a new charter in 1887. Pius XI designated the Casina of Pope Pius IV in the Vatican Gardens as the site of academy headquarters in 1922 and gave it its present title and status in 1936. In 1940, Pius XII gave the title of Excellency to its members; John XXIII extended the privilege to honorary members in 1961.

Members in U.S.

Scientists in the U.S. who presently hold membership in the Academy are listed below according to year of appointment. Nobel prize-winners are indicated by an asterisk.

Christian de Duve,* professor of biochemistry at the International Institute of Cellular and Molecular Pathology at Brussels, Belgium, and Rockefeller University, NY (Apr. 10, 1970);

Marshall Warren Nirenberg,* director of Laboratory on genetics and biochemistry at the National Institutes of Health, Bethesda, MD (June 24, 1974).

George Palade,* professor of cellular biology at University of California, San Diego and Victor Weisskopf, professor of physics at the Massachusetts Institute of Technology, Cambridge, Mass. (Dec. 2, 1975); David Baltimore,* professor of biology at the Massachusetts Institute of Technology, Cambridge, MA; Har Gobind Khorana,* professor of biochemistry, and Alexander Rich, professor of biophysics, both at the Massachusetts Institute of Technology, Cambridge, MA (Apr. 17, 1978).

Charles Townes,* professor emeritus of physics at the University of California at Berkeley (Jan. 26, 1983); Beatrice Mintz, senior member of the Cancer Research Institute of Philadelphia and Maxine Singer, biochemist, president of Carnegie Institution, Washington, DC (June 9, 1986). Roald Z. Sagdeev, professor of physics at University of Maryland, College Park and Peter Hamilton Raven, professor of biology at the Missouri Botanical Garden of St. Louis, MO (Oct. 4, 1990); Luis Angel Caffarelli, professor of mathematics at New York University and Luigi

Luca Cavalli-Sforza, professor of genetics at Stanford University (Aug. 2, 1994). Joshua Lederberg, professor of genetics at Rockefeller University, NY (Mar. 4, 1996); Joseph Edward Murray, professor of plastic surgery at Harvard Medical School, Cambridge, MA; Paul Berg, professor of biochemistry at Stanford Univ. and Vera C. Rubin, professor of astronomy at Carnegie Institution of Washington (June 25, 1996); Gary S. Becker,* professor of economics at the University of Chicago (Mar. 3, 1997); Chen-ning Yang,* professor of physics and director of the Institute of Theoretical Physics at the State University of NY at Stony Brook (Apr. 18,1997); Frank Press, professor of geophysics and director of the Washington Advisory Group (Sept. 3, 1999); Ahmed Zewail, professor of Chemistry and Physics, California Institute of Technology, Pasadena (Sept. 3, 1999); Mario Jose Molina, professor of atmospheric chemistry at the Massachusetts Institute of Technology (Nov. 9, 2000); Günter Blobel,* professor of cellular biology of the Rockefeller University, NY (Sept. 28, 2001); Fotis C. Kafatos, professor of molecular biology at Harvard University (Jan. 23, 2003); Tsung-Dao Lee, professor of Physics at Columbia University in New York (Apr. 14, 2003); William D. Phillips,* professor of physics at the University of Maryland and the National Institute of Standards and Technology, Gaithersburg, PA (Oct. 23, 2004); Veerabhadran (Ram) Ramanathan, professor of atmospheric science at the University of California, San Diego, and director of the Center for Atmospheric Science at Scripps Institution of Oceanography, La Jolla (Oct. 23, 2004); Edward Witten, professor of Physics at the Institute for Advanced Study, Princeton, NJ (June 21, 2006); Francis S. Collins, director of the National Institutes of Health, Bethesda, MD (Oct. 10, 2009); Edward M. De Robertis, professor of chemical biology at the Howard Hughes Institute of Medicine of the University of California, CA (Oct. 10, 2009); Miguel A. L. Nicolelis, professor of neuroscience at Duke University, NC (Jan. 5, 2011).

There is also one honorary member from the U.S.: Robert J. White, professor of neurosurgery at Case Western Reserve University, Cleveland (Mar. 29, 1994).

Members in Other Countries

Listing includes place and date of selection. Nobel prize winners are indicated by an asterisk.

Argentina: Antonio M. Battro (Sept. 21, 2002).

Armenia: Rudolf M. Muradian (Oct. 16, 1994).

Austria: Hans Tuppy (Apr. 10, 1970); Walter Thirring (June 9, 1986).

Belgium: Paul Adriaan Jan Janssen (June 25, 1990); Thierry Boon-Falleur (April 9, 2002).

Brazil: Carlos Chagas, former president of the academy (Aug. 18, 1961); Johanna Döbereiner (Apr. 17, 1978); Crodowaldo Pavan (Apr. 17, 1978); Rudolf Muradian (Oct. 16, 1994).

Canada: John Charles Polanyi* (June 9, 1986).

Chile: Héctor Rezzio Croxatto (Dec. 2, 1975); Rafael Vicuna (Nov. 10, 2000).

Congo (formerly Zaire): Felix wa Kalengo Malu (Sept. 26, 1983).

Denmark: Aage Bohr* (Apr. 17, 1978).
France: André Blanc-LaPierre (Apr. 17, 1978); Paul Germain (June 9, 1986); Jacques-Louis Lions (Oct. 4, 1990); Jean-Marie Lehn (May 30, 1996); Claude Cohen-Tannoudji (May 17, 1999); Nicole M. Le Douarin (Sept. 3, 1999); Pierre Jean Léna (Jan. 18, 2001); Yves Quéré (Dec. 20, 2003).
Germany: Rudolf L. Mössbauer* (Apr. 10, 1970); Manfred Eigen* (May 12, 1981); Wolf Joachim Singer (Sept. 18, 1992); Paul Joseph Crutzen (June 25, 1996); Yuri Ivanovich Manin (June 26, 1996); Jürgen Mittelstrass (Sept. 21, 2002); Theodor Wolfgang Hänsch (June 21, 2006); Klaus von Klitzing (Oct. 9, 2007).
Ghana: Daniel Adzei Bekoe (Sept. 26, 1983).
Great Britain: Hermann Alexander Brück (Apr. 5, 1955); George Porter* (June 24, 1974); Max Ferdinand Perutz* (May 12, 1981); Stephen William Hawking (Jan. 9, 1986); Martin John Rees (June 25, 1990); Sir Richard Southwood (Sept. 18, 1992); Raymond Hide (June 25, 1996).
India: Mambillikalathil Govind Kumar Menon (May 12, 1981); Chintamani N.R. Rao (June 25, 1990).
Israel: Michael Sela (Dec. 2, 1975); Aaron J. Ciechanover (March 13, 2007).
Italy: Giampietro Puppi (Apr. 17, 1978); Nicola Cabibbo (June 9, 1986), President; Nicola Dallaporta (Oct. 5, 1989), honorary member; Bernardo Maria Colombo (Sept. 18, 1992); Antonino Zichichi (Nov. 9, 2000); Enrico Berti (Sept. 28, 2001).
Japan: Minoru Oda (Sept. 18, 1992); Ryoji Noyori* (Oct. 1, 2002); Takashi Gojobori, Jan. 31, 2008.
Kenya: Thomas R. Odhiambo (May 12, 1981).
Mexico: Marcos Moshinsky (June 9, 1986).
Nigeria: Thomas Adeoye Lambo (June 24, 1974).
Poland: Stanislaw Lojasiewicz (Jan. 28, 1983); Czeslaw Olech (June 9, 1986); Michal Heller (Oct. 4, 1990); Andrzej Szezeklik (Oct. 16, 1994).
Russia: Vladimir Isaakovich Keilis-Borok (Oct. 16, 1994); Sergei Petrovich Novikov (June 25, 1996), also teaches at University of Maryland).
Spain: Manuel Lora-Tamayo (Sept. 24, 1964); Garcia-Bellido, Antonio (June 24, 2003).
Sweden: Sune Bergström* (Dec. 14, 1985); Kai Siegbahn* (Dec. 14, 1985).
Switzerland: Werner Arber* (May 12, 1981); Carlo Rubbia* (Dec. 14, 1985); Albert Eschenmoser (June 9, 1986).
Taiwan: Te-tzu Chang (Apr. 18, 1997); Yuan Tseh Lee (Oct. 9, 2007).
Vatican City State: Cottier, Card. George, O.P. (Oct. 28, 1992; honorary member); Rev. Enrico do Rovasenda, O.P. (Nov. 13, 1968), honorary member.
Venezuela: Marcel Roche (Apr. 10, 1970); Ignacio Rodríguez-Iturbe (Jan. 10, 2008).
Ex officio members: Rev. George V. Coyne, S.J., director of Vatican Observatory (Sept. 2, 1978); Raffaele Cardinal Farina, S.D.B., prefect of the Vatican Library (May 24, 1997); Most Rev. Sergio B. Pagano, prefect of the Secret Vatican Archives (Jan. 7, 1997). President: Werner Arber, professor emeritus of microbiology at the University of Basel, Switzerland (app. Jan. 13, 2011). Chancellor: Most Rev. Marcelo Sánchez Sorondo.
Honorary members: Rev. Jean-Michel Maldame, O.P., Dean of Faculty, Catholic Institute of Toulouse.

Pontifical Academy of Social Sciences

Founded by John Paul II, Jan. 1, 1994 (*motu proprio Socialium Scientiarum Investigationes*), to promote the study and the progress of social sciences, to advise the Vatican on social concerns and to foster research aimed at improving society. The number of members is not less than 20 nor more than 40. Five of the 32 members of the Academy (as of Jan. 1, 2013) were from the United States: Kenneth J. Arrow of Stanford University, Mary Ann Glendon of Harvard University, Kevin Ryan of Boston University, Joseph Stiglitz of Columbia University, and Russell Hittinger of the University of Tulsa. President, Mary Ann Glendon; Chancellor, Most Rev. Marcelo Sánchez Sorondo. Address: Casino Pio IV, Vatican Gardens.

Pontifical Academy for Life

Established by John Paul II, Feb. 11, 1994 (*motu proprio Vitae Mysterium*), "to fulfill the specific task of study, information and formation on the principal problems of biomedicine and law relative to the promotion and defense of life, especially in the direct relationship they have with Christian morality and the directives of the Church's magisterium."

Members, appointed by the pope without regard to religion or nationality, represent the various branches of "the biomedical sciences and those that are most closely related to problems concerning the promotion and protection of life." Membership, as of Jan. 1, 2013, included the following from the United States:

Prof. Carl Anderson, Vice-President of the Pontifical John Paul II Institute for Studies of Marriage and the Family; Mrs. Mercedes Arzu-Wilson, founder and president of the Foundations Family of the Americas and founder and director of the Commission at the World Organization for the Family; Dr. Thomas Hilgers, founder and director of the Institute "Paul VI," Omaha, NE; Mrs. Christine de Vollmer, president of the World Organization for the Family; Prof. Denis Cavanagh, professor of obstetrics and gynecology, University of South Florida College of Medicine; Prof. John M. Finnis, professor of philosophy of law, University of Oxford and the University Notre Dame; Dr. A.J. Luke Gormally, director emeritus of Linacre Centre for Health Care Ethics in England and research professor at Ave Maria School of Law; Prof. John Haas, professor of Moral Theology and the Pontifical College Josephinum, president of the National Catholic Bioethics Center and the International Institute of Culture. President: Msgr. Ignacio Carrasco de Paula.

Hierarchy of the Catholic Church

ORGANIZATION AND GOVERNMENT

As a structured society, the Catholic Church is organized and governed along lines corresponding mainly to the jurisdictions of the pope and bishops. The pope is the supreme head of the Church. He has primacy of jurisdiction as well as honor over the entire Church. Bishops, in union with and in subordination to the pope, are the successors of the Apostles for care of the Church and for the continuation of Christ's mission in the world. They serve the people of their own dioceses, or particular churches, with ordinary authority and jurisdiction. They also share, with the pope and each other, common concern and effort for the general welfare of the whole Church.

Bishops of exceptional status are patriarchs of Eastern Catholic Churches who, subject only to the pope, are heads of the faithful belonging to their rites throughout the world.

Subject to the Holy Father and directly responsible to him for the exercise of their ministry of service to people in various jurisdictions or divisions of the Church throughout the world are: resident archbishops and metropolitans (heads of archdioceses), diocesan bishops, vicars and prefects apostolic (heads of vicariates apostolic and prefectures apostolic), certain abbots and prelates, and apostolic administrators. Each of these, within his respective territory and according to the provisions of canon law, has ordinary jurisdiction over pastors (who are responsible for the administration of parishes), priests, religious and lay persons. Also subject to the Holy Father are titular archbishops and bishops, religious orders and congregations of pontifical right, pontifical institutes and faculties, papal nuncios and apostolic delegates. Assisting the pope and acting in his name in the central government and administration of the Church are cardinals and other officials of the Roman Curia.

THE HIERARCHY

The ministerial hierarchy is the orderly arrangement of the ranks and orders of the clergy to provide for the spiritual care of the faithful, the government of the Church, and the accomplishment of the Church's total mission in the world. Persons belong to this hierarchy by virtue of ordination and canonical mission.

The term hierarchy is also used to designate an entire body or group of bishops; for example, the hierarchy of the Church, the hierarchy of the United States.

Hierarchy of Order: Consists of the pope, bishops, priests and deacons. Their purpose, for which they are ordained to holy orders, is to carry out the sacramental and pastoral ministry of the Church.

Hierarchy of Jurisdiction: Consists of the pope and bishops by divine institution, and other church officials by ecclesiastical institution and mandate, who have authority to govern and direct the faithful for spiritual ends.

The Pope

His Holiness the Pope is the Bishop of Rome, Vicar of Jesus Christ, successor of St. Peter, Prince of the Apostles, Supreme Pontiff of the Universal Church, Primate of Italy, Archbishop and Metropolitan of the Roman Province, Sovereign of the State of Vatican City, Servant of the Servants of God.

Cardinals

(*See* **p. 276**, and **Index**)

Patriarchs

Patriarch, a term which had its origin in the Eastern Church, is the title of a bishop who, second only to the pope, has the highest rank in the hierarchy of jurisdiction. He is the incumbent of one of the sees listed below. Subject only to the pope, a patriarch of the Eastern Church is the head of the faithful belonging to his rite throughout the world. The patriarchal sees are so called because of their special status and dignity in the history of the Church.

The Council of Nicaea (325) recognized three patriarchs — the Bishops of Alexandria and Antioch in the East, and of Rome in the West. The First Council of Constantinople (381) added the bishop of Constantinople to the list of patriarchs and gave him rank second only to that of the pope, the bishop of Rome and patriarch of the West; this action was seconded by the Council of Chalcedon (451) and was given full recognition by the Fourth Lateran Council (1215). The Council of Chalcedon also acknowledged patriarchal rights of the bishop of Jerusalem.

Eastern patriarchs are as follows: one of Alexandria, for the Copts; three of Antioch, one each for the Syrians, Maronites and Greek Melkites (the latter also has the personal title of Greek Melkite patriarch of Alexandria and of Jerusalem). The patriarch of Babylonia, for the Chaldeans, and the patriarch of Sis, or Cilicia, for the Armenians, should be called, more properly, *Katholikos* — that is, a prelate delegated for a universality of causes. These patriarchs are elected by bishops of their churches; they receive approval and the pallium, symbol of their office, from the pope.

Latin Rite patriarchates were established for Antioch, Jerusalem, Alexandria and Constantinople during the Crusades; afterwards, they became patriarchates in name only. Jerusalem, however, was reconstituted as a patriarchate by Pius IX, in virtue of the bull *Nulla Celebrior* of July 23, 1847. In 1964, the Latin titular patriarchates of Constantinople, Alexandria and Antioch, long a bone of contention in relations with Eastern Churches, were abolished.

As of Aug. 15, 2013, the patriarchs in the Church were: Card. Antonios Naguib, of Alexandria, for the Copts; Card. Gregory III Laham, of Antioch, for the Greek Melkites (the patriarch also has personal titles of Alexandria and Jerusalem for the Greek Melkites); Card. Bechara Rai, of Antioch, for the Maronites; Nerses Bedros XIX Tarmouni, of Cilicia, for the Armenians; Card. Emmanuel III Delly, of Babylon of the Chaldeans; Ignace Joseph III Younan, of Antioch, for the Syrians. (For biographical information on the patriarchs, see **Eastern Catholics**, p. 343.)

The titular patriarchs (in name only) of the Latin Rite were: Card. José da Cruz Policarpo of Lisbon; Abp. Francesco Moraglia of Venice; Abp. Filipe Neri António do Rosário Ferrão of the East Indies (archbishop of Goa and Damao, India); and Abp. Fouad Twal of Jerusalem. The patriarchate of the West Indies has been vacant since 1963.

Major Archbishops

A major archbishop has the prerogatives but not the title of a patriarch. As of May 15, 2012, there were four major archbishops: Abp. Sviatoslav Schevchuk, of the major archbishopric of Kiev and Halych of the Ukrainian Catholic Church (Ukraine); Card. George Alencherry, of the major archbishopric of Ernakulam-Angomaly of the Syro-Malabar Church (India); Card. Isaac Mar Cleemis Thottunkal of the major archbishopric of Trivandrum of the Syro-Malankara Catholic Church (India), whose election was confirmed on Feb. 8, 2007, by Pope Benedict XVI); and Card. Lucian Muresan of the major archbishopric of Fagaras and Alba Julia for the Romanian Greek Catholic Church (Romania) who was promoted to the rank of major archbishop on Dec. 16, 2005.

Archbishops, Metropolitans

Archbishop: A bishop with the title of an archdiocese.

Coadjutor Archbishop: An assistant archbishop with right of succession.

Metropolitan: Archbishop of the principal see, an archdiocese, in an ecclesiastical province consisting of several dioceses. He has the full powers of bishop in his own archdiocese and limited supervisory jurisdiction and influence over the other (suffragan) dioceses in the province. The pallium, conferred by the pope, is the symbol of his status as a metropolitan.

Titular Archbishop: Has the title of an archdiocese that formerly existed in fact but now exists in title only. He does not have ordinary jurisdiction over an archdiocese. Examples are archbishops in the Roman Curia, papal nuncios, apostolic delegates.

Archbishop *ad personam*: A title of personal honor and distinction granted to some bishops. They do not have ordinary jurisdiction over an archdiocese.

Primate: A title of honor given to the ranking prelate of some countries or regions.

Bishops

Diocesan Bishop: A bishop in charge of a diocese.

Coadjutor Bishop: An assistant (auxiliary) bishop to a diocesan bishop, with right of succession to the see.

Titular Bishop: A bishop with the title of a diocese that formerly existed in fact but now exists in title only; an assistant (auxiliary) bishop to a diocesan bishop.

Episcopal Vicar: An assistant, who may or may not be a bishop, appointed by a residential bishop as his deputy for a certain part of a diocese, a determined type of apostolic

work, or the faithful of a certain rite.

Eparch, Exarch: Titles of bishops of Eastern churches.

Nomination of Bishops: Nominees for episcopal ordination are selected in several ways. Final appointment and/or approval in all cases is subject to decision by the pope.

In the U.S., bishops periodically submit the names of candidates to the archbishop of their province. The names are then considered at a meeting of the bishops of the province, and those receiving a favorable vote are forwarded to the nuncio for transmission to the Holy See and consideration for possible vacancies. Bishops are free to seek the counsel of priests, religious and lay persons with respect to nominees. For the selection of diocesan bishops or archbishops, the nuncio consults with appropriate bishops of the ecclesiastical province and all other relevant officials. Normally, three names are submitted on what is termed a *terna* from the nuncio to the Congregation for Bishops. The bishop members of the Congregation, including the Cardinals, will study the *terna* and submit a complete dossier to the Holy Father for each along with their preference. The pope makes the final decision on the appointment.

Eastern Catholic churches have their own procedures and synodal regulations for nominating and making final selection of candidates for episcopal ordination. Such selection is subject to approval by the pope. The Code of Canon Law concedes no rights or privileges to civil authorities with respect to the election, nomination, presentation or designation of candidates for the episcopate.

Ad Limina Visit: Diocesan bishops and apostolic vicars are obliged to make an ad limina visit ("to the threshold" of the Apostles) every five years to the tombs of Sts. Peter and Paul, have audience with the Holy Father and consult with appropriate Vatican officials. They are required to send a report on conditions in their jurisdiction to the Cong. for bishops approximately six — and not less than three — months in advance of the scheduled visit.

Others with Ordinary Jurisdiction

Ordinary: One who has the jurisdiction of an office: the pope, diocesan bishops, vicars general, prelates of missionary territories, vicars apostolic prefects apostolic, vicars capitular during the vacancy of a see, superiors general, abbots primate and other major superiors of men religious.

Some prelates and abbots, with jurisdiction like that of diocesan bishops, are pastors of the people of God in territories (prelatures and abbacies) not under the jurisdiction of diocesan bishops.

Vicar Apostolic: Usually a titular bishop who has ordinary jurisdiction over a mission territory.

Prefect Apostolic: Has ordinary jurisdiction over a mission territory.

Apostolic Administrator: Usually a bishop appointed to administer an ecclesiastical jurisdiction temporarily. Administrators of lesser rank are also appointed on occasion and have more restricted supervisory duties.

Vicar General: A bishop's deputy for the administration of a diocese; does not have to be a bishop.

Prelates Without Jurisdiction

The title of protonotary apostolic was originally given by the fourth century or earlier to clergy who collected accounts of martyrdom and other church documents, or who served the Church with distinction in other ways. Other titles — e.g., domestic prelate, papal chamberlain, prelate of honor — are titles of clergy in service to the pope and the papal household, or of clergy honored for particular rea-

sons. All prelates without jurisdiction are appointed by the pope, and have designated ceremonial privileges and the title of Rev. Monsignor.

SYNOD OF BISHOPS

The Synod of Bishops was chartered by Pope Paul VI Sept. 15, 1965, in a document he issued on his own initiative under the title *Apostolica Sollicitudo*. Provisions of this *motu proprio* are contained in Canons 342 to 348 of the Code of Canon Law. According to major provisions of the Synod charter:

• The purposes of the Synod are "to encourage close union and valued assistance between the Sovereign Pontiff and the bishops of the entire world; to insure that direct and real information is provided on questions and situations touching upon the internal action of the Church and its necessary activity in the world of today; to facilitate agreement on essential points of doctrine and on methods of procedure in the life of the Church."

• The Synod is a central ecclesiastical institution, permanent by nature.

• The Synod is directly and immediately subject to the pope, who has authority to assign its agenda, to call it into session, and to give its members deliberative as well as advisory authority.

• In addition to a limited number of ex officio members and a few heads of male religious institutes, the majority of the members are elected by and representative of national or regional episcopal conferences. The pope reserved the right to appoint the general secretary, special secretaries and no more than 15 percent of the total membership.

The pope is president of the Synod. The secretary general is Abp. Nikola Eterovic, of Croatia. Address: Palazzo del Bramante, Via della Conciliazione 34, 00193 Rome, Italy.

Assemblies

1. First Assembly: The first assembly was held from Sept. 29 to Oct. 29, 1967. Its objectives, as stated by Pope Paul VI, were "the preservation and strengthening of the Catholic faith, its integrity, its force, its development, its doctrinal and historical coherence."

2. Pope-Bishop Relations: The second assembly, held Oct. 11 to 28, 1969, was extraordinary in character. It opened the way toward greater participation by bishops with the pope and each other in the governance of the Church.

3. Priesthood and Justice: The ministerial priesthood and justice in the world were the principal topics under discussion at the second ordinary assembly, Sept. 30 to Nov. 6, 1971.

4. Evangelization: The assembly of Sept. 27 to Oct. 26, 1974, produced a general statement on evangelization of the modern world, covering the need for it and its relationship to efforts for total human liberation from personal and social evil.

5. Catechetics: The fourth ordinary assembly, Sept. 30 to Oct. 29, 1977, focused attention on catechetics, with special reference to children and young people.

6. Family: "A Message to Christian Families in the Modern World" and a proposal for a "Charter of Family Rights" were produced by the assembly held Sept. 26 to Oct. 25, 1980.

7. Reconciliation: Penance and reconciliation in the mission of the Church was the theme of the assembly held Sept. 29 to Oct. 29, 1983.

8. Vatican II Review: The second extraordinary assembly was convened Nov. 24 to Dec. 8, 1985, for the purposes of: (1) recalling the Second Vatican Council; (2) evaluating the implementation of its enactments during the 20 years since its conclusion; (3) seeking ways and means of promoting renewal in the Church in accordance with the spirit and letter of the council.

9. Vocation and Mission of the Laity in the Church and in the World 20 years after the Second Vatican Council: The seventh ordinary assembly, Oct. 1 – 30, 1987, produced a set of 54 propositions which were presented to the pope for consideration in the preparation of a document of his own on the theme of the assembly. He responded with the apostolic exhortation, *Christifideles Laici*, "The Christian Faithful Laity," released by the Vatican Jan. 30, 1989.

10. Formation of Priests in Circumstances of the Present Day: The eighth general assembly, Sept. 30 – Oct. 28, 1990, dealt principally with the nature and mission of the priesthood. Pope John Paul issued an apostolic exhortation entitled *Pastores Dabo Vobis* ("I Will Give You Shepherds") Apr. 7, 1992.

11. The Consecrated Life and Its Role in the Church and in the World: The ninth general assembly was held Oct. 2 – 29, 1994. Pope John Paul's reflections on the proceedings of the assembly and the recommendations of the bishops were the subjects of his apostolic exhortation entitled *Vita Consecrata* ("Consecrated Life"), issued Mar. 25, 1996.

12. The Bishop: Servant of the Gospel of Jesus Christ for the Hope of the World: The 10th ordinary general assembly was held from Sept. 30 – Oct. 27, 2001. Pope John Paul II's reflections on the proceedings of the assembly and the recommendations of the bishops was the subject of the apostolic exhortation *Ecclesia in Europa*, issued on June 28, 2003.

13. The Eucharist: Source and Summit of the Life and Mission of the Church: The 11th ordinary general assembly was held from Oct. 2 – Oct. 23, 2005. Pope Benedict XVI's reflections on the proceedings of the assembly and the recommendations of the bishops were the subject of an apostolic exhortation, *Sacramentum Caritatis* issued on Mar. 13, 2007.

14. The Word of God in the Life and Mission of the Church: The 12th ordinary general assembly was from Oct. 5 – Oct. 26, 2008. Pope Benedict XVI's reflections on the proceedings of the assembly and the recommendations of the Bishops was the subject of an apostolic exhortation, *Verbum Domini*, issued on Nov. 11, 2010.

15. The New Evangelization for the Transmission of the Christian Faith: The 13th ordinary general assembly was held in Oct. 2012. [See under Special Reports.]

Recent Special Assemblies of the Synod of Bishops: Special Synods have been held for Europe (Nov. 28 – Dec. 14, 1991, on the theme "So that we might be witnesses of Christ who has set us free"); for Africa (Apr. 10 – May 8, 1994, on the theme "The Church in Africa and Her Evangelizing Mission Toward the Year 2000: 'You Shall Be My Witnesses' (Acts 1:8)"); for Lebanon (Nov. 27 – Dec. 14, 1995, on the theme "Christ is Our Hope: Renewed by His Spirit, in Solidarity We Bear Witness to His Love"); the Americas (Nov. 16 – Dec. 12, 1997, on the theme, "Encounter with the Living Jesus Christ: Way to Conversion, Community and Solidarity"); for Asia (Apr. 19 – May 14, 1998, on the theme "Jesus Christ the Savior and His Mission of Love and Service in Asia: '... That They May Have Life, and Have it Abundantly' (Jn 10:10)"; for Oceania (Nov. 12 – Dec. 12, 1998, on the theme "Jesus Christ and the Peoples of Oceania: Walking His Way, Telling His Truth, Living His Life"; a special assembly for Europe (Oct. 1–23, 1999), on the theme "Jesus Christ, Alive in His Church, Source of Hope for Europe"; a Second Special Assembly for Africa (Oct. 5–25, 2009); and a Special Assembly for the Middle East (Oct. 10–24, 2010).

COLLEGE OF CARDINALS

Cardinals are chosen by the pope to serve as his principal assistants and advisers in the central administration of church affairs. Collectively, they form the College of Cardinals. Provisions regarding their selection, rank, roles and prerogatives are detailed in Canons 349 to 359 of the Code of Canon Law.

History of the College

The College of Cardinals was constituted in its present form and categories of membership in the 12th century. Before that time the pope had a body of advisers selected from among the bishops of dioceses neighboring Rome, priests and deacons of Rome. The college was given definite form in 1150, and in 1179 the selection of cardinals was reserved exclusively to the pope. Sixtus V fixed the number at 70, in 1586. Bl. John XXIII set aside this rule when he increased membership at the 1959 and subsequent consistories. The number was subsequently raised by Paul VI. The number of cardinals entitled to participate in papal elections was limited to 120 by Paul VI in 1973. The limit on the number of cardinals was set aside by Pope John Paul II three times, in 1998, 2001 and 2003. As of Aug. 1, 2013, 112 of the 202 cardinals were eligible to vote.

In 1567 the title of cardinal was reserved to members of the college; previously it had been used by priests attached to parish churches of Rome and by the leading clergy of other notable churches. The Code of Canon Law promulgated in 1918 decreed that all cardinals must be priests. Previously there had been cardinals who were not priests (e.g., Cardinal Giacomo Antonelli, d. 1876, Secretary of State to Pius IX, was a deacon). John XXIII provided in the *motu proprio Cum Gravissima* Apr. 15, 1962, that cardinals would henceforth be bishops; this provision is included in the revised Code of Canon Law.

Age Limits

Pope Paul VI placed age limits on the functions of cardinals in the apostolic letter *Ingravescentem Aetatem,* dated Nov. 21, 1970, and effective Jan. 1, 1971. At 80, they cease to be members of curial departments and offices, and become ineligible to take part in papal elections. They retain membership in the College of Cardinals, however, with relevant rights and privileges.

Three Categories

All cardinals except Eastern patriarchs are aggregated to the clergy of Rome. This aggregation is signified by the assignment to each cardinal, except the patriarchs, of a titular church in Rome. The three categories of members of the college are cardinal bishops, cardinal priests and cardinal deacons.

Cardinal bishops include the six titular bishops of the suburbicarian sees and Eastern patriarchs. First in rank are the titular bishops of the suburbicarian sees neighboring Rome: Ostia, Palestrina, Porto-Santa Rufina, Albano, Velletri-Segni, Frascati, Sabina-Poggio Mirteto. The dean of the college holds the title of the See of Ostia as well as his other suburbicarian see. These cardinal bishops are engaged in full-time service in the central administration of church affairs in departments of the Roman Curia.

Full recognition is given in the revised Code of Canon Law to the position of Eastern patriarchs as the heads of sees of apostolic origin with ancient liturgies. They are assigned rank among the cardinals in order of seniority, following the suburbicarian titleholders.

Cardinal priests, who were formerly in charge of leading churches in Rome, are bishops whose dioceses are outside Rome.

Cardinal deacons, who were formerly chosen according to regional divisions of Rome, are titular bishops assigned to full-time service in the Roman Curia.

The dean and sub-dean of the college are elected by the cardinal bishops — subject to approval by the pope — from among their number. The dean, or the sub-dean in his absence, presides over the college as the first among equals. Cardinals Angelo Sodano and Roger Etchegeray were elected dean and vice-dean, respectively, on Apr. 30, 2005. The Secretary to the College of Cardinals is Abp. Lorenzo Baldisseri, sec. of the Cong. for Bishops.

Selection and Duties

Cardinals are selected by the pope and are inducted into the college in appropriate ceremonies. Cardinals under the age of 80 elect the pope when the Holy See becomes vacant (*see* **Index: Papal Election, see also below under Conclave**); and are major administrators of church affairs, serving in one or more departments of the Roman Curia. Cardinals in charge of agencies of the Roman Curia and Vatican City are asked to submit their resignation from office to the pope on reaching the age of 75. All cardinals enjoy a number of special rights and privileges. Their title, while symbolic of high honor, does not signify any extension of the powers of holy orders. They are called princes of the Church.

A cardinal *in pectore (petto)* is one whose selection has been made by the pope but whose name has not been disclosed; he has no title, rights or duties until such disclosure is made, at which time he takes precedence from the time of the secret selection.

BIOGRAPHIES OF CARDINALS

Biographies of the cardinals, as of Sept. 15, 2013, are given below in alphabetical order. For historical notes, order of seniority and geographical distribution of cardinals, see separate entries. An * asterisk indicates cardinals ineligible to take part in papal elections.

Abril y Castello, Santos: b. Sept. 21, 1935, Alfambra,

diocese of Teruel, Spain; Rome; ord. priest, Mar. 19, 1960; entered the diplomatic service of the Holy See in 1967 and served in the nunciatures in Pakistan and Turkey and in the Secretariat of State; ord. titular abp. of Tamada and app. nuncio in Bolivia, Apr. 29, 1985; pro-nuncio in Cameroon, Gabon and Equatorial Guinea, Oct. 2, 1989; nuncio in the Federal Republic of Yugoslavia, Feb. 24, 1996; nuncio to Argentina, Mar. 4, 2000; nuncio to Slovenia, Bosnia and Hercegovina, and Macedonia in 2003; app. vice camerlengo of the Holy Roman Church, Jan. 22, 2011; app. archpriest of the papal Liberian basilica, Rome, Nov. 21, 2011; cardinal, Feb. 18, 2012, with the deaconry of S. Ponziano.

Curial membership: Bishops, Education, Evangelization, Saints (Congregation); Eucharistic Congresses.

Agré,* Bernard: b. Mar. 2, 1926, Monga, Côte d'Ivoire; ord., July 20, 1953; headmaster in Dabou; vicar general of Abidjan archdio.; app. bp. of Man, June 8, 1968; app. first bp. of Yamoussoukro, Mar. 6, 1992; abp. of Abidjan, 1994-2006; ret. May 2, 2006; pres. of the Episcopal Conferences of Francophone West Africa (CERAO) and chair of the Pan-African Episcopal Committee for Social Communications (CEPACS); card., Feb. 21, 2001; titular church, St. John Chrysostom in Monte Sacro Alto.

Agustoni,* Gilberto: b. July 26, 1922, Schaffhausen, Switzerland; ord., Apr. 20, 1946; called to Rome in 1950 to work under Card. Ottaviani in the Cong. for the Holy Office; a Prelate Auditor of the Roman Rota, 1970-86; ord. titular abp. of Caorle Jan. 6, 1987; sec. of the Cong. for the Clergy, 1986-92; pro-prefect of the Apostolic Signatura, 1992-94; card. deacon, Nov. 26, 1994; titular church Sts. Urban and Laurence at Prima Porta. Prefect of Supreme Tribunal of Apostolic Signatura, 1994-98.

Alencherry, George: b. Apr. 19, 1945, Kottayam, archiepiscopal of Changanacherry of the Syro-Malabars, India; ord. priest, Nov. 19, 1972; ord. first eparch of Thuckalay of the Syro-Malbars, Feb. 2, 1997; elected archbishop major of Ernakulam-Changanacherry by the Syro-Malabar Synod, May 24, 2011; election was confirmed by Pope Benedict XVI, May 25, 2011; cardinal, Feb. 18, 2012, with the title of S. Bernardo alle Terme Diocleziane.

Curial membership: Doctrine of the Faith, Oriental Churches (Congregations).

Álvarez Martínez,* Francisco: b. July 14, 1925, Santa Eulalia de Ferroñes Llanera, Spain; ord., June 11, 1950; app. bp. of Tarazona, Apr. 13, 1973; cons., June 3, 1973; bp. of Calahorra and La Calzado-Logroño, Dec. 20, 1976; transferred to Orihuela-Alicante, May 12, 1989; abp. of Toledo, 1995-2002; member of the Standing Committee and the Executive Committee of the Spanish Episcopal Conference; card., Feb. 21, 2001; titular church, St. Mary Regina Pacis in Monte Verde.

Amato, S.D.B., Angelo: b. June 8, 1938, Molfetta, Italy; studied at the Pontifical Salesian Univ. and the Pontifical Gregorian Univ. in Rome and the Salesian Univ. in Brindisi; ord. Dec. 22, 1967, for the Salesians; ord. titular abp. of Sila, Jan. 6, 2003; sec. of the Cong. for the Doctrine of the Faith, 2002-2008; app. prefect of the Cong. for the Causes of the Saints, July 9, 2008; created card. deacon, Nov. 20, 2010; deaconry of S. Maria in Aquiro.

Curial membership: Divine Worship, Doctrine (congregations); Christian Unity (council).

Amigo Vallejo, O.F.M., Carlos: b. Aug. 23, 1934, Medina de Rioseco, Spain; joined Order of Friars Minor and ord. Aug. 17, 1960; ord. abp. of Tanger, Morocco, Apr. 28, 1974; abp. of Toledo, 1974-84; abp. of Seville,

1984-2009; card., Oct. 21, 2003; titular church, St. Mary of Monserrat of the Spanish.

Curial membership: Health Care Workers (council); Latin America (commission).

Angelini,* Fiorenzo: b. Aug. 1, 1916, Rome, Italy; ord., Feb. 3, 1940; master of pontifical ceremonies, 1947-54; ord. bp. (titular see of Messene) July 29, 1956, and head of Rome Vicariate's section for apostolate to health care workers; abp, 1985; pres. of newly established Curia agency for health care workers; card. deacon, June 28, 1991, deaconry, Holy Spirit (in Sassio). President of Pontifical Council for Pastoral Assistance to Health Care Workers, 1989-96.

Antonelli, Ennio: b. Nov. 18, 1936, Todi, Italy; ord., Apr. 2, 1960; bp. of Gubbio, Aug. 29, 1982; abp. of Perugia-Città della Pieve, 1988-2001; secretary-general of the Italian Episcopal Conference, 1995; abp. of Florence, Mar. 21, 2001-June 7, 2008; pres. of the Pont. Council for the Family, 2008-2012; card., Oct. 21, 2003; titular church, St. Andrew delle Fratte.

Curial membership: Laity, Social Communications (councils).

Arinze,* Francis: b. Nov. 1, 1932, Eziowelle, Nigeria; ord., Nov. 23, 1958; ord. titular bp. of Fissiana and aux. bp. of Onitsha, Aug. 29, 1965; abp. of Onitsha, 1967-84; pro-president of Secretariat for Non–Christians (now the Council for Interreligious Dialogue), 1984; card. deacon, May 25, 1985; deaconry, St. John (della Pigna); transferred to the order of card. priests, Jan. 29, 1996; transferred to the order of card. bishops, Apr. 25, 2005, with Suburbicarian See of Veletri-Segni; President of Council for Interreligious Dialogue, 1985-2002; Prefect of the Cong. for Divine Worship and the Discipline of the Sacraments, 2002-2008.

Curial membership: Doctrine of the Faith, Oriental Churches, Evangelization of Peoples, Causes of Saints (congregations); Laity, Christian Unity (councils); International Eucharistic Congresses (committee).

Arns,* O.F.M., Paulo Evaristo: b. Sept. 14, 1921, Forquilhinha, Brazil; ord., Nov. 30, 1945; held various teaching posts; director of *Sponsa Christi,* monthly review for religious, and of the Franciscan publication center in Brazil; ord. titular bp. of Respetta and aux. bp. of São Paulo, July 3, 1966; abp. of São Paulo, 1970-98; card., Mar. 5, 1973; titular church, St. Anthony of Padua (in Via Tuscolana).

Assis, Raymundo Damasceno: b. Feb. 15, 1937, Capela Nova, Brazil; studied at the Major Seminary of Mariana, Pontifical Gregorian Univ., Rome, the Superior Institute of Catechesis in Münich, Germany, and the Univ. of Brasília and the Pontifical Catholic Univ. of Mina Gerais; ord. Mar. 19, 1968; ord. titular bp. of Novapietra and aux. bp. of Brasília, Sept. 15, 1986; sec. general of the Episcopal Council of Latin America (CELAM), 1991-1995; app. abp. of Aparecida, Jan. 28, 2004; pres. of CELAM, 2007-2011; created card. priest, Nov. 20, 2010; titular church of Immacolata al Tiburtino.

Curial membership: Social Communications (council); Latin America (commission).

Backis, Audrys Juozas: b. Feb. 1, 1937, Kaunas, Lithuania; ord., Mar. 18, 1961; entered Holy See diplomatic service in 1964 and posted to the Philippines, Costa Rica, Turkey, Nigeria, and the Council for Public Affairs of the Church; undersecretary to the Council for the Public Affairs of the Church, 1979-88; app. titular abp. of Meta and nuncio to the Netherlands, Aug. 5, 1988;

app. abp. of Vilnius Dec. 24, 1991; pres. of the Lithuanian Bishops' Conference; card., Feb. 21, 2001; titular church, Nativity of Our Lord Jesus Christ in Via Gallia.

Curial membership: Education (congregation); Social Communication (council).

Bagnasco, Angelo: b. Feb. 14, 1943, Pontevico, Italy; ord. June 29, 1966; earned a doctorate in philosophy from the State Univ. of Genoa in 1979 and served in pastoral ministry from 1966-1985; professor of metaphysics and contemporary atheism at the Theological Faculty of Northern Italy, 1980-1998; cons. bp. of Pesaro, Feb. 7, 1998; promoted to archbishop when the diocese was elevated to the rank of metropolitan see, Mar. 11, 2000; app. military ordinary for Italy, June 20, 2003; app. abp. of Genoa, Aug. 29, 2006; app. by Pope Benedict XVI president of the Italian Episcopal Conference on Mar. 7, 2007 (re-appointed, Mar. 17, 2012); card., Nov. 24, 2007, titular church, Great Mother of God.

Curial membership: Bishops, Oriental Churches, Sacraments (congregation).

Barbarin, Philippe: b. Oct. 17, 1950, Rabat, Morocco; ord. Dec. 17, 1977; from 1994 to 1998, served in Madagascar as pastor and professor in the island's seminary; ord. bp. of Moulins, France, Nov. 22, 1998; abp. of Lyon, July 16, 2002, card., Oct. 21, 2003; titular church, Most Holy Spirit al Monte Pincio.

Curial membership: Sacraments, Consecrated Life and Societies of Apostolic Life (congregations).

Bartolucci,* Domenico: b. May 7, 1917, Borgo San Lorenzo, Italy; studied at the Archiepiscopal Seminary of Florence, Conservatory of Florence, Pontifical Institute of Sacred Music, and Accademia Nazionale di S. Cecilia; ord. Dec. 23, 1939; dir. of the choir of the cathedral of Florence; app. maestro of the Cappella Musicale Liberiana of the basilica of Sta. Maria Maggiore, 1947; app. vice-maestro of the Sistine Chapel, 1952; app. dir. of the Cappella Musicale Pontificia Sistina, 1956; replaced in 1997, he was recalled in 2006 by Pope Benedict XVI; created card. deacon, Nov. 20, 2010; deaconry of SS. Nomi de Gesù e Maria in via Lata.

Baum,* William Wakefield: b. Nov. 21, 1926, Dallas, TX; moved to Kansas City, MO, at an early age; ord. (Kansas City-St. Joseph diocese), May 12, 1951; executive director of U.S. Bishops' Commission for Ecumenical and Interreligious Affairs, 1964-69; attended Second Vatican Council as *peritus* (expert adviser); ord. bp. of Springfield-Cape Girardeau, MO, Apr. 6, 1970; abp. of Washington, DC, 1973-80; cardinal, May 24, 1976; titular church, Holy Cross on the Via Flaminia; prefect of Cong. for Catholic Education (Seminaries and Institutes of Study), 1980-90. Major Penitentiary, 1990-2001; res., Nov. 22, 2001.

Becker,* S.J., Karl Josef: b. Apr. 18, 1928, Cologne, Germany; entered the Society of Jesus (Jesuits) and ord. priest July 31, 1958, for the Society; served as professor of dogmatic theology at the Pontifical Gregorian University, Rome, from 1969 to 2003; consultor of the Cong. for the Doctrine of the Faith from 1977; cardinal, Feb. 18, 2012, but was exempted from episcopal consecration; deaconry of S. Giuliano Martire.

Bertello, Giuseppe: b. Oct. 1, 1942, Foglizzo, Italy; earned a doctorate in canon law and studied diplomacy at the Pontifical Ecclesiastical Academy, Rome; ord. priest, June 29, 1966, and entered the diplomatic service of the Holy See in 1971; served in Sudan, Turkey, Venezuela and in the Office of the Organization of the United Nations in Geneva; ord. titular abp. of Urbisaglia and named pro-nuncio in Ghana, Togo and Benin, Oct. 17, 1987;

nuncio in Rwanda, 1991, app. permanent Observer of Office of the United Nations and Specialized Institutions in Geneva in 1995; nuncio to Mexico in 2000; nuncio in Italy and in the Republic of San Marino in 2007; app. president of the Pontifical Commission for Vatican City State and of the Governorate of Vatican City State, Sept. 3, 2011; cardinal Feb.18, 2012 with the deaconry of Ss. Vito, Modesto e Crescenzia.

Curial membership: Bishops, Evangelization (congregations); Justice and Peace (council).

Bertone, S.D.B., Tarcisio: b. Dec. 2, 1934, Romano Canavese, entered the Society of St. Francis de Sales of St. John Bosco (Salesians); ord., July 1, 1960; prof. of Special Moral Theology, Pontifical Salesian Athenaeum (later Pontifical Salesian Univ. in 1973), 1967-76; prof. of Canon Law, 1976-1991; vice-rector, Pontifical Salesian Univ. of Rome, 1987–1989; ord. abp. of Vercelli, Aug. 1, 1991; sec. of the Cong. for the Doctrine of the Faith, 1995-2002; abp. of Genoa, Dec. 10, 2002; card., Oct. 21, 2003; titular church, St. Mary, Helper in Via Tuscolana; transferred to the order of card. bishops (with the suburbicarian see of Frascati), May 10, 2008; app. Secretary of State, Sept. 15, 2006; app. Chamberlain (Camerlengo) of the Holy Roman Church, Apr. 4, 2007; res. Oct. 15, 2013.

Curial membership: Bishops, Clergy, Doctrine of the Faith, Eastern Churches, Evangelization, Sacraments (congregations); Institute for Works of Religion (commission).

Betori, Giuseppe: b. Feb. 25, 1947, Foligno, Italy; earned a doctorate in Sacred Scripture from the Pontifical Biblical Institute; ord. priest, Sept. 26, 1970; ord. titular bp. of Falerone, May 6, 2001, and served as sec. general of the Italian Bishops' Conference; app. abp. of Florence, Sept. 8, 2008; survived an assassination attempt in November 2011; cardinal on Feb. 18, 2012, with the title of S. Marcello.

Curial membership: Education (congregation); Culture (council).

Biffi,* Giacomo: b. June 13, 1928, Milan, Italy; ord., Dec. 23, 1950; ord. titular bp. of Fidene and aux. of Milan, Jan. 11, 1976; abp. of Bologna, 1984-2003; card., May 25, 1985; titular church, Sts. John the Evangelist and Petronius.

Bozanic, Josip: b. Mar. 20, 1949, Rijeka, Yugoslavia; ord., June 29, 1975; prof. of canon law and dogmatic theology in the Seminary of Rijeka, 1988-1997; ord. bp. of Krk, Veglia, June 25, 1989; abp. of Zagreb, Croatia, July 5, 1997; pres. of the Croatian Conference of Bishops and vice-pres. of the Council of European Bishops' Conferences; card., Oct. 21, 2003; titular church, St. Jerome of the Croatians. Abp. of Zagreb.

Curial membership: Sacraments (congregation); Laity (council).

Brady, Seán Baptist: b. Aug. 16, 1939, Drumcalpin, diocese of Kilmore, Ireland; ord. Feb. 22, 1964; served from 1964-1993 as a faculty member in the Minor Seminary, Kilmore and then vice-rector and rector of the Pontifical Irish College in Rome; cons. coadj. abp. of Armagh, Ireland, Feb. 19, 1995 and acceded to the metropolitan and primatial see of Armagh, Oct. 1, 1996; has been a leading voice for peace in Northern Ireland and has warned against secularism in the country; card., Nov. 24, 2007, titular church, Sts. Quirico and Giulitta.

Curial membership: Christian Unity (council); Culture (commission).

Brandmüller,* Walter: b. Jan. 5, 1929, Ansbach, Germany; studied at the Ludwig-Maximilians University,

Münich; ord. July 26, 1953; served as a professor of Church History and Patrology; app. canon of the chapter of St. Peter's Basilica, 1997, and pres. of the Pontifical Committee for Historical Sciences, 1998-2009; ord. titular abp. of Cesarea di Mauretania, Nov. 13, 2010; created cardinal deacon, Nov. 20, 2010; deaconry of S. Giuliano dei Fiaminghi.

Bráz de Aviz, João: b. Apr. 24, 1947, Mafra, Brazil; earned a doctorate in theology at the Pontifical Lateran University, Rome; ord. priest, Nov. 26, 1972; ord. titular bp. of Flenucleta and aux. bp. of Vitória, Apr. 6, 1994; app. bp. of Ponta Grossa, Aug. 12, 1998; took possession on Oct. 15, 1999 and abp. of Maringá, July 17, 2002; app. abp. of Brasília, Jan. 28, 2004; app. prefect of the Congregation for the Institutes of Consecrated Life and the Societies of Apostolic Life, Jan. 4, 2011; cardinal, Feb. 18, 2012, with the deaconry of S. Elena fuori Porta Prenestina.

Curial membership: Clergy (congregation).

Burke, Raymond Leo: b. June 30, 1948, Richland Center, WI; studied at Holy Cross Seminary, La Crosse, WI, Catholic Univ., Washington, DC, North American College and Gregorian Univ., Rome; holds a diploma in Latin Letters and a doctorate in Canon Law; ord. for the La Crosse diocese, June 29, 1975; served in the Supreme Tribunal of the Apostolic Signatura (the highest court in the Church) and was the first American to hold the position of Defender of the Bond of the Supreme Tribunal of the Apostolic Signatura; app. bishop of La Crosse, Dec. 10, 1994; ord. Jan. 6, 1995, pres. of the board of directors, National Catholic Rural Life Conference, 1996-2001; app. abp. of St. Louis, Dec. 2, 2003; app. prefect of the Supreme Tribunal of the Apostolic Signatura, June 27, 2008; he is considered one of the greatest living experts on canon law; created card. deacon, Nov. 20, 2010; deaconry of S. Agatha le Goths.

Curial membership: Secretariat of State; Bishops, Divine Worship (congregations); Texts (council).

Cacciavillan,* Agostino: b. Aug. 14, 1926, Novale de Valdagno (Vicenza), Italy; ord., June 26, 1949; attended Pont. Ecclesiastical Academy; entered Holy See diplomatic service; posted to the Philippines, Spain, Portugal, and Secretariat of State; pro-nuncio in Kenya and apostolic delegate to Seychelles, 1976; titular abp. of Amiternum, Feb. 28, 1976; nuncio to India, 1981; pro-nuncio to Nepal, 1985; nuncio to United States and permanent observer at the Org. of American States, 1990; pres., Admin. of the Patrimony of the Apostolic See (APSA), 1998-2002; card. deacon, Feb. 21, 2001; protodeacon, Mar. 2, 2008; deaconry, Holy Guardian Angels in Città Giardino.

Caffarra, Carlo: b. June 1, 1938, Samboseto di Busseto, in the province of Parma, Italy; ord. July 2, 1961; studied at the Pontifical Lombard Seminary, Gregorian Univ., where he earned a doctorate in canon law, and the Pontifical Accademia Alfonsiana, with a diploma for a specialization in Moral Theology; after holding a variety of teaching positions, he was named to the International Theological Commission in 1974; founded in 1981 the John Paul II Pontifical Institute for Studies on Marriage and the Family; consultor to the Cong. for the Doctrine of the Faith, 1983-88; app. Sept. 8, 1995, abp. of Ferrara-Comacchio; app. Dec. 16, 2003, abp. of Bologna; pres. of the Episcopal Conference of Emilia Romagna; card. Mar. 24, 2006; titular church, San Giovanni Battista dei Fiorentini.

Curial membership: Evangelization of People (con gregation); Family (council); Pontifical Academy of Life;

Apostolic Signatura.

Calcagno, O.F.M., Domenico: b. Feb. 3, 1943, Parodi Ligure, province of Alessandria, Italy; earned a doctorate in Sactred Theology from the Pontifical Gregorian University, Rome; ord. priest, Feb. 25, 1967, ord. bp. of Savona-Noli, Mar. 9, 2002; app. sec. of the Administration of the Patrimony of the Apostolic See, Aug. 31, 2007 and elevated to the rank of archbishop; app. president of the Administration of the Patrimony of the Apostolic See, July 7, 2011; cardinal, Feb. 18, 2012, with the deaconry of Annunciazione della Beata Vergine Maria a Via Ardeatina.

Curial membership: Evangelization (congregation); Health Care (council); Vatican City State (commission).

Canestri,* Giovanni: b. Sept. 30, 1918, Castelspina, Italy; ord., Apr. 12, 1941; spiritual director of Rome's seminary, 1959; ord. titular bp. of Tenedo and aux. to the card. vicar of Rome, July 30, 1961; bp. of Tortona, 1971–75; titular bp. of Monterano (personal title of abp.) and vice regent of Rome, 1975–84; abp. of Cagliari, 1984–87; abp. of Genoa, July 6, 1987–95; card., June 28, 1988; titular church, St. Andrew of the Valley.

Cañizares Llovera, Antonio: b. Oct. 10, 1945, Utiel, Spain; after studies in the diocesan seminary of Valencia, he earned a doctorate in theology from the Pontifical Univ. of Salamanca in 1971; ord. June 21, 1970; sec. of the Episcopal Commission for the Doctrine of the Faith, 1985-92; founder and first presdent of the Spanish Assoc. of Catechists, 1977-89; app. bp. of Ávila, Mar. 6, 1992; contributed to the compilation of the Spanish-language edition of the *Catechism of the Catholic Church*; app. abp. of Granada, Dec. 10, 1996; founder and first grand chancellor of the Catholic Univ., "Santa Teresa de Jesús" in Ávila, 1994-97; app. metropolitan abp. of Toledo and primate of Spain, Oct. 24, 2002; card., Mar. 24, 2006; titular church, di San Pancrazio; app. Prefect of the Cong. for Divine Worship and the Discipline of the Sacraments, Dec. 9, 2008. Prefect of the Cong. for Divine Worship and the Discipline of the Sacraments.

Curial membership: Bishops, Doctrine of the Faith (congregations); Ecclesia Dei, Latin America (commissions).

Carles Gordó,* Ricardo Maria: b. Sept. 24, 1926, Valencia, Spain; ord., June 29, 1951; ord. bp. of Tortosa, Aug. 3, 1969; abp. of Barcelona, 1990-2004; card., Nov. 26, 1994; titular church, St. Mary of Consolation in Tiburtino.

Cassidy,* Edward Idris: b. July 5, 1924, Sydney, Australia; ord., July 23, 1949; entered Vatican diplomatic service in 1955; served in nunciatures in India, Ireland, El Salvador and Argentina; ord. titular bp. of Amantia with personal title of abp., Nov. 15, 1970; pro-nuncio to Republic of China (Taiwan), 1970-79 and pro-nuncio to Bangladesh and apostolic delegate in Burma, 1973-79; pro-nuncio to Lesotho and apostolic delegate to southern Africa, 1979-84; pro-nuncio to the Netherlands, 1984-88; substitute of the Secretary of State for General Affairs, 1988-89; pres. of Pontifical Council for Promoting Christian Unity, 1989-2001; card. deacon, June 28, 1991; deaconry, St. Mary (in via Lata).

Castrillón Hoyos,* Darío: b. July 4, 1929, Medellín, Colombia; ord., Oct. 26, 1952; dir. local Cursillo Movement; delegate for Catholic Action; taught canon law at the Free Civil Univ.; gen. sec. of the Colombian Bishops' Conference; coadj. bp. of Pereira, June 2, 1971; bp. of Pereira, 1976-1992; gen. sec. of Latin American Episcopal Council (CELAM), 1983-87; pres. CELAM,

1987-91; abp. of Bucaramanga, 1992-96; pro-prefect Cong. for the Clergy, 1996-98; Pref. Cong. for the Clergy, 1998-2006; Protodeacon, 2007- 2008; card. deacon, Feb. 21, 1998; card. priest, Mar. 2, 2008; titular church, Holy Name of Mary on the Forum Traiani.

Curial membership: Bishops, Education, Evangelization of Peoples, Sacraments (congregations); Texts (councils); Latin America (commission).

Cé,* Marco: b. July 8, 1925, Izano, Italy; ord., Mar. 27, 1948; taught sacred Scripture and dogmatic theology at seminary in his home diocese of Crema; rector of seminary, 1957; presided over diocesan liturgical commission, preached youth retreats; ord. titular bp. of Vulturia, May 17, 1970; aux. bp. of Bologna, 1970-76; gen. ecclesiastical assistant of Italian Catholic Action, 1976-78; patriarch of Venice, 1978-2001; ret., Jan. 5, 2002; card., June 30, 1979; titular church, St. Mark. Patriarch emeritus of Venice.

Cheong-Jin-Suk,* Nicolas: b. Dec. 7, 1931, Supyo Dong, near Seoul, Korea; raised in the faith, he survived the tumult of the Korean War and then entered the Major Seminary of Song Shin; ord. Mar. 18, 1961; after pastoral service, he was sent to Rome for studies in canon law; app. bp. of Cheongju, June 25; member of the Executive Committee of the Korean Episcopal Conference, 1975-99; pres. of the Korean Episcopal Conference, 1996-99; abp. of Seoul, 1998-2012 and administrator of the diocese of P'yong-yang; card., Mar. 24, 2006; titular church, Sta. Maria Immacolata di Lourdes a Boccea.

Curial membership: Family, Social Communications (councils).

Cipriani Thorne, Juan Luis: b. Dec. 28, 1943, Lima, Peru; champion basketball player and student in industrial engineering, he joined Opus Dei in 1962; ord. for the prelature, Aug. 21, 1977; after a doctorate in theology at the Univ. of Navarre and pastoral work in Lima, he taught moral theology at the Pontifical Faculty of Theology, Lima, and was regional vicar for Peru and vice-chancellor of the Univ. of Piura; app. titular bp. of Turuzi and aux. bp. of Ayacucho, May 23, 1988; cons. July 3, 1988; app. abp. of Ayacucho, May 13, 1995; tried to negotiate a peaceful resolution to the siege of the Japanese ambassador's residence in Lima, Dec. 1996-Apr. 1997 and ministered to Japanese and Peruvian hostages; app. abp. of Lima, Jan. 9, 1999; card., Feb. 21, 2001; titular church St. Camillus de Lellis.

Curial membership: Causes of Saints, Sacraments (congregation); Latin America (commission); Economic Affairs (prefecture).

Clancy,* Edward Bede: b. Dec. 13, 1923, Lithgow, New South Wales, Australia; ord., July 23, 1949; ord. titular bp. of Ard Carna and aux. of Sydney, Jan. 19, 1974; abp. of Canberra, 1978-83; abp. of Sydney, Feb. 12, 1983; res., Mar. 26, 2001; card., June 28, 1988; titular church, Holy Mary of Vallicella.

Coccopalmerio, Francesco: b. Mar. 6, 1938, San Giuliano Milanese, Italy; earned a doctorate in canon law from the Pontifical Gregorian Univ. and a doctorate in jurisprudence at the Catholic Univ. of the Sacred Heart in Milan; ord. priest, June 29, 1962 and served as a professor of canon law at the Theological Faculty of Northern Italy from 1966 until 1999; ord. titular bishop of Celiana and appointed aux. bp. of Milan, April 8, 1993; app. pres. of the Pontifical Council of Legislative Texts and promoted to the rank of archbishop, Feb. 15, 2007; cardinal Feb. 18, 2012, with the deaconry of S. Giuseppe dei Falegnami.

Curial membership: Doctrine of the Faith (congrega-

tion); Christian Unity (council); Signatura (tribunal)

Collins, Thomas C.: b. Jan. 16, 1947, Guelph, Ontario; earned a doctorate in theology at the Pontifical Gregorian Univ., Rome; ord. priest, May 5, 1973 and served as rector of St. Peter's Seminary, London, Ontario, 1995 until 1997; cons. coadjutor bishop of St. Paul in Alberta, May 14, 1997; acceded to the see of St. Paul in Alberta, June 30, 1997; app. coadj. abp. of Edmonton, Feb. 18, 1999; acceded to the see of Edmonton, June 7, 1999; app. metropolitan abp. of Toronto, Dec. 16, 2006; cardinal, Feb. 18, 2012 with the title of S. Patrizio.

Curial membership: Education (congregation); Social Communications (council).

Comastri, Angelo: b. Sept. 17, 1943, Sorano, diocese of Sovana-Pitigliano (now Pitigliano-Sovana-Orbetello), Italy; ord. Mar. 11, 1967; after many years of pastoral work, served as bp. of Massa Marittima-Piombo, 1990-1994; pres. of the National Italian Committee for the Jubilee of the year 2000; app. prelate of Loreto and pontifical delegate for the Lauretano shrine, and promoted to the rank of archbishop, Nov. 9, 1996; app. coadj. of the archpriest of the papal basilica of St. Peter in the Vatican, vicar general of His Holiness for the State of Vatican City, and pres. of the Fabric of St. Peter's, Feb. 5, 2005; succeeded to the post of archpriest of the papal Vatican basilica, Oct. 31, 2006; card., Nov. 24, 2007, deaconry, San Salvatore in Lauro.

Curial membership: Saints (congregation).

Connell,* Desmond: b. Mar. 24, 1926, Phibsboro, Ireland; ord., May 19, 1951; taught at Univ. College Dublin, 1953-72; dean of the faculty of Philosophy and Sociology, 1983; chaplain to the Poor Clares in Donnybrook and Carmelites in Drumcondra and Blackrock; app. abp. of Dublin, Jan. 21, 1988; cons., Mar. 6, 1988; ret. Apr. 26, 2004; card., Feb. 21. 2001; titular church, St. Sylvester in Capite.

Coppa,* Giovanni: b. Nov. 9, 1925, Alba, Italy; ord. Jan. 2, 1949; entered the Roman Curia in 1952 and held various posts; app. titular abp. of Serta and delegate for the pontifical representations in the Secretariat of State, Dec. 1, 1979; cons. Jan. 6, 1980; nuncio to the Czech Republic and Slovakia, Jan. 1, 1993; ceased in his functions of nuncio in Slovakia, Mar. 2, 1994; resigned as nuncio to the Czech Republic, May 19, 2001; card., Nov. 24, 2007; deaconry, St. Linus.

Cordero Lanza di Montezemolo,* Andrea: b. Aug. 27, 1925, Turin, Italy; ord. Mar. 13, 1954; entered diplomatic service after studies at the Pontifical Ecclesiastical Academy in 1959; served for 42 years in various diplomatic posts; app. undersecretary and secretary of the Pont. Comm. Justice and Peace; app. nuncio and titular abp. of Anglona, Apr. 5, 1977; nuncio to Papau New Guinea and apostolic delegate to Solomon Islands, 1977; app. apostolic delegate in Jerusalem, Palestine, and Jordan, Apr. 28, 1990; transf. to see of Tuscania, Apr. 13, 1991, and first nuncio to Israel, 1994-98; nuncio to Italy and San Marino, 1998-2001; app. archpriest of the basilica of St. Paul Outside-the-Walls, 2005-2009; an expert ecclesiastical herald, he assisted the design of the papal coat-of-arms for Pope Benedict XVI in 2005; card., Mar. 24, 2006; titular church, Diaconia di Santa Maria in Portico.

Cordes, Paul-Josef: b. Sept. 5, 1934, Kirchhundem, Paderborn, Germany; ord. Dec. 21, 1961; served in the seminary for the dioceses of Paderborn and Münster, 1962-1969, and after doctoral studies was in the secretariat of the Episcopal Conference of Germany; titular bp of Naisso and aux. bp. of Paderborn, Oct. 27, 1975; cons., Feb. 1, 1976, vice-president of the Pontifical Council for the Laity, 1980-1995; promoted to abp., 1995; pres. Pontifical Council Cor Unum, 1995-2010; card., Nov. 24, 2007, deaconry, San Lorenzo in Piscibus.

Curial membership: Clergy, Evangelization, Saints (congregations); Justice and Peace (council).

Cottier,* O.P., Georges: b. Apr. 25, 1922; ord. July 2, 1951; theologian of the Papal Household theologian, 1989; secretary general of the International Theological Commission, 1989-2004; cons. titular abp. of Tullia, Oct. 20, 2003; card., Oct. 21, 2003; titular church, Sts. Dominic and Sixtus.

Danneels,* Godfried: b. June 4, 1933, Kanegem, Belgium; ord., Aug. 17, 1957; professor of liturgy and sacramental theology at Catholic Univ. of Louvain, 1969-77; ord. bp. of Antwerp, Dec. 18, 1977; abp. of Mechelen-Brussel, 1979-2010; installed, Jan. 4, 1980; card., Feb. 2, 1983; titular church, St. Anastasia.

Curial membership: Secretariat of State (second section); Divine Worship and Sacraments, Education, Evangelization of Peoples, Oriental Churches (congregations).

Darmaatmadja, S.J., Julius Riyadi: b. Dec. 20, 1934, Muntilan, Mageland, Central Java, Indonesia; entered Society of Jesus in 1957; ord., Dec. 18, 1969; ord. abp. of Semarang, June 29, 1983; abp. of Jakarta, 1996-2010; card., Nov. 26, 1994; titular church, Sacred Heart of Mary.

Curial membership: Interreligious Dialogue (councils).

De Giorgi,* Salvatore: b. Sept. 6, 1930 Vernole, Italy; ord., June 28, 1953; diocesan chaplain to the Teachers' Movement of Catholic Action; dir. Diocesan Pastoral Office; app. titular bp. of Tulana and aux. bp. of Oria, Nov. 21, 1973; bp. of Oria, Mar. 17, 1978; abp. of Foggia, Apr. 4, 1981; abp. of Taranto, Oct. 10, 1987 (resigned, 1990); general president of Catholic Action, 1990-96; abp. of Palermo, 1996-2006; president of the Sicilian Episcopal Conference; card., Feb. 21, 1998; titular church, St. Mary in Ara Caeli.

Curial membership: Bishops, Sacraments (congregations); Laity, Family (councils).

Delly,* Emmanuel III: b. Oct. 6, 1927, Telkaif, Iraq; ord. Dec. 21, 1952; elected titular bp. of Palempoli di Asia and aux. of Babylon of the Chaldeans, Dec. 7, 1962, (confirmed by the pope, Dec. 26, 1962, and cons., Apr. 19, 1963); aux. emeritus of Babylon of the Chaldeans, Oct. 24, 2002; elected patriarch of Babylon of the Chaldeans, Dec. 3, 2003, by the Synod of Bishops of the Chaldean Church, and took the name Emmanuel III; granted *ecclesiastica communio* by Pope John Paul II, Dec. 3, 2003; card., Nov. 24, 2007; as a patriarch, he did not receive a titular church.

Curial membership: Eastern Churches.

De Paolis, C.S., Velasio: b. Sept. 19, 1935, Sonnino, Italy; made his profession for the Cong. of the Missionaries of St. Charles Borromeo (Scalabrinians) in 1955 and studied at the Pontifical Gregorian Univ., the Univ. of St Thomas (Angelicum), La Sapienza Univ., and Alphonsianum, Rome; ord. Mar. 18, 1961; held various academic posts; respected expert in canon law; app. titular bp. of Telepte and sec. of the Supreme Tribunal of the Apostolic Signatura, Dec. 30, 2003; ord., Feb. 21, 2004; app. pres. of the prefecture for the Economic Affairs of the Holy See and promoted to the rank of abp., Apr. 12, 2008; app. pontifical delegate for the Cong. of the Legionaries of Christ, July 9, 2010; created card. deacon, Nov. 20, 2010; deaconry of Gesù Buon Pastore alla Montagnola.

Curial membership: Divine Worship, Saints (congregation); Legislative Texts (council); Signatura (tribunal).

Dias, Ivan: b. Apr. 14, 1936, Bandra, India; ord., Dec. 8, 1958; entered the Holy See diplomatic service and was posted to Indonesia, Madagascar, Reunion, the Comorros, Mauritius, and Secretariat of State; app. titular abp. of Rusubisir and pro-nuncio in Ghana, Togo and Benin, May 8, 1982; cons., June 19, 1982; nuncio in Korea, 1987-91; nuncio in Albania, 1991-97; abp. of Bombay, Jan. 22, 1997-May 22, 2006; cons., Mar. 13, 1997; card., Feb. 21, 2001; titular church, Holy Spirit in Ferratella; app. Prefect of the Cong. for the Evang. of Peoples, May 20, 2006.

Curial membership: Doctrine of the Faith, Eastern Churches, Education, Sacraments, (congregations); Christian Unity, Culture, Interreligious Dialogue, Legislative Texts, Social Comm. (councils); Cultural Heritage of the Church, Latin America (commission).

DiNardo, Daniel N.: b. May 23, 1949, Steubenville, OH; ord. July 16, 1977; studied at the Catholic Univ. of America, in Washington, DC, the North American College, Pontifical Gregorian Univ., and the Augustinianum in Rome; served at the Cong. for Bishops in the Roman Curia, 1984 to 1991 and also as director of Villa Stritch and adjunct professor at the Pontifical North American College; app. coadj. Bp. of Sioux City, Aug. 19, 1997, cons., Oct. 7, 1997; acceded as bp. of Sioux City, Nov. 28, 1998; app. coadj. bp. of Galveston-Houston, Jan. 16, 2004; inst. Mar. 26, 2004; app. coadj. abp. of Galveston-Houston, Dec. 29, 2004; abp. of Galveston-Houston, Feb. 28, 2006; card., Nov. 24, 2007; titular church, St. Eusebius.

Curial membership: Cultural Heritage, Migrants (councils).

Dolan, Timothy M.: b. Feb. 6, 1950, St. Louis, MO; studied at St. Louis Preparatory Seminary, Cardinal Glennon College, the North American College, Rome, and the Pontifical Univ. of St. Thomas Aquinas (Rome); earned a doctorate in Church History from The Catholic Univ. of America in Washington, DC; ord. priest for the archdiocese of St. Louis, June 19, 1976; served on the staff of apostolic nunciature (Washington, DC); rector, North American College, Rome, 1994-2001; app. titular bp. of Natchez and aux. bp. of St. Louis, June 19, 2001; ord., Aug. 15, 2001; app. abp. of Milwaukee, June 25, 2002; inst., Aug. 28, 2002; app. abp. of New York, Feb. 23, 2009; inst. Apr. 15, 2009; elected pres of the USCCB, Nov. 2011; cardinal, Feb. 18, 2012, with the titular church of Nostra Signora di Guadalupe a Monte Mario.

Curial membership: Evangelization of Peoples (congregation); New Evangelization, Social Communications (councils).

do Nascimento,* Alexandre: b. Mar. 1, 1925, Malanje, Angola; ord., Dec. 20, 1952, in Rome; forced into exile in Lisbon, Portugal, 1961-71; returned to Angola, 1971; active with student and refugee groups; professor at Pius XII Institute of Social Sciences; ord. bp. of Malanje, Aug. 31, 1975; abp. of Lubango and apostolic administrator of Onjiva, 1977-86; held hostage by Angolan guerrillas, Oct. 15 to Nov. 16, 1982; card., Feb. 2, 1983; titular church, St. Mark in Agro Laurentino. Abp. of Luanda, 1986.

Duka, O.P., Dominik: b. Apr. 26, 1943, Hradec Králové, East Bohemia, Czech Republic (then Czechoslovakia); entered the Order of Preachers (Dominicans) secretly in 1968 and took the name Dominik; ord. priest, June 22, 1970, and made his solemn profession in the Order of Preachers in 1971; deprived of the state authorization to exercise his priestly ministry by the Czech communist government and worked in a factory for 15 years but served secretly as vicar provincial and master of the novices;

arrested in 1981-1982 and imprisoned; ord. bp. of Hradec Králové, Sept. 26, 1998, awarded the First Grade Medal of Merit for the Czech Republic, 2001; app. metropolitan abp. of Prague, Feb. 13, 2010; elected pres. of the Czech Bishops Conference, 2010; Cardinal, Feb. 18, 2012 with the title of Ss. Marcellino e Pietro.

Curial membership: Consecrated Life (congregation); Justice and Peace (council).

Dziwisz, Stanislaw: b. Apr. 27, 1939, in Raba Wyzna, Poland; ord. June 23, 1963; secretary to Card. Karol Wojtyla, 1966-78; with election of Wojtyla as Pope John Paul II in 1978, he became papal secretary, a post he held until John Paul II's death in 2005; named a prelate of his holiness in 1985, titular bishop of San Leone e Prefetto and adjunct prefect of the Papal Household on Feb. 7, 1998, and named titular abp. on Sept. 29, 2003; app. abp. of Cracow, June 3, 2005; card. Mar. 24, 2006; titular church, Titolo di Santa Maria del Popolo.

Curial membership: Education (congregation); Laity, Social Communications (councils).

Egan,* Edward Michael: b. Apr. 2, 1932, Oak Park, IL; ord., Dec. 15, 1957, in Rome; sec. to Card. Albert Meyer, 1958-60; assistant vice-rector of the North American College, 1960-64; vice-chancellor of the archdiocese of Chicago, 1964-68; co-chancellor for human relations and ecumenism, 1968-72; judge of Roman Rota, 1972–85; ord. titular bp. of Allegheny and aux. bp. of New York, May 22, 1985; app. bp. of Bridgeport, Nov. 5, 1988; abp. of New York, May 11, 2000, inst., June 19, 2000; ret. Feb. 23, 2009; card., Feb. 21, 2001; titular church, Ss. John and Paul.

Curial membership: Eastern Churches (congregation), Family (council); Signatura (tribunal); Economic Affairs (office); Cultural Heritage (commission).

Eijk, Willem J.: b. June 22, 1953, Duivendrecht, Netherlands; earned doctorates in medicine at the University of Leiden and moral philosophy at the Pontifical University of St. Thomas Aquinas, Rome; ord. priest, June 1, 1985; professor of moral theology, 1997 to 1999; member of the International Theological Commission; ord. bp. of Groningen-Leeuwarden, Nov. 6, 1999; app. abp. of Utrecht, Dec. 11, 2007; cardinal, Feb. 18, 2012, with the title of S. Callisto.

Curial membership: Clergy, Education (congregations).

Erdö, Peter: b. June 25, 1952, Budapest, Hungary; ord. June 18, 1975 and earned doctorates in Theology and Canon Law from the Lateran Univ., Rome; professor of Theology and Canon Law, seminary of Esztergom, 1980-1988; guest professor, in Canon Law, Pontifical Gregorian Univ., 1986; rector of the Catholic Univ. Péter Pázmány, 1998; ord. Jan. 6, 2000, titular bp. of Puppi and aux. bp. of Szikesfehirvar; app. abp. of Esztergom-Budapest, Dec. 7, 2002; card., Oct. 21, 2003; titular church, St. Balbina.

Curial membership: Education, Sacraments (congregation); Culture, Legislative Texts (council); Signatura (tribunal).

Errázuriz Ossa,* Francisco Javier: b. Sept. 5, 1933, Santiago, Chile; ord. for the Schönstatt Fathers, July 16, 1961; chaplain to students and professionals of the Schönstatt Movement and regional superior; elected superior general of the Schönstatt Fathers, 1974; app. titular abp. of Hólar and sec. of the Cong. For Institutes of Consecrated Life and Societies of Apostolic Life, Dec. 22, 1990; app. abp. of Valparaiso, Sept. 24, 1996; transferred to archdio. of Santiago, Apr. 24, 1998; pres. of the Episcopal Conference of Chile and first vice-pres. of CELAM; card., Feb. 21, 2001; titular church, St. Mary of Peace.

Curial membership: Consecrated Life (congregation);

Culture, Family (council); Latin America (commission).

Estepa Llaurens,* José Manuel: b. Jan. 1, 1926, Andújar, Spain; ord. Jan. 27, 1954; ord. titular bp. of Tisili and aux. bp. of Madrid, Oct. 15, 1972; app. general military vicar of Spain and promoted to titular abp. of Velebusdo, July 30, 1983; transf. to the titular see of Italica, with personal title of abp., Nov. 18, 1989; res. Oct. 30, 2003; created card. priest, Nov. 20, 2010; titular church of S. Gabriele Arcangelo all'Acqua Traversa.

Etchegaray,* Roger: b. Sept. 25, 1922, Espelette, France; ord., July 13, 1947; deputy director, 1961-66, and secretary general, 1966-70, of French Episcopal Conference; ord. titular bp. of Gemelle di Numidia and aux. of Paris, May 27, 1969; abp. of Marseilles, 1970-84; prelate of Mission de France, 1975-82; president of French Episcopal Conference, 1979-81; card., June 30, 1979; titular church, St. Leo I. President of Council Cor Unum, 1984-95; pres. of Council for Justice and Peace (1984-98) and president of Central Committee for the Jubilee of the Holy Year 2000 (1994-98); transferred to order of card. bishops, June 24, 1998 (suburbicarian see of Porto-Santa Rufina); Vice-dean of the Sacred College of Cardinals, Apr. 30, 2005.

Falcão,* José Freire: b. Oct. 23, 1925, Erere, Brazil; ord., June 19, 1949; ord. titular bp. of Vardimissa and coadj. of Limoeiro do Norte, June 17, 1967; bp. of Limoeiro do Norte, Aug. 19, 1967; abp. of Teresina, Nov. 25, 1971; abp. of Brasilia, 1984-2004; res. Jan. 28, 2004; card., June 28, 1988; titular church, St. Luke (Via Prenestina).

Farina,* S.D.B., Raffaele: b. Sept. 24, 1933, Buonalbergo, Italy; ord. July 1, 1958; entered the Salesians in 1949 and took his final vows in 1954; earned a doctorate in Ecclesiastical History from the Pontifical Gregorian Univ. in Rome and served as a prof. of Church History and also rector at the Theological Faculty of the Pontifical Salesian Univ.; sec. of the Pontifical Committee of Historical Science and under-sec. of the Pontifical Council for Culture; app. prefect of the Apostolic Vatican Library, May 25, 1997; cons. titular bp. of Oderzo, Dec. 16, 2006; app. archivist and librarian of the Holy Roman Church, June 25, 2007; card., Nov. 24, 2007; deaconry, San Giovanni della Pigna.

Curial membership: Education, Saints (congregation); Cultural Heritage (commission).

Fernandes de Araújo,* Serafim: b. Aug. 13, 1924, Minas Novas, Brazil; ord., Mar. 12, 1949; taught canon law at provincial seminary of Diamantina; titular bp. of Verinopolis and aux. bp. of Belo Horizonte, Jan. 19, 1959; co-adjutor abp. of Belo Horizonte, 1982; abp. Belo Horizonte, 1986-2004; res. Jan. 28, 2004; co-president of the Fourth General Conference of the Latin American Episcopate, 1992; card., Feb. 21, 1998; titular church, St. Louis Marie Grignion de Montfort.

Filoni, Fernando: b. Apr. 15, 1946, Manduria, Italy; earned a doctorate in canon law from the Pontifical Lateran University, Rome, and a doctorate in philosophy at the State Univ. La Sapienza, in Rome; ord. priest, July 3, 1970 and entered the diplomatic service of the Holy See on Apr. 3, 1981; served in Sri Lanka, Iran, Brazil, and Hong Kong; ord. titular abp. of Volturno and appointed nuncio in Jordan and Iraq, Jan. 17, 2001; app. nuncio in Philippines, Feb. 25, 2006; app. sostituto for the General Affairs of the Church of the Secretariat of State, June 9, 2007, app. prefect of the Congregation for the Evangelization of Peoples on May 10, 2011; cardinal, Feb. 18, 2012, with the deaconry of Nostra Signora di Coromoto in S. Giovanni di Dio.

Curial membership: Doctrine of the Faith, Education, Oriental Churches

Furno,* Carlo: b. Dec. 2, 1921, Bairo Canavese, Italy; ord., June 25, 1944; entered diplomatic service of the Holy See in the 1950s; served in Colombia, Ecuador and Jerusalem; worked in Secretariat of State for 11 years; ord. titular bp. of Abari with personal title of abp., Sept. 16, 1973; nuncio in Peru, 1973-78, Lebanon, 1978-82, Brazil, 1982-92, Italy, 1992-94; card. deacon, Nov. 26, 1994; deaconry, Sacred Heart of Christ the King. Grand Master of the Equestrian Order of the Holy Sepulchre, 1995-2007; pontifical delegate for Patriarchal Basilica of St. Francis in Assisi, 1996; archpriest emeritus of the patriarchal basilica of Santa Maria Maggiore, Rome, 2004-2004.

George, O.M.I., Francis E.: b. Jan. 16, 1937, Chicago, IL; ord., Dec. 21, 1963; provincial of central region of Oblates of Mary Immaculate, 1973-74, vicar general, 1974-86; ord. bp. of Yakima, Sept. 21, 1990; abp. of Portland, OR, Apr. 30, 1996, installed, May 27, 1996; abp. of Chicago, Apr. 8, 1997, installed, May 7, 1997; card., Feb. 21, 1998; titular church, St. Bartholomew on Tiber Island.

Curial membership: Divine Worship and the Discipline of the Sacraments, Institutes of Consecrated Life, Oriental Churches, Evangelization (congregations); Cor Unum, Culture (council); Cultural Heritage of the Church (commission).

Gracias, Oswald: b. Dec. 24, 1944, Bombay (now Mumbai), India; ord. Dec. 20, 1970; earned a doctorate in canon law and a diploma in jurisprudence from the Pontifical Urbanian Univ. in Rome, 1982; served as chancellor and secretary to the bishop of Jamshedpur, 1971-1976; chancellor, judge of the metropolitan tribunal, and judicial vicar of Bombay from 1982-1997; cons. titular bp. of Bladia and aux. bp. of Bombay, Sept. 16, 1997; abp. of Agra, 2000-2006; app. abp. of Bombay, Oct. 14, 2006; card., Nov. 24, 2007; titular church, St. Paul of the Cross at Corviale.

Curial membership: Sacraments (congregation); Texts (council)

Grech,* O.S.A., Prosper: b. Dec. 24, 1925, Vittoriosa, Malta; entered the Augustinians in 1943; earned a doctorate a doctorate in theology at the Pontifical Gregorian University, Rome and a licentiate in Sacred Scriptures from the Pontifical Biblical Institute, Rome; ord. priest, Mar. 25, 1950; served as a professor of Scripture from 1971 to 1989 at the Pontifical Lateran Univ.; member of the Pontifical Theological Academy and the Pontifical Biblical Commission; cons. titular abp. of San Leone, Feb. 8, 2012; cardinal, Feb. 18, 2012, with the deaconry of S. Maria Goretti.

Grocholewski, Zenon: b. Oct. 11, 1939, Bródki, Poland; ord., May 26, 1963; earned a doctorate in canon law; served in the Supreme Tribunal of the Apostolic Signatura, 1972-1999; prefect of the Supreme Tribunal of the Apostolic Signatura; member of the commission studying the 1983 Code of Canon Law; titular bp. of Agropoli, Dec. 21, 1982; titular abp., Dec. 16, 1991; prefect of the Cong. for Catholic Education, Nov. 15, 1999; card. deacon, Feb. 21, 2001; titular church, deaconry, St. Nicholas in Carcere. Prefect of the Cong. for Catholic Education.

Curial membership: Bishops, Doctrine of the Faith, Evangelization, Sacraments (congregations); Texts (council); Apostolic Signatura (tribunal).

Gulbinowicz,* Henryk Roman: b. Oct. 17, 1923, Szukiszki, Poland; ord., June 18, 1950; ord. titular bp. of Acci and apostolic administrator of Polish territory in Lithuanian archdio. of Vilnius (Vilna), Feb. 8, 1970; abp. of Wroclaw, Poland. 1976-2004; card., May 25, 1985; titular church, Immaculate Conception of Mary (a Grottarosa).

Herranz Casado,* Julián: b. Mar. 31, 1930, Baena, Spain; joined the personal prelature of Opus Dei and ord. Aug. 7, 1955; ord. titular bp. of Vertara, Jan. 6, 1991; pres. of the Pontifical Council for the Interpretation of the Legislative Texts, 1994-2007; president of the Disciplinary Commission of the Roman Curia, Dec. 3, 1999; card. deacon, Oct. 21, 2003; titular church, St. Eugene.

Curial membership: Bishops, Causes of Saints, Doctrine of the Faith, Evangelization of Peoples (congregations); Apostolic Signatura (Tribunal); Laity (Council); Ecclesia Dei (commission).

Harvey, James M.: b. Oct. 20, 1949, Milwaukee, Wisc.; studied at De Sales Preparatory Seminary in Milwaukee, Saint Francis Seminary of Milwaukee, the Pontifical North American College and Pontifical Gregorian University in Rome, where he earned a doctorate in canon law; he also studied at the Pontifical Ecclesiastical Academy; ord. a priest, June 29, 1975, for the archdiocese of Milwaukee; entered the diplomatic service of the Holy See in 1980 and served in various posts; assessor of the Secretariat of State, July 22, 1997; elected titular bishop of Memfi and app. prefect of the Pontifical Household, Feb. 7, 1998; cons. a bishop, March 19, 1998, promoted to the rank of archbishop, Sept. 20, 2003; app. archpriest of the papal basilica of S. Paolo fuori le mura on Nov. 23, 2012; created cardinal deacon in the consistory of November 24, 2012, with the deaconry of S. Pio V a Villa Carpegna.

Curial membership: Causes of the Saints, Evangelization of Peoples (Congregations); Administration of the Patrimony of the Apostolic See (APSA).

Hummes, O.F.M., Cláudio: b. Aug. 8, 1934, Montenegro, Brazil; ord., priest for the Franciscans, Aug. 3, 1958; specialist in ecumenism; taught philosophy at the Franciscan seminary in Garibaldi, at the major seminary of Viamão and the Pontifical Catholic Univ. of Porto Alegre; adviser for ecumenical affairs to the National Bishops' Conference of Brazil; Provincial of Rio Grande do Sul, 1972-75; pres. of the Union of Latin American Conferences of Franciscans; app. coadj. bp. of Santo André, Mar. 22, 1975; cons., May 25, 1975; succeeded to see, Dec. 29, 1975; app. abp. of Fortaleza, July 21, 1996; Abp. of São Paulo, 1998-2006; card., Feb. 21, 2001; titular church, St. Anthony of Padua in Via Merulana; prefect of the Cong. for Clergy, 2006-2010.

Curial membership: Bishops, Doctrine of the Faith, Education, Evangelization, Sacraments (congregation); Cor Unum, Culture, Family, Interreligious Dialogue, Laity (councils); Latin America (commission).

Husar,* M.S.U., Lubomyr: b. Feb. 26, 1933, Lviv, Ukraine; family fled to Austria because of the war and then to the U.S.; ord. for the eparchy of Stamford for Ukrainians, U.S., Mar. 30, 1958; entered the Studite Monks after completing a doctorate in theology in Rome; superior of the Studion in Grottaferrata, Italy; ord. bp. Apr. 2, 1977; app. archimandrite of Studite Monks residing outside Ukraine; organized a new Studite monastery in Ternopil, Ukraine, 1994; elected exarch of Kyiv-Vyshorod, 1995; app. aux. bp. to major abp. of Lviv, 1996; elected major abp. of Lviv for Ukrainians, Jan. 25, 2001; title changed to major abp. of Kiev and Halych, Aug. 21, 2005; ret. Feb. 10, 2011; card., Feb. 21, 2001; titular church, Holy Wisdom in Via Boccea.

Curial membership: Oriental Churches (congregation); Christian Unity, Culture, Texts (councils).

Jaworski,* Marian: b. Aug. 21, 1926, Lwów, Poland

(modern Lviv, Ukraine); ord., June 25, 1950; taught at the Catholic Theological Academy of Warsaw and Pontifical Theological faculty of Kraków; first rector of the Pontifical Theological Academy, Kraków, 1981-87; app. titular bp. of Lambaesis and apostolic admin. of Lubaczów, May 21, 1984; cons., June 23, 1984; app. abp. of Lviv for Latins, Jan. 16, 1991; ret. Oct. 21, 2008; pres. of the Ukrainian Episcopal Conference, 1992; card. (*in pectore*), Feb. 21, 1998; titular church, St. Sixtus.

Curial membership: Clergy (congregation); Family (council).

Karlic,* Estanislao Esteban: b. Feb. 7, 1926; Oliva, Argentina; ord. Dec. 8, 1954; ord. titular bp. of Castro, Aug. 15, 1977; promoted to coadj. abp. and apostolic administrator of Paraná, Jan. 19, 1983; acceded to the see of Paraná, Apr. 1, 1986; pres. of the Episcopal Conference of Argentina, 1996-1999 and 1999-2002; ret., Apr. 29, 2003; card., Nov. 24, 2007; titular church, Santa Maria Addolorata on Piazza Buenos Aires.

Kasper,* Walter: b. Mar. 5, 1933, Heidenheim/Brenz, Germany; ord., Apr. 6, 1957; taught theology and later dean of the theological faculty in Münster and Tübingen; app. bp. of Rottenburg-Stuttgart, Apr. 17, 1989, cons., June 17, 1989; co-chair of the International Commission for Lutheran/Catholic Dialogue, 1994; sec. of the Pontifical Council for Promoting Christian Unity, June 1, 1999; pres. Pontifical Council for Promoting Christian Unity, 2001-2010; card. deacon, Feb. 21, 2001; deaconry, All Saints in Via Appia Nuova.

Curial membership: Doctrine of the Faith, Oriental Churches (congregations); Interreligious Dialogue (council); Apostolic Signatura (tribunal); Culture, Legislative Texts (council).

Keeler,* William Henry: b. Mar. 4, 1931, San Antonio, TX; ord., (Harrisburg diocese) July 17, 1955; secretary to Bp. Leech at Vatican II, named peritus by Pope John XXIII; ord. titular bp. of Ulcinium and aux. bp. of Harrisburg, Sept. 21, 1979; bp. of Harrisburg, 1983-1989, abp. of Baltimore, 1989-2007; card., Nov. 26, 1994; titular church, St. Mary of the Angels.

Curial membership: Oriental Churches (congregation); Christian Unity (council).

Kitbunchu,* Michael Michai: b. Jan. 25, 1929, Samphran, Thailand; ord., Dec. 20, 1959, in Rome; rector of metropolitan seminary in Bangkok, 1965-72; ord. abp. of Bangkok, June 3, 1973; card., Feb. 2, 1983, the first from Thailand; ret. May 14, 2009, titular church, St. Laurence in Panisperna.

Curial membership: Evangelization of Peoples (congregation).

Koch, Kurt: b. Mar. 15, 1950, Emmenbrücke, Switzerland; studied at the Univ. of Lucerne, Switzerland and Ludwig-Maximilians-Universität, Münich, Germany; dissertation on philosophy of history in Wolfhart Pannenberg; ord. June 20, 1982, held various academic posts; ord. bp. of Basel, Jan. 6, 1996; member of the International Catholic-Orthodox Theological Commission and a member of the International Catholic-Lutheran Dialogue Commission; pres. of the Swiss Bishops Conference, 2007-2010; app. pres. of the Pontifical Council for the Promotion of Christian Unity and promoted to the rank of abp., July 1, 2010; created card. deacon, Nov. 20, 2010; deaconry of Nostra Signora del Sacro Cuore in Circo Agonale.

Curial membership: Doctrine, Oriental Churches, Saints (congregations); Interreligious Dialogue (council).

Korec,* S.J., Ján Chryzostom: b. Jan. 22, 1924, Bosany, Slovakia; entered Society of Jesus in 1939; ord., Oct. 1, 1950;

ord. bp. secretly, Aug. 24, 1951; sentenced to 12 years in prison in 1960 for helping seminarians with their study and ordaining priests; paroled in 1968; appointed bp. of Nitra, Feb. 6, 1990; ret. June 9, 2005; card., June 28, 1991; titular church, Sts. Fabian and Venantius (a Villa Forelli).

Lajolo, Giovanni: b. Jan. 3, 1935, Novara, Italy; ord., Apr. 29, 1960; studied at the Pontifical Gregorian Univ. in Rome, earned a doctorate in canon law from the Univ. of Munich, and studied at Pontifical Ecclesiastical Academy; entered service of Secretariat of State in 1970 and served in nunciature of Germany and then Secretariat of State; named titular abp. of Cesariana and sec. of the Admin. of the Patrimony of the Apostolic See, Oct. 3, 1988; cons. Jan. 6, 1989; nuncio in Germany from 1995-2003; sec. of the secretariat of State for the Relations with the States, 2003-2006; pres. of the Pontifical Commission for the State of Vatican City and president of the Governatorato, June 22, 2006; card., Nov. 24, 2007; deaconry, Sta. Maria Liberatrice on Monte Testaccio.

Curial membership: Bishops (congregation); Culture (council), APSA, Signatura (offices).

Law,* Bernard F.: b. Nov. 4, 1931, Torreon, Mexico, the son of U.S. Air Force colonel; ord., (Jackson diocese), May 21, 1961; editor of Natchez-Jackson, MS, diocesan paper, 1963-68; director of NCCB Committee on Ecumenical and Interreligious Affairs, 1968-71; ord. bp. of Springfield-Cape Girardeau, MO, Dec. 5, 1973; abp. of Boston, Jan. 11, 1984; card., May 25, 1985; titular church, St. Susanna; res., Dec.13, 2002; archpriest of the patriarchal basilica of Sta. Maria Maggiore, Rome, 2004-2012.

Curial membership: Bishops, Clergy, Consecrated Life and Societies of Apostolic Life, Divine Worship and Sacraments, Education, Evangelization of Peoples, Oriental Churches; (congregations); Family (council).

Lehmann, Karl: b. May 16, 1936, Sigmaringen, Germany; ord., Oct. 10, 1963; earned doctorates in theology and philosophy; assistant to Fr. Karl Rahner at Univ. of Münster; taught dogmatic theology at the Johannes Gutenberg Univ., Mainz; member of the Central Committee of German Catholics and the Jaeger-Stählin Ecumenical Circle; taught at the Albert Ludwig Univ., Freiburg im Breisgau; member of the International Theological Commission; edited the official publication of the documents of the Joint Synod of the Dioceses in the Federal Republic of Germany, Synod of Würzburg, 1971-75; app. bp. of Mainz, June 21, 1983; cons., Oct. 2, 1983; pres. of the German Bishops' Conference; card., Feb. 21, 2001; titular church, St. Leo I.

Curial membership: Bishops, Oriental Churches (congregations); Christian Unity (council); APSA (office).

Levada, William J.: b. June 15, 1936, Long Beach, CA; studied at St. John's College, Camarillo, CA, and the Gregorian Univ. in Rome; ord., Dec. 20, 1961; ord. titular bp. of Capri and aux. bp. of Los Angeles, May 12, 1983; app. abp. of Portland, OR, July 3, 1986; coadj. abp. of San Francisco, Aug. 17, 1995; abp. of San Francisco, Dec. 27, 1995; ret. and app. Prefect for the Cong. for the Doctrine of the Faith, May 13, 2005; ret, July 2, 2012; card., Mar. 24, 2006; titular church, Diaconia di Sta. Maria in Dominica.

Curial membership: Bishops, Causes of Saints, Eastern Churches, Education, Evangelization (congregations); Christian Unity (council); Ecclesial Dei, Latin America (commissions); Synod of Bishop (special council).

López Rodríguez, Nicolás de Jesús: b. Oct. 31, 1936, Barranca, Dominican Republic; ord., Mar. 18, 1961; sent to Rome for advanced studies at Angelicum and Gregorian Univ.; served in various diocesan offices after returning to home diocese of La Vega; ord. first bp. of San Francisco de Macoris, Feb. 25, 1978; abp. of Santo Domingo and Military Ordinary for Dominican Republic, Nov. 15, 1981; card., June 28, 1991; titular church, St. Pius X (alla Balduina).

Curial membership: Clergy, Institutes of Consecrated Life and Societies of Apostolic Life (congregations); Social Communications (council); Latin America (commission).

Lourdusamy,* D. Simon: b. Feb. 5, 1924, Kalleri, India; ord., Dec. 21, 1951; ord. titular bp. of Sozusa and aux. of Bangalore, Aug. 22, 1962; titular abp. of Filippi and coadj. abp. of Bangalore, Nov. 9, 1964; abp. of Bangalore, 1968-71; assoc. secretary, 1971-73, and secretary, 1973-85, of Cong. for Evangelization of Peoples; card. deacon, May 25, 1985; deaconry, St. Mary of Grace; transferred to the order of card. priests, Jan. 29, 1996; prefect of Cong. for Oriental Churches, 1985-91.

Lozano Barragán,* Javier: b. Jan. 26, 1933, Toluca, Mexico; ord. Oct. 30, 1955; pres. of the Mexican Theological Society and dir. of the Institute of Pastoral Theology of the Episcopal Conference of Latin America (CELAM); ord. titular bp. of Tinisia di Numidia and aux. bp. of Mexico, Aug. 15, 1979; bp. of Zacatecas, 1984-96; pres. of Pontifical Council for Health Care Workers, 1996-2009; named abp. 1997; card. deacon, Oct. 21, 2003, deaconry, St. Michael the Archangel. Pres. emeritus of Pontifical Council for Health Care Workers.

Curial membership: Bishops, Causes of Saints, Evangelization (congregations); Eucharistic Congresses, Latin America (commissions).

McCarrick,* Theodore E.: b. July 7, 1930, New York, NY; ord., May 31, 1958; dean of students Catholic Univ. of America, 1961-63; pres., Catholic Univ. of Puerto Rico, 1965-69; secretary to Card. Cooke, 1970; ord. titular bp. of Rusubisir and aux. bp. of New York, June 29, 1977; app. first bp. of Metuchen, NJ, Nov. 19, 1981, installed, Jan. 31, 1982; app. abp. of Newark, June 3, 1986, installed, July 25, 1986; abp. of Washington, Nov. 21, 2000; ins., Jan. 3, 2001, card. priest, Feb. 21, 2001; titular church, Sts. Nereus and Achilleus; ret. May 16, 2006.

Curial membership: Christian Unity (council); APSA (office).

Macharski,* Franciszek: b. May 20, 1927, Kraków, Poland; ord., Apr. 2, 1950; engaged in pastoral work, 1950-56; abp. of Kraków, 1979-2005; card., June 30, 1979; titular church, St. John at the Latin Gate. Abp. emeritus of Kraków.

Curial membership: Secretariat of State (second sec tion); Bishops, Clergy, Consecrated Life and Societies of Apostolic Life, Education, Evangelization of Peoples (congregations).

Mahony, Roger M.: b. Feb. 27, 1936, Hollywood, CA; ord., (Fresno diocese) May 1, 1962; ord. titular bp. of Tamascani and aux. bp. of Fresno, Mar. 19,1975; bp. of Stockton, Feb. 15, 1980, installed, Apr. 25, 1980; abp. of Los Angeles, July 16, 1985, installed, Sept. 5, 1985; ret. Mar. 1, 2011; card., June 28, 1991; titular church, Four Crowned Saints.

Curial membership: Eastern Churches (congregation), Social Communications (council); Economic Affairs (office).

Maida,* Adam Joseph: b. Mar. 18, 1930, East Vandergrift, PA; ord., (Pittsburgh diocese), May 26, 1956; ord. bp. of Green Bay, Jan. 25, 1984; app. abp. of Detroit, Apr. 28, 1990, installed, June 12, 1990; ret. Jan. 5, 2009; card., Nov. 26, 1994; titular church, Sts. Vitalis, Valeria, Gervase and Protase.

Curial membership: Education (congregation); Migrants and Itinerant Peoples (council); Institute for Works of Religion (commission).

Majella Agnelo,* Geraldo: b. Oct. 19, 1933, Juiz de Fora, Brazil; ord. June 29, 1957; taught at the seminary of Aparecida, Immaculate Conception Seminary, and Pius XI Theological Institute; rector of Our Lady of the Assumption Seminary; bp. of Toledo, May 5, 1978; cons., Aug. 6, 1978; app. abp. of Londrina, Oct. 27, 1982; pres. of the Brazilian Bishops' Liturgical Commission; app. sec. of the Cong. For Divine Worship and the Discipline of Sacraments, Sept. 16, 1991; app. abp. of São Salvador da Bahia, Jan. 13, 1999; card., Feb. 21, 2001; titular church, St. Gregory the Great in Magliana Nuova.

Curial membership: Pastoral Care of Migrants and Itinerant People (council); Cultural Heritage of the Church (commission).

Marchisano,* Francesco: b. June 25, 1929, Racconigi, Italy; ord. June 29, 1952; ord. titular bp. of Populonia, Jan. 6, 1989; secr. of the Pontifical Commission for the Preservation of the Artistic and Cultural Patrimony of the Church, 1988-91; pres. of the Pontifical Commission of Sacred Archeology, 1991; pres. of the Pontifical Commission for the Cultural Patrimony of the Church, 1993-2003; named abp., 1994; archpriest of the Patriarchal Vatican Basilica, vicar general for the State of Vatican City, and president of the Fabric of St. Peter, 2002-2006; pres. of the Permanent Commission for the Care of the Historical and Artistic Monuments of the Holy See, 2003-2009; card. deacon, Oct. 21, 2003; deaconry, St. Lucy of Gonfalone; pres. of the Labor Office of the Apostolic See, 2005-2009. Archpriest emeritus of the Patriarchal Vatican Basilica, vicar general emeritus for the State of Vatican City, and pres. emeritus of the Labor Office of the Apostolic See; pres. emeritus of the Fabric of St. Peter.

Curial membership: Education (congregation); Christian Unity (council).

Martínez Sistach, Lluís: b. Apr. 29, 1937, Barcelona, Spain; ord. Sept. 17, 1961; doctorate in utroque iure, both canon and civil law, from the Pontifical Lateran Univ., Rome, in 1967; professor of canon law at the Theological Faculty of Catalonia and at the Superior Institute of Religious Sciences of Barcelona, 1975-1987; cons. titular bp. of Aliezira and aux. bp. of Barcelona, Dec. 27, 1987; bp. of Tortosa, 1991-1997; abp. of Tarragona, 1997-2004; app. abp. of Barcelona, June 15, 2004; card., Nov. 24, 2007; titular church, St. Sebastian in the Catacombs.

Curial membership: Laity, Texts (councils); Signatura (tribunal); Economic Affairs (prefecture).

Martínez Somalo,* Eduardo: b. Mar. 31, 1927, Baños de Rio Tobia, Spain; ord., Mar. 19, 1950; ord. titular bp. of Tagora with personal title of abp., Dec. 13, 1975; in secretariat of state from 1956; substitute (assistant) secretary of state, 1979-88; card. deacon, June 28, 1988; deaconry, Most Holy Name of Jesus (raised pro hac vice to presbyteral title); promoted to card. priest, Jan. 9, 1999; prefect of Cong. for Divine Worship and Sacraments, 1988-92. Prefect of Cong. for Institutes of Consecrated Life and Societies of Apostolic Life, 1992-2004; Chamberlain (Camerlengo) of the Holy Roman Church, 1993-2007; Protodeacon, 1996-99.

Curial membership: Secretariat of State (second sec tion); Bishops, Causes of Saints, Clergy, Divine Worship and Sacraments, Education, Evangelization of Peoples (congregations); Legislative Texts (council); Latin America, Institute for Works of Religion (commissions).

Martino,* Renato: b. Nov. 23, 1932, Salerno, Italy; ord.

June 27, 1957; entered the diplomatic service of the Holy See, July 1, 1962; served in various diplomatic postings, 1962-80; ord. titular abp. of Segerme, Dec. 14, 1980; pro-nuncio in Thailand and apostolic delegate in Laos, Malaysia and Singapore, 1980-86; permanent observer of the Holy See to the U.N., 1986-2002; pres. of the Pontifical Council Justice and Peace, 2002-2006; card. deacon, Oct. 21, 2003, titular church, St. Francis of Paola ai Monti; Pres. of the Pontifical for Council for Pastoral Care of Migrants and Itinerants, Mar. 11, 2006.

Curial membership: Evangelization of Peoples (congregation); "Cor Unum" (council); Vatican City State (commission); Admin. of the Patrimony of the Apostolic See (APSA).

Marx, Reinhard: b. Sept. 21, 1953, Geseke, Germany; studied at the Theological Faculty of Paderborn, Institut Catholique de Paris, Ruhr-Universität Bochum, and Westfälische Wilhelms-Universität Münster; ord. June 2, 1979; ord. titular bp. of Pedena and auxiliary bp. of Paderborn, Sept. 21, 1996; app. bp. of Trier, Dec. 20, 2001; app. abp. of München und Freising, Nov. 30, 2007; he is the author of a number of books and is ranked among the foremost European social scientists; created card. priest, Nov. 20, 2010; titular church of S. Corbiniano.

Curial membership: Education, Oriental Churches (congregations); Justice (council).

Mazombwe,* Medardo Joseph: b. Sept. 24, 1931, Chundamira, Northern Rhodesia (modern Zambia); studied at St. Mary's Seminar in Kasina, Nyasaland (modern Malawi), the Regional Major Seminary of Kachebere, Nyasaland, Lovanium Univ., Leopoldville (modern Kinshasa), and Univ. of Lusaka; ord. Sept. 4, 1960; ord. bp. of Chipata, Feb. 7, 1971; chair of the regional conferences under the Association of Member Episcopal Conferences in Eastern Africa (A.M.E.C.E.A.), 1979-1986; app. abp. of Lusaka, Nov. 30 1996; res. Oct. 28, 2006; created card. priest, Nov. 20, 2010; titular church of S. Emerenziana a Tor Fiorenza.

Curial membership: Evangelization (congregation); Cor Unum (council).

Medina Estévez,* Jorge Arturo: b. Dec. 23, 1926, Santiago, Chile; ord., June 12, 1954; ord. abp., Jan. 6, 1985, Santiago, Chile; appointed pro-Prefect, Cong. for Divine Worship and the Discipline of the Sacraments, 1996-98; prefect of the Cong. for Divine Worship and the Discipline of the Sacraments, 1998-2002; card. deacon, Feb. 21, 1998; card. priest, Mar. 2, 2008; titular church, St. Sabas; Protodeacon, 2005-2007.

Meisner, Joachim: b. Dec. 25, 1933, Breslau, Silesia, Germany (present-day Wroclaw, Poland); ord., Dec. 22, 1962; regional director of Caritas; ord. titular bp. of Vina and aux. of apostolic administration of Erfurt-Meiningen, E. Germany, May 17, 1975; bp. of Berlin, 1980-88; card., Feb. 2, 1983; titular church, St. Prudenziana. Abp. of Cologne, Dec. 20, 1988.

Curial membership: Bishops, Clergy, Divine Worship and Sacraments (congregations); Legislative Texts (council); Economic Affairs of Holy See (office).

Mejía,* Jorge María: b. Jan. 31, 1923, Buenos Aires, Argentina; ord., Sept. 22, 1945; *peritus* at Second Vatican Council; sec. of CELAM's Department of Ecumenism, 1967-77; sec. of Pontifical Commission for Religious Relations with Jews, 1977-86; vice-president of the Pontifical Commission Justice and Peace and titular bp. of Apollonia, Apr. 12, 1986; sec. of the Cong. for Bishops and titular abp., Mar. 1994; Archivist and Librarian of the Holy

Roman Church, 1998-2003; cardinal deacon, Feb. 21, 2001; deaconry, St. Jerome della Carità.

Monsengwo Pasinya, Laurent: b. Oct. 7, 1939, Mongobele, Congo (modern Democratic Republic of Congo); he is a member of the royal lines of Basakata; studied at the Major Seminary of Kabwe, Pontifical Urban Univ., Pontifical Biblical Institute, Rome, and the Pontifical Biblical Institute in Jerusalem; he was the first African to obtain a doctorate in biblical studies; ord. Dec. 21, 1963; ord. titular bishop of Acque nuove di Proconsulare and aux. bp. of Inongo, May 4, 1980; transferred to aux. bp. of Kisangani, Apr. 7, 1981; app. abp. of Kisangani, Sept. 1, 1988, and was noted for his efforts to help guide his country during a civil war and the dictatorship of Mobutu Sese Seko into a democracy; app. abp. of Kinshasa, Dec. 2007; created card. priest, Nov. 20, 2010; titular church of S. Maria Regina Pacis in Ostra mare.

Curial membership: Education (congregation); Justice (council).

Monteiro de Castro, Manuel: b. Mar. 29, 1938, Santa Eufémia de Prazins, Guimarães, Portugal; earned a doctorate in canon law at the Pontifical Gregorian Univ., Rome, and a diploma in diplomacy from the Pontifical Ecclesiastical Academy, Rome; ord. priest, July 9, 1961; entered the diplomatic service of the Holy See in 1967 and served in Panama, Guatemala, Vietnam and Cambodia, Australia, Mexico, and Belgium; ord. titular abp. of Benevento and app. pro-nuncio to Trinidad and Tobago, Bahamas, Barbados, Belize, Dominica, Jamaica, Grenada, St. Lucia; and apostolic delegate in The Antilles, Feb. 16, 1985; app. nuncio to El Salvador and Honduras, Aug. 21, 1990; app. nuncio to South Africa, Nambia and Swaziland, Feb. 2, 1998 and nuncio to Lesotho, Mar. 7, 1998; app. nuncio to Spain and Andorra, Mar. 1, 2000; permanent observer of the Holy See at the World Tourism Organization, 1997-2009; app. sec. of the Congregation for Bishops, July 3, 2009 and sec. of the College of Cardinals, Oct. 21, 2009; app. penitentiary major on Jan. 5, 2012; cardinal Feb. 18, 2012 with the deaconry of S. Domenico di Guzman.

Curial membership: Bishops, Saints (congregations); Migrants (council).

Monterisi, Francesco: b. May 28, 1934, Barletta, Italy; studied at the Pontifical Major Seminary and the Pontifical Lateran Univ., Rome; later studied diplomacy at the Pontifical Ecclesiastical Academy; ord. Mar. 16, 1957 and entered the diplomatic service of the Holy See in 1964; served in various diplomatic posts and was named titular abp. of Alba marittima and nuncio in South Korea, Dec. 24, 1982; ord. Jan. 6, 1983; delegate for the pontifical representations on Aug. 28, 1990; nuncio to Bosnia-Herzegovina 1993-1998; app. sec. of the Cong. for Bishops and of the College of Cardinals, Mar. 7, 1998; sec. of the 2005 conclave; app. archpriest of the papal basilica of S. Paolo fouri le Mura, July 3, 2009; created cardinal deacon, Nov. 20, 2010; deaconry of S. Paolo alla Regola.

Curial membership: Oriental Churches, Saints (congregation); Latin America (commission).

Muresan,* Lucian: b. May 23, 1931, village of Ferneziu, eparchy of Maramures, Romania; endured severe persecution under the Romanina Communist regime and worked in various jobs as religion was banned by the government; ord. priest, Dec. 19, 1964, and served in secret; elected eparch of Maramures of the Romanians, Mar. 14, 1990, and cons., May 27, 1990; opened the Baia Mare Theological Institute, 1990-1991; app. abp. of Fagaras si Alba Iulia of the Romanians, July 4, 1994; welcomed Pope John Paul II during his visit to Romania in 1999; promoted to the rank of archbishop major on Dec. 16, 2005; cardinal Feb. 18, 2012, with the title of S. Atanasio.

Curial membership: Oriental Churches (congregation).

Murphy-O'Connor,* Cormac: b. Aug. 24, 1932, Reading, Great Britain; ord., Oct. 28, 1956; dir. of vocations and secretary to the bp.; rector of the Venerable English College, Rome, 1971-77; app. bp. of Arundel and Brighton, Nov. 17, 1977; cons., Dec. 21, 1977; co-chairman of the Anglican-Roman Catholic International Commission (ARCIC), 1982-2000; chairman of several committees of the Bishop's Conference of England and Wales; app. abp. of Westminster, Feb. 15, 2000; ret. Apr. 3, 2009; card., Feb. 21, 2001; titular church, St. Mary sopra Minerva.

Naguib, Antonios: b. Mar. 18, 1935, Samalout, eparchy of Minya of the Copts, Egypt; studied Pontifical Urban College and the Pontifical Biblical Institute, Rome; ord. Oct. 30, 1960 and ord. bp. of Minya of the Copts, Sept. 9, 1977; elected patriarch of Alexandria of the Copts, Mar. 30, 2006 and granted ecclesiastical communio, Apr. 7, 2006; pres. of the Synod of the Coptic-Catholic Church in Egypt and president of the Catholic Bishops Conference of Egypt; created card. patriarch, Nov. 20, 2010.

Curial membership: Oriental Churches (congregation); Migrants (council).

Napier, O.F.M., Wilfrid Fox: b. Mar. 8, 1941, Swartberg, South Africa; ord., for the Franciscans, July 25, 1970; app. apostolic admin. of Kokstad, 1978; app. bp. of Kokstad, Nov. 29, 1980; cons., Feb. 28, 1981; deeply involved in the mediation and negotiations surrounding the ending of apartheid in South Africa and subsequent South African politics; pres. of the Southern African Catholic Bishops' Conference, 1987-94; app. abp. of Durban, May 29, 1992; apostolic admin. sede vacante et ad nutum Sanctae Sedis of Umzimkulu, 1994; card., Feb. 21, 2001; titular church, St. Francis of Assisi in Acilia.

Curial membership: Evangelization, Consecrated Life (congregations); Culture (council); Health Care (commission); Economic Affairs (office).

Nicora, Attilio: b. Mar. 16, 1937, Varese, Italy; ord. June 27, 1964; ord. titular bp. of Fornos minore and aux. bp. of Milan, May 28, 1977; bp. of Verona, 1992-2002; pres. of the Administration of the Patrimony of the Apostolic See (APSA) and abp., Sept. 2002; card. deacon, Oct. 21, 2003; deaconry, St. Philip Neri in Eurosia. Pres. of the Administration of the Patrimony of the Apostolic See.

Curial membership: Secretariat of State (second section), Bishops, Evangelization of Peoples (congregation); Apostolic Signatura (tribunal); Texts (council); Vatican City, Works of Religion (commission).

Njue, John: b. 1944, Embu, Kenya; ord. Jan. 6, 1973; after studies in Rome, he served as a professor of philosophy and rector at the National Seminary of Bungoma, diocese of Kakmega, 1975; cons. the first bp. of Embu, Sept. 20, 1986; app. coadj. abp. of Nyeri, Jan. 23, 2002; app. abp. of Nairobi, Oct. 6, 2007; card., Nov. 24, 2007; titular church, Most Precious Blood of Our Lord Jesus Christ.

Curial Membership: Clergy, Evangelization (congregation).

Nycz, Kazimierz: b. Feb. 1, 1950, Stara Wies, Poland; studied at the Major Seminary of Kraków, Pontifical Academy of Theology of Kraków, and the Catholic University of Lublin; ord., May 20, 1973; ord. titular bp. of Villa del re and auxiliary bp. of Kraków, June 4, 1988; app. bp. of Koszalin-Kołobrzeg, June 9, 2004; app. abp. of Warsaw, Mar. 3, 2007; created cardinal priest, Nov. 20, 2010; titular church of Ss.

Silvestro e Martino ai Monti.

Curial membership: Clergy, Divine Worship (congregation).

Obando Bravo,* S.D.B., Miguel: b. Feb. 2, 1926, La Libertad, Nicaragua; ord., Aug. 10, 1958; ord. titular bp. of Puzia di Bizacena and aux. of Matagalpa, Mar. 31, 1968; abp. emeritus of Managua, 1970-2005; card., May 25, 1985; titular church, St. John the Evangelist (a Spinaceta).

Curial membership: Clergy, Consecrated Life and Societies of Apostolic Life, Divine Worship and Sacraments, (congregations).

O'Brien, Edwin F.: b. Apr. 8, 1939, Bronx, NY; earned a doctorate in Sacred Theology at the Pontifical Univ. of St. Thomas Aquinas, Rome; ord. priest for New York archdio., May 29, 1965; served as a military chaplain; rector of the Pontifical North American College, Rome, 1990-1994; ord. titular bp. of Tizica and aux. bp. of New York, Mar. 25, 1996; app. coadjutor abp. for Military Services Archdiocese, Apr. 8, 1997; abp. of Military Services Archdiocese, Aug. 12, 1997; app. abp. of Baltimore, July 12, 2007; app. grand master of the Equestrian Order of the Holy Sepulchre of Jerusalem, Aug. 29, 2011; cardinal, Feb. 18, 2012, with the deaconry of S. Sebastiano al Palatino.

Curial membership: Education, Oriental Churches (congregations); "Cor Unum" (council)

O'Brien, Keith Michael Patrick: b. Mar. 17, 1938, Ballycastle, Ireland; ord. Apr. 3, 1965; ord. abp. of St. Andrews and Edinburgh, May 30, 1985; card., Oct. 21, 2003; titular church, Sts. Joachim and Anne at the Tuscolano; res., Feb. 2013.

Curial membership: Migrants and Itinerant People, Social Communications (councils).

Okogie, Anthony Olubunmi: b. June 16, 1935, Lagos, Nigeria; ord. Dec. 11, 1966; ord. titular bp. of Mascula, June 5, 1971; abp. of Lagos, Apr. 13, 1973; card., Oct. 21, 2003; titular church, Blessed Virgin Mary of Mt. Carmel of Mostacciano.

Curial membership: Evangelization of Peoples (congregation); Social Communications (council).

O'Malley, O.F.M. Cap., Sean P.: b. June 29, 1944, Lakewood, OH; studied at St. Fidelis Seminary, Capuchin College, and Catholic Univ., Washington, DC; ord. Aug. 29, 1970; episcopal vicar of priests serving Spanish speaking in Washington archdio., 1974-84; executive director of Spanish Catholic Center, Washington from 1973; ord. coadj. bp. of St. Thomas, Virgin Islands, Aug. 2, 1984; bp. of St. Thomas, Oct. 16, 1985; app. bp. of Fall River, June 16, 1992; app. bp. of Palm Beach, Sept. 3, 2002; app. abp. of Boston, July 1, 2003; card., Mar. 24, 2006; titular church, Sta. Maria della Vittoria.

Curial membership: Clergy; Consecrated Life (congregation).

Onaiyekan, John Olorunfemi: b. Jan. 29, 1944, Kabba, Nigeria; studied at Ss. Peter and Paul Major Seminary, in Bodija, Ibadan, Pontifical Urbanian University, in Rome, and Pontifical Biblical Institute, Rome; earned a doctorate in 1976 from the Urbanian University; ord. a priest, Aug. 3, 1969; app. titular bp. of Tunusuda and aux. bp. of Ilorin, Sept. 10, 1982; cons. on Jan. 6, 1983; app. bp. of Ilorin, Oct. 20, 1984; app. coadjutor of Abuja, July 7, 1990; acceded to the see of Abuja, Sept. 28, 1992; promoted to metropolitan archbishop of Abuja, March 26, 1995; in 2012, he was a nominee for the Nobel Peace Prize, with the Muslim Sultan of Sokoto, Alhaji Muhammed Sa'ad Abubakar III; created cardinal priest in the consistory of Nov. 24, 2012, with the title of S. Saturnino.

Curial membership: Doctrine of the Faith (congregation), Family (council).

Ortega y Alamino, Jaime Lucas: b. Oct. 18, 1936, Jagüey Grande, Cuba; ord., Aug. 2, 1964 detained in work camps (UMAP), 1966-67; parish priest; ord. bp. of Pinar del Rio, Jan. 14, 1979; app. abp. of Havana, Nov. 20, 1981; card., Nov. 26, 1994; titular church, Sts. Aquila and Priscilla.

Curial membership: Clergy (congregation); Health Care Workers (council); Latin America (commission).

Ouellet, P.S.S., Marc: b. June 8, 1944, Lamotte, Canada; ord. May 25, 1968; entered the Society of Priests of Saint-Sulpice, 1972; rector and prof., Major Seminary of Montréal, 1989-1994 and Major Seminary of Edmonton, 1994-1997; prof., John Paul II Institute of Studies on Marriage and the Family, 1997-2001; ord. titular bp. of Agropoli, Mar. 19, 2001; sec. of the Pont. Council for the Promotion of Christian Unity, 2001-2002; abp. of Québec, Nov. 15, 2002-June 30, 2010; card., Oct. 21, 2003; titular church, St. Mary in Traspontina; prefect of the Cong. of Bishops and pres. of the Pont. Comm. for Latin America, June 30, 2010.

Curial membership: Clergy, Education, Oriental Churches, Sacraments (congregation); Culture, Legislative Texts (councils); Latin America, Eucharistic Congresses (commissions); Economic Affairs (office).

Panafieu,* Bernard: b. Jan. 26, 1931, Châtellerault, France; ord. Apr. 22, 1956; ord. titular bp. of Tibili, June 9, 1974, and aux. bp. of Annecy, 1974-78; abp. of Aix, 1978-94; coadj. abp. of Marseilles, Aug. 24, 1994; abp. of Marseilles, 1995-2006; metropolitan abp. when Marseille was elevated to that rank, Dec. 16, 2002; card., Oct. 21, 2003; titular church, St. Gregory Barbarigo alle Tre Fontane.

Curial membership: Interreligious Dialogue, Justice and Peace (councils).

Paskai,* O.F.M., László: b. May 8, 1927, Szeged, Hungary; ord., Mar. 3, 1951; ord., titular bp. of Bavagaliana and apostolic administrator of Veszprem, Apr. 5, 1978; bp. of Veszprem, Mar. 31, 1979; coadj. abp. of Kalocsa, Apr. 5, 1982; abp. of Esztergom (renamed Esztergom–Budapest, 1993), 1987-2002; card., June 28, 1988; titular church, St. Theresa (al Corso d'Italia).

Curial membership: Consecrated Life and Societies of Apostolic Life, Oriental Churches (congregations).

Patabendige Don, Albert Malcolm Ranjith: b. Nov. 15, 1947, Polgahawela, Sri Lanka; studied at the National Seminary in Kandy, Pontifical Urban Univ. and the Pontifical Biblical Institute, Rome, and the Hebrew Univ. of Jerusalem; ord. June 29, 1975; ord. titular bp. of Cabarsussi and aux. of Colombo, Aug. 31, 1991; app. nuncio to Indonesia and East Timor and transferred to the titular see of Umbriatica, Apr. 29, 2004; app. sec. of the Cong. for Divine Worship and the Discipline of the Sacraments, Dec. 10, 2005; app. abp. of Colombo, June 16, 2009; created card. priest, Nov. 20, 2010; titular church of S. Lorenzo in Lucina.

Curial membership: Divine Worship, Evangelization (congregations)

Pell, George: b. Apr. 8, 1941, Ballarat, Australia; ord. Dec. 16, 1966; episcopal vicar for Education, diocese of Ballarat, 1973-1984; rector of Corpus Christi College, the Provincial Seminary for Victoria and Tasmania, 1985-1987; ord. titular bp. of Scala, May 21, 1987; aux. bp. of Melbourne, 1987-96; abp. of Melbourne, 1996-2001; abp. of Sydney, Mar. 26, 2001; grand prior of the Equestrian Order of the Holy Sepulchre of Jerusalem, Australian Lieutenancy, Southern, 1998; card., Oct. 21, 2003; titular church, St. Mary Dominic Mazzarello.

Curial membership: Sacraments (congregation); Family, Justice and Peace (councils).

Pengo, Polycarp: b. Aug. 5, 1944, Mwayze, Tanzania; ord., Aug. 5, 1971; taught moral theology at the major seminary in Kipalapala, Tanzania, 1977; rector of the major seminary in Segerea, 1978-83; ord. bp. of Nachingwea, Jan. 6, 1984; bp. of Tunduru-Masasi 1986-90; coadj. abp. of Dar-es-Salaam, Jan. 22, 1990; abp. of Dar-es-Salaam, July 22, 1992, in succession to Laurean Card. Rugambwa; card., Feb. 21, 1998; titular church, Our Lady of La Salette.

Curial membership: Clergy, Doctrine of the Faith, Evangelization of Peoples (congregation); Culture, Family, Interreligious Dialogue (council).

Pham Minh Man, Jean Baptiste: b. 1934, Ca Mau, Vietnam; ord. May 25, 1965; ord. coadj. bp. of My Tho, Aug. 11, 1993; abp. of Thàn-Phô Hô Chi Minh (Hô Chi Minh City), Mar. 1, 1998; card., Oct. 21, 2003; titular church, St. Justin.

Curial membership: Sacraments, Evangelization of Peoples (congregation).

Piacenza, Mauro: b. Sept. 15, 1944, Genoa, Italy; studied at the Major Archiepiscopal Seminary of Genoa and the Pontifical Lateran Univ.; ord. Dec. 21, 1969; professor of canon law and theology and entered Roman Curia in 1990; app. titular bp. of Vittoriana and pres. of the Pontifical Commission for the Cultural Heritage of the Church, Oct. 13, 2003; ord. Nov. 15, 2003; app. pres. of the Pontifical Commission for Sacred Archeology, Aug. 28, 2004; app. sec. of the Cong. for the Clergy and promoted to the rank of abp., May 7, 2007; app. prefect of the Cong. for the Clergy on Oct. 7, 2010; card. deacon, Nov. 20, 2010; deaconry of S. Paolo alle Tre Fontane.

Curial membership: Clergy, Divine Worship, Education (congregations); Social Communications (council)

Piovanelli,* Silvano: b. Feb. 21, 1924, Ronta di Mugello, Italy; ord., July 13, 1947; ord. titular bp. of Tubune di Mauretania and aux. of Florence, June 24, 1982; abp. of Florence, 1983-2001; card., May 25, 1985; titular church, St. Mary of Graces (Via Trionfale).

Poletto,* Severino: b. Mar. 18, 1933, Salgareda (Treviso), Italy; ord., June 29, 1957; pref. of discipline at the diocesan seminary and vocation director; founded Diocesan Centre for Family Ministry, 1973; coordinated city mission for the 500th anniversary of the foundation of the diocese of Casale Monferrato; app. coadj. bp. of Fossano, Apr. 3, 1980; cons., May 17, 1980; succeeded to see on Oct. 29, 1980; app. bp. of Asti, Mar. 16, 1989; app. abp. of Turin, June 19, 1999; card., Feb. 21, 2001; titular church, St. Joseph in Via Trionfale.

Curial membership: Economic Affairs of the Holy See (office).

Policarpo,* José Da Cruz: b. Feb. 26, 1936, Alvorninha, Portugal; ord., priest, Aug. 15, 1961; dir. of the seminary in Penafirme, rector of the seminary in Olivais and dean of the Theological Faculty of the Portuguese Catholic Univ.; served two terms as rector of the Portuguese Catholic Univ., 1988-96; app. titular bp. of Caliabria and aux. bp. of Lisbon, May 26, 1978; cons., June 29, 1978; app. coadj. abp. of Lisbon, Mar. 5, 1997; succeeded as patriarch of Lisbon, Mar. 24, 1998; grand chancellor of the Portuguese Catholic Univ., pres. of the Portuguese Episcopal Conference; card., Feb. 21, 2001; titular church, St. Anthony in Campo Formio.

Curial membership: Education (congregation), Culture, Laity (councils).

Poupard,* Paul: b. Aug. 30, 1930, Bouzille, France; ord., Dec. 18, 1954; ord. titular bp. of Usula and aux.

of Paris, Apr. 6, 1979; title of abp. and pro-president of the Secretariat for Non-Believers, 1980; card. deacon, May 25, 1985; transferred to order of card. priests, Jan. 29, 1996; titular church, St. Praxedes; president of Pontifical Council for Dialogue with Non-Believers, 1985-93. President of Pontifical Council for Culture, 1988; President of the Pontifical Council for Interreligious Dialogue, 2006-2007.

Curial membership: Divine Worship and Sacraments, Education, Evangelization of Peoples (congregations); Christian Unity, Interreligious Dialogue, Laity (council).

Pujats,* Janis: b. Nov. 14, 1930, the Rezekne district of Latvia; ord., Mar. 29, 1951; taught art history and liturgy at the Catholic Theological Seminary, Riga; vicar general in the Metropolitan Curia, Riga, 1979-84; declared persona non grata by the KGB, 1984; abp. of Riga, 1991-2010; pres. of the Latvian Bishops' Conference; card. (in pectore), Feb. 21, 1998, titular church, St. Sylvia.

Puljic, Vinko: b. Sept. 8, 1945, Prijecani, Bosnia–Herzegovina; ord., June 29, 1970; spiritual director of minor seminary of Zadar, 1978-87; parish priest; app. vice-rector of Sarajevo major seminary, 1990; ord. abp. of Vrhbosna (Sarajevo), Jan. 6, 1991, in Rome; card., Nov. 26, 1994; titular church, St. Clare in Vigna Clara.

Curial membership: Evangelization of Peoples (congregation); Interreligious Dialogue (council).

Rai, O.M.M., Béchara Boutros: b. Feb. 25, 1940, Himlaya, Lebanon; studied at the Pontifical Lateran University, in Rome, where he obtained a licentiate in theology and a doctorate in canon law; entered the Maronite Order of the Blessed Virgin Mary (Mariamita) (O.M.M.); ord. a priest, Sept. 3, 1967; elected patriarchal vicar and titular bishop of Cesarea di Filippo by the Maronite Patriarchal Synod, May 2, 1986; app. eparch of Jbeil (Byblos), June 9, 1990; elected patriarch of Antioch of the Maronites, March 15, 2011; confirmed by Pope Benedict XVI on March 25, 2011; created cardinal patriarch in the consistory of Nov. 24, 2012.

Curial membership: Oriental Churches (congregation); Supreme Tribunal of the Apostolic Signatura; Migrants and Itinerants, Social Communications (councils).

Ravasi, Gianfranco: b. Oct. 18, 1942, Merate, Italy; studied at the Major Seminary of Milan, Pontifical Gregorian Univ. and Pontifical Biblical Institute; ord. June 28, 1966, and served as a professor of Scripture; prefect of the Ambrosian Library, Milan, 1989-2007; app. member of the Pontifical Biblical Commission, 1995; wrote the meditations for the Way of the Cross on Good Friday 2007; app. titular abp. of Villamagna di Proconsolare and president of the Pontifical Council of Culture and president of the Pontifical Commission for the Cultural Patrimony of the Church, and of the Pontifical Commission for Sacred Archeology, Sept. 3, 2007; ord. Sept. 29, 2007; prolific author and renowned biblical scholar; created card. deacon, Nov. 20, 2010; deaconry of S. Giorgio in Velabro.

Curial membership: Education (congregation); Interreligious Dialogue, New Evangelization (councils).

Re, Giovanni Battista: b. Jan. 30, 1934, Borno (Brescia), Italy; ord., Mar. 3, 1957; earned doctorate in canon law and taught in the Brescia Seminary; entered Holy See diplomatic service, served in Panama and Iran; recalled for service in Secretariat of State; sec. for Cong. for Bishops, 1987; titular abp., Nov. 7, 1987; sostituto for Secretariat of State, 1989; prefect of the Cong. of Bishops and pres. of the Pont. Comm. for Latin America, 2000-2010; card., Feb. 21, 2001; titular church, Twelve Holy Apostles;

transferred to order of card. bishops as titular bp. of suburbicarian see of Sabina-Poggio Mirteto.

Curial membership: Secretariat of State (second section); Doctrine of the Faith, Eastern Churches, Evangelization (congregations); Texts (council); Vatican City State (commission); APSA (office).

Ricard, Jean-Pierre: b. Sept. 26, 1944, Marseille, France; studied at Institut Catholique in Paris; ord. Oct. 5, 1968; app. titular bp. of Pulcheriopoli and aux. bp. of Grenoble, Apr. 17, 1993; app. coadj. bp. of Montpellier, July 4, 1996; bp. of Montpellier, Sept. 6, 1996; promoted close relations with the Church in Africa and visited Peru in 1999 to meet a fidei donum priest of the diocese; visited Lebanon in 2000; major supporter of dialogue with the Jews; elected pres. of the Episcopal Conference of France, Nov. 6, 2001; app. abp. of Bordeaux, Dec. 21, 2001; in 2003 authored book, *Sept défis pour l'Eglise* (*Seven Challenges for the Church*); card., Mar. 24, 2006; titular church, Sant'Agostino.

Curial membership: Doctrine of the Faith, Sacraments (congregations); Culture (council); Ecclesia dei (commission).

Rigali, Justin Francis: b. Apr. 19, 1935, Los Angeles, CA; educ. St. John's Seminary (Camarillo, CA); ord. priest (Los Angeles*), Apr. 25, 1961; in Vatican diplomatic service from 1964; ord. titular abp. of Bolsena, Sept. 14, 1985, by Pope John Paul II; president of the Pontifical Ecclesiastical Academy, 1985-89; secretary of Cong. for Bps., 1989-94; and the College of Cardinals, 1990-94; app. abp. of St. Louis, Jan. 25, 1994, inst., Mar. 16, 1994; app. abp. of Philadelphia, July 15, 2003; ret. July 19, 2011; card., Oct. 21, 2003; titular church, St. Prisca.

Curial membership: Bishops, Sacraments (congregation); APSA (office).

Rivera Carrera, Norberto: b. June 6, 1942, La Purísima, Mexico; ord., July 3, 1966; taught dogmatic theology at the major seminary of Mexico City; professor of ecclesiology at Pontifical Univ. of Mexico; bp. of Tehuacán, Nov. 5, 1985; abp. of Mexico City, June 13,1995; app. member of the Council for the Study of the Organizational and Economic Problems of the Holy See, Oct. 23, 2010; card., Feb. 21, 1998; titular church, St. Francis of Assisi at Ripa Grande.

Curial membership: Clergy, Divine Worship and the Discipline of Sacraments (congregation); Family (council); Latin America (commission).

Robles Ortega, Francisco: b. Mar. 2, 1949, Mascota, México; ord. July 20, 1976; vicar general of Autlán and prof. of philosophy and theology at its seminary; cons. titular bp. of Bossa and aux. bp. of Toluca, June 5, 1991; bp. of Toluca, 1996-2003; app. abp. of Monterrey, Jan. 25, 2003; card., Nov. 24, 2007; app. abp. of Guadalajara, Dec. 7, 2011; titular church, St. Mary of the Presentation.

Curial membership: Latin America (commission).

Rodé, C.M., Franc: b. Sept. 23, 1934, Jarse, Ljubljana, Slovenia; the family left for Austria and then Argentina during World War II; entered the Cong. of the Missions (Vincentians), Mar. 6, 1952 and took his perpetual vows in 1957; studied at the Gregorian Univ. in Rome and the Institut Catholique in Paris; ord. June 29, 1960; returned to Slovenia and after parish ministry, he taught at the Faculty of Theology in Ljubljana; his work in support of Catholic education caused him to be placed under surveillance by state authorities; app. undersecretary of the Secretariat for Non-Believers and then secretary of the Pont. Council for Culture; app. abp. of Ljubljana, Mar. 5, 1997; prefect of the Cong. for the Institutes of Consecrated Life and Societies of Apostolic Life, 2004-2010; card. Mar. 24, 2006; titular church, Diaconia di San

Francesco Saverio alla Garbatella.

Curial membership: Bishops, Doctrine of the Faith, Education, Evangelization, Sacraments (congregations); Culture (council); Ecclesia Dei (commission).

Rodríguez Maradiaga, S.D.B., Oscar Andrés: b. Dec. 29, 1942, Tegucigalpa, Honduras; ord., for the Salesians June 28, 1870; taught Salesian colleges in El Salvador, Honduras and Guatemala; prof. at the Salesian Theological Institute, Guatemala, and rector Salesian Philosophical Institute, Guatemala; app. titular bp. of Pudentiana and aux. bp. of Tegucigalpa, Oct. 28, 1978; app. abp. of Tegucigalpa, Jan. 8, 1993; pres. of CELAM, 1995-99; pres. of the Episcopal Conference of Honduras; card. priest, Feb. 21, 2001; titular church, St. Mary of Hope.

Curial membership: Clergy (congregation); Justice and Peace, Social Communication (councils); Latin America (commission).

Romeo, Paolo: b. Feb. 20, 1938, Acireale, Italy; studied at the Seminary of Acireale, Pontifical Gregorian Univ., and Pontifical Lateran Univ., Rome; ord. Mar. 18, 1961, he studied at the Pontifical Ecclesiastical Academy, entered the diplomatic service of the Holy See in 1967; ord. titular abp. of Vulturia, Jan. 6, 1984; nuncio to Haiti, 1983-1990, Colombia, 1990-1999, Canada, 1999-2001, and Italy and San Marino, 2001-2006; app. abp. of Palermo, Dec. 19, 2006; created card. priest, Nov. 20, 2010; titular of S. Maria Odigitria dei Siciliani, deaconry elevated *pro hac vice* to titular church.

Curial membership: Laity (council); Latin America (commission).

Rosales,* Gaudencio: b. Aug. 10, 1932, Batangas City; ord. Mar. 23, 1958; app. titular bp. of Esco and aux. bp. of Manila, Aug. 12, 1974; app. coadj. bp. of Malaybalay, June 9, 1982; bp. of Malaybalay, Sept. 14, 1984; app. abp. of Lipa, Dec. 30, 1992; app. abp. of Manila, Sept. 15, 2003; card., Mar. 24, 1006, titular church, Santissimo Nome di Maria a Via Latina.

Curial membership: Interreligious Dialogue; Social Communications (councils).

Rouco Varela, Antonio María: b. Aug. 24, 1936, Villalba, Spain; ord., Mar. 28, 1959; taught fundamental theology and canon law at the Mondoñedo seminary; adjunct prof. at the Univ. of Munich; taught ecclesiastical law at Pontifical Univ. of Salamanca; vice-rector of Pontifical Univ. of Salamanca; titular bp. of Gergis and aux. bp. of Santiago de Compostela, Sept. 17, 1976; abp. of Santiago de Compostela, May 9,1984; abp. of Madrid June 29, 1994; card., Feb. 21, 1998, titular church, St. Laurence in Damaso.

Curial membership: Bishops, Clergy, Education (congregations); "Cor Unum," Culture, Texts (councils); Supreme Tribunal of the Apostolic Signatura (tribunal); Economic Affairs (office).

Rubiano Sáenz,* Pedro: b. Sept. 13, 1932, Cartago, Colombia; ord., July 8, 1956; chaplain to Marco Fidel Suárez Air Force Academy, St. Liberata National College, and Our Lady of Remedies Clinic; app. bp. of Cúcuta, June 2, 1971; cons., June 11, 1971; app. coadj. abp. of Cali, Mar. 26, 1983; abp. of Cali, 1985-1994; apost. admin. of Popayán; abp. of Bogota, 1994-2010; card. priest, Feb. 21, 2001; titular church, Transfiguration of Our Lord Jesus Christ.

Curial membership: Education (congregation); Migrants and Itinerant Peoples (council).

Ruini,* Camillo: b. Feb. 19, 1931, Sassuolo, Italy; ord., Dec. 8, 1954; taught at seminaries in central Italy; ord. titular bp. of Nepte and aux. bp. of Reggio Emilia and Guastella, June 29, 1983; secretary general of Italian Bishops' Conference, 1986-91; abp. Jan. 17, 1991 and pro-vicar general of the Pope for the Rome diocese; pro-Archpriest of Patriarchal Lateran Archbasilica; card., June 28, 1991; titular church, St. Agnes outside the Wall. Vicar General of the Pope for the Diocese of Rome and Archpriest of Patriarchal Lateran Basilica, and grand chancellor of Pontifical Lateran Univ., 1991-2008; President of the Peregrinatio ad Petri Sedem, 1992–96.

Curial membership: Bishops (congregation); Laity (council).

Rylko, Stanislaw: b. July 4, 1945, Andrychów, Poland; ord. Mar. 30, 1969; earned a doctorate in social sciences from the Pontifical Gregorian Univ., Rome and served as a professor at the Pontifical Theological Academy of Kraków; app. titular bp. of Novica and sec. of the Pontifical Council for the Laity, Dec. 20, 1995; pres. of the Pont. Council for the Laity and promoted to the rank of archbishop, Oct. 4, 2003; card., Nov. 24, 2007; deaconry, Sacred Heart of Christ the King.

Curial Membership: Bishops, Saints (congregation); Latin America (commission).

Salazar Gomez, Rubén: b. Sept. 22, 1942, Bogotá, Colombia; studied at San Joaquín of Ibagué Minor Seminary, Pontifical Gregorian University, Rome, and Pontifical Biblical Institute, Rome; ord. a priest, May 20, 1967; app. bp. of Cúcuta, Feb. 11, 1992; ord. Mar. 25, 1992; app. metropolitan abp. of Barranquilla, Mar. 18, 1999; pres. of the episcopal conference of Colombia for the triennium 2008-2011; app. metropolitan abp. of Bogotá, July 8, 2010; created cardinal priest in the consistory of Nov. 24, 2012, with the title of S. Gerardo Maiella.

Curial membership: Latin America (commission), Justice and Peace (council).

Sandoval Íñiguez,* Juan: b. Mar. 28, 1933, Yahualica, Mexico; ord., Oct. 27, 1957; ord. coadj. bp. of Ciudad Juárez, Apr. 30, 1988; bp. of Ciudad Juarez, July 11, 1992; app. abp. of Guadalajara, Apr. 21, 1994; card., Nov. 26, 1994; ret., Dec. 7, 2011; titular church, Our Lady of Guadalupe and St. Philip the Martyr on Via Aurelia.

Curial membership: Institutes of Consecrated Life and Societies of Apostolic Life, Catholic Education (congregations); Culture, Latin America (commission); Economic Affairs of the Holy See (office); Works of Religion (commission).

Sandri, Leonardo: b. Nov. 18, 1943, Buenos Aires, Argentina; ord., Dec. 2, 1967; earned a doctorate in canon law at the Pontifical Gregorian Univ., Rome and studied at the Pontifical Ecclesiastical Academy; entered the diplomatic service of the Holy See in 1974 and served in the nunciatures in Madagascar and Maurice and the U.S.; held several posts in the Secretariat of State; elected titular abp. of Cittanova and nuncio in Venezuela, July 22, 1997; cons., Oct. 11, 1997; nuncio to México, Nov. 1, 2000; sostituto of the Secretariat of State for General Affairs, Sept. 16, 2000; card. Nov. 24, 2007; deaconry, Sts. Biagio and Carlo at Catinari; Prefect of Cong. for Oriental Churches, June 9, 2007.

Curial membership: Doctrine, Evangelization (congregations), Christian Unity, Vatican City (commission)

Santos,* O.F.M., Alexandre José Maria dos: b. Mar. 18, 1924, Zavala, Mozambique; ord., July 25, 1953; first Mozambican black priest; ord. abp. of Maputo, Mar. 9, 1975; card., June 28, 1988; titular church, St. Frumentius (ai Prati Fiscali).

Sarah, Robert: b. June 15, 1945, Ourous, Guinea; studied at the Grand Seminary of Nancy, France, the

Pontifical Gregorian Univ., Rome, and Studium Biblicum Franciscanum of Jerusalem; ord. July 20, 1969, app. abp. of Conakry, Aug. 13, 1979 and ord. Dec. 8, 1979; app. sec. of the Cong. for the Evangelization of Peoples, Oct. 1, 2001; app. pres. of the Pontifical Council Cor Unum, Oct. 7, 2010; created card. deacon, Nov. 20, 2010 with the deaconry of S. Giovanni Bosco in via Tuscolana.

Curial membership: Evangelization (congregation); Justice, Laity (council).

Saraiva Martins,* C.M.F., José: b. Jan. 6, 1932, Gagos do Jarmelo, Portugal; ord., for the Claretians, Mar. 16, 1957; taught at Claretian seminary in Marino, Italy; taught at Claretianum, Rome; taught at the Pontifical Urbanian Univ. and served as rector, 1977-80, 1980-83, 1986-88; sec. of the Cong. for Catholic Education and titular abp. of Thuburnica, May 26, 1988; cons. abp., July 2, 1988; pref. of Cong. for the Causes of Saints, 1998-2008; card. deacon, Feb. 21, 2001; deaconry of Our Lady of the Sacred Heart; promoted to card. bishop, Feb. 24, 2009, suburbicarian see of Palestrina.

Curial membership: Bishops, Sacraments (congregations); Health Care (council); Vatican City (commission).

Sardi, Paolo: b. Sept. 1, 1934, Ricaldone, Italy; studied at the Major Seminary in Torino, Pontifical Gregorian Univ., Rome, and Università Cattolica del Sacro Cuore, Milan; ord. June 29, 1958; appointed to the Secretariat of State, 1976; app. titular abp. of Sutri and apostolic nuncio with special responsibilities, Dec. 10, 1996; ord. Jan. 6, 1997; vice-camerlengo of the Holy Roman Church, 2004-2011; app. pro-patron of the Sovereign Military and Hospitaller Order of St. John of Jerusalem of Rhodes and of Malta, June 6, 2009 and patron Nov. 30, 2010; created card. deacon, Nov. 20, 2010; deaconry of S. Maria Ausiliatrice in via Tuscolana.

Curial membership: Consecrated Life, Saints (congregations); Laity (council).

Sarr, Théodore-Adrien: b. Nov. 28, 1936, Fadiouth, Sénégal; ord. May 28, 1964; pastoral ministry and prof. of the Minor Seminary of N'Gasobil and superior, 1970-1974; cons. bp. of Kaolack, Nov. 24, 1974; app. abp. of Dakar, June 2, 2000; well known voice for peace in western Africa; card., Nov. 24, 2007; titular church, St. Lucy at the Piazza d'Armi.

Curial membership: Evangelization, Sacraments (congregation); Culture (council).

Scheid, Eusebio Oscar: b. Dec. 8, 1932, Luzerna, Brazil; ord. July 3, 1960; joined the Cong. of Priests of the Sacred Heart of Jesus (S.C.J.); ord. bp. of São José dos Campos, May 1, 1981; app. abp. of Florianapolis, Jan. 23, 1991; app. abp. of São Sebastião do Rio de Janeiro, July 25, 2001; ret. Feb. 27, 2009; card., Oct. 21, 2003; titular church, Sts. Boniface and Alexis.

Curial membership: Latin America (commission).

Scherer, Odilo: b. Sept. 21, 1949, São Francisco, Brazil; ord. Dec. 7, 1976; doctorate in theology Pontifical Gregorian Univ. in Rome; rector and professor in several seminaries and universities; 1994–2001 Cong. for Bishops; cons. titular bp. of Novi and aux. bp. of São Paulo, Nov. 28, 2001; elected sec. general of the National Conference of Bishops of Brazil, 2003; app. abp. of São Paulo, Mar. 21, 2007; card., Nov. 24, 2007; titular church, St. Andrea at the Quirinale.

Curial membership: Clergy (congregation); Latin America, Works of Religion (commission); Economic Affairs (office).

Schönborn, O.P., Christoph: b. Jan. 22, 1945, Skalsko, Bohemia (fled to Austria in Sept. 1945); entered Dominican Order in 1963; ord., 1970; student pastor in Graz Univ.,

1973-75; assoc. professor of dogma in the Univ. of Fribourg, 1976; professor theology, 1978; professor dogmatic theology, 1981-91; Orthodox-Roman Catholic Dialogue Commission of Switzerland, 1980–87; International Theological Commission, 1980–; foundation, "Pro Oriente" since 1984; Secretary for the Draft Commission of the *Catechism of the Catholic Church*, 1987–1992; ord. aux. bp. (Sutri) of Vienna, Sept. 29, 1991; coadj. of Vienna, Apr. 13, 1995; abp. Vienna, Sept. 14, 1995; card., Feb. 21, 1998; titular church, Jesus the Divine Worker.

Curial membership: Doctrine of the Faith, Education, Oriental Churches (congregations); Culture (council); Cultural Heritage of the Church (commission).

Schwery,* Henri: b. June 14, 1932, Saint-Leonard, Switzerland; ord., July 7, 1957; director of minor seminary and later rector of the College in Sion; bp. of Sion, 1977–95; card., June 28, 1991; titular church, Protomartyrs (a via Aurelia Antica).

Scola, Angelo: b. Nov. 7, 1941, Malgrate, Italy; ord., July 18, 1970; professor of theological anthropology Pontifical John Paul II Institute for Studies on Marriage and the Family at the Pontifical Lateran Univ., Rome; later, professor of Contemporary Christology at the Faculty of Theology, Pontifical Lateran Univ., Rome; ord. bp. of Grosseto, Sep. 21, 1991; rector of the Pontifical Lateran Univ., 1995-2002; patriarch of Venice, Jan. 5, 2002; card., Oct. 21, 2003; titular church, the Seven Most Holy Apostles; app. abp. of Milan, June 28, 2011.

Curial membership: Clergy, Doctrine of the Faith, Oriental Churches, Sacraments (congregations); Culture, Family, Laity(council); Economic Affairs (office).

Sebastiani,* Sergio: b. Apr. 11, 1931, Montemonaco (Ascoli Piceno), Italy; ord., 1956; entered Holy See diplomatic service and posted to Peru, Brazil, and Chile; recalled to Secretariat of State; app. titular abp. of Caesarea in Mauretania and pro-nuncio in Madagascar and Mauritius and apostolic delegate to Reunion and Comorros; nuncio to Turkey, 1985; sec. to Central Committee for the Great Jubilee of the Year 2000, 1994; pres. Prefecture for the Economic Affairs of the Holy See, Nov. 3, 1997; card., Feb. 21, 2001; titular church, Deaconry of St. Eustace. Pres. of the Prefecture for the Economic Affairs of the Holy See.

Curial membership: Bishops, Causes of Saints, Clergy, Evangelization (congregations); Christian Unity (council); Apostolic Signatura (tribunal).

Sepe, Crescenzio: b. June 2, 1943, Carinaro (Caserta), Italy; ord., Mar. 12, 1967; taught at Lateran and Urbanian Universities; studied at Pontifical Ecclesiastical Academy; entered Holy See diplomatic service and posted to Brazil; recalled to Secretariat of State, 1987; pres. of Commission for Vatican Telecommunications; app. titular abp. of Grado and sec. of the Cong. for the Clergy, Apr. 2, 1992; cons. Apr. 26, 1992; General Secretary of the Central Committee for the Great Jubilee of the Year 2000, 1997-2001; Pref. Cong. for the Evangelization of Peoples, 2001-2006; card. deacon, Feb. 21, 2001; deaconry, God the Merciful Father; app. abp. of Naples, May 20, 2006.

Curial membership: Clergy, Doctrine of the Faith (congregation); Legislative Texts (councils).

Sfeir,* Nasrallah Pierre: b. May 15, 1920, Reyfoun, in Maronite diocese of Sarba, Lebanon; ord., May 7, 1950; secretary of Maronite patriarchate, 1956-61; taught Arabic literature and philosophy at Marist Fathers College, Jounieh, 1951–61; ord. titular abp. of Tarsus for the Maronites, July 16, 1961; elected Patriarch of Antioch

for Maronites, Apr. 19, 1986; granted ecclesial communion by John Paul II May 7, 1986; card., Nov. 26, 1994.
Patriarch of Antioch for Maronites.

Curial membership: Oriental Churches (congregation).

Sgreccia,* **Elio**: b. June 6, 1928, Nidastore Arcevia,
Italy; studied at the Theological Seminary of Fano and
the Univ. of Bologna; ord. June 29, 1951; director of
Bioethics Center of the Catholic Univ. Sacro Cuore of
Milan, 1985-2006; ord. titular bp. of Zama Minor, Jan. 6,
1993; sec. of the Pontifical Council for the Family, 1992-
1996; vice-president of the Pontifical Academy for Life,
1994-2005; pres. of the Academy, 2005-2008; key voice for
responsible bioethics in modern era; created card. deacon,
Nov. 20, 2010; deaconry of S. Angelo in Pescheria.

Silvestrini,* **Achille**: b. Oct. 25, 1923, Brisighella, Italy;
ord., July 13, 1946; official in Secretariat of State from
1953; ord. titular bp. of Novaliciana with personal title
of abp., May 27, 1979; undersecretary, 1973-79, and
secretary, 1979-88, of the Council for Public Affairs of
the Church (now the second section of the Secretariat
of State); card., June 28, 1988; deaconry, St. Benedict
Outside St. Paul's Gate, promoted to card. priest, Jan.
9, 1999; prefect of Apostolic Signatura, 1988-91. Prefect
of Cong. for Oriental Churches, 1991-2001; Grand
Chancellor of Pontifical Oriental Institute.

Simonis,* **Adrianus J.**: b. Nov. 26, 1931, Lisse,
Netherlands; ord., June 15, 1957; ord. bp. of Rotterdam,
Mar. 20, 1971; coadj. abp. of Utrecht, June 27, 1983; abp.
of Utrecht, 1983-2007; card., May 25, 1985; titular church,
St. Clement.

Curial membership: Consecrated Life and Societies
of Apostolic Life, Education (congregations); Christian
Unity (council).

Sodano,* **Angelo**: b. Nov. 23, 1927, Isola d'Asti, Italy;
ord., Sept. 23, 1950; entered diplomatic service of the
Holy See in 1959; served in Ecuador and Uruguay; ord.
titular abp. of Nova di Cesare, Jan. 15, 1978; nuncio to
Chile, 1978-88; secretary of the Council for Relations with
States, 1988-90; pro-Secretary of State, 1990-1991; card.
June 28, 1991; titular church, S. Maria Nuova; transferred
to order of card. bishops, Jan 10, 1994, as titular bp. of
suburbicarian see of Albano (while retaining title to S.
Maria Nuova). Secretary of State, June 29, 1991-Sept.
15, 2006; Vice-dean of the Sacred College of Cardinals,
2002-05; dean of the College of Cardinals (Apr. 30, 2005).

Stafford,* **James Francis**: b. July 26, 1932, Baltimore,
MD; ord., (Baltimore*) Dec. 15, 1957; ord. titular bp.
of Respetta and aux. bp. of Baltimore, Feb. 29, 1976;
app. bp. of Memphis, Nov. 17, 1982; app. abp. of Denver,
June 3, 1986, installed July 30, 1986; app. President
of Pontifical Council for the Laity, 1996-2003; Major
Penitentiary of the Apostolic Penitentiary, Oct. 4, 2003-
June 2, 2009; card. deacon, Feb. 21, 1998; card. priest,
Mar. 2, 2008; titular church, S. Pietro in Montorio.

Curial membership: Bishops, Doctrine of the Faith,
Causes of Saints, Evangelization of Peoples (congregations); Texts (council).

Szoka,* **Edmund C.**: b. Sept. 14, 1927, Grand Rapids,
MI; ord., (Marquette diocese), June 5, 1954; ord. first bp.
of Gaylord, MI, July 20, 1971; abp. of Detroit, 1981–90;
card., June 28, 1988; titular church, Sts. Andrew and
Gregory (al Monte Celio). President of Prefecture for
Economic Affairs of the Holy See, 1990-97. Pres. Pont.
Comm. for Vatican City State, 1997-2006. Pres. emeritus
of the Pont. Comm. for Vatican City State.

Tagle, Luis Antonio Gokim: b. June 21, 1957, Manila,

Philippines; has the nickname "Chito"; studied at St.
Jose Seminary, Manila, Ateneo de Manila University,
and The Catholic University of America, Washington,
D.C., where he earned a doctorate in theology, summa
cum laude; ord. priest, for Manila, Feb. 27, 1982, member
of the International Theological Commission, 1997-2002
and served on the editorial board of the Bologna-based
"History of Vatican II" project founded by Giuseppe
Alberigo; app. bp. of Imus, Oct. 22, 2001; ord. bp., Dec. 12,
2001; app abp of Manila, Oct. 13, 2011; created cardinal
priest in the consistory of Nov. 24, 2012, with the title of S.
Felice da Cantalice a Centocelle.

Curial membership: Family and Pastoral of Migrants and
Itinerants (councils).

Tauran, Jean-Louis: b. Apr. 3, 1943, Bordeaux, France;
ord. Sep. 20, 1969; entered the diplomatic service of the
Holy See in 1975; app. titular abp. of Telepte and appointed
secretary of the Secretariat of State for the Relations with
the States, 1990-2003; Archivist and Librarian of the Holy
Roman Church, 2003; card. deacon, Oct. 21, 2003, titular
church, St. Apollinaris alle Terme Neroniane-Alessandrine;
Pres. of the Pont. Council for Interreligious Dialogue, 2007.

Curial membership: Secretariat of State (second sec
tion), Bishops, Doctrine of the Faith, Oriental Churches
(Congregations); Culture (council); Supreme Tribunal of
the Apostolic Signatura (tribunal); Vatican City State,
Works of Religion (commission); APSA (office).

Terrazas Sandoval, C.SS.R., Julio: b. Mar. 7, 1936,
Vallegrande, Bolivia; ord., for the Redemptorists July
29, 1962; superior of the Redemptorist community in
Vallegrande and vicar forane; app. aux. bp. of La Paz
and cons., Apr. 15, 1978; transferred to the see of Oruro,
Jan. 9, 1982; pres. of the Bolivian Episcopal Conference
in 1985 and 1988; app. abp. of Santa Cruz, Feb. 6, 1991;
card., Feb. 21, 2001; titular church, St. John Baptist Rossi.

Curial membership: Laity (council); Latin America
(commission).

Tettamanzi, Dionigi: b. Mar. 14, 1934, Renate, Italy; ord.,
June 28, 1957; taught fundamental theology at the major
seminary of Lower Venegono, pastoral theology at the
Priestly Institute of Mary Immaculate and the Lombard
Regional Institute of Pastoral Ministry, Milan; rector of
the Pontifical Lombard Seminary, Rome; abp. of Ancona-
Osimo, July 1,1989 (res. 1991); general secretary of the Italian
Episcopal Conference, 1991-95; Vice-President of the Italian
Episcopal Conference, May 25, 1995; abp. of Genoa Apr. 20,
1995; card., Feb. 21, 1998; titular church, Sts. Ambrose and
Charles; app. abp. of Milan, July 11, 2002; ret. June 28, 2011.

Curial membership: Clergy, Education, Oriental
Churches (congregations).

Thottunkal, Baselios Cleemis: b. June 15, 1959,
Nedungadapally, India; studied at the Infant Jesus Minor
Seminary of the Eparchy of Tiruvalla, St. Berchman's
College, Changanacherry, St. Joseph's Pontifical Seminary,
Aluva, Pontifical Seminary of Pune, Dharmaram College,
Bangalore, Pontifical University of St. Thomas Aquinas in
Rome, where he earned a doctorate in theology; ord. a priest,
June 11, 1986, for the eparchy of Battery; app. titular bp. of
Chayal of the Syro-Malankars and auxiliary of Trivandrum
of the Syro-Malankars, June 18, 2001; cons. August 15, 2001;
app. bp. of Tiruvalla of the Syro-Malankars, Sept. 11, 2003;
app. first metropolitan of Tiruvalla, May 15, 2006; elected,
unanimously elected him archbishop major, Feb. 8, 2007;
confirmed on Feb. 10, by Pope Benedict XVI; created cardinal priest in the consistory of Nov.24, 2012, with the title
of S. Gregorio VII.

Curial membership: Oriental Churches (congregation), Inter-religious Dialogue (council).

Tomko,* Jozef: b. Mar. 11, 1924, Udavske, Slovakia; ord., Mar. 12, 1949; ord. titular abp. of Doclea, Sept. 15, 1979; secretary-general of the Synod of Bishops, 1979-85; card. deacon, May 25, 1985; transferred to order of card. priests, Jan. 29, 1996; titular church, St. Sabina. Prefect of the Cong. for the Evangelization of Peoples, 1985-2001; Grand Chancellor of Pontifical Urban Univ.; President of Pontifical Committee for International Eucharistic Congresses, 2001.

Tong Hon, John: b. July 31, 1939, Hong Kong; earned a doctorate in theology at the Pontifical Urbanian Univ.; ord, priest, Jan. 6, 1966; ord. titular bp. of Bossa and aux. of Hong Kong, Dec. 9, 1996; app. coadj. bp. of Hong Kong, Jan. 30, 2008; acceded to the see of Hong Kong, Apr. 15, 2009; cardinal, Feb. 18, 2012 with the title of Regina Apostolorum.

Curial membership: Evengelization (congregation); Interreligious Dialogue (council).

Toppo, Telesphore Placidus: b. Oct. 15, 1939, Chainpur, India, to tribal family that had converted to Christianity; ord. May 3, 1969; ord. bp. of Dumka, June 8, 1979; abp. of Ranchi, Aug. 7, 1985; supported programs to assist tribes in Jharkhand; card., Oct. 21, 2003; titular church, Sacred Heart of Jesus in Agony at Vitinia.

Curial membership: Evangelization of Peoples (congregation); Culture, Interreligious Dialogue (council); Works of Religion (commission).

Tucci,* S.J., Roberto: b. Apr. 19, 1921, Naples, Italy; ord., for the Jesuits, Aug. 24, 1950; editor of *La Civiltà Cattolica*; member of the Preparatory Commission on the Apostolate of the Laity for Vatican II and *peritus* involved in drafting *Ad Gentes* and *Gaudium et Spes*; consultor to the Pontifical Council for Social Communications, 1965-89; vice-pres. of the Italian Catholic Union of the Press, 1961–82; general sec. of the Italian Province of the Jesuits, 1967–69; app. general manager of Vatican Radio, 1973; since 1982, he has been responsible for all papal visits outside Italy; app. chairman of the Administrative Committee of Vatican Radio, 1986; card., Feb. 21, 2001; titular church, Deaconry of St. Ignatius Loyola in Campo Marzio. Chairman of the Administrative Committee of Vatican Radio.

Tumi,* Christian Wiyghan: b. Oct. 15, 1930, Kikaikelaki, Cameroon; ord., Apr. 17, 1966; ord. bp. of Yagoua, Jan. 6, 1980; coadj. abp. of Garoua, Nov. 19, 1982; abp. of Garoua, 1984–91; abp. of Douala, Aug. 31, 1991; card., June 28, 1988; titular church, Martyrs of Uganda (a Poggio Ameno).

Curial membership: Divine Worship and Sacraments, Education, Evangelization of Peoples (congregations); Cor Unum, Family (councils).

Turcotte, Jean–Claude: b. June 26, 1936, Montreal, Canada; ord., May 24, 1959; ord. titular bp. of Suas and aux. of Montreal, June 29, 1982; abp. of Montreal, Mar. 17, 1990; card., Nov. 26, 1994; titular church, Our Lady of the Blessed Sacrament and the Holy Canadian Martyrs.

Curial membership: Evangelization, Causes of Saints (congregation); Social Communications (council).

Turkson, Peter Kodwo Appiah: b. Oct. 11, 1948, Wassaw Nsuta, Ghana; ord. July 20, 1975; abp. of Cape Coast, Jan. 6, 1992-Oct. 24, 2009; pres. of the Catholic Bishops' Conference and Chancellor of the Catholic Univ. College of Ghana; card. priest, Oct. 21, 2003; titular church, St. Liborius; pres. of the Pontifical Council for Justice and Peace, Oct. 24, 2009.

Curial membership: Evangelization, Sacraments (con-

gregation); Christian Unity (council); Cultural Heritage of the Church (commission).

Urosa Savino, Jorge Liberato: b. Aug. 28, 1942, Caracas, Venezuela; ord. Aug. 15, 1967; doctorate in theology Gregorian Univ., 1971; rector several Venezuelan seminaries, 1974–82 and prof. of philosophical anthropology and dogmatic theology; pres. of the organization of Venezuelan Seminaries, 1974–77; vice-pres. of Organization of Latin American Seminaries, 1976–82; app. titular bp. of Vegesela in Byzacena and aux. bp. of Caracas, July 13, 1982; app. abp. of Valencia in Venezuela, Mar. 17, 1990; app. abp. of Caracas, Sept. 19, 2005; card., Mar. 24, 2006, titular church, Sta. Maria ai Monti.

Curial membership: Clergy (congregation); Culture, Justice and Peace (council); Latin America (commission); Economic Affairs (office).

Vallini, Agostino: b. Apr. 17, 1940, Poli, Italy; ord. July 19, 1964; study of canon law Pontifical Lateran Univ.; doctorate *in utroque iure*; taught in Naples, 1969–71; called back to Rome 1971 to teach public ecclesiastical law at the Lateran, with the task of reorganizing the field in keeping with the Second Vatican Council; rector Major Seminary of Naples, 1978; app. titular bp. of Tortibulum and aux. bp. of Naples, Mar. 23, 1989; app. suburbicarian bp. of Albano, Nov. 13, 1999; app. prefect of the Supreme Tribunal of the Apostolic Signatura, 2004–2008; pres. of the Court of Causation of the Vatican City State, 2004–2008; card., Mar. 24, 2006; titular church, Diaconia di San Pier Damiani ai Monti di San Paolo; card. priest, retaining titular church, *pro hac vice*, Feb. 24, 2009; app. Vicar General of Rome, Archpriest of the Archbasilica of St. John Lateran, and grand chancellor of the Pontifical Lateran Univ., June 27, 2008.

Curial membership: Consecrated Life, Evangelization, Saints (Congregation); Texts (council); APSA; Economic Affairs (office).

Vanhoye,* S.J., Albert: b. July 24, 1923, Hazebrouck, France; entered the Jesuits, Sept. 11, 1941 and ord. July 24, 1954; professor at Pontifical Biblical Institute, the Biblicum, Rome 1963–; dean of biblical faculty, 1969–75 and rector, 1984–90; taught at Gregorian Univ. and Lateran Univ., Rome; assisted in the preparation of the apostolic constitution, *Sapientia Christiana*; served as member of the Pontifical Biblical Commission, 1984–2001 and sec. of the commission, 1990–2001; consultor to the Congs. of Catholic Education from 1978 and Doctrine of the Faith from 1990; card., Mar. 24, 2006; titular church, diaconia di Sta. Maria della Mercede e Sant'Adriano a Villa Albani.

Vegliò, Antonio Maria: b. Feb. 3, 1938, Macerata Feltria, Italy; earned a doctorate in canon law and studied at the Pontifical Ecclesiastical Academy, Rome; ord. priest, Mar. 18, 1962; entered the diplomatic service of the Holy See in 1968 and served in the nunciatures in Peru, Philippines, Senegal, and Great Britain; ord. titular abp. of Eclano and app. pro-nuncio in Papua New Guinea and Solomon Islands, July 27, 1985; app. pro-Nuncio in Cape Verde, Guinea-Bissau, Mali and Senegal in 1989, nuncio in Cape Verde, Guinea-Bissau, Mali and Senegal in 1994, nuncio in Kuwait in 1998, and nuncio in Lebanon, 1997-2001; ap. sec. of Congregation for the Oriental Churches, Apr. 11, 2001; app. president of the Pontifical Council for Pastoral Care of Migrants and Itinerant Peoples, Feb. 28, 2009; cardinal Feb. 18, 2012 with the deaconry of S. Cesareo in Palatio.

Curial membership: Divine Worship (congregation); Family, Laity (councils).

Vela Chiriboga, Raúl Eduardo: b. Jan. 1, 1934, Riobamba, Ecuador; studied at the Major Seminary of Quito; ord. July 28, 1957, general sec. of the episcopal conference of Ecuador, 1970-1975; ord. titular bp. Ausafa and aux. bp. Guayaquil, May 21, 1972; bp. Azogues, 1975-1989; transf. to the titular see of Pauzera and app. military ordinary of Ecuador, July 8, 1989; app. abp. of Quito, Mar. 21, 2003; res., Sept. 11, 2010; created card. priest, Nov. 20, 2010; titular church of S. Maria in Via.

Curial membership: Family (council); Latin America (commission).

Versaldi, Giuseppe: b. July 30, 1943, Villarboit, Italy; earned a doctorate in canon law from the Pontifical Gregorian Univ. and was advocate at the Sacred Roman Rota; ord. priest June 29, 1967; ord. bp. of Alessandria, May 26, 2007; app. apostolic visitor to the Legionaires of Christ, June 27, 2009; app. president of the Prefecture for the Economic Affairs of the Holy See and named archbishop Sept. 21, 2010; cardinal, Feb. 18, 2012, with the deaconry of Sacro Cuore di Gesù a Castro Pretorio.

Curial membership: Bishops, Consecrated Life (congregations); Signatura (tribunal).

Vidal,* Ricardo J.: b. Feb. 6, 1931, Mogpoc, Philippines; ord., Mar. 17, 1956; ord. titular bp. of Claterna and coadj. of Melalos, Nov. 30, 1971; abp. of Lipa, 1973-81; coadj. abp. of Cebu, Apr. 13, 1981; abp. of Cebu, Aug. 24, 1982; card., May 25, 1985; titular church, Sts. Peter and Paul (in Via Ostiensi).

Curial membership: Education, Evangelization of Peoples (congregations); Family, Health Care Workers (councils).

Vingt-Trois, André: b. Nov. 7, 1942, Paris, France; ord. June 28, 1969; served as professor of theology and in a variety of pastoral positions, including diocesan formation; cons. titular bp. of Tibili and aux. of Paris, Oct. 14, 1988; abp. of Tours, 1999-2005; app. abp. of Paris and ordinary of the Catholics of Oriental rite in France, Feb. 11, 2005; elected pres. Episcopal Conference of France, Nov. 5, 2007; card., Nov. 24, 2007; titular church, St. Louis of the French.

Curial membership: Bishops, Clergy, Oriental Churches (congregations); Family, Migrants (councils).

Vlk,* Miloslav: b. May 17, 1932, Lisnice, Czech Republic; during communist persecution when theological studies were impossible he studied archival science at Charles Univ. and worked in various archives in Bohemia; ord., June 23, 1968, during "Prague Spring"; sent to isolated parishes in Bohemian Forest by State authorities in 1971; state authorization to exercise his priestly ministry was cancelled in 1978; from then until 1986 he worked as a window-washer in Prague, carrying out his priestly ministry secretly; the situation changed with the "velvet revolution"; ord. bp. Ceske Budejovice, Mar. 31, 1990; abp. Prague, 1991–2010; card., Nov. 26, 1994; titular church, Holy Cross in Jerusalem; President of the Council of European Episcopal Conferences, 1993–.

Curial membership: Oriental Churches (congregation); Social Communications (council).

Wamala,* Emmanuel: b. Dec. 15, 1926, Kamaggwa, Uganda; ord., Dec. 21, 1957; ord. bp. of Kiyinda-Mityana, Nov. 22, 1981; coadj. abp. Kampala, June 21, 1988; abp. Kampala, 1990-2006; card., Nov. 26, 1994; titular church, St. Hugh.

Wetter,* Friedrich: b. Feb. 20, 1928, Landau, Germany; ord., Oct. 10, 1953; ord. bp. of Speyer, June 29, 1968; abp. of Munich and Freising, 1982-2007; card., May 25, 1985; titular church, St. Stephen (al Monte Celio).

Williams,* Thomas Stafford: b. Mar. 20, 1930, Wellington, New Zealand; ord., Dec. 20, 1959, in Rome; studied in Ireland after ordination, receiving degree in social sciences; served in various pastoral assignments on his return to New Zealand; missionary in Western Samoa to 1976; abp. of Wellington, New Zealand, 1979-2005; ret. Mar. 20, 2005; card., Feb. 2, 1983; titular church, Jesus the Divine Teacher (at Pineda Sacchetti).

Curial membership: Evangelization of Peoples (congregation).

Woelki, Rainer Maria: b. Aug. 18, 1956, Cologne-Mülheim, Germany; earned a doctorate in theology from the Pontifical University della Santa Croce, Rome; ord. priest, June 14, 1985, for the archdiocese of Cologne; ord. titular bp. of Scampa and aux. bp. of Cologne, Mar. 30, 2003; app. abp. of Berlin, July 2, 2011; cardinal, Feb. 18, 2012, with the title of S. Giovanni Maria Vianney.

Curial membership: Education (congregation); Christan Unity (council).

Wuerl, Donald W.: b. Nov. 12, 1940, Pittsburgh, PA; studied at Catholic Univ., Washington, DC); North American College, Pontifical Gregorian Univ., and Pontifical Univ. of St. Thomas Aquinas (Angelicum), Rome; earned doctorate in theology from the Angelicum; ord. for Pittsburgh, Dec. 17, 1966, in Rome; ord. titular bp. of Rosemarkie Jan. 6, 1986, in Rome; served as aux. bp. of Seattle, 1986 87; app. bp. of Pittsburgh, Feb. 11, 1988, inst., Mar. 25, 1988; app. abp. of Washington, May 16, 2006; a prolific writer, he has authored numerous books; created card. priest, Nov. 20, 2010; titular church of S. Pietro in Vincoli.

Curial membership: Clergy, Doctrine of the Faith (congregations); Christian Unity (council).

Zen Ze-Kiun,* S.D.B., Joseph: b. Jan. 13, 1932, Yang King-pang, Shanghai, China; parents were converts and survived great hardships during World War II; profession in the Salesians, Aug. 16, 1949, perpetual vows, Aug. 16, 1955; ord. in Turin, Italy, Feb. 11, 1961; app, coadj. bp. Hong Kong, Sept. 13, 1996; bp. Hong Kong, Sept. 23, 2002; card. Mar. 24, 2006; titular church, Sta. Maria Madre del Redentore a Tor Bella Monaca.

Curial membership: Evangelization; Sacraments (congregations); Synod of Bishops.

Zubeir Wako, Gabriel: b. Feb. 27, 1941, Mboro, diocese of Wau, Sudan; ord. July 21, 1963; ord. bp. of Wau, Apr. 6, 1975; coadj. abp. of Khartoum, Oct. 30, 1979; abp. of Khartoum, Oct. 10, 1981; card., Oct. 21, 2003; titular church, St. Anthanasius in Via Tiburtina. Abp. of Khartoum.

Curial membership: Evangelization of Peoples (congregation); "Cor Unum," Migrants (councils).

CATEGORIES OF CARDINALS

(As of Sept. 1, 2013.) Information below includes categories of cardinals listed according to seniority or order of precedence. Seniority or precedence usually depends on order of elevation. It is customary for cardinal deacons to be promoted eventually to the rank of cardinal priest.

Order of Bishops

Titular Bishops of Suburbicarian Sees: Angelo Sodano, dean (June 28, 1991, Albano and Ostia); Roger Etchegaray (June 24, 1998, Porto-Santa Rufina; vice-dean); Giovanni Battista Re (Oct. 1, 2002, Sabina-Poggio Mirteto); Francis Arinze (Apr. 25, 2005, Velletri-Segni); Tarcisio Bertone, (May 10, 2008, Frascati); José Saraiva Martins (Feb. 24, 2009, Palestrina). Eastern Rite Patriarchs: Nasrallah Pierre Sfeir (Nov. 26, 1994); Emmanuel III Delly (Nov. 24. 2007); Antonios Naguib (Nov. 20, 2010); Bechara Rai, O.M.M. (Nov. 24, 2012).

Order of Priests

Paulo Evaristo Arns, O.F.M., William W. Baum, Marco Cé, Franciszek Macharski, Michael Michai Kitbunchu, Alexandre do Nascimento, Godfried Danneels, Thomas Stafford Williams, Joachim Meisner, Simon D. Lourdusamy, Miguel Obando Bravo, S.D.B., Ricardo Vidal, Henryk Roman Gulbinowicz, Jozef Tomko, Andrzej Maria Deskur, Paul Poupard, Louis-Albert Vachon, Friedrich Wetter, Silvano Piovanelli, Adrianus J. Simonis, Bernard F. Law, Giacomo Biffi, Eduardo Martinez Somalo, Achille Silvestrini, José Freire Falcão, Alexandre José Maria dos Santos, O.F.M., Giovanni Canestri, Antonio Maria Javierre Ortas, S.D.B., Edward Bede Clancy, Edmund C. Szoka, László Paskai, O.F.M., Christian Wiyghan Tumi, Edward I. Cassidy, Frédéric Etsou-Nzabi-Bamungwabi, C.I.C.M., Nicolás de Jesús López Rodriguez, Virgilio Noè, Fiorenzo Angelini, Roger Mahony, Camillo Ruini, Ján Chryzostom Korec, S.J., Henri Schwery, Miloslav Vlk, Carlo Furno, Julius Riyadi Darmaatmadja, S.J., Jaime Lucas Ortega y Alamino, Gilberto Agustoni,Emmanuel Wamala, William Henry Keeler, Jean-Claude Turcotte, Ricardo Maria Carles Gordó, Adam Joseph Maida, Vinko Puljic, Juan Sandoval Íñiguez, Kazimierz Swiàtek, Ersilio Tonino, Salvatore de Giorgi, Serafim Fernandes de Araújo, Antonio Maria Rouco Varela, Dionigi Tettamanzi, Polycarp Pengo, Christoph Schönborn, O.P., Norberto Rivera Carrera, Francis George, O.M.I., Marian Jaworski, Janis Pujats, Agostino Cacciavillan, Sergio Sebastiani, Zenon Grocholewski, Crescenzio Sepe, Jorge María Mejía, Walter Kasper, Roberto Tucci, S.J., Ivan Dias, Geraldo Majella Agnelo, Pedro Rubiano Sáenz, Theodore E. McCarrick, Desmond Connell, Audrys Juozas Backis, Francisco Javier Errázuriz Ossa, Juan Julio Terrazas Sandoval, C.SS.R., Wilfrid Fox Napier, O.F.M., Oscar Andres Rodríguez Maradiaga, S.D.B., Bernard Agré, Luis Cipriani Thorne, Francisco Álvarez Martínez, Cláudio Hummes, O.F.M., José Da Cruz Policarpo, Severino Poletto, Cormac Murphy-O'Connor, Edward Michael Egan, Lubomyr Husar, Karl Lehmann, Angelo Scola, Anthony Olubunmi Okogie, Bernard Panafieu, Gabriel Zubeir Wako, Carlos Amigo Vallejo, Justin Francis Rigali, Keith Michael O'Brien, Eusebio Oscar Scheid, Ennio Antonelli, Tarcisio Bertone, Peter Kodwo Appiah Turkson, Telesphore Placidus Toppo, George Pell, Josip Bozanic, Jean Baptiste Pham Minh Man, Philippe Barbarin, Peter Erdõ, Marc Ouellet, P.S.S., Urosa Savino, Rosales, Ricard, Cañizares Llovera, Cheong-Jin-Suk, O'Malley, Dziwisz, Caffara, Zen Ze-Kiun, Seán Brady, Lluís Martínez Sistach, André Vingt-Trois, Angelo Bagnasco, Théodore-Adrien Sarr, Oswald Gracias, Francisco Lopez Ortega, Daniel Nicholas DiNardo, Odilo Scherer, John Njue, Darío Castrillón Hoyos, Jorge Medina Estévez, James Francis Stafford, Estanislao Esteban Karlic, Medardo Joseph Mazombwe, Raúl Eduardo Vela Chiriboga, Monsengwo Pasinya, Paolo Romeo, Donald Wuerl, Raymundo Damasceno Assis, Kazimierz Nycz, Albert Malcolm Ranjith Patabendige Don, Reinhard Marx, José Manuel Estepa Llaurens, José Manuel Estepa Llaurens, George Alencherry, Thomas C. Collins, Dominik Duka, Willem J. Eijk, Giuseppe Betori, Timothy M. Dolan, Rainer Maria Woelki, John Tong Hon, Lucian Muresan, Baselios Cleemis Thottunkal, John Onaiyekan, Ruben Salazar Gomez, Luis Tagle.

Order of Deacons

Jean-Louis Tauran, Renato Martino, Francesco Marchisano, Julián Herranz, Javier Lozano Barragán, Attilio Nicora, Georges Cottier, O.P., Levada, Rodé, Vallini, Montezemolo, Vanhoye, Leonardo Sandri Giovanni Lajolo, Paul-Josef Cordes, Stanislaw Rylko, Angelo Comastri, Raffaele Farina S.D.B. Giovanni Coppa, Angelo Amato, Antonios Naguib, Robert Sarah, Francesco Monterisi, Raymond Leo Burke, Kurt Koch, Paolo Sardi, Mauro Piacenza,Velasio De Paolis, Gianfranco Ravasi, Elio Sgreccia, Walter Brandmuller, Domenico Bartolucci, Fernando Filoni, Manuel Monteiro de Castro, Santos y Abril Castello, Antonio Maria Veglio, Giuseppe Bertello, Francesco Coccopalmerio, Joao Braz de Aviz, Edwin F. O'Brien, Domenico Calcagno, Giuseppe Versaldi, Prosper Grech, Karl Josef Becker, James M. Harvey.

CONSISTORIES

(As of Sept. 1, 2013.) Information below includes dates of consistories at which the current cardinals were created. They are listed according to seniority. Of these 202 cardinals, 2 were named by Paul VI (consistories of Mar. 5, 1973 and May 24, 1976); 117 by John Paul II (consistories of June 30, 1979, Feb. 2, 1983, May 25, 1985, June 28, 1988, June 28, 1991, Nov. 26, 1994, Feb. 21, 1998, Feb. 21, 2001, and Oct. 21, 2003), and 83 by Benedict XVI (Mar. 24, 2006, Nov. 24, 2007, Nov. 20, 2010, Feb. 19, 2012, Nov. 24, 2012).

Pope Paul VI

1973 (Mar. 5): Paulo Evaristo Arns, O.F.M.

1976 (May 24): William W. Baum.

Pope John Paul II

1979 (June 30): Marco Cé, Roger Etchegaray, Franciszek Macharski.

1983 (Feb. 2): Michael Michai Kitbunchu, Alexandre do Nascimento, Godfried Danneels, Thomas Stafford Williams, Carlo Maria Martini, Józef Glemp, Joachim Meisner.

1985 (May 25): Simon D. Lourdusamy, Francis A. Arinze, Miguel Obando Bravo, S.D.B., Ricardo Vidal, Henryk Roman Gulbinowicz, Jozef Tomko, Andrzej Maria Deskur, Paul Poupard, Friedrich Wetter, Silvano Piovanelli, Adrianus J. Simonis, Bernard F. Law, Giacomo Biffi.

1988 (June 28): Eduardo Martinez Somalo, Achille Silvestrini, José Freire Falcão, Alexandre José Maria dos Santos, O.F.M., Giovanni Canestri, Edward Bede Clancy, Edmund C. Szoka, László Paskai, O.F.M., Christian Wiyghan Tumi.

1991 (June 28): Angelo Sodano, Edward I. Cassidy, Nicolás de Jesús López Rodriguez, Fiorenzo Angelini Roger Mahony, Camillo Ruini, Ján Chryzostom Korec, S.J., Henri Schwery.

1994 (Nov. 26): Nasrallah Pierre Sfeir, Miloslav Vlk, Carlo Furno, Julius Riyadi Darmaatmadja, S.J., Jaime Lucas Ortega y Alamino, Gilberto Agustoni, Emmanuel Wamala, William Henry Keeler, Jean-Claude Turcotte, Ricardo Maria Carles Gordó, Adam Joseph Maida, Vinko Puljic, Juan Sandoval Íñiguez.

1998 (Feb. 21): Jorge Medina Estévez, Darío Castrillón Hoyos, James F. Stafford, Salvatore de Giorgi, Serafim Fernandes de Araújo, Antonio Maria Rouco Varela, Dionigi Tettamanzi, Polycarp Pengo, Christoph Schönborn, O.P., Norberto Rivera Carrera, Francis George, O.M.I., Giovanni Cheli, Marian Jaworski, Janis Pujats.

2001 (Feb. 21): Giovanni Battista Re, Agostino Cacciavillan, Sergio Sebastiani, Zenon Grocholewski, José Saraiva Martins, C.M.F., Crescenzio Sepe, Jorge María Mejía, Walter Kasper, Ivan Dias, Geraldo

Majella Agnelo, Pedro Rubiano Sáenz, Theodore E. McCarrick, Desmond Connell, Audrys Juozas Backis, Francisco Javier Errázuriz Ossa, Juan Julio Terrazas Sandoval, C.SS.R., Wilfrid Fox Napier, O.F.M., Oscar Andres Rodríguez Maradiaga, S.D.B., Bernard Agré, Luis Cipriani Thorne, Francisco Álvarez Martínez, Cláudio Hummes, Jorge Mario Bergoglio, S.J., José Da Cruz Policarpo, Severino Poletto, Cormac Murphy-O'Connor, Edward M. Egan, Lubomyr Husar, Karl Lehmann, Jean Honoré, O.F.M., Roberto Tucci, S.J.

2003 (Oct. 21): Jean-Louis Tauran, Renato Martino, Francesco Marchisano, Julián Herranz, Javier Lozano Barragán, Attilio Nicora, Angelo Scola, Anthony Olubunmi Okogie, Bernard Panafieu, Gabriel Zubeir Wako, Carlos Amigo Vallejo, Justin Francis Rigali, Keith Michael O'Brien, Eusebio Oscar Scheid, Ennio Antonelli, Tarcisio Bertone, Peter Kodwo Appiah Turkson, Telesphore Placidus Toppo, George Pell, Josip Bozanic, Jean Baptiste Pham Minh Man, Philippe Barbarin, Peter Erdő, Marc Ouellet, P.S.S., Georges Cottier, O.P.

Pope Benedict XVI

2006 (Mar. 24): William Levada, Franc Rodé, C.M., Agostino Vallini, Jorge Liberato Urosa Savino, Gaudencio Rosales, Jean-Pierre Ricard, Antonio Cañizares Llovera, Cheong Jin-Suk, Sean Patrick O'Malley, O.F.M. Cap., Stanislaw Dziwisz, Carlo Caffarra, Joseph Zen Ze-Kiun, S.D.B., Andrea Cordero Lanza di Montezemolo, Albert Vanhoye, S.J.

2007 (Nov. 24): Leonardo Sandri, John P. Foley, Giovanni Lajolo, Paul-Josef Cordes, Stanislaw Rylko, Angelo Comastri, Raffaele Farina SDB, Seán Brady, Lluís Martínez Sistach, André Vingt-Trois, Angelo Bagnasco, Théodore-Adrien Sarr, Oswald Gracias, Francisco Lopez Ortega, Daniel Nicholas DiNardo, Odilo Scherer, John Njue, Emmanuel III Delly, Giovanni Coppa, Estanislao Esteban Karlic.

2010 (Nov. 20): Angelo Amato, Antonios Naguib, Robert Sarah, Francesco Monterisi, Fortunato Baldelli, Raymond Leo Burke, Kurt Koch, Paolo Sardi, Mauro Piacenza, Velasio De Paolis, Gianfranco Ravasi, Medardo Joseph Mazombwe, Raúl Eduardo Vela Chiriboga, Monsengwo Pasinya, Paolo Romeo, Donald Wuerl, Raymundo Damasceno Assis, Kazimierz Nycz, Albert Malcolm Ranjith Patabendige Don, Reinhard Marx, José Manuel Estepa Llaurens, Elio Sgreccia, Walter Brandmuller, Domenico Bartolucci.

2012 (Feb. 19): Fernando Filoni, Manuel Monteiro de Castro, Santos Abril Castello, Antonio Maria Veglio, Giuseppe Bertello, Francesco Coccopalmerio, Joao Braz de Aviz, Edwin F. O'Brien, Domenico Calcagno, Giuseppe Versaldi, George Alencherry, Thomas C. Collins, Dominik Duka, Willem J. Eijk, Giuseppe Betori, Timothy M. Dolan, Rainer Maria Woelki, John Tong Hon, Lucian Muresan, Julien Ries, Prosper Grech, Karl Josef Becker; (Nov. 24): James M. Harvey, Bechara Boutros Rai, O.M.M., Baselios Cleemis Thottunkal, John Onaiyekan, Ruben Salazar Gomez, Luis Tagle.

DISTRIBUTION OF CARDINALS

As of Aug. 15, 2013, there were 202 cardinals from 68 countries or areas. Listed below are areas, countries, number and last names. Names with asterisks are cardinals ineligible to vote.

Europe — 110

Italy (47): Amato, Angelini,* Antonelli, Bagnasco,

Bartolucci,* Bertello, Bertone, Betori, Biffi,* Cacciavillan,* Caffarra, Calcagno, Canestri,* Cé,* Coccopalmerio, Comastri, Coppa,* Cordero Lanza di Montezemolo,* de Giorgi,* De Paolis, Farina, Filoni, Furno,* Lajolo, Marchisano,* Martino, Monterisi, Nicora, Noè,* Piacenza, Piovanelli,* Poletto, Ravasi, Re, Romeo, Ruini,* Sardi, Scola, Sebastiani,* Sepe, Sgreccia,* Silvestrini,* Sodano,* Tettamanzi, Tucci,* Vallini, Veglio, Versaldi.

Spain (10): Abril Castello, Alvarez Martinez,* Amigo Vallejo, Cañizares Llovera, Carles Gordó,* Estepa Llaurens,* Herranz Casado,* Martínez Sistach, Martinez Somalo,* Rouco Varela.

Germany (9): Becker,* Brandmüller,* Cordes, Kasper, Lehmann, Marx, Meisner, Wetter,* Woelki.

France (8): Barbarin, Etchegaray,* Panafieu,* Poupard,* Ricard, Tauran, Vanhoye,* Vingt-Trois.

Poland (6): Dziwisz, Grocholewski, Gulbinowicz,* Macharski,* Nycz, Rylko.

Switzerland (4): Agustoni,* Cottier,* Koch, Schwery.

Portugal (3): Policarpo, Monteiro de Castro, Saraiva Martins*

Czech Republic (2): Duka, Vlk*

Hungary (2): Erdő, Paskai.*

Ireland (2): Brady, Connell.*

Netherlands (2): Eijk, Simonis*

Slovakia (2): Korec,* Tomko.*

Ukraine (2): Husar, Jaworski.*

One from each of the following countries: **Austria**, Schönborn; **Belgium**, Danneels; **Bosnia Herzegovina**, Puljic; Croatia, Bozanic; **England**, Murphy-O'Connor; **Latvia**, Pujats*; **Lithuania**, Backis; **Malta**, Grech*; **Romania**, Murasyn*; **Scotland**, O'Brien; **Slovenia**, Rodé.

Asia — 19

India (6): Alencherry, Dias, Gracias, Lourdusamy,* Thottunkal, Toppo.

Philippines (3): Rosales, Tagle, Vidal.*

Hong Kong (2): Tong Hon, Zen Ze-kiun.*

Lebanon (2), Bechara Rai, Sfeir.*

One from each of the following countries: **Indonesia**, Darmaatmadja; **Iraq**, Delly*; **Korea**, Cheong Jin-Suk*; **Sri Lanka**, Ranjith Patabendige; **Thailand**, Kitbunchu*; **Vietnam**, Pham Minh Man.

Oceania — 4

Australia (3): Cassidy,* Clancy,* Pell.

One from **New Zealand**, Williams.*

Africa — 18

Nigeria (3): Arinze,* Okogie, Onaiyekan.

One from each of the following countries: **Angola**, do Nascimento*; **Cameroon**, Tumi*; **Congo**, Pasinya; **Egypt**, Naguib; **Ghana**, Turkson; **Guinea**, Sarah; **Ivory Coast**, Agre*; **Kenya**, Njue; **Mozambique**, Santos*; **Senegal**, Sarr; **South Africa**, Napier; **Sudan**, Wako; **Tanzania**, Pengo; **Uganda**, Wamala*; **Zambia**, Mozombwe.*

North America – 26

United States (19): Baum,* Burke, DiNardo, Dolan, Egan,* George, Harvey, Keeler,* Law,* Levada, McCarrick,* Mahony, Maida,* O'Brien, O'Malley, Rigali, Stafford,* Szoka,* Wuerl.

Mexico (4): Lozano Barragán, Rivera Carrera, Robles Ortega, Sandoval Iñiguez.

Canada (3): Collins, Ouellet, Turcotte.

Central and South America – 25

Brazil (9): Arns,* Braz de Aviz, Damasceno Assis, Falcão,* Fernandes de Araújo,* Hummes, Majella Agnelo, Scheid,* Scherer.
Argentina (3): Karlic,* Mejia,* Sandri.
Colombia (3): Castrillón Hoyos,* Rubiano Saenz, Salazar Gomez.
Chile (2): Errazuriz Ossa, Medina Estévez.*
.One each from the following countries: **Bolivia**, Sandoval; **Cuba**, Ortega y Alamino; **Dominican Republic**, Lopez Rodriguez; **Ecuador**, Vela Chiriboga; **Honduras**, Rodriguez Maradiaga; **Nicaragua**, Obando Bravo*; **Peru**, Cipriani Thorne; **Venezuela**, Urosa Savino

Cardinal Electors

As of August 1, 2013, there were 112 Cardinal-electors: 58 are from Europe, 16 from North America, 12 from South America, 3 from Central America, 11 from Africa, 11 from Asia and 1 from Oceania. The Electors are from 49 countries.
Total Cardinals
As of Aug. 1, 2013, there were 202 Cardinals: 110 are from Europe, 26 from North America, 21 from South America, 4 from Central America, 18 from Africa, 19 from Asia and 4 from Oceania. The Cardinals are from 68 countries.
Ineligible to Vote
As of Aug. 1, 2013, 90 of the 202 cardinals were ineligible to take part in a papal election in line with the apostolic letter *Ingravescentem Aetetem* effective Jan. 1, 1971, which limited the functions of cardinals after completion of their 80th year.

Cardinals affected are: Agré, Agustoni, Álvarez Martínez, Angelini, Araujo Sales, Arinze, Arns, Bartolucci, Baum, Becker, Biffi, Brandmüller, Cacciavillan, Canestri, Carles Gordó, Cassidy, Castrillón Hoyos, Cé, Cheli, Cheong Jin-suk, Clancy, Connell, Coppa, Cordero Lanza di Montezemolo, Cottier, Danneels, De Giorgi, Delly, do Nascimento, Egan, Errázuriz Ossa, Estepa Llaurens, Etchegaray, Falcão, Farina, Furno, Glemp, Grech, Gulbinowicz, Herranz Casado, Husar, Jaworski, Karlic, Kasper, Keeler. Kitbunchu, Korec, Law, Lourdusamy, Lozano Barragán, McCarrick, Macharski, Maida, Marchisano, Martinez Somalo, Martino, Mazombwe, Medina Estévez, Mejia, Muresan, Murphy-O'Connor, Obando Bravo, Panafieu, Paskai, Piovanelli, Poletto, Poupard, Pujats, Ries, Rosales, Rubiano Saenz, Ruini, Sandoval Iñiguez, Santos, Saraiva Martins, Scheid; Schwery, Sebastiani, Sfeir, Sgreccia, Silvestrini, Simonis, Sodano, Stafford, Szoka, Tomko, Tucci, Tumi, Vanhoye, Vidal, Vlk, Wamala, Wetter, Williams, Zen.

Cardinals who complete their 80th year in 2013-14 and who become ineligible to vote: 2013: Majella Agnelo, Meisner; 2014: Bertone, Cordes, Darmaatmadja, Hummes, Monterisi, Pham Minh Man, Re, Rodé, Sardi, Tettamanzi, Vela Chiriboga,

Cardinals of the United States

As of Aug. 15, 2013, the following cardinals were in service, according to their years of elevation (for biographies, see **College of Cardinals** above):
1976: **William W. Baum** (major penitentiary emeritus); 1985: **Bernard F. Law** (abp. emeritus of Boston); 1988: **Edmund C. Szoka** (governor emeritus of the Vatican City State); 1991: **Roger M. Mahony** (abp. emeritus of Los Angeles); 1994: **William H. Keeler** (abp. emeritus of Baltimore), **Adam J. Maida** (abp. emeritus of Detroit); 1998: **Francis E. George, O.M.I.** (abp. of Chicago), **James F. Stafford** (Major Penitentiary emeritus of the Apostolic Penitentiary); 2001: **Edward M. Egan** (abp. emeritus of New York), **Theodore E. McCarrick** (abp. emeritus of Washington), 2003: **Justin F. Rigali** (abp. emeritus of Philadelphia); 2006: **William J. Levada** (prefect emeritus of the Cong. for the Doctrine of the Faith), **Sean P. O'Malley, O.F.M. Cap.** (abp. of Boston). 2007: **Daniel N. DiNardo** (abp. of Galveston-Houston); 2010: **Raymond L. Burke** (prefect of the Apostolic Signatura); **Donald W. Wuerl** (abp. of Washington, D.C.); 2012: **Timothy M. Dolan** (abp. of New York); **Edwin F. O'Brien** (Grand Master of the Knights of the Holy Sepulchre); **James M. Harvey** (archpriest of the papal basilica of S. Paolo fuori le mura, Rome). **Lubomyr Husar, M.S.U.**, major abp. emeritus of Lviv for Ukrainians, is also an American citizen.

U.S. Cardinals of the Past (according to year of elevation; for biographical data, see **American Catholics of the Past** at www.catholicalmanac.com): 1875: John McCloskey; 1886: James Gibbons; 1911: John Farley, William O'Connell; 1921: Dennis Dougherty; 1924: Patrick Hayes, George Mundelein; 1946: John Glennon, Edward Mooney, Francis Spellman, Samuel Stritch; 1953: James F. McIntyre; 1958: John O'Hara, C.S.C., Richard Cushing; 1959: Albert Meyer, Aloysius Muench; 1961: Joseph Ritter; 1965: Lawrence J. Shehan; 1967: Francis Brennan, John P. Cody, Patrick A. O'Boyle, John J. Krol; 1969: John J. Wright, Terence J. Cooke, John F. Dearden, John J. Carberry; 1973: Humberto S. Medeiros, Timothy Manning; 1983: Joseph L. Bernardin; 1985: John J. O'Connor; 1988: James A. Hickey; 1994: Anthony J. Bevilacqua; 2001: Avery Dulles, S.J.; 2007: John P. Foley. (Myroslav Lubachivsky, major abp. of Lviv of the Ukrainians (Ukraine), was made a card. in 1985. He was a citizen of the United States and metropolitan of the Philadelphia Ukrainian Rite Archeparchy, from 1979-81.)

Prelates who became cardinals after returning to their native countries: John Lefebvre de Chevrus, first bp. of Boston (1808-23) and apostolic administrator of New York (1810-15), elevated to the cardinalate, 1836, in France. Ignatius Persico, O.F.M. Cap., bp. of Savannah (1870-72), elevated to the cardinalate, 1893, in Italy; Diomede Falconio, O.F.M. ord. a priest in Buffalo, NY, missionary in U.S., apostolic delegate to the U.S. (1902-11), elevated to cardinalate, 1911, in Italy.

The Universal Church

THE CHURCH IN COUNTRIES THROUGHOUT THE WORLD

(Principal sources for statistics: *Annuarium Statisticum Ecclesiae*, Statistical Yearbook of the Church, 2011 — the most recent edition; *Annuario Pontificio*, 2013; and Agenzia Internazionale FIDES. Figures are as of Jan. 1, 2012, except for cardinals [as of Aug. 30, 2013] and others which are indicated. For 2012-2013 developments, see **Index** entries for individual countries.)

An asterisk indicates that the country has full diplomatic relations with the Holy See (see **Diplomats to the Holy See** in the **Holy See** section).

Abbreviations (in order in which they appear): archd. – archdiocese; dioc. – diocese; ap. ex. – apostolic exarchate; prel. – prelature; abb. – abbacy; v.a. – apostolic vicariate; p.a. – apostolic prefecture; a.a. – apostolic administration; mil. ord. – military ordinariate; card. – cardinal; abp. – archbishops; bp. – bishops (diocesan and titular); priests (dioc. – diocesan or secular priests; rel. – those belonging to religious orders); p.d. – permanent deacons; sem. – major seminarians, diocesan and religious; bros. – brothers; srs. – sisters; bap. – baptisms; Caths. – Catholic population; tot. pop. – total population; (AD) – apostolic delegate (see **Index**: Papal Representatives).

Afghanistan

Republic in south-central Asia; capital, Kabul. Christianity antedated Muslim conquest in the seventh century but was overcome by it. All inhabitants are subject to the law of Islam (Shariah). Under Afghan's Taliban regime, religious freedom was severely restricted, and proselytizing was forbidden. In January 2002, Italian and English chaplains celebrated the first public Mass in nearly 10 years in Kabul, at the Italian Embassy.

Albania*

Archd., 2; dioc., 3; a.a., 1; abp., 3; bp., 5; parishes, 122; priests, 154 (57 dioc., 97 rel.); p.d., 1; sem., 36; bros., 14; srs., 495; bap., 4,265; Caths., 516,000 (16.1%); tot. pop., 3,218,000.

Republic in the Balkans, bordering the Adriatic Sea; capital, Tirana. Christianity was introduced in apostolic times. The northern part of the country remained faithful to Rome while the South broke from unity following the schism of 1054. A large percentage of the population became Muslim following the invasion (15th century) and long centuries of occupation by the Ottoman Turks. Many Catholics fled to southern Italy, Sicily and Greece. In 1945, at the time of the communist takeover, an estimated 68 percent of the population was Muslim; 19 percent was Orthodox and 13 percent Roman Catholic. The Catholic Church prevailed in the north. During 45 years of communist dictatorship, the Church fell victim, as did all religions, to systematic persecution.

In 1967, the government, declaring it had eliminated all religion in the country, proclaimed itself the first atheist state in the world. The right to practice religion was restored in late 1990. In March 1991, a delegation from the Vatican was allowed to go to Albania; later in the year diplomatic relations were established with the Holy See at the request of the Albanian prime minister. Pope John Paul II made a one-day visit to the country Apr. 25, 1993, during which he ordained four bishops appointed by him in December 1992 to fill long-vacant sees. The first Albanian cardinal was named in November 1994. Albanians welcomed hundreds of thousands of ethnic Albanians from Kosovo during Yugoslav persecution in 1999.

Algeria*

Archd., 1; dioc., 3; abp., 3; bp., 4; parishes, 39; priests, 74 (21 dioc., 53 rel.); p.d., 1; sem., 4; bros., 17; srs., 158; bap., 7; Caths., 9,000 (.01%); tot. pop., 36,717,000.

Republic in northwest Africa; capital, Algiers. Christianity, introduced at an early date, succumbed to Vandal devastation in the fifth century and Muslim conquest in 709, but survived in small communities into the 12th century. Missionary work was unsuccessful except in service to traders, military personnel and captives along the coast. Church organization was established after the French gained control of the territory in the 1830s. A large number of Catholics were among the estimated million Europeans who left the country after it secured independence from France, July 5, 1962. Islam is the state religion. Armed Islamic militants and guerrillas have caused terror and unrest in Algeria since 1992. Among the more than 80,000 people killed were seven Trappist monks and the Catholic bishop of Oran, all in 1996.

Andorra*

Parishes, 7; priests, 16 (10 dioc., 6 rel.); srs., 10; bap., 331; Caths., 79,000 (99%); tot. pop., 85,000.

Parliamentary state (1993) in the Pyrenees; capital, Andorra la Vella. From 1278-1993, it was a co-principality under the rule of the French head of state and the bishop of Urgel, Spain, who retain their titles. Christianity was introduced at an early date. Catholicism is the state religion. Ecclesiastical jurisdiction is under the Spanish Diocese of Urgel. The constitution calls for freedom of religion, but also guarantees "the Roman Catholic Church free and public exercise of its activities and the preservation of the relations of special cooperation with the state."

Angola*

Archd., 5; dioc., 14; card., 1; abp., 5; bp., 21; parishes, 313; priests, 914 (531 dioc., 383 rel.); sem., 1,292; bros., 93; srs., 2,260; catechists, 37,737; bap., 146,911; Caths., 9,576,000 (55.5%); tot. pop., 17,229,000.

Republic in southwest Africa; capital, Luanda. Evangelization by Catholic missionaries from Portugal, dat ing from 1491, reached high points in the 17th and 18th centuries. Independence from Portugal in 1975 and the long civil war that followed (peace accord signed in 1991) left the Church with a heavy loss of personnel resulting from the departure of about half the foreign missionaries and the persecution and martyrdom experienced by the Church during the war. Renewed fighting following elections in late 1992 brought repeated appeals for peace from the nation's bishops and religious in 1993 and 1994.

Despite another peace accord signed by the rebels and the government in late 1994, conditions have remained unsettled. One effect of the fighting was to cut off Church leaders from large groups of the faithful. In an attempt to encourage peace efforts, the Vatican established diplomatic relations with Angola in 1997. Attacks on Church workers, however, continued in 1998 and 1999. In 2000, Church leaders began an active peace movement, holding national and diocesan congresses and beginning a consultation with Angolan political leaders. Government and rebel representatives signed a peace agreement in 2002, after the government killed rebel leader Jonas Savimbi, and the Church offered humanitarian aid and helped to rebuild the country.

Antigua and Barbuda*

Dioc., 1; bp., 1; parishes, 2; priests, 10 (5 dioc., 5 rel.); p.d, 5; sem., 1; srs., 9; bap., 69; Caths., 9,000 (12.5%); tot. pop., 86,000.

Independent (1981) Caribbean island nation; capital, St. John's, Antigua. The Diocese of St. John's-Basseterre includes Antigua and Barbuda, St. Kitts and Nevis, Anguilla, the British Virgin Islands and Montserrat.

Argentina*

Archd., 14; dioc., 51; prel., 4; ap. ex., 3 (for Armenians of Latin America); mil. ord., 1; card., 3; abp., 20; bp., 93; parishes, 2,780; priests, 5,909 (4,012 dioc., 1,897 rel.); p.d., 824; sem., 1,473; bros., 774; srs., 7,937; bap., 553,657; catechists, 95,017; Caths., 38,016,000 (93%); tot. pop., 41,282,000

Republic in southeast South America, bordering on the Atlantic; capital, Buenos Aires. Priests were with the Magellan exploration party and the first Mass in the country was celebrated Apr. 1, 1519. Missionary work began in the 1530s, diocesan organization in the late 1540s, and effective evangelization about 1570. Independence from Spain was proclaimed in 1816. Since its establishment in the country, the Church has been influenced by Spanish cultural and institutional forces, antagonistic liberalism, government interference and opposition; the latter reached a climax during the last five years of the first presidency of Juan Peron (1946-55).

Widespread human rights violations, including the disappearance of thousands of people, marked the "Dirty War," the period of military rule from 1976 to December 1983, when an elected civilian government took over. In 1996 the Argentine bishops said they did not do enough to stop human rights violations during the "Dirty War." In the late 1990s, the bishops spoke out against government corruption and have worked to find solutions to the country's crises. In 2013, Cardinal Jorge Mario Bergoglio of Buenos Aires was elected Pope Francis, an event that has galvanized the Church in Argentina.

Armenia*

Ord., 1 (for Catholic Armenians of Eastern Europe, with seat in Armenia); parishes, 11; abp., 2; priests, 11 (7 dioc., 4 rel.); sem., 10; bros., 5; srs., 26; bap., 220; Caths.,

200,000 (4%); tot. pop., 3,274,000.

Republic in Asia Minor; capital Yerevan. Part of the USSR from 1920 until it declared its sovereignty in September 1991. Ancient Armenia, which also included territory annexed by Turkey in 1920, was Christianized in the fourth century. Diplomatic relations were established with the Holy See on May 23, 1992. Pope John Paul II visited Armenia in late September 2001 to help mark the 1,700th anniversary of Christianity in the nation. The small Catholic community in Armenia has good relations with the predominant Armenian Apostolic Church, an Oriental Orthodox Church.

Australia*

Archd., 7; dioc., 25; mil. ord., 1; card., 3; abp., 10; bp., 52; parishes, 1,370; priests, 3,117 (1,881 dioc., 1,236 rel.); p.d., 127; sem., 312; bros., 897; srs., 6,152; catechists, 7,344; bap., 64,507; Caths., 6,179,000 (27.5%); tot. pop. 22,621,000.

Commonwealth; island continent southeast of Asia; capital, Canberra. The first Catholics in the country were Irish under penal sentence, 1795-1804; the first public Mass was celebrated May 15, 1803. Official organization of the Church dates from 1820. The country was officially removed from mission status in March 1976.

Near the end of the 20th century, the Church in Australia was rocked by allegations of sexual abuse from previous decades. In 1996 the Australian bishops published a plan for dealing with such cases. In 1998 the bishops also apologized to aboriginal children their support of harsh government policy in the 1970s.

In an unusual move, in mid-November 1998, just before the Synod of Bishops for Oceania and after the Australian bishops' ad limina visits, Vatican officials met with Church leaders from Australia to discuss doctrinal and pastoral issues. In December 1998, the Vatican and representatives of Australian Church leaders signed a document, later endorsed by the Australian bishops' conference, that spoke of a "crisis of faith" in the Catholic Church on the continent. The Australian Church, like many others in the late 20th and early 21st century, struggled with cases of clergy sexual abuse. Pope Benedict XVI made a memorable visit in 2008.

Austria*

Archd., 2; dioc., 7; abb., 1; ord., 1; mil. ord., 1; card., 1; abp., 3; bp., 21; parishes, 3,102; priests, 4,178 (2,544 dioc., 1,634 rel.); p.d., 627; sem., 288; bros., 577; srs., 4,206; catechists, 1,701; bap., 49,613; Caths., 6,123,000 (73%); tot. pop., 8,423,000.

Republic in central Europe; capital, Vienna. Christianity was introduced by the end of the third century, strengthened considerably by conversion of the Bavarians from about 600, and firmly established in the second half of the eighth century. Catholicism survived and grew stronger as the principal religion in the country in the post-Reformation period, but suffered from Josephinism in the 18th century. Although liberated from much government harassment in the aftermath of the Revolution of 1848, the Church came under pressure again some 20 years later in the Kulturkampf. The Church faced strong opposition from Socialists after WW I and suffered persecution from 1938 to 1945 during the Nazi regime. Some Church-state matters are regulated by a concordat originally concluded in 1934.

At the turn of the century, the Church in Austria was beset by internal difficulties, including a seminary pornography scandal and the launch of a global movement seeking more lay participation in Church decision-making and changes in

Church policy on ordination of women and priestly celibacy. In 1995, Card. Hans Hermann Gröer resigned as archbishop of Vienna amid charges of sexual misconduct. His successor, Card. Christoph Schönborn, has worked to restore a sense of unity to the Church and to bring healing.

Azerbaijan*

Mission. Independent republic (1991) on the Caspian Sea; formerly part of the USSR; capital, Baku. Islam is the prevailing religion. Soviet rulers destroyed Baku's one Catholic church in the late 1930s; in the 21st century, the church was rebuilt and was dedicated in 2007. A small Catholic community of Polish and Armenian origin near the capital is ministered to by two missionaries. Latin-rite Catholics are under the apostolic administration of Caucasus (seat in Georgia), established in December 1993. The Holy See reached an agreement with the government in 2011 to regulate relations.

Bahamas*

Dioc., 1; bp., 1; parishes, 30; priests, 29 (14 dioc., 15 rel.); p.d., 1; sem., 5; srs., 18; catechists, 235; bap., 430; Caths., 50,000 (15%); tot. pop., 340,000.

Independent (July 10, 1973) island group consisting of some 700 (30 inhabited) small islands southeast of Florida and north of Cuba; capital, Nassau. On Oct. 12, 1492, Columbus landed on one of these islands, where the first Mass was celebrated in the New World. Organization of the Catholic Church in the Bahamas dates from about the middle of the 19th century. The Church was under the jurisdiction on the Archdiocese of New York until 1960, when Nassau became a diocese. From 1891 to 1981, Benedictines from St. John's Abbey in Collegeville, MN, were responsible for episcopal leadership. After that time, Benedictine priests and brothers continued working in the Bahamas until 2005; local Benedictine nuns continue their work there. Nassau became an archdiocese in 1999.

Bahrain*

Parish, 1; priests, 7 (1 dioc., 6 rel.); srs., 6 bap., 143; Caths., 110,000 (4.3%); tot. pop., 1,268,000. (AD)

Island state in Persian Gulf; capital, Manama. Population is Muslim; Catholics are foreign workers, under ecclesiastical jurisdiction of Arabia apostolic vicariate. Diplomatic relations were established between Bahrain and the Holy See in January 2000.

Bangladesh*

Archd., 1; dioc., 5; abp., 3; bp., 9; parishes, 97; priests, 360 (196 dioc., 164 rel.); p.d., 2; sem., 105; bros., 101 srs., 1,100; catechists, 1,546; bap., 8,088; Caths., 340,000 (.20%); tot. pop. 150,668,000.

Formerly the eastern portion of Pakistan. Officially constituted as a separate nation Dec. 16, 1971; capital, Dhaka. Jesuit, Dominican and Augustinian missionaries were in the area in the 16th century. An apostolic vicariate (of Bengali) was established in 1834; the hierarchy was erected in 1950. Islam, the principal religion, was declared the state religion in 1988; freedom of religion is granted. Church-run humanitarian and development agencies have been instrumental in responding to natural disasters, such as flooding. The bishops have emphasized inculturation and Church social doctrine.

Barbados*

Dioc., 1; bp., 2; parishes, 6; priests, 11 (4 dioc., 7 rel.);

p.d., 1; srs., 9; bap., 99; sem., 1; Caths., 11,000 (3.6%); tot. pop., 277,000.

Parliamentary democracy (independent since 1966), easternmost of the Caribbean islands; capital, Bridgetown. About 70 % of the population are Anglican.

Belarus*

Archd., 1; dioc., 3; card., 1; abp., 2; bp., 4; parishes, 629; priests, 480 (288 dioc., 192 rel.); sem., 129; bros., 6; srs., 314; bap., 7,787; Caths., 1,418,000 (14%); tot. pop., 10,404,000.

Independent republic (1991) in Eastern Europe; former Soviet republic (Byelorussia); capital, Minsk. Slow recovery of the Church was reported after years of repression in the Soviet Union, although in the mid-1990s under the authoritarian rule of President Alexander Lukashenka, the Church encountered tensions, especially in refusal of permits for foreign religious workers. In December 2000, the nation's bishops asked forgiveness for the "human weaknesses" of Church members throughout the centuries and said the Church forgave acts of Soviet-era persecution. In October 2002, Belarus adopted one of the most restrictive religion laws in the former Soviet Union, but by April 2003 government officials had granted the Catholic Church full legal status.

Belgium*

Archd., l; dioc., 7; mil. ord., 1; card., 2; abp., 3; bp., 17; parishes, 3,905; priests, 5,804 (3,359 dioc., 2,445 rel.); p.d., 604; sem., 227; bros., 855; srs., 9,408; catechists, 8,699; bap., 80,121; Caths., 7,900,000 (73%); tot. pop., 10,996,000.

Constitutional monarchy in northwestern Europe; capital, Brussels. Christianity was introduced about the first quarter of the fourth century and major evangelization was completed about 730. During the rest of the medieval period the Church had firm diocesan and parochial organization, generally vigorous monastic life and influential monastic and cathedral schools. Lutherans and Calvinists made some gains during the Reformation period but there was a strong Catholic restoration in the first half of the 17th century, when the country was under Spanish rule. Jansenism disturbed the Church from about 1640 into the 18th century. Josephinism, imposed by an Austrian regime, hampered the Church late in the same century. Repressive and persecutory measures were enforced during the Napoleonic conquest. Freedom came with separation of Church and state in the wake of the Revolution of 1830, which ended the reign of William I. Thereafter, the Church encountered serious problems with philosophical liberalism and political socialism.

Catholics have long been engaged in strong educational, social and political movements. In 1990, in an unprecedented political maneuver, King Baudouin temporarily gave up his throne, saying his Catholic conscience would not allow him to sign a law legalizing abortion. In the mid- and late-1990s, Church leaders expressed concern that Belgians dissented from Church teachings. Therapeutic in vitro fertilization for stable married couples continued at a leading Belgian Catholic hospital despite Vatican objections. The bishops fought a losing battle against the 2002 legalization of euthanasia and faced new allegations of sexual abuse of minors by clergy. Controversy surrounded the massive seizure of records and files from the residence and chancery of the Abp. of Mechelen-Brussels in 2010.

Belize*

Dioc., 1; abp.; bp., 2; parishes, 14; priests, 44 (11 dioc.,

33 rel.); p.d., 7; sem., 2; bros., 5; srs., 53 catechists, 495; bap., 2,431; Caths., 158,000 (76%); tot. pop., 319,000.

Independent (Sept. 21, 1981) constitutional monarchy on eastern coast of Central America; capital, Belmopan. Its history has points in common with Guatemala, where evangelization began in the 16th century. The Church in Belize worked with refugees during the decades of Central American civil wars.

Benin*

Archd., 2; dioc., 8; abp., 4; bp., 7; parishes, 338; priests, 866 (730 dioc., 136 rel.); sem., 536; bros., 113; srs., 1,247; catechists, 10,630; bap., 55,444; Caths., 3,067,000 (29%); tot. pop., 9,067,000.

Democratic republic in West Africa, bordering on the Atlantic; capital, Porto Novo. Missionary work was very limited from the 16th to the 18th centuries. Effective evangelization dates from 1861. The hierarchy was established in 1955. In the 1970s, Benin's Marxist-Leninist government nationalized Catholic schools, expelled foreign missionaries and jailed some priests. After the government dropped the one-party system in 1989, Abp. Isidore de Souza of Cotonou presided over the 1990 national conference that drew up a new constitution and prepared the way for elections. One challenge facing the Church as it entered the 21st century was maintaining peace with people of other faiths. Pope Benedict XVI visited the country in November 2011.

Bermuda

Dioc., 1; bp., 1; parishes, 6; priests, 8 (1 dioc., 7 rel.); sem., 7; srs., 2; bap., 94; Caths., 10,000 (16%); tot. pop., 65,000. (AD)

British dependency, consisting of 360 islands (20 of them inhabited), nearly 600 miles east of Cape Hatteras; capital, Hamilton. Catholics were not permitted until about 1800. Occasional pastoral care was provided the few Catholics there by visiting priests during the 19th century. Early in the 1900s priests from Nova Scotia began serving the area. An apostolic prefecture was set up in 1953. The first bishop assumed jurisdiction in 1956, when it was made an apostolic vicariate; diocese established, 1967.

Bhutan

Parish; bap., 1; Caths., 1,000 (approx.); tot. pop., 2,664,000.

Kingdom in the Himalayas, northeast of India; capital, Thimphu. Buddhism is the state religion; Christians, including Catholics, are free to worship in private homes but cannot erect religious buildings, proselytize or congregate in public. Jesuits (1963) and Salesians (1965) were invited to the country to direct schools. Salesians were expelled in February 1982, on disputed charges of proselytism. The only Catholic missionary allowed to stay in the country was Canadian Jesuit Father William Mackey, who served Catholics there from 1963 until his death in 1995. Ecclesiastical jurisdiction is under the Darjeeling (India) Diocese, which ordained the first indigenous Bhutanese priest in 1995.

Bolivia*

Archd., 4; dioc., 6; prel., 2; mil. ord., 1; v.a., 5; card., 1; abp., 6; bp., 23; parishes, 624; priests, 1,231 (629 dioc., 602 rel.); p.d., 102; sem., 639; bros., 233; srs., 2,435; catechists, 17,722; bap., 160,584; Caths., 9,050,000 (83%); tot. pop., 10,624,000.

Republic in central South America; capital, Sucre; seat of government, La Paz. Catholicism, the official religion, was introduced in the 1530s, and the first diocese was established in 1552. Effective evangelization among the Indians, slow to start, reached high points in the middle of the 18th and the beginning of the 19th centuries and was resumed about 1840. Independence from Spain was proclaimed in 1825, at the end of a campaign that started in 1809. Church-state relations are regulated by a 1951 concordat with the Holy See. Catholics have worked against social poverty and corruption. Early in the 21st century, amid social and economic turmoil, surveys showed the Catholic Church was seen as the most credible institution in the country.

Bosnia and Herzegovina*

Archd., 1; dioc., 2; card., 1; abp., 2; bp., 3; parishes, 303; priests, 651 (306 dioc., 345 rel.); sem., 141; bros., 18; srs., 536; bap., 4,734; Caths., 451,000 (12%); tot. pop., 3,843,000.

Independent republic (1992) in southeastern Europe; formerly part of Yugoslavia; capital, Sarajevo. During the three years of fighting that erupted after Bosnia-Herzegovina declared its independence, some 450,000 Catholics were driven from their homes; many fled to Croatia or southern Bosnia. Sarajevo Card. Vinko Puljic, named a cardinal in 1994, has led the bishops in calls for the safe return of all refugees from the war and acknowledged that in some areas Croatian Catholics were responsible for atrocities. Although the bishops worked to rebuild the Church, they said ethnic discrimination and violence still plagued the nation more than a decade after the war ended.

Botswana

Dioc., 1; v.a., 1; bp., 2; parishes, 40; priests, 63 (14 dioc., 49 rel.); p.d., 5; sem., 20; bros., 5; srs., 82; catechists, 362; bap., 1,300; Caths., 98,000 (5%); tot. pop., 1,850,000.

Republic (independent since 1966) in southern Africa; capital, Gaborone. The first Catholic mission was opened in 1928 near Gaborone; earlier attempts at evangelization dating from 1879 were unsuccessful. The Church in Botswana gave strong support to tens of thousands of South African refugees from apartheid. As Botswana's diamond industry grew, Church leaders worked to minimize the effects of social changes such as pockets of unemployment and competition for jobs.

Brazil*

Archd., 44; dioc., 215; prel., 12; abb., 1; exarch., 1; mil. ord., 1; card., 9; abp., 75; bp., 370; parishes, 10,802; priests, 20,701 (13,121 dioc., 7,580 rel.); p.d., 2,903; sem., 8,956; bros., 2,702; srs., 30,528; catechists, 483,104; bap., 1,571,872; Caths., 164,780,000 (85%); tot. pop., 195,041,000.

Federal republic in northeastern South America; capital, Brasilia. One of several priests with the discovery party celebrated the first Mass in the country Apr. 26, 1500. Evangelization began some years later, and the first diocese was erected in 1551. During the colonial period, which lasted until 1822, evangelization made some notable progress — especially in the Amazon region between 1680 and 1750 — but was seriously hindered by government policy and the attitude of colonists regarding Amazon Indians the missionaries tried to protect from exploitation and slavery. The Jesuits were suppressed in 1782 and other missionaries expelled as well. Liberal anti-Church influence grew in strength. The government exercised maximum control over the Church. After the proclamation of independence from Portugal in 1822 and throughout the regency, government control was tightened and the Church suffered greatly from dissident actions of ecclesiastical brotherhoods, Masonic anticlericalism and general decline in religious life. Church and state were separated by the constitution of 1891, proclaimed two years after the end of the empire.

The Church carried into the 20th century problems associated with increasingly difficult political, economic and social conditions affecting the majority of the population. Many Afro-Brazilians indiscriminately mixed African-based rites such as candomble with Catholic rituals. In the second half of the 20th century, the bishops became known for their liberal stances on social and some theological issues. In the 1980s, Vatican officials had a series of meetings with Brazilian bishops to discuss liberation theology and other issues. The Brazilian bishops' conference took the lead in advocating for land reform in the country. Members of the Church's Pastoral Land Commission often faced threats, harassment and murder. The Church-founded Indigenous Missionary Council worked for the rights of the country's Indians. Pope Francis visited Brazil in July 2013 for World Youth Day in Rio de Janeiro.

Brunei

P.a., 1; parishes, 3; priests, 4 (3 dioc., 1 rel); sem., 1; srs. 1; bap., 200; Caths., 1,900 (0.6%); tot. pop., 418,000.

Independent state (1984) on the northern coast of Borneo; formal name, Brunei Darussalam; capital, Bandar Seri Begawan. Islam is the official religion; other religions are allowed with some restrictions. Most of the Catholics are technicians and skilled workers from other countries who are not permanent residents; under ecclesiastical jurisdiction of Miri Diocese, Malaysia.

Bulgaria*

Dioc., 2; ap. ex., 1; abp., 1; bp., 3; parishes, 56; priests, 67 (25 dioc., 42 rel.); sem., 5; bros., 7; srs., 85; bap., 360; Caths., 73,000 (1%); tot. pop., 7,327,000.

Republic in southeastern Europe on the eastern part of the Balkan peninsula; capital, Sofia. Most of the population is Orthodox. Christianity was introduced before 343 but disappeared with the migration of Slavs into the territory. The baptism of Boris I about 865 ushered in a new period of Christianity, which soon became involved in switches of loyalty between Constantinople and Rome. Through it all the Byzantine, and later Orthodox, element remained stronger and survived under the rule of Ottoman Turks into the 19th century.

In 1947 the constitution of the new republic decreed the separation of Church and state. Catholic schools and institutions were abolished and foreign religious banished in 1948. A year later the apostolic delegate was expelled. Ivan Romanoff, vicar general of Plovdiv, died in prison in 1952. Bp. Eugene Bossilkoff, imprisoned in 1948, was sentenced to death in 1952; his fate remained unknown until 1975, when the Bulgarian government informed the Vatican that he had died in prison shortly after being sentenced. He was beatified in 1998. Although Church leaders were permitted to attend the Second Vatican Council, all Church activity was under surveillance and/or control by the government, which professed to be atheistic. Pastoral and related activities were strictly limited. There was some improvement in Bulgarian-Vatican relations in 1975. In 1979, the Sofia-Plovdiv apostolic vicariate was raised to a diocese, and a bishop was appointed for the vacant see of Nicopoli.

Diplomatic relations with the Holy See were established in 1990. In the late 1990s, the government instituted religion classes in state schools, but Church leaders had no input into the curriculum and that teachers were mostly Orthodox. In 2002, Pope John Paul II visited Bulgaria.

Burkina Faso*

Archd., 3; dioc., 11; abps., 6; bp., 13; parishes, 162; priests, 925 (770 dioc., 155 rel.); sem., 439; bros., 263; srs., 1,469; catechists, 7,747; bap., 89,925; Caths., 2,374,000 (13.3%); tot. pop., 16,254,000.

Republic inland in West Africa; capital, Ouagadougou. Missionaries of Africa started the first missions in 1900 and 1901. Their sisters began work in 1911. A minor and a major seminary were established in 1926 and 1942, respectively. The hierarchy was established in 1955. The first indigenous bishop in modern times from West Africa was ordained in 1956 and the first cardinal created in 1965. In 1980 and 1990, Pope John Paul II's visits to the country were used to launch appeals for an end to desertification of sub-Saharan Africa and an end to poverty in the region. In later years, the pope encouraged increased evangelization and interreligious harmony.

Burma (See Myanmar)

Burundi*

Archd., 2; dioc., 6; abp., 3; bp., 8; parishes, 164; priests, 677 (579 dioc., 98 rel.); sem., 609; bros., 210; srs., 1,642; catechists, 5,593; bap., 92,886; Caths., 5,838,000 (68%); tot. pop., 8,668,000.

Republic (1966), near the equator in east-central Africa; capital, Bujumbura. The first permanent Catholic mission station was established late in the 19th century. Large numbers were received into the Church following the ordination of the first Burundian priests in 1925. The first indigenous bishop was appointed in 1959.

In 1972-73, the country was torn by tribal warfare between the Tutsis, the ruling minority, and the Hutus. In 1979, the government began expelling foreign missionaries, and in 1986, seminaries were nationalized. A gradual resumption of Church activity since 1987 has been hampered by continuing ethnic violence, which began in 1993 and left more than 150,000 Burundians dead. The bishops repeatedly have called for peace and for an end to sanctions imposed by the Organization of African Unity in 1996. Missionaries continued to be the target of violent attacks, and the papal nuncio was killed after being shot in an ambush in 2003.

Cambodia*

V.a., 1; p.a., 2; bp., 2; parishes, 39 (there were also 28 mission stations without resident priests); priests, 96 (38 dioc., 58 rel.); sem., 9; bros., 26; srs., 99; catechists, 253; baptisms, 583; Caths., 22,000 (.16%); tot. pop., 15,342,000.

Constitutional monarchy in Southeast Asia; capital, Phnom Penh. Evangelization dating from the second half of the 16th century had limited results, more among Vietnamese than Khmers. Thousands of Catholics of Vietnamese origin were forced to flee in 1970 because of Khmer hostility. Most indigenous priests and nuns were killed under the 1975-79 Pol Pot regime. During those years, the Vietnamese invasion in 1979 and the long civil war that followed, foreign missionaries were expelled, local clergy and religious were sent to work the land and a general persecution followed. Religious freedom was re-established in 1990. Diplomatic relations with the Holy See were established in March 1994. Despite a lack of vocations, many Catholics maintain their faith through small Christian communities led by lay catechists. In the 21st century, Church leaders described their congregations as young and vibrant, involved in such things as AIDS ministry.

Cameroon*

Archd., 5; dioc., 19; card., 1; abp., 7; bp., 24; parishes, 938; priests, 2,128 (1,480 dioc., 648 rel.); p.d., 24; sem., 1,543; bros., 430; srs., 2,556; catechists, 26,100; bap., 125,837; Caths., 5,529,000 (26%); tot. pop., 20,387,000.

Republic in West Africa; capital, Yaounde. Effective evangelization began in 1890, although Catholics had been in the country long before that time. In the 40-year period from 1920 to 1960, the number of Catholics increased from 60,000 to 700,000. The first black priests were ordained in 1935. Twenty years later the first indigenous bishops were ordained and the hierarchy established. The first Cameroonian cardinal (Christian Wiyghan Tumi) was named in 1988. Around that same time, unknown people began persecuting Church personnel. Among those murdered was Abp. Yves Plumy of Garoua in 1991. Some felt the government did not do enough to investigate.

Canada* (See Catholic Church in Canada; see also Statistics of the Church in Canada)

Cape Verde*

Dioc., 2; bp., 2; parishes, 35; priests, 62 (21 dioc., 41 rel.); sem., 27; bros., 5; srs., 115; catechists, 2,768; bap., 5,573; Caths., 531,000 (93%); tot. pop., 566,000.

Independent (July 5, 1975) island group in the Atlantic 300 miles west of Senegal; formerly a Portuguese overseas province; capital, Praia, São Tiago Island. Evangelization began some years before the establishment of a diocese in 1532. The Church languished from the 17th to the 19th centuries, and for two long periods there was no resident bishop. Portugal's anti-clerical government closed the only minor seminary in 1910. Missionaries returned in the 1940s. Cape Verde has faced massive emigration of youth because of perennial drought and a weak economy.

Central African Republic*

Archd., 1; dioc., 8; abp., 2; bp., 11; parishes, 116; priests, 322 (187 dioc., 135 rel.); sem., 218; bros., 49; srs., 336; catechists, 4,127; bap., 20,786; Caths., 1,479,000 (24%); tot. pop., 4,380,000.

Former French colony (independent since 1960) in central Africa; capital, Bangui. Effective evangelization dates from 1894. The region was organized as a mission territory in 1909. The first indigenous priest was ordained in 1938. The hierarchy was organized in 1955. The Church in the country has expressed concern about the growing number of sects. Frequent military coups and attempted coups have left the nation divided, and church leaders have worked for reconciliation; including heading the national dialogue coordination team. Hundreds of thousands of people remain displaced, and sporadic fighting continues.

Chad*

Archd., 1; dioc., 6; v.a., 1; abp., 2; bp., 7; parishes, 122; priests, 266 (151 dioc., 115 rel.); sem., 127; p.d.; bros., 41; srs., 379; catechists, 6,991; bap., 19,450; Caths., 1,074,000 (9.5%); tot. pop., 11,036,000.

Republic (independent since 1960) in north-central Africa; former French possession; capital, N'Djamena. Evangelization began in 1929, leading to firm organization in 1947 and establishment of the hierarchy in 1955. Many catechists, who often were local community leaders, were killed during Chad's 1982-87 civil war. The Vatican established diplomatic relations with Chad in 1988. After the government established more freedoms in the early 1990s, the Church worked to teach people, including Catholics, that solidarity must extend across religious, ethnic and regional boundaries. Church workers were involved in ministering to hundreds of thousands of refugees displaced during the conflict in the Darfur region of Sudan.

Chile*

Archd., 5; dioc., 19; prel., 1; v.a., 1; mil. ord., 1; card., 2; abp., 8; bp., 39; parishes, 950; priests, 2,455 (1,204 dioc., 1,251 rel.); p.d., 1,011; sem., 659; bros., 397; srs., 4,442; catechists, 48,454; bap., 133,239; Caths., 12,768,000 (74%); tot. pop., 17,248,000.

Republic on the southwest coast of South America; capital, Santiago. Priests were with the Spanish on their entrance into the territory early in the 16th century. The first parish was established in 1547 and the first diocese in 1561. Overall organization of the Church took place later in the century. By 1650, most of the peaceful Indians in the central and northern areas were evangelized. Missionary work was more difficult in the southern region. Church activity was hampered during the campaign for independence, 1810-18, and through the first years of the new government, to 1830. Later, Church activity increased but was hampered by shortages of indigenous personnel and attempts by the government to control Church administration through the patronage system. Separation of Church and state was decreed in the constitution of 1925.

Church-state relations were strained during the regime of Marxist President Salvador Allende (1970-73). In the mid-1970s, the Adio. of Santiago established the Vicariate of Solidarity to counter human-rights abuses under the rule of Gen. Augusto Pinochet. The Chilean bishops issued numerous statements strongly critical of human rights abuses by the military dictator, who remained in power until 1990, when an elected president took office. The Church was praised for its role in educating and registering voters in the 1988 plebiscite that rejected another term for Pinochet. In 1999, when a British court ruled that Pinochet could be extradited from Britain to Spain to face trial for torture and murder, Chilean bishops said the ruling damaged Chilean democracy.

China, People's Republic of

Archd., 20; dioc., 92; p.a., 29. No Roman Catholic statistics are available. In 1949 there were between 3,500,000-4,000,000 Catholics, about .7% of the total population; current total is unknown. Tot. pop. 1,346,028,000. **Hong Kong:** Dioc., 1; card., 2; bps., 2; parishes, 51; priests, 317 (75 dioc., 242 rel.); p.d., 16; sem., 42; bros., 54; srs., 489; catechists, 1,456; bap., 6,249; Caths., 507,000 (5.2%); tot. pop., 7,072,000. **Macau:** Dioc., 1; bp., 2; parishes, 9; priests, 77 (26 dioc., 51 rel.); sem., 21; bros., 25; srs., 194; bap., 360; catechists, 128; Caths., 29,000; tot. pop. 558,000.

People's republic in eastern part of Asia; capital, Beijing. Christianity was introduced by the Church of the East monks called "Nestorians," who had some influence on part of the area from 635 to 845 and again from the 11th century until 1368. John of Monte Corvino started a Franciscan mission in 1294; he was ordained an archbishop about 1307. Missionary activity involving more priests increased for a while thereafter, but the Franciscan mission ended in 1368. Jesuit Matteo Ricci initiated a remarkable period of activity in the 1580s. In what became known as the Chinese rites controversy, the Jesuits argued that Confucian veneration of ancestors was compatible with Catholicism, but Dominican and Franciscan missionaries viewed it as idolatry. The controversy even was debated in Europe throughout the 17th century, and the Vatican ruled against the rites in the early 1800s. In the mid-19th century, the Opium War forced China to open its doors, accept free trade and allow Christian missionaries in. Progress in evangelization resumed with an extension of legal and social tolerance. At the turn of the 20th century, however, Christian missionary activity helped provoke the Boxer Rebellion against foreign influence in China.

Missionary work in the 20th century reached a new high. The hierarchy was instituted by Pope Pius XII, Apr. 11, 1946 (Apostolic Constitution *Quotidie Nos*). Then followed persecution initiated by communists, before and especially after they established the republic in 1949. The government outlawed missionary work and pastoral activity; expelled more than 5,000 foreign missionaries; arrested, imprisoned and harassed Chinese Church officials; closed more than 4,000 schools, clinics and social service institutions; denied the free exercise of religion; detained hundreds of priests, religious and lay people in jail or in slave labor; proscribed Catholic movements for "counterrevolutionary activities" and "crimes against the new China."

The government formally established the Chinese Catholic Patriotic Association, independent of the Holy See, in July 1957. Initially, relatively few priests and lay people joined the organization, which was condemned by Pius XII in 1958. Many of the Catholics who then joined the Patriotic Association indicated they chose to cooperate with the government and work within its restrictions, but remained loyal to the Vatican. The government formed the nucleus of what it hoped might become the hierarchy of a national Chinese Catholic Church in 1958 by "electing" 26 bishops and having them consecrated validly but illicitly between Apr. 13, 1958, and Nov. 15, 1959. Additional bishops were subsequently ordained. Catholics continued to practice the faith clandestinely and face persecution.

From 1966 to 1978, the Cultural Revolution declared religions to be dangerous and illegal in China. The Catholic registered communities were forbidden to exist. Total persecution of the Catholics followed for more than 10 years.

In the 1980s, although bishops on the mainland were asked to register with the government and join the Patriotic Association, many began to reconcile secretly with the Vatican. Gradually, and in some regions more than others, clandestine and registered Catholic communities began to mingle. By the early 21st century, nearly all of the government-approved bishops in the Patriotic Association had reconciled with the Vatican. Although Chinese officials continued to insist on the right to name bishops, in most cases bishops also were approved by the Vatican.

In 2007, Pope Benedict XVI issued a historic letter to Chinese Catholics urging reconciliation between the clandestine and registered Catholic communities. The letter said registration with the government was permissible as long as it did not compromise the faith. It also formally revoked all Vatican pastoral directives and special faculties previously granted to address pastoral necessities in difficult times. However, it said the Patriotic Association's idea of an independent Chinese church that self-manages itself democratically was "incompatible with Catholic doctrine," and it criticized government limits on the church's activities. The last year has also brought a sharp increase in the persecution of the Church.

Colombia*

Archd., 13; dioc., 52; v.a., 10; mil. ord., 1; card., 3; abp., 24; bp., 83; parishes, 3,996; priests, 8,976 (6,630 dioc., 2,346 rel.); p.d., 503; sem., 4,241; bros., 1,216 srs., 14,997; catechists, 55,187; bap., 620,732; Caths., 43,524,000 (87%); tot. pop., 46,581,000.

Republic in northwest South America; capital, Bogotá. Evangelization began in 1508. The first two dioceses were established in 1534. Vigorous development of the Church was reported by the middle of the 17th century despite obstacles posed by the multiplicity of Indian languages, government interference through patronage rights, rivalry among religious orders and the small number of native American priests among the predominantly Spanish clergy. Some persecution, including the confiscation of property, followed in the wake of the proclamation of independence from Spain in 1819. Guerrilla warfare aimed at Marxist-oriented radical social reform and redistribution of land, along with violence related to drug traffic, has plagued the country since the 1960s, posing problems for the Church, which backed reforms but rejected actions of radical groups. In the late 20th and early 21st centuries, the Church worked as a mediator between the government and guerrillas, but Church leaders suffered threats, attacks, and sometimes death, including from paramilitaries. For example, on Mar. 16, 2002, Abp. Isaias Duarte Cancino of Cali was shot to death for speaking out about the political situation; he was one of at least 10 Church workers killed in 2002.

Comoros

A.a., 1; bp.; parishes, 4; missions, 4; priests, 4 (1 dioc.; 3 rel.); bros., 1; srs., 7; catechists, 20; bap., 28; Caths., 6,000 (.02%); tot. pop., 875,000. (AD)

Consists of main islands of Grande Comore, Anjouan and Moheli in Indian Ocean off southeast coast of Africa; capital, Moroni, Grande Comore Island. Former French territory; independent (July 6, 1975). The majority of the population is Muslim. An apostolic administration was established in 1975.

Congo, Democratic Republic of *

Archd., 6; dioc., 41; Card., 1; abp., 8; bp., 41; parishes, 1,391; priests, 5,453 (3,450 dioc., 2,003 rel.); p.d., 4, sem., 3,376; bros., 1,580; srs., 9,037; catechists, 83,220; bap., 447,274; Caths., 38,528,000 (53%); tot. pop., 73,673,000.

Republic in south central Africa; capital, Kinshasa. Christianity was introduced in 1484 and evangelization began about 1490. The first bishop from black Africa was ordained in 1518. Subsequent missionary work was hindered by factors including 18th- and 19th-century anticlericalism. Modern evangelization started in the second half of the 19th century. The hierarchy was established in 1959. In the civil disorders that followed independence in 1960, some missions and other Church installations were abandoned, thousands of people reverted to tribal religions and many priests and religious were killed.

Church-state tensions developed in the late 1980s and 1990s because of the Church's criticism of President Mobutu Sese Seko. In 1992, Abp. Laurent Monswengo Pasinya was named president of a council charged with drafting a new constitution and overseeing a transition to democracy, but Mobutu supporters blocked effective change, and the archbishop resigned in 1994. As government and rebel forces battled in the Bukavu region of the country in 1996, Abp. Christophe Munzihirwa Mwene Ngabo was killed in unclear circumstances. In the ensuing years of civil war, Church personnel worked to meet humanitarian needs and to promote peace.

Congo, Republic of *

Archd., 1; dioc., 6; p.a., 1; abp., 2; bp., 5; parishes, 160; priests, 440 (328 dioc., 102 rel.); p.d., 1; sem., 339; bros., 109; srs., 479; catechists, 3,695; bap., 27,984; Caths., 2,866,000 (57%); tot. pop., 5,090,000.

Republic (independent since 1960) in west central Africa; former French possession; capital, Brazzaville. Small-scale missionary work with little effect preceded modern evangelization dating from the 1880s. The work of the Church has been affected by political instability, communist influence, tribalism and hostility to foreigners. The hierarchy was established in 1955. In 1992 Bp. Ernest Kombo of Owando was appointed chief organizer of the country's parliamentary elections. In 1994, the Church canceled independence day celebrations after more than 142 Catholics, mostly children, were crushed or suffocated in a rain-induced stampede at a Catholic church in Brazzaville. During renewed violence in the late 1990s, the bishops appealed for peace and stability.

Costa Rica*

Archd., 1; dioc., 7; abp., 2; bp., 9; parishes, 292; priests, 796 (591 dioc., 205 rel.); sem., 269; p.d., 13; bros., 96; srs., 864; catechists, 23,947; bap., 40,870; Caths., 3,817,000 (83%); tot. pop., 4,616,000.

Republic in Central America; capital, San José. Evangelization began about 1520 and proceeded by degrees to real development and organization of the Church in the 17th and 18th centuries. The republic became independent in 1838. Twelve years later Church jurisdiction also became independent with the establishment of a diocese in the present capital.

Côte d'Ivoire (Ivory Coast)*

Archd., 4; dioc., 11; card., 1; abp., 5; bp., 16; parishes, 438; priests, 1,312 (1,050 dioc., 273 rel.); p.d., 6; sem., 670; bros.405, ; srs., 1,112; catechists, 21,052; bap., 59,703; Caths., 5,351,000 (17%); tot. pop., 22,618,000.

Republic in western Africa; capital, Abidjan. The Holy Ghost Fathers began systematic evangelization in 1895. The first priests from the area were ordained in 1934. The hierarchy was set up in 1955; the first indigenous cardinal (Bernard Yago) was named in 1983. In 1990 Pope John Paul II consecrated the continent's biggest, most costly and most controversial cathedral in Yamoussoukro. The pope only agreed to accept the cathedral after convincing the country's president to build an adjacent hospital and youth center.

Croatia*

Archd., 5; dioc., 11; mil. ord., 1; card., 1; abp., 6; bp., 16; parishes, 1,621; priests, 2,378 (1,590 dioc., 788 rel.); p.d., 22; sem., 430; bros., 73; srs., 3,433; catechists, 1,879; bap., 37,727; Caths., 3,926,000 (89%); tot. pop., 4,414,000.

Independent (1991) republic in southeastern Europe; capital Zagreb; formerly a constituent republic of Yugoslavia. Christianity was introduced in the seventh century. On-again, off-again fighting from 1991 to 1995 pitted mostly Catholic Croats against mostly Orthodox Serbs. In 1995, Croatian bishops issued guidelines for rebuilding the nation including suppressing feelings of vengeance toward Serbs. However, in 1996 the head of Croatia's Helsinki human rights committee criticized the bishops for taking a weak stance on Croat abuses after

the 1995 Croatian recapture of the Serb-occupied Krajina region. The 1998 beatification of Croatian Cardinal Alojzije Stepinac generated controversy among some Serb and Jewish leaders, who considered the cardinal a Nazi sympathizer. Pope Benedict XVI visited in June 2011.

Cuba*

Archd., 3; dioc., 8; card., 1; abp., 4; bp., 13; parishes, 305; priests, 404 (227 dioc., 177 rel.); p.d., 73; sem., 78; bros., 33; srs., 620; catechists, 4,127; bap., 80,483; Caths. 6,767,000 (60%); tot. pop., 11,245,000.

Republic under Communist dictatorship, south of Florida; capital, Havana. Effective evangelization began about 1514, leading eventually to the predominance of Catholicism on the island. Vocations to the priesthood and religious life were unusually numerous in the 18th century but declined in the 19th. The island became independent of Spain in 1902 following the Spanish-American War.

Fidel Castro took control of the government Jan. 1, 1959. In 1961, after Cuba was officially declared a socialist state, the University of Villanueva was closed, 350 Catholic schools were nationalized and 136 priests expelled. A greater number of foreign priests and religious had already left the country. Freedom of worship and religious instruction were limited to Church premises and no social action was permitted by the Church, which survived under surveillance. A new constitution approved in 1976 guaranteed freedom of conscience but restricted its exercise. Small improvements in Church-state relations occurred in the late 1980s and early 1990s. In December 1997, just before Pope John Paul II's historic visit, the government allowed public celebration of Christmas, banned for 30 years. Although the pope's January 1998 visit was seen as a new dawn for the Church on the islands, Cuban Catholics say change has come slowly. Church leaders say the government has made concessions on public worship and restoration of church buildings. Some progress has been made on visas for foreign Church personnel and in Church-run media. In 2007, representatives of the Latin American bishops' council (CELAM) met on the island for the first time. Pope Benedict XVI visited in March 2012; after his trip, Cuba declared Good Friday a national holiday, and it was hoped that further progress would be achieved in the areas of human rights and economic freedom.

Cyprus*

Archd., 1 (Maronite); abp., 2; parishes, 16; priests, 42 (11 dioc., 31 rel.); sem., 1; bros., 10; srs., 47; bap., 89; Caths., 25,000 (2.2%); tot. pop., 813,000.

Republic in the eastern Mediterranean; capital, Nicosia. Christianity was preached on the island in apostolic times and has a continuous history from the fourth century. Latin and Eastern rites were established but the latter prevailed and became Orthodox after the schism of 1054. Christians have suffered under many governments, particularly during the period of Turkish dominion from late in the 16th to late in the 19th centuries, and from differences between the 80 percent Greek majority and the Turkish minority. About 80 percent of the population are Orthodox.

Czech Republic*

Archd., 2; dioc., 6; ap. ex., 1; card., 2; abp., 3; bp., 17; parishes, 2,439; priests, 1,907 (1,330 dioc., 577 rel.); p.d., 197; sem., 166; bros., 136; srs., 1,382; catechists, 1,103; bap., 22,782; Caths., 3,147,000 (32%); tot. pop., 10,504,000.

Independent state (Jan. 1, 1993); formerly part of Czechoslovakia; capital, Prague. The martyrdom of Prince Wenceslaus in 929 triggered the spread of Christianity. Prague has had a continuous history as a diocese since 973. A parish system was organized about the 13th century in Bohemia and Moravia. Mendicant orders strengthened relations with the Latin rite in 13th century. In the following century the teachings of John Hus in Bohemia brought trouble to the Church in the forms of schism and heresy and initiated a series of religious wars that continued for decades following his death at the stake in 1415. So many of the faithful joined the Bohemian Brethren that Catholics became a minority. In the 1560s, a Counter-Reformation got under way and led to a gradual restoration through the thickets of Josephinism, the Enlightenment, liberalism and troubled politics. St. Jan Sarkander, a priest accused of helping an invading Polish army, was killed by Protestants in 1620. (His 1995 canonization caused strains with the Protestant community.)

In 1920, two years after the establishment of the Republic of Czechoslovakia, the schismatic Czechoslovak Church was proclaimed at Prague, resulting in numerous defections from the Catholic Church in the Czech region. Following the accession of the Gottwald regime to power early in 1948, perse cution began in the Czech part of Czechoslovakia. A number of theatrical trials of bishops and priests were staged in 1950. Pressure was applied on Eastern Catholics in Slovakia to join the Orthodox Church. Diplomatic relations with the Holy See were terminated in 1950. In the following decade, thousands of priests were arrested and hundreds were deported, and attempts were made to force government-approved "peace priests" on the people. Pope Pius XII granted the Czech Church emergency powers to appoint clergy during the communist persecution.

From January to October 1968, Church-state relations improved to some extent under the Dubcek regime: a number of bishops were reinstated; some priests were still barred from priestly work; the "peace priests" organization was disbanded. The Eastern Catholic Church was re-established. In 1969, rehabilitation trials for priests and religious ended, but there was no wholesale restoration of priests and religious to their proper ways of life and work. Government restrictions continued to hamper the work of priests and nuns. Signatories of the human rights declaration Charter 77 were particular objects of government repression and retribution.

In December 1983, the Czechoslovakian foreign minister met with the pope at Vatican City; it was the first meeting of a high Czech official with a pope since the country had been under communist rule. In 1988, three new bishops were ordained in Czechoslovakia, the first since 1973. The communist government fell in late 1989. In 1990, bishops were appointed to fill vacant sees; diplomatic relations between the Holy See and Czechoslovakia were re-established, and Pope John Paul II visited the country. In 1997 the issue of married Czech priests secretly ordained under communist rule was resolved when they began work in the country's new Eastern Catholic jurisdiction. Under a 1949 communist decree declaring priests Culture Ministry employees, Czech priests were still paid by the state. A Church spokesman said confiscation of Church property under communist rule left priests still financially dependent on the state. Pope Benedict XVI visited in Sept. 2009.

Denmark*

Dioc., 1; bp., 2; parishes, 47; priests, 72 (39 dioc., 33

rel.); p.d., 5; sem., 20; bros., 2; srs., 187; bap., 646; Caths., 40,000 (.6%); tot. pop., 5,581,000.

Includes the Faroe Islands and Greenland. Constitutional monarchy in northwestern Europe; capital, Copenhagen. Christianity was introduced in the ninth century and the first diocese for the area was established in 831. Intensive evangelization and full-scale organization of the Church occurred from the second half of the 10th century and ushered in a period of great development and influence in the 12th and 13th centuries. Decline followed, resulting in almost total loss to the Church during the Reformation, when Lutheranism became the national religion. A few Catholic families practiced the faith secretly until religious freedom was legally assured in the mid-1800s. Since then, immigration has increased the number of Catholics. About 95 percent of the population are Evangelical Lutherans.

Catholicism was introduced in Greenland, a Danish island province northeast of North America, about 1000. The first diocese was established in 1124 and a line of bishops dated from then until 1537. The first known churches in the Western Hemisphere, dating from about the 11th century, were on Greenland. The departure of Scandinavians and spread of the Reformation reduced the Church to nothing. The Moravian Brethren evangelized the Inuit from the 1720s to 1901. By 1930 the Danish Church — Evangelical Lutheran — was in full possession. Since 1930, priests have been in Greenland, which is part of the Copenhagen Dio.

Djibouti*

Dioc., 1; bp., 1; parishes, 5; priests, 3 (1 dioc., 2 rel.); bros., 6; srs., 25; catechists, 10; sem., 1; bap., 15; Caths., 7,000 (1%); tot. pop., 801,000. (AD)

Independent (1977) republic in East Africa; capital, Djibouti. Christianity in the area, formerly part of Ethiopia, antedated but was overcome by the Arab invasion of 1200. Modern evangelization, begun in the latter part of the 19th century, had meager results. The hierarchy was established in 1955. Formal diplomatic relations with the Holy See were established in May 2000.

Dominica*

Dioc., 1; bp., 1; parishes, 15; priests, 23 (12 dioc., 11 rel.); sem., 10; bros., 5; srs., 14; catechists, 315; bap., 512; Caths., 42,000 (79%); tot. pop., 69,000.

Independent (Nov. 3, 1978) state in Caribbean; capi tal, Roseau. Evangelization began in 1642.

Dominican Republic*

Archd., 2; dioc., 9; mil. ord., 1; v.a., 1; card., 1; abp., 3; bp., 17; parishes, 648; priests, 1,066 (599 dioc., 467 rel.); p.d., 535; sem., 693; bros., 270; srs., 3,136; catechists, 50,086; bap., 99,916; Caths., 8,825,000 (88%); tot. pop., 10,011,000.

Caribbean republic on the eastern two-thirds of the island of Hispaniola, bordering on Haiti; capital, Santo Domingo. Evangelization began shortly after discovery by Columbus in 1492 and Church organization, the first in America, was established by 1510. Catholicism is the state religion. Pope John Paul II visited the country in 1992 to mark the quincen tennial celebrations of Columbus' discovery. The pope also opened the Fourth General conference of the Latin American Episcopate there. Church leaders worked to end social injustices, including the plight of mistreated sugar cane workers.

East Timor*

Dioc., 2; bp., 2; parishes, 56; priests, 199 (90 dioc., 109

rel.); sem., 191; p.d., 1; bros., 50; srs., 499; catechists, 1,555; bap., 22,275; Caths., 1,124,000 (89%); tot. pop., 1,169,000.

Independent (May 2002) state; capital, Dili. The pre dominantly Catholic former Portuguese colony was invaded by Indonesia in 1975 and annexed the follow ing year. Most countries did not recognize the annexation. The Catholic Church worked to bring peace between the Indonesian government and guerrilla forces seeking independence. Bp. Carlos Filipe Ximenes Belo, former apostolic administrator of Dili, was a co-winner of the 1996 Nobel Peace Prize for his peace efforts. In 1999, dozens of civilians— including more than two dozen at a Catholic church — were killed during a terror campaign waged by pro-Indonesia para-militaries in the run-up to an August vote on independence for East Timor. Indonesian troops withdrew, and in August 2001, East Timor held elections for a transitional govern-ment. The Church has worked on peace and reconciliation issues to raise awareness of social issues.

Ecuador*

Archd., 4; dioc., 12; v.a., 8; mil. ord., 1; Card., 1; abp., 8; bp., 38; parishes, 1,246; priests, 2,174 (1,369 dioc., 805 rel.); p.d., 89; sem., 587; bros., 493; srs., 5,276; catechists, 49,501; bap., 281,322; Caths., 13,203,000 (91%); tot. pop., 15,248,000.

Republic on the west coast of South America, includes Galápagos Islands; capital, Quito. Evangelization began in the 1530s. The first diocese was established in 1545. Multi-phased missionary work, spreading from the coastal and mountain regions into the Amazon, made the Church highly influential during the colonial period. The Church was practically enslaved by the constitution enacted in 1824, two years after Ecuador, as part of Colombia, gained independence from Spain. Some change for the better took place later in the century, but from 1891 until the 1930s the Church labored under serious liabilities imposed by liberal governments. Foreign missionaries were barred from the country for some time; the property of religious orders was confiscated; education was taken over by the state; tradi-tional state support was refused; legal standing was denied; attempts to control Church offices were made through insistence on rights of patronage. A period of harmony and independence for the Church began after agreement was reached on Church-state relations in 1937. In 1998, the Church was actively involved in peace talks that ended a border dispute of some 170 years with Peru. At the begin-ning of the 21st century, Ecuador's bishops were working to fight social turmoil and the results of severe economic austerity measures. They also were working to support fam-ily members left behind as up to 2.5 million of the country's residents emigrated to foreign lands for work.

Egypt*

Patriarchates, 2 (Alexandria for the Copts and for the Melkites); dioc., 1; v.a., 1; ex., 1; patriarch, 1; Card., 1; abp., 3; bp., 15; parishes, 204; priests, 465 (230 dioc., 235 rel.); p.d., 8; sem., 94; bros., 61; srs., 1,078; catechists, 1,985; bap., 2,139; Caths., 240,000 (.29%); tot. pop., 80,410,000.

Arab Republic in northeastern Africa; capital, Cairo. Alexandria was the influential hub of a Christian com-munity established by the end of the second centu-ry; it became a patriarchate and the center of the Coptic Church and had great influence on the spread of Christianity in various parts of Africa. Monasticism

developed from desert communities of hermits in the third and fourth centuries. Arianism was first preached in Egypt in the 320s. In the fifth century, the Coptic Church went Monophysite through failure to accept doctrine for-mulated by the Council of Chalcedon in 451 with respect to the two natures of Christ. The country was thoroughly Arabized after 640 and was under the rule of Ottoman Turks from 1517 to 1798.

Islam, the religion of some 90 percent of the population, is the state religion. The Christian population faced the upheaval that toppled Pres. Hosni Mubarak in early 2011 with fear given the increase in anti-Christian violence. Concern continues to grow about the safety of Christians as Islamic extremists have expanded their attacks on Christian churches and houses.

El Salvador*

Archd., 1; dioc., 7; mil. ord., 1; abp., 3; bp., 11 parishes, 492, priests, 863 (625 dioc., 238 rel.); p.d., 1; sem., 525; bros., 63; srs., 1,654; catechists, 16,373; bap., 64,278; Cath., 4,963,000 (80%); tot. pop., 6,213,000.

Republic in Central America; capital, San Salvador. Evangelization affecting the whole territory followed Spanish occupation in the 1520s. The country was admin-istered by the captaincy general of Guatemala until 1821, when independence from Spain was declared and it was annexed to Mexico. El Salvador joined the Central American Federation in 1825, declared independence in 1841 and became a republic formally in 1856.

During the country's 1980-92 civil war, Church lead ers worked to achieve social justice. The San Salvador Archdiocese's human rights office, Tutela Legal, document-ed abuses and political killings and offered legal support to victims, despite Church persecution. Abp. Oscar Romero of San Salvador, peace advocate and outspoken champion of human rights, was murdered Mar. 24, 1980, while celebrat-ing Mass. Four U.S. Church women were murdered the same year. Six Jesuits and two lay women were assassinated Nov. 16, 1989, at Central American University in El Salvador. Church leaders, particularly Abp. Romero's successor, Abp. Arturo Rivera Damas, were active in the peace process. In the 1990s, Church-government relations cooled. Church leaders often urged the U.S. government not to deport the hundreds of thousands of Salvadoran refugees who lived, often illegally, in the United States, and sent money to their families in El Salvador. The situation worsened after the destruction caused by Hurricane Mitch in 1998.

England*

Archd., 4; dioc., 15; ap. ex., 1; mil. ord. (Great Britain), 1; card., 1; abp., 6; bp., 34; parishes, 2,219; priests, 4,446 (3,075 dioc., 1,371 rel.); p.d., 727; sem., 269; bros., 1,281; srs., 5,157; catechists, 30,860; bap., 67,613; Caths., 4,344,000 (8.7%; tot. Catholic pop. for Great Britain: 5,254,000); tot. pop., 51,040,000 (tot. pop. for Great Britain: 59,947,000). Note: England and Wales share a joint Episcopal Conference; see also Scotland and Wales.

Center of the United Kingdom of Great Britain (England, Scotland, Wales) and Northern Ireland, off the northwestern coast of Europe; capital, London. The arrival of St. Augustine of Canterbury and a band of monks in 597 marked the beginning of evangelization. Real organization of the Church took place some years after the Synod of Whitby, held in 663. Heavy losses were sustained in the wake of the Danish invasion in the 780s, but recovery starting from the time of Alfred the Great and dating especially from the middle of the 10th century led to Christianization of the whole country and close Church-state relations. The Norman Conquest of 1066 opened the Church in England to European influence. The Church began to decline in numbers in the 13th century. In the 14th century, John Wycliff presaged the Protestant Reformation.

Henry VIII, failing in 1529 to gain annulment of his marriage to Catherine of Aragon, refused to acknowl edge papal authority over the Church in England, had himself proclaimed its head, suppressed all houses of religious, and persecuted people — Sts. Thomas More and John Fisher, among others — for not subscribing to the Oath of Supremacy and Act of Succession. He held the line on other-than-papal doctrine, however, until his death in 1547. Doctrinal aberrations were introduced during the reign of Edward VI (1547-53), through the Order of Communion, two books of Common Prayer, and the Articles of the Established Church. Mary Tudor's attempted Catholic restoration (1553-58) was a disaster, resulting in the deaths of more than 300 Protestants. Elizabeth (1558-1603) firmed up the established Church with the aid of Matthew Parker, archbishop of Canterbury, with formation of a hierarchy, legal enactments and multi-phased persecution. More than 100 priests and 62 lay persons were among the casualties of persecution during the underground Catholic revival that followed the return to England of missionary priests from France and the Lowlands.

Several periods of comparative tolerance ensued after Elizabeth's death. The first of several apostolic vicariates was established in 1685; this form of Church government was maintained until the restoration of the hierarchy and diocesan organization in 1850. The revolution of 1688 and subsequent developments to about 1781 subjected Catholics to a wide variety of penal laws and disabilities in religious, civic and social life. The situation began to improve in 1791, and from 1801 Parliament frequently considered proposals for the repeal of penal laws against Catholics.

The Act of Emancipation restored citizenship rights to Catholics in 1829. Restrictions remained in force for some time afterward, however, on public religious worship and activity. The hierarchy was restored in 1850. Since then the Catholic Church, existing side by side with the established Churches of England and Scotland, has followed a general pattern of growth and development. After the Church of England began ordaining women priests in 1994, hundreds of Anglican priests and four Anglican bishops have been received into the Catholic Church, although many said ordination of women was not their primary reason for leaving. In the late 20th and early 21st centuries, the Church was active in the prolife movement and was outspoken on bioethical issues. Pope Benedict XVI visited in Sept. 2010 for the beatification of John Henry Cardinal Newman. Recent studies have revealed that nearly a quarter of Britons now profess no reigious affiliation, a mark of secularization in the country. (See also **Ireland, Northern**)

Equatorial Guinea*

Archd., 1; dioc., 2; abp., 1; bp., 1; parishes, 72; priests, 150 (84 dioc., 66 rel.); p.d. 1; sem., 53; bros., 28; srs., 225; catechists, 1,114; bap., 21,385; Caths., 684,000 (93%); tot. pop., 708,000.

Republic on the west coast of Africa, consisting of Rio Muni on the mainland and the islands of Bioko

and Annobon in the Gulf of Guinea: capital, Malabo. Evangelization began in 1841. The country became independent of Spain in 1968. The Church was severe ly repressed during the 11-year rule of President Macias Nguema. Developments since his overthrow in 1979 indicated some measure of improvement. An ecclesiastical province was established in October 1982.

In the 1990s, bishops worked to educate Catholics about the need for social justice and respect for human rights. In mid-1998, the government expelled three foreign missionaries involved in development programs partially funded by the United States.

Eritrea*

Dioc., 3; bp., 4; parishes, 121; priests, 507 (101 dioc., 406 rel); sem., 549; p.d., 3, bros., 107; srs., 999; catechists, 183; bap., 3,806; Caths., 191,000 (3.1%); tot. pop., 5,388,000.

Independent state (May 24, 1993) in northeast Africa; formerly a province of Ethiopia. Christianity was introduced in the fourth century. Population is evenly divided between Christians and Muslims. Catholics form a small minority; most of the population is Orthodox or Muslim. In 1995, two new dioceses were established, but because of three decades of civil war, the dioceses had no facilities and little staffing. In 1998 the government announced plans to take over private schools and health clinics, most of which were run by the Church. Eritrean bishops form an episcopal conference with Ethiopia, and the bishops of the two countries frequently appealed for peace during their governments' border war.

Estonia*

A.a., 1; abp., 1 (nuncio is apostolic administrator); parishes, 9; priests, 14 (12 dioc., 2 rel); sem., 1; srs., 20; bap., 66; Caths., 6,000 (.43%); tot. pop., 1,340,000.

Independent (1991) Baltic republic; capital, Tallinn. (Forcibly absorbed by the USSR in 1940, it regained inde pendence in 1991.) Catholicism was introduced in the 11th and 12th centuries. Jurisdiction over the area was made directly subject to the Holy See in 1215. Lutheran penetration was general in the Reformation period, and Russian Orthodox influence was strong from early in the 18th century until 1917, when independence was attained. The first of several apostolic administrators was appointed in 1924. The small Catholic community was hard-hit during the 1940-91 Soviet occupation (not recognized by the Holy See or the United States). Since its independence, the small Catholic community in Estonia has worked to re-establish Catholic theology and education. In 1999 the Holy See and government of Estonia reached agreement on a number of issues, including guarantees that the Church could name its own bishops and that priests from abroad would be able to continue to work in the country.

Ethiopia*

Archd., 1; dioc., 2; v.a., 8; abp., 2; bp., 12; parishes, 297; priests, 548 (274 dioc., 274 rel.); p.d., 3; sem., 275; bros., 78; srs., 758; catechists, 2,699; bap., 27,072; Caths., 903,000 (1%); tot. pop., 85,847,000.

People's republic in northeast Africa; capital, Addis Ababa. The country was evangelized by missionaries from Egypt in the fourth century and had a bishop by about 340. Following the lead of its parent body, the Egyptian (Coptic) Church, the Church in the area suc cumbed to the Monophysite heresy in the sixth century. An apostolic delegation was set up in Addis Ababa in

1937 and several jurisdictions were organized, some under Vatican congregations. The northern Church jurisdictions follow the Alexandrian rite, while the southern part of the country is Latin rite. The small Church has good relations with Orthodox and Protestant Churches, all of which face the task of helping people move from a rural society to a more modern society without losing Christian identity. Although the constitution calls for religious freedom, treatment of the churches can vary in different localities.

Falkland Islands

P.a., 1; parish, 1; srs., 1; bap., 1; priest; Caths., 300 (approx.) (10%); tot. pop., 3,000 (approx).

British colony off the southern tip of South America; capital, Port Stanley. The islands are called Islas Malvinas by Argentina, which also claims sovereignty.

Fiji*

Archd., 1; abp., 1; parishes, 35; priests, 133 (35 dioc., 98 rel.); p.d., sem., 55; bros., 51; srs., 140; bap., 2,000; catechists, 550; Caths., 103,000 (9%); tot. pop., 1,309,000.

Independent island group (100 inhabited) in the southwest Pacific; capital, Suva. Marist missionaries began work in 1844 after Methodism had been firmly established. An apostolic prefecture was organized in 1863. The hierarchy was established in 1966.

Finland*

Dioc., 1; bp., 1; parishes, 7; priests, 23 (13 dioc., 10 rel.); p.d., 1; sem., 14; srs., 34; bap., 250; Caths., 11,000 (.01%); tot. pop., 5,337,000.

Republic in northern Europe; capital, Helsinki. Swedes evangelized the country in the 12th century. The Reformation swept the country, resulting in the prohibition of Catholicism in 1595, general reorganization of ecclesiastical life and affairs, and dominance of the Evangelical Lutheran Church. Catholics were given religious liberty in 1781 but missionaries and conversions were forbidden by law. The first Finnish priest since the Reformation was ordained in 1903 in Paris. An apostolic vicariate for Finland was erected in 1920 (made a diocese in 1955). A law on religious liberty, enacted in 1923, banned the foundation of monasteries.

France*

Archd., 24; dioc., 71; prel., 1; ap. ex., 2; mil. ord., 1; card., 8; abp., 38; bp., 144; parishes, 16,442; priests, 18,804 (14,006 dioc., 4,798 rel.); p.d., 2,474; sem., 1,297; bros., 2,949; srs., 33,662; catechists, 57,407; bap., 294,991; Caths., 47,512,000 (77%); tot. pop., 63,461,000.

Republic in Western Europe; capital, Paris. Christianity was known around Lyons by the middle of the second century. By 250 there were 30 dioceses. The hierarchy reached a fair degree of organization by the end of the fourth century. Vandals and Franks subsequently invaded the territory and caused barbarian turmoil and doctrinal problems because of their Arianism. The Frankish nation was converted following the baptism of Clovis about 496. Christianization was complete by some time in the seventh century. From then on the Church, its leaders and people, figured in virtually every important development — religious, cultural, political and social — through the periods of the Carolingians, feudalism, the Middle Ages and monarchies to the end of the 18th century. The University of Paris became one of the intellectual centers of the 13th century. Churchmen and secular rulers were involved with developments surrounding the Avignon residence of the popes and curia from 1309 until near the end of the 14th century and with the disastrous Western Schism that followed.

Strong currents of Gallicanism and conciliarism ran through ecclesiastical and secular circles in France; the former was an ideology and movement to restrict papal control of the Church in the country, the latter sought to make the pope subservient to a general council. Calvinism entered the country about the middle of the 16th century and won a strong body of converts. Jansenism appeared in the next century, to be followed by the highly influential Enlightenment. The Revolution, which started in 1789 and was succeeded by the Napoleonic period, completely changed the status of the Church, taking a toll of numbers by persecution and defection and disenfranchising the Church in practically every way. Throughout the 19th century the Church was caught up in the whirl of imperial and republican developments and was made the victim of official hostility, popular indifference and liberal opposition.

In the 20th century, the Church struggled with problems involving the heritage of the Revolution and its aftermath. In the 1990s, French bishops fought a racist backlash that resulted from large-scale emigration from Africa. Pope Benedict XVI visited in Sept. 2008.

Gabon*

Archd., 1; dioc., 4; p.a., 1; abp., 1; bp., 4; parishes, 70; priests, 171 (89 dioc., 82 rel.); p.d., 2; sem., 185; bros., 43; srs., 186; catechists, 2,242; bap., 12,044; Caths., 820,000 (50%); tot. pop., 1,602,000.

Republic on the west coast of central Africa; capital Libreville. Sporadic missionary effort took place before 1881 when effective evangelization began. The hierarchy was established in 1955. In 1993, Gabon's president defeated a Catholic priest in presidential elections. In the late 1990s, the government and the Holy See signed an agreement setting out the rights of the Church in society.

Gambia*

Dioc., 1; bp., 3; parishes, 39; priests, 26 (16 dioc., 10 rel.); sem., 9; bros., 1; srs., 57; bap., 1,076; Caths., 44,000 (2%); tot. pop., 1,932,000.

Republic (1970) on the northwestern coast of Africa; capital, Banjul. Christianity was introduced by Portuguese explorers in the 15th century; effective evangelization began in 1822. The country was under the jurisdiction of an apostolic vicariate until 1931. The hierarchy was established in 1957.

Georgia*

A.a., 1; parishes, 31; abp., 1; bp., 1; priests, 24 (13 dioc., 11 rel); sem., 12; brs. 4; srs., 40; bap, 112; Caths., 110,000 (2%); tot. pop., 4,469,000.

Independent (1991) state in the Caucasus; former Soviet republic; capital, Tbilisi. Christianity came to the area under Roman influence and, according to tradition, was spread through the efforts of St. Nino (or Christiana), a maiden who was brought as a captive to the country and is venerated as its apostle. The apostolic administration of the Caucasus (with seat in Georgia) was established in December 1993 for Latin-rite Catholics of Armenia, Azerbaijan and Georgia. Chaldean- and Armenian-rite Catholics also are present. Differences between Catholicism and Orthodoxy often are blurred on the parish level. The Catholic Church and the Armenian Orthodox Church have been unable to secure the return of Churches closed during the Soviet period, many of which were later given to the Georgian Orthodox Church. Early in the 21st century, many denominations, including Catholics, reported attacks and harassment from Orthodox mobs.

Germany*

Archd., 7; dioc., 20; ap. ex., 1; mil. ord., 1; card., 9; abp., 9; bp., 100; parishes, 11,273; priests, 17,007 (12,857 dioc., 4,150 rel.); p.d., 3,118; sem., 1,110; bros., 1,515; srs., 26,085; catechists, 9,345; bap., 169,931; Caths., 25,150,000 (31.2%); tot. pop., 81,844,000.

Country in northern Europe; capital, Berlin. From 1949-90 it was partitioned into the Communist German Democratic Republic in the East (capital, East Berlin) and the German Federal Republic in the West (capital, Bonn). Christianity was introduced in the third century, if not earlier. Trier, which became a center for missionary activity, had a bishop by 400. Visigoth invaders introduced Arianism in the fifth century but were converted in the seventh century by the East Franks, Celtic and other missionaries. St. Boniface, the apostle of Germany, established real ecclesiastical organization in the eighth century.

Beginning in the Carolingian period, bishops began to act in dual roles as pastors and rulers, a state of affairs that inevitably led to confusion and conflict in Church-state relations and perplexing problems of investiture. The Church developed strength and vitality through the Middle Ages but succumbed to abuses that antedated and prepared the ground for the Reformation. Martin Luther's actions from 1517 made Germany a confessional battleground. Religious strife continued until the conclusion of the Peace of Westphalia at the end of the Thirty Years' War in 1648. Nearly a century earlier the Peace of Augsburg (1555) had been designed, without success, to assure a degree of tranquility by recognizing the legitimacy of different religious confessions in different states, depending on the decisions of princes. The implicit principle that princes should control the churches emerged in practice into the absolutism and Josephinism of subsequent years. St. Peter Canisius and his fellow Jesuits spearheaded a Counter Reformation in the second half of the 16th century. Before the end of the century, however, 70 percent of the population of north and central Germany were Lutheran. Calvinism also had established a strong presence.

The Church suffered some impoverishment as a result of shifting boundaries and the secularization of property shortly after 1800. It came under direct attack in the Kulturkampf of the 1870s but helped to generate the opposition that resulted in a dampening of the campaign of Bismarck against it. Despite action by Catholics on the social front and other developments, discrimination against the Church spilled over into the 20th century and lasted beyond World War I. Catholics in politics struggled with others to pull the country through numerous postwar crises. The dissolution of the Center Party, agreed to by the bishops in 1933 without awareness of the ultimate consequences, contributed in part to the rise of Hitler to supreme power. Church officials protested the Nazi anti-Church and anti-Semitic actions, but to no avail.

After World War II East Germany, compelled to communism under Soviet domination, initiated a program of control and repression of the Church. The regime eliminated religious schools, curtailed freedom for religious instruction and formation, and restricted the religious press. Beginning in the mid-1950s, the communists substituted youth initiation and Communist ceremonies for many sacraments. Bishops were generally forbidden to travel outside the Republic. The number of priests decreased, partly because of reduced seminary enrollments ordered by the East German government.

The official reunification of Germany took place Oct. 3, 1990, and the separate episcopal conferences were merged to form one conference in November. During the 1990s, the united German bishops fought against introduction of the former East Germany's more liberal abortion law. When a high-court decision allowed a woman to obtain an abortion after visiting a state-approved counseling center and obtaining proof she had been counseled, German Church leaders searched for a compromise position, since they ran more than 250 such centers. In 1999, Pope John Paul II asked the German bishops to include a line on the proof-of-counseling certificate that said it could not be used for abortion, but some German states said they would not consider the line valid. Eventually, most of the bishops withdrew their centers from the system. As the 20th century came to an end, German Church leaders also spoke on behalf of immigrants, refugees and asylum seekers and against a surge in racist and anti-Semitic attacks. Early in the 21st century, a change in the country's tax rate and growing unemployment led to a severe budget crisis for many German dioceses. Recent sexual abuse cases caused a major scandal in the country, compounded by the controversial resignation of Bp. Walter Mixa of Ausgburg. Pope Benedict XVI visited Germany in 2011 in his first official trip as pope.

Ghana*

Archd., 4; dioc., 15; p.a.; Card., 1; abp., 8; bp., 15; parishes, 460; priests, 1,381 (1,112 dioc., 269 rel.); p.d., 2; sem., 792; bros., 226; srs., 1,061; catechists, 6,523; bap., 55,175; Caths., 3,302,000 (12%); tot. pop., 24,619,000.

Republic on the western coast of Africa; capital, Accra. Priests visited the country in 1482, 11 years after discovery by the Portuguese, but missionary effort, hindered by the slave trade and other factors, was slight until 1880 when systematic evangelization began. An apostolic prefecture was set up in 1879. The hierarchy was established in 1950.

In 1985, the government shut down the Church's newspaper, *The Catholic Standard*, for criticizing the government; in 1989 the government ordered religious bodies to register. However, in 1992 the paper resumed publication, and five new dioceses were established in 1995. In 1997 the bishops issued a pastoral letter urging an end to political corruption and ethnic tension.

Gibraltar

Dioc., 1; bp., 2; parishes, 5; priests, 12 (12 dioc.); sem., 1; bros., 2; srs., 5; bap., 354; Caths., 23,000 (72%); tot. pop., 29,000.

British dependency on the tip of the Spanish Peninsula on the Mediterranean. Evangelization took place after the Moors were driven out near the end of the 15th century. The Church was hindered by the British, who acquired the colony in 1713. Most of the Catholics were, and are, Spanish and Italian immigrants and their descendants. An apostolic vicariate was organized in 1817. The diocese was erected in 1910.

Great Britain

(See separate entries for England, Scotland, Wales, Northern Ireland)

Greece*

Archd., 4; dioc., 4; v.a., 1; ap. ex., 2; abp., 4; bp., 4; parishes, 81; priests, 100 (61 dioc., 39 rel.); p.d., 3; sem., 3; bros., 28; srs., 118; bap., 686; Caths., 141,000 (1%); tot. pop., 11,334,000.

Republic in southeastern Europe on the Balkan Peninsula; capital, Athens. St. Paul preached the Gospel at Athens and Corinth on his second missionary journey and visited the country again on his third tour. Other Apostles may have passed through. Two bishops from Greece attended the First Council of Nicaea. After the division of the Roman Empire, the Church remained Eastern in rite and later broke ties with Rome as a result of the schism of 1054. A Latin-rite jurisdiction was set up during the period of the Latin Empire of Constantinople, 1204-61, but crumbled afterward. Unity efforts of the Council of Florence had poor results and failed to save the Byzantine Empire from conquest by the Ottoman Empire in 1453. The country now has Latin, Byzantine and Armenian rites. The Greek Orthodox Church is predominant. The Catholic Church continues to work to obtain full legal rights. In May 2001, during the first papal visit to Greece since the eighth century, Pope John Paul II apologized for past wrongs against the Orthodox, including the 13th-century sack of Constantinople.

Greenland (Statistics for Greenland are included in Denmark)

Grenada*

Dioc., 1; bp., 2; parishes, 20; priests, 32 (10 dioc., 22 rel.); p.d., 4; sem., 3; bros., 4; srs., 33; catechists, 102; bap., 373; Caths., 46,000 (54%); tot. pop., 102,000.

Independent island state in the West Indies; capital, St. George's.

Guam

Archd., 1; abp., 1; parishes, 24; priests, 49 (39 dioc., 10 rel.); p.d., 21; sem., 37; srs., 108; bap., 1,953; catechists, 471; Caths., 144,000 (85%); tot. pop., 169,000.

Outlying area of U.S. in the southwest Pacific; capital, Agana. The first Mass was offered in the Mariana Islands in 1521. The islands were evangelized by the Jesuits, from 1668, and other missionaries. The first Micronesian bishop was ordained in 1970. The Agana Diocese, which had been a suffragan of San Francisco, was made a metropolitan see in 1984.

Guatemala*

Archd., 2; dioc., 10; prel., 1; v.a., 2; abp., 3; bp., 18; parishes, 486; priests, 1,076 (621 dioc., 455 rel.); p.d., 7; sem., 483; bros., 215; srs., 2,749; catechists, 60,290; bap., 163,605; Caths. 11,757,000 (81%); tot. pop. 14,729,000.

Republic in Central America; capital, Guatemala City. Evangelization dates from the beginning of Spanish occupation in 1524. The first diocese, for all Central American territories administered by the captaincy general of Guatemala, was established in 1534. The country became independent in 1839, following annexation to Mexico in 1821, secession in 1823 and membership in the Central American Federation from 1825. In 1870, a government installed by a liberal revolution repudiated the concordat of 1853 and took active measures against the Church. Separation of Church and state was decreed; religious orders were suppressed and their property seized; priests and religious were exiled; schools were secularized. Full

freedom was subsequently granted.

During the nation's 36-year civil war, which ended in 1996, Church officials spoke out against atrocities and illegal drafting of youths and often were persecuted. The Guatemala City archbishop's human rights office, established after decades of war, was one of the few agencies able to document abuses. Bishops participated in the country's peace process, at times withdrawing in an effort to force government and guerrilla leaders back to the table.

After the war, the archbishop's human rights office began an extensive project to help document abuses during the war. Two days after the report was released in April 1998, Aux. Bp. Juan Gerardi Conedera of Guatemala City, who headed the project, was murdered. In 2001, a priest who lived with the bishop and three military officers were convicted of involvement in the murder, but said they would appeal the decision. One of the three officers was killed in a Guatemala City prison riot in 2003. Church leaders mobilized to help Guatemalans after mudslides and flooding from Hurricane Stan in 2005 made it the country's worst natural disaster in nearly 30 years.

Guinea*

Archd., 1; dioc., 2; Card., 1; abp. 2; bp., 3; parishes, 64; priests, 137 (115 dioc., 22 rel.); sem., 68; bros., 27; srs., 76; catechists, 519; bap., 2,385; Caths., 250,000 (3%); tot. pop., 10,813,000.

Republic on the west coast of Africa; capital, Conakry. Occasional missionary work followed exploration by the Portuguese about the middle of the 15th century; organized effort dates from 1877. The hierarchy was established in 1955. Following independence from France in 1958, Catholic schools were nationalized, youth organizations banned and missionaries restricted. Foreign missionaries were expelled in 1967. Abp. Raymond-Marie Tchidimbo of Conakry, sentenced to life imprisonment in 1971 on a charge of conspiring to overthrow the government, was released in August 1979; he resigned his see. Private schools, suppressed by the government for more than 20 years, again were authorized in 1984.

Guinea-Bissau*

Dioc., 2; bp., 2; parishes, 33; priests, 88 (20 dioc., 68 rel.); sem., 32; bros., 15; srs., 144; bap., 1,817; catechists, 1,150; Caths., 202,000 (13%); tot. pop., 1,558,000.

Independent state on the west coast of Africa; capital, Bissau. Catholicism was introduced in the second half of the 15th century but limited missionary work, hampered by the slave trade, had meager results. Missionary work in the 20th century began in 1933. An apostolic prefecture was made a diocese in 1977. In 1998, Bp. Settimio Ferrazzetta of Bissau worked to mediate a crisis between the government and military leaders.

Guyana*

Dioc., 1; bp., 2; parishes, 24; priests, 31 (4 dioc., 27 rel.); p.d., 3; sem., 8; bros., 3; srs., 56; catechists, 580; bap., 1,022; Caths., 62,000 (10.2%); tot. pop., 787,000.

Republic on the north coast of South America; capital, Georgetown. In 1899 the Catholic Church and other churches were given equal status with the Church of England and the Church of Scotland. Most of the Catholics are Portuguese. The Georgetown Diocese was established in 1956, 10 years before Guyana became independent of England. The first indigenous bishop was appointed in 1971. Schools were nationalized in

1976. In the late 1970s and in the 1980s, *The Catholic Standard* newspaper was cited by the Inter-American Press Association as the "sole independent voice" in Guyana.

Haiti*

Archd., 2; dioc., 8; abp., 4; bp., 12; parishes, 397; priests, 855 (529 dioc., 326 rel.); p.d., 3; sem., 492; bros., 331; srs., 1,924; catechists, 3,283; bap., 123,673; Caths., 7,453,000 (80%); tot. pop., 10,248,000.

Caribbean republic on the western third of Hispaniola adjacent to the Dominican Republic; capital, Port-au-Prince. Evangelization followed discovery by Columbus in 1492. Capuchins and Jesuits did most of the missionary work in the 18th century. From 1804, when independence was declared, until 1860, the country was in schism. Relations were regularized by a concordat concluded in 1860, when an archdiocese and four dioceses were established.

In the second half of the 20th century, the Church worked to develop the small nation, considered among the poorest in the Western Hemisphere. In the 1980s and 1990s, priests and religious often were targets of political violence, which resulted in a series of coups. The Church was sometimes seen as the lone voice for the people and, at times, was seen as backing the government. A Salesian priest, Fr. Jean-Bertrand Aristide, known for his fiery, anti-government sermons, won the December 1990 president election, considered the first genuinely democratic vote in Haitian history. A 1991 military coup forced him into exile for three years and resulted in an international trade embargo against Haiti. Aristide was laicized by the Vatican and married in January 1996. In the late 1990s, the Church continued its service in the social field through programs in basic literacy and operation of schools and health facilities. On Jan. 12, 2010, a 7.0 magnitude earthquake struck Haiti and devastated Port-au-Prince. More than 150,000 people were killed, with exact numbers still unknown. The Archbp. of Port-au-Prince, Joseph Serge Miot, was among those killed.

Honduras*

Archd., 1; dioc., 8; card., 1; abp., 1; bp., 12; parishes, 224; priests, 446 (267 dioc., 179 rel.); sem., 189; bros., 37; srs., 905; catechists, 17,546; bap., 60,915; Caths., 6,687,000 (82%); tot. pop., 8,215,000.

Republic in Central America; capital, Tegucigalpa. Evangelization preceded establishment of the first diocese in the 16th century. Under Spanish rule and after independence from 1823, the Church held a favored position until 1880, when equal legal status was given to all religions. Harassment of priests and nuns working among indigenous peasants and Salvadoran refugees was reported during the years of Central American civil unrest in the late 20th century. In 1998 Hurricane Mitch killed more than 6,000 Hondurans and forced more than 2 million in the country to evacuate their homes. The Church took a lead role in post-hurricane relief and development efforts.

Hungary*

Archd., 4; dioc., 9; abb., 1; ap. ex., 1; mil. ord. 1; card., 2; abp., 8; bp., 23; parishes, 2,155; priests, 2,219 (1,784 dioc., 435 rel.); p.d., 110; sem., 327; bros., 60; srs., 920; catechists, 2,091; bap., 40,573; Caths., 6,069,000 (59%); tot. pop., 10,299,000.

Republic in east central Europe; capital, Budapest. The early origins of Christianity in the country, whose territory was subject to a great deal of change, is not known.

Magyars accepted Christianity about the end of the 10th century. St. Stephen I promoted its spread and helped to organize some of its historical dioceses. Bishops became influential in politics as well as in the Church.

For centuries the country served as a buffer for the Christian West against barbarians from the East, notably the Mongols in the 13th century. Hussites and Waldensians prepared the way for the Reformation, which struck at almost the same time as the Turks. The Reformation made considerable progress after 1526, resulting in the conversion of large numbers to Lutheranism and Calvinism by the end of the century. Turks repressed the Churches, Protestant as well as Catholic, during a reign of 150 years, but they managed to survive. Domination of the Church was one of the objectives of government policy during the reigns of Maria Theresa and Joseph II in the second half of the 18th century; their Josephinism affected Church-state relations until World War I.

Secularization increased in the second half of the 19th century, which also witnessed the birth of many new Catholic organizations and movements. Catholics were involved in the social chaos and anti-religious atmosphere of the years following World War I, struggling with their compatriots for religious as well as political survival.

After World War II, the communist campaign against the Church started with the disbanding of Catholic organizations in 1946. In 1948, Caritas, the Catholic charitable organization, was taken over, and all Catholic institutions were suppressed. Interference in Church administration and attempts to split the bishops preceded the arrest of Card. Jozsef Mindszenty Dec. 26, 1948, and his sentence to life imprisonment in 1949. (He was free for a few days during the unsuccessful uprising of 1956. He then took up residence at the U.S. Embassy in Budapest, where he remained until September 1971, when he was permitted to leave the country. He died in 1975 in Vienna.)

In 1950, religious orders and congregations were suppressed and 10,000 religious were interned. Several dozen priests and monks were assassinated, jailed or deported. About 4,000 priests and religious were confined in jail or concentration camps. The government sponsored a national "Progressive Catholic" Church and captive organizations for priests. Despite a 1964 agreement with the Holy See regarding episcopal appointments, bishops remained subject to government surveillance and harassment.

On Feb. 9, 1990, an accord was signed between the Holy See and Hungary re-establishing diplomatic relations. Pope John Paul II reorganized the ecclesiastical structure of the country in May 1993. In 1997, the Vatican and Hungary signed an agreement that restored some Church property confiscated under communism and provided some sources of funding for Church activities. Hungary's bishops have said social conflicts, political changes and economic strains have put new pressures on the Church.

Iceland*

Dioc., 1; bp., 1; parishes, 5; priests, 14 (4 dioc., 10 rel.); sem., 1; bros., 1; srs., 34; bap., 183; Caths., 16,000 (2.2%); tot. pop., 320,000.

Island republic between Norway and Greenland; capital, Rekjavik. Irish hermits were there in the eighth century. Missionaries subsequently evangelized the island and Christianity was officially accepted about 1,000. The first bishop was ordained in 1056. The Black Death had dire effects, and spiritual decline set in during the 15th century. Lutheranism was introduced from Denmark between 1537 and 1552 and made the official religion. Some Catholic missionary work was done in the 19th century. Religious freedom was granted to the few Catholics in 1874. A vicariate was erected in 1929 and was made a diocese in 1968.

India*

Patriarchate, 1 (titular of East Indies); major archbishoprics (Syro-Malabar and Syro-Malankara), 2; archd., 30; dioc., 136; Card., 7; patr., 2; abp., 41; bp., 171; parishes, 9,972; priests, 27,228 (14,478 dioc., 12,750 rel.); p.d., 51; sem., 15,363; bros. 4,288; srs., 98,381; catechists, 76,313; bap., 351,968; Caths., 19,431,000 (1.6%); tot. pop. 1,193,000,000.

Republic on the subcontinent of south central Asia; capital, New Delhi. Long-standing tradition credits the Apostle Thomas with the introduction of Christianity in the Kerala area. Evangelization followed the establishment of Portuguese posts and the conquest of Goa in 1510. Jesuits, Franciscans, Dominicans, Augustinians and members of other religious orders figured in the early missionary history. An archdio. for Goa, with two suffragan sees, was set up in 1558.

Missionaries had some difficulties with the British East India Co., which exercised virtual government control from 1757 to 1858. They also had trouble because of a conflict that developed between policies of the Portuguese government, which pressed its rights of patronage in episcopal and clerical appointments, and the Vatican Congregation for the Propagation of the Faith, which sought greater freedom of action in the same appointments. This struggle resulted in the schism of Goa between 1838 and 1857. In 1886, when the number of Catholics was estimated to be 1 million, the hierarchy for India and Ceylon was restored.

Jesuits contributed greatly to the development of Catholic education from the second half of the 19th century. A large percentage of the Catholic population is located around Goa and Kerala and farther south. The country is predominantly Hindu. Anti-conversion laws in effect in several states have had a restrictive effect on pastoral ministry and social service.

Recent years have seen tensions within the Syro-Malabar rite over liturgy and tradition. In addition, there have been tensions between the Latin-rite and Eastern-rite Catholic churches in India over the care of Catholics outside the traditional boundaries of their rites. In the late 20th and early 21st centuries, Church leaders campaigned for the rights of low-caste Indians. Religious also faced a series of attacks, including murders, by extremist Hindus who claimed they were trying to convert people to Christianity

Indonesia*

Archd., 10; dioc., 27; mil. ord. 1; card., 1; abp., 13; bps. 34; parishes, 1,234; priests, 4,140 (1,819 dioc., 2,321 rel.) p.d., 12; sem., 3,903; bros., 1,328; srs., 9,091; catechists 26,588; bap., 211,925; Caths., 7,539,000 (3%); tot. pop. 241,492,000.

Republic in the Malay Archipelago, consisting of some 3,000 islands; capital, Jakarta. Evangelization by the Portuguese began about 1511. St. Francis Xavier spen: some 14 months in the area. Christianity was strongly rooted in some parts of the islands by 1600. Islam's rise to dominance began at this time. The Dutch East Indies Co., which gained effective control in the 17th century, banned evangelization by Catholic missionaries for some time, but Dutch secular and religious priests managed to resume the

work. A vicariate of Batavia for all the Dutch East Indies was set up in 1841. About 90 percent of the population is Muslim. The hierarchy was established in 1961.

From 1981 to about 1996, Catholics and Protestants clashed more than 40 times over what Catholics perceived as Communion host desecration. At least three Protestants died from beatings by Catholics after the incidents.

In the late 1990s, as the Indonesian economy took a nose-dive, Muslim-Christian violence increased, especially in the Molucca Islands. Church leaders continued to urge calm and dialogue, and at one point a bishop sought U.N. intervention to prevent what he saw as a potential genocide of Christians. A militant Muslim group charged with inciting much of the violence disbanded in late 2002, Church leaders expressed hope for peace. The Church worked for years to help victims of the December 2004 tsunami and subsequent earthquakes and tsunamis, offering its services to people regardless of religious affiliation.

Iran*

Archd., 4; dioc., 2; abp., 4; parishes, 18; priests, 15 (8 dioc., 7 rel.); p.d., 3; sem., 3; srs., 26; bap., 41; Caths., 6,000 (.02%); tot. pop., 75,591,000.

Islamic republic (Persia until 1935) in southwestern Asia; capital, Teheran. Some of the earliest Christian communities were established in this area outside the Roman Empire. They suffered persecution in the fourth century and were then cut off from the outside world. Nestorianism was generally professed in the late fifth century. Islam became dominant after 640. Some later missionary work was attempted but without success. Religious liberty was granted in 1834, but Catholics were the victims of a massacre in 1918. Islam is the religion of perhaps 98 percent of the population. Catholics belong to the Latin, Armenian and Chaldean rites.

After Iran nationalized many Church-run social institutions in 1980, about 75 Catholic missionaries left the country, by force or by choice. In recent years, however, Iranian authorities have shown more cooperation regarding entry visas for Church personnel. Although freedom of worship is guaranteed in Iran, Church sources said Catholic activities are monitored carefully by authorities. Since Pope John Paul II and Iranian President Mohammed Khatami met in 1999, the Holy See and Iran have had several high-level diplomatic exchanges.

Iraq*

Patriarchate, 1; archd., 9; dioc., 5; ap. ex., 2; card, 1; patriarch, 1; abp., 9; bp., 3; parishes, 114; priests, 174 (123 dioc., 51 rel.); sem., 63; bros., 10; srs., 286; catechists, 784; bap., 2,565; Caths., 297,000 (1%); tot. pop., 33,402,000.

Republic in southwestern Asia; capital, Baghdad. Some of the earliest Christian communities were established in the area, whose history resembles that of Iran. Catholics belong to the Armenian, Chaldean, Latin and Syrian rites; Chaldeans are most numerous. Islam is the religion of some 90 percent of the population. Iraq's Chaldean Catholic patriarch was outspoken against the international embargo against Iraq, saying it especially hurt children and the sick. In early 2003, Vatican officials met separately with U.S. and Iraqi leaders in an effort to prevent the U.S.-led war; the Vatican embassy in Baghdad remained open throughout the conflict, and Church aid agencies treated wounded. Catholic aid organizations geared up relief efforts after the war but were frustrated by lawlessness and looting. According to estimates, the

Christian population in Iraq has declined from a prewar population of 1.2 million to a current estimate of several hundred thousand. Refugee agencies said Christians, including Catholics, were targeted for persecution marked by violence, murder and restrictions on religious freedom; some Christians in Baghdad were told to convert to Islam, pay higher taxes or leave their homes. The U.N. High Commissioner for Refugees reported over 40% of Iraqi refugees are Christian even though they represent only about 4% of Iraq's total population.

After the war, Catholic leaders were among those expressing alarm at the growing number of Christians leaving the country or fleeing to northern Iraq, where Christians banded together in an effort to gain more of a political voice. Church leaders said Christians in the Baghdad area were threatened with conversion to Islam, paying higher taxes or leaving their homes. The kidnappings and violence led Pope Benedict XVI to say in 2007 that Iraqi Christians were experiencing an "authentic martyrdom." In 2008 the archbishop of Mosul was kidnapped and later found dead.

Ireland*

Archd., 4; dioc., 22; card., 2; abp., 7; bp., 42; parishes, 1,360; priests, 4,911 (2,830 dioc., 1,918 rel.); p.d., 3; sem., 195; bros., 651; srs., 7,063; bap., 72,228 (preceding figures include Northern Ireland); Caths., 5,316,000 (76%); tot. 6,984,000 (population numbers include Northern Ireland; in Republic of Ireland, Catholics comprise 95% of the pop.).

Republic in the British Isles; capital, Dublin. St. Patrick, who is venerated as the apostle of Ireland, evangelized parts of the island for some years after the middle of the fifth century. Conversion of the island was not accomplished, however, until the seventh century or later. Celtic monks were the principal missionaries. The Church was organized along monastic lines at first, but a movement developed in the 11th century for the establishment of jurisdiction along episcopal lines. The Church gathered strength during the period from the Norman Conquest of England to the reign of Henry VIII despite a wide variety of rivalries, wars, and other disturbances.

Henry introduced an age of repression of the faith, which continued for many years under several of his successors. The Irish suffered from proscription of the Catholic faith, economic and social disabilities, subjection to absentee landlords and a plantation system designed to keep them from owning property, and actual persecution which took an uncertain toll of lives up until about 1714. Some penal laws remained in force until emancipation in 1829. Nearly 100 years later Ireland was divided in two, making Northern Ireland, consisting of six counties, part of the United Kingdom (1920) and giving dominion status to the Irish Free State, made up of the other 26 counties (1922). This state (Eire, in Gaelic) was proclaimed the Republic of Ireland in 1949. The Catholic Church pre dominates but religious freedom is guaranteed for all. The Irish Republic and Northern Ireland share a bishops' conference, which has worked for peace in Northern Ireland. Recent years have witnessed a decrease in vocations and growing turmoil over issues such as priestly pedophilia, divorce, and abortion. Ireland was also convulsed in 2009 and 2010 by the Murphy and Ryan reports detailing the extent of sex abuse among schools run by religious communities and the archdiocese of Dublin. Pope Benedict summoned the Irish bishops to the Vatican in early 2010 and in March 2010 issued the "Letter to the Catholics of Ireland" in which he apologized to the victims and promised reform and renewal for the Church in the country. (See **News in Depth for updates**.) In 2012, the Irish Parliament defeated by a vote of 109-20 a bill that would have expanded the availiability of abortions in the country.

Ireland, Northern

Tot. pop., 1,610,000; Catholics comprise more than one third. (Other statistics are included in **Ireland**).

Part of the United Kingdom, it consists of six of the nine counties of Ulster in the northeast corner of Ireland; capital, Belfast. Early history is given under **Ireland**.

Nationalist-unionist tensions fall primarily along Catholic-Protestant lines, with nationalists, mainly Catholics, advocating an end to British rule. Violence and terrorism began in the late 1960s and, by the late 1990s, more than 3,000 people had been killed.

On Apr. 10, 1998, the governments of the Irish Republic and Great Britain and the political parties of Northern Ireland reached an agreement known as the Good Friday agreement. Irish bishops supported it, and it was endorsed by the voters in Ireland and Northern Ireland. However, the agreement or the coalition government established as a result of the agreement was suspended several times, and Northern Ireland's bishops spoke out in support of continuing democratic structures.

For years, Catholics claimed discrimination in the workplace and harassment from the Royal Ulster Constabulary, Northern Ireland's police force that was disbanded and reformed as the Police Service of Northern Ireland. In 2002 some 40 percent of the new force was Catholic, compared to 8 percent in 2001.

Israel*

Patriarchates, 2 (Jerusalem for Latins; patriarchal vicariate for Greek-Melkites); archd., 2; ap.ex., 5; patriarch, 2; abp., 5; bp., 3; parishes, 87; priests, 431 (91 dioc., 340 rel.); p.d., 13; sem., 148; bros., 203; srs., 1,030; bap., 1,806; Caths., 162,000 (1.7%); tot. pop., 7,759,000.

Parliamentary democracy in the Middle East; capitals, Jerusalem and Tel Aviv (diplomatic). Israel was the birthplace of Christianity, the site of the first Christian communities. Some persecution was suffered in the early Christian era and again during the several hundred years of Roman control. Muslims conquered the territory in the seventh century and, except for the period of the Kingdom of Jerusalem established by Crusaders, remained in control most of the time up until World War I. The Church survived in the area, sometimes just barely, but it did not prosper greatly or show any notable increase in numbers. The British took over the protectorate of the area after World War I.

Partition into Israel for the Jews and Palestine for the Arabs was approved by the United Nations in 1947. War broke out a year later with the proclamation of the Republic of Israel. The Israelis won the war and 50 percent more territory than they had originally been ceded. War broke out again for six days in June 1967, and in October 1973.

Judaism is the faith professed by about 85 percent of the inhabitants; approximately one-third of them are considered observant. Israeli-Holy See relations improved in 1994 with the implementation of full diplomatic relations, and the Church gained legal status in 1997, although some taxation issues remained unresolved.

The Holy See repeatedly has asked for an internationally guaranteed statute to protect the sacred nature of Jerusalem, which is holy to Christians, Muslims and Jews.

It has underlined that this means more than access to specific holy places and that the political and religious dimensions of Jerusalem are interrelated. During the Palestinian intifada, the Vatican and Holy Land Church leaders defended Israeli rights to live without the threat of terrorism and the Palestinians' right to a homeland, saying both would only be achieved through a negotiated settlement.

Italy*

Patriarchate, 1 (Venice); archd. 60 (40 are metropolitan sees); dioc., 156; prel., 3; abb., 6; mil. ord. 1; pat., 1 (Venice); card., 48; abp., 175; bps., 536 (hierarchy includes 218 residential, 16 coadjutors or auxiliaries, 115 in Curia offices, remainder in other offices or retired); parishes, 25,572; priests, 48,333 (32,476 dioc., 15,857 rel.); p.d., 4,052; sem., 5,761; bros., 3,392; srs., 89,299; catechists, 243,538; bap., 420,553; Caths., 57,834,000 (96%); tot. pop., 60,851,000.

Republic in southern Europe; capital, Rome. A Christian community was formed early in Rome, probably by the middle of the first century. St. Peter established his see there. He and St. Paul suffered death for the faith in the 60s. The early Christians were persecuted at various times, as in other parts of the empire, but the Church developed in numbers and influence, gradually spreading out from towns and cities in the center and south to rural areas and the north.

Church organization began in the second century. The Church emerged from underground in 313, with the Edict of Milan, and rose to a position of prestige and lasting influence on politics and culture until well into the 19th century. In the 1870s, the Papal States were annexed by the Kingdom of Italy. The 1929 Lateran Pacts included a treaty recognizing the Vatican as an independent state, a financial agreement by which Italy agreed to compensate the Vatican for loss of the papal states, and a concordat regulating Church-state relations. In 1984 the Vatican and Italy signed a revised concordat, reducing some of the Church's privileges and removing Catholicism as the state religion.

The Church strongly opposed Italy's abortion law in 1978 and forced a 1981 referendum on the issue. Abortion remained legal, and the Italian Church has taken a more low-profile stance. The Church has been active in social issues, including helping unprecedented numbers of illegal immigrants in the late 1990s. Church leaders have expressed concern about Italy's low birth rate.

Jamaica*

Archd., 1; dioc., 2; abp., 3; bp., 3; parishes, 61; priests, 102 (74 dioc., 28 rel.); p.d., 47; sem., 10; bros., 188; srs., 131; catechists, 480; bap., 842; Caths., 70,000 (4.3%); tot. pop., 2,706,000.

Republic in the West Indies; capital, Kingston. Franciscans and Dominicans evangelized the island from about 1512 until 1655. Missionary work was interrupted after the English took possession but was resumed by Jesuits about the turn of the 19th century. An apostolic vicariate was organized in 1837. The hierarchy was established in 1967. In the late 1990s, Church leaders spoke out against violence; more than 800 people were murdered in Jamaica in 1997 alone.

Japan*

Archd., 3; dioc., 13; abp., 6; bp., 18; parishes, 893; priests, 1,505 (525 dioc., 980 rel.); p.d., 27; sem., 132;

bros., 212; srs., 5,791; catechists, 1,840; bap., 6,302; Caths., 546,000 (.4%); tot. pop., 127,817,000.

Archipelago in the northwest Pacific; capital, Tokyo. Jesuits began evangelization in the middle of the 16th century and about 300,000 converts, most of them in Kyushu, were reported at the end of the century. The Nagasaki Martyrs were victims of persecution in 1597. Another persecution took some 4,000 lives between 1614 and 1651. Missionaries, banned for two centuries, returned about the middle of the 19th century and found Christian communities still surviving in Nagasaki and other places in Kyushu. A vicariate was organized in 1866. Religious freedom was guaranteed in 1889. The hierarchy was established in 1891. Several Japanese bishops at the 1998 Synod of Bishops for Asia said Catholicism has grown slowly in the region because the Church is too Western.

Since the 1980s, on several occasions Church leaders have apologized and asked forgiveness for the Church's complicity in the nation's aggression during the 1930s and 1940s. At the end of the 20th century, bishops and religious superiors suggested that during the 21st century the Japanese Church focus on pastoral care for migrant workers, concern for the environment and interreligious dialogue.

Japan's Catholic prime minister, Taro Aso, met with Pope Benedict XVI in a private audience at the Vatican on July 7, 2009. He is the third Catholic prime minister; the others were Hara Takashi (1918-1921) and Hosokowa Morihiro (1993-94). In March 2009, Abp. Dominique Mamberti, the Vatican secretary for relations with states, met his counterpart in Tokyo, marking the first time a Vatican foreign minister had visited the country since diplomatic relations were established in 1942. The earthquake that struck in early 2011 caused immense damage; Catholic resources were used to help the victims.

Jordan*

Archd., 1; ex. pat., 2; abp., 2; bp., 1; parishes, 65; priests, 131 (55 dioc., 76 rel.); sem., 3; bros., 9; srs., 158; bap., 877; Caths., 111,000 (1.9%); tot. pop., 6,249,000.

Constitutional monarchy in the Middle East; capital, Amman. Christianity there dates from apostolic times. Survival of the faith was threatened many times under the rule of Muslims from 636 and Ottoman Turks from 1517 to 1918, and in the Islamic Emirate of Trans-Jordan from 1918 to 1949. In the years following the creation of Israel, some 500,000 Palestinian refugees, including Christians, moved to Jordan. Islam is the state religion, but religious freedom is guaranteed for all. The Greek Melkite Archdiocese of Petra and Filadelfia is located in Jordan. Latin-rite Catholics are under the jurisdiction of the Latin Patriarchate of Jerusalem. Jordan established diplomatic relations with the Holy See in 1994. In the late 20th and especially in the early 21st centuries, an influx of Iraqi refugees strained the resources of the Jordanian Catholic community, which offered aid, including housing, counseling and schooling.

Kazakhstan

Archd. 1, dioc., 2; a.a.; 1; abp., 3; bp., 3; parishes, 68; priests, 91(48 dioc., 43 rel.); sem., 11; bros., 9; srs., 134; bap., 596; Caths., 150,000 (1.3%); tot. pop., 16,790,000.

Independent republic (1991); formerly part of USSR; capital, Astana. About 47 percent of the population is Muslim, and about 44 percent is Orthodox. The Catholic population is mainly of German, Polish and Ukrainian origin, descendants of those deported during the Stalin regime. A Latin-rite apostolic administration was established in 1991. In 1998, the Vatican and the Kazakh government signed an agreement guaranteeing the Church legal rights. Diocesan structure was established in 1999, and the Vatican created the first archdiocese and diocese in 2003. The country had its first priestly ordinations on Kazakh soil in 2006.

Kenya*

Archd. 4; dioc., 20; v.a., 1; mil. ord., 1; card. 1; abp. 6; bp., 20; parishes, 845; priests, 2,430 (1,606 dioc., 824 rel.); p.d., 1; sem., 1,691; bros., 713; srs., 4,935; catechists, 11,170; bap., 355,519; Caths., 11,770,000 (27%); tot. pop., 41,745,000.

Republic in East Africa on the Indian Ocean; capital, Nairobi. Systematic evangelization by the Holy Ghost Missionaries began in 1889, nearly 40 years after the start of work by Protestant missionaries. The hierarchy was established in 1953. Three metropolitan sees were established in 1990. Kenyan Catholics were in the forefront of ministering to victims of the 1998 explosion at the U.S. Embassy in Nairobi. The Kenyan bishops have been outspoken against ethnic violence, poverty, government corruption and mismanagement, and the need for a constitutional review. In some rural areas, Church workers, including foreign missionaries, were targeted for their work with the poor.

Kiribati*

Dioc., 1; bp., 1; parishes, 22; priests, 29 (19 dioc., 10 rel.); p.d. 2; sem., 13; bros., 12; srs., 96; catechists, 220; bap., 1,894; Caths., 59,000 (54.2%); tot. pop., 108,000.

Former British colony (Gilbert Islands) in Oceania; became independent July 12, 1979; capital, Bairiki on Tarawa. French Missionaries of the Sacred Heart began work in the islands in 1888. A vicariate for the islands was organized in 1897. The hierarchy was established in 1966.

Korea, North

Tot. pop., 24,136,000. No recent Catholic statistics available; there were an estimated 100,000 Catholics reported in 1969.

Northern part of peninsula in eastern Asia; formal name Democratic People's Republic of Korea (May 1, 1948); capital, Pyongyang. See **South Korea** for history before country was divided. After liberation from Japan in 1945, the Soviet regime in the North systematically punished all religions. After the 1950-53 Korean war, Christian worship was not allowed outside of homes until 1988, when the country's one Catholic Church was built in Pyongyang. A 1999 South Korean government report said North Korea clearly restricts religious practices and churches in the North exist only for show.

Korea, South*

Archd., 3; dioc., 12; mil. ord. 1; card., 1; abp., 6; bp., 24; parishes, 1,646; priests, 4,098 (3,452 dioc., 646 rel.); sem., 1,739; p.d., 5; bros., 631; srs., 9,360; catechists, 16,333; bap., 134,853; Caths., 5,220,000 (10%); tot. pop., 50,111,000.

Southern part of peninsula in eastern Asia; formal name, Republic of Korea (1948); capital, Seoul. Some Catholics may have been in Korea before it became a "hermit kingdom" toward the end of the 16th century and closed its borders to foreigners. The modern introduction to Catholicism came in 1784 through lay converts. A priest arriving in the country in 1794 found 4,000 Catholics there who had never seen a priest. A vicariate was erected in 1831 but was not manned for several years thereafter. There were 15,000 Catholics by 1857. Four persecutions in the 19th century took a terrible toll; several thousand died in the last one, 1866-69. (In 1984, 103 of these martyrs were canonized.) Freedom of religion was granted in 1883, when Korea opened its borders. During World War II, most foreign priests were arrested and expelled, seminaries were closed and churches were taken over. After liberation from Japan in 1945, the Church in the South had religious freedom. Since the 1950-53 Korean war, the Church in South Korea has flourished. Church leaders in the South have worked at reconciliation with the North and to alleviate famine in the North.

Kuwait*

V.a., 1; pat. ex., 1; abp., 1; bp., 1; parishes, 4; priests, 23 (7 dioc., 16 rel.); p.d., 1; bros., 12; bap., 549; Caths., 310,000 (12%); tot. pop., 2,766,000.

Constitutional monarchy (sultanate or sheikdom) in southwest Asia bordering on the Persian Gulf. Remote Christian origins probably date to apostolic times. Islam is the predominant and official religion. Catholics are mostly foreign workers; the Church enjoys religious freedom.

Kyrgyzstan*

A.a., 1; parishes, 3; priests, 8 (2 dioc., 6 rel.); sem., 1; bros., 1; srs., 6; bap., 10; Caths., 1,000; tot. pop., 5,260,000.

Independent republic bordering China; former Soviet republic; capital, Bishkek (former name, Frunze). Most of the people are Sunni Muslim. Established diplomatic relations with the Holy See in August 1992; became apostolic administration in March 2006. The country received its first bishop in July 2006.

Laos

V.a., 4; bp., 3; parishes, 67; priests, 17 (17 dioc.); p.d., 1; sem., 20; srs., 93; catechists, 294; bap., 909; Caths., 46,000 (.7%); tot. pop., 6,385,000. (AD)

People's republic in southeast Asia; capital, Vientiane. Systematic evangelization by French missionaries started about 1881; earlier efforts ended in 1688. The first mission was established in 1885; an apostolic vicariate was organized in 1899. Most of the foreign missionaries were expelled following the communist takeover in 1975. Catholic schools remain banned, and the government lets foreign missionaries into the country only as "social workers." A Laotian bishop at the 1998 Synod of Bishops for Asia said religious practice was nearly normal in two of the country's four apostolic vicariates, but elsewhere was more controlled and sometimes difficult. Buddhism is the state religion.

Latvia*

Archd., 1; dioc., 3; card., 1; bp., 5; parishes, 274; priests, 149 (124 dioc., 25 rel.); p.d., 1; sem., 24; srs., 95; catechist, 327; bap., 5,763; Caths., 419,000 (19%); tot. pop., 2,112,000.

Independent (1991) Baltic republic; capital, Riga. (Forcibly absorbed by the USSR in 1940; it regained independence in 1991). Catholicism was introduced late in the 12th century. Lutheranism became the dominant religion after 1530. Catholics were free to pracice their faith during the long period of Russian control and during independence from 1918 to 1940. The relatively small Catholic community in Latvia was repressed during the 1940-91 Soviet takeover.

After Latvia declared its independence, the Church began to flourish, including among people who described themselves as nonreligious. In the late 1990s, one archbishop urged the Russian government not to interfere in disputes over citizenship for the country's ethnic Russians, who make up about one-third of the country's population.

Lebanon*

Patriarchates, 3; archd., 12 (1 Armenian, 4 Maronite, 7 Greek Melkite); dioc., 8 (1 Chaldean, 6 Maronite); v.a., 1 (Latin); card., 2 (patriarch and emeritus of the Maronites); patriarchs, 4 (patriarchs of Antioch of the Maronites, Antioch of the Syrians and Cilicia of the Armenians who reside in Lebanon); abp., 24; bp., 18; parishes, 1,126; priests, 1,585 (868 dioc., 717 rel.); p.d., 32; sem., 390; bros., 147; srs., 2,553; catechists, 483; bap., 11,069; Caths., 2,148,000 (52%); tot. pop., 4,050,000.

Republic in the Middle East; capital, Beirut. Christianity, introduced in apostolic times, was firmly established by the end of the fourth century and has remained so despite heavy Muslim influence since early in the seventh century. The country is the center of the Maronite rite, and the presidency is reserved for a Maronite Catholic. In the 1980s, the country was torn by violence and often heavy fighting among rival political-religious factions drawn along Christian-Muslim lines. A 1995 Synod of Bishops for Lebanon provoked controversy by directly criticizing Israeli occupation of southern Lebanon and Syria's continued deployment of troops in the area. After Syria withdrew the majority of its troops in 2005, Lebanon's bishops were outspoken in calling for free and fair elections. The Catholic Church has multiple rites in Lebanon and has been seen as influential with politicians.

Lesotho*

Archd., 1; dioc., 3; abp., 1; bp., 3; parishes, 95; priests, 249 (92 dioc., 157 rel.); sem., 70; bros., 26; srs., 624; catechists, 1,194; bap., 15,211; Caths., 1,271,000 (52%); tot. pop., 2,342,000.

Constitutional monarchy, an enclave in the southeastern part of South Africa; capital, Maseru. Oblates of Mary Immaculate, the first Catholic missionaries in the area, started evangelization in 1862. Fr. Joseph Gerard, beatified in 1988, worked 10 years before he made his first conversion. An apostolic prefecture was organized in 1894. The hierarchy was established in 1951. Under the military government of the late 1980s, Lesotho's Catholics pressed for democratic reforms. In the 1990s, they gave special pastoral care to families whose breadwinners had to travel to South Africa to work, often for weeks at a time.

Liberia*

Archd., 1; dioc., 2; abp., 1; bp., 2; parishes, 56; priests, 63 (42 dioc., 21 rel.); sem., 44; bros., 14; srs., 67; catechists, 207; bap. 1,784; Caths., 313,000 (8%); tot. pop., 3,892,000.

Republic in West Africa; capital, Monrovia. Missionary work and influence, dating intermittently from the 16th century, were slight before the Society of African Missions undertook evangelization in 1906. The hierarchy was established in 1982. Fighting within the country, which began in 1989, culminated in 1996 and resulted in the evacuation of most Church workers and the archbishop of Monrovia. The war claimed the lives of 150,000 and made refugees of or displaced another million. Most Church institutions in Monrovia were destroyed. Monrovia Archbp. Michael Francis was among leaders calling for U.S.-led intervention

to quell chaos in the country in mid-2003.

Libya*

V.a., 3; p.a.; bp., 2; parishes, 7; priests, 14 (2 dioc., 13 rel.); srs., 62; bap., 85; Caths., 130,000 (1.8%); tot. pop., 6,790,000.

Arab state in North Africa; capital, Tripoli. Christianity was probably preached in the area at an early date but was overcome by the spread of Islam from the 630s. Islamization was complete by 1067, and there has been no Christian influence since then. Almost all Catholics are foreign workers. Islam is the state religion. After implementation of a U.N. embargo against the country in 1992, the government removed most limitations on entry of Catholic religious orders, especially health care workers. Libya established diplomatic relations with the Holy See in 1997. Vatican officials called for peace in the face of the country's severe civil upheaval in 2011, and Christians have been under attack in the chaotic political climate that followed the fall and execution of Muammar Qadafi.

Liechtenstein*

Archd. 1; abp., 1; parishes, 10; priests, 35 (24 dioc., 11 rel); sem., 8; srs., 52; bap., 298; Caths., 27,000 (80%); tot. pop., 36,000.

Constitutional monarchy in central Europe; capital, Vaduz. Christianity in the country dates from the fourth century. The Reformation had hardly any influence in the country. Catholicism is the state religion, but religious freedom for all is guaranteed by law.

Lithuania*

Archd., 2; dioc., 5; mil. ord., 1; card., 1; abp., 1; bp., 10; parishes, 712; priests, 846 (735 dioc., 111 rel.); p.d., 8; sem., 94; bros., 13; srs., 550; catechists, 1,358; bap., 29,946; Caths., 2,715,000 (78%); tot. pop., 3,471,000.

Baltic republic forcibly absorbed and under Soviet domination from 1940; regained independence, 1991; capital, Vilnius. Catholicism was introduced in 1251 and a short-lived diocese was established by 1260. Effective evangelization took place between 1387 and 1417, when Catholicism became the state religion. Efforts of czars to "russify" the Church between 1795 and 1918 were strongly resisted. Concordat relations with the Vatican were established in 1927, nine years after independence from Russia and 13 years before Russia annexed Lithuania. The Russians closed convents and seminaries; in Kaunas, men needed government approval to attend the seminary. Priests were restricted in pastoral ministry and subject to appointment by government officials; no religious services were allowed outside churches; religious press and instruction were banned. Some bishops and hundreds of priests and laity were imprisoned or detained in Siberia between 1945 and 1955. Two bishops — Vincentas Sladkevicius and Julijonas Steponavicius — were forbidden to act as bishops and relegated to remote parishes in 1957 and 1961, respectively. Despite such conditions, a vigorous underground Church flourished in Lithuania.

In the 1980s, government pressure eased, and some bishops were allowed to return to their dioceses. In 1989, Pope John Paul II appointed bishops in all six Lithuanian dioceses. The Church strongly supported the 1990 independence movement, and Lithuanian independence leaders urged young men to desert the Russian army and seek sanctuary in churches. However, communist rule had nearly destroyed the Church's infrastructure. In 2000 the

Church and government signed a series of agreements regularizing the Church's position.

Luxembourg*

Archd., 1; abp., 2; parishes, 275; priests, 207 (151 dioc., 56 rel.); p.d., 6; sem., 5; bros., 21; srs., 566; bap., 2,641; Caths. 398,000 (85%); tot. pop., 504,000.

Constitutional monarchy in Western Europe; capital, Luxembourg. Christianity, introduced in the fifth and sixth centuries, was firmly established by the end of the eighth century. A full-scale parish system was in existence in the ninth century. Monastic influence was strong until the Reformation, which had minimal influence in the country. The Church experienced some adverse influence from the currents of the French Revolution. In recent years, the Church has restructured its adult formation program to involve more lay workers.

Macedonia*

Dioc., 1; bp., 2; parishes, 9; priests, 21 (14 dioc., 7 rel.); sem., 13; srs., 31; bap., 82; Caths., 15,000 (.9%); tot. pop., 2,350,000.

Former Yugoslav Republic of Macedonia; declared independence in 1992; capital, Skopje. The Diocese of Skopje-Prizren includes the Yugoslav province of Kosovo, so the Macedonian Church helped with ethnic Albanians during the period of ethnic cleansing by Serb forces and retaliatory NATO air strikes.

Madagascar*

Archd., 5; dioc., 16; abp., 8; bp., 24; parishes, 328; priests, 1,469 (687 dioc., 782 rel.); p.d., 2; sem., 1,087; bros., 540; srs., 4,796; catechists, 13,613; bap., 149,926; Caths., 6,872,000 (30%); tot. pop. 20,696,000.

Republic (Malagasy Republic) off the eastern coast of Africa; capital, Antananarivo. Missionary efforts were gener ally fruitless from early in the 16th century until the Jesuits were permitted to start open evangelization about 1845. An apostolic prefecture was set up in 1850 and an apostolic vicariate in the North was under the charge of the Holy Ghost Fathers in 1898. There were 100,000 Catholics by 1900. The first indigenous bishop was ordained in 1936. The hierarchy was established in 1955. In the late 1980s and early 1990s, the Church joined opposition calls for renewal of social institutions. Today, the Church in Madagascar runs hundreds of schools and dozens of orphanages and is active in the island's social justice concerns; some consider it the largest landowner, after the government.

Malawi*

Archd., 2; dioc., 6; abp., 1; bp., 11 parishes, 149; priests, 443 (323 dioc., 120 rel.); sem., 327; bros., 70; srs., 898; catechists, 2,240; bap., 125,713; Caths., 4,961,000 (29%); tot. pop., 15,034,000.

Republic in the interior of East Africa; capital, Lilongwe. Missionary work, begun by Jesuits in the late 16th and early 17th centuries, was generally ineffective until the end of the 19th century. The Missionaries of Africa (White Fathers) arrived in 1889 and later were joined by others. A vicariate was set up in 1897. The hierarchy was established in 1959. In the late 1980s, the Church in Malawi helped hundreds of thousands of refugees from the war in Mozambique. Malawi's churches, especially the Catholic Church, were instrumental in bringing about the downfall of President Hastings Kamuzu Banda, who ruled for 30 years. A 1992 bishops' pastoral letter criticized Banda's rule and the nation's poverty and galvanized Malawians into pro-democracy protests. Banda responded by summoning the country's bishops, seizing copies of the letter and expelling an Irish member of the Malawi hierarchy. Western donors called off aid, and in 1994 Banda was forced to call multi-party elections, which he lost. In 2002, Church officials were outspoken against plans by Banda's successor, President Bakili Muluzi, to seek a third term of office; Church officials said they were threatened and attacked for that criticism.

Malaysia

Archd., 3; dioc., 6; abp., 6; bp., 8; parishes, 168; priests, 270 (207 dioc., 63 rel.); p.d., 10; sem., 68; bros., 81; srs., 509; catechists, 2,812; bap., 19,289; Caths., 995,000 (3%); tot. pop., 28,855,000. (AD)

Parliamentary democracy and elective monarchy in Southeast Asia; capital, Kuala Lumpur. Christianity, introduced by Portuguese colonists about 1511, was confined almost exclusively to Malacca until late in the 18th century. The effectiveness of evangelization increased from then on because of the recruitment and training of indigenous clergy. Singapore (see separate entry), founded in 1819, became a center for missionary work. Effective evangelization in Sabah and Sarawak began in the second half of the 19th century. The hierarchy was established in 1973. In accordance with government wishes for Bahasa Malaysia to be the national language, the Church has tried to introduce it into its liturgies. For more than a decade, Church leaders campaigned against the Internal Security Act, which allows renewable 30-day detentions without trial. Proselytizing Muslims is illegal, but the government allows conversions from other religions. In 2011, Malaysia normalized relations with the Holy See.

Maldives

Republic, an archipelago 400 miles southwest of India and Ceylon; capital, Male. No serious attempt was ever made to evangelize the area, which is completely Muslim. Population, 310,000.

Mali*

Archd., 1; dioc., 5; abp., 1; bp., 5; parishes, 43; priests, 177 (117 dioc., 60 rel.); sem., 72; bros., 14; srs., 270; catechists, 1,098; bap., 4,034; Caths., 365,000 (.2%); tot. pop., 16,182,000.

Republic, inland in western Africa; capital, Bamako. Catholicism was introduced late in the second half of the 19th century. Missionary work made little progress in the midst of the predominantly Muslim population. A vicariate was set up in 1921. The hierarchy was established in 1955. In recent years, the Church has promoted the role of women in society. Catholics have cordial relations with Muslims.

Malta*

Archd., 1; dioc., 1; card., 1; abp., 6; bp., 4; parishes, 85; priests, 805 (437 dioc., 368 rel.); sem., 83; bros., 61; srs., 1,006; catechists, 11,234; bap., 3,105; Caths., 412,000 (94%); tot. pop., 446,000.

Republic south of Sicily; capital, Valletta. Catacombs and inscriptions are evidence of the early introduction of Christianity. St. Paul was shipwrecked on Malta in 60. Saracens controlled the islands from 870 to 1090, a period of difficulty for the Church. The line of bishops extends from 1090 to the present. Late in the 20th century, Church-state conflict developed over passage of government-sponsored legislation affecting Catholic schools and

Church-owned property. An agreement reached in 1985 ended the dispute. An influx of several thousand African migrants early in the 21st century strained Maltese hospitality, and Jesuit priests were targeted with arson because of their advocacy for the groups. Pope Benedict XVI visited in April 2010.

Marshall Islands*

P.a., 1; parishes, 4; priests, 6 (5 dioc., 1 rel.); p.d., 1; sem., 2; brs., 1; srs., 12; bap., 211; Caths., 5,000 (12.5%); tot. pop., 57,000.

Island republic in central Pacific Ocean; capital, Majura. Formerly administered by United States as part of U.N. Trust Territory of the Pacific; independent nation, 1991. An apostolic prefecture was erected May 25, 1993 (formerly part of Carolines-Marshall Diocese), with Fr. James Gould, a U.S. Jesuit, as its first apostolic prefect.

Mauritania*

Dioc., 1; bp., 1; parishes, 6; priests, 12 (3 dioc., 9 rel.); brs. 1; srs., 36; sem., 2; bap., 34; Caths., 5,000 (.2%); tot. pop., 3,433,000. (AD)

Islamic republic on the northwest coast of Africa; capital, Nouakchott. With few exceptions, the Catholics in the country are foreign workers. At the 1994 Synod of Bishops for Africa, a bishop from Mauritania reported increasing problems with fundamentalist Muslims, but cautioned Church leaders against generalizing about Muslims.

Mauritius*

Dioc., 1; v.a., 1; bp., 2; parishes, 51; priests, 101 (52 dioc., 49 rel.); sem., 12; bros., 25; srs., 225; catechists, 1,509; bap., 5,520; Caths., 347,000 (26%); tot. pop., 1,286,000.

Island republic in the Indian Ocean; capital, Port Louis. Catholicism was introduced by Vincentians in 1722. Port Louis, made a vicariate in 1819 and a diocese in 1847, was a jumping-off point for missionaries to Australia, Madagascar and South Africa. During a 1989 visit to Mauritius, Pope John Paul II warned against sins that accompanied its rapid economic development and booming tourism industry.

Mexico* (See Catholic Church in Mexico; see also Statistics of the Church in Mexico)

Micronesia*

Dioc., 1; bp., 1; parishes, 26; priests, 19 (9 dioc., 10 rel.); p.d., 40. sem., 10; bros., 1; srs., 55; catechists, 541; bap., 1,604; Caths., 76,000 (54%); tot. pop., 129,000.

Federated States of Micronesia (Caroline archipel ago) in southwest Pacific; capital, Palikir; former U.N. trust territory under U.S. administration; became independent nation September 1991. Effective evangelization began in the late 1880s. The government established diplomatic relations with the Holy See in 1994.

Moldova*

Dioc., 1; bp., 1; parishes, 17; priests, 34 (17 dioc., 17 rel.); p.d., 2; sem., 11; bros., 2; srs., 40; bap., 68; Caths., 20,000 (.5%); tot. pop., 3,566,000.

Independent republic, former constituent republic of the USSR; capital, Kishinev. The majority of people belong to the Orthodox Church. Catholics are mostly of Polish or German descent.

Monaco*

Archd., 1; abp., 1; parishes, 6; priests, 21 (15 dioc., 6 rel.); p.d., 3; sem., 2; srs., 9; bap., 176; Caths., 30,000 (90%); tot. pop., 33,000.

Constitutional monarchy, an enclave on the Mediterranean coast of France; capital, Monaco. Christianity was introduced before 1000. Catholicism is the official religion but religious freedom is guaranteed for all.

Mongolia*

Bp., 1; parishes, 4; priests, 20 (5 dioc., 20 rel.); sem., 4; bros., 6; srs., 58; bap., 118; Caths., 1,000 (.08%); tot. pop., 2,781,000.

Republic in north central Asia; formerly under com munist control; capital, Ulan Bator. Christianity was introduced by Oriental Orthodox. Some Franciscans were in the country in the 13th and 14th centuries, en route to China. Freedom of worship is guaranteed under the new constitution, which went into effect in 1992. The government established relations with the Holy See in 1992 and indicated that missionaries would be welcome to help rebuild the country. The first Catholic parish was established in 1994, and by 1997 the Church had extended its work beyond the capital. In 2003 a missionary from the Philippines became Mongolia's first bishop.

Montenegro

Archd., 1, Dioc. 1; abp., 1; bp., 1; parishes, 44; priests, 37 (25 dioc., 12 rel.); sem., 2; brs. 1; srs., 150; bap., 241; Caths., 21,000 (4%); tot. pop., 731,000.

Independent nation (July 2006) in southeastern Europe; formerly part of Yugoslavia and Serbia and Montenegro; capital Podgorica. Church history coincides with much of Serbia. Montenegro and the Vatican announced diplomatic ties in December 2006.

Morocco*

Archd., 2; abp., 4; bp., 14; parishes, 36; priests, 42 (13 dioc., 29 rel.); bros., 12; srs., 222; bap., 58; Caths., 23,000 (.08%); tot. pop., 32,245,000.

Constitutional monarchy in North Africa; capital, Rabat. Christianity was known in the area by the end of the third century. Bishops from Morocco attended a council at Carthage in 484. Catholic life survived under Visigoth and, from 700, Arab rule; later it became subject to influence from the Spanish, Portuguese and French. Islam is the state religion. The hierarchy was established in 1955.

Mozambique*

Archd., 3; dioc., 9; card., 1; abp. 4; bp., 13; parishes, 308; priests, 623 (240 dioc., 383 rel.); p.d. 2, sem., 479; bros., 102; srs., 1,136; catechists, 44,318; bap., 102,673; Caths., 5,867,000 (24%); tot. pop., 22,370,000. (AD)

Republic in southeast Africa; capital, Maputo. Christianity was introduced by Portuguese Jesuits about the middle of the 16th century. Evangelization continued from then until the 18th century, when it went into decline largely because of the Portuguese government's expulsion of the Jesuits. Conditions worsened in the 1830s, improved after 1881, but deteriorated again during the anticlerical period from 1910 to 1925.

Conditions improved in 1940, the year Portugal concluded a new concordat with the Holy See and the hierarchy was established. Missionaries' outspoken criticism of Portuguese policies in Mozambique resulted in Church-state tensions in the years immediately preceding independence. The first two indigenous bishops were ordained Mar. 9, 1975. Two ecclesiastical provinces were established in 1984. Mozambican bishops and members of the Rome-based Sant' Egidio Community were official mediators in the talks that ended 16 years of civil war in 1992. Since then, Church participation has flourished, with high attendance at Mass, a boom in vocations and active catechists at the parish level.

Myanmar

Archd., 3; dioc., 13; abp., 4; bp., 19; parishes, 358; priests, 793 (714 dioc., 79 rel.); sem., 393; bros., 139; srs., 1,819; catechists, 3,180; bap., 17,456; Caths., 657,000 (1.2%); tot. pop., 60,821,000. (AD)

Socialist republic in Southeast Asia, formerly Burma; name changed to Myanmar in 1989; capital, Yangon (Rangoon). Christianity was introduced about 1500. Small-scale evangelization had limited results from the middle of the 16th century until the 1850s, when effective organization of the Church began. The hierarchy was established in 1955. Buddhism was declared the state religion in 1961, but the state is now officially secular. In 1965, Church schools and hospitals were nationalized. In 1966, all foreign missionaries who had entered the country for the first time after 1948 were forced to leave when the government refused to renew their work permits. The Church is involved primarily in pastoral and social activities.

Namibia*

Archd., 1; dioc., 1; v.a., 1; abp., 1; bp., 2; parishes, 102; priests, 94 (22 dioc., 72 rel.); p.d., 49; sem., 32; bros., 21; srs., 509; catechists, 1,393; bap., 7,836; Caths., 439,000 (18%); tot. pop., 2,183,000. (AD)

Independent (March 21, 1990) state in southern Africa; capital, Windhoek. The area shares the history of South Africa. The hierarchy was established in 1994. The Church is hindered by a lack of priests.

Nauru*

Parishes, 2; priest, 1 (rel); p.d., 2; srs., 3; bap., 154; Caths., 5,000 (37%); tot. pop., 14,000.

Independent republic in western Pacific; capital, Yaren. Forms part of the Tarawa and Nauru Diocese (Kiribati). Established diplomatic relations with the Holy See in 1992.

Nepal*

P.a., 1; parishes, 8; priests, 67 (14 dioc.; 53 rel.); sem., 24; bros., 13; srs., 160; bap., 201; Caths., 8,000 (.2%); tot. pop., 28,585,000.

Constitutional monarchy in central Asia; capital, Katmandu. Little is known of the country before the 15th century. Some Jesuits passed through from 1628 and some sections were evangelized in the 18th century, with minimal results, before the country was closed to foreigners. Conversions from Hinduism, the state religion, are not recognized in law and are punishable by imprisonment. The Church has established an effective charitable network in Nepal, which officially declared itself a secular state in 2006.

Netherlands*

Archd., 1; dioc., 6; mil ord., 1; card., 2; abp., 2; bp., 14; parishes, 1,179; priests 2,475 (1,115 dioc., 1,360 rel.); p.d., 374; sem., 179; bros., 752; srs., 6,112; bap., 24,213; Caths., 4,649,000 (30%); tot. pop., 16,730,000.

Constitutional monarchy in northwestern Europe; capital, Amsterdam (seat of government, The Hague). Evangelization, begun about the turn of the sixth century by Irish, Anglo-Saxon and Frankish missionaries, resulted in Christianization of the country by 800 and subsequent strong influence on the Lowlands. Invasion by French Calvinists in 1572 brought serious losses to the Catholic Church and made the Reformed Church dominant. Catholics suffered a practical persecution of official repression and social handicap in the 17th century. The schism of Utrecht occurred in 1724. Only one-third of the population was Catholic in 1726. The Church had only a skeletal organization from 1702 to 1853, when the hierarchy was re-established.

Despite this upturn, cultural isolation was the experience of Catholics until about 1914. From then on new vigor came into the life of the Church, and a whole new climate of interfaith relations began to develop. Before and for some years following the Second Vatican Council, the thrust and variety of thought and practice in the Dutch Church moved it to the vanguard position of "progressive" renewal. A synod of Dutch bishops held at the Vatican in January 1980 discussed ideological differences among Catholics with the aim of fostering unity and restoring some discipline within the nation's Church. However, even into the 1990s Church leaders spoke of a polarization among Catholics over issues such as sexual morality, ministries for women and priestly celibacy. The bishops also spoke out against permissive laws on euthanasia and assisted suicide.

New Zealand*

Archd., 1; dioc., 5; mil. ord., 1; card., 1; abp., 2; bp., 10; parishes, 271; priests, 499 (317 dioc., 182 rel.); p.d., 22; sem., 27; bros., 138; srs., 828; bap., 8,188; Caths. 542,000 (12%); tot. pop., 4,368,000.

Parliamentary democracy in southwestern Pacific Ocean; capital, Wellington. Protestant missionaries were the first evangelizers. On North Island, Catholic missionaries started work before the establishment of two dioceses in 1848; their work among the Maoris was not organized until about 1881. On South Island, whose first resident priest arrived in 1840, a diocese was established in 1869. These three jurisdictions were joined in a province in 1896. The Marists were the predominant Catholic missionaries in the area. The first Maori bishop was named in 1988. In 1998, Pope John Paul II urged New Zealand's bishops not to allow the Church to fall prey to the practices and values of prevailing culture.

Nicaragua*

Archd., 1; dioc., 6; v.a., 1; card., 1; abp., 3; bp., 12; parishes, 322; priests, 588 (424 dioc., 164 rel.); p.d., 32; sem., 302; bros., 56; srs., 867; catechists, 46,352; bap., 58,288; Caths., 5,246,000 (89%); tot. pop., 5,889,000.

Republic in Central America: capital, Managua. Evangelization began shortly after the Spanish con quest, about 1524, and eight years later the first bish op took over jurisdiction of the Church in the country. Jesuits were leaders in missionary work during the colonial period, which lasted until the 1820s. Evangelization increased after establishment of the republic in 1838 and extended to the Atlantic coastal area, where Protestant missionaries began work about the middle of the 1900s.

Many Church leaders, clerical and lay, supported the aims but not necessarily all the methods of the Sandinista revolution, which forced the resignation and flight July 17, 1979, of Anastasio Somoza, whose family had controlled the government since the early 1930s. During the Sandinista period that followed, four priests accepted government posts. Some Nicaraguan Catholics threw their energies behind the Sandinista program of land reform and socialism, forming what some called a "popular church" based on liberation theology, while others strongly opposed the government. Managua Card. Miguel Obando Bravo helped mediate cease-fire talks during the war between the Sandinistas and U.S.-backed guerrillas. Land distribution, exacerbated by a wide gap in incomes, continued to be an issue, and in the late 1990s the Nicaraguan bishops continued to call for compromise between the government and former government officials. Despite an influx of aid after Hurricane Mitch killed more than 2,500 Nicaraguans and forced 900,000 to evacuate in 1998, Church leaders still cited poverty as a major issue.

Niger*

Archd., 1; dioc.; 1; bp., 2; parishes, 21; priests, 60 (28 dioc., 32 rel.); p.d., 1; sem., 10; bros., 9; srs., 96; catechists, 248; bap., 440; Caths., 22,000 (.13%); tot. pop., 15,731,000. Republic in west central Africa; capital, Niamey. The first mission was set up in 1831. An apostolic prefecture was organized in 1942, and the first diocese was established in 1961. The country is predominantly Muslim. The Church is active in the fields of health and education.

Nigeria*

Archd., 9; dioc., 41; v.a., 2; card., 3; abp., 13; bp., 43; parishes, 2,891; priests, 6,343 (5,346 dioc., 997 rel.); p.d., 4; sem., 6,411; bros., 498; srs., 5,087; catechists, 24,338; bap., 429,567; Caths., 24,934,000 (15%); tot. pop., 157,225,000.

Republic in West Africa; capital, Lagos. The Portuguese introduced Catholicism to the coastal region in the 15th century. Capuchins did some evangelization in the 17th century but systematic mission ary work did not get under way along the coast until about 1840. A vicariate for this area was organized in 1870. A prefecture was set up in 1911 for missions in the northern part of the country, where Islam was strongly entrenched. The hierarchy was established in 1950. From 1967, when Biafra seceded, until early in 1970 the country was torn by civil war. Under the 1993-99 rule of Gen. Sani Abacha, Church leaders spoke out on behalf of human rights and democracy. After Abacha announced elections, the bishops said the country needed "new leading actors and fresh vision." As the 21st century began, bishops spoke out against imposition of Islamic law in individual states within the country. Recent years have seen a severe increase in attacks on Christians by Islamic extremist groups, including Boko Haram.

Norway*

Dioc., 1; prel., 2; bp., 3; parishes, 37; priests, 83 (47 dioc., 36 rel.); p.d., 2; sem., 7; bros., 5; srs., 143; bap., 1,053; Caths., 116,000 (1.1%); tot. pop., 4,988,000.

Constitutional monarchy in northern Europe; capital, Oslo. Evangelization begun in the ninth century by missionaries from England and Ireland put the Church on a firm footing about the turn of the 11th century. The first diocese was set up in 1153 and development of the Church progressed until the Black Death in 1349 inflicted losses from which it never recovered. Lutheranism, introduced from outside in 1537 and furthered cautiously, gained general acceptance by about 1600 and was made the state religion. Legal and other measures crippled the Church, forcing priests to flee the country and completely disrupting normal activity. Changes for the better came in the 19th century, with the granting of religious liberty in 1845 and the repeal of many legal disabilities in 1897. Norway was administered as a single apostolic vicariate from 1892 to 1932, when it was divided into three jurisdictions.

Oman

Parishes, 4; priests, 9 (1 dioc., 8 rel.); bap., 157; Caths., 80,000 (2.7%); tot. pop., 2,975,000.

Independent monarchy in eastern corner of Arabian Peninsula; capital, Muscat. Under ecclesiastical jurisdiction of Arabia apostolic vicariate.

Pakistan*

Archd., 2; dioc., 4; p.a., 1; abp., 2; bp., 7; parishes, 123; priests, 280 (153 dioc., 127 rel.); sem., 175; bros., 65; srs., 803; catechists, 663; bap., 21,311; Caths., 1,194,000 (.07%); tot. pop., 170,854,000.

Islamic republic in southwest Asia; capital, Islamabad. Islam, firmly established in the eighth century, is the state religion. Christian evangelization of the native population began about the middle of the 19th century, years after earlier scattered attempts. The hierarchy was established in 1950. A series of death sentences against Christians accused of blasphemy resulted in acquittals during appeal processes, but in 1998 Bp. John Joseph of Faisalabad committed suicide to protest the strict blasphemy laws, which continued to be used as reasons for Christian arrests. In early 2002, the government did away with the system under which religious minorities, such as Catholics, could only vote in elections for members of their religious group. Pakistani Christians, including Catholics, have been the target of several terrorist incidents since the United States attacked Afghanistan in October 2001 and have grown more violent in the last few years.

Palau*

Parishes, 3; priests, 4 (2 dioc., 2 rel.); p.d., 1; srs., 5; bap., 327; Caths., 13,000 (52%); tot. pop., 23,000.

Independent (1994) nation in western Pacific; capital, Koror; part of Caroline chain of Islands. Under ecclesiastical jurisdiction of diocese of Caroline Islands, Federated States of Micronesia.

Panama*

Archd., 1; dioc., 5; prel., 1; v.a., 1; abp., 3; bp., 10; parishes, 199; priests, 218 (213 dioc., 205 rel.); p.d., 67; sem., 152; bros., 54; srs., 437; catechists, 5,050; bap., 34,034; Caths., 3,183,000 (85%); tot. pop., 3,643,000.

Republic in Central America; capital, Panama City. Catholicism was introduced by Franciscan missionaries and evangelization started in 1514. The Panama Diocese, oldest in the Americas, was set up at the same time. The Catholic Church has favored status and state aid for missions, charities and parochial schools, but freedom is guaranteed to all religions. In May 1989, Panama's bishops accused the government of thwarting the presidential elections and of attempting to intimidate the Church. The elections' legitimate leader, Guillermo Endara, temporarily sought refuge at the Vatican Embassy in Panama City. After increasing unrest and violence, on Dec. 24, 1989, the country's dictator, Gen. Manuel Noriega, sought refuge at the Vatican Embassy. Ten days later, after U.S. troops spent days blasting the embassy with loud rock music and after meetings with Church diplomatic officials, Noriega surrendered.

Papua New Guinea*

Archd., 4; dioc., 15; abp., 2; bp., 25; parishes, 390; priests, 617 (265 dioc., 352 rel.); p.d., 4; sem., 457; bros., 198; srs., 914; catechists, 3,668; bap., 34,452; Caths., 1,905,000 (31%); tot. pop., 6,205,000.

Independent (Sept. 16, 1975) republic in southwest Pacific; capital, Port Moresby. Marists began evangelization about 1844 but were handicapped by many factors, including "spheres of influence" laid out for Catholic and Protestant missionaries. An apostolic prefecture was set up in 1896 and placed in charge of the Divine Word Missionaries. The territory suffered greatly during World War II. Hierarchy was established for New Guinea and adjacent islands in 1966. A decade-long war that began in the Bougainville area in the late 1980s left many churches, schools and health centers destroyed. At the end of the century, the Church fought social disintegration marked by violence, poverty and corruption.

Paraguay*

Archd., 1; dioc., 11; v.a., 2; mil. ord. 1; abp., 2; bp., 18; parishes, 363; priests, 776 (337 dioc., 439 rel.); p.d., 168; sem., 488; bros., 149; srs., 1,538; bap., 100,989; catechists, 48,060; Caths., 6,117,000 (91%); tot. pop., 6,563,000.

Republic in central South America; capital, Asunción. Catholicism was introduced in 1542, evangelization began almost immediately. A diocese erected in 1547 was occupied for the first time in 1556. On many occasions thereafter, dioceses in the country were left unoccupied because of political and other reasons. Jesuits who came into the country after 1609 devised the reductions system for evangelizing the Indians, teaching them agriculture, husbandry, trades and other arts, and giving them experience in property use and community life. The reductions were communes of Indians only, and had an average population of 3,000-4,000, under the direction of the missionaries. At their peak, some 30 reductions had a population of 100,000. Political officials regarded the reductions with disfavor because politicians did not control them and feared that the Indians trained in them might foment revolt and upset the established colonial sys tem under Spanish control. The reductions lasted until about 1768, when the Jesuits were expelled.

Church-state relations following independence from Spain in 1811 were often tense because of government efforts to control the Church through continued exercise of Spanish patronage rights and by other means. The Church as well as the whole country suffered during the War of the Triple Alliance, 1865-70. After that time, the Church had the same kind of experience in Paraguay as in the rest of Latin America, with forces of liberalism, anticlericalism, massive educational needs, poverty, and a shortage of priests and other personnel.

In the 1980s, Church-state tensions increased as Catholic leaders spoke out against President Alfredo Stroessner's decades of one-man rule. A 1988 papal visit seemed to increase the Church's confidence, as bishops repeatedly spoke out against Stroessner. The army general who overthrew Stroessner in 1989 said he did so in part to defend the Catholic Church.

Retired Bp. Fernando Lugo, who campaigned on a platform of equality for Paraguay's poor farmers and indigenous people, was elected president of Paraguay in 2008, ending the six-decade rule of the Colorado Party.

Peru*

Archd., 7; dioc., 19; prel., 10; v.a., 8; mil. ord. 1; card., 1; abp., 12; bp., 58; parishes, 1,592; priests, 3,297 (1,976 dioc., 1,321 rel.); p.d., 64; sem., 1,959; bros., 544; srs., 5,609; catechists, 49,546; bap., 361,127; Caths., 26,511,000 (88%); tot. pop., 30,136,000.

Republic on the west coast of South America; capital, Lima. An effective diocese became operational in 1537, five years after the Spanish conquest. Evangelization, already under way, developed for some time after 1570 but deteriorated before the end of the colonial period in the 1820s. The first American saint of the new world was a Peruvian, Rose of Lima, a Dominican tertiary who died in 1617 and was canonized in 1671.

In the new republic founded after the wars of independence the Church experienced problems of adjustment, government efforts to control it through continuation of the patronage rights of the Spanish crown; suppression of houses of religious and expropriation of Church property; religious indifference and outright hostility. In the 20th century, liberation theology was born in Peru under the leadership of Father Gustavo Gutierrez. In the 1980s and early 1990s, the Maoist Sendero Luminoso guerrillas often targeted Church workers, who also found themselves prone to false charges of terrorism. A Peruvian cardinal was credited with much of the success of an early 1990s government effort to win the surrender of the rebels. When the government initiated a drastic economic program in 1990, Peruvian Church leaders worked to help feed and clothe the poor. In the late '90s, the Church successfully fought a government program of sterilization.

Early in the 21st century, Church leaders became more outspoken on environmental issues and took the lead in reconstruction after the 2007 earthquake hit coastal areas.

Philippines*

Archd., 16; dioc., 58; prel., 4; v.a., 7; mil. ord. 1; card., 3; abp., 24; bp., 133; parishes, 3,169; priests, 9,089 (6,065 dioc., 3,024 rel.); p.d.,55; sem., 8,096; bros., 1,347; srs., 12,858 catechists, 94,752; bap., 1,640,551; Caths., 78,900,000 (81.5%); tot. pop., 95,834,000.

Republic, an archipelago of 7,000 islands off the southeast coast of Asia; capital, Manila. Systematic evangelization was begun in 1564 and resulted in firm establishment of the Church by the 19th century. During the period of Spanish rule, which lasted from the discovery of the islands by Magellan in 1521 to 1898, the Church experienced difficulties with the patronage system under which the Spanish crown tried to control ecclesiastical affairs through episcopal and other appointments. This system ended in 1898 when the United States gained possession of the islands and instituted a policy of separation of Church and state. Anticlericalism flared late in the 19th century. The Aglipayan schism, an attempt to set up a nationalist Church, occurred in 1902.

Church leaders and human rights groups constantly criticized abuses under former president and dictator Ferdinand Marcos. Church newspapers were among those censored or closed after he declared martial law, and religious and lay people were arrested and held without formal charges for long periods of time. After Marcos declared himself the victor in the 1986 elections and international observers declared his win a fraud, the Philippine bishops' call for a nonviolent struggle for justice was seen as the catalyst for the nation's "people power" revolution. Corazon Aquino, Marcos's successor, took refuge with Carmelite nuns during the revolution. At the turn of the century, Church workers often found themselves unintentional victims of violence spurred by Muslim separatists' fight for autonomy in the southern Philippines. Church social action focused on the poor, overseas workers, ecology, corruption, and a fight against the death penalty. There was also much controversy over a proposed changes to the contraception laws.

Poland*

Archd., 15; dioc., 28; mil. ord., 1; ordinariate, 1; cards., 6; abps., 26; bps., 103; parishes, 10,315; priests, 29,961 (23,446 dioc., 6,515 rel.); p.d., 23; sem., 4,388; bros., 1,054; srs., 21,464; catechists, 14,094; bap., 383,486; Caths., 36,709,000 (96%); tot. pop., 38,209,000.

Republic in Eastern Europe; capital, Warsaw. The first traces of Christianity date from the second half of the ninth century. Its spread was accelerated by the union of the Slavs in the 10th century. The first diocese was set up in 968. The Reformation, supported mainly by city dwellers and the upper classes, peaked from about the middle of the 16th century, resulting in numerous conversions to Lutheranism, the Reformed Church and the Bohemian Brethren. A successful Counter-Reformation, with the Jesuits in a position of leadership, was completed by about 1632. The movement served a nationalist as well as religious purpose; in restoring religious unity to a large degree, it united the country against potential invaders, the Swedes, Russians and Turks. The Counter-Reformation had bad side effects, leading to the repression of Protestants long after it was over and to prejudice against Eastern-rite Catholics. The Church, in the same manner as the entire country, was adversely affected by the partitions of the 18th and 19th centuries. Russification hurt the Eastern- and Latin-rite Catholics.

In the republic established after World War I the Church reorganized itself, continued to serve as a vital force in national life, and enjoyed generally harmonious relations with the state. Progressive growth was strong until 1939, when German and Russian forces invaded and World War II began. In 1945, seven years before the adoption of a Soviet-type of constitution, the communist-controlled government initiated a policy that included a constant program of atheistic propaganda; a strong campaign against the hierarchy and clergy; the imprisonment in 1948 of 700 priests and even more religious; rigid limitation on the activities of the Catholic press and religious movements.

Regular contacts on a working level were initiated by the Vatican and Poland in 1974; regular diplomatic relations were established in 1989. Cardinal Karol Wojtyla of Krakow was elected to the papacy in 1978. Church and papal support was strong for the independent labor movement, Solidarity, which was recognized by the government in August 1980 but outlawed in December 1981, when martial law was imposed (martial law was suspended in 1982). In May 1989, following recognition of Solidarity and a series of political changes, the Catholic Church was given legal status for the first time since the communists took control of the government in 1944. In 1990, a new constitution was adopted, declaring Poland a democratic state. In 1992, the pope restructured the Church in Poland, adding 13 new dioceses. A new concordat between the Polish government and the Holy See was signed in 1993.

Since the end of communist rule, Poland's Church has struggled with anti-Semitism among some clergy. A dispute over a Carmelite convent outside the former Nazi death camp at Auschwitz resulted in the convent's removal, but several years later the Church was forced to speak against Catholic protesters who posted hundreds of crosses outside the camp. A nearly eight-year national synod process concluded in 1999 with calls for priests to live less luxurious lifestyles and to keep parishes finances open. The Polish Church continued to be a source of missionary priests in more than 90 countries. Church leaders also were dogged by allegations of spying under the communist regime, a charge that led the newly appointed archbishop of Warsaw to resign in early 2007 shortly before his installation. The country celebrated Pope John Paul II's beatification in May 2011.

Portugal*

Patriarchate (Lisbon), 1; archd., 2; dioc., 17; mil. ord., 1; patriarch, 1; card., 3; abp., 6; bp., 36; parishes, 4,420; priests, 3,663 (2,705 dioc., 958 rel.); p.d., 293; sem., 452; bros., 255; srs., 5,190; catechists, 62,640; bap., 68,876; Caths., 9,453,000 (88%); tot. pop., 10,682,000.

Republic in the western part of the Iberian penin sula; capital, Lisbon. Christianity was introduced before the fourth century. From the fifth century to early in the eighth century the Church experienced difficulties from the physical invasion of barbarians and the intellectual invasion of doctrinal errors in the forms of Arianism, Priscillianism and Pelagianism. The Church survived under the rule of Arabs from about 711 and of the Moors until 1249. Ecclesiastical life was fairly vigorous from 1080 to 1185, and monastic influence became strong. A decline set in about 1450. Several decades later Portugal became the jumping-off place for many missionaries to newly discovered colonies. The Reformation had little effect in the country.

In the early 1700s, King John V broke relations with Rome and required royal approval of papal acts. His successor,

Joseph I, expelled the Jesuits from Portugal and the colonies. Liberal revolutionaries with anti-Church policies made the 19th century a difficult one for the Church. Similar policies prevailed in Church-state relations in the 20th century until the accession to power of Premier Antonio de Oliveira Salazar in 1928; the hierarchy was seen as closely aligned with him. In 1940 Salazar concluded a concordat with the Holy See that regularized Church-state relations but still left the Church in a subservient condition.

In 1930, after lengthy investigation, the Church authorized devotion to Our Lady of Fátima, who appeared to three Portuguese children in 1917. Pope John Paul II, who credited Our Lady of Fátima with saving his life during a 1981 assassination attempt on her feast day, visited Portugal several times, including in May 2000 to beatify two of the Fátima visionaries. At that time, he had his Secretary of State, Cardinal Angelo Sodano, announce that the so-called third secret of Fátima would be published. The following month, the Vatican published the secret and said the message predicted the struggles of the Church with Nazism and communism and foretold the shooting of Pope John Paul.

Puerto Rico

Archd., 1; dioc., 5; abp., 1; bp., 8; parishes, 329; priests, 676 (350 dioc., 326 rel.); p.d., 455; sem., 93; bros., 49; srs., 885; catechists, 6,614; bap., 21,109; Caths., 3,129,000 (78%); tot. pop., 3,988,000. (AD)

A U.S. commonwealth, the smallest of the Greater Antilles, 885 miles southeast of the southern coast of Florida; capital, San Juan. Following its discovery by Columbus in 1493, the island was evangelized by Spanish missionaries and remained under Spanish ecclesiastical as well as political control until 1898, when it became a possession of the United States. The original diocese, San Juan, was erected in 1511. The present hierarchy was established in 1960.

Qatar

Parish; priest, 7 (1 dioc., 6 rel.); p.d., 1; bap., 348; Caths., 124,000 (10.6%); tot. pop., 1,625,000.

Independent state in the Persian Gulf; capital, Doha. Under ecclesiastical jurisdiction of Arabia apostolic vicariate.

Réunion

Dioc., 1; bp., 1; parishes, 71; priests, 127 (65 dioc., 62 rel.); p.d., 20; sem., 16; bros., 12; srs., 293; catechists, 2,890; bap., 9,821; Caths., 671,000 (82.6%); tot. pop., 839,000. (AD)

French overseas department, 450 miles east of Madagascar; capital, Saint-Denis. Catholicism was introduced in 1667 and some intermittent missionary work was done through the rest of the century. An apostolic prefecture was organized in 1712. Vincentians began work there in 1817 and were joined later by Holy Ghost Fathers. In 1998 the bishops joined their counterparts in Guadeloupe, French Guiana and Martinique to call slavery "an immense collective sin."

Romania*

Archd., 3; dioc., 8; ord., 1; ex., 1; abp., 5; bp., 14; parishes, 1,907; priests, 1,962 (1,691 dioc., 271 rel.); p.d., 4; sem., 603; bros., 145; srs., 1,226; catechists, 522; bap., 10,482; Caths., 1,619,000 (8.4%); tot. pop., 21,448,000.

Republic in southeastern Europe; capital, Bucharest. Latin Christianity, introduced in the third century, all but disappeared during the barbarian invasions. The Byzantine rite was introduced by the Bulgars about the beginning of the eighth century and established firm roots. It eventually became Orthodox, but a large number of its adherents returned later to union with Rome.

Communists took over the government following World War II, forced the abdication of Michael I in 1947, and enacted a Soviet type of constitution in 1952. By that time a campaign against religion was already in progress. In 1948 the government denounced a concordat concluded in 1929, nationalized all schools and passed a law on religions that resulted in the disorganization of Church administration. The 1.5 million-member Romanian Byzantine-rite Church, by government decree, was incorporated into the Romanian Orthodox Church, and Catholic properties were given to the Orthodox. Five of the six Latin-rite bishops were immediately disposed of by the government, and the last was sentenced to 18 years' imprisonment in 1951. Religious orders were suppressed in 1949.

Some change for the better in Church-state relations was reported after the middle of the summer of 1964, although restrictions were still in effect. The Eastern Church regained liberty in 1990 with the change of government. The hierarchy was restored and diplomatic relations with the Holy See were re-established. Today, most Latin-rite Catholics are ethnic Hungarians residing in Transylvania. Pope John Paul II visited Romania May 7-9, 1999. Church leaders said the historic visit led to a deeper openness and understanding between Catholics and Orthodox.

Russia*

Archd., 2; dioc. 3 (2 for European Russia, 1 for Siberia); ap. ex., 1; abp., 2; bp., 2; parish, 235; priests, 320 (114 dioc., 206 rel.); p.d., 3; sem., 63; bros., 23; srs 412; bap., 1,174; Caths., 928,000 (.07%); tot. pop., 143,056,000.

Federation in Europe and Asia; capital, Moscow. The Orthodox Church has been predominant in Russian history. It developed from the Byzantine Church before 1064. Some of its members subsequently established communion with Rome as the result of reunion movements, but most remained Orthodox. The government has always retained some kind of general or particular control of this Church.

From the beginning of the Communist government in 1917, all churches of whatever kind became the targets of official campaigns designed to negate their influence on society and/or to eliminate them entirely. An accurate assessment of the situation of the Catholic Church in Russia was difficult to make. Research by a Polish priest, reported in 1998, documented the arrests, trials and fabricated confessions of priests in the 1920s and 1930s. A report by a team of research specialists made public by the Judiciary Committee of the U.S. House of Representatives in 1964 said: "The fate of the Catholic Church in the USSR and countries occupied by the Russians from 1917 to 1959 shows the following: (a) the number killed: 55 bishops; 12,800 priests and monks; 2.5

million Catholic believers; (b) imprisoned or deported: 199 bishops; 32,000 priests and 10 million believers; (c) 15,700 priests were forced to abandon their priesthood and accept other jobs; and (d) a large number of seminaries and religious communities were dissolved." Despite repression, Lithuania and Ukraine remained strongholds of Catholicism. During his 1985-91 presidency, Soviet President Mikhail Gorbachev met twice with Pope John Paul II — meetings later credited with the return of religious freedom in the Soviet Union. In 1991, the pope established two Latin-rite apostolic administrations in the Russian Republic: one in Moscow and one based in Novosibirsk, Siberia. Catholic communities in Europe and the United States have been instrumental in helping to rebuild the Church in Russia. Under a 1997 religion law, every religious organization in Russia had to register on a national level, then re-register each parish by the end of 1999 to enjoy full legal benefits such as owning property and publishing religious literature. The apostolic administrations registered with no problems, but after the Russian government rejected the Jesuits' registration application, they were forced to take the matter to the country's constitutional court, which ruled that they qualified.

The Vatican's upgrading of Russia's four apostolic administrations to dioceses in early 2002 provoked new tensions with the Orthodox, who accused the Catholic Church of trying to convert its members. Russian authorities refused to readmit five prominent Church leaders, including one bishop, after they left the country. The Vatican eventually appointed a new bishop for the vacant Russian diocese and transferred the expelled bishop. Formal diplomatic relations were established between Russia and the Holy See in 2009.

Rwanda*

Archd., 1; dioc., 3; abp., 2; bp., 9; parishes, 162; priests, 701 (555 dioc., 146 rel.); sem., 553; bros., 184; srs., 1,644; catechists, 3,485; bap., 119,111; Caths., 4,975,000 (49%); tot. pop., 10,718,000.

Republic in east central Africa; capital, Kigali. Catholicism was introduced about the turn of the 20th century. The hierarchy was established in 1959. Intertribal warfare between the ruling Hutus (90 percent of the population) and the Tutsis (formerly the ruling aristocracy) plagued the country for a number of years. In April 1994, the deaths of the presidents of Rwanda and Burundi in a suspicious plane crash sparked the outbreak of a ferocious civil war. Among the thousands of victims — mostly Tutsis — were three bishops and about 25 percent of the clergy. Thousands more fled the country.

Although in 1996 Pope John Paul II said that all members of the Church who participated in the genocide must face the consequences, in 1997 the Vatican donated $50,000 to help ensure that certain people — including priests and religious — received fair trials. Two nuns accused of participating in the genocide were sent to prison in Belgium, but a bishop was acquitted after a nine-month trial in Rwanda. The bishop later said Marian apparitions in his diocese in the 1980s foretold the genocide.

Saint Lucia*

Archd., 1; abp., 1; parishes, 22; priests, 28 (17 dioc., 11 rel.); sem., 3; bros., 4; srs., 46; catechists, 262; bap., 1,505; Caths., 106,000 (63%); tot. pop., 159,000.

Independent (Feb. 22, 1979) island state in West Indies; capital, Castries.

Saint Vincent and the Grenadines*

Dioc., 1; bp., 1; parishes, 9; priests, 12 (7 dioc., 5 rel.); sem., 1; srs., 15; catechists, 31; bap., 97; Caths., 15,000 (13%); tot. pop., 118,000.

Independent state (1979) in West Indies; capital, Kingstown. The Kingstown diocese (St. Vincent) was established in 1989; it was formerly part of Bridgetown-Kingstown Diocese with see in Barbados. The Vatican established diplomatic relations with St. Vincent and the Grenadines in 1990. The Church is recognized for its role in education and health care.

Samoa, American

Dioc., 1; bp., 1; parishes, 17; priests, 20 (17 dioc., 3 rel.); p.d., 32; sem., 6; srs., 11; bap., 521; Caths., 14,000 (22%); tot. pop., 68,000.

Unincorporated U.S. territory in southwestern Pacific, consisting of six small islands; seat of government, Pago Pago on the Island of Tutuila. Samoa-Pago Pago Diocese established in 1982.

Samoa, Western*

Archd., 1; abp., 1; parishes, 38; priests, 52 (35 dioc., 17 rel.); p.d., 19; sem., 10; bros., 14; srs., 70; catechists, 146; bap., 1,332; Caths., 43,000 (19%); tot. pop., 189,000.

Independent state in the southwestern Pacific; capital, Apia. Catholic missionary work began in 1845. Most of the missions now in operation were established by 1870 when the Catholic population numbered about 5,000. Additional progress was made in missionary work from 1896. The first Samoan priest was ordained in 1892. A diocese was established in 1966; elevated to a metropolitan see in 1982.

San Marino*

Parishes, 12; priests, 23 (8 dioc., 14 rel.); p.d. 1; bros., 1; srs 19; bap., 243; Caths., 29,000 (97%); tot. pop., 31,000.

Republic, a 24-square-mile enclave in northeastern Italy; capital, San Marino. The date of initial evangelization is not known, but a diocese was established by the end of the third century. Ecclesiastically, it forms part of the Diocese of San Marino-Montefeltro in Italy.

São Tome and Principe*

Dioc., 1; bp., 2; parishes, 12; priests, 13 (6 dioc., 7 rel.); sem. 8; bros., 3; srs., 34; catechists, 545; bap., 3,549; Caths., 125,000 (73%); tot. pop., 185,000.

Independent republic (July 12, 1975), consisting of two islands off the western coast of Africa in the Gulf of Guinea; former Portuguese territory; capital, São Tome. Evangelization was begun by the Portuguese who discovered the islands in 1471-72. The São Tome Diocese was established in 1534. In a 1992 visit to São Tome, a major transport center for slaves until the mid-1800s, Pope John Paul II condemned slavery as "a cruel offense" to African dignity.

Saudi Arabia

Parishes, 3; priests, 7 (1 dioc., 6 rel.); p.d., bap., 406; Caths., 1,530,000; total pop., 26,417,000.

Monarchy occupying four-fifths of Arabian peninsula; capital, Riyadh. Population is Muslim; all other religions are banned. Christians in the area are workers from other countries. The Church falls under the ecclesiastical jurisdiction of the Arabian apostolic vicariate. In May 1999, Pope John Paul II met with the crown prince of Saudi Arabia at the Vatican. In 2007, Pope Benedict XVI met with King Abdullah in the Vatican; human rights and religious freedom were major topics of discussion.

Scotland*

Archd., 2; dioc., 6; card., 1; abp., 1; bp., 9; parishes, 470; priests, 655 (495 dioc., 160 rel.); p.d., 92; sem., 36; bros., 335; srs., 410; bap., 7,683; Caths., 701,850 (12%); tot. pop., 5,834,000.

Part of the United Kingdom, in the northern British Isles; capital, Edinburgh. St. Ninian's arrival in 397 marked the beginning of Christianity in Scotland. The arrival of St. Columba and his monks in 563 inaugurated a new era of evangelization that reached to remote areas by the end of the sixth century. He was extremely influential in determining the character of the Church, which was tribal, monastic, and in union with Rome. Considerable disruption of Church activity resulted from Scandinavian invasions in the late eighth and ninth centuries. By 1153 the Scottish Church took a turn away from its insularity and was drawn into closer contact with the European community. Anglo-Saxon religious and political relations, complicated by rivalries between princes and ecclesiastical superiors, were not always the happiest.

From shortly after the Norman Conquest of England to 1560 the Church suffered adverse effects from the Hundred Years' War, the Black Death, the Western Schism and other developments. In 1560 Parliament abrogated papal supremacy over the Church in Scotland and committed the country to Protestantism in 1567. The Catholic Church was proscribed, to remain that way for more than 200 years, and the hierarchy was disbanded. Defections made the Church a minority religion from that time on. Presbyterian Church government was ratified in 1690. Priests launched the Scottish Mission in 1653, incorporating themselves as a mission body under an apostolic prefecture and working underground to serve the faithful in much the same way their confreres did in England. Catholics got some relief from legal disabilities in 1793 and more relief later. Many left the country about that time. Some of their numbers were filled subsequently by immigrants from Ireland. About 100 heather priests, trained in clandestine places in the heather country, were ordained by the early 19th century. The hierarchy was restored in 1878. In a 1997 message to celebrations marking 1,600 years of Christianity in Scotland, Pope John Paul II urged Catholics to make new efforts at evangelization and ecumenism.Pope Benedict XVI visited in 2011.

Senegal*

Archd., 1; dioc., 6; card. 1; abp., 1; bp., 6; parishes, 133; priests, 473 (342 dioc., 131 rel.); p.d., 1; sem., 183; bros., 189; srs., 797; catechists, 2,085; bap., 11,003; Caths., 684,000 (5%); tot. pop., 12,842,000.

Republic in West Africa; capital, Dakar. The country had its first contact with Catholicism through the Portuguese some time after 1460. Some incidental missionary work was done by Jesuits and Capuchins in the 16th and 17th centuries. A vicariate for the area was placed in charge of the Holy Ghost Fathers in 1779. More effective evangelization efforts were accomplished after the Senegambia vicariate was erected in 1863; the hierarchy was established in 1955. During a 1992 trip to the predominantly Muslim country, Pope John Paul II praised the small Catholic community for its contributions, especially in the areas of health care and education.

Serbia*

Archd., 2; dioc., 3; ex., 1; a.a., 1; abp., 2; bp., 4; parishes, 241; priests, 273 (237 dioc., 36 rel.); p.d., 11; sem., 51; bros., 49; srs., 255; bap., 3,425; Caths., 519,000 (5%); tot. pop., 7,428,000.

Independent nation in southeastern Europe; part of the former Yugoslavia; capital, Belgrade.

Christianity was introduced from the seventh to ninth centuries in the regions combined to form Yugoslavia after World War I. Since these regions straddled the original line of demarcation for the Western and Eastern Empires (and churches), and since the Reformation had little lasting effect, the Christians are nearly all either Latin- or Eastern-rite Catholics or Orthodox. Yugoslavia was proclaimed a Socialist republic in 1945, and persecution of the Catholic Church began. In an agreement signed June 25, 1966, the government recognized the Holy See's spiritual jurisdiction over the Church in the country and guaranteed to bishops the possibility of maintaining contact with Rome in ecclesiastical and religious matters. During early 1990s the split of the Yugoslav republic, Catholic leaders joined Orthodox and, in some cases, Muslim leaders in calling for peace.

Seychelles*

Dioc., 1; bp., 1; parishes, 19; priests, 24 (10 dioc., 14 rel.); p.d., 1; sem., 3; bros. 5; srs., 57; catechists, 209; bap., 1,098; Caths., 75,000 (85%); tot. pop., 88,000.

Independent (1976) group of 92 islands in the Indian Ocean; capital, Victoria. Catholicism was introduced in the 18th century. An apostolic vicariate was organized in 1852. All education in the islands was conducted under Catholic auspices until 1954. In 1991, Bp. Felix Paul of Port Victoria said the country's one-party socialist government was an affront to the rights and dignity of its people, but President France-Albert René continued to lead the government into the 21st century. Pope John Paul II warned Seychelles to beware of the dark side of tourism, a main industry in the country.

Sierra Leone*

Archd., 1; dioc., 2; abp., 1; bp., 3; parishes, 70; priests, 161 (95 dioc., 66 rel.); sem., 62; bros., 50; srs., 101; catechists, 659; bap., 10,493; Caths., 299,000 (5%); tot. pop., 5,890,000.

Republic on the west coast of Africa; capital, Freetown. Catholicism was introduced in 1858. Members of the African Missions Society, the first Catholic missionaries in the area, were joined by Holy Ghost Fathers in 1864. Protestant missionaries were active in the area before their Catholic counterparts. Educational work had a major part in Catholic endeavor. The hierarchy was established in 1950. Most of the inhabitants are followers of traditional African religions.

Church leaders suffered at the hands of rebel soldiers in the late 1990s, when a military coup ousted the country's democratically elected government. Although some Church workers fled to neighboring Guinea, some remained. Rebels kidnapped several foreign missionaries and, shortly before West African intervention forces ousted them from power in 1998, rebels forced the archbishop of Freetown to strip naked while they plundered his office. As the war lessened and later ended, the Church worked for reconciliation, to rehabilitate child soldiers and to rebuild damaged Church property.

Singapore*

Archd., 1; abp., 2; parishes, 31; priests, 138 (75 dioc., 63 rel.); sem., 27; bros., 92; srs., 188; catechists, 1,805; bap., 3,886; Caths., 193,000 (3.7%); tot. pop., 5,184,000.

Independent island republic off the southern tip of the Malay Peninsula; capital, Singapore. Christianity was introduced in the area by Portuguese colonists about 1511. Singapore was founded in 1819; the first parish Church was built in 1846. Freedom of religion is generally respected, although in the late 1980s nearly a dozen people involved in Catholic social work were arrested and detained without trial under the Internal Security Act.

Slovakia*

Archd., 4; dioc., 7; mil. ord.; card., 2; abp., 7; bp., 19; parishes, 1,557; priests, 2,840 (2,218 dioc., 622 rel.); p.d., 18; sem., 476; bros., 163, srs., 2,369; catechists, 1,558; bap., 42,450; Caths., 4,031,000 (74%); tot. pop., 5,469,000.

Independent state (Jan. 1, 1993); formerly part of Czechoslovakia; capital, Bratislava. Christianity was introduced in Slovakia in the eighth century by Irish and German missionaries, and the area was under the jurisdiction of German bishops. In 863, Sts. Cyril and Methodius began pastoral and missionary work in the region, ministering to the people in their own language. A diocese established at Nitra in 880 had a continuous history (except for one century ending in 1024). The Church in Slovakia was severely tested by the Reformation and political upheavals. After World War I, when it became part of the Republic of Czechoslovakia, it was 75 percent Catholic.

Vigorous persecution of the Church began in Slovakia in 1944, when communists mounted an offensive against bishops, priests and religious. Msgr. Josef Tiso, a Catholic priest who served as president of the Slovak Republic from 1939-45, was tried for "treason" in December 1946 and was executed the following April.

In 1972, the government ordered the removal of nuns from visible but limited apostolates to farms and mental hospitals. In 1973, the government allowed the ordination of three bishops in the Slovak region.

When Slovakia split from Czechoslovakia in 1993, the country slid into economic difficulties. Church-state tensions increased, and the Slovakian government eventually apologized to Bp. Rudolf Balaz of Banska Bystrica, whose house had been raided

in a government investigation of stolen art. In an attempt to fight the effects of decades of communism, in 1996 the bishops said all adult Catholics who had not received confirmation must undergo a special two-year catechism course. In 2000, the government and Vatican signed an accord establishing the Church's legal status. The country is remarkably Pro-Life, including the celebration of an annual Day of the Unborn Child.

Slovenia*

Archd., 2; dioc., 4; abp., 2; bp., 6; parishes, 787; priests, 1,102 (798 dioc., 304 rel.); p.d., 27; sem., 97; bros., 43; srs., 591; catechists, 605; bap., 13,747; Caths., 1,608,000 (78.8%); tot. pop., 2,049,000.

Independent republic (1991) in southeastern Europe; formerly part of Yugoslavia; capital, Ljubljana. Established diplomatic relations with the Holy See in 1992. After independence, Church leaders found themselves in repeated skirmishes with Slovenia's governing coalition over religious education, restitution of Church property and the Church's proper social role.

Solomon Islands*

Archd., 1; dioc., 2; abp., 1; bp., 3; parishes, 30; priests, 72 (39 dioc., 33 rel.); sem., 72; bros., 24; srs., 98; catechists, 775; bap., 4,177; Caths., 109,000 (21%); tot. pop., 540,000.

Independent (July 7, 1978) island group in Oceania; capital, Honiara, on Guadalcanal. After violence interrupted the Marists' evangelization of the Southern Solomons, they resumed their work in 1898. An apostolic vicariate was organized in 1912. A similar jurisdiction was set up for the Western Solomons in 1959. World War II caused a great deal of damage to mission installations.

Somalia

Dioc., 1; parish, 1; priests, 3 (1 dioc., 2 rel.); srs., 4; Caths., 100; tot. pop., 8,695,000. (AD)

Republic on the eastern coast of Africa; capital, Mogadishu. The country has been Muslim for centuries. Pastoral activity has been confined to immigrants. Schools and hospitals were nationalized in 1972, resulting in the departure of some foreign missionaries.

South Africa*

Archd., 5; dioc., 20; v.a., 1; mil. ord., 1; card., 1; abp., 8; bp., 20; parishes, 788; priests, 1,233 (558 dioc., 675 rel.); p.d., 250; sem., 413; bros., 166; srs., 2,127; catechists, 11,486; bap., 56,358; Caths., 3,647,000 (7%); tot. pop., 50,587,000.

Republic in the southern part of Africa; capitals, Cape Town (legislative), Pretoria (administrative) and Bloemfontein (judicial). Christianity was introduced by the Portuguese who discovered the Cape of Good Hope in 1488. Boers, who founded Cape Town in 1652, expelled Catholics from the region. There was no Catholic missionary activity from that time until the 19th century. A bishop established residence in 1837, and evangelization got under way thereafter among the Bantus and white immigrants. The hierarchy was established in 1951.

Under South Africa's apartheid regime, the Church found itself the victim of attacks, from the parish level to the headquarters of the bishops' conference in Pretoria. Some Church leaders were detained, tortured and deported, particularly in the 1970s and 1980s. However, in a 1997 statement to South Africa's Truth Commission, the Catholic Church said the complicity of some Catholics with apartheid was an "act of omission rather than commission." Since the end of apartheid, Catholic leaders have spoken out against an increase in violence and anti-Muslim sentiment and have worked to combat the growing AIDS problem. Reports of clergy sexual abuse became public in 2003.

South Sudan*

Archd., 1; dioc., 6; abp., 1; bp., 8; parishes, 89; priests, 256 (184 dioc., 72 rel.); sem., 368; bros., 45; srs., 159; catechists, 3,512; bap., 57,457; Caths., 5,440,000 (39%); tot. pop., 13,614,000.

Republic in North Africa, previously known as Southern Sudan, in east-central Africa; capital, Juba. It was established officially in 2011 after breaking off from Sudan, the result of two civil wars.

The Holy See and the Republic of South Sudan established diplomatic relations in Feb. 2013, including the establishment of an apostolic nunciature. The Republic of South Sudan is also a UN member state, as well as a member state of the African Union and the Intergovernmental Authority on Development. The country is majority Christian, with Catholics comrpising the largest religious group; Muslims comprise 18% of the population.

Spain*

Archd., 14; dioc., 55; mil. ord., 1; card., 10; abp., 22; bp., 98; parishes, 22,915; priests, 24,353 (16,499 dioc., 7,854 rel.); p.d., 375; sem., 1,983; bros., 3,746; srs., 48,557; catechists, 97,143; bap., 291,589; Caths., 42,830,000 (93%); tot. pop., 46,196,000.

Constitutional monarchy on the Iberian peninsula in southwestern Europe; capital, Madrid. Christians were on the peninsula by 200; some of them suffered martyrdom during persecutions of the third century. A council held in Elvira about 305 enacted the first legislation on clerical celibacy in the West. Vandals invaded the peninsula in the fifth century, bringing with them an Arian brand of Christianity that they retained until their conversion following the baptism of their king, Reccared, in 589.

In the seventh century, Toledo was established as the primatial see. The Visigoth kingdom lasted to the time of the Arab invasion, 711-14. The Church survived under Muslim rule but experienced some doctrinal and disciplinary irregularities as well as harassment. Re-evangelization of most of the peninsula was accomplished by 1248; unification was achieved during the reign of Ferdinand and Isabella. The discoveries of Columbus and other explorers ushered in an era of colonial expansion in which Spain became one of the greatest missionary-sending countries in history. In 1492, in repetition of anti-Semitic actions of 694, the expulsion of unbaptized Jews was decreed, leading to mass baptisms but a questionable number of real conversions in 1502. Activity by the Inquisition followed. Spain was not seriously affected by the Reformation.

Ecclesiastical decline set in about 1650.

Anti-Church actions authorized by a constitution enacted in 1812 resulted in the suppression of religious and other encroachments on the leaders, people and goods of the Church. Political, religious and cultural turmoil recurred during the 19th century and into the 20th. A revolutionary republic was proclaimed in 1931, triggering a series of developments that led to civil war from 1936 to 1939. During the conflict, which pitted leftist Loyalists against the forces of Francisco Franco, more than 6,600 priests and religious and an unknown number of lay people were massacred. One-man, one-party rule, established after the civil war and with rigid control policies with respect to personal liberties and social and economic issues, continued for more than 35 years before giving way after the death of Franco to democratic reforms. Since the 1970s, the Catholic Church has not been the established religion; the constitution guarantees freedom for other religions as well. In the late 20th century, Spanish Church leaders fought a growing feeling of indifference among many Catholics. After the March 2004 al-Qaida bombings led to the election of a Socialist government, Spanish Church leaders were appalled by the series of social policy changes being proposed. Pope Benedict XVI visited in 2010 and 2011.

Sri Lanka*

Archd., 1; dioc., 10; card., 1; abp., 3; bp., 14; parishes, 428; priests, 1,269 (811 dioc., 458 rel.); p.d., 1; sem., 480; bros., 194; srs., 2,363; catechists, 13,347; bap., 25,129; Caths., 1,505,000 (7%); tot. pop., 20,858,000.

Independent socialist republic, island southeast of India; capital, Colombo. The Portuguese began evangelizing in the 16th century. In 1638, the Dutch began forcing Portuguese from the coastal areas. The Dutch outlawed Catholicism, banished priests and confiscated buildings, forcing people to become Calvinists. Blessed Joseph Vaz, an Oratorian priest, is credited with almost single-handedly reviving the Catholic Church toward the end of the 17th century.

Anti-Catholic laws were repealed by the British in 1806. The hierarchy was established in 1886; the country gained independence in 1948. In an unusual move in January 1998, Archbp. Nicholas M. Fernando of Colombo, authorized by the Vatican Congregation for the Doctrine of the Faith, lifted the excommunication of a prominent Sri Lankan theologian, Oblate Father Tissa Balasuriya. Sri Lankan bishops repeatedly called for reconciliation in the decades-long war between the Liberation Tigers of Tamil Eelam and the Sinhalese-dominated government.

Sudan*

Archd., 2; dioc., 7; ap. ex., 1; card., 1; abp., 2; bp., 14; parishes, 44; priests, 407 (277 dioc., 130 rel.); p.d., 5; sem., 245; bros., 82; srs., 357; catechists, 4,637; bap., 59,963; Caths., 836,000 (3%); tot. pop., 27,149,000

Republic in northeastern Africa, the largest country on the continent; capital Khartoum. Christianity was introduced from Egypt and gained acceptance in the sixth century. Under Arab rule, it was eliminated in the northern region. No Christians were in the country in 1600.

Evangelization attempts begun in the 19th century in the south yielded hard-won results. By 1931 there were nearly 40,000 Catholics there, and considerable progress was made by missionaries after that time. In 1957, a year after the republic was established, Catholic schools were nationalized. An act restrictive of religious freedom went into effect in 1962, resulting in the harassment and expulsion of foreign missionaries. By 1964 all but a few Sudanese missionaries had been forced out of the southern region. The northern area, where Islam predominates, is impervious to Christian influence.

Late in 1971 some missionaries were allowed to return to work in the South. The hierarchy was established in 1974. The most recent fighting, which began in 1983, originally pitted the mostly Arab and Muslim North against the mostly black African Christian and animist South, but it has since evolved into a nationwide conflict fueled by religion, ethnicity, oil and ideology. The imposition of Islamic penal codes in 1984 was a cause of concern to all Christian Churches. Recent government policies have denied Christians the right to places of worship and authorization to gather for prayer. Bishops from the South have condemned human rights violations — aggravated by famine and war — in their area. They have said they want peace but cannot accept an Islamic state and were hopeful that terms of a 2005 peace agreement would hold. The agreement would allow southerners to vote on independence after a six-year period of power-sharing. A widespread conflict in the western Darfur region resulted in a massive exodus of Sudanese, who were cared for in neighboring countries by international – including church-run – agencies.

Surinam*

Dioc., 1; bp., 1; parishes, 33; priests, 22 (6 dioc., 16 rel.); sem., 1; bros., 4; srs., 9; bap., 1,444; Caths., 133,000 (25%); tot. pop., 540,000.

Independent (Nov. 25, 1975) state in northern South America; capital, Paramaribo. Catholicism was introduced in 1683. Evangelization began in 1817.

Swaziland*

Dioc., 1; bp., 1; parishes, 17; priests, 30 (14 dioc., 16 rel.); sem., 15; bros., 3; srs., 49; bap., 664; Caths., 58,000 (5%); tot. pop., 1,118,000.

Monarchy in southern Africa, almost totally surrounded by South Africa; capital, Mbabane. Missionary work was entrusted to the Servites in 1913. An apostolic prefecture was organized in 1923. The hierarchy was established in 1951. Swaziland established diplomatic relations with the Holy See in 1992. In the 1990s, Swazi Catholics worked to help transform the country to a democracy but to retain the traditions of the people.

Sweden*

Dioc., 1; abp., 1; bp., 3; parishes, 44; priests, 178 (83 dioc., 95 rel.); p.d., 22; sem., 16; bros., 12; srs.,

217 catechists, 347; bap., 1,376; Caths., 143,000 (1.5%); tot. pop., 9,374,000.

Constitutional monarchy in northwestern Europe; capital, Stockholm. Christianity was introduced by St. Ansgar, a Frankish monk, in 829-830. The Church became well-established in the 12th century and was a major influence at the end of the Middle Ages. Political and other factors favored the introduction and spread of the Lutheran Church, which became the state religion in 1560. The Augsburg Confession of 1530 was accepted by the government; all relations with Rome were severed; monasteries were suppressed; the very presence of Catholics in the country was forbidden in 1617. A decree of tolerance for foreign Catholics was issued about 1781. Two years later an apostolic vicariate was organized for the country. In 1873 Swedes were given the legal right to leave the Lutheran church and join another Christian church. Membership in the Lutheran church is presumed by law unless notice is given of membership in another church.

Since 1952 Catholics have enjoyed almost complete religious freedom. The hierarchy was re-established in 1953. Hindrances to growth of the Church are the strongly entrenched established church, limited resources, a clergy shortage and the size of the country. In the 1960s, an influx of guest workers increased the number of Catholics, and in the 1970s and 1980s, refugees helped increase Church numbers. In 1998, the pope named the first Swedish bishop in more than 400 years. In the early 21st century, the government worked to give the Church and other minority faiths the right to operate as legal entities, including owning property.

Switzerland*

Dioc., 6; abb., 2; card., 4; abp., 3; bp., 17; parishes, 1,627; priests, 2,602 (1,566 dioc., 1,036 rel.); p.d., 249; sem., 186; bros., 335; srs., 5,100; catechists, 1,389; bap., 28,260; Caths., 3,421,000 (44%); tot. pop., 7,843,000.

Confederation in central Europe; capital, Bern. Christianity was introduced in the fourth century or earlier and was established on a firm footing before the barbarian invasions of the sixth century. Constance, established as a diocese in the seventh century, was a stronghold of the faith against the pagan Alamanni, in particular, who were not converted until some time in the ninth century. During this period of struggle with the barbarians, a number of monasteries of great influence were established.

The Reformation in Switzerland was triggered by Zwingli in 1519 and furthered by him at Zurich until his death in battle against the Catholic cantons in 1531. Calvin set in motion the forces that made Geneva the international capital of the Reformation and transformed it into a theocracy. Catholics mobilized a Counter-Reformation in 1570, six years after Calvin's death. Struggle between Protestant and Catholic cantons was a fact of Swiss life for several hundred years. The Helvetic Constitution enacted at the turn of the 19th century embodied anti-Catholic measures and consequences, among them the dissolution of 130 monasteries. The Church was reorganized later in the century to meet the threats of liberalism, radicalism and the Kulturkampf. In the process, the Church, even though on the defensive, gained the strength and cohesion that characterizes it to the present time. In 1973, constitutional articles banning Jesuits from the country and prohibiting the establishment of convents and monasteries were repealed. In the 1990s, Swiss bishops battled internal divisions and sought forgiveness for any anti-Semitism on behalf of the Church.

Syria*

Patriarchates, 1 (Greek Melkites; patriarchs of Antioch of Maronites and Syrians reside in Lebanon); archd., 12 (1 Armenian, 2 Maronite, 5 Greek Melkite, 4 Syrian); dioc., 3 (Armenian, Chaldean, Maronite); v.a., 1 (Latin); ap.ex., 1; patriarch, 1; card., 1; abp., 15; bp., 4; parishes, 216; priests, 286 (208 dioc., 78 rel.); p.d., 15; sem., 71; bros., 33; srs., 520; catechists, 1,148; bap., 2,158; Caths., 432,000 (2%); tot. pop., 21,124,000.

Arab socialist republic in southwest Asia; capital, Damascus. Christian communities were formed in apostolic times. It is believed that St. Peter established a see at Antioch before going to Rome. Damascus became a center of influence. The area was the place of great men and great events in the early history of the Church. Monasticism developed there in the fourth century; so did the Monophysite and Monothelite heresies to which a portion of the Church succumbed. Byzantine Syrians who remained in communion with Rome were given the name Melkites. Christians of various persuasions — Jacobites, Orthodox and Melkites — were subject to various degrees of harassment from the Arabs who took over in 638 and from the Ottoman Turks who isolated the country and remained in control from 1516 to the end of World War II.

Syrian Catholics are members of the Armenian, Chaldean, Greek-Melkite, Latin, Maronite and Syrian rites. During a visit to Syria in May 2001, Pope John Paul II became the first pontiff in history to enter a mosque. Early in the 21st century, growing instability in neighboring countries, including Iraq, led to an influx of Christians and challenges for the small but flourishing Catholic community. Christians have faced severe violence in the country over the last year owing to the bloody civil war in the country, with rebel groups committing attacks and massacres of Christian villages. Many fear for the future of the Christian population in the country.

Taiwan*

Archd., 2; dioc., 8; card., 1; abp., 3; bp., 9; parishes, 449; priests, 639 (231 dioc., 408 rel.); p.d., 1; sem., 59; bros., 61; srs., 1,050; catechists, 279; bap., 3,298; Caths., 302,000 (1.3%); tot. pop., 23,975,000.

Democratic island state, 100 miles off the southern coast of mainland China; capital, Taipei. Attempts to introduce Christianity in the 17th century were unsuccessful. Evangelization in the 19th century resulted in some 1,300 converts in 1895. Missionary endeavor was hampered by the Japanese, who occupied the island following the Sino-Japanese war of 1894-95. Great progress was made in missionary endeavor among the Chinese who emigrated to the island (seat of the Nationalist Government of the Republic of China) following the Communist takeover of the mainland in 1949. The hierarchy was established in 1952. Many Taiwanese Catholics have worked to form a bridge to Catholics in mainland China.

Tajikistan*

Mission, 3; parishes, 3; priests, 4 (4 rel.); srs., 8; bap., 14; Cath., 3,000; tot. pop. 7,695,000.

Independent republic (1992) in Asia; formerly part of the USSR; capital, Dushanbe. The majority of the population is Sunni Muslim. When the Vatican established diplomatic relations in 1996, Church officials estimated most of the country's Catholics had fled. In 1997, the Vatican established a mission in the country.

Tanzania*

Archd., 5; dioc., 29; card., 1; abp., 5; bp., 37; parishes, 945; priests, 2,643 (1,779 dioc., 864 rel.); p.d. 1; sem., 1,260; bros., 826; srs., 10,404; catechists, 15,580; bap., 333,113; Caths., 13,626,000 (30%); tot. pop., 44,516,000.

Republic on and off the eastern coast of Africa; capital, Dar es Salaam. The first Catholic mission in the former Tanganyikan portion of the republic was manned by Holy Ghost Fathers in 1868. The hierarchy was established there in 1953. Zanzibar was the landing place of Augustinians with the Portuguese in 1499. Some evangelization was attempted between then and 1698 when the Arabs expelled all priests from the territory. There was no Catholic missionary activity from then until the 1860s. The Holy Ghost Fathers arrived in 1863 and were entrusted with the mission in 1872. Zanzibar was important as a point of departure for missionaries to Tanganyika, Kenya and other places in East Africa. A vicariate for Zanzibar was set up in 1906.

In the late 20th century the Church in Tanzania saw an increase in vocations and an active Church life. The bishops assisted hundreds of thousands of refugees from Rwanda, Burundi and Mozambique. More recently, Church leaders worked to stem the AIDS pandemic and to improve education.

Thailand*

Archd., 2; dioc., 8; card., 1; abp., 3; bp., 14; parishes, 479; priests, 830 (519 dioc., 311 rel.); sem., 347; bros., 149; srs., 1,450; catechists, 1,661; bap., 7,250; Caths., 363,000 (.5%); tot. pop., 67,912,000.

Constitutional monarchy in southeast Asia; capital, Bangkok. The first Christians in the region were Portuguese traders who arrived early in the 16th century. A number of missionaries began arriving in the mid-1500s, but pastoral care was confined mostly to the Portuguese until the 1660s, when evangelization began. A seminary was organized in 1665, a vicariate was set up four years later, and a point of departure was established for China. Persecution and death for some of the missionaries ended evangelization efforts in 1688. It was resumed, however, and made progress from 1824 onward. In 1881 missionaries were sent from Siam to neighboring Laos. The hierarchy was established in 1965. Archbp. Michael Michai Kitbunchu was named the first Thai cardinal in 1983. The Church is recognized for its social justice efforts, including work with refugees.

Togo*

Archd., 1; dioc., 6; abp., 3; bp., 8; parishes, 207; priests, 651 (491 dioc., 160 rel.); sem., 572; bros., 216; srs., 901; catechists, 5,926; bap., 31,285; Caths., 1,815,000 (30%); tot. pop., 6,012,000.

Republic on the west coast of Africa; capital, Lome. The first Catholic missionaries in the area, where slave raiders operated for nearly 200 years, were members of the African Missions Society who arrived in 1563. They were followed by Divine Word Missionaries in 1914, when an apostolic prefecture was organized. At that time the Catholic population numbered about 19,000. The African Missionaries returned after their German predecessors were deported following World War I. The first indigenous priest was ordained in 1922. The hierarchy was established in 1955. In the early 1990s, Archbp. Philippe Fanoko Kossi Kpodzro of Lome served as president of the transitional legislative assembly.

Tonga*

Dioc., 1; bp., 1; parishes, 14; priests, 36 (29 dioc., 7 rel.); sem., 27; bros., 2; srs., 37; bap., 523; Caths., 14,000 (14.5%); tot. pop., 102,000.

Polynesian monarchy in the southwestern Pacific, consisting of about 150 islands; capital, Nuku'alofa. Marists started missionary work in 1842, some years after Protestants had begun evangelization. By 1880 the Catholic population numbered about 1,700. A vicariate was organized in 1937. The hierarchy was established in 1966. Tonga established diplomatic relations with the Holy See in 1994.

Trinidad and Tobago*

Archd., 1; abp., 2; bp., 1; parishes, 61; priests, 109 (48 dioc., 61 rel.); sem., 19; bros., 5; srs., 152; catechists, 700; bap., 3,812; Caths., 337,000 (30%); tot. pop., 1,318,000.

Independent nation, consisting of two islands in the Caribbean; capital, Port-of-Spain. The first Catholic Church in Trinidad was built in 1591, years after several missionary ventures had been launched and a number of missionaries killed. Capuchins were there from 1618 until about 1802. Missionary work continued after the British gained control early in the 19th century. Cordial relations have existed between the Church and state, both of which have manifested their desire for the development of indigenous clergy. In 1999, Church leaders protested reinstatement of the death penalty.

Tunisia*

Dioc., 1; abp., 1; parishes, 10; priests, 32 (10 dioc., 22 rel.); bros., 5; sem., 2; srs., 121; bap., 42; Caths., 25,000 (.02%); tot. pop., 10,674,000.

Republic on the northern coast of Africa; capital, Tunis. Ancient Carthage, now a site outside the capital city of Tunis, hosted early Church councils and was home to Church fathers like St. Augustine. Carthage was devastated by Vandals in the fifth century and invaded by Muslims in the seventh century, after which it had few Christians

until the 19th century. An apostolic vicariate was organized in 1843, and the Carthage Archdiocese was established in 1884. The Catholic population in 1892 consisted of most of the approximately 50,000 Europeans in the country. When Tunis became a republic in 1956, most of the Europeans left the country. A 1964 agreement with the Vatican and Holy See suppressed the Archdiocese of Carthage and replaced it with the Territorial Prelature of Tunis. In 1995 the prelature was made a diocese. Today Tunisia's Catholics are predominantly foreign nationals. The Church's social presence is seen in schools, hospitals and institutions for the disabled.

Turkey*

Archd., 3; v.a., 2; ord., 1; ap. ex., 1; abp., 2; bp., 3; parishes, 56; priests, 72 (13 dioc., 59 rel.); p.d., 3; sem., 5; bros., 15; srs., 61; bap., 132; Caths., 37,000 (.05%); tot. pop., 74,224,000.

Republic in Asia Minor and southeastern Europe; capital, Ankara. Christian communities were established in apostolic times, as attested in the Acts of the Apostles, some of the Letters of St. Paul, and Revelation. The territory was the scene of heresies and ecumenical councils, the place of residence of Fathers of the Church, and the area in which ecclesiastical organization reached the dimensions of more than 450 sees in the middle of the seventh century. The region remained generally Byzantine except for the period of the Latin occupation of Constantinople from 1204 to 1261, but was conquered by the Ottoman Turks in 1453 and remained under their domination until establishment of the republic in 1923. Christians, always a minority, numbered more Orthodox than Catholics; they all were under some restrictions during the Ottoman period. They suffered persecution in the 19th and 20th centuries, the Armenians being the most numerous victims. Turkey is overwhelmingly Muslim. Catholics are tolerated to a degree.

Turkmenistan*

Mission, 1; parish, 1; priests, 2 (rel.); bap., 6; Caths., 1,000; tot. pop., 5,110,000.

Former constituent republic of USSR; independent, 1991; capital, Ashgabat. Almost all the population is Sunni Muslim. The Vatican established diplomatic relations with the country in 1996 and set up a mission in 1997.

Tuvalu

Mission, 1; parish, 1; priest, 2 (rel.); bap., 2; Caths., 100; tot. pop., 10,000.

Independent state (1978) in Oceania, consisting of 9 islands; capital, Funafuti.

Uganda*

Archd., 4; dioc., 15; mil. ord., 1; card., 1; abp., 6; bp., 27; parishes, 508; priests, 2,015 (1,674 dioc., 341 rel.); p.d., 2; sem., 1,381; bros., 620; srs., 3,454; catechists, 14,412; bap., 513,242; Caths., 14,934,000 (44%); tot. pop., 32,940,000.

Republic in East Africa; capital, Kampala. The Missionaries of Africa (White Fathers) were the first Catholic missionaries, starting in 1879. Persecution broke out from 1885 to 1887, taking a toll of 22 Catholic martyrs, who were canonized in 1964, and a number of Anglican victims. (Pope Paul VI honored all those who died for the faith during a visit to Kampala in 1969.) By 1888, there were more than 8,000 Catholics. Evangelization was resumed in 1894, after being interrupted by war, and proceeded thereafter. The first African bishop was ordained in 1939. The hierarchy was established in 1953.

The Church was suppressed during the erratic regime of President Idi Amin, who was deposed in the spring of 1979. Guerrilla activity in northern and southwestern Uganda has hampered Church workers. The Church has devoted much of its resources to caring for the many victims of HIV/AIDS in the country. In northern Uganda as a guerrilla war continued, church officials worked to protect children from being inducted into military or guerrilla service.

Ukraine*

Major archbishopric, 2 (Ukrainian); archd., 4 (Metropolitans); dioc., 12; pat. ex., 3; card., 2; abp., 3; bp., 32; parishes, 4,632; priests, 3,672 (3,049 dioc., 623 rel.); p.d., 25; sem., 1,082; bros., 206; srs., 1,274; catechists, 2,394; bap., 39,224; Caths., 4,847,000 (10%); tot. pop., 45,779,000.

Independent republic bordering on the Black Sea; former USSR republic; capital, Kiev. The baptism of Vladimir and his people in 988 marked the beginning of Christianity in the territory of Kievan Rus, which is included in today's Ukraine. The 1596 Union of Brest brought the Ukrainian Byzantine-rite community back into communion with Rome. The Eastern Catholic Church was officially suppressed and underground in the USSR from the late 1940s; all of its bishops were killed or imprisoned and its property seized by the government and given to the Orthodox. Some Catholic priests continued to minister clandestinely under communist rule.

As the Eastern Church regained its legal status under Soviet President Mikhail Gorbachev, serious tensions arose with the Orthodox over ownership of property and the allegiance of priests and lay people. Latin-rite dioceses were re-established in 1991. In the late 1990s, rising inflation and weakening currency, aggravated by the government's and some companies' failure to pay wages, led Ukrainian Church leaders to fight homelessness and hunger. Despite opposition from Ukraine's largest Orthodox Church, Pope John Paul II visited Ukraine in June 2001. He challenged Ukrainians to talk to each other and focus on unity, despite religious, ethnic and political tensions. Despite Russian Orthodox objections, the Ukrainian Catholic Church moved its headquarters from Lviv to Kiev and Halych in 2005.

United Arab Emirates*

V.a, 1; bp., 2; parishes, 8; priests, 32 (4 dioc., 28 rel.); srs., 38; bap., 1,997; Caths., 750,000 (11%); tot. pop., 8,328,000.

Independent state along Persian Gulf; capital, Abu Dhabi. The apostolic vicariate of Arabia has its seat in Abu Dhabi. It includes the states of Bahrain, Oman, Qatar, Saudi Arabia and Yemen

(see separate entries) as well as United Arab Emirates. Diplomatic relations with the Holy See were established in May 2007.

United States*

(See **Catholic Church in the U.S.**; see also **Chronology of American Catholic History**; and **Statistics of the Church in the U.S.**)

Uruguay*

Archd., 1; dioc., 9; abp., 2; bp., 13; parishes, 235; priests, 501 (257 dioc., 244 rel.); p.d., 103; sem., 75; bros., 92; srs., 876; catechists, 4,257; bap., 20,489; Caths., 2,594,000 (75%); tot. pop., 3,369,000.

Republic on the southeast coast of South America; capital, Montevideo. The Spanish established a settle ment in 1624 and evangelization followed. Missionaries followed the reduction pattern to reach the Indians, form them in the faith and train them in agriculture, husbandry, other arts, and the experience of managing property and living in community. The constitution of 1830 made Catholicism the religion of the state and subsidized some of its activities, principally the missions to the Indians. Separation of Church and state was provided for in the constitution of 1917. In 1997, despite a court decision halting further investigations, the Church pledged to make one last effort to help search for people who remained missing from the 1973-85 military dictatorship.

Uzbekistan*

A.a, 1; parishes, 5; priests, 9 (1 dioc., 8 rel.); bros., 2; sem., 1; srs.,10; bap., 16; Caths. 4,000; tot. pop. 27,490,000.

Former republic of USSR; independent, 1991; capital, Tashkent. The communist government confiscated Catholic properties in 1917 and severely repressed the practice of religion in the country. The country won its independence in 1991. The majority of the population is Sunni Muslim. A small number of Catholics live in Tashkent. The Vatican established a mission in 1997. In 2005 the Church became an apostolic administration and received its first Catholic bishop.

Vanuatu*

Dioc., 1; bp., 1; parishes, 31; priests, 27 (17 dioc., 10 rel.); p.d.; sem., 14; bros., 17; srs., 51; catechists, 300; bap., 530; Caths., 33,000 (16%); tot. pop., 243,000.

Independent (July 29, 1980) island group in the southwest Pacific; capital, Vila. Effective, though slow, evangelization by Catholic missionaries began about 1887. An apostolic vicariate was set up in 1904. The hierarchy was established in 1966.

Vatican City State (See separate entry)

Venezuela*

Archd., 9; dioc., 24; ord.; v.a., 4; ap. ex., 2; mil. ord. 1; card., 1; abp., 11; bp., 42; parishes, 1,378; priests, 2,720 (1,816 dioc., 904 rel.); p.d., 231; sem., 1,207; bros., 189; srs., 3,270; catechists, 30,656; bap., 399,389; Caths., 25,709,000 (87%); tot. pop., 29,278,000.

Republic in northern South America; capital,

Caracas. Evangelization began in 1513-14 and involved members of a number of religious orders who worked in assigned territories, developing missions into pueblos or villages of Indian converts. Nearly 350 towns originated as missions. The first diocese was established in 1531. Fifty-four missionaries met death by violence from the start of missionary work until 1817. Missionary work was seriously hindered during the wars of independence in the second decade of the 19th century and continued in decline through the rest of the century as dictator followed dictator in a period of political turbulence. Restoration of the missions got under way in 1922. In mid-2005, amid increasing poverty, several surveys found the Catholic Church had the highest respect of any of the nation's institutions. The Church faced hostility from the late Pres. Hugo Chavez, including attacks on the offices of the papal nuncio.

Vietnam

Archd., 3; dioc., 23; card., 1; abp., 2; bp., 40; parishes, 2,675; priests, 3,980 (3,007 dioc., 973 rel.); p.d., 2; sem., 3,172; bros., 2,179; srs., 14,797; catechists, 56,203; bap., 173,596, Caths., 6,404,000 (6.8%); tot. pop., 86,928,000.

Country in southeast Asia, reunited officially July 2, 1976, as the Socialist Republic of Vietnam; capital, Hanoi.

Catholicism was introduced in 1533, but missionary work was intermittent until 1615, when Jesuits arrived to stay. Two vicariates were organized in 1659. A seminary was set up in 1666, and two Vietnamese priests were ordained two years later. A congregation of native women religious formed in 1670 is still active. Severe persecution broke out in 1698, three times in the 18th century, and again in the 19th. Up to 300,000 people suffered in some way from persecution during the 50 years before 1883, when the French moved in to secure religious liberty for the Catholics. Most of the 117 beatified Martyrs of Vietnam were killed during this 50-year period. After the French were forced out of Vietnam in 1954, the country was partitioned at the 17th parallel. The North became Communist and the Viet Cong, joined by North Vietnamese regular army troops in 1964, fought to gain control of the South. In 1954 there were approximately 1.1 million Catholics in the North and 480,000 in the South. More than 650,000 fled to the South to avoid the government repression. In South Vietnam, the Church continued to develop during the war years.

After the end of the war in 1975, the government exercised control over virtually all aspects of Church life. In the late 1980s, bishops noted some softening of the government's hard line. In the 1990s, the Vatican and Vietnam held intermittent talks on Church-state issues, with sporadic progress reported, but in 1997, the government censored the section of the "Catechism of the Catholic Church" that dealt with human rights. Although at times the Vatican was forced to wait years for government approval of bishops' appointments, in the late 20th and early 21st century, Vatican delegations made regular visits to Vietnam to discuss the appointments and other Church-related issues. Early in the 21st century, the government approved a series of bishops' appointments in northern Vietnam, and Church leaders said they saw a rejuvenation of the faith there. Recent years have also seen government seizures of Catholic property, including the old nunciature. Catholic protests have resulted in arrests and threats. The Vietnam-Holy See Joint Working Group has held several meetings in the Vatican to strengthen and develop bilateral relations between Vietnam and the Holy See. In Jan. 2013, then-Pope Benedict XVI met with the head of the Vietnamese Communist Party in the Vatican.

Virgin Islands (U.S.)

Dioc., 1 (St. Thomas, suffragan of Washington, DC); bp., 2; parishes, 8; priests, 23 (15 dioc., 8 rel.); p.d., 27; sem., 6; bros., 3; srs., 24; bap., 256; Caths., 30,000 (29%); tot. pop., 109,000.

Organized unincorporated U.S. territory in Atlantic Ocean; capital, Charlotte Amalie on St. Thomas (one of the three principal islands). The islands were discovered by Columbus in 1493 and named for St. Ursula and her virgin companions. Missionaries began evangelization in the 16th century. A church on St. Croix dates from about 1660; another, on St. Thomas, from 1774. The Baltimore archdiocese had jurisdiction over the islands from 1804 to 1820, when it was passed on to the first of several places in the Caribbean area. Some trouble arose over a pastoral appointment in the 19th century, resulting in a small schism. The Redemptorists took over pastoral care in 1858; normal conditions have prevailed since.

Wales*

Archd., 1; dioc., 2; abp., 1; bp., 4; parishes, 156; priests, 193 (119 dioc., 74 rel.); p.d., 33; sem., 8; bros., 84; srs., 319; bap, 2,159; Caths., 208,779 (.7%); tot. pop., 3,073,000.

Part of the United Kingdom, on the western part of the island of Great Britain. Celtic missionaries completed evangelization by the end of the sixth century, the climax of what has been called the age of saints. Welsh Christianity received its distinctive Celtic character at this time. Some conflict developed when attempts were made — and proved successful later — to place the Welsh Church under the jurisdiction of Canterbury; the Welsh opted for direct contact with Rome.

The Church made progress despite the depredations of Norsemen in the eighth and ninth centuries. Norman infiltration occurred near the middle of the 12th century, resulting in a century-long effort to establish territorial dioceses and parishes to replace the Celtic organizational plan of monastic centers and satellite churches. The Western Schism produced split views and allegiances. Actions of Henry VIII in breaking away from Rome had serious repercussions. Proscription and penal laws crippled the Church, resulted in heavy defections and touched off a 150-year period of repression. Methodism prevailed by 1750. Modern Catholicism came to Wales with Irish immigrants in the 19th century, when the number of Welsh Catholics was negligible. Catholic emancipation was granted in 1829. The hierarchy was restored in 1850. Wales shares a bishops' conference with England.

Yemen*

Parishes, 4; priests, 4 (rel.); srs., 22; bap., 2; Caths., 4,000; tot. pop., 23,154,000.

Republic on southern coast of Arabian peninsula; capital, Sana. Formerly North Yemen (Arab Republic of Yemen) and South Yemen (People's Republic of Yemen); formally reunited in 1990. Christians perished in the first quarter of the sixth century. Muslims have been in control since the seventh century. The state religion is Islam; the Church is under the ecclesiastical jurisdiction of Arabia apostolic vicariate. In the early 1990s, Salesians reported some harassment of Church workers in the South. In early 1998, three Missionaries of Charity nuns were murdered. The Vatican established diplomatic relations with Yemen in October 1998.

Zambia*

Archd., 2; dioc., 9; Card., 1; abp., 3; bp., 9; parishes, 316; priests, 860 (462 dioc., 398 rel.); sem., 567; bros., 201; srs., 2,021; catechists, 7,117; bap., 46,533; Caths., 4,510,000 (33%); tot. pop., 13,655,000.

Republic in central Africa; capital, Lusaka. Portuguese priests did some evangelizing in the 16th and 17th centuries but no results of their work remained in the 19th century. Jesuits began work in the South in the 1880s and White Fathers in the North and East in 1895. Evangelization of the western region began for the first time in 1931. The number of Catholics doubled in the 20 years following World War II. Zambian Catholics have welcomed tens of thousands of refugees from the region. In the 1990s, Zambian Church leaders worked caring for victims of HIV/AIDS and spoke out against foreign debt. In 2003, the

bishops urged parishes to set up civic education programs to help with the nation's constitutional review process.

Zimbabwe*

Archd., 2; dioc., 6; abp., 4; bp., 6; parishes, 238; priests, 491 (280 dioc., 211 rel.); p.d., 22; sem., 494; bros., 96; srs., 1,010; catechists, 5,919; bap., 24,658; Caths., 1,776,000 (10%); tot. pop., 15,806,000.

Independent republic (1980) in south central Africa; capital, Harare. Earlier unsuccessful missionary ventures preceded the introduction of Catholicism in 1879. Missionaries began to make progress after 1893. The hierarchy was established in 1955; the first black bishop was ordained in 1973.

In 1969, four years after the government of Ian Smith made a unilateral declaration of independence from England, a new constitution was enacted for the purpose of assuring continued white supremacy over the black majority. Catholic and Protestant prelates in the country protested. The Smith regime was ousted in 1979 after seven years of civil war in which at least 25,000 people were killed.

In 1997, the bishops published a report detailing more than 7,000 cases of killings, torture and human rights abuses by government troops in western Zimbabwe from 1981-87. As the Church entered the 21st century, it was devoting tremendous resources toward palliative care of AIDS victims and work with AIDS orphans. Some lay Church leaders were outspoken against government-backed campaigns of violence against white landowners and the poor; Bp. Pius Ncube of Bulawayo was targeted for speaking against government abuses. In 2007, the bishops issued a strong pastoral letter condemning Robert Mugabe's regime, and, after Mugabe failed to win a majority in the 2008 presidential election, spoke out against post-election violence.

CATHOLIC WORLD STATISTICS

(Principal sources: *Statistical Yearbook of the Church*, 2011 (the latest edition); figures are as of Jan. 1, 2011, unless indicated otherwise.)

	Africa	North America[1]	South America	Asia	Europe	Oceania	WORLD TOTALS
Patriarchates[2]	2	–	–	8	2	–	12
Archdioceses	94	92	102	124	181	18	610
Dioceses	404	365	450	351	511	56	2,108
Prelatures	–	7	29	4	6	–	46
Abbacies	–	–	–	–	10	–	10
Exarchates/Ords.	–	2	6	1	17	1	27
Military Ords.	3	4	9	3	15	2	36
Vicariates Apostolic	22	5	37	21	1	–	86
Prefectures	4	–	1	4	1	1	11
Apostolic Admin.	–	–	1	3	4	–	8
Independent Missions	1	2	–	3	–	2	8
Cardinals[3]	18	25	26	20	111	4	205
Patriarchs[2]	1	–	–	9	2	–	10
Archbishops	146	154	167	195	375	27	1,064[4]
Bishops	544	761	791	544	1,123	104	3,867[4]
Priests	39,057	72,171	48,839	58,678	187,864	4,805	413,418
Diocesan	26,586	49,104	31,369	34,135	132,375	2,754	278,346
Religious	12,471	23,067	17,470	24,543	55,489	2,010	135,072
Perm. Deacons	421	20,312	6,003	267	13,519	387	40,914
Brothers	8,592	9,339	6,794	11,557	17,437	1,373	55,085
Sisters	67,863	113,681	77,002	167,423	278,583	8,654	713,206
Maj. Seminarians	27,483	16,226	20,239	35,297	20,296	1,075	120,616
Sec. Inst. Mbrs. (Men)	75	49	184	51	360	1	713
Sec. Inst. Mbrs. (Women)	814	1,704	4,045	1,765	16,189	46	24,564
Lay Missionaries	7,773	61,495	274,702	31,020	6,385	347	381,722
Catechists	400,834	967,722	882,475	303,807	554,219	16,189	3,125,235
Parishes	14,602	32,899	24,050	23,937	123,267	2,421	221,176[5]
Kindergartens	14,379	10,231	7,416	13,701	24,157	1,598	71,482
Students	1,412,316	454,935	827,365	1,899,290	1,918,591	79,990	6,720,545
Elem./PrimarySchools	35,821	13,171	10,528	16,355	16,091	3,172	94,411
Students	15,692,697	3,336,898	3,212,171	6,071,936	2,900,826	696,887	31,939,415
Secondary Schools	11,882	4,394	6,646	10,567	9,628	660	43,777
Students	5,024,553	1,633,936	2,112,760	6,115,601	3,648,597	417,529	18,952,976
Students, Higher Insts[6]	97,738	613,190	206,544	1,237,767	324,168	14,704	2,494,111
Social Service Facilities	15,907	20,053	21,117	21,132	36,778	2,132	117,119
Hospitals	1,284	997	704	1,125	1,137	188	5,435
Dispensaries	5,398	3,003	2,208	3,828	2,557	530	17,524
Leprosaria	211	20	45	281	6	4	567
Homes for Aged/Handic.	615	2,023	1,850	2,440	8,271	545	15,784
Orphanages	1,435	1,096	1,648	3,911	2,321	123	10,534
Nurseries	2,010	1,110	2,629	3,286	2,447	110	11,592
Matrimonial Advice Ctrs.	1,722	3,912	2,318	972	5,819	265	15,008
Social Educ. Ctrs.	3,232	7,892	9,675	5,286	14,219	367	40,671
Other Institutions	–	–	–	3	1	–	4
Baptisms	3,731,007	3,779,893	4,207,335	2,680,805	2,229,881	123,589	16,752,510
Under Age 7	2,518,907	3,461,126	3,583,366	2,228,835	2,143,518	109,455	14,045,207
Over Age 7	1,212,100	318,767	623,969	451,970	86,363	14,134	2,707,303
Marriages	347,956	629,672	547,822	597,546	678,153	20,853	2,822,002
Between Catholics	303,233	565,547	532,754	531,724	615,981	13,403	2,575,363
Mixed Marriages	44,723	51,404	15,068	65,822	62,172	7,450	246,636
Catholic Pop[7]	193,667,000	249,658,000	342,652,000	132,238,000	285,746,000	9,630,000	1,213,591,000
World Population	1,039,476,000	541,398,000	396,934,000	4,202,786,000	715,729,000	36,987,000	6,933,310,000

1. Includes Central America. 2. For listing and description, see Index. 3. As of Aug. 30, 2013. 4. Figures for the hierarchy (cardinals, abps. and bps.) include 2,730 ordinaries, 559 coadjutors or aux., 285 with offices in the Roman Curia, 15 in other offices, 1,543 ret. 5. 172,405 have parish priests; 45,026 are administered by other priests; 599 are entrusted to perm. deacons; 170 to bros; 488 to women rel.; 1,206 to lay people; 1,282 vacant. 6. There are also approximately 468,457 in univs. for ecclesiastical studies and 3,039,684 other univ. students. 7. Percentages of Catholics in world pop.: Africa, 18.6; North America (Catholics 85,535,000; tot. pop., 346,307,000), 24.7; Central America (Catholics, 164,123,000; tot. pop., 195,091,000), 84; South America, 86; Asia, 3.1; Europe, 40; Oceania, 26; world, 17.5 (Catholic totals do not include those in areas that could not be surveyed, est. to be approx. 9 million).

EPISCOPAL CONFERENCES

(*Principal sources:* Annuario Pontificio *and* Catholic Almanac *survey.*)

Episcopal conferences, organized and operating under general norms and particular statutes approved by the Holy See, are official bodies in and through which the bishops of a given country or territory act together as pastors of the Church. Listed according to countries or regions are titles and addresses of conferences, telephone numbers (where possible), and names and sees of presidents.

Africa, Northern: Conference Episcopale Regionale du Nord de l'Afrique (CERNA), 13 rue KhelifaBoukhalfa, 16000 Algiers, Algeria; (021) 63-35-62. Abp. Vincent Landel (Rabat).

Africa, Southern: Southern African Catholic Bishops' Conference (SACBC), 140 Visagie St., P.O. Box 941, Pretoria 0001, S. Africa; (021) 65-35-62. Abp. Stephen Brislin (Cape Town).

Albania: Conferenza Episcopale dell'Albania, Tirane, Rruga Don Bosco 1, Kulia Postare 2950; (042) 47-159. Abp. Angelo Massafra, O.F.M. (Shkodre-Pult).

Angola and São Tome: Conferencia Episcopal de Angola e HR Tome (CEAST), C.P. 3579 Luanda, Angola; (02) 44-36-86. Abp. Gabriel Mbilingi (Lubango).

Antilles: Antilles Episcopal Conference (AEC), P.O. Box 3086, St. James (Trinidad and Tobago), W.I.; (868) 622-2932. Abp. Patrick PInder (Nassau).

Arab Countries: Conférence des Evêques Latins dans les Régions Arabes (CELRA), Latin Patriarchate, P.O. Box 14152, Jerusalem (Old City); (02) 628-85-54. Patriarch Fouad Twal (Jerusalem).

Argentina: Conferencia Episcopal Argentina (CEA), C1008AAV, Calle Suipacha 1034, 1008 Buenos Aires; (011) 4328-95-70. Abp. Jose Maria Arancedo (Santa Fe de la Vera Cruz).

Australia: Australian Catholic Bishops' Conference, 63 Currong St., Braddon, A.C.T. 2601; (02) 6201-9845; www.catholic.org.au. Abp. Denis Hart (Melbourne).

Austria: Österreichische Bischofskonferenz, Wollzeile 2, A1010 Vienna; 01-516-11-32.80. Christoph Card. Schönborn, O.P. (Vienna).

Balkans: Int'l. Conference of Bishops of Sts. Cyril and Methodius, 11000 Beograd (Srbija), Visegradska 23; (011) 303-22-46. Abp. Zef Gashi, S.D.B. (Bar).

Bangladesh: Catholic Bishops' Conference of Bangladesh (CBCB), P.O. Box 3, Dhaka1000; (02) 40-88-79. Abp. Patrick D'Rozario, C.S.C. (Dhaka).

Belgium: Bisschoppenconferentie van België — Conférence Episcopale de Belgique, Rue Guimard 1, B1040 Brussels; (02) 509-96-93; www.catho. be, www.kerknet.be. Abp. Andre-Joseph Leonard (Mechelen-Brussel).

Belarus: Conferentia Episcoporum Catholicorum, 220030 Minsk, pl. Swobody 9; (017) 26.61.27. Bp. Aleksander Kaszkiewicz (Grodno).

Benin: Conférence Episcopale du Bénin, 01 B.P. 491; 30.01.45. Abp. Antoine Ganye (Cotonou).

Bolivia: Conferencia Episcopal Boliviana (CEB), Casilla 2309, Calle Potosi 814, La Paz; (02) 40-67-98. Bp. Oscar Aparicio Cespedes (Military Ordinary).

Bosnia and Herzegovina: Biskupska Konferencija Bosne i Hercegovine (B.K. B.i.H.), Nadbiskupski Ordinariat, Kaptol 7, 71000 Sarajevo; (071) 47-21-78. Bp. Franjo Komarica (Banja Luka).

Brazil: Conferência Nacional dos Bispos do Brasil (CNBB), C.P. 02067, SE/Sul Quadra 801, Conjunto "B," 70259970 Brasilia, D.F.; (061) 313-8300. Card. Raymondo Damasceno Assis (Aparecida).

Bulgaria: Mejduritual Episcopska Konferenzia vâv Bâlgaria, Ul. Liulin Planina 5, 1606 Sofia; (0) 540-406. Bp. Christo Proykov (Briula, titular see).

Burkina Faso and Niger: Conférence des Evêques de Burkina Faso et du Niger, B.P. 1195, Ouagadougou, Burkina Faso; 30-60-26. Abp. Seraphim François Rouamba (Koupela).

Burma: See **Myanmar**.

Burundi: Conférence des Evêques catholiques du Burundi (C.E.CA.B.), B. P. 1390, 5 Blvd. de l'Uprona, Bujumbura; 223-263. Bp. Gervais Banshimiyubusa (Ngozi).

Cameroon: Conférence Episcopale Nationale du Cameroun (CENC), BP 1963, Yaoundé; 231-15-92. Abp. Joseph Atanga, S.J. (Bertoua).

Canada: See **Canadian Conference of Catholic Bishops** in **Catholic Church in Canada**.

Central African Republic: Conférence Episcopale Centrafricaine (CECA), B.P. 1518, Bangui; 50-24-84. Abp. Paulin Pomodimo (Bangui).

Chad: Conférence Episcopale du Tchad, B.P. 456, N'Djaména; (235) 51-74-44. Bp. Jean-Claude Bouchard, O.M.I. (Pala).

Chile: Conferencia Episcopal de Chile (CECH), Casilla 517V, Correo 21, Cienfuegos 47, Santiago; (02) 671-77-33. Abp. Andrello Ricardo Ezzati, S.D.B. (Santiago de Chile).

China: Chinese Regional Episcopal Conference, 34 Lane 32, KuangFu South Rd., Taipeh 10552, Taiwan; (02) 578-2355. Abp. John Hung Shan-chuan (Taipei).

Colombia: Conferencia Episcopal de Colombia, Apartado 7448, Carrera 8ª 47, N. 8485, Santafé de Bogotá D.E.; (91) 311-42-77. Abp. Rubén Salazar Gómez (Barranquila).

Congo: Conférence Episcopale du Congo, B.P. 200, Brazzaville; (83) 06-29. Bp. Louis Portella Mbuyu (Kinkala).

Congo, Democratic Republic (formerly Zaire): Conférence Episcopale du Zaïre (CEZ), B.P. 3258, KinshasaGombe; 012-33-992. Bp. Nicolas Djomo Lola (Tshumbe).

Costa Rica: Conferencia Episcopal de Costa Rica (CECOR), Apartado 497, 1000 San Jose; 221-30-53. Abp. Hugo Barrantes Ureña (San Jose de Costa Rica).

Côte d'Ivoire: Conference Episcopale de la Côte d'Ivoire, B.P. 1287, Abidjan 01. Bp. Alexis Touabli Youlo (Agboville).

Croatia: Hrvatska Biskupska Konferencija, Kaptol 22, HR10000 Zagreb; 385-01-481-18-93; www.hbk.hr. Bp. Marin Srakic (Djakovo-Osijek).

Cuba: Conferencia de Obispos Católicos de Cuba (COCC), Apartado 594, Calle 26 n. 314 Miramar, 10100 Havana 1; (07) 22-3868. Abp. Guillermo Garcia Ibanez Dionisio (Santiago de Cuba).

Czech Republic: Ceská Biskupská Konference, Sekretariat, Thakurova 3, 160 00 Praha (Prague) 6; (02) 33-15-421. Abp. Dominik Duca, O.P. (Prague).

Dominican Republic: Conferencia del Episcopado Dominicano (CED), Apartado 186, Santo Domingo; (809) 685-3141. Nicolas de Jesus Card. Lopez Rodriguez (Santo Domingo).

Ecuador: Conferencia Episcopal Ecuatoriana, Apartado 1081, Avenida América 1805 y Lagasca, Quito; (02) 23-82-21. Abp. Antonio Arregui Yarza (Guayaquil).

El Salvador: Conferencia Episcopal de El Salvador (CEDES). 15 Av. Norte 1420, Col. Layco, Apartado 1310, San Salvador; 25-8997. Abp. Jose Luis Escobar Alas (San Salvador).

Equatorial Guinea: Conferencia Episcopal de Guinea Ecuatorial, Apartado 106, Malabo. Abp. Ildefonso Obama Obono (Malabo).

Ethiopia: Ethiopian Episcopal Conference, P.O. Box 21322, Addis Ababa; (01) 55-03-00. Abp. Berhaneyesus Demerew Souraphiel, C.M. (Addis Ababa).

France: Conférence des Evêques de France, 106 rue du Bac, 75341 Paris CEDEX 07; 33-01-45-49-69-70; www. cef.fr. André Cardinal Vingt-Trois (Paris).

Gabon: Conférence Episcopale du Gabon, B.P. 2146, Libreville; 72-20-73. Bp. Timothée Modibo-Nzockena (Franceville).

Gambia, Liberia and Sierra Leone: InterTerritorial Catholic Bishops' Conference of the Gambia, Liberia and Sierra Leone (ITCABIC), Santanno House, P.O. Box 893, Freetown, Sierra Leone; (022) 22-82-40. Bp. Daniel Koroma (Kenema).

Germany: Deutsche Bischofskonferenz, Postfach 2962, Kaiserstrasse 163, D53019 Bonn; (0049) 228-103-290. Abp. Robert Zollitsch (Freiburg im Breisgau).

Ghana: Ghana Bishops' Conference, National Catholic Secretariat, P.O. Box 9712 Airport, Accra; (021) 500-491. Bp. Joseph Osei-Bonsu (Konongo-Mampong).

Great Britain: Bishops' Conference of England and Wales, General Secretariat, 39 Eccleston Square, London, SWIV IBX; (020) 7630-8220. Abp. Vincent Nichols (Westminster).

Greece: Conferentia Episcopalis Graeciae, Odos Homirou 9, 106 72 Athens; (01) 3642-311. Bp. Fragkiskos Papamanolis, O.F.M. Cap, (Syros, Santorini, and Milos).

Guatemala: Conferencia Episcopal de Guatemala (CEG), Apartado 1698, 01901 Ciudad de Guatemala; 543-18-27/8. Bp. Rodolfo Valenzuela Nunez (Vera Paz).

Guinea: Conférence Episcopale de la Guinée, B.P. 1006 bis, Conkary. Bp. Emmanuel Felemou (Kankan).

Guinea Bissau: See **Senegal**.

Haiti: Conférence Episcopale de Haïti (CEH). B.P. 1572, Angle rues Piquant et Lammarre, Port-au-Prince; 222-5194. Bp. Chibly Langlois (Les Cayes).

Honduras: Conferencia Episcopal de Honduras (CEH), Apartado 847, Blvd. Estadio Suyapa, Tegucigalpa; (504) 32-40-43. Oscar Andrés Card. Rodríguez Maradiaga (Tegucigalpa).

Hungary: Magyar Katolikus Püspöki Konferencia, H-1071 Budapest VII, Városligeti fasor 45; 1-342-69-59. Peter Card. Erdö (Esztergom-Budapest).

India: Catholic Bishops' Conference of India (CBCI), CBCI Centre, Ashok Place, Goldakkhana, New Delhi110001; (011) 334-44-70. Oswald Card. Gracias (Mumbai).

Conference of Catholic Bishops of India – Latin Rite (CCBI L.R.), Bangalore-560084, Karnataka, D'Costa Lay out, 2nd Cross, Wheeler's Rd., St. Mary's Town; (080)

2549.8081. Card. Telesphore Toppo (Ranchi).

Indian Ocean: Conférence Episcopale de l'Océan Indien (CEDOI) (includes Islands of Mauritius, Seychelles, Comore and La Réunion), 13 rue Msgr. Gonin, Port Louis, Mauritius; (230) 208-3068. Bp. Denis Wiehe (Victoria).

Indonesia: Konperensi Waligereja Indonesia (KWI), Jl. Cut Mutiah 10, Tromolpos 3044, Jakarta 10002; (021) 33-64-22. Ignatius Suharyo Hardjoatmodjo (Jakarta).

Ireland: Irish Episcopal Conference, "Ara Coeli," Armagh BT61 7QY; 028-3752-2045. Sean Card. Brady (Armagh).

Italy: Conferenza Episcopale Italiana (CEI), Circonvallazione Aurelia, 50, 00165 Rome; 06-663-981. Angelo Card. Bagnasco (Genoa).

Ivory Coast: See **Côte d'Ivoire**.

Japan: Catholic Bishops' Conference of Japan, Shiomi 21010, KotoKu, Tokyo, 135; (03) 56324411. Abp. Leo Jun Ikenaga, S.J. (Osaka).

Kazakstan: Episcopal Conference of Kazakstan, 473003 Astana, 3 Tashenova St., P.O. Box 622; (3172) 37.29.35. Abp. Tomash Peta (Most Blessed Mary, Astana).

Kenya: Kenya Episcopal Conference (KEC), The Kenya Catholic Secretariat, P.O. Box 13475, Nairobi; (020) 444-3133. John Card. Njue (Nairobi).

Korea: Catholic Bishops' Conference of Korea, Box 16, Seoul 100600; (02) 466-3417. Bp. Peter Kang U-il (Cheju).

Laos and Cambodia: Conférence Episcopale du Laos et du Cambodge, c/o Msgr. Pierre Bach, Paris Foreign Missions, 254 Silom Rd., Bangkok 10500; (02) 234-1714. Louis-Marie Ling Mangkhanekoun (Acque nuove di Proconsolare).

Latvia: Latvijas Biskapu Konference, Maza Pils iela 2/a, LV-1050, Riga; (7) 22-72-66. Bp. Janis Bulis (Rezekne-Aglona).

Lesotho: Lesotho Catholic Bishops' Conference, Catholic Secretariat, P.O. Box 200, Maseru 100; (0501) 31-25-25. Abp. Gerard Tlali Lerotholi, O.M.I. (Maseru).

Liberia: Catholic Bishops' Conference of Liberia, 1000 Monrovia 10, P.O. Box 10-2078; 227-245. Bp. Lewis Zeigler (Gbarnga).

Lithuania: Conferentia Episcopalis Lituaniae, Sventaragio, 4, 2001 Vilnius; (5) 212-54-55. Abp. Sigitas Tamkevicius, S.J. (Kaunas).

Madagascar: Conférence Episcopale de Madagascar, 102 bis Av. Maréchal Joffre, Antanimena, B. P 667, Antananarivo; (02) 2220-478. Abp. Desire Tsarahazana (Toamasina).

Malawi: Episcopal Conference of Malawi, Catholic Secretariat of Malawi, P.O. Box 30384, Lilongwe 3; 782-066. Bp. Joseph Mukasa Zuza (Mzuzu).

Malaysia-Singapore-Brunei: Catholic Bishops' Conference of Malaysia, Singapore and Brunei (BCMSB), Xavier Selangor Darul Ehsan, 46000 Petaling Jaya, Malaysia; (03) 758-1371. Abp. John Ha Tiong Hock (Kuching).

Mali: Conférence Episcopale du Mali, B.P. 298, Bamako; 225-499. Bp. Jean-Baptiste Tiama (Sikasso).

Malta: Konferenza Episkopali Maltija, Archbishop's Curia, Floriana; (356) 234317; www.maltachurch.org.mt. Abp. Paul Cremona, O.P. (Malta).

Mexico: See the Conferencia del Episcopado Mexicano (CEM), in the section on the **Catholic**

Church in Mexico.
Mozambique: Conferência Episcopal de Moçambique (CEM), Av. Paulo Samuel Kankhomba 188/RC, C.P. 286; (01) 49-07-66. Bp. Lucio Andrice Muandula (Xai-Xai).

Myanmar: Myanmar Catholic Bishops' Conference (MCBC), 292 Pyi Rd., P.O. Box 1080, Yangon; (01) 23-71-98. Bp. John Hsane Hgyi (Pathein).

Namibia: Namibian Catholic Bishops' Conference (NCBC). P.O. Box 11525 W., Windhoek; (061) 22-47-98. Abp. Ndumbukuti Nashenda Liborius, O.M.I. (Windhoek).

Netherlands: Nederlandse Bisschoppenconferentie, Postbus 13049, NL3507 LA, Utrecht; (31)-30-232-69-00; www.omroep.nl/rkk. Card. Willem Eijk (Utrecht).

New Zealand: New Zealand Catholic Bishops Conference, P.O. Box 1937, Wellington 6015; (04) 496-1747. Abp. John Dew (Wellington).

Nicaragua: Conferencia Episcopal de Nicaragua (CEN), Apartado Postal 2407, de Ferretería Lang 1 cuadro al Norte y 1 cuadro al Este, Managua; (02) 666-292. Bp. Rene Jiron Socrates (Juigalpa).

Niger: See **Burkina Faso**.

Nigeria: Catholic Bishops Conference of Nigeria, P.O. Box 951, 6 Force Rd., Lagos; (01) 263-58-49. Abp. Ignatius Ayau Kaigama (Jos).

Pacific: Conferentia Episcopalis Pacifici (CE PAC), P.O. Box 289, Suva (Fiji); 300-340. Bp. Mafi Soane Patita Paini (Togo).

Pakistan: Pakistan Episcopal Conference, P.O. Box 909, Lahore 54000; (042) 6366-137. Abp. Lawrence J. Saldanha (Lahore).

Panama: Conferencia Episcopal de Panamá (CEP), Apartado 870033, Panama 7; 223-0075. Bp. José Luis Lacunza Maestrojuán, O.A.R. (Goroka).

Papua New Guinea and Solomon Islands: Catholic Bishops' Conference of Papua New Guinea and Solomon Islands, P.O. Box 398, Waigani, N.C.D., Papua New Guinea; 25-9577. Abp. John Ribat, M.S.C. (Port Moresby).

Paraguay: Conferencia Episcopal Paraguaya (CEP), Alberdi 782, Casilla Correo 1436, Asunción; (021) 490-920. Bp. Claudio Gimenez Medina Catalino (Caacupe).

Peru: Conferencia Episcopal Peruana, Apartado 310, Rio de Janeiro 488, Lima 100; (01) 463-10-10. Abp. Salvador Pineiro Garcia-Calderon (Ayacucho).

Philippines: Catholic Bishops' Conference of the Philippines (CBCP), P.O. Box 3601, 470 General Luna St., 1099 Manila; (02) 527-4054. Abp. Jose Palma (Cebu).

Poland: Konferencja Episkopatu Polski, Skwer Kardynala Stefana Wyszynskiego 6, 01015 Warsaw; (022) 838-92-51. Jozef Michalik (Przemysl of the Latins).

Portugal: Conferência Episcopal Portuguesa, Campo dos Mártires da Pátria, 431 Esq., 1100 Lisbon; 21-885-21-23. Card. Jose da Cruz Policarop (Lisbon).

Puerto Rico: Conferencia Episcopal Puertorriqueña (CEP), P.O. Box 40682, Estacion Minillas, San Juan 009400682; (787) 728-1650. Abp. Roberto Octavio Gonzalez Nieves, O.F.M. (San Juan).

Romania: Conferinte Episcopala Românâ, Via Popa Tatu 58, Bucharest; (01) 311-12-89. Abp. Ioan Robu (Bucharest).

Russian Federation: Conference of Catholic Bishops of the Russian Federation (C.V.C.F.R.), 101031 Moskva, Via Pietrovka, d. 19 str., 5Kv. 35; (095) 923-16-97. Bp. Joseph Werth, S.J. (Transfiguration at Novosibirsk).

Rwanda: Conférence Episcopale du Rwanda (C.Ep.R.), B.P. 357, Kigali; 75439. Bp. Smaragde Mbonyintege (Kabgayi).

Scandinavia: Conferentia Episcopalis Scandiae, Trollbärsvägen 16, S426 55 Västra Frölunda (Sweden); (031) 709-64-87. Bp. Anders Arborelius, O.C.D. (Stockholm).

Scotland: Bishops' Conference of Scotland, 64 Aitken St., Airdrie, ML6; 44-1236-764-061. Abp. Philip Tartaglia (Glasgow).

Senegal, Mauritania, Cape Verde and Guinea Bissau: Conférence des Evêques du Sénégal, de la Mauritanie, du CapVert et de GuinéeBissau, B.P. 941, Dakar, Senegal. Bp. Benjamin Ndiaye (Kaolack).

Serbia and Montenegro: Biskupska konferecija Srbije I Crne Gore, 11000 Beograd, Visegradska 23; (011) 303.22.46. Bp. Stanslav Hocevar, S.D.B. (Beograd).

Sierra Leone: See **Gambia, Liberia and Sierra Leone**.

Slovakia: Biskupská Konferencia Slovenska, Kapitulská 11, 81521 Bratislava; (07) 733-54-50. Abp. Stanislav Zvolensky (Bratislava).

Slovenia: Slovenska Skofovska Konferenca, CirilMetodov trg 4, p.p.1990, 1001 Ljubljana; (386) 1-2342612. Abp. Anton Stres, C.M. (Ljubljana).

Spain: Conferencia Episcopal Española, Apartado 29075, Calle Añastro 1, 28080 Madrid; 91-343-96-15. Antonio Maria Card. Rouco Varela (Madrid).

Sri Lanka: Catholic Bishops' Conference of Sri Lanka, 19 Balcombe Place, Cotta Rd., Borella, Colombo 8; (01) 95-091; 59-70-62. Albert Ranjith Card. Patabendige (Colombo).

Sudan: Sudan Catholic Bishops' Conference (SCBC), P.O. Box 6011, Khartoum; (011) 225-075-9. Card. Zubeir Wako (Khartoum).

Switzerland: Conférence des Evêques Suisses, Secretariat, C.P. 22, av. Moléson 21, CH1706 Fribourg; (026) 322-47-94; www.kath.ch. Bp. Marcus Buchel (Sankt Gallen).

Tanzania: Tanzania Episcopal Conference (TEC), P.O. Box 2133, Mansfield St., DaresSalaam; (022) 51-075. Bp. Ngalalekumtwa Tarcisius (Iringa).

Thailand: Bishops' Conference of Thailand, 122-67 Soi Naaksuwan, Nonsi Road, Yannawa, Bangkok; 02-6815361-8. Abp. Louis Chamniern Santisukniran (Thare and Nonseng).

Togo: Conférence Episcopale du Togo, B.P. 348, Lomé; 21-22-72. Bp. Comlan Messan Alowonou Benoit (Kpalime).

Turkey: Turkish Episcopal Conference, Ölçek Sokak 83, Harbiye, 80230 Istanbul; (212) 248-07-75. Abp. Ruggero Franceschini, O.F.M. Cap. (Izmir).

Uganda: Uganda Episcopal Conference, P.O. Box 2886, Kampala; (041) 510-398. Abp. John Baptist Odama (Gulu).

Ukraine: Ukraine Episcopal Conference, 79008 Lviv, Mytropolycha Kuria Latynskoho Obriadu, Pl. Katedralna 1; (0322) 76-94-15. Abp. Mieczyslaw

Mokrzycki (Lviv of the Latins).
United States: See **National Conference of Catholic Bishops**.
Uruguay: Conferencia Episcopal Uruguaya (CEU), Avenida Uruguay 1319, 11100 Montevideo; (02) 900-26-42. Bp. Rodolfo Pedro Wirz Kraemer (Maldonado-Punta del Este).
Venezuela: Conferencia Episcopal de Venezuela (CEV), Apartado 4897, Torre a Madrices, Edificio Juan XXIII, Piso 4, Caracas 1010A; (0212) 4432-23-65. Abp. Rafael Padron Sanchez Diego (Cumana).
Vietnam: Conferenza Episcopale del Viêt Nam, Nha Trang, Khán Hoà, 22 Tran Phu; (058) 822-842. Bp. Pierre Nguyen Van Nhon (Da Lat).
Yugoslavia: Biskupska Konferencija Savezne Republike Jugoslavije, 11000 Beograd, Visegradska 23; (011) 642-280. Abp. Stanislav Hocevar, S.D.B. (Beograd).
Zambia: Zambia Episcopal Conference, P.O. Box 31965, 20201 Lusaka; (01) 212-070. Bp. George Cosmas Zumaire Lungu (Chipata).
Zimbabwe: Zimbabwe Catholic Bishops' Conference (ZCBC), Causeway, P.O. Box 8135, Harare; (14) 705-368. Angel Floro Martinez, I.E.M.E. (Gokwe).

Regional Conferences

(*Sources:* Almanac *survey*; Annuario Pontificio.)
Africa: Symposium of Episcopal Conferences of Africa and Madagascar (SECAM) (Symposium des Conférences Episcopales d'Afrique et de Madagascar, SCEAM): Polycarp Card. Pengo, abp. of Dar-es-Salaam, president. Address: Secretariat, P.O. Box 9156 Airport, Accra, Ghana.

Association of Episcopal Conferences of Central Africa (Association des Conférences Episcopales de l'Afrique Centrale, ACEAC): Comprises Burundi, Rwanda and Zaire. Bp. Simon Ntamwana, abp. of Gitega, president. Address: B.P. 20511, Kinshasa, Democratic Republic of Congo.

Association of Episcopal Conferences of the Region of Central Africa (Association des Conférences Episcopales de la Région de l'Afrique Central, ACERAC): Comprises Cameroon, Chad, Congo, Equatorial Guinea, Central African Republic and Gabon. Bp. Timothée Modibo-Nzockena, bp. of Franceville, president. Address: Secretariat, B.P. 200, Brazzaville, Republic of the Congo.

Association of Episcopal Conferences of Anglophone West Africa (AECAWA): Comprises Gambia, Ghana, Liberia, Nigeria and Sierra Leone. Bp. John Olorunfemi Onaiyekan, abp. of Abuja, president. Address: P.O. Box 11, Santasi, Ghana.

Association of Member Episcopal Conferences in Eastern Africa (AMECEA): Represents Eritrea, Ethiopia, Kenya, Malawi, Sudan, Tanzania, Uganda and Zambia. Affiliate members: Seychelles (1979), Somalia (1994). Abp. Tarcisius Gervazio Ziyaye, Abp. of Blantyre, president. Address: P.O. Box 21191, Nairobi, Kenya.

Regional Episcopal Conference of French Speaking West Africa (Conférence Episcopale Régionale de l'Afrique de l'Ouest Francophone, CERAO): Comprises Benin, Burkina Faso, Cape Verde, Côte d'Ivoire, Guinea, Guinea Bissau, Mali, Mauritania, Niger, Senegal and Togo. Peter Card. Turkson, abp. of Cape Town, president. Address: Secretariat General, B.P.470 CIDEX 1, Abidjan — Côte d'Ivoire.

InterRegional Meeting of Bishops of Southern Africa (IMBISA): Bishops of Angola, Botswana, Lesotho, Mozambique, Namibia, São Tome e Principe, South Africa, Swaziland and Zimbabwe. Abp. Gabriel Mbilingi, C.S.Sp., abp. of Lubango, president. Address: 88 Broadlands Rd., Avondale, Harare, Zimbabwe.

Asia: Federation of Asian Bishops' Conferences (FABC): Represents 14 Asian episcopal conferences and four independent jurisdictions (Hong Kong, Macau, Nepal, Mongolia) as regular members (excluding the Middle East). Established in 1970; statutes approved experimentally Dec. 6, 1972. Abp. Orlando B. Quevedeo, O.M.B., abp. of Cotabato, secretary general. Address: 16 Caine Road, Hong Kong; 25258021; www.fabc.org.ph.

Oceania: Federation of Catholic Bishops' Conferences of Oceania (FCBCO). Statutes approved Dec. 25, 1997. Bp. Peter Ingham, bp. of Wollongong in Australia, president. Address: P.O. Box 1937, 22-30 Hill St., Wellington, New Zealand 6015.

Europe: Council of European Bishops' Conferences (Consilium Conferentiarum Episcoporum Europae, CCEE): Reorganized in 1993 in accordance with suggestions made during the 1991 Synod of Bishops on Europe. Peter Card. Erdö, abp. of Esztergom-Budapest, president. Address of secretariat: Gallusstrasse 24, CH9000 Sankt Gallen, Switzerland; (0041) 71-227-33-74; www.kath.ch/ccee.

Commission of the Episcopates of the European Community (Commissio Episcopatuum Communitatis Europaeae, COMECE): Established in 1980; represents episcopates of states belonging to European Community. Card. Reinhard Marx, abp. of Munich-Freising, president. Address of secretariat: 42, Rue Stévin, B1000 Brussels, Belgium; (02) 230-73-16.

Central and South America: Latin American Bishops' Conference (Consejo Episcopal Latino-Americano, CELAM): Established in 1956; statutes approved Nov. 9, 1974. Represents 22 Latin American national bishops' conferences. Abp. Carlos Aguiar Retes, president. Address of the secretariat: Carrera 5 No. 11831, Usaquén, Bogotá, Colombia; (91) 612-16-20.

Episcopal Secretariat of Central America and Panama (Secretariado Episcopal de America Central y Panama, SEDAC): Statutes approved experimentally Sept. 26, 1970. Abp. José Francisco Ulloa, abp. of Panama, president. Address of secretary general: Calle 20 y Av Mexico 24-45, Apartado 6386, Panama 5, Panama; 262-7802.

INTERNATIONAL CATHOLIC ORGANIZATIONS

(Principal sources: Sr. Dorothy Farley, Executive Director, ICO Information Center; Pontifical Council for the Laity; Catholic Almanac survey.)

Guidelines

International organizations wanting to call themselves "Catholic" are required to meet standards set by the Vatican's Council for the Laity and to register with and get the approval of the Papal Secretariat of State, according to guidelines dated Dec. 3 and published in *Acta Apostolicae Sedis* under the date of Dec. 23, 1971.

Among conditions for the right of organizations to "bear the name Catholic" are:
• leaders "will always be Catholics," and candidates for office will be approved by the Secretariat of State
• adherence by the organization to the Catholic Church, its teaching authority and the teachings of the Gospel
• evidence that the organization is really international with a universal outlook and that it fulfills its mission through its own management, meetings and accomplishments.

The guidelines also stated that leaders of the organizations "will take care to maintain necessary reserve as regards taking a stand or engaging in public activity in the field of politics or trade unionism. Abstention in these fields will normally be the best attitude for them to adopt during their term of office."

The guidelines were in line with a provision stated by the Second Vatican Council: "No project may claim the name 'Catholic' unless it has obtained the consent of the lawful Church authority."

They made it clear that all organizations are not obliged to apply for recognition, but that the Church "reserves the right to recognize as linked with her mission and her aims those organizations or movements which see fit to ask for such recognition."

Conference of International Catholic Organizations

A permanent body for collaboration among various organizations the conference seeks to promote the development of international life along the lines of Christian principles. Eleven international Catholic organizations participated in its foundation and first meeting in 1927 at Fribourg, Switzerland. In 1951, the conference established its general secretariat and adopted governing statutes that were approved by the Vatican Secretariat of State in 1953.

The permanent secretariat is located at 3739 rue de Vermont, CH1202 Geneva, Switzerland. Other office addresses are: 1 rue Varembe, CH1211 Geneva 20, Switzerland (International Catholic Center of Geneva); 9, rue Cler, F75007 Paris, France (International Catholic Center for UNESCO); ICO Information Center, 323 East 47th St., New York, NY 10017.

Charter

According to its charter (adopted in November 1997), the conference "responds to the challenge of *Christifideles Laici*: Open to the saving power of Christ the frontiers of States, economic and political systems, the vast domains of culture, civilization and development (No. 34)."

In a universal vision of those problems, these organizations have the following responsibilities to their members:
• to make them increasingly aware of the compexities of the situations in which they live and work
• to help them to grow in discernment and critical analysis
• to facilitate the search for solutions to concrete difficulties.

The Conference is open to any organization which is acting and is involved recognizably Catholic in its work in the international world, which accepts the present Charter, respects its principles in practice and adheres to its Statutes. The Conference witnesses to the organized presence of Catholics in the international world.

Fundamental Convictions

• Their desire to announce Jesus Christ to the women and men of our time, and their vocation to serve the world, are indivisible; faith calls for action
• Their wish to contribute to the building of the Kingdom of God is demonstrated by solidarity with all women and men of good will
• Their desire for participation in decision-making in the Church in areas which concern their competence and in which they are involved.

A Unique Spirituality

In its desire to live fully its faith in Jesus Christ, the Conference stresses:
• The need to be rooted in reality, through a relationship with God lived out in the world
• An experience of community nourished by group sharing and exchange
• Openness to the international dimension, validated by experiences at the local level to which it gives meaning
• Adaptation to different human groups and to different sensibilities
• The witness of Christian freedom to initiate, as well as willingness to live in "solid and strong communion" with the Church
• Desire to serve the universal Church through insertion in the local Churches by respecting diverse pastoral programs, but also to participate in major events in the life of the universal Church.

Members

Members of the Conference of International Catholic Organizations are listed below. Information includes name, date and place of establishment (when available), address of general secretariat. Approximately 30 of the organizations have consultative status with other international or regional non-governmental agencies.

Caritas Internationalis (1951, Rome, Italy): Piazza San Calisto 16, I00153, Rome, Italy. Coordinates and represents its 146 national member organizations (in 194 countries) operating in the fields of development, emergency aid, social action.

Catholic International Education Office (1952): 60, rue des Eburons, B1000 Brussels, Belgium.

Catholic International Union for Social Service (1925, Milan, Italy): rue de la Poste 111, B1210 Brussels, Belgium (general secretariat).

Christian Life Community (CVX) (1953): Borgo Santo Spirito 8, C.P. 6139, I00195 Rome, Italy. First Sodality of Our Lady founded in 1563.

International Ascent, The: 84, rue Charles Michels, F93206 Saint Denis Cedex, France. Member of ICO.

International Association of Charities (1617, Chatillon les Dombes, France): Rue Joseph Brand, 118, B1030 Brussels, Belgium.

International Catholic Child Bureau (1948, in Paris): 63, rue de Lausanne, CH1202 Geneva, Switzerland.

International Catholic Committee of Nurses and MedicoSocial Assistants (ICCN) (1933): Square Vergote, 43, B1040 Brussels, Belgium.

International Catholic Conference of Scouting (1948): Piazza Pasquale Paoli, 18, I-00186 Rome, Italy.

International Catholic Migration Commission (1951): 3739 rue de Vermont, C.P. 96, CH1211 Geneva 20, Switzerland. Coordinates activities worldwide on behalf of refugees and migrants, both administering programs directly and supporting the efforts of national affiliated agencies.

International Catholic Organization for Cinema and Audiovisual (1928, The Hague, The Netherlands): Rue du Saphir, 15, B1040 Brussels, Belgium (general secretariat). Federation of National Catholic film offices.

International Catholic Society for Girls (1897): 3739, rue de Vermont, CH1202 Geneva, Switzerland.

International Catholic Union of the Press: 3739 rue de Vermont, Case Postale 197, CH1211 Geneva 20 CIC, Switzerland. Coordinates and represents at the international level the activities of Catholics and Catholic federations or associations in the field of press and information. Has seven specialized branches: International Federation of Catholic Journalists; International Federation of Dailies; International Federation of Periodicals; International Federation of Catholic News Agencies; International Catholic Federation of Teachers and Researchers in the Science and Techniques of Information; International Federation of Church Press Associations; and International Federation of Book Publishers.

International Conference of Catholic Guiding (1965): c/o Mlle Francoise Parmentier, rue de la Tour 64, 75016 Paris. Founded by member bodies of interdenominational World Association of Guides and Girl Scouts.

International Coordination of Young Christian Workers (YCYCW): via dei Barbieri 22, I-00186 Rome, Italy.

International Council of Catholic Men (ICCM) (Unum Omnes) (1948): Wahringer Str. 24, A.1090 Vienna IX, Austria.

International Federation of Catholic Medical Associations (1954): Palazzo San Calisto, I-00120 Vatican City.

International Federation of Catholic Parochial Youth Communities (1962, Rome, Italy): St. Kariliquai 12, 6000 Lucerne 5, Switzerland.

International Federation of Catholic Pharmacists (1954): Bosdorf 180, 9190 Stekene, Belgium.

International Federation of Rural Adult Catholic Movements (1964, Lisbon, Portugal): Rue Jaumain 15, B5330 Assesse, Belgium.

International Federation of Catholic Universities (1949): 21, rue d'Assas, F75270 Paris 06, France.

International Federation of the Catholic Associations of the Blind: Avenue Dailly 90, B1030 Brussels, Belgium. Coordinates actions of Catholic groups and associations for the blind and develops their apostolate.

International Independent Christian Youth (IICY): 11, rue Martin Bernard, 75013 Paris, France.

International Military Apostolate (1967): Breite Strasse 25, D53111 Bonn, Germany. Comprised of organizations of military men.

International Movement of Apostolate of Children (1929, France): 24, rue Paul Rivet, F92350 Le Plessis Robinson, France.

International Movement of Apostolate in the Independent Social Milieux (MIAMSI) (1963): Piazza San Calisto 16, 00153 Rome, Italy.

International Movement of Catholic Agricultural and Rural Youth (1954, Annevoie, Belgium): 53, rue J. Coosemans, B1030 Brussels, Belgium (permanent secretariat).

International Young Catholic Students (1946, Fribourg, Switzerland; present name, 1954): 171 rue de Rennes, F75006 Paris, France.

Pax Romana (1921, Fribourg, Switzerland, divided into two branches, 1947): **Pax Romana IMCS (International Movement of Catholic Students)** (1921): 171, rue de Rennes, F-75006, Paris, France, for undergraduates; **Pax Romana ICMICA (International Catholic Movement for Intellectual and Cultural Affairs)** (1947): rue du Grand Bureau 15, CH-1227 Geneva, Switzerland, for Catholic intellectuals and professionals.

Society of St. Vincent de Paul (1833, Paris): 5, rue du Pré-aux-Clercs, F-75007 Paris, France.

Unda: International Catholic Association for Radio and Television (1928, Cologne, Germany): rue de l'Orme, 12, B-1040 Brussels, Belgium.

World Movement of Christian Workers (1961): Blvd. du Jubilé 124, 1080 Brussels, Belgium.

World Organization of Former Pupils of Catholic Education (1967, Rome): 48, rue de Richelieu, F-75001 Paris, France.

World Union of Catholic Teachers (1951): Piazza San Calisto 16, 00153 Rome, Italy.

World Union of Catholic Women's Organizations (1910): 18, rue Notre Dame des Champs, F-75006 Paris, France.

Other Catholic Organizations

Apostleship of Prayer (1849): Borgo Santo Spirito 5, I-00193 Rome, Italy. National secretariat in most countries.

Apostolatus Maris (Apostleship of the Sea) (1922, Glasgow, Scotland): Pontifical Council for

Migrants and Itinerant People, Piazza San Calisto 16, 00153 Rome, Italy. (See **Index**.)

L'Arche Communities: B.P. 35, 60350 Cuise Lamotte, France.

Associationes Juventutis Salesianae (Associations of Salesian Youth) (1847): Via della Pisana, 1111, 00163 Rome, Italy.

Blue Army of Our Lady of Fatima: P.O. Box 976, Washington, NJ, 07882.

Catholic International Federation for Physical and Sports Education (1911; present name, 1957): 5, rue Cernuschi, 75017 Paris, France.

Christian Fraternity of the Sick and Handicapped: 9, Avenue de la Gare, CH1630, Bulle, Switzerland.

"Communione e Liberazione" Fraternity (1955, Milan, Italy): Via Marcello Malpighi 2, 00161 Rome, Italy. Catholic renewal movement.

"Focolare Movement" (Work of Mary) (1943, Trent, Italy): Via di Frascati, 306, I-00040 Rocca di Papa (Rome), Italy.

Foi et Lumiere: 8 rue Serret, 75015 Paris, France.

Franciscans International: 345 E. 47th St., New York, NY 10017. A nongovernmental organization at the UN.

Inter Cultural Association (ICA, 1937, Belgium) and **Association Fraternelle Internationale** (AFI): 91, rue de la Servette, CH-1202 Geneva, Switzerland.

International Association of Children of Mary (1847): 67 rue de Sèvres, F-75006 Paris, France.

International Catholic Rural Association (1962, Rome): Piazza San Calisto, 00153 Rome, Italy. International body for agricultural and rural organizations. Invited member of ICO.

International Catholic Union of Esperanto: Via Berni 9, 00185 Rome, Italy.

International Centre for Studies in Religious Education LUMEN VITAE (193435, Louvain, Belgium, under name Catechetical Documentary Centre; present name, 1956): 184, rue Washington, B1050 Brussels, Belgium. Also referred to as Lumen Vitae Centre; concerned with all aspects of religious formation.

International Young Christian Workers (1925, Belgium): 11, rue Plantin, B1070 Brussels, Belgium. Associate member of ICO.

Legion of Mary (1921, Dublin, Ireland): De Montfort House, North Brunswick St., Dublin, Ireland. (See **Index**.)

Medicus Mundi Internationalis (1964, Bensberg, Germany FR): P.O. Box 1547, 6501 BM Nijmegen, Netherlands. To promote health and medicosocial services, particularly in developing countries; recruit essential health and medical personnel for developing countries; contribute to training of medical and auxiliary personnel; undertake research in the field of health.

NOVALIS, Marriage Preparation Center: University of St. Paul, 1 rue Stewart, Ottawa 2, ON, Canada.

Our Lady's Teams (Equipes NotreDame) (1937, France): 49, rue de la Glacière, 75013 Paris, France. Movement for spiritual formation of couples.

Pax Christi International (1950): rue du Vieux Marché aux grains 21, B1000 Brussels, Belgium. International Catholic peace movement. Originated in Lourdes, France, in 1948 by French and German Catholics to reconcile enemies from World War II; spread to Italy and Poland and acquired its international title when it merged with the English organization Pax. Associate member of ICO.

Pro Sanctity Movement: Piazza S. Andrea della Valle 3, 00166 Rome, Italy.

St. Joan's International Alliance (1911, in England, as Catholic Women's Suffrage Society): Quai Churchill 19, Boite 061, B4020 Liège, Belgium. Associate member of ICO.

Salesian Cooperators (1876, Turin, Italy): **Salesian Cooperators**: Founded by St. John Bosco; for lay men and women and diocesan clergy. A public association of the faithful, members commit themselves to apostolates in the local Church, especially on behalf of the young, in the Salesian spirit and style. Address: 174 Filors Lane, Stony Point, NY 10980-2645; (845) 947-2200.

Secular Franciscan Order (1221, first Rule approved): Via Piemonte, 70, 00187, Rome, Italy.

Secular Fraternity of Charles de Foucauld: Katharinenweg 4, B-4700 Eupen, Belgium.

Serra International (1953, in U.S.): 65 E. Wacker Pl. Suite 1210, Chicago, IL 60601.

Unio Internationalis Laicorum in Servitio Ecclesiae (1965, Aachen, Germany): Postfach 990125, Am Kielshof 2, 5000 Cologne, Germany 91. Consists of national and diocesan associations of persons who give professional services to the Church.

Union of Adorers of the Blessed Sacrament (1937): Largo dei Monti Parioli 3, I-00197, Rome, Italy.

World Catholic Federation for the Biblical Apostolate (1969, Rome): Mittelstrasse, 12, P.O. Box 601, D-7000, Stuttgart 1, Germany.

Regional Organizations

European Federation for Catholic Adult Education (1963, Lucerne, Switzerland): Hirschengraben 13, P.B. 2069, CH-6002 Lucerne, Switzerland.

European Forum of National Committees of the Laity (1968): 169, Booterstown Av., Blackrock, Co. Dublin, Ireland.

Movimiento Familiar Cristiano (194950, Montevideo and Buenos Aires): Carrera 17 n. 4671, Bogotá, D.E., Colombia. Christian Family Movement of Latin America.

Eastern Catholic Churches

Sources: Fr. Ronald Roberson, C.S.P., Associate Director, Ecumenical and Interreligious Affairs, USCCB.; Annuario Pontificio; Official Catholic Directory.

The Second Vatican Council, in its Decree on Eastern Catholic Churches (*Orientalium Ecclesiarum*), stated the following points regarding Eastern heritage, patriarchs, sacraments and worship.

Venerable Churches: The Catholic Church holds in high esteem the institutions of the Eastern Churches, their liturgical rites, ecclesiastical traditions, and Christian way of life. For, distinguished as they are by their venerable antiquity, they are bright with that tradition which was handed down from the Apostles through the Fathers, and which forms part of the divinely revealed and undivided heritage of the universal Church (No. 1). That Church, Holy and Catholic, which is the Mystical Body of Christ, is made up of the faithful who are organically united in the Holy Spirit through the same faith, the same sacraments, and the same government and who, combining into various groups held together by a hierarchy, form separate Churches or rites. It is the mind of the Catholic Church that each individual Church or rite retain its traditions whole and entire, while adjusting its way of life to the various needs of time and place (No. 2).

Such individual Churches, whether of the East or of the West, although they differ somewhat among themselves in what are called rites (that is, in liturgy, ecclesiastical discipline, and spiritual heritage) are, nevertheless, equally entrusted to the pastoral guidance of the Roman Pontiff, the divinely appointed successor of St. Peter in supreme government over the universal Church. They are consequently of equal dignity, so that none of them is superior to the others by reason of rite (No. 3).

Eastern Heritage: Each and every Catholic, as also the baptized of every non-Catholic Church or community who enters into the fullness of Catholic communion, should everywhere retain his proper rite, cherish it, and observe it to the best of his ability (No. 4). The Churches of the East, as much as those of the West, fully enjoy the right, and are in duty bound, to rule themselves. Each should do so according to its proper and individual procedures (No. 5). All Eastern rite members should know and be convinced that they can and should always preserve their lawful liturgical rites and their established way of life, and that these should not be altered except by way of an appropriate and organic development (No. 6).

Patriarchs: The institution of the patriarchate has existed in the Church from the earliest times and was recognized by the first ecumenical Synods. By the name Eastern Patriarch is meant the bishop who has jurisdiction over all bishops (including metropolitans), clergy, and people of his own territory or rite, in accordance with the norms of law and without prejudice to the primacy of the Roman Pontiff (No. 7). Though some of the patriarchates of the Eastern Churches are of later origin than others, all are equal in patriarchal dignity. Still the honorary and lawfully established order of precedence among them is to be preserved (No. 8). In keeping with the most ancient tradition of the Church, the Patriarchs of the Eastern Churches are to be accorded exceptional respect, since each presides over his patriarchate as father and head.

This sacred Synod, therefore, decrees that their rights and privileges should be re-established in accord with the ancient traditions of each Church and the decrees of the ecumenical Synods. The rights and privileges in question are those which flourished when East and West were in union, though they should be somewhat adapted to modern conditions.

The Patriarchs with their synods constitute the superior authority for all affairs of the patriarchate, including the right to establish new eparchies and to nominate bishops of their rite within the territorial bounds of the patriarchate, without prejudice to the inalienable right of the Roman Pontiff to intervene in individual cases (No. 9).

What has been said of Patriarchs applies as well, under the norm of law, to major archbishops, who preside over the whole of some individual Church or rite (No. 10).

Sacraments: This sacred Ecumenical Synod endorses and lauds the ancient discipline of the sacraments existing in the Eastern Churches, as also the practices connected with their celebration and administration (No. 12).

With respect to the minister of holy chrism (confirmation), let that practice be fully restored which existed among Easterners in most ancient times. Priests, therefore, can validly confer this sacrament, provided they use chrism blessed by a Patriarch or bishop (No. 13).

In conjunction with baptism or otherwise, all Eastern-Rite priests can confer this sacrament validly on all the faithful of any rite, including the Latin; licitly, however, only if the regulations of both common and particular law are observed. Priests of the Latin rite, to the extent of the faculties they enjoy for administering this sacrament, can confer it also on the faithful of Eastern Churches, without prejudice to rite. They do so licitly if the regulations of both common and particular law are observed (No. 14).

The faithful are bound on Sundays and feast days to attend the divine liturgy or, according to the regulations or custom of their own rite, the celebration of the Divine Praises. That the faithful may be able to satisfy their obligation more easily, it is decreed that this obligation can be fulfilled from the Vespers of the vigil to the end of the Sunday or the feast day (No. 15). Because of the everyday intermingling of the communicants of diverse Eastern Churches in the same Eastern region or territory, the faculty for hearing confession, duly and unrestrictedly granted by his proper bishop to a priest of any rite, is applicable to the entire territory of the grantor, also to the places and the faithful belonging to any other rite in the same territory, unless an Ordinary of the place explicitly decides otherwise with respect to the places pertaining to his rite (No. 16).

This sacred Synod ardently desires that where it has fallen into disuse the office of the permanent diaconate be restored. The legislative authority of each individual church should decide about the subdiaconate and the minor orders (No. 17).

By way of preventing invalid marriages between Eastern Catholics and baptized Eastern non-Catholics, and in the interests of the permanence and sanctity of marriage and of domestic harmony, this sacred Synod decrees that the canonical 'form' for the celebration of such marriages obliges only for lawfulness. For their validity, the presence of a sacred minister suffices, as long as the other requirements of law are honored (No. 18).

Worship: Henceforth, it will be the exclusive right of an ecumenical Synod or the Apostolic See to establish, transfer, or suppress feast days common to all the Eastern Churches. To establish, transfer, or suppress feast days for any of the individual Churches is within the competence not only of the Apostolic See but also of a patriarchal or archiepiscopal synod, provided due consideration is given to the entire region and to other individual Churches (No. 19). Until such time as all Christians desirably concur on a fixed day for the celebration of Easter, and with a view meantime to promoting unity among the Christians of a given area or nation, it is left to the Patriarchs or supreme authorities of a place to reach a unanimous agreement, after ascertaining the views of all concerned, on a single Sunday for the observance of Easter (No. 20). With respect to rules concerning sacred seasons, individual faithful dwelling outside the area or territory of their own rite may conform completely to the established custom of the place where they live. When members of a family belong to different rites, they are all permitted to observe sacred seasons according to the rules of any one of these rites (No. 21). From ancient times the Divine Praises have been held in high esteem among all Eastern Churches. Eastern clerics and religious should celebrate these Praises as the laws and customs of their own traditions require. To the extent they can, the faithful too should follow the example of their forebears by assisting devoutly at the Divine Praises (No. 22).

Restoration of Ancient Practices

An "Instruction for the Application of the Liturgical Prescriptions of the Code of Canons of the Eastern Churches" was published by the Congregation for the Oriental Churches in January, 1996. It has been published in several languages. Msgr. Alan Detscher, then executive director of the U.S. bishops' Secretariat for the Liturgy, said it was the first instruction on liturgical renewal of the Eastern Catholic Churches since the Second Vatican Council (1962-65).

JURISDICTIONS AND FAITHFUL OF THE EASTERN CATHOLIC CHURCHES

Introduction

The Church originated in Palestine, whence it spread to other regions of the world where certain places became key centers of Christian life with great influence on the local churches in their respective areas. These centers developed into the ancient patriarchates of Constantinople, Alexandria, Antioch and Jerusalem in the East, and Rome in the West. The main lines of Eastern Church patriarchal organization and usages were drawn before the Roman Empire became two empires, East (Byzantine) and West (Roman), in 292. Other churches with distinctive traditions grew up beyond the boundaries of the Roman Empire in Persia, Armenia, Syria, Egypt, Ethiopia, and India. The "nestorian" church in Persia, known today as the Assyrian Church of the East, broke communion with the rest of the church in the wake of the Council of Ephesus (431) whose teachings it did not accept. The "monophysite" churches of Armenia, Syria, Egypt, Ethiopia, Eritrea and India (known today as the Oriental Orthodox Churches) did not accept the christological teachings of the Council of Chalcedon (451) and so broke away from the church within the Roman Empire. And finally, in the wake of the mutual excommunications of 1054 between the Patriarch of Constantinople and the papal legate, the church within the empire divided into what would become the Catholic Church in the West and the Orthodox Church in the East. This was a lengthy process of estrangement that culminated only in 1204 and the sack of Constantinople by the Latin Crusaders.

In the following centuries, attempts to overcome these divisions took place, most notably at the Second Council of Lyons in 1274 and the Council of Ferrara-Florence in 1438-39. Both failed. Subsequently, the Catholic Church began to send missionaries to work with separated Eastern Christians, and some groups within those churches spontaneously asked to enter into full communion with Rome. Thus began the formation of the Eastern Catholic Churches, which retained most of the liturgical, canonical, spiritual and theological patrimony of their non-Catholic counterparts.

The Code of Canons of the Eastern Churches groups these churches today into four categories: patriarchal, major archepiscopal, metropolitan, and other churches *sui iuris*. In common usage, an eparchy is equivalent to a diocese in the Latin rite.

STATISTICS

Principal source: 2013 Annuario Pontificio.

The following statistics are the sum of those reported for Eastern Catholic jurisdictions only, and do not include Eastern Catholics under the jurisdiction of Latin bishops. Some of the figures reported are only approximate. The churches are grouped according to their liturgical traditions.

PATRIARCHS

The current Patriarchs of the Eastern Catholic Churches (as of July 15, 2013) are as follows:

Sidrak, Ibrahim Isaac: b. Aug. 19, 1955; ord. Feb. 7, 1980; cons. bp. Nov. 15, 2002; Patriarch of Alexandria of the Copts, Jan. 15, 2013; granted "ecclesiastical communion" with Pope Benedict XVI, Jan. 18, 2013.

Sako, Louis Raphael I: b. July 4, 1948; ord. June 1, 1974; cons. bp. Nov. 14, 2003; Patriarch of Babylon of the Chaldeans, Jan. 31, 2013; granted "ecclesiastical communion" with Pope Benedict XVI, Feb. 1, 2013.

Laham, Gregory III: b. Dec. 15, 1933; ord. Feb. 15, 1959; cons. bp. Nov. 27, 1981; patriarch of Greek Melkites, Nov. 29, 2000; granted "ecclesiastical communion" with Pope John Paul II, Dec. 5, 2000.

Bechara Rai: b. Feb. 25, 1940; ord. Sept. 3, 1967; cons. bp. July 12, 1986; patriarch of Antioch, for the Maronites, Mar. 15, 2011; granted "ecclesiastical communion" with Pope Benedict XVI, Mar. 24, 2011.

Tarmouni, Nerses XIX Bedros: b. Jan. 17, 1940, in Cairo, Egypt; ord. Aug. 15, 1965; cons. bp. Feb. 18, 1990; patriarch of Cilicia of the Armenians, Oct. 7, 1999; granted "ecclesiastical communion" with the Pope John Paul II, Oct. 13, 1999.

Younan, Joseph: b. Nov. 11, 1944; ord. Sept. 12, 1971; cons. bp. Jan. 7, 1996; patriarch of Antioch of the Syrians, Jan. 20, 2009; granted "ecclesiastical communion" with Pope Benedict XVI, Jan. 23, 2009.

ALEXANDRIAN

The liturgical tradition of Egypt, in particular that of the early Patriarchate of Alexandria. In the Egyptian desert monasteries the rite evolved in a distinctive way and eventually became that of the Coptic Orthodox Church. The Greek Patriarchate of Alexandria adopted the Byzantine rite by the 12th century. The Coptic rite, with its Alexandrian origins, spread to Ethiopia in the fourth century where it underwent substantial modifications under strong Syrian influence. The Catholic Churches in this group are:

The Coptic Catholic Church (Patriarchate): Seven eparchies in Egypt; 165,923. Catholic missionaries were present since the 17th century. The Patriarchate was established first in 1824 and renewed in 1895. Liturgical languages are Coptic and Arabic.

The Ethiopian Catholic Church (Metropolitanate): Three eparchies in Ethiopia and three in Eritrea; 227,078. Catholic missionary activity began in the 19th century, and the present ecclesiastical structure dates from 1961. The liturgical languages are Ge'ez and Amharic.

ANTIOCHIAN

The liturgical tradition of Antioch, one of the great centers of the early Christian world, also known as West Syrian. In Syria it developed under strong influence of Jerusalem, especially the Liturgy of St. James, into the form used by today's Syrian Orthodox and Catholics in the Middle East and India. The Maronites of Lebanon developed their own variation of the West Syrian rite which later came under Latin influence.

The Catholic Churches of this group are:

The Syro-Malankara Catholic Church (Major Archbishopric): Eight eparchies in India and one Apostolic Exarchate in the United States; 438,387. Began in 1930 when two bishops, a priest, a deacon and a layman of the Malankara Orthodox Church were received into full communion with Rome. Raised to Major Archepiscopal status in 2005. The liturgical language is Malayalam.

The Maronite Catholic Church (Patriarchate): Ten eparchies in Lebanon, three in Syria, two in the United States, and one each in Cyprus, Egypt, Argentina, Brazil, Australia, the Holy Land, Canada, and Mexico, plus patriarchal exarchates in Jordan and Jerusalem; 3,381,733.

Founded by followers of St. Maron in the fourth century, the Maronites claim to have always been in communion with Rome. They have no counterpart among the separated Eastern churches. The patriarchate dates to the eighth century, and was confirmed by Pope Innocent III in 1216. Liturgical language is Arabic.

The Syrian Catholic Church (Patriarchate): Four eparchies in Syria, two in Iraq, and one each in Lebanon, Egypt, and North America, and patriarchal exarchates in Turkey, Venezuela, and Iraq/Kuwait; 266,461.

Catholic missionary activity among the Syrian Orthodox began in the 17th century, and there has been an uninterrupted series of Catholic patriarchs since 1783. The liturgical languages are Syriac/Aramaic and Arabic.

ARMENIAN

The liturgical tradition of the Armenian Apostolic and Armenian Catholic Churches. It contains elements of the Syriac, Jerusalem, and Byzantine rites. From the fifth to the seventh centuries there was strong influence from Syria and Jerusalem. More Byzantine usages were adopted later, and in the Middle Ages elements of the Latin tradition were added.

Three eparchies in Syria, one each in Lebanon, Iran, Iraq, Egypt, Turkey, Ukraine, France, Argentina and the United States/Canada, and Ordinariates in Greece, Romania, and Eastern Europe (Armenia); 566,015.

Catholic missionaries had been working among the Armenians since the 14th century, and an Armenian Catholic patriarchate was established in Lebanon in 1742. The liturgical language is classical Armenian. His Beatitude Nerses Bedros XIX Tarmouni, canonically elected as patriarch of Cilicia of the Armenians, by the Synod of Bishops of the Armenian Catholic Church was approved by Pope John Paul II on Oct. 18, 1999.

BYZANTINE

The tradition of the Eastern Orthodox and Byzantine Catholic Churches which originated in the Orthodox Patriarchate of Constantinople (Byzantium). Its present form is a synthesis of Constantinopolitan and Palestinian elements that took place in the monasteries between the ninth and 14th centuries. It is by far the most widely used Eastern liturgical tradition. The Catholic Churches of this group are:

Belarusans (formerly Byelorussian, also known as White Russian): No hierarchy, Apostolic Visitator. Most Belarusan Orthodox became Catholic with the Union of Brest in 1595-6, but this union was short lived. A modest revival has taken place since the end of communism. The liturgical language is Belarusan.

The Bulgarian Catholic Church: One apostolic exarchate in Bulgaria; 10,000. Originated with a group of Bulgarian Orthodox who became Catholic in 1861; liturgical language is Old Slavonic.

Greek Catholics in Former Yugoslavia: One eparchy (Krizevci) located in Zagreb with jurisdiction over Slovenia, Croatia, and Bosnia-Herzegovina; Apostolic Exarchates in Serbia-Montenegro and in Macedonia; 58,337. A bishop for former Serbian Orthodox living in Catholic Croatia was first appointed in 1611; liturgical languages are Old Slavonic and Croatian.

The Greek Catholic Church: Apostolic exarchates in Greece and Turkey; 6,025. Catholic missionaries in Constantinople formed a small group of Byzantine Catholics there in the mid-19th century. Most of them moved to Greece in the 1920s. The liturgical language is Greek.

The Hungarian Catholic Church: One eparchy and one apostolic exarchate in Hungary; 327,200.

Descendants of groups of Orthodox in Hungary who became Catholic in the 17th century and after. The liturgical language is Hungarian.

The Italo-Albanian Catholic Church: Two eparchies, one territorial abbey in Italy; 61, 814

Descended mostly from Albanian Orthodox who came to southern Italy and Sicily in the 15th century and eventually became Catholic; liturgical languages are Greek and Italian.

The Melkite Greek Catholic Church (Patriarchate): Five eparchies in Syria, seven in Lebanon, one each in Jordan, Israel, Brazil, U.S., Canada, Mexico, and Australia. Apostolic Exarchates in Venezuela and Argentina, and patriarchal exarchates in Iraq and Kuwait; 1,651,500.

Catholic missionaries began work within the Greek Orthodox Patriarchate of Antioch in the mid-17th century. In 1724 it split into Catholic and Orthodox counterparts, the Catholics becoming known popularly as Melkites. Liturgical languages are Greek and Arabic.

The Romanian Greek Catholic Church (Major Archbishopric): Five eparchies in Romania and one in the US and Canada; 535,171.

Romanian Orthodox in Transylvania formally entered into union with Rome in 1700; the liturgical language is Romanian. In December 2005, the Romanian Greek Catholic Church was raised to the rank of Major Archbishopric.

Russians: An apostolic exarchate was established for Russia in 1917 and for Russians in China in 1928, but neither is functioning today. There are now at least eight parishes in Russia and 13 in the diaspora. In 2004 Pope John Paul II appointed Bishop Joseph Werth of the Diocese of the Transfiguration in Novosibirsk as Ordinary Bishop for Catholics of the Byzantine rite throughout Russia, but no other ecclesial structures were established.

The Ruthenian Catholic Church (Metropolitanate in the United States): One eparchy in Ukraine, one Archeparchy and three eparchies in the United States, and an apostolic exarchate in the Czech Republic. Originated with the reception of 63 Orthodox priests into the Catholic Church at the Union of Uzhhorod in 1646. Liturgical languages are Old Slavonic and English; 486,627.

The Slovak Catholic Church (Metropolitanate): Three eparchies in Slovakia, and one eparchy in Canada; 233,386.

Also originated with the Union of Uzhhorod in 1646; eparchy of Presov was established for them in 1818. Liturgical languages are Old Slavonic and Slovak. Organized as a Metropolitan church on January 30, 2008.

The Ukrainian Greek Catholic Church (Major Archbishopric): Nine eparchies and three archepiscopal exarchates in Ukraine, two eparchies in Poland, five eparchies in Canada, four in the United States, one each in France, Great Britain, Australia, Brazil and Argentina, apostolic exarchate in Germany; 4,345,599.

Originated with the Union of Brest between the Orthodox Metropolitanate of Kiev and the Catholic Church in 1595-6. Liturgical languages are Old Slavonic and Ukrainian.

CHALDEAN

Also called East Syrian, the liturgical tradition of the Chaldean Catholic and Syro-Malabar Catholic Churches as well as the Assyrian Church of the East. Descends from the ancient rite of the church of Mesopotamia in the Persian Empire. It is celebrated in the eastern dialect of classical Syriac. The Catholic Churches of this tradition are:

The Chaldean Catholic Church (Patriarchate): Ten eparchies in Iraq, three in Iran, two in the U.S., one each in Lebanon, Egypt, Syria, and Turkey; 536,525.

A group of disaffected members of the ("Nestorian") Assyrian Church of the East asked for union with Rome in 1553. In that year Pope Julius III ordained their leader a bishop and named him Patriarch; liturgical languages are Syriac, Arabic.

The Syro-Malabar Catholic Church (Major Archbishopric): 28 eparchies in India, one in the U.S.; 3,893,334.

Descended from Thomas Christians of India who became Catholic in the wake of Portuguese colonization; the diocese of Ernakulam-Angamaly was raised to Major Archepiscopal status in 1993; the liturgical language is Malayalam.

EASTERN JURISDICTIONS

For centuries Eastern Churches were identifiable with a limited number of nationality and language groups in certain countries of the Middle East, Eastern Europe, Asia and Africa. The persecution of religion in the former Soviet Union since 1917 and in communist-controlled countries for more than 40 years following World War II — in addition to decimating and destroying the Church in those places — resulted in the emigration of many Eastern Catholics from their homelands. This forced emigration, together with voluntary emigration, has led to the spread of Eastern Churches to many other countries.

Europe

Bp. Krikor Ghabroyan, of the Armenian Eparchy of Sainte-Croix-de-Paris, France, is apostolic visitor for Armenian Catholics in Western Europe who do not have their own bishop. Bp. Youssef Ibrahim Sarraf of Cairo of the Chaldeans is apostolic visitor for Chaldeans in Europe. Bp. Samis Mazloum is apostolic visitor for Maronites in Western and Northern Europe. Archimandrite Jan Sergiusz Gajek is Apostolic Visitator for Greek Catholics in Belarus.

Austria: Byzantine ordinariate.

Bulgaria: Bulgarian apostolic exarchate.

Croatia: Eparchy of Krizevci.

Czech Republic: Ruthenian apostolic exarchate.

France: Ukrainian eparchy (2013). Armenian eparchy (1986). Maronite eparchy (2012). Ordinariate for all other Eastern Catholics.

Germany: Ukrainian apostolic exarchate.

Great Britain: Ukrainian eparchy (2013).

Greece: Byzantine apostolic exarchate. Armenian ordinariate.

Hungary: Hungarian Byzantine eparchy, apostolic exarchate.

Italy: Two Italo-Albanian eparchies, one abbacy.
Macedonia: One apostolic exarchate.
Poland: Ukrainian metropolitan see (1996), one eparchy. Ordinariate for all other Eastern Catholics.
Romania: Romanian Byzantine major archbishopric, four eparchies; Armenian ordinariate.
Russia: Russian apostolic exarchate (for Byzantine Catholics).
Serbia and Montenegro: One apostolic exarchate.
Slovakia: Slovak Byzantine metropolitan see, two eparchies.
Ukraine: Armenian archeparchy; Ruthenian eparchy; Ukrainian major archbishopric, eight eparchies, two archepiscopal exarchates.

Asia
Armenia: Armenian ordinariate (for Armenians of Eastern Europe).
China: Russian Byzantine apostolic exarchate.
Cyprus: Maronite archeparchy.
India: Syro-Malankara metropolitan see, five eparchies. Syro-Malabar major archbishopric (1993), four metropolitan sees, 24 eparchies.
Iran: Two Chaldean metropolitan sees, one archeparchy, one eparchy; Armenian eparchy.
Iraq: Two Syrian archeparchies; Melkite patriarchal exarchate; Chaldean patriarchate, two metropolitan sees, three archeparchies and five eparchies; Armenian archeparchy.
Israel (including Jerusalem): Syrian patriarchal exarchate; Maronite archeparchy; Melkite archeparchy, patriarchal exarchate; Chaldean patriarchal exarchate; Armenian patriarchal exarchate.
Jordan: Melkite archeparchy.
Kuwait: Melkite patriarchal exarchate; Syrian patriarchal exarchate.
Syria: Two Maronite archeparchies, one eparchy; two Syrian metropolitan and two archeparchal sees; Melkite patriarchate, four metropolitan sees, one archeparchy; Chaldean eparchy; Armenian archeparchy, one eparchy .
Turkey: Syrian patriarchal exarchate; Greek apostolic exarchate; Chaldean archeparchy; Armenian archeparchy.

Oceania
Australia: Ukrainian eparchy; Melkite eparchy (1987); Maronite eparchy.

Africa
Egypt: Coptic patriarchate, six eparchies; Maronite eparchy; Syrian eparchy; Melkite patriarchal dependency; Chaldean eparchy; Armenian eparchy.
Eritrea: Three Ethiopian eparchies.
Ethiopia: Ethiopian metropolitan see, two eparchies.
Sudan: Melkite patriarchal dependency.

North America
Canada: One Ukrainian metropolitan, four eparchies; Slovak eparchy; Melkite eparchy; Armenian eparchy for Canada and the U.S. (New York is see city); Maronite eparchy.
United States: Two Maronite eparchies; Syrian eparchy (1995); one Ukrainian metropolitan see,

three eparchies; one Ruthenian metropolitan see, three eparchies; Melkite eparchy; Romanian eparchy; Syro-Malabar eparchy based in Chicago; Belarusan apostolic visitator; Armenian eparchy for Canada and U.S. (New York is see city); two Chaldean eparchies; other Eastern Catholics are under the jurisdiction of local Latin bishops. See **Eastern Catholics in the United States.**)
Mexico: Melkite eparchy; Maronite eparchy (1995).

South America
Armenian Catholics in Latin America (including Mexico and excluding Argentina) are under the jurisdiction of an apostolic exarchate.
Argentina: Ukrainian eparchy; Maronite eparchy; Armenian eparchy; Melkite apostolic exarchate; ordinariate for all other Eastern Catholics.
Brazil: Maronite eparchy; Melkite eparchy; Ukrainian eparchy; ordinariate for all other Eastern Catholics.
Venezuela: Melkite apostolic exarchate.

Synods, Assemblies
These assemblies are collegial bodies that have pastoral authority over members of the Eastern Catholic Churches. (Canons 102-113, 152-153, 322 of Oriental Code of Canon Law.)
Patriarchal Synods:
Synod of the Coptic Catholic Church: Antonios Naguib, patriarch of Alexandria of the Copts.
Synod of the Greek-Melkite Catholic Church: Gregory III Laham, patriarch of Antioch of the Greek Catholics-Melkites.
Synod of the Syrian Catholic Church: Joseph Younan, patriarch of Antioch of the Syrians.
Synod of the Maronite Church: Bechara Rai, patriarch of Antioch of the Maronites.
Synod of the Chaldean Church: Louis Raphael Sako, patriarch of Babylonia of the Chaldeans.
Synod of the Armenian Catholic Church: Nerses Bedros XIX Tarmouni, patriarch of Cilicia of the Armenians.

Major Archiepiscopal Synods:
The Synod of the Ukrainian Greek Catholic Church (raised to major archiepiscopal status Dec. 23, 1963): Sviatoslav Schevchuk, major archbishop of Kiev and Halych, president.
The Synod of the Syro-Malabar Catholic Church (raised to major archiepiscopal status, Jan. 29, 1993): Card. Mar George Alencherry, major archbishop of Ernakulam-Angamaly of the Syro-Malabars, president.
The Synod of the Syro-Malankara Catholic Church (raised to major archiepiscopal status Feb. 10, 2005): Card. Isaac Mar Cleemis Thottunkal of Trivandrum of the Syro-Malankarese, president.
The Synod of the Romanian Greek Catholic Church (raised to major archiepiscopal status December 16, 2005): Card. Lucian Muresan of Fagaras and Alba Julia, president.

Councils, Assemblies, Conferences
Council of Ethiopian Churches: Most Rev. Berhane-Yesus Demerew Souraphiel, C.M., Archbishop of Addis Ababa, president.

Council of Ruthenian Churches, U.S.A.: Abp. William C. Skurla, Metropolitan of Pittsburgh of the Byzantines, president.

Assembly of the Catholic Hierarchy of Egypt (Dec. 5, 1983): His Beatitude Ibrahim Isaac Sidrak, Patriarch of Alexandria of the Copts, president.

Assembly of Catholic Patriarchs and Bishops of Lebanon: His Beatitude Bechara Rai, patriarch of Antioch of the Maronites, president.

Assembly of Ordinaries of the Syrian Arab Republic: His Beatitude Gregory III Laham, patriarch of Antioch of the Greek Melkites, president.

Assembly of Catholic Ordinaries of the Holy Land (Jan. 27, 1992): His Beatitude Fouad Twal, patriarch of Jerusalem of the Latins, president.

Interritual Union of the Bishops of Iraq: His Beatitude Louis Raphael Sako, patriarch of Babylonia of the Chaldeans, president.

Iranian Episcopal Conference (Aug. 11, 1977): Most Rev. Ignatius Bedini, SDB, Archbishop of Ispahan of the Latins, president.

Episcopal Conference of Turkey (Nov. 30, 1987): Most Rev. Ruggero Franceschini, O.F.M.Cap., Archbishop of Izmir, president.

EASTERN CATHOLIC CHURCHES IN THE U.S.

Statistics, from the 2013 Annuario Pontificio unless noted otherwise, are membership figures reported by Eastern jurisdictions. Additional Eastern Catholics are included in statistics for Latin dioceses.

Byzantine Tradition

Ukrainians: There were 50,247 reported in four jurisdictions in the U.S.: the metropolitan see of Philadelphia (1924, metropolitan 1958) and the suffragan sees of Stamford, CN (1956), St. Nicholas of Chicago (1961) and St. Josaphat in Parma (1983).

Ruthenians: There were 84,227 reported in four jurisdictions in the U.S.: the metropolitan see of Pittsburgh (est. 1924 at Pittsburgh; metropolitan and transferred to Munhall, 1969; transferred to Pittsburgh, 1977) and the suffragan sees of Passaic, NJ (1963), Parma, OH (1969) and Holy Mary of Protection in Phoenix, AZ (est. 1981 at Van Nuys, transferred to Phoenix, 2009). Hungarian and Croatian Byzantine Catholics in the U.S. are also under the jurisdiction of Ruthenian bishops.

Melkites: There were 24,000 reported under the jurisdiction of the Melkite eparchy of Newton, MA (established as an exarchate, 1965; eparchy, 1976).

Romanians: There were 6,240 reported in 14 Romanian Catholic Byzantine Rite parishes in the U.S., under the jurisdiction of the Romanian eparchy of St. George Martyr, Canton, OH (established as an exarchate, 1982; eparchy, 1987).

Russians: In the United States, there are parishes in New York City (St. Michael) and in El Segundo in the Los Angeles area (St. Andrew). They are under the jurisdiction of local Latin bishops.

Alexandrian Tradition

Copts: Have a Catholic Chapel—Resurrection, in Brooklyn, NY, and St. Mary's Coptic Catholic parish, Los Angeles, CA.

Antiochian Tradition

Maronites: There were 85,100 reported in two jurisdictions in the U.S.: the eparchy of St. Maron, Brooklyn (established at Detroit as an exarchate, 1966; eparchy, 1972; transferred to Brooklyn, 1977) and the eparchy of Our Lady of Lebanon of Los Angeles (resident in St. Louis, MO, established Mar. 1, 1994).

Syrians: The eparchy of Our Lady of the Deliverance of Newark with 22,000 faithful was established in 1995 for Syrian Catholics of the U.S. and Canada.

Syro-Malankarese: A new Apostolic Exarchate was established for the 10,100 Syro-Malankara faithful in the United States in 2010. It has twelve parishes served by twelve priests. The headquarters is in New Hyde Park, New York.

Armenian Tradition

An apostolic exarchate for Canada and the United States was established July 3, 1981; raised to status of eparchy on Sept. 12, 2005; 36,000 in the two countries.

Chaldean Tradition

Chaldeans: There were 169,800 reported under the jurisdictions of the eparchy of St. Thomas the Apostle of Detroit (established as an exarchate, 1982; eparchy, 1986) and the eparchy of St. Peter the Apostle of San Diego (established on May 21, 2002).

Syro-Malabarese (Malabar): The eparchy of Saint Thomas the Apostle in Chicago (established Feb. 16, 2001) has eight parishes around the country. Estimated 100,700 faithful with 39 diocesan priests.

Eastern Catholic Associates

Eastern Catholic Associates is the association of all Eastern Catholic bishops and their equivalents in law in the United States, representing the Armenian, Chaldean, Maronite, Melkite, Syriac, Romanian, Ruthenian, Syro-Malabar and Ukrainian churches. President: Abp. William C. Skurla, Metropolitan Archbishop of Pittsburgh of the Byzantines. Vice President: Most Rev. John Kudrick, Bishop of Parma of the Byzantines.

The association meets at the same time as the United States Conference of Catholic Bishops in the fall of each year.

BYZANTINE DIVINE LITURGY

The Divine Liturgy in all rites is based on the consecration of bread and wine by the narration-reactualization of the actions of Christ at the Last Supper, and the calling down of the Holy Spirit. Aside from this fundamental usage, there are differences between the Roman (Latin) Rite and Eastern Rites, and among the Eastern Rites themselves. Following is a general description of the Byzantine Divine Liturgy which is in widest use in the Eastern Churches.

In the Byzantine, as in all Eastern Rites, the bread and wine are prepared at the start of the Liturgy. The priest does this in a little niche or at a table in the sanctuary. Taking a round loaf of leavened bread stamped with religious symbols, he cuts out a square host and other particles while reciting verses expressing the symbolism of the action. When the bread and wine are ready, he says a prayer of offering and incenses the oblations, the altar, the icons and the people.

Liturgy of the Catechumens: At the altar a litany for all classes of people is sung by the priest. The congregation answers, "Lord, have mercy." The Little Entrance comes next. In procession, the priest leaves the sanctuary carrying the Book of the Gospels, and then returns. He sings prayers especially selected for the day and the feast. These are followed by the solemn singing of the prayer, "Holy God, Holy Mighty One, Holy Immortal One." The Epistle follows. The Gospel is sung or read by the priest facing the people at the middle door of the sanctuary.

An interruption after the Liturgy of the Catechumens, formerly an instructional period for those learning the faith, is clearly marked. Catechumens, if present, are dismissed with a prayer. Following this are a prayer and litany for the faithful.

Great Entrance: The Great Entrance or solemn Offertory Procession then takes place. The priest first says a long silent prayer for himself, in preparation for the great act to come. Again he incenses the oblations, the altar, the icons and people. He goes to the table on the Gospel side for the veil-covered paten and chalice. When he arrives back at the sanctuary door, he announces the intention of the Mass in the prayer: "May the Lord God remember all of you in his kingdom, now and forever." After another litany, the congregation recites the Nicene Creed.

Consecration: The most solemn portion of the sacrifice is introduced by the preface, which is very much like the preface of the Roman Rite. At the beginning of the last phrase, the priest raises his voice to introduce the singing of the Sanctus. During the singing he reads the introduction to the words of consecration. The words of consecration are sung aloud, and the people sing "Amen" to both consecrations. As the priest raises the Sacred Species in solemn offering, he sings: "Thine of Thine Own we offer unto Thee in behalf of all and for all." A prayer to the Holy Spirit is followed by the commemorations, in which special mention is made of the all-holy, most blessed and glorious Lady, the Mother of God and ever-Virgin Mary. The dead are remembered and then the living.

Holy Communion: A final litany for spiritual gifts precedes the Our Father. The Sacred Body and Blood are elevated with the words, "Holy Things for the Holy." The Host is then broken and commingled with the Precious Blood. The priest recites preparatory prayers for Holy Communion, consumes the Sacred Species, and distributes Holy Communion to the people under the forms of both bread and wine. During this time the choir or congregation sings a communion verse.

The Liturgy closes quickly after this. The consecrated Species of bread and wine are removed to the side table to be consumed later by the priest. A prayer of thanksgiving is recited, a prayer for all the people is said in front of the icon of Christ, a blessing is invoked upon all, and the people are dismissed.

BYZANTINE CALENDAR

The Byzantine calendar has many distinctive features of its own, although it shares common elements with the Roman calendar — e.g., general purpose, commemoration of the mysteries of faith and of the saints, identical dates for some feasts. Among the distinctive things are the following. The liturgical year begins on Sept. 1, the Day of Indiction, in contrast with the Latin or Roman start on the First Sunday of Advent late in November or early in December. The Advent season begins on Dec. 10.

Cycles of the Year

As in the Roman usage, the dating of feasts follows the Gregorian Calendar. Formerly, until well into this century, the Julian Calendar was used. (The Julian Calendar, which is now about 13 days late, is still used by some Eastern Churches.) The year has several cycles, which include proper seasons, the feasts of saints, and series of New Testament readings. All of these elements of worship are contained in liturgical books of the rite. The ecclesiastical calendar, called the *Menologion*, explains the nature of feasts, other observances and matters pertaining to the liturgy for each day of the year. In some cases, its contents include the lives of saints and the history and meaning of feasts.

The Divine Liturgy (Mass) and Divine Office for the proper of the saints, fixed feasts, and the Christmas season are contained in the Menaion. The *Triodion* covers the pre-Lenten season of preparation for Easter; Lent begins two days before the Ash Wednesday observance of the Roman Rite. The *Pentecostarion* contains the liturgical services from Easter to the Sunday of All Saints, the first after Pentecost. The *Evangelion* and *Apostolos* are books in which the Gospels, and Acts of the Apostles and the Epistles, respectively, are arranged according to the order of their reading in the Divine Liturgy and Divine Office throughout the year.

The cyclic progression of liturgical music throughout the year, in successive and repetitive periods of eight weeks, is governed by the *Oktoechos*, the *Book of Eight Tones*.

Sunday Names

Many Sundays are named after the subject of the Gospel read in the Mass of the day or after the name of a feast falling on the day — e.g., Sunday of the Publican and Pharisee, of the Prodigal Son, of the Samaritan Woman, of St. Thomas the Apostle, of the Fore-Fathers (Old Testament Patriarchs).

Other Sundays are named in the same manner as in the Roman calendar e.g., numbered Sundays of Lent and after Pentecost.

Holy Days

The calendar lists about 28 holy days. Many of the major holy days coincide with those of the Roman calendar, but the feast of the Immaculate Conception is observed on Dec. 9 instead of Dec. 8, and the feast of All Saints falls on the Sunday after Pentecost rather than on Nov. 1. Instead of a single All Souls' Day, there are five All Souls' Saturdays. According to regulations in effect in the Byzantine

(Ruthenian) Archeparchy of Pittsburgh and its suffragan sees of Passaic, Parma and Van Nuys, holy days are obligatory, solemn and simple, and attendance at the Divine Liturgy is required on five obligatory days — the feasts of the Epiphany, the Ascension, Sts. Peter and Paul, the Assumption of the Blessed Virgin Mary, and Christmas. Although attendance at the liturgy is not obligatory on 15 solemn and seven simple holy days, it is recommended. In the Byzantine (Ukrainian) Archeparchy of Philadelphia and its suffragan sees of St. Josaphat in Parma, St. Nicholas (Chicago) and Stamford, the obligatory feasts are the Epiphany, Annunciation, Ascension, Sts. Peter & Paul, Dormition, and Christmas.

Lent

The first day of Lent — the Monday before Ash Wednesday of the Roman Rite — and Good Friday are days of strict abstinence for persons in the age bracket of obligation. No meat, eggs, or dairy products may be eaten on these days. All persons over the age of 14 must abstain from meat on Fridays during Lent, Holy Saturday, and the vigils of the feasts of Christmas and Epiphany; abstinence is urged, but is not obligatory, on Wednesdays of Lent. The abstinence obligation is not in force on certain "free" or "privileged" Fridays.

Synaxis

An observance without a counterpart in the Roman calendar is the synaxis. This is a commemoration, on the day following a feast, of persons involved with the occasion for the feast — e.g., Sept. 9, the day following the feast of the Nativity of the Blessed Virgin Mary, is the Synaxis of Joachim and Anna, her parents.

Holy Week

In the Byzantine Rite, Lent is liturgically concluded with the Saturday of Lazarus, the day before Palm Sunday, which commemorates the raising of Lazarus from the dead. On the following Monday, Tuesday and Wednesday, the Liturgy of the Presanctified is prescribed.

On Holy Thursday, the Liturgy of St. Basil the Great is celebrated together with Vespers.

The Divine Liturgy is not celebrated on Good Friday. On Holy Saturday, the Liturgy of St. Basil the Great is celebrated along with Vespers.

BYZANTINE FEATURES

Art: Named for the empire in which it developed, Byzantine art is a unique blend of imperial Roman and classic Hellenic culture with Christian inspiration. The art of the Greek Middle Ages, it reached a peak of development in the 10th or 11th century. Characteristic of its products, particularly in mosaic and painting, are majesty, dignity, refinement and grace. Its sacred paintings, called icons, are reverenced highly in all the Eastern Churches of the Byzantine tradition.

Church Building: The classical model of Byzantine church architecture is the Church of the Holy Wisdom (*Hagia Sophia*), built in Constantinople in the first half of the sixth century and still standing.

The square structure, extended in some cases in the form of a cross, is topped by a distinctive onion-shaped dome and surmounted by a triple-bar cross. The altar is at the eastern end of building, where the wall bellies out to form an apse. The altar and sanctuary are separated from the body of the church by a fixed or movable screen, the iconostas, to which icons or sacred pictures are attached (see below).

Clergy: The Byzantine Churches have married as well as celibate priests. In places other than the U.S., where married candidates have not been accepted for ordination since about 1929, men already married can be ordained to the diaconate and priesthood and can continue in marriage after ordination. Celibate deacons and priests cannot marry after ordination; neither can a married priest remarry after the death of his wife. Bishops must be unmarried.

Iconostasis: A large screen decorated with sacred pictures or icons that separates the sanctuary from the nave of a church; its equivalent in the Roman Rite, for thus separating the sanctuary from the nave, is an altar rail. An iconostas has three doors through which the sacred ministers enter the sanctuary during the Divine Liturgy: smaller (north and south) Deacons' Doors and a large central Royal Door. The Deacons' Doors usually feature the icons of Sts. Gabriel and Michael; the Royal Door, the icons of the Evangelists — Matthew, Mark, Luke and John. To the right and left of the Royal Door are the icons of Christ the Teacher and of the Blessed Virgin Mary with the Infant Jesus. To the extreme right and left are the icons of the patron of the church and St. John the Baptist (or St. Nicholas of Myra). Immediately above the Royal Door is a picture of the Last Supper. To the right are six icons depicting the major feasts of Christ, and to the left are six icons portraying the major feasts of the Blessed Virgin Mary. Above the picture of the Last Supper is a large icon of Christ the King. Some icon screens also have pictures of the 12 Apostles and the major Old Testament prophets surmounted by a crucifixion scene.

Liturgical Language: In line with Eastern tradition, Byzantine practice has favored the use of the language of the people in the liturgy. Two great advocates of the practice were Sts. Cyril and Methodius, apostles of the Slavs, who devised the Cyrillic alphabet and pioneered the adoption of Slavonic in the liturgy.

Sacraments: Baptism is administered by immersion, and confirmation (Chrismation) is conferred at the same time. The Eucharist is administered by intinction, i.e., by giving the communicant a piece of consecrated leavened bread that has been dipped into the consecrated wine. When giving absolution in the sacrament of penance, the priest holds his stole over the head of the penitent. Distinctive marriage ceremonies include the crowning of the bride and groom. Ceremonies for anointing the sick closely resemble those of the Roman Rite. Holy orders are conferred by a bishop.

Sign of the Cross: The sign of the cross in conjunction with a deep bow expresses reverence for the presence of Christ in the Blessed Sacrament. (*See* entry in **Glossary**, p. 156.)

VESTMENTS, APPURTENANCES

Antimension: A silk or linen cloth laid on the altar for the Liturgy; it may be decorated with a picture of the burial of Christ and the instruments of his passion; the relics of martyrs are sewn into the front border.

Asteriskos: Made of two curved bands of gold or silver which cross each other to form a double arch; a star depends from the junction, which forms a cross; it is placed over the diskos holding the consecrated bread and is covered with a veil.

Diskos: A shallow plate, which may be elevated on a small stand, corresponding to the Roman-Rite paten.

Eileton: A linen cloth that corresponds to the Roman-Rite corporal.

Epimanikia: Ornamental cuffs; the right cuff symbolizing strength, the left, patience and good will.

Epitrachelion: A stole with ends sewn together, having a loop through which the head is passed; its several crosses symbolize priestly duties.

Lance: A metal knife used for cutting up the bread to be consecrated during the Liturgy.

Phelonion: An ample cape, long in the back and sides and cut away in front; symbolic of the higher gifts of the Holy Spirit.

Poterion: A chalice or cup that holds the wine and Precious Blood.

Spoon: Used in administering Holy Communion by intinction; consecrated leavened bread is dipped into consecrated wine and spooned onto the tongue of the communicant.

Sticharion: A long white garment of linen or silk with wide sleeves and decorated with embroidery; formerly the vestment for clerics in minor orders, acolytes, lectors, chanters, and subdeacons; symbolic of purity.

Veils: Three are used, one to cover the poterion, the second to cover the diskos, and the third to cover both.

Zone: A narrow clasped belt made of the same material as the *epitrachelion*; symbolic of the wisdom of the priest, his strength against enemies of the Church and his willingness to perform holy duties.

CODE OF CANONS OF THE EASTERN CHURCHES

The **Code of Canons of the Eastern Churches** serves as the legal corpus for the Eastern Churches, providing the legal principles for the preservation of the rich heritage of these Churches. The overarching theological structure for the Code was enunciated by the Second Vatican Council in its declaration in *Orientalium Ecclesiarum* (3):

These individual Churches, whether of the East or the West, although they differ somewhat among themselves in rite (to use the current phrase), that is, in liturgy, ecclesiastical discipline, and spiritual heritage, are, nevertheless, each as much as the others, entrusted to the pastoral government of the Roman Pontiff, the divinely appointed successor of St. Peter in primacy over the universal Church. They are consequently of equal dignity, so that none of them is superior to the others as regards rite and

they enjoy the same rights and are under the same obligations, also in respect of preaching the Gospel to the whole world (cf. Mark 16:15) under the guidance of the Roman Pontiff.

Background

The creation and promulgation of the Code for the Eastern Churches began during the pontificate of Pope Pius XI (1922-39) when he established a commission of cardinals in 1929 to examine the requirements for a code. This preparatory commission was succeeded in 1935 by a new commission with the task of undertaking the actual composition of the Code. What followed was a gradual process of promulgations. Pope Pius XII (1939-58) issued a series of apostolic letters as different elements of the Eastern Code were completed. This method of promulgation continued until 1972 when Pope Paul VI (1963-78) established the Pontifical Commission for the Revision of the Code of Eastern Canon Law.

The commission approached the initial stages of its work quite deliberately. Extensive consultation was made with canonists as well as many bishops of the Eastern Churches. These efforts culminated in November 1988 with the unanimous vote of the commission's members accepting the draft of the new Code. On Oct. 18, 1990, Pope John Paul II officially promulgated the Code of Canons of the Eastern Churches. The Code became effective on Oct. 1, 1991. As the decree makes clear, in accordance with this universal legislation, each Eastern Catholic Church is to develop its own particular law. This stands in contrast to the Code of Canon Law that applies only to the single Latin Church.

Contents and Structure

The Code of Canons of the Eastern Churches marked a significant milestone in the history of Church law. It represented the long process in the development of Canon Law for the Eastern Churches throughout the 20th century and was an eloquent means of both respecting and preserving the proper discipline of those Churches. It was noted from the start that the Code for the Eastern Catholics was organized differently in comparison with the Code of Canon Law for the Latin Rite. There are different elements to Eastern Law, and the Code presents the independence of these laws from the Latin Rite, save, of course, for those canons that give reference to the Pope. Nevertheless, while safeguarding the centuries' old traditions and heritage of the Eastern Catholic Churches, the differences are not disruptive to the unity of the Church. Rather, the Code is an instrument in moving toward appropriate unity. As the 1996 document, "Applying the Liturgical Prescriptions of the Code of Canons of the Eastern Catholic Churches" (9), by the Congregation for the Eastern Churches states:

The Code of Canons of the Eastern Churches, in can. 28 § 1 which refers to *Lumen Gentium*, No. 23, and *Orientalium Ecclesiarum*, No. 3, elucidates the important areas which articulate the heritage of each of the Churches *sui iuris*: liturgy, theology, spirituality and discipline. It is necessary to note that these particular fields penetrate and condition one another in turn inside a global vision of divine revelation which pervades all life and which culminates in the praise of the most holy Trinity.

The Catholic Church in the United States

CHRONOLOGY OF U.S. CATHOLIC HISTORY

The following are key dates in U.S. Catholic History. Reprinted from Our Sunday Visitor's Encyclopedia of American Catholic History.

1492 Christopher Columbus sailed to the New World and reached San Salvador (probably Watlings Island in the Bahamas). He subsequently made three voyages and established a Spanish presence on Santo Domingo (Hispaniola).

1497 John Cabot, a Genoese sailing under the English flag, reached the coasts of Labrador and Newfoundland.

1499 Alonso de Ojeda and Amerigo Vespucci reached Venezuela and explored the South American coast.

1500 Pedro Cabral reached Brazil.

1511 Diocese of Puerto Rico established as suffragan of Seville, Spain. Bishop Alonso Manso, sailing from Spain in 1512, became first bishop to take up residence in New World.

1513 Juan Ponce de León reached Florida and sailed as far north as the Carolinas.

1519 Hernando Cortes began the conquest of Mexico; by the next year, the Aztec Empire had been conquered and the Spanish rule over Mexico was established.

1521 Missionaries accompanying Ponce de León and other explorers probably said first Masses within present limits of US.

1526 Lucas Vázquez de Ayllón attempted to establish a colony in South Carolina; it later failed.

1534-36 Jacques Cartier explored the Newfoundland area and sailed up the St. Lawrence River.

1539 Hernando de Soto journeyed through Florida and as far north as Arkansas.

1540 Francisco Coronado set out to find the Seven Cities of Gold, journeying through Texas, Kansas and New Mexico. Franciscans Juan de Padilla and Marcos de Niza accompanied Coronado expedition through the territory. They celebrated the first Mass within territory of 13 original colonies.

c. 1540 Juan de Padilla, the first martyr of the United States, was murdered on the plains of Kansas by local Indians.

1565 City of St. Augustine, oldest in U.S., founded by Pedro Menendez de Aviles, who was accompanied by four secular priests. America's oldest mission, Nombre de Dios, was established. Fr. Martin Francisco Lopez de Mendoza Grajales became the first parish priest of St. Augustine, where the first parish in the U.S. was established.

1602 Carmelite Anthony of the Ascension offered first recorded Mass in Calif. on shore of San Diego Bay.

1608 Samuel de Champlain established the first permanent French colony at Québec.

1606 Bishop Juan de las Cabeyas de Altamirano, O.P., conducted the first episcopal visitation in the U.S.

1609 Henry Hudson entered New York Bay and sailed up the Hudson River. Santa Fe established as a mission in New Mexico. It later served as a headquarters for missionary efforts in the American Southwest.

1611 Pierre Biard, S.J., and Ennémond Massé, S.J., began missionary labors among the Indians of Maine.

1612 First Franciscan province in U.S. erected under title of Santa Elena; it included Georgia, South Carolina and Florida.

1613 Four Jesuits attempted to establish permanent French settlement near mouth of Kennebec River, Maine.

1619 French Franciscans began work among settlers and Indians. They were driven out by English in 1628.

1620 The Mayflower Compact drawn up by the Pilgrims. The chapel of *Nombre de Dios* was dedicated to *Nuestra Senora de la Leche y Buen Parto* (Our Nursing Mother of the Happy Delivery) in Florida; oldest shrine to the Blessed Mother in the U.S.

1622 Pope Gregory XV established the Congregation de Propaganda Fide to oversee all mission territories. The Catholics of America remained under its jurisdiction until 1908.

1630 New England made a prefecture apostolic in charge of French Capuchins.

1634 Ark and Dove reached Maryland with the first settlers. Maryland established by Lord Calvert; two Jesuits were among first colonists. First Mass offered on Island of St. Clement in Lower Potomac by Jesuit Fr. Andrew White.

1638 Jean Nicolet discovered the water route to the Mississippi.

1642 Jesuits Isaac Jogues and René Goupil were mutilated by Mohawks; Goupil was killed shortly afterwards. Dutch Calvinists rescued Fr. Jogues. The colony of Virginia outlawed priests and disenfranchised Catholics.

1646 Jesuit Isaac Jogues and John Lalande were martyred by Iroquois at Ossernenon, now Auriesville.

1647 Massachusetts Bay Company enacted an anti-priest law.

1649 The General Assembly of Maryland passed an act of religious toleration for the colony.

1653 Jesuits opened a school at Newton Manor, the first school in the American English colonies.

1654 Following the English Civil War and the deposition of King Charles I, the installed Puritan regime in Maryland repealed the act of religious toleration in Maryland.

1656 Church of St. Mary erected on Onondaga Lake, in first French settlement within the state. Kateri Tekakwitha, "Lily of the Mohawks," was born at Ossernenon, now Auriesville (d. in Canada, 1680). She was beatified in 1980; canonized Oct. 21, 2012.

1660 Jesuit René Menard opened first regular mission in Lake Superior region.

1668 Fr. Marquette founded Sainte Marie Mission at Sault Sainte Marie.

1671 Sieur de Lusson and Claude Allouez, S.J., arrived at Mackinac Island and claimed possession of the western country in the name of France.

1673 Louis Joliet and Jacques Marquette, S.J., began their expedition down the Mississippi River.

1674 Fr. Marquette set up a cabin for saying Mass in what later became the city of Chicago.

1675 Fr. Marquette established Mission of the Immaculate Conception among Kaskaskia Indians, near present site of Utica; transferred to Kaskaskia, 1703.

1678 Franciscan Recollect Louis Hennepin, first white man to describe Niagara Falls, celebrated Mass there.

1680 Louis Hennepin followed the Mississippi to its source. The missions of New Mexico destroyed by a local Indian uprising.

1682 Mission Corpus Christi de Isleta (Ysleta) founded by Franciscans near El Paso, first mission in present-day Texas.

1682 Religious toleration extended to members of all faiths in Pennsylvania.

1683 The New York colony passed the Charter of Liberties providing for religious freedom for believers in Christ.

1687 Eusebio Kino, S.J., launched the missions in Arizona at Pimería Alta.

1688 Maryland became royal colony as a result of the so-called Glorious Revolution in England; Anglican Church became the official religion (1692). Toleration Act repealed; Catholics disenfranchised and persecuted until 1776. Hanging of Ann Glover, an elderly Irish-Catholic widow, who refused to renounce her Catholic religion.

1689 Jesuit Claude Allouez died after 32 years of missionary activity among Indians of midwest; he had evangelized Indians of 20 different tribes. Jesuit Jacques Gravier succeeded Allouez as vicar general of Illinois.

1690 Mission San Francisco de los Tejas founded in east Texas.

1692 The Church of England officially established in Maryland. New Mexico re-subjugated by the Spanish and the missions re-opened.

1697 Religious liberty granted to all except "papists" in South Carolina.

1700 Jesuit Eusebio Kino, who first visited the area in 1692, established mission at San Xavier del Bac, near Tucson. In 1783, under Franciscan administration, construction was begun on the Mission Church of San Xavier del Bac near the site of the original mission; it is still in use as a parish church. Although the New York Assembly enacted a bill calling for religious toleration for all Christians in 1683, other penal laws were now enforced against Catholics; all priests were ordered out of the province.

1701 Tolerance granted to all except "papists" in New Jersey.

1703 Mission San Francisco de Solano founded on Rio Grande; rebuilt in 1718 as San Antonio de Valero, or the Alamo.

1704 Destruction of Florida's northern missions by English and Indian troops led by Governor James Moore of South Carolina. Franciscans Juan de Parga, Dominic Criodo, Tiburcio de Osorio, Augustine Ponze de León, Marcos Delgado and two Indians, Anthony Enixa and Amador Cuipa Feliciano, were slain by the invaders.

1709 French Jesuit missionaries obliged to give up their central New York missions.

1716 Antonio de Margil, O.F.M., began his missionary labors in Texas.

1718 The Catholics in Maryland officially disenfranchised. City of New Orleans founded by Jean Baptiste Le Moyne de Bienville.

1727 Ursuline Nuns founded convent in New Orleans, oldest convent in what is now U.S.; they conducted a school, hospital and orphan asylum.

1735 Bishop Francis Martinez de Tejadu Diaz de Velasco, auxiliary of Santiago, was the first bishop to take up residence in U.S., at St. Augustine.

1740s The First Great Awakening among Protestants.

1741 Because of an alleged popish plot to burn the city of New York, four whites were hanged and 11 blacks burned at the stake.

1744 Mission church of the Alamo built in San Antonio.

1751 First Catholic settlement founded among Huron Indians near Sandusky, Ohio, by Jesuit Fr. de la Richardie.

1754-63 The French and Indian War (The Seven Years War in Europe), the first world war; the conflict ended with the defeat of France and the loss of their American colonies.

1755 Fifty-six Catholics of Acadia expelled to the American colonies; those landing in Boston were denied the services of a Catholic priest.

1763 The Jesuits banished from the territories of Louisiana and Illinois. Spain ceded Florida to England. The English also gained control of all French territories east of the Mississippi following the cessation of the French and Indian War.

1765 The Quartering Act imposed on the colonies by the British as a means of paying the cost of colonial defense. It was followed by the Stamp Act, sparking the rise of the Sons of Liberty and the convening of the Stamp Act Congress.

1767 Jesuits expelled from Spanish territory. Spanish Crown confiscated their property, including the Pious Fund for Missions. Upper California missions entrusted to Franciscans.

1769 Franciscan Junípero Serra, missionary in Mexico for 20 years, began establishment of Franciscan missions in California, in present San Diego. He was beatified in 1988.

1770 The Boston Massacre resulted in the deaths of five colonists in Boston.

1773 The Tea Act sparked the Boston Tea Party. The British responded with the Intolerable Acts in 1774. Charles Carroll of Carrollton published the "First Citizen" letter in defense of the Church and Catholics against Daniel Dulany and the royal colonial government in Maryland.

1774 Elizabeth Bayley Seton, foundress of the American Sisters of Charity, was born in New York City on Aug. 28. She was canonized in 1975. The British Parliament passed the Quebec Act granting the French in the region the right to their own religion, language and customs. The first Continental Congress is convened.

1775-1781 The American Revolution, in which Catholics played a major role. In 1790, newly elected President George Washington wrote to American Catholics to thank them for their instrumental role in the war for American freedom.

1775 The Continental Congress denounced the rampant anti-Catholicism of the colonies to King George III. General Washington discouraged Guy Fawkes Day procession, in which pope was carried in effigy.

1776 Charles Carroll received appointment with Samuel Chase and Benjamin Franklin to a commission of the Continental Congress seeking aid from Canada; Fr. John Carroll accompanied them on their mission. Virginia became the first state to vote for full religious freedom in the new state's bill of rights. Similar provisions were passed by Maryland and Pennsylvania. The Continental Congress passed the Declaration of Independence (Charles Carroll was also the longest surviving signer). The New Jersey State Constitution tacitly excluded Catholics from office.

1777 The New York State Constitution gave religious liberty, but the naturalization law required an oath to renounce allegiance to any foreign ruler, ecclesiastical as well as civil.

1778 Fr. Gibault aided George Rogers Clark in campaign against British in conquest of Northwest Territory.

1780 The Massachusetts State Constitution granted religious liberty, but required a religious test to hold public office and provided for tax to support Protestant teachers of piety, religion and morality.

1781 Expedition from San Gabriel Mission founded present city of Los Angeles, Pueblo "de Nuestra Senora de los Angeles." British General Cornwallis surrendered at Yorktown, ending the Revolutionary War.

1783 The Treaty of Paris ended the American Revolution; Great Britain recognized the independence of the United States.

1784 The Vatican appointed Fr. John Carroll to the post of superior of the American Catholic missions. The State Constitution of New Hampshire included a religious test that barred Catholics from public office; local support was provided for public Protestant teachers of religion.

1787 Daniel Carroll of Maryland and Thomas FitzSimons of Pennsylvania signed the Constitution of the United States.

1788 First public Mass said in Boston on Nov. 2 by Abbé de la Poterie, first resident priest.

1789 Pope Pius VI erected the first United States diocese, Baltimore; John Carroll is named the first bishop.

1790 Catholics given right to vote in South Carolina.

1791 French Sulpicians opened the first seminary in the United States, St. Mary's in Baltimore.

Georgetown Academy is established and begins holding classes. Bishop Carroll convoked the first synod of the clergy of the diocese. The Bill of Rights ratified by the Congress. Pierre Charles L'Enfant designed the Federal City of Washington. His plans were not fully implemented until the early 1900s.

1792 James Hoban designed the White House.

1793 Rev. Stephen T. Badin first priest ordained by Bishop Carroll; he soon began missionary work in Kentucky.

1799 Prince Demetrius Gallitzin (Fr. Augustine Smith) arrived in the Allegheny Mountains. He labored there for the next 40 years and established the Church in western Pennsylvania, at Loretto.

1800 Jesuit Leonard Neale became first bishop consecrated in present limits of U.S.

1801 Start of the Second Great Awakening among Protestants.

1802 First mayor of Washington, appointed by President Jefferson, was Catholic Judge Robert Brent.

1803 The Louisiana Purchase resulted in the acquisition by the United States of all French lands from the Mississippi River to the Rocky Mountains for $15 million.

1804-06 President Jefferson sponsored the expedition of Lewis and Clark into the Louisiana Territory.

1806 New York anti-Catholic 1777 Test Oath for naturalization repealed.

1808 Pope Pius VII declared Baltimore the first metropolitan see of the United States, erecting at the same time the new dioceses of Bardstown (KY), Boston, New York, and Philadelphia as suffragans.

1809 Mother Elizabeth Ann Seton established the first native American congregation of sisters, at Emmitsburg, Maryland.

1810 The United States annexed West Florida under the pretext that it was included in the Louisiana Purchase.

1811 Catholic Canadian trappers and traders with John J. Astor expedition founded first American settlement, Astoria. Fr. Guy I. Chabrat becomes first priest ordained west of the Allegheny Mountains.

1812 The War of 1812; it was ended by the Treaty of Ghent in 1814.

1814 St. Joseph's Orphanage, Philadelphia, opened, the first Catholic asylum for children in the United States.

1818 Religious freedom established by new constitution in Connecticut, although the Congregational Church remained, in practice, the state church. Bp. Dubourg arrived at St. Louis, with Vincentians Joseph Rosati and Felix de Andreis. Rose Philippine Duchesne arrived at St. Charles; founded first American convent of the Society of the Sacred Heart. She was beatified in 1940 and canonized in 1988.

1822 Bp. John England founded the *United States Catholic Miscellany*, the first Catholic newspaper in the country of a strictly religious nature. The Society for the Propagation of the Faith is founded in France; it sent missionaries throughout the world. Vicariate Apostolic of Mississippi and Alabama established.

1823 President Monroe proposed the Monroe Doctrine of foreign policy. Fr. Gabriel Richard elected delegate to Congress from Michigan territory; he was the first priest elected to the House of Representatives.

1828 New York State Legislature enacted a law upholding sanctity of seal of confession. The first hospital opened west of the Mississippi in St. Louis, staffed by the Sisters of Charity from Emmitsburg, Maryland.

1829 The First Provincial Council of Baltimore convoked. The Oblate Sisters of Providence, the first African-American congregation of women religious in the United States was established in Baltimore.

1831 Xavier University founded.

1833 Fr. Frederic Baraga celebrated first Mass in present Grand Rapids.

1834 First native New Yorker to become a secular priest, Rev. John McCloskey, was ordained. Indian missions in Northwest entrusted to Jesuits by Holy See. A mob of Nativists attacked and burned down the Ursuline Convent at Charlestown, Mass.

1835 Samuel F.B. Morse published *The Foreign Conspiracy Against the Liberties of the United States.*

1836 Texans under Stephen F. Austin declared their independence from Mexico; the Battle of the Alamo in San Antonio resulted in the deaths of 188 Texans, including the commander William B. Travis and perhaps Davy Crockett. Texas soon won its independence and was annexed in 1845. John Nepomucene Neumann arrived from Bohemia and was ordained a priest in Old St. Patrick's Cathedral, New York City. He was canonized in 1977. The infamous work of Maria Monk's *Awful Disclosures of the Hotel Dieu Nunnery of Montreal*, detailing supposed scandals of Catholic religious, was published. President Jackson nominated Roger Brooke Taney as chief justice of the Supreme Court.

1838 Fathers Blanchet and Demers, "Apostles of the Northwest," sent to territory by Abp. of Québec.

1839 Pope Gregory XVI condemned the slave trade in his decree *In Supremo Apostolatus.*

1840 Mother Theodore Guérin founded the Sisters of Providence of St.-Mary-of-the-Woods in Indiana.

1842 Fr. Augustine Ravoux began ministrations to French and Indians at Fort Pierre, Vermilion and Prairie du Chien; printed devotional book in Sioux language the following year. Henriette Delille and Juliette Gaudin began the Sisters of the Holy Family in New Orleans, the second African-American community of women religious. University of Notre Dame founded by Holy Cross Fr. Edward Sorin and Brothers of St. Joseph on land given the diocese of Vincennes by Fr. Stephen Badin.

1844 Thirteen persons killed, two churches and a school burned in Know-Nothing riots at Philadelphia. Orestes Brownson received into the Church; he subsequently founded *Brownson's Quarterly Review.*

1845 Nativists opposed to Catholics and Irish immigration, established the Native American Party. Issac Hecker received into the Church. The potato famine began in Ireland, causing in part the mass migration of Irish to the United States. The St. Vincent de Paul Society founded in the United States.

1846-48 The Mexican-American War was caused by a border dispute between the United States and Mexico. Catholic chaplains were appointed to the army, to minister to Mexican Catholics.

1846 Peter H. Burnett, who became first governor of California in 1849, received into Catholic Church. First Benedictine Abbey in New World founded near Latrobe by Fr. Boniface Wimmer.

1847 The Bishops of the United States requested Pope Pius IX to name the Immaculate Conception patron of the United States.

1848 The first permanent American Trappist foundation established, in Kentucky. Jacob L. Martin named the first American representative to the Vatican.

1852 The First Plenary Council of Baltimore held. Redemptorist John Nepomucene Neumann became fourth bishop of Philadelphia. He was beatified in 1963 and canonized in 1977.

1853 Calling for the exclusion of Catholics and foreigners from office and a 21-year residence requirement, the American Party was founded, known also as the Know-Nothing Party.

1854 Members of the Benedictine Swiss-American congregation established a community at St. Meinrad in southern Indiana.

1855 The German Catholic Central Verein founded. The "Bloody Monday" Riots in Louisville, Kentucky, leave 20 dead.

1857 The Supreme Court issued the Dred Scott Decision; Chief Justice Roger Taney stated that Congress could not exclude slavery from the territories since, according to the Constitution, slaves were property and could be transported anywhere. The American College at Louvain opened; closed June 2011.

1858 Jesuit Fr. De Smet accompanied General Harney as chaplain on expedition sent to settle troubles between Mormons and U.S. government. The Paulists, the first native religious community for men, established. Cornerstone of second (present) St. Patrick's Cathedral, New York City, was laid; the cathedral was completed in 1879.

1859 The North American College founded in Rome as a training center for American seminarians.

1860 South Carolina seceded from the Union.

1861-65 The American Civil War. Catholics participated in large numbers on both sides. There were approximately 40 Catholic chaplains in the Union army and 28 in the Confederate army. More than 500 Catholic nuns ministered to the sick and wounded. Over 20 generals in the Union army and 11 generals in the Confederate army were Catholics.

1861 The Confederacy was formed after 11 states seceded from the Union. Jefferson Davis was elected president of the Confederacy.

1865 *Catholic World* founded. A Test Oath law passed by state legislature (called Drake Convention) to crush Catholicism in Missouri. Law declared unconstitutional by Supreme Court in 1866. Rev. H. H. Spalding, a Protestant missionary, published the Whitman Myth to hinder work of Catholic missionaries in Oregon. President Lincoln was assassinated. The murder sparked anti-Catholicism, including charges that Jesuits orchestrated his death. Congress passed the Thirteenth Amendment abolishing slavery.

1866 The Second Plenary Council of Baltimore.

1867 Reconstruction launched in the South; the presence of Federal troops did not end until 1877. The Ku Klux Klan founded to defeat

Reconstruction, oppose Catholicism, and establish white supremacy in the post-war South. The U.S. purchased Alaska for $7.2 million; organized by Secretary of State William Seward, the purchase was called "Seward's Folly."

1869-70 The Fist Vatican Council convoked. Most of the bishops of the United States took part in the deliberations of the council.

1869 The Transcontinental Railroad completed, with the two tracks meeting at Promontory, near Ogden, Utah. The Knights of Labor founded.

1870 The Holy Name Society organized in the U.S.

1873 Blessed Fr. Damien de Veuster of the Sacred Hearts Fathers arrived in Molokai and spent the remainder of his life working among lepers. He was beatified in 1995.

1875 James A. Healy, first bishop of Negro blood consecrated in U.S., became second Bishop of Portland, Maine. Abp. John McCloskey of New York became the first American prelate to be elevated to the College of Cardinals.

1876 George Armstrong Custer killed at the Battle of Little Bighorn (in the Second Sioux War) in Montana. *The American Catholic Quarterly Review* is established. James Gibbons publishes *Faith of Our Fathers*.

1878 Franciscan Sisters of Allegany becomes first native American community to send members to foreign missions.

1880 William R. Grace becomes the first Catholic mayor of New York City.

1882 Knights of Columbus founded by Fr. Michael J. McGivney.

1884 The Third Plenary Council of Baltimore held. John Gilmary Shea began the U.S. Catholic Historical Society.

1886 Abp. Charles J. Seghers, "Apostle of Alaska," was murdered by a guide; he had surveyed southern and northwest Alaska in 1873 and 1877. Abp. James Gibbons of Baltimore is named the second American cardinal. Augustus Tolton is ordained the first African-American priest for the United States. The Knights of St. John was established.

1887 The American Protective Association (APA) was established to resist the growth of immigration. The Dawes Act was passed, dissolving all Indian tribes and distributing their lands among their former members, who were not permitted to dispose of their property for 25 years.

1889 The Catholic University of America opened. The first African-American Lay Congress was held in Washington, D.C.; subsequent congresses held in Cincinnati (1890), Philadelphia (1892), Chicago (1893), and Baltimore (1894). Mother Frances Xavier Cabrini arrived in New York City to begin work among Italian immigrants. She was canonized in 1946. *American Ecclesiastical Review* begun.

1890 Archbishop Ireland delivered an address on public and private schools at the gathering of the National Education Association in St. Paul, Minnesota.

1891 Vicariate Apostolic of Oklahoma and Indian Territory was established. Katharine Drexel founded Sisters of Blessed Sacrament for Indians and Colored Peoples. She was canonized in 2000. The Rosary Society organized.

1893 The Apostolic Delegation under Abp. Francesco Satolli established in Washington, D.C.; it became an Apostolic Nunciature in 1984 with the establishment of full diplomatic relations between the U.S. and the Holy See. The first Catholic college for women in the United States, College of Notre Dame of Maryland, was established. *St. Anthony Messenger* launched.

1898 Puerto Rico ceded to U.S. (became self-governing Commonwealth in 1952); inhabitants granted U.S. citizenship in 1917. The United States annexed Hawaii; the monarchy had been overthrown in 1897.

1898 The Spanish-American War.

1899 Pope Leo XIII issued *Testem Benevolentiae*.

1901 President McKinley assassinated.

1904 The National Catholic Education Association (NCEA) founded. First publication of the *Catholic Almanac*.

1905 The Catholic Church Extension Society for home missions established.

1907 The first volume of the *Catholic Encyclopedia* was published by the Catholic University of America.

1908 Pope St. Pius X published *Pascendi Domini Gregis* against Modernism. Pope Pius issued the bull *Sapienti Consilio*, by which the Church in the U.S. was removed from mission status and the jurisdiction of the Congregation de Propaganda Fide. First American Missionary Congress held in Chicago.

1909 The Holy Name Society was established. *America* Magazine founded by the Jesuits.

1911 The Catholic Foreign Mission Society of America (Maryknoll) founded. Katharine Drexel founded the Sisters of the Blessed Sacrament.

1912 *Our Sunday Visitor* founded.

1914-18 World War I.

1917 The United States entered the First World War. The National Catholic War Council was founded. Over one million Catholics served in the Armed Forces (over 20% of the total U.S. military).

1919 The Bishops' *Program of Social Reconstruction* published. The National Catholic Welfare Council was founded. Peter Guilday began the American Catholic Historical Association.

1920 The National Catholic News Service (NC, now the Catholic News Service, CNS) was established.

1924 The Federated Colored Catholics of the United States was established. *Commonweal* magazine was founded by Michael Williams.

1925 The Supreme Court declares the Oregon school law unconstitutional. The Scopes Trial, also called the Dayton Monkey Trial, took place in Dayton, Ohio.

1926 The Twenty-Eighth International Eucharistic Congress was held in Chicago.

1928 Alfred E. Smith of New York nominated for president by the Democratic Party; he was the first Catholic ever chosen to head a major-party national ticket. He was defeated by Herbert Hoover, in part because of his opposition to Prohibition and his faith.

1929 The stockmarket crash signaled the start of the Great Depression. The Catholic Church devoted enormous resources to alleviating the suffering of those afflicted by the global Depression.

1932 Franklin Delano Roosevelt was elected president, launching the New Deal period (1933-45).

1933 The Catholic Worker Movement was established by Dorothy Day and Peter Maurin.

1934 John LaFarge, S.J., begins the first Catholic Interracial Council in New York.

1937 The Association of Catholic Trade Unionists (ACTU) established.

1939 Myron C. Taylor named personal representative of President Roosevelt to Pope Pius XII.

1939-45 World War II.

1941 Pearl Harbor was attacked by Japan; the U.S. entered World War II. Catholics comprised over 25% of the Armed Forces.

1945 End of World War II. Delegates from 50 nations established the Charter of the United Nations.

1947 The Christian Family Movement was begun by Pat and Patty Crowley. The Supreme Court issued the decision *Everson v. Board of Education* approving the use of public school buses to carry Catholic students to parochial schools.

1948 Protestants and Other Americans for Separation of Church and State (POAU) founded.

1951 President Truman nominates General Mark Clark as Ambassador to Vatican City. The nomination later withdrawn in the face of anti-Catholic protests.

1954 The Sisters Formation Conference was founded. The Supreme Court decided *Brown v. Board of Education of Topeka*; the decision declared that segregation in the public schools was unconstitutional.

1955 John Tracy Ellis published *American Catholics and the Intellectual Life.*

1956 Leadership Conference of Women Religious and Conference of Major Superiors of Men was founded.

1957 The Civil Rights Act was passed, the first since 1875.

1958 Christopher Dawson was named the first holder of the Chauney Stillman Chair of Roman Catholic Studies at the Harvard Divinity School.

1959 Pope John XXIII announced his intention to convoke the Second Vatican Council.

1960 John F. Kennedy elected president of the United States; he was the first Catholic president.

1962-65 The Second Vatican Council.

1962 Gustave Weigel, S.J., appointed by the Vatican to be one of the five Catholic observers at the third general assembly of the World Council of Churches at New Delhi. Archbishop Joseph Rummel of New Orleans announced the integration of archdiocesan Catholic schools.

1963 The Catholic University of America prohibited Hans Küng, John Courtney Murray, S.J., Gustave Weigel, S.J., and Godfrey Diekmann, O.S.B., from speaking at the school. Elizabeth Ann Seton, the first American to be beatified. President Kennedy assassinated in Dallas.

1964 The Civil Rights Act passed.

1965 Pope Paul VI visited the United Nations, the first pope to visit the U.S. Gommar A. De Pauw organizes the Catholic Traditionalist movement.

1966 The National Conference of Catholic Bishops and the United States Catholic Conference were organized. Harold Perry, S.V.D., became the second African-American to be named a bishop.

1967 The Land O' Lakes Statement issued. The Catholic Charismatic Movement began. The Catholic Committee on Urban Ministry (CCUM) was established.

1968 Pope Paul VI issued *Humanae Vitae*. The National Black Catholic Clergy Caucus, the National Black Sisters' Conference, the National Black Catholic Seminarians Association, and the National Federation of Priests' Council were formed. Catholics United for the Faith established.

1969 The Organization of Priests Associated for Religious, Educational, and Social Rights (PADRES) established. The Campaign for Human Development established.

1970 Patricio Flores, the first modern Latino bishop, ordained.

1971 The Leadership Conference of Women Religious established.

1972 Religious Brothers Conference established.

1973 Roe v. Wade Decision handed down by the Supreme Court, legalizing abortion.

1975 Pope Paul VI canonized the first American saint, Elizabeth Ann Seton.

1976 The U.S. celebrated the Bicentennial. The 41st International Eucharistic Congress in Philadelphia.

1977 Fellowship of Catholic Scholars established.

1979 Pope John Paul II visited the U.S.

1983 The NCCB issued the *Challenge of Peace.*

1986 The NCCB issued *Economic Justice for All.* The Vatican and Catholic University of America removed Fr. Charles Curran from teaching theology at the university.

1987 Pope John Paul II visited the U.S. for the second time. The National Black Catholic Congress convoked in Washington, D.C.

1991 The U.S. played a major role in the Gulf War.

1992 Council of Major Superiors of Women Religious founded.

1993 World Youth Day held in Denver.

1995 Pope John Paul II visited the United Nations, Baltimore, and New York.

1997 U.S. Bishops took part in a special assembly of the Synod of Bishops on the Church in the Americas.

1999 Pope John Paul II visited St. Louis.

2001 The U.S. attacked on Sept. 11. The NCCB and USSC merged to form the United States Conference of Catholic Bishops (USCCB); Bishop Wilton Gregory of Belleville was elected the first black president of the USCCB.

2002 The pedophilia crisis erupted across the country; the USCCB passed a series of protective norms.

2003 The U.S. launched the Iraq War to topple Saddam Hussein.

2004 Pres. George W. Bush re-elected president. The Democratic nominee, Sen. John Kerry, a Catholic, caused considerable controversy because of his pro-abortion position. The issue sparked a national debate over the issue of Catholic politicians and abortion.

2008 Pope Benedict XVI visited Washington, D.C. and New York, his first apostolic voyage to the United States as pope. Sen. Barack Obama elected the first African-American president; his running-mate, Sen. Joseph Biden of Delaware became the first nominally Catholic vice-president.

2012 The Bishops of the United States speak out publicly against the Mandate issued by the Obama Administration that would require Catholic employers to provide their employees with insurance that includes contraception, sterilization, and abortion-inducing drugs. The mandate is the cause of immense conteoversy over the limitations being placed upon religious liberty.

U.S. CATHOLIC HISTORY

Courtesy Rev. Clyde Crews, Ph.D.

The starting point of the mainstream of Catholic history in the U.S. was in Baltimore at the end of the Revolutionary War. Long before that time, however, Catholic explorers had traversed much of the country and missionaries had done considerable work among Indians in the Southeast, Northeast and Southwest. (*See* **Index, Chronology of Church in U.S.**)

Spanish and French Missions

Missionaries from Spain evangelized Indians in Florida (which included a large area of the Southeast), New Mexico, Texas and California. Franciscan Juan de Padilla, killed in 1542 in what is now central Kansas, was the first of numerous martyrs among the early missionaries. The city of St. Augustine, settled by the Spanish in 1565, was the first permanent settlement in the United States and also the site of the first parish, established the same year with secular Fr. Martin Francisco Lopez de Mendoza Grajales as pastor. Italian Jesuit Eusebio Kino (1645-1711) established Spanish missions in lower California and southern Arizona, where he founded San Xavier del Bac mission in 1700. Bl. Junípero Serra (1713-84), who established nine of the famous chain of 21 Franciscan missions in California, was perhaps the most noted of the Spanish missionaries. He was beatified in 1988.

French missionary efforts originated in Canada and extended to parts of Maine, New York and areas around the Great Lakes and along the Mississippi River as far south as Louisiana. Sts. Isaac Jogues, René Goupil and John de Brébeuf, three of eight Jesuit missionaries of New France martyred between 1642 and 1649 (canonized in 1930), met their deaths near Auriesville, New York. Jesuit explorer Jacques Marquette (1637-75), who founded St. Ignace Mission at the Straits of Mackinac in 1671, left maps and a diary of his exploratory trip down the Mississippi River with Louis Joliet in 1673. Claude Allouez (1622-89), another French Jesuit, worked for 32 years among Indians in the Midwest, baptizing an estimated 10,000. French Catholics founded the colony in Louisiana in 1699. In 1727, Ursuline nuns from France founded a convent in New Orleans, the oldest in the United States.

English Settlements

Catholics were excluded by penal law from English settlements along the Atlantic coast.

The only colony established under Catholic leadership was Maryland, granted to George Calvert (Lord Baltimore) as a proprietary colony in 1632; its first settlement at St. Mary's City was established in 1634 by a contingent of Catholic and Protestant colonists who had arrived from England on the *Ark and the Dove*. Jesuits Andrew White and John Altham, who later evangelized Indians of the area, accompanied the settlers. The principle of religious freedom on which the colony was founded was enacted into law in 1649 as the Act of Toleration. It was the first such measure passed in the colonies

and, except for a four-year period of Puritan control, remained in effect until 1688, when Maryland became a royal colony and the Anglican Church was made the official religion in 1692. Catholics were disenfranchised and persecuted until 1776.

The only other colony where Catholics were assured some degree of freedom was Pennsylvania, founded by the Quaker William Penn in 1681.

One of the earliest permanent Catholic establishments in the English colonies was St. Francis Xavier Mission, Old Bohemia, in northern Maryland, founded by the Jesuits in 1704 to serve Catholics of Delaware, Maryland and southeastern Pennsylvania. Its Bohemia Academy, established in the 1740s, was attended by sons of prominent Catholic families in the area.

Catholics and the Revolution

Despite their small number, which accounted for about one percent of the population, Catholics made significant contributions to the cause for independence from England.

Fr. John Carroll (1735-1815), who would later become the first bishop of the American hierarchy, and his cousin, Charles Carroll (1737-1832), a signer of the Declaration of Independence, were chosen by the Continental Congress to accompany Benjamin Franklin and Samuel Chase to Canada to try to secure that country's neutrality. Fr. Pierre Gibault (1737-1804) gave important aid in preserving the Northwest Territory for the revolutionaries. Thomas FitzSimons (1741-1811) of Philadelphia gave financial support to the Continental Army, served in a number of campaigns and later, with Daniel Carroll of Maryland, became one of the two Catholic signers of the Constitution. John Barry (1745-1803), commander of the *Lexington*, the first ship commissioned by Congress, served valiantly and is considered a founder of the U.S. Navy. There is no record of the number of Catholics who served in Washington's armies, although 38 to 50 percent had Irish surnames.

Casimir Pulaski (1748-79) and Thaddeus Kosciusko (1746-1817) of Poland served the cause of the Revolution. Assisting also were the Catholic nations of France, with a military and naval force, and Spain, with money and the neutrality of its colonies.

Acknowledgment of Catholic aid in the war and the founding of the Republic was made by General Washington in his reply to a letter from prominent Catholics seeking justice and equal rights: "I presume your fellow citizens of all denominations will not forget the patriotic part which you took in the accomplishment of our Revolution and the establishment of our government or the important assistance which they received from a nation [France] in which the Roman Catholic faith is professed."

In 1789, religious freedom was guaranteed under the First Amendment to the Constitution. Discriminatory laws against Catholics remained in force in many of the states, however, until well into the 19th century.

Beginning of Organization

Fr. John Carroll's appointment as superior of the American missions on June 9, 1784, was the first step toward organization of the Church in this country. According to a report he made to Rome the following year, there were 24 priests and approximately 25,000 Catholics, mostly in Maryland and Pennsylvania, in a general population of four million. Many of them had been in the Colonies for several generations. For the most part, however, they were an unknown minority laboring under legal and social handicaps.

Establishment of the Hierarchy

Fr. Carroll was named the first American bishop in 1789 and placed in charge of the Diocese of Baltimore, whose boundaries were coextensive with those of the United States. He was ordained in England on Aug. 15, 1790, and installed in his see the following Dec. 12.

Ten years later, Fr. Leonard Neale became his coadjutor and the first bishop ordained in the U.S. Bishop Carroll became an archbishop in 1808 when Baltimore was designated a metropolitan see and the new dioceses of Boston, New York, Philadelphia and Bardstown (now Louisville) were established. These jurisdictions were later subdivided, and by 1840 there were, in addition to Baltimore, 15 dioceses, 500 priests and 663,000 Catholics in the general population of 17 million.

Priests and First Seminaries

The original number of 24 priests noted in Bishop Carroll's 1785 report was gradually augmented with the arrival of others from France and other countries. Among arrivals from France after the Civil Constitution of the Clergy went into effect in 1790 were Jean Louis Lefebvre de Cheverus and Sulpicians Ambrose Maréchal, Benedict Flaget and William Dubourg, who later became bishops.

The first seminary in the country was St. Mary's, established in 1791 in Baltimore, and placed under the direction of the Sulpicians. French seminarian Stephen T. Badin (1768-1853), who fled to the U.S. in 1792 and became a pioneer missionary in Kentucky, Ohio and Michigan, was the first priest ordained (1793) in the U.S. Demetrius Gallitzin (1770-1840), a Russian prince and convert to Catholicism who did pioneer missionary work in western Pennsylvania, was ordained to the priesthood in 1795; he was the first to receive all his orders in the U.S. By 1815, St. Mary's Seminary had 30 ordained alumni.

Two additional seminaries, Mt. St. Mary's at Emmitsburg, Maryland, and St. Thomas at Bardstown, Kentucky, were established in 1809 and 1811, respectively. These and similar institutions founded later played key roles in the development and growth of the American clergy.

Early Schools

Early educational enterprises included the establishment in 1791 of a school at Georgetown that later became the first Catholic university in the U.S.; the opening of a secondary school for girls, conducted by Visitation Nuns, in 1799 at Georgetown; and the start of a similar school in the first decade of the 19th century at Emmitsburg, Maryland, by St. Elizabeth Ann Seton.

By the 1840s, which saw the beginnings of the present public school system, more than 200 Catholic elementary schools, half of them west of the Alleghenies, were in operation. From this start, the Church subsequently built the greatest private system of education in the world.

Sisterhoods

Institutes of women Religious were largely responsible for the development of educational and charitable institutions. Among them were Ursuline Nuns in Louisiana from 1727 and Visitation Nuns at Georgetown in the 1790s.

The first contemplative foundation in the country was established in 1790 at Fort Tobacco, Maryland, by three American-born Carmelites trained at an English convent in Belgium.

The first community of American origin was the Sisters of Charity of St. Joseph, founded in 1808 at Emmitsburg, Maryland, by Mother Elizabeth Ann Bayley Seton (canonized in 1975). Other early American communities were the Sisters of Loretto and the Sisters of Charity of Nazareth, both founded in 1812 in Kentucky, and the Oblate Sisters of Providence, a black community founded in 1829 in Baltimore by Mother Mary Elizabeth Lange.

Among pioneer U.S. foundresses of European communities were Mother Rose Philippine Duchesne (canonized in 1980), who established the Religious of the Sacred Heart in Missouri in 1818, and Mother Theodore Guérin, who founded the Sisters of Providence of St.-Mary-of-the-Woods in Indiana in 1840.

The number of sisters' communities, most of them branches of European institutes, increased apace with needs for their missions in education, charitable service and spiritual life.

Trusteeism

The initial lack of organization in ecclesiastical affairs, nationalistic feeling among Catholics and the independent action of some priests were factors involved in several early crises.

In Philadelphia, some German Catholics, with the reluctant consent of Bp. Carroll, founded Holy Trinity, the first national parish in the U.S. They refused to accept the pastor appointed by the bishop and elected their own. This and other abuses led to formal schism in 1796, a condition that existed until 1802, when they returned to canonical jurisdiction. Philadelphia was also the scene of the Hogan Schism, which developed in the 1820s when Fr. William Hogan, with the aid of lay trustees, seized control of St. Mary's Cathedral. His movement, for churches and parishes controlled by other than canonical procedures and run in extralegal ways, was nullified by a decision of the Pennsylvania Supreme Court in 1822.

Similar troubles seriously disturbed the peace of the Church in other places, principally New York, Baltimore, Buffalo, Charleston and New Orleans.

Dangers arising from the exploitation of lay control were gradually diminished with the extension and enforcement of canonical procedures and with changes in civil law about the middle of the century.

Anti-Catholicism

Bigotry against Catholics waxed and waned during the 19th century and into the 20th. The first major campaign of this kind, which developed in the wake of the panic of 1819 and lasted for about 25 years, was mounted in 1830 when the number of Catholic immigrants began to increase to a noticeable degree. Nativist anti-Catholicism generated a great deal of violence, represented by loss of life and property in Charlestown, Massachusetts, in 1834, and in Philadelphia 10 years later. Later bigotry was fomented by the Know-Nothings, in the 1850s; the Ku Klux Klan, from 1866; the American Protective Association, from 1887; and the Guardians of Liberty. Perhaps the last eruption of virulently overt anti-Catholicism occurred during the campaign of Alfred E. Smith for the presidency in 1928. Observers feel the issue was muted to a considerable extent in the political area with the election of John F. Kennedy to the presidency in 1960.

The Catholic periodical press had its beginnings in response to the attacks of bigots. The *U.S. Catholic Miscellany* (1822-61), the first Catholic newspaper in the U.S., was founded by Bishop John England of Charleston to answer critics of the Church. This remained the character of most of the periodicals published in the 19th and into the 20th century.

Growth and Immigration

Between 1830 and 1900, the combined factors of natural increase, immigration and conversion raised the Catholic population to 12 million. A large percentage of the growth figure represented immigrants: some 2.7 million, largely from Ireland, Germany and France, between 1830 and 1880; and another 1.25 million during the 1880s when Eastern and Southern Europeans came in increasing numbers. By the 1860s the Catholic Church, with most of its members concentrated in urban areas, was probably the largest religious body in the country.

The efforts of progressive bishops to hasten the acculturation of Catholic immigrants occasioned a number of controversies, which generally centered around questions concerning national or foreign-language parishes. One of them, called Cahenslyism, arose from complaints that German Catholic immigrants were not being given adequate pastoral care.

Eastern Rite Catholics

The immigration of the 1890s included large numbers of Eastern Rite Catholics with their own liturgies and tradition of a married clergy, but without their own bishops. The treatment of their clergy and people by some of the U.S. (Latin Rite) hierarchy and the prejudices they encountered resulted in the defection of thousands from the Catholic Church.

In 1907, Basilian monk Stephen Ortynsky was ordained the first bishop of Byzantine Rite Catholics in the U.S. Eventually jurisdictions were established for most Byzantine and other Eastern Rite Catholics in the country.

Councils of Baltimore

The bishops of the growing U.S. dioceses met at Baltimore for seven provincial councils between 1829 and 1849.

In 1846, they proclaimed the Blessed Virgin Mary patroness of the United States under the title of the Immaculate Conception, eight years before the dogma was proclaimed in Rome.

After the establishment of the Archdiocese of Oregon City in 1846 and the elevation to metropolitan status of St. Louis, New Orleans, Cincinnati and New York, the first of the three plenary councils of Baltimore was held.

The first plenary assembly was convoked on May 9, 1852, with Abp. Francis P. Kenrick of Baltimore as papal legate. The bishops drew up regulations concerning parochial life, matters of church ritual and ceremonies, the administration of church funds and the teaching of Christian doctrine.

The second plenary council, meeting from Oct. 7 to 21, 1866, under the presidency of Abp. Martin J. Spalding, formulated a condemnation of several current doctrinal errors and established norms affecting the organization of dioceses, the education and conduct of the clergy, the management of ecclesiastical property, parochial duties and general education.

Abp. (later Cardinal) James Gibbons called into session the third plenary council which lasted from Nov. 9 to Dec. 7, 1884. Among highly significant results of actions taken by this assembly were the preparation of the line of Baltimore catechisms that became a basic means of religious instruction in this country; legislation that fixed the pattern of Catholic education by requiring the building of elementary schools in all parishes; the establishment of the Catholic University of America in Washington, D.C., in 1889; and the determination of six holy days of obligation for observance in this country.

The enactments of the three plenary councils have had the force of particular law for the Church in the U.S.

The Holy See established the Apostolic Delegation in Washington, D.C., on Jan. 24, 1893.

Slavery

In the Civil War period, as before, Catholics reflected attitudes of the general population with respect to the issue of slavery. Some supported it, some opposed it, but none were prominent in the Abolition Movement. Pope Gregory XVI had condemned the slave trade in 1839, but no contemporary pope or American bishop published an official document on slavery itself. The issue did not split Catholics in schism as it did Baptists, Methodists and Presbyterians.

Catholics fought on both sides in the Civil War. Five hundred members of 20 or more sisterhoods served the wounded of both sides.

One hundred thousand of the four million slaves emancipated in 1863 were Catholics; the highest concentrations were in Louisiana, about 60,000, and Maryland, 16,000. Three years later, their pastoral care was one of the subjects covered in nine decrees issued by the Second Plenary Council of Baltimore. The measures had little practical effect with respect to integration of the total Catholic community, predicated as they were on the proposition that individual bishops should handle questions regarding segregation in churches and related matters as best they could in the pattern of local customs.

Long-entrenched segregation practices continued in force through the rest of the 19th century and well into the 20th. The first effective efforts to alter them were initiated by Card. Joseph Ritter of St. Louis in 1947, Card. (then Abp.) Patrick O'Boyle of Washington in 1948, and Bp. Vincent Waters of Raleigh in 1953.

Friend of Labor

The Church became known during the 19th century as a friend and ally of labor in seeking justice for the working man. Cardinal Gibbons journeyed to Rome in 1887, for example, to defend and prevent a condemnation of the Knights of Labor by Leo XIII. The encyclical *Rerum Novarum* (1891) was hailed by many American bishops as a confirmation, if not vindication, of their own theories. Catholics have always formed a large percentage of union membership, and some have served unions in positions of leadership.

Americanism

Near the end of the century some controversy developed over what was characterized as Americanism or the phantom heresy. It was alleged that Americans were discounting the importance of contemplative virtues, exalting the practical virtues, and watering down the purity of Catholic doctrine for the sake of facilitating convert work.

The French translation of Fr. Walter Elliott's *Life of Isaac Hecker*, which fired the controversy, was one of many factors that led to the issuance of Leo XIII's *Testem Benevolentiae* in January 1899, in an attempt to end the matter. It was the first time the orthodoxy of the Church in the U.S. was called into question.

Schism

In the 1890s, serious friction developed between Poles and Irish in Scranton, Buffalo and Chicago, resulting in schism and the establishment of the Polish National Catholic Church. A central figure in the affair was Fr. Francis Hodur, who was excommunicated by Bp. William O'Hara of Scranton in 1898. Nine years later, his ordination by an Old Catholic Abp. of Utrecht gave the new church its first bishop.

Another schism of the period led to formation of the American Carpatho-Russian Orthodox Greek Catholic Church.

Coming of Age

In 1900, there were 12 million Catholics in the total U.S. population of 76 million, 82 dioceses in 14 provinces, and 12,000 priests and members of about 40 communities of men Religious. Many sisterhoods, most of them of European origin and some of American foundation, were engaged in Catholic educational and hospital work, two of their traditional apostolates.

The Church in the U.S. was removed from mission status with promulgation of the apostolic constitution *Sapienti Consilio* by Pope St. Pius X on June 29, 1908.

Before that time, and even into the early 1920s, the Church in this country received financial assistance from mission-aid societies in France, Bavaria and Austria. Already, however, it was making increasing contributions of its own. At the present time, it is one of the major national contributors to the worldwide Society for the Propagation of the Faith.

American foreign missionary personnel increased from 14 or less in 1906 to an all-time high in 1968 of 9,655 priests, brothers, sisters, seminarians, and lay persons. The first missionary seminary in the U.S. was in operation at Techny, Illinois, in 1909, under the auspices of the Society of the Divine Word. Maryknoll, the first American missionary society,

was established in 1911 and sent its first priests to China in 1918. Despite these contributions, the Church in the U.S. has not matched the missionary commitment of some other nations.

Bishops' Conference

A highly important apparatus for mobilizing the Church's resources was established in 1917 under the title of the National Catholic War Council. Its name was changed to National Catholic Welfare Conference several years later, but its objectives remained the same: to serve as an advisory and coordinating agency of the American bishops for advancing works of the Church in fields of social significance and impact — education, communications, immigration, social action, legislation, youth and lay organizations.

The forward thrust of the bishops' social thinking was evidenced in a program of social reconstruction they recommended in 1919. By 1945, all but one of their 12 points had been enacted into legislation — including many later social security programs.

The NCWC was renamed the United States Catholic Conference (USCC) in November 1966, when the hierarchy also organized itself as a territorial conference with pastoral-juridical authority under the title, National Conference of Catholic Bishops. The USCC carried on the functions of the former NCWC until July 2001, when it merged with the National Conference of Catholic Bishops to create the USCCB.

Catholic Press

The establishment of the National Catholic News Service (NC) — now the Catholic News Service (CNS) — in 1920 was an important event in the development of the Catholic press, which had its beginnings about 100 years earlier. Early in the 20th century there were 63 weekly newspapers. The 2013 Catholic Press Directory, published by the Catholic Press Association, reported a total of 243 periodicals in North America, with a circulation of 10,330,011. The figures included 141 newspapers, with a circulation of 4,994,063; 70 magazines, with a circulation of 3,774,301; 19 newsletters, with a circulation of 891,147; and 13 other language periodicals (newspapers and magazines), with a circulation of 373,500.

Lay Organizations

A burst of lay organizational growth occurred from the 1930s onwards with the appearance of Catholic Action types of movements and other groups and associations devoted to special causes, social service and assistance for the poor and needy. Several special apostolates developed under the aegis of the National Catholic Welfare Conference (now the U.S. Catholic Conference); the outstanding one was the Confraternity of Christian Doctrine.

Nineteenth-century organizations of great influence included: The St. Vincent de Paul Society, whose first U.S. office was set up in 1845 in St. Louis; the Catholic Central Union (*Verein*), dating from 1855; the Knights of Columbus, founded in 1882; the Holy Name Society, organized in the U.S. in 1870; the Rosary Society (1891); and scores of chapters of the Sodality of the Blessed Virgin Mary.

Pastoral Concerns

The potential for growth of the Church in this country by immigration was sharply reduced but not entirely curtailed after 1921 with the passage of restrictive federal legislation. As a result, the Catholic population became more stabilized and, to a certain extent and for many reasons, began to acquire an identity of its own.

Some increase from outside has taken place in the past 50 years, however, from Canada, from Central and Eastern European countries, and from Puerto Rico and Latin American countries since World War II. This influx, while not as great as that of the 19th century and early 20th, has enriched the Church here with a sizable body of Eastern Rite Catholics for whom 12 ecclesiastical jurisdictions have been established. It has also created a challenge for pastoral care of millions of Hispanics in urban centers and in agricultural areas where migrant workers are employed.

The Church continues to grapple with serious pastoral problems in rural areas, where about 600 counties have no priests in ministry. The National Catholic Rural Life Conference was established in 1922 in an attempt to make the Catholic presence felt on the land, and the Glenmary Society since its foundation in 1939 has devoted itself to this single apostolate. Religious communities and diocesan priests are similarly engaged.

Other challenges lie in the cities and suburbs, where 75 percent of the Catholic population lives. Conditions peculiar to each segment of the metropolitan area have developed in recent years as the flight to the suburbs has not only altered some traditional aspects of parish life but has also, in combination with many other factors, left behind a complex of special problems in inner city areas.

A Post-War World

In the years after the Second World War, Catholics increasingly assumed a mainline role in American life. This was evidenced especially in the 1960 election of John F. Kennedy as the nation's first Catholic president. Catholic writers and thinkers were making a greater impact in the nation's life. One example of this was Trappist Thomas Merton's runaway best-selling book of 1948, *The Seven Storey Mountain*; another was the early television success of Bp. Fulton Sheen's "Life is Worth Living" series, begun in 1952. Meanwhile, lay leader Dorothy Day, founder of the Catholic Worker movement, continued to challenge American society with her views on pacifism and evangelical poverty.

A Post-Conciliar World

Catholic life in the United States was profoundly affected by the Second Vatican Council (1962-65). In the post-conciliar generation, American Catholicism grew both in numbers and complexity. Lay ministry and participation expanded; extensive liturgical changes (including the use of English) were implemented; and the numbers of priests, vowed religious and seminarians declined.

The Church has taken a high profile in many social issues. This has ranged from opposition to abortion, capital punishments and euthanasia to support for civil rights, economic justice and international peace and cooperation. Meanwhile Catholics have been deeply involved in inter-faith and ecumenical relationships. The bishops have issued landmark pastoral statements, including "The Challenge of Peace" (1983) and "Economic Justice for All" (1986).

In these years after the Council, the Catholics in America have known something of alienation, dissent and polarity. They also found new intensity and maturity. New U.S. saints have been declared by the universal church, such as Elizabeth Ann Seton (1975), John Nepomucene Neumann (1977), and Rose Philippine Duchesne (1988). Especially at the time of visits to America by Pope John Paul II (e.g., in 1979, 1987, 1993, 1995, and 1999), U.S. Catholics have given evidence – in their personal and corporate lives – of the ongoing power of faith, liturgy and the primal call of the Gospel in its many dimensions.

Modern U.S. Catholicism

In the decades after Vatican Council II, the American Church confronted a variety of challenges, including the increasing age of American religious, especially in the Religious Institutes of Women; the decline in vocations; the presence of nominally Catholic organizations that nevertheless work to counter or alter Catholic teaching on such issues as abortion, contraception, papal supremacy, collegiality, women's ordination, clerical celibacy, and homosexuality; the societal decay precipitated by a proliferation of an abortion culture; the weakening of the family structure and the destructive effects of unrestrained materialism and secular humanism; the spread of religious apathy and indifferentism; the needs of Catholic immigrants; and the lamentable state of American education. The varied difficulties, however, were overshadowed from late 2001 by the sexual scandal involving child molestation by a small number of priests in the country and the resulting legal cases, lawsuits, and media frenzy. While perpetrated by only a few hundred priests over nearly 40 years, the cases of child molestation (the vast majority of cases involved teenage boys) created the most severe scandal faced by the Church in the U.S. in the previous century. Compounding the legal and financial problems caused by the actions of the priests was the failure on the part of many bishops to recognize the severity of the scandal and the willingness of some bishops to move pedophile priests from one pastoral assignment to another.

At the summer meeting of the USCCB, the American bishops drafted a series of documents to insure the safety of children and to improve oversight of the situation. The bishops approved a Charter for the Protection of Children and Young People and Essential Norms for Diocesan/ Eparchial Policies Dealing With Allegations of Sexual Abuse of Minors by Priests, Deacons, or Other Church Personnel. Officials of the Holy See rejected initially certain elements of canonical details of the norms, but the subsequent changes made by the bishops were given full Vatican approval. Nevertheless, the scandal created crushing financial difficulties for many dioceses facing a host of lawsuits, as well as a crisis of confidence among American Catholics.ears have also brought significant controversies regarding restrictions on religious liberty, including the mandate issued by the Department of Health and Human Services compelling all religious-based employers (with a very narrow exception) to provide insurance coverage to employees that includes contraception, sterilization, and abortion-inducing drugs. In May 2012, 43 Catholic institutions began lawsuits against the HHS Mnadates.

Even in the face of these problems, there are a number of positive developments that give reason for guarded optimism: the progress in ecumenism; the rise of new religious congregations; the increase in conversions (over 400,000 a year); the marked sophistication of Catholic communications, centered in the USCCB; the Church's active role in social issues (human rights, poverty, health care, race relations, abortion and economic justice); and the greater involvement of the laity - especially women - in the life of the Church. Today, the membership in the U.S. is approximately 23% (69 million) of the U.S. population.

MISSIONARIES TO THE AMERICAS

An asterisk with a feast date indicates that the saint or blessed is listed in the General Roman Calendar or the proper calendar for U.S. dioceses.

Allouez, Claude Jean (1622-89): French Jesuit; missionary in Canada and midwestern U.S.; preached to 20 different tribes of Indians and baptized over 10,000; vicar general of Northwest.

Altham, John (1589-1640): English Jesuit; missionary among Indians in Maryland.

Amadeus of the Heart of Jesus (1846-1920): Provincial Superior of the Ursulines in the United States and missionary in Montana, Wyoming, and Alaska; founded 12 Ursuline missions for the Native Americans.

Anchieta, José de, Bl. (1534-97): Portuguese Jesuit, born Canary Islands; missionary in Brazil; writer; beatified 1980; feast, June 9.

Andreis, Felix de (1778-1820): Italian Vincentian; missionary and educator in western U.S.

Aparicio, Sebastian, Bl. (1502-1600): Franciscan brother, born Spain; settled in Mexico, c. 1533; worked as road builder and farmer before becoming Franciscan at about the age of 70; beatified, 1787; feast, Feb. 25.

Badin, Stephen T. (1768-1853): French missioner; came to U.S., 1792, when Sulpician seminary in Paris was closed; ordained, 1793, Baltimore, the first priest ordained in U.S.; missionary in Kentucky, Ohio and Michigan; bought land on which Notre Dame University now stands; buried on its campus.

Baraga, Frederic (1797-1868): Slovenian missionary bishop in U.S.; studied at Ljubljana and Vienna, ordained, 1823; came to U.S., 1830; missionary to Indians of Upper Michigan; first bishop of Marquette, 1857-1868; wrote Chippewa grammar, dictionary, prayer book and other works.

Bauer, Benedicta (1803-65): Missionary Dominican sister who helped establish convents and schools for German-speaking immigrants in New Jersey, California, Missouri, Washington and Kansas.

Bertran, Louis, St. (1526-81): Spanish Dominican; missionary in Colombia and Caribbean, 1562-69; canonized, 1671; feast, Oct. 9.

Betancur, Pedro de San José, Bl. (1626-67): Secular Franciscan, born Canary Islands; arrived in Guatemala, 1651; established hospital, school and homes for poor; beatified 1980; feast, Apr. 25.

Bourgeoys, Marguerite, St. (1620-1700): French foundress, missionary; settled in Canada, 1653; founded Congregation of Notre Dame, 1658; beati-

fied, 1950; canonized 1982; feast, Jan. 12.

Brébeuf, Jean de, St. (1593-1649): French Jesuit; missionary among Huron Indians in Canada; martyred by Iroquois, Mar. 16, 1649; canonized, 1930; one of Jesuit North American martyrs; feast, Oct. 19* (U.S.).

Cancer de Barbastro, Louis (1500-49): Spanish Dominican; began missionary work in Middle America, 1533; killed at Tampa Bay, Florida.

Castillo, John de, St. (1596-1628): Spanish Jesuit; worked in Paraguay Indian mission settlements (reductions); martyred; beatified, 1934; canonized, 1988; feast, Nov. 16.

Catala, Magin (1761-1830): Spanish Franciscan; worked in California mission of Santa Clara for 36 years.

Chabanel, Noel, St. (1613-49): French Jesuit; missionary among Huron Indians in Canada; murdered by renegade Huron, Dec. 8, 1649; canonized, 1930; one of Jesuit North American martyrs; feast, Oct. 19* (U.S.).

Chaumonot, Pierre Joseph (1611-93): French Jesuit; missionary among Indians in Canada.

Clarke, Mary Frances (1803-87): Founder of the Sisters of Charity of the Blessed Virgin Mary; went to Iowa to start schools for children of white farmers and Native Americans; in Iowa Women's Hall of Fame.

Claver, Peter, St. (1581-1654): Spanish Jesuit; missionary among Negroes of South America and West Indies; canonized, 1888; patron of Catholic missions among black people; feast, Sept. 9*.

Cope, Marianne, St. (1838-1918): German-born immigrant; entered Sisters of St. Francis; led sisters to Hawaii to take over a hospital and then to Molokai to care for lepers, including Bl. Damien de Veuster; she cared for women and young girls with the disease; she was beatified in May 2005 and canonized in Oct. 2012; feast, Jan. 23.

Daniel, Anthony, St. (1601-48): French Jesuit; missionary among Huron Indians in Canada; martyred by Iroquois, July 4, 1648; canonized, 1930; one of Jesuit North American martyrs; feast, Oct. 19* (U.S.).

De Smet, Pierre Jean (1801-73): Belgian-born Jesuit; missionary among Indians of northwestern U.S.; served as intermediary between Indians and U.S. government; wrote on Indian culture.

Duchesne, Rose Philippine, St. (1769-1852): French nun; educator and missionary in the U.S.; established first convent of the Society of the Sacred Heart in the U.S., at St. Charles, Missouri; founded schools for girls; did missionary work among Indians; beatified, 1940; canonized, 1988; feast, Nov. 18* (U.S.).

Farmer, Ferdinand (family name, Steinmeyer) (1720-86): German Jesuit; missionary in Philadelphia, where he died; one of the first missionaries in New Jersey.

Flaget, Benedict J. (1763-1850): French Sulpician bishop; came to U.S., 1792; missionary and educator in U.S.; first bishop of Bardstown, Kentucky (now Louisville), 1810-32; 1833-50.

Frances Xavier Cabrini: *See under* **Saints**.

Friess, Caroline (1824-92): Mother Superior of the School Sisters of Notre Dame in America from 1850-92; through her labors, the sisters opened 265 parochial schools in 29 diocese and four institutes of higher education for women.

Gallitzin, Demetrius (1770-1840): Russian prince, born The Hague; convert, 1787; ordained priest at Baltimore, 1795; frontier missionary, known as Fr. Smith; Gallitzin, PA, named for him; his cause for canonization was opened in 2007.

Garnier, Charles, St. (c. 1606-49): French Jesuit; missionary among Hurons in Canada; martyred by Iroquois, Dec. 7, 1649; canonized, 1930; one of Jesuit North American martyrs; feast, Oct. 19* (U.S.).

Gibault, Pierre (1737-1804): Canadian missionary in Illinois and Indiana; aided in securing states of Ohio, Indiana, Illinois, Michigan and Wisconsin for the Americans during Revolution.

Gonzalez, Roch, St. (1576-1628): Paraguayan Jesuit; worked in Paraguay Indian mission settlements (reductions); martyred; beatified, 1934; canonized, 1988; feast, Nov. 16.

Goupil, René, St. (1607-42): French lay missionary; had studied surgery at Orleans, France; missionary companion of St. Isaac Jogues among the Hurons; martyred, Sept. 29, 1642; canonized, 1930; one of Jesuit North American martyrs; feast, Oct. 19* (U.S.).

Gravier, Jacques (1651-1708): French Jesuit; missionary among Indians of Canada and midwestern U.S.

Guérin, St. Theodore (1798-1856): Pioneer educator and Sister of Providence; arrived in U.S. in 1830 and founded St. Mary-of the-Woods in Vincennes, Indiana. Canonized on Oct. 15, 2006; feast, Oct. 3.

Hennepin, Louis (d. c. 1701): Belgian-born Franciscan missionary and explorer of Great Lakes region and Upper Mississippi, 1675-81, when he returned to Europe.

Ireland, Seraphine (1842-1930): Mother Superior of the Sisters of St. Joseph in the upper Midwest; opened 30 schools, five hospitals, and the College of St. Catherine, the second Catholic college for women in the U.S.

Jesuit North American Martyrs: Isaac Jogues, Anthony Daniel, John de Brébeuf, Gabriel Lalemant, Charles Garnier, Noel Chabanel (Jesuit priests), and René Goupil and John Lalande (lay missionaries) who were martyred between Sept. 29, 1642, and Dec. 9, 1649, in the missions of New France; canonized June 29, 1930; feast, Oct. 19* (U.S.). See separate entries.

Jogues, Isaac, St. (1607-46): French Jesuit; missionary among Indians in Canada; martyred near present site of Auriesville, NY, by Mohawks, Oct. 18, 1646; canonized, 1930; one of Jesuit North American Martyrs; feast, Oct. 19* (U.S.).

Kino, Eusebio (1645-1711): Italian Jesuit; missionary and explorer in U.S.; arrived Southwest, 1681; established 25 Indian missions, took part in 14 exploring expeditions in northern Mexico, Arizona and southern California; helped develop livestock raising and farming in the area. He was selected in 1965 to represent Arizona in Statuary Hall.

Lalande, John, St. (d. 1646): French lay missionary, companion of Isaac Jogues; martyred by Mohawks at Auriesville, NY, Oct. 19, 1646; canonized, 1930; one of Jesuit North American Martyrs; feast, Oct. 19* (U.S.).

Lalemant, Gabriel, St. (1610-49): French Jesuit; missionary among the Hurons in Canada; martyred by the Iroquois, Mar. 17, 1649; canonized, 1930; one of Jesuit North American Martyrs; feast, Oct. 19* (U.S.).

Lalor, Teresa (d. 1846): Co-founder, with Bp. Neale of Baltimore, of the Visitation Order in the U.S.; helped establish houses in Mobile, Kaskaskia, and Baltimore.

Lamy, Jean Baptiste (1814-88): French prelate; came to U.S., 1839; missionary in Ohio and Kentucky; bishop in Southwest from 1850; first bishop (later Abp.) of Santa Fe, 1850-85. He was nominated in 1951 to represent New Mexico in Statuary Hall.

Las Casas, Bartolome (1474-1566): Spanish Dominican; missionary in Haiti, Jamaica and Venezuela; reformer of abuses against Indians and black people; bishop of Chalapas, Mexico, 1544-47; historian.

Laval, Françoise de Montmorency, Bl. (1623-1708): French-born missionary bishop in Canada; named vicar apostolic of Canada, 1658; first bishop of Québec, 1674; jurisdiction extended over all French-claimed territory in New World; beatified 1980; feast, May 6.

Manogue, Patrick (1831-95): Missionary bishop in U.S., born Ireland; migrated to U.S.; miner in California; studied for priesthood at St. Mary's of the Lake, Chicago, and St. Sulpice, Paris; ordained, 1861; missionary among Indians of California and Nevada; coadj. bishop, 1881-84, and bishop, 1884-86, of Grass Valley; first bishop of Sacramento, 1886-95, when see was transferred there.

Margil, Antonio, Ven. (1657-1726): Spanish Franciscan; missionary in Middle America; apostle of Guatemala; established missions in Texas.

Marie of the Incarnation, St. (Marie Guyard Martin) (1599-1672): French widow; joined Ursuline Nuns; arrived in Canada, 1639; first superior of Ursulines in Québec; missionary to Indians; writer; beatified 1980; feast, Apr. 30.

Marquette, Jacques (1637-75): French Jesuit; missionary and explorer in America; sent to New France, 1666; began missionary work among Ottawa Indians on Lake Superior, 1668; accompanied Joliet down the Mississippi to mouth of the Arkansas, 1673, and returned to Lake Michigan by way of Illinois River; made a second trip over the same route; his diary and map are of historical significance. He was selected in 1895 to represent Wisconsin in Statuary Hall.

Massias (Macias), John de, St. (1585-1645): Dominican brother, a native of Spain; entered Dominican Friary at Lima, Peru, 1622; served as doorkeeper until his death; beatified, 1837; canonized 1975; feast, Sept. 16.

Mazzuchelli, Samuel C. (1806-64): Italian Dominican; missionary in midwestern U.S.; called builder of the West; writer. A decree advancing his beatification cause was promulgated July 6, 1993.

Membre, Zenobius (1645-87): French Franciscan; missionary among Indians of Illinois; accompanied LaSalle expedition down the Mississippi (1681-82) and Louisiana colonizing expedition (1684) that landed in Texas; murdered by Indians.

Mozcygemba, Leopold (1824-91): Polish Franciscan priest and missionary, the patriarch of American Polonia; labored as a missionary in Texas and 11 other states for nearly 40 years; co-founded the Polish seminary of Sts. Cyril and Methodius in Detroit (1885) and served as confessor at Vatican Council I.

Nerinckx, Charles (1761-1824): Belgian priest; missionary in Kentucky; founded Sisters of Loretto at the Foot of the Cross.

Nobrega, Manoel (1517-70): Portuguese Jesuit; leader of first Jesuit missionaries to Brazil, 1549.

Padilla, Juan de (d. 1542): Spanish Franciscan; missionary among Indians of Mexico and southwestern U.S.; killed by Indians in Kansas; protomartyr of the U.S.

Palou, Francisco (c. 1722-89): Spanish Franciscan; accompanied Junípero Serra to Mexico, 1749;

founded Mission Dolores in San Francisco; wrote history of the Franciscans in California.

Pariseau, Mary Joseph (1833-1902): Canadian Sister of Charity of Providence; missionary in state of Washington from 1856; founded first hospitals in Northwest Territory; artisan and architect. Represents Washington in National Statuary Hall.

Peter of Ghent (d. 1572): Belgian Franciscan brother; missionary in Mexico for 49 years.

Porres, Martin de, St. (1579-1639): Peruvian Dominican oblate; his father was a Spanish soldier and his mother a black freedwoman from Panama; called wonder worker of Peru; beatified, 1837; canonized, 1962; feast, Nov. 3*.

Quiroga, Vasco de (1470-1565): Spanish missionary in Mexico; founded hospitals; bishop of Michoacan, 1537.

Ravalli, Antonio (1811-84): Italian Jesuit; missionary in far-western U.S., mostly Montana, for 40 years.

Raymbaut, Charles (1602-43): French Jesuit; missionary among Indians of Canada and northern U.S.

Richard, Gabriel (1767-1832): French Sulpician; missionary in Illinois and Michigan; a founder of University of Michigan; elected delegate to Congress from Michigan, 1823; first priest to hold seat in the House of Representatives.

Riepp, Benedicta (1825-62): Founder of the first Benedictine community of nuns in the U.S.; by the time of her death, the order had founded convents in Illinois, Kentucky, Minnesota, and New Jersey.

Rodriguez, Alfonso, St. (1598-1628): Spanish Jesuit; missionary in Paraguay; martyred; beatified, 1934; canonized, 1988; feast, Nov. 16.

Rosati, Joseph (1789-1843): Italian Vincentian; missionary bishop in U.S. (vicar apostolic of Mississippi and Alabama, 1822; coadj. of Louisiana and the Two Floridas, 1823-26; administrator of New Orleans, 1826-29; first bishop of St. Louis, 1826-1843).

Russell, Mary Baptist (1829-98): Mother Superior of the Sisters of Mercy in San Francisco from 1854-98; founded St. Mary's Hospital in 1857, schools, and homes the aged and former prostitutes.

Sahagun, Bernardino de (c. 1500-90): Spanish Franciscan; missionary in Mexico for over 60 years; expert on Aztec archaeology.

Seelos, Bl. Francis X. (1819-67): Redemptorist missionary, born Bavaria; ordained, 1844, at Baltimore; missionary in Pittsburgh and New Orleans. Beatified by Pope John Paul II on April 8, 2000.

Seghers, Charles J. (1839-86): Belgian missionary bishop in North America; Apostle of Alaska; Abp. of Oregon City (now Portland), 1880-84; murdered by berserk companion while on missionary journey.

Serra, Junípero, Bl. (1713-84): Spanish Franciscan, born Majorca; missionary in America; arrived Mexico, 1749, where he did missionary work for 20 years; began work in Upper California in 1769 and established nine of the 21 Franciscan missions along the Pacific coast; baptized some 6,000 Indians and confirmed almost 5,000; a cultural pioneer of California Represents California in Statuary Hall. He was declared venerable May 9, 1985, and was beatified Sept. 25, 1988; feast, July l* (U.S.).

Solanus, Francis, St. (1549-1610): Spanish Franciscan; missionary in Paraguay, Argentina and Peru; wonder worker of the New World; canonized,

1726; feast, July 14.

Sorin, Edward F. (1814-93): French priest; member of Congregation of Holy Cross; sent to U.S. in 1841; founder and first president of the University of Notre Dame; missionary in Indiana and Michigan.

Todadilla, Anthony de (1704-46): Spanish Capuchin; missionary to Indians of Venezuela; killed by Motilones.

Turibius de Mogrovejo, St. (1538-1606): Spanish Abp. of Lima, Peru, c. 1580-1606; canonized 1726; feast, Mar. 23*.

Twelve Apostles of Mexico (early 16th century): Franciscan priests who arrived in Mexico, 1524: Fathers Martin de Valencia (leader), Francisco de Soto, Martin de la Coruna, Juan Suares, Antonio de Ciudad Rodrigo, Toribio de Benevente, Garcia de Cisneros, Luis de Fuensalida, Juan de Ribas, Francisco Ximenes; Brothers Andres de Coroboda, and Juan de Palos.

Valdivia, Luis de (1561-1641): Spanish Jesuit; defender of Indians in Peru and Chile.

Vasques de Espiñosa, Antonio (early 17th century): Spanish Carmelite; missionary and explorer in Mexico, Panama and western coast of South America.

Vieira, Antonio (1608-87): Portuguese Jesuit; preacher; missionary in Peru and Chile; protector of Indians against exploitation by slave owners and traders; considered foremost prose writer of 17th-century Portugal.

Ward, Mary Francis Xavier (1810-84): Established the Sisters of Mercy in U.S.; arrived in Pittsburgh in 1843; founded convents in 10 states to care for the sick and poor and provide education.

White, Andrew (1579-1656): English Jesuit; missionary among Indians in Maryland.

Wimmer, Boniface (1809-87): German Benedictine; missionary among German immigrants in the U.S.

Youville, Marie Marguerite d', St. (1701-71): Canadian widow; foundress of Sisters of Charity (Grey Nuns), 1737, at Montréal: beatified, 1959; canonized 1990, first native Canadian saint; feast, Dec. 23.

Zumarraga, Juan de (1468-1548): Spanish Franciscan; missionary; first bishop of Mexico; introduced first printing press in New World, published first book in America, a catechism for Aztec Indians; extended missions in Mexico and Central America; vigorous opponent of exploitation of Indians; approved of devotions at Guadalupe; leading figure in early church history in Mexico.

FRANCISCAN MISSIONS

The 21 Franciscan missions of Upper California were established during the 54-year period from 1769 to 1822. Located along the old El Camino Real, or King's Highway, they extended from San Diego to San Francisco and were the centers of Indian civilization, Christianity and industry in the early history of the state.

Junípero Serra (beatified 1988) was the great pioneer of the missions of Upper California He and his successor as superior of the work, Fermin Lasuen, each directed the establishment of nine missions. One hundred and 46 priests of the Order of Friars Minor, most of them Spaniards, labored in the region from 1769 to 1845; 67 of them died at their posts, two as martyrs. The regular time of mission service was 10 years.

The missions were secularized by the Mexican government in the 1830s but were subsequently restored to the Church by the U.S. government. They are now variously used as the sites of parish churches, a university, houses of study and museums.

The names of the missions and the order of their establishment were as follows:

San Diego de Alcala, San Carlos Borromeo (El Carmelo), San Antonio de Padua, San Gabriel Arcangel, San Luis Obispo de Tolosa, San Francisco de Asis (Dolores), San Juan Capistrano; Santa Clara de Asis, San Buenaventura, Santa Barbara, La Purisima Concepcion de Maria Santisima, Santa Cruz, Nuestra Señora de la Soledad, San José de Guadalupe, San Juan Bautista, San Miguel Arcangel, San Fernando Rey de España, San Luis Rey de Francia, Santa Ínes, San Rafael Arcangel, San Francisco Solano de Sonoma (Sonoma).

Find more material at: www.CatholicAlmanac.com.

CHURCH-STATE RELATIONS IN THE UNITED STATES

CHURCH-STATE DECISIONS OF THE SUPREME COURT

Among sources of this selected listing of U.S. Supreme Court decisions was *The Supreme Court on Church and State*, Joseph Tussman, editor; Oxford University Press, New York, 1962.

Watson v. Jones, 13 Wallace 679 (1872): The Court declared that a member of a religious organization may not appeal to secular courts against a decision made by a church tribunal within the area of its competence.

Reynolds v. United States, 98 US 145 (1879): Davis v. Beason, 133 US 333 (1890); Church of Latter-Day Saints v. United States, 136 US 1 (1890). The Mormon practice of polygamy was at issue in three decisions and was declared unconstitutional.

Bradfield v. Roberts, 175 US 291 (1899): The Court denied that an appropriation of government funds for an institution (Providence Hospital, Washington, DC) run by Roman Catholic sisters violated the No Establishment Clause of the First Amendment.

Pierce v. Society of Sisters, 268 US 510 (1925): The Court denied that a state can require children to attend public schools only. The Court held that the liberty of the Constitution forbids standardization by such compulsion, and that the parochial schools involved had claims to protection under the Fourteenth Amendment.

Cochran v. Board of Education, 281 US 370 (1930): The Court upheld a Louisiana statute providing textbooks at public expense for children attending public or parochial schools. The Court held that the children and state were beneficiaries of the appropriations, with incidental secondary benefit going to the schools.

United States v. MacIntosh, 283 US 605 (1931): The Court denied that anyone can place allegiance to the will of God above his allegiance to the government since such a person could make his own interpretation of God's will the decisive test as to whether he would or would not obey the nation's law. The Court stated that the nation, which has a duty to survive, can require citizens to bear arms in its defense.

Everson v. Board of Education, 330 US 1 (1947): The Court upheld the constitutionality of a New Jersey statute authorizing free school bus trans-

portation for parochial as well as public school students. The Court expressed the opinion that the benefits of public welfare legislation, included under such bus transportation, do not run contrary to the concept of separation of Church and State.

McCollum v. Board of Education, 333 US 203 (1948): The Court declared unconstitutional a program for releasing children, with parental consent, from public school classes so they could receive religious instruction on public school premises from representatives of their own faiths.

Zorach v. Clauson, 343 US 306 (1952): The Court upheld the constitutionality of a New York statute permitting, on a voluntary basis, the release during school time of students from public school classes for religious instruction given off public school premises.

Torcaso v. Watkins, 367 US 488 (1961): The Court declared unconstitutional a Maryland requirement that one must make a declarati on of belief in the existence of God as part of the oath of office for notaries public.

McGowan v. Maryland, 81 Sp Ct 1101; Two Guys from Harrison v. McGinley, 81 Sp Ct 1135; Gallagher v. Crown Kosher Super Market, 81 Sp Ct 1128; Braunfeld v. Brown, 81 Sp Ct 1144 (1961): The Court ruled that Sunday closing laws do not violate the No Establishment of Religion Clause of the First Amendment, even though the laws were religious in their inception and still have some religious overtones. The Court held that, "as presently written and administered, most of them, at least, are of a secular rather than of a religious character, and that presently they bear no relationship to establishment of religion as those words are used in the Constitution of the United States."

Engel v. Vitale, 370 US 42 (1962): The Court declared that the voluntary recitation in public schools of a prayer composed by the New York State Board of Regents is unconstitutional on the ground that it violates the No Establishment of Religion Clause of the First Amendment.

Abington Township School District v. Schempp and Murray v. Curlett, 83 Sp Ct 1560 (1963): The Court ruled that Bible reading and recitation of the Lord's Prayer in public schools, with voluntary participation by students, are unconstitutional on the ground that they violate the No Establishment of Religion Clause of the First Amendment.

Chamberlin v. Dade County, 83 Sp Ct 1864 (1964): The Court reversed a decision of the Florida Supreme Court concerning the constitutionality of prayer and devotional Bible reading in public schools during the school day, as sanctioned by a state statute which specifically related the practices to a sound public purpose.

Board of Education v. Allen, No. 660 (1968): The Court declared constitutional the New York school-book-loan law that requires local school boards to purchase books with state funds and lend them to parochial and private school students.

Walz v. Tax Commission of New York (1970): The Court upheld the constitutionality of a New York statute exempting church-owned property from taxation.

Earle v. DiCenso, Robinson v. DiCenso, Lemon v. Kurtzman, Tilton v. Richardson (1971): In Earle v. DiCenso and Robinson v. DiCenso, the Court ruled unconstitutional a 1969 Rhode Island statute that provided salary supplements to teachers of secular subjects in parochial schools; in Lemon v. Kurtzman, the Court ruled unconstitutional a 1968 Pennsylvania statute that authorized the state to purchase services for the teaching of secular subjects in nonpublic schools. The principal argument against constitutionality in these cases was that the statutes and programs at issue entailed excessive entanglement of government with religion. In Tilton v. Richardson, the Court held that this argument did not apply to a prohibitive degree with respect to federal grants, under the Higher Education Facilities Act of 1963, for the construction of facilities for nonreligious purposes by four church-related institutions of higher learning, three of which were Catholic, in Connecticut.

Yoder, Miller and Yutzy (1972): In a case appealed on behalf of Yoder, Miller and Yutzy, the Court ruled that Amish parents were exempt from a Wisconsin statute requiring them to send their children to school until the age of 16. The Court said in its decision that secondary schooling exposed Amish children to attitudes, goals and values contrary to their beliefs, and substantially hindered "the religious development of the Amish child and his integration into the way of life of the Amish faith-community at the crucial adolescent state of development."

Committee for Public Education and Religious Liberty, et al., v. Nyquist, et al., No. 72-694 (1973): The Court ruled that provisions of a 1972 New York statute were unconstitutional on the grounds that they were violative of the No Establishment Clause of the First Amendment and had the "impermissible effect" of advancing the sectarian activities of church-affiliated schools. The programs ruled unconstitutional concerned: (1) maintenance and repair grants, for facilities and equipment, to ensure the health, welfare and safety of students in nonpublic, nonprofit elementary and secondary schools serving a high concentration of students from low income families; (2) tuition reimbursement ($50 per grade school child, $100 per high school student) for parents (with income less than $5,000) of children attending nonpublic elementary or secondary schools; tax deduction from adjusted gross income for parents failing to qualify under the above reimbursement plan, for each child attending a nonpublic school.

Sloan, Treasurer of Pennsylvania, et al., v. Lemon, et al., No. 72-459 (1973): The Court ruled unconstitutional a Pennsylvania Parent Reimbursement Act for Nonpublic Education which provided funds to reimburse parents (to a maximum of $150) for a portion of tuition expenses incurred in sending their children to nonpublic schools. The Court held that there was no significant difference between this and the New York tuition reimbursement program (above), and declared that the Equal Protection Clause of the Fourteenth Amendment cannot be relied upon to sustain a program held to be violative of the No Establishment Clause.

Levitt, et al., v. Committee for Public Education and Religious Liberty, et al., No. 72-269 (1973): The Court ruled unconstitutional the Mandated Services Act of 1970 under which New York provided $28 million ($27 per pupil from first to seventh grade, $45 per pupil from seventh to 12th grade) to reimburse nonpublic schools for testing, recording and reporting services required by the state. The Court declared that the act provided "impermissible aid" to religion in contravention of the No Establishment Clause.

In related decisions handed down June 25, 1973, the Court: (1) affirmed a lower-court decision against the

constitutionality of an Ohio tax credit law benefiting parents with children in nonpublic schools; (2) reinstated an injunction against a parent reimbursement program in New Jersey; (3) affirmed South Carolina's right to grant construction loans to church-affiliated colleges, and (4) dismissed an appeal contesting its right to provide loans to students attending church-affiliated colleges (Hunt v. McNair, Durham v. McLeod).

Wheeler v. Barrera (1974): The Court ruled that nonpublic school students in Missouri must share in federal funds for educationally deprived students on a comparable basis with public school students under Title I of the Elementary and Secondary Education Act of 1965.

Norwood v. Harrison 93 S. Ct. 2804: The Court ruled that public assistance that avoids the prohibitions of the "effect" and "entanglement" tests (and which therefore does not substantially promote the religious mission of sectarian schools) may be confined to the secular functions of such schools.

Wiest v. Mt. Lebanon School District (1974): The Court upheld a lower court ruling that invocation and benediction prayers at public high school commencement ceremonies do not violate the principle of separation of Church and State.

Meek v. Pittenger (1975): The Court ruled unconstitutional portions of a Pennsylvania law providing auxiliary services for students of nonpublic schools; at the same time, it ruled in favor of provisions of the law permitting textbook loans to students of such schools. In denying the constitutionality of auxiliary services, the Court held that they had the "primary effect of establishing religion" and involved "excessive entanglement" of Church and state officials with respect to supervision; objection was also made against providing such services only on the premises of nonpublic schools and only at the request of such schools.

TWA, Inc., v. Hardison, 75-1126; International Association of Machinists and Aero Space Workers v. Hardison, 75-1385 (1977): The Court ruled that federal civil-rights legislation does not require employers to make more than minimal efforts to accommodate employees who want a particular working day of as their religion's Sabbath Day, and that an employer cannot accommodate such an employee by violating seniority systems determined by a union collective bargaining agreement. The Court noted that its ruling was not a constitutional judgment but an interpretation of existing law.

Wolman v. Walter (1977): The Court ruled constitutional portions of an Ohio statute providing tax-paid textbook loans and some auxiliary services (standardized and diagnostic testing, therapeutic and remedial services, off school premises) for nonpublic school students. It decided that other portions of the law, providing state funds for nonpublic school field trips and instructional materials (audio-visual equipment, maps, tape recorders), were unconstitutional.

Byrne v. Public Funds for Public Schools (1979): The Court decided against the constitutionality of a 1976 New Jersey law providing state income tax deductions for tuition paid by parents of students attending parochial and other private schools.

Student Bus Transportation (1979): The Court upheld a Pennsylvania law providing bus transportation at public expense for students to nonpublic schools up to 10 miles away from the boundaries of the public school districts in which they lived.

Reimbursement (1980): The Court upheld the constitutionality of a 1974 New York law providing direct cash payment to nonpublic schools for the costs of state-mandated testing and record-keeping.

Ten Commandments (1980): The Court struck down a 1978 Kentucky law requiring the posting of the Ten Commandments in public school classrooms in the state.

Widmar v. Vincent (1981): The Court ruled that the University of Missouri at Kansas City could not deny student religious groups the use of campus facilities for worship services. The Court also, in Brandon v. Board of Education of Guilderland Schools, declined without comment to hear an appeal for reversal of lower court decisions denying a group of New York high school students the right to meet for prayer on public school property before the beginning of the school day.

Lubbock v. Lubbock Civil Liberties Union (1983): By refusing to hear an appeal in this case, the Court upheld a lower court ruling against a public policy of permitting student religious groups to meet on public school property before and after school hours.

Mueller v. Allen (1983): The Court upheld a Minnesota law allowing parents of students in public and nonpublic (including parochial) schools to take a tax deduction for the expenses of tuition, textbooks and transportation. Maximum allowable deductions were $500 per child in elementary school and $700 per child in grades seven through 12.

Lynch v. Donnelly (1984): The Court ruled 5-to-4 that the First Amendment does not mandate "complete separation of church and state," and that, therefore, the sponsorship of a Christmas nativity scene by the City of Pawtucket, RI, was not unconstitutional. The case involved a scene included in a display of Christmas symbols sponsored by the city in a park owned by a non-profit group. The majority opinion said "the Constitution (does not) require complete separation of church and state; it affirmatively mandates accommodation, not merely tolerance, of all religions and forbids hostility toward any. Anything less" would entail callous indifference not intended by the Constitution. Moreover, "such hostility would bring us into 'war with our national tradition as embodied in the First Amendment's guaranty of the free exercise of religion.'" (The additional quotation was from the 1948 decision in McCollum v. Board of Education.)

Christmas Nativity Scene (1985): The Court upheld a lower court ruling that the Village of Scarsdale, NY, must make public space available for the display of privately sponsored nativity scenes.

Wallace v. Jaffree, No. 83-812 (1985): The Court ruled against the constitutionality of a 1981 Alabama law calling for a public-school moment of silence that specifically included optional prayer.

Grand Rapids v. Ball, No. 83-990, and **Aguilar v. Felton, No. 84-237** (1985): The Court ruled against the constitutionality of programs in Grand Rapids and New York City allowing public school teachers to teach remedial entitlement subjects (under the Elementary and Secondary Education Act of 1965) in private schools, many of which were Catholic.

Bender v. Williamsport Area School District (1986): The Court let stand a lower federal-court decision allowing a public high school Bible study group the same "equal access" to school facilities as that enjoyed by other extra-curricular clubs. A similar decision was handed down

in 1990 in Board of Education v. Mergens, involving Westside High School in Omaha.

County of Allegheny v. American Civil Liberties Union (1989): The Court ruled (1) that the display of a Christmas nativity scene in the Allegheny County Courthouse in Pittsburgh, PA, violated the principle of separation of church and state because it appeared to be a government-sponsored endorsement of Christian belief; (2) and that the display of a Hanukkah menorah outside the Pittsburgh-Allegheny city-county building was constitutional because of its "particular physical setting" with secular symbols.

Unemployment Division v. Smith (1990): The Court ruled that religious use of the hallucinogenic cactus peyote is not covered by the First Amendment protection of religious freedom.

Lee v. Weisman (1992): The Court banned officially organized prayer at public school graduation ceremonies.

Lamb's Chapel v. Center Moriches Union School District (1993): The Court reversed a ruling by the 3rd U.S. Circuit Court of Appeals, declaring that the school district was wrong in prohibiting the congregation of Lamb's Chapel from using public school meeting space after hours to show a film series addressing family problems from a religious perspective. In view of the variety of organizations permitted to use school property after school hours, said the Court's opinion: "There would have been no realistic danger that the community would think that the district was endorsing religion or any particular creed, and any benefit to religion or to the church would have been no more than incidental."

5th U.S. Circuit Court of Appeals (1993): The Court let stand a ruling by the 5th U.S. Circuit Court of Appeals, permitting students in Texas, Mississippi and Louisiana to include student-organized and student-led prayers in graduation exercises.

Church of Lukumi Babalu Aye v. City of Hialeah (1993): The Court ruled that municipal laws that effectively prohibit a single church from performing its religious rituals are unconstitutional. The ordinances at issue singled out one religion, Santeria, for the purpose of restricting its members from the practice of ritual animal sacrifices.

Zobrest v. Catalina Foothills School District (1993): The Court ruled that a public school district may provide a sign-language interpreter for a deaf student attending a Catholic school without violating constitutional separation of church and state. The majority opinion said: "Handicapped children, not sectarian schools are the primary beneficiaries of the Disabilities Education Act; to the extent sectarian schools benefit at all from (the act), they are only incidental beneficiaries."

Fairfax County, Va., school district (1994): The Court upheld lower court rulings against a Fairfax County, VA, school district's practice of charging churches more rent than other entities for the use of school buildings.

Board of Education of Kiryas Joel Village School District v. Grumet (1994): The Court ruled in 1994 that a school district created to meet the special education needs of an Hasidic Jewish community violated the Establishment Clause of the Constitution. The Court said the New York Legislature effectively endorsed a particular religion when it established a public school district for the Satmar Hasidic Village of Kiryas Joel.

Agostino v. Felton (1997): The court reversed, 5 to 4, its 1985 Aguilar v. Felton ruling, which had declared it unconstitutional for teachers employed by public school districts to hold Title I remedial programs for low-income students on the property of church-related schools.

Boerne v. Flores (1997): The court ruled, 6 to 3, that the Religious Freedom Restoration Act (1993) was unconstitutional because Congress overstepped its constitutional authority in enacting the law. Congress "has been given the power to 'enforce,' not the power to determine what constitutes a constitutional violation," said the majority opinion.

Mitchell v. Helms (2000): The court ruled, 6 to 3, that a Louisiana parish can distribute money for instructional equipment — including computers, books, maps, and film strip projectors — to private schools as long as it is done in a "secular, neutral and non-ideological" way. The court's decision overturns two previous Supreme Court bans on giving public materials to parochial schools.

Santa Fe Independent School District v. Doe (2000): The court affirmed a lower court ruling that said prayer in public schools must be private and that such prayers at high school football games violate the constitutionally required separation of church and state. At issue in the Santa Fe case was a Texas school policy which permitted students selected by their peers to deliver an inspirational message of their own design at football games and the graduation ceremony. In 1999, the Santa Fe policy was struck down by the U.S. Court of Appeals for the Fifth Circuit. The Court of Appeals held that the policy violated the Establishment Clause of the First Amendment, even though the government played no role in creating the message or selecting the messenger.

Chandler v. Siegelman (2001): The court let stand a lower court ruling that students may participate in group prayers at school functions such as football games or graduations.

The Good News Club v. Milford Central Schools (2001): The court ruled that if the Boy Scouts and 4-H can use a public school as a meeting hall, a children's Bible study class can also.

Brown v. Gilmore (2001): The court declined to hear a challenge to Virginia's mandatory minute of silence in schools.

Children's Health Care is a Legal Duty Inc. v. McMullan (2001): The court turned down an appeal that claimed Medicare and Medicaid payments to church-run health centers violate the constitutional separation of church and state.

Gentala v. Tucson (2001): The court ordered a federal appeals court to take another look at a case that asked whether taxpayers must cover $340 in expenses from a prayer rally in a city park, saying it should be reconsidered in light of the high court's earlier ruling that a Bible club cannot be excluded from meeting at a public school so long as other groups with a moral viewpoint are allowed to gather there.

Cleveland Voucher Program (2002): By a 5-4 ruling, the court upheld the Cleveland voucher program that had been implemented in 1995 to assist the improvement of one of the worst public school systems in the country.

Ten Commandments (2005): By a 5-4 vote, the court prohibited the posting of the Ten Commandments in court houses; at the same time, the court permitted their posting in state houses.

Gonzales v. Carhart and Gonzales v. Planned Parenthood (2007): By a 5-4 vote, the court upheld the Partial Birth Abortion Ban Act that Congress passed and President George W. Bush signed into law in 2003, saying that the prohibition does not violate the constitutional right to an abortion.

RELIGION IN PUBLIC SCHOOLS

Based on a Catholic News Service article by Carol Zimmermann.

A diverse group of religious and civil rights organizations issued a joint statement Apr. 13, 1995, in an effort to clarify the confusing issue of prayer and religious observances or discussions in public schools. Their six-page statement outlines what is and what is not currently permissible in expressing religious beliefs in public schools.

The statement says, for example: "Students have the right to pray individually or in groups, or to discuss their religious views with their peers so long as they are not disruptive." But, the statement specifies that such prayers or discussions do not include "the right to have a captive audience listen or to compel other students to participate."

Prayer at Graduations

Regarding prayer at graduation ceremonies, the document says school officials may not mandate or organize prayer, but fails to set the record straight about student-led prayer at these services.

"The courts have reached conflicting conclusions under the federal Constitution" in this area, says the statement, recommending that schools consult their lawyers for the rules that apply to them, "until the issue is authoritatively resolved."

Since the Supreme Court's 1992 Lee v. Weisman opinion prohibited school authorities from even arranging for a speaker to present a prayer, lower courts in different states have made various rulings about student-led prayer at commencement exercises.

In Virginia, the state's Attorney General and the Board of Education proposed guidelines in mid-April to allow student-led prayer at graduations, despite a 1994 ruling by a U.S. district judge banning all prayer at graduations.

Religion in the Classroom

"It is both permissible and desirable to teach objectively about the role of religion in the history of the United States and other countries," but public school teachers may not specifically teach religion.

The same rules apply to the recurring controversy surrounding theories of evolution. Teachers may discuss explanations of the beginnings of life, but only within the confines of classes on religion or social studies. Public school teachers are required, according to the statement, to teach only scientific explanations of life's beginnings in science classes. And, just as teachers may not advance a religious view, they should not ridicule a student's religious belief.

Constitutional Protection

The statement says that students' expressions of religious beliefs in reports, homework or artwork are constitutionally protected. Likewise, students have the right to speak to and attempt to persuade their peers on religious topics. "But school officials should intercede to stop student religious speech if it turns into religious harassment aimed at a student or a small group of students."

The statement also says:

• Students have the right to distribute religious literature to their schoolmates, subject to reasonable restrictions for any non-school literature.

• Student religious clubs in secondary schools "must be permitted to meet and to have equal access" to school media for announcing their events.

• Religious messages on T-shirts and the like cannot be singled out for suppression.

• Schools can use discretion about dismissing students for off-site religious instruction.

The 35 organizations that endorsed the statement included the National Association of Evangelicals, the American Jewish Congress, the Christian Legal Society, the National Council of Churches, the Baptist Joint Committee on Public Affairs, the American Muslim Council, the Presbyterian Church (USA) and the American Civil Liberties Union.

Purpose of the Statement

"By making this document available," said Phil Baum, executive director of the American Jewish Congress, "the organizations are attempting to clarify what has become one of the most divisive issues of our time: religion in the public schools."

He said the document attempts to "ensure that the rights of all students are respected in the public schools."

Baum noted that the American Jewish Congress, which initiated the effort to draft the statement, had a long-standing commitment to ensuring that public schools are themselves religiously neutral.

"We believe, however, that it is inconsistent with that historic commitment to ask the public schools to root out private expressions of religious faith."

CHURCH TAX EXEMPTION

The exemption of church-owned property was ruled constitutional by the U.S. Supreme Court May 4, 1970, in the case of Walz v. The Tax Commission of New York.

Suit in the case was brought by Frederick Walz, who purchased in June 1967, a 22-by-29-foot plot of ground in Staten Island valued at $100 and taxable at $5.24 a year. Shortly after making the purchase, Walz instituted a suit in New York State, contending that the exemption of church property from taxation authorized by state law increased his own tax rate and forced him indirectly to support churches in violation of his constitutional right to freedom of religion under the First Amendment. Three New York courts dismissed the suit, which had been instituted by mail. The Supreme Court, judging that it had probable jurisdiction, then took the case.

In a 7-1 decision affecting Church-state relations in every state in the nation, the Court upheld the New York law under challenge.

For and Against

Chief Justice Warren E. Burger, who wrote the majority opinion, said that Congress from its ear-

liest days had viewed the religion clauses of the Constitution as authorizing statutory real estate tax exemption to religious bodies. He declared: "Nothing in this national attitude toward religious tolerance and two centuries of uninterrupted freedom from taxation has given the remotest sign of leading to an established church or religion, and on the contrary it has operated affirmatively to help guarantee the free exercise of all forms of religious beliefs."

Justice William O. Douglas wrote in dissent that the involvement of government in religion as typified in tax exemption may seem inconsequential but: "It is, I fear, a long step down the establishment path. Perhaps I have been misinformed. But, as I read the Constitution and the philosophy, I gathered that independence was the price of liberty."

Burger rejected Douglas' "establishment" fears. If tax exemption is the first step toward establishment, he said, "the second step has been long in coming."

The basic issue centered on the following question: Is there a contradiction between federal constitutional provisions against the establishment of religion, or the use of public funds for religious purposes, and state statutes exempting church property from taxation? In the Walz decision, the Supreme Court ruled that there is no contradiction.

Legal Background

The U.S. Constitution makes no reference to tax exemption. There was no discussion of the issue in the Constitutional Convention nor in debates on the Bill of Rights.

In the Colonial and post-Revolutionary years, some churches had established status and were state-supported. This changed with enactment of the First Amendment, which laid down no-establishment as the federal norm. This norm was adopted by the states which, however, exempted churches from tax liabilities.

No establishment, no hindrance, was the early American view of Church-State relationships.

This view, reflected in custom law, was not generally formulated in statute law until the second half of the 19th century, although specific tax exemption was provided for churches in Maryland in 1798, in Virginia in 1800, and in North Carolina in 1806.

The first major challenge to church property exemption was initiated by the Liberal League in the 1870s. It reached the point that President Grant included the recommendation in a State of the Union address in 1875, stating that church property should bear its own proportion of taxes. The plea fell on deaf ears in Congress, but there was some support for the idea at state levels. The exemption, however, continued to survive various challenges.

About 36 state constitutions contain either mandatory or permissive provisions for exemption. Statutes provide for exemption in all other states.

There has been considerable litigation challenging this exemption, but most of it focused on whether a particular property satisfied statutory requirements. Few cases before Walz focused on the strictly constitutional question, whether directly under the First Amendment or indirectly under the Fourteenth.

Objections

Objectors to the tax exempt status of churches feel that churches should share, through taxation, in the cost of the ordinary benefits of public services they enjoy, and/or that the amount of "aid" enjoyed through exemption should be proportionate to the amount of social good they do.

According to one opinion, exemption is said to weaken the independence of churches from the political system that benefits them by exemption.

In another view, exemption is said to involve the government in decisions regarding what is and what is not religion.

The Wall of Separation

Thomas Jefferson, in a letter written to the Danbury (Connecticut) Baptist Association Jan. 1, 1802, coined the metaphor, "a wall of separation between Church and State," to express a theory concerning interpretation of the religion clauses of the First Amendment: "Congress shall make no law respecting an establishment of religion or prohibiting the free exercise thereof."

The metaphor was cited for the first time in judicial proceedings in 1879, in the opinion by Chief Justice Waite in Reynolds v. United States. It did not, however, figure substantially in the decision.

Accepted as Rule

In 1947 the wall of separation gained acceptance as a constitutional rule, in the decision handed down in Everson v. Board of Education. Associate Justice Black, in describing the principles involved in the No Establishment Clause, wrote:

"Neither a state nor the Federal Government can set up a church. Neither can pass laws which aid one religion, aid all religions, or prefer one religion over another. Neither can force nor influence a person to go to or to remain away from church against his will or force him to profess a belief or disbelief in any religion. No person can be punished for entertaining or professing religious beliefs or disbeliefs, for church attendance or non-attendance. No tax in any amount, large or small, can be levied to support any religious activities or institutions, whatever they may be called, or whatever form they may adopt to teach or practice religion. Neither a state nor the Federal Government can, openly or secretly, participate in the affairs of any religious organizations or groups and vice versa. In the words of Jefferson, the clause against establishment of religion by law was intended to erect 'a wall of separation between Church and State.' "

Mr. Black's associates agreed with his statement of principles, which were framed without reference to the Freedom of Exercise Clause. They disagreed, however, with respect to application of the principles, as the split decision in the case indicated. Five members of the Court held that the benefits of public welfare legislation — in this case, free bus transportation to school for parochial as well as public school students — did not run contrary to the concept of separation of Church and State embodied in the First Amendment.

(For coverage of the recent Supreme Court decision pertaining to vouchers, see **Education**.)

CATHOLICS IN THE U.S. GOVERNMENT

CATHOLICS IN PRESIDENTS' CABINETS

From 1789 to 1940, nine Catholics were appointed to cabinet posts by six of 32 presidents. The first was Roger Brooke Taney (later named first Catholic Supreme Court Justice) who was appointed in 1831 by Andrew Jackson. Catholics have been appointed to cabinet posts from the time of Franklin D. Roosevelt to the present. Listed below in chronological order are presidents, Catholic cabinet officials, posts held, dates.

Andrew Jackson: Roger B. Taney, Attorney General, 1831-33, Secretary of Treasury, 1833-34.

Franklin Pierce: James Campbell, Postmaster General, 1853-57.

James Buchanan: John B. Floyd, Secretary of War, 1857-61.

William McKinley: Joseph McKenna, Attorney General, 1897-98.

Theodore Roosevelt: Robert J. Wynne, Postmaster General, 1904-05; Charles Bonaparte, Secretary of Navy, 1905-06, Attorney General, 1906-09.

Franklin D. Roosevelt: James A. Farley, Postmaster General, 1933-40; Frank Murphy, Attorney General, 1939-40; Frank C. Walker, Postmaster General, 1940-45.

Harry S. Truman: Robert E. Hannegan, Postmaster General, 1945-47; J. Howard McGrath, Attorney General, 1949-52; Maurice J. Tobin, Secretary of Labor, 1948-53; James P. McGranery, Attorney General, 1952-53.

Dwight D. Eisenhower: Martin P. Durkin, Secretary of Labor, 1953; James P. Mitchell, Secretary of Labor, 1953-61.

John F. Kennedy: Robert F. Kennedy, Attorney General, 1961-63; Anthony Celebrezze, Secretary of Health, Education and Welfare, 1962-63; John S. Gronouski, Postmaster General, 1963.

Lyndon B. Johnson: Robert F. Kennedy, 1963-64, Anthony Celebrezze, 1963-65, and John S. Gronouski, 1963-65, reappointed to posts held in Kennedy Cabinet; John T. Connor, Secretary of Commerce, 1965-67; Lawrence O'Brien, Postmaster General, 1965-68.

Richard M. Nixon: Walter J. Hickel, Secretary of Interior, 1969-71; John A. Volpe, Secretary of Transportation, 1969-72; Maurice H. Stans, Secretary of Commerce, 1969-72; Peter J. Brennan, Secretary of Labor, 1973-74; William E. Simon, Secretary of Treasury, 1974.

Gerald R. Ford: Peter J. Brennan, 1974-75, and William E. Simon, 1974-76, reappointed to posts held above.

Jimmy Carter: Joseph Califano, Jr., Secretary of Health, Education and Welfare, 1977-79; Benjamin Civiletti, Attorney General, 1979-81; Moon Landrieu, Secretary of Housing and Urban Development, 1979-81; Edmund S. Muskie, Secretary of State, 1980-81.

Ronald Reagan: Alexander M. Haig, Secretary of State, 1981-82; Raymond J. Donovan, Secretary of Labor, 1981-84; Margaret M. Heckler, Secretary of Health and Human Services, 1983-85; William J. Bennett, Secretary of Education, 1985-88; Ann Dore McLaughlin, Secretary of Labor, 1988-89; Lauro F. Cavazos, Secretary of Education, 1988-89; Nicholas F. Brady, Secretary of

Treasury, 1988-89.

George Bush: Lauro F. Cavazos (reappointed), Secretary of Education, 1989-90; Nicholas F. Brady (reappointed), Secretary of Treasury, 1989-93; James D. Watkins, Secretary of Energy, 1989-93; Manuel Lujan, Jr., Secretary of Interior, 1989-93; Edward J. Derwinski, Secretary of Veteran Affairs, 1989-92; Lynn Martin, Secretary of Labor, 1990-93; Edward Madigan, Secretary of Agriculture, 1991-93; William P. Barr, Attorney General, 1991-93.

Bill Clinton: Henry G. Cisneros, Secretary of Housing and Urban Development, 1993-97; Federico F. Peña, Secretary of Transportation, 1993-97; Donna Shalala, Secretary of Health and Human Services, 1993-2001; William M. Daley, Secretary of Commerce, 1997-2000; Andrew Cuomo, Secretary of Housing and Urban Development, 1997-2001; Alexis H. Herman, Secretary of Labor, 1997-2001.

George W. Bush: Paul O'Neill, Secretary of the Treasury, 2001-03; Tommy Thompson, Secretary of Health and Human Services, 2001-05; Mel Martinez, Secretary of Housing and Urban Development, 2001-05; Anthony Principi, Secretary of Veterans Affairs, 2001-05; Jim Nicholson, Secretary of Veterans Affairs, 2005-07; Alberto Gonzalez, Attorney General, 2005-07; Carlos Gutierrez, Commerce Secretary, 2005-08.

Barack H. Obama: Sen. John Kerry, Secretary of State, 2013-; Tom Vilsack, Secretary of Agriculture, 2009-; Kathleen Sebelius, Secretary of Health and Human Services, 2009-; Ray Lahood, Secretary of Transportation, 2009-; Shaun Donovan, Secretary of Housing and Urban Development, 2009-; Janet Napolitano, Secretary of Homeland Security, 2009-; Sen. Ken Salazar, Secretary of the Interior, 2009-12; Hilda Solis, Secretary of Labor, 2009-12.

[It is noted that while nominally Catholic, members of the Obama Cabinet uniformly hold positions that are in strong opposition to the Church's teachings, particularly regarding abortion.]

Cabinet members who became Catholics after leaving their posts were: Thomas Ewing, Secretary of Treasury under William H. Harrison and Secretary of Interior under Zachary Taylor; Luke E. Wright, Secretary of War under Theodore Roosevelt; Albert B. Fall, Secretary of Interior under Warren G. Harding.

Catholics in the 113th Congress

As of the start of the 113th Congress in 2013, there were 163 Catholic members, comprising approximately 25% of the total Congressional membership and therefore the largest faith group in that body (Baptists were second, with 73 House and Senate members; there are also 46 Methodists). There are presently 136 Catholics in the House (61 Republicans and 75 Democrats) and 27 Catholics in the Senate (18 Democrats and 9 Republicans), according to the Pew Forum and Congressional Quarterly. In the 112th Congress, there were 63 Republicans and 69 Democrats, meaning that the number of Catholic Republicans in the House has declined. Among congressional leaders, three are Catholics (Speaker of the House John Boehner, R-Ohio; and House Minority Leader Nancy Pelosi, D-Calif.; Senate Majority Whip Richard Durbin, D-Ill.). It is noted, however, that Catholic representatives and senators do not vote as a bloc, nor do many vote consistently in line with the teachings of the Church. There are also 34 members who are of the Jewish faith,

as well as three practicing Buddhists, and two Muslims, and one Hindu. Six members of the new Congress said they have no religious affiliation. In addition, there are 43 Presbyterians, 39 Episcopalians, 23 Lutherans, 15 Mormons, and five members of the Orthodox Churches. Ten said they had no religious affiliation or did not know.

Catholic Supreme Court Justices

Roger B. Taney, Chief Justice 1836-64; app. by Andrew Jackson.

Edward D. White, Associate Justice 1894-1910, app. by Grover Cleveland; Chief Justice 1910-21; app. by William H. Taft.

Joseph McKenna, Associate Justice 1898-1925; app. by William McKinley.

Pierce Butler, Associate Justice 1923-39; app. by Warren G. Harding.

Frank Murphy, Associate Justice 1940-49; app. by Franklin D. Roosevelt.

William Brennan, Associate Justice 1956-90; app. by Dwight D. Eisenhower.

Antonin Scalia, Associate Justice 1986-; app. by Ronald Reagan.

Anthony M. Kennedy, Associate Justice 1988-; app. by Ronald Reagan.

Clarence Thomas, Associate Justice 1991-; app. by George H. W. Bush.

John Roberts, Chief Justice 2005-; app. by George W. Bush.

Samuel Alito, Associate Justice 2005-; app. George W. Bush.

Sonia Sotomayor, Associate Justice 2009-; app. Barack Obama.

Sherman Minton, Associate Justice from 1949 to 1956; became a Catholic several years before his death in 1965.

Catholics in Statuary Hall

Statues of 13 Catholics deemed worthy of national commemoration are among those enshrined in National Statuary Hall and other places in the U.S. Capitol. The Hall, formerly the chamber of the House of Representatives, was erected by Act of Congress July 2, 1864.

Donating states, names and years of placement are listed.

Arizona: Rev. Eusebio Kino, S.J., missionary, 1965.

California: Rev. Junípero Serra, O.F.M. missionary, 1931. (Beatified 1988.)

Hawaii: Fr. Damien, missionary, 1969. (Canonized 2009.)

Illinois: Gen. James Shields, statesman, 1893.

Louisiana: Edward D. White, Justice of the U.S. Supreme Court (1894-1921), 1955.

Maryland: Charles Carroll, statesman, 1901.

Nevada: Patrick A. McCarran, statesman, 1960.

New Mexico: Dennis Chavez, statesman, 1966. (Abp. Jean B. Lamy, pioneer prelate of Santa Fe, was nominated for Hall honor in 1951.)

North Dakota: John Burke, U.S. treasurer, 1963.

Oregon: Dr. John McLoughlin, pioneer, 1953.

Washington: Mother Mary Joseph Pariseau, pioneer missionary and humanitarian.

West Virginia: John E. Kenna, statesman, 1901.

Wisconsin: Rev. Jacques Marquette, S.J., missionary, explorer, 1895.

United States Hierarchy

U.S. CATHOLIC JURISDICTIONS, HIERARCHY, STATISTICS

According to the United States Conference of Catholic Bishops, the organizational structure of the Catholic Church in the United States consists of 195 archdioceses/dioceses, one Apostolic Exarchate, and one Personal Ordinariate. Specifically, there are: 145 Latin Catholic dioceses, 33 Latin Catholic archdioceses, 15 Eastern Catholic dioceses, 2 Eastern Catholic archdioceses, one Apostolic Exarchate for the Syro-Malankara Catholic Church, one Personal Ordinariate of the Chair of St. Peter. The current number of archdioceses reflects the creation of the archdiocese of Galveston-Houston on Dec. 29, 2004; the current number of suffragan sees reflects the creation of the new diocese of Laredo, TX, on July 3, 2000, the eparchy of St. Peter the Apostle of San Diego of the Chaldeans on May 21, 2002, and the elevation of the Apostolic Exarchate for Armenian Catholics in the United States and Canada to the rank of eparchy on Sept. 13, 2005. The eparchy of Our Lady of Deliverance of Newark for Syrian-rite Catholics in the U.S. and Canada has its seat in Newark, NJ. The Armenian apostolic eparchy for the United States and Canada has its seat in New York. On July 14, 2010, Pope Benedict XVI created an apostolic exarchate for the Syro-Malankara Catholic Church in the United States. On Jan. 1, 2012, Pope Benedict XVI established the Personal Ordinariate of the Chair of St. Peter for those groups of Anglicans in the U.S. who seek to enter into full communion with the Catholic Church. On April 23, 2013, Pope Francis extended the jurisdiction of the Romanian Catholic Eparchy of St. George the Martyr in Canton, Ohio, over all the Romanian Greek-Catholics residing in Canada. On Nov. 14, 2006, the Bishops of the USCCB approved a new non-geographic 15th USCCB region, composed of the bishops of Eastern-rite Catholic Churches. The structure includes the territorial episcopal conference known as the United States Conference of Catholic Bishops (USCCB). The representative of the Holy See to the Church in the United States is an Apostolic Nuncio (presently Archbishop Carlo Maria Viganò, J.C.D.).

ECCLESIASTICAL PROVINCES

(Sources: The Official Catholic Directory, *Catholic News Service.)*

The 34 ecclesiastical provinces bear the names of archdioceses, i.e., of metropolitan sees.

Anchorage: Archdiocese of Anchorage and suffragan sees of Fairbanks, Juneau. Geographical area: Alaska.

Atlanta: Archdiocese of Atlanta (GA) and suffragan sees of Savannah (GA); Charlotte and Raleigh (NC), Charleston (SC). Geographical area: Georgia, North Carolina, South Carolina.

Baltimore: Archdiocese of Baltimore (MD) and suffragan sees of Wilmington (DE); Arlington and Richmond (VA); Wheeling-Charleston (WV). Geographical area: Maryland (except five counties), Delaware, Virginia, West Virginia.

Boston: Archdiocese of Boston (MA) and suffragan sees of Fall River, Springfield and Worcester (MA); Portland (ME); Manchester (NH); Burlington (VT). Geographical area: Massachusetts, Maine, New Hampshire, Vermont.

Chicago: Archdiocese of Chicago and suffragan sees of Belleville, Joliet, Peoria, Rockford, Springfield. Geographical area: Illinois.

Cincinnati: Archdiocese of Cincinnati and suffragan sees of Cleveland, Columbus, Steubenville, Toledo, Youngstown. Geographical area: Ohio.

Denver: Archdiocese of Denver (CO) and suffragan sees of Colorado Springs and Pueblo (CO); Cheyenne (WY). Geographical area: Colorado, Wyoming.

Detroit: Archdiocese of Detroit and suffragan sees of Gaylord, Grand Rapids, Kalamazoo, Lansing, Marquette, Saginaw. Geographical area: Michigan.

Dubuque: Archdiocese of Dubuque and suffragan sees of Davenport, Des Moines, Sioux City. Geographical area: Iowa.

Galveston-Houston: Archdiocese of Galveston-Houston and suffragan sees of Austin, Beaumont, Brownsville, Corpus Christi, Tyler, and Victoria. Geographical area: Southeast Texas.

Hartford: Archdiocese of Hartford (CT) and suffragan sees of Bridgeport and Norwich (CT); Providence (RI). Geographical area: Connecticut, Rhode Island.

Indianapolis: Archdiocese of Indianapolis and suffragan sees of Evansville, Fort Wayne-South Bend, Gary, Lafayette. Geographical area: Indiana.

Kansas City (KS): Archdiocese of Kansas City and suffragan sees of Dodge City, Salina, Wichita. Geographical area: Kansas.

Los Angeles: Archdiocese of Los Angeles and suffragan sees of Fresno, Monterey, Orange, San Bernardino, San Diego. Geographical area: Southern and Central California.

Louisville: Archdiocese of Louisville (KY) and suffragan sees of Covington, Lexington and Owensboro (KY); Knoxville, Memphis and Nashville (TN). Geographical area: Kentucky, Tennessee.

Miami: Archdiocese of Miami and suffragan sees of Orlando, Palm Beach, Pensacola-Tallahassee, St. Augustine, St. Petersburg, Venice. Geographical area: Florida.

Milwaukee: Archdiocese of Milwaukee and suffragan sees of Green Bay, La Crosse, Madison, Superior. Geographical area: Wisconsin.

Mobile: Archdiocese of Mobile, AL, and suffragan sees of Birmingham (AL); Biloxi and Jackson (MS). Geographical area: Alabama, Mississippi.

Newark: Archdiocese of Newark and suffragan sees of Camden, Metuchen, Paterson, Trenton. Geographical area: New Jersey.

New Orleans: Archdiocese of New Orleans and suffragan sees of Alexandria, Baton Rouge, Houma-Thibodaux, Lafayette, Lake Charles and Shreveport. Geographical area: Louisiana.

New York: Archdiocese of New York and suffragan sees of Albany, Brooklyn, Buffalo, Ogdensburg, Rochester, Rockville Centre, Syracuse. Geographical area: New York.

Oklahoma City: Archdiocese of Oklahoma City (OK) and suffragan sees of Tulsa (OK) and Little Rock (AR). Geographical area: Oklahoma, Arkansas.

Omaha: Archdiocese of Omaha and suffragan sees of Grand Island, Lincoln. Geographical area: Nebraska.

Philadelphia: Archdiocese of Philadelphia and suffragan sees of Allentown, Altoona-Johnstown, Erie, Greensburg, Harrisburg, Pittsburgh, Scranton. Geographical area: Pennsylvania.

Philadelphia (Byzantine, Ukrainians): Metropolitan See of Philadelphia (Byzantine) and Eparchies of St. Josaphat in Parma (OH), St. Nicholas of the Ukrainians in Chicago and Stamford, CT The jurisdiction extends to all Ukrainian Catholics in the U.S. from the ecclesiastical province of Galicia in the Ukraine.

Pittsburgh (Byzantine, Ruthenians): Metropolitan See of Pittsburgh, PA and Eparchies of Passaic (NJ), Parma (OH), Van Nuys (CA).

Portland: Archdiocese of Portland (OR) and suffragan sees of Baker (OR); Boise (ID); Great Falls-Billings and Helena (MT). Geographical area: Oregon, Idaho, Montana.

St. Louis: Archdiocese of St. Louis and suffragan sees of Jefferson City, Kansas City-St. Joseph, Springfield-Cape Girardeau. Geographical area: Missouri.

St. Paul and Minneapolis: Archdiocese of St. Paul and Minneapolis (MN) and suffragan sees of Crookston, Duluth, New Ulm, St. Cloud and Winona (MN); Bismarck and Fargo (ND); Rapid City and Sioux Falls (SD). Geographical area: Minnesota, North Dakota, South Dakota.

San Antonio: Archdiocese of San Antonio (TX) and suffragan sees of Amarillo, Dallas, El Paso, Fort Worth, Laredo, Lubbock, and San Angelo. Geographical area: Texas.

San Francisco: Archdiocese of San Francisco (CA) and suffragan sees of Oakland, Sacramento, San Jose, Santa Rosa and Stockton (CA); Honolulu (HI); Reno (NV); Las Vegas (NV); Salt Lake City (UT). Geographical area: Northern California, Nevada, Utah, Hawaii.

Santa Fe: Archdiocese of Santa Fe (NM) and suffragan sees of Gallup and Las Cruces (NM); Phoenix and Tucson (AZ). Geographical area: New Mexico, Arizona.

Seattle: Archdiocese of Seattle and suffragan sees of Spokane, Yakima. Geographical area: Washington.

Washington: Archdiocese of Washington, DC, and suffragan see of St. Thomas (VI). Geographical area: District of Columbia, five counties of Maryland, Virgin Islands.

ARCHDIOCESES, DIOCESES, ARCHBISHOPS, BISHOPS

(Sources: *Official Catholic Directory*; Catholic News Service; *L'Osservatore Romano*. As of Aug. 20, 2013.)

Information includes name of diocese, year of foundation (as it appears on the official document erecting the see), present ordinaries (year of installation), auxiliaries and former ordinaries (for biographies, *see* Index).

Archdioceses are indicated by an asterisk.

Albany, NY (1847): Howard J. Hubbard, bishop, 1977.

Former bishops: John McCloskey, 1847-64; John J. Conroy, 1865-77; Francis McNeirny, 1877-94; Thomas M. Burke, 1894-1915; Thomas F. Cusack, 1915-18; Edmund F. Gibbons, 1919-54; William A. Scully, 1954-69; Edwin B. Broderick, 1969-76.

Alexandria, LA (1853): Ronald P. Herzog, bishop, 2004.

Established at Natchitoches, transferred to Alexandria, 1910; title changed to Alexandria-Shreveport, 1977; redesignated Alexandria, 1986, when Shreveport was made a diocese.

Former bishops: Augustus M. Martin, 1853-75; Francis X. Leray, 1877-79, administrator, 1879-83; Anthony Durier, 1885-1904; Cornelius Van de Ven, 1904-32; Daniel F. Desmond, 1933-45; Charles P. Greco, 1946-73; Lawrence P. Graves, 1973-82; William B. Friend, 1983-86; John C. Favalora, 1986-89; Sam G. Jacobs, 1989-2003.

Allentown, PA (1961): John O. Barres, bishop, 2009.

Former bishop: Joseph McShea, 1961-83; Thomas J. Welsh, 1983-97; Edward P. Cullen, 1997-2009.

Altoona-Johnstown, PA (1901): Mark L. Bartchak, bishop, 2011.

Established as Altoona, name changed, 1957.

Former bishops: Eugene A. Garvey, 1901 20; John J. McCort, 1920 36; Richard T. Guilfoyle, 1936 57; Howard J. Carroll, 1958 60; J. Carroll McCormick, 1960 66; James J. Hogan, 1966 86; Joseph V. Adamec, 1987-2011.

Amarillo, TX (1926): Patrick J. Zurek, bishop, 2008.

Former bishops; Rudolph A. Gerken, 1927-33; Robert E. Lucey, 1934-41; Laurence J. Fitzsimon, 1941-58; John L. Morkovsky, 1958-63; Lawrence M. De Falco, 1963-79; Leroy T. Matthiesen, 1980-97; John W. Yanta, 1997-2008.

Anchorage,* Alaska (1966): Roger Lawrence Schwietz O.M.I., archbishop, 2001.

Former archbishop: Joseph T. Ryan, 1966-75; Francis T. Hurley, 1976-2001.

Arlington, VA (1974): Paul S. Loverde, bishop, 1999.

Former bishop: Thomas J. Welsh, 1974-83; John R. Keating, 1983-98.

Atlanta,* GA (1956; archdiocese, 1962): Wilton Daniel Gregory, archbishop, 2004. Luis R. Zarama, David P. Talley, auxiliaries.

Former ordinaries: Francis E. Hyland, 1956-61; Paul J. Hallinan, first archbishop, 1962-68; Thomas A. Donnellan, 1968-87; Eugene A. Marino, S.S.J., 1988-90; James P. Lyke, 1991-92; John F. Donoghue, 1993-2004.

Austin, TX (1947): Joe Steve Vazquez, bishop, 2010.

Former bishops: Louis J. Reicher, 1947-71; Vincent M. Harris, 1971-86; John E. McCarthy, 1986-2001; Gregory Michael Aymond, 2001-2009.

Baker, OR (1903): Liam S. Cary, bishop, 2012.

Established as Baker City, name changed, 1952.

Former bishops: Charles J. O'Reilly, 1903 18; Joseph F. McGrath, 1919 50; Francis P. Leipzig, 1950 71; Thomas J. Connolly, 1971-99; Robert Vasa, 1999-2011.

Baltimore,* MD (1789; archdiocese, 1808): William Edward Lori, archbishop, 2012; Mitchell Thomas Rozanski, Denis James Madden, auxiliaries.

Former ordinaries: John Carroll, 1789-1815, first archbishop; Leonard Neale, 1815-17; Ambrose Marechal, S.S., 1817-28; James Whitfield, 1828-34; Samuel Eccleston, S.S., 1834-51; Francis P. Kenrick, 1851-63; Martin J. Spalding, 1864-72; James R. Bayley, 1872-77; Cardinal James Gibbons, 1877-1921; Michael J. Curley, 1921-47; Francis P. Keough, 1947-61; Cardinal Lawrence J. Shehan, 1961-74; William D. Borders, 1974-89; Cardinal William H. Keeler, 1989-2007; Cardinal Edwin F. O'Brien, 2007-2011.

Baton Rouge, LA (1961): Robert W. Muench, bishop, 2001.

Former bishops: Robert E. Tracy, 1961-74; Joseph V. Sullivan, 1974-82; Stanley J. Ott, 1983-93; Alfred C. Hughes, 1993-2001.

Beaumont, TX (1966): Curtis J. Guillory, S.V.D., bishop, 2000.

Former bishops: Vincent M. Harris, 1966-71; Warren L. Boudreaux, 1971-77; Bernard J. Ganter, 1977-93; Joseph A. Galante, 1994-2000.

Belleville, IL (1887): Edward Braxton, bishop, 2005.

Former bishops: John Janssen, 1888-1913; Henry Althoff, 1914-47; Albert R. Zuroweste, 1948-76; William M. Cosgrove, 1976-81; John N. Wurm, 1981-84; James P. Keleher, 1984-93; Wilton D. Gregory, 1994-2004.

Biloxi, MS (1977): Roger Paul Morin, 2009.

Former bishop: Joseph Lawson Howze, 1977-2001; Thomas John Rodi, 2001-2008.

Birmingham, AL (1969): Robert J. Baker, bishop, 2007.

Former bishops: Joseph G. Vath, 1969-87; Raymond J. Boland, 1988-93; David E. Foley, 1994-2005.

Bismarck, ND (1909): David D. Kagan, bishop, 2011.

Former bishops: Vincent Wehrle, O.S.B., 1910-39; Vincent J. Ryan, 1940-51; Lambert A. Hoch, 1952-56; Hilary B. Hacker, 1957-82; John F. Kinney, 1982-95; Paul A. Zipfel, 1996-2011.

Boise, ID (1893): Michael P. Driscoll, 1999.

Former bishops: Alphonse J. Glorieux, 1893-1917; Daniel M. Gorman, 1918-27; Edward J. Kelly, 1928-56; James J. Byrne, 1956-62; Sylvester Treinen, 1962-88; Tod David Brown, 1989-98.

Boston,* MA (1808; archdiocese, 1875): Sean O'Malley, O.F.M. Cap., 2003. Walter James Edyvean, John A. Dooher, Robert F. Hennessey, Arthur L. Kennedy, Peter J. Uglietto, Robert Deeley, auxiliaries.

Former ordinaries: John L. de Cheverus, 1810-23; Benedict J. Fenwick, S.J., 1825-46; John B. Fitzpatrick, 1846-66; John J. Williams, 1866-1907, first archbishop; Cardinal William O'Connell, 1907-44; Cardinal Richard Cushing, 1944-70; Cardinal Humberto Medeiros, 1970-83; Cardinal Bernard F. Law, 1984-2002.

Bridgeport, CT (1953): Frank Caggiano, bishop, 2013.

Former bishops: Lawrence J. Shehan, 1953-61; Walter W. Curtis, 1961-88; Edward M. Egan, 1988-2000; William Edward Lori, 2001-2012.

Brooklyn, NY (1853): Nicholas A. DiMarzio, 2003. Octavio Cisneros, Raymond Chappetto, Paul R. Sanchez, auxiliaries.

Former bishops: John Loughlin, 1853-91; Charles E. McDonnell, 1892-1921; Thomas E. Molloy, 1921-56; Bryan J. McEntegart, 1957-68; Francis J. Mugavero, 1968-90; Thomas V. Daily, 1990-2003.

Brownsville, TX (1965): Daniel E. Flores, bishop, 2010.

Former bishops: Adolph Marx, 1965; Humberto S. Medeiros, 1966-70; John J. Fitzpatrick, 1971-91; Enrique San Pedro, S.J., 1991-94; Raymundo J. Peña, 1995-2010.

Buffalo, NY (1847): Richard Joseph Malone, bishop, 2012. Edward M. Grosz, auxiliary.

Former bishops: John Timon, C.M., 1847-67; Stephen V. Ryan, C.M., 1868-96; James E. Quigley, 1897-1903; Charles H. Colton, 1903-15; Dennis J. Dougherty, 1915-18; William Turner, 1919-36; John A. Duffy, 1937-44; John F. O'Hara, C.S.C., 1945-51; Joseph A. Burke, 1952-62; James McNulty, 1963-72; Edward D. Head, 1973-95 Henry J. Mansell, 1995-2003; Edward U. Kmiec, 2004-2012.

Burlington, VT (1853): Salvatore R. Matano, bishop, 2005.

Former bishops: Louis De Goesbriand, 1853-99; John S. Michaud, 1899-1908; Joseph J. Rice, 1910-38; Matthew F. Brady, 1938-44; Edward F. Ryan, 1945-56; Robert F. Joyce, 1957-71; John A. Marshall, 1972-91. Kenneth A. Angell, bishop, 1992-2005.

Camden, NJ (1937): Dennis J. Sullivan, bishop, 2013.

Former bishops: Bartholomew J. Eustace, 1938-56; Justin J. McCarthy, 1957-59; Celestine J. Damiano, 1960-67; George H. Guilfoyle, 1968-89; James T. McHugh, 1989-98; Nicholas A. DiMarzio, 1999-2003; Joseph Galante, 2004-2012.

Charleston, SC (1820): Robert E. Guglielmone, bishop, 2009.

Former bishops: John England, 1820-42; Ignatius W. Reynolds, 1844-55; Patrick N. Lynch, 1858-82; Henry P. Northrop, 1883-1916; William T. Russell, 1917-27; Emmet M. Walsh, 1927-49; John J. Russell, 1950-58; Paul J. Hallinan, 1958-62; Francis F. Reh, 1962-64; Ernest L. Unterkoefler, 1964-90; David B. Thompson, 1990-99; Robert J. Baker, 1999-2007.

Charlotte, NC (1971): Peter J. Jugis, bishop, 2003.

Former bishops: Michael J. Begley, 1972-84; John F. Donoghue, 1984-93; William G. Curlin, 1994-2002.

Cheyenne, WY (1887): Paul D. Etienne, bishop, 2009.

Former bishops: Maurice F. Burke, 1887-93; Thomas M. Lenihan, 1897-1901; James J. Keane, 1902-11; Patrick A. McGovern, 1912-51; Hubert M. Newell, 1951-78; Joseph Hart, 1978-2001; David Laurin Ricken, 2001-2008.

Chicago,* IL (1843; archdiocese, 1880): Cardinal Francis E. George, archbishop, 1997. John R. Manz, Joseph N. Perry, Francis J. Kane, George J. Rassas, Alberto Rojas, Andrew P. Wypych, auxiliaries.

Former ordinaries: William Quarter, 1844-48; James O. Van de Velde, S.J., 1849-53; Anthony O'Regan, 1854-58; James Duggan, 1859-70; Thomas P. Foley, administrator, 1870-79; Patrick A. Feehan, 1880-1902, first archbishop; James E. Quigley, 1903-15; Cardinal George Mundelein, 1915-39; Cardinal Samuel Stritch, 1939-58; Cardinal Albert Meyer, 1958-65; Cardinal John Cody, 1965-82; Cardinal Joseph L. Bernardin, 1982-96.

Cincinnati,* OH (1821; archdiocese, 1850): Dennis M. Schnurr, co-adjutor, 2008, archbishop, 2009. Joseph R. Binzer, auxiliary.

Former ordinaries: Edward D. Fenwick, O.P., 1822-32; John B. Purcell, 1833-83, first archbishop; William H.

Elder, 1883-1904; Henry Moeller, 1904-1925; John T. McNicholas, O.P., 1925-50; Karl J. Alter, 1950-69; Paul F. Leibold, 1969-72; Joseph L. Bernardin, 1972-82; Daniel E. Pilarczyk, 1982-2009.

Cleveland, OH (1847): Richard Gerard Lennon, bishop, 2006. Roger W. Gries, O.S.B., auxiliary.

Former ordinaries: L. Amadeus Rappe, 1847-70; Richard Gilmour, 1872-91; Ignatius F. Horstmann, 1892-1908; John P. Farrelly, 1909-21; Joseph Schrembs, 1921-45; Edward F. Hoban, 1945-66; Clarence G. Issenmann, 1966-74; James A. Hickey, 1974-80; Anthony M. Pilla, 1980-2006.

Colorado Springs, CO (1983): Michael J. Sheridan, bishop, 2003.

Former ordinaries: Richard C. Hanifen, 1984-2003.

Columbus, OH (1868): Frederick Francis Campbell, bishop, 2004.

Former bishops: Sylvester H. Rosecrans, 1868-78; John A. Watterson, 1880-99; Henry Moeller, 1900-03; James J. Hartley, 1904-44; Michael J. Ready, 1944-57; Clarence Issenmann, 1957-64; John J. Carberry, 1965-68; Clarence E. Elwell, 1968-73; Edward J. Herrmann, 1973-82; James A. Griffin, 1983-2004.

Corpus Christi, TX (1912): William M. Mulvey, bishop, 2010.

Former bishops: Paul J. Nussbaum, C.P., 1913-20; Emmanuel B. Ledvina, 1921-49; Mariano S. Garriga, 1949-65; Thomas J. Drury, 1965-83; Rene H. Gracida, 1983-97. Roberto O. Gonzalez, O.F.M., 1997-99; Edmond Carmody, 2000-2010

Covington, KY (1853): Roger J. Foys, bishop, 2002.

Former bishops: George A. Carrell, S.J., 1853-68; Augustus M. Toebbe, 1870-84; Camillus P. Maes, 1885-1914; Ferdinand Brossart, 1916-23; Francis W. Howard, 1923-44; William T. Mulloy, 1945-59; Richard Ackerman, C.S.Sp., 1960-78; William A. Hughes, 1979-95; Robert W. Muench, 1996-2001.

Crookston, MN (1909): Michael J. Hoeppner, bishop, 2007.

Former bishops: Timothy Corbett, 1910-38; John H. Peschges, 1938-44; Francis J. Schenk, 1945-60; Laurence A. Glenn, 1960-70; Kenneth J. Povish, 1970-75; Victor H. Balke, 1976-2007.

Dallas, TX (1890): Kevin J. Farrell, bishop, 2007. John D. Deshotel, auxiliary.

Established 1890, as Dallas, title changed to Dallas-Ft. Worth, 1953; redesignated Dallas, 1969, when Ft. Worth was made a diocese.

Former bishops: Thomas F. Brennan, 1891-92; Edward J. Dunne, 1893-1910; Joseph P. Lynch, 1911-54; Thomas K. Gorman, 1954-69; Thomas Tschoepe, 1969-90; Charles V. Grahmann, 1990-2007.

Davenport, IA (1881): Martin John Amos, bishop, 2006.

Former bishops: John McMullen, 1881-83; Henry Cosgrove, 1884-1906; James Davis, 1906-26; Henry P. Rohlman, 1927-44; Ralph L. Hayes, 1944-66; Gerald F. O'Keefe, 1966-93; William E. Franklin, 1993-2006.

Denver,* CO (1887; archdiocese, 1941): Samuel J. Aquila, archbishop, 2012.

Former ordinaries: Joseph P. Machebeuf, 1887-89; Nicholas C. Matz, 1889-1917; J. Henry Tihen, 1917-31; Urban J. Vehr, 1931-67, first archbishop; James V. Casey, 1967-86; J. Francis Stafford, 1986-96; Charles J. Chaput, O.F.M. Cap., 1997-2011.

Des Moines, IA (1911): Richard Edmund Pates, bishop, 2008.

Former bishops: Austin Dowling, 1912-19; Thomas W. Drumm, 1919-33; Gerald T. Bergan, 1934-48; Edward C. Daly, O.P., 1948-64; George J. Biskup, 1965-67; Maurice J. Dingman, 1968-86; William H. Bullock, 1987-93; Joseph L. Charron, C.PP.S., 1993-2007.

Detroit,* MI (1833; archdiocese, 1937): Allen H. Vigneron, archbishop, 2009. Francis R. Reiss, Michael J. Byrnes, Donald F. Hanchon, José A. Cepeda Escobedo, auxiliaries.

Former ordinaries: Frederic Rese, 1833-71; Peter P. Lefevere, administrator, 1841-69; Caspar H. Borgess, 1871-88; John S. Foley, 1888-1918; Michael J. Gallagher, 1918-37; Cardinal Edward Mooney, 1937-58, first archbishop; Cardinal John F. Dearden, 1958-80; Cardinal Edmund C. Szoka, 1981-90; Cardinal Adam J. Maida, 1990-2009.

Dodge City, KS (1951): John B. Brungardt, bishop, 2010.

Former bishops: John B. Franz, 1951 59; Marion F. Forst, 1960 76; Eugene J. Gerber, 1976 82; Stanley G. Schlarman, 1983-98; Ronald M. Gilmore, 1998-2010.

Dubuque,* Iowa (1837; archdiocese, 1893): Michael O. Jackels, archbishop, 2013.

Former ordinaries: Mathias Loras, 1837-58; Clement Smyth, O.C.S.O., 1858-65; John Hennessy, 1866-1900, first archbishop; John J. Keane, 1900-11; James J. Keane, 1911-29; Francis J. Beckman, 1930-46; Henry P. Rohlman, 1946-54; Leo Binz, 1954-61; James J. Byrne, 1962-83; Daniel W. Kucera, O.S.B., 1984-95; Jerome Hanus, O.S.B., 1995-2013.

Duluth, MN (1889): Paul D. Sirba, bishop, 2009.

Former bishops: James McGolrick, 1889-1918; John T. McNicholas, O.P., 1918-25; Thomas A. Welch, 1926-59; Francis J. Schenk, 1960-69; Paul F. Anderson, 1969-82; Robert H. Brom, 1983-89; Roger L. Schwietz, O.M.I., 1990-2000; Dennis M. Schnurr, 2001-2008.

El Paso, TX (1914): Mark J. Seitz, bishop, 2013.

Former bishops: Anthony J. Schuler, S.J., 1915-42; Sidney M. Metzger, 1942-78; Patrick F. Flores, 1978-79; Raymundo J. Pena, 1980-95; Armando X. Ochoa, 1996-2011.

Erie, PA (1853): Lawrence T. Persico, bishop, 2012.

Former bishops: Michael O'Connor, 1853-54; Josue M. Young, 1854-66; Tobias Mullen, 1868-99; John E. Fitzmaurice, 1899-1920; John M. Gannon, 1920-66; John F. Whealon, 1966-69; Alfred M. Watson, 1969-82; Michael J. Murphy, 1982-90; Donald W. Trautman, 1990-2012.

Evansville, IN (1944): Charles C. Thompson, 2011, bishop.

Former bishops: Henry Joseph Grimmelsman, 1944-1965; Paul Francis Leibold, 1966-1969; Francis Raymond Shea, 1969-1989; Gerald Andrew Gettelfinger, 1989-2011.

Fairbanks, Alaska (1962): Donald Kettler, bishop, 2002.

Former bishops: Francis D. Gleeson, S.J., 1962-68; Robert L. Whelan, S.J., 1968-85; Michael J. Kaniecki, S.J., 1985-2000.

Fall River, MA (1904): George William Coleman, bishop, 2003.

Former bishops: William Stang, 1904-07; Daniel F. Feehan, 1907-34; James E. Cassidy, 1934-51; James L. Connolly, 1951-70; Daniel A. Cronin, 1970-91; Sean O'Malley, O.F.M. Cap., 1992-2002.

Fargo, ND (1889): John F. Folda, bishop, 2013.

Established at Jamestown, transferred, 1897.

Former bishops: John Shanley, 1889-1909; James

O'Reilly, 1910-34; Aloysius J. Muench, 1935-59; Leo F. Dworschak, 1960-70; Justin A. Driscoll, 1970-84; James S. Sullivan, 1985-2002; Samuel J. Aquila, 2002-2012.

Fort Wayne-South Bend, IN (1857): Kevin C. Rhoades, bishop, 2009.
Established as Fort Wayne, name changed, 1960.
Former bishops: John H. Luers, 1858-71; Joseph Dwenger, C.Pp.S., 1872-93; Joseph Rademacher, 1893-1900; Herman J. Alerding, 1900-24; John F. Noll, 1925-56; Leo A. Pursley, 1957-76; William E. McManus, 1976-85; John M. D'Arcy, 1985-2009.

Fort Worth, TX (1969): Vacant.
Former bishop: John J. Cassata, 1969-80; Joseph P. Delaney, 1981-2005; Kevin W. Vann, 2005-2012.

Fresno, CA (1967): Armando X. Ochoa, bishop, 2011.
Formerly Monterey-Fresno, 1922.
Former bishops (Monterey-Fresno): John J. Cantwell, administrator, 1922-24; John B. MacGinley, first bishop, 1924-32; Philip G. Sher, 1933-53; Aloysius J. Willinger, 1953-67.
Former bishops (Fresno): Timothy Manning, 1967-69; Hugh A. Donohoe, 1969-80; Joseph J. Madera, M.Pp.S., 1980-91. John T. Steinbock, 1991-2010.

Gallup, NM (1939): James S. Wall, bishop, 2009.
Former bishops: Bernard T. Espelage, O.F.M., 1940-69; Jerome J. Hastrich, 1969-90; Donald Pelotte, S.S.S., 1990-2008.

Galveston-Houston, TX* (1847; archdiocese, 2004): Card. Daniel N. DiNardo, archbishop, 2006. George A. Sheltz, auxiliary.
Established as Galveston, name changed, 1959.
Former bishops: John M. Odin, C.M., 1847-61; Claude M. Dubuis, 1862-92; Nicholas A. Gallagher, 1892-1918; Christopher E. Byrne, 1918-50; Wendelin J. Nold, 1950-75; John L. Morkovsky, 1975-84; Joseph A. Fiorenza, 1985-2004, first archbishop, 2004-2006.

Gary, IN (1956): Dale J. Melczek, bishop, 1996.
Former bishops: Andrew G. Grutka, 1957-84; Norbert F. Gaughan, 1984-96.

Gaylord, MI (1971): Bernard A. Hebda, bishop, 2009.
Former bishops: Edmund C. Szoka, 1971-81; Robert J. Rose, 1981-89; Patrick R. Cooney, 1989-2009.

Grand Island, NE (1912): William J. Dendinger, bishop, 2004.
Established at Kearney, transferred, 1917.
Former bishops: James A. Duffy, 1913-31; Stanislaus V. Bona, 1932-44; Edward J. Hunkeler, 1945-51; John L. Paschang, 1951-72; John J. Sullivan, 1972-77; Lawrence J. McNamara, 1978-2004.

Grand Rapids, MI (1882): David J. Walkowiak, bishop, 2013.
Former bishops: Henry J. Richter, 1883-1916; Michael J. Gallagher, 1916-18; Edward D. Kelly, 1919-26; Joseph G. Pinten, 1926-40; Joseph C. Plagens, 1941-43; Francis J. Haas, 1943-53; Allen J. Babcock, 1954-69; Joseph M. Breitenbeck, 1969-89; Robert J. Rose, 1989-2003; Kevin M. Britt, 2003-2004; Walter A. Hurley, 2005-2013.

Great Falls-Billings, MT (1904): Michael W. Warfel, bishop, 2007.
Established as Great Falls, name changed, 1980.
Former bishops: Mathias C. Lenihan, 1904-30; Edwin V. O'Hara, 1930-39; William J. Condon, 1939-67; Eldon B. Schuster, 1968-77; Thomas J. Murphy, 1978-87; Anthony M. Milone, 1988-2006.

Green Bay, WI (1868): David Laurin Ricken,

bishop, 2008. Robert F. Morneau, auxiliary.
Former bishops: Joseph Melcher, 1868-73; Francis X. Krautbauer, 1875-85; Frederick X. Katzer, 1886-91; Sebastian G. Messmer, 1892-1903; Joseph J. Fox, 1904-14; Paul P. Rhode, 1915-45; Stanislaus V. Bona, 1945-67; Aloysius J. Wycislo, 1968-83; Adam J. Maida, 1984-90. Robert J. Banks, 1990-2003; David A. Zubic, 2003-2007.

Greensburg, PA (1951): Lawrence E. Brandt, bishop, 2004.
Former bishops: Hugh L. Lamb, 1951-59; Willam G. Connare, 1960-87; Anthony G. Bosco, 1987-2004.

Harrisburg, PA (1868): Vacant.
Former bishops: Jeremiah F. Shanahan, 1868-86; Thomas McGovern, 1888-98; John W. Shanahan,1899-1916; Philip R. McDevitt, 1916-35; George L. Leech, 1935-71; Joseph T. Daley, 1971-83; William H. Keeler, 1984-89; Nicholas C. Dattilo, 1990-2004; Kevin C. Rhoades, 2004-2009; Joseph Patrick McFadden, 2010-2013.

Hartford,* CT (1843; archdiocese, 1953): Henry J. Mansell, archbishop, 2003. Christie A. Macaluso, auxiliary.
Former ordinaries: William Tyler, 1844-49; Bernard O'Reilly, 1850-56; F. P. MacFarland, 1858-74; Thomas Galberry, O.S.A., 1876-78; Lawrence S. McMahon, 1879-93; Michael Tierney, 1894-1908; John J. Nilan, 1910-34; Maurice F. McAuliffe, 1934-44; Henry J. O'Brien, 1945-68, first archbishop; John F. Whealon, 1969-91; Daniel A. Cronin, 1991-2003.

Helena, MT (1884): George L. Thomas, bishop, 2004.
Former bishops: John B. Brondel, 1884-1903; John P. Carroll, 1904-25; George J. Finnigan, C.S.C., 1927-32; Ralph L. Hayes, 1933-35; Joseph M. Gilmore, 1936-62; Raymond Hunthausen, 1962-75; Elden F. Curtiss, 1976-93; Alexander J. Brunett, 1994-97; Robert C. Morlino, 1999-2003.

Honolulu, HI (1941): Clarence L. Silva, bishop, 2005.
Former bishops: James J. Sweeney, 1941-68; John J. Scanlan, 1968-81; Joseph A. Ferrario, 1982-93; Francis X. DiLorenzo (apostolic administrator, 1993), 1994-2004.

Houma-Thibodaux, LA (1977): Sam G. Jacobs, 2003.
Former bishop: Warren L. Boudreaux, 1977-92; C. Michael Jarrell, 1993-2002.

Indianapolis,* IN (1834; archdiocese, 1944): Joseph W. Tobin, C.Ss.R., archbishop; Christopher J. Coyne, auxiliary.
Established at Vincennes, transferred, 1898.
Former ordinaries: Simon G. Bruté, 1834-39; Celestine de la Hailandiere, 1839-47; John S. Bazin, 1847-48; Maurice de St. Palais, 1849-77; Francis S. Chatard, 1878-1918; Joseph Chartrand, 1918-33; Joseph E. Ritter, 1934-46, first archbishop; Paul C. Schulte, 1946-70; George J. Biskup, 1970-79; Edward T. O'Meara, 1980-92; Daniel M. Buechlein, O.S.B., 1992-2011.

Jackson, MS (1837): Joseph Latino, bishop, 2003.
Established at Natchez, title changed to Natchez-Jackson, 1956; transferred to Jackson, 1977 (Natchez made titular see).
Former bishops: John J. Chanche, S.S., 1841-52; James Van de Velde, S.J., 1853-55; William H. Elder, 1857-80; Francis A. Janssens, 1881-88; Thomas Heslin, 1889-1911; John E. Gunn, S.M., 1911-24; Richard O. Gerow, 1924-67; Joseph B. Brunini, 1968-84; William R. Houck, 1984-2003.

Jefferson City, MO (1956): John R. Gaydos, bishop, 1997.
Former bishops: Joseph Marling, C.Pp.S., 1956-69;

Michael F. McAuliffe, 1969-97.

Joliet, IL (1948): Robert D. Conlon, bishop, 2011. Joseph Siegel, auxiliary.

Former bishops: Martin D. McNamara, 1949-66; Romeo Blanchette, 1966-79; Joseph L. Imesch, 1979-2006; James Peter Sartain, 2006-2010.

Juneau, Alaska (1951): Edward J. Burns, bishop, 2009.

Former bishops: Dermot O'Flanagan, 1951-68; Joseph T. Ryan, administrator, 1968-71; Francis T. Hurley, 1971-76, administrator, 1976-79; Michael H. Kenny, 1979-95; Michael W. Warfel, 1996-2007.

Kalamazoo, MI (1971): Paul J. Bradley, bishop, 2009.

Former bishop: Paul V. Donovan, 1971-94; Alfred J. Markiewicz, 1995-97; James A. Murray, 1997-2009.

Kansas City,* KS (1877; archdiocese, 1952): Joseph F. Naumann, archbishop, 2005.

Established as vicariate apostolic, 1850, became Diocese of Leavenworth, 1877, transferred to Kansas City, 1947.

Former ordinaries: J. B. Miege, vicar apostolic, 1851-74; Louis M. Fink, O.S.B., vicar apostolic, 1874-77, first bishop, 1877-1904; Thomas F. Lillis, 1904-10; John Ward, 1910-29; Francis Johannes, 1929-37; Paul C. Schulte, 1937-46; George J. Donnelly, 1946-50; Edward Hunkeler, 1951-69, first archbishop; Ignatius J. Strecker, 1969-93; James P. Keleher, 1993-2005.

Kansas City-St. Joseph, MO (Kansas City, 1880, St. Joseph, 1868, united 1956): Robert W. Finn, bishop, 2005.

Former bishops: John J. Hogan, 1880-1913; Thomas F. Lillis, 1913-38; Edwin V. O'Hara, 1939-56; John P. Cody, 1956-61; Charles H. Helmsing, 1962-77; John J. Sullivan, 1977-93; Raymond J. Boland, 1993-2005.

Former bishops (St. Joseph): John J. Hogan, 1868-80, administrator, 1880-93; Maurice F. Burke, 1893-1923; Francis Gilfillan, 1923-33; Charles H. Le Blond, 1933-56.

Knoxville, TN (1988): Richard Stika, bishop, 2009.

Former bishops: Anthony J. O'Connell, bishop, 1988-98; Joseph E. Kurtz, 1999-2007.

La Crosse, WI (1868): William Callahan, OFM Conv., 2010.

Former bishops: Michael Heiss, 1868-80; Kilian C. Flasch, 1881-91; James Schwebach, 1892-1921; Alexander J. McGavick, 1921-48; John P. Treacy, 1948-64; Frederick W. Freking, 1965-83; John J. Paul, 1983-94; Raymond L. Burke, 1995-2003; Jerome E. Listecki, 2004-2009.

Lafayette, IN (1944): Timothy Doherty, bishop, 2010.

Former bishops: John G. Bennett, 1944-57; John J. Carberry, 1957-65; Raymond J. Gallagher, 1965-82; George A. Fulcher, 1983-84 William L. Higi, 1984-2010.

Lafayette, LA (1918): C. Michael Jarrell, bishop, 2002.

Former bishops: Jules B. Jeanmard, 1918-56; Maurice Schexnayder, 1956-72; Gerard L. Frey, 1973-89; Harry J. Flynn, 1989-94; Edward J. O'Donnell, 1994-2002.

Lake Charles, LA (1980): Glen J. Provost, bishop, 2007

Former bishop: Jude Speyrer, 1980-2000; Edward Braxton, 2000-2005.

Lansing, MI (1937): Earl Boyea, bishop, 2008.

Former bishops: Joseph H. Albers, 1937-65; Alexander Zaleski, 1965-75; Kenneth I. Povish, 1975-95; Carl F. Mengeling, 1995-2008.

Laredo, Tx. (2000): James A. Tamayo, bishop, 2000.

Las Cruces, NM (1982): Oscar Cantu, bishop, 2013.

Former bishops: Ricardo Ramirez, C.S.B., 1982-2013.

Las Vegas, NV (1995): Joseph Pepe, 2001.

Formerly Reno-Las Vegas, 1976; made separate diocese 1995.

Former bishops: Daniel F. Walsh, 1995-2000.

Lexington, KY (1988): Ronald William Gainer, bishop, 2002.

Former bishops: James Kendrick Williams, 1988-2002.

Lincoln, NE (1887): James Douglas Conley, bishop, 2012.

Former bishops: Thomas Bonacum, 1887-1911; J. Henry Tihen, 1911-17; Charles J. O'Reilly, 1918-23; Francis J. Beckman, 1924-30; Louis B. Kucera, 1930-57; James V. Casey, 1957-67; Glennon P. Flavin, 1967-92; Fabian W. Bruskewitz, 1992-2012

Little Rock, AR (1843): Anthony Basil Taylor, bishop, 2008.

Former bishops: Andrew Byrne, 1844-62; Edward Fitzgerald, 1867-1907; John Morris, 1907-46; Albert L. Fletcher, 1946-72; Andrew J. McDonald, 1972-2000; James Peter Sartain, 2000-2006.

Los Angeles,* CA (1840; archdiocese, 1936): José H. Gomez, archbishop, 2011. Thomas J. Curry, Gerald E. Wilkerson, Edward William Clark, Oscar Azarcon Solis, Alexander Salazar, auxiliaries.

Founded as diocese of Two Californias, 1840; became Monterey diocese, 1850; Baja California detached from Monterey diocese, 1852; title changed to Monterey Los Angeles, 1859, Los Angeles San Diego, 1922; became archdiocese under present title, 1936 (San Diego became separate see).

Former ordinaries: Francisco Garcia Diego y Moreno, O.F.M., 1840 46; Joseph S. Alemany, O.P., 1850-53; Thaddeus Amat, C.M., 1854-78; Francis Mora, 1878-96; George T. Montgomery, 1896-1903; Thomas J. Conaty, 1903-15; John J. Cantwell, 1917-47, first archbishop; Cardinal James McIntyre, 1948-70; Cardinal Timothy Manning, 1970-85; Cardinal Roger M. Mahony, 1985-2011.

Louisville,* KY (1808; archdiocese, 1937): Joseph E. Kurtz, archbishop, 2007.

Established at Bardstown, transferred, 1841.

Former ordinaries: Benedict J. Flaget, S.S., 1810-32; John B. David, S.S., 1832-33; Benedict J. Flaget, S.S., 1833-50; Martin J. Spalding, 1850-64; Peter J. Lavialle, 1865-67; William G. McCloskey, 1868-1909; Denis O'Donaghue, 1910-24; John A. Floersh, 1924-67, first archbishop; Thomas J. McDonough, 1967-81; Thomas C. Kelly, O.P., 1982-2007.

Lubbock, TX (1983): Placido Rodriguez, C.M.F., bishop, 1994.

Former bishop: Michael J. Sheehan, 1983-93.

Madison, WI (1946): Robert C. Morlino, bishop, 2003.

Former bishops: William P. O'Connor, 1946-67; Cletus F. O'Donnell, 1967-92, William H. Bullock, 1993-2003.

Manchester, NH (1884): Peter A. Libasci, bishop, 2011; Francis J. Christian, auxiliary.

Former bishops: Denis M. Bradley, 1884-1903; John B. Delany, 1904-06; George A. Guertin, 1907-32; John B. Peterson, 1932-44; Matthew F. Brady, 1944-59; Ernest J. Primeau, 1960-74; Odore J. Gendron, 1975-90; Leo E. O'Neil, 1990-97; John B. McCormack, 1998-2011.

Marquette, MI (1857): Vacant.

Founded as Sault Ste. Marie and Marquette;

changed to Marquette, 1937.

Former bishops: Frederic Baraga, 1857-68; Ignatius Mrak, 1869-78; John Vertin, 1879-99; Frederick Eis, 1899-1922; Paul J. Nussbaum, C.P., 1922-35; Joseph C. Plagens, 1935-40; Francis Magner, 1941-47; Thomas L. Noa, 1947-68; Charles A. Salatka, 1968-77; Mark F. Schmitt, 1978-92; James H. Garland, 1992-2005; Alexander K. Sample, 2005-2013.

Memphis, TN (1970): J. Terry Steib, S.V.D., bishop, 1993.

Former bishops: Carroll T. Dozier, 1971-82; J. Francis Stafford, 1982-86; Daniel M. Buechlein, O.S.B.,1987-92.

Metuchen, NJ (1981): Paul G. Bootkoski, bishop, 2002.

Former bishops: Theodore E. McCarrick, 1981-86; Edward T. Hughes, 1987-97; Vincent DePaul Breen, 1997-2002.

Miami,* FL (1958; archdiocese, 1968): Thomas G. Wenski, archbishop, 2010.

Former ordinaries: Coleman F. Carroll, 1958-77, first archbishop; Edward A. McCarthy, 1977-94; John C. Favalora, 1994-2010.

Milwaukee,* WI (1843; archdiocese, 1875): Jerome E. Listecki, archbishop, 2009. Donald J. Hying, auxiliary.

Former ordinaries: John M. Henni, 1844-81, first archbishop; Michael Heiss, 1881-90; Frederick X. Katzer, 1891-1903; Sebastian G. Messmer, 1903-30; Samuel A. Stritch, 1930-39; Moses E. Kiley, 1940-53; Albert G. Meyer, 1953-58; William E. Cousins, 1959-77; Rembert G. Weakland, O.S.B., 1977-2002; Timothy M. Dolan, 2002-2009.

Mobile,* AL (1829; archdiocese, 1980): Thomas John Rodi, archbishop, 2008.

Founded as Mobile, 1829, title changed to Mobile-Birmingham, 1954; redesignated Mobile, 1969.

Former bishops: Michael Portier, 1829-59; John Quinlan, 1859-83; Dominic Manucy, 1884; Jeremiah O'Sullivan, 1885-96; Edward P. Allen, 1897-1926; Thomas J. Toolen, 1927-69; John L. May, 1969-80; Oscar H. Lipscomb, first archbishop, 1980-2008.

Monterey in California (1967): Richard J. Garcia, bishop, 2006.

Formerly Monterey-Fresno, 1922. (Originally established in 1850, see Los Angeles listing.)

Former bishops (Monterey-Fresno): John J. Cantwell, administrator, 1922-24; John B. MacGinley, first bishop, 1924-32; Philip G. Sher, 1933-53; Aloysius J. Willinger, 1953-67.

Former bishops (Monterey): Harry A. Clinch, 1967-82; Thaddeus A. Shubsda, 1982-91; Sylvester D. Ryan, 1992-2006

Nashville, TN (1837): David Choby, bishop, 2005.

Former bishops: Richard P. Miles, O.P., 1838-60; James Whelan, O.P., 1860-64; Patrick A. Feehan, 1865-80; Joseph Rademacher, 1883-93; Thomas S. Byrne, 1894-1923; Alphonse J. Smith, 1924-35; William L. Adrian, 1936-69; Joseph A. Durick, 1969-75; James D. Niedergeses, 1975-92; Edward U. Kmiec, 1992-2004.

Newark,* NJ (1853; archdiocese, 1937): John J. Myers, 2001. Edgar M. da Cunha, Thomas A. Donato, John W. Flesey, Manuel Cruz, auxiliaries.

Former ordinaries: James R. Bayley, 1853-72; Michael A. Corrigan, 1873-80; Winand M. Wigger, 1881-1901; John J. O'Connor, 1901-27; Thomas J. Walsh, 1928-52, first archbishop; Thomas

A. Boland, 1953-74; Peter L. Gerety, 1974-86; Theodore E. McCarrick, 1986-2000.

New Orleans,* LA (1793; archdiocese, 1850): Gregory Michael Aymond, archbishop, 2009. Shelton Fabre, auxiliary.

Former ordinaries: Luis Penalver y Cardenas, 1793-1801; John Carroll, administrator, 1805-15; W. Louis Dubourg, S.S., 1815-25; Joseph Rosati, C.M., administrator, 1826-29; Leo De Neckere, C.M., 1829-33; Anthony Blanc, 1835-60, first archbishop; Jean Marie Odin, C.M., 1861-70; Napoleon J. Perche, 1870-83; Francis X. Leray, 1883-87; Francis A. Janssens, 1888-97; Placide L. Chapelle, 1897-1905; James H. Blenk, S.M., 1906-17; John W. Shaw, 1918-34; Joseph F. Rummel, 1935-64; John P. Cody, 1964-65; Philip M. Hannan, 1965-88; Francis B. Schulte, 1988-2002; Alfred Hughes, 2002-2009.

Newton, MA (Melkite) (1966; eparchy, 1976): Nicholas J. Samra, eparch, 2011.

Former ordinaries: Justin Najmy, exarch, 1966-68; Joseph Tawil, exarch, 1969-76, first eparch, 1976-89; Ignatius Ghattas, B.S.O., 1990-92; John A. Elya, B.S.O., 1993-2004; Cyrille Salim Bustros, S.M.S.P., 2004.

New Ulm, MN (1957): John LeVoir, bishop, 2008.

Former bishop: Alphonse J. Schladweiler, 1958-75; Raymond A. Lucker, 1975-2000; John Clayton Nienstedt, 2001-2007.

New York,* NY (1808; archdiocese, 1850): Cardinal Timothy M. Dolan, archbishop, 2009. Robert J. Iriondo, Dominick J. Lagonegro, Gerald T. Walsh, auxiliaries.

Former ordinaries: Richard L. Concanen, O.P., 1808-10; John Connolly, O.P., 1814-25; John Dubois, S.S., 1826-42; John J. Hughes, 1842-64, first archbishop; Cardinal John McCloskey, 1864-85; Michael A. Corrigan, 1885-1902; Cardinal John Farley, 1902-18; Cardinal Patrick Hayes, 1919-38; Cardinal Francis Spellman, 1939-67; Cardinal Terence J. Cooke, 1968-83; Cardinal John J. O'Connor, 1984-2000; Cardinal Edward M. Egan, 2000-2009.

Norwich, CT (1953): Michael R. Cote, bishop, 2003.

Former bishops: Bernard J. Flanagan, 1953-59; Vincent J. Hines, 1960-75; Daniel P. Reilly, 1975-94; Daniel A. Hart, 1995-2003.

Oakland, CA (1962): Michael C. Barber, S.J., bishop, 2013.

Former bishop: Floyd L. Begin, 1962-77; John S. Cummins, 1977-2003; Allen H. Vigneron, 2003-2009; Salvatore Cordileone, 2009-2012.

Ogdensburg, NY (1872): Terry R. LaValley, bishop, 2010.

Former bishops: Edgar P. Wadhams, 1872-91; Henry Gabriels, 1892-1921; Joseph H. Conroy, 1921-39; Francis J. Monaghan, 1939-42; Bryan J. McEntegart, 1943-53; Walter P. Kellenberg, 1954-57; James J. Navagh, 1957-63; Leo R. Smith, 1963; Thomas A. Donnellan, 1964-68; Stanislaus J. Brzana, 1968-93; Paul S. Loverde, 1993-99; Gerald M. Barbarito, 1999-2003; Robert Joseph Cunningham, 2004-2009.

Oklahoma City,* OK (1905; archdiocese, 1972): Paul S. Coakley, archbishop, 2010.

Former ordinaries: Theophile Meerschaert, 1905-24; Francis C. Kelley, 1924-48; Eugene J. McGuinness, 1948-57; Victor J. Reed, 1958-71; John R. Quinn, 1971-77, first archbishop; Charles A. Salatka, 1977-92; Eusebius J. Beltran, 1993-2011.

Omaha,* NE (1885; archdiocese, 1945): George J. Lucas, archbishop, 2009.

Former ordinaries: James O'Gorman, O.C.S.O., 1859-74, vicar apostolic; James O'Connor, vicar apostolic, 1876-85, first bishop, 1885-90; Richard Scannell, 1891-1916; Jeremiah J. Harty, 1916-27; Francis Beckman, administrator, 1926-28; Joseph F. Rummel, 1928-35; James H. Ryan, 1935-47, first archbishop; Gerald T. Bergan, 1948-69; Daniel E. Sheehan, 1969-93; Elden F. Curtiss, 1993-2009

Orange, CA (1976): Kevin W. Vann, bishop, 2012; Dominic Mai Luong, auxiliary.

Former bishop: William R. Johnson, 1976-86; Norman F. McFarland, 1986-98; Tod D. Brown, 1998-2012

Orlando, FL (1968): John G. Noonan, bishop, 2010.

Former bishops: William Borders, 1968-74; Thomas J. Grady, 1974-89; Thomas G. Wenski, 2005-2010.

Our Lady of Deliverance of Newark (for Syrian-rite Catholics of the U.S. and Canada, 1995): Yousif Benham Habash, bishop, 2010.

Former bishop: Joseph Younan, 1996-2009.

Our Lady of Lebanon of Los Angeles, CA (Maronite) (1994): Abdallah E. Zaidan, M.L., bishop, 2013.

Former eparch: John G. Chedid, 1994-2000; Robert J. Shaheen, 2000-2013.

Our Lady of Nareg (Apostolic Eparchy for Armenian Catholics in the United States and Canada), New York, NY (1981, eparchy, 2005): Mikael A. Mouradian, I.C.P.B., 2011.

Former exarchs: Nerses Mikael Setian, 1981-93; Hovhannes Tertzakian, O.M. Ven., 1995-2000; Manuel Batakian, 2000; first eparch, 2005.

Owensboro, KY (1937): William F. Medley, bishop, 2009.

Former bishops: Francis R. Cotton, 1938-60; Henry J. Soenneker, 1961-82; John J. McRaith, 1982-2009.

Palm Beach, FL (1984): Gerald Michael Barbarito, 2003.

Former bishop: Thomas V. Daily, 1984-90; J. Keith Symons, 1990-98; Anthony J. O'Connell, 1998-2002; Sean O'Malley, O.F.M. Cap., 2002-2003.

Parma, OH (Byzantine, Ruthenian) (1969): John Kudrick, bishop, 2002.

Former bishops: Emil Mihalik, 1969-84; Andrew Pataki, 1984-95; Basil Schott, O.F.M., 1996-2002.

Passaic, NJ (Byzantine, Ruthenian) (1963): Vacant.

Former bishops: Stephen Kocisko, 1963-68; Michael J. Dudick, 1968-95; Andrew Pataki, 1996-2007; William C. Skurla, 2007-2012.

Paterson, NJ (1937): Arthur J. Serratelli, bishop, 2004.

Former bishops: Thomas H. McLaughlin, 1937-47; Thomas A. Boland, 1947-52; James A. McNulty, 1953-63; James J. Navagh, 1963-65; Lawrence B. Casey, 1966-77; Frank J. Rodimer, 1978-2004.

Pensacola-Tallahassee, FL (1975): Gregory L. Parkes, bishop, 2012.

Former bishops: Rene H. Gracida, 1975-83; J. Keith Symons, 1983-90; John M. Smith, 1991-95; John H. Ricard, S.S.J., 1997-2011.

Peoria, IL (1877): Daniel R. Jenky, C.S.C., bishop, 2002. Former bishops: John L. Spalding, 1877-1908; Edmund

M. Dunne, 1909-29; Joseph H. Schlarman, 1930-51; William E. Cousins, 1952-58; John B. Franz, 1959-71; Edward W. O'Rourke, 1971- 90; John J. Myers, 1990-2001.

Philadelphia,* PA (1808; archdiocese, 1875): Charles J. Chaput, archbishop, 2011. Daniel E. Thomas, Timothy C. Senior, John J. McIntyre, Michael J. Fitzgerald, auxiliaries.

Former ordinaries: Michael Egan, O.F.M., 1810-14; Henry Conwell, 1820-42; Francis P. Kenrick, 1842-51; John N. Neumann, C.SS.R., 1852-60; James F. Wood, 1860-83, first archbishop; Patrick J. Ryan, 1884-1911; Edmond F. Prendergast, 1911-18; Cardinal Dennis Dougherty, 1918-51; Cardinal John O'Hara, C.S.C., 1951-60; Cardinal John Krol, 1961-88; Cardinal Anthony J. Bevilacqua, 1988-2003; Cardinal Justin F. Rigali, 2003-2011.

Philadelphia,* PA (Byzantine, Ukrainian) (1924; metropolitan, 1958): Stephen Soroka, archbishop, 2001. John Bura, auxiliary.

Former ordinaries: Stephen Ortynsky, O.S.B.M., 1907-16; Constantine Bohachevsky, 1924-61; Ambrose Senyshyn, O.S.B.M., 1961-76; Joseph Schmondiuk, 1977-78; Myroslav J. Lubachivsky, 1979-80, apostolic administrator, 1980-81; Stephen Sulyk, 1981-2000.

Phoenix, AZ (1969): Thomas J. Olmsted, bishop, 2003. Eduardo A. Nevares, auxiliary.

Former bishops: Edward A. McCarthy, 1969-76; James S. Rausch, 1977-81; Thomas J. O'Brien, 1982-2003.

Pittsburgh,* PA (Byzantine, Ruthenian) (1924; metropolitan, 1969): William C. Skurla, achbishop, 2012.

Former ordinaries: Basil Takach 1924-48; Daniel Ivancho, 1948-54; Nicholas T. Elko, 1955-67; Stephen J. Kocisko, 1968-91, first metropolitan; Thomas V. Dolinay, 1991-93; Judson M. Procyk, 1995-2001; Basil Schott, O.F.M., 2002-2010.

Pittsburgh, PA (1843): David A. Zubic, bishop, 2007. William J. Walterscheid, auxiliary.

Former bishops: Michael O'Connor, 1843-53, 1854-60; Michael Domenec, C.M., 1860-76; J. Tuigg, 1876-89; Richard Phelan, 1889-1904; J.F. Regis Canevin, 1904-20; Hugh C. Boyle, 1921-50; John F. Dearden, 1950-58; John J. Wright, 1959-69; Vincent M. Leonard, 1969-83; Anthony J. Bevilacqua, 1983-88; Donald W. Wuerl, 1988-2006.

Portland, ME (1853): Vacant.

Former bishops: David W. Bacon, 1855-74; James A. Healy, 1875-1900; William H. O'Connell, 1901-06; Louis S. Walsh, 1906-24; John G. Murray, 1925-31; Joseph E. McCarthy, 1932-55; Daniel J. Feeney, 1955-69; Peter L. Gerety, 1969-74; Edward C. O'Leary, 1974-88, Joseph J. Gerry, O.S.B., 1989-2004; Richard Joseph Malone, 2004-2012.

Portland,* OR (1846): Alexander K. Sample, 2013. Established as Oregon City, name changed, 1928.

Former ordinaries: Francis N. Blanchet, 1846-80 vicar apostolic, first archbishop; Charles J. Seghers, 1880-84; William H. Gross, C.SS.R., 1885-98; Alexander Christie, 1899-1925; Edward D. Howard, 1926-66; Robert J. Dwyer, 1966-74; Cornelius M. Power, 1974-86; William J. Levada, 1986-95; Francis E. George, 1996-97; John G. Vlazny, 1997-2013.

Providence, RI (1872): Thomas J. Tobin, bishop, 2005. Robert E. Evans, auxiliary.

Former bishops: Thomas F. Hendricken, 1872-86; Matthew Harkins, 1887-1921; William A. Hickey,'

1921-33; Francis P. Keough, 1934-47; Russell J. McVinney, 1948-71; Louis E. Gelineau, 1972-97; Robert E. Mulvee, 1997-2005.

Pueblo, CO (1941): Vacant.

Former bishops: Joseph C. Willging, 1942-59; Charles A. Buswell, 1959-79; Arthur N. Tafoya, 1980-2009; Fernando Isern, 2009-2013.

Raleigh, NC (1924): Michael F. Burbidge, bishop, 2006.

Former bishops: William J. Hafey, 1925-37; Eugene J. McGuinness, 1937-44; Vincent S. Waters, 1945-75; F. Joseph Gossman, 1975-2006.

Rapid City, SD (1902): Robert D. Gruss, bishop, 2011. Established at Lead, transferred, 1930.

Former bishops: John Stariha, 1902-09; Joseph F. Busch, 1910-15; John J. Lawler, 1916-48; William T. McCarty, C.SS.R., 1948-69; Harold J. Dimmerling, 1969-87; Charles J. Chaput, O.F.M., Cap., 1988-97; Blase Cupich, 1998-2010.

Reno, NV (1931): Randolph R. Calvo, bishop, 2005. Established at Reno, 1931; title changed to Reno-Las Vegas, 1976, redesignated Reno, 1995, when Las Vegas was made a separate diocese.

Former bishops (Reno/Reno-Las Vegas): Thomas K. Gorman, 1931-52; Robert J. Dwyer, 1952-66; Joseph Green, 1967-74; Norman F. McFarland, 1976-86; Daniel F. Walsh, 1987-95; Phillip F. Straling, 1995-2005.

Richmond, VA (1820): Francis X. DiLorenzo, 2004.

Former bishops: Patrick Kelly, 1820-22; Ambrose Marechal, S.S., administrator, 1822-28; James Whitfield, administrator, 1828-34; Samuel Eccleston, S.S., administrator, 1834-40; Richard V. Whelan, 1841-50; John McGill, 1850-72; James Gibbons, 1872-77; John J. Keane, 1878-88; Augustine Van de Vyver, 1889-1911; Denis J. O'Connell, 1912-26; Andrew J. Brennan, 1926-45; Peter L. Ireton, 1945-58; John J. Russell, 1958-73; Walter F. Sullivan, 1974-2003.

Rochester, NY (1868): Vacant.

Former bishops: Bernard J. McQuaid, 1868-1909; Thomas F. Hickey, 1909-28; John F. O'Hern, 1929-33; Edward F. Mooney, 1933-37; James E. Kearney, 1937-66; Fulton J. Sheen, 1966-69; Joseph L. Hogan, 1969-78; Matthew H. Clark, 1979-2012.

Rockford, IL (1908): David J. Malloy, bishop, 2012.

Former bishops: Peter J. Muldoon, 1908-27; Edward F. Hoban, 1928-42; John J. Boylan, 1943-53; Raymond P. Hillinger, 1953-56; Loras T. Lane, 1956-68; Arthur J. O'Neill, 1968-94; Thomas G. Doran, 1994-2012.

Rockville Centre, NY (1957): William Francis Murphy, bishop, 2001. Paul H. Walsh, Robert J. Brennan, Nelson J. Perez, auxiliaries.

Former bishop: Walter P. Kellenberg, 1957-76; John R. McGann, 1976-2000; James McHugh, 2000.

Sacramento, CA (1886): Jaime Soto, coadjutor bishop, 2007, bishop, 2008.

Former bishops: Patrick Manogue, 1886-95; Thomas Grace, 1896-1921; Patrick J. Keane, 1922-28; Robert J. Armstrong, 1929-57; Joseph T. McGucken, 1957-62; Alden J. Bell, 1962-79; Francis A. Quinn, 1979-93; William K. Weigand, 1993-2008.

Saginaw, MI (1938): Joseph Robert Cistone, bishop, 2009.

Former bishops: William F. Murphy, 1938-50; Stephen S. Woznicki, 1950-68; Francis F. Reh, 1969-80; Kenneth

E. Untener, 1980-2004; Robert J. Carlson, 2004-09.

St. Augustine, FL (1870): Felipe de Jesús Estevez, bishop, 2011.

Former bishops: Augustin Verot, S.S., 1870-76; John Moore, 1877-1901; William J. Kenny, 1902-13; Michael J. Curley, 1914-21; Patrick J. Barry, 1922-40; Joseph P. Hurley, 1940-67; Paul F. Tanner, 1968-79; John J. Snyder, 1979-2000; Victor Benito Galeone, 2001-2011.

St. Cloud, MN (1889): John F. Kinney, bishop, 1995.

Former bishops: Otto Zardetti, 1889-94; Martin Marty, O.S.B., 1895-96; James Trobec, 1897-1914; Joseph F. Busch, 1915-53; Peter Bartholome, 1953-68; George H. Speltz, 1968-87; Jerome Hanus, O.S.B.,1987-94.

St. George's in Canton, OH (Byzantine, Romanian) (1982; eparchy, 1987): John Michael Botean, bishop, 1996.

Former bishop: Vasile Louis Puscas, 1983-93.

St. Josaphat in Parma, OH (Byzantine, Ukrainians) (1983): Vacant.

Former bishops: Robert M. Moskal, 1984-2009.

St. Louis,* MO (1826; archdiocese, 1847): Robert J. Carlson, archbishop, 2009. Edward Rice, auxiliary.

Former ordinaries: Joseph Rosati, C.M., 1827-43; Peter R. Kenrick, 1843-95, first archbishop; John J. Kain, 1895-1903; Cardinal John Glennon, 1903-46; Cardinal Joseph Ritter, 1946-67; Cardinal John J. Carberry, 1968-79; John L. May, 1980-92; Justin F. Rigali, 1994-2003; Raymond L. Burke, 2003-2008.

St. Maron, Brooklyn, NY (Maronite) (1966; diocese, 1971): Gregory John Mansour, eparch, 2004. Established at Detroit, transferred to Brooklyn, 1977.

Former eparchs: Francis Zayek, exarch 1966-72, first eparch 1972-97; Hector Y. Doueihi, 1997-2004.

St. Nicholas in Chicago (Byzantine Eparchy of St. Nicholas of the Ukrainians) (1961): Richard Stephen Seminack, 2003.

Former bishops: Jaroslav Gabro, 1961-80; Innocent H. Lotocky, O.S.B.M., 1981-93; Michael Wiwchar, C.SS.R., 1993-2000.

St. Paul and Minneapolis,* MN (1850; archdiocese, 1888): John C. Nienstedt, coadjutor, 2007, archbishop, 2008. Lee Anthony Piché, auxiliary.

Former ordinaries: Joseph Crétin, 1851-57; Thomas L. Grace, O.P., 1859-84; John Ireland, 1884-1918, first archbishop; Austin Dowling, 1919-30; John G. Murray, 1931-56; William O. Brady, 1956-61; Leo Binz, 1962-75; John R. Roach, 1975-95; Harry J. Flynn, 1995-2008.

St. Peter the Apostle of San Diego (Chaldean) (2002, eparchy): Sarhad Jammo, first eparch, 2002.

St. Petersburg, FL (1968): Robert N. Lynch, bishop, 1996.

Former bishops: Charles McLaughlin, 1968-78; W. Thomas Larkin, 1979-88; John C. Favalora, 1989-94.

St. Thomas the Apostle of Detroit (Chaldean) (1982; eparchy, 1985): Ibrahim N. Ibrahim, exarch, 1982; first eparch, 1985.

St. Thomas of the Syro-Malabars of Chicago (Syro-Malabars) (2001, eparchy): Jacob Angadiath, first eparch, 2001.

Salina, KS (1887): Edward J. Weisenburger, bishop, 2012.

Established at Concordia, transferred, 1944.

Former bishops: Richard Scannell, 1887-91; John J. Hennessy, administrator, 1891-98; John F. Cunningham, 1898-1919; Francis J. Tief, 1921-38; Frank A. Thill, 1938-57; Frederick W. Freking, 1957-64; Cyril J. Vogel, 1965-79; Daniel W. Kucera, O.S.B., 1980-84; George K. Fitzsimons, 1984-2004, Paul S. Coakley, 2004-11.

Salt Lake City, UT (1891): John C. Wester, bishop, 2007.
Former bishops: Lawrence Scanlan, 1891-1915; Joseph S. Glass, C.M., 1915-26; John J. Mitty, 1926-32; James E. Kearney, 1932-37; Duane G. Hunt, 1937-60; J. Lennox Federal, 1960-80; William K. Weigand, 1980-93; George H. Niederauer, 1995-2005.

San Angelo, TX (1961): Michael D. Pfeifer, O.M.I., bishop, 1985.
Former bishops: Thomas J. Drury, 1962-65; Thomas Tschoepe, 1966-69; Stephen A. Leven, 1969-79; Joseph A. Fiorenza, 1979-84.

San Antonio,* TX (1874; archdiocese, 1926): Gustavo Garcia-Siller, M.Sp.S., 2010.
Former ordinaries: Anthony D. Pellicer, 1874-80; John C. Neraz, 1881-94; John A. Forest, 1895-1911; John W. Shaw, 1911-18; Arthur Jerome Drossaerts, 1918-40, first archbishop; Robert E. Lucey, 1941-69; Francis Furey, 1969-79; Patrick F. Flores, 1979-2004; José H. Gomez, 2004-2010.

San Bernardino, CA (1978): Gerald R. Barnes, bishop, 1995. Rutilio J. Del Riego, auxiliaries.
Former bishop: Phillip F. Straling, 1978-95.

San Diego, CA (1936): Robert H. Brom, bishop, 1990; Cirilo Flores, coadjutor, 2012.
Former bishops: Charles F. Buddy, 1936-66; Francis J. Furey, 1966-69; Leo T. Maher, 1969-90.

San Francisco,* CA (1853): Salvatore J. Cordileone, archbishop, 2012. William J. Justice, Robert W. McElroy, auxiliaries.
Former ordinaries: Joseph S. Alemany, O.P., 1853-84; Patrick W. Riordan, 1884-1914; Edward J. Hanna, 1915-35; John Mitty, 1935-61; Joseph T. McGucken, 1962-77; John R. Quinn, 1977-95; William J. Levada, 1995-2005; George H. Niederauer, 2005-2012.

San Jose, CA (1981): Patrick J. McGrath, bishop, 1999. Thomas A. Daly, auxiliary
Former ordinaries: R. Pierre DuMaine, 1981-98.

Santa Fe*, NM (1850; archdiocese, 1875): Michael J. Sheehan, archbishop, 1993.
Former ordinaries: John B. Lamy, 1850-85; first archbishop; John B. Salpointe, 1885-94; Placide L. Chapelle, 1894-97; Peter Bourgade, 1899-1908; John B. Pitaval, 1909-18; Albert T. Daeger, O.F.M., 1919-32; Rudolph A. Gerken, 1933-43; Edwin V. Byrne, 1943-63; James P. Davis, 1964-74; Robert F. Sanchez, 1974-93.

Santa Rosa, CA (1962): Robert Francis Vasa, coadjutor bp., 2010, bishop, 2011.
Former bishops: Leo T. Maher, 1962 69; Mark J. Hurley, 1969 86; John T. Steinbock, 1987 91; G. Patrick Ziemann, 1992-99; Daniel Walsh, 2000-2011.

Savannah, GA (1850): Gregory J. Hartmayer, O.F.M. Conv., bishop, 2011.
Former bishops: Francis X. Gartland, 1850-54; John Barry, 1857-59; Augustin Verot, S.S., 1861-70; Ignatius Persico, O.F.M. Cap., 1870-72; William H. Gross, C.SS.R., 1873-85; Thomas A. Becker,

1886-99; Benjamin J. Keiley, 1900-22; Michael Keyes, S.M., 1922-35; Gerald P. O'Hara, 1935-59; Thomas J. McDonough, 1960-67; Gerard L. Frey, 1967-72; Raymond W. Lessard, 1973-95; John Kevin Boland, 1995-2011.

Scranton, PA (1868): Joseph C. Bambera, bishop, 2010.
Former bishops: William O'Hara, 1868-99; Michael J. Hoban, 1899-1926; Thomas C. O'Reilly, 1928-38; William J. Hafey, 1938-54; Jerome D. Hannan, 1954-65; J. Carroll McCormick, 1966-83; John J. O'Connor, 1983-84; James C. Timlin, 1984-2003; Joseph F. Martino, 2003-2009.

Seattle,* WA (1850; archdiocese, 1951): James Peter Sartain, archbishop, 2010. Eusebio Elizondo, M.Sp.S., auxiliary.
Established as Nesqually, name changed, 1907.
Former ordinaries; Augustin M. Blanchet, 1850-79; Aegidius Junger, 1879-95; Edward J. O'Dea, 1896-1932; Gerald Shaughnessy, S.M., 1933-50; Thomas A. Connolly, first archbishop, 1950-75; Raymond G. Hunthausen, 1975-91; Thomas J. Murphy, 1991-97; Alexander J. Brunett, 1997-2011

Shreveport, LA (1986): Michael G. Duca, bishop, 2008.
Former bishops: William B. Friend, 1986-2006.

Sioux City, IA (1902): Ralph W. Nickless, bishop, 2005.
Former bishops: Philip J. Garrigan, 1902-19; Edmond Heelan, 1919-48; Joseph M. Mueller, 1948-70; Frank H. Greteman, 1970-83; Lawrence D. Soens, 1983-98; Daniel N. DiNardo, 1998-2004.

Sioux Falls, SD (1889): Paul J. Swain, bishop, 2006.
Former bishops: Martin Marty, O.S.B., 1889-94; Thomas O'Gorman, 1896-1921; Bernard J. Mahoney, 1922-39; William O. Brady, 1939-56; Lambert A. Hoch, 1956-78; Paul V. Dudley, 1978-95; Robert J. Carlson, 1995-2004.

Spokane, WA (1913): Blase Cupich, bishop, 2010.
Former bishops: Augustine F. Schinner, 1914-25; Charles D. White, 1927-55; Bernard J. Topel, 1955-78; Lawrence H. Welsh, 1978-90. William S. Skylstad, 1990-2010.

Springfield, IL (1853): Thomas J. Paprocki, bishop, 2010.
Established at Quincy, transferred to Alton, 1857; transferred to Springfield, 1923.
Former bishops: Henry D. Juncker, 1857-68; Peter J. Baltes, 1870-86; James Ryan, 1888-1923; James A. Griffin, 1924-48; William A. O'Connor, 1949-75; Joseph A. McNicholas, 1975-83; Daniel L. Ryan, bishop, 1984-99.

Springfield, MA (1870): Timothy A. McDonnell, bishop, 2004.
Former bishops: Patrick T. O'Reilly, 1870-92; Thomas D. Beaven, 1892-1920; Thomas M. O'Leary, 1921-49; Christopher J. Weldon, 1950-77; Joseph F. Maguire, 1977-91; John A. Marshall, 1991-94; Thomas L. Dupre, 1995-2004.

Springfield-Cape Girardeau, MO (1956): James Vann Johnston, Jr., bishop, 2008.
Former bishops: Charles Helmsing, 1956-62; Ignatius J. Strecker, 1962-69; William Baum, 1970-73; Bernard F. Law, 1973-84; John J. Leibrecht, 1984-2008.

Stamford, CT (Byzantine, Ukrainian) (1956): Paul

P. Chomnycky, O.S.B.M., eparch, 2006.
Former eparchs: Ambrose Senyshyn, O.S.B.M., 1956-61; Joseph Schmondiuk, 1961-77; Basil Losten, 1977-2006.
Steubenville, OH (1944): Jeffrey M. Monforton, 2012.
Former bishops: John K. Mussio, 1945-77; Albert H. Ottenweller, 1977-92; Gilbert I. Sheldon, 1992-2002; Robert Daniel Conlon, 2002-11.
Stockton, CA (1962): Stephen E. Blaire, bishop, 1999.
Former bishops: Hugh A. Donohoe, 1962-69; Merlin J. Guilfoyle, 1969-79; Roger M. Mahony, 1980-85; Donald W. Montrose, 1986-99.
Superior, WI (1905): Peter F. Christensen, bishop, 2007.
Former bishops: Augustine F. Schinner, 1905-13; Joseph M. Koudelka, 1913-21; Joseph G. Pinten, 1922-26; Theodore M. Reverman, 1926-41; William P. O'Connor, 1942-46; Albert G. Meyer, 1946-53; Joseph Annabring, 1954-59; George A. Hammes, 1960-85; Raphael M. Fliss, 1985-2007.
Syracuse, NY (1886): Vacant.
Former bishops: Patrick A. Ludden, 1887-1912; John Grimes, 1912-22; Daniel J. Curley, 1923-32; John A. Duffy, 1933-37; Walter A. Foery, 1937-70; David F. Cunningham, 1970-76; Frank J. Harrison, 1976-87; Joseph T. O'Keefe, 1987-95; James M. Moynihan, 1995-2009; Robert Joseph Cunningham, 20012.
Toledo, OH (1910): Leonard P. Blair, bishop, 2003.
Former bishops: Joseph Schrembs, 1911-21; Samuel A. Stritch, 1921-30; Karl J. Alter, 1931-50; George J. Rehring, 1950-67; John A. Donovan, 1967-80; James R. Hoffman, 1980-2003.
Trenton, NJ (1881): David M. O'Connell, C.M., bishop, 2010.
Former bishops: Michael J. O'Farrell, 1881-94; James A. McFaul, 1894-1917; Thomas J. Walsh, 1918-28; John J. McMahon, 1928-32; Moses E. Kiley, 1934-40; William A. Griffin, 1940-50; George W. Ahr, 1950-79; John C. Reiss, 1980-97; John M. Smith, 1997-2010.
Tucson, AZ (1897): Gerald F. Kicanas, bishop, 2003.
Former bishops: Peter Bourgade, 1897-99; Henry Granjon, 1900-22; Daniel J. Gercke, 1923-60; Francis J. Green, 1960-81; Manuel D. Moreno, 1982-2003.
Tulsa, OK (1972): Edward J. Slattery, bishop, 1993.
Former bishops: Bernard J. Ganter, 1973-77; Eusebius J. Beltran, 1978-92.
Tyler, TX (1986): Vacant.
Former bishop: Charles E. Herzig, 1987 91; Edmond Carmody, 1992-2000; Alvaro Corrada del Rio, S.J., 2000-11.
Van Nuys, CA (Byzantine, Ruthenian) (1981): Gerald N. Dino, eparch, 2007.
Former bishop: Thomas V. Dolinay, 1982-90; George M. Kuzma, 1991-2000; William C. Skurla, 2002-2007.
Venice, FL (1984): Frank J. Dewane, bishop, 2007.
Former bishops: John J. Nevins, 1984-2007.
Victoria, TX (1982): David E. Fellhauer, bishop, 1990.
Former bishops: Charles V. Grahmann, 1982-89.
Washington,* DC (1939): Cardinal Donald W.

Wuerl, archbishop. Francisco González Valer, S.F., Martin D. Holley, Barry C. Knestout, auxiliaries.
Former ordinaries: Michael J. Curley, 1939-47; Cardinal Patrick O'Boyle, 1948-73; Cardinal William Baum, 1973-80; Cardinal James A. Hickey, 1980-2000; Cardinal Theodore E. McCarrick, 2000-2006
Wheeling-Charleston, WV (1850): Michael J. Bransfield, bishop, 2004.
Established as Wheeling, name changed, 1974.
Former bishops: Richard V. Whelan, 1850-74; John J. Kain, 1875-93; Patrick J. Donahue, 1894-1922; John J. Swint, 1922-62; Joseph H. Hodges, 1962-85; Francis B. Schulte, 1985-88; Bernard W. Schmitt, 1989-2004.
Wichita, KS (1887): Vacant.
Former bishops: John J. Hennessy, 1888-1920; Augustus J. Schwertner, 1921-39; Christian H. Winkelmann, 1940-46; Mark K. Carroll, 1947-67; David M. Maloney, 1967-82; Eugene J. Gerber, 1982-2001; Thomas J. Olmsted, 2001-2003; Michael Owen Jackels, 2005-2013.
Wilmington, DE (1868): William Francis Malooly, bishop, 2008.
Former bishops: Thomas A. Becker, 1868-86; Alfred A. Curtis, 1886-96; John J. Monaghan, 1897-1925; Edmond Fitzmaurice, 1925-60; Michael Hyle, 1960-67; Thomas J. Mardaga, 1968-84; Robert E. Mulvee, 1985-95; Michael A. Saltarelli, 1995-2008.
Winona, MN (1889): John M. Quinn, co-adjutor, 2008, bishop, 2009.
Former bishops: Joseph B. Cotter, 1889-1909; Patrick R. Heffron, 1910-27; Francis M. Kelly, 1928-49; Edward A. Fitzgerald, 1949-69; Loras J. Watters, 1969-86; John G. Vlazny, 1987-97; Bernard J. Harrington, 1998-2009.
Worcester, MA (1950): Robert McManus, bishop, 2004.
Former bishops: John J. Wright, 1950-59; Bernard J. Flanagan, 1959-83; Timothy J. Harrington, 1983-94; Daniel P. Reilly, 1994-2004.
Yakima, WA (1951): Joseph J. Tyson, bishop, 2011.
Former bishops: Joseph P. Dougherty, 1951-69; Cornelius M. Power, 1969-74; Nicolas E. Walsh, 1974-76; William S. Skylstad, 1977-90; Francis E. George, O.M.I., 1990-96; Carlos A. Sevilla, S.J., 1996-2011.
Youngstown, OH (1943): George V. Murry, S.J., bishop, 2007
Former bishops: James A. McFadden, 1943-52; Emmet M. Walsh, 1952-68; James W. Malone, 1968-95; Thomas J. Tobin, 1995-2005.
Apostolic Exarchate for the Syro-Malankara Catholics in the United States (created July 14, 2010): Thomas Naickamparampil, first exarch.
Archdiocese for the Military Services, U.S.A., Washington, DC (1957; restructured, 1985): Timothy M. Broglio, archbishop, 2007. Richard Brendan Higgins, Joseph Walter Estabrook, F. Richard Spencer, Neal J, Buckon, Robert J. Coyle, auxiliaries.
Military vicar appointed, 1917; canonically established, 1957, as U.S. Military Vicariate under jurisdiction of New York archbishop; name changed, restructured as independent jurisdiction, 1985.
Former military vicars: Cardinal Patrick Hayes,

1917-38; Cardinal Francis Spellman, 1939-67; Cardinal Terence J. Cooke, 1968-83; Cardinal John J. O'Connor, apostolic administrator, 1984-85.

Former military ordinaries: Archbishop Joseph T. Ryan, 1985-91; Joseph T. Dimino, 1991-97; Edwin F. O'Brien, 1997-2007.

(Note: For coverage of **Missionary Bishops**, *see* under **Missionary Activity of the Church in the U.S.**)

CHANCERY OFFICES OF U.S. ARCHDIOCESES AND DIOCESES

A chancery office, under this or another title, is the central administrative office of an archdiocese or dio cese. (Archdioceses are indicated by asterisk.) As of Aug. 15, 2013.

Albany, NY: Pastoral Center, 40 N. Main Ave., 12203. (518) 453-6611; www.rcda.org.

Alexandria, LA: The Chancery Office, P.O. Box 7417, 71306. (318) 445-2401; www.diocesealex.org.

Allentown, PA: The Chancery Office, P.O. Box F, 18105-1538. (610) 437-0755; www.allentown diocese.org.

Altoona-Johnstown, PA: The Chancery, 927 S. Logan Blvd., Hollidaysburg, 16648. (814) 695-5579; www.dioceseialtjtn.org.

Amarillo, TX: Pastoral Center, 1800 N. Spring St., P.O. Box 5644, 79117-5644. (806) 383-2243; www.amarillodiocese.org.

Anchorage,* AK: The Chancery Office, 225 Cordova St., 99501. (907) 297-7700; www.archdioceseofanchorage.org

Arlington, VA: The Chancery Office, Suite 914, 200 N. Glebe Rd., 22203. (703) 841-2500; www.arlington diocese.org.

Atlanta,* GA: Catholic Center, 680 W. Peachtree St. N.W., 30308. (404) 888-7802; www.archatl.com.

Austin, TX: The Chancery Office, 1600 N. Congress Ave., P.O. Box 13327, 78711. (512) 476-4888; www.austindiocese.org.

Baker, OR: Diocesan Pastoral Office, P.O. Box 5999, Bend, 97708. (541) 388-4004; www.dioceseof baker.org.

Baltimore,* MD: The Chancery Office, 320 Cathedral St., 21201. (410) 547-5446; www.archbalt.org.

Baton Rouge, LA: Catholic Life Center, P.O. Box 2028. 70821-2028. (225) 387-0561; www.diobr.org.

Beaumont, TX: Diocesan Pastoral Office, 70Archie St., P.O. Box 3948, 77704-3948. (409) 838-0451; www.dioceseofbmt.org.

Belleville, IL: The Chancery, 222 S. Third St. 62220-1985, (618) 277-8181; www.diobelle.org.

Biloxi, MS: Administration Offices, P.O. Box 6489, 39522-6489. (228) 702-2100; www.biloxidiocese.org.

Birmingham, AL: Catholic Life Center, P.O. Box 12047, 35202-2047. (205) 838-8322; www.bhmdiocese.org.

Bismarck, ND: The Chancery Office, 420 Raymond St., Box 1575, 58502-1575. (701) 223-1347; www.bismarckdiocese.com.

Boise, ID: The Chancery Office, 303 Federal Way, 83705-5925. (208) 342-1311; www.catholicidaho.org.

Boston,* MA: The Chancery Office, 2121 Commonwealth Ave., Brighton, 02135. (617) 254-0100; www.rcab.or.

Bridgeport, CT: The Catholic Center, 238 Jewett Ave., 06606-2892. (203) 372-4301; www.bridgeportdiocese.com

Brooklyn, NY: The Chancery Office, 75 Greene Ave., P.O. Box C, 11238. (718) 399-5970; www.dioceseofbrooklyn.org.

Brownsville, TX: The Catholic Pastoral Center, P.O. Box 2279, 1910 E. Elizabeth St., 78522-2279. (956) 542-2501; www.cdob.org.

Buffalo, NY: The Chancery Office, 795 Main St., 14203. (716) 847-5500; www.buffalodiocese.org

Burlington, VT: The Chancery Office, P.O. Box 489,Buirlington,VT.05402-0489. (802) 658-6110; www.vermontcatholic.org.

Camden, NJ: Camden Diocesan Center, 631 Market St., P.O. Box 708, 08102. (856) 756-7900; www.camden diocese.org.

Charleston, SC: The Chancery Office, 119 Broad St., P.O. Box 818, 29402. (843) 723-3488; www.catholic-doc.org.

Charlotte, NC: The Pastoral Center, P.O. Box 36776, 28236. (704) 370-6299; www.charlottedio cese.org.

Cheyenne, WY: The Chancery Office, Box 1468, 82003-0426. (307) 638-1530; www.dioceseof cheyenne.

Chicago,* IL: Pastoral Center, P.O. Box 1979, 60690. (312) 751-7999; www.archdiocese-chgo.org

Cincinnati,* OH: The Chancery Office, 100 E. 8th St. 45202. (513) 421-3131; www.catholiccincinnati.org.

Cleveland, OH: The Chancery Office, 1027 Superior Ave., 44114. (216) 696-6525; www.dioceseofcleveland.org

Colorado Springs, CO: Pastoral Center, 228 N. Cascade Ave., 80903-1498; (719) 636-2345; www.diocs.org.

Columbus, OH: Chancery Office, 198 E. Broad St., 43215. (614) 224-2251; www.colsdioc.org

Corpus Christi, TX: The Chancery Office, 620 Lipan St., P.O. Box 2620, 78403-2620. (512) 882-6191; www.diocesecc.org.

Covington, KY: Catholic Center, P.O. Box 15550, 41015. (859) 392-1500; www.covingtondiocese.org.

Crookston, MN: Chancery Office, 1200 Memorial Dr., 56716. (218) 281-4533; www.crookston.org.

Dallas, TX: Chancery Office, 3725 Blackburn St., 75219. (214) 528-2240; www.cathdal.org.

Davenport, IA: Chancery Office, 2706 N. Gaines St., 52804-1998. (563) 324-1911; www.davenport diocese.org.

Denver,* CO: Catholic Pastoral Center, 1300 South Steele St., 80210. (303) 722-4687; www.archden.org.

Des Moines, IA: Chancery Office, 601 Grand Ave., 50309;. (515) 243-7653; www.dmdiocese.org

Detroit,* MI: Chancery Office, 1234 Washington Blvd., 48226. (313) 237-5800; www.aodonline.org.

Dodge City, KS: Chancery Office, 910 Central Ave., 67801-4905. (620) 227-1500; www.dcdiocese.org.

Dubuque,* IA: Chancery Office, 1229 Loretta Ave., 52003; (563) 556-2580; www.arch.pvt.k12.ia.us/home.

Duluth, MN: Pastoral Center, 2830 E. 4th St., 55812. (218) 724-9111; www.dioceseduluth.org.

El Paso, TX: The Chancery Office, 499 St. Matthews St., 79907. (915) 872-8400; www.elpasodi ocese.org.

Erie, PA: St. Mark Catholic Center, P.O. Box 10397, 16514-0397. (814) 824-1135; www.eriecd.org.

Evansville, IN: Chancery Office, P.O. Box 4169, 47724-0169. (812) 424-5536; www.evansville-diocese.org.

Fairbanks, AK: Chancery Office, 1316 Peger Rd., 99709. (907) 374-9500; www.cbna.info.

Fall River, MA: Chancery Office, 450 Highland

Ave., Box 2577, 02722. (508) 675-1311.

Fargo, ND: Chancery, 5201 Bishop Blvd., Suite A, 58104-7605; (701) 356-7900; www.fargodiocese.org.

Fort Wayne-South Bend, IN: Chancery, 1103 S. Calhoun St., Fort Wayne, 46801. (260) 422-4611; South Bend Chancery, 114 W. Wayne St., South Bend, 46601; (574) 234-0687;www.diocesefwsb.org.

Fort Worth, TX: Catholic Center, 800 W. Loop 820 South, 76108. (817) 560-3300; www.fwdioc.org.

Fresno, CA: Chancery Office, 1550 N. Fresno St., 93703-3788. (559) 488-7400; www.diocesoffresno.org.

Gallup, NM: Chancery, 711 S. Puerco Dr., P.O. Box 1338, 87305. (505) 863-4406; www.diocesofgallup.org.

Galveston-Houston, TX: Chancery Office, 1700 San Jacinto, 77002-8291; (713) 659-5461; www.diogh.org.

Gary, IN: The Chancery Office, 9292 Broadway, Merrillville, 46410. (219) 769-9292; www.dcgary.org.

Gaylord, MI: Diocesan Pastoral Center, 611 North St., 49735. (989) 732-5147; www.diocesofgaylord.org.

Grand Island, NE: Chancery Office, P.O. Box 5131, 2708 Old Fair Rd., 68802. (308) 382-6565; www.gidiocese.org.

Grand Rapids, MI: Chancery, 360 Division Ave. S., 49503. (616) 243-0491; www.diocesofgrandrapids.org.

Great Falls-Billings, MT: Chancery, P.O. Box 1399, Great Falls, 59401. (406) 727-6683; www.diocesofgfb.org.

Green Bay, WI: Chancery, P.O. Box 23825, 1910 S. Webster Ave., 54305-3825. (920) 437-7531; www.gbdioc.org.

Greensburg, PA: Chancery, 723 E. Pittsburgh St., 15601. (724) 837-0901; www.diocesofgreensburg.org.

Harrisburg, PA: Chancery, 4800 Union Deposit Rd., 17111-3710. (717) 657-4804; www.hbgdiocese.org.

Hartford,* CT: Chancery, 134 Farmington Ave., 06105-3784. (860) 541-6491; www.archdiocesofhartford.org.

Helena, MT: Chancery, 515 N. Ewing, P.O. Box 1729, 59624-1729. (406) 442-5820; www.diocesehelena.org.

Honolulu, HI: Chancery, 1184 Bishop St., 96813; (808) 585-3300; www.catholichawaii.com.

Houma-Thibodaux, LA: Pastoral Center, 2779 Highway 311, Schriever, 70395-3273. (985) 868-7720; www.htdiocese.org.

Indianapolis,* IN: Archbishop Edward T. O'Meara Catholic Center, 1400 N. Meridian St., 46202. (317) 236-1405; www.archindy.org.

Jackson, MS: Chancery, 237 E. Amite St., P.O. Box 2248, 39225-2248. (601) 969-1880; www.jacksondiocese.org.

Jefferson City, MO: Chancery, 2207 W. Main St., P.O. Box 104900, 65110-4900. (573) 635-9127; www.diojeffcity.org.

Joliet, IL: Chancery, 425 Summit St., 60435. (815) 722-6606; www.diocesofjoliet.org.

Juneau, AK: Chancery, 414 6th St., No. 300, 99801; (907) 586-2227; www.diocesofjuneau.org.

Kalamazoo, MI: Chancery, 215 N. Westnedge Ave., 49007-3760. (269) 349-8714; www.diocesofkalamazoo.

Kansas City,* KS: Chancery, 12615 Parallel Pkwy., 66109. (913) 721-1570; www.archkck.org.

Kansas City-St. Joseph, MO: The Chancery Office, P.O. Box 419037, Kansas City, 64141-6037. (816) 756-1850; www.diocese-kcsj.org.

Knoxville, TN: Chancery, 805 Northshore Dr., SW, P.O. Box 11127; 37939-1127. (865) 584-3307; www.diocesofknoxville.org.

La Crosse, WI: The Chancery Office, 3710 East Ave. S., Box 4004, 54602-4004. (608) 788-7700; www.dioceseoflacrosse.com

Lafayette, IN: Bishop's Office, P.O. Box 260, 610 Lingle Ave.,47901. (765) 742-0275; www.dioceseoflafayette. org.

Lafayette, LA: Chancery, 1408 Carmel Ave., 70501. (337) 261-5652; www.diolaf.org.

Lake Charles, LA: Chancery, 414 Iris St., 70601. (318) 439-7400; www.lcdiocese.org.

Lansing, MI: Chancery, 300 W. Ottawa St., 48933-1577. (517) 342-2440; www.dioceseoflansing.org.

Laredo, TX: Chancery, 1901 Corpus Christi St., 78043. (956) 727-2140; www.thediocesoflaredo. org.

Las Cruces, NM: Chancery, 1280 Med Park Dr., 88005-3239. (575) 523-7577; www.dioceseoflascruces.org.

Las Vegas, NV: Chancery, 336 Cathedral Way, [P.O. Box 18316, 89114-8316]. (702) 735-3500; www.lasvegas-diocese.org.

Lexington, KY: Catholic Center, 1310 Main St., 40508-2048. (859) 253-1993; www.cdlex.org.

Lincoln, NE: Chancery, 3400 Sheridan Blvd. [P.O. Box 80328, 68501-0328]. (402) 488-0921; www.diocesofloincoln.org.

Little Rock, AR: Chancery, 2500 N. Tyler St., [P.O. Box 7565; 72217-7565]. (501) 664-0340; www.dolr.org

Los Angeles,* CA: Archdiocesan Catholic Center, 3424 Wilshire Blvd., 90010-2202. (213) 637-7000; www.archdiocese.la

Louisville,* KY: Chancery, 212 E. College St., [P.O. Box 1073, 40201-1073]. (502) 585-3291; www.archlou.org.

Lubbock, TX: The Catholic Center, P.O. Box 98700, 79499. (806) 792-3943; www.catholiclubbock.org.

Madison, WI: Bishop O'Connor Catholic Pastoral Center, 3577 High Point Rd., [P.O. Box 44983, 53719-4983]. (608) 821-3000; www.madisondiocese.org.

Manchester, NH: Chancery, 153 Ash St., [P.O. Box 310, 03105-0310]. (603) 669-3100; www.diocesemanch.org.

Marquette, MI: Chancery, 117 W. Washington St., P.O. Box 1000, 49855. (906) 227-9111; www.diocesof marquette.org.

Memphis, TN: The Catholic Center, 5825 Shelby Oaks Dr., 38134. (901) 373-1200; www.cdom.org.

Metuchen, NJ: Chancery, 146 Metlars Ln., Piscataway, NJ 08854-4303; [P.O. Box 191, 08840-0191]; (732) 562-1990; www.diometuchen.org.

Miami,* FL: Chancery, 9401 Biscayne Blvd., Miami Shores, 33138. (305) 757-6241; www.miamiarch.org.

Milwaukee,* WI: Archbishop Cousins Catholic Center, P.O. Box 70912, 53207-0912. (414) 769-3300; www.archmil.org.

Mobile,* AL: Chancery, 400 Government St., P.O. Box 1966, 36633. (251) 434-1585; www.mobilearchdiocese.org.

Monterey, CA: Chancery, P.O. Box 2048, 93942-2048. (831) 373-4345; www.diocesofmonterey.org.

Nashville, TN: Chancery, 2400 21st Ave. S., 37212-5387. (615) 383-6393; www.diocesofnashville.org.

Newark,* NJ: Chancery, 171 Clifton Ave., P.O. Box 9500, 07104-0500. (973) 497-4000; www.rcan.org.

New Orleans,* LA: Chancery, 7887 Walmsley Ave., 70125. (504) 861-9521; www.arch-no.org.

Newton, MA (Melkite): Chancery, 3 VFW Pkwy., Roslindale, 02131. (617) 323-9922; www.melkite. org.

New Ulm, MN: Catholic Pastoral Center, 1400 Sixth St. N., 56073-2099. (507) 359-2966; www.dnu.org.

New York,* NY: Chancery, 1011 First Ave., 10022-

4134. (212) 371-1000; www.ny-archdiocese.org.

Norwich, CT: Chancery, 201 Broadway, 06360-4328. (860) 887-9294; www.norwichdiocese.org

Oakland, CA: Chancery, 2121 Harrison St. Suite 100, 94612; (510) 893-4711; www.oakdiocese.org

Ogdensburg, NY: Chancery, 604 Washington St., P.O. Box 369, 13669. (315) 393-2920; www.dioogdensburg.org

Oklahoma City,* OK: Pastoral Center, 7501 NW Expressway, 73132. (405) 721-5651; www.catharch dioceseokc.org

Omaha,* NE: Chancery, 100 N. 62nd St., 68132-2795. (402) 558-3100; www.archomaha.com

Orange, CA: Chancery, 2811 E. Villa Real Dr., 92867, [P.O. Box 14195, 92863-1595]. (714) 282-3000; www.rcbo.org.

Orlando, FL: Chancery, P.O. Box 1800, 32802-1800. (407) 246-4800; www.orlandodiocese.org.

Our Lady of Deliverance of Newark, for Syrian rite Catholics of the U.S. and Canada: P.O. Box 8366, Union City, NJ, 07087-8262. (201) 583-1067; www.syriac-catholic.org.

Our Lady of Lebanon, Eparchy, USA (Maronite): Chancery, 1021 South Tenth St., St. Louis, MO 63104; (314) 231-1021; www.usamaronite.org.

Owensboro, KY: Catholic Pastoral Center, 600 Locust St., 42301-2130. (270) 683-1545; www.owensborodio.org.

Palm Beach, FL: Pastoral Center, 9995 N. Military Trail, Palm Beach Gardens, 33410. (561) 775-9500; www.diocesepb.org.

Parma, OH (Byzantine): Chancery, 1900 Carlton Rd., 44134-3129. (216) 741-8773; www.parma.org.

Passaic, NJ (Byzantine): Chancery, 445 Lackawanna Ave., West Paterson, 07424. (973) 890-7777; www.eparchyof passaic.com

Paterson, NJ: Diocesan Pastoral Center, 777 Valley Rd., Clifton, 07013. (973) 777-8818; www.paterson diocese.org.

Pensacola-Tallahassee, FL: Pastoral Center, 11 N. B. St., Pensacola, 32501. (850) 435-3500; www.ptdiocese.org

Peoria, IL: Chancery, 607 N.E. Madison Ave., 61603. (309) 671-1550; www.cdop.org

Philadelphia,* PA: Chancery, 222 N. 17th St., 19103. (215) 587-3600; www.archphila.org.

Philadelphia,* PA (Byzantine): Chancery, 827 N. Franklin St., 19123-2097. (215) 627-0143; www. ukrarcheparchy.us.

Phoenix, AZ: Chancery, 400 E. Monroe St., 85004-2376. (602) 354-2000; www.diocesephoenix.org.

Pittsburgh,* PA (Byzantine): Chancery, 66 Riverview Ave., 15214. (412) 231-4000; www.archeparchy.org

Pittsburgh, PA: Pastoral Center, 111 Blvd. of the Allies, 15222. (412) 456-3000; www.diopitt.org.

Portland, ME: Chancery, 510 Ocean Ave., P.O. Box 11559, 04103. (207) 773-6471; www.portlanddiocese.net.

Portland, OR*: Pastoral Center, 2838 E. Burnside St., 97214. (503) 234-5334; www.archdpdx.org.

Providence, RI: Chancery, One Cathedral Sq., 02903. (401) 278-4500; www.dioceseofprovidence.org

Pueblo, CO: Catholic Pastoral Center, 1001 N. Grand Ave., 81003. (719) 544-9861; www.dioceseofpueblo.com.

Raleigh, NC: Catholic Center, 715 Nazareth St., 27606. (919) 821-9700; www.dioceseofraleigh.org

Rapid City, SD: Chancery, 606 Cathedral Dr., P.O. Box 678, 57709. (605) 343-3541; www.rapidcitydiocese.org

Reno, NV: Pastoral Center, 290 Arlington Ave., Suite 200, 89501. (775) 329-9274; www.catholi creno.org

Richmond, VA: Pastoral Center, 7800 Carousel Lane, 23294-4201. (804) 359-5661; www.richmonddiocese.org

Rochester, NY: The Pastoral Center, 1150 Buffalo Rd., 14624. (585) 328-3210; www.dor.org

Rockford, IL: Chancery, 555 Colman Center Drive 61108, [P.O. Box 7044, 61125-7044]. (815) 399-4300 www.rockforddiocese.org.

Rockville Centre, NY: Chancery, 50 N. Park Ave. P.O. Box 9023, 11571-9023. (516) 678-5800; www drvc.org.

Sacramento, CA: Pastoral Center, 2110 Broadway. 95818. (916) 733-0100; www.diocese-sacramento. org.

Saginaw, MI: Chancery, 5800 Weiss St., 48603-2799. (989) 799-7910; www. saginaw.org

St. Augustine, FL: Catholic Center, 11625 Old St. Augustine Rd., Jacksonville, 32258. (904) 262-3200; www.dosafl.com

St. Cloud, MN: Chancery, 214 Third Ave. S., 56301; [P.O. Box 1248, 56302-1248]. (320) 251-2340; www.stclouddiocese.org

St. George's in Canton, OH (Byzantine, Romanian): Chancery 1123 44th St. N.E., 44714, [P.O. Box 7189, 44705-0189]. (330) 493-9355; www.romaniancatholic.org.

St. Josaphat in Parma, OH (Byzantine): Chancery, P.O. Box 347180, 44134-7180. (440) 888-1522; www.stjosaphateparchy.org

St. Louis,* MO: Catholic Center, 4445 Lindell Blvd., 63108-2497. (314) 633-2222; www.archstl. org.

St. Maron of Brooklyn (Maronite): Pastoral Center, 109 Remsen St., 11201. (718) 237-9913; www.stmaron.org

St. Nicholas in Chicago (Byzantine): Chancery, 2245 W. Rice St., 60622. (773) 276-5080; www.stni cholaseparchy.org

St. Paul and Minneapolis,* MN: Chancery, 226 Summit Ave., St. Paul, 55102-2197. (651) 291-4400; www.archspm.org

St. Peter the Apostle of San Diego (Chaldean): Chancery Office, 1627 Jamacha Way, El Cajon, CA 92019. (619) 590-9028; www.kaldu.org

St. Petersburg, FL: Chancery, 6363 9th Ave. N, 33710, [P.O. Box 40200, 33743-0200]. (727) 344-1611; www.dioceseofstpete.org.

St. Thomas of Chicago (Syro-Malabar): Diocesan Office, 717 N. Eastland, Elmhurst, IL 60126. (630) 530-8399; www.stthomasdiocese.org

St. Thomas the Apostle of Detroit (Chaldean Catholic Diocese – USA): Chancery, 25603 Berg Rd., Southfield, MI 48034. (248) 351-0440; www..

Salina, KS: Chancery, 103 N. 9th St., 67401, [P.O. Box 980, 67402-0980]. (785) 827-8746; www.salinadiocese.org

Salt Lake City, UT: Pastoral Center, 27 C St., 84103. (801) 328-8641; www.utahcatholicdiocese. org

San Angelo, TX: Chancery, P.O. Box 1829, 76902-1829. (915) 651-7500; www.san-angelo-diocese.org.

San Antonio,* TX: Chancery, 2718 W. Woodlawn, [P.O. Box 28410, 78228-0410]. (210) 734-2620; www.archdiosa.org.

San Bernardino, CA: Chancery, 1201 E. Highland Ave., 92404. (909) 475-5300; www.sbdiocese.org.

San Diego, CA: Pastoral Center, 3888 Paducah Dr., 92117 [P.O. Box 85728, 92186-5728], (858) 490-8200; www.diocese-sdiego.org.

San Francisco,* CA: Chancery, One Peter Yorke Way 94109. (415) 614-5500; www.sfarchdiocese.org

San Jose, CA: Chancery, 1150 N. First St., Suite 100, 95112-4966. (408) 983-0100; www.dsj.org.

Santa Fe,* NM: Catholic Center, 4000 St. Joseph's Pl. N.W., Albuquerque, 87120-1741. (505) 831-8100.

Santa Rosa, CA: Chancery, P.O. Box 1297, 95402-1297. (707) 545-7610; www.santarosacatholic.org.

Savannah, GA: Pastoral Center, 601 E. Liberty St., 31401-5196. (912) 201-4100; www.diosav.org.

Scranton, PA: Chancery, 300 Wyoming Ave., 18503-1279. (570) 207-2216; www.dioceseofscranton.org.

Seattle,* WA: Chancery, 910 Marion St., 98104-1299. (206) 382-4560; www.seattlearch.org.

Shreveport, LA: Catholic Center, 3500 Fairfield Ave. 71104. (318) 868-4441; www.dioshpt.org.

Sioux City, IA: Chancery, 1821 Jackson St., P.O. Box 3379, 51102-3379. (712) 255-7933; www.scdiocese.org.

Sioux Falls, SD: Pastoral Center, 523 N. Duluth Ave., 57104-2714. (605) 334-9861; www.sfcatholic.org.

Spokane, WA: Pastoral Center, 1023 W. Riverside Ave., P.O. Box 1453, 99201. (509) 358-7300; www.dioceseofspokane.org.

Springfield, IL: Pastoral Center, 1615 W. Washington, P.O. Box 3187, 62708-3187. (217) 698-8500; www.dio.org.

Springfield, MA: Chancery, P.O. Box 1730, 01102. (413) 732-3175; www.diospringfield.org.

Springfield-Cape Girardeau, MO: The Catholic Center, 601 S. Jefferson Ave., Springfield. 65806-3143. (417) 866-0841; home.catholicweb.com/diocspfdcape/index.cfm

Stamford, CT (Byzantine): Chancery, 14 Peveril Rd., 06902-3019. (203) 324-7698

Steubenville, OH: Chancery, 422 Washington St., P.O. Box 969, 43952. (740) 282-3631; www.diosteub.org.

Stockton, CA: Chancery, 1125 N. Lincoln St., 95203. (209) 472-1008; www.stocktondiocese.org

Superior, WI: Chancery, 1201 Hughitt Ave., Box 969, 54880. (715) 392-2937; www.catholicdos.org.

Syracuse, NY: Chancery, 240 E. Onondaga St., P.O. Box 511, 13201-0511. (315) 422-7203; wwwsyrdioc.org.

Toledo, OH: Chancery, 1933 Spielbusch Ave., 43604 [P.O. Box 985, 43697-0895]. (419) 244-6711; www.toledodiocese.org

Trenton, NJ: Chancery, 701 Lawrenceville Rd., P.O. Box 5147, 08638. (609) 406-7400; www.dioceseoftrenton.org.

Tucson, AZ: Pastoral Center, 111 S. Church Ave., Box 31, 85702. (520) 792-3410; www.diocesetucson.org

Tulsa, OK: Chancery, 12300 E. 91st St. S, Broken Arrow, 74102 [P.O. Box 690240, Tulsa 74169]. (918) 294-1904; www.dioceseoftulsa.org

Tyler, TX: Chancery, 1015 E.S.E. Loop 323, 75701-9663. (903) 534-1077; www.dioceseoftyler.org

Van Nuys, CA (Byzantine): Chancery, 8105 N. 16th St., Phoenix, AZ 85020. (602) 861-9778; www.eparchy-of-vannuys.org.

Venice, FL: Catholic Center, P.O. Box 2006, 34284. (941) 484-9543; www.dioceseofvenice.org.

Victoria, TX: Chancery, 1505 E. Mesquite Ln., 77901 [P.O. Box 4070, 77903]. (361) 573-0828; www.victoriadiocese.org

Washington,* DC: Pastoral Center, 5001 Eastern Ave., Hyattsville, MD 20782 [P.O. Box 29260, DC 20017-0260]. (301) 853-4500; www.adw.org.

Wheeling-Charleston, WV: Chancery, 1300 Byron St., P.O. Box 230, Wheeling, 26003. (304) 233-0880; www.dwc.org.

Wichita, KS: Chancery, 424 N. Broadway, 67202. (316) 269-3900; www.cdowk.org

Wilmington, DE: Chancery, 1925 Delaware Ave., P.O. Box 2030, 19899-2030. (302) 573-3100; www.cdow.org.

Winona, MN: Chancery, 55 W. Sanborn St., P.O. Box 588, 55987. (507) 454-4643; www.dow.org.

Worcester, MA: Chancery, 49 Elm St., 01609-2597. (508) 791-7171; www.worcesterdiocese.org.

Yakima, WA: Chancery, 5301-A Tieton Dr., 98908-3493. (509) 965-7119; www.yakimadiocese.org.

Youngstown, OH: Chancery, 144 W. Wood St., 44503. (330) 744-8451; www.doy.org.

Military Archdiocese: P.O. Box 4469, Washington, DC 20017-0469; 3311 Toledo Terrace, Suite A201, Hyattsville, MD 20782-4135. (202) 269-9100; www.milarch.org.

Armenian Apostolic Exarchate for the United States and Canada: 110 E. 12th St., New York, NY 10003. (212) 477-2030.

Apostolic Exarchate for the Syro-Malankara Catholics in the United States: Mar Ivanios Malankara Catholic Centre, 950 Hill Side Avenue, New Hyde Park, New York 11004.

CATHEDRALS, BASILICAS, AND SHRINES IN THE U.S.

CATHEDRALS IN THE UNITED STATES

A cathedral is the principal church in a diocese, the one in which the bishop has his seat (cathedra). He is the actual pastor, although many functions of the church, which usually serves a parish, are the responsibility of a priest serving as the rector. Because of the dignity of a cathedral, the dates of its dedication and its patronal feast are observed throughout a diocese. The pope's cathedral, the Basilica of St. John Lateran, is the highest-ranking church in the world.

(Archdioceses are indicated by asterisk.)

Albany, NY: Immaculate Conception.

Alexandria, LA: St. Francis Xavier.

Allentown, PA: St. Catherine of Siena.

Altoona-Johnstown, PA: Blessed Sacrament (Altoona); St. John Gualbert (Johnstown).

Amarillo, TX: St. Laurence.

Anchorage,* AK: Holy Family.

Arlington, Va: St. Thomas More.

Atlanta,* GA: Christ the King.

Austin, TX: St. Mary (Immaculate Conception).

Baker, OR: St. Francis de Sales.

Baltimore,* MD: Mary Our Queen; Basilica of the National Shrine of the Assumption of the Blessed Virgin Mary (Co-Cathedral).

Baton Rouge, LA: St. Joseph.

Beaumont, TX: St. Anthony (of Padua).

Belleville, IL: St. Peter.

Biloxi, MS: Nativity of the Blessed Virgin Mary.

Birmingham, AL: St. Paul.

Bismarck, N.D.: Holy Spirit.

Boise, Id.: St. John the Evangelist.

Boston,* MA: Holy Cross.

Bridgeport, CT: St. Augustine.

Brooklyn, NY: St. James (Minor Basilica).
Brownsville, TX: Immaculate Conception.
Buffalo, NY: St. Joseph.
Burlington, VT: Immaculate Conception; St. Joseph (Co-Cathedral).
Camden, NJ: Immaculate Conception.
Charleston, SC: St. John the Baptist.
Charlotte, NC: St. Patrick.
Cheyenne, WY: St. Mary.
Chicago,* IL: Holy Name (of Jesus).
Cincinnati,* OH: St. Peter in Chains.
Cleveland, OH: St. John the Evangelist.
Colorado Springs, Colo: St. Mary.
Columbus, OH: St. Joseph.
Corpus Christi, TX: Corpus Christi.
Covington, KY: Basilica of the Assumption.
Crookston, MN: Immaculate Conception.
Dallas, TX: Cathedral-Santuario de Guadalupe.
Davenport, IA: Sacred Heart.
Denver,* CO: Immaculate Conception (Minor Basilica).
Des Moines, IA: St. Ambrose.
Detroit,* MI: Most Blessed Sacrament.
Dodge City, KS: Our Lady of Guadalupe.
Dubuque,* IA: St. Raphael.
Duluth, MN: Our Lady of the Rosary.
El Paso, TX: St. Patrick.
Erie, PA: St. Peter.
Evansville, IN: Most Holy Trinity (Pro-Cathedral).
Fairbanks, AK: Sacred Heart.
Fall River, MA: St. Mary of the Assumption.
Fargo, N.D.: St. Mary.
Fort Wayne-S. Bend, IN: Immaculate Conception (Fort Wayne); St. Matthew (South Bend).
Fort Worth, TX: St. Patrick.
Fresno, CA: St. John (the Baptist).
Gallup, NM: Sacred Heart.
Galveston-Houston, TX: St. Mary (Minor Basilica, Galveston); Sacred Heart Co-Cathedral (Houston).
Gary, IN: Holy Angels.
Gaylord, MI: St. Mary, Our Lady of Mt. Carmel.
Grand Island, NE: Nativity of Blessed Virgin Mary.
Grand Rapids, MI: St. Andrew.
Great Falls-Billings, MT: St. Ann (Great Falls); St. Patrick Co-Cathedral (Billings).
Green Bay, WI: St. Francis Xavier.
Greensburg, PA: Blessed Sacrament.
Harrisburg, PA: St. Patrick.
Hartford,* CT: St. Joseph.
Helena, MT: St. Helena.
Honolulu, HI: Our Lady of Peace; St. Theresa of the Child Jesus (Co-Cathedral).
Houma-Thibodaux, LA: St. Francis de Sales (Houma); St. Joseph Co-Cathedral (Thibodaux).
Indianapolis,* IN: Sts. Peter and Paul.
Jackson, MS: St. Peter.
Jefferson City, MO: St. Joseph.
Joliet, IL: St. Raymond Nonnatus.
Juneau, AK: Nativity of the Blessed Virgin Mary.
Kalamazoo, MI: St. Augustine.
Kansas City,* KS: St. Peter the Apostle.
Kansas City-St. Joseph, MO: Immaculate Conception (Kansas City); St. Joseph Co-Cathedral (St. Joseph).
Knoxville, TN: Sacred Heart of Jesus.

La Crosse, WI: St. Joseph the Workman.
Lafayette, IN: St. Mary.
Lafayette, LA: St. John the Evangelist.
Lake Charles, LA: Immaculate Conception.
Lansing, MI: St. Mary.
Laredo, TX: San Augustin.
Las Cruces, NM: Immaculate Heart of Mary.
Las Vegas, NV: Guardian Angel.
Lexington, KY: Christ the King.
Lincoln, NE: Cathedral of the Risen Christ.
Little Rock, AR: St. Andrew.
Los Angeles,* CA: Cathedral of Our Lady of the Angels of Los Angeles (opened in 2002).
Louisville,* KY: Assumption.
Lubbock, TX: Christ the King.
Madison, WI: St. Raphael.
Manchester, NH: St. Joseph.
Marquette, MI: St. Peter.
Memphis, TN: Immaculate Conception.
Metuchen, NJ: St. Francis (of Assisi).
Miami,* FL: St. Mary (Immaculate Conception).
Milwaukee,* WI: St. John.
Mobile,* AL: Immaculate Conception (Minor Basilica).
Monterey, CA: San Carlos Borromeo.
Nashville, TN: Incarnation.
Newark,* NJ: Sacred Heart (Minor Basilica).
New Orleans,* LA: St. Louis. (Minor Basilica)
Newton, MA (Melkite): Our Lady of the Annunciation (Boston).
New Ulm, MN: Holy Trinity.
New York,* NY: St. Patrick.
Norwich, CT: St. Patrick.
Oakland, CA: St. Francis de Sales.
Ogdensburg, NY: St. Mary (Immaculate Conception).
Oklahoma City,* OK: Our Lady of Perpetual Help.
Omaha,* NE: St. Cecilia.
Orange, CA: Holy Family.
Orlando, FL: St. James.
Our Lady of Deliverance of Newark, New Jersey for Syrian Rite Catholics in the U.S. and Canada: Our Lady of Deliverance.
Our Lady of Lebanon of Los Angeles, CA (Maronite): Our Lady of Mt. Lebanon-St. Peter.
Owensboro, KY: St. Stephen.
Palm Beach, FL: St. Ignatius Loyola, Palm Beach Gardens.
Parma, OH (Byzantine): St. John the Baptist.
Passaic, NJ (Byzantine): St. Michael.
Paterson, NJ: St. John the Baptist.
Pensacola-Tallahassee, FL: Sacred Heart (Pensacola); Co-Cathedral of St. Thomas More (Tallahassee).
Peoria, IL: St. Mary.
Philadelphia,* PA: Sts. Peter and Paul (Minor Basilica).
Philadelphia,* PA (Byzantine): Immaculate Conception of Blessed Virgin Mary.
Phoenix, AZ: Sts. Simon and Jude.
Pittsburgh,* PA (Byzantine): St. John the Baptist, Munhall.
Pittsburgh, PA: St. Paul.
Portland, ME: Immaculate Conception.
Portland,* OR: Immaculate Conception.
Providence, RI: Sts. Peter and Paul.

Pueblo, CO: Sacred Heart.
Raleigh, NC: Sacred Heart.
Rapid City, SD: Our Lady of Perpetual Help.
Reno, NV: St. Thomas Aquinas.
Richmond, VA: Sacred Heart.
Rochester, NY: Sacred Heart.
Rockford, IL: St. Peter.
Rockville Centre, NY: St. Agnes.
Sacramento, CA: Blessed Sacrament.
Saginaw, MI: St. Mary.
St. Augustine, FL: St. Augustine (Minor Basilica).
St. Cloud, MN: St. Mary.
St. George's in Canton, OH (Byzantine, Romanian): St. George.
St. Josaphat in Parma, OH (Byzantine): St. Josaphat.
St. Louis,* MO: St. Louis.
St. Maron, Brooklyn, NY (Maronite): Our Lady of Lebanon.
St. Nicholas in Chicago (Byzantine): St. Nicholas.
St. Paul and Minneapolis,* MN: St. Paul (St. Paul); Basilica of St. Mary Co-Cathedral (Minneapolis).
St. Petersburg, FL: St. Jude the Apostle.
St. Thomas the Apostle of Detroit (Chaldean): Our Lady of Chaldeans Cathedral (Mother of God Church), Southfield, MI
St. Thomas of Chicago (Syro-Malabar): Mar Thoma Shleeha Church.
Salina, KS: Sacred Heart.
Salt Lake City, UT: The Madeleine.
San Angelo, TX: Sacred Heart.
San Antonio,* TX: San Fernando.
San Bernardino, CA: Our Lady of the Rosary.
San Diego, CA: St. Joseph.
San Francisco,* CA: St. Mary (Assumption).
San Jose, CA: St. Joseph (Minor Basilica); St. Patrick, Proto-Cathedral.
Santa Fe,* NM: San Francisco de Asis (Minor Basilica).
Santa Rosa, CA: St. Eugene.
Savannah, GA: St. John the Baptist.
Scranton, PA: St. Peter.
Seattle,* WA: St. James.
Shreveport, LA: St. John Berchmans.
Sioux City, IA: Epiphany.
Sioux Falls, SD: St. Joseph.
Spokane, WA: Our Lady of Lourdes.
Springfield, IL: Immaculate Conception.
Springfield, MA: St. Michael.
Springfield-Cape Girardeau, MO: St. Agnes (Springfield); St. Mary (Cape Girardeau).
Stamford, CT (Byzantine): St. Vladimir.
Steubenville, OH: Holy Name.
Stockton, CA: Annunciation.
Superior, WI: Christ the King.
Syracuse, NY: Immaculate Conception.
Syro-Malankara Exarchate: St. John Chrysostom Pro-Cathedral
Toledo, OH: Queen of the Most Holy Rosary.
Trenton, NJ: St. Mary (Assumption).
Tucson, AZ: St. Augustine.
Tulsa, OK: Holy Family.
Tyler, TX: Immaculate Conception.
Van Nuys, CA (Byzantine): St. Mary (Patronage of the Mother of God), Van Nuys; St. Stephen's (Pro-Cathedral), Phoenix, AZ

Venice, Fla: Epiphany.
Victoria, TX: Our Lady of Victory.
Washington,* DC: St. Matthew.
Wheeling-Charleston, WV: St. Joseph (Wheeling); Sacred Heart (Charleston).
Wichita, KS: Immaculate Conception.
Wilmington, DE: St. Peter.
Winona, MN: Sacred Heart.
Worcester, MA: St. Paul.
Yakima, WA: St. Paul.
Youngstown, OH: St. Columba.
Apostolic Exarchate for Armenian Catholics in the U.S. and Canada: St. Ann (110 E. 12th St., New York, NY 10003).

BASILICAS IN THE UNITED STATES

Basilica is a title assigned to certain churches because of their antiquity, dignity, historical importance or significance as centers of worship. Major basilicas have the papal altar and holy door, which is opened at the beginning of a Jubilee Year; minor basilicas enjoy certain ceremonial privileges.

Among the major basilicas are the patriarchal basilicas of St. John Lateran, St. Peter, St. Paul Outside the Walls and St. Mary Major in Rome; St. Francis and St. Mary of the Angels in Assisi, Italy. The patriarchal basilica of St. Lawrence, Rome, is a minor basilica. The dates in the listings below indicate when the churches were designated as basilicas.

Minor Basilicas in U.S., Puerto Rico, Guam

Alabama: Mobile, Cathedral of the Immaculate Conception (Mar. 10, 1962).

Arizona: Phoenix, St. Mary's (Immaculate Conception) (Sept. 2, 1985).

California: San Francisco, Mission Dolores (Feb. 6, 1952); Carmel, Old Mission of San Carlos (Feb. 5, 1960); Alameda, St. Joseph (Jan. 21, 1972); San Diego, Mission San Diego de Alcala (Nov. 17, 1975); San Jose, St. Joseph (Jan. 28, 1997); San Juan Capistrano, Mission Basilica of San Juan Capistrano (Feb. 14, 2000).

Colorado: Denver, Cathedral of the Immaculate Conception (Nov. 3, 1979).

Connecticut: Waterbury, Basilica of the Immaculate Conception (Feb. 9, 2008); Bridgeport, Basilica of St. John the Evangelist (June 16, 2009).

District of Columbia: National Shrine of the Immaculate Conception (Oct. 12, 1990).

Florida: St. Augustine, Cathedral of St. Augustine (Dec. 4, 1976); Daytona Beach, Basilica of St. Paul (Jan. 25, 2006); Orlando, Basilica of the National Shrine of Mary, Queen of the Universe (June 3, 2009).

Illinois: Chicago, Our Lady of Sorrows (May 4, 1956); Queen of All Saints (Mar. 26, 1962); Basilica of St. Hyacinth (Nov. 30, 2003).

Indiana: Vincennes, Old Cathedral (Mar. 14, 1970); Notre Dame, Basilica of the Most Sacred Heart, Univ. of Notre Dame (Nov. 23, 1991).

Iowa: Dyersville, St. Francis Xavier (May 11, 1956); Des Moines, St. John the Apostle (Aug. 10, 1989).

Kentucky: Trappist, Our Lady of Gethsemani (Mar. 22, 1949); Covington, Cathedral of

Assumption (Oct. 19, 1953); Bardstown, St. Joseph Proto-Cathedral Basilica (2001).

Louisiana: Alexandria, Basilica of the Immaculate Conception (Feb. 22, 2009); New Orleans, St. Louis King of France (Dec. 9, 1964).

Maine: Lewiston, Basilica of Sts. Peter and Paul (May 22, 2005).

Maryland: Baltimore, Assumption of the Blessed Virgin Mary (July 14, 1937; designated national shrine, 1993); Emmitsburg, Shrine of St. Elizabeth Ann Seton (Feb. 13, 1991).

Massachusetts: Boston, Perpetual Help ("Mission Church") (Sept. 8, 1954); Chicopee, St. Stanislaus (June 25, 1991); Webster, St. Joseph (Oct. 1998).

Michigan: Grand Rapids, St. Adalbert (Aug. 22, 1979).

Minnesota: Minneapolis. St. Mary (Jan. 18, 1926).

Mississippi: Natchez, St. Mary Basilica (Sept. 8, 1998).

Missouri: Conception, Basilica of Immaculate Conception (Aug. 8, 1940); St. Louis, St. Louis King of France (Jan. 27, 1961).

New Jersey: Newark, Cathedral Basilica of the Sacred Heart (Dec. 22, 1995).

New Mexico: Mesilla, Basilica of San Albino (June 2008); Santa Fe, Cathedral Basilica of St. Francis of Assisi (Oct. 4, 2005).

New York: Brooklyn, Our Lady of Perpetual Help (Sept. 5, 1969), Cathedral-Basilica of St. James (May 6, 1982); Buffalo, St. Adalbert's Basilica (Aug. 11, 1907); Lackawanna, Our Lady of Victory (July 14, 1926); Youngstown, Blessed Virgin Mary of the Rosary of Fatima (Oct. 7, 1975); Syracuse, Sacred Heart of Jesus (Aug. 27, 1998).

North Carolina: Asheville, St. Lawrence (Apr. 6, 1993; ceremonies, Sept. 5, 1993); Belmont, Our Lady Help of Christians (July 27, 1998).

North Dakota: Jamestown, St. James (Oct. 26, 1988).

Ohio: Carey, Shrine of Our Lady of Consolation (Oct. 21, 1971).

Pennsylvania: Latrobe, St. Vincent Basilica, Benedictine Archabbey (Aug. 22, 1955); Conewago, Basilica of the Sacred Heart (June 30, 1962); Philadelphia, Sts. Peter and Paul (Sept. 27, 1976); Danville, Sts. Cyril and Methodius (chapel at the motherhouse of the Sisters of Sts. Cyril and Methodius) (June 30, 1989); Loretto, St. Michael the Archangel (Sept. 9, 1996); Scranton, National Shrine of St. Ann (Oct. 18, 1997).

Texas: Galveston, St. Mary Cathedral (Aug. 2, 1979); San Antonio, Basilica of the National Shrine of the Little Flower (Sept. 27, 1931); Basilica of Our Lady of San Juan del Valle-National Shrine (May 2, 1954); Beaumont, Saint Anthony Cathedral Basilica (August 2006).

Virginia: Norfolk, St. Mary of the Immaculate Conception (July 9, 1991).

West Virginia: Wheeling, Basilica of the Co-Cathedral of the Sacred Heart (Nov. 9, 2009).

Wisconsin: Milwaukee, St. Josaphat (Mar. 10, 1929); Hubertus, Holy Hill National Shrine of Mary, Help of Christians (Nov. 19, 2006).

Puerto Rico: San Juan, Cathedral of San Juan (Jan. 25, 1978).

Guam: Agana, Cathedral of Dulce Nombre de Maria (Sweet Name of Mary) (1985).

BASILICA OF THE NATIONAL SHRINE OF THE IMMACULATE CONCEPTION

The Basilica of the National Shrine of the Immaculate Conception is dedicated to the honor of the Blessed Virgin Mary, declared patroness of the United States under this title in 1846, eight years before the proclamation of the dogma of the Immaculate Conception. The church was designated a minor basilica by Pope John Paul II Oct. 12, 1990. The church is the eighth largest religious building in the world and the largest Catholic church in the Western Hemisphere, with numerous special chapels and with normal seating and standing accommodations for 6,000 people. Open daily, it is adjacent to The Catholic University of America, at Michigan Ave. and Fourth St. N.E., Washington, DC 20017; (202) 526-8300; www.nationalshrine.com. Rev. Msgr. Walter R. Rossi is the rector.

SHRINES AND PLACES OF HISTORIC INTEREST IN THE U.S.

(Principal source: Catholic Almanac *survey.)*

Listed below, according to state, are shrines, other centers of devotion and some places of historic interest with special significance for Catholics. The list is necessarily incomplete because of space limitations.

Information includes, where possible: name and location of shrine or place of interest, date of foundation, sponsoring agency or group, and address for more information.

Alabama: Our Lady of the Angels, Hanceville; Birmingham Diocese. Address: Our Lady of the Angels Monastery, 3222 County Road 548, Hanceville, 35077; (256) 352-6267.

• St. Jude Church of the City of St. Jude, Montgomery (1934; dedicated, 1938); Mobile Archdiocese. Address: 2048 W. Fairview Ave., Montgomery, 36108; (334) 265-1390.

• Shrine of the Most Blessed Trinity, Holy Trinity (1924); Missionary Servants of the Most Blessed Trinity. Address: Holy Trinity, 36859.

Arizona: Chapel of the Holy Cross, Sedona (1956); Phoenix Diocese: P.O. Box 1043, W. Sedona 86339.

• Mission San Xavier del Bac, near Tucson (1692); National Historic Landmark; Franciscan Friars and Tucson Diocese; Address: 1950 W. San Xavier Rd., Tucson, 85746-7409; (520) 294-2624.

• Shrine of St. Joseph of the Mountains, Yarnell (1939); erected by Catholic Action League; currently maintained by Board of Directors. Address: P.O. Box 267, Yarnell, 85362.

California: Mission San Diego de Alcala (July 16, 1769); first of the 21 Franciscan missions of Upper California; Minor Basilica; National Historic Landmark; San Diego Diocese. Address: 10818 San Diego Mission Rd., San Diego, 92108; (619) 283-7319.

• Carmel Mission Basilica (Mission San Carlos Borromeo del Rio Carmelo), Carmel by the Sea (June 3, 1770); Monterey Diocese. Address: 3080 Rio Rd., Carmel, 93923; (831) 624-1271.

• Old Mission San Luis Obispo de Tolosa, San Luis Obispo (Sept. 1, 1772); Monterey Diocese (Parish Church). Address: Old Mission Church, 751 Palm St., San Luis Obispo, 93401.

• San Gabriel Mission, San Gabriel (Sept. 8,

1771); Los Angeles Archdiocese (Parish Church, staffed by Claretians). Address: 537 W. Mission, San Gabriel, 91776.

• Mission San Francisco de Asis (Oct. 9, 1776) and Mission Dolores Basilica (1860s); San Francisco Archdiocese. Address: 3321 Sixteenth St., San Francisco, 94114.

• Old Mission San Juan Capistrano, San Juan Capistrano (Nov. 1, 1776); Orange Diocese. Address: P.O. Box 697, San Juan Capistrano, 92693; (949) 248-2026; www.missionsjc.com.

• Old Mission Santa Barbara, Santa Barbara (Dec. 4, 1786); National Historic Landmark; Parish Church, staffed by Franciscan Friars. Address: 2201 Laguna St., Santa Barbara, 93105; (805) 682-4713.

• Old Mission San Juan Bautista, San Juan Bautista (June 24, 1797); National Historic Landmark; Monterey Diocese (Parish Church). Address: P.O. Box 400, San Juan Bautista, 95045.

• Mission San Miguel, San Miguel (July 25, 1797); Parish Church, Monterey diocese; Franciscan Friars. Address: P.O. Box 69, San Miguel, 93451; (805) 467-3256.

• Old Mission Santa Inés, Solvang (1804); Historic Landmark; Los Angeles Archdiocese (Parish Church, staffed by Capuchin Franciscan Friars). Address: P.O. Box 408, Solvang, 93464; (805) 688-4815; www.missionsantaines.org.

Franciscan Friars founded 21 missions in California. (See Index: **Franciscan Missions**.)

• Shrine of Our Lady of Sorrows, Sycamore (1883); Sacramento Diocese. Address: c/o Our Lady of Lourdes Church, 745 Ware Ave., Colusa, 95932.

Colorado: Mother Cabrini Shrine, Golden; Missionary Sisters of the Sacred Heart. Address: 20189 Cabrini Blvd., Golden, 80401.

Connecticut: Shrine of Our Lady of Lourdes, Litchfield (1958); Montfort Missionaries. Address: P.O. Box 667, Litchfield, 06759.

• Shrine of the Infant of Prague, New Haven (1945); Dominican Friars. Address: P.O. Box 1202, 5 Hillhouse Ave., New Haven, 06505.

District of Columbia: Mount St. Sepulchre, Franciscan Monastery of the Holy Land (1897; church dedicated, 1899); Order of Friars Minor. Address: 1400 Quincy St. N.E., Washington, DC 20017.

• Basilica of the National Shrine of the Immaculate Conception. See Index for separate entry.

Florida: Mary, Queen of the Universe Shrine, Orlando (1986, temporary facilities; new shrine dedicated, 1993); Orlando diocese. Address: 8300 Vineland Ave., Orlando, 32821; (407) 239-6600; www.maryqueenoftheuniverse.org.

• Our Lady of La Leche Shrine (Patroness of Mothers and Mothers-to-be) and Mission of Nombre de Dios, Saint Augustine (1565); Angelus Crusade Headquarters; St. Augustine Diocese. Address: 30 Ocean Ave., St. Augustine 32084.

Illinois: Holy Family Log Church, Cahokia (1799; original log church erected 1699); Belleville Diocese (Parish Church). Address: 116 Church St., Cahokia, 62206; (618) 337-4548.

• Marytown/Shrine of St. Maximilian Kolbe and Retreat Center, Libertyville; Our Lady of the Blessed Sacrament Sanctuary of Perpetual Eucharistic Adoration (1930) and Archdiocesan Shrine to St. Maximilian Kolbe (1989), conducted by Conventual Franciscan Friars, 1600 West Park Ave., Libertyville, 60048; (847) 367-7800.

• National Shrine of Our Lady of the Snows, Belleville (1958); Missionary Oblates of Mary Immaculate. Address: 442 S. De Mazenod Dr., Belleville, 62223.

• National Shrine of St. Jude, Chicago (1929); located in Our Lady of Guadalupe Church, founded and staffed by Claretians. Address: 3200 E. 91st St., Chicago, 60617; (312) 236-7782.

• National Shrine of St. Therese and Museum, Darien (1930, at St. Clara's Church, Chicago; new shrine, 1987, after original destroyed by fire); Carmelites of Most Pure Heart of Mary Province. Address: Carmelite Visitor Center, 8501 Bailey Rd., Darien, 60561; (630) 969-3311; www.saint-therese.org.

• Shrine of St. Jude Thaddeus, Chicago (1929) located in St. Pius V Church; staffed by Dominicans, Central Province. Address: 1909 S. Ashland Ave., Chicago, 60608; (312) 226-0020; www.op.org/dom-central/places/stjude.

Indiana: Our Lady of Monte Cassino Shrine, St. Meinrad (1870); Benedictines. Address: Saint Meinrad Archabbey, Highway 62, St. Meinrad, 47577; (812) 357-6585; www.saintmeinrad.edu/abbey/shrine.

• Old Cathedral (Basilica of St. Francis Xavier), Vincennes (1826, parish records go back to 1749); Evansville Diocese. Minor Basilica, 1970. Address: 205 Church St., Vincennes, 47591; (812) 882-5638.

Iowa: Grotto of the Redemption, West Bend (1912); Sioux City Diocese. Life of Christ in stone. Mailing address: P.O. Box 376, West Bend, 50597; (515) 887-2371; www.aw-cybermall.com/grotto.htm.

Louisiana: National Votive Shrine of Our Lady of Prompt Succor, New Orleans (1810); located in the Chapel of the Ursuline Convent (a National Historic Landmark). Address: 2635 State St., New Orleans, 70118.

• Shrine of St. Ann. Mailing address: 4920 Loveland St., Metaire, 70006; (504) 455-7071.

• Shrine of St. Roch, New Orleans (1876); located in St. Roch's Campo Santo (Cemetery); New Orleans Archdiocese. Address: 1725 St. Roch Ave., New Orleans, 70117.

Maryland: Basilica of the National Shrine of the Assumption of the Blessed Virgin Mary, Baltimore (1806). Mother Church of Roman Catholicism in the U.S. and the first metropolitan cathedral. Designed by Benjamin Henry Latrobe (architect of the Capitol) it is considered one of the finest examples of neoclassical architecture in the world. The church hosted many of the events and personalities central to the growth of Roman Catholicism in the U.S. Address: Cathedral and Mulberry Sts., Baltimore, MD 21201.

• National Shrine Grotto of Our Lady of Lourdes, Emmitsburg (1809, Grotto of Our Lady; 1875, National Shrine Grotto of Lourdes); public oratory, Archdiocese of Baltimore. Address: Mount St. Mary's College and Seminary, Emmitsburg, 21727; (301) 447-5318; www.msmary.edu/grotto/.

• National Shrine of St. Elizabeth Ann Seton, Emmitsburg. Foundation of Sisters of Charity (1809); first parochial school in America (1810); dedicated as Minor Basilica (1991). Address: 333 South Seton Ave., Emmitsburg, 21727; (301) 447-6606; www.setonshrine.org.

• St. Francis Xavier Shrine, "Old Bohemia,"

near Warwick (1704); located in Wilmington Diocese; restoration under aupices of Old Bohemia Historical Society, Inc. Address: P.O. Box 61, Warwick, 21912.
• St. Jude Shrine (1873), Archdiocese of Baltimore. Address: 308 N. Paca St., P.O. Box 1455, Baltimore, 21203.
Massachusetts: National Shrine of Our Lady of La Salette, Ipswich (1945); Missionaries of Our Lady of La Salette. Address: 251 Topsfield Rd., Ipswich, 01938.
• Our Lady of Fatima Shrine, Holliston (1950); Xaverian Missionaries. Address: 101 Summer St., Holliston, 01746; (508) 429-2144.
• St. Anthony Shrine, Boston (1947); downtown Service Church with shrine; Boston Archdiocese and Franciscans of Holy Name Province. Address: 100 Arch St., Boston, 02107.
• St. Clement's Eucharistic Shrine, Boston (1945); Boston Archdiocese, staffed by Oblates of the Virgin Mary. Address: 1105 Boylston St., Boston, 02215.
• National Shrine of The Divine Mercy, Stockbridge (1960); Congregation of Marians. Address: National Shrine of The Divine Mercy, Eden Hill, Stockbridge, 01262.
Michigan: Cross in the Woods-Parish, Indian River (1947); Gaylord diocese; staffed by Franciscan Friars of Sacred Heart Province, St. Louis. Address: 7078 M-68, Indian River, 49749; (231) 238-8973; www.rc.net/gaylord/crossinwoods.
• Shrine of the Little Flower, Royal Oak (c. 1929, by Father Coughlin); Detroit archdiocese. Address: 2123 Roseland, Royal Oak, 48073.
Minnesota: National Shrine of St. Odilia; St. Cloud Diocese. Address: P.O. Box 500, Onamia, 56359.
Missouri: Memorial Shrine of St. Rose Philippine Duchesne, St. Charles; Religious of the Sacred Heart of Jesus. Address: 619 N. Second St., St. Charles, 63301; (314) 946-6127.
• National Shrine of Our Lady of the Miraculous Medal, Perryville; located in St. Mary of the Barrens Church (1837); Vincentians. Address: 1811 W. St. Joseph St., Perryville, 63775; (573) 547-8343; www.amm.org.
• Old St. Ferdinand's Shrine, Florissant (1819, Sacred Heart Convent; 1821, St. Ferdinand's Church); Friends of Old St. Ferdinand's, Inc. Address: No. 1 Rue St. Francois, Florissant, 63031.
• Shrine of Our Lady of Sorrows, Starkenburg (1888; shrine building, 1910); Jefferson City Diocese. Address: c/o Church of the Risen Savior, 605 Bluff St., Rhineland, 65069; (573) 236-4390.
Nebraska: The Eucharistic Shrine of Christ the King (1973); Lincoln Diocese and Holy Spirit Adoration Sisters. Address: 1040 South Cotner Blvd., Lincoln, 68510; (402) 489-0765.
New Hampshire: Shrine of Our Lady of Grace, Colebrook (1948); Missionary Oblates of Mary Immaculate. Address: R.R. 1, Box 521, Colebrook, 03576-9535; (603) 237-5511.
• Shrine of Our Lady of La Salette, Enfield (1951); Missionaries of Our Lady of La Salette. Address: Rt. 4A, P.O. Box 420, Enfield, 03748.
New Jersey: Blue Army Shrine of the Immaculate Heart of Mary (1978); National Center of the Blue Army of Our Lady of Fatima, USA, Inc. Address: Mountain View Rd. (P.O. Box 976), Washington, 07882-0976; (908) 689-1701; www.bluearmy

• Shrine of St. Joseph, Stirling (1924); Missionary Servants of the Most Holy Trinity. Address: 1050 Long Hill Rd., Stirling, 07980; (908) 647-0208; www.STShrine.org.
New Mexico: St. Augustine Mission, Isleta (1613); Santa Fe Archdiocese. Address: P.O. Box 463, Isleta, Pueblo, 87022.
• Santuario de Nuestro Senor de Esquipulas, Chimayo (1816); Santa Fe archdiocese, Sons of the Holy Family; National Historic Landmark, 1970. Address: Santuario de Chimayo, P.O. Box 235; Chimayo, 87522.
• Shrine of St. Bernadette (2003); Santa Fe archdiocese, St. Bernadette parish. Address: 1800 Martha St., N.E., Albuquerque, NM 87112-3161; (505) 298-7557; www.shrineofstbernadette.com.
New York: National Shrine of Bl. Kateri Tekakwitha, Fonda (1938); Order of Friars Minor Conventual. Address: P.O. Box 627, Fonda, 12068.
• Marian Shrine (National Shrine of Mary Help of Christians), West Haverstraw (1953); Salesians of St. John Bosco. Address: 174 Filors Lane, Stony Point, NY 10980-2645; (845) 947-2200; www.MarianShrine.org.
• National Shrine Basilica of Our Lady of Fatima, Youngstown (1954); designated a national shrine in 1994; Barnabite Fathers. Address: 1023 Swann Rd., Youngstown, 14174; (716) 754-7489.
• Original Shrine of St. Ann in New York City (1892); located in St. Jean Baptiste Church; Blessed Sacrament Fathers. Address: 184 E. 76th St., NY 10021; (212) 288-5082.
• Our Lady of Victory National Shrine, Lackawanna (1926); Minor Basilica. Address: 767 Ridge Rd., Lackawanna, 14218.
• Shrine Church of Our Lady of Mt. Carmel, Brooklyn (1887); Brooklyn Diocese (Parish Church). Address: 275 N. 8th St., Brooklyn, 11211; (718) 384-0223.
• Shrine of Our Lady of Martyrs, Auriesville (1885); Society of Jesus. Address: Auriesville, 12016; (518) 853-3033; www.klink.net/~jesuit.
• Shrine of Our Lady of the Island, Eastport (1975); Montfort Missionaries. Address: Box 26, Eastport, 11941; (516) 325-0661.
• Shrine of St. Elizabeth Ann Seton, New York City (1975); located in Our Lady of the Rosary Church. Address: 7 State St., NY 10004.
• Shrine of St. Frances Xavier Cabrini, New York (1938; new shrine dedicated 1960); Missionary Sisters of the Sacred Heart. Address: 701 Fort Washington Ave., 10040; (212) 923-3536; www.cabrinishrineny.org
Ohio: Basilica and National Shrine of Our Lady of Consolation, Carey (1867); Minor Basilica; Toledo Diocese; staffed by Conventual Franciscan Friars. Address: 315 Clay St., Carey, 43316; (419) 396-7107.
• National Shrine of Our Lady of Lebanon, North Jackson (1965); Eparchy of Our Lady of Lebanon of Los Angeles. Address: 2759 N. Lipkey Rd., N. Jackson, 44451; (330) 538-3351; www.nationalshrine.org.
• National Shrine and Grotto of Our Lady of Lourdes, Euclid (1926); Sisters of the Most Holy Trinity. Address: 21281 Chardon Rd., Euclid,

44117-2112; (216) 481-8232.
• National Shrine of St. Dymphna, Massillon (1938), Youngstown diocese. Address: 3000 Erie St. S., Massillon, 44648-0004.
• Our Lady of Czestochowa Shrine, Garfield Heights (1939); Sisters of St. Joseph, Third Order of St. Francis. Address: 12215 Granger Rd., Garfield Hts., 44125; (216) 581-3535.
• Our Lady of Fatima, Ironton (1954); Address: Old Rt. 52, Haverhill, OH. Mailing address: St. Joseph Church, P.O. Box 499, Ironton, 45638-0499; (740) 429-2144.
• St. Anthony Shrine, Cincinnati (1888); Franciscan Friars, St. John Baptist Province. Address: 5000 Colerain Ave., Cincinnati, 45223.
• Shrine and Oratory of the Weeping Madonna of Mariapoch, Burton (1956); Social Mission Sisters. Parma Diocese (Byzantine). Address: 17486 Mumford Rd., Burton, 44021.
• Shrine of the Holy Relics (1892); Sisters of the Precious Blood. Address: 2291 St. Johns Rd., Maria Stein, 45860; (419) 925-4532.
• Sorrowful Mother Shrine, Bellevue (1850); Society of the Precious Blood. Address: 4106 State Rt. 269, Bellevue, 44811; (419) 483-3435.
Oklahoma: National Shrine of the Infant Jesus of Prague, Prague (1949); Oklahoma City Archdiocese. Address: P.O. Box 488, Prague ,74864.
Oregon: The Grotto (National Sanctuary of Our Sorrowful Mother), Portland (1924); Servite Friars. Address: P.O. Box 20008, Portland, 97294; www.thegrotto.com.
Pennsylvania: Basilica of the Sacred Heart of Jesus, Conewago Township (1741; present church, 1787); Minor Basilica; Harrisburg Diocese. Address: 30 Basilica Dr., Hanover, 17331.
• National Shrine Center of Our Lady of Guadalupe, Allentown (1974); located in Immaculate Conception Church; Allentown Diocese. Address: 501 Ridge Ave., Allentown, 18102; (610) 433-4404.
• National Shrine of Our Lady of Czestochowa (1955); Order of St. Paul the Hermit (Pauline Fathers). Address: P.O. Box 2049, Doylestown, 18901.
• National Shrine of St. John Neumann, Philadelphia (1860); Redemptorist Fathers, St. Peter's Church. Address: 1019 N. 5th St., Philadelphia, 19123.
• National Shrine of the Sacred Heart, Harleigh (1975); Scranton Diocese. Address: P.O. Box 500, Harleigh (Hazleton), 18225; (570) 455-1162.
• Old St. Joseph's National Shrine, Philadelphia (1733); Philadelphia Archdiocese (Parish Church). Address: 321 Willings Alley, Philadelphia, 19106; (215) 923-1733; www.oldstjoseph.org.
• St. Ann's Basilica Shrine, Scranton (1902); Passionist Community. Designated a minor basilica Aug. 29, 1996. Address: 1230 St. Ann's St.,

Scranton, 18504; (570) 347-5691.
• St. Anthony's Chapel, Pittsburgh (1883); Pittsburgh Diocese. Address: 1700 Harpster St., Pittsburgh, 15212.
• Shrine of St. Walburga, Greensburg (1974); Sisters of St. Benedict. Address: 1001 Harvey Ave., Greensburg, 15601; (724) 834-3060.
South Dakota: Fatima Family Shrine, Alexandria; St. Cloud Diocese. Address: St. Mary of Mercy Church, Box 158, Alexandria, 57311.
Texas: Mission Espiritu Santo de Zuniga, Goliad (1749). Victoria Diocese.
• Mission Nuestra Senora de la Purisma Concepcion, San Antonio. San Antonio Archdiocese. Address: 807 Mission Rd., 78210.
• Mission San Francisco de la Espada, San Antonio (1731); San Antonio Archdiocese. Address: 10040 Espada Rd., 78214; (210) 627-2064.
• Mission San Jose y San Miguel de Aguayo, San Antonio (1720); San Antonio Archdiocese. Address: 701 E. Pyron Ave., 78214; (210) 922-0543.
• Mission San Juan Capistrano, San Antonio (1731); San Antonio Archdiocese. Address: 9101 Graf Rd., 78214.
• National Shrine of Our Lady of San Juan Del Valle, San Juan (1949); Brownsville Diocese; staffed by Oblates of Mary Immaculate. Address: P.O. Box 747, San Juan, 78589; (956) 787-0033.
• Nuestra Senora de la Concepcion del Socorro, Socorro, El Paso (1692).
• Oblate Lourdes Grotto Shrine of the Southwest, Tepeyac de San Antonio, San Antonio Archdiocese. Address: P.O. Box 96, San Antonio, 78291-0096; (210) 342-9864; www.oblatemissions.org.
• Old Mission San Francisco de los Tejas, Weches (1690); San Antonio Archdiocese.
• Presidio La Bahia, Goliad (1749); Victoria Diocese. Address: P.O. Box 57, Goliad, 77963; (361) 645-3752.
• San Elizario Presidio Chapel, El Paso (1789); El Paso Diocese. Address: El Paso Co., San Elceario, P.O. Box 398, 79855.
• Ysleta Mission (Nuestra Senora del Carmen), Ysleta, El Paso (1744). El Paso Diocese.
Vermont: St. Anne's Shrine, Isle La Motte (1666); Burlington Diocese, conducted by Edmundites. Address: West Shore Rd., Isle La Motte, 05463; (802) 928-3362.
Wisconsin: Holy Hill — National Shrine of Mary, Help of Christians (1857); Discalced Carmelite Friars. Address: 1525 Carmel Rd., Hubertus, 53033.
• National Shrine of St. Joseph, De Pere (1889); Norbertine Fathers. Address: 1016 N. Broadway, De Pere, 54115.
• Shrine of Mary, Mother Thrice Admirable Queen and Victress of Schoenstatt (1965), Address: W284 N698 Cherry Lane, Waukesha, 53188-9402; (414) 547-7733.

Biographies of American Bishops

(*Sources:* Catholic Almanac *survey,* The Official Catholic Directory, Annuario Pontificio, *Catholic News Service. As of Aug. 20, 2013. For notable former bp.s of the U.S., see* **American Catholics of the Past** *at www.CatholicAlmanac.com.*)

Information includes: date and place of birth; educational institutions attended; date of ordination to the priesthood with, where applicable, name of archdiocese (*) or diocese in parentheses; date of episcopal ordination; episcopal appointments; date of resignation/retirement.

A

Adamec, Joseph V.: b. Aug. 13, 1935, Bannister, MI; educ. Michigan State Univ. (East Lansing), Nepomucene College and Lateran Univ. (Rome); ord. priest (for Nitra diocese, Slovakia), July 3, 1960; served in Saginaw diocese; ord. bp. of Altoona-Johnstown, May 20, 1987; ret. Jan. 14, 2011.

Adams, Edward J.: b. Aug. 24, 1944, Philadelphia, PA; educ. St. Charles Borromeo Seminary (Philadelphia), Pontifical Ecclesiastical Academy (Rome); ord. priest (Philadelphia*), May 16, 1970; in Vatican diplomatic service from 1976; ord. titular abp. of Scala, Oct. 23, 1996; app. papal nuncio to Greece, Feb. 22, 2011.

Allué, Emilio S., S.D.B.: b. Feb. 18, 1935, Huesca, Spain; educ. Salesian schools (Huesca, Spain) Don Bosco College/Seminary (Newton, NJ); Salesian Pontifical Univ. (Rome), Fordham Univ. (New York); ord. priest Dec. 22, 1966, in Rome; ord. titular bp. of Croe and aux. bp. of Boston, Sept. 17, 1996; ret. June 30, 2010.

Amos, Martin J.: b. Dec. 8, 1941, Cleveland; educ. St. Mary Seminary Cleveland; ord. priest (Cleveland), May 25, 1968; app. aux. bp. of Cleveland April 3, 2001, ord., June 7, 2001; app. bp. of Davenport Oct. 12, 2006.

Anderson, Moses B., S.S.E.: b. Sept. 9, 1928, Selma, AL; educ. St. Michael's College (Winooski, VT), St. Edmund Seminary (Burlington, VT), Univ. of Legon (Ghana); ord. priest, May 30, 1958; ord. titular bp. of Vatarba and aux. bp. of Detroit, Jan. 27, 1983; ret. Oct. 24, 2003.

Angadiath, Jacob: b. Oct. 26, 1945, Periappuram, Kerala, India; educ. St. Thomas Apostolic Seminary, Vadavathoor, Kottayam, India, Univ. of Kerala, India, Univ. of Dallas (U.S.); ord. priest (Palai, Kerala) Jan. 5, 1972; Director, Syro-Malabar Catholic Mission, Archdiocese of Chicago 1999-2001; app. bp. of Eparchy of St. Thomas of Chicago of the Syro-Malabarians and Permanent Apostolic Visitator in Canada, Mar. 13, 2001; inst., July 1, 2001.

Angell, Kenneth A.: b. Aug. 3, 1930, Providence, RI; educ. St. Mary's Seminary (Baltimore, MD); ord. priest (Providence) May 26, 1956; ord. titular bp. of Septimunicia and aux. bp. of Providence, RI, Oct. 7, 1974; bp. of Burlington, Oct. 6, 1992; inst., Nov. 9, 1992; ret. Nov. 9, 2005.

Apuron, Anthony Sablan, O.F.M. Cap.: b. Nov. 1, 1945, Agana, Guam; educ. St. Anthony College and Capuchin Seminary (Hudson, NH), Capuchin Seminary (Garrison, NY), Maryknoll Seminary (New York), Univ. of Notre Dame (Notre Dame, IN); ord. priest, Aug. 26, 1972, in Guam; ord. titular bp. of Muzuca in Proconsulari and aux. bp. of Agana, Guam (unincorporated U.S. territory), Feb. 19, 1984; abp. of Agana, Mar. 10, 1986.

Aquila, Samuel J.: b. Sept. 24, 1950, Burbank, CA; educ. St. Thomas Seminary, Denver, San Anselmo (Rome); ord. priest (Denver*), June 5, 1976; rector, St. John Vianney Seminary (Denver), 1999-2001; app. coadjutor bp. of Fargo, June 12, 2001; ord., Aug. 24, 2001; bp. of Fargo, Mar. 19, 2002; app. abp. of Denver, May 29, 2012; inst. July 18, 2012.

Arias, David, O.A.R.: b. July 22, 1929, Leon, Spain; educ. St. Rita's College (San Sebastian, Spain), Our Lady of Good Counsel Theologate (Granada, Spain), Teresianum Institute (Rome, Italy); ord. priest, May 31, 1952; ord. titular bp. of Badie and aux. bp. of Newark, Apr. 7, 1983; episcopal vicar for Hispanic affairs; ret. May 21, 2004.

Aymond, Gregory M.: b. Nov. 12, 1949, New Orleans, LA; educ. St. Joseph Seminary College, Notre Dame Seminary (New Orleans, LA); ord. priest (New Orleans*), May 10, 1975; ord. titular bp. of Acolla and aux. bp. of New Orleans, Jan. 10, 1997; co-adjutor bp. of Austin, June 2, 2000, ins., Aug. 3, 2000; bp. of Austin, Jan. 2, 2001; app. abp. of New Orleans, June 12, 2009; inst. Aug. 20, 2009.

Azarcon Solis, Oscar: b. Oct. 13, 1953, San Jose, Philippines; educ. Divine Word Seminary, Tagaytay City, Univ. of St. Thomas Seminary, Manila; ord. Apr. 28, 1979 (Cabanatuan, Philippines); incard. Houma-Thibodaux 1992; app. tit. bp. of Urci and aux. bp. of Los Angeles, Dec. 1, 2003; ord. Feb. 10, 2004.

B

Baker, Robert J.: b. June 4, 1944, Fostoria, OH; educ. Pontifical College Josephinum, Columbus, OH, Gregorian Univ., Rome; ord. (St. Augustine), Mar. 21, 1970; app. bp of Charleston, July 13, 1999; ord., Sept. 29, 1999; app. bp. of Birmingham; inst. Oct. 23, 2007.

Balke, Victor H.: b. Sept. 29, 1931, Meppen, IL; educ. St. Mary of the Lake Seminary (Mundelein, IL), St. Louis Univ. (St. Louis, MO); ord. priest (Springfield, IL), May 24, 1958; ord. bp. of Crookston, Sept. 2, 1976; ret. Sept. 28, 2007.

Baltakis, Paul Antanas, O.F.M.: b. Jan. 1, 1925, Troskunai, Lithuania; educ. seminaries of the Franciscan Province of St. Joseph (Belgium); ord. priest, Aug. 24, 1952, in Belgium; served in U.S. as director of Lithuanian Cultural Center, New York, and among Lithuanian youth; head of U.S. Lithuanian Franciscan Vicariate, Kennebunkport, ME, from 1979; ord. titular bp. of Egara, Sept. 24, 1984; assigned to pastoral assistance to Lithuanian Catholics living outside Lithuania (resides in Brooklyn).

Balvo, Charles Daniel: b. June 29, 1951, Brooklyn, NY; educ. North American College and Pontifical Gregorian Univ. (Rome) and Catholic Univ. of America (Washington, DC); ord. priest (New York*), June 6, 1976; studied at the Pontifical Ecclesiastical Academy and entered the diplomatic service of the Holy See; served in nunciatures in Africa, South America, and Eastern Europe; ord. titular abp. of Castello, June 29, 2005 and appointed apostolic nuncio to New Zealand, Cook Islands, Fiji, Marshall Islands, Kiribati, Fed. States Micronesia, Nauru, Western Samoa, Tonga, Palau and Vanuatu, and Apostolic Delegate to the Pacific Ocean, Apr. 1, 2005; app. nuncio to Kenya, Jan. 17, 2013.

Bambera, Joseph C.: b. Mar. 21, 1956, Carbondale, PA; educ., Univ. of Pittsburgh (Pittsburgh, PA); St. Pius X Seminary (Dalton, PA), Mary Immaculate Seminary (Northhampton, PA), St. Paul Univ. (Ottawa); ord. priest, Nov. 5, 1983 (Scranton); app. bp. of Scranton, Feb. 23, 2010; ord. bp., Apr. 26, 2010.

Banach, Michael W.: b. Nov. 19, 1962, Worcester, Mass.; educ. College of the Holy Cross (Mass.), Pontifical North American College and Pontifical Gregorian University (Rome); ord. priest July 2, 1988 (Worcester, Mass.); entered papal diplomatic corps and served in numerous nunciatures and as the Holy See permanent representative to the International Atomic Energy Agency (AIEA), to the Organization for Security and Cooperation in Europe (OSCE), and to the Preparatory Commission for the Comprehensive Nuclear-Test-Ban Treaty Organization (CTBTO) and Holy See permanent observer to the United Nations Organization for Industrial Development (ONUDI) and to the Office of the United Nations in Vienna, Austria; app. apostolic nuncio and titular abp. of Memphis, Feb. 22, 2013.

Banks, Robert J.: b. Feb. 26, 1928, Winthrop, MA; educ. St. John's Seminary (Brighton, MA), Gregorian Univ., Lateran Univ. (Rome); ord. priest (Boston*), Dec. 20, 1952, in Rome; rector of St. John's Seminary, Brighton, MA, 1971 81; vicar general of Boston, 1984; ord. titular bp. of Taraqua and aux. bp. of Boston, Sept. 19, 1985; bp. of Green Bay, Oct. 16, 1990, inst., Dec. 5, 1990; ret. Oct. 10, 2003.

Barbarito, Gerald M.: b. Jan. 4, 1950, Brooklyn, NY; educ. Cathedral College (Douglaston, NY), Immaculate Conception Seminary (Huntington, NY), Catholic Univ. (Washington, DC); ord. priest (Brooklyn), Jan. 31, 1976; ord. titular bp. of Gisipa and aux. bp. of Brooklyn, Aug. 22, 1994; bp. of Ogdensburg, Oct. 27, 1999; inst., Jan. 7, 2000; app. bp. of Palm Beach, July 1, 2003.

Barber, S.J., Michael C.: b. July 13, 1954, Salt Lake City, UT; educ. Loyola Marymount Univ., Gonzaga Univ. (Spokane, WA), Regis College at the University of Toronto, Pontifical Gregorian University (Rome); ord. priest for the Society of Jesus, June 8, 1985; held posts in Western Samoa, the Gregorian, the University of Oxford, England, St. Patrick's Seminary in Menlo Park, CA, and Saint John's Seminary, Brighton, MA; app. bp. of Oakland, May 3, 2013; ord. bp., May 25, 2013.

Barnes, Gerald R.: b. June 22, 1945, Phoenix, AZ, of Mexican descent; educ. St. Leonard Seminary (Dayton, OH), Assumption St. John's Seminary (San Antonio, TX); ord. priest (San Antonio*), Dec. 20, 1975; ord. titular bp. of Montefiascone and aux. bp. of San Bernardino, Mar. 18, 1992; bp. of San Bernardino, Dec. 28, 1995.

Barres, John O.: b. Sept. 20, 1960, Port Chester, NY; educ. Princeton Univ. (Princeton, NJ), New York Univ. Graduate School of Business (New York, NY), Catholic Univ. of America (Washington, D.C.), Pontifical Univ. della Santa Croce (Rome); ord priest, Oct. 21, 1989 (Wilmington); app. bp. of Allentown, May 27, 2009; ord. bp. July 30, 2009.

Bartchak, Mark L.: b. Jan. 1, 1955, Cleveland, OH; educ.

St. Mark Seminary and Gannon Univ. (Erie, PA), Christ the King Seminary (East Aurora, NY), The Catholic Univ. of America (Washington, D.C.); ord. priest (Erie), May 15, 1981; app. consultant for the USCCB Committee on Canonical Affairs and Church Governance, 2007; judge for the Congregation for the Doctrine of the Faith; visiting judge in various diocesan tribunals; lecturer on canon law at Catholic Univ. of America, The Catholic Univ. of Lublin, Poland, and St. Paul Univ., Ottawa, Canada; pres. of the Canon Law Society of America; app. bp. of Altoona-Johnstown, Jan. 14, 2011; ord. Apr. 19, 2011.

Batakian, Manuel: b. Nov. 5, 1929, Greece; moved with his family to Lebanon during World War II; educ. philosophy and theology studies in Rome; ord. priest (as a member of the Institute of the Clergy of Bzommar, an Armenian patriarchal religious order), Dec. 8, 1954; patriarchal vicar of the Institute and superior of its motherhouse in Bzommar, 1978-84; pastor of the Armenian Catholic Cathedral, Paris, 1984-90; rector of the Armenian Pontifical College, Rome, 1990-94; elected auxiliary of the patriarchate, Dec. 8, 1994, ordained bp., Mar. 12, 1995; trans. Our Lady of Nareg in New York Sept. 12, 2005; ret. May 21, 2011.

Baum, William W.: (See **Cardinals, Biographies**.)

Beltran, Eusebius J.: b. Aug. 31, 1934, Ashley, PA; educ. St. Charles Seminary (Philadelphia, PA); ord. priest (Atlanta*), May 14, 1960; ord. bp. of Tulsa, Apr. 20, 1978; app. abp. of Oklahoma City, Nov. 24, 1992; inst., Jan 22, 1993; ret. Dec. 16, 2010.

Bennett, Gordon D., S.J.: b. Oct. 21, 1946, Denver; educ. Mount St. Michael's (Spokane, WA), Jesuit School of Theology (Berkeley, CA), Fordham Univ. (NY); entered Society of Jesus, 1966; ord priest, June 14, 1975; app. titular bp. of Nesqually and aux. bp. of Baltimore, Dec. 23, 1997, ord. Mar. 3, 1998; app. bp. of Mandeville (Jamaica), July 6, 2004; ret. Aug. 6, 2006.

Bevard, Herbert A., b. Feb. 24, 1946, Baltimore; educ. St. Charles Borromeo Seminary (Wynnewood, PA), Dickinson College (Carlisle, PA); ord. pr. May 20, 1972 (Philadelphia); app. bp. of St. Thomas, July 7, 2008; ord. bp. Sept. 3, 2008.

Binzer, Joseph R.: b. Apr. 26, 1955, Cincinnati, OH; educ. Miami Univ. (Ohio), Mount St. Mary's Seminary of the West (Cincinnati), Athenaeum of Ohio, The Catholic Univ. of America (Washington, D.C.); ord. priest (Cincinnati*), June 4, 1994; app. titular bp. Subbur and aux. bp. of Cincinnati, Apr. 6, 2011; ord. bp., June 9, 2011.

Blair, Leonard P.: b. Apr. 12, 1949, Detroit; educ. Sacred Heart Seminary, Detroit, MI; Pontifical North American College, Gregorian Univ., and the Angelicum, Rome; ord. priest (Detroit*), June 26, 1976; at Vatican Secretariat of State, 1986-1991; Secretary to the President of the Prefecture for the Economic Affairs of the Holy See, 1994-1997; app. aux. of Detroit, July 9, 1999, ord., Aug. 24, 1999; app. bp. of Toledo, Oct. 7, 2003.

Blaire, Stephen E.: b. Dec. 22, 1941, Los Angeles, CA; educ. St. John's Seminary (Camarillo, CA); ord. priest (Los Angeles*), Apr. 29, 1967; ord. titular bp. of Lamzella and aux. of Los Angeles, May 31, 1990; app. bp. of Stockton, Jan. 19, 1999, inst., Mar. 16, 1999.

Blume, Michael A., S.V.D.: b. May 30, 1946, South Bend, IN; educ. Gregorian Univ. (Rome); ord. priest Dec. 23, 1972 (Divine Word Fathers); Under-Sec. of the Pont. Council for the Pastoral Care of Migrants and Itinerants, Apr. 6, 2000; app. abp. (nuncio to Benin and Togo) and titular abp. of Alessano, Alexanum Aug. 24, 2005; cons. Sept. 30, 2005; app. nuncio to Uganda, Feb. 2, 2013.

Boland, Ernest B., O.P.: b. July 10, 1925, Providence, RI; educ. Providence College (RI), Dominican Houses of Study (Somerset, OH; Washington, DC); ord. priest, June 9, 1955; ord. bp. of Multan, Pakistan, July 25, 1966; res., Oct. 20, 1984.

Boland, J.(John) Kevin: b. Apr. 25, 1935, Cork, Ireland (brother of Bp. Raymond J. Boland); educ. Christian Brothers School (Cork), All Hallows Seminary (Dublin); ord. priest (Savannah), June 14, 1959; ord. bp. of Savannah, Apr. 18, 1995; ret. July 19, 2011.

Boland, Raymond J.: b. Feb. 8, 1932, Tipperary, Ireland; educ. National Univ. of Ireland and All Hallows Seminary (Dublin); ord. priest (Washington*), June 16, 1957, in Dublin; vicar general and chancellor of Washington arch-dio.; ord. bp. of Birmingham, Mar. 25, 1988; app. bp. of Kansas City St. Joseph, June 22, 1993; ret. May 24, 2005.

Boles, John P.: b. Jan. 21, 1930, Boston, MA; educ. St. John Seminary, Boston College (Boston, MA); ord. priest (Boston*), Feb. 2, 1955; ord. titular bp. of Nova Sparsa and aux. bp. of Boston, May 21, 1992; ret. Oct. 12, 2006.

Bootkoski, Paul G.: b. July 4, 1940, Newark, NJ; educ. Seton Hall Univ. (South Orange, NJ), Immaculate Conception Seminary (Darlington, NJ); ord. priest, (Newark*), May 29, 1966; ord. titular bp. of Zarna and aux. bp. of Newark, Sept. 5, 1997; app. bp. of Metuchen, Jan. 4, 2002.

Botean, John Michael: b. July 9, 1955, Canton, OH; educ. St. Fidelis Seminary (Herman, PA), Catholic Univ. of America (Washington, DC), St. Gregory Melkite Seminary (Newton Centre, MA), Catholic Theological Union (Chicago, IL); ord. priest (Romanian rite St. George's in Canton), May 18, 1986; ord. bp. of St. George's in Canton for Romanians, Aug. 24, 1996.

Boyea, Earl: b. Apr. 10, 1951, Pontiac, MI; educ. Sacred Heart Seminary (Detroit), North American College and Pontifical Gregorian Univ. (Rome), Wayne State Univ. (Detroit), Catholic Univ. of America (Washington, DC); ord., May 20, 1978 (Detroit*); rector and president of the Pontifical College Josephinum (Columbus, OH), 2000-2002; app. titular bp. of Siccenna and aux. bp. of Detroit, July 22, 2002, ord., Sept. 13, 2002; app. bp. of Lansing, Feb. 27, 2008; inst. Apr. 29, 2008.

Bradley, Paul J.: b. Oct. 18, 1945, Glassport, PA; educ. St. Meinrad Seminary (St. Meinrad, IN); ord. priest May 1, 1971 (Pittsburgh); app. aux. bp. of Pittsburgh and tit. bp. of Afufenia Dec. 16, 2004; ord. Feb. 2, 2005; app. bp. of Kalamazoo, Apr. 6, 2009, inst. June 5, 2009.

Brandt, Lawrence E.: b. Mar. 27, 1939, Charleston, WV; educ. Pontifical College Josephinum (Worthington, OH), North American College (Rome), Univ. of Innsbruck (Austria), Pontifical Lateran Univ. (Rome); ord. priest (Rapid City), Dec. 19, 1969; after studies in the Pontifical Ecclesiastical Academy, entered into the diplomatic ser-vice of the Holy See, 1973 and held posts in Madagascar, Germany, Ecuador and Algeria; incardinated in Erie diocese in 1981; app. bp. of Greensburg of Jan. 2, 2004.

Bransfield, Michael J.: b. Sept. 8, 1943; educ. St. Charles Borromeo Sem. (Wynnewood, PA), Catholic Univ. of America (Washington); ord. priest May 15, 1971 (Philadelphia); app. bp. of Wheeling-Charleston Dec. 9, 2004; ord. Feb. 22, 2005.

Braxton, Edward K.: b. June 28, 1944, Chicago, IL; educ. Loyola Univ. of Chicago, Univ. of St. Mary of the Lake and Mundelein Seminary (Chicago), Louvain Univ. (Belgium); ord. priest (Chicago*), May 13, 1970; ord. titular bp. of Macomades rusticiana and aux. bp. of St. Louis, May 17, 1995; app. bp. of Lake Charles, Dec. 11,

2000; inst., Feb. 22, 2001; app. bp. of Belleville, Mar. 16, 2005; inst. June 22, 2005.

Brennan, Robert J.: b. June 7, 1962, Bronx, NY; educ. Saint John's University, Seminary of the Immaculate Conception (Huntington, NY); ord. priest (Rockville Center), May 27, 1989; Secretary to the Bishop (1994-2002); Vicar General and Moderator of the Curia, 2002-2010; app. aux. bp. of Rockville Center and titular bp. of Erdonia, June 8, 2012; ord. bp., July 25, 2012.

Broglio, Timothy M.: b. Dec. 22, 1951, Cleveland, OH; educ. Boston College (Boston, MA), North American College and Gregorian Univ. (Rome); ord. May 19, 1977; graduate of the Pontifical Ecclesiastical Academy; entered the diplomatic corps in 1983; chief of staff to the Vatican Secretary of State; app. titular abp. (Amiternum) and papal nuncio to the Dominican Republic and apostolic delegate to Puerto Rico, Feb. 27, 2001; ord., Mar. 19, 2001; app. abp. for Military Services, Nov. 19, 2007; inst. Jan. 25, 2008.

Brom, Robert H.: b. Sept. 18, 1938, Arcadia, WI; educ. St. Mary's College (Winona, MN), Gregorian Univ. (Rome); ord. priest (Winona), Dec. 18, 1963, in Rome; ord. bp. of Duluth, May 23, 1983; coadj. bp. of San Diego, May, 1989; bp. of San Diego, July 10, 1990.

Brown, Charles J.: Oct. 13, 1959, New York, N.Y.; educ. University of Notre Dame (Notre Dame, IN), University of Oxford (Oxford, England), University of Toronto (Toronto, Canada), Pontifical University of St. Anselmo (Rome, Italy); ord. priest, May 13, 1989 (New York*); official of the Congregation for the Doctrine of the Faith, 1994-2011; app. nuncio to Ireland, Nov. 26, 2011; ord. titular abp. of Aquileia, Jan. 6, 2012.

Brown, Tod D.: b. Nov. 15, 1936, San Francisco, CA; educ. St. John's Seminary (Camarillo, CA), North American College (Rome); ord. priest (Monterey-Fresno), May 1, 1963; ord. bp. of Boise, Apr. 3, 1989; app. bp. of Orange, June 30, 1998; ret. Sept. 21, 2012.

Brucato, Robert A.: b. Aug. 14, 1931, New York, NY; educ. Cathedral College (Douglaston, NY), St. Joseph's Seminary (Dunwoodie, NY), Univ. of Our Lady of the Lake (San Antonio, TX); ord. priest (New York*), June 1, 1957; air force chaplain for 22 years; ord. titular bp. of Temuniana and aux. of New York, Aug. 25, 1997; ret. Oct. 31, 2006.

Brunett, Alexander J.: b. Jan. 17, 1934, Detroit, MI; educ. Gregorian Univ. (Rome), Sacred Heart Seminary, Univ. of Detroit (Detroit, MI), Marquette Univ. (Milwaukee, WI); ord. priest (Detroit*), July 13, 1958; ord. bp. of Helena, July 6, 1994; app. abp. of Seattle, Oct. 28, 1997, inst., Dec. 18, 1997.

Brungardt, John B.: b. July 10, 1958, Salina, KS; educ. Benedictine College (Atchison, KS), Kansas State Univ.; Pontifical College Josephinum (Columbus, OH); ord. priest (Wichita), May 23, 1998; app. bp. of Dodge City, Dec. 15, 2010; ord. Feb. 2, 2011.

Bruskewitz, Fabian W.: b. Sept. 6, 1935, Milwaukee, WI; educ. North American College, Gregorian Univ. (Rome); ord. priest (Milwaukee*), July 17, 1960; ord. bp. of Lincoln, May 13, 1992; ret. Sept. 14, 2012.

Buckon, Neal J.: b. Sept. 3, 1953, Columbus, OH; educ. John Carroll Univ. (Univ. Heights, OH), Cleveland State Univ., Borromeo College (Wycliffe, OH), St. Mary's Seminary (Cleveland, OH); ord. priest (Cleveland), May 25, 1995; served in the U.S. Army, 1975-1982; Army chaplain from 1998; app. titular bp. of Vissalsa and aux. bp. of the Archdio. for the Military Services, Jan. 3, 2011; ord. Feb. 22, 2011.

Buechlein, Daniel M., O.S.B.: b. Apr. 20, 1938; educ.

St. Meinrad College and Seminary (St. Meinrad, IN), St. Anselm Univ. (Rome); solemn profession as Benedictine monk, Aug. 15, 1963; ord. priest (St. Meinrad Archabbey) May 3, 1964; ord. bp. of Memphis, Mar. 2, 1987; app. abp. of Indianapolis, July 14, 1992; inst., Sept. 9, 1992; res. Sept. 21, 2011.

Bura, John: b. June 12, 1944, Wegeleben, Germany; educ. St. Basil College Seminary (Stamford), St. Josaphat Ukrainian Catholic Seminary, The Catholic Univ. of America, Washington; ord. priest Feb. 14, 1971 (Philadelphia/Ukrainian); ap. aux. bp. Ukrainian Arch. of Philadelphia and tit. bp. of Limisa Jan. 3, 2006; inst. Feb. 21, 2006; Apostolic Admin. of St. Josaphat in Parma (Ukrainians), July 29, 2009.

Burbidge, Michael F.: b. June 16, 1957, Philadelphia; educ. St. Charles Borromeo Seminary; ord. priest (Philadelphia*), May 19, 1984; app. titular bp. of Cluain Iraird and aux. bp. of Philadelphia, June 21, 2002, ord., Sept. 5, 2002; app. bp. of Raleigh, June 8, 2006.

Burke, John J., O.F.M.: b. Mar. 16, 1935, River Edge, NJ; educ. St. Joseph Seminary (Callicoon, NY), St. Bonaventure Univ. (St. Bonaventure, NY), Holy Name College (Washington, DC); solemnly professed in Franciscan Order, Aug. 20, 1958; ord. priest, Feb. 25, 1961; missionary in Brazil from 1964; ord. coadjutor bp. of Miracema do Tocantins, Brazil, Mar. 25, 1995; bp. of Miracema do Tocantins, Feb. 14, 1996.

Burke, Raymond L.: (See **Cardinals' Biographies**).

Burns, Edward J.: b. Oct. 7, 1957, Pittsburgh, PA; educ. Duquesne Univ. (Pittsburgh, PA), Mount St. Mary Seminary (Emmitsburg, MD); ord. priest (Pittsburgh), June 25, 1983; Exec. Dir. of the Secretariat for Clergy, Consecrated Life and Vocations, USCCB (1999-2008); app. bp. of Juneau, Jan. 19, 2009; ord. bp. Mar. 3, 2009; inst. Apr. 2, 2009.

Bustros, Cyrille Salim, S.M.S.P.: b. Jan. 26, 1939, Ain-Bourday, Lebanon; educ. Missionaries of St. Paul and Seminary of St.e-Anne of Jerusalem (Jerusalem), Univ. of Louvain (Louvain, Belgium); ord. June 29, 1962 (Society of the Missionaries of St. Paul); elected abp. of Baalbeck, Lebanon, Oct. 25, 1988; app. eparch of Newton, June 22, 2004; confirmed as abp. of Beirut, June 15, 2011.

Byrnes, Michael J.: b. Aug. 23, 1958; educ. Univ. of Michigan, Sacred Heart Seminary (Detroit), Pontifical Gregorian Univ. (Rome); faculty of Sacred Heart Seminary, 2003; vice-rector and dean of formation, Sacred Heart Seminary, and pastor Presentation/Our Lady of Victory Parish, 2004-11; app. titular bp. of Eguga and aux. bp. of Detroit, Mar. 22, 2011; ord. May 5, 2011.

C

Caggiano, Frank J.: b. Mar. 29, 1959, Brooklyn; educ. Immaculate Conception Seminary (Huntington, NY), Gregorian Univ. (Rome); ord. priest May 16, 1987 (Brooklyn); appointed aux. bp. of Brooklyn and tit. bp. of Inis Cathaig June 6, 2006; ord. Aug. 22, 2006; app. bp. of Bridgeport, July 31, 2013; inst. Sept. 19, 2013.

Callahan, William P., O.F.M. Conv.: b. June 17, 1950, Chicago, Ill.; educ. St. Mary Minor Seminary (Crystal Lake, Ill.), Loyola Univ. (Chicago), Univ. of St. Michael's College, Univ. of Toronto (Toronto, Canada); entered the Conventual Franciscans and made his first profession, Aug. 11, 1970; ord. priest, Apr. 30, 1977; spiritual director of the North American College, 2005-2007; app. titular bp. of Lares and aux. bp. of Milwaukee, Oct. 30, 2007; cons. bp. Dec. 21, 2007; app. bp. of La Crosse, June 11,

2010; inst. Aug. 11, 2010.

Calvo, Randolph R.: b. Aug. 28, 1950, Agana, Guam; educ. St. Patrick's Seminary and Univ. (Menlo Park, CA), Angelicum (Rome); ord. priest May 21, 1977 (San Francisco); app. bp of Reno Dec. 23, 2005; ord. bp. Feb. 17, 2006.

Camacho, Tomas Aguon: b. Sept. 18, 1933, Chalon Kanoa, Saipan; educ. St. Patrick's Seminary (Menlo Park, CA); ord. priest, June 14, 1961; ord. first bp. of Chalan Kanoa, Northern Marianas (U.S. Commonwealth), Jan. 13, 1985.

Campbell, Frederick F.: b. Aug. 5, 1943, Elmira, NY; educ. Ohio State Univ., St. Paul Seminary, St. Paul, MN; ord. priest (St. Paul and Minneapolis*), May 31, 1980; app. titular bp. of Afufenia and aux. bp. of St. Paul and Minneapolis, Mar. 2, 1999, ord., May 14, 1999; app. bp. of Columbus, Oct. 14, 2004; inst. Jan. 13, 2005.

Cantú, Oscar: b. Dec. 5, 1966, Houston, TX; educ. Holy Trinity Seminary and Univ. of Dallas (Dallas, TX), St. Mary's Seminary, (Houston, TX), Gregorian Univ. (Rome); ord. priest, May 21, 1994 (Galveston-Houston*); app. titular bp. of Dardano and aux. bp. of San Antonio, Apr. 10, 2008; ord. bp., June 2, 2008; app. bp. of Las Cruces, Jan. 10, 2013.

Carlson, Robert J.: b. June 30, 1944, Minneapolis, MN; educ. Nazareth Hall and St. Paul Seminary (St. Paul, MN), Catholic Univ. (Washington, DC): ord. priest (St. Paul Minneapolis*), May 23, 1970; ord. titular bp. of Avioccala and aux. bp. of St. Paul and Minneapolis, Jan. 11, 1984; app. coadjutor bp. of Sioux Falls, Jan. 13, 1994; succeeded as bp. of Sioux Falls, Mar. 21, 1995; app. bp. of Saginaw, Dec. 29, 2004; inst. Feb. 24, 2005; app. abp. of St. Louis, Apr. 21, 2009; inst. June 10, 2009.

Carmody, Edmond: b. Jan. 12, 1934, Ahalena, Kerry, Ireland; educ. St. Brendan's College (Killarney), St. Patrick Seminary (Carlow); ord. priest (San Antonio*), June 8, 1957; missionary in Peru 1984 89; ord. titular bp. of Mortlach and aux. bp. of San Antonio, Dec. 15, 1988; app. bp. of Tyler, 1992-2000; app. bp. of Corpus Christi, Feb. 3, 2000; inst., Mar. 17, 2000.

Carmon, Dominic, S.V.D.: b. Dec. 13, 1930, Opelousas, LA; entered Society of Divine Word, 1946; ord. priest, Feb. 2, 1960; missionary in Papua New Guinea, 1961 68; ord. titular bp. of Rusicade and aux. bp. of New Orleans, Feb. 11, 1993; ret. Dec. 13, 2006.

Cary, Liam S.: b. Aug. 21, 1947, Portland, OR; educ. Mount Angel Seminary and St. Patrick Seminary (Portland, OR), Pontifical North American College and Pontifical Gregorian University (Rome, Italy); ord. priest, Sept. 5, 1992 (Portland*); app. bp. of Baker, Mar. 8, 2012; ord. bp. May 18, 2012.

Casey, Luis Morgan: b. June 23, 1935, Portageville, MO; ord. priest (St. Louis*), Apr. 7, 1962; missionary in Bolivia from 1965; ord. titular bp. of Mibiarca and aux. of La Paz, Jan. 28, 1984; vicar apostolic of Pando, Bolivia, Jan. 18, 1988, and apostolic administrator (1995) of La Paz.

Cepeda Escobedo, José A.: b. San Luis Potosi, Mexico, May 15, 1969; educ., Seminario Arquidiocesano Guadalupano Josefino (San Luis Potosi), Our Lady of the Lake University (San Antonio), College Seminary of the Immaculate Heart of Mary (Santa Fe, NM), St. Mary's University (San Antonio), Pontifical University of St. Thomas Aquinas (Rome); ord. priest (San Antonio*), June 1, 1996; rector, Assumption Seminary, San Antonio, 2010; app. titular bp. of Tagase and aux. bp. Detroit, Apr. 18, 2011; ord. May 5, 2011.

Chappetto, Raymond F.: b. Aug. 20, 1945, Astoria, NY; educ. Our Lady of Angels Seminary (Albany, NY), St.

John's University; ord. priest (Brooklyn), May 29, 1971; served in various pastoral assignments and was named by the National Catholic Education Association Pastor of the Year in 2008; app. aux. bp. of Brooklyn and titular bp. of Citium, May 2, 2012; ord. bp., July 11, 2012.

Chaput, Charles J., O.F.M. Cap.: b. Sept. 26, 1944, Concordia, KS; educ. St. Fidelis College (Herman, PA), Capuchin College and Catholic Univ. (Washington, DC), Univ. of San Francisco; solemn vows as Capuchin, July 14, 1968; ord. priest, Aug. 29, 1970; ord. bp. of Rapid City, SD, July 26, 1988, the second priest of Native American ancestry (member of Prairie Band Potawatomi Tribe) ordained a bp. in the U.S.; app abp. of Denver, inst., Apr. 7, 1997; app. abp. of Philadelphia, July 19, 2011; inst., Sept. 8, 2011.

Charron, Joseph L., C.PP.S.: b. Dec. 30, 1939, Redfield, SD; educ. St. John's Seminary (Collegeville, MN); ord. priest, June 3, 1967; ord. titular bp. of Bencenna and aux. bp. of St. Paul and Minneapolis, Jan. 25, 1990; app. bp. of Des Moines, Nov. 12, 1993; res. Apr. 10, 2007.

Chavez, Gilbert Espinoza: b. May 9, 1932, Ontario, CA; educ. St. Francis Seminary (El Cajon, CA), Immaculate Heart Seminary (San Diego), Univ. of CA; ord. priest (San Diego). Mar. 19, 1960; ord. titular bp. of Magarmel and aux. of San Diego, June 21, 1974; ret. June 1, 2007.

Choby, David R.: b. Jan. 17, 1947, Nashville, TN; educ. St. Ambrose College (Davenport, IA), Catholic Univ. of America (Washington), and the Angelicum (Rome); ord. priest Sept. 6, 1974 (Nashville); app. bp of Nashville Dec. 20, 2005; ord. bp. Feb. 27, 2006.

Chomnycky, Paul P.: b. May 19, 1954, Vancouver, B.C; educ. Univ. of British Columbia (Vancouver), Pont. St. Anselm Univ., Pont. Gregorian Univ. (Rome); ord. Oct. 1, 1988 (Basilians); app. bp for Ukrainian Catholics living in Great Britain April 5, 2002; ord. bp. June 11, 2002; trans. Ukrainian Dio. of Stamford Jan. 3, 2006; inst. Feb. 20, 2006.

Christensen, Peter F.: b. Dec. 24, 1952, Pasadena, CA; educ. College of the Redwoods (Eureka, CA), Univ. of Montana (Missoula, MT), St. John Vianney Seminary, Univ. of St. Thomas, and St. Paul Seminary (St. Paul, MN); ord. May 25, 1985 (St. Paul and Minneapolis*); app. bp. of Superior, June 28, 2007; ord. Sept. 14, 2007.

Christian, Francis J.: b. Oct. 8, 1942, Peterborough, NH; educ. St. Anselm College (Manchester, NH), St. Paul Seminary (Ottawa), American College in Louvain (Belgium); ord. priest (Manchester), June 29, 1968; ord titular bp. of Quincy and aux. of Manchester, May 14, 1996.

Cisneros, Octavio: b. July 19, 1945, Cuba; educ.: Immaculate Conception Sem. (Huntington, N.Y.); ord. priest Mary 29, 1971; app. aux. bp. of Brooklyn and tit bp. of Eanach Duin June 6, 2006; ord. Aug. 22, 2006.

Cistone, Joseph R.: b. May 18, 1949, Philadelphia, PA. educ. St. Charles Borromeo Seminary (Overbrook, PA); ord. priest (Philadelphia*), May 17, 1975; app. titular bp. of Case mediane and aux. bp. of Philadelphia, June 8, 2004; ord. July 28, 2004; app. bp. of Saginaw, May 20, 2009; inst. July 28, 2009.

Clark, Edward W.: b. Nov. 30, 1946, Minneapolis; educ. Our Lady Queen of Angels Seminary (San Fernando, CA), St. John's Seminary College (Camarillo, CA), Gregorian Univ. (Rome); ord. priest (Los Angeles*), May 9, 1972; President/Rector, St. John's Seminary College (Camarillo, CA), 1994-2001; app. titular bp. of Gardar and aux. bp. of Los Angeles, Jan. 16, 2001, ord., Mar. 26, 2001.

Clark, Matthew H.: b. July 15, 1937, Troy, NY; educ. St. Bernard's Seminary (Rochester, NY), Gregorian Univ. (Rome); ord. priest (Albany) Dec. 19, 1962; ord. bp. of

Rochester, May 27, 1979; inst., June 26, 1979; ret. Sept. 21, 2012.

Coakley, Paul S.: b. June 3, 1955, Norfolk, VA; educ. Univ. of Kansas (Lawrence), St. Pius X Seminary (Erlanger, KY), Mount St. Mary's Seminary (Emmitsburg, MD); ord. Priest May 21, 1983 (Wichita); app. bp. of Salina Oct. 21, 2004; ord. Dec. 28, 2004; app. abp. of Oklahoma City, Dec. 16, 2010; inst. Feb. 11, 2011.

Coleman, George W.: b. Feb. 1, 1939, Fall River, MA; educ. Holy Cross College (Worcester, MA), Fall River, St. John's Seminary (Boston, MA), North American College and Gregorian Univ. (Rome), Brown Univ. (Providence, RI); ord. priest, Dec. 16, 1964; app. bp. of Fall River, Apr. 30, 2003; ord. bp., July 22, 2003.

Conley, James Douglas: b. Mar. 19, 1955, Kansas City, MO; educ., Univ. of Kansas (Lawrence, KS), St. Pius X Seminary (Erlanger, KY), Mt. St. Mary's Seminary (Emmitsburg, MD), Pont. North American College and Accademia Alfonsiana (Rome); ord. priest May 18, 1985 (Wichita); served in Congregation for Bps. in Rome, 1996-2006; Chaplain of His Holiness, Feb. 9, 2001; app. titular bp. of Cissa and aux. bp. of Denver, Apr. 10, 2008; ord. bp., May 30, 2008; app. bp. of Lincoln, Sept. 14, 2012; inst. Nov. 20, 2012.

Conlon, Robert D.: b. Dec. 4, 1948, Cincinnati; educ. Mount St. Mary's Seminary of the West, Univ. of St. Paul, Ottawa; ord. priest (Cincinnati*), Jan. 15, 1977; app. bp. of Steubenville, May 31, 2002; app. bp. of Joliet, May 17, 2011; inst. July 14, 2011.

Connolly, Thomas J.: b. July 18, 1922, Tonopah, NV; educ. St. Patrick's Seminary (Menlo Park, CA), Catholic Univ. (Washington, DC), Lateran Univ. (Rome); ord. priest (Reno Las Vegas), Apr. 8, 1947; ord. bp. of Baker, June 30, 1971; res., Nov. 19, 1999.

Cooney, Patrick R.: b. Mar. 10, 1934, Detroit, MI; educ. Sacred Heart Seminary (Detroit), Gregorian Univ. (Rome), Univ. of Notre Dame (Notre Dame, IN); ord. priest (Detroit*), Dec. 20, 1959; ord. titular bp. of Hodelm and aux. bp. of Detroit, Jan. 27, 1983; app. bp. of Gaylord, Nov. 6, 1989; inst., Jan. 28, 1990; ret. Oct. 3, 2009.

Cordileone, Salvatore: b. June 5, 1956, San Diego, CA.; educ. St. Francis Seminary (San Diego), Univ. of San Diego (San Diego), North American College (Rome), Pontifical Gregorian Univ. (Rome); ord. July 9, 1982; official of the Supreme Tribunal of the Apostolic Signatura in Roma, 1995-2002 and vice-director of Villa Stritch in Rome; app. titular bp. of Natchez and aux. bp. of San Diego, July 5, 2002, ord., Aug. 21, 2002; app. bp. of Oakland, Mar. 23, 2009; inst. May 5, 2009; app. abp. of San Francisco, July 27, 2012; inst. Oct. 4, 2012.

Corrada del Rio, Alvaro, S.J.: b. May 13, 1942, Santurce, Puerto Rico; entered Society of Jesus, 1960, at novitiate of St. Andrew on Hudson (Poughkeepsie, NY); educ. Jesuit seminaries, Fordham Univ. (New York), Institut Catholique (Paris); ord. priest, July 6, 1974, in Puerto Rico; pastoral coordinator of Northeast Catholic Hispanic Center, New York, 1982-85; ord. titular bp. of Rusticiana and aux. bp. of Washington, DC, Aug. 4, 1985; app. apostolic administrator of Caguas, Puerto Rico, Aug. 5, 1997 (retained his title as aux. bp. of Washington); app. bp. of Tyler, Dec. 5, 2000; inst., Jan. 30, 2001; app. bp. of Mayaguez, Puerto Rico, July 6, 2011.

Costello, Thomas J.: b. Feb. 23, 1929, Camden, NY; educ. Niagara Univ. (Niagara Falls, NY), St. Bernard's Seminary (Rochester, NY), Catholic Univ. (Washington, DC); ord. priest (Syracuse), June 5, 1954; ord. titular bp. of Perdices and aux. bp. of Syracuse, Mar. 13, 1978; ret. Mar. 23, 2004.

Cote, Michael R.: b. June 19, 1949, Sanford, ME; educ. Our Lady of Lourdes Seminary (Cassadaga, NY), St. Mary's Seminary College (Baltimore, MD); Gregorian Univ. (Rome), Catholic Univ. (Washington, DC); ord. priest (Portland, ME), June 29, 1975, by Pope Paul VI in Rome; secretary, 1989-94 at apostolic nunciature, Washington; ord. titular bp. of Cebarades and aux. of Portland, ME, July 27, 1995; app. bp. of Norwich, Mar. 11, 2003; inst., May 13, 2003.

Cotey, Arnold R., S.D.S.: b. June 15, 1921, Milwaukee, WI; educ. Divine Savior Seminary (Lanham, MD), Marquette Univ. (Milwaukee, WI); ord. priest, June 7, 1949; ord. first bp. of Nachingwea (now Lindi), Tanzania, Oct. 20, 1963; ret., Nov. 11, 1983.

Coyle, Robert J.: b: Sept. 23, 1964, Brooklyn, N.Y.; educ. Fordham University (New York), Immaculate Conception Seminary (Huntington, N.Y.); ord. priest May 25, 1991 (Rockville Centre); joined the U.S. Navy, June 3, 1988 and served for 24 years; app. titular bp. of Zabi and aux. bp. of the Military Archdiocese, Feb. 11, 2013; ord. bishop Apr. 25, 2013.

Coyne, Christopher J.: b. June 17, 1958, Woburn, MA; educ. Univ. of Mass. (Lowell), St. John Seminary (Brighton), Pont. Liturgical Institute (Rome); ord. priest (Boston*), June 7, 1986; app. aux. bp. of Indianapolis and titular bp. of Mopta, Jan. 14, 2011; ord. Mar. 2, 2011.

Cronin, Daniel A.: b. Nov. 14, 1927, Newton, MA; educ. St. John's Seminary (Boston, MA), North American College and Gregorian Univ. (Rome); ord. priest (Boston*), Dec. 20, 1952; attaché apostolic nunciature (Addis Ababa), 1957 61; served in papal Secretariat of State, 1961 68; ord. titular bp. of Egnatia and aux. bp. of Boston, Sept. 12, 1968; bp. of Fall River, Dec. 16, 1970; abp. of Hartford, Dec. 10, 1991; ret. Oct. 23, 2003.

Cruz, Manuel A.: b. Dec. 2, 1953, Havana, Cuba; educ. Seton Hall Univ. (South Orange, NJ), Immaculate Conception Seminary (South Orange, NJ); ord. priest, May 31, 1980 (Newark*); app. aux. bp. of Newark and titular bp. of Gaguari, June 9, 2008; ord. bp. Sept. 9, 2008.

Cullen, Edward P.: b. Mar. 15, 1933, Philadelphia, PA; educ. St. Charles Borromeo Seminary (Overbrook, PA), Univ. of Pennsylvania and LaSalle Univ. (Philadelphia), Harvard Graduate School of Business; ord. priest (Philadelphia*), May 19, 1962; ord. titular bp. of Paria in Proconsolare and aux. of Philadelphia, Feb. 8, 1994; app. bp. of Allentown, Dec. 16, 1997, inst., Feb. 9, 1998; res. May 27, 2009.

Cummins, John S.: b. Mar. 3, 1928, Oakland, CA; educ. St. Patrick's Seminary (Menlo Park, CA), Catholic Univ. (Washington, DC), Univ. of CA; ord. priest (San Francisco*), Jan. 24, 1953; exec. dir. of the CA Catholic Conference 1971-76; ord. titular bp. of Lambaesis and aux. bp. of Sacramento, May 16, 1974; app. bp. of Oakland, inst., June 30, 1977; ret. Oct. 1, 2003.

Cunningham, Robert J.: b. June 18, 1943, Buffalo, N.Y.; educ. St. John Vianney Seminary (East Aurora, N.Y.), Catholic Univ. of America (Washington, D.C.); ord. May 24, 1969 (Buffalo); bp. of Ogdensburg Mar. 9, 2004; ord. May 18, 2004; app. bp. of Syracuse, Apr. 21, 2009; inst. May 26, 2009.

Cupich, Blase: b. Mar. 19, 1949, Omaha, NE; educ. College of St. Thomas (St. Paul, MN), Gregorian Univ. (Rome), Catholic Univ. of America (Washington, DC); ord. priest (Omaha*), Aug. 16, 1975; service at the apostolic nunciature, Washington, DC, 1981-87; rector, Pontifical College Josephinum (Columbus, OH), 1989-97; app. bp. of Rapid City, SD, July 7, 1998; ord., Sept. 21, 1998.

Curlin, William G.: b. Aug. 30, 1927, Portsmouth, VA; educ. Georgetown Univ. (Washington, DC), St. Mary's Seminary (Baltimore, MD); ord. priest (Washington*), May 25, 1957; ord. titular bp. of Rosemarkie and aux. bp. of Washington, Dec. 20, 1988; app. bp. of Charlotte, Feb. 22, 1994, ret., Sept. 16, 2002.

Curry, Thomas J.: b. Jan. 17, 1943, Drumgoon, Ireland; educ. Patrician College (Ballyfin), All Hallows Seminary (Dublin); ord. priest (Los Angeles*), June 17, 1967; ord. titular bp. of Ceanannus Mór and aux. of Los Angeles, Mar. 19, 1994.

Curtiss, Elden F.: b. June 16, 1932, Baker, OR; educ. St. Edward Seminary College and St. Thomas Seminary (Kenmore, WA); ord. priest (Baker), May 24, 1958; ord. bp. of Helena, MT, Apr. 28, 1976; app. abp. of Omaha, NE, May 4, 1993; ret. June 3, 2009.

D

Da Cunha, Edgar M., S.D.V.: b. Aug. 21, 1953, Riachão do Jacuípe Bahia, Brazil; educ. Catholic Univ. of Salvador (Brazil), Immaculate Conception Seminary (Newark, NJ); professed perpetual vows, Feb. 11, 1979, and ord., priest Mar. 27, 1982; app. titular bp. of Ucres and aux. of Newark, June 27, 2003.

Daily, Thomas V.: b. Sept. 23, 1927, Belmont, MA; educ. Boston College, St. John's Seminary (Brighton, MA); ord. priest (Boston*), Jan. 10, 1952; missionary in Peru for five years as a member of the Society of St. James the Apostle; ord. titular bp. of Bladia and aux. bp. of Boston, Feb. 11, 1975; app. first bp. of Palm Beach, FL, July 17, 1984; app. bp. of Brooklyn, Feb. 20, 1990; inst., Apr. 18, 1990; ret., Aug. 1, 2003.

Daly, James: b. Aug. 14, 1921, New York, NY; educ. Cathedral College (Brooklyn, NY), Immaculate Conception Seminary (Huntington, L.I.); ord. priest (Brooklyn), May 22, 1948; ord. titular bp. of Castra Nova and aux. bp. of Rockville Centre, May 9, 1977; ret., July 1, 1996.

Daly, Thomas: b. Apr. 30, 1960, San Francisco, CA; educ. Univ. of San Francisco, St. Patrick's Seminary (Menlo Park, CA), Boston College; ord. priest, May 9, 1987 (San Francisco*); app. titular bp. of Tabalta and aux. bp. of San Jose, Mar. 16, 2011; ord. May 25, 2011.

Deeley, Robert: b. June 18, 1946, Cambridge, Mass.; Catholic University of Americ (Washington, D.C.), Pontifical Gregorian University (Rome); ord. priest July 14, 1973 (Boston*); app. titular bp. of Kearney and aux. bp. of Boston, Nov. 9, 2012; ord. bishop, Jan. 4, 2013.

Del Riego, Rutilio: b. Sept. 21, 1940, Valdesandinas (Leon), Spain; educ. Diocesan Laborer Priests seminary (Salamanca, Spain), Catholic Univ. of America; ord. priest June 5, 1965, (Diocesan Laborer Priests); app. aux. bp. San Bernardino and tit. bp. of Daimlaig July 26, 2005; ord. Sept. 20, 2005.

Dendinger, William J.: b. May 20, 1939, Omaha; educ. Conception College Seminary (Conception, Missouri), Aquinas Institute (Iowa); ord. priest May 29, 1965; U.S. Air Force chaplain, 1970-2002, achieving the rank of Major General; app. bp. of Grand Island Oct. 14, 2004; ord. Dec. 13, 2004.

Deshotel, John D.: b. Jan. 6, 1952, Basile, LA; educ. Univ. of Dallas (Dallas, TX); ord. priest (Dallas), May 13, 1978; app. titular bp. of Cova and aux. bp. of Dallas, March 13, 2010; ord. bp., Apr. 27, 2010.

De Simone, Louis A.: b. Feb. 21, 1922, Philadelphia, PA; educ. Villanova Univ. (Villanova, PA), St. Charles Borromeo Seminary (Overbrook, PA); ord. priest (Philadelphia*),

May 10, 1952; ord. titular bp. of Cillium and aux. bp. of Philadelphia, Aug. 12, 1981; ret., Apr. 5, 1997.

DeWane, Frank J.: b. March 9, 1950, Green Bay, Wis.; educ. Univ. of Wisconsin (Oshkosh), American Univ., George Washington Univ. (Washington, DC), North American College, Pont. Gregorian Univ., Angelicum (Rome); ord. priest July 16, 1988 (Green Bay); app. coadj. bp. of Venice April 25, 2006; ord. bp. July 25, 2006; bp. of Venice, Jan. 19, 2007.

Di Lorenzo, Francis X.: b. Apr. 15, 1942, Philadelphia, PA; educ. St. Charles Borromeo Seminary (Philadelphia), Univ. of St. Thomas (Rome); ord. priest (Philadelphia*), May 18, 1968; ord. titular bp. of Tigia and aux. bp. of Scranton, Mar. 8, 1988; app. apostolic administrator of Honolulu, Oct. 12, 1993; bp. of Honolulu, Nov. 29, 1994; app. bp. of Richmond, Mar. 31, 2004.

DiMarzio, Nicholas: b. June 16, 1944, Newark, NJ; educ. Seton Hall Univ. (South Orange, NJ), Immaculate Conception Seminary (Darlington, NJ), Catholic Univ. (Washington, DC), Fordham Univ. (New York), Rutgers Univ. (New Brunswick, NJ); ord. priest (Newark*), May 30, 1970; ord. titular bp. of Mauriana and aux. bp. of Newark, Oct. 31, 1996, app. Bp. of Camden, June 8, 1999, inst., July 22, 1999; app. bp. of Brooklyn, Aug. 1, 2003.

Dimino, Joseph T.: b. Jan. 7, 1923, New York, NY; educ. Cathedral College (Douglaston, NY), St. Joseph's Seminary (Yonkers, NY), Catholic Univ. (Washington, DC); ord. priest (New York*), June 4, 1949; ord. titular bp. of Carini and aux. bp. of the Military Services archdiocese, May 10, 1983; app. ordinary of Military Services archdiocese, May 14, 1991; ret., Aug. 12, 1997.

DiNardo, Daniel N.: (See **Cardinals' Biographies**).

DiNoia, Joseph Augustine, O.P.: b. July 10, 1943, New York, NY; educ. Dominican House of the Studies in Washington, DC, Yale Univ., New Haven, CT; ord. priest for the Dominicans, June 4, 1970; served as exec. dir. of the Secretariat for Doctrine and Pastoral Practices for the NCCB; member of the Int. Theol. Comm., 1997-2002 and undersec. of the Cong. for the Doctrine of the Faith, 2002-2009; in 1998 he was granted the title Magister in Sacra Theologia by the Dominicans; app. sec. of the Congr. of Divine Worship and Discipline of the Sacraments, June 16, 2009; ord. titular abp. of Oregon City, July 11, 2009; app. Vice Pres. of the Pntifical Commission "Eclesia Dei," June 26, 2012.

Dino, Gerald N.: b. Jan. 11, 1940, Binghamton, NY; educ. Duquesne Univ. (Pittsburgh, PA), Byzantine Catholic Seminary of Sts. Cyril and Methodius (Pittsburgh, PA), Pontifical Oriental Inst. (Rome); ord. priest, Mar. 21, 1965 (Passaic); app. protosincellus of the eparchy of Passaic of the Ruthenians, U.S.A., and pastor in Linden, New Jersey; app. bp. of the eparchy of Van Nuys of the Ruthenians, Dec. 6, 2007; ord. bp. Mar. 27, 2008.

Doherty, Timothy L.: b. Sept. 29, 1950, Rockford, IL; educ.: St. Mary's Minor Seminary (Crystal Lake, IL), St. Ambrose College (Davenport, IA), North American College and Pontifical Lateran Univ. (Rome), Loyola Univ. (Chicago, IL); ord. priest (Rockford), 1976; diocesan ethicist for health care, 1995-2010; app bp. of Lafayette, IN, May 12, 2010.

Dolan, Timothy M.: (See **Cardinals' Biographies**).

Donato, Thomas A.: b. Oct. 1, 1940, Jersey City, NJ; educ. Seton Hall Univ. (South Orange, NJ), Immaculate Conception Seminary (Darlington, NJ); ord. priest (Newark*), May 29, 1965; app. aux. bp. of Newark and tit. bp of Jamestown, May 21, 2004; ord. Aug. 4, 2004.

Donnelly, Robert William: b. Mar. 22, 1931, Toledo, OH; educ. St. Meinrad Seminary College (St. Meinrad, IN), Mount St. Mary's in the West Seminary (Norwood, OH); ord. priest (Toledo), May 25, 1957; ord. titular bp. of Garba and aux. bp. of Toledo, May 3, 1984; ret. May 30, 2006.

Dooher, John A.: b. May 3, 1943, Dorchester, MA; educ. St. John's Seminary (Brighton, MA); ord. May 21, 1969 (Boston); app. aux. bp. of Boston and tit. bp. of Teveste Oct. 12, 2006; ord. Dec. 12, 2006.

Doran, Thomas George: b. Feb. 20, 1936, Rockford, IL; educ. Loras College (Dubuque, IA), Gregorian Univ. (Rome), Rockford College (Rockford, IL); ord. priest (Rockford), Dec. 20, 1961; ord. bp. of Rockford, June 24, 1994; ret. Mar. 20, 2012.

Doueihi, Stephen Hector: b. June 25, 1927, Zghorta, Lebanon; educ. Univ. of St. Joseph (Beirut, Lebanon), Propaganda Fide, Gregorian Univ. and Institute of Oriental Study (Rome); ord. priest, Aug. 14, 1955; came to U.S. in 1973; ord. eparch of Eparchy of St. Maron of Brooklyn, Jan 11, 1997; ret. Jan. 10, 2004.

Dougherty, John Martin: b. Apr. 29, 1932, Scranton, PA; educ. St. Charles College (Catonsville, MD), St. Mary's Seminary (Baltimore), Univ. of Notre Dame (South Bend, IN); ord. priest (Scranton), June 15, 1957; ord. titular bp. of Sufetula and aux. bp. of Scranton, Mar. 7, 1995; ret. Aug. 31, 2009.

Driscoll, Michael P.: b. Aug. 8, 1939, Long Beach, CA; educ. St. John Seminary (Camarillo, CA), Univ. of Southern CA; ord. priest (Los Angeles*), May 1, 1965; ord. titular bp. of Massita and aux. bp. of Orange, Mar. 6, 1990; app. bp. of Boise, Jan. 19, 1999, inst., Mar. 18, 1999.

Duca, Michael Gerard: b. June 5, 1952, Dallas, TX; educ. Holy Trinity Seminary, Irving, TX, Pontifical Univ. of St. Thomas Aquinas, Rome; ord. priest, Apr. 29, 1978 (Dallas); rector of Holy Trinity Seminary (1996-2008); app. bp. of Shreveport, Apr. 1, 2008; ord. bp. May 19, 2008.

Duffy, Paul, O.M.I.: b. July 25, 1932, Norwood, MA; educ Oblate houses of study in Canada and Washington, DC; ord. priest, 1962; missionary in Zambia from 1984; app. first bp. of Mongu, Zambia, July 1, 1997; ret. Feb. 15, 2011.

DuMaine, (Roland) Pierre: b. Aug. 2, 1931, Paducah, KY; educ. St. Joseph's College (Mountain View, CA), St. Patrick's College and Seminary (Menlo Park, CA), Univ. of CA (Berkeley), Catholic Univ. (Washington, DC); ord. priest (San Francisco), June 15, 1957; ord. titular bp. of Sarda and aux. bp. of San Francisco, June 29, 1978; app. first bp. of San Jose, Jan. 27, 1981; inst., Mar. 18, 1981; res, Nov. 27, 1999.

Dunne, John C.: b. Oct. 30, 1937, Brooklyn, NY; educ. Cathedral College (Brooklyn, NY), Immaculate Conception Seminary (Huntington, NY), Manhattan College (New York); ord. priest (Rockville Centre), June 1, 1963; ord. titular bp. of Abercorn and aux. bp. of Rockville Centre, Dec. 13, 1988; ret. June 22, 2013.

Dupre, Thomas L.: b. Nov. 10, 1933, South Hadley Falls, MA; educ. College de Montreal, Assumption College (Worcester, MA), Catholic Univ. (Washington, DC), ord. priest (Springfield, MA), May 23, 1959; ord. titular bp. of Hodelm and aux. bp. of Springfield, MA, May 31, 1990; bp. of Springfield, Mar. 14, 1995; res. Feb.11, 2004.

E

Edyvean, Walter J.: b. Oct. 18, 1938, Medford, MA; educ. Boston College, St. John's Seminary (Brighton, MA), the North American College and the Gregorian Univ. (Rome); ord. priest (Boston*), Dec. 16, 1964; served on staff of Congregation for Catholic Education, 1990-

2001; app. titular bp. of Elie and aux. bp. of Boston, June 29, 2001, ord., Sept. 14, 2001

Egan, Edward M.: (See **Cardinals, Biographies**).

Elizondo, Eusebio: b. Aug. 8, 1954, Victoria, Mexico; educ. Missionaries of the Holy Spirit seminary, (Jalisco, Mexico), Gregorian Univ. (Rome); ord. priest (Missionaries of Holy Spirit) Aug. 18, 1984; app. auxiliary bp. of Seattle and titular bp. of Acolla May 12, 2005; ord. bp. June 6, 2005.

Elya, John A., B.S.O.: b. Sept. 16, 1928, Maghdouche, Lebanon; educ. diocesan monastery (Sidon, Lebanon), Gregorian Univ. (Rome, Italy); professed as member of Basilian Salvatorian Order, 1949; ord. priest, Feb. 17, 1952, in Rome; came to U.S., 1958; ord. titular bp. of Abilene of Syria and aux. bp. of Melkite diocese of Newton, MA, June 29, 1986; app. bp. of Newton (Melkites), Nov. 25, 1993, res. Jun. 22, 2004.

Estevez, Felipe de Jesus: b. Feb. 5, 1946, Betancourt, Cuba; educ: Grand Seminary, Montreal, Gregorian Univ., Rome; ord. May 30, 1970 (Matanzas, Cuba); incard. Miami Feb. 1979; app. aux. bp. of Miami and tit. bp. of Kearney Nov. 21, 2003; ord. Jan. 7, 2004; app. bp. of St. Augustine, Apr. 27, 2011; inst. June 2, 2011.

Etienne, Paul D.: b. June 15, 1959, Tell City, IN; educ. Bellarmine College (Louisville, KY), Univ. of St. Thomas/St. John Vianney Seminary (St. Paul, Minnesota), North American College and Pontifical Gregorian Univ. (Rome); ord. priest, June 27, 1992 (Indianapolis*); app. bp. of Cheyenne, Oct. 19, 2009; ord. Dec. 9, 2009.

Evans, Robert C.: b. Sept. 2, 1947, Moultri, GA; educ. Our Lady of Providence (Warwick, RI), North American College, Pontifical Gregorian Univ., and Pontifical Univ. of St. Thomas Aquinas (Rome); ord. priest (providence), July 2, 1973; sec. at the apostolic nunciature in Washington, DC (2005-2007); app. aux. bp. of Providence, titular bp. of Aquae Regiae, Oct. 15, 2009; ord. Jan. 5, 2010.

F

Fabre, Shelton J.: b. Oct. 25, 1963, New Roads, LA; educ. St. Joseph Seminary College (Covington, LA) and American College (Louvain, Belgium);ord. Aug. 5, 1989 (Baton Rouge, LA); app. aux. bp. of New Orleans and tit. bp. of Pudenzuana Dec. 13, 2006; ord. Feb. 28, 2007.

Farrell, Kevin J.: b. Dublin, Ireland, Sept. 2, 1947; educ. Univ. of Salamanca (Spain), Gregorian Univ. and Univ. of St. Thomas Aquinas (Rome), Univ. of Notre Dame (South Bend, IN); ord. priest (of the Legionaries of Christ), Dec. 24, 1978; incardinated into Archdiocese of Washington, 1984; app. titular bp. of Rusuccuru and aux. bp. of Washington, Dec. 28, 2001; app. bp. of Dallas, Mar. 6, 2007.

Favalora, John C.: b. Dec. 5, 1935, New Orleans, LA; educ. St. Joseph Seminary (St. Benedict, LA), Notre Dame Seminary (New Orleans, LA), Gregorian Univ. (Rome), Catholic Univ. of America (Washington, DC), Xavier Univ. and Tulane Univ. (New Orleans); ord. priest (New Orleans*), Dec. 20, 1961; ord. bp. of Alexandria, LA, July 29, 1986; bp. of St. Petersburg, Mar. 14, 1989; app. abp. of Miami, inst., Dec. 20, 1994; ret. Apr. 20, 2010.

Fellhauer, David E.: b. Aug. 19, 1939, Kansas City, MO; educ. Pontifical College Josephinum (Worthington, OH), St. Paul Univ. (Ottawa); ord. priest (Dallas), May 29, 1965; ord. bp. of Victoria, May 28, 1990.

Finn, Robert W.: b. April 2, 1953, St. Louis; educ. Kenrick-Glennon Seminary (St. Louis), North American College and Angelicum Univ. (Rome); ord. July 7, 1979 (St. Louis); coad. bp. Kansas City-St. Joseph, Mo., Mar. 9, 2004; ord. May 3, 2004; bp. of Kansas City-St. Joseph,

Mo., May 24, 2005.

Fiorenza, Joseph A.: b. Jan. 25, 1931, Beaumont, TX; educ. St. Mary's Seminary (LaPorte, TX); ord. priest (Galveston Houston), May 29, 1954; ord. bp. of San Angelo, Oct. 25, 1979; app. bp. of Galveston Houston, Dec. 18, 1984, inst., Feb. 18, 1985; vice president, NCCB/USCC, 1995-1998, President, 1998-2001; app. first abp. of Galveston Houston, Dec. 29, 2004; ret. Feb. 28, 2006.

Fitzgerald, Michael J.: b. May 23, 1948, Montclair, NJ; educ. Temple Univ. (Philadelphia, PA), Villanova Univ. (Philadelphia, PA), St. Charles Borromeo Seminary (Overbrook, PA), Catholic Univ. of America (Washington, D.C.), Gregorian Univ. (Rome); ord. priest, May 17, 1980 (Philadelphia*); app. titular bp. of Tamallula and aux. bp. of Philadelphia, June 22, 2010; ord. bp., Aug. 6, 2010.

Flanagan, Thomas Joseph: b: Oct. 23, 1930, Rathmore, Ireland; educ. St. Patrick's College, Thurles, Ireland; ord priest (San Antonio*), June 10, 1956; app. titular bp. of Bavagaliana and aux. bp. of San Antonio, Jan. 5, 1998, ord., Feb. 16, 1998; ret. Dec. 15, 2005.

Flesey, John W.: b. Aug. 6, 1942, Jersey City (NJ); educ. St. Peter's College (Jersey City), Immaculate Conception Seminary (South Orange, NJ), Catholic Univ. of America (Washington, DC), Iona College (New Rochelle, NY), Pontifical Gregorian Univ., Pontifical Univ. of St. Thomas Aquinas (Rome); ord. priest (Newark*), May 31, 1969; dean of the School of Theology, Seton Hall Univ.; app. aux. bp. of Newark and tit. bp. of Allegheny May 21, 2004; ord. Aug. 4, 2004.

Fliss, Raphael M.: b. Oct. 25, 1930, Milwaukee, WI; educ. St. Francis Seminary (Milwaukee, WI), Catholic Univ. (Washington, DC), Pontifical Lateran Univ. (Rome); ord. priest (Milwaukee*), May 26, 1956; ord. coadj. bp. of Superior with right of succession, Dec. 20, 1979; bp. of Superior, June 27, 1985; ret. June 28, 2007.

Flores, Cirilo: b. June 20, 1948, Corona, CA; educ. Loyola Marymount Univ. (Los Angeles, CA), Stanford Univ. (Palo Alto, CA); St. John's Seminary (Camarillo, CA); ord. priest (Orange), June 8, 1991; app. titular bp. of Quiza and aux. bp. of Orange, Jan. 5, 2009; ord. bp. Mar. 19, 2009; app. coadjutor bp. of San Diego, Jan. 4, 2012.

Flores, Daniel E.: b. Aug. 28, 1961, Palacios, Texas; educ. Univ. of Dallas, Holy Trinity Seminary (Dallas), Pont. Univ. of St. Thomas Aquinas (Rome); ord. priest Jan. 30, 1988 (Corpus Christi); app. aux. bp. of Detroit and tit. bp. of Cozila Oct. 28, 2006; ord. Nov. 29, 2006; app. bp. of Brownsville, Dec. 29, 2009; inst. Feb. 2, 2010.

Flores, Patrick F.: b. July 26, 1929, Ganado, TX; educ. St. Mary's Seminary (Houston, TX); ord. priest (Galveston Houston), May 26, 1956; ord. titular bp. of Itolica and aux. bp. of San Antonio, May 5, 1970 (first Mexican American bp.); app. bp. of El Paso, Apr. 4, 1978, inst., May 29, 1978; app. abp. of San Antonio, 1979; inst., Oct. 13, 1979; ret. Dec. 29, 2004.

Flynn, Harry J.: b. May 2, 1933, Schenectady, NY; educ. Siena College (Loudonville, NY), Mt. St. Mary's College (Emmitsburg, MD); ord. priest (Albany), May 28, 1960; ord. coadjutor bp. of Lafayette, LA, June 24, 1986; bp. of Lafayette, LA, May 15, 1989; app. coadj. abp. of St. Paul and Minneapolis, Feb. 24, 1994, inst., Apr. 27, 1994; abp. of St. Paul and Minneapolis, Sept. 8, 1995; ret. May 2, 2008.

Folda, John T.: b. August 8, 1961, Omaha, Neb.; educ.: University of Nebraska, St. Charles Borromeo Seminary (Philadelphia), Pontifical University of St. Thomas Aquinas (Rome); ord. priest (Lincoln), May 27, 1989; app. bp. of Fargo, Apr. 8, 2013; ord. bp. June 19, 2013.

Foley, David E.: b. Feb. 3, 1930, Worcester, MA; educ. St. Charles College (Catonsville, MD), St. Mary's Seminary (Baltimore, MD); ord. priest (Washington*), May 26, 1952; ord. titular bp. of Octaba and aux. bp. of Richmond, June 27, 1986; app. bp. of Birmingham, Mar. 22, 1994; ret. May 10, 2005.

Foys, Roger J.: b. July 27, 1945, Chicago; educ. Univ. of Steubenville, St. John Vianney Seminary, (Bloomingdale, OH), the Catholic Univ. of America, Washington, DC; ord. priest (Steubenville), May 16, 1973; Knight Commander of the Equestrian Order of the Holy Sepulchre of Jerusalem, 1986; app. bp. of Covington, May 31, 2002.

Franklin, William Edwin: b. May 3, 1930, Parnell, IA; educ. Loras College and Mt. St. Bernard Seminary (Dubuque, IA); ord. priest (Dubuque*), Feb. 4, 1956; ord. titular bp. of Surista and aux. bp. of Dubuque, Apr. 1, 1987; app. bp. of Davenport, Nov. 12, 1993, inst., Jan. 20, 1994; ret. Oct. 12, 2006.

Friend, William B.: b. Oct. 22, 1931, Miami, FL; educ. St. Mary's College (St. Mary, KY), Mt. St. Mary Seminary (Emmitsburg, MD), Catholic Univ. (Washington, DC), Univ. of Notre Dame (South Bend, IN); ord. priest (Mobile*), May 7, 1959; ord. titular bp. of Pomaria and aux. bp. of Alexandria Shreveport, LA, Oct. 30, 1979; app. bp. of Alexandria Shreveport, Nov. 17, 1982, inst., Jan 11, 1983; app. first bp. of Shreveport, June, 1986; inst., July 30, 1986; ret. Dec. 20, 2006.

G

Gainer, Ronald W.: b. Aug. 24, 1947, Pottsville, PA; educ. St. Charles Borromeo Seminary (Philadelphia), Gregorian Univ. (Rome); ord. priest (Allentown), May 19, 1973; app. bp. of Lexington, KY, ord. bp., Feb. 22, 2003.

Galante, Joseph A.: b. July 2, 1938, Philadelphia, PA; educ. St. Joseph Preparatory School, St. Charles Seminary (Philadelphia, PA); Lateran Univ., Angelicum, North American College (Rome); ord. priest (Philadelphia*), May 16, 1964; on loan to diocese of Brownsville, TX, 1968-72, where he served in various diocesan posts; returned to Philadelphia, 1972; assistant vicar (1972-79) and vicar (1979-87) for religious; undersecretary of Congregation for Institutes of Consecrated Life and Societies of Apostolic Life (Rome), 1987-92; ord. titular bp. of Equilium and aux. bp. of San Antonio, Dec. 11, 1992; app. bp. of Beaumont, Apr. 5, 1994; app. co-adjutor bp. of Dallas, Nov. 23, 1999; app. bp. of Camden, Mar. 23, 2004; ret. Jan. 8, 2013.

Galeone, Victor Benito: b. Sept. 13, 1935, Philadelphia; educ. St. Charles College (Baltimore), North American College, Pontifical Gregorian Univ. (Rome), ord. priest (Baltimore*), Dec. 18, 1960; served as missionary in Peru, 1970-75, 1978-85; app. bp. of St. Augustine, June 25, 2001, ord., Aug. 21, 2001; ret. Apr. 27, 2011.

Garcia, Richard J.: b. Apr. 24, 1947, San Francisco; educ. St. Patrick's Seminary (Menlo Park, CA), Pontifical Univ. of St. Thomas Aquinas (Rome); ord priest (San Francisco*), May 13, 1973; app. Titular bp. of Bapara and aux. bp. of Sacramento, Nov. 25, 1997, ord., Jan. 28, 1998; app. bp. of Monterey in California, Dec. 19, 2006.

Garcia-Siller, Gustavo, M.Sp.S.: b. Dec. 21, 1956, San Luis Potosi, Mexico, educ. St. John's Seminary (Camarillo, Calif.), Western Jesuit Univ. (Guadalajara, Mexico), Gregorian Univ. (Rome); ord. priest, June 22, 1984; app. aux. bp of Chicago and titular bp. of Esco, Jan. 24, 2003; ord., Mar. 19, 2003; app. abp. of San Antonio, Oct. 14, 2010; inst. Nov. 23, 2010.

Garland, James H.: b. Dec. 13, 1931, Wilmington, OH; educ. Wilmington College (OH), Ohio State Univ. (Columbus, OH); Mt. St. Mary's Seminary (Cincinnati, OH), Catholic Univ. (Washington, DC); ord. priest (Cincinnati*), Aug. 15, 1959; ord. titular bp. of Garriana and aux. bp. of Cincinnati, July 25, 1984; app. bp. of Marquette, Oct. 6, 1992; inst., Nov. 11, 1992; ret. Dec. 13, 2005.

Gaydos, John R.: b. Aug. 14, 1943, St. Louis, MO; educ Cardinal Glennon College (St. Louis, MO), North American College, Gregorian Univ. (Rome); ord. priest (St. Louis*), Dec. 20, 1968; ord. bp. of Jefferson City, Aug. 27, 1997.

Gelineau, Louis E.: b. May 3, 1928, Burlington, VT; educ. St. Michael's College (Winooski, VT), St. Paul's Univ. Seminary (Ottawa), Catholic Univ. (Washington, DC); ord. priest (Burlington), June 5, 1954; ord. bp. of Providence, RI, Jan. 26, 1972; ret., June 11, 1997.

Gendron, Odore J.: b. Sept. 13, 1921, Manchester, NH; educ. St. Charles Borromeo Seminary (Sherbrooke, QC), Univ. of Ottawa, St. Paul Univ. Seminary (Ottawa, Ont., Canada); ord. priest (Manchester), May 31, 1947; ord. bp. of Manchester, Feb. 3, 1975; res., June 12, 1990.

George, Cardinal Francis E., O.M.I.: (See **Cardinals, Biographies**).

Gerber, Eugene J.: b. Apr. 30, 1931, Kingman, KS; educ. St. Thomas Seminary (Denver, CO), Wichita State Univ.; Catholic Univ. (Washington, DC), Angelicum (Rome); ord. priest (Wichita), May 19, 1959; ord. bp. of Dodge City, Dec. 14, 1976; app. bp. of Wichita, Nov. 17, 1982, inst., Feb. 9, 1983; res. Oct. 4, 2001.

Gerety, Peter L.: b. July 19, 1912, Shelton, CT; educ. Sulpician Seminary (Paris, France); ord. priest, (Hartford*), June 29, 1939; ord. titular bp. of Crepedula and coadjutor bp. of Portland, ME, with right of succession, June 1, 1966; app. apostolic administrator of Portland, 1967; bp. of Portland, ME, Sept. 15, 1969; app. abp. of Newark, Apr. 2, 1974; inst., June 28, 1974; ret., June 3, 1986.

Gerry, Joseph J., O.S.B.: b. Sept. 12, 1928, Millinocket, ME; educ. St. Anselm Abbey Seminary (Manchester, NH), Univ. of Toronto (Canada), Fordham Univ. (New York); ord. priest, June 12, 1954; abbot of St. Anselm Abbey, Manchester, NH, 1972; ord. titular bp. of Praecausa and aux. of Manchester, Apr. 21, 1986; bp. of Portland, ME, Dec. 27, 1988, inst., Feb. 21, 1989; ret. Feb. 10, 2004.

Gettelfinger, Gerald A.: b. Oct. 20, 1935, Ramsey, IN; educ. St. Meinrad Seminary (St. Meinrad, IN), Butler Univ. (Indianapolis, IN); ord. priest (Indianapolis*), May 7, 1961; ord. bp. of Evansville, Apr. 11, 1989; ret. Apr. 26, 2011.

Gilbert, Edward J., C.SS.R.: b. Dec. 26, 1936, Brooklyn, NY; educ. Mt. St. Alphonsus Seminary (Esopus, NY), Catholic Univ. (Washington, DC); ord. priest (Redemptorists, Baltimore Province), June 21, 1964; ord. bp. of Roseau, Dominica, Sept. 7, 1994; ret. Dec. 26, 2011.

Gilmore, Ronald W.: b. Apr. 23, 1942, Wichita, KS; educ. Univ. Seminary (Ottawa), St. Paul Univ. (Ottawa); ord. priest (Wichita), June 7, 1969; app. Bp. of Dodge City, May 11, 1998, ord., July 16, 1998; ret. Dec. 15, 2010.

Goedert, Raymond E.: b. Oct. 15, 1927, Oak Park, IL; educ. Quigley Preparatory Seminary (Chicago, IL), St. Mary of the Lake Seminary and Loyola Univ. (Chicago, IL), Gregorian Univ. (Rome); ord. priest (Chicago*), May 1, 1952; ord. titular bp. of Tamazeni and aux. bp. of Chicago, Aug. 29, 1991; ret., Jan. 24, 2003.

Gomez, José H.: b. Dec. 26, 1951, Monterrey, Mexico (became U.S. citizen 1995); educ. National Univ., Mexico, Univ. of Navarre (Spain); ord. priest of the Prelature of Opus Dei, Aug. 15, 1978; Vicar of Opus Dei for State of Texas, 1999-2001; app. titular bp. of Belali and aux. bp of Denver, Jan. 23, 2001, ord., Mar. 26, 2001; app. abp. of San Antonio, Dec. 29, 2004; inst. Feb. 15, 2005; app. coadjutor abp. of Los Angeles, Apr. 6, 2010; acceded to the see, Mar. 1, 2011.

Gonzalez, Roberto O., O.F.M., b. June 2, 1950, Elizabeth, NJ; educ. St. Joseph Seminary (Callicoon, NY), Siena College, (Loudonville, NY), Washington Theological Union (Silver Spring, MD), Fordham Univ. (New York, NY); solemnly professed in Franciscan Order, 1976; ord. priest, May 8, 1977; ord. titular bp. of Ursona and aux. bp. of Boston, Oct. 3, 1988; app. coadj. bp. of Corpus Christi, May 16 1995; bp. of Corpus Christi, Apr. 1, 1997; app. abp. of San Juan de Puerto Rico, Mar. 26, 1999, inst., May 8, 1999.

Gonzalez Valer, S.F., Francisco: b. Arcos de Jalon, Spain, May 22, 1939; educ. Missionary Seminary of the Holy Family, Barcelona (Spain), Catholic Univ. of America (Washington, DC); ord. priest (of the Congregation of the Sons of the Holy Family), May 1, 1964; Episcopal Vicar for Hispanic Catholics, Archdiocese of Washington, 1997; app. titular bp. of Lamfua and aux. bp. of Washington, Dec. 28, 2001.

Gorman, John R.: b. Dec. 11, 1925, Chicago, IL; educ, St. Mary of the Lake Seminary (Mundelein, IL), Loyola Univ. (Chicago, IL); ord. priest (Chicago*), May 1, 1956; ord. titular bp. of Catula and aux. bp. of Chicago, Apr. 11, 1988; ret., Jan. 24, 2003.

Gracida, Rene H.: b. June 9, 1923, New Orleans, LA; educ. Rice Univ. and Univ. of Houston (Houston, TX), Univ. of Fribourg (Switzerland); ord. priest (Miami*), May 23, 1959; ord. titular bp. of Masuccaba and aux. bp. of Miami, Jan. 25, 1972; app. first bp. of Pensacola Tallahassee, Oct. 1, 1975, inst., Nov. 6, 1975; app. bp. of Corpus Christi, May 24, 1983, inst., July 11, 1983; ret., Apr. 1, 1997.

Grahmann, Charles V.: b. July 15, 1931, Halletsville, TX; educ. The Assumption St. John's Seminary (San Antonio, TX); ord. priest (San Antonio*), Mar. 17, 1956; ord. titular bp. of Equilium and aux. bp. of San Antonio, Aug. 20, 1981; app. first bp. of Victoria, TX, Apr. 13, 1982; app. coadj. bp. of Dallas, Dec. 9, 1989; bp. of Dallas, July 14, 1990; ret. Mar. 6, 2007.

Green, James P.: b. May 30, 1950, Philadelphia, PA; educ. St. Charles Borromeo Seminary (Overbrook, PA), Pontifical Ecclesiastical Academy (Rome); ord. priest (Philadelphia*), May 15, 1976; after studies at the Pontifical Ecclesiastical Academy, entered the diplomatic service of the Holy See in 1987 and served in Papua New Guinea, Korea, the Netherlands, Spain, Scandinavia, and Taiwan; head of the English-language section in the Secretariat of State 2002-2006; app. nuncio to South Africa, Lesotho, and Namibia, and apostolic delegate in Botswana, Aug. 17, 2006; cons. Sept. 6, 2006; app. nuncio to Peru, Oct. 15, 2011

Gregory, Wilton D.: b. Dec. 7, 1947, Chicago, IL; educ. Quigley Preparatory Seminary South, Niles College of Loyola Univ. (Chicago, IL), St. Mary of the Lake Seminary (Mundelein IL), Pontifical Liturgical Institute, Sant'Anselmo (Rome); ord. priest, (Chicago*), May 9, 1973; ord. titular bp. of Oliva and aux. bp. of Chicago, Dec. 13, 1983; app. bp. of Belleville, Dec. 29, 1993; inst., Feb. 10, 1994 vice president, NCCB/USCC, 1998-2001; president, USCCB, 2001-2004; app. abp. of Atlanta, Dec. 9, 2004; inst. Jan. 17, 2005.

Gries, Roger W., O.S.B.: b. Mar. 26, 1937, Cleveland; educ. St. John Univ., (Collegeville, MN), St. Joseph's Seminary, Cleveland, Loyola Univ., Chicago; ord. priest (Order of St. Benedict), May 16, 1963; Abbot, St. Andrew

Abbey, Cleveland, 1981-2001; app. aux. bp. of Cleveland, April 3, 2001, ord., June 7, 2001.

Griffin, James A.: b. June 13, 1934, Fairview Park, OH; educ. St. Charles College (Baltimore, MD), Borromeo College (Wicklife, OH); St Mary Seminary (Cleveland, OH); Lateran Univ. (Rome); Cleveland State Univ.; ord. priest (Cleveland), May 28, 1960; ord. titular bp. of Holar and aux. bp. of Cleveland, Aug. 1, 1979; app. bp. of Columbus, Feb. 8, 1983; ret. Oct. 14, 2004.

Grosz, Edward M.: b. Feb. 16, 1945, Buffalo, NY; educ. St. John Vianney Seminary (East Aurora, NY), Univ. of Notre Dame (Notre Dame, IN); ord. priest (Buffalo), May 29, 1971; ord. titular bp. of Morosbisdus and aux. bp. of Buffalo, Feb. 2, 1990.

Gruss, Robert D.: b. June 25, 1955, Texarkana, AR; Madison Area Technical College (Madison, WI), Spartan School of Aeronautics (Tulsa, OK), St. Ambrose University (Davenport, IA), Pontifical North American College and Pontifical University of St. Thomas (Rome); ord. priest, July 2, 1994 (Davenport); vice-rector, North American College, Rome, 2007-2010; app. bp. of Rapid City, May 26, 2011; ord. bp. July 28, 2011.

Guglielmone, Robert E.: b. Dec. 30, 1945, New York, NY; St. John's Univ. (Jamaica, NY); Seminary of the Immaculate Conception (Huntington, NY); ord. priest, Apr. 8, 1978; app. bp. of Charleston, Jan. 24, 2009; ord. bp. Mar. 25, 2009.

Guillory, Curtis J., S.V.D.: b. Sept. 1, 1943, Mallet, LA; educ. Divine Word College (Epworth, IA), Chicago Theological Union (Chicago), Creighton Univ. (Omaha, NE); ord. priest, Dec. 16, 1972; ord. titular bp. of Stagno and aux. bp. of Galveston-Houston, Feb. 19, 1988; bp. of Beaumont, June 2, 2000, inst., July 28, 2000.

Gullickson, Thomas E.: b. Aug. 14, 1950, Sioux Falls, SD; educ. North American College and Pontifical Gregorian Univ. (Rome, Italy); ord. priest, June 27, 1976 (Sioux Falls); after studies in the Pontifical Ecclesiastical Academy, he entered the diplomatic service of the Holy See in 1985 and served in the nunciatures in Rwanda, Austria, Czechoslovakia, Jerusalem, and Germany; app. titular abp. of Bomarzo, Oct. 2, 2004; cons. Nov. 11, 2004; Apostolic Nuncio to Trinidad and Tobago, Bahamas, Dominica, St. Kitts and Nevis, Santa Lucia, San Vincenzo and Grenadine; app. nuncio to Ukraine, May 21, 2011.

Gumbleton, Thomas J.: b. Jan. 26, 1930, Detroit, MI; educ. St. John Provincial Seminary (Detroit, MI), Pontifical Lateran Univ. (Rome); ord. priest (Detroit*), June 2, 1956; ord. titular bp. of Ululi and aux. bp. of Detroit, May 1, 1968; ret. Feb. 2, 2006.

H

Habash, Yousif Benham: b. June 1, 1951, Qaraqosh, Iraq; educ. Seminary of St. John of the Dominicans (Mosul), Seminary of Charfet (Lebanon), Pontifical Univ. of the Holy Spirit (Kaslik, Lebanon); ord. priest, Aug. 31, 1975; served in the U.S. in the mission for Our Lady of Deliverance of Newark and then in Chicago and Los Angeles; app. Our Lady of Deliverance of Newark, Apr. 12, 2010.

Hanchon, Donald F.: b. Oct. 9, 1947, Wayne, MI educ. St. John Provincial Seminary, Univ. of Detroit, Univ. of Notre Dame; ord. priest (Detroit*), Oct. 19, 1974; app. titular bp. of Horreomargum and aux. bp. of Detroit, Mar. 22, 2011; ord. May 5, 2011.

Hanifen, Richard C.: b. June 15, 1931, Denver, CO; educ. Regis College and St. Thomas Seminary (Denver, CO), Catholic Univ. (Washington, DC), Lateran Univ. (Rome);

ord. priest (Denver*), June 6, 1959; ord. titular bp. cf Abercorn and aux. bp. of Denver, Sept. 20, 1974; app. first bp. of Colorado Springs, Nov. 10, 1983; inst., Jan. 30, 1984; ret., Jan. 30, 2003.

Hanus, Jerome George, O.S.B.: b. May 25, 1940, Brainard, NE; educ. Conception Seminary (Conception, MO), St. Anselm Univ. (Rome), Princeton Theological Seminary (Princeton, NJ); ord. priest (Conception Abbey, MO), July 30, 1966; abbot of Conception Abbey, 1977-87; president of Swiss American Benedictine Congregation, 1984-87; ord. bp. of St. Cloud, Aug. 24, 1987; app. coadjutor abp. of Dubuque, Aug. 23, 1994; abp. of Dubuque, Oct. 16, 1995; ret. Apr. 8, 2013.

Harrington, Bernard J.: b. Sept. 6, 1933, Detroit, MI; educ. Sacred Heart Seminary (Detroit), St. John's Provincial Seminary (Plymouth, MI), Catholic Univ. of America (Washington, DC), Univ. of Detroit; ord. priest (Detroit*), June 6, 1959; ord. titular bp. of Uzali and aux. bp. of Detroit, Jan. 6, 1994; app. Bp. of Winona, Nov. 5, 1998, inst., Jan. 6, 1999; ret. May 7, 2009.

Hart, Joseph: b. Sept. 26, 1931, Kansas City, MO; educ. St. John Seminary (Kansas City, MO), St. Meinrad Seminary (Indianapolis, IN); ord. priest (Kansas City St. Joseph), May 1, 1956; ord. titular bp. of Thimida Regia and aux. bp. of Cheyenne, WY, Aug. 31, 1976; app. bp. of Cheyenne, inst., June 12, 1978; ret., Sept. 26, 2001.

Hartmayer, Gregory J., O.F.M. Conv.: b. Nov. 21, 1951, Buffalo, NY; educ. Franciscan novitiate in Ellicott City (MD), St. Hyacinth College and Seminary (MA), St. Anthony-on-Hudson (Rensselaer, NY), Emmanuel College (Boston), Boston College; solemn profession in the Conventual Franciscans, Aug. 15, 1973; ord. priest, May 5, 1979; app. bp. of Savannah, July 19, 2011; ord. Oct. 18, 2011

Harvey, James M.: (See Cardinals' Biographies).

Hebda, Bernard A.: b. Sept. 3, 1959, Pittsburgh, PA; educ. Harvard Univ. (Cambridge, MA), Columbia Law School, Parker School of Foreign and Comparative Law, St. Paul Seminary (Pittsburgh, PA), North American College and Gregorian Univ. (Rome); ord. priest, July 1, 1989 (Pittsburgh); served in the Pontifical Council for Legislative Texts (1996-2003) and assistant spiritual director at the North American College; app. bp. of Gaylord, Oct. 7, 2009; ord. Dec. 1, 2009.

Heim, Capistran F., O.F.M.: b. Jan. 21, 1934, Catskill, NY; educ. Franciscan Houses of Study; ord. priest, Dec. 18, 1965; missionary in Brazil; ord. first bp. of prelature of Itaituba, Brazil, Sept. 17, 1988; inst., Oct. 2, 1988.

Hennessey, Robert F.: b. April 20, 1952 (Boston); educ. St. John's Seminary (Brighton, Mass.), Moreau Seminary (Notre Dame, Ind.); ord. May 20, 1978 (Boston); app. aux. bp. of Boston and tit. bp. of Tigia Oct. 12, 2006; ord. Dec. 12, 2006.

Hermann, Robert J.: b. Aug. 12, 1934, Weingarten, MO; educ. Cardinal Glennon College (Shrewsbury, MO.), St. Louis Univ.; ord. priest (St. Louis), Mar. 30, 1963; aux. bp. St. Louis and tit. bp. of Zerta, Oct. 16, 2002; ord., Dec. 12, 2002; ret. Dec. 1, 2010.

Hermes, Herbert, O.S.B.: b. May 25, 1933, Scott City, KS; ord. priest (St. Benedict Abbey, Atchison, KS), May 26, 1960; missionary in Brazil; ord. bp. of territorial prelature of Cristalandia, Brazil, Sept. 2, 1990; ret. Feb. 25, 2009.

Herzog, Ronald P.: b. April 22, 1942, Akron, OH; educ. St. Joseph Seminary (St. Benedict, LA), Pontifical College Josephinum (Worthington, OH); ord. priest June 1, 1968 (Natchez-Jackson, MS; now Biloxi); app. bp. of Alexandria Nov. 4, 2004; ord. Jan. 5, 2005.

Higgins, Richard B.: b. Feb. 22, 1944, Longford, Ireland; educ. Pontifical Lateran Univ. (Rome); ord. priest (Sacramento), Mar. 9, 1968; entered the Air Force as a chaplain, 1974; app. titular bp. of Case Calane and aux. bp. of the Archdiocese for the Military Services, May 7, 2004.

Higi, William L.: b. Aug. 29, 1933, Anderson, IN; educ. Our Lady of the Lakes Preparatory Seminary (Wawasee, IN), Mt. St. Mary of the West Seminary and Xavier Univ. (Cincinnati, OH); ord. priest, (Lafayette, IN) May 30, 1959; ord. bp. of Lafayette, IN, June 6, 1984; ret. May 12, 2010.

Hoeppner, Michael J.: b. June 1,1949, Winona, MN; educ. Immaculate Heart of Mary Seminary (Winona), Pontifical North American College and Pontifical Gregorian Univ. (Rome), St. Paul Univ. (Ottawa, Canada), Winona State Univ. (Winona); ord. priest, June 29, 1975 (Winona); app. bp. of Crookston, Sept. 28, 2007; inst. Nov. 30, 2007.

Holley, Martin D.: b. Dec. 31, 1954, Pensacola, FL; educ. Alabama State Univ. (Montgomery, AL), Catholic Univ. of America (Washington, DC), St. Vincent de Paul Regional Seminary (Boynton Beach); ord. priest (Pensacola-Tallahassee), May 8, 1987; app. titular bp. of Rusibisir and aux. bp. of Washington, May 18, 2004; ord. July 2, 2004.

Houck, William Russell: b. June 26, 1926, Mobile, AL; educ. St. Bernard Jr. College (Cullman, AL), St. Mary's Seminary College and St. Mary's Seminary (Baltimore, MD), Catholic Univ. (Washington, DC); ord. priest (Mobile*), May 19, 1951; ord. titular bp. of Alessano and aux. bp. of Jackson, MS, May 27, 1979, by Pope John Paul II; app. bp. of Jackson, Apr. 11, 1984, inst., June 5, 1984; ret., Jan. 3, 2003.

Howze, Joseph Lawson: b. Aug. 30, 1923, Daphne, AL; convert to Catholicism, 1948; educ. St. Bonaventure Univ. (St. Bonaventure, NY); ord. priest (Raleigh), May 7, 1959; ord. titular bp. of Massita and aux. bp. of Natchez Jackson, Jan. 28, 1973; app. first bp. of Biloxi, Mar. 8, 1977; inst., June 6, 1977; res. May 15, 2001.

Hubbard, Howard J.: b. Oct. 31, 1938, Troy, NY; educ. St. Joseph's Seminary (Dunwoodie, NY); North American College and Gregorian Univ. (Rome), Catholic Univ. (Washington, DC); ord. priest (Albany), Dec. 18, 1963; ord. bp. of Albany, Mar. 27, 1977.

Hughes, Alfred C.: b. Dec. 2, 1932, Boston, MA; educ. St. John Seminary (Brighton, MA), Gregorian Univ. (Rome); ord. priest (Boston*), Dec. 15, 1957, in Rome; ord. titular bp. of Maximiana in Byzacena and aux. bp. of Boston, Sept. 14, 1981; app. bp. of Baton Rouge, Sept. 7, 1993; coadj. abp. of New Orleans, Feb. 16, 2001; abp. of New Orleans, Jan. 3, 2002; ret. June 12, 2009.

Hughes, Edward T.: b. Nov. 13, 1920, Lansdowne, PA; educ. St. Charles Seminary, Univ. of Pennsylvania (Philadelphia); ord. priest (Philadelphia*), May 31, 1947; ord. titular bp. of Segia and aux. bp. of Philadelphia, July 21, 1976; app. bp. of Metuchen, Dec. 11, 1986, inst., Feb. 5, 1987; ret., July 8, 1997.

Hunthausen, Raymond G.: b. Aug. 21, 1921, Anaconda, MT; educ. Carroll College (Helena, MT), St. Edward's Seminary (Kenmore, WA), St. Louis Univ. (St. Louis, MO), Catholic Univ. (Washington, DC), Fordham Univ. (New York City), Univ. of Notre Dame (Notre Dame, IN); ord. priest (Helena), June 1, 1946; ord. bp. of Helena, Aug. 30, 1962; app. abp. of Seattle, Feb. 25, 1975; ret., Aug. 21, 1991.

Hurley, Francis T.: b. Jan. 12, 1927, San Francisco, CA; educ. St. Patrick's Seminary (Menlo Park, CA), Catholic Univ. (Washington, DC); ord. priest (San Francisco*), June 16, 1951; assigned to NCWC in Washington, DC, 1957; assistant (1958) and later (1968) associate secretary of NCCB and USCC; ord. titular bp. of Daimlaig and aux. bp. of Juneau, AK, Mar. 19, 1970; app. bp. of Juneau, July 20, 1971, inst., Sept. 8, 1971; app. abp. of Anchorage, May 4, 1976, inst., July 8, 1976; res., Mar. 3, 2001.

Hurley, Walter A.: b. May 30, 1937, Fredericton, New Brunswick; educ. Sacred Heart Seminary, St. John Provincial Seminary, Catholic Univ. of America; ord. priest, June 5, 1965 (Detroit); app. aux. bp. of Detroit and titular bp. of Cunavia, July 7, 2003; app. bp. of Grand Rapids, June 21, 2005; inst. Aug. 5, 2005; ret. Apr. 18, 2013.

Hying, Donald J.: b. Aug. 18, 1963, West Allis, WI; educ. Marquette Univ. (Marquette), St. Francis de Sales Seminary (St. Francis, WI); St. Mary of the Lake Seminary (Mundelein, IL); ord. priest, May 20, 1989 (Milwaukee*); rector, St. Francis de Sales Seminary, 2007-2011; app. titular bp. of Regiae and aux. bp. of Milwaukee, May 26, 2011; ord. bp. July 20, 2011.

I J

Ibrahim, Ibrahim N.: b. Oct. 1, 1937, Telkaif, Mosul, Iraq.; educ. Patriarchal Seminary (Mosul, Iraq), St. Sulpice Seminary (Paris, France); ord. priest, Dec. 30, 1962, in Baghdad, Iraq; ord. titular bp. of Anbar and apostolic exarch for Chaldean Catholics in the United States, Mar. 8, 1982, in Baghdad; inst., in Detroit, Apr. 18, 1982; app. first eparch, Aug. 3, 1985, when exarchate was raised to eparchy of St. Thomas Apostle of Detroit.

Imesch, Joseph L.: b. June 21, 1931, Detroit, MI; educ. Sacred Heart Seminary (Detroit, MI), North American College, Gregorian Univ. (Rome); ord. priest (Detroit*), Dec. 16, 1956; ord. titular bp. of Pomaria and aux. bp. of Detroit, Apr. 3, 1973; app. bp. of Joliet, June 30, 1979; ret. May 16, 2006.

Iriondo, Robert J.: b. Dec. 19, 1938, Legazti, Spain; educ. Collegio San Vittore and Pontifical Gregorian Univ., Rome; ord. priest (of the Canons Regular of the Lateran), Dec. 22, 1962; incardinated into Archdio. of New York, 1996; Vicar for Hispanics, 1997; ord. titular bp. of Alton and aux. of New York, Dec. 12, 2001.

Irwin, Francis X.: b. Jan 9, 1934, Medford, MA; educ. Boston College High School, Boston College, St. John's Seminary (Brighton, MA), Boston College School of Social Service; ord. priest (Boston*), Feb. 2, 1960; ord. titular bp. of Ubaza and aux. bp. of Boston, Sept. 17, 1996; ret. Oct. 20, 2009.

Isern, Fernando: b. Sept. 22, 1958, Havana, Cuba; educ. Florida International Univ. (Miami, FL), St. John Vianney College Seminary (Miami), St. Vincent De Paul Regional Seminary (Boynton Beach); ord. priest (Miami*), Apr. 16, 1993; app. bp. of Pueblo, Oct. 15, 2009; ord. Dec. 10, 2009; res. June 13, 2013.

Jackels, Michael O.: b. April 13, 1954, Rapid City, S.D.; educ. Univ. of Nebraska-Lincoln, St. Pius X Seminary (Erlanger, KY), Mt. St. Mary's (Emmitburg, MD); ord. priest May 30, 1981 (Lincoln, NE); app. bp. of Wichita Jan. 29, 2005; ord. Apr. 4, 2005; app. abp. of Dubuque, Apr. 8, 2013; inst. May 30, 2013.

Jacobs, Sam Gallip: b. Mar. 4, 1938, Greenwood, MS; educ. Immaculata Seminary (Lafayette, LA), Catholic Univ. (Washington, DC); ord. priest (Lafayette), June 6, 1964; became priest of Lake Charles diocese, 1980, when that see was established; ord. bp. of Alexandria, LA, Aug. 24, 1989; app. bp. of Houma-Thibodaux, Aug. 1, 2003.

Jammo, Sarhad: b. March 14, 1941, Baghdad, Iraq; educ. Patriarchal Seminary of Mosul, Urban College of the Propaganda Fide Pontifical Oriental Institute (Rome);

ord. priest (Baghdad*), Dec. 19, 1964; rector, Chaldean Seminary, Baghdad; after service in Iraq, transferred in 1977 to the Eparchy of St. Thomas the Apostle of Detroit for Chaldeans; app. first eparch of the eparchy of St. Peter the Apostle of San Diego (Chaldean), May 21, 2002.

Jarrell, C. Michael: b. May 15, 1940, Opelousas, LA; educ. Immaculata Minor Seminary (Lafayette, LA); Catholic Univ. (Washington, DC); ord. priest (Lafayette, LA), June 3, 1967; ord. bp. of Houma-Thibodaux, Mar. 4, 1993; app. bp. of Lafayette, Nov. 8, 2002.

Jenky, Daniel R., C.S.C.: b. Mar. 3, 1947, Chicago; educ. Univ. of Notre Dame; ord. priest, Apr. 6, 1974; Religious Superior of the Holy Cross religious at Notre Dame, 1985-1990; app.titular bp. of Amanzia and aux. of Ft. Wayne-South Bend, Oct. 21, 1997, ord., Dec. 16, 1997, bp. of Peoria, Feb. 12, 2002, inst. Apr. 10, 2002.

Johnston, James Vann: b. Oct. 16, 1959, Knoxville, TN; educ. Univ. of Tennessee (Knoxville, TN), St. Meinrad Seminary (St.Meinrad, IN), Catholic Univ. of America (Washington, DC.); ord. priest, June 9, 1990 (Knoxville); app. bp. of Springfield-Cape Girardeau, Jan. 24, 2008; ord. bp., Mar. 31, 2008.

Jugis, Peter J.: b. March 3, 1957, Charlotte, NC; educ. Univ. of North Carolina at Charlotte, North American College and Gregorian Univ. (Rome), Catholic Univ. of America (Washington, DC); ord. priest, June 12, 1983; app. bp. of Charlotte, Aug. 1, 2003; ord. Oct. 24, 2003.

Justice, William J.: b. May 8, 1942; educ., St. Patrick Seminary (Menlo Park, CA), Univ. of San Francisco (San Francisco, CA); ord. priest, May 17, 1968 (San Francisco*); app. titular bp. of Matara di Proconsolare and aux. bp. of San Francisco, Apr. 10, 2008; ord. bp., May 28, 2008.

K

Kagan, David D.: b. Nov. 9, 1949, Waukegan, IL; educ. Loras College/St. Pius X Seminary (Dubuque, IA), Pontifical North American Colege and Gregorian University (Rome, Italy); ord. priest, June 14, 1975 (Rockford); app. Protonotary Apostolic, 2011; app. bp. of Bismarck. Oct. 19, 2011; ord. bp. Nov. 30, 2011; res. Apr. 8, 2013.

Kane, Francis Joseph: b. Oct. 30, 1942, Chicago, IL; educ. Quigley Preparatory Seminary (Chicago, IL), Niles College Seminary (Chicago, IL), St. Mary of the Lake Seminary (Chicago, IL); ord. priest, May 14, 1969 (Chicago*); app. aux. bp. of Chicago and titular bp. of Sault Ste Marie, MI Jan. 24, 2003; ord., Mar. 19, 2003.

Keeler, Cardinal William Henry: (See **Cardinals, Biographies.**)

Keleher, James P.: b. July 31, 1931, Chicago, IL; educ. Quigley Preparatory Seminary (Chicago, IL), St. Mary of the Lake Seminary (Mundelein, IL); ord. priest (Chicago*), Apr. 12, 1958; ord. bp. of Belleville, Dec. 11, 1984; app. abp. of Kansas City, KS, June 28, 1993; ret. Jan. 15, 2005.

Kennedy, Arthur L.: b. Jan. 9, 1942, Boston, MA; educ., St. John Seminary (Brighton, MA), Pontifical North American College and Pontifical Gregorian Univ. (Rome), Boston Univ. (Boston, MA); ord. priest (Boston*); rector of St. John Seminary in Brighton, 2007-2010; app. titular bp. of Timidana and aux. bp. of Boston, June 30, 2010.

Kettler, Donald J.: b. Nov. 26, 1944, Minneapolis; educ. St. John's Seminary Collegeville, Minnesota; ord. priest (Sioux Falls), May 29, 1970; app. bp. of Fairbanks, Alaska, June 7, 2002, ord., Aug. 22, 2002.

Kicanas, Gerald F.: b. Aug. 18, 1941, Chicago, IL;

educ. Quigley Preparatory Seminary, St. Mary of the Lake Seminary and Loyola Univ. in Chicago; ord. priest (Chicago*), Apr. 27, 1967; ord. titular bp. of Bela and aux. of Chicago, Mar. 20, 1995; app. coadj. bp. of Tucson, Oct. 30, 2001; inst. as coadj. bp. of Tuscon, Jan. 17, 2002; bp. of Tucson, Mar. 7, 2003.

Kinney, John F.: b. June 11, 1937, Oelwein, IA; educ. Nazareth Hall and St. Paul Seminaries (St. Paul, MN); Pontifical Lateran Univ. (Rome); ord. priest (St. Paul Minneapolis*), Feb. 2, 1963; ord. titular bp. of Caorle and aux. bp. of St. Paul and Minneapolis, Jan. 25, 1977; app. bp. of Bismarck June 30, 1982; app. bp. of St. Cloud, May 9, 1995.

Kmiec, Edward U.: b. June 4, 1936, Trenton, NJ; educ. St. Charles College (Catonsville, MD), St. Mary's Seminary (Baltimore, MD), Gregorian Univ. (Rome); ord. priest (Trenton), Dec. 20, 1961; ord. titular bp. of Simidicca and aux. bp. of Trenton, Nov. 3, 1982; app. bp. of Nashville, Oct. 13, 1992; inst., Dec. 3, 1992; app. bp. of Buffalo, Aug. 12, 2004; ret. May 29, 2012.

Knestout, Barry C.: b. June 11, 1962, Cheverly (MD), Univ. of Maryland (College Park, MD), Mount St. Mary's Seminary (Emmitsburg, MD); ord. priest (Washington*), June 24, 1989; app. titular bp. of Leavenworth and aux. bp. of Washington, Nov. 18, 2008; ord. bp. Dec. 29, 2008.

Kucera, Daniel W., O.S.B.: b. May 7, 1923, Chicago, IL; educ. St. Procopius College (Lisle, IL), Catholic Univ. (Washington, DC); professed in Order of St. Benedict, June 16, 1944; ord. priest, May 26, 1949; abbot, St. Procopius Abbey, 1964 71; pres. Illinois Benedictine College, 1959 65 and 1971 76; ord. titular bp. of Natchez and aux. bp. of Joliet, July 21, 1977; app. bp. of Salina, Mar. 5, 1980; app. abp. of Dubuque, inst., Feb. 23, 1984; ret., Oct. 16, 1995.

Kudrick, John M.: b. Dec. 23, 1947, Lloydell, PA; educ Third Order Regular of St. Francis, 1967; ord. priest May 3, 1975; granted bi-ritual faculties for service in the Byzantine Rite, 1978; app. bp. of Parma, May 3, 2002.

Kurtz, Joseph E.: b. Aug. 18, 1946, Shenandoah, PA.; educ. St. Charles Borromeo Seminary, Philadelphia, Marywood College, Scranton; ord. priest (Allentown), Mar. 18, 1972; app. bp. of Knoxville, Oct. 26, 1999, ord., Dec. 8, 1999; app. abp. of Louisville, June 12, 2007.

Kurtz, Robert, C.R.: b. July 25, 1939, Chicago, IL; ord. priest, Mar. 11, 1967; ord. bp. of Hamilton, Bermuda, Sept. 15, 1995; inst. Aug. 15, 2007.

L

LaValley, Terry R.: b. Mar. 26, 1956, Plattsburgh, NY; educ. State Univ. of New York (Plattsburgh, NY), Wadhams Hall Seminary (Ogdensburg, NY), Christ the King Seminary (East Aurora, NY), St. Paul Univ. (Ottawa); ord. priest, Sept. 24, 1988 (Ogdensburg); app. bp. of Ogdensburg, Feb. 23, 2010; ord. bp. Apr. 30, 2010.

Lagonegro, Dominick J.: b. Mar. 6, 1943, White Plains, NY; educ. Cathedral College, (Douglaston), St. Joseph Seminary, Yonkers; ord. priest (New York*), May 31, 1969; ord. titular bp. of Modrus and aux. of New York, Dec. 12, 2001.

Latino, Joseph: b. Oct. 21, 1937, New Orleans, LA; educ. St. Joseph College Seminary (Covington, LA), Notre Dame Seminary (New Orleans, LA); ord. priest, May 25, 1963; app. bp. Jackson, Jan. 3, 2003; ord., March 7, 2003.

Law, Bernard F.: (See **Cardinals, Biographies**.)

Leibrecht, John J.: b. Aug. 30, 1930, Overland, MO; educ. Catholic Univ. (Washington, DC); ord. priest (St. Louis*), Mar. 17, 1956; superintendent of schools of St. Louis archdiocese, 1962 1981; ord. bp. of Springfield Cape Girardeau, MO, Dec. 12, 1984; ret. Jan. 24, 2008.

Lennon, Richard G.: b. Mar. 26, 1947, Arlington, (MA); educ. St. John's Seminary, Brighton; ord. priest (Boston*), May 19, 1973; rector, St. John's Seminary 1999-2001; app. titular bp. of Sufes and aux. bp. of Boston, June 29, 2001, ord., Sept. 14, 2001; apost. admin. of Boston, 2002-03; app. bp. of Cleveland, Apr. 4, 2006.

Lessard, Raymond W.: b. Dec. 21, 1930, Grafton, ND; educ. St. Paul Seminary (St. Paul, MN), North American College (Rome); ord. priest (Fargo), Dec. 16, 1956; served on staff of the Congregation for Bps. in the Roman Curia, 1964 73; ord. bp. of Savannah, Apr. 27, 1973; ret., Feb. 7, 1995.

Levada, William J.: (See **Cardinals, Biographies**).

LeVoir, John: b. Feb. 7, 1946, Minneapolis, Minnesota; educ., Univ. of St. Thomas (Houston, TX), Dallas Univ. (Dallas, TX), St. Paul Seminary (St. Paul and Minneapolis, MN); ord. priest, May 30, 1981 (St. Paul and Minneapolis*); co-author of *Covenant of Love: John Paul II on Sexuality, Marriage, and Family in the Modern World, Faith for Today*, and the series *Image of God*; app. bp. of New Ulm, July 14, 2008.

Libasci, Peter A.: b. Nov. 9, 1951, Jackson Heights (NY); educ. St. John's Univ. (Queens, NY), St. Meinrad School of Theology (St. Meinrad, IN); ord. priest (Rockville Center, NY), Apr. 1, 1978; app. titular bp. of Satafis and aux. bp. of Rockville Center, Apr. 3, 2007; app. bp. of Manchester, Sept. 19, 2011; inst. Dec. 8, 2011.

Lippert, Donald, O.F.M. Cap.: b. June 12, 1957, Pittsburgh, PA; professed perpetual vows for the Capuchin Franciscans, Aug. 20, 1983; ord. priest, June 8, 1985, for the Capuchin Franciscans; app. bp. pf Mendi, Paula, New Guinea, Nov. 22, 2011; ord. bp., Feb. 4, 2012.

Lipscomb, Oscar H.: b. Sept. 21, 1931, Mobile, AL; educ. McGill Institute, St. Bernard College (Cullman AL), North American College and Gregorian Univ. (Rome), Catholic Univ. (Washington, DC); ord. priest (Mobile*), July 15, 1956; ord. first abp. of Mobile, Nov. 16, 1980; ret. Apr. 2, 2008.

Listecki, Jerome E.: b. Mar. 12, 1949, Chicago; educ. Loyola Univ. and St. Mary of the Lake Seminary, Mundelein, IL, De Paul Univ. College of Law, Univ. of St. Thomas Aquinas and Pontifical Gregorian Univ., Rome; ord. priest (Chicago*), June 1, 1975; app. titular bp. of Nara and aux bp. of Chicago, Nov. 7, 2000, ord., Jan. 8, 2001; app. bp. of La Crosse, Dec. 29, 2004; inst. Mar. 1, 2005; app. abp. of Milwaukee, Nov. 14, 2009; inst. Jan. 15, 2010.

Lohmuller, Martin N.: b. Aug. 21, 1919, Philadelphia, PA; educ. St. Charles Borromeo Seminary (Philadelphia, PA), Catholic Univ. (Washington, DC); ord. priest (Philadelphia*), June 3, 1944; ord. titular bp. of Ramsbury and aux. bp. of Philadelphia, Apr. 2, 1970; ret., Oct. 11, 1994.

Lori, William E.: b. May 6, 1951, Louisville, KY; educ. St. Pius X College (Covington, KY), Mount St. Mary's Seminary (Emmitsburg, MD), Catholic Univ. (Washington, DC); ord. priest (Washington*), May 14, 1977; ord. titular bp. of Bulla and aux. bp. of Washington, DC, Apr. 20, 1995; app. bp. of Bridgeport, Jan. 23, 2001; inst., Mar. 19, 2001; app. abp. of Baltimore, Mar. 20, 2012; inst. May 16, 2012.

Losten, Basil: b. May 11, 1930, Chesapeake City, MD; educ. St. Basil's College (Stamford, CT), Catholic Univ. (Washington, DC); ord. priest (Philadelphia* Ukrainian Byzantine), June 10, 1957; ord. titular bp. of Arcadiopolis in Asia and aux. bp. of Ukrainian archeparchy of Philadelphia, May 25, 1971; app. apostolic administrator of archeparchy, 1976; app. bp. of Ukrainian eparchy of Stamford, Sept. 20, 1977; ret. Jan. 3, 2006.

Loverde, Paul S.: b. Sept. 3, 1940, Framingham, MA; educ. St. Thomas Seminary (Bloomfield, CT), St. Bernard Seminary (Rochester, NY), Gregorian Univ. (Rome), Catholic Univ. (Washington, DC); ord. priest (Norwich), Dec. 18, 1965; ord. titular bp. of Ottabia and aux. bp. of Hartford, Apr. 12, 1988; app. bp. of Ogdensburg, Nov. 11, 1993; inst., Jan. 17, 1994; app. bp. of Arlington, Jan. 25, 1999, inst., Mar. 25, 1999.

Lucas, George J.: b. June 12, 1949, St. Louis, MO; educ. Major Seminary of St. Louis, Univ. of St. Louis; ord. priest (St. Louis*), May 24, 1975; rector, Kenrick-Glennon Seminary, 1995-1999; app. bp. of Springfield in Illinois, Oct. 19, 1999, ord., Dec. 14, 1999; app. abp. of Omaha, June 3, 2009; inst. July 26, 2009.

Luong, Dominic Dinh Mai: b: Dec. 20, 1940, Minh Cuong, Vietnam; educ. seminary (Buffalo, N.Y.), and St. Bernard Seminary (Rochester, N.Y.), Canisius College (Buffalo); ord. priest in Buffalo for Diocese of Danang, Vietnam, May 21, 1966; incardinated into New Orleans 1986; named aux. bp. of Orange, CA, and titular bp. of Cebarades, April 25, 2003; ord., June 11, 2003.

Lynch, Robert N.: b. May 27, 1941, Charleston, WV; educ. Pontifical College Josephinum (Columbus, OH); John XXIII National Seminary (Weston, MA); ord. priest (Miami*), May 13, 1978; assoc. gen. secretary (1984 89) and gen. secretary (1989 95) of the NCCB/USCC; app. bp. of St. Petersburg, Dec. 5, 1995; ord. and inst., Jan. 26, 1996; app. apostolic administrator of Palm Beach (while continuing as bp. of St. Petersburg), June 2, 1998.

Lyne, Timothy J.: b. Mar. 21, 1919, Chicago, IL; educ. Quigley Preparatory Seminary, St. Mary of the Lake Seminary (Mundelein, IL); ord. priest (Chicago*), May 1, 1943; ord. titular bp. of Vamalla and aux. bp. of Chicago, Dec. 13, 1983; ret., Jan. 24, 1995.

M

Macaluso, Christie Albert: b. June 12, 1945, Hartford, CT; educ. St. Thomas Seminary (Bloomfield, CT), St. Mary's Seminary (Baltimore, Md), Trinity College (Hartford, CT), New York Univ.; ord. priest (Hartford*), May 21, 1971; ord. titular bp. of Grass Valley and aux. bp. of Hartford, June 10, 1997.

McCarrick, Theodore E.: (See **Cardinals, Biographies**.)

McCarthy, James F.: b. July 9, 1942, Mount Kisco, NY; educ. Cathedral College and St. Joseph's Seminary, New York; ord. priest (New York*), June 1, 1968; app. titular bp. of Veronna and aux. bp. of New York, May 11, 1999, inst., June 29, 1999; res., June 12, 2002.

McCarthy, John E.: b. June 21, 1930, Houston, TX; educ. Univ. of St. Thomas (Houston, TX); ord. priest (Galveston Houston), May 26, 1956; assistant director Social Action Dept. USCC, 1967 69; executive director Texas Catholic Conference; ord. titular bp. of Pedena and aux. bp. of Galveston Houston, Mar. 14, 1979; app. bp. of Austin, Dec. 19, 1985, inst., Feb. 25, 1986; res., Jan. 2, 2001.

McCormack, John B.: b Aug. 12, 1935, Winthrop, MA; educ. St. John Seminary College and St. John Seminary Theologate (Boston, MA); ord. priest (Boston*), Feb. 2, 1960; ord. titular bp. of Cerbali and aux. bp. of Boston, Dec. 27, 1995; app. bp. of Manchester, NH, July 21, 1998, inst., Sept. 22, 1998.

McCormack, William J.: b. Jan. 24, 1924, New York, NY; educ. Christ the King Seminary, St. Bonaventure Univ. (St. Bonaventure, NY); ord. priest (New York*),

Feb. 21, 1959; national director of Society for the Propagation of the Faith, 1980; ord. titular bp. of Nicives and aux. bp. of New York, Jan. 6, 1987; res., Oct. 31, 2001.

McDonald, Andrew J.: b. Oct. 24, 1923, Savannah, GA; educ. St. Mary's Seminary (Baltimore, MD), Catholic Univ. (Washington, DC), Lateran Univ. (Rome); ord. priest (Savannah), May 8, 1948; ord. bp. of Little Rock, Sept. 5, 1972; res., Jan. 4, 2000.

McDonnell, Charles J.: b. July 7, 1928, Brooklyn, NY; educ. Seton Hall Univ. (South Orange, NJ), Immaculate Conception Seminary (Darlington, NJ), Long Island Univ. (Brooklyn, NY); ord. priest (Newark*), May 29, 1954; U.S. Army Chaplain, 1965 89; ret., from active duty with rank of Brigadier General; ord. titular bp. of Pocofelto and aux. bp. of Newark, May 12, 1994; ret. May 21, 2004.

McDonnell, Timothy A.: b. Dec. 23, 1937, New York City; educ. St. Joseph Seminary, Yonkers, Iona College, New Rochelle; ord. priest (New York*), June 1, 1963; ord. titular bp. of Semina and aux. bp. of New York, Dec. 12, 2001; app. bp. of Springfield in Massachusetts, Mar. 9, 2004.

McElroy, Robert W.: b. Feb. 5, 1954, San Francisco, CA; educ. St. Patrick Seminary (Menlo Park, CA), Harvard Univ. (Cambridge, MA), Stanford Univ. (Palo Alto, CA), Jesuit School of Theology (Berkeley, CA), North American College (Rome); ord. priest, Apr. 12, 1980 (San Francisco*); app. titular bp. of Gemellae in Byzacena and aux. bp. of San Francisco, July 6, 2010; ord. bp. Sept. 7, 2010.

McGrath, Patrick J.: b. July 11, 1945, Dublin, Ire.; educ. St. John's College Seminary (Waterford), Lateran Univ. (Rome, Italy); ord. priest in Ireland, June 7, 1970; came to U.S. same year and became San Francisco archdiocesan priest; ord. titular bp. of Allegheny and aux. bp. of San Francisco, Jan. 25, 1989; app. coadj. bp. of San Jose, June 30, 1998; bp. of San Jose, Nov. 29, 1999.

McIntyre, John J.: b. Aug. 20, 1963, Philadelphia, PA; educ. St. Alphonsus Seminary (Suffield, CT), St. Charles Borromeo Seminary (Obervbrook, PA); ord. priest, May 16, 1992 (Philadelphia*); sec. to Card. Justin Rigali, 1999-2010; app. titular bp. of Bononia and aux. bp. of Philadelphia, June 8, 2010; ord. bp. Aug. 6, 2010.

McLaughlin, Bernard J.: b. Nov. 19, 1912, Buffalo, NY; educ. Urban Univ. (Rome, Italy); ord. priest (Buffalo), Dec. 21, 1935, at Rome; ord. titular bp. of Mottola and aux. bp. of Buffalo, Jan. 6, 1969; res., Jan. 5, 1988.

McManus, Robert J.: b. July 5, 1951, Warwick, RI; educ. Our Lady of Providence Seminary, Catholic Univ. (Washington, DC), Seminary of Toronto, Canada, Pontifical Gregorian Univ. (Rome); ord. priest (Providence), May 27, 1978; diocesan Vicar for Education and Rector of Our Lady of Providence; app. titular bp. of Allegheny and aux. of Providence, Dec. 1, 1998, ord., Feb. 22, 1999; app. bp. of Worcester, Mar. 9, 2004.

McNabb, John C., O.S.A.: b. Dec. 11, 1925, Beloit, WI; educ. Villanova Univ. (Villanova, PA), Augustinian College and Catholic Univ. (Washington, DC), De Paul Univ. (Chicago, IL); ord. priest, May 24, 1952; ord. titular bp. of Saia Maggiore, June 17, 1967 (resigned titular see, Dec. 27, 1977); prelate of Chulucanas, Peru, 1967; first bp. of Chulucanas, Dec. 12, 1988; ret. Oct. 28, 2000.

McNaughton, William J., M.M.: b. Dec. 7, 1926, Lawrence, MA; educ. Maryknoll Seminary (Maryknoll, NY); ord. priest, June 13, 1953; ord. titular bp. of Thuburbo Minus and vicar apostolic of Inchon, Korea, Aug. 24, 1961; first bp. of Inchon, Mar. 10, 1962, when vicariate was raised to diocese; ret. Apr. 25, 2002.

McRaith, John Jeremiah: b. Dec. 6, 1934, Hutchinson,

MN; educ. St. John Preparatory School (Collegeville, MN), Loras College, St. Bernard Seminary (Dubuque, IA); ord. priest (New Ulm), Feb. 21, 1960; exec. dir. of Catholic Rural Life Conference, 1971 78; ord. bp. of Owensboro, KY, Dec. 15, 1982; ret. Jan. 5, 2009.

Madden, Denis J.: b. Mar. 8, 1940, Carbondale, Pa.; educ. Univ. of Notre Dame, Univ. of Maryland; ord. priest Apr. 1, 1967 (Benedictines); inc. Baltimore Nov. 4, 1976; app. aux. bp. of Baltimore and tit. bp. of Baia, May 10, 2005; ord. bp. Aug. 24, 2005.

Madera, Joseph J., M.Sp.S.: b. Nov. 27, 1927, San Francisco, CA; educ. Domus Studiorum of the Missionaries of the Holy Spirit (Coyoacan, D.F. Mexico); ord. priest, June 15, 1957; ord. coadj. bp. of Fresno, Mar. 4, 1980; bp. of Fresno, July 1, 1980; app. titular bp. of Orte and aux. of Military Services archdiocese, June 30, 1991; ret. Sept. 15, 2004.

Maginnis, Robert P.: b. Dec. 22, 1933, Philadelphia, PA; educ. St. Charles Borromeo Seminary (Overbrook, PA), ord. priest (Philadelphia*), May 13, 1961; ord. titular bp. of Siminina and aux. bp. of Philadelphia, Mar. 11, 1996.

Maguire, Joseph F.: b. Sept. 4, 1919, Boston, MA; educ. Boston College, St. John's Seminary (Boston, MA); ord. priest (Boston*), June 29, 1945; ord. titular bp. of Macteris and aux. bp. of Boston, Feb. 2, 1972; app. coadj. bp. of Springfield, MA, Apr. 13, 1976; succeeded as bp. of Springfield, MA, Oct. 15, 1977; ret., Dec. 27, 1991.

Mahony, Roger M.: (See **Cardinals, Biographies.**)

Maida, Adam J.: (See **Cardinals, Biographies.**)

Malloy, David J.: b. Feb. 3, 1956, Milwaukee, WI; educ. St. Francis de Sales Seminary (Milwaukee, WI), North American College, Pontifical University of St. Thomas, and Pontifical Gregorian University (Rome, Italy); ord. priest (Milwaukee*), July 1, 1983; entered the Pontifical Ecclesiastical Academy and served as secretary to the apostolic nunciatures in Pakistan and Syria and the Mission of the Holy See to the United Nations in New York; served in the Prefecture of the Papal Household in Rome, 1998-2001; USCCB Associate General Secretary, 2001-2006; USCCB General Secretary, 2006-2011; app. bp. of Rockford, Mar. 20, 2012; ord. bp., May 14, 2012.

Malone, Richard J.: b. Mar. 19, 1946, Salem, MA; educ. St. John's Seminary, Brighton, Boston Univ., ord. priest (Boston*), May 20, 1972; app. titular bp. of Aptuca and aux. bp. of Boston, Jan. 27, 2000, ord., Mar. 1, 2000; app. bp. of Portland, ME, Feb. 10, 2004; app. bp. of Buffalo, May 29, 2012.

Malooly, William Francis: b. Jan. 18, 1944, Baltimore; educ. St. Charles Minor Seminary, St. Mary's Seminary (Baltimore); ord priest (Baltimore*), May 7, 1970, app. titular bp. of Flumenzer and aux. bp. of Baltimore, Dec. 12, 2000, ord., Mar. 1, 2001; app. bp. of Wilmington, July 7, 2008.

Manning, Elias (James), O.F.M. Conv.: b. Apr. 14, 1938, Troy, NY; educ. Sao José Seminary (Rio de Janeiro, Brazil); ord. priest, Oct. 30, 1965, in New York; ord. bp. of Valença, Brazil, May 13, 1990.

Manning, Thomas R., O.F.M.: b. Aug. 29, 1922, Baltimore, MD; educ. Duns Scotus College (Southfield, MI), Holy Name College (Washington, DC); ord. priest, June 5, 1948; ord. titular bp. of Arsamosata, July 14, 1959 (res. titular see, Dec. 30, 1977); prelate of Coroico, Bolivia, July 14, 1959; became first bp., 1983, when prelature was raised to diocese; ret., Oct. 9, 1996.

Mansell, Henry J.: b. Oct. 10, 1937, New York, NY; educ. Cathedral College, St. Joseph's Seminary and College (New York); North American College, Gregorian Univ. (Rome); ord. priest (New York*), Dec. 19, 1962; ord. titular bp. of Marazane and aux. bp. of New York, Jan. 6, 1993, by John Paul II in Vatican City; app. bp. of Buffalo, Apr. 18, 1995; inst., June 12, 1995; app. abp. of Hartford, Oct. 20, 2003.

Mansour, Gregory John: b. Nov. 11, 1955, Flint, MI; educ. Univ. of Michigan (Kalamazoo, MI), Catholic Univ. of America (Washington, DC), North American College and Pontifical Gregorian Univ. (Rome); ord. priest (Eparchy of St. Maron of Brooklyn), Sept. 18, 1982; app. bp. of the Eparchy of St. Maron, Brooklyn, NY, Jan. 10, 2004.

Manz, John R.: b. Nov. 14, 1945, Chicago, IL; educ. Niles College Seminary (Niles, IL), Univ. of St. Mary of the Lake Mundelein Seminary (Chicago); ord. priest (Chicago*), May 12, 1971; ord. titular bp. of Mulia and aux. bp. of Chicago, Mar. 5, 1996.

Marconi, Dominic A.: b. Mar. 13, 1927, Newark, NJ; educ. Seton Hall Univ. (S. Orange, NJ), Immaculate Conception Seminary (Darlington, NJ), Catholic Univ. (Washington, DC); ord. priest (Newark*), May 30, 1953; ord. titular bp. of Bure and aux. bp. of Newark, June 25, 1976; res., July 1, 2002.

Marino, Joseph: b. Jan. 23, 1953, Birmingham, AL; educ. Pontifical North American College and Pontifical Gregorian Univ. (Rome); ord. priest, Aug. 25, 1979 (Birmingham); studies at the Pontifical Ecclesiastical Academy, entered papal diplomatic service in 1988; diplomatic posts in the Philippines, Uruguay, Nigeria, Great Britain, and the Secretariat of State in Rome; app. apostolic nuncio to Bangladesh and titular abp. of Natchitoches, Jan. 12, 2008; ord. Mar. 29, 2008; app. nuncio to Malaysia, East Timor, and Brunei.

Martino, Joseph F.: b. May 1, 1946, Philadelphia, PA; educ. St. Charles Borromeo Seminary (Overbrook, PA), Gregorian Univ. (Rome); ord. priest (Philadelphia*), Dec. 18, 1970; ord. titular bp. of Cellae in Mauretania and aux. bp. of Philadelphia, Mar. 11, 1996; app. bp. of Scranton, July 25, 2003; res. Aug. 31, 2009.

Matano, Salvatore R.: b. Sept. 15, 1946, Providence, RI; educ. Our Lady of Providence Seminary College (Warwick, RI), Gregorian Univ. (Rome); ord. priest Dec. 17, 1971 (Providence); served on staff of apostolic nunciature (Washington, DC); app. coadj. bp. of Burlington Mar. 3, 2005; ord. Apr. 19, 2005; bp. of Burlington, Nov. 9, 2005.

Medley, William F.: b. Sept. 17, 1952, Marion County, Kentucky; educ. Bellarmine Univ. (Louisville, KY), St. Meinrad School of Theology (St. Meinrad, IN); ord. priest (Louisville), May 22, 1982; app. bp. of Owensboro, Dec. 15, 2009; ord. Feb. 10, 2010.

Melczek, Dale J.: b. Nov. 9, 1938, Detroit, MI; educ. St. Mary's College (Orchard Lake, MI), St. John's Provincial Seminary (Plymouth, MI), Univ. of Detroit; ord. priest (Detroit*), June 6, 1964; ord. titular bp. of Trau and aux. bp. of Detroit, Jan. 27, 1983; apostolic administrator of Gary, Aug. 19, 1992; coadjutor bp. of Gary, Oct. 28, 1995; bp. of Gary, June 1, 1996.

Mengeling, Carl F.: b. Oct. 22, 1930, Hammond, IN; educ. St. Meinrad College and Seminary (St. Meinrad, IN), Alphonsianum Univ. (Rome); ord. priest (Gary), May 25, 1957; ord. bp. of Lansing, Jan. 25, 1996; ret. Feb. 27, 2008.

Michaels, James E., S.S.C.: b. May 30, 1926, Chicago, IL; educ. Columban Seminary (St. Columban, NE), Gregorian Univ. (Rome); ord. priest, Dec. 21, 1951; ord. titular bp. of Verbe and aux. bp. of Kwang Ju, Korea, Apr. 14, 1966; app. aux. bp. of Wheeling, Apr. 3, 1973 (title of see changed to Wheeling-Charleston, 1974); res., Sept. 22, 1987.

Miller, J. Michael, C.S.B.: b. July 9, 1946, Ottawa, Canada; educ. St. Michael's College, Univ. of Toronto (Toronto, Canada), Gregorian Univ. (Rome); ord. priest (Congregation of St. Basil), June 29, 1975, Congregation of St. Basil; official in Secretariat of State, Rome, 1992-97; pres. of Univ. of St. Thomas Aquinas, Houston, Texas, 1997-2004; 2004; app.titular abp. of Vertara and sec. of the Cong. for Catholic Education, Rome, Nov. 25, 2003; app. coadj. abp. of Vancouver, June 1, 2007.

Milone, Anthony M.: b. Sept. 24, 1932, Omaha, NE; educ. North American College (Rome); ord. priest (Omaha*), Dec. 15, 1957, in Rome; ord. titular bp. of Plestia and aux. bp. of Omaha, Jan. 6, 1982; app. bp. of Great Falls Billings, Dec. 14, 1987, inst., Feb. 23, 1988; ret. July 12, 2006.

Monforton, Jeffrey M.: b. May 5, 1963, Detroit, MI; educ. Wayne State University, Sacred Heart Major Seminary (Detroit, MI), Pontifical North American College and Pontifical Gregorian University (Rome); ord. priest (Detroit*), June 25, 1994; sec. to Cardinal Adam Maida, 1998-2005; served as an apostolic visitor by the Congregation for Catholic Education in the apostolic visitation of U.S. seminaries and houses of formation, 2005-2006; rector of Sacred Heart Major Seminary, 2006; app. bp. of Steubenville, July 3, 2012; ord., Sept. 12, 2012.

Morin, Roger Paul: b. Mar. 7, 1941, Lowell, MA; educ. Notre Dame Seminary (New Orleans, LA), Tulane Univ. (New Orleans, LA); ord. priest, Apr. 15, 1971 (New Orleans*); app. aux. bp. of New Orleans and titular bp. of Aulona, Feb. 11, 2003; ord., Apr. 22, 2003; bp. of Biloxi, Mar. 2, 2009.

Morlino, Robert C.: b. Dec. 31, 1946, Scranton, PA; educ. Fordham Univ., Univ. of Notre Dame, Weston School of Theology, Cambridge, MA, Gregorian Univ., Rome; ord. priest for the Society for Jesus, Maryland Province, June 1, 1974, incardinated into the Diocese of Kalamazoo, MI, Oct. 26, 1983, app. bp. of Helena, July 6, 1999, inst,. Sept. 21, 1999; app. bp. of Madison, May 23, 2003.

Morneau, Robert F.: b. Sept. 10, 1938, New London, WI; educ. St. Norbert's College (De Pere, WI), Sacred Heart Seminary (Oneida, WI), Catholic Univ. (Washington, DC); ord. priest (Green Bay), May 28, 1966; ord. titular bp. of Massa Lubrense and aux. bp. of Green Bay, Feb. 22, 1979.

Moskal, Robert M.: b. Oct. 24, 1937, Carnegie, PA; educ. St. Basil Minor Seminary (Stamford, CT), St. Josaphat Seminary and Catholic Univ. (Washington, DC); ord. priest (Philadelphia*, Byzantine Ukrainian), Mar. 25, 1963; ord. titular bp. of Agatopoli and aux. bp. of the Ukrainian archeparchy of Philadelphia, Oct. 13, 1981; app. first bp. of St. Josaphat in Parma, Dec. 5, 1983; ret. July 29, 2009.

Mouradian, Mikael A.: b. July 5, 1961, Beirut, Lebanon; ord. priest, (Institute of the Patriarchal Clergy of Bzommar, Oct. 24, 1987; app. eparch of Our Lady of Nareg, May 21, 2011; ord. bp. Oct. 2, 2011; inst. Oct. 2, 2011.

Moynihan, James M.: b. July 16, 1932, Rochester, NY; educ. St. Bernard's Seminary (Rochester, NY), North American College and Gregorian Univ. (Rome); ord. priest (Rochester), Dec. 15, 1957, in Rome; ord. bp. of Syracuse, May 29, 1995; ret. Apr. 21, 2009.

Muench Robert W.: b. Dec. 28, 1942, Louisville, KY; educ. St. Joseph Seminary and Notre Dame Seminary (New Orleans, LA), Catholic Univ. (Washington, DC); ord. priest (New Orleans*), June 18, 1968; ord. titular bp of Mactaris and aux. bp. of New Orleans, June 29, 1990; app. bp. of Covington Jan., 1996; inst., Mar. 19, 1996 app. bp. of Baton Rouge, Dec. 15, 2001.

Mulvee, Robert E.: b. Feb. 15, 1930, Boston, MA; educ

St. Thomas Seminary (Bloomfield, CT), Univ. Seminary (Ottawa, ON), American College (Louvain, Belgium), Lateran Univ. (Rome); ord. priest (Manchester), June 30, 1957; ord. titular bp. of Summa and aux. bp. of Manchester, NH, Apr. 14, 1977; app. bp. of Wilmington, Del., Feb. 19, 1985; app. coadj. bp. of Providence, Feb. 9, 1995; bp. of Providence, June 11, 1997; ret. Mar. 31, 2005.

Mulvey, William M.: b. Aug. 23, 1949, (Houston, TX); educ. St. Edward's Univ. (Austin, TX), North American College, Pontifical Univ. of St. Thomas Aquinas, and Pontifical Gregorian Univ. (Rome); ord. priest (Austin), July 29, 1975; app. bp. of Corpus Christi, Jan. 10, 2010; ord. Mar. 25, 2010.

Murphy, William F.: b. May 14, 1940, Boston MA; educ. Boston Latin School (Boston), Harvard College, St. John's Seminary (Boston), Gregorian Univ. (Rome); ord. priest (Boston*), Dec. 16, 1964; ord. titular bp. of Saia Maggiore and aux. bp. of Boston, Dec. 27, 1995; app. bp. of Rockville Centre, June 25, 2001, inst., Sept. 5, 2001.

Murray, James A.: b. July 5, 1932, Jackson, MI; educ. Sacred Heart Seminary Detroit, St. John Provincial Seminary (Plymouth, MI), Catholic Univ. of America; ord. priest (Lansing), June 7, 1958; app. bp. of Kalamazoo, Nov. 18, 1997, ord., Jan. 27, 1998; ret. Apr. 6, 2009.

Murry, George V., S.J.: b. Dec. 28, 1948, Camden, NJ; educ. St. Joseph's College (Philadelphia, PA), St. Thomas Seminary (Bloomfield, CT), St. Mary Seminary (Baltimore, MD), Jesuit School of Theology (Berkeley, CA), George Washington Univ. (Washington, DC); entered Jesuits 1972; ord. priest, June 9, 1979; ord. titular bp. of Fuerteventura and aux. bp. of Chicago, Mar. 20, 1995; app. co-adjutor of St. Thomas in the Virgin Islands, May 5, 1998; bp. of St. Thomas in the Virgin Islands, June 30, 1999; bp. of Youngstown, Jan. 30, 2007.

Myers, John Joseph: b. July 26, 1941, Ottawa, IL; educ. Loras College (Dubuque, IA), North American College and Gregorian Univ. (Rome), Catholic Univ. of America (Washington, DC); ord. priest (Peoria), Dec. 17, 1966, in Rome; ord. coadj. bp. of Peoria, Sept. 3, 1987; bp. of Peoria, Jan. 23, 1990; app. abp. of Newark, July 24, 2001.

N

Naickamparampil, Thomas: b. Mylapra, India, June 6, 1961; educ. St. Aloysious Minor Seminary, (Pattom, Trivandrum, India), Papal Seminary of Pune (Pune, India); Gregorian Univ. (Rome); ord. priest (Trivandrum*), Dec. 29, 1986; app. first apostolic exarchate for the Syro-Malankara Catholic Church in the United States and apostolic visitor for the Syro-Malankara Catholics in Canada and Europe; ord. bp. Sept. 21, 2010.

Naumann, Joseph F.: b. June 4, 1949, St. Louis, MO; educ. Cardinal Glennon Seminary College and Kenrick Seminary (St. Louis, MO); ord. priest (St. Louis*), 1975; app. titular bp. of Caput Cilla and aux. bp. of St. Louis, July 9, 1997; app. coadj. abp. of Kansas City, Jan. 7, 2004; abp. of Kansas City, Jan. 15, 2005.

Nevares, Eduardo: b. Feb. 19, 1954, San Antonio, TX; educ.: LaSalette Minor Seminary (Jefferson City, MO), St. Henry Preparatory Seminary (Belleville, IL), LaSalette Junior College Seminary and LaSalette Senior College Seminary (Ipswich, MA), Univ. of St. Thomas (Houston, TX); entered the novitiate of the Missionaries of Our Lady of LaSalette in 1976, professed first vows in 1977, and final vows in 1980; ord. priest, July 18, 1981; app. auxiliary bp. of Phoenix and titular bp. of Natchez, May 11, 2010.

Nevins, John J.: b. Jan. 19, 1932, New Rochelle, NY; educ. Iona College (New Rochelle, NY), Catholic Univ. (Washington, DC); ord. priest (Miami*), June 6, 1959; ord. titular bp. of Rusticana and aux. bp. of Miami, Mar. 24, 1979; app. first bp. of Venice, FL, July 17, 1984; inst., Oct. 25, 1984; ret. Jan. 19, 2007.

Newman, William C.: b. Aug. 16, 1928, Baltimore, MD; educ. St. Mary Seminary (Baltimore, MD), Catholic Univ. (Washington, DC), Loyola College (Baltimore, MD); ord. priest (Baltimore*), May 29, 1954; ord. titular bp. of Numluli and aux. bp. of Baltimore, July 2, 1984; ret. Aug. 28, 2003.

Nickless, R. Walker: b. May 28, 1947, Denver; educ. St. Thomas Seminary, Univ. of Denver, Gregorian Univ. (Rome); ord. priest Aug. 4, 1973 (Denver); app. bp. of Sioux City, Iowa, Nov. 10, 2005; ord. bp. Jan. 20, 2006.

Niederauer, George H.: b. June 14, 1936, Los Angeles, CA; educ. St. John's Seminary (Camarillo, CA), Catholic Univ. (Washington, DC), Loyola Univ. of Los Angeles, Univ. of Southern CA, Loretta Heights College (Denver, CO); ord. priest (Los Angeles*), Apr. 30, 1962; app. bp. of Salt Lake City, Nov. 3, 1994, ord., Jan. 25, 1995; app. Abp. of San Francisco, Dec. 15, 2005; ret. July 27, 2012.

Nienstedt, John C.: b. Mar. 18, 1947, Detroit, MI; educ. Sacred Heart Seminary (Detroit), North American College, Gregorian Univ., Alphonsianum (Rome); ord. priest (Detroit*), July 27, 1974; served in Vatican Secretariat of State, 1980 86; rector of Sacred Heart Seminary (Detroit), 1988 94; pastor of the Shrine of the Little Flower (Royal Oak, MI), 1994; ord. titular bp. of Alton and aux. bp. of Detroit, July 9, 1996; app. bp. of New Ulm, June 12, 2001, inst., Aug. 6, 2001; app. coadj. abp. of St. Paul-Minneapolis, Apr. 24, 2007; acceded to the see, May 2, 2008.

Noonan, John G.: b. Feb. 26, 1951, Limerick, Ireland; educ. St. John Vianney College Seminary (Miami), St. Vincent de Paul Seminary (Boynton Beach, Fla.); app. aux. bp. Miami June 21, 2005; ord. bp. Aug. 24, 2005; app. bp. Of Orlando, Dec. 16, 2010.

Novak, Alfred, C.Ss.R.: b. June 2, 1930, Dwight, NE; educ. Immaculate Conception Seminary (Oconomowoc, WI); ord. priest, July 2, 1956; ord. titular bp. of Vardimissa and aux. bp. of Sao Paulo, Brazil, May 25, 1979; bp. of Paranagua, Brazil, Mar. 14, 1989; ret. Aug. 2, 2006.

O

O'Brien, Edwin F.: (See **Cardinals' Biographies**).

O'Brien, Thomas Joseph: b. Nov. 29, 1935, Indianapolis, IN; educ. St. Meinrad High School Seminary, St. Meinrad College Seminary (St. Meinrad, IN); ord. priest (Tucson), May 7, 1961; ord. bp. of Phoenix, Jan. 6, 1982; res., June 18, 2003.

Ochoa, Armando: b. Apr. 3, 1943, Oxnard, CA; educ. Ventura College (Ventura, CA), St. John's College and St. John's Seminary (Camarillo, CA); ord. priest (Los Angeles*), May 23, 1970; ord. titular bp. of Sitifi and aux. bp. of Los Angeles, Feb. 23, 1987; app. bp. of El Paso, Apr. 1, 1996; inst., June 26, 1996; app. bp. of Fresno, Dec. 1, 2011; inst. Feb. 2, 2012.

O'Connell, C.M., David M.: b.: Apr. 21, 1955, Philadelphia, PA; educ.: Niagara Univ. (Niagara, NY), Mary Immaculate Seminary (Northhampton, PA); Catholic Univ. of America (Washington, D.C.); ord. priest for the Congregation of the Missions, May 29, 1982; held various academic posts at Mary Immaculate Seminary and St. John's Univ.; president of Catholic Univ. of America 1998-2010; app. coadj. bp. of Toledo,

June 4, 2010; acceded to see, Dec. 1, 2010.

Olivier, Leonard J., S.V.D.: b. Oct. 12, 1923, Lake Charles, LA; educ. St. Augustine Major Seminary (Bay St. Louis, MS), Catholic Univ. (Washington, DC), Loyola Univ. (New Orleans, LA); ord. priest, June 29, 1951; ord. titular bp. of Leges in Numidia and aux. bp. of Washington, Dec. 20, 1988; ret. May 18, 2004.

Olmsted, Thomas J.: b. Jan. 21, 1947, Oketo, KS; educ. St. Thomas Seminary (Denver), North American College and Pontifical Gregorian Univ. (Rome); ord. priest (Lincoln), July 2, 1973; served in Vatican Secretariat of State, 1979-1988; Dean of Formation, Pontifical College Josephinum, Columbus, OH, 1993, President and Rector, Pontifical College, Josephinum, 1997; app. coadjutor bp. of Wichita, Feb. 16, 1999, ord., Apr. 20, 1999; bp. of Wichita, Oct. 4, 2001; app. bp. of Phoenix, Nov. 25, 2003.

O'Malley, Sean, O.F.M.Cap.: (See **Cardinals' Biographies**).

Ottenweller, Albert H.: b. Apr. 5, 1916, Stanford, MT; educ. St. Joseph's Seminary (Rensselaer, IN), Catholic Univ. (Washington, DC); ord. priest (Toledo), June 19, 1943; ord. titular bp. of Perdices and aux. bp. of Toledo, May 29, 1974; app. bp. of Steubenville, OH, Oct. 11, 1977, inst., Nov. 22, 1977; ret., Jan. 28, 1992.

P

Paprocki, Thomas J.: b. Aug. 5, 1952, Chicago, IL; educ. Niles College of Loyola (Chicago, IL), St. Mary of the Lake Seminary (Chicago, IL), DePaul Univ. College of Law (Chicago, IL), Gregorian Univ. (Rome); ord. priest, May 10, 1978 (Chicago*); app. aux. bp. of Chicago and titular bp. of Vulturara, Jan. 24, 2003; ord., Mar. 19, 2003; app. bp. of Springfield, Apr. 20, 2010; inst. June 22, 2010.

Parkes, Gregory L.: b. Apr. 2, 1964, Mineola, New York; educ. Florida State University (Tallahassee, FL), St. Vincent de Paul Seminary (Boynton Beach, FL), Pontifical North American College and Pontifical Gregorian University (Rome, Italy); ord. priest (Orlando), June 26, 1999; app. bp. of Pensacola-Tallahassee, Mar. 20, 2012; ord. bp., June 12, 2012.

Pates, Richard E.: b. Feb. 12, 1943, St. Paul; educ. St. Paul Seminary, North American College (Rome); ord. priest (St. Paul and Minneapolis*), Dec. 20, 1968; staff, Apostolic Nunciature, Washington, 1975-81; app. titular bp. of Suacia and aux. bp. of St. Paul and Minneapolis, Dec. 22, 2000, ord., Mar. 26, 2001; app. bp. of Des Monies, Apr. 10, 2008; inst. May 29, 2008.

Pearce, George H., S.M.: b. Jan. 9, 1921, Brighton, MA; educ. Marist College and Seminary (Framington, MA); ord. priest, Feb. 2, 1947; ord. titular bp. of Attalea in Pamphylia and vicar apostolic of the Samoa and Tokelau Islands, June 29, 1956; title changed to bp. of Apia, June 21, 1966; app. abp. of Suva, Fiji Islands, June 22, 1967; res., Apr. 10, 1976.

Peña, Raymundo J.: b. Feb. 19, 1934, Robstown, TX; educ. Assumption Seminary (San Antonio, TX); ord. priest (Corpus Christi), May 25, 1957; ord. titular bp. of Trisipa and aux. bp. of San Antonio, Dec. 13, 1976; app. bp. of El Paso, Apr. 29, 1980; app. bp. of Brownsville, May 23, 1995; ret. Dec. 9, 2009.

Pepe, Joseph A.: b. June 18, 1942, Philadelphia; educ. St. Charles Borromeo Seminary, Univ. of St. Thomas (Rome); ord. priest (Philadelphia*), May 16, 1970; app. bp. of Las Vegas, April 6, 2001, ord., May 31, 2001.

Perez, Nelson J.: b. Miami, FL, June 16, 1961; educ. Montclair State College, St. Charles Borromeo Seminary (Philadelphia, PA); ord. priest. (Philadelphia*), May 20, 1989; app. aux. bp. of Rockville Center and titular bp. of

Catrum, June 8, 2012; ord. bp., July 25, 2012.

Perry, Joseph N.: b. Apr. 18, 1948, Chicago, IL; educ. Capuchin Seminary of St. Lawrence, (Milwaukee), St. Mary Capuchin Seminary, Crown Point, (IN), St. Francis Seminary (Milwaukee), Catholic Univ. of America (Washington, DC); ord. priest (Milwaukee*), May 24, 1975; app. titular bp. of Lead and aux. bp. of Chicago, May 5, 1998; ord., June 29, 1998.

Persico, Lawrence T.: b. Monessesn, PA, Nov. 21, 1950; educ. Seminary of St. Pius X (Erlanger, KY), St. Vincent Seminary (Latrobe, PA), The Catholic University of America, Washington, D.C.; ord. priest, Apr. 30, 1977 (Greensburg); served as chancellor and vicar general of Greensburg and also vice-president of the Pennsylvania Catholic Conference (2006-2012); app. bp. of Erie, July 31, 2012; ord., Oct. 1, 2012.

Pevec, A. Edward: b. Apr. 16, 1925, Cleveland, OH; educ. St. Mary's Seminary, John Carroll Univ. (Cleveland, OH); ord. priest (Cleveland), Apr. 29, 1950; ord. titular bp. of Mercia and aux. bp. of Cleveland, July 2, 1982; res., Apr. 3, 2001.

Pfeifer, Michael, O.M.I.: b. May 18, 1937, Alamo, TX; educ. Oblate school of theology (San Antonio, TX); ord. priest, Dec. 21, 1964; provincial of southern province of Oblates of Mary Immaculate, 1981; ord. bp. of San Angelo, July 26, 1985.

Piché, Lee Anthony: b. May 8, 1958, Minneapolis, MN; educ. St. Paul Seminary and St. Thomas College (St. Paul, MN), St. Joseph Seminary (Princeton N.J.), Columbia Univ. (New York); ord. priest, May 26, 1984 (St. Paul and Minneapolis*); app. aux. bp. of Minneapolis and St. Paul and titular bp. of Tamata, May 27, 2009; ord. June 29, 2009.

Pilarczyk, Daniel E.: b. Aug. 12, 1934, Dayton, OH; educ. St. Gregory's Seminary (Cincinnati, OH), Urban Univ. (Rome), Xavier Univ. and Univ. of Cincinnati (Cincinnati, OH); ord. priest (Cincinnati*), Dec. 20, 1959; ord. titular bp. of Hodelm and aux. bp. of Cincinnati, Dec. 20, 1974; app. abp. of Cincinnati, Oct. 30, 1982; inst., Dec. 20, 1982; president of NCCB/USCC, 1989 92; ret. Dec. 21, 2009.

Pilla, Anthony M.: b. Nov. 12, 1932, Cleveland, OH; educ. St. Gregory College Seminary (Cincinnati, OH), Borromec College Seminary (Wickliffe, OH), St. Mary Seminary and John Carroll Univ. (Cleveland, OH); ord. priest (Cleveland) May 23, 1959; ord. titular bp. of Scardona and aux. bp of Cleveland, Aug. 1, 1979; app. apostolic admin. of Cleveland, 1980; bp. of Cleveland, Nov. 13, 1980. President of NCCB/USCC, 1995 98; res. Apr. 4, 2006.

Popp, Bernard F.: b. Dec. 6, 1917, Nada, TX; educ. St. John's Seminary and St. Mary's Univ. (San Antonio, TX); ord. priest (San Antonio*), Feb. 24, 1943; ord. titular bp. of Capsus and aux. bp. of San Antonio, July 25, 1983; ret., Mar. 23, 1993.

Potocnak, Joseph J., S.C.J.: b. May 13, 1933, Berwick, PA; educ. Dehon Seminary (Great Barrington, MA), Kilroe Seminary (Honesdale, PA), Sacred Heart (Hales Corners, WI); ord. priest, Sept 21, 1966; missionary in South Africa from 1973; ord. bp. of De Aar, South Africa, May 1, 1992.

Provost, Glen J.: b. Aug. 9, 1949, Lafayette, La.; educ. Immaculata Seminary (Lafayette), St. Joseph Seminary College (St. Benedict, La.), Pontifical North America College (Rome), Univ. of South Louisiana (Lafayette, La.); ord. June 29, 1975 (Lafayette); app. bp. of Lake Charles, Mar. 6, 2007; ord. bp. Apr. 23, 2007.

Q

Quinn, Alexander James: b. Apr. 8, 1932, Cleveland,

OH; educ. St. Charles College (Catonsville, MD), St. Mary Seminary (Cleveland, OH), Lateran Univ. (Rome), Cleveland State Univ.; ord. priest (Cleveland), May 24, 1958; ord. titular bp. of Socia and aux. bp. of Cleveland, Dec. 5, 1983; ret. June 14, 2008.

Quinn, Francis A.: b. Sept. 11, 1921, Los Angeles, CA; educ. St. Joseph's College (Mountain View, CA), St. Patrick's Seminary (Menlo Park, CA), Catholic Univ. (Washington, DC); Univ. of CA (Berkeley); ord. priest (San Francisco*), June 15, 1946; ord. titular bp. of Numana and aux. bp. of San Francisco, June 29, 1978; app. bp. of Sacramento, Dec. 18, 1979; ret., Nov. 30, 1993.

Quinn, John M.: b. Dec. 17, 1945, Detroit; educ. Sacred Heart Seminary, St. John Provincial Seminary, Univ. of Detroit and Catholic Univ. of America (Washington, D.C.); ord. priest, Mar. 17, 1972; app. aux. bp. of Detroit and titular bp. of Ressiana, July 7, 2003; app. coadj. bp. of Winona, Oct. 15, 2008; bp. of Winona, May 7, 2009.

Quinn, John R.: b. Mar. 28, 1929, Riverside, CA; educ. St. Francis Seminary (El Cajon, CA), North American College (Rome); ord. priest (San Diego), July 19, 1953; ord. titular bp. of Thisiduo and aux. bp. of San Diego, Dec. 12, 1967; bp. of Oklahoma City and Tulsa, Nov. 30, 1971; first abp. of Oklahoma City, Dec. 19, 1972; app. abp. of San Francisco, Feb. 22, 1977, inst., Apr. 26, 1977; president NCCB/USCC, 1977 80; res., see Dec. 27, 1995.

R

Ramirez, Ricardo, C.S.B.: b. Sept. 12, 1936, Bay City, TX; educ. Univ. of St. Thomas (Houston, TX), Univ. of Detroit (Detroit, MI), St. Basil's Seminary (Toronto, ON), Seminario Concilium (Mexico City, Mexico), East Asian Pastoral Institute (Manila, Philippines); ord. priest, Dec. 10, 1966; ord titular bp. of Vatarba and aux. of San Antonio, Dec. 6, 1981; app. first bp. of Las Cruces, NM, Aug. 17, 1982; inst., Oct. 18, 1982; ret. Jan. 10, 2013.

Rassas, George J.: b. Baltimore May 26, 1942; educ. Univ. of St. Mary of the Lake (Mundelein, IL), Loyola Univ. (Chicago); ord. priest May 2, 1968 (Chicago); app. aux. bp. Chicago and tit. bp. of Reperi Dec. 1, 2005; ord. bp. Feb. 2, 2006.

Reichert, Stephen J., O.F.M. Cap.: b. May 14, 1943, Leoville, KS; educ. Capuchin minor seminary (Victoria, KS), St. Fidelis College (Hermann, PA), Capuchin College (Washington, DC); ord. priest, Sept. 27, 1969; missionary in Papua New Guinea since 1970; ord. bp. of Mendi, Papua New Guinea, May 7, 1995; app. abp. of Madang, Papua New Guinea, Nov. 30, 2010; inst. Feb. 2, 2011.

Reilly, Daniel P.: b. May 12, 1928, Providence, RI; educ. Our Lady of Providence Seminary (Warwick, RI), St. Brieuc Major Seminary (Cotes du Nord, France); ord. priest (Providence), May 30, 1953; ord. bp. of Norwich, Aug. 6, 1975; app. bp. of Worcester, Oct. 27, 1994, inst., Nov. 8, 1994; ret. Mar. 9, 2004.

Reiss, Francis R.: b. Nov. 11, 1940, Detroit; educ. Sacred Heart Seminary, St. John Provincial Seminary, Univ. of Detroit, Gregorian Univ.; ord. priest, June 4, 1966; app. aux. bp. of Detroit and titular bp. of Remesiana, July 7, 2003.

Rhoades, Kevin C.: b. Nov. 26, 1957, Mahanoy City, PA; educ. Mt. St. Mary's College (Emmitsburg, MD), St. Charles Borromeo Seminary (Wynnewood, PA); Gregorian Univ. (Rome); ord. priest July 9, 1983 (Harrisburg); app. bp. of Harrisburg Oct. 14, 2004; ord. Dec. 9, 2004; app. bp. of Ft. Wayne-South Bend, Nov. 14, 2009; inst. Jan. 13, 2010.

Riashi, Georges, B.C.O.: b. Nov. 25, 1933, Kaa el Rim, Lebanon; ord. priest, Apr. 4, 1965; parish priest of Our

Lady of Redemption Parish, Warren, MI (Newton Greek Catholic Melkite eparchy); U.S. citizen; ord. first bp. of eparchy of St. Michael's of Sydney (Australia) for Greek Catholic Melkites, July 19, 1987; app. abp. of archeparchy of Tripoli of Lebanon for Greek-Melkites, Aug. 5, 1995.

Ricard, John H., S.S.J.: b. Feb. 29, 1940, Baton Rouge, LA; educ. St. Joseph's Seminary (Washington, DC), Tulane Univ. (New Orleans, LA); ord. priest, May 25, 1968; ord. titular bp. of Rucuma and aux. of Baltimore, July 2, 1984; urban vicar, Baltimore; app. bp. of Pensacola Tallahassee, Jan 21, 1997; ret. Mar. 11, 2011.

Rice, Edward M.: b. July 28, 1960, St. Louis, MO; educ. Cardinal Glennon College and Kenrick-Glennon Seminary, St. Louis, MO; ord. priest Jan. 3, 1987 (St. Louis*); titular bp. of Sufes and aux. bp. of St. Louis, Dec. 1, 2010; ord. Jan. 13, 2011.

Ricken, David L.: b. Nov. 9, 1952, Dodge City, KS; educ. Conception Seminary College, MO, Univ. of Louvain (Belgium), Pontifical Gregorian Univ., Rome; ord. priest (Pueblo), Sept. 12, 1980; official of the Congregation for the Clergy, 1996-1999; app. coadj. Bp. of Cheyenne, Dec. 14, 1999, ord. bp. by Pope John Paul II at the Vatican, Jan. 6, 2000; bp. of Cheyenne, Sept. 26, 2001; app. bp. of Green Bay, July 9, 2008; inst. Aug. 28, 2008.

Rigali, Justin F.: (See **Cardinals, Biographies.**)

Rizzotto, Vincent M.: b. Sept. 9, 1931, Houston, TX; educ. St. Mary Seminary (Houston), the Catholic Univ. of America (Washington, DC), ord. priest, (Galveston, now Galveston-Houston) May 26, 1956; Vicar General of Galveston-Houston, 1994; app. titular bp. of Lamasba and aux. bp. of Galveston-Houston June 22, 2001, ord., July 31, 2001; ret. Oct. 30, 2006.

Rodi, Thomas J: b. Mar. 27, 1949, New Orleans, LA; educ. Georgetown Univ. (Washington, D.C.), Tulane Univ. School of Law (New Orleans), Notre Dame Seminary (New Orleans); ord. priest, (New Orleans*), May 20, 1978; app. bp. of Biloxi, May 15, 2001, ord., July 2, 2001; app. abp. of Mobile, Apr. 2, 2008; inst. June 6, 2008.

Rodimer, Frank J.: b. Oct. 25, 1927, Rockaway, NJ; educ. Seton Hall Prep (South Orange, NJ), St. Charles College (Catonsville, MD), St. Mary's Seminary (Baltimore, MD), Immaculate Conception Seminary (Darlington, NJ), Catholic Univ. (Washington, DC); ord. priest (Paterson), May 19, 1951; ord. bp. of Paterson, Feb. 28, 1978; ret. June 1, 2004.

Rodriguez, Migúel, C.SS.R.: b. Apr. 18, 1931, Mayaguez, P.R.; educ. St. Mary's Minor Seminary (North East, PA), Mt. St. Alphonsus Major Seminary (Esopus, NY); ord. priest, June 22, 1958; ord. bp. of Arecibo, P.R., Mar. 23, 1974; res., Mar. 20, 1990.

Rodriguez, Placido, C.M.F.: b. Oct. 11, 1940, Celaya, Guanajuato, Mexico; educ. Claretian Novitate (Los Angeles, CA), Claretville Seminary College (Calabasas, CA), Catholic Univ. (Washington, DC), Loyola Univ. (Chicago, IL); ord. priest, May 23, 1968; ord. titular bp. of Fuerteventura and aux. bp. of Chicago, Dec. 13, 1983; app. bp. of Lubbock, TX, Apr. 5, 1994.

Roque, Francis X.: b. Oct. 9, 1928, Providence RI; educ. St. John's Seminary (Brighton, MA); ord. priest, (Providence) Sept. 19, 1953; became chaplain in U.S. Army 1961; ord. titular bp. of Bagai and aux. bp. of Military Services archdiocese, May 10, 1983; ret. Sept. 15, 2004.

Rosazza, Peter Anthony: b. Feb. 13, 1935, New Haven, CT; educ. St. Thomas Seminary (Bloomfield, CT), Dartmouth College (Hanover, NH), St. Bernard's Seminary (Rochester, NY), St. Sulpice (Issy, France); ord. priest (Hartford*), June 29, 1961; ord. titular bp. of Oppido Nuovo and aux. bp. of

Hartford, June 24, 1978; ret., June 30, 2010.

Rose, Robert John: b. Feb. 28, 1930, Grand Rapids, MI; educ. St. Joseph's Seminary (Grand Rapids, MI), Seminaire de Philosophie (Montreal, Canada), Urban Univ. (Rome), Univ. of Michigan; ord. priest (Grand Rapids), Dec. 21, 1955; ord. bp. of Gaylord, Dec. 6, 1981; app. bp. of Grand Rapids, inst., Aug. 30, 1989; ret. Oct. 13, 2003.

Rozanski, Mitchell Thomas: b. Aug. 6, 1958, Baltimore, MD; educ. Catholic Univ. of America (Washington, DC); ord. priest (Baltimore*), Nov. 24, 1984; app. titular bp. of Walla Walla and aux. bp. of Baltimore, July 2, 2004; ord. Aug. 24, 2004.

Rueger, George E.: b. Sept. 3, 1933, Framingham, MA; educ. Holy Cross College (Worcester, MA), St. John's Seminary (Brighton), Harvard Univ. (Cambridge, MA); ord. priest (Worcester), Jan. 6, 1958; ord. titular bp. of Maronana and aux. bp. of Worcester, Feb. 25, 1987; ret. Jan. 25, 2005.

Ryan, Daniel L.: b. Sept. 28, 1930, Mankato, MN; educ. St. Procopius Seminary (Lisle, IL), Lateran Univ. (Rome); ord. priest (Joliet), May 3, 1956; ord. titular bp. of Surista and aux. bp. of Joliet, Sept. 30, 1981; app. bp. of Springfield, IL, Nov. 22, 1983, inst., Jan. 18, 1984; res. Oct. ,19, 1999.

Ryan, Sylvester D.: b. May 3, 1930, Catalina Is., CA; educ. St. John's Seminary (Camarillo, CA); ord. priest (Los Angeles*), May 3, 1957; ord. titular bp. of Remesiana and aux. bp. of Los Angeles, May 31, 1990; app. bp. of Monterey, Jan. 28, 1992; ret. Dec. 19, 2006.

S

Salazar, Alexander: b. Nov. 28, 1949, San Jose, Costa Rica; educ. California State Univ. and Immaculate Heart College (Los Angeles), St. John's Seminary (Camarillo, CA); ord. priest June 16, 1984; appointed auxiliary bp. of Los Angeles and titular bp. of Nesqually Sept. 7, 2004; ord. Nov. 4, 2004.

Sample, Alexander K.: b. Nov. 7, 1960, Kalispell, Mont.; educ. Michigan Technological Univ. (Houghton), St. Thomas College (St. Paul, Minn.), Pontifical College Josephinum (Columbus, Ohio), Angelicum (Rome); ord. priest June 1, 1990 (Marquette); app. bp of Marquette Dec. 13, 2005; ord. bp. Jan. 25, 2006; app. abp. of Portland in Oregon, Jan. 29, 2013; inst. Apr. 2, 2013.

Samra, Nicholas J.: b. Aug. 15, 1944, Paterson, NJ; educ. St. Anselm College (Manchester, NH), St. Basil Seminary (Methuen, MA), St. John Seminary (Brighton, MA); ord. priest (Newton), May 10, 1970; ord. titular bp. of Gerasa and aux. bp. of Melkite diocese of Newton, July 6, 1989; res. Jan. 11, 2005; app. eparch of Newton, June 15, 2011.

Sanchez, Paul R.: b. Nov. 26, 1946, Brooklyn, NY; St. Bonaventure's University (New York), University of Notre Dame (South Bend, IN), Pontifical Gregorian University (Rome); ord. priest (Brooklyn), Dec. 17, 1971; served in various pastoral assignments and was an adjunct faculty member at Saint John's University and the Seminary of the Immaculate Conception, Huntington, NY; app. aux. bp. of Brooklyn and titular bp. of Coeliana, May 2, 2012; ord. bp., July 11, 2012

Sansaricq, Guy A.: b. Oct. 6, 1934, Jeremie, Haiti; educ. St. Paul College (Ottawa); ord. priest June 29, 1960 (Les Cayes, Haiti); incard. Brooklyn 1991; appointed aux. bp. of Brooklyn and tit. bp. of Glenndalocha June 6, 2006; ord. Aug. 22, 2006.

Sartain, James P.: b. June 6, 1952, Memphis, TN; educ. St. Meinrad Seminary, (IN), North American College, (Rome), Pontifical Univ. of St. Thomas (the Angelicum), Pontifical Institute of St. Anselm (Rome); ord. priest

(Memphis), July 15, 1978; app. bp. of Little Rock, Jan. 4, 2000, ord., Mar. 6, 2000; app. bp. of Joliet, May 16, 2006; app. abp. of Seattle, Dec. 1, 2010.

Sartoris, Joseph M.: b. July 1, 1927, Los Angeles, CA; educ. St. John's Seminary (Camarillo, CA); ord. priest (Los Angeles*), May 30, 1953; ord. titular bp. of Oliva and aux. bp. of Los Angeles, Mar. 19, 1994; ret., Dec. 31, 2002.

Scarpone Caporale, Gerald, O.F.M.: b. Oct. 1, 1928, Watertown, MA; ord. priest, June 24, 1956; ord. coadj. bp. of Comayagua, Honduras, Feb. 21, 1979; succeeded as bp. of Comayagua, May 30, 1979.

Schlarman, Stanley Gerard: b. July 27, 1933, Belleville, IL; educ. St. Henry Prep Seminary (Belleville, IL), Gregorian Univ. (Rome), St. Louis Univ. (St. Louis, MO); ord. priest (Belleville), July 13, 1958, Rome; ord. titular bp. of Capri and aux. bp. of Belleville, May 14, 1979; app. bp. of Dodge City, Mar. 1, 1983; res., May 12, 1998.

Schmitz Simon, Paul, O.F.M. Cap.: b. Dec. 4, 1943, Fond du Lac, WI; ord. priest, Sept. 3, 1970; missionary in Nicaragua from 1970; superior of vice province of Capuchins in Central America (headquartered in Managua), 1982-84; ord. titular bp. of Elepla and aux. of the vicariate apostolic of Bluefields, Nicaragua, Sept. 17, 1984; app. bp. of vicariate apostolic of Bluefields, Aug. 17, 1994.

Schnurr, Dennis M.: b. June 21, 1948, Sheldon, IA; educ. Loras College (Dubuque), Gregorian Univ. (Rome), Catholic Univ. of America (Washington, DC); ord. priest (Sioux City), July 20, 1974; Staff, Apostolic Nunciature, Washington, DC, 1985-1989; Assoc. Gen. Secretary, National Conference of Catholic Bps./United States Catholic Conference (NCCB/USCC), 1989-1995; National Executive Director, World Youth Day 1993, Denver, 1991-1993; General Secretary, NCCB/USCC, 1995-2001; app. bp. of Duluth, Jan. 18, 2001, ord., Apr. 2, 2001; app. co-adj. abp. of Cincinnati, Oct. 17, 2008; acceded to the see, Dec. 21, 2009.

Schulte, Francis B.: b. Dec. 23, 1926, Philadelphia, PA; educ. St. Charles Borromeo Seminary (Overbrook, PA); ord. priest (Philadelphia*), May 10, 1952; ord. titular bp. of Afufenia and aux. bp. of Philadelphia, Aug. 12, 1981; app. bp. of Wheeling-Charleston, June 4, 1985; abp. of New Orleans, Dec. 6, 1988, inst., Feb. 14, 1989; ret., Jan. 3, 2002.

Schwietz, Roger L., O.M.I.: b. July 3, 1940, St. Paul, MN; educ. Univ. of Ottawa (Canada), Gregorian Univ. (Rome); ord. priest, Dec. 20, 1967; ord. bp. of Duluth Feb. 2, 1990; bp. of Duluth, 1990-2000; coadj. abp. of Anchorage, Jan. 18, 2000; abp. of Anchorage, Mar. 3, 2001.

Seitz, Mark J.: b. Jan. 10, 1954, Milwaukee, WI; educ. Univ. of Dallas (Dallas, TX), St. John's Univ. (Collegeville, MN), National Catholic Bioethics Center (Philadelphia, PA); ord. priest (Dallas), May 17, 1980; ord. titular bp. of Cozila and aux. bp. of Dallas, Mar. 11, 2010; ord. bp. Apr. 27, 2010; app. bp. of El Paso, May 6, 2013; inst. July 9, 2013.

Seminack, Richard: b. Mar. 3, 1942, Philadelphia; educ. St. Basil Seminary College (Stamford, CT), St. Josaphat Major Seminary and Catholic Univ. of America (Washington), Oriental Institute (Rome); ord. priest, May 25, 1967 (archeparchy of Philadelphia); incard. Eparchy of St. Josaphat (Parma) 1983; app. bp. of St. Nicholas of Chicago for Ukrainians, Mar. 25, 2003; ord., June 4, 2003.

Senior, Timothy C.: b. Mar. 22, 1960, Philadelphia, PA; educ. St. Charles Seminary Overbrook, PA), Boston College (Boston, MA); ord. priest (Philadelphia*), May 18, 1985; sec. for archdiocesan Catholic Human Services (1997-2004); app. titular bp. of Floriana and aux. bp. of Philadelphia, June 8, 2009; ord. bp. July 31, 2009.

Serratelli, Arthur J.: b. Apr. 18, 1944, Newark, NJ; educ. Seton Preparatory School (NJ), Seton Hall Univ. (NJ), North American College and Gregorian Univ. (Rome), Pontifical Biblical Institute (Rome); ord. priest (Newark*), Dec. 20, 1968; prof. of Sacred Scripture, Immaculate Conception Seminary; rector of the College Seminary, Seton Hall Univ.; prelate of honor, 1998; app. titular bp. of Enera and aux. bp. of Newark, July 3, 2000; app. bp. of Paterson, June 1, 2004.

Sevilla, Carlos A., S.J.: b. Aug. 9, 1935, San Francisco, CA; entered Jesuits Aug. 14, 1953; educ. Gonzaga Univ. (Spokane, WA), Santa Clara Univ. (Santa Clara, CA), Jesuitenkolleg (Innsbruck, Austria), Catholic Institute of Paris (France); ord. priest, June 3, 1966; ord. titular bp. of Mina and aux. bp. of San Francisco, Jan. 25, 1989; bp. of Yakima, Dec. 31, 1996; ret. Apr. 12, 2011.

Shaheen, Robert J.: b. June 3, 1937, Danbury, CT; ord., May 2, 1964; elected eparch of Our Lady of Lebanon of Los Angeles of the Maronites (U.S.A.), Dec. 5, 2000; ret. July 10, 2013.

Sheehan, Michael J.: b. July 9, 1939, Wichita, KS; educ. Assumption Seminary (San Antonio, TX), Gregorian Univ. and Lateran Univ. (Rome); ord. priest (Dallas), July 12, 1964; ord. first bp. of Lubbock, TX, June 17, 1983; apostolic administrator of Santa Fe, Apr. 6, 1993; app. abp. of Santa Fe, Aug. 17, 1993.

Sheldon, Gilbert I.: b. Sept. 20, 1926, Cleveland, OH; educ. John Carroll Univ. and St. Mary Seminary (Cleveland, OH); ord. priest (Cleveland), Feb. 28, 1953; ord. titular bp. of Taparura and aux. bp. of Cleveland, June 11, 1976; app. bp. of Steubenville, Jan. 28, 1992, ret., May 31, 2002.

Sheltz, George A.: b. Apr. 20, 1946, Houston, TX; University of St. Thomas and St. Mary's Seminary (Houston, TX); ord. priest, May 15, 1971 (Galveston-Houston*); app. titular bp. of Hirina and aux. bp. of Galveston-Houston, Feb. 21, 2012; ord. bp., May 2, 2012.

Sheridan, Michael J.: b. Mar. 4, 1945, St. Louis, MO; educ. Glennon College, Kenrick Seminary (St. Louis, MO), Angelicum (Rome); ord. priest (St. Louis*), 1971; app. titular bp. of Thibiuca and aux. bp. of St. Louis, July 9, 1997; coadj. bp. of Colorado Springs, Dec. 4, 2001; bp. of Colorado Springs, Jan. 30, 2003.

Silva, Clarence: b. Aug. 6, 1949, Honolulu; educ. St. Patrick Seminary (Menlo Park, Calif.); ord. priest May 2, 1975 (Oakland); app. bp. of Honolulu May 17, 2005; ord. bp. July 21, 2005.

Siegel, Joseph M.: b. July 18, 1963, Joliet, IL; educ. St. Meinrad Seminary College, North American College, Pontifical Univ. of St. Thomas Aquinas and Pontifical Gregorian Univ. (Rome), Univ. of St. Mary of the Lake/Mundelein Seminary; ord. priest (Joliet), June 4, 1988; app. aux. bp. of Joliet and titular bp. of Pupiana, Oct. 28, 2009; ord. Jan. 19, 2010.

Sirba, Paul D.: b. Sept. 2, 1960, St. Paul, MN; educ. Archdiocesan Seminary (St. Paul and Minneapolis), Notre Dame Institute for Catechetics (Alexandria, VA); ord. priest (St. Paul and Minneapolis*), May 31, 1986; app. bp. of Duluth, Oct. 15, 2009; ord. Dec. 14, 2009.

Sklba, Richard J.: b. Sept. 11, 1935, Racine, WI; educ. Old St. Francis Minor Seminary (Milwaukee, WI), North American College, Gregorian Univ., Pontifical Biblical Institute, Angelicum (Rome); ord. priest (Milwaukee*), Dec. 20, 1959; ord. titular bp. of Castra and aux. bp. of Milwaukee, Dec. 19, 1979; ret. Oct. 18, 2010.

Skurla, William C.: b. June 1, 1956, Duluth; educ. Columbia Univ., New York, Mary Immaculate Seminary,

Northhampton, PA; ord. priest (Franciscan), 1987; incardinated into Eparchy of Van Nuys, 1996; app. bp. of Van Nuys Byzantine Catholic Eparchy in California, Feb. 19, 2002; app. bp. of Ruthenian Byzantine diocese of Passaic, Dec. 6, 2007; app. abp. of Pittsburgh for the Ruthenians, Jan. 19, 2012; inst. Apr. 18, 2012.

Skylstad, William S.: b. Mar. 2, 1934, Omak, WA; educ. Pontifical College Josephinum (Worthington, OH), Washington State Univ. (Pullman, WA), Gonzaga Univ. (Spokane, WA); ord. priest (Spokane), May 21, 1960; ord. bp. of Yakima, May 12, 1977; app. bp. of Spokane, Apr. 17, 1990; vice-pres. of USCCB, 2001-2004; pres. of USCCB, 2004-2007; app. apostolic admin. of Baker, Jan. 24, 2011.

Slattery, Edward J.: b. Aug. 11, 1940, Chicago, IL; educ. Quigley Preparatory, St. Mary of the Lake Seminary (Mundelein, IL), Loyola Univ. (Chicago); ord. priest (Chicago*), Apr. 26, 1966; vice president, 1971-76, and president, 1976-94, of the Catholic Church Extension Society; ord. bp. of Tulsa, Jan. 6, 1994.

Smith, John M.: b. June 23, 1935, Orange, NJ; educ. Immaculate Conception Seminary (Darlington, NJ), Seton Hall Univ. (South Orange, NJ), Catholic Univ. (Washington, DC); ord. priest (Newark*), May 27, 1961; ord. titular bp. of Tre Taverne and aux. bp. of Newark, Jan. 25, 1988; app. bp. of Pensacola-Tallahassee, FL, June 25, 1991; app. coadj. bp. of Trenton, Nov. 21, 1995; bp. of Trenton, July 1, 1997; ret. Dec. 1, 2010.

Snyder, John J.: b. Oct. 25, 1925, New York, NY; educ. Cathedral College (Brooklyn, NY), Immaculate Conception Seminary (Huntington, NY); ord. priest (Brooklyn), June 9, 1951; ord. titular bp. of Forlimpopli and aux. bp. of Brooklyn, Feb. 2, 1973; app. bp. of St. Aug.ine, inst., Dec. 5, 1979; res., Dec. 11, 2000.

Soens, Lawrence D.: b. Aug. 26, 1926, Iowa City, IA; educ. Loras College (Dubuque, IA), St. Ambrose College (Davenport, IA), Kenrick Seminary (St. Louis, MO), Univ. of Iowa; ord. priest (Davenport), May 6, 1950; ord. bp. of Sioux City, Aug. 17, 1983, res., Nov. 28, 1998.

Soroka, Stephen: b. Nov. 13, 1951, Winnipeg, Manitoba; educ. Univ. of Manitoba, Ukrainian Seminary, Washington, DC, Catholic Univ. of America, ordained (Ukrainian Archdiocese of Winnipeg*), June 13, 1982; Chancellor and financial administrator of the Winnipeg archdiocese, 1994, auxiliary bp., Winnipeg, 1996; metropolitan abp. of Philadelphia for the Ukrainians, Nov. 29, 2000; inst., Feb. 27, 2001.

Soto, Jaime: b. Dec. 31, 1955, Inglewood, CA; educ. St. John's Seminary, Camarillo, CA, Columbia Univ. School of Social Work, New York; ord. priest (Orange), June 12, 1982; Episcopal Vicar for Hispanic Ministry, 1989; app. titular bp. of Segia and aux. bp. of Orange, Mar. 23, 2000, ord., May 31, 2000; app. coadj. bp. of Sacramento, Oct. 11, 2007; inst. Nov. 19, 2007; bp. of Sacramento, Nov. 29, 2008.

Sowada, Alphonse A., O.S.C.: b. June 23, 1933, Avon, MN; educ. Holy Cross Scholasticate (Ft. Wayne, IN), Catholic Univ. (Washington, DC), ord. priest, May 31, 1958; missionary in Indonesia from 1958; ord. bp. of Agats, Indonesia, Nov. 23, 1969; ret. May 9, 2001.

Spencer, F. Richard: b. June 10, 1951, Sylacauga, AL; educ.: Jacksonville State Univ., (AL), Univ. of Wisconsin (LaCrosse, WI), St. Mary's Seminary and Univ. (Baltimore, MD), and military training courses; ord. priest, May 14, 1988 (Baltimore*); commissioned an Army Officer in 1973 and began serving active duty in

1974; returned to active duty ministry in Jan. 1999; selected to attend the National War College, Class 2010; app. titular bp. of Auzia and auxiliary bp. of the Archdiocese for the Military Services, May 22, 2010.

Stafford, James Francis: (See Cardinals, Biographies).

Steib, J. (James) Terry, S.V.D.: b. May 17, 1940, Vacherie, LA; educ. Divine Word seminaries (Bay St. Louis, MS, Conesus, NY, Techny, IL), Xavier Univ. (New Orleans, LA); ord. priest, Jan. 6, 1967; ord. titular bp. of Fallaba and aux. bp. of St. Louis, Feb. 10, 1984; app. bp. of Memphis, Mar. 24, 1993.

Steiner, Kenneth Donald: b. Nov. 25, 1936, David City, NE; educ. Mt. Angel Seminary (St. Benedict, OR), St. Thomas Seminary (Seattle, Wash); ord. priest (Portland,* OR), May 19, 1962; ord. titular bp. of Avensa and aux. bp. of Portland, Mar. 2, 1978; ret. Nov. 25, 2011.

Stika, Richard F.: b. July 4, 1957, St. Louis, MO; educ. St. Louis Univ. (St. Louis, MO), Cardinal Glennon College (St. Louis), Kenrick Seminary (St. Louis); ord. priest (St. Louis), Dec. 14, 1985; possesses bi-ritual faculties of the Maronite Church; in 1999 he coordinated for the archdiocese the visit of Pope John Paul II to St. Louis; app. bp. of Knoxville, Jan. 12, 2009; ord. bp., Mar. 19, 2009.

Straling, Phillip F.: b. Apr. 25, 1933, San Bernardino, CA; educ. Immaculate Heart Seminary, St. Francis Seminary, Univ. of San Diego and San Diego State Univ. (San Diego, CA), North American College (Rome); ord. priest (San Diego), Mar. 19, 1959; ord. first bp. of San Bernardino, Nov. 6, 1978; app. first bp. of Reno, Mar. 21, 1995, when Reno Las Vegas diocese was made two separate dioceses; res. Jun. 21, 2005.

Sullivan, Dennis J.: b. Mar. 17, 1945, New York, NY; educ. Iona College (New Rochelle, NY), St. Joseph Seminary (Dunwoodie, NY); ord. May 29, 1971; app. titular bp. of Enera and aux. bp. of New York, June 28, 2004; ord. Sept. 21, 2004; app. bp. of Camden, Jan. 8, 2013; inst. Feb. 12, 2013.

Sulyk, Stephen: b. Oct. 2, 1924, Balnycia, Western Ukraine; migrated to U.S. 1948; educ. Ukrainian Catholic Seminary of the Holy Spirit (Hirschberg, Germany), St. Josaphat's Seminary and Catholic Univ. (Washington, DC); ord. priest (Philadelphia,* Byzantine), June 14, 1952; ord. abp. of the Ukrainian archeparchy of Philadelphia, Mar. 1, 1981; res., Nov. 29, 2000.

Swain, Paul J.: b. Sept. 12, 1943, Newark, N.Y.; educ. Univ. of Wisc.-Madison, Univ. of Wisc. Law School, John XXIII Seminary (Weston, Mass.); ord. May 27, 1988 (Madison); app. bp. of Sioux Falls, S.D., Aug. 31, 2006; ord. Oct. 26, 2006.

Symons, J. Keith: b. Oct. 14, 1932, Champion, MI; educ. St. Thomas Seminary (Bloomfield, CT), St. Mary Seminary (Baltimore, MD); ord. priest (St. Augustine), May 18, 1958; ord. titular bp. of Siguitanus and aux. bp. of St. Petersburg, Mar. 19, 1981; app. bp. of Pensacola Tallahassee, Oct. 4, 1983, inst., Nov. 8, 1983; app. bp. of Palm Beach, June 12, 1990; res., June 2, 1998.

Szoka, Edmund C.: (See Cardinals, Biographies.)

T

Tafoya, Arthur N.: b. Mar. 2, 1933, Alameda, NM; educ. St. Thomas Seminary (Denver, CO), Conception Seminary (Conception, MO); ord. priest (Santa Fe*), May 12, 1962; ord. bp. of Pueblo, Sept. 10, 1980; ret. Oct. 15, 2009.

Talley, David P.: b. Sept. 11, 1950, Columbus, Georgia; educ. St. Meinrad Seminary (Indiana), Pontifical Gregorian University (Rome); app. titular bp. of Lambaesis and aux. bp. of Atlanta, Jan. 3, 2013; ord. bishop Apr. 2, 2013.

Tamayo, James A.: b. Oct. 23, 1949, Brownsville, TX; educ. Del Mar College (Corpus Christi, TX), Univ. of St. Thomas and Univ. of St. Thomas School of Theology (Houston); ord. priest (Corpus Christi), June 11, 1976; ord. titular bp. of Ita and aux. bp. of Galveston Houston, Mar. 10, 1993; app. first bp. of Laredo, TX, July 3, 2000, ins., Aug. 9, 2000.

Taylor, Anthony Basil: b. Apr. 24, 1954, Forth Worth, TX; educ. Univ. of Oklahoma (Enid, OK), St. Meinrad Seminary (IN), Pontifical North American College and Gregorian Univ. (Rome, Italy), Fordham Univ. (New York, NY); ord. priest (Oklahoma City*), Aug. 2, 1980; app. bp. of Little Rock, Apr. 10, 2008; inst. June 5, 2008.

Thomas, Daniel E.: b. June 11, 1959, Philadelphia; educ. St. Charles Borromeo Sem. (Philadelphia), Gregorian Univ. (Rome); ord. priest May 18, 1985 (Philadelphia); appointed aux. bp. of Philadelphia and tit. bp. of Bardstown June 8, 2006; ord. July 26, 2006.

Thomas, Elliott G.: b. July 15, 1926, Pittsburgh, PA; educ. Howard Univ. (Washington, DC), Gannon Univ. (Erie, PA), St. Vincent de Paul Seminary (Boynton Beach, FL); ord. priest (St. Thomas, Virgin Islands), June 6, 1986; ord. bp. of St. Thomas in the Virgin Islands, Dec. 12, 1993; res., June 30, 1999.

Thomas, George L.: b. May 19, 1950, Anaconda, MT, educ. St. Thomas Seminary, Seattle, Univ. of Washington, Seattle; ord. priest (Seattle*), May 22, 1976; chancellor and vicar general, 1988-1999, diocesan administrator of Seattle, 1996-1997; app. titular bp. of Vagrauta and aux. bp. of Seattle, Nov. 19, 1999, inst., Jan. 28, 2000; app. bp. of Helena, Mar. 23, 2004.

Thompson, Charles C.: b. Apr. 11, 1961, Louisville, KY; educ. Bellarmine College (Louisville), St. Meinrad School of Theology (Meinrad, IN), St. Paul University (Ottawa); ord. priest (Louisville), May 30, 1987; app. bp. of Evansville, Apr. 26, 2011; ord. bp. June 29, 2011.

Thompson, David B.: b. May 29, 1923, Philadelphia, PA; educ. St. Charles Seminary (Overbrook, PA), Catholic Univ. (Washington, DC); ord. priest (Philadelphia*), May 27, 1950; ord. coadjutor bp. of Charleston, May 24, 1989; bp. of Charleston, Feb. 22, 1990; res., July 13, 1999.

Tiedemann, Neil, C.P.: b. Mar. 5, 1948, Brooklyn, New York; educ. Passionist seminary; entered Congregation of the Passionists in 1970 and took his perpetual vows on Aug. 22, 1974; ord. priest, May 16, 1975; app. bp. of Mandeville, Jamaica, May 20, 2008.

Timlin, James C.: b. Aug. 5, 1927, Scranton, PA; educ. St. Charles College (Catonville, MD), St. Mary's Seminary (Baltimore, MD), North American College (Rome); ord. priest (Scranton), July 16, 1951; ord. titular bp. of Gunugo and aux. bp. of Scranton, Sept. 21, 1976; app. bp. of Scranton, Apr. 24, 1984; ret., July 25, 2003.

Tobin, Joseph William, C.SS.R.: b. May 3, 1952, Detroit, MI,; educ. Holy Redeemer College (Waterford, WI), Mount St. Alphonsus Major Seminary (New York); ord. priest, Redemptorists, June 1, 1978; Superior General of the Redemptorists, 1997-2009; app. titular abp. of Obba and Sec. of the Congregation for Institutes of Consecrated Life and Societies of Apostolic Life, Aug. 2, 2010; app. abp. of Indianapolis, Oct. 18, 2012; inst. Dec. 3, 2012.

Tobin, Thomas J.: b. Apr. 1, 1948, Pittsburgh, PA; educ.

St. Mark Seminary High School, Gannon Univ. (Erie, PA), St. Francis College (Loretto, PA), North American College (Rome); ord. priest (Pittsburgh), July 21, 1973; ord. titular bp. of Novica and aux. bp. of Pittsburgh, Dec. 27, 1992; app. bp. of Youngstown Dec. 5, 1995; inst., Feb. 2, 1996; app. bp. of Providence, Mar. 31, 2005; inst May 31, 2005.

Trautman, Donald W.: b. June 24, 1936, Buffalo, NY; educ. Our Lady of Angels Seminary (Niagara Falls, NY), Theology Faculty (Innsbruck, Austria), Pontifical Biblical Institute (Rome), Catholic Univ. (Washington, DC); ord. priest (Buffalo), Apr. 7, 1962, in Innsbruck; ord. titular bp. of Sassura and aux. of Buffalo, Apr. 16, 1985; app. bp. of Erie, June 12, 1990; ret. July 31, 2012.

Turley Murphy, Daniel T. , O.S.A.: b. Jan. 25, 1943, Chicago, IL; ord. priest, Dec. 21, 1961; ord. coadj. bp. of Chulucanas, Peru, Aug. 17, 1996.

Tyson, Joseph J.: b. Oct. 16, 1957, Moses Lake, Wash.; educ. Univ. of Washington, Catholic Univ. of America; ord. priest June 10, 1989 (Seattle); app. auxiliary bp. of Seattle and titular bp. of Migirpa May 12, 2005; ord. bp. June 6, 2005, app. bp. of Yakima, Apr. 12, 2011; inst. May 31, 2011.

U V

Uglietto, Peter J.: b. Sept. 24, 1951, Cambridge, MA; educ., St. John Seminary (Brighton, MA), Creighton Univ. (Omaha, NE), John Paul II Institute for Marriage and Family (Washington D.C.); ord. priest, May 21, 1977 (Boston*); rector, Blessed John XXIII National Seminary, 2005-2010; app. titular bp. of Thubursicum and aux. bp. of Boston, June 30, 2010.

Valero, René A.: b. Aug. 15, 1930, New York, NY; educ. Cathedral College, Immaculate Conception Seminary (Huntington, NY), Fordham Univ. (New York); ord. priest (Brooklyn), June 2, 1956; ord. titular bp. of Turris Vicus and aux. bp. of Brooklyn, Nov. 24, 1980; ret. Oct. 27, 2005.

Vann, Kevin W.: b. May 10, 1951, Springfield, IL; educ. Milikin Univ. (Decatur, Ill.), Immaculate Conception Seminary (Springfield), Kenrick Seminary (St. Louis), Univ. of St. Thomas Aquinas (Rome); ord. May 30, 1981 (Springfield); app. coadjutor bp. Forth Worth May 17, 2005; ord. bp. July 13, 2005; app. bp. of Orange, Sept. 21, 2012; inst. Dec. 12, 2012.

Vasa, Robert F.: b. May 7, 1951, Lincoln, NE, educ. St. Thomas Seminary, Denver, Holy Trinity Seminary, Dallas, Pontifical Gregorian Univ. (Rome, Italy); ord. priest (Lincoln), May 22,1976; Vicar General and Moderator of the Curia, 1996; app. bp. of Baker, OR Nov. 19, 1999, inst., Jan. 26, 2000; app. coadjutor bp. of Santa Rosa, Jan. 24, 2011; inst. Mar. 6, 2011; acceded to see June 30, 2011.

Vasquez, José S.: b. July 9, 1957, Stamford, Texas; educ. St. Mary Seminary, Houston, Univ. of St. Thomas, North American College and Pontifical Gregorian Univ. (Rome); ord. priest (San Angelo), June 30, 1984; app. titular bp. of Cova and aux. of Galveston-Houston, Nov. 30, 2001, ord., Jan. 23, 2002; app. bp. of Austin, Jan. 26, 2010; inst. Mar. 8, 2010.

Vigneron, Allen H.: b. Oct. 21, 1948, Detroit, MI; educ. Sacred Heart Seminary (Detroit, MI), North American College, Gregorian Univ. (Rome), Catholic Univ. (Washington, DC); ord. priest (Detroit*), July 26, 1975; served in Vatican Secretariat of State, 1991 94; rector of Sacred Heart Seminary (Detroit), 1994; ord. titular bp. of Sault Ste Marie and aux. bp. of Detroit, July 9, 1996; app. coadj. bp. of Oakland, Jan. 10, 2003; bp. of

Oakland Oct. 1, 2003; app. abp. of Detroit, Jan. 5, 2009; inst. Jan. 28, 2009.

Vlazny, John G.: b. Feb. 22, 1937, Chicago, IL; educ. Quigley Preparatory Seminary (Chicago, IL), St. Mary of the Lake Seminary (Mundelein, IL), Gregorian Univ. (Rome), Univ. of Michigan, Loyola Univ. (Chicago, IL); ord. priest (Chicago*), Dec. 20, 1961; ord. titular bp. of Stagno and aux. bp. of Chicago, Dec. 13, 1983; app. bp. of Winona, MN, May 19, 1987; app. abp. of Portland in Oregon, Oct. 28, 1997, inst., Dec. 19, 1997; ret. Jan. 29, 2013.

W

Walkowiak, David J.: b. June 18, 1953, Cleveland, OH; educ. University of Notre Dame, St. Mary Seminary (Wickliffe, OH), The Catholic University of America (Washington, DC); ord. priest June 9, 1979 (Cleveland); app. bp. of Grand Rapids, Apr. 18, 2013; ord. bp. June 18, 2013.

Wall, James S.: b. Oct. 11, 1964, Ganado, AZ; educ. Arizona State Univ. (Phoenix, AZ); St. John's Seminary (Camarillo, CA), Mundelein Seminary (Chicago, IL); ord. priest (Phoenix), June 6, 1998; member of the National Advisory Council of the USCCB, 2003-2007; app. bp. of Gallup, Feb. 5, 2009; ord. bp. Apr. 23, 2009.

Walsh, Daniel Francis: b. Oct. 2, 1937, San Francisco, CA; educ. St. Joseph Seminary (Mountain View, CA), St. Patrick Seminary (Menlo Park, CA) Catholic Univ. (Washington, DC); ord. priest (San Francisco*), Mar. 30, 1963; ord. titular bp. of Tigia and aux. bp. of San Francisco, Sept. 24, 1981; app. bp. of Reno-Las Vegas, June 9, 1987; app. first bp. of Las Vegas, Mar. 21, 1995, when the Reno-Las Vegas diocese was made two separate dioceses; app. bp. Santa Rosa, Apr. 11, 2000; ret. June 30, 2011.

Walsh, Gerald T.: b. Apr. 25, 1942, New York, NY; educ. Iona College (New Rochelle, NY), St. Joseph Seminary (Dunwoodie, NY), Fordham Univ. (New York, NY); ord. May 27, 1967; app. titular bp. of Altiburo and aux. bp. of New York, June 28, 2004; ord. Sept. 21, 2004.

Walsh, Paul H.: b. Aug. 17, 1937, Brooklyn; educ. Providence College (R.I.), St. Stephen's College (Dover, MA), Dominican House of Studies (Washington); ord. Dominican, June 9, 1966; incard. Rockville Centre, Dec. 13, 1984; app. aux. bp. of Rockville Centre and titular bp. of Abtugni, Apr. 3, 2003; ord. bp., May 29, 2003.

Walterscheid, William J.: b. Nov. 18, 1956, Ashland, PA; educ. St. John Seminary College (Brighton, MA), Pontifical Gregorian Univ. (Rome); ord. priest (Harrisburg), July 11, 1992; dir. of Pastoral Formation, North American College, Rome, 1999-2000; vice rector, North American College, 2000-2003; app. aux. bp. of Pittsburgh and titular bp. of Califonria, Feb. 25, 2011; ord. Apr. 25, 2011.

Wang, Ignatius: b. Feb. 27, 1934, Beijing, China; educ. Urbanian Univ. and Gregorian Univ. (Rome); ord. priest (for apostolic vicariate in southern China) July 4, 1959; unable to return home, he served in the Antilles and transferred to San Francisco in 1974; auxiliary bp. of San Francisco and titular bp. of Sitipa, Dec. 13, 2002; ord., Jan. 30, 2003; ret. May 16, 2009.

Warfel, Michael William: b. Sept 16, 1948, Elkhart, IN; educ. Indiana Univ, St. Gregory's College Seminary, Mt. St. Mary's Seminary of the West (Cincinnati, OH); ord. priest, Apr. 26, 1980; ord. bp. of Juneau, Dec. 17, 1996; app. bp. of Great-Fall-Billings, Nov. 20, 2007.

Wcela, Emil A.: b. May 1, 1931, Bohemia, NY; educ.

St. Francis College (Brooklyn, NY), Immaculate Conception Seminary (Huntington, NY), Catholic Univ. (Washington, DC), Pontifical Biblical Institute (Rome, Italy); ord. priest (Brooklyn), June 2, 1956; ord. titular bp. of Filaca and aux. bp. of Rockville Centre, Dec. 13, 1988; ret. Apr. 3, 2007.

Weakland, Rembert G., O.S.B.: b. Apr. 2, 1927, Patton, PA; joined Benedictines, 1945; ord. priest, June 24, 1951; abbot primate of Benedictine Confederation, 1967 77; ord. abp. of Milwaukee, Nov. 8, 1977; res., May 24, 2002.

Weigand, William K.: b. May 23, 1937, Bend, OR; educ. Mt. Angel Seminary (St. Benedict, OR), St. Edward's Seminary and St. Thomas Seminary (Kenmore, WA); ord. priest (Boise), May 25, 1963; ord. bp. of Salt Lake City, Nov. 17, 1980; app. bp. of Sacramento, Nov. 30, 1993, inst., Jan. 27, 1994; ret. Nov. 29, 2008

Weisenburger, Edward J.: b. Dec. 23, 1960, Alton, IL; educ. Conception Seminary College (Conception, MO), American College Seminary at the Catholic University of Louvain (Leuven, Belgium), University of St. Paul (Ottawa, Canada); ord. priest, Dec. 19, 1987 (Oklahoma City*); aside from pastoral service and duties in the archdiocese, he served as on-site chaplain in 1995 during the recovery after the Oklahoma City Bombing; app. bp. of Salina, Feb. 6, 2012; ord. bp., May 1, 2012.

Weitzel, John Quinn, M.M.: b. May 10, 1928, Chicago, IL; educ. Maryknoll Seminary (Maryknoll, NY); ord. priest, Nov. 5, 1955; missionary to Samoa, 1979; ord. bp. of Samoa-Pago Pago, American Samoa, Oct. 29, 1986; ret. May 31, 2013.

Wenski, Thomas G.: b. Oct. 18, 1950, West Palm Beach, FL; educ. St. John Vianney College Seminary, St. Vincent de Paul Regional Seminary, Fordham Univ.; ord. priest (Miami*), May 15, 1976; director of Miami Haitian Apostolate; app. titular bp. of Kearney and aux. of Miami, June 24, 1997; app. coadj. bp. of Orlando, July 1, 2003; bp. of Orlando, Nov. 13, 2004; app. abp. of Miami, Apr. 20, 2010.

Wester, John Charles: b. Nov. 5, 1950, San Francisco; educ.St. John's Seminary, Camarillo, CA, St. Patrick's Seminary, Menlo Park, CA, Univ. of San Francisco; ord. priest (San Francisco*), May 15, 1976; app. titular bp. of Lamiggiga and aux. bp. of San Francisco, June 30, 1998; app. bp. of Salt Lake City, Jan. 8, 2007.

Wilkerson, Gerald E.: b. Oct. 21, 1939, Des Moines, IA; educ. St. John's Seminary (Camarillo, CA); ord. priest (Los Angeles*), Jan. 5, 1965; app. titular bp. of Vincennes and aux. bp. of Los Angeles, Nov. 5, 1997, ord., Jan. 21, 1998.

Williams, James Kendrick: b. Sept. 5, 1936, Athertonville, KY; educ. St. Mary's College (St. Mary's, KY), St. Maur's School of Theology (South Union, KY); ord. priest (Louisville*), May 25, 1963; ord. titular bp. of Catula and aux. bp. of Covington, June 19, 1984; first bp. of Lexington, KY, inst., Mar. 2, 1988; res., June 11, 2002.

Winter, William J.: b. May 20, 1930, Pittsburgh, PA; educ. St. Vincent College and Seminary (Latrobe, PA), Gregorian Univ. (Rome, Italy); ord. priest (Pittsburgh), Dec. 17, 1955; ord. titular bp. of Uthina and aux. bp. of Pittsburgh, Feb. 13, 1989; ret. May 20, 2005.

Wiwchar, Michael, C.Ss.R.: b. May 9, 1932, Komarno, Manitoba, Can.; educ. Redemptorist Seminary (Windsor, Ontario); made solemn vows as Redemptorist, 1956; ord. priest, June 28, 1959; pastor St. John the Baptist Parish, Newark, NJ, 1990-93; ord. bp. of St. Nicholas of Chicago for the Ukrainians, Sept. 28, 1993; bp. of Saskatoon of Ukrainians, Nov. 29, 2000.

Wuerl, Donald W.: (See **Cardinals' Biographies**).

Y Z

Yanta, John W.: b. Oct. 2, 1931, Runge, TX; educ. St. John's Preparatory Seminary and Assumption Seminary (San Antonio); ord. priest (San Antonio*), Mar. 17, 1956; ord. titular bp. of Naratcata and aux. bp. of San Antonio, Dec. 30, 1994; app. bp. of Amarillo, Jan. 21,1997, inst., Mar. 17, 1997; ret. Jan. 3, 2008.

Younan, Joseph: b. Nov. 15, 1944, Hassakeh, Syria; educ. Our Lady of Deliverance Seminary (Charfet, Lebanon), Pontifical College of the Propagation of the Faith (Rome); ord. priest, Sept. 12, 1971; came to U.S., 1986; served Syrian Catholics in U.S.; ord. first bp. Our Lady of Deliverance of Newark for Syrian Catholics in the U.S. and Canada, Jan. 7, 1996, in Kamisly, Syria; ret. Jan. 20, 2009; elected patriarch of Antioch for the Syrians, Jan. 20, 2009; inst. Feb. 15, 2009.

Zaidan, Abdallah E.: b. March 10, 1963, Kseibe, Lebanon; educ. Holy Spirit University (Kaslik, Lebanon), St. John's Univ. (NY), Pepperdine Univ. (CA); entered the Congregation of Maronite Lebanese Missionaries and ord. priest, July 20, 1986; contributed to the establishment of Maronite missions in Dallas and Houston; app. eparch of the Maronite Eparchy of Our Lady of Lebanon of Los Angeles, July 10, 2013; ord. bp. Sept. 28, 2013.

Zarama Pasqualetto, Luis R.: b. Nov. 28, 1958, Pasto, Colombia; educ. Seminary of Pasto, Universidad Mariana (Pasto, Colombia), Universidad Javeriana (Bogota, Colombia); ord. priest (Atlanta*), Nov. 27, 1993; became an American citizen on July 4, 2004; app. aux. bp. of Atlanta and titular bp. of Baranus, July 27, 2009; ord. bp. Sept. 29, 2009.

Zavala, Gabino: b. Sept. 7, 1951, Guerrero, Mexico; became U.S. citizen, 1976; educ. St. John's Seminary (Los Angeles), Catholic Univ. (Washington, DC); ord. priest (Los Angeles*), May 28, 1977; ord. titular bp. of Tamascani and aux. bp. of Los Angeles, Mar. 19, 1994; ret. Jan. 4, 2012.

Zayek, Francis: b. Oct. 18, 1920, Manzanillo, Cuba; ord. priest, Mar. 17, 1946; ord. titular bp. of Callinicum and aux. bp. for Maronites in Brazil, Aug. 5, 1962; named apostolic exarch for Maronites in U.S., with headquarters in Detroit; inst., June 11. 1966; first eparch of St. Maron of Detroit, Mar. 25, 1972; see transferred to Brooklyn, June 27, 1977; given personal title of abp., Dec. 22, 1982; ret., Nov. 23, 1996.

Zipfel, Paul A.: b. Sept. 22, 1935, St. Louis, MO; educ. Cardinal Glennon College, Kenrick Seminary (St. Louis, MO), Catholic Univ. (Washington, DC), St. Louis Univ. (St. Louis, MO); ord. priest (St. Louis*), Mar. 18, 1961; ord. titular bp. of Walla Walla and aux. bp. of St. Louis, June 29, 1989; app. bp. of Bismarck, Dec. 31, 1996; ret. Oct. 19, 2012.

Zubic, David A.: b. Sept. 4, 1949, Sewickley, PA; educ. St. Paul Seminary Duquesne Univ. (Pittsburgh), St. Mary's Seminary (Baltimore), Duquesne Univ. (Pittsburgh); ord. priest (Pittsburgh), May 3, 1975; ord. titular bp. of Jamestown and aux. of Pittsburgh, Apr. 6, 1997; app. bp. of Green Bay, Oct. 10, 2003; app. bp. of Pittsburgh, July 18, 2007.

Zurek, Patrick J.: b. Aug. 17, 1948, Wallis, TX; educ. Univ. of St. Thomas (Houston), Angelicum and Alphonsian Academy (Rome); ord priest (Austin), June 29, 1975; app. titular bp. of Tamugadi and aux. bp. of San Antonio, Jan. 5, 1998, ord., Feb. 16, 1998; app. bp. of Amarillo, Jan. 3, 2008.

BISHOP-BROTHERS

(The asterisk indicates brothers who were bishops at the same time.)

There have been 10 pairs of brother-bishops in the history of the U.S. hierarchy.

Living: Francis T. Hurley,* abp. of Anchorage and Mark J. Hurley,* bp. emeritus of Santa Rosa (deceased). Raymond J. Boland,* bp. emeritus of Kansas City-St. Joseph, MO and John Kevin Boland,* bp. of Savannah.

Deceased: Francis Blanchet* of Oregon City (Portland) and Augustine Blanchet* of Walla Walla; John S. Foley of Detroit and Thomas P. Foley of Chicago; Francis P. Kenrick,* apostolic administrator of Philadelphia, bp. of Philadelphia and Baltimore, and Peter R. Kenrick* of St. Louis; Matthias C. Lenihan of Great Falls and Thomas M. Lenihan of Cheyenne; James O'Connor, vicar apostolic of Nebraska and bp. of Omaha, and Michael O'Connor of Pittsburgh and Erie; Jeremiah F. and John W. Shanahan, both of Harrisburg; Sylvester J. Espelage, O.F.M.* of Wuchang, China, who died 10 days after the ordination of his brother, Bernard T. Espelage, O.F.M.* of Gallup; Coleman F. Carroll* of Miami and Howard Carroll* of Altoona-Johnstown.

U.S. BISHOPS OVERSEAS

Edwin Cardinal O'Brien, Grand Master of the Equestrian Order of the Holy Sepulchre of Jerusalem; Raymond Leo Cardinal Burke, Prefect of the Apostolic Signatura, Roman Curia; James Michael Cardinal Harvey, Prefect of the Prefecture of the Papal Household, Roman Curia; William Joseph Cardinal Levada, Prefect emeritus of the Congregation for the Doctrine of the Faith, Roman Curia; James Francis Cardinal Stafford, Major Penitentiary Emeritus of the Apostolic Penitentiary, Roman Curia; Edmund Casimir Cardinal Szoka, President Emeritus of the Governatorate of Vatican City State, Roman Curia; Lubomyr Cardinal Husar, Major Archbishop emeritus of Kyiv-Halyc, Kiev, Ukraine. Abp. Joseph Augustine Di Noia, O.P., Secretary of the Commission Ecclesia Dei, Roman Curia.

Abp. Edward J. Adams, apostolic nuncio to Greece; Abp. Charles Balvo, nuncio to Kenya; Abp. Michael August Blume, S.V.D., Apostolic Nuncio to Uganda; Abp. Thomas Edward Gullickson, Apostolic Nuncio to Ukraine; Abp. Joseph Salvador Marino, Apostolic Nuncio to Malaysia, East Timor, and Brunei; Abp. James P. Green, nuncio to Peru; Abp. Charles Brown, nuncio to Ireland; Abp. Edward Joseph Gilbert, C.SS.R., Archbishop emeritus of Port of Spain, Trinidad and Tobago, Antilles; Abp. Roberto Octavio González Nieves, O.F.M., Archbishop of San Juan de Puerto Rico; Abp Abp. George Hamilton Pearce, S.M., Archbishop Emeritus of Suva, Fiji, Pacific (Oceania); Abp. George Riashi, B.C.O., Archbishop of archeparchy of Tripoli of Lebanon (Lebanon) for Greek Catholic Melkites; Abp. Rrok Kola Mirdita, Archbishop of Tiranë-Durrës, Albania; Abp. Stephen Joseph Reichert, O.F.M. Cap., archbishop of Madang, Papua New Guinea; Abp. Ignace Joseph III (Ephrem) Younan, Patriarch of Antioch,

Lebanon; Abp. Cyril Bustros, S.M.S.P., abp. of Beirut; Abp. Michael Banach, Holy See permanent representative to the International Atomic Energy Agency (AIEA), to the Organization for Security and Cooperation in Europe (OSCE), and to the Preparatory Commission for the Comprehensive Nuclear-Test-Ban Treaty Organization (CTBTO) and Holy See permanent observer to the United Nations Organization for Industrial Development (ONUDI) and to the Office of the United Nations in Vienna, Austria.

Bp. Gordon Dunlap Bennett, S.J., Bishop Emeritus of Mandeville, Jamaica, Antilles; Bp. Herbert Armstrong Bevard, Bishop of Saint Thomas, American Virgin Islands; Bp. Ernest Bertrand Boland, O.P., Bishop Emeritus of Multan, Pakistan; Bp. Christopher Cardone, O.P., Bishop of Auki, Solomon Islands; Bp. Luis Morgan Casey, Vicar Apostolic emeritus of Pando, Bolivia; Bp. Nicholas D'Antonio Salza, O.F.M., Prelate Emeritus of Inmaculada Concepción de la B.V.M. en Olancho, Honduras; Bp. Paul Francis Duffy, O.M.I., Bishop emeritus of Mongu, Zambia; Bp. Daniel Fernández Torres, Auxiliary Bishop of San Juan de Puerto Rico; Bp. Capistran Heim, O.F.M., Bishop of the Prelacy of Itaituba; Bp. Robert Bever, aux. bp. of Cochabamba, Bolivia; Bp. Hlib Lonchyna, M.S.U., bp. of Holy Family, London (Ukrainian); Bp. Boris Gudziak, bp. of Saint Wladimir-le-Grand de Paris (Ukrainian);

Bp. Heriberto Hermes, O.S.B., Prelate Emeritus of Cristalândia, Goias, Brazil; Bp. Henry Theophilus Howaniec, O.F.M., Bishop of Santissima Trinità in Almaty, Kazakhstan; Bp. Antons Justs, Bishop of Jelgava, Latvia; Bp. Robert Joseph Kurtz, C. R., Bishop of Hamilton in Bermuda, Antilles; Bp. Miguel La Fay Bardi, O. Carm., Prelate of Sicuani, Peru; Bp. Hlib Lonchyna, M.S.U., Auxiliary Bishop of Lviv (Ukrainian), Ukraine; Bp. Elias James Manning, O.F.M. Conv., Bishop of Valença, Brazil; Bp. Adalberto Martínez Flores, Bishop of San Pedro, Paraguay; Bp. Juan Conway McNabb, O.S.A., Bishop Emeritus of Chulucanas, Peru; Bp. William John McNaughton, M.M., Bishop Emeritus of Inchon, South Korea; Bp. William Dermott Molloy McDermott, Bishop Emeritus of Huancavélica, Peru; Bp. Tomás Andrés Mauro Muldoon, O.F.M., Bishop of Juticalpa, Honduras; Bp. Alfredo Ernest Novak, C.SS.R., Bishop Emeritus of Paranaguá, Parana, Brazil; Bp. Donald Joseph Leo Pelletier, M.S., Bishop of Morondava, Madagascar; Bp. Miguel Romano Gómez, Auxiliary Bishop of Guadalajara, Jalisco, México; Bp. Geraldo Scarpone Caporale, O.F.M., Bishop Emeritus of Comayagua, Honduras; Bp. Pablo Ervin Schmitz Simon, O.F.M. Cap., Vicar Apostolic of Bluefields, Nicaragua; Bp. Alphonsus Augustus Sowada, O.S.C., Bishop Emeritus of Agats, Indonesia; Bp. Neil Tiedemann, C.P., Bishop of Mandeville, Jamaica, Antilles; Bp. Daniel Thomas Turley Murphy, O.S.A., Bishop of Chulucanas, Peru; Bp. David Albin Zywiec Sidor, O.F.M. Cap., Auxiliary Bishop of Bluefields, Nicaragua; Bp. William Fey, O.F.M. Cap., Bishop of Kimbe, Papua New Guinea; Bp. Henry Theophilus Howaniec, O.F.M., Bishop emeritus of Santissima Trinita in Almaty; Christopher J. Glancy, C.S.V., aux. bp. of Belize City-Belmopan, Belize. (See **Missionary Bishops**.)

DECEAESED BISHOPS, 2012-2013

Anderson, Bp. Moses B., 84, Jan. 7, auxiliary bishop of Detroit from 1983-2003.

Bosco, Bp. Anthony G., 85, July 2, bishop of Greensburg from 1987 to 2004.

Catanello, Bp. Ignatius A., 74, March 11, auxiliary bp. of Brooklyn from 1994.

Cooney, Bp. Patrick R. 78, Oct. 15, bishop of Gaylord from 1989-2009.

D'Arcy, Bp. John M., 80, Feb. 3, bishop of Fort Wayne-South Bend from 1985-2009.

Dorsey, Bp. Norbert M., C.P.: 83, Feb. 21, bishop of Orlando from 1990-2004.

Fitzsimons, Bp. George K., 84, July 21, bp. of Salina from 1984-2004.

Gossman, Bp. F. Joseph, 83, Aug. 12, bp. of Raleigh from 1975-2006.

Hughes, Bp. Edward T., 92, Dec. 25, bishop of Metuchen from 1986-97.

Hughes, Bp. William A., 91, Feb. 7, bishop of Covington from 1979-1995.

Jakubowski, Bp. Thad J., 89, July 14, auxiliary bishop of Chicago from 1988-2003.

Lotocky, Innocent Hilarius, O.S.B.M., July 4, bp. of St. Nicholas of Chicago for the Ukrainians from 1981-1993.

McFadden, Bp. Joseph P., 65, May 2, bishop of Harrisburg from 2010-2013.

O'Neill, Bp. Arthur J., 95, April 27, bishop of Rockford from 1968 to 1994.

Ottenweller, Bp. Albert H., 96, Sept. 23, bishop of Steubenville from 1977-1992.

Sullivan, Bp. Joseph M., 83, June 7, auxiliary bishop of Brooklyn from 1980-2005.

Sullivan, Bp. Walter, 84, Dec. 11, bishop of Richmond from 1974-2003.

RETIRED/RESIGNED U.S. PRELATES

Information, as of Aug. 20, 2013, includes name of the prelate and see held at the time of retirement or resignation; abps. are indicated by an asterisk. Most of the prelates listed below resigned their sees because of age in accordance with church law. See **Index: Biographies, U.S. Bishops**

Forms of address of retired residential prelates (unless they have a titular see): Abp. or Bp. Emeritus of (last see held); Former Abp. or Bp. of (last see held).

Joseph V. Adamec (Altoona-Johnstown), Emilio S. Allue S.D.B. (Boston, aux.), Kenneth A. Angell (Burlington), Juan Arzube (Los Angeles, aux.), Victor H. Balke (Crookston), Robert J. Banks (Green Bay), Eusebius J. Beltran* (Oklahoma City), Gordon D. Bennett (Mandeville, Jamaica), Ernest B. Boland, O.P. (Multan, Pakistan), Kevin Boland (Savannah), Raymond J. Boland (Kansas-City-St. Joseph), John P. Boles (Boston, aux.), William D. Borders* (Baltimore), Paul M. Boyle, C.P. (Mandeville, Jamaica), Joseph M. Breitenbeck (Grand Rapids), Tod Brown (Orange), Robert A. Brucato (New York, aux.), Fabian Bruskewitz (Lincoln), Daniel Buechlein, O.S.B.* (Indianapolis).

Edmond Carmody (Corpus Christi), Dominic Carmon (New Orleans, aux.), Joseph L. Charron, C.PP.S. (Des Moines), Gilbert E. Chavez (San Diego, aux.), Matthew Clark (Rochester), John W. Comber, M.M. (Foratiano, titular see), Thomas Connolly (Baker), Ronald G. Connors, C.SS.R. (San Juan de la Maguana, Dominican Republic), Patrick Cooney (Gaylord), Thomas J. Costello (Syracuse, aux.), Arnold R. Cotey, S.D.S. (Nachingwea, now Lindi, Tanzania), Daniel A. Cronin* (Hartford), Edward Cullen (Allentown), John Stephen Cummins (Oakland), William G. Curlin (Charlotte), James J. Daly (Rockville Centre, aux.), Thomas V. Daily (Brooklyn), Nicholas D'Antonio,

O.F.M. (Olancho, Honduras).

Louis A. DeSimone (Philadelphia, aux.), Joseph T. Dimino* (Military Services archdiocese), Robert W. Donnelly (Toledo, aux.), Thomas G. Doran (Rockford), Stephen Hector Doueihi (St. Maron of Brooklyn), John Dougherty (aux. Scranton), Michael J. Dudick (Passaic, Byzantine rite), Paul Duffy (Mongu, Zambia), Roland Pierre DuMaine (San Jose), Thomas L. Dupre (Springfield), Dennis V. Durning, C.S.Sp. (Arusha, Tanzania), Edward Cardinal Egan* (New York), John Elya (Newton), John Favalora (Miami*), J. Lennox Federal (Salt Lake City), Joseph A. Fiorenza* (Galveston-Houston), Thomas J. Flanagan (San Antonio, aux.), Raphael M. Fliss (Superior), Patrick F. Flores* (San Antonio), Harry Flynn* (St. Paul-Minneapolis), David E. Foley (Birmingham), Marion F. Forst (Dodge City), William E. Franklin (Davenport), William B. Friend (Shreveport).

Joseph Galante (Camden), Victor Galeone (St. Augustine), James H. Garland (Marquette), Louis E. Gelineau (Providence), Odore Gendron (Manchester), Peter L. Gerety* (Newark), Joseph J. Gerry, O.S.B. (Portland, ME), Gerald Gettelfinger (Evansville), Ronald Gilmore (Dodge City), Raymond E. Goedert (Chicago, aux.), John R. Gorman (Chicago, aux.), Rene H. Gracida (Corpus Christi), Charles V. Grahmann (Dallas), James Griffin (Columbus), Thomas J. Gumbleton (Detroit, aux.), Richard C. Hanifen (Colorado Springs), Jerome Hanus (Dubuque*), Henry Harrington (Winona), Joseph Hart (Cheyenne), Edward D. Head (Buffalo), Herbert Hermes, O.S.B. (Cristalandia, Brazil), William Higi (Lafayette).

Joseph L. Hogan (Rochester), William Russell Houck (Jackson), Henry Howaniec, O.F.M. (Santissima Trinita in Almaty), Joseph Lawson Howze (Biloxi), Alfred Hughes* (New Orleans), Edward T. Hughes (Metuchen), Raymond G. Hunthausen* (Seattle), Walter A. Hurley (Grand Rapids), Joseph L. Imesch (Joliet), Francis Irwin (Boston, aux.), Fernando Isern (Pueblo), Cardinal William Keeler* (Baltimore), James P. Keleher* (Kansas City), Thomas C. Kelly, O.P.* (Louisville), Edward Kmiec (Buffalo), Daniel W. Kucera, O.S.B.* (Dubuque), Bernard Cardinal Law* (Boston), John J. Leibrecht (Springfield-Cape Girardeau), Raymond W. Lessard (Savannah), Card. William J. Levada (prefect for the Cong. of the Doctrine of the Faith), Oscar Lipscomb* (Mobile), Martin N. Lohmuller (Philadelphia, aux.), Basil Losten (Stamford), Timothy J. Lyne (Chicago, aux.).

Robert P. Maginnis (Philadelphia, aux.), Cardinal Adam Maida* (Detroit), Cardinal Theodore McCarrick* (Washington, D.C.), James F. McCarthy (New York, aux.) John McCarthy (Austin), William J. McCormack (New York, aux.), Andrew McDonald (Little Rock), Charles J. McDonnell (Newark, aux.), John B. McDowell (Pittsburgh, aux.), Norman McFarland (Orange, CA), Bernard J. McLaughlin (Buffalo, aux.), John C. McNabb, O.S.A. (Chulucanas), William J. McNaughton (Inchon),

John J. McRaith (Owensboro), Joseph Madera (Military Archdiocese, aux.), Joseph F. Maguire (Springfield, MA), Cardinal Roger Mahony* (Los Angeles), Thomas R. Manning, O.F.M. (Coroico, Bolivia), Dominic Anthony Marconi (Newark, aux.), Joseph Martino (Scranton), Leroy T. Matthiesen (Amarillo), Carl F. Mengeling (Lansing), Anthony F. Mestice (New York, aux.), James E. Michaels (Wheeling Charleston, aux.), Anthony M. Milone (Great Falls-Billings), Michail Moskal (St. Josaphat), James M. Moynihan (Syracuse), Robert E. Mulvee (Providence), James A. Murray (Kalamazoo), John J. Nevins (Venice), William C. Newman (Baltimore, aux.), Alfredo Ernest Novak, C.SS.R. Paranaguá, Brazil), Thomas Joseph O'Brien (Phoenix), Leonard James Olivier, S.V.D. (Washington, aux.).

George H. Pearce, S.M.* (Suva, Fiji Islands), Raymundo J. Peña (Brownsville), Edward Pevec (Cleveland, aux.), Daniel Pilarczyk (Cincinnati*), Anthony M. Pilla (Cleveland), Bernard F. Popp (San Antonio, aux.), Alexander James Quinn (aux., Cleveland), Francis A. Quinn (Sacramento), John R. Quinn* (San Francisco), Ricardo Ramirez (Las Cruces), Daniel P. Reilly (Worcester), John Ricard, S.S.J. (Pensacola), Cardinal Justin Rigali* (Philadelphia), Vincent M. Rizzotto (Galveston-Houston, aux.), Francis X. Roque (Military Archdiocese, aux.), Peter A. Rosazza (aux. Hartford), Robert John Rose (Grand Rapids), George E. Rueger (Worcester, aux.), Daniel Ryan (Springfield, IL), Sylvester Ryan (Monterey).

Michael A. Saltarelli (Wilmington), Nicholas J. Samra (Melkite eparchy of Newton, aux.), Joseph Sartoris (Los Angeles, aux.), Stanley G. Schlarman (Dodge City), Walter J. Schoenherr (Detroit, aux.), Francis B. Schulte* (New Orleans), Carlos A. Sevilla (Yakima), Daniel E. Sheehan* (Omaha), Robert J. Shaheen (Our Lady of Lebanon), Gilbert I. Sheldon (Steubenville), William Skylstad (Spokane), John Snyder (St. Augustine), Kenneth D. Steiner (Portland, aux.), Philip Straling (Reno), Stephen Sulyk* (Philadelphia, Ukrainians), J. Keith Symons (Palm Beach).

Arthur Tafoya (Pueblo), Elliott Thomas (Virgin Islands), David B. Thompson (Charleston), James C. Timlin (Scranton), Donald Trautman (Erie), René A. Valero (Brooklyn, aux.), George Vlazny (Portland*), Daniel Walsh (Santa Rosa), Ignatius Wang (San Francisco, aux.), Emil A. Wcela (Rockville Center, aux.), Rembert G. Weakland, O.S.B.* (Milwaukee), William K. Weigand (Sacramento), James Kendrick Williams (Lexington), George O. Wirz (Madison, aux.), John W. Yanta (Amarillo), Joseph Younan (Our Lady of Deliverance), Gabino Zavala (Los Angeles, aux.), Francis Zayek (St. Maron of Brooklyn), Paul A. Zipfel (Bismarck).

American Bishops of the Past: For coverage of the deceased bishops who served in the United States, please visit www.CatholicAlmanac.com.

The United States Conference of Catholic Bishops

Courtesy USCCB

According to the United States Conference of Catholic Bishops, the USCCB is an assembly of the hierarchy of the United States and the U.S. Virgin Islands who jointly exercise certain pastoral functions on behalf of the Christian faithful of the United States. The purpose of the Conference is to promote the greater good which the Church offers humankind, especially through forms and programs of the apostolate fittingly adapted to the circumstances of time and place. This purpose is drawn from the universal law of the Church and applies to the episcopal conferences which are established all over the world for the same purpose.

The bishops themselves constitute the membership of the Conference and are served by a staff of over 350 lay people, priests, deacons, and religious located at the Conference headquarters in Washington, DC. There is also a small Office of Film and Broadcasting in New York City and a branch office of Migration and Refugee Services in Miami.

The Conference is organized as a corporation in the District of Columbia. Its purposes under civil law are: "To unify, coordinate, encourage, promote and carry on Catholic activities in the United States; to organize and conduct religious, charitable and social welfare work at home and abroad; to aid in education; to care for immigrants; and generally to enter into and promote by education, publication and direction the objects of its being."

History

When the bishops merged their two national organizations into the United States Conference of Catholic Bishops (USCCB) on July 1, 2001, it marked the latest chapter in the evolution of the bishops' national structure, which was established 82 years ago in the aftermath of the First World War. Like its immediate predecessors — the National Conference of Catholic Bishops (NCCB) and United States Catholic Conference (USCC) — the USCCB is an organization staffed by lay people, priests, and members of religious orders, but whose members are the bishops of the United States, and it is the bishops who direct its activities.

The concept of the bishops acting together on matters of mutual interest can be traced back to 1919 when, in their first national meeting since 1884, they agreed to meet annually and to form the National Catholic Welfare Council (NCWC) to serve as their organized voice on the national scene. The word "Council" was replaced by the word "Conference" in 1922.

In 1966, following the Second Vatican Council, NCWC was reorganized into two parallel conferences. The National Conference of Catholic Bishops — sometimes referred to as the canonical arm — would deal with matters connected to the internal life of the Church, such as liturgy and priestly life and ministry. The U.S. Catholic Conference — in effect the civil arm — would represent the bishops as they related to the "secular" world, in areas such as social concerns, education, communications and public affairs. During the period from 1992 to 1996, a Conference committee on mission and structure, headed by the late Card. Joseph L. Bernardin of Chicago, led the bishops in extensive consultation on restructuring. A primary purpose of this undertaking was to provide more of the nation's approximately 300 bishops with an opportunity to be directly involved in the work of the Conference, which operates primarily through a committee structure.

In 1997 the bishops voted to combine NCCB-USCC into one conference, to be called the U.S. Conference of Catholic Bishops. They decided that in the future only bishops would be voting members of committees, but non-bishops could serve on some committees as consultants or advisers. A new committee on statutes and bylaws, headed by Abp. Daniel E. Pilarczyk of Cincinnati, which was formed to lead the rest of the reorganization process, completed its work last year. The new statutes and bylaws were subsequently approved by the Holy See.

It is unlikely that persons outside the bishops' conference will notice any immediate difference in the new structure. Many of the same concerns that motivated the bishops in 1919 — like the welfare of immigrants, communicating through the Catholic press, and defending the legal rights of the Church — are still pressing today, as evidenced in the departments which carry out these functions, though many others have been added as well. In a May 23, 2001, letter sent to organizations which have dealings with the Conference, its General Secretary, Msgr. William P. Fay, said the renaming "will not affect any change in the activities or programs of the Conference but simply how the Conference is identified."

USCCB Restructuring

At their fall general meeting on Nov. 14, 2006, the bishops of the USCCB approved a plan to restructure national operations of the USCCB and to cut diocesan assessments by 16 percent, eliminate more than 60 jobs at the USCCB headquarters in Washington and satellite offices, and trim the number of USCCB committees. The comprehensive plan of reorganization and strategic planning for 2008-2011 was approved by a 213-19 vote. Diocesan heads then voted 158-6 to adopt the proposal to reduce diocesan funding of the USCCB in 2008 by 16 percent. Diocesan assessments, covering nearly $11.9 million of the USCCB's overall budget of $139.5 million in 2007, will be reduced in 2008 to just under $10 million.

The restructuring plan was overseen by the bishops' Committee on Priorities and Plans, in the last few years under the chairmanship of Archbishop Michael J. Sheehan of Santa Fe, NM, who also served as secretary of the conference.

Central to the reorganization was the plan for the conference to concentrate on top priorities discerned by the bishops. Those chosen for the 2008-2011 planning cycle:

• Implementation of the pastoral initiative on marriage.
• Faith formation focused on sacramental practice.
• Priestly and religious vocations.
• The Life and dignity of the human person.
• Recognition of cultural diversity, with special emphasis on Hispanic ministry, "in the spirit of Encuentro."

Mission Statement

Preamble

Evangelizing is in fact the grace and vocation proper to the Church, her deepest identity. She exists to evangelize. (*Evangelii Nuntiandi*, No. 14)

The mission of evangelization is entrusted by Christ to his Church to be carried out in all her forms of ministry, witness, and service. By evangelizing, the Church seeks to bring about in all Catholics such an enthusiasm for their faith that, in living their faith in Jesus and strengthened by the sacraments, most especially the celebration of the Eucharist, they freely share that faith with others to transform the world. (Based on Go and Make Disciples, A National Plan and Strategy for Catholic Evangelization in the United States, 1990).

Mission

The mission of the United States Conference of Catholic Bishops (see CIC, c. 447) is to support the ministry of bishops with an emphasis on evangelization, by which the bishops exercise in a communal and collegial manner certain pastoral functions entrusted to them by the Lord Jesus of sanctifying, teaching, and governing (see *Lumen Gentium*, No. 21).

This mission calls the Conference to:

-Act collaboratively and consistently on vital issues confronting the Church and society (see *Christus Dominus*, No. 38.1)

-Foster communion with the Church in other nations, within the Church universal, under the leadership of its supreme pastor, the Roman Pontiff

-Offer appropriate assistance to each bishop in fulfilling his particular ministry in the local Church (Cf. *Apostolos Suos*, 1998.)

Administration

The principal officers of the conference are: Card. Timothy M. Dolan, president; Abp. Joseph Kurtz, vice president; Bp. Michael Bransfield, treasurer; Abp. Peter Sartain, secretary; ; Msgr. Ronny Jenkins, J.C.D., general secretary. Headquarters of the conferences are located at 3211 Fourth St. N.E., Washington, D.C. 20017; (202) 541-3000; www.usccb.org.

USCCB REGIONS

I. Maine, Vermont, New Hampshire, Massachusetts, Rhode Island, Connecticut. II. New York. III. New Jersey, Pennsylvania. IV. Delaware, District of Columbia, Maryland, Virgin Islands, Virginia, West Virginia, Military Archdiocese. V. Alabama, Kentucky, Louisiana, Mississippi, Tennessee. VI. Michigan, Ohio. VII. Illinois, Indiana, Wisconsin. VIII. Minnesota, North Dakota, South Dakota. IX. Iowa, Kansas, Missouri, Nebraska. X. Arkansas, Oklahoma, Texas. XI. California, Hawaii, Nevada. XII. Idaho, Montana, Alaska, Washington, Oregon. XIII. Utah, Arizona, New Mexico, Colorado, Wyoming, including El Paso. XIV. Florida, Georgia, North Carolina, South Carolina. XV: Eastern Catholic Churches (non-geographic; approved on Nov. 14, 2006).

Pastoral Council

The conference, one of many similar territorial conferences envisioned in the conciliar Decree on the Pastoral Office of Bishops in the Church (No. 38), is "a council in which the bishops of a given nation or territory [in this case, the United States] jointly exercise their pastoral office to promote the greater good which the Church offers mankind, especially through the forms and methods of the apostolate fittingly adapted to the circumstances of the age."

Its decisions, "provided they have been approved legitimately and by the votes of at least two-thirds of the prelates who have a deliberative vote in the conference, and have been recognized by the Apostolic See, are to have juridically binding force only in those cases prescribed by the common law or determined by a special mandate of the Apostolic See, given either spontaneously or in response to a petition of the conference itself."

All bishops who serve the Church in the U.S., its territories and possessions, have membership and voting rights in the USCCB. Retired bishops cannot be elected to conference offices nor can they vote on matters that by law are binding by two-thirds of the membership. Only diocesan bishops can vote on diocesan quotas, assessments or special collections.

Officers, Committees

The conference operates through a number of bishops' committees with functions in specific areas of work and concern. Their basic assignments are to prepare materials on the basis of which the bishops, assembled as a conference, make decisions, and to put suitable action plans in effect.

The officers, with several other bishops, hold positions on executive-level committees — Administrative, Executive, the Committee on Budget and Finance, the Committee on Personnel, and the Committee on Priorities and Plans. They also, with other bishops, serve on the USCCB Administrative Committee.

STANDING COMMITTEES

The standing committees and their chairmen (Cardinals, Archbishops, and Bishops), as of Aug. 15, 2013 are as follows (chairmen elect are in parentheses):

Canonical Affairs and Church Governance – Abp. Timothy Broglio
Catholic Education – Bp. Joseph McFadden
Child and Youth Protection – Bp. R. Daniel Conlon
Clergy, Consecrated Life, and Vocations – Bp. Michael F. Burbidge
Committee on Communications – Bp. John Wester
Cultural Diversity in the Church – Bp. Jaime Soto
• Subcommittee on African American Affairs (Permanent) – Bp. Martin D. Holley
• Subcommittee on Asian and Pacific Island Affairs (Permanent) – Bp. Randolph R. Calvo
• Subcommittee on Hispanics Affairs – Bp. Gerald R. Barnes
• Subcommittee on Native American Catholics (Permanent) – Abp. Charles J. Chaput, O.F.M. Cap.
• Subcommittee on Pastoral Care of Migrants, Refugees, and Travelers (Permanent) – Bp. Rutilio J. Del Riego
Divine Worship – Card. Daniel DiNardo
• Subcommittee on Hispanics and the Liturgy (Permanent) – Bp. Octavio Cisneros
Doctrine – Abp. John Nienstedt
• Subcommittee on the Translation of Scripture Text (Permanent) – Bp. Arthur J. Serratelli
Domestic Justice and Human Development – Abp. Thomas Wenski
• Subcommittee on the Catholic Campaign for Human Development (Permanent) – Bp. Jaime Soto
Ecumenical and Interreligious Affairs – Bp. Denis Madden
Evangelization and Catechesis – Bp. David Ricken
• Subcommittee on the Catechism (Permanent) – Bp. Leonard P. Blair
International Justice and Peace – Bp. Richard E. Pates
Laity, Marriage, Family Life, and Youth – Bp. Richard Malone
Migration – Bp. Eusebio Elizondo, M.Sp.S.
National Collections – Abp. Dennis Schnurr
• Subcommittee on Catholic Home Missions (Permanent) – Bp. Michael Warfel
• Subcommittee on the Church in Africa (Permanent) – Bp. John H. Ricard, S.S.J.
• Subcommittee on the Church in Central and Eastern Europe (Permanent) – Cardinal Justin Rigali
• Subcommittee on the Church in Latin America (Permanent) – Abp. José H. Gomez
Pro-Life Activities – Cardinal Sean O'Malley
Ad Hoc Committee for the Defense of Marriage – Abp. Salvatore Cordileone

Executive Level and Management Committees

Administrative Committee – Card. Timothy M. Dolan
Budget and Finance – Bp. Kevin J. Farrell
• Audit Subcommittee– Bp. Kevin J. Farrell
Priorities and Plans – Bp. George V. Murry, S.J.
Executive Committee – Card. Timothy M. Dolan

Task Forces, Boards and Related Organizations

Task Force on Health Care – Bp. Kevin C. Rhoades
Task Force on Spanish Language Bible – Abp. José H. Gomez
American College of Louvain – Bp. David L. Ricken
North American College, Rome – Abp. John J. Myers
Board of Directors: Catholic Legal Immigration Network, INC – Bp. Jaime Soto
Board of Directors: Catholic Relief Services – Bp. Gerald Kicanas
Board of Trustees: CCD, INC – Card. Timothy M. Dolan
National Review Board – Francesco Cesareo, Ph.D.

STATE CATHOLIC CONFERENCES

These conferences are agencies of bishops and dioceses in the various states. Their general purposes are to develop and sponsor cooperative programs designed to cope with pastoral and common-welfare needs, and to represent the dioceses before governmental bodies, the public, and in private sectors. Their membership consists of representatives from the dioceses in the states — bishops, clergy and lay persons in various capacities.

The National Association of State Catholic Conference Directors maintains liaison with the general secretariat of the United States Conference of Catholic Bishops.

Alaska Catholic Conference, 225 Cordova St., Anchorage. AK 99501; (907) 297-7700; Exec. Dir., Mary Gore.
Arizona Catholic Conference, 400 E. Monroe St., Phoenix, AZ 85004-2376; (602) 354-2391; Exec. Dir., Ron Johnson.
California Catholic Conference, 1119 K St., 2nd Floor, Sacramento, CA 95814; (916) 443-4851; Exec. Dir., Edward Dolejsi.
Colorado Catholic Conference, 1535 Logan St., Denver, CO 80203; (303) 894-8808; Exec. Dir. Jennifer Kraska.
Connecticut Catholic Conference, 134 Farmington Ave., Hartford, CT 06105; (860) 524-7882; Exec. Dir., Michael Culhane.
Florida Catholic Conference, 201 W. Park Ave., Tallahassee, FL 32301; (850) 222-3803; Exec. Dir., Dr. D. Michael McCarron, Ph.D.
Georgia Catholic Conference, Office Bldg., 3200 Deans Bridge Rd., Augusta, GA 30906; (706) 798-1719; Exec. Dir., Francis J. Mulcahy, Esq.
Hawaii Catholic Conference, Stephen Diocesan Center, 6301 Pali Hwy., Kaneohe, HI 96744; (808) 585-3341; Exec. Dir., Dcn. Walter Yoshimitsu.
Illinois, Catholic Conference of, 65 E. Wacker Pl., Ste. 1620, Chicago, IL 60601; (312) 368-1066. 108 E. Cook, Springfield, IL 62701; (217) 528-9200; Exec. Dir., Robert Gilligan.
Indiana Catholic Conference, 1400 N. Meridian St., P.O. Box 1410, Indianapolis, IN 46206; (317) 236-1455; Exec. Dir., Glenn Tebbe.
Iowa Catholic Conference, 530-42nd St., Des Moines, IA 50312-2707; (515) 243-6256; Exec. Dir., Thomas Chapman.
Kansas Catholic Conference, 6301 Antioch, Merriam, KS 66202; (913) 722-6633; Exec. Dir.,

Michael Schuttloffel.

Kentucky, Catholic Conference of, 1042 Burlington Lane, Frankfort, KY 40601; (502) 875-4345; Interim Exec. Dir., Rev. Patrick Delahanty.

Louisiana Catholic Conference, 3423 Hundred Oaks Ave., Baton Rouge, LA 70808; (225) 344-7120; Exec. Dir., Daniel J. Loar.

Maryland Catholic Conference, 188 Duke of Gloucester St., Annapolis, MD 21401; (410) 269-1155; Exec. Dir., Mary Ellen Russell.

Massachusetts Catholic Conference, 150 Staniford St., West End Pl., Boston, MA 02114-2511; (617) 367-6060; Acting Exec. Dir., James F. Driscoll.

Michigan Catholic Conference, 510 N. Capitol Ave., Lansing, MI 48933; (517) 372-9310; President and CEO, Paul Long.

Minnesota Catholic Conference, 475 University Ave. W., St. Paul, MN 55103; (651) 227-8777; Interim Exec. Dir., Jason Adkins.

Missouri Catholic Conference, P.O. Box 1022, 600 Clark Ave., Jefferson City, MO 65102; (573) 635-7239; Exec. Dir., J. Micheal Hoey.

Montana Catholic Conference, P.O. Box 1708, Helena, MT 59624; (406) 442-5761; www.mt.net/~mcc; Exec. Dir., Moe Wosepka.

Nebraska Catholic Conference, 215 Centennial Mall South, Suite 410, Lincoln, NE 68508-1890; (402) 477-7517; Exec. Dir., James R. Cunningham.

Nevada Catholic Conference, 290 South Arlington Ave., Ste. 200, Reno, NV 89501-1713; (775) 322-7412; Exec. Dir., John Cracchiolo.

New Jersey Catholic Conference, 149 N. Warren St., Trenton, NJ 08608; (609) 989-1120; Exec. Dir., Patrick R. Brannigan.

New York State Catholic Conference, 465 State St., Albany, NY 12203; (518) 434-6195; www.nyscatholicconference.org; Exec. Dir., Richard E. Barnes.

North Dakota Catholic Conference, 103 3rd St., Ste. 2, Bismarck, ND 58501; (701) 223-2519; www.ndcatholic.org; Exec. Dir., Christopher T. Dodson.

Ohio, Catholic Conference of, 9 E. Long St., Suite 201, Columbus, OH 43215; (614) 224-7147; Exec. Dir., Carolyn Jurkowitz.

Oregon Catholic Conference, 2838 E. Burnside, Portland, OR 97214; (503) 233-8387; General Counsel and Exec. Dir., Msgr. Denis O'Donovan.

Pennsylvania Catholic Conference, 223 North St., Box 2835, Harrisburg, PA 17105; (717) 238-9613; (717) 238-9613; Exec. Dir., Dr. Robert J. O'Hara, Jr.

Texas Catholic Conference, 1625 Rutherford Lane, Bldg. D, Austin, TX 78754; (512) 339-9882; Exec. Dir., Andrew Rivas.

Washington State Catholic Conference, 508 2nd Ave. West, Seattle, WA 98119-3928; (206) 301-0556; Exec. Dir., Sr. Sharon Park, O.P.

West Virginia State Catholic Conference, P.O. Box 230, Wheeling, WV 26003; (304) 233-0880; Dir., Rev. Brian P. O'Donnell, S.J., Ph.D.

Wisconsin Catholic Conference, 30 W. Mifflin St., Suite 302, Madison, WI 53703; (608) 257-0004; Exec. Dir., John A. Huebscher.

Background

The National Conference of Catholic Bishops (NCCB), was established by action of the U.S. hierarchy Nov. 14, 1966, as a strictly ecclesiastical body with defined juridical authority over the Church in this country. It was set up with the approval of the Holy See and in line with directives from the Second Vatican Council. Its constitution was formally ratified during the November 1967 meeting of the U.S. hierarchy. The NCCB was a development from the Annual Meeting of the Bishops of the United States, whose pastoral character was originally approved by Pope Benedict XV, Apr. 10, 1919.

The USCC, as of Jan. 1, 1967, took over the general organization and operations of the former National Catholic Welfare Conference, Inc., whose origins dated back to the National Catholic War Council of 1917. The council underwent some change after World War I and was established on a permanent basis on Sept. 24, 1919, as the National Catholic Welfare Council to serve as a central agency for organizing and coordinating the efforts of U.S. Catholics in carrying out the social mission of the Church in this country. In 1923, its name was changed to National Catholic Welfare Conference, Inc., and clarification was made of its nature as a service agency of the bishops and the Church rather than as a conference of bishops with real juridical authority in ecclesiastical affairs.

The Official Catholic Directory stated that the USCC assisted "the bishops in their service to the Church in this country by uniting the people of God where voluntary collective action on a broad interdiocesan level is needed. The USCC provided an organizational structure and the resources needed to insure coordination, cooperation, and assistance in the public, educational and social concerns of the Church at the national, regional, state and, as appropriate, diocesan levels."

CATHOLIC RELIEF SERVICES

Catholic Relief Services is the official overseas aid and development agency of U.S. Catholics; it is a separately incorporated organization of the U.S. Conference of Catholic Bishops.

CRS was founded in 1943 by the bishops of the United States to help civilians in Europe and North Africa caught in the disruption and devastation of World War II. As conditions in Europe improved in the late 1940s and early 1950s, the works conducted by CRS spread to other continents and areas — Asia, Africa and Latin America.

Although best known for its record of disaster response, compassionate aid to refugees and commitment to reconstruction and rehabilitation, CRS places primary focus on long-term development projects designed to help people to help themselves and to determine their own future. Administrative funding for CRS comes largely from the American Bishops' Overseas Appeal (ABOA). Major support is derived from private, individual donors and through programs such as Operation Rice Bowl and the new Global Village Project.

Carolyn Y. Woo is Executive Director. CRS headquarters are located at 209 W. Fayette St., Baltimore, MD 21201; (410) 625-2220; www.catholicrelief.org.

Cultural Diversity in the Church

The increasing and vibrant diversity of the Catholic Church in the United States is both a vital strength and immense pastoral challenge to the American Catholic community. Much as the history of American Catholicism in the 19th and 20th centuries was profoundly shaped by the contributions of immigrants from Ireland, Germany, Italy, and Eastern Europe, so too will the Church in the United States be impacted significantly by the contributions of Hispanics, African Americans, Asians and Pacific Islanders, Europeans, and Native Americans in the 21st century and beyond.

Secretariat of Cultural Diversity in the Church

The Secretariat of Cultural Diversity in the Church of the United States Conference of Catholic Bishops is the primary instrument for the U.S. bishops in organizing pastoral care for the many different groups of Catholics in the country. The Secretariat has four subcommittees: Hispanic Catholics, African American Catholics, Native American Catholics, Asian Catholics, African Catholics, Pacific Islander Catholics, Catholic migrants and refugees. It was created officially on Jan. 1, 2008 as part of the wider reorganization of the USCCB by uniting several different secretariats.

According to its own stated mandate, the Secretariat of Cultural Diversity in the Church assists the bishops in instilling the vision of *Encuentro* 2000 and *Ecclesia in America* throughout the Church by working collaboratively with all the committees of the Conference and with bishops and their dioceses to bring Catholics from various culturally diverse communities into a fuller participation in the faith, life, and evangelizing mission of the Church. The committee especially works to promote an awareness of cultural diversity within all the committees and offices of the USCCB. This mandate includes the following responsibilities: Pastoral care of Hispanic Catholics, African American Catholics, Native American Catholics, Asian Catholics, African Catholics, Pacific Islander Catholics, Catholic migrants and refugees and people on the move.

Most Rev. Daniel Flores, Bp. of Brownsville, is current Chairman of the Secretariat. María del Mar Muñoz-Visoso is the Executive Director. She is assisted by Alejandro Aguilera-Titus, Assistant Director of Hispanic Affairs; Donna Toliver Grimes, Assistant Director of African American Affairs; Sister Anna Nguyen, S.C.C., Assistant Director of Asian Pacific Affairs, and Sr. Myrna Tordillo, MSCS, Program Coordinator for Pastoral Care for Migrants, Refugees, and Travelers. Contact information: 3211 Fourth St. N.E., Washington, DC, 20017, (202) 541-3000, www.usccb.org.

HISPANIC CATHOLICS IN THE UNITED STATES

The nation's Hispanic population totaled 50.5 million in 2010, according to figures reported by the U.S. Census Bureau. It is estimated that 71 percent of the Hispanics were baptized Catholics. Perhaps 100,000 Catholic Hispanics a year are being lost, principally to fundamentalist and pentecostal sects.

Subcommittee on Hispanic Affairs

The national secretariat for Hispanics was established by the U.S. Catholic Conference for service promoting and coordinating pastoral ministry to the Spanish-speaking. Its basic orientation is toward integral evangelization, combining religious ministry with development efforts in programs geared to the culture and needs of Hispanics. Its concerns are urban and migrant Spanish-speaking people; communications and publications in line with secretariat purposes and the service of people; bilingual and bicultural religious and general education; liaison for and representation of Hispanics with church, civic and governmental agencies.

The mandate of the subcommittee declares that the subcommittee on Hispanic Affairs is under the direction of and assists the Committee on Cultural Diversity within the Church by working collaboratively with the committee and other USCCB committees to affirm the gifts and contributions of Hispanic Catholics and to provide more opportunities for Hispanic Catholics to engage in the life of the Church and help shape its evangelization mission. This mandate includes the following areas of responsibility: The subcommittee is directly responsible for outreach to Hispanic communities and to work closely with the subcommittee on Pastoral Care of Migrants and Refugees.

The Subcommittee states that its key mission priorities are:

• Promote the vision for Hispanic/Latino(a) ministry articulated in the National Pastoral Plan for Hispanic Ministry.

• Promote the implementation of Encuentro and Mission: A New Pastoral Framework for Hispanic Ministry at the national and local level.

• Provide support and technical assistance to dioceses, key national Catholic organizations, and institutions on issues related to the Hispanic/Latino presence and the Encuentro process.

• Collaborate with USCCB committees, secretariats, and offices in the implementation of the five priorities as they relate to Hispanics/Latinos(as) in the area of vocations, marriage and family life, faith formation, life and dignity of the human person, and cultural diversity.

• Develop means to share news and information periodically with the Hispanic ministry network through a newsletter and/or website.

• Follow up on the National Encuentro for Hispanic Youth and Young Adult Ministry and the National Symposium on Lay Ecclesial Ministry.

• Continue ongoing relationship with CELAM, particularly in regard to the implementation of Ecclesia in America and the conclusions of the Fifth Conference of the Latin-American Episcopate and of the Caribbean held in Aparecida, Brazil.

Bp. Gerald Barnes is currently the Chairman of the Subcommittee of Bishops for Hispanic/Latino Affairs. Alejandro Aguilera-Titus is the assistant director of the subcommittee. Address: 3211 Fourth St. N.E., Washington, DC, 20017, (202) 541-3000, www. usccb.org.

Pastoral Patterns

Pastoral ministry to Hispanics varies, depending on cultural differences and the availability of personnel to carry it out. The pattern in cities with large numbers of Spanish-speaking people is built around special and bilingual churches, centers or other agencies where pastoral and additional forms of service are provided in a manner suited to the needs, language and culture of the people. Pastoral ministry to Hispanics was the central concern of three national meetings, Encuentros, held in 1972, 1977 and 1985. The third National Encuentro in 1985 produced a master pastoral plan for ministry which the National Conference of Catholic Bishops approved in 1987. Its four keys are collaborative ministry; evangelization; a missionary option regarding the poor, the marginalized, the family, women and youth; and the formation of lay leadership. A National Encuentro was held in 2000. In 2002, the Secretariat published *Encuentro and Mission: A New Pastoral Framework for Hispanic Ministry.*

The U.S. bishops, at their annual meeting in November 1983, approved and subsequently published a pastoral letter on Hispanic Ministry under the title, "The Hispanic Presence: Challenge and Commitment." (For text, see pp. 46-49 of the *1985 Catholic Almanac.*)

Bishops

As of Aug. 1, 2013, there were 42 (28 active) bishops of Hispanic origin in the United States; all were named since 1970 (for biographies, see Index). Fourteen were heads of archdioceses or dioceses: Abp. José H. Gomez (Los Angeles) and Abp. Gustavo Garcia-Siller, M.Sp.S. (San Antonio); Bishops Gerald R. Barnes (San Bernardino), Oscar Cantú (Las Cruces), Felipe de Jesús Estevez (St. Augustine), Daniel E. Flores (Brownsville), Richard J. Garcia (Monterey in California), Fernando Isern (Pueblo), Armando X. Ochoa (Fresno), Placido Rodriguez, C.M.F. (Lubbock), Jaime Soto (Sacramento), James A. Tamayo (Laredo), José S. Vasquez (Austin); Bp. Cirilo B. Flores is coadjutor of San Diego.

Fourteen were auxiliary bishops: Octavio Cisneros (Brooklyn), Manuel Cruz (Newark), Edgar M. Da Cunha, S.D.V. (Newark), Rutilio del Riego (San Bernardino), Eusebio Elizondo, M.Sp.S. (Seattle), José Cepeda Escobedo (Detroit), Francisco Gonzalez Valer, S.F. (Washington, DC), Robert J. Iriondo (New York), Eduardo Nevares (Phoenix), Nelson Perez (Rockville Center), Alberto Rojas (Chicago), Alexander Salazar (Los Angeles), Paul Sanchez (Brooklyn), Luis Zarama (Atlanta), Paul Sanchez (Brooklyn), and Nelson Perez (Rockville Center).

Resigned/retired prelates: Abp. Patrick F. Flores

(San Antonio); Bps. Emilio Simeon Allué (Boston), Bishop David Arias, O.A.R. (Newark), Bishop Joseph J. Madera (Military Services), Bishop Raymundo J Peña (Brownsville), Bishop Rene H. Gracida (Corpus Christi), Bishop Agustin Roman (Miami), Bishop Rene Valero (Brooklyn), Gilbert Espinoza Chavez (San Diego), Carlos A. Sevilla, S.J. (Yakima), Arthur N. Tafoya (Pueblo), Ricardo Ramirez, C.S.B. (Las Cruces), and Gabino Zavala (Los Angeles), Bishop Roberto O. Gonzalez, O.F.M. (Corpus Christi), was appointed archbishop of San Juan de Puerto Rico on Mar. 26, 1999, by Pope John Paul II. Bp. Alvaro Corrada del Rio, S.J. (Tyler) was appointed bp. of Mayaguez, Puerto Rico, on July 6, 2011.

Hispanic priests and nuns in the U.S. number about 1,600 and 3,000, respectively, according to revent estimates.

The National Pastoral Plan for Hispanic Ministry

The National Pastoral Plan for Hispanic Ministry was approved by the NCCB in November 1987. This plan is addressed to the entire Church in the United States. It focuses on the pastoral needs of the Hispanic Catholic, but it challenges all Catholics as members of the Body of Christ.

General Objective: To live and promote by means of a Pastoral de Conjunto, a model of Church that is: communitarian, evangelizing, and missionary, incarnate in the reality of the Hispanic people and open to the diversity of cultures, a promoter and example of justice ... that develops leadership through integral education ... that is leaven for the Kingdom of God in society.

Catholic Hispanic Organizations

Academy of Catholic Hispanic Theologians of the United States – ACHTUS. Dr. Carmen Nanko-Fernández, Assistant Professor of Pastoral Ministry, Catholic Theological Union, 5401 S. Cornell Ave., Chicago, Il 60615; (773) 371-5533.

Asociación Nacional de Diáconos Hispanos – ANDH. Deacon Jorge Benavente, 818 N. East Ave., Waukesha, WI 53186; (262) 542-2589.

Asociación Nacional de Sacerdotes Hispanos – ANSH Rev. Heberto M. Diaz, Diocese of Brownsville, 1910 University Blvd., Brownsville, TX 78522-2279; (956) 550-1517.

Catholic Association of Latino Leaders – CALL. Mr. Mario Paredes, 2718 W. Woodlawn Ave., P. O. Box 28410, San Antonio, TX; (210) 734-2620.

Catholic Migrant Farmworker Network – CMFN. Sr. Karen Bernhardt HM, CMFN President, P.O. Box 50026, Boise, ID 83705.

Federación de Institutos Pastorales – FIP. Sr. Ruth Bolarte, President, 7700 SW 56 St., Miami, FL 33155; (305) 279-2333.

Instituto Nacional Hispano de Liturgia – INHL. Rev. Juan J. Sosa, St. Catherine of Siena, 9200 SW 107th Ave., Miami. FL 33176; (305) 274-6333.

Mexican American Catholic College – MACC. Dr. Arturo Chavez, 3115 W Ashby, San Antonio, TX 78228; (210) 732-2156.

National Catholic Association of Diocesan Directors for Hispanic Ministry – NCADDHM Rev. Hector Madrigal, President, Diocese of Amarillo, TX.

National Catholic Network de Pastoral Juvenil Hispana – NCNPJH, Diocese of Beaumont, P. O. Box 3948; Beaumont, TX 77701; (409) 838-0451.

National Catholic Council for Hispanic Ministry (NCCHM)

The council is a volunteer federation of Roman Catholic organizations, agencies and movements committed to the development of Hispanics/Latinos in Church and society. It was established June 17, 1990, at a gathering at Mundelein College, Chicago; its by-laws were adopted in January 1991 at Mercy Center, Burlingame, CA. Currently, there are 56 members. Carmen F. Aguinaco, Pres., 205 W. Monroe Chicago, IL 60606; (312) 544-8153; www.ncchm.org.

Statistics

(Courtesy, Secretariat for Hispanic Affairs, USCCB.)

According to the most recent official Census estimates (as of 2010), there is a population of 50.5 million Hispanics, or about 16 percent of the total population. They are the fastest growing minority group in the United States, and the Hispanic population in the country is the second largest one in the world, after only Mexico. The nation's Hispanic Catholic population (not including Puerto Rico) has increased by 71 percent since 1960, and approximately 68 percent are Catholic. Hispanics also account for 71 percent of the U.S. Catholic population growth since 1960. The total Hispanic Catholic population as a percentage of the U.S. Catholic population is approximately 40 percent. Of these Hispanic Catholics, 64 percent attend church services regularly.

According to statistics based on the 2010 Census, 4,800 U.S. parishes have Hispanic ministry; approximately 21 percent of U.S. parishes have a majority Hispanic presence. There are approximately 3,000 Hispanic priests (7.45 percent of the total) and 29 active Hispanic bishops. Over the past few years, 20% of all new priests ordained in the United States have been of Hispanic/Latino(a) descent. Hispanics/Latinos(as) constitute 43% of all laypeople engaged in diocesan ministry programs. The 10 metropolitan areas with the largest Hispanic populations are: Los Angeles, New York, Chicago, Miami, Houston, Riverside-San Bernardino, Orange County, Phoenix, San Antonio, and Dallas. Eight states in 2011 had more than one million Hispanic residents: Arizona, California, Colorado, Florida, Illinois, New Jersey, New York, and Texas. Approximately one half of the Hispanic population lived in just two states: California and Texas. In New Mexico, Hispanics made up 47 percent of the state's total population, the highest for any state.

Current U.S. Census figures reveal that Hispanics accounted for 56 percent of the nation's increase in population over the decade from 2000-2010. Data demonstrate that the Hispanic population in the U.S. is young. The median age of the Hispanic population in 2009 is 27.4 years, compared with 36.8 years for the general population. The Hispanic population comprises 26 percent of the children under the age of five; Hispanics comprise 22 percent of children younger than 18. Only 4.8 percent of Hispanics are older than 65. More than 50% of all Millennial Catholics in the United States under age 25 are of Hispanic/Latino(a) descent. The poverty rate in the general population in 1999 was 7.7 percent among non-Hispanic whites; the poverty rate among Hispanics was 21.2 percent or 7.2 million people. This is a record low matching that of the 1970s. It is projected that Hispanics/ Latinos(as) will surpass the 132.8 million mark by the year 2050. Hispanics will comprise 30 percent of the total population.

AFRICAN-AMERICAN CATHOLICS IN THE UNITED STATES

The Subcommittee for African-American Catholics reports that there are presently approximately three million African-American Catholics in the United States out of 36 million total African-Americans (13 percent of the total population).

Subcommittee on African-American Catholics

(Courtesy, Subcommittee for African-American Catholics, USCCB.)

The Subcommittee on African American Affairs is the officially recognized voice of the African-American Catholic community as it articulates the needs and aspirations regarding ministry, evangelization, social justice issues, and worship. According to the Subcommittee:

The subcommittee attends the needs and aspirations of African American Catholics in regard to issues of ministry, evangelization, social justice, worship and other areas of concern. The subcommittee also seeks to be a resource for the all the Bishops and the entire Catholic Church in the U.S. It aims to articulate the socio-cultural dimension of the African American Catholic community and identify or create resources that would allow for an authentic integration of the richness of the African American Catholic culture and the Catholic Church in the United States.

The Subcommittee for African-American Catholics was established initially as a committee and secretariat by the National Conference of Catholic Bishops in 1987. It was reorganized as a subcommittee in Jan. 2008 and is part of the Bishop's Committee for Cultural Diversity in the Church. The purpose of the subcommittee is to assist the bishops in their evangelization efforts to the African-American community. The subcommittee is under the direction of and assists the Committee on Cultural Diversity in the Church by working collaboratively with the committee and other USCCB committees to affirm the gifts and contributions of African American Catholics and to provide more opportunities for African American Catholics to engage in the life of the Church and help shape its evangelizing mission. This mandate includes the following areas of responsibility: The subcommittee is directly responsible for outreach to the African American communities and to work closely with the subcommittee on Pastoral Care of Migrants and Refugees.

The subcommittee is chaired by Bp. Martin D. Holley, aux. bp. of Washington. Beverly Carroll is the assistant director of the subcommittee. Address: 3211 Fourth St. N.E., Washington, DC, 20017, (202) 541-3000, www. usccb.org.

Bishops

There were 15 (8 active) black bishops as of Sept. 1, 2013. Five were heads of dioceses: Abp. Wilton D. Gregory (Atlanta, president of the USCCB, 2001-2004); Bishops Curtis J. Guillory, S.V.D. (Beaumont), George V. Murry, S.J. (Youngstown), Edward K. Braxton (Belleville), J. Terry Steib, S.V.D. (Memphis). Four were auxiliary bishops: Shelton J. Fabre (New Orleans), Joseph N. Perry (Chicago), and Martin D. Holley (Washington). Elliott G. Thomas, of St. Thomas, Virgin Islands (res.,

June 30, 1999), Joseph L. Howze of Biloxi (res., May 15, 2001), Leonard J. Olivier, S.V.D., Washington aux. (ret., May 18, 2004), John H. Ricard, S.S.J (ret. March 11, 2011), Gordon D. Bennett (ret. Aug. 8, 2006), and Dominic Carmon, S.V.D., New Orleans aux. (ret., Dec. 13, 2006), and Guy A. Sansaricq, Brooklyn (ret. Oct. 6, 2010), are retired. African-American Bishops of the Past: James August Healy (1830-1900); Joseph A. Francis, S.V.D. (1923-1997); Eugene A. Marino, S.S.J. (1934-2000); Raymond Rodly Caeser, S.V.D. (1932-1987); James Lyke, O.F.M. (1939-1992); Carl A. Fisher, S.S.J. (1945-1993); Emerson J. Moore (1938-1995); Harold R. Perry, S.V.D. (1916-1991), and Moses Anderson, S.S.E. (1928-2013),

Statistics

The Subcommittee for African-American Catholics reports that there are presently approximately three million African-American Catholics in the United States out of 36 million total African-Americans. They are served by 798 parishes, 75 African-American pastors, and 71 Diocesan Offices for African American Catholic Ministry. There are approximately 250 African-American priests, 400 African-American sisters, 50 African-American brothers, 437 African-American deacons, and 26 African-American Seminarians. It is projected that the Black population will increase to 62 million by 2050, or 16% of the total population.

African-American Catholic Organizations

Black Catholic Catechetical Network A network intended to assist and revitalize catechesis for Black Catholics throughout the United States. Address: Mrs. Therese Wilson Favors, Office of African American Catholic Ministries, Archdiocese of Baltimore, 320 Cathedral St., Baltimore, Maryland 21201; (410) 625-8471.

Black Catholic Theological Symposium A national interdisciplinary theological society of the Roman Catholic tradition that was established "to foster among Black Catholics an ethical community of scholarly dialogue; to publish reports, the Symposium's discussions, and the research of Symposium members; to encourage the teaching and discussion of Black Catholic religious and cultural experiences." Address: Dr. M. Shawn Copeland, Convener, Associate Professor, Theology Department, Boston College, 140 Commonwealth Ave., Chestnut Hill, MA 02467; www.bcts.org.

Institute for Black Catholic Studies Founded in 1980, the IBCS of Xavier University of Louisiana offers programs in pastoral ministries, religious education and pastoral theology taught from the perspective of the Christian faith expressed in the Black religious community. Address: Sr. Jamie Phelps, OP, Ph.D., Dir., Xavier University, 1 Drexel Dr., New Orleans, LA 70125; (504) 483-7691; www.xula.edu/IBCS.html.

Josephite Fathers and Brothers The Josephite Pastoral Center was established in Sept. 1968 as an educational and pastoral service agency for the Josephites in their mission work, specifically in the black community, subsequently to all those who minister in the African-American community. St. Joseph's Society of the Sacred Heart, the sponsoring body, has about 134 priests and 11 brothers in 64 mostly southern parishes in 17 dioceses. Contact: 1130 N. Calvert St., Baltimore, MD 21202; (410) 727-3386; www.josephite.com and Josephite Pastoral Center, St. Joseph Seminary, 1200 Varnum St. NE, Washington, DC 20017; (202) 526-9270.

Knights of Peter Claver and Knights of Peter Claver, Ladies Auxiliary. The largest Black Catholic organization in the United States, the Knights are a fraternal and aid society. The Knights were begun in 1909 and the Ladies Auxiliary was authorized and their constitution adopted in August 1922; it was recognized as a Division of the National Council in 1926. The Junior Daughters was established in 1930 and the Junior Knights were established in 1935. Address: Mr. Anthanase Jones, Exec. Dir., 1825 Orleans Ave., New Orleans, LA 70116; (504) 821-4225; www.knightsofpeterclaver.com.

National African American Catholic Youth Ministry Network An affiliate of the National Federation for Catholic Youth Ministry, the NAACYMN provides assists the needs of youth and youth ministers in the African American community. The National African American Catholic Youth Ministry Network was founded in 1986. Address: Mr. Michael Youngblood, Office of Black Catholic Ministries, 1933 Spielbusch Ave., P.O. Box 958, Toledo, OH 43697-0985; (419) 244-6711; www.nbccongress.org.

National Association of African American Catholic Deacons Founded in 1993, (NAAACD) promotes unity among African American deacons, assists the professional spiritual growth of its members, and develops relationships with the National Black Catholic Congress, the National Black Catholic Clergy Caucus, and the Bishops' Committee on the Diaconate in relevant matters. Address: Rev. Mr. Marvin T. Threatt, Ph.D.,10125 Fabled Water Ct., Spring Valley, CA 91977; (619) 670-8339.

National Association of Black Catholic Administrators Established in 1976, the NABCA works to address issues and concerns facing African American communities and promote and support African American leadership. Address: Mrs. Annette Turner, President, Office of Multicultural Ministry, Archdiocese of Louisville, 1200 South Shelby St., Louisville, KY 40203-2600; (502) 636-0296.

The National Black Catholic Apostolate for Life Founded in 1997, the National Black Catholic Apostolate for Life is a ministry committed to promote the culture of life and defending unconditionally human life from the moment of conception to natural death. Address: Fr. James E. Goode, OFM, Ph.D., Pres., 440 West 36th St., New York, NY 10018-6326; (212) 868-1847; www.blackcatholicsforlife.org

National Black Catholic Clergy Caucus The National Black Catholic Clergy Caucus, founded in 1968 in Detroit, is a fraternity of several hundred black priests, permanent deacons and brothers pledged to mutual support in their vocations and ministries. Address: Deacon Dunn Cumby, DDS, President, 603 North East 17, Oklahoma City, OK 73105; (405) 524-7214.

National Black Catholic Congress The National Black Catholic Congress, Inc., was formed in 1985 exclusively to assist in the development of the Roman Catholic Church in the African-American community and to devise effective means of evangelization of African-American peoples in the United States. Address: Valerie E. Washington, President, Archdiocese of Baltimore Catholic Center, 320 Cathedral St., 3rd Floor, Baltimore, MD 21201, (410) 547-8496, www.nbccongress.org.

National Black Catholic Seminarians Association The NBCSA promotes the bonds of brotherhood among Black Catholic Seminarians and focuses on vocations of Black men and those who work with Black persons. Address: Br. Damian Harris, SVD, President, Divine Word Seminary, P.O. Box 0380, Epworth, IA 52045; (563) 876-3057; www.bcvp.org.

National Black Sisters' Conference The NBSC provides support to its membership of Black Catholic women religious through prayer, study, solidarity, and programs. Address: Sr. Patricia Haley, SCN, President, National Office,101 Q St., NE, Washington, DC 20002; (202) 529-9520.

National Office for Black Catholics The National Office for Black Catholics, organized in July 1970, is a central agency with the general purposes of promoting active and full participation by black Catholics in the Church and of making more effective the presence and ministry of the Church in the black community. Address: The Paulist Center, 3025 Fourth St. N.E., Washington, DC, 20017; (202) 635-1778.

Xavier University of Louisiana Founded by Saint Katherine Drexel and the Sisters of Blessed Sacrament in 1925, Xavier University of Louisiana is the only predominately Black Catholic university in the world. Dr. Norman C. Francis, President,1 Drexel Dr., New Orleans, LA 70125; (504) 520-7541; www.xula.edu.

ASIAN AND PACIFIC ISLANDER CATHOLICS IN THE UNITED STATES

One of the most challenging areas of ministry in the United States today is meeting the pastoral needs of Asian and Pacific Islander communities in the United States. As of 2010, 14.6 million (5% of the total U.S. population) people are Asian and 540,000 Pacific Islanders, including Hawaiians (0.3% of total U.S. population.)

Subcommittee on Asian and Pacific Islanders

The pastoral care of Asian and Pacific communities was coordinated nationally from the 1980s through the Office for the Pastoral Care of Migrants and Refugees (PCMR) of the Migration and Refugee Services Department at USCCB. When, however, the USCCB underwent its restructuring, a permanent bishops' subcommittee on Asian and Pacific Affairs was formed in 2008 as part of the Committee on Cultural Diversity in the Church. The subcommittee states that its priorities include:

• Assist dioceses in building capacities to welcome and integrate Asian and Pacific Catholics in parish life.

• Increase availability of sacraments, pastoral services, and appropriate religious education materials in the languages and cultural idioms of Asian and Pacific Island communities who cannot sufficiently make use of the common and ordinary pastoral services of local parishes.

• Promote the formation of Asian and Pacific Island Catholic pastoral leaders so they become evangelizers of their families, ethnic communities, and local churches.

• Assist Asian and Pacific Island Catholics in strengthening their faith communities and building communion with each other, with diverse members of the Church, and with their local bishops and pastors through diocesan, regional, and national gatherings.

• Promote the implementation of recommendations in Asian and Pacific Presence: Harmony in Faith at the local and national level.

The subcommittee is currently chaired by Bp. Raldolph Calvo, Bishop of Reno. Sister Anna Nguyen, S.C.C., is the assistant director of the subcommittee. Address: 3211 Fourth St. N.E., Washington, DC, 20017, (202) 541-3000, www. usccb.org.

Statistics

The Subcommittee for Asians and Pacific Islanders reports that there are presently approximately 14.6 million (5% of the total U.S. population) people in the United States who are Asian and 540,000 Pacific Islanders, including Hawaiians (0.3% of total U.S. population.) The largest Asian U.S. populations are Chinese (including mainland China, Hong Kong and Taiwan), Filipino, Indian, Vietnamese, followed by Korean, and Japanese. The largest Pacific Islander populations in the U.S. are Hawaiian, Micronesian, Guamanian, Samoan and Tongan. Except for the Filipinos, the majority of Asian and Pacific people in the U.S. are followers of Buddhism, Hinduism, and Islam.

The U.S. Asian Pacific populations with the largest number of Catholics are the Filipinos, followed by the Vietnamese, Chinese, Indian and Korean. The USCCB estimated in 1999 that Asian Pacific Catholics made up the third largest group of people of color, accounting for about 2.6% of all Catholics in the U.S.The Subcommittee also states that Asian Catholics also include members of Eastern Catholic Churches of the Syro-Malabar, Syro-Malankara, and Midle-Eastern Catholic rites.

In 2001 the USCCB issued a pastoral statement, Asian and Pacific Presence: Harmony in Faith. It was notable for being the first time that the bishops of the United States collectively issued a letter devoted to Asian and Pacific people in the Church. The full text of the document is available at: www.usccb.org/apa/statement.shtml.

NATIVE-AMERICAN CATHOLICS IN THE UNITED STATES

According to the United States Conference of Catholic Bishops' report, "Native American Catholics at the Millennium," there are nearly half a million Native American Catholics in the U.S. They are served by a variety of ministries, including the Bureau of Catholic Indian Missions and the USCCB Subcommittee of Native American Catholics.

Bureau of Catholic Indian Missions

Established in 1874 as the representative of Catholic Indian missions before the federal government and the public, the bureau was made a permanent organization in 1884 by the Third Plenary Council of Baltimore. After a remarkable history of rendering important services to the Indian people, the bureau continues to represent the Catholic Church in the U.S. in her apostolate to the American Indian. Its primary concerns are evangelization, catechesis, liturgy, family life, education, and advocacy. Address: 2021 H Street N.W., Washington, DC, 20006-4207, (202) 331-8542.

Subcommittee of Native American Catholics

The Subcommittee on Native American Affairs is part of the USCCB Committee on Cultural Diversity within the Church and works directly with the standing committee and other USCCB committees to address the pastoral needs of Native American Catholics. The key mission priorities are:

• Continue to support and collaborate with key national organizations, including the Bureau of Catholic Indian Missions and the Tekakwitha Conference.

• Continue to identify and/or develop culturally and ethnically specific resources in the areas of catechesis, lay ministry formation, liturgy, evangelization, and the diaconate.

• Continue to collaborate with other USCCB offices, including Laity, Marriage, Family Life, and Youth; Education; Evangelization and Catechesis; Vocations; Liturgy; and Pastoral Practices.

The subcommittee is currently chaired by Abp. Charles J. Chaput of Philadelphia. Address: 3211 Fourth St. N.E., Washington, DC, 20017, (202) 541-3000, www. usccb.org.

Kateri Tekakwitha Conference

The Kateri Tekakwitha Conference is so named in honor of Blessed Kateri Tekakwitha, "Lily of the Mohawks," who was born in 1656 at Ossernenon (Auriesville), NY, in 1656, baptized in 1676, lived near Montreal, died in 1680, and was beatified in 1980. The conference was established in 1939 as a missionary-priest advisory group in the Diocese of Fargo. It was a missionary-priest support group from 1946 to 1977. Since 1977 it has been a gathering of Catholic Native peoples and the men and women — clerical, religious and lay persons — who minister to Native Catholic communities.

Conferences and local Kateri Circles serve as occasions for the exchange of ideas, prayer and mutual support. Since 1980, the national center has promoted and registered 130 Kateri Circles in the U.S. and Canada. Publications include a quarterly newsletter.

The conference has a board of 12 directors, the majority of whom are Native people. Abp. Charles Chaput, O.F.M. Cap., is the episcopal moderator. Address: Tekakwitha Conference National Center, P.O. Box 6768, Great Falls, MT, 59406, (406) 727-0147.

Statistics

On June 19, 2003, the United States Conference of Catholic Bishops issued a report, "Native American Catholics at the Millennium," on the current state of Native American Catholics in the U.S. There are 4.1 million people who identify themselves as Native American. Of these, 493,615 Native Americans, or 12% of the total population, are considered Catholic. Native Americans comprise 3.5% of all Catholics in the U.S. More than 340 parishes in the United States serve predominantly Native American congregations.

Bishops

There is presently one Native American bishop in the United States: Abp. Charles J. Chaput, O.F.M. Cap. of Philadelphia.

PASTORAL CARE OF MIGRANTS, REFUGEES, AND TRAVELERS

As a result of globalization, modern travel, and economic and political unrest, men, women, and children are forced to be constantly on the move. They are still in need of pastoral care, and the Church has a long history of reaching out to all of the populations of migrants, refugees, and travelers. There are two primary bodies charged with the immediate pastoral needs of these groups. The first is the Pontifical Council for the Pastoral Care of Migrants and Itinerant Peoples and the other is the Subcommittee on the Pastoral Care of Migrants, Refugees and Travelers.

Pontifical Council for Pastoral Care of Migrants and Itinerant Peoples

For details, see under the Roman Curia in the section on the Holy See.

The Subcommittee on the Pastoral Care of Migrants, Refugees and Travelers

The Subcommittee on the Pastoral Care of Migrants, Refugees and Travelers is part of the Committee on Cultural Diversity within the Church by and works both with the other subcommittees and other USCCB committees to support the pastoral care of migrants, refugees and travelers. According to the subcommittee, People on the Move ministries include:

Airport and airline workers and travelers; Circus and Carnival Workers; Gypsies and Irish Travelers; Port and ship chaplains, seafarers and fishers; Migrant Farm Workers; Race Car drivers in conjunction with Championship Auto Racing Team Ministries; Tourism – National Parks, Tourist Centers, pilgrimage groups, and workers in the Tourist industry; Truckers, highway travelers and workers at truck stops, bus stations and rest stops in conjunction with the National Diaconate Office.

The subcommittee is currently chaired by Bp. Rutilio Del Riego, aux. bp. of San Bernardino. Sr. Myrna Tordillo, MSCS, is the assistant director of the subcommittee. Address: 3211 Fourth St. N.E., Washington, DC, 20017, (202) 541-3000, www. usccb.org.

MISSIONARY ACTIVITY OF THE U.S. CHURCH

Sources: U.S. Catholic Mission Handbook 2010: Mission Inventory 2008-2009 *(the most recent issue), reproduced with permission of the United States Catholic Mission Council, 3029 Fourth St. N.E., Washington, DC.*

OVERSEAS MISSIONS

Field Distribution, 2008-2009

Africa: 418 (213 men; 205 women). Largest numbers in Kenya, 112; Tanzania, 60; Zambia, 35; Uganda, 35; Ghana, 25; South Africa, 25; Nigeria, 21.

Asia: 395 (254 men; 141 women). Largest numbers in Philippines, 86; Japan, 62; Taiwan, 52; China PRC Hong Kong SAR, 48; India, 43; Korea, 21; Bangladesh, 19; Thailand, 12. (Those present in China were there for professional services.)

Caribbean: 154 (63 men; 91 women). Largest numbers in Puerto Rico, 36; Jamaica, 34; Dominican Republic 23; Belize, 26; Haiti, 11.

Eurasia (Kazakhstan, Russia, Siberia): 6 (5 men; 1 women). Largest group, Russia, 3.

Europe: 85 (25 men; 60 women). Largest numbers in Italy, 33; Ireland, 15; England, 10; Germany, 4.

Latin America: 567 (215 men; 352 women). Largest numbers in Peru, 106; Mexico, 77; Brazil, 90; Bolivia, 55; Guatemala, 60; Chile, 55.

Middle East: 11 (7 men; 4 women). Largest numbers in Jordan, 4; Israel, 3; Lebanon, 3.

North America (Canada and United States): 1,629 (313 men; 1,316 women). Largest number in the United States, 1,605.

Oceania: 87 (56 men; 31 women). Largest numbers in

Papua New Guinea, 26; Micronesia, 23; Marshall Island, 8; Australia, 6; Guam, 4.
TOTAL: 3,352 (1,151 men; 2,201 women).

Missionary Personnel, 2008-2009

Bishops: 22.

Religious Priests: 50 mission sending groups had 784 priests in overseas assignments. Listed below are those with 15 or more members abroad.

Jesuits, 169; Maryknoll Fathers and Brothers, 152; Oblates of Mary Immaculate, 113; Society of Divine Word, 72; Order of Friars Minor, 54; Holy Cross Fathers, 41; Columbans, 29; Franciscans (O.F.M. Cap), 29; Oblates of Francis de Sales, 26; Glenmary Home Missoners, 26; Dominicans, 16; Marianists, 15.

Diocesan Priests: There were 49 priests from 25 dioceses. The majority were in Latin American countries.

Religious Brothers: 34 mission sending groups had 171 brothers in overseas assignments. Those with 15 or more members: Jesuits, 314; Marianists, 36; Franciscans (O.F.M.), 20; Holy Cross Congregation, 17.

Religious Sisters: 130 mission sending communities of women Religious had 1,962 sisters in overseas missions. Those with 15 or more members: Maryknoll Mission Sisters, 185; Franciscan Missionaries of Mary, 130; School Sisters of Notre Dame, 112; Missionaries of Charity, 92; Medical Mission Sisters, 51; Dominicans, 45; Congregation of Sisters of St. Agnes, 45; St. Joseph Sisters, 45; Franciscan Sisters, 39; Sisters of Charity of the BVM, 38; Ursulines, 37; Providence Sisters, 37; Daughters of Charity, 34; Holy Cross, Cong. of Sisters, 30; Sisters of Mercy (various communities), 25; Sisters of Notre Dame de Namur, 24; Medical Missionaries of Mary, 22; Franciscan Sisters of Little Falls, 21; IHM Sisters of Immaculata, 21; Little Sisters of the Poor, 20; Sisters of St. Joseph of Carondelet, 17; Apostles of the Sacred Heart, 18; Mission Sisters of the Immaculate Heart of Mary, 17; Franciscan Sisters of Atonement, 16.

Lay Persons: 45 mission-sending groups had 358 members in overseas missions. Those with 15 or more members:

Jesuit Volunteer Corps, 98; Jesuit Volunteers International, 40; Salesian Lay Missionaries, 24; Catholic Medical Mission Board, 22; Mercy Corps, 20; LAMP Ministries, 17; Red Cloud Volunteers, 16.

Seminarians: There were 9 from 2 groups. Jesuits, 7; Maryknoll, 2.

U.S. MISSIONARY BISHOPS

The following is a list of missionary bishops from the United States in active service around the world. This list does not include retired bishops. As of July 15, 2011:

Africa

Madagascar: Morondava (diocese), Donald Pelletier, M.S

Zambia: Mongu (diocese), Paul F. Duffy, O.M.I.

Asia

Kazakhstan: Almaty (diocese), Henry Howaniec, O.F.M

Central America, West Indies

Honduras: Juticalpa (diocese), Thomas Maurus Muldoon, O.F.M.

Nicaragua: Bluefields (vicariate apostolic), Paul Simon Schmitz, O.F.M.Cap.; David Albin Zywiec Sidor, O.F.M. Cap. (aux. bp.).

Puerto Rico: San Juan (archdiocese), Roberto Octavio González Nieves, O.F.M., Daniel Fernández Torres (aux. bp.); Mayaguez (diocese), Alvaro Corrado del Rio, S.J.

Trinidad and Tobago: Port of Spain (archdiocese), Edward J. Gilbert, C.SS.R.

North America

Bermuda: Hamilton (diocese), Robert Kurtz, C.R.

Jamaica: Mandeville (diocese), Neil Tiedemann, C.P.

Mexico: Nuevo Laredo (diocese), Ricardo Watty Urquidi, M.Sp.S., first bishop; Guadalajara; Miguel Romano Gómez (aux. bp.).

St. Thomas, American Virgin Islands: Hamilton: Herbert Armstrong Bevard.

United States: Gallup (diocese), James S. Wall.

Oceania

American Samoa: Samoa-Pago Pago (diocese), John Quinn Weitzel, M.M. (emeritus, May 31, 2013); successor: Peter Brown, C.Ss.R., ord. bp. Aug. 22, 2013.

Papua New Guinea: Kimbe (diocese), William Fey, O.F.M. Cap.; Mendi (diocese), Stephen J. Reichert, O.F.M.Cap.

Solomon Islands: Gizo (diocese), Christopher Cardone, O.P., aux. bp.

South America

Bolivia: Pando (vicariate apostolic), Luis Morgan Casey.

Brazil: Itaituba (prelacy), Capistran Heim, O.F.M.; Miracema do Tocantins (diocese); Valença (diocese), Elias James Manning, O.F.M. Conv.

Paraguay: San Pedro: Adalberto Martínez Flores;

Peru: Chulucanas (diocese), Daniel Thomas Turley Murphy, O.S.A.; Sicuani (prelacy), Michael La Fay Bardi, O.Carm.

U.S. CATHOLIC MISSION ASSOCIATION

This is a voluntary association of individuals and organizations for whom the missionary presence of the universal Church is of central importance. It is a nonprofit religious, educational and charitable organization which exists to promote global missions. Its primary emphasis is on cross-cultural evangelization and the promotion of international justice and peace. The association is also responsible for gathering and publishing annual statistical data on U.S. missionary personnel overseas. President: Teresita Gonzalez de la Maza; Executive Director, Fr. Michael Montoya, M.J. Address: 3029 Fourth St. N.E., Washington, DC, 20017, (202) 832-3112, www.uscatholicmission.org.

Mission Statement

In its 1996-97 handbook, the association included the following in a mission statement.

"In the Church, our understanding of the mission of evangelization is evolving to embrace dialogue, community building, struggles for justice, efforts to model justice and faith in our lifestyles, activities and structures, in addition to the teaching/preaching/witnessing role traditionally at the heart of the mission enterprise. Still, the contemporary 'identity-confusion' about 'mission' stands forth as a major challenge for USCMA as we move toward the 21st century.

"The larger context of mission is the Spirit moving in

the Signs of our Times: the liberation movements, the women's movements, the economy movements, the rising awareness and celebration of cultural diversity, the search for ways to live peacefully and creatively with great pluralism, rapid technological change, the emergence of the global economy, the steady increase in poverty and injustice, the realigning of the global political order - and the many ripples radiating out from each of these."

Home Missions

The expression "home missions" is applied to places in the U.S. where the local church does not have its own resources, human and otherwise. These areas share the name "missions" with their counterparts in foreign lands because they too need outside help to provide the personnel and means for making the Church present and active there in carrying out its mission for the salvation of people.

Dioceses in the southeast, the southwest, and the far west are most urgently in need of outside help to carry on the work of the Church. Millions of people live in counties in which there are no resident priests. Many others live in rural areas beyond the reach and influence of a Catholic center. According to recent statistics compiled by the Glenmary Research Center, there are more than 500 priestless counties in the United States.

Mission Workers

A number of forces are at work to meet the pastoral needs of these missionary areas and to establish permanent churches and operating institutions where they are required. In many dioceses, one or more missions and stations are attended from established parishes and are gradually growing to independent status. Priests, brothers and sisters belonging to scores of religious institutes are engaged full-time in the home missions. Lay persons, some of them in affiliation with special groups and movements, are also involved.

The Society for the Propagation of the Faith, which conducts an annual collection for mission support in all parishes, allocates 40% of this sum for disbursement to home missions through the American Board of Catholic Missions.

Various mission-aid societies frequently undertake projects on behalf of the home missions.

The Glenmary Home Missioners, founded by Fr. W. Howard Bishop in 1939, is the only home mission society established for the sole purpose of carrying out the pastoral ministry in small towns and rural districts of the U.S. Glenmary serves in many areas where at least 20 per cent of the people live in poverty and less than one per cent are Catholic. With 61 priests and 19 professed brothers as of January 1998 the Glenmary Missioners had missions in the archdioceses of Atlanta and Cincinnati, and in the dioceses of Birmingham, Charlotte, Covington, Jackson, Lexington, Little Rock, Nashville, Owensboro, Richmond, Savannah, Tulsa, Tyler and Wheeling-Charleston. National headquarters are located at 4119 Glenmary Trace, Fairfield, OH. The mailing address is P.O. Box 465618, Cincinnati, OH, 45246, (513) 874-8900.

Organizations

Black and Indian Mission Office (The Commission for Catholic Missions among the Colored People and the Indians): Organized officially in 1885 by decree of the Third Plenary Council of Baltimore. Provides financial support for religious works among Blacks and Native Americans in 133 archdioceses and dioceses through funds raised by an annual collection in all parishes of the U.S. on the first Sunday of Lent, the designated Sunday.

Bureau of Catholic Indian Missions See under Native American Catholics above.

Catholic Negro-American Mission Board (1907): Supports priests and sisters in southern states and provides monthly support to sisters and lay teachers in the poorest black schools. Address: 2021 H St. N.W., Washington, DC, 20006-4207, (202) 331-8542.

The Catholic Church Extension Society (1905): Established with papal approval for the purpose of preserving and extending the Church in rural and isolated parts of the U.S. and its dependencies through the collection and disbursement of funds for home mission work. Since the time of its founding, more than $400 million has been received and distributed for church construction, religious education and seminary formation, campus and outreach ministries, evangelization, and salaries for missionaries. The Society celebrated its 100th anniversary in 2005. Works of the society are supervised by a 14-member board of governors: Card. Francis George of Chicago, chancellor; Fr. John Wall, president; three archbishops, three bishops and six lay people. Headquarters: 150 S. Wacker Dr., 20th Floor, Chicago, IL, 60601, (312) 236-7240; www.catholicextension.org.

National Catholic Rural Life Conference: Founded in 1923 through the efforts of Bp. Edwin V. O'Hara. Applies the Gospel message to rural issues through focus on rural parishes and the provision of services including distribution of educational materials development of prayer and worship resources, advocacy for strong rural communities. Bp. Frank J. Dewane, president; James F. Ennis, exec. dir. National headquarters: 4625 Beaver Ave., Des Moines, IA, 50310, (515) 270-2634, www.ncrlc.com.

Bishops' Committee On The Home Missions

Established in 1924, the Committee on the Home Missions of the U.S. Conference of Catholic Bishops provides financial support for missionary activities that strengthen and extend the presence of the Church in the United States and its island territories in the Caribbean and the Pacific. Funding for mission dioceses and national organizations engaged in home mission work is provided through the annual Catholic Home Missions Appeal, which is nationally scheduled on the last weekend of April. For 2006-2007, $8.4 million was allocated to mission dioceses and mission organizations thanks to the faithfulness and sustained generosity of Catholics. Since 1924, close to $300 million has been collected and disbursed for home missions. The committee's work is supervised by seven bishops and a small national staff. Bp. Peter F. Christensen, Bishop of Superior, is chairperson; Mary Mencarini Campbell, Dir. National headquarters: U. S. Conference of Catholic Bishops, 3211 4th NE, Washington, DC, 20017-1194, (202) 541-3450, www.usccb.org.

U.S. Catholic Statistics

U.S. STATISTICAL SUMMARY

(Principal sources: The Official Catholic Directory, 2013, *Almanac survey comparisons, where given, are with figures reported in the previous edition of the Directory. Totals below do not include statistics for Outlying Areas of U.S. unless otherwise noted. These are given in tables on the preceding pages and elsewhere in the* Catholic Almanac; *see Index.)*

Catholic Population: 69,436,660; increase, 326,054. Percent of total population: 22%.

Jurisdictions: In the United States, there are 196 archdioceses and dioceses: 33 Latin Catholic archdioceses, 145 Latin Catholic dioceses, 15 Eastern Catholic dioceses, and 2 Eastern Catholic archdioceses; there is also 1 apostolic exarchate (New York based Armenian exarchate for U.S. and Canada) and 1 personal ordinariate of the Chair of St. Peter. The current number of dioceses reflects the elevation of the diocese of Galveston-Houston to an archdiocese on Dec. 29, 2004, and the creation on July 3, 2000, of the new diocese of Laredo. There are also the eparchies of St. Maron and Our Lady of Lebanon of Los Angeles (Maronites), Newton (Melkites), St. Thomas Apostle of Detroit (Chaldeans), St. George Martyr of Canton, Ohio (Romanians), St. Thomas of Chicago (Syro-Malabars), the Eparchy of St. Peter the Apostle of San Diego, and the creation of the Syro-Malankara apostolic exarchate on June 14, 2010. The personal ordinariate of the Chair of St. Peter was established on Jan. 1, 2012. The eparchy of Our Lady of Deliverance of Newark has its seat in Newark, NJ. The Armenian apostolic exarchate for the United States and Canada has its seat in New York. Vacant jurisdictions (as of Aug. 15, 2013): Ft. Worth, Harrisburg, Marquette, Passaic, Portland in Maine, Pueblo, Rochester, St. Josaphat, Wichita.

Cardinals: 19 (5 head archiepiscopal sees in U.S.; three are Roman Curia officials; 11 are retired). As of July 10, 2013.

Archbishops: 54. Diocesan, in U.S., 30 (does not include 5 cardinals and military archbishop); retired, 24; there are also 16 archbishops serving outside U.S. As of July 15, 2013.

Bishops: 371. Diocesan, in U.S. (and Virgin Islands), 151; auxiliaries, 75; retired, 145; there are also 20 bishops serving outside U.S. As of Jul. 15, 2013.

Priests: 39,368; decrease, 336. Diocesan, 26,979 (decrease, 157); religious order priests (does not include those assigned overseas), 12,389 (decrease, 230). There were 471 newly ordained priests; decrease, 16.

Permanent Deacons: 18,121; increase, 305

Brothers: 4,459; decrease, 59.

Sisters: 52,557; decrease, 2,488.

Seminarians: 5,153. Diocesan seminarians, 3,441, religious order seminarians, 1,712.

Receptions into Church: 876,708. Includes 763,208 infant baptisms; 41,918 adult baptisms and 71,582 already baptized persons received into full communion with the Church.

First Communions: 784,927.

Confirmations: 600,136.

Marriages: 163,976.

Deaths: 412,581.

Parishes: 17,990.

Seminaries, Diocesan: 71.

Religious Seminaries: 93.

Colleges and Universities: 232. **Students,** 818,331.

High Schools: 1,314. **Students,** 612,616.

Elementary Schools: 5,672. **Students,** 1,440,232.

Non Residential Schools for Handicapped: 53. **Students,** 6,047.

Teachers: 171,634 (priests, 1,219; brothers, 687; scholastics, 515; sisters, 4,421; laity, 164,792).

Public School Students in Religious Instruction Programs: 3,411,919. High school students, 635,142; elementary school students, 2,776,777.

Hospitals: 542; patients treated, 88,377,290.

Health Care Centers: 422; patients treated, **5,663,747.**

Specialized Homes: 1,534; patients assisted, 639,162.

Residential Care of Children (Orphanages): 113; children assisted, 20,894.

Day Care and Extended Day Care Centers: 989; children assisted, 110,492.

Special Centers for Social Services: 3,294; assisted annually, 32,316,136.

PERCENTAGE OF CATHOLICS IN TOTAL POPULATION IN U.S.

(Source: The Official Catholic Directory, 2013; *figures are as of Jan. 1, 2013. Total general population figures at the end of the table are U.S. Census Bureau esimates for Jan. 1 of the respective years. Archdioceses are indicated by an asterisk; for dioceses marked +, see Dioceses with Interstate Lines.)*

State Diocese	Catholic Pop.	Total Pop.	Cath. Pct.	State Diocese	Catholic Pop.	Total Pop.	Cath. Pct.
Alabama	**158,215**	**4,712,547**	**3.5**	**Illinois,** cont.			
*Mobile	67,488	1,772,873	4	Springfield	149,833	1,150,549	13
Birmingham	90,727	2,939,674	3	**Indiana**	**752,182**	**6,499,353**	**12**
Alaska	**50,681**	**639,355**	**8**	*Indianapolis	220,565	2,621,455	8
*Anchorage	26,742	400,000	7	Evansville	82,492	510,752	16
Fairbanks	13,939	164,355	8	Ft.Wayne-S.Bend	159,812	1,275,094	13
Juneau	10,000	75,000	13	Gary	184,000	795,668	23
Arizona	**1,018,636**	**6,279,287**	**16**	Lafayette	105,313	1,296,384	8
Phoenix	795,027	4,428,994	18	**Iowa**	**494,533**	**3,059,534**	**16**
Tucson	223,609	1,850,293	12	*Dubuque	200,588	998,638	20
Arkansas				Davenport	95,727	763,844	13
Little Rock	142,050	2,937,979	5	Des Moines	103,430	837,773	12
California	**12,346,923**	**38,020,554**	**32**	Sioux City	94,788	459,279	21
*Los Angeles	4,263,990	11,816,567	36	**Kansas**	**407,106**	**2,734,003**	**15**
*San Francisco	550,600	1,795,066	31	*Kansas City	205,243	1,193,425	17
Fresno	1,074,944	2,845,903	38	Dodge City	45,513	217,486	21
Monterey	202,847	1,014,237	20	Salina	43,831	334,858	13
Oakland	406,253	2,604,689	16	Wichita	112,499	988,234	11
Orange	1,304,582	3,055,745	43	**Kentucky**	**376,763**	**4,342,936**	**9**
Sacramento	980,171	3,526,143	28	*Louisville	192,485	1,368,911	14
San Bernardino	1,596,160	4,304,997	37	Covington	92,456	513,971	18
San Diego	986,499	3,127,045	32	Lexington	45,514	1,578,749	3
San Jose	590,000	1,890,909	31	Owensboro	46,308	881,305	5
Santa Rosa	174,357	891,101	20	**Louisiana**	**1,264,684**	**4,482,346**	**28**
Stockton	216,520	1,330,152	16	*New Orleans	520,056	1,238,228	42
Colorado	**785,976**	**5,052,394**	**16**	Alexandria	43,520	383,421	11
*Denver	557,049	3,352,228	17	Baton Rouge	198,828	976,018	20
Colo. Springs	165,213	1,032,580	16	Houma-			
Pueblo	63,714	667,586	10	Thibodaux	96,719	202,000	48
Connecticut	**1,240,727**	**3,580,945**	**35**	Lafayette	292,019	568,154	51
*Hartford	591,528	1,944,607	30	Lake Charles	72,253	296,402	24
Bridgeport	410,834	925,899	44	Shreveport	41,289	818,123	5
Norwich+	238,365	710,439	34	**Maine**			
Delaware+				Portland	187,912	1,328,361	14
Wilmington	239,638	1,358,080	18	**Maryland**			
District of Columbia				*Baltimore	489,109	3,170,447	15
*Washington+	621,476	2,824,893	22	**Massachusetts**	**2,739,440**	**6,571,479**	**42**
Florida	**2,279,306**	**18,993,275**	**12**	*Boston	1,906,372	4,138,274	46
*Miami	742,608	4,408,811	17	Fall River	302,484	824,551	37
Orlando	380,924	4,249,507	9	Springfield	229,584	823,662	28
Palm Beach	259,000	1,963,000	13	Worcester	301,000	784,992	38
Pensacola-				**Michigan**	**2,008,445**	**9,766,758**	**21**
Tallahassee	64,400	1,373,621	5	*Detroit	1,310,915	4,248,127	31
St. Augustine	173,110	2,031,392	9	Gaylord	60,471	508,658	12
St. Petersburg	432,209	2,924,479	15	Grand Rapids	182,000	1,283,717	14
Venice	227,055	2,042,465	11	Kalamazoo	109,358	949,011	12
Georgia	**1,086,939**	**9,923,399**	**11**	Lansing	194,963	1,792,445	11
*Atlanta	1,000,000	6,998,399	13	Marquette	48,207	311,629	15
Savannah	86,939	2,925,000	3	Saginaw	102,531	673,171	15
Hawaii				**Minnesota**	**1,243,990**	**5,341,635**	**23**
Honolulu	229,099	1,374,810	17	*St. Paul and			
Idaho				Minneapolis	825,000	3,203,382	26
Boise	174,348	1,584,985	11	Crookston	34,410	260,616	13
Illinois	**3,771,104**	**13,363,539**	**28**	Duluth	56,417	446,956	13
*Chicago	2,321,000	5,950,693	39	New Ulm	60,391	283,536	21
Belleville	93,795	860,658	11	St. Cloud	136,727	561,685	24
Joliet	604,175	1,916,361	32	Winona	131,045	585,460	22
Peoria	132,351	1,492,335	9	**Mississippi**	**110,665**	**2,911,758**	**4**
Rockford	469,950	1,992,943	24	Biloxi	62,941	800,165	8

State / Diocese	Catholic Pop.	Total Pop.	Cath. Pct.
Missippi, cont.			
Jackson	47,724	2,111,593	2
Missouri	**801,700**	**6,012,924**	**13**
*St. Louis	524,908	2,225,000	24
Jefferson City	80,262	913,815	9
Kansas City			
St. Joseph	129,515	1,520,250	9
Springfield			
C. Girardeau	67,015	1,353,859	5
Montana	**80,674**	**1,030,656**	**8**
Great Falls			
Billings	36,261	450,673	8
Helena	44,413	579,983	8
Nebraska	**378,494**	**1,805,011**	**21**
*Omaha	230,680	902,447	26
Grand Island	50,262	307,587	16
Lincoln	97,552	594,977	16
Nevada	**645,069**	**2,663,086**	**24**
Las Vegas	551,397	1,969,274	28
Reno	93,672	693,812	14
New Hampshire			
Manchester	280,627	1,318,194	21
New Jersey	**3,777,486**	**8,867,489**	**43**
*Newark	1,352,000	2,859,850	47
Camden	518,219	1,461,315	35
Metuchen	631,946	1,373,796	46
Paterson	426,000	1,145,500	37
Trenton	849,321	2,027,028	42
New Mexico	**516,531**	**2,316,503**	**22**
*Santa Fe	321,885	1,292,284	25
Gallup+	62,000	475,000	13
Las Cruces	132,646	549,219	24
New York	**7,189,530**	**20,219,984**	**36**
*New York	2,618,755	5,819,455	45
Albany	330,000	1,392,464	24
Brooklyn	1,400,000	4,780,493	29
Buffalo	631,409	1,542,113	41
Ogdensburg	93,994	498,302	19
Rochester	311,427	1,512,046	21
Rockville Ctr.	1,531,445	3,504,737	44
Syracuse	272,500	1,170,374	23
North Carolina	**411,716**	**9,697,705**	**4**
Charlotte	180,130	4,967,591	4
Raleigh	231,586	4,730,114	5
North Dakota	**135,519**	**683,932**	**20**
Bismarck	61,862	290,738	21
Fargo	73,657	393,194	19
Ohio	**1,976,989**	**11,282,312**	**18**
*Cincinnati	471,457	3,000,267	16
Cleveland	698,450	2,775,879	25
Columbus	266,776	2,336,923	11
Steubenville	36,030	511,522	7
Toledo	319,189	1,465,561	22
Youngstown	185,087	1,192,160	16
Oklahoma	**173,135**	**3,719,649**	**5**
*Oklahoma City	113,857	2,069,649	6
Tulsa	59,278	1,650,000	4
Oregon	**452,880**	**3,857,743**	**12**
*Portland	417,614	3,345,270	12
Baker	35,266	512,473	7
Pennsylvania	**3,323,254**	**12,716,146**	**26**
*Philadelphia	1,462,975	4,030,926	36
Allentown	270,469	1,272,212	21
Altoona J'town	87,525	652,258	14

State / Diocese	Catholic Pop.	Total Pop.	Cath. Pct.
Pennsylvania, cont.			
Erie	187,500	836,222	22
Greensburg	151,221	658,434	23
Harrisburg	234,822	2,236,085	11
Pittsburgh	636,683	1,915,768	33
Scranton	292,059	1,110,241	26
Rhode Island			
Providence	620,268	1,051,302	59
South Carolina			
Charleston	192,422	4,679,230	4
South Dakota	**143,185**	**797,137**	**18**
Rapid City	24,183	227,211	11
Sioux Falls	119,002	569,926	21
Tennessee	**201,703**	**6,388,542**	**3**
Knoxville	61,793	2,381,842	3
Memphis	61,210	1,562,650	4
Nashville	78,700	2,444,050	3
Texas	**7,189,310**	**25,925,301**	**28**
*Galveston			
Houston	1,181,398	6,249,904	19
*San Antonio	723,305	2,386,218	30
Amarillo	43,355	432,849	10
Austin	536,183	2,902,992	18
Beaumont	77,672	620,434	13
Brownsville	1,074,477	1,264,091	85
Corpus Christi	397,500	572,000	69
Dallas	1,165,582	3,847,430	30
El Paso+	689,549	877,940	79
Fort Worth	680,000	3,356,669	20
Laredo	306,354	360,416	85
Lubbock	72,527	494,458	15
San Angelo	77,230	859,701	9
Tyler	61,318	1,411,976	4
Victoria	102,860	288,223	36
Utah			
Salt Lake City	277,000	2,817,222	10
Vermont			
Burlington	118,000	625,000	19
Virginia	**681,626**	**8,522,803**	**8**
Arlington	454,382	2,968,486	15
Richmond	227,244	5,554,317	4
Washington	**758,045**	**6,768,115**	**11**
*Seattle	579,000	5,299,770	11
Spokane	107,271	825,161	13
Yakima	71,774	643,184	11
West Virginia			
Wheeling			
Charleston	72,913	1,855,364	4
Wisconsin	**1,457,755**	**5,699,300**	**26**
*Milwaukee	603,514	2,329,288	26
Green Bay	323,790	1,011,845	32
La Crosse	174,369	901,157	19
Madison	282,444	1,017,792	28
Superior	73,638	439,218	17
Wyoming			
Cheyenne	55,777	563,626	10
East. Churches	**594,626**	**–**	**–**
Military Arch.('99)	**1,194,000**	**–**	**–**
Outlying Areas	**2,710,479**	**4,314,466**	**63**
Total 2013	**68,436,660**	**317,235,394**	**22**
Total 2012	69,110,606	314,040,483	22
Total 2003	66,407,105	290,446,533	23

CATHOLIC POPULATION OF THE UNITED STATES

(Source: The Official Catholic Directory, 2013*; figures as of Jan. 1, 2013. Archdioceses are indicated by an asterisk; for dioceses marked +, see Dioceses with Interstate Lines.)*

State Diocese	Cath. Pop.	Dioc. Priests	Rel. Priests	Total Priests	Perm. Deac.	Bros.	Sisters	Par ishes
Alabama	**158,215**	**180**	**60**	**240**	**101**	**32**	**223**	**130**
*Mobile	67,488	97	31	128	50	10	107	76
Birmingham	90,727	83	29	112	51	22	116	54
Alaska	**50,681**	**44**	**19**	**63**	**44**	**2**	**32**	**78**
*Anchorage	26,742	24	10	34	16	–	18	23
Fairbanks	13,939	10	7	17	25	2	12	46
Juneau	10,000	10	2	12	3	–	2	9
Arizona	**1,018,636**	**226**	**168**	**394**	**430**	**35**	**342**	**171**
Phoenix	795,027	131	92	223	240	13	163	93
Tucson	223,609	95	76	171	190	22	179	78
Arkansas, Little Rock	**142,050**	**74**	**28**	**102**	**116**	**22**	**158**	**89**
California	**12,346,923**	**2,022**	**1,497**	**3,519**	**1,299**	**363**	**4,042**	**1,069**
*Los Angeles	4,263,990	512	531	1,043	370	80	1,581	287
*San Francisco	550,600	181	160	341	85	32	725	90
Fresno	1,074,944	138	39	177	66	1	102	89
Monterey	202,847	76	35	111	3	33	26	56
Oakland	406,253	158	175	333	112	96	337	83
Orange	1,304,582	170	80	250	102	9	326	57
Sacramento	980,171	192	59	251	145	10	166	102
San Bernardino	1,596,160	106	118	224	115	19	137	91
San Diego	986,499	166	85	251	157	18	230	98
San Jose	590,000	164	192	356	34	45	294	50
Santa Rosa	174,357	89	12	101	37	24	36	42
Stockton	216,520	70	11	81	43	3	52	34
Colorado	**785,976**	**283**	**135**	**418**	**291**	**21**	**352**	**214**
*Denver	557,049	190	103	293	186	17	211	123
Colo. Springs	165,213	39	16	55	57	3	98	39
Pueblo	63,714	54	16	70	48	1	43	52
Connecticut	**1,240,727**	**635**	**175**	**810**	**484**	**53**	**1,128**	**371**
*Hartford	591,528	304	92	396	307	30	628	213
Bridgeport	410,834	226	32	258	1	112	–	325
Norwich+	238,365	105	51	156	65	23	175	76
Delaware, Wilmington+	**239,638**	**124**	**64**	**188**	**104**	**19**	**201**	**57**
D.C.,*Washington+	**621,476**	**287**	**359**	**646**	**208**	**116**	**503**	**139**
Florida	**2,279,306**	**910**	**374**	**1,284**	**779**	**117**	**809**	**465**
*Miami	742,608	233	63	296	151	48	264	102
Orlando	380,924	138	77	215	186	7	75	79
Palm Beach	259,000	108	30	138	106	2	95	50
Pensacola–Tallahassee	64,400	72	14	86	59	5	25	49
St. Augustine	173,110	94	16	110	75	2	105	52
St. Petersburg	432,209	154	114	268	108	36	172	74
Venice	227,055	111	60	171	94	17	73	59
Georgia	**1,086,939**	**289**	**107**	**396**	**309**	**32**	**166**	**143**
*Atlanta	1,000,000	208	84	292	235	30	86	88
Savannah	86,939	81	23	104	74	2	80	55
Hawaii, Honolulu	**229,099**	**62**	**61**	**123**	**63**	**32**	**122**	**66**
Idaho, Boise	**174,348**	**78**	**15**	**93**	**75**	**5**	**71**	**52**
Illinois	**3,771,104**	**1,564**	**965**	**2,529**	**1,089**	**353**	**3,288**	**981**
*Chicago	2,321,000	789	697	1,486	660	254	1,739	356
Belleville	93,795	107	38	145	1	4	139	114
Joliet	604,175	179	114	293	211	52	467	120
Peoria	132,351	182	34	216	148	11	189	157
Rockford	469,950	202	41	243	–	11	108	104
Springfield	149,833	105	41	146	45	21	646	130
Indiana	**752,182**	**507**	**332**	**839**	**195**	**151**	**1,389**	**416**
*Indianapolis	220,565	140	82	222	46	30	580	136
Evansville	82,492	72	6	78	48	–	238	69
Ft. Wayne–South Bend	159,812	78	196	274	20	107	456	81
Gary	184,000	98	35	133	64	11	74	68
Lafayette	105,313	119	13	132	17	3	41	62

State Diocese	Cath. Pop.	Dioc. Priests	Rel. Priests	Total Priests	Perm. Deac.	Bros.	Sisters	Par ishes
Iowa	**494,533**	**492**	**42**	**534**	**271**	**24**	**925**	**441**
*Dubuque	200,588	183	30	213	103	23	658	167
Davenport	95,727	97	3	100	39	1	154	80
Des Moines	103,430	84	9	93	85	–	50	81
Sioux City	94,788	128	–	128	44	–	63	112
Kansas	**407,106**	**310**	**80**	**390**	**43**	**16**	**934**	**332**
*Kansas City	205,263	106	55	161	25	15	489	108
Dodge City	45,513	32	5	37	8	–	73	48
Salina	43,831	56	19	75	6	1	132	86
Wichita	112,499	116	1	117	4	–	240	90
Kentucky	**376,763**	**341**	**108**	**449**	**270**	**64**	**1,129**	**276**
*Louisville	192,485	139	50	189	140	55	598	102
Covington	92,456	81	16	97	34	6	292	47
Lexington	45,514	50	18	68	73	3	67	48
Owensboro	46,308	71	24	95	–	23	172	79
Louisiana*	**1,264,684**	**638**	**265**	**903**	**500**	**116**	**747**	**450**
*New Orleans	520,056	201	151	352	233	74	424	108
Alexandria	43,520	53	10	63	20	3	29	50
Baton Rouge	198,828	72	26	98	66	15	90	67
Houma-Thibodaux	202,000	62	9	71	39	4	23	39
Lafayette	292,019	161	40	201	98	14	141	121
Lake Charles	72,253	56	13	69	26	1	10	38
Shreveport	41,289	33	16	49	18	5	30	27
Maine, Portland	**187,912**	**141**	**27**	**168**	**41**	**12**	**268**	**57**
Maryland, *Baltimore	**489,109**	**244**	**196**	**440**	**159**	**55**	**803**	**145**
Massachusetts	**2,739,440**	**1,180**	**688**	**1,868**	**558**	**232**	**2,529**	**561**
*Boston	1,906,372	703	475	1,178	280	139	1,765	288
Fall River	302,484	148	84	232	81	14	147	89
Springfield	229,584	146	39	185	85	13	350	81
Worcester	301,000	183	90	273	112	66	267	103
Michigan	**2,008,445**	**932**	**293**	**1,225**	**482**	**53**	**2,031**	**729**
*Detroit	1,310,915	372	194	566	211	48	858	260
Gaylord	60,471	64	6	70	22	–	27	80
Grand Rapids	182,000	101	23	124	37	1	370	82
Kalamazoo	109,358	61	10	71	45	2	192	46
Lansing	194,963	163	48	211	104	2	457	84
Marquette	48,207	77	6	83	48	–	42	72
Saginaw	102,531	94	6	100	17	–	85	105
Minnesota	**1,243,990**	**809**	**209**	**1,046**	**342**	**124**	**1,335**	**673**
*St.Paul & Minneapolis	825,000	401	84	485	184	52	617	195
Crookston	34,410	45	3	48	15	–	71	66
Duluth	56,417	78	8	86	51	–	97	91
New Ulm	60,391	67	–	67	14	–	49	76
St. Cloud	136,727	109	103	212	51	68	440	131
Winona	131,045	109	11	120	27	4	61	114
Mississippi	**110,665**	**103**	**58**	**161**	**36**	**18**	**190**	**116**
Biloxi	62,941	53	24	77	31	12	36	42
Jackson	47,724	50	34	84	5	6	154	74
Missouri	**801,700**	**573**	**429**	**1,002**	**410**	**183**	**1,742**	**435**
*St. Louis	524,908	331	282	613	268	115	1,425	187
Jefferson City	80,262	82	7	89	64	2	44	95
Kansas City-St. Joseph	129,515	100	84	184	61	29	204	87
Springfield-Cape Girardeau	67,015	60	56	116	17	37	69	66
Montana	**80,674**	**144**	**17**	**161**	**51**	**2**	**79**	**103**
Great Falls Billings	36,261	63	12	75	9	–	45	46
Helena	44,413	81	5	86	42	2	34	57
Nebraska	**378,494**	**397**	**88**	**485**	**254**	**20**	**473**	**302**
*Omaha	230,680	185	78	263	245	20	266	132
Grand Island	50,262	62	–	62	7	–	56	36
Lincoln	97,552	150	10	160	2	–	151	134
Nevada	**645,069**	**73**	**24**	**97**	**60**	**6**	**24**	**57**
Las Vegas	551,397	37	18	55	31	3	–	29
Reno	93,672	36	6	42	29	3	23	28
New Hampshire, Manchester	**280,627**	**164**	**54**	**218**	**49**	**19**	**400**	**90**

State Diocese	Cath. Pop.	Dioc. Priests	Rel. Priests	Total Priests	Perm. Deac.	Bros.	Sisters	Par- ishes
New Jersey	**3,777,486**	**1,684**	**413**	**2,097**	**1,010**	**221**	**2,403**	**603**
*Newark	1,352,000	723	152	875	181	90	853	218
Camden	518,219	272	39	311	150	10	264	71
Metuchen	631,946	189	39	228	166	19	286	94
Paterson	426,000	262	124	386	205	48	677	111
Trenton	849,321	238	59	297	308	54	323	109
New Mexico	**516,531**	**218**	**134**	**352**	**290**	**59**	**266**	**190**
*Santa Fe	321,885	140	80	220	219	51	146	92
Gallup+	62,000	45	18	63	25	7	87	52
Las Cruces	132,646	33	36	69	46	1	33	46
New York	**7,189,530**	**2,459**	**1,181**	**3,640**	**1,386**	**754**	**6,766**	**1,304**
*New York	2,618,755	614	729	1,343	382	433	2,589	368
Albany	330,000	212	59	271	111	56	608	127
Brooklyn	1,400,000	490	162	652	211	106	800	186
Buffalo	631,409	314	98	412	126	36	852	164
Ogdensburg	93,994	108	5	113	67	6	107	107
Rochester	311,427	166	46	212	143	31	449	95
Rockville Centre	1,531,445	345	48	393	275	77	1,070	133
Syracuse	272,500	210	34	244	71	9	291	132
North Carolina	**411,716**	**214**	**82**	**296**	**175**	**12**	**169**	**151**
Charlotte	180,130	126	41	167	119	7	129	73
Raleigh	231,586	88	41	129	56	5	40	78
North Dakota	**135,519**	**199**	**27**	**226**	**123**	**17**	**197**	**230**
Bismarck	61,862	68	18	86	78	17	83	98
Fargo	73,657	131	9	140	45	–	114	132
Ohio	**1,976,989**	**1,222**	**430**	**1,652**	**801**	**205**	**2,759**	**776**
*Cincinnati	471,457	269	228	497	196	116	819	214
Cleveland	698,450	394	83	477	208	51	978	185
Columbus	266,776	152	30	182	118	11	230	106
Steubenville	36,030	77	33	110	12	7	48	58
Toledo	319,189	191	38	229	190	8	462	126
Youngstown	185,087	139	18	157	77	12	222	87
Oklahoma	**173,135**	**149**	**55**	**204**	**161**	**37**	**143**	**140**
*Oklahoma City	113,857	75	29	104	95	9	89	63
Tulsa	59,278	74	26	100	66	28	54	77
Oregon	**452,880**	**195**	**195**	**390**	**83**	**64**	**416**	**155**
*Portland	417,614	159	189	348	73	64	397	124
Baker	35,266	36	6	42	–	10	19	31
Pennsylvania	**3,323,254**	**1,927**	**697**	**2,624**	**698**	**202**	**5,282**	**1,064**
*Philadelphia	1,462,975	530	311	841	275	100	2,631	257
Allentown	270,469	199	67	266	105	17	340	104
Altoona Johnstown	87,525	118	52	170	37	10	70	87
Erie	187,500	187	8	195	62	–	313	117
Greensburg	151,221	106	67	173	2	32	198	85
Harrisburg	234,822	133	33	166	66	1	319	89
Pittsburgh	636,683	387	99	486	83	34	948	204
Scranton	292,059	267	60	327	68	8	463	121
Rhode Island, Providence	**620,268**	**270**	**99**	**369**	**87**	**74**	**408**	**142**
South Carolina, Charleston	**192,422**	**86**	**47**	**133**	**127**	**20**	**110**	**95**
South Dakota	**143,185**	**153**	**42**	**195**	**64**	**9**	**306**	**233**
Rapid City	24,183	37	16	53	27	3	36	87
Sioux Falls	119,202	116	26	142	37	6	270	146
Tennessee	**201,703**	**171**	**61**	**232**	**187**	**38**	**90**	**142**
Knoxville	61,793	61	17	78	58	10	37	47
Memphis	61,210	65	15	80	60	28	51	42
Nashville	78,700	45	29	74	69	2	2	53
Texas	**7,189,310**	**1,301**	**742**	**2,043**	**1,766**	**209**	**2,154**	**1,060**
*Galveston-Houston	1,180,398	204	205	409	386	12	449	146
*San Antonio	723,305	152	168	320	341	88	714	139
Amarillo	43,355	39	4	43	56	–	88	38
Austin	536,183	134	55	189	165	51	94	101
Beaumont	77,672	45	23	68	40	3	18	44
Brownsville	1,074,477	92	28	120	4	90	16	92
Corpus Christi	397,500	131	25	156	102	4	160	32

State Diocese	Cath. Pop.	Dioc. Priests	Rel. Priests	Total Priests	Perm. Deac.	Bros.	Sisters	Par ishes
Texas, cont.								
Dallas	1,165,582	105	79	184	144	12	104	69
El Paso	689,549	73	43	116	26	12	118	57
Fort Worth	680,000	68	54	122	105	5	71	89
Laredo	306,354	23	21	44	29	6	62	32
Lubbock	72,527	50	8	58	71	–	23	62
San Angelo	77,230	54	13	67	84	–	20	47
Tyler	61,318	80	8	88	89	–	52	48
Victoria	102,860	51	8	59	38	1	89	50
Utah, Salt Lake City	**277,000**	**57**	**12**	**69**	**76**	**–**	**34**	**48**
Vermont, Burlington	**118,000**	**91**	**32**	**123**	**43**	**21**	**86**	**73**
Virginia	**681,626**	**304**	**85**	**389**	**185**	**17**	**296**	**213**
Arlington	454,382	164	55	219	67	10	133	68
Richmond	227,244	140	30	170	118	7	163	145
Washington	**758,045**	**348**	**169**	**517**	**229**	**28**	**546**	**246**
*Seattle	579,000	197	95	292	124	19	373	147
Spokane	107,271	80	72	152	62	7	146	58
Yakima	71,774	71	2	73	43	2	27	41
West Virginia								
Wheeling-Charleston	**72,913**	**100**	**47**	**147**	**45**	**5**	**135**	**110**
Wisconsin	**1,457,755**	**868**	**482**	**1,350**	**464**	**116**	**2,344**	**746**
*Milwaukee	603,514	333	343	676	186	73	1,047	204
Green Bay	323,790	178	105	283	133	28	454	157
La Crosse	174,369	154	9	163	60	2	387	164
Madison	282,444	132	19	151	17	12	387	117
Superior	73,638	71	6	77	68	1	69	104
Wyoming, Cheyenne+	**55,777**	**57**	**5**	**62**	**39**	**1**	**15**	**33**
EASTERN CHURCHES	**594,626**	**644**	**101**	**745**	**343**	**20**	**276**	**603**
*Philadelphia	15,689	50	4	54	7	–	49	67
*Pittsburgh	57,951	52	9	61	22	1	64	75
St. Nicholas	10,400	45	10	55	–	11	–	38
Stamford	13,783	38	10	48	10	1	40	51
St. Josaphat (Parma)	8,489	52	1	53	2	11	2	38
Parma	8,609	37	–	37	16	–	6	29
Passaic	14,356	67	10	77	26	1	15	84
Holy Prot. of Mary	2,399	23	1	24	13	2	4	19
St. Maron (Maronites)	33,000	48	13	61	16	7	2	34
Our Lady of Lebanon (Maronites)	46,000	34	15	49	19	–	6	32
Newton (Melkites)	21,000	46	–	60	1	–	5	43
St. Peter the Apostle of San Diego	60,000	18	–	18	10	–	10	10
St. Thomas Apostle of Detroit (Chaldean)	150,000	24	–	24	120	–	10	9
St. Thomas (Syro-Malabrs)	87,000	58	15	73	–	–	–	21
St. George Martyr (Romanian)	5,675	21	2	23	7	5	4	14
Our Lady of Deliverance (Syrians, U.S. Canada)	22,600	13	–	13	4	–	–	9
Armenian Ex.(U.S. Canada)	37,500	5	10	15	1	–	10	9
Syro-Malankara Ex.(U.S.)	6,000	13	1	14	–	–	33	13
Military Archd. ('99)[1]	**1,194,000**	**–**	**–**	**–**	**–**	**–**	**–**	**–**
Outlying Areas								
Puerto Rico	2,415,893	353	278	631	493	30	773	329
Samoa-Pago Pago	14,200	17	1	18	23	–	4	18
Caroline Islands	77,733	13	15	28	65	2	34	29
Chalan Kanoa (N. Mariana Is.)	43,000	14	1	15	–	–	–	12
Guam, *Agana	135,454	25	10	35	16	1	83	25
Marshall Islands	4,950	1	5	6	1	–	10	5
Virgin Islands, St. Thomas	30,000	15	4	19	29	1	17	8
TOTAL 2013	**69,436,660**	**26,979**	**12,389**	**39,368**	**18,121**	**4,459**	**52,557**	**17,990**
TOTAL 2012	69,110,606	27,136	12,598	39,734	17,816	4,518	55,045	18,061
TOTAL 2003	66,407,105	29,715	14,772	44,487	14,106	5,568	74,698	19,484

1288 diocesan and 62 religious-order chaplains are on loan to the military (*2013 Annuario Pontificio*).

RECEPTIONS INTO THE CHURCH IN THE UNITED STATES

(Source: The Official Catholic Directory, 2013; *figures as of Jan. 1, 2013. Archdioceses are indicated by an asterisk; for dioceses marked +, see Dioceses with Interstate Lines. Information includes infant and adult baptisms and those received into full communion.)*

State Diocese	Infant Baptisms	Adult Bapts.	Rec'd into Full Com.	State Diocese	Infant Baptisms	Adult Bapts.	Rec'd into Full Com.
Alabama	**3,182**	**334**	**649**	**Indiana,** cont.			
*Mobile	1,189	134	229	Lafayette	1,656	170	306
Birmingham	1,993	200	420	**Iowa**	**6,657**	**458**	**458**
Alaska	**652**	**52**	**87**	*Dubuque	2,590	116	260
*Anchorage	352	30	45	Davenport	1,314	142	138
Fairbanks	249	18	34	Des Moines	1,522	115	222
Juneau	51	4	8	Sioux City	1,231	85	216
Arizona	**13,073**	**598**	**2,264**	**Kansas**	**7,668**	**522**	**1,118**
Phoenix	8,612	610	1,781	*Kansas City	3,509	184	367
Tucson	4,461	288	483	Dodge City	1,007	48	64
Arkansas, Lit. Rock	**2,560**	**222**	**435**	Salina	918	51	123
California	**161,291**	**4,660**	**13,605**	Wichita	2,234	239	564
*Los Angeles	66,424	1,281	5,267	**Kentucky**	**4,677**	**607**	**826**
*San Francisco	6,003	243	818	*Louisville	2,213	170	376
Fresno	16,935	428	501	Covington	963	195	100
Monterey	6,582	157	459	Lexington	678	94	163
Oakland	7,834	342	491	Owensboro	823	148	187
Orange	13,893	510	933	**Louisiana**	**12,379**	**656**	**1,725**
Sacramento	8,162	360	1,419	*New Orleans	3,804	239	252
San Bernardino	9,728	351	1,222	Alexandria	493	44	100
San Diego	8,647	354	870	Baton Rouge	2,097	122	390
San Jose	7,212	299	572	Houma-Thibodaux	1,089	47	86
Santa Rosa	3,198	131	240	Lafayette	3,448	117	430
Stockton	6,673	204	813	Lake Charles	959	55	328
Colorado	**11,448**	**639**	**941**	Shreveport	453	32	139
*Denver	9,244	471	599	**Maine,** Portland	**1,171**	**95**	**102**
Colorado Springs	1,139	85	183	**Maryland,** *Baltimore	**5,456**	**465**	**413**
Pueblo	1,065	83	159	**Massachusetts**	**20,322**	**635**	**1,007**
Connecticut	**11,079**	**359**	**1,047**	*Boston	13,222	369	465
*Hartford	5,400	137	276	Fall River	2,800	70	163
Bridgeport	4,195	170	590	Springfield	2,052	90	200
Norwich+	1,484	52	181	Worcester	2,248	106	179
Delaware, Wilm.+	**2,266**	**101**	**224**	**Michigan**	**15,657**	**1,391**	**2,513**
D.C., *Washington+	**4,216**	**700**	**502**	*Detroit	8,084	603	1,008
Florida	**29,145**	**1,848**	**4,316**	Gaylord	501	64	160
*Miami	11,254	506	1,189	Grand Rapids	2,231	181	429
Orlando	5,003	301	498	Kalamazoo	1,131	118	134
Palm Beach	3,527	206	960	Lansing	2,334	245	470
Pensacola-				Marquette	507	37	73
Tallahassee	733	118	250	Saginaw	867	143	239
St. Augustine	1,901	184	581	**Minnesota**	**11,367**	**780**	**1,055**
St. Petersburg	3,385	391	477	*St. Paul and			
Venice	3,342	142	361	Minneapolis	6,039	623	495
Georgia	**11,907**	**663**	**1,032**	Crookston	541	11	76
*Atlanta	10,167	522	725	Duluth	592	34	112
Savannah	1,740	141	307	New Ulm	808	19	65
Hawaii, Honolulu	**2,380**	**119**	**157**	St. Cloud	1,875	32	121
Idaho, Boise	**2,530**	**188**	**316**	Winona	1,512	61	186
Illinois	**50,172**	**2,603**	**2,856**	**Mississippi**	**1,717**	**203**	**408**
*Chicago	31,277	1,597	974	Biloxi	869	123	176
Belleville	2,100	119	203	Jackson	848	80	232
Joliet	7,241	244	695	**Missouri**	**9,195**	**785**	**1,234**
Peoria	2,137	266	316	*St. Louis	5,400	319	481
Rockford	5,759	191	324	Jefferson City	1,038	150	255
Springfield	1,658	186	344	Ks. City-St. Joe	1,851	186	314
Indiana	**10,638**	**907**	**1,638**	Springfield-			
*Indianapolis	3,807	381	526	Cape Girardeau	906	130	184
Evansville	1,085	84	121	**Montana**	**1,092**	**76**	**215**
Ft. Wayne-S. Bend	2,650	197	489	Great Falls-Billings	525	46	144
Gary	1,440	75	196	Helena	567	30	71

State Diocese	Infant Baptisms	Adult Bapts.	Rec'd into Full Com.	State Diocese	Infant Baptisms	Adult Bapts.	Rec'd into Full Com.
Nebraska	**5,864**	**401**	**892**	**Tennessee**, cont.			
*Omaha	3,996	222	461	Memphis	1,273	92	332
Grand Island	826	59	163	Nashville	1,749	154	339
Lincoln	1,042	120	268	**Texas**	**74,010**	**5,460**	**4,925**
Nevada	**6,604**	**263**	**1,055**	*Galv.-Houston	9,883	2,216	833
Las Vegas	5,041	173	851	*San Antonio	9,170	586	751
Reno	1,563	90	204	Amarillo	955	59	116
New Hampshire				Austin	8,472	376	671
Manchester	**1,923**	**173**	**125**	Beaumont	1,339	134	–
New Jersey	**36,685**	**1,173**	**870**	Brownsville	7,993	171	800
*Newark	13,743	286	110	Corpus Christi	2,083	159	246
Camden	5,047	–	–	Dallas	15,142	767	465
Metuchen	4,350	105	212	El Paso	4,769	154	289
Paterson	6,355	148	273	Fort Worth	7,082	336	–
Trenton	7,190	634	275	Laredo	2,610	43	47
New Mexico	**6,786**	**332**	**632**	Lubbock	842	66	152
*Santa Fe	4,343	181	383	San Angelo	1,654	244	236
Gallup+	589	93	114	Tyler	826	101	193
Las Cruces	1,854	58	135	Victoria	1,190	48	126
New York	**64,650**	**2,236**	**2,134**	**Utah**, Salt Lake City	**7,167**	**269**	**1,210**
*New York	21,990	1,152	990	**Vermont**, Burlington	**682**	**84**	**118**
Albany	2,582	18	148	**Virginia**	**10,575**	**579**	**1,429**
Brooklyn	14,980	560	49	Arlington	7,414	382	558
Buffalo	3,679	172	247	Richmond	3,161	197	871
Ogdensburg	927	48	46	**Washington**	**10,597**	**647**	**846**
Rochester	2,460	178	–	*Seattle	6,111	414	434
Rockville Centre	15,211	–	417	Spokane	1,272	124	148
Syracuse	2,821	108	236	Yakima	3,214	109	264
North Carolina	**10,898**	**500**	**1,051**	**West Virginia**			
Charlotte	6,028	311	697	Wheeling Chas.	**685**	**121**	**128**
Raleigh	4,870	189	354	**Wisconsin**	**14,941**	**513**	**1,021**
North Dakota	**2,064**	**80**	**239**	*Milwaukee	6,539	169	345
Bismarck	970	55	114	Green Bay	3,353	138	176
Fargo	1,094	25	125	La Crosse	1,790	101	237
Ohio	**19,209**	**1,777**	**3,901**	Madison	2,486	78	183
*Cincinnati	5,523	412	656	Superior	773	27	80
Cleveland	6,099	385	1,092	**Wyoming**, Chey.+	**857**	**75**	**155**
Columbus	3,361	310	372	**Eastern Churches**	**4,082**	**117**	**374**
Steubenville	388	70	531	*Philadelphia	230	7	7
Toledo	2,315	471	943	*Pittsburgh	156	12	40
Youngstown	1,523	129	307	St. Nicholas	242	4	6
Oklahoma	**3,618**	**306**	**721**	Stamford	193	11	7
*Okla. City	2,169	176	486	St. Josaphat (Parma)	27	–	31
Tulsa	1,449	130	255	Parma	53	–	12
Oregon	**6,239**	**453**	**565**	Passaic	119	1	48
*Portland	5,413	408	503	Holy Protect. of Mary	66	13	18
Baker	826	45	62	St. Maron (Maronites)	360	7	23
Pennsylvania	**27,666**	**2,510**	**2,029**	Our Lady of Lebanon			
*Philadelphia	12,448	418	352	(Maronites)	393	29	–
Allentown	2,684	132	3,345	Newton (Melkites)	172	11	70
Altoona-Johnstn.	919	64	115	St. Peter the Apostle	353	2	16
Erie	1,350	110	70	St. Thomas Apostle of			
Greensburg	1,125	1,151	191	Detroit (Chaldeans)	1,084	5	–
Harrisburg	1,771	285	323	St. Thomas (Syro-Mal.)	372	13	61
Pittsburgh	4,828	227	535	St. George Martyr			
Scranton	2,541	123	139	(Romanian)	40	2	7
Rhode Island, Providence	**3,228**	**151**	**398**	Our Lady of Deliverance (Syrians,			
South Carolina				U.S. Can.)	55	–	55
Charleston	**2,701**	**180**	**358**	Arme. Ex. (U.S. Can.)	167	–	–
South Dakota	**2,047**	**27**	**443**	Syro-Malankara Ex.(U.S.)	–	–	–
Rapid City	447	27	72	**Military Archd.**	**3,450**	**992**	**306**
Sioux Falls	1,570	–	371	**Outlying Areas**	**18,041**	**14,259**	**3,209**
Tennessee	**4,042**	**345**	**927**	**Total 2013**	**763,208**	**41,918**	**71,582**
Knoxville	1,020	99	256	Total 2012	793,103	43,692	76,588

The Catholic Church in Canada

Background

The first date in the remote background of the Catholic history of Canada is July 7, 1534, when a priest in the exploration company of Jacques Cartier celebrated Mass on the Gaspe Peninsula.

Successful colonization and the significant beginnings of the Catholic history of the country date from the foundation of Québec in 1608 by Samuel de Champlain and French settlers. Montréal was established in 1642.

The earliest missionaries were Franciscan Récollets (Recollects) and Jesuits who arrived in 1615 and 1625, respectively. They provided some pastoral care for the settlers but worked mainly among the 100,000 Indians — Algonquins, Hurons and Iroquois — in the interior and in the Lake Ontario region. Eight of the Jesuit missionaries, killed in the 1640s, were canonized in 1930. (*See* **Index: Jesuit North American Martyrs.**) Sulpician Fathers, who arrived in Canada late in the 1640s, played a part in the great missionary period, which ended about 1700.

St. Kateri Tekakwitha, "Lily of the Mohawks," who was baptized in 1676 and died in 1680, was declared "Blessed" in 1980 and canonized in 2012.

The communities of women religious with the longest histories in Canada are the Canonesses of St. Augustine and the Ursulines, since 1639; and the Hospitallers of St. Joseph, since 1642. Communities of Canadian origin are the Congregation of Notre Dame, founded by St. Marguerite Bourgeoys in 1658, and the Grey Nuns, formed by St. Marie Marguerite d'Youville in 1737.

Mother Marie (Guyard) of the Incarnation, an Ursuline nun, was one of the first three women missionaries to New France; called "Mother of the Church in Canada," she was declared "Blessed" on June 22, 1980.

Start of Church Organization

Ecclesiastical organization began with the appointment in 1658 of François De Montmorency-Laval, "Father of the Church in Canada," as vicar apostolic of New France. He was the first bishop of Québec from 1674 to 1688, with jurisdiction over all French-claimed territory in North America. He was declared "Blessed" on June 22, 1980.

In 1713, the French Canadian population numbered 18,000. In the same year, the Treaty of Utrecht ceded Acadia, Newfoundland and the Hudson Bay Territory to England. The Acadians were scattered among the American colonies in 1755.

The English acquired possession of Canada and its 70,000 French-speaking inhabitants by virtue of the Treaty of Paris in 1763. Anglo-French and Anglican-Catholic differences and tensions developed. The pro-British government at first refused to recognize the titles of church officials, hindered the clergy in their work and tried to install a non-Catholic educational system. Laws were passed that guaranteed religious liberties to Catholics (Québec Act of 1774, Constitutional Act of 1791, legislation approved by Queen Victoria in 1851), but it took some time before actual respect for these liberties matched the legal enactments. The initial moderation of government antipathy toward the Church was caused partly by the loyalty of Catholics to the Crown during the American Revolution and the War of 1812.

Growth

The 15 years following the passage in 1840 of the Act of Union, which joined Upper and Lower Canada, were significant. New communities of men and women religious joined those already in the country. The Oblates of Mary Immaculate, missionaries par excellence in Canada, advanced the penetration of the West that had been started in 1818 by Abbé Provencher. New jurisdictions were established, and Québec became a metropolitan see in 1844. The first Council of Québec was held in 1851. The established Catholic school system enjoyed a period of growth.

Laval University was inaugurated in 1854 and canonically established in 1876.

Archbishop Elzear-Alexandre Taschereau of Québec was named Canada's first cardinal in 1886. The apostolic delegation to Canada was set up in 1899. It became a nunciature October 16, 1969, with the establishment of diplomatic relations with the Vatican. The present Apostolic Nuncio is Archbishop Pedro López Quintana, appointed on Dec. 10, 2009.

Early in this century, Canada had eight ecclesiastical provinces, 23 dioceses, three vicariates apostolic, 3,500 priests, 2 million Catholics, about 30 communities of men religious, and 70 or more communities of women religious. The Church in Canada was phased out of mission status and removed from the jurisdiction of the Congregation for the Propagation of the Faith in 1908.

Diverse Population

The greatest concentration of Catholics is in the eastern portion of the country. In the northern and western portions, outside metropolitan centers, there are some of the most difficult parish and mission areas in the world. Bilingual (English-French) differences in the general population are reflected in the Church; for example, in the parallel structures of the Canadian Conference of Catholic Bishops, which was established in 1943. Québec is the center of French cultural influence. Many language groups are represented among Catholics, who include more than 257,000 members of Eastern Rites in one metropolitan see, seven eparchies and an apostolic exarchate.

Education, a past source of friction between the Church and the government, is administered by the civil provinces in a variety of arrangements authorized by the Canadian Constitution. Denominational schools have tax support in one way in Québec and Newfoundland, and in another way in Alberta, Ontario and Saskatchewan. Several provinces provide tax support only for public schools, making private financing necessary for separate church-related schools.

ECCLESIASTICAL JURISDICTIONS OF CANADA

Provinces

Names of ecclesiastical provinces and metropolitan sees in bold face; suffragan sees in parentheses.

Edmonton (Calgary, St. Paul).

Gatineau-Hull (Amos, Mont-Laurier, Rouyn Noranda).

Grouard-McLennan (Mackenzie-Ft. Smith, Prince George, Whitehorse).

Halifax (Antigonish, Charlottetown).

Keewatin-LePas (Churchill-Hudson Bay, Labrador-Schefferville, Moosonee).

Kingston (Alexandria-Cornwall, Peterborough, Sault Ste. Marie).

Moncton (Bathurst, Edmundston, St. John).

Montréal (Joliette, St. Jean-Longueuil, St. Jerome, Valleyfield).

Ottawa (Hearst, Pembroke, Timmins).

Québec (Chicoutimi, Ste.-Anne-de-la-Pocatiere, Trois Rivieres).

Regina (Prince Albert, Saskatoon, Abbey of St. Peter).

Rimouski (Baie-Comeau, Gaspe).

St. Boniface (no suffragan).

St. John's (Grand Falls, St. George).

Sherbrooke (Nicolet, St. Hyacinthe).

Toronto (Hamilton, London, St. Catharines, Thunder Bay).

Vancouver (Kamloops, Nelson, Victoria).

Winnipeg-Ukrainian (Edmonton, New Westminster, Saskatoon, Toronto).

Jurisdictions immediately subject to the Holy See: Roman-Rite Archdiocese of Winnipeg, Byzantine Eparchy of Sts. Cyril and Methodius for Slovaks, Byzantine Eparchy of St. Sauveur de Montréal for Greek Melkites; Antiochene Eparchy of St. Maron of Montréal for Maronites.

JURISDICTIONS, HIERARCHY

(Principal sources: Information office, Canadian Conference of Catholic Bishops; Rev. Mr. William Kokesch, Dir., Communications Service, Canadian Conference of Catholic Bishops; Annuaire, Conférence des Évêques Catholiques du Canada;

Catholic Almanac *survey;* Annuario Pontificio; L'Osservatore Romano; *Catholic News Service. As of June 1, 2013.)*

Information includes names of archdioceses (indicated by asterisk) and dioceses, date of foundation, present ordinaries and auxiliaries; addresses of chancery office/bishop's residence; cathedral.

Alexandria-Cornwall, ON (1890 as Alexandria; name changed to Alexandria-Cornwall, 1976): Marcel Damphousse, bishop, 2012.

Diocesan Center: 220, chemin Montréal, C.P. 1388, Cornwall, ON K6H 5V4; (613) 933-1138; www.alexandria-cornwall.ca/. Cathedral: St. Finnans (Alexandria); Nativity Co-Cathedral (Cornwall).

Amos, QC (1938): Gilles Lemay, bishop, 2011.

Bishop's Residence: 450, rue Principale Nord, Amos, QC J9T 2M1; (819) 732-6515; www.dioceseamos.org. Cathedral: St. Teresa of Ávila.

Antigonish, NS (Arichat, 1844; transferred, 1886): Brian J. Dunn, bishop, 2010.

Chancery Office: 168 Hawthorne St., P.O. Box 1330, Antigonish, NS B2G 2L7; (902) 863-3335; www.antigonishdiocese.com/title.htm. Cathedral: St. Ninian.

Baie-Comeau, QC (p.a., 1882; v.a., 1905; diocese Gulf of St. Lawrence, 1945; name changed to Hauterive, 1960; present title, 1986): Jean Pierre Blais, bishop.

Bishop's Residence: 639, rue de Bretagne, Baie-Comeau, QC G5C 1X2; (418) 589-5744; www.diocese-bc.org. Cathedral: Paroisse St. Jean-Eudes.

Bathurst, NB (Chatham, 1860; transferred, 1938): Daniel Jodoin, bishop, 2013.

Bishop's Residence: 645, avenue Murray, C.P. 460, Bathurst, NB E2A 3Z4; (506) 546-1420; www.diocesebathurst.com. Cathedral: Sacred Heart of Jesus.

Calgary, AB (1912): Frederick Henry, bishop, 1997.

Address: Room 290, The Iona Building, 120 17 Ave. SW, Calgary, AB T2S 2T2; (403) 218-5526; www.rcdiocese-calgary.ab.ca. Cathedral: St. Mary.

Charlottetown, PEI (1829): Richard Grecco, bishop, 2009.

Bishop's Residence: P.O. Box 907, Charlottetown, PEI C1A 7L9; (902) 368-8005; www.dioceseofcharlottetown/com. Cathedral: St. Dunstan's.

Chicoutimi, QC (1878): André Rivest, bishop, 2004. Roch Pedneault, aux.

Bishop's Residence: 602, Racine Est, Chicoutimi, QC G7H 6J6; (418) 543-0783; www.evechedechicoutimi.qc.ca. Cathedral: St. Francois-Xavier.

Churchill-Hudson Bay, MB (p.a., 1925; v.a. Hudson Bay, 1931; diocese of Churchill, 1967; present title, 1968): Anthony W. Krotki, O.M.I, bishop, 2013.

Diocesan Office: P.O. Box 10, Churchill, MB R0B 0E0; (204) 675-2252. Cathedral: Holy Canadian Martyrs.

Corner Brook and Labrador, QC (formerly Labrador City-Schefferville; v.a. Labrador, 1946; diocese, 1967): Peter Joseph Hundt, bishop, 2011.

Bishop's Residence: Sutton House, 320 avenue Elizabeth, C.P. 545, Labrador City, Labrador, NL A2V 2L3; (709) 944-2046; www.labdiocese.com. Cathedral: Our Lady of Perpetual Help.

Edmonton,* AB (St. Albert, 1871; archdiocese,

transferred Edmonton, 1912): Richard W. Smith, archbishop, 2007. Gregory Bittman, auxiliary.

Archdiocesan Office: 8421-101 Avenue, Edmonton, Alta. T6A 0L1; (780) 469-1010; www.edmontoncatholicchurch.com. Cathedral: Basilica of St. Joseph.

Edmonton, AB (Ukrainian Byzantine) (ap. ex. of western Canada, 1948; eparchy, 1956): David Motiuk, bishop, 2007.

Eparch's Residence: 9645 108th Ave., Edmonton, Alta. T5H 1A3; (780) 424-5496. Cathedral: St. Josaphat.

Edmundston, NB (1944): Claude Champagne, O.M.I., bishop, 2009.

Diocesan Center: 60, rue Bouchard, Edmundston, NB E3V 3K1; (506) 735-5578; www.diocese-edmunston.ca. Cathedral: Immaculate Conception.

Gaspé, QC (1922): Jean Gagnon, bishop, 2002.

Bishop's House: 172, rue Jacques-Cartier, Gaspé, QC G4X 1M9; (418) 368-2274; www.gaspesie.net/ diocesegaspe. Cathedral: Christ the King.

Gatineau,* QC (1963, as Hull; name changed, 1982; archdiocese, 1990): Paul-André Durocher, archbishop, 2011.

Diocesan Center: 180 Boulevard Mont-Bleu, Hull, QC J8Z 3J5; (819) 771-8391; www.diocesegatineau-hull.qc.ca.

Grand Falls, NL (Harbour Grace, 1856; present title, 1964): Robert Anthony Daniels, bishop, 2011.

Chancery Office: 8A Church Rd., P.O. Box 771, Grand Falls-Windsor, NL A2A 2M4; (709) 489-2778; www.rcdiocesegrandfalls.ca/. Cathedral: Immaculate Conception.

Grouard-McLennan,* AB (v.a. Athabaska-Mackenzie, 1862; Grouard, 1927; archdiocese Grouard-McLennan, 1967); Gerard Pettipas, C.Ss.R., archbishop, 2006.

Archbishop's Residence: 210-1 Street West, C.P. 388, McLennan, AB T0H 2L0; (780) 324-3820. Cathedral: St. Jean-Baptiste (McLennan).

Halifax-Yarmouth,* NS (1842; archdiocese, 1852; united with Yarmouth diocese, 2009): Anthony Mancini, archbishop, 2007; archbishop of Halifax-Yarmouth, 2009.

Chancery Office: 1531 Grafton St., P.O. Box 1527, Halifax, NS B3J 2Y3; (902) 429-9800; www. catholichalifax.org.

Hamilton, ON (1856): David Crosby, O.M.I., bishop, 2010. Daniel Miehm, auxiliary.

Chancery Office: 700 King St. West, Hamilton, ON L8P 1C7; (905) 528-7988; www.hamiltondiocese.com/. Cathedral: Christ the King.

Hearst, ON (p.a., 1918; v.a., 1920; diocese, 1938): Vincent Cadieux, O.M.I., bishop, 2007.

Bishop's Residence: 76 7e rue, C.P. 1330, Hearst, ON P0L 1N0; (705) 362-4903; www.hearstdiocese.com. Cathedral: Notre Dame de la Assumption.

Joliette, QC (1904): Gilles Lussier, bishop, 1991.

Bishop's Residence: 2 rue Saint-Charles-Borromée Nord, C.P. 470, Joliette, QC J6E 6H6; (450) 753-7596; www.diocesedejoliette.org. Cathedral: St. Charles Borromeo.

Kamloops, BC (1945): David Monroe, bishop, 2002.

Bishop's Residence: 635-A Tranquille Rd., Kamloops, BC V2B 3H5; (250) 376-3351. Cathedral: Sacred Heart.

Keewatin-Le Pas,* MB (v.a., 1910; archdiocese, 1967): Murray Chatlain, archbishop, 2012.

Archbishop's Residence: 76 1st St. W., P.O. Box 270, The Pas, MB R9A 1K4; (204) 623-6152. Cathedral: Our Lady of the Sacred Heart.

Kingston,* ON (1826; archdiocese, 1889): Brendan Michael O'Brien, archbishop, 2007.

Chancery Office: 390 Palace Rd., Kingston, ON K7L 4T3; (613) 548-4461; www.romancatholic.kingston.on.ca. Cathedral: St. Mary of the Immaculate Conception.

London, ON (1855; transferred Sandwich, 1859; London, 1869): Ronald P. Fabbro, C.S.B., bishop, 2002. Robert Anthony Daniels, auxiliary.

Bishop's Residence: 1070 Waterloo St., London, ON N6A 3Y2; (519) 433-0658; www.rcec.london. on.ca. Cathedral: St. Peter's Cathedral Basilica.

Mackenzie-Fort Smith, NT (v.a. Mackenzie, 1902; diocese Mackenzie-Fort Smith, 1967): Murray Chatlain, coadjutor bishop, 2007; bishop, 2008.

Diocesan Office: 5117-52nd St., Yellowknife, NT X1A 1T7; (867) 920-2129. Cathedral: St. Joseph (Ft. Smith).

Moncton,* NB (1936): Valery Vienneau, archbishop, 2012.

Archbishop's Residence: 452, rue Amirault, Dieppe, NB E1A 1G3; (506) 857-9531. Cathedral: Our Lady of the Assumption.

Mont-Laurier, QC (1913): Paul Lortie, bishop, 2012.

Bishop's Residence: 435, rue de la Madone, Mont-Laurier, QC J9L 1S1; (819) 623-5530. Cathedral: Notre Dame de Fourvières.

Montréal,* QC (1836; archdiocese, 1886): Christian Lépine, archbishop, 2012. Thomas Dowd, auxiliary.

Archbishop's Residence: 2000, rue Sherbrooke Ouest, Montréal, QC H3H 1G4; (514) 931-7311; www.diocesemontreal.org. Cathedral: Basilica of Mary Queen of the World and Saint James.

Montréal, QC (Sauveur de Montréal, Eparchy of Greek Melkites) (ap. ex. 1980; eparchy, 1984): Ibrahim M. Ibrahim, 2003.

Address: 34 rue Maplewood, Montréal, QC H2V 2MI; (514) 272-6430.

Montréal, QC (St. Maron of Montréal, Maronites) (1982): Paul-Marwan Tabet, C.M.L., bishop, 2013.

Chancery Office: 12 475 rue Grenet, Montréal, QC H4J 2K4; (514) 331-2807. Cathedral: St. Maron.

Moosonee, ON (v.a. James Bay, 1938; diocese Moosonee, 1967): Vincent Cadieux, O.M.I., bishop, 1992.

Bishop's Residence: 2 Bay Rd., C.P. 40, Moosonee, ON P0L 1Y0; (705) 336-2908. Cathedral: Christ the King.

Nelson, BC (1936): John Corriveau, O.F.M. Cap., bishop, 2007.

Bishop's Residence: 402 West Richards St., Nelson, BC VIL 3K3; (250) 354-6921; www.diocese. nelson.bc.ca/. Cathedral: Mary Immaculate.

New Westminster, BC (Ukrainian Byzantine) (1974): Kenneth Nowakowski, eparch, 2007

Eparch's address: 502 5th Ave., New Westminster, BC V3L 1S2; (604) 524-8824; www.vcn.bc.ca/ ucepnw.

Nicolet, QC (1885): André Gazaille, bishop, 2011.

Bishop's Residence: 49, rue Mgr Brunault, Nicolet, QC J3T 1X7; (819) 293-4696. Cathedral: St. Jean-Baptiste.

Ottawa,* ON (Bytown, 1847, name changed, 1854; archdiocese, 1886): Terrence Prendergast, S.J., archbishop, 2007.

Archbishop's Residence: 1247 Place Kilborn, Ottawa, ON K1H 6K9; (613) 738-5025; www.ecclesia-ottawa.org. Cathedral: Basilica of Notre Dame-of-Ottawa.

Pembroke, ON (v.a. 1882; diocese, 1898): Michael Mulhall, bishop, 2007. Bishop's Residence: 188 Renfrew St., P.O. Box 7, Pembroke, ON K8A 6X1; (613) 732-7933; www.diocesepembroke.org. Cathedral: St. Columbkille.

Peterborough, ON (1882): Nicola De Angelis, C.F.I.C., bishop 2002.

Bishop's Residence: 350 Hunter St. West, P.O. Box 175, Peterborough, ON K9J 6Y8; (705) 745-5123; www.peterboroughdiocese.org. Cathedral: St. Peter-in-Chains.

Prince Albert, SK (v.a., 1890; diocese, 1907): Albert Thévenot, M. Afr., bishop, 2008.

Address: 1415 4th Ave. West, Prince Albert, SK S6V 5H1; (306) 922-4747; www.padiocese.sk.ca. Cathedral: Sacred Heart.

Prince George, BC (p.a., 1908; v.a. Yukon and Prince Rupert, 1944; diocese Prince George, 1967): Stephen A. Jensen, bishop, 2013.

Chancery Office: 6500 Southbridge Ave., P.O. Box 7000, Prince George, BC V2N 3Z2; (250) 964-4424; www.pgdiocese.bc.ca. Cathedral: Sacred Heart.

Québec,* QC (v.a., 1658; diocese, 1674; archdiocese, 1819; metropolitan, 1844; primatial see, 1956): Gérard Cyprien Lacroix, I.S.P.X., archbishop, 2011. Denis Grondin, Gaetan Proulx, O.S.M., auxiliaries.

Chancery Office: 1073, boul. René-Lévesque ouest, Québec, QC G1S 4R5; (418) 688-1211; www.diocesequebec.qc.ca/. Cathedral: Notre-Dame-de-Québec (Basilica).

Regina,* SK (1910; archdiocese, 1915): Daniel Bohan, archbishop, 2005.

Chancery Office: 445 Broad St. North, Regina, SK S4R 2X8; (306) 352-1651; www.archregina.sk.ca. Cathedral: Our Lady of the Most Holy Rosary.

Rimouski,* QC (1867; archdiocese, 1946): Pierre-André Fournier, archbishop, 2008.

Archbishop's Residence: 34, rue de l'Évêché Ouest, C.P. 730, Rimouski, QC G5L 7C7; (418) 723-3320; www.dioceserimouski.com.

Rouyn-Noranda, QC (1973): Dorylas Moreau, bishop, 2001.

Bishop's Residence: 515, avenue Cuddihy, C.P. 1060, Rouyn-Noranda, QC J9X 4C5; (819) 764-4660; www.dioc-cath-rouyn-noranda.org. Cathedral: St. Michael the Archangel.

Saint-Boniface,* MB (1847; archdiocese, 1871): Albert LeGatt, archbishop, 2009.

Archbishop's Residence: 151, avenue de la Cathédrale, Saint-Boniface, MB R2H 0H6; (204) 237-9851. Cathedral: Basilica of St. Boniface.

St. Catharine's, ON (1958): Gerard P. Bergie, bishop, 2010.

Bishop's Residence: P.O. Box 875, St. Catharines, ON L2R 6Y3; (905) 684-0154; www.romancatholic.niagara.on.ca. Cathedral: St. Catherine of Alexandria.

Saint-Hyacinthe, QC (1852): François Lapierre, P.M.E., bishop, 1998.

Bishop's Residence: 1900, rue Girouard Ouest, C.P. 190, Saint-Hyacinthe, QC J2S 7B4; (450) 773-8581; www.diocese-st-hyacinthe.qc.ca. Cathedral: St. Hyacinthe the Confessor.

Saint-Jean-Longueuil, QC (1933 as St.-Jean-de-Québec; named changed, 1982): Lionel Gendron, P.S.S., bishop, 1996. Louis Dicaire, auxiliary.

Bishop's Residence: 740, boulevard Sainte-Foy, C.P. 40, Longueuil, QC J4K 4X8; (450) 679-1100; www.diocese-st-jean-longueuil.org. Cathedral: St. John the Evangelist.

St. Jérôme, QC (1951): Pierre Morissette, bishop, 2008.

Bishop's Residence: 355, Place du Curé Labelle, Saint-Jerome, QC J7Z 5A9; (450) 432-9742; www.diocese-stjerome.qc.ca. Cathedral: St. Jerome.

Saint John, NB (1842): Robert Harris, bishop, 2007; Raymond Poisson, auxiliary.

Chancery Office: 1 Bayard Dr., Saint John, NB E2L 3L5; (506) 653-6800; www.dioceseofsaintjohn.org. Cathedral: Immaculate Conception.

St. John's,* NL (p.a., 1784; v.a., 1796; diocese, 1847; archdiocese, 1904): Martin W. Currie, archbishop, 2007.

Chancery Office: P.O. Box 37, St. John's, NL. A1C 5N5; (709) 726-3660; www.stjohnsarchdiocese.nf.ca. Cathedral: St. John the Baptist.

St. Paul in AB (1948): Paul Terrio, bishop.

Bishop's Residence: 4410, 51e avenue, Saint Paul, AB T0A 3A2; (780) 645-3277. Cathedral: St. Paul.

Sainte-Anne-de-la-Pocatière, QC (1951): Yvon-Joseph Moreau, O.C.S.O., bishop, 2008.

Bishop's Residence: 1200, 4e avenue, C.P. 430, La Pocatière, QC G0R 1Z0; (418) 856-1811. Cathedral: St. Anne.

Saskatoon, SK (1933): Donald Bolen, bishop, 2009.

Chancery Office: 100-5th Ave. North, Saskatoon, SK S7K 2N7; (306) 242-1500; www.saskatoonrcdiocese.com. Cathedral: St. Paul.

Saskatoon, SK (Ukrainian Byzantine) (ap. ex., 1951; diocese, 1956): P. Bryan Bayda, C.SS.R, 2008.

Address: 866 Saskatchewan Crescent East, Saskatoon, SK S7N 0L4; (306) 653-0138.

Sault Ste. Marie, ON (1904): Jean-Louis Plouffe, bishop, 1990, Noël Simard, auxiliary.

Chancery Office: 30, chemin Ste. Anne, Sudbury, ON P3C 5E1, (705) 674-2727; www.isys.ca/cathcom.htm. Cathedral: Pro-Cathedral of the Assumption, North Bay.

Sherbrooke,* QC (1874; archdiocese, 1951): Luc Cyr, archbishop, 1996.

Archbishop's Residence: 130, rue de la Cathédrale, C.P. 430, Sherbrooke, QC J1H 5K1; (819) 563-9934; www.diosher.org. Cathedral: St. Michel.

Thunder Bay, ON (Ft. William, 1952; transferred, 1970): Frederick J. Colli, bishop, 1999.

Bishop's Office: 1222 Reaume St., P.O. Box 10400, Thunder Bay, ON P7B 6T8; (807) 343-9313; www.dotb.ca. Cathedral: St. Patrick.

Timmins, ON (v.a. Temiskaming, 1908; diocese Haileybury, 1915; present title, 1938): Serge Poitras, bishop, 2012.

Address: 65, Ave. Jubilee Est, Timmins, ON

P4N 5W4; www.nt.net/~dioctims/. Cathedral: St. Anthony of Padua.

Toronto,* ON (1841; archdiocese, 1870): Cardinal Thomas C. Collins, archbishop, 2006. John A. Boissonneau, Peter Joseph Hundt, Vincent Nguyen, William Terrence McGrattan, Wayne J. Kirkpatrick, auxiliaries.

Chancery Office: Catholic Pastoral Centre, 1155 Yonge St., Toronto, ON M4T 1W2; (416) 934-0606; www.archtoronto.org. Cathedral: St. Michael.

Toronto, ON (Eparchy for Slovakian Byzantine) (1980): John Pazak, C.Ss.R., 2000.

Eparch's Residence: 223 Carlton Rd., Unionville, ON L3R 3M2; (905) 477-4867.

Toronto, ON (Eparchy for Ukrainian Byzantine) (ap. ex., 1948; eparchy, 1956): Stephen Victor Chmilar eparch, 2003.

Chancery Office: 3100-A Weston Rd., Weston, ON M9M 2S7; (416) 746-0154; www.ucet.ca. Cathedral: St. Josaphat.

Trois-Rivières, QC (1852): Joseph Luc André Bouchard, bishop, 2012.

Bishop's Residence: 362, rue Bonaventure, C.P. 879, Trois-Rivières, QC G9A 5J9; (819) 374-9847; www.diocese-tr.qc.ca/. Cathedral: The Assumption.

Valleyfield, QC (1892): Noel Simard, bishop, 2011.

Bishop's Residence: 11, rue de l'Eglise, Salaberry-de-Valleyfield, QC J6T 1J5; (450) 373-8122; www.rocler.qc.ca/diocese-valleyfield/. Cathedral: St. Cecilia.

Vancouver,* BC (v.a. British Columbia, 1863; diocese New Westminster, 1890; archdiocese Vancouver, 1908): J. Michael Miller, C.S.B., archbishop, 2009.

Chancery Office: 150 Robson St., Vancouver, BC V6B 2A7; (604) 683-0281; www.rcav.bc.ca. Cathedral: Holy Rosary.

Victoria, BC (diocese Vancouver Is., 1846; archdiocese, 1903; diocese Victoria, 1908): Richard Gagnon, 2004.

Chancery Office: Diocesan Pastoral Centre, #1-4044 Nelthorpe St., Victoria, BC V8X 2A1; (250) 479-1331; www.rcdvictoria.org. Cathedral: St. Andrew.

Whitehorse, YT (v.a., 1944; diocese 1967): Gary Gordon, bishop, 2006.

Chancery Office: 5119 5th Ave., Whitehorse, YT Y1A 1L5; (867) 667-2052. Cathedral: Sacred Heart.

Winnipeg,* MB (1915): V. James Weisgerber, archbishop, 2000.

Chancery Office: Catholic Centre, 1495 Pembina Highway, Winnipeg, MB R3T 2C6; (204) 452-2227; www.archwinnipeg.ca. Cathedral: St. Mary.

Winnipeg,* MB (Ukrainian Byzantine) (Ordinariate of Canada, 1912; ap. ex. Central Canada, 1948; ap. ex. Manitoba, 1951; archeparchy Winnipeg, 1956): Lawrence Huculak, O.S.B.M., archeparch, 1993. Archeparchy Office: 233 Scotia St., Winnipeg, MB R2V 1V7; (204) 338-7801; www. archeparchy.ca. Cathedral: Sts. Vladimir and Olga.

Military Ordinariate of Canada (1951): Donald J. Thériault, bishop, 1998.

Address: Canadian Forces Support Unit (Ottawa), Uplands Site – Bldg. 469, Ottawa, ON K1A 0K2; (613) 990-7824.

An Apostolic Exarchate for Armenian-Rite

Catholics in Canada and the United States was established in July 1981 with headquarters in New York City (110 E. 12th St., New York, NY 10003); (212) 477-2030. Manuel Batakian, exarch, 1995.

The Eparchy of Our Lady of Deliverance of Newark for Syrian-rite Catholics in the United States and Canada was established Nov. 6, 1995. Address: 502 Palisade Ave., Union City, NJ 08087-5213; (201) 583-1067; www.Syriac-Catholic.org. Vacant.

Hungarian Emigrants throughout the world, resides in Canada: Most Rev. Attila Mikloshazy, S.J., titular bishop of Cast'el Minore. Address: 2661 Kingston Rd., Scarborough, ON M1M 1M3; (416) 261-7207.

Note: The diocese of **Gravelbourg**, in Saskatchewan, was dissolved in September 1998 as part of a reorganization of Canadian dioceses. The regions under the jurisdiction of **Gravelbourg** were integrated into the neighboring dioceses of **Regina** and **Saskatoon**. The **Territorial Abbacy of St. Peter,** Muenster, SK, was also dissolved.

Dioceses with Interprovincial Lines

The following dioceses, indicated by + in the table, have interprovincial lines.

Churchill-Hudson Bay includes part of Northwest Territories.

Keewatin-LePas includes part of Manitoba and Saskatchewan provinces.

Corner Brook and Labrador includes the Labrador region of Newfoundland and the northern part of Québec province.

Mackenzie-Fort Smith, Northwest Territories, includes part of Alberta and Saskatchewan provinces.

Moosonee, Ontario, includes part of Québec province.

Pembroke, Ontario, includes one county of Québec province.

Whitehorse, Yukon Territory, includes part of British Columbia.

CANADIAN CONFERENCE OF CATHOLIC BISHOPS

The Canadian Conference of Catholic Bishops was established Oct. 12, 1943, as a permanent voluntary association of the bishops of Canada, was given official approval by the Holy See in 1948, and acquired the status of an episcopal conference after the Second Vatican Council.

The CCCB acts in two ways: (1) as a strictly ecclesiastical body through which the bishops act together with pastoral authority and responsibility for the Church throughout the country; (2) as an operational secretariat through which the bishops act on a wider scale for the good of the Church and society.

At the top of the CCCB organizational table are the president, an executive committee, a permanent council and a plenary assembly. The membership consists of all the bishops of Canada.

Departments and Offices

The CCCB's work is planned and coordinated by the Programmes and Priorities Committee composed of the six chairmen of the national episcopal commissions and the two general secretaries. It is chaired by the vice-president of the CCCB.

The CCCB's 12 episcopal commissions undertake study and projects in special areas of pastoral work. Six serve nationally (justice and peace; canon law/inter-rite; relations with associations of clergy, consecrated life and laity; evangelization of peoples; ecumenism; doctrine); three relate to French sectors (*communications sociale, éducation Chrétienne, liturgie*); and three relate to corresponding English sectors (social communications, Christian education, liturgy).

The general secretariat consists of a general secretary and assistants and directors of public relations. The current general secretary is Msgr. Patrick Powers, P.H.

Administrative services for purchasing, archives and library, accounting, personnel, publications, printing and distribution are supervised by directors who relate to the general secretaries.

Various advisory councils and committees with mixed memberships of lay persons, religious, priests and bishops also serve the CCCB on a variety of topics.

Operations

Meetings for the transaction of business are held at least once a year by the plenary assembly, six times a year by the executive committee, and four times a year by the permanent council.

Abp. Richard Smith of Edmonton is president of the CCCB, and Abp. Paul-André Durocher of Gatineau is vice-president for the 2011-2013 term.

The Conference headquarters is located at 2500 Don Reid Dr., Ottawa, K1H 2J2, Canada; (613) 241-9461; www.cccb.ca.

CANADIAN SHRINES

Our Lady of the Cape (Cap de la Madeleine), Queen of the Most Holy Rosary: The Three Rivers, Québec, parish church, built in 1714 and considered the oldest stone church on the North American continent preserved in its original state, was rededicated June 22, 1888, as a shrine of the Queen of the Most Holy Rosary. The site increased in importance as a pilgrimage and devotional center, and in 1904 St. Pius X decreed the crowning of a statue of the Blessed Virgin which had been donated 50 years earlier to commemorate the dogma of the Immaculate Conception. In 1909, the First Plenary Council of Québec declared the church a shrine of national pilgrimage. In 1964, the church at the shrine was given the status and title of minor basilica.

St. Anne de Beaupre: The devotional history of this shrine in Québec began with the reported cure of a cripple, Louis Guimont, on Mar. 16, 1658, the starting date of construction work on a small chapel of St. Anne. The original building was successively enlarged and replaced by a stone church, which was given the rank of minor basilica in 1888. The present structure, a Romanesque-Gothic basilica, houses the shrine proper in its north transept, including an eight-foot-high oaken statue and a relic of St. Anne, a portion of her forearm.

St. Joseph's Oratory: The massive oratory basilica standing on the western side of Mount Royal and overlooking the city of Montréal had its origin in a primitive chapel erected there by Blessed André Bessette, C.S.C., in 1904. Eleven years later, a large crypt was built to accommodate an increasing number of pilgrims, and in 1924 construction work was begun on the large church. A belfry, housing a 60-bell carillon and standing on the site of the original chapel, was dedicated May 15, 1955, as the first major event of the jubilee year observed after the oratory was given the rank of minor basilica.

Martyrs' Shrine: A shrine commemorating several of the Jesuit Martyrs of North America who were killed between 1642 and 1649 in the Ontario and northern New York area is located on the former site of old Fort Sainte Marie. Before its location was fixed near Midland, ON, in 1925, a small chapel had been erected in 1907 at old Mission St. Ignace to mark the martyrdom of Fathers Jean de Brebeuf and Gabriel Lalemant. This sanctuary has a U.S. counterpart in the Shrine of the North American Martyrs near Auriesville, NY, under the care of the Jesuits.

Others

In Québec City: Basilica of Notre Dame (1650), once the cathedral of a diocese stretching from Canada to Mexico; Notre Dame des Victoires (1690); the Ursuline Convent (1720), on du Parloir St.

Near Montréal: Hermitage of St. Anthony, La Bouchette; Ste. Anne de Micmacs, Restigouche; Chapel of Atonement, Pointe aux Trembles; Our Lady of Lourdes, Rigaud; St. Benoît du Lac, near Magog.

In Montréal: Notre Dame Basilica (1829).

Near Montréal: Chapel of St. Marie Marguerite d'Youville, foundress of the Grey Nuns; Notre Dame de Lourdes, at Rigaud.

STATISTICAL SUMMARY OF THE CATHOLIC CHURCH IN CANADA

(*Principal source:* 2013 Directory of the Canadian Conference of Catholic Bishops; *figures as of Jan. 2013.*) Catholic population statistics are those reported in the 2001 Canadian Census. Archdioceses are indicated by an asterisk. For dioceses marked +, *see* **Canadian Dioceses with Interprovincial Lines**.

Canada's 10 civil provinces and two territories are divided into 18 ecclesiastical provinces consisting of 18 metropolitan sees (archdioceses) and 44 suffragan sees; there are also eight Oriental Rite dioceses, one archdiocese and three eparchies immediately subject to the Holy See, and the Military Ordinariate.

This table presents a regional breakdown of Catholic statistics. In some cases, the totals are approximate because diocesan boundaries fall within several civil provinces.

Civil Province Diocese	Cath. Pop.	Dioc. Priests	Rel. Priests	Total Priests	Perm. Deacs.	Bro- thers	Sis- ters	Lay Assts.	Par- ishes[1]
Newfoundland	**188,089**	**129**	**13**	**142**	**4**	**9**	**420**	**25**	**220**
St. John's*	111,605	40	7	47	2	8	170	2	70
Corner Brook & Lab.+	40,624	22	3	25	–	–	15	4	28
Grand Falls	35,860	19	1	20	1	–	19	1	70
Prince Edward Island									
Charlottetown	**63,240**	**48**	**2**	**50**	**1**	**1**	**108**	**18**	**52**
Nova Scotia	**327,945**	**171**	**20**	**197**	**38**	**11**	**404**	**9**	**215**
Halifax-Yarmouth	198,215	72	17	89	38	–	179	9	97
Antigonish	129,730	99	3	102	–	11	225	0	118
New Brunswick	**385,985**	**167**	**41**	**211**	**4**	**13**	**517**	**109**	**228**
Moncton*	110,895	41	22	63	1	13	228	84	56
Bathurst	107,655	44	5	49	–	–	144	–	57
Edmundston	52,035	23	7	30	–	–	54	15	32
St. John	115,400	59	7	66	3	–	91	20	83
Québec	**5,926,191**	**2,104**	**1,408**	**3,447**	**456**	**849**	**9,454**	**728**	**1,403**
Gatineau*	234,725	43	20	63	1	5	135	17	53
Montréal*	1,494,132	422	576	998	94	244	3,078	113	208
Québec*	917,045	386	254	640	96	102	2,891	70	207
Rimouski*	143,640	86	6	92	15	19	512	15	104
Sherbrooke*	245,495	158	85	243	23	65	629	38	70
Amos	95,506	10	12	22	–	2	57	–	64
Baie Comeau	90,130	39	11	50	11	0	32	17	55
Chicoutimi	263,950	137	25	162	43	20	387	55	67
Gaspé	85,840	45	3	48	3	2	112	10	65
Joliette	206,981	56	53	109	7	74	133	45	53
Mont Laurier	77,340	34	6	40	2	4	29	19	19
Montréal, St. Maron (Maronites)	4,100	10	4	14	2	–	5	–	16
Montréal, St. Sauveur (Greek Melkites)	9,200	6	8	14	–	–	–	–	6
Nicolet	184,625	108	14	122	24	44	267	46	60
Rouyn Noranda	56,380	26	5	31	–	1	72	19	39
Ste Anne de la Pocatière	87,700	82	1	83	7	–	120	16	56
St.-Hyacinthe	336,445	100	102	202	32	115	551	54	87
St.-Jean Long	553,470	82	37	119	4	88	284	92	46
St. Jérôme	407,112	65	21	86	19	6	115	43	36
Trois Rivières	232,985	87	67	154	32	56	369	37	67
Valleyfield	199,390	77	11	88	17	22	36	22	25
Ontario	**3,930,075**	**1,106**	**790**	**1,896**	**518**	**118**	**2,506**	**286**	**1,073**
Kingston*	116,845	71	10	81	22	–	150	–	51
Ottawa*	392,635	137	48	185	86	18	573	15	108
Toronto*	1,626,465	296	412	708	134	51	556	75	244
Alexandria–Corn.	55,570	32	1	33	18	4	22	–	27
Hamilton	559,290	102	103	205	36	10	240	42	152

Civil Province Diocese	Cath. Pop.	Dioc. Priests	Rel. Priests	Total Priests	Perm. Deacs.	Bro thers	Sis ters	Lay Assts.	Par- ishes[1]
Ontario, cont.									
Hearst	31,790	28	–	28	2	–	2	17	28
London	444,310	110	58	168	51	6	473	59	116
Moosonee+	3,830	0	3	3	1	1	–	3	8
Pembroke+	67,870	45	4	49	9	3	163	2	58
Peterborough	99,785	89	9	98	7	–	93	–	64
St. Catharine's	153,565	61	31	92	19	3	30	7	46
Sault Ste. Marie	206,405	76	12	88	92	1	180	2	96
Thunder Bay	73,780	31	12	43	33	–	9	–	43
Timmins	50,605	20	4	24	7	4	14	7	27
Toronto (Ukr.)	42,330	79	4	83	18	1	17	1	57
Toronto (Slovaks)	5,000	4	–	4	–	–	–	–	5
Manitoba	**344,845**	**171**	**87**	**258**	**56**	**11**	**373**	**14**	**370**
Keewatin Le Pas*+	37,380	4	11	15	–	–	7	–	45
St. Boniface*	113,495	70	38	108	25	10	230	11	97
Winnipeg*	158,095	61	23	84	18	1	110	-	89
Winnipeg (Ukrainians)*	29,760	34	10	44	13	–	23	–	122
Churchill Hud. Bay+	6,115	2	5	7	–	–	3	3	17
Saskatchewan+	**286,625**	**169**	**82**	**251**	**9**	**16**	**291**	**55**	**416**
Regina*#	126,980	86	21	107	2	7	67	–	156
Prince-Albert	55,450	38	17	55	2	–	66	9	86
Saskatoon#	86,645	36	34	70	2	9	139	46	95
Saskatoon (Ukrainians)	17,550	19	10	29	3	–	19	–	79
Alberta	**783,940**	**269**	**157**	**426**	**75**	**25**	**385**	**61**	**409**
Edmonton*	333,545	90	87	177	20	17	254	43	126
Grouard McLellan*	44,470	18	8	26	2	–	12	8	66
Calgary	320,425	105	41	146	43	4	79	–	79
Edmonton (Ukrainians)	28,845	28	12	40	4	4	20	–	83
St. Paul	56,655	28	9	37	6	–	20	10	55
British Columbia	**672,515**	**217**	**135**	**352**	**3**	**28**	**211**	**6**	**299**
Vancouver*	402,310	106	102	208	1	19	109	–	89
Kamloops	51,435	15	5	20	1	1	15	–	67
Nelson	67,025	29	4	33	–	–	11	–	53
New Westminster (Ukrainians)	7,780	9	1	10	-	–	2	–	12
Prince George	49,500	17	7	24	1	4	11	5	37
Victoria	94,465	41	16	57	–	4	63	–	41
Yukon Territory									
Whitehorse+	**8,150**	**7**	**3**	**10**	**–**	**–**	**2**	**7**	**22**
Northwest Territories									
MacKenzie–Ft. Smith+	**20,110**	**7**	**3**	**10**	**1**	**1**	**6**	**1**	**37**
Military Ordinariate	**13,400**	**48***	**0****	**48**	**7**	**0**	**–**	**39**	**23****
TOTALS	**12.951.1102**	**4.500**	**2.739**	**7.239**	**1.171**	**1.081**	**13.857**	**1.338**	**4.715**

1. Denotes both parishes and missions.
2. Catholics comprise about 43% of the total population. According to the 2011 *Annuarium Statisticum Ecclesiae* (the most recent edition), there were 110,059 baptisms and 20,143 marriages.
* The Canadian Military Ordinariate does not incardinate clerics.
** Not included in the total.

The Catholic Church in Mexico

BACKGROUND

Start of Church Organization

The history of the Catholic Church in Mexico began in 1519 with the capture of Mexico's native civilization, the Aztec Empire, by the Spanish *conquistadores* under Hernándo Cortés. The Spanish army besieged the Aztec capital of Tenochtitlan, massacred most of the inhabitants, strangled the Aztec emperor Montezuma, and crushed the rest of the empire. Mexico City became the chief city of New Spain and the cultural and religious center of colonial Mexico; it was declared a diocese in 1530.

The record of Colonial Spanish treatment of the native peoples of Mexico is a grim one. The Indians suffered exploitation, slavery, and rapid depletion of their population from disease; they were forced to labor in inhuman conditions in mines and endured servitude in the *encomienda* system.

In sharp contrast to the treatment of the natives by the government was the effort to evangelize Mexico by the religious orders, who followed the command of Pope Alexander VI in the 1494 Treaty of Tordesillas to convert all peoples who would be encountered in the coming age of exploration. A papal bull, dated Apr. 25, 1521, gave the Franciscans the permission of the Holy See to preach in New Spain. They were joined by the Dominicans and, later, by the Jesuits. The missionary orders soon distinguished themselves by their resistance to the brutal enslavement of the Indians, their mastery of native languages, and their willingness to endure enormous hardships in bringing the faith to the distant corners of Mexico.

As the Church became more established, however, the missionary priests and friars came increasingly into conflict with the secular clergy, who desired full control over ecclesiastical affairs, resented the extensive powers of religious orders, and normally identified closely with the interests of the crown. The government thus decreed that the missionaries were to have 10 years in which to convert the Indians, after which control would pass to the diocesan clergy. This was protested by the missionary orders, and the conflict was resolved in favor of the diocesan priests in 1640 thanks to the efforts of Bishop Juan de Palafox de Mendoza of Puebla.

The alliance of the secular clergy with the government was a reflection of the control enjoyed by the Spanish Crown over the Church in Mexico. The Holy See had granted to the kings of Spain royal patronage over the Church in Mexico, and the practice of the *Patronato Real* meant that the king nominated all Church officials in New Spain and held authority over the Church's temporal concerns.

A major element in this policy was the forced conversion of the local peoples. Coerced into adopting the faith, many Indians were insincere or hesitant to embrace the faith. To insure the full embrace of the faith, Spanish authorities received permission from King Philip II in 1569 to introduce the Inquisition to Mexico. Indians who had survived the mines, diseases, and brutality of the colonial rulers were now subjected to tribunals to test their faith. This practice was eventually ended when authorities decided that the natives were not culpable because of limited intelligence. Nevertheless, the close identification of the diocesan clergy with the interests and policies of the Spanish crown created a hostility toward the Church in Mexico by the lower classes that endures today.

On the positive side, the Church did much through its missionaries to save many Indians from death and enslavement and to preserve vital portions of Mesoamerican culture, art, and history. Friars also traveled to northern Mexico and beyond, bringing the faith into California, Texas, and New Mexico.

The native peoples were given a profound encouragement to embrace the Catholic faith in 1531 by the appearance of Our Lady of Guadalupe to the farmer Juan Diego (beatified in 1990 and canonized in 2002 by Pope John Paul II) on the Tepeyac hill just outside of Mexico City. The shrine built in her honor remains the most important religious site in Mexico. Enshrined within it is the mantle brought by Juan Diego to Bishop Zumaragga to convince him of the genuine nature of the apparition. Miraculously emblazoned upon it is the life-size image of the Virgin Mary.

MEXICAN INDEPENDENCE

The Spanish domination of Mexico endured for nearly three centuries, deteriorating gradually throughout the 1700s as the gulf widened between the Spanish ruling class and the native classes that were joined by the *mestizos* and *creoles* (descendants of Native Americans and Europeans). Unrest broke out into a full-scale rebellion in 1810 with the uprising of many priests led by Father Miguel Hidalgo y Costilla and, after his execution, by Father José Maria Morelos y Pavón. While suppressed in 1816 by the colonial regime with the support of the upper classes and most of the diocesan clergy, it proved only the first of several revolts, culminating in the 1821 declaration of Mexican independence. By the terms of the independence, the Church received a special status and had enormous sway in political life.

A republic was proclaimed in 1834 and various liberal regimes came to power. Anticlericalism became commonplace, made even more strident by the lingering hostility over the Church's activities with Spanish colonial government. Much influenced by the ideals of the European revolutions then taking place, the Mexican republican movements were strongly anti-Catholic. For more than a decade, power was in the hands of Antonio López de Santa Anna (also known for his victory at the Alamo) and Valentin Gómez Farías. After the Mexican-American War (1846-1848), the political instability led to the dictatorship of Santa Anna.

Santa Anna was toppled in 1855 by a liberal regime whose anti-Church legislation sparked an armed struggle called the War of the Reform (1858-1861). The laws issued by the government included the *Ley Juárez*, abolishing all ecclesiastical courts, and the *Ley Lerdo*, forcing the Church to sell all of its lands. Deprived of its properties, the Church lost control of education and schools, and Mexico's educational system became often bitterly anti-Catholic.

While the liberal forces won the War of the Reform, the conflict had so debilitated Mexico that the French were able to intervene in 1861 and install their puppet, the Austrian duke Maximilian, on the Mexican throne. As the United States was embroiled in its own civil war from 1861-1865, it was unable to respond to French imperialist ambitions in Mexico. Maximilian initially enjoyed the support of the conservative elements and the Church, but his liberal reforms alienated the mistrustful conservatives and he soon clung to power only with French support. When France finally withdrew its troops in 1867, Maximilian was deposed by republican forces and executed.

MODERN MEXICO

The fall of Emperor Maximilian signaled a restoration of the anticlerical constitution of 1857 and the elevation of Benito Juárez – the republican leader long recognized by the United States – as president. His successor, Sebastián Lerdo de Tijada, was toppled in 1876 by Porfirio Díaz, who remained dictator for 34 years. A civil war ended his regime, and more bloodshed ensued. Finally, a constitution was issued in 1917 that placed severe restrictions on the Church: there could be no criticism of the government, only Mexicans could be clergy, the Church was not permitted to own property, and any privileges were stripped away.

The situation became worse after 1923, when the papal legate was expelled. The administration of Plutarco Calles (1924-1928) launched a wave of persecution that sparked a popular but ultimately unsuccessful uprising called the Cristero Rebellion. Coupled with the repressive measures of local governments, the Calles regime and its successors forced the Church into very difficult circumstances, with only a few priests remaining in the country. The tragedy was deepened by the execution of dozens of priests and nuns by republican forces for assorted and imaginary crimes or for speaking out on behalf of the poor or oppressed Catholics. A number of the executed clergy have been beatified and canonized since the tragedy, most so during the pontificate of Pope John Paul II. The persecution prompted Pope Pius XI to issue the encyclicals *Iniquis afflictisque* (1926) and *Acerba animi* (1932).

An easing of the situation began in 1940 as the rigid anticlerical laws ceased to be enforced with enthusiasm. A rapprochement was visible in the 1958 elections, when the Church received conciliatory gestures from the ruling Revolutionary Party and its presidential candidate Adolfo López Mateos. The Church continued to exist under numerous legal disabilities and was oppressed in a number of the Mexican states.

Gradual improvement in relations between Mexico and the Holy See led to the exchange in 1990 of personal representatives between the Mexican president and Pope John Paul II. The Holy Father's efforts to build a further diplomatic bridge culminated in the establishment of full diplomatic ties in 1992. This was followed by the final easing of many of the handicaps under which the Church had long suffered.

The faith of the Mexican people is profoundly deep, as was seen in the nearly frenzied greeting given to Pope John Paul II in 1979, 1990, 1993, and 1999. However, social unrest, poverty, economic challenges, the violence of drug cartels, and corruption still plague the country. Church leaders — especially religious orders — have been outspoken in their criticism of government human rights abuses and corruption. During the mid-1990s, the Jesuits said they were the target of a "campaign of intimidation" because of their human rights work.

On May 24, 1993, Cardinal Juan Jesus Posadas Ocampo of Guadalajara was killed during a supposed shoot-out among rival drug cartels. The murder remained unsolved, although Cardinal Posadas' successor, Cardinal Juan Sandoval Íñiguez, continued to claim that high-ranking officials, including the Mexican attorney general at the time, lied to protect others involved in a plot. In 2001 Cardinal Sandoval said he would seek a reopening of the case because he had new evidence contradicting the findings of the official investigation; he also claimed he had been almost fatally poisoned in 1999 during a dinner with federal officials angry with his insistence that the murder was not accidental.

In the 1970s and 1980s, one of Mexico's most prominent proponents of liberation theology was Bishop Samuel Ruiz Garcia of San Cristobal de las Casas. In the early 1990s the Vatican began investigating his views, but because he had the trust of indigenous peasants, in 1994 he was thrown into the role of mediator between the government and the mostly native Zapatista National Liberation Army in Chiapas. He continued that role until 1998, when he resigned after accusing the government of "dismantling any possible means or effort to solve the crisis in Chiapas." Mexico's bishops said at that time that they would provide support to the peace process but would not seek to mediate the conflict.

On July 2, 2000, Vicente Fox Quesada, head of the National Action Party and a practicing Catholic, won the Mexican presidential election, marking the first time since 1929 that the country was not ruled by the Institutional Revolutionary Party. Mexico City Cardinal Norberto Rivera Carrera told reporters the election was "not a miracle, as some have suggested, but it is an extraordinary act." Church officials emphasized that they expected no special privileges from the new government, but the general climate was one of optimism for an improvement in church-state relations.

Within weeks, Fox – with news cameras flashing – received Communion in his hometown parish. However, in July 2001, the Vatican said he failed to have his first marriage annulled before marrying his spokeswoman in a civil ceremony; thus, he would be prohibited from receiving the sacraments. In June 2001, federal and state officials participated in a public Mass at the Basilica of Our Lady of Guadalupe, breaking a taboo on government officials publicly practicing their religion. On July 31, 2002, during his fifth pastoral visit to Mexico, Pope John Paul II canonized St. Juan Diego. In recent years, the country has suffered enormously from the violence of the drug cartels and the rampant corruption in the government. Pope Benedict XVI made an apostolic visit to Leon, Mexico, in March, 2012.

ORGANIZATION

Presently, the Church in Mexico is organized into 18 provinces. There are 18 archdioceses (including the promotion of Tijuana, León, Tuxtla Gutierrez, and Tulancingo as metropolitan sees), 67 dioceses, 5 prelacies, and 2 eparchs, for the Greek Melkites and Maronites. In 2009, the new diocese of Tenancingo (a suffragan of Mexico City) was established. As of Aug. 15, 2013, there were four Mexican members of the College of Cardinals: Norberto Rivera Carrera, Juan Sandoval Íñiguez, Javier Lozano Barragán, and Adolfo Antonio Suárez Rivera. (For statistical information on the Church in Mexico, see below.)The current apostolic delegation to Mexico was set up in 1992 as a nunciature with the establishment of renewed formal diplomatic relations with the Vatican. The present Apostolic Nuncio is Archbishop Christophe Pierre, J.C.D., who was appointed in 2007.

ECCLESIASTICAL JURISDICTIONS OF MEXICO

Provinces

Names of ecclesiastical provinces and metropolitan sees in bold face: suffragan sees in parentheses. The current listing reflects the restructuring of Mexico's provinces in 2009.

Acapulco (Chilpancingo-Chilapa, Ciudad Altamirano, Tlapa).

Antequera, Oaxaca (Puerto Escondido, Tehuantepec, Tuxtepec; Prelacies of Mixes and Huautla).

Chihuahua (Ciudad Juárez, Cuauhtémoc-Madera, Nuevos Casas Grandes, Parral, Tarahumara).

Durango (Mazatlán, Torreón, El Salto, Gómez Palacio).

Guadalajara (Aguascalientes, Autlán, Ciudad Guzmán, Colima, San Juan de los Lagos, Tepic; Prelature of Jesús Maria del Nayar).

Hermosillo (Ciudad Obregón, Culiacán).

León (Celaya, Irapuato, Querétaro

México (Atlacomulco, Cuernavaca, Tenancingo, Toluca).

Monterrey (Ciudad Victoria, Linares, Matamoros, Nuevo Laredo, Piedras Negras, Saltillo, Tampico).

Morelia (Apatzingán, Ciudad Lázaro Cárdenas, Tacámbaro, Zamora).

Puebla de los Angeles (Huajuapan de León, Tehuacán, Tlaxcala).

San Luis Potosi (Matehuala, Ciudad Valles, Zacatecas).

Tijuana (La Paz, Mexicali, Ensenada).

Tlalnepantla (Texcoco, Cuautitlán, Netzahualcóyotl, Ecatepec, Valle de Chalco, Teotihuacan).

Tulancingo (Huejutla and Tula)

Tuxtla Gutierrez (San Cristóbal de las Casas and Tapachula).

Xalapa (Papantla, San Andrés Tuxtla, Coatzacoalcos, Tuxpan, Veracruz, Orizaba, Córdoba).

Yucatán (Campeche, Tabasco, Prelacy of Cancún-

Chetumal; Eparchy of Nuestra Señora del Paraiso).

Jurisdictions, Hierarchy

(Principal sources: Information office, Mexican Conference of Catholic Bishops; Catholic Almanac survey; Annuario Pontificio; L'Osservatore Romano; Catholic News Service. *As of July 1, 2013. Addresses and phone numbers are provided by the* Annuario Pontificio.*)*

Information includes names of archdioceses (indicated by asterisk) and dioceses, date of foundation, present ordinaries and auxiliaries; addresses of chancery office/bishop's residence.

Acapulco* (1958; promoted to archdiocese, 1983): Carlos Garfias Merlos, archbishop, 2010; Juan Navarro Castellanos, auxiliary.

Diocesan Address: Apartado Postal 201, Quebrada 16, 39850 Acapulco, Guerrero; (748) 2-07-63.

Aguascalientes (1899): José María De la Torre Martín, bishop, 2008.

Diocesan Address: Apartado 167, Galeana 105 Norte, 20000 Aquascalientes, Aguascalientes; (449) 9-15-32-61.

Apatzingán (1962): Miguel Patiño Velázquez, M.S.F., bishop, 1981.

Diocesan Address: Calle Esteban Vaca Calderón 100, 60600 Apatzingán, Mich.; (453) 5-34-17-87.

Atlacomulco (1984): Odilón Martínez García, bishop, 2010.

Diocesan Address: Hidalgo Sur 1, Apartado 22, 50450 Atlacomulco, Méx.; (712) 1-22-05-53.

Autlán (1961): Gonzalo Galván Castillo, bishop, 2004.

Diocesan Address: Apartado 8, Hidalgo 74, 48900 Autlán, Jal., Mex.; (317) 3-82-12-28.

Campeche (1895): Ramón Castro Castro, bishop, 2006.

Diocesan Address: Calle 53 # 1-B Entre 8 y 10 Centro Apdo. Postal # 12724000 - Campeche, Camp.; (981) 8-16-25-24.

Cancún-Chetumal, Prelacy of (1970, as Chetumal; name changed in 1996): Pedro Pablo Elizondo Cárdenas, L.C., bishop, 2004.

Diocesan Address: Apartado Postal 165, Othón P. Blanco 150, 77000 Chetumal, Quintana Roo; (983) 2-06-38.

Celaya (1973): Benjamin Castillo Plascencia, bishop, 2010.

Diocesan Address: Curia Diocesana, Apartado 207, Manuel Doblado 110, 38000 Celaya, Gto.; (461) 6-12-48-35.

Chihuahua* (1891; promoted to archdiocese, 1958): Constancio Miranda Weckmann, archbishop, 2010.

Diocesan Address: Av. Cuauhtémoc # 1828 Col. Cuauhtémoc, Apartado Postal 7, 31000 Chihuahua, Chihuahua; (614) 4-10-32-02.

Chilpancingo-Chilapa (1863 as Chilpancingo; name changed to Chilpancingo-Chilapa, 1989): Alejo Zavala Castro, bishop, 2008.

Diocesan Address: Abasolo e Hidalgo, Apartado Postal #185, 39000 Chilpancingo, Gro.; (747) 4-71-05-92.

Ciudad Altamirano (1964): Maximino Martínez Miranda, bishop, 2006.

Diocesan Address: Juárez 18 Oriente, Centro, Apdo 17, 40680 Ciudad Altamirano, Gro.; (767) 6-72-17-74.

Ciudad Guzmán (1972): Braulio Rafael León Villegas, bishop, 1999.
Diocesan Address: Ramón Corona 26, Apartado 86, 49000 Ciudad Guzman, Jal.; (341) 4-12-19-94.
Ciudad Juárez (1957): Renato Ascencio León, bishop, 1994; José Guadalupe Torres Campos, auxiliary.
Diocesan Address: Apartado Postal 188, 32000 Cuidad Juárez, Chih.; (16) 15-09-22.
Ciudad Lázaro Cárdenas (1985): Fabio Martínez Castilla, bishop, 2007.
Diocesan Address: Apartado 500, Andador Ciudad del Carmen #4, Fideicomiso 2° Sector, 60950 Lázaro Cardenas, Mich.; (753) 5-41-64-07.
Ciudad Obregón (1959): Felipe Padilla Cardona, bishop, 2010.
Diocesan Address: Apartado 402, Sonora 161 Norte, 85000 Ciudad Obregón, Son.; (644) 4-13-20-98.
Ciudad Valles (1960): Roberto Octavio Balmori Cinta, M.J., bishop, 2002.
Diocesan Address: 16 de Septiembre 726, Apartado 170, 79000 Ciudad Valles, S.L.P.; (138) 2-25-97
Ciudad Victoria (1964): Antonio González Sánchez, bishop, 1995.
Diocesan Address: 15 Hidalgo y Juárez, Centro, Apartado Postal #335, 87000 Ciudad Victoria, Tamps.; (834) 3-12-87-16.
Coatzacoalcos (1984): Rutilo Muñoz Zamora, bishop, 2002.
Diocesan Address: Apartado 513 y 513, Aldama 502, 96400 Coatzacoalcos, Ver.; (921) 2-12-23-99.
Colima (1881): José Luis Amezcua Melgoza, bishop, 2005.
Diocesan Address: Hidalgo 135, Apartado 1, 28000 Colima, Colima; (312) 3-12-02-62.
Cordoba (2000): Eduardo Porfirio Patiño Leal, bishop, 2000.
Diocesan Address: Avenida 11-1300, Esquina con Calle 13, Apartado 154, Zona Centro, 94500 Cordoba, Ver., Mexico; (271) 7-14-91-56.
Cuauhtémoc-Madera (1966): Juan Guillermo López Soto, bishop, 1995.
Diocesan Address: Reforma y 4ª # 479, Apartado Postal 209, 31500 Cuauhtemoc, Chih.; (625) 5-81-57-22.
Cuautitlán (1979): Rodrigo Guillermo Ortiz Mondragón, bishop, 2005.
Diocesan Address: Apartado 14-21, Sor Juana Inés de la Cruz 208, Anexo a Catedral, 54800 Cuautitlán de Romero Rubio; (55) 58-72-19-96.
Cuernavaca (1891): Ramon Castro Castro, bishop, 2013.
Diocesan Address: Apartado 13, Hidalgo #17, 62000 Cuernavaca, Mor.; (777) 3-18-45-90.
Culiacán (1883 as Sinaloa; name changed 1959): Jonás Guerrero Corona, bishop, 2011; Emigdio Duarte Figueroa, auxiliary.
Diocesan Address: Apartado Postal 666, Av. Las Palmas #26 Oriente, 80220 Culiacán, Sinaloa; (667) 7-12-32-72.
Durango* (1620, promoted to archdiocese, 1891): Hector González Martínez, archbishop, 2003; Enrique Sanchez Martinez, aux.
Diocesan Address: Apartado Postal 116, 34000 Durango, Durango; (618) 8-11-42-42
Ecatepec (1995): Óscar Roberto Dominguez Couttolenc, M.G., bishop, 2012.
Diocesan Address: Plaza Principal s/n, San

Cristóbal Centro, Apartado Postal 95, 55000 Ecatepec de Morelos; (5) 116-09-76.
El Salto, Prelacy of (1968): Juan Maria Huerta Muro, O.F.M., bishop, 2012.
Prelature Address: Mons. Francisco Medina s/n, Apartado Postal 58, 34950 El Salto, Durango; (675) 8-76-00-70.
Ensenada (2007): Rafael Valdez Torres, bishop, 2013.
Diocesan Address: Av. Guadalupe 565, Col. Obrera, 22830 Ensenada, B.C.; (646) 176-37-40.
Gómez Palacio (Nov. 25, 2008): José Guadalupe Torres Campos, bishop, 2008.
Diocesan Address: N/A
Guadalajara* (1548; promoted to archdiocese, 1863): Cardinal Francisco Robles Ortega, archbishop, 2011; José Trinidad González Rodriguez, Miguel Romano Gómez, José Leopoldo González González, José Francisco González González, auxiliaries.
Diocesan Address: Arzobispado, Apartado Postal 1-331, Calle Liceo 17, 44100 Guadalajara, Jal.; (33) 36-14-55-04; www.arquidiocesisgdl.org.mx.
Hermosillo* (1779, as Sonora, promoted to an archdiocese, 1963): José Ulises Macias Salcedo, archbishop, 1996.
Diocesan Address: Apartado 1, Dr. Paliza 81, 83260 Hermosillo, Son.; (662) 2-13-21-38.
Huajuapan de Leon (1903): Teodoro Enrique Pino Miranda, 2000.
Diocesan Address: Apartado 43, Anexos de Catedral, 69000 Huajuapan de León, Oax.; (953) 5-32-07-97.
Huautla, Prelacy of (1972): Jose Armando Alvarez Cano, prelate, 2011.
Diocesan Address: Casa Prelaticia Calle 5 de Feb. # 15, Apartado 2, 68500 Huautla de Jiménez, Oaxaca; (236) 3-78-00-19.
Huejutla (1922): Salvador Rangel Mendoza O.F.M., bishop, 1994.
Diocesan Address: Obispado, Apartado 8, Ave. Corona del Rosal s/n, Col. Tecoluco, 43000 Huejutla, Hgo.; (789) 8-96-01-85.
Irapuato (2004): José de Jesús Martínez Zepeda, first bishop, 2004.
Diocesan Address: Juarez 138-407, Apatado 13, 36500 Irapuato, Gto.; 462-625-61-04.
Jesús María de Nayar, Prelature of (1962): José de Jesús González Hernández, O.F.M., bishop, 2010.
Diocesan Address: Curia Prelaticia de Jesús María, Belén #24, Apartado 33-B, 63150 Tepic, Nayar; (311) 2-13-88-80.
La Paz en la Baja California Sur (1988): Miguel Angel Alba Díaz, 2001.
Diocesan Address: Apartado 25, Revolución y 5 de Mayo, 23000 La Paz, B.C.S.; (112) 2-25-96.
León* (1863, promoted to archdiocese, 2006): Alfonso Cortes Contreras, archbishop, 2012; Juan Frausto Pallares, auxiliary.
Diocesan Address: Pedro Moreno #312, Apartado 108, 37000 León, Gto.; (477) 7-13-27-47; www.diocesisleon.org.mx.
Linares (1962): Ramón Calderón Batres, bishop, 1988.
Diocesan Address: Morelos y Zaragoza s/n, Apartado 70, 67700 Linares, N.L.; (821) 2-00-54.
Matamoros (1958): Ruy Rendon Leal, bishop, 2011.
Diocesan Address: Apartado 70, Calle 5 y

Morelos, 87351 Matamoros, Tamps.; (88) 13-55-11; www.communion.org.mx.

Matehuala (1997): Rodrigo Aguilar Martínez, bishop, 1997.

Diocesan Address: Rayón #200 Centro, Apartado 40, 78700 Matehuala, S.L.P.; (01) 488-2-51-42.

Mazatlán (1958): Mario Espinosa Contreras, bishop, 2005.

Diocesan Address: Apartado Postal 1, Canizales y Benito Juárez s/n, 82000 Mazatlán, Sin.; (69) 81-33-52.

Mexicali (1966): José Isidro Guerrero Macías, bishop, 1997.

Diocesan Address: Av. Morelos #192, Col. Primera sécción, Apartado 3-547, 21100 Mexicali, B.C. Norte; (686) 5-52-40-09.

México* (1530, promoted to an archdiocese, 1546): Cardinal Norberto Rivera Carrera, archbishop, 1995; José de Jesús Martinez Zepeda, Marcelino Hernández Rodríguez, Luis Fletes Santana, Rogelio Esquivel Medina, Antonio Ortega Franco, C.O., Carlos Briseño Arch, O.A.R., Florencio Armando Colín Cruz, Jesús Antonio Lerma Nolasco, Andrés Vargas Peña, Adolfo Miguel Castaño Fonseca, Crispin Ojeda Marquez, Jorge Estrada Solorzano, auxiliaries.

Diocesan Address: Curia Arzobispal, Apartado Postal 24-433, Durango 90, Col. Roma, 06700 - México, D. F.; (55) 55-25-11-10; www.arzobispadomexico.org.mx.

Mixes, Prelacy of (1964): Don Héctor Guerrero Córdova, S.D.B., bishop, 2007

Diocesan Address: Casa del Señor Obispo, 70283, Ayutla, Mixes, Oax.; (951) 5-58-20-98.

Monterrey* (1777, as Linares o Nuevo León, promoted to an archdiocese, 1891; name changed 1922): Rogelio Cabrera Lopez, archbishop, 2012; Gustavo Rodríguez Vega, Jorge Alberto Cavazos Arizpe, auxiliaries.

Diocesan Address: Apartado 7, Zuazua 1110 Sur con Ocampo, 64000 Monterrey, N.L.; (81) 83-45-24-66; www.pixel.com.mx/info-gral/info-nl/religion/catolica/arqui.html.

Morelia* (1536, as Michoacan, promoted to an archdiocese 1863, name changed in 1924): Alberto Suárez Inda, archbishop, 1995; Enrique Díaz Díaz, Octavio Villegas Aguilar, Juan Esponosa Jimenez, auxiliaries.

Diocesan Address: Apartado 17, 58000 Morelia, Mich.; (443) 3-12-05-23.

Netzahualcóyotl (1979): Héctor Luis Morales Sánchez, bishop, 2011.

Diocesan Address: Apartado 89, 4 Avenida esq. Bellas Artes, Col. Evolución, 57700 Cuidad Netzahualcóyotl; (55) 57-97-61-32.

Nuestra Señora de los Mártires del Libano, Eparchy of (Maronites, 1995): Georges M. Saad Abi Younes, O.L.M., eparch, 2003.

Diocesan address: Ntra. Sra. de Balvarena Correo Mayor #65, 06060 — México, D. F.; (55) 55-21-20-11.

Nuestra Señora del Paraiso, Eparchy of (Greek Melkites, 1988): Vacant.

Diocesan Address: Matías Romero 1014, Dpto. 601, Col. Del Valle, 3100 Mexico, D.F.; (5) 542-0225.

Nuevo Casas Grandes (1977): Gerardo de Jesús Rojas López, bishop, 2004.

Diocesan Address: Apartado Postal 198, Av. Hidalgo #105, 31700 Nuevo Casas Grandes, Chih.; (636) 6-94-05-20.

Nuevo Laredo (1989): Jesus Herrera Quinonez, bishop, 2011.

Diocesan Address: Saltillo 206, Apartado Postal #20-B, Col. México, 88280 Nuevo Laredo, Tamps.; (867) 7-15-29-28.

Oaxaca* (Also Antequera, 1535, promoted to archdiocese, 1891): José Luis Chávez Botello, archbishop, 2003; Miguel Ángel Alba Díaz, Gonzalo Calzada Guerrero, auxiliaries.

Diocesan Address: Apartado Postal #31, Garcia Vigil #600, 68000 Oaxaca, Oax.; (951) 6-20-49.

Orizaba (2000): Marcelino Hernández Rodríguez, bishop, 2008. Diocesan Address: Templo de Ntra. Sra. del Carmen, Sur 9 # 142 esq. Oriente 4, Apdo. Postal # 151, 94300 - Orizaba, Ver.; (272) 7-24-17-33.

Papantla (1922): Jorge Carlos Patron Wong, bishop, 2012.

Diocesan Address: Apartado 27, Juárez 1102, 73800 Teziutlán, Pue.; (231) 3-24-30.

Parral (1992): Eduardo Carmona Ortega, O.R.C., bishop, 2012.

Diocesan Address: Apartado Postal 313, Fray Bartolomé de las Casas #13, 33800 Parral, Chih.; (152) 2-03-71.

Piedras Negras (2003): Alonso Gerardo Garza Treviño, first bishop, 2003. Diocesan address: Hidalgo Sur # 404 Centro 26000 - Piedras Negras, Coah.; (878) 7-82-94-80.

Puebla de los Angeles* (1525, as Tlaxcala, renamed in 1903): Victor Sánchez Espinosa, archbishop, 2009. Eugenio Lira Rugarcia, Dagoberto Sosa Arriaga, auxiliaries.

Diocesan Address: Apartado 235, Av. 2, Sur N. 305, 72000 Puebla, Pue.; (222) 2-32-62-12.

Puerto Escondido (2003): Pedro Vazquez Villalobos, first bishop, 2012.

Diocesan Address: Felipe Merklin s/n, Col. Centro Puerto Escondido, Oax; 954-582-36-77.

Querétaro (1863): Faustino Armendariz Jimenez, bishop, 2011.

Diocesan Address: Apartado Postal 49, Reforma #48, 76000 Querétaro, Qro.; (42) 12-10-33.

Saltillo (1891): Raul Vera López, O.P., bishop, 1999.

Diocesan Address: Hidalgo Sur 166, Apartado 25, 25000 Saltillo, Coah.; (844) 4-12-37-84.

San Andrés Tuxtla (1959): José Trinidad Zapata Ortiz, bishop, 2004.

Diocesan Address: Constitución y Morelos, 95700 San Andrés Tuxtla, Ver.; (294) 9-42-03-74.

San Cristóbal de las Casas (1539, as Chiapas, renamed in 1964): Felipe Arizmendi Esquivel, bishop, 2000.

Diocesan Address: 5 de Feb. y 20 de Nov. # 1 Centro 29200 — San Cristóbal las Casas, Chis; (967) 6-78-00-53; www.laneta.apc.org/curiasc.

San Juan de los Lagos (1972): Felipe Salazar Villagrana, bishop, 2008.

Diocesan Address: Morelos 30, Apartado #1, 47000 San Juan de los Lagos, Jal.; (395) 7-85-05-70; www.redial.com.mx/obispado/index.htm.

San Luis Potosí* (1854, promoted to an archdiocese, 1988): Jesus Cabrero Romero, archbishop, 2012.

Diocesan Address: Madero #300, Apartado N. 1, 78000 - San Luis Potosí, S.L.P.; (444) 8-12-45-55.

Tabasco (1880): Gerardo de Jesús Rojas López, bishop, 2010.
Diocesan Address: Apartado Postal 97, Fidencia 502, 86000 Villahermosa, Tab.; (93) 12-13-97.

Tacámbaro (1913): Luis Castro Medellín, M.S.F., bishop, 2002.
Diocesan Address: Apartado 4, Professor Enrique Aguilar 49, 61650 Tacámbaro, Mich.; (459) 6-00-44.

Tampico (1870, as Ciudad Victoria o Tamaulipas, renamed in 1958): José Luis Dibildox Martinez, bishop, 2003.
Diocesan Address: Apartado 545, Altamira 116 Oriente, 89000 Tampico, Tamps.; (12) 12-28-02.

Tapachula (1957): Leopoldo González González, bishop, 2005.
Diocesan Address: Apartado 70, Av. Primera Sur 1, 30700 Tapachula, Chiapas; (962) 6-15-03; www.diocesistapachula.org.mx.

Tarahumara (1958, as a vicariate apostolic, promoted to diocese, 1993): Rafael Sandoval Sandoval, M.N.M., bishop, 2005.
Diocesan Address: Apartado Postal 11, Av. López Mateos #7, 33190 Guachochi, Chih.; (649) 5-43-02-23.

Tehuacán (1962): Rodrigo Aguilar Martínez, bishop, 2006.
Diocesan Address: Apartado Postal 137, Agustin A. Cacho 107, 75700 Tehuacán, Pue.; (238) 3-83-14-68.

Tehuantepec (1891): Oscar Armando Campos Contreras, bishop, 2010.
Diocesan Address: Apartado Postal 93, Mina s/n. Anexos de Catedral, 70760 Tehuantepec, Oax.; (971) 7-15-00-60.

Tenancingo (2009): Raul Gomez Gonzalez, first bishop, 2009.
Diocesan Address: N/A.

Teotihuacan (2008): Francisco Escobar Galicia, bishop, 2008.
Diocesan Address: N/A.

Tepic (1891): Luis Flores Calzada, bishop, 2012.
Diocesan Address: Apartado 15, Av. de las Flores 10, Fracciónamiento Residencial La Loma, 63137 Tepic, Nay.; (311) 2-14-46-45.

Texcoco (1960): Juan Manuel Mancilla Sanchez, bishop, 2009; Víctor René Rodríguez Gómez, auxiliary.
Diocesan Address: Apartado Postal 35, Fray Pedro de Gante 2, 56100 Texcoco, Méx.; (595) 4-08-69.

Tijuana* (1963, promoted to archdiocese, 2006): Rafael Romo Muñoz, bishop, 1996-2006, first archbishop, 2006.
Diocesan Address: Apartado 226, Calle 10ª y Av. Ocampo # 1049, 22000 Tijuana, B.C.N.; (664) 6-84-84-11 y 12; www.iglesiatijuana.org.

Tlalnepantla* (1964, promoted to archdiocese, 1989): Carlos Aguiar Retes, archbishop, 2009; Francisco Ramírez Navarro, Efrain Mendoza Cruz, auxiliary.
Diocesan Address: Apartado 268 y 270, Av. Juárez 42, 54000 Tlalnepantla, Méx.; (55) 55-65-39-44.

Tlapa (1992): Dagoberto Sosa Arriaga, bishop, 2013.
Diocesan Address: Anexo Catedral, Centro, 41300 Tlapa de Comonfort, Gro.; (757) 4-76-08-35.

Tlaxcala (1959): Francisco Moreno Barrón, bishop, 2001.
Diocesan Address: Apartado 84, Lardizábal 45, 90000 Tlaxcala, Tlax.; (246) 4-62-32-43.

Toluca (1950): Francisco Javier Chavolla Ramos, bishop, 2003.
Diocesan Address: Apartado 82, Portal Reforma Norte 104, 50000 Toluca, Méx.; (72) 15-25-35; www.diocesistoluca.org.mx.

Torreón (1957): Vacant.
Diocesan Address: Apartado Postal 430, Av. Morelos 46 Poniente, 27000 Torreón, Coah.; (871) 7-12-30-43.

Tula (1961): Juan Pedro Juárez Meléndez, bishop, 2006.
Diocesan Address: 5 de Mayo, #5, Apartado 31, 42800 Tula de Allende, Hgo.; (773) 7-32-02-75.

Tulancingo* (1863, promoted to archdiocese, 2006): Domingo Díaz Martínez, archbishop, 2008.
Diocesan Address: Apartado #14, Plaza de la Constitución, 43600 Tulancingo, Hgo.; (775) 3-10-10.

Tuxpan (1962): Juan Navarro Castellanos, bishop, 2009.
Diocesan Address: Independencia #56, 92870 Tuxpan, Ver.; (783) 4-16-36.

Tuxtepec (1979): José Antonio Fernández Hurtado, bishop, 2005.
Diocesan Address: Bonfil #597, entre Juárez y Villa Col. Santa Fe Apartado Postal 9, 68320 — Tuxtepec, Oax.; (287) 5-00-42.

Tuxtla Gutiérrez* (1964, promoted to archdiocese, 2006): Fabio Martinez Castilla, archbishop, 2013. José Mendoza Corzo, auxiliary.
Diocesan Address: Uruguay #500 A Col. El Retiro Apdo. Postal # 36529040 - Tuxtla Gutiérrez, Chis.; (961) 6-04-06-44; www.chisnet.com.mx/~cosi/obispado.

Valle de Chalco (2003): Victor Rene Rodriguez Gomez, first bishop, 2012.
Diocesan Address: Calle Colorines 12, Col. Granjas, 56600 Chalco, Mex.

Veracruz (1962): Luis Felipe Gallardo Martín del Campo, S.D.B., bishop, 2006.
Diocesan Address: Insurgentes Veracruzanos #470, Paseo del Malecón, 91700 Veracruz, Ver.; (229) 9-31-24-13.

Xalapa* (1962; originally Veracruz and Xalapa, 1863; promoted to archdiocese, 1951): Hipolito Reyes Larios, archbishop, 2007.
Diocesan Address: Apartado 359, Av. Manuel Avila Camacho #73, 91000 Xalapa, Ver.; (228) 8-12-05-79.

Yucatán* (1561, promoted to archdiocese, 1906): Emilio Carlos Berlie Belaunzarán, archbishop, 1995; José Rafael Palma Capetillo, auxiliary.
Diocesan Address: Calle 58 N. 501, 97000 Mérida, Yuc.; (99) 23-79-83; www.geocities.com/SoHo/207/principa.html.

Zacatecas (1863): Sigifredo Moriega Barcelo, bishop, 2012.
Diocesan Address: Apartado #1, Miguel Auza #219, 98000 Zacatecas, Zacatecas; (492) 9-22-02-32; www.logicnet.com.mx/obispado.

Zamora (1863): Javier Navarro Rodríguez, bishop, 2007; Jaime Calderon Calderon, auxiliary.
Diocesan Address: Altos de Catedral (Calle Hidalgo), Apartado Postal #18, 59600 Zamora, Mich.; (351) 5-12-12-08.

CONFERENCIA DEL EPISCOPADO MEXICANO

(Sources: *Annuario Pontificio;* Pbro. Jorge Fco. Vázquez M., Secretario Adjunto, Conferencia del Episcopado Mexicano; *Conferencia del Episcopado Mexicano, Directorio, 2012*; translation courtesy Suzanne Lea.)

STRUCTURE

The Mexican Conference of Bishops (CEM, *Conferencia del Episcopado Mexicano*) is the permanent body of Mexican bishops. The bishops adhere to the guidelines of the conference in specific fulfillment of their pastoral labors. They do this in order to obtain the greatest good for the people that the church can achieve. The conference proposes: 1) To study the problems that occur in pastoral work, and to seek solutions. 2) To initiate, with a common end in mind and a common course of action, the forms and methods of preaching that best suit the needs of the country. 3) In regard to the collective salvific mission of the church: To look for and to teach the best way in which the respective activities of the deacons, priests, religious, and lay person will be most efficient. 4) To facilitate relations with the civil authority and with other organizations in specific cases. 5) To write to the Episcopal commission regarding patrimonial and proprietary matters, and give counsel on determined financial or labor related points.

All those elected to the body of the CEM will have three years of service and will not be reelected to the same position after two three-year sessions have been completed consecutively.

The address of the conference headquarters is: Prolongación Misterios No. 26, Col. Tepeyac Insurgentes, 07020 México, D.F. Tels. (01-55) 5577-5401; www.cem.org.mx.

Permanent Assembly

The Permanent Assembly is the representative arm of the bishops belonging to the CEM. Its function is to ensure the continuation of the works of the conference and the fulfillment of its accords.

The Permanent Assembly is comprised of the Presidential Assembly and the Assembly of Pastoral Regions. It meets four times per year in ordinary session. It meets in extraordinary sessions whenever the majority of its members or those of the Presidential Assembly determine it to be necessary. A session is valid if two-thirds of the members are present.

Officers
President: Archbp. Carlos Aguiar Retes of Tlalnepantla
Vice-President: Archbp. Rogelio Cabrera López of Tuxtla.
Secretary General: Bp. Víctor René Rodríguez Gómez, aux. bishop of Texcoco.
General Treasurer: Bp. Oscar Roberto Domínguez Couttolenc of Tlapa.
Spokesmen: Archbishop José Luis Chávez Botello of Antequera Oaxaca; Bishop Faustino Armendáriz Jiménez of Matamoros.

Commissions
Biblical Studies: Bishop Florencio Colin Cruz.
Doctrine: Bishop José Guadalupe Martin Rabago.
Culture: Bishop Felipe Arizmendi Esquivel.
Education: Bishop Alfonso Cortes Contreras.
Health Care: Bishop Emigdio Duarte Figueroa.
Liturgy: Bishop Victor Sanchez Espinosa.
Missions: Bishop Rafael Sandoval Sandoval.
Pastoral Sanctuaries: Bishop Felipe Salazar Villagrana.
Catechesis: Bishop José Antonio Fernandez Hurtado.
Social Justice: Bishop Ramon Castro.
Clergy: Bishop Marcelino Hernández.
Social Communications: Bishop Luis Artemio Calzada Flores.
Interreligious Dialogue: Card. Francisco Robles Ortega.
Consecrated Life: Bishop Roberto Balmori Cinta, M.J.
Diaconate: Bishop José Trinidad Zapata Ortiz.
Lay Apostolates: Bishop Eduardo Carmona Ortega.
Priestly Formation: Bishop José Francisco Gonzalez.
Seminaries and Vocations: Bishop José Luis Amezcua.

STATISTICAL SUMMARY OF THE CATHOLIC CHURCH IN MEXICO

(Principal sources: *Annuario Pontificio, 2013; Annuarium Statisticum Ecclesiae, 2011* (the most recent edition); Conferencia del Espicopado Mexicano, Directorio, 2012 figures as of January 2012. Catholic population statistics are those reported in the most recent *Annuario* population estimates. Archdioceses are indicated by an asterisk.)

Includes 18 provinces: 18 archdioceses, 68 dioceses, 5 prelacies, and two eparchies. There are 159 total prelates: 4 Cardinals, 16 Archbishops, 67 Bishops, 31 Auxiliary Bishops, 39 Retired Bishops, and 2 Eparchs. The Catholic population of Mexico comprises approximately 92% of the overall Mexican population of 109,308,000 according to the *Conferencia del Episcopado Mexicano, Directorio, 2013* (the most recent edition). In 2012, there were 2,016,167 baptisms and 376,921 marriages. This table presents a provincial breakdown of Catholic statistics. The population totals are approximate.

Province Diocese	Cath. Pop.	Dioc. Priests	Rel. Priests	Total Priests	Perm. Deacs.	Bro- thers	Sis- ters	Par- ishes
Acapulco	**5,324,000**	**336**	**58**	**394**	**24**	**94**	**507**	**220**
Acapulco*	3,074,000	106	20	126	21	37	187	84
Chilpancingo-Chilapa	882,000	125	16	141	1	16	188	75
Ciudad Altamirano	935,000	68	5	73	–	20	76	34
Tlapa	477,000	37	17	54	2	21	56	27
Baja California	**4,260,000**	**385**	**122**	**507**	**12**	**210**	**889**	**216**
Tijuana*	2,205,000	156	64	220	10	105	510	99
Ensenada	443,000	32	16	48	–	18	87	28

Province Diocese	Cath. Pop.	Dioc. Priests	Rel. Priests	Total Priests	Perm. Deacs.	Bro- thers	Sis- sters	Par- ishes
Baja California, con't.								
La Paz	523,000	56	24	80	1	25	151	36
Mexicali	1,122,000	141	18	159	1	62	141	53
Bajío	**7,034,637**	**733**	**333**	**1,066**	**15**	**419**	**2,414**	**368**
León*	2,564,000	233	120	353	12	128	754	121
Celaya	1,502,000	163	69	232	–	78	503	68
Irapuato	1,179,000	123	37	160	3	43	237	67
Querétaro	1,848,000	214	107	321	–	170	920	112
Chiapas	**3,804,000**	**255**	**70**	**325**	**320**	**79**	**605**	**166**
Tuxtla Gutiérrez*	1,005,000	110	19	129	–	19	267	67
San Cristobal	1,368,000	56	43	99	320	52	201	54
Tapachula	1,462,000	89	8	97	–	8	137	45
Chihuahua	**4,598,426**	**320**	**104**	**424**	**35**	**137**	**625**	**224**
Chihuahua*	1,250,000	111	39	150	9	48	161	66
Ciudad Juárez	2,297,000	93	21	114	13	29	179	73
Cuauhtémoc-Madera	349,789	32	9	41	–	9	58	26
Nuevo Casas Grandes	135,000	35	2	37	1	2	44	24
Parral	295,000	38	13	51	10	22	69	20
Tarahumara	301,000	11	20	31	2	27	114	15
Durango	**3,400,987**	**407**	**69**	**478**	**2**	**99**	**515**	**258**
Durango*	1,160,000	157	22	179	–	37	214	91
El Salto	334,000	27	–	27	2	2	16	15
Mazatlán	767,000	78	8	86	–	11	111	47
Torreón	702,034	94	38	132	–	39	91	66
Gómez Palacio	464,000	51	1	52	–	10	83	39
Guadalajara	**11,892,692**	**2,232**	**450**	**2,682**	**10**	**895**	**2,698**	**897**
Guadalajara*	5,265,000	1,127	354	1,481	4	633	831	450
Aguascalientes	1,709,230	267	39	306	1	57	669	108
Autlán	334,000	116	–	116	3	–	192	46
Ciudad Guzmán	455,000	92	18	110	–	54	112	59
Colima	621,000	116	5	121	–	9	221	53
San Juan los Lagos	1,095,000	298	16	314	–	107	413	77
Tepic	1,151,000	206	4	210	–	8	213	88
Jesús María of Nayar	138,000	10	14	24	2	27	47	16
Hermosillo	**4,420,765**	**420**	**23**	**443**	**5**	**49**	**479**	**214**
Hermosillo*	1,075,260	127	3	130	1	7	150	75
Ciudad Obregón	938,000	111	16	127	–	31	139	65
Culiacán	2,443,000	182	4	186	4	11	190	74
Hidalgo	**3,120,360**	**331**	**25**	**356**	**2**	**38**	**326**	**178**
Tulancingo	*1,562,000	155	6	161	1	19	179	88
Huejutla	542,000	96	6	102	–	6	53	41
Tula	1,041,000	80	13	93	1	13	94	49
Mexico	**13,355,688**	**1,279**	**1,157**	**2,436**	**148**	**2,263**	**6,134**	**783**
Mexico*	8,038,000	759	1,030	1,789	146	2,041	5,170	453
Atlacomulco	941,000	111	3	114	1	4	103	66
Cuernavaca	1,919,000	128	74	202	1	149	437	109
Tenancingo	364,503	42	15	57	–	20	99	30
Toluca	2,212,346	239	35	274	–	49	325	125
Monterrey	**12,253,000**	**922**	**330**	**1,252**	**53**	**670**	**1,587**	**498**
Monterrey*	5,910,000	389	206	595	44	495	733	188
Ciudad Victoria	408,000	50	13	63	–	19	89	34
Linares	357,000	37	3	40	–	3	55	22
Matamoros	1,810,000	109	8	117	1	11	114	55
Nuevo Laredo	877,000	55	19	74	8	26	94	41
Piedras Negras	496,000	49	11	60	–	13	89	32

Province Diocese	Cath. Pop.	Dioc. Priests	Rel. Priests	Total Priests	Perm. Deacs.	Bro-thers	Sis-ters	Par-ishes
Monterrey, cont.								
Saltillo	1,193,000	127	54	292	1	84	292	61
Tampico	1,168,000	106	16	122	–	19	121	65
Morelia	**5,695,878**	**922**	**179**	**1,101**	**–**	**408**	**2,244**	**478**
Morelia*	2,415,868	431	131	562	–	308	1,144	236
Apatzingán	370,000	62	–	62	–	–	127	27
Ciudad Lázaro Cárdenas	787,000	32	11	43	–	14	68	24
Tacámbaro	352,000	86	2	88	–	2	137	41
Zamora	1,489,000	311	35	346	–	84	768	140
Oaxaca	**3,986,200**	**319**	**89**	**408**	**51**	**109**	**447**	**253**
Oaxaca*	1,246,000	148	33	181	23	37	229	122
Huautla1	133,600	21	6	27	1	9	7	9
Mixes1	140,800	14	28	42	16	35	31	18
Puerto Escondido	454,000	38	8	46	–	8	56	29
Tehuantepec	1,377,000	54	7	61	–	11	89	47
Tuxtepec	724,000	44	7	51	11	9	35	28
Puebla de los Angeles	**7,199,000**	**734**	**189**	**924**	**4**	**247**	**1,178**	**480**
Puebla de los Angeles*	4,447,000	388	160	548	2	208	720	277
Huajuapan de León	761,000	111	–	111	1	–	157	72
Tehuacán	1,003,450	90	8	98	–	8	131	57
Tlaxcala	1,073,000	145	21	166	1	31	170	74
San Luis Potosi	**4,219,000**	**513**	**90**	**603**	**11**	**233**	**1,521**	**286**
San Luis Potosi*	1,875,000	216	62	278	11	201	807	113
Ciudad Valles	1,010,000	59	17	76	–	17	155	47
Matehuala	248,000	32	3	35	–	3	36	17
Zacatecas	1,140,000	206	8	214	–	12	523	109
Tlalnepantla	**17,801,244**	**934**	**185**	**1,109**	**51**	**356**	**857**	**595**
Tlalnepantla*	1,926,753	271	76	347	10	46	138	200
Cuautitlan	3,976,000	163	37	200	–	58	260	67
Ecatepec	1,474,962	153	7	160	23	25	72	95
Netzahualcóyotl	3,598,235	105	29	134	–	65	42	83
Teotihuacan	792,000	61	–	61	11	–	95	22
Texcoco	1,467,000	114	13	127	7	139	159	70
Valle de Chalco	2,340,000	67	23	80	–	23	91	58
Xalapa	**9,230,365**	**755**	**51**	**806**	**47**	**90**	**1,068**	**449**
Xalapa*	1,195,000	146	5	151	–	16	284	83
Coatzacoalcos	887,000	60	1	61	1	3	76	25
Cordoba	690,000	84	1	85	–	8	182	44
Orizaba	584,000	76	13	89	–	18	123	43
Papantla	1,729,000	89	–	89	1	–	128	55
San Andrés Tuxtla	1,026,000	94	3	97	33	10	94	59
Tuxpan	1,270,000	97	–	97	1	1	20	61
Veracruz	1,924,000	109	28	137	11	34	161	79
Yucatán	**5,527,000**	**424**	**164**	**588**	**71**	**240**	**863**	**294**
Yucatán*	1,771,000	174	38	212	35	62	413	108
Campeche	647,000	86	22	108	3	62	155	57
Tabasco	1,506,000	138	13	151	15	19	162	79
Cancún-Chetumal1	1,019,000	18	84	102	17	90	130	47
Nuestra Sra. de los Mártires2	153,000	6	4	10	1	4	–	3
Nuestra Sra. del Paraiso2	4,700	2	3	5	–	3	3	–
Totals:	**100,446,0003**	**12,221**	**3,688**	**15,909**	**853**	**6,636**	**24,957**	**6,857**

Note: 1. Prelacy. 2. Eparchy. 3. According to the Conferencia del Episcopado Mexicano and the *Annuarium Statisticum Ecclesiae.*

Consecrated Life

INSTITUTES OF CONSECRATED LIFE

Religious institutes and congregations are special societies in the Church — institutes of consecrated life — whose members, called Religious, commit them selves by public vows to observance of the evangelical counsels of poverty, chastity and obedience in a community kind of life in accordance with rules and constitutions approved by Church authority.

Secular institutes (covered in their own *Almanac* entries) are also institutes of consecrated life.

The particular goal of each institute and the means of realizing it in practice are stated in the rule and constitutions proper to the institute. Local bishops can give approval for rules and constitutions of institutes of diocesan rank. Pontifical rank belongs to institutes approved by the Holy See. General jurisdiction over all religious is exercised by the Congregation for Institutes of Consecrated Life and Societies of Apostolic Life. General legislation concerning religious is contained in Canons 573 to 709 in Book II, Part III, of the Code of Canon Law.

All institutes of consecrated life are commonly called religious orders, despite the fact that there are differences between orders and congregations. The best known orders include the Benedictines, Trappists, Franciscans, Dominicans, Carmelites and Augustinians, for men; and the Carmelites, Benedictines, Poor Clares, Dominicans of the Second Order and Visitation Nuns, for women. The orders are older than the congregations, which did not appear until the 16th century.

Contemplative institutes are oriented to divine worship and service within the confines of their communities, by prayer, penitential practices, other spiritual activities and self-supporting work. Examples are the Trappists and Carthusians, the Carmelite and Poor Clare nuns. Active institutes are geared for pastoral ministry and various kinds of apostolic work. Mixed institutes combine elements of the contemplative and active ways of life. While most institutes of men and women can be classified as active, all of them have contemplative aspects.

Clerical communities of men are those whose membership is predominantly composed of priests. Non-clerical or lay institutes of men are the various brotherhoods.

"The Consecrated Life and Its Role in the Church and in the World" was the topic of the ninth general assembly of the Synod of Bishops held Oct. 2-29, 1994.

Societies of Apostolic Life

Some of the institutes listed below have a special kind of status because their members, while living a common life characteristic of religious, do not profess the vows of religious. Examples are the Maryknoll Fathers, the Oratorians of St. Philip Neri, the Paulists and Sulpicians. They are called societies of apostolic life and are the subject of Canons 731 to 746 of the Code of Canon Law.

RELIGIOUS INSTITUTES OF MEN IN THE UNITED STATES

Sources: Annuario Pontificio, The Official Catholic Directory; Catholic Almanac *survey. As of June 1, 2013.*

Africa, Missionaries of, M. Afr.: Founded 1868 at Algiers by Cardinal Charles M. Lavigerie; known as White Fathers until 1984. Generalate, Rome, Italy. U.S. headquarters, 1624 21st St. N.W., Washington, DC 20009, (202) 232-5154. Missionary work in Africa.

African Missions, Society of, S.M.A.: Founded 1856, at Lyons, France, by Bishop Melchior de Marion Brésillac. Generalate, Rome, Italy. American province (1941), 23 Bliss Ave., Tenafly, NJ 07670, (201) 567-9085, www.smafathers.com. Missionary work.

Alexian Brothers, C.F.A.: Founded 14th century in western Germany and Belgium during the Black Plague. Motherhouse, Aachen, Germany. Generalate, 198 James Blvd., Signal Mountain, TN 37377, (423) 886-0380. Hospital and general health work.

Apostolic Life Community of Priests in the Opus Spiritus Sancti, A.L.C.P./O.S.S. (Holy Spirit Fathers): Founded 1974 in Moshi, Tanzania, by German Fr. Bernard Bendel; In US, 1992; US address, Immaculate Heart Church, 2926 North Williams Ave. Portland, OR 97227, (503) 287-3724. educational and foreign mission work.

Assumptionists (Augustinians of the Assumption), A.A.: Founded 1845, at Nimes, France, by Rev. Emmanuel d'Alzon; in U.S., 1946. General House, Rome, Italy. U.S. province, 330 Market St., Brighton, MA 02135, (617) 783-0400, www. assumption.us. Educational, parochial, ecumenical, retreat, foreign mission work.

Atonement, Franciscan Friars of the, S.A.: Founded as an Anglican Franciscan community in 1898 at Garrison, NY, by Fr. Paul Wattson. Community corporately received into the Catholic Church in 1909. Generalate, St. Paul's Friary, Graymoor, Rte. 9, PO Box 300, Garrison, NY 10524, (914) 424-2113; www.atonementfriars.org Ecumenical, mission, retreat and charitable works.

Augustinian Recollects, O.A.R.: Founded 1588; in U.S., 1944. General motherhouse, Rome, Italy. Monastery of St. Cloud (formerly St. Augustine Province, 1944), 29 Ridgeway Ave., West Orange, NJ 07052-3217, (973) 731-0616, www.augustinianrecollects.us. St. Nicholas of Tolentino Province (U.S. Delegation), St. Nicholas of Tolentino Monastery,

3201 Central Ave., Union City, NJ 07087, (201) 422-7550. Missionary, parochial, education work.

Augustinians (Order of St. Augustine), O.S.A.: Established canonically in 1256 by Pope Alexander IV; in U.S., 1796. General motherhouse, Rome, Italy. St. Thomas Monastery, 800 Lancaster Ave., Villanova, PA 19085-1687, (610) 519-7548, www.augustinians.org., (1796). Our Mother of Good Counsel Province (1941), 5401 S. Cornell Ave., Chicago, IL 60615, (773) 595-4000, www.midweststaugustinians.org. St. Augustine, Province of (1969), 1605 28th St., San Diego, CA 92102-1417, (619) 235-0247.

Barnabites (Clerics Regular of St. Paul), C.R.S.P.: Founded 1530, in Milan, Italy, by St. Anthony M. Zaccaria; approved 1533; in U.S., 1952. Historical motherhouse, Church of St. Barnabas (Milan). Generalate, Rome, Italy. North American province, 981 Swann Rd, PO Box 167, Youngstown, NY 14174, (716) 754-7489, www.barnabites.com. Parochial, educational, mission work.

Basil the Great, Order of St. (Basilian Order of St. Josaphat), O.S.B.M.: General motherhouse, Rome, Italy. U.S. province, 29 Peacock Ln., Locust Valley, NY 11560, (516) 609-3262. Parochial work among Byzantine Ukrainian Rite Catholics.

Basilian Fathers (Congregation of the Priests of St. Basil), C.S.B.: Founded 1822, at Annonay, France. General motherhouse, Toronto, ON, Canada. U.S. address: 1910 W. Alabama, Houston, TX 77098, (713) 522-1736. Educational, parochial work.

Basilian Salvatorian Fathers, B.S.O.: Founded 1684, at Saida, Lebanon, by Eftimios Saifi; in U.S., 1953. General motherhouse, Saida, Lebanon. American headquarters, 30 East St., Methuen, MA 01844. Educational, parochial work among Eastern Rite peoples.

Benedictine Monks (Order of St. Benedict), O.S.B.: Founded 529, in Italy, by St. Benedict of Nursia; in U.S., 1846.

• **American Cassinese Congregation (1855).** Pres., Rt. Rev. Melvin J. Valvano, O.S.B., Newark Abbey, 528 Dr. Martin Luther King Blvd., Newark, NJ 07102, (973) 733-2822. Abbeys and priories belonging to the congregation:

St. Vincent Archabbey, 300 Fraser Purchase Rd., Latrobe, PA 15650, (724) 805-2503, www.benedictine.stvincent.edu. Saint John's Abbey, P.O. Box 2015, Collegeville, MN 56321, (320) 363-2548, www.saintjohnsabbey.org. St. Benedict's Abbey, 1020 North Second St., Atchison, KS 66002, (913) 367-7853, www.kansasmonks.org. St. Mary's Abbey, 230 Mendham Rd., Morristown, NJ 07960, (973) 538-3231, www.osbmonks.org. Newark Abbey, 528 Dr. Martin Luther King, Jr., Blvd., Newark, NJ 07102, (973) 643-4800. Belmont Abbey, 100 Belmont Mt. Holly Rd., Belmont, NC 28012, (704) 461-6675, www.belmontabbey.org. St. Bernard Abbey, 1600 Saint Bernard Dr., Cullman, AL 35055, (256) 734-8291. St. Gregory's Abbey, 1900 W. MacArthur, Shawnee, OK 74804, (405) 878-5491, www.monksok.org. St. Leo Abbey, St. Leo, FL 33574, (352) 588-8624, www.saintleoabbey.org. Assumption Abbey, P.O. Box A, Richardton, ND 58652, (701) 974-3315. St. Bede Abbey, Peru, IL 61354, (815) 223-3140, www.theramp.net/stbede/

index.html. St. Martin's Abbey, 5000 Abbey Way, E.E., Lacey, WA 98503-1297, (360) 438-4440, www.stmartin.edu. Holy Cross Abbey, P.O. Box 1510, Canon City, CO 81215, (719) 275-8631, www.holycrossabbey.org. St. Anselm's Abbey, 100 St. Anselm Dr., Manchester, NH, 03102, (603) 641-7651, www.anselm.edu. Holy Trinity Priory, P.O. Box 990, Butler, PA 16003, (724) 287-4461. Benedictine Priory, 6502 Seawright Dr., Savannah, GA 31406, (912) 644-7001, www.bcsav.net. Woodside Priory, 302 Portola Rd., Portola Valley, CA 94028, (650) 851-6133. Mary Mother of the Church Abbey, 12829 River Rd., Richmond, VA 23233, (804) 784-3508, www.richmondmonks.org. Abadia de San Antonio Abad, P.O. Box 729, Humacao, PR 00792, (787) 852-1616; St. Procopius Abbey, 5601 College Rd., Lisle, IL 60532, (630) 969-6410, www.Procopius.org.

• **Swiss-American Congregation (1870)**. Abbeys and priory belonging to the congregation:

St. Meinrad Archabbey, 100 Hill Dr., St. Meinrad, IN 47577-1003, (812) 357-6514, www.saintmeinrad.edu. Conception Abbey, 37174 State Hwy., VV, Conception, MO 64433-0501, (660) 944-3100, www.conceptionabbey.org. Mt. Michael Abbey, 22520 Mt. Michael Rd., Elkhorn, NE 68022-3400, (402) 289-2541, www.mountmichael.org. Subiaco Abbey, Subiaco, AR 72865, (479) 934-1001, www.subi.org. St. Joseph's Abbey, St. Benedict, LA 70457, (504) 892-1800. Mt. Angel Abbey, St. Benedict, OR 97373, (503) 845-3030. Marmion Abbey, 850 Butterfield Rd., Aurora, IL 60502 (630) 897-7215. St. Benedict's Abbey, 12605 224th Ave., Benet Lake, WI 53102, (262) 396-4311, www.benetlake.org. Glastonbury Abbey, 16 Hull St., Hingham, MA 02043, (781) 749-2155, www.glastonburyabbey.org. Blue Cloud Abbey, Marvin, SD 57251-0098, (605) 398-9200, www.bluecloud.org. Corpus Christi Abbey, 101 South Vista Dr., Sandia, TX 78383, (361) 547-3257, www.geocities.com/Athens/styx/8125/ccabbey.html. Prince of Peace Abbey, 650 Benet Hill Rd., Oceanside, CA 92054, (760) 967-4200, www.princeofpeaceabbey.org. St. Benedict Abbey, 254 Still River Rd., PO Box 22, Still River (Harvard), MA 01467, (978) 456-8017.

• **Congregation of St. Ottilien for Foreign Missions:** St. Paul's Abbey, PO Box 7, 289 Rt. 206 South, Newton, NJ 07860, (973) 383-2470. Christ the King Priory, PO Box 528, Schuyler, NE 68661, (402) 352-2177, www.benedictinemissionhouse.com

• **Congregation of the Annunciation**, St. Andrew Abbey, P.O. Box 40, Valyermo, CA 93563-0040, (661) 944-2178, www.valyermo.com.

• **English Benedictine Congregation**: St. Anselm's Abbey, 4501 S. Dakota Ave. N.E., Washington, DC 20017, (202) 269-2300. Abbey of St. Gregory the Great, Cory's Lane, Portsmouth, RI 02871-1352, (401) 683-2000. Abbey of St. Mary and St. Louis, 500 S. Mason Rd., St. Louis, MO 63141-8500, (314) 434-3690, www.priory.org, www.stlouisabbey.org.

• **Houses Not in Congregations**: Mount Saviour Monastery, 231 Monastery Rd., Pine City, NY 14871-9787, (607) 734-1688, www.servtech.com/~msaviour; Weston Priory, 58 Priory Hill Rd., Weston, VT 05161-6400, (802) 824-5409, www.westonpriory.org.

Benedictines, Camaldolese Hermits of America, O.S.B. Cam.: Founded 1012, at Camaldoli, near Arezzo, Italy, by St. Romuald; in U.S., 1958. General motherhouse, Arezzo, Italy. U.S. foundation, New Camaldoli Hermitage, 62475 Highway 1, Big Sur, CA 93920, (831) 667-2456, www.contemplation.org.

Benedictines, Olivetan, O.S.B.: General motherhouse, Siena, Italy. U.S. monasteries: Our Lady of Guadalupe Abbey, PO Box 1080, Pecos, NM 87552, (505) 757-6600, www.pecosabbey.org. Holy Trinity Monastery, P.O. Box 298, St. David, AZ 85630-0298, (520) 720-4642, www.holytrinitymonastery.org. Monastery of the Risen Christ, P.O. Box 3931, San Luis Obispo, CA 93403-3931, (805) 544-1810. Benedictine Monastery of Hawaii, PO Box 490, Waialua, HI 96791, (808) 637-7887, www.Hawaiibenedictines.org.

Benedictines, Subiaco Congregation, O.S.B.: Independent priory, 1983. Monastery of Christ in the Desert, Abiquiu, NM 87510, (505) 470-6668, www.christdesert.org. St. Mary's Monastery, P.O. Box 345, Petersham, MA 01366, (978) 724-3350.

Benedictines, Sylvestrine, O.S.B.: Founded 1231, in Italy, by Sylvester Gozzolini. General motherhouse, Rome, Italy. U.S. foundations: 17320 Rosemont Rd., Detroit, MI 48219, (313) 531-0140. 2711 E. Drahner Rd., Oxford, MI 48370, (248) 628-2249, www.benedictinemonks.org. 1697 State Highway 3, Clifton, NJ 07012, (201) 778-1177.

Blessed Sacrament, Congregation of the, S.S.S.: Founded 1856, at Paris, France, by St. Pierre Julien Eymard; in U.S., 1900. General motherhouse, Rome, Italy. U.S. province, 5384 Wilson Mills Rd., Cleveland, OH 44143-3092, (440) 442-6311, www.blessedsacrament.com. Eucharistic apostolate.

Brigittine Monks (Order of the Most Holy Savior), O.Ss.S.: Monastery of Our Lady of Consolation, 23300 Walker Lane, Amity, OR 97101, (503) 835-8080, www.brigittine.org.

Camaldolese Hermits of the Congregation of Monte Corona, Er. Cam.: Founded 1520, from Camaldoli, Italy, by Bl. Paul Giustiniani; in U.S., 1959; motherhouse, Frascati (Rome), Italy. U.S. foundation, Holy Family Hermitage, 1501 Fairplay Rd., Bloomingdale, OH 43910-7971, (740) 765-4511.

Camillian Fathers and Brothers (Order of St. Camillus; Order of Servants of the Sick), O.S.Cam.: Founded 1582, at Rome, by St. Camillus de Lellis; in U.S., 1923. General motherhouse, Rome, Italy. North American province, 3345 South 1st St., Milwaukee, WI 53215, (414) 481-3696, www.camillians.org.

Carmelites (Order of Our Lady of Mt. Carmel), O. Carm.: General motherhouse, Rome, Italy. Most Pure Heart of Mary Province (1864), 1317 Frontage Rd., Darien, IL 60559, (630) 971-0050. North American Province of St. Elias (1931), PO Box 3079, Middletown, NY 10940-0890, (845) 344-2225; www.carmelitefriars.org. Mt. Carmel Hermitage, Pineland, R.R. 1, Box 330 C, Bolivar, PA, 15923, (724) 238-0423. Educational, charitable work.

Carmelites, Order of Discalced, O.C.D.: Established 1562, a Reform Order of Our Lady of Mt. Carmel; in U.S., 1924. Generalate, Rome, Italy. Western Province (1983), 926 E. Highland Ave., P.O. Box 2178, Redlands, CA 92373, (909) 793-0424; www.ocdwest.org. Province of

St. Thérèse (Oklahoma,1935), 515 Marylake Dr., Little Rock AR 72206, (501) 888-5827. Immaculate Heart of Mary Province (1947), 1233 S. 45th St., Milwaukee, WI 53214, (414) 672-7212. Our Lady of Mt. Carmel Monastery, 1628 Ridge Rd., Munster, IN 46321, (219) 838-7111, www.carmelitefathers.com. Spiritual direction, retreat, parochial work.

Carmelites of Mary Immaculate, C.M.I.: Founded 1831, in India, by Bl. Kuriakose Elias Chavara and two other Syro-Malabar priests; canonically established, 1855. Generalate, Kerala, India. North American headquarters, St. Anthony Church, 862 Manhattan Ave, Brooklyn, NY 11222, (718) 388-4866.

Carthusians, Order of, O. Cart.: Founded 1084, in France, by St. Bruno; in U.S., 1951. General motherhouse, St. Pierre de Chartreuse, France. U.S., Charterhouse of the Transfiguration, Carthusian Monastery, 1084 Ave Maria Way, Arlington, VT 05250, (802) 362-2550, www.transfiguration.chartreux.org. Cloistered contemplatives; semi-eremitic.

Charity, Brothers of, F.C.: Founded 1807, in Belgium, by Canon Peter J. Triest. General motherhouse, Rome, Italy. American District (1963), 7720 Doe Lane, Laverock, PA 19038.

Charity, Servants of (Guanellians), S.C.: Founded 1908, in Italy, by Bl. Luigi Guanella. General motherhouse, Rome, Italy. U.S. headquarters, St. Louis School, 16195 Old U.S. 12, Chelsea, MI 48118, (734) 475-8430, www.stlouiscenter.org.

Christ, Society of, S.Ch.: Founded 1932. General Motherhouse, Poznan, Poland; U.S.-Canadian Province, 3000 Eighteen Mile Rd., Sterling Heights, MI 48311.

Christian Brothers, Congregation of, C.F.C. (formerly Christian Brothers of Ireland): Founded 1802 at Waterford, Ireland, by Bl. Edmund Ignatius Rice; in U.S., 1906. General motherhouse, Rome, Italy. American Province, Eastern U.S. (1916), 33 Pryer Terr., New Rochelle, NY 10804, (914) 712-7580. Brother Rice Province, Western U.S. (1966), 958 Western Ave., Joliet, IL 60435, (815) 723-5464. Educational work.

Christian Instruction, Brothers of (La Mennais Brothers), F.I.C.: Founded 1817, at Ploermel, France, by Abbe Jean Marie de la Mennais and Abbe Gabriel Deshayes. General motherhouse, Rome, Italy. American province, Notre Dame Institute, P.O. Box 159, Alfred, ME 04002, (207) 324-0067, www.ficbrothers.org.

Christian Schools, Brothers of the (Christian Brothers), F.S.C.: Founded 1680, at Reims, France, by St. Jean Baptiste de la Salle. General motherhouse, Rome, Italy. U.S. Conference, 4351 Garden City Dr., Suite 200, Landover, MD 20785, (301) 459-9410, www.cbconf.org. Baltimore Province (1845), Box 29, Adamstown, MD 21710-0029, (301) 874-5188, www.fscbaltimore.org. Brothers of the Christian Schools (Midwest Province) (1995), 7650 S. County Line Rd., Burr Ridge, IL 60527-4718, (630) 323-3725, www.cbmidwest.org. New York Province (1848), 444 A Route 35 South, Eatontown, NJ 07724, (732) 380-7926, www.fscdena.org. Long Island-New England Province (1957), Christian Brothers Center, 635 Ocean Rd., Narragansett, RI 02882-1314, (401) 789-0244, www.cbline.org. San Francisco Province (1868), P.O. Box 3720, Napa, CA 94558, (707) 252-0222, www.delasalle.org. Fe Province (1921), De La Salle Christian Brothers, 1522 Carmel Dr., Lafayette, LA 70501, (337)

234-1973. Educational, charitable work.

Cistercians, Order of, O.Cist.: Founded 1098, by St. Robert. Headquarters, Rome, Italy. Our Lady of Spring Bank Abbey, 17304 Havenwood Rd., Sparta, WI 54656-8177, (608) 269-8138. Our Lady of Dallas Abbey, 3550 Cistercian Rd., Irving, TX 75039, (972) 438-2044. Cistercian Monastery of Our Lady of Fatima, 564 Walton Ave., Mt. Laurel, NJ 08054, (856) 235-1330. Cistercian Conventual Priory, St. Mary's Priory, 70 Schuylkill Rd., New Ringgold, PA 17960, (570) 943-2645. www.cistercian.org.

Cistercians of the Strict Observance, Order of (Trappists), O.C.S.O.: Founded 1098, in France, by St. Robert; in U.S., 1848. Generalate, Rome, Italy.

Abbey of Gethsemani (1848), 3642 Monks Rd., KY 40051, (502) 549-3117. Our Lady of New Melleray Abbey (1849), 6632 Melleray Circle, Peosta, IA 52068-7079, (563) 588-2319. Holy Spirit Monastery (1944), 2625 Hwy. 212 S.W., Conyers, GA 30094-4044, (770) 483-8705 (fax), www.trappist.net. Our Lady of Guadalupe Abbey (1947), P.O. Box 97, Lafayette, OR 97127, (503) 852-7174, www.trappistabbey.org. Abbey of Our Lady of the Holy Trinity (1947), 1250 South 9500 East, Huntsville, UT 84317, (801) 745-3784, www.xmission.com~hta. Abbey of the Genesee (1951), PO Box 900, Piffard, NY 14533, (585) 243-0660, www.geneseeabbey.org. Mepkin Abbey (1949), 1098 Mepkin Abbey Rd., Moncks Corner, SC 29461-4796, (843) 761-8509, www.mepkinabbey.org. Our Lady of the Holy Cross Abbey (1950), 901 Cool Spring Lane, Berryville, VA 22611-2900, (540) 955-4383, www.heava.org. Assumption Abbey (1950), Rt. 5, Box 1056, Ava, MO 65608-9142, (417) 683-5110. Abbey of New Clairvaux (1955), 26240 7th St., Vina, CA 96092, (530) 839-2161, www.newclairvaux.org. St. Benedict's Monastery (1956), 1012 Monastery Rd., Snowmass, CO 81654, (970) 927-3311, www.snowmass.org.

Claretians (Missionary Sons of the Immaculate Heart of Mary), C.M.F.: Founded 1849, at Vich, Spain, by St. Anthony Mary Claret. General headquarters, Rome, Italy. Western Province, 414 S. Mission Dr., San Gabriel, CA 91776, (626) 289-2009. Eastern Province, 400 N. Euclid Ave, Oak Park, IL 60302, (708) 848-2076. Missionary, parochial, educational, retreat work.

Clerics Regular Minor (Adorno Fathers) C.R.M.: Founded 1588, at Naples, Italy, by Ven. Augustine Adorno and St. Francis Caracciolo. General motherhouse, Rome, Italy. U.S. address, 575 Darlington Ave., Ramsey, NJ 07446, (201) 327-7375, members. tripod.com/~adornofathers.

Columban, Missionary Society of St. (St. Columban Foreign Mission Society), S.S.C.: Founded 1918. General headquarters, Dublin, Ireland. U.S. headquarters., PO Box 10, St. Columbans, NE 68056, (402) 291-1920, www.columban.org. Foreign mission work.

Comboni Missionaries of the Heart of Jesus (Verona Fathers), M.C.C.J.: Founded 1867, in Italy by Bl. Daniel Comboni; in U.S., 1939. General motherhouse, Rome, Italy. North American headquarters, Comboni Mission Center, 1318 Nagel Rd., Cincinnati, OH 45255, (513) 474-4997. Mission work in Africa and the Americas.

Consolata Missionaries, I.M.C.: Founded 1901, at Turin, Italy, by Bl. Joseph Allamano. General motherhouse, Rome, Italy. U.S. headquarters, PO Box 5550, 2301 Rt. 27, Somerset, NJ 08875, (732) 297-9191.

Crosier Fathers (Canons Regular of the Order of the Holy Cross), O.S.C.: Founded 1210, in Belgium by Bl. Theodore De Celles. Generalate, Rome, Italy. U.S. Province of St. Odilia, 3510 Vivian Ave., Shoreview, MN 55126-3852, (651) 486-7456, www.crosier.org. Mission, retreat, educational work.

Cross, Brothers of the Congregation of Holy, C.S.C.: Founded 1837, in France, by Fr. Basil Moreau; U.S. province, 1841. Generalate, Rome, Italy. Midwest Province (1841), Box 460, Notre Dame, IN 46556-0460, (574) 631-2912, www.brothersofholycross.com. Southwest Province (1956), 1101 St. Edward's Dr., Austin, TX 78704-6512, (512) 442-7856, www.holycross-sw.org. Eastern Province (1956), 85 Overlook Circle, New Rochelle, NY 10804, (914) 632-4468, www.holycrossbrothers. org. Educational, social work, missions.

Cross, Congregation of Holy, C.S.C.: Founded 1837, in France; in U.S., 1841. Generalate, Rome, Italy. Indiana Province (1841), 54515 State Rd. 933, North, PO Box 1064, Notre Dame, IN 46556-1064, (574) 631-6196. Southern Province (1968), 2111 Brackenridge St., Austin, TX 78704, (512) 443-3886, www.southerncsc. org. Educational and pastoral work; home missions and retreats; foreign missions; social services and apostolate of the press.

Divine Word, Society of the, S.V.D.: Founded 1875, in Holland, by Bl. Arnold Janssen. General motherhouse, Rome, Italy. North American Province founded 1897 with headquarters in Techny, IL. Province of Bl. Joseph Freinademetz (Chicago Province) (1985, from merger of Eastern and Northern provinces), 1985 Waukegan Rd., Techny, IL 60082, (847) 272-2700. St. Augustine (Southern Province) (1940), 201 Ruella Ave., Bay St. Louis, MS 39520, (228) 467-4322, www.svdsouth.com. St. Therese of the Child Jesus (Western Province) (1964), 2737 Pleasant St., Riverside, CA 92507, (323) 735-8130.

Dominicans (Order of Friars Preachers), O.P.: Founded early 13th century by St. Dominic de Guzman. General headquarters, Santa Sabina, Rome, Italy. Eastern Province of St. Joseph (1805), 869 Lexington Ave., New York, NY 10065, (212) 737-5757, www.dominicanfriars. org. Most Holy Name of Jesus (Western) Province (1912), 5877 Birch Ct., Oakland, CA 94618-1626, (510) 658-8722, www.opwest.org. St. Albert the Great (Central) Province (1939), 2005 S. Ashland Ave., Chicago, IL 60608, (312) 243-0011, www.domcentral.org. St. Martin de Porres Province (1979), 1421 N. Causeway Blvd., Suite 200, Metairie, LA 70001-4144, (504) 837-2129, www.opsouth. org. Spanish Province, U.S. foundation (1926), PO Box 279, San Diego, TX 78384, (512) 279-3596. Preaching, teaching, missions, research, parishes.

Edmund, Society of St., S.S.E.: Founded 1843, in France, by Fr. Jean Baptiste Muard. General motherhouse, Edmundite Generalate, 270 Winnoski Park, Colchester, VT 05439-0270, (802) 654-3400, www.sse.org. Educational, missionary work.

Eudists (Congregation of Jesus and Mary), C.J.M.: Founded 1643, in France, by St. John Eudes. General motherhouse, Rome, Italy. North American province, 6125 Premiere Ave., Charlesbourg, QC G1H 2V9, Canada, (418) 626-6494; U.S. community, 36 Flohr Ave., W. Seneca, NY 14224, (716) 825-4475; www.eudistes.org. Parochial, educational, pastoral, missionary work.

Francis, Brothers of Poor of St., C.F.P.: Founded 1857. Motherhouse, Aachen, Germany. International Office, PO Box 35, Wever, IA 52658, (319) 752-4000, brothersofthe poorofstfrancis.org. U.S. province, 239 W. Robbins

St., Covington, KY 41011, www.brothersofthepoorofst-francis.org. Educational work, especially with poor and neglected youth.

Francis, Third Order Regular of St., T.O.R.: Founded 1221, in Italy; in U.S., 1910. General motherhouse, Rome, Italy. Most Sacred Heart of Jesus Province (1910), 128 Woodshire Dr., Pittsburgh, PA 15215-1714, (412) 781-8333. Immaculate Conception Province (1925), 3811 Emerson Ave. N., Minneapolis, MN 55412, (612) 529-7779, www.franciscanfriarstor. com. Franciscan Commissariat of the Spanish Province (1924), 301 Jefferson Ave., Waco, TX 76701-1419, (254) 752-8434. Educational, parochial, missionary work.

Francis de Sales, Oblates of St., O.S.F.S.: Founded 1871, by Fr. Louis Brisson. General motherhouse, Rome, Italy. Wilmington-Philadelphia Province (1906), 2200 Kentmere Parkway, Wilmington, DE 19806, (302) 656-8529, www.oblates.org. Toledo-Detroit Province (1966), 2043 Parkside Blvd., Toledo, OH 43607, (419) 724-9851. Educational, missionary, parochial work.

Francis Xavier, Brothers of St. (Xaverian Brothers), C.F.X.: Founded 1839, in Belgium, by Theodore J. Ryken. Generalate, 4409 Frederick Ave., Baltimore, MD, 21229, (410) 644-0034; xaverianbrothers.org. Educational work.

Franciscan Brothers of Brooklyn, O.S.F.: Founded in Ireland; established at Brooklyn, 1858. Generalate, 135 Remsen St., Brooklyn, NY 11201, (718) 858-8217, www.franciscanbros.org. Educational work.

Franciscan Brothers of the Holy Cross, F.F.S.C.: Founded 1862, in Germany. Generalate, Hausen, Linz Rhein, Germany; U.S. region, 2500 St. James Rd., Springfield, IL 62707, (217) 528-4757; www.franciscanbrothers.net. Educational work.

Franciscan Brothers of the Third Order Regular, O.S.F.: Generalate, Mountbellew, Ireland. U.S. region, 2117 Spyglass Trail W., Oxnard, CA 93030, (805) 485-5002. (Mailing address: 4522 Gainsborough Ave., Los Angeles, CA 90029.)

Franciscan Friars of the Immaculate, F.F.I: Founded 1990, Italy. General motherhouse, Benevento, Italy. U.S. addresses, 600 Pleasant St., New Bedford, MA. 02740; 22 School Hill Rd., Baltic, CT 06330, (508) 996-8274.

Franciscan Friars of the Renewal, C.F.R.: Community established under jurisdiction of the archbishop of New York. Central House, St. Crispin Friary, 420 E. 156th St., Bronx, NY 10455, (718) 402-8255, www.franciscanfriars.com.

Franciscan Missionary Brothers of the Sacred Heart of Jesus, O.S.F.: Founded 1927, in the St. Louis archdiocese. Motherhouse, St. Joseph Rd., Eureka, MO 63025, (314) 587-3661. Care of aged, infirm, homeless men and boys.

Franciscans (Order of Friars Minor), O.F.M.: A family of the First Order of St. Francis (of Assisi) founded in 1209 and established as a separate jurisdiction in 1517; in U.S., 1844. General headquarters, Rome, Italy. English-speaking conference: 1615 Vine St., Cincinnati, OH 45210-1200, (513) 721-4700.

Immaculate Conception Province (1855), 125 Thompson St., New York, NY 10012, (212) 674-4388, icprovince.org. Sacred Heart Province, Franciscan Missionary Union (1858), 3140 Meramec St., St. Louis, MO 63118-4339,

(314) 655-0532. Assumption of the Blessed Virgin Mary Province (1887), P.O. Box 100, 165 East Pulaski St., Pulaski, WI 54162-0100. Holy Name Province (1901), 129 W. 31st St., 2nd Floor, New York, NY 10001, (646) 473-0265, www.hnp.org. St. Barbara Province (1915), 1500 34th Ave., Oakland, CA 94601, (510) 536-3722, www.sbfranciscans.org.

Our Lady of Guadalupe Province (1985), 1204 Stinson. S.W., Albuquerque, NM 87121, (505) 831-9199; OLGofm.org. Commissariat of the Holy Cross (1912), P.O. Box 608, Lemont, IL 60439-0608, (630) 257-2494. Mt. Alverna Friary, 517 S. Belle Vista Ave., Youngstown, OH 44509, (330) 799-1888. Holy Family Croatian Custody (1926), 4851 S. Drexel Blvd., Chicago, IL 60615-1703, (773) 536-0552.

St. Casimir Lithuanian Vice-Province, PO Box 980, Kennebunkport, ME 04046, (207) 967-2011. Holy Gospel Province (Mexico), U.S. foundation, 2400 Marr St., El Paso, TX 79903, (915) 565-2921. Commissariat of the Holy Land, 1400 Quincy St. N.E., Washington, DC 20017, (202) 269-5430, myfranciscan.com. Holy Dormition Friary, Byzantine Slavonic Rite, PO Box 270, Rt. 93, Sybertsville, PA 18251, (570) 788-1212, www.hdbf.com. Academy of American Franciscan History, 1712 Euclid Ave., Berkeley, CA 94709. Preaching, missionary, educational, parochial, charitable work.

Franciscans (Order of Friars Minor Capuchin), O.F.M. Cap.: A family of the First Order of St. Francis (of Assisi) founded in 1209 and established as a separate jurisdiction in 1528. St. Joseph Province/St. Bonaventure Monastery (1857), 1740 Mt. Elliott Ave., Detroit, MI 48207-3427, (313) 579-2100. Province of St. Augustine (1873), 220 37th St., Pittsburgh, PA 15201, (412) 682-6011, www.capuchin.com. St. Mary Province (1952), 30 Gedney Park Dr., White Plains, NY 10605, (914) 761-3008. Province of the Stigmata of St. Francis (1918), P.O. Box 809, Union City, NJ 07087-0809, (201) 865-0611. Western American Capuchin Province, Our Lady of the Angels, 1345 Cortez Ave., Burlingame, CA 94010, (650) 342-1489, www.beafriar.com.

St. Stanislaus Friary (1948), 2 Manor Dr., Oak Ridge, NJ 07438, (973) 697-7757. Province of Mid-America (1977), 3613 Wyandot St., Denver, CO 80211, (303) 477-5436, www.midamcaps.org. Vice-Province of Texas, 604 Bernal Dr., Dallas, TX 75212, (214) 631-1937. St. John the Baptist Vice-Province, P.O. Box 21350, Rio Piedras, Puerto Rico 00928-1350, (787) 764-3090. General motherhouse, Rome, Italy. Missionary, parochial work, chaplaincies.

Franciscans (Order of Friars Minor Conventual), O.F.M. Conv.: A family of the First Order of St. Francis (of Assisi) founded in 1209 and established as a separate jurisdiction in 1517; first U.S. foundation, 1852. General curia, Rome, Italy. Immaculate Conception Province (1852), Immaculate Conception Friary, P.O. Box 629, Rensselaer, NY 12144, (518) 472-1000, www.franciscanseast. St. Anthony of Padua Province (1906), 12300 Folly Quarter Rd., Ellicott City, MD 21042, (410) 531-1400,www.stanthonyprovince.org. St. Bonaventure Province (1939), 6107 Kenmore Ave., Chicago, IL 60660, (773) 274-7681. Our Lady of Consolation Province (1926), 101 St. Anthony Dr., Mt. St. Francis, IN 47146, (812) 923-8444. St. Joseph of Cupertino Province (1981), P.O. Box 820, Arroyo Grande, CA 93421-0820, (805) 489-1012, franciscansusa.org. Missionary, educational, parochial work.

Glenmary Missioners (The Home Missioners of

America): Founded 1939, in U.S.. General headquarters, P.O. Box 465618, Cincinnati, OH 45246, (513) 881-7442, www.glenmary.org. Home mission work.

Good Shepherd, Little Brothers of the, B.G.S.: Founded 1951, by Bro. Mathias Barrett. Foundation House, P.O. Box 389, Albuquerque, NM 87103, (505) 243-4238. General headquarters, Hamilton, ON, Canada. Operate shelters and refuges for aged and homeless; homes for handicapped men and boys, alcoholic rehabilitation center.

Holy Eucharist, Brothers of the, F.S.E.: Founded in U.S., 1957. Generalate, P.O. Box 25, Plaucheville, LA 71362, (318) 922-3630. Teaching, social, clerical, nursing work.

Holy Family, Congregation of the Missionaries of the, M.S.F.: Founded 1895, in Holland, by Rev. John P. Berthier. General motherhouse, Rome, Italy. U.S. provincialate, 3014 Oregon Ave., St. Louis, MO, 63118-1498, (314) 577-6300, www.msfamerica.org. Belated vocations for the missions.

Holy Family, Sons of the, S.F.: Founded 1864, at Barcelona, Spain, by Bl. Jose Mañanet y Vives; in U.S., 1920. General motherhouse, Barcelona, Spain. U.S. address, 401 Randolph Rd., P.O. Box 4138, Silver Spring, MD 20914-4138, (301) 622-1184, www.manyanet.us/www.manyanet.org.

Holy Ghost Fathers, C.S.Sp.: Founded 1703, in Paris, France, by Claude Francois Poullart des Places; in U.S., 1872. Generalate, Rome, Italy. Eastern Province (1872), 6230 Brush Run Rd., Bethel Park, PA 15102, (412) 831-0302, www.spiritans.org.Western Province (1964), 1700 W. Alabama St., Houston, TX 77098-2808, (713) 522-2882, www.spiritans.org. Missions, education.

Holy Ghost Fathers of Ireland: Founded 1971. U.S. delegates: 4849 37th St., Long Island City, NY 11101 (East); St. Dunstan's Church, 1133 Broadway, Mill Brae, CA 94030 (West).Holy Spirit, Missionaries of the, M.Sp.S.: Founded 1914, at Mexico City, Mexico, by Felix Rougier. General motherhouse, Mexico City. U.S. headquarters, 9792 Oma Place, Garden Grove, CA 92841, (714) 534-5476, www.christthepriest.org; charity work.

Immaculate Heart of Mary, Brothers of the, I.H.M.: Founded 1948, at Steubenville, Ohio, by Bishop John K. Mussio. Villa Maria Generalate, 609 N. 7th St., Steubenville, OH 43952, (740) 283-2462. Educational, charitable work.

Jesuits (Society of Jesus), S.J.: Founded 1534, in France, by St. Ignatius of Loyola; received papal approval, 1540; suppressed in 1773 and revived in 1814 by Pope Pius VII; first U.S. province, 1833. The Jesuits remain the largest single order in the Church. Generalate, Rome, Italy. U.S. national office, Jesuit Conference, 1016 16th Street, N.W., Fourth Floor, Washington, DC 20036-1420, (202) 462-0400, www.jesuit.org. Maryland Province (1833), 8600 La Salle Rd., Ste. 620, Towson, MD 21286, (443) 921-131039 www.mdsj.org. New York Province (1943), East 83rd St., New York, NY 10028, (212) 774-5500, www.nysj.org. Missouri Province (1863), 4511 W. Pine Blvd., St. Louis, MO 63108-2191, (314) 361-7765, www.jesuits-mis. org. New Orleans Province (1907), 710 Baronne St., Suite B, New Orleans, LA 70113, (504) 788-1719.

California Province (1909), 300 College Ave., P.O. Box 519, Los Gatos, CA 95031, (408) 884-1600, www.jesuit-scalifornia.org. New England Province (1926), 85 School St., Watertown, MA 02472; (617) 607-2800. Chicago Province (1928), 2050 N. Clark St., Chicago, IL 60614, (773) 975-6363, www.jesuits-chi.org. Oregon Province (1932), 2222 N.W. Hoyt, Portland, OR 97210, (503) 226-6977. Detroit Province (1955), 2050 N. Clark St., Chicago, IL 60614, (773) 975-6888, www.detprovejesuit-det.org. Wisconsin Province (1955), PO Box 080288, Milwaukee, WI 53208-0288, (414) 937-6949, www.jesuitwisprov.org. Province of the Antilles (1947), U.S. address, 12725 S.W. 6th St., Miami, FL 33184, (305) 559-9044. Missionary, educational, literary work.

John of God, Brothers of the Hospitaller Order of St., O.H.: Founded 1537, in Spain. General motherhouse, Rome, Italy. American province, 2425 S. Western Ave., Los Angeles, CA 90018, (323) 731-0233, www.hospitallers.org. Nursing and related fields.

Joseph, Congregation of St., C.S.J.: General motherhouse, Rome, Italy. U.S. vice-province, 338 North Grand Ave., San Pedro, CA 90731-2006, (310) 831-5360. Parochial, missionary, educational work.

Joseph, Oblates of St., O.S.J.: Founded 1878, in Italy, by Bl. Joseph Marello; in U.S., 1929. General motherhouse, Rome, Italy. Our Lady of Sorrows Province, 1880 Hwy 315, Pittston, PA 18640, (570) 654-7542. California Province, 544 W. Cliff Dr., Santa Cruz, CA 95060, (831) 457-1868, www.osjoseph.org. Parochial, educational work.

Josephite Fathers, C.J.: General motherhouse, Ghent, Belgium; U.S. foundation, 5075 Harp Rd., Santa Maria, CA 93455, (805) 937-4555; www.josephiteweb.org.

Josephites (St. Joseph's Society of the Sacred Heart), S.S.J.: Established 1893, in U.S. as American congregation (originally established in U.S., in 1871 by Mill Hill Josephites from England). General motherhouse, 1130 N. Calvert St., Baltimore, MD 21202-3802, (410) 727-3386, www.josephite.com. Evangelization in African-American community.

LaSalette, Missionaries of Our Lady of: Province of Mary, Mother of the Americas, P.O. Box 777, Twin Lakes, WI 53181, (262) 877-3111.

Lateran, Canons Regular of the, C.R.L.: General House, Rome, Italy. U.S. address: 2317 Washington Ave., Bronx, NY 10458, (212) 295-9600.

Legionaries of Christ, L.C.: Founded 1941, in Mexico, by Rev. Marcial Maciel; in U.S., 1965. General headquarters, Rome, Italy. U.S. headquarters, 475 Oak Ave., Cheshite, CT 06410, novitiate, 475 Oak Ave., Cheshire, CT 06410, (203) 271-0805, www.legionofchrist.org.

Little Brothers of St. Francis, L.B.S.F.: Founded 1970 in Archdiocese of Boston by Bro. James Curran. General fraternity, 785 789 Parker St., Boston, MA 02120-3021, (617) 442-2556, www. littlebrothersofstfrancis.org. Combine contemplative life with evangelical street ministry.

Mariannhill, Congregation of the Missionaries of, C.M.M.: Trappist monastery, begun in 1882 by Abbot Francis Pfanner in Natal, South Africa, became an independent modern congregation in 1909; in U.S., 1920. Generalate, Rome, Italy. U.S. Canadian province (1938), Our Lady of Grace Monastery, 23715 Ann Arbor Trail, Dearborn Hts., MI 48127-1449, (313) 561-2330, www. rc.net/detroit/marianhill. Foreign mission work.

Marians of the Immaculate Conception, Congregation of, M.I.C.: Founded 1673; U.S. foundation, 1913. General motherhouse, Rome, Italy. Mother of Mercy Province, Eden Hill, Stockbridge, MA 01262. Educational, parochial, mission, publication work.

Marist Brothers, F.M.S.: Co-founded 1817, in France, by St. Marcellin Champagnat. Generalate, Rome, Italy. U.S. Province, 1241 Kennedy Blvd., Bayonne, NJ 07002, (201) 823-1115; www.societyofmaryusa.org. Educational, social, catechetical work.

Marist Fathers (Society of Mary), S.M.: Founded 1816, at Lyons, France, by Jean Claude Colin; in U.S., 1863. General motherhouse, Rome, Italy. United States Province: 815 Varnum St., NE, Washington, D.C. 20017, (202) 529-2821, www.societyofmaryusa.org. Educational, foreign mission, pastoral work.

Maronite Lebanese Missionaries, Congregation of, C.M.L.M.: Founded in Lebanon 1865; established in the U.S., 1991. U.S. foundation, Our Lady of the Cedars Maronite Mission, 11935 Bellfort Village, Houston, TX 77031, (281) 568-6800.

Maronite Monks of Most Holy Trinity Monastery: Founded in 1978 and canonically approved by John Paul II and established in the Eparchy of St. Maron in 1989. A community of contemplative monks dedicated to a life of prayer and Eucharistic Adoration. Most Holy Trinity Monastery, 67 Dugway Road, Petersham, MA 01366-9725, (978) 724-3347, www.maronitemonks.org.

Mary, Society of (Marianist Fathers and Brothers; Brothers of Mary), S.M.: Founded 1817, at Bordeaux, France, by Fr. William-Joseph Chaminade; in U.S., 1849. General motherhouse, Rome, Italy. Marianist Province of the U.S., 4425 West Pine Blvd., St. Louis, MO 63108, (314) 533-1207, www.marianist.com. The Marianist provinces of Cincinnati, St. Louis, Pacific, and New York have merged to form one province. Educational work.

Mary Immaculate, Missionary Oblates of, O.M.I.: Founded 1816, in France, by St. Charles Joseph Eugene de Mazenod; in U.S., 1849. General House, Rome, Italy. U.S. Province: 327 Oblate Dr., San Antonio, TX 78216-6602, (210) 349-1475, www.omiusa.org. Parochial, foreign mission, educational work, ministry to marginal.

Maryknoll (Catholic Foreign Mission Society of America), M.M.: Founded 1911, in U.S., by Frs. Thomas F. Price and James A. Walsh. General Center, Maryknoll, NY 10545, (914) 941-7590.

Mercedarians (Order of Our Lady of Mercy), O. de M.: Founded 1218, in Spain, by St. Peter Nolasco. General motherhouse, Rome, Italy. U.S. headquarters, 3205 Fulton Rd., Cleveland, OH 44109 (216) 961-8331.

Mercy, Brothers of, F.M.M.: Founded 1856, in Germany. General motherhouse, Montabaur, Germany. American headquarters, 4520 Ransom Rd., Clarence, NY 14031, (716) 759-8341. Hospital work.

Mercy, Brothers of Our Lady, Mother of, C.F.M.M.: Founded 1844, in the Netherlands by Abp. Jan Zwijsen. Generalate, Tilburg, the Netherlands. U.S. region, 7140 Ramsgate Ave., Los Angeles, CA 90045, (310) 338-5954, www.cmmbrothers.nl.

Mercy, Congregation of Priests of (Fathers of Mercy), C.P.M.: Founded 1808, in France, by Rev. Jean Baptiste Rauzan; in U.S., 1839. General mission house, Auburn, KY 42206, (270) 542-4164; www.fathersofmercy.com. Mission work.

Mill Hill Missionaries (St. Joseph's Society for Foreign Missions), M.H.M.: Founded 1866, in England, by Cardinal Vaughan; in U.S., 1951. International headquarters, London, England. American headquarters, 222 W. Hartsdale Ave., Hartsdale, NY 10530, (914) 682-0645.

Minim Fathers, O.M.: General motherhouse, Rome, Italy. North American delegation (1970), 3431 Portola Ave., Los Angeles, CA 90032, (213) 223-1101.

Missionaries of St. Charles, Congregation of the (Scalabrinians), C.S.: Founded 1887, at Piacenza, Italy, by Bl. John Baptist Scalabrini. General motherhouse, Rome, Italy. St. Charles Borromeo Province (1888), 27 Carmine St., New York, NY 10014, (212) 675-3993. St. John Baptist Province (1903), 546 N. East Ave., Oak Park, IL 60302, (708) 386-4430.

Missionaries of the Holy Apostles, M.Ss.A.: Founded 1962, Washington, DC, by Very Rev. Eusebe M. Menard. North American headquarters, 24 Prospect Hill Rd., Cromwell, CT 06416, (860) 632-3039, www.msagen.org.

Missionarii Franciscani Verbi Aeterni, Franciscan Missionaries of the Eternal Word, 5821 Old Leeds Rd., Irondale, AL 35210, www.mfva.info.

Missionary Servants of Christ, M.S.C.: Founded 1979 in U.S. by Bro. Edwin Baker. Headquarters, P.O. Box 270, 305 S. Lake St., Aurora, IL 60507-0270, (630) 892-2371, www.misacor-usa.org.

Missionhurst-CICM (Congregation of the Immaculate Heart of Mary): Founded 1862, at Scheut, Brussels, Belgium, by Very Rev. Theophile Verbist. General motherhouse, Rome, Italy. U.S. province, 4651 N. 25th St., Arlington, VA 22207, (703) 528-3800, www.missionhurst.org. Home and foreign mission work.

Montfort Missionaries (Missionaries of the Company of Mary), S.M.M.: Founded 1715, by St. Louis Marie Grignon de Montfort; in U.S., 1948. General motherhouse, Rome, Italy. U.S. province, 101-18 104th St., Ozone Park, NY 11416, (718) 849-5885. Mission work.

Mother Co-Redemptrix, Congregation of, C.M.C.: Founded 1953 at Lein-Thuy, Vietnam (North), by Fr. Dominic Mary Tran Dinh Thu; in U.S., 1975. General house, Hochiminhville, Vietnam. U.S. provincial house, 1900 Grand Ave., Carthage, MO 64836, (417) 358-7787, www.dongcong.net. Work among Vietnamese Catholics in U.S.

Oblates of the Virgin Mary, O.M.V.: Founded 1815, in Italy; in U.S., 1976; Generalate, Rome, Italy. U.S. provincialate: 2 Ipswich St., Boston, MA 02215, (617) 536-4141.

Oratorians (Congregation of the Oratory of St. Philip Neri), C.O.: Founded 1575, at Rome, by St. Philip Neri. A confederation of autonomous houses. U.S. addresses: PO Box 11586, Rock Hill, SC 29731, (803) 327-2097, www.rockhilloratory.org. PO Box 1688, Monterey, CA 93940, (831) 373-0476. 4450 Bayard St., Pittsburgh, PA 15213, (412) 681-3181. P.O. Drawer II, Pharr, TX 78577, (956) 843-8217. 109 Willoughby St., Brooklyn, NY 11201, (718) 788-5693.

Pallottines (Society of the Catholic Apostolate), S.A.C.: Founded 1835, at Rome, by St. Vincent Pallotti. Generalate, Rome, Italy. Immaculate Conception Province (1953), PO Box 979, South Orange, NJ 07079, (201) 762-2926. Mother of God Province (1946), 5424 W. Blue Mound Rd., Milwaukee, WI 53208, (414) 259-0688. Irish Province (1909), U.S. address: 3352 4th St., Wyandotte, MI 48192, www.irishpallottines.com. Queen of Apostles Province (1909), 448 E. 116th St., New York, NY 10029, (212) 534-0681. Christ the King Province, 3452 Niagara Falls, Blvd., N. Tonawanda, NY 14120, (716) 694-4313, www.pallottines.org. Charitable, educational, parochial, mission work.

Paraclete, Servants of the, S.P.: Founded 1947, Santa Fe, NM, archdiocese. Generalate and U.S. motherhouse, 13270 Maple Dr., St. Louis, MO 63127, (314) 965-0860; www.theservants.org. Dedicated to ministry to priests and Brothers with personal difficulties.

Paris Foreign Missions Society, M.E.P.: Founded 1662, at Paris, France. Headquarters, Paris, France; U.S. establishment, 930 Ashbury St., San Francisco, CA 94117, (415) 664-6747. Mission work and training of native clergy.

Passionists (Congregation of the Passion), C.P.: Founded 1720, in Italy, by St. Paul of the Cross. General motherhouse, Rome, Italy. St. Paul of the Cross Province (Eastern Province) (1852), 80 David St., South River, NJ 08882, (732) 257-7177, www.thepassionists.org. Holy Cross Province (Western Province), 5700 N. Harlem Ave., Chicago, IL 60631, (773) 631-6336.

Patrician Brothers (Brothers of St. Patrick), F.S.P.: Founded 1808, in Ireland, by Bp. Daniel Delaney. U.S. novitiate, 7820 Bolsa Ave., Midway City, CA 92655, (714) 897-8181. Educational work.

Patrick's Missionary Society, St., S.P.S.: Founded 1932, at Wicklow, Ireland, by Msgr. Patrick Whitney; in U.S., 1953. International headquarters, Kiltegan Co., Wicklow, Ireland. U.S. foundations: 70 Edgewater Rd., Cliffside Park, NJ 07010, (201) 943-6575, 19536 Eric Dr., Saratoga, CA 95070, (408) 253-3135, www.spms.org; 8422 W. Windsor Ave., Chicago, IL 60656, (773) 887-4741.

Pauline Fathers (Order of St. Paul the First Hermit), O.S.P.P.E.: Founded 1215; established in U.S., 1955. General motherhouse, Czesto-chowa, Jasna Gora, Poland; U.S. province, P.O. Box 2049, Doylestown, PA 18901, (215) 345-0600; www.czestochowa.us.

Pauline Fathers and Brothers (Society of St. Paul for the Apostolate of Communications), S.S.P.: Founded 1914, by Very Rev. James Alberione; in U.S., 1932. Motherhouse, Rome, Italy. New York province (1932), P.O. Box 139, Ellsworth, OH 44416-0139, (330) 533-7427. Social communications work.

Paulists (Missionary Society of St. Paul the Apostle), C.S.P.: Founded 1858, in New York, by Fr. Isaac Thomas Hecker. Motherhouse: 86-11 Midland Pkwy, Jamaica Estates, NY 11432, (718) 291-5995, www.paulist.org. Missionary, ecumenical, pastoral work.

Piarists (Order of the Pious Schools), Sch.P.: Founded 1617, at Rome, Italy, by St. Joseph Calasanctius. General motherhouse, Rome, Italy. U.S. province, 363 N. Valley Forge Rd., Devon, PA 19333, (610) 688-7337, www.devonprep.com. New York-Puerto Rico vice-province (Calasanzian Fathers), P.O. Box 7760, Ponce, PR 00732-7760, (787) 840-0610. California vice province, 3940 Perry St., Los Angeles, CA 90063, (323) 261-1386. Educational work.

Pius X, Brothers of St., C.S.P.X.: Founded 1952, at La Crosse, WI, by Bishop John P. Treacy. Motherhouse, PO Box 217, De Soto, WI 54624. Education.

Pontifical Institute for Foreign Missions, P.I.M.E.: Founded 1850, in Italy, at request of Pope Pius IX. General motherhouse, Rome, Italy. U.S. province, 17330 Quincy Ave., Detroit, MI 48221, (313) 342-4066, www.pimeusa.org work.

Precious Blood, Society of, C.P.P.S.: Founded 1815, in Italy, by St. Gaspar del Bufalo. General motherhouse, Rome, Italy. Cincinnati Province, 431 E. Second St., Dayton, OH 45402, (937) 228-9263, www.cpps-preciousblood.org. Kansas City Province, P.O. Box 339, Liberty, MO 64069-0339, (816) 781-4344, www.kcprovince.org. Pacific Province, 2337 134th Ave. W., San Leandro, CA 94577, (510) 357-4982, www.rc.net/oakland/cpps. Atlantic Province 100 Pelmo Cres., Toronto, ON M9N 2Y1, (416) 614-7096, www.precious-blood.org.

Premonstratensians (Order of the Canons Regular of Premontre; Norbertines), O. Praem.: Founded 1120, at Premontre, France, by St. Norbert; in U.S., 1893. Generalate, Rome, Italy. St. Norbert Abbey, 1016 N. Broadway, DePere, WI 54114, (920) 337-4300, www.snc.edu/norbertines. Daylesford Abbey, 220 S. Valley Rd., Paoli, PA 19301, (610) 647-2530, www.daylesford.org. St. Michael's Abbey, 19292 El Toro Rd., Silverado, CA 92676, (949) 858-0222, www.abbeynews.com. Immaculate Conception Priory (1997), 3600 Philadelphia Pike, Claymont, DE 19703, (302) 792-2791. Educational, parish work.

Priestly Fraternity of St. Peter, F.S.S.P.: Founded and approved Oct. 18, 1988; first foundation in U.S., 1991. U.S. headquarters, St. Peter's House, 119 Griffin Rd., Elmhurst, PA 18444, (570) 842-4000, www.fssp.com. Pastoral and sacramental ministry using the 1962 liturgical books.

Providence, Sons of Divine, F.D.P.: Founded 1893, at Tortona, Italy, by Bl. Luigi Orione; in U.S., 1933. General motherhouse, Rome, Italy. U.S. address, 111 Orient Ave., E. Boston, MA 02128, (617) 569-2100.

Redemptorist Fathers and Brothers (Congregation of the Most Holy Redeemer), C.SS.R.: Founded 1732, in Italy, by St. Alphonsus Mary Liguori. Generalate, Rome, Italy. Baltimore Province (1850), 7509 Shore Rd., Brooklyn, NY 11209, (718) 833-1900. Redemptorist-Denver Province (1875), 1230 South Parker Rd., Denver, CO 80203-0399, (303) 370-0035, www.redemptorists-denver.org. Richmond Vice-Province (1942), 313 Hillman St., PO Box 1529, New Smyrna Beach, FL 32168, (386) 427-3094. Mission work.

Resurrectionists (Congregation of the Resurrection), C.R.: Founded 1836, in France, under direction of Bogdan Janski. Motherhouse, Rome, Italy. U.S. Province, 7050 N. Oakley Ave., Chicago, IL 60645-3426, (773) 465-8320, www.resurrectionists.com. Ontario Kentucky Province, U.S. address, 338 N. 25th St., Louisville, KY 40212, (502) 772-3694.

Rogationist Fathers, R.C.J.: Founded by Bl. Annibale (Hannibal) di Francia, 1887. General motherhouse, Rome, Italy. U.S. delegation: 2688 S. Newmark Ave., Sanger, CA 91343, (209) 875-5808. Charitable work.

Rosary, Brothers of Our Lady of the Holy, F.S.R.: Founded 1956, in U.S. motherhouse and novitiate, 232 Sunnyside Dr., Reno, NV 89503-3510, (775) 326-9429.

Rosminians (Institute of Charity), I.C.: Founded 1828, in Italy, by Antonio Rosmini-Serbati. General motherhouse, Rome, Italy. U.S. address, 2327 W. Heading Ave., Peoria, IL 61604, (309) 676-6341. Charitable work.

Sacred Heart, Brothers of the, S.C.: Founded 1821, in France, by Fr. Andre Coindre. General motherhouse, Rome, Italy. New Orleans Province (1847), 4600 Elysian Fields Ave., New Orleans, LA 70122, (504) 282-5693. New England Province (1945), 219 MacArthur Ave.,

Sayreville, NJ 08872, (732) 718-8559, www.brothersofthesacredheart.org. New York Province (1960), 141-11 123 Ave., South Ozone Park, NY 11436-1426, (718) 322-3309. Educational work.

Sacred Heart, Missionaries of the, M.S.C.: Founded 1854, by Fr. Jules Chevelier. General motherhouse, Rome, Italy. U.S. province, 305 S. Lake St., Aurora, IL 60507-0271, (630) 892-8400.

Sacred Heart of Jesus, Congregation of the (Sacred Heart Fathers and Brothers), S.C.J.: Founded 1877, in France. General motherhouse, Rome, Italy. U.S. provincial office, PO Box 289, Hales Corners, WI 53130-0289, (414) 425-6910, www.sacredheartusa.org. Educational, preaching, mission work.

Sacred Hearts of Jesus and Mary, Congregation of (Picpus Fathers), SS.CC.: Founded 1805, in France, by Fr. Coudrin. General motherhouse, Rome, Italy. Eastern Province (1946), 77 Adams St. (Box 111), Fairhaven, MA 02719, (508) 993-2442, www.sscc.org. Western Province (1970), 2150 Damien Ave., La Verne, CA 91750, (909) 593-5441. Hawaii Province, Box 797, Kaneohe, Oahu, HI 96744, (808) 247-5035. Mission, educational work.

Sacred Hearts of Jesus and Mary, Missionaries of the, M.SS.CC.: Founded 1833, in Naples, Italy, by Cajetan Errico. General motherhouse, Rome, Italy. U.S. headquarters, 2249 Shore Rd., Linwood, NJ 08221, (609) 927-5600.

Salesians of St. John Bosco (Society of St. Francis de Sales), S.D.B.: Founded 1859, by St. John (Don) Bosco. Generalate, Rome, Italy. St. Philip the Apostle Province (1902), 148 Main St., New Rochelle, NY 10802-0639, (914) 636-4225. San Francisco Province (1926), 1100 Franklin St., San Francisco, CA 94109, (415) 441-7144; www.salesians.org

Salvatorians (Society of the Divine Savior), S.D.S.: Founded 1881, in Rome, by Fr. Francis Jordan; in U.S., 1896. General headquarters, Rome, Italy. U.S. province, 1735 N. Hi-Mount Blvd., Milwaukee, WI 53208-1720, (414) 258-1735, www.salvatorians.com. Educational, parochial, mission work; campus ministries, chaplaincies.

Scalabrinians: See **Missionaries of St. Charles.**

Servites (Order of Friar Servants of Mary), O.S.M.: Founded 1233, at Florence, Italy, by Seven Holy Founders. Generalate, Rome, Italy. United States Province (1967), 3121 W. Jackson Blvd., Chicago, IL 60612, (773) 533-0360. General apostolic ministry.

Somascan Fathers, C.R.S.: Founded 1534, at Somasca, Italy, by St. Jerome Emiliani. General motherhouse, Rome, Italy. U.S. address, Pine Haven Boys Center, River Rd., P.O. Box 162, Suncook, NH 03275, (603) 485-7141, www.somascans.org.

Society of Our Lady of the Most Holy Trinity, S.O.L.T.: Headquarters, Casa San Jose, 109 W. Ave. F, PO Box 152, Robstown, TX 78380, (512) 387-2754.

Sons of Mary (Sons of Mary, Health of the Sick), F.M.S.I.: Founded 1952, in the Boston archdiocese, by Fr. Edward F. Garesche, S.J. Headquarters, 567 Salem End Rd., Framingham, MA 01701-5599, (508) 879-2541, www.sonsofmary.com.

Stigmatine Fathers and Brothers (Congregation of the Sacred Stigmata), C.S.S.: Founded 1816, by St. Gaspar Bertoni. General motherhouse, Rome, Italy. North American Province, 554 Lexington St., Waltham, MA 02452-3097, (781) 209-3100, www.stigmatines.com. Parish work.

Sulpicians (Society of Priests of St. Sulpice), S.S.: Founded 1641, in Paris, by Fr. Jean Jacques Olier. General motherhouse, Paris, France; U.S. province, 5408 Roland Ave., Baltimore, MD 21210, (410) 323-5070, www.sulpicians.org. Education of seminarians and priests.

Theatines (Congregation of Clerics Regular), C.R.: Founded 1524, in Rome, by St. Cajetan. General motherhouse, Rome, Italy. U.S. headquarters, 1050 S. Birch St., Denver, CO 80246, (303) 756-5522.

Trappists: See **Cistercians of the Strict Observance.**

Trinitarians (Order of the Most Holy Trinity), O.SS.T.: Founded 1198, by St. John of Matha; in U.S., 1911. General motherhouse, Rome, Italy. U.S. headquarters, P.O. Box 5742, Baltimore, MD 21282, (410) 486-5171.

Trinity Missions (Missionary Servants of the Most Holy Trinity), S.T.: Founded 1929, by Fr. Thomas Augustine Judge. Generalate, PO Box 7130, Silver Springs, MD 20907-7130, (301) 434-6761, www.trinitymissions.org. Home mission work.

Viatorian Fathers (Clerics of St. Viator), C.S.V.: Founded 1831, in France, by Fr. Louis Joseph Querbes. General motherhouse, Rome, Italy. Province of Chicago (1882), 1212 E. Euclid Ave., Arlington Hts., IL 60004, (847) 398-1353. Educational work.

Vincentians (Congregation of the Mission; Lazarists), C.M.: Founded 1625, in Paris, by St. Vincent de Paul; in U.S., 1818. General motherhouse, Rome, Italy. Eastern Province (1867), 500 E. Chelten Ave., Philadelphia, PA 19144, (215) 848-1985. Western Province (1888), 13663 Rider Trail North, Earth City, MO 63045, (314) 344-1184; www.vincentian.org. New England Province (1975), 234 Keeney St., Manchester, CT 06040-7048, (860) 643-2828. American Italian Branch, Our Lady of Pompei Church, 3600 Claremont St., Baltimore, MD 21224, (410) 675-7790. American Spanish Branch (Barcelona, Spain), 118 Congress St., Brooklyn, NY 11201-6045, (718) 624-5670. American Spanish Branch (Zaragoza, Spain), Holy Agony Church, 1834 3rd Ave., New York, NY 10029, (212) 289-5589. Southern Province (1975), 3826 Gilbert Ave., Dallas, TX 75219, (214) 526-0234, www.cmsouth.org. Educational work.

Vocationist Fathers (Society of Divine Vocations), S.D.V.: Founded 1920, in Italy; in U.S., 1962. Generalate, Rome, Italy. U.S. headquarters, 90 Brooklake Rd., Florham Park, NJ 07932, (973) 966-6262, www.vocationist.org.

Xaverian Missionary Fathers, S.X.: Founded 1895, by Bl. Guido Conforti, at Parma, Italy. General motherhouse, Rome, Italy. U.S. province, 12 Helene Ct., Wayne, NJ 07470, (973) 942-2975, www.xaviermissionaries.org. Foreign mission work.

MEMBERSHIP OF RELIGIOUS INSTITUTES OF MEN

Principal source: Annuario Pontificio. *Statistics as of Jan. 1, 2013, unless indicated otherwise.* Listed below are world membership statistics of institutes of men of pontifical right with 500 or more members; the number of priests is in parentheses. Also listed are institutes with less than 500 members with houses in the U.S.

Jesuits (12,534)	17,676
Salesians (10,571)	15,573
Franciscans (Friars Minor) (9,735)	14,123
Franciscans (Capuchins) (7,057)	10,786
Benedictines (3,796)	7,231
Society of the Divine Word (4,152)	6,015
Dominicans (4,459)	5,947
Redemptorists (4,047)	5,338
Brothers of Christian Schools	4,736
Franciscans (Conventuals) (2,921)	4,289
Oblates of Mary Immaculate (3,024)	4,149
Discalced Carmelites (O.C.D.) (2,837)	3,994
Vincentians (3,024)	3,691
Marist Brothers	3,667
Claretians (2,167)	3,024
Holy Spirit (Holy Ghost), Vincentians Congregation of (2,177)	2,979
Augustinians (2,026)	2,810
Carmelites of the BVM (1,721)	2,448
Pallottines (1,679)	2,364
Priests of the Sacred Heart (1,677)	2,333
Passionists (1,618)	2,123
Trappists (782)	2,009
Carmelites (O.Carm.) (1,332)	2,007
Legionaries of Christ (923)	1,993
Missionaries of the Sacred Heart of Jesus (1,341)	1,872
Combonian Missionaries of the Heart of Jesus (1,253)	1,732
Cistercians (Common Observance) (731)	1,709
Missionaries of Africa (1,314)	1,656
Missionaries of St. Francis de Sales of Annecy (954)	1,531
Holy Cross, Congregation of (737)	1,474
Piarists (986)	1,327
Premonstratensians (935)	1,280
Marianists (403)	1,279
Brothers of Christian Instruction of St. Gabriel (25)	1,248
Christian Brothers	1,239
Salvatorians (836)	1,170
Augustinians (Recollects) (924)	1,145
Hospitallers of St. John of God (129)	1,138
Ministers of the Sick (Camillians) (672)	1,132
Brothers of the Sacred Heart (30)	1,121
Society of St. Paul (550)	1,018
Consolata Missionaries (751)	1,007
Little Workers of Divine Providence (654)	962
LaSalette Missionaries (698)	960
Society of African Missions (782)	947
Marists (803)	943
Blessed Sacrament, Congregation of (603)	906
Immaculate Heart of Mary, Congregation of Missionhurst; Scheut Missionaries) (728)	900
Montfort Missionaries (643)	892
Assumptionists (540)	882
Brothers of Christian Instruction	
of Ploërmel (5)	875
Franciscans (Third Order Regular) (576)	870
Missionaries of the Holy Family (658)	860
Servants of Mary (581)	827
Sacred Hearts, Congregation of (Picpus) (659)	808
Xaverian Missionaries (630)	795
Blessed Sacrament, Miss. Congr. (322)	765
Scalabrinians (582)	726
Mercedarians (503)	695
Most Precious Blood (515)	671
Missionaries of the Mill Hill (363)	659
Canons Regular of St. Augustine (547)	654
Vincentian Cong. (460)	652
Trinitarians (407)	621
Brothers of Charity (Ghent)	599
Oblates of St. Joseph (395)	598
Heralds of Good News (352)	592
St. Joseph, Congregation of (414)	579
Pontifical Institute for Foreign Missions (447)	567
Servants of Charity (333)	557
Oblates of St. Francis de Sales (429)	555
Oratorians (414)	552
Order of St. Basil the Great (Basilians of St. Josaphat) (348)	524
Order of St. Paul the First Hermit (351)	520
Viatorians (216)	516
Rogationists (300)	502
Columbans (435)	479
Somascans (350)	476
Marian Fathers and Brothers (349)	471
Eudists (354)	469
Society of Christ (397)	462
Vocationist Fathers (227)	434
Stigmatine Fathers and Brothers (337)	433
Immaculate Conception, Sons of (174)	429
Maryknollers (354)	416
Charity, Missionaries of (1)	407
Crosiers (Order of the Holy Cross) (250)	399
Capuchin Tertiaries (199)	392
Barnabites (285)	392
Priestly Fraternity of St. Peter (222)	384
Resurrection, Congregation of the (322)	376
Mariannhill Missionaries (212)	370
St. Patrick's Mission Society (293)	361
Missionaries of the Holy Spirit (237)	348
Michael the Archangel (265)	343
Brothers of the Immaculate Conception (2)	329
Rosminians (212)	310
Carthusians (149)	310
Sulpicians (290)	290
Paris Foreign Mission Society (237)	270
St. Basil, Congr. of (250)	222
Little Brothers of Jesus (58)	215
Discalced Augustinians (132	213
Brothers of St. Patrick	200
Rosarians (74)	201
Paulists (62)	187
Xaverian Brothers	185
Minim Fathers (120)	184
Oblates of the Virgin Mary (139)	181
Theatines (138)	174

RELIGIOUS INSTITUTES OF WOMEN IN THE UNITED STATES

Sources: The Official Catholic Directory; Catholic Almanac *survey. As of June 1, 2013.*

Adorers of the Blood of Christ, A.S.C.: Founded 1834, in Italy; in U.S., 1870. General motherhouse, Rome, Italy. U.S. region: 4233 Sulphur Ave., St. Louis, MO 63109, (314) 351-6294,; 3950 Columbia Ave., Columbia, PA 17512, (717) 285-4536; www.adorers.org. Education, retreats, social services, pastoral ministry.

Africa, Missionary Sisters of Our Lady of (Sisters of Africa), M.S.O.L.A.: Founded 1869, at Algiers, Algeria, by Cardinal Lavigerie; in U.S., 1929. General motherhouse, Rome, Italy. U.S. headquarters, 47 W. Spring St., Winooski, VT 05404-1397, (802) 655-4003, www.smnda.org. Medical, educational, catechetical and social work in Africa.

Agnes, Sisters of St., C.S.A.: Founded 1858, in U.S., by Rev. Caspar Rehrl. General motherhouse, 320 County Rd., Fond du Lac, WI 54935, (920) 907-2321, www.csasisters.org. Education, health care, social services.

Ann, Sisters of St., S.S.A.: Founded 1834, in Italy; in U.S., 1952. General motherhouse, Rome, Italy. U.S. headquarters, Mount St. Ann, Ebensburg, PA 15931, (814) 472-9354.

Anne, Sisters of St., S.S.A.: Founded 1850, at Vaudreuil, QC, Canada; in U.S., 1866. General motherhouse, Lachine, QC, Canada. U.S. address, 720 Boston Post Rd., Marlborough, MA 01752, (508) 597-0204, www.sistersofsaintanne. org. Retreat work, pastoral ministry, religious education.

Anthony, Missionary Servants of St., M.S.S.A.: Founded 1929, in U.S., by Fr. Peter Basque. General motherhouse, 100 Peter Baque Rd., San Antonio, TX 78209, (210) 824-4553. Social work.

Antoine Maronite Sisters: Founded in Beirut, Lebanon. Motherhouse, Couvent Mar-Doumith, Roumieh, El-Metn, B.P. 84, Borumana, Lebanon. U.S. house, 2691 North Lipkey Rd., North Jackson, OH 44451, (330) 538-9822; www.antoinesisters.com.

Assumption, Little Sisters of the, L.S.A.: Founded 1865, in France; in U.S., 1891. General motherhouse, Paris, France. U.S. provincialate, 100 Gladstone Ave., Walden, NY 12586, (914) 778-0667, www.little sisters.org. Social work, nursing, family life education.

Assumption, Religious of the, R.A.: Founded 1839, in France; in U.S., 1919. Generalate, Paris, France. North American province, 11 Old English Rd., Worcester, MA 01609, (508) 791-2936; www.assumptionsisters.org.

Assumption of the Blessed Virgin, Sisters of the, S.A.S.V.:

Founded 1853, in Canada; in U.S., 1891. General motherhouse, Nicolet, QC, Canada. U.S. province, 2 Buchanan Rd., Salem, MA 01970, (978) 744-2757. Education, mission, pastoral ministry.

Augustinian Nuns of Contemplative Life, O.S.A.: Established in Spain in 13th century. U.S. foundation, Convent of Our Mother of Good Counsel, 440 Marley Rd., New Lenox, IL, 60451, (815) 463-9662; www.lampsalight.org.

Augustinian Sisters, Servants of Jesus and Mary, Congregation of, O.S.A.: Generalate, Rome, Italy. U.S. foundation, St. John School, 513 E. Broadway, Brandenburg, KY 40108, (270) 422-2088, www.stjohnonline.org.

Basil the Great, Sisters of the Order of St. (Byzantine Rite), O.S.B.M.: Founded fourth century, in Cappadocia, by St. Basil the Great and his sister, St. Macrina; in U.S., 1911. Generalate, Rome, Italy. U.S. motherhouses: Philadelphia Ukrainian Byzantine Rite, 710 Fox Chase Rd., Philadelphia, PA 19046-4198, (215) 379-3998, www. basilianfoxchase.org. Pittsburgh Ruthenian Byzantine Rite, Mount St. Macrina, PO Box 878, Uniontown, PA 15401, (724) 438-8644. Education, health care.

Benedict, Sisters of the Order of St., O.S.B.: Our Lady of Mount Caritas Monastery (founded 1979, Ashford, CT), 54 Seckar Rd., Ashford, CT 06278, (860) 429-7457, www.mountcaritasmonastery.org. Contemplative.

Benedictine Nuns, O.S.B.: St. Scholastica Priory, Box 606, Petersham, MA 01366, (978) 724-3213; www.stscholasticapriory.org. Cloistered.

Benedictine Nuns of the Congregation of Solesmes, O.S.B.: U.S. establishment, 1981, in Burlington diocese. Monastery of the Immaculate Heart of Mary, 4103 Vt. Rte 100, Westfield, VT 05874, (802) 744-6525, www. ihmwest field.com. Cloistered, papal enclosure.

Benedictine Nuns of the Primitive Observance, O.S.B.: Founded c. 529, in Italy; in U.S., 1948. Abbey of Regina Laudis, Flanders Rd., Bethlehem, CT 06751, (203) 266-7727, www.abbeyofreginalaudis.com. Cloistered.

Benedictine Sisters, O.S.B.: Founded c. 529, in Italy; in U.S., 1852. General motherhouse, Eichstatt, Bavaria, Germany. U.S. addresses: St. Emma Monastery, motherhouse and novitiate, 1001 Harvey Ave., Greensburg, PA 15601, (724) 834-3060, www.stemma.org. Abbey of St. Walburga, 32109 N. U.S. Highway 287, Virginia Dale, CO 80536, (970) 472-0612, www.walburga.org.

Benedictine Sisters, Missionary, O.S.B.: Founded 1885. Generalate, Rome, Italy. U.S. motherhouse, 300 N. 18th St., Norfolk, NE 68701-3687, (402) 371-3438, www.norfolksb.org.

Benedictine Sisters, Olivetan, O.S.B.: Founded 1887, in U.S. General motherhouse, Holy Angels Convent, P.O. Box 1209, Jonesboro, AR 72403- 0130, (870) 935-5810, www.olivben.org. Educational, hospital work.

Benedictine Sisters of Perpetual Adoration of Pontifical Jurisdiction, Congregation of the, O.S.B.: Founded in U.S., 1874, from Maria Rickenbach, Switzerland. General motherhouse, 8300 Morganford Rd., St. Louis, MO 63123, (314) 638-6427.

Benedictine Sisters of Pontifical Jurisdiction, O.S.B.: Founded c. 529, in Italy. No general mother house in U.S. Three federations:

• **Federation of St. Scholastica** (1922). Pres., Sister Esther Fangman, O.S.B., 3741 Forest Ave., Kansas City, MO 64109, (816) 753-2514. Motherhouses belonging to the federation:

MOUNT ST. SCHOLASTICA, 801 S. 8th St., Atchison, Kans. 66002, (913) 360-6210, www.mountosb.org. Benedictine Sisters of Elk Co., ST. JOSEPH'S MONASTERY, St. Mary's, PA 15857, (814) 834-2267, www.osbnuns.org. Benedictine Sisters of Erie, 6101 E. Lake Rd., Erie, PA 16511, (814) 899- 0614, www.eriebenedictines.org. Benedictine Sisters of Chicago, ST. SCHOLASTICA PRIORY, 7430 N. Ridge Blvd., Chicago, IL 60645, (773) 764-2413, www.osbchicago.org. Benedictine Sisters of the Sacred Heart, 1910 Maple Ave., Lisle, IL 60532-2164, (630) 725-6000, www.shmlisle.org. Benedictine Sisters of Elizabeth, ST. WALBURGA MONASTERY, 851 N. Broad St., Elizabeth, NJ 07208-2593, (201) 352-4278, www.catholic-forum.com/bensisnj. Benedictine Sisters of Pittsburgh, 4530 Perrysville Ave., Pittsburgh, PA 15229, (412) 931-2844, www.osbpgh.org.

ST. JOSEPH'S MONASTERY, 2200 S. Lewis, Tulsa, OK 74114, (918) 742-4989, www.stjosephmonastery.org. ST. GERTRUDE'S MONASTERY, 14259 Benedictine Lane, Ridgely, MD 21660, (410) 634-2497. ST. WALBURGA MONASTERY, 2500 Amsterdam Rd., Villa Hills, KY 41017, (859) 331-6771, www.stwalburg.org. SACRED HEART MONASTERY, P.O. Box 2040, Cullman, AL 35056, (256) 734-4622, www.shmon. org. Benedictine Sisters of Virginia, 9535 Linton Hall Rd., Bristow, VA 20136-1217, (703) 361-0106, www.osbva.org. ST. SCHOLASTICA MONASTERY, 416 W. Highland Dr., Boerne, TX 78006, (830) 816-8504, www.boernebenedictines.com. ST. LUCY'S PRIORY, 19045 E. Sierra Madre Ave., Glendora, CA 91741, (626) 335-1682. Benedictine Sisters of Florida, HOLY NAME MONASTERY, P.O. Box 2450, St. Leo, FL 33574-2450, (352) 588-8320, www.floridabenedictines.com. BENET HILL MONASTERY, 2555 N. Chelton Rd., Colorado Springs, CO 80909, (719) 633-0655, www.benethillmonastery.org. QUEEN OF HEAVEN MONASTERY (Byzantine Rite), 169 Kenmore Ave., #305, Warren, OH 44483, (330) 856-1813, www.benedictinebyzantine.org. QUEEN OF ANGELS MONASTERY, 23615 N.E. 100th St., Liberty, MO 64068, (816) 750-4618.

• **Federation of St. Gertrude the Great** (1937). Office: St. Benedict of Ferdinand, Indiana, 802 E. 10th St., Ferdinand, IN 47532, (812) 367-1411, www.thedo me.org. Pres., Sister Kathryn Huber, O.S.B. Motherhouses belonging to the federation:

MOTHER OF GOD MONASTERY, 110 28th Ave., S.E., Watertown, SD 57201, (605) 882-6633, www.watertown benedictines. org. SACRED HEART MONASTERY, 1005 W. 8th St., Yankton, SD 57078-3389, (605) 668-6000, www. yank tonbenedictines.org. MT. ST. BENEDICT MONASTERY, 620 E. Summit Ave., Crookston, MN 56716, (218) 281-3441, www.msb.net. SACRED HEART MONASTERY, P.O. Box 364, Richardton, ND 58652, (701) 974-2121, www.

sacredheart monastery.com. ST. MARTIN MONASTERY, 1851 City Springs Rd., Rapid City, SD 57702-9613, (605) 343-8011, www.blackhillsbenedictine.com. MONASTERY OF IMMACULATE CONCEPTION, 802 E. 10th St., Ferdinand, IN 47532, (812) 367-2313. MONASTERY OF ST. GERTRUDE, 465 Keuterville Rd., Cottonwood, ID 83522-5183, (208) 962-3224, www.stgertrudes.org.

MONASTERY OF ST. BENEDICT CENTER, Box 5070, Madison, WI 53705-0070, (608) 836-1631, www.sbcenter.org. QUEEN OF ANGELS MONASTERY, 840 S. Main St., Mt. Angel, OR 97362, (503) 845-6141, www.benedictine-srs.org. ST. SCHOLASTICA MONASTERY, P.O. Box 3489, Fort Smith, AR 72913-3489, (479) 783-4147, www.stgcho.org. OUR LADY OF PEACE MONASTERY, 3710 W. Broadway, Columbia, MO 65203, (573) 446-2300, www.benedictinesister.org. QUEEN OF PEACE MONASTERY, Box 370, Belcourt, ND 58316, (701) 477-6167. OUR LADY OF GRACE MONASTERY, 1402 Southern Ave., Beech Grove, IN 46107, (317) 787-3287, www.benedictine.com. SPIRIT OF LIFE MONASTERY, 10760 W. Glennon Dr., Lakewood, CO 80226, (303) 986-9234. ST. BENEDICT'S MONASTERY 225 Masters Ave., Winnipeg, MB, R4A 2A1, Canada, (204) 338-4601, www.stbens.ca. THE DWELLING PLACE MONASTERY, 150 Mt. Tabor Rd., Martin, KY 41649, (606) 886-9624.

• **Federation of St. Benedict** (1947). Pres., Sister Colleen Haggerty, O.S.B., St. Benedict Convent, 104 Chapel Lane, St. Joseph, MN 56374-0220, (320) 363- 7100, www.sbm. osb.org. Motherhouses in U.S. belonging to the federation:

ST. BENEDICT'S CONVENT, St. Joseph, MN 56374, (320) 363-7013. ST. SCHOLASTICA MONASTERY, 1001 Kenwood Ave., Duluth, MN 55811-2300, (218) 723-7001, www.duluthbenedictines.org. ST. BEDE MONASTERY, 1190 Priory Rd., Eau Claire, WI 54702, (715) 834-3176, www.saintbede.org. ST. MARY MONASTERY, 2200 88th Ave. W., Rock Island, IL 61201, (309) 283-2101, www.smmsis ters.org; ANNUNCIATION MONASTERY, 7520 University Dr., Bismarck, ND 58504, (701) 255-1520, www.annunciation monastery.org. ST. PAUL'S MONASTERY, 2675 Larpenteur Ave. E., St. Paul, MN 55109, (651) 777-8181, www.osb.org/spm. ST. PLACID PRIORY, 500 College St. N.E., Lacey, WA 98516, (360) 438-1771, www.stplacid.org. MOUNT BENEDICT MONASTERY, 6000 South 1075 East, Ogden, UT 84405-4945, (801) 479-6030, www.mbutah.org.

Bethany, Sisters of, C.V.D.: Founded 1928, in El Salvador; in U.S. 1949. General motherhouse, Santa Tecla, El Salvador. U.S. address: 850 N. Hobart Blvd., Los Angeles, CA 90029, (213) 669-9411.

Bethlemita Sisters, Daughters of the Sacred Heart of Jesus (Beth.): Founded 1861, in Guatemala. Motherhouse, Bogota, Colombia. U.S. address, St. Joseph Residence, 330 W. Pembroke St., Dallas, TX 75208, (214) 948-3597.

Bon Secours, Congregation of, C.B.S.: Founded 1824, in France; in U.S., 1881. Generalate, Rome, Italy. U.S. provincial house, 1525 Marriottsville Rd., Marriottsville, MD 21104, (410) 442-1333, www.bonsecours.org. Hospital work.

Brigid, Congregation of St., C.S.B.: Founded 1807, in Ireland; in U.S., 1953. U.S. regional house, 5118 Loma Linda Dr., San Antonio, TX 78201, (210) 733-0701, www.brigidine.org.au.

Brigittine Sisters (Order of the Most Holy Savior), O.SS.S.: Founded 1344, at Vadstena, Sweden, by St. Bridget; in U.S., 1957. General motherhouse, Rome, Italy. U.S. address, Vikingsborg, 4 Runkenhage Rd., Darien, CT 06820, (203) 655-1068.

Canossian Daughters of Charity (Fd.C.C.): Founded 1808 in Verona, Italy, by St. Magdalen of Canossa. General motherhouse, Rome, Italy. U.S. provincial house, 5625 Isleta Blvd. S.W., Albuquerque, NM 87105, (505) 873-2854, www.fdcc.org.

Carmel, Congregation of Our Lady of Mount, O. Carm.: Founded 1825, in France; in U.S., 1833. Generalate, PO Box 476, Lacombe, LA 70445, (504) 882-7577, www. mountcarmel.home.mindspring.com. Education, social services, pastoral ministry, retreat work.

Carmel, Institute of Our Lady of Mount, O. Carm.: Founded 1854, in Italy; in U.S., 1947. General motherhouse, Rome, Italy. U.S. novitiate, 5 Wheatland St., Peabody, MA 01960, (978) 531-4733; www.carmeliteoreschool.com. Apostolic work.

Carmelite Community of the Word, C.C.W.: Motherhouse and novitiate, 394 Bem Rd., Gallitzin, PA 16641, (814) 886-4098 (fax).

Carmelite Nuns, Discalced, O.C.D.: Founded 1562, Spain. First foundation in U.S. in 1790, at Charles County, MD; this monastery was moved to Baltimore. Monasteries in U.S. are listed below by state.
Alabama: 716 Dauphin Island Pkwy., Mobile 36606, (334) 471-3991. Arkansas: 7201 W. 32nd St., Little Rock 72204, (501) 565-5121, www.littlerockcarmel.org. California: 215 E. Alhambra Rd., Alhambra 91801, (626) 282-2387, www.carmelites.org/teresacarmel; 27601 Highway 1, Carmel 93923, (831) 624-3043, www.carmelitesistersbythesea.net; 6981 Teresian Way, Georgetown 95634, (530) 333-1617; 5158 Hawley Blvd., San Diego 92116, (619) 280-5424, www.carmelsandiego.com; 721 Parker Ave., San Francisco 94118; 530 Blackstone Dr., San Rafael 94903, (415) 479-6872; 1000 Lincoln St., Santa Clara 95050-5285, (408) 296-8412, www.members.aol.com/ santaclaracarmel.
Colorado: 6138 S. Gallup St., Littleton 80120, (303) 798- 4176. Georgia: Coffee Bluff, 11 W. Back St., Savannah 31419, (912) 925-8505, www.savannahcarmel.org. Hawaii: 6301 Pali Hwy., Kaneohe 96744, (808) 261-6542; Illinois: 949 N. River Rd., Des Plaines 60016, (847) 298-4241. Indiana: 2500 Cold Spring Rd., Indianapolis 46222-2323, (317) 926-5654, www.praythenews.com; 59 Allendale Pl., Terre Haute 47802, (812) 299-1410; www.heartsawake.org. Iowa: 17937 250th St., Eldridge 52748, (319) 285-8387; 2901 S. Cecilia St., Sioux City 51106, (712) 276-1680. Kentucky: 1740 Newburg Rd., Louisville 40205, (502) 451- 6796. Louisiana: 1250 Carmel Ave., Lafayette 70501, (337) 232-4651; 73530 River Rd., Covington 70435, (985) 898-0923.
Maryland: 1318 Dulaney Valley Rd., Towson, Baltimore 21286, (410) 823-7415, www.geocities.com/ baltimorecarmel; 5678 Mt. Carmel Rd., La Plata, 20646, (301) 934-1654, www.carmelofporttobacco@erols.com. Massachusetts: 61 Mt. Pleasant Ave., Roxbury, Boston 02119, (617) 442-1411, www.carmelitesofboston.org; 15 Mt. Carmel Rd., Danvers 01923, (978) 774-3008. Michigan: 4300 Mt. Carmel Dr. NE, Ada 49301, (616) 691-7625; 35750 Moravian Dr., Clinton Township 48035, (586) 790-7255, www.rc.net/detroit/carmelite; U.S. 2 Highway N 4028, PO Box 397, Iron Mountain 49801, (906) 774-0561; 3501 Silver Lake Rd., Traverse City 49684, (231) 946-4960. Minnesota: 8251 De Montreville Trail N., Lake Elmo 55042-9547, (651) 777-3882. Mississippi: 2155 Terry Rd., Jackson 39204, (601) 373-1460.
Missouri: 2201 W. Main St., Jefferson City 65101, (573) 636-3364; 9150 Clayton Rd., Ladue, St. Louis Co. 63124, (314) 993-3494, www.stormpages.com/mtcarmel;

424 E. Monastery Rd., Springfield 65807, (417) 881-2115. Nevada: 1950 La Fond Dr., Reno 89509-3099, (775) 323-3236. New Hampshire: 275 Pleasant St., Concord, 03301-2590, (603) 225-5791. New Jersey: 26 Harmony School Rd., Flemington 08822-2606, www.flemingtoncarmel.org. ingtoncarmel.htm; 189 Madison Ave., Morristown 07960, (973) 538-2886. New Mexico: 49 Mt. Carmel Rd., Santa Fe 87505-0352, (505) 983-7232, carmelofsantafe.org. New York: c/o Chancery Office, Diocese of Brooklyn, 361 Highland Blvd., Brooklyn 11207, (718) 235- 0422; 89 Hiddenbrook Dr., Beacon, 12508, (914) 831-5572; 75 Carmel Rd., Buffalo 14214, (716) 837-6499; 1931 W. Jefferson Rd., Pittsford, NY 14534, (585) 427-7094, www. carmelitesofrochester.org.
Ohio: 3176 Fairmount Blvd., Cleveland Heights 44118, (216) 321-6568; www.clevelandcarmel.org. Oklahoma: 20000 N. County Line Rd., Piedmont 73078, (405) 348- 3947, www.okcarmel.org. Oregon: 87609 Green Hill Rd., Eugene 97402, (541) 345-8649. Pennsylvania: 1 Maria Hall Dr., Danville 17821, (570) 275-4682, www. carmelelysburg. org; 510 E. Gore Rd., Erie 16509-3799, (814) 825-0846, erieRDC.org/Carmelites.asp; 5206 Center Dr., Latrobe 15650, (724) 539-1056, www.latrobecarmel. org; P.O. Box 57, Loretto 15940-0057, (814) 472-8620, lorettocarmel.org; Byzantine Rite, 403 West County Rd., Sugarloaf 18249-9998, (570) 788-1205; 66th and Old York Rd., Philadelphia 19126, (215) 424-6143. Rhode Island: 25 Watson Ave., Barrington 02806, (401) 245-3421. South Dakota: 221 5th St., W., Alexandria, 57311, (605) 239-4382.
Texas: 600 Flowers Ave., Dallas 75211; 5801 Mt. Carmel Dr., Arlington 76017, (817) 468-1781; 1100 Parthenon Pl., Roman Forest, New Caney 77357-3276, (281) 399-0270, www.icansurf.com/ocdnewcaney; 6301 Culebra and St. Joseph Way, San Antonio 78238-4909, (210) 680-1834, www.carmelsanantonio.org. Utah: 5714 Holladay Blvd., Salt Lake City 84121, (801) 277-6075, www.carmelslc.org. Vermont: 94 Main St., Montpelier, 05601, (914) 831-5572. Washington: 2215 N.E. 147th St., Shoreline 98155, (206) 363-7150. Wisconsin: W267 N2517 Meadowbrook Rd., Pewaukee 53072, (262) 691-0336, www.geocities.com/ pewaukeecarmel.org; 6100 Pepper Rd., Denmark 54208, (920) 863-5055.

Carmelite Nuns of the Ancient Observance (Calced Carmelites), O. Carm.: Founded 1452, in the Netherlands; in U.S., 1930, from Naples, Italy, convent (founded 1856). U.S. monasteries: Carmelite Monastery of St. Therese and St. Mary Magdalen di Pazzi, 3551 Lanark Rd., Coopersburg, PA 18036, (610) 797-3721. Carmel of Mary, Wahpeton, ND 58075. Our Lady of Grace Monastery, 6202 CR 339 Via Maria, Christoval, TX 76935 (325) 853-1722. Carmel of the Sacred Heart, 430 Laurel Ave., Hudson, WI 54016, (715) 862-2156, www.carmelite-nuns. com. Papal enclosure.

Carmelite Sisters (Corpus Christi), O. Carm.: Founded 1908, in England; in U.S., 1920. General motherhouse, Tunapuna, Trinidad, W.I. U.S. address: Mt. Carmel Home, 412 W. 18th St., Kearney, NE 68845, (308) 237-2287, www.corpuschristicarmelites.org. Home and foreign mission work.

Carmelite Sisters for the Aged and Infirm, O. Carm.: Founded 1929, at New York, by Mother M. Angeline Teresa, O. Carm. Motherhouse, 600 Woods Rd., Avila-on-Hudson, Germantown, NY 12526, (518) 537-5000, www.carmelitesisters.com. Social work, nursing and educating in the field of gerontology.

Carmelite Sisters of Charity, C.a.Ch.: Founded 1826 at Vich, Spain, by St. Joaquina de Vedruna. Generalate, Rome, Italy. U.S. address, 701 Beacon Rd., Silver Spring, MD 20903, (301) 434-6344.

Carmelite Sisters of St. Therese of the Infant Jesus, C.S.T.: Founded 1917, in U.S. General mother house, 1300 Classen Dr., Oklahoma City, OK 73103, (405) 232-7926, www.oksister.com. Educational work.

Carmelite Sisters of the Divine Heart of Jesus, Carmel D.C.J.: Founded 1891, in Germany; in U.S., 1912. General motherhouse, Sittard Netherlands. U.S. provincial houses: Northern Province, 1230 Kavanaugh Pl., Milwaukee, WI 53213, (414) 453- 4040, www.carmelitedcjnorth.org. Central Province, 10341 Manchester Rd., St. Louis, MO 63122, (314) 965-7616, www.carmelitesdcj.org. South Western Province, 8585 La Mesa Blvd., La Mesa, CA 91941-3901, (619) 335-7265. Social services, mission work.

Carmelite Sisters of the Most Sacred Heart of Los Angeles, O.C.D.: Founded 1904, in Mexico. General mother house and novitiate, 920 E. Alhambra Rd., Alhambra, CA 91801-2799, (626) 289-1353, wwwcarmelmsh.org. Social services, retreat and educational work.

Carmelites, Calced, O. Carm.: Founded 1856 in Naples, Italy. U.S. address: Carmelite Monastery of St. Therese, 3551 Lanark Rd., Coopersburg, PA 18036.

Carmelites of St. Theresa, Congregation of Missionary, C.M.S.T.: Founded 1903, in Mexico. General motherhouse, Mexico City, Mexico. U.S. foundation, 9548 Deer Trail Dr., Houston, TX 77038, (281) 445-5520.

Casimir, Sisters of St., S.S.C.: Founded 1907, in U.S., by Mother Maria Kaupas. General motherhouse, 2601 W. Marquette Rd., Chicago, IL 60629, (773) 776- 1324. Education, missions, social services.

Cenacle, Congregation of Our Lady of the Retreat in the, R.C.: Founded 1826, in France; in U.S., 1892. Generalate, Rome, Italy. Eastern Province, Cenacle Rd., Lake Ronkonkoma, NY 11779, (516) 471-6270. Midwestern Province, 513 W. Fullerton Pkwy., Chicago, IL 60614-6428, (773) 528-6300, www.cenaclesisters.org.

Charity, Daughters of Divine, F.D.C.: Founded 1868, at Vienna, Austria; in U.S., 1913. General moth erhouse, Rome, Italy. U.S. province: 205 Major Ave., Staten Island, NY 10305, (718) 720-4377, www.godslovefdc.org. Education, social services.

Charity, Missionaries of, M.C.: Founded 1950, in Calcutta, India, by Mother Teresa; first U.S. foundation, 1971. General motherhouse, 54A, A.J.C. Bose Rd., Calcutta 700016, India. U.S. address, 335 E. 145th St., Bronx, NY 10451, (718) 292-0019. Service of the poor.

Charity, Religious Sisters of, R.S.C.: Founded 1815, in Ireland; in U.S., 1953. Motherhouse, Dublin, Ireland. U.S. headquarters, 10668 St. James Dr., Culver City, CA 90230, (310) 559-1654.

Charity, Sisters of (of Seton Hill), S.C.: Founded 1870, at Altoona, PA, from Cincinnati foundation. Generalate, De Paul Center, 463 Mt. Thor Rd., Greensburg, PA 15601, (724) 836-0406, www.scsh.org. Educational, hospital, social, for eign mission work.

Charity, Sisters of (Grey Nuns of Montréal), S.G.M.: Founded 1737, in Canada, by St. Marie Marguerite d'Youville; in U.S., 1855. General administration, Montréal, QC H2Y 2L7, Canada. U.S. provincial house, 10 Pelham Rd., Ste. 1000, Lexington, MA 02421, (781) 674-7407, www.sqmlex.org.

Charity, Sisters of (of Leavenworth), S.C.L.: Founded 1858, in U.S. Motherhouse, 4200 S. 4th St., Leavenworth,

KS 66048, (913) 758-6508, www.scls.org/.

Charity, Sisters of (of Nazareth), S.C.N.: Founded 1812, in U.S. General motherhouse, SCN Center, P.O. Box 172, Nazareth, KY 40048, (502) 348-1561; 8200 McKnight Rd., Pittsburgh, PA 15237, (412) 364-3000, www.scnazareth.org. Education, health services. Merged with the Vincentian Sisters of Charity in Nov. 2008.

Charity, Sisters of (of St. Augustine), C.S.A.: Founded 1851, at Cleveland, Ohio. Motherhouse, 5232 Broadview Rd., Richfield, OH 44286, (330) 659-5100, www.srsofcharity.org.

Charity, Sisters of Christian, S.C.C.: Founded 1849, in Paderborn, Germany, by Bl. Pauline von Mallinckrodt; in U.S., 1873. Generalate, Rome, Italy. U.S. provinces: Mallinckrodt Convent, 350 Bernardsville Rd., Mendham, NJ 07945, (973) 543-6528, www.scceast.org. 2041 Elmwood Ave., Wilmette, IL 60091-1431, (847) 920-9341, www.sccwilmette.org. Education, health services, other apostolic work.

Charity, Vincentian Sisters of, V.S.C.: Founded 1928, at Bedford, Ohio. General motherhouse, 1160 Broadway, Bedford, OH 44146, (440) 232-4755.

Charity of Cincinnati, Ohio, Sisters of, S.C.: Founded 1809; became independent community, 1852. General motherhouse, 5900 Delhi Rd., Mt. St. Joseph, OH 45051, (513) 347-5201, www.srcharitycinti.org. Educational, hospital, social work.

Charity of Ottawa, Sisters of (Grey Nuns of the Cross), S.C.O.: Founded 1845, at Ottawa, Canada; in U.S., 1857. General motherhouse, Ottawa, Canada. U.S. provincial house, 559 Fletcher St., Lowell, MA 01854, (978) 453-4993. Educational, hospital work, extended health care.

Charity of Our Lady, Mother of Mercy, Sisters of, S.C.M.M.: Founded 1832, in Holland; in U.S., 1874. General motherhouse, Den Bosch, the Netherlands. U.S. provincialate, 520 Thompson Ave., East Haven, CT 06512, (203) 469-7872.

Charity of Our Lady, Mother of the Church, S.C.M.C: U.S. foundation, 1970. General mother house, 520 Thompson Ave., East Haven, CT 06512, (203) 469-7872.

Charity of Our Lady of Mercy, Sisters of, O.L.M.: Founded 1829, in Charleston, SC. Generalate and motherhouse, 424 Fort Johnson Rd., P. O. Box 12410, Charleston, SC 29422, (843) 795-6083. Education, campus ministry, social services.

Charity of Quebec, Sisters of (Grey Nuns), S.C.Q.: Founded 1849, at Quebec; in U.S., 1890. General motherhouse, 2655 Le Pelletier St., Beauport, QC GIC 3X7, Canada. U.S. address, 359 Summer St., New Bedford, MA 02740, (508) 996-6751. Social work.

Charity of Saint Elizabeth, Sisters of (Convent Station, N.J.), S.C.: Founded 1859, at Newark, NJ. General motherhouse, P.O. Box 476, Convent Station, NJ 07961-0476, (973) 290-5450, www.scnj.org. Education, pastoral ministry, social services.

Charity of St. Hyacinthe, Sisters of (Grey Nuns), S.C.S.H.: Founded 1840, at St. Hyacinthe, Canada; in U.S., 1878. General motherhouse, 16470 Avenue Bourdages, SUD, St. Hyacinthe, QC J2T 4J8, Canada. U.S. regional house, 98 Campus Ave., Lewiston, ME 04240, (207) 797-8607.

Charity of St. Joan Antida, Sisters of, S.C.S.J.A.: Founded 1799, in France; in U.S., 1932. General moth erhouse, Rome, Italy. U.S. provincial house, 8560 N. 76th

Pl., Milwaukee, WI 53223, (414) 354-9233, www.scsja.org.

Charity of St. Louis, Sisters of, S.C.S.L.: Founded 1803, in France; in U.S., 1910. Generalate, Rome, Italy. U.S. provincialate, 60 Club Rd., Unit 204, Plattsburgh, NY 12901, (518) 563-7410.

Charity of St. Vincent de Paul, Daughters of, D.C.: Founded 1633, in France; in U.S., 1809, at Emmitsburg, MD, by St. Elizabeth Ann Seton. General motherhouse, Paris, France. U.S. provinces: 333 South Seton Ave., Emmitsburg, MD 21727, (301) 447-2900, www.daughtersofcharity- emmitsburg.org. 7800 Natural Bridge Rd., St. Louis, MO 63121, (314) 382-2800. 9400 New Harmony Rd., Evansville, IN 47720-8912, (812) 963-3341, www.doc-ecp.org. 96 Menands Rd., Albany, NY 12204, (518) 462-5593, www.dc- northeast.org. 26000 Altamont Rd., Los Altos Hills, CA 94022, (650) 949-8865, www.daughtersofcharity.com.

Charity of St. Vincent de Paul, Sisters of, V.Z.: Founded 1845, in Croatia. in U.S., 1955. General motherhouse, Zagreb, Croatia; U.S. foundation, 171 Knox Ave., West Seneca, NY 14224, (716) 825-5859.

Charity of St. Vincent de Paul, Sisters of, Halifax, S.C.: Founded 1856, at Halifax, NS, from Emmitsburg foundation. Generalate, Mt. St. Vincent, Halifax, NS, Canada. U.S. addresses: Commonwealth of Massachusetts, 125 Oakland St., Wellesley Hills, MA 02481-5338, (781) 997-1165, www.schalifax.ca. Boston Province, 26 Phipps St., Quincy, MA 02169, (617) 773-6085. New York Province, 85-10 61st Rd., Rezo Park, NY 11374, (718) 651-1684. Educational, hospital, social work.

Charity of St. Vincent de Paul, Sisters of, New York, SC.: Founded 1817, from Emmitsburg foundation. General motherhouse, Mt. St. Vincent on Hudson, 6301 Riverdale Ave., Bronx, NY 10471, (718) 549-9200, www.scny.org. Educational, hospital work.

Charity of the Blessed Virgin Mary, Sisters of, B.V.M.: Founded 1833, in U.S. by Mary Frances Clarke. General motherhouse, BVM Center, 1100 Carmel Dr., Dubuque, IA 52003, (563) 588-2351, www.bvmcong.com. Education, pastoral ministry, social services.

Charity of the Immaculate Conception of Ivrea, Sisters of, S.C.I.C.: Founded 18th century, in Italy; in U.S., 1961. General motherhouse, Rome, Italy. U.S. address, Immaculate Virgin of Miracles Convent, 268 Prittstown Rd., Mt. Pleasant, PA 15666, (724) 887-6753.

Charity of the Incarnate Word, Congregation of the Sisters of, C.C.V.I.: Founded 1869, at San Antonio, TX, by Bp. C. M. Dubuis. Generalate, 3200 McCullough, San Antonio, TX 78212, (210) 734-8310, www.incarnatewordsisters.org.

Charity of the Incarnate Word, Congregation of the Sisters of (Houston, TX), C.C.V.I.: Founded 1866, in U.S., by Bp. C. M. Dubuis. General motherhouse, P.O. Box 230969, Houston, TX 77223, (713) 928-6053. Educational, hospital, social work.

Charity of the Sacred Heart, Daughters of, F.C.S.C.J.: Founded 1823, at La Salle de Vihiers, France; in U.S., 1905. General motherhouse, La Salle de Vihiers, France. U.S. address, Sacred Heart Province, 226 Grove St., PO Box 642, Littleton, NH 03561, (603) 444-3970.

Charles Borromeo, Missionary Sisters of St. (Scalabrini Srs.): Founded 1895, in Italy; in U.S., 1941. American novitiate, 1414 N. 37th Ave., Melrose Park, IL 60160; (708) 343-2162.

Child Jesus, Sisters of the Poor, P.C.J.: Founded

1844, at Aix-la-Chapelle, Germany; in U.S., 1924. General motherhouse, Simpelveld, the Netherlands. American provincialate, 4567 Olentangy River Rd., Columbus, OH 43214, (614) 459-8285; www.ourladyofbethlehem.org.

Chretienne, Sisters of Ste., S.S.Ch.: Founded 1807, in France; in U.S., 1903. General motherhouse, Metz, France. U.S. provincial house, 297 Arnold St., Wrentham, MA 02093, (508) 384-8066, www.sistersofstchretienne.org. Educational, hospital, mission work.

Christ the King, Missionary Sisters of, M.S.C.K.: Founded 1959 in Poland; in U.S., 1978. General moth erhouse, Poznan, Poland. U.S. address, 3000 18-Mile Rd., Sterling Heights, MI 48314.

Christ the King, Sister Servants of, S.S.C.K.: Founded 1936, in U.S. General motherhouse, Loretto Convent, N8114 Calvary St., Mt. Calvary, WI 53057, (920) 753-3211. Social services.

Christian Doctrine, Sisters of Our Lady of, R.C.D.: Founded 1910, in New York. Marydell Convent, 110 Larchdale Ave., Nyack, NY 10960; (845) 727-1011.

Christian Education, Religious of, R.C.E.: Founded 1817, in France; in U.S., 1905. General motherhouse, France. U.S. provincial residence, 55 Parkwood Dr., Milton, MA 02186, (617) 696-7732, www.holyunionsisters.org.

Cistercian Nuns, O. Cist.: Headquarters, Rome, Italy. U.S. address, Valley of Our Lady Monastery, E. 11096 Yanke Dr., Prairie du Sac, WI 53578, www.nunocist.org.

Cistercian Nuns of the Strict Observance, Order of, O.C.S.O.: Founded 1125, in France, by St. Stephen Harding; in U.S., 1949. U.S. addresses: MT. ST. MARY'S ABBEY, 300 Arnold St., Wrentham, MA 02093, (508) 528-1282, www.msmabbey.org. 14200 E Fish Canyon Rd., Sonoita, AZ 85637, (520) 455-5595, www.santaritabbey.org. OUR LADY OF THE REDWOODS ABBEY, 18104 Briceland Thorn Rd., Whitethorn, CA 95589, (707) 986-7419, www.redwoodsabbey.org. OUR LADY OF THE MISSISSIPPI ABBEY, 8400 Abbey Hill Rd., Dubuque, IA 52003, (563) 582-2595, www.mis sissippiabbey.org/. OUR LADY OF THE ANGELS MONASTERY, 3365 Monastery Dr., Crozet, VA 22932, (434) 823-1452, www.olamonastery.org.

Clare, Sisters of St., O.S.C.: General motherhouse, Dublin, Ireland. U.S. foundation, St. Francis Convent, 1974 Cherrywood St., Vista, CA 92083, (760) 945-8040.

Claretian Missionary Sisters (Religious of Mary Immaculate), R.M.I.: Founded 1855, in Cuba; in U.S., 1956. Generalate, Rome, Italy. U.S. address, 7080 SW 99 Ave., Miami, FL 33173, (305) 274-5695 (fax), www.claretiansisters.org.

Clergy, Congregation of Our Lady, Help of the, C.L.H.C.: Founded 1961, in U.S. Motherhouse, Maryvale Convent, 2522 June Bug Rd., Vale, NC 28168, (704) 276-2626.

Clergy, Servants of Our Lady Queen of the, S.R.C.: Founded 1929, in Canada; in U.S., 1934. General mother house, 57 Jules A. Brillant, Rimouski, QC G5L 1X1 Canada, (418) 724-0508. Domestic work.

Colettines: *See* **Franciscan Poor Clare Nuns**.

Columban, Missionary Sisters of St., S.S.C.: Founded 1922, in Ireland; in U.S., 1930. General motherhouse, Wicklow, Ireland. U.S. region, 73 Mapleton St., Brighton, MA 02135, (617) 782-5683.

Comboni Missionary Sisters (Missionary Sisters of Verona), C.M.S.: Founded 1872, in Italy; in U.S., 1950. U.S. address, 5405 Loch-Raven Blvd., Baltimore, MD

21239, (410) 323-1469, www.combonisrs.com.

Consolata Missionary Sisters, M.C.: Founded 1910, in Italy, by Bl. Giuseppe Allamano; in U.S., 1954. General motherhouse, Turin, Italy. U.S. headquarters, 6801 Belmont Rd., P.O. Box 97, Belmont, MI 49306 (616) 361-9609, www.consolatasisters.org.

Cross, Daughters of the, D.C.: Founded 1640, in France; in U.S., 1855. General motherhouse, 411 E. Flournoy-Lucas Rd., Shreveport, LA 71115, (318) 797-0887. Educational work.

Cross, Daughters of, of Liege, F.C.: Founded 1833, in Liege, Belgium; in U.S., 1958. U.S. address, 165 W. Eaton Ave., Tracy, CA 95376.

Cross, Sisters of the Holy, C.S.C.: Founded 1841, at Le Mans, France; established in Canada, 1847; in U.S., 1881. General motherhouse, St. Laurent, Montreal, QC, Canada. U.S. regional office, 377 Island Pond Rd., Manchester, NH 03109, (603) 622-9504. Educational work.

Cross, Sisters of the Holy, Congregation of, C.S.C.: Founded 1841, at Le Mans, France; in U.S., 1843. General motherhouse, 101 Bertrand Hall – Saint Mary's, Notre Dame, IN 46556, (574) 384-5572, www.cscsisters.org. Education, health care, social services, pastoral ministry.

Cross and Passion, Sisters of the (Passionist Sisters), C.P.: Founded 1852; in U.S., 1924. Generalate, Northampton, England. U.S. address: Holy Family Convent, One Wright Lane, N. Kingstown, RI 02852, (401) 294-3554; www.passionistsisters.org.

Cyril and Methodius, Sisters of Sts., SS.C.M.: Founded 1909, in U.S., by Rev. Matthew Jankola. General mother house, Villa Sacred Heart, Danville, PA 17821, (570) 275-4929, www.sscm.org. Education, care of aged.

Disciples of the Lord Jesus Christ, D.L.J.C.: Founded 1972; canonically erected 1991. P.O. Box 17, Channing, TX 79018, (806) 534-2312, www.dljc.org.

Divine Compassion, Sisters of, R.D.C.: Founded 1886, in U.S. General motherhouse, 52 N. Broadway, White Plains, NY 10603, (914) 949-2950. Education, other ministries.

Divine Love, Daughters of, D.D.L.: Founded 1969, in Nigeria; in U.S., 1990. General house, Enugu, Nigeria. U.S. regional house, 2601 N. Sayre Ave., Chicago, IL 60707, (773) 622-2434.

Divine Spirit, Congregation of the, C.D.S.: Founded 1956, in U.S., by Archbishop John M. Gannon. Motherhouse, 409 W. 6th St., Erie, PA 16507, (330) 453-8137. Education, social services.

Divine Zeal, Daughters of, F.D.Z.: Founded 1887 in Italy by Bl. Hannibal Maria DiFrancia; in U.S., 1951. Generalate, Rome. U.S. headquarters, Hannibal House Spiritual Center, 1526 Hill Rd., Reading, PA 19602, (610) 375-1738.

Dominicans

Dominican Nuns: Nuns of the Order of Preachers, O.P.: Founded 1206 by St. Dominic at Prouille, France. Cloistered, contemplative. Two branches in the United States:

• **Dominican Nuns having Perpetual Adoration.** First monastery established 1880, in Newark, NJ, from Oullins, France, foundation (1868). Autonomous monasteries:

ST. DOMINIC'S MONASTERY 2636 Monastery Rd., Linden, VA 22642, (540) 635-3259, www.lindenopnuns.org; CORPUS CHRISTI MONASTERY, 1230 Lafayette Ave., Bronx, NY 10474, (718) 328-6996. BLESSED SACRAMENT, 29575 Middlebelt Rd., Farmington Hills, MI 48334-2311,

(248) 626-8321, www.opnuns-fh.org. MONASTERY OF THE ANGELS, 1977 Carmen Ave., Los Angeles, CA 90068-4098, (323) 466-2186, www.op-stjoseph.org/ nuns/angels/. CORPUS CHRISTI MONASTERY, 215 Oak Grove Ave., Menlo Park, CA 94025-3272, (650) 322-1801, www.nunsmenlo. org. INFANT JESUS, 1501 Lotus Lane, Lufkin, TX 75904-2699, (936) 634-4233, www.lufkintxnuns.org.

Dominican Nuns devoted to the Perpetual Rosary. First monastery established 1891, in Union City, NJ, from Calais, France, foundation (1880). Autonomous monasteries (some also observe Perpetual Adoration):

DOMINICAN NUNS OF PERPETUAL ROSARY, 605 14th and West Sts., Union City, NJ 07087, (201)866-7004. 217 N. 68th St., Milwaukee, WI 53213, (414) 258-0579, www.dsopr.org. PERPETUAL ROSARY, 1500 Haddon Ave., Camden, NJ 08103, (856) 342-8340. OUR LADY OF THE ROSARY, 335 Doat St., Buffalo, NY 14211. OUR LADY OF THE ROSARY, 543 Spingfield Ave., Summit, NJ 07901, (908) 273-1228, www.op.org/nunsopsummit. MONASTERY OF THE MOTHER OF GOD, 1430 Riverdale St., W. Springfield, MA 01089-4698, (413) 736-3639, www.op- stjoseph.org/nuns/ ws. DOMINICAN MONASTERY OF THE PERPETUAL ROSARY, 802 Court St., Syracuse, NY 13208- 1766. MONASTERY OF THE IMMACULATE HEART OF MARY, 1834 Lititz Pike, Lancaster, PA 17601-6585, (717) 569-2104. MARY THE QUEEN, 1310 W. Church St., Elmira, NY 14905, (607) 734-9506, www.oporg/maryqueen. ST. JUDE, P.O. Box 170, Marbury, AL 36051-0170, (205) 755-1322, www. stjude monastery.org. OUR LADY OF GRACE MONASTERY, 11 Race Hill Rd., North Guilford, CT 06437, (203) 345-0599, www.ourladyofgracemonastery.org. ST. DOMINIC'S MONASTERY, 4901 16th St. N.W., Washington, DC 20011, (202) 726-2107.

Dominican Sisters of Charity of the Presentation, O.P.: Founded 1696, in France; in U.S., 1906. General mother house, Tours, France. U.S. headquarters, 3012 Elm St., Dighton, MA 02715, (508) 669-5425, www. dominicansister softhepresentation.org. Hospital work.

Dominican Sisters of Hope, O.P.: Formed 1995 through merger of Dominican Sisters of the Most Holy Rosary, Newburgh, NY, Dominican Sisters of the Sick Poor, Ossining, NY, and Dominican Sisters of St. Catherine of Siena, Fall River, MA. General Offices: 299 N. Highland Ave., Ossining, NY 10562, (914) 941-4420, www.ophope.org.

Dominican Sisters of Our Lady of the Rosary and of St. Catherine of Siena (Cabra): Founded 1644 in Ireland. General motherhouse, Cabra, Dublin, Ireland. U.S. regional house, 1930 Robert E. Lee Rd., New Orleans, LA 70122, (504) 288-1593.

Dominican Sisters of Peace, O.P.: Founded in 2009 through the merger of seven Dominican communities: Eucharistic Missionaries of St. Dominic, 3801 Canal St., Suite 400, New Orleans, LA 70119, (504) 486-1133, www.emdsisters.org. St. Rose of Lima, 775 Drahner Rd., #124, Oxford, MI 48371, (248) 628-2872, www. domlife.org. St. Mary, 7300 St. Charles Ave., New Orleans, LA 70118, (504) 861-8183, www.dominican-sisters.net/stmarys; Dominican Sisters of Great Bend, 3600 Broadway, Great Bend, KS 67530, (316) 792-1232, www.ksdom.org. St. Mary of the Springs, 2320 Airport Dr., Columbus, OH 43219- 2098, (614) 416-1038, www. oppeace.org; St. Catherine of Siena, 2645 Bardstown Rd., St. Catharine, KY 40061, (606) 336-9303, www. opkentucky.org. Immaculate Heart of Mary, 1929. 1230 W. Market St., Akron, OH 44313-7108, (330) 836-4908, www.akrondominicans.org.

Dominican Sisters of the Perpetual Rosary, O.P.: 217 N. 68th St., Milwaukee, WI 53213, (414) 258-0579; www.dsopr.org. Cloistered, contemplative.

Dominican Sisters of the Roman Congregation of St. Dominic, O.P.: Founded 1621, in France; in U.S., 1904. General motherhouse, Rome, Italy. U.S. province, 123 Dumont Ave., Lewiston, ME 04240, (207) 786-5058; www.crsdop.org. Educational work.

Religious Missionaries of St. Dominic, O.P.: General motherhouse, Rome, Italy. U.S. address (Spanish province), 2237 Waldron Rd., Corpus Christi, TX 78418, (361) 939-8102.

Sisters of St. Dominic, O.P.: Names of congregations are given below, followed by the date of foundation, and location of motherhouse. Most Holy Rosary, 1847. Sinsinawa, WI 53824, (608) 748-4411. Most Holy Name of Jesus, 1850. 1520 Grand Ave., San Rafael, CA 94901, (415) 453-8303, www.sanrafaelop.org. Holy Cross, 1853. 555 Albany Ave., Amityville, NY 11701, (631) 842-6000, www.amityvilleop. org. St. Cecilia, 1860. 801 Dominican Dr., Nashville, TN 37228, (615) 256-5486, www.nashville-dominican.org.

St. Catherine of Siena, 1862. 5635 Erie St., Racine, WI 53402, (262) 639-4100, www.racinedominicans.org. Sacred Heart Convent, 1873. 1237 W. Monroe St., Springfield, IL 62704, (217) 787-0481, www.springfieldop.org. Sisters of Our Lady of the Rosary, Dominican Convent, 175 Route 340, Sparkill, NY 10976, (845) 359-4088, www.sparkill.org. Dominican Sisters of Mission San Jose,. 43326 Mission Blvd., Mission San Jose, CA 94539, (510) 657-2468, www. msjdominicans.org. Most Holy Rosary, 1892. 1257 Siena Heights Dr., Adrian, MI 49221, (517) 266-3570.

Our Lady of the Sacred Heart, 1877. 2025 E. Fulton St., Grand Rapids, MI 49503, (616) 643-0130. St. Dominic, 1878. 496 Western Hwy., Blauvelt, NY 10913, (845) 359-0696, www.opblauvelt.org. St. Catherine de Ricci, 1880. 131 Copley Rd., Upper Darby, PA 19082, (215) 635-6027. Sisters of St. Dominic, 1881. 1 Ryerson Ave., Caldwell, NJ 07006, (973) 403-3331, www.caldwellop.org. Dominican Sisters of Houston, 1882. 6501 Almeda Rd., Houston, TX 77021-2095, (713) 747-3310, www.houstonop.org. Tacoma Dominican Center, 1888. 935 Fawcett Ave., Tacoma, WA 98402, (253) 272-9688.

St. Rose of Lima (Servants of Relief for Incurable Cancer) 1896. 600 Linda Ave., Hawthorne, NY 10532, (914) 769- 0114, www.hawthorne-dominicans.org. St. Catherine of Siena of Kenosha, 119 Brooks St., Taos, NM 87571, (575) 751-1237. Immaculate Conception, 1929. 9000 W. 81st St., Justice, IL 60458, (708) 458-3040.

Dominican Sisters of Oakford (St. Catherine of Siena), 1889. Motherhouse, Oakford, Natal, South Africa; U.S. regional house, 1965. 980 Woodland Ave., San Leandro, CA 94577, (510) 638-2822.

Dorothy, Institute of the Sisters of St., S.S.D.: Founded 1834, in Italy, by St. Paola Frassinetti; in U.S., 1911. General motherhouse, Rome, Italy. U.S. provincialate, St. Dorothy Convent, 1305 Hylan Blvd., Si, NY, 10305; (718) 987-2604.

Eucharist, Religious of the, R.E.: Founded 1857, in Belgium; in U.S., 1900. General motherhouse, Belgium. U.S. foundation, 2907 Ellicott Terr., N.W., Washington, DC 20008, (202) 966-3111.

Felix, Congregation of the Sisters of St. (Felician Sisters), C.S.S.F.: Founded 1855, in Poland by Bl. Mary Angela Truszkowska; in U.S., 1874. General motherhouse, Rome,

Italy. U.S. provinces: 36800 Schoolcraft Rd., Livonia, MI 48150, (734) 591-1730, www.feliciansisters.org. 600 Doat St., Buffalo, NY 14211, (716) 892-4141, www.cssbuffalo. org. 3800 W. Peterson Ave., Chicago, IL 60659-3116, (773) 463-3020, www.felicianschicago.org. 871 Mercer Rd., Beaver Falls, PA 15010, (724) 384-5302, www.feliciansistersna.org; 1500 Woodcrest Ave., Coraopolis, PA 15108, (412) 264- 2890, www.felicianspa.org. 1315 Enfield St., Enfield, CT 06082, (860) 745-7791. 4210 Meadowlark Lane, S.E., Rio Rancho, NM 87124-1021, (505) 892-8862; southwestfeliciansisters.org.

Filippini, Religious Teachers, M.P.F.: Founded 1692, in Italy; in U.S., 1910. General motherhouse, Rome, Italy. U.S. provinces: St. Lucy Filippini Province, Villa Walsh, Morristown, NJ 07960, (973) 538-2886. Queen of Apostles Province, 474 East Rd., Bristol, CT 06010, (860) 584-2138, www.queenofapostles.com. Educational work.

Francis de Sales, Oblate Sisters of St., O.S.F.S.: Founded 1866, in France; in U.S., 1951. General motherhouse, Troyes, France. U.S. headquarters, Villa Aviat Convent, 399 Childs Rd., MD 21916, (410) 398-3699; (410) 398-3699. Educational, social work.

Franciscans

Bernardine Sisters of the Third Order of St. Francis, O.S.F.: Founded 1457, at Cracow, Poland; in U.S., 1894. Generalate, 450 St. Bernardine St., Reading, PA 19607; (484) 334-6976; www.bfrancis can.org. Educational, hospital, social work.

Capuchin Poor Clares, O.S.C. Cap: U.S. establishment, 1981, Amarillo diocese. Convent of the Blessed Sacrament and Our Lady of Guadalupe, 4201 N.E. 18th St., Amarillo, TX 79107, (806) 383-9877. Cloistered.

Congregation of the Servants of the Holy Child Jesus, O.S.F.: Founded 1855, in Germany; in U.S., 1929. General motherhouse, Würzburg, Germany. American motherhouse, Villa Maria, 641 Somerset St., North Plainfield, NJ 07060-4909, (908) 757-3050.

Congregation of the Third Order of St. Francis of Mary Immaculate, O.S.F.: Founded 1865, in U.S., by Fr. Pamphilus da Magliano, O.F.M. General mother house, 520 Plainfield Ave., Joliet, IL 60435, (815) 727-3686. Educational and pastoral work.

Daughters of St. Francis of Assisi, D.S.F.: Founded 1894, in Hungary; in U.S., 1946. Provincial mother house, 507 N. Prairie St., Lacon, IL 61540, (309) 246- 2175. Nursing, CCD work.

Eucharistic Franciscan Missionary Sisters, E.F.M.S.: Founded 1943, in Mexico. Motherhouse, 943 S. Soto St., Los Angeles, CA 90023, (323) 264-6556.

Franciscan Handmaids of the Most Pure Heart of Mary, F.H.M.: Founded 1916, in U.S. General moth erhouse, 15 W. 124th St., New York, NY 10027-5634, (212) 289-5655. Educational, social work.

Franciscan Hospitaller Sisters of the Immaculate Conception, F.H.I.C.: Founded 1876, in Portugal; in U.S., 1960. General motherhouse, Lisbon, Portugal. U.S. novitiate, 300 S. 17th St., San Jose, CA 95112, (408) 998-3407.

Franciscan Missionaries of Mary, F.M.M.: Founded 1877, in India; in U.S., 1904. General motherhouse, Rome, Italy. U.S. provincialate, 3305 Wallace Ave., Bronx, NY 10467, (718) 547-4693, www.fmmusa.org. Mission work.

Franciscan Missionaries of Our Lady, O.S.F.: Founded 1854, at Calais, France; in U.S., 1913. General motherhouse, Desvres, France. U.S. provincial house, 4200 Essen Lane, Baton Rouge, LA 70809, (225) 926-1627. Hospital work.

Franciscan Missionaries of St. Joseph (Mill Hill Sisters), F.M.S.J.: Founded 1883, at Rochdale, Lancashire, England; in U.S., 1952. Generalate, Manchester, England. U.S. head quarters, Franciscan House, 1006 Madison Ave., Albany, NY 12208, (518) 482-1991.

Franciscan Missionary Sisters for Africa, O.S.F.: American foundation, 1953. Generalate, Ireland. U.S. headquarters, 172 Foster St., Brighton, MA 02135, (617) 254-4343.

Franciscan Missionary Sisters of Assisi, F.M.S.A.: First foundation in U.S., 1961. General motherhouse, Assisi, Italy. U.S. address, St. Francis Convent, 1039 Northampton St., Holyoke, MA 01040, (413) 532-8156; www.sistersofassisi.org.

Franciscan Missionary Sisters of Our Lady of Sorrows, O.S.F.: Founded 1939, in China, by Bishop Rafael Palazzi, O.F.M.; in U.S., 1949. 3600 S.W. 170th Ave., Beaverton, OR 97006, (503) 649-7127. Educational, social, domestic, retreat and foreign mission work.

Franciscan Missionary Sisters of the Divine Child, F.M.D.C.: Founded 1927, at Buffalo, NY, by Bishop William Turner. General motherhouse, 6380 Main St., Williamsville, NY 14221, (716) 632-3144. Educational, social work.

Franciscan Missionary Sisters of the Infant Jesus, F.M.I.J.: Founded 1879, in Italy; in U.S., 1961. Generalate, Rome, Italy. U.S. provincialate, 1215 Kresson Rd., Cherry Hill, NJ 08003, (609) 428-8834.

Franciscan Missionary Sisters of the Sacred Heart, F.M.S.C.: Founded 1860, in Italy; in U.S., 1865. Generalate, Rome, Italy. U.S. provincialate, 250 South St., Peekskill, NY 10566-4419, (914) 737-5409, www.fmsc.org. Educational and social welfare apostolates.

Franciscan Poor Clare Nuns (Poor Clares, Order of St. Clare, Poor Clares of St. Colette), P.C., O.S.C., P.C.C.: Founded 1212, at Assisi, Italy, by St. Francis of Assisi; in U.S., 1875. Proto-monastery, Assisi, Italy. Addresses of autonomous motherhouses in U.S. are listed below.

8650 Russell Ave., S., Minneapolis, MN 55431, (952) 881-4766, www.poorclare.com. 3626 N. 65th Ave., Omaha, NE 68104-3299, (402) 558-4916, www.oma-hapoorclare.org. 720 Henry Clay Ave., New Orleans, LA 70118-5891, (504) 895-2019, www.poorclarenuns. com. 6825 Nurrenbern Rd., Evansville, IN 47712-8518, (812) 425-4396, www.poorclare.org. 1310 Dellwood Ave., Memphis, TN 38127-6399, (901) 357-6662, www.poor-clare.org/memphis. 920 Centre St., Jamaica Plain, MA 02130-3099, (617) 524-1760, www.stanthonyshrine.org/ poorclares. 327 S. Broad St., Trenton, NJ 08608, (609) 392-7673. 1271 Langhorne- Newtown Rd., Langhorne, PA 19047-1297, (215) 968-5775. 4419 N. Hawthorne St., Spokane, WA 99205, (509) 327- 4479, www.calledbyjoy. com. 86 Mayflower Ave., New Rochelle, NY, 10801-1615, (914) 632-5227, www.poorclaresny.com. 421 S. 4th St., Sauk Rapids, MN 56379-1898, (612) 251-3556. 3501 Rocky River Dr., Cleveland, OH 44111, (216) 941-2821.

1671 Pleasant Valley Rd., Aptos, CA 95001, (831) 761- 9659. 2111 S. Main St., Rockford, IL 61102, (815) 963-7343, www.poorclare.org/rockford. 215 E. Los Olivos St., Santa Barbara, CA 93105-3605, (805) 682-7670, www. poorclaressantabarbara.org. 445 River Rd., Andover, MA 01810, (978) 683-7599. 809 E. 19th St., Roswell, NM 88201-7514, (575) 622-0868, www.poorclares-roswell.org. 28210 Natoma Rd., Los Altos Hills, CA 94022, (650) 948-2947, www.chcweb. com. 37 McCauley Rd., Travelers

Rest, SC 29690 (864) 834-8015. 5500 Holly Fork Rd., Barhamsville, VA 23011, (757) 566-1684, www.poor-clares.org. 1175 N. 300 W., Kokomo, IN 46901-1799, (765) 457-5743, www.thepoorclares.org. 3900 Sherwood Blvd., Delray Beach, FL 33445, (561) 498-3294. 200 Marycrest Dr., St. Louis, MO 63129, (314) 846-2618. 6029 Estero Blvd., Fort Myers Beach, FL 33931, (239) 463-5599, www. poor clares-fmb.org. 9300 Hwy 105, Brenham, TX 77833, (409) 836-2444, www.franciscanpoorclares.org.

Franciscan Sisters, Daughters of the Sacred Hearts of Jesus and Mary, O.S.F.: Founded 1860, in Germany; in U.S., 1872. Generalate, Rome, Italy. U.S. motherhouse, P.O. Box 667, Wheaton, IL 60189-0667, (630) 909-6677, www.wheatonfranciscan.org. Educational, hospital, foreign mission, social work.

Franciscan Sisters Daughters of Mercy, F.H.M.: Founded 1856, in Spain; in U.S., 1962. General moth erhouse, Palma de Mallorca, Spain. U.S. address, 612 N. 3rd St., Waco, TX 76701, (254) 753-5565.

Franciscan Sisters of Allegany, O.S.F.: Founded 1859, at Allegany, NY, by Fr. Pamphilus da Magliano, O.F.M. General motherhouse, P.O. Box W, 115 East Main St., Allegany, NY 14706, (716) 373-0200, www.alleganyfran-ciscans.org. Hospital, foreign mission work.

Franciscan Sisters of Baltimore, O.S.F.: Founded 1868, in England; in U.S., 1881. General mother-house, 3725 Ellerslie Ave., Baltimore, MD 21218, (410) 235- 0139. Educational work; social services.

Franciscan Sisters of Chicago, O.S.F.: Founded 1894, in U.S., by Mother Mary Therese (Josephine Dudzik). General motherhouse, 11500 Theresa Dr., Lemont, IL 60439, (630) 243-3550. Educational work, social services.

Franciscan Sisters of Christian Charity, O.S.F.: Founded 1869, in U.S. Motherhouse, Holy Family Convent, 2409 S. Alverno Rd., Manitowoc, WI 54220, (920) 682-7728, www.fscc-calledtobe.org. Hospital work.

Franciscan Sisters of Little Falls, MN, O.S.F.: Founded 1891, in U.S. General motherhouse, 116 8th Ave., S.E., Little Falls, MN 56345, (320) 632-0612, www.fslf.org. Health, education, social services, pastoral ministry, mission work.

Franciscan Sisters of Mary, F.S.M.: Established, 1987, through unification of the Sisters of St. Mary of the Third Order of St. Francis (founded 1872, St. Louis) and the Sisters of St. Francis of Maryville, MO (founded 1894). Address of general superior: 3221 McKelvey Rd., Suite 107, Bridgeton, MO 63044, (314) 768-1833, www. fsmonline.org. Health care, social services.

Franciscan Sisters of Mary Immaculate of the Third Order of St. Francis of Assisi, F.M.I.: Founded 16th century, in Switzerland; in U.S., 1932. General motherhouse, Bogota, Colombia. U.S. provincial house, 4301 N.E. 18th Ave., Amarillo, TX 79107-7220, (806) 383-5769. Education.

Franciscan Sisters of Our Lady of Perpetual Help, O.S.F.: Founded 1901, in U.S., from Joliet, IL, founda tion. General motherhouse, 335 South Kirkwood Rd., St. Louis, MO 63122, (314) 965-3700, www.franciscansisters-olph.org. Educational, hospital work.

Franciscan Sisters of Peace, F.S.P.: Established 1986, in U.S., as archdiocesan community, from Franciscan Missionary Sisters of the Sacred Heart. Congregation Center, 20 Ridge St., Haverstraw, NY 10927, (845) 942-2527, www.fspnet.org.

Franciscan Sisters of Ringwood, F.S.R.: Merged with the Sisters of St. Francis of Philadelphia in 2003.

Franciscan Sisters of St. Elizabeth, F.S.S.E.: Founded

1866, at Naples, Italy, by Bl. Ludovico of Casorio; in U.S., 1919. General motherhouse, Rome, Italy. U.S. delegate house, 499 Park Rd., Parsippany, NJ 07054, (973) 539-3797, www.franciscansisters.com. Educational work, social services.

Franciscan Sisters of St. Joseph, F.S.S.J.: Founded 1897, in U.S. General motherhouse, 5229 South Park Ave., Hamburg, NY 14075, (716) 649-1205, www.franciscansistersofsaintjoseph.org. Educational, hospital work.

Franciscan Sisters of St. Joseph (of Mexico): U.S. foundation, St. Paul College, 3015 4th St. N.E., Washington, DC 20017, (202) 832-6262.

Franciscan Sisters of the Atonement (Graymoor Sisters), S.A.: Founded 1898, in U.S., as Anglican community; entered Church, 1909. General mother house, St. Francis Convent-Graymoor, 41 Old Highland Turnpike, Garrison, NY 10524, (914) 424- 3624, www.graymoor.org. Mission work.

Franciscan Sisters of the Immaculate Conception, O.S.F.: Founded in Germany; in U.S., 1928. General mother house, Kloster, Bonlanden, Germany. U.S. province, 291 North St., Buffalo, NY 14201, (716) 881-2323.

Franciscan Sisters of the Immaculate Conception, O.S.F.: Founded 1874, in Mexico; in U.S., 1926. U.S. provincial house, 11306 Laurel Canyon Blvd., San Fernando, CA 91340, (818) 365-2582.

Franciscan Sisters of the Immaculate Conception and St. Joseph for the Dying, O.S.F.: Founded 1919, in U.S. General motherhouse, 1249 Joselyn Canyon Rd., Monterey, CA 93940, (408) 372-3579.

Franciscan Sisters of the Poor, S.F.P.: Founded 1845, at Aachen, Germany, by Bl. Frances Schervier; in U.S., 1858. Congregational office, 133 Remsen St., Brooklyn, NY 11201, (718) 643-1919, www.franciscansisters.org. Hospital, social work and foreign missions.

Franciscan Sisters of the Sacred Heart, O.S.F.: Founded 1866, in Germany; in U.S., 1876. General motherhouse, St. Francis Woods, 9201 W. St. Francis Rd., Frankfort, IL 60423- 8335, (815) 469-4895, www.fssh.net. Education, health care, other service ministries.

Hospital Sisters of the Third Order of St. Francis, O.S.F.: Founded 1844, in Germany; in U.S., 1875. General motherhouse, Muenster, Germany. U.S. motherhouse, 4849 La Verna Rd., Springfield, IL 62707, (217) 522-3386, www.hospitalsisters.org. Hospital work.

Institute of the Franciscan Sisters of the Eucharist, F.S.E.: Founded 1973. Motherhouse, 405 Allen Ave., Meriden, CT 06451, (203) 237-0841, www.fscommunity.org.

Little Franciscans of Mary, P.F.M.: Founded 1889, in U.S. General motherhouse, Baie St. Paul, QC, Canada. U.S. region, 55 Moore Ave., Worcester, MA 01602, (508) 755- 0878. Educational, hospital, social work.

Missionary Franciscan Sisters of the Immaculate Conception, M.F.I.C.: Founded 1873, in U.S. General motherhouse, Rome, Italy. U.S. address, 790 Centre St., Newton, MA 02458, (617) 527-1004, www.mficusa.org. Educational work.

Missionary Sisters of the Immaculate Conception of the Mother of God, S.M.I.C.: Founded 1910, in Brazil; in U.S., 1922. U.S. provincialate, P.O. Box 3026, Paterson, NJ 07509, (973) 279-3790, www.smic-missionarysisters.com. Mission, educa tional, health work, social services.

Mothers of the Helpless, M.D.: Founded 1873,

in Spain; in U.S., 1916. General motherhouse, Valencia, Spain. U.S. address, Sacred Heart Residence, 432 W. 20th St., New York, NY 10011, (212) 929-5790; www.sacredheartresidence.com.

Poor Clares of Perpetual Adoration, P.C.P.A.: Founded 1854, at Paris, France; in U.S., 1921, at Cleveland, OH. U.S. monasteries: 4200 N. Market Ave., Canton, OH 44714. 2311 Stockham Lane, Portsmouth, OH 45662-3049, (740) 353-4713. 4108 Euclid Ave., Cleveland, OH 44103, (216) 361-0783. 3900 13th St. N.E., Washington, DC 20017, (202) 526- 6808, www.poorclareswdc.org. 5817 Old Leeds Rd., Birmingham, AL 35210, (205) 271-2917. 3222 County Rd. 548, Hanceville, AL 35077, (256) 352-6267, www.olamshrine.com. Contemplative, clois tered, perpetual adoration.

St. Francis Mission Community, O.S.F.: Autonomous province of Franciscan Sisters of Mary Immaculate. 4305 54th St., Lubbock, TX 79413, (806) 793-9859.

School Sisters of St. Francis, O.S.F.: Founded 1874, in U.S. General motherhouse, 1501 S. Layton Blvd., Milwaukee, WI 53215, (414) 384-4105, www.sssf.org.

School Sisters of St. Francis, (Pittsburgh, PA), O.S.F.: Established 1913, in U.S. Motherhouse, Mt. Assisi Convent, 934 Forest Ave., Pittsburgh, PA 15202-1199, (412) 761-2855, www.franciscansisters-pa.org. Education, health care servic es and related ministries.

School Sisters of the Third Order of St. Francis (Bethlehem, PA), O.S.F.: Founded in Austria, 1843; in U.S., 1913. General motherhouse, Rome, Italy. U.S. province, 395 Bridle Path Rd., Bethlehem, PA 18017, (610) 866-2597. Educational, mission work.

School Sisters of the Third Order of St. Francis (Panhandle, TX), O.S.F.: Established 1931, in U.S., from Vienna, Austria, foundation (1845). General motherhouse, Vienna, Austria. U.S. center and novitiate, P.O. Box 906, Panhandle, TX 79068, (806) 537-3182, www.panhandlefranciscans.org. Educational, social work.

Sisters of Mercy of the Holy Cross, S.C.S.C.: Founded 1856, in Switzerland; in U.S. 1912. General motherhouse, Ingenbohl, Switzerland. U.S. provincial residence, 1400 O'Day St., Merrill, WI 54452, (715) 539-1460, www.holycrosssisters.org.

Sisters of Our Lady of Mercy (Mercedarians), S.O.L.M.: General motherhouse, Rome, Italy. U.S. address: Most Precious Blood, 133-157 27th Ave., Brooklyn, NY 11214, (718) 373-7343.

Sisters of St. Francis (Clinton, IA), O.S.F.: Founded 1868, in U.S. General motherhouse, 588 N. Bluff Blvd., Clinton, IA 57232-3953, (563) 242-7611, www.clintonfranciscans.com. Educational, hospital, social work.

Sisters of St. Francis (Millvale, PA), O.S.F.: Founded 1865, Pittsburgh. General motherhouse, 146 Hawthorne Rd., Millvale PO, Pittsburgh, PA 15209, (412) 821-2200. Educational, hospital work.

Sisters of St. Francis (Hastings-on-Hudson), O.S.F.: Founded 1893, in New York. General mother house, 49 Jackson Ave., Hastings-on-Hudson, NY 10706-3217, (914) 478-3930. Education, parish ministry, social services.

Sisters of St. Francis of Assisi, O.S.F.: Founded 1849, in U.S. General motherhouse, 3221 S. Lake Dr., St. Francis, WI 53235-3799, (414) 744-3150, www.lakeosfs.org. Education, other ministries.

Sisters of St. Francis of Christ the King, O.S.F.: Founded 1864, in Austria; in U.S., 1909. General motherhouse,

Rome, Italy. U.S. provincial house, 13900 Main St., Lemont, IL 60439, (630) 257-7495. Educational work, home for aged.

Sisters of St. Francis of Penance and Christian Charity, O.S.F.: Founded 1835, in Holland; in U.S., 1874. General motherhouse, Rome, Italy. U.S. provinces: 4421 Lower River Rd., Stella Niagara, NY 14144-1001, (716) 754-2193, www.franciscans-stella-niagara.org. 5314 N. Columbine Rd., Denver, CO 80221, (303) 458-6270; 3910 Bret Harte Dr., PO Box 1028, Redwood City, CA 94064, (650) 369-1725.

Sisters of St. Francis of Philadelphia, O.S.F.: Founded 1855, at Philadelphia, by Mother Mary Francis Bachmann and St. John N. Neumann. General motherhouse, Convent of Our Lady of the Angels, Aston, PA 19014, (610) 558-7701, www.osfphila.org. Education, health care, social services.

Sisters of St. Francis of Savannah, MO, O.S.F.: Founded 1850, in Austria; in U.S., 1922. Provincial house, La Verna Heights, Box 488, 104 E. Park, Savannah, MO 64485-0488, (816) 324-3179. Educational, hospital work.

Sisters of St. Francis of the Holy Cross, O.S.F.: Founded 1881, in U.S., by Rev. Edward Daems, O.S.C. General moth erhouse, 3110 Nicolet Dr., Green Bay, WI 54311, (920) 884- 2700, www.gbfranciscans.org. Educational, nursing work, pastoral ministry, foreign missions.

Sisters of St. Francis of the Holy Eucharist, O.S.F.: Founded 1378, in Switzerland; in U.S., 1893. General motherhouse, 2100 N. Noland Rd., Independence, MO 64050, (816) 252-1673; www.osfholyeucharist.org. Education, health care, social services, foreign missions.

Sisters of St. Francis of the Holy Family, O.S.F.: U.S. foundation, 1875. Motherhouse, Mt. St. Francis, 3390 Windsor Ave., Dubuque, IA 52001, (563) 583-9786, www.osfdbq.org. Varied apostolates.

Sisters of St. Francis of the Immaculate Conception, O.S.F.: Founded 1890, in U.S. General motherhouse, 2408 W. Heading Ave., West Peoria, IL 61604-5096, (309) 674-6168, www.westpeoriasis ters.org. Education, care of aging, pastoral ministry.

Sisters of St. Francis of the Immaculate Heart of Mary, O.S.F.: Founded 1241, in Bavaria; in U.S., 1913. General motherhouse, Rome, Italy. U.S. motherhouse, 102 6th St., S.E., Hankinson, ND 58041, (701) 242-7195, www.dillingenfranciscansusa.org. Education, social services.

Sisters of St. Francis of the Martyr St. George, O.S.F.: Founded 1859, in Germany; in U.S., 1923. General motherhouse, Thuine, Germany. U.S. provincial house, St. Francis Convent, 2120 Central Ave., Alton, IL 62002, (618) 463-2750, www.altonfranciscans.org. Education, social services, foreign mission work.

Sisters of St. Francis of the Perpetual Adoration, O.S.F.: Founded 1863, in Germany; in U.S., 1875. General mother house, Olpe, Germany. U.S. provinces: Box 766, Mishawaka, IN 46546-0766, (574) 259-5427, www.ssfpa.org. 7665 Assisi Heights, Colorado Springs, CO 80919, (719) 955-7015, www.stfrancis.org.

Sisters of St. Francis of the Providence of God, O.S.F.: Founded 1922, in U.S., by Msgr. M. L. Krusas. General motherhouse, 3603 McRoberts Rd., Pittsburgh, PA 15234, (412) 885-7407. Education, varied apostolates.

Sisters of St. Joseph of the Third Order of St. Francis, S.S.J.: Founded 1901, in U.S. Administrative office, P.O. Box 305, Stevens Pt., WI 54481-0305, (715) 341-8457, www.ssj-tosf.org. Education, health care, social services.

Sisters of the Infant Jesus, I.J.: Founded 1662, at Rouen, France; in U.S., 1950. Motherhouse, Paris, France. Generalate, Rome, Italy. U.S. address: 20 Reiner St., Colma, CA 94014.

Sisters of the Sorrowful Mother (Third Order of St. Francis), S.S.M.: Founded 1883, in Italy; in U.S., 1889. General motherhouse, Rome, Italy. U.S. address: 17600 E. 51st St., Broken Arrow, OK 74012, (918) 355-1148, www.ssmfranciscans.org. Educational, hos pital work.

Sisters of St. Franciscan of the Neumann Communities, O.S.F.: Founded 1860, at Syracuse, NY. Generalate offices, 2500 Grant Blvd., Syracuse, NY 13208, (315) 624-7000, www.sosf.org.

Sisters of the Third Order of St. Francis, O.S.F.: Founded 1877, in U.S., by Bishop John L. Spalding. Motherhouse, 1175 St. Francis Lane, E. Peoria, IL 61611-1299, (309) 699-7215, www.franciscansisterpeoria.org. Hospital work.

Sisters of the Third Order of St. Francis (Oldenburg, IN), O.S.F.: Founded 1851, in U.S. General motherhouse, Sisters of St. Francis, PO Box 100, Oldenburg, IN 47036-0100, (812) 934-2475, www.oldenburgfranciscans.org. Education, social services, pastoral ministry, foreign missions.

Sisters of the Third Order of St. Francis of Penance and Charity, O.S.F.: Founded 1869, in U.S., by Fr. Joseph Bihn. Motherhouse, 200 St. Francis Ave., Tiffin, OH 44883, (419) 447-0435, www.tiffinfranciscans.org. Education, social services.

Sisters of the Third Order of St. Francis of the Perpetual Adoration, F.S.P.A.: Founded 1849, in U.S. Generalate, 912 Market St., La Crosse, WI 54601, (608) 782-5610, www.fspa.org. Education, health care.

Sisters of the Third Order Regular of St. Francis of the Congregation of Our Lady of Lourdes, O.S.F.: Founded 1877, in U.S. General motherhouse, Assisi Heights, 1001 14th St., NW, Rochester, MN 55901, (507) 282-7441; www.rochesterfranciscan.org. Education, health care, social services.

Good Shepherd Sisters (Servants of the Immaculate Heart of Mary), S.C.I.M.: Founded 1850, in Canada; in U.S., 1882. General motherhouse, QC, Canada. In U.S., Provincial House, Bay View, 313 Seaside Ave., Saco, Maine 04072, (207) 284-6429. Educational, social work.

Good Shepherd, Sisters of the, R.G.S.: Founded 1835, in France, by St. Mary Euphrasia Pelletier; in U.S., 1843. Generalate, Rome, Italy. U.S. provinces: 2108 Hatmaker St., Cincinnati, OH 45204, (513) 921-5923. 25-30 21st Ave., Astoria, NY 11105, (718) 278-1155, www.goodshepherdsistersna.org. 504 Hexton Hill Rd., Silver Spring, MD 20904, (301) 384-1169. 7654 Natural Bridge Rd., St. Louis, MO 63121, (314) 381-3400, www.goodshepherdsis-ters.org. 5100 Hodgson Rd., St. Paul, MN 55126, (651) 484-0221, www.bounpastorint.org. Active and contemplative (Contemplative Sisters of the Good Shepherd, C.G.S.).

Graymoor Sisters: See Franciscan Sisters of the Atonement.

Grey Nuns of the Sacred Heart, G.N.S.H.: Founded 1921, in U.S. General motherhouse, 1750 Quarry Rd., Yardley, PA 19067-3998, (215) 968-4236, www.greynun.org.

Guadalupan Missionaries of the Holy Spirit, M.G.Sp.S.: Founded 1930 in Mexico by Rev. Felix de Jesus Rougier, M.Sp.S. General motherhouse, Mexico. U.S. delegation: 2483 S.W. 4th St. Miami, FL 33135- 2907, (305) 642-9544.

Guardian Angel, Sisters of the, S.A.C.: Founded 1839,

in France. General motherhouse, Madrid, Spain. U.S. foundation, 1245 S. Van Ness, Los Angeles, CA 90019, (213) 732-7881.

Handmaids of the Precious Blood, Congregation of, H.P.B.: Founded 1947, at Jemez Springs, NM. Motherhouse and novitiate, Cor Jesu Monastery, P.O. Box 90, Jemez Springs, NM 87025, (505) 829-3906.

Helpers, Society of, H.H.S.: Founded 1856, in France; in U.S., 1892. General motherhouse, Paris, France. American province, 3206 S. Aberdeen, Chicago, IL 60657, (773) 523-8638.

Hermanas Catequistas Guadalupanas, H.C.G.: Founded 1923, in Mexico; in U.S., 1950. General motherhouse, Mexico. 4110 S. Flores, San Antonio, TX 78214, (210) 533-9344.

Hermanas Josefinas, H.J.: General motherhouse, Mexico. U.S. foundation, Assumption Seminary, 2600 W. Woodlawn Ave., PO Box 28240, San Antonio, TX 78284, (210) 734-0039. Domestic work.

Holy Child Jesus, Society of the, S.H.C.J.: Founded 1846, in England; in U.S., 1862. General motherhouse, Rome, Italy. U.S. province, 460 Shadeland Ave., Drexel Hill, PA 19026, (610) 626-1400, www.shcj.org.

Holy Faith, Congregation of the Sisters of the, C.H.F.: Founded 1856, in Ireland; in U.S., 1953. General motherhouse, Dublin, Ireland. U.S. province, 12322 S. Paramount Blvd., Downey, CA 90242, (562) 869-6092.

Holy Family, Congregation of the Sisters of the, S.S.F.: Founded 1842, in Louisiana, by Henriette Delille and Juliette Gaudin. General motherhouse, 6901 Chef Menteur Hwy., New Orleans, LA 70126, (504) 242-8315, www.sistersoftheholyfamily.com. Hospital work.

Holy Family, Sisters of the, S.H.F.: Founded 1872, in U.S. General motherhouse, P.O. Box 3248, Fremont, CA 94539, (510) 624-4500 www.holyfamilysisters. com. Educational, social work.

Holy Family of Nazareth, Sisters of the, C.S.F.N.: Founded 1875, in Italy; in U.S., 1885. General mother house, Rome, Italy. U.S. provinces: Sacred Heart, 310 N. River Rd., Des Plaines, IL 60016-1211, (847) 298-6760. Immaculate Conception BVM, 4001 Grant Ave., Philadelphia, PA 19114, (215) 268-1035, www.philacsfn.org. St. Joseph, 285 Bellevue Rd., Pittsburgh, PA 15229-2195, (412) 931-4778, www.csfn.org. Immaculate Heart of Mary, Marian Heights, 1428 Monroe Turnpike, Monroe, CT 04648, (203) 268-7646. Bl. Frances Siedliska Provincialate, 1814 Egyptian Way, Box 530959, Grand Prairie, TX 75053, (972) 641-4496, www.csfn.org.

Holy Heart of Mary, Servants of the, S.S.C.M.: Founded 1860, in France; in U.S., 1889. General moth erhouse, Montreal, QC, Canada. U.S. province, 15 Elmwood Dr., Kankakee, IL 60901, (815) 937-2380, www.sscm-usa.org. Educational, hospital, social work.

Holy Names of Jesus and Mary, Sisters of the, S.N.J.M.: Founded 1843, in Canada by Bl. Marie Rose Durocher; in U.S., 1859. Generalate, Longueuil, QC, Canada. U.S.-Ontario Province was formed in 2006 by uniting the five predominantly English-speaking provinces of the Congregation. Address: Box 25, Marylhurst, OR 97036, (503) 675-2449, www.snjm.org.

Holy Spirit, Community of the, C.H.S.: Founded 1970 in San Diego, CA. 6151 Rancho Mission Rd., No. 205, San Diego, CA 92108, (619) 584-0809.

Holy Spirit, Daughters of the, D.H.S.: Founded 1706, in France; in U.S., 1902. Generalate, Bretagne, France. U.S. motherhouse, 72 Church St., Putnam, CT 06260-

1817, (860) 928-0891. Educational work, dis trict nursing, pastoral ministry.

Holy Spirit, Mission Sisters of the, M.S.Sp.: Founded 1932, at Cleveland, OH. Motherhouse, 1030 N. River Rd., Saginaw, MI 48603, (517) 781-0934.

Holy Spirit, Missionary Sisters, Servants of the: Founded 1889, in Holland; in U.S., 1901. Generalate, Rome, Italy. U.S. motherhouse, Convent of the Holy Spirit, PO Box 6026, Techny, IL 60082-6026, (847) 441-0126, www.sspsusa.org. International congregation for the spread of the Gospel *ad gentes*.

Holy Spirit, Sisters of the, C.S.Sp.: Founded 1890, in Rome, Italy; in U.S. as independent diocesan community, 1929. General motherhouse, 10102 Granger Rd., Garfield Hts., OH 44125, (216) 581-2900, www.sistersoftheholyspirit.org. Educational, social, nursing work.

Holy Spirit, Sisters of the, S.H.S.: Founded 1913, in U.S., by Most Rev. J. F. Regis Canevin. General moth erhouse, 5246 Clarwin Ave., Ross Township, Pittsburgh, PA 15229-2208, (412) 931-1917. Educational, nursing work, care of aged.

Holy Spirit and Mary Immaculate, Sisters of, S.H.Sp.: Founded 1893, in U.S. Motherhouse, 301 Yucca St., San Antonio, TX 78203, (210) 533-5149. Education, hospital work.

Holy Spirit of Perpetual Adoration, Sister Servants of the, S.Sp.S.deA.P.: Founded 1896, in Holland; in U.S., 1915. Generalate, Bad Driburg, Germany. U.S. novitiate, 2212 Green St., Philadelphia, PA 19130, (215) 567-0123, www.adorationsisters.org.

Home Mission Sisters of America (Glenmary Sisters), G.H.M.S.: Founded 1952, in U.S. Glenmary Center, PO Box 22264, Owensboro, KY 42304-2264, (270) 686-8401; www.glenmarysisters.org.

Home Visitors of Mary, Sisters, H.V.M.: Founded 1949, in Detroit, MI. Motherhouse, 121 E. Boston Blvd., Detroit, MI 48202, (313) 869-2160.

Hospitallers of St. Joseph, Religious, R.H.S.J.: Founded in 1636, in France; in U.S., 1894. Motherhouse, 2450, Chemin de la Côte Sainte-Catherine, Montréal, Canada H3T 1B1. U.S. address: 644, Langlade Road, Antigo, WI 54409, (715) 623- 4615; www.rhsj.org.

Humility of Mary, Congregation of, C.H.M.: Founded 1854, in France; in U.S., 1864. U.S. address, Humility of Mary Center, Davenport IA, 52804, (563) 323-9466, www. chmiowa.org.

Humility of Mary, Sisters of the, H.M.: Founded 1854, in France; in U.S., 1864. U.S. address, Villa Maria Community Center, Villa Maria, PA 16155, (724) 964-8861, www.humilityofmary.org.

Immaculate Conception, Little Servant Sisters of the, L.S.I.C.: Founded 1850, in Poland; in U.S., 1926. General motherhouse, Poland. U.S. provincial house, 1000 Cropwell Rd., Cherry Hill, NJ 08003, (609) 424-1962. Education, social services, African missions.

Immaculate Conception, Sisters of the, R.C.M.: Founded 1892, in Spain; in U.S., 1962. General moth erhouse, Madrid, Spain. U.S. address, 2230 Franklin, San Francisco, CA 94109, (415) 474-0159, www.rc.net/conception.

Immaculate Conception, Sisters of the, C.I.C.: Founded 1874, in U.S. General motherhouse, P.O. Box 50426, New Orleans, LA 70185, (504) 486-7426.

Immaculate Conception of the Blessed Virgin Mary, Sisters of the (Lithuanian): Founded 1918, at Mariampole, Lithuania; in U.S., 1936. U.S. headquar ters, Immaculate

Conception Convent, 600 Liberty Hwy., Putnam, CT 06260, (860) 928-7955.

Immaculate Heart of Mary, Missionary Sisters, I.C.M.: Founded 1897, in India; in U.S., 1919. Generalate, Rome, Italy. U.S. province, 283 E. 15th St., New York, NY 10003, (212) 260-8567. Educational social, foreign mission work.

Immaculate Heart of Mary, Sisters of the, I.H.M.: Founded 1848, in Spain; in U.S., 1878. General moth erhouse, Rome, Italy. U.S. province, 3820 Sabino Canyon Rd., Tucson, AZ 85750, (520) 886-4273. Educational work.

Immaculate Heart of Mary, Sisters, Servants of the, I.H.M.: Founded 1845. SSIHM Leadership Council, 610 W. Elm, Monroe, MI 48162, (734) 340- 9700, www.sistersihm.org.

Immaculate Heart of Mary, Sisters, Servants of the, I.H.M.: Founded 1845; established in Scranton, PA, 1871. General motherhouse, 2300 Adams Ave., Scranton, PA 18509, (570) 346-5404, www.sistersofihm.org.

Immaculate Heart of Mary, Sisters Servants of the, I.H.M.: Founded 1845; established in West Chester, PA, 1872. General motherhouse, Villa Maria, Immaculata, PA 19345, (610) 647-2160, www.ihmimmaculata.org.

Immaculate Heart of Mary of Wichita, Sisters of, I.H.M.: Established at Wichita, KS. 1979. Address: 145 S. Millwood St., Wichita, KS 67213, (316) 722-9316, www.sistersofwichita.org.

Incarnate Word, Religious of, C.V.I.: General motherhouse, Mexico City, Mexico. U.S. address, 153 Rainier Ct., Chula Vista, CA 92011, (619) 420-0231.

Incarnate Word and Blessed Sacrament, Congregation of, C.V.I.: Founded 1625, in France; in U.S., 1853. Incarnate Word Convent, 3400 Bradford Pl., Houston, TX 77025, (713) 668-0423; www.incarnateword.org/cvi.

Incarnate Word and Blessed Sacrament, Congregation of the, I.W.B.S.: Motherhouse, 1101 Northeast Water St., Victoria, TX 77901, (361) 575-2266, www.iwbsvictoria.org.

Incarnate Word and Blessed Sacrament, Congregation of the, I.W.B.S.: Motherhouse, 2930 S. Alameda, Corpus Christi, TX 78404, (361) 882-5413, www.iwbscc.org.

Incarnate Word and Blessed Sacrament, Sisters of the, S.I.W.: Founded 1625, in France; in U.S. 1853. Motherhouse, 6618 Pearl Rd., Parma Heights, Cleveland, OH 44130, (440) 886-6440, www.incar natewordorder.org.

Infant Jesus, Congregation of the (Nursing Sisters of the Sick Poor), C.I.J.: Founded 1835, in France; in U.S., 1905. General motherhouse, 310 Prospect Park W., Brooklyn, NY 11215, (718) 965-7300.

Institute of the Blessed Virgin Mary (Loretto Sisters), I.B.V.M.: Founded 17th century in Belgium; in U.S., 1954. Motherhouse, Rathfarnham, Dublin, Ireland. U.S. address: 2521 W. Maryland Ave., Phoenix, AZ 85017, (602) 522-2544.

Institute of the Blessed Virgin Mary (Loretto Sisters), I.B.V.M.: Founded 1609, in Belgium; in U.S., 1880. Loretto Convent, Box 508, Wheaton, IL 60189, (630) 665-3814. Educational work.

Jesus, Daughters of (*Filles de Jesus*), F.J.: Founded 1834, in France; in U.S., 1904. General mother-house, Kermaria, Locmine, France. U.S. address, 4209 3rd Ave. S., Great Falls, MT 59405, (406) 452-7231. Educational, hospital, parish and social work.

Jesus, Little Sisters of, L.S.J.: Founded 1939, in Sahara; in U.S., 1952. General motherhouse, Rome, Italy. U.S. headquarters, 400 N. Streeper St., Baltimore, MD 21224, www.rc.net/org/littlesisters.

Jesus, Society of the Sisters, Faithful Companions of, F.C.J.: Founded 1820, in France; in U.S., 1896. General motherhouse, Kent, England. U.S. province, St. Philomena Convent, Cory's Lane, Portsmouth, RI 02871, (401) 683-2222, www.portsmouthabbey.org.

Jesus and Mary, Little Sisters of, L.S.J.M.: Founded 1974 in U.S. Joseph House, P.O. Box 1755, Salisbury, MD 21802, (410) 742-9590, www.thejosephhouse.org.

Jesus and Mary, Religious of, R.J.M.: Founded 1818, at Lyons, France; in U.S., 1877. General mother house, Rome, Italy. U.S. province, 821 Varnum St., NE, Washington, DC 20017, (202) 526-3203. Educational work.

Jesus Crucified, Congregation of: Founded 1930, in France; in U.S., 1955. General motherhouse, Brou, France. U.S. foundation: Benedictines of Jesus Crucified, Monastery of the Glorious Cross, 61 Burban Dr., Branford, CT 06405-4003, (203) 315- 9964, www.bene-dictinesjc.org.

Jesus Crucified and the Sorrowful Mother, Poor Sisters of, C.J.C.: Founded 1924, in U.S., by Rev. Alphonsus Maria, C.P. Motherhouse, 261 Thatcher St., Brockton, MA 02402. Education, nursing homes, catechetical centers.

Jesus, Mary and Joseph, Missionary Sisters of, M.J.M.J.: Founded 1942, in Spain; in U.S., 1956. General motherhouse, Madrid, Spain. U.S. regional house, 12940 Leopard St., Corpus Christi, TX 78410, (361) 241-1955.

John the Baptist, Sisters of St., C.S.J.B.: Founded 1878, in Italy; in U.S., 1906. General motherhouse, Rome, Italy. U.S. provincialate, 3308 Campbell Dr., Bronx, NY 10465, (718) 518-7820, www.home.att. net/~baptistines. Education, parish and retreat work; social services.

Joseph, Congregation of Saint, C.S.J.: Founded in 2007 through the formation of seven congregations in the central United States. 1515 W. Ogden Ave., La Grange Park, IL, 60526, (708) 354-9200. 3700 E. Lincoln St., Wichita, KS 67218, (316) 689-4040. Medaille, 4010 Executive Park Dr Ste. 320, Cincinnati, OH 45241, (513)761-2888. Mount St. Joseph, 137 Mount St. Joseph Rd., Wheeling, WV 26003, (304) 232-8160. Nazareth Community Center, 3427 Gull Road, PO Box 34, Nazareth, MI 49074- 0034, (269) 381-6290.St. Joseph Center, 3430 Rocky River Drive, Cleveland, OH 44111-2997, (216) 252- 0440.

Joseph, Poor Sisters of St., P.S.S.J.: Founded 1880, in Argentina. General motherhouse, Muniz, Buenos Aires, Argentina. U.S. addresses: Casa Belen, 305 E. 4th St., Bethlehem, PA 78015, (610) 867-4030. Casa Nazareth, 5321 Spruce St., Reading, PA 19602, (610) 378-1947. St. Gabriel Convent, 4319 Sano St., Alexandria, VA 22312, (703) 354-0395.

Joseph, Religious Daughters of St., F.S.J.: Founded 1875, in Spain. General motherhouse, Spain. U.S. foundation, 319 N. Humphreys Ave., Los Angeles, CA 90022.

Joseph, Servants of St., S.S.J.: Founded 1874, in Spain; in U.S., 1957. General motherhouse, Salamanca, Spain. U.S. address, 203 N. Spring St., Falls Church, VA 22046, (703) 533-8441.

Joseph, Sisters of St., C.S.J. or S.S.J.: Founded 1650, in France; in U.S., 1836, at St. Louis. Independent mother-houses in U.S.: 637 Cambridge St., Brighton, MA 02135, (617) 783-9090, www.csjboston.org. 480 S. Batavia St., Orange, CA 92868, (714) 633-8121, www.sistersofstjo-sephorange.org. St. Joseph Convent, 1725 Brentwood Rd., Brentwood, NY 11717-5587, (516) 273-4531. 23 Agassiz Circle, Buffalo, NY 14214, (716) 838-4400. 1425 Washington St., Watertown, NY 13601, (315) 782-3460, www.ssjwa tertown.org. 1020 State St., Baden, PA 15005-1342, (724) 869-2151, www.stjosephbaden.org. 5031 W. Ridge Rd., Erie, PA 16506, (814) 836-4193, www.ssjerie.org. 150 French Rd., Rochester, NY 14618, (585) 641-8119, www.ssjrochester.org. Mont Marie, 34 Lower Westfield Rd. Holyoke, MA 01040, (413) 536-0853. PO Box 279, Concordia, KS 66901, (785) 243-2149, www.csjkansas.org.

Joseph, Sisters of St., of Peace, C.S.J.P.: Founded 1884, in England; in U.S. 1885. Generalate, 399 Hudson Terrace, Englewood Cliffs, NJ 07632, (201) 608-5401. Educational, hospital, social service work.

Joseph of Carondelet, Sisters of St., C.S.J.: Founded 1650, in France; in U.S., 1836, at St. Louis, MO. U.S. headquarters, 2311 S. Lindbergh Blvd., St. Louis, MO 63131, (314) 966-4048, www.csjcarondolet.org.

Joseph of Chambery, Sisters of St.: Founded 1650, in France; in U.S., 1885. Generalate, Rome, Italy. U.S. provincial house, 27 Park Rd., West Hartford, CT 06119, (860) 233-5126. Educational, hospital, social work.

Joseph of Chestnut Hill, Sisters of St., S.S.J.: Founded 1650; Philadelphia foundation, 1847. Motherhouse, Mt. St. Joseph Convent, 9701 Germantown Ave., Philadelphia, PA 19118, (215) 248- 7200, www.ssjphila.org.

Joseph of Cluny, Sisters of St., S.J.C.: Founded 1807, in France. Generalate, Paris, France. U.S. provincial house, 7 Restmere Terrace, Middletown, RI 02842, (401) 846-4826.

Joseph of Medaille, Sisters of, C.S.J.: See under Joseph, Congregation of St.

Joseph of St. Augustine, Florida, Sisters of St., S.S.J.: General motherhouse, 241 St. George St., P.O. Box 3506, St. Augustine, FL 32085, (904) 824-1752, www.ssjfl.org. Educational, hospital, pastoral, social work.

Joseph of St. Mark, Sisters of St., S.J.S.M.: Founded 1845, in France; in U.S., 1937. General motherhouse, 21800 Chardon Rd., Euclid, Cleveland, OH 44117, (216) 531-7426. Nursing homes.

Joseph the Worker, Sisters of St., S.J.W.: General motherhouse, St. William Convent, 1 St. Joseph Lane, Walton, KY 41094, (859) 485-4256.

Lamb of God, Sisters of the, A.D.: Founded 1945, in France; in U.S., 1958. General motherhouse, France. U.S. address, 2063 Wyandotte Ave., Owensboro KY 42301, (502) 281-5450.

Life, Sisters of, S.V. (*Sorer Vitae*): Founded by Cardinal John J. O'Connor, 1991, to protect life. St. Frances de Chantal Convent, 198 Hollywood Ave., Bronx, NY 10465, (718) 863-2264. Our Lady of New York, 1955 Needham Ave., Bronx, NY, 10466, (718) 881-8008. Sacred Heart Convent, 450 W. 51st St., New York, NY, (212) 397-1386.

Little Sisters of the Gospel, L.S.G.: Founded 1963 in France by Rev. Rene Voillaume; in U.S., 1972. Box 305, Mott Haven Sta., Bronx, NY 10454, (718) 292- 2867.

Little Workers of the Sacred Hearts, P.O.S.C.: Founded 1892, in Italy; in U.S., 1948. General House, Rome, Italy. U.S. address, Our Lady of Grace Convent, 635 Glenbrook Rd., Stamford, CT 06906, (203) 348- 5531.

Living Word, Sisters of the, S.L.W.: Founded 1975, in U.S. Motherhouse, Living Word Center, 800 N. Fernandez Ave. B, Arlington Heights, IL 60004-5316, (847) 577-5972, www.slw.org. Education, hospital, parish ministry work.

Loretto at the Foot of the Cross, Sisters of, S.L.:

Founded 1812 in U.S., by Rev. Charles Nerinckx. General motherhouse, 4000 S. Wadsworth Blvd., Littleton, CO 80123, (303) 783-0450, www.loretto community.org. Educational work.

Louis, Juilly-Monaghan, Congregation of Sisters of St., S.S.L.: Founded 1842, in France; in U.S., 1949. General motherhouse, Monaghan, Ireland. U.S. regional house, 22300 Mulholland Dr., Woodland Hills, CA 91364, (818) 883-1678. Educational, med ical, parish, foreign mission work.

Lovers of the Holy Cross Sisters (Phat Diem), L.H.C.: Founded 1670, in Vietnam; in U.S. 1976. U.S. address, Holy Cross Convent, 14700 South Van Ness Ave., Gardena, CA 90249, (310) 516-0271.

Mantellate Sisters, Servants of Mary, of Blue Island, O.S.M.: Founded 1861, in Italy; in U.S., 1916. Generalate, Rome, Italy. U.S. motherhouse, 13811 S. Western Ave., Blue Island, IL 60406, (708) 385-2103. Educational work.

Mantellate Sisters Servants of Mary, of Plainfield, O.S.M.: Founded 1861 in Italy; in U.S., 1916. 16949 S. Drauden Rd., Plainfield, IL 60586, (815) 436-5796.

Marian Sisters of the Diocese of Lincoln: Founded 1954. Marycrest Motherhouse, 6905 N. 112th St., Waverly, NE 68462-9690, (402) 786-2750.

Marianites of Holy Cross, Congregation of the Sisters, M.S.C.: Founded 1841, in France; in U.S., 1843. Motherhouse, Le Mans, Sarthe, France. North American headquarters, 1011 Gallier St., New Orleans, LA 70117-6111, (504) 945-1620, www.marianites.org.

Marist Sisters, Congregation of Mary, S.M.: Founded 1824, in France. General motherhouse, Rome, Italy. U.S. foundation: 810 Peach, Abilene, TX 79602, (915) 675-5806.

Mary, Company of, O.D.N.: Founded 1607, in France; in U.S., 1926. General motherhouse, Rome, Italy. U.S. motherhouse, 16791 E. Main St., Tustin, CA 92680-4034, (714) 541-3125, www.companyof mary.com.

Mary, Daughters of the Heart of, D.H.M.: Founded 1790, in France; in U.S., 1851. Generalate, Paris, France. U.S. provincialate, 1339 Northampton St., Holyoke, MA 01040, (413) 533-6681, www.dhmna. org. Education, retreat work.

Mary, Missionary Sisters of the Society of (Marist Sisters), S.M.S.M.: Founded 1845, at St. Brieuc, France; in U.S., 1922. General motherhouse, Rome, Italy. U.S. provincial house, 349 Grove St., Waltham, MA 02453, (781) 893-0149, www.maristmissionary smsm.org.

Mary, Servants of, O.S.M.: Founded 13th century, in Italy; in U.S., 1893. General motherhouse, England. U.S. provincial motherhouse, 7400 Military Ave., Omaha, NE 68134, (402) 571-2547.

Mary, Servants of (Servite Sisters), O.S.M.: Founded 13th century, in Italy; in U.S., 1912. General motherhouse, Servants of Mary Convent, 1000 College Ave., Ladysmith, WI 54848, (715) 532-3364, www.servitesisters.org.

Mary, Sisters of St., of Oregon, S.S.M.O.: Founded 1886, in Oregon, by Bishop William H. Gross, C.Ss.R. General motherhouse, 4440 S.W. 148th Ave., Beaverton, OR 97007, (503) 644-9181, www.ssmo.org. Educational, nursing work.

Mary, Sisters of the Little Company of, L.C.M.: Founded 1877, in England; in U.S., 1893. Generalate, London, England. U.S. provincial house, 9350 S. California Ave., Evergreen Park, IL 60805, (708) 229-5490, www.lcmglobal.org.

Mary, Sisters Servants of (Trained Nurses), S.M.: Founded 1851, at Madrid, Spain; in U.S., 1914. General motherhouse, Rome, Italy. U.S. motherhouse, 800 N. 18th St., Kansas City, KS 66102, (913) 371-3423. Home nursing.

Mary and Joseph, Daughters of, D.M.J.: Founded 1817, in Belgium; in U.S., 1926. Generalate, Rome, Italy. American provincialate, 5300 Crest Rd., Rancho Palos Verdes, CA 90274, (310) 541-8194.

Mary Help of Christians, Daughters of (Salesian Sisters of St. John Bosco), F.M.A.: Founded 1872, in Italy, by St. John Bosco and St. Mary Dominic Mazzarello; in U.S., 1908. General motherhouse, Rome, Italy. U.S. provinces: 655 Belmont Ave., Haledon, NJ 07508, (937) 790-7963. 6019 Buena Vista St., San Antonio, TX 78237, (210) 432-0089. Education, youth work.

Mary Immaculate, Daughters of (Marianist Sisters), F.M.I.: Founded 1816, in France, by Very Rev. William-Joseph Chaminade. General mother house, Rome, Italy. U.S. foundation, 251 W. Ligustrum Dr., San Antonio, TX 78228-4092, (210) 433-5501, www.marianistsisters.org. Educational work.

Mary Immaculate, Religious of, R.M.I.: Founded 1876, in Spain; in U.S., 1954. Generalate, Rome, Italy. U.S. foundation, 719 Augusta St., San Antonio, TX 78215, (210) 226-0025.

Mary Immaculate, Sisters Minor of, S.M.M.I.: Established in U.S., 1989. 138 Brushy Hill Rd., Danbury, CT 06818, (203) 744-8041.

Mary Immaculate, Sisters of, S.M.I.: Founded 1948, in India, by Bp. Louis LaRavoire Morrow; in U.S., 1981. General motherhouse, Bengal, India. U.S. address, 118 Park Rd., Leechburg, PA 15656, (724) 845-2828.

Mary Immaculate, Sisters Servants of, S.S.M.I.: Founded 1878 in Poland. General motherhouse, Mariowka-Opoczynska, Poland; American provincialate, 1220 Tugwell Dr., Catonsville, MD 21228, (410) 747-1353.

Mary Immaculate, Sisters Servants of, S.S.M.I: Founded 1892, in Ukraine; in U.S., 1935. General motherhouse, Rome, Italy. U.S. address, 9 Emmanuel Dr., PO Box 9, Sloatsburg, NY 10974-0009, (845) 753-2840. Educational, hospital work.

Mary of Namur, Sisters of St., S.S.M.N.: Founded 1819, at Namur, Belgium; in U.S., 1863. General motherhouse, Namur, Belgium. U.S. provinces: 241 Lafayette Ave., Buffalo, NY 14213-1453, (716) 884- 8221, www.ssmn.us. 909 West Shaw St., Ft. Worth, TX 76110, (817) 923-8393, web2.airmail.net/ssmn.

Mary of Providence, Daughters of St., D.S.M.P.: Founded 1872, at Como, Italy; in U.S., 1913. General motherhouse, Rome, Italy. U.S. provincial house, 4200 N. Austin Ave., Chicago, IL 60634, (773) 545-8300. Special education for mentally handicapped.

Mary of the Immaculate Conception, Daughters of, D.M.: Founded 1904, in U.S., by Msgr. Lucian Bojnowski. General motherhouse, 314 Osgood Ave., New Britain, CT 06053, (860) 225-9406. Educational, hospital work.

Mary Queen, Congregation of, C.M.R.: Founded in Vietnam; established in U.S., 1979. U.S. region, 625 S. Jefferson, Springfield, MO 65806.

Mary Reparatrix, Society of, S.M.R.: Founded 1857, in France; in U.S., 1908. Generalate, Rome, Italy. U.S. province, 225 E. 234th St., Bronx NY 10470.

Maryknoll Sisters, M.M.: Founded in 1912 in U.S. by Mother Mary Joseph. General motherhouse: PO Box 311, Maryknoll, NY 10545-0311, (914) 941-7575, www.maryknoll.org.

Medical Mission Sisters (Society of Catholic Medical Missionaries, Inc.), M.M.S.: Founded 1925, in U.S., by Mother Anna Dengel. Generalate, London, England. U.S. headquarters, 8400 Pine Rd., Philadelphia, PA 19111, (215) 742-6100, www.medicalmissionsisters.org. Medical work, health education, especially in mission areas.

Medical Missionaries of Mary, M.M.M.: Founded 1937, in Ireland, by Mother Mary Martin; in U.S., 1950. General motherhouse, Dublin, Ireland. U.S. headquarters, 563 Minneford Ave., City Island, Bronx, NY 10464, (718) 885-0945. Medical aid in missions.

Medical Sisters of St. Joseph, M.S.J.: Founded 1946, in India; first U.S. foundation, 1985. General motherhouse, Kerala, S. India. U.S. address, 3435 E. Funston, Wichita, KS 67218, (316) 689-5360. Health care apostolate.

Mercedarian Sisters of the Blessed Sacrament, H.M.S.S.: Founded 1910, in Mexico; first U.S. foun dation, 1926. Regional House, 227 Keller St., San Antonio, TX 78204, (210) 223-5013.

Mercy, Daughters of Our Lady of, D.M.: Founded 1837, in Italy, by St. Mary Joseph Rossello; in U.S., 1919. General motherhouse, Savona, Italy. U.S. motherhouse, Villa Rossello, 1009 Main Rd., Newfield, NJ 08344, (856) 697-2983. Educational, hospital work.

Mercy, Missionary Sisters of Our Lady of, M.O.M.: Founded 1938, in Brazil; in U.S., 1955. General motherhouse, Brazil. U.S. address, 388 Franklin St., Buffalo, NY 14202, (716) 854-5198.

Mercy, Religious Sisters of, R.S.M.: Founded 1973 in U.S. Motherhouse, 1835 Michigan Ave., Alma, MI 48801, (517) 463-6035.

Mercy, Sisters of, of the Americas: Formed in July, 1991, through union of nine provinces and 16 regional communities of Sisters of Mercy which previously were independent motherhouses or houses which formed the Sisters of Mercy of the Union. Mother Mary Catherine McAuley founded the Sisters of Mercy in Dublin, Ireland, in 1831; first established in the U.S., 1843, in Pittsburgh. Administrative office: 8300 Colesville Rd., No. 300, Silver Spring, MD 20910, (301) 587-0423.

Mill Hill Sisters: *See* **Franciscan Missionaries of St. Joseph.**

Minim Daughters of Mary Immaculate, C.F.M.M.: Founded 1886, in Mexico; in U.S., 1926. General motherhouse, Leon, Guanajuato, Mexico. U.S. address, 555 Patagonia Hwy., Nogales, AZ 85621, (520) 287-3377.

Misericordia Sisters, S.M.: Founded 1848, in Canada; in U.S., 1887. General motherhouse, 12435 Ave. Misericorde, Montreal, QC H4J 2G3, Canada. U.S. address, 225 Carol Ave., Pelham, NY 10803. Social work with unwed mothers and their children; hospital work.

Mission Helpers of the Sacred Heart, M.H.S.H.: Founded 1890, in U.S. General motherhouse, 1001 W. Joppa Rd., Baltimore, MD 21204, (410) 823-8585, www.missionhelpers.org. Religious education, evangelization.

Missionary Catechists of the Sacred Hearts of Jesus and Mary (Violetas), M.C.S.H.: Founded 1918, in Mexico; in U.S., 1943. Motherhouse, Tlalpan, Mexico. U.S. address, 805 Liberty St., Victoria, TX 77901, (512) 578-9302.

Missionary Daughters of the Most Pure Virgin Mary, M.D.P.V.M.: Founded in Mexico; in U.S., 1916. 919 N. 9th St., Kingsville, TX 78363, (512) 595-1087.

Mother of God, Missionary Sisters of the, M.S.M.G.: Byzantine, Ukrainian Rite, Stamford. Motherhouse, 711 N. Franklin St., Philadelphia, PA 19123, (215) 627-7808.

Mother of God, Sisters Poor Servants of the, S.M.G.: Founded 1869, in London, England; in U.S., 1947. General motherhouse, Maryfield, Roehampton, London.

U.S. address: Maryfield Nursing Home, Greensboro Rd., High Point, NC 27260, (336) 886-2444, www.greensboro.com/mnh. Hospital, educational work.

Nazareth, Poor Sisters of, P.S.N.: Founded in England; U.S. foundation, 1924. General mother house, Hammersmith, London, England. U.S. novi tiate, 3333 Manning Ave., Los Angeles, CA 90064, (310) 839-2361. Social services, education.

Notre Dame, School Sisters of, S.S.N.D.: Founded 1833, in Germany; in U.S., 1847. General mother-house, Rome, Italy. U.S. province: 320 E. Ripa Ave., St. Louis, MO 63125, (314) 633-7006, www.ssndcentralpacific.org.

Notre Dame, Sisters of, S.N.D.: Founded 1850, at Coesfeld, Germany; in U.S., 1874. General mother house, Rome, Italy. U.S. provinces: 13000 Auburn Rd., Chardon, OH 44024, (440) 286-7101. 1601 Dixie Highway, Covington, KY 41011, (606) 291-2040. 3837 Secor Rd., Toledo, OH 43623, (419) 474-5485. 1776 Hendrix Ave., Thousand Oaks, CA 91360, (805) 496-3243.

Notre Dame, Sisters of the Congregation of, C.N.D.: Founded 1658, in Canada, by St. Marguerite Bourgeoys; in U.S., 1860. General motherhouse, Montréal, QC, Canada. U.S. province, 223 West Mountain Rd., Ridgefield, CT 06877-3627, (203) 438- 3115, www.cnd-m.com. Education.

Notre Dame de Namur, Sisters of, S.N.D.deN.: Founded 1804, in France; in U.S., 1840. General motherhouse, Rome, Italy. U.S. provinces: 351 Broadway, Everett, MA 02149, (617) 387-2500, www.SNDdeN. org. 30 Jeffrey's Neck Rd., Ipswich, MA 01938, (978) 356-2159. 468 Poquonock Ave., Windsor, CT 06095-2473, (860) 688-1832, www.sndden.org. 1531 Greenspring Valley Rd., Stevenson, MD 21153, (410) 486-5599. 305 Cable St., Baltimore, MD 21210, (410) 243-1993, www.sndden.org. 701 E. Columbia Ave., Cincinnati, OH 45215, (513) 761-7636. 1520 Ralston Ave., Belmont, CA 94002-1908, (650) 593-2045. SND Base Communities, 125 Michigan Ave., N.E., Washington, DC 20017, (202) 884-9750; www.snd den.org. Educational work.

Notre Dame de Sion, Congregation of, N.D.S.: Founded 1850, in France; in U.S., 1892. Generalate, Rome, Italy. U.S. province, 3823 Locust St., Kansas City, MO 64109, (816) 531-1374. Creation of better understanding between Christians and Jews.

Notre Dame Sisters: Founded 1853, in Czechoslo- vakia; in U.S., 1910. General motherhouse, Javornik, Czech Republic. U.S. motherhouse, 3501 State St., Omaha, NE 68112, (402) 455-2994, www.notredame sisters.org. Educational work.

Oblates of the Mother of Orphans, O.M.O: Founded 1945, in Italy. General motherhouse, Milan, Italy. U.S. address, 20 E. 72 St., New York, NY 10021.

Our Lady of Charity, Sisters of (Eudist Sisters, Sisters of Our Lady of Charity of the Refuge), N.A.U.-O.L.C.: Founded 1641, in Caen, France, by St. John Eudes; in U.S., 1855. Autonomous houses were federated in 1944 and in March 1979 the North American Union of the Sisters of Our Lady of Charity was established. General mother-house, 620 Roswell Rd. NW, PO Box 340, Carrollton, OH 44615-0340, (330) 627-1641; www.nauolc.org. Primarily devoted to re-education and rehabilitation of women and girls in residential and non-residential settings.

Our Lady of Sorrows, Sisters of, O.L.S.: Founded 1839, in Italy; in U.S., 1947. General motherhouse, Rome, Italy.

U.S. headquarters, 9894 Norris Ferry Rd., Shreveport, LA 71106.

Our Lady of the Holy Rosary, Daughters of, F.M.S.R. (*Filiae Mariae Sacri Rosarii*): Founded 1946, in North Vietnam; foundation in U.S., 1968. General Motherhouse, Saigon, Vietnam. U.S. Province, 1492 Moss St., New Orleans, LA 70119, (504) 486-0039.

Our Lady of Victory Missionary Sisters, O.L.V.M.: Founded 1922, in U.S. Motherhouse, Victory Noll, 1900 W. Park Dr., PO Box 109, Huntington, IN 46752, (260) 356-0628, www.olvm.org. Educational, social work.

Pallottine Missionary Sisters (Missionary Sisters of the Catholic Apostolate), S.A.C.: Founded in Rome, 1838; in U.S., 1912. Generalate, Rome, Italy. U.S. provincialate, 15270 Old Halls Ferry Rd., Florissant, MO 63034, (314) 837-7100, www.geocities.com/pallottinerenewal.

Pallottine Sisters of the Catholic Apostolate, C.S.A.C.: Founded 1843, at Rome, Italy; in U.S., 1889. General motherhouse, Rome. U.S. motherhouse, St. Patrick's Villa, Harriman Heights, Harriman, NY 10926, (914) 783-9007. Educational work.

Parish Visitors of Mary Immaculate, P.V.M.I.: Founded 1920, in New York. General motherhouse, Box 658, Monroe, NY 10949, (845) 783-2251, www.parishvisitors.org. Mission work.

Passionist Nuns (Passion of Jesus Christ, Religious of), C.P.: Founded 1771, in Italy, by St. Paul of the Cross; in U.S., 1910. U.S. convents: 2715 Churchview Ave., Pittsburgh, PA 15227-2141, (412) 881-1155. 631 Griffin Pond Rd., Clarks Summit, PA 18411-8899, (570) 586-2791, www.intiques.net/cpnuns. 8564 Crisp Rd., Whitesville, KY 42378-9729, (270) 233-4571, www.passionistnuns.org. 1151 Donaldson Hwy., Erlanger, KY 41018, (859) 371-8568. 15700 Clayton Rd., Ellisville, MO 63011, (314) 227-5275. Contemplatives.

Passionist Sisters: *See* Cross and Passion, Sisters of the

Paul, Daughters of St. (Missionary Sisters of the Media of Communication), D.S.P.: Founded 1915, at Alba, Piedmont, Italy; in U.S., 1932. General motherhouse, Rome, Italy. U.S. provincial house, 50 St. Paul's Ave., Boston, MA 02130-3491, (617) 522-8911, www.pauline.org. Apostolate of the communications arts.

Paul of Chartres, Sisters of St., S.P.C.: Founded 1696, in France. General House, Rome, Italy. U.S. address, 2920 Third Ave., So., Escanaba, MI 49828; (906) 399-0420.

Perpetual Adoration of Guadalupe, Sisters of, A.P.G.: U.S. foundation, 2403 W. Travis, San Antonio, TX 78207, (956) 227-7785.

Peter Claver, Missionary Sisters of St., S.S.P.C.: Founded 1894 in Austria by Bl. Maria Teresa Ledochowska; in U.S., 1914. General motherhouse, Rome, Italy. U.S. address, 667 Woods Mill Rd. S., Chesterfield, MO 63006, (314) 469-4923.

Pious Disciples of the Divine Master, P.D.D.M.: Founded 1924 in Italy; in U.S., 1948. General motherhouse, Rome, Italy. U.S. headquarters, 60 Sunset Ave., Staten Island, NY 10314, (718) 494-8597.

Pious Schools, Sisters of the, Sch. P.: Founded 1829 in Spain; in U.S., 1954. General motherhouse, Rome, Italy. U.S. headquarters, 17601 Nordhoff St., Northridge, CA 91325, (818) 882-6265.

Poor, Little Sisters of the, L.S.P.: Founded 1839, in France, by Bl. Jeanne Jugan; in U.S., 1868. General moth-erhouse, St. Pern, France. U.S. provinces: 110-30 221st St.,

Queens Village, NY 11429, (718) 464-1800. 601 Maiden Choice Lane, Baltimore, MD 21228, (410) 744-9367; www.littlesistersofthepoor.org. 80 W. Northwest Hwy., Palatine, IL 60067, (847) 358-5700, www.littlesistersofthe poor.org. Care of aged.

Poor Clare Missionary Sisters (Misioneras Clarisas), M.C.: Founded in Mexico. General motherhouse, Rome, Italy. U.S. novitiate, 1019 N. Newhope, Santa Ana, CA 92703-1534, (714) 554-8850.

Poor Clare Nuns: *See* **Franciscan Poor Clare Nuns**.

Poor Handmaids of Jesus Christ (Ancilla Domini Sisters), P.H.J.C.: Founded 1851, in Germany by Bl. Mary Kasper; in U.S., 1868. General motherhouse, Dernbach, Westerwald, Germany. U.S. motherhouse, Ancilla Domini Convent, Donaldson, IN 46513, (219) 936-9936. Educational, hospital work, social services.

Precious Blood, Daughters of Charity of the Most, D.C.P.B.: Founded 1872, at Pagani, Italy; in U.S., 1908. General motherhouse, Rome, Italy. U.S. convent, 1482 North Ave., Bridgeport, CT 06604, (203) 334- 7000.

Precious Blood, Missionary Sisters of the, C.P.S.: Founded 1885, at Mariannhill, South Africa; in U.S., 1925. Generalate, Rome, Italy. U.S. novitiate, PO Box 97, Reading, PA 19607, (610) 777-1624. Home and foreign mission work.

Precious Blood, Sisters Adorers of the, A.P.B.: Founded 1861, in Canada; in U.S., 1890. General motherhouse, Canada. U.S. autonomous monasteries: 5400 Fort Hamilton Pkwy., Brooklyn, NY 11219, (718) 438-6371, www.sisterspreciousblood.org. 700 Bridge St., Manchester, NH 03104-5495, (603) 623-4264. 166 State St., Portland, ME 04101. 400 Pratt St., Watertown, NY 13601, (315) 782-5119, www.sisters preciousblood.org. Cloistered, contemplative.

Precious Blood, Sisters of the, C.PP.S.: Founded 1834, in Switzerland; in U.S., 1844. Generalate, 4000 Denlinger Rd., Dayton, OH 45426, (937) 837-3302. Education, health care, other ministries.

Precious Blood, Sisters of the Most, C.PP.S.: Founded 1845, in Steinerberg, Switzerland; in U.S., 1870. General motherhouse, 204 N. Main St., O'Fallon, MO 63366-2203, (636) 240-3420. Education, other ministries.

Presentation, Sisters of Mary of the, S.M.P.: Founded 1829, in France; in U.S., 1903. General motherhouse, Broons, Côtes-du-Nord, France. U.S. address, Maryvale Novitiate, 11550 River Rd., Valley City, ND 58072, (701) 845-2864, www.sistersofmaryofthepresentation.com. Hospital work.

Presentation of Mary, Sisters of the, P.M.: Founded 1796, in France by Bl. Marie Rivier; in U.S., 1873. General motherhouse, Castel Gandolfo, Italy. U.S. provincial houses: 495 Mammoth Rd., Manchester, NH 03104, (603) 669-1080, www.presentationofmary-usa.org. 209 Lawrence St., Methuen, MA 01844, (978) 687-1369, www.presmarymethuen.org.

Presentation of the B.V.M., Sisters of the, P.B.V.M.: Founded 1775, in Ireland; in U.S., 1854, in San Francisco. U.S. motherhouses: 2360 Carter Rd., Dubuque, IA 52001, (563) 588-2008, www.dubuquepresentations.org. 880 Jackson Ave., New Windsor, NY 12553, (845) 564-0513. 281 Masonic Ave, San Francisco, CA 94118, (415) 422-5013, www.presentationsisterssf.org. St. Colman's Convent, Watervliet, NY 12189, (518) 273-4911. 1101

32nd Ave., S., Fargo ND 58103, (701) 237-4857, www. presetnationsistersfargo.org. Presentation Convent, Aberdeen, SD 57401, (605) 229-8419, Leominster, MA 01453. 419 Woodrow Rd., Staten Island, NY 10312, (718) 966- 2365.

Presentation of the Blessed Virgin Mary, Sisters of, of Union: Founded in Ireland, 1775; union established in Ireland, 1976; first U.S. vice province, 1979. Generalate, Kildare, Ireland. U.S. provincialate, 729 W. Wilshire Dr., Phoenix, AZ 85007, (602) 271-9687.

Providence, Daughters of Divine, F.D.P.: Founded 1832, Italy; in U.S., 1964. General motherhouse, Rome, Italy. U.S. address, 74684 Airport Rd., Covington, LA 70435, (985) 809-8836 (fax).

Providence, Missionary Catechists of Divine, M.C.D.P.: Administrative house, 2318 Castroville Rd., San Antonio, TX 78237, (210) 432-0113.

Providence, Oblate Sisters of, O.S.P.: Founded 1829, in U.S., by Mother Mary Elizabeth Lange and Father James Joubert, S.S. First order of black nuns in U.S. General motherhouse, 701 Gun Rd., Baltimore, MD 21227, (410) 242-8500. Educational work.

Providence, Sisters of, S.P.: Founded 1861, in Canada; in U.S., 1873. General motherhouse, Our Lady of Victory Convent, 5 Gamelin St., Holyoke, MA 01040, (413) 536-7511, wwwsisofprov.org.

Providence, Sisters of, S.P.: Founded 1843, in Canada; in U.S., 1854. General motherhouse, Montreal, QC, Canada. U.S. province, Mother Joseph Province, 506 Second Ave., #1200, Seattle, WA 98104, (206) 464-3394, www.sistersofprovidence.net.

Providence, Sisters of (of St. Mary-of-the-Woods), S.P.: Founded 1806, in France; in U.S., 1 Sisters of Providence, St. Mary-of-the-Woods, IN 47876, (812) 535-3131, www. sistersofprovidence.org.

Providence, Sisters of Divine, C.D.P.: Founded 1762, in France; in U.S., 1866. Generalate, 515 SW 24th St., San Antonio, TX 78207, (210) 434-1866. Educational, hospital work.

Providence, Sisters of Divine, C.D.P.: Founded 1851, in Germany; in U.S., 1876. Generalate, Rome, Italy. U.S. provinces: 9000 Babcock Blvd., Allison Park, PA 15101-2793, (412) 931-5241, www.divineprovidenceweb. org. 3415 Bridgeland Dr., Bridgetown, MO 63044, (314) 209-9181, www.divineprovi denceweb.org. 363 Bishops Hwy., Kingston, MA 02364, (781) 585-7707. Educational, hospital work.

Providence, Sisters of Divine (of Kentucky), C.D.P.: Founded 1762, in France; in U.S., 1889. General motherhouse, Fenetrange, France. U.S. province, St. Bartholomew Parish, Cincinnati, OH 45231, (513) 728-3146, www.cdpkentucky.org. Education, social services, other ministries.

Redeemer, Oblates of the Most Holy, O.SS.R.: Founded 1864, in Spain. General motherhouse, Spain. U.S. foundation, 60-80 Pond St., Jamaica Plain, MA 02130, (617) 524-1640.

Redeemer, Order of the Most Holy, O.SS.R.: Founded 1731, by Ven. Mother Marie Celeste Crostarosa, with the help of St. Alphonsus Liguori; in U.S., 1957. U.S. addresses: Mother of Perpetual Help Monastery, PO Box 220, Esopus, NY 12429, (845) 384-6533, www.redemptor-istinenunsofnewyork.org. Monastery of St. Alphonsus, 200 Ligouri Dr., Liguori, MO 63057, (636) 464-1093, www.redemptoristine nuns.org.

Redeemer, Sisters of the Divine, S.D.R.: Founded

1849, in Niederbronn, France; in U.S., 1912. General motherhouse, Rome, Italy. U.S. province, 999 Rock Run Road, Elizabeth, PA 15037, (412) 751-8600. Educational, hospital work; care of the aged.

Redeemer, Sisters of the Holy, C.S.R.: Founded 1849, in Alsace; in U.S., 1924. General motherhouse, Wurzburg, Germany. U.S. provincial house, 521 Moredon Rd., Huntingdon Valley, PA 19006, (215) 914-4101. Personalized medical care in hospitals, homes for aged, private homes; retreat work.

Reparation of the Congregation of Mary, Sisters of, S.R.C.M.: Founded 1903, in U.S. Motherhouse, St. Zita's Villa, Monsey, NY 10952, (845) 356-2011.

Reparation of the Sacred Wounds of Jesus, Sisters of, S.R.: Founded 1959 in U.S. General motherhouse, 2120 S.E. 24th Ave., Portland, OR 97214-5504, (503) 236-4207.

Resurrection, Sisters of the, C.R.: Founded 1891, in Italy; in U.S., 1900. General motherhouse, Rome, Italy. U.S. provinces: 7432 Talcott Ave., Chicago, IL 60631, (773) 792-6363. Mt. St. Joseph, 35 Boltwood Ave., Castleton-on-Hudson, NY 12033, (518) 732-2429, www.resurrectionsisters.org. Education, nursing.

Rita, Sisters of St., O.S.A.: General motherhouse, Wurzburg, Germany. U.S. foundation, St. Monica's Convent, 3920 Green Bay Rd., Racine, WI 53404, (262) 639-5050, www.srsofstrita.org.

Rosary, Congregation of Our Lady of the Holy, R.S.R.: Founded 1874, in Canada; in U.S., 1899. General motherhouse, Rimouski, QC, Canada. U.S. regional house, 20 Portland Ave., Old Orchard Beach, ME 04964, (207) 934-0592, www.soeursdu-saintrasaire.org. Educational work.

Rosary, Missionary Sisters of the Holy, M.S.H.R.: Founded 1924, in Ireland; in U.S., 1954. Motherhouse, Dublin, Ireland. In U.S., 741 Polo Rd., Bryn Mawr, PA 19010, (610) 520-1976, www.holyrosarymissionarysisters. org. African missions.

Sacrament, Missionary Sisters of the Most Blessed, M.SS.S.: General motherhouse, Madrid, Spain. U.S. foundation, 1111 Wordin Ave., Bridgeport, CT 06605.

Sacrament, Nuns of the Perpetual Adoration of the Blessed, A.P.: Founded 1807 in Rome, Italy; in U.S., 1925. U.S. monasteries: 145 N. Cotton Ave., El Paso, TX 79901, (915) 533-5323. 771 Ashbury St., San Francisco, CA 94117, (415) 566-2743.

Sacrament, Oblate Sisters of the Blessed, O.S.B.S.: Founded 1935, in U.S. Motherhouse, St. Sylvester Convent, PO Box 217, Marty, SD 57361, (605) 384-3305. Care of American Indians.

Sacrament, Servants of the Blessed, S.S.S.: Founded 1858, in France, by St. Pierre Julien Eymard; in U.S., 1947. General motherhouse, Rome, Italy. American provincial house, St. Charles Borromeo Parish, 1818 Coal Pl. SE, Albuquerque, NM 87106, (505) 242-3692. Contemplative.

Sacrament, Sisters of the Blessed, for Indians and Colored People, S.B.S.: Founded 1891, in U.S., by St. Katharine Drexel. General motherhouse, 1663 Bristol Pike, PO Box 8502, Bensalem, PA 19020, (215) 244- 9900, www.katharinedrexel.org.

Sacrament, Sisters of the Most Holy, M.H.S.: Founded 1851, in France; in U.S., 1872. Generalate, 313 Corona Dr. (P.O. Box 90037), Lafayette, LA 70509, (337) 981-8475.

Sacrament, Sisters Servants of the Blessed, S.J.S.: Founded 1904, in Mexico; in U.S., 1926. General motherhouse, Mexico. U.S. address: 215 Lomita St., El Segundo, CA 90245, (310) 615-0766.

Sacramentine Nuns (Religious of the Order of the Blessed Sacrament and Our Lady), O.S.S.: Founded 1639, in France; in U.S., 1912. U.S. monasteries: 235 Bellvale Lakes Rd., Warwick NY 10990. 2798 US 31 N, PO Box 86, Conway, MI 49722, (231) 347-0447. Perpetual adoration of the Holy Eucharist.

Sacred Heart, Daughters of Our Lady of the, F.D.N.S.C.: Founded 1882, in France; in U.S., 1955. General motherhouse, Rome, Italy. U.S. address, 424 E. Browning Rd., Bellmawr, NJ 08031, (609) 931- 8973. Educational work.

Sacred Heart, Missionary Sisters of the (Cabrini Sisters), M.S.C.: Founded 1880, in Italy, by St. Frances Xavier Cabrini; in U.S., 1889. General motherhouse, Rome, Italy. U.S. provincial office, 222 E. 19th St., 5B, New York, NY 10003. Educational, health, social and catechetical work.

Sacred Heart, Society Devoted to the, S.D.S.H.: Founded 1940, in Hungary; in U.S., 1956. U.S. motherhouse, 9814 Sylvia Ave., Northridge, CA 91324, (818) 831-9710; www. sacredheartsisters.com. Educational work.

Sacred Heart, Society of the, R.S.C.J.: Founded 1800, in France; in U.S., 1818. Generalate, Rome, Italy. U.S. provincial house, 4389 W. Pine Blvd., St. Louis, MO 63108, (314) 652-1500, www.rscj.org. Educational work.

Sacred Heart of Jesus, Apostles of, A.S.C.J.: Founded 1894, in Italy; in U.S., 1902. General motherhouse, Rome, Italy. U.S. motherhouse, 295 Benham St., Hamden, CT 06514, (203) 248-4225, www.ascjus.org. Pastoral ministry, nursing and health care, legal assistance, elderly day care.

Sacred Heart of Jesus, Handmaids of the, A.C.J.: Founded 1877, in Spain. General motherhouse, Rome, Italy. U.S. province, 616 Coopertown Rd., Haverford, PA 19041, (610) 642-5715, www.acjusa.org. Educational, retreat work.

Sacred Heart of Jesus, Missionary Sisters of the Most (Hiltrup), M.S.C.: Founded 1899, in Germany; in U.S., 1908. General motherhouse, Rome, Italy. U.S. province, 2811 Moyers Lane, Reading, PA 19605, (610) 929-5944; www.mscrdg.org. Education, health care, pastoral ministry.

Sacred Heart of Jesus, Oblate Sisters of the, O.S.H.J.: Founded 1894; in U.S., 1949. General motherhouse, Rome, Italy. U.S. headquarters, 50 Warner Rd., Hubbard, OH 44425, (330) 759-9329, www.oblatesister.com. Educational, social work.

Sacred Heart of Jesus, Servants of the Most, S.S.C.J.: Founded 1894, in Poland; in U.S., 1959. General motherhouse, Cracow, Poland. U.S. address, 866 Cambria St., Cresson, PA 16630, (814) 886-4223, www.sacredheartsis-ters.org. Education, health care, social services.

Sacred Heart of Jesus, Sisters of the, S.S.C.J.: Founded 1816, in France; in U.S., 1903. General motherhouse, St. Jacut, Brittany, France. U.S. provincial house, 11931 Radium St., San Antonio, TX 78216, (210) 344-7203. Educational, hospital, domestic work.

Sacred Heart of Jesus and of the Poor, Servants of the (Mexican), S.S.H.J.P.: Founded 1885, in Mexico; in U.S., 1907. General motherhouse, Apartado 92, Puebla, Mexico. U.S. address, 3310 S. Zapata Hwy, Laredo, TX 78046, (956) 723-3343.

Sacred Heart of Jesus and Our Lady of Guadalupe, Missionaries of the, M.S.C.Gpe.: U.S. address, 1212 E.

Euclid Ave., Arlington Heights, IL 60004, (708) 398-1350.

Sacred Heart of Jesus for Reparation, Congregation of the Handmaids of the, A.R.: Founded 1918, in Italy; in U.S., 1958. U.S. address, 36 Villa Dr., Steubenville, OH 43953, (740) 282-3801.

Sacred Heart of Mary, Religious of the, R.S.H.M.: Founded 1848, in France; in U.S., 1877. Generalate, Rome, Italy. U.S. provinces; 50 Wilson Park Dr., Tarrytown, NY 10591, (914) 631-8872, www.rshm.org. 441 N. Garfield Ave., Montebello, CA 90640, (323) 887-8821, www.rshm.org.

Sacred Hearts and of Perpetual Adoration, Sisters of the, SS.CC.: Founded 1797, in France; in U.S., 1908. General motherhouse, Rome, Italy. U.S. provinces: 1120 Fifth Ave., Honolulu, HI 96816, (808) 737-5822, www.ssccpicpus.com (Pacific). 35 Huttleston Ave., Fairhaven, MA 02719, (508) 994-9341 (East Coast). Varied ministries.

Sacred Hearts of Jesus and Mary, Sisters of the, S.H.J.M.: Established 1953, in U.S. General mother house, Essex, England. U.S. address, 2150 Lake Shore Ave., Oakland CA 94606, (510) 832-2935.

Savior, Company of the, C.S.: Founded 1952, in Spain; in U.S., 1962. General motherhouse, Madrid, Spain. U.S. foundation, 820 Clinton Ave., Bridgeport, CT 06604, (203) 368-1875.

Savior, Sisters of the Divine, S.D.S.: Founded 1888, in Italy; in U.S., 1895. General motherhouse, Rome, Italy. U.S. province, 4311 N. 100th St., Milwaukee, WI 53222, (414) 466-0810, www.salvatoriansisters.org. Educational, hospital work.

Social Service, Sisters of, S.S.S.: Founded in Hungary, 1923, by Sr. Margaret Slachta. U.S. generalate, 296 Summit Ave., Buffalo, NY 14214, (716) 834-0197, www.sistersofsocialservicebuffalo.org. Social work.

Social Service, Sisters of, S.S.S.: Founded 1908, in Hungary; in U.S., 1926. General motherhouse, 4316 Lanai Rd., Encino, CA 91436, (818) 285-3359, www.sistersofsocialservice.com

Teresa of Jesus, Society of St., S.T.J.: Founded 1876, in Spain; in U.S., 1910. General motherhouse, Rome, Italy. U.S. provincial house, 18080 St. Joseph's Way, Covington, LA 70435, (985) 893-1470, www.teresians.org.

Thomas of Villanova, Congregation of Sisters of St., S.S.T.V.: Founded 1661, in France; in U.S., 1948. General motherhouse, Neuilly-sur-Seine, France. U.S. foundation, W. Rocks Rd., Norwalk, CT 06851, (203) 847-5893.

Trinity, Missionary Servants of the Most Blessed, M.S.B.T.: Founded 1912, in U.S., by very Rev. Thomas A. Judge. General motherhouse, 3501 Solly Ave., Philadelphia, PA 19136, (215) 335-7550, www.msbt.org. Educational, social work, health services.

Trinity, Sisters Oblates to the Blessed, O.B.T.: Founded 1923, in Italy. U.S. novitiate, Beekman Rd., P.O. Box 98, Hopewell Junction, NY 12533, (914) 226-5671.

Trinity, Sisters of the Most Holy, O.Ss.T.: Founded 1198, in Rome; in U.S., 1920. General motherhouse, Rome, Italy. U.S. address, Immaculate Conception Province, 21281 Chardon Rd., Euclid, OH 44117, (216) 481-8232, www.srstrinity.org. Educational work.

Trinity, Society of Our Lady of the Most Holy, S.O.L.T.: Motherhouse, 1200 Lantana St., Corpus Christi, TX 78407, (361) 387-9095.

Ursula of the Blessed Virgin, Society of the Sisters of St., S.U.: Founded 1606, in France; in U.S., 1902. General motherhouse, France. U.S. novitiate, 50 Linnwood Rd.,

Rhinebeck, NY 12572, (845) 876-2341, www.societyofstursula.org. Educational work.

Ursuline Nuns (Roman Union), O.S.U.: Founded 1535, in Italy; in U.S., 1727. Generalate, Rome, Italy. U.S. provinces: 1338 North Avenue, New Rochelle, NY 10804, (914) 712-0060. 353 S. Sappington Rd., Kirkwood, MO 63122, (314) 821-6884, www.osucen tral.org. 639 Angela Dr., Santa Rosa, CA 95401, (707) 545-6811. St. Mary's Residences, 100 Campus Ave., #211, Lewiston, ME 04240, (207) 786-9312.

Ursuline Sisters of Mount Saint Joseph, O.S.U.: Founded 1535, in Italy; in U.S., 1727, in New Orleans. U.S. motherhouses: 20860 St, Rte. 251, St. Martin, OH 45518-9705, (513) 875-2020. 901 E. Miami St., Paola, KS 66071, (913) 557-2349. 8001 Cummings Rd., Maple Mount, KY 42356, (270) 229-4200, www.ursuineslou.org. 2600 Lander Rd., Cleveland, OH 44124, (440) 449-1200, www. ursulinesisters.org. 8001 Cummings Rd., Maple Mount, KY 42356, (270) 229-4200, www.ursu-linesmsj.org. 4045 Indian Rd., Toledo, OH 43606, (419) 536-9587, www.toledoursulines.org. 4250 Shields Rd., Canfield, OH 44406, (330) 792-7636. 1339 E. McMillan St., Cincinnati, OH 45206, (513) 961-3410.

Ursuline Sisters of the Congregation of Tildonk, Belgium, O.S.U.: Founded 1535, in Italy; Tildonk con gregation, 1832; in U.S., 1924. Generalate, Brussels, Belgium. U.S. address, 81-15 Utopia Parkway, Jamaica, NY 11432, (718) 591-0681, www.tressy.tripod.com. Educational, foreign mission work.

Ursuline Sisters of Belleville, O.S.U.: Founded 1535, in Italy; in U.S., 1910; established as diocesan community, 1983. Central house, 1026 N. Douglas Ave., Belleville, IL 62220, (618) 235-3444. Educational work.

Venerini Sisters, Religious, M.P.V.: Founded 1685, in Italy; in U.S., 1909. General motherhouse, Rome, Italy. U.S. provincialate; 23 Edward St., Worcester, MA 01605, (508) 754-1020, www.venerinisisters.org.

Vietnamese Adorers of the Holy Cross, M.T.G.: Founded 1670 in Vietnam; in U.S. 1976. General motherhouse 7408 S.E. Adler St., Portland, OR 97215, (503) 254-3284.

Vincent de Paul, Sisters: *See* **Charity of St. Vincent de Paul, Sisters of.**

Visitation Nuns, V.H.M.: Founded 1610, in France; in U.S. (Georgetown, DC), 1799. Contemplative, educational work. Two federations in U.S:

• First Federation of North America. Major pontifical enclosure. Pres., Mother Mary Jozefa Kowalewski, Monastery of the Visitation, 2055 Ridgedale Dr., Snellville, GA 30078, (770) 972-1060. Addresses of monasteries belonging to the federation: 2300 Springhill Ave., Mobile, AL 36607, (251) 473-2321. 14 Beach Rd., Tyringham, MA, 01264, (413) 243- 3995. 12221 Bievenue Rd, Rockville, VA 23146, (804) 749-4885. 5820 City Ave., Philadelphia, PA 19131, (215) 473-5888. 1745 Parkside Blvd., Toledo, OH 43607, (419) 536-1343. 2055 Ridgedale Dr., Snellville, GA 30078-2443, (770) 972-1060.

• Second Federation of North America. Constitutional enclosure. Pres., Sr. Anne Madeleine Godefroy, Monastery of the Visitation, 3020 N. Ballas Rd., St. Louis, MO 63131, (314) 432-5353, www.visitationmonastery.org/stlouis. Addresses of monasteries belonging to the federation: 1500 35th St., Washington, DC 20007, (202) 337-0305. 3020 N. Ballas Rd., St. Louis, MO

63131, (314) 432-5353. 200 E. Second St., Frederick, MD 21701, (301) 622-3322. Mt. de Chantal Monastery of the Visitation, 410 Washington Ave., Wheeling, WV 26003, (304) 232-1283; www.mountdechan tal.org. 8902 Ridge Blvd., Brooklyn, NY 11209, (718) 745- 5151, www.visitationsisters.org. 2455 Visitation Dr., Mendota Heights, MN 55120, (651) 683-1700.

Visitation of the Congregation of the Immaculate Heart of Mary, Sisters of the, S.V.M.: Founded 1952, in U.S. Motherhouse, 2950 Kaufmann Ave., Dubuque, IA 52001, (563) 588-7256. Educational work, parish ministry.

Vocationist Sisters (Sisters of the Divine Vocations), S.V.D.: Founded 1921, in Italy; in U.S., 1967 General motherhouse, Naples, Italy. U.S. founda tion, Perpetual Help Nursery, 172 Broad St., Newark, NJ 07104, (973) 484-3535.

Wisdom, Daughters of, D.W.: Founded 1703, in France, by St. Louis Marie Grignion de Montfort; in U.S., 1904. General motherhouse, Vendee, France. U.S. province, 385 Ocean Ave., Islip, NY 11751, (631) 277-2660, www. daughtersofwisdom.org. Education, health care, parish ministry, social services.

Xaverian Missionary Society of Mary, Inc., X.M.M.: Founded 1945, in Italy; in U.S., 1954. General motherhouse, Parma, Italy. U.S. address, 242 Salisbury St., Worcester, MA 01609, (508) 757-0514.

MEMBERSHIP OF RELIGIOUS INSTITUTES OF WOMEN

Principal source: Annuario Pontificio. *Statistics as of Jan. 1, 2013, unless indicated otherwise.* Listed below are world membership statistics of institutes of women with 500 or more members. Numbers in parentheses reflect the number of houses. For statistical information of institutes in the United States, *see* **Statistics**.

Salesian Srs. (1,436)	13,653	Joseph Benedetto, Srs. of St. (118)	1,691
Calced Carmelites (712)	9,181	Apostolic Carmel, Srs. of (177)	1,674
Franciscan Clarist Congr. (758)	7,129	Joseph, Srs. of St. (Chambéry) (267)	1,665
Claretians (534)	6,799	Mission, Carmelites (247)	1,658
Carmel, Srs. of the Mother of (664) 6,587		Wisdom, Daught. of (227)	1,609
Franciscan Missionaries of Mary (748) 6,452		Felician Srs. (207)	1,607
Charity, Mission. of (766)	5,314	Franciscans of the Penance and	
Ador. of the Bl. Sacrament. (603)	4,750	Christian Charity (222)	1,600
Charity of St. Bartholomew of Capitanio (415)	4,406	Mary, Minister of the Infirm, Servants of (115)	1,571
Benedictine Nuns (236)	4,153	Cistercian Nuns (Strict Observance) (70)	1,559
Paul of Chartres, Srs. of St. (594)	4,000	Mary Our Lady, Company of (185)	1,510
Our Lady of Charity of the Good Shepherd (486) 3,669		Adorers of the Blood of Christ (226)	1,507
Sacred Heart Congregation (463)	3,648	Notre Dame de Namur, Srs. of (546)	1,486
Mercy of the Americas, Srs. of (1,728)	3,627	Destitute, Srs. of the (211)	1,450
Holy Cross, Srs. of Mercy of the (403)	3,581	Salesian Missionaries of Mary Immaculate (172)	1,448
Holy Spirit, Mission Servants of the (423)	3,249	Holy Savior, Srs. of the (166)	1,443
Immaculate Heart of Mary, Mission.		Cross, Srs. of the (204)	1,434
Srs. (163)	3,248 (2009)	Comboni Missionary Srs. (178)	1,413
Notre Dame, School Srs. of (467)	3,162	Teresa of Jesus, Society of St. (204)	1,412
Joseph, Srs. of St. (Cluny) (424)	2,809	Divine Master, Pious Disciples of (170)	1,410
Dominicans (198)	2,705	Elizabeth, Srs. of St. (201)	1,411
Canossian Daught. of Charity (326)	2,691	Dorothy, Srs. of St. (166)	1,405
Poor, Little Sisters of the (195)	2,503	Teresian Carmelites of Verapoly (166)	1,403
Sacred Heart of Jesus "Sophie Barat,"		Benedictines, Missionary (142)	1,395
Society of the (389)	2,443	Little Flower of Bethany, Srs. of the (170)	1,382
Paul, Daught. of St. (239)	2,401	Joseph, Srs. of St. (Carondolet) (564)	1,362
Charity of St. Joan Antida, Srs. of (292)	2,356	Franciscan Hospitallers	
Dominicans of the Presentation		of the Immaculate Conception (157)	1,361
of the Virgin (328)	2,323	Holy Family of Nazareth, Srs. of (159)	1,328
Mercy, Srs. of (Ireland) (682)	2,307	Heart of Mary, Soc. of Daught. of (139)	1,313
Ancianos Desamparados, Hermanitas de		Jesus and Mary, Religious of (178)	1,303
los (205)	2,275	Charity of Jesus and Mary, Srs. of (178)	1,303
Anne, Srs. of Charity of St. (280)	2,200	Anne, Daughters of Saint (205)	1,294
Notre Dame, Srs. of (275)	2,182	Immaculate Conception, Little Srs. of the (232)	1,285
Claretian Capuchins (150)	1,965	Jesus, Mary, and Joseph, Society of (160)	1,273
Visitandine Nuns (134)	1,964	Capuchin Tertiaries of the Holy Family (209)	1,245
Ursulines of the Roman Union (233)	1,948	Anne, Srs. of Saint (172)	1,236
Holy Family Sisters (224)	1,933	Union of the Srs. of the Presentation (241)	1,234
Carmelites of Charity of Vedruna (258)	1,904	Franciscans of George the Martyr (142)	1,227
Cross, Srs. of the (Swiss) (250)	1,873	Mary Immaculate, Religious of (122)	1,194
Carmelites, Scalced (124)	1,820	Fraternity of Little Sisters of Jesus (254)	1,184
B.V.M., Inst. of the (English) (290)	1,818	Divine Providence,	
Jesus, Congr. of (290)	1,818	Srs. of (St. Maurice) (230)	1,171
Holy Family, Srs. of the (Bordeaux) (267)	1,817	Our Lady of the Sacred Heart, Daughters	
Concezioniste (Franciscan Concessionists) (143)	1,710	of (194)	1,171

Sacred Heart of Jesus, Apostles of (165)	1,168
Presentation of Mary, Srs. of the (170)	1,154
Salvatorians (200)	1,152
Adorers of the Blessed Sacrament and Charity (158)	1,154
Mary Help of Christians, Mission. Srs. (179)	1,143
Charity, Dtrs. of Divine (162)	1,132
Servants of Mary, Srs. of Our Lady of Sorrows (156)	1,130
Hospitallers of the Sacred Heart of Jesus (106)	1,126
Sacred Heart of Jesus, Ancelle (124)	1,122
Anne, Srs. of, Tiruchchirappalli (188)	1,107
Assumption, Religious of the (152)	1,107
Holy Spirit, Daughters of the (153)	1,102
Jesus, Daught. of (St. Joseph of Kermaria) (153)	1,102
Mary, Mother of Mercy, Daught. of (212)	1,094
Ursulines of Tildonk (141)	1,093
Anne, Daught. of Saint (Ranchi) (130)	1,082
Franciscans of the Family of Mary (140)	1,054
Franciscan Srs. (Pondicherry) (181)	1,053
Notre Dame, Srs. of the Cong. of (121)	1,050
Franciscans of Christ the King (143)	1,051
Franciscans of the Immaculate Conception (147)	1,044
Holy Names of Jesus and Mary, Srs. of the (73)	1,031
Caritas Srs. of Miyazaki (166)	1,009
Mercedarians of Charity (137)	1,001
Cross and Passion, Srs. of the (Passionist Srs.) (162)	999
Religious Dominicans of the Annunciation (136)	992
Infirm of St. Francis, Srs. of (95)	990
Jesus, Daught. of (Salamanca) (122)	962
Queen of Apostles (128)	961
Dorothy of Frassinetti, Srs. of St. (134)	958
Mercy of Australia, Inst. of Srs. (287)	951
Immaculate Heart of Mary, Mother of Christ (136)	950
Franciscan Srs. of Notre Dame de Bon Secours of Madras (120)	944 (2010)
School Srs. of St. Francis of Milwaukee (288)	941
Our Lady of the Missions, Srs. of (232)	939
Immaculate, Mission. of (116)	937
Cistercian Nuns, O. Cist. (59)	934
Mary, Daught. of (167)	921
Handmaids of the Holy Child Jesus (138)	914
Servants of Jesus of Charity (93)	914
Claretian (Urban) (79)	912
Mercy, Srs. of (Verona) (90)	911
Clarist Franciscan Mission (150)	910
Joseph, Srs. of St. (Philadelphia) (134)	900
Precious Blood, Mission. Srs. of the (99)	901
Joseph of the Apparition, Srs. of St. (157)	891
Divine Love, Daughters of (170)	883
Charity (Ancelle della) (90)	879
B.V.M., Inst. of the (140)	879
Our Lady of Mercy, Daught. of (154)	878
Sacred Heart of Jesus, Daught. of Charity of the (128)	869
Ursuline Franciscans (121)	868
Medical Srs. of St. Joseph (80)	866
Servants of the Imm. Hrt. Of Mary, Srs. (76)	860
Sacramentines (Perp. Ador. of the Blessed Sacrament) (60)	850
Carmelite Sisters of St. Teresa (120)	847
Franciscan Sisters of the Presentation of Mary (142)	847

Providence, Srs. of (Portieux) (152)	845
Imitation of Christ, Srs. of the (180)	840
Mary Immaculate / Catherine of Siena (149)	835
Camillus, Dtrs. of St. (98)	833
Elizabethan Franciscans (97)	831
Cross, Daughters of, of Liege (113)	827
Love of God, Sisters of the (107)	820
Joseph, Srs. of St. (207)	829
Joseph of the Sacred Heart of Jesus, Srs. of St. (278)	822
Dominicans of the Most Holy Rosary (312)	816
Immaculate Conception, Srs. of the (163)	814
Baptistine Srs., Srs. of St. John the Baptist (122)	804
Ursulines of the Sacred Heart of Jesus (98)	801
Charity, Srs. of (Thrissur) (107)	801
Immaculate Heart of Mary (144)	797
Immaculate Heart of Mary, Miss. Srs. (144)	797
Ursulines of Mary Immaculate (104)	797
Sacred Heart of Mary Virgin Immaculate, Srs. of the (126)	793
Vincent de Paul, Srs. of Charity of (108)	792
Assumption, Little Srs. of the (118)	791
Charity, Srs. of, Our Lady of Mercy (69)	791
Our Lady of Africa, Mission. Srs. of (110)	783
Joseph, Inst. of Srs. of St. (174)	779
Franciscan Srs. of Dillingen (81)	772
Sacred Heart of Jesus, Mission. Srs. (147)	771
Poor of the Inst. Palazzolo, Srs. of the (104)	766
Mary Immaculate, Sisters of the B.V.M. (112)	766
Augustinians (78)	763
Franciscans of Gonzaga (134)	763
Immaculate Conception, Srs. of Charity (93)	757
Our Lady of the Apostles, Missionary Sisters of (126)	756
Joseph, Srs. of St. (Cantaous) (135)	756
Benedictine Srs., Fed. of St. Scholastica (21)	744
B.V.M., Religious of the (117)	744
Franciscans Third Order Regular (51)	742
Immaculate Conc. of the B.V.M. (116)	740
Missionary Srs. of Mary Imm. (101)	734
Franciscans of the Blessed Sacrament (43)	733 (2004)
Joseph, Srs. of St. (Lyon) (191)	726
Assisi Srs. of Mary Immaculate (100)	722
Franciscan Mission. of Mary, Auxiliatrix (121)	718
Dominicans of the Rosary (132)	718
Holy Family, Little Srs. of the (93)	708
Mary Immaculate of Guadalupe (76)	707
Little Srs. of Mary Immaculate (143)	705
Our Lady Mother of Mercy (153)	701
Carmelite Nuns, Discalced, O.C.D. (68)	700
Consolata Missionary Sisters (110)	700
Benedictine Srs., Federation of St. Gertrude the Great (15)	699
Sacramentine Srs. (100)	694
Sacred Heart of Jesus and Mary, Sisters of (84)	692
Scalabrinians (141)	691
Charity, Little Mission. Srs. of (104)	688
Bethlemite Srs., Daughters of the Sacred Heart of Jesus (90)	687
Franciscan Missionaries of the Sacred Heart (102)	686
Providence of S. Gaetano da Thiene (82)	686
Jesus Crucified, Missionary Sisters of (154)	681
Providence, Srs. of (79)	672
Ann, Srs. of St. (93)	670
Mary, Dtrs. of (65)	668

Maestre Pie Filippini (94)   667
Teresian Carmelite Mission. (95)   659
Franciscan Mission. of Baby Jesus (94)   664
Anne, Srs. of (Chennai) (121)   664
Pious Schools, Religious of (104)   663
Mary, Daught. of, Bannabikira Srs. (75)   663
Mary Immaculate, Srs. of (77)   660
Mary Most Holy of the Word, Daughters
of (113)   659
Servants of Jesus Sacramentado (75)   655
Mercedarians of the Blessed Sacrament (86)   652
Charles Borromeo, Srs. of Charity of (78)   648
Jesus Christ, Poor Srs. of (104)   648
Divine Providence, Daught. of Mary of the (112)   643
Catherine Virgin and Martyr, Srs. of St. (116)   641
Enfant-Jesus, Soeurs de l' (122)   641
Mother of Mercy (151)   641
Mary Reparatrix, Society of (90)   639
Charity of Nazareth, Srs. of (218)   638
Sacred Heart of Jesus and the Poor, Srs. of (85) 633
Providence of Gap, Srs. of the (114)   630
Franciscan Missionaries of the Mother of the
Divine Pastor (100)   627
Servants of the Poor (90)   626
Seraphic Sisters (70)   622
Sacred Heart of Jesus and the Poor (83)   619
Claretians, Sacramentarian (63)   611
Franciscan Mission., I.H.M., of Egypt (85)   605
Dominican Missionary Srs. (65)   604
Medical Mission Srs. (103)   603
Charity of St. Louis, Srs. of (76)   602
Our Lady of the Consolation, Srs. of (94)   600
Franc. Dtrs. of the Sacred Hearts (64)   599
Joseph, Servants of St. (89)   599
Cross, Srs. of the Company of the (53)   599
Marcellina, Srs. of St. (49)   595
Pallottine Srs. of the Catholic Apostolate,
Mission. (79)   595
Catholic Apostle, Srs. of (79)   595
Franciscans of Mary Imm. (106)   595
Divine Zeal, Daughters of (75)   593
Sacred Hearts and of Perp. Ador.,
Srs. of the (95)   592
Brigid, Srs. of (51)   589
Reparation, Srs. of (83)   589
Srs. of Notre Dame (122)   586
St. Joseph of St. Mark, Srs. of (96)   586
Joseph, Srs. of (Mexico) (83)   582
Dominican Srs. of Peace (188)   582
Charles Borromeo, Srs. of (85)   582
Claretian Colettines (52)   580
Basil the Great, Srs. of the
Order of St. (Byzantine Rite) (74)   580
Benedictine Srs. Fed. of St. Benedict (10) 578
Charity of Ottawa, Srs. of (64)   578

Our Lady of Perp. Help (144)   579
Ursuline Daught. of Mary Immaculate (69)   576
Missionary Srs. of the Immaculate
Conception (88)   576
Imm. Conc., Sr. Servants (88)   575
Immaculate Conc., Missionary Srs. (56)   575
Albertine Srs. (73)   570
Jesus the Good Shepherd, Srs. of (123) 568
Franciscans of St. Joseph (93)   568
Franciscan Missionaries of Assisi (89)   565
Auxiliatrices des Ames du Purgatoire (110)   565
Holy Cross and Seven Dolors, Srs. of the (136)   556
Carmelites of Trivandrum (74)   556
Teresa of the Baby Jesus (71)   555
Annunciation, Little Sisters of (122)   552
Carmelite Missionaries of St. Teresa (122)   552
Francis of Assisi, Srs. (69)   552
Sacred Heart of Jesus, Srs. of the (90)   547
Franciscan Tertiaries (62)   545
Anne de Lachine, Srs. of Saint (51)   543
Dominican Srs. of the Rosary (Sinsinawa) (213)   541
Franciscan Srs. of the Imm. Heart (66)   541
Christian Charity, Dtrs. of (54)   540
Joseph, Srs. of (Annecy) (78)   538
Sacred Heart of Jesus, Santa Verzeri (85)   537
Immaculate Hrt. of Mary (43)   536
St. Francis, Srs. of (Glen Riddle) (178)   536
Poor Baby Jesus, Srs. of....(62)   534
Oblates of the Assumption (78)   534
Catherine of Siena, Srs. of (80)   529
Imm. Conc. Srs. of the Mother of God (84)   528
Sacred Heart of Jesus (Ragusa) (59)   528
Sacramentary Claretians (35)   520
Marianne of Jesus, Inst. of (102)   517
Sacred Heart of Jesus, Servants of the (69)   517
Perpetual Adoration, Benedictines(39)   516
Cross, Daught. of, of St. André (97)   515
Precious Blood, Dtrs. of....(63)   515
Ann, Srs. of (50)   515
Divine Providence, Srs. of
(St.-Jean-de-Bassel) (105)   513
Holy Redeemer, Oblate Srs. of the (80)   512
Mary of the Heart of Jesus (32) 511
Holy Family, Srs. of the (Villefranche) (80)   508
Olivetan Benedictines (1)   508
Guardian Angel, Srs. of (86)   508
Handmaids of the Lord (61)   508
Srs. Servants of the Imm. Hrt. Of Mary (89)   507
Immaculate Heart of Mary (89)   507
Dorothy, Srs. of St. (65)   504
Handmaids of Mary (70)   503
Franciscan Missionaries of Our Lord (82)   502
Martha, Srs. of (61)   501
Franciscans of Syracuse (93)   500

ORGANIZATIONS OF RELIGIOUS

Conferences

Conferences of major superiors of religious institutes, dating from the 1950s, are encouraged by the Code of Canon Law (Code 708) "so that joining forces they can work toward the achievement of the purpose of their individual institutes more fully, transact common business and foster suitable coordination and cooperation with conferences of bishops and also with individual bishops." Statutes of the conferences must be approved by the Holy See "by which alone they are erected" (Canon 709). Conferences have been established in 24 countries of Europe, 14 in North and Central America, 10 in South America, 35 in Africa and 19 in Asia and Oceania.

Listed below are U.S. and international conferences.

Conference of Major Superiors of Men: Founded in 1956; canonically established Sept. 12, 1957. Membership, 269 major superiors representing institutes with a combined membership of approximately 24,000. Pres., John Edmunds, S.T.; Secr. John Pavlik, O.F.M. Cap. National office: 8808 Cameron St., Silver Spring, MD 20910, (301) 588-4030, www.cmsm.org.

Leadership Conference of Women Religious: Founded in 1956; canonically established Dec. 12, 1959. Membership, nearly 1,000 (Dec. 31, 1996), representing approximately 400 religious institutes. Pres., Sr. Florence Deacon, O.S.F.; Carol Zinn, S.S.J., president-elect; exec. dir., Sr. Janet Mock, C.S.J. National office: 8808 Cameron St., Silver Spring, MD 20910, (301) 588-4955, www.lcwr.org.

Council of Major Superiors of Women Religious: Canonically erected June 13, 1992. Membership, 141 superiors of 103 religious congregations. Chairperson, Sr. Regina Marie Gorman, O.C.D. National office: PO Box 4467, Washington, DC 20017-0467, (202) 832-2575, www.cmswr.org.

International Union of Superiors General (Women): Established Dec. 8, 1965; approved, 1967. Pres., Sr. Mary Lou Wirtz, F.C.J.M. Address: Piazza Ponte S. Angelo, 28, 00186, Rome, Italy, 06-684-00-20.

Union of Superiors General (Men): Established in 1957. President, Fr. Jose Carballo Rodriguez; general secretary, David Glenday, M.C.C.J. Address: Via dei Penitenzieri 19, 00193 Rome, Italy, 06-686-82-29.

Latin American Confederation of Religious (Confederacion Latinoamericana de Religiosos — CLAR): Established in 1959; statutes reformed in 1984. President, Mercedes Casas Sanchez, F.Sp.S.; secretary general, Gabriel Narajno Salazar, C.M. Address: Calle 64 No 10-45, Piso 5°, Apartado Aéreo 56804, Santafé de Bogotá, D.C., Colombia, 57-1-310-0481/310-0392, www.clar.org.

Union of European Conferences of Major Superiors (UCESM): Established Dec. 25, 1983. President: Rev. Giovanni Peragine. Rue de Pascal 4, B-1040, Bruxelles, Belgium, 02 230 86 22.

Other Organizations

Institute on Religious Life (1974). To foster more effective understanding and implementation of teachings of the Church on religious life, promote vocations to religious life and the priesthood, and promote growth in sanctity of all the faithful according to their state in life. Fr. Thomas Nelson, O.Praem., Nat. Dir. National office, PO Box 7500, Libertyville, IL 60048; (847) 573-8975; www.religiouslife.com. Publishes Religious Life magazine and Consecrated

Life periodical.

Religious Brothers Conference (1972): To publicize the unique vocations of brothers, to further communication among brothers and provide liaison with various organizations of the Church. 5401 S. Cornell Avenue, Chicago, IL 60615; (773) 595-4023, www.brothersonline.org.

National Black Sisters' Conference (1968): Black Catholic women religious and associates networking to provide support through prayer, study, solidarity and programs. Address: 101 Q. St., N.E., Washington, DC 20002, (202) 529-9250.

National Conference of Vicars for Religious (1967): National organization of diocesan officials concerned with relations between their respective dioceses and religious communities engaged therein. President, Sr. Therese Sullivan, SP, 9292 Broadway, Merrillville, IN 46410; secretary, Eymard Flood, OSC. Address: 2811 East Villareal Dr., PO Box 14195, Orange, CA, 92863-1595, (714) 282-3114.

National Religious Vocation Conference (NRVC) (1988, with merger of National Sisters Vocation Conference and National Conference of Religious Vocation Directors.) Service organization of men and women committed to the fostering and discernment of vocations. Executive director, Br. Paul Bednarczyk, CSC. Address: 5401 S. Cornell Avenue, Chicago, IL 60615; (773) 363-5454, www.nrvc.net.

Religious Formation Conference (1953): Originally the Sister Formation Conference; membership includes women and men Religious and non-canonical groups. Facilitates the ministry of formation, both initial and ongoing, in religious communities. Co-Chairs, Dennis Wermert S.C., Clarice Suchy S.T.J.; National office: 8820 Cameron St., Silver Spring, MD 20910-4152, (301) 588-4938, www.relforcon.org.

SECULAR INSTITUTES

Sources: *Catholic Almanac* survey; United States Conference of Secular Institutes; *Annuario Pontificio*.

Secular institutes are societies of men and women living in the world who dedicate themselves to observe the evangelical counsels and to carry on apostolic works suitable to their talents and opportunities in the areas of their everyday life.

"Secular institutes are not religious communities but they carry with them in the world a profession of evangelical counsels which is genuine and complete, and recognized as such by the Church. This profession confers a consecration on men and women, laity and clergy, who reside in the world. For this reason they should chiefly strive for total self-dedication to God, one inspired by perfect charity. These institutes should preserve their proper and particular character, a secular one, so that they may everywhere measure up successfully to that apostolate which they were designed to exercise, and which is both in the world and, in a sense, of the world" ("Decree on the Appropriate Renewal of Religious Life," No. 11; Second Vatican Council).

Secular institutes are under the jurisdiction of the Congregation for Institutes of Consecrated Life and Societies of Apostolic Life. General legislation concerning them is contained in Canons 710 to 730 of the Code of Canon Law.

A secular institute reaches maturity in several stages. It begins as an association of the faithful, technically called a pious union, with the approval of a local bishop. Once it has proved its viability, he can give it the status of an institute of diocesan right, in accordance with norms and permission emanating from the Congregation for Institutes of Consecrated Life and Societies of Apostolic Life. On issuance of a separate decree from this congregation, an institute of diocesan right becomes an institute of pontifical right.

Secular institutes, which originated in the latter part of the 18th century, were given full recognition and approval by Pius XII Feb. 2, 1947, in the apostolic constitution Provida Mater Ecclesia. On Mar. 25 of the same year a special commission for secular institutes was set up within the Congregation for Religious. Institutes were commended and confirmed by Pius XII in a motu proprio of Mar. 12, 1948, and were the subject of a special instruction issued a week later, Mar. 19, 1948.

The World Conference of Secular Institutes (CMIS) was approved by the Vatican May 23, 1974. Address: Piazza San Calisto, 16, 00153 Roma, Italy: 0039-06-69887100; cmisroma@tin.it; www.cmis-int.org.

The United States Conference of Secular Institutes (USCSI) was established following the organization of the World Conference of Secular Institutes in Rome. Its membership is open to all canonically erected secular institutes with members living in the United States. The conference was organized to offer secular institutes an opportunity to exchange experiences, to do research in order to help the Church carry out its mission, and to search for ways and means to make known the existence of secular institutes in the U.S. Address: 38 Locke St., Saco, ME 04072, (207) 284-8966, www.secularinstitutes.org; Pres.: Beatrice Caron.

Institutes in the U.S.

Apostolic Oblates: Founded in Rome, Italy, 1947; established in the U.S., 1962; approved as a secular institute of pontifical right Dec. 8, 1994; for women. To promote the universal call to holiness through the specific apostolate of the Pro Sanctity Movement. Address: Teresa Monaghen, 11002 N 204th St, Elkhorn, NE 68022; (402) 289-2670; www.prosanctity.org.

Apostolic Sodales: Founded in Rome, Italy, 1992 by Bp. Giaquinta; for priests. Established to promote a spirit of fraternity among diocesan priests gathered around their bishop in ready availability in the two-fold universal vocation—the call to holiness and brotherhood. Address: Fr. Thomas Weisbecker, 1565 18th Ave, Columbus, NE 68601; (402) 564-7151; www.prosanctity.org.

Caritas Christi: Originated in Marseilles, 1937; for women. Established as a secular institute of pontifical right Mar. 19, 1955. To form and give to the Church women who strive to love God and make him loved where he has placed them in the midst of the world. Address: Mary Sue Brueneman, PO Box 9604, Cincinnati, OH 45209, (513) 271-7894; www.ccinfo.org.

Catechists of the Sacred Heart of Jesus (*Ukrainian*): Founded in Parana, Brazil, 1940, by Christopher Meskiv, OSBM; approved as a secular institute of pontifical right, 1971; for women. Established for religious instruction, to assist clerics in missionary work, to help the Church and to maintain the Ukrainian rite and culture. Address: Elvira Julek, 195 Glenbrook Rd, Stamford, CT 06902; (203) 327-6374; egardasz@yahoo.com.

Company of St. Paul: Originated in Milan, Italy, 1920; approved as a secular institute of pontifical right, June 30, 1950; for lay people and priests. To practice the evangelical counsels as an expression of consecration to God. Professional work becomes the main means of the apostolate. Address: Fr. Stuart Sandberg, 52 Davis Ave, White Plains, NY 10605; (914) 946-1019; jssandberg@optonline.net.

Company of St. Ursula: Founded in Brescia, Italy, 1535, by Angela Merici; an international federation linking most Companies was approved as a secular institute, 1958; began in the U.S. in 2000; for women. By life-long promises, members commit to share God's love for the world, making Christ better known, and infusing the spirit of the Gospel into our surroundings. Address: Mary-Cabrini Durkin, 2718 Hackberry St, Cincinnati, OH 45206; www.companyofstursula.org.

Crusaders of St. Mary: Founded 1947 in Madrid, Spain; approved as a secular institute of diocesan right, 1988; for men. To focus on the formation of young people toward integrating the spiritual with the secular through application of Ignatian spiritual exercises with Marian devotion. Address: Antonio Pérez-Alcalá, 2001 Great Falls St, McLean, VA 22101; (703) 536-3546; aperezalca@cox.net; www.secularinstitutes.org/directory.htm.

Don Bosco Volunteers: Founded 1917 by Bl. Philip Rinaldi; approved as a secular institute of pontifical right, Aug. 5, 1978; for women. Following the charism of St. John Bosco, in an effort to renew society from within, members bring their talents to a variety of apostolates, particularly on behalf of the youth. Address: 169 Bell Rd., Scarsdale, NY 10583; (914) 723-0239; seculardbv@aol.com.

Family of Mary of the Visitation: Founded in Saigon, Vietnam, 1976; approved as a secular institute of pontifical right, 1993; for women. As faith-filled vowed women, help people to protect their faith and meet social needs, with a preferential option for the poor. Address: Mary Lien Do, 615 S Euclid St, 1-2, Santa Anna, CA 92704; liendo2004@yahoo.com.

Father Kolbe Missionaries of the Immaculata: Founded in Bologna, Italy, in 1954, by Fr. Luigi Faccenda, OFM Conv; approved as a secular institute of pontifical right, Mar. 25, 1992; for women. Live the fullness of baptismal consecration, strive for perfect charity and promote the knowledge and veneration of Mary. Address: Rumela Camanga, 531 E Merced Ave, West Covina, CA 91790; (626) 917-0040; fkmissionaries@gmail.com; www.kolbemission.org/en.

Handmaids of Divine Mercy: Founded in Bari, Italy, 1951; approved as a secular institute of pontifical right, 1972; for women. To promote the riches, the graces, the vital life stream of Divine Mercy for our world of today. Address: 2410 Hughes Ave, Bronx, NY 10458; (718) 295-3770; Spiritual Director Rev. Msgr. John A. Ruvo (914) 632-0675.

Institute of the Heart of Jesus: Founded by a Jesuit priest in Paris, France, 1791; approved as a secular institute of pontifical right, Feb 2, 1952; for diocesan priests who wish to pursue holiness through the evangelical vows, prolonged prayer, and fraternal support. Formation is fundamentally Ignatian but priests may embrace spiritualities of other Catholic traditions. Address: Fr. Enrique Sera, St. Joachim Parish, 1964 Orange Ave, Costa Mesa, CA 92627; (949) 574-7400; CorUnumPriests@gmail.com; www.corunumusa.org.

Institute of the Heart of Jesus (*Women*): approved as a secular institute of pontifical right in 1999. Single women or widows consecrate themselves to God through the evangelical vows, prolonged prayer, mutual support in regular gatherings for discernment and accountability. Formation is fundamentally Ignatian but members may embrace spiritualities of other Catholic traditions. Address: Karen Ceckowski, PO Box 501, Conception, MO 64433; (660) 944-2842; karen@conception.edu; www.isfcj.com.

Institute of the Heart of Jesus (*Men*): Founded by a Jesuit priest in Paris, France, 1791. The Institute was erected as a secular institute of diocesan right by Bp. William Weigand in 2008; for single men and widowers who consecrate themselves to God through the evangelical vows, prolonged prayer, and fraternal discernment accountability. Fundamentally formation is Ignatian but members may embrace other Catholic spiritualities. Address: David Bland, 6135 Verner Ave, Sacramento, CA 95841; (213) 952-3755; david-bland@att.net.

Jesus Caritas Fraternity: Founded in France, 1952; approved as a secular institute of diocesan right, 1996; for women. To form members in the contemplative tradition of Brother Charles de Foucauld, bringing God's love especially to neglected children. Members strive to live the Gospel message in their daily life. Address: Mary Christensen, 4 Curran Ct, Apt 1R, Yonkers, NY 10710; (914) 961-0050.

Lay Missionaries of the Passion (*Men*): Founded by a Passionist priest under the charism of St. Paul of the Cross, in Sicily, 1980; approved as a secular institute of diocesan right, 2001. Men take vows of poverty, chastity and obedience, together with a promise to live the spirit of the Passion of our Lord according to St. Paul of the Cross. Address: James Beers, 830 Howard Ave, Apt 3-D, Staten Island, NY 10301; (718) 720-2194; beers153@verizon.net.

Lay Missionaries of the Passion (*Women*): Founded in Catania, Sicily; approved as a secular institute of pontifical right, 1999; for women. To be fully responsible to shape this world, to transform it, and to live in the spirit of the Passion. Address: Constance Leist, 311 Leonard St, Brooklyn, NY 11211; (718) 387-3619; leo31lc@aol.com.

Mission of Our Lady of Bethany: Founded in France in 1948; approved as a secular institute of diocesan right in 1965; for women. To bring the mystery of redemptive love to the most rejected of society – the imprisoned and the prostitute – in a true fraternity of love and hope to help the Church to build the kingdom of Christ. Address: Estelle Nichols, 109 Rollins Rd, Nottingham, NH 03290; estellenichols@comcast.net.

Missionaries of the Kingship of Christ (*Men*): Founded in Assisi, Italy, 1928, by Agostino Gemelli; approved as a secular institute of pontifical right, 1997. To spread the social reign of Christ through individual professions lived with the spirit of St. Francis of Assisi. Address: Fr. Gene Pistacchio, OFM, 100 Arch St, Boston, MA 02110; (617) 542-6440; gpistacchio@stanthonyshrine.org.

Missionaries of the Kingship of Christ (*Women*): Founded in Assisi, Italy, 1919, by Agostino Gemelli and Armida Barelli as a Franciscan secular institute for women; approved as a secular institute of pontifical right, 1948. To give witness to Gospel values in work, family, civic, social, and spiritual environments in the spirit of St. Francis of Assisi. Address: Angela Ricciardelli, Hecker Center for Ministry, 3025 Fourth St NE #10, Washington, DC 20017; (202) 525-1267; simKingship10@comcast.net; www.simkc.org.

Notre-Dame De Vie: In the spirit of Carmel, founded by Fr. Marie-Eugene of the Child Jesus, OCD, and Marie Pila, in Venasque, France, 1932; approved as a secular institute of pontifical right, 1962; for women, men, and priests. Address: Anne Giuliani, 1419 37th St NW #260, Washington, DC 20007; (202) 687-1912; ndv_washington@yahoo.com.

Oblate Missionaries of Mary Immaculate: Founded in Canada, 1952; approved as a secular institute of pontifical right, 1984; for women. Like Christ, to manifest the unconditional love of God the Father to everyone by revealing the signs of his presence at the heart of daily life. Address: Pauline Labbe, 56 Brookfield St, Lawrence, MA 01843; (978) 687-9399; pjlabbe1@juno.com; www.ommi-is.org.

Opus Spiritus Sancti: Founded in Germany, 1950; approved as a secular institute of diocesan right, 1970; for priests. To live our charism in fraternal community, stamped by the Easter-Pentecost event. Priests work and pray for a new Pentecost through lives shared with one another, by our hope-filled vision, reconciling love, and missionary zeal. Address: Fr. Bruce Lawler, PO Box 1106, Storm Lake, IA 50588; (712) 723-3110; www.opus-spiritus-sancti.de.

Pius X Secular Institute: Founded in New Hampshire, 1939; approved in Quebec, Canada, as a secular institute of diocesan right, 1959; for priests and single laymen; associate members are priests, single lay men and women, and married couples. Totally dedicated to the evangelization of the working class by our presence in the world through apostolic works and bringing the Gospel to all. Address: Fr. Marcel Caron, 27 Cove St, Goffstown, NH 03045; (418) 626-5882; info@ispx.org; www.ispx.org.

Schoenstatt Fathers: Founded in 1965, but with roots back to Oct. 18, 1914, founding day of the Schoenstatt Movement by Fr. Joseph Kentenich; approved as a secular institute of pontifical right, June 24, 1988; for priests. To serve the needs of the Schoenstatt Family in all their different communities, promoting and cultivating Schoenstatt's original spirituality with priestly inspiration and guidance. Addresses: Fr. Francisco Rojas, W284N746 Cherry Ln., Waukesha, WI 53188; (262) 548-9061; father.francisco@gmail.com and Fr. Christian Christensen, 225 Addie Roy Rd., Austin, TX 78746; (512) 301-8762; pchri02@sbcglobal.net.

Schoenstatt Sisters of Mary: Founded in Germany, Oct. 1, 1926, by Fr. Joseph Kentenich; approved as a secular institute of pontifical right, May 20, 1948; for women. For the moral and religious renewal of society, to be Mary for our world today. Members practice a Marian spirituality as a means of growing in love for God and consecrating the world to him. Addresses: Joanna Buckley, W284N404 Cherry Ln, Waukesha, WI 53188; (262) 522-4200; vocation@schsrsmary.org and Gabriella Maschita, 130 Front St, Rockport, TX 78382; (361) 729-1868; confprov@cobridge.tv.

Secular Institute of St Francis de Sales: Founded in Vienna, Austria, 1947; approved as a secular institute of pontifical right, 1964; for women. The personal sanctification of its members living in the world according to the spirituality of St. Francis de Sales and the application of this spirituality in institute, missionary, parish, and community apostolates depending on our different life situations. Address: Dana Elzi, 104 West Main St, Middletown, PA 17057; 717-948-5009; dana.elzi104@gmail.com; www.secularinstituteofsaintfrancisdesales.org.

Servite Secular Institute: Founded in 1947, by Joan Bartlett, OBE, in London, England; approved as a secular institute of pontifical right, 1979; for single or widowed women. To be genuine leaven in the world for strengthening and enlarging Christ's body by contemplation and service in kindness, compassion, and hospitality. Address: Mary Power, 44 Stirling Ave, Ottawa, Ontario K1Y 1P8, Canada; (613) 722-0302; mpower1661@rogers.com; www.ssi.org.uk.

Servitium Christi: Founded in Holland, 1952; approved as a secular institute of diocesan right, 1963; for women. To live the mystery of the Eucharist fully as consecrated lay persons and to make known its meaning so that the glory of God may be revealed in the world. Address: Olympia Panagatos, 1550 York Ave #17A, New York, NY 10028; (212) 734-9748.

Madonna della Strada/Society of Our Lady of the Way: Founded in Vienna, Austria, 1936; approved as a secular institute of pontifical right, 1953; for women. Members pursue individual apostolates, seeking to manifest Christ in life and work with Mary and St. Ignatius in the spirit of thanksgiving with the guidance of the Holy Spirit. Address: Mary Ann Tady, 1064 Oxford Rd., Cleveland Heights, OH 44121, (216) 381-5502; matslow@aol.com; www.saecimds.com.

Voluntas Dei Institute: Founded in Trois-Rivieres, Canada, on July 2, 1958, by Fr. Louis-Marie Parent, OMI; approved as a secular institute of pontifical right, 1987; for priests, laymen, and married couples. Members share in the Church's mission that has been sent by Christ to make known and to communicate to all peoples God's unconditional love. Address: Fr. Anthony Ciorra, 244 Fifth Ave., Suite P250, NY, NY 10001; (212) 726-2286; www.voluntasdeiusa.org.

The Annuario Pontificio *lists the following secular institutes of pontifical right that are not established in the U.S.:*

For men: Christ the King; Institute of Our Lady of Life; Institute of Prado; Priests of the Sacred Heart of Jesus. Community of St. John and Our Lady of Altagracia

For women: Alliance in Jesus through Mary; Apostles of the Sacred Heart; Catechists of Mary, Virgin and Mother; Community of St. John; Cordimarian Filiation; Daughters of the Nativity of Mary; Daughters of the Queen of the Apostles; Daughters of the Sacred Heart; Evangelical Crusade; Faithful Servants of Jesus; Handmaids of Our Mother of Mercy; Institute of Notre Dame du Travail; Institute of Our Lady of Life; Institute of St. Boniface; Little Apostles of Charity.

Life and Peace in Christ Jesus; Missionaries of Royal Priesthood; Missionaries of the Sick; Oblates of Christ the King; Oblates of the Sacred Heart of Jesus; Our Lady of Altagracia; Servants of Jesus the Priest; Union of the Daughters of God; Workers of Divine Love; Workers of the Cross; Handmaids of Holy Church; Augustinian Auxiliary Missionaries; Heart of Jesus; Apostolic Missionaries of Charity; Combonian Secular Missionaries; Missionaries of the Gospel; Secular Servants of Jesus Christ Priest; Women of Schoenstatt; Missionaries of Infinite Love.

Aspiring to Become Secular Institutes in the U.S.:

Blessed Trinity Missionary Institute: Founded in Philadelphia, 1950, by Dr. Margaret Healy according to the inspiration of Fr. Thomas Augustine Judge, CM; approved as a pious union, 1964; for women. To preserve the faith among people who are spiritually neglected and to develop a missionary spirit in the laity. Addresses: Rosa

Tirado, 154-14 Ash Ave, Flushing, NY 11355; (718) 359-5910; roniltirado@earthlink.net and Vocation Chair, 8570 Vaughn Rd, Montgomery, AL 36117; (334) 207-0324; mnpecot@aol.com; www.btmi.info.

Franciscan Missionaries of Jesus Crucified: Founded in 1987, in New York by Louise Principe; approved as an association of the faithful, 1992; for women and men. To provide an opportunity for persons with disabilities, to live a life of total consecration in the pursuit of holiness, and the apostolate of service to the Church and to those who suffer in any way. Address: Bonnie Fagan, 11 Dahlem Blvd, Niskayuna, NY 12309; (518) 452-1696; bjffmjc@aol.com; www.fmjccommunity.com.

Holy Family Institute (aggregated to the Society of St. Paul): Founded by Fr. James Alberione in 1963 for married couples who wish to commit themselves to seeking evangelical perfection in marriage; definitively approved by the Holy See in 1993. Address: Fr. Tom Fogarty, 9531 Akron-Canfield Rd, Box 498, Canfield OH 44406; (330) 533-6646; www.hficoncord.com.

Schoenstatt Family Institute: Founded July 16, 1942, in the Dachau concentration camp by Father Joseph Kentenich for married couples, which now number 600 persons in 12 countries. Marriage is a way to holiness; a sacrament, a realization and school of Divine love. Members contribute toward the renewal of marriage and family life, the Church and society through living the three evangelical counsels according to their state of life, and through a lived covenant of love with Mary and Jesus. Address: Michael and Margaret Fenelon, 1719 Orchard Ln, McHenry IL 60050; (815) 385-3152; m.j.fenelon.ill@gmail.com; www.schoenstatt-familien.de.

Volunteers with Don Bosco: Founded in 1994, in Rome by Fr. Egidio Viganò, Rector Major of the Salesians of Don Bosco; approved as an association of the faithful in 1998; for celibate men. Drawing inspiration from the charism of St. John Bosco, members strive to imitate his pastoral style and follow Christ radically through consecration in secular life. Their aim is to build a better society following the Gospel and living the Salesian spirit. Address: Fr. John Puntino, SDB, 148 Main St., New Rochelle, NY 10802; (914) 636-4225; www.volontaricdb.altervista.org.

Associations

Association of Mary Help of Christians: Founded by St. John Bosco in Turin, Italy, in 1869, for men and women. Public association of the faithful. Members encourage participation in the liturgical life of the Church, emphasizing frequent reception of the Eucharist and the Sacrament of Reconciliation. They also live and spread devotion to Mary Help of Christians according to the spirit of St. John Bosco. Address: 148 Main St., P.O. Box 639, New Rochelle, NY 10802, (614) 440-0202.

Caritas: Originated in New Orleans, 1950; for women. Follows guidelines of secular institutes. Small self supporting groups who live and work with poor and oppressed; in Louisiana and Guatemala. Address: Box 308, Abita Springs, LA 70420, (985) 892-4345.

Daughters of Our Lady of Fatima: Originated in Lansdowne, PA, 1949; for women. Received diocesan approval, Jan. 1952. Address: Fatima House, P.O. Box 116, Bedminster 18910, (215) 795-2947.

Focolare Movement: Founded in Trent, Italy, in 1943, by Chiara Lubich; for men and women. Approved as an association of the faithful, 1962. It is not a secular institute by statute; however, vows are observed by its totally dedicated core membership of 4,000 who live in small communities called Focolare (Italian word for "hearth") centers. There are 17 resident centers in the U.S. and four in Canada. GEN (New Generation) is the youth organization of the movement. An estimated 75,000 are affiliated with the movement in the U.S. and Canada, 2,000,000 worldwide. Publications include Living City, monthly; GEN II and GEN III for young people and children. Five week long summer conventions, called "Mariapolis" ("City of Mary"), are held annually. Address for information: Mariopolis Luminosa, 257 Peace Ave., Hyde Park, NY 12538, (845) 229-9712 (men's or women's branch), www. focolare.us.

Jesus-Caritas Fraternity of Priests: An international association of diocesan priests who strive to combine an active life with a contemplative calling by their membership in small fraternities. U.S. address for information: Rev. Greg Pawloski, St. Patrick's Church, P.O. Box 96, 126 E. 7th St., Imperial, NE 69033-0096, (308) 882-4995, www. rc.net/org/jesuscaritas.

Madonna House Apostolate: Originated in Toronto, Canada, 1930; for priests and lay persons. Public association of the Christian faithful. Address: Madonna House, 2888 Dafoe Rd., Combermere, ON, Canada K0J 1L0, (613) 756-3713, www.madonnahouse.org. Directors General: Jean Fox (women), Albert Osterberger (men), Fr. Robert Pelton (priests). International membership and missions.

Pax Christi: Lay institute of men and women dedicated to witnessing to Christ, with special emphasis on service to the poor in Mississippi. Addresses: St. Francis Center, 709 Ave. I, Greenwood, MS 38930. LaVerna House, 2108 Alta Woods Blvd., Jackson, MS 39204, (601) 373-4463.

Rural Parish Workers of Christ the King: Founded in 1942; for women. A secular institute of the Archdiocese of St. Louis. Dedicated to the glory of God in service of neighbor, especially in rural areas. Address: 15540 Cannon Mines Rd., Cadet, MO 63630, (636) 586-5171; rpwck.com.

Salesian Cooperators: Founded by St. John Bosco in Turin, Italy, in 1876; for lay men and women and diocesan clergy. Public association of the faithful, members commit themselves to apostolates in the local Church, especially on behalf of the young, in the Salesian spirit and style. Address: 6400 E. Chelsea St., Tampa, FL 33610; (813) 626-6191. Contact person: Fr. Dennis Donovan.

Society of Evangelical Life of the Heart of Jesus: presently an Association of the Faithful, this society was definitively approved in 1996, developing since the 1970s with the three Secular Institutes of the Heart of Jesus. In 1996 a federation Cor Unum Family was formed of the four groups. The association (for married couples, single men and women, and priests) follows the same Rule of Life as the institutes. Members live the evangelical counsels as they pursue holiness of life in their married or celibate state, committing to prolonged prayer, communal discernment and accountability, and adopt Ignatian principles of formation. Address: Bob and Cindy Kodis; 1820 76th St, Windsor Heights IA 50324; (515) 251-3930; ckodis@ishsi.com.

Teresian Institute: Founded in Spain 1911 by Pedro Poveda. Approved as an association of the faithful of pontifical right, Jan. 11, 1924. Mailing Address: 3400 S. W. 99th Ave., Miami, FL 33165, (305) 553-8567.

THIRD ORDERS

Augustine, Third Order Secular of St.: Founded 13th century; approved Nov. 7, 1400.

Carmelites, Lay (Third Order of Our Lady of Mt. Carmel): Rule for laity approved by Pope Nicholas V, Oct. 7, 1452; new statutes, January 1991. Addresses: 8501 Bailey Rd., Darien, IL 60561. PO Box 613, Williamston, MA 01267. PO Box 27, Tappan, NY 10983-0027, (845) 359-0535. Approximately 270 communities and 10,000 members in the U.S. and Canada.

Carmelites, The Secular Order of Discalced (formerly the Third Order Secular of the Blessed Virgin Mary of Mt. Carmel and of St. Teresa of Jesus): Rule based on the Carmelite reform established by St. Teresa and St. John of the Cross; approved Mar. 23, 1594. Revised rule approved May 10, 1979. Office of National Secretariat, USA: PO Box 3079, San Jose, CA 95156-3079, (408) 251-1361. Approximately 24,445 members throughout the world; 130 groups/communities and 5,200 members in the US and Canada.

Dominican Laity (formerly known as Third Order of St. Dominic): Founded in the 13th century. Addresses of provincial promoters in the United States: St. Dominic Priory, 3601 Lindell Blvd., St. Louis, MO 63108-3393, (314) 977-2588, www.op.org /domcentral. Eastern Province, 487 Michigan Ave., N.E., Washington, DC, 20017, (202) 529-5300. Priory of St. Martin de Porres, P.O. Box 12927, Raleigh, NC 27605, (919) 833-1893. Western Province, 2005 Berryman St., Berkeley, CA 94709, (510) 526-4811. Midwest Province, 3904 Golfside Dr., Ypsilanti, MI 48197, (734) 434-0195.

Franciscan Order, Secular (SFO): Founded 1209 by St. Francis of Assisi; approved Aug. 30, 1221. Vocation Director, 37430 Stonegate Circle, Clinton Township, MI 48036, (800) FRANCIS, www.NAFRA-SFO.org. International Secretariate, Via Pomponia Grecina, 31, 00145 Rome. Tau USA, quarterly. Approximately 780,000 throughout the world; 18,000 in the U.S.

Mary, Third Order of (Marist Laity): Founded, Dec. 8, 1850; rule approved by the Holy See, 1857. Addresses of provincial directors: Marist Laity Center, 1706 Jackson Ave., New Orleans, LA 70113-1510, (504) 524-5192, www.maristlaity.org. Marist Fathers, 698 Beacon St., Boston, MA 02115, (617) 262-2271. Marist Fathers, 2335 Warring St., Berkeley, CA 94704. Approximately 14,000 in world, 5,600 in U.S

Mary, Secular Order of Servants of (Servite): Founded 1233; approved 1304. Revised rule approved 1995. Address: National Assistant for the Secular Order, 3121 W. Jackson Blvd., Chicago, IL 60612-2729, (773) 638-5800.

Mercy, Secular Third Order of Our Lady of (Mercedarian): Founded 1219 by St. Peter Nolasco; approved the same year.

Norbert, Third Order of St.: Founded 1122 by St. Norbert; approved by Pope Honorius II in 1126.

Oblates of St. Benedict: Lay persons affiliated with a Benedictine abbey, or monastery, who strive to direct their lives, as circumstances permit, according to the spirit and Rule of St. Benedict.

Trinity, Third Order Secular of the Most: Founded 1198; approved 1219.

Apostolates and Ministries

RIGHTS AND OBLIGATIONS OF ALL THE FAITHFUL

The following rights are listed in Canons 208-223 of the revised Code of Canon Law; additional rights are specified in other canons.
• Because of their baptism and regeneration, there is equality regarding dignity and action for the building up of the Body of Christ.
• They are bound always to preserve communion with the Church.
• According to their condition and circumstances, they should strive to lead a holy life and promote the growth and holiness of the Church.
• They have the right and duty to work for the spread of the divine message of salvation to all peoples of all times and places.
• They are bound to follow with Christian obedience those things which the bishops, as they represent Christ, declare as teachers of the faith or establish as rulers of the Church.
• They have the right to make known their needs, especially their spiritual needs, to pastors of the Church.
• They have the right, and sometimes the duty, of making known to pastors and others of the faithful their opinions about things pertaining to the good of the Church.
• They have the right to receive help from their pastors, from the spiritual goods of the Church and especially from the word of God and the sacraments.
• They have the right to divine worship performed according to prescribed rules of their rite, and to follow their own form of spiritual life in line with the doctrine of the Church.
• They have the right to freely establish and control associations for good and charitable purposes, to foster the Christian vocation in the world, and to hold meetings related to the accomplishment of these purposes.
• They have the right to promote and support apostolic action but may not call it "Catholic" unless they have the consent of competent authority.
• They have a right to a Christian education.
• They have a right to freedom of inquiry in sacred studies, in accordance with the teaching authority of the Church.
• They have a right to freedom in the choice of their state of life.
• No one has the right to harm the good name of another person or to violate his or her right to maintain personal privacy.
• They have the right to vindicate the rights they enjoy in the Church, and to defend themselves in a competent ecclesiastical forum.
• They have the obligation to provide for the needs of the Church, with respect to things pertaining to divine worship, apostolic and charitable works, and the reasonable support of ministers of the Church.
• They have the obligation to promote social justice and to help the poor from their own resources.
• In exercising their rights, the faithful should have regard for the common good of the Church and for the rights and duties of others.
• Church authority has the right to monitor the exercise of rights proper to the faithful, with the common good in view.

RIGHTS AND OBLIGATIONS OF LAY PERSONS

In addition to rights and obligations common to all the faithful and those stated in other canons, lay persons are bound by the obligations and enjoy the rights specified in these canons (224-231).
• Lay persons, like all the faithful, are called by God to the apostolate in virtue of their baptism and confirmation. They have the obligation and right, individually or together in associations, to work for the spread and acceptance of the divine message of salvation among people everywhere; this obligation is more urgent in those circumstances in which people can hear the Gospel and get to know Christ only through them (lay persons).
• They are bound to bring an evangelical spirit to bear on the order of temporal things and to give Christian witness in carrying out their secular pursuits.
• Married couples are obliged to work for the building up of the people of God through their marital and family life.
• Parents have the most serious obligation to provide for the Christian education of their children according to the doctrine handed down by the Church.
• Lay persons have the same civil liberty as other citizens. In the use of this liberty, they should take care that their actions be imbued with an evangelical spirit. They should attend to the doctrine proposed by the magisterium of the Church but should take care that, in questions of opinion, they do not propose their own opinion as the doctrine of the Church.
• Qualified lay persons are eligible to hold and perform the duties of ecclesiastical offices open to them in accord with the provisions of law.
• Properly qualified lay persons can assist pastors of the Church as experts and counselors.
• Lay persons have the obligation and enjoy the right to acquire knowledge of doctrine commensurate with their capacity and condition.
• They have the right to pursue studies in the sacred sciences in pontifical universities or facilities and in institutes of religious sciences, and to obtain

academic degrees.

• If qualified, they are eligible to receive from ecclesiastical authority a mandate to teach sacred sciences.

• Laymen can be invested by liturgical rite and in a stable manner in the ministries of lector and acolyte.

• Lay persons, by temporary assignment, can fulfill the office of lector in liturgical actions; likewise, all lay persons can perform the duties of commentator or cantor.

• In cases of necessity and in the absence of the usual ministers, lay persons — even if not lectors or acolytes — can exercise the ministry of the word, lead liturgical prayers, confer baptism and distribute Communion, according to the prescripts of law.

• Lay persons who devote themselves permanently or temporarily to the service of the Church are obliged to acquire the formation necessary for carrying out their duties in a proper manner.

• They have a right to remuneration for their service which is just and adequate to provide for their own needs and those of their families; they also have a right to insurance, social security and health insurance.

(*See* **Canon Law** *for details on the* **Code**.)

DIRECTORY OF LAY GROUPS

The U.S. Conference of Catholic Bishops' Secretariat for Family, Laity, Women and Youth released its 2007-2008 *Directory of Lay Movements, Organizations, and Professional Associations* (the most recent edition).

The directory contains listings for more than 100 national lay movements, professional associations, and organizations. Each listing includes a brief description of the group and the name, address, phone number of a contact person, and web/email information if available. The groups listed are national in scope, but not all are solely lay. Some are included because their work affects the life and mission of the laity and/or because their membership has a significant lay component. The secretariat acknowledges that the listing is a partial one and welcomes suggestions for groups to be included in future editions. Copies may be ordered from the USCCB Secretariat for Family, Laity, Women, and Youth, 3211 4th St., N.E., Washington, DC 20017; (202) 541-3040 (phone); (202) 541-3176 (fax).

SPECIAL APOSTOLATES AND GROUPS

Apostleship of the Sea (1920, Glasgow, Scotland; 1947 in U.S.): 1500 Jefferson Dr., Port Arthur, TX 77642; (409) 985-4545; 3211 Fourth St. N.E., Washington, DC 20017 (national office); (202) 541-3035; www.aos-usa.org. An international Catholic organization for the moral, social and spiritual welfare of seafarers and those involved in the maritime industry. Formally instituted by the Holy See in 1952 (apostolic constitution *Exul Familia*), it is a sector of the Pontifical Council for Migrants and Itinerant Peoples. Its norms were updated by Pope John Paul II in a *motu proprio* dated Jan. 31, 1997. The U.S. unit, an affiliate of the USCCB, serves port chaplains in 63 U.S. ports. Pres., Fr. Sinclair Oubre.

Auxiliaries of Our Lady of the Cenacle (1878,

France): 1114 Iowa Dr., LeClaire, IA 52753; (563) 289-9975; www.cenaclesisters.org. An association of consecrated Catholic laywomen, under the direction of the Congregation of Our Lady of the Cenacle. They profess annually the evangelical counsels of celibacy, poverty and obedience and serve God through their own professions and life styles and pursue individual apostolates. Reg. Dir., Carol Gantenbein.

Catholic Central Verein (Union) of America (1855): 3835 Westminster Pl., St. Louis, MO 63108; (314) 371-1653; www.socialjusticereview.org. One of the oldest Catholic lay organizations in the U.S. and the first given an official mandate for Catholic Action by a committee of the American bishops (1936); *Social Justice Review*, bimonthly.

Catholic Medical Mission Board (1928): 10 W. 17th Street, New York, NY 10011-5765; (212) 242-7757; www.cmmb.org. A charitable, nonprofit organization dedicated to providing health care supplies and support for the medically disadvantaged in developing and transitional countries. CMMB depends upon the financial generosity of over 25,000 individual donors and through product contributions by major pharmaceutical corporations. In 2012, CMMB received support from 37,188 individuals, 47 foundations, 54 corporations, 38 trusts and estates, 190 health and religious-affiliated organizations, and administered two grants from the U.S. government. CMMB also receives substantial in-kind donations from pharmaceutical companies. "The importance of the role of faith-based organizations in delivering solutions to the HIV/AIDS pandemic in the developing countries cannot be overstated. The faith-based network within many countries is often the most trusted source of refuge for those seeking help in any way, regardless of creed or color. Zambia is a prime example. CMMB's partnership with the Churches Health Association of Zambia (CHAZ) provides it with the opportunity to partner with clinics on the ground to prevent the transmission of HIV. Similarly, in Latin America and the Caribbean, CMMB has partnered with Catholic health care networks in five countries to lower childhood mortality by teaching basic health care." Pres., Bruce Wilkinson.

Catholic Movement for Intellectual and Cultural Affairs: 3025 Fourth St., N.E., Washington, DC, 20017; (202) 269-6672. The U.S. affiliate of Pax Romana-ICMICA (see International Catholic Organizations); *The Notebook*, quarterly. Pres., Joseph Kirchner.

Catholic Volunteer Network (1963; formerly, International Liaison of Lay Volunteers in Mission): 6930 Carroll Ave., Suite 820, Takoma Park, MD 201912; (301) 270-0900; www.cnvs.org. Membership organization of 235 faith-based volunteer programs, placing persons in all fifty states and 120 countries; *The Response*, annual directory. Exec. Dir., James Lindsay.

Catholic Volunteers in Florida (1983): P.O. Box 536476, Orlando, FL 32853-6476; (407) 382-7071; www.cvif.org. Co-sponsored by the bishops of Florida to promote values of social justice by direct service to farm workers, homeless, hungry, low-income people, single mothers and others in need. Volunteers, 20 years of age and older, serve for a one year period in urban and rural settings. Exec. Dir., Richard Galentino.

Center for Applied Research in the Apostolate (CARA): 2300 Wisconsin Ave., N.W., Suite 400, Washington, DC 20007; (202) 687-8080; www.cara.georgetown.edu. A nonprofit research center serving the planning needs of the Catholic Church. CARA gathers empirical data for use by bishops, diocesan agencies, parishes, congregations of men and women religious and Catholic organizations. The *CARA Report*, quarterly; *CARA Catholic Ministry Formation Directory*, annually. Exec. Dir., Rev. Thomas Gaunt, S.J., Ph.D.

Christian Family Movement (CFM) (1947): National office, P.O. Box 540550, Omaha, NE 68154; (800) 581-9824; www.cfm.org. Originated in Chicago to Christianize family life and create communities conducive to Christian family life. Since 1968, CFM in the U.S. has included couples from all Christian churches.

Christian Life Communities (1971, promulgation of revised norms by Pope Paul VI; originated, 1563, as Sodalities of Our Lady, at the Jesuit College in Rome): 3601 Lindell Blvd., St. Louis, MO 63108 (national office); (314) 542-1335; www.clc-usa.org. The world CLC office is in Rome. Small communities of primarily lay persons who come together to form committed individuals for service to the world and the Church.

Cursillo Movement (1949, in Spain; in U.S., 1957): National Cursillo Center, P.O. Box 210226, Dallas, TX 75211. An instrument of Christian renewal designed to form and stimulate persons to engage in evangelizing their everyday environments.

Franciscan Mission Service of North America, an Overseas Lay Ministry Program (1990): P.O. Box 29034, Washington, DC 20017; (202) 832-1762; www.franciscanmissionservice.catholic.edu. Lay missioners work with Franciscan sisters, brothers and priests for a minimum of three years in underdeveloped countries. Co-Dir. Joseph Nangle, OFM, and Megeen White.

Grail, The (1921, in The Netherlands, by Rev. Jacques van Ginneken, SJ; 1940, in U.S.): Grailville, 932 O'Bannonville Rd., Loveland, OH 45140 (U. S. headquarters); (513) 683-5750; www.grail-us.org. Duisburger Strasse 442, 45478 Mulheim, Germany, (international secretariat). An international movement of women concerned about the full development of all peoples, working in education, religious, social, cultural and ecological areas.

Jesuit Volunteer Corps (1956): 18th and Thompson Sts., Philadelphia, PA 19121 (address for information); (215) 232-0300; www.jesuitvolunteers.org. Sponsored by the Society of Jesus in the U.S. Men and women volunteers work throughout the U.S. serving the poor directly and working for structural change.

LAMP Ministries (Lay Apostolic Ministries with the Poor): 2704 Schurz Ave., Bronx, NY 10465; (718) 409-5062; www.lampministries.org. Missionary service of evangelization with the materially poor and homeless in the larger metropolitan New York/New Jersey area. Newsletter, two times a year. Directors, Drs. Tom and Lyn Scheuring.

Lay Mission-Helpers Association (1955): 3435 Wilshire Blvd., #1035, Los Angeles, CA 90010; (213) 368-1870; www.laymissionhelpers.org. Trains and assigns men and women for work in overseas apostolates for periods of two to three years. Approximately 700 members of the association have served in overseas assignments since

its founding. Director, Janice England. **The Mission Doctors Association:** (same address; (213) 637-7499; www.missiondoctors.org) recruits, trains and sends Catholic physicians and their families to mission hospitals and clinics throughout the world for tours of two to three years. Additionally, MDA has a short-term program for volunteer physicians with a term of service of 12 months. Program Dir., Elise Frederick.

Legion of Mary (1921, in Dublin, Ireland, by Frank Duff): Maria Center, 326 E. Ripa, St. Louis, MO 63125 (U.S. address); (314) 631-3447. De Montfort House, Dublin 7, Ireland (headquarters). Membership: active Catholics of all ages, under the direction of local bishops and priests, for the work of conversion, conservation and consolation. Pres., Mary T. Budde.

Movimiento Familiar Cristiano-USA (MFC) (1969): St. Mary Seminary, 9845 memorial Dr., Houston, TX 77024; (713) 686-4345. Movement of Catholic Hispanic families united in their efforts to promote the human and Christian virtues of the family so that it may become a force that forms persons, transmits the faith and contributes to the total development of the community. Rev. Rafael Davila, national spiritual director.

Pax Christi USA (1972): 1225 Otis St., NE, Washington, DC 20017; (202) 635-2741; www.paxchristiusa.org. Pax Christi (see International Catholic Organizations). Founded to establish peacemaking as a priority for the American Catholic Church. *Pax Christi USA*, quarterly.

Schoenstatt Lay Movement (1914): International Schoenstatt Center, W284 N 698 Cherry Lane, Waukesha, WI 53188; (262) 547-7733. Lay movement founded in Germany by Fr. Joseph Kentenich. A Marian and apostolic way of life, Schoenstatt is present on all continents and includes people of all ages and walks of life, men and women, young and old, priests and laity. The Schoenstatt Shrine, dedicated to Mary, Mother Thrice Admirable, Queen and Victress of Schoenstatt, is an integral part of the spirituality of Schoenstatt. There are over 160 shrines around the world, 6 of them in the U.S., in Minnesota, New York, Texas, and Wisconsin.

Volunteer Missionary Movement (1969): 5980 W. Loomis Rd., Milwaukee, WI 53129; (414) 423-8660; www.vmmusa.org. Independent lay international mission organization with origins in the Catholic tradition but ecumenical and open to all Christian denominations. *Bridges*, quarterly. Exec. Dir., Julie Pagenkopf.

CATHOLIC YOUTH ORGANIZATIONS

Camp Fire Boys and Girls: 4601 Madison Ave., Kansas City, MO 64112; (816) 756-1950; www.campfireusa.org. The National Catholic Committee for Girl Scouts and Camp Fire, a standing committee of the National Federation for Catholic Youth Ministry, cooperates with Camp Fire Boys and Girls.

Catholic Forester Youth Program, Catholic Order of Foresters: Naperville, IL 60566; (800) 552-0145. To develop Christian leadership and promote the moral, intellectual, social and physical growth of its youth members. Membership: youth up to 16 years of age; over 19,046 in 610 local courts in U.S. Catholic Forester. High Chief Ranger-Pres., Robert Ciesla.

Catholic Youth Organization (CYO): Name of parish-centered diocesan Catholic youth programs throughout the country. CYO promotes a program of spiritual, social and physical activities. The original CYO was organized in 1930 by Bishop Bernard Sheil, auxiliary bishop of Chicago.

Columbian Squires (1925): 1 Columbus Plaza, New Haven, CT 06510-3326; (203) 752-4401; www.kofc. org. The official youth organization of the Knights of Columbus. To train and develop leadership through active participation in a well-organized program of spiritual, service, social, cultural and athletic activities. Membership: Catholic young men, 12-18 years old. More than 25,000 in over 1,000 circles (local units) active in the U.S., Canada, Puerto Rico, Philippines, Mexico, the Bahamas, Virgin Islands and Guam. Squires Newsletter, monthly.

Girl Scouts: 830 Third Ave., New York, NY 10022. Girls from archdioceses and dioceses in the U.S. and its possessions participate in Girl Scouting through the collaboration of Girl Scouts of the U.S.A., with the National Catholic Committee for Girl Scouts and Camp Fire, a standing committee of the National Federation for Catholic Youth Ministry.

Holy Childhood Association (Pontifical Association of the Holy Childhood) (1843): 366 Fifth Ave., New York, NY 10001; (212) 563-8700; www.worldmissions-catholicchurch.org. The official children's mission-awareness society of the Church. Provides mission awareness for elementary-grade students in parochial schools and religious education programs and financial assistance to children in more than 100 developing countries. Publishes It's Our World, three times a year, in two grade levels. Nat. Dir., Rev. Francis W. Wright, CSSp.

The National Catholic Committee on Scouting: P.O. Box 152079, Irving, TX 75015-2079; (972) 580-2114; www.catholic-church.org/catholicscouting; www.nccs-bsa.org. Works with the Boy Scouts of America in developing the character and spiritual life of members in units chartered to Catholic and non-Catholic organizations. National Committee Chairman, Robert Runnels of Leawood, KS. Admin. Sec., Barbara Nestel.

National Catholic Forensic League (1952): 21 Nancy Rd., Milford, MA 01757; (508) 473-0431. To develop articulate Catholic leaders through an inter-diocesan program of speech and debate activities. Newsletter, quarterly. Membership: 925 schools; membership open to Catholic, private and public schools through the local diocesan league. Exec. Sec.-Treas., Richard Gaudette.

National Catholic Young Adult Ministry Association (1982): P.O. Box 32253, Washington, DC 20007; (888) NCYAMA1; www.ncyama.org. A response to the needs of young adults, an invitation to share their gifts with the larger community and a challenge to live gospel values in the world. A national network for single and married young adults. Exec. Dir., Michelle M. Miller.

National Federation for Catholic Youth Ministry, Inc. (1981): 415 Michigan Ave., N.E., Washington, DC 20017; (202) 636-3825; www.nfcym.org. To fos-

ter the development of youth ministry in the United States. Exec. Dir., Robert McCarty.

Young Christian Students: 19666 W. Dunlap Rd., Dennison, IL 62423; (217) 826-5708. A student movement for Christian personal and social change.

CAMPUS MINISTRY

Campus ministry is an expression of the Church's special desire to be present to all who are involved in higher education and to further dialogue between the Church and the academic community. In the words of the U.S. bishops' 1985 pastoral letter entitled "Empowered by the Spirit," this ministry is "the public presence and service through which properly prepared baptized persons are empowered by the Spirit to use their talents and gifts on behalf of the Church in order to be sign and instrument of the Kingdom in the academic world."

Campus ministry, carried on by lay, Religious and ordained ministers, gathers members of the Church on campus to form the faith community, appropriate the faith, form Christian consciences, educate for justice and facilitate religious development.

The dimensions and challenge of this ministry are evident from, among other things, the numbers involved: approximately 550,000 Catholics on more than 230 Catholic college and university campuses; about four million in several thousand non-Catholic private and public institutions; 1,200 or more campus ministers. In many dioceses, the activities of ministers are coordinated by a local diocesan director. Two professional organizations serve the ministry on the national level:

The National Association of Diocesan Directors of Campus Ministry: Ms. Krista Bajoka (contact), 305 Michigan Ave., Detroit, MI 48226; (313) 237-5962.

The Catholic Campus Ministry Association: 1,200 members. 1118 Pendleton St., Suite 300, Cincinnati, OH 45202; (513) 842-0167; www.ccmanet.org. Exec. Dir., Austin Fragomen, Jane G. Belford.

COLLEGE SOCIETIES

Alpha Sigma Nu (1915): Marquette University, Brooks 201, P.O. Box 1881, Milwaukee, WI 53201-1881 (national headquarters); (414) 288-7542; www.alphasigmanu.org. National honor society of the 30 Jesuit institutions of higher education in the U.S. and a chapter at Sogany University in Korea; members chosen on the basis of scholarship, loyalty and service; 1,575 student and 38,000 alumni members. Member, Association of College Honor Societies. Gamma Pi Epsilon (1925) merged with Alpha Sigma Nu in 1973 to form society for men and women. Exec. Dir., Kate Greatner.

Delta Epsilon Sigma (1939): Barry University, 11300 NE Second Ave., Miami Shores, FL 33161; (305) 899-3020; www.des.barry.edu. National scholastic honor society for students, faculty and alumni of colleges and universities with a Catholic tradition. Delta Epsilon Sigma Journal, three times a year. Membership: 60,000 in 116 chapters. Sec., Dr. J. Patrick Lee.

Kappa Gamma Pi (1926): KGP National Office,

7250 Overcliff Rd, Cincinnati, OH, 45233-1038; (305) 525-3744; www.kappagammapi.org. A national Catholic college honor society for graduates who, in addition to academic excellence, have shown outstanding leadership in extracurricular activities. Also offers Cornaro Scholarship for Graduate Studies. *Kappa Gamma Pi News*, five times a year. Membership: more than 37,000 in 139 colleges; 20 alumnae chapters in metropolitan areas. Nat. Coord. Judy Gelwicks.

Phi Kappa Theta: 3901 W. 86th St., Suite 425, Indianapolis, IN 46268. National social fraternity with a Catholic heritage. Merger (1959) of Phi Kappa Fraternity, founded at Brown University in 1889, and Theta Kappa Phi Fraternity, founded at Lehigh University in 1919. *The Temple Magazine*, semi-annually, and newsletters. Membership: 2,800 undergraduate and 50,500 alumni in 63 collegiate and 40 alumni chapters. Exec. Dir., Mark T. McSweeney.

National Catholic Student Coalition (1988); 45 Lovett Ave., Newark, DE 19717; www.catholicstudent.org. National coalition of Catholic campus ministry groups at public and private institutions of higher education. Formed after National Newman Club Federation and the National Federation of Catholic College Students dissolved in the 1960s. The U.S. affiliate of Pax Romana-IMCS (see International Catholic Organizations). *The Catholic Collegian*, four times a year. Membership: 200 campus groups. Exec. Dir., Jamie Williams; contact, Kim Zitzner.

ASSOCIATIONS, MOVEMENTS, SOCIETIES IN THE U.S.

Principal source: Catholic Almanac *survey.*

Academy of American Franciscan History (1944): 1712 Euclid Ave., Berkeley, CA 94709; (510) 548-1755; www.aafh.org. To encourage the study of the Franciscan Order in the New World. Dir., Dr. Jeffrey M. Burns.

Adoremus-Society for the Renewal of the Sacred Liturgy (1995): P.O. Box 3286, St. Louis, MO 63130; (314) 863-8385; www.adoremus.org. Promotes authentic renewal of Catholic liturgy. Publishes *Adoremus Bulletin*, 10 times a year; editor, Helen Hull Hitchcock.

Aid to the Church in Need (1947): U.S. office, 725 Leonard St., Brooklyn, N.Y. 11222; (718) 609-0939; www.churchinneed.org. Assists the pastoral activities of the church in Third World countries and Eastern Europe. *Mirror*, newsletter, 9 times a year. Pres./Exec. Dir., Joseph Donnelly.

American Benedictine Academy (1947): Saint Meinrad Archabbey, Guest House, 100 Hill Dr. Saint Meinrad, IN, 47577; (800) 581-6905. To promote Benedictine values in contemporary culture. Pres., Eugene Hensell, O.S.B.

American Catholic Correctional Chaplains Association (1952): 100 E. Eighth St., Cincinnati, OH 45202; (513) 771-1877; www.catholiccorrection alchaplains.org. Pres., Rev. Mark. Schmieder.

American Catholic Historical Association (1919): Dealy Hall, Room 637, 441 E. Fordham Rd., Bronx, NY 10458; (718) 817-3830; www.achahistory.org. *The Catholic Historical Review*, quarterly. Sec.-Treas., Rev. Dr. R. Bentley Anderson, S.J.

American Catholic Philosophical Association (1926): Administration Building, Fordham University, 441 E. Fordham Rd., Bronx, NY, 10458; (718) 817-3295; www.acpa-main.org. *American Catholic Philosophical Quarterly; Proceedings*, annually.

American Committee on Italian Migration (1952): 25 Carmine St., New York, NY 10014; (212) 247-5419; www.acimmmigra.org. *ACIM Newsletter* and *ACIM Nuova Via*, 6 times a year.

American Friends of the Vatican Library (1981): 3535 Indian Trail, Orchard Lake, MI 48324; (248) 683-0311. AMICI, newsletter. Sponsored by the Catholic Library Association. To assist in supporting the Vatican Library. Pres., Rev. Msgr. Charles G. Kosanke.

American Life League, Inc. (1979), P.O. Box 1350, Stafford, VA 22555; (540) 659-4171; www.all.org. *Celebrate Life*, six times a year, and the *ABAC Quarterly*, for the American Bioethics Advisory Commission. Pres., Judie Brown.

Ancient Order of Hibernians in America, Inc. (1836): 31 Logan St., Auburn, NY 13021. National *Hibernian Digest*, bimonthly. 120,000 members. Nat. Sec., Thomas McNabb.

Apostleship of Prayer (1844, France; 1861, U.S.): 3211 South Lake Dr., Suite 216, Milwaukee, WI 53235; (414) 486-1152; www.apostleshipofprayer. org. Promotes Daily Offering and Sacred Heart devotion. Contact: Rev. James Kubicki.

Apostolate for Family Consecration (1975): 3375 County Rd. 36, Bloomingdale, OH 43910; (740) 765-5500; www.familyland.org. Pope John Paul II Holy Family Center, known as Catholic Familyland. To transform families and parishes and nourish families through the Catholic faith. Pres., Jerome F. Coniker.

Archconfraternity of Christian Mothers (Christian Mothers) (1881): 220 37th St., Pittsburgh, PA 15201; (412) 683-2400; www.capuchin.com. Over 3,500 branches. Dir., Rev. Bertin Roll, O.F.M. Cap.

Archconfraternity of the Holy Ghost (1912): Holy Ghost Fathers, 6230 Brush Run Rd., Bethel Park, PA 15102; (412) 831-0302; www.spiritans.org (U.S. headquarters).

Archdiocese for the Military Services Seminary Education Fund (1988): P.O. Box 4469, Washington, D.C., 20017-0469; (202) 269-9100; www.milarch. org.

Association for Social Economics (formerly the Catholic Economic Association) (1941): Marquette University, Milwaukee, WI 53233. *Review of Social Economy*, quarterly. 1,300 members.

Association of Catholic Diocesan Archivists (1979): P.O. Box 818, Charleston, SC 29402; (843) 577-1017; www.diocesanarchivists.org. To work for establishment of an archival program in every American diocese. *ACDA Bulletin*, quarterly. Treas. Brian P. Fahey.

Association of Marian Helpers (1944): Eden Hill, 2 Prospect Rd., Stockbridge, MA 01263; (413) 298-3691; www.marian.org. *Marian Helpers Bulletin*, quarterly. 900,000 members, mostly in U.S. To promote vocations to Church service and support world wide apostolates of Marians of the Immaculate Conception. Exec. Dir., Rev. Joseph, M.I.C.

Assumption Guild — Mass Cards: 330 Market St., Brighton, MA 02135; (617) 783-0495; www.mass cardsaa.com.

Beginning Experience (1974): International Ministry Center, 1657 Commerce Dr., Suite 2B, South

Bend, IN 46628; (574) 283-0279; www.beginningex perience.org. Programs to help divorced, widowed and separated. Pres., Kathleen Murphy.

Calix Society (1947): 2555 Hazelwood St., St. Paul, MN 55109; www.calixsociety.org. Association of Catholic alcoholics maintaining their sobriety through 12-step program. Sec. Jim Billigmeier.

Canon Law Society of America (1939): 3025 Fourth St., NE, Hecker Center, Suite 111, Washington, DC 20017; (202) 832-2350; www.clsa.org. To further research and study in canon law. 1,600 members. Exec. Coord., Sister Sharon Euart, R.S.M., J.C.D.

Cardinal Mindszenty Foundation (CMF) (1958): P.O. Box 11321, St. Louis, MO 63105-0121; (314) 727-6279; www.mindszenty.org. To uphold and defend the Catholic Church, family life and freedom for all under God. *The Mindszenty Report*, monthly. Pres., Eleanor Schlafly.

Catholic Academy for Communication Arts Professionals (2002): 1645 Brook Lynn Dr., Ste. 2, Dayton, OH 45432; (937) 229-2303; www.catholica cademy.org; the U.S. affiliate of SIGNIS, the Vatican approved organization for communication.

Catholic Answers (1982): 2020 Gillespie Way, El Cajon, CA 92020; (619) 387-7200; www.catholic.com. Apologetics and evangelization organization. *This Rock*, monthly. Founder and dir., Karl Keating.

Catholic Association of Diocesan Ecumenical and Interreligious Officers (CADEIO): 303 S. Poplar St., Carbondale, IL 62901; (618) 457-4556. To promote the work of ecumenical officers in their efforts to fos ter Christian unity and interreligious dialogue. Pres., Very Rev. Robert Flannery.

Catholic Biblical Association of America (1936): The Catholic University of America, Washington, DC 20064; (202) 319-5519; www.cba.cua.edu. The *Catholic Biblical Quarterly, Old Testament Abstracts*, CBQ monograph series. Exec. Sec., Joseph Jensen, O.S.B.

Catholic Book Publishers Association, Inc. (1987): 8404 Jamesport Dr., Rockford, IL 61108; (815) 332-3245; www.cbpa.org. Exec. Dir., Terry Wessels.

Catholic Cemetery Conference (1949): 1400 S. Wolf Rd., Building 3, Hillside, IL 60162; (888) 850-8131. Exec. Dir., Sidney Cristol.

Catholic Coalition on Preaching: Madonna University, 36600 Schoolcraft Rd. Livonia, MI 48150-1173; (734) 432-5538. Pres., Rev. Francis Tebbe, OFM.

Catholic Committee of Appalachia (1970): 885 Orchard Run Rd., Spencer, WV 25276; (304) 927-5798; ccappal.org. Dir., Fr. John Rausch.

Catholic Communications Foundation (CCF): 6363 St. Charles Ave., New Orleans, LA 70118. Established to assist the communications apostolate of the Catholic Church in the U.S.

Catholic Daughters of the Americas (1903): 10 W. 71st St., New York, NY 10023; (212) 877-3041; www.catholicdaughters.org. *Share Magazine*. 125,000 members. Nat. Regent, M. Joan McKenna.

Catholic Death Row Ministry (1990): P.O. Box 1328, Howe, Texas 75459-1328; (903)892-9411; to share the Catholic Faith with Death Row Inmates; also assist victims and families of Death Row inmates. Founder and director, Michael Denson.

Catholic Familyland (1975): 3375 County Rd. Bloomingdale, OH 43910; (740) 765-5500; www.family land.org. Canonically named the John Paul II Holy Family Center; functions under the auspices of the Apostolate for Family Consecration. Pres., Jerome F. Coniker.

Catholic Golden Age (1975): P.O. Box 3658, Scranton, PA 18505-0658; (800) 836-5699. *CGA World*, quarterly. For Catholics over 50 years of age.

Catholic Guardian Society and Home Bureau (1913): 1011 First Ave., New York, NY 10022; (212) 371-1000. Exec. Dir., John J. Frein.

Catholic Home Bureau (1899): 1011 First Ave., New York, NY 10022; (212) 371-1000; www.catholi chomebureau.com. Exec. Dir., Philip Georgini.

Catholic Home Study Service (1936): P.O. Box 363, Perryville, MO 63775-0363; (573) 547-4084; www.amm.org/chss.htm. Provides instruction in the Catholic faith by mail free of charge. Dir., Rev. James Ward, C.M.

Catholic Interracial Council of New York, Inc. (1934): 899 Tenth Ave., New York, NY 10019; (212) 237-8600; www.amm.org/chss.htm. To promote racial and social justice.

Catholic Knights of America (1877): Publication Office, 1850 Dalton St., Cincinnati, OH 45214. Fraternal insur ance society. *CK of A Journal*, monthly. 7,800 members.

Catholic Knights of Ohio (1891): 22005 Mastick Rd., Fairview Park, OH 44126; (440) 777-5355. Fraternal insur ance society. *The Messenger*, monthly. 8,000 members in Ohio and Kentucky. Mr. Tom Welsh, General Secretary.

Catholic Kolping Society of America (1849): 1223 Van Houten, Clifton, NJ 07013. International soci ety concerned with spiritual and educational devel opment of members. *Kolping Banner*, monthly. Nat. Admin., Patricia Farkas.

Catholic Lawyers' Guild: Organization usually on a diocesan basis, under different titles.

Catholic League for Religious Assistance to Poland (1943): 6002 W. Berteau Ave., Chicago, IL 60634-1630; (773) 202-7720. Exec. Dir., Most Rev. Thad Jakubowski.

Catholic League for Religious and Civil Rights (1973): 450 Seventh Ave., 34th Floor, New York, NY 10123; (212) 371-3191; www.catholicleague.org. Local chapters through out U.S. Serves Catholic community as an anti-defama tion and civil rights agency. *Catalyst*, league journal. Pres., William A. Donohue, Ph.D.

Catholic Library Association (1921): 205 W. Monroe St., Suite 314, Chicago, IL 60606. www. cathla.org; *Catholic Library World, Catholic Periodical and Literature Index*, quarterlies. Pres. Malachy McCarthy, Pres.

Catholic Marketing Network (1955): 111 Ferguson Court, #102, Irving, TX 75062; (800) 506-6333; www. catholicmarketing.com. A trade association founded to encourage the most effective production and distribu tion of Catholic goods and provide a common forum for mutual interchange of ideas. *Catholic Marketing Network*, quarterly. Exec. Dir., Cherylann Tucker.

Catholic Near East Welfare Association (1926): 1011 First Ave., Suite 1552, New York, NY 10022; (212) 826-1480; www.cnewa.org. A papal agency for humanitarian and pastoral support serving the churches and peoples of the Middle East, Northeast Africa, India and Eastern Europe, with offices in New York, Vatican City, Addis Ababa, Amman, Jerusalem and Beirut. Chair., Abp. Timothy M. Dolan; pres, Msgr. John Kozar.

Catholic Order of Foresters (1883): 355 Shuman Blvd., P.O. Box 3012, Naperville, IL 60566; (630) 983-4900; www.catholicforester.com. Fraternal insur ance society. *The Catholic Forester*, bimonthly. 136,685 members. High Chief Ranger, Robert Ciesla.

Catholic Press Association of the U.S. and Canada, Inc. (1911): 205 W. Monroe, Suite 470, Chicago, IL 60606; (312) 380-6789; www.catholic press.org. *The Catholic Journalist*, monthly; *Catholic Press Directory*, annually. Exec. Dir., Timothy Walter.

Catholic Theological Society of America (1946): John Carroll University, 20700 North Park Blvd., University Hgts., OH, 44118; (216) 397-3980; www. jcu.edu/ctsa. Proceedings, annually. Exec. Sec., Mary Jane Ponyik.

Catholic Union of Texas, The K.J.T. (1889): 214 E. Colorado St., La Grange, TX 78945-0297; (979) 968-5877; www.kjtnet.org. Fraternal and insurance society. *Nasinec*, weekly, and *K. J. T. News*, monthly. 18,226 members. Pres., Elo J. Goerig.

Catholic United Financial (1878): 3499 Lexington Ave., North, St. Paul, MN 55126; (651) 490-0170; www.catho-licunited.org. Fraternal life insurance society; formerly called Catholic Aid Association. *Catholic Aid News*, monthly. Chairman of the Board, Michael McGovern.

Catholic War Veterans (1935): 441 N. Lee St., Alexandria, VA 22314; (703) 549-3622; www.cwv. org. *Catholic War Veteran*, bimonthly. 500 posts.

Catholic Worker Movement (1933): 36 E. 1st St., New York, NY 10003. Lay apostolate founded by Peter Maurin and Dorothy Day; has Houses of Hospitality in over 60 U.S. cities and several commu nal farms in various parts of the country. *The Catholic Worker*, 8 times a year.

Catholic Workman (Katolicky Delnik) (1891): 111 West Main St., New Prague, MN 56071; (612) 758-2229. Fraternal and insurance society. *Catholic Workman*, monthly. 16,405 members.

Catholics Against Capital Punishment (1992): P.O. Box 5706, Bethesda, MD 20824-5706; (301) 652-1125; www.cacp.org. Promotes greater awareness of papal and episcopal statements against the death penalty. *CACP News* Notes, bimonthly. Nat. Coord., Frank McNeirney.

Catholics United for the Faith (1968): 827 N. Fourth St., Steubenville, OH 43952; (740) 283-2484; www.cuf.org. 23,000 members worldwide. Lay apos tolic group concerned with spiritual and doctrinal for mation of members. *Lay Witness*, monthly. Mike Sullivan, Dir. of Communications.

Center of Concern (1971): 1225 Otis St., N.E., Washington, DC 20017; (202) 635-2757; www.coc. org. Exec. Dir., Rev. James E. Hug, S.J.

Central Association of the Miraculous Medal (1915): 475 E. Chelten Ave., Philadelphia, PA 19144; (800) 523-3674; www.cammonline.org. *Miraculous Medal*, quarterly. Dir., Rev. James O. Kiernan, C.M.

Chaplains' Aid Association, Inc. (1917): 3311 Toledo Terrace, Hyattsville, MD 20780. To receive and administer funds toward education of seminar-ians to become priest-chaplains in military services.

Christian Foundation for Children and Aging: One Elmwood Ave., Kansas City, KS 66103; (913) 384-6500; www.cfcausa.org. Grassroots movement dedi-cated to improving through sponsorship the lives of children and aging at Catholic mission sites around the world. Exec. Dir., Paco Wertin.

Christophers, Inc., The (1945): 12 E. 48th St.,

New York, NY 10017; (212) 759-4050; www.chris-tophers.org. Founded by Rev. James Keller, M.M. The Christophers stimulate personal initiative and responsible action in line with Judeo-Christian principles through broadcast of Christopher radio and TV programs; free distribution of *Christopher News Notes*, ten times a year; publication of a weekly Christopher column in over 200 newspapers; Spanish literature; annual media awards; youth outreach. Pres., Dennis W. Heaney.

Citizens for Educational Freedom (1959): 9333 Clayton Road, St. Louis, MO 63124-1511; (314) 997-6361; www.educational-freedom.org. Nonsectarian group concerned with parents' right to educational choice by means of tuition tax cred-its and vouchers. Exec. Dir., Mae Duggan.

Coming Home Network (1993): P.O. Box 8290, Zanesville, OH 43702; (740) 450-1175; www. chnetwork.org. Founded by Marcus Grodi (a former presbyterian pastor), *The Coming Home Network International* (CHNetwork) pro vides fellowship, encouragement and support for Protestant pastors and laymen who are somewhere along the journey or have already been received into the Catholic Church. Pres. Marcus Grodi.

Conference of Slovak Clergy (1985): 126 Logan Blvd., Hollidaysburg, PA, 16648; (814) 695-5579. Founded in 1985 and incorporated in 2000, the Conference seeks to associate priests and deacons of Slovak ancestry in the United States and to assist those preparing themselves for priestly min-istry in the Church; provides financial assistance to the Slovak Pontifical College of Saints Cyril and Methodius in Rome and scholarships to individual students. Chair., Bp.Joseph V. Adamec.

Confraternity of Bl. Junipero Serra (1989): P.O. Box 7125, Mission Hills, CA 91346. Founded in Monterey (CA) diocese to help promote process of canonization of Bl. Junipero Serra and increase spiri tual development of members. 3,500 members in U.S. and foreign countries. Dir., Rev. Thomas L. Davis, Jr.; Spiritual Dir., Rev. Noel F. Moholy, O.F.M.

Confraternity of Catholic Clergy (1976): 4445 W. 64th St., Chicago, IL 60629; (773) 581-8904. Association of priests pledged to pursuit of per-sonal holiness, loyalty to the pope, theological study and adherence to authentic teachings of the Catholic faith. Sec., Rev. L. Dudley Day, OSA.

Confraternity of Christian Doctrine, Inc.: 3211 Fourth St., N.E., Washington, DC 20017; (202) 541-3098; www.usccb.org/nab. A distinct entity, separately incorporated and directed by a Board of Trustees from the United States Catholic Conference of Bishops. Its purpose is to foster and promote the teaching of Christ as understood and handed down by the Roman Catholic Church. To this end it licenses use of the Lectionary for Mass and the *New American Bible (NAB), the Revised Psalms of the NAB* and the *Revised New Testament of the NAB*, translations made from the original languages in accordance with the papal encyclical *Divino Afflante Spiritu* (1943) of Pope Pius XII.

Confraternity of the Immaculate Conception of Our Lady of Lourdes (1874): Box 561, Notre Dame, IN 46556; (574) 631-6562. Distributors of Lourdes water.

Confraternity of the Most Holy Rosary: See Dominican

Rosary Apostolate.

Courage (1980): c/o St. John the Baptist Church and Friary, 210 West 31st St., New York, NY 10001; (212) 268-1010; www.couragerc.org. Ministry to men and women who experience same-sex attractions and desire to live Christian chastity in accordance with the teachings of the Catholic Church. Newsletter, 4 times a year. Nat. Dir., Rev. John F. Harvey, O.S.F.S.

CUSA (Catholics United for Spiritual Action, Inc.) — An Apostolate of the Sick or Disabled (1947): 176 W. 8th St., Bayonne, NJ, 07002-1227; (201) 437-0412; www.cusan.org. A group-correspon dence apostolate for the disabled and chronically ill. Admin. Ms. Anna Marie Sopko.

Damien-Dutton Society for Leprosy Aid, Inc. (1944): 616 Bedford Ave., Bellmore, NY 11710; (516) 221-5829; www.damien-duttonleprosysociety. org. Provides medicine, rehabilitation and research for conquest of leprosy. *Damien Dutton Call*, quarterly. 25,000 members. Vice Pres., Elizabeth Campbell.

Daniel Dajani, S.J., Albanian Catholic Institute (1992): University of San Francisco, Xavier Hall, 650 Parker Ave., San Francisco, CA 94118; (415) 422-6966; www.albanian-catholic-institute.org. To assist the rebuilding of the Catholic Church in Albania and to promote the dissemination of knowledge of Albania's national, religious and cultural heritage. Exec. Dir., Raymond Frost.

Daughters of Isabella (1897): P.O. Box 9585, New Haven, CT 06535; www.daughtersofisabella. To unite Catholic women into a fraternal order for spiritual benefits and to pro mote higher ideals within society. 100,000 members.

Disaster Response Office (1990): Catholic Charities USA, 1731 King St., Suite 200, Alexandria, VA 22314; (703) 549-1390; www.catholiccharitiesusa.org. Promotes and facilitates Catholic disaster response in the U.S. Dir., Jane A. Gallagher.

Dismas Ministry: P.O. Box 070363, Milwaukee, WI 53207; (414) 977-5064; www.dismasministry.org; out reach to inmates, their families, and the community; services include spiritual ministry to inmates, victim support, and faith-based rehabilitation.

Dominican Rosary Apostolate (1806): Dominican Province of St. Joseph, 280 N. Grant Ave., Columbus, OH 43215, (614) 240-5915. Contact: Rev. André-Joseph LaCasse, O.P., Promoter of the Rosary, Dominican Province of St. Joseph.

Edith Stein Guild, Inc. (1955): Church of St. John the Baptist, 210 W. 31st St., New York, NY 10001-2876; (212) 567-8230. Assists and encourages Jewish Catholics; fosters among Catholics a better understanding of their Jewish heritage; promotes spread of knowledge of life and writings of St. Edith Stein; fosters better understanding between Jews and Christians and supports the Church's spirit of ecumenism. Pres., Sr. Marie Goldstein, R.S.H.M.

Enthronement of the Sacred Heart in the Home (1907): P.O. Box 111, Fairhaven, MA 02719; (508) 999-2680.

Federation of Diocesan Liturgical Commissions (FDLC) (1969): P.O. Box 29039, Washington, DC 20017; (202) 635-6990; www.fdlc.org. Voluntary association of personnel from diocesan liturgical commissions and worship offices. The main purpose is promotion of the liturgy as the heart of Christian life, especially in the parish community. Exec. Dir., Rev. Michael J. Spillane.

Federation of Seminary Spiritual Directors (1972): Cardinal Muench Seminary, 100 35th Ave., N.E., Fargo, ND 58102; (701) 232-8969. Responsible for priestly spiritual formation in high school and college seminaries, novitiates, theologates and houses of formation in the U.S. and Canada. Pres., Dennis Skonseng.

Fellowship of Catholic Scholars (1977): Ave Maria School of Law, 3475 Plymouth Rd., Ann Arbor, Michigan 48105; (734) 827-8043. Interdisciplinary research and publications of Catholic scholars in accord with the magisterium of the Catholic Church. 1,000 members. Pres., Bernard Dobranski.

First Catholic Slovak Ladies' Association, USA (1892): 24950 Chagrin Blvd., Beachwood, OH 44122; (800) 464-4642; www.fcsla.com. *Fraternally Yours*, monthly. 102,000 members. Fraternal insurance society. Pres., Cynthia Maleski.

First Catholic Slovak Union (Jednota) (1890): FCSU Corporate Center, 6611 Rockside Rd., Independence, OH 44131; (216) 642-9406; www. fcsu.com. *Jednota*, biweekly. 96,206 members.

Foundation for the Family (1986): P.O. Box 111184, Cincinnati, OH 45211; (800) 745-8252; www.ccli. org. Established by Couple to Couple League (see entry above) to provide materials for family not relating to Natural Family Planning, Exec. Dir., Mark Hayden.

Foundations and Donors Interested in Catholic Activities, Inc. (FADICA): 1350 Connecticut Ave. N.W., Suite 303, Washington, DC 20036; (202) 223-3550; www.FADICA.org. A consortium of private foundations providing continuing education and research to members to make churchrelated philanthropy more effective. Pres., Francis J. Butler.

Franciscan Apostolate of the Way of the Cross (1949): P.O. Box 23, Boston, MA 02112; (617) 542-6659. Distributes religious materials to the sick and shut-in. Dir., Rev. Robert Lynch, O.F.M.

Free The Fathers (1983): 845 Oak St. Chattanooga, TN 37403; (423) 756-9660; www.ftf.org. To work for the freedom of bishops and priests imprisoned in China. Pres., John M. Davies.

Friends of the Holy Land, Inc. (1974): 370 Mile Square Rd., Yonkers, NY 10701. To provide spiritual and material support for the Christian communities in the Holy Land. *Friends of the Holy Land* Newsletter. 300 members. Gen. Dir., Ernest F. Russo.

Gabriel Richard Institute (1949): 3641 Estates Dr., Troy, MI 48084; (248) 643-8887. Conducts Christopher Leadership Course. Exec. Dir., Dolores Ammar.

Guard of Honor of the Immaculate Heart of Mary (1932): 135 West 31st St., New York, NY 10001; (212) 736-8500; www.hnp.org. An archconfraternity approved by the Holy See whose members cultivate devotion to the Blessed Virgin Mary, particularly through a daily Guard Hour of Prayer. Dir., Rev. Cassian A. Miles, O.F.M.

Holy Cross Family Ministries (formerly The Family Rosary, Inc.) (1942): 518 Washington St.,

North Easton, MA, 02356-1200; (508) 238-4095; www.hcfm.org. Founded by Fr. Patrick Peyton, C.S.C. Encourages family prayer, especially the Rosary. Pres., Fr. John Phalen, C.S.C.

Holy Name Society: P.O. Box 12012, Baltimore, MD 21281; (410) 325-1523; www.holynamesociety.info. Founded in 1274 by Blessed John Vercelli, master general of the Dominicans, to promote reverence for the Holy Name of Jesus; this is still the principal purpose of the society, which also develops lay apostolic programs in line with directives of the Second Vatican Council. Introduced in the U.S. in 1870-71 by Dominican Fr. Charles H. McKenna, the society has about 5 million members on diocesan and parochial levels. With approval of the local bishop and pastor, women as well as men may be members.

Holy Name Society, National Association (NAHNS) (1970): P.O. Box 12012, Baltimore, MD 21281; (410) 276-1166; www.members.aol.com/nahns. Association of diocesan and parochial Holy Name Societies. *Holy Name Newsletter*, monthly.

Hungarian Catholic League of America, Inc. (1945): One Cathedral Sq., Providence, RI 02903-3695; (401) 278-4520. Chair., Rev. Msgr. William I. Varsanyi.

International Catholic Stewardship Council (1962): 1275 K St. N.W., Suite 880, Washington, DC 20005-4083; (800) 352-3452; www.catholicstewardship.org. A professional association which fosters an environment in which stewardship is understood, accepted and practiced throughout the church. Moderator, Alex R. Carrion.

International Catholic Charismatic Renewal Services: Palazzo della Cancelleria, 00120 Vatican City; 39 06 698 87538; www.iccrs.org. The ICCRS provides leadership and vision to the Catholic Charismatic Renewal throughout the world in harmony with the Pontifical Council for the Laity which has established ICCRS as a Private Association of the Faithful. *See* National Catholic Charismatic Renewal Services.

Italian Catholic Federation (1924): 675 Hegenberger Rd., #230, Oakland, CA 94621; (888) 423-1924; www.icf.org. Fraternal organization of Italian-American Catholics. 19,000 members.

John Carroll Society, The (1951): P.O. Box 50188, Washington, DC 20091; (703) 573-3043; www.johncarrollsociety.org. Exec. Asst., Mary Ann Dmochowski, Ph.D.

Judean Society, Inc., The (1966): 1075 Space Park Way No. 336, Mountain View, CA 94043.

Knights of Peter Claver (1909), and Knights of Peter Claver, Ladies Auxiliary (1926): 1825 Orleans Ave., New Orleans, LA 70116; (504) 821-4225; www.knightsofpeterclaver.com. Fraternal and aid society. *The Claverite*, biannually. National Chaplain, Most Rev. Curtis J. Guillory, S.V.D.

Knights of St. John, International Supreme Commandery (1886): 89 So. Pine Ave., Albany, NY 12208; (518) 453-5675; www.members.tripod.com/ksji/knights/ksji.html. Supreme Sec., Maj. Gen. Joseph Hauser, Jr.

Ladies of Charity of the United States of America (1960): PO Box 31697, St. Louis, MO 63131; (314)

344-1184; www.famvin.org/lcusa. International Association founded by St. Vincent de Paul in 1617. 25,000 members in U.S.; 250,000 worldwide.

Latin Liturgy Association (1975): P. O. Box 3017, Bethlehem, PA, 18017; www.latinliturgy.com. To promote the use of the Latin language and music in the approved rites of the Church. Quarterly journal. 850 members. Pres., James F. Pauer.

Legatus (1987): 30 Frank Lloyd Wright Dr., P.O. Box 997, Ann Arbor, MI 48106; (734) 930-3854. To apply Church's moral teaching in business and personal lives of members. *Legatus Newsletter*, monthly.

Lithuanian Groups: Ateitininkai, members of Lithuanian Catholic Federation Ateitis (1910), 1209 Country Lane, Lemont, IL 60439. *Ateitis*, bimonthly. Pres., Juozas Polikaitis. Knights of Lithuania (1913): Roman Catholic educational-fraternal organization. Vytis, monthly. Pres., Evelyn Ozelis, 2533 W. 45th St., Chicago, IL 60632.

Lithuanian Catholic Alliance (1886), 7173 S. Washington St., Wilkes-Barre, PA 18701. Fraternal insurance organization. Pres., Thomas E. Mack.

Lithuanian Roman Catholic Federation of America (1906): 4545 W. 63rd St., Chicago, IL 60629; (312) 585-9500. Umbrella organization for Lithuanian parishes and organizations. *The Observer*, bimonthly. Pres., Saulius Kuprys.

Lithuanian Catholic Religious Aid, Inc. (1961): 64-25 Perry Ave., Maspeth, NY 11378-2441; (718) 326-5202. To assist Catholics in Lithuania. Chairman and Pres., Most Rev. Paul Baltakis, O.F.M.

Lithuanian Roman Catholic Priests' League (1909): P.O. Box 1025, Humarock, MA 02047-1025; (781) 834-4079. Religious-professional association. Pres., Rev. Albert Contons.

Little Flower Mission League (1957), P.O. Box 25, Plaucheville, LA 71362; (318) 922-3630. Sponsored by the Brothers of the Holy Eucharist. Dir., Bro. André M. Lucia, F.S.E.

Little Flower Society (1923): 1313 Frontage Rd. Darien, IL 60561. 200,000 members. Nat. Dir., Rev. Robert E. Colaresi, O. Carm.

Liturgical Conference, The: 415 Michigan Ave., NE, #65, Washington, DC 20017; (202) 832-6520; www.litconf.org. Liturgy, homily service. Education, research and publication programs for renewing and enriching Christian liturgical life. Ecumenical.

Loyal Christian Benefit Association (1890): P.O. Box 13005, Erie, PA 16514; (814) 453-4331; www.icba.com. Fraternal benefit and insurance society. *The Fraternal Leader*, quarterly. Pres., Jackie Sobania-Robison.

Marian Movement of Priests (1972): P.O. Box 8, St. Francis, ME 04774-0008 (U.S.); (207) 398-3375; www.mmp-usa.net. Via Mercalli, 23, 20122 Milan, Italy (international headquarters). Spiritual renewal through consecration to the Immaculate Heart of Mary. 4,000 clergy members, 53,000 religious and laity (U.S.). Contact: Tammy Ouellette.

Mariological Society of America (1949): Marian Library, #1390, University of Dayton, Dayton, OH 45469; (937) 229-4214; www.udayton.edu/mary. Founded by Rev. Juniper B. Carol, O.F.M., to promote greater appreciation of and scientific research in Marian theology. Marian Studies, annually. Sec., Rev. Thomas A. Thompson, S.M.

Marriage Encounter, National: 4704 Jamerson Pl., Orlando, FL 32807. The national office of Worldwide Marriage Encounter is located at 2210 East Highland Ave., #106, San Bernardino, CA 92404; (909) 863-9963. Brings couples together for a weekend program of events directed by a team of several couples and a priest, to develop their abilities to communicate with each other as husband and wife.

Maryheart Crusaders, The (1964): 22 Button St., Meriden, CT 06450; (203) 239-5979; www.maryheartcrusaders.org. Pres., Louise D'Angelo.

Men of the Sacred Heart (1964): National Shrine of the Sacred Heart, P.O. Box 500, Harleigh, PA 18225; (570) 455-1162. Promotes enthronement of Sacred Heart.

Militia Immaculate National Center — Marytown (1917): 1600 W. Park Ave., Libertyville, IL 60048; (847) 367-7800; www.consecration.com. Canonically established with international headquarters in Rome. A pious association to promote total consecration to Mary in the spirit of St. Mximilian Kolbe. Pres., Fr. Patrick Greenough, OFM Conv.

Missionary Association of Catholic Women (1916): 3501 S. Lake Dr., P.O. Box 07212, Milwaukee, WI 53207-0912; (414) 769-3406.

Missionary Vehicle Association, Inc. (MIVA America) (1971): 1400 Michigan Ave., N.E., Washington, DC 20017-7234; (202) 635-3444; www.miva.org. To raise funds and distribute them annually as vehicle grants to missionaries working with the poor in Third World countries. Nat. Dir., Rev. Philip De Rea, MSC; Exec. Dir., Rev. Anthony F. Krisak.

Morality in Media, Inc. (1962): 475 Riverside Dr., Suite 1264, New York, NY 10115; (212) 870-3222; www.moralityinmedia.org. Interfaith national organization. Works by constitutional means to curb the explosive growth of hard-core pornography and to turn back the tide of grossly offensive, indecent media. A major project is the National Obscenity Law Center which provides legal information for prosecutors and other attorneys. Newsletter, bimonthly. Pres., Robert W. Peters.

National Association of African American Catholic Deacons: 1418 Glen View Rd., Yellow Springs, OH 45387; (937) 974-1588. To assist and promote permanent deacons of Africn American heritage. Pres. Deacon Paul E. Richardson.

National Assembly of Religious Women (NARW): 529 S. Wabash Ave., Suite 404, Chicago, IL 60605; (312) 663-1980. Founded as the National Assembly of Women Religious, 1970; title changed, 1980. A movement of feminist women committed to prophetic tasks of giving witness, raising awareness and engaging in public action and advocacy for justice in church and society.

National Association for Lay Ministry (1977): 6896 Laurel St., N.W., Washington, DC 20012; (202) 291-4100; www.nalm.org. Acts as advocate and support for lay people who respond to a call to ministry in the Church. Exec. Dir., Christopher Anderson.

National Association of Catholic Chaplains: 5007 S. Howell Ave., Ste. 120, Milwaukee, WI 532-7; (414) 483-4898; www.nacc.org. Supports the work and ministry of Catholic chaplains; publishes newsletter, Vision, and e-mail newsletter, NACC Now.

National Association of Catholic Family Life Ministers: 300 College Park, Dayton, OH 45469; (937) 431-5443; www.nacflm.org. Strives to be a voice and advocate for families and family ministry in Church and society. Pres., Lorrie Gramer.

National Association of Catholic Home Educators (1993): 6102 Saints Hill Lane, Broad Run, VA 20137; (540) 349-4314; www.nache.com. Promotion of home-schooling. The Catholic Home Educator, quarterly.

National Association of Church Personnel Administrators (1971): 100 E. 8th St., Cincinnati, OH 45202; (513) 421-3134; www.nacpa.org. Association for human resource and personnel directors dedicated to promotion and development of just personnel practices for all church employees. Exec. Dir., Sr. Ellen Doyle, OSU.

National Association of Diaconate Directors (1977): 7625 N. High St., Columbus, OH 43215; (614) 985-2276; www.nadd.org. Deacon Thomas R. Dubois, Exec. Dir.

National Association of Diocesan Ecumenical Officers: 7800 Kenrick Rd., St. Louis, MO 63119; (314) 961-4320. Network of Catholics involved in ecumenical and interreligious work. Pres., Vincent A. Heier.

National Association of Pastoral Musicians (1976): 962 Wayne Ave., Suite 210, Silver Spring, MD 20910; (240) 247-3000; www.npm.org. 9,000 members. Dedicated to fostering the art of musical liturgy. Pastoral Music, six times a year. Exec. Dir., Dr. J. Michael McMahon.

National Association of Priest Pilots (1964): 481 N. Shore Dr., Apt. 301, Clear Lake IA 50428-1368; (641) 357-4539. Pres., Rev. Msgr. John Hemann.

National Catholic AIDS Network: P.O. Box 422984, San Francisco, CA 94142; (707) 874-3031; www.ncan.org. Exec. dir., Rev. Rodney DeMartini; Board Pres., Rev. Robert J. Vitillo.

National Catholic Band Association (1953): 3334 N. Normandy, Chicago, IL 60634; (773) 282-9153; www.catholicbands.org.

National Catholic Conference for Interracial Justice (NCCIJ) (1960): 1200 Varnum St. N.E., Washington, DC 20017; (202) 529-6480. Exec. Dir., Rev. Mr. Joseph M. Conrad, Jr.

National Catholic Conference for Seafarers: 4219 Constance St., New Orleans, LA 70115; (504) 891-6677. Association of chaplains and laity serving in the pastoral care of seafarers.

National Catholic Council on Addiction: 1601 Joslyn Rd., Lake Orion, MI 48360; (800) 626-6910; www.nccatoday.com. An affiliate of the USCCB. Committed to assisting members in a greater awareness of alcoholism, other chemical addictions and prevention issues. Coordinator: Louise Westcott.

National Catholic Development Conference (1968): 86 Front St., Hempstead, NY 11550; (516) 481-6000. Professional association of organizations and individuals engaged in raising funds for Catholic charitable activities. Pres., Sr. Georgette Lehmuth, OSF.

National Catholic Ministry to the Bereaved (NCMB) (1990): 28700 Euclid Ave., Wickliffe, OH, 44092-2527; (440) 943-3480; www.griefwork.org.

Offers ongoing education, resources and assistance to dioceses, parishes and caregivers in their ministry to the bereaved. Coordinator: Mary Ann Wachtel, SFCC.

National Catholic Pharmacists Guild of the United States (1962): 1012 Surrey Hills Dr., St. Louis, MO 63117; (314) 645-0085. *The Catholic Pharmacist.* Co-Pres., Exec. Dir. and Editor, John P. Winkelmann.

National Catholic Society of Foresters (1891): 320 S. School St., Mt. Prospect, IL 60056; (847) 342-4500; www.ncsf.com. A fraternal insurance society. *National Catholic Forester*, quarterly. National Pres., Margaret Babinat.

National Catholic Women's Union (1916): 3835 Westminster Pl., St. Louis, MO 63108; (314) 371-1653; www.socialjusticereview.org. 7,000 members.

National Center for the Laity (1977): P.O. Box 291102, Chicago, IL 60629; (708) 974-5221; www.catholiclabor.org/ncl.htm. To promote and implement the vision of Vatican II: That the laity are the Church in the modern world as they attend to their occupational, family and neighborhood responsibilities. *Initiatives*, six times a year.

National Center for Urban Ethnic Affairs (1971): P.O. Box 20, Cardinal Station, Washington, DC 20064; (202) 232-3600. Research and action related to the Church's concern for cultural pluralism and urban neighborhoods. An affiliate of the USCCB. Pres., Dr. John A. Kromkowski.

National Christ Child Society Inc. (1887): 6900 Wisconsin Ave. N.W., Suite 604, Bethesda, MD 20815; (800) 814-2149; www.NationalChristChildSoc.org. Founder, Mary V. Merrick. A nonprofit Catholic association of volunteers of all denominations dedicated to the service of needy children and youth regardless of race or creed. Approximately 7,000 adult members in 38 chapters in U.S. Exec. Dir., Margaret Saffell.

National Committee of Catholic Laymen, The (1977): 215 Lexington Ave., Fourth Floor, New York, NY 10016; (212) 685-6666. Lobbying and publishing organization representing "orthodox" Catholics who strongly support Pope John Paul II. *Catholic Eye*, monthly; editor, Mrs. Anne Conlon.

National Conference of Catechetical Leadership (formerly, National Conference of Diocesan Directors of Religious Education) (1936): 125 Michigan Ave., N.E., Washington, DC 20017; (202) 884-9753; www.nccl.org. To promote catechetical ministry at the national diocesan and parish levels. 1,300 members. Exec. Dir., Leland Nagel.

National Conference of Catholic Airport Chaplains (1986): P.O. Box 66353, Chicago, IL 60666; (773) 686-2636; www.nccac.us. Provides support and communication for Catholics performing pastoral ministry to airport and airline workers and Catholic travelers; affiliated with Bishops' Committee on Migration, USCCB. Pres., Deacon Rev. Michael Zaniolo, STL, CAC.

National Conference of Diocesan Vocation Directors (NCDVD) (1961): 440 W. Neck Rd., Huntington, NY 11743; (631) 645-8210. Professional organization for diocesan vocation personnel providing resources and on-going edu-

cation in their promoting, assessing and forming of candidates for the diocesan priesthood. Pres., Fr. Leonard Plazewski.

National Council for Catholic Evangelization (1983): 415 Michigan Ave, NE, Suite 90, Washington, DC, 20017; 1-800-786-NCCE; www.catholicevangelization.org. To promote evangelization as the "primary and essential mission of the Church," in accordance with *Evangelii Nuntiandi*, the 1975 apostolic exhortation of Pope Paul VI. Exec. Dir., Sr. Priscilla Lemire, RJM.

National Council of Catholic Women (1920): 200 N. Glebe Rd., Suite 703, Arlington, VA 22203; (703) 224-0990; www.nccw.org. A federation of some 7,000 organizations of Catholic women in the U.S. NCCW unites Catholic organizations and individual Catholic women of the U.S., develops their leadership potential, assists them to act upon current issues in the Church and society, provides a medium through which Catholic women may speak and act upon matters of common interest, and relates to other national and international organizations in the solution of presentday problems. It is an affiliate of the World Union of Catholic Women's Organizations. *Catholic Woman*, bimonthly. Exec. Dir., Sheila McCarron.

National Evangelization Teams (NET): 110 Crusader Ave., West St. Paul, MN 55118-4427; (651) 450-6833; www.netusa.org. Trains Catholic young adults to be evangelists to peers and high school/junior high youth through traveling retreat teams.

National Federation of Catholic Physicians' Guilds (1927): P.O. Box 757, Pewaukee, WI 53072; (262) 523-6201; www.cathmed.com. *Linacre* Quarterly. Exec. Dir., Robert H. Herzog.

National Federation of Priests' Councils (1968): 333 N. Michigan Ave., Ste. 1205, Chicago, IL 60601; (312) 442-9700; www.nfpc.org. To give priests' councils a representative voice in matters of presbyteral, pastoral and ministerial concern to the U.S. and the universal Church. *Touchstone*, quarterly. Pres., Rev. Richard Vega.

National Institute for the Word of God (1972): 487 Michigan Ave. N.E., Washington, DC 20017; (203) 562-6193; www.wordofgodinstitute.org. For renewed biblical preaching, Bible sharing and evangelization. Dir., Rev. John Burke, OP.

National Life Center, Inc.: 686 N. Broad St., Woodbury, NJ 08096; (856) 848-1819, (800) 848-LOVE; www.nationallifecenter.com. Interdenominational guidance and referral service organization offering pregnant women alternatives to abortion. Pres., Denise F. Cocciolone.

National Organization for Continuing Education of Roman Catholic Clergy, Inc. (1973): 333 N. Michigan Ave., Ste. 1205, Chicago, IL 60601; (312) 781-9450; www.nocercc.org. Membership: 152 dioceses, 66 religious provinces, 46 institutions, 49 individuals in U.S., 18 associates outside U.S. Pres., Fr. Mark R. Hession.

National Pastoral Life Center: 18 Bleecker St., New York, NY 10012-2404; (212) 431-7825; www.nplc.org. *Church*, quarterly. Dir., Fr. John Hurley, CSP.

National Service Committee of the Catholic Charismatic Renewal: Charismcenter USA, PO Box 628, Locust Grove, VA 22508; (540) 972-0225; www.nsc-hariscenter.org, www.iccrs.org. The mission of the National Service

Committee is "to stir into flame the grace of Pentecost within and beyond the Church, to broaden and deepen the understanding that baptism in the Holy Spirit is the Christian inheritance of all, and to strengthen the Catholic Charismatic Renewal." Exec. Dir., Walter Matthews.

NETWORK, A Catholic Social Justice Lobby (1971): 22 E St. NW, Suite 200, Washington, DC 20001; (202) 347-9797; www.networklobby.org. A national Catholic social justice lobby. *NETWORK Connection*, bimonthly. Exec. Dir., Simone Campbell.

Nocturnal Adoration Society of the United States (1882): 184 E. 76th St., New York, NY 10021; (212) 288-5082. Nat. Dir., Rev. Mario Marzocchi, S.S.S.

North American Academy of Liturgy: c/o CSSR Executive Office, Valparaiso University, Valparaiso, IN 46383. Foster ecumenical and interreligious liturgical research, publication and dialogue on a scholarly level. Proceedings, annually. Pres., Alan Barthel.

North American Conference of Separated and Divorced Catholics (1972): P.O. Box 360, Richland, OR 97870; (541) 893-6089; www.nacsdc.com. Exec. Dir., Irene Varley.

North American Forum on the Catechumenate: 125 Michigan Ave. NE, Washington, DC 20017; (202) 884-9758; www.naforum.org. An international network committed to the implementation of the Order of Christian Initiation of Adults. Exec. Dir., James Schellman.

Order of the Alhambra (1904): 4200 Leeds Ave., Baltimore, MD 21229; (410) 242-0660; www.OrderAlhambra.org. Fraternal society dedicated to assisting developmentally disabled and handicapped children. 7,000 members in US and Canada. Exec. Dir., Roger J. Reid.

Our Lady's Rosary Makers (1949): 4611 Poplar Level Rd., Louisville, KY 40233; www.olrm.org. To supply missionaries with free rosaries for distribution throughout the world. *News Bulletin*, monthly. Pres., Michael Ford.

Papal Foundation, The: 150 Monument Rd., Ste. 609, Bala Cynwyd, PA 19004; (610) 535-6340; V. Pres., James V. Coffey.

Paulist National Catholic Evangelization Association (1977): 3031 Fourth St., NE, Washington, DC 20017-1102; (202) 832-5022; www.pncea.org. To work with unchurched and alienated Catholics; to develop, test and document contemporary ways in which Catholic parishes and dioceses can evangelize the unchurched and inactive Catholics. Share the Word, bimonthly magazine; *Evangelization Update*, bimonthly newsletter. Dir., Fr. Kenneth Boyack, CSP.

Philangeli (Friends of the Angels) (1949 in England; 1956 in U.S.): Viatorian Fathers, 1115 E. Euclid St., Arlington Heights, IL 60004.

Pious Union of Prayer (1898): St. Joseph's Home, P.O. Box 288, Jersey City, NJ 07303; (201) 798-4141. St. Joseph's Messenger and *Advocate of the Blind*, quarterly.

Polish Roman Catholic Union of America (1887): 984 N. Milwaukee Ave., Chicago, IL 60622; (773) 728-2600; www.prcua.org. Fraternal benefit society. *Narod Polski*, bimonthly. Sec.-Treas. Josephine Szarowicz.

Pontifical Mission for Palestine (1949): 1011 First Ave., New York, NY 10022-4195; (212) 826-1480; www.cnewa.org. A papal relief and development agency of the Holy See for the Middle East, with offices in New York, Vatican City, Amman, Beirut and Jerusalem. Pres., Msgr. Archim; Robert L. Stern, JCD.

Pontifical Mission Societies (1916): 70 West 36th St., 8th Floor, New York, NY 10018; (212) 563-8700; www.worldmissions-catholicchurch.org. To promote mission awareness among clergy, religious, candidates, and others engaged in pastoral ministry. Nat. Dir., Fr. Andrew Small, O.M.I.

Population Research Institute (1989): 1190 Progress Drive, Suite 2D, P.O. Box 1559, Front Royal, VA 22630; (540) 622-5240; www.pop.org. Non-profit research and educational organization dedicated to objectively presenting the truth about population-related issues. *PRI Review*, a bimonthly newsletter, which reports on population news of interest from around the world. Pres., Steven W. Mosher.

Priests' Eucharistic League (1887): 5384 Wilson Mills Rd., Highland Heights, OH 44143. *Emmanuel*, 10 issues a year. Nat. Dir., Very Rev. Norman Pelletier, SSS.

Pro Ecclesia Foundation (1970): 350 Fifth Ave., New York, NY 10118. *Pro Ecclesia Magazine*. Pres., Dr. Timothy A. Mitchell.

ProLife Across America (1989): P.O. Box 18669, Minneapolis, MN 55418; (612) 781-0410; www.prolifeacrossamerica.org. A non-profit organization that uses various media to promote the culture of life. Contact: Mary Ann Kuharski.

Pro Maria Committee (1952): 112 Norris Rd. Tyngsboro, MA 01879; (978) 649-1813. Promotes devotion to Our Lady of Beauraing (*see* Index).

Pro Sanctity Movement: Pro Sanctity Spirituality Center, 205 S. Pine Dr., Fullerton, CA 92833; (714) 956-1020. 45-30 195th St., Flushing, NY 11358; (718) 649-0324. 6762 Western Ave., Omaha, NE 68132; (402) 553-4418. 1102 N. 204 St. Elkhorn, NE 68022; (402) 289-2670; www.prosanctity.org. Organized to spread God's call of all persons to holiness.

Project Children (1975): P.O. Box 933, Greenwood Lake, NY 10925; (845) 477-3472; www.interwebinc.com/children. Nonsectarian volunteer group; provides children of Northern Ireland with a six-week summer vacation with host families in the U.S.

The Providence Association of the Ukrainian Catholics in America (Ukrainian Catholic Fraternal Benefit Society) (1912): 817 N. Franklin St., Philadelphia, PA 19123; (215) 627-4984.

Queen of the Americas Guild, Inc. (1979): P.O. Box 851, St. Charles, IL 60174; (630) 584-1822; www.queenoftheamericasguild.org. To build English information center and retreat center near Basilica in Mexico City and spread the message of Guadalupe. 7,000 members. Nat. Coord. Rebecca Nichols.

Raskob Foundation for Catholic Activities, Inc. (1945): P.O. Box 4019, Wilmington, DE 19807-0019; (302) 655-4440; www.rfca.org. Exec. Pres., Frederick Perella, Jr.

Reparation Society of the Immaculate Heart of Mary, Inc. (1946): 100 E. 20th St., Baltimore, MD 21218. *Fatima Findings*, monthly.

Retrouvaille: P.O.Box 25, Kelton, PA 19346. A ministry to hurting marriages, Retrouvaille consists of a weekend experience with follow-up sessions designed to provide couples with ways and means of healing and reconciling. Emphasis is placed on communication, enabling husband and wife to rediscover each other and to examine their lives in a new and positive way. The ministry is neither a retreat nor a sensitivity group, nor does it include group dynamics or discussions. The program is conducted by trained couples and priests, with programs offered under the auspices of diocesan family life agencies. International Coordinating Team: Bill and Peg Swaan.

Sacred Heart League: 6050 Hwy 61 N, P.O. Box 190, Walls, MS 38680. Pres., Fr. Robert Hess, S.C.J.

St. Ansgar's Scandinavian Catholic League (1910): 160 Cornelison Ave., Jersey City, NJ 07304; (201) 333-2525. Prayers and financial support for Church in Scandinavia. *St. Ansgar's Bulletin*, annually. 1,000 members. Pres., Astrid M. O'Brien.

St. Anthony's Guild (1924): P.O. 2948, Paterson, NJ 07509-2948; (973) 777-3737. Promotes devotion to St. Anthony of Padua and support for formation programs, infirm friars and ministries of the Franciscans of Holy Name Province. *The Anthonian*, quarterly. Dir., Fr. Joseph Hertel, OFM.

St. Bernadette Institute of Sacred Art (1993): P.O. Box 8249, Albuquerque, NM 87198-8249; (505) 265-9126; www.nmia.com/~paulos. To promote, initiate, encourage interest and sustain projects and persons engaged in sacred art.

St. Gregory Foundation for Latin Liturgy (1989): Newman House, 601 Buhler Ct., Pine Beach, NJ 08741; (732) 914-1222. To promote within the Church in the U.S. the use of the Latin language in the Mass in accordance with the teachings of Vatican II. Founder and Pres., Rev. Peter M.J. Stravinskas, Ph.D., S.T.D.

St. Margaret of Scotland Guild, Inc. (1938): Graymoor, P.O. Box 300, Garrison, NY 10524-0300; (845) 424-3671. Moderator, Bro. Pius MacIsaac.

St. Martin de Porres Guild (1935): 141 E. 65th St., New York, NY 10021; (212) 744-2410; www.opstjoseph.org. Dir., Rev. Raymond F. Halligan, O.P.

Serra International (1934): 220 S. State St., Suite 1703, Chicago, IL 60604; (312) 588-0700; www.serrainternational.org. Fosters vocations to the priesthood, and religious life, trains Catholic lay leadership. Formally aggregated to the Pontifical Society for Priestly Vocations, 1951. *Serran*, bimonthly. 21,000 members in 673 clubs in 35 countries. Exec. Dir., John W. Woodward.

Slovak Catholic Federation (1911): 301 S. State St., Clarks Summit, PA 18411; (570) 585-7382; www.slovakcatholicfederation.org. Founded by Rev. Joseph Murgas to promote and coordinate religious activities among Slovak Catholic fraternal societies, religious communities and Slovak ethnic parishes in their effort to address themselves to the special needs of Slovak Catholics in the U.S. and Canada. Pres., Rev. Philip A. Altavilla.

Slovak Catholic Sokol (1905): 205 Madison St., Passaic, NJ 07055; (800) 886-7656; www.slovak-

catholicsokol.org. Fraternal benefit society. *Slovak Catholic Falcon*, weekly. 38,000 members.

Society for the Propagation of the Faith (1822): 70 West 36th St., 8th Floor, New York, NY 10018; (212) 563-8700; www.worldmissions-catholic-church.org. Established in all dioceses. Church's principal instrument for promoting mission awareness and generating financial support for the missions. General fund for ordinary and extraordinary subsidies for all mission dioceses. Is subject to Congregation for the Evangelization of Peoples. Mission, four times a year; *Director's Newsletter*, monthly. Nat. Dir., Fr. Andrew Small, O.M.I.

Society of St. Monica (1986): 215 Falls Ave., Cuyahoga Falls, OH 44221. Confident, daily prayer for the return of inactive Catholics and Catholics who have left the Church. More than 10,000 members worldwide. Founder and Spir. Dir., Fr. Dennis M. McNeil.

Society of St. Peter Apostle (1889): 70 West 36th St., 8th Floor, New York, NY 10018; (212) 563-8700; www.world missions-catholicchurch.org. Church's central fund for support of seminaries, seminarians and novices in all mission dioceses. Nat. Dir., Fr. Andrew Small, O.M.I.

Society of the Divine Attributes (1974): 2905 Castlegate Ave., Pittsburgh, PA 15226; (412) 456-3114. Contemplative prayer society. 3,000 members worldwide (lay, clerical and religious). Spir. Dir. Rev. Ronald D. Lawler, OFM Cap.

Spiritual Life Institute of America (1960): Box 219, Crestone, CO 81131; (719) 256-4778; www.spiritualifeinstitute.org. An eremetical movement to foster the contemplative spirit in America. *Forefront*, seasonal. Founder, Fr. William McNamara, O.C.D. Second foundation: Nova Nada, Primitive Wilderness Hermitage, Kemptville, Nova Scotia, Canada B0W 1Y0. Third foundation, Holy Hill Hermitage, Skreen, Co. Sligo, Ireland.

Support Our Aging Religious (SOAR) (1986): 1400 Spring St., Suite 320, Silver Spring, MD 20910-2755; (301) 589-9811; www.soar-usa.org. Laity-led campaign to raise funds for retired religious. Pres., Timothy P. Hamer.

Theresians of the United States (1961): 1237 W. Monroe, Springfield, IL 62704; (217) 726-5484; www.theresians.org. Spiritual, educational and ministerial organization of Christian women. Exec. Dir., Victoria S. Schmidt. International division: Theresian World Ministry (1971), same address.

United Societies of U.S.A. (1903): 613 Sinclair St., McKeesport, PA 15132. *Prosvita-Enlightenment*, bimonthly newspaper. 3,755 members.

United States Catholic Historical Society (1884): St. Joseph's Seminary, 201 Seminary Ave., Yonkers, NY 10704; (914) 337-8381; www.uschs.com. Exec. Vice-Pres., John T. Gildea.

Western Catholic Union (1877): 510 Maine St., Quincy, IL 62301; (217) 223-9721; www.wculife.com. 19,000 members. A fraternal benefit society. *Western Catholic Union Record*, quarterly. Pres., Mark A. Wiewel.

Women for Faith and Family (1984): P.O. Box 8326, St. Louis, MO 63132; (314) 863-8385; www.wf-f.org. An international movement to promote Catholic teachings especially on all issues involving the family and roles for women. 60,000 signers worldwide of the Affirmation for Catholic Women. Members sign an eight-point statement of fidelity to the Church. *Voices,* quarterly. Dir., Helen Hull Hitchcock.

Word on Fire (1999): 1167 Asbury Ave, Winnetka, IL 60093; (847) 224-4670; www.wordonfire.org; a global media organization in support of Catholic evangelical preaching, particularly the work of Father Robert Barron. Contact: Nancy Ross.

World Apostolate of Fatima, USA (The Blue Army of Our Lady of Fatima, 1947): P.O. Box 976, Washington, NJ 07882; (908) 689-1700; www.bluearmy.com. Soul, bimonthly; Hearts Aflame, quarterly. U.S. branch of the World Apostolate of Fatima. Promote the Fatima Message. Fatima shrine. Exec. Dir.: Michael La Corte.

Worldwide Seminarian Support, Inc. (1993) Northeast 28th Ave. Unit C, Portland, Oregon 97232; Tel: 888-437-8508; www.SeminarianSupport.org. To raise financial support for Catholic seminarians worldwide in need of educational funding. President John L. Becker Jr.

Young Ladies' Institute (1887): 1111 Gough St., San Francisco, CA 94109-6606; (415) 346-4367. *Voice of YLI,* bimonthly. 13,000 members. Pres., Joan Vandehey.

Young Men's Institute (1883): YMI Grand Council, P.O. Box 281047 San Francisco, CA 94128-1047; (800-964-9646); www.ymiusa.org. *Institute Journal,* bimonthly. 4,500 members. Grand Sec., Mike Amato.

PERSONAL PRELATURE OF THE HOLY SEE: OPUS DEI

Founded in Madrid in 1928 by Msgr. Josemaría Escrivá de Balaguer (beatified in 1992 and canonized in October 2002), Opus Dei has the aim of spreading throughout all sectors of society a profound awareness of the universal call to holiness and apostolate (of Christian witness and action) in the ordinary circumstances of life, and, more specifically, through one's professional work. On Nov. 28, 1982, Pope John Paul II established Opus Dei as a personal prelature with the full title, Prelature of the Holy Cross and Opus Dei. The 2013 edition of the Annuario Pontificio reported that the prelature had 2,051 priests (35 newly ordained) and 320 major seminarians. Also, there were 89,909 lay persons — men and women, married and single, of every class and social condition — of about 80 nationalities, as well as 1,955 churches and pastoral centers.

Further, the prelature operates the Pontifical University of the Holy Cross (Pontificia Università della Santa Croce) in Rome; it was established in 1985 and received approval as a pontifical institution in 1995. Courses of study include theology, philosophy, canon law, and social communications.

In the United States, members of Opus Dei, along with cooperators and friends, conduct apostolic works corporately in major cities in the East and Midwest, Texas and on the West Coast. Elsewhere, corporate works include universities, vocational institutes, training schools for farmers and numerous other apostolic initiatives. Opus Dei information offices are located at: 99 Overlook Cir., New Rochelle, NY 10804; (914) 235-6128 (office of the New York chaplain); and 655 Levering Ave., Los Angeles, CA 90024; (310) 208-0941; www.opusdei.org.

KNIGHTS OF COLUMBUS

The Knights of Columbus, a fraternal benefit society of Catholic men, is a family service organization founded by Fr. Michael J. McGivney and chartered by the General Assembly of Connecticut on Mar. 29, 1882.

Currently, there are over 1.8 million Knights, more than ever before in the Order's history. Together with their families, the Knights are nearly 6 million strong. From the first local council in New Haven, the Order has grown to more than 13,485 councils in the United States, Canada, Mexico, the Philippines, Puerto Rico, Cuba, the Dominican Republic, Panama, the Virgin Islands, Guatemala, Guam, Saipan, and Poland. The Knights of Columbus insurance program passed a major milestone when total insurance in force exceeded $90 billion in June 2013.

In keeping with their general purpose to be of service to the Church, the Knights and their families are active in many apostolic works and community programs. The Knights cooperate with the U.S. bishops in pro-life activities and are engaged in other apostolic endeavors as well. They have been especially active in promoting wide awareness of issues related to religious liberty and

According to the Knights' Annual Survey of Fraternal Activity for the year ending Dec. 31, 2012, record amounts of money and hours — more than $167.5 million and 70 million hours — were donated to charitable causes. The Knights financial contribution for the year grew by more than $9.4 million to $167,549,817. Contributions increased for the 13th consecutive year. The number of volunteer service hours also rose by nearly 64,000 hours from the 2011 total to 70,113,207 hours. At an average value of $22.14 per service hour as estimated by Independent Sector, the value of the Knights' service hours last year exceeded $1.55 billion.

Cumulative figures show that during the past decade the Knights of Columbus donated $1.475 billion to charity and provided more than 673 million hours of volunteer service in support of charitable initiatives.

The Knights of Columbus headquarters address is One Columbus Plaza, New Haven, CT 06510-3326; (203) 752-4350; www.kofc.org. The Grand Knight is Carl Anderson.

Catholic Social Services

Catholic Charities USA (formerly National Conference of Catholic Charities): 66 Canal Center Plaza, Ste. 600, Alexandria, VA 22314; (703) 549-1390; www.catholiccharitiesusa.org. Founded in 1910 by Most Rev. Thomas J. Shahan and Rt. Rev. Msgr. William J. Kerby in cooperation with lay leaders of the Society of St. Vincent de Paul to help advance and promote the charitable programs and activities of Catholic community and social service agencies in the United States. As the central and national organization for this purpose, it services a network of more than 1,400 agencies and institutions by consultation, information and assistance in planning and evaluating social service programs under Catholic auspices.

Diocesan member agencies provide shelter, food, counseling, services to children, teen parents and the elderly, and a variety of other services to people in need — without regard to religion, gender, or national origin. Each year millions of people receive help from Catholic Charities; in 2005 (the latest statistics available), more than $32 million were spent in activities by Catholic Charities agencies. In addition, Catholic Charities is an advocate for persons and families in need.

Catholic Charities USA serves members through national and regional meetings, training programs, literature and social policy advocacy on the national level. It is charged by the U.S. bishops with responding to disasters in this country. Catholic Charities USA's president represents North America before *Caritas Internationalis*, the international conference of Catholic Charities, and thus maintains contact with the Catholic Charities movement throughout the world. Publications include *Charities USA*, a quarterly membership magazine, and a directory of U.S. Catholic Charities agencies and institutions. Pres., Fr. Larry Snyder.

Society of St. Vincent de Paul, Council of the United States (originally called the Conference of Charity): National Council, 58 Progress Parkway, St. Louis, MO 63043; (314) 576-3993; www.svdpuscouncil.org. An association of Catholic lay men and women devoted to personal service to the poor through the spiritual and corporal works of mercy. The first conference was formed at Paris in 1833 by Bl. Frederic Ozanam and his associates.

The first conference in the U.S. was organized in 1845 at St. Louis. There are now approximately 4,400 units of the society in this country, with a membership of more than 60,000. The society operates world wide in more than 130 countries and has more than 800,000 members.

Besides person-to-person assistance, increasing emphasis is being given to stores and rehabilitation workshops of the society through which persons with marginal income can purchase refurbished goods at minimal cost. Handicapped persons are employed in renovating goods and store operations. The society also operates food centers, shelters, criminal justice and other programs. Publications include *The Ozanam News*, a biannual membership magazine, and *The United States Councilor*, a quarterly newsletter. Exec. Dir., Roger Playwin.

Catholic Health Association of the United States (CHA): National Headquarters, 4455 Woodson Road, St. Louis, MO 63134; (314) 427-2500; www.chausa.org. Represents more than 1,200 Catholic-sponsored facilities and organizations, works with its members to promote justice and compassion in healthcare, influence public policy, shape a continuum of care through integrated delivery, and strengthen ministry presence and influence in the U.S. healthcare system. CHA supports and strengthens the Catholic health ministry by being a catalyst through research and development (leading edge tools for sustaining a faithbased ministry in price competitive markets), education and facilitation (annual assembly, conferences, and other methods for engaging the ministry), and advocacy (a united ministry voice for public policy). CHA members make up the nation's largest group of not-for-profit healthcare facilities under a single form of sponsorship. Pres., Sr. Carol Keehan, DC.

National Association of Catholic Chaplains: 3501 S. Lake Dr., Milwaukee, WI 53207; (414) 483-4898. Founded in 1965. Membership is over 3,500.

SOCIAL SERVICE ORGANIZATIONS

(See separate article for a listing of facilities for the handicapped.)

The Carroll Center for the Blind (formerly the Catholic Guild for All the Blind): 770 Centre St., Newton, MA 02458; (617) 969-6200; www.carroll.org. The center conducts diagnostic evaluation and rehabilitation programs for blind people over 16 years of age, and provides computer training and other services. Pres., Rachel Rosenbaum.

International Catholic Deaf Association: 8002 S. Sawyer Rd., Darian, IL 60561; TTY (630) 887-9472. Established by deaf adults in Toronto, Canada, in 1949, the association has more than 8,000 members in 130 chapters, mostly in the U.S. It is the only international lay association founded and controlled by deaf Catholic adults. The ICDA publishes *The Deaf Catholic*, bimonthly, sponsors regional conferences, workshops and an annual convention. Pres., Kathleen Kush.

National Apostolate for Inclusion Ministry (NAfIM): P.O. Box 218, Riverdale, MD, 20738; (301) 699-9500; www.nafim.org. Formerly known as the National Apostolate for Persons with Mental Retardation (NAPMR). Established in 1968 to promote the full participation by persons with mental retardation in the life of the Church. Exec. Dir., Barbara Lampe.

National Catholic Office for the Deaf: 7202 Buchanan St., Landover Hills, MD 20784; (301) 577-1684; www. ncod.org. Formally established in 1971, at Washington, DC, to provide pastoral service to those who teach deaf children and adults, to the parents of deaf children, to pastors of deaf persons, and to organizations of the deaf. Publishes *Vision*, a quarterly magazine. Exec. Dir., Consuelo Wild.

National Catholic Office Partnership on Disability (NCPD): 415 Michigan Ave., N.E., Suite 240, Washington, DC 20017; (202) 529-2933; www. ncpd.org. NCPD's mission is to provide resources and consultation to a national network of diocesan directors who oversee access and inclusion at the parish level; to collaborate with other national Catholic organizations, advocating for inclusion within all their programs and initiatives and to work with Catholic organizations addressing the concerns and needs of those with various disabilities. Established in 1982 as a result of the 1978 Pastoral Statement of the U.S. Catholic Bishops on People with Disabilities, the office continues to press for words and actions which promote meaningful participation and inclusion at all levels of the Church. Exec. Dir., Mary Jane Owen, M.S.W.

Xavier Society for the Blind: 154 E. 23rd St., New York, NY 10010-4595; (212) 473-7800; www.xaviersociety.com. Founded in 1900 by Rev. Joseph Stadelman, S.J., it is a center for publications for the blind and partially sighted. Acting Dir., Kathleen Lynch.

OTHER SOCIAL SERVICES

Cancer Hospitals or Homes: The following homes or hospitals specialize in the care of cancer patients. Capacities are in parentheses.

Our Lady of Perpetual Help Home, Servants of Relief for Incurable Cancer, 760 Pollard Blvd., S.W., Atlanta, GA 30315; (404) 688-9515 (52).

Rose Hawthorne Lathrop Home, Servants of Relief for Incurable Cancer, 1600 Bay St., Fall River, MA 02724; (508) 673-2322 (35).

Our Lady of Good Counsel Home, Servants of Relief for Incurable Cancer, 2076 St. Anthony Ave., St. Paul, MN 55104; (651) 646-2797.

Calvary Hospital, Inc., 1740 Eastchester Rd., Bronx, NY 10461; (718) 863-6900 (200). Operated in connection with Catholic Charities, Department of Health and Hospitals, Archdiocese of New York.

St. Rose's Home, Servants of Relief for Incurable Cancer, 71 Jackson St., New York, NY 10002; (212) 677-8132 (60).

Rosary Hill Home, Servants of Relief for Incurable Cancer, 600 Linda Ave., Hawthorne, NY 10532; (914) 769-0114 (72).

Holy Family Home, Servants of Relief for Incurable Cancer, 6753 State Rd., Parma, OH 44134; (440) 845-7700; www.cle-dioc.org (50).

Sacred Heart Free Home for Incurable Cancer, Servants of Relief for Incurable Cancer, 1315 W. Hunting Park Ave., Philadelphia, PA 19140; (215) 329-3222 (45).

Substance Abuse: Facilities for substance abuse (alcohol and other drugs) include:

Daytop Village, Inc., 54 W. 40th St., New York, NY 10018; (212) 354-6000; www.daytop.org. Twenty-eight residential and ambulatory sites in New York, New Jersey, Pennsylvania, Florida, Texas and California. Msgr. William B. O'Brien, president.

Good Shepherd Gracenter, Convent of the Good Shepherd, 1310 Bacon St., San Francisco, CA 94134; (415) 586-2822. Residential program for chemically dependent women.

New Hope Manor, 35 Hillside Rd., Barryville, NY 12719; fax (914) 557-6603. Residential substance abuse treatment center for teen-age girls and women ages 13-40. Residential; half-way house and after-care program totaling 6 months or more.

St. Joseph's Hospital, L.E. Phillips Libertas Center for the Chemically Dependent, 2661 County Road, Hwy. I, Chippewa Falls, WI 54729; (715) 723-1811 (46). Residential and outpatient. Adult and adolescent programs. Hospital Sisters of the Third Order of St. Francis.

St. Joseph's Hospital (Chippewa Falls, WI) Libertas Center for the Treatment of Chemical Dependency, 1701 Dousman St., Green Bay, WI 54302 (23). Residential and outpatient adolescent programs. Hospital Sisters of the Third Order of St. Francis.

St. Luke's Addiction Recovery Services, 7707 NW 2nd Ave., Miami, FL 33150; (305) 795-0077; www.catholiccharitiesadm.org/stluke. A program of Catholic Community Services, Miami. Adult residential and family outpatient recovery services for drug, alcohol addiction and DUI.

Miami Substance Abuse Prevention Programs, 7707 N.W. Second Ave., Miami, FL 33150; (305) 795-0077; www.catholiccharitiesadm.org/stluke. Trains parents, youth, priests and teachers as prevention volunteers in the area of substance abuse.

Transitus House, 1830 Wheaton St., Chippewa Falls, WI 54729; (715) 723-1155. Two programs for chemically dependent: adult intensive residential (15 beds, women); adolescent intensive residential (5 beds, girls 15-18 yrs.). Hospital Sisters of the Third Order of St. Francis.

Matt Talbot Inn, 2270 Professor Ave., Cleveland, OH 44113; (216) 781-0288. Two programs: Chemical dependency Residential Treatment/Halfway House (capacity 27) and outpatient treatment/aftercare. Serves male clients 18 years and over.

Sacred Heart Rehabilitation Center, Inc., 2203 St. Antoine, Detroit, MI 48201 (admissions/assessment, outpatient). 400 Stoddard Rd., P.O. Box 41038, Memphis, MI 48041 (12 beds, detoxification; 70 beds residential treatment). 28573 Schoenherr, Warren, MI 48093 (outpatient). All facilities serve male and female clients 18 and over.

Straight and Narrow, Inc., 396 Straight St., Paterson, NJ 07501. Facilities and services include (at various locations): Straight and Narrow Hospital (Mount Carmel Guild), substance abuse, detoxification (20 beds); Alpha House for Drug and Alcohol Rehabilitation (women; 30 beds — 25 adults, 5 children; Dismas House for Drug and Alcohol Rehabilitation (men; 78 beds); The Guild for Drug and Alcohol Rehabilitation (men, 56 beds); juvenile residential units; outpatient services and facility; three halfway houses; counseling services; employment assistance; intoxicated driver's resource center; medical day care center (available to HIV infected persons and persons diagnosed with AIDS); methadone clinic.

The National Catholic Council on Alcoholism and Related Drug Problems, Inc., 1550 Hendrickson St., Brooklyn, NY 11234. Offers educational material to those involved in pastoral ministry on ways of dealing with problems related to alcoholism and medication dependency.

Convicts: Priests serve as full- or part-time chaplains in penal and correctional institutions throughout the country. Limited efforts have been made to assist in the rehabilitation of released prisoners in Halfway House establishments.

• *Dining Rooms:* Facilities for homeless: Representative of places where meals are provided, and in some cases lodging and other services as well, are:

St. Anthony Foundation, 121 Golden Gate Ave., San Francisco, CA 94102; (415) 241-2600; www.stanthonyfdn. org. Founded in 1950 by the Franciscan Friars. Multiprogram social service agency serving people who are poor and homeless. Dining room serves up to 2,100 meals daily; more than 25 million since its founding. Other services include free clothing and furniture; free medical clinic; residential drug and alcohol rehabilitation programs; employment program; emergency shelter, housing and daytime facility for homeless women; residence for lowincome senior women; free hygiene services; case management for seniors; social services.

St. Vincent de Paul Free Dining Room, 675 23rd St., Oakland, CA 94612; (510) 451-7676. Administered by Daughters of Charity of St. Vincent de Paul, under sponsorship of St. Vincent de Paul Society. Hot meals served at lunch time 7 days a week. Also provides counseling, referral/information services.

St. Vincent's Dining Room, P.O. Box 5099, Reno, NV 89513; (775) 329-5363. St. Vincent Dining Room, 1501 Las Vegas Blvd., Las Vegas, NV 89101. Structured program for 275 men in which job development office works with homeless to enable them to find employment. For non-residents, there is a hot meal every day at noon. Emergency overnight shelter facility for families, women and men.

Good Shepherd Center, Little Brothers of the Good Shepherd, 218 Iron St. S.W., P.O. Box 749, Albuquerque, NM 87103; (505) 243-2527.

Holy Name Centre for Homeless Men, Inc., 18 Bleecker St., New York, NY 10012. A shelter for alcoholic, homeless men. Provides social services and aid to transients and those in need. Affiliated with New York Catholic Charities.

St. Francis Inn, 2441 Kensington Ave., Philadelphia, PA 19125. Serves hot meals. Temporary shelter for men. Day center for women. Thrift shop.

St. John's Hospice for Men, staffed by Little Brothers of the Good Shepherd, 1221 Race St., Philadelphia, PA 19107. Hot meals served daily; 36-bed shelter; clothing distribution, showers, mail distribution, drug/alcohol rehabilitation and work programs. Good Shepherd Program of St. John's Hospice, 1225 Race St., Philadelphia, PA 19107. Tenbed facility for homeless men with AIDS.

Camillus House, Little Brothers of the Good Shepherd, P.O. Box 11829, Miami, FL 33101; (305) 374-1065; www.camillus.org. Free comprehensive services for the poor and homeless including daily dinner; night lodging for 70; clothing distribution; showers; mail distribution; drug/alcohol rehabilitation program. Forty-eight units of single-room housing for employed formerly homeless women and men who have completed drug and alcohol rehabilitation programs.

Camillus Health Concern, P.O. Box 12408, Miami, FL 33101; (305) 577-4840. Free comprehensive medical and social services for the homeless.

• *Shelters:* Facilities for runaways, the abused, exploited and homeless include:

Anthony House, supported by St. Anthony's Guild (*see* Index). 38 E. Roosevelt Ave., Roosevelt, NY 11575 (with St. Vincent de Paul Society — for homeless men). 128 W. 112th St., New York, NY 10026 (emergency food and clothing). 6215 Holly St., P.O. Box 880, Zellwood, FL 32798 (for migrant workers and their families).

Good Shepherd Shelter-Convent of the Good Shepherd. Office, 2561 W. Venice Blvd., Los Angeles, CA 90019; (323) 737-6111. Non-emergency longterm shelter for battered women and their children.

Covenant House, 346 W. 17th St., New York, NY 10011; (212) 727-4973. Pres., Sr. Mary Rose McGeady, D.C. Provides crisis care — food, shelter, clothing, medical treatment, job placement and counseling — for homeless youth without regard to race, creed, color and national origin. Locations: New York, New Jersey (Newark, Atlantic City), Houston, Ft. Lauderdale, New Orleans, Anchorage, Los Angeles, Detroit, Orlando, Washington, DC; Toronto (Canada), Tegucigalpa (Honduras), Guatemala City (Guatemala), Mexico City (Mexico).

Crescent House, 1000 Howard Ave., Suite 1200, New Orleans, LA 70113. Provides temporary shelter, counseling and advocacy for battered women and their children.

The Dwelling Place, 409 W. 40th St., New York, NY 10018; (212) 564-7887. For homeless women 30 years of age and over.

Gift of Hope, Missionaries of Charity, 724 N.W. 17th St., Miami, FL 33136; (305) 326-0032. Shelter for women and children; soup kitchen for men.

House of the Good Shepherd, 1114 W. Grace St., Chicago, IL 60613; (773) 935-3434. For abused women with children.

Mercy Hospice, 334 S. 13th St., Philadelphia, PA 19107; (215) 545-5153. Temporary shelter and relocation assistance for homeless women and children.

Mt. Carmel House, Carmelite Sisters, 471 G Pl., N.W., Washington, DC 20001. For homeless women.

Ozanam Inn, 843 Camp St., New Orleans, LA 70130. Under sponsorship of the St. Vincent de Paul Society. Hospice for homeless men.

St. Christopher Inn, P.O. Box 150, Graymoor, Garrison, NY 10524; (845) 424-3616; www.atonementfriars.org. Temporary shelter (21 days) for alcohol- and drug-free homeless and needy men.

Siena-Francis House, Inc., P.O. Box 217 D.T.S., Omaha, NE 68102. Two units, both at 1702 Nicholas St., Omaha, NE 68101; (402) 341-1821. Siena House (for homeless and abused women or women with children; provides 24-hour assistance and advocacy services); and Francis House (temporary shelter for homeless men). Also at this location: a 50-bed residential substance abuse program.

• *Unwed Mothers:* Residential and care services for unwed mothers are available in many dioceses.

FACILITIES FOR RETIRED AND AGED PERSONS

Sources: *Catholic Almanac* survey, *The Official Catholic Directory.*
This list covers residence, health care and other facilities for the retired and aged under Catholic auspices. Information includes name, type of facility if not evident from the title, address, and total capacity (in parentheses); unless noted otherwise, facilities are for both men and women. Many facilities for the aged offer intermediate nursing care.

Alabama: Allen Memorial Home (skilled nursing), 735 S. Washington Ave., Mobile 36603; (251) 433-2642 (119).
Cathedral Place Apartments (retirement complex), 351 Conti St., Mobile 36602; (334) 434-1590 (184).
Mercy Medical (acute rehabilitation hospital, skilled and post-acute nursing, hospice, home Health and assisted and independent living), P.O. Box 1090, Daphne 36526; (334) 626-2694 (162). Not restricted to elderly.
Sacred Heart Residence Little Sisters of the Poor, 1655 McGill Ave., Mobile 36604; (251) 476-6335 (84).
Seton Haven (retirement complex), 3721 Wares Ferry Rd., Montgomery 36193; (334) 272-4000 (114).

Arizona: Guadalupe Senior Village, 222 W. Thomas Rd., Ste. 214, Phoenix, 85103; (602) 406-6218.

California: Alexis Apartments of St. Patrick's Parish, 756 Mission St. 94103; 390 Clementina St., San Francisco 94103; (415) 495-3690 (240).
Casa Manana Inn, 3700 N. Sutter St., Stockton 95204; (209) 466-4046 (162). Non-profit housing for low-income elderly over 62.
Cathedral Plaza, 1551 Third Ave., San Diego 92101; (619) 234-0093 (222 apartments).
Guadalupe Plaza, 4142 42nd St., San Diego 92105; (619) 584-2414 (147 apartments).
Jeanne d'Arc Manor, 85 S. Fifth St., San Jose 95112; (408) 288-7421 (145). For low income elderly and handicapped.
La Paz Villas, P.O. Box 1962, Palm Desert 92261; (760) 772-1382 (24 units).
Little Flower Haven (residential care facility for retired), 8585 La Mesa Blvd., La Mesa 91941; (619) 466-3163 (85).
Little Sisters of the Poor, St. Anne's Home, 300 Lake St., San Francisco 94118; (415) 751-6510 (90).
Little Sisters of the Poor, Jeanne Jugan Residence, 2100 South Western Ave., San Pedro 90732; (310) 548-0625 (100).
Madonna Senior Center and Residence, St. Anthony Foundation, 500 Golden Gate Ave., San Francisco 94102; (415) 592-2864; www.stanthonysf.org (37).
Marian Residence (retirement home), 124 S. College Dr., Santa Maria 93454; (805) 922-7731 (32).
Mercy McMahon Terrace (residential care facility), 3865 J St., Sacramento 95816; (916) 733-6510;

www.mercysacramento.org (118 units).
Mercy Retirement and Care Center, 3431 Foothill Blvd., Oakland 94601; (510) 534-8540; www.mercyretirementcenter.org (59).
Mother Gertrude Home for Senior Citizens, 11320 Laurel Canyon Blvd., San Fernando 91340; (818) 898-1546 (98).
Nazareth House (residential and skilled care), 2121 N. 1st St., Fresno 93703; (559) 237-2257 (65 residential; 39 skilled nursing).
Nazareth House (residential and skilled nursing), 3333 Manning Ave., Los Angeles 90064; (310) 839-2361 (123).
Nazareth House (retirement home), 245 Nova Albion Way, San Rafael 94903; (415) 479-8282 (151).
Nazareth House Retirement Home, 6333 Rancho Mission Rd., San Diego 92108; (619) 563-0480 (354).
O'Connor Woods, 3400 Wagner Heights Rd., Stockton 95209; (209) 956-3400; www.oconnorwoods.org, (48).
Our Lady of Fatima Villa (skilled nursing facility), 20400 Saratoga-Los Gatos Rd., Saratoga 95070; (408) 741-2950; www.fatimavilla.org; (85).
St. Bernardine Plaza (retirement home), 550 W. 5th St., San Bernardino 92401; (909) 888-0153 (150 units).
St. John of God (retirement and care center), 2468 S. St. Andrew Place, Los Angeles 90018; (323) 731-0641; www.hospitallers.org, (215).
Vigil Light Apartments, 1945 Long Dr., Santa Rosa 95405; (707) 544-2810 (54).
Villa Scalabrini (retirement center and skilled nursing Care), 10631 Vinedale St., Sun Valley 91352; (818) 768-6500; www.villascalabrini.com (130 residence; 58 skilled nursing).
Villa Siena (residence and skilled nursing care), 1855 Miramonte Ave., Mountain View 94040; (650) 961-6484; www.villasiena.org (56, residence; 20, skilled nursing care).

Colorado: Francis Heights, Inc., 2626 Osceola St., Denver 80212; (303) 433-6268 (384 units; 411 residents).
Gardens at St. Elizabeth (congregate housing and assisted living), 2835 W. 32nd Ave., Denver 80211; (303) 964-2005 (320).
Little Sisters of the Poor, 3629 W. 29th Ave., Denver 80211; (303) 433-7221 (70).

Connecticut: Augustana Homes (residence), Simeon Rd., Bethel 06801; (203) 743-2508.
Carmel Ridge, 6454 Main St., Trumbull 06611; (203) 261-2229.
Holy Family Home and Shelter, Inc., 88 Jackson St., P.O. Box 884, Willimantic 06226; (860) 423-7719; www.holyfamilywillimantic.org (155).
Monsignor Bojnowski Manor, Inc. (skilled nursing facility), 50 Pulaski St., New Britain 06053; (860) 229-0336 (60).
Notre Dame Convalescent Home, 76 West Rocks Rd., Norwalk 06851; (203) 847-5893 (60).
St. Joseph Living Center, 14 Club Rd., Windham 06280; (860) 456-1107 (120).
St. Joseph's Manor (health care facility; home for aged), Carmelite Srs. for Aged and Infirm, 6448 Main St., Trumbull 06611; (203) 268-6204; www.

harborsidehealthcare.com; (297).

St. Joseph's Residence, Little Sisters of the Poor, 1365 Enfield St., Enfield 06082; (860) 741-0791 (84).

St. Lucian's Home for the Aged, 532 Burritt St., New Britain 06053; (860) 223-2123 (42).

St. Mary's Home (residence and health care facility) 2021 Albany Ave., W. Hartford 06117; (860) 570-8200 (26).

Delaware: The Antonian, 1701 W. 10th St., Wilmington 19805; (302) 421-3758 (136 apartments).

Jeanne Jugan Residence, Little Sisters of the Poor, 185 Salem Church Rd., Newark 19713; (302) 368-5886 (80).

Marydale Retirement Village, 135 Jeandell Dr., Newark 19713; (302) 368-2784 (118 apartments).

St. Patrick's House, Inc., 115 E. 14th St., Wilmington 19801; (302) 654-6908 (12).

District of Columbia: Jeanne Jugan Residence-St. Joseph Villa, Little Sisters of the Poor, 4200 Harewood Rd., N.E., Washington 20017; (202) 269-1831; www.littlesistersofthepoorwashingtondc. org (97).

Florida: All Saints Home, 5888 Blanding Blvd., Jacksonville 32244; (904) 772-1220; www.allsaints. org (118).

Casa Calderon, Inc. (retirement apartments), 800 W. Virginia St., Tallahassee 32304; (850) 222-4026 (111).

Haven of Our Lady of Peace (assisted living and nursing home), 5203 N. 9th Ave., Pensacola 32504; (850) 477-0531 (89).

Palmer House, Inc., 1225 S.W. 107th Ave., Miami 33174; (305) 221-9566 (120 apartments).

St. Andrew Towers (retirement apartments), 2700 N.W. 99th Ave., Coral Springs 33065 (432).

St. Catherine Labouré (skilled and intermediate care), 1750 Stockton St., Jacksonville 32204; (904) 308-4700 (239).

St. Dominic Gardens (retirement apartments), 5849 N.W. 7th St., Miami 33126 (149 apartments).

St. Elizabeth Gardens, Inc. (retirement apartments), 801 N.E. 33rd St., Pompano Beach 33064 (150).

St. John's Rehabilitation Hospital and Nursing Center, Inc., 3075 N.W. 35th Ave., Lauderdale Lakes 33311.

Stella Maris House, Inc., 8636 Harding Ave., Miami Beach 33141 (136 apartments).

Illinois: Addolorata Villa (sheltered intermediate, skilled care facility; apartments), 555 McHenry Rd., Wheeling 60090; (847) 808-6168 (100 apartments).

Alvernia Manor (sheltered care), 13950 Main St., Lemont 60439; (630) 257-7721 (50).

Bishop Conway Residence, 1900 N. Karlov Ave., Chicago 60639; (773) 252-9941.

Carlyle Healthcare Center, 501 Clinton St., Carlyle 62231; (618) 594-3112 (131).

Carmelite Carefree Village, 8419 Bailey Rd., Darien 60561; (630) 960-4060 (98).

Cortland Manor Retirement Home, 1900 N. Karlov, Chicago 60639; (773) 235-3670 (48).

Holy Family Nursing and Rehabilitation Center, 2380 Dempster, Des Plaines 60016; (847) 296-3335 (362).

Holy Family Villa (intermediate care facility), 12395 McCarthy Rd., Lemont 60439; (630) 257-7721 (50).

Jugan Terrace, Little Sisters of the Poor, 2300 N. Racine, Chicago 60614; (773) 935-9600 (50 apartments).

Little Sisters of the Poor, St. Joseph's Home for the Elderly, 80 W. Northwest Hwy., Palatine 60067; (847) 358-5700 (61).

Little Sisters of the Poor Center for the Aging, 2325 N. Lakewood Ave., Chicago 60614; (773) 935-9600 (71).

Marian Heights Apartments (elderly, handicapped), 20 Marian Heights Dr., Alton 62002; (618) 462-0363 (130).

Marian Park, Inc., 26 W. 171 Roosevelt Rd., Wheaton 60187; (630) 665-9100 (470).

Maryhaven, Inc. (skilled and intermediate care facility, 1700 E. Lake Ave., Glenview 60025; (847) 729-1300 (138).

Mayslake Village (retirement apartments), 1801 35th St., Oak Brook 60523; (630) 850-8232; www. mayslake.com (630 apartments).

Meredith Memorial Home, 16 S. Illinois St., Belleville 62220; (618) 233-8780 (86).

Merkle-Knipprath Countryside (apartments and nursing facility), 1190 E. 2900 N. Rd., Clifton 60927; (815) 694-2306 (130).

Mother Theresa Home (skilled, intermediate and sheltered care), 1270 Franciscan Dr., Lemont 60439; (630) 257-5801; www.franciscancommunities.com. (150).

Nazarethville (intermediate and sheltered care), 300 N. River Rd., Des Plaines 60016; (847) 297-5900; www.nazarethvillereshealth.com. (83).

Our Lady of Angels Retirement Home, 1201 Wyoming, Joliet 60435; (815) 725-6631; www.olar-etirement.org (101).

Our Lady of the Snows, Apartment Community, 9500 West Illinois Highway 15, Belleville 62223; (618) 397-6700 (201).

Our Lady of Victory Nursing Home (intermediate and skilled care), 20 Briarcliff Lane, Bourbonnais 60914; (815) 937-2022 (107).

Pope John Paul Apartments (elderly and handicapped), 1 Pope John Paul Plaza, Springfield 62703; (217) 528-1771; www.dio.org (160).

Provena Cor Mariae Center (assisted living and nursing home), 3330 Maria Linden Dr., Rockford 61107; (815) 877-7416 (146).

Provena St. Anne Center (nursing home), 4405 Highcrest Rd., Rockford 61107; (815) 229-1999 (179).

Provena St. Joseph's Home for the Aged, 659 E. Jefferson St., Freeport 61032; (815) 232-6181 (120).

Provena Villa Franciscan (skilled care), 210 N. Springfield, Joliet 60435; (815) 725-3400; www. provenahealth.com.

Queen of Peace Center, 1910 Maple Ave., Lisle 60532; (630) 852-5360; www.qopc.net (32).

Red Bud Regional Nursing Home (skilled intermediary facility), 350 W. S. First St., Red Bud 62278; (618) 282-3891 (115).

Resurrection Nursing Pavilion (skilled care), 1001 N. Greenwood, Park Ridge 60068; (847) 692-5600 (295).

Resurrection Retirement Community, 7262 W. Peterson Ave., Chicago, 60631; (773) 792-7930;

www.reshealth.org (472 apartments).

Rosary Hill Home (women), 9000 W. 81st St., Justice 60458; (708) 458-3040 (48).

St. Andrew Life Center (retirement residence), 7000 N. Newark Ave., Niles 60714; (847) 647-8332 (99).

St. Anne Place (retirement apartments), 4444 Brendenwood Rd., Rockford 61107; (815) 399-6167 (120).

St. Benedict Home, 6930 W. Touhy Ave., Niles 60714; (847) 647-0003. (99).

St. Elizabeth Home (residence), 704 W. Marion St., Joliet 60436; (815) 727-0125 (11). Group living for Senior women.

St. James Manor, 1251 East Richton Rd., Crete 60417; (708) 672-6700 (110).

St. Joseph's Home (sheltered and intermediate care), 3306 S. 6th St. Rd., Springfield 62703; (217) 529-5596 (110).

St. Joseph Home of Chicago, Inc. (skilled care), 2650 N. Ridgeway Ave., Chicago 60647; (773) 235-8600; www.franciscancommunities.com (173).

St. Patrick's Residence, 1400 Brookdale Rd., Naperville 60563-2125; (630) 416-6565; www.stpatricksresidence.org

Villa Scalabrini (sheltered, intermediate and skilled), 480 N. Wolf Rd., Northlake 60164; (708) 562-0040 (259).

Indiana: Albertine Home, 1501 Hoffman St., Hammond 46327; (219) 937-0575 (35).

Provena LaVerna Terrace, 517 N. Main St., Avilla 46710; (260) 897-2093 (51).

Provena Sacred Heart Home (comprehensive nursing), 515 N. Main St., Avilla 46710; (260) 897-2841, (133).

Regina Continuing Care Center (intermediate care Facility), 3900 Washington Ave., Evansville 47714; (812) 485-4226; www.stmarys.org (137).

St. Anne Home (Residential and Comprehensive nursing), 1900 Randallia Dr., Ft. Wayne 46805; (219) 484-5555 (254).

St. Anthony Home, Inc., 203 Franciscan Dr., Crown Point 46307; (219) 661-5100; www.stanthonyhome.com (219).

St. Augustine Home for the Aged, Little Sisters of the Poor, 2345 W. 86th St., Indianapolis 46260; (317) 872-6420 (92).

St. John's Home for the Aged, Little Sisters of the Poor, 1236 Lincoln Ave., Evansville 47714; (812) 464-3607 (70).

St. Paul Hermitage (residential and intermediate care nursing), 501 N. 17th Ave., Beech Grove 46107; (317) 786-2261; www.stpaulhermitage.org; (100).

Iowa: The Alverno Health Care Facility (nursing care), 849 13th Ave. N., Clinton 52732; (563) 242-1521; www.alvernohealthcare.com (194).

Bishop Drumm Retirement Center, 5837 Winwood Dr., Johnston 50131; (515) 270-1100 (64).

Hallmar-Mercy Medical Center, 701 Tenth St. S.E., Cedar Rapids 52403; (319) 369-4638 (57).

Holy Spirit Retirement Home (intermediate care), 1701 W. 25th St., Sioux City 51103; (712) 252-2726 (95).

Kahl Home for the Aged and Infirm (skilled and intermediate care facility), 1101 W. 9th St., Davenport 52804; (319) 324-1621; www.kahlhome-dav.com (135).

The Marian Home, 2400 6th Ave. North, Fort Dodge 50501; (515) 576-1138 (116).

St. Anthony Nursing Home (intermediate care), 406 E. Anthony St., Carroll 51401; (712) 792-3581 (79).

St. Francis Continuation Care and Nursing Home Center, Burlington 52601; (319) 752-4564 (170).

Stonehill Adult Center (day care), 3485 Windsor, Dubuque 52001; (319) 557-7180 (35).

Kansas: Catholic Care Center (skilled and intermediate care facility), 6700 E. 45th St, Wichita 67226; (316) 744-2020 (294).

Mt. Joseph Senior Village (intermediate care facility), 1110 W. 11, Concordia 66901; (785) 143-1347 (16 apartments).

St. John Rest Home (nursing facility), 701 Seventh St., Victoria 67671; (785) 735-2208 (90).

St. John's New Horizons, 2225 Canterbury, Hays 67601; (785) 628-8742 (43).

Villa Maria, Inc. (intermediate care facility), 116 S. Central, Mulvane 67110; (316) 777-1129 (99).

Kentucky: Bishop Soenneker Personal Care Home, 9545 Ky. 144, Knottsville, KY 42366; (270) 281-4881 (55).

Carmel Home (residence, adult day care, respite care and nursing care), 2501 Old Hartford Rd., Owensboro 42303; (270) 683-0227 (101).

Carmel Manor (skilled, intermediate and personal care home), 100 Carmel Manor Rd., Ft. Thomas, 41075; (859) 781-5111; (145).

Madonna Manor Nursing Home, 2344 Amsterdam Rd., Villa Hills 41017; (606) 341-3981 (60).

Marian Home, 3105 Lexington Rd., Louisville 40206; (502) 893-0121 (69).

Nazareth Home, 2000 Newburg Rd., Louisville 40205; (502) 459-9681; www.nazhome.org (168).

St. Charles Care Center and Village, 500 Farrell Dr., Covington 41011; (606) 331-3224; www.stcharlescare.org (149). Nursing home; adult day health program. Independent living cottages (44); assisted living (60); independent living apartments (12).

Louisiana: Annunciation Inn, 1220 Spain St., New Orleans 70117; (504) 944-0512 (111).

Bethany M.H.S. Health Care Center (women), P.O. Box 2308, Lafayette 70502; (337) 234-2459. (200).

Château de Notre Dame (residence and nursing home), 2832 Burdette St., New Orleans 70125; (504) 866-2741 (103).

Christopher Inn Apartments, 2110 Royal St., New Orleans 70116; (504) 949-0312 (144).

Christus St. Joseph's Home (nursing home), 2301 Sterlington Rd., Monroe 71211; (318) 323-3426 (150).

Consolata Home (nursing home), 2319 E. Main St., New Iberia 70560; (337) 365-8226 (114).

Haydel Heights Apartments, 4402 Reynes St., New Orleans 70126; (504) 242-4438 (65 units).

Lafon Nursing Home of the Holy Family, 6900 Chef Menteur Hwy., New Orleans 70126; (504) 246-1100 (171).

Metairie Manor, 4929 York St., Metairie 70001; (504) 456-1467 (287).

Nazareth Inn, 9630 Hayne Blvd., New Orleans 70127; (504) 241-9630 (158).

Ollie Steele Burden Manor (nursing home), 4250 Essen Lane, Baton Rouge 70809; (225) 926-0091 (184).

Our Lady of Prompt Succor Home, 954 East Prudhomme St., Opelousas 70570; (337) 948-3634 (80).

Our Lady's Manor, Inc., 402 Monroe St., Alexandria 71301; (318) 473-2560 (114).

Place Dubourg, 201 Rue Dubourg, LaPlace 70068; (504) 652-1981 (115).

Rouquette Lodge, 4300 Hwy 22, Mandeville 70471; (504) 626-5217 (51).

St. John Berchmans Manor, 3400 St. Anthony Ave., New Orleans 70122; (504) 943-9342 (157).

St. Margaret's Daughters Home (nursing home), 3419 St. Claude Ave., New Orleans 70117; (504) 279-6414; www.stmargaretno.org; (139).

St. Martin Manor, 1501 N. Johnson St., New Orleans 70116; (504) 945-7728 (145).

Villa St. Maurice 500 St. Maurice Ave., New Orleans 70117; (504) 277-8477 (193).

Villa St. Maurice II, 6101 Douglas St., New Orleans 70117; (504) 277-8731 (80).

Village du Lac, Inc., 1404 Carmel Ave., Lafayette 70501; (337) 234-5106 (200).

Wynhoven Apartments and Wynhoven II (residence for senior citizens), 1000 Howard Ave., Suite 100, New Orleans, 70113; (504) 596-3460 (375).

Maine: Deering Pavilion (apartments for senior citizens), 880 Forest Ave., Portland 04103; (207) 797-8777 (232 units).

Maison Marcotte (independent living community), 100 Campus Ave., Lewiston 04240; (207) 786-0062 (128 apartments).

Mt. St. Joseph Holistic Care Community, Highwood St., Waterville 04901; (207) 873-0705 (138).

St. Andre Health Care Facility, Inc. (nursing facility), 407 Pool St., Biddeford 04005; (207) 282-5171 (96).

St. Joseph's Manor (nursing care facility), 1133 Washington Ave., Portland 04103; (207) 797-0600; www.saintjosephsmanor.org. (200).

St. Marguerite D'Youville Pavilion, 102 Campus Ave., Lewiston 04240; (207) 777-4200 (280).

St. Xavier's Home (apartments), 199 Somerset St., Bangor 04401; (207) 942-4815 (19 units).

Seton Village, Inc., 1 Carver St., Waterville 04901; (207) 873-0178 (140 housing units).

Maryland: Little Sisters of the Poor, St. Martin's Home (for the aged), 601 Maiden Choice Lane, Baltimore 21228; (410) 744-9367 (104).

Sacred Heart Home, 5805 Queens Chapel Rd., Hyattsville 20782; (301) 277-6500; www.sacredhearthome.org (102).

St. Joseph Nursing Home, 1222 Tugwell Dr., Baltimore 21228; (410) 747-0026 (51).

Villa Rosa Nursing Home, 3800 Lottsford Vista Rd., Mitchellville 20721; (301) 459-4700 (100).

Massachusetts: Catholic Memorial Home (nursing home), 2446 Highland Ave., Fall River 02720; (508) 679-0011 (300).

Don Orione Nursing Home, 111 Orient Ave., East Boston 02128; (617) 569-2100 (185).

D'Youville Manor (nursing home), 981 Varnum Ave., Lowell 01854; (978) 454-5681; www.dyouville.com (203).

Jeanne Jugan Pavilion, 190 Highland Ave., Somerville 02143; (617) 776-4420 (30).

Jeanne Jugan Residence, Little Sisters of the Poor (home for the elderly), 190 Highland Ave., Somerville 02143; (617) 776-4420; www.littlesistersofthepoor.org (84).

Madonna Manor (nursing home), 85 N. Washington St., N. Attleboro 02760; (508) 699-2740; www.dhfo.org (129).

Marian Manor, for the Aged and Infirm (nursing home), 130 Dorchester St., S. Boston, 02127; (617) 268-3333; www.marianmanor.org (366).

Marian Manor of Taunton (nursing home), 33 Summer St., Taunton 02780; (508) 822-4885 (184).

Maristhill Nursing Home, 66 Newton St., Waltham 02154; (781) 893-0240 (154).

MI Nursing/Restorative Center, 172 Lawrence St., Lawrence 01841; (978) 685-6321; www.mihcs.com (335).

Our Lady's Haven (nursing home), 71 Center St., Fairhaven 02719; (508) 999-4561; www.dhfo.org (158).

Sacred Heart Home, 359 Summer St., New Bedford 02740; (508) 996-6751; www.dhfo.org (217).

St. Joseph Manor Health Care, Inc., 215 Thatcher St., Brockton 02302; (508) 583-5834 (118).

St. Joseph's Nursing Care Center, 321 Centre St., Dorchester, Boston 02122; (617) 825-6320 (191).

St. Patrick's Manor (nursing home), 863 Central St., Framingham 01701; (508) 879-8000; www.stpatricksmanor.org (460).

Michigan: Bishop Noa Home for Senior Citizens (nursing home and residence), 2900 3rd Ave. S., Escanaba 49829; (906) 786-5810 (123).

Lourdes Nursing Home (skilled facility), 2300 Watkins Lake Rd., Waterford 48328; (248) 674-2241; www.lourdescampus.com (108).

Marycrest Manor (skilled nursing facility), 15475 Middlebelt Rd., Livonia 48154; (313) 427-9175 (55).

Ryan Senior Residences of the Archdiocese of Detroit: Casa Maria, 600 Maple Vista, Imlay City 48444; (810) 724-6300 (84). Kundig Center, 3300 Jeffries Freeway, Detroit 48208; (313) 894-0555 (160). Lourdes Senior Community, 2450 Watkins Lake Rd., Waterford 48328; (248) 674-2241; www.lourdescampus.com (6). Marian-Oakland West, 29250 W. Ten Mile Rd., Farmington Hills 48336; (248) 474-7204 (87). Marian Place, 408 W. Front St., Monroe 48161; (734) 241-2414 (53). Marydale Center, 3147 Tenth Ave., Port Huron 48060; (810) 985-9683 (56). Maryhaven, 11350 Reeck Rd., Southgate 48195; (734) 287-2111 (90). Sanctuary at Clinton Villa, 17825 Fifteen Mile Rd., Clinton Twp. 48035; (586) 792-0358 (86). Stapleton Center, 9341 Agnes St., Detroit 48214; (313) 822-0397 (59). Villa Marie, 15131 Newburgh Rd., Livonia 48154; (734) 464-9494 (86). St. Ann's Home, (residence and nursing home), 2161 Leonard St. N.W., Grand Rapids 49504; (616) 453-7715; www.stannshome.com (140). St. Catherine House, 1641 Webb Ave., Detroit 48206; (313) 868-4505 (12). St. Elizabeth Briarbank (women, residence), 1315 N. Woodward Ave., Bloomfield Hills 48304; (248) 644-1011 (44).

St. Francis Home (nursing home), 915 N. River Rd., Saginaw 48609; (989) 781-3150 (100).

St. Joseph's Home, 4800 Cadieux Rd., Detroit 48224; (313) 882-3800 (104).

Minnesota: Alverna Apartments, 300 8th Ave. S.E., Little Falls 56345; (320) 632-1246; www.unityfamily.com (68).

Assumption Home, 715 North First St., Cold Spring 56320; (320) 685-4110 (34).

Benedictine Health Center, 935 Kenwood Ave., Duluth, MN 55811; (218) 723-6408; www.benedictinehealthcenter.org.

Divine Providence Community Home (skilled nursing care) and Lake Villa Maria Senior Housing, 702 Third Ave. N.W., Sleepy Eye 56085; (507) 794-5333 (58).

Franciscan Health Community, 1925 Norfolk Ave., St. Paul 55116; (651) 696-8400 (223).

John Paul Apartments, 200 8th Ave. N., Cold Spring 56320; (320) 685-4429 (41).

Little Sisters of the Poor, Holy Family Residence (skilled nursing and intermediate care), 330 S. Exchange St., St. Paul 55102; (651) 227-0336 (73). Independent living apartments (32).

Madonna Towers (retirement apartments and nursing home), 4001 19th Ave. N.W., Rochester 55901; (507) 288-3911; www.madonnatowers.org (184).

Mary Rondorf Retirement Home of Sacred Heart Parish, Inc., 222 5th St., N.E., Staples 56479; (218) 894-2124 (45). Board and lodging with special services.

Mother of Mercy Nursing Home and Retirement Center, 230 Church Ave., Box 676, Albany 56307; (320) 845-2195 (114).

Regina Nursing Home and Retirement Residence Center, 1175 Nininger Rd., Hastings 55033; (651) 480-6836; www.reginamedical.com. Nursing home (61); retirement home (43); boarding care (32). Admin., Juliane M. Saxon.

Sacred Heart Hospice (skilled nursing home, adult day care, home health care) 1200 Twelfth St. S.W., Austin 55912; (507) 433-1808 (59).

St. Ann's Residence, 330 E. 3rd St., Duluth 55811; (218) 727-8831; www.stanns.com (185).

St. Anne of Winona (skilled nursing home), 1347 W. Broadway, Winona 55987; (507) 454-3621; www.saintanneofwinona.org (74).

St. Benedict's Center, 1810 Minnesota Blvd. S.E., St. Cloud 56304; (320) 252-0010; www.centracare.com (198 bed skilled nursing care; adult day care, respite care). Benedict Village(retirementt apartments), 2000 15th Ave. S.E., St. Cloud 56304; (320) 252-0010; www.centracare.com. Benedict Homes (Alzheimer residential care) and Benedict Court (assisted living), 1980 15th Ave. S.E., St. Cloud 56304; (320) 252-0010.

St. Benedict's Senior Community (independent and assisted living), 1301 East 7th St., Monticello, MN 55362; (763) 295-4051; www.centracare.com.

St. Elizabeth's Health Care Center, 1200 Grant Blvd., Wabasha 55981; (651) 565-4531; www.stelizabethswabasha.org (106).

St. Elizabeth's Medical Center, 626 Shields Ave., Wabasha, MN 55981; (651) 565-4581; www.stelizabethswabasha.org.

St. Francis Home, 2400 St. Francis Dr., Breckenridge 56520; (218) 643-3000; www.sfcare.org (124).

St. Mary's Regional Health Center, 1027 Washington Ave., Detroit Lakes 56501; (218) 847-5611 (100).

St. Otto's Care Center (nursing home), 920 S.E. 4th St., Little Falls 56345; (320) 632-9281 (150).

St. William's Nursing Home, P.O. Box 30, Parkers Prairie 56361; (218) 338-4671 (90).

Villa St. Vincent (skilled nursing home and residence), 516 Walsh St., Crookston 56716; (218) 281-3424. Skilled nursing home (80); special care unit (24); apartments (27); board and care (34).

West Wind Village, 1001 Scotts Ave., Morris 56267; (320) 589-1133; www.sfhs.org (128).

Westwood Senior Apartments, 925 Kenwood Ave., Duluth 55811; (218) 733-2238; www.westwoodduluth.org (70).

Mississippi: Notre Dame de la Mer Retirement Apartments, 292 Hwy. 90, Bay St. Louis 39520; (228) 467-2885 (61).

Santa Maria Retirement Apartments, 674 Beach Blvd., Biloxi, 39530; (228) 432-1289 (223).

Villa Maria Retirement Apartments, 921 Porter Ave., Ocean Springs 39564; (228) 875-8811 (225).

Missouri: Cathedral Square Towers, 444 W. 12th St., Kansas City 64105; (816) 471-6555 (167).

Chariton Apartments (retirement apartments), 4249 Michigan Ave., St. Louis 63111; (314) 352-7600 (122 units; 143 residents).

LaVerna Village Nursing Home, 904 Hall Ave., Savannah 64485; (816) 324-3185; lavernavillage.com (133).

Little Sisters of the Poor (home for aged), 3225 N. Florissant Ave., St. Louis 63107; (314) 421-6022; www;littlesistersofthepoorstlouis.org (114).

Mary, Queen and Mother Center (nursing care), 7601 Watson Rd., St. Louis 63119; (314) 961-8000; www.cardinalcarberry.org (230).

Mother of Good Counsel Home (skilled nursing, women), 6825 Natural Bridge Rd., Northwoods, 63121; (314) 383-4765; www.mogch.org (114).

Our Lady of Mercy Country Home, 2205 Hughes Rd., Liberty 64068; (816) 781-7276; www.ourladyofmercy.net (105).

Price Memorial skilled nursing facility, Forby Rd., P.O. Box 476, Eureka 63025; (636) 587-3200 (120).

St. Agnes Home for the Elderly, 10341 Manchester Rd., Kirkwood 63122; (314) 965-7616; www.stagneshome.com (124).

St. Joseph Hill Infirmary, Inc., (nursing care facility, men), St. Joseph Road, Eureka 63025; (636) 587-3661 (120).

St. Joseph's Home (residential and intermediate care), 723 First Capitol Dr., St. Charles 63301; (314) 946-4140; (110).

St. Joseph's Home (residential and intermediate care facility), 1306 W. Main St., Jefferson City 65109; (573) 635-0166 (90).

Nebraska: Madonna Rehabilitation Hospital, 5401 South St., Lincoln 68506; (402) 489-7102; www.madonna.org (252).

Mercy Care Center (skilled nursing facility for chronic, complex and subacute levels of care and rehabilitation), 1870 S. 75th St., Omaha 68124; (402) 343-8500 (246).

Mercy Villa, 1845 S. 72nd St., Omaha 68124; (402) 391-6224.

Mt. Carmel Home, Keens Memorial (nursing home), 412 W. 18th St., Kearney 68847; (308) 237-2287 (75).

New Cassel Retirement Center, 900 N. 90th St., Omaha 68114; (402) 393-2277; www.newcassel.org (165).

St. Joseph's Rehabilitation and Care Center, 401 N. 18th St., Norfolk 68701; (402) 644-7375 (99).

St. Joseph's Retirement Community, 320 E. Decatur St., West Point 68788; (402) 372-3477 (90).

St. Joseph's Villa (nursing home), 927 7th St., David City 68632; (402) 367-3045; www.saintjosephvilla.org (65).

New Hampshire: Mount Carmel Healthcare Center, 235 Myrtle St., Manchester 03104; (603) 627-3811 (120).

St. Ann Home (nursing home), 195 Dover Point Rd., Dover 03820; (603) 742-2612 (54).

St. Francis Rehabilitation and Nursing Center (nursing home), 406 Court St., Laconia 03246; (603) 524-0466 (51).

St. Teresa Rehabilitation and Nursing Center (nursing home), 519 Bridge St., Manchester 03104; (603) 668-2373; www.nh-cc.org; (5).

St. Vincent de Paul Healthcare Center, 29 Providence Ave., Berlin 03570; (603) 752-1820 (80).

New Jersey: McCarrick Care Center, 15 Dellwood Lane, Somerset 08873; (732) 545-4200 (142).

Mater Dei Nursing Home, 176 Rt. 40, Newfield 08344; (856) 358-2061 (64).

Morris Hall (St. Joseph Skilled Nursing Center, St. Mary Assisted Living), 1 Bishops' Dr., Lawrenceville 08648-2050; (609) 896-0006; www.morrishall.org (100).

Mount St. Andrew Villa (residence), 55 W. Midland Ave., Paramus 07652; (201) 261-5950 (55).

Our Lady's Residence (nursing home), 1100 Clematis Ave., Pleasantville 08232; (609) 646-2450 (236).

St. Ann's Home for the Aged (akilled and intermediate nursing care home, women), 198 Old Bergen Rd., Jersey City 07305; (201) 433-0950; www.saintannshome.com; (106).

St. Francis Health Resort (residence), 122 Diamond Spring Rd., Denville 07834; (973) 627-5560; www.saintfrancisres.com (150).

St. Joseph's Home for the Elderly, Little Sisters of the Poor, 140 Shepherd Lane, Totowa 07512; (973) 942-0300 (134).

St. Joseph's Rest Home for Aged Women, 46 Preakness Ave., Paterson 07522; (973) 956-1921 (35).

St. Joseph's Assisted Living Residence, 1 St. Joseph Terr., Woodbridge, 07095; (732) 634-0004 (60).

St. Joseph's Nursing Home, 3 St. Joseph Terr., Woodbridge, 07095; (732) 750-0077.

St. Mary's, 210 St. Mary's Dr., Cherry Hill 08003; (856) 424-9521 (215).

The Manor at St. Mary's, 220 St. Mary's Dr., Cherry Hill 08003; (856) 424-5344 (739).

St. Vincent's Nursing Home, 45 Elm St., Montclair 07042; (973) 754-4800 (220).

Villa Maria (residence and infirmary, women), 641 Somerset St., N. Plainfield 07061; (908) 757-3050 (86).

New York: Bernardine Apartments, 417 Churchill Ave., Syracuse 13205; (315) 469-7786.

Brothers of Mercy Sacred Heart Home (residence) 4520 Ransom Rd., Clarence 14031; (716) 759-6985 (80). Brothers of Mercy Nursing Home, 10570 Bergtold Rd., Clarence 14031; (716) 759-6985; www.brothersofmercy.org (240). Brothers of Mercy Housing Co., Inc. (apartments), 10500 Bergtold Rd., Clarence 14031; (716) 759-2122 (110).

Carmel Richmond Nursing Home, 88 Old Town Rd., Staten Island 10304; (718) 979-5000 (300).

Ferncliff Nursing Home, 21 Ferncliff Dr., Rhinebeck 12572; (845) 876-2011 (328).

Franciscan Health System of New York, 2975 Independence Ave., Bronx 10463; (718) 548-1700.

Good Samaritan Nursing Home (skilled nursing), 101 Elm St., Sayville 11782; (631) 244-2400 (100).

The Heritage (apartments with skilled nursing care), 1450 Portland Ave., Rochester 14621; (716) 342-1700; www.stannsrochester.org (237)

Holy Family Home, 174084th St., Brooklyn 11214; (718) 232-3666 (200).

Kateri Residence (skilled nursing), 150 Riverside Dr., New York 10024; (646) 505-3500; www.catholichealthcaresystem.org/kateri (610).

Little Sisters of the Poor, Jeanne Jugan Residence (Skilled Nursing and Health Related; Adult Care), 3200 Baychester Ave., Bronx 10475; (718) 671-2120 (60).

Little Sisters of the Poor, Queen of Peace Residence, 110-30 221st St., Queens Village 11429; (718) 464-1800.

Mary Manning Walsh Home (nursing home), 1339 York Ave., New York 10021; (212) 628-2800 (362).

Mercy Healthcare Center (skilled nursing facility), 114 Wawbeek Ave., Tupper Lake 12986; (518) 359-3355; www.muhc.org (80).

Mt. Loretto Nursing Home, (skilled nursing home), Sisters of the Resurrection, 302 Swart Hill Rd., Amsterdam 12010; (518) 842-6790 (120).

Nazareth Nursing Home (women), 291 W. North St., Buffalo 14201; (716) 881-2323 (125).

Our Lady of Consolation Nursing and Rehabilitation Care Center (skilled nursing) 111 Beach Dr., West Islip 11795; (631) 587-1600; www.olc.chsli.org (450).

Our Lady of Hope Residence (home for the aged), Little Sisters of the Poor, 1 Jeanne Jugan Lane, Latham 12210; (518) 785-4551 (117).

Ozanam Hall of Queens Nursing Home, Inc., 42-41 201st St., Bayside 11361; (718) 423-2000 (432).

Providence Rest , 3304 Waterbury Ave., Bronx 10465; (718) 931-30000; www.providencerest.org (242).

Resurrection Nursing Home (skilled nursing facility), Castleton 12033; (518) 732-7617 (80).

St. Ann's Community (skilled nursing facility), 1500 Portland Ave., Rochester 14621; (585) 697-6000; www.stannscommunity.com (354).

St. Cabrini Nursing Home, 115 Broadway, Dobbs Ferry 10522; (914) 693-6800 (304).

St. Clare Manor (nursing home), 543 Locust St., Lockport 14094; (716) 434-4718 (28).

St. Columban's on the Lake (retirement home), 2546 Lake Rd., Silver Creek 14136; (716) 934-4515 (50).

St. Elizabeth Home (adult home), 5539 Broadway, Lancaster 14086; (716) 683-5150 (117).

St. Francis Home (skilled nursing facility), 147

Reist St., Williamsville 14221; (716) 633-5400 (142).

St. Joseph Manor (nursing home), 2211 W. State St., Olean 14760; (716) 372-7810 (22).

St. Joseph Nursing Home, 2535 Genesee St., Utica 13501; (315) 797-1230; www.stjosephnh.org.

St. Joseph's Guest Home, Missionary Sisters of St. Benedict, 350 Cuba Hill Rd., Huntington 11743; (631) 368-9528.

St. Joseph's Home (nursing home), 420 Lafayette St., Ogdensburg 13669; (315) 393-3780; www.stjh.org (117).

St. Joseph's Villa (adult home), 38 Prospect Ave., Catskill 12414; (518) 943-5701.

St. Luke Manor, 17 Wiard St., Batavia 14020; (585) 343-8806 (20).

St. Mary's Manor, 515 Sixth St., Niagara Falls 14301; (716) 285-3236 (165).

St. Patrick's Home, 66 Van Cortlandt Park S., Bronx NY 10463; (718) 519-2800; www.stpatrickshome.org (264).

St. Teresa Nursing Home, 120 Highland Ave., Middletown 10940; (914) 342-1033 (98).

St. Vincent's Home for the Aged, 319 Washington Ave., Dunkirk 14048; (716) 366-2066 (40).

Terence Cardinal Cooke Health Care Center (skilled nursing), 1249 Fifth Ave., New York 10029; (212) 360-1000 (523).

Teresian House, 200 Washington Ave. Extension, Albany 12203; (518) 456-2000; www.teresianhouse.com (300).

Uihlein Mercy Center (nursing home), 185 Old Military Rd., Lake Placid 12946; (518) 523-2464 (220).

North Carolina: Maryfield Nursing Home, 1315 Greensboro Rd., High Point 27260; (336) 886-2444 (115).

North Dakota: Manor St. Joseph (basic care facility), 404 Fourth Ave., Edgeley 58433; (701) 493-2477 (40).

Marillac Manor Retirement Center, 1016 28th St., Bismarck 58501-3139; (701) 258-8702; www.marillac-manor.org (78 apartments).

St. Anne's Guest Home, 524 N. 17th St., Grand Forks 58203; (701) 746-9401 (86).

St. Vincent's Care Center (nursing facility), 1021 N. 26th St., Bismarck 58501; (701) 323-1999 (101).

Ohio: Archbishop Leibold Home for the Aged, Little Sisters of the Poor, 476 Riddle Rd., Cincinnati 45220; (513) 281-8001 (100).

The Assumption Village, 9800 Market St., North Lima 44452; (330) 549-0740 (120).

Francesca Residence (retirement), 39 N. Portage Path, Akron 44303; (330) 867-6334 (40).

House of Loreto (nursing home), 2812 Harvard Ave. N.W., Canton 44709; (330) 453-8137 (76).

Jennings Center for Older Adults (nursing care), 10204 Granger Rd., Cleveland 44125; (216) 581-2900; www.jenningscenter.org (150).

Little Sisters of the Poor, Sacred Heart Home, 930 Wynn Rd. Oregon 43616; (419) 698-4331 (81).

Little Sisters of the Poor, Sts. Mary and Joseph Home for Aged, 4291 Richmond Rd., Cleveland 44122; (216) 464-1222 (125).

The Maria-Joseph Living Care Center, 4830 Salem Ave., Dayton 45416; (937) 278-2692; www.mariajoseph.org (440).

Mercy Franciscan Terrace, 100 Compton Rd., Cincinnati 45215; (513) 761-9036 (148).

Mercy St. Theresa Center, 7010 Rowan Hill Dr., Cincinnati 45227; (513) 527-0105; www.e-mercy.com (157).

Mercy Siena Retirement Community, 6125 N. Main St., Dayton 45415; (937) 278-8211; www.mercysiena.com; (99).

Mount Alverna Village (intermediate care nursing facility), 6765 State Rd., Cleveland 44134; (440) 843-7800; www.franciscanservices.com/facilities/ (203).

Mt. St. Joseph (skilled nursing facility, dual certified), 21800 Chardon Rd., Euclid 44117; (216) 531-7426 (100).

Nazareth Towers, 300 E. Rich St., Columbus 43215; (614) 464-4780 (229).

St. Augustine Manor (skilled nursing facility), 7801 Detroit Ave., Cleveland 44102; (216) 634-7400 (248).

St. Francis Health Care Centre, 401 N. Broadway St., Green Springs 44836; (419) 639-2626; www.sfhcc.org (186).

St. Francis Home, Inc. (residence and nursing care), 182 St. Francis Ave., Tiffin 44883; (419) 447-2723 (173).

St. Joseph's Care Center, 2308 Reno Dr., Louisville 44641; (330) 875-5562 (100, nursing home; 40 assisted living).

St. Margaret Hall (rest home and nursing facility), Carmelite Sisters for the Aged and Infirm, 1960 Madison Rd., Cincinnati 45206; (513) 751-5880 (133).

St. Raphael Home (nursing home), 1550 Roxbury Rd., Columbus 43212; (614) 486-0436 (78).

St. Rita's Home (skilled nursing home), 880 Greenlawn Ave., Columbus 43223; (614) 443-9433 (100).

Schroder Manor Retirement Community (residential care, skilled nursing care and independent living units), Franciscan Sisters of the Poor, 1302 Millville Ave., Hamilton 45013; (513) 867-1300 (125).

The Villa Sancta Anna Home for the Aged, Inc., 25000 Chagrin Blvd., Beachwood 44122; (216) 464-9250 (68).

The Village at St. Edward (apartments, nursing care and assisted living), 3131 Smith Rd., Fairlawn 44333; (330) 666-1183; www.vased.org (160).

Oklahoma: St. Ann's Home, 9400 St. Ann's Dr., Oklahoma City 73162; (405) 728-7888 (120).

Westminster Village, Inc. (residence), 1601 Academy, Ponca City 74604; (580) 762-0927 (131).

Oregon: Evergreen Court Independent Retirement Living, 451 O'Connell St., North Bend 97459; (541) 751-7658; www.baycrest-village.com.

Maryville Nursing Home, 14645 S.W. Farmington, Beaverton 97007; (503) 643-8626; www.ssmo.org.

Mt. St. Joseph, 3060 S.E. Stark St., Portland 97214; (503) 535-4700 (347).

St. Catherine's Residence and Nursing Center, 3959 Sheridan Ave., North Bend 97459; (541) 756-4151 (200).

Pennsylvania: Antonian Towers, 1318 Spring St., Bethlehem, PA 18018; (610) 865-3963.

Ascension Manor I (senior citizen housing), 911 N. Franklin St., Philadelphia 19123; (215) 922-1116.

Ascension Manor II (senior citizen housing), 970

N. 7th St., Philadelphia 19123; (215) 922-1116.

Benetwood Apartments, Benedictine Sisters of Erie, 641 Troupe Rd., Harborcreek 16421; (814) 899-0088 (80).

Bethlehem Retirement Village, 100 W. Wissahickon Ave., Flourtown 19031; (215) 233-0998.

Catholic Senior Housing Development and Management, 1318 Spring St., Bethlehem 18018; (610) 865-3963; hfmanor.com/html/independent_living.html (50).

Christ the King Manor, 1100 W. Long Ave., Du Bois 15801; (814) 371-3180 (160).

D'Youville Manor (residential care facility), 1750 Quarry Rd., Yardley 19067; (215) 579-1750 (49).

Garvey Manor and Our Lady of the Allegheny Residence (nursing home), 128 Logan Blvd., Hollidaysburg 16648-2693; (814) 695-5571; www.garveymanor.org (150).

Grace Mansion (personal care facility), Holy Family Residential Services, 1200 Spring St., Bethlehem; (610) 865-6748; www.hfmanor.org (33).

Holy Family Home, Little Sisters of the Poor, 5300 Chester Ave., Philadelphia 19143; (215) 729-5153 (105).

Holy Family Manor (skilled and intermediate nursing facility), 1200 Spring St., Bethlehem 18018; (610) 865-5595; www.hfmanor.com (208).

Immaculate Mary Home (nursing care facility), 2990 Holme Ave., Philadelphia 19136; (215) 335-2100 (296).

John XXIII Home (skilled, intermediate and personal care), 2250 Shenango Freeway, Hermitage 16148; (724) 981-3200; www.johnxxiiihome.org (196).

Little Flower Manor (residence, women), 1215 Springfield Rd., Darby 19023; (610) 534-6000 (180).

Little Flower Manor Nursing Home (skilled nursing), 1201 Springfield Rd., Darby 19023; (610) 534-6000 (185).

Little Flower Manor of Diocese of Scranton, (long-term skilled nursing care facility), 200 S. Meade St., Wilkes-Barre 18702; (570) 823-6131.

Little Sisters of the Poor, 1028 Benton Ave., Pittsburgh 15212; (412) 307-1100; www.littlesistersofthepoor-pittsburgh.org (40).

Little Sisters of the Poor, Holy Family Residence, 2500 Adams Ave., Scranton 18509; (570) 343-4065 (58).

Maria Joseph Manor (skilled nursing, personal care facility and independent living cottages), 875 Montour Blvd., Danville 17821; (570) 275-4221 (135).

Marian Hall Home for the Aged (women), 934 Forest Ave., Pittsburgh 15202; (412) 761-1999 (49).

Marian Manor (intermediate care), 2695 Winchester Dr., Pittsburgh 15220; (412) 563-6866 (194).

Mount Macrina Manor (skilled nursing facility), 520 W. Main St., Uniontown 15401; (724) 437-1400 (141).

Neumann Apartments (low income), 25 N. Nichols St., St. Clair 17970; (570) 429-0699 (25).

Queen of Angels Apartments, 22 Rothermel St., Hyde Park, Reading 19605; (610) 921-3115 (45 units).

Queen of Peace Apartments (low income), 1318 Spring St., Bethlehem 18018; (610) 865-3963 (65).

Redeemer Village II, 1551 Huntingdon Pike, Huntingdon Valley 19006; (215) 947-8168; www.holyredeemer.com (151).

Sacred Heart Manor (nursing home and independent living), 6445 Germantown Ave., Philadelphia 19119; (215) 438-5268 (171 nursing home; 48 personal care; 48 independent living).

St. Anne's Retirement Community, 3952 Columbia Ave., Columbia 17512; (717) 285-5443; www.stannesrc.org (121).

St. Anne Home (nursing facility), 685 Angela Dr., Greensburg 15601; (724) 837-6070 (125).

St. Ignatius Nursing Home, 4401 Haverford Ave., Philadelphia 19104; (215) 349-8800 (176).

St. John Neumann Nursing Home, 10400 Roosevelt Blvd., Philadelphia 19116; (215) 248-7200 (107).

St. Joseph Home for the Aged (Residential and skilled nursing facility), 1182 Holland Rd., Holland 18966; (215) 357-5511 (76).

St. Joseph Nursing and Health Care Center (skilled nursing facility), 5324 Penn Ave., Pittsburgh 15224; (412) 665-5100 (153).

St. Leonard's Home Inc. (personal care facility), 601 N. Montgomery St., Hollidaysburg 16648; (814) 695-9581 (30).

St. Mary of Providence Center, R.D. 2, Box 145, Elverson 19520; (610) 942-4166; www.stmaryofprov-pa.org (52).

Saint Mary's Home of Erie, 607 E. 26th St., Erie 16504-2813; (814) 459-0621; www.stmaryshome.org (131).

St. Mary's at Asbury Ridge, 4855 West Ridge Rd., Erie, PA 16506; (814) 836-5300.

St. Mary's Manor (residential, personal care, shortterm rehabilitation and nursing care), 701 Lansdale Ave., Lansdale 19446; (215) 368-0900; www.smmphl.org (200).

St. Mary's Villa Nursing Home, 675 St. Mary's Villa Rd., Moscow 18444; (570) 842-7621 (176).

Trexler Pavilion (personal care facility), 1220 Prospect Ave., Bethlehem 18018; (610) 868-7776 (30).

Vincentian de Marillac Nursing Home, 5300 Stanton Ave., Pittsburgh 15206; (412) 361-2833 (52).

Vincentian Home (nursing facility), 111 Perrymont Rd., Pittsburgh 15237; (412) 366-5600 (217).

Rhode Island: Jeanne Jugan Residence of the Little Sisters of the Poor, 964 Main St., Pawtucket 02860; (401) 723-4314 (95).

Saint Antoine Residence (skilled nursing facility), 10 Rhodes Ave., North Smithfield 02896; (401) 767-3500; www.stantoine.net (416).

St. Clare Home (nursing facility), 309 Spring St., Newport 02840; (401) 849-3204 (47).

Scalabrini Villa (convalescent, rest-nursing home), 860 N. Quidnessett Rd., North Kingstown 02852; (401) 884-1802; www.freeyellow.com/members3/scalabrini (175).

South Carolina: Carter-May Home/St. Joseph Residence, 1660 Ingram Rd., Charleston 29407; (843) 556-8314 (15).

South Dakota: Avera Brady Health and Rehabilitation (skilled nursing facility), 500 S. Ohlman St., Mitchell 57301; (605) 966-7701 (83).

Mother Joseph Manor (skilled nursing facility), 1002 N. Jay St., Aberdeen 57401; (605) 622-5850 (81).

Prince of Peace Retirement Community, 4500 Prince of Peace Pl., Sioux Falls 57103; (605) 322-5600 (204).

St. William's Care Center (intermediate care), 100

South 9th St., Milbank 57252; (605) 432-5811 (60).

Tekakwitha Nursing Home (skilled and intermediate care), 6 E. Chestnut St., Sisseton 57262; (605) 698-7693 (101).

Tennessee: Alexian Village of Tennessee, 100 James Blvd., Signal Mountain 37377; (423) 886-0100 (277).

St. Mary Manor, 1771 Highway 45 Bypass, Jackson 38305; (731) 668-5633.

St. Peter Manor (retirement community), 108 N. Auburndale, Memphis 38104; (901) 278-8200.

St. Peter Villa (intermediate and skilled care), 141 N. McLean, Memphis 38104; (901) 276-2021.

Villa Maria Manor, 32 White Bridge Rd., Nashville 37205; (615) 352-3084 (230).

Texas: Casa, Inc., Housing for Elderly and Handicapped, 3201 Sondra Dr., Fort Worth 76107; (817) 332-7276 (200).

Casa Brendan Housing for the Elderly and Handicapped (56 apartments) and Casa II, Inc. (30 apartments), 1300 Hyman St., Stephenville 76401; (254) 965-6964 (83).

John Paul II Nursing Home (intermediate care and personal care), 209 S. 3rd St., Kenedy 78119; (830) 583-9841.

Mother of Perpetual Help Home (intermediate care facility), 519 E. Madison Ave., Brownsville 78520; (956) 546-6745 (38).

Mt. Carmel Home (personal care home), 4130 S. Alameda St., Corpus Christi 78411; (512) 855-6243 (92).

Nuestro Hogar Housing for Elderly and Handicapped, 709 Magnolia St., Arlington 76012; (817) 261-0608 (63).

St. Ann's Nursing Home, P.O. Box 1179, Panhandle 79068; (806) 537-3194 (56).

St. Dominic Residence Hall, 2401 Holcombe Blvd., Houston 77021; (713) 741-8700 (149).

St. Francis Nursing Home (intermediate care facility), 630 W. Woodlawn, San Antonio 78212; (210) 736-3177 (152).

St. Francis Village, Inc. (retired and elderly), 1 Chapel Plaza, Crowley 76036; (817) 292-5786 (420).

San Juan Nursing Home, Inc. (skilled and intermediate care facility), P.O. Box 1238, San Juan 78589; (956) 787-1771 (127).

Villa Maria (home for aged women-men), 920 S. Oregon St., El Paso 79901; (915) 533-5152 (17 units).

Villa Maria, Inc. (apartment complex), 3146 Saratoga Blvd., Corpus Christi 78415; (361) 857-6171 (59).

Utah: Christus Health Utah (Christus St. Joseph Villa and Christus Marian Center), 451 Bishop Federal Lane, Salt Lake City 84115; (801) 487-7557; www.stjosephvilla.com (300).

Vermont: Loretto Home, 59 Meadow St., Rutland 05701; (802) 773-8840 (57).

Michaud Memorial Manor (residential home for elderly), Derby Line 05830; (802) 873-3152 (34).

St. Joseph's Residential Care Home, 243 N. Prospect St., Burlington 05401; (802) 864-0264 (32).

Virginia: Madonna Home (home for aged), 814 W. 37th St., Norfolk 23508; (757) 623-6662 (16).

Marian Manor (assisted living, nursing care), 5345 Marian Lane, Virginia Beach 23462; (757) 456-5018; marian-manor.com (100).

Marywood Apartments, 1261 Marywood Lane, Richmond 23229; (804) 740-5567 (126).

McGurk House Apartments, 2425 Tate Springs Rd., Lynchburg 24501; (434) 846-2425 (89).

Our Lady of the Valley Retirement Community, 650 N. Jefferson St., Roanoke 24016; (540) 345-5111.

Russell House Apartments, 900 First Colonial Rd., Virginia Beach 23454; (757) 481-0770 (126).

St. Francis Home, 2511 Wise St., Richmond 23225; (804) 231-1043 (34).

St. Joseph's Home for the Aged, Little Sisters of the Poor, 1503 Michaels Rd., Henrice 23221; (804) 288-6245; www.littlesistersofthepoorvirginia.org (72).

St. Mary's Woods (independent and assisted living apartments), 1257 Marywood Lane, Richmond 23229; (804) 741-8624; www.stmaryswood.com (118 apartments).

Seton Manor (apartments), 215 Marcella Rd., Hampton 23666; (757) 827-6512 (112).

Washington: Cathedral Plaza Apartments (retirement apartments), W. 1120 Sprague Ave., Spokane 99204 (150).

Chancery Place (retirement apartments), 910 Marion, Seattle 98104; (206) 343-9415; www.ccsww.org.

The Delaney, W. 242 Riverside Ave., Spokane 99201; (509) 747-5081 (83).

Elbert House, 16000 N.E. 8th St., Bellevue 98008; (206) 747-5111.

Emma McRedmond Manor, 7960-169th N.E., Redmond 98052; (206) 869-2424 (31).

Fahy Garden Apartments, W. 1403-11 Dean Ave., Spokane 99201; (509) 326-6759 (31).

Fahy West Apartments, W. 1523 Dean Ave., Spokane 99201 (55).

The Franciscan (apartments), 15237-21stAve. S.W., Seattle 98166; (206) 431-8001.

Providence Mt. St. Vincent (nursing center and retirement apartments), 4831 35th Ave. S.W., Seattle 98126; (206) 937-3700 (174).

Tumwater Apartments, 57016th Ave. S.W., Tumwater 98501; (360) 352-4321.

West Virginia: Welty Home for the Aged, 21 Washington Ave., Wheeling 26003; (304) 242-5233 (46).

Wisconsin: Alexian Village of Milwaukee (retirement community/skilled nursing home), 9301 N. 76th St., Milwaukee 53223; (414) 355-9300; www.alexianvillage.org (327).

Bethany-St. Joseph Health Care Center, 2501 Shelby Rd., La Crosse 54601; (608) 788-5700 (226).

Clement Manor (retirement community and skilled nursing), 3939 S. 92nd St., Greenfield 53228; (414) 321-1800 (162).

Divine Savior Nursing Home, 715 W. Pleasant St., Portage 53901; (608) 742-4131 (124).

Felician Village (independent living), 1700 S. 18th St., Manitowoc 54020; (920) 683-8811 (134 apartments).

Franciscan Care Center, 500 S. Oakwood Rd., Oshkosh, WI 54901; (920) 223-0110.

Mayo Health System: Arcadia Campus Nursing Home, 464 S. St. Joseph Ave., Arcadia 54612; (608) 323-3341 (75).

McCormick Memorial Home, 212 Iroquois St., Green Bay 54301; (920) 437-0883 (60).

Marian Catholic Home (skilled care nursing home), 3333 W. Highland Blvd., Milwaukee 53208; (414) 344-8100 (215).

Marian Franciscan Center, 9632 W. Appleton Ave., Milwaukee 53225; (414) 461-8850 (310).

Marian Housing Center (independent living), 4105 Spring St., Racine 53405; (262) 633-5807 (40).

Maryhill Manor Nursing Home (skilled nursing facility), 501 Madison Ave., Niagara 54151; (715) 251-3178 (75).

Milwaukee Catholic Home (continuing care retirement community), 2462 N. Prospect Ave., Milwaukee 53211-4462; (414) 224-9700; www.milwaukeecatholichome.org (131).

Nazareth House (skilled nursing facility), 814 Jackson St., Stoughton 53589; (608) 873-6448 (99).

St. Ann Rest Home (intermediate care facility, women), 2020 S. Muskego Ave., Milwaukee 53204; (414) 383-2630 (50).

St. Anne's Home for the Elderly, 3800 N. 92nd St., Milwaukee 53222; (414) 463-7570; www.wahsa.org/st.anne (106).

St. Camillus Campus (continuing care retirement community), 10100 West Blue Mound Road, Wauwatosa 53226; (414) 258-1814; www.stcam.com (386).

St. Elizabeth Nursing Home, 109 S. Atwood Ave., Janesville 53545; (608) 752-6709 (43).

St. Francis Home (skilled nursing facility), 1416 Cumming Ave., Superior 54880; (715) 394-5591.

St. Francis Home (skilled nursing), 33 Everett St., Fond du Lac 54935; (920) 923-7980 (106).

St. Joseph's Home, 9244 29th Ave., Kenosha 53143; (262) 925-8124; www.stjosephs.com (93).

St. Joseph's Rehabilitation Center, 2902 East Ave. S., La Crosse 54601; (608) 788-9870; www.crsinc.org (80).

St. Joseph's Nursing Home of St. Joseph Community Health Services, Inc. P.O. Box 527, Hillsboro 54634; (608) 489-8000.

St. Joseph Residence, Inc. (nursing home), 107 E. Beckert Rd., New London 54961; (920) 982-5354 (107).

St. Mary's Home for the Aged (skilled nursing, Alzheimer's unit, respite care), 2005 Division St., Manitowoc 54220; (920) 684-7171; www.feliciancommunity.org (266).

St. Mary's Nursing Home, 3515 W. Hadley St., Milwaukee 53210; (414) 873-9250 (88).

St. Monica's Senior Citizens Home, 3920 N. Green Bay Rd., Racine 53404; (262) 639-5050; www.srsofstrita.org (110).

St. Paul Home Elder Services (intermediate and skilled nursing home), 1211 Oakridge Ave., Kaukauna 54130; (920) 766-6020; www.stpaulelders.org (129).

Villa Loretto Nursing Home, N8114 Calvary St., Mount Calvary 53057; (920) 753-3211; www.villalorettonh.org (52).

Villa St. Francis, Inc., 1910 W. Ohio Ave., Milwaukee 53215; (414) 649-2888 (142).

FACILITIES FOR CHILDREN AND ADULTS WITH DISABILITIES

Sources: Catholic Almanac *survey*; The Official Catholic Directory.

This listing covers facilities and programs with educational and training orientation. Information about other services for the handicapped can generally be obtained from the Catholic Charities Office or its equivalent (c/o Chancery Office) in any diocese. (See Index for listing of addresses of chancery offices in the U.S.)

Abbreviation code: b, boys; c, coeducational; d, day; g, girls; r, residential. Other information includes age for admission. The number in parentheses at the end of an entry indicates total capacity or enrollment.

Deaf and Hearing Impaired

California: St. Joseph's Center for Deaf and Hard of Hearing, 3880 Smith St., Union City 94587.

Louisiana: Chinchuba Institute (d,c; birth through 18 yrs.), 1131 Barataria Blvd., Marrero 70072.

Missouri: St. Joseph Institute for the Deaf (r,d,c; birth to 14 years), 1809 Clarkson Rd., Chesterfield, MO 63107; (636) 532-3211 (Voice/TDD).

New York: Cleary School for the Deaf (d,c; infancy through 21), 301 Smithtown Blvd., Nesconset, NY 11767-2077; (516) 588-0530; www.clearyschool.org (70).

St. Francis de Sales School for the Deaf (d,c; infant through elementary grades), 260 Eastern Parkway, Brooklyn 11225; (718) 636-4573 (150).

St. Joseph's School for the Deaf (d,c; parent-infant through 14 yrs.), 1000 Hutchinson River Pkwy, Bronx 10465; (718) 828-9000 (140).

Ohio: St. Rita School for the Deaf (r,d,c; birth to 12th grade), 1720 Glendale-Milford Rd., Cincinnati 45215; (513) 771-7600; www.srsdeaf.org (130).

Pennsylvania: Archbishop Ryan School for Hearing Impaired Children (d,c; parent-infant programs through 8th grade), 233 Mohawk Ave., Norwood, PA 19074; (610) 586-7044 (49).

De Paul Institute (d,c; birth through 21 yrs.), 2904 Castlegate Ave., Pittsburgh 15226; (412) 561-4848 (77).

Abused, Abandoned, and Neglected

This listing includes facilities for abused, abandoned and neglected as well as emotionally disturbed children and youth.

Alabama: St. Mary's Home for Children (r,c; referred from agencies), 4350 Moffat Rd., Mobile 36618; (251) 344-7733.

California: Hanna Boys Center (r,b; 10-15 yrs. at intake; school, 4th to 10th grade), Box 100, Sonoma 95476; (707)996-6767 (107). Treatment center and therapeutic special school for boys with emotional problems, behavior disorders, learning disabilities.

Rancho San Antonio (r,b; 13-17 yrs.), 21000 Plummer St., Chatsworth 91311; (818) 882-6400.

St. Vincent's (r,d,g; 12-17 yrs.), 4200 Calle Real, Santa Barbara 93110-1454; (805) 683-6381.

Colorado: Mt. St. Vincent Home (r,c; 5-13 yrs.), 4159 Lowell Blvd., Denver 80211; (303) 458-7220; www.nahse.org/member/st.vincent.

Connecticut: St. Francis Home for Children (r,d,c;

4-17 yrs.), 651 Prospect St., New Haven 06511; (203) 777-5513. Exec. Dir., Peter Salerno.

Mt. St. John Home and School for Boys (r,b; 11-16 yrs.), 135 Kirtland St., Deep River 06417; (860) 526-5391; www.mtstjohn.org (77).

Delaware: Our Lady of Grace Home for Children (r,d,c; 6-12 yrs.), 487 E. Chestnut Hill Rd., Newark 19713; (302) 738-4658.

Seton Villa, Siena Hall and Children's Home (r,c; group home; 12-18 yrs,; mothers and their children), c/o 2307 Kentmere Pkwy, Wilmington 19806; (302) 656-2183.

Florida: Boystown of Florida (r,b; 12-16 yrs.; group home), 11400 S.W. 137th Court, Miami 33186.

Georgia: Village of St. Joseph (r,c; 6-16 yrs.), 1961 Druid Hills Rd., Ste. 205-B, 30329; (404) 321-2900.

Illinois: Guardian Angel Community Services (d,c; r,b), 1550 Plainfield Rd., Joliet 60435; (815) 729-0930 (35).

Maryville Academy (r,c; 6-18 yrs.), 1150 North River Rd., Des Plaines 60016; (708) 824-1893.

Mission of Our Lady of Mercy, Mercy Home for Boys and Girls (r,d,c; 15-18 yrs.), 1140 W. Jackson Blvd., Chicago 60607; (312) 738-7560; www.mercyhome.org.

Indiana: Gibault School for Boys (r; 10-18 yrs.), 6401 South U.S. Highway 41, Terre Haute 47802; (812) 299-1156; www.gibault.org.

Campagna Academy (r; 10-18 yrs.), 7403 Cline Ave., Schererville 46375; (219) 322-8614.

Kentucky: Boys' Haven (r; 12-18 yrs.), 2301 Goldsmith Lane, Louisville 40218; (502) 458-1171; www.boyshaven.org.

Louisiana: Hope Haven Center (r,c; 5-18 yrs.), 1101 Barataria Blvd., Marrero 70072; (504) 347-5581.

Maryland: Good Shepherd Center (r,g; 13-18 yrs.), 4100 Maple Ave., Baltimore, 21227; (410) 247-2770; www.goodshepherdcenter.com.

Massachusetts: The Brightside for Families and Children (r,d,c; 6-16 yrs.), 1233 Main St., Holyoke, MA 01040; (413) 539-2484; www.brightsidecares.com.

McAuley Nazareth Home for Boys (r; 6-13 yrs.), 77 Mulberry St., Leicester 01524; (508) 892-4886; www.nazareth-home.org (16). Residential treatment center.

St. Vincent Home (r,c 5-22 yrs.), 2425 Highland Ave., Fall River 02720; (508) 679-8511.

Michigan: Don Bosco Hall (r,b; 13-17 years.), 10001 Petoskey Ave., Detroit 48204; (313) 834-8677.

Holy Cross Children's Services (r,d,c; 13-17 yrs.), 8759 Clinton-Macon Rd., Clinton 49236; (517) 423-7451; www.hccsnet.org (650). Facilities located throughout the state and northern Ohio.

Vista Maria (r,g; 11-18 yrs.), 20651 W. Warren Ave., Dearborn Heights 48127; (313) 271-6250; www.community.milive.com/cc/girls.

Minnesota: St. Cloud Children's Home (r,c; 8-18 yrs.), RTC Campus, Bld. 4-D, P.O. Box 1006, Fergus Falls, MN 56538; (218) 739-9325. Day Treatment Program (d,c; 7-14 yrs.), same address.

St. Elizabeth Home (r,c; 18 yrs. and older), 306 15th Ave. N., St. Cloud 56301; (320) 252-8350.

Missouri: Child Center of Our Lady (r,d,c; 5-14 yrs.), 7900 Natural Bridge Rd., St. Louis 63121; (314) 383-0200.

Child Center-Marygrove (r,d,c; 6-21 yrs.) (97); intense treatment unit (r,b; 13-18 yrs) (13); overnight crises care (r,d,c; birth to 18 yrs.) (8), 2705 Mullanphy Lane, Florissant, 63031; (314) 830-6201; www.marygroveservices.org.

Nebraska: Father Flanagan's Boys' Home (r,c; 10-16 yrs.), 14100 Crawford St., Boys Town 68010; (402) 498-1000; www.boystown.org (556). Boys Town National Research Hospital (r,d,c; 1-18 yrs.), 555 N. 30th St., Omaha 68131; (402) 498-6362; www.boystownhospital.org. Center for abused handicapped children, diagnosis of speech, language and hearing problems in children. Boys Town also has various facilities or programs in Brooklyn, NY; Portsmouth, RI; Philadelphia, PA; Washington, DC; Tallahassee, Orlando and Delray Beach, FL; Atlanta, GA; New Orleans, LA; San Antonio, TX; Las Vegas, NV; and southern CA.

New Jersey: Catholic Community Services/Mt. Carmel Guild, 1160 Raymond Blvd., Newark 07102; (973) 596-4084.

Collier High School (d,c; 13-18 yrs.), 160 Conover Rd., Wickatunk 07765; (732) 946-4771; www.collierservices.com.

Collier Group Home, 180 Spring St., Red Bank, NJ 07701; (732) 842-8337.

Collier House (transitional living), 386 Maple Pl., Keyport, NJ 07735; (732) 264-3222.

New York: The Astor Home for Children (r,d,c; 5-12 yrs.), 6339 Mill St., P.O. Box 5005, Rhinebeck 12572-5005; (845) 871-1000; www.astorservices.org. Child Guidance Clinics/Day Treatment (Rhinebeck, Poughkeepsie, Beacon, Bronx). Head Start Day Care (Poughkeepsie, Beacon, Red Hook, Dover, Millerton).

Baker Victory Services, 780 Ridge Rd. Lackawanna 14218; (716) 828-9500; www.ourladyofvictory.org.

Good Shepherd Services (r,d,c), 305 Seventh Ave., New York, NY 10001; (212) 243-7070; www.goodshepherds.org. City-wide residential programs or adolescents (12-21 yrs.); foster care and adoption services (infant-21 yrs.); training institute for human services workers; day treatment program (13-18 yrs.); community-based neighborhood family services in South Brooklyn Community (infant-adult),

LaSalle School (r,d,b; 12-18 yrs.), 391 Western Ave., Albany 12203; (518) 242-4731.

Madonna Heights Services (r,d,g; 12-18 yrs.), 151 Burrs Lane, Dix Hills 11746; (631) 643-8800; www.sco.org (110). Also conducts group homes on Long Island and outpatient programs.

St. Anne Institute (r,d,g; 12-18 yrs.), 160 N. Main Ave., Albany 12206; (518) 437-6500.

St. Catherine's Center for Children (r,d,c; birth through 12 yrs.), 40 N. Main Ave., Albany 12203; (518) 453-6700; www.st-cath.org.

St. John's of Rockaway Beach (r,b; 9-21 yrs.), 144 Beach 111th St., Rockaway Park 11694; (718) 945-2800. Programs include diagnostic centers and independent living programs.

North Dakota: Home on the Range (r,c; 10-18 yrs.), 16351 I-94, Sentinel Butte 58654; (701) 872-3745; www.hotrnd.org (79). Residential and emergency shelter therapeutic programs.

Home on the Range-Red River Victory Ranch (r,b; 10-18 yrs.), P.O. Box 9615, Fargo 58106; (701) 293-6321; www.hotr.org (12). Residential chemical addictions program.

Ohio: St. Vincent Family Centers (d,c; preschool) Outpatient counseling program (c; 2-18 yrs.), 1490 East Main St., Columbus 43205; (614) 252-0731; www.svfc.org.

Marycrest (r,g; 13-18 yrs.), 7800 Brookside Rd., Independence 44131.

Catholic Charities Services/Parmadale (r,c; 12-18 yrs.), 6753 State Rd., Parma 44134; (440) 845-7700.

Rosemont (r,g;d,c; 11-18 yrs.), 2440 Dawnlight Ave., Columbus 43211; (614) 471-2626.

Oregon: St. Mary's Home for Boys (r; 10-18 yrs.), 16535 S.W. Tualatin Valley Highway, Beaverton 97006; (503) 649-5651; www.stmaryshomeforboys.org.

Pennsylvania: Auberle (r,c; 7-18 yrs.), 1101 Hartman St., McKeesport 15132-1500; (412) 673-5800; www.auberle.org (181). Residential treatment for boys; emergency shelter care, foster care, group home for girls and family preservation program.

De LaSalle in Towne (d,b; 14-17 yrs.), 25 S. Van Pelt St., Philadelphia 19103; (215) 567-5500.

De LaSalle Vocational (b; 15-18 yrs.), 1265 Street Rd., Bensalem 19020; (215) 464-0344.

Gannondale (r,g; 12-17 yrs.), 4635 E. Lake Rd., Erie 16511; (814) 899-7659.

Harborcreek Youth Services (r,d,c; 10-17 yrs.), 5712 Iroquois Ave., Harborcreek 16421; (814) 899-7664; www.hys-erie.org.

Holy Family Institute (r,d,c; 0-18 yrs.), 8235 Ohio River Blvd., Emsworth 15202; (412) 766-4030; www.hfi-pgh.org.

Lourdesmont Good Shepherd Youth and Family Services (r,g;d,c; 12-17 yrs.), 537 Venard Rd., Clarks Summit 18411; (507) 587-4741; www.lourdesmont.com. Sponsored by the Sisters of the Good Shepherd. John A. Antognoli.

St. Gabriel's Hall (r,b; 10-18 yrs.), P.O. Box 7280, Audubon 19407; (215) 247-2776.

St. Michael's School (r,b; d,c; 12-17 yrs.), Box 370, Tunkhannock 18657; (570) 388-6155.

Texas: St. Joseph Adolescent and Family Counseling Center (c; 13-17 yrs.), 5415 Maple Ave., #320, Dallas 75235; (214) 631-TEEN.

Washington: Morning Star Boys Ranch (Spokane Boys' Ranch, Inc.) (r,b; 10-18 yrs.), Box 8087, Spokane 99203-0087; (509) 448-1411; www.morningstarboysranch.org. Dir. Joseph M. Weitensteiner.

Wisconsin: North American Union Sisters of Our Lady of Charity Center (r,c; 10-17 yrs.), 154 Edgington Lane, Wheeling, WV 26003-1535; (304) 242-0042.

St. Charles Youth and Family Services (r,d,b; 12-18 yrs.), 151 S. 84th St., Milwaukee 53214; (414) 476-3710; www.stcharlesinc.org.

Wyoming: St. Joseph's Children's Home (r,c; 6-18 yrs.), P.O. Box 1117, Torrington 82240; (307) 532-4197.

Developmentally Challenged

This listing includes facilities for children, youth, and adults with learning disabilities.

Alabama: Father Purcell Memorial Exceptional Children's Center (r, c; birth to 10 yrs.), 2048 W. Fairview Ave., Montgomery 36108; (334) 834-5590; www.mnw.net/fpm.

California: Child Study Center of St. John's Hospital (d,c; birth-18 yrs.), 1339-20th St., Santa Monica 90404; (310) 829-8921.

St. Madeleine Sophie's Center (d,c; 18 yrs. and older), 2111 E. Madison Ave., El Cajon 92019.

Tierra del Sol Foundation (d,c; 18 yrs. and older), 9919 Sunland Blvd., Sunland 91040; (818) 352-1419. 14547 Gilmore St., Van Nuys 91411; (818) 904-9164.

Connecticut: Gengras Center (d,c; 3-21 yrs.), St. Joseph College, 1678 Asylum Ave., W. Hartford 06117.

Villa Maria Education Center (d,c; 6-14 yrs.), 161 Sky Meadow Dr., Stamford 06903-3400; (203) 322-5886; www.villamariaedcenter.org.

District of Columbia: Lt. Joseph P. Kennedy, Jr., Institute (d,c; 6 weeks to 5 yrs. for Kennedy Institute for Child Development Center; 6-21 yrs. for Kennedy School; 18 yrs. and older for training and employment, therapeutic and residential services). Founded in 1959 for people of all ages with developmental disabilities and their families in the Washington archdiocese. Heaquarters: 801 Buchanan St. N.E., Washington 20017; (202) 529-7600; www.kennedyinstitute.org. Other locations in D.C. and Maryland. No enrollment limit.

Florida: L'Arche Harbor House, (c; 20 yrs. and older; community home), 700 Arlington Rd., Jacksonville 32211; (904) 721-5992.

Marian Center Services for Developmentally Handicapped and Mentally Retarded (r,d,c; 2-21 yrs.), 15701 Northwest 37th Ave., Opa Locka 33054; (305) 625-8354; www.mariancenterschool.org. Pre-school, school, workshop residence services.

Morning Star School (d,c; 4-16 yrs.), 725 Mickler Rd., Jacksonville, 32211; (904) 421-2144.

Morning Star School (d,c; school age), 954 Leigh Ave., Orlando 32804.

Morning Star School (d,c; 6-14 yrs.), 4661-80th Ave. N., Pinellas Park 33781; (727) 544-6036; www.morningstarschool.org.

Morning Star Catholic School (d,c; 6-16 yrs.), 210 E. Linebaugh Ave., Tampa 33612; (813) 935-0232; www.morningstartampa.org..

Georgia: St. Mary's Home (r,c), 2170 E. Victory Dr., Savannah 31404; (912) 236-7164.

Illinois: Bartlett Learning Center (r,d,c; 3-21 yrs.), 801 W. Bartlett Rd., Bartlett 60103; (630) 289-4221.

Brother James Court (r, men over 18 yrs.), 2508 St. James Rd., Springfield 62707; (217) 544-4878.

Good Shepherd Manor (men; 18 yrs. and older), Little Brothers of the Good Shepherd, P.O. Box 260, Momence 60954; (815) 472-3700; www.goodshepherdmanor.org. Resident care for developmentally disabled men.

Misericordia Home South (r,c), 2916 W. 47th St., Chicago 60632; (773) 254-9595. For severely and profoundly impaired children.

Misericordia Home — Heart of Mercy Village (r,c; 6-45 yrs.), 6300 North Ridge, Chicago 60660; (773) 973-6300; www.misericordia.com.

Mt. St. Joseph (developmentally disabled women; over age 21), 24955 N. Highway 12, Lake Zurich 60047; (847) 438-5050.

Provena St. Vincent Community Living Facility

(r,c; adults, over 18 yrs.) (20), and St. Vincent Supported Living Arrangement (r,c; adults, over 18 yrs.) (20), 659 E. Jefferson St., Freeport 61032; (815) 232-6181.

St. Coletta's of Illinois (r,d,; 6 to adult), 123rd and Wolf Rd., Palos Park 60464; (708) 448-6520.

St. Mary of Providence (r,women; 18 yrs. and older), 4200 N. Austin Ave., Chicago 60634; (773) 545-8300.

Springfield Developmental Center (m; 21 yrs. and over), 4595 Laverna Rd., Springfield 62707; (217) 525-8271.

Massachusetts: Cardinal Cushing Centers (d,c; 3-22 yrs.), 85 Washington St., Braintree 02184; (781) 848-6250; www.coletta.org.

Vocational Training

Indiana: Marian Day School (d,c; 6-16 yrs.), 700 Herndon Dr., Evansville 47711; (812) 422-5346.

Kansas: Lakemary Center, Inc. (r,d,c), 100 Lakemary Dr., Paola 66071; (913) 557-4000; www.lakemaryctr.org.

Kentucky: Pitt Academy (d,c), 6010 Preston Hwy., Louisville 40219; (502) 966-6979; www.pitt.com.

Louisiana: Department of Special Education, Archdiocese of New Orleans, St. Michael Special School (d,c; 6-21 yrs.), 1522 Chippewa St., New Orleans 70130.

Holy Angels Residential Facility (r,c; teenage, 14 yrs. and older), 10450 Ellerbe Rd., Shreveport 71106; (318) 797-8500.

Ocean Avenue Community Home, 361 Ocean Ave., Gretna 70053; (504) 361-0674.

Padua Community Services (r,c; birth-25 yrs.), 200 Beta St., Belle Chasse 70037.

St. Jude the Apostle, 1430 Claire Ave., Gretna 70053; (504) 361-8457.

St. Mary's Residential Training School (r,c; 3-22 yrs.), P.O. Drawer 7768, Alexandria 71306; (318) 445-6443.

St. Peter the Fisherman, 62269 Airport Dr., Slidell 70458; (504) 641-4914.

St. Rosalie (r; men 18 and up), 119 Kass St., Gretna 70056; (504) 361-8320.

Sts. Mary and Elizabeth, 720 N. Elm St., Metairie 70003; (504) 738-6959.

Maryland: The Benedictine School for Exceptional Children (r,c; 6-21 yrs.), 14299 Benedictine Lane, Ridgely 21660; (410) 634-2112; www.benschool.com.

Francis X. Gallagher Services (r), 2520 Pot Spring Rd., Timonium 21093.

St. Elizabeth School and Habilitation Center (d,c; 11-21 yrs.), 801 Argonne Dr., Baltimore 21218; (410) 889-5054; www.stelizabeth-school.org.

Massachusetts: Cardinal Cushing School and Training Center (r,d,c; 16-22 yrs.), Hanover 02339 (116 r; 28 d).

Mercy Centre (d,c; 3-22 yrs. and over), 25 West Chester St., Worcester 01605-1136; (508) 852-7165; www.mercycentre.com.

Michigan: Our Lady of Providence Center (r,g; 11-30 yrs., d,c; 26 yrs. and older), 16115 Beck Rd., Northville 48118; (734) 453-1300.

St. Louis Center and School (r,d,b; 6-18 yrs. child care; 18-36 yrs. adult foster care), 16195 Old U.S.

12, Chelsea 48118-9646; (734) 475-8430; www.stlouiscenter.org.

Minnesota: Mother Teresa Home (r,c; 18 yrs. and older), 101-10th Ave. N., Cold Spring 56320.

St. Francis Home (r,c; 18 yrs. and older), P.O. Box 326, Waite Park 56387; (320) 251-7630.

St. Luke's Home (r; 18 yrs. and older), 411 8th Ave. N., Cold Springs 56320.

Missouri: Department of Special Education, Archdiocese of St. Louis, 4472 Lindell Blvd., St. Louis. 63108; (314) 533-3454. Serves children with developmental disabilities, mental retardation or learning disabilities; services include special ungraded day classes in 8 parish schools.

Good Shepherd Homes (residential for developmentally disabled men; 18 yrs. and up), The Community of the Good Shepherd, 10101 James A. Reed Rd., Kansas City 64134; (816) 767-8090.

St.Mary's Special School (r,c; 5-21 yrs.), 4445 Lindell Blvd., St. Louis 63108; (314) 792-7320. St. Mary's Supported Living (r,c) (24); supervised homes for adolescents or adults. St. Mary's Early Intervention (d,c) (30); early intervention for toddlers.

Nebraska: Madonna School for Exceptional Children (d,c; 5-21 yrs.), 2537 N. 62nd St., Omaha 68104; (402) 556-1883; www.madonnaschool.org. Children with learning problems.

Villa Marie School and Home for Exceptional Children (r,d,c; 6-18 yrs.), 3700 Sheridan Blvd., Ste. 3, Lincoln 68506; (402) 488-2040.

New Jersey: Archbishop Damiano School (d,c; 3-21 yrs.), 1145 Delsea Dr., Westville Grove 08093.

Catholic Community Services, Archdiocese of Newark, 1160 Raymond Blvd., Newark 07102.

Department of Special Education, Diocese of Camden, 5609 Westfield Ave., Pennsauken, NJ 08110-1836; (609) 488-7123; www.catholiccharities.org. Services include: Archbishop Damiano School (above), and full time programs (d,c; 6-21 yrs.) at 4 elementary (96) and 2 high schools (60) and some religious education programs.

Department for Persons with Disabilities, Diocese of Paterson, 1 Catholic Charities Way, Oak Ridge, N.J. 07438; (973) 697-4395; www.dpd.org. Services include 8 residential programs for adults, one adult training center, family support services.

Felician School for Exceptional Children (d,c; 5-21 yrs.), 260 S. Main St., Lodi 07644; (973) 777-5355.

McAuley School for Exceptional Children (d,c; 5-21 yrs.), 107 Westervelt Ave., North Plainfield, NJ 07060; (908) 754-4114.

Mt. Carmel Guild Special Education School (d,c; 6-21 yrs.), 60 Kingsland Ave., Kearny 07032; (201) 995-3280.

St. Anthony's Special Education School (d,c), 25 N. 7th St., Belleville 07109; (973) 844-3700.

Sister Georgine School (d,c; 6-17 yrs.), 544 Chestnut Ave., Trenton 08611; (609) 396-5444.

St. Patrick's Special Education School (d,c), 72 Central Ave., Newark 07102.

New York: Baker Victory Services (r), 780 Ridge Rd., Lackawanna, N.Y. 14218; (716) 828-9500; www.bakervictoryservices.org. Residential care for handicapped and retarded children; nursery school program for emotionally disturbed pre-school children.

Bishop Patrick V. Ahern High School (d,c; 15-21 yrs.), 100 Merrill Ave., Staten Island 10314.

Cantalician Center for Learning (d,c; birth-21 yrs.), 3233 Main St., Buffalo 14214; (716) 833-5353; www.cantalician.org. Infant and pre-school; elementary and secondary; workshop (426). Three group homes. Rehabilitation, day treatment and senior rehabilitation programs.

Catholic Charities Residential Services, Rockville Centre Diocese, 269 W. Main St., Bay Shore 11706. Residences for developmentally disabled adults (88).

Cobb Memorial School (r,d,c; 5-21 yrs.), 100-300 Mt. Presentation Way, Altamont 12009; (518) 861-6446.

Joan Ann Kennedy Memorial Preschool (d,c; 3-5 yrs.), 26 Sharpe Ave., Staten Island 10302.

L'Arche Syracuse (r, adults), 1232 Teall Ave., Syracuse 13206-3468; (315) 479-8088; www.larch-esyracuse.com (12). Homes where assistants and persons with developmental disabilities share life, following the philosophy of Jean Vanier. Member of International L'Arche Federation, Exec. Dir., Frank Woolever.

Maryhaven Center of Hope (r,d,c; school age to adult), 51 Terryville Rd., Port Jefferson 11776; (631) 474-4120; www.maryhaven.org.

Mercy Home for Children (r,c), 243 Prospect Park West, Brooklyn 11215; (718) 832-1075. Residences for adolescents and young adults who are developmentally disabled: Visitation, Warren, Vincent Haire, Santulli and Littlejohn residences (Brooklyn), Kevin Keating Residence (Queens).

Office for Disabled Persons, Catholic Charities, Diocese of Brooklyn, 191 Joralemon St., Brooklyn 11201; (718) 722-6000; www.ccbg.org. Services include: adult day treatment center; community residences for mentally retarded adults; special events for disabled children (from age 3) and adults.

Office for Disabled Persons, Archdiocese of New York, 1011 First Ave., New York 10022; (212) 371-1000. Services include consultation and referral, variety of services for deaf, blind, mentally retarded, mentally ill.

Seton Foundation for Learning (d,c; 5-15 yrs.), 104 Gordon St., Staten Island 10304; (718) 447-1750.

North Carolina: Holy Angels (r,c; birth to adult), 6600 Wilkinson Blvd., P.O. Box 710, Belmont 28012; (704) 825-4161; www.holyangelsnc.org.

North Dakota: Friendship, Inc. (r,d,c; all ages), 3004 11th St. South, Fargo 58103; (701) 235-8217.

Ohio: Julie Billiart School (d,c; 6-12 yrs.), 4982 Clubside Rd., Cleveland 44124; (216) 381-1191; www.juliebilliartschool.org.

Mary Immaculate School (d,c; 6-14 yrs.), 3835 Secor Rd., Toledo 43623; (419) 474-1688; www.maryimmaculatetoledo.org

OLA/St. Joseph Center (d,c; 6-16 yrs.), 2346 W. 14th St., Cleveland 44113; (216) 621-3451.

Rose Mary, The Johanna Graselli Rehabilitation and Education Center (r,c; 5 yrs. and older), 19350 Euclid Ave., Cleveland 44117.

St. John's Villa (r,c; continued care and training,

15 yrs. and over), P.O. Box 457, Carrollton 44615; (330) 627-9789.

Oregon: Providence Montessori School Early Intervention Program (d,c; 3-5 yrs.), 830 N.E. 47th Ave., Portland 97213; (503) 215-2409.

Pennsylvania: Clelian Heights School for Exceptional Children (r,d,c; 5-21 yrs.), R.D. 9, Box 607, Greensburg 15601; (724) 837-8120 (95). Also conducts resocialization program (r,d,c; young adults).

Divine Providence Village (adults), 686 Old Marple Rd., Springfield 19064; (610) 328-7730. Admin., Sr. Esther Leroux.

Don Guanella Village: Don Guanella School (r,d,b; 6-21 yrs.) and Cardinal Krol Center (r; adults, postschool age), 1797 S. Sproul Rd., Springfield 19602; (610) 543-3380. Admin. Rev. Dennis Weber, S.C.

John Paul II Center (d,c; 3-21 yrs.), 1092 Welsh Rd., Shillington, PA 19607; (610) 777-0605; www.JohnPaulIICenter.org.

McGuire Memorial (r,d,c; 18 mos. to adult.), 2119 Mercer Rd., New Brighton 15066; (724) 843-3400; www.mcguirememorial.org.

Mercy Special Learning Center (d,c; 3-21 yrs. and early intervention), 830 S. Woodward St., Allentown 18103; (610) 797-8242.

Our Lady of Confidence Day School (d,c; 4½-21 yrs.), 10th and Lycoming Sts., Philadelphia 19140.

Queen of the Universe Day Center (d,c; 4½-16 yrs.), 2479 Trenton Rd., Levittown 19056; (215) 945-6090; www.qudaycenter.org.

St. Anthony School Programs (d,c; 5-21 yrs.), 2718 Custer Ave., Pittsburgh 15227; (412) 882-1333.

St. Joseph Center for Special Learning (d,c; 4-21 yrs.), 2075 W. Norwegian St., Pottsville 17901; (570) 622-4638; www.pottsville.com/stjosephctr.

St. Joseph's Center (r,d,c; birth-10 yrs.), 2010 Adams Ave., Scranton 18509; (570) 342-8379; www.stjosephcenter.org.

St. Katherine Day School (d,c; 4½-21 yrs.), 930 Bowman Ave., Wynnewood 19096; (610) 667-3958; www.stkatherinedayschool.org.

Tennessee: Madonna Learning Center, Inc., for Retarded Children (d,c; 5-16 yrs.), 7007 Poplar Ave., Germantown 38138.

Texas: Notre Dame of Dallas School (d,c; 3-21 yrs.), 2018 Allen St., Dallas 75204; (214) 720-3911.

Virginia: St. Coletta School (d,c; 5-22 yrs.), 207 S. Peyton St., Alexandria, 22314; (703) 683-3686. For developmentally disabled. Services include: occupational, physical and language therapy; vocational program with job search, placement, training and follow-up services.

St. Mary's Infant Home (r,c; birth to 14 yrs.), 317 Chapel St., Norfolk 23504; (757) 622-2208. For multiple handicapped.

Wisconsin: St Coletta of Wisconsin, W4955 Hwy 18, Jefferson 53549; (920) 674-4330; www.stcolettawi.org. Year-round special education programs for adolescents and adults; prevocational and vocational skills training; residential living alternatives. Young adult population. Employment opportunities for those who qualify.

St. Coletta Day School (c; 8-17 yrs.), 1740 N. 55th St., Milwaukee 53208; (414) 453-1850.

Orthopedically/Physically Challenged

Pennsylvania: St. Edmond's Home for Children (r,c; 1-21 yrs.)., 320 S. Roberts Rd., Rosemont 19010; (610) 525-8800.

Virginia: St. Joseph Villa Housing Corp. (adults), 8000 Brook Rd., Richmond 23227; (804) 553-3283.

Visually Challenged

Maine: Educational Services for Blind and Visually Impaired Children (Catholic Charities, Maine), 1066 Kenduskeag Ave., Bangor 04401. 66 Western Ave., Fairfield 04937. 15 Westminster St., Lewiston 04240. P.O. Box 378, Fairfield, ME 04937; (800) 660-5231. Itinerant teachers, instructional materials center.

New Jersey: St. Joseph's School for the Blind (r,d,c; 3-21 yrs.), 257 Baldwin Ave., Jersey City 07306; (201) 653-0578; www.sjsb.net.

New York: Lavelle School for the Blind (d,c; 3-21 yrs.), East 221st St. and Paulding Ave., Bronx 10469; (718) 882-1212. For visually impaired, multiple handicapped.

Pennsylvania: St. Lucy Day School (d,c; pre-K to 8th grade), 130 Hampden Rd., Upper Darby 19082; (610) 352-4550; www.stlucydayschool.org. For children with visual impairments.

HOUSES OF RETREAT AND RENEWAL

There is great variety in retreat and renewal programs, with orientations ranging from the traditional to teen encounters. Central to all of them are celebration of the liturgy and deepening of a person's commitment to faith and witness in life. Features of many of the forms are as follows.

Traditional Retreats: Centered around conferences and the direction of a retreat master; oriented to the personal needs of the retreatants; including such standard practices as participation in Mass, reception of the sacraments, private and group prayer, silence and meditation, discussions.

Team Retreat: Conducted by a team of several leaders or directors (priests, religious, lay persons) with division of subject matter and activities according to their special skills and the nature and needs of the group.

Closed Retreat: Involving withdrawal for a period of time — overnight, several days, a weekend — from everyday occupations and activities.

Open Retreat: Made without total disengagement from everyday involvements, on a part-time basis.

Private Retreat: By one person, on a kind of do-it-yourself basis with the one-to-one assistance of a director.

Special Groups: With formats and activities geared to particular groups; e.g., members of Alcoholics Anonymous, vocational groups and apostolic groups.

Marriage Encounters: Usually weekend periods of husband-wife reflection and dialogue; introduced into the U.S. from Spain in 1967.

Charismatic Renewal: Featuring elements of the movement of the same name; "Spirit-oriented," communitarian and flexible, with spontaneous and shared prayer, personal testimonies of faith and witness.

Christian Community: Characterized by strong community thrust.

Teens Encounter Christ (TEC), SEARCH: Formats adapted to the mentality and needs of youth, involving experience of Christian faith and commitment in a community setting.

Christian Maturity Seminars: Similar to teen encounters in basic concept but different to suit persons of greater maturity.

RENEW International: Spiritual renewal process involving the entire parish. Office, 1232 George St., Plainfield, NJ 07062; (908) 769-5400. Director, Msgr. Thomas A. Kleissler.

Cursillo: *See separate entry.*

Conference

Retreats International Inc.: National Office, Box 1067, Notre Dame, IN 46556; (574) 247-4443. An organization for promoting retreats in the U.S. was started in 1904 in New York. Its initial efforts and the gradual growth of the movement led to the formation in 1927 of the National Catholic Laymen's Retreat Conference, the forerunner of the men's division of Retreats International. The women's division developed from the National Laywomen's Retreat Movement that was founded in Chicago in 1936. The men's and women's divisions merged July 9, 1977. The services of the organization include an annual summer institute for retreat and pastoral ministry, regional conferences for retreat center leadership and area meetings of directors and key leadership in the retreat movement. The officers are: Episcopal advisor, Auxiliary Bishop Robert Morneau of Green Bay; Pres., Sr. Mary Elizabeth Imler, O.S.F.; Exec. Dir., Anne M. Luther.

Houses of Retreat and Renewal

Principal sources: Catholic Almanac *survey*; The Official Catholic Directory.

Abbreviation code: m, men; w, women; mc, married couples; y, youth. Houses and centers without code generally offer facilities to most groups. An asterisk after an abbreviation indicates that the facility is primarily for the group designated but that special groups are also accommodated. Houses furnish information concerning the types of programs they offer.

Alabama: Blessed Trinity Shrine Retreat and Cenacle, 107 Holy Trinity Rd., Holy Trinity 36856, (334) 855-4474; Visitation Sacred Heart Retreat House, 2300 Spring Hill Ave., Mobile 36607, (334) 473-2321.

Alaska: Holy Spirit Center, 10980 Hillside Dr., Anchorage 99507, (907) 346-2343, home.gci.net/~hsrh.

Arizona: Franciscan Renewal Center, 5802 E. Lincoln Dr., Scottsdale 85253, (480) 948-7460; Holy Trinity Monastery, P.O. Box 298, St. David 85630, Benedictine community, selfdirected/Spiritdirected monastic retreat, (520) 720-4642; Mount Claret Retreat Center, 4633 N. 54th St., Phoenix 85018, (602) 840-5066; Our Lady of Solitude House of Prayer, P.O. Box 1140, Black Canyon City 85324,

(623) 374-9204; Redemptorist Picture Rocks Retreat House, 7101 W. Picture Rocks Rd., Tucson 85743, (520) 744-3400, www.desertrenewal.org.

Arkansas: Brothers and Sisters of Charity, Little Portion Hermitage, 350 CR 248, Berryville, 72616-8505, (479) 253-7710, www.johnmichaeltalbot.com; Little Portion Retreat and Training Center, Rt. 4, Box 430, Eureka Springs 72632, (501) 253-7379; St. Scholastica Retreat Center, P.O. Box 3489, Ft. Smith 72913, (479) 783-1135, www. scholastica-fortsmith.org; Hesychia House of Prayer, 204 St. Scholastica Rd., New Blaine, Shoal Creek, 72851, (501) 938-7375.

California: Angela Center, 535 Angela Dr., Santa Rosa 95403, (707) 528-8578; Christ the King Retreat Center, 6520 Van Maren Lane, Citrus Heights 95621, (916) 725-4720, www.passionist. org; Claretian Retreat Center, 1119 Westchester Pl., Los Angeles 90019, (323) 737-8464; El Carmelo Retreat House, P.O. Box 446, Redlands 92373, (909) 792-1047, www.elcarmelo.org; Heart of Jesus Retreat Center, 2927 S. Greenville St., Santa Ana 92704, (714) 557-4538; Holy Spirit Retreat Center, 4316 Lanai Rd., Encino 91436, (818) 784-4515; Holy Transfiguration Monastery (m*), Monks of Mt. Tabor (Byzantine Ukrainian), 17001 Tomki Rd., P.O. Box 217, Redwood Valley 95470, (707) 485-8959; Jesuit Retreat House, 300 Manresa Way, Los Altos 94022, (650) 917-4000, www.elretiro.org; Madonna of Peace Renewal Center (y), P.O. Box 71, Copperopolis 95228, (209) 785-2157; Marian Retreat Center, 535 Sacramento St., Auburn 95603, (916) 887-2019; Mary and Joseph Retreat Center, 5300 Crest Rd., Rancho Palos Verdes 90275, (310) 377-4867, www.maryjoseph.org.

Marywood Retreat Center, 2811 E. Villa Real Dr., Orange 92863-1595, (714) 282-3000, www.rcbo.org; Mater Dolorosa Retreat Center, 700 N. Sunnyside Ave., Sierra Madre 91024, (626) 355-7188, www. passionist.org; Mercy Center, 2300 Adeline Dr., Burlingame 94010, (650) 340-7474, www.mercy-center.org; Mission San Luis Rey Retreat, 4050 Mission Ave., Oceanside, 92057-6402, (760) 757-3659, www.sanluisrey.org; Mount Alverno Retreat and Conference Center, 3910 Bret Harte Dr., Redwood City 94061, (650) 369-0798, www.moun-talverno.com; New Camaldoli Hermitage, Big Sur 93920, (831) 667-2456, www.contemplation. com; Our Lady of the Oaks Villa, P.O. Box 128, Applegate 95703, (530) 878-2776.

Poverello of Assisi Retreat House, 1519 Woodworth St., San Fernando 91340, (818) 365-1071; Presentation Education and Retreat Center, 19480 Bear Creek Rd., Los Gatos 95033, (408) 354-2346, www.prescenter.org; Prince of Peace Abbey, 650 Benet Hill Rd., Oceanside 92054, (760) 430-1305; Pro Sanctity Spirituality Center, 205 S. Pine St., Fullerton 92633 (for day use), www.caprosanctity.org; Sacred Heart Retreat House (w*), 920 E. Alhambra Rd., Alhambra 91801, (626) 289-1353; St. Andrew's Abbey Retreat House, P.O. Box 40, Valyermo 93563, (661) 944-2178, www.valyermo.com; St. Anthony Retreat, P.O. Box 249, Three Rivers 93271, (559) 561-4595, www.stanthonyretreat. org; St. Clare's Retreat, 2381 Laurel Glen Rd.,

Soquel 95073, (831) 423-8093, www.infoteam. com/nonprofit/stclaresretreat/index.html; St. Francis Retreat, P.O. Box 970, San Juan Bautista 95045, (831) 623-4234,www.stfrancis retreat.com; St. Francis Youth Center (y), 2400 E. Lake Ave., Watsonville 95076; St. Joseph's Salesian Youth Center, P.O. Box 1639, 8301 Arroyo Dr., Rosemead 91770, (626) 280-8622, www.stjoescenter.org; St. Mary's Seminary and Retreat House, 1964 Las Canoas Rd., Santa Barbara 93105, (805) 966-4829; San Damiano Retreat, P.O. Box 767, Danville 94526, (925) 837-9141, www.sandamiano.org.

San Miguel Retreat House, P.O. Box 69, San Miguel 93451, (805) 467-3256; Santa Sabina Center, 25 Magnolia Ave., San Rafael 94901, (415) 457-7727; Serra Retreat, 3401 S. Serra Rd., Box 127, Malibu 90265, (310) 456-6631, www.serraretreat. com; Starcross Community, 34500 Annapolis Rd., Annapolis 95412, (707) 886-1919, www.starcross. org; Villa Maria del Mar, Santa Cruz, 21918 E. Cliff Dr., Santa Cruz 95062, (831) 475-1236, www. villamariadelmar.org; Villa Maria – House of Prayer (w), 1252 N. Citrus Dr., La Habra 90631, (562) 691-5838.

Colorado: Benet Pines Retreat Center, 15880 Highway 83, Colorado Springs 80921, (719) 495-2574, www.geocities.com; Camp St. Malo Religious Retreat and Conference Center, 10758, Hwy. 7, Allenspark 80510, (303) 747-2892; Sacred Heart Retreat House, Box 185, Sedalia 80135, (303) 688-4198, www.gabrielmedia.org/shjrh; Spiritual Life Institute (individuals only), Nada Hermitage, P.O. Box 219, Crestone 81131, (719) 256-4778. www. spirituallifeinstitute.org.

Connecticut: St. Edmund's Retreat, P.O. Box 399, Mystic 06355, (860) 536-0565, www.sse.org/enders; Emmaus Spiritual Life Center, 24 Maple Ave., Uncasville 06382, (860) 848-3427; Holy Family Retreat, 303 Tunxis Rd., Farmington 06107, (860) 521-0440; Immaculata Retreat House, P.O. Box 55, Willimantic 06226, (860) 423-8484, www.immacu-lateretreat.org; Mercy Center at Madison, P.O. Box 191, 167 Neck Rd., Madison 06443, (203) 245-0401, www.mercybythesea.org; My Father's House, Box 22, 39 North Moodus Rd., Moodus 06469, (860) 873-1906, www.myfathershouse.com; Our Lady of Calvary Retreat (w*), 31 Colton St., Farmington 06032, (860) 677-8519, www.ourladyofcalvary.com; Trinita Retreat Center, 595 Town Hill Rd., Rt. 219, New Hartford 06057, (860) 379-4329; Villa Maria Guadalupe Retreat House, 159 Sky Meadow Dr., Stamford 06903, (203) 329-1492; Wisdom House Retreat Center, 229 E. Litchfield Rd., 06759, (860) 567-3163, www.wisdomhouse.org.

Delaware: St. Francis Renewal Center, 1901 Prior Rd., Wilmington 19809, (302) 798-1454.

District of Columbia: Washington Retreat House, 4000 Harewood Rd. N.E., Washington 20017, (202) 529-1111.

Florida: Cenacle Retreat House, 1400 S. Dixie Highway, Lantana 33462-5492, (561) 582-2534, www.cenaclesisters.org; Dominican Retreat House, Inc., 7275 S.W. 124th St., Miami 33156-5324, (305) 238-2711; Franciscan Center, 3010 Perry Ave., Tampa 33603, (813) 229-2695, www.slleganyfranciscans.org/franciscancenter.htm; John Paul II Retreat House, 720 N.E. 27th St., Miami 33137, (305) 576-2748, www.acu-adsum.org; Our Lady of Divine Providence, 702 S. Bayview Ave., Clearwater, 33759, (727) 797-7412, www.divineprovidence.org; Our Lady of Perpetual Help Retreat and Spirituality Center, 3989 S. Moon Dr., Venice 34292, (941) 486-0233, www.olph-retreat.org; Saint John Neumann Renewal Center, 685 Miccosukee Rd., Tallahassee 32308, (850) 224-2971; St. Leo Abbey Retreat Center, P.O. Box 2350, St. Leo 33574, (352) 588-2009.

Georgia: Ignatius House, 6700 Riverside Dr. N.W., Atlanta 30328, (404) 255-0503.

Idaho: Nazareth Retreat Center, 4450 N. Five Mile Rd., Boise 83713, (208) 375-2932.

Illinois: Bellarmine Jesuit Retreat House (mc), 420 W. County Line Rd, Barrington 60010, (847) 381-1261, www.bellarminehall.org; Bishop Lane Retreat House, 7708 E. McGregor Rd., Rockford 61102, (815) 965-5011; Cabrini Retreat Center, 9430 Golf Rd., Des Plaines 60016, (847) 297-6530; Carmelite Spiritual Center, 8433 Bailey Rd., Darien 60561, (630) 969-4141; Cenacle Retreat House, 513 Fullerton Parkway, Chicago 60614, (773) 528-6300; Cenacle Retreat House, P.O. Box 797, Warrenville 60555, (630) 393-1231, www.cenacle.org; King's House Retreat and Renewal Center, 700 N. 66th St., Belleville 62223-3949, (618) 397-0584; La Salle Manor, Christian Brothers Retreat House, 12480 Galena Rd., Plano 60545, (630) 552-3224, www.lasallemanor.org; St. Mary's Retreat House, P.O. Box 608, 14230 Main St., Lemont 60439, (630) 257-5102.

Indiana: Archabbey Guest House, St. Meinrad Archabbey, St. Meinrad 47577, (800) 581-6905, www.saintmeinrad.edu; Benedict Inn Retreat and Conference Center, 1402 Southern Ave., Beech Grove 46107, (317) 788-7581, www.benedictinn.org; Bethany Retreat House, 2202 Lituanica Ave., 46312, (219) 398-5047; Fatima Retreat House, 5353 E. 56th St., Indianapolis 46226-1486, (317) 545-7681, www.archindy.org; John XXIII Retreat Center, 407 W. McDonald St., Hartford City 47348, (765) 348-4008, www.netusa1.net/~john23rd; Kordes Retreat Center, 841 E. 14th St., Ferdinand 47532, (812) 367-1411, www.thedome.org/kordes; Lindenwood, PHJC Ministry Center, P.O. Box 1, Donaldson 46513, (574) 935-1780; Mount Saint Francis Retreat Center and Friary, 101 St. Anthony Dr., Mount Saint Francis 47146, (812) 923-8817, www.mountsaintfrancis.org; Sarto Retreat House, 4200 N. Kentucky Ave., Evansville 47724, (812) 424-5536.

Iowa: American Martyrs Retreat House, 2209 N. Union Rd., P.O. Box 605, Cedar Falls 50613-0605, (319) 266-3543, www.americanmartyrs.tripod.com; Emmanuel House of Prayer Country Retreat and Solitude Center, 4427 Kotts Rd. N.E., Iowa City 52240; New Melleray Guest House, 6632 Melleray Circle, Dubuque 52068, (319) 588-2319, www.new-melleray.org; Shalom Retreat Center, 1001 Davis Ave., Dubuque 52001, (319) 582-3592, members.aol.com/dbqshalom.

Kansas: Heartland Center for Spirituality, 3600 Broadway, Great Bend 67530, (316) 792-1232; Manna House of Prayer, 323 East 5th St., Box 675,

Concordia 66901, (785) 243-4428; Spiritual Life Center, 7100 E. 45th St., N. Wichita 67226, (316) 744-0167, www.slcwichita.org.

Kentucky: Bethany Spring, 115 Dee Head Rd., New Haven, 40051, (502) 549-8277; Flaget Center, 1935 Lewiston Dr., Louisville 40216, (502) 448-8581; Marydale Retreat Center, 945 Donaldson Hwy., Erlanger 41018, (606) 371-4224; Mt. St. Joseph Retreat Center, 8001 Cummings Rd., Maple Mount 42356-9999, (229) 229-0200, www.msjcenter.org; Our Lady of Gethsemani (m, w, private), The Guestmaster, Abbey of Gethsemani, Trappist, 40051; Passionist Nuns, 8564 Crisp Rd, Whitesville 42378, (270) 233-4571.

Louisiana: Abbey Christian Life Center, St. Joseph's Abbey, St. Benedict 70457, (504) 892-3473; Ave Maria Retreat House, 8089 Barataria Blvd., Crown Point, 70072, (504) 689-3837; Cenacle Retreat House (w*), 5500 St. Mary St., P.O. Box 8115, Metairie 70006, (504) 887-1420, www.cenaclesisters.org/metairie.htm; Jesuit Spirituality Center (m,w; directed), P.O. Box C, Grand Coteau 70541-1003, (337) 662-5251, www.jesuitspiritualitycenter.org; Lumen Christi Retreat Center, 100 Lumen Christi Lane, Hwy. 311, Schriever 70395, (504) 868-1523; Magnificat Center of the Holy Spirit, 23629 Faith Rd., Ponchatoula 70454, (504) 362-4356.

Manresa House of Retreats (m), P.O. Box 89, Convent 70723, (225) 562-3596; Maryhill Renewal Center, 600 Maryhill Rd., Pineville 71360, (318) 640-1378, www.diocesealex.org; Our Lady of the Oaks Retreat House, P.O. Box D, 214 Church St., Grand Coteau 70541, (318) 662-5410; Regina Coeli Retreat Center, 17225 Regina Coeli Rd., Covington 70433, (504) 892-4110; Sophie Barat House, 1719 Napoleon Ave., New Orleans 70115, (504) 899-6027.

Maine: Bay View Villa, 187 Bay View Rd., Saco 04072, (207) 286-8762; Marie Joseph Spiritual Center, 10 Evans Rd., Biddeford 04005, (207) 284-5671, www.mariejosephspiritual.org; Mother of the Good Shepherd Monastery by the Sea, 235 Pleasant Ave., Peaks Island 04108, (207) 766-2717; Notre Dame Retreat & Spiritual Center, P.O. Box 159, Alfred 04002, (207) 324-6160; St. Paul Retreat and Cursillo Center, 136 State St., Augusta 04330, (207) 622-6235.

Maryland: Bon Secours Spiritual Center, Marriottsville 21104, (410) 442-1320, www.bonsecours.org/bssc; Christian Brothers Spiritual Center (m,w,y), P.O. Box 29, 2535 Buckeyestown Pike, Adamstown 21710, (301) 874-5180; Loyola on the Potomac Retreat House, Faulkner 20632, (301) 870-3515, www.loyolaretreat.org; Msgr. Clare J. O'Dwyer Retreat House (y*), 15523 York Rd., P.O. Box 310, Sparks 21152, (410) 666-2400; Our Lady of Mattaponi Youth Retreat and Conference Center, 11000 Mattaponi Rd., Upper Marlboro 20772, (301) 952-9074; Seton Retreat Center, 333 S. Seton Ave., Emmitsburg 21727, (301) 447-6021.

Massachusetts: Boston Cenacle Society, 25 Avery St., Dedham 02026; Calvary Retreat Center, 59 South St., P.O. Box 219, Shrewsbury 01545, (508) 842-8821, www.calvaryretreat.org; Campion Renewal Center, 319 Concord Rd., Weston 02193, (781) 788-6810; Community of Teresian

Carmelites, 30 Chrome St., 01613, (508) 752-5734; Don Orione Center, P.O. Box 205, Old Groveland Rd., Bradford 01835, (508) 373-0461; Eastern Point Retreat House, Gonzaga Hall, 37 Niles Pond Rd., Gloucester 01930, (978) 283-0013; Espousal Center, 554 Lexington St., Waltham 02452, (781) 209-3120, www.espousal.org; Esther House of Spiritual Renewal, Sisters of St. Anne, 1015 Pleasant St., Worcester 01602-1338.

Franciscan Center — Retreat House, 459 River Rd., Andover 01810, (978) 851-3391, www.franrcent.org; Genesis Spiritual Life Center, 53 Mill St., Westfield 01085, (413) 562-3627; Glastonbury Abbey (Benedictine Monks), 16 Hull St., Hingham 02043, (701) 749-2155, www.glastonburyabbey.org; Holy Cross Fathers Retreat House, 490 Washington St., N. Easton 02356, (508) 238-2051; La Salette Retreat Center, 947 Park St., Attleboro 02703, (508) 222-8530, www.lasaletteretreatcenter.com; Marian Center, 1365 Northampton St., Holyoke 01040-1913, (413) 534-4502 (day and evening programs); Marist House, 518 Pleasant St., 01701, (508) 879-1620; Miramar Retreat Center, P.O. Box M, Duxbury, 02331-0614, (781) 585-2460, www. miramarretreat.org; Mt. Carmel Christian Life Center, Oblong Rd., Box 613, Williamstown 01267, (413) 458-3164.

Sacred Heart Retreat Center, Salesians of St. John Bosco, P.O. Box 567, Ipswich 01938; St. Benedict Abbey (Benedictine Monks), 252 Still River Rd., P.O. Box 67, Still River 01467, (978) 456-3221; St. Joseph Villa Retreat Center, Sisters of St. Joseph, 339 Jerusalem Rd., Cohasset 02025, (781) 383-6024; St. Joseph's Abbey Retreat House (m) (Trappist Monks), 167 North Spencer Rd., Spencer 01562, (508) 885-8710, www.spencerabbey.org; St. Stephen Priory Spiritual Life Center (Dominican), 20 Glen St., Box 370, Dover 02030, (508) 785-0124, www. ststephenpriory.org.

Michigan: Augustine Center Retreat House, 2798 U.S. 31 North, Box 84, Conway 49722, (231) 347-3657, www.dioceseofgaylord.org; Capuchin Retreat, 62460 Mt. Vernon, Box 396, Washington 48094, (248) 651-4826; Colombiere Conference and Retreat Center, 9075 Big Lake Rd., Clarkston 48346, (248) 620-2534, www.colombiere.com; Manresa Jesuit Retreat House, 1390 Quarton Rd., Bloomfield Hills 48304, (248) 644-4933; Marygrove Retreat Center, Garden 49835, (906) 644-2771; Queen of Angels Retreat, 3400 S. Washington Rd., P.O. Box 2026, Saginaw 48605, (517) 755-2149, www.rc.net/saginaw/retreat.

St. Francis Retreat Center, 703 E. Main St., De Witt 48820-9499, (517) 669-8321, www.stfrancis.ws; St. Lazare Retreat House, 18600 W. Spring Lake Rd., Spring Lake 49456, (616) 842-3370, stlazareretreat.net; St. Mary's Retreat House (w*), 775 W. Drahner Rd., Oxford 48371, (248) 628-3894, www. op.org/oxford; St. Paul of the Cross Retreat Center (m*), 23333 Schoolcraft, Detroit 48223, (313) 535-9563; Weber Retreat Center, 1257 Siena Hghts. Dr., Adrian 49221, (517) 266-4000.

Minnesota: Benedictine Center, St. Paul's Monastery, 2675 Larpenteur Ave. East, St. Paul 55106, (651) 777-7251, www.osb.org/spm; The Cenacle, 1221 Wayzata Blvd., Wayzata 55391;

Center for Spiritual Development, 211 Tenth St. S., P.O. Box 538, Bird Island 55310, (320) 365-3644, www.centerbi.com; Christ the King Retreat Center, 621 First Ave. S., Buffalo 55313, (763) 682-1394, www.kingshouse.com; Dunrovin Christian Brothers' Retreat Center, 15525 St. Croix Trail North, Marine on St. Croix 55047, (651) 433-2486, www.dunrovin.org.

Franciscan Retreats, Conventual Franciscan Friars, 16385 St. Francis Lane, Prior Lake 55372, (952) 447-2182, www.franciscanretreats.net; Holy Spirit Retreat House, 3864 420th Ave., Janesville, 56048, (507) 234-5712; Jesuit Retreat House (m), 8243 DeMontreville Trail North, Lake Elmo 55042, (651) 777-1311; Maryhill (m,w*), 1988 Summit Ave., St. Paul 55105, (651) 696-2970, www.sdhm. net; Villa Maria Center, Villa Maria Center, 29847 County 2 Blvd., Frontenac 55026, (651) 345-4582.

Missouri: Assumption Abbey, Rte. 5, Box 1056, Ava 65608, (417) 683-5110, www.assumptionabbey.org; The Cenacle, 3393 McKelvey Rd., Apt. 211, Bridgeton, 63044-2544, (314) 387-2211; Cordis House, 648 S. Assisi Way, Republic 65738, (417) 732-6684; Il Ritiro The Little Retreat, P.O. Box 38, Eime Rd., Dittmer 63023, (636) 274-0554; La Salle Institute, 2101 Rue de la Salle, Wildwood 63038, (636) 938-5374; Maria Fonte Solitude (private; individual hermitages), P.O. Box 322, High Ridge 63049, (314) 677-3235.

Marianist Retreat and Conference Center, P.O. Box 718, Eureka 63025-0718, (636) 938-5390; Mercy Center, 2039 N. Geyer Rd., St. Louis 63131, (314) 909-4629; Our Lady of Assumption Abbey (m,w), Trappists, Rt. 5, Box 1056, Ava 65608-9142, (417) 683-5110; Pallottine Renewal Center, 15270 Old Halls Ferry Rd., Florissant 63034, (314) 837-7100, members.aol.com/prcrenewal/home.html; Society of Our Mother of Peace (private, individual hermitages), 6150 Antire Rd., High Ridge 63049, (636) 677-3235; White House Retreat, 3601 Lindell Blvd., St. Louis 63108, (314) 846-2575, www.whretreat.org; Windridge Solitude, 1932 W. Linda Lane, Lonedell 63060; (636) 629-4449.

Montana: Sacred Heart Retreat Center, 26 Wyoming Ave., P.O. Box 153, Billings 59103, (406) 252-0322; Ursuline Retreat Centre, 2300 Central Ave., Great Falls 59401, (406) 452-8585.

Nebraska: Our Lady of Good Counsel retreat House, R.R. 1, Box 110, 7303 N. 112th St., Waverly 68462, (402) 786-2705.

New Hampshire: Epiphany Monastery, 96 Scobie Rd., P.O. Box 60, New Boston 03070; La Salette Shrine (private and small groups), 410 NH, Route 4A, P.O. Box 420, Enfield 03748, (603) 632-7087.

New Jersey: Bethany Ridge, P.O. Box 241, Little York 08834, (908) 995-9758; Bethlehem Hermitage, 82 Pleasant Hill Rd., Chester 07930-2135, (908) 879-7059; Cenacle Retreat House, 411 River Rd., Highland Park 08904, (732) 249-8100, www.cenacle.sisters.org; Emmaus House, 101 Center St., Perth Amboy 08861, (732) 442-7688; Father Judge Apostolic Center (young adults), 1292 Long Hill Rd., Stirling 07980; Felician Retreat House, 35 Windemere Ave., Mt. Arlington 07856, (973) 398-9806; John Paul II Retreat Center, 414 S. 8th St., Vineland 08360; Loyola House of Retreats, 161

James St., Morristown 07960, (973) 539-0740, www.
loyola.org.
Marianist Family Retreat Center (families*), 417
Yale Ave., Box 488, Cape May Point 08212-0488;
Maris Stella (Retreat and Vacation Center), 7201
Long Beach Blvd., P.O. Box 3135, Harvey Cedars
08008, (609) 474-1182; Mount Paul Retreat Center,
243 Mt. Paul Rd., Oak Ridge 07438, (973) 697-
6341; Franciscan Spiritual Center, 474 Sloatsburg
Rd., Ringwood 07456-1978, (973) 962-9778; Queen
of Peace Retreat House, St. Paul's Abbey, P.O. Box
7, Newton 07860, (973) 383-2470, www.newtonsb.
org; Sacred Heart Renewal Center, P.O. Box 68,
Belvidere 07823, (908) 475-4694; Sacred Heart
Retreat Center (y*, m,w), 20 Old Swartswood
Rd., Newton 07860, (973) 383-2620; St. Joseph
by the Sea Retreat House, 400 Rte. 35 N., South
Mantoloking 08738-1309, (732) 892-8494, www.
sjbsea.org.
St. Pius X Spiritual Life Center, P.O. Box 216,
Blackwood 08012, (856) 227-1436; San Alfonso
Retreat House, P.O. Box 3098, 755 Ocean Ave.,
Long Beach 07740, (732) 222-2731, www.sanalfons-
oretreats.org; Sanctuary of Mary, Pilgrimage Place,
Branchville 07826, (973) 875-7625; Stella Maris
Retreat House, 981 Ocean Ave., Elberon 07740,
(732) 229-0602, www.stellamarisretreatcenter.org;
Villa Pauline Retreat House, 350 Bernardsville
Rd., Mendham 07945, (973) 543-9058; Vincentian
Renewal Center, 75 Mapleton Rd., P.O. Box 757,
Plainsboro 08536, (609) 520-9626; Vocationist
Fathers Retreat, 90 Brooklake Rd., Florham Park
07932, (973) 966-6262, www.vocationist.org; Xavier
Retreat and Conference Center, P.O. Box 211,
Convent Station 07961, (973) 290-5100, www.
xaviercenter.org.
New Mexico: Holy Cross Retreat, Conventual
Franciscan Friars, 600 Holy Cross Rd., Mesilla Park
88047, (505) 524-3688, www.zianet.com/franciscan;
Immaculate Heart of Mary Retreat and Conference
Center, Mt. Carmel Rd., Santa Fe 87501, (505)
988-1975; Madonna Retreat Center, Inc., 4040 St.
Joseph Pl., N.W., 87120, (505) 831-8196; Pecos
Benedictine Monastery, Pecos 87552, (505) 757-
6600, www.pecosabbey.org; Spiritual Renewal
Center, 6400 Coors Rd., NW, Albuquerque 87120;
(505) 890-4110; www.spiritualretreats.com; Sacred
Heart Retreat, P.O. Box 1989, Gallup 87301.
New York: Bethany Spirituality Center, 202
County Road 105, Box 1003, Highland Mills 10930,
(845) 460-3061, www.bthanysirituualitycnter.org.
Bethlehem Retreat House, Abbey of the Genesee,
Piffard 14533, (585) 243-2220, www.abbeyretreats.
org; Bishop Molloy Retreat House, 8645 Edgerton
Blvd., Jamaica 11432, (718) 739-1229, www.bish-
opmolloy.org; National Kateri Tekakwitha Shrine,
P.O. Box 627, Fonda 12068, (518) 853-3646, www.
katerishrine.com; Cardinal Spellman Retreat
House, Passionist Community, 5801 Palisade Ave.,
Bronx (Riverdale) 10471, (718) 549-6500, www.pas-
sionists.org; Cenacle Center for Spiritual Renewal,
310 Cenacle Rd., Ronkonkoma 11779-2203, (631)
588-8366 www.cenaclesisters.org.
Cenacle Retreat House, State Rd., P.O. Box 467,
Bedford Village 10506, (914) 234-3344; Christ the
King Retreat and Conference Center, 500 Brookford

Rd., Syracuse 13224, (315) 446-2680; Cormaria
Retreat House, Sag Harbor, L.I. 11963, (631) 725-
4206; Dominican Retreat and Conference Center,
1945 Union St., Niskayuma, (518) 393-4169, www.
dslcny.org; Marian Shrine and Don Bosco Retreat
Center, 174 Filors Lane, Stony Point, 10980-2645,
(845) 947-2200, www.marianshrine.org; Graymoor
Spiritual Life Center, Graymoor, Route 9, P.O. Box
300, Garrison 10524, (845) 424-2111, www.gray-
moorcenter.org; Jesuit Retreat House, Auriesville,
(518) 853-3033; Monastery of the Precious Blood
(w), Ft. Hamilton Parkway and 54th St., Brooklyn
11219 (single day retreats); Mount Alvernia Retreat
Center, Box 858, Wappingers Falls 12590, (845)
297-5706, www.mtalvernia.org.
Mount Irenaeus Franciscan Mountain Retreat,
Holy Peace Friary, P.O. Box 100, West Clarksville,
NY 14786, (716) 973-2470; Mount Manresa Retreat
House, 239 Fingerboard Rd., Staten Island 10305,
(718) 727-3844; Mt. St. Alphonsus Redemptorist
Retreat Ministry, P.O. Box 219, Esopus 12429,
(845) 384-8000, www.msaretreat.org; Notre
Dame Retreat House, Box 342, 5151 Foster Rd.,
Canandaigua 14424, (585) 394-5700, www.notre-
dameretreathouse.org; Our Lady of Hope Center,
434 River Rd., Newburgh 12550, (914) 568-0780;
Regina Maria Retreat House, 77 Brinkerhoff
St., Plattsburgh 12901-2701, (518) 561-3421; St.
Andrew's House, 257 St. Andrew's Rd., Walden
12586, (845) 778-5941; St. Columban Center,
Diocese of Buffalo, 6892 Lake Shore Rd., P.O. Box
816, Derby 14047, (716) 947-4708, www.stcolum-
bacenter.org.
St. Francis Retreat, 1 Pryer Manor Rd.,
Larchmont 10538, (914) 235-6839; St. Francis
Center for Spirituality, 500 Todt Hill Rd., Staten
Island, NY 10304, (718) 981-3131, www.st-francis-
center-for-spirituality.org; St. Gabriel's Spiritual
Center for Youth (y, mc), 64 Burns Rd., P.O. Box
3015, Shelter Island Heights 11965, (631) 749-3154
(fax); St. Ignatius Retreat House, 251 Searingtown
Rd., Manhasset 11030, (516) 621-8300, www.inis-
fada.net; St. Josaphat's Retreat House, Basilian
Monastery, 1 East Beach Dr., Glen Cove 11542,
(516) 671-8980; St. Joseph Center (Spanish Center),
275 W. 230th St., Bronx 10463, (718) 796-4340;
St. Mary's Villa, 150 Sisters Servants Lane, P.O.
Box 9, Sloatsburg 10974-0009, (914) 753-5100;
St. Paul Center, 2135 Crescent St., Astoria 11105,
(718) 932-0752; St. Ursula Retreat Center, 186
Middle Rd., Blue Point 11715, (631) 363-2422,
www.ursulinesofbluepoint.org; Stella Maris Retreat
Center, 130 E. Genesee St., Skaneateles 13152, (315)
685-6836; Tagaste Monastery, 220 Lafayette Ave.,
Suffern 10901; Trinity Retreat, 1 Pryer Manor Rd.,
Larchmont 10538, (914) 235-6839.
North Carolina: Avila Retreat Center, 711 Mason
Rd., Durham 27712, (919) 477-1285; Madonna
House, 424 Rose Ln., Raleigh 27610.
North Dakota: Presentation Prayer Center, 1101
32nd Ave. S., Fargo 58103, (701) 237-4857; Queen
of Peace Retreat, 1310 Broadway, Fargo 58102,
(701) 293-9286.
Ohio: Bergamo Center for Lifelong Learning,
4400 Shakertown Rd., Dayton 45430, (937)
426-2363, www.bergamocenter.org; Friarhurst

Retreat House, 8136 Wooster Pike, Cincinnati 45227, (513) 561-2270; Jesuit Retreat House, 5629 State Rd., Cleveland 44134-2292, (440) 884-9300, www.jrh-cleveland.org; Jesuit Spiritual Center at Milford, 5361 S. Milford Rd., Milford 45150, (513) 248-3500, www.milfordspiritual-center.org; Loyola of the Lakes, 700 Killinger Rd., Clinton 44216-9653, (330) 896-2315, www.loyolaofthelakes.com; Maria Stein Spiritual Center, 2365 St. Johns Rd., Maria Stein 45860, (419) 925-7625, www.spiritualcenter.net; Our Lady of Consolation Retreat House, 321 Clay St., Carey 43316, (419) 396-7970, www.olcshrine.com; Our Lady of the Pines, 1250 Tiffin St., Fremont 43420, (419) 332-6522, www.pinesretreat.org.

Sacred Heart Retreat and Renewal Center, 3128 Logan Ave., P.O. Box 6074, Youngstown 44501, (330) 759-9539; St. Joseph Christian Life Center, 18485 Lake Shore Blvd., Cleveland 44119, (216) 531-7370, www.enterthecenter.org; St. Francis Spirituality Center, 200 St. Francis Ave., Tiffin 44883, (419) 443-1485, www.stfrancisspirituality-center.org; St. Therese Retreat Center, 5277 E. Broad St., Columbus, OH 43213, (614) 866-1611, www.cathedral-bookshop.com.

Oklahoma: St. Gregory's Abbey, 1900 W. MacArthut, Shawnee 74804, (405) 878-5491, www.sgc.edu.

Oregon: The Jesuit Spirituality Center, 424 S.W. Mill St., Portland 97201, (503) 242-1973; Mount Angel Abbey Retreat House, 1 Abbey Dr., St. Benedict 97373, (503) 845-3027, www.mtangel.edu; Our Lady of Peace Retreat, 3600 S. W. 170th Ave., Beaverton 97006, (503) 649-7127, www.geocities.com/ourladyofpeaceretreat; St. Rita Retreat Center, P.O. Box 310, Gold Hill 97525, (541) 855-1333; Shalom Prayer Center, Benedictine Sisters, 840 S. Main St., Mt. Angel 97362-9527, (503) 845-6773, www.benedict-srs.org; St. Palmetto Lodge, 56630 North Bank Rd., McKenzie Bridge 97413, (541) 822-3572; Trappist Abbey Guesthouse (m,w), 9200 N.E. Abbey Rd., Lafayette 97127, (503) 852-0107; www.trappistabbey.org.

Pennsylvania: Avila Retreat Center, 61 E. High St., Union City 16438, (814) 438-7020; Dominican Retreat House, 750 Ashbourne Rd., Elkins Park 19027, (215) 782-8520; Ecclesia Center, 9101 Ridge Rd., Erie 16417, (814) 774-9691; Fatima Renewal Center, 1000 Seminary Rd., Dalton 18414, (570) 563-8500; Fatima House Retreat Center, P.O. Box 116, Bedminster 18910, (215) 579-2947.

Franciscan Spirit and Life Center, 3605 McRoberts Rd., Pittsburgh 15234, (412) 881-9207; Gilmary Diocesan Center, 601 Flaugherty Run Rd., Coraopolis 15108-3899, (412) 264-8400, www.diopitt.org.

Jesuit Center, 501 N. Church Rd., Wernersville 19565, (610) 670-3676, www.jesuitcenter.org; Kearns Spirituality Center, 9000 Babcock Blvd., Allison Park 15101, (412) 366-1124, www.divineprovidenceweb.org; Mariawald Renewal Center, P.O. Box 97 (1094 Welsh Rd.), Reading 19607, (610) 777-0135, www.hometown.aol.com/mariawald/index.html; Martina Spiritual

Renewal Center, 5244 Clarwin Ave., Pittsburgh 15229, (412) 931-9766; Mt. Saint Macrina House of Prayer, 510 W. Main St., Box 878, Uniontown 15401, (724) 438-7149, www.sistersofstbasil.org; St. Emma Guest House and St. Emma Retreat House, 1001 Harvey Ave., Greensburg 15601-1494, (724) 834-3060, www.stemm.org; St. Francis Center for Renewal, Monocacy Manor, 395 Bridle Path Rd., Bethlehem 18017, (610) 867-8890, www.catholic-church.org/stfranciscfn; St. Francis Retreat House, 3918 Chipman Rd., Easton 18045, (610) 258-3053; St. Gabriel's Retreat House, 631 Griffin Pond Rd., Clarks Summit 18411-8899, (570) 586-4957, www.intiques.com/cpnuns.

St. Joseph's in the Hills, 315 S. Warren Ave., Malvern 19355-0315, (610) 644-0400, www.malvernretreat.com; St. Paul of the Cross Retreat Center, 148 Monastery Ave., Pittsburgh 15203, (412) 381-7676, www.stpaulsretreatcenter-pittsburgh.org; Saint Raphaela Center, 616 Coopertown Rd., Haverford 19041, (610) 642-5715; St. Vincent Summer Retreat Program (m,w,mc; summers only), Latrobe 15650, (724) 805-2139; Urban House of Prayer, 1919 Cambridge St., Philadelphia 19130, (215) 236-8328; Villa of Our Lady Retreat Center (w, mc, y), HCR No. 1, Box 41, Mt. Pocono 18344, (570) 839-7217.

Rhode Island: Bethany Renewal Center, 397 Fruit Hill Ave., N. Providence 02911, (401) 353-5860; Father Marot CYO Center (y), P.O. Box 518, Woonsocket 02895, (401) 762-3252, www.frmaryotcyo.org; Our Lady of Peace Spiritual Life Center, 333 Ocean Rd., Box 507, Narragansett 02882, (401) 884-7676; St. Paul Priory Guest House, 61 Narrangansett Ave., Newport 02840, (401) 847-2423.

South Carolina: Sea of Peace House of Prayer, 59 Palmetto Pointe Rd., Edisto Island 29438, (843) 869-0513; Springbank Retreat for Eco-Spirituality and the Arts, 1345 Springbank Rd., Kingstree 29556, (843) 382-9777, www.springbankspirit.org.

South Dakota: St. Martin's Community Center, 2110C St. Martin's Dr., Rapid City 57702, (605) 343-8011; Sioux Spiritual Center, 20100 Center Rd., Howes, SD 57748, (605) 985-5906.

Tennessee: Carmelites of Mary Immaculate Center of Spirituality, 610 Bluff Rd., Liberty 37095, (615) 536-5177.

Texas: Benedictine Retreat Center, HC#2, Box 6300, Sandia 78383; Bishop DeFalco Retreat Center, 2100 N. Spring, Amarillo 79107-7274, (806) 383-1811, www.bdrc.org; Bishop Rene H. Gracida Retreat Center, 3036 Saratoga Blvd., Corpus Christi 78415, (512) 851-1443; Catholic Renewal Center of North Texas, 4503 Bridge St., Ft. Worth 76103, (817) 429-2920; Cenacle Retreat House, 420 N. Kirkwood, Houston 77079, (281) 497-3131, www.cenacleretreathouse.org; Christian Renewal Center (Centro de Renovacion Cristiana), Oblates of Mary Immaculate, P.O. Box 699, Dickinson 77539, (281) 337-1312, www.retreatcenterrc.org.

Holy Family Retreat Center, 9920 N. Major Dr.,

Beaumont 77713-7618, (409) 899-5617, www.dioceseofbmt.org/holyfamily/index/html; Holy Name Retreat Center, 430 Bunker Hill Rd., Houston 77024, (713) 464-0211; Holy Spirit Retreat and Conference Center, 501 Century Dr. S., Laredo 78040, (956) 726-4352, www.stjean.com/laredo/hsrc/holy.htm; Lebh Shomea House of Prayer, La Parra Ranch, P.O. Box 9, Sarita 78385; Montserrat Retreat House, P.O. Box 1390, Lake Dallas 75065, (940) 321-6020, www.montserratretreat.org; Moye Center, 600 London, Castroville 78009, (830) 931-2233, www.moyecenter.org; Oblate Renewal Center, 5700 Blanco Rd., San Antonio 78216, (210) 349-4173.

Omega Retreat Center, 216 W. Highland Dr., Boerne 78006, (830) 816-8471; Our Lady of Mercy Retreat Center, P.O. Box 744, 19th & Division, Slaton 79364, (806) 828-6428; Prayer Town Emmanuel Retreat House, P.O. Box 17, Channing 79018, (806) 534-2312; San Juan Retreat House (St. Eugene de Mazenod Retreat Center), P.O. Box 747, San Juan 78589, (956) 787-0033.

Utah: Abbey of Our Lady of the Holy Trinity (m), 1250 S 9500 E, Huntsville 84317, (801) 745-3784, www.xmission.com/~hta; Our Lady of the Mountains, 1794 Lake Rd., Ogden 84401, (801) 392-9231.

Virginia: Benedictine Retreat and Conf. Center, Mary Mother of the Church Abbey, 12829 River Rd., 23233, (804) 784-3508; Dominican Retreat, 7103 Old Dominion Dr., McLean 22101-2799, (703) 356-4243, www.dominicanretreat.org; The Dwelling Place, 601 Holly Grove Ln., Richmond 23235, (804) 323-3360; Holy Family Retreat House, P.O. 3151, 1414 N. Mallory St., Hampton 23663, (757) 722-3997; Madonna House, 828 Campbell Ave., S.W., Roanoke 24016, (540) 343-8464.

Retreat House, Holy Cross Abbey, 901 Cool Spring Lane, Berryville 22611, (540) 955-4383; Shalom House, P.O. Box 196, Montpelier 23192, (804) 883-6149; Tabor Retreat Center, 2125 Langhorne Rd., Lynchburg 24501, (804) 846-6475; The Well, 18047 Quiet Way, Smithfield 23430, (757) 255-2366, www.thewellretreatcenter.org.

Washington: Immaculate Heart Retreat Center, 6910 S. Ben Burr Rd., Spokane 99223, (509) 448-1224, www.ihrc.net; House of the Lord Retreat Center, P.O. Box 1034, Tum Tum 99034, (509) 276-2219; KAIROS House of Prayer, 1714 W. Stearns Rd., Spokane 99208, (509) 466-2187; Palisades Retreat House, 4700 SW Dash Point Rd., #100, Federal Way 98023, (206) 748-7991, www.seattlearch.org/formationandeducation; St. Peter Retreat Center, 15880 Summitview Rd., Cowiche 98923, (509) 678-4935.

West Virginia: Bishop Hodges Pastoral Center, Rt. 1, Box 9D, Huttonsville, 26273, (304) 335-2165; Good Counsel Friary, 493 Tyrone Rd., Morgantown 26508, (304) 594-1714; John XXIII Pastoral Center, 100 Hodges Rd., Charleston 25314, (304) 342-0507; Paul VI Pastoral Center, 667 Stone and Shannon Rd., Wheeling 26003, (304) 277-3300; Priest Field Pastoral Center, Rt. 51, Box 133, Kearneysville 25430, (304) 725-1435; West Virginia Institute for Spirituality, 1414 Virginia St. E., Charleston, WV 25301, (304) 345-0926, www.wvis.ws.

Wisconsin: Archdiocesan Retreat Center, 3501 S. Lake Dr., P.O. Box 07912, Milwaukee 53207, (414) 769-3491, www.archmil.org; The Dwelling Place, 528 N. 31st St., Milwaukee 53208, (414) 933-1100; Franciscan Spirituality Center, 920 Market St., La Crosse 54601, (608) 791-5295, www.fspa.org; Holy Name Retreat House, Chambers Island, mailing address: 1825 Riverside Drive, P.O. Box 23825, Green Bay 54305, (920) 437-7531; Jesuit Retreat House, 4800 Fahrnwald Rd., Oshkosh 54902, (920) 231-9060, www.jesuitretreathouse.org; Marywood Franciscan Spirituality Center (FSPA), 3560 Hwy. 51 N., Arbor Vitae 54568, (715) 385-3750, www.fspa.org.

Monte Alverno Retreat Center, 1000 N. Ballard Rd., Appleton 54911, (920) 733-8526; Mount Carmel Hermitage, 897 U.S. Hwy. 8, 54001, (715) 268-9313; Mount Tabor, 522 2 St., Menasha 54952, (920) 722-8918; Norbertine Center for Spirituality, St. Norbert Abbey, 1016 N. Broadway, De Pere 54115, (920) 337-4315, www.norbertines.org; Redemptorist Retreat Center, 1800 N. Timber Trail Lane, Oconomowoc 53066-4897, (262) 567-6900, www.redemptoristretreat.org; St. Anthony Retreat Center, 300 E. 4th St., Marathon 54448, (715) 443-2236, www.sarcenter.com.

Saint Benedict Center (monastery and ecumenical retreat and conference center), P.O. Box 5070, Madison 53705-0070, (608) 836-1631, www.sbcenter.org; St. Benedict's Retreat Center, 12605 224th Avenue, Benet Lake, WI 53102-0333, (262) 396-4311, www.benetlake.org; St. Clare Center for Spirituality, 7381 Church St., Custer 54423, (715) 592-4099; St. Joseph's Retreat Center, 3035 O'Brien Rd., Bailey's Harbor 54202, (920) 839-2391, www.stjosephretreat.org; St. Vincent Pallotti Center, N6409 Bowers Rd., Elkhorn 53121, (262) 723-2108, (877) 220-3306, www.elknet.net/vpallelk; Schoenstatt Center, W. 284 N. 698 Cherry Lane, Waukesha 53188, (262) 522-4300.

Catholic Education

LEGAL STATUS OF CATHOLIC EDUCATION

The right of private schools to exist and operate in the United States is recognized in law. It was confirmed by the U.S. Supreme Court in 1925 when the tribunal ruled (Pierce v. Society of Sisters, see **Church-State Decisions of the Supreme Court**, p. 366) that an Oregon state law requiring all children to attend public schools was unconstitutional.

Private schools are obliged to comply with the education laws in force in the various states regarding such matters as required basic curricula, periods of attendance, and standards for proper accreditation.

The special curricula and standards of private schools are determined by the schools themselves. Thus, in Catholic schools, the curricula include not only the subject matter required by state educational laws but also other fields of study, principally, education in the Catholic faith.

The Supreme Court has ruled that the First Amendment to the U.S. Constitution, in accordance with the No Establishment of Religion Clause of the First Amendment, prohibits direct federal and state aid from public funds to church-affiliated schools. (See several cases in **Church-State Decisions of the Supreme Court.**)

Public Aid

This prohibition does not extend to all child-benefit and public-purpose programs of aid to students of non-public elementary and secondary schools.

Statutes authorizing such programs have been ruled constitutional on the grounds that they:
• have a "secular legislative purpose"
• neither inhibit nor advance religion as a "principal or primary effect"
• do not foster "excessive government entanglement with religion."

Aid programs considered constitutional have provided bus transportation, textbook loans, school lunches and health services, and "secular, neutral or non-ideological services, facilities and materials provided in common to all school children," public and non-public.

The first major aid to education program in U.S. history containing provisions benefiting non-public school students was enacted by the 89th Congress and signed into law by President Lyndon B. Johnson on Apr. 11, 1965. The Elementary and Secondary Education Act was designed to avoid the separation of Church and state impasse which had blocked all earlier aid proposals pertaining to non-public, and especially church-affiliated, schools. The objective of the program, under public control, is to serve the public purpose by aiding disadvantaged pupils in non-public as well as public schools.

With respect to college and university education in church-affiliated institutions, the Supreme Court has upheld the constitutionality of statutes providing student loans and, under the Federal Higher Education Facilities Act of 1963, construction loans and grants for secular-purpose facilities.

Catholic schools are exempt from real estate taxation in all of the states. Since Jan. 1, 1959, nonprofit parochial and private schools have also been exempt from several federal excise taxes.

NCEA

The National Catholic Educational Association, founded in 1904, is a voluntary organization of educational institutions and individuals concerned with Catholic education in the U.S. Its objectives are to promote and encourage the principles and ideals of Christian education and formation by suitable service and other activities. The NCEA serves approximately 200,000 Catholic educators at all levels from pre-K through university. Numerous service publications are issued to members. Archbishop Wilton Gregory of Atlanta, chairman of the Board of Directors; Dr. Karen Ristau, president. Address: 1077 30th St. N.W., Washington, DC 20007; (202) 337-6232; www.ncea.org.

Association of Catholic Colleges and Universities

The ACCU, founded in 1899, is an association intended to promote and strengthen the missions and character of Catholic higher education in the United States and to serve as its collective voice. It became an independently incorporated organization separate from the NCEA in 2000. ACCU's journal, *Current Issues in Catholic Higher Education* is published semi-annually, and its electronic newsletter, Update, quarterly. ACCU serves approximately 220 colleges/universities, and the association gathers at its annual meeting fpcused on special Catholic higher education topics. Dr. Michael Galligan-Stierle, president. Address: 1 Dupont Circle, NW, Suite 650, Washington, DC 20036; (202) 457-0650; www.accunet.org.

EDUCATIONAL VOUCHERS

Although 41 educational voucher programs funded by private philanthropy were operating in the United States by 1998-99, discussion of vouchers as a political, legal, and educational issue primarily concerns publicly-funded plans allowing parents to send their children to the school of their choice. At present there are three educational voucher programs of this kind — in Milwaukee, Cleveland, and the state of Florida.

The Vouchers Debate

Proponents of vouchers argue that they are not merely consistent with parental rights but an appropriate, even necessary, practical means of realizing them. In particular, it is said, they enable low-income parents to exercise a choice about schools. Another pro-vouchers argument is that they create an incentive for self-improvement by public schools that is lacking when they enjoy a near monopoly.

Arguments against vouchers are that they take funds away from public schools and encourage highly motivated parents and competent students to abandon failing public institutions in favor of private ones. Using vouchers at church-related schools also is said to violate the First Amendment ban on an establishment of religion. The chief opponents of educational vouchers are teacher unions — the National Education Association, the American Federation of Teachers, and their affiliates — and other public school groups, church-state separationists, and some mainline African-American organizations. Phi Delta Kappa/Gallup polls in 1998 and 1999 found 51% of the respondents, including 60% of public school parents in the latter year, were in favor of total or partial government-paid tuition for children in private or church-related schools, although support declined when vouchers were specified.

Recent Developments

On June 27, 2002, the U.S. Supreme Court upheld the Cleveland voucher program in a 5-4 ruling, saying it is "entirely neutral with respect to religion." The majority opinion, written by Chief Justice William Rehnquist, said the program is therefore "a program of true private choice" and does not violate the Establishment Clause of the First Amendment.

Cleveland established the voucher program in 1995 to help address problems in what was considered one of the worst public school systems in the country. The state Legislature created the system after a federal judge declared the schools were being mismanaged and put them under the authority of the state superintendent of public instruction. The program provides for vouchers of up to $4,000 annually for children in low-income families to attend other public or private schools or pay for tutors. The vast majority of participants use their vouchers to pay tuition at church-affiliated schools, nearly all of them Catholic.

The case came to the Supreme Court after the 6th U.S. Circuit Court of Appeals ruled in 2000 that the program was unconstitutional because the vouchers are primarily used at religious schools. The U.S. Conference of Catholic Bishops in a friend-of-the-court brief argued that the program should not be considered unconstitutional because most voucher recipients choose to attend church schools.

Opponents of the program who filed briefs included the National Association for the Advancement of Colored People, an association of Ohio school boards and several groups of public schools from around the country. Opponents call vouchers a fraud meant to siphon tax money from struggling public schools. The Ohio school boards argued that the state has ignored its responsibility to provide a good education and is merely shifting the burden to religious schools.

Central to the court's reasoning was that children in the Cleveland program have a theoretical choice of attending religious schools, secular private academies, suburban public schools, or charter schools run by parents or others outside the education establishment. The fact that only a handful of secular schools and no suburban public schools have signed up to accept voucher students is not the fault of the program itself, Ohio authorities say. "We believe that the program challenged here is a program of true private choice," Chief Justice William H. Rehnquist wrote for himself and Justices Sandra Day O'Connor, Antonin Scalia, Anthony M. Kennedy and Clarence Thomas.

The Cleveland program goes too far toward state-sponsored religion, the dissenting justices said. It does not treat religion neutrally, as Rehnquist contended, wrote Justice David H. Souter. The majority is also wrong about the question of whether parents have a true choice among schools, Souter wrote for himself and Justices John Paul Stevens, Ruth Bader Ginsburg and Stephen Breyer. "There is, in any case, no way to interpret the 96.6 percent of current voucher money going to religious schools as reflecting a free and genuine choice by the families that apply for vouchers," Souter wrote.

President George W. Bush was a staunch advocate of school vouchers, and emphasized the issue in his campaign for the White House. Congress shelved that effort, but Bush resurrected the idea, proposing in his 2003 budget to give families up to $2,500 per child in tax credits if they choose a private school rather than a failing neighborhood public school. Following the court's hearing on arguments in February 2002, Education Secretary Rod Paige said he would continue advocating on behalf of both improved public schools and school choice. Republican lawmakers in Congress agreed with Bush's stance. The Bush administration sided with Ohio, arguing that the program is constitutional because parents control where the money goes. In Cleveland, the public money flows to parents, not directly to the church-run schools, the program's supporters noted.

On April 4, 2011, the U.S. Supreme Court upheld an Arizona law that provides tax vouchers for private-school tuition. By a 5-4 decision, the high court rejected arguments that the voucher program violates the First Amendment by providing state support to religious schools. Recipients receive a $500 voucher for use in paying tuition at religious schools. Reportedly, most use it for religious high schools.

EX CORDE ECCLESIAE

On Nov. 17, 1999, the Catholic Bishops of the United States approved *The Application of Ex corde Ecclesiae for the United States,* implementing the Apostolic Constitution *Ex corde Ecclesiae.* This action received the recognitio from the Congregation for Bishops on May 3, 2000. Bp. Joseph Fiorenza, President of the National Conference of Catholic Bishops, decreed that the application would have the force of particular law for the United States on May 3, 2001. Guidelines concerning the Academic Mandatum in Catholic Universities were subsequently issued, based on Canon 812. The following is the first guidelines.

Pope John Paul II's Constitution *Ex corde Ecclesiae* of 1990 fostered a productive dialogue between the Bishops of the United States and the leaders of our Catholic colleges and universities. It is anticipated that this recently approved *Application of Ex corde Ecclesiae for the United States* would further that dialogue and build a community of trust between bishops and theologians. Both bishops and theologians are engaged in a necessary though complementary service to the Church that requires ongoing and mutually respectful conversation.

Article 4, 4, e, iv of the Application states that "a detailed procedure will be developed outlining the process of requesting and granting (or withdrawing) the mandatum." These guidelines are intended to explain and serve as a resource for the conferral of the mandatum. Only those guidelines herein which repeat a norm of the Application have the force of particular law. They were approved for distribution to the members of NCCB by the Conference's general membership.

Nature of the *mandatum*.
• The mandatum is fundamentally an acknowledgment by Church authority that a Catholic professor of a theological discipline is a teacher within the full communion of the Catholic Church (Application: Article 4,4,e,i).
• The mandatum, therefore, recognizes the professor's commitment and responsibility to teach authentic Catholic doctrine and to refrain from putting forth as Catholic teaching anything contrary to the Church's magisterium (cf. Application: Article 4,4,e, iii).
• The mandatum should not be construed as an appointment, authorization, delegation or approbation of one's

teaching by Church authorities. Those who have received a mandatum teach in their own name in virtue of their baptism and their academic and professional competence, not in the name of the bishop or of the Church's magisterium (Application: Article 4,4,e,ii).

Cardinal Newman Society
The Cardinal Newman Society is a national organization established in 1993 and dedicated to the renewal of Catholic identity in Catholic higher education in the United States. CNS has more than 18,000 members nationwide who share a common concern for the future of Catholic higher education and urge fidelity to the Magisterium. The society seeks to: promote discussion and understanding of the message of the Catholic Church concerning the nature and value of Catholic higher education; assist college leaders, educators, students, and alumni in their efforts to preserve the religious identity of Catholic institutions of higher learning; and advocate the faithful implementation of *Ex Corde Ecclesiae* by facilitating an active dialogue among members of the Catholic university community. **J. Laurence McCarty,** Chairman of the Board; **Patrick J. Reilly,** president. Address: 10562 Associates Court, Manassas, VA 20109; (703) 367-0333; www.cardinalnewmansociety.org.

SUMMARY OF SCHOOL STATISTICS

Status and figures (as of Jan. 1, 2013) reported by The Official Catholic Directory.

Colleges and Universities: 232 (U.S., 226; outlying areas, 6).

College and University Students: 818,331 (U.S., 794,854; outlying areas, 23,477).

High Schools: 1,314 (721 diocesan and parochial; 593 private). U.S., 1,212 (670 diocesan and parochial; 542 private). Outlying areas, 102 (51 diocesan and parochial; 51 private).

High School Students: 612,616 (319,164 diocesan and parochial; 293,452 private). U.S., 594,754 (310,376 diocesan and parochial; 284,378 private). Outlying areas, 17,862 (8,788 diocesan and parochial; 9,074 private).

Public High School Students Receiving Religious Instruction: 635,142 (U.S., 624,973; outlying areas, 10,169).

Elementary Schools: 5,672 (5,291 diocesan and parochial; 381 private). U.S., 5,531 (5,214 diocesan and parochial; 317 private). Outlying areas, 141 (77 diocesan and parochial; 64 private).

Elementary School Students: 1,440,232 (1,347,016 diocesan and parochial; 93,216 private) U.S., 1,400,698 (1,327,283 diocesan and parochial; 73,415 private). Outlying areas, 39,534 (19,733 diocesan and parochial; 19,801 private).

Public Elementary School Students Receiving Religious Instruction: 2,776,777 (U.S., 2,745,390; outlying areas, 31,387).

Non-Residential Schools for Handicapped: 53 (U.S., 52, Outlying areas, 1). Students: 6,047 (U.S., 5,967, Outlying areas, 80).

Teachers: 168,363, U.S., 163,532 (lay persons, 160,745; sisters, 4,011; priests, 1,180; brothers, 659; scholastics, 210). Outlying areas, 4,831 (lay persons, 4,047; sisters, 410; priests, 39; brothers, 28; scholastics, 307).

Seminaries: 164 (71 diocesan; 93 religious). U.S.: 151 (66 diocesan; 85 religious). Outlying areas: 13 (5 diocesan; 8 religious).

Seminarians: 5,153 (3,441 diocesan; 1,712 religious). U.S., 5,110 (3,416 diocesan; 1,694 religious). Outlying areas: 43 (25 diocesan; 18 religious).

CATHOLIC SCHOOLS AND STUDENTS IN THE UNITED STATES

(*Source:* Official Catholic Directory, *2013; figures as of Jan. 1, 2013; Archdioceses are indicated by an asterisk.*)

State Diocese	Universities/ Colleges	Students	High Schools	Students	Elem. Schools	Students
Alabama	1	1,867	8	3,182	37	9,126
*Mobile	1	1,867	3	1,583	19	4,584
Birmingham	–	–	5	1,599	18	4,542
Alaska	–	–	3	294	6	738
*Anchorage	–	–	2	106	4	394
Fairbanks	–	–	1	188	1	251
Juneau	–	–	–	–	1	93
Arizona	1	36	12	6,837	57	14,618
Phoenix	1	36	6	4,808	38	9,202
Tucson	–	–	6	2,029	19	5,416
Arkansas						
Little Rock	–	–	6	1,675	27	3,010
California	12	49,313	116	69,505	553	143,029
*Los Angeles	4	14,370	50	27,249	217	51,375
*San Francisco	3	12,017	14	7,838	60	17,291
Fresno	–	–	2	1,180	20	4,524
Monterey	–	–	5	1,607	14	3,331
Oakland	2	5,449	9	5,666	45	11,759
Orange	–	–	7	6,482	34	12,702
Sacramento	–	–	6	4,045	39	9,921
San Bernardino	–	–	3	1,309	26	6,294
San Diego	2	8,677	6	4,147	47	11,267
San Jose	1	8,800	6	6,713	29	9,366
Santa Rosa	–	–	6	1,934	11	2,289
Stockton	–	–	2	1,335	11	2,910
Colorado	2	14,971	8	4,217	47	11,073
*Denver	2	14,971	7	3,887	38	9,128
Colorado Springs	–	–	1	330	5	1,096
Pueblo	–	–	–	–	4	849
Connecticut	6	16,783	21	10,367	101	21,458
*Hartford	2	4,384	9	4,589	54	11,004
Bridgeport	3	12,162	7	3,537	34	8,144
Norwich	1	237	6	2,241	13	2,310
Delaware, Wilmington	–	–	8	3,987	22	7,052
District of Columbia, *Wash., DC	3	26,858	20	10,238	78	17,688
Florida	5	27,847	37	24,013	170	58,856
*Miami	3	11,407	13	12,511	53	21,559
Orlando	–	–	5	2,708	31	9,870
Palm Beach	–	–	3	1,376	15	4,772
Pensacola-Tallahassee	–	–	2	758	7	1,869
St. Augustine	–	–	4	2,189	27	8,265
St. Petersburg	1	15,564	6	2,951	27	9,660
Venice	1	876	3	1,520	11	2,861
Georgia	–	–	12	5,269	34	11,794
*Atlanta	–	–	7	4,187	18	7,483
Savannah	–	–	5	1,422	14	3,665
Hawaii, Honolulu	1	2,850	7	3,141	23	5,874
Idaho, Boise	–	–	1	690	13	2,329
Illinois	11	68,633	70	39,674	408	109,095
*Chicago	5	49,322	40	24,014	211	60,813
Belleville	–	–	3	1,086	28	4,039
Joliet	3	16,463	7	5,550	48	16,181
Peoria	1	390	6	2,828	39	8,932
Rockford	–	–	8	4,067	40	10,163
Springfield	2	2,458	6	2,129	41	8,878
Indiana	11	31,493	27	12,832	158	42,712
*Indianapolis	2	3,824	12	6,099	59	17,346
Evansville	–	–	4	1,438	24	5,907
Ft.Wayne-S. Bend	5	17,010	4	3,185	41	10,701
Gary	1	1,275	4	1,332	17	5,203

State Diocese	Universities/ Colleges	Students	High Schools	Students	Elem. Schools	Students
Indiana, cont.						
Lafayette	3	13,430	2	1,094	18	4,089
Iowa	**6**	**10,281**	**22**	**6,570**	**90**	**22,144**
*Dubuque	3	4,616	7	2,353	46	9,292
Davenport	1	3,671	5	974	13	3,465
Des Moines	1	844	2	1,589	15	4,824
Sioux City	1	1,150	8	1,654	16	4,563
Kansas	**4**	**8,070**	**16**	**6,951**	**93**	**22,474**
*Kansas City	3	4,962	7	3,555	41	11,840
Dodge City	–	–	–	–	7	908
Salina	–	–	5	801	11	1,650
Wichita	1	3,108	4	2,595	34	8,076
Kentucky	**5**	**9,431**	**23**	**11,047**	**95**	**24,643**
*Louisville	3	6,759	9	6,155	38	12,130
Covington	1	1,832	9	3,257	29	6,969
Lexington	–	–	2	892	14	2,816
Owensboro	1	840	3	743	14	2,728
Louisiana	**4**	**9,381**	**50**	**25,201**	**143**	**55,541**
*New Orleans	3	7,624	23	13,072	61	25,009
Alexandria	–	–	3	955	7	1,388
Baton Rouge	1	1,757	8	4,156	23	11,011
Houma-Thib.	–	–	3	1,905	10	3,748
Lafayette	–	–	10	3,813	32	11,192
Lake Charles	–	–	1	585	6	1,949
Shreveport	–	–	2	715	4	1,244
Maine, Portland	**1**	**3,375**	**3**	**868**	**11**	**2,192**
Maryland,*Baltimore	**4**	**11,158**	**20**	**10,651**	**48**	**16,467**
Massachusetts	**11**	**35,310**	**47**	**22,368**	**138**	**37,524**
*Boston	6	22,289	30	15,723	80	24,847
Fall River	1	2,620	5	2,848	21	4,471
Springfield	1	1,538	3	739	14	3,535
Worcester	3	8,863	9	3,058	22	4,671
Michigan	**5**	**18,308**	**43**	**15,852**	**191**	**38,980**
*Detroit	3	13,337	24	10,416	66	21,185
Gaylord	–	–	4	495	16	1,882
Grand Rapids	1	2,281	4	1,695	27	1,954
Kalamazoo	–	–	3	628	21	2,434
Lansing	1	2,690	5	2,019	35	7,473
Marquette	–	–	–	–	9	1,335
Saginaw	–	–	3	599	17	2,717
Minnesota	**6**	**24,860**	**22**	**11,761**	**165**	**35,724**
*St.Paul and Minn.	2	15,391	12	9,211	80	23,045
Crookston	–	–	1	131	8	1,152
Duluth	1	4,144	–	–	12	1,587
New Ulm	–	–	3	358	15	1,692
St. Cloud	2	4,053	2	965	27	4,237
Winona	1	1,272	4	1,096	23	4,011
Mississippi	**2**	**24**	**9**	**2,658**	**24**	**5,975**
Biloxi	–	–	5	1,477	10	2,729
Jackson	2	24	4	1,181	14	3,246
Missouri	**4**	**21,321**	**42**	**18,106**	**200**	**46,771**
*St.Louis	2	16,605	28	12,612	113	29,497
Jefferson City	–	–	3	1,004	37	6,094
Kansas City-St. Joseph	2	4,716	8	4,508	27	7,588
Springfield-Cape Girar.	–	–	3	982	23	3,592
Montana	**2**	**2,577**	**5**	**885**	**16**	**2,866**
Great Falls-Billings	1	1,075	3	582	12	2,039
Helena	1	1,502	2	303	4	827
Nebraska	**2**	**8,773**	**27**	**7,808**	**87**	**20,152**
*Omaha	2	8,773	17	5,598	54	13,807
Grand Island	–	–	4	493	6	1,059
Lincoln	–	–	6	1,717	27	5,286

State Diocese	Universities/ Colleges	Students	High Schools	Students	Elem. Schools	Students
Nevada	–	–	2	1,924	11	3,774
Las Vegas	–	–	1	1,318	7	2,729
Reno	–	–	1	606	4	1,045
New Hampshire, Manchester	4	4,469	5	2,304	23	4,311
New Jersey	7	22,901	63	32,319	210	54,090
*Newark	4	18,199	30	13,336	74	16,613
Camden	–	–	10	5,492	32	7,394
Metuchen	–	–	5	2,934	28	7,883
Paterson	2	2,147	7	3,642	37	8,677
Trenton	1	2,555	11	6,915	39	13,523
New Mexico	1	387	6	1,571	29	4,992
*Santa Fe	1	387	2	1,398	14	3,254
Gallup	–	–	2	164	12	1,178
Las Cruces	–	–	2	9	3	560
New York	26	104,609	116	65,612	479	126,680
*New York	9	44,412	50	24,930	195	50,045
Albany	4	10,000	7	1,852	21	4,723
Brooklyn	3	30,755	19	14,458	100	31,138
Buffalo	7	17,902	15	5,207	52	11,254
Ogdensburg	–	–	2	318	12	1,871
Rochester	–	–	5	2,996	22	4,191
Rockville Centre	1	3,037	10	12,155	47	17,797
Syracuse	1	3,533	6	2,294	18	2,862
North Carolina	1	1,710	6	3,470	45	13,394
Charlotte	1	1,710	3	1,997	16	5,751
Raleigh	–	–	3	1,473	29	7,643
North Dakota	2	3,195	4	954	22	3,302
Bismarck	1	2,895	3	638	10	1,724
Fargo	1	300	1	316	12	1,578
Ohio	13	40,655	78	38,860	339	93,940
*Cincinnati	4	20,303	23	13,281	93	29,432
Cleveland	3	7,224	21	12,873	102	33,271
Columbus	2	4,023	11	4,663	42	11,580
Steubenville	1	2,587	3	480	10	1,647
Toledo	2	3,568	14	5,489	63	12,610
Youngstown	1	2,950	6	2,074	29	5,400
Oklahoma	1	734	4	2,455	32	6,994
*Oklahoma City	1	734	2	1,086	20	3,921
Tulsa	–	–	2	1,369	12	3,073
Oregon	2	5,707	10	5,639	45	9,543
*Portland	2	5,707	10	5,639	40	9,015
Baker	–	–	–	–	5	528
Pennsylvania	26	98,551	77	39,500	421	102,894
*Philadelphia	11	46,559	34	22,652	181	54,031
Allentown	2	7,142	7	3,453	40	8,799
Altoona-Johnstown	2	4,042	4	1,022	20	3,407
Erie	2	8,306	7	2,281	31	5,001
Greensburg	2	3,860	2	644	17	2,534
Harrisburg	–	–	7	3,272	36	8,034
Pittsburgh	3	13,630	11	3,931	83	16,561
Scranton	4	15,012	5	2,245	13	4,500
Rhode Island, Providence	2	7,346	8	5,071	34	8,264
South Carolina, Charleston	–	–	4	1,802	28	5,260
South Dakota	2	1,909	5	1,531	24	5,090
Rapid City	–	–	2	445	3	881
Sioux Falls	2	1,909	3	1,086	21	4,209
Tennessee	2	2,428	12	5,548	50	10,310
Knoxville	–	–	2	1,092	8	2,118
Memphis	1	1,598	7	2,644	24	3,714
Nashville	1	830	3	1,812	18	4,478
Texas	9	26,828	54	20,722	220	58,506
*Galveston Houston	1	3,711	9	4,762	50	13,833
*San Antonio	5	15,847	11	3,850	33	9,850
Amarillo	–	–	1	102	4	646

State Diocese	Universities/ Colleges	Students	High Schools	Students	Elem. Schools	Students
Texas, cont.						
Austin	1	5,285	6	1,585	17	3,834
Beaumont	–	–	1	423	5	1,107
Brownsville	–	–	3	916	11	3,108
Corpus Christi	–	–	2	666	15	2,701
Dallas	1	1,951	7	4,743	30	9,935
El Paso	–	–	3	1,164	10	2,857
Fort Worth	1	34	4	1,310	17	4,365
Laredo	–	–	1	350	6	1,795
Lubbock	–	–	1	53	2	381
San Angelo	–	–	–	–	3	773
Tyler	–	–	1	276	5	780
Victoria	–	–	3	522	12	2,431
Utah, Salt Lake City	–	–	**3**	**1,787**	**13**	**3,772**
Vermont, Burlington	**2**	**2,800**	**4**	**452**	**11**	**1,648**
Virginia	**5**	**5,438**	**14**	**7,004**	**65**	**17,732**
Arlington	5	5,438	6	4,374	40	10,743
Richmond	–	–	8	2,630	25	6,989
Washington	**3**	**17,121**	**15**	**7,473**	**83**	**21,682**
*Seattle	2	9,284	11	6,150	62	16,548
Spokane	1	7,837	3	1,151	14	3,253
Yakima	–	–	1	172	5	1,881
West Virginia, Wheeling Chas.	**1**	**1,579**	**7**	**1,394**	**27**	**4,409**
Wisconsin	**9**	**32,975**	**29**	**10,651**	**278**	**50,279**
*Milwaukee	5	23,910	13	6,200	102	25,978
Green Bay	2	3,407	6	2,217	54	8,184
La Crosse	1	3,000	7	1,565	63	7,138
Madison	1	2,658	3	669	44	6,578
Superior	–	–	–	–	15	2,401
Wyoming, Cheyenne	**–**	**–**	**–**	**–**	**7**	**931**
EASTERN CHURCHES	**1**	**982**	**3**	**910**	**14**	**1,734**
*Philadelphia	1	982	1	312	3	426
St. Nicholas (Chicago)	–	–	–	–	2	335
Stamford	–	–	1	212	2	198
St. Josaphat (Parma)	–	–	–	–	–	–
*Pittsburgh	–	–	–	–	–	–
Parma	–	–	–	–	1	165
Passaic	–	–	–	–	–	–
Holy Protection	–	–	–	–	1	15
St. Maron (Maronites)	–	–	–	–	–	–
Our Lady of Deliverance (Syriacs)	–	–	–	–	–	–
Our Lady of Lebanon (Maronites)	–	–	–	–	1	39
Newton (Melkites)	–	–	–	–	–	–
St. George Martyr (Romanians)	–	–	–	–	–	–
St. Peter the Apostle (Chaldeans)	–	–	–	–	–	–
St. Thomas Apostle of Detroit (Chaldeans)	–	–	–	–	–	–
St. Thomas (Syro-Malabars)	–	–	–	–	–	–
Armenians (Ap. Ex.)	–	–	1	384	4	542
SCHOOLS AND STUDENTS IN OUTLYING AREAS						
American Samoa	–	–	1	264	2	372
Caroline Islands	–	–	4	795	4	1,221
Guam	–	–	4	1,181	7	3,032
Marshall Islands	–	–	2	162	3	559
Marianas	–	–	1	87	3	170
Puerto Rico	6	23,477	90	14,871	119	33,792
Virgin Islands	–	–	2	502	3	388
TOTAL 2013	**232**	**818,331**	**1,314**	**612,616**	**5,672**	**1,440,232**
TOTAL 2012	233	812,098	1,326	623,613	5,764	1,489,511
TOTAL 2003	237	749,512	1,376	686,651	7,142	1,971,394

CATHOLIC UNIVERSITIES AND COLLEGES IN THE UNITED STATES

(*Sources*: Catholic Almanac *survey*; The Official Catholic Directory.)

Listed below are institutions of higher learning established under Catholic auspices. Some of them are now independent.

Information includes: name of each institution; indication of male (m), female (w), coeducational (c) student body; name of founding group or group with which the institution is affiliated; year of foundation; total number of students in parentheses.

Albertus Magnus College (c): 700 Prospect St., New Haven, CT 06511; (203) 773-8550; www.albertus.edu. Dominican Sisters; 1925; independent (2,065).

Alvernia College (c): 400 Saint Bernardine St., Reading, PA 19607; (610) 796-8200; www.alvernia. edu. Bernardine Sisters; 1958 (2,457).

Alverno College (w): 3400 S. 43th St., P.O. Box 343922, Milwaukee, WI 53234; (414) 382-6000; www.alverno.edu. School Sisters of St. Francis; 1887; independent (2,000).

Anna Maria College (c): 50 Sunset Lane, Paxton, MA 01612; (508) 849-3300; www.annamaria.edu. Sisters of St. Anne;1946; independent (1,244).

Aquinas College (c): 1607 Robinson Rd. S.E., Grand Rapids, MI 49506; (616) 459-8281. Sisters of St. Dominic; 1922; independent (2,571).

Aquinas College (c): 4210 Harding Rd., Nashville, TN 37205; (615) 297-7545; www.aquinas-tn.edu. Dominican Sisters; 1961 (506).

Aquinas Institute of Theology (c): 3642 Lindell Boulevard, St. Louis, MO 63108; (314) 977-3869; www.op.org/aquinas. Dominicans, 1961; graduate theology; offers distance learning program in pastoral studies and specializations in preaching (200).

Assumption College (c): 500 Salisbury St., Worcester, MA 01615-0005; (508) 767-7000; www.assumption.edu. Assumptionist Religious; 1904 (2,766).

Augustine Institute, The (c): 3001 S. Federal Blvd. Box 1126 Denver CO, 80236 Phone: (303) 937-4420 FAX: (303) 468-293; www.augustineinstitute.org; 2005. (264). Offers graduate programs leading to the M.A., with specializations in biblical theology, sacred Scripture, and evangelization and catechesis.

Ave Maria School of Law (c): 3475 Plymouth Rd., Ann Arbor, MI 48105; (734) 930-4408.

Ave Maria University (c): 5050 Ave Maria Blvd. Ave Maria, fl 34142-9505; 877-283-8648; www.avemaria.edu

Avila University (c): 11901 Wornall Rd., Kansas City, MO 64145-1698; (816) 942-8400; www.avila.edu. Sisters of St. Joseph of Carondelet; 1916 (2,658).

Barry University (c): 11300 N.E. 2nd Ave., Miami Shores, FL 33161; (305) 899-3000; www.barry.edu. Dominican Sisters (Adrian, MI); 1940 (8,691).

Bellarmine College (c): 2001 Newburg Rd., Louisville, KY 40205; (502) 452-8211; www.bellarmine.edu. Louisville archdiocese; independent (2,323).

Belmont Abbey College (c): 100 Belmont-Mt. Holly Rd., Belmont, NC 28012; (704) 825-6700; www.belmontabbeycollege.edu. Benedictine Fathers; 1876 (883).

Benedictine College (c): 1020 N. Second St., Atchison, KS 66002; (913) 367-5340; www.benedictine.edu. Benedictines; 1859; independent (1,375).

Benedictine University (formerly Illinois Benedictine College) (c): 5700 College Rd., Lisle, IL 60532-0900; (630) 829-600 0; www.ben.edu. Benedictine Monks of St. Procopius Abbey; 1887 (2,809).

Boston College (University status) (c): Chestnut Hill, MA 02167; (617) 552-8000; www.bc.edu. Jesuit Fathers; 1863 (14,297).

Brescia University (c): 717 Frederica St., Owensboro, KY 42301; (270) 685-3131; www.brescia.edu. Ursuline Sisters; 1950 (820).

Briar Cliff College (c): 3303 Rebecca St., Sioux City, IA 51104; (712) 279-5405; www.briarcliff.edu. Sisters of St. Francis of the Holy Family; 1930 (994).

Cabrini College (c): 610 King of Prussia Rd., Radnor, PA 19087; (610) 902-8100; www.cabrini.edu. Missionary Srs. of Sacred Heart; 1957; private (2,669).

Caldwell College (c): 9 Ryerson Ave., Caldwell, NJ 07006; (973) 618-3000; www.caldwell.edu. Dominican Sisters; 1939 (2,270).

Calumet College of St. Joseph (c): 2400 New York Ave., Whiting, IN 46394; (219) 473-7770; www.ccsj. edu. Society of the Precious Blood, 1951 (1,141).

Canisius College (c): 2001 Main St., Buffalo, NY 14208; (716) 883-7000; www.canisius.edu. Jesuit Fathers; 1870; independent (4,995).

Cardinal Stritch University (c): 6801 N. Yates Rd., Milwaukee, WI 53217; (414) 410-4000; www.stritch. edu. Sisters of St. Francis of Assisi; 1937 (5,855).

Carlow College (w): 3333 5th Ave., Pittsburgh, PA 15213; (412) 578-6059; www.carlow.edu. Sisters of Mercy; 1929 (2,199).

Carroll College (c): 1601 N. Benton Ave., Helena, MT 59625; (406) 447-4300. Diocesan; 1909 (1,400).

Catholic Distance University (c): 120 East Colonial Highway, Hamilton, VA 20158-9012; www.cdu. edu. Offers External Degree programs, including Masters degrees in Religious Studies (7,000).

Catholic Theological Union (c): 5401 South Cornell Ave., Chicago, IL 60615; (773) 324-8000; www.ctu.edu (348).

Catholic University of America, The (c): Michigan Ave. & Fourth St., NE, Washington, DC 20064; (202) 319-5000; www.cua.edu. Hierarchy of the United States; 1887. Pontifical University (5,777).

Chaminade University of Honolulu (c): 3140 Waialae Ave., Honolulu, HI 96816; (808) 735-4711; www.chaminade.edu. Marianists; 1955 (2,788).

Chestnut Hill College (w): 9601 Germantown Ave., Philadelphia, PA 19118; (215) 248-7000; www.chc.edu. Sisters of St. Joseph; 1924 (1,645).

Christendom College (c): 134 Christendom Dr., Front Royal, VA 22630; (540) 636-2900. Independent, 1977 (477).

Christian Brothers University (c): 650 E. Parkway S., Memphis, TN 38104; (901) 321-3000. Brothers of the Christian Schools; 1871 (2,027).

Clarke College (c): 1550 Clarke Dr., Dubuque, IA 52001; (563) 588-6300; www.clarke.edu. Sisters of Charity, BVM; 1843; independent (1,126).

Creighton University (c): 2500 California Plaza, Omaha, NE 68178; (402) 280-2700; www.creighton. edu. Jesuit Fathers; 1878; independent (6,297).

Dallas, University of (c): 1845 E. Northgate, Irving, TX 75062; (972) 721-5000. Dallas diocese; 1956; independent (3,518).

Dayton, University of (c): 300 College Park, Dayton, OH 45469-1660; (937) 229-1000; www.udayton.edu. Marianists; 1850 (10,248).

DePaul University (c): One E. Jackson Blvd., Chicago, IL 60604; (312) 362-8000; www.depaul.edu. Vincentians; 1898 (23,174).

De Sales University (c): 2755 Station Ave., Center Valley, PA 18034; (610) 282-1100; www.desales.edu. Oblates of St. Francis de Sales; 1965 (1,339).

Detroit Mercy, University of (c): 4001 W. McNichols Rd., Detroit, MI, 48221; 8200 W. Outer Dr., Detroit MI 48219; (313) 993-1000. Society of Jesus and Sisters of Mercy; 1877; independent (5,843).

Dominican College (c): 470 Western Hwy., Orangeburg, NY 10962; (845) 359-7800; www.dc.edu. Dominican Sisters; 1952; independent (1,700).

Dominican University of California (c): 50 Acacia Ave., San Rafael, CA 94901-2298; (415) 457-4440; www.dominican.edu. Dominican Sisters; 1890; independent (1,578).

Dominican University (formerly Rosary College) (c): 7900 W. Division St., River Forest, IL 60305; (708) 366-2490; www.dom.edu. Sinsinawa Dominican Sisters; 1901 (2,533).

Duquesne University (c): 600 Forbes Ave., Pittsburgh, PA 15282; (412) 396-6000; www.duq.edu. Congregation of the Holy Ghost; 1878 (9,600).

D'Youville College (c): 320 Porter Ave., Buffalo, NY 14201; (716) 881-3200; www.dyc.edu. Grey Nuns of the Sacred Heart; 1908; independent (2,453).

Edgewood College (c): 1000 Edgewood College Dr., Madison, WI 53711; (608) 663-4861. Sinsinawa Dominican Sisters; 1927 (2,258).

Emmanuel College (w): 400 The Fenway, Boston, MA 02115; (617) 735-9715; www.emmanuel.edu. Sisters of Notre Dame de Namur; 1919; independent (1,549).

Fairfield University (c): 1073 North Benson Rd., Fairfield, CT 06430; (203) 254-4000; www.fairfield.edu. Jesuits; 1942 (6,001).

Felician College (c): 262 S. Main St., Lodi, NJ 07644; (201) 559-6000; www.felician.edu. Felician Sisters; 1942; independent (1,400).

Fontbonne University (c): 6800 Wydown Blvd., St. Louis, MO 63105; (314) 862-3456; www.fontbonne.edu. Sisters of St. Joseph of Carondelet; 1917; independent (2,344).

Fordham University (c): Fordham Rd. and Third Ave., New York, NY 10458; (718) 817-3040. Society of Jesus (Jesuits); 1841; independent (13,800).

Franciscan University of Steubenville (c): 1235 University Blvd., Steubenville, OH 43952; (740) 283-3771; www.franuniv.edu. Franciscan TOR Friars; 1946 (2,208). Also offers distance learning programs.

Gannon University (c): 109 University Square, Erie, PA 16541-0001; (814) 871-7000; www.gannon.edu. Diocese of Erie; 1933 (3,404).

Georgetown University (c): 37th and O Sts. N.W., Washington, DC 20057; (202) 687-0100; www.georgetown.edu. Jesuit Fathers; 1789 (12,688).

Georgian Court College (w/c): 900 Lakewood Ave., Lakewood, NJ 08701; (732) 364-2200; www.georgian.edu. Sisters of Mercy; 1908 (3,561).

Gonzaga University (c): E. 502 Boone Ave., Spokane, WA 99258; (509) 328-4220. Jesuit Fathers; 1887 (4,515).

Graduate School of Theology (c): 5890 Birch Ct., Oakland, CA 94618; (510) 652-1651; www.satgtu.org. Affiliate of the Graduate Theological Union.

Great Falls, University of (c): 1301 20th St. S., Great Falls, MT 59405; (406) 761-8210; www.ugf.edu. Sisters of Providence; 1932; independent (825).

Gwynedd-Mercy College (c): Gwynedd Valley, PA 19437; (215) 646-7300; www.gmc.edu. Sisters of Mercy; 1948; independent (2,198).

Hilbert College (c): 5200 S. Park Ave., Hamburg, NY 14075; (716) 649-7900; www.hilbert.edu. Franciscan Sisters of St. Joseph; 1957; independent (970).

Holy Cross, College of the (c): Worcester, MA 01610; (508) 793-2011; www.holycross.edu. Jesuits; 1843 (2,811).

Holy Family College (c): Grant and Frankford Aves., Philadelphia, PA 19114 and One Campus Dr., Newtown, PA 18940; (215) 637-7700; www.hfc.edu. Sisters of Holy Family of Nazareth; 1954; independent (2,559).

Holy Names College (c): 3500 Mountain Blvd., Oakland, CA 94619; (510) 436-1000; www.hnc.edu. Sisters of the Holy Names of Jesus and Mary; 1868; independent (947).

Immaculata College (w): Immaculata, PA 19345; (610) 647-4400; www.immaculata.edu. Sisters, Servants of the Immaculate Heart of Mary; 1920 (3,062).

Incarnate Word, University of the (c): 4301 Broadway, San Antonio, TX 78209; (210) 829-6000; www.uiw.edu. Sisters of Charity of the Incarnate Word; 1881 (4,264).

Iona College (c): 715 North Ave., New Rochelle, NY 10801; (914) 633-2000; www.iona.edu. Congregation of Christian Brothers; 1940; independent (4,897).

John Carroll University (c): 20700 N. Park Blvd., Cleveland, OH 44118; (216) 397-1886; www.jcu.edu. Jesuits; 1886 (4,294).

John Paul the Great Catholic University (c): 10174 Old Grove Road, Suite 200, San Diego, CA 92131; (858) 653-6740; www.jpcatholic.com.

King's College (c): 133 North River St., Wilkes-Barre, PA 18711; (570) 208-5900; www.kings.edu. Holy Cross Fathers; 1946 (2,178).

La Roche College (c): 9000 Babcock Blvd., Pittsburgh, PA 15237; (412) 367-9300; www.laroche.edu. Sisters of Divine Providence; 1963 (1,981).

La Salle University (c): 1900 W. Olney Ave., Philadelphia, PA 19141; (215) 951-1000. Christian Brothers; 1863 (5,567).

Le Moyne College (c): 1419 Salt Springs Rd., Syracuse, NY 13214; (315) 445-4100; www.lemoyne.edu. Jesuit Fathers; 1946; independent (approx. 3,129, full-time, part-time, graduate).

Lewis University (c): Romeoville, IL 60446; (815) 838-0500; www.lewisu.edu. Christian Brothers; 1932 (4,348).

Loras College (c): 1450 Alta Vista St., Dubuque, IA 52004; (563) 588-7100. Archdiocese of Dubuque; 1839 (1,736).

Lourdes College (c): 6832 Convent Blvd., Sylvania, OH 43560; (419) 885-3211; www.lourdes.edu. Sisters of St. Francis; 1958 (1,356).

Loyola College (c): 4501 N. Charles St., Baltimore, MD 21210; (410) 617-2000; www.loyola.edu. Jesuits; 1852; combined with Mt. St. Agnes College, 1971 (6,144).

Loyola Marymount University (c): 7900 Loyola Blvd., Los Angeles, CA 90045-2699; (310) 338-2700; www.lmu. edu. Society of Jesus; Religious of Sacred Heart of Mary, Sisters of St. Joseph of Orange, 1911 (6,591).

Loyola University (c): 6363 St. Charles Ave., New Orleans, LA 70118; (504) 865-2011. Jesuit Fathers; 1912 (5,842).

Loyola University Chicago (c): 820 N. Michigan Ave., Chicago, IL 60611; (312) 915-6000; www.luc. edu. Society of Jesus; 1870 (12,604).

Madonna University (c): 36600 Schoolcraft Rd., Livonia, MI 48150; (734) 432-5300. Felician Sisters; 1947 (3,979).

Magdalen College (c): 511 Kearsarge Mountain Rd., Warner, NH 03278; (603) 456-2656; www.magdalen.edu. Magdalen College Corporation; 1973 (81).

Manhattan College (c): Manhattan College Pkwy., Bronx, NY 11201; (718) 862-7200; www.manhattan.edu. De La Salle Christian Brothers; 1835; independent (2,744). Cooperative program with College of Mt. St. Vincent.

Marian College of Fond du Lac (c): 45 S. National Ave., Fond du Lac, WI 54935; (920) 923-7600; www.mariancollege.edu. Sisters of St. Agnes; 1936 (2,558).

Marian College (c): 3200 Cold Spring Rd., Indianapolis, IN 46222; (317) 955-6000; www.marian.edu. Sisters of St. Francis (Oldenburg, IN); 1851; independent (1,425).

Marquette University (c): P.O. Box 1881, Milwaukee, WI 53201-1881; (414) 288-7250; www.marquette.edu. Jesuit Fathers; 1881; independent (10,832).

Mary, University of (c): 7500 University Dr., Bismarck, ND 58504; (701) 255-7500; www.umary. edu. Benedictine Sisters; 1959 (2,546).

Marygrove College (c): 8425 W. McNichols Rd., Detroit, MI 48221; (313) 927-1200. Sisters, Servants of the Immaculate Heart of Mary; 1905; independent (6,459).

Marylhurst College (c): P.O. Box 261, Marylhurst, OR 97036-0261; (503) 636-8141; www.marylhurst. edu. Sisters of Holy Names of Jesus and Mary; 1893; independent (1,579).

Marymount College (w): Tarrytown, NY 10591; (914) 631-3200; www.marymt.edu. Religious of the Sacred Heart of Mary; 1907; independent (842). Coed in weekend degree programs.

Marymount University (c): 2807 N. Glebe Rd., Arlington, VA 22207; (703) 522-5600; www.marymount.edu. Religious of the Sacred Heart of Mary; 1950; independent (3,672).

Marywood College (c): Scranton, PA 18509; (570) 348-6211; www.marywood.edu. Sisters, Servants of the Immaculate Heart of Mary; 1915; independent (3,087).

Mercy College of Health Sciences (c): 928-6th Ave., Des Moines, IA 50309-1239; (515) 643-3180; www.mchs.edu. Sisters of Mercy of the Americas (552).

Mercyhurst College (c): 501 E. 38th St., Erie, PA 16546; (814) 824-2000; www.mercyhurst.edu. Sisters of Mercy; 1926 (3,404).

Merrimack College (c): North Andover, MA 01845; (978) 837-5000; www.merrimack.edu. Augustinians;1947 (2,108).

Misericordia (College Misericordia) (c): 301 Lake St., Dallas, PA 18612-1098; (570) 674-6400; www.miseri.edu. Religious Sisters of Mercy of the Union; 1924 (1,983).

Molloy College (c): 1000 Hempstead Ave., P.O. Box 5002, Rockville Centre, NY 11570-5002; (516) 678-5000. Dominican Sisters; 1955; independent (2,500).

Mount Aloysius College (c): 7373 Admiral Peary Hwy., Cresson, PA 16630; (814) 886-4131; www. mtaloy.edu. Sisters of Mercy; 1939 (2,000).

Mount Marty College (c): 1105 W. 8th St., Yankton, SD 57078; (800) 658-4552; www.mtmc. edu. Benedictine Sisters; 1936 (1,168).

Mount Mary College (w): 2900 N. Menomonee River Pkwy., Milwaukee, WI 53222; (414) 258-4810. School Sisters of Notre Dame; 1913 (1,368).

Mount Mercy College (c): 1330 Elmhurst Dr. N.E., Cedar Rapids, IA 52402; (319) 363-8213; www.mtmercy.edu. Sisters of Mercy; 1928; independent (1,432).

Mount St. Clare College (c): 400 N. Bluff Blvd., Clinton, IA 52732; (319) 242-4023; www.clare.edu. Sisters of St. Francis of Clinton, Iowa; 1918 (appr. 497).

Mount St. Joseph, College of (c): 5701 Delhi Rd., Cincinnati, OH 45233-1670; (513) 244-4200; www. msj.edu. Sisters of Charity; 1920 (5,527).

Mount Saint Mary College (c): Newburgh, NY 12550; (914) 561-0800; www.msmc.edu.. Dominican Sisters; 1954; independent (2,541).

Mount St. Mary's College (c): Emmitsburg, MD 21727; (301) 447-6122; www.msmary.edu. Founded by Fr. John DuBois, 1808; independent (1,821).

Mount St. Mary's College (w/c): 12001 Chalon Rd., Los Angeles, CA 90049 and 10 Chester Pl., Los Angeles, CA 90007 (Doheny Campus); (310) 954-4010; www.msmc.la.edu. Sisters of St. Joseph of Carondelet; 1925. Coed in music, nursing and graduate programs (1,965).

Mount Saint Vincent, College of (c): 6301 Riverdale Ave., New York, NY 10471; (718) 405-3200; www.cmsv.edu. Sisters of Charity; 1847; independent (1,515). Cooperative program with Manhattan College.

Neumann College (c): One Neumann Dr., Aston, PA 19014; (610) 459-0905; www.neumann.edu. Sisters of St. Francis; 1965; independent (2,221).

Newman University (c): 3100 McCormick Ave., Wichita, KS 67213; (316) 942-4291; www.newmanu. edu. Sisters Adorers of the Blood of Christ; 1933 (1,929).

New Rochelle, College of (w/c): 29 Castle Pl., New Rochelle, NY 10805 (main campus); (914) 654-5000; www.cnr.edu. Ursuline Order; 1904; independent (6,084). Coed in nursing, graduate, new resources divisions.

Niagara University (c): Lewiston Rd. Niagara Univ., NY 14109-2015; (716) 285-1212; www.niagara.edu. Vincentian Fathers and Brothers; 1856 (3,446).

Notre Dame de Namur University (c): 1500 Ralston Ave., Belmont, CA 94002; (650) 593-1601; www. cnd.edu. Sisters of Notre Dame de Namur; 1851; independent (1,799).

Notre Dame, University of (c): (University of Notre Dame du Lac) Notre Dame, IN 46556; (219) 631-5000; www.nd.edu. Congregation of Holy Cross; 1842 (11,054).

Notre Dame College of Ohio (w): 4545 College

Rd., Cleveland, OH 44121; (216) 381-1680; www.ndc.edu. Sisters of Notre Dame; 1922 (1,093).

Notre Dame of Maryland, College of (w): 4701 N. Charles St., Baltimore, MD 21210; (410) 435-0100; www.ndm.edu. School Sisters of Notre Dame; 1873 (3,077).

Oblate School of Theology (c): 285 Oblate Dr., San Antonio, TX 78216-6693; (210) 341-1366; www.ost.edu. Oblates of Mary Immaculate; 1903 (264). Graduate theology programs.

Ohio Dominican College (c): 1216 Sunbury Rd., Columbus, OH 43219-2099; (614) 253-2741; www.odc.edu. Dominican Sisters of St. Mary of the Springs; 1911 (2,300).

Our Lady of Holy Cross College (c): 4123 Woodland Dr., New Orleans, LA 70131; (504) 394-7744; www.olhcc.edu. Congregation of Sisters Marianites of Holy Cross; 1916 (3,994).

Our Lady of the Elms, College of (w): Chicopee, MA 01013; (413) 594-2761; www.elms.edu. Sisters of St. Joseph; 1928 (866).

Our Lady of the Lake College (c): 5345 Brittany Dr., Baton Rouge, LA 70808-4398; (225) 768-1710; www.ololcollege. Independent (1,421).

Our Lady of the Lake University (c): 411 S.W. 24th St., San Antonio, TX 78207; (210) 434-6711; www.ollusa.edu. Sisters of Divine Providence; 1895 (3,324).

Our Lady Seat of Wisdom Academy: 18 Karol Wojtyla Square, P.O. Box 249, Barry's Bay, Ontario K0J 1B0, Canada; (613) 756-3082; www.seatofwisdom.org.

Pontifical Catholic University of Puerto Rico (c): 2250 Avenida de las Americas, Ponce, PR 00717-0777; (787) 841-2000; www.pucpr.edu. Hierarchy of Puerto Rico; 1948; Pontifical University (9,912).

Portland, University of (c): 5000 N. Willamette Blvd., Portland, OR 97203; (503) 943-7911; www.up.edu. Holy Cross Fathers; 1901; independent (3,234).

Presentation College (c): Aberdeen, SD 7401; (605) 225-1634. Sisters of the Presentation; 1951 (615).

Providence College (c): 549 River Ave., Providence, RI 02918; (401) 865-1000; www.providence.edu. Dominican Friars; 1917 (5,742, day, evening, and graduate).

Queen of the Holy Rosary College (c): P.O. Box 3908, Mission San Jose, CA 94539; (510) 657-2468. Dominican Sisters of Mission San Jose, independent (200).

Quincy University (c): 1800 College Ave., Quincy, IL 62301; (217) 222-8020; www.quincy.edu. Franciscan Friars; 1860 (1,146).

Regis College (w): 235 Wellesley St., Weston, MA 02493-1571; (781) 768-7000; www.regiscollege.edu. Sisters of St. Joseph; 1927; independent (1,300).

Regis University (c): 3333 Regis Blvd. Denver, CO 80221; (303) 458-4100. Jesuits; 1887 (11,240).

Rivier College (c): Nashua, NH 03060; (603) 888-1311; www.rivier.edu. Sisters of the Presentation of Mary; 1933; independent (2,572).

Rockhurst College (c): 1100 Rockhurst Rd., Kansas City, MO 64110; (816) 501-4000; www.rockhurst.edu. Jesuit Fathers; 1910 (3,536).

Rosemont College of the Holy Child Jesus (w): Rosemont, PA 19010-1699; (610) 526-2984; www.rosemont.edu. Society of the Holy Child Jesus; 1921 (1,210).

Sacred Heart University (c): 5151 Park Ave., Fairfield, CT 06432; (203) 371-7999; www.sacredheart.edu. Diocese of Bridgeport; 1963; independent (6,001).

St. Ambrose University (c): Davenport, IA 52803; (319) 333-6300; www.sau.edu. Diocese of Davenport; 1882 (3,500).

Saint Anselm College (c): Manchester NH 03102-1030; (603) 641-7000; www.anselm.edu. Benedictines; 1889 (1,985).

St. Basil College (m): 195 Glenbrook Rd., Stamford, CT 06902; (203) 324-4578; UkrCathSem@aol.com. The Ukrainian Catholic Diocese of Stamford.

Saint Benedict, College of (w): 37 S. College Ave., St. Joseph, MN 56374; (320) 363-5407; www.csbsju.edu. Benedictine Sisters; 1913 (2,072). Sister college of St. John's University, Collegeville.

St. Bonaventure University (c): St. Bonaventure, NY 14778; (716) 375-2000; www.sbu.edu. Franciscan Friars; 1858; independent (2,719).

St. Catherine, College of (w): St. Paul: 2004 Randolph Ave., St. Paul, MN 55105; (651) 690-6000; Minneapolis; www.stkate.edu. Sisters of St. Joseph of Carondelet; 1905 (4,622).

St. Edward's University (c): 3001 S. Congress Ave., Austin, TX 78704; (512) 448-8400; www.stedwards.edu. Holy Cross Brothers; 1881; independent (4,267).

Saint Elizabeth, College of (w): 2 Convent Rd., Morristown, NJ 07960-6989; (973) 290-4000; www.st-elizabeth.edu. Sisters of Charity; 1899; independent (1,766). Coed in adult undergraduate and graduate programs.

St. Francis College (c): 180 Remsen St., Brooklyn Heights, NY 11201; (718) 489-5200. Franciscan Brothers; 1884; private, independent in the Franciscan tradition (2,505).

St. Francis University (c): P.O. Box 600, Loretto, PA 15940-0600; (814) 472-3000; www.sfcpa.edu. Franciscan Friars; 1847; independent (2,012).

St. Francis, University of (c): 500 N. Wilcox, Joliet, IL 60435; (815) 740-3360; www.stfrancis.edu. Sisters of St. Francis of Mary Immaculate (3,920).

St. Francis, University of (c): 2701 Spring St., Fort Wayne, IN 46808-3994; (219) 434-3100; www.sf.edu. Sisters of St. Francis; 1890 (1,740).

St. Gregory's University (c): 1900 W. MacArthur, Shawnee, OK 74801; (405) 878-5100; www.sgc.edu. Benedictine Monks; 1876 (805).

St. John's University (c): 8000 Utopia Pkwy., Jamaica, NY 11439 (Queens Campus); 300 Howard Ave., Staten Island, NY 10301 (Staten Island Campus); (718) 990-6161; www.stjohns.edu. Vincentians; 1870 (18,523).

St. John's University (m): Collegeville, MN 56321; (320) 363-2011; www.csbsju.edu. Benedictines; 1857 (2,072). All classes and programs are coeducational with College of St. Benedict.

St. Joseph in Vermont, College of (c): 71 Clement Rd., Rutland, VT 05701; (802) 773-5900; www.csj.edu. Sisters of St. Joseph; 1950; independent (482).

Saint Joseph College (w/c): 1678 Asylum Ave., West Hartford, CT 06117-2700; (860) 232-4571; www.sjc.edu. Sisters of Mercy; 1932 (1,965). Women's college in undergraduate liberal arts. Coed in graduate school and Weekend College.

Saint Joseph's College (c): 278 Whites Bridge Rd., Standish, ME 04084-5263; (207) 893-7711; www.sjcme.edu. Sisters of Mercy; 1912 (4,197 total; 1,609 graduate). Offers extensive distance education programs.

Saint Joseph's College (c): P.O. Box 909, Rensselaer, IN 47978; (219) 866-6000; www.stjoe.edu. Society of the Precious Blood; 1891 (1,101).

St. Joseph's College (c): 245 Clinton Ave., Brooklyn, NY 11205; (718) 636-6800 and 155 W. Roe Blvd., Patchogue, NY 11772; (631) 447-3200; www.sjcny.edu. Sisters of St. Joseph; 1916; independent (3,444).

St. Joseph's University (c): 5600 City Ave., Philadelphia, PA 19131; (610) 660-1000; www.sju.edu. Jesuit Fathers; 1851 (6,850).

Saint Leo University (c): P.O. Box 6665, MC 2186, Saint Leo, FL 33574; (352) 588-8200; www.saintleo.edu. Order of St. Benedict; 1889; independent (9,931).

Saint Louis University (c): 221 N. Grand Blvd., St. Louis, MO 63103; (314) 977-2222; www.slu.edu. Society of Jesus; 1818; independent (11,274).

Saint Martin's College (c): 5300 Pacific Ave. SE, Lacey, WA 98503-1297; (360) 438-4311; www.stmartin.edu. Benedictine Monks; 1895 (1,474 main and extension campuses).

Saint Mary, College of (w): 1901 S. 72nd St., Omaha, NE 68124; (402) 399-2400; www.csm.edu. Sisters of Mercy; 1923; independent (981).

Saint Mary, University of (c): 4100 S. 4th Street, Leavenworth, KS 66048; (913) 682-5151. Sisters of Charity of Leavenworth; 1923 (888).

Saint Mary-of-the-Woods College (w): St. Mary-of-the-Woods, IN 47876; (812) 535-5151; www.smwc.edu. Sisters of Providence; 1840 (1,510).

Saint Mary's College (w): Notre Dame, IN 46556; (219) 284-4556; www.saintmarys.edu. Sisters of the Holy Cross; 1844 (1,473).

Saint Mary's College (c): 3535 Indian Trail, Orchard Lake, MI 48324; (248) 683-0521; www.stmarys-avemaria.edu. 1885 (510).

St. Mary's College (c): Moraga, CA 94575; (510) 631-4000. Brothers of the Christian Schools; 1863 (4,127).

Saint Mary's University of Minnesota (c): 700 Terrace Heights, Winona, MN 55987-1399; (507) 452-4430; www.smumn.edu. Brothers of the Christian Schools; 1912 (1,376).

St. Mary's University of San Antonio (c): One Camino Santa Maria, San Antonio, TX 78228-8607; (210) 436-3011; www.stmarytx.edu. Society of Mary (Marianists). 1852 (4,264).

Saint Meinrad School of Theology (c): 200 Hill Dr., St. Meinrad, IN 47577; (812) 357-6611; www.saintmeinrad.edu. Benedictines (91 full- and part-time lay students.) Graduate-level theological studies.

St. Michael's College (c): Winooski Park, Colchester, VT 05439; (802) 654-2211; www.smcvt.edu. Society of St. Edmund; 1904 (2,630).

St. Norbert College (c): De Pere, WI 54115; (920) 403-3181; www.snc.edu. Norbertine Fathers; 1898; independent (2,045).

Saint Peter's College (c): 2641 Kennedy Blvd., Jersey City, NJ 07306; (201) 915-9000; www.spc.

edu. Society of Jesus; 1872; independent (4,201).

Saint Rose, College of (c): 432 Western Ave., Albany, NY 12203; (518) 454-5111. Sisters of St. Joseph of Carondelet; 1920; independent (4,441).

St. Scholastica, The College of (c): 1200 Kenwood Ave., Duluth, MN 55811; (218) 723-6000. Benedictine Sisters; 1912; independent (2,518).

St. Thomas, University of (c): 2115 Summit Ave., St. Paul, MN 55105; (651) 962-5000; www.stthomas.edu. Archdiocese of St. Paul and Minneapolis; 1885 (11,366).

St. Thomas, University of (c): 3800 Montrose Blvd., Houston, TX 77006-4696; (713) 522-7911; www.stthom.edu. Basilian Fathers; 1947 (7,174).

St. Thomas Aquinas College (c): Sparkill, NY 10976; (914) 398-4000; www.stac.edu. Dominican Sisters of Sparkill; 1952; independent, corporate board of trustees (2,200).

St. Thomas More, College of (c): 3020 Lubbock Street, Fort Worth, Texas 76109; (817) 923-8459; www.cstm.edu.

St. Thomas University (c): 16400 N.W. 32nd Ave., Miami, FL 33054; (305) 625-6000; www.stu.edu. Archdiocese of Miami; 1962 (3,677).

Saint Vincent College (c): 300 Fraser Purchase Rd., Latrobe, PA 15650-2690; (724) 539-9761; www.benedictine.stvincent.edu/seminary. Benedictine Fathers; 1846 (1,222).

Saint Vincent's College (c): 2800 Main St., Bridgeport, CT 06606; (203) 576-5235; www.stvincentscollege.edu. (345).

St. Xavier University (c): 3700 W. 103rd St., Chicago, IL 60655; (773) 298-3000. Sisters of Mercy; chartered 1847 (4,100).

Salve Regina University (c): Ochre Point Ave., Newport, RI 02840-4192; (401) 847-6650; www.salve.edu. Sisters of Mercy; 1934 (1,542). Offers distance learning programs in graduate studies.

San Diego, University of (c): 5998 Alcala Park, San Diego, CA 92110; (619) 260-4600. San Diego diocese and Religious of the Sacred Heart; 1949; independent (7,062).

San Francisco, University of (c): 2130 Fulton St., San Francisco, CA 94117; (415) 422-5555. Jesuit Fathers; 1855 (8,130).

Santa Clara University (c): 500 El Camino Real, Santa Clara, CA 95053; (408) 554-4000; www.scu.edu. Jesuit Fathers; 1851; independent (7,368).

Santa Fe, College of (c): 1600 St. Michael's Dr., Santa Fe, NM 87505; (505) 473-6011. Brothers of the Christian Schools; 1947 (1,588).

Scranton, University of (c): Scranton, PA 18510; (570) 941-7533; www.uofs.edu. Society of Jesus; 1888; independent (4,728).

Seattle University (c): 900 Broadway, Seattle, WA 98122; (206) 296-6000; www.seattleu.edu. Society of Jesus; 1891 (6,337).

Seton Hall University (c): 400 South Orange Ave., South Orange, NJ 07079; (973) 761-9000. Diocesan Clergy; 1856 (9,760).

Seton Hill College (w): Seton Hill Dr., Greensburg, PA 15601-1599; (724) 834-2200; www.setonhill.edu. Sisters of Charity of Seton Hill; 1883 (1,521).

Siena College (c): 515 Loudon Rd., Loudonville, NY 12211; (518) 783-2300; www.siena.edu. Franciscan Friars; 1937 (3,379).

Siena Heights University (c): 1247 E. Siena Heights Dr., Adrian, MI 49221; (517) 263-0731; www.sienahts.edu. Adrian Dominican Sisters; 1919 (2,124).

Silver Lake College of the Holy Family (c): 2406 S. Alverno Rd., Manitowoc, WI 54220-9319; (920) 684-6691. Franciscan Sisters of Christian Charity; 1935 (2,969).

Spalding University (c): 851 S. 4th Ave., Louisville, KY 40203; (502) 585-9911; www.spalding.edu. Sisters of Charity of Nazareth; 1814; independent (1,670).

Spring Hill College (c): 4000 Dauphin St., Mobile, AL 36608; (334) 380-4000; www.shc.edu. Jesuit Fathers; 1830 (1,050).

Stonehill College (c): North Easton, MA 02357; (508) 565-1000; www.stonehill.edu. Holy Cross Fathers; 1948; independent (2,550).

Thomas Aquinas College (c): 10000 N. Ojai Rd., Santa Paula, CA 93060; (805) 525-4417; www.thomasaquinas.edu. Founded 1971 (331).

Thomas More College (c): 333 Thomas More Pkwy., Crestview Hills, Covington, KY 41017; (859) 341-5800; www.thomasmore.edu. Diocese of Covington; 1921 (1,555).

Thomas More College of Liberal Arts (c): Six Manchester Street, Merrimack, NH 03054; (603) 880-8308; www.thomasmorecollege.edu.

Trinity College (w): 125 Michigan Ave. NE, Washington, DC 20017; (202) 939-5000. Sisters of Notre Dame de Namur; 1897 (1,600). Coed graduate school.

Ursuline College (w): 2550 Lander Rd., Pepper Pike, OH 44124; (440) 449-4200; www.ursuline.edu. Ursuline Nuns; 1871 (1,319).

Villanova University (c): Villanova, PA 19085; (610) 519-7499; www.villanova.edu. Order of St. Augustine; 1842 (10,396).

Viterbo College (c): 815 S. 9th, La Crosse, WI 54601; (608) 796-3000; www.viterbo.org. Franciscan Sisters of Perpetual Adoration; 1890 (2,200).

Walsh University (c): 2020 Easton St. N.W., North Canton, Ohio 44720-3396; (330) 490-7090; www.walsh.edu. Brothers of Christian Instruction; 1958 (1,648).

Washington Theological Union (c): 6896 Laurel Street N.W., Washington, DC 20012-2016; (202) 726-8800; www.wtu.edu. Coalition of Religious Seminaries; 1968 (263).

Wheeling Jesuit University (c): 316 Washington Ave., Wheeling, WV 26003-6295; (304) 243-2000; www.wju.edu. Jesuit Fathers; 1954 (1,703).

Wyoming Catholic College (c): P.O. Box 750, Lander, WY 82520; (877) 332-2930; www.wyomingcatholiccollege.com; liberal arts college that stresses the Great Books; 2005.

Xavier University (c): 3800 Victory Pkwy., Cincinnati, OH 45207; (513) 745-3000; www.xu.edu. Jesuit Fathers; 1831 (2,631).

Xavier University of Louisiana (c): 1 Drexel Dr., New Orleans, LA 70125; (504) 486-7411; www.xula.edu. Sisters of Blessed Sacrament; 1925 (3,787).

Catholic Two-Year Colleges

Ancilla Domini College (c): P.O. Box 1, Donaldson, IN 46513; (219) 936-8898; www.ancilla.edu. Ancilla Domini Sisters; 1937 (546).

Assumption College for Sisters: Mendham, NJ 07945; (973) 543-6528. Sisters of Christian Charity; 1953 (24).

Chatfield College (c): St. Martin, OH 45118; (937) 875-3344; www.chatfield.edu. Ursulines; 1971 (273).

The College of St. Catherine-Minneapolis (c): 601 25th Ave. S., Minneapolis, MN 55454; (651) 690-7702. Sisters of St. Joseph of Carondelet (918).

Donnelly College (c): 608 N. 18th St., Kansas City, KS 66102; (913) 621-6070; www.donnelly.cc.ks.us. Archdiocesan College; 1949 (645).

Don Bosco Technical Institute (m): 1151 San Gabriel Blvd., Rosemead, CA 91770; (626) 307-6500; www.boscotech.tec.ca.us. Salesians; 1969 (994).

Holy Cross College (c): 54515 State Rd., 933 N., Notre Dame, IN 46556-0308; (219) 239-8400; www.hcc-nd.edu. Brothers of Holy Cross; 1966 (503).

Manor College (c): 700 Fox Chase Road, Jenkintown, PA 19046; (215) 885-2360; www.manor.edu. Sisters of St. Basil the Great; 1947.

Maria College (c): 700 New Scotland Ave., Albany, NY 12208. Sisters of Mercy; 1963 (1,048).

Marymount College Palos Verdes (c): 30800 Palos Verdes Dr., E., Rancho Palos Verdes, CA 90275-6299; (310) 377-5501; www.marymountpv.edu. Religious of the Sacred Heart of Mary; independent (840).

St. Catharine College (c): 2735 Bardstown Rd., St. Catharine, KY 40061; (859) 336-5082. Dominican Sisters; 1931 (742).

Springfield College in Illinois (c): 1500 N. Fifth St., Springfield, IL 62702-2694; (217) 525-1420; www.sci.edu. Ursuline Sisters; 1929 (300).

Trocaire College (c): 360 Choate Ave., Buffalo, NY 14220; (716) 827-2423; www.trocaire.edu. Sisters of Mercy; 1958; independent (780).

Villa Maria College of Buffalo (c): 240 Pine Ridge Rd., Buffalo, NY 14225; (716) 896-0700; www.villa.edu. Felician Sisters 1960; independent (475).

DIOCESAN AND INTERDIOCESAN SEMINARIES

(*Sources*: Catholic Almanac *survey*; The Official Catholic Directory; Catholic News Service.)

Information, according to states, includes names of archdioceses and dioceses, and names and addresses of seminaries. Types of seminaries, when not clear from titles, are indicated in most cases. Interdiocesan seminaries are generally conducted by religious orders for candidates for the priesthood from several dioceses. The list does not include houses of study reserved for members of religious communities. Archdioceses are indicated by an asterisk.

California: Los Angeles* – St. John's Seminary (major), 5118 Seminary Rd., Camarillo 93012-2599; (805) 482-2755; www.stjohnsem.edu.

San Diego – St. Francis Seminary (college and pretheology formation program), 1667 Santa Paula Dr.,

92111; (619) 291-7446.

San Francisco* – St. Patrick's Seminary (major), 320 Middlefield Rd., Menlo Park 94025; (650) 325-5621; www.stpatricksseminary.org..

Colorado: Denver* – St. John Vianney Theological Seminary (college and pre-theology formation program), 1300 S. Steele St., 80210; (303) 282-3427; Redemptoris Mater Archdiocesan Missionary Seminary (seminary, house of formation), 1300 S. Steele St., 80210; (303) 282-3427.

Connecticut: Hartford* – St. Thomas Seminary (college formation program), 467 Bloomfield Ave., Bloomfield 06002-2999; (860) 242-5573.

Norwich – Holy Apostles College and Seminary (adult vocations; minor and major), 33 Prospect Hill Rd., Cromwell 06416; (860) 632-3000; www.holyapostles.edu.

Stamford – Byzantine Rite: Ukrainian Catholic Seminary: St. Basil College Seminary (minor), 195 Glenbrook Rd., Stamford 06902-3099; (203) 324-4578.

District of Columbia: Washington, DC* – Theological College (national, major), The Catholic University of America, 401 Michigan Ave., N.E., 20017; (202) 756-4900; www.theologicalcollege.org. St. Josaphat's Seminary, 201 Taylor St. N.E., 20017; (202) 529-1177. (Major house of formation serving the four Ukrainian Byzantine-rite dioceses in the U.S.)

Florida: Miami* – St. John Vianney College Seminary, 2900 S.W. 87th Ave., 33165; (305) 223-4561.

Palm Beach – St. Vincent de Paul Regional Seminary (major), 10701 S. Military Trail, Boynton Beach 33436; (561) 732-4424; www.svdp.edu.

Illinois: Chicago* – St. Joseph Seminary (college), 6551 N. Sheridan Rd., Chicago 60626; (773) 973-9700; www.stjoseph.luc.edu. University of St. Mary of the Lake Mundelein Seminary (School of Theology), 1000 E. Maple Ave., Mundelein 60060; (847) 566-6401; www.vocations.org.

Indiana: Indianapolis* – Saint Meinrad Seminary, College and School of Theology (interdiocesan), St. Meinrad 47577; (812) 357-6611; www.saintmeinrad.edu.

Iowa: Davenport – St. Ambrose University Seminary (interdiocesn), 518 W. Locust St., 52803; (319) 333-6151; www.davenportdiocese.org.

Dubuque* – Seminary of St. Pius X (interdiocesan), Loras College, 52004-0178; (319) 588-7782.

Louisiana: New Orleans* – Notre Dame Seminary Graduate School of Theology, 2901 S. Carrollton Ave., 70118; (504) 866-7426; St. Joseph Seminary College (interdiocesan), St. Benedict 70457-9999; (504) 892-1800; www.stjosephabbey.org.

Maryland: Baltimore* – Mt. St. Mary's Seminary and University, 5400 Roland Ave., 21210; (410) 864-4000; www.stmarys.edu. Mt. St. Mary's Seminary, Emmitsburg 21727-7797; (301) 447-5295; www.msmary.edu.

Massachusetts: Boston* – St. John's Seminary, School of Theology, 127 Lake St., Brighton 02135; (617) 254-2610. St. John's Seminary, College of Liberal Arts, 127 Lake St., Brighton 02135; (617) 746-5450. Pope John XXIII National Seminary (for ages 30-60), 558 South Ave., Weston 02943; (781) 899-5500; www.blessedjohnXXIII.org.

Newton – Melkite Greek Catholic: St. Gregory the Theologian Seminary, 3 VFW Parkway, Roslindale, MA 02131; (617) 323-9922. Seminary of St. Basil the Great, 30 East St., 01844; (978) 683-2471.

Michigan: Detroit* – Sacred Heart Major Seminary (college/theologate and institute for ministry), 2701 Chicago Blvd., Detroit 48206; (313) 883-8500. Sts. Cyril

and Methodius Seminary, St. Mary's College (theologate and college) independent, primarily serving Polish-American community, 3535 Indian Trail, Orchard Lake 48324; (248) 683-0311.

Grand Rapids – Christopher House, 723 Rosewood Ave., S.E., East Grand Rapids 49506; (616) 243-6538.

Minnesota: St. John's School of Theology and Seminary, St. John's University, P.O. Box 7288, Collegeville 56321-7288; (320) 363-2100; www.csbsju.edu/sot.

St. Paul and Minneapolis* – St. Paul Seminary School of Divinity, University of St. Thomas, St. Paul 55101; (612) 962-5050; www.stthomas.edu. St. John Vianney Seminary (college residence), 2115 Summit Ave., St. Paul 55105; (651) 962-6825; www.stthomas.edu/sjv.

Winona – Immaculate Heart of Mary Seminary, St. Mary's University, No. 43, 700 Terrace Heights, 55987; (507) 457-7373; www.ihmseminary.org.

Missouri: St. Louis* – Kenrick-Glennon Seminary (St. Louis Roman Catholic Theological Seminary). Kenrick School of Theology and Cardinal Glennon College, 5200 Glennon Dr., 63119; (314) 792-6100.

Nebraska: Seward – St. Gregory the Great Seminary (pre-theology), 1301 280th Rd., 68434; (402) 643-4052, www.stgregoryseminary.org. Our Lady of Guadalupe Seminary, P.O. Box 147, Denton, NE 68339; (402) 797-7700; www.fssp.com.

New Jersey: Newark* – Immaculate Conception Seminary – college seminary; major seminary; graduate school – Seton Hall University, 400 South Orange Ave., South Orange 07079; (973) 761-9575; www.shu.edu. Redemptoris Mater, Archdiocesan Missionary Seminary, 672 Passaic Ave., 07032; (201) 997-3220.

New York: Brooklyn – Cathedral Seminary Residence of the Immaculate Conception (college and pre-theology), 7200 Douglaston Parkway, Douglaston 11362; (718) 229-8001. Cathedral Preparatory Seminary, 56-25 92nd St., Elmhurst 11373; (718) 592-6800. St. Alphonsus Formation Residence, 22-04 Parsons Blvd., 11357-3440; (718) 321-1096.

Buffalo – Christ the King Seminary (interdiocesan theologate), P.O. Box 607, 711 Knox Rd., East Aurora 14052; (716) 652-8900. Pope John Paul II Residence, 217 Winston Rd., 14216; (716) 836-5526.

New York* – St. Joseph's Seminary (major), 201 Seminary Ave., Dunwoodie, Yonkers 10704; (914) 968-6200. St. John Neumann Residence (college and pre-theology), 201 Seminary Ave., Yonkers, N.Y., 10704-1896; (914) 964-3025. Cathedral Preparatory Seminary, 946 Boston Post Rd., Rye 10580; (914) 968-6200; www.cathedralprep.com.

Rockville Centre – Seminary of the Immaculate Conception (major), 440 West Neck Rd., Huntington, 11743; (631) 423-2346.

St. Maron Eparchy, Brooklyn – Our Lady of Lebanon Maronite Seminary, 7164 Alaska Ave. N.W., Washington, DC 20012; (202) 723-8831; www.maroniteseminary.org.

North Dakota: Fargo – Cardinal Muench Seminary (interdiocesan high school, college and pre-theology), 100 35th Ave. N.E., Fargo 58102; (701) 232-8969; www.cardinalmuench.org.

Ohio: Cincinnati* – Mt. St. Mary's Seminary of the West (division of the Athenaeum of Ohio), 6616 Beechmont Ave., 45230; (513) 231-2223; www.mtsm.org..

Cleveland – St. Mary Seminary and Graduate School of Theology, 28700 Euclid Ave. Wickliffe 44092; (440) 943-7600. Borromeo Seminary, 28700 Euclid Ave., 44092-2585; (440) 943-7600; www.a-full-life.com.

Columbus – Pontifical College Josephinum (national),

theologate and college, 7625 North High St., 43235-1498; (614) 885-5585; www.pcj.edu.

Oregon: Portland* – Mt. Angel Seminary (interdiocesan, college, pre-theology program, graduate school of theology), 1 Abbey Dr., St. Benedict 97373; (503) 845-3951. Felix Rougier House of Studies, 585 E. College St., 97362. Jesuit Novitiate of St. Francis Xavier, 3301 S.E. 45th Ave., 97206.

Pennsylvania: Erie – St. Mark Seminary, P.O. Box 10397, Erie 16514; (814) 824-1200.

Greensburg – St. Vincent Seminary (interdiocesan; pre-theology program; theologate; graduate programs in theology; religious education), 300 Fraser Purchase Rd., Latrobe 15650-2690; (724) 539-9761; www.stvincent.edu.

Philadelphia* – Theological Seminary of St. Charles Borromeo (College, pre-theology program, spirituality year pogram, theologate), 100 East Wynnewood Rd., Wynnewood 19096; (610) 667-3394; www.scs.edu.

Pittsburgh* (Byzantine-Ruthenian) – Byzantine Catholic Seminary of Sts. Cyril and Methodius (college, pre-theology program, theologate), 3605 Perrysville Ave., 15214; (412) 321-8383; www.byzcath.org/seminary.

Pittsburgh – St. Paul Seminary (interdiocesan, college and pre-theology), 2900 Noblestown Rd., 15205; (412) 921-5800; www.diopitt.org.

Scranton – St. Pius X Seminary (college and pre-theology formation; interdiocesan), 1000 Seminary Rd., Dalton 18414; (570) 563-1131. Affiliated with the University of Scranton.

Rhode Island: Providence — Seminary of Our Lady of Providence (House of Formation; college students and pre-theology), 485 Mount Pleasant Ave., 02908; (401) 331-1316; www.catholicpriest.com.

Texas: Dallas – Holy Trinity Seminary (college and pre-theology; English proficiency and academic foundation programs), P.O. Box 140309, Irving 75014; (972) 438-2212.

El Paso – St. Charles Seminary College, P.O. Box 17548, 79917; (915) 591-9821.

Galveston-Houston – St. Mary's Seminary (theologate), 9845 Memorial Dr., Houston 77024; (713) 686-4345.

San Antonio* – Assumption Seminary (theologate and pre-theology, Hispanic ministry emphasis), 2600 W. Woodlawn Ave., 78228; (210) 734-2324.

Washington: Spokane – Bishop White Seminary, College Formation Program, E. 429 Sharp Ave., 99202; (509) 326-3255; www.bishopwhiteseminary.org.

Wisconsin: Milwaukee* – St. Francis Seminary, 3257 S. Lake Dr., St. Francis 53235; (414) 747-6400; www.sfs.edu. College Program, 2497 N. Murray Ave., Milwaukee, 53211; (414) 964-6982. Sacred Heart School of Theology (interdiocesan seminary for second-career vocations), P.O. Box 429, Hales Corners, 53130-0429; (414) 425-8300.

North American College

Founded by the U.S. Bishops in 1859, the North American College serves as a residence and house of formation for U.S. seminarians and graduate students in Rome. The first ordination of an alumnus took place June 14, 1862. Pontifical status was granted the college by Pope Leo XIII Oct. 25, 1884. Students pursue theological and related studies principally at the Pontifical Gregorian University, the Pontifical University of Saint Thomas Aquinas, and the Pontifical University della Santa Croce. The current rector is Msgr. James F. Checcio, J.C.D., M.B.A. Address: 00120 Città del Vaticano; 011-39-06-684-931; www.pnac.org.

American College of Louvain

Founded by U.S. Bishops in 1857, the American College of Louvain, Belgium, was a seminary for U.S. students. It also served as a community for English-speaking graduate-student priests and religious priests pursuing studies at the Catholic University of Louvain (Université Catholique de Louvain, founded 1425). The college was administered by an American rector and faculty, and operated under the auspices of a committee of the national Conference of Catholic Bishops. The seminary closed in June 2011.

WORLD AND U.S. SEMINARY STATISTICS

The *2011 Statistical Yearbook of the Church* (the most recent edition) reports the following comparative statistics for the years 1996 to 2011 of candidates in Philosophy and Theology (major seminarians). World totals are given first; U.S. statistics are given in parentheses.

Year	Total Major Seminarians	Diocesan	Religious
1996	105,870 (4,785)	70,034 (3,268)	35,836 (1,517)
1997	108,517 (4,729)	70,534 (3,311)	37,983 (1,418)
1998	109,171 (4,830)	70,564 (3,436)	38,607 (1,394)
1999	110,021 (5,024)	70,989 (3,428)	39,032 (1,596)
2000	110,583 (5,109)	71,756 (3,479)	38,827 (1,630)
2001	112,244 (5,080)	72,241 (3,404)	40,003 (1,676)
2002	113,199 (5,169)	72,977 (3,578)	40,222 (1,591)
2003	112,373 (4,676)	72,266 (3,181)	40,107 (1,495)
2004	113,044 (5,642)	71,841 (3,929)	41,203 (1,713)
2005	114,439 (5,180)	72,188 (3,383)	42,251 (1,797)
2006	115,480 (4,913)	71,878 (3,214)	43,602 (1,699)
2007	115,919 (4,901)	71,225 (3,366)	44,602 (1,699)
2008	117,024 (5,453)	71,176 (3,804)	45,484 (1,649)
2009	117,978 (5,181)	71,219 (3,573)	46,759 (1,608)
2010	118,890 (5,321)	71,974 (3,677)	47,016 (1,644)
2011	**120,616 (5,775)**	**72,277 (3,893)**	**48,339 (1,882)**

PONTIFICAL UNIVERSITIES

(*Principal source*: Annuario Pontificio.)

These universities, listed according to country of location, have been canonically erected and authorized by the Congregation for Catholic Education to award degrees in stated fields of study. New laws and norms governing ecclesiastical universities and faculties were promulgated in the apostolic constitution *Sapientia Christiana*, issued Apr. 15, 1979. Phone numbers are listed where possible.

Argentina: Pontifical Catholic University of S. Maria of Buenos Aires (June 16, 1960): Av. Alicia Moreau de Justo 1400, 1107 Buenos Aires.

Belgium: Catholic University of Louvain (founded Dec. 9, 1425; canonically erected, 1834), with autonomous institutions for French- (Louvain) and Flemish-(Leuven) speaking: Place de l'Universite I, B-1348 Louvain-La-Neuve (French); Naamsestraat 22/b, B-3000 Leuven (Flemish).

Brazil: Pontifical Catholic University of Rio de Janeiro (Jan. 20, 1947): Rua Marquês de São Vicente 225, 22451-000 Rio de Janeiro, RJ.

Pontifical Catholic University of Minas Gerais (June 5, 1983): Av. Dom José Gaspar 500, C.P. 2686, 30161-000 Belo Horizonte, MG.; (031) 319-1127.

Pontifical Catholic University of Parana (Aug. 6, 1985): Rua Imaculada Conceição, 1155, Prado Velho, C.P. 670, 80001-000 Curitiba, PR; (041) 223-0922.

Pontifical Catholic University of Rio Grande do Sul (Nov. 1, 1950): Av. Ipiranga 6681, C.P.1429,90001-000 Porto Alegre, RS.

Pontifical Catholic University of São Paulo (Jan. 25, 1947): Rua Monte Alegre 984, 05014-901 São Paulo SP.

Pontifical University of Campinas (Sept. 8, 1956): Rua Marechal Deodoro 1099, 13020-000 Campinas, SP.; (0192) 27-001.

Canada: Laval University (Mar. 15, 1876): Case Postale 460, QC G1K 7P4.

St. Paul University (formerly University of Ottawa) (Feb. 5, 1889): 223 Rue Main, Ottawa, ON K1S 1C4;

University of Sherbrooke (Nov. 21, 1957): Chemin Ste.-Catherine, 2500, boulevard de l'Université, Sherbrooke, QC J1K 12R1.

Chile: Pontifical Catholic University of Chile (June 21, 1888): Avenida Bernardo O'Higgins, 340, Casilla 114D, Santiago.

Catholic University of Valparaíso (Nov. 1, 1961): Avenida Brasil 2950, Casilla 4059, Valparaíso.

Colombia: Bolivarian Pontifical Catholic University (Aug. 16, 1945): Circular 1a, N.70-01, Apartado 56006, Medellín.

Pontifical Xaverian University (July 31, 1937): Carrera 7, N. 40-62, Apartado 56710, Santafé de Bogota D.C.; Apartado 26239, Calle 18, N. 118-250, Cali (Cali campus).

Cuba: Catholic University of St. Thomas of Villanueva (May 4, 1957): Avenida Quenta 16,660, Marianao.

Dominican Republic: Pontifical Catholic University "Mother and Teacher" (Sept. 9, 1987): Apartado 822, Santiago de Los Caballeros.

Ecuador: Pontifical Catholic University of Ecuador (July 16, 1954): Doce de Octubre, N. 1076, Apartado 17-01-2184, Quito.

France: Catholic University of Lille (Nov. 18, 1875): Boulevard Vauban 60, 59016 Lille.

Catholic Faculties of Lyon (Nov. 22, 1875): 25, Rue du Plat, 69288 Lyon 02.

Catholic Institute of Paris (Aug. 11, 1875): 21, Rue d'Assas, 75270 Paris 06.

Catholic Institute of Toulouse (Nov. 15, 1877): Rue de la Fonderie 31, 31068 Toulouse.

Catholic University of the West (Sept. 16, 1875): 3, Place André Leroy, B.P. 808, 49005 Angers; 2-41-81-66-00.

Germany: Catholic University Eichstätt (Apr. 1, 1980): Ostenstrasse 26, D-85072, Eichstätt, Federal Republic of Germany; (08421) 201.

Guatemala: Rafael Landívar University (Oct. 18, 1961): Vista Hermosa III, Zona 16, Guatemala; (02) 69-21-51.

Hungary: Catholic University Pázmány Péter (March 25, 1999): Papnövelde Utea 7, H-1053 Budapest, Hungary; (01) 11-73-701.

Ireland: St. Patrick's College (Mar. 29, 1896): Maynooth, Co. Kildare.

Italy: Catholic University of the Sacred Heart (Dec. 25, 1920): Largo Gemelli 1, 20123 Milan.

Libera University Mary of the Assumption (Oct. 26, 1939): Via della Transpontina 21, 00193 Rome, Italy.

Japan: Jochi Daigaku (Sophia University) (Mar. 29, 1913): Chiyoda-Ku, Kioi-cho 7, Tokyo 102.

Lebanon: St. Joseph University of Beirut (Mar. 25, 1881): Rue de l'Université St.-Joseph, Boite Postale 293, Beyrouth (Beirut), Liban; (01) 42-64-56.

Netherlands: Catholic University of Nijmegen (June 29, 1923): P.B. 9102, Comeniuslaam 4, 6500 HC, Nijmegen.

Panama: University of S. Maria La Antigua (May 27, 1965): Apartado 6-1696, Panama 6.

Paraguay: Catholic University of Our Lady of the Assumption (Feb. 2, 1965): Independencia Nacional y Comuneros, Casilla 1718, Asunción; (021) 44-10-44.

Peru: Pontifical Catholic University of Peru (Sept. 30, 1942): Av. Universitaria, s/n. San Miguel, Apartado 1761, Lima 100. [Stripped of its Catholic title on July 21, 2012 by the Holy See.]

Philippines: Pontifical University of Santo Tomás (Nov. 20, 1645): España Street, 1008 Manila.

Poland: Catholic University of Lublin (July 25, 1920): Aleje Racùawickie 14, Skr. Poczt. 129, 20-950, Lublin.

Catholic Theological Academy (June 29, 1989): Ul. Dewajtis 5, 01-815, Warsaw.

Pontifical Academy of Theology of Krakow (Dec. 8, 1981): Ul. Kanonicza, 25, 31-002 Kraków; (014) 22-33-31.

Portugal: Portuguese Catholic University (Nov. 1, 1967): Palma de Cima, 1 600 Lisbon.

Puerto Rico: Pontifical Catholic University of Puerto Rico (Aug. 15, 1972): 2250 Ave. Las Américas Suite 523, Ponce, Puerto Rico 00731-6382.

Spain: Catholic University of Navarra (Aug. 6, 1960): Campus Universitario, E-31080 Pamplona.

Pontifical University "Comillas" (Mar. 29, 1904): Campus de Cantoblanco, 28049 Madrid.

Pontifical University of Salamanca (Sept. 25, 1940): Compañía 5, 37002 Salamanca.

University of Deusto (Aug. 10, 1963): Avenida de las Universidades, 28, 48007 Bilbao o Apartado 1, 48080 Bilbao; 94-445-31-00.

Taiwan (China): Fu Jen Catholic University (Nov. 15, 1923, at Peking; reconstituted at Taipeh, Sept. 8,

1961): Hsinchuang, Taipeh Hsien 24205.

United States: The Catholic University of America (Mar. 7, 1889): 620 Michigan Ave. N.E., Washington, DC 20064.

Georgetown University (Mar. 30, 1833): 37th and O Sts. N.W., Washington, DC 20057.

Niagara University (June 21, 1956): Lewiston Rd., Niagara Falls, NY 14109.

Uruguay: Catholic University of Uruguay "Dámaso Antonio Larrañaga" (Jan. 25, 1985): Avda. 8 de Octubre 2738, 11.600 Montevideo.

Venezuela: Catholic University "Andrés Bello" (Sept. 29, 1963): Esquina Jesuitas, Apartado 29068, Caracas 1021; (02) 442-21-20.

ECCLESIASTICAL FACULTIES

(*Principal source*: Annuario Pontificio.) These faculties in Catholic seminaries and universities, listed according to country of location, have been canonically erected and authorized by the Congregation for Catholic Education to award degrees in stated fields of study.

Argentina: Faculties of Philosophy and Theology, San Miguel (Sept. 8, 1932).

Australia: Catholic Institute of Sydney, Sydney (Feb. 2, 1954).

Austria: Theological Faculty, Linz (Dec. 25, 1978).

International Theological Institute for Family Studies (Oct. 1, 1996).

Brazil: Philosophical and Theological Faculties of the Company of Jesus, Belo Horizonte (July 15, 1941 and Mar. 12, 1949).

Ecclesiastical Faculty of Philosophy "John Paul II," Rio de Janeiro (Aug. 6, 1981).

Cameroon: Catholic Institute of Yaoundé (Nov. 15, 1991).

Canada: College of Immaculate Conception — Montréal Section of Jesuit Faculties in Canada (Sept. 8, 1932). Suspended.

Pontifical Institute of Medieval Studies, Toronto (Oct. 18, 1939).

Dominican Faculty of Theology of Canada, Ottawa (1965; Nov. 15, 1975).

Regis College, Toronto Section of the Jesuit Faculty of Theology in Canada, Toronto (Feb. 17, 1956; Dec. 25, 1977).

Congo (formerly Zaire): Catholic Faculties of Kinshasa, Kinshasa (theology, Apr. 25, 1957; philosophy, Nov. 25, 1987).

Côte d'Ivoire (Ivory Coast): Catholic Institute of West Africa, Abidjan (Aug. 12, 1975).

Croatia: Philosophical Faculty, Zagreb (July 31, 1989).

France: Centre Sèvres, Faculties of Theology and Philosophy of the Jesuits, Paris (Sept. 8, 1932).

Germany: Theological Faculty of the Major Episcopal Seminary, Trier (Sept. 8, 1955).

Theological Faculty, Paderborn (June 11, 1966).

Theological-Philosophical Faculty, Frankfurt (1932; June 7, 1971).

Philosophical Faculty, Munich (1932; Oct. 25, 1971).

Theological Faculty, Fulda (Dec. 22, 1978).

Philosophical-Theological School of Salesians, Benediktbeuern (May 24, 1992).

Philosphical-Theological School, Vallendar (Oct. 7, 1993).

Great Britain: Heythrop College, University of London, London (Nov. 1, 1964). Theology, philosophy.

Hungary: Faculty of Theology (1635), Institute on Canon Law (Nov. 30, 1996), Budapest.

India: Jnana Deepa Vidyapeeth (Pontifical Athenaeum), Institute of Philosophy and Religion, Poona (July 27, 1926).

Vidyajyoti, Institute of Religious Studies, Faculty of Theology, Delhi (1932; Dec. 9, 1974).

Satya Nilayam, Institute of Philosophy and Culture. Faculty of Philosophy, Madras (Sept. 8, 1932; Dec. 15, 1976).

Pontifical Institute of Theology and Philosophy at the Pontifical Interritual Seminary of St. Joseph, Alwaye, Kerala (Feb. 24, 1972).

Dharmaram Vidya Kshetram, Pontifical Athenaeum of Theology and Philosophy, Bangalore (theology, Jan. 6, 1976; philosophy, Dec. 8, 1983).

Pontifical Oriental Institute of Religious Studies, Kottayam (July 3, 1982). Faculty of Theology, Ranchi (Aug. 15, 1982).

St. Peter's Pontifical Institute of Theology, Bangalore (Jan. 6, 1985).

Indonesia: Wedabhakti Pontifical Faculty of Theology, Yogyakarta (Nov. 1, 1984).

Ireland: The Milltown Institute of Theology and Philosophy, Dublin (1932).

Israel: French Biblical and Archeological School, Jerusalem (founded 1890; approved Sept. 17, 1892; canonically approved to confer Doctorate in Biblical Science, June 29, 1983).

Italy: Theological Faculty of Southern Italy, Naples. Two sections: St. Louis Posillipo (Mar. 16, 1918) and St. Thomas Aquinas Capodimonte (Oct. 31, 1941).

Pontifical Theological Faculty of Sardinia, Cagliari, (Aug. 5, 1927).

Interregional Theological Faculty, Milan (Aug. 8, 1935; restructured 1969).

Faculty of Philosophy "Aloisianum," Gallarate (1937; Mar. 20, 1974).

Pontifical Ambrosian Institute of Sacred Music, Milan (Mar. 12, 1940).

Theological Faculty of Sicily, Palermo (Dec. 8, 1980).

Theological Institute Pugliese, Molfetta (June 24, 1992).

Theological Institute Calabro, Catanzaro (Jan. 28, 1993).

Theological Faculty of Central Italy, Florence (Sep. 9, 1997).

Japan: Faculty of Theology, Nagoya (May 25, 1984).

Kenya: Catholic Higher Institute of Eastern Africa, Nairobi (May 2, 1984).

Lebanon: Faculty of Theology, University of the Holy Spirit, Kaslik (May 30, 1982).

Madagascar: Superior Institute of Theology and Philosophy, at the Regional Seminary of Antananarivo, Ambatoroka-Antananarivo (Apr. 21, 1960).

Malta: Faculty of Theology, Tal-Virtù (Nov. 22, 1769), with Institute of Philosophy and Human Studies (Sept. 8, 1984).

Mexico: Theological Faculty of Mexico (June 29, 1982) and Philosophy (Jan. 6, 1986), Institute of Canon Law (Sept. 4, 1995), Mexico City.

Nigeria: Catholic Institute of West Africa, Port

Harcourt (May 9, 1994).
Peru: Pontifical and Civil Faculty of Theology, Lima (July 25, 1571).
Poland: Pontifical Theological Faculty, Warsaw (May 3, 1988) with two sections: St. John Baptist (1837, 1920, Nov. 8, 1962) at the Metropolitan Seminary Duchowne, and St. Andrew Bobola – Bobolanum (Sept. 8, 1932).
Philosophical Faculty, Krakow (1932; Sept. 20, 1984).
Theological Faculty, Poznan (1969; pontifical designation, June 2, 1974).
Spain: Theological Faculty, Granada (1940; July 31, 1973).
Theological Faculty of San Esteban, Salamanca (1947; Oct. 4, 1972).
Theological Faculty of the North, of the Metropolitan Seminary of Burgos and the Diocesan Seminary of Vitoria (Feb. 6, 1967).
Theological Faculty of Catalunya, (Mar. 7, 1968), with the Institutes of Fundamental Theology (Dec. 28, 1984), Liturgy (Aug. 15, 1986) and Philosophy (July 26, 1988), Barcelona.
Theological Faculty "San Vicente Ferrer" (two sections), Valencia (Jan. 23, 1974).
Theological Faculty "San Damaso" (Sept. 19, 1996), Madrid.
Switzerland: Theological Faculty, Lucerne (Dec. 25, 1973).
Theological Faculty, Chur (Jan. 1, 1974).
Theological Faculty, Lugano (Nov. 20, 1993).
United States: St. Mary's Seminary and University, School of Theology, Baltimore (May 1, 1822).
St. Mary of the Lake Faculty of Theology, Mundelein, IL (Sept. 30, 1929).
Weston Jesuit School of Theology, Cambridge, MA (Oct. 18, 1932).
The Jesuit School of Theology, Berkeley, CA (Feb. 2, 1934, as "Alma College," Los Gatos, CA).
Faculty of Philosophy and Letters, St. Louis, MO (Feb. 2, 1934).
St. Michael's Institute, Jesuit School of Philosophy and Letters, Spokane, WA (Feb. 2, 1934).
Pontifical Faculty of Theology of the Immaculate Conception, Dominican House of Studies, Washington, DC (Nov. 15, 1941).
Also located in the **United States** are:
The Marian Library/International Marian Research Institute (IMRI), U.S. branch of Pontifical Theological Faculty "Marianum," University of Dayton, Dayton, OH 45469 (affil. 1976, inc. 1983).
John Paul II Institute for Studies on Marriage and the Family, U.S. section of Pontifical John Paul II Institute for Studies on Marriage and Family at the Pontifical Lateran University, 487 Michigan Ave. N.E., Washington, DC 20017 (Aug. 22, 1988).
Pontifical College Josephinum (Theologate and College) at Columbus, OH, is a national pontifical seminary. Established Sept. 1, 1888, it is directly under the auspices of the Vatican through the Apostolic Nuncio to the U.S., who serves as the seminary's chancellor.
Vietnam: Theological Faculty of the Pontifical National Seminary of St. Pius X, Dalat (July 31, 1965). Activities suppressed.
In addition to those listed above, there are other faculties of theology or philosophy in state universities and for members of certain religious orders only. These include:
Austria: Katholisch-Theologische Fakultät (1619), Universitätsstrasse, 1, A-5010 Salzburg, Österreich.
Katholisch-Theologische Fakultät (1365), Dr. Karl-Lueger-Ring, 1, A-1010 Wien, Österreich.
Theologische Fakultät (1586), Karl-Franzens-Universität, Universitätsplatz, 3, A-8010 Graz, Österreich.
Theologische Fakultät (1669), Leopold-Franzens-Universität, Karl-Rahner-Platz 1, A-6020 Innsbruck, Österreich.
Canada: Faculté de Theologie et Institut Supérieur de Science Religieuses (1878), University of Montreal, 3034, Bd. Edouard-Montpetit, C.P. 6128, Montral, QC H3C 3J7, Canada.
Croatia: Facolta di Teologia Cattolica nell'Università Statale de Split (1999), Zrinsko-Frankopanska, 19, 21000 Split, Hrvatska.
Katolicki Bogoslovni Fakultet u Zagrebu (1669), Vlaska 38, 10000 Zagreb, Hrvatska.
Czech Republic: Cyrilometodejska teologicka fakulta (1570), Univerzitni 22, 771-11 Olomouc, Ceska Republika.
Katolicka teologicka fakulta University Karlovy (1347), Thakurova 3, 160 00 Praha 6/Dejvice, Ceska Republika.
France: Faculté de Theologie Catholique (1567), 9, Place de l'Université, 67084 Strasbourg, France.
Germany: Katholisch-Theologische Fakultät, Universität Augsburg (1970), Universitätsstrasse 10, D-86159 Augsburg, Bundesrepublik Deutschland.
Katholisch-Theologische Fakultät, Universität Bamberg (1972), An der Universität 2, D-96045 Bamberg, Bundesrepublik Deutschland.
Katholisch-Theologische Fakultät (1965), Universität Ruhr, Universitätsstrasse 150, Postfach 102148, D-44801 Bochum, Bundesrepublik Deutschland.
Katholisch-Theologische Fakultät Universität Bonn (1818), Am Hof 1, D-53113 Bonn, Bundesrepublik Deutschland.
Theologische Fakultät (1657), Albert-Ludwigs Universität, Erbprinzstrasse 13, D-79098 Freiburg im Breisgau, Bundesrepublik Deutschland.
Fachbereich Katholische Theologie (1946), Johannes Gutenberg-Universität, Saarstrasse 21, D-55122, Mainz, Bundesrepublik Deutschland.
Katholisch-Theologische Fakultät (1472), Ludwig-Maximilians-Universität, Geschw.-Scholl-Platz 1, D-80539, München, Bundesrepublik Deutschland.
Katholisch-Theologische Fakultät (1780), WestfälischeWilhelms-Universität, Johannisstrasse 8-10, D-48143, Münster, Bundesrepublik Deutschland.
Katholisch-Theologische Fakultät (1978), Michaeligasse 13, D-94032, Passau, Bundesrepublik Deutschland.
Fachbereich Katholische Theologie (1962), Universitätsstrasse 31, D-93053 Regensburg, Bundesrepublik Deutschland.
Katholisch-Theologische Fakultät (1477), Eberhard-Karls-Universität Tübingen, Libermeisterstr., 18, D-72076 Tübingen,

Bundesrepublik Deutschland.

Katholisch-Theologische Fakultät (1402), Bayerische Julius-Maximilians-Universität, Sanderring 2, D-97070 Würzburg, Bundesrepublik Deutschland.

Lithuania: Kataliku Teologijos Fakultetas (1922), Vilniaus 29, LT-3000 Kaunas, Lietuva.

Poland: Wydzial Teologiczny, Wydzial Prawa Kanonicznego, Wydzial Filozofii Chrzescijanskiej (1999), ul. Dewajtis, 5, 01-815 Warszawa, Polska.

Wydzial Teologiczny Uniwersytetu Slaskiego w Katowicach (2000), ul. Wita Stwosza 17 A, 40-042 Katowice, Polska.

Wydzial Teologii Uniwersytetu Warminsko-Mazurskiego w Olsztynie (1999), ul. Stanislawa Kard. Hozjusza, 15, 11-041 Olsztyn, Polska.

Wydzial Teologiczny (1994), ul. Drzymaly, 1/a, 45-342 Opole, Polska.

Wydzial Teologiczny Uniwersytetu Mikolaja Kopernika w. Toruniu (2001), pl. Bl. Ks. S. Frelichowskiego 1, 87-100, Torun, Polska.

Slovakia: Rimskokatolicka cyrilo-metodska bohoslovecka fakulta (1919), Archdiocese of Bratislava-Trnava, Kapitulska 26, 814-58 Bratislava, Slovenska Republika.

Slovenia: Teoloska Fakulteta v. Ljublana (1920), p.p. 2007, 1001 Ljubljana, Slovenia.

Switzerland: Theologische Fakultät (1889), University of Fribourg, Misericorde, CH-1700 Fribourg, Switzerland.

PONTIFICAL UNIVERSITIES AND INSTITUTES IN ROME

(*Source*: Annuario Pontificio.)

Pontifical Gregorian University (Gregorian) (1552): Piazza della Pilotta, 4, 00187 Rome. Associated with the university are: **Pontifical Biblical Institute** (May 7, 1909): Via della Pilotta, 25, 00187 Rome; **Pontifical Institute of Oriental Studies** (Oct. 15, 1917): Piazza S. Maria Maggiore, 7, 00185 Rome.

Pontifical Lateran University (1773): Piazza S. Giovanni in Laterano, 4, 00184 Rome. Attached to the university is the **Pontifical Institute of Studies of Marriage and the Family**, erected by Pope John Paul II, Oct 7, 1982; a section of the Institute was established at the Dominican House of Studies, Washington, DC, by a decree dated Aug. 22, 1988; sections were opened in Mexico in 1992 and Valencia, Spain, in 1994.

Pontifical Urbaniana University (1627): Via Urbano VIII, 16, 00165 Rome.

Pontifical University of St. Thomas Aquinas (Angelicum) (1580), of the Order of Preachers: Largo Angelicum, 1, 00184 Rome.

Pontifical University *Salesianum* (May 3, 1940; university designation May 24, 1973), of the Salesians of Don Bosco: Piazza dell' Ateneo Salesiano, 1, 00139 Rome. Associated with the university is the **Pontifical Institute of Higher Latin Studies**, known as the Faculty of Christian and Classical Letters (June 4, 1971).

Pontifical University *della Santa Croce* (of the Holy Cross) (Jan. 9, 1985), of the Personal Prelature of Opus Dei: Piazza S. Apollinare, 49, 00186 Rome.

Pontifical University *Antonianum* (of St. Anthony) (May 17, 1933), of the Order of Friars Minor: Via Merulana, 124, 00185 Rome. Pontifical University status granted in 2005.

Pontifical Athenaeum of St. Anselm (1687) of the Benedictines: Piazza Cavalieri di Malta, 5, 00153 Rome.

Pontifical Athenaeum *Regina Apostolorum* (Queen of the Apostles), of the Legionaries of Christ: Via Aurelia Antica, 460, 00165 Rome.

Pontifical Institute of Sacred Music (1911; May 24, 1931): Via di Torre Rossa, 21, 00165 Rome.

Pontifical Institute of Christian Archeology (Dec. 11, 1925): Via Napoleone III, 1, 00185 Rome.

Pontifical Theological Faculty *St. Bonaventure* (Dec. 18, 1587), of the Order of Friars Minor Conventual: Via del Serafico, 1, 00142 Rome.

Pontifical Theological Faculty, Pontifical Institute of Spirituality *Teresianum* (1935), of the Discalced Carmelites: Piazza San Pancrazio, 5-A, 00152 Rome.

Pontifical Theological Faculty *Marianum* (1398), of the Servants of Mary: Viale Trente Aprile, 6, 00153 Rome. Attached to the university is **The Marian Library/International Marian Research Institute** (IMRI), U.S. branch of Pontifical Theological Faculty Marianum, University of Dayton, Dayton, OH, 45469 (affil. 1976, inc. 1983).

Pontifical Institute of Arabic and Islamic Studies (1926), of the Missionaries of Africa: Viale di Trastevere, 89, 00153 Rome.

Pontifical Faculty of Educational Science *Auxilium* (June 27, 1970), of the Daughters of Mary, Help of Christians: Via Cremolino, 141, 00166 Rome.

Pontifical Ecclesiastical Academy

The Pontifical Ecclesiastical Academy (*Pontificia Ecclesiastica Academia*) is one of the various Roman Academies (not to be confused with the Pontifical Universities that are also in Rome). The Academy has as its purpose to prepare future Vatican diplomats for service around the world and in the Secretariat of State. The Academy was founded in 1701 by Pope Clement XI to prepare students for diplomatic service on behalf of the Holy See. It bore the original name of the Pontifical Academy of Noble Ecclesiastics and was open only to members of noble families in Europe (undisputed noble lineage was expressly required). This requirement was eventually phased out, and young men of promise from all walks of life are now eligible, providing that they meet the strict requirements of admission. The name was changed to the present title to reflect the changed circumstances of admission.

Those chosen are most often already recipients of assorted degrees, including but not limited to doctorates in the sacred sciences, especially theology, Church History, and especially canon law from pontifical universities. Once admitted, these young priests undergo a very demanding program of studies that includes all aspects of ecclesiastical diplomacy and diplomatic history, Church history, diplomatic law, and also intensive study of modern languages. The current president of the Academy is Abp. Beniamino Stella.

Catholic Communications

CATHOLIC PRESS

Statistics

The 2013 Catholic Press Directory, published by the Catholic Press Association, reported a total of 243 periodicals in North America, with a circulation of 10,330,011. The figures included 141 newspapers, with a circulation of 4,994,063; 70 magazines, with a circulation of 3,774,301; 19 newsletters, with a circulation of 891,147; and 13 other language periodicals (newspapers and magazines), with a circulation of 373,500.

Newspapers in the U.S.

There were 138 newspapers in the United States, with a circulation of 4,928,061. Four of these had national circulation totaling 121,505; 133 were diocesan newspapers with a total circulation of 4,783,556. There was one other miscellaneous newspaper with a total circulation of 23,000.

National papers included: *National Catholic Register*, founded 1900; *Our Sunday Visitor*, founded 1912; *National Catholic Reporter*, founded 1964; *The Wanderer*, founded 1867. In addition there were *The Adoremus Bulletin*, founded 1995; and the English-language weekly edition of *L'Osservatore Romano*, established in the U.S. in 1998. In 2012 The oldest U.S. Catholic newspaper is *The Pilot* of Boston, established in 1829 (under a different title).

Magazines in the U.S.

The Catholic Press Directory reported 70 magazines in the U.S., Canada, and International with a circulation of 3,774,301. In addition, there were 19 newsletters, with a circulation of 891,147.

America and *Commonweal* are the only weekly and biweekly magazines, respectively, of general interest.

The monthly magazines with the largest circulation are *Columbia* (250,000), the official organ of the Knights of Columbus, *Catholic Digest* (285,000) and *St. Anthony's Messenger* (135,000).

Other-language publications: There were an additional 12 publications (newspapers and magazines) in the U.S. in languages other than English, with a circulation of 371,000.

Canadian Statistics

There were three newspapers in Canada with a circulation of 66,002. These included one national newspaper (*The Catholic Register*, founded 1893) and two diocesan (*The B.C. Catholic* and *Western Catholic Reporter*). There were 4 magazines, with a circulation of approximately 24,000.

CATHOLIC NEWSPAPERS, MAGAZINES, AND NEWSLETTERS IN THE U.S.

(*Sources:* Catholic Press Directory; The Catholic Journalist; Catholic Almanac *survey; Catholic News Service.*) *Abbreviation code: a, annual; bm, bimonthly; m, monthly; q, quarterly; w, weekly; bw, bi-weekly.*

Newspapers

Our Sunday Visitor, w; 200 Noll Plaza, Huntington, IN 46750; (260) 356-8400; www.osv.com; national.

Acadiana Catholic, m; 1408 Carmel Ave., Lafayette, LA 70501; (337) 261-5511; www.dollouisiana.org; Lafayette diocese.

A.D. Times, bw; P.O. Box F, Allentown, PA 18105-1538; (610) 871-5200; Allentown diocese.

Adoremus Bulletin, The, 10 times a year; P.O. Box 3286, St. Louis, MO 63130; (314) 863-8385; www.adoremus.org; national liturgical journal.

Agua Viva, m; 1280 Med Park Dr., Las Cruces, NM 88005-3239; (575) 523-5777; www.dioceseoflascruces.org; Las Cruces diocese.

Alaskan Shepherd, bm; 1312 Peger Rd., Fairbanks, AK 99709; (904) 374-9532; www.cbna.info; Fairbanks diocese.

America (Ukrainian-English), 2 times a week; 817 N. Franklin St., Philadelphia, PA 19123; (215) 627-4519; Providence Association of Ukrainian Catholics in America.

Anchor, The, w; P.O. Box 7, Fall River, MA 02722; (508) 675-7151; Fall River diocese.

Arkansas Catholic, w; P.O. Box 7417, Little Rock, AR 72217; (501) 664-0125; www.arkansas-catholic.org. Little Rock diocese.

Arlington Catholic Herald, w; 200 N. Glebe Rd., Suite 607, Arlington, VA 22203; (703) 841-2590; www.catholicherald.com; Arlington diocese.

Bayou Catholic, The, w; P.O. Box 505, Schriever, LA 70395; (985) 850-3132; www.htdiocese.org; Houma-Thibodaux diocese.

Beacon, The, w; P.O. Box 1887, Clifton, NJ 07015-1887; (973) 279-8845; www.patersondiocese.org; Paterson diocese.

Bishop's Bulletin, m; 523 N. Duluth Ave., Sioux Falls, SD 57104-2714; (605) 988-3791; www.sfcatholic.org; Sioux Falls diocese.

Bolletino, m; 675 Hegenberger Rd., Suite 110, Oakland, CA 94621; (510) 633-9058; www.icf.org; Italian Catholic Federation.

Byzantine Catholic World, bw; 66 Riverview Ave., Pittsburgh, PA 15214; (412) 231-4000; www.archeparchy.org; Pittsburgh Byzantine archdiocese.

Catholic Accent, 40 times a year; 725 E. Pittsburgh St., Greensburg, PA 15601; (724) 834-4010; www.dioceseofgreensburg.org; Greensburg diocese.

Catholic Advance, The, w; 424 N. Broadway,

Wichita, KS 67202-2377; (316) 269-3965; www. catholicadvance.org; Wichita diocese.

Catholic Advocate, The, w; 171 Clifton Ave., Newark, NJ 07104-9500; (973) 497-4200; www. rcan.org/advocate; Newark archdiocese.

Catholic Aid News, m; 3499 N. Lexington Ave., St. Paul, MN 55126; (651) 490-0170; www.catholicaid.com.

Catholic Anchor, w; 225 Cordova St., Anchorage, AK 99501; (907) 297-7708; www.catholicanchor. org. Anchorage diocese.

Catholic Calendar, semi-monthly; 411 Iris St., Lake Charles, LA 70601; (337) 439-7426; www.lcdiocese.org; one page in local newspaper semi-monthly; Lake Charles diocese.

Catholic Chronicle, bw; P.O. Box 985, Toledo, OH 43697; (419) 244-6711; www.catholicchronicle.org; Toledo diocese.

Catholic Commentator, The, bw; P.O. Box 14746, Baton Rouge, LA 70898-4746; (225) 387-0983; www.diobr.com; Baton Rouge diocese.

Catholic Courier, w; P.O. Box 24379, Rochester, NY 14624-0379; (585) 529-9530; www.catholiccourier.com; Rochester diocese.

Catholic East Texas, bw; 1015 ESE Loop 323, Tyler, TX 75701-9663; (903) 534-1077; Tyler diocese.

Catholic Exponent, bw; P.O. Box 6787, Youngstown, OH 44501-6787; (330) 744-5251; www.cathexpo.org; Youngstown diocese.

Catholic Free Press, w; 51 Elm St., Worcester, MA 01609; (508) 757-6387; www.catholicfreepress.org; Worcester diocese.

Catholic Health World, semi-monthly; 4455 Woodson Rd., St. Louis, MO 63134-3797; (314) 253-3410; www. chausa.org; Catholic Health Association; national.

Catholic Herald, The Colorado, m; 228 N. Cascade Ave., Colorado Springs, CO 80903; (719) 636-2345; www. coloradocatholicherald.com; Colorado Springs diocese.

Catholic Herald, w; P.O. Box 070913, Milwaukee, WI 53207-0913; (414) 769-3500; www.chnonline.org; Milwaukee archdiocese; also publishes editions for Madison and Superior dioceses.

Catholic Herald: Madison Edition, w; 702 S. High Point Rd., Madison, WI 53719; (608) 821-3070; www.madisoncatholicherald.org; Madison diocese.

Catholic Herald: Superior Edition, w; P.O. Box 969, Superior, WI 54880; (715) 392-8268; www. catholicherald.org; Superior diocese.

Catholic Herald, bw; 5890 Newman Ct., Sacramento, CA 95819; (916) 452-3344; www.diocese-sacramento.org; Sacramento diocese.

Catholic Islander, m; P.O. Box 301825, St. Thomas, USVI, 00803-1825; (340) 774-3166; www. catholicislander.com; Virgin Islands diocese.

Catholic Journalist, The, m; 205 West Monroe St., Suite 470, Chicago, IL 60606; (312) 380-6789; www. catholicpress.org; Catholic Press Association.

Catholic Key, 44 times a year; P.O. Box 419037, Kansas City, MO 64141-6037; (816) 756-1850; www.catholickey. org; Kansas City-St. Joseph diocese.

Catholic Light, bw; 300 Wyoming Ave., Scranton, PA 18503; (570) 207-2229; www.dioceseofscranton. org; Scranton diocese.

Catholic Lighthouse, m; P.O. Box 4070, Victoria, TX 77903; (361) 573-0828; www.victoriadiocese. org; Victoria diocese.

Catholic Messenger, w; P.O. Box 460, Davenport, IA 52805; (563) 323-9959; www.catholicmessenger. org; Davenport diocese.

Catholic Mirror The, m; 601 Grand Ave., Des Moines, IA 50309; (515) 237-5046; www.dmdiocese. org; Des Moines diocese.

Catholic Miscellany, The, w; 119 Broad St., Charleston, SC 29401; (843) 724-8375; www.the-miscellany.org; Charleston diocese.

Catholic Missourian, w; P.O. Box 104900, Jefferson City, MO 65110-4900; (573) 635-9127; www.diojef-fcity.org; Jefferson City diocese.

Catholic Moment, The, w; P.O. Box 1603, Lafayette, IN 47902; (765) 742-2050; www.the-catholicmoment.org; Lafayette diocese.

Catholic New World, The, w; 3525 S. Lake Park Ave., Chicago, IL 60653; (312) 534-7324; www. catholicnewworld.com; Chicago archdiocese.

Catholic New York, w; 1011 First Ave., New York, NY 10022; (212) 688-2399; www.cny.org; New York archdiocese.

Catholic News, w; P.O. Box 85, Independence Square, Port-of-Spain, Trinidad, West Indies; (868) 623-6093; www.catholicnews-tt.net.

Catholic News and Herald, The, w; P.O. Box 37267, Charlotte, NC 28237; (704) 370-3333; www. charlottediocese.org; Charlotte diocese.

Catholic Northwest Progress, The, w; 710 9th Ave., Seattle, WA 98104; (206) 382-4850; www.seattlee-arch.org/progress; Seattle archdiocese.

Catholic Observer, bw; Box 1730, Springfield, MA 01101-1730; (413) 737-4744; www.iobserve.org; Springfield diocese.

Catholic Peace Voice, q.; 532 W. Eighth St., Erie, PA 16502-1343; (814) 453-4955; www.paxchristiusa. org; published by Pax Christi.

Catholic Post, The, w; P.O. Box 1722, Peoria, IL 61656; (309) 671-1550; www.thecatholicpost.com; Peoria diocese.

Catholic Register, bw; P.O. Box 413, Hollidaysburg, PA 16648; (814) 695-7563; www.cathregaj.org; Altoona-Johnstown diocese.

Catholic Review, w; P.O. Box 777, Baltimore, MD 21203; (443) 524-3150; www.catholicreview. org; Baltimore archdiocese.

Catholic San Francisco, bw; One Peter Yorke Way, San Francisco, CA 94109; (415) 614-5632; www. catholic-sf.org; San Francisco archdiocese.

Catholic Sentinel, w; P.O. Box 18030, Portland, OR 97218-0030; (503) 281-1191; www.sentinel.org; Portland archdiocese, Baker diocese.

Catholic Spirit, The, w; 244 Dayton Ave., Ste. 2, St. Paul, MN 55102-1893; (651) 291-4444; www.thecatholicspirit. com; St. Paul & Minneapolis archdiocese.

Catholic Spirit, The, w; P.O. Box 191, Metuchen, NJ 08840; (732) 562-2424; www.catholicspirit.com; Metuchen diocese.

Catholic Spirit, The, m; P.O. Box 15405, Austin, TX 78761; (512) 949-2443; www.austindiocese.org; Austin diocese.

Catholic Spirit, The, m; P.O. Box 230, Wheeling, WV 26003-0119; (304) 233-0880; www.dwc.org; Wheeling-Charleston diocese.

Catholic Standard, w; P.O. Box 4464, Washington, DC, 20017; (202) 281-2410; www.cathstan.org; Washington archdiocese.

Catholic Standard and Times, w; 222 N. 17th St., Philadelphia, PA 19103; (215) 587-3660; www.cst-phl.com; Philadelphia archdiocese.

Catholic Star Herald, w; 15 North 7th St., Camden, NJ 08102; (856) 583-6142; www.catholicstarherald.org; Camden diocese.

Catholic Sun, The, semi-monthly; P.O. Box 13549, Phoenix, AZ 85002; (602) 354-2139; www.catholicsun.org; Phoenix diocese.

Catholic Sun, The, w; 421 S. Warren St., Syracuse, NY 13202; (315) 422-8153; www.syrdio.org; Syracuse diocese.

Catholic Telegraph, w; 100 E. 8th St., Cincinnati, OH 45202; (513) 421-3131; www.catholiccincinnati.org; Cincinnati archdiocese.

Catholic Times, w; 197 E. Gay St., Columbus, OH 43215-3229; (614) 224-5195; www.ctonline.org; Columbus diocese.

Catholic Times, The, w; P.O. Box 1405, Saginaw, MI 48605; (810) 659-4670; www.catholictimesmi.org; Lansing diocese.

Catholic Times, The, w; P.O. Box 4004, La Crosse, WI 54602-4004; (608) 788-1524; www.dioceseoflacrosse.com; La Crosse diocese.

Catholic Times, w; P.O. Box 3187, Springfield, IL 62708-3187; (217) 698-8500; www.ct.dio.org; Springfield diocese.

Catholic Transcript, w; 467 Bloomfield Ave., Bloomfield, CT 06002; (860) 286-2828; Hartford archdiocese, Bridgeport and Norwich dioceses.

Catholic Universe Bulletin, bw; 1027 Superior Ave. NE, Cleveland, OH 44114-2556; (216) 696-6525; www.catholicuniversebulletin.org; Cleveland diocese.

Catholic Virginian, bw; 7800 Carousel Lane, Richmond, VA 23294; (804) 359-5654; www.catholicvirginian.org; Richmond diocese.

Catholic Voice, The, bw; 3014 Lakeshore Ave., Oakland, CA 94610; (510) 893-5339; www.catholicvoiceoakland.org; Oakland diocese.

Catholic Voice, The, bw; P.O. Box 4010, Omaha, NE 68104-0010; (402) 558-6611; www.catholicvoiceomaha.com; Omaha archdiocese.

Catholic War Veteran, bm; 441 N. Lee St., Alexandria, VA 22314-2344; (703) 549-3622; www.cwv.org.

Catholic Week, w; P.O. Box 349, Mobile, AL 36601; (251) 434-1544; Mobile archdiocese.

Catholic Weekly, The, w; P.O. Box 1405, Saginaw, MI 48605; (989) 793-7661; www.catholicweekly.org; Saginaw diocese.

Catholic Weekly, The, w; P.O. Box 1405, Saginaw, MI 48602; (989) 793-7661; Gaylord diocese.

Catholic Witness, The, w; P.O. Box 2555, Harrisburg, PA 17105; (717) 657-4804; www.hbgdiocese.org; Harrisburg diocese.

Central Washington Catholic, bm; 5301-A Tieton Dr., Yakima, WA 98908; (509) 965-7117; Yakima diocese.

Chicago Catolico (Spanish), m; 721 N. La Salle St., 4th Floor, Chicago, IL 60610; (312) 655-7880; Chicago archdiocese.

Chronicle of Catholic Life, bm; 1001 North Grand Ave., Pueblo, CO 81003; (719) 685-9617; www.dioceseofpueblo.com; Pueblo diocese.

Church Today, twice a month; P.O. Box 7417, Alexandria, LA 71306-0417; (318) 445-2401; www.diocesealex.org; Alexandria diocese.

Clarion Herald, bw; P.O. Box 53247, New Orleans, LA 70153; (504) 596-3035; www.clarionherald.org; New Orleans archdiocese.

Compass, The, w; P.O. Box 23825, Green Bay, WI 54305-3825; (920) 437-7531; www.thecompassnews.org; Green Bay diocese.

Courier, The, m; P.O. Box 949, Winona, MN 55987-0949; (507) 454-4643; www.dow.org; Winona diocese.

Criterion, The, w; P.O. Box 1717, Indianapolis, IN 46206; (317) 236-1570; www.criteriononline.com; Indianapolis archdiocese.

Cross Roads, bw; 1310 W. Main St., Lexington, KY 40508-2040; (859) 253-1993; Lexington diocese.

Dakota Catholic Action, m (except July); P.O. Box 1137, Bismarck, ND 58502-1137; (701) 222-3035; www.bismarckdiocese.com; Bismarck diocese.

Denver Catholic Register, w; 1300 S. Steele St., Denver, CO 80210-2599; (303) 715-3215; www.archden.org; Denver archdiocese.

Dialog, The, w; P.O. Box 2208, Wilmington, DE 19899; (302) 573-3109; www.cdow.org/dialog.html; Wilmington diocese.

East Tennessee Catholic, The, bw; P.O. Box 11127, Knoxville, TN 37939-1127; (865) 584-3307; www.dioceseofknoxville.org; Knoxville diocese.

East Texas Catholic, semi-monthly; P.O. Box 3948, Beaumont, TX 77704-3948; (409) 832-3944; Beaumont diocese.

Eastern Catholic Life, bw; 445 Lackawanna Ave., W. Paterson, NJ 07424; (973) 890-7777; Passaic Byzantine eparchy.

Eastern Oklahoma Catholic, bw; Box 690240, Tulsa, OK 74169-0240; (918) 294-1904; www.dioceseoftulsa.org; Tulsa diocese.

Eternal Flame (Armenian-English), 167 North 6th St., Brooklyn, NY 11211; (212) 477-2030; Armenian exarchate.

Evangelist, The, w; 40 N. Main Ave., Albany, NY 12203; (518) 453-6688; www.evangelist.org; Albany diocese.

Fairfield County Catholic, m; 238 Jewett Ave., Bridgeport, CT 06606; (203) 416-1461; www.bridgeportdiocese.org; Bridgeport diocese.

FaithLife, bw; 429 E. Grandview Blvd., Erie, PA 16504; (814) 824-1161; www.eriecd.org; Erie diocese.

Florida Catholic, The, w; P.O. Box 4993, Orlando, FL 32802-4993; (407) 373-0075; www.thefloridacatholic.org; Orlando diocese; publishes editions for Miami archdiocese and Palm Beach, Pensacola-Tallahassee, St. Petersburg and Venice dioceses.

Florida Catholic: Miami Edition, w; 9401 Biscayne Blvd., Miami, FL 33138; (305) 762-1131; www.thefloridacatholic.org.

Florida Catholic: Palm Beach Edition, w; P.O. Box 109650, Palm Beach Gardens, FL 33410; (561) 775-9528; www.thefloridacatholic.org; Palm Beach diocese.

Florida Catholic: Pensacola-Tallahassee Edition, w; 11 North B St., Pensacola, FL 32501; (850) 435-3500; www.thefloridacatholic.org.

Florida Catholic: St. Petersburg Edition, w; P.O. Box 43022, St. Petersburg, FL 33743; (727) 345-3338.

Florida Catholic: Venice Edition, w; 1000 Pinebrook Rd., Venice, FL 34292; (941) 486-4701; www.thefloridacatholic.org.

Four County Catholic, m; 31 Perkins Ave., Norwich, CT 06360; (860) 886-3613; www.norwichdiocese.org; Norwich diocese.

Georgia Bulletin, w; 680 W. Peachtree St. NW, Atlanta, GA 30308; (404) 877-5500; www.archatl.com; Atlanta archdiocese.

Glasilo KSKJ Amerikanski Slovenec (Slovenian), bw; 708 E. 159th, Cleveland, OH 44110; (216) 541-7243; American Slovenian Catholic Union.

Globe, The, w; P.O. Box 5079, Sioux City, IA 51102; (712) 255-2550; www.catholicglobe.org; Sioux City diocese.

Good News for the Diocese of Kalamazoo, The, m; 215 N. Westnedge, Kalamazoo, MI 49007-3760; (269) 349-8714; www.dioceseofkalamazoo.org; Kalamazoo diocese.

Gulf Pine Catholic, w; 1790 Popps Ferry Rd., Biloxi, MS 39532; (228) 702-2126; Biloxi diocese.

Harvest, The, 121 23rd St. South, Great Falls, MT 59405; (406) 727-6683; www.dioceseofgfb.org; Great Falls diocese.

Hawaii Catholic Herald, bw; 1184 Bishop St., Honolulu, HI 96813; (808) 585-3300; www. hawaiicatholicherald.com; Honolulu diocese.

Hlas Naroda (Voice of the Nation) (Czech-English), bw; P.O. Box 159, Berwyn, IL 60402; (708) 484-0583.

Horizons, twice a month; 1900 Carlton Rd., Parma, OH 44134-3129; (216) 741-3312; www. parma.org; Parma Byzantine eparchy.

Idaho Catholic Register, twice a month; 1501 S. Federal Way, Boise, ID 83705; (208) 342-1311; www.catholicidaho.org/icr.cfm; Boise diocese.

Inland Register, every 3 weeks; P.O. Box 48, Spokane, WA 99210; (509) 358-7340; www.dioce-seofspokane.org; Spokane diocese.

Inside Passage, bw; 415 6th St., Juneau, AK 99801; (907) 586-2227; www.dioceseofjuneau.org; Juneau diocese.

Intermountain Catholic, w; P.O. Box 2489, Salt Lake City, UT 84110-2489; (801) 328-8641; www. icatholic.org; Salt Lake City diocese.

Jednota (Slovak-Eng.), w; 6611 Rockside Rd., Independence, OH 44131; (216) 642-9406; First Catholic Slovak Union.

Leaven, The, w; 12615 Parallel Parkway, Kansas City, KS 66109; (913) 721-1570; www.theleaven.com; Kansas City archdiocese.

Long Island Catholic, The, w; P.O. Box 9000, Rockville Centre, NY 11575-9000; (516) 594-1000; www.licatholic.org; Rockville Centre diocese.

L'Osservatore Romano, w; 200 Noll Plaza, Huntington, IN 46750; (800) 348-2440; www.osv. com. English edition of the Vatican newspaper (published by Our Sunday Visitor).

Maronite Voice, The, m; 4611 Sadler Rd., Glen Allen, VA 23060; (804) 270-7234; www.stmaron. org; Eparchy of St. Maron of Brooklyn.

Message, The, w; P.O. Box 4169, Evansville, IN 47724-0169; (812) 424-5536; Evansville diocese.

Messenger, The, w; 2620 Lebanon Ave., Belleville, IL 62221; (618) 233-8670; www.bellevillemessenger. org; Belleville diocese.

Messenger, The, 45 times a year; P.O. Box 15550, Erlanger, KY 41015; (859) 392-1570; www.coving-tondiocese.org; Covington diocese.

Michigan Catholic, The, w; 305 Michigan Ave., 4th Floor, Detroit, MI 48226; (313) 224-8000; Detroit archdiocese.

Mirror, The, w; 601 S. Jefferson Ave., Springfield, MO 65806-3143; (417) 866-0841; www.the-mirror. org; Springfield-Cape Girardeau diocese.

Mississippi Catholic, w; P.O. Box 2130, Jackson, MS 39225-2130; (601) 969-1880; www.mississip-picatholic.org; Jackson diocese.

Monitor, The, w; P.O. Box 5147, Trenton, NJ 08638; (609) 406-7404; www.dioceseoftrenton.org; Trenton diocese.

Montana Catholic, The, 16 times a year; P.O. Box 1729, Helena, MT 59624; (406) 442-5820; www. diocesehelena.org/mtcath; Helena diocese.

Narod Polski (Polish Nation) (Polish-Eng.) semi-monthly; 984 Milwaukee Ave., Chicago, IL 60622-4101; (773) 782-2600; www.prcua.com; Polish Roman Catholic Union of America.

National Catholic Register, w; 432 Washington Ave., North Haven, CT 06473; (203) 230-3800; www.ncregister.com; national.

National Catholic Reporter, w; P.O. Box 411009, Kansas City, MO 64141; (816) 531-0538; www. ncronline.org; national.

National Jesuit News, m; 1616 P St. NW, Suite 300, Washington, DC 20036; (202) 462-0400; www.jesuit.org.

New Earth, The, m; 5201 Bishops Blvd., Ste. A, Fargo, ND 58104; (701) 356-7958; www.fargidi-ocese.org; Fargo diocese.

New Star, The, every 3 weeks; 2208 W. Chicago Ave., Chicago, IL 60622; (312) 772-1919; St. Nicholas of Chicago Ukrainian diocese.

New Vision/La Nueva Vision, m.; P.O. Box 31, Tucson, AZ 85702; (520) 792-3410; www.newvision-online.org; Tucson diocese.

North Country Catholic, w; P.O. Box 326, Ogdensburg, NY 13669; (315) 393-2540; www. northcountrycatholic.org; Ogdensburg diocese.

North Texas Catholic, w; 800 West Loop 820 South, Fort Worth, TX 76108; (817) 560-3300; www.fwdioc.org; Fort Worth diocese.

Northern Cross, The, m.; 2830 E. 4th St., Duluth, MN 55812; (218) 724-9111; www.dioceseduluth. org; Duluth diocese.

Northern Nevada Catholic, m; 290 S. Arlington Ave., #200, Reno, NV 89501; (775) 326-9410; Reno diocese.

Northwest Indiana Catholic, w; 9292 Broadway, Merrillville, IN 46410-7088; (219) 769-9292; www. nwicatholic.com; Gary diocese.

Oblate World, The and Voice of Hope, twice a month; P.O. Box 680, Tewksbury, MA 01876; (978) 851-7258; www.omiusa.org; published by the Missionary Oblates of Mary Immaculate.

Observer, The, m; P.O. Box 2079, Monterey, CA 93942; (831) 373-2919; www.dioceseofmonterey.org; Monterey diocese.

Observer, The, m; 4545 W. 63rd St., Chicago, IL 60629; (312) 585-9500; Lithuanian Roman Catholic Federation of America.

Observer, The, twice a month; P.O. Box 7044, Rockford, IL 61125; (815) 399-4300; www.rockford-diocese.org; Rockford diocese.

One Voice, w; P.O. Box 10822, Birmingham, AL 35202; (205) 838-8305; Birmingham diocese.

Orange County Catholic, m.; P.O. Box 14195, Orange, CA 92863-1595; (714) 282-3022; Orange diocese.

Our Northland Diocese, semi-monthly; P.O. Box 610, Crookston, MN 56716; (218) 281-4553; www. crookston.org; Crookston diocese.

People of God, m; 4000 St. Joseph Pl. NW, Albuquerque, NM 87120; (505) 831-8180; www.archdiocesesantafe.org; Santa Fe archdiocese.

Pilot, The, w; 2121 Commonwealth Ave., Brighton, MA 02135-3193; (617) 746-5889; www. thebostonpilot.com; Boston archdiocese.

Pittsburgh Catholic, w; 135 First Ave., Suite 200, Pittsburgh, PA 15222; (412) 471-1252; www.pittsburghcatholic.org; Pittsburgh diocese.

Prairie Catholic, m; 1400 6th St. North, New Ulm, MN 56073-2099; (507) 359-2966; www.dnu.org; New Ulm diocese.

Record, The, w; Maloney Center, 1200 S. Shelby St., Louisville, KY 40203-2600; (502) 636-0296; www.archlou.org; Louisville archdiocese.

Register, The, w; P.O. Box 1038, Salina, KS 67402; (785) 827-8746; www.salinadiocese.org; Salina diocese.

RI Catholic, The, w; 184 Broad St., Providence, RI 02903; (401) 272-1010; www.thericatholic.com; Providence diocese.

Rio Grande Catholic, The, m; 499 St. Matthews St., El Paso, TX 79907; (915) 872-8414; www.elpasodiocese.org; El Paso diocese.

St. Louis Review, w; 20 Archbishop May Dr., St. Louis, MO 63119; (314) 792-7500; www.stlouisreview.com; St. Louis archdiocese.

Seasons, q; 5800 Weiss St., Saginaw, MI 48603-2799; (989) 797-6666; www.dioceseofsaginaw.org; Saginaw diocese.

Slovak Catholic Falcon (Slovak-English), w; 205 Madison St., P.O.Box 899, Passaic, NJ 07055; (973) 777-4010; Slovak Catholic Sokol.

Sooner Catholic, The, bw; P.O. Box 32180, Oklahoma City, OK 73123; (405) 721-1810; www.catharchdioceseok.org; Oklahoma City archdiocese.

Sophia, q; 200 E. North Ave., Northlake, IL 60164; (708) 865-7050; Newton Melkite eparchy.

South Plains Catholic, twice a month; P.O. Box 98700, Lubbock, TX 79499-8700; (806) 792-3943; www.catholiclubbock.org; Lubbock diocese.

South Texas Catholic, twice a month; P.O. Box 2620, Corpus Christi, TX 78403-2620; (361) 882-6191; www.goccn.org; Corpus Christi diocese.

Southern Cross, semi-monthly; P.O. Box 81869, San Diego, CA 92138; (858) 490-8266; www.thesoutherncross.org; San Diego diocese.

Southern Cross, The, w; 601 E. Liberty Street, Savannah, GA 31401-5196; (912) 201-4100; www.diosav.org; Savannah diocese.

Southern Nebraska Register, w; P.O. Box 80329, Lincoln, NE 68501; (402) 488-0090; Lincoln diocese.

Southwest Catholic, The, m; P.O. 411 Iris St., Lake Charles, LA 70601; (337) 439-7426; www.lcdiocese.org; Lake Charles diocese.

Southwest Kansas Register, bw; P.O. Box 137, Dodge City, KS 67801; (620) 227-1519; www.dcdiocese.org/swkregister; Dodge City diocese.

Sower (Ukrainian and English), bw; 14 Peveril Rd., Stamford, CT 06902; (203) 324-7698; www.thesower@adcus.com; Stamford Ukrainian diocese.

Star of Chaldeans (Arabic and English), bm; 25585 Berg Rd., Southfield, MI 48034; St. Thomas the Apostle Chaldean diocese.

Steubenville Register, bw; P.O. Box 160, Steubenville, OH 43952; (740) 282-3631; www.diosteub.org; Steubenville diocese.

Tablet, The, w; 310 Prospect Park West, Brooklyn, NY 11215-6214; (718) 965-7333; www.dioceseofbrooklyn.org/tablet; Brooklyn diocese.

Tautai, bw; P.O. Box 532, Feiloaimauso Hall, Apia, Samoa; Samoa-Apia archdiocese.

Tennessee Register, The, bw; 2400 21st Ave. S., Nashville, TN 37212; (615) 783-0770; www.dioceseofnashville.org; Nashville diocese.

Texas Catholic, The, bw; P.O. Box 190346, Dallas, TX 75219; (214) 528-8792; www.texascatholic.com; Dallas diocese.

Texas Catholic Herald, The, twice a month; 1700 San Jacinto St., Houston, TX 77001-0907; (713) 659-5461; Galveston-Houston diocese.

Tidings, The, w; 3424 Wilshire Blvd, Los Angeles, CA 90010; (213) 637-7360; www.the-tidings.com; Los Angeles archdiocese.

Today's Catholic, w; P.O. Box 11169, Fort Wayne, IN 46856; (260) 456-2824; www.diocesefwsb.org; Fort Wayne-South Bend diocese.

Today's Catholic, bw; P.O. Box 28410, San Antonio, TX 78228-0410; (210) 734-1690; www.satodayscatholic.org; San Antonio archdiocese.

UNIREA (The Union) (Romanian) 10 times a year; 4309 Olcott Ave., East Chicago, IN 46312; (219) 398-3760; Romanian diocese of Canton.

U. P. Catholic, The, semi-monthly; P.O. Box 548, Marquette, MI 49855; (906) 227-9131; www.dioceseofmarquette.org; Marquette diocese.

Valley Catholic, m; 900 Lafayette St., Suite 301, Santa Clara, CA 95050-4966; (408) 983-0260; www.valleycatholiconline.com; San Jose diocese.

Vermont Catholic Tribune, bw; P.O. Box 489, Burlington, VT 05402; (802) 658-6110; www.vermontcatholic.org; Burlington diocese.

Vida Nueva; 3424 Wilshire Blvd., Los Angeles, CA 90010-2241; (213) 637-7310.

Visitor, The, w; 305 N. 7th Ave., Ste. 206, St. Cloud, MN 56303; (320) 251-3022; www.stclouddiocese.org/visitor; St. Cloud diocese.

Voice of the Southwest, m; 711 S. Puerco, Gallup, NM 87301; (505) 863-4406; www.dioceseofgallup.org; Gallup diocese.

Wanderer, The, w; 201 Ohio St., St. Paul, MN 55107; (651) 224-5733; national.

Way, The (Ukrainian-Eng.), bw; 827 N. Franklin St., Philadelphia, PA 19123; (215) 922-5231; Philadelphia archeparchy.

West Nebraska Register, w; P.O. Box 608, Grand Island, NE 68802; (308) 382-4660; Grand Island diocese.

West River Catholic, m; P.O. Box 678, Rapid City, SD 57709; (605) 343-3541; www.rapidcitydiocese.org; Rapid City diocese.

West Tennessee Catholic, w; P.O. Box 341669, Memphis, TN 38184-1669; (901) 373-1213; www.cdom.org; Memphis diocese.

West Texas Angelus, m; P.O. Box 1829, San Angelo, TX 76902; (325) 651-7500; www.sanangelodiocese.org; San Angelo diocese.

West Texas Catholic, bw; P.O. Box 5644, Amarillo, TX 79117-5644; (806) 383-2243; www.amarillodiocese.org; Amarillo diocese.

Western Kentucky Catholic, m; 600 Locust St., Owensboro, KY 42301; (270) 683-1545; Owensboro diocese.

Western New York Catholic, m; 795 Main St., Buffalo, NY 14203-1250; (716) 847-8727; www.wnycatholic.org; Buffalo diocese.

Witness, The, w; P.O. Box 917, Dubuque, IA 52004-0917; (563) 588-0556; Dubuque archdiocese.
Wyoming Catholic Register, m; P.O. Box 1468, Cheyenne, WY 82003; (307) 638-1530; www.wyo-cathregister.org; Cheyenne diocese.

Magazines

Abbey Banner, The, 3 times a year; Saint John's Abbey, Collegeville, MN 56321; (320) 363-2011; www.saintjohnsabbey.org/banner/index.html.
AIM: Liturgy Resources, q; 3708 River Rd., Ste. 400, Franklin Park, IL 60131; (800) 566-6150; www.wlp.jspaluch.com/8062.htm.
America, w; 106 W. 56th St., New York, NY 10019; (212) 581-4640; www.americamagazine.org; Jesuits of U.S. and Canada.
American Benedictine Review, q; Assumption Abbey, Box A, Richardton, ND 58652; (701) 974-3315; www.osb.org/abr/.
American Catholic Philosophical Quarterly (formerly *The New Scholasticism*), Philosophy Documentation Center, P. O. Box 7147, Charlottesville, Virginia 22906-7147; (800) 444-2419; www.acpa-main.org; American Catholic Philosophical Assn.
American Catholic Studies; Villanova University, 800 Lancaster Ave., Villanova, PA 19085; (610) 519-5470.
The Annals of St. Anne de Beaupre, m; 9795 Boul, Ste.Anne, St. Anne de Beaupre, Quebec, GOA 3CO; (418) 827-4538.
Anthonian, The, q; c/o St. Anthony's Guild, Paterson, NJ 07509; (212) 924-1451; www.hnp.org/publications; St. Anthony's Guild.
Apostolate of the Little Flower, bm; P.O. Box 5280, San Antonio, TX 78201-0280; (210) 736-3889; Discalced Carmelite Fathers.
Augustinian, The, q; P.O. Box 340, Villanova, PA 19085; (610) 527-3330; www.augustinian.org; published by the Province of St. Thomas of Villanova.

Barry Magazine, 2 times a year; 11300 NE 2nd Ave., Miami Shores, FL 33161; (305) 899-3188; www.barry.edu/barrymagazine. Barry University.
Benedictine Sisters and Friends, 3 times a year, 104 Chapel Lane, St. Joseph,MN 56374; (320) 363-7100; www.sbm.osb.org.
Benedictines, 44 N. Mill St., Kansas City, KS 66101; (913) 342-0938; www.mountosb.org.
Bread of Life, 6 times a year, P.O. Box 127, Burlington, Ontario, L7R 3X8, Canada; (905) 632-5433; www.thebreadoflife.ca.
Bright Ideas; P.O. Box 510817, New Berlin, WI, 53151-0817; (800) 950-9952; www.lpiresourcecenter.com.
Canticle: The Voice of Women of Grace, 6 times a year, 325 Scarlet Blvd., Oldsmar, FL 34677; (813) 854-1518; www.canticlemagazine.com.
Carmelite Digest q; Carmelite Digest, PO Box 3898, Yountville CA 94599; 707-944-9007; www.carmelitedigest.com.
Carmelite Review, q; 8501 Bailey Rd., Darien, IL, 60561; (630) 971-0724; www.carlemitereview.org; published by the Province of the Most Pure Heart of Mary of the Carmelite Order.
Catechist, The, 7 times a year; 2621 Dryden Rd., Dayton, OH 45439; (937) 293-1415; www.pflaum.com.
Catechumenate: A Journal of Christian Initiation, bm; 1800 N. Hermitage Ave., Chicago, IL 60622-1101; (773) 486-8970; www.ltp.org.

Catholic Answer, The, bm; 200 Noll Plaza, Huntington, IN 46750; (260) 356-8400; www.osv.com; Our Sunday Visitor, Inc.
Catholic Biblical Quarterly; Catholic University of America, Washington, DC 20064; (202) 319-5519; cba.cua.edu/CBQ.cfm; Catholic Biblical Assn.
Catholic Cemetery, The, m; 1400 S. Wolf Rd., Bldg. 3, Hillside,IL 60162; (708) 202-1242; National Catholic Cemetery Conference.
Catholic Connection, The, m.; 3500 Fairfield Ave., Shreveport, LA 71104; (318) 868-4441; www.dioshpt.org; diocese of Shreveport.
Catholic Digest, m; 1 Montauk Ave., Ste. 200, New London, CT 06320; (860) 437-3012; www.catholicdigest.org.
Catholic Family News, m.; MPO Box 743, Niagara Falls, NY 14302; (905) 871-6292; www.cfnews.org/cfn.htm.
Catholic Historical Review, q; 2715 North Charles Street, Baltimore, Maryland 21218; (410) 516-6989; muse.jhu.edu/journals/cat.
Catholic Lawyer, q; St. John's Law Review, St. John's University School of Law, Room 3-40, 8000 Utopia Parkway, Jamaica, NY 11439; (718) 990-6655; St. Thomas More Institute for Legal Research.
Catholic Library World, q; 100 North St., #224, Pittsfield, MA 01201-5109; (413) 443-2252; www.cathla.org; Catholic Library Association.
Catholic Missions in Canada, q; 201-1155 Yonge St., Toronto, Ontario, M4T 1W2, Canada; (416) 934-3424; www.cmic.info.
Catholic Press Directory, a; 205 W. Monroe St., Ste. 470, Chicago, IL 60606; (312) 380-6789; www.catholicpress.org; Catholic Press Assn.
Catholic Response, m.; 601 Buhler Ct., Pine Beach, NJ 08741; (732) 914-1222; www.jhcnewman.org.
Catholic Review (Braille, tape, large print), bm; 154 E. 23rd St., New York, NY 10010; (212) 473-7800; Xavier Society for the Blind.
Catholic Southwest: A Journal of History and Culture, a; 1625 Rutherford Lane, Bldg. D, Austin, TX, 78754-5105; (512) 339-9882.
Catholic Woman, bm; 200 N. Glebe Rd., Suite 703, Arlington, VA 22203; (202) 224-0990; www.nccw.org; National Council of Catholic Women.
Catholic Worker, 7 times a year; 36 E. First St., New York, NY 10003; (212) 677-8627; Catholic Worker Movement.
Catholic World Report, The, 11 times a year; P.O. Box 2512, Alexandria, VA 22301; (800) 353-2324; www.catholicworldreport.com; Ignatius Press.
Celebrate!, six times a year, Novalis, 10 Lower Spadina Ave., Ste. 400, Toronto, ON M5V 2Z2; (780) 451-2228; www.celebrate-liturgy.ca; Novalis, Saint Paul University.
Charities USA, q; 1731 King St., Suite 200, Alexandria, VA 22314; (703) 549-1390; www.catholiccharitiesusa.org.
Chesterton Review, The, q; Seton Hall University, 400 South Orange Ave., South Orange, NJ 07079; (973) 275-2431; academic.shu.edu/Chesterton. G.K. Chesterton Society.
Chicago Studies, 3 times a year; 1800 N. Hermitage Ave., Chicago, IL 60622-1101; (800) 933-1800; www.ltp.org.
Christian Renewal News, q.; P.O. Box 6164, Santa Maria, CA 93456; (805) 524-5890; www.theservantsandhandmaids.net; published by The Servants and Handmaids of the Sacred Heart of Jesus.
Christianity and the Arts, q; P.O. Box 118088, Chicago,

IL 60611; (312) 642-8606; www.christianarts.net.

Church, q; 18 Bleeker St., New York, NY 10012; (212) 431-7825; www.nplc.org; National Pastoral Life Center.

CMMB Today, q., 10 West 17th St., New York, N.Y. 10011; (212) 242-7757; www.cmmb.org; Catholic Medical Mission Board publication.

CNEWA Connections, bm; 1011 First Ave., New York, NY 10022; (800) 442-6392; www.cnewa.org; Catholic Near East Welfare.

Columban Mission, 8 times a year; St. Columbans, NE 68056; (402) 291-1920; www.columban.org; Columban Fathers.

Columbia, m; One Columbus Plaza, New Haven, CT 06510; (203) 752-4398; www.kofc.org; Knights of Columbus.

Commonweal, bw; 475 Riverside Dr., Room 405, New York, NY 10115; (212) 662-4200; www.commonwealmagazine.org.

Communio: International Catholic Review, q; P.O. Box 4557, Washington, DC 20017-0557; (202) 526-0251; www.communio-icr.com.

Company, q; P.O. Box 60790, Chicago, IL 60660-0790; (773) 760-9432; www.companymagazine.com; Jesuit magazine.

CONNECT!, Liturgical Publications, Inc., P.O. Box 510817, New Berlin, WI 53151; (800) 950-9952; www.lpiresourcecenter.com.

Consecrated Life, semi-annually; P.O. Box 7500, Libertyville, IL 60048-7500; (847) 573-8975; www.religiouslife.com; Institute on Religious Life. English edition of *Informationes*, official publication of Congregation for Institutes of Consecrated Life and Societies of Apostolic Life.

Consolata Missionaries, bm; P.O. Box 5550, Somerset, NJ 08875-5550; (732) 297-9191; www.consolata.org.

Cord, The, m; Franciscan Institute, St. Bonaventure University, St. Bonaventure, NY 14778; (716) 375-2160; www.sbu.edu; Franciscan Institute.

Counseling and Values, 3 times a year; College of Educational, Southern Illinois University, Carbondale, IL 62901; (618) 537-7791.

Crisis, Morley Publishing Group Inc., 2100 M Street NW, #170-339, Washington, D.C. 20037; www.insidecatholic.com; journal of lay Catholic opinion.

Cross Currents, q; College of New Rochelle, New Rochelle, NY 10805; (914) 235-1439; www.aril.org; inter-religious; Assn. for Religion and Intellectual Life.

Crusade Magazine, bm; P.O. Box 341, Hanover, PA 17331; (717) 225-7147; The American Society for the Defense of Tradition, Family and Property (TFP).

CUA Magazine, 3 times a year; 620 Michigan Ave. N.E., Washington, DC 20064; (202) 319-5600; www.cua.edu; Catholic University of America.

Culture Wars, (formerly *Fidelity Magazine*), m; 206 Marquette Ave., South Bend, IN 46617; (219) 289-9786.

Darbininkas (The Worker) (Lithuanian), w; 341 Highland Blvd., Brooklyn, NY 11207; (718) 827-1352; Lithuanian Franciscans.

Desert Call, q.; P.O. Box 219, Crestone, CO 81131-0219; (719) 256-4778; www.spirituallifeinstitute.org; published by the Spiritual Life Institute.

Diakonia, 3 times a year; University of Scranton, Scranton, PA 18510-4643; (570) 941-6141; www.nyssa.cecs.uofs.edu/diaktoc.html; Center for Eastern Christian Studies.

Dominican Torch, The, q; 141 East 65th St., N.Y.,N.Y. 10021; (212) 744-2080.

Don Bosco Alive/The Salesian Bulletin; 148 Main Street,

New Rochelle, NY 10802-0639; (914) 636-4225; www.salesians.org.

Eastern Oklahoma Catholic, 10 times a year; Box 690240, Tulsa, OK 74169-0240; (918) 307-4946; www.dioceseoftulsa.org; Tulsa diocese.

Ecumenical Trends, m (except Aug.); Graymoor, Route 9, P.O. Box 306, Garrison, NY 10524-0306; (845) 424-2109; www.atonementfriars.org; Graymoor Ecumenical Institute.

Eglute (The Little Fir Tree) (Lithuanian), m; 13648 Kikapoo Trail, Lockport, IL 60441; (708) 301-6410; for children ages 5-10.

Emmanuel, 10 times a year; 5384 Wilson Mills Rd., Cleveland, OH 44143; (440) 449-2103; www.blessedsacrament.com; Congregation of Blessed Sacrament.

Envoy, bm; P.O. Box 585, Granville, OH 43023; (740) 345-2705; www.envoymagazine.com; journal of Catholic apologetics and evangelization.

EWTN Religious Catalogue, two times a year; 5817 Old Leeds Rd., Irondale, AL 35210, (205) 271-2900, www.ewtn.com, printed catalogue of select new and favorite "holy reminders" for the Easter and Christmas seasons. Circ. 700,000.

Extension, m; 150 S. Wacker Dr., 20th Floor, Chicago, IL 60606; (312) 236-7240; www.catholicextension.org; Catholic Church Extension Society.

Faith, 209 Seymour Ave., Lansing, MI 48933-1577; (517) 342-2595; www.faithmag.com.

Faith-Diocese of Erie, 429 E. Grandview Blvd., Erie, PA 16504; (814) 824-1160; www.eriecd.org.

Faith-Diocese of Grand Rapids, 360 Division Ave. S., Grand Rapids, MI 49503; (616) 475-1240; www.dioceseofgrandrapids.org.

Faith and Family, bm; 432 Washington Ave., North Haven, CT 06473; (203) 230-3800; formerly *Catholic Twin Circle*.

Family Digest, The, bm; P.O. Box 40137, Fort Wayne, IN 46804 (editorial address); (952) 929-6765.

Family Foundations Magazine, P.O. Box 111184, Cincinnati, OH 45211; (513) 471-2000; www.ccli.org; published by the Couple to Couple League.

Family Friend, q; P.O. Box 11563, Milwaukee, WI 53211; (414) 961-0500; www.cfli.org; Catholic Family Life Insurance.

Fatima Crusader, The, q; P.O. Box 602, Fort Erie, ON, L2A 4M7, Canada; (905) 871-7607; www.fatima.org.

F.M.A. Focus, q; P.O. Box 598, Mt. Vernon, NY 10551; (914) 664-5604; Franciscan Mission Associates.

Franciscan Studies, a; Franciscan Institute, St. Bonaventure, NY 14778; (716) 375-2105; www.franinst.sbu.edu; Franciscan Institute.

Franciscan Way, q; 1235 University Blvd., Steubenville, OH 43952; (740) 283-6450; www.franciscan.edu.

Fraternal Leader, q; P.O. Box 13005; Erie, PA 16514-1302; (814) 453-4331; Loyal Christian Benefit Association.

Fraternally Yours (Engish-Slovak), m; 24950 Chagrin Blvd., Beachwood, OH 44122; (216) 464-8015; First Catholic Slovak Ladies Assn.

Fuente de Misericordia, q; Eden Hill, Stockbridge, MA 01263; (413) 298-3691; www.marian.org; Congregation of Marians of the Immaculate Conception.

Glenmary Challenge, The, q; P.O. Box 465618, Cincinnati, OH 45246-5618; (513) 874-8900; www.glenmary.org; Glenmary Home Missioners.

God's Word Today, m; 1 Montauk Ave., Ste. 200, New

London, CT 06320; (860) 437-3012; www.godswordtoday. org; Daily Scripture readings.

Good News for Children, 32 times during school year; 2621 Dryden Rd., Dayton, OH 45439; (800) 543-4383; www.pflaum.com.

Good Shepherd (Dobry Pastier) (Slovak-English), a; 8200 McKnight Rd., Pittsburgh, PA 15237; (412) 364-3000.

Greyfriars Review, 3 times a year; Franciscan Institute, St. Bonventure University, St. Bonaventure, NY 14778; (716) 375-2105; www.franinst.sbu.edu; Franciscan Institute.

Growing with the Gospel, w; Liturgical Publications, P.O. Box 510817, New Berlin, WI, 53151; (800) 950-9952.

Guide to Religious Ministries for Catholic Men and Women, A, a; 210 North Ave., New Rochelle, NY 10801; (914) 632-1220; www.religiousministries.com.

Health Progress, bm; 4455 Woodson Rd., St. Louis, MO 63134-3797; (314) 427-2500; www.chausa.org; Catholic Health Association.

Heart, 4389 West Pine Blvd., St. Louis, MO 63108; (314) 652-1500; www.rscj.org.

Homiletic and Pastoral Review, m; 70 Lake Street, P.O. Box 297, Ramsey, NJ 07446; (800) 353-2324; www.hprweb.com.

Horizon, q; 5401 S. Cornell Ave., Chicago, IL 60615-5604; (773) 363-5454.

Horizons, 2 times a year; Villanova University, Villanova, PA 19085; (610) 519-7302; College Theology Society.

ICSC Resource; 1275 K St. N.W., Suite 980, Washington, DC, 20005-4006; (202) 289-1093; www.catholicstewardship.org; published by International Catholic Stewardship Council.

Immaculate Heart Messenger, q; P.O. Box 269, Hanceville, AL 35077; (800) 213-5541; www.fatimafamily.org.

In a Word, m; 199 Seminary Dr., Bay Saint Louis, MS 39520-4626; (601) 467-1097; www.inaword.com; Society of the Divine Word.

Inside the Vatican, 10 times a year; Rome office: Via della Mura Aurelio 7c, 00165 Rome, Italy; U.S. office: St. Martin de Porres Lay Dominican Community, 3050 Gap Knob Rd., New Hope, KY 40052; (270) 325-5499; www.insidethevatican.com. The only current journal that focuses exclusively on Rome, the impact of the papacy worldwide, and the functioning, travels, and activities of the Holy Father and the Roman Curia.

Jesuit Bulletin, 3 times a year; 3601 Lindell Blvd., St. Louis, MO 63108; (314) 633-4610; www.jesuitsmis.org; Jesuit Seminary Aid Association.

Jesuit Journeys, 3 times a year; 3400 W. Wisconsin Ave., Milwaukee, WI 53208-0288; (414) 727-6236; www.jesuitswisprov.org.

Josephinum Journal of Theology, twice a year; 7625 N. High St., Columbus, OH 43235; (614) 885-5585; www.pcj.edu.

Josephite Harvest, The, q; 1130 N. Calvert St., Baltimore, MD 21202-3802; (410) 727-2233; www.josephite.com; Josephite Missionaries.

Journal of Catholic Legal Studies, St. John's University, 8000 Utopia Parkway, Jamaica, NY 11439; (718) 990-6655.

Jurist, The, semi-annually; Catholic University of America, Washington, DC 20064; (202) 319-5439; canon-law.cua.edu/links. Department of Canon Law.

Kinship, q; P.O. Box 22264, Owensboro, KY 42304; (270) 686-8401; www.glenmarysisters.org; Glenmary Sisters.

Law Briefs, m; 3211 Fourth St. N.E., Washington, DC 20017; (202) 541-3300; Office of General Counsel, USCCB.

Lay Witness, m; 827 North Fourth St., Steubenville, OH, 43952; (740) 283-2484; www.cuf.org; Catholics United for the Faith.

Leaflet Missal, 16565 South State St., S. Holland, IL 60473; (708) 331-5485; www.americancatholicpress.org/leafletmissal.html.

Leaves, bm; P.O. Box 87, Dearborn, MI 48121-0087; (313) 561-2330; www.rc.net/detroit/marianhill/leaves.htm; Mariannhill Mission Society.

Legatus, 10 times a year, 5072 Annunciation Circle, Ste. 202, Ave Maria, FL 34142; (239) 435-3852; www.legatus.org. Published by Legatus International.

Liguorian, m; 1 Liguori Dr., Liguori, MO 63057; (636) 464-2500; www.liguorian.org; Redemptorists.

Linacre Quarterly; 333 E. Lancaster Avenue, #348, Wynnewood, PA 19096; (215) 877-9099; www.cathmed.org; Catholic Medical Association (National Federation of Catholic Physicians Guilds).

Liturgia y Cancion (Spanish and English), q; 5536 NE Hassalo, Portland, OR 97213; (800) 548-8749; Oregon Catholic Press.

Liturgical Catechesis, 6 times a year; 160 E. Virginia St., San Jose, CA 95112; (408) 286-8505; www.rpinet.com/lc.

Liturgy Planner, The, semi-annual; P.O. Box 13071, Portland, OR 97213; (503) 331-2965.

Living City, m; 202 Comforter Blvd., Hyde Park, NY 12538; (845) 229-0230; www.livingcitymagazine.com; Focolare Movement.

Living Faith: Daily Catholic Devotions, q; 1564 Fencorp Dr., Fenton, MO 63026-2942; (636) 305-9777; www.livingfaith.com.

Magnificat, m.; Dunwoodie, P.O. Box 834, Yonkers, NY 10702; (914) 502-1820; www.magnificat.net.

Marian Helper, q.; Eden Hill, Stockbridge, MA 01263; (413) 298-3691; www.marian.org.

Marriage, bm; 955 Lake Dr., St. Paul, MN 55120; (651) 454-7947; www.marriagemagazine; International Marriage Encounter.

Maryknoll, m; Maryknoll, NY 10545-0308; (914) 941-7590; www.maryknoll.org; Catholic Foreign Mission Society.

Matrimony, q; 215 Santa Rosa Pl., Santa Barbara, CA 93109; (805) 965-9541; Worldwide Marriage Encounter.

Ministry & Liturgy, m.; 160 E. Virginia St., #290, San Jose, CA 95112; (408) 286-8505; www.rpinet.com.

Mission, q; 1663 Bristol Pike, Bensalem, PA 19020-8502; (215) 244-9900; www.katharinedrexel.org; Sisters of the Blessed Sacrament.

Mission, q., 10582 Associates Court, Manassas, VA 20109; (703) 367-0333; www.cardinalnewmansociety.org; Cardinal Newman Society to promote Catholic higher education.

   Mission, 300 College Ave., Los Gatos, CA 95031; (408) 884-1634; www.jesuitscalifornia.org.

MISSION Magazine, q; 366 Fifth Ave., New York, NY 10001; (212) 563-8700; www.onefamilymission.org; Society for Propagation of the Faith.

Mission Helper, The, q; 1001 W. Joppa Rd., Baltimore, MD 21204-3787; (410) 823-8585; Mission Helpers of the Sacred Heart.

Missionhurst, bm; 4651 N. 25th St., Arlington, VA 22207; (703) 528-3804; www.missionhurst.org.

Modern Schoolman, The, q; St. Louis University, P.O. Box 56907, St. Louis, MO 63156; (314) 997-3149; St. Louis University Philosophy Department.

Momento Catolico, El; 205 W. Monroe St., Chicago, IL, 60606; (312) 236-7782; www.hmrc.claretianpubs.org.

Momentum, q; Suite 100, 1077 30th St. N.W., Washington, DC 20007-3852; (202) 337-6232; www.ncea. org; National Catholic Educational Association.

Mountain Spirit, The, bm; P.O. Box 55911, Lexington, KY 40555-5911; (866) 270-4227; www. chrisapp.org; Christian Appalachian Project.

My Daily Visitor, bm; 200 Noll Plaza, Huntington, IN 46750; (260) 356-8400; www.osv.com; Our Sunday Visitor, Inc.

National Apostolate for Inclusion Ministry, q; P.O. Box 218, Riverdale, MD, 20738-0218; (301) 699-9500; www.nafim.org.

National Catholic Forester, q; 320 S. School St., Mt. Prospect, IL 60056; (847) 342-4500; www.ncsf.com.

National Catholic Rural Life, bi-annual; 4625 Beaver Ave., Des Moines, IA 50310; (515) 270-2634; www.ncrlc. com.

NC Catholics, 715 Nazareth, Raleigh, NC 27606; (919) 821-9736; www.nccatholics.org; diocese of Raleigh.

NETWORK Connection, bm; 25 E St. NW, Washington, DC 20001; (202) 347-9797; www.net-worklobby.org; Network.

New England Province of Jesuits, P.O. Box 9199, Watertown, MA 02471; (617) 607-2895; www.sjnen. org; New England Province of the Society of Jesus.

New Oxford Review, 10 issues a year; 1069 Kains Ave., Berkeley, CA 94706; (510) 526-5374; www. newoxfordreview.org.

Notebook, The, q; CMICA-USA, 3049 4 St. N.E., Washington, DC 20017; (202) 269-6672; www.pax-romana.org; Catholic Movement for Intellectual and Cultural Affairs.

Nova-Voice of Ministry, bm; P.O. Box 432, Milwaukee, WI 53201; (800) 876-4574; www.execpc.com/~lpi; Liturgical Publications.

Oblates Magazine, six times a year, 9480 North De Mazenod Dr., Belleville, IL 62223-1160; (618) 398-4848; www.oblatesusa.org.

Old Testament Abstracts, 3 times a year; 320 Caldwell Hall, Catholic University of America, Washington, DC 20064; (202) 319-5519.

ONE, bm., 1011 First Ave., New York, NY 10022; (800) 442-6329; www.cnewa.org. Catholic Near East Welfare Association.

Ozanam News, The, twice a year; 58 Progress Parkway, St. Louis, MO 63043-3706; (314) 576-3993; www.svdpus-council.org; Society of St. Vincent de Paul.

Palabra Entre Nosotros, La, bm; 9639 Dr. Perry Rd., Unit 126N, Jamesville, MD, 21754; (301) 831-1262; www.wau.org.

Parable Magazine, P.O. Box 310, Manchester, NH 03105; (603) 669-0377;www.parablemag..com.

Parish Liturgy, q; 16565 S. State St., S. Holland, IL 60473; (708) 331-5485; www.parishliturgy.com.

Partners Magazine: Chicago Province of the Society of Jesus, 3 times a year; 2059 N. Sedgwick St., Chicago, IL 60614; (773) 975-8181; www.jesuits-chi.org.

Passionists Compassion, The, q; 526 Monastery Pl.,

Union City, NJ 07087; (201) 864-0018; www.cptryon.org.

Pastoral Life, m; Box 595, Canfield, OH 44406; (330) 533-5503; www.albahouse.org; Society of St. Paul.

Pastoral Music, bm; 962 Wayne Ave., Suite 210, Silver Spring, MD 20910-4433; (240) 247-3000; www.npm.org; National Association of Pastoral Musicians.

Pax Romana/CMICA-USA, q; 3049 4th St., N.E., Washington, DC 20017; (202) 269-6672; www.pax-romana.org.

Philosophy Today, q; 2352 N.Clifton Ave., Chicago, IL 60614; (773) 325-7267; Philosophy Department.

PIME World, m (except July-Aug.); 17330 Quincy St., Detroit, MI 48221; (313) 342-4066; www.pimeysa.org; PIME Missionaries.

Poverello, The, 10 times a year; 6832 Convent Blvd., Sylvania, OH 43560; (419) 824-3627; www.sistersosf; Sisters of St. Francis of Sylvania.

Prayers for Worship, q; P.O. Box 510817, New Berlin, WI 53151; (800) 950-9952; www.lpiresourcecenter.com.

Preach: Enlivening the Pastoral Art, 6 times a year, 3708 River Rd., Ste. 400, Franklin Park, IL 60131; (800) 566-6150; www.wlpmusic.com; published by World Library Publications.

Priest, The, m; 200 Noll Plaza, Huntington, IN 46750; (260) 356-8400; www.osv.com; Our Sunday Visitor, Inc.

Proceedings, a; Fordham University, Adm. Bldg., Bronx, NY 10458; (718) 817-4081; www.acpa-main.org; Journal of the American Catholic Philosophical Association.

Promise, 32 times a year; 2621 Dryden Rd., Suite 300, Dayton, OH 45439; (937) 293-1415; www.pflaum.com.

Queen of All Hearts, bm; 26 S. Saxon Ave., Bay Shore, NY 11706; (631) 665-0726; www.montfortmissionaries. com; Montfort Missionaries.

Reign of the Sacred Heart, q; 6889 S. Lovers Lane, Hales Corners, WI 53130; (414) 425-3383; www.poshusa.org.

Religion Teacher's Journal, m (Sept.-May); P.O. Box 6015, New London, CT 06320; (860) 437-3012; www.religionteachersjournal.com.

Religious Life, bm., P.O. Box 410007, Chicago, IL 60641; (773) 267-1195; www.religiouslife.com.

Renascence, q; P.O. Box 1881, Marquette University, Milwaukee, WI 53201-1881; (414) 288-6725.

Report on U.S. Catholic Overseas Mission, bi-annually; 3029 Fourth St. N.E., Washington, DC 20017; (202) 832-3112; www.catholicmission.org; United States Catholic Mission Association.

Response: Directory of Volunteer Opportunities, a; 6930 Carroll Ave., Suite 820, Takoma Park, MD 20912; (301) 270-0900; www.cnvs.org; Catholic Network of Volunteer Service.

Review for Religious, bm; 3601 Lindell Blvd., St. Louis, MO 63108; (314) 633-4610; www.reviewforreligious.org.

Review of Social Economy, q; University of Groningen, School of Economics & Business, P.O. Box 800, Groningen, 9700 AV, Netherlands; 31-50-3632789; www.socialeconomic.org.

Revista Maryknoll (Spanish-English), m; Maryknoll, NY 10545; (914) 941-7590; www.maryknoll.org; Catholic Foreign Mission Society of America.

RITE, 8 times a year; 1800 North Hermitage Ave., Chicago, IL 60622-1101; (773) 486-8970; www.ltp.org.

Roze Maryi (Polish), m; Eden Hill, Stockbridge, MA 01263; (413) 298-3691; www.marian.org; Marian Helpers Center.

Sacred Music, q; 134 Christendom Dr., c/o K. Poterack, Front Royal, VA 22630; (540) 636-2900.

St. Anthony Messenger, m; 28 W. Liberty St., Cincinnati,

OH 45210-1298; (513) 241-5615; www.americancatholic. org; Franciscan Friars.

St. Augustine Catholic, bm (Sept-May); 11625 Old St. Augustine Rd., Jacksonville, FL 32258; (904) 262-3200; www.staugcatholic.org; St. Augustine diocese.

St. Joseph's Messenger and Advocate of the Blind, bi-annual; St. Joseph Home, 537 Pavonia Ave., Jersey City, NJ 07303; (201) 798-4141.

St. Paul's Family Magazine, q; 14780 W. 159th St., Olathe, KS 66062; (913) 780-0405.

Salesian Bulletin, q; 148 Main St., New Rochelle, NY 10802; (914) 636-4225; www.salesians.org; Salesians of Don Bosco.

SALT/Sisters of Charity, BVM, q; 1100 Carmel Dr., Dubuque, IA 52001; (563) 588-2351; www.bvmcong.org.

Scalabrinians, q; 209 Flagg Pl., Staten Island, NY 10304; (718) 351-0257.

Scarboro Missions, 7 times a year, 2685 Kingston Rd., Scarborough, ON M1M 1M4, Canada; (416) 261-7135; www.scarboromissions.ca.

School Guide, a; 210 North Ave., New Rochelle, NY 10801; (914) 632-7771; www.schoolguides.com.

SCN Journey, bm; SCN Office of Communications, P.O. Box 9, Nazareth, KY 40048; (502) 348-1564; www.scnazarethky.org; Sisters of Charity of Nazareth.

Seeds, 32 times a year; 2621 Dryden Rd., Dayton, OH 45439; (937) 293-1415; www.pflaum.com.

Serenity, q; 601 Maiden Choice Lane, Baltimore, MD 21228; (410) 744-9367; Little Sisters of the Poor.

SerraUSA, The, bm; 65 E. Wacker Pl., #802, Chicago, IL 60601-7203; (312) 201-6549; www.serraus.org; Serra International.

Share Magazine, q; 10 W. 71st St., New York, NY 10023; (212) 877-3041; www.catholicdaughters.com; Catholic Daughters of the Americas.

Share the Word, bm; 3031 Fourth St. N.E., Washington, DC 20017-1102; (202) 832-5022; www.sharetheword.net; Paulist Catholic Evangelization Association.

Silent Advocate, q; St. Rita School for the Deaf, 1720 Glendale-Milford Rd., Cincinnati, OH 45215; (513) 771-7600; www.srsdeaf.org.

Social Justice Review, bm; 3835 Westminster Pl., St. Louis, MO 63108-3409; (314) 371-1653; www.socialjusticereview.com; Catholic Central Union of America.

SOUL Magazine, bm; P.O. Box 976, Washington, NJ 07882; (908) 213-2223; www.bluearmy.com; The Blue Army of Our Lady of Fatima, USA, Inc.

Spirit, w; 1884 Randolph Ave., St. Paul, MN 55105; (612) 690-7012; www.goodgroundpress.com; for teens.

Spirit, bi-annually; Seton Hall University, South Orange, NJ 07079; (201) 761-9000.

Spirit & Life, bm; 800 N. Country Club Rd., Tucson, AZ 85716; (520) 325-6401; www.benedictinesisters.org; Benedictine Srs. of Perpetual Adoration.

Spiritan Missionary News, q; 121 Victoria Park Ave., Toronto, ON, M4E 3S2, Canada; (416) 691-9319; www.spiritans.com.

Spiritual Life, q; 2131 Lincoln Rd. N.E., Washington, DC 20002; (888) 616-1713; Discalced Carmelite Friars.

Star, 10 times a year; 22 W. Kiowa, Colorado Springs, CO 80903.

Studies in the Spirituality of Jesuits, 5 times a year; 3601 Lindell Blvd., St. Louis, MO 63108; (314) 633-4622.

Sunday by Sunday, w; 1884 Randolph Ave., St. Paul, MN 55105; (651) 690-7012; www.goodgroundpress.com.

Sword Magazine, 2 times a year; 2097 Town Hall Terrace, #3, Grand Island, NY 14072-1737; (716) 773-0992; Carmelite Fathers.

Take Out, 10 times a year; Our Sunday Visitor, 200 Noll Plaza, Huntington, IN 46750; (800) 348-2440; www.osv.com.

Theological Studies, q; Marquette University, 100 Coughlin Hall, Milwaukee, WI 53201-1881; (414) 288-3164; www.ts.mu.edu.

Theology Digest, q; P.O. Box 56907, St. Louis, MO 63156-0907; (314) 977-3410; St. Louis University.

This Rock Magazine, 10 times a year; 2020 Gillespie Way, El Cajon, CA 92020; (619) 387-7200; www.catholic.com; Catholic apologetics.

Thomist, The, q; 487 Michigan Ave. N.E., Washington, DC 20017; (202) 529-5300; www.thomist.org; Dominican Fathers.

Today's Catholic Teacher, m (Sept.-April); 2621 Dryden Rd., Dayton, OH 45439; (937) 293-1415; www.catholic-teacher.com.

Today's Liturgy, q; 5536 NE Hassalo, Portland, OR 97213; (800) 548-8749; www.ocp.org.

Today's Parish Minister, m (Sept.-May); 1 Montauk Ave., New London, CT 06320; (860) 437-3012; www.twentythirdpublications.com.

Together in the Word, bi-annual; Box 577, Techny, IL 60082-0577; (708) 272-2700; www.divineword.org; Chicago province, Society of Divine Word.

The Tower, w; The Catholic University of America, University Center, 127 Pryzbyla Center, Washington, DC 20064; (202) 319-5778.

Traces, m; 125 Maiden Lane, 15th Floor, N.Y., N.Y. 10038; (212) 337-3580; www.traces-cl.com.

Tracings, q; 5 Gamelin St., Holyoke, MA 01040; (413) 536-7511; www.sisofprov.org; Sisters of Providence.

Ultreya Magazine, bm; 4500 W. Davis St., P.O. Box 210226, Dallas, TX 75211; (214) 339-6321; Cursillo Movement.

L'Union (French and English), q; P.O. Box F, Woonsocket, RI 02895; (401) 769-0520.

Universitas, q; 221 N. Grand, Room 39, St. Louis, MO 63103; (314) 977-2537; www.slu.edu; St. Louis University.

U.S. Catholic, m; 205 W. Monroe St., Chicago, IL 60606; (312) 236-7782; www.uscatholic.org; Claretians.

Venture, 32 times during school year; 2621 Dryden Rd., Suite 300, Dayton, OH 45439; (937) 293-1415; www.pflaum.com; intermediate grades.

Vida Catolica, La, m.; 40 Green St., Lynn, MA 01902; (781) 586-0197; www.la-vida.org/catolica; Boston archdiocese Hispanic community.

Vincentian Heritage, twice a year; 2233 N. Kenmore Ave., Chicago, IL 60614; (773) 325-7348; www.depaul.edu/~vstudies.

Vision, a, 205 W. Monroe St., Chicago, IL 60606; (312) 236-7782; www.visionguide.org; Claretian Publications in conjunction with National Religious Vocation Conference.

Vision, 3 times a year; 7202 Buchanan St., Landover Hills, MD 20784; (301) 577-1684; www.ncod.org; National Catholic Office for the Deaf.

Vision (Spanish-English), P.O. Box 28185, San Antonio, TX 78228; (210) 732-2156; www.maccsa.org; Mexican American Cultural Center.

Visions, 32 times during school year; 2621 Dryden Rd., Suite 300, Dayton, OH 45439; (937) 293-1415; www.pflaum.com; for students in grades 7-9.

Vocations and Prayer, q; 6635 Tobias Ave., Van Nuys, CA 91405; (818) 782-1765; www.vocationsandprayer.com; Rogationist Fathers.

Voice Crying in the Wilderness, A, q; 4425 Schneider Rd., Filmore, NY 14735; (716) 567-4433; Most Holy Family Monastery.

Waif's Messenger, q; 1140 W. Jackson Blvd., Chicago, IL 60607; (312) 738-9522; Mission of Our Lady of Mercy.

Way of St. Francis, bm; 1500 34th Ave., Oakland, CA 94601; (916) 443-5717; www.sbfranciscans.org; Franciscan Friars of California, Inc.

Wheeling Jesuit University Chronicle, 3 times a year; 316 Washington Ave., Wheeling, WV 26003; (304) 243-2296.

Word Among Us, The, m; 9639 Dr. Perry Rd., No. 126N, Jamesville, MD 21754; (301) 831-1262; www.wau.org.

Word and Witness, P.O. Box 510817, Wisconsin, WI, 53151-0817; (800) 950-9952; www.lpiresourcecenter.com.

World Lithuanian Catholic Directory, P.O. Box 1025, Humarock , MA 02047; (781) 834-4079.

Worship, bm; St. John's Abbey, Collegeville, MN 56321; (612) 363-3883.

Newsletters

ACT, 10 times a year; Box 925, Evansville, IN 47706-0925; (812) 962-5508; www.cfm.org; Christian Family Movement.

Action News, q; Pro-Life Action League, 6160 N. Cicero Ave., Chicago, IL 60646; (773) 777-2900; www.prolifeaction.org.

Annual Report, The, 2021 H St. N.W., Washington, DC 20006; (202) 331-8542; Black and Indian Mission Office.

Archdiocesan Bulletin, bm; 827 N. Franklin St., Philadelphia, PA 19123; (215) 627-0143; Philadelphia archeparchy.

Baraga Bulletin, The, q; P.O. Box 550, Marquette, MI 49855; (906) 227-9117; www.dioceseofmarquette.org; Bishop Baraga Association.

Bringing Home the Word, w; 28 W. Liberty St., Cincinnati, OH 45202; (513) 241-5615; www.americancatholic.org; lectionary-based resource from St. Anthony's Messenger Press.

Brothers' Voice, 5420 South Cornell Ave., #205, Chicago, IL 60615-5604; (773) 493-2306.

Called By Joy, three times a year; 4419 N. Hawthorne St., Spokane, WA 99205; (509) 327-4479; Franciscan Monastery of St. Clare.

Campaign Update, bm; 1513 Sixteenth St. N.W., Ste. 400, Washington, DC 20036; (202) 833-4999; www.cathcamp.org; Catholic Campaign for America.

Canticle, The, four times a year, 146 Hawthorne Rd., Pittsburgh, PA 15209; (412) 821-2200; www.millvalefranciscans.org; Sisters of St. Francis of Millvale.

Capuchin Chronicle, q.; P.O. Box 15099, Pittsburgh, PA 15237-0099; (412) 367-2222; www.capuchin.org.

CARA Report, The, bm; Georgetown University, Washington, DC 20057-1203; (202) 687-8080; www.cara.georgetown.edu; Center for Applied Research in the Apostolate.

Caring Community, The, m; 115 E. Armour Blvd., Kansas City, MO 64111; (816) 968-2278; www.ncrpub.com.

Catalyst, 10 times a year; 450 Seventh Ave., New York, NY, 10123; (212) 371-3191; www.catholicleague.org; Catholic League for Civil and Religious Rights.

Catechist's Connection, The, 10 times a year; 115 E. Armour Blvd., Kansas City, MO 64111; (816)

968-2278; www.ncrpub.com.

Catholic Communicator, The, q; 120 East Colonial Hgwy., Hamilton, VA 20158-9012; (540) 338-2700; Catholic Distance University Newsletter.

Catholic Indian Missions, 10 times a year; 2021 H St., NW, Washington, DC 20006; (202) 331-8542. Bureau of Catholic Indian Missions.

Catholic Trends, bw; 3211 Fourth St. N.E., Washington, DC 20017; (202) 541-3290; Catholic News Service.

Catholic Update, m; 28 W. Liberty St., Cincinnati, OH 45202-6498; (513) 241-5615; www.americancatholic.org.

CCHD News, q; 3211 Fourth St. N.E., Washington, DC 20017-1194; (202) 541-3210; www.povertyusa.org; Catholic Campaign for Human Development.

Celebration, Sisters of Charity of Seaton Hill, q; DePaul Center, 463 Mount Thor Rd., Greensburg, PA 15601; (724) 836-0406; www.scsh.org.

Christ the King Seminary Newsletter, 3 times a year; 711 Knox Rd., Box 607, E. Aurora, NY 14052; (716) 652-8900.

Christian Brothers Today, twice a year; 33 Pryor Terrace, New Rochelle, NY 10804; (914) 712-7580. Christian Brothers.

Christian Response Newsletter, P.O. Box 125, Staples, MN 56479-0125; (218) 894-1165.

Christopher News Notes, 10 times a year; 12 E. 48th St., New York, NY 10017; (212) 759-4050; www.christophers.org; The Christophers.

Clarion, The, 5 times a year; Box 159, Alfred, ME 04002-0159; (207) 324-0067; Brothers of Christian Instruction.

CMSM Bulletin, m; 8808 Cameron St., Silver Spring, MD 20910; (301) 588-4030; www.cmsm.org.

Comboni Mission Newsletter, q; 1318 Nagel Rd., Cincinnati, OH 45255-3194; (513) 474-4997; www.combonimissionaries.org.

Connections, five times a year, 610 W. Elm, Monroe, MI 48161; (734) 240-9745; IHM Sisters.

Context, 22 issues a year; 205 W. Monroe St., Chicago, IL 60606; (312) 236-7782; www.contextonline.org; Claretians.

CPN Newsletter, twice a month; 1318 Nagel Rd., Cincinnati, OH, 45255-3120; (513) 474-4997; www.combonimissionaries.org.

Cross and Feathers (Tekakwitha Conference Newsletter), q; P.O. Box 6768, Great Falls, MT 59406; (406) 727-0147; www.tekconf.org; Tekakwitha Conference.

Crossroads, 8 times a year; 1118 Pendleton St., #300, Cincinnati, OH 45202; (888) 714-0171; www.ccmanet.org; Catholic Campus Ministry Association.

CrossRoads, q; 370 W. Camino Gardens Blvd., Boca Raton, FL 33432; www.crossinternational.org. Cross International Catholic Outreach.

CRUX of the News, w; P.O. Box 758, Latham, NY 12110-0758; (518) 783-0058.

Cycles of Faith, P.O. Box 510817, New Berlin, WI 53201; (800) 950-9952; www.lpiresourcecenter.com.

Damien-Dutton Call, q; 616 Bedford Ave., Bellmore, NY 11710.

Dimensions, m; 86 Front St., Hempstead, NY 11550; (516) 481-6000; www.ncdc.org; National Catholic Development Conference.

Diocesan Dialogue, two times a year; 16565 South State St., South Holland, IL 60473; (708) 331-5485; www.americancatholicpress.org.

Diocesan Newsletter, The, m; P.O. Box 2147, Harlingen, TX

78551; (956) 421-4111; www.cdob.org; Brownsville diocese.

Environment and Art Letter, m; 1800 N. Hermitage Ave., Chicago, IL 60622-1101; (773) 486-8970; www.ltp.org; Liturgy Training Publications.

E-Proclaim, 10 times a year; 3211 Fourth St., N.E., Washington, DC, 20017-1194; (202) 541-3204; www.usccb.org/ccc.

Ethics and Medics, m; 6399 Drexel Rd., Philadelphia, PA 19151; (215) 877-2660; www.ncbcenter.org; National Catholic Bioethics Center.

Eucharistic Minister, m; 115 E. Armour, Kansas City, MO 64111; (816) 968-2278; www.ncrpub.com.

Every Day Catholic, m; 28 W. Liberty St., Cincinnati, OH 45202-6498; (513) 241-5615; www.everydaycatholic.org; St. Anthony Messenger Press.

EWTN Family Newsletter, 13 times a year; 5817 Leeds Rd., Irondale, AL 35210; (205) 271-2900; www.ewtn.com; Eternal Word Television Network.

EWTN Monthly Programming Guide, 13 times a year for each satellite; 5817 Old Leeds Road, Irondale, AL 35210, 205-271-2900; www.ewtn.com; EWTN Global Catholic Network, lists monthly programming and schedule for each satellite coverage area, including special end-of-year Christmas schedule.

Explorations, q; American Interfaith Institute, 321 Chestnut St., Philadelphia, PA, 19106; (215) 238-5345.

Faith Extra, 26 times a year; P.O. Box 10668, Erie, PA 16514; www.eriecd.org; diocese of Erie.

Family Connection, The, bm; 3753 MacBeth Dr., San Jose, CA 95127; (408) 258-8534.

Father Flood, q; P.O. Box 51087, New Berlin, WI 53151-0817; (800) 950-9952; www.lpireesourcecenter.com; Liturgical Publications.

Fellowship of Catholic Scholars Newsletter Quarterly, P.O. Box 495, Notre Dame, IN 46556; www.catholicscholars.org.

Fonda Tekakwitha News, P.O. Box 627, Fonda, NY 12068; (518) 853-3636; www.katerishrine.com; Order Minor Conventuals.

Food for the Poor, 3 times a year; 550 SW 12th Ave., Deerfield Beach, FL 33442; (954) 427-2222; www.foodforthepoor.org.

FOOTSTEPS: Walking with Edmund, q; 145 Huguenot Ave., Ste. 402; (914) 712-7580; Christian Brothers Foundation.

Forum Focus, q; P.O. Box 542, Hudson, WI 54016; (651) 276-1429; www.focusonfaith.org; The Wanderer Forum Foundation.

Foundations Newsletter for Newly Married Couples, bm; P.O. Box 1632, Portland, ME, 04104-1632; (207) 775-4757.

Franciscan Foundation for the Holy Land, three or four times a year; 9924 Cedar Ridge Dr., Carmel, IN 46032; (317) 574-4191; www.ffhl.org.

Franciscan World Care, q; P.O. Box 29034, Washington, DC 20017; (202) 832-1762; www.franciscanmissionservice.catholic.edu; Franciscan Mission Service.

Frontline Report, bm; 23 Bliss Ave., Tenafly, NJ 07670; (201) 567-0450; www.smafathers.org; Society of African Missions.

Graymoor Today, m; P.O. Box 301, Garrison, NY 10524-0301; (845) 424-3671; www.atonementfriars.org.

Happiness, q; 567 Salem End Rd., Framingham, MA 01702-5599; (508) 879-2541; www.sonsofmary.com; Sons of Mary, Health of the Sick.

Harmony, 3 times a year; 800 N. Country Club Rd., Tucson, AZ 85716; (520) 325-6401; Benedictine Srs. of Perpetual Adoration.

Healing & Hope, 9480 North De Mazenod Dr., Belleville, IL 62223-1160; (618) 398-4848; www.snows.org.

Heart Beats, 169 Cummins Hwy., Roslindale, MA 02131; (617) 325-3322.

Heart to Heart, twice a year; St. Vincent Archabbey, 300 Fraser Purchase Rd., Latrobe, PA 15650; (724) 805-2601; www.stvincentstore.com; Benedictines of St. Vincent Archabbey.

HLI Reports, m; 4 Family Life, Front Royal, VA 22630; Human Life International.

HN People, bm; 158 W. 27th St., New York, NY 10001; (212) 924-1451; www.hnp.org/publications; Franciscans of Holy Name Province.

HNP Today, w; 158 W. 27th St., New York, NY 10001; (212) 924-1451; www.hnp.org/publications; Franciscans of Holy Name Province.

ICSC Commitment, 1275 K St. N.W., Suite 980, Washington, DC 20005-4006; (202) 289-1093; www.catholicstewardship.org.

Immaculate Heart of Mary Shrine Bulletin, 3 times a year; Mountain View Road, P.O. Box 976, Washington, NJ 07882-0976; (908) 689-1700; www.ewtn.com/bluearmy.

Initiatives, bm; P.O. Box 291102, Chicago, IL 60629; (773) 776-9036; www.catholiclabor.org/ncl.htm; National Center for the Laity.

Interchange, Assisi Heights, 1001 14 St., NW, #100, Rochester, MN 55901-2525; (507) 529-3523; www.rochesterfranciscan.org; Rochester Franciscan Sisters.

It's Our World, 4 times during school year; 366 Fifth Ave., New York, NY 10001; (212) 563-8700; www.hcakids.org; Young Catholics in Mission.

Journey, The, q; 210 W. 31st St., New York, NY 10001-2876; (212) 714-0950; www.capuchin.org; Province of St. Mary of Capuchin Order.

Joyful Noiseletter, The, m; P.O. Box 895, Portage, MI 49081-0895; (616) 324-0990; www.joyfulnoiseletter.com; Fellowship of Merry Christians.

Jubilee, q; 3900 Harewood Rd., NE, Washington, DC 20017; (202) 635-5400; www.jp2cc.org; John Paul II Cultural Center.

Knightline, 18 times a year; 1 Columbus Plaza, New Haven, CT 06510-3326; (203) 772-2130; www.kofc.org; Knights of Columbus Supreme Council.

Laity and Family Life Updates, bm; 20 Archbishop May Dr., St. Louis, MO, 63119; (314) 792-7173; www.stlcatholics.org.

Land of Cotton, q; 2048 W. Fairview Ave., Montgomery, AL 39196; (205) 265-6791; City of St. Jude.

Law Reports, q; 4455 Woodson Rd., St. Louis, MO 63134; (314) 427-2500; Catholic Health Association.

LCWR Update, m; 8808 Cameron St., Silver Spring, MD 20910; (301) 588-4955; www.lcwr.org; Leadership Conference of Women Religious.

Legatus, m; P.O. Box 511, Ann Arbor, MI 48106; (734) 930-3854; www.legatus.org; Legatus.

Let's Talk! (English edition), **Hablemos!** (Spanish edition), bm; 3031 Fourth St. N.E., Washington, DC 20017-1102; (202) 832-5022; www.prison-ministry.org; prison ministries of Paulist National Catholic Evangelization Assn.

Letter to the Seven Churches, bm; 1516 Jerome St., Lansing, MI 48912; (517) 372-6222; Catholic Charismatics.

Life at Risk, 10 times a year; 3211 Fourth St. N.E., Washington, DC 20017; (202) 541-3070; Pro-Life Activities Committee, USCCB.

Life Insight, m; 3211 Fourth St. N.E., Washington, DC 20017; (202) 541-3070; Committee for Pro-Life Activities, USCCB.

Liturgical Images, m; P.O. Box 2225, Hickory, NC 28603; (828) 327-3225.

Loyola World, 22 times a year; 820 North Michigan Ave., Chicago, IL, 60611; (312) 915-6157; www.luc.edu.

Magnificat, three times a year; 6559 State Hwy. M-26, Eagle Harbor, MI, 49950; (906) 289-4388 (fax); www.societystjohn.com.

Malvern Retreat House, q; P.O. Box 315, Malvern, PA 19355-0315; (610) 644-0400; www.malvernretreat.org; Laymen's Retreat League.

Maronite Voice, The, annual; 4611 Salder Rd. Glen Allen, VA 23060; (804) 270-7234; www.stmaron.org. Maronite eparchies of Brooklyn and Our Lady of Lebanon.

Maronites Today, m; P.O. Box 1891, Austin, TX 78767-1891; (512) 458-3693; www.eparchyla.org; Eparchy of Our Lady of Los Angeles.

Martyrs' Shrine Message, twice a year; P.O. Box 7, Hwy. 12, Midland, ON L4R 4K6, Canada; www.martyrs-shrine.com.

Medical Mission Sisters News, q; 8400 Pine Road, Philadelphia, PA 19111; (215) 742-6100; www.medicalmissionsisters.org.

Messenger of St. Joseph's Union, The, 3 times a year; 108 Bedell St., Staten Island, NY 10309; (718) 984-9296.

Mission, The, three times a year; 90 Cherry Lane, Hicksville, NY 11801-6299; (516) 733-7042; www.catholicharities.cc; Catholic Charities.

Mission Messenger, The, q; P.O. Box 610, Thoreau, NM, 87323; (505) 862-7847; www.stbonaventuremission.org; St. Bonaventure Indian Mission and School.

Missionaries of Africa Report, q; 1624 21st St. N.W., Washington, DC 20009; (202) 232-5154; Society of Missionaries of Africa (White Fathers).

Mission Update, bm; 3029 Fourth St. N.E., Washington, DC 20017; (202) 832-3112; www.uscatholicmission.org.

Mountain View, q.; 8501 Bailey Rd., Darien, IL 60561; (630) 969-5050; Lay Carmelite Headquarters.

National Holy Name Newsletter, bm; 53 Laux Street, Buffalo, NY 14206-2218; (716) 847-6419; www.members.aol.com/nahns.

NCPD National Update, q; 415 Michigan Ave. N.E., #240, Washington, DC 20017; (202) 529-2933; www.ncpd.org; National Catholic Office for Persons with Disabilities.

Neighbors, Committee on Home Missions, q.; 3211 Fourth St. N.E., Washington, D.C. 20017; (202) 541-5400; Bishops' Committee on Home Missions.

News and Ideas, q.; 9480 North De Mazenod Dr., Belleville, IL 62223; (618) 398-4848; www.snows.org; Missionary Oblates of Mary Immaculate.

News and Views, q; 3900 Westminster Pl., St. Louis, MO 63108; (314) 533-0320; www.sacredheartprogram.org; Sacred Heart Program.

Newsletter of the Bureau of Catholic Indian Missions, 10 times a year; 2021 H St. N.W., Washington, DC 20006; (202) 331-8542.

North Coast Catholic, bi-monthly; P.O. Box 1297, Santa Rosa, CA 95402; (707) 566-3302; www.santarosacatholic.org; Santa Rosa diocese.

Nuestra Parroquia (Spanish-English), m; 205 W. Monroe St., Chicago, IL 60606; (312) 236-7782; www.hmrc.claretianpubs.org; Claretians.

Oblates Mission Friendship Club News, q; 9480 North De Mazenod Dr., Belleville, IL 62223-1160; (618) 398-4848; www.oblatesusa.org; Missionary Oblates of Mary Immaculate.

Origins, 48 times a year; 3211 Fourth St. N.E., Washington, DC 20017; (202) 541-3284; Catholic News Service.

Overview, m; 205 W. Monroe St., 6th Floor, Chicago, IL 60606; (312) 609-8880; Thomas More Assn.

Paulist, Today, q; 415 W. 59th St., New York, NY 10019; (212) 265-3209; www.paulist.org.

Peace Times, 3-4 times a year; P.O. Box 248, Bellevue, WA 98009-0248; (425) 451-1770.

Pentecost Today, q; P.O. Box 628, Locust Grove, VA 22508-0628; (540) 972-0225; www.nsc-chariscenter.org.

Perspectives, q; 912 Market St., La Crosse, WI 54601; (608) 791-5289; www.fspa.org.

Pilgrim, The, q; 136 Shrine Rd., Auriesville, NY 12016; (518) 853-3033; Shrine of North American Martyrs.

Poverello, q; 220 37th St., Pittsburgh, PA 15201; (412) 682-1300; www.capuchin.com; Capuchin Franciscans.

Priests for Life, bm; P.O. Box 141172, Staten Island, NY 10314; (718) 980-4400; www.priestsforlife.org.

Proclaim, 10 times a year; 3211 Fourth St. N.E., Washington, DC 20017-1194; (202) 541-3237; www.usccb.org.

Quarterly, The, q; 209 W. Fayette St., Baltimore, MD 21201; (410) 951-7455; www.catholicrelief.org; Catholic Relief Services.

Religious Life, m (bm, May-Aug.); P.O. Box 41007, Chicago, IL 60641; (312) 267-1195; www.ewtn.com/religious life; Institute on Religious Life.

RSCJ Newsletter, m; 1235 Otis St. N.E., Washington, DC 20017-2516; (202) 526-6258; www.rscj.org; Religious of Sacred Heart.

St. Anthony's Newsletter, m; 103 St. Francis Blvd., Mt. St. Francis, IN 47146; (812) 923-5250; Conventual Franciscans.

St. Joseph's Parish Life Quarterly, q; 1382 Highland Ave., Needham, MA 02192; (617) 444-0245.

Sacred Ground, three times a year; 1 Elmwood Ave., Kansas City, KS 66103-3719; (913) 384-6500; www.cfcusa.org; Christian Foundation for Children and Aging.

San Francisco Charismatics, m; 2555 17th Ave., San Francisco, CA 94116; (415) 664-8481; www.sfspirit.com.

SCJ News, 9 times a year; P.O. Box 289, Hales Corners, WI 53130-0289; (414) 427-4266; www.scjusa.net. Sacred Heart Fathers and Brothers.

SCRC Spirit, The, bm; 9795 Cabrini Dr., #105, Burbank, CA, 91504-1739; (818) 771-1361; www.scrc.org.

Sharing & Caring, q; 4960 Salem Ave., Dayton,

OH 45416; (937) 274-2707; www.preciousbloodsistersdayton.org. Precious Blood Sisters.

Shrine Advocates Newsletter, q; 9480 N. De Mazenod Dr., Belleville, IL 62223; (618) 398-4848; www.oblatesusa.org.

Spirit & The Bide, The, m; 8300 Morganford Rd., St. Louis, MO 63123; (314) 792-7070; www.stlcharismatic.org.

Spiritual Book Associates, 8 times a year; Notre Dame, IN 46556-0428; (219) 287-2838; www.spiritualbookassoc.org.

Squires Newsletter, m; One Columbus Plaza, New Haven, CT 06510-3326; (203) 752-4402; Columbian Squires.

SSpS Mission, q; P.O. Box 6026, Techny, IL 60082-6026; (847) 441-0126; www.ssps-usa.org; Holy Spirit Missionary Sisters.

Tidings, Washington Theological Union, 3 times a year; 6896 Laurel St. N.W., Washington, DC 20012; (202) 726-8800; www.wtu.edu.

Touchstone, q; NFPC Office, 333 N. Michigan Ave., Suite 1205, Chicago, IL 60601; (312) 442-9700; www.nfpc.org; National Federation of Priests' Councils.

Trinity Missions Report, q; 9001 New Hampshire Ave., Silver Spring, MD 20903; (301) 434-6761.

Triumph of the Past, m.; P.O. Box 29535, Columbus, OH 43229; (614) 261-1300.

Unda USA Newsletter, q; 901 Irving Ave., Dayton, OH 45409-2316; (937) 229-2303; www.undausa.org.

Vision: National Association of Catholic Chaplains, 10 times a year; P.O. Box 070473, Milwaukee, WI 53207-0473; (414) 483-4898; www.nacc.org.

Voices, 2 times a year; 1625 Rutherford Lane, Bldg. D, Austin, TX 78754-5105; (512) 339-7123; Volunteers for Educational and Social Services.

Voices in Mission and Ministry, q.; 1257 E. Siena Heights Dr., Adrian, MI 49221; (517) 266-3400; www.adriansisters.org; Adrian Dominicans.

Woodstock Report, q; Georgetown University, Box 571137, Washington, DC 20057; (202) 687-3532; www.georgetown.edu/centers/woodstock; Woodstock Theological Center.

Word One, 5 times a year; 205 W. Monroe St., Chicago, IL 60606; (312) 236-7782; www.wordone.org; Claretians.

Xaverian Missions Newsletter, bm; P.O. Box 5857, Holliston, MA 01746; (508) 429-2144; Xaverian Missionary Fathers.

Your Edmundite Missions Newsletter, bm; 1428 Broad St., Selma, AL 36701; (334) 872-2359; www.edmunditemissions.com; Southern Missions of Society of St. Edmund.

Youth Update, m; 28 W. Liberty St., Cincinnati, OH 45210; (513) 241-5615; www.americancatholic.org.

Zeal Newsletter, 3 times a year; P.O. Box 86, Allegany, NY 14706; (716) 373-1130; Franciscan Sisters of Allegany.

BOOKS

The Catholic Almanac, a; Our Sunday Visitor, Inc., 200 Noll Plaza, Huntington, IN 46750, publisher; editorial offices, 200 Noll Plaza, Huntington, IN 46750; (260) 444-4398; www.catholicalmanac.com; first edition, 1904.

The Official Catholic Directory, a; P.J. Kenedy & Sons in association with R.R. Bowker, a Reed Reference Publishing Company, 121 Chanlon Rd., New Providence, NJ 07974; (847) 966-8278; first edition, 1817.

BOOK CLUBS

Catholic Book Club (1928), 106 W. 56th St., New York, NY 10019; (212) 581-4640; www.americapress.org/cbc.htm; sponsors the Campion Award.

Catholic Digest Book Club (1954), 2115 Summit Ave., St. Paul, MN 55105-1081; (651) 962-6748.

Spiritual Book Associates (1934), Ave Maria Press Building, P.O. Box 428, Notre Dame, IN 46556; (219) 287-2838.

Thomas More Book Club (1939), Thomas More Association, 205 W. Monroe St., Sixth Floor, Chicago, IL 60606; (312) 609-8880.

General Publishers

(*Source:* Catholic Press Directory, Almanac *Survey.*)

Our Sunday Visitor Publishing: 200 Noll Plaza, Huntington IN 46750; (800) 348-2440, (260) 356-8400; e-mail: booksed@osv.com.

Abbey Press: One Caring Place, Saint Meinrad, IN 47577; (812) 357-8215; www.carenotes.com.

Abingdon Press: 201 8th Ave. South, Nashville, TN 37202; (615) 749-6615; www.abingdonpress.com.

ACTA Publications: 5559 Howard St., Skokie, IL 60077; (847) 676-2282; www.actapublications.com.

Alba House/St. Pauls: 2187 Victory Blvd. Staten Island, NY 10314; (718) 698-2759; www.alba-house.com

Alleluia Press: P.O. Box 103, Allendale, NJ 07401; (201) 327-3513.

American Catholic Press: 16565 South State St., South Holland, IL 60473; (708) 331-5485; www.acpress.org.

AMI Press, The Blue Army of Our Lady of Fatima: Mountain View Rd., Washington, NJ 07882; (908) 213-2223.

Apostolate for Family Consecration: 3375 County Rd. 36, Bloomingdale, OH 43910; (740) 765-5500; www.familyland.org.

Ascension Press: P.O. Box 1990, West Chester, PA 19380; 610-696-7795; www.ascensionpress.com

Ave Maria Press, Inc.: PO Box 428, Notre Dame IN 46556; (574) 287-2831; e-mail: avemariapress.1@nd.edu.

Angelus Press: 2915 Forest Ave., Kansas City, MO 64109; (816) 753-3150; www.angeluspress.org.

BlueBridge: 240 W. 35th St., Suite 509, N.Y., N.Y. 10001; (212) 244-4166; www.bluebridgebooks.com.

Cathedral Foundation Press: P.O. Box 777, Baltimore, MD 21203; (443) 263-0248; www.catholicfoundation.org.

Catholic Health Assoc.: 4455 Woodson Rd., St. Louis, MO 63134; (314) 253-3477; www.chusa.org.

Catholic Library Assoc.: 100 N. St., Suite 224, Pittsfield, MA 01201; (413) 443-2252; www.cathla.org.

Catholic News Agency: 1300 S. Steele St., Denver, CO 80210; (303) 715-3265; www.catholicnewsagency.com.

Catholic News Service: 3211 Fourth St N.E., Washington DC 20017; (202) 541-3250; www.catholicnews.com.

Catholic Relief Services: 209 West Fayette St., Baltimore MD 21201; (410) 625-2220.

Catholic University of America Press: 620 Michigan Ave. NE, Washington, DC 20064; (202) 319-5052; www.cuapress.cua.edu.

The Christophers: 5 Hanover Sq., 11th Floor, New York NY 10004; (212) 759-4050; www.christophers.org.

Cistercian Publ.: St. John's Abbey, P.O. Box 7500, Collegeville, MN 56321; (320) 363-3096; www.cistercianpublications.org.

Claretian Publications: 205 West Monroe St., Chicago IL 60606; (800) 328-6515, (312) 236-7782; e-mail: editors@uscatholic.org.

Clarity Publishing, Inc.: PO Box 758, Latham NY 12110-3510; (518) 783-0058.

Couple to Couple League: P.O. Box 111184, Cincinnati, OH 45211; (513) 471-2000; www.ccli.org.

Doubleday: 1540 Broadway, New York, NY 10036; (212) 782-9392; www.randomhouse.com.

Eerdmans: 255 Jefferson Ave., SE, Grand Rapids, 49503; (616) 459-4591; www.eerdmans.com.

Emmaus Road: 827 N. Fourth St., Steubenville, OH 43952; (740) 283-2880.

Franciscan Mission Associates: PO Box 598, Mount Vernon NY 10551-0598; (914) 664-5604.

Franciscan Press: Quincy University, 1800 College Ave., Quincy, IL 62301; (217) 228-5670; www.qufranciscanpress.com.

Georgetown University Press: 3240 Prospect St., NW, Washington, DC 20007; (202) 687-5889; www.press.georgetown.edu.

Gingerbread House: 602 Montauk Hwy., Westhampton Beach, NY 11978; (631) 288-5119; www.gingerbreadbooks.com.

ICS Publ.: 2131 Lincoln Rd. NE, Washington, DC 20002; (202) 832-8489; www.icspublications.org.

Ignatius Press: 2515 McAllister St., San Francisco, CA 94118; (415) 387-2324; www.ignatius.com.

Liguori Publications: One Liguori Drive, Liguori MO 63057; (636) 464-2500; www.liguori.org.

Liturgical Press: St. John's Abbey, P.O. Box 7500, Collegeville, MN 56321; (320) 363-2213; www.litpress.org.

Little Books: P.O. Box 6009, Saginaw, MI 48608; (989) 797-6653; www.littlebooks.org.

Liturgical Press: St. John's Abbey, P.O. Box 7500, Collegeville, MN 56321; (320) 363-2213; www.litpress.org.

Liturgical Publications Inc. Resource Center: 2875 S. James Dr., New Berlin, WI 53151; (262) 785-2469; www.4lpi.com.

Loyola Press: 3441 North Ashland Avenue, Chicago, IL 60657; (800) 621-1008; www.loyolapress.org.

Marquette University Press: 1415 West Wisconisn Ave., Milwaukee, WI 53233; (414) 288-1564; www.marquette.edu/mupress/.

Missionary Oblates of Mary Immaculate: 9480 North De Mazenod Dr., Belleville, IL 62223-1160; (888) 330-6264; e-mail: mami@oblatesusa.org.

National Catholic Bioethics Center (NCBC): 6399 Drexel Rd., Philadelphia, PA 19151; (215) 877-2660; www.ncbcenter.org.

Notre Dame Press, University of: 310 Flanner Hall, Notre Dame, IN 46556; (219) 631-6346; www.undpress.edu.

Orbis Books: P.O. Box 308, Maryknoll, NY 10545; (914) 941-7636; www.orbisbooks.com.

Pauline Books & Media: 50 St. Paul's Avenue, Boston MA 02130; (617) 522-8911; www.pauline.org.

Paulist National Catholic Evangelization Association: 3031 Fourth Street N.E., Washington DC 20017; (800) 237-5515, (202) 832-5022; e-mail: pncea@pncea.org.

Paulist Press: 997 Macarthur Blvd. Mahwah, NJ 07430; (201) 825-7300; www.paulistpress.com.

Pittsburgh Press, University of: 3400 Forbes Ave., 5th Floor Eureka, Pittsburgh, PA 15260; (412) 383-2456; www.pitt.edu/~press.

Pontifical Mission Societies in the United States: 366 Fifth Ave., New York NY 10001; (800) 431-2222, (212) 563-8700; e-mail: propfaith@aol.com.

Resource Publications, Inc.: 160 E. Virginia St., #290,

San Jose, CA 95112; (408) 286-8505; www.rpinet.com.

Resurrection Press: 77 West End Rd., Totowa, NJ 07512; (973) 890-2400; www.catholicbookpublishing.com.

St. Anthony Messenger Press: 28 W Liberty St, Cincinnati OH 45202; (513) 241-5615; www.americancatholic.org.

St. Joseph's University Press: 5600 City Ave., Philadelphia, PA 19131; (610) 660-3400; www.sju.edu/sjupress.

Scepter: P.O. Box 211, New York, NY 10018; (212) 354-0670; www.scepterpublishers.org.

Servant Publications: 1143 Highland Dr., Suite E, Ann Arbor, MI 48108; (734) 677-6490; www.servantpub.com.

Sophia Institute Press: Box 5284, Manchester, NH 03108; (603) 641-9344; www.sophiainstitute.com.

Twenty-Third Publications: P.O. Bix 180, Mystic, CT 06355; (860) 437-3012; www.twentythirdpublications.com.

USCCB Publishing: 3211 Fourth St. NE, Washington, DC 20017; (202) 541-3090; www.usccb.org.

CANADIAN CATHOLIC PUBLICATIONS

(*Principal source*: *2012 Catholic Press Directory*.)

Newspapers

B. C. Catholic, The, w; 150 Robson St., Vancouver, BC V6B 2A7; (604) 683-0281; www.bcc.rcav.org.

Catholic Register, The (national), w; 1155 Younge St., Suite 401, Toronto, ON M4T 1W2; (416) 934-3410; www.catholicregister.org; lay edited.

Western Catholic Reporter, w.; 8421 101 Ave. NW, Edmonton, AB T6A 0L1; (780) 465-8030; www.wcr.ab.ca.

Magazines, Other Periodicals

L'Almanach Populaire Catholique, a; 9795 St. Anne Blvd., St. Anne de Beaupre, QC G0A3C0; (418) 827-4538.

ANNALS of St. Anne de Beaupre, The, m; Box 1000, Ste. Anne de Beaupre, QC G0A 3C0; (418) 827-4538; Basilica of St. Anne.

Apostolat, bm; 8844 Notre-Dame Est, Montréal, QC H1L 3M4; (514) 351-9310; Oblates of Mary Immaculate, CMO (*Centre Missionnaire Oblat*).

Bread of Life, The, bm; P.O. Box 395, Hamilton, ON L8N 3H8; (905) 529-4496; www.breadoflife.ca.

Canadian Catholic Review, The, St. Joseph's College, University of Alberta, Edmonton, AB T6G 2J5; (403) 492-7681.

Canadian League, The, q; 1-160 Murray Park Rd., Winnipeg, MB R3J 3X5; (204) 927-2310; www.cwl.ca; Catholic Women's League of Canada.

Caravan, q; 90 Parent Ave., Ottawa, ON K1N 7B1; (613) 241-9461; www.cccb.ca; Canadian Conference of Catholic Bishops.

Celebrate! (Novalis), bm; St. Paul University, 223 Main St., Ottawa, ON K1S 1C4; (780) 451-2228.

Companion Magazine, m; 695 Coxwell Ave., Suite 600, Toronto, ON M4C 5R6; (416) 690-5611; www.franciscan.on.ca; Conventual Franciscan Fathers.

Compass — A Jesuit Journal, bm (Jan.-Nov.); Box 400, Stn. F, 50 Charles St. East, Toronto, ON M4Y 2L8; (416) 921-0653; www.io.org/ngvanv/compass/com-phome.html.

CRC Bulletin (French-English), q; 219 Argyle Ave., Ottawa, ON K2P 2H4; (613) 236-0824; www.crcn.ca; Canadian Religious Conference.

L'Église Canadienne (French), 11 times a year; 6255 rue Hutchison, Bureau 103, Montreal, QC H2V 4C7; (514)

278-3020; www.novalis.ca.

Fatima Crusader, q; P.O. Box 602, Fort Erie, ON L2A 4M7; (905) 871-7607; www.fatima.org.

Global Village Voice, The, q; 10 St. Mary St., Suite 420, Toronto, ON M4Y 1P9; (416) 922-1592; Canadian Organization for Development and Peace.

Kateri (English-French), q; P.O. Box 70, Kahnawake, QC J0L 1B0; (450) 638-1546.

Le Messager de Saint Antoine (French), 10 times a year; Lac-Bouchette, QC G0W 1V0; (418) 348-6344.

Messenger of the Sacred Heart, m; 661 Greenwood Ave., Toronto, ON M4J 4B3; (416) 466-1195; Apostleship of Prayer.

Mission Canada, q; 201-1155 Younge St., Toronto, ON M4T 1W2; (416) 934-3424; www.missioncanada.ca.

Missions Étrangères (French), bm; 180 Place Juge-Desnoyers, Laval, QC H7G 1A4; (450) 667-4190; www.smelaval.org.

Nouvel Informateur Catholiqué, Le, semi-monthly; 6550 Rte 125, Rawdon, QC J0K 1S0; (450) 834-8503.

Oratory, bm; 3800 Ch. Queen Mary, Montreal, QC H3V 1H6; (514) 733-8211; www.saint-joseph.org.

Our Family, m; P.O. Box 249, Battleford, SK; S0M 0E0; (306) 937-7771; www.ourfamilymagazine.com; Oblates of Mary Immaculate.

Prêtre et Pasteur (French), m; 4450 St. Hubert St., #500, Montreal, QC H2J 2W9; (514) 525-6210.

Prieres Missionaires, m; Missionaires de la Consolata, 2505 Boulevard Gouin ouest, Montréal, QC H3M 1B5; (514) 334-1910; www.consolata.org.

Relations (French), 10 times a year; 25 Rue Jarry Ouest, Montreal, QC H2P 1S6; (514) 387-2541.

Reveil Missionaire, bm; Missionaire de la Consolata, 2505 Boulevard Gouin ouest, Montréal, QC H3M 1B5; (514) 334-1910; www.consolata.org.

La Revue d'Sainte Anne de Beaupre (French), m; P.O. Box 1000, Ste. Anne de Beaupre, Québec G0A 3C0; (418) 827-4538.

Scarboro Missions, 9 times a year; 2685 Kingston Rd., Scarboro, ON M1M 1M4; (416) 261-7135; www.web.net/~sfms.

Spiritan Missionary News, q; 121 Victoria Park Ave., Toronto, ON M4E 3S2; (416) 698-2003; www.spiritans.com.

Unity, q; 308 Young St., Montréal, QC H3C 2G2; (514) 937-5973.

INTERNATIONAL CATHOLIC PERIODICALS

(Principal source: Catholic Almanac *survey. Included are English-language Catholic periodicals published outside the U.S.)*

African Ecclesial Review (AFER), bm; Gaba Publications, P.O. Box 4002, Eldoret, Kenya.

Australasian Catholic Record, q; 99 Albert Rd., Strathfield 2135, New South Wales, Australia.

Christ to the World, 5 times a year; Via di Propaganda 1-C, 00187, Rome, Italy.

Christian Orient, q; P.B. 1 Vadavathoor, Kottayam 686010, Kerala, India.

Doctrine and Life, m; Dominican Publications, 42 Parnell Sq., Dublin 1, Ireland.

Downside Review, q; Downside Abbey, Stratton on the Fosse, Bath, BA3 4RH, England.

East Asian Pastoral Review, q; East Asian Pastoral Institute, P.O. Box 221, U.P. Campus, 1101 Quezon City, Philippines.

Furrow, The, m; St. Patrick's College, Maynooth, Ireland.

Heythrop Journal, q; Heythrop College, Kensington Sq., London W8 5HQ, England (editorial office); published by Blackwell Publishers, 108 Cowley Rd., Oxford, OX4 1JF, England.

Holy Land Magazine, q; P.O. Box 186, 91001 Jerusalem, Israel; illustrated.

Irish Biblical Studies, The, q; Union Theological College, 108 Botanic Ave., Belfast BT7 1JT, N. Ireland.

Irish Journal of Sociology, The, a; St. Patrick's College, Maynooth, Ireland.

Irish Theological Quarterly, q; St. Patrick's College, Maynooth, Ireland.

L'Osservatore Romano, w; Vatican City. (*See above* under **U.S. Newspapers.**)

Louvain Studies, q; Peeters Publishers, Bondgenotenlaan 153, B-3000, Leuven, Belgium.

Lumen Vitae (French, with English summaries), q; International Center for Studies in Religious Education, 186, rue Washington, B-1050 Brussels, Belgium.

Mediaeval Studies, a; Pontifical Institute of Mediaeval Studies, 59 Queen's Park Crescent East, Toronto, ON M5S 2C4, Canada.

Month, m; 114 Mount St., London WIY 6AH, England.

Music and Liturgy, bm; The Editor, 33 Brockenhurst Rd., Addiscombe Croydan, Surrey CRO 7DR, England.

New Blackfriars, m; edited by English Dominicans, Blackfriars, Oxford OX1 3LY, England.

Omnis Terra (English Edition), m; Pontifical Missionary Union, Congregation for the Evangelization of Peoples, Via di Propaganda 1/c, 00187 Rome, Italy.

One in Christ, q; Edited at Turvey Abbey, Turvey, Bedfordshire MK43 8DE, England.

Priests & People (formerly **The Clergy Review**), 11 times a year; Blackfriars, Buckingham Rd., Cambridge CB3 0DD, England.

Recusant History, bi-annual; Catholic Record Society, 12 Melbourne Pl., Wolsingham, Durham DL13 3EH, England.

Religious Life Review, bm; Dominican Publications, 42 Parnell Sq., Dublin 1, Ireland.

Scripture in Church, q; Dominican Publications, 42 Parnell Sq., Dublin 1, Ireland.

Southwark Liturgy Bulletin, q; The Editor, 10 Claremont Rd., Maidstone, Kent ME14 5L2, England.

Spearhead, 5 times a year; Gaba Publications, P.O. Box 4002, Eldoret, Kenya.

Spirituality, bm; Dominican Publications, 42 Parnell Sq., Dublin 1, Ireland.

Tablet, The, w; 1 King Street Cloisters, Clifton Walk, London W60QZ, England; 44(1)-20-8748-8484.

Way, The, q; 114 Mount St., London W1Y6AN, England.

CATHOLIC NEWS AGENCIES

(Sources: International Catholic Union of the Press, Geneva; Catholic Press Association, U.S.)

Argentina: *Agencia Informativa Catolica Argentina* (AICA), av. Rivadavia, 413, 40 Casilla de Correo Central 2886, 1020 Buenos Aires.

Austria: *Katholische Presse-Agentur* (Kathpress), Singerstrasse 7/6/2, 1010 Vienna 1.

Belgium: *Centre d'Information de Presse* (CIP), 35 Chausée de Haecht, 1030 Brussels.

Bolivia: *Agencia Noticias Fides*, ANF, Casilla 5782, La Paz. *ERBOL*, Casilla 5946, La Paz.

Chile: *Agencia informativa y de comunicaciones* (AIC Chile), Brasil 94, Santiago.

Croatia: *Christian Information Service*, Marulicev 14, PP 434, 410001 Zagreb.

Germany: *Katholische Nachrichten Agentur* (KNA), Adenauer Allee 134, 5300 Bonn 1.

Greece: *Agence TYPOS*, Rue Acharnon 246, Athens 815.

Hong Kong: *UCA-News*, P.O. Box 69626, Kwun Tong (Hong Kong).

Hungary: *Magyar Kurir*, Milkszath ter 1, 1088, Budapest.

India: *South Asian Religious News* (SAR-News), PB 6236, Mazagaon, Bombay 400 010.

Italy: *Servizio Informazioni Religiosa* (SIR), Via di Porta Cavalleggeri 143, I-00165 Roma.

Centrum Informationis Catolicae (CIC-Roma), via Delmonte de la Farina, 30/4, 00186 Roma.

Rome Reports: a private and independent international television news agency based in Rome, Italy, specializing in covering the Pope and the Vatican; produces a weekly program called "Rome Reports, The World seen from the Vatican." Address: Via della Conciliazione 44, 00193, Rome, Italy; www.romereports.com.

Zenit, a non-profit international news agency that covers the life of the Church. Innovative Media Inc. is listed officially as the publisher and editor of ZENIT in all language-editions.

Peru: ACI-PRENSA, A.P. 040062, Lima.

Switzerland: *Katholische Internationale Presse-Agentur* (KIPA), Case Postale 1054 CH 1701, Fribourg.

Centre International de Reportages et d'Information Culturelle (CIRIC), Chemin Clochetons 8, P.O. Box 1000, Lausanne.

United States of America: *Catholic News Service* (CNS), 3211 Fourth St. N.E., Washington, DC 20017; (202) 541-3250; www.catholicnews.com.

Catholic News Agency (CNA), 3392 S. Broadway, Englewood, CO 80113; (303) 997-8563; www.catholic-newsagency.com

Vatican City State: Vatican Information Service (VIS), a news service, established by the Holy See Press Office in 1991, that provides information on the activities of the Holy Father and the Roman Curia. The VIS transmits news from Monday through Friday throughout the year, except during the month of August. It is available in English, Italian, Spanish, and French; press.catholica.va.

U.S. PRESS SERVICES

Catholic News Service (CNS), established in 1920 (NC News Service), provides a worldwide daily news report by satellite throughout the U.S. and Canada and by wire and computer links into several foreign countries, and by mail to other clients, serving Catholic periodicals and broadcasters including Vatican Radio in about 40 countries. CNS also provides feature and photo services and publishes "Origins," a weekly documentary service and Catholic Trends, a fortnightly newsletter, the weekly TV and Movie Guide and Movie Guide Monthly. CNS maintains a full time bureau in Rome. It is a division of the United States Catholic Conference. Address: 3211 Fourth St. N.E., Washington, DC 20017; (202) 541-3250; www.catholicnews.com.

Catholic News Agency (CNA), established in 2004 in response to Pope John Paul II's call for a "New Evangelization. CNA provides coverage of events in the life of the Church and offers free access to Catholic dioceses, parishes, and websites. The agency is funded chiefly by donations and gifts from readers and benefactors. Address: 3392 S. Broadway, Englewood, CO 80113; (303) 997-8563; www.catholicnewsagency.com

EWTNews, 5817 Old Leeds Road, Irondale, AL 35210; 205-271-2900; www.ewtn.com. Exclusive interviews, investigative reports, live coverage of special events and cultural reporting weekly on the World Over Live newsmagazine. Daily coverage of world news from a Catholic perspective.

Spanish-Language Service, A weekly news summary provided by Catholic News Service, used by a number of Catholic newspapers. Some papers carry features of their own in Spanish.

Religion News Service (RNS) provides coverage of all religions as well as ethics, spirituality and moral issues. Founded in 1934 (as the Religious News Service) by the National Conference of Christian and Jews as an independent agency, RNS became an editorially independent subsidiary of the United Methodist Reporter, an interfaith publishing company, in 1983. It was acquired by Newhouse News Service in 1994. Address: 1930 18th Street NW, Suite B2, Washington, DC 20009; (202) 463.8777; www.religionnews.com.

RADIO, TELEVISION, THEATER

(The following listings are as of June 1, 2013. Sources, Catholic Almanac survey. Telephone and web addresses are listed as available.)

Radio

Catholic Radio Association: an association comprised primarily of the majority of Catholic radio stations in the United States and Catholic program providers united to advance the apostolate of Catholic radio. The Mission Statement states: "The Catholic Radio Association seeks to bring together Catholic radio apostolates, program providers and the hierarchy of the Catholic Church in order that this means of social communication be used effectively and in obedience to the decrees of the Second Vatican Council and the magisterium of the Church, especially as expressed in the words of Pope John Paul II." The Catholic Radio Association, 121 Broad St., Charleston, SC 29401; 843) 853-2300; www.catholicradioassociation.org.

Ave Maria Radio: Ave Maria Radio employs radio, internet and other media to offer news, analysis, teaching, devotions and music. Programs include Teresa Tomeo and Al Kresta. Ave Maria Radio, P.O. Box 504, Ann Arbor, MI 48106; (734) 930-5200; www.avemariaradio.com.

Catholic Answers Radio: Produced by Catholic Answers; programming includes "Catholic Answers Live" is a two hour, daily, call-in radio program, hosted by Patrick Coffin. Catholic Answers, 2020 Gillespie Way, El Cajon, CA 92020 USA Main: 619-387-7200; www.catholic.com.

EWTN Global Catholic Radio Network (formerly known as WEWN), 5817 Old Leeds Road, Irondale, AL 35210; 205-271-2900; www.ewtn.com; the first 24-hour U.S. Catholic radio network, launched in 1996.

Relevant Radio: Relevant Radio exists to assist the Church in the New Evangelization by providing relevant programming through a media platform to help people bridge the gap between faith and everyday life. Programming includes "Morning Air" and the "The Drew Mariani Show." Relevant Radio PO Box 10707, Green Bay, WI 54307-0707; (920) 884-1460; www.relevantradio.com.

Immaculate Heart Radio: A network of approximately 30 radio stations in the western part of the United States; started in 1997 with K-IHM, named for the Immaculate Heart of Mary, in Reno, Nevada. Programming includes an extensive array of EWTN programs. Immaculate Heart Radio, 3256 Penryn Road, Suite 100, Loomis, CA 95650-8052; (888) 887-7120; (916) 535-0500, ihradio.com

Radio Maria: Part of the international Radio Maria Association founded in Milan, Italy, in 1987. Radio Maria in the U.S. began in 2000 with a station in Alexandria, LA; it has grown to more than ten stations and offers a variety of programming. Radio Maria, 601 Washington St., Alexandria, LA 71301; 888-408-0201; radiomaria.us.

Vatican Radio: *See* under **Vatican City State**.

Stations and Programs

Christopher Radio Program: 14-minute interview series, "Christopher Closeup" weekly and "Christopher Minutes" daily, on 400 stations. 12 E. 48th St., New York, NY 10017; (212) 759-4050; www.christophers.org.

Journeys Thru Rock: Produced in cooperation with the Department of Communication, USCCB. A 15-minute weekly program currently employing a youth-oriented music and commentary format (ABC).

Sirius Satellite Radio: Offers the Catholic Channel (Channel 129) through the Archdiocese of New York; programs include, "Busted Halo with Father Dave Dwyer," "The Catholic Guy with Lino Rulli," and "Conversation with Cardinal Dolan."

Television and Communications Services

Catholic Familyland: A ministry of the Apostolate for Family Consecration. Established in 1975, FL-TV produces television and video programs and operates in Asia, Latin America, Europe and Africa. Familyland Television Network, 3375 County Rd. 36, Bloomingdale, OH 43910; (740) 765-5500; www.familyland.org.

Catholic Academy for Communication Arts Professionals: The U.S. affiliate of SIGNIS, a Vatican-approved organization for Catholic communication professionals; membership is open to those professionally involved in Catholic church-related communications and to Catholic communicators working in secular organizations. President: Sally Oberski, Catholic Academy for Communication Arts Professionals, 1645 Brook Lynn Dr., Ste 2, Dayton, OH 45432-1944; (937) 458-0265; www.catholicacademy.org.

Catholic Communication Campaign (CCC): A U.S. Catholic bishops' program that produces, distributes and supports Catholic media projects, including a weekly television talk show, "Personally Speaking," television documentaries and public service messages. Ellen McCloskey, 3211 4th St. N.E., Washington, DC 20017; (202) 541-3204; www.usccb.org/ccc.

Catholic Communications Foundation (CCF): A foundation established by the Catholic Fraternal Benefit Societies in 1966 to lend support and assistance to development of the communications apostolate of the Church. The CCF promotes diocesan communications capabilities and funds a scholarship program at the Annual Institute for Religious Communications. 303 W. Lancaster Ave., PMB 333, Wayne, PA 19087.

CatholicTV: A Catholic broadband network delivering a variety of programs. CatholicTV, PO Box 9196, 34 Chestnut St., Watertown MA 02471; catholictv.com., 617-923-0220.

Christopher TV Series, "Christopher Closeup": Originated in 1952. Half-hour interviews, weekly, on commercial TV and numerous cable outlets. 12 E. 48th St., New York, NY

10017; (212) 759-4050; www.christophers.org.

Clemons Productions, Inc.: Produces "That's the Spirit," a family show for television; "Thoughts for the Week," on the ABC Satellite Network, and "Spirituality for Today" on the internet. Available to dioceses, organizations or channels. P.O. Box 7466, Greenwich, CT 06830; www.spirituality.org.

EWTN Global Catholic Network (EWTN): 5817 Old Leeds Road, Irondale, AL 35210; 205-271-2900; www.ewtn.com. America's largest religious cable network, features 24 hours of spiritual growth programming for the entire family. Offers documentaries, weekly teaching series and talk shows, including the award-winning "Mother Angelica Live." Nightly live programs include *The Journey Home, Threshold of Hope, EWTN Live, Life on the Rock* and *The World Over*. Daily live radio programming includes the popular call-in shows, *Open Line*. Also features live Church events from around the world and devotional programs such as "The Holy Rosary." Mother M. Angelica, P.C.P.A., Foundress.

Family Theater Productions: Founded by Father Peyton. Videocassettes, films for TV. 7201 Sunset Blvd., Hollywood, CA 90046; (323) 874-6633; www.familytheater.org. Nat. Dir., Fr. Wilfred J. Raymond, C.S.C.

Franciscan Media: Producer of video and print resources for pastoral ministry; St. Anthony Messenger Press, 28 W. Liberty St., Cincinnati, OH 45210; (513) 241-5615; www.Franciscanmedia.org.

Hispanic Telecommunications Network, Inc. (HTN): Produces "Nuestra Familia," a national weekly Spanish-language TV series; 1405 N. Main, Suite 240, San Antonio, TX 78212.

Mary Productions: Originated in 1950. Offers royalty-free scripts for stage, film, radio and tape production. Audio and video tapes of lives of the saints and historical characters. Traveling theater company; Mary Productions, 212 Oakdale Dr., Tomaso Plaza, Middletown, NJ 07748; (732) 617-8144.

National Interfaith Cable Coalition: A 28-member consortium representing 64 faith groups from Roman Catholic, Jewish, Protestant and Eastern Orthodox traditions; works with faith groups to present programming on the Faith and Values Media; 74 Trinity Place, Suite 1550, New York, NY 10006; (212) 406-4121; www.faithandvalues.com.

Oblate Media and Communication Corporation: Producers, Broadcast syndicators and distributors of Catholic and value-centered video programming. 7315 Manchester Rd., St. Louis, MO 63143.

Passionist Communications, Inc.: Presents Sunday Mass on TV seen in U.S. and available to dioceses and channels; publishes "TV Prayer Guide," semi-annually. P.O. Box 440, Pelham, NY 10803-0440.

Paulist Media Works: Full service audio production in syndication to dioceses, religious communities and church groups; 3015 4th St. N.E., Washington, DC 20017; (202) 269-6064. Rev. John Geaney, exec. prod.

Paulist Productions: Producers and distributors of the INSIGHT Film Series (available for TV) and educational film series. 17575 Pacific Coast Hwy., Pacific Palisades, CA 90272; (310) 454-0688; www.paulistproductions.org.

SIGNIS (World Catholic Association for Communication): A Vatican approved non-governmental organization that includes members from 140 countries and brings together radio, television, cinema, video, media education, Internet, and new technology professionals. SIGNIS was established in November 2001 from the merger between Unda (for radio and television) and OCIC (for cinema and audiovisual); both had been created in 1928. Its varied initiatives cover fields such as the promotion of films or television programs (including juries at festivals such as Cannes, Berlin, Monte Carlo, Venice, etc.), the creation of radio, video, and television studios, production and distribution of programs, training professionals in the field, and supplying specialized equipment. General Secretariat, 15, rue du Saphir, 1030 Brussels, Belgium; 00 32 (0)2 7349708; www.signis.net/.

Telecare: non-profit, state-of-the-art television and production facility of the Diocese of Rockville Centre. Broadcasts seven days a week to almost a million homes served by Cablevision, Telecare works through a partnership with WLNY/Channel 55. Programming includes the popular *God Squad* program that reaches 12 million viewers in New York, New Jersey and Connecticut every weekday. Msgr. Thomas Hartman, Director. 1200 Glen Curtiss Blvd., Uniondale, 11553; (516) 538-4108; www.telecaretv.org.

Theater
Catholic Actors' Guild of America, Inc.: Established in 1914 to provide material and spiritual assistance to people in the theater. Has more than 500 members; publishes *The Call Board*. 1501 Broadway, Suite 510, New York, NY 10036; (212) 398-1868 (fax).

FILM

Best Films of 2012
Catholic film critic Steven Greydanus released his 2012 Best Films List in January 2013 that was published in the National Catholic Register.

The Kid With a Bike; Barbara; Argo; The Avengers; The Secret World of Arrietty; Lincoln; Damsels in Distress; Planet of Snail; I Wish; Anna Karenina;

Runners-Up (in alphabetical order): Beasts of the Southern Wild; Brave; The Dark Knight Rises; Elena; Jiro Dreams of Sushi; Les Misérables; Moonrise Kingdom; The Queen of Versailles; Skyfall; Zero Dark Thirty.

Honorable Mentions (in alphabetical order): Arbitrage; A Cat in Paris; First Position; For Greater Glory; Frankenweenie; The Impossible; Monsieur Lazhar; The Pirates! Band of Misfits; Ruby Sparks; The Turin Horse.

Vatican List of the Greatest Films of the 20th Century
On the occasion of the 100th anniversary of cinema in 1995, the Vatican compiled this list of "great films." The 45 movies are divided into three categories: "Religion," "Values," and "Art."

Religion
"Andrei Rublev" (1969); "Babette's Feast" (1988); "Ben-Hur" (1959); "The Flowers of St. Francis" (1950); "Francesco" (1989); "The Gospel According to St. Matthew" (1966); "La Passion de Notre Seigneur Jesus-Christ" (1905); "A Man for All Seasons" (1966); "The Mission" (1986); "Monsieur Vincent" (1947); "Nazarin" (1958); "Ordet" (1954); "The Passion of Joan of Arc" (1928); "The Sacrifice" (1986); "Thérèse" (1986).

Values
"Au Revoir les Enfants" (1988); "The Bicycle Thief" (1949); "The Burmese Harp" (1956); "Chariots of Fire" (1981); "Decalogue" (1988); "Dersu Uzala" (1978); "Gandhi" (1982); "Intolerance" (1916); "It's a Wonderful Life" (1946); "On the Waterfront" (1954); "Open City" (1945); "Schindler's List" (1993); "The Seventh Seal" (1956); "The Tree of Wooden Clogs" (1978); "Wild Strawberries" (1958).

Art
"Citizen Kane" (1941); "8-1/2" (1963); "Fantasia" (1940); "Grand Illusion" (1937); "La Strada" (1956); "The Lavender Hill Mob" (1951); "The Leopard" (1963); "Little Women" (1933); "Metropolis" (1926); "Modern Times" (1936); "Napoleon" (1927); "Nosferatu" (1922); "Stagecoach" (1939); "2001: A Space Odyssey" (1968); "The Wizard of Oz" (1939).

CATHOLIC INTERNET SITES

Website addresses change periodically. Find this list online at www.CatholicAlmanac.com. Visit Our Sunday Visitor's web site at www.osv.com.

Holy See Sites
Vatican News Portal: www.news.va
Vatican: www.vatican.va
L'Osservatore Romano: www.vatican.va/news_services/or/or_eng/index.html
Vatican Radio: www.vatican.va/news_services/radio

Catholic Megasites, Directories and Links
Catholic Almanac: www.CatholicAlmanac.com
Catholic Canada: www.catholicanada.com
Catholic Community Forum: www.catholic-forum.com
Catholic Goldmine!: www.catholicgoldmine.com
Catholic Hotlinks: www.cathinsight.com
Catholic Information Center on the Internet: www.catholic.net
Catholic Information Network: www.cin.org
Catholic Internet Directory: www.catholic-church.org
Catholic Internet Yellow Pages: www.monksofadoration.org/directory.html
Catholic Kiosk: www.aquinas-multimedia.com/arch
Catholic.Net Periodicals: www.catholic.net/RCC/Periodicals
Catholic Pages: www.catholic-pages.com
Catholic Press Association: www.catholicpress.org
Catholicity Internet Directory: www.catholicity.com
Catholic Exchange: www.catholicexchange.com
Ecclesia Web Service for Catholics: www.catholic-church.org
El Directorio Catolico en Internet: www.iglesia.org
New Advent: www.newadvent.org
Our Sunday Visitor: www.OSV.com
PetersNet: www.catholicculture.org
RCNet: www.rc.net
St. Jane's: www.stjane.org
The Internet Padre: www.internetpadre.com
Theology Library Search Engines: www.shc.edu/theolibrary/engines.htm

Catholic Internet Service Providers
Catholic Families Network: www.catholicfamilies.net
Catholic Online: www.catholiconline.com

FamiLink (ISP for the family): www.familink.com

Catholic Movements and Organizations
Adoremus: www.adoremus.org
Catholic Charismatic Center: www.garg.com/ccc
Catholic Doctrinal Concordance: www.infpage.com/concordance
Catholic Family and Human Rights Institute: www.c-fam.org
Catholic Health Association USA: www.chausa.org
Catholic League: www.catholicleague.org
Focolare Movement: www.rc.net/focolare
Madonna House: www.madonnahouse.org
Nat'l Bioethics Center: www.ncbcenter.org
Opus Dei: www.opusdei.org
Pax Christi International: www.paxchristi.net
Pax Christi USA: www.paxchristiusa.org
Saints Alive: www.ichrusa.com/saintsalive
Schoenstatt (information): www.catholiclinks.org/schoenstattunitedstates.htm
Seton Home Study School: www.setonhome.org

Catholic Newspapers and Magazines
Catholic Digest: www.catholicdigest.org
Catholic New York Online: www.cny.org
Catholic Worker: www.catholicworker.org
First Things: www.firstthings.com
Houston Catholic Worker: www.cjd.org
Our Sunday Visitor: www.osv.com
The Tablet, U.K.: www.thetablet.co.uk
The Universe, U.K.: www.totalcatholic.com
The Wanderer: www.thewandererpress.com

Religious Orders and Apostolates
Apostolates/Orders: www.catholic-forum.com/links/pages/Religious_Orders
EWTN: www.ewtn.com
RCNet-Apostolates: www.rc.net/org

Colleges and Universities (Links To)
Colleges: www.shc.edu/theolibrary/edu.htm
Assocation of Catholic Colleges and Universities: www.accunet.org

Useful and Informative Sites
Mass Times: www.masstimes.org
Mass in Transit: www.massintransit.com
Christworld: www.christworld.com
Catholic-Pages: www.catholic-pages.com
PetersVoice: www.petersvoice.com
Rosary Center: www.rosary-center.org
Daily E-pistle (e-newsletter) Signup Page: www.catholic-forum.com/e-pistle.html
Grace In Action Stewardship: www.GraceInAction.org

For Kids and Families
Catholic Kids Net: www.catholickidsnet.org
Global Schoolhouse: www.gsn.org
My Friend: www.myfriendmagazine.com
Teaching Catholic Kids: www.TeachingCatholicKids.com
Apostolate for Family Consecration: www.familyland.org
Catholic Family and Human Rights Institute: www.c-fam.org
Catholic Fathers: www.dads.org
Catholic Parent Magazine: www.CatholicParent.com
Natural Family Planning: www.ccli.org
Domestic Church: www.domestic-church.com

DEVELOPMENTS IN COMMUNICATIONS 2012-13

The following are significant developments or documents in the field of Catholic communications in 2012-13.

Message of His Holiness Pope Benedict XVI for the 47th World Communications Day,
issued on Jan. 24, 2013, Feast of Saint Francis de Sales:

"Social Networks: portals of truth and faith; new spaces for evangelization."

Dear Brothers and Sisters,

As the 2013 World Communications Day draws near, I would like to offer you some reflections on an increasingly important reality regarding the way in which people today communicate among themselves. I wish to consider the development of digital social networks which are helping to create a new "agora," an open public square in which people share ideas, information and opinions, and in which new relationships and forms of community can come into being.

These spaces, when engaged in a wise and balanced way, help to foster forms of dialogue and debate which, if conducted respectfully and with concern for privacy, responsibility and truthfulness, can reinforce the bonds of unity between individuals and effectively promote the harmony of the human family. The exchange of information can become true communication, links ripen into friendships, and connections facilitate communion. If the networks are called to realize this great potential, the people involved in them must make an effort to be authentic since, in these spaces, it is not only ideas and information that are shared, but ultimately our very selves.

The development of social networks calls for commitment: people are engaged in building relationships and making friends, in looking for answers to their questions and being entertained, but also in finding intellectual stimulation and sharing knowledge and know-how. The networks are increasingly becoming part of the very fabric of society, inasmuch as they bring people together on the basis of these fundamental needs. Social networks are thus nourished by aspirations rooted in the human heart.

The culture of social networks and the changes in the means and styles of communication pose demanding challenges to those who want to speak about truth and values. Often, as is also the case with other means of social communication, the significance and effectiveness of the various forms of expression appear to be determined more by their popularity than by their intrinsic importance and value. Popularity, for its part, is often linked to celebrity or to strategies of persuasion rather than to the logic of argumentation. At times the gentle voice of reason can be overwhelmed by the din of excessive information and it fails to attract attention which is given instead to those who express themselves in a more persuasive manner. The social media thus need the commitment of all who are conscious of the value of dialogue, reasoned debate and logical argumentation; of people who strive to cultivate forms of discourse and expression which appeal to the noblest aspirations of those engaged in the communication process. Dialogue and debate can also flourish and grow when we converse with and take seriously people whose ideas are different from our own. "Given the reality of cultural diversity, people need not only to accept the existence of the culture of others, but also to aspire to be enriched by it and to offer to it whatever they possess that is good, true and beautiful" (Address at the meeting with the World of Culture, Bélem, Lisbon, May 12, 2010).

The challenge facing social networks is how to be truly inclusive: thus they will benefit from the full participation of believers who desire to share the message of Jesus and the values of human dignity which his teaching promotes. Believers are increasingly aware that, unless the Good News is made known also in the digital world, it may be absent in the experience of many people for whom this existential space is important. The digital environment is not a parallel or purely virtual world, but is part of the daily experience of many people, especially the young. Social networks are the result of human interaction, but for their part they also reshape the dynamics of communication which builds relationships: a considered understanding of this environment is therefore the prerequisite for a significant presence there.

The ability to employ the new languages is required, not just to keep up with the times, but precisely in order to enable the infinite richness of the Gospel to find forms of expression capable of reaching the minds and hearts of all. In the digital environment the written word is often accompanied by images and sounds. Effective communication, as in the parables of Jesus, must involve the imagination and the affectivity of those we wish to invite to an encounter with the mystery of God's love. Besides, we know that Christian tradition has always been rich in signs and symbols: I think for example of the Cross, icons, images of the Virgin Mary, Christmas cribs, stained-glass windows and pictures in our churches. A significant part of mankind's artistic heritage has been created by artists and musicians who sought to express the truths of the faith.

In social networks, believers show their authenticity by sharing the profound source of their hope and joy: faith in the merciful and loving God revealed in Christ Jesus. This sharing consists not only in the explicit expression of their faith, but also in their witness, in the way in which they communicate "choices, preferences and judgements that are fully consistent with the Gospel, even when it is not spoken of specifically" (Message for the 2011 World Communications Day). A particularly significant way of offering such witness will be through a willingness to give oneself to others by patiently and respectfully engaging their questions and their doubts as they advance in their search for the truth and the meaning of human existence. The growing dialogue in social networks about faith and belief confirms the importance and relevance of religion in public debate and in the life of society.

For those who have accepted the gift of faith with an open heart, the most radical response to mankind's questions about love, life and the meaning of life – questions certainly not absent from social networks – are found in the person of Jesus Christ. It is natural for those who have faith to desire to share it, respectfully and tactfully, with those they meet in the digital forum. Ultimately, however, if our efforts to share the Gospel bring forth good fruit, it is always because of the power of the word of God itself to touch hearts, prior to any of our own efforts. Trust in the power of God's work must always be greater than any confidence we place in human means. In the digital environment, too, where it is easy for heated and divisive voices to be raised and where sensationalism can at times prevail, we are called to attentive discernment. Let us recall in this regard that Elijah recognized the voice of God not in the great and strong wind, not in the earthquake or the fire, but in "a still, small voice" (1 Kg 19:11-12). We need to trust in the fact that the basic human desire to love and to be loved, and to find meaning and truth – a desire which God himself has placed in the heart of every man and woman – keeps our contemporaries ever open to what Blessed Cardinal Newman called the "kindly light" of faith.

Social networks, as well as being a means of evangelization, can also be a factor in human development. As an example, in some geographical and cultural contexts where Christians feel isolated, social networks can reinforce their sense of real unity with the worldwide community of believers. The networks facilitate the sharing of spiritual and liturgical resources, helping people to pray with a greater sense of closeness to those who share the same faith. An authentic and interactive engagement with the questions and the doubts of those who are distant from the faith should make us feel the need to nourish, by prayer and reflection, our faith in the presence of God as well as our practical charity: "If I speak in the tongues of men and of angels, but have not love, I am a noisy gong or a clanging cymbal" (1 Cor 13:1).

In the digital world there are social networks which offer our contemporaries opportunities for prayer, meditation and sharing the word of God. But these networks can also open the door to other dimensions of faith. Many people are actually discovering, precisely thanks to a contact initially made online, the importance of direct encounters, experiences of community and even pilgrimage, elements which are always important in the journey of faith. In our effort to make the Gospel present in the digital world, we can invite people to come together for prayer or liturgical celebrations in specific places such as churches and chapels. There should be no lack of coherence or unity in the expression of our faith and witness to the Gospel in whatever reality we are called to live, whether physical or digital. When we are present to others, in any way at all, we are called to make known the love of God to the furthest ends of the earth.

I pray that God's Spirit will accompany you and enlighten you always, and I cordially impart my blessing to all of you, that you may be true heralds and witnesses of the Gospel. "Go into all the world and preach the Gospel to the whole creation" (Mk 16:15).

— From the Vatican, Jan. 24, 2013, Feast of St. Francis de Sales.

PONTIFICAL HONORS AND AWARDS

Pontifical Orders

The Pontifical Orders of Knighthood are secular orders of merit whose membership depends directly on the pope.

Supreme Order of Christ (Militia of Our Lord Jesus Christ): The highest of the five pontifical orders of knighthood, the Supreme Order of Christ was approved Mar. 14, 1319, by John XXII as a continuation in Portugal of the suppressed Order of Templars. Members were religious with vows and a rule of life until the order lost its religious character toward the end of the 15th century. Since that time it has existed as an order of merit. Paul VI, in 1966, restricted awards of the order to Christian heads of state.

Order of the Golden Spur (Golden Militia): Although the original founder is not certainly known, this order is one of the oldest knighthoods. Indiscriminate bestowal and inheritance diminished its prestige, however, and in 1841 Gregory XVI replaced it with the Order of St. Sylvester and gave it the title of Golden Militia. In 1905 St. Pius X restored the Order of the Golden Spur in its own right, separating it from the Order of St. Sylvester. Paul VI, in 1966, restricted awards of the order to Christian heads of state.

Order of Pius IX: Founded by Pius IX June 17, 1847, the order is awarded for outstanding services for the Church and society, and may be given to non-Catholics as well as Catholics. The title to nobility formerly attached to membership was abolished by Pius XII in 1939. In 1957 Pius XII instituted the Class of the Grand Collar as the highest category of the order; in 1966, Paul VI restricted this award to heads of state "in solemn circumstances." The other three classes are of Knights of the Grand Cross, Knight Commanders with and without emblem, and Knights. The new class was created to avoid difficulties in presenting papal honors to Christian or non Christian leaders of high merit.

Order of St. Gregory the Great: First established by Gregory XVI in 1831 to honor citizens of the Papal States, the order is conferred on persons who are distinguished for personal character and reputation, and for notable accomplishment. The order has civil and military divisions, and three classes of knights.

Order of St. Sylvester: Instituted Oct. 31, 1841, by Gregory XVI to absorb the Order of the Golden Spur, this order was divided into two by St. Pius X in 1905, one retaining the name of St. Sylvester and the other assuming the title of Golden Militia. Membership consists of three degrees: Knights of the Grand Cross, Knight Commanders with and without emblem, and Knights.

Papal Medals

Pro Ecclesia et Pontifice: This decoration ("For the Church and the Pontiff") had its origin in 1888 as a token of the golden sacerdotal jubilee of Leo XIII; he bestowed it on those who had assisted in the observance of his jubilee and on persons responsible for the success of the Vatican Exposition. The medal, cruciform in shape, bears the likenesses of Sts. Peter and Paul, the tiara and the papal keys, the words Pro Ecclesia et Pontifice, and the name of the present pontiff, all on the same side; it is attached to a ribbon of yellow and white, the papal colors. Originally, the medal was issued in gold, silver or bronze. It is awarded in recognition of service to the Church and the papacy.

Benemerenti: Several medals ("To a well-deserving person") have been conferred by popes for exceptional accomplishment and service. The medals, which are made of gold, silver or bronze, bear the likeness and name of the reigning pope on one side; on the other, a laurel crown and the letter "B." These two medals may be given by the pope to both men and women. Their bestowal does not convey any title or honor of knighthood.

ECCLESIASTICAL ORDERS

Equestrian Order of the Holy Sepulchre of Jerusalem

The order traces its origin to Godfrey de Bouillon who instituted it in 1099. It took its name from the Basilica of the Holy Sepulchre where its members were knighted. After the fall of the Latin Kingdom of Jerusalem and the consequent departure of the knights from the Holy Land,

national divisions were established in various countries.

The order was re-organized by Pius IX in 1847 when he reestablished the Latin Patriarchate of Jerusalem and placed the order under the jurisdiction of its patriarch. In 1888, Leo XIII confirmed permission to admit women — Ladies of the Holy Sepulchre — to all degrees of rank. Pius X reserved the office of grand master to himself in 1907; Pius XII gave the order a cardinal patron in 1940 and, in 1949, transferred the office of grand master from the pope to the cardinal patron. Pope John XXIII approved updated constitutions in 1962; the latest statutes were approved by Paul VI in 1977.

The purposes of the order are strictly religious and charitable. Members are committed to sustain and aid the charitable, cultural and social works of the Catholic Church in the Holy Land, particularly in the Latin Patriarchate of Jerusalem. The order is composed of knights and ladies grouped in three classes: class of Knights of the Collar and Ladies of the Collar; Class of Knights (in four grades); Class of Ladies (in four grades). Members are appointed by the cardinal grand master according to procedures outlined in the constitution.

Under the present constitution the order is divided into national lieutenancies, largely autonomous, with international headquarters in Rome. Then Abp. Edwin O'Brien, abp. of Baltimore since 2007, was appointed Pro-Grand Master on Aug. 29, 2011. He succeeded Card. John P. Foley, who had served as Grand Master since 2007. O'Brien was named to the College of Cardinals on Feb. 18, 2012, and became Grand Master on Mar. 12, 2012. The address of the headquarters is: Grand Magisterium of the Equestrian Order of the Holy Sepulchre of Jerusalem, Borgo Spirito Santo, 73, 00193 Roma, Italia; Tel. 39066828121; www.vatican.va/roman_curia/institutions_connected/oessh/index.htm.

As of the end of 2008 (the latest available figures), the Order had a total of 25,835 Members (14,432 were Knights of all grades, 8,159 were Ladies, and 3,244 were religious. Geographical distribution: approximayely 12,500 (almost 48%) are resident in the United States; the largest Lieutenancy is that of Central Italy and Sardinia, with a total of 2,590 Members; this was followed by two US Lieutenancies: USASouthwestern with 2,540 and USA-Eastern with 2,306 Knights, Ladies and religious. The USA is the only area where the Order has more Ladies than Knights. (Source: Newsletter, *Ordo Sequestris Sancti Sepulcri Hierosolymitani*, XVII, Dec. 2009).

There are nine lieutenancies of the order in the United States and one in Puerto Rico. The U.S. lieutenancies are: USA Eastern, 1011 First Ave. - 7th Floor, New York, NY 10022; USA Middle Atlantic, P.O. Box 29260, Washington, DC, 20017-0260; USA North Central, 939 Londmeadow Ct., Lake Barrington, IL 60010; USA North Eastern, 340 Main St., Suite 906, Worcester, MA 01608; USA North Western, 8 Lenox Way, San Francisco, CA 94127; USA Northern, 848 Drakes Dream Dr., Gravois Mills, MO 65037; USA South Eastern, 2955 Ridgelake Dr., Suite 205, Metaire, LA 70002; USA South Western, 2001 Kirby Dr., Suite 902, Houston, TX 77019; USA Western, 8141 East Kaiser Bld., Suite 300, Anaheim Hills, CA 92808.

Order of Malta

The Sovereign Military Hospitaller Order of St. John of Jerusalem of Rhodes and of Malta traces its origin to a group of men who maintained a Christian hospital in the Holy Land in the 11th century. The group was approved as a religious order – the Hospitallers of St. John – by Paschal

II in 1113.

The order, while continuing its service to the poor, principally in hospital work, assumed military duties in the 12th century and included knights, chaplains and sergeants-at-arms among its members. All the knights were professed monks with the vows of poverty, chastity and obedience. Headquarters were located in the Holy Land until the last decade of the 13th century and on Rhodes after 1308 (whence the title, Knights of Rhodes).

After establishing itself on Rhodes, the order became a sovereign power like the sea republics of Italy and the Hanseatic cities of Germany, flying its own flag, coining its own money, floating its own navy, and maintaining diplomatic relations with many nations.

The order was forced to abandon Rhodes in 1522 after the third siege of the island by the Turks under Sultan Suleyman I. Eight years later, the Knights were given the island of Malta, where they remained as a bastion of Christianity until near the end of the 18th century. Headquarters have been located in Rome since 1834.

The title of Grand Master of the Order, in abeyance for some time, was restored by Leo XIII in 1879. A more precise definition of both the religious and the sovereign status of the order was embodied in a new constitution of 1961 and a code issued in 1966.

The four main classifications of members are: Knights of Justice, who are religious with the vows of poverty, chastity and obedience; Knights of Obedience, who make a solemn promise to strive for Christian perfection; Knights of Honor and Devotion and of Grace and Devotion, all of noble lineage; and Knights of Magistral Grace. There are also chaplains, Dames and Donats of the order.

The order, with six grand priories, three sub-priories and 40 national associations, is devoted to hospital and charitable works of all kinds in some 100 countries.

Under the provisions of international law, the order maintains full diplomatic relations with the Holy See – on which, in its double nature, it depends as a religious Order, but of which, as a sovereign Order of Knighthood, it is independent – and 68 countries throughout the world.

The Grand Master, who is the head of the order, has the title of Most Eminent Highness with the rank of Cardinal. He must be of noble lineage and under solemn vows for a minimum period of 10 years, if under 50 and holds the position for life.

The present and 79th Grand Master is Fra' Matthew Festing, an Englishman. He was the Grand Prior of England since the Priory's re-establishment in 1993 after a period of 450 years. In 1977 Fra' Matthew became a member of the Order of Malta, taking solemn religious vows in 1991.

Fra' Andrew Willoughby Ninian Bertie, member of the British aristocracy who elected for life as Grand Master on Apr. 8, 1988 by the Council of State, died on Feb. 7, 2008.

The patron of the Knights is Cardinal Paolo Sardi, a long-time Vatican diplomat.

The headquarters of the order is at Via Condotti, 68, Palazzo Malta, 00187 Rome, Italy; (011) 39.06.67581.1; www.orderofmalta.org. U.S. addresses: American Association, 1011 First Ave., New York, NY 10022; (212) 371.1522, www.maltausa.org; Western Association of U.S.A., 465 California St., Suite 818, San Francisco, CA 94104, (415) 788-4550, www.orderofmaltausawestern. org; Federal Association of U.S.A., 1730 M St. N.W., Suite 403, Washington, D.C. 20036; (202) 331-2494, www. orderofmalta-federal.org.

Order of St. George

The Sacred Military Constantinian Order of St. George was established by Pope Clement XI in 1718. The purposes of the order are to work for the preaching and defense of the Catholic faith and to promote the spiritual and physical welfare of sick, disabled, homeless and other unfortunate persons. The principal officer is Prince Carlo of Bourbon-Two Sicilies, duke of Calabria. Addresses: Via Sistina 121, 00187 Rome, Italy; Via Duomo 149, 80138 Naples, Italy; American Delegation, 302 Gessner Rd., Houston, TX 77024; (713) 888-0242.

2013 CATHOLIC PRESS ASSOCIATION AWARDS

The winners of the 2013 Catholic Press Awards were announced on Friday, June 21, 2013, at the Catholic Media Convention in Denver, Colorado.

Newspapers — General Excellence

National First Place: *The Catholic Register*, Toronto, ON; Second Place: *National Catholic Reporter*, Kansas City, MO; Third Place: *Our Sunday Visitor*, Huntington, IN; Honorable Mention: *Catholic Health World*, St. Louis, MO. **40-000+ Diocesan paper** First Place: *Catholic New York*, New York, NY; Second Place: *The Catholic Review*, Baltimore, MD; Third Place: *Catholic News Herald*, Charlotte, NC; Honorable Mention: *Catholic Transcript*, Bloomfield, CT; *FaithLife*, Erie, PA. **17,001-40,000 Diocesan paper** First Place: Tennessee Register, Nashville, TN; Second Place: *The Catholic Spirit*, Metuchen, NJ; Third Place: *Catholic Herald*, Diocese of Madison, Madison, WI; Honorable Mention: *The Valley Catholic*, San Juan, TX; *The Compass*, Green Bay, WI. **1-17,000 Diocesan paper** First Place: *The Catholic Northwest Progress*, Seattle, WA; Second Place: *Catholic Anchor*, Anchorage, AK; Third Place: *The Florida Catholic*, Orlando, FL; Honorable Mention: *Idaho Catholic Register*, Boise, ID; *The Message*, Evansville, IN.

Newsletters

General interest newsletters First Place: *Catholic Update*, Cincinnati, OH; Second Place: *I Believe*, Cincinnati, OH; **Special interest newsletters** First Place: *At Home with Our Faith*, Chicago, IL; Second Place: *Nuestra Parroquia*, Chicago, IL; Third Place: *Dimensions*, Hempstead, NY.

Magazines

General interest First Place: *St. Anthony Messenger*, Cincinnati, OH; Second Place: *Columbia Magazine*, New Haven, CT; Third Place: *U.S. Catholic*, Chicago, IL; Honorable Mention: *Liguorian Magazine*, Ligouri, MO. Diocesan magazines First Place: *Bayou Catholic*, Schriever, LA; Second Place: *Vermont Catholic*, South Burlington, VT; Third Place: *North Texas Catholic*, Fort Worth, TX. **Mission magazines (overseas and home)** First Place: *One Magazine*, New York, NY; Second Place: *Maryknoll*, Maryknoll, NY; Third Place: *Glenmary Challenge*, Cincinnati, OH; Honorable Mention: *Catholic Missions In Canada*, Toronto, Ontario, ON. **Religious order magazines** First Place: *The Augustinian*, Villanova, PA; Second Place: *Congregation of Holy Cross*, United States Province, Notre Dame, IN; Third Place: *Marian Helper*, Stockbridge, MA; Honorable Mention:

Plentiful Redemption, Annapolis, MD. **Professional & special-interest magazines including clergy & religious** First Place: *Catholic Health World*, St. Louis, MO; Second Place: *Ecumenical Trends - Graymoor*, Garrison, NY; Third Place: *Catholic Library World*, Chicago, IL; Honorable Mention: *Today's Catholic Teacher*, Dayton, OH.

Scholarly magazines First Place: *American Catholic Studies*, Villanova, PA; Second Place: *Horizons*, Villanova, PA; Third Place: *Catholic Southwest: Journal*, Baton Rouge, LA. **Prayer & spirituality magazines** First Place: *Spiritual Life*, Washington, DC; Second Place: *Magnificat*, Yonkers, NY; Third Place: *Soul - World Apostolate of Fatima*, Washington, NJ.

Books

Popular Presentation of the Catholic Faith First Place: *Saved by Beauty*, by Brother Michael O'Neill McGrath, OSFS; Second Place: *Journey to the Heart*, by Kim Nataraja, Orbis Books, Maryknoll, NY; Third Place: *The Chapels of Notre Dame*, by Lawrence Cunningham, University of Notre Dame Press, Notre Dame, IN.

Spirituality – softcover First Place: *Eternal Consciousness*, by John S. Dunne, University of Notre Dame Press, Notre Dame, IN; Second Place: *Genius Born of Anguish: The Life and Legacy of Henri Nouwen*, by Michael W. Higgins & Kevin Burns , Paulist Press, Mahwah, NJ; Third Place: *Saints As They Really Are: Voices of Holiness in Our Time*, by Michael Plekon, University of Notre Dame Press, Notre Dame, IN.

Spirituality – hardcover First Place: *Messages of Glory: The Narrative Art of Roman Catholicism*, by Robert A. Flischel, Joe Simon, Jay Yocis, Anne Husted Burleigh, Rev. Christopher Armstrong, Msgr. William Cleves and Margo Warminski, David-Flischel Enterprises, Cincinnati, OH; Second Place: *A World of Prayer*, by Rosalind Bradley, Orbis Books, Maryknoll, NY; Third Place: *A Rhythm of Life: The Monastic Way*, by Brother Victor-Antoine D'Avila-Latourrette, Liguori Publications, Liguori, MO.

Theology First Place: *If These Walls Could Talk*, by Maureen H. O'Connell, Liturgical Press, Collegeville, MN; Second Place: *Balthasar: A (Very) Critical Introduction*, by Karen Kilby, William B. Eerdmans Publishing Company, Grand Rapids, MI; Third Place: *Dust Bound for Heaven: Explorations in the Theology of Thomas Aquinas*, by Reinhard Hutter, William B. Eerdmans Publishing Company, Grand Rapids, MI.

Scripture First Place: *First Corinthians*, by Pheme Perkins, Baker Academic, Ada, MI; Second Place: *God's Saving Grace: A Pauline Theology*, by Frank J. Matera, William B. Eerdmans Publishing Company, Grand Rapids, MI; Third Place: *Jesus of Nazareth: What He Wanted, Who He Was*, by Gerhard Lohfink, Liturgical Press, Collegeville, MN.

Liturgy First Place: *Liturgy: The Illustrated History*, by Keith F. Pecklers, Paulist Press, Mahwah, NJ; Second Place: *Baptismal Imagery in Early Christianity: Ritual, Visual, and Theological Dimensions*, by Robin M. Jensen, Baker Academic, Ada, MI; Third Place: *Hunger and You Fed Me, Homilies and Reflections for Cycle C*, by Deacon Jim Knipper, Editor featuring James Martin, S.J. and Richard Rohr, OFM, Clear Vision Publishing, Manalpan, NJ.

Pastoral Ministry First Place: *Embracing the End of*

Life: Help for Those Who Accompany the Dying, by Michelle O'Rourke and Eugene Dufour, Novalis, Toronto, ON; Second Place: *Nourishing the Spirit*, by James D. Whitehead, Evelyn Eaton Whitehead, Orbis Books, Maryknoll, NY; Third Place: *My Neighbor's Faith*, by Jennifer How Peace, Or N. Rose, Gregory Mobley, Orbis Books, Maryknoll, NY.

Professional First Place: *God's Mission and PostModern Culture*, by John C. Sivalon, MM, Orbis Books, Maryknoll, NY; Second Place: *The Inner Life of Priests*, by Gerard J. McGlone, SJ and Len Sperry, Liturgical Press, Collegeville, MN; Third Place: *Same Call, Different Men*, by Mary L. Gautier, Paul M. Peri, Rev. Stephen J. Fichter, Liturgical Press, Collegeville, MN.

Design and Production First Place: *Notre Dame's Happy Returns*, by Brian O'Conchubhair, Susan Mullen Guibert, Photography: Matt Cashore, University of Notre Dame Press, Notre Dame, IN; Second Place: *A Call to Vision: A Jesuits Perspective on the World*, by Don Doll, S.J., Magis Productions, Creighton University Press, Omaha, NE; Third Place: *Journey to the Heart*, by Kim Nataraja, Orbis Books, Maryknoll, NY.

Children's Books/Teens First Place: *Mary's Song*, by Lee Bennett Hopkins, author; Stephen Alcorn, illustrator, William B. Eerdmans Publishing Company, Grand Rapids, MI; Second Place: *I Wasn't Dead When I Wrote This*, by Lisa-Marie Calderone-Stewart, Loyola Press, Chicago, IL; Third Place: *Forever You – A Book About Your Soul and Body*, by Nicolle Lataiff; illustrated by Mary Rojas, Pauline Books & Media, Boston, MA.

First Time Author First Place: *The Infertility Companion for Catholics*, by Angelique Ruhi-Lopez and Carmen Santamaria, Ave Maria Press, Notre Dame, IN; Second Place: *Living Celibacy: Healthy Pathways for Priests*, by Gerdnio Sonny Manuel, SJ, Paulist Press, Mahwah, NJ; Third Place: *What's So Funny About Faith*, by Jake Martin, S.J., Loyola Press, Chicago, IL.

Family Life First Place: *Getting the Marriage Conversation Right*, by William B. May, Emmaus Road Publishing, Steubenville, OH; Second Place: *Catholic and Newly Married*, by Kathy and Steve Beirne, ACTA Publications, Chicago, IL; Third Place: *Build Your House Upon Rock: A Bible Study for Catholics Peparing for the Sacrament of Marriage*, by Nancy Humes, Emmaus Road Publishing, Steubenville, OH.

History First Place: *Latin Catholicism: Transformation in America's Largest Church*, by Timothy Matovina, Princeton University Press, Princeton, NJ; Second Place: *History of the World Christian Movement, Volume II Modern Christianity from 1545-1800*, by Dale T. Irvin, Scott W. Sundquist, Orbis Books, Maryknoll, NY; Third Place: *Were the Popes Against the Jews? Tracking the Myths, Confronting the Ideologies*, by Justus George Lawler, William B. Eerdmans Publishing Company, Grand Rapids, MI.

Biography First Place: *Redeeming the Past*, by Father Michael Lapsley with Stephen Karakashian, Orbis Books, Maryknoll, NY; Second Place: *Leonardo and The Last Supper*, by Ross King, Walker Books, New York, NY; Third Place: *The Pope and I*, by Jerzy Kluger, Orbis Books, Maryknoll, NY.

Gender Issues First Place: *She Who Imagines*, by Laurie Cassidy and Maureen H. O'Connell, Liturgical Press, Collegeville, MN; Second Place: *Woman-Killing in Juarez*, by Rafael Luevano, Orbis Books, Maryknoll, NY; Third Place: *The Catholic Girl's Survival Guide for* *the Single Years: The Nuts and Bolts of Staying Sane and Happy While Waiting for Mr. Right*, by Emily Stimpston, Emmaus Road Publishing, Steubenville, OH.

Diocesan Directory First Place: *Catholic Diocese of Rockford 2012-2013 Directory*, by Gwen LaShock, Catholic Diocese of Rockford, Rockford, IL; Second Place: *2012-2014 Official Directory of the Catholic Diocese of Beaumont*, by Staff, Catholic Diocese of Beaumont, Beaumont, TX; Third Place: *Catholic Directory, Diocese of Buffalo 2012*, by Gregg Prince, Kevin Keenan, Patrick J. Buechi, Kristina Connell, Diana Damstetter, Carolyn Luick, Kathy Luppi, Patrick McPartland, Sr. M. Loriette Tokasz, CSSF, Office of Communications, Diocese of Buffalo, Buffalo, NY.

Seasonal Catalog First Place: *Fall Catalog*, copy and layout by Gina Buckley; design by Chris Broquet, World Library Publications, Franklin Park, IL; Second Place: *Fall Catalog*, by Amanda Modelski – marketing, Patricia Lynch – designer, ACTA Publications, Chicago, IL; Third Place: *Summer Catalog*, by OCP Marketing Staff, Oregon Catholic Press, Portland, OR.

Best Book by Small Publisher First Place: *Eli's Reach: On the Value of Human Life and the Power of Prayer*, by Chad Judice, Acadian House Publishing, Lafayette, LA; Second Place: *Hunger, And You Fed Me: Homilies and Reflections for Cycle C*, by Deacon Jim Knipper, editor, featuring James Martin, S.J. and Richard Rohr, OFM, Clear Vision Publishing, Manalpan, NJ; Third Place: *Reading God's Handwriting: Poems*, by Philip C. Kolin, Kaufmann Publishing, St. Simons Island, GA.

Catholic Social Teaching First Place: *Option for the Poor and for the Earth*, by Donal Dorr, Orbis Books, Maryknoll, NY; *Gandhi and the Unspeakable*, by James W. Douglass, Orbis Books, Maryknoll, NY; Third Place: *Kinship Across Borders: A Christian Ethic of Immigration*, by Kristin E. Heyer, Georgetown University Press, Washington, DC.

Faith and Science First Place: *In the Beginning was the Spirit*, by Diarmuid O' Murchu, Orbis Books, Maryknoll, NY; Second Place: *Vast Universe*, by Thomas F. O'Mera, OP, Liturgical Press, Collegeville, MN; Third Place: *God and Evolution? Science Meets Faith*, by Dr. Gerard M. Verschuuren, Pauline Books and Media, Boston, MA.

50th Anniversary of Vatican II First Place: *My Journal of the Council*, by Yves Congar, OP, Liturgical Press, Collegeville, MN; Second Place: *Vatican II: 50 Personal Stories*, by William Madges & Michael J. Daley, Orbis Books, Maryknoll, NY; Third Place: *After Vatican II: Trajectories and Hermenutics*, by James L. Heft, William B. Eerdmans Publishing Company, Grand Rapids, MI.

The Year of Faith First Place: *Christian Spirituality*

for Seekers, by Roger Haight, Orbis Books, Maryknoll, NY; Second Place: *Friends in Christ*, by Brother John of Taize, Orbis Books, Maryknoll, NY; Third Place: *Along the Way Lessons for an Authentic Journey of Faith*, by Randy Hain, Liguori Publications, Liguori, MO.

Faithful Citizenship First Place: *Law's Virtues: Fostering Autonomy and Solidarity in American Society*, by Cathleen Kaveny, Georgetown University Press, Washington, DC; Second Place: *Seek First the Kingdom*, by Cardinal Donald Wuerl, Our Sunday Visitor, Huntington, IN; Third Place: *The Gospel of Rutba*, by Greg Barrett, Orbis Books, Maryknoll, NY.

Francis de Sales Award: Peter Finney, Jr.; **Bishop John England Award:** Bishop David Kagan.

2013 Christopher Awards

Christopher Awards recognize the creative writers, producers and directors who have achieved artistic excellence in films, books and television specials. The 2013 awards were presented May 23, 2013, in New York.

Books: *Carly's Voice* (Touchstone Books/Simon & Schuster); *Fearless* (Waterbrook Multnomah Publishing Group/Random House); *A Good Man* (Henry Holt and Company); *My Sisters the Saints* (Image Books/Random House); *Road to Valor* (Crown Publishing Group/Random House). Books for Young People: *Forever You: A Book About Your Soul and Body* (Pauline Books and Media); *The Fantastic Flying Books of Mr. Morris Lessmore* (Atheneum Books for Young Readers/Simon and Schuster); *The House on Dirty-Third Street* (Peachtree Publishers); *The One and Only Ivan* (Harper Collins Children's Books); *Wonder* (Alfred A. Knopf/Random House Children's Books); *Outcasts United* (Delacorte Press/Random House Children's Books).

Films: "Les Misérables" (Working Title Films/Universal Pictures); "Lincoln" (DreamWorks Studios/Touchstone Pictures); "Undefeated" (Spitfire Pictures/The Weinstein Company).

Television and Cable: "60 Minutes: Joy in the Congo" (CBS News); "The Call the Midwife Holiday Special" (Neal Street Production/BBC/PBS); "God Is the Bigger Elvis" (HBO Documentary Films); "NY Med: Season 1" (ABC News); "Under African Skies" (@radical.media/A&E Indie Films).

2013 Christopher Lifetime Achievement Award: Mother Dolores Hart.

Ecumenism and Interreligious Dialogue

ECUMENISM

Edited in consultation with the staff of the Secretariat for Ecumenical and Interreligious Affairs, USCCB.

The modern ecumenical movement, with roots in 19th-century scholars and individuals began its institutional life in 1910 among Protestants and Orthodox and led to formation of the World Council of Churches in 1948, developed outside the mainstream of Catholic interest until the 1950s. It has now become for Catholics as well one of the great religious facts of our time.

The *magna carta* of ecumenism for Catholics is a complex of several documents which include, in the first place, *Unitatis Redintegratio*, the "Decree on Ecumenism," promulgated by the Second Vatican Council Nov. 21, 1964. Other enactments underlying and expanding this decree are *Lumen Gentium* ("Dogmatic Constitution on the Church"), *Orientalium Ecclesiarum* ("Decree on Eastern Catholic Churches"), and *Gaudium et Spes* ("Pastoral Constitution on the Church in the Modern World").

The Holy See has more recently brought together Catholic ecumenical priorities in *Directory for the Application of Principles and Norms on Ecumenism* (1993) and *The Ecumenical Dimension in the Formation of Pastoral Workers* (1998). These, in addition to Pope John Paul II's encyclical letter, *Ut Unum Sint* (1995), provide a guide for Catholic ecumenical initiatives.

POPE FRANCIS (2013-)

On March 20, 2013, Pope Francis met with representatives of Christian churches, ecclesial communities and other world religions who had come to Rome for his inaugural Mass the previous day. He received them seated on an armchair at floor level, rather than on the customary raised throne.

After he was greeted by Ecumenical Patriarch Bartholomew of Constantinople, Pope Francis thanked him for his remarks, referring to him as "my brother Andrew." This was significant because Andrew is the patron saint of Constantinople and Peter is that of Rome; the two represent two ancient churches who are trying to retrieve the fraternal relationship that the two brother apostles had. This was most probably the first time ever that an ecumenical patriarch was present at the inaugural Mass of a pope.

Pope Francis recalled the significance of the Second Vatican Council for ecumenism, and quoted Pope John XXIII who said at the opening session of the council, "The Catholic Church considers it her duty to actively work so as to bring about the great mystery of that unity for which Jesus Christ prayed so ardently to His Father in heaven on the eve of his sacrifice." He went on to say that, "For my part, I wish to assure you, following in the path of my predecessors, of my firm will to continue on the path of ecumenical dialogue."

The new pope also reminded the representatives of the Jewish communities of "the very special spiritual bond" that links Jews and Christians. He quoted from Vatican II's Decree on Non-Christian Religions, which states: "The Church of Christ acknowledges that, according to God's saving design, the beginnings of her faith and her election are found already among the Patriarchs, Moses and the prophets." The pope said that he looked forward to the continuation of the fruitful dialogue that has accomplished so much in recent years.

The Holy Father then turned to the representatives of other world religions who were present, especially the Muslims who, again quoting the Council, "adore the one, living and merciful God and who call upon Him in prayer." He said that the Catholic Church is– and he repeated this twice for emphasis – "aware of the importance of the promotion of friendship and respect between men and women of different religious traditions." He went on to say that the Church "is also aware of the responsibility that we all bear to this our world, to all of creation, which we should love and protect. And we can do much for the good of the poorest, of the weak and suffering, to promote justice and reconciliation, to build peace. But, above all, we must keep alive the thirst for the Absolute in the world, not allowing a one-dimensional vision of the human person, in which humanity is reduced to that which it produces and consumes, to prevail. This is one of the most dangerous pitfalls of our times."

In this brief address, Pope Francis has made it clear that he intends to continue the path of dialogue that the Catholic Church has followed since the Second Vatican Council. (Courtesy, USCCB Blog entry by Fr. Ronald Roberson, CSP, March 20, 2013.)

POPE BENEDICT XVI (2005-2013)

Pope Benedict XVI reaffirmed the irreversible commitment of the Catholic Church to the ecumenical movement, and stated that ecumenism would be the "primary task" of his pontificate. This is an excerpt from his address to the Cardinals at the end of a Mass he celebrated with them the day after his election, on April 20, 2005:

"Nourished and sustained by the Eucharist, Catholics cannot but feel encouraged to strive for the full unity for which Christ expressed so ardent a hope in the Upper Room. The Successor of Peter knows that he must make himself especially responsible for his Divine Master's supreme aspiration. Indeed, he is entrusted with the task of strengthening his brethren (cf. Lk 22:32).

With full awareness, therefore, at the beginning of his

ministry in the Church of Rome which Peter bathed in his blood, Peter's current Successor takes on as his primary task the duty to work tirelessly to rebuild the full and visible unity of all Christ's followers. This is his ambition, his impelling duty. He is aware that good intentions do not suffice for this. Concrete gestures that enter hearts and stir consciences are essential, inspiring in everyone that inner conversion that is the prerequisite for all ecumenical progress.

Theological dialogue is necessary; the investigation of the historical reasons for the decisions made in the past is also indispensable. But what is most urgently needed is that 'purification of memory,' so often recalled by John Paul II, which alone can dispose souls to accept the full truth of Christ. Each one of us must come before him, the supreme Judge of every living person, and render an account to him of all we have done or have failed to do to further the great good of the full and visible unity of all his disciples. The current Successor of Peter is allowing himself to be called in the first person by this requirement and is prepared to do everything in his power to promote the fundamental cause of ecumenism. Following the example of his Predecessors, he is fully determined to encourage every initiative that seems appropriate for promoting contacts and understanding with the representatives of the different Churches and Ecclesial Communities. Indeed, on this occasion he sends them his most cordial greeting in Christ, the one Lord of us all."

VATICAN II DECREE

The following excerpts from Unitatis Redintegratio *cover the broad theological background and principles and indicate the thrust of the Church's commitment to ecumenism.*

Men who believe in Christ and have been properly baptized are brought into a certain, though imperfect, communion with the Catholic Church. Undoubtedly, the differences that exist in varying degrees between them and the Catholic Church — whether in doctrine and sometimes in discipline, or concerning the structure of the Church — do indeed create many and sometimes serious obstacles to full ecclesiastical communion. These the ecumenical movement is striving to overcome (No. 3).

Elements Common to Christians

Moreover some, even very many, of the most significant elements or endowments which together go to build up and give life to the Church herself can exist outside the visible boundaries of the Catholic Church: the written word of God; the life of grace; faith, hope, and charity, along with other interior gifts of the Holy Spirit and visible elements. All of these, which come from Christ and lead back to Him, belong by right to the one Church of Christ (No. 3).

[In a later passage, the decree singled out a number of elements which the Catholic Church and other churches have in common but not in complete agreement: confession of Christ as Lord and God and as mediator between God and man; belief in the Trinity; reverence for Scripture as the revealed word of God; baptism and the Lord's Supper; Christian life and worship; faith in action; concern with moral questions.]

The brethren divided from us also carry out many of the sacred actions of the Christian religion. Undoubtedly, in ways that vary according to the condition of each church or community, these actions can truly engender a life of grace, and can be rightly described as capable of providing access to the community of salvation.

It follows that these separated Churches and Communities, though we believe they suffer from defects already mentioned, have by no means been deprived of significance and importance in the mystery of salvation. For the Spirit of Christ has not refrained from using them as means of salvation which derive their efficacy from the very fullness of grace and truth entrusted to the Catholic Church (No. 3).

Unity Lacking

Nevertheless, our separated brethren, whether considered as individuals or as Communities and Churches, are not blessed with that unity which Jesus Christ wished to bestow on all those whom he has regenerated and vivified into one body and newness of life — that unity which the holy Scriptures and the revered tradition of the Church proclaim. For it is through Christ's Catholic Church alone, which is the all-embracing means of salvation, that the fullness of the means of salvation can be obtained. It was to the apostolic college alone, of which Peter is the head, that we believe our Lord entrusted all the blessings of the New Covenant, in order to establish on earth the one Body of Christ into which all those should be fully incorporated who already belong in any way to God's People (No. 3).

In the 1995 encyclical of Pope John Paul II, *Ut Unum Sint* the language of Separate Brethren has been put aside for the designation of "fellow Christian" to speak of Christians not in full communion with the Catholic Church.

What the Movement Involves

Today, in many parts of the world, under the inspiring grace of the Holy Spirit, multiple efforts are being expended through prayer, word, and action to attain that fullness of unity which Jesus Christ desires. This sacred Synod, therefore, exhorts all the Catholic faithful to recognize the signs of the times and to participate skillfully in the work of ecumenism.

The "ecumenical movement" means those activities and enterprises which, according to various needs of the Church and opportune occasions, are started and organized for the fostering of unity among Christians. These are:

• First, every effort to eliminate words, judgments, and actions which do not respond to the condition of separated brethren with truth and fairness and so make mutual relations between them more difficult.

• Then, "dialogue" between competent experts from different Churches and Communities [scholarly ecumenism].

• In addition, these Communions cooperate more closely in whatever projects a Christian conscience demands for the common good [social ecumenism].

• They also come together for common prayer, where this is permitted [spiritual ecumenism].

• Pope John Paul urged that the results of (now) 45 years of dialogue become a "common heritage," therefore all Catholic catechetical and ministry formation programs are to be informed by the progress of ecumenical relations.[ecumenical formation]

• Finally, all are led to examine their own faithfulness to Christ's will for the Church and, wherever necessary, undertake with vigor the task of renewal and reform.

It is evident that the work of preparing and reconciling those individuals who wish for full Catholic communion is of its nature distinct from ecumenical action. But there is no opposition between the two, since both proceed from the wondrous providence of God (No. 4).

Primary Duty of Catholics

In ecumenical work, Catholics must assuredly be concerned for their separated brethren, praying for them, keeping them informed about the Church, making the first approaches toward them. But their primary duty is to make an honest and careful appraisal of whatever needs to be renewed and achieved in the Catholic household itself, in order that its life may bear witness more loyally and luminously to the teachings and ordinances which have been handed down from Christ through the Apostles.

Every Catholic must aim at Christian perfection (cf. Jas 1:4; Rom 12:1-2) and, each according to his station, play his part so that the Church may daily be more purified and renewed, against the day when Christ will present her to himself in all her glory, without spot or wrinkle (cf. Eph 5:27).

Catholics must joyfully acknowledge and esteem the truly Christian endowments from our common heritage which are to be found among our separated brethren.

Nor should we forget that whatever is wrought by the grace of the Holy Spirit in the hearts of our separated brethren can contribute to our own edification. Whatever is truly Christian never conflicts with the genuine interests of the faith; indeed, it can always result in a more ample realization of the very mystery of Christ and the Church (No. 4).

Participation in Worship

Norms concerning participation by Catholics in the worship of other Christian Churches were sketched in this conciliar decree and elaborated in a number of other documents such as: the Decree on Eastern Catholic Churches, promulgated by the Second Vatican Council in 1964; Interim Guidelines for Prayer in Common, issued June 18, 1965, by the U.S. Bishops' Committee for Ecumenical and Interreligious Affairs; a Directory on Ecumenism and Guidelines on Ecumenical Formation published in 1967, 1970, 1993 and 1998 by the Pontifical Council for Promoting Christian Unity; additional communications from the U.S. Bishops' Committee, and numerous sets of guidelines issued locally by and for dioceses throughout the U.S.

The norms encourage common prayer services for Christian unity and other intentions. Beyond that, they draw a distinction between separated churches of the Reformation tradition and of the Anglican Communion, and separated Eastern churches, in view of doctrine and practice the Catholic Church has in common with the separated Eastern churches concerning the apostolic succession of bishops, holy orders, liturgy and other creedal matters.

Full participation by Catholics in official Protestant Eucharistic liturgies is prohibited, because it implies profession of the faith expressed in the liturgy. Reception of communion by Catholics at Protestant liturgies is prohibited. Under certain conditions, Protestants may be given Holy Communion in the Catholic Church. A Catholic may stand as a witness, but not as a sponsor, in baptism, and as a witness in the marriage of separated Christians. Similarly, a Protestant may stand as a witness, but not as a sponsor, in a Catholic baptism, and as a witness in the marriage of Catholics.

The principal norms regarding liturgical participations with separated Eastern Churches are included under Eastern Ecumenism.

DIRECTORY ON ECUMENISM

A Directory for the Application of the Principles and Norms of Ecumenism was approved by Pope John Paul II on Mar. 25, 1993, and published early in June. The Pontifical Council for Promoting Christian Unity said on release of the document that revision of Directories issued in 1967 and *1970 was necessary in view of subsequent developments. These included promulgation of the Code of Canon Law for the Latin Church in 1983 and of the Code of Canons of the Eastern Churches in 1990; publication of the Catechism of the Catholic Church in 1992; additional documents and the results of theological dialogues. In 1998, The Ecumenical Dimension in the Formation of Pastoral Workers was published by the Holy See to give practical and detailed guidance in the implementation of Chapter 3 of the Directory.*

The following excerpts are from the text published in the June 16, 1993, English edition of L'Osservatore Romano.

Address and Purpose

"The Directory is addressed to the pastors of the Catholic Church, but it also concerns all the faithful, who are called to pray and work for the unity of Christians, under the direction of their bishops."

"At the same time, it is hoped that the Directory will also be useful to members of churches and ecclesial communities that are not in full communion with the Catholic Church."

"The new edition of the Directory is meant to be an instrument at the service of the whole Church, and especially of those who are directly engaged in ecumenical activity in the Catholic Church. The Directory intends to motivate, enlighten and guide this activity, and in some particular cases also to give binding directives in accordance with the proper competence of the Pontifical Council for Promoting Christian Unity."

Outline

Principles and norms of the document are covered in five chapters.

"I. The Search for Christian Unity. The ecumenical commitment of the Catholic Church based on the doctrinal principles of the Second Vatican Council.

"II. Organization in the Catholic Church at the Service of Christian Unity. Persons and structures involved in promoting ecumenism at all levels, and the norms that direct their activity.

"III. Ecumenical Formation in the Catholic Church. Categories of people to be formed, those responsible for formation; the aims and methods of formation; its doctrinal and practical aspects.

"IV. Communion in Life and Spiritual Activity among the Baptized. The communion that exists with other Christians on the basis of the sacramental bond of baptism, and the norms for sharing in prayer and other spiritual activities, including, in particular cases, sacramental sharing.

"V. Ecumenical Cooperation, Dialogue and Common Witness. Principles, different forms and norms for cooperation between Christians with a view to dialogue and common witness in the world."

ECUMENICAL AGENCIES

Pontifical Council

The top-level agency for Catholic ecumenical efforts is the Pontifical Council for Promoting Christian Unity (formerly the Secretariat for Promoting Christian Unity), which originated in 1960 as a preparatory commission for the Second Vatican Council. Its purposes are to provide guidance and, where necessary, coordination for ecumenical endeavor by Catholics, and to establish and maintain relations with representatives of other Christian Churches for ecumenical dialogue and action.

The council, under the direction of Card. Kurt Koch (successor to Card. Walter Kasper, has established firm working relations with representative agencies of other churches, the Global Christian Forum and the World Council of Churches. It has joined in dialogue with the Eastern and Oriental Orthodox Churches, the Anglican Communion, the Lutheran World Federation, the World Alliance of Reformed Churches, the World Methodist Council, Baptist World Alliance, World Evangelical Alliance, the Pentecostals, Mennonites, Seventh-day Adventists and other religious bodies. In the past several years, staff members and representatives of the council have been involved in one way or another in nearly every significant ecumenical enterprise and meeting held throughout the world.

While the council and its counterparts in other churches have focused primary attention on common mission, theological and other related problems of Christian unity, they have begun, and in increasing measure, to emphasize the responsibilities of the churches for greater unity of effort in areas of humanitarian need. With the Congregation of the Doctrine of the Faith, the Council carries responsibility for official Catholic action on the results of the dialogue and shepherding the process of reception in the Catholic Church.

Bishops' Committee

The Committee for Ecumenical and Interreligious Affairs of the United States Conference of Catholic Bishops was established by the American hierarchy in 1964. Its purposes are to maintain relationships with other Christian churches and religious communities at the national level, to help other offices of the Conference do their work ecumenically, to advise and assist dioceses in developing and applying ecumenical policies, and to maintain liaison with corresponding Vatican offices – the Pontifical Councils for Christian Unity and for Interreligious Dialogue and other bishops conferences when needed.

This standing committee of the United States Conference of Catholic Bishops is chaired by Aux. Bp. Denis J. Madden of the Archdiocese of Baltimore. Operationally, the committee is assisted by a secretariat overseen by Executive Director is Fr. John Crossin, O.S.F.S., along with Associate Directors Fr. Ronald Roberson, C.S.P., and Dr. Anthony Cirelli. The committee co-sponsors several national consultations with other churches and ecclesial communities. These bring together Catholic representatives and counterparts from the Episcopal Church, the Evangelical Lutheran Church in America and Lutheran Church – Missouri Synod, the Polish National Catholic Church, the United Methodist Church, the Orthodox Churches, the Oriental Orthodox Churches, and the Reformed Churches (which include the United Church of Christ, the Presbyterian Church, the Christian Reformed Church, and the Reformed Church in America). There is also a history of engagement with the National Association of Evangelicals, the Pentecostal churches in the context of the Society for Pentecostal Studies, and – until 2001 – a 30 year conversation with the Southern Baptist Convention. (*See* **Ecumenical Dialogues.**)

The committee relates to the National Council of Churches of Christ through membership in the Faith and Order Commission and helping to produce materials for the annual Week of Prayer for Christian Unity. It also sponsored a joint study committee investigating the possibility of Roman Catholic membership in the NCCC in the 1970s. Collaboration in multiple areas of church life has proved to be more fruitful than membership given the disparity of numbers and diversity of program priorities of the Bishop's Conference and the Council.

The USCCB participates in a new ecumenical entity, Christian Churches Together in the USA. It includes representatives from the five major families of Christian churches in the United States which, in addition to the Catholic Church, include the historic Protestant, Orthodox, Evangelical/Pentecostal, and African American churches.

Advisory and other services are provided by the committee to ecumenical commissions and agencies in dioceses throughout the country.

Through its Section for Catholic-Jewish Relations, the committee is in contact with several national Jewish agencies and bodies. Issues of mutual interest and shared concern are reviewed for the purpose of furthering deeper understanding between the Catholic and Jewish communities.

The committee also co-sponsors interreligious activities and programs. By late 2009, there were three regional dialogues with Muslims and regular contacts with Buddhists, Hindus and Sikhs.

Offices of the committee are located at 3211 Fourth St. N.E., Washington, DC 20017; www.usccb.org/seia.

World Council of Churches

The World Council of Churches is a fellowship of churches which acknowledge "Jesus Christ as Lord and Savior." It is a permanent organization providing constituent members — 330 churches with some 450 million communicants in 100 countries — with opportunities for meeting, consultation and cooperative action with respect to doctrine, worship, practice, social mission, evangelism and missionary work, and other matters of mutual concern.

The WCC was formally established Aug. 23, 1948, in Amsterdam with ratification of a constitution by 147 communions. This action merged two previously existing movements — Life and Work (social mission), Faith and Order (doctrine) — which had initiated practical steps toward founding a fellowship of Christian churches at meetings held in Oxford, Edinburgh and Utrecht in 1937 and 1938. A third movement for cooperative missionary work, which originated about 1910 and, remotely, led to formation of the WCC, was incorporated into the council in 1961 under the title of the International Missionary Council.

Additional WCC General Assemblies that have been held since the charter meeting of 1948 include Evanston, Ill. (1954), New Delhi, India (1961), Uppsala, Sweden (1968), Nairobi, Kenya (1975), Vancouver, British Columbia, Canada (1983) and Canberra, Australia (1991). The 1998 general assembly was held in Harare, Zimbabwe, with the regular Catholic delegation in attendance, led by Abp. Mario Conti of Glasgow, Scotland. The Ninth General Assembly took place in Porto Alegre, Brazil, Feb. 14–23, 2006. A Catholic delegation headed by Card. Walter Kasper, President of the Pontifical Council for Promoting Christian Unity, was present. The 10th General Assembly is set to take place in Busan, South Korea, Oct. 30–Nov. 8, 2013.

The council continues the work of the International Missionary Council, the Commission on Faith and Order, and the Commission on Church and Society. The work of the council is carried out through four program units: unity and renewal; mission, education and witness; justice, peace and creation; sharing and service.

Liaison between the council and the Vatican has been maintained since 1966 through a Joint Working Group. The Joint Commission on Society, Development and Peace (SODEPAX) was an agency of the council and the

Pontifical Commission for Justice and Peace from 1968 to Dec. 31, 1980, after which another working group was formed. Roman Catholics serve as full members of the Commission on Faith and Order since 1968, the Holy See provides staff to mission, education and witness unit of the Council, and the Catholic Church is engaged in various capacities on other program committees of the council.

WCC headquarters are located in Geneva, Switzerland. The WCC also maintains fraternal relations with regional, national and local councils of churches throughout the world. Web site: http://www.oikoumene.org/

National Council of Churches

The National Council of the Churches of Christ in the U.S.A., the largest ecumenical body in the United States, is an organization of 36 Protestant, Orthodox and Anglican communions, with an aggregate membership of about 50 million in 140,000 congregations.

The NCC, established by the churches in 1950, was structured through the merger of 12 separate cooperative agencies. Presently, the NCC carries on work in behalf of member churches in overseas ministries, Christian education, domestic social action, communications, disaster relief, refugee assistance, rehabilitation and development, biblical translation, international affairs, theological dialogue, inter-faith activities, worship and evangelism, and other areas.

NCC president: Kathryn Mary Lohre. Interim General Secretary: Clare Chapman, Esq. NCC headquarters are located at 475 Riverside Drive, New York, NY 10115; (212) 870-2141; www.ncccusa.org.

Christian Churches Together in the USA

In early 2001, discussions began in earnest among church leaders in the United States about the possibility of forming a new ecumenical organization. There was an acute awareness that since the members of the current National Council of Churches (NCC) represent only about one third of the Christians in the United States, a much broader ecumenical witness was needed. Thus in the summer of 2001 letters were sent out to various American church leaders inviting them to attend a meeting at St. Mary's Seminary and University in Baltimore on Sept. 7-8. The letter was signed by Bp. Tod Brown, Card. William Keeler, Rev. Wesley Granberg-Michaelson (General Secretary of the Reformed Church in America), and Rev. Dr. Robert Edgar (NCC General Secretary). The meeting was to explore whether or not the time had come to "create a new, more inclusive ecumenical table and/or body." The most striking result was the unanimous strong desire among the participants for a broader structure of some kind that would include all the major groupings of churches, including the Catholic Church and major Evangelical and Pentecostal groups that do not now belong to the NCC. Subsequent organizational meetings were held in Chicago (April 2002), Pasadena (January 2003), and Navasota, Texas (January 2004). The name chosen for the new entity is "Christian Churches Together in the USA" (CCT).

In November 2004, the Catholic Bishops of the United States took an historic ecumenical step by voting to participate in CCT. Bp. Stephen E. Blaire of Stockton, California, chairman of the Committee on Ecumenical and Interreligious Affairs, presented the proposal to the body of bishops and urged its adoption, calling CCT a "fresh and creative initiative to broaden the ecumenical table." The bishops approved the proposal to join CCT by a vote of 151-73, slightly more than a 2-to-1 margin.

From June 1-3, 2005, 67 national Christian leaders from five Christian families–Evangelical/Pentecostal, Historic Protestant, Historic Racial/Ethnic, Orthodox and Catholic–met in their fifth and largest CCT organizational meeting at the Jesuit Conference Center in Los Altos, California. The gathering at Los Altos brought together a wider, more diverse circle of Christian church leaders than at any of the previous four meetings. Through two and a half days of sharing, prayer and worship, the participants wrestled with difficult and complex issues in a spirit of love and good will. Relationships with the Historic Black Churches were deepened through intensive dialogue and sharing.

It was decided at Los Altos to delay a formal launch planned for September 2005 in order to continue the productive and positive conversation with churches and organizations actively considering joining. Participants enthusiastically reaffirmed their commitment to "grow closer together in Christ in order to strengthen our Christian witness in the world." The Rev. Wesley Granberg-Michaelson was unanimously reelected as moderator to lead an expanded Steering Committee.

Another plenary meeting of CCT took place at Simpsonwood Conference and Retreat Center near Atlanta, Ga., from Mar. 28-31, 2006. At this meeting the new By-laws of CCT were adopted and the new organization formally came into existence. Subsequent plenaries were held in February 2007 (Pasadena, Calif.), January 2008 (Baltimore, Md.) January 2009 (Baltimore, Md.), and January 2010 (Seattle, Wash.). The January 2011 plenary in Birmingham, Ala. With 43 churches and national organizations participating, CCT is now the broadest, most inclusive fellowship of Christian churches and traditions that has ever existed in the USA. The main focus of recent meetings has been poverty in the United States, evangelization and racism. The next plenary is scheduled to take place in Memphis, Tenn., in February 2012. Moderator (elected 2008): Rev. Leonid Kishkovsky; Catholic President: Aux. Bp. Denis J. Madden of Baltimore; Executive Director: Rev. Carlos Malave; www.christianchurchestogether.org.

Churches Uniting in Christ

Churches Uniting in Christ (CUIC) is a relationship among Christian communions that have pledged to live more closely together in expressing their unity in Christ with a primary focus upon combating racism both within the church and in society. CUIC is both an outgrowth of and successor to the Consultation on Church Union (COCU), an organization that worked for more than 40 years toward the day when Christians can become more fully reconciled to each other. After a two year pause to reassess the vision and structure of the organization, CUIC members announced their recommitment to a "New Way Forward" in 2010.

The eight marks of communion in the CUIC partnership are: mutual recognition of each other as authentic expressions of the one church of Jesus Christ, mutual recognition of members in one Baptism, mutual recognition that each affirms the apostolic faith of Scripture and tradition which is expressed in the Apostles' and Nicene Creeds, and that each seeks to give witness to the apostolic faith in its life and mission, provision for celebration of the Eucharist together with intentional regularity, engagement together in Christ's mission on a regular and intentional basis, especially a shared mission to combat racism, intentional commitment to promote unity with wholeness and to oppose marginalization and exclusion in church and society based on such things as race, age, gender, forms of disability, sexual orientation, and class, appropriate structures of accountability and appropriate means for consultation and decision making, an ongoing process of theological dialogue.

The member communions, representing 25 million Christians, are the African Methodist Episcopal Church, the Christian Church (Disciples of Christ), the Christian Methodist Episcopal Church, the Episcopal Church, the Presbyterian Church (U.S.A), the United Church of Christ, the United Methodist Church, the Moravian Church Northern Province, and the International Council of Community Churches. The Evangelical Lutheran Church in America is a partner in mission and dialogue and the Secretariat of Ecumenical and Interreligious Affairs of the United States Conference of Catholic Bishops maintains observer status. Catholic participation includes a staff representative to the CUIC coordinating council, with a voice but no vote, and Catholic membership on the task forces, with a voice and a vote. Catholic theologians have made a significant contribution by serving on the Ministry Task Force and offering insights from the Catholic perspective.

At the January 2011 plenary meeting in Ft. Lauderdale, CUIC expressed its commitment to seek reconciliation with the African Methodist Episcopal Zion (AME Zion) Church, a member communion that suspended its membership with CUIC over concerns that the organization had not been fully committed to addressing issues of racial justice.

The final day of the 2011 plenary included consideration of recommended actions CUIC member communions might take to address racism in three specific contexts: international, national, and within the member churches. The plenary concluded with a service of recommitment to CUIC's initial goals and marks of visible unity.

Currently the President of CUIC is Rev. Robina Winbush of the Presbyterian Church (USA), the Vice President is Mrs. Jacqueline Dupont Walker of the African Methodist Episcopal Church, the Secretary is Rev. Jean Hawxhurst of the United Methodist Church, and the Treasurer is Rev. Dr. Robert Welsh of the Disciples of Christ. churchesunitinginchrist.org

Graymoor Institute

The Graymoor Ecumenical and Interreligious Institute is a forum where issues that confront the Christian Churches are addressed, the spiritual dimensions of ecumenism are fostered, and information, documentation and developments within the ecumenical movement are published through Ecumenical Trends, a monthly journal. GEII also produces the annual materials for the Week of Prayer for Christian Unity.

Director: Fr. James Loughran, SA. Address: 475 Riverside Dr., Rm. 1960, New York, NY 10115-1999. http://www.geii.org/

INTERNATIONAL BILATERAL COMMISSIONS

Anglican Roman Catholic International Commission, sponsored by the Pontifical Council for Promoting Christian Unity and the Lambeth Conference, from 1970 to 1981; succeeded by a **Second Anglican Roman Catholic International Commission,** called into being by the Common Declaration of Pope John Paul and the Archbishop of Canterbury in 1982. It completed its work in 2005. A new International Anglican-Roman

Catholic Commission for Unity and Mission, set up in 2000, has summarized the main conclusions of ARCIC and proposed ways to grow together in mission and witness. When Dr. Rowan Williams, the Archbishop of Canterbury, met with Pope Benedict XVI in Rome in November 2009, they announced preparations for the establishment of a **Third Anglican-Roman Catholic International Commission.** It met for the first time at a Catholic monastery in Bose, Italy, from May 17–27, 2011, and is examining the Church as Communion, local and universal, and how in communion the local and universal Church come to discern right ethical teaching.

The International Theological Colloquium between Baptists and Catholics, established in 1984 by the Pontifical Council for Promoting Christian Unity and the Commission for Faith and Interchurch Cooperation of the Baptist World Alliance.

The Disciples of Christ-Roman Catholic Dialogue, organized by the Council of Christian Unity of the Christian Church (Disciples of Christ) and the U.S. Bishops' Committee for Ecumenical and Interreligious Affairs, along with participation by the Disciples' Ecumenical Consultative Council and the Unity Council; since 1977.

The Evangelical-Roman Catholic Dialogue on Mission, organized by Evangelicals and the Pontifical Council for Promoting Christian Unity; from 1977. This dialogue is now sponsored by the World Evangelical Alliance, on the evangelical side.

The Lutheran-Roman Catholic Commission on Unity, established by the Pontifical Council for Promoting Christian Unity and the Lutheran World Federation; from 1967.

The Joint International Commission for Theological Dialogue between the Orthodox Church and the Catholic Church, established by the Holy See and 14 autocephalous Orthodox Churches, began its work at a first session held at Patmos/Rhodes in 1980. Subsequent sessions have been held at Munich (1982), Crete (1984), Bari (1987), Valamo (1988), Freising (1990), Balamand (1993), and Emmitsburg, Maryland (2000); Belgrade, Serbia (2006); Ravenna, Italy (2007); Paphos, Cyprus (2009), and Vienna, Austria (2010).

Pentecostal-Roman Catholic Conversations, since 1972.

The Reformed-Roman Catholic Conversations, inaugurated in 1970 by the Pontifical Council for Promoting Christian Unity and the World Alliance of Reformed Churches.

The International Joint Commission between the Catholic Church and the Coptic Orthodox Church, since 1974. Established officially in the Common Declaration signed by Pope Paul VI and Coptic Pope Shenouda III in Rome in 1973. Superseded in 2003 by the international dialogue with the Oriental Orthodox.

The Joint International Commission between the Roman Catholic Church and the Malankara Orthodox Syrian Church, since 1989.

The Joint Commission between the Catholic Church and the Malankara Jacobite Syrian Orthodox Church, since 1990.

The Assyrian Church of the East-Roman Catholic Dialogue, officially established in the Common Declaration signed by Pope John Paul II and Mar Dinkha IV in November 1994.

Catholic Church-Oriental Orthodox Churches International Joint Commission for Dialogue was planned at a Preparatory Meeting held in Rome in January 2003. The first meeting of the Joint Commission took place in Cairo in January 2004. Subsequent meetings have taken place in Rome (2005), Etchmiadzin, Armenia (2006),

Rome (2007), near Damascus, Syria (2008), Rome (2009), Antelias, Lebanon (2010), and Rome (2011).

Dialogue between the World Evangelical Alliance and the Catholic Church begun in 1990 issued a statement in 2002.

Dialogue with the Mennonite World Conference begun in 1998 produced an agreed statement in 2003.

U.S. ECUMENICAL DIALOGUES

Representatives of the Bishops' Committee for Ecumenical and Interreligious Affairs, United States Conference of Catholic Bishops, have met in dialogue with representatives of other churches since the 1960s, for discussion of a wide variety of subjects related to the quest for unity among Christians. Following is a list of dialogue groups and the years in which dialogue began.

Anglican-Roman Catholic Consultation, 1965; North American Orthodox-Catholic Theological Consultation, 1965; Joint Committee of Orthodox and Catholic Bishops, 1981; Lutheran Consultation, 1965; Oriental Orthodox Consultation (with Armenian, Coptic, Ethiopian, Indian Malabar and Syrian Orthodox Churches), 1978; Polish National-Catholic Consultation, 1984; Presbyterian/ Reformed Consultation, 1965; Southern Baptist Conversations, 1969; United Methodist Consultation, 1966; Faith and Order National Council of Churches, 1968; National Association of Evangelicals, 2003-2008.

COMMON DECLARATIONS OF POPES, OTHER CHURCH LEADERS

(*Source: Secretariat for Ecumenical and Interreligious Affairs, United States Conference of Catholic Bishops.*)

The following Common Declarations, issued by several popes and heads, carry the authority given them by their signators.

Paul VI and Orthodox Ecumenical Patriarch Athenagoras I, First Common Declaration, Dec. 7, 1965: They hoped the differences between the churches would be overcome with the help of the Holy Spirit, and that their "full communion of faith, brotherly concord and sacramental life" would be restored.

Paul VI and Anglican Abp. Michael Ramsey of Canterbury, Mar. 24, 1966: They stated their intention "to inaugurate between the Roman Catholic Church and the Anglican Communion a serious dialogue which, founded on the Gospels and on the ancient common traditions, may lead to that unity in truth for which Christ prayed."

Paul VI and Patriarch Athenagoras I, Second Common Declaration, Oct. 27, 1967: They wished "to emphasize their conviction that the restoration of full communion (between the churches) is to be found within the framework of the renewal of the Church and of Christians in fidelity to the traditions of the Fathers and to the inspirations of the Holy Spirit who remains always with the Church."

Paul VI and Vasken I, Orthodox Catholicos-Patriarch of All Armenians, May 12, 1970: They called for closer collaboration "in all domains of Christian life…. This collaboration must be based on the mutual recognition of the common Christian faith and the sacramental life, on the mutual respect of persons and their churches."

Paul VI and Mar Ignatius Jacob III, Syrian Orthodox Patriarch of Antioch, Oct. 27, 1971: They declared themselves to be "in agreement that there is no difference in

the faith they profess concerning the mystery of the Word of God made flesh and become really man, even if over the centuries difficulties have arisen out of the different theological expressions by which this faith was expressed."

Paul VI and Shenouda III, Coptic Orthodox Pope of Alexandria, May 10, 1973: Their common declaration recalls the common elements of the Catholic and Coptic Orthodox faith in the Trinity, the divinity and humanity of Christ, the seven sacraments, the Virgin Mary, the Church founded upon the Apostles, and the Second Coming of Christ. It recognizes that the two churches "are not able to give more perfect witness to this new life in Christ because of existing divisions which have behind them centuries of difficult history" dating back to the year A.D. 451. In spite of these difficulties, they expressed "determination and confidence in the Lord to achieve the fullness and perfection of that unity which is his gift."

Paul VI and Anglican Abp. Donald Coggan of Canterbury, Apr. 29, 1977: They stated many points on which Anglicans and Roman Catholics hold the faith in common and called for greater cooperation between Anglicans and Roman Catholics.

John Paul II and Orthodox Ecumenical Patriarch Dimitrios I, First Common Declaration, Nov. 30, 1979: "Purification of the collective memory of our churches is an important fruit of the dialogue of charity and an indispensable condition of future progress." They announced the establishment of the Catholic-Orthodox Theological Commission.

John Paul II and Anglican Abp. Robert Runcie of Canterbury, May 29, 1982: They agreed to establish a new Anglican-Roman Catholic commission with the task of continuing work already begun toward the eventual resolution of doctrinal differences.

John Paul II and Ignatius Zakka I, Syrian Orthodox Patriarch of Antioch, June 23, 1984: They recalled and solemnly reaffirmed the common profession of faith made by their predecessors, Paul VI and Mar Ignatius Jacob III, in 1971. They said: "The confusions and the schisms that occurred between the churches, they realize today, in no way affect or touch the substance of their faith, since these arose only because of differences in terminology and culture, and in the various formulae adopted by different theological schools to express the same matter. Accordingly, we find today no real basis for the sad divisions which arose between us concerning the doctrine of the Incarnation." On the pastoral level, they declared: "It is not rare for our faithful to find access to a priest of their own church materially or morally impossible. Anxious to meet their needs and with their spiritual benefit in mind, we authorize them in such cases to ask for the sacraments of penance, Eucharist and anointing of the sick from lawful priests of either of our two sister churches, when they need them."

John Paul II and Orthodox Ecumenical Patriarch Dimitrios I, Second Common Declaration, Dec. 7, 1987: Dialogue conducted since 1979 indicated that the churches can already profess together as common faith about the mystery of the Church and the connection between faith and the sacraments. They also stated that, "when unity of faith is assured, a certain diversity of expressions does not create obstacles to unity, but enriches the life of the Church and the understanding, always imperfect, of the revealed mystery.

John Paul II and Anglican Abp. Robert Runcie of Canterbury, Oct. 2, 1989: They said: "We solemnly re-commit ourselves and those we represent to the restoration of visible unity and full ecclesial communion in the confidence that to seek anything less would be to betray our Lord's intention for the unity of his people."

John Paul II and His Holiness Mar Dinkha IV, Catholicos-Patriarch of the Assyrian Church of the East, Nov. 11, 1994: Following is the text of the "Common Christological Declaration" between the Catholic Church and the Assyrian Church of the East, signed Nov. 11, 1994, by Pope John Paul II and His Holiness Mar Dinkha IV, Catholicos-Patriarch of the Assyrian Church of the East. The declaration acknowledges that, despite past differences, both churches profess the same faith in the real union of divine and human natures in the divine Person of Christ. Providing background to the declaration was the Assyrian Church's adherence to the teaching of Nestorius who, in the fifth century, denied the real unity of divine and human natures in the single divine Person of Christ.

Pope John Paul II with Ecumenical Orthodox Patriarch Bartholomew I, June 29, 1995: Pope John Paul and Ecumenical Orthodox Patriarch Bartholomew I, after several days of meetings, signed a common declaration June 29, 1995, declaring: "Our meeting has followed other important events which have seen our Churches declare their desire to relegate the excommunications of the past to oblivion and to set out on the way to establishing full communion. "Our new-found brotherhood in the name of the Lord has led us to frank discussion, a dialogue that seeks understanding and unity. This dialogue — through the Joint International (Catholic-Orthodox) Commission — has proved fruitful and has made substantial progress.

Pope John Paul II with Anglican Abp. George Carey, Common Ecumenical Declaration, Dec. 5, 1996: The pontiff and archbishop praised the work of the Anglican-Roman Catholic International Commission and stated that "In many parts of the world Anglicans and Catholics attempt to witness together in the face of growing secularism, religious apathy and moral confusion."

Pope John Paul II with Karekin I, Catholicos of All Armenians, Dec. 13, 1996. Pope John Paul and His Holiness Karekin I, Supreme Patriarch and Catholicos of All Armenians, signed Dec. 13, 1996, a common declaration in which they said in part: "Pope John Paul II and Catholicos Karekin I recognize the deep spiritual communion which already unites them and the bishops and clergy and lay faithful of their churches. It is a communion which finds its roots in the common faith in the holy and life-giving Trinity proclaimed by the Apostles and transmitted down the centuries.... They rejoice in the fact that recent developments of ecumenical relations and theological discussions ... have dispelled many misunderstandings inherited from the controversies and dissensions of the past. Such dialogues and encounters have prepared a healthy situation of mutual understanding and recovery of the deeper spiritual communion based on the common faith in the holy Trinity that they have been given through the Gospel of Christ and in the holy tradition of the Church.

Pope John Paul II with Aram I, Armenian Catholicos of Cilicia, Jan. 25, 1997: The common declaration stated, "the two spiritual leaders stress the vital importance of sincere dialogue. The Catholic Church and the Catholicate of Cilicia also have an immense field of constructive cooperation before them."

Card. Edward Cassidy with Bishop Christian Krause, President of the Lutheran World Federation, Oct. 31, 1999: "Joint Declaration on Justification by Faith." (*See* **Special Section.**)

Pope John Paul II with Karekin II, Catholicos of All Armenians, Nov. 10, 2000, in Rome: His Holiness Pope John Paul II, Bishop of Rome, and His Holiness Karekin II, Supreme Patriarch and Catholicos of All Armenians, give thanks to the Lord and Savior Jesus Christ, for enabling them to meet together on the occasion of the Jubilee of the Year 2000 and on the threshold of the 1700th anniversary of the proclamation of Christianity as the state religion of Armenia.

Pope John Paul II with Christodoulos, Archbishop of Athens, May 4, 2001: The common declaration stated: We are anguished to see that wars, massacres, torture and martyrdom constitute a terrible daily reality for millions of our brothers. We commit ourselves to struggle for the prevailing of peace throughout the whole world, for the respect of life and human dignity, and for solidarity toward all who are in need.

John Paul II and Karekin II, Catholicos of All Armenians, Sept. 27, 2001, in Etchmiadzin, Armenia: The celebration of the 1700th anniversary of the proclamation of Christianity as the religion of Armenia has brought us together – John Paul II, Bishop of Rome and Pastor of the Catholic Church, and Karekin II, the Supreme Patriarch and Catholicos of All Armenians – and we thank God for giving us this joyous opportunity to join again in common prayer, in praise of his all-holy Name. Blessed be the Holy Trinity – Father, Son and Holy Spirit – now and forever.

Pope John Paul II and Ecumenical Patriarch Bartholomew I signed a Common Declaration on Environmental Ethics, June 10, 2002: We are gathered here today in the spirit of peace for the good of all human beings and for the care of creation. At this moment in history, at the beginning of the third millennium, we are saddened to see the daily suffering of a great number of people from violence, starvation, poverty and disease. We are also concerned about the negative consequences for humanity and for all creation resulting from the degradation of some basic natural resources such as water, air and land, brought about by an economic and technological progress which does not recognize and take into account its limits. *Rome — Venice, 10 June 2002*

Pope John Paul II and Patriarch Teoctist of the Romanian Orthodox Church signed a Joint Declaration in Rome on Oct. 12, 2002: The glory which you have given me I have given to them, that they may be one even as we are one, I in them and you in me, that they may become perfectly one, so that the world may know that you have sent me and have loved them even as you have loved me" (Jn 17:22-23).

In the deep joy of being together again in the city of Rome, close to the tombs of the holy Apostles Peter and Paul, we exchange the kiss of peace under the gaze of the One who watches over his Church and guides our steps; and we meditate anew on these words, which the Evangelist John transmitted to us and which constitute Christ's heartfelt prayer on the eve of his Passion.

Pope John Paul II and Ecumenical Patriarch Bartholomew I signed a Common Declaration in Rome on June 29, 2004: Unity and Peace! The hope kindled by that historic encounter has lit up our journey in these last decades. Aware that the Christian world has suffered the tragedy of separation for centuries, our Predecessors and we ourselves have persevered in the 'dialogue of charity,' our gaze turned to that blessed, shining day on which it will be possible to communicate with the same cup of the precious Blood and the holy Body of the Lord (cf. Patriarch Athenagoras I, Address to Pope Paul VI [Jan. 5, 1964], ibid., No. 48, p. 109).

Despite our firm determination to journey on towards full communion, it would have been unrealistic not to expect obstacles of various kinds: doctrinal, first of all, but also the result of conditioning by a troubled history. In addition, the new problems which have emerged from the radical changes that have occurred in political and social structures have not failed to make themselves felt in relations between the Christian Churches. With the return to freedom of Christians in Central and Eastern Europe, old fears have also been reawakened, making dialogue difficult. Nonetheless, St. Paul's exhortation to the Corinthians: let all things be done in charity, must always be vibrant within us and between us…

Abp. Rowan Williams of Canterbury and Pope Benedict XVI in Rome on Nov. 23, 2006: Forty years ago, our predecessors, Pope Paul VI and Abp. Michael Ramsey, met together in this city sanctified by the ministry and the blood of the Apostles Peter and Paul. They began a new journey of reconciliation based on the Gospels and the ancient common traditions. Centuries of estrangement between Anglicans and Catholics were replaced by a new desire for partnership and co-operation, as the real but incomplete communion we share was rediscovered and affirmed. Pope Paul VI and Abp. Ramsey undertook at that time to establish a dialogue in which matters which had been divisive in the past might be addressed from a fresh perspective with truth and love.

True ecumenism goes beyond theological dialogue; it touches our spiritual lives and our common witness. As our dialogue has developed, many Catholics and Anglicans have found in each other a love for Christ which invites us into practical co-operation and service. This fellowship in the service of Christ, experienced by many of our communities around the world, adds a further impetus to our relationship. The International Anglican–Roman Catholic Commission for Unity and Mission (IARCCUM) has been engaged in an exploration of the appropriate ways in which our shared mission to proclaim new life in Christ to the world can be advanced and nurtured. Their report, which sets out both a summary of the central conclusions of ARCIC and makes proposals for growing together in mission and witness, has recently been completed and submitted for review to the Anglican Communion Office and the Pontifical Council for Promoting Christian Unity, and we express our gratitude for their work.

In this fraternal visit, we celebrate the good which has come from these four decades of dialogue. We are grateful to God for the gifts of grace which have accompanied them. At the same time, our long journey together makes it necessary to acknowledge publicly the challenge represented by new developments which, besides being divisive for Anglicans, present serious obstacles to our ecumenical progress. It is a matter of urgency, therefore, that in renewing our commitment to pursue the path towards full visible communion in the truth and love of Christ, we also commit ourselves in our continuing dialogue to address the important issues involved in the emerging ecclesiological and ethical factors making that journey more difficult and arduous.

As Christian leaders facing the challenges of the new millennium, we affirm again our public commitment to the revelation of divine life uniquely set forth by God in the divinity and humanity of Our Lord Jesus Christ. We believe that it is through Christ and the means of salvation found in him that healing and reconciliation are offered to us and to the world.

There are many areas of witness and service in which we can stand together, and which indeed call for closer co-operation between us: the pursuit of peace in the Holy Land and in other parts of the world marred by conflict and the threat of terrorism; promoting respect for life from conception until natural death; protecting the sanctity of marriage and the well-being of children in the context of healthy family life; outreach to the poor, oppressed and the most vulnerable, especially those who are persecuted for their faith; addressing the negative effects of materialism; and care for creation and for our environment. We also commit ourselves to inter-religious dialogue through which we can jointly reach out to our non-Christian brothers and sisters.

Mindful of our 40 years of dialogue, and of the witness of the holy men and women common to our traditions, including Mary the Theotókos, Sts. Peter and Paul, Benedict, Gregory the Great, and Augustine of Canterbury, we pledge ourselves to more fervent prayer and a more dedicated endeavour to welcome and live by that truth into which the Spirit of the Lord wishes to lead his disciples (cf. Jn 16:13). Confident of the apostolic hope "that he who has begun this good work in you will bring it to completion"(cf. Phil 1:6), we believe that if we can together be God's instruments in calling all Christians to a deeper obedience to our Lord, we will also draw closer to each other, finding in his will the fullness of unity and common life to which he invites us. — *From the Vatican, Nov. 23, 2006*

Pope Benedict XVI and Ecumenical Patriarch Bartholomew I signed a Common Declaration in Constantinople (Istanbul) on Nov. 30, 2006: This fraternal encounter which brings us together, Pope Benedict XVI of Rome and Ecumenical Patriarch Bartholomew I, is God's work, and in a certain sense his gift. We give thanks to the Author of all that is good, who allows us once again, in prayer and in dialogue, to express the joy we feel as brothers and to renew our commitment to move towards full communion. This commitment comes from the Lord's will and from our responsibility as Pastors in the Church of Christ. May our meeting be a sign and an encouragement for us to share the same sentiments and the same attitudes of fraternity, cooperation and communion in charity and truth. The Holy Spirit will help us to prepare the great day of the re-establishment of full unity, whenever and however God wills it. Then we shall truly be able to rejoice and be glad.

As far as relations between the Church of Rome and the Church of Constantinople are concerned, we cannot fail to recall the solemn ecclesial act effacing the memory of the ancient anathemas which for centuries have had a negative effect on relations between our Churches. We have not yet drawn from this act all the positive consequences which can flow from it in our progress towards full unity, to which the mixed Commission is called to make an important contribution. We exhort our faithful to take an active part in this process, through prayer and through significant gestures. — *From the Phanar, Nov. 30, 2006*

Common Declaration signed by Pope Benedict XVI and H.B. Christolodoulos, Archbishop of Athens and All Greece, Dec. 14, 2006:

The Common Declaration was signed by Pope Benedict XVI and Archbishop Christodoulos of Athens and All Greece during the Archbishop's visit to Rome on Dec. 14, 2006:

We, Benedict XVI, Pope and Bishop of Rome, and Christodoulos, Archbishop of Athens and All Greece, in this sacred place of Rome, renowned for the preaching of the Gospel and the martyrdom of the Apostles Peter and Paul, desire to live ever more intensely our mission to offer an apostolic witness, to pass on the faith to those both near and far and to proclaim to them the Good News of the Savior's birth, which we will both be celebrating shortly. It is also our common responsibility to overcome the many problems and painful experiences of the past *in love and truth*, for the glory of God, the Blessed Trinity, and of his Holy Church.

Our meeting *in charity* makes us ever more conscious of our common task: to travel together along the arduous route of a *dialogue in truth* with a view to re-establishing the full communion of faith in the bond of love. Thus, we will be obeying the divine commandment and will put into practice the prayer of Our Lord Jesus Christ. In addition, enlightened by the Holy Spirit, who accompanies Christ's Church and never abandons her, we will persevere in our commitment on this path, following the example of the Apostles and demonstrating our mutual love and spirit of reconciliation.

With regard to our relations, we recognize the important steps that have been taken in the dialogue of charity and by the decisions of the Second Vatican Council. Furthermore, we hope that the bilateral theological dialogue will carry forward these positive elements to formulate proposals accepted by both parties in a spirit of reconciliation, after the example of our illustrious Father of the Church, St. Basil the Great, who, in a period of manifold divisions in the Ecclesial Body, declared his conviction *"that by extended communication and mutual experience without strife, if anything more requires to be added by way of explanation, the Lord, who works all things together for the good of those who love him, will grant it"* (cf. Letter, No. 113)... — *From the Vatican, Dec. 14, 2006.*

Common Declaration Signed By Pope Benedict XVI and Chrysostomos II, Archbishop of Nea Justiniana and All Cyprus, June 16, 2007:

"Blessed be God and Father of Our Lord Jesus Christ, who has blessed us in Christ with every spiritual blessing in the heavenly places" (Eph 1:3).

On the happy occasion of our fraternal encounter at the tombs of Sts. Peter and Paul, the "coryphaei of the Apostles," as liturgical tradition says, we would like to declare of common accord our sincere and firm willingness, in obedience to the desire of Our Lord Jesus Christ, to intensify our search for full unity among all Christians, making every possible effort deemed useful to the life of our Communities. We desire that the Catholic and Orthodox faithful of Cyprus live a fraternal life in full solidarity, based on our common faith in the Risen Christ. We also wish to sustain and encourage the theological dialogue which is preparing through the competent International Commission to address the most demanding issues that marked the historical event of the division.

For full communion in the faith, the sacramental life and the exercise of the pastoral ministry, it is necessary to reach substantial agreement. To this end, we assure our faithful of our fervent prayers as Pastors in the Church and ask them to join us in a unanimous invocation "that they may all be one... so that the world may believe" (Jn 17: 21).

At our meeting, we reviewed the historical situations in which our Churches are living. In particular, we examined the situation of division and tensions that have marked the Island of Cyprus for more than 30 years, with its tragic daily problems which impair the daily life of our communities and of individual families. More generally, we considered the situation in the Middle East, where the war and conflicts between peoples risk spreading with disastrous consequences. We prayed for the peace that "comes from the heavenly places." It is the intention of our Churches to play a role of peacemaking in justice and solidarity and, to achieve all this, it is our constant wish to foster fraternal relations among all Christians and loyal dialogue between the different religions present and active in the Region. May faith in the one God help the people of these ancient and celebrated regions to rediscover friendly coexistence, in reciprocal respect and constructive collaboration... — *From the Vatican, June 16, 2007*

ECUMENICAL STATEMENTS

The ecumenical statements listed below, and others like them, reflect the views of participants in the dialogues which produced them. They have not necessarily been accepted by the respective churches as formulations of doctrine or points of departure for practical changes in discipline. (For other titles, see U.S. Ecumenical Dialogues, Ecumenical Reports.)

• The "Windsor Statement" on Eucharistic doctrine, published Dec. 31, 1971, by the Anglican-Roman Catholic International Commission of theologians. (For text, see pages 132-33 of the *1973 Catholic Almanac*.)

• The "Canterbury Statement" on ministry and ordination, published Dec. 13, 1973, by the same commission. (For excerpts, see pages 127-30 of the 1975 *Catholic Almanac*.)

• "Papal Primacy/Converging Viewpoints," published Mar. 4, 1974, by the dialogue group sanctioned by the U.S.A. National Convention of the World Lutheran Federation and the U.S. Bishops' Committee for Ecumenical and Interreligious Affairs. (For excerpts, see pages 130-31 of the 1975 *Catholic Almanac*.)

• An "Agreed Statement on the Purpose of the Church," published Oct. 31, 1975, by the Anglican-Roman Catholic Consultation in the U.S.

• "Christian Unity and Women's Ordination," published Nov. 7, 1975, by the same consultation, in which it was said that the ordination of women (approved in principle by the Anglican Communion but not by the Catholic Church) would "introduce a new element" in dialogue but would not mean the end of consultation nor the abandonment of its declared goal of full communion and organic unity.

• "Holiness and Spirituality of the Ordained Ministry," issued early in 1976 by theologians of the Catholic Church and the United Methodist Church; the first statement resulting from dialogue begun in 1966.

• "Mixed Marriages," published in the spring of 1976 by the Anglican-Roman Catholic Consultation in the U.S.

• "Bishops and Presbyters," published in July, 1976, by the Orthodox-Roman Catholic Consultation in the U.S. on the following points of common understanding: (1) Ordination in apostolic succession is required for pastoral office in the Church. (2) Presiding at the Eucharistic Celebration is a task belonging to those ordained to pastoral service. (3) The offices of bishop and presbyter are different realizations of the sacrament of order. (4) Those ordained are claimed permanently for the service of the Church.

• "The Principle of Economy," published by the body named above at the same time, concerning God's plan and activities in human history for salvation.

• "Venice Statement" on authority in the Church, published Jan. 20, 1977, by the Anglican-Roman Catholic International Commission of theologians.

• "Response to the Venice Statement," issued Jan. 4, 1978, by the Anglican-Roman Catholic Consultation in the U.S.A., citing additional questions.

• "An Ecumenical Approach to Marriage," published in January, 1978, by representatives of the Catholic Church, the Lutheran World Federation

and the World Alliance of Reformed Churches.
• "Teaching Authority and Infallibility in the Church," released in October 1978, by the Catholic-Lutheran dialogue group in the U.S.
• "The Eucharist," reported early in 1979, in which the Roman Catholic-Lutheran Commission indicated developing convergence of views.
• "The Holy Spirit," issued Feb. 12, 1979, by the International Catholic-Methodist Commission.
• A statement on "Ministry in the Church," published in March 1981, by the International Roman Catholic-Lutheran Joint Commission, regarding possible mutual recognition of ministries.
• The Final Report of the Anglican-Roman Catholic International Commission, 1982, on the results of 12 years of dialogue.
• "The Mystery of the Church and of the Eucharist in the Light of the Mystery of the Holy Trinity," issued by the Mixed International Commission for Theological Dialogue between the Catholic Church and the Orthodox Church at Munich, Germany, in July 1982.
• The Final Report of the Anglican-Roman Catholic International Commission, 1982, on the results of 12 years of dialogue.
• "Justification by Faith," issued Sept. 30, 1983, by the U.S. Lutheran-Roman Catholic dialogue group, claiming a "fundamental consensus on the Gospel."
• "Images of God: Reflections on Christian Anthropology," released Dec. 22, 1983, by the Anglican-Roman Catholic Dialogue in the United States.
• "The Journeying Together in Christ – The Report of the Polish National Catholic-Roman Catholic Dialogue (1984-89)."
• "Salvation and the Church," issued Jan. 22, 1987, by the Second Anglican-Roman Catholic International Commission.
• "Faith, Sacraments and the Unity of the Church," issued by the Mixed International Commission for Theological Dialogue between the Catholic Church and the Orthodox Churches in June 1987.
• "The Sacrament of Order in the Sacramental Structure of the Church, with Particular Reference to the Importance of Apostolic Succession for the Sanctification and Unity of the People of God," issued by the Mixed International Commission for Theological Dialogue between the Catholic Church and the Orthodox Church in Valamo, Finland, in 1988.
• "The Presence of Christ in Church and World" and "Toward a Common Understanding of the Church" (developed between 1984 and 1990), by the Reformed-Roman Catholic Conversations, under the auspices of the Pontifical Council for Promoting Christian Unity and the World Alliance of Reformed Churches.
• "The Church as Communion," issued by the Second Anglican-Roman Catholic International Commission, 1991.
• "Uniatism, Method of Union of the Past, and the Present Search for Full Communion," issued by the Joint International Commission for Theological Dialogue between the Catholic Church and the Orthodox Church at Balamand, Lebanon, in 1993.
• "Life in Christ: Morals, Communion and the Church," issued by the Second Anglican-Roman Catholic International Commission, 1994.
• "Common Response to the Aleppo Statement on the Date of Easter/Pacha," issued by the North American Orthodox-Catholic Theological Consultation

in Washington, DC, Oct. 31, 1998.
• "The Gift of Authority," issued by the Second Anglican-Roman Catholic International Commission, May 12, 1999.
• "Baptism and 'Sacramental Economy,'" issued by the North American Orthodox-Catholic Theological Consultation at Crestwood, NY, in June 1999.
• "Guidelines Concerning the Pastoral Care of Oriental Orthodox Students in Catholic Schools," issued by the Oriental Orthodox-Roman Catholic Theological Consultation in the United States at New Rochelle, NY, in June 1999.
• "Joint Declaration of the Catholic Church and the Lutheran World Federation on the Doctrine of Justification," issued July 8, 1999, by the International Roman Catholic-Lutheran Joint Commission.
• "Agreed Report on the Local/Universal Church," issued by the United States Anglican-Roman Catholic Consultation, Nov. 12, 1999.
• "Communion in Mission" and "Action Plan to Implement 'Communion in Mission,'" issued by a special consultation of Anglican and Roman Catholic bishops in Mississauga, Ontario, Canada, May 19, 2000.
• "Sharing the Ministry of Reconciliation: A Statement on the Orthodox-Catholic Dialogue and the Ecumenical Movement," issued June 1, 2000, by the North American Orthodox-Catholic Theological Consultation in Brookline, MA.
• "Methodist-Catholic Dialogues: Thirty Years of Mission and Witness," issued by the U.S. dialogue in 2001.
• "Doing the Truth in Charity," issued in July 2001 by the World Methodist Council and the Pontifical Council for Promoting Unity's Methodist-Catholic International Commission.
• "Interchurch Families: Resources for Ecumenical Hope," issued by the Catholic/Reformed Dialogue in the United States in 2002.
Response of the Anglican-Roman Catholic Consultation in the USA to the Anglican-Roman Catholic International Commission's "The Gift of Authority" (Mar. 29, 2003).
• "Called Together to be Peacemakers," Mennonite World Conference Catholic Dialogue 2003.
• "Church, Evangelization, and *Koinonia*," World Evangelical Alliance – Pontifical Council for Promoting Christian Unity 2003.
• "Journeying Together in Christ: The Journey Continues — The Report of the Polish National Catholic Roman Catholic Dialogue (1989-2002)."
• "The *Filioque*: A Church-Dividing Issue?" issued by the North American Orthodox-Catholic Theological Consultation, October 2003.
• "The Church as *Koinonia* of Salvation: Its Structures and Ministries," May 2004, Lutheran Catholic Dialogue in the US.
• "Mary: Grace and Hope in Christ," Anglican Roman Catholic Commission, 2004.
• "Journey in Faith: Forty Years of Reformed-Catholic Dialogue: 1965-2005," 2005.
• "Through Divine Love: The Church in Each Place and All Places," April 2005, United Methodist Roman Catholic Dialogue in the US. "Joint Declaration on Unity" by the Polish National Catholic – Roman Catholic Dialogue (May 17, 2006).
• ARCUSA Response to "Mary: Grace & Hope in Christ," October 2007, Anglican-Roman Catholic Consultation in the USA.
• "Ecclesiological and Canonical Consequences of the

Sacramental Nature of the Church: Ecclesial Communion, Conciliarity and Authority," issued by the Joint International

Commission for Theological Dialogue between the Catholic Church and the Orthodox Church at Ravenna, Italy, on Oct 13, 2007.
• "Nature, Constitution and Mission of the Church," International Oriental Orthodox-Roman Catholic Dialogue, Jan. 29, 2009.
• "A Common Response to the Joint International Commission for the Theological Dialogue Between the Roman Catholic Church and the Orthodox Church Regarding the Ravenna Document: 'Ecclesiological and Canonical.
• "Consequences of the Sacramental Nature of the Church: Ecclesial Communion, Conciliarity and Authority" by the North American Orthodox-Catholic Theological Consultation, Oct. 24, 2009.
• "Celebrating Easter/Pascha Together," by the North American Orthodox-Catholic Theological Consultation, Oct. 1, 2010.
• "Steps toward a Reunited Church: A Sketch of an Orthodox-Catholic Vision for the Future," by the North American Orthodox-Catholic Theological Consultation, Oct. 2, 2010.
• "These Living Waters," by the Catholic-Reformed Dialogue in the US, Oct. 8, 2010.
• "This Bread of Life," by the Catholic-Reformed Dialogue in the US, Oct. 8, 2010.
• "The Hope of Eternal Life," by the United States Lutheran-Catholic Dialogue, Oct. 17, 2010.
• "Heaven and Earth are Full of your Glory: A United Methodist and Roman Catholic Statement on the Eucharist and Ecology," by the U.S. United Methodist-Catholic Dialogue, April 2012.
• "The Importance of Sunday," by the North American Orthodox-Catholic Theological Consultation, Oct.27, 2012.
See online: www.prounione.urbe.it/dia-int/e_dialogues. html, or http://www.usccb.org/seia/

RELATIONS WITH THE ORTHODOX CHURCH

This is a group of Eastern churches of the Byzantine tradition that were in full communion with Rome during the first millennium, and which all recognize the Patriarch of Constantinople as the first Orthodox bishop. In spite of the division between Catholics and Orthodox, often symbolized by the mutual excommunications of 1054, the Catholic Church considers itself to be in almost full communion with the Orthodox Churches. According to Vatican II, they "are still joined to us in closest intimacy" in various ways, especially in the priesthood and Eucharist. The Orthodox Churches recognize the first seven ecumenical councils as normative to their faith, along with the Scriptures and other local councils that took place in later centuries.

The Orthodox Churches are organized in approximately 15 autocephalous (independent) churches that correspond in most cases to nations or ethnic groups. The Ecumenical Patriarch of Constantinople (modern Istanbul) has a primacy of honor among the patriarchs, but his actual jurisdiction is limited to his own patriarchate. As the spiritual head of worldwide Orthodoxy, he serves as a point of unity, and has the right to call Pan-Orthodox assemblies.

Top-level relations between the Churches have improved in recent years through the efforts of Ecumenical Patriarch

Athenagoras I, Bl. John XXIII, Paul VI and Patriarch Dimitrios I. Pope Paul met with Athenagoras three times before the latter's death in 1972. The most significant action of both spiritual leaders was their mutual nullification of excommunications imposed by the two Churches on each other in 1054. Development of better relations with the Orthodox was a priority of John Paul II, as well as Benedict XVI. Both Pope Benedict and Orthodox Ecumenical Patriarch Bartholomew have made known their commitment to better relations, despite contentions between Eastern Catholic and Orthodox Churches over charges of proselytism and rival property claims in places liberated from anti-religious communist control in the recent past.

The largest Orthodox body in the United States is the Greek Orthodox Archdiocese of America consisting of nine dioceses; it has an estimated membership of 1.9 million. The second largest is the Orthodox Church in America, with more than one million members; it was given autocephalous status by the Patriarchate of Moscow May 18, 1970, without the consent of the Patriarchate of Constantinople. An additional 650,000 or more Orthodox belong to smaller national and language jurisdictions.

JURISDICTIONS

The Autocephalous Orthodox Churches

Patriarchate of Constantinople (Ecumenical Patriarchate), with jurisdiction in Turkey, Crete, the Dodecanese, and Greeks in the rest of the world outside Greece and Africa. Autonomous churches linked to the Ecumenical Patriarchate exist in Finland and Estonia. Several other jurisdictions of various ethnicities in the diaspora are also directly under the Patriarchate.

Patriarchate of Alexandria, with jurisdiction in Egypt and the rest of Africa; it includes a native African Orthodox Church centered in Kenya and Uganda.

Patriarchate of Antioch, with jurisdiction in Syria, Lebanon, Iraq, Australia, the Americas.

Patriarchate of Jerusalem, with jurisdiction in Israel and Jordan. The autonomous church of Mount Sinai is linked to the Jerusalem Patriarchate.

Russian Orthodox Church, the Patriarchate of Moscow with jurisdiction over most of the former Soviet Union. Autonomous churches in Japan and China are linked to the Moscow Patriarchate, and since the breakup of the Soviet Union, a certain autonomy has been granted to the Orthodox churches in the newly independent republics of Ukraine, Belarus, Estonia, Moldova and Latvia.

The Serbian Orthodox Church, a patriarchate with jurisdiction in all of former Yugoslavia, Western Europe, North America and Australia.

The Romanian Orthodox Church, a patriarchate with jurisdiction in Romania, Western Europe and North America.

The Bulgarian Orthodox Church, a patriarchate with jurisdiction in Bulgaria, Western Europe and North America.

The Georgian Orthodox Church, a patriarchate with jurisdiction in the republic of Georgia.

The Orthodox Church of Cyprus, an archbishopric with jurisdiction in Cyprus.

The Orthodox Church of Greece, an archbishopric with jurisdiction in most of Greece.

The Orthodox Church of Poland, a metropolitanate with jurisdiction in Poland.

The Orthodox Church of Albania, an archbishopric with jurisdiction in Albania.

The Orthodox Church in the Czech and Slovak Republics, a metropolitanate with jurisdiction in the Czech and Slovak Republics. Its autocephalous status was granted by Moscow in 1951 but by Constantinople only in 1998.

The Orthodox Church in America, a metropolitanate with jurisdiction in North America and a few parishes in Latin America and Australia. Its autocephalous status was granted by Moscow in 1970; Constantinople and most other Orthodox churches have not recognized this.

Population

The Center for the Study of Global Christianity estimates that in 2004 there were a total of 216,574,000 Orthodox Christians worldwide. Some Orthodox claim a total membership of as many as 300 million.

Standing Conference of Orthodox Bishops

The Standing Conference of the Canonical Orthodox Bishops in the Americas was established in 1960 to achieve cooperation among the various Orthodox jurisdictions in the Americas. Member churches were: Albanian Orthodox Diocese of America (Ecumenical Patriarchate), American Carpatho-Russian Orthodox Diocese in the U.S.A. (Ecumenical Patriarchate), Antiochian Orthodox Christian Archdiocese of North America, Bulgarian Eastern Orthodox Church, Greek Orthodox Archdiocese of America (Ecumenical Patriarchate), Orthodox Church in America, Romanian Orthodox Archdiocese in America and Canada, Serbian Orthodox Church in the United States and Canada, Ukrainian Orthodox Church in the United States (Ecumenical Patriarchate), and the Representation of the Moscow Patriarchate in the United States of America.

At a meeting of representatives of the Orthodox Churches in Switzerland in June 2009, it was decided to establish "Episcopal Assemblies" in various parts of the Orthodox diaspora, including one for North and Central America. It replaces SCOBA as the primary structure coordinating the life of the Orthodox Churches in that region. The Assembly met in plenary for the first time in New York May 2010 and again in Chicago in May 2011. a third plenary was planned for Chicago in September 2012. A Committee for Ecumenical Relations has been established, headed by Bishop Demetrios of Mokissos, Chancellor of the Greek Orthodox Metropolis of Chicago. Assembly Office: 8-10 East 79th St., New York, NY 10021; www.assemblyofbishops.org/.

EASTERN ECUMENISM

The Second Vatican Council, in *Orientalium Ecclesiarum*, the "Decree on Eastern Catholic Churches," pointed out the special role they have to play "in promoting the unity of all Christians." The document also stated in part as follows.

The Eastern Churches in communion with the Apostolic See of Rome have a special role to play in promoting the unity of all Christians, particularly Easterners, according to the principles of this sacred Synod's Decree on Ecumenism first of all by prayer, then by the example of their lives, by religious fidelity to ancient Eastern traditions, by greater mutual knowledge, by collaboration, and by a brotherly regard for objects and attitudes (No. 24).

If any separated Eastern Christian should, under the guidance of grace of the Holy Spirit, join himself to Catholic unity, no more should be required of him than what a simple profession of the Catholic faith demands. A valid priesthood is preserved among Eastern clerics. Hence, upon joining themselves to the unity of the Catholic Church, Eastern clerics are permitted to exercise the orders they possess, in accordance with the regulations established by the competent authority (No. 25).

Divine Law forbids any common worship (communicatio in sacris) that would damage the unity of the Church, or involve formal acceptance of falsehood or the danger of deviation in the faith, of scandal, or of indifferentism. At the same time, pastoral experience clearly shows that with respect to our Eastern brethren there should and can be taken into consideration various circumstances affecting individuals, wherein the unity of the Church is not jeopardized nor are intolerable risks involved, but in which salvation itself and the spiritual profit of souls are urgently at issue.

Hence, in view of special circumstances of time, place, and personage, the Catholic Church has often adopted and now adopts a milder policy, offering to all the means of salvation and an example of charity among Christians through participation in the sacraments and in other sacred functions and objects. With these considerations in mind, and "lest because of the harshness of our judgment we prove an obstacle to those seeking salvation," and in order to promote closer union with the Eastern Churches separated from us, this sacred Synod lays down the following policy:

In view of the principles recalled above, Eastern Christians who are separated in good faith from the Catholic Church, if they ask of their own accord and have the right dispositions, may be granted the sacraments of penance, the Eucharist, and the anointing of the sick. Furthermore, Catholics may ask for these same sacraments from those non-Catholic ministers whose Churches possess valid sacraments, as often as necessity or a genuine spiritual benefit recommends such a course of action, and when access to a Catholic priest is physically or morally impossible (Nos. 26, 27).

Again, in view of these very same principles, Catholics may for a just cause join with their separated Eastern brethren in sacred functions, things, and places (No. 28). Bishops decide when and if to follow this policy.

THE ORTHODOX CHURCHES

Pope John Paul II Returns Icon of the Mother of God of Kazan to the Russian Orthodox Church.

In August 2004 Pope John Paul II returned to the Russian Orthodox Church an icon of the Mother of God of Kazan that had hung over his desk in his personal study for eleven years. The icon was believed to have been taken out of Russia at the time of the Bolshevik Revolution, and had been given to the Holy Father by the Blue Army in 1993.

Pope John Paul II Returns Relics of Sts John Chrysostom and Gregory Nazianzen to the Patriarchate of Constantinople.

In November 2004 Pope John Paul II returned relics of Sts. John Chrysostom and Gregory Nazianzus to the Ecumenical Patriarchate. Patriarch Bartholomew traveled to Rome to receive the relics in a special service in St Peter's Basilica on Nov. 27.

Joint International Commission for Theological Dialogue.

The 12th meeting of the Joint International Commission for Theological Dialogue between the Orthodox Church and the Roman Catholic Church took place in Vienna, Austria, a city with a long history, a bridge between West and East, with a rich ecumenical life. The meeting, generously and fraternally hosted by the Roman Catholic Archdiocese of Vienna, from Sept. 20-27, 2010, in the Kardinal König Haus.

Twenty-three Catholic members were present, a few were unable to attend. All the Orthodox churches, with the exception of the Patriarchate of Bulgaria, were represented, namely the Ecumenical Patriarchate, the Patriarchate of Alexandria, the Patriarchate of Antioch, the Patriarchate of Jerusalem, the Patriarchate of Moscow, the Patriarchate of Serbia, the Patriarchate of Romania, the Patriarchate of Georgia, the Church of Cyprus, the Church of Greece, the Church of Poland, the Church of Albania and the Church of the Czech Lands and Slovakia.

The Commission worked under the direction of its two co-presidents, Archbp. Kurt Koch and Metropolitan Prof. Dr. John of Pergamon, assisted by the co-secretaries, Metropolitan Prof. Dr Gennadios of Sassima (Ecumenical Patriarchate) and Rev. Andrea Palmieri (Pontifical Council for Promoting Christian Unity).

At the opening plenary session on Wed., Sept. 22, the Commission was welcomed very warmly by the host, Card. Christoph Schönborn of Vienna, and by Metropolitan Michael of Austria of the Ecumenical Patriarchate on behalf of all Orthodox Churches present in Austria. Both emphasized the importance of holding the meeting in Vienna, which occupies a particular place in the history of the whole of Christianity. In the evening a reception was given by the Mayor of Vienna, Dr. Michael Häupl, at the Vienna Town Hall. The co-presidents announced that Pope Benedict XVI had urged intense prayer for the Commission meeting at his Wednesday General Audience and they read a Message to the participants from His All Holiness the Ecumenical Patriarch Bartholomew. A letter was sent by the co-presidents on behalf of the Joint Commission to the former President of the Pontifical Council for Promoting Christian Unity and co-president of the dialogue, Card. Walter Kasper, expressing gratitude and appreciation for his service and for his significant contribution.

On Thursday, Sept. 23, the Ecumenical Council of Churches in Austria met the members of the Joint Commission at Kardinal König Haus. On Saturday, Sept. 25, the Catholic members celebrated the Eucharist in the Stephansdom in Vienna presided over by Card. Christoph Schönborn, in the presence of the Orthodox members. In his homily he said that "we have and we need a primacy in the canonical sense, but above all there is the primacy of charity. All canonical dispositions in the Church serve this primacy of love (*agape*)." Afterwards a reception was offered in the Courtyard of the Archiepiscopal Palace of Vienna.

On Sunday, Sept. 26, the Orthodox members celebrated the Divine Liturgy in the Cathedral of the Holy Trinity of the Greek Orthodox Metropolitanate of Austria in Vienna, presided over by Metropolitan John of Pergamon, in the presence of the Catholic members. In addressing those present, Metropolitan Michael of Austria conveyed "the greetings of the Ecumenical Patriarch Bartholomew and underlined the role and the contribution of the Greek Metropolitanate to the history of Vienna with great eminent personalities." He also referred to "the close collaboration between Orthodox and Catholics in Austria and in Vienna in particular, expressing the wish that the Lord's prayer 'that all may be one' (Jn 17:21) be a reality in the search for the unity of His Church."

During the afternoon, the members paid a visit to the Cistercian Abbey of Heiligenkreuz and attended the service of Vespers. Later in the evening, they visited the Russian Orthodox Cathedral of St. Nikolaus.

On the first day of the meeting, as is customary, the Roman Catholic and Orthodox members met separately to coordinate their work. The Orthodox meeting discussed among other things the unfinished draft text produced by the 11th plenary session in Paphos, Cyprus last year, and much time was given to the methodology of the dialogue. The Catholic meeting also considered the draft text, seeking specific ways to improve the text, and reflected on methodological questions.

As was decided at the 10th plenary session in Ravenna, 2007, the Commission is studying the theme "The Role of the Bishop of Rome in the Communion of the Church in the First Millennium," on the basis of a draft text prepared by the Joint Coordinating Committee, which met in Aghios Nikolaos/Crete, Greece, 2008. During its meeting in Vienna, the Commission continued the detailed consideration of the text which began at last year's plenary session in Paphos, Cyprus. At this stage, the Commission is discussing this text as a working document and it decided that the text must be further revised. It was also decided to form a sub-commission to begin consideration of the theological and ecclesiological aspects of Primacy in its relation to Synodality. The sub-commission will submit its work to the Joint Coordinating Committee of the Commission which will meet next year.

During the meeting the members received the sad news that Msgr. Eleuterio Fortino, co-secretary of the Joint Commission since its inception, passed away, after a long period of illness, and prayers were offered for the repose of his soul.

The meeting of the Joint Commission was marked by a spirit of friendship and trustful collaboration. All members greatly appreciated the generous hospitality of the host Church, and they strongly commend the continuing work of the dialogue to the prayers of the faithful. Vienna, Austria, Sept. 26, 2010.

North American Orthodox-Catholic Theological Consultation Issues Agreed Statement on Filioque, a Question that Divided the Two Communions for Many Centuries.

(Courtesy, USCCB.) The North American Orthodox-Catholic Theological Consultation concluded a four-year study of the *Filioque* on Oct. 25, 2003, when it unanimously adopted an agreed text on this difficult question that has divided the two communions for many centuries. This important development took place at the 65th meeting of the Consultation, held at St. Paul's College in Washington, DC, under the joint chairmanship of Metropolitan Maximos of the Greek Orthodox Metropolis of Pittsburgh and Abp. Daniel E. Pilarczyk of Cincinnati.

The original version of the Creed most Christian churches accept as the standard expression of their faith dates from the First Council of Constantinople, in 381, and has been used by Orthodox Christians since that time. Toward the end, this Creed states that the Holy Spirit "proceeds from the Father." The word *Filioque* ("and the Son") was later added to the Latin version of this Creed used in the West, so that the phrase as most western Christians know it reads that the Holy Spirit "proceeds from the Father and the Son." This modification appeared in some areas of Western Europe as early as the 6th century but was accepted in Rome only in the 11th century. This change in the wording of the Creed and the underlying variations in understanding the origin and procession of the Holy Spirit within the Trinity have long been considered a church-dividing issue between Catholics and Orthodox. The Consultation had been studying this question since 1999 in the hope of eventually releasing an agreed statement.

Entitled "The Filioque: A Church-Dividing Issue?," the 10,000 word text has three major sections. The first, "The Holy Spirit in the Scriptures," summarizes references to the Spirit in both the Old and New Testaments. The more lengthy second section, "Historical Considerations," provides an overview of the origins of the two traditions concerning the eternal procession of the Spirit and the slow process by which the *Filioque* was added to the Creed in the West. It also shows how this question concerning Trinitarian theology became entwined with disputes regarding papal jurisdiction and primacy, and reviews recent developments in the Catholic Church which point to a greater awareness of the unique and normative character of the original Greek version of the Creed as an expression of the faith that unites the Orthodox East and Catholic West. The third section, "Theological Reflections," emphasizes our limited ability to speak of the inner life of God, points out that both sides of the debate have often caricatured the positions of the other, and lists areas in which the traditions agree. It then explores the differences that have developed regarding terminology, and identifies both theological and ecclesiological divergences that have arisen over the centuries.

In a final section, the Consultation makes eight recommendations to the members and bishops of the two churches. It recommends that they "enter into a new and earnest dialogue concerning the origin and person of the Holy Spirit." It also proposes that in the future both Catholics and Orthodox "refrain from labeling as heretical the traditions of the other side" on this subject, and that the theologians of both traditions make a clearer distinction between the divinity of the Spirit, and the manner of the Spirit's origin, "which still awaits full and final ecumenical resolution." The text also urges theologians to distinguish, as far as possible, the theological issues concerning the origin of the Holy Spirit from ecclesiological issues, and suggests that attention be paid in the future to the status of councils of both our churches that took place after the seven ecumenical councils of the first millennium. And finally, in view of the fact that the Vatican has affirmed the "normative and irrevocable dogmatic value of the Creed of 381" in its original Greek version, the Consultation recommends that the Catholic Church use the same text (without the *Filioque*) "in making translations of that Creed for catechetical and liturgical use," and declare that the anathema pronounced by the Second Council of Lyons against those who deny that the Spirit proceeds eternally from the Father and the Son is no longer applicable.

The North American Orthodox-Catholic Theological Consultation is sponsored jointly by the Standing Conference of Canonical Orthodox Bishops of the Americas (SCOBA), the Bishops' Committee for Ecumenical and Interreligious Affairs of the USCCB, and the Canadian Conference of Catholic Bishops. Since its establishment in 1965, the Consultation has now issued 22 agreed statements on various topics. All these texts are now available on the website of the U.S. Catholic Conference at: www.usccb.org/seia/dialogues.htm. The full text of the document is available on the USCCB website at: www.usccb.org/seia/filioque.htm.

Orthodox-Catholic Dialogue Lays Out a Vision of Unity in Unprecedented Document

Representatives of the Orthodox and Catholic Churches have issued two new documents outlining immediate steps they can take to overcome their thousand-year separation. The North American Orthodox-Catholic Theological Consultation finalized these agreed statements when it met at Georgetown University in Washington, Sept. 30 to Oct. 2, 2010. The Consultation is co-chaired by Abp. Gregory M. Aymond of New Orleans and Metropolitan Maximos of Pittsburgh.

The first statement, "Steps Toward a Reunited Church: A Sketch of an Orthodox-Catholic Vision for the Future," is an unprecedented effort to begin to visualize the shape of a reunited Catholic and Orthodox Church that would result from the reestablishment of full communion. The text acknowledges that the role of the Bishop of Rome in the Church is a central point of disagreement and outlines the history of this divergence between East and West. It goes on to summarize the many elements of the Christian faith and ecclesial life that the two churches share, and emphasizes the urgency of overcoming our divisions.

"Clearly, this cannot be achieved without new, better harmonized structures of leadership on both sides: new conceptions of both synodality and primacy in the universal Church, new approaches to the way primacy and authority are exercised in both our communions," the document says.

The agreed statement lists some of the features that would characterize a fully reunited Church and then focuses on the role the papacy would play within it. This role would need to be carefully defined, "both in continuity with the ancient structural principles of Christianity and in response to the need for a unified Christian message in the world of today." The document then suggests several aspects of the Pope's ministry in a reunited Church that could be both faithful to Catholic teaching and acceptable to the Orthodox. The document also lists several "preparatory steps" that could be taken even now as a prelude to the future unity of the churches, such as shared prayer and social ministry, and enumerates several questions and problems that remain outstanding.

The text concludes that "The challenge and the invitation to Orthodox and Catholic Christians ... is now to see Christ authentically present in each other, and to find in those structures of leadership that have shaped our communities through the centuries a force to move us beyond disunity, mistrust, and competition, towards that oneness in his Body, that obedience to his Spirit, which will reveal us as his disciples before the world."

The complete text of this statement is available here: www.usccb.org/seia/steps-towards-reunited-church.shtml

The second statement, "Celebrating Easter/Pascha Together," is a re-affirmation of the Consultation's 1998 document, "A Common Response to the Aleppo Statement on the Date of Easter/Pascha." In this new text, the members emphasize the importance of a united witness to the Resurrection of Christ, which lies at the very center of the Christian faith, and the scandal caused by the inability to celebrate this feast day consistently on the same date.

The Consultation joins many other expressions of support for a recent proposal that would re-calculate the date of Easter for all Christians based strictly on the teaching of the First Council of Nicaea (325), which determined that Easter be celebrated on the first Sunday following the first full moon after the Spring Equinox. Determining the Equinox from the Jerusalem meridian and using the most accurate scientific instruments and astronomical data available would require a change for both traditions, but would also represent greater faithfulness to the teaching of Nicaea.

"For the mission of the Church," the document states, "a common celebration would support the unity we already share and help to build it further in the future."

The full text is available at: www.usccb.org/seia/easter.shtml This 79th session of the Consultation was hosted by the Office of the President of Georgetown University, which made the historic Riggs Library available for the meeting. The members were the guests of Fr. John P. Langan, SJ, rector of the Georgetown Jesuit Community for dinner on Sept. 30, and Dr. John J. DeGioia, the president of the university, hosted a dinner for the Consultation and several members of the faculty and staff in the Philodemic Room on Friday evening Oct. 1.

Since its establishment in 1965, the North American Consultation has now issued 25 agreed statements on various topics. (USCCB Press Release, Oct. 7, 2010.)

Orthodox-Catholic Dialogue Issues Joint Statement On The Importance Of Sunday In The Lives Of Christians

The North American Orthodox-Catholic Theological Consultation issued an agreed statement on the importance of Sunday in the lives of Christians at its Oct. 25-27 meeting at St. Paul's College in Washington. Abp. Gregory M. Aymond of New Orleans and Metropolitan Methodios of Boston jointly chaired the meeting.

The pastoral statement on the importance of Sunday calls for Orthodox and Catholic Christians to recover the theological significance of a day that for many "has become less a day of worship and family and more like an ordinary work day." It ends with a call to clergy and laity "to work cooperatively within their communities to stress the importance of Sunday for worship and family." The full text of the statement is available online: www.usccb.org/beliefs-and-teachings/dialogue-with-others/ecumenical/orthodox/the-importance-of-sunday.cfm (USCCB Press Release, Nov. 19, 2012).

RELATIONS WITH THE ORIENTAL ORTHODOX CHURCHES

The Tenth Meeting of the International Joint Commission for Theological Dialogue Between the Catholic Church and the Oriental Orthodox Churches

The tenth meeting of the International Joint Commission for Theological Dialogue between the Catholic Church and the Oriental Orthodox Churches took place in Rome from Jan. 23–27, 2013, hosted by the Pontifical Council for Promoting Christian Unity. It was chaired jointly by Card. Kurt Koch, President of the Pontifical Council for Promoting Christian Unity, and by His Eminence Metropolitan Bishoy of Damiette.

Joining delegates from the Catholic Church were representatives of the following Oriental Orthodox Churches: the Antiochian Syrian Orthodox Church, the Armenian Apostolic Church (Catholicosate of All Armenians), the Armenian Apostolic Church (Holy See of Cilicia), the Coptic Orthodox Church, the Ethiopian Orthodox Tewahedo Church, and the Malankara Orthodox Syrian Church. No representative of the Eritrean Orthodox Tewahdo Church was able to attend.

The two delegations met separately on the morning of Jan. 23. The Joint Commission held plenary sessions on Jan. 23–26, each of which began with a brief prayer service using material prepared for the Week of Prayer for Christian Unity.

At the beginning of the first session, Card. Koch noted with sadness that the heads of two of the Oriental Orthodox Churches had passed away since the last meeting: His Holiness Shenouda III, Pope of Alexandria and Patriarch of the See of St. Mark, and His Holiness Abuna Paulos I, Patriarch of the Ethiopian Orthodox Tewahedo Church who had hosted the 2012 meeting of the dialogue. The members observed a moment of silent prayer for the repose of the two patriarchs, and also for Bp. Mikhael Al-Jamil, Procurator General of the Syrian Catholic Patriarchate, a member of the dialogue who died in December 2012. Prayers were also offered for the new Coptic Orthodox Patriarch, His Holiness Pope Tawadros II, and for the new Coptic Catholic Patriarch, His Beatitude Ibrahim Isaac Sidrak. The members congratulated Most Reverend Paul Rouhana on his ordination as Maronite Bishop of Sarba in July 2012, and regretted very much that Armenian Catholic Abp. Peter Marayati of Aleppo was not able to attend because of the dramatic situation in his city.

At this 10th meeting, the members continued their study of the ways in which full communion among our churches was expressed in the first five centuries. In particular, the role of mutual recognition of saints was examined. His Eminence Dr. Gabriel Mar Gregorios presented a paper, "Saints as an Element of Communion and Communication in the Early Church: A Biblical-Theological Perspective," and Fr. Mark Sheridan, OSB, read his parallel study, "The Saints as an Element in the Communion and Communication in the Early Church." The commission also considered the procedures employed by their churches to recognize new saints. Fr. Ronald Roberson, CSP, offered a paper entitled "The Process of Recognition/Canonization of Saints in the Catholic Church in History and Today," which was coupled with a study by Abp. Nareg Alemezian, "The Procedure for Introducing a Saint into the Church Directory of Feasts - Recognition/Canonization in the Armenian Apostolic Church." Briefer summaries of the canonization/recognition procedures in their own churches were offered by Metropolitan Bishoy (Coptic Orthodox Church), His Eminence Metropolitan Theophilus George Saliba (Syrian Orthodox Church of Antioch), Fr. Daniel Seifemichael Feleke (Ethiopian Orthodox Tewahedo Church), His Eminence Metropolitan Youhanon Mar Demetrios (Malankara Orthodox Syrian Church), and His Eminence Metropolitan Theophilose Kuriakose (Malankara Syrian Orthodox Church). Based on these studies, the members noted that the mutual recognition of saints – which in the first five centuries was largely a local phenomenon – was a constitutive element in the expression of full communion at that time.

On Sept. 13–14, 2012, a drafting committee met in Rome and produced an initial draft document entitled, "The Exercise of Communion in the Life of the Early Church and its Implications for our Search for Communion Today." The bulk of the commission's time at this tenth meeting was spent carefully examining this draft text, to which a section on the mutual recognition of saints will also be added. The comments and observations of the members were noted by the drafting committee and will be taken into account as it prepares a more ample text for consideration at the next meeting.

On Jan. 25, the Commission was received in audience by Pope Benedict XVI. Metropolitan Bishoy extended greetings to the Holy Father on behalf of the members of the commission. He thanked him for the condolences he expressed upon the recent deaths of the Coptic and Ethiopian patriarchs, and for his congratulatory message to Pope Tawardos II. He also presented him with a hand painted icon of the Blessed Virgin St. Mary the Mother of God as a gift.

Pope Benedict then addressed the Commission in these words: "It is with joy in the Lord that I welcome you, the members of the Joint International Commission for Theological Dialogue between the Catholic Church and the Oriental Orthodox Churches. Through you I extend fraternal greetings to the heads of all the Oriental Orthodox Churches. In a particular way I greet His Eminence Anba Bishoy, Co-President of the Commission, and I thank him for his kind words. Before all else I would like to recall with appreciation the memory of His Holiness Shenouda III, Pope of Alexandria and Patriarch of the See of St. Mark, who died recently. I also remember with gratitude His Holiness Abuna Paulos, Patriarch of the Ethiopian Tewahedo Orthodox Church, who last year hosted the Ninth Meeting of the International Joint Commission for Theological Dialogue in Addis Ababa, Ethiopia. I was saddened, too, to learn of the death of the Most Reverend Jules Mikhael Al-Jamil, Titular Archbishop of Takrit and Procurator of the Syrian Catholic Patriarchate in Rome and a member of your Commission. I join you in prayer for the eternal rest of these dedicated servants of the Lord. Our meeting today affords us an opportunity to reflect together with gratitude on the work of the International Joint Commission, which began ten years ago, in January 2003, as an initiative of the ecclesial authorities of the family of the Oriental Orthodox Churches and the Pontifical Council for Promoting Christian Unity. In the past decade the Commission has examined from an historical perspective the various ways in which the Churches expressed their communion in the early centuries. During this week devoted to prayer for the unity of all Christ's followers, you have met to explore more fully the communion and communication which existed between the Churches in the first five centuries of Christian history. In acknowledging the progress which has been made, I express my hope that relations between the Catholic Church and the Oriental Orthodox Churches will continue to develop in a fraternal spirit of cooperation, particularly through the growth of a theological dialogue capable of helping all the Lord's followers to grow in communion and to bear witness before the world to the saving truth of the Gospel. Many of you come from areas where Christians, as individuals and communities, face painful trials and difficulties which are a source of deep concern to us all. Through you, I would like to assure all the faithful of the Middle East of my spiritual closeness and my prayer that this land, so important in God's plan of salvation, may be led, through constructive dialogue and cooperation, to a future of justice and lasting peace. All Christians need to work together in mutual acceptance and trust in serving the cause of peace and justice in fidelity to the Lord's will. May the example and intercession of the countless martyrs and saints who down the ages have borne courageous witness to Christ in all our Churches, sustain and strengthen all of us in meeting the challenges of the present with confidence and hope in the future which the Lord is opening before us. Upon you, and upon all those associated with the work of the Commission, I cordially invoke a fresh outpouring of the Holy Spirit's gifts of wisdom, joy and peace. Thank you for your attention."

Later on the same day, the members attended the Vespers Service presided over by Pope Benedict XVI in the Basilica of St. Paul the Apostle Outside the Walls for the conclusion of the Week of Prayer for Christian Unity.

Card. Koch hosted a meal at the Domus Sanctae Marthae in the Vatican on Thursday evening, Jan. 24 for the members of the dialogue commission and the staff of the Pontifical Council for Promoting Christian Unity. Card. Leonardo Sandri, Prefect of the Congregation for the Oriental Churches, also attended the dinner.

The 11th meeting of the International Joint Commission will take place in Kerala, India, hosted by the Malankara Orthodox Syrian Church. The members will plan to arrive on Monday, Jan. 27, 2014. Separate family meetings will take place on Jan. 28, followed by plenary sessions on Jan. 29– Feb. 1.

The members concluded with joyful thanks to God, the Father, the Son and the Holy Spirit, for what has been accomplished at this meeting.

RELATIONS WITH THE POLISH NATIONAL CATHOLIC CHURCH

The Roman Catholic-Polish National Catholic Dialogue issued this Joint Declaration on Unity on May 17, 2006, in Fall River, Mass.:

With thankfulness to God, the members of the Roman Catholic-Polish National Catholic dialogue in the United States look back on 22 years of theological and canonical reflection concerning the nature of our division and the possibility of reaching full communion. Because of a new outpouring of the Holy Spirit that affected both our churches following the celebration of the Second Vatican Council (1962-1965) and a similar renewal within the Polish National Catholic Church, our faithful have been rediscovering one another increasingly as brothers and sisters in the Lord. At this time we wish to review the progress that we have achieved over the past two decades, and reaffirm our intention to continue our efforts to achieve that unity for which Christ prayed.

Calls for a dialogue between our churches go back as far as 1966, when Bp. Leon Grochowski, Prime Bishop of the Polish National Catholic Church, courageously proposed such a dialogue to the Roman Catholic Bishop of Scranton. Later, in 1980, Pope John Paul II of blessed memory expressed the desire that the conference of bishops of the United States examine the relationship that exists with the Polish National Catholic Church and explore the possibility of dialogue. This resulted in an exchange of correspondence between the leaders of our churches that would culminate in the first meeting of an official dialogue in Passaic, NJ, on Oct. 23, 1984.

In view of the fact that most of the ecumenical dialogues began in the 1960s and 1970s, the establishment of our dialogue was late in coming. This was the result of the particularly painful history of our relationship and the circumstances of the origins of the Polish National Catholic Church among ethnic Polish and other Roman Catholics in the United States at the end of the 19th and the beginning of the 20th century. The disputes of that time, we now realize, were more concerned with matters of church governance than points of doctrine. Nevertheless, the complicated series of events that led to our division caused much hurt and anguish even within families whose members often found themselves on opposite sides of the dispute. The consequences of those events can still be felt among us more than a century later, and must be addressed.

For this purpose, a number of highly symbolic gestures of reconciliation have taken place, perhaps most notably at the Service of Healing that was held in St. Stanislaus Polish National Catholic Cathedral in Scranton, Pa., on

Feb. 15, 1992. Leaders of our two churches, including Card. Edward I. Cassidy (President of the Pontifical Council for Promoting Christian Unity), His Grace John F. Swantek, Prime Bishop of the Polish National Catholic Church, and the two co-chairmen of the dialogue, asked for forgiveness, and pledged to work to overcome our divisions definitively. In 1997 Bp. James C. Timlin, then the Roman Catholic Co-Chairman of the dialogue, reiterated this request for forgiveness in a letter he issued on the occasion of the centenary of the organization of the Polish National Catholic Church.

Our dialogue has achieved much. For example, in a 1989 report summarizing the first five years of the dialogue's progress, we affirmed our agreement on the seven sacraments of the Church, in spite of some differences in practice that do not touch upon our basic common faith. The report also examined two areas of divergence – our understandings of the Word of God and the life to come – and discovered that here too there are broad areas of agreement. In sum, the report was able to look back over five years of dialogue and state that "we have thus far discovered no doctrinal obstacle that would impede the further growth of our churches toward that unity which we believe is Christ's will." A second report dealing with developments in our dialogue from 1989 to 2002 was published in 2003.

In view of this progress, concrete steps have been taken. In response to an inquiry from the Archbishop of Baltimore, Card. William Keeler, then President of the National Conference of Catholic Bishops, Card. Edward Cassidy, President of the Pontifical Council for Promoting Christian Unity, stated in 1993 that members of the Polish National Catholic Church in the United States and Canada may receive the sacraments of Penance, Holy Communion and Anointing of the Sick from Roman Catholic priests if they ask for them on their own, are properly disposed and not otherwise excluded from the sacraments in line with the provisions of canon 844 §3 of The Code of Canon Law. This was followed in 1996 by a letter by Abp. Oscar H. Lipscomb, the Chairman of the Bishops' Committee for Ecumenical and Interreligious Affairs, to the bishops of the United States spelling out in more detail the conditions under which Polish National Catholics may receive the aforementioned sacraments in the Roman Catholic Church. In 1998 the Polish National Catholic Church issued Guidelines for the Reception by Polish National Catholics of Sacraments in the Roman Catholic Church. Canon 844 §2 of The Code of Canon Law also specifies conditions under which Roman Catholics may receive the sacraments in the Polish National Catholic Church.

In light of these concrete steps toward unity, we have much for which to be thankful. Furthermore, we recognize each other's ecclesial character and sacraments, allow a certain amount of sacramental sharing, and maintain many of the same traditions. These facts bear witness to how much we have rediscovered as our common heritage. Our mutual esteem clearly rules out inappropriate actions such as proselytism among each other's faithful or the re-ordination of clergy who pass from one church to the other.

During our century-long division we have grown apart in ways that at first glance make reconciliation appear to be difficult. The Polish National Catholic Church, which during most of its existence was a member of the Union of Utrecht, has developed a strong sense of autonomy and the desire to preserve its distinctive traditions, including the vital role played by the laity in church governance. Even though the primacy and infallibility of the Bishop of Rome was not an issue at the time of our division, our churches today have different understandings of the Pope's role in the Church. Another complicating factor is the presence of a significant number of former Roman Catholic priests in the ranks of the Polish National Catholic clergy. Such is the legacy of the divisions of the past that remain with us today.

At this point in our relationship, therefore, we the members of the Polish National Catholic-Roman Catholic dialogue wish to reaffirm our resolve to overcome what still divides us, and to state clearly that our goal is full communion between our churches. We wish to emphasize that "full communion" does not imply absorption or uniformity, but a unity that fully recognizes differing traditions that are consistent with our common apostolic faith. It must still be determined if any of our divergent traditions are truly church-dividing, or simply examples of legitimate diversity which, in the words of Pope John Paul II, "is in no way opposed to the Church's unity, but rather enhances her splendor and contributes greatly to the fulfillment of her mission" (*Ut Unum Sint*, No. 50). We plan to give further consideration to other concrete steps concerning reciprocity in regard to the sacraments, acting as godparents, and the requirement of canonical form for lawfulness only in mixed marriages. We are equally committed to a thorough examination of the theological concepts of primacy and conciliarity. This will include searching for a common understanding of the ministry of the Bishop of Rome in the Church.

As members of a commission authorized to engage in this ecumenical dialogue, our role is not to speak definitively for either of our churches. Nevertheless, we hope to propose new incremental steps that will make concrete the growing unity between us, and we wish our faithful to know of our conviction that a way can be found to overcome this regrettable division that took place among Catholics here in the United States. We know that the goal of unity is nothing less than the will of Christ for us. Therefore we ask the faithful of both our churches to join us in fervent prayer that, with a new outpouring of the Holy Spirit, the barriers between us will fall and we will one day soon find ourselves joined again in that perfect unity that befits the disciples of our Lord Jesus Christ.

The 2013 meeting of the Polish National Catholic-Roman Catholic Dialogue

The 2013 session of the Polish National Catholic (PNCC) – Roman Catholic Dialogue took place at the PNCC's National Church Center in Scranton, Pennsylvania, on May 20–21. The meeting was chaired jointly by Aux. Bp. Mitchell T. Rozanski of the Archdiocese of Baltimore and Bp. John Mack of the PNCC Buffalo-Pittsburgh diocese.

During the course of the meeting, the members examined a number of ecumenical developments and major events in the lives of their churches. These included the Special PNCC General Synod that was held on June 22, 2012, in Scranton, Pa. that elected two new bishops; Card. Walter Kasper's 2009 book, *Harvesting the Fruits: Basic Aspects of Christian Faith in Ecumenical Dialogue*; the Union of Scranton and the Nordic Catholic Church; two documents of the international Orthodox-Catholic Dialogue: "Ecclesiological and Canonical Consequences of the Sacramental Nature of the Church: Ecclesial Communion, Conciliarity and Authority (The 2007 Ravenna Document), and the 2008 draft text, "The Role of the Bishop of Rome in the Communion of the Church in the First

Millennium" (the Crete Document); PNCC Reactions to Anglicanorum Coetibus; the 2010 "Vision Statement" of the North American Orthodox-Catholic Theological Consultation, "Steps Toward a Reunited Church: A Sketch of an Orthodox-Catholic Vision for the Future"; and the 2003 U.S. Faith and Order Commission's response to *Ut Unum Sint* on Petrine Ministry

All these texts and developments were discussed at some length. The members were particularly grateful for the "Vision Statement" of the North American Orthodox-

Catholic dialogue because it offered creative ideas regarding the ministry of the Bishop of Rome in the event of a full reconciliation among our churches.

Bp. Rozanski announced that Bp. Matthew Ustrzycki, Aux. Bp. of Hamilton, Ontario, had resigned from the dialogue. Bp. Rozanski expressed his gratitude for Bp. Ustrzycki's service, and looked forward to the nomination of a new representative of the Canadian Conference of Catholic Bishops in time for the 2014 meeting. It is due to take place on Feb. 24–25, 2014, in Miami.

REFORMATION CHURCHES
LEADERS AND DOCTRINES OF THE REFORMATION

Some of the leading figures, doctrines and churches of the Reformation are covered below. A companion article covers Major Protestant Churches in the U.S.

LEADERS

John Wycliff (c. 1320-1384): English priest and scholar who advanced one of the leading Reformation ideas nearly 200 years before Martin Luther — that the Bible alone is the sufficient rule of faith — but had only an indirect influence on the 16th century Reformers. Supporting belief in an inward and practical religion, he denied the divinely commissioned authority of the pope and bishops of the Church; he also denied the Real Presence of Christ in the Holy Eucharist, and wrote against the sacrament of penance and the doctrine of indulgences. Nearly 20 of his propositions were condemned by Gregory XI in 1377; his writings were proscribed more extensively by the Council of Constance in 1415. His influence was strongest in Bohemia and Central Europe.

John Hus (c. 1369-1415): A Bohemian priest and preacher of reform who authored 30 propositions condemned by the Council of Constance. Excommunicated in 1411 or 1412, he was burned at the stake in 1415. His principal errors concerned the nature of the Church and the origin of papal authority. He spread some of the ideas of Wycliff but did not subscribe to his views regarding faith alone as the condition for justification and salvation, the sole sufficiency of Scripture as the rule of faith, the Real Presence of Christ in the Eucharist, and the sacramental system. In 1457 some of his followers founded the Church of the Brotherhood which later became known as the United Brethren or Moravian Church and is considered the earliest independent Protestant body.

Martin Luther (1483-1546): An Augustinian friar, priest and doctor of theology, the key figure in the Reformation. In 1517, as a special indulgence was being preached in Germany, and in view of needed reforms within the Church, he published at Wittenberg 95 theses concerning matters of Catholic belief and practice. Leo X condemned 41 statements from Luther's writings in 1520. Luther, refusing to recant, was excommunicated the following year. His teachings strongly influenced subsequent Lutheran theology; its statements of faith are found in the Book of Concord (1580).

Luther's doctrines included the following: The sin of Adam, which corrupted human nature radically (but not substantially), has affected every aspect of man's being. Justification, understood as the forgiveness of sins and the state of righteousness, is by grace for Christ's sake through faith. Faith involves not merely intellectual assent but an act of confidence by the will. Good works are indispensably necessary concomitants of faith, but do not merit salvation. Of the sacraments, Luther retained baptism, penance and

the Holy Communion as effective vehicles of the grace of the Holy Spirit; he held that in the Holy Communion the consecrated bread and wine are the Body and Blood of Christ. The rule of faith is the divine revelation in the Sacred Scriptures. He rejected purgatory, indulgences and the invocation of the saints, and held that prayers for the dead have no efficacy. Catholics clarified their positions at the Council of Trent. The 1999 Joint Declaration indicates that the condemnations of doctrine by the Council of Trent and the Book of Concord do not apply to present day Catholic and Lutheran teaching respectively.

Ulrich Zwingli (1484-1531): A priest who triggered the Reformation in Switzerland with a series of New Testament lectures in 1519, later disputations and by other actions. He held the Gospel to be the only basis of truth; rejected the Mass (which he suppressed in 1525 at Zurich), penance and other sacraments; denied papal primacy and doctrine concerning purgatory and the invocation of saints; rejected celibacy, monasticism and many traditional practices of piety. His symbolic view of the Eucharist, which was at odds with Catholic doctrine, caused an irreconcilable controversy with Luther and his followers. Zwingli was killed in a battle between the forces of Protestant and Catholic cantons in Switzerland.

John Calvin (1509-64): French leader of the Reformation in Switzerland, whose key tenet was absolute predestination of some persons to heaven and others to hell. He rejected Catholic doctrine in 1533 after becoming convinced of a personal mission to reform the Church. In 1536 he published the first edition of Institutes of the Christian Religion, a systematic exposition of his doctrine which became the classic textbook of Reformed – as distinguished from Lutheran – theology. To Luther's principal theses – regarding Scripture as the sole rule of faith, the radical corruption of human nature, and justification by faith alone – he added absolute predestination, certitude of salvation for the elect, and the incapability of the elect to lose grace. Calvin's Eucharist teaching, while affirming Christ's true presence, was not able to find agreement with that of Luther. However, in our own time, agreement has been reached between Lutherans and Reformed (Calvinists), and considerable progress has been made with Catholics and Orthodox toward a common understanding of Christ's presence in Communion.

CHURCHES AND MOVEMENTS

Adventists: Members of several Christian groups whose doctrines are dominated by belief in a more or less imminent second advent or coming of Christ upon earth for a glorious 1,000-year reign of righteousness. This reign, following victory by the forces of good over evil in a final Battle of Armageddon, will begin with the resurrection of the chosen and will end with the resurrection of all others and the annihilation of the wicked. Thereafter, the just will live forever in a renewed heaven and earth. A sleep of the soul takes place between the time of death and the day of judgment. There is no hell. The Bible, in literalist interpretation, is regarded as the only rule of faith and practice. About six churches have developed in the course of the Adventist movement which originated with William Miller (1782-1849) in the U.S. Miller, on the basis of calculations made from the Book of Daniel, predicted that the second advent of Christ would occur between 1843 and 1844. After the prophecy went unfulfilled, divisions occurred in the movement and the Seventh Day Adventists, whose actual formation dates from 1860, emerged as the largest single body. The observance of Saturday instead of Sunday as the Lord's Day dates from 1844.

Anabaptism: Originated in Saxony in the first quarter of the 16th century and spread rapidly through southern Germany. Its doctrine included several key Lutheran tenets but was not regarded with favor by Luther, Calvin or Zwingli. Anabaptists believed that baptism is for adults only and that infant baptism is invalid. Their doctrine of the Inner Light, concerning the direct influence of the Holy Spirit on the believer, implied rejection of Catholic doctrine concerning the sacraments and the nature of the Church. Eighteen artcles of faith were formulated in 1632 in Holland. Mennonites are Anabaptists.

Arminianism: A modification of the rigid predestinationism of Calvin, set forth by Jacob Arminius (1560-1609) and formally stated in the Remonstrance of 1610. Arminianism influenced some Calvinist bodies.

Baptists: So called because of their doctrine concerning baptism. They reject infant baptism and consider only baptism by immersion as valid. Leaders in the formation of the church were John Smyth (d. 1612) in England and Roger Williams (d. 1683) in America. Baptists are congregational in church government, and therefore are gathered into a variety of groupings, often called Conventions, the largest Protestant community in the US being the Southern Baptist Convention.

Congregationalists: Evangelical in spirit and seeking a return to forms of the primitive church, they uphold individual freedom in religious matters, do not require the acceptance of a creed as a condition for communion, and regard each congregation as autonomous. Robert Browne influenced the beginnings of Congregationalism.

Disciples: From a 19th century revival movement and desire for the unity of the Christian churches, a network of congregations developed which desired to be called simply "Christian churches." These churches opened their communion and membership to all, celebrated the Eucharist each Sunday and baptized only adults. From this movement the Christian Church/Disciples of Christ, the Churches of Christ and the independent Christian Churches emerged.

Methodists: A group who broke away from the Anglican Communion under the leadership of John Wesley (1703-1791), although some Anglican beliefs were retained. Doctrines include the witness of the Spirit to the individual and personal assurance of salvation. The largest Methodist body in the United States is the United Methodist Church. There are three Black Methodist bodies: African Methodist Episcopal, African Methodist Episcopal Zion, and Christian Methodist Episcopal Churches. There are also several Holiness Churches in the Wesleyan tradition: i.e., Nazarene, Free Methodist, Wesleyan Church.

Pentecostals: Churches that grew up after the 1906 enthusiastic revival, accompanied by the phenomena of speaking in foreign tongues and the experience of baptism in the Holy Spirit. From this revival churches of a Methodist or Baptist theological emphasis emerged, such as the Church of God in Christ or the Assemblies of God. In the mid-20th century, the charismatic experience began to be shared by some members of the classical churches, including Roman Catholic.

Puritans: Congregationalists who sought church reform along Calvinist lines in severe simplicity. (Use of the term was generally discontinued after 1660.)

Presbyterians: Basically Calvinistic, called Presbyterian because church polity centers around assemblies of presbyters or elders. John Knox (c. 1513-1572) established the church in Scotland.

Quakers: Their key belief is in internal divine illumination, the inner light of the living Christ, as the only source of truth and inspiration. George Fox (1624-1691) was one of their leaders in England. Called the Society of Friends, the Quakers are noted for their pacifism.

Unitarianism: A 16th century doctrine which rejected the Trinity and the divinity of Christ in favor of a uni-personal God. It claimed scriptural support for a long time but became generally rationalistic with respect to "revealed" doctrine as well as in ethics and its world-view. One of its principal early proponents was Faustus Socinus (1539-1604), a leader of the Polish Brethren. A variety of communions developed in England in the Reformation and post-Reformation periods.

Universalism: A product of 18th-century liberal Protestantism in England. The doctrine is not Trinitarian and includes a tenet that all men will ultimately be saved.

Anglican Communion: This communion, which regards itself as the same apostolic Church as that which was established by early Christians in England, derived not from Reformation influences but from the renunciation of papal jurisdiction by Henry VIII (1491-1547). His Act of Supremacy in 1534 called Christ's Church an assembly of local churches subject to the prince, who was vested with fullness of authority and jurisdiction. In spite of Henry's denial of papal authority, this Act did not reject substantially other principal articles of faith. Notable changes, proposed and adopted for the reformation of the church, took place in the subsequent reigns of Edward VI and Elizabeth, with respect to such matters as Scripture as the rule of faith, the sacraments, the nature of the Mass, and the constitution of the hierarchy. There are more than 27 provinces (national churches with their own canon law, primate and hierarchy) in the Anglican Communion. (See Episcopal Church, Anglican Orders, Anglican-Catholic Final Report.)

MAJOR PROTESTANT CHURCHES IN THE UNITED STATES

There are more than 250 Protestant church bodies in the U.S.

The majority of U.S. Protestants belong to the following denominations: Baptist, Methodist, Lutheran, Presbyterian, Episcopal, the United Church of Christ, the Christian Church (Disciples of Christ), Pentecostals and a variety of evangelical congregations and denominations.

See Ecumenical Dialogues, Reports and related entries for coverage of relations between the Catholic Church and other Christian churches.

Baptist Churches

Baptist churches, comprising the largest of all American Protestant denominations, were first established by John Smyth near the beginning of the 17th century in England. The first Baptist church in America was founded at Providence by Roger Williams in 1639.

Largest of the nearly 30 Baptist bodies in the U.S. are: The Southern Baptist Convention, 901 Commerce St., Suite 750, Nashville, TN 37203, with 16 million members. The National Baptist Convention, U.S.A., Inc., 915 Spain St., Baton Rouge, LA 70802, with 5.1 million members. The National Baptist Convention of America, Inc., 1320 Pierre Ave., Shreveport, LA 71103, with 3.5 million members. The American Baptist Churches in the U.S.A., P.O. Box 851, Valley Forge, PA 19482, with 1.3 million members. The total number of U.S. Baptists is more than 29 million. The world total is 33 million.

Proper to Baptists is their doctrine on baptism. Called an "ordinance" rather than a sacrament, baptism by immersion is a sign that one has experienced and decided in favor of the salvation offered by Christ. It is administered only to persons who are able to make a responsible decision. Baptism is not administered to infants.

Baptists do not have a formal creed but generally subscribe to two professions of faith formulated in 1689 and 1832 and are in general agreement with classical Protestant theology regarding Scripture as the sole rule of faith, original sin, justification through faith in Christ, and the nature of the Church. Their local churches are autonomous.

Worship services differ in form from one congregation to another. Usual elements are the reading of Scripture, a sermon, hymns, vocal and silent prayer. The Lord's Supper, called an "ordinance," is celebrated at various times during the year.

Christian Church (Disciples of Christ)

The Christian Church (Disciples of Christ) originated early in the 1800s from two movements against rigid denominationalism led by Presbyterians Thomas and Alexander Campbell in western Pennsylvania and Barton W. Stone in Kentucky. The two movements developed separately for about 25 years before being merged in 1832.

The church, which identifies itself with the Protestant mainstream, has nearly one million members in almost 3,600 congregations in the U.S. and Canada. The greatest concentration of members in the U.S. is located roughly along the old frontier line, in an arc sweeping from Ohio and Kentucky through the Midwest and down into Oklahoma and Texas.

The general offices of the church are located at 130 E. Washington St., Indianapolis, IN 46204. The church's persistent concern for Christian unity is based on a conviction expressed in a basic document, Declaration and Address, dating from its founding. The document states: "The church of Christ upon earth is essentially, intentionally and constitutionally one."

The Disciples have no official doctrine or dogma. Their worship practices vary widely from more common informal services to what could almost be described as "high church" services. Membership is granted after a simple statement of belief in Jesus Christ and baptism by immersion; most congregations admit un-immersed transfers from other denominations. The Lord's Supper or Eucharist, generally called Communion, is always open to Christians of all persuasions. Lay men and women routinely preside over the Lord's Supper, which is celebrated each Sunday; they often preach and perform other pastoral functions as well. Distinction between ordained and non-ordained members is blurred somewhat because of the Disciples' emphasis on all members of the church as ministers.

The Christian Church is oriented to congregational government, and has a unique structure in which three sections of polity (general, regional and congregational) operate as equals rather than in a pyramid of authority. At the national or international level, it is governed by a general assembly which has voting representation direct from congregations and regions as well as all ordained and licensed clergy.

Episcopal Church

The Episcopal Church, which includes over 100 dioceses in the United States, Central and South America, and elsewhere overseas, regards itself as part of the same apostolic church which was established by early Christians in England. Established in this country during the colonial period, it became independent of the jurisdiction of the Church of England when a new constitution and Prayer Book were adopted at a general convention held in 1789. It has approximately two million members worldwide.

Offices of the presiding bishop and the executive council are located at 815 Second Ave., New York, NY 10017.

The presiding bishop is chief pastor and primate; he or she is elected by the House of Bishops and confirmed by the House of Deputies for a term of nine years.

The Episcopal Church, which is a part of the Anglican Communion, regards the Archbishop of Canterbury as the "First among Equals," though not under his authority.

The Anglican Communion, worldwide, has 85 million members in more than 165 countries and 38 self governing churches.

Official statements of belief and practice are found in the Book of Common Prayer. Scripture has primary importance with respect to the rule of faith, and authority is also attached to tradition.

An episcopal system of church government prevails, but presbyters, deacons and lay persons also have an active voice in church affairs. The levels of government are the general convention, and executive council, dioceses, and local parishes. At the parish level, the congregation has the right to select its own rector, with the consent of the bishop.

Liturgical worship is according to the Book of Common Prayer as adopted in 1979, but details of ceremonial practice vary from one congregation to another.

Lutheran Churches

The origin of Lutheranism is generally traced to Oct. 31, 1517, when Martin Luther — Augustinian friar, priest, doctor of theology — tacked "95 Theses" to the door of the castle church in Wittenberg, Germany. This call to debate on the subject of indulgences and related concerns has come to symbolize the beginning of the Reformation. Luther and his supporters intended to reform the Church they knew. Though Lutheranism has come to be visible in separate denominations and national churches, at its heart it professes itself to be a confessional movement within the one, holy, catholic and apostolic Church.

The world's 75 million Lutherans form the third largest grouping of Christians, after Roman Catholics and Orthodox. 70.5 million of them belong to church bodies which make up the Lutheran World Federation, headquartered in Geneva.

There are around 8 million Lutherans in the United States, making them the fourth largest Christian grouping, after Roman Catholics, Baptists and Methodists. There are nearly 20 U.S. Lutheran church bodies. The largest is the Evangelical Lutheran Church in America (with 4.2 million members and headquarters at 8765 W. Higgins Rd., Chicago, IL 60631), The Lutheran Church Missouri Synod (with 2.2 million members and headquarters at 1333 S. Kirkwood Rd., St. Louis, MO 63122), the Wisconsin Evangelical Lutheran Synod (with 385,000 members and headquarters at 2929 N. Mayfair Rd., Milwaukee, WI 53222) and two newer Lutheran Church bodies established after the year 2,000 (Congregations in Mission for Christ with 321,000 members, with headquarters at 7000 N Sheldon Rd, Canton, MI 48187; and the North American Lutheran Church with 125,000 members with headquarters at 3500 Mill Run Dr., Hilliard, OH 43026).

The Evangelical Lutheran Church in America and the Lutheran Church Missouri Synod carry out some work together through inter Lutheran agencies such as Lutheran World Relief, Lutheran Immigration and Refugee Services located at 700 Light Street, Baltimore, MD 21230; and Lutheran Services in America located at 100 Maryland Avenue, NE Suite 500, Washington, DC 20002.

The statements of faith which have shaped the confessional life of Lutheranism are found in the Book of Concord. This 1580 collection includes the three ancient ecumenical creeds (Apostles', Nicene and Athanasian), Luther's Large and Small Catechisms (1529), the Augsburg Confession (1530) and the Apology in defense of it (1531), the Smalkald Articles (including the "Treatise on the Power and Primacy of the Pope") (1537), and the Formula of Concord (1577).

The central Lutheran doctrinal proposition is that Christians "receive forgiveness of sins and become righteous before God by grace, for Christ's sake." The Joint Declaration on the Doctrine of Justification between the Vatican and the Lutheran World Federation is valued for its ecumenical and historical agreement. Foundational work for the JDDJ was done at the ELCA-US Conference of Catholic Bishops dialogue. The Methodist World Council has also affirmed the JDDJ. In preparation for the 500th Anniversary of the Reformation, the LWF and Vatican dialogue produced "From Conflict to Communion," as a common statement on history and developing relationships between Lutherans and Catholics.

Baptism and the Lord's Supper (Holy Communion, the Eucharist) are universally celebrated among Lutherans as sacramental means of grace. Lutherans also treasure the Word proclaimed in the reading of the Scriptures, preaching and absolution.

In the ELCA, the bishop is the minister of ordination. Much of Lutheranism continues what it understands as the historic succession of bishops (though without considering the historic episcopate essential for the church). All of Lutheranism is concerned to preserve apostolic succession in life and doctrine. Lutheran churches in Scandinavia and the Baltics, in the U.S., and in Canada have moved into full communion with their Anglican counterparts.

Lutheran jurisdictions corresponding to dioceses are called districts or synods in North America. There are more than 100 of them; each of them is headed by a bishop or president. The Evangelical Lutheran Church in America moved into full communion with the three Reformed Churches (Presbyterian Church, United Church of Christ and Reformed Church in America) in 1997, and in 2000 into full communion with the Episcopal Church, all of its bishops being ordained by bishops including those in the apostolic succession as understood by Anglicans. It moved into full communion with the Moravian Church in 1999. In 2009, the ELCA and the United Methodist Church entered full communion.

Methodist Churches

John Wesley (1703 1791), an Anglican priest, was the founder of the 'Arminian' branch of Methodism (distinguished from a much smaller, parallel Calvinistic Methodism – most notably represented by the revivalistic preacher, George Whitefield (1714-1770) – that rejected Wesley's core emphases on free will and the doctrine of Christian perfection). The earliest expressions of Methodism manifested at Oxford University during Wesley's time there. Subsequently, in 1738, following a period of missionary work in America and a significant encounter with the Moravians, he had his Aldersgate conversion experience in which he received assurance of his salvation and shortly thereafter became a key leader in a religious awakening in England. By the end of the 18th century, Methodism had also taken root in America and many other parts of the world into which the British Empire was expanding. By the middle of the 19th century, the (then) Methodist Episcopal Church was the single largest denomination in the American republic.

The United Methodist Church, formed in 1968 by a merger of the Methodist Church and the Evangelical United Brethren Church, is one of the largest Protestant denominations in the U.S., with more than eight million members (and over eleven million members worldwide); its principal agencies are located in New York, Evanston, IL, Nashville, TN, and Washington, DC. The second largest Methodist body, with just under two million members, is the African Methodist Episcopal Church. Five other major Wesleyan Methodist churches in the U.S. are the African Methodist Episcopal Zion Church, Christian Methodist Episcopal Church, Free Methodist Church, Wesleyan Church, and the Salvation Army. The total Methodist membership in the U.S. is about 15.5 million.

Worldwide, there are more than 73 autonomous Methodist/Wesleyan churches in 107 countries, with a membership of more than 33 million. Many of them participate in the World Methodist Council (P.O. Box 518, Lake Junaluska, NC 28745), which serves as an ecumenical expression of similar and shared Wesleyan Methodist perspectives on the Christian faith. Significantly, Wesleyan Methodism is also a forerunner of many branches of Pentecostalism worldwide.

Wesleyan Methodism rejects predestination and maintains that Christ offers grace freely to all persons, not just to an elect. In addition to a strong emphasis upon free will and personal assurance of salvation, John Wesley stressed a doctrine of Christian perfection (in which the justified believer lived out their faith in Christ by seeking to be conformed to the image of God as embodied in the perfect love of Jesus). Thus, while Methodists expected a conversion – like many other Evangelical churches of the 18th and 19th centuries – they also placed strong emphasis upon the importance of sanctification. Methodists are in general agreement with many points of Protestant theology regarding Scripture as the sole rule of faith, original sin, justification through faith in Christ, and the sacraments of baptism and the Lord's Supper; while also stressing the significance of tradition and experience of the Holy Spirit in their role in illumining the meaning of Scripture. In The United Methodist Church, polity is a hybrid of a presbyterian conference structure (Annual Conferences over geographic areas and a General Conference to govern the denomination) with bishops who are specialized elders (presbyters) set aside for certain specific functions such as presiding over meetings of Conference, officiating at ordinations, and appointing ministers to local churches. Churches stemming from British Methodism do not have bishops but vest appointive powers within an appropriate conference. Clergy serving local congregations are generally free to choose various forms of worship services; typical elements include readings from Scripture, sermons, hymns and prayers. In 2006 the World Methodist Council signed on to the Joint Declaration on the Doctrine of Justification with Lutherans and Catholics.

Presbyterian Churches

Presbyterians are so called because of their tradition of governing the church through a system of representative bodies composed of elders (presbyters).

Presbyterianism is a part of the Reformed Family of Churches that grew out of the theological work of John Calvin following the Lutheran Reformation, to which it is heavily indebted. Countries in which it acquired early strength and influence were Switzerland, France, Holland, Scotland and England. Presbyterianism spread widely in this country in the latter part of the 18th century and afterwards. Presently, it has approximately 4.5 million communicants in nine bodies. The two largest Presbyterian bodies in the country – the United Presbyterian Church in the U.S.A. and the Presbyterian Church in the United States – were reunited in June 1983, to form the Presbyterian Church (U.S.A.), with a membership of 2.7 million. Its national offices are located at 100 Witherspoon St., Louisville, KY 40202. The church is closely allied with the Reformed Church in America, the Christian Reformed Church – both of Dutch background, the United Church of Christ, the Cumberland Presbyterian Churches, the Korean Presbyterian Church in America and the Associate Reformed Presbyterian Church.

In Presbyterian doctrine, baptism and the Lord's Supper, viewed as seals of the covenant of grace, are regarded as sacraments. Baptism, which is not necessary for salvation, is conferred on infants and adults The Lord's Supper is celebrated as a covenant of the Sacrifice of Christ. In both sacraments, a doctrine of the real presence of Christ is considered the central theological principle. The Church is twofold, being invisible and also visible; it consists of all of the elect and all those Christians who are united in Christ as their immediate head.

Presbyterians are in general agreement with classical Protestant theology regarding Scripture as the sole rule of faith and practice, salvation by grace, and justification through faith in Christ. Presbyterian congregations are governed by a council called a session composed of elders elected by the communicant membership. On higher levels there are other councils called presbyteries, synods and a general assembly with various degrees of authority over local bodies; all such representative bodies are composed of elected ruling elders and teaching elders (ministers) in approximately equal numbers. The church elects a moderator every other year who presides at the General Assembly and travels throughout the church to speak to and hear from the members. Worship services, simple and dignified, include sermons, prayer, reading of the Scriptures

and hymns. The Lord's Supper is celebrated at intervals. Doctrinal developments of the past several years included approval in May, 1967, by the General Assembly of the United Presbyterian Church of a contemporary confession of faith to supplement the historic Westminster Confession. A statement entitled "The Declaration of Faith" was approved in 1977 by the Presbyterian Church in the U.S. for teaching and liturgical use. The reunited church adopted "A Brief Statement of Reformed Faith" in 1991 regarding urgent concerns of the church. The Presbyterian Church, USA, along with the Reformed Church in America and the United Church of Christ, has moved into full communion with the Evangelical Lutheran Church in America in 1997.

United Church of Christ

The 1,058,423 member (in 2010) United Church of Christ was formed in 1957 by a union of the Congregational Christian and the Evangelical and Reformed Churches. The former was originally established by the Pilgrims, the Puritans of the Massachusetts Bay Colony, while the latter was founded in Pennsylvania in the early 1700s by settlers from Central Europe. It considers itself "a united and uniting church" and keeps itself open to all ecumenical options. Its headquarters are located at 700 Prospect, Cleveland, OH 44115.

Its statement of faith recognizes Jesus Christ as "our crucified and risen Lord (who) shared our common lot, conquering sin and death and reconciling the world to himself." It believes in the life after death, and the fact that God "judges men and nations by his righteous will declared through prophets and apostles."

The United Church further believes that Christ calls its members to share in his baptism "and eat at his table, to join him in his passion and victory." Each local church is free to adopt its own methods of worship and to formulate its own covenants and confessions of faith. Some celebrate communion weekly; others, monthly or on another periodical basis. The United Church is governed along congregational lines, and each local church is autonomous. However, the actions of its biennial General Synod are taken with great seriousness by congregations. Between synods, a 44-member executive council oversees the work of the church. In 1989 the UCC moved into full communion with the Christian Church (Disciples of Christ) and in 1997 with the Evangelical Lutheran Church in America.

Evangelicalism

The revivalist evangelical movement, dating from 1735 in England (the Evangelical Revival) and after 1740 in the United States (the Great Awakening), has had and continues to have widespread influence in Protestant churches. It has been estimated that about 45 million American Protestants – communicants of both large denominations and small bodies – are evangelicals.

The Bible is their rule of faith and religious practice. Being born again in a life-changing experience through faith in Christ is the promise of salvation. Missionary work for the spread of the Gospel is a normal and necessary activity.

Additional matters of belief and practice are generally of a conservative character. Fundamentalists, numbering perhaps 4.5 million, comprise an extreme right-wing subculture of evangelicalism. They are distinguished mainly by militant biblicism, belief in the absolute inerrancy of the Bible and emphasis on the Second Coming of Christ. Fundamentalism developed early in the 20th century in reaction against liberal theology and secularizing trends in mainstream and other Protestant denominations.

The Holiness or Perfectionist wing of evangelicalism evolved from Methodist efforts to preserve, against a contrary trend, the personal-piety and inner-religion concepts of John Wesley. There are at least 30 Holiness bodies in the U.S.

Pentecostals, probably the most demonstrative of evangelicals, are noted for speaking in tongues and the stress they place on healing, prophecy and personal testimony to the practice and power of evangelical faith. There are strong charismatic movements within many of the historic Protestant churches and Roman Catholicism.

The evangelical communities have national and international ecumenical bodies. Black and white Pentecostal churches belong to the Pentecostal and Charismatic Fellowship of North America. Over 40 Pentecostal, Holiness and evangelical churches belong to the US National Association of Evangelicals. Internationally, these national evangelical associations collaborate in the World Evangelical Alliance.

Assemblies of God

Assemblies (Churches) of God form the largest body (more than 2 million members) in the Pentecostal Movement which developed from (1) the Holiness Revival in the Methodist Church after the Civil War and (2) the Apostolic Faith Movement at the beginning of the 20th century. Members share with other Pentecostals belief in the religious experience of conversion and in the baptism by the Holy Spirit that sanctifies. Distinctive is the emphasis placed on the charismatic gifts of the apostolic church, healing and speaking in tongues, which are signs of the "second blessing" of the Holy Spirit.

The Assemblies are conservative and biblicist in theology; are loosely organized in various districts, with democratic procedures; are vigorously evangelistic. The moral code is rigid.

RELATIONS WITH ANGLICANS AND PROTESTANTS

ANGLICAN-ROMAN CATHOLIC FINAL REPORT

The Anglican Roman Catholic International Commission issued a Final Report in 1982 on 12 years of dialogue on major issues of concern, especially the Eucharist and ordained ministry.

In 1988 the Lambeth Conference called parts of the report on these two subjects "consonant in substance with the faith of Anglicans." In 1991 the Congregation for the Doctrine of the Faith and the Pontifical Council for Promoting Christian Unity called the Report a significant milestone not only in relations between the Catholic Church and the Anglican Communion but in the ecumenical movement as a whole. They said, however, that it was not yet possible to state that substantial agreement had been reached on all the questions studied by the commission, and that important differences still remained with respect to essential matters of Catholic doctrine regarding the Eucharist, ordination and other subjects. Clarifications were requested.

The Anglican Roman Catholic Commission II responded in 1994, saying that its members were in agreement regarding:

• the substantial and sacramental presence of Christ in the Eucharist;

• the propitiatory nature of the Eucharistic Sacrifice, which can also be applied to the deceased;

• institution of the sacrament of order from Christ;

• the character of priestly ordination, implying configuration to the priesthood of Christ.

In 1994 Card. Edward I. Cassidy, president of the Pontifical Council for Interreligious Dialogue addressed a letter to the Catholic and Anglican co chairmen of the commission, responding to the clarifications, stating that "no further work" seems to be necessary at this time on Eucharist and ministry. Questions still remained to be answered about a number of subjects, including the authority in the Church, ordination of women, infallibility and Marian doctrine.

THE RELATIONSHIP BETWEEN ANGLICANS AND ROMAN CATHOLICS

By Dr. John Borelli, assistant to the President, Georgetown University.

A special consultation of Roman Catholic and Anglican bishops from 13 regions around the world met in Mississauga, Ontario, May 14-20, 2000, to review and evaluate the accomplishment of thirty years of dialogue between the two traditions and to reflect on how the special relationship has been developing in various parts of the world. Bishops attended from New Zealand, Canada, England, United States, Ireland, India, Nigeria, Papua New Guinea, Southern Africa, Uganda, Australia, Brazil and the West Indies.

The meeting was convened by Card. Edward Cassidy, then President of the Pontifical Council Promoting Christian Unity, and Archbp. George Carey of Canterbury. Also participating were the two recently appointed co-chairman for the Anglican-Roman Catholic International Commission: the Most Rev. Frank T. Griswold, Presiding Bishop of the Episcopal Church (U. S.) and Bp. Alexander J. Brunett, Archbishop of Seattle.

The meeting grew out of the visit of Archbishop Carey with Pope John Paul II in Advent 1996 and was suggested in their Common Declaration of Dec. 5, 1996, "it may be opportune at this stage in our journey to consult further about how the relationship between the Anglican Communion and the Catholic Church is to progress." With consensus yet to be achieved on authority in the church and with the new situation created by ordination of women as priests and bishops in some provinces of the Anglican Communion becoming increasingly evident, a certain amount of risk was involved in calling for a special consultation. The meeting could end in a standoff on certain issues and might even conclude with a simple acknowledgment of past achievements, current good will, and hope that the future will be brighter. These scenarios would be viewed as evidence that the dialogue is deadlocked or, at best, lost in a maze of seemingly endless study of details and differences and no certain direction towards reconciliation. Over three years were spent in preparations for the special consultation. Independent provinces of the Anglican Communion and national conferences of Catholic bishops were asked twice in the course of the planning to advise on agenda and other aspects of the proposed meeting. It was postponed once from May 1999 to May 2000 so that careful reflection and thorough preparation could take place first, and conveniently the meeting did not coincide other developments related to restoration of unity between Anglicans and Catholics.

In the meantime, the Lambeth Conference met in July 1998. The Lambeth Conference is a meeting of Anglican bishops, currently from 36 provinces and other churches in the communion worldwide, and one of its actions in 1998 was to receive "the Virginia Report," prepared by the Inter-Anglican Theological and Doctrinal Commission. This study is a response to the particular need recognized by the Lambeth Conference of 1988 for exploration of the meaning and nature of communion and how the Anglican Communion makes authoritative decisions while maintaining unity and interdependence among the independent provinces. The Lambeth Conference of 1998 recommended the report for study throughout the Communion. Also, in May 1999, the Anglican-Roman Catholic International Commission released its third agreed statement on authority in the Church, "The Gift of Authority," which among other suggestions lists eleven advances points of consensus on authority (See page 102 of the *2000 Catholic Almanac*). In a dramatic gesture of unity, on Jan. 18, 2000, Abp. Carey assisted Pope John Paul II in opening the holy door at St. Paul-Outside-the-Walls Basilica. Thus there was a certain momentum building up to the Mississauga meeting. The second Anglican Roman Catholic International Commission completed its work with the publication of "Mary: Grace and Hope in Christ" in 2004.

On May 20, 2000, Card. Cassidy and Archbp. Carey released two short documents resulting from the meeting and a press release: "Communion in Mission" and "Action Plan to Implement 'Communion in Mission." They reported that the bishops had spent a week in prayer together, worship, and reflection. They focused on the relationship between their communions which the Second Vatican Council said "occupies a special place" (Decree on Ecumenism, No. 13). They also reported how the participants came to see that the relationship is no longer to be viewed in minimal terms but has reached a significant new place. The texts acknowledge unresolved differences and challenges, but they felt that these did not compare with all that Anglicans and Catholics hold in common. They also list the essentials of the faith and common practices to which the faithful hold fast and noted areas of theological convergence that have been achieved. They also express a common vision of full and visible unity.

Communique from the Meeting of ARCIC III in Brazil

The Anglican-Roman Catholic International Commission, the official body appointed by the two communions to engage in theological dialogue, has held the third meeting of its new phase (ARCIC III) at the Mosteiro de São Bento, Rio de Janeiro, Brazil (29 April-7 May 2013). This is the first time in its 40-year history that ARCIC has met in Latin America and, indeed, in the southern hemisphere.

Members of the Commission are grateful to Dom Filipe da Silva, OSB, the Abbot, and to his community for their gracious hospitality. The Commission participated in daily vespers and in the Sunday Eucharist at the monastery church, and were held in prayer throughout by the monastic community.

A wide range of papers was prepared for the meeting and discussed, taking the Commission further towards its goal of producing an agreed statement. The mandate for this third phase of ARCIC is to explore the Church as Communion, local and universal, and how in communion the local and universal Church come to discern right ethical teaching. In exploring this mandate, the members of the Commission engaged in theological analysis and shared reflection on the nature of the Church and those

structures which contribute to discernment and decision-making. Time was spent considering some case studies of ethical issues which members had prepared, and analysing the ways in which the two communions have come to their present teaching on these matters.

Over the forty years of its work, ARCIC has produced a number of Agreed Statements. The work of ARCIC I received official responses from the two communions. The Commission continued its task of preparing the documents of ARCIC II for presentation to the respective communions to assist with their reception. Members reviewed responses already given to each of the five Agreed Statements and will prepare introductions for them that place each of these documents within the current ecumenical situation.

The Commission welcomed at a meal leaders of the local Anglican and Roman Catholic churches, including Anglican Bishop Filadelfo Oliveira and Roman Catholic Bishop Francisco Biasin, and members of the local Anglican-Roman Catholic Dialogue of Brazil. ARCIC is keen to deepen its relationship with such local and regional ARCs and rejoices that both communions are exploring concrete ways of sharing documents and discussion about ARCIC's work.

Members of the Commission visited the City of God (*Cidade de Deus*), one of the many favelas (neighbourhoods housing large numbers of the poor and displaced) that surround Rio de Janeiro. They were warmly welcomed by the Roman Catholic parish and their priest, Fr. Marcio José de Assis Macedo, MSC. Fr. Nicholas Wheeler, the Anglican parish priest of the City of God, arranged for the Commission to visit three projects in the community (a day centre for seniors, a community development centre, and a mural project that portrays the community's history and provides a vision of the City of God from Revelation), and to learn from the local police how officers engage positively with the community. The evening concluded with ecumenical vespers. In offering thanks, one of the bishops said he was trying to think of a phrase to sum up our visit, and could only think of "City of Hope." Hope sprang from real ecumenical activity (unashamedly from a Christian base but working to support any community good), and the sheer hard work and organising by local people.

The Commission will prepare further papers, expand the case studies, and continue its work in preparation for its next meeting, 12–20 May 2014.

U.S. Anglican-Catholic Dialogue Looks at Moral Discernment, Homosexuality

Anglican and Catholic ecumenical leaders examined moral discernment and homosexuality at their current round of dialogue where they explore the positions of the Catholic and Episcopalian churches on theological issues.

The meeting of the Anglican-Roman Catholic Theological Consultation in the USA (ARC-USA) held the sixth meeting of its current dialogue in Berkeley, California, Feb. 28-Mar. 1. Bp. Ronald P. Herzog of the Catholic Diocese Alexandria, La. and Bp. John Bauerschmidt of the Episcopal Diocese of Tennessee chaired the meeting.

Dialogue members continued to study the theme of the current round, "Ecclesiology and Moral Discernment: Common Ground and Divergences," and considered a preliminary draft of some sections of a statement on this theme that they expect to adopt. Members also heard a paper by Rev. Matthew S.C. Olver summarizing the discussions so far in this round and outlining areas of disagreement and convergence.

Members also examined statements by both churches on the question of homosexuality. These included "To Set Our Hope on Christ, A Response to the Invitation of Windsor Report 135," a 2005 unofficial response by The Episcopal Church to a request from the Anglican Consultative Council and "Same-Sex Relationships in the Life of the Church," an unofficial statement prepared in 2010 by the Theology Committee of the House of Bishops of The Episcopal Church. Two Catholic statements also were studied, including "Always Our Children: A Pastoral Message to Parents of Homosexual Children and Suggestions for Pastoral Ministers," by the United States Conference of Catholic Bishops' Committee on Marriage and Family (1997) and the USCCB's "Ministry to Persons with a Homosexual Inclination: Guidelines for Pastoral Care," which was adopted by the full body of bishops in 2006.

"One of the primary tasks of this round of dialogue is to examine what has led our churches to come to very different conclusions regarding the morality of certain actions, especially in the area of human sexuality," Bishop Herzog explained. "We also acknowledge that we agree on many other moral questions. I have been impressed by the way in which both sides have been listening to each other with a spirit of patience and generosity as we search for common ground on these vexing moral issues."

At the meeting the dialogue team welcomed The Rev. Canon Dr. Beverly F. Gibson, Sub Dean of Christ Church Cathedral in Mobile, Alabama, as a new member from the Episcopal Church. In addition, Dr. Christopher Wells, Ex. Dir. of The Living Church Foundation in Milwaukee, attended as a theological consultant. Two faculty members of local Catholic theological schools also attended as consultants: Jesuit Fr. William O'Neill, Associate Professor of Social Ethics at the Jesuit School of Theology, and Holy Cross Sr. Marianne Farina, Assistant Professor at the Dominican School of Philosophy and Theology. (USCCB Press Release, Mar. 11, 2011).

Note: ARC-USA continues to meet, and hopes to finish work on an agreed statement in late 2013 or 2014.

JOINT DECLARATION ON JUSTIFICATION WITH THE LUTHERAN WORLD FEDERATION

By Russell Shaw

Hailed by Pope John Paul II as a "milestone" on the road to Christian unity, a Lutheran-Catholic Joint Declaration on the Doctrine of Justification was signed Oct. 31, 1999, in Augsburg, Germany, by representatives of the Catholic Church and the Lutheran World Federation.

"This document represents a sound basis for continuing the ecumenical theological research and for addressing the remaining problems with a better founded hope of resolving them in the future," Pope John Paul said the same day in Rome in a talk accompanying the recitation of the Angelus. "It is also a valuable contribution to the purification of historical memory and to our common witness."

The Joint Declaration states a "consensus" shared by the signers regarding the doctrine of justification. The key passage formulating this consensus says:

"In faith we together hold the conviction that justification is the work of the triune God. The Father sent his Son into the world to save sinners. The foundation and presupposition of justification is the incarnation, death, and resurrection of Christ. Justification thus means that Christ himself is our righteousness, in which we share through the Holy Spirit in accord with the will of the Father.

"Together we confess: By grace alone, in faith in Christ's saving work and not because of any merit on our part, we are accepted by God and receive the Holy Spirit, who renews our hearts while equipping and calling us to good works."

The signers of the Joint Declaration were Card. Edward I. Cassidy, President of the Vatican's Pontifical Council for Promoting Christian Unity, and Bp. Christian Krause, President of the Lutheran World Federation, which represents 58 million of the world's 61 million Lutherans. Most, but not all, of the churches within the federation have accepted the Joint Declaration.

Both the date and the place of the signing had symbolic significance. Oct. 31 is observed by Protestants as Reformation Day, commemorating Martin Luther's nailing of his 95 Theses on the castle church door in Wittenberg on that date in 1517. The city of Augsburg is associated with the Augsburg Confession, a document authored in 1530 by the Protestant Reformer Philipp Melancthon in an attempt to bring about reconciliation between Lutherans and Catholics.

From a theological perspective, the doctrine of justification was of central importance in the Reformation and in the mutual condemnations exchanged by Catholics and Lutherans in the 16th century via the Council of Trent and the Lutheran Confessions.

The Joint Declaration stresses that the churches "neither take the condemnations lightly nor do they disavow their own past." But, it insists, as a result of ecumenical dialogue during the last 30 years, they have come to "new insights" that transcend the mutual polemics of the Reformation era and make it clear that neither party's understanding of justification, as it is expressed in the Joint Declaration, now merits condemnation by the other, while the differences about the doctrine that continue to exist between them "are acceptable."

The Council for Promoting Christian Unity and the Lutheran World Federation reached basic agreement on the document in June 1998, but further clarifications were required on both sides before official approval was forthcoming. These clarifications are embodied in an "Annex" to the text.

In 2006 the World Methodist Council also entered into the signing of the *Joint Declaration* with the Catholic Church and the Lutheran World Federation, adding their distinctive emphasis within the internally differentiated consensus.

U.S. Lutheran-Catholic Dialogue Completes Statement on Death and Eternal Life

Members of the Lutheran-Roman Catholic Dialogue in the United States approved by unanimous consent on Oct. 17, 2010, the dialogue's final report on "The Hope of Eternal Life." The 65-page report represents the fruit of the dialogue's four-and-a-half-year study. It explores issues related to the Christian's life beyond death, such as the communion of saints, resurrection of the dead, and final judgment, as well as historically divisive issues such as purgatory, indulgences, and prayers for the dead.

U.S. Catholic-Lutheran Dialogue Begins Round XII, Theme: Ministries of Teaching

The Catholic-Lutheran dialogue began in 1965 and has continued since that time. The Twelfth Round has completed three meetings.

Bishop Lee Piché, auxiliary bishop of Minneapolis-St. Paul, Minnesota is serving as the Catholic co-chairman of Round XII, the topic of which is, "Ministries of Teaching: Sources, Shapes, and Essential Contents." The topic began to come into focus after the two initial meetings.

The third meeting took place April 11-14, 2013, at St. Paul's College. The meeting began with a Service of Thanksgiving in remembrance of Dr. Margaret O'Gara, a long-time Roman Catholic member of the Dialogue, who died in August 2012. The Lutheran Co-Chair Rev. Dr. Lowell G. Almen offered a personal reflection on the experience of being fortuitously in Rome for the election of Pope Francis. The numerous scholarly presentations which followed led to serious and insightful discussions by the dialogue participants. Numerous formal and informal discussions characterized the four days of the meeting. The topic is focusing more and more. The next meeting is scheduled for Feb. 20-23 2014, at St. Paul's College.

RELATIONS WITH THE REFORMED CHURCHES

Catholics, Reformed Christians Publicly Sign Historic Agreement to Recognize Each Other's Baptisms

Representatives of the U.S. Conference of Catholic Bishops (USCCB) and four Reformed Christian denominations publicly signed an agreement on baptism on Jan. 29, 2013, in Austin, Texas. The agreement affirmed that all of the churches involved recognize the validity of each other's baptisms.

Significantly, the signing took place at the opening of the annual meeting of the ecumenical association Christian Churches Together, which includes over 40 Christian communions and groups. Each member group received a copy of the agreement, which Catholic ecumenical leaders hope will encourage them to consider how and whether they too will respond.

"There has already been a strong response from CCT members who have said this represents healing," said Fr. John Crossin, OSFS, Executive Director for the USCCB's Secretariat for Ecumenical and Interreligious Affairs. "Our hope is that this would be a model for similar agreements."

The Common Agreement on the Mutual Recognition of Baptism is the result of the seventh round of the Catholic-Reformed Dialogue in the United States, from 2003-2010, which found that the agreed formula for a valid baptism is that it include flowing water and be performed in the name of the Father, the Son and the Holy Spirit.

The signing, which occurred during a prayer service at St. Mary Cathedral, included the Presbyterian Church-USA, the Christian Reformed Church in North America, the Reformed Church in America and the United Church of Christ.

The U.S. bishops voted to accept the agreement at the annual Fall General Assembly in Baltimore in November 2010. In 2011, members of the Catholic-Reformed Dialogue privately signed the agreement. The Jan. 29 signing was a ceremonial representation of the growing unity between Christians and the progress of the ecumenical movement.

"We are overjoyed at this historic recognition of one another's baptism and are committed to move forward in a new round exploring a common vision of the church," said Bp. Denis Madden, auxiliary bishop of Baltimore and chairman of the USCCB Committee on Ecumenical and Interreligious Affairs.

More information on the Common Agreement on the Mutual Recognition of Baptism is available online: www.usccb.org/beliefs-and-teachings/ecumenical-and-interreligious/ecumenical/reformed/baptism.cfm (USCCB Press Release, Jan. 31, 2013).

Catholic-Reformed Dialogue Commences Round VIII on Mission and Identity of Church in Modern World

Participants of the Catholic-Reformed dialogue convened in Austin, Texas on Jan. 28-29 to begin a multi-year study on the mission and identity of the church in the modern world. The dialogue is chaired by Bp. Tod Brown of the Diocese of Orange, CA and the Rev. Cynthia Campbell, Ph.D., Pastor, Highland Presbyterian Church, Louisville and president emerita of McCormick Theological Seminary.

This comprehensive study, which follows an historical round in which a common agreement on Baptism was signed, will explore the Reformed and Catholic understandings of the identity of the church in terms of mission. Importantly, a major source for this study is the 2012 report "The Church—Towards a Common Vision," which was produced by the World Council of Churches (WCC), Faith and Order Commission. Topics that will be addressed in this study include unity and diversity in the church, the nature and role of authority and episcopacy (which is a direct response to Pope John Paul II's invitation in Ut Unum Sint for church leaders to help the pope think about the ministerial role of the Bishop of Rome), and the origins and current interpretations of ministry and ordination. Abp. Wilton Gregory, chairman of the USCCB's committee for ecumenical and interreligious affairs at the time of the common agreement, affirmed the work of the dialogue: "Our work together has been and will be of service to all Christian communities in ways that we cannot foresee. The Holy Spirit continues to guide us in ways unseen."

The Catholic co-chair, Bp. Brown, indicated that "there is an opportunity for greater cooperation between Catholics and Reformed in this study of the church precisely because the identity of church as a mission entails a shared understanding of identity that both are called to serve." Rev. Campbell, the Reformed co-chair, commented: "What a privilege it will be to work on this Eighth Round of the dialogue as we build on the truly historic consensus achieved on Baptism. We now have the opportunity to reflect together on what it means to be the Church – Christ's Body in and for the world. I know that this will be an opportunity for spiritual growth for the participants, and we pray, for the Church as a whole."

The significance of this round, it is hoped, will be a positive step in the direction of ecumenical unity. The next scheduled meeting will take place Sept. 16-17 in Louisville, KY.

Catholic dialogue participants included Bp. Tod Brown of Orange, CA, co-chair; Bp. Denis Madden, CEIA chair; Fr. Thomas Weinandy, Fr. John A. Radano, Kristin Colberg, Ph.D., Fr. John Crossin, Anthony Cirelli, Ph.D.

Reformed Church in America participants included Rev. Dr. Wes Granberg-Michaelson, Rev. Dr. Leanne van Dyk, and Rev. Dr. Allan Janssen; Christian Reformed Church participants included Dr. Sue Rozeboom, Rev. Peter Choi, and Rev. Dr. Ronald Feenstra; Presbyterian Church USA participants included Rev. Dr. Cynthia Campbell (co-chair), Rev. David Gambrell, and Rev. Robina Winbush. United Church of Christ participants included Rev. Dr. Sidney D. Fowler, Rev. Dr. Randi Walker, and Rev. Karen Georgia Thompson. (USCCB Press Release, Feb. 1, 2013).

INTERRELIGIOUS DIALOGUE

JUDAISM

Judaism is the religion of the Hebrew Bible and of contemporary Jews. Divinely revealed and with a patriarchal background (Abraham and Sarah, Isaac and Jacob), it originated with the Mosaic Covenant, was identified with the Israelites, and achieved distinctive form and character as the religion of the Torah (Law, "The Teaching") from this Covenant and reforms initiated by Ezra and Nehemiah after the Babylonian Exile.

Judaism does not have a formal creed but its principal points of belief are clear. Basic is belief in one transcendent God who reveals himself through the Torah, the prophets, the life of his people and events of history. The fatherhood of God involves the brotherhood of all humanity. Religious faith and practice are equated with just living according to God's Law. Moral conviction and practice are regarded as more important than precise doctrinal formulation and profession. Formal worship, whose principal act was sacrifice from the Exodus times to A.D. 70, is by prayer, reading and meditating upon the sacred writings, and observance of the Sabbath and festivals.

Judaism has messianic expectations of the complete fulfillment of the Covenant, the coming of God's kingdom, the ingathering of his people, and final judgment and retribution for all. Views differ regarding the manner in which these expectations will be realized – through a person, the community of God's people, an evolution of historical events, an eschatological act of God himself. Individual salvation expectations also differ, depending on views about the nature of immortality, punishment and reward, and related matters.

Sacred Books

The sacred books are the 24 books of the Masoretic Hebrew Text of The Law, the Prophets and the Writings (see The Bible). Together, they contain the basic instruction or norms for just living. In some places, the term Law or Torah refers only to the Pentateuch (Genesis, Exodus, Leviticus, Numbers, Deuteronomy); in others, it denotes all the sacred books and/or the whole complex of written and oral tradition.

Also of great authority are two Talmuds, which were composed in Palestine and Babylon in the fourth and fifth centuries A.D., respectively. They consist of the Mishna, a compilation of oral laws, and the Gemara, a collection of rabbinical commentary on the Mishna. Midrash are collections of scriptural comments and moral counsels.

Priests were the principal religious leaders during the period of sacrificial and temple worship. Rabbis were originally teachers; today they share with cantors the function of leaders of prayer. The synagogue is the place of community worship. The family and home are focal points of many aspects of Jewish worship and practice.

Of the various categories of Jews, Orthodox are the most conservative in adherence to strict religious traditions. Others – Reformed, Conservative, Reconstructionist – are liberal in comparison with the Orthodox. They favor greater or less modification of religious practices in accommodation to contemporary culture and living conditions.

Principal events in Jewish life include the circumcision of males, according to prescriptions of the Covenant; the bar and bat mitzvah that marks the coming-of-age of boys and girls in Judaism at age 13; marriage; and observance of the Sabbath and festivals.

Observances of the Sabbath and festivals begin at sundown of the previous calendar day and continue until the following sundown.

Sabbath: Saturday, the weekly day of rest prescribed in the Decalogue.

Sukkoth (Tabernacles): A seven-to-nine-day festival in the month of Tishri (Sept.-Oct.), marked by some Jews with Covenant-renewal and reading of The Law. It originated as an agricultural feast at the end of the harvest and got its name from the temporary shelters used by workers in the fields.

Hanukkah (The Festival of Lights, the Feast of Consecration and of the Maccabees): Commemorates the dedication of the new altar in the Temple at Jerusalem by Judas Maccabeus in 165 B.C. The eight-day festival, during which candles in an eight-branch candelabra are lighted in succession, one each day, occurs near the winter solstice, close to Christmas time.

Pesach (Passover): A seven-day festival commemorating the liberation of the Israelites from Egypt. The narrative of the Exodus, the Haggadah, is read at ceremonial Seder meals on the first and second days of the festival, which begins on the 14th day of Nisan (Mar.-Apr.).

Shavuoth, Pentecost (Feast of Weeks): Observed 50 days after Passover, commemorating the anniversary of the revelation of the Law to Moses.

Purim: A joyous festival observed on the 14th day of Adar (Feb.-Mar.), commemorating the rescue of the Israelites from massacre by the Persians through the intervention of Esther. The festival is preceded by a day of fasting. A gift- and alms-giving custom became associated with it in medieval times.

Rosh Hashana (Feast of Trumpets, New Year): Observed on the first day of Tishri (Sept.-Oct.), the festival focuses attention on the ways of life and the ways of death. It is second in importance only to the most solemn observance of Yom Kippur.

Yom Kippur (Day of Atonement): The highest holy day, observed with strict fasting. It occurs 10 days after Rosh Hashana.

Yom HaShoah (Holocaust Memorial Day): Observed in the week after Passover; increasingly observed with joint Christian-Jewish services of remembrance.

CATHOLIC-JEWISH RELATIONS

The Second Vatican Council, in addition to the Decree on Ecumenism (concerning the movement for unity among Christians, stated the mind of the Church on a similar matter in Nostra Aetate, a" Declaration on the Relationship of the Church to Non-Christian Religions." This document, as the following excerpts indicate, backgrounds the reasons and directions of the Church's regard for the Jews. (Other portions of the document refer to Hindus, Buddhists and Muslims.)

Excerpt from Nostra Aetate on the Spiritual Bond between Jews and Catholics

As this sacred Synod searches into the mystery of the Church, it recalls the spiritual bond linking the people of the New Covenant with Abraham's stock.

For the Church of Christ acknowledges that, according to the mystery of God's saving design, the beginnings of her faith and her election are already found among the patriarchs, Moses, and the prophets. She professes that all who believe in Christ, Abraham's sons according to faith (cf. Gal 3:7), are included in the same patriarch's call, and likewise that the salvation of the Church was mystically foreshadowed by the Chosen People's exodus from the land of bondage.

The Church, therefore, cannot forget that she received the revelation of the Old Testament through the people with whom God in his inexpressible mercy deigned to establish the Ancient Covenant. Nor can she forget that she draws sustenance from the root of that good olive tree onto which have been grafted the wild olive branches of the Gentiles (cf. Rom 11:17-24). Indeed, the Church believes that by his cross Christ, our Peace, reconciled Jew and Gentile, making them both one in himself (cf. Eph 2:14-16).

The Jews still remain most dear to God because of their fathers, for he does not repent of the gifts he makes nor of the calls he issues (cf. Rom 11:28-29). In company with the prophets and the same Apostle (Paul), the Church awaits that day, known to God alone, on which all peoples will address the Lord in a single voice and "serve him with one accord" (Zeph 3:9; cf. Is 66:23; Ps 65:4; Rom 11:11-32).

Since the spiritual patrimony common to Christians and Jews is thus so great, this sacred Synod wishes to foster and recommend that mutual understanding and respect which is the fruit above all of biblical and theological studies, and of brotherly dialogues.

True, authorities of the Jews and those who followed their lead pressed for the death of Christ (cf. Jn 19:6); still, what happened in his passion cannot be blamed upon all the Jews then living, without distinction, nor upon the Jews of today. Although the Church is the new People of God, the Jews should not be presented as repudiated or cursed by God, as if such views followed from the holy Scriptures. All should take pains, then, lest in catechetical instruction and in the preaching of God's Word they teach anything out of harmony with the truth of the Gospel and the spirit of Christ.

The Church repudiates all persecutions against any person. Moreover, mindful of her common patrimony with the Jews, and motivated by the Gospel's spiritual love and by no political considerations, she deplores the hatred, persecutions, and displays of anti-Semitism directed against the Jews at any time and from any source (No. 4).

The Church rejects, as foreign to the mind of Christ, any discrimination against men or harassment of them because of their race, color, condition of life, or religion (No. 5).

Bishops' Secretariat

The American hierarchy's first move toward implementation of the Vatican II "Declaration on the Relationship of the Church to Non-Christian Religions" (*Nostra Aetate*) was to establish, in 1965, a Subcommission for Catholic-Jewish Relations in the framework of its Commission for Ecumenical and Interreligious Affairs. Its moderator is Card. William H. Keeler of Baltimore. The Secretariat for Ecumenical and Interreligious Relations is located at 3211 Fourth St. N.E., Washington, DC 20017.

Its Catholic-Jewish efforts were directed by Dr. Eugene J. Fisher from 1977 until his retirement in 2007; at present, the Executive Director of the Secretariat handles these same assignments.

According to the key norm of a set of guidelines issued by the secretariat Mar. 16, 1967, and updated Apr. 9, 1985: "The general aim of all Catholic-Jewish meetings (and relations) is to increase our understanding both of Judaism and the Catholic faith, to eliminate sources of tension and misunderstanding, to initiate dialogue or conversations on different levels, to multiply intergroup meetings between Catholics and Jews, and to promote cooperative social action."

Vatican Guidelines

In a document issued Jan. 3, 1975, the Vatican Commission for Religious Relations with the Jews offered a number of suggestions and guidelines for implementing the Christian-Jewish portion of the Second Vatican Council's Declaration on Relations with Non-Christian Religions. Among "suggestions from experience" were those concerning dialogue, liturgical links between Christian and Jewish worship, the interpretation of biblical texts, teaching and education for the purpose of increasing mutual understanding, and joint social action.

Notes on Preaching and Catechesis

On June 24, 1985, the Vatican Commission for Religious Relations with the Jews promulgated its "Notes on the Correct Way to Present Jews and Judaism in Preaching and Catechesis in the Roman Catholic Church," with the intent of providing "a helpful frame of reference for those who are called upon in the course of their teaching assignments to speak about Jews and Judaism and who wish to do so in keeping with the current teaching of the Church in this area."

The document states emphatically that, since the relationship between the Church and the Jewish people is one "founded on the design of the God of the Covenant," Judaism does not occupy "an occasional and marginal place in catechesis," but an "essential" one that "should be organically integrated" throughout the curriculum on all levels of Catholic education.

The Notes discuss the relationship between the Hebrew Scriptures and the New Testament, focusing especially on typology, which is called "the sign of a problem unresolved." Underlined is the "eschatological dimension," that "the people of God of the Old and the New Testament are tending toward a like end in the future: the coming or return of the Messiah." Jewish witness to God's kingdom, the Notes declare, challenges Christians to "accept our responsibility to prepare the world for the coming of the Messiah by working together for social justice and reconciliation."

The Notes emphasize the Jewishness of Jesus' teaching, correct misunderstandings concerning the portrayal of Jews in the New Testament and describe the Jewish origins of Christian liturgy. One section addresses the "spiritual fecundity" of Judaism to the present, its continuing "witness — often heroic — of its fidelity to the one God," and mandates the development of Holocaust curricula and a positive approach in Catholic education to the "religious attachment which finds its roots in biblical tradition " between the Jewish people and the Land of Israel, affirming the "existence of the State of Israel" on the basis of "the common principles of international law."

WE REMEMBER: A REFLECTION ON THE SHOAH

On Mar. 16, 1998, the Commission for Religious Relations with the Jews under Card. Edward Idris Cassidy, issued a long-awaited white paper on the Holocaust, entitled "We Remember: Reflections on the Shoah."

The document offered repentance for the failures of many Christians to oppose the policies of Nazi Germany and to resist the extermination of the Jews during the years of the Third Reich. It analyzed the history of anti-Semitism in the Church, while distinguishing between the historical anti-Judaism of Christian teaching over the centuries and the modern, racial ideology of Nazism that climaxed with the Holocaust.

"We Remember" defends Pope Pius XII and his efforts on behalf of the Jews during World War II, and at the same time acknowledges the need for a "call to penitence" by the Church as a whole "for the failures of her sons and daughters in every age." Card. Cassidy, in an address given in May of 1998 to the American Jewish Committee responding to criticisms of the text, stated clearly that terms such as "sons and daughters" and "members of the Church" are not restricted to a single category, "but can include popes cardinals, bishops, priests and laity," and he acknowledged that Christian anti-Judaism paved the way for Nazi anti-Semitism, though distinct from it.

We Remember begins with a letter from Pope John Paul II expressing his hope that the document will indeed help to heal the wounds of past misunderstandings and injustices and enable memory to play its necessary part in the process of shaping a future in which the unspeakable iniquity of the Shoah will never again be possible."

The U.S. Conference of Catholic Bishops' Committee for Ecumenical and Interreligious Relations in 1998 published the text of "We Remember" along with the statements of European and American bishops' conferences similarly expressing repentance for Christian sins of omission and commission during the Shoah in a volume entitled, Catholics Remember the Holocaust. In 2001 the U.S. Bishops issued Catholic Teaching on the Shoah: Implementing the Holy See's "We Remember" urging and giving guidelines for Holocaust education in all Catholic schools, from elementary through college and university education.

PAPAL STATEMENTS

(Courtesy The USCCB's Secretariat for Ecumenical and Interreligious Affairs.)

Pope John Paul II

Pope John Paul II was deeply loved and admired by the Jewish people worldwide over his long tenure. The Jewish outpouring of grief and condolence was deep and widespread, and save for that when the beloved Bl. John XXIII died, entirely without precedent. The prayers and statements of Jewish groups can be seen on their websites. Pope John Paul II, in a remarkable series of addresses

beginning in 1979, sought to promote and give shape to the development of dialogue between Catholics and Jews.

In a homily delivered June 7, 1979, at Auschwitz, which he called the "Golgotha of the Modern World," he prayed movingly for "the memory of the people whose sons and daughters were intended for total extermination."

In a key address delivered Nov. 17, 1980, to the Jewish community in Mainz, the Pope articulated his vision of the three "dimensions" of the dialogue: (1) "the meeting between the people of God of the Old Covenant and the people of the New Covenant"; (2) the encounter of "mutual esteem between today's Christian churches and today' s people of the Covenant concluded with Moses"; (3) the "holy duty" of witnessing to the one God in the world and "jointly to work for peace and justice."

During his historic visit to the Great Synagogue in Rome Apr. 13, 1986, the Pope affirmed that God's covenant with the Jewish people is "irrevocable," and stated: "The Jewish religion is not 'extrinsic' to us, but in a certain way is 'intrinsic' to our own religion. With Judaism, therefore, we have a relationship which we do not have with any other religion."

Meeting with the Jewish community in Sydney, Australia, Nov. 26, 1986, the Holy Father termed the 20th century "the century of the Shoah" (Holocaust) and called "sinful" any "acts of discrimination or persecution against Jews."

On June 14, 1987, meeting with the Jewish community of Warsaw, the pope called the Jewish witness to the Shoah (Holocaust) a "saving warning before all of humanity" which reveals "your particular vocation, showing you (Jews) to be still the heirs of that election to which God is faithful."

Meeting with Jewish leaders Sept. 11, 1987, in Miami, the Pope praised the efforts in theological dialogue and educational reform implemented in the U.S. since the Second Vatican Council; affirmed the existence of the State of Israel "according to international law," and urged "common educational programs on the Holocaust so that never again will such a horror be possible. Never again!"

On Apr. 7, 1994, the eve of Yom HaShoah, the Jewish day of prayer commemorating the victims of the Holocaust, Pope John Paul II hosted a memorial concert at the Vatican. It was, he noted, a moment of "common meditation and shared prayer," as the Kaddish, the prayer for the dead, and the Kol Nidre, the prayer for forgiveness and atonement, were recited.

Pope Benedict XVI

Because he had already built up an impressive series of positive reflections on Catholic-Jewish relations over the years, including a book, the election of Card. Joseph Ratzinger to the papacy was greeted with joy by all involved in Catholic-Jewish relations. In a major article in *L'Osservatore Romano* in December 2000, for example, Card. Ratzinger clarified and synthesized Catholic teaching on Jews and Judaism. With regard to the Shoah, for example, he stated: "Even if the most recent, loathsome experience of the Shoah was perpetrated in the name of an anti-Christian ideology, which tried to strike the Christian faith at its Abrahamic roots in the people of Israel, it cannot be denied that a certain insufficient resistance to this atrocity on the part of Christians can be explained by an inherited anti-Judaism present in the hearts of not a few Christians." The dialogue, he said, "must begin with a prayer to our God, first of all that he might grant to us Christians a greater esteem and love for that people, the people of Israel, to whom belong 'the adoption as sons, the glory, the covenants, the giving of the law, the worship, and the promises; theirs are the patriarchs, and from them comes Christ according to the flesh, he who is over all, God, blessed forever. Amen' (Rom 9:4-5), and this not only in the past, but still today, "for the gifts and the call of God are irrevocable" (Rom 11:29)."

In his first meeting with the International Jewish Committee for Interreligious Consultations, Benedict reassured many by affirming the direction of his predecessor: "At the very beginning of my Pontificate, I wish to assure you that the Church remains firmly committed, in her catechesis and in every aspect of her life, to implementing this decisive teaching."

Similarly, in his meeting with Jews in the Synagogue in Cologne, Benedict stated that "I make my own the words written by my venerable Predecessor on the occasion of the 60th anniversary of the liberation of Auschwitz and I too say: 'I bow my head before all those who experienced this manifestation of the mysterium iniquitatis.' The terrible events of that time must 'never cease to rouse consciences, to resolve conflicts, to inspire the building of peace'"

In his review of the year 2005 with the Vatican Curia in December of that year, the Holy Father discussed the proper understanding of the Second Vatican Council. He spoke of the "hermeneutics of continuity and discontinuity" in three key areas: faith and science, Church and State (religious freedom), and "the relationship between the Church and the faith of Israel."

Greeting the chief rabbi of Rome in January 2006, Benedict, in a remarkable formulation, emphasized God's enduring and saving love for the Jewish People: "Your visit brings me great joy, and induces me to renew with you this song of gratitude for the salvation we have received. The people of Israel have been liberated many times from the hands of their enemies and, in times of antisemitism, in the dramatic moments of the Shoah, the hand of the Almighty has supported and guided them. The favor of the God of the Covenant has always accompanied them, giving them the strength to overcome trials. To this divine loving attention your Jewish community, present in the city of Rome for more than 2,000 years, can also render testimony.

While affirming the necessity of Jewish, Christian, Muslim dialogue, Benedict emphasized in meeting with the American Jewish Committee in March 2007 that "Jews and Christians have a rich common patrimony. In many ways this distinguishes our relationship as unique among the religions of the world. The Church can never forget that chosen people with whom God entered into a holy covenant (cf. *Nostra Aetate*, 4)."

In May 2006, Benedict visited Auschwitz. "In a place like this," he said, "words fail; in the end, there can only be a dread silence – a silence which is itself a heartfelt cry to God: Why, Lord, did you remain silent? How could you tolerate all this? In silence, then, we bow our heads before the endless line of those who suffered and were put to death here; yet our silence becomes in turn a plea for forgiveness and reconciliation, a plea to the living God never to let this happen again." Returning to Rome and reflecting on the visit at the General Audience, he stated that "At the death camp of Auschwitz-Birkenau, a place of horror and godless inhumanity, I paid homage to the victims, including over a million Jews and many Poles... May modern humanity not forget Auschwitz and the other 'factories of death' where the Nazi regime attempted to eliminate God in order to take his place. May it not give in to the temptation of racial hatred, which is the origin of the worst forms of anti-Semitism."

MILLENNIUM EVENTS

During 2000 the London Philharmonic conducted by Maestro Gilbert Levine played a special series of concerts of Haydn's "Creation" for interreligious audiences in Baltimore, Paris, Jerusalem and, finally in Rome to celebrate the Holy Father's 80th birthday. In London, the Holy See and the World Union for Progressive Judaism sponsored a theological dialogue, wht papers of which have been published as *He Kissed Him and They Wept* (London: SCM Press) co-edited by Tony Bayfield, Sydney Brichto and Eugene Fisher. A second theological conference on Revelation and Covenant was held in London in 2003.

Pope John Paul II determined that the year marking the beginning of the 3rd millennium would be a year of repentance by the Church for the sins of its members during the 2nd millennium. On the first Sunday of Lent, during Mass in St. Peter's, he lead the Church in a liturgy of repentance in seven categories of Christian sins, one of which was the mistreatment of Jews and Judaism over the centuries including, especially the Shoah in the 20th century.

A high point of the millennium year was the pope's pilgrimage to the Holy Land. In Israel, he visited not only Christian holy places, but places central to Jewish memory as well. At Yad VaShem in Jerusalem, Israel's memorial to the six million Jews murdered by Nazi Germany, he prayed for the deceased and embraced Jewish survivors, some of them from his own home town of Wadowice. The prime minister of Israel, Ehud Barak, spoke movingly for his people and his country in a warm response. At the Western Wall (the Kotel, the last remnant of the ancient Temple of Jerusalem), the Pope not only prayed but inserted into the Wall a written petition just as the humblest of Jews have done ever since the Temple's destruction in 70 C.E. Its wording summarizes one of the major themes of the millennium year and of the remarkable pontificate of Karol Wojtyla. Addressing the "God of our fathers," the pope prayed in the name of the whole Church: "We are deeply saddened by the behavior of those who in the course of history have caused these children of yours to suffer and, asking your forgiveness, we wish to commit ourselves to genuine brotherhood with the People of the Covenant." The note was reverently taken from the wall for permanent display at Yad VaShem.

Pontifical Biblical Commission

In 2002 the Pontifical Biblical Commission issued "The Jewish People and Their Sacred Scriptures in the Christian Bible," a 205-page volume fulfilling the pope's 1997 mandate to the Commission. The first section of the report stresses, contrary to Marcionism, that the Jewish Scriptures are a fundamental part of the Christian Bible. The second section shows how the New Testament attests "conformity" (continuity) to the Jewish Bible in "fulfilling the Scriptures" but also presents a "newness" ("discontinuity, progression") in the life and certain teachings of Christ (IIA). Still, major " fundamental themes" of revelation are shared by both testaments (IIB). Jewish readings of the Bible, from rabbinic times to the present, maintain their own integrity and validity based upon the integrity and validity of the Jewish Scriptures understood in their own terms.

The third section outlines the historical setting of the New Testament as a document of "post-exilic Judaism" (IIIA) and describes the portrait of Jews in each gospel (IIIB) and of Judaism in the Pauline Letters and other apostolic writings (IIIC). The document concludes with "pastoral orientations" urging Jews and Christians to continued dialogue over the "inexhaustible riches" of our shared sacred texts.

INTERNATIONAL LIAISON COMMITTEE

The International Catholic-Jewish Liaison Committee (ILC) was formed in 1971 and is the official link between the Commission for Religious Relations with the Jewish People and the International Jewish Committee for Interreligious Consultations. The committee meets every 18 months to examine matters of common interest.

Topics under discussion have included: mission and witness (Venice, 1977), religious education (Madrid, 1978), religious liberty and pluralism (Regensburg, 1979), religious commitment (London, 1981), the sanctity of human life in an age of violence (Milan, 1982), youth and faith (Amsterdam, 1984), the Vatican Notes on Preaching and Catechesis (Rome, 1985), the Holocaust (Prague, 1990), education and social action (Baltimore, 1992), family and ecology (Jerusalem, 1994), the Catholic Church and the Shoah (Rome, 1998), theological understandings of one another and their implications for our teaching about each other (New York, 2001), Tsedek and Tsedakah (Righteousness and Charity (Buenos Aires, 2004), Healing and Health (Cape Town, 2006).

Pope John Paul, addressing in Rome a celebration of Nostra Aetate (the Second Vatican Council's "Declaration on the Relationship of the Church to Non-Christian Religions") by the Liaison Committee, stated: "What you are celebrating is nothing other than the divine mercy which is guiding Christians and Jews to mutual awareness, respect, cooperation and solidarity. The universal openness of Nostra Aetate is anchored in and takes its orientation from a high sense of the absolute singularity of God's choice of a particular people. The Church is fully aware that Sacred Scripture bears witness that the Jewish people, this community of faith and custodian of a tradition thousands of years old, is an intimate part of the mystery of revelation and of salvation."

Family Rights and Obligations

The Liaison Committee, at its May 1994, meeting in Jerusalem, issued its first joint statement, on the family, in anticipation of the UN Cairo Conference subsequently held in September.

The statement affirmed that "the rights and obligations of the family do not come from the State but exist prior to the State and ultimately have their source in God the Creator. The family is far more than a legal, social or economic unit. For both Jews and Christians, it is a stable community of love and solidarity based on God's covenant."

Caring for God's Creation

During its Mar. 23-26, 1998, meeting in the Vatican, the Liaison Committee issued its second joint statement, on the environment. Drawing deeply on the shared sacred text of Genesis, the Committee affirmed that "concern for the environment has led both Catholics and Jews to reflect on the concrete implications of their belief in God, creator of all things," especially "a recognition of the mutual dependence between the land and the human person." "Care for creation," the document concluded "is also a religious act."

In its April 2001, meeting, the Liaison Committee issued two statements, one affirming the need to preserve the sacred character of Christian and Jewish holy places, as well as the communities who give witness to them, and one urging review and revision where necessary of curriculum and course materials teaching about each other's traditions especially in institutions of theological education.

Protecting Religious Freedom and Holy Sites

At its May 2001, meeting in New York, the Liaison Committee issued a joint declaration on a subject of increasing concern, not only in the Middle East, but in Asia and Africa as well. With regard to the obligation of states, the document notes: "Government and political authorities bear special responsibility for protecting human and religious rights. Those responsible for law, order, and public security should feel themselves obligated to defend religious minorities and to use available legal remedies against those who commit crimes against religious liberty and the sanctity of holy places. Just as they are prohibited from engaging in anti-religious acts, governments must also be vigilant lest by inaction they effectively tolerate religious hatred or provide impunity for the perpetrators of anti-religious actions."

On Education in Catholic and Jewish Seminaries and Theological Schools

Also in New York, the Liaison Committee issued a statement calling on Catholic and Jewish seminaries to provide understanding of the other. In addition to expanding course work and examining existing courses for the treatment of the other, the statement concluded that "educational institutions in both our communities should make every effort to expose students to living Jewish and Christian communities through guest lecturers, field trips, involvement in local national and international dialogue groups and conferences."

Tzedeq and Tzedaqah

The 18th International Catholic-Jewish Liaison Committee Meeting was held in Buenos Aires, from July 5-8, 2004. This encounter, convened for the first time in Latin America, was devoted to the subject of Tzedeq and Tzedaqah (Justice and Charity). The group renewed its "total rejection of anti-Semitism in all its forms, including anti-Zionism as a more recent manifestation of anti-Semitism," noting that while anti-Zionism can be distinguished from anti-Semitism, it can serve as a "screen" for it and lead to it.

Healing in Our Two Traditions

The 19th International Catholic-Jewish Liaison Committee Meeting, held in Madrid, centered on Healing in the Catholic and Jewish traditions, with a special focus on the AIDS epidemic that is a scourge of the continent. Also discussed, in a spirit of frankness and trust, was the fact that the State of Israel has failed to implement its commitment in the Fundamental Agreement of 1993 to resolve issues of the legal status of the Catholic Church and consequent taxation requirements of Church properties such as hospitals and schools.

Dialogue with the Chief Rabbinate of Israel

After two meetings, in Jerusalem (June 2002) and Grottaferrata/Rome (February 2003) the respective high ranking delegations convened in Jerusalem to discuss the theme of "The Relevance of Central Teachings In the Holy Scriptures Which We Share for Contemporary Society and the Education of Future Generations Accordingly." The Feb. 27, 2003 meeting in Rome issued statements on "The Sanctity of Human Life" and "Family Values." In Jerusalem in June 2005, the Bi-Lateral Commission discussed "The Relationship between Religious and Civil Authority in the Jewish and Christian Traditions," agreeing on the following principles based upon biblical values: At the February 2006 meeting in Rome, the Commission issued a statement on "human Life and Technology," stating among other principle that "The conviction that we share, that life on earth is but one stage in the soul's existence, must only lead us to a greater respect for the vessel – the human form – in which the soul resides in this world. Accordingly we totally reject the idea that the temporary nature of human existence on earth allows us to instrumentalise it. In this regard we strongly condemn any kind of bloodshed to promote any ideology – especially if this is done in the name of Religion. Such action is nothing less than a desecration of the Divine Name."

Vatican-Israel Accord

On Dec. 30, 1993, a year of dramatic developments in the Middle East was capped by the signing in Jerusalem of a "Fundamental Agreement" between representatives of the Holy See and the State of Israel. The agreement acknowledged in its preamble that the signers were "aware of the unique nature of the relationship between the Catholic Church and the Jewish people, and of the historic process of reconciliation and growth in mutual understanding and friendship between Catholics and Jews." Abp. (later Card.) William H. Keeler, president of the National Conference of Catholic Bishops, welcomed the accord together with the Israeli Ambassador to the United States at a ceremony at the NCCB headquarters in Washington. In 1996, the Anti-Defamation League published a set of documents related to the accord, entitled "A Challenge Long Delayed," edited by Eugene Fisher and Rabbi Klenicki.

Catholic-Jewish Dialogue in the United States

The National Workshop on Christian-Jewish Relations, begun in 1973 by the NCCB Secretariat, draws more than 1,000 participants from around the world. Recent workshops have been held in Baltimore (1986), Minneapolis (1987), Charleston, SC (1989), Chicago (1990), Pittsburgh (1992), Tulsa (1994), Stamford (1996), and Houston (1999).

In October 1987, the Bishops' Committee for Ecumenical and Interreligious Affairs began a series of twice-yearly consultations with representatives of the Synagogue Council of America. Topics of discussion have included education, human rights, respect for life, the Middle East. The consultation has issued several joint statements: "On Moral Values in Public Education" (1990), "On Stemming the Proliferation of Pornography" (1993), "On Dealing with Holocaust Revisionism" (1994).

Ongoing relationships are maintained by the USCCB Secretariat with such Jewish agencies as the American Jewish Committee, the Anti-Defamation League, B'nai B'rith International, and the National Jewish Council for Public Affairs.

In June 1988, the Bishops' Committee for Ecumenical and Interreligious Affairs published in Spanish and English Criteria for the Evaluation of Dramatizations of the Passion, providing for the first time Catholic guidelines for passion plays.

In January 1989, the Bishops' Committee for the Liturgy issued guidelines for the homiletic presentation of Judaism under the title, "God's Mercy Endures Forever."

When the Synagogue Council of America dissolved in 1995, the Bishops' Committee for Ecumenical and Interreligious Affairs initiated separate consultations with the new National Council of Synagogues (Reform and Conservative), chaired by Card. William H. Keeler, and the Orthodox Union/Rabbinical Council, chaired by Card. John J. O'Connor, of blessed memory. The bishops have issued several joint statements with the National Council of Synagogues: "Reflections on the Millennium" (1998), "To End the Death Penalty" (1999), and "Children and the Environment" (2001), "Filled with Sadness, Charged with Hope" (2001), and "Reflections on Covenant and Mission" (2002), More recent topics have included the relationship of the Covenant and the land of Israel (2013). Joint communiqués on issues of common concern, such as the Middle East and Catholic teaching on the Jews and the death of Jesus, have been issued since then. These documents, as well as those with Orthodox Jews can be found on the website of the USCCB on the webpage of the SEIA.

Bp. William Murphy (Diocese of Rockville Center) succeeded Card. O' Connor as co-chair of the dialogue with Orthodox Judaism. This ongoing consultation has also issued joint communiqués and a joint statement on aid for private education. It has collaborated on a statement on marriage and continues to meet, examining such topics as the possibility and limits of inter-religious dialogue (2013).

RECENT DEVELOPMENTS

In December 1999, the Holy See's Commission and the International Jewish Committee for Interreligious Consultations announced the establishment of a committee of three Catholic and three Jewish scholars to look into the many complex historical and moral issues involving the Church and the Shoah beginning with an analysis of the thousands of archival documents for the period of

World War II already made public by the Holy See in its 12 volume *Actes et Documents* (1965-80). The Committee met in New York in December 1999, in London in May 2000, in Baltimore in July 2000, and finally in Rome in October 2000, where it issued its "Preliminary Report." The report affirmed the objectivity of the original team of four Jesuit scholars who selected the tens of thousands of texts from the Vatican archives for inclusion in the 11 volumes of the *Actes et Documents du Saint Siege Relatives a la Seconde Guerre Mondiale* (Libreria Editrice Vaticana, 1965-80), but also raised numerous questions for further study and documentation. The Joint Commission's Catholic Coordinator, Dr. Eugene Fisher praised the group's "achievement of so much consensus between Catholic and Jewish scholars on what are the questions that need to be faced today. Such solid consensus could by no means be presumed when the group started its work, so emotional and complex are the issues.... The scholarly successors of this group will be forever in their debt" (*Catholic International*, May 2002, p. 68). Card. Jorge Mejia, then Vatican Archivist, announced a major increase in the number of archivists working on preparing the remaining material for scholarly review, a process that already resulted in the release of tens of thousands of documents in 2003.

In 2004, the film, *The Passion of the Christ*, precipitated great controversy in the media. Jews, given the often violent history of Passion Plays, with which The Passion has much in common, expressed various concerns. Catholic leaders, whatever their personal feelings on the artistic merits of the movie, were strong in condemning any possible anti-Semitic use of it, pointing teachers and preachers to resources where the full and accurate teaching of the Church can be found, such as the BCEIA's *The Bible, the Jews and the Death of Jesus*.

40TH ANNIVERSARY OF *NOSTRA AETATE*

Card. Keeler, Fr. Kennedy, and Dr. Fisher represented the BCEIA at the meeting of representatives of bishops conferences held at the Pontifical Commission on Religious Relations with the Jews on Oct. 27, 2005, in conjunction with its celebration of the 40th anniversary of *Nostra Aetate*. The group reported on current efforts and future hopes for the implementation of the document, especially in the area of education. The celebration that evening featured addresses by Cards. Kasper and Lustiger, and Rabbi David Rosen, International Interfaith Affairs Director of the American Jewish Committee. Ancillary to the main event were dinners hosted by the Ambassador of Great Britain to the Quirinale and the Ambassador of Israel to the Holy See.

Celebrations also took place on the national level and in many dioceses throughout the country as well.

UPDATE OF GUIDELINES

In 2007, the BCEIA issued an updated version of its Guidelines for Catholic-Jewish Relations. The Guidelines were first published in 1967, and were the first guidelines issued after the Second Vatican Council. The Vatican's own Guidelines for Implementing *Nostra Aetate*, No. 4 did not come out until 1975, so the U.S. bishops' were the first such guidelines ever issued in the history of the Church. The 2007 version takes into account the numerous statements of the Holy See, Popes John Paul II and Benedict XVI, and the USCCB itself since the last update in 1985.

Pope Francis and Catholic-Jewish Relations

On Feb. 28, 2013, Pope Benedict XVI resigned the papacy and thereby opened the process for a conclave of cardinals to choose his replacement. Mar. 13, 2013 saw the election of Jose Maria Bergolio, Archbishop of Buenos Aires, as the 266th successor to St. Peter as Bishop of Rome. His choice was immediately hailed by the Jewish communities as one signaling the kind of friendship that Bergolio himself had practiced with Jews while in Argentina. Outspoken in defense of Jews, the then Archbishop of Buenos Aires had condemned the 1994 bombing of a Jewish institution by anti-Semitic terrorists. Frequently attending prayer services in synagogues, Jose Mario Bergolio was a popular figure to Jews in Argentina, befriending Rabbi Abraham Skorka with whom he co-authored, *On Heaven and Earth* (Random House, 2013) as a series of dialogues in 2010 on current issues between the two faith communities. His election has been widely acknowledged by both Jewish and Catholic groups associated with inter-religious dialogue as a positive sign of continued growth between Catholics and Jews.

ISLAM

Edited in consultation with the staff of the Secretariat for Ecumenical and Interreligious Affairs, USCCB.

Islam literally means submission (to God). As a distinct religion, Islam originated with Muhammad (A.D. 570-633) and with the revelation he is believed to have received. Muslims acknowledge that this revelation, recorded in the *Quran*, is from the one God and do not view Islam as a new religion. They profess that Muhammad was the last in a long series of prophets, most of whom are named in the Hebrew Bible and the New Testament, beginning with Adam and continuing through Noah, Abraham, Moses, Jesus and down to Muhammad. Muslims believe in the virgin birth of Jesus Christ and have great reverence for Mary, the mother of Jesus, to whom an entire chapter of the Quran is devoted.

Muslims believe in the one God, Allah in Arabic, and cognate with the Hebrew Elohim and the ancient Aramaic Elah. According to the Quran, God is one and transcendent, Creator and Sustainer of the universe, all-merciful and all-compassionate Ruler and Judge. God possesses numerous other titles, known collectively by His 99 attributes. The profession of faith states: "There is no god but the God and Muhammad is the messenger of God."

There are five pillars of Islam, the essential duties of Muslims: to witness the faith in one God and the prophethood of Muhammad and of the prophets who came before him; to worship five times a day facing in the direction of the holy Kaaba in Mecca, a sanctuary believed to have been dedicated by Abraham to belief in one God; give alms; fast daily from dawn to dusk during the month of Ramadan; make a pilgrimage to Mecca once in a lifetime if affordable.

Muslims believe in the final judgment, the resurrection

of the body, and heaven and hell. Following divinely prescribed moral norms are extremely important to Muslims. Some dietary regulations (e.g. avoiding alcoholic beverages and pork) are in effect. On Fridays, the noon prayer is a congregational (juma) prayer. The general themes of prayer are adoration and thanksgiving. The imam gives a sermon to the congregation, but unlike Judeo-Christian tradition, the day is not a "day of rest." Muslims do not have an ordained ministry.

The basis of Islamic belief is the Quran, believed to be the word of God revealed to Muhammad through the angel Gabriel over a period of 23 years. The contents of this sacred book are supplemented by the Sunna, a collection of sacred traditions from the life of the prophet Muhammad, and reinforced by Ijma, the consensus of scholars of Islamic Law (Shariah) which shields them against errors in matters of belief and practice.

Conciliar Statement

The attitude of the Church toward Islam was stated in the Second Vatican Council's "Constitution on the Church" (*Lumen Gentium*, No. 16): "But the plan of salvation also includes those who acknowledge the Creator, in the first place among whom are the Muslims: these profess to hold the faith of Abraham, and together with us they adore the one, merciful God, mankind's judge on the last day." The Council's "Declaration on the Relation of the Church to Non-Christian Religions" (*Nostra Aetate*, No. 3) stated the position in further detail:

"The Church has a high regard for the Muslims. They worship God, who is one, living and subsistent, merciful and almighty, the Creator of heaven and earth, who has also spoken to men. They strive to submit themselves without reserve to the hidden decrees of God, just as Abraham submitted himself to God's plan, to whose faith Muslims eagerly link their own. Although not acknowledging him as God, they venerate Jesus as a prophet, his virgin Mother they also honor, and even at times devoutly invoke. Further, they await the day of judgment and the reward of God following the resurrection of the dead. For this reason, they highly esteem an upright life and worship God, especially by way of prayer, alms-deeds and fasting.

Over the centuries many quarrels and dissensions have arisen between Christians and Muslims. The sacred Council now pleads with all to forget the past, and urges that a sincere effort be made to achieve mutual understanding; for the benefit of all men, let them together preserve and promote peace, liberty, social justice and moral values."

Dialogue

Pope John Paul II met with Muslim leaders and delegations both in Rome and during his trips abroad. He addressed large gatherings of Muslims in Morocco, Indonesia, Mali and elsewhere. In 1979 on a pastoral visit to Turkey, he suggested to the Catholic community: "My brothers, when I think of the spiritual patrimony [of Islam] and of the value it has for man and for society, its capacity of offering a direction in life particularly for the young, filling the gap left by materialism, and giving a secure foundation to the social and legal order, I wonder if it is not urgent, precisely today when Christians and Muslims have entered a new period of history, to recognize and develop the spiritual bonds that unite us, in order 'to promote and defend together peace, liberty, social justice and moral values for the benefit of all men,' as the Council calls us to do (*Nostra Aetate*, No. 3). In

Tertio Millennio Adveniente (1999), he recommended that "the dialogue with Jews and the Muslims ought to have a pre-eminent place" involving "meetings in places of significance for the great monotheistic religions." On Feb. 24, 2000, John Paul II traveled to Egypt as part of his Jubilee Year pilgrimages and was received by Grand Sheik Mohammed Sayyid Tantawi at al-Azhar University, the most influential Islamic university in the world. On a pastoral visit to Syria in May 2001, John Paul II spoke of the significant relationship that exists between Muslims and Christians citing his first letter of the new millennium: "I am thinking too of the great cultural influence of Syrian Islam, which under the Umayyad caliphs reached the farthest shores of the Mediterranean. Today, in a world that is increasingly complex and interdependent, there is a need for a new spirit of dialogue and cooperation between Christians and Muslims. Together we acknowledge the one indivisible God, the Creator of all that exists. Together we must proclaim to the world that the name of the one God is 'a name of peace and a summons to peace' (*Novo Millennio Ineunte*, No. 55)!" On the same trip to Syria, on May 6, 2001, John Paul II made the first papal visit to a mosque when he was received at the Umayyad Mosque in Damascus by the Minister of the Waqf and the Grand Mufti of Syria. On Nov. 18, 2001, John Paul II asked Catholics to fast and pray for peace on Friday, Dec. 14, the last Friday of the Ramadan fast that year. He also announced that he was intending to invite representatives of various world religions to Assisi for a day of prayer which was held on Jan. 24, 2002.

The Pontifical Council for Interreligious Dialogue holds formal dialogues with several Islamic organizations on a regular basis; these are regularly reported in the official bulletin, *Pro Dialogo* and in *Islamochristiana*, a journal published by the Pontifical Institute for Arabic and Islamic Studies.

At the beginning of the pontificate of Pope Benedict XVI, a meeting with Muslims in Cologne, France, was added to the Holy Father's participation in the 2005 World Youth Day. In a university lecture at Regensburg, Germany, on Sept. 12, 2006, Pope Benedict cited a 14th century Byzantine Emperor, Manuel Palaeologos, remarking on how the emperor had once entered into a discussion with "a startling brusqueness, a brusqueness that we find unacceptable, on the central question about the relationship between religion and violence in general, saying: 'Show me just what Mohammed brought that was new, and there you will find things only evil and inhuman, such as his command to spread by the sword the faith he preached.'" Pope Benedict concluded this reference, noting that "The emperor, after having expressed himself so forcefully, goes on to explain in detail the reasons why spreading the faith through violence is something unreasonable. Violence is incompatible with the nature of God and the nature of the soul." Although the actual subject of this lecture was an analysis of the intellectual crisis of European civilization, and the need to recover both faith and reason in contemporary discourse, unfortunately, the quote about Muhammad attracted world media attention. Violent protests broke out in Muslim-majority countries, churches were burned, and several people lost their lives, in spite of the fact that the Pope had not expressed any personal agreement with the citation. A group of 39 Muslim scholars responded to the crisis in October 2006 with an insightful written discussion of some points in the Pope's lecture. The Holy Father visited Turkey from Nov. 28–Dec. 1, 2006; in the course of his visit he met several times with Muslim leaders and prayed silently in the Blue Mosque in Istanbul. The visit to Turkey considerably improved Muslim responses to the current pontificate.

In October 2007, a group of 138 Muslim scholars convened by the Royal Academy of The Royal Aal al-Bayt Institute for Islamic Thought in Jordan, under the Patronage of H.M. King Abdullah II, composed "A Common Word Between Us and You" addressed to Christian leaders of various churches and ecclesial communities around the world. The theme of this document is the love of God and the love of neighbor, known to Christians from the words of Jesus in the New Testament. The Muslim scholars cited texts from the Quran and from the Bible to show how love of God and neighbor can constitute a common ground for Muslims and Christians to work together for mutual understanding and world peace. A number of Christian scholars have replied to "A Common Word" on the website: www.acommonword. com. The Holy See has formed The Catholic-Muslim Forum which will be meeting on Nov. 4-6, 2008 with Muslim signatories in order to formulate together an in-depth response to "A Common Word."

During the visit of Pope Benedict XVI to the United States (Apr. 15-20, 2008), the Pope John Paul II Cultural Center hosted an interreligious gathering for over 180 Jews, Muslims, Hindus, Buddhists, and Jains entitled "Peace Our Hope." The Holy Father encouraged the communities of dialogue in the United States, reminding them that "The broader purpose of dialogue is to discover the truth. What is the origin and destiny of mankind? What are good and evil? What awaits us at the end of our earthly existence? Only by addressing these deeper questions can we build a solid basis for the peace and security of the human family, for 'wherever and whenever men and women are enlightened by the splendor of truth, they naturally set out on the path of peace' (Message for the 2006 World Day of Peace, No. 3)." Pope Benedict also pointed out that dialogue not only serves the members of the respective religious communities, but also bears valuable witness to the larger society of the perennial value of religious faith.

In the U.S., the Bishops' Committee for Ecumenical and Interreligious Affairs holds regular regional bilateral dialogues with Muslims. Dialogue on a national level with the participation of Catholics and Muslims from several U.S. cities was initiated in October 1991. A series of conversations with Muslims on international and domestic issues were co-sponsored with the American Muslim Council. In the late 1990s, the Bishops' Committee initiated the following three regional dialogues with Muslims.

In 1996, an annual regional dialogue in the Midwest with the co-sponsorship of the Islamic Society of North America in Plainfield, IN, was initiated. This dialogue concluded several years of discussion on revelation with a report, Revelation: Catholic and Muslim Perspectives, published by USCCB Publishing (2006). This dialogue has continued to examine the role of virtues and values in our communities in view of the challenges that Catholics and Muslims face in American society. A mission statement was adopted in 2007:

"Catholics and Muslims engage in interreligious dialogue because it is part of our core identities as people of faith. Our common belief in the one God of mercy and love calls us into relationship with one another; therefore we see our dialogue as a spiritual journey. Common ethical concerns compel us to take responsibility for our relationship within U.S. American society. The United States Conference of Catholic Bishops and the Islamic Society of North America sponsor our annual gathering of official representatives for formal dialogue on topics of mutual concern. Our Dialogue provides a forum for Muslim-Catholic discussion, critique, and exchange of information that is supportive of the programs of our respective institutions."

In 1998, an annual dialogue in the Mid-Atlantic region with the co-sponsorship of the Islamic Circle of North America in Queens, New York, held its first meeting. The group has been working on a common document on marriage, which should be of great value for mosque and parish leaders responsible for marriage preparation. In 2007, a new round of this dialogue began work on a study of interreligious education in order to make recommendations to the education communities that serve our churches and mosques.

In 2000, the West Coast Dialogue of Muslims and Catholics began meeting in Orange, CA, with the co-sponsorship of several Islamic councils. The West Coast Dialogue issued a report in December 2003, Friends and Not Adversaries, a Catholic-Muslim Spiritual Journey. Since 2004, the West Coast dialogue has focused on a study of comparative narratives from the Bible and from the Quran; in each case, the moral, cultural, and catechetical principles of these narratives have allowed us to explore the immigrant experience of Catholics and Muslims in American society.

All three regional dialogues are co-chaired by bishops and Islamic leaders. Also in 1995 a dialogue between representatives of the ministry of W.D. Mohammed and the United States Conference of Catholic Bishops began. Since then, the relationship between Imam W.D. Mohammad's American Society of Muslims and the Catholic Church has been served by the Focolare Movement. The Pope John Paul II Cultural Center in Washington, DC, has also been the at the service of Muslim-Catholic dialogue, hosting a dialogue on "The Primordial Relationship Between God and the Human Person in Catholicism and Islam" on Jan. 16, 2007, with Card. Angelo Scola, Patriarch of Venice, and Dr. Muzammil Siddiqi, head of the Islamic Society of Orange County, CA. On May 16, 2007, the Center sponsored a one-day dialogue on "Sin, Forgiveness, Repentance, Reparation, and Mercy" with Prof. Zeki Saritoprak of John Carroll University and Fr. Francis Tiso of the Secretariat for Ecumenical and Interreligious Affairs of the USCCB. On Oct. 3-5, 2012, a national plenary of the three regional dialogues was held at the Catholic Theological Union in Chicago, IL. The theme of the plenary was "Living our faiths together" and featured keynote addresses by Fr. Tom Michel, S.J., and Dr. Jamal Badawi.

Catholic, Muslim Leaders Celebrate Past Accomplishments, Pledge Continued Support in Public Square at National Gathering

Leading Catholic and Muslim scholars and religious leaders convened a national plenary at the Catholic Theological Union in Chicago, Oct. 3-5. Participants from the three regional Catholic-Muslim dialogues sponsored by the U.S. Conference of Catholic Bishops (USCCB) celebrated the work and public impact of the dialogues, received formal updates on the status of regional projects, and voiced a future vision for the dialogues.

In his opening address, retired Abp. Alexander Brunett of Seattle presented a narrative of the dialogues, praised the solidarity and friendship of the participants, especially following the events of 9/11, and urged his listeners to cooperate on projects of common concern in the public square. Referencing Pope John Paul II's address to Muslim youth in Morroco, he urged the audience never to lose sight of the fact that, despite the differences between religions, the unity of the human community is the more fundamental reality.

In service to this unity, Catholic and Muslim leaders must advance dialogue by approaching it as a spiritual exercise that requires the cultivation of virtues, especially meekness, humility, and trust.

In response, Sayyid Syeed, Ph.D., of the Islamic Society of North America (ISNA) remarked that if the last millennium witnessed the spilling of blood, this new period of emerging multiculturalism is an opportunity for the Catholic-Muslim dialogue in the United States to lead the way as a witness of harmony and peaceful coexistence.

A panel delivered commentary on the present status and future hopes of the dialogues. The co-chairs of the Mid-Atlantic dialogue, auxiliary Bp. Denis Madden of Baltimore (who also chairs the USCCB Committee on Ecumenical and Interreligious Affairs) and Talat Sultan, Ph.D., of the Islamic Circle of North America (ICNA) expressed gratitude to the dialogue participants for their work on the defense of family, marriage and interreligious education. Both leaders interpreted these works as important contributions to the formation of individual conscience, especially among the young.

Midwest co-chair Syeed remarked that the work of these regional dialogues is conveyed to the international Muslim community and thus serves to promote greater understanding and peace between Muslims and Christians around the world. His Catholic counterpart, aux. Bp. Francis Reiss of Detroit, emphasized this point by remarking that the reality of multiculturalism in society entails that "we live in a moment in history that is significantly and profoundly unique," to the extent that Muslims and Catholics can show the world how to live in peace and harmony with persons of different religious affiliation.

West Coast co-chair, retired Bp. Carlos Sevilla, S.J., of Yakima, Wash., encouraged dialogue participants to "cast our nets wider, so as to include in our work a wider audience, especially the youth." His Muslim co-chair, Muzammil Siddiqi, Ph.D., of the Fiqh Council of North America, urged the participants to consider publishing to a wider audience, generating more joint statements, and expanding the Catholic-Muslim network through the enhanced use of technology.

The plenary keynote addresses were delivered by scholars Jamal Badawi, Ph.D., and Jesuit Fr. Tom Michel, Ph.D. Speaking to the plenary theme of living our faiths together, Badawi drew attention to the role of language, specifically translation of religious texts and the dissemination of opinion based on particular translations, in determining the possibility and extent of harmony and/or tension between Muslims and Christians. Fr. Michel, whose address was highlighted by reflections from his experience living abroad in Muslim majority countries, argued that effective and truthful dialogue requires faithfulness to one's tradition. "Muslims must glory in the prophethood of Muhammad and the Quranic message that he brought," he said, "just as Christians must glory in the cross of Jesus Christ and our faith in what God has accomplished in him for all human-kind." But, he continued, this faithfulness need not lead to enmity but rather mutual affection and encouragement since, "we worship and confess the same God" (USCCB Press Release, Oct. 10, 2012).

West Coast Muslim-Catholic Dialogue Continues Comparative Study of Sacred Texts with Discussion of After-Life in Islam and Christianity

The 14th annual West Coast Muslim-Catholic Dialogue convened for a close study of the after-life in Christianity and Islam. Presentations focused on a comparative study of

Christ's return and the judgment of nations in Mt 25:31-46 and the corresponding Muslim version of the judgment in Sahih Muslim Hadith 1172. The meeting was held at the Mary and Joseph Retreat Center in Rancho Palos Verdes, CA, on May 29-39, 2013. Bp. Carlos Sevilla, S.J., of the Diocese of Yakima, WA, and Imam Muzammil H. Siddiqi, Ph.D., of the Islamic Society of Orange County, presided.

In the first part of the meeting, a general overview on the question of the after-life in Islam and Christianity was provided by Imam Moustafa al-Qazwini of the Islamic Educational Center of Orange County and Bishop Sevilla. Imam Qazwini's presentation, entitled "Aspects of the Day of Reckoning," provided an account of the Muslim perspective on the after-life gleaned from salient passages in the Quran. With respect to the after-life, he contended, two aspects stand-out. First, we will experience the materialization of our deeds, which will take "specific forms" that manifest the status of one's soul. "The Quran stresses that all deeds are going to be transformed into a form or substance. Thus, good deeds, such as acts of kindness, generosity, and charity would turn into serene entities which surround and protect us." Second, the reality of the after-life entails for Muslims a strong "belief in the unseen." Qazwini asserted that "...the universe man has so far discovered is very small compared to the one that has not been seen yet. God created this vast cosmos and made our knowledge and vision of it limited for a reason: so that we understand that this life is not the eternal life...This life is only a test," calling us to exercise belief.

In his presentation, largely culled from passages in the *Catechism of the Catholic Church,* Bp. Sevilla provided a summary description of the rudiments of Catholic understanding on the after-life. Beginning his presentation with reference to the Creed, which identifies the God Christians believe in and follow, he proceeded to focus his attention on Christ as Redeemer, that is, as the one alone who saves humanity from sin whose effect is death. Christians begin their journey with Christ through Baptism, which is the door to eternal redeemed life, Sevilla noted. He then completed his presentation with reference to the meaning of "judgment" and the status of beings after death, i.e., heaven, hell, and purgatory. He completed his talk with a brief description of the Last Judgment in Christian tradition.

In the second part of the meeting, Fr. Al Baca of the Diocese of Orange, CA presented on the particular dimensions of the after-life in Matthew 25:31-46, while Imam Siddiqi presented on Hadith 1172. Fr. Baca provided a line-by-line exegesis of the passage. He first situated it in the context of the earlier gospel parable of the 10 wise and 10 foolish virgins, as well as the parable of the talents. In his explanation of the meaning of each verse, he was able to treat the important topics of the eschatological roots of Jesus as the Son of Man, the close connection of corporal works of mercy in the determination of one's eternal status, the importance of cultivating virtues, the nature of heaven and hell, and the meaning of everlasting punishment. In order to provide a modern interpretation of how Christians are to live in the world with one eye oriented to the eternal destiny of the soul, Fr. Baca referenced germane passages from the Second Vatican Council's *Gaudium et Spes* and *Lumen Gentium.* Imam Siddiqi closed the series of presentations with an address on the Hadith 1172 entitled "Ethical Implications of Belief in Life after Death." His understanding of the passage is two-fold: on the one hand, there is an ethical dimension to our eternal status in the Hadith as those "who do not care for the poor and needy, regardless of their so-called faith," will be judged negatively by Allah; on the other hand, Siddiqi argued, there is a theological dimension in that "Allah is encountered and understood precisely with the needy." To know God, to see his face, is to encounter it in those who suffer. He closed his presentation with the recognition of the close parallels between the Gospel passage and the Hadith.

In addition to the co-chairs, those present at the meeting included Muslim participants Imam Mostafa Al-Qazwini of the Islamic Educational Center of Orange County; Mr. Kalim Farooki of Corona; Mr. Iftekhar A. Hai of United Muslims of America Interfaith Alliance; Imam Taha Hassane of the Islamic Center of San Diego; Ms. Sherrel A. Johnson, Community Relations Manager and Assistant to the Director of CAIR, Greater Los Angeles Area; Imam Jerrel Abdul Salaam of Paramount, CA; Mrs. Maria Khani; Ms. Fatma Saleh of the Islamic Educational Center of Orange County; and Dr. Ejaz Naqvi of San Francisco, CA. Additional Catholic participants included incoming co-chair (2014) Bp. Robert McElroy of the Archdiocese of San Francisco; Fr. Al Baca, Diocese of Orange; Msgr. Dennis L. Mikulanis, Diocese of San Diego; Fr. Jose A. Rubio, Diocese of San Jose; Rt. Rev. Alexei Smith, Archdiocese of Los Angeles; and, Dr. Anthony Cirelli, Associate Director, USCCB SEIA. The next meeting is scheduled to take place 20-21 May 2014. (USCCB Press Release, May 31, 2013)

STATEMENTS AND MESSAGES

Message from Pope Francis for the End of Ramadan, 2013

To Muslims throughout the World

It gives me great pleasure to greet you as you celebrate 'Id al-Fitr, so concluding the month of Ramadan, dedicated mainly to fasting, prayer and almsgiving.

It is a tradition by now that, on this occasion, the Pontifical Council for Interreligious Dialogue sends you a message of good wishes, together with a proposed theme for common reflection. This year, the first of my Pontificate, I have decided to sign this traditional message myself and to send it to you, dear friends, as an expression of esteem and friendship for all Muslims, especially those who are religious leaders.

As you all know, when the Cardinals elected me as Bishop of Rome and Universal Pastor of the Catholic Church, I chose the name of "Francis," a very famous saint who loved God and every human being deeply, to the point of being called "universal brother." He loved, helped and served the needy, the sick and the poor; he also cared greatly for creation.

I am aware that family and social dimensions enjoy a particular prominence for Muslims during this period, and it is worth noting that there are certain parallels in each of these areas with Christian faith and practice.

This year, the theme on which I would like to reflect with you and with all who will read this message is one that concerns both Muslims and Christians: Promoting Mutual Respect through Education.

This year's theme is intended to underline the importance of education in the way we understand each other, built upon the foundation of mutual respect. "Respect" means an attitude of kindness toward people for whom we have consideration and esteem. "Mutual" means that this is not a one-way process, but something shared by both sides.

What we are called to respect in each person is first of all his life, his physical integrity, his dignity and the rights deriving from that dignity, his reputation, his property, his ethnic and cultural identity, his ideas and his political choices. We are therefore called to think, speak and write respectfully of the other, not only in his presence, but always and everywhere, avoiding unfair criticism or defamation. Families, schools, religious teaching and all forms of media have a role to play in achieving this goal.

Turning to mutual respect in interreligious relations, especially between Christians and Muslims, we are called to respect the religion of the other, its teachings, its symbols, its values. Particular respect is due to religious leaders and to places of worship. How painful are attacks on one or other of these!

It is clear that, when we show respect for the religion of our neighbours or when we offer them our good wishes on the occasion of a religious celebration, we simply seek to share their joy, without making reference to the content of their religious convictions.

Regarding the education of Muslim and Christian youth, we have to bring up our young people to think and speak respectfully of other religions and their followers, and to avoid ridiculing or denigrating their convictions and practices.

We all know that mutual respect is fundamental in any human relationship, especially among people who profess religious belief. In this way, sincere and lasting friendship can grow.

When I received the Diplomatic Corps accredited to the Holy See on Mar. 22, 2013, I said: "It is not possible to establish true links with God, while ignoring other people. Hence it is important to intensify dialogue among the various religions, and I am thinking particularly of dialogue with Islam. At the Mass marking the beginning of my ministry, I greatly appreciated the presence of so many civil and religious leaders from the Islamic world." With these words, I wished to emphasize once more the great importance of dialogue and cooperation among believers, in particular Christians and Muslims, and the need for it to be enhanced.

With these sentiments, I reiterate my hope that all Christians and Muslims may be true promoters of mutual respect and friendship, in particular through education.

Finally, I send you my prayerful good wishes, that your lives may glorify the Almighty and give joy to those around you.

Happy Feast to you all!

From the Vatican, July 10, 2013

HINDUISM, BUDDHISM, AND SIKHISM

(Edited in consultation with the staff of the Secretariat for Ecumenical and Interreligious Affairs, USCCB.)

In its *Declaration on the Relation of the Church to Non-Christian Religions*, the Second Vatican Council stated: "In Hinduism men explore the divine mystery and express it both in the limitless riches of myth and the accurately defined insights of philosophy. They seek release from the trials of the present life by ascetical practices, profound meditation and recourse to God in confidence and love." (2)

Catholics, especially in India, have sought good relations with Hindus and have engaged in numerous dialogues and conferences. In visits to India, Paul VI in 1964 and John Paul II in 1986 and 1999, popes have addressed words of respect for Indian, particularly Hindu, religious leaders. Pope John

Paul II said to Hindus in India in 1986: "Your overwhelming sense of the primacy of religion and of the greatness of the Supreme Being has been a powerful witness against a materialistic and atheistic view of life." In 1987, he said of Hinduism: "I hold in esteem your concern for inner peace and for the peace of the world, based not on purely mechanistic or materialistic political considerations, but on self-purification, unselfishness, love and sympathy for all."

In 1995, the Pontifical Council for Interreligious Dialogue began sending a general message to Hindus on the occasion of Diwali, a feast commemorating the victory of light over darkness. When Pope John Paul II was in India during Diwali in 1999, he addressed the religious leaders of India: "On the occasion of Diwali, the festival of lights, which symbolizes the victory of life over death, good over evil, I express the hope that this meeting will speak to the world of the things that unite us all: our common human origin and destiny, our shared responsibility for people's well-being and progress, our need of the light and strength that we seek in our religious convictions." Pope John Paul II also encouraged an intellectual exchange with Indian philosophy in his encyclical, *Fides et Ratio* (1998): "A great spiritual impulse leads Indian thought to seek an experience which would liberate the spirit from the shackles of time and space and would therefore acquire absolute value. The dynamic of this quest for liberation provides the context for great metaphysical systems" Nos. 72-73.

In the United States, dialogues between Catholics and Hindus focus on common themes of spirituality and theological philosophy. A series of informal consultations with the Vaishnava Hindu traditions over the past 10 years, since 1998, has explored the problem of evil, the mystical expression of divine love, the relationship between love and fear, and the theological rationales in our traditions for interreligious dialogue. New consultations have germinated since the Apr. 15-20, 2008, visit of Pope Benedict XVI, involving the Swadhyaya Pariwar activist movement, founded by Rev. Pandurang Shastri Athavale, and with the Vishwa Madhva Sangha in New Jersey. Leaders from the Hindu Temple Society and from the InterFaith Conference of Metropolitan Washington, DC, have been available to assist with Hindu-Catholic relations in recent years.

The Second Vatican Council, in its Declaration on the Relation of the Church to Non-Christian Religions, stated: "Buddhism in its multiple forms acknowledges the radical insufficiency of this shifting world. It teaches a path by which men, in a devout and confident spirit, can either reach a state of absolute freedom or attain supreme enlightenment by their own efforts or by higher assistance."

Numerous delegations of Buddhists and leading monks have been received by the popes, and John Paul II has met with Buddhist leaders on many of his trips. Paul VI said to a group of Japanese Buddhists in 1973: "Buddhism is one of the riches of Asia: you teach men to seek truth and peace in the kingdom of the Eternal, beyond the horizon of visible things. You likewise strive to encourage the qualities of goodness, meekness and non-violence." In 1995, while in Sri Lanka, John Paul II said to Buddhists: "I express my highest regard for the followers of Buddhism,...with its four great values of loving kindness, compassion, sympathy, and equanimity; with its 10 transcendental virtues and the joys of the Sangha [the monastic community].... At the 1986 World Day of Prayer for Peace at Assisi, the Dalai Lama, principal teacher of the Gelugpa lineage, was placed immediately to the Holy Father's left. Numerous dialogues and good relations between Catholics and Buddhists exist in many countries.

In 1995, the Pontifical Council for Interreligious Dialogue organized a Buddhist-Christian colloquium hosted by the Fo Kuang Shan Buddhist order in Taiwan. A second colloquium was held in Bangalore, India, in 1998. A third was held in Tokyo in 2002. These grew out of the perceived need for greater ongoing contact between the Pontifical Council and Buddhist leaders and scholars. Each of these meetings has produced a report. Also in 1995, the council began sending a message to Buddhists on the feast of Vesakh, the celebration of Gautama Buddha's birth, enlightenment, and final entry into Nirvana.

A meeting of great significance between Buddhist and Catholic monastics took place at Our Lady of Gethsemani Abbey, Kentucky, in July 1996, which was organized and facilitated by Monastic Interreligious Dialogue, a network formed in 1981 mostly of monasteries of men and women following the rule of St. Benedict. The Gethsemani Encounter, the result of several formal visits and hospitality between Catholic and Buddhist monks and nuns, focused on various aspects of monastic life. There were 25 participants on each side with numerous observers. The Buddhists represented the Theravada, Tibetan, and Zen traditions. A second Gethsemani Encounter took place in April 2002, the proceedings of which have been published as Transforming Suffering: Reflections on Finding Peace in Troubled Times. In 2008, a third Gethsemani Encounter on "Monasticism and the Environment" addressed ethical concerns raised by the world ecological and food crisis, taking into consideration the witness value to the wider world of simplicity of life as practiced by monastic communities.

In 1998, an ongoing dialogue between Buddhists and Catholics in Los Angeles hosted a retreat dialogue for 50 Catholic and Buddhist participants from different regions of the U.S. The retreat/dialogue was co-planned with the Faiths in the World Committee of the National Association of Diocesan Ecumenical Officers (now called CADEIO), a network of Catholic diocesan staff responsible for ecumenical and interreligious relations. A second retreat/dialogue, co-planned by the Faiths in the World Committee, met at Graymoor, a spiritual life center at the headquarters of the Society of the Atonement, in Garrison, NY, in 2003. This second retreat/dialogue was a "two monastery dialogue," co-hosted by Graymoor and Chuang Yen Buddhist Monastery in nearby Carmel, NY.

In 1996, Card. Arinze, in a letter to "Dear

Buddhist Friends," wrote: "The pluralistic society in which we live demands more than mere tolerance. Tolerance is usually thought of as putting up with the other or, at best, as a code of public conduct. Yet, this resigned, lukewarm attitude does not create the right atmosphere for true harmonious coexistence. The spirit of our religions challenges us to go beyond this. We are commanded, in fact, to love our neighbors as ourselves."

Formal dialogues continue in the Archdiocese of Los Angeles and formal relations are developing in a few other dioceses. In 1989 and 1990, the Bishops' Committee for Ecumenical and Interreligious Affairs convened its earliest national consultations on relations with Buddhists. After a series of meetings in the San Francisco area, the Bishops' Committee inaugurated a Buddhist-Catholic dialogue in March 2003, following the model of its regional dialogues, with the Dharma Realm Buddhist Association and the San Francisco Zen Center as partners. The theme of the first dialogue was "Walking the Bodhisattva Path/Walking the Christ Path." The Northern California Chan/Zen-Catholic Dialogue met again in March 2004 to discuss the theme "Transformation of Hearts and Minds: Chan/Zen-Catholic Approaches to Precepts." In 2005, the theme was "Practice: Means Towards Transformation," at the San Francisco Zen Center. The theme of the 2006 meeting was "Meeting on the Path." The theme for the 2007 meeting was "Taking Refuge in the Buddha / Abiding in Christ," with particular attention to the stages of initiation into Buddhist and Christian life. In 2008, the dialogue topic, "Abiding in Christ; Taking Refuge in the Buddha: Then What?" focused on the stages of the spiritual life from the perspective of the training programs for lay and ordained religious teachers. Attention was directed not only to the stages formation in contemplative communities, but also in active religious orders, lay associations such as the St. Vincent de Paul Society, and the Engaged Buddhist movement.

In an effort to further the bishops' interest in interreligious dialogue, planning for a new outreach to the Sikh community began in 2005. In May 2006 the first meeting of a Sikh-Catholic Consultation comprised of representatives of the World Sikh Council–America Region and the U.S. Conference of Catholic Bishops was held in New York. At the consultation, the Sikh and Catholic communities expressed shared concerns over the challenges faced by immigrant communities in the U.S., the curtailment of religious freedom and human rights in South Asia, and the challenges of secularism to both religious communities. The consultation has also explored the spiritual teachings of Sikhism and Christianity and discussed personal paths to holiness as exemplified by Catholic saints and Sikhs revered as holy people.

The new consultation with the Sikhs arose in part from previous years of collaboration with religious organizations working together for world peace. The World Conference on Religions for Peace and Religions for Peace-USA have provided a vital forum for peace making. Religions for Peace-USA has fostered closer ties with the Sikh, Hindu, Buddhist, and Jain communities, as well as our ecumenical partners and non-governmental organizations addressing issues of the international community.

Programs for Bishops

In 2006 and 2007, on the Sunday morning before the Plenary Meeting of the United States Conference of Catholic Bishops, the Secretariat for Ecumenical and Interreligious Affairs sponsored a breakfast for the bishops with Abp. Pietro Sambi, the Apostolic Nunzio to the United States, an expert on Middle Eastern affairs. In 2007, Abp. Sambi was joined by Dr. Sayyid M. Syeed, National Director of the Islamic Society of North America, for a Muslim-Catholic conversation that engaged questions from the Bishops in attendance.

In the recent restructuring of the USCCB, the former Subcommittee on Interreligious Dialogue will be reabsorbed into the Committee for Ecumenical and Interreligious Affairs as of 2008. In order to enhance its ability to take up interreligious concerns, the Committee has suggested the formation of an advisory group of bishops to work with the Secretariat.

STATEMENTS AND MESSAGES

Message to Buddhists for the Feast of Vesakh/Hanamatsuri, 2013, Pontifical Council for Interrelgious Dialogue

Christians and Buddhists: loving, defending and promoting human life

1. On behalf of the Pontifical Council for Interreligious Dialogue, I would like to extend my heartfelt greetings and good wishes to all of you, as you celebrate the feast of Vesakh which offers us Christians an occasion to renew our friendly dialogue and close collaboration with the different traditions that you represent.

2. Pope Francis, at the very beginning of his ministry, has reaffirmed the necessity of dialogue of friendship among followers of different religions. He noted that "The Church is [...] conscious of the responsibility which all of us have for our world, for the whole of creation, which we must love and protect. There is much that we can do to benefit the poor, the needy and those who suffer, and to favour justice, promote reconciliation and build peace" (Audience with Representatives of the Churches and Ecclesial Communities and of the Different Religions, Mar. 20, 2013). The Message of the World Day of Peace in 2013 entitled "Blessed are the Peacemakers," notes that "The path to the attainment of the common good and to peace is above all that of respect for human life in all its many aspects, beginning with its conception, through its development and up to its natural end. True peacemakers, then, are those who love, defend and promote human life in all its dimensions, personal, communitarian and transcendent. Life in its fullness is the height of peace. Anyone who loves peace cannot tolerate attacks and crimes against life" (Message for the World Day of Peace in 2013, No. 4).

3. I wish to voice that the Catholic Church has

sincere respect for your noble religious tradition. Frequently we note a consonance with values expressed also in your religious books: respect for life, contemplation, silence, simplicity (cf. *Verbum Domini*, No. 119). Our genuine fraternal dialogue needs to foster what we Buddhists and Christians have in common especially a shared profound reverence for life.

4. Dear Buddhist friends, your first precept teaches you to abstain from destroying the life of any sentient being and it thus prohibits killing oneself and others. The cornerstone of your ethics lies in loving kindness to all beings. We Christians believe that the core of Jesus' moral teaching is twofold: love of God and love of neighbor. Jesus says: "As the Father has loved me, so have I loved you; abide in my love." And again: 'This is my commandment, that you love one another as I have loved you" (*Catechism of the Catholic Church,* No. 1823).The fifth Christian Commandment, "You shall not kill" harmonizes so well with your first precept. Nostra Aetate teaches that "the Catholic Church rejects nothing of what is true and holy in these religions" (NA, No. 2). I think, therefore, that it is urgent for both Buddhists and Christians on the basis of the genuine patrimony of our religious traditions to create a climate of peace to love, defend and promote human life.

5. As we all know, in spite of these noble teachings on the sanctity of human life, evil in different forms contributes to the dehumanization of the person by mitigating the sense of humanity in individuals and communities. This tragic situation calls upon us, Buddhists and Christians, to join hands to unmask the threats to human life and to awaken the ethical consciousness of our respective followers to generate a spiritual and moral rebirth of individuals and societies in order to be true peacemakers who love, defend and promote human life in all its dimensions.

6. Dear Buddhist friends, let us continue to collaborate with a renewed compassion and fraternity to alleviate the suffering of the human family by fostering the sacredness of human life. It is in this spirit that I wish you once again a peaceful and joyful feast of Vesakh.

Message to Hindus for the Feast of Deepavali, 2012, Pontifical Council for Interrelgious Dialogue

1. The Pontifical Council for Interreligious Dialogue sends its warmest greetings and congratulations on the occasion of this year's Deepavali celebrations. May fellowship and fraternity shine forth more and more in your families and communities.

2. At this point in time in human history, when various negative forces threaten the legitimate aspirations in many regions of the world for peaceful co-existence, we would like to use this cherished tradition of sharing with you a reflection to explore the responsibility that Hindus, Christians and others have in doing everything possible to form all people, especially the young generation, into peacemakers.

3. Peace is not merely absence of war, nor is it a pact or treaty which ensures a tranquil life; rather,

it is being complete and intact, a restoration of harmony (cf. Benedict XVI, *Ecclesia in Medio Oriente*, No. 9) and a fruit of charity. Parents, teachers, elders, religious and political leaders, peace-workers, those in the world of communications and all those who have the cause of peace at heart are called to educate the young generation, and are called to foster such wholeness.

4. To form young men and women into people of peace and builders of peace is an urgent summons to collective engagement and common action. If peace is to be authentic and enduring, it must be built on the pillars of truth, justice, love and freedom (cf. John XXIII, *Pacem in Terris*, No. 35), and all young men and women need to be taught above all to act truthfully and justly in love and freedom. Furthermore, in all education for peace, cultural differences ought surely to be treated as a richness rather than a threat or danger.

5. The family is the first school of peace and the parents the primary educators for peace. By their example and teachings, they have the unique privilege of forming their children in values that are essential for peaceful living: mutual trust, respect, understanding, listening, sharing, caring and forgiving. In schools, colleges and universities, as young people mature by relating, studying and working with others from different religions and cultures, their teachers and others responsible for their training have the noble task of ensuring an education that respects and celebrates the innate dignity of all human beings and promotes friendship, justice, peace and cooperation for integral human development. With spiritual and moral values as the bedrock of education, it becomes their ethical imperative also to caution the students against ideologies that cause discord and division.

While states and individual leaders in the social, political and cultural fields, generally have their own important roles to play in strengthening the education of the young, religious leaders in particular, by reason of their vocation to be spiritual and moral leaders, must continue to inspire the young generation to walk the path of peace and to become messengers of peace. Since all means of communication greatly shape the way people think, feel and act, those involved in these fields must, to the utmost possible extent, contribute to promoting thoughts, words, and works of peace. Indeed, young people themselves ought to live up to the ideals they set for others, by employing their freedom responsibly and by promoting cordial relationships for a culture of peace.

6. Evidently, the wholeness which peace conveys will shape a more fraternal world and a "new kind of fraternity" among people in which "a shared sense of the greatness of each person" will prevail. (cf. Benedict XVI, Apostolic Journey to Lebanon, Meeting with Members of the Government, Institutions of the Republic, the Diplomatic Corps, Religious leaders and Representatives from the world of culture, Sept. 15, 2012).

7. May all of us seek, always and everywhere, to adhere to the moral and religious imperative to inspire the young as they strive to become peacemakers. Wish you all a Blessed Deepavali!

INDEX